Graduate School GUIDES

GRADUATE PROGRAMS IN Social Sciences 2004

THOMSON
PETERSON'S

Australia • Canada • Mexico • Singapore • Spain • United Kingdom • United States

THOMSON
PETERSON'S

About The Thomson Corporation and Peterson's

With revenues of US$7.8 billion, The Thomson Corporation (www.thomson.com) is a leading global provider of integrated information solutions for business, education, and professional customers. Its Learning businesses and brands (www.thomsonlearning.com) serve the needs of individuals, learning institutions, and corporations with products and services for both traditional and distributed learning.

Peterson's, part of The Thomson Corporation, is one of the nation's most respected providers of lifelong learning online resources, software, reference guides, and books. The Education Supersite℠ at www.petersons.com—the Internet's most heavily traveled education resource—has searchable databases and interactive tools for contacting U.S.-accredited institutions and programs. In addition, Peterson's serves more than 105 million education consumers annually.

For more information, contact Peterson's, 2000 Lenox Drive, Lawrenceville, NJ 08648; 800-338-3282; or find us on the World Wide Web at www.petersons.com/about.

ISSN 1528-5987
ISBN 0-7689-1196-6

Printed in Canada

10 9 8 7 6 5 4 3 2 1 05 04 03

Table of Contents

How to Use This Book

The *Decision Guides* are a collaborative effort between Peterson's and Educational Testing Service (ETS) and the Graduate Record Examinations (GRE) Board. This collaboration builds upon Peterson's survey research and publication capabilities and the GRE Program's long-term relationship with the graduate education community, including administration of the Graduate Record Examinations. This collaboration enables a greater range of potential graduate students to access comprehensive information as they make decisions about pursuing graduate education. At the same time, it enables institutions to achieve greater promotion and awareness of their graduate offerings.

The graduate and professional programs in this *Decision Guide* are offered by colleges, universities, and professional schools and specialized institutions in the United States and U.S. territories. They are accredited by U.S. accrediting bodies recognized by the Department of Education or the Council on Higher Education Accreditation. Most are regionally accredited.

This volume is divided into three major sections, Library and Information Studies; Social Sciences; and Social Work. Within these broad subject areas, there are many sections that represent the subject fields in which graduate degrees are offered. The Social Sciences section has eleven individual subject areas: Area and Cultural Studies; Conflict Resolution and Mediation; Criminology and Forensics; Economics; Family and Consumer Sciences; Geography; Military and Defense Studies; Political Science and International Affairs; Public, Regional, and Industrial Affairs; Social Sciences; and Sociology, Anthropology, and Archaeology.

How Information Is Organized

Graduate program information in this *Decision Guide* is presented in profile form. The format of the profiles is consistent throughout the book, making it easy to compare one institution with another and one program with another. Any item that does not apply to or was not provided by a graduate unit is omitted from its listing. The following outline describes the profile information.

Identifying Information. In the conventional university-college-department organizational structure, the parent institution's name is followed by the name of the administrative unit or units under which the degree program is offered and then the specific unit that offers the degree program. (For example, University of Notre Dame, College of Arts and Letters, Division of Humanities, Department of Art, Art History, and Design, Concentration in Design.) The last unit listed is the one to which all information in the profile pertains. The institution's city, state, and postal code follow.

Awards. Each postbaccalaureate degree awarded is listed; fields of study offered by the unit may also be listed. Frequently, fields of study are divided into subspecializations, and those appear following the degrees awarded. Students enrolled in the graduate program would be able to specialize in any of the fields mentioned.

Part-Time and Evening/Weekend Programs. When information regarding the availability of part-time or evening/weekend study appears in the profile, it means that students are able to earn a degree exclusively through such study.

Postbaccalaureate Distance Learning Degrees. A postbaccalaureate distance learning degree program signifies that course requirements can be fulfilled with minimal or no on-campus study.

Faculty. Figures on the number of faculty members actively involved with graduate students through teaching or research are separated into full- and part-time as well as men and women whenever the information has been supplied.

Students. Figures for the number of students enrolled in graduate and professional programs pertain to the semester of highest enrollment from the 2001–02 academic year. These figures are divided into full- and part-time and men and women whenever the data have been supplied. Information on the number of students who are members of a minority group or are international students appears here. The average age of the students is followed by the number of applicants, the percentage accepted, and the number enrolled for fall 2001. This section also includes the number of degrees awarded in calendar year 2001. Many doctoral programs offer a terminal master's degree if students leave the program after completing only part of the requirements for a doctoral degree; that is indicated here. All degrees are classified into one of four types: master's, doctoral, first-professional, and other advanced degrees. A unit may award one or several degrees at a given level; however, the data are only collected by type and may therefore represent several different degree programs.

Degree Requirements. The information in this section is also broken down by type of degree, and all information for a degree level pertains to all degrees of that type unless otherwise specified. Degree requirements are collected in a simplified form to provide some very basic information on the nature of the program and on foreign language, thesis or dissertation, comprehensive exam, and registration requirements. Some units may also provide a short list of additional requirements, such as fieldwork or internships. Information on the median amount of time required to earn the degree for full-time and part-time students is presented here. For complete information on graduation requirements, contact the graduate school or program directly.

Entrance Requirements. Entrance requirements are divided into the levels of master's, doctoral, first-professional, and other advanced degrees. Within each level, information may be provided in two basic categories, entrance exams and other requirements. The entrance exams use the standard acronyms used by the testing agencies, unless they are not well known. Other entrance requirements are quite varied, but they often contain an undergraduate or graduate grade point average (GPA). Unless otherwise stated, the GPA is calculated on a 4.0 scale and is listed as a minimum required for admission.

Application. The standard application **deadline**, any nonrefundable application **fee**, and whether electronic applications are accepted may be listed here. Note that the deadline should be used for reference only; these dates are subject to change, and students interested in applying should contact the graduate unit directly about application procedures and deadlines.

Expenses. Cost of study may be quite complex at a graduate institution. There are often sliding scales for part-time study, a different cost for first-year students, and other variables that make it impossible to completely cover the cost of study for each graduate program. To provide the most usable information, figures are given for full-time study for a full year where available and for part-time study in terms of a per-unit rate (per credit, per semester hour, etc.) **if** these costs are reported to be the **same** as the parent institution. If specific program costs have been reported as different from the parent institution, the reader is advised to contact the institution for expense information. Because expenses are always subject to change, this is good advice at any time.

Financial Support. This section contains data on the number of awards administered by the institution and given to graduate students during the 2001–02 academic year. The first figure given represents the total number of students enrolled in that unit who received financial aid. If the unit has provided information on graduate appointments, these are broken down into three major categories: *fellowships* give money to graduate students to cover the cost of study and living expenses and are not based on a work obligation or research commitment, *research assistantships* provide stipends to graduate students for assistance in a formal research project with a faculty member, and *teaching assistantships* provide stipends to graduate students for teaching or for assisting faculty members in teaching undergraduate classes.

In addition to graduate appointments, the availability of several other financial aid sources is covered in this section. *Career-related internships* or *fieldwork* offer money to students who are participating in a formal off-campus research project or practicum. *Federal Work-Study* is made available to students who demonstrate need and meet the federal guidelines; this form of aid normally includes 10 or more hours of work per week in an office of the institution or off campus in a nonprofit agency. *Tuition waivers* are routinely part of a graduate appointment, but units sometimes waive part or all of a student's tuition even if a graduate appointment is not available. *Institutionally sponsored loans* are low-interest loans available to graduate students to cover both educational and living expenses. The availability of grants, scholarships, traineeships, unspecified assistantships, and financial aid to part-time students is also indicated here.

Some programs list the financial aid application deadline and the forms that need to be completed for students to be eligible for financial aid. There are two forms: FAFSA, the Free Application for Federal Student Aid, which is required for federal aid; and the CSS Financial Aid PROFILE.

Faculty Research. Each unit has the opportunity to list several keyword phrases describing the current research involving faculty members and graduate students. Space limitations prevent the unit from listing complete information on all research programs. The total expenditure for funded research from the previous academic year may also be included.

Unit Head and Application Contact. The head of the graduate program for each unit is listed with the academic title and telephone and fax numbers and e-mail addresses, if available. In addition to the unit head, many graduate programs list separate contacts for application and admission information. Unit Web sites are provided, if available. If no unit head or application contact is given, you should contact the overall institution for information.

For Further Information

Many programs offer more in-depth, narrative style information that can be located at www.petersons.com/gradchannel. There is a notation to this effect at the end of those program profiles.

How This Information Was Gathered

The information published in this book was collected through *Peterson's Annual Survey of Graduate and Professional Institutions.* Each spring and summer, this survey is sent to more than 1,800 institutions offering postbaccalaureate degree programs, including accredited institutions in the United States and U.S. territories. (See article entitled "Accreditation and Accrediting Agencies.") Deans and other administrators provide information on specific programs as well as overall institutional information. Peterson's editorial staff then goes over each returned survey carefully and verifies or revises responses after further research and discussion with administrators at the institutions.

While every effort is made to ensure the accuracy and completeness of the data, information is sometimes unavailable or changes occur after publication deadlines. The omission of any particular item from a directory or profile signifies either that the item is not applicable to the institution or program or that information was not available.

The Admissions Process

Generalizations about graduate admissions practices are not always helpful because each institution has its own set of guidelines and procedures. Nevertheless, some broad statements can be made about the admissions process that may help you plan your strategy.

General Requirements

Graduate schools and departments have requirements that applicants for admission must meet. Typically, these requirements include undergraduate transcripts (which provide information about undergraduate grade point average and course work applied toward a major), admission test scores, and letters of recommendation. Most graduate programs also ask for an essay or personal statement that describes your personal reasons for seeking graduate study. In some fields, such as art and music, portfolios or auditions may be required in addition to other evidence of talent. Some institutions require that the applicant have an undergraduate degree in the same subject as the intended graduate major.

Most institutions evaluate each applicant on the basis of the applicant's total record, and the weight accorded any given factor varies widely from institution to institution and from program to program.

Admission Tests

The major testing program used in graduate admissions is the Graduate Record Examinations (GRE) testing program, sponsored by the GRE Board and administered by Educational Testing Service, Princeton, New Jersey.

The Graduate Record Examinations testing program consists of a General Test and eight Subject Tests. The General Test measures verbal reasoning, quantitative reasoning, and analytical writing skills. It is offered as a computer-adaptive test (CAT) in the United States, Canada, and many other countries. In the CAT, the computer determines which question to present next by adjusting to your previous responses. Paper-based General Test administrations are offered in some parts of the world.

The computer-adaptive General Test consists of a 30-minute verbal section, a 45-minute quantitative section, and a 75-minute analytical writing section. In addition, an unidentified verbal or quantitative section that doesn't count toward a score may be included and an identified research section that is not scored may also be included.

The paper-based General Test consists of two 30-minute verbal sections, two 30-minute quantitative sections, and a 75-minute analytical writing section. In addition, an unidentified verbal or quantitative section that doesn't count toward a score may be included.

The Subject Tests measure achievement and assume undergraduate majors or extensive background in the following eight disciplines:

- Biochemistry, Cell and Molecular Biology
- Biology
- Chemistry
- Computer Science
- Literature in English
- Mathematics
- Physics
- Psychology

The Subject Tests are available at regularly scheduled paper-based administrations at test centers around the world. Testing time is approximately 2 hours and 50 minutes. You can obtain more information about the GRE tests by visiting the GRE Web site at www.gre.org or consulting the *GRE Information and Registration Bulletin*. The *Bulletin* can be obtained at many undergraduate colleges. You can also download it from the GRE Web site or obtain it by contacting Graduate Record Examinations, Educational Testing Service, Princeton, NJ 08541-6000, telephone 1-609-771-7670.

If you expect to apply for admission to a program that requires any of the GRE tests, you should select a test date well in advance of the application deadline. Scores on the computer-adaptive General Test are reported within ten to fifteen days; however, if you choose to handwrite your essay responses on the analytical writing section, score reporting will take approximately six weeks. Scores on the paper-based General Test and the Subject Tests are reported within six weeks.

Another testing program, the Miller Analogies Test (MAT), is administered at more than 600 licensed testing centers in the United States, Canada, and other countries. Testing time is 50 minutes. The test consists entirely of analogies. You can obtain the *Candidate Information Booklet*, which contains a list of test centers and instructions for taking the test, by calling The Psychological Corporation, Controlled Test Center, at 1-800-622-3231.

Check the specific requirements of the programs to which you are applying.

Factors Involved in Selecting a Graduate School or Program

Selecting a graduate school and a specific program of study is a complex matter. Quality of the faculty; program and course offerings; the nature, size, and location of the institution; admission requirements; cost; and the availability of financial assistance are among the many factors that affect one's choice of institution. Other considerations are job placement and achievements of the program's graduates and the institution's resources, such as libraries, laboratories, and computer facilities. If you are to make the best possible choice, you need to learn as much as you can about the schools and programs you are considering before you apply.

The following steps may help you narrow your choices.

- Talk to alumni of the programs or institutions you are considering to get their impressions of how well they were prepared for work in their fields of study.
- Remember that graduate school requirements change, so be sure to get the most up-to-date information possible.
- Talk to department faculty and the graduate adviser at your undergraduate institution. They often have information about programs of study at other institutions.
- Visit the Web sites of the graduate schools in which you are interested to request a graduate catalog. Contact the department chair in your chosen field of study for additional information about the department and the field.
- Visit as many campuses as possible. Call ahead for an appointment with the graduate adviser in your field of interest and be sure to check out the facilities and talk to students.

Tips for Minority Students: Indicators of a university's values in terms of diversity are found both in its recruitment programs and its resources directed to student success. Important questions: Does the institution vigorously recruit minorities for its graduate programs? Is there funding available to help with the costs associated with visiting the school? Are minorities represented in the institution's brochures or Web site or on their faculty rolls? What campus-based resources or services (including assistance in locating housing or career counseling and placement) are available? Is funding available to members of underrepresented groups?

At the program level, it is particularly important for minority students to investigate the "climate" of a program under consideration. How many minority students are enrolled and how many have graduated? What opportunities are there to work with diverse faculty and mentors whose research interests match yours? How are conflicts resolved or concerns addressed? How interested are faculty in building strong and supportive relations with students? "Climate" concerns should be addressed by posing questions to various individuals, including faculty members, current students, and alumni.

Information is also available through various organizations, such as the Hispanic Association of Colleges and Universities (HACU), and publications, such as *Black Issues in Higher Education* and *Hispanic Outlook* magazine. There are also books devoted to this topic, such as *The Multicultural Student's Guide to Colleges* by Robert Mitchell.

When and How to Apply

You should begin the application process at least one year before you expect to begin your graduate study. Find out the application deadline for each institution (many are provided in the profile section of this volume). Go to the institution Web site and find out if you can apply online. If not, request a paper application form. Fill out this form thoroughly and neatly. Assume that the school needs all the information it is requesting and that the admissions officer will be sensitive to the neatness and overall quality of what you submit. Do not supply more information than the school requires.

The institution may ask at least one question that will require a three- or four-paragraph answer. Compose your response on the assumption that the admissions officer is interested in both what you think and how you express yourself. Keep your statement brief and to the point, but, at the same time, include all pertinent information about your past experiences and your educational goals. Individual statements vary greatly in style and content, which helps admissions officers to differentiate among applicants. Many graduate departments give considerable weight to the statement in making their admissions decisions, so be sure to take the time to prepare a thoughtful and concise statement.

If recommendations are a part of the admissions requirements, choose carefully the individuals you ask to write them. It is generally best to ask current or former professors to write the recommendations, provided they are able to attest to your intellectual ability and motivation for doing the work required of a graduate student. It is advisable to provide stamped, preaddressed envelopes to people being asked to submit recommendations on your behalf.

Completed applications, including references and transcripts and admission test scores, should be received at the institution by the specified date.

Be advised that institutions do not usually make admissions decisions until all materials have been received. Enclose a self-addressed postcard with your application, requesting confirmation of receipt. Allow at least 10 days for the return of the postcard before making further inquiries.

If you plan to apply for financial support, it is imperative that you file your application early.

How Admission Decisions Are Made

The program you apply to is directly involved in the admissions process. Although the final decision is usually made by the graduate dean (or an associate) or by the faculty admissions committee, recommendations from faculty members in your intended field are important. At some institutions, an interview is incorporated into the decision process.

A Special Note for International Students

In addition to the steps already described, there are some special considerations for international students who intend to apply for graduate study in the United States. All graduate schools require an indication of competence in English. The purpose of the Test of English as a Foreign Language (TOEFL) is to evaluate the English proficiency of people who are nonnative speakers of English and want to study at colleges and universities where English is the language of instruction. The TOEFL is administered by Educational Testing

Service (ETS) under the general direction of a policy board established by the College Board and the Graduate Record Examinations Board.

The TOEFL is administered as a computer-based test throughout most of the world and is available year-round by appointment only. It is not necessary to have previous computer experience to take the test. The test consists of four sections—listening, reading, structure, and writing. Total testing time is approximately 4 hours.

The TOEFL is offered in the paper-based format in areas of the world where computer-based testing is not available. The paper-based TOEFL consists of three sections—listening comprehension, structure and written expression, and reading comprehension. Testing time is approximately 3 hours. The Test of Written English (TWE) is also given. TWE is a 30-minute essay that measures the examinee's ability to compose in English. Examinees receive a TWE score separate from their TOEFL score. The *Information Bulletin* contains information on local fees and registration procedures.

Additional information and registration materials are available from TOEFL Services, Educational Testing Service, P.O. Box 6151, Princeton, New Jersey 08541-6151. Telephone: 1-609-771-7100. E-mail: toefl@ets.org. World Wide Web: http://www.toefl.org.

International students should apply especially early because of the number of steps required to complete the admissions process. Furthermore, many United States graduate schools have a limited number of spaces for international students, and many more students apply than the schools can accommodate.

International students may find financial assistance from institutions very limited. The U.S. government requires international applicants to submit a certification of support, which is a statement attesting to the applicant's financial resources. In addition, international students *must* have health insurance coverage.

Financial Support

The range of financial support at the graduate level is very broad. The following descriptions will give you a general idea of what you might expect and what will be expected of you as a financial support recipient.

Fellowships, Scholarships, and Grants

These are usually outright awards of a few hundred to many thousands of dollars with no service to the institution required in return. Fellowships and scholarships are usually awarded on the basis of merit and are highly competitive. Grants are made on the basis of financial need or special talent in a field of study. Many grants not only cover tuition, fees, and supplies but also include stipends for living expenses with allowances for dependents. However, the terms of each grant should be examined because some do not permit recipients to supplement their income with outside work. Fellowships, scholarships, and grants may vary in the number of years for which they are awarded.

In addition to the availability of these funds at the university or program level, many excellent fellowship programs are available at the national level and may be applied for before and during enrollment in a graduate program. A listing of many of these programs can be found at the Council of Graduate Schools' Web site: http://www.cgsnet.org/ResourcesForStudents/fellowships.htm.

Assistantships and Internships

As described here, many graduate students receive financial support through assistantships, particularly involving teaching or research duties. It is important to recognize that such appointments should not be simply employment relationships but rather should constitute an integral and important part of a student's graduate education. As such, the appointments should be accompanied by strong faculty mentoring and increasingly responsible apprenticeship experiences (these are often lacking for teaching assistantships). The specific nature of these appointments in a given program should be factor considered in selecting that graduate program.

Teaching Assistantships

These usually provide a salary and full or partial tuition remission, and they may also provide health benefits. Unlike fellowships, scholarships, and grants, which require no service to the institution, teaching assistantships require recipients to provide the institution with a specific amount of undergraduate teaching, ideally related to the student's field of study. Some teaching assistants are limited to grading papers, compiling bibliographies, or monitoring laboratories. At some graduate schools, teaching assistants must carry lighter course loads than regular full-time students.

Research Assistantships

These are very similar to teaching assistantships in the manner in which financial assistance is provided. The difference is that recipients are given basic research assignments in their disciplines rather than teaching responsibilities. The work required is normally related to the student's field of study; in most instances, the assistantship supports the student's thesis or dissertation research.

Administrative Internships

These are similar to assistantships in application of financial assistance funds, but the student is given an assignment on a part-time basis, usually as a special assistant to one of the university's administrative officers. The assignment may not necessarily be directly related to the recipient's discipline.

Residence Hall and Counseling Assistantships

These are frequently assigned to graduate students in psychology, counseling, and social work. Duties can vary from being available in a dean's office for a specific number of hours for consultation with undergraduates to living in campus residences and being responsible for both counseling and administrative tasks or advising student activity groups. Residence hall assistantships sometimes include room and board in addition to tuition and stipends.

Health Insurance

The availability and affordability of health insurance is an important issue and one that should be considered in an applicant's choice of institution and program. While often included with assistantships and fellowships, this is not always the case and, even if provided, the benefits may be very limited. It is important to note that the U.S. government requires international students to have health insurance.

The GI Bill

This provides financial assistance for students who are veterans of the United States armed forces. If you are a veteran, contact your local Veterans Administration office to determine your eligibility and to get full details about benefits.

Federal Work-Study Program (FWS)

Employment is another way some students finance their graduate studies. The federally funded Federal Work-Study Program provides eligible students with employment opportunities, usually in public and private nonprofit organizations. Federal funds pay up to 75 percent of the wages, with the remainder paid by the employing agency. FWS is available to graduate students who demonstrate financial need. Not all schools have these funds, and some only award them to undergraduates. Each school sets its application deadline and work-study earnings limits. Wages vary and are related to the type of work done.

Loans

Many graduate students borrow to finance their graduate programs when other sources of assistance (which do not have to be repaid) prove insufficient. You should always read and understand the terms of any loan program before submitting your application.

Federal Loans

Federal Stafford Loans. The Federal Stafford Loan Program offers government-sponsored, low-interest loans to students through a private lender such as a bank, credit union, or savings and loan association.

There are two components of the Federal Stafford Loan program. Under the *subsidized* component of the program, the federal government pays the interest accruing on the loan while you are enrolled in graduate school on at least a half-time basis. Under the *unsubsidized* component of the program, you pay the interest on the loan from the day proceeds are issued. Eligibility for the federal subsidy is based on demonstrated financial need as determined by the financial aid office from the information you provide on the Free Application for Federal Student Aid (FAFSA). (See "Applying for Need-Based Financial Aid" for more information on the FAFSA.) A cosigner is not required, since the loan is not based on creditworthiness.

Although *unsubsidized* Federal Stafford Loans may not be as desirable as *subsidized* Federal Stafford Loans from the consumer's perspective, they are a useful source of support for those who may not qualify for the subsidized loans or who need additional financial assistance.

Graduate students may borrow up to $18,500 per year through the Stafford Loan Program, up to a cumulative maximum of $138,500, including undergraduate borrowing. This may include up to $8500 in Subsidized Stafford Loans annually, depending on eligibility, up to a cumulative maximum of $65,500, including undergraduate borrowing. The amount of the loan borrowed through the *unsubsidized* Stafford Program equals the total amount of the loan (as much $18,500) minus your eligibility for a Subsidized Stafford Loan (as much as $8500). You may borrow up to the cost of the school in which you are enrolled or will attend, minus estimated financial assistance from other federal, state, and private sources, up to a maximum of $18,500.

The interest rate for the Federal Stafford Loans varies annually and is set every July. The rate during in-school, grace, and deferment periods is based on the 91-Day U.S. Treasury Bill rate plus 1.7 percent, capped at 8.25 percent. The rate during repayment is based on the 91-Day U.S. Treasury Bill rate plus 2.3 percent, capped at 8.25 percent. The 2002–03 rate is 4.06 percent.

Two fees may be deducted from the loan proceeds upon disbursement: a guarantee fee of up to 1 percent, which is deposited in an insurance pool to ensure repayment to the lender if the borrower defaults, and a federally mandated 3 percent origination fee, which is used to offset the administrative cost of the Federal Stafford Loan Program.

Under the *subsidized* Federal Stafford Loan Program, repayment begins six months after your last enrollment on at least a half-time basis. Under the *unsubsidized* program, repayment of interest begins within thirty days from disbursement of the loan proceeds, and repayment of the principal begins six months after your last enrollment on at least a half-time basis. Some borrowers may choose to defer interest payments while they are in school. The accrued interest is added to the loan balance when the borrower begins repayment. There are several repayment options.

Federal Direct Loans. Some schools participate in the Department of Education's Direct Lending Program instead of offering Federal Stafford Loans. The two programs are essentially the same except that with the Direct Loans, schools themselves generate the loans with funds provided from the federal government. Terms and interest rates are virtually the same except that there are a few more repayment options with Federal Direct Loans.

Federal Perkins Loans. The Federal Perkins Loan is available to students demonstrating financial need and is administered directly by the school. Not all schools have these funds, and some may award them to undergraduates only. Eligibility is determined from the information you provide on the FAFSA. The school will notify you of your eligibility.

Eligible graduate students may borrow up to $6000 per year, up to a maximum of $40,000, including undergraduate borrowing (even if your previous Perkins Loans have been repaid). The interest rate for Federal Perkins Loans is 5 percent, and no interest accrues while you remain in school at least half-time. There are no guarantee, loan, or disbursement fees. Repayment begins nine months after your last enrollment on at least a half-time basis and may extend over a maximum of ten years with no prepayment penalty.

Deferring Your Federal Loan Repayments. If you borrowed under the Federal Stafford Loan Program or the Federal Perkins Loan Program for previous undergraduate or graduate study, your repayments may be deferred when you return to graduate school, depending on when you borrowed and under which program.

There are other deferment options available if you are temporarily unable to repay your loan. Information about these deferments is provided at your entrance and exit interviews. If you believe you are eligible for a deferment of your loan repayments, you must contact your lender to complete a deferment form. The deferment must be filed prior to the time your repayment is due, and it must be refiled when it expires if you remain eligible for deferment at that time.

Supplemental (Private) Loans

Many lending institutions offer supplemental loan programs and other financing plans, such as the ones described below, to students seeking additional assistance in meeting their educational expenses. Some loan programs target all types of graduate students; others are designed specifically for business, law, or medical students. In addition, you can use private loans not specifically designed for education to help finance your graduate degree.

If you are considering borrowing through a supplemental or private loan program, you should carefully consider the terms and be sure to "read the fine print." Check with the program sponsor for the most current terms that will be applicable to the amounts you intend to borrow for graduate study. Most supplemental loan programs for graduate study offer unsubsidized, credit-based loans. In general, a credit-ready borrower is one who has a satisfactory credit history or no credit history at all. A creditworthy borrower generally must pass a credit test to be eligible to borrow or act as a cosigner for the loan funds.

Many supplemental loan programs have a minimum annual loan limit and a maximum annual loan limit. Some offer amounts equal to the cost of attendance minus any other aid you will receive for graduate study. If you are planning to borrow for several years of graduate study, consider whether there is a cumulative or aggregate limit on the amount you may borrow. Often this cumulative or aggregate limit will include any amounts you borrowed and have not repaid for undergraduate or previous graduate study.

The combination of the annual interest rate, loan fees, and the repayment terms you choose will determine how much you will repay over time. Compare these features in combination before you decide which loan program to use. Some loans offer interest rates that are adjusted monthly, some quarterly, some annually. Some offer interest rates that are lower during the in-school, grace, and deferment periods, and then increase when you begin repayment. Most programs include a loan "origination" fee, which is usually deducted from the principal amount you receive when the loan is disbursed, and must be repaid along with the interest and other principal when you graduate, withdraw from school, or drop below half-time study. Sometimes the loan fees are reduced if you borrow with a qualified cosigner. Some programs allow you to defer interest and/or principal payments while you are enrolled in graduate school. Many programs allow you to capitalize your interest payments; the interest due on your loan is added to the outstanding balance of your loan, so you don't have to repay immediately, but this increases the amount you owe. Other programs allow you to pay the interest as you go, which will reduce the amount you later have to repay.

Some examples of supplemental programs follow.

CitiAssist Loans. Offered by Citibank, these no-fee loans help graduate students fill the gap between the financial aid they receive and the money they need for school. Visit www.studentloan.com for more loan information from Citibank.

EXCEL Loan. This program, sponsored by Nellie Mae, is designed for students who are not ready to borrow on their own and wish to borrow with a creditworthy cosigner. Visit www.nelliemae.com for more information.

Key Alternative Loan. This loan can bridge the gap between education costs and traditional funding. Visit www.keybank.com for more information.

Graduate Access Loan. Sponsored by the Access Group, this is for graduate students enrolled at least half-time. The Web site is www.accessgroup.com.

Signature Student Loan. A loan program for students who are enrolled at least half-time, this is sponsored by Sallie Mae. Visit www.salliemae.com for more information.

Remember that these are generalized statements about financial assistance at the graduate level. Because each institution allots its aid differently, you should communicate directly with the school and the specific department of interest to you. It is not unusual, for example, to find that an endowment vested within a specific department supports one or more fellowships. You may fit its requirements and specifications precisely.

Applying for Need-Based Financial Aid

Schools that award federal and institutional financial assistance based on need will require you to complete the FAFSA and, in some cases, an institutional financial aid application.

If you are applying for federal student assistance, you **must** complete the FAFSA. A service of the U.S. Department of Education, it is free to all applicants. You must send the FAFSA to the address listed in the FAFSA instructions or you can apply online at http://www.fafsa.ed.gov.

After your FAFSA information has been processed, you will receive a Student Aid Report (SAR). If you are an entering student, you may want to make copies of the SAR and send them to the school(s) to which you are applying. If you are a continuing student, you should make a copy of the SAR and forward the original document to the school you are attending.

Follow the instructions on the SAR if your situation changes and you need to correct information reported on your original application.

If you would like more information on federal student financial aid, visit the FAFSA Web site or request *The Student Guide 2003–2004* from the following address: Federal Student Aid Information Center, P.O. Box 84, Washington, DC 20044.

The U.S. Department of Education also has a toll-free number for questions concerning federal student aid programs. The number is 1-800-4-FED AID (1-800-433-3243). If you are hearing impaired, call toll-free, 1-800-730-8913.

Accreditation and Accrediting Agencies

Colleges and universities in the United States, and their individual academic and professional programs, are accredited by nongovernmental agencies concerned with monitoring the quality of education in this country. Agencies with both regional and national jurisdictions grant accreditation to institutions as a whole, while specialized bodies acting on a nationwide basis—often national professional associations—grant accreditation to departments and programs in specific fields.

Institutional and specialized accrediting agencies share the same basic concerns: the purpose an academic unit—whether university or program—has set for itself and how well it fulfills that purpose, the adequacy of its financial and other resources, the quality of its academic offerings, and the level of services it provides. Agencies that grant institutional accreditation take a broader view, of course, and examine university-wide or college-wide services that a specialized agency may not concern itself with.

Both types of agencies follow the same general procedures when considering an application for accreditation. The academic unit prepares a self-evaluation, which focuses on the concerns mentioned above and includes an assessment of both its strengths and weaknesses; a team of representatives of the accrediting body reviews this evaluation, visits the campus, and makes its own report; and finally, the accrediting body makes a decision on the application. Often, even when accreditation is granted, the agency makes a recommendation regarding how the institution or program can improve. All institutions and programs are reviewed every few years to determine whether they continue to meet established standards; if they do not, they may lose their accreditation.

Accrediting agencies themselves are reviewed and evaluated periodically by the U.S. Department of Education and the Council for Higher Education Accreditation (CHEA). Agencies recognized adhere to certain standards and practices, and their authority in matters of accreditation is widely accepted in the educational community.

This does not mean, however, that accreditation is a simple matter, either for schools wishing to become accredited or for students deciding where to apply. Indeed, in certain fields the very meaning and methods of accreditation are the subject of a good deal of debate. **Those who are applying to graduate school should be aware of the safeguards provided by regional accreditation, especially in terms of degree acceptance and institutional longevity. Indeed, many institutions that offer graduate study will accept only those applicants whose undergraduate degree is from a regionally accredited institution.** (NOTE: Most institutions profiled in the *Decision Guides* are regionally accredited.) Beyond this, applicants should understand the role that specialized accreditation plays in their field, as this varies considerably from one discipline to another. In certain professional fields, it is necessary to have graduated from a program that is accredited in order to be eligible for a license to practice, and, in some fields, the federal government also makes this a hiring requirement.

Institutions and programs that present themselves for accreditation are sometimes granted the status of candidate for accreditation, or what is known as "preaccreditation." This may happen, for example, when an academic unit is too new to have met all the requirements for accreditation. Such status signifies initial recognition and indicates that the school or program in question is working to fulfill all requirements; it does not, however, guarantee that accreditation will be granted.

Readers are advised to contact agencies directly for answers to their questions about accreditation. The names and addresses of all agencies recognized by the U.S. Department of Education and the Council for Higher Education Accreditation are listed below.

Institutional Accrediting Agencies—Regional

MIDDLE STATES ASSOCIATION OF COLLEGES AND SCHOOLS

Accredits institutions in Delaware, District of Columbia, Maryland, New Jersey, New York, Pennsylvania, Puerto Rico, and the Virgin Islands.

Jean Avnet Morse, Executive Director
Commission on Higher Education
3624 Market Street
Philadelphia, Pennsylvania 19104-2680
Telephone: 215-662-5606
Fax: 215-662-5501
E-mail: jamorse@msache.org
World Wide Web: http://www.msache.org

NEW ENGLAND ASSOCIATION OF SCHOOLS AND COLLEGES

Accredits institutions in Connecticut, Maine, Massachusetts, New Hampshire, Rhode Island, and Vermont.

Charles M. Cook, Director
Commission on Institutions of Higher Education
209 Burlington Road
Bedford, Massachusetts 01730-1433
Telephone: 781-271-0022
Fax: 781-271-0950
E-mail: CIHE@neasc.org
World Wide Web: http://www.neasc.org

NORTH CENTRAL ASSOCIATION OF COLLEGES AND SCHOOLS

Accredits institutions in Arizona, Arkansas, Colorado, Illinois, Indiana, Iowa, Kansas, Michigan, Minnesota, Missouri, Nebraska, New Mexico, North Dakota, Ohio, Oklahoma, South Dakota, West Virginia, Wisconsin, and Wyoming.

Steven D. Crow, Executive Director
The Higher Learning Commission
30 North LaSalle, Suite 2400
Chicago, Illinois 60602-2504
Telephone: 312-263-0456
Fax: 312-263-7462
E-mail: scrow@hlcommission.org
World Wide Web: http://www.ncahigherlearningcommission.org

NORTHWEST ASSOCIATION OF SCHOOLS AND COLLEGES

Accredits institutions in Alaska, Idaho, Montana, Nevada, Oregon, Utah, and Washington.

Sandra E. Elman, Executive Director
Commission on Colleges and Universities
8060 165th Avenue, NE, Suite 100
Redmond, Washington 98052
Telephone: 425-558-4224
Fax: 425-376-0596
E-mail: pjarnold@nwccu.org
World Wide Web: http://www.nwccu.org

SOUTHERN ASSOCIATION OF COLLEGES AND SCHOOLS

Accredits institutions in Alabama, Florida, Georgia, Kentucky, Louisiana, Mississippi, North Carolina, South Carolina, Tennessee, Texas, and Virginia.

James T. Rogers, Executive Director
Commission on Colleges
1866 Southern Lane
Decatur, Georgia 30033
Telephone: 404-679-4500
Fax: 404-679-4528
E-mail: jrogers@sacscoc.org
World Wide Web: http://www.sacscoc.org

WESTERN ASSOCIATION OF SCHOOLS AND COLLEGES

Accredits institutions in California, Guam, and Hawaii.

Ralph A. Wolff, Executive Director
The Senior College Commission
985 Atlantic Avenue, Suite 100
Alameda, California 94501
Telephone: 510-748-9001
Fax: 510-748-9797
E-mail: rwolff@wascsenior.org
World Wide Web: http://www.wascweb.org

Institutional Accrediting Agencies—Other

ACCREDITING COUNCIL FOR INDEPENDENT COLLEGES AND SCHOOLS

Dr. Steven A. Eggland, Executive Director
750 First Street, NE, Suite 980
Washington, D.C. 20002-4241
Telephone: 202-336-6780
Fax: 202-842-2593
E-mail: steve@acics.org
World Wide Web: http://www.acics.org

DISTANCE EDUCATION AND TRAINING COUNCIL

Michael P. Lambert, Executive Secretary
1601 Eighteenth Street, NW
Washington, D.C. 20009
Telephone: 202-234-5100
Fax: 202-332-1386
E-mail: detc@detc.org
World Wide Web: http://www.detc.org

Specialized Accrediting Agencies

LIBRARY

Ann L. O'Neill, Director
Office for Accreditation
American Library Association
50 East Huron Street
Chicago, Illinois 60611
Telephone: 800-545-2433 Ext.2435
Fax: 312-280-2433
E-mail: aoneill@ala.org
World Wide Web: http://www.ala.org/education

PLANNING

Beatrice Clupper, Executive Director
American Institute of Certified Planners/Association of Collegiate Schools of Planning
Merle Hay Tower, Suite 302
3800 Merle Hay Road
Des Moines, Iowa 50310
Telephone: 515-252-0729/0733
Fax: 515-252-7404
E-mail: fi_pab@netins.net
World Wide Web: http://netins.net/showcase/pab_fi66

PUBLIC AFFAIRS AND ADMINISTRATION

Laurel L. McFarland, Managing Director
Commission on Peer Review and Accreditation
National Association of Schools of Public Affairs and Administration
1120 G Street, NW, Suite 730
Washington, D.C. 20005
Telephone: 202-628-8965
Fax: 202-626-4978
E-mail: naspaa@naspaa.org
World Wide Web: http://www.naspaa.org

SOCIAL WORK

Ann Johnson, Interim Director
Division of Standards and Accreditation
Council on Social Work Education
1725 Duke Street, Suite 500
Alexandria, Virginia 22314
Telephone: 703-683-8080 Ext. 205
Fax: 703-739-9048
E-mail: ajohnson@cswe.org
World Wide Web: http://www.cswe.org

Graduate Programs in Library and Information Studies

INFORMATION STUDIES

■ THE CATHOLIC UNIVERSITY OF AMERICA

School of Library and Information Science, Washington, DC 20064

AWARDS MSLS, JD/MSLS, MSLS/MA, MSLS/MS. Part-time and evening/weekend programs available. Postbaccalaureate distance learning degree programs offered (minimal on-campus study).

Faculty: 7 full-time (all women), 18 part-time/adjunct (11 women).
Students: 25 full-time (22 women), 175 part-time (134 women); includes 28 minority (23 African Americans, 3 Asian Americans or Pacific Islanders, 2 Hispanic Americans), 10 international. Average age 38. 111 applicants, 77% accepted, 52 enrolled. In 2001, 63 degrees awarded.
Degree requirements: For master's, comprehensive exam.
Entrance requirements: For master's, GRE General Test. *Application deadline:* For fall admission, 7/1 (priority date); for spring admission, 11/1. Applications are processed on a rolling basis. *Application fee:* $55. Electronic applications accepted.
Expenses: Contact institution.
Financial support: Fellowships, research assistantships, career-related internships or fieldwork, Federal Work-Study, institutionally sponsored loans, tuition waivers (full and partial), and unspecified assistantships available. Support available to part-time students. Financial award application deadline: 2/1.
Faculty research: Information transfer, archives and manuscripts, legal libraries, information seeking, information storage and retrieval, special collections, information systems.
Dr. Peter Liebscher, Dean, 202-319-5085, *E-mail:* liebscher@cua.edu.

■ CENTRAL CONNECTICUT STATE UNIVERSITY

School of Graduate Studies, School of Arts and Sciences, Department of Information Design, New Britain, CT 06050-4010

AWARDS Graphic information design (MA).

Faculty: 4 full-time (3 women), 2 part-time/adjunct (1 woman).
Students: 6 full-time (4 women), 2 part-time (1 woman); includes 1 minority (Asian American or Pacific Islander). Average age 34. 3 applicants, 100% accepted.
Entrance requirements: For master's, minimum GPA of 2.7. *Application deadline:* For fall admission, 8/10 (priority date); for spring admission, 12/10. Applications are processed on a rolling basis. *Application fee:* $40.
Expenses: Tuition, state resident: full-time $2,772; part-time $245 per credit. Tuition, nonresident: full-time $7,726; part-time $245 per credit. Required fees: $2,102. Tuition and fees vary according to course level and degree level.
Financial support: Application deadline: 3/15.
Susan Vial, Chair, 862-832-2623.

■ CENTRAL MISSOURI STATE UNIVERSITY

School of Graduate Studies, Department of Library Science and Information Services, Warrensburg, MO 64093

AWARDS Human services/learning resources (Ed S); library information technology (MS); library science and information services (MS). Part-time programs available.

Faculty: 2 full-time (1 woman).
Students: 7 full-time (all women), 72 part-time (70 women); includes 3 minority (2 African Americans, 1 Hispanic American), 1 international. Average age 37. 9 applicants, 89% accepted. In 2001, 10 degrees awarded.
Degree requirements: For master's and Ed S, thesis or alternative.
Entrance requirements: For master's, minimum GPA of 2.75, interview, 2 years of teaching experience; for Ed S, minimum GPA of 3.25, master's degree, teaching certificate. *Application deadline:* Applications are processed on a rolling basis. *Application fee:* $25 ($50 for international students).
Expenses: Tuition, area resident: Full-time $4,200; part-time $175 per credit hour. Tuition, nonresident: full-time $8,352; part-time $348 per credit hour.
Financial support: In 2001–02, 1 research assistantship with tuition reimbursement (averaging $4,000 per year), 2 teaching assistantships with partial tuition reimbursements (averaging $5,875 per year) were awarded. Federal Work-Study, scholarships/grants, unspecified assistantships, and administrative assistantship also available. Support available to part-time students. Financial award application deadline: 3/1; financial award applicants required to submit FAFSA.
Faculty research: Library services for distance learners, information seeking in context, entrepreneurial library management, library services for children, library financial management.
Dr. Linda Lillard, Chair, 660-543-8633, *Fax:* 660-543-8001. *Web site:* http://www.cmsu.edu/

■ CLARK ATLANTA UNIVERSITY

School of Library and Information Studies, Atlanta, GA 30314

AWARDS MSLS, SLS. Part-time and evening/weekend programs available.

Degree requirements: For master's, one foreign language, thesis optional; for SLS, one foreign language, thesis.
Entrance requirements: For master's, GRE, TOEFL.
Faculty research: Comparative/international librarianship, African American bibliography, school library media services.

■ COLLEGE OF ST. CATHERINE

Graduate Program, Program in Library and Information Science, St. Paul, MN 55105-1789

AWARDS MA. Part-time and evening/weekend programs available.

Faculty: 3 full-time (all women).
Students: 107 full-time (91 women), 93 part-time (79 women); includes 10 minority (1 African American, 5 Asian Americans or Pacific Islanders, 3 Hispanic Americans, 1 Native American). Average age 37. 88 applicants, 82% accepted, 59 enrolled.
Degree requirements: For master's, microcomputer competency.
Entrance requirements: For master's, Michigan English Language Assessment Battery or TOEFL, minimum GPA of 3.2 or GRE. *Application deadline:* For fall admission, 2/15. *Application fee:* $25.
Expenses: Tuition: Part-time $375 per credit. Required fees: $60; $60 per year. Tuition and fees vary according to program.
Financial support: In 2001–02, 39 students received support. Institutionally sponsored loans available. Support available to part-time students. Financial award application deadline: 4/1; financial award applicants required to submit FAFSA.
Mary Wagner, Director, 651-690-6802.
Application contact: 651-690-6505.

■ DOMINICAN UNIVERSITY

Graduate School of Library and Information Science, River Forest, IL 60305-1099

AWARDS MLIS, MSMIS, CSS, MBA/MLIS, MLIS/M Div, MLIS/MA, MLIS/MM. Part-time and evening/weekend programs available. Postbaccalaureate distance learning degree programs offered (minimal on-campus study).

Entrance requirements: For master's, TOEFL, minimum GPA of 3.0 or GRE General Test or MAT.
Expenses: Contact institution.
Faculty research: Productivity and the information environment, bibliometrics,

library history, subject access, library materials and services for children. *Web site:* http://www.dom.edu/

■ DREXEL UNIVERSITY

Graduate School, College of Information Science and Technology, Program in Information Systems, Philadelphia, PA 19104-2875

AWARDS MSIS. Part-time and evening/weekend programs available.

Faculty: 27 full-time (13 women), 11 part-time/adjunct (2 women).
Students: 49 full-time (23 women), 259 part-time (91 women); includes 49 minority (18 African Americans, 29 Asian Americans or Pacific Islanders, 2 Hispanic Americans), 57 international. Average age 32. 172 applicants, 72% accepted, 61 enrolled. In 2001, 120 degrees awarded. *Application deadline:* For fall admission, 8/21. Applications are processed on a rolling basis. *Application fee:* $50. Electronic applications accepted.
Expenses: Tuition: Full-time $20,088; part-time $558 per credit. Required fees: $78 per term. One-time fee: $200. Tuition and fees vary according to course load, degree level and program.
Financial support: Research assistantships, teaching assistantships, career-related internships or fieldwork, Federal Work-Study, institutionally sponsored loans, tuition waivers (partial), and unspecified assistantships available. Support available to part-time students. Financial award application deadline: 2/1.
Application contact: Director of Graduate Admissions, 215-895-6700, *Fax:* 215-895-5939, *E-mail:* enroll@drexel.edu.

■ EMPORIA STATE UNIVERSITY

School of Graduate Studies, School of Library and Information Management, Emporia, KS 66801-5087

AWARDS Library and information science (PhD); library science (MLS). Part-time programs available.

Faculty: 19 full-time (11 women), 41 part-time/adjunct (30 women).
Students: 48 full-time (37 women), 219 part-time (187 women); includes 8 minority (2 African Americans, 2 Asian Americans or Pacific Islanders, 4 Hispanic Americans), 2 international. 123 applicants, 85% accepted. In 2001, 78 master's, 3 doctorates awarded.
Degree requirements: For master's, comprehensive exam or thesis; for doctorate, thesis/dissertation.
Entrance requirements: For master's, GRE General Test, TOEFL; for doctorate, GRE General Test, TOEFL, interview, minimum graduate GPA of 3.5. *Application deadline:* For fall admission, 8/15 (priority date). Applications are processed on a rolling basis. *Application fee:* $30 ($75 for international students). Electronic applications accepted.
Expenses: Tuition, state resident: full-time $2,632; part-time $119 per credit hour. Tuition, nonresident: full-time $6,734; part-time $290 per credit hour.
Financial support: In 2001–02, 1 research assistantship (averaging $5,632 per year), 17 teaching assistantships with full tuition reimbursements (averaging $5,273 per year) were awarded. Career-related internships or fieldwork, Federal Work-Study, institutionally sponsored loans, health care benefits, and unspecified assistantships also available. Financial award application deadline: 3/15; financial award applicants required to submit FAFSA.
Faculty research: Information management in corporate environment.
Dr. Robert J. Grover, Dean, 800-552-4770, *Fax:* 620-341-5233, *E-mail:* groverro@emporia.edu.
Application contact: Daniel Rowland, Director of Communications, 800-552-4770, *Fax:* 620-341-5233, *E-mail:* sliminfo@emporia.edu. *Web site:* http://slim.emporia.edu/

Find an in-depth description at www.petersons.com/gradchannel.

■ FLORIDA STATE UNIVERSITY

Graduate Studies, School of Information Studies, Tallahassee, FL 32306

AWARDS Information studies (PhD); library and information studies (MS, PhD, Specialist). Part-time and evening/weekend programs available. Postbaccalaureate distance learning degree programs offered (minimal on-campus study).

Faculty: 18 full-time (8 women), 7 part-time/adjunct (4 women).
Students: 171 full-time, 386 part-time. Average age 38. 270 applicants, 88% accepted. In 2001, 92 master's, 9 doctorates, 11 other advanced degrees awarded.
Degree requirements: For doctorate, thesis/dissertation.
Entrance requirements: For master's, GRE General Test, minimum GPA of 3.0; for doctorate, GRE General Test, minimum graduate GPA of 3.5. *Application deadline:* For fall admission, 7/16 (priority date). *Application fee:* $20.
Expenses: Tuition, state resident: part-time $163 per credit hour. Tuition, nonresident: part-time $570 per credit hour. Tuition and fees vary according to program.
Financial support: In 2001–02, 57 students received support, including 14 fellowships with full tuition reimbursements available, 45 research assistantships with full tuition reimbursements available, 19 teaching assistantships with full tuition reimbursements available; career-related internships or fieldwork, Federal Work-Study, scholarships/grants, and unspecified assistantships also available. Financial award application deadline: 4/1; financial award applicants required to submit FAFSA.
Faculty research: Community information service, needs assessment, information policy, usability analysis, human information behavior.
Dr. Jane B. Robbins, Dean, 850-644-5775, *Fax:* 850-644-9763, *E-mail:* robbins@lis.fsu.edu.
Application contact: Marion Davis, Program Assistant, 850-644-8103, *Fax:* 850-644-9763, *E-mail:* grad@slis-two.lis.fsu.edu. *Web site:* http://www.fsu.edu/~lis/

Find an in-depth description at www.petersons.com/gradchannel.

■ INDIANA UNIVERSITY–PURDUE UNIVERSITY INDIANAPOLIS

School of Library and Information Science, Indianapolis, IN 46202-2896

AWARDS MIS, MLS, M PI/MIS. Part-time and evening/weekend programs available.

Faculty: 1 (woman) full-time.
Students: 24 full-time (19 women), 155 part-time (120 women); includes 4 minority (all African Americans), 1 international. Average age 37. In 2001, 67 degrees awarded.
Entrance requirements: For master's, GRE General Test, TOEFL, English language proficiency. *Application deadline:* For fall admission, 5/15 (priority date). Applications are processed on a rolling basis. *Application fee:* $45 ($55 for international students).
Expenses: Tuition, state resident: full-time $4,480; part-time $187 per credit. Tuition, nonresident: full-time $12,926; part-time $539 per credit. Required fees: $177.
Financial support: Career-related internships or fieldwork available.
Dr. Blaise Cronin, Dean, 317-278-2375.
Application contact: Dr. Debora Shaw, Associate Dean, 317-278-2375, *Fax:* 317-278-1807, *E-mail:* shawd@indiana.edu. *Web site:* http://www.slis.indiana.edu/

■ LONG ISLAND UNIVERSITY, C.W. POST CAMPUS

College of Information and Computer Science, Palmer School of Library and Information Science, Brookville, NY 11548-1300

AWARDS Archives (Certificate); information studies (PhD); library and information science (MS); records management (Certificate); schooll library media specialist (MS). Part-time and evening/weekend programs available. Postbaccalaureate distance learning degree programs offered (minimal on-campus study).

Faculty: 14 full-time (3 women), 30 part-time/adjunct (10 women).
Students: 72 full-time (37 women), 333 part-time (233 women). 133 applicants, 88% accepted. In 2001, 113 master's, 1 doctorate, 1 other advanced degree awarded.

Long Island University, C.W. Post Campus (continued)
Degree requirements: For master's, internship, thesis optional; for doctorate, thesis/dissertation, qualifying exam.
Entrance requirements: For master's, GRE or MAT, minimum undergraduate GPA of 3.0, resumé. *Application deadline:* For fall admission, 2/15; for spring admission, 10/15. *Application fee:* $30. Electronic applications accepted.
Expenses: Tuition: Full-time $10,296; part-time $572 per credit. Required fees: $380; $190 per semester.
Financial support: Fellowships, research assistantships, career-related internships or fieldwork, Federal Work-Study, institutionally sponsored loans, and tuition waivers (partial) available. Support available to part-time students. Financial award application deadline: 5/15; financial award applicants required to submit CSS PROFILE or FAFSA.
Faculty research: Information retrieval, digital libraries, scientometric and infometric studies, preservation/archiving and electronic records.
Dr. Michael E. D. Koening, Dean, 516-299-2866, *Fax:* 516-299-4168, *E-mail:* palmer@cwpost.liu.edu.
Application contact: Rosemary Chu, Graduate Admissions, 516-299-2866, *Fax:* 516-299-4168, *E-mail:* palmer@cwpost.liu.edu. *Web site:* http://www.liu.edu/palmer/

■ LOUISIANA STATE UNIVERSITY AND AGRICULTURAL AND MECHANICAL COLLEGE

Graduate School, School of Library and Information Science, Baton Rouge, LA 70803

AWARDS MLIS, CAS. Evening/weekend programs available.

Faculty: 9 full-time (5 women).
Students: 55 full-time (40 women), 109 part-time (99 women); includes 27 minority (23 African Americans, 2 Hispanic Americans, 2 Native Americans), 10 international. Average age 36. 64 applicants, 64% accepted, 25 enrolled. In 2001, 61 master's, 3 other advanced degrees awarded.
Degree requirements: For master's, thesis optional.
Entrance requirements: For master's, GRE General Test, minimum GPA of 3.0. *Application deadline:* For fall admission, 1/25 (priority date). Applications are processed on a rolling basis. *Application fee:* $25.
Expenses: Tuition, state resident: full-time $2,551. Tuition, nonresident: full-time $5,551. Required fees: $854. Part-time tuition and fees vary according to course load.
Financial support: In 2001–02, 16 students received support, including 11 research assistantships with partial tuition reimbursements available (averaging $8,588 per year), 2 teaching assistantships with partial tuition reimbursements available (averaging $10,338 per year); fellowships, career-related internships or fieldwork and unspecified assistantships also available. Support available to part-time students. Financial award applicants required to submit FAFSA.
Faculty research: Information retrieval, management, collection development, public libraries.
Dr. Beth M. Paskoff, Dean, 225-578-3158, *Fax:* 225-578-4581, *E-mail:* lspask@lsu.edu.
Application contact: Admissions Secretary, 225-578-3158. *Web site:* http://adam.slis.lsu.edu/

■ MANSFIELD UNIVERSITY OF PENNSYLVANIA

Graduate Studies, Program in School Library and Information Technologies, Mansfield, PA 16933

AWARDS MS.

Faculty: 1 (woman) full-time, 11 part-time/adjunct (10 women).
Students: 6 full-time, 68 part-time. Average age 34. In 2001, 9 degrees awarded.
Entrance requirements: For master's, minimum GPA of 3.0. *Application deadline:* Applications are processed on a rolling basis. *Application fee:* $25. Electronic applications accepted.
Expenses: Tuition, state resident: full-time $2,300; part-time $256 per credit. Tuition, nonresident: full-time $3,777; part-time $470 per credit. Required fees: $230.
Financial support: Application deadline: 5/1.
Dr. Larry Nesbit, Head, 670-662-4672.
Application contact: Dr. Doris Dorwant, Program Director, 570-662-4676, *E-mail:* ddorwant@mnsfld.edu.

■ METROPOLITAN STATE UNIVERSITY

College of Management, St. Paul, MN 55106-5000

AWARDS Finance (MBA); human resource management (MBA); information management (MMIS); international business (MBA); law enforcement (MPNA); management information systems (MBA); marketing (MBA); nonprofit management (MPNA); organizational studies (MBA); public administration (MPNA); purchasing management (MBA); systems management (MMIS). Part-time and evening/weekend programs available.

Degree requirements: For master's, computer language (MMIS), thesis optional.
Entrance requirements: For master's, GMAT (MBA), resumé.
Faculty research: Yugoslav economic system, workers' cooperatives, participative management and job enrichment, global business systems. *Web site:* http://www.metrostate.edu/

■ MONTANA STATE UNIVERSITY–BILLINGS

College of Business, Program in Information Processing and Communications, Billings, MT 59101-0298

AWARDS MSIPC.

Entrance requirements: For master's, GMAT or GRE, minimum GPA of 3.0 (undergraduate), 3.25 (graduate).
Expenses: Tuition, state resident: full-time $3,560; part-time $1,164 per semester. Tuition, nonresident: full-time $8,498; part-time $2,810 per semester.

■ NORTH CAROLINA CENTRAL UNIVERSITY

Division of Academic Affairs, School of Library and Information Sciences, Durham, NC 27707-3129

AWARDS MIS, MLS. Part-time and evening/weekend programs available.

Faculty: 7 full-time (3 women), 7 part-time/adjunct (2 women).
Students: 72 full-time (44 women), 128 part-time (107 women); includes 107 minority (83 African Americans, 18 Asian Americans or Pacific Islanders, 6 Native Americans). Average age 36. 79 applicants, 99% accepted. In 2001, 96 degrees awarded.
Degree requirements: For master's, one foreign language.
Entrance requirements: For master's, 90 hours in liberal arts, minimum B average. *Application deadline:* For fall admission, 8/1. *Application fee:* $30.
Expenses: Tuition, state resident: full-time $1,424. Tuition, nonresident: full-time $9,492. Required fees: $1,054.
Financial support: Fellowships, research assistantships, career-related internships or fieldwork, institutionally sponsored loans, and scholarships/grants available. Support available to part-time students. Financial award application deadline: 5/1.
Faculty research: African-American resources, planning and evaluation, analysis of economic and physical resources, geography of information, artificial intelligence.
Dr. Benjamin F. Speller, Dean, 919-560-6485, *Fax:* 919-560-6402, *E-mail:* bspeller@wpo.nccu.edu.

■ PRATT INSTITUTE

School of Information and Library Science, Brooklyn, NY 11205-3899

AWARDS MS, Adv C, JD/MS, MS/MS. Part-time and evening/weekend programs available.

Degree requirements: For master's, thesis.
Entrance requirements: For master's, TOEFL. Electronic applications accepted.
Expenses: Contact institution.

Faculty research: Development of urban libraries and information centers, medical and law librarianship, information management.

Find an in-depth description at www.petersons.com/gradchannel.

■ QUEENS COLLEGE OF THE CITY UNIVERSITY OF NEW YORK

Division of Graduate Studies, Social Science Division, Graduate School of Library and Information Studies, Flushing, NY 11367-1597

AWARDS MLS, AC. Part-time and evening/weekend programs available.

Faculty: 8 full-time (5 women).
Students: 23 full-time (17 women), 364 part-time (267 women). 201 applicants, 95% accepted. In 2001, 146 degrees awarded.
Degree requirements: For master's, thesis; for AC, thesis optional.
Entrance requirements: For master's, TOEFL, minimum GPA of 3.0; for AC, TOEFL, master's degree or equivalent. *Application deadline:* For fall admission, 4/1; for spring admission, 11/1. Applications are processed on a rolling basis. *Application fee:* $40.
Expenses: Tuition, state resident: full-time $2,175; part-time $185 per credit. Tuition, nonresident: full-time $3,800; part-time $320 per credit. Required fees: $114; $57 per semester. Tuition and fees vary according to course load.
Financial support: Career-related internships or fieldwork, Federal Work-Study, institutionally sponsored loans, and tuition waivers (partial) available. Support available to part-time students. Financial award application deadline: 4/1; financial award applicants required to submit FAFSA.
Faculty research: Multimedia and video studies, ethnicity and librarianship, information science and computer applications.
Dr. Marianne Cooper, Director and Chair, 718-997-3790, *E-mail:* marianne_cooper@qc.edu.
Application contact: Dr. Karen Smith, Graduate Adviser, 718-997-3790, *E-mail:* karen_smith@qc.edu.

■ RUTGERS, THE STATE UNIVERSITY OF NEW JERSEY, NEW BRUNSWICK

Graduate School, Program in Communication and Information Studies, New Brunswick, NJ 08901-1281

AWARDS PhD. Part-time programs available.

Degree requirements: For doctorate, thesis/dissertation, qualifying exams.
Entrance requirements: For doctorate, GRE General Test.
Faculty research: Information science, information policy, communication, media studies, library studies. *Web site:* http://www.scils.rutgers.edu/

■ RUTGERS, THE STATE UNIVERSITY OF NEW JERSEY, NEW BRUNSWICK

School of Communication, Information and Library Studies, Program in Communication and Information Studies, New Brunswick, NJ 08901-1281

AWARDS MCIS. Part-time programs available.

Degree requirements: For master's, thesis optional.
Entrance requirements: For master's, GRE General Test, TOEFL. Electronic applications accepted.
Faculty research: Communication processes and systems, information process and systems, human information and communication behavior.

■ ST. JOHN'S UNIVERSITY

St. John's College of Liberal Arts and Sciences, Division of Library and Information Science, Jamaica, NY 11439

AWARDS Library and information science (MLS, Adv C);). Part-time and evening/weekend programs available.

Faculty: 5 full-time (all women), 6 part-time/adjunct (2 women).
Students: 10 full-time (7 women), 64 part-time (49 women); includes 11 minority (5 African Americans, 3 Asian Americans or Pacific Islanders, 3 Hispanic Americans), 11 international. Average age 37. 50 applicants, 76% accepted, 21 enrolled. In 2001, 25 degrees awarded.
Degree requirements: For master's, comprehensive exam.
Entrance requirements: For master's, interview, minimum GPA of 3.0. *Application deadline:* Applications are processed on a rolling basis. *Application fee:* $40.
Expenses: Contact institution.
Financial support: Research assistantships with full tuition reimbursements, career-related internships or fieldwork and scholarships/grants available. Support available to part-time students. Financial award application deadline: 3/1; financial award applicants required to submit FAFSA.
Faculty research: On-line database management, public library patronage, medieval monastic libraries and archives, children's literature, indexing.
Dr. Sherry Vellucci, Acting Director, 718-990-6735.
Application contact: Matthew Whelan, Director, Office of Admission, 718-990-2000, *Fax:* 718-990-2096, *E-mail:* admissions@stjohns.edu. *Web site:* http://www.stjohns.edu/

■ SAN JOSE STATE UNIVERSITY

Graduate Studies, Graduate Studies Program, School of Library and Information Science, San Jose, CA 95192-0001

AWARDS MLIS. Part-time and evening/weekend programs available.

Faculty: 6 full-time (3 women), 4 part-time/adjunct (3 women).
Students: 87 full-time (66 women), 341 part-time (269 women); includes 83 minority (15 African Americans, 39 Asian Americans or Pacific Islanders, 27 Hispanic Americans, 2 Native Americans), 5 international. Average age 38. 352 applicants, 77% accepted. In 2001, 211 degrees awarded.
Degree requirements: For master's, comprehensive exam.
Entrance requirements: For master's, minimum GPA of 3.0. *Application deadline:* For fall admission, 6/29; for spring admission, 11/30. Applications are processed on a rolling basis. *Application fee:* $59. Electronic applications accepted.
Expenses: Tuition, nonresident: part-time $246 per unit. Required fees: $678 per semester. Tuition and fees vary according to course load.
Financial support: In 2001–02, 4 fellowships, 4 teaching assistantships were awarded. Career-related internships or fieldwork, Federal Work-Study, and institutionally sponsored loans also available. Support available to part-time students. Financial award application deadline: 8/20; financial award applicants required to submit FAFSA.
Faculty research: Evaluation of information services online, search strategy, organizational behavior.
Dr. Blanche Woolls, Director, 408-924-2491, *Fax:* 408-924-2476.

■ SIMMONS COLLEGE

Graduate School of Library and Information Science, Boston, MA 02115

AWARDS Archives management (MS); competitive intelligence (MS, Certificate); library and information science (DA); school library media specialist (MS, Certificate). MS/DA and MS/MA offered jointly with Department of History. Part-time and evening/weekend programs available.

Faculty: 17 full-time (8 women), 29 part-time/adjunct (20 women).
Students: 550. Average age 34. 307 applicants, 70% accepted, 141 enrolled. In 2001, 374 master's, 3 doctorates awarded.
Degree requirements: For master's, technology competency.
Entrance requirements: For master's, GRE General Test or minimum GPA of 3.0; interview; for doctorate, GRE General Test or MAT, interview. *Application deadline:* For fall admission, 7/1 (priority

Simmons College (continued)
date); for spring admission, 11/1. Applications are processed on a rolling basis. *Application fee:* $35. Electronic applications accepted.
Financial support: In 2001–02, 462 students received support, including 4 research assistantships (averaging $18,900 per year); teaching assistantships, career-related internships or fieldwork, Federal Work-Study, institutionally sponsored loans, scholarships/grants, and tuition waivers (full and partial) also available. Support available to part-time students. Financial award application deadline: 3/1; financial award applicants required to submit FAFSA.
Faculty research: Optical technology, visual communications, database management, information policy.
Dr. James Matarazzo, Dean, 617-521-2806, *Fax:* 617-521-3192, *E-mail:* matarazz@simmons.edu.
Application contact: Judith J. Beal, Director of Admissions, 617-521-2141, *Fax:* 617-521-3045, *E-mail:* judy.beal@simmons.edu. *Web site:* http://www.simmons.edu/graduate/gslis/

Find an in-depth description at www.petersons.com/gradchannel.

■ SOUTHERN CONNECTICUT STATE UNIVERSITY

School of Graduate Studies, School of Communication, Information and Library Science, Department of Library Science and Instructional Technology, New Haven, CT 06515-1355

AWARDS Instructional technology (MS); library science (MLS); library/information studies (Diploma). Part-time and evening/weekend programs available.

Faculty: 6 full-time (4 women).
Students: 27 full-time (23 women), 175 part-time (149 women); includes 6 minority (5 African Americans, 1 Hispanic American), 1 international. 244 applicants, 32% accepted. In 2001, 76 master's, 2 other advanced degrees awarded.
Degree requirements: For master's and Diploma, thesis or alternative.
Entrance requirements: For master's, GRE General Test, interview, minimum QPA of 2.7, introductory computer science course; for Diploma, master's degree in library science or information science. *Application deadline:* For fall admission, 7/15 (priority date). Applications are processed on a rolling basis. *Application fee:* $40.
Financial support: Research assistantships available. Financial award application deadline: 4/15; financial award applicants required to submit FAFSA.
Nancy Disbrow, Chairperson, 203-392-5781, *Fax:* 203-392-5780, *E-mail:* disbrow@southernct.edu.

■ SYRACUSE UNIVERSITY

Graduate School, School of Information Studies, Information Management Program, Syracuse, NY 13244-0003

AWARDS MS, JD/MS. Part-time and evening/weekend programs available. Postbaccalaureate distance learning degree programs offered (minimal on-campus study).

Faculty: 33 full-time (12 women), 42 part-time/adjunct (12 women).
Students: 45 full-time (18 women), 152 part-time (67 women); includes 14 minority (9 African Americans, 4 Hispanic Americans, 1 Native American), 99 international. Average age 34. In 2001, 129 degrees awarded.
Entrance requirements: For master's, GRE General Test. *Application deadline:* For fall admission, 2/15 (priority date); for spring admission, 11/1 (priority date). *Application fee:* $50. Electronic applications accepted.
Expenses: Tuition: Full-time $15,528; part-time $647 per credit. Required fees: $420; $38 per term. Tuition and fees vary according to program.

Find an in-depth description at www.petersons.com/gradchannel.

■ SYRACUSE UNIVERSITY

Graduate School, School of Information Studies, Information Transfer Program, Syracuse, NY 13244-0003

AWARDS PhD.

Faculty: 33 full-time (12 women), 42 part-time/adjunct (12 women).
Students: 24 full-time (13 women), 16 part-time (8 women), 21 international. Average age 38. In 2001, 1 degree awarded.
Degree requirements: For doctorate, thesis/dissertation.
Entrance requirements: For doctorate, GRE General Test. *Application deadline:* For fall admission, 2/15 (priority date); for spring admission, 11/1 (priority date). *Application fee:* $50. Electronic applications accepted.
Expenses: Tuition: Full-time $15,528; part-time $647 per credit. Required fees: $420; $38 per term. Tuition and fees vary according to program.

Find an in-depth description at www.petersons.com/gradchannel.

■ UNIVERSITY AT BUFFALO, THE STATE UNIVERSITY OF NEW YORK

Graduate School, School of Informatics, Department of Library and Information Studies, Buffalo, NY 14260

AWARDS MLS, PhD, Certificate. Part-time and evening/weekend programs available.

Faculty: 9 full-time (4 women), 1 part-time/adjunct (0 women).
Students: 113 full-time (86 women), 161 part-time (131 women); includes 17 minority (8 African Americans, 6 Asian Americans or Pacific Islanders, 2 Hispanic Americans, 1 Native American), 11 international. Average age 34. 109 applicants, 86% accepted. In 2001, 115 degrees awarded.
Degree requirements: For master's, thesis optional; for Certificate, thesis.
Entrance requirements: For master's, minimum GPA of 3.0. *Application deadline:* For fall admission, 4/1 (priority date); for spring admission, 10/15 (priority date). Applications are processed on a rolling basis. *Application fee:* $35. Electronic applications accepted.
Expenses: Tuition, state resident: full-time $6,118. Tuition, nonresident: full-time $9,434.
Financial support: In 2001–02, 5 fellowships (averaging $10,000 per year), 2 research assistantships with full tuition reimbursements (averaging $5,000 per year) were awarded. Teaching assistantships, career-related internships or fieldwork, Federal Work-Study, institutionally sponsored loans, tuition waivers (full and partial), and unspecified assistantships also available. Support available to part-time students. Financial award application deadline: 3/1; financial award applicants required to submit FAFSA.
Faculty research: Information user behavior, storage and information retrieval, digital libraries, information management services to information users. *Total annual research expenditures:* $202,000.
Dr. Judith Robinson, Chair, 716-645-2412, *Fax:* 716-645-3775, *E-mail:* ub-lis@buffalo.edu.
Application contact: Carolynn Krupp, Student Services Coordinator, 716-645-2412 Ext. 1170, *Fax:* 716-645-3775, *E-mail:* cjk2@buffalo.edu. *Web site:* http://www.informatics.buffalo.edu/dlis/

■ THE UNIVERSITY OF ALABAMA

Graduate School, College of Communication and Information Sciences, School of Library and Information Studies, Tuscaloosa, AL 35487

AWARDS Book arts (MFA); library and information studies (MLIS, PhD, Ed S).

Faculty: 7 full-time (3 women), 2 part-time/adjunct (1 woman).
Students: 54 full-time (40 women), 118 part-time (103 women); includes 17 minority (13 African Americans, 2 Asian Americans or Pacific Islanders, 1 Hispanic American, 1 Native American). Average age 34. 86 applicants, 73% accepted, 49 enrolled. In 2001, 96 master's, 1 doctorate, 2 other advanced degrees awarded.
Entrance requirements: For master's, GRE General Test or MAT, minimum GPA of 3.0. *Application deadline:* For fall admission, 2/15 (priority date); for spring admission, 11/1. Applications are processed

on a rolling basis. *Application fee:* $25. Electronic applications accepted.
Expenses: Tuition, state resident: full-time $3,292; part-time $183 per credit hour. Tuition, nonresident: full-time $8,912; part-time $495 per credit hour. Tuition and fees vary according to course load, campus/location and program.
Financial support: In 2001–02, 67 students received support, including 9 research assistantships with full tuition reimbursements available, 17 teaching assistantships with full tuition reimbursements available; fellowships, career-related internships or fieldwork and Federal Work-Study also available. Financial award application deadline: 2/15.
Faculty research: Instructional design, information equity, youth services, rural information services.
Dr. Joan Atkinson, Director, 205-348-1522, *Fax:* 205-348-3746, *E-mail:* jatkinso@slism.slis.ua.edu.
Application contact: Dr. Margaret Dalton, Professor, Graduate Coordinator, 205-348-1524, *E-mail:* mdalton@slis.ua.edu.

■ THE UNIVERSITY OF ARIZONA

Graduate College, College of Social and Behavioral Sciences, School of Information Resources and Library Science, Tucson, AZ 85721

AWARDS MA, PhD. Part-time programs available.

Degree requirements: For master's, proficiency in disk operating system (DOS); for doctorate, thesis/dissertation.
Entrance requirements: For master's, GRE, TOEFL, minimum GPA of 3.0; for doctorate, GRE General Test, TOEFL.
Expenses: Tuition, state resident: full-time $2,490; part-time $436 per unit. Tuition, nonresident: full-time $10,300; part-time $436 per unit. Full-time tuition and fees vary according to degree level and program.
Faculty research: Microcomputer applications; quantitative methods systems; information transfer, planning, evaluation, and technology.

■ UNIVERSITY OF CALIFORNIA, BERKELEY

Graduate Division, School of Information Management and Systems, Berkeley, CA 94720-1500

AWARDS MIMS, PhD.

Degree requirements: For doctorate, thesis/dissertation, qualifying exam.
Entrance requirements: For master's, GRE General Test, TOEFL, minimum GPA of 3.0, previous course work in java or C programming; for doctorate, GRE General Test, minimum GPA of 3.0.
Expenses: Tuition, nonresident: full-time $10,704. Required fees: $4,349.
Faculty research: Information retrieval research, design and evaluation of information systems, work practice-based design of information systems, economics of information, intellectual property law.

■ UNIVERSITY OF CALIFORNIA, LOS ANGELES

Graduate Division, Graduate School of Education and Information Studies, Department of Information Studies, Los Angeles, CA 90095

AWARDS Archival studies (MLIS); informatics (MLIS); library and information science (PhD, Certificate); library studies (MLIS). Part-time programs available.

Faculty: 14 full-time (9 women), 10 part-time/adjunct (7 women).
Students: 171 (139 women); includes 38 minority (1 African American, 18 Asian Americans or Pacific Islanders, 17 Hispanic Americans, 2 Native Americans) 16 international. Average age 33. 172 applicants, 59% accepted, 56 enrolled. In 2001, 53 master's, 4 doctorates awarded. Terminal master's awarded for partial completion of doctoral program.
Degree requirements: For master's, thesis or alternative, professional portfolio; for doctorate, thesis/dissertation, oral and written qualifying exams, professional portfolio.
Entrance requirements: For master's, GRE General Test, TOEFL, TWE, previous course work in computer programming and statistics; for doctorate, GRE General Test, TOEFL, TWE, previous course work in statistics, 2 samples of research writing in English. *Application deadline:* For fall admission, 12/15 (priority date). Applications are processed on a rolling basis. *Application fee:* $60. Electronic applications accepted.
Expenses: Tuition, nonresident: full-time $10,244. Required fees: $3,609. Full-time tuition and fees vary according to program.
Financial support: In 2001–02, 12 research assistantships, 2 teaching assistantships were awarded. Fellowships, career-related internships or fieldwork, Federal Work-Study, institutionally sponsored loans, scholarships/grants, tuition waivers (full and partial), and federal fellowships also available. Support available to part-time students. Financial award application deadline: 3/1; financial award applicants required to submit FAFSA.
Faculty research: Multimedia, digital libraries, archives and electronic records, interface design, information technology and policy, preservation, access.
Dr. Michele V. Cloonan, Chair, 310-825-8799, *Fax:* 310-206-3076, *E-mail:* mcloonan@ucla.edu.
Application contact: Susan S. Abler, Student Affairs Officer, 310-825-5269, *Fax:* 310-206-4460, *E-mail:* abler@gseis.ucla.edu. *Web site:* http://is.gseis.ucla.edu/

■ UNIVERSITY OF DENVER

University College, Denver, CO 80208

AWARDS Applied communication (MSS); computer information systems (MCIS); environmental policy and management (MEPM); healthcare systems (MHS); liberal studies (MLS); library and information services (MLIS); public health (MPH); technology management (MoTM); telecommunications (MTEL). Part-time and evening/weekend programs available. Postbaccalaureate distance learning degree programs offered (no on-campus study).

Faculty: 167 part-time/adjunct (52 women).
Students: 1,244 (618 women); includes 177 minority (65 African Americans, 53 Asian Americans or Pacific Islanders, 54 Hispanic Americans, 5 Native Americans) 76 international. 54 applicants, 85% accepted. In 2001, 274 degrees awarded.
Entrance requirements: For master's, minimum undergraduate GPA of 3.0. *Application deadline:* For fall admission, 7/15 (priority date); for winter admission, 10/14 (priority date); for spring admission, 2/10 (priority date). Applications are processed on a rolling basis. *Application fee:* $25.
Expenses: Contact institution.
Financial support: In 2001–02, 174 students received support. *Total annual research expenditures:* $59,206.
Mike Bloom, Dean, 303-871-3141.
Application contact: Cindy Kraft, Admission Coordinator, 303-871-3969, *Fax:* 303-871-3303. *Web site:* http://www.du.edu/ucol/

■ UNIVERSITY OF HAWAII AT MANOA

Graduate Division, College of Arts and Sciences, College of Natural Sciences, Department of Information and Computer Sciences, Library and Information Science Program, Honolulu, HI 96822

AWARDS Advanced library and information science (Certificate); communication and information science (PhD); library and information science (MLI Sc). Part-time programs available. Postbaccalaureate distance learning degree programs offered (minimal on-campus study).

Degree requirements: For master's, thesis optional.
Entrance requirements: For master's, GRE General Test, TOEFL. Electronic applications accepted.
Expenses: Tuition, state resident: full-time $2,160; part-time $1,980 per year. Tuition, nonresident: full-time $5,190; part-time $4,829 per year.
Faculty research: Information behavior, evaluation of electronic information

University of Hawaii at Manoa (continued)
sources, online learning, history of libraries. *Web site:* http://www.hawaii.edu/slis/

■ UNIVERSITY OF ILLINOIS AT URBANA–CHAMPAIGN

Graduate College, Graduate School of Library and Information Science, Champaign, IL 61820

AWARDS MS, PhD, CAS.

Faculty: 16 full-time, 2 part-time/adjunct.
Students: 321 full-time (243 women); includes 22 minority (12 African Americans, 4 Asian Americans or Pacific Islanders, 6 Hispanic Americans), 45 international. Average age 31. 354 applicants, 38% accepted. In 2001, 162 master's, 3 doctorates awarded.
Degree requirements: For doctorate, thesis/dissertation; for CAS, project.
Entrance requirements: For master's, GRE General Test, minimum GPA of 3.0; for doctorate, interview; for CAS, master's degree in library and information science or related field, minimum GPA of 3.0. *Application deadline:* For fall admission, 6/1 (priority date); for spring admission, 10/1. Applications are processed on a rolling basis. *Application fee:* $40 ($50 for international students). Electronic applications accepted.
Expenses: Tuition, state resident: part-time $3,227 per degree program. Tuition, nonresident: part-time $7,169 per degree program. Tuition and fees vary according to program.
Financial support: In 2001–02, 38 fellowships, 151 research assistantships, 16 teaching assistantships were awarded. Tuition waivers (full and partial) also available. Financial award application deadline: 2/1.
Dr. Linda Smith, Interim Dean, 217-333-3281, *Fax:* 217-244-3102, *E-mail:* lcsmith@uiuc.edu.
Application contact: Carol DeVoss, Officer, 217-333-7197, *Fax:* 217-244-3302, *E-mail:* devoss@uiuc.edu. *Web site:* http://alexia.lis.uiuc.edu/

Find an in-depth description at www.petersons.com/gradchannel.

■ THE UNIVERSITY OF IOWA

Graduate College, School of Library and Information Science, Iowa City, IA 52242-1316

AWARDS MA, JD/MA, MBA/MA.

Faculty: 4 full-time.
Students: 40 full-time (32 women), 41 part-time (35 women); includes 4 minority (3 Asian Americans or Pacific Islanders, 1 Native American), 6 international. 46 applicants, 70% accepted, 13 enrolled. In 2001, 27 degrees awarded.
Degree requirements: For master's, exam, thesis optional.
Entrance requirements: For master's, GRE General Test, TOEFL. *Application deadline:* For fall admission, 3/1 (priority date); for spring admission, 10/1 (priority date). *Application fee:* $30 ($50 for international students). Electronic applications accepted.
Expenses: Tuition, state resident: full-time $3,702; part-time $206 per semester hour. Tuition, nonresident: full-time $11,924; part-time $206 per semester hour. Required fees: $101 per semester. Tuition and fees vary according to course load and program.
Financial support: In 2001–02, 12 research assistantships, 7 teaching assistantships were awarded. Fellowships available. Financial award applicants required to submit FAFSA.
Joseph Kearney, Director, 319-335-5707.

■ UNIVERSITY OF MARYLAND, COLLEGE PARK

Graduate Studies and Research, College of Information Studies, College Park, MD 20742

AWARDS MLS, PhD, MA/MLS. Part-time and evening/weekend programs available.

Faculty: 11 full-time (6 women), 13 part-time/adjunct (6 women).
Students: 136 full-time (114 women), 143 part-time (109 women); includes 36 minority (20 African Americans, 12 Asian Americans or Pacific Islanders, 2 Hispanic Americans, 2 Native Americans), 14 international. 209 applicants, 54% accepted, 73 enrolled. In 2001, 111 master's, 1 doctorate awarded. Terminal master's awarded for partial completion of doctoral program.
Degree requirements: For doctorate, thesis/dissertation, 1 year residency, comprehensive exam.
Entrance requirements: For master's and doctorate, GRE General Test, minimum GPA of 3.0. *Application deadline:* For fall admission, 4/1; for spring admission, 11/1. Applications are processed on a rolling basis. *Application fee:* $50 ($70 for international students). Electronic applications accepted.
Expenses: Tuition, state resident: part-time $289 per credit hour. Tuition, nonresident: part-time $448 per credit hour. One-time fee: $436 part-time. Full-time tuition and fees vary according to course load, campus/location and program.
Financial support: In 2001–02, 8 fellowships with full tuition reimbursements (averaging $5,963 per year), 21 teaching assistantships with tuition reimbursements (averaging $10,575 per year) were awarded. Career-related internships or fieldwork, Federal Work-Study, scholarships/grants, and tuition waivers (full and partial) also available. Support available to part-time students. Financial award application deadline: 2/1; financial award applicants required to submit FAFSA. *Total annual research expenditures:* $190,051.
Dr. Bruce Dearstyne, Acting Dean, 301-405-2033, *Fax:* 301-314-9145, *E-mail:* ap57@umail.umd.edu.
Application contact: Trudy Lindsey, Director, Graduate Admissions and Records, 301-405-6991, *Fax:* 301-314-9305, *E-mail:* grschool@deans.umd.edu.

Find an in-depth description at www.petersons.com/gradchannel.

■ UNIVERSITY OF MICHIGAN

Horace H. Rackham School of Graduate Studies, School of Information, Ann Arbor, MI 48109

AWARDS Archives and records management (MS); human-computer interaction (MS); information (PhD); information economics, management and policy (MS); library and information services (MS). Part-time programs available.

Entrance requirements: For master's and doctorate, GRE General Test. *Web site:* http://www.si.umich.edu/

Find an in-depth description at www.petersons.com/gradchannel.

■ UNIVERSITY OF MISSOURI–COLUMBIA

Graduate School, College of Education, School of Information Science and Learning Technologies, Columbia, MO 65211

AWARDS Educational technology (M Ed, Ed S); information science and learning technology (PhD); library science (MA). Part-time and evening/weekend programs available.

Faculty: 14 full-time (6 women).
Students: 47 full-time (20 women), 102 part-time (67 women); includes 4 minority (1 African American, 2 Asian Americans or Pacific Islanders, 1 Hispanic American), 47 international. 45 applicants, 87% accepted. In 2001, 47 master's, 5 doctorates, 1 other advanced degree awarded.
Entrance requirements: For master's, GRE General Test or MAT, minimum GPA of 3.0. *Application deadline:* For fall and spring admission, 3/1 (priority date); for winter admission, 10/1 (priority date). Applications are processed on a rolling basis. *Application fee:* $25 ($50 for international students).
Expenses: Tuition, state resident: part-time $179 per credit hour. Tuition, nonresident: part-time $539 per credit hour. Required fees: $122 per semester. Tuition and fees vary according to program.
Financial support: Fellowships, teaching assistantships available.
Dr. John M. Budd, Director of Graduate Studies, 573-882-3258, *E-mail:* buddj@missouri.edu. *Web site:* http://www.coe.missouri.edu/~sislt/

■ THE UNIVERSITY OF NORTH CAROLINA AT CHAPEL HILL

Graduate School, School of Information and Library Science, Chapel Hill, NC 27599

AWARDS MSIS, MSLS, PhD, CAS. Part-time programs available.

Faculty: 17 full-time (9 women), 20 part-time/adjunct (10 women).
Students: 189 full-time (142 women), 63 part-time (40 women); includes 29 minority (12 African Americans, 14 Asian Americans or Pacific Islanders, 3 Hispanic Americans), 33 international. Average age 30. 281 applicants, 58% accepted, 88 enrolled. In 2001, 80 master's, 3 doctorates, 1 other advanced degree awarded.
Degree requirements: For master's, paper or project; for doctorate, thesis/dissertation.
Entrance requirements: For master's and doctorate, GRE General Test. *Application deadline:* For fall admission, 1/1 (priority date); for spring admission, 10/15. Applications are processed on a rolling basis. *Application fee:* $60. Electronic applications accepted.
Expenses: Tuition, state resident: full-time $2,864. Tuition, nonresident: full-time $12,030.
Financial support: In 2001–02, 54 fellowships with full tuition reimbursements, 69 research assistantships with full tuition reimbursements (averaging $10,000 per year), 10 teaching assistantships with full tuition reimbursements (averaging $14,000 per year) were awarded. Career-related internships or fieldwork, Federal Work-Study, institutionally sponsored loans, health care benefits, and unspecified assistantships also available. Financial award application deadline: 1/1; financial award applicants required to submit FAFSA.
Faculty research: Information retrieval, digital libraries, multimedia networking, management of information resources, archives and cultural heritage, information management.
Dr. Joanne Gard Marshall, Dean, 919-962-8366, *Fax:* 919-962-8071, *E-mail:* info@ils.unc.edu.
Application contact: Lucia Zonn, Student Services Manager, 919-962-8366, *Fax:* 919-962-8071, *E-mail:* info@ils.unc.edu. *Web site:* http://ils.unc.edu/

■ THE UNIVERSITY OF NORTH CAROLINA AT GREENSBORO

Graduate School, School of Education, Department of Library and Information Studies, Greensboro, NC 27412-5001

AWARDS MLIS. Part-time and evening/weekend programs available. Postbaccalaureate distance learning degree programs offered (no on-campus study).

Faculty: 8 full-time (5 women), 9 part-time/adjunct (7 women).
Students: 21 full-time (14 women), 282 part-time (247 women). Average age 30. 45 applicants, 84% accepted. In 2001, 84 degrees awarded.
Degree requirements: For master's, portfolio.
Entrance requirements: For master's, GRE General Test, TOEFL. *Application deadline:* For fall admission, 7/1 (priority date); for spring admission, 11/1. Applications are processed on a rolling basis. *Application fee:* $35.
Expenses: Tuition, state resident: part-time $344 per course. Tuition, nonresident: part-time $2,457 per course.
Financial support: In 2001–02, fellowships (averaging $6,000 per year), research assistantships (averaging $10,750 per year) were awarded. Teaching assistantships, career-related internships or fieldwork, institutionally sponsored loans, and unspecified assistantships also available. Financial award application deadline: 3/1.
Faculty research: Library history, gender studies, children's literature, web design, homeless technical services.
Kieth C. Wright, Chair, 336-334-3481, *Fax:* 336-334-5060, *E-mail:* kieth_wright@uncg.edu.
Application contact: Dr. James Lynch, Director of Graduate Recruitment and Information Services, 336-334-4881, *Fax:* 336-334-4424. *Web site:* http://www.uncg.edu/LIS/

■ UNIVERSITY OF NORTH TEXAS

Robert B. Toulouse School of Graduate Studies, School of Library and Information Sciences, Denton, TX 76203

AWARDS Information science (MS, PhD); library science (MS). Part-time and evening/weekend programs available.

Faculty: 14.
Students: 73 full-time (61 women), 324 part-time (277 women); includes 47 minority (17 African Americans, 5 Asian Americans or Pacific Islanders, 22 Hispanic Americans, 3 Native Americans), 6 international. Average age 37. In 2001, 118 master's, 16 doctorates awarded.
Degree requirements: For master's, comprehensive exam; for doctorate, one foreign language, thesis/dissertation, comprehensive exam.
Entrance requirements: For master's and doctorate, GRE General Test. *Application deadline:* For fall admission, 7/17; for spring admission, 11/30. Applications are processed on a rolling basis. *Application fee:* $25 ($50 for international students).
Expenses: Tuition, state resident: part-time $186 per hour. Tuition, nonresident: part-time $319 per hour. Required fees: $88; $21 per hour.
Financial support: Fellowships, research assistantships, teaching assistantships, career-related internships or fieldwork, Federal Work-Study, institutionally sponsored loans, and library assistantships available. Financial award application deadline: 4/1.
Faculty research: Information resources and services, information management and retrieval, computer-based information systems.
Dr. Philip M. Turner, Dean, 940-565-2445, *Fax:* 940-565-3110, *E-mail:* turner@lis.admin.unt.edu.
Application contact: Dr. Herman Totten, Graduate Adviser, 940-565-2445, *Fax:* 940-565-3110, *E-mail:* totten@lis.admin.unt.edu.

■ UNIVERSITY OF OKLAHOMA

Graduate College, College of Arts and Sciences, School of Library and Information Studies, Norman, OK 73019-0390

AWARDS MLIS, Certificate, M Ed/MLIS, MBA/MLIS. Part-time programs available.

Faculty: 10 full-time (7 women), 2 part-time/adjunct (1 woman).
Students: 29 full-time (23 women), 127 part-time (113 women); includes 15 minority (5 African Americans, 1 Asian American or Pacific Islander, 1 Hispanic American, 8 Native Americans), 1 international. 34 applicants, 100% accepted, 23 enrolled. In 2001, 46 degrees awarded.
Degree requirements: For master's, comprehensive exam (MLIS), thesis (MALIS).
Entrance requirements: For master's, GRE, TOEFL, minimum GPA of 3.2 in last 60 hours or 3.0 overall. *Application deadline:* For fall admission, 3/1 (priority date); for spring admission, 10/15. Applications are processed on a rolling basis. *Application fee:* $25 ($50 for international students).
Expenses: Tuition, state resident: full-time $2,208; part-time $92 per credit hour. Tuition, nonresident: part-time $297 per credit hour. Tuition and fees vary according to course level, course load and program.
Financial support: In 2001–02, 37 students received support, including 6 research assistantships with partial tuition reimbursements available (averaging $8,220 per year), 7 teaching assistantships with partial tuition reimbursements available (averaging $8,033 per year); fellowships, career-related internships or fieldwork, Federal Work-Study, scholarships/grants, and tuition waivers (full and partial) also available. Support available to part-time students. Financial award applicants required to submit FAFSA.
Faculty research: School library media, reader's advisory services, networked information systems, multicultural librarianship, knowledge management. *Total annual research expenditures:* $31,121.
Danny Wallace, Director, 405-325-3921, *Fax:* 405-325-7648.

University of Oklahoma (continued)
Application contact: Maggie Ryan, Student Program Specialist, 405-325-3921, *Fax:* 405-325-7648, *E-mail:* mryan@ou.edu.

■ UNIVERSITY OF PITTSBURGH

School of Information Sciences, Department of Library and Information Science, Pittsburgh, PA 15260

AWARDS MLIS, PhD, Certificate. Part-time programs available. Postbaccalaureate distance learning degree programs offered (minimal on-campus study).

Faculty: 12 full-time (8 women), 2 part-time/adjunct (both women).
Students: 118 full-time (82 women), 153 part-time (127 women); includes 33 minority (23 African Americans, 6 Asian Americans or Pacific Islanders, 4 Hispanic Americans), 24 international. 142 applicants, 94% accepted, 76 enrolled. In 2001, 91 master's, 8 doctorates awarded.
Degree requirements: For master's, thesis optional; for doctorate, variable foreign language requirement, thesis/dissertation.
Entrance requirements: For master's, minimum GPA of 3.0; for doctorate, GRE General Test, minimum GPA of 3.0. *Application deadline:* For fall admission, 7/1 (priority date); for spring admission, 11/1 (priority date). Applications are processed on a rolling basis. *Application fee:* $40. Electronic applications accepted.
Expenses: Tuition, state resident: full-time $9,410; part-time $385 per credit. Tuition, nonresident: full-time $19,376; part-time $797 per credit. Required fees: $480; $90 per term. Tuition and fees vary according to program.
Financial support: In 2001–02, 45 students received support, including 5 fellowships (averaging $21,292 per year), 20 research assistantships, 20 teaching assistantships; scholarships/grants, tuition waivers (full and partial), and unspecified assistantships also available. Support available to part-time students. Financial award application deadline: 1/15; financial award applicants required to submit FAFSA.
Faculty research: Archives, electronic records and preservation, children's resources and services, medical informatics, management.
Dr. Christinger Tomer, Chair, 412-624-9448, *Fax:* 412-648-7001, *E-mail:* ctomer@pitt.edu.
Application contact: Ninette Kay, Admissions Coordinator, 412-624-5146, *Fax:* 412-624-5231, *E-mail:* nkay@mail.sis.pitt.edu. *Web site:* http://www.sis.pitt.edu/~isdept/

■ UNIVERSITY OF PUERTO RICO, RÍO PIEDRAS

Graduate School of Librarianship, San Juan, PR 00931

AWARDS Librarianship (Post-Graduate Certificate); librarianship and information services (MLS). Part-time and evening/weekend programs available.

Faculty: 9.
Students: 36 full-time (30 women), 99 part-time (70 women); all minorities (all Hispanic Americans). Average age 29. 49 applicants, 61% accepted. In 2001, 20 degrees awarded.
Degree requirements: For master's, thesis, comprehensive exam.
Entrance requirements: For master's, PAEG, interview, minimum GPA of 3.0. *Application deadline:* For fall admission, 2/1. *Application fee:* $17.
Expenses: Tuition, state resident: full-time $1,200; part-time $70 per credit. Tuition, nonresident: full-time $3,500; part-time $219 per credit. Required fees: $70; $35 per semester.
Financial support: Fellowships, research assistantships, teaching assistantships, Federal Work-Study, institutionally sponsored loans, and tuition waivers (partial) available. Financial award application deadline: 5/31.
Faculty research: Evaluation of journals published by the Puerto Rican system.
Dr. Consuelo Figueras-Alvarez, Director, 787-764-0000 Ext. 5207, *Fax:* 787-764-2311.
Application contact: Migdalia Dávila, Student Affairs Officer, 787-764-0000 Ext. 5827, *Fax:* 787-764-2311.

■ UNIVERSITY OF RHODE ISLAND

Graduate School, Graduate Library School, Kingston, RI 02881

AWARDS MLIS.

Students: In 2001, 64 degrees awarded. *Application deadline:* For fall admission, 4/15 (priority date). Applications are processed on a rolling basis. *Application fee:* $35.
Expenses: Tuition, state resident: full-time $3,756; part-time $209 per credit. Tuition, nonresident: full-time $10,774; part-time $599 per credit. Required fees: $1,586; $76 per credit. One-time fee: $60 full-time.
Dr. W. Michael Havener, Director, 401-874-2947.

■ UNIVERSITY OF SOUTH CAROLINA

The Graduate School, College of Library and Information Science, Columbia, SC 29208

AWARDS MLIS, Certificate, Specialist, MLIS/MA. Part-time programs available. Postbaccalaureate distance learning degree programs offered (no on-campus study).

Faculty: 14 full-time (8 women), 7 part-time/adjunct (4 women).
Students: 85 full-time (70 women), 361 part-time (318 women); includes 27 minority (22 African Americans, 2 Asian Americans or Pacific Islanders, 3 Hispanic Americans), 5 international. Average age 37. 147 applicants, 76% accepted. In 2001, 170 master's, 19 other advanced degrees awarded.
Degree requirements: For master's and other advanced degree, registration.
Entrance requirements: For master's, GRE General Test, TOEFL, or MAT; for other advanced degree, GRE General Test or MAT, TOEFL. *Application deadline:* For fall admission, 4/1 (priority date); for spring admission, 10/1 (priority date). Applications are processed on a rolling basis. *Application fee:* $40. Electronic applications accepted.
Expenses: Tuition, state resident: full-time $4,434. Tuition, nonresident: full-time $9,854. Tuition and fees vary according to program.
Financial support: In 2001–02, 9 fellowships with partial tuition reimbursements (averaging $9,500 per year), 30 research assistantships with partial tuition reimbursements were awarded. Career-related internships or fieldwork, scholarships/grants, and unspecified assistantships also available. Support available to part-time students. Financial award application deadline: 4/1; financial award applicants required to submit FAFSA.
Faculty research: Information technology management, distance education, library services for children and young adults, special libraries.
Dr. Fred W. Roper, Dean, 803-777-3858, *Fax:* 803-777-7938.
Application contact: Sharon Allen, Admissions Contact, 803-777-3887, *Fax:* 803-777-0457, *E-mail:* sharona@gwm.sc.edu. *Web site:* http://www.libsci.sc.edu/

■ UNIVERSITY OF SOUTH FLORIDA

College of Graduate Studies, College of Arts and Sciences, School of Library and Information Science, Tampa, FL 33620-9951

AWARDS Library and information sciences (MA); school library media (MA). Part-time and evening/weekend programs available. Postbaccalaureate distance learning degree programs offered (minimal on-campus study).

Faculty: 17 full-time (12 women).
Students: 68 full-time (52 women), 291 part-time (239 women); includes 52 minority (8 African Americans, 6 Asian Americans or Pacific Islanders, 37 Hispanic Americans, 1 Native American), 2 international. Average age 32. 158 applicants, 71% accepted, 76 enrolled. In 2001, 63 degrees awarded.
Entrance requirements: For master's, GRE General Test, minimum GPA of 3.0 in last 60 hours. *Application deadline:* For fall admission, 6/1; for spring admission, 10/15. Applications are processed on a rolling basis. *Application fee:* $20. Electronic applications accepted.
Expenses: Tuition, state resident: part-time $166 per credit hour. Tuition,

nonresident: part-time $573 per credit hour. Required fees: $17 per term.
Financial support: Fellowships, research assistantships, teaching assistantships, career-related internships or fieldwork, Federal Work-Study, and institutionally sponsored loans available. Support available to part-time students. Financial award applicants required to submit FAFSA. *Total annual research expenditures:* $42,668.
Vicki L. Gregory, Chairperson and Program Director, 813-974-3520, *Fax:* 813-974-6840, *E-mail:* gregory@luna.cas.usf.edu.
Application contact: Information Contact, 813-974-6837, *Fax:* 813-974-6840, *E-mail:* lis@luna.cas.usf.edu. *Web site:* http://www.cas.usf.edu/lis/

■ THE UNIVERSITY OF TENNESSEE

Graduate School, School of Information Sciences, Knoxville, TN 37996

AWARDS MS. Part-time programs available. Postbaccalaureate distance learning degree programs offered (no on-campus study).

Faculty: 11 full-time (6 women), 1 part-time/adjunct (0 women).
Students: 47 full-time (38 women), 137 part-time (105 women); includes 7 minority (4 African Americans, 3 Asian Americans or Pacific Islanders), 6 international. 128 applicants, 69% accepted. In 2001, 86 degrees awarded.
Degree requirements: For master's, thesis or alternative.
Entrance requirements: For master's, GRE General Test, TOEFL, minimum GPA of 2.7. *Application deadline:* For fall admission, 2/1 (priority date). Applications are processed on a rolling basis. *Application fee:* $35. Electronic applications accepted.
Expenses: Tuition, state resident: full-time $4,280; part-time $233 per hour. Tuition, nonresident: full-time $12,066; part-time $666 per hour. Tuition and fees vary according to program.
Financial support: In 2001–02, 1 fellowship, 16 teaching assistantships were awarded. Research assistantships, Federal Work-Study, institutionally sponsored loans, and unspecified assistantships also available. Financial award application deadline: 2/1; financial award applicants required to submit FAFSA.
Dr. Elizabeth Aversa, Head, 865-974-2148, *Fax:* 865-974-4967, *E-mail:* aversa@utk.edu.
Application contact: Dr. Kristie Atwood, Graduate Representative, *E-mail:* katwood@utk.edu.

Find an in-depth description at www.petersons.com/gradchannel.

■ THE UNIVERSITY OF TEXAS AT AUSTIN

Graduate School, Graduate School of Library and Information Science, Austin, TX 78712-1111

AWARDS MLIS, PhD. Part-time programs available.

Faculty: 20 full-time, 9 part-time/adjunct.
Students: 305 (243 women); includes 41 minority (2 African Americans, 5 Asian Americans or Pacific Islanders, 33 Hispanic Americans, 1 Native American) 35 international. Average age 27. 164 applicants, 74% accepted. In 2001, 137 master's, 3 doctorates awarded.
Degree requirements: For doctorate, 2 foreign languages, thesis/dissertation.
Entrance requirements: For master's and doctorate, GRE General Test. *Application deadline:* For fall admission, 2/1 (priority date); for winter admission, 5/1; for spring admission, 10/1. Applications are processed on a rolling basis. *Application fee:* $50 ($75 for international students). Electronic applications accepted.
Expenses: Tuition, state resident: full-time $3,159. Tuition, nonresident: full-time $6,957. Tuition and fees vary according to program.
Financial support: Fellowships, research assistantships, teaching assistantships, career-related internships or fieldwork, Federal Work-Study, and tuition waivers (partial) available. Support available to part-time students. Financial award application deadline: 2/1.
Faculty research: Information retrieval and artificial intelligence, library history and administration, classification and cataloguing.
Andrew I. Dillon, Dean, 512-471-3828, *Fax:* 512-471-3971.
Application contact: Dr. Philip Doty, Graduate Adviser, 512-471-3746, *Fax:* 512-471-3971, *E-mail:* pdoty@gslis.utexas.edu. *Web site:* http://www.gslis.utexas.edu

■ UNIVERSITY OF WISCONSIN–MADISON

Graduate School, College of Letters and Science, School of Library and Information Studies, Madison, WI 53706-1380

AWARDS MA, PhD, Certificate. Part-time programs available.

Faculty: 7 full-time (4 women), 4 part-time/adjunct (1 woman).
Students: 114 full-time (88 women), 83 part-time (59 women); includes 15 minority (4 African Americans, 8 Asian Americans or Pacific Islanders, 3 Hispanic Americans), 15 international. Average age 29. 164 applicants, 62% accepted. In 2001, 70 master's, 1 doctorate, 1 other advanced degree awarded.
Degree requirements: For doctorate, thesis/dissertation, comprehensive exam. *Median time to degree:* Master's–2 years full-time, 7 years part-time; doctorate–5 years full-time, 7 years part-time.
Application deadline: For fall admission, 12/15 (priority date). Applications are processed on a rolling basis. *Application fee:* $45. Electronic applications accepted.
Expenses: Tuition, state resident: full-time $7,361; part-time $399 per credit. Tuition, nonresident: full-time $20,499; part-time $1,282 per credit. Required fees: $34 per credit. Full-time tuition and fees vary according to course load, program, reciprocity agreements and student level.
Financial support: In 2001–02, 26 students received support, including 6 fellowships with full and partial tuition reimbursements available (averaging $8,700 per year), 2 teaching assistantships with full tuition reimbursements available; career-related internships or fieldwork, Federal Work-Study, scholarships/grants, and unspecified assistantships also available. Financial award application deadline: 12/15.
Faculty research: Intellectual freedom, children's literature, print culture history, information systems design and evaluation, school library media centers. *Total annual research expenditures:* $125,207.
Louise S. Robbins, Director, 608-263-2908, *Fax:* 608-263-4849, *E-mail:* lrobbins@slis.wisc.edu.
Application contact: Barbara J. Arnold, Admissions and Placement Adviser, 608-263-2909, *Fax:* 608-263-4849, *E-mail:* bjarnold@facstaff.wisc.edu. *Web site:* http://www.slis.wisc.edu/

■ UNIVERSITY OF WISCONSIN–MILWAUKEE

Graduate School, School of Information Studies, Milwaukee, WI 53201-0413

AWARDS MLIS, CAS, MLIS/MA, MLIS/MM, MLIS/MS. Part-time programs available.

Faculty: 10 full-time (5 women).
Students: 52 full-time (39 women), 99 part-time (81 women); includes 7 minority (3 African Americans, 1 Asian American or Pacific Islander, 2 Hispanic Americans, 1 Native American), 6 international. Average age 36. 151 applicants, 70% accepted. In 2001, 85 degrees awarded.
Entrance requirements: For master's, GRE General Test or MAT. *Application deadline:* For fall admission, 1/1 (priority date); for spring admission, 9/1. Applications are processed on a rolling basis. *Application fee:* $45 ($75 for international students).
Expenses: Tuition, state resident: full-time $6,180; part-time $535 per credit. Tuition, nonresident: full-time $19,482; part-time $1,366 per credit. Tuition and fees vary according to course load, program and reciprocity agreements.
Financial support: In 2001–02, 2 fellowships, 6 teaching assistantships were awarded. Research assistantships, career-related internships or fieldwork, Federal

University of Wisconsin–Milwaukee (continued)
Work-Study, and unspecified assistantships also available. Support available to part-time students. Financial award application deadline: 4/15.
Dietmar Wolfram, Representative, 414-229-4707, *Fax:* 414-229-4848, *E-mail:* dwolfram@uwm.edu. *Web site:* http://www.uwm.edu/Dept/SLIS/

■ VALDOSTA STATE UNIVERSITY

Graduate School, Program in Library and Information Science, Valdosta, GA 31698

AWARDS MLIS.

Faculty: 4 full-time (2 women).
Students: 1 (woman) full-time, 10 part-time (6 women); includes 3 minority (1 African American, 1 Asian American or Pacific Islander, 1 Hispanic American). 18 applicants, 100% accepted.
Degree requirements: For master's, comprehensive exam.
Entrance requirements: For master's, GRE. *Application deadline:* For fall admission, 5/1. *Application fee:* $20.
Expenses: Tuition, state resident: full-time $1,746; part-time $97 per hour. Tuition, nonresident: full-time $6,966; part-time $387 per hour. Required fees: $594; $297 per semester.
Financial support: In 2001–02, 2 research assistantships with full tuition reimbursements (averaging $2,452 per year) were awarded; institutionally sponsored loans, scholarships/grants, and unspecified assistantships also available. Support available to part-time students. Financial award application deadline: 7/1; financial award applicants required to submit FAFSA.
Dr. George Gaumond, University Librarian, 229-333-5860, *E-mail:* ggaumond@valdosta.edu.
Application contact: Dr. Wallace Koehler, Director, 229-333-5860.

■ WAYNE STATE UNIVERSITY

Graduate School, Library and Information Science Program, Detroit, MI 48202

AWARDS Archives administration (Certificate); library and information science (MLIS, Spec). Part-time and evening/weekend programs available.

Faculty: 11 full-time.
Students: 62 full-time (46 women), 403 part-time (336 women); includes 53 minority (42 African Americans, 7 Asian Americans or Pacific Islanders, 3 Hispanic Americans, 1 Native American), 5 international. 232 applicants, 70% accepted, 113 enrolled. In 2001, 121 degrees awarded.
Application deadline: For fall admission, 7/1. Applications are processed on a rolling basis. *Application fee:* $20 ($30 for international students). Electronic applications accepted.
Expenses: Tuition, state resident: full-time $3,764. Tuition and fees vary according to degree level and program.
Financial support: In 2001–02, 4 research assistantships were awarded; career-related internships or fieldwork, Federal Work-Study, institutionally sponsored loans, and scholarships/grants also available. Support available to part-time students. Financial award application deadline: 5/15.
Faculty research: Management, infometrics, imaging processes, library history, bibliographic control.
Joseph J. Mika, Director, 313-577-6196, *Fax:* 313-577-7563, *E-mail:* aa2500@wayne.edu.
Application contact: Nancy Johnson, Education Director, 313-577-8541. *Web site:* http://www.wayne.edu/xisp/lishome.html

LIBRARY SCIENCE

■ APPALACHIAN STATE UNIVERSITY

Cratis D. Williams Graduate School, College of Education, Department of Leadership and Educational Studies, Program in Library Science, Boone, NC 28608

AWARDS MA, MLS, Ed S.

Faculty: 18 full-time (4 women).
Students: 19 full-time (12 women), 40 part-time (39 women); includes 2 minority (1 African American, 1 Asian American or Pacific Islander). In 2001, 24 degrees awarded.
Degree requirements: For master's, thesis or alternative, comprehensive exam; for Ed S, thesis optional.
Entrance requirements: For master's, GRE General Test or MAT; for Ed S, GRE General Test. *Application deadline:* For fall admission, 7/15 (priority date). *Application fee:* $35.
Expenses: Tuition, state resident: full-time $1,286. Tuition, nonresident: full-time $9,354. Required fees: $1,116.
Financial support: In 2001–02, research assistantships (averaging $6,250 per year), teaching assistantships (averaging $6,250 per year) were awarded. Fellowships, career-related internships or fieldwork, scholarships/grants, and unspecified assistantships also available. Support available to part-time students. Financial award application deadline: 7/1.
Faculty research: Multicultural issues in library science curriculum.
Dr. Carol Truett, Adviser, 828-262-3115, *E-mail:* truettca@appstate.edu.

■ THE CATHOLIC UNIVERSITY OF AMERICA

School of Library and Information Science, Washington, DC 20064

AWARDS MSLS, JD/MSLS, MSLS/MA, MSLS/MS. Part-time and evening/weekend programs available. Postbaccalaureate distance learning degree programs offered (minimal on-campus study).

Faculty: 7 full-time (all women), 18 part-time/adjunct (11 women).
Students: 25 full-time (22 women), 175 part-time (134 women); includes 28 minority (23 African Americans, 3 Asian Americans or Pacific Islanders, 2 Hispanic Americans), 10 international. Average age 38. 111 applicants, 77% accepted, 52 enrolled. In 2001, 63 degrees awarded.
Degree requirements: For master's, comprehensive exam.
Entrance requirements: For master's, GRE General Test. *Application deadline:* For fall admission, 7/1 (priority date); for spring admission, 11/1. Applications are processed on a rolling basis. *Application fee:* $55. Electronic applications accepted.
Expenses: Contact institution.
Financial support: Fellowships, research assistantships, career-related internships or fieldwork, Federal Work-Study, institutionally sponsored loans, tuition waivers (full and partial), and unspecified assistantships available. Support available to part-time students. Financial award application deadline: 2/1.
Faculty research: Information transfer, archives and manuscripts, legal libraries, information seeking, information storage and retrieval, special collections, information systems.
Dr. Peter Liebscher, Dean, 202-319-5085, *E-mail:* liebscher@cua.edu.

■ CENTRAL MISSOURI STATE UNIVERSITY

School of Graduate Studies, Department of Library Science and Information Services, Warrensburg, MO 64093

AWARDS Human services/learning resources (Ed S); library information technology (MS); library science and information services (MS). Part-time programs available.

Faculty: 2 full-time (1 woman).
Students: 7 full-time (all women), 72 part-time (70 women); includes 3 minority (2 African Americans, 1 Hispanic American), 1 international. Average age 37. 9 applicants, 89% accepted. In 2001, 10 degrees awarded.
Degree requirements: For master's and Ed S, thesis or alternative.
Entrance requirements: For master's, minimum GPA of 2.75, interview, 2 years of teaching experience; for Ed S, minimum GPA of 3.25, master's degree, teaching certificate. *Application deadline:* Applications are processed on a rolling basis. *Application fee:* $25 ($50 for international students).
Expenses: Tuition, area resident: Full-time $4,200; part-time $175 per credit hour. Tuition, nonresident: full-time $8,352; part-time $348 per credit hour.
Financial support: In 2001–02, 1 research assistantship with tuition reimbursement (averaging $4,000 per year), 2 teaching

assistantships with partial tuition reimbursements (averaging $5,875 per year) were awarded. Federal Work-Study, scholarships/grants, unspecified assistantships, and administrative assistantship also available. Support available to part-time students. Financial award application deadline: 3/1; financial award applicants required to submit FAFSA.
Faculty research: Library services for distance learners, information seeking in context, entrepreneurial library management, library services for children, library financial management.
Dr. Linda Lillard, Chair, 660-543-8633, *Fax:* 660-543-8001. *Web site:* http://www.cmsu.edu/

■ CHICAGO STATE UNIVERSITY

Graduate Studies, College of Education, Department of Early Childhood and Elementary Education, Program in Library Science and Communications Media, Chicago, IL 60628

AWARDS MS.

Faculty: 3 full-time (2 women).
Students: 50 (45 women); includes 25 minority (24 African Americans, 1 Native American).
Entrance requirements: For master's, minimum GPA of 2.75. *Application deadline:* For fall admission, 7/1; for spring admission, 11/10. *Application fee:* $25.
Financial support: Research assistantships available.

■ CLARION UNIVERSITY OF PENNSYLVANIA

College of Graduate Studies, College of Education and Human Services, Department of Library Science, Clarion, PA 16214

AWARDS MSLS, CAS. Part-time programs available.

Faculty: 6 full-time (3 women).
Students: 20 full-time (14 women), 137 part-time (111 women); includes 7 minority (3 African Americans, 3 Asian Americans or Pacific Islanders, 1 Hispanic American). 74 applicants, 84% accepted. In 2001, 51 degrees awarded.
Degree requirements: For master's, thesis or alternative.
Entrance requirements: For master's, minimum QPA of 3.0. *Application deadline:* For fall admission, 8/1 (priority date); for spring admission, 12/1 (priority date). Applications are processed on a rolling basis. *Application fee:* $30.
Expenses: Tuition, state resident: full-time $4,600; part-time $256 per credit. Tuition, nonresident: full-time $7,554; part-time $420 per credit. Required fees: $908; $72 per credit.
Financial support: In 2001–02, 14 research assistantships with partial tuition reimbursements (averaging $2,001 per year) were awarded. Financial award application deadline: 3/1.
Dr. Andrea Miller, Chair, 814-393-2271, *Fax:* 814-393-2150, *E-mail:* vavrek@clarion.edu.

■ CLARK ATLANTA UNIVERSITY

School of Library and Information Studies, Atlanta, GA 30314

AWARDS MSLS, SLS. Part-time and evening/weekend programs available.

Degree requirements: For master's, one foreign language, thesis optional; for SLS, one foreign language, thesis.
Entrance requirements: For master's, GRE, TOEFL.
Faculty research: Comparative/international librarianship, African American bibliography, school library media services.

■ COLLEGE OF ST. CATHERINE

Graduate Program, Program in Library and Information Science, St. Paul, MN 55105-1789

AWARDS MA. Part-time and evening/weekend programs available.

Faculty: 3 full-time (all women).
Students: 107 full-time (91 women), 93 part-time (79 women); includes 10 minority (1 African American, 5 Asian Americans or Pacific Islanders, 3 Hispanic Americans, 1 Native American). Average age 37. 88 applicants, 82% accepted, 59 enrolled.
Degree requirements: For master's, microcomputer competency.
Entrance requirements: For master's, Michigan English Language Assessment Battery or TOEFL, minimum GPA of 3.2 or GRE. *Application deadline:* For fall admission, 2/15. *Application fee:* $25.
Expenses: Tuition: Part-time $375 per credit. Required fees: $60; $60 per year. Tuition and fees vary according to program.
Financial support: In 2001–02, 39 students received support. Institutionally sponsored loans available. Support available to part-time students. Financial award application deadline: 4/1; financial award applicants required to submit FAFSA.
Mary Wagner, Director, 651-690-6802.
Application contact: 651-690-6505.

■ DOMINICAN UNIVERSITY

Graduate School of Library and Information Science, River Forest, IL 60305-1099

AWARDS MLIS, MSMIS, CSS, MBA/MLIS, MLIS/M Div, MLIS/MA, MLIS/MM. Part-time and evening/weekend programs available. Postbaccalaureate distance learning degree programs offered (minimal on-campus study).

Entrance requirements: For master's, TOEFL, minimum GPA of 3.0 or GRE General Test or MAT.
Expenses: Contact institution.
Faculty research: Productivity and the information environment, bibliometrics, library history, subject access, library materials and services for children. *Web site:* http://www.dom.edu/

■ DREXEL UNIVERSITY

Graduate School, College of Information Science and Technology, Philadelphia, PA 19104-2875

AWARDS Information science and technology (PhD); information studies (PhD, CAS); information systems (MSIS); library and information science (MS). Part-time and evening/weekend programs available. Postbaccalaureate distance learning degree programs offered (no on-campus study).

Faculty: 27 full-time (13 women), 11 part-time/adjunct (2 women).
Students: 67 full-time (38 women), 460 part-time (235 women); includes 68 minority (31 African Americans, 34 Asian Americans or Pacific Islanders, 3 Hispanic Americans), 61 international. Average age 34. 298 applicants, 76% accepted, 118 enrolled. In 2001, 178 master's awarded.
Degree requirements: For doctorate, thesis/dissertation.
Entrance requirements: For master's, GRE General Test, TOEFL; for doctorate, GRE General Test, TOEFL, master's degree. *Application deadline:* For fall admission, 8/21. Applications are processed on a rolling basis. *Application fee:* $50. Electronic applications accepted.
Expenses: Contact institution.
Financial support: Research assistantships, teaching assistantships, career-related internships or fieldwork, Federal Work-Study, institutionally sponsored loans, traineeships, tuition waivers (partial), and unspecified assistantships available. Support available to part-time students. Financial award application deadline: 2/1.
Faculty research: Bibliometric analysis, information management, scientific communication, expert systems, man-machine interfaces in information transfer.
Dr. Tom Childers, Associate Dean, 215-895-2474.
Application contact: Director of Graduate Admissions, 215-895-6700, *Fax:* 215-895-5939, *E-mail:* info@cis.drexel.edu.

Find an in-depth description at www.petersons.com/gradchannel.

■ EAST CAROLINA UNIVERSITY

Graduate School, School of Education, Department of Librarianship, Educational Technology, and Distance Instruction, Greenville, NC 27858-4353

AWARDS Instruction technology specialist (MA Ed); library science (MLS, CAS). Part-time and evening/weekend programs available.

Faculty: 6 full-time (4 women).
Students: 15 full-time (8 women), 114 part-time (99 women); includes 13 minority (12 African Americans, 1 Native American), 1 international. Average age 37.

East Carolina University (continued)
65 applicants, 86% accepted. In 2001, 44 master's, 1 other advanced degree awarded.
Degree requirements: For master's, thesis optional.
Entrance requirements: For master's, GRE General Test or MAT, TOEFL. *Application deadline:* For fall admission, 6/1 (priority date). Applications are processed on a rolling basis. *Application fee:* $45.
Expenses: Tuition, state resident: full-time $2,636. Tuition, nonresident: full-time $11,365.
Financial support: Research assistantships, teaching assistantships, Federal Work-Study available. Support available to part-time students. Financial award application deadline: 6/1.
Dr. Dianne Kester, Chair, 252-328-4939, *Fax:* 252-328-4368, *E-mail:* kesterd@mail.ecu.edu.
Application contact: Dr. Paul D. Tschetter, Senior Associate Dean of the Graduate School, 252-328-6012, *Fax:* 252-328-6071, *E-mail:* gradschool@mail.ecu.edu.

■ EMPORIA STATE UNIVERSITY

School of Graduate Studies, School of Library and Information Management, Emporia, KS 66801-5087

AWARDS Library and information science (PhD); library science (MLS). Part-time programs available.

Faculty: 19 full-time (11 women), 41 part-time/adjunct (30 women).
Students: 48 full-time (37 women), 219 part-time (187 women); includes 8 minority (2 African Americans, 2 Asian Americans or Pacific Islanders, 4 Hispanic Americans), 2 international. 123 applicants, 85% accepted. In 2001, 78 master's, 3 doctorates awarded.
Degree requirements: For master's, comprehensive exam or thesis; for doctorate, thesis/dissertation.
Entrance requirements: For master's, GRE General Test, TOEFL; for doctorate, GRE General Test, TOEFL, interview, minimum graduate GPA of 3.5. *Application deadline:* For fall admission, 8/15 (priority date). Applications are processed on a rolling basis. *Application fee:* $30 ($75 for international students). Electronic applications accepted.
Expenses: Tuition, state resident: full-time $2,632; part-time $119 per credit hour. Tuition, nonresident: full-time $6,734; part-time $290 per credit hour.
Financial support: In 2001–02, 1 research assistantship (averaging $5,632 per year), 17 teaching assistantships with full tuition reimbursements (averaging $5,273 per year) were awarded. Career-related internships or fieldwork, Federal Work-Study, institutionally sponsored loans, health care benefits, and unspecified assistantships also available. Financial award application deadline: 3/15; financial award applicants required to submit FAFSA.
Faculty research: Information management in corporate environment.
Dr. Robert J. Grover, Dean, 800-552-4770, *Fax:* 620-341-5233, *E-mail:* groverro@emporia.edu.
Application contact: Daniel Rowland, Director of Communications, 800-552-4770, *Fax:* 620-341-5233, *E-mail:* sliminfo@emporia.edu. *Web site:* http://slim.emporia.edu/

Find an in-depth description at www.petersons.com/gradchannel.

■ FLORIDA STATE UNIVERSITY

Graduate Studies, School of Information Studies, Tallahassee, FL 32306

AWARDS Information studies (PhD); library and information studies (MS, PhD, Specialist). Part-time and evening/weekend programs available. Postbaccalaureate distance learning degree programs offered (minimal on-campus study).

Faculty: 18 full-time (8 women), 7 part-time/adjunct (4 women).
Students: 171 full-time, 386 part-time. Average age 38. 270 applicants, 88% accepted. In 2001, 92 master's, 9 doctorates, 11 other advanced degrees awarded.
Degree requirements: For doctorate, thesis/dissertation.
Entrance requirements: For master's, GRE General Test, minimum GPA of 3.0; for doctorate, GRE General Test, minimum graduate GPA of 3.5. *Application deadline:* For fall admission, 7/16 (priority date). *Application fee:* $20.
Expenses: Tuition, state resident: part-time $163 per credit hour. Tuition, nonresident: part-time $570 per credit hour. Tuition and fees vary according to program.
Financial support: In 2001–02, 57 students received support, including 14 fellowships with full tuition reimbursements available, 45 research assistantships with full tuition reimbursements available, 19 teaching assistantships with full tuition reimbursements available; career-related internships or fieldwork, Federal Work-Study, scholarships/grants, and unspecified assistantships also available. Financial award application deadline: 4/1; financial award applicants required to submit FAFSA.
Faculty research: Community information service, needs assessment, information policy, usability analysis, human information behavior.
Dr. Jane B. Robbins, Dean, 850-644-5775, *Fax:* 850-644-9763, *E-mail:* robbins@lis.fsu.edu.
Application contact: Marion Davis, Program Assistant, 850-644-8103, *Fax:* 850-644-9763, *E-mail:* grad@slis-two.lis.fsu.edu. *Web site:* http://www.fsu.edu/~lis/

Find an in-depth description at www.petersons.com/gradchannel.

■ GRATZ COLLEGE

Graduate Programs, Program in Judaica Librarianship, Melrose Park, PA 19027

AWARDS Certificate, MIS/Certificate. Part-time programs available.

Faculty: 8 full-time (3 women), 11 part-time/adjunct (7 women).
Degree requirements: For Certificate, one foreign language.
Application deadline: Applications are processed on a rolling basis. *Application fee:* $50.
Expenses: Tuition: Full-time $9,950; part-time $466 per credit.
Financial support: Application deadline: 4/1.
Eli Wise, Coordinator, 215-635-7300 Ext. 159, *Fax:* 215-635-7320.
Application contact: Adena E. Johnston, Director of Admissions, 215-635-7300 Ext. 140, *Fax:* 215-635-7320, *E-mail:* admissions@gratz.edu.

■ INDIANA UNIVERSITY BLOOMINGTON

School of Library and Information Science, Bloomington, IN 47405

AWARDS MIS, MLS, PhD, Spec, JD/MLS, MIS/MA, MLS/MA, MPA/MIS, MPA/MLS. PhD offered through the University Graduate School. Part-time programs available.

Faculty: 13 full-time (5 women), 1 part-time/adjunct (0 women).
Students: 168 full-time (105 women), 104 part-time (75 women); includes 30 minority (12 African Americans, 10 Asian Americans or Pacific Islanders, 7 Hispanic Americans, 1 Native American), 20 international. Average age 31. In 2001, 115 master's, 7 doctorates awarded.
Degree requirements: For doctorate, thesis/dissertation.
Entrance requirements: For master's, GRE General Test, TOEFL, minimum GPA of 3.0; for doctorate, GRE General Test, minimum GPA of 3.5. *Application deadline:* For fall admission, 5/15 (priority date); for spring admission, 11/1 (priority date). Applications are processed on a rolling basis. *Application fee:* $45 ($55 for international students).
Expenses: Tuition, state resident: full-time $4,720; part-time $197 per credit. Tuition, nonresident: full-time $13,748; part-time $573 per credit. Required fees: $642.
Financial support: In 2001–02, fellowships with partial tuition reimbursements (averaging $9,811 per year); career-related internships or fieldwork and tuition waivers (partial) also available.
Faculty research: Scholarly communication, interface design, public library policy,

computer-mediated communication, information retrieval. *Total annual research expenditures:* $179,634.
Dr. Blaise Cronin, Dean, 812-855-2018, *Fax:* 812-855-6166.
Application contact: Rhonda Spencer, Information Contact, 812-855-2018, *Fax:* 812-855-6166. *Web site:* http://www.slis.indiana.edu/

Find an in-depth description at www.petersons.com/gradchannel.

■ INDIANA UNIVERSITY–PURDUE UNIVERSITY INDIANAPOLIS

School of Library and Information Science, Indianapolis, IN 46202-2896

AWARDS MIS, MLS, M PI/MIS. Part-time and evening/weekend programs available.

Faculty: 1 (woman) full-time.
Students: 24 full-time (19 women), 155 part-time (120 women); includes 4 minority (all African Americans), 1 international. Average age 37. In 2001, 67 degrees awarded.
Entrance requirements: For master's, GRE General Test, TOEFL, English language proficiency. *Application deadline:* For fall admission, 5/15 (priority date). Applications are processed on a rolling basis. *Application fee:* $45 ($55 for international students).
Expenses: Tuition, state resident: full-time $4,480; part-time $187 per credit. Tuition, nonresident: full-time $12,926; part-time $539 per credit. Required fees: $177.
Financial support: Career-related internships or fieldwork available.
Dr. Blaise Cronin, Dean, 317-278-2375.
Application contact: Dr. Debora Shaw, Associate Dean, 317-278-2375, *Fax:* 317-278-1807, *E-mail:* shawd@indiana.edu. *Web site:* http://www.slis.indiana.edu/

■ INTER AMERICAN UNIVERSITY OF PUERTO RICO, SAN GERMÁN CAMPUS

Graduate Programs, Department of Education, Program in Library Science, San Germán, PR 00683-5008

AWARDS MA. Part-time and evening/weekend programs available.

Faculty: 2 full-time (0 women).
Students: 8 full-time (4 women), 39 part-time (36 women). Average age 37. In 2001, 11 degrees awarded.
Degree requirements: For master's, comprehensive exam.
Entrance requirements: For master's, minimum GPA of 3.0, GRE General Test, or PAEG. *Application deadline:* For fall admission, 4/30 (priority date); for spring admission, 11/15. Applications are processed on a rolling basis. *Application fee:* $31.
Expenses: Tuition: Part-time $165 per credit. Required fees: $390; $195 per semester. Tuition and fees vary according to degree level and program.
Financial support: Teaching assistantships available.
Application contact: Dr. Waldemar Velez, Director of Graduate Program Center, 787-892-4300 Ext. 7358, *Fax:* 787-892-6350, *E-mail:* wvelez@sg.inter.edu.

■ KENT STATE UNIVERSITY

College of Fine and Professional Arts, School of Library and Information Science, Kent, OH 44242-0001

AWARDS MLS, MS.

Degree requirements: For master's, thesis optional.
Entrance requirements: For master's, GRE General Test, minimum GPA of 2.75.

■ KUTZTOWN UNIVERSITY OF PENNSYLVANIA

College of Graduate Studies and Extended Learning, College of Education, Program in Library Science, Kutztown, PA 19530-0730

AWARDS MLS, Certificate. Part-time and evening/weekend programs available.

Faculty: 3 part-time/adjunct (2 women).
Students: 5 full-time (4 women), 54 part-time (42 women), 1 international. Average age 33. In 2001, 25 degrees awarded.
Degree requirements: For master's, comprehensive exam.
Entrance requirements: For master's, GRE General Test, TOEFL, TSE. *Application deadline:* Applications are processed on a rolling basis. *Application fee:* $35.
Expenses: Tuition, state resident: full-time $4,600; part-time $256 per credit. Tuition, nonresident: full-time $7,554; part-time $420 per credit. Required fees: $835.
Financial support: Career-related internships or fieldwork, Federal Work-Study, and unspecified assistantships available. Financial award application deadline: 3/15; financial award applicants required to submit FAFSA.
Dr. M. Kathryn Holland, Chairperson, 610-683-4300, *Fax:* 610-683-4636, *E-mail:* holland@kutztown.edu. *Web site:* http://www.kutztown.edu/acad/

■ LONG ISLAND UNIVERSITY, C.W. POST CAMPUS

College of Information and Computer Science, Palmer School of Library and Information Science, Brookville, NY 11548-1300

AWARDS Archives (Certificate); information studies (PhD); library and information science (MS); records management (Certificate); schooll library media specialist (MS). Part-time and evening/weekend programs available. Postbaccalaureate distance learning degree programs offered (minimal on-campus study).

Faculty: 14 full-time (3 women), 30 part-time/adjunct (10 women).
Students: 72 full-time (37 women), 333 part-time (233 women). 133 applicants, 88% accepted. In 2001, 113 master's, 1 doctorate, 1 other advanced degree awarded.
Degree requirements: For master's, internship, thesis optional; for doctorate, thesis/dissertation, qualifying exam.
Entrance requirements: For master's, GRE or MAT, minimum undergraduate GPA of 3.0, resumé. *Application deadline:* For fall admission, 2/15; for spring admission, 10/15. *Application fee:* $30. Electronic applications accepted.
Expenses: Tuition: Full-time $10,296; part-time $572 per credit. Required fees: $380; $190 per semester.
Financial support: Fellowships, research assistantships, career-related internships or fieldwork, Federal Work-Study, institutionally sponsored loans, and tuition waivers (partial) available. Support available to part-time students. Financial award application deadline: 5/15; financial award applicants required to submit CSS PROFILE or FAFSA.
Faculty research: Information retrieval, digital libraries, scientometric and infometric studies, preservation/archiving and electronic records.
Dr. Michael E. D. Koening, Dean, 516-299-2866, *Fax:* 516-299-4168, *E-mail:* palmer@cwpost.liu.edu.
Application contact: Rosemary Chu, Graduate Admissions, 516-299-2866, *Fax:* 516-299-4168, *E-mail:* palmer@cwpost.liu.edu. *Web site:* http://www.liu.edu/palmer/

■ LOUISIANA STATE UNIVERSITY AND AGRICULTURAL AND MECHANICAL COLLEGE

Graduate School, School of Library and Information Science, Baton Rouge, LA 70803

AWARDS MLIS, CAS. Evening/weekend programs available.

Faculty: 9 full-time (5 women).
Students: 55 full-time (40 women), 109 part-time (99 women); includes 27 minority (23 African Americans, 2 Hispanic Americans, 2 Native Americans), 10 international. Average age 36. 64 applicants, 64% accepted, 25 enrolled. In 2001, 61 master's, 3 other advanced degrees awarded.
Degree requirements: For master's, thesis optional.
Entrance requirements: For master's, GRE General Test, minimum GPA of 3.0. *Application deadline:* For fall admission, 1/25 (priority date). Applications are processed on a rolling basis. *Application fee:* $25.
Expenses: Tuition, state resident: full-time $2,551. Tuition, nonresident: full-time $5,551. Required fees: $854. Part-time tuition and fees vary according to course load.

Louisiana State University and Agricultural and Mechanical College (continued)

Financial support: In 2001–02, 16 students received support, including 11 research assistantships with partial tuition reimbursements available (averaging $8,588 per year), 2 teaching assistantships with partial tuition reimbursements available (averaging $10,338 per year); fellowships, career-related internships or fieldwork and unspecified assistantships also available. Support available to part-time students. Financial award applicants required to submit FAFSA.
Faculty research: Information retrieval, management, collection development, public libraries.
Dr. Beth M. Paskoff, Dean, 225-578-3158, *Fax:* 225-578-4581, *E-mail:* lspask@lsu.edu.
Application contact: Admissions Secretary, 225-578-3158. *Web site:* http://adam.slis.lsu.edu/

■ MANSFIELD UNIVERSITY OF PENNSYLVANIA

Graduate Studies, Program in School Library and Information Technologies, Mansfield, PA 16933

AWARDS MS.

Faculty: 1 (woman) full-time, 11 part-time/adjunct (10 women).
Students: 6 full-time, 68 part-time. Average age 34. In 2001, 9 degrees awarded.
Entrance requirements: For master's, minimum GPA of 3.0. *Application deadline:* Applications are processed on a rolling basis. *Application fee:* $25. Electronic applications accepted.
Expenses: Tuition, state resident: full-time $2,300; part-time $256 per credit. Tuition, nonresident: full-time $3,777; part-time $470 per credit. Required fees: $230.
Financial support: Application deadline: 5/1.
Dr. Larry Nesbit, Head, 670-662-4672.
Application contact: Dr. Doris Dorwant, Program Director, 570-662-4676, *E-mail:* ddorwant@mnsfld.edu.

■ MCDANIEL COLLEGE

Graduate Studies, Department of Education, Program in Media/Library Science, Westminster, MD 21157-4390

AWARDS MS. Part-time and evening/weekend programs available.

Faculty: 1 (woman) full-time, 7 part-time/adjunct (6 women).
Students: 2 full-time (both women), 59 part-time (55 women); includes 3 minority (2 African Americans, 1 Hispanic American). Average age 37. 4 applicants, 100% accepted, 3 enrolled. In 2001, 15 degrees awarded.
Degree requirements: For master's, thesis optional.
Entrance requirements: For master's, GRE General Test, MAT, or NTE/Praxis I, letters of reference (3). *Application deadline:* Applications are processed on a rolling basis. *Application fee:* $40.
Expenses: Tuition: Part-time $240 per course. Required fees: $315 per year. Tuition and fees vary according to campus/location.
Financial support: Career-related internships or fieldwork available. Financial award application deadline: 3/1.
Dr. Ramona Kerby, Coordinator, 410-857-2507, *Fax:* 410-857-2515, *E-mail:* rkerby@wmdc.edu.
Application contact: Crystal L. Perry, Administrator of Graduate Records, 410-857-2513, *Fax:* 410-857-2515, *E-mail:* cperry@wmdc.edu.

■ NORTH CAROLINA CENTRAL UNIVERSITY

Division of Academic Affairs, School of Library and Information Sciences, Durham, NC 27707-3129

AWARDS MIS, MLS. Part-time and evening/weekend programs available.

Faculty: 7 full-time (3 women), 7 part-time/adjunct (2 women).
Students: 72 full-time (44 women), 128 part-time (107 women); includes 107 minority (83 African Americans, 18 Asian Americans or Pacific Islanders, 6 Native Americans). Average age 36. 79 applicants, 99% accepted. In 2001, 96 degrees awarded.
Degree requirements: For master's, one foreign language.
Entrance requirements: For master's, 90 hours in liberal arts, minimum B average. *Application deadline:* For fall admission, 8/1. *Application fee:* $30.
Expenses: Tuition, state resident: full-time $1,424. Tuition, nonresident: full-time $9,492. Required fees: $1,054.
Financial support: Fellowships, research assistantships, career-related internships or fieldwork, institutionally sponsored loans, and scholarships/grants available. Support available to part-time students. Financial award application deadline: 5/1.
Faculty research: African-American resources, planning and evaluation, analysis of economic and physical resources, geography of information, artificial intelligence.
Dr. Benjamin F. Speller, Dean, 919-560-6485, *Fax:* 919-560-6402, *E-mail:* bspeller@wpo.nccu.edu.

■ OLD DOMINION UNIVERSITY

Darden College of Education, Program in Elementary/Middle Education, Norfolk, VA 23529

AWARDS Educational media (MS Ed); elementary education (MS Ed); instructional technology (MS Ed); library science (MS Ed); middle school education (MS Ed). Part-time and evening/weekend programs available.

Faculty: 28 full-time (11 women).
Students: 69 full-time (50 women), 257 part-time (165 women); includes 72 minority (52 African Americans, 3 Asian Americans or Pacific Islanders, 13 Hispanic Americans, 4 Native Americans). Average age 38. 69 applicants, 93% accepted. In 2001, 231 degrees awarded.
Degree requirements: For master's, comprehensive exam.
Entrance requirements: For master's, GRE General Test or MAT, PRAXIS I, minimum GPA of 2.75, teaching certificate. *Application deadline:* For fall admission, 6/1 (priority date); for winter admission, 11/1 (priority date); for spring admission, 3/1 (priority date). Applications are processed on a rolling basis. *Application fee:* $30.
Expenses: Tuition, state resident: part-time $202 per credit. Tuition, nonresident: part-time $534 per credit. Required fees: $76 per semester.
Financial support: In 2001–02, 180 students received support, including 4 research assistantships with tuition reimbursements available (averaging $4,131 per year); fellowships, teaching assistantships, career-related internships or fieldwork, Federal Work-Study, institutionally sponsored loans, scholarships/grants, and tuition waivers (partial) also available. Support available to part-time students. Financial award application deadline: 2/15; financial award applicants required to submit FAFSA.
Faculty research: Education pre-K to 6, middle school education, school librarianship, instructional technology.
Dr. Katherine Bucher, Graduate Program Director, 757-683-3283, *Fax:* 757-683-5862, *E-mail:* eciegpd@odu.edu. *Web site:* http://www.odu.edu/webroot/orgs/Educ/ECI/eci.nsf./pages/home/

■ OLD DOMINION UNIVERSITY

Darden College of Education, Programs in Secondary Education, Norfolk, VA 23529

AWARDS Biology (MS Ed); chemistry (MS Ed); English (MS Ed); instructional technology (MS Ed); library science (MS Ed); mathematics (MS Ed); secondary education (MS Ed); social studies (MS Ed). Part-time and evening/weekend programs available. Postbaccalaureate distance learning degree programs offered (minimal on-campus study).

Faculty: 28 full-time (11 women).
Students: 42 full-time (25 women), 127 part-time (72 women); includes 28 minority (20 African Americans, 3 Asian Americans or Pacific Islanders, 2 Hispanic Americans, 3 Native Americans). Average age 37. 44 applicants, 95% accepted. In 2001, 100 degrees awarded.
Degree requirements: For master's, candidacy exam, thesis optional. *Median time to degree:* Master's–1.5 years full-time, 3 years part-time.
Entrance requirements: For master's, GRE General Test, or MAT, PRAXIS 1

for master's with licensure, minimum GPA of 3.0, teaching certificate. *Application deadline:* Applications are processed on a rolling basis. *Application fee:* $30. Electronic applications accepted.
Expenses: Tuition, state resident: part-time $202 per credit. Tuition, nonresident: part-time $534 per credit. Required fees: $76 per semester.
Financial support: In 2001–02, 58 students received support, including 2 research assistantships with tuition reimbursements available (averaging $6,777 per year), 3 teaching assistantships with tuition reimbursements available (averaging $5,333 per year); fellowships, career-related internships or fieldwork, Federal Work-Study, institutionally sponsored loans, scholarships/grants, and tuition waivers (partial) also available. Support available to part-time students. Financial award application deadline: 2/15; financial award applicants required to submit FAFSA.
Faculty research: Mathematics retraining, writing project for teachers, geography teaching, reading.
Dr. Murray Rudisill, Graduate Program Director, 757-683-3283, *Fax:* 757-683-5862, *E-mail:* ecisgpd@odu.edu. *Web site:* http://www.odu.edu/webroots/orgs/educ/ECI/eci.nsf/pages/home

■ PRATT INSTITUTE

School of Information and Library Science, Brooklyn, NY 11205-3899

AWARDS MS, Adv C, JD/MS, MS/MS. Part-time and evening/weekend programs available.

Degree requirements: For master's, thesis.
Entrance requirements: For master's, TOEFL. Electronic applications accepted.
Expenses: Contact institution.
Faculty research: Development of urban libraries and information centers, medical and law librarianship, information management.

Find an in-depth description at www.petersons.com/gradchannel.

■ QUEENS COLLEGE OF THE CITY UNIVERSITY OF NEW YORK

Division of Graduate Studies, Social Science Division, Graduate School of Library and Information Studies, Flushing, NY 11367-1597

AWARDS MLS, AC. Part-time and evening/weekend programs available.

Faculty: 8 full-time (5 women).
Students: 23 full-time (17 women), 364 part-time (267 women). 201 applicants, 95% accepted. In 2001, 146 degrees awarded.
Degree requirements: For master's, thesis; for AC, thesis optional.
Entrance requirements: For master's, TOEFL, minimum GPA of 3.0; for AC, TOEFL, master's degree or equivalent. *Application deadline:* For fall admission, 4/1; for spring admission, 11/1. Applications are processed on a rolling basis. *Application fee:* $40.
Expenses: Tuition, state resident: full-time $2,175; part-time $185 per credit. Tuition, nonresident: full-time $3,800; part-time $320 per credit. Required fees: $114; $57 per semester. Tuition and fees vary according to course load.
Financial support: Career-related internships or fieldwork, Federal Work-Study, institutionally sponsored loans, and tuition waivers (partial) available. Support available to part-time students. Financial award application deadline: 4/1; financial award applicants required to submit FAFSA.
Faculty research: Multimedia and video studies, ethnicity and librarianship, information science and computer applications.
Dr. Marianne Cooper, Director and Chair, 718-997-3790, *E-mail:* marianne_cooper@qc.edu.
Application contact: Dr. Karen Smith, Graduate Adviser, 718-997-3790, *E-mail:* karen_smith@qc.edu.

■ RUTGERS, THE STATE UNIVERSITY OF NEW JERSEY, NEW BRUNSWICK

School of Communication, Information and Library Studies, Department of Library and Information Science, New Brunswick, NJ 08901-1281

AWARDS MLS. Part-time programs available.

Entrance requirements: For master's, GRE General Test, TOEFL. Electronic applications accepted.
Faculty research: Information science, library services, management of information services. *Web site:* http://scils.rutgers.edu/

■ ST. JOHN'S UNIVERSITY

St. John's College of Liberal Arts and Sciences, Division of Library and Information Science, Jamaica, NY 11439

AWARDS Library and information science (MLS, Adv C);). Part-time and evening/weekend programs available.

Faculty: 5 full-time (all women), 6 part-time/adjunct (2 women).
Students: 10 full-time (7 women), 64 part-time (49 women); includes 11 minority (5 African Americans, 3 Asian Americans or Pacific Islanders, 3 Hispanic Americans), 11 international. Average age 37. 50 applicants, 76% accepted, 21 enrolled. In 2001, 25 degrees awarded.
Degree requirements: For master's, comprehensive exam.
Entrance requirements: For master's, interview, minimum GPA of 3.0. *Application deadline:* Applications are processed on a rolling basis. *Application fee:* $40.
Expenses: Contact institution.
Financial support: Research assistantships with full tuition reimbursements, career-related internships or fieldwork and scholarships/grants available. Support available to part-time students. Financial award application deadline: 3/1; financial award applicants required to submit FAFSA.
Faculty research: On-line database management, public library patronage, medieval monastic libraries and archives, children's literature, indexing.
Dr. Sherry Vellucci, Acting Director, 718-990-6735.
Application contact: Matthew Whelan, Director, Office of Admission, 718-990-2000, *Fax:* 718-990-2096, *E-mail:* admissions@stjohns.edu. *Web site:* http://www.stjohns.edu/

■ SAM HOUSTON STATE UNIVERSITY

College of Education and Applied Science, Department of Library Science, Huntsville, TX 77341

AWARDS MLS. Part-time and evening/weekend programs available.

Students: 2 full-time (1 woman), 136 part-time (132 women); includes 35 minority (2 African Americans, 33 Hispanic Americans). Average age 38. In 2001, 55 degrees awarded.
Entrance requirements: For master's, GRE General Test, minimum GPA of 2.8. *Application deadline:* For fall admission, 8/1; for spring admission, 12/1. Applications are processed on a rolling basis. *Application fee:* $20.
Expenses: Tuition, area resident: Part-time $69 per credit. Tuition, state resident: full-time $1,380; part-time $69 per credit. Tuition, nonresident: full-time $5,600; part-time $280 per credit. Required fees: $748. Tuition and fees vary according to course load.
Financial support: Teaching assistantships, career-related internships or fieldwork and Federal Work-Study available. Support available to part-time students. Financial award application deadline: 5/31; financial award applicants required to submit FAFSA.
Dr. Mary Berry, Chair, 936-294-1150, *Fax:* 936-294-1153, *E-mail:* lis_mab@shsu.edu. *Web site:* http://www.shsu.edu/lis_www/

■ SAN JOSE STATE UNIVERSITY

Graduate Studies, Graduate Studies Program, School of Library and Information Science, San Jose, CA 95192-0001

AWARDS MLIS. Part-time and evening/weekend programs available.

Faculty: 6 full-time (3 women), 4 part-time/adjunct (3 women).
Students: 87 full-time (66 women), 341 part-time (269 women); includes 83 minority (15 African Americans, 39 Asian Americans or Pacific Islanders, 27

San Jose State University (continued)
Hispanic Americans, 2 Native Americans), 5 international. Average age 38. 352 applicants, 77% accepted. In 2001, 211 degrees awarded.
Degree requirements: For master's, comprehensive exam.
Entrance requirements: For master's, minimum GPA of 3.0. *Application deadline:* For fall admission, 6/29; for spring admission, 11/30. Applications are processed on a rolling basis. *Application fee:* $59. Electronic applications accepted.
Expenses: Tuition, nonresident: part-time $246 per unit. Required fees: $678 per semester. Tuition and fees vary according to course load.
Financial support: In 2001–02, 4 fellowships, 4 teaching assistantships were awarded. Career-related internships or fieldwork, Federal Work-Study, and institutionally sponsored loans also available. Support available to part-time students. Financial award application deadline: 8/20; financial award applicants required to submit FAFSA.
Faculty research: Evaluation of information services online, search strategy, organizational behavior.
Dr. Blanche Woolls, Director, 408-924-2491, *Fax:* 408-924-2476.

■ SIMMONS COLLEGE

Graduate School of Library and Information Science, Boston, MA 02115

AWARDS Archives management (MS); competitive intelligence (MS, Certificate); library and information science (DA); school library media specialist (MS, Certificate). MS/DA and MS/MA offered jointly with Department of History. Part-time and evening/weekend programs available.

Faculty: 17 full-time (8 women), 29 part-time/adjunct (20 women).
Students: 550. Average age 34. 307 applicants, 70% accepted, 141 enrolled. In 2001, 374 master's, 3 doctorates awarded.
Degree requirements: For master's, technology competency.
Entrance requirements: For master's, GRE General Test or minimum GPA of 3.0; interview; for doctorate, GRE General Test or MAT, interview. *Application deadline:* For fall admission, 7/1 (priority date); for spring admission, 11/1. Applications are processed on a rolling basis. *Application fee:* $35. Electronic applications accepted.
Financial support: In 2001–02, 462 students received support, including 4 research assistantships (averaging $18,900 per year); teaching assistantships, career-related internships or fieldwork, Federal Work-Study, institutionally sponsored loans, scholarships/grants, and tuition waivers (full and partial) also available. Support available to part-time students. Financial award application deadline: 3/1; financial award applicants required to submit FAFSA.
Faculty research: Optical technology, visual communications, database management, information policy.
Dr. James Matarazzo, Dean, 617-521-2806, *Fax:* 617-521-3192, *E-mail:* matarazz@simmons.edu.
Application contact: Judith J. Beal, Director of Admissions, 617-521-2141, *Fax:* 617-521-3045, *E-mail:* judy.beal@simmons.edu. *Web site:* http://www.simmons.edu/graduate/gslis/

Find an in-depth description at www.petersons.com/gradchannel.

■ SOUTHERN ARKANSAS UNIVERSITY–MAGNOLIA

Graduate Programs, Magnolia, AR 71753

AWARDS Agency counseling (M Ed); education (M Ed), including counseling and development, educational administration and supervision, elementary education, kinesiology, secondary education; library media and information specialist (M Ed); teaching (MAT). Part-time programs available.

Faculty: 35 full-time (16 women), 4 part-time/adjunct (3 women).
Students: 24 full-time (15 women), 93 part-time (72 women); includes 17 minority (15 African Americans, 1 Asian American or Pacific Islander, 1 Hispanic American), 1 international. 63 applicants, 38% accepted. In 2001, 45 degrees awarded.
Degree requirements: For master's, thesis optional.
Entrance requirements: For master's, GRE, minimum GPA of 2.75. *Application deadline:* For fall admission, 8/15. Applications are processed on a rolling basis. *Application fee:* $0.
Expenses: Tuition, state resident: full-time $2,322; part-time $129 per hour. Tuition, nonresident: full-time $3,366; part-time $187 per hour. Required fees: $48; $1 per hour. $15 per semester.
Financial support: In 2001–02, 70 students received support, including 35 research assistantships with full tuition reimbursements available (averaging $3,091 per year); career-related internships or fieldwork, Federal Work-Study, scholarships/grants, and unspecified assistantships also available. Financial award application deadline: 8/15; financial award applicants required to submit FAFSA.
Faculty research: Alternative certification for teachers, supervision of instruction, instructional leadership, counseling.
Dr. John R. Jones, Associate Dean, Graduate Studies, 870-235-4055, *Fax:* 870-235-5035, *E-mail:* jrjones@saumag.edu.

■ SOUTHERN CONNECTICUT STATE UNIVERSITY

School of Graduate Studies, School of Communication, Information and Library Science, Department of Library Science and Instructional Technology, New Haven, CT 06515-1355

AWARDS Instructional technology (MS); library science (MLS); library/information studies (Diploma). Part-time and evening/weekend programs available.

Faculty: 6 full-time (4 women).
Students: 27 full-time (23 women), 175 part-time (149 women); includes 6 minority (5 African Americans, 1 Hispanic American), 1 international. 244 applicants, 32% accepted. In 2001, 76 master's, 2 other advanced degrees awarded.
Degree requirements: For master's and Diploma, thesis or alternative.
Entrance requirements: For master's, GRE General Test, interview, minimum QPA of 2.7, introductory computer science course; for Diploma, master's degree in library science or information science. *Application deadline:* For fall admission, 7/15 (priority date). Applications are processed on a rolling basis. *Application fee:* $40.
Financial support: Research assistantships available. Financial award application deadline: 4/15; financial award applicants required to submit FAFSA.
Nancy Disbrow, Chairperson, 203-392-5781, *Fax:* 203-392-5780, *E-mail:* disbrow@southernct.edu.

■ SPALDING UNIVERSITY

Graduate Studies, School of Education, Program in School Media Librarianship, Louisville, KY 40203-2188

AWARDS MA. Part-time and evening/weekend programs available.

Faculty: 10 full-time (8 women), 4 part-time/adjunct (2 women).
Students: 6 full-time (all women), 31 part-time (28 women); includes 2 minority (1 African American, 1 Asian American or Pacific Islander). Average age 27. In 2001, 6 degrees awarded.
Degree requirements: For master's, comprehensive exam.
Entrance requirements: For master's, GRE General Test or MAT, portfolio. *Application deadline:* For fall admission, 8/15 (priority date). Applications are processed on a rolling basis. *Application fee:* $30.
Expenses: Tuition: Full-time $6,000; part-time $400 per credit hour. Required fees: $96.
Financial support: In 2001–02, 12 students received support; research assistantships, career-related internships or fieldwork, Federal Work-Study, and scholarships/grants available. Support available to part-time students. Financial

award application deadline: 3/15; financial award applicants required to submit FAFSA.
Application contact: 502-585-7105, *Fax:* 502-585-7158, *E-mail:* gradadmissions@spalding.edu. *Web site:* http://www.spalding.edu/

■ STATE UNIVERSITY OF NEW YORK AT ALBANY

School of Information Science and Policy, Albany, NY 12222-0001

AWARDS Information science (MS, PhD); information science and policy (CAS); library science (MLS). Part-time and evening/weekend programs available.

Students: 127 full-time (96 women), 102 part-time (81 women); includes 8 minority (4 African Americans, 3 Hispanic Americans, 1 Native American), 29 international. Average age 35. 172 applicants, 76% accepted. In 2001, 81 master's, 5 doctorates awarded.
Degree requirements: For doctorate, thesis/dissertation.
Entrance requirements: For doctorate, GRE General Test. *Application deadline:* For fall admission, 7/1; for spring admission, 11/1. *Application fee:* $50.
Expenses: Tuition, state resident: full-time $2,550; part-time $213 per credit. Tuition, nonresident: full-time $4,208; part-time $351 per credit. Required fees: $470; $470 per year.
Financial support: Fellowships, Federal Work-Study available. Financial award application deadline: 4/1.
Philip Eppard, Dean, 518-442-5115.
Application contact: Florance Bolton, Assistant to the Dean of Graduate Studies, 518-442-5200.

■ SYRACUSE UNIVERSITY

Graduate School, School of Information Studies, Information and Library Science Program, Syracuse, NY 13244-0003

AWARDS MLS, CAS, JD/MLS. Part-time and evening/weekend programs available. Postbaccalaureate distance learning degree programs offered (minimal on-campus study).

Faculty: 33 full-time (12 women), 42 part-time/adjunct (12 women).
Students: 17 full-time (11 women), 149 part-time (130 women); includes 7 minority (4 African Americans, 2 Asian Americans or Pacific Islanders, 1 Hispanic American), 26 international. Average age 38. In 2001, 84 degrees awarded.
Degree requirements: For master's, fieldwork or research paper.
Entrance requirements: For master's, GRE General Test; for CAS, 2 years of work experience, MLS or related degree. *Application deadline:* For fall admission, 2/15 (priority date); for spring admission, 11/1 (priority date). *Application fee:* $50. Electronic applications accepted.
Expenses: Tuition: Full-time $15,528; part-time $647 per credit. Required fees: $420; $38 per term. Tuition and fees vary according to program.

Find an in-depth description at www.petersons.com/gradchannel.

■ TENNESSEE TECHNOLOGICAL UNIVERSITY

Graduate School, College of Education, Department of Curriculum and Instruction, Program in Library Science, Cookeville, TN 38505

AWARDS MA.

Students: 1 (woman) full-time, 5 part-time (all women). 2 applicants, 100% accepted. *Application deadline:* For fall admission, 3/1 (priority date); for spring admission, 8/1. *Application fee:* $25 ($30 for international students).
Expenses: Tuition, state resident: full-time $4,000; part-time $215 per hour. Tuition, nonresident: full-time $10,500; part-time $495 per hour. Required fees: $1,971 per semester.
Financial support: Application deadline: 4/1.
Application contact: Dr. Francis O. Otuonye, Associate Vice President for Research and Graduate Studies, 931-372-3233, *Fax:* 931-372-3497, *E-mail:* fotuonye@tntech.edu.

■ TEXAS WOMAN'S UNIVERSITY

Graduate Studies and Research, College of Professional Education, School of Library and Information Studies, Denton, TX 76201

AWARDS Library science (MA, MLS, PhD). Part-time and evening/weekend programs available. Postbaccalaureate distance learning degree programs offered (minimal on-campus study).

Faculty: 11 full-time (9 women).
Students: 36 full-time (34 women), 204 part-time (195 women); includes 33 minority (18 African Americans, 1 Asian American or Pacific Islander, 14 Hispanic Americans), 2 international. Average age 39. In 2001, 95 master's, 1 doctorate awarded.
Degree requirements: For doctorate, thesis/dissertation.
Entrance requirements: For master's, minimum GPA of 3.0; for doctorate, interview, minimum GPA of 3.0, master's degree in library science. *Application deadline:* Applications are processed on a rolling basis. *Application fee:* $30.
Expenses: Tuition, state resident: part-time $90 per semester hour. Tuition, nonresident: part-time $303 per semester hour. Required fees: $24 per credit hour. $79 per semester.
Financial support: In 2001–02, 5 fellowships with partial tuition reimbursements, 6 teaching assistantships with partial tuition reimbursements were awarded. Research assistantships with partial tuition reimbursements, career-related internships or fieldwork, Federal Work-Study, institutionally sponsored loans, and scholarships/grants also available. Support available to part-time students. Financial award application deadline: 4/1; financial award applicants required to submit FAFSA.
Dr. Laurie Bonnici, Director, 940-898-2602, *Fax:* 940-898-2611, *E-mail:* lbonnici@twu.edu. *Web site:* http://www.libraryschool.net/

■ UNIVERSITY AT BUFFALO, THE STATE UNIVERSITY OF NEW YORK

Graduate School, School of Informatics, Department of Library and Information Studies, Buffalo, NY 14260

AWARDS MLS, PhD, Certificate. Part-time and evening/weekend programs available.

Faculty: 9 full-time (4 women), 1 part-time/adjunct (0 women).
Students: 113 full-time (86 women), 161 part-time (131 women); includes 17 minority (8 African Americans, 6 Asian Americans or Pacific Islanders, 2 Hispanic Americans, 1 Native American), 11 international. Average age 34. 109 applicants, 86% accepted. In 2001, 115 degrees awarded.
Degree requirements: For master's, thesis optional; for Certificate, thesis.
Entrance requirements: For master's, minimum GPA of 3.0. *Application deadline:* For fall admission, 4/1 (priority date); for spring admission, 10/15 (priority date). Applications are processed on a rolling basis. *Application fee:* $35. Electronic applications accepted.
Expenses: Tuition, state resident: full-time $6,118. Tuition, nonresident: full-time $9,434.
Financial support: In 2001–02, 5 fellowships (averaging $10,000 per year), 2 research assistantships with full tuition reimbursements (averaging $5,000 per year) were awarded. Teaching assistantships, career-related internships or fieldwork, Federal Work-Study, institutionally sponsored loans, tuition waivers (full and partial), and unspecified assistantships also available. Support available to part-time students. Financial award application deadline: 3/1; financial award applicants required to submit FAFSA.
Faculty research: Information user behavior, storage and information retrieval, digital libraries, information management services to information users. *Total annual research expenditures:* $202,000.
Dr. Judith Robinson, Chair, 716-645-2412, *Fax:* 716-645-3775, *E-mail:* ub-lis@buffalo.edu.
Application contact: Carolynn Krupp, Student Services Coordinator, 716-645-2412 Ext. 1170, *Fax:* 716-645-3775, *E-mail:* cjk2@buffalo.edu. *Web site:* http://www.informatics.buffalo.edu/dlis/

■ THE UNIVERSITY OF ALABAMA

Graduate School, College of Communication and Information Sciences, School of Library and Information Studies, Tuscaloosa, AL 35487

AWARDS Book arts (MFA); library and information studies (MLIS, PhD, Ed S).

Faculty: 7 full-time (3 women), 2 part-time/adjunct (1 woman).
Students: 54 full-time (40 women), 118 part-time (103 women); includes 17 minority (13 African Americans, 2 Asian Americans or Pacific Islanders, 1 Hispanic American, 1 Native American). Average age 34. 86 applicants, 73% accepted, 49 enrolled. In 2001, 96 master's, 1 doctorate, 2 other advanced degrees awarded.
Entrance requirements: For master's, GRE General Test or MAT, minimum GPA of 3.0. *Application deadline:* For fall admission, 2/15 (priority date); for spring admission, 11/1. Applications are processed on a rolling basis. *Application fee:* $25. Electronic applications accepted.
Expenses: Tuition, state resident: full-time $3,292; part-time $183 per credit hour. Tuition, nonresident: full-time $8,912; part-time $495 per credit hour. Tuition and fees vary according to course load, campus/location and program.
Financial support: In 2001–02, 67 students received support, including 9 research assistantships with full tuition reimbursements available, 17 teaching assistantships with full tuition reimbursements available; fellowships, career-related internships or fieldwork and Federal Work-Study also available. Financial award application deadline: 2/15.
Faculty research: Instructional design, information equity, youth services, rural information services.
Dr. Joan Atkinson, Director, 205-348-1522, *Fax:* 205-348-3746, *E-mail:* jatkinso@slism.slis.ua.edu.
Application contact: Dr. Margaret Dalton, Professor, Graduate Coordinator, 205-348-1524, *E-mail:* mdalton@slis.ua.edu.

■ THE UNIVERSITY OF ARIZONA

Graduate College, College of Social and Behavioral Sciences, School of Information Resources and Library Science, Tucson, AZ 85721

AWARDS MA, PhD. Part-time programs available.

Degree requirements: For master's, proficiency in disk operating system (DOS); for doctorate, thesis/dissertation.
Entrance requirements: For master's, GRE, TOEFL, minimum GPA of 3.0; for doctorate, GRE General Test, TOEFL.
Expenses: Tuition, state resident: full-time $2,490; part-time $436 per unit. Tuition, nonresident: full-time $10,300; part-time $436 per unit. Full-time tuition and fees vary according to degree level and program.
Faculty research: Microcomputer applications; quantitative methods systems; information transfer, planning, evaluation, and technology.

■ UNIVERSITY OF CALIFORNIA, LOS ANGELES

Graduate Division, Graduate School of Education and Information Studies, Department of Information Studies, Los Angeles, CA 90095

AWARDS Archival studies (MLIS); informatics (MLIS); library and information science (PhD, Certificate); library studies (MLIS). Part-time programs available.

Faculty: 14 full-time (9 women), 10 part-time/adjunct (7 women).
Students: 171 (139 women); includes 38 minority (1 African American, 18 Asian Americans or Pacific Islanders, 17 Hispanic Americans, 2 Native Americans) 16 international. Average age 33. 172 applicants, 59% accepted, 56 enrolled. In 2001, 53 master's, 4 doctorates awarded. Terminal master's awarded for partial completion of doctoral program.
Degree requirements: For master's, thesis or alternative, professional portfolio; for doctorate, thesis/dissertation, oral and written qualifying exams, professional portfolio.
Entrance requirements: For master's, GRE General Test, TOEFL, TWE, previous course work in computer programming and statistics; for doctorate, GRE General Test, TOEFL, TWE, previous course work in statistics, 2 samples of research writing in English. *Application deadline:* For fall admission, 12/15 (priority date). Applications are processed on a rolling basis. *Application fee:* $60. Electronic applications accepted.
Expenses: Tuition, nonresident: full-time $10,244. Required fees: $3,609. Full-time tuition and fees vary according to program.
Financial support: In 2001–02, 12 research assistantships, 2 teaching assistantships were awarded. Fellowships, career-related internships or fieldwork, Federal Work-Study, institutionally sponsored loans, scholarships/grants, tuition waivers (full and partial), and federal fellowships also available. Support available to part-time students. Financial award application deadline: 3/1; financial award applicants required to submit FAFSA.
Faculty research: Multimedia, digital libraries, archives and electronic records, interface design, information technology and policy, preservation, access.
Dr. Michele V. Cloonan, Chair, 310-825-8799, *Fax:* 310-206-3076, *E-mail:* mcloonan@ucla.edu.
Application contact: Susan S. Abler, Student Affairs Officer, 310-825-5269, *Fax:* 310-206-4460, *E-mail:* abler@gseis.ucla.edu. *Web site:* http://is.gseis.ucla.edu/

■ UNIVERSITY OF CENTRAL ARKANSAS

Graduate School, College of Education, Department of Middle/Secondary Education and Instructional Technologies, Program in Education Media and Library Science, Conway, AR 72035-0001

AWARDS MS. Part-time programs available.

Faculty: 4.
Students: 5 full-time (4 women), 67 part-time (65 women); includes 9 minority (all African Americans). In 2001, 34 degrees awarded.
Degree requirements: For master's, comprehensive exam.
Entrance requirements: For master's, GRE General Test, minimum GPA of 2.7. *Application deadline:* For fall admission, 3/1 (priority date); for spring admission, 10/1 (priority date). Applications are processed on a rolling basis. *Application fee:* $25 ($40 for international students).
Expenses: Tuition, state resident: full-time $3,303; part-time $184 per hour. Tuition, nonresident: full-time $5,922; part-time $329 per hour. Required fees: $68; $24 per semester.
Financial support: In 2001–02, 22 students received support, including 6 research assistantships with partial tuition reimbursements available (averaging $5,700 per year); Federal Work-Study, scholarships/grants, and tuition waivers (partial) also available. Financial award application deadline: 2/15.
Application contact: Jane Douglas, Co-Admissions Secretary, 501-450-5064, *Fax:* 501-450-5066, *E-mail:* janed@ecom.uca.edu.

■ UNIVERSITY OF DENVER

University College, Denver, CO 80208

AWARDS Applied communication (MSS); computer information systems (MCIS); environmental policy and management (MEPM); healthcare systems (MHS); liberal studies (MLS); library and information services (MLIS); public health (MPH); technology management (MoTM); telecommunications (MTEL). Part-time and evening/weekend programs available. Postbaccalaureate distance learning degree programs offered (no on-campus study).

Faculty: 167 part-time/adjunct (52 women).
Students: 1,244 (618 women); includes 177 minority (65 African Americans, 53 Asian Americans or Pacific Islanders, 54 Hispanic Americans, 5 Native Americans) 76 international. 54 applicants, 85% accepted. In 2001, 274 degrees awarded.
Entrance requirements: For master's, minimum undergraduate GPA of 3.0. *Application deadline:* For fall admission,

7/15 (priority date); for winter admission, 10/14 (priority date); for spring admission, 2/10 (priority date). Applications are processed on a rolling basis. *Application fee:* $25.
Expenses: Contact institution.
Financial support: In 2001–02, 174 students received support. *Total annual research expenditures:* $59,206.
Mike Bloom, Dean, 303-871-3141.
Application contact: Cindy Kraft, Admission Coordinator, 303-871-3969, *Fax:* 303-871-3303. *Web site:* http://www.du.edu/ucol/

■ UNIVERSITY OF HAWAII AT MANOA

Graduate Division, College of Arts and Sciences, College of Natural Sciences, Department of Information and Computer Sciences, Library and Information Science Program, Honolulu, HI 96822

AWARDS Advanced library and information science (Certificate); communication and information science (PhD); library and information science (MLI Sc). Part-time programs available. Postbaccalaureate distance learning degree programs offered (minimal on-campus study).

Degree requirements: For master's, thesis optional.
Entrance requirements: For master's, GRE General Test, TOEFL. Electronic applications accepted.
Expenses: Tuition, state resident: full-time $2,160; part-time $1,980 per year. Tuition, nonresident: full-time $5,190; part-time $4,829 per year.
Faculty research: Information behavior, evaluation of electronic information sources, online learning, history of libraries. *Web site:* http://www.hawaii.edu/slis/

■ UNIVERSITY OF ILLINOIS AT URBANA–CHAMPAIGN

Graduate College, Graduate School of Library and Information Science, Champaign, IL 61820

AWARDS MS, PhD, CAS.

Faculty: 16 full-time, 2 part-time/adjunct.
Students: 321 full-time (243 women); includes 22 minority (12 African Americans, 4 Asian Americans or Pacific Islanders, 6 Hispanic Americans), 45 international. Average age 31. 354 applicants, 38% accepted. In 2001, 162 master's, 3 doctorates awarded.
Degree requirements: For doctorate, thesis/dissertation; for CAS, project.
Entrance requirements: For master's, GRE General Test, minimum GPA of 3.0; for doctorate, interview; for CAS, master's degree in library and information science or related field, minimum GPA of 3.0. *Application deadline:* For fall admission, 6/1 (priority date); for spring admission, 10/1. Applications are processed on a rolling basis. *Application fee:* $40 ($50 for international students). Electronic applications accepted.
Expenses: Tuition, state resident: part-time $3,227 per degree program. Tuition, nonresident: part-time $7,169 per degree program. Tuition and fees vary according to program.
Financial support: In 2001–02, 38 fellowships, 151 research assistantships, 16 teaching assistantships were awarded. Tuition waivers (full and partial) also available. Financial award application deadline: 2/1.
Dr. Linda Smith, Interim Dean, 217-333-3281, *Fax:* 217-244-3102, *E-mail:* lcsmith@uiuc.edu.
Application contact: Carol DeVoss, Officer, 217-333-7197, *Fax:* 217-244-3302, *E-mail:* devoss@uiuc.edu. *Web site:* http://alexia.lis.uiuc.edu/

Find an in-depth description at www.petersons.com/gradchannel.

■ THE UNIVERSITY OF IOWA

Graduate College, School of Library and Information Science, Iowa City, IA 52242-1316

AWARDS MA, JD/MA, MBA/MA.

Faculty: 4 full-time.
Students: 40 full-time (32 women), 41 part-time (35 women); includes 4 minority (3 Asian Americans or Pacific Islanders, 1 Native American), 6 international. 46 applicants, 70% accepted, 13 enrolled. In 2001, 27 degrees awarded.
Degree requirements: For master's, exam, thesis optional.
Entrance requirements: For master's, GRE General Test, TOEFL. *Application deadline:* For fall admission, 3/1 (priority date); for spring admission, 10/1 (priority date). *Application fee:* $30 ($50 for international students). Electronic applications accepted.
Expenses: Tuition, state resident: full-time $3,702; part-time $206 per semester hour. Tuition, nonresident: full-time $11,924; part-time $206 per semester hour. Required fees: $101 per semester. Tuition and fees vary according to course load and program.
Financial support: In 2001–02, 12 research assistantships, 7 teaching assistantships were awarded. Fellowships available. Financial award applicants required to submit FAFSA.
Joseph Kearney, Director, 319-335-5707.

■ UNIVERSITY OF KENTUCKY

Graduate School, College of Communications and Information Studies, Program in Library and Information Science, Lexington, KY 40506-0032

AWARDS Library science (MA, MSLS). Part-time programs available.

Faculty: 10 full-time (2 women).
Students: 56 full-time (40 women), 119 part-time (106 women); includes 5 minority (3 African Americans, 2 Asian Americans or Pacific Islanders), 2 international. 95 applicants, 81% accepted. In 2001, 78 degrees awarded.
Degree requirements: For master's, variable foreign language requirement, comprehensive exam.
Entrance requirements: For master's, GRE General Test, minimum undergraduate GPA of 2.75. *Application deadline:* For fall admission, 7/15; for spring admission, 11/1. Applications are processed on a rolling basis. *Application fee:* $30 ($35 for international students).
Expenses: Tuition, state resident: full-time $4,075; part-time $213 per credit hour. Tuition, nonresident: full-time $11,295; part-time $614 per credit hour.
Financial support: In 2001–02, 5 fellowships, 27 research assistantships, 2 teaching assistantships were awarded. Career-related internships or fieldwork, Federal Work-Study, and unspecified assistantships also available. Financial award application deadline: 4/1.
Faculty research: Information retrieval systems, information-seeking behavior, organizational behavior, computer cataloging, library resource sharing. *Total annual research expenditures:* $24,000.
Dr. Timothy Sineath, Director of Graduate Studies, 859-257-8100, *Fax:* 859-257-4205.
Application contact: Dr. Jeannine Blackwell, Associate Dean, 859-257-4905, *Fax:* 859-323-1928.

■ UNIVERSITY OF MARYLAND, COLLEGE PARK

Graduate Studies and Research, Interdepartmental Programs, Program in Geography, Library, and Information Services, College Park, MD 20742

AWARDS MA/MLS.

Students: 3 full-time (2 women). 3 applicants, 67% accepted, 1 enrolled.
Application deadline: For fall admission, 1/15. Applications are processed on a rolling basis. *Application fee:* $50 ($70 for international students). Electronic applications accepted.
Expenses: Tuition, state resident: part-time $289 per credit hour. Tuition, nonresident: part-time $448 per credit hour. One-time fee: $436 part-time. Full-time tuition and fees vary according to course load, campus/location and program.
Financial support: Fellowships, research assistantships, teaching assistantships available. Financial award application deadline: 2/1; financial award applicants required to submit FAFSA.
Dr. Diane Barlow, Assistant Dean, 301-405-2038, *Fax:* 301-314-9145.
Application contact: Trudy Lindsey, Director, Graduate Admissions and

University of Maryland, College Park (continued)
Records, 301-405-6991, *Fax:* 301-314-9305, *E-mail:* grschool@deans.umd.edu.
Find an in-depth description at www.petersons.com/gradchannel.

■ UNIVERSITY OF MARYLAND, COLLEGE PARK

Graduate Studies and Research, Interdepartmental Programs, Program in History, Library, and Information Services, College Park, MD 20742

AWARDS MA/MLS.

Students: 15 full-time (11 women), 4 part-time (2 women); includes 1 minority (Asian American or Pacific Islander). 12 applicants, 67% accepted, 4 enrolled. *Application deadline:* For fall admission, 1/15. Applications are processed on a rolling basis. *Application fee:* $50 ($70 for international students). Electronic applications accepted.
Expenses: Tuition, state resident: part-time $289 per credit hour. Tuition, nonresident: part-time $448 per credit hour. One-time fee: $436 part-time. Full-time tuition and fees vary according to course load, campus/location and program.
Financial support: Fellowships, research assistantships, teaching assistantships available. Financial award applicants required to submit FAFSA.
Dr. Diane Barlow, Assistant Dean, 301-405-2038, *Fax:* 301-314-9145.
Application contact: Trudy Lindsey, Director, Graduate Admissions and Records, 301-405-6991, *Fax:* 301-314-9305, *E-mail:* grschool@deans.umd.edu.
Find an in-depth description at www.petersons.com/gradchannel.

■ UNIVERSITY OF MICHIGAN

Horace H. Rackham School of Graduate Studies, School of Information, Ann Arbor, MI 48109

AWARDS Archives and records management (MS); human-computer interaction (MS); information (PhD); information economics, management and policy (MS); library and information services (MS). Part-time programs available.

Entrance requirements: For master's and doctorate, GRE General Test. *Web site:* http://www.si.umich.edu/
Find an in-depth description at www.petersons.com/gradchannel.

■ UNIVERSITY OF MISSOURI–COLUMBIA

Graduate School, College of Education, School of Information Science and Learning Technologies, Columbia, MO 65211

AWARDS Educational technology (M Ed, Ed S); information science and learning technology (PhD); library science (MA). Part-time and evening/weekend programs available.

Faculty: 14 full-time (6 women).
Students: 47 full-time (20 women), 102 part-time (67 women); includes 4 minority (1 African American, 2 Asian Americans or Pacific Islanders, 1 Hispanic American), 47 international. 45 applicants, 87% accepted. In 2001, 47 master's, 5 doctorates, 1 other advanced degree awarded.
Entrance requirements: For master's, GRE General Test or MAT, minimum GPA of 3.0. *Application deadline:* For fall and spring admission, 3/1 (priority date); for winter admission, 10/1 (priority date). Applications are processed on a rolling basis. *Application fee:* $25 ($50 for international students).
Expenses: Tuition, state resident: part-time $179 per credit hour. Tuition, nonresident: part-time $539 per credit hour. Required fees: $122 per semester. Tuition and fees vary according to program.
Financial support: Fellowships, teaching assistantships available.
Dr. John M. Budd, Director of Graduate Studies, 573-882-3258, *E-mail:* buddj@missouri.edu. *Web site:* http://www.coe.missouri.edu/~sislt/

■ THE UNIVERSITY OF NORTH CAROLINA AT CHAPEL HILL

Graduate School, School of Information and Library Science, Chapel Hill, NC 27599

AWARDS MSIS, MSLS, PhD, CAS. Part-time programs available.

Faculty: 17 full-time (9 women), 20 part-time/adjunct (10 women).
Students: 189 full-time (142 women), 63 part-time (40 women); includes 29 minority (12 African Americans, 14 Asian Americans or Pacific Islanders, 3 Hispanic Americans), 33 international. Average age 30. 281 applicants, 58% accepted, 88 enrolled. In 2001, 80 master's, 3 doctorates, 1 other advanced degree awarded.
Degree requirements: For master's, paper or project; for doctorate, thesis/dissertation.
Entrance requirements: For master's and doctorate, GRE General Test. *Application deadline:* For fall admission, 1/1 (priority date); for spring admission, 10/15. Applications are processed on a rolling basis. *Application fee:* $60. Electronic applications accepted.
Expenses: Tuition, state resident: full-time $2,864. Tuition, nonresident: full-time $12,030.
Financial support: In 2001–02, 54 fellowships with full tuition reimbursements, 69 research assistantships with full tuition reimbursements (averaging $10,000 per year), 10 teaching assistantships with full tuition reimbursements (averaging $14,000 per year) were awarded. Career-related internships or fieldwork, Federal Work-Study, institutionally sponsored loans, health care benefits, and unspecified assistantships also available. Financial award application deadline: 1/1; financial award applicants required to submit FAFSA.
Faculty research: Information retrieval, digital libraries, multimedia networking, management of information resources, archives and cultural heritage, information management.
Dr. Joanne Gard Marshall, Dean, 919-962-8366, *Fax:* 919-962-8071, *E-mail:* info@ils.unc.edu.
Application contact: Lucia Zonn, Student Services Manager, 919-962-8366, *Fax:* 919-962-8071, *E-mail:* info@ils.unc.edu. *Web site:* http://ils.unc.edu/

■ THE UNIVERSITY OF NORTH CAROLINA AT GREENSBORO

Graduate School, School of Education, Department of Library and Information Studies, Greensboro, NC 27412-5001

AWARDS MLIS. Part-time and evening/weekend programs available. Postbaccalaureate distance learning degree programs offered (no on-campus study).

Faculty: 8 full-time (5 women), 9 part-time/adjunct (7 women).
Students: 21 full-time (14 women), 282 part-time (247 women). Average age 30. 45 applicants, 84% accepted. In 2001, 84 degrees awarded.
Degree requirements: For master's, portfolio.
Entrance requirements: For master's, GRE General Test, TOEFL. *Application deadline:* For fall admission, 7/1 (priority date); for spring admission, 11/1. Applications are processed on a rolling basis. *Application fee:* $35.
Expenses: Tuition, state resident: part-time $344 per course. Tuition, nonresident: part-time $2,457 per course.
Financial support: In 2001–02, fellowships (averaging $6,000 per year), research assistantships (averaging $10,750 per year) were awarded. Teaching assistantships, career-related internships or fieldwork, institutionally sponsored loans, and unspecified assistantships also available. Financial award application deadline: 3/1.
Faculty research: Library history, gender studies, children's literature, web design, homeless technical services.
Kieth C. Wright, Chair, 336-334-3481, *Fax:* 336-334-5060, *E-mail:* kieth_wright@uncg.edu.
Application contact: Dr. James Lynch, Director of Graduate Recruitment and Information Services, 336-334-4881, *Fax:* 336-334-4424. *Web site:* http://www.uncg.edu/LIS/

■ UNIVERSITY OF NORTH TEXAS

Robert B. Toulouse School of Graduate Studies, School of Library and Information Sciences, Denton, TX 76203

AWARDS Information science (MS, PhD); library science (MS). Part-time and evening/weekend programs available.

Faculty: 14.
Students: 73 full-time (61 women), 324 part-time (277 women); includes 47 minority (17 African Americans, 5 Asian Americans or Pacific Islanders, 22 Hispanic Americans, 3 Native Americans), 6 international. Average age 37. In 2001, 118 master's, 16 doctorates awarded.
Degree requirements: For master's, comprehensive exam; for doctorate, one foreign language, thesis/dissertation, comprehensive exam.
Entrance requirements: For master's and doctorate, GRE General Test. *Application deadline:* For fall admission, 7/17; for spring admission, 11/30. Applications are processed on a rolling basis. *Application fee:* $25 ($50 for international students).
Expenses: Tuition, state resident: part-time $186 per hour. Tuition, nonresident: part-time $319 per hour. Required fees: $88; $21 per hour.
Financial support: Fellowships, research assistantships, teaching assistantships, career-related internships or fieldwork, Federal Work-Study, institutionally sponsored loans, and library assistantships available. Financial award application deadline: 4/1.
Faculty research: Information resources and services, information management and retrieval, computer-based information systems.
Dr. Philip M. Turner, Dean, 940-565-2445, *Fax:* 940-565-3110, *E-mail:* turner@lis.admin.unt.edu.
Application contact: Dr. Herman Totten, Graduate Adviser, 940-565-2445, *Fax:* 940-565-3110, *E-mail:* totten@lis.admin.unt.edu.

■ UNIVERSITY OF OKLAHOMA

Graduate College, College of Arts and Sciences, School of Library and Information Studies, Norman, OK 73019-0390

AWARDS MLIS, Certificate, M Ed/MLIS, MBA/MLIS. Part-time programs available.

Faculty: 10 full-time (7 women), 2 part-time/adjunct (1 woman).
Students: 29 full-time (23 women), 127 part-time (113 women); includes 15 minority (5 African Americans, 1 Asian American or Pacific Islander, 1 Hispanic American, 8 Native Americans), 1 international. 34 applicants, 100% accepted, 23 enrolled. In 2001, 46 degrees awarded.
Degree requirements: For master's, comprehensive exam (MLIS), thesis (MALIS).
Entrance requirements: For master's, GRE, TOEFL, minimum GPA of 3.2 in last 60 hours or 3.0 overall. *Application deadline:* For fall admission, 3/1 (priority date); for spring admission, 10/15. Applications are processed on a rolling basis. *Application fee:* $25 ($50 for international students).
Expenses: Tuition, state resident: full-time $2,208; part-time $92 per credit hour. Tuition, nonresident: part-time $297 per credit hour. Tuition and fees vary according to course level, course load and program.
Financial support: In 2001–02, 37 students received support, including 6 research assistantships with partial tuition reimbursements available (averaging $8,220 per year), 7 teaching assistantships with partial tuition reimbursements available (averaging $8,033 per year); fellowships, career-related internships or fieldwork, Federal Work-Study, scholarships/grants, and tuition waivers (full and partial) also available. Support available to part-time students. Financial award applicants required to submit FAFSA.
Faculty research: School library media, reader's advisory services, networked information systems, multicultural librarianship, knowledge management. *Total annual research expenditures:* $31,121.
Danny Wallace, Director, 405-325-3921, *Fax:* 405-325-7648.
Application contact: Maggie Ryan, Student Program Specialist, 405-325-3921, *Fax:* 405-325-7648, *E-mail:* mryan@ou.edu.

■ UNIVERSITY OF PITTSBURGH

School of Information Sciences, Department of Library and Information Science, Pittsburgh, PA 15260

AWARDS MLIS, PhD, Certificate. Part-time programs available. Postbaccalaureate distance learning degree programs offered (minimal on-campus study).

Faculty: 12 full-time (8 women), 2 part-time/adjunct (both women).
Students: 118 full-time (82 women), 153 part-time (127 women); includes 33 minority (23 African Americans, 6 Asian Americans or Pacific Islanders, 4 Hispanic Americans), 24 international. 142 applicants, 94% accepted, 76 enrolled. In 2001, 91 master's, 8 doctorates awarded.
Degree requirements: For master's, thesis optional; for doctorate, variable foreign language requirement, thesis/dissertation.
Entrance requirements: For master's, minimum GPA of 3.0; for doctorate, GRE General Test, minimum GPA of 3.0. *Application deadline:* For fall admission, 7/1 (priority date); for spring admission, 11/1 (priority date). Applications are processed on a rolling basis. *Application fee:* $40. Electronic applications accepted.
Expenses: Tuition, state resident: full-time $9,410; part-time $385 per credit. Tuition, nonresident: full-time $19,376; part-time $797 per credit. Required fees: $480; $90 per term. Tuition and fees vary according to program.
Financial support: In 2001–02, 45 students received support, including 5 fellowships (averaging $21,292 per year), 20 research assistantships, 20 teaching assistantships; scholarships/grants, tuition waivers (full and partial), and unspecified assistantships also available. Support available to part-time students. Financial award application deadline: 1/15; financial award applicants required to submit FAFSA.
Faculty research: Archives, electronic records and preservation, children's resources and services, medical informatics, management.
Dr. Christinger Tomer, Chair, 412-624-9448, *Fax:* 412-648-7001, *E-mail:* ctomer@pitt.edu.
Application contact: Ninette Kay, Admissions Coordinator, 412-624-5146, *Fax:* 412-624-5231, *E-mail:* nkay@mail.sis.pitt.edu. *Web site:* http://www.sis.pitt.edu/~isdept/

■ UNIVERSITY OF PUERTO RICO, RÍO PIEDRAS

Graduate School of Librarianship, San Juan, PR 00931

AWARDS Librarianship (Post-Graduate Certificate); librarianship and information services (MLS). Part-time and evening/weekend programs available.

Faculty: 9.
Students: 36 full-time (30 women), 99 part-time (70 women); all minorities (all Hispanic Americans). Average age 29. 49 applicants, 61% accepted. In 2001, 20 degrees awarded.
Degree requirements: For master's, thesis, comprehensive exam.
Entrance requirements: For master's, PAEG, interview, minimum GPA of 3.0. *Application deadline:* For fall admission, 2/1. *Application fee:* $17.
Expenses: Tuition, state resident: full-time $1,200; part-time $70 per credit. Tuition, nonresident: full-time $3,500; part-time $219 per credit. Required fees: $70; $35 per semester.
Financial support: Fellowships, research assistantships, teaching assistantships, Federal Work-Study, institutionally sponsored loans, and tuition waivers (partial) available. Financial award application deadline: 5/31.
Faculty research: Evaluation of journals published by the Puerto Rican system.
Dr. Consuelo Figueras-Alvarez, Director, 787-764-0000 Ext. 5207, *Fax:* 787-764-2311.
Application contact: Migdalia Dávila, Student Affairs Officer, 787-764-0000 Ext. 5827, *Fax:* 787-764-2311.

■ UNIVERSITY OF RHODE ISLAND

Graduate School, Graduate Library School, Kingston, RI 02881

AWARDS MLIS.

Students: In 2001, 64 degrees awarded. *Application deadline:* For fall admission, 4/15 (priority date). Applications are processed on a rolling basis. *Application fee:* $35.
Expenses: Tuition, state resident: full-time $3,756; part-time $209 per credit. Tuition, nonresident: full-time $10,774; part-time $599 per credit. Required fees: $1,586; $76 per credit. One-time fee: $60 full-time.
Dr. W. Michael Havener, Director, 401-874-2947.

■ UNIVERSITY OF SOUTH CAROLINA

The Graduate School, College of Library and Information Science, Columbia, SC 29208

AWARDS MLIS, Certificate, Specialist, MLIS/MA. Part-time programs available. Postbaccalaureate distance learning degree programs offered (no on-campus study).

Faculty: 14 full-time (8 women), 7 part-time/adjunct (4 women).
Students: 85 full-time (70 women), 361 part-time (318 women); includes 27 minority (22 African Americans, 2 Asian Americans or Pacific Islanders, 3 Hispanic Americans), 5 international. Average age 37. 147 applicants, 76% accepted. In 2001, 170 master's, 19 other advanced degrees awarded.
Degree requirements: For master's and other advanced degree, registration.
Entrance requirements: For master's, GRE General Test, TOEFL, or MAT; for other advanced degree, GRE General Test or MAT, TOEFL. *Application deadline:* For fall admission, 4/1 (priority date); for spring admission, 10/1 (priority date). Applications are processed on a rolling basis. *Application fee:* $40. Electronic applications accepted.
Expenses: Tuition, state resident: full-time $4,434. Tuition, nonresident: full-time $9,854. Tuition and fees vary according to program.
Financial support: In 2001–02, 9 fellowships with partial tuition reimbursements (averaging $9,500 per year), 30 research assistantships with partial tuition reimbursements were awarded. Career-related internships or fieldwork, scholarships/grants, and unspecified assistantships also available. Support available to part-time students. Financial award application deadline: 4/1; financial award applicants required to submit FAFSA.
Faculty research: Information technology management, distance education, library services for children and young adults, special libraries.
Dr. Fred W. Roper, Dean, 803-777-3858, *Fax:* 803-777-7938.
Application contact: Sharon Allen, Admissions Contact, 803-777-3887, *Fax:* 803-777-0457, *E-mail:* sharona@gwm.sc.edu. *Web site:* http://www.libsci.sc.edu/

■ UNIVERSITY OF SOUTHERN MISSISSIPPI

Graduate School, College of Liberal Arts, School of Library and Information Science, Hattiesburg, MS 39406

AWARDS MLIS, SLS. Part-time and evening/weekend programs available. Postbaccalaureate distance learning degree programs offered (minimal on-campus study).

Faculty: 8 full-time (5 women), 6 part-time/adjunct (3 women).
Students: 31 full-time (21 women), 55 part-time (46 women); includes 24 minority (18 African Americans, 1 Asian American or Pacific Islander, 5 Hispanic Americans). Average age 36. 27 applicants, 85% accepted. In 2001, 35 master's, 1 other advanced degree awarded.
Degree requirements: For master's, thesis or alternative, research project; for SLS, field project.
Entrance requirements: For master's, GRE General Test, minimum GPA of 3.0; for SLS, GRE General Test, MLIS, minimum graduate GPA of 3.25. *Application deadline:* For fall admission, 8/6 (priority date). Applications are processed on a rolling basis. *Application fee:* $0 ($25 for international students). Electronic applications accepted.
Expenses: Tuition, state resident: full-time $3,416; part-time $190 per credit hour. Tuition, nonresident: full-time $7,932; part-time $441 per credit hour.
Financial support: In 2001–02, 8 students received support, including 4 fellowships with tuition reimbursements available (averaging $14,000 per year), 8 research assistantships with full and partial tuition reimbursements available (averaging $3,400 per year); career-related internships or fieldwork, Federal Work-Study, institutionally sponsored loans, scholarships/grants, tuition waivers (full and partial), and unspecified assistantships also available. Financial award application deadline: 3/15.
Faculty research: Printing, library history, children's literature, telecommunications, management. *Total annual research expenditures:* $14,185.
Dr. Tom Walker, Director, 601-266-4228, *Fax:* 601-266-5774.

■ UNIVERSITY OF SOUTH FLORIDA

College of Graduate Studies, College of Arts and Sciences, School of Library and Information Science, Tampa, FL 33620-9951

AWARDS Library and information sciences (MA); school library media (MA). Part-time and evening/weekend programs available. Postbaccalaureate distance learning degree programs offered (minimal on-campus study).

Faculty: 17 full-time (12 women).
Students: 68 full-time (52 women), 291 part-time (239 women); includes 52 minority (8 African Americans, 6 Asian Americans or Pacific Islanders, 37 Hispanic Americans, 1 Native American), 2 international. Average age 32. 158 applicants, 71% accepted, 76 enrolled. In 2001, 63 degrees awarded.
Entrance requirements: For master's, GRE General Test, minimum GPA of 3.0 in last 60 hours. *Application deadline:* For fall admission, 6/1; for spring admission, 10/15. Applications are processed on a rolling basis. *Application fee:* $20. Electronic applications accepted.
Expenses: Tuition, state resident: part-time $166 per credit hour. Tuition, nonresident: part-time $573 per credit hour. Required fees: $17 per term.
Financial support: Fellowships, research assistantships, teaching assistantships, career-related internships or fieldwork, Federal Work-Study, and institutionally sponsored loans available. Support available to part-time students. Financial award applicants required to submit FAFSA. *Total annual research expenditures:* $42,668.
Vicki L. Gregory, Chairperson and Program Director, 813-974-3520, *Fax:* 813-974-6840, *E-mail:* gregory@luna.cas.usf.edu.
Application contact: Information Contact, 813-974-6837, *Fax:* 813-974-6840, *E-mail:* lis@luna.cas.usf.edu. *Web site:* http://www.cas.usf.edu/lis/

■ THE UNIVERSITY OF TENNESSEE

Graduate School, School of Information Sciences, Knoxville, TN 37996

AWARDS MS. Part-time programs available. Postbaccalaureate distance learning degree programs offered (no on-campus study).

Faculty: 11 full-time (6 women), 1 part-time/adjunct (0 women).
Students: 47 full-time (38 women), 137 part-time (105 women); includes 7 minority (4 African Americans, 3 Asian Americans or Pacific Islanders), 6 international. 128 applicants, 69% accepted. In 2001, 86 degrees awarded.
Degree requirements: For master's, thesis or alternative.
Entrance requirements: For master's, GRE General Test, TOEFL, minimum

GPA of 2.7. *Application deadline:* For fall admission, 2/1 (priority date). Applications are processed on a rolling basis. *Application fee:* $35. Electronic applications accepted.
Expenses: Tuition, state resident: full-time $4,280; part-time $233 per hour. Tuition, nonresident: full-time $12,066; part-time $666 per hour. Tuition and fees vary according to program.
Financial support: In 2001–02, 1 fellowship, 16 teaching assistantships were awarded. Research assistantships, Federal Work-Study, institutionally sponsored loans, and unspecified assistantships also available. Financial award application deadline: 2/1; financial award applicants required to submit FAFSA.
Dr. Elizabeth Aversa, Head, 865-974-2148, *Fax:* 865-974-4967, *E-mail:* aversa@utk.edu.
Application contact: Dr. Kristie Atwood, Graduate Representative, *E-mail:* katwood@utk.edu.

Find an in-depth description at www.petersons.com/gradchannel.

■ THE UNIVERSITY OF TEXAS AT AUSTIN

Graduate School, Graduate School of Library and Information Science, Austin, TX 78712-1111

AWARDS MLIS, PhD. Part-time programs available.

Faculty: 20 full-time, 9 part-time/adjunct.
Students: 305 (243 women); includes 41 minority (2 African Americans, 5 Asian Americans or Pacific Islanders, 33 Hispanic Americans, 1 Native American) 35 international. Average age 27. 164 applicants, 74% accepted. In 2001, 137 master's, 3 doctorates awarded.
Degree requirements: For doctorate, 2 foreign languages, thesis/dissertation.
Entrance requirements: For master's and doctorate, GRE General Test. *Application deadline:* For fall admission, 2/1 (priority date); for winter admission, 5/1; for spring admission, 10/1. Applications are processed on a rolling basis. *Application fee:* $50 ($75 for international students). Electronic applications accepted.
Expenses: Tuition, state resident: full-time $3,159. Tuition, nonresident: full-time $6,957. Tuition and fees vary according to program.
Financial support: Fellowships, research assistantships, teaching assistantships, career-related internships or fieldwork, Federal Work-Study, and tuition waivers (partial) available. Support available to part-time students. Financial award application deadline: 2/1.
Faculty research: Information retrieval and artificial intelligence, library history and administration, classification and cataloguing.
Andrew I. Dillon, Dean, 512-471-3828, *Fax:* 512-471-3971.
Application contact: Dr. Philip Doty, Graduate Adviser, 512-471-3746, *Fax:* 512-471-3971, *E-mail:* pdoty@gslis.utexas.edu. *Web site:* http://www.gslis.utexas.edu

■ UNIVERSITY OF WASHINGTON

Graduate School, The Information School, Seattle, WA 98195

AWARDS Information management (MSIM); information science (PhD); library and information science (MLIS). Part-time and evening/weekend programs available. Postbaccalaureate distance learning degree programs offered.

Faculty: 10 full-time (5 women), 10 part-time/adjunct (6 women).
Students: 173 full-time (130 women), 130 part-time (96 women); includes 41 minority (6 African Americans, 26 Asian Americans or Pacific Islanders, 8 Hispanic Americans, 1 Native American), 8 international. Average age 33. 308 applicants, 63% accepted, 142 enrolled. In 2001, 86 degrees awarded.
Degree requirements: For master's, thesis optional; for doctorate, thesis/dissertation.
Entrance requirements: For master's, GRE General Test, TOEFL, GMAT, minimum GPA of 3.0; for doctorate, GRE General Test, TOEFL, minimum GPA of 3.0. *Application deadline:* For fall admission, 1/15. *Application fee:* $50.
Expenses: Tuition, state resident: full-time $5,539. Tuition, nonresident: full-time $14,376. Required fees: $390. Tuition and fees vary according to course load and program.
Financial support: In 2001–02, 71 students received support, including 28 fellowships with tuition reimbursements available (averaging $11,340 per year), 8 research assistantships with tuition reimbursements available (averaging $11,340 per year), 4 teaching assistantships with tuition reimbursements available (averaging $11,340 per year); career-related internships or fieldwork, Federal Work-Study, institutionally sponsored loans, scholarships/grants, health care benefits, tuition waivers (full and partial), and unspecified assistantships also available. Financial award application deadline: 2/28; financial award applicants required to submit FAFSA.
Faculty research: Metadata, impact of networked information, augmented reality, human factors in information and communication technology, delivery of information resources in a networked environment. *Total annual research expenditures:* $664,080.
Michael B. Eisenberg, Dean, 206-685-9937, *Fax:* 206-616-3152, *E-mail:* mbe@u.washington.edu.
Application contact: Student Services, 206-543-1794, *Fax:* 206-616-3152, *E-mail:* studentservices@ischool.washington.edu. *Web site:* http://www.ischool.washington.edu/

■ UNIVERSITY OF WISCONSIN–MADISON

Graduate School, College of Letters and Science, School of Library and Information Studies, Madison, WI 53706-1380

AWARDS MA, PhD, Certificate. Part-time programs available.

Faculty: 7 full-time (4 women), 4 part-time/adjunct (1 woman).
Students: 114 full-time (88 women), 83 part-time (59 women); includes 15 minority (4 African Americans, 8 Asian Americans or Pacific Islanders, 3 Hispanic Americans), 15 international. Average age 29. 164 applicants, 62% accepted. In 2001, 70 master's, 1 doctorate, 1 other advanced degree awarded.
Degree requirements: For doctorate, thesis/dissertation, comprehensive exam. *Median time to degree:* Master's–2 years full-time, 7 years part-time; doctorate–5 years full-time, 7 years part-time.
Application deadline: For fall admission, 12/15 (priority date). Applications are processed on a rolling basis. *Application fee:* $45. Electronic applications accepted.
Expenses: Tuition, state resident: full-time $7,361; part-time $399 per credit. Tuition, nonresident: full-time $20,499; part-time $1,282 per credit. Required fees: $34 per credit. Full-time tuition and fees vary according to course load, program, reciprocity agreements and student level.
Financial support: In 2001–02, 26 students received support, including 6 fellowships with full and partial tuition reimbursements available (averaging $8,700 per year), 2 teaching assistantships with full tuition reimbursements available; career-related internships or fieldwork, Federal Work-Study, scholarships/grants, and unspecified assistantships also available. Financial award application deadline: 12/15.
Faculty research: Intellectual freedom, children's literature, print culture history, information systems design and evaluation, school library media centers. *Total annual research expenditures:* $125,207.
Louise S. Robbins, Director, 608-263-2908, *Fax:* 608-263-4849, *E-mail:* lrobbins@slis.wisc.edu.
Application contact: Barbara J. Arnold, Admissions and Placement Adviser, 608-263-2909, *Fax:* 608-263-4849, *E-mail:* bjarnold@facstaff.wisc.edu. *Web site:* http://www.slis.wisc.edu/

■ UNIVERSITY OF WISCONSIN–MILWAUKEE

Graduate School, School of Information Studies, Milwaukee, WI 53201-0413

AWARDS MLIS, CAS, MLIS/MA, MLIS/MM, MLIS/MS. Part-time programs available.

Faculty: 10 full-time (5 women).

University of Wisconsin–Milwaukee (continued)

Students: 52 full-time (39 women), 99 part-time (81 women); includes 7 minority (3 African Americans, 1 Asian American or Pacific Islander, 2 Hispanic Americans, 1 Native American), 6 international. Average age 36. 151 applicants, 70% accepted. In 2001, 85 degrees awarded.
Entrance requirements: For master's, GRE General Test or MAT. *Application deadline:* For fall admission, 1/1 (priority date); for spring admission, 9/1. Applications are processed on a rolling basis. *Application fee:* $45 ($75 for international students).
Expenses: Tuition, state resident: full-time $6,180; part-time $535 per credit. Tuition, nonresident: full-time $19,482; part-time $1,366 per credit. Tuition and fees vary according to course load, program and reciprocity agreements.
Financial support: In 2001–02, 2 fellowships, 6 teaching assistantships were awarded. Research assistantships, career-related internships or fieldwork, Federal Work-Study, and unspecified assistantships also available. Support available to part-time students. Financial award application deadline: 4/15.
Dietmar Wolfram, Representative, 414-229-4707, *Fax:* 414-229-4848, *E-mail:* dwolfram@uwm.edu. *Web site:* http://www.uwm.edu/Dept/SLIS/

■ VALDOSTA STATE UNIVERSITY

Graduate School, Program in Library and Information Science, Valdosta, GA 31698

AWARDS MLIS.

Faculty: 4 full-time (2 women).
Students: 1 (woman) full-time, 10 part-time (6 women); includes 3 minority (1 African American, 1 Asian American or Pacific Islander, 1 Hispanic American). 18 applicants, 100% accepted.
Degree requirements: For master's, comprehensive exam.
Entrance requirements: For master's, GRE. *Application deadline:* For fall admission, 5/1. *Application fee:* $20.
Expenses: Tuition, state resident: full-time $1,746; part-time $97 per hour. Tuition, nonresident: full-time $6,966; part-time $387 per hour. Required fees: $594; $297 per semester.
Financial support: In 2001–02, 2 research assistantships with full tuition reimbursements (averaging $2,452 per year) were awarded; institutionally sponsored loans, scholarships/grants, and unspecified assistantships also available. Support available to part-time students. Financial award application deadline: 7/1; financial award applicants required to submit FAFSA.
Dr. George Gaumond, University Librarian, 229-333-5860, *E-mail:* ggaumond@valdosta.edu.
Application contact: Dr. Wallace Koehler, Director, 229-333-5860.

■ WAYNE STATE UNIVERSITY

Graduate School, Library and Information Science Program, Detroit, MI 48202

AWARDS Archives administration (Certificate); library and information science (MLIS, Spec). Part-time and evening/weekend programs available.

Faculty: 11 full-time.
Students: 62 full-time (46 women), 403 part-time (336 women); includes 53 minority (42 African Americans, 7 Asian Americans or Pacific Islanders, 3 Hispanic Americans, 1 Native American), 5 international. 232 applicants, 70% accepted, 113 enrolled. In 2001, 121 degrees awarded.
Application deadline: For fall admission, 7/1. Applications are processed on a rolling basis. *Application fee:* $20 ($30 for international students). Electronic applications accepted.
Expenses: Tuition, state resident: full-time $3,764. Tuition and fees vary according to degree level and program.
Financial support: In 2001–02, 4 research assistantships were awarded; career-related internships or fieldwork, Federal Work-Study, institutionally sponsored loans, and scholarships/grants also available. Support available to part-time students. Financial award application deadline: 5/15.
Faculty research: Management, infometrics, imaging processes, library history, bibliographic control.
Joseph J. Mika, Director, 313-577-6196, *Fax:* 313-577-7563, *E-mail:* aa2500@wayne.edu.
Application contact: Nancy Johnson, Education Director, 313-577-8541. *Web site:* http://www.wayne.edu/xisp/lishome.html

■ WRIGHT STATE UNIVERSITY

School of Graduate Studies, College of Education and Human Services, Department of Teacher Education, Programs in Business, Technology, and Vocational Education, Dayton, OH 45435

AWARDS Business education (M Ed, MA); computer/technology education (M Ed, MA); library/media (M Ed, MA); vocational education (M Ed, MA).

Students: 5 full-time (3 women), 30 part-time (27 women), 1 international. 17 applicants, 94% accepted. In 2001, 14 degrees awarded.
Degree requirements: For master's, thesis (for some programs).
Entrance requirements: For master's, GRE General Test, MAT, TOEFL. *Application fee:* $25.
Expenses: Tuition, state resident: full-time $7,161; part-time $225 per quarter hour. Tuition, nonresident: full-time $12,324; part-time $385 per quarter hour. Tuition and fees vary according to course load, degree level and program.
Financial support: Available to part-time students. Applicants required to submit FAFSA.
Dr. Bonnie K. Mathies, Associate Dean and Program Adviser, 937-775-2822, *Fax:* 937-775-4855, *E-mail:* bonnie.mathies@wright.edu.
Application contact: Gerald C. Malicki, Assistant Dean and Director of Graduate Admissions and Records, 937-775-2976, *Fax:* 937-775-2453, *E-mail:* jerry.malicki@wright.edu.

Graduate Programs in Social Sciences

Area and Cultural Studies

AFRICAN-AMERICAN STUDIES

■ BOSTON UNIVERSITY

Graduate School of Arts and Sciences, Program in African American Studies, Boston, MA 02215

AWARDS MA.

Degree requirements: For master's, one foreign language, comprehensive exam, registration.
Entrance requirements: For master's, GRE General Test, TOEFL. *Application deadline:* For fall admission, 7/1. *Application fee:* $60.
Expenses: Tuition: Full-time $25,872; part-time $340 per credit. Required fees: $40 per semester. Part-time tuition and fees vary according to class time, course level and program.
Financial support: Career-related internships or fieldwork and Federal Work-Study available. Support available to part-time students. Financial award application deadline: 1/15; financial award applicants required to submit FAFSA.
Ronald K. Richardson, Director, 617-353-2796, *Fax:* 617-353-4975, *E-mail:* rrichard@bu.edu.

■ CLARK ATLANTA UNIVERSITY

School of Arts and Sciences, Department of African-American Studies, Atlanta, GA 30314

AWARDS MA. Part-time programs available.

Degree requirements: For master's, one foreign language, thesis.
Entrance requirements: For master's, GRE General Test, minimum GPA of 2.5.

■ CLARK ATLANTA UNIVERSITY

School of Arts and Sciences, Department of Africana Women's Studies, Atlanta, GA 30314

AWARDS MA, DA.

Degree requirements: For master's, one foreign language, thesis; for doctorate, 2 foreign languages, thesis/dissertation.
Entrance requirements: For master's, GRE General Test, minimum GPA of 2.5; for doctorate, GRE General Test, minimum graduate GPA of 3.0.
Faculty research: Concerns of women of African descent globally.

■ COLUMBIA UNIVERSITY

Graduate School of Arts and Sciences, Program in African-American Studies, New York, NY 10027

AWARDS MA. Part-time programs available.

Expenses: Tuition: Full-time $27,528. Required fees: $1,638.
Application contact: Robert Furno, Assistant Dean for Admissions, 212-854-4737, *Fax:* 212-854-2863, *E-mail:* jc12@columbia.edu.

■ CORNELL UNIVERSITY

Graduate School, Graduate Fields of Arts and Sciences, Field of Africana Studies, Ithaca, NY 14853-0001

AWARDS African studies (MPS); African-American studies (MPS).

Faculty: 17 full-time.
Students: 15 full-time (10 women); includes 13 minority (all African Americans). 33 applicants, 27% accepted. In 2001, 4 degrees awarded.
Degree requirements: For master's, thesis.
Entrance requirements: For master's, GRE General Test (recommended), TOEFL, 3 letters of recommendation. *Application deadline:* For fall admission, 1/30. *Application fee:* $65. Electronic applications accepted.
Expenses: Tuition: Full-time $25,970. Required fees: $50.
Financial support: In 2001–02, 14 students received support, including 7 fellowships with full tuition reimbursements available, 7 teaching assistantships with full tuition reimbursements available; research assistantships, institutionally sponsored loans, scholarships/grants, tuition waivers (full and partial), and unspecified assistantships also available. Financial award applicants required to submit FAFSA.
Faculty research: African-American literature, art, cinema and theater; African-American politics and public policy; African history, politics and art; Caribbean politics and Africana Diaspora.
Application contact: Graduate Field Assistant, 607-255-4626, *Fax:* 607-2550784, *E-mail:* spt1@cornell.edu. *Web site:* http://www.gradschool.cornell.edu/grad/fields_1/africana.html

■ INDIANA UNIVERSITY BLOOMINGTON

Graduate School, College of Arts and Sciences, Department of Afro-American Studies, Bloomington, IN 47405

AWARDS MA. Part-time programs available.

Faculty: 3 full-time (1 woman).
Students: 3 full-time (0 women), 5 part-time (4 women); includes 7 minority (6 African Americans, 1 Asian American or Pacific Islander). Average age 40. In 2001, 3 degrees awarded.
Entrance requirements: For master's, GRE, TOEFL, minimum GPA of 3.0. *Application deadline:* For fall admission, 1/15 (priority date); for spring admission, 9/1. Applications are processed on a rolling basis. *Application fee:* $45 ($55 for international students). Electronic applications accepted.
Expenses: Tuition, state resident: full-time $4,720; part-time $197 per credit. Tuition, nonresident: full-time $13,748; part-time $573 per credit. Required fees: $642.
Prof. John McCluskey, Chairman, 812-855-3874, *Fax:* 812-855-4869, *E-mail:* afroamer@indiana.edu.
Application contact: Dr. Portia Maultsby, Graduate Adviser, 812-855-2708, *E-mail:* maultsby@indiana.edu. *Web site:* http://www.indiana.edu/~afroamer/afroamer.home.html

■ MORGAN STATE UNIVERSITY

School of Graduate Studies, College of Liberal Arts, Department of History and Geography, Baltimore, MD 21251

AWARDS African-American studies (MA); history (MA, PhD). Part-time and evening/weekend programs available.

Faculty: 5 full-time (3 women).
Students: 27 (12 women); includes 24 minority (all African Americans). 20 applicants, 75% accepted. In 2001, 2 degrees awarded.
Degree requirements: For master's and doctorate, thesis/dissertation, comprehensive exam.
Entrance requirements: For master's, minimum GPA of 2.5; for doctorate, GRE or MAT. *Application deadline:* For fall admission, 2/1; for spring admission, 10/1. Applications are processed on a rolling basis. *Application fee:* $0.
Expenses: Tuition, state resident: part-time $193 per credit. Tuition, nonresident: part-time $364 per credit. Required fees: $40 per credit.
Financial support: In 2001–02, 2 fellowships were awarded. Financial award application deadline: 4/1.
Faculty research: Women's history, African diaspora history, urban history.
Dr. Annette Palmer, Chair, 443-885-3190, *Fax:* 443-319-3473, *E-mail:* apalmer@moac.morgan.edu.
Application contact: Dr. James E. Waller, Admissions Officer, 410-319-3185, *Fax:* 410-319-3837, *E-mail:* jwaller@moac.morgan.edu.

■ NORTH CAROLINA AGRICULTURAL AND TECHNICAL STATE UNIVERSITY

Graduate School, College of Arts and Sciences, Department of English, Program in English and Afro-American Literature, Greensboro, NC 27411

AWARDS MA. Part-time and evening/weekend programs available.

Degree requirements: For master's, qualifying exam.
Entrance requirements: For master's, GRE General Test, minimum GPA of 3.0.

■ THE OHIO STATE UNIVERSITY

Graduate School, College of Humanities, Department of African-American and African Studies, Columbus, OH 43210

AWARDS MA.

Degree requirements: For master's, internship, or thesis.
Entrance requirements: For master's, GRE General Test.

■ PRINCETON UNIVERSITY

Graduate School, Program in African-American Studies, Princeton, NJ 08544-1019

AWARDS PhD. Offered through the Departments of Anthropology, Art and Archaeology, Economics, English, History, Philosophy, Politics, Psychology, Religion and Sociology, the School of Architecture, and the Woodrow Wilson School of Public and International Affairs.

Degree requirements: For doctorate, thesis/dissertation.
Entrance requirements: For doctorate, GRE General Test, sample of written work.

■ STATE UNIVERSITY OF NEW YORK AT ALBANY

College of Arts and Sciences, Department of Africana Studies, Albany, NY 12222-0001

AWARDS African studies (MA); Afro-American studies (MA). Part-time and evening/weekend programs available.

Students: 15 full-time (8 women), 1 part-time; includes 6 minority (all African Americans), 5 international. Average age 29. 12 applicants, 83% accepted. In 2001, 7 degrees awarded.
Application deadline: For fall admission, 7/15; for spring admission, 11/1. Applications are processed on a rolling basis. *Application fee:* $50.
Expenses: Tuition, state resident: full-time $2,550; part-time $213 per credit. Tuition, nonresident: full-time $4,208; part-time $351 per credit. Required fees: $470; $470 per year.
Financial support: Fellowships, teaching assistantships, Federal Work-Study available. Financial award application deadline: 5/1.
Faculty research: The black family, Afrocentricity in poetry, black women in U.S. literature.
Dr. Leonard Slade, Chair, 518-442-4730.

■ TEMPLE UNIVERSITY

Graduate School, College of Liberal Arts, Department of African-American Studies, Philadelphia, PA 19122-6096

AWARDS MA, PhD. Terminal master's awarded for partial completion of doctoral program.

Degree requirements: For master's, comprehensive exam; for doctorate, one foreign language, thesis/dissertation, oral and written qualifying exams.
Entrance requirements: For doctorate, MA in African-American studies. Electronic applications accepted.
Expenses: Tuition, state resident: full-time $8,487; part-time $369 per credit hour. Tuition, nonresident: full-time $12,282; part-time $534 per credit hour. Required fees: $350. Tuition and fees vary according to course load, program and reciprocity agreements.
Faculty research: Afrocentric theory; African-American youth; centered drama, literature, and history; comparative analysis; South and West Africa, Nile Valley.

■ UNIVERSITY OF CALIFORNIA, BERKELEY

Graduate Division, College of Letters and Science, Department of African American Studies, Berkeley, CA 94720-1500

AWARDS PhD.

Degree requirements: For doctorate, thesis/dissertation.
Entrance requirements: For doctorate, GRE General Test, minimum GPA of 3.0.
Expenses: Tuition, nonresident: full-time $10,704. Required fees: $4,349.
Faculty research: Black influence on U.S. foreign policy, black intellectuals, ethnic space in urban society, representation in museums of African-Americans and British Americans during slavery.

■ UNIVERSITY OF CALIFORNIA, LOS ANGELES

Graduate Division, College of Letters and Science, Program in Afro-American Studies, Los Angeles, CA 90095

AWARDS MA.

Students: 14 full-time (8 women); includes 11 minority (10 African Americans, 1 Hispanic American). 15 applicants, 47% accepted, 5 enrolled. In 2001, 6 degrees awarded.
Degree requirements: For master's, one foreign language.
Entrance requirements: For master's, GRE General Test, minimum GPA of 3.0, sample of written work. *Application deadline:* For fall admission, 12/15. *Application fee:* $60. Electronic applications accepted.
Expenses: Tuition, nonresident: full-time $10,244. Required fees: $3,609. Full-time tuition and fees vary according to program.
Financial support: In 2001–02, 7 research assistantships, 6 teaching assistantships were awarded. Fellowships, Federal Work-Study, institutionally sponsored loans, and tuition waivers (full and partial) also available. Financial award application deadline: 3/1.
Dr. Romeria Tidwell, Chair, 310-825-3776.
Application contact: Departmental Office, 310-825-3776, *E-mail:* kgriffin@caas.ucla.edu.

■ THE UNIVERSITY OF IOWA

Graduate College, College of Liberal Arts and Sciences, Program in African American World Studies, Iowa City, IA 52242-1316

AWARDS MA.

Faculty: 3 full-time.
Students: 3 full-time (1 woman), 2 part-time (1 woman); includes 3 minority (2 African Americans, 1 Hispanic American), 2 international. 7 applicants, 43% accepted, 1 enrolled. In 2001, 2 degrees awarded.
Degree requirements: For master's, exam, thesis optional.
Entrance requirements: For master's, GRE General Test, TOEFL. *Application deadline:* For fall admission, 3/1. *Application fee:* $30 ($50 for international students). Electronic applications accepted.
Expenses: Tuition, state resident: full-time $3,702; part-time $206 per semester hour. Tuition, nonresident: full-time $11,924; part-time $206 per semester hour. Required fees: $101 per semester. Tuition and fees vary according to course load and program.
Financial support: In 2001–02, 4 research assistantships, 1 teaching assistantship were awarded. Fellowships available. Financial award applicants required to submit FAFSA.
Horace A. Porter, Chair, 319-335-0317.

■ UNIVERSITY OF MASSACHUSETTS AMHERST

Graduate School, College of Humanities and Fine Arts, Department of Afro-American Studies, Amherst, MA 01003

AWARDS MA, PhD.

University of Massachusetts Amherst (continued)
Faculty: 10 full-time (1 woman).
Students: 26 full-time (13 women), 3 part-time (2 women); includes 21 minority (19 African Americans, 2 Hispanic Americans), 3 international. Average age 33. 38 applicants, 13% accepted.
Degree requirements: For master's, thesis or alternative; for doctorate, thesis/dissertation.
Entrance requirements: For doctorate, writing sample. *Application deadline:* For fall admission, 2/1. Applications are processed on a rolling basis. *Application fee:* $40 ($50 for international students).
Expenses: Tuition, state resident: full-time $1,980; part-time $110 per credit. Tuition, nonresident: full-time $7,456; part-time $414 per credit. Required fees: $4,112. One-time fee: $115 full-time.
Financial support: In 2001–02, 23 fellowships with full tuition reimbursements (averaging $7,400 per year), 2 research assistantships with full tuition reimbursements (averaging $9,839 per year), 12 teaching assistantships with full tuition reimbursements (averaging $6,243 per year) were awarded. Career-related internships or fieldwork, Federal Work-Study, scholarships/grants, traineeships, and unspecified assistantships also available. Support available to part-time students. Financial award application deadline: 2/1.
Dr. Esther Terry, Head, 413-545-2751, *Fax:* 413-545-0628.

■ UNIVERSITY OF WISCONSIN–MADISON

Graduate School, College of Letters and Science, Department of Afro-American Studies, Madison, WI 53706-1380

AWARDS MA.

Faculty: 8 full-time (2 women), 4 part-time/adjunct (2 women).
Students: 15 full-time (10 women), 1 part-time; includes 9 minority (all African Americans). Average age 25. 12 applicants, 50% accepted. In 2001, 3 degrees awarded.
Degree requirements: For master's, thesis or alternative.
Entrance requirements: For master's, TOEFL, bachelor's degree in related field, minimum GPA of 3.0. *Application deadline:* For fall admission, 1/15. *Application fee:* $45. Electronic applications accepted.
Expenses: Tuition, state resident: full-time $7,361; part-time $399 per credit. Tuition, nonresident: full-time $20,499; part-time $1,282 per credit. Required fees: $34 per credit. Full-time tuition and fees vary according to course load, program, reciprocity agreements and student level.
Financial support: In 2001–02, 7 students received support, including 3 fellowships with tuition reimbursements available (averaging $13,446 per year), 6 teaching assistantships with tuition reimbursements available (averaging $4,190 per year); Federal Work-Study and unspecified assistantships also available.
Faculty research: Afro American art, history, music, literature, and culture. *Total annual research expenditures:* $616,087.
Stanlie M. James, Chair, 608-263-7978, *Fax:* 608-263-7198.
Application contact: Nellie Y. McKay, Professor, 608-263-2472, *Fax:* 608-263-7198, *E-mail:* nymckay@facstaff.wisc.edu. *Web site:* http://polyglot.lss.wisc.edu/aas/

■ WEST VIRGINIA UNIVERSITY

Eberly College of Arts and Sciences, Department of History, Morgantown, WV 26506

AWARDS African history (MA, PhD); African-American history (MA, PhD); American history (MA, PhD); Appalachian/regional history (MA, PhD); East Asian history (MA, PhD); European history (MA, PhD); history of science and technology (MA, PhD); Latin American history (MA). Part-time programs available.

Faculty: 19 full-time (4 women), 2 part-time/adjunct (1 woman).
Students: 35 full-time (13 women), 29 part-time (10 women); includes 5 minority (2 African Americans, 1 Asian American or Pacific Islander, 1 Hispanic American, 1 Native American), 5 international. Average age 34. 86 applicants, 44% accepted. In 2001, 4 master's, 1 doctorate awarded.
Degree requirements: For master's, one foreign language; for doctorate, one foreign language, comprehensive exam, dissertation defense.
Entrance requirements: For master's, GRE General Test, TOEFL, minimum GPA of 3.0; for doctorate, GRE General Test, TOEFL, MA or equivalent. *Application deadline:* For spring admission, 11/1. Applications are processed on a rolling basis. *Application fee:* $45.
Expenses: Tuition, state resident: full-time $2,791. Tuition, nonresident: full-time $8,659. Required fees: $1,002. Tuition and fees vary according to program.
Financial support: In 2001–02, 43 students received support, including 2 research assistantships, 23 teaching assistantships; fellowships, career-related internships or fieldwork, Federal Work-Study, institutionally sponsored loans, tuition waivers (full and partial), and graduate administrative assistantships also available. Financial award application deadline: 2/1; financial award applicants required to submit FAFSA.
Faculty research: U.S., Appalachia, modern Europe, Africa, science and technology.
Dr. Robert M. Maxon, Chair, 304-293-2421 Ext. 5223, *Fax:* 304-293-3616, *E-mail:* robert.maxon@mail.wvu.edu.
Application contact: Dr. Robert E. Blobaum, Director of Graduate Studies, 304-293-2421 Ext. 5241, *Fax:* 304-293-3616, *E-mail:* robert.blobaum@mail.wvu.edu. *Web site:* http://www.as.wvu.edu/history/

■ YALE UNIVERSITY

Graduate School of Arts and Sciences, Interdisciplinary Program in African-American Studies, New Haven, CT 06520

AWARDS MA, PhD.

Degree requirements: For master's, one foreign language, thesis.
Entrance requirements: For master's and doctorate, GRE General Test.

AFRICAN STUDIES

■ BOSTON UNIVERSITY

Graduate School of Arts and Sciences, Department of International Relations, Boston, MA 02215

AWARDS African studies (Certificate); international relations (MA); international relations and environmental policy management (MA); international relations and international communication (MA).

Students: 65 full-time (30 women), 11 part-time (5 women); includes 4 minority (1 Asian American or Pacific Islander, 3 Hispanic Americans), 25 international. Average age 28. 299 applicants, 61% accepted, 42 enrolled. In 2001, 27 degrees awarded.
Degree requirements: For master's, one foreign language, thesis, comprehensive exam, registration.
Entrance requirements: For master's, GRE General Test, TOEFL, 3 letters of recommendation; for Certificate, GRE General Test, TOEFL. *Application deadline:* For fall admission, 4/15; for spring admission, 10/15. *Application fee:* $60.
Expenses: Tuition: Full-time $25,872; part-time $340 per credit. Required fees: $40 per semester. Part-time tuition and fees vary according to class time, course level and program.
Financial support: In 2001–02, 25 students received support. Federal Work-Study, scholarships/grants, and unspecified assistantships available. Support available to part-time students. Financial award application deadline: 1/15; financial award applicants required to submit FAFSA.
Dr. Erik Goldstein, Chairman, 617-353-9280, *Fax:* 617-353-9290, *E-mail:* goldstee@bu.edu.
Application contact: David E. Clark, Graduate Program Administrator, 617-353-9349, *Fax:* 617-353-9290, *E-mail:* ir@bu.edu. *Web site:* http://www.bu.edu/IR/

■ COLUMBIA UNIVERSITY

School of International and Public Affairs, Institute of African Studies, New York, NY 10027

AWARDS Certificate. Students must be enrolled in a separate graduate degree program at Columbia University.

Faculty: 22 full-time, 14 part-time/adjunct.
Application deadline: For fall admission, 1/5 (priority date); for spring admission, 10/15 (priority date). *Application fee:* $75. Electronic applications accepted.
Financial support: Application deadline: 1/15.
Prof. Mahmood Mamdani, Director, 212-854-4633, *Fax:* 212-854-4639, *E-mail:* mm1124@columbia.edu.
Application contact: Robert Garris, Associate Director, 212-854-6216, *Fax:* 212-854-3010, *E-mail:* sipa_admission@columbia.edu.

■ CORNELL UNIVERSITY

Graduate School, Graduate Fields of Arts and Sciences, Field of Africana Studies, Ithaca, NY 14853-0001

AWARDS African studies (MPS); African-American studies (MPS).

Faculty: 17 full-time.
Students: 15 full-time (10 women); includes 13 minority (all African Americans). 33 applicants, 27% accepted. In 2001, 4 degrees awarded.
Degree requirements: For master's, thesis.
Entrance requirements: For master's, GRE General Test (recommended), TOEFL, 3 letters of recommendation. *Application deadline:* For fall admission, 1/30. *Application fee:* $65. Electronic applications accepted.
Expenses: Tuition: Full-time $25,970. Required fees: $50.
Financial support: In 2001–02, 14 students received support, including 7 fellowships with full tuition reimbursements available, 7 teaching assistantships with full tuition reimbursements available; research assistantships, institutionally sponsored loans, scholarships/grants, tuition waivers (full and partial), and unspecified assistantships also available. Financial award applicants required to submit FAFSA.
Faculty research: African-American literature, art, cinema and theater; African-American politics and public policy; African history, politics and art; Caribbean politics and Africana Diaspora.
Application contact: Graduate Field Assistant, 607-255-4626, *Fax:* 607-2550784, *E-mail:* spt1@cornell.edu. *Web site:* http://www.gradschool.cornell.edu/grad/fields_1/africana.html

■ FLORIDA INTERNATIONAL UNIVERSITY

College of Arts and Sciences, Program in African-New World Studies, Miami, FL 33199

AWARDS MA.

Faculty: 2 full-time (0 women).
Students: 5 full-time (4 women), 6 part-time (4 women); includes 10 minority (9 African Americans, 1 Asian American or Pacific Islander). 15 applicants, 80% accepted, 6 enrolled.
Degree requirements: For master's, one foreign language, thesis optional.
Entrance requirements: For master's, GRE General Test, TOEFL. *Application fee:* $20.
Expenses: Tuition, state resident: full-time $2,916; part-time $162 per credit hour. Tuition, nonresident: full-time $10,245; part-time $569 per credit hour. Required fees: $168 per term.
Dr. Carole Boyce-Davies, Director, 305-919-5521, *Fax:* 305-919-5267, *E-mail:* cboyced@fiu.edu.

■ HOWARD UNIVERSITY

Graduate School of Arts and Sciences, Department of African Studies, Washington, DC 20059-0002

AWARDS MA, PhD. Part-time programs available.

Faculty: 7.
Students: 54; includes 39 minority (all African Americans), 10 international. In 2001, 2 master's, 6 doctorates awarded.
Degree requirements: For master's, one foreign language, thesis, internship, comprehensive exam; for doctorate, 2 foreign languages, thesis/dissertation, field research, comprehensive exam. *Median time to degree:* Master's–2 years full-time, 5 years part-time; doctorate–5 years full-time, 7 years part-time.
Entrance requirements: For master's, GRE General Test, minimum GPA of 3.0; for doctorate, GRE General Test, minimum GPA of 3.5. *Application deadline:* For fall admission, 4/1; for spring admission, 11/1. Applications are processed on a rolling basis. *Application fee:* $45.
Financial support: Fellowships with full and partial tuition reimbursements, research assistantships with full and partial tuition reimbursements, teaching assistantships with full and partial tuition reimbursements, career-related internships or fieldwork, Federal Work-Study, institutionally sponsored loans, scholarships/grants, tuition waivers (full and partial), and unspecified assistantships available. Support available to part-time students. Financial award application deadline: 4/1.
Faculty research: African literature, economics of Africa, international relations, public policy analysis.
Dr. Robert Cummings, Chair, 202-238-2328, *Fax:* 202-238-2326, *E-mail:* rcummings@howard.edu. *Web site:* http://www.howard.edu/

■ JOHNS HOPKINS UNIVERSITY

Paul H. Nitze School of Advanced International Studies, Washington, DC 20036

AWARDS Emerging markets (Certificate); interdisciplinary studies (MA, PhD), including African studies, American foreign policy (MA), Asian studies, Canadian studies, conflict resolution and mediation (MA), environmental policy and resource management (MA), European studies, international business (MA), international development (MA), international economics (MA), international relations (MA), Latin American studies, Middle Eastern studies (MA), military and defense studies (MA), Russian area and East European studies (MA), social change and development (MA); international public policy (MIPP). MBA/MA offered jointly with the University of Pennsylvania–Wharton School and INSEAD in France.

Faculty: 44 full-time (13 women), 113 part-time/adjunct (29 women).
Students: 567 full-time (275 women), 17 part-time (8 women); includes 71 minority (14 African Americans, 46 Asian Americans or Pacific Islanders, 10 Hispanic Americans, 1 Native American). Average age 27. 1,288 applicants, 35% accepted. In 2001, 294 master's, 13 doctorates, 34 other advanced degrees awarded. Terminal master's awarded for partial completion of doctoral program.
Degree requirements: For master's, one foreign language, comprehensive exam; for doctorate, 2 foreign languages, thesis/dissertation.
Entrance requirements: For master's, GMAT or GRE General Test or TOEFL, previous course work in economics, foreign language; for doctorate, GRE General Test or TOEFL; for Certificate, TOEFL. *Application deadline:* For fall admission, 1/15. *Application fee:* $75. Electronic applications accepted.
Expenses: Contact institution.
Financial support: In 2001–02, 431 fellowships (averaging $5,500 per year) were awarded; career-related internships or fieldwork and Federal Work-Study also available. Financial award application deadline: 2/1; financial award applicants required to submit FAFSA.
Faculty research: Comparative politics, regional studies, language and linguistics.
Dr. Jessica Einhorn, Dean, 202-663-5624, *Fax:* 202-663-5621.
Application contact: Bonnie Wilson, Associate Dean of Student Affairs, 202-663-5700, *Fax:* 202-663-7788, *E-mail:* admissions.sais@jhu.edu. *Web site:* http://www.sais-jhu.edu/

Find an in-depth description at www.petersons.com/gradchannel.

■ NEW YORK UNIVERSITY

Graduate School of Arts and Science, Program in Africana Studies, New York, NY 10012-1019

AWARDS MA.

Faculty: 3 full-time (1 woman), 3 part-time/adjunct.
Students: 5 full-time (3 women), 5 part-time (4 women); includes 3 minority (all Hispanic Americans), 5 international. Average age 25. 29 applicants, 34% accepted, 5 enrolled. In 2001, 1 degree awarded.
Degree requirements: For master's, thesis or alternative.
Entrance requirements: For master's, GRE, TOEFL, sample of written work. *Application deadline:* For fall admission, 1/4 (priority date). *Application fee:* $60.
Expenses: Tuition: Full-time $19,536; part-time $814 per credit. Required fees: $1,330; $38 per credit. Tuition and fees vary according to course load and program.
Financial support: Fellowships with tuition reimbursements, Federal Work-Study and institutionally sponsored loans available. Financial award application deadline: 1/4; financial award applicants required to submit FAFSA.
Faculty research: Pan-Africanism, black urban studies, film and literature of black diaspora, cultural politics and theory, politics of identity.
Manthia Diawara, Director, 212-998-2130, *Fax:* 212-995-4109.
Application contact: Robert Hinton, Director of Graduate Studies, 212-998-2130, *Fax:* 212-995-4109. *Web site:* http://www.nyu.edu/gsas/dept/africana/

■ NORTHWESTERN UNIVERSITY

The Graduate School, Program in African Studies, Evanston, IL 60208

AWARDS Certificate.

Application fee: $50 ($55 for international students).
Expenses: Tuition: Full-time $26,526.
Financial support: In 2001–02, 3 fellowships with full tuition reimbursements were awarded
Dr. David Lee Schoenbrun, Interim Director, 847-491-7323, *Fax:* 847-491-3739, *E-mail:* dls@northwestern.edu.
Application contact: Dr. Akbar Virmani, Associate Director, 847-491-7323, *Fax:* 847-491-3739, *E-mail:* a-virmani@northwestern.edu. *Web site:* http://www.northwestern.edu/african-studies/

■ THE OHIO STATE UNIVERSITY

Graduate School, College of Humanities, Department of African-American and African Studies, Columbus, OH 43210

AWARDS MA.

Degree requirements: For master's, internship, or thesis.
Entrance requirements: For master's, GRE General Test.

■ OHIO UNIVERSITY

Graduate Studies, Center for International Studies, Program in African Studies, Athens, OH 45701-2979

AWARDS MA. Part-time programs available.

Faculty: 21 full-time (7 women).
Students: 23 full-time (7 women), 1 (woman) part-time; includes 5 minority (all African Americans), 13 international. 66 applicants, 88% accepted.
Degree requirements: For master's, one foreign language, thesis optional.
Entrance requirements: For master's, GRE, TOEFL (for foreign language area studies), minimum GPA of 3.0. *Application deadline:* For fall admission, 3/1 (priority date). *Application fee:* $30.
Expenses: Tuition, state resident: full-time $6,585. Tuition, nonresident: full-time $12,254.
Financial support: In 2001–02, 6 fellowships with tuition reimbursements (averaging $11,000 per year), 12 research assistantships with tuition reimbursements (averaging $9,000 per year), 1 teaching assistantship with tuition reimbursement (averaging $9,000 per year) were awarded. Federal Work-Study, institutionally sponsored loans, scholarships/grants, and tuition waivers (full) also available. Financial award application deadline: 1/15.
Faculty research: Institute for the African child.
Dr. William Stephen Howard, Director, 740-593-1834, *Fax:* 740-593-1837, *E-mail:* showard1@ohio.edu.
Application contact: Joan Kraynanski, Administrative Assistant, 740-593-1840, *Fax:* 740-593-1837, *E-mail:* kraynans@ohio.edu. *Web site:* http://www.ohiou.edu/~intsdept/international studies/

■ ST. JOHN'S UNIVERSITY

St. John's College of Liberal Arts and Sciences, Institute of Asian Studies, Jamaica, NY 11439

AWARDS Asian and African cultural studies (Adv C); Asian studies (Adv C); Chinese studies (MA, Adv C); East Asian culture studies (Adv C); East Asian studies (MA). Part-time and evening/weekend programs available.

Faculty: 1 (woman) full-time, 5 part-time/adjunct (4 women).
Students: 4 full-time (3 women), 9 part-time (7 women); includes 6 minority (5 Asian Americans or Pacific Islanders, 1 Hispanic American), 6 international. Average age 34. 11 applicants, 4 enrolled. In 2001, 4 degrees awarded.
Degree requirements: For master's, one foreign language, comprehensive exam.
Entrance requirements: For master's, 18 hours in the field, minimum GPA of 3.0. *Application deadline:* Applications are processed on a rolling basis. *Application fee:* $40.
Expenses: Tuition: Full-time $14,520; part-time $605 per credit. Required fees: $150; $75 per term. Tuition and fees vary according to class time, course load, degree level, campus/location, program and student level.
Financial support: Research assistantships with full tuition reimbursements, scholarships/grants available. Support available to part-time students. Financial award application deadline: 3/1; financial award applicants required to submit FAFSA.
Faculty research: East Asian philosophy and religion, Chinese language and literature, Japanese language, modern Japan, Chinese art and history.
Dr. John Lin, Director, 718-990-6582, *E-mail:* linj@stjohns.edu.
Application contact: Matthew Whelan, Director, Office of Admission, 718-990-2000, *Fax:* 718-990-2096, *E-mail:* admissions@stjohns.edu. *Web site:* http://www.stjohns.edu/

■ STATE UNIVERSITY OF NEW YORK AT ALBANY

College of Arts and Sciences, Department of Africana Studies, Albany, NY 12222-0001

AWARDS African studies (MA); Afro-American studies (MA). Part-time and evening/weekend programs available.

Students: 15 full-time (8 women), 1 part-time; includes 6 minority (all African Americans), 5 international. Average age 29. 12 applicants, 83% accepted. In 2001, 7 degrees awarded.
Application deadline: For fall admission, 7/15; for spring admission, 11/1. Applications are processed on a rolling basis. *Application fee:* $50.
Expenses: Tuition, state resident: full-time $2,550; part-time $213 per credit. Tuition, nonresident: full-time $4,208; part-time $351 per credit. Required fees: $470; $470 per year.
Financial support: Fellowships, teaching assistantships, Federal Work-Study available. Financial award application deadline: 5/1.
Faculty research: The black family, Afrocentricity in poetry, black women in U.S. literature.
Dr. Leonard Slade, Chair, 518-442-4730.

■ UNIVERSITY OF CALIFORNIA, LOS ANGELES

Graduate Division, College of Letters and Science, Program in African Studies, Los Angeles, CA 90095

AWARDS MA, MFA/MA, MPH/MA.

Students: 12 full-time (8 women); includes 4 minority (all African Americans), 3

international. 24 applicants, 71% accepted, 11 enrolled. In 2001, 7 degrees awarded.
Degree requirements: For master's, one foreign language.
Entrance requirements: For master's, GRE General Test, minimum GPA of 3.0, sample of research writing. *Application deadline:* For fall admission, 12/15. *Application fee:* $60. Electronic applications accepted.
Expenses: Tuition, nonresident: full-time $10,244. Required fees: $3,609. Full-time tuition and fees vary according to program.
Financial support: In 2001–02, 10 fellowships, 3 research assistantships, 5 teaching assistantships were awarded. Federal Work-Study, institutionally sponsored loans, scholarships/grants, and tuition waivers (full and partial) also available. Financial award application deadline: 3/1.
Russell Schuh, Chair, 310-825-2944.
Application contact: Departmental Office, 310-825-2944, *E-mail:* maas@isop.ucla.edu.

■ UNIVERSITY OF CONNECTICUT

Graduate School, College of Liberal Arts and Sciences, Field of African Studies, Storrs, CT 06269

AWARDS MA.

Entrance requirements: For master's, GRE General Test.

■ UNIVERSITY OF FLORIDA

Graduate School, College of Liberal Arts and Sciences, Center for African Studies, Gainesville, FL 32611-5560

AWARDS Certificate. Part-time programs available.

Expenses: Tuition, state resident: part-time $164 per hour. Tuition, nonresident: part-time $571 per hour. Tuition and fees vary according to course level and program.
Faculty research: Governance, human rights, African archaeology, southern African history, wildlife conservation and natural resources. *Web site:* http://www.africa.ufl.edu/

■ UNIVERSITY OF ILLINOIS AT URBANA–CHAMPAIGN

Graduate College, College of Liberal Arts and Sciences, Center for African Studies, Champaign, IL 61820

AWARDS AM.

Faculty: 1 full-time.
Students: 7 full-time (4 women); includes 1 minority (African American), 2 international. 10 applicants, 30% accepted. In 2001, 8 degrees awarded.
Degree requirements: For master's, one foreign language, thesis optional.
Entrance requirements: For master's, minimum GPA of 3.0. *Application deadline:* For fall admission, 2/21. Applications are processed on a rolling basis. *Application fee:* $40 ($50 for international students). Electronic applications accepted.
Expenses: Tuition, state resident: part-time $3,227 per degree program. Tuition, nonresident: part-time $7,169 per degree program. Tuition and fees vary according to program.
Financial support: In 2001–02, 5 fellowships, 1 research assistantship, 1 teaching assistantship were awarded. Career-related internships or fieldwork, Federal Work-Study, institutionally sponsored loans, and tuition waivers (partial) also available. Financial award application deadline: 2/15.
Ezekiel Kalipeni, Acting Director, 217-333-6335, *Fax:* 217-244-2429, *E-mail:* kalipeni@uiuc.edu.
Application contact: Sue Swisher, Director of Graduate Studies, 217-244-4713, *Fax:* 217-244-2429, *E-mail:* swisher@uiuc.edu. *Web site:* http://www.wsi.cso.uiuc.edu/CAS/

■ UNIVERSITY OF LOUISVILLE

Graduate School, College of Arts and Sciences, Department of Pan-African Studies, Louisville, KY 40292-0001

AWARDS MA.

Students: 1 full-time (0 women); minority (African American).
Application fee: $25.
Expenses: Tuition, state resident: full-time $4,134. Tuition, nonresident: full-time $11,486.
Dr. J. Blaine Hudson, Department Chair, 502-852-5506, *Fax:* 502-852-5954.

■ UNIVERSITY OF WISCONSIN–MADISON

Graduate School, College of Letters and Science, Department of African Languages and Literature, Madison, WI 53706-1380

AWARDS MA, PhD. Part-time programs available.

Faculty: 10 full-time (4 women), 1 part-time/adjunct (0 women).
Students: 18 full-time (7 women), 6 part-time (5 women); includes 5 minority (4 African Americans, 1 Hispanic American), 5 international. Average age 26. 15 applicants, 80% accepted, 8 enrolled. In 2001, 1 master's, 2 doctorates awarded.
Degree requirements: For master's, one foreign language, thesis; for doctorate, 2 foreign languages, thesis/dissertation, comprehensive exam.
Entrance requirements: For master's, BA in African language and literature; for doctorate, MA in African language and literature. *Application deadline:* Applications are processed on a rolling basis. *Application fee:* $45. Electronic applications accepted.
Expenses: Tuition, state resident: full-time $7,361; part-time $399 per credit. Tuition, nonresident: full-time $20,499; part-time $1,282 per credit. Required fees: $34 per credit. Full-time tuition and fees vary according to course load, program, reciprocity agreements and student level.
Financial support: In 2001–02, 9 students received support, including 3 fellowships with tuition reimbursements available, 1 research assistantship, 5 teaching assistantships with tuition reimbursements available Financial award application deadline: 11/15.
Faculty research: Oral traditions, language pedagogy, stylistics, sociolinguistics, literary criticism.
Magadalena Hauner, Chair, 608-262-2487, *Fax:* 608-265-4151, *E-mail:* hauner@facstaff.wisc.edu.
Application contact: Dustin Cowell, Admissions Chair, 608-262-2487, *Fax:* 608-265-4151, *E-mail:* afrlang@macc.wisc.edu. *Web site:* http://african.lss.wisc.edu/all/

■ WEST VIRGINIA UNIVERSITY

Eberly College of Arts and Sciences, Department of History, Morgantown, WV 26506

AWARDS African history (MA, PhD); African-American history (MA, PhD); American history (MA, PhD); Appalachian/regional history (MA, PhD); East Asian history (MA, PhD); European history (MA, PhD); history of science and technology (MA, PhD); Latin American history (MA). Part-time programs available.

Faculty: 19 full-time (4 women), 2 part-time/adjunct (1 woman).
Students: 35 full-time (13 women), 29 part-time (10 women); includes 5 minority (2 African Americans, 1 Asian American or Pacific Islander, 1 Hispanic American, 1 Native American), 5 international. Average age 34. 86 applicants, 44% accepted. In 2001, 4 master's, 1 doctorate awarded.
Degree requirements: For master's, one foreign language; for doctorate, one foreign language, comprehensive exam, dissertation defense.
Entrance requirements: For master's, GRE General Test, TOEFL, minimum GPA of 3.0; for doctorate, GRE General Test, TOEFL, MA or equivalent. *Application deadline:* For spring admission, 11/1. Applications are processed on a rolling basis. *Application fee:* $45.
Expenses: Tuition, state resident: full-time $2,791. Tuition, nonresident: full-time $8,659. Required fees: $1,002. Tuition and fees vary according to program.
Financial support: In 2001–02, 43 students received support, including 2 research assistantships, 23 teaching assistantships; fellowships, career-related internships or fieldwork, Federal Work-Study, institutionally sponsored loans, tuition waivers (full and partial), and graduate administrative assistantships also available. Financial award application deadline: 2/1; financial award applicants required to submit FAFSA.

West Virginia University (continued)
Faculty research: U.S., Appalachia, modern Europe, Africa, science and technology.
Dr. Robert M. Maxon, Chair, 304-293-2421 Ext. 5223, *Fax:* 304-293-3616, *E-mail:* robert.maxon@mail.wvu.edu.
Application contact: Dr. Robert E. Blobaum, Director of Graduate Studies, 304-293-2421 Ext. 5241, *Fax:* 304-293-3616, *E-mail:* robert.blobaum@mail.wvu.edu. *Web site:* http://www.as.wvu.edu/history/

■ YALE UNIVERSITY

Graduate School of Arts and Sciences, Interdisciplinary Program in African Studies, New Haven, CT 06520

AWARDS MA.

Degree requirements: For master's, one foreign language, thesis.
Entrance requirements: For master's, GRE General Test.

AMERICAN STUDIES

■ APPALACHIAN STATE UNIVERSITY

Cratis D. Williams Graduate School, College of Arts and Sciences, Center for Appalachian Studies, Boone, NC 28608

AWARDS MA. Part-time programs available.

Faculty: 23 full-time (4 women).
Students: 12 full-time (11 women), 1 (woman) part-time. Average age 27. 11 applicants, 91% accepted, 7 enrolled. In 2001, 5 degrees awarded.
Degree requirements: For master's, one foreign language, thesis, comprehensive exam.
Entrance requirements: For master's, GRE General Test. *Application deadline:* For fall admission, 7/1 (priority date); for spring admission, 11/1. Applications are processed on a rolling basis. *Application fee:* $35.
Expenses: Tuition, state resident: full-time $1,286. Tuition, nonresident: full-time $9,354. Required fees: $1,116.
Financial support: In 2001–02, fellowships (averaging $1,000 per year), 6 research assistantships (averaging $6,250 per year), 3 teaching assistantships were awarded. Career-related internships or fieldwork, scholarships/grants, and unspecified assistantships also available. Support available to part-time students. Financial award application deadline: 7/1; financial award applicants required to submit FAFSA.
Dr. Pat Beaver, Director, 828-262-2550.

■ BAYLOR UNIVERSITY

Graduate School, College of Arts and Sciences, Department of American Studies, Waco, TX 76798

AWARDS MA.

Students: 7 full-time (5 women), 2 part-time (both women), 3 international.
Degree requirements: For master's, thesis, final oral exam.
Entrance requirements: For master's, GRE General Test, 24 semester hours of course work in subjects with American content. *Application deadline:* For fall admission, 8/1. Applications are processed on a rolling basis. *Application fee:* $25.
Expenses: Tuition: Part-time $379 per semester hour. Required fees: $42 per semester hour. $101 per semester. Tuition and fees vary according to program.
Financial support: Fellowships, Federal Work-Study and institutionally sponsored loans available. Financial award application deadline: 4/15.
Dr. Donald Greco, Director of Graduate Studies, 254-710-3434, *Fax:* 254-710-3600, *E-mail:* donald_greco@baylor.edu.
Application contact: Suzanne Keener, Administrative Assistant, 254-710-3588, *Fax:* 254-710-3870, *E-mail:* graduate_school@baylor.edu. *Web site:* http://www.baylor.edu/~American_Studies/

■ BOSTON UNIVERSITY

Graduate School of Arts and Sciences, Program in American and New England Studies, Boston, MA 02215

AWARDS American and New England studies (PhD).

Students: 33 full-time (25 women), 6 part-time (all women); includes 1 minority (Asian American or Pacific Islander), 1 international. Average age 34. 50 applicants, 34% accepted, 8 enrolled. In 2001, 2 doctorates awarded.
Degree requirements: For doctorate, one foreign language, thesis/dissertation, oral exams.
Entrance requirements: For doctorate, GRE General Test, TOEFL, scholarly writing sample, 3 letters of recommendation. *Application deadline:* For fall admission, 1/15. *Application fee:* $60.
Expenses: Tuition: Full-time $25,872; part-time $340 per credit. Required fees: $40 per semester. Part-time tuition and fees vary according to class time, course level and program.
Financial support: In 2001–02, 37 students received support, including 1 fellowship (averaging $14,000 per year), 2 research assistantships with full tuition reimbursements available, 3 teaching assistantships with full tuition reimbursements available (averaging $12,500 per year); career-related internships or fieldwork, Federal Work-Study, and unspecified assistantships also available. Support available to part-time students. Financial award application deadline: 1/15; financial award applicants required to submit FAFSA.
Bruce J. Schulman, Director, 617-353-9912, *Fax:* 617-353-2556, *E-mail:* bjschulm@bu.edu.
Application contact: Samantha M. Khosla, Staff Coordinator, 617-353-2948, *Fax:* 617-353-2556, *E-mail:* skhosla@bu.edu. *Web site:* http://www.bu.edu/AMNESP/

■ BOWLING GREEN STATE UNIVERSITY

Graduate College, College of Arts and Sciences, American Culture Studies Program, Bowling Green, OH 43403

AWARDS MA, MAT, PhD. Part-time programs available.

Students: 54 full-time (30 women), 14 part-time (7 women); includes 12 minority (6 African Americans, 1 Asian American or Pacific Islander, 4 Hispanic Americans, 1 Native American), 6 international. Average age 35. 66 applicants, 70% accepted, 19 enrolled. In 2001, 11 master's, 15 doctorates awarded.
Degree requirements: For master's, thesis or alternative; for doctorate, thesis/dissertation, comprehensive exam.
Entrance requirements: For master's and doctorate, GRE General Test, TOEFL. *Application deadline:* For fall admission, 2/1. *Application fee:* $30. Electronic applications accepted.
Expenses: Tuition, state resident: full-time $7,376; part-time $342 per credit hour. Tuition, nonresident: full-time $13,628; part-time $640 per credit hour.
Financial support: In 2001–02, 8 research assistantships with full tuition reimbursements (averaging $10,368 per year), 39 teaching assistantships with full tuition reimbursements (averaging $9,198 per year) were awarded. Federal Work-Study and unspecified assistantships also available. Financial award applicants required to submit FAFSA.
Faculty research: Race and ethnicity, gender, popular culture.
Dr. Don McQuarie, Chair, 419-372-0586.

■ BOWLING GREEN STATE UNIVERSITY

Graduate College, College of Arts and Sciences, Department of Popular Culture, Bowling Green, OH 43403

AWARDS MA. Part-time programs available.

Faculty: 8.
Students: 15 full-time (4 women), 2 international. Average age 27. 22 applicants, 50% accepted, 8 enrolled. In 2001, 7 degrees awarded.
Degree requirements: For master's, thesis or alternative.
Entrance requirements: For master's, GRE General Test, TOEFL. *Application fee:* $30. Electronic applications accepted.

Expenses: Tuition, state resident: full-time $7,376; part-time $342 per credit hour. Tuition, nonresident: full-time $13,628; part-time $640 per credit hour.
Financial support: In 2001–02, 15 teaching assistantships with full tuition reimbursements (averaging $7,300 per year) were awarded; research assistantships with full tuition reimbursements, career-related internships or fieldwork, Federal Work-Study, institutionally sponsored loans, and unspecified assistantships also available. Financial award applicants required to submit FAFSA.
Faculty research: Mass media (popular film, TV, and music); folklore/folklife; ritual, festival, celebration, and holidays; global, international, and popular culture; nineteenth-century everyday life.
Dr. Chris Geist, Chair (Interim), 419-372-7863.
Application contact: Dr. Carl Holmberg, Graduate Coordinator, 419-372-8172.

■ BRANDEIS UNIVERSITY

Graduate School of Arts and Sciences, Department of History, Program in American History, Waltham, MA 02454-9110

AWARDS MA, PhD. Part-time programs available.

Faculty: 7 full-time (3 women), 1 part-time/adjunct (0 women).
Students: 31 full-time (17 women); includes 2 minority (1 African American, 1 Asian American or Pacific Islander), 1 international. Average age 25. 35 applicants, 14% accepted, 5 enrolled. In 2001, 1 master's, 3 doctorates awarded. Terminal master's awarded for partial completion of doctoral program.
Degree requirements: For master's, one foreign language, registration; for doctorate, 2 foreign languages, thesis/dissertation, colloquia, directed research, comprehensive exam, registration.
Entrance requirements: For master's, GRE General Test, resumé, sample of written work, letters of recommendation; for doctorate, GRE General Test, resumé, sample of written work. *Application deadline:* For spring admission, 2/15. *Application fee:* $60. Electronic applications accepted.
Expenses: Tuition: Full-time $27,392. Required fees: $35.
Financial support: In 2001–02, 13 fellowships with full tuition reimbursements (averaging $15,000 per year), 18 teaching assistantships (averaging $3,000 per year) were awarded. Research assistantships, scholarships/grants and tuition waivers (full and partial) also available. Support available to part-time students. Financial award application deadline: 4/15; financial award applicants required to submit CSS PROFILE or FAFSA.
Faculty research: American polity, social history, cultural, legal, colonial.
Dr. David Engerman, Chair, 781-736-2281, *Fax:* 781-736-2273, *E-mail:* engerman@brandeis.edu. *Web site:* http://www.brandeis.edu/gsas/viewbk2/socsci.html

■ BRIGHAM YOUNG UNIVERSITY

The David M. Kennedy Center for International and Area Studies, Provo, UT 84602-1001

AWARDS American studies (MA); ancient Near Eastern studies (MA); Asian studies (MA); international development (MA); international relations (MA).

Faculty: 21 full-time (2 women), 2 part-time/adjunct (0 women).
Students: 16 full-time (8 women), 13 part-time (9 women); includes 1 minority (Hispanic American), 4 international. Average age 25. 62 applicants, 31% accepted. In 2001, 17 degrees awarded.
Degree requirements: For master's, one foreign language, thesis.
Entrance requirements: For master's, GRE General Test, minimum GPA of 3.55 in last 60 hours. *Application deadline:* For fall admission, 2/1. *Application fee:* $50. Electronic applications accepted.
Expenses: Tuition: Full-time $3,860; part-time $214 per hour.
Financial support: In 2001–02, 18 research assistantships (averaging $3,500 per year), 2 teaching assistantships (averaging $3,500 per year) were awarded. Fellowships with full tuition reimbursements, career-related internships or fieldwork and tuition waivers (full) also available. Financial award application deadline: 2/1.
Faculty research: Comparative education, education for development, comparative economics. *Total annual research expenditures:* $100,000.
Dr. Donald B. Holsinger, Director, 801-422-3378, *Fax:* 801-378-8748, *E-mail:* donald_holsinger@byu.edu.
Application contact: Dr. Phillip J. Bryson, Director of Graduate Studies, Associate Director, 801-422-7402, *Fax:* 801-378-8748, *E-mail:* phillip_bryson@byu.edu.

■ BROWN UNIVERSITY

Graduate School, Department of American Civilization, Providence, RI 02912

AWARDS AM, PhD.

Degree requirements: For doctorate, thesis/dissertation, preliminary exam.

■ CALIFORNIA STATE UNIVERSITY, FULLERTON

Graduate Studies, College of Humanities and Social Sciences, Department of American Studies, Fullerton, CA 92834-9480

AWARDS MA. Part-time programs available.

Faculty: 8 full-time (3 women), 10 part-time/adjunct.
Students: 17 full-time (10 women), 28 part-time (17 women); includes 10 minority (3 African Americans, 3 Asian Americans or Pacific Islanders, 4 Hispanic Americans), 6 international. Average age 35. 31 applicants, 61% accepted, 13 enrolled. In 2001, 6 degrees awarded.
Degree requirements: For master's, comprehensive exam or thesis.
Entrance requirements: For master's, minimum GPA of 3.0 in major, 2.5 in last 60 hours. *Application fee:* $55.
Expenses: Tuition, nonresident: part-time $246 per unit. Required fees: $964.
Financial support: Teaching assistantships, Federal Work-Study, institutionally sponsored loans, and scholarships/grants available. Support available to part-time students. Financial award application deadline: 3/1.
Dr. Jesse Battan, Chair, 714-278-2441.
Application contact: Dr. John Ibson, Adviser, 714-278-3625.

■ CASE WESTERN RESERVE UNIVERSITY

School of Graduate Studies, Department of Theater Arts, Program in American Studies, Cleveland, OH 44106

AWARDS MA, PhD. Terminal master's awarded for partial completion of doctoral program.

Degree requirements: For master's, thesis optional; for doctorate, thesis/dissertation.
Entrance requirements: For master's and doctorate, GRE General Test, TOEFL.
Faculty research: American regionalism, American theater and drama.

■ CLAREMONT GRADUATE UNIVERSITY

Graduate Programs, Center for the Humanities, Department of English, Claremont, CA 91711-6160

AWARDS American studies (MA); English (M Phil, MA, PhD); literature and creative writing (MA); literature and film (MA); literature and theatre (MA). Part-time programs available.

Faculty: 3 full-time (2 women), 7 part-time/adjunct (2 women).
Students: 60 full-time (45 women), 45 part-time (26 women); includes 25 minority (6 African Americans, 10 Asian Americans or Pacific Islanders, 7 Hispanic Americans, 2 Native Americans). Average age 33. In 2001, 15 master's, 3 doctorates awarded.
Degree requirements: For master's, one foreign language, comprehensive exam; for doctorate, 2 foreign languages, thesis/dissertation, comprehensive exam.
Entrance requirements: For master's, GRE General Test; for doctorate, GRE General Test, MA in literature. *Application*

Claremont Graduate University (continued)

deadline: For fall admission, 2/15 (priority date); for spring admission, 11/15. Applications are processed on a rolling basis. *Application fee:* $50. Electronic applications accepted.
Expenses: Tuition: Full-time $22,984; part-time $1,000 per unit. Required fees: $160; $80 per semester.
Financial support: Fellowships, Federal Work-Study and institutionally sponsored loans available. Support available to part-time students. Financial award application deadline: 2/15; financial award applicants required to submit FAFSA.
Faculty research: American, comparative, and English Renaissance literature; modernism; feminist literature and theory.
Wendy Martin, Chair, 909-607-3335, *Fax:* 909-607-7938, *E-mail:* wendy.martin@cgu.edu.
Application contact: Cynda Boland, Secretary, 909-607-3335, *Fax:* 909-621-8390, *E-mail:* english@cgu.edu. *Web site:* http://www.cgu.edu/hum/eng/index.html

■ CLAREMONT GRADUATE UNIVERSITY

Graduate Programs, Center for the Humanities, Department of History, Claremont, CA 91711-6160

AWARDS American studies (MA, PhD); European studies (MA, PhD); history (MA, PhD).

Faculty: 2 full-time (1 woman), 2 part-time/adjunct (both women).
Students: 55 full-time (32 women), 24 part-time (9 women); includes 17 minority (3 African Americans, 4 Asian Americans or Pacific Islanders, 10 Hispanic Americans), 3 international. Average age 37. In 2001, 11 master's, 5 doctorates awarded.
Degree requirements: For master's, 2 foreign languages, thesis/dissertation; for doctorate, 2 foreign languages, thesis/dissertation, comprehensive exam.
Entrance requirements: For master's and doctorate, GRE General Test. *Application deadline:* For fall admission, 2/15 (priority date). Applications are processed on a rolling basis. *Application fee:* $50. Electronic applications accepted.
Expenses: Tuition: Full-time $22,984; part-time $1,000 per unit. Required fees: $160; $80 per semester.
Financial support: Fellowships, research assistantships, Federal Work-Study and institutionally sponsored loans available. Support available to part-time students. Financial award application deadline: 2/15; financial award applicants required to submit FAFSA.
Faculty research: Intellectual and social history, cultural studies, gender studies, Western history, Chicano history.
Janet Farrell Brodie, Chair, 909-621-8172, *Fax:* 909-621-8609.
Application contact: Elisabeth Flores Griffith, Secretary, 909-621-8172, *Fax:* 909-621-8390, *E-mail:* history@cgu.edu. *Web site:* http://www.cgu.edu/hum/his/index.html

■ THE COLLEGE OF WILLIAM AND MARY

Faculty of Arts and Sciences, Program in American Studies, Williamsburg, VA 23187-8795

AWARDS MA, PhD, JD/MA. Part-time programs available.

Faculty: 5 full-time (3 women), 2 part-time/adjunct (both women).
Students: 43 full-time (32 women), 6 part-time (2 women); includes 11 minority (9 African Americans, 1 Asian American or Pacific Islander, 1 Hispanic American), 4 international. Average age 32. 94 applicants, 37% accepted. In 2001, 9 master's, 7 doctorates awarded. Terminal master's awarded for partial completion of doctoral program.
Degree requirements: For master's, thesis defense; for doctorate, one foreign language, comprehensive exam, dissertation defense.
Entrance requirements: For master's, minimum GPA of 2.5. *Application deadline:* For fall admission, 1/15. *Application fee:* $30.
Expenses: Tuition, state resident: full-time $3,262; part-time $175 per credit hour. Tuition, nonresident: full-time $14,768; part-time $550 per credit hour. Required fees: $2,478.
Financial support: In 2001–02, 26 students received support, including 5 fellowships with full tuition reimbursements available (averaging $12,000 per year), 17 research assistantships with full tuition reimbursements available (averaging $12,000 per year), 4 teaching assistantships with full tuition reimbursements available (averaging $12,000 per year); career-related internships or fieldwork, Federal Work-Study, and institutionally sponsored loans also available. Financial award application deadline: 3/15; financial award applicants required to submit FAFSA.
Faculty research: Antebellum intellectual history, black autobiography, philanthropy and society, nineteenth-century literature, material culture, film studies.
Dr. David P. Aday, Director, 757-221-1275.
Application contact: Dr. Richard Lowry, Director of Graduate Studies, 757-221-1285, *Fax:* 757-221-1287, *E-mail:* rslowr@wm.edu.

■ COLUMBIA UNIVERSITY

Graduate School of Arts and Sciences, Program in Liberal Studies, New York, NY 10027

AWARDS American studies (MA); East Asian studies (MA); human rights studies (MA); Islamic culture studies (MA); Jewish studies (MA); medieval studies (MA); modern European studies (MA); South Asian studies (MA). Part-time and evening/weekend programs available.

Faculty: 5 part-time/adjunct (2 women).
Students: 7 full-time (2 women), 75 part-time (51 women); includes 5 minority (1 African American, 3 Asian Americans or Pacific Islanders, 1 Hispanic American), 8 international. Average age 41. 39 applicants, 77% accepted. In 2001, 20 degrees awarded.
Degree requirements: For master's, thesis.
Application deadline: For fall admission, 4/1; for spring admission, 11/1. *Application fee:* $65.
Expenses: Tuition: Full-time $27,528. Required fees: $1,638.
Steve Laymon, Assistant Dean, 212-854-4932, *Fax:* 212-854-4912.
Application contact: Director of Admissions, 212-854-3331.

Find an in-depth description at www.petersons.com/gradchannel.

■ EAST CAROLINA UNIVERSITY

Graduate School, College of Arts and Sciences, Department of History, Greenville, NC 27858-4353

AWARDS American history (MA, MA Ed); European history (MA, MA Ed); maritime history (MA). Part-time and evening/weekend programs available.

Faculty: 22 full-time (3 women).
Students: 32 full-time (9 women), 40 part-time (13 women); includes 4 minority (1 African American, 2 Asian Americans or Pacific Islanders, 1 Native American), 1 international. Average age 31. 36 applicants, 69% accepted. In 2001, 17 degrees awarded.
Degree requirements: For master's, one foreign language, thesis, comprehensive exam.
Entrance requirements: For master's, GRE General Test, GRE Subject Test, MAT (MA Ed), TOEFL. *Application deadline:* For fall admission, 6/1 (priority date); for spring admission, 10/15. Applications are processed on a rolling basis. *Application fee:* $45.
Expenses: Tuition, state resident: full-time $2,636. Tuition, nonresident: full-time $11,365.
Financial support: Fellowships, research assistantships with partial tuition reimbursements, teaching assistantships with partial tuition reimbursements, Federal Work-Study available. Support available to part-time students. Financial award application deadline: 6/1.
Dr. Michael Palmer, Chairperson, 252-328-6155, *Fax:* 252-328-6774, *E-mail:* palmerm@mail.ecu.edu.
Application contact: Dr. Carl Swanson, Director of Graduate Studies, 252-328-6485, *E-mail:* swansonc@mail.ecu.edu.

■ EASTERN MICHIGAN UNIVERSITY

Graduate School, College of Arts and Sciences, Department of History and Philosophy, Program in Social Science and American Culture, Ypsilanti, MI 48197

AWARDS MLS.

Degree requirements: For master's, thesis optional.
Entrance requirements: For master's, TOEFL. *Application deadline:* For fall admission, 5/15; for spring admission, 3/15. Applications are processed on a rolling basis. *Application fee:* $30.
Expenses: Tuition, state resident: part-time $285 per credit hour. Tuition, nonresident: part-time $510 per credit hour.
Financial support: Fellowships, teaching assistantships available. Support available to part-time students. Financial award application deadline: 3/15; financial award applicants required to submit FAFSA.
Dr. JoEllen Vinyard, Coordinator, 734-487-0053.

■ FAIRFIELD UNIVERSITY

College of Arts and Sciences, Program in American Studies, Fairfield, CT 06824

AWARDS MA. Part-time and evening/weekend programs available.

Faculty: 22 full-time (6 women).
Students: Average age 41. 12 applicants, 100% accepted, 11 enrolled. In 2001, 3 degrees awarded.
Degree requirements: For master's, capstone research project.
Entrance requirements: For master's, minimum GPA of 3.0. *Application deadline:* For fall admission, 7/1; for spring admission, 12/1. Applications are processed on a rolling basis. *Application fee:* $55.
Expenses: Tuition: Full-time $9,550; part-time $390 per credit hour. Required fees: $25 per term. Tuition and fees vary according to program.
Financial support: Tuition waivers (partial) available. Financial award applicants required to submit FAFSA.
Dr. Leo O'Connor, Director, 203-254-4000 Ext. 2801, *Fax:* 203-254-4119, *E-mail:* lfoconnor@fair1.fairfield.edu.
Application contact: Sue Peterson, Assistant to the Dean, 203-254-4000 Ext. 2246, *Fax:* 203-254-4119, *E-mail:* speterson@mail.fairfield.edu. *Web site:* http://www.fairfield.edu/

■ FLORIDA STATE UNIVERSITY

Graduate Studies, College of Arts and Sciences, Program in American and Florida Studies, Tallahassee, FL 32306

AWARDS MA. Part-time programs available. Postbaccalaureate distance learning degree programs offered (minimal on-campus study).

Faculty: 7 full-time (3 women).
Students: 15 full-time (8 women); includes 1 minority (African American). Average age 25. 8 applicants, 100% accepted. In 2001, 1 degree awarded.
Degree requirements: For master's, one foreign language, thesis or alternative.
Entrance requirements: For master's, GRE General Test, minimum GPA of 3.0. *Application deadline:* For fall admission, 7/13; for spring admission, 11/1. Applications are processed on a rolling basis. *Application fee:* $20. Electronic applications accepted.
Expenses: Tuition, state resident: part-time $163 per credit hour. Tuition, nonresident: part-time $570 per credit hour. Tuition and fees vary according to program.
Financial support: In 2001–02, 3 students received support, including fellowships with tuition reimbursements available (averaging $20,000 per year), 1 research assistantship with tuition reimbursement available (averaging $7,500 per year), 2 teaching assistantships with tuition reimbursements available (averaging $7,500 per year); career-related internships or fieldwork, Federal Work-Study, and unspecified assistantships also available. Support available to part-time students. Financial award applicants required to submit FAFSA.
Faculty research: American intellectual history, religion in America, aging studies.
Dr. John J. Fenstermaker, Director, 850-644-1352, *Fax:* 850-644-2140, *E-mail:* jfenstermaker@english.fsu.edu.
Application contact: 850-644-0202, *Fax:* 850-644-2140. *Web site:* http://www.fsu.edu/~ams/

■ FORDHAM UNIVERSITY

Graduate School of Arts and Sciences, Department of History, New York, NY 10458

AWARDS History (MA, PhD), including American (MA), early modern Europe (PhD), medieval Europe, modern Europe (MA). Part-time and evening/weekend programs available.

Faculty: 27 full-time (11 women).
Students: 14 full-time (8 women), 25 part-time (11 women); includes 4 minority (1 African American, 3 Hispanic Americans), 3 international. Average age 30. 40 applicants, 55% accepted. In 2001, 13 master's, 5 doctorates awarded. Terminal master's awarded for partial completion of doctoral program.
Degree requirements: For master's, one foreign language; for doctorate, 2 foreign languages, thesis/dissertation, comprehensive exam.
Entrance requirements: For master's and doctorate, GRE General Test. *Application deadline:* For fall admission, 1/15 (priority date); for spring admission, 12/1. *Application fee:* $65. Electronic applications accepted.
Expenses: Tuition: Part-time $720 per credit. Required fees: $135 per semester.
Financial support: In 2001–02, 20 students received support, including 1 fellowship with tuition reimbursement available (averaging $15,000 per year), research assistantships with tuition reimbursements available (averaging $11,000 per year), 6 teaching assistantships with tuition reimbursements available (averaging $14,000 per year); institutionally sponsored loans, tuition waivers (full and partial), and unspecified assistantships also available. Financial award application deadline: 1/16.
Dr. Richard Gyug, Chair, 718-817-3925, *Fax:* 718-817-4680, *E-mail:* gyug@fordham.edu.
Application contact: Dr. Craig W. Pilant, Assistant Dean, 718-817-4420, *Fax:* 718-817-3566, *E-mail:* pilant@fordham.edu. *Web site:* http://www.fordham.edu/gsas/

■ THE GEORGE WASHINGTON UNIVERSITY

Columbian College of Arts and Sciences, Department of American Studies, Washington, DC 20052

AWARDS American studies (MA, PhD); folklife (MA); historic preservation (MA); material culture (MA). Part-time and evening/weekend programs available.

Faculty: 6 full-time (2 women), 1 (woman) part-time/adjunct.
Students: 14 full-time (9 women), 37 part-time (27 women); includes 7 minority (4 African Americans, 2 Asian Americans or Pacific Islanders, 1 Hispanic American), 2 international. Average age 33. 75 applicants, 53% accepted. In 2001, 11 master's, 2 doctorates awarded. Terminal master's awarded for partial completion of doctoral program.
Degree requirements: For master's, comprehensive exam; for doctorate, one foreign language, thesis/dissertation, general exam.
Entrance requirements: For master's and doctorate, GRE General Test, minimum GPA of 3.0. *Application fee:* $55.
Expenses: Tuition: Part-time $810 per credit. Required fees: $1 per credit.
Financial support: In 2001–02, 16 students received support, including 16 fellowships (averaging $7,600 per year), 10 teaching assistantships (averaging $4,100 per year); research assistantships, career-related internships or fieldwork, Federal Work-Study, and institutionally sponsored loans also available. Financial award application deadline: 2/1.
Teresa Murphy, Chair, 202-994-6071, *Fax:* 202-994-8651.
Application contact: Monica Turcich, Executive Aide, 202-994-6070, *Fax:* 202-994-8651, *E-mail:* amst@gwu.edu. *Web site:* http://www.gwu.edu/~amst/index.htm/

■ HARVARD UNIVERSITY

Graduate School of Arts and Sciences, Committee on History of American Civilization, Cambridge, MA 02138

AWARDS PhD.

Degree requirements: For doctorate, 2 foreign languages, thesis/dissertation.
Entrance requirements: For doctorate, GRE General Test, GRE Subject Test (recommended), TOEFL.
Expenses: Tuition: Full-time $23,370. Required fees: $816. Full-time tuition and fees vary according to program and student level.
Faculty research: American history, literature, and religion in the Colonial era; twentieth-century American history, literature, and law; Southern literature, history, and sociology.

■ LEHIGH UNIVERSITY

College of Arts and Sciences, Program in American Studies, Bethlehem, PA 18015-3094

AWARDS MA.

Entrance requirements: For master's, TOEFL. *Application deadline:* For fall admission, 6/1. *Application fee:* $40. Electronic applications accepted.
Expenses: Tuition: Part-time $468 per credit hour. Required fees: $200; $100 per semester. Tuition and fees vary according to program.
Financial support: Fellowships available.
Application contact: Prof. John Pettegrew, Director, 610-758-3355, *Fax:* 610-758-6554, *E-mail:* jcp5@lehigh.edu.

Find an in-depth description at www.petersons.com/gradchannel.

■ MICHIGAN STATE UNIVERSITY

Graduate School, College of Arts and Letters, American Studies Program, East Lansing, MI 48824

AWARDS MA, PhD.

Students: 41 (23 women); includes 9 minority (3 African Americans, 1 Asian American or Pacific Islander, 3 Hispanic Americans, 2 Native Americans) 9 international. 35 applicants, 43% accepted.
Degree requirements: For master's, thesis optional; for doctorate, thesis/dissertation.
Entrance requirements: For master's, GRE General Test, TOEFL; for doctorate, GRE General Test. *Application deadline:* For fall admission, 1/1; for spring admission, 12/29 (priority date). Applications are processed on a rolling basis. *Application fee:* $30 ($40 for international students). Electronic applications accepted.
Expenses: Tuition, state resident: part-time $244 per credit hour. Tuition, nonresident: part-time $494 per credit hour. Required fees: $268 per semester. Tuition and fees vary according to course load, degree level and program.
Financial support: Fellowships, teaching assistantships, Federal Work-Study and institutionally sponsored loans available. Financial award application deadline: 1/1; financial award applicants required to submit FAFSA.
Faculty research: Cultural studies, social history, Native American studies, women's studies, African-American studies.
Dr. Stephen D. Rachman, Director, 517-353-1645, *E-mail:* amstudys@pilot.msu.edu.
Application contact: Information Contact, 517-353-9821, *Fax:* 517-432-1460. *Web site:* http://pilot.msu.edu/user/amstudys/

■ MICHIGAN STATE UNIVERSITY

Graduate School, College of Arts and Letters, Department of English, East Lansing, MI 48824

AWARDS American studies (PhD); creative writing (MA); critical studies (MA); English (MA, PhD); English and American literature (MA); literature in English (MA); secondary school/community college teaching (MA); teaching English in secondary school (MA); teaching of English to speakers of other languages (MA). Part-time and evening/weekend programs available.

Faculty: 46.
Students: 77 full-time (49 women), 82 part-time (52 women); includes 19 minority (15 African Americans, 2 Asian Americans or Pacific Islanders, 1 Hispanic American, 1 Native American), 45 international. Average age 33. 171 applicants, 40% accepted. In 2001, 18 master's, 14 doctorates awarded.
Degree requirements: For master's, one foreign language, thesis (for some programs); for doctorate, one foreign language.
Entrance requirements: For master's, GRE General Test, GRE Subject Test, TOEFL, minimum GPA of 3.5, 2 years of a foreign language, writing sample or portfolio; for doctorate, GRE General Test, GRE Subject Test, minimum GPA of 3.5. *Application deadline:* For fall admission, 1/10 (priority date). Applications are processed on a rolling basis. *Application fee:* $30 ($40 for international students). Electronic applications accepted.
Expenses: Tuition, state resident: part-time $244 per credit hour. Tuition, nonresident: part-time $494 per credit hour. Required fees: $268 per semester. Tuition and fees vary according to course load, degree level and program.
Financial support: In 2001–02, 36 fellowships with tuition reimbursements (averaging $2,883 per year), 26 teaching assistantships with tuition reimbursements (averaging $10,541 per year) were awarded. Research assistantships with tuition reimbursements Financial award application deadline: 2/1; financial award applicants required to submit FAFSA.
Faculty research: Literary theory, feminist studies, postcolonial literature, African-American literature. *Total annual research expenditures:* $15,413.
Dr. Patrick O'Donnell, Chairperson, 517-355-7570, *Fax:* 517-353-3755, *E-mail:* engdept@msu.edu.
Application contact: Dr. Judith Stoddart, Associate Chairperson, Graduate Studies, 517-355-7570, *Fax:* 517-353-3755, *E-mail:* engdept@msu.edu. *Web site:* http://www.cal.msu.edu/english/

■ NEW MEXICO HIGHLANDS UNIVERSITY

Graduate Studies, College of Arts and Sciences, Program in Southwest Studies, Las Vegas, NM 87701

AWARDS Anthropology (MA); Hispanic language and literature (MA); history and political science (MA). Program is interdisciplinary. Part-time programs available.

Faculty: 16 full-time (5 women).
Students: 6 full-time (4 women), 15 part-time (9 women); includes 10 minority (all Hispanic Americans). Average age 39. In 2001, 3 degrees awarded.
Degree requirements: For master's, thesis or alternative.
Entrance requirements: For master's, minimum undergraduate GPA of 3.0. *Application deadline:* For fall admission, 8/1 (priority date). Applications are processed on a rolling basis. *Application fee:* $15.
Expenses: Tuition, state resident: full-time $2,238. Tuition, nonresident: full-time $9,366.
Financial support: Research assistantships with full and partial tuition reimbursements, Federal Work-Study available. Financial award application deadline: 3/1.
Dr. Tomas Salazar, Dean, 505-454-3080, *Fax:* 505-454-3389, *E-mail:* salazar_t@nmhu.edu.
Application contact: Dr. Linda LaGrange, Associate Dean of Graduate Studies, 505-454-3266, *Fax:* 505-454-3558, *E-mail:* lagrange_l@nmhu.edu.

■ NEW YORK UNIVERSITY

Graduate School of Arts and Science, Program in American Studies, New York, NY 10012-1019

AWARDS MA, PhD. Part-time programs available.

Faculty: 4 full-time (1 woman), 2 part-time/adjunct.
Students: 41 full-time (23 women), 14 part-time (7 women); includes 25 minority (13 African Americans, 9 Asian Americans or Pacific Islanders, 2 Hispanic Americans, 1 Native American), 3 international. Average age 29. 155 applicants, 10% accepted, 8 enrolled. In 2001, 2 master's, 5 doctorates awarded.

Degree requirements: For master's, one foreign language, thesis; for doctorate, 2 foreign languages, thesis/dissertation.
Entrance requirements: For master's and doctorate, GRE General Test, TOEFL, sample of written work. *Application deadline:* For fall admission, 1/4. *Application fee:* $60.
Expenses: Tuition: Full-time $19,536; part-time $814 per credit. Required fees: $1,330; $38 per credit. Tuition and fees vary according to course load and program.
Financial support: Fellowships with tuition reimbursements, teaching assistantships with tuition reimbursements, Federal Work-Study and institutionally sponsored loans available. Financial award application deadline: 1/4; financial award applicants required to submit FAFSA.
Faculty research: Cultural politics; race, gender, and sexuality studies; nationalism and transnationalism; science and technology; urban and suburban studies.
Andrew Ross, Director, 212-998-8538.
Application contact: Phil Harper, Director of Graduate Studies, 212-998-8800, *Fax:* 212-995-4019, *E-mail:* gsas.admissions@nyu.edu. *Web site:* http://www.nyu.edu/gsas/dept/amerstu/

■ NORTHEASTERN STATE UNIVERSITY

Graduate College, College of Behavioral and Social Sciences, Program in American Studies, Tahlequah, OK 74464-2399

AWARDS MA. Part-time and evening/weekend programs available.

Students: 7 full-time (5 women), 4 part-time (2 women); includes 3 minority (all Native Americans), 1 international. In 2001, 5 degrees awarded.
Degree requirements: For master's, thesis, written and oral examinations.
Entrance requirements: For master's, minimum GPA of 2.5. *Application deadline:* For fall admission, 6/1 (priority date). Applications are processed on a rolling basis. *Application fee:* $0.
Expenses: Tuition, area resident: Part-time $87 per credit hour. Tuition, state resident: part-time $206 per credit hour.
Financial support: Teaching assistantships, Federal Work-Study available. Financial award application deadline: 3/1.
Dr. Brad Agnew, Coordinator, 918-456-5511 Ext. 3519, *Fax:* 918-458-2390, *E-mail:* agnew@cherokee.nsuok.edu.

■ THE PENNSYLVANIA STATE UNIVERSITY HARRISBURG CAMPUS OF THE CAPITAL COLLEGE

Graduate Center, School of Humanities, Program in American Studies, Middletown, PA 17057-4898

AWARDS MA. Evening/weekend programs available.

Students: 9 full-time (6 women), 54 part-time (35 women). Average age 33. In 2001, 24 degrees awarded.
Degree requirements: For master's, thesis.
Application deadline: For fall admission, 7/26. *Application fee:* $45.
Expenses: Tuition, state resident: full-time $7,882; part-time $333 per credit. Tuition, nonresident: full-time $14,384; part-time $600 per credit.
Financial support: Career-related internships or fieldwork available.
Faculty research: Gettysburg, Civil War diaries, American architecture and painting, museology.
Dr. Simon J. Bronner, Coordinator, 717-948-6470.

■ PEPPERDINE UNIVERSITY

Seaver College, Division of Interdisciplinary Studies, Malibu, CA 90263-0002

AWARDS American studies (MA). Part-time and evening/weekend programs available.

Faculty: 4 full-time (2 women).
Students: Average age 38. 16 applicants, 75% accepted. In 2001, 8 degrees awarded.
Degree requirements: For master's, comprehensive exam.
Entrance requirements: For master's, GRE General Test, TOEFL, bachelor's degree in English, economics, history, or political science. *Application deadline:* For fall admission, 5/1; for spring admission, 9/1. Applications are processed on a rolling basis. *Application fee:* $55.
Expenses: Tuition: Full-time $15,700; part-time $785 per unit. Tuition and fees vary according to degree level and program.
Financial support: Fellowships, scholarships/grants available. Support available to part-time students. Financial award application deadline: 2/15; financial award applicants required to submit FAFSA.
Dr. James Thomas, Director, 310-506-4747.
Application contact: Paul Long, Dean of Enrollment Management, 310-506-4392, *Fax:* 310-506-4861, *E-mail:* admission-seaver@pepperdine.edu. *Web site:* http://www.pepperdine.edu/

■ PURDUE UNIVERSITY

Graduate School, School of Liberal Arts, Program in American Studies, West Lafayette, IN 47907

AWARDS MA, PhD.

Faculty: 16 full-time (6 women).
Students: 23 full-time (13 women), 14 part-time (8 women); includes 8 minority (6 African Americans, 2 Hispanic Americans), 4 international. Average age 32. 36 applicants, 56% accepted. In 2001, 3 master's, 1 doctorate awarded.
Degree requirements: For master's, essay; for doctorate, one foreign language, thesis/dissertation.
Entrance requirements: For master's and doctorate, GRE General Test, TOEFL, TWE, sample of written work. *Application deadline:* For fall admission, 1/15 (priority date); for spring admission, 9/1. Applications are processed on a rolling basis. *Application fee:* $30. Electronic applications accepted.
Expenses: Tuition, state resident: full-time $4,164; part-time $149 per credit hour. Tuition, nonresident: full-time $13,872; part-time $458 per credit hour. Tuition and fees vary according to campus/location and program.
Financial support: In 2001–02, 34 students received support, including 10 fellowships, 24 teaching assistantships Support available to part-time students. Financial award application deadline: 1/15; financial award applicants required to submit FAFSA.
Faculty research: American history, literature, politics, sociology, women's studies, African-American studies, mass culture.
Dr. S. K. Curtis, Chair, 765-494-4159, *Fax:* 765-496-1755, *E-mail:* curtis@purdue.edu.
Application contact: Jennifer E. Redden, Graduate Secretary, 765-494-4126, *Fax:* 765-496-1755, *E-mail:* grad-fhs@sla.purdue.edu.

■ SAINT LOUIS UNIVERSITY

Graduate School, College of Arts and Sciences, Department of American Studies, St. Louis, MO 63103-2097

AWARDS MA, MA(R), PhD.

Faculty: 12 full-time (5 women), 1 (woman) part-time/adjunct.
Students: 9 full-time (6 women), 25 part-time (11 women); includes 6 minority (2 African Americans, 4 Hispanic Americans). Average age 35. 22 applicants, 77% accepted, 8 enrolled. In 2001, 4 master's, 6 doctorates awarded.
Degree requirements: For master's, comprehensive written and oral exams, thesis optional; for doctorate, one foreign language, thesis/dissertation, preliminary exams.
Entrance requirements: For master's and doctorate, GRE General Test. *Application deadline:* For fall admission, 7/1; for spring

Saint Louis University (continued)
admission, 11/1. Applications are processed on a rolling basis. *Application fee:* $40.
Expenses: Tuition: Part-time $630 per credit hour.
Financial support: In 2001–02, 17 students received support, including 1 fellowship with tuition reimbursement available, 2 research assistantships with tuition reimbursements available; teaching assistantships, tuition waivers (partial) and unspecified assistantships also available. Financial award application deadline: 4/1; financial award applicants required to submit FAFSA.
Faculty research: Urban studies, American religion, intellectual history, southern culture, African-American literature, visual culture.
Dr. Matthew J. Mancini, Chairperson, 314-977-2911, *Fax:* 314-977-1806, *E-mail:* mancini@slu.edu.
Application contact: Dr. Marcia Buresch, Associate Dean of the Graduate School, 314-977-2240, *Fax:* 314-977-3943, *E-mail:* bureschm@slu.edu.

■ STATE UNIVERSITY OF NEW YORK COLLEGE AT CORTLAND

Graduate Studies, Program in American Civilization and Culture, Cortland, NY 13045

AWARDS CAS. Part-time and evening/weekend programs available.

Application deadline: For fall admission, 8/1; for spring admission, 1/1. *Application fee:* $50.
Financial support: Career-related internships or fieldwork, Federal Work-Study, and tuition waivers (partial) available. Support available to part-time students. Financial award application deadline: 3/31; financial award applicants required to submit FAFSA.
Dr. John Ryder, Dean, 607-753-4312, *E-mail:* ryderj@cortland.edu.
Application contact: Mark Yacavone, Assistant Director of Admissions, 607-753-4711, *Fax:* 607-753-5998, *E-mail:* marky@em.cortland.edu.

■ STONY BROOK UNIVERSITY, STATE UNIVERSITY OF NEW YORK

School of Professional Development and Continuing Studies, Stony Brook, NY 11794

AWARDS Art and philosophy (Certificate); biology 7-12 (MAT); chemistry-grade 7-12 (MAT); coaching (Certificate); computer integrated engineering (Certificate); cultural studies (Certificate); earth science-grade 7-12 (MAT); educational computing (Certificate); English-grade 7-12 (MAT); environmental/occupational health and safety (Certificate); French-grade 7-12 (MAT); German-grade 7-12 (MAT); human resource management (Certificate); industrial management (Certificate); information systems management (Certificate); Italian-grade 7-12 (MAT); liberal studies (MA); liberal studies online (MA); Long Island regional studies (Certificate); oceanic science (Certificate); operation research (Certificate); physics-grade 7-12 (MAT); Russian-grade 7-12 (MAT); school administration and supervision (Certificate); school district administration (Certificate); social science and the professions (MPS), including labor management, public affairs, waste management; social studies 7-12 (MAT); waste management (Certificate); women's studies (Certificate). Part-time and evening/weekend programs available. Postbaccalaureate distance learning degree programs offered.

Faculty: 1 full-time, 101 part-time/adjunct.
Students: 240 full-time (133 women), 1,307 part-time (868 women); includes 101 minority (43 African Americans, 13 Asian Americans or Pacific Islanders, 43 Hispanic Americans, 2 Native Americans), 9 international. Average age 28. In 2001, 478 master's, 157 other advanced degrees awarded.
Degree requirements: For master's, one foreign language, thesis or alternative.
Application deadline: Applications are processed on a rolling basis. *Application fee:* $50.
Expenses: Tuition, state resident: full-time $5,100; part-time $213 per credit. Tuition, nonresident: full-time $8,416; part-time $351 per credit. Required fees: $496.
Financial support: In 2001–02, 1 fellowship, 7 teaching assistantships were awarded. Research assistantships, career-related internships or fieldwork also available. Support available to part-time students.
Dr. Paul J. Edelson, Dean, 631-632-7052, *Fax:* 631-632-9046, *E-mail:* paul.edelson@sunysb.edu.
Application contact: Sandra Romansky, Director of Admissions and Advisement, 631-632-7050, *Fax:* 631-632-9046, *E-mail:* sandra.romansky@sunysb.edu. *Web site:* http://www.sunysb.edu/spd/

■ TRINITY COLLEGE

Graduate Programs, Program in American Studies, Hartford, CT 06106-3100

AWARDS MA. Part-time and evening/weekend programs available.

Faculty: 5 full-time (2 women), 2 part-time/adjunct (1 woman).
Students: Average age 38. In 2001, 7 degrees awarded.
Degree requirements: For master's, thesis or alternative.
Entrance requirements: For master's, minimum GPA of 3.0. *Application deadline:* For fall admission, 4/1; for spring admission, 11/1. *Application fee:* $50.
Expenses: Tuition: Part-time $900 per course. Required fees: $25 per term.
Financial support: In 2001–02, 4 students received support, including 4 fellowships; tuition waivers (full) also available. Support available to part-time students. Financial award application deadline: 4/1.
Dr. Paul Lauter, Graduate Adviser, 860-297-2303.

■ UNIVERSITY AT BUFFALO, THE STATE UNIVERSITY OF NEW YORK

Graduate School, College of Arts and Sciences, Center for the Americas, Buffalo, NY 14260

AWARDS MA, PhD. Part-time programs available.

Faculty: 5 full-time (3 women), 1 part-time/adjunct (0 women).
Students: 29 full-time (21 women), 14 part-time (12 women); includes 14 minority (7 African Americans, 1 Asian American or Pacific Islander, 4 Hispanic Americans, 2 Native Americans), 8 international. Average age 35. 12 applicants, 50% accepted. In 2001, 5 master's, 3 doctorates awarded. Terminal master's awarded for partial completion of doctoral program.
Degree requirements: For master's, project or thesis; for doctorate, one foreign language, thesis/dissertation, oral exam and dissertation.
Entrance requirements: For master's and doctorate, TOEFL, writing sample.
Application deadline: For fall admission, 12/15. *Application fee:* $35.
Expenses: Tuition, state resident: full-time $6,118. Tuition, nonresident: full-time $9,434.
Financial support: In 2001–02, 23 students received support, including 2 teaching assistantships with full tuition reimbursements available; fellowships with full tuition reimbursements available, research assistantships, career-related internships or fieldwork, Federal Work-Study, institutionally sponsored loans, tuition waivers (full and partial), and unspecified assistantships also available. Financial award application deadline: 2/28; financial award applicants required to submit FAFSA.
Faculty research: Native American studies, intercultural studies, indigenous people's studies, multiculturalism, border theory. *Total annual research expenditures:* $17,438.
Dr. Dennis Tedlock, Co-Director, 716-645-2546 Ext. 1224, *Fax:* 716-645-5977, *E-mail:* dtedlock@ascu.buffalo.edu.
Application contact: Yvonne Dion-Buffalo, Administrative Assistant, 716-645-2546 Ext. 1228, *Fax:* 716-645-5977, *E-mail:* ydb@ascu.buffalo.edu. *Web site:* http://www.cas.buffalo.edu/centers/americas/

■ THE UNIVERSITY OF ALABAMA

Graduate School, College of Arts and Sciences, Department of American Studies, Tuscaloosa, AL 35487

AWARDS MA. Part-time programs available.

Faculty: 7 full-time (2 women).
Students: 11 full-time (3 women); includes 1 minority (African American), 3 international. Average age 27. 17 applicants, 59% accepted, 7 enrolled. In 2001, 7 degrees awarded.
Degree requirements: For master's, thesis optional.
Entrance requirements: For master's, GRE General Test, TOEFL, minimum GPA of 3.0. *Application deadline:* For fall admission, 7/6. Applications are processed on a rolling basis. *Application fee:* $25.
Expenses: Tuition, state resident: full-time $3,292; part-time $183 per credit hour. Tuition, nonresident: full-time $8,912; part-time $495 per credit hour. Tuition and fees vary according to course load, campus/location and program.
Financial support: In 2001–02, 9 students received support, including fellowships with tuition reimbursements available (averaging $10,000 per year), 2 research assistantships with partial tuition reimbursements available (averaging $3,933 per year), 7 teaching assistantships with tuition reimbursements available (averaging $7,866 per year); career-related internships or fieldwork and tuition waivers (full) also available. Financial award application deadline: 7/14.
Faculty research: Social and cultural history, popular music, African-American culture, visual arts, women.
Dr. James M. Salem, Chairperson, 205-348-5940, *E-mail:* jsalem@tenhoor.as.ua.edu.

■ UNIVERSITY OF CENTRAL OKLAHOMA

College of Graduate Studies and Research, College of Liberal Arts, Department of History, Edmond, OK 73034-5209

AWARDS History (MA); museum studies (MA); social studies teaching (MA); Southwestern studies (MA). Part-time programs available.

Degree requirements: For master's, thesis optional.
Faculty research: China, Russia, civil war, American naval logistics. *Web site:* http://www.libarts.ucok.edu/history

■ UNIVERSITY OF DALLAS

Braniff Graduate School of Liberal Arts, Program in American Studies, Irving, TX 75062-4736

AWARDS MAS. Part-time programs available.

Faculty: 10 full-time (1 woman).
Students: Average age 26. 5 applicants, 100% accepted, 1 enrolled. In 2001, 4 degrees awarded.
Degree requirements: For master's, comprehensive exam.
Entrance requirements: For master's, GRE General Test. *Application deadline:* For fall admission, 2/15 (priority date); for spring admission, 11/15. Applications are processed on a rolling basis. *Application fee:* $40.
Expenses: Tuition: Full-time $3,807; part-time $423 per credit.
Financial support: Scholarships/grants, tuition waivers, and tuition remissions available. Financial award application deadline: 2/15.
Faculty research: Shakespeare, Milton, Melville, Hawthorne, liberty and American literature.
Dr. John Alvis, Director, 972-721-5365, *Fax:* 972-721-4007, *E-mail:* alvis@udallas.edu.
Application contact: 972-721-5106, *Fax:* 972-721-5280, *E-mail:* graduate@acad.udallas.edu. *Web site:* http://www.udallas.edu/bgs/amerstudies.hmtl/

■ UNIVERSITY OF DELAWARE

College of Arts and Science, Winterthur Program in Early American Culture, Newark, DE 19716

AWARDS MA.

Faculty: 17 full-time (8 women).
Students: 21 full-time (15 women). Average age 26. 38 applicants, 29% accepted, 10 enrolled. In 2001, 8 degrees awarded.
Degree requirements: For master's, thesis. *Median time to degree:* Master's–4 years full-time.
Entrance requirements: For master's, GRE General Test, minimum GPA of 3.0. *Application deadline:* For fall admission, 1/15. *Application fee:* $45.
Expenses: Tuition, state resident: full-time $4,770; part-time $265 per credit. Tuition, nonresident: full-time $13,860; part-time $770 per credit. Required fees: $414.
Financial support: In 2001–02, 20 students received support, including 20 fellowships with full tuition reimbursements available (averaging $12,180 per year); career-related internships or fieldwork also available. Financial award application deadline: 1/15.
Faculty research: American material culture, American studies, decorative arts.
Dr. James C. Curtis, Director, 302-831-2678, *E-mail:* jcurtis@udel.edu. *Web site:* http://www.udel.edu/admissions/majors.html

■ UNIVERSITY OF HAWAII AT MANOA

Graduate Division, College of Arts and Sciences, College of Arts and Humanities, Department of American Studies, Honolulu, HI 96822

AWARDS MA, PhD. Part-time programs available.

Faculty: 12 full-time (3 women), 4 part-time/adjunct (0 women).
Students: 40 full-time (24 women), 22 part-time (17 women); includes 13 Asian Americans or Pacific Islanders, 2 Hispanic Americans, 2 Native Americans. Average age 38. 77 applicants, 45% accepted, 19 enrolled. In 2001, 3 master's, 5 doctorates awarded.
Degree requirements: For master's, thesis (for some programs); for doctorate, thesis/dissertation. *Median time to degree:* Master's–1.67 years full-time; doctorate–5.67 years full-time.
Entrance requirements: For master's and doctorate, GRE General Test, TOEFL. *Application deadline:* For fall admission, 3/1; for spring admission, 9/1. *Application fee:* $25 ($50 for international students).
Expenses: Tuition, state resident: full-time $2,160; part-time $1,980 per year. Tuition, nonresident: full-time $5,190; part-time $4,829 per year.
Financial support: In 2001–02, 2 research assistantships (averaging $15,567 per year), 4 teaching assistantships (averaging $13,830 per year) were awarded. Institutionally sponsored loans and tuition waivers (full and partial) also available. Support available to part-time students. Financial award application deadline: 3/31.
Faculty research: Ethnicity and race, popular culture, historic preservation, arts and culture, international relations.
Dr. Paul Hooper, Chairperson, 808-956-8570, *Fax:* 808-956-4733, *E-mail:* hooper@hawaii.edu.

■ THE UNIVERSITY OF IOWA

Graduate College, College of Liberal Arts and Sciences, Department of American Studies, Iowa City, IA 52242-1316

AWARDS MA, PhD.

Faculty: 4 full-time.
Students: 8 full-time (2 women), 22 part-time (15 women); includes 3 minority (all African Americans), 4 international. 34 applicants, 38% accepted, 5 enrolled. In 2001, 3 master's, 4 doctorates awarded.
Degree requirements: For master's, exam, thesis optional; for doctorate, thesis/dissertation, comprehensive exam.
Entrance requirements: For master's, GRE General Test, TOEFL; for doctorate, GRE General Test, TOEFL, minimum GPA of 3.0. *Application deadline:* For fall admission, 2/1 (priority date). *Application fee:* $30 ($50 for international students). Electronic applications accepted.

The University of Iowa (continued)
Expenses: Tuition, state resident: full-time $3,702; part-time $206 per semester hour. Tuition, nonresident: full-time $11,924; part-time $206 per semester hour. Required fees: $101 per semester. Tuition and fees vary according to course load and program.
Financial support: In 2001–02, 5 fellowships, 3 research assistantships, 19 teaching assistantships were awarded. Financial award applicants required to submit FAFSA.
Dr. Lauren Rabinovitz, Chair, 319-335-0320, *Fax:* 319-335-0314.

■ UNIVERSITY OF KANSAS

Graduate School, College of Liberal Arts and Sciences, Program in American Studies, Lawrence, KS 66045

AWARDS MA, PhD, MUP/MA. Part-time programs available.

Faculty: 13.
Students: 34 full-time (17 women), 31 part-time (14 women); includes 11 minority (6 African Americans, 1 Asian American or Pacific Islander, 2 Hispanic Americans, 2 Native Americans), 16 international. Average age 33. 29 applicants, 31% accepted, 9 enrolled. In 2001, 5 master's, 12 doctorates awarded. Terminal master's awarded for partial completion of doctoral program.
Degree requirements: For master's, thesis or alternative; for doctorate, variable foreign language requirement, thesis/dissertation.
Entrance requirements: For master's and doctorate, GRE General Test, TOEFL. *Application deadline:* For fall admission, 5/1. Applications are processed on a rolling basis. *Application fee:* $35 ($40 for international students).
Expenses: Tuition, state resident: full-time $2,722; part-time $113 per credit. Tuition, nonresident: full-time $8,586; part-time $358 per credit. Required fees: $551; $46 per credit. Tuition and fees vary according to campus/location, program and reciprocity agreements.
Financial support: In 2001–02, 7 teaching assistantships with full and partial tuition reimbursements (averaging $9,363 per year) were awarded; fellowships, research assistantships with partial tuition reimbursements, Federal Work-Study also available. Financial award application deadline: 1/10.
Faculty research: Race and ethnicity, popular culture, contemporary America, gender, social and cultural theory.
Norman Yetman, Chair, 785-864-4011, *Fax:* 785-864-5742.
Application contact: Information Contact, 785-864-4011, *Fax:* 785-864-5742, *E-mail:* amerst@ku.edu. *Web site:* http://www.ku.edu/~amerst/

■ UNIVERSITY OF LOUISIANA AT LAFAYETTE

Graduate School, College of Liberal Arts, Department of Modern Languages, Program in Francophone Studies, Lafayette, LA 70504

AWARDS PhD.

Faculty: 9 full-time (4 women).
Students: 15 full-time (12 women), 6 part-time (4 women); includes 3 minority (1 African American, 1 Asian American or Pacific Islander, 1 Native American), 11 international. 13 applicants, 62% accepted, 4 enrolled. In 2001, 5 degrees awarded.
Degree requirements: For doctorate, 2 foreign languages, thesis/dissertation or alternative.
Entrance requirements: For doctorate, GRE General Test, minimum GPA of 2.75. *Application deadline:* For fall admission, 5/15. *Application fee:* $20 ($30 for international students).
Expenses: Tuition, state resident: full-time $2,317; part-time $79 per credit. Tuition, nonresident: full-time $8,882; part-time $369 per credit. International tuition: $9,018 full-time.
Financial support: In 2001–02, 4 fellowships with full tuition reimbursements (averaging $12,000 per year), 8 teaching assistantships with full tuition reimbursements (averaging $10,000 per year) were awarded. Financial award application deadline: 5/1.
Faculty research: Louisiana folklore, eighteenth-century French literature, contemporary criticism.
Application contact: Dr. Dominique Ryon, Graduate Coordinator, 337-482-6816.

■ UNIVERSITY OF MARYLAND, COLLEGE PARK

Graduate Studies and Research, College of Arts and Humanities, Department of American Studies, College Park, MD 20742

AWARDS MA, PhD.

Faculty: 8 full-time (4 women).
Students: 39 full-time (24 women), 40 part-time (26 women); includes 23 minority (18 African Americans, 3 Asian Americans or Pacific Islanders, 1 Hispanic American, 1 Native American), 4 international. 64 applicants, 47% accepted, 16 enrolled. In 2001, 6 master's, 3 doctorates awarded.
Degree requirements: For master's, thesis or scholarly paper and exam; for doctorate, variable foreign language requirement, thesis/dissertation, 3 comprehensive exams.
Entrance requirements: For master's, GRE General Test, minimum GPA of 3.0, writing sample; for doctorate, GRE General Test. *Application deadline:* For fall admission, 1/15. Applications are processed on a rolling basis. *Application fee:* $50 ($70 for international students). Electronic applications accepted.
Expenses: Tuition, state resident: part-time $289 per credit hour. Tuition, nonresident: part-time $448 per credit hour. One-time fee: $436 part-time. Full-time tuition and fees vary according to course load, campus/location and program.
Financial support: In 2001–02, 5 fellowships with full tuition reimbursements (averaging $12,361 per year), 12 teaching assistantships with tuition reimbursements (averaging $11,675 per year) were awarded. Career-related internships or fieldwork, Federal Work-Study, and scholarships/grants also available. Support available to part-time students. Financial award applicants required to submit FAFSA.
Faculty research: Material culture, modes of culture, cultural movements, popular culture, ethnography.
Dr. John Caughey, Acting Chairman, 301-405-1354, *Fax:* 301-314-9453, *E-mail:* amstgrad@deans.umd.edu.
Application contact: Trudy Lindsey, Director, Graduate Admissions and Records, 301-405-6991, *Fax:* 301-314-9305, *E-mail:* grschool@deans.umd.edu.

■ UNIVERSITY OF MASSACHUSETTS BOSTON

Office of Graduate Studies and Research, College of Arts and Sciences, Faculty of Arts, Program in American Studies, Boston, MA 02125-3393

AWARDS MA. Part-time and evening/weekend programs available.

Degree requirements: For master's, thesis or capstone project, thesis optional.
Entrance requirements: For master's, minimum GPA of 2.75.
Faculty research: War in American culture, immigration history, Latin Americans, history of race and popular music, education and Asian Americans.

■ UNIVERSITY OF MICHIGAN

Horace H. Rackham School of Graduate Studies, Interdepartmental Program in American Culture, Ann Arbor, MI 48109

AWARDS AM, PhD.

Faculty: 14 full-time (6 women).
Students: 70 full-time; includes 33 minority (8 African Americans, 11 Asian Americans or Pacific Islanders, 12 Hispanic Americans, 2 Native Americans), 1 international. 72 applicants, 26% accepted, 8 enrolled. In 2001, 7 master's, 5 doctorates awarded. Terminal master's awarded for partial completion of doctoral program.
Degree requirements: For doctorate, field and preliminary exams, oral defense of dissertation.

Entrance requirements: For master's, GRE General Test; for doctorate, GRE General Test, sample of written work. *Application deadline:* For fall admission, 12/15. *Application fee:* $55. Electronic applications accepted.
Financial support: Fellowships, research assistantships, teaching assistantships, Federal Work-Study and tuition waivers (partial) available. Support available to part-time students. Financial award application deadline: 2/1.
Faculty research: Cultural studies; ethnic studies, American culture methodology, literature, history.
Alan Wald, Director, 734-763-1460, *Fax:* 734-936-1967, *E-mail:* ac.inq@umich.edu.
Application contact: Marlene Moore, Graduate Assistant, 734-647-9533, *Fax:* 734-936-1967, *E-mail:* ac.inq@umich.edu. *Web site:* http://www.lsa.umich.edu/ac/

■ UNIVERSITY OF MICHIGAN–FLINT

Graduate Programs, Program in American Culture, Flint, MI 48502-1950

AWARDS MLS. Part-time and evening/weekend programs available.

Faculty: 8 full-time (1 woman).
Students: 6 full-time (3 women), 39 part-time (24 women). Average age 36. 10 applicants, 100% accepted. In 2001, 11 degrees awarded.
Degree requirements: For master's, thesis.
Entrance requirements: For master's, minimum GPA of 3.0, 24 undergraduate credits in humanities and social sciences. *Application deadline:* For fall admission, 7/15; for winter admission, 11/15; for spring admission, 3/15. *Application fee:* $55.
Expenses: Tuition, area resident: Part-time $386 per credit. Tuition, nonresident: full-time $6,950; part-time $386 per credit. Required fees: $113 per term. Full-time tuition and fees vary according to program. Part-time tuition and fees vary according to course load.
Financial support: In 2001–02, 2 fellowships were awarded; Federal Work-Study and scholarships/grants also available. Support available to part-time students. Financial award application deadline: 4/1.
Dr. Bruce Rubenstein, Director, 810-762-9366, *E-mail:* rubenste@umflint.edu.
Application contact: Ann Briggs, Administrative Associate, 810-762-3171, *Fax:* 810-766-6789, *E-mail:* ahb@umich.edu.

■ UNIVERSITY OF MINNESOTA, TWIN CITIES CAMPUS

Graduate School, College of Liberal Arts, Department of American Studies, Minneapolis, MN 55455-0213

AWARDS PhD. Part-time programs available.

Faculty: 10 full-time (7 women), 48 part-time/adjunct (27 women).
Students: 67; includes 15 minority (2 African Americans, 5 Asian Americans or Pacific Islanders, 5 Hispanic Americans, 3 Native Americans), 5 international. Average age 25. 98 applicants, 17% accepted. In 2001, 5 degrees awarded.
Degree requirements: For doctorate, one foreign language, thesis/dissertation, comprehensive exam.
Entrance requirements: For doctorate, GRE General Test, sample of written work, minimum GPA of 3.5. *Application deadline:* For fall admission, 12/15. *Application fee:* $40 ($50 for international students).
Expenses: Tuition, state resident: full-time $2,932; part-time $489 per credit. Tuition, nonresident: full-time $5,758; part-time $960 per credit. Part-time tuition and fees vary according to course load, program and reciprocity agreements.
Financial support: In 2001–02, 6 fellowships with full tuition reimbursements (averaging $14,000 per year), 1 research assistantship with partial tuition reimbursement (averaging $12,000 per year), 10 teaching assistantships with full and partial tuition reimbursements (averaging $12,000 per year) were awarded. Federal Work-Study, institutionally sponsored loans, health care benefits, and tuition waivers (full and partial) also available. Financial award application deadline: 1/5.
Faculty research: Popular culture, nationalism/transnationalism, gender and sexuality, race and ethnicity.
Jean O'Brien, Chair, 612-624-4190, *Fax:* 612-624-3858.
Application contact: Jennifer L. Pierce, Director of Graduate Studies, 612-624-0852, *Fax:* 612-624-3858, *E-mail:* pierc012@tc.umn.edu.

■ UNIVERSITY OF MISSISSIPPI

Graduate School, College of Liberal Arts, Interdisciplinary Program in Southern Studies, Oxford, University, MS 38677

AWARDS MA.

Faculty: 4.
Students: 22 full-time (16 women), 3 part-time; includes 1 minority (African American), 1 international. In 2001, 6 degrees awarded.
Entrance requirements: For master's, GRE General Test, TOEFL, minimum GPA of 3.0. *Application deadline:* For fall admission, 8/1. Applications are processed on a rolling basis. *Application fee:* $0 ($25 for international students).
Expenses: Tuition, state resident: full-time $3,626; part-time $202 per hour. Tuition, nonresident: full-time $8,172; part-time $454 per hour.
Financial support: Application deadline: 3/1.
Dr. Charles R. Wilson, Director, 662-915-5993, *Fax:* 662-915-5814, *E-mail:* cssc@olemiss.edu.

■ UNIVERSITY OF NEW MEXICO

Graduate School, College of Arts and Sciences, Department of American Studies, Albuquerque, NM 87131-2039

AWARDS MA, PhD. Part-time programs available.

Faculty: 4 full-time (2 women), 3 part-time/adjunct (2 women).
Students: 34 full-time (20 women), 27 part-time (20 women); includes 21 minority (2 African Americans, 2 Asian Americans or Pacific Islanders, 13 Hispanic Americans, 4 Native Americans), 1 international. Average age 41. 34 applicants, 38% accepted, 5 enrolled. In 2001, 4 master's, 5 doctorates awarded. Terminal master's awarded for partial completion of doctoral program.
Degree requirements: For master's, thesis optional; for doctorate, one foreign language, thesis/dissertation.
Entrance requirements: For master's and doctorate, minimum GPA of 3.0. *Application deadline:* For fall admission, 2/1. *Application fee:* $40.
Expenses: Tuition, state resident: full-time $2,771; part-time $115 per credit hour. Tuition, nonresident: full-time $11,207; part-time $467 per credit hour. Required fees: $570; $24 per credit hour. Part-time tuition and fees vary according to course load and program.
Financial support: In 2001–02, 36 students received support, including 3 fellowships (averaging $4,000 per year), 12 research assistantships with partial tuition reimbursements available (averaging $2,600 per year), 12 teaching assistantships with partial tuition reimbursements available (averaging $2,700 per year); career-related internships or fieldwork, Federal Work-Study, institutionally sponsored loans, scholarships/grants, health care benefits, tuition waivers (full), and unspecified assistantships also available. Support available to part-time students. Financial award application deadline: 3/1; financial award applicants required to submit FAFSA.
Faculty research: Culture studies environment/science/technology, gender, race/class/ethnicity, popular culture, Southwest studies.
Dr. Gabriel Melendez, Chair, 505-277-6356, *Fax:* 505-277-1208, *E-mail:* gabriel@unm.edu.
Application contact: Gloria G. Gomez, Administrator, 505-277-0820, *Fax:* 505-277-1208, *E-mail:* gomez@law.edu. *Web site:* http://www.unm.edu/~amstudy/

■ UNIVERSITY OF PENNSYLVANIA

School of Arts and Sciences, Graduate Group in American Civilization, Philadelphia, PA 19104

AWARDS AM, PhD, JD/AM, JD/PhD.

Expenses: Tuition: Part-time $12,875 per semester.

University of Pennsylvania (continued)
Faculty research: Cultural history, historic ethnography, material culture studies.

■ UNIVERSITY OF SOUTHERN MAINE

College of Arts and Science, Program in American and New England Studies, Portland, ME 04104-9300

AWARDS MA. Part-time and evening/weekend programs available.

Faculty: 4 full-time (1 woman), 5 part-time/adjunct (2 women).
Students: 7 full-time, 36 part-time; includes 1 minority (Asian American or Pacific Islander). 20 applicants, 80% accepted. In 2001, 6 degrees awarded.
Degree requirements: For master's, thesis optional.
Entrance requirements: For master's, GRE General Test or MAT. *Application deadline:* For fall admission, 3/15 (priority date); for spring admission, 10/1. *Application fee:* $25.
Expenses: Tuition, state resident: part-time $200 per credit. Tuition, nonresident: part-time $560 per credit.
Financial support: In 2001–02, 3 research assistantships were awarded
Faculty research: Social history, regional culture, landscape of literature, material culture, art and architecture.
Dr. Kent Ryden, Director, 207-780-4920.
Application contact: Mary Sloan, Director of Graduate Admissions, 207-780-4236, *Fax:* 207-780-4969, *E-mail:* msloan@usm.maine.edu.

■ UNIVERSITY OF SOUTH FLORIDA

College of Graduate Studies, College of Arts and Sciences, Department of Humanities and American Studies, Tampa, FL 33620-9951

AWARDS American studies (MA); liberal arts (MLA). Part-time and evening/weekend programs available.

Faculty: 8 full-time (5 women).
Students: 11 full-time (7 women), 33 part-time (21 women); includes 3 minority (2 African Americans, 1 Hispanic American), 1 international. In 2001, 2 degrees awarded.
Degree requirements: For master's, thesis.
Entrance requirements: For master's, GRE General Test, minimum GPA of 3.0 in last 60 hours. *Application deadline:* For fall admission, 6/1 (priority date); for spring admission, 10/15 (priority date). *Application fee:* $20.
Expenses: Tuition, state resident: part-time $166 per credit hour. Tuition, nonresident: part-time $573 per credit hour. Required fees: $17 per term.
Financial support: Research assistantships with partial tuition reimbursements, teaching assistantships with partial tuition reimbursements, Federal Work-Study and institutionally sponsored loans available. Support available to part-time students. Financial award applicants required to submit FAFSA.
Faculty research: American South, American autobiography, material culture, critical theory, cultural studies. *Total annual research expenditures:* $5,603.
Priscilla Patricia, Chairperson, 813-974-2431, *Fax:* 813-974-9409, *E-mail:* brewer@luna.cas.usf.edu. *Web site:* http://www.cas.usf.edu/humanities/index.html

■ THE UNIVERSITY OF TEXAS AT AUSTIN

Graduate School, College of Liberal Arts, Department of American Studies, Austin, TX 78712-1111

AWARDS MA, PhD. Part-time programs available.

Faculty: 11 full-time (4 women), 2 part-time/adjunct (both women).
Students: 80 (43 women); includes 11 minority (4 African Americans, 5 Asian Americans or Pacific Islanders, 1 Hispanic American, 1 Native American) 6 international. Average age 28. 67 applicants, 37% accepted. In 2001, 6 master's, 10 doctorates awarded.
Degree requirements: For master's, thesis; for doctorate, one foreign language, thesis/dissertation, qualifying oral exam.
Entrance requirements: For master's and doctorate, GRE General Test, minimum GPA of 3.5. *Application deadline:* For fall admission, 1/15 (priority date). *Application fee:* $50 ($75 for international students). Electronic applications accepted.
Expenses: Tuition, state resident: full-time $3,159. Tuition, nonresident: full-time $6,957. Tuition and fees vary according to program.
Financial support: In 2001–02, 15 students received support, including 8 teaching assistantships; fellowships, Federal Work-Study, institutionally sponsored loans, and assistant instructorships also available. Financial award application deadline: 2/1; financial award applicants required to submit CSS PROFILE or FAFSA.
Faculty research: Race, gender, and ethnicity; history of the American West; American design and archaeology; literary cultural history; religion and psychology in American culture.
Dr. Jeffrey L. Meikle, Chair, 512-471-7277.
Application contact: Cynthia Frese, Graduate Coordinator, 512-471-7277. *Web site:* http://www.dla.utexas.edu/cola/depts/ams

■ UNIVERSITY OF WYOMING

Graduate School, College of Arts and Sciences, American Studies Program, Laramie, WY 82071

AWARDS MA. Part-time programs available.

Faculty: 3 full-time (1 woman).
Students: 17 full-time (11 women), 12 part-time (8 women); includes 2 minority (1 Hispanic American, 1 Native American), 3 international. 17 applicants, 100% accepted. In 2001, 11 degrees awarded.
Degree requirements: For master's, thesis optional.
Entrance requirements: For master's, GRE General Test, minimum GPA of 3.0. *Application deadline:* For fall admission, 4/1 (priority date). Applications are processed on a rolling basis. *Application fee:* $40.
Expenses: Tuition, state resident: full-time $2,895; part-time $161 per credit hour. Tuition, nonresident: full-time $8,367; part-time $465 per credit hour. Required fees: $491; $10 per credit hour. $2 per credit hour. Tuition and fees vary according to course load and program.
Financial support: In 2001–02, 10 research assistantships with tuition reimbursements, 7 teaching assistantships with tuition reimbursements were awarded. Career-related internships or fieldwork, Federal Work-Study, and tuition waivers (partial) also available. Financial award application deadline: 3/1.
Faculty research: Material culture, American culture, ethnicity, cultural environments, public culture. *Total annual research expenditures:* $25,000.
Dr. Eric Sandeen, Director, 307-766-3898.

■ UTAH STATE UNIVERSITY

School of Graduate Studies, College of Humanities, Arts and Social Sciences, Department of English and Department of History, Program in American Studies, Logan, UT 84322

AWARDS Folklore (MA, MS). Part-time and evening/weekend programs available.

Faculty: 12 full-time (5 women).
Students: 5 full-time (3 women), 26 part-time (17 women); includes 1 minority (Native American), 2 international. Average age 32. 17 applicants, 94% accepted. In 2001, 7 degrees awarded.
Degree requirements: For master's, thesis or alternative.
Entrance requirements: For master's, GRE General Test or MAT, TOEFL, minimum GPA of 3.0. *Application deadline:* For fall admission, 2/15 (priority date); for spring admission, 10/15. *Application fee:* $40.
Expenses: Tuition, state resident: full-time $1,693. Tuition, nonresident: full-time $4,233. Required fees: $501. Tuition and fees vary according to program.
Financial support: In 2001–02, teaching assistantships with partial tuition reimbursements (averaging $7,200 per year); fellowships with partial tuition

reimbursements, career-related internships or fieldwork, Federal Work-Study, institutionally sponsored loans, and tuition waivers (partial) also available. Financial award application deadline: 2/15.
Faculty research: Folklore and folklife, American culture, regional studies, material culture, Jewish folklore, Native American folklore.
Barre Toelken, Graduate Adviser, 435-797-2737, *Fax:* 435-797-3797, *E-mail:* btoelken@english.usu.edu.
Application contact: Dr. Keith A. Grant-Davie, Director of Graduate Studies, 435-797-2733, *Fax:* 435-797-3797, *E-mail:* dept@english.usu.edu. *Web site:* http://english.usu.edu/dept/

■ WASHINGTON STATE UNIVERSITY

Graduate School, College of Liberal Arts, Department of English and Department of History, Program in American Studies, Pullman, WA 99164

AWARDS MA, PhD.

Faculty: 23.
Students: 21 full-time (11 women), 4 part-time (3 women); includes 10 minority (1 African American, 8 Hispanic Americans, 1 Native American), 2 international. In 2001, 2 master's, 1 doctorate awarded.
Degree requirements: For master's, one foreign language, oral exam, thesis optional; for doctorate, one foreign language, thesis/dissertation, oral exam.
Entrance requirements: For master's and doctorate, GRE General Test, TOEFL, minimum GPA of 3.0. *Application deadline:* For fall admission, 2/1 (priority date). Applications are processed on a rolling basis. *Application fee:* $35.
Expenses: Tuition, state resident: full-time $6,088; part-time $304 per semester. Tuition, nonresident: full-time $14,918; part-time $746 per semester. Tuition and fees vary according to program.
Financial support: In 2001–02, 7 research assistantships with full and partial tuition reimbursements, 28 teaching assistantships with full and partial tuition reimbursements were awarded. Career-related internships or fieldwork, Federal Work-Study, institutionally sponsored loans, tuition waivers (partial), and teaching associateships also available. Financial award application deadline: 3/1; financial award applicants required to submit FAFSA.
Faculty research: The American West in multicultural perspective; nineteenth-century historical, literary, and cultural studies; comparative American ethnic literatures and cultures; American cultures and the environment; American rhetoric.
Dr. T. V. Reed, Director, 509-335-1560. *Web site:* http://www.wsu.edu:8080/~amerstu/

■ WASHINGTON STATE UNIVERSITY

Graduate School, College of Liberal Arts, Department of History, Pullman, WA 99164

AWARDS American studies (MA, PhD); history (MA, PhD).

Faculty: 22 full-time (9 women).
Students: 38 full-time (16 women), 8 part-time (3 women); includes 5 minority (2 African Americans, 1 Hispanic American, 2 Native Americans), 2 international. Average age 33. 49 applicants, 67% accepted, 5 enrolled. In 2001, 5 master's, 8 doctorates awarded.
Degree requirements: For master's, oral exam, thesis optional; for doctorate, one foreign language, thesis/dissertation, oral and written exam.
Entrance requirements: For master's, GRE General Test, minimum GPA of 3.3; for doctorate, GRE General Test, minimum GPA of 3.7. *Application deadline:* For fall admission, 3/1 (priority date); for spring admission, 12/1. Applications are processed on a rolling basis. *Application fee:* $35. Electronic applications accepted.
Expenses: Tuition, state resident: full-time $6,088; part-time $304 per semester. Tuition, nonresident: full-time $14,918; part-time $746 per semester. Tuition and fees vary according to program.
Financial support: In 2001–02, 1 fellowship, 27 teaching assistantships with full and partial tuition reimbursements were awarded. Research assistantships with full and partial tuition reimbursements, career-related internships or fieldwork, Federal Work-Study, institutionally sponsored loans, and scholarships/grants also available. Financial award application deadline: 4/1; financial award applicants required to submit FAFSA.
Faculty research: Public, world, environmental. *Total annual research expenditures:* $15,390.
Dr. Roger Schlesinger, Chair, 509-335-5816, *Fax:* 509-335-4171, *E-mail:* schlesin@wsu.edu. *Web site:* http://www.libarts.wsu.edu/history/

■ WESTERN CAROLINA UNIVERSITY

Graduate School, College of Arts and Sciences, Department of History, Cullowhee, NC 28723

AWARDS American history (MA); comprehensive education (MA Ed), including social sciences; social sciences (MAT). Part-time and evening/weekend programs available.

Faculty: 18 full-time (3 women).
Students: 13 full-time (6 women), 18 part-time (9 women); includes 2 minority (1 African American, 1 Native American), 1 international. 18 applicants, 67% accepted, 3 enrolled. In 2001, 11 degrees awarded.
Degree requirements: For master's, one foreign language, thesis (for some programs), comprehensive exam.
Entrance requirements: For master's, GRE General Test. *Application deadline:* For fall admission, 5/1 (priority date); for spring admission, 10/1 (priority date). Applications are processed on a rolling basis. *Application fee:* $35.
Expenses: Tuition, state resident: full-time $1,072. Tuition, nonresident: full-time $8,704. Required fees: $1,171.
Financial support: In 2001–02, 11 students received support, including 4 research assistantships with full and partial tuition reimbursements available (averaging $4,064 per year), 7 teaching assistantships with full and partial tuition reimbursements available (averaging $4,289 per year); fellowships, Federal Work-Study, institutionally sponsored loans, and scholarships/grants also available. Financial award application deadline: 3/15; financial award applicants required to submit FAFSA.
Dr. James Lewis, Head, 828-227-7243, *E-mail:* lewis@email.wcu.edu.
Application contact: Josie Bewsey, Assistant to the Dean, 828-227-7398, *Fax:* 828-227-7480, *E-mail:* jbewsey@email.wcu.edu. *Web site:* http://www.wcu.edu/as/history/

■ WEST VIRGINIA UNIVERSITY

Eberly College of Arts and Sciences, Department of History, Morgantown, WV 26506

AWARDS African history (MA, PhD); African-American history (MA, PhD); American history (MA, PhD); Appalachian/regional history (MA, PhD); East Asian history (MA, PhD); European history (MA, PhD); history of science and technology (MA, PhD); Latin American history (MA). Part-time programs available.

Faculty: 19 full-time (4 women), 2 part-time/adjunct (1 woman).
Students: 35 full-time (13 women), 29 part-time (10 women); includes 5 minority (2 African Americans, 1 Asian American or Pacific Islander, 1 Hispanic American, 1 Native American), 5 international. Average age 34. 86 applicants, 44% accepted. In 2001, 4 master's, 1 doctorate awarded.
Degree requirements: For master's, one foreign language; for doctorate, one foreign language, comprehensive exam, dissertation defense.
Entrance requirements: For master's, GRE General Test, TOEFL, minimum GPA of 3.0; for doctorate, GRE General Test, TOEFL, MA or equivalent. *Application deadline:* For spring admission, 11/1. Applications are processed on a rolling basis. *Application fee:* $45.
Expenses: Tuition, state resident: full-time $2,791. Tuition, nonresident: full-time $8,659. Required fees: $1,002. Tuition and fees vary according to program.

West Virginia University (continued)
Financial support: In 2001–02, 43 students received support, including 2 research assistantships, 23 teaching assistantships; fellowships, career-related internships or fieldwork, Federal Work-Study, institutionally sponsored loans, tuition waivers (full and partial), and graduate administrative assistantships also available. Financial award application deadline: 2/1; financial award applicants required to submit FAFSA.
Faculty research: U.S., Appalachia, modern Europe, Africa, science and technology.
Dr. Robert M. Maxon, Chair, 304-293-2421 Ext. 5223, *Fax:* 304-293-3616, *E-mail:* robert.maxon@mail.wvu.edu.
Application contact: Dr. Robert E. Blobaum, Director of Graduate Studies, 304-293-2421 Ext. 5241, *Fax:* 304-293-3616, *E-mail:* robert.blobaum@mail.wvu.edu. *Web site:* http://www.as.wvu.edu/history/

■ WHEATON COLLEGE

Graduate School, Department of Biblical and Theological Studies, Program in Religion in American Life, Wheaton, IL 60187-5593

AWARDS Biblical and theological studies (MA). Part-time programs available.

Degree requirements: For master's, thesis optional.
Entrance requirements: For master's, GRE General Test, MAT. *Application deadline:* For fall admission, 3/1 (priority date); for spring admission, 11/1. Applications are processed on a rolling basis. *Application fee:* $30.
Expenses: Tuition: Part-time $410 per hour.
Financial support: Scholarships/grants and unspecified assistantships available. Financial award application deadline: 6/1; financial award applicants required to submit FAFSA.
Dr. Mark Noll, Coordinator, 630-752-3797.
Application contact: Julie A. Huebner, Director of Graduate Admissions, 630-752-5195, *Fax:* 630-752-5935, *E-mail:* gradadm@wheaton.edu.

■ YALE UNIVERSITY

Graduate School of Arts and Sciences, Interdisciplinary Program in American Studies, New Haven, CT 06520

AWARDS MA, PhD.

Degree requirements: For doctorate, one foreign language, thesis/dissertation.
Entrance requirements: For doctorate, GRE General Test.

ASIAN-AMERICAN STUDIES

■ CALIFORNIA STATE UNIVERSITY, LONG BEACH

Graduate Studies, College of Liberal Arts, Department of Asian and Asian American Studies, Long Beach, CA 90840

AWARDS Asian American studies (Certificate); Asian studies (MA). Part-time programs available.

Faculty: 24 full-time (7 women), 4 part-time/adjunct (2 women).
Students: 4 full-time (2 women), 10 part-time (8 women); includes 5 minority (all Asian Americans or Pacific Islanders), 3 international. Average age 41. 16 applicants, 56% accepted. In 2001, 2 degrees awarded.
Degree requirements: For master's, one foreign language.
Application deadline: For fall admission, 8/1; for spring admission, 12/1. Applications are processed on a rolling basis. *Application fee:* $55. Electronic applications accepted.
Financial support: Federal Work-Study, institutionally sponsored loans, and scholarships/grants available. Financial award application deadline: 3/2.
Faculty research: South Asia, China, Japan, Southeast Asia, Asian-American in the U.S.
Dr. Cassandra Kao, Chair, 562-985-7530, *Fax:* 562-985-1535, *E-mail:* ckao@csulb.edu.
Application contact: Information Contact, 562-985-7530, *Fax:* 562-985-1535.

■ UNIVERSITY OF CALIFORNIA, LOS ANGELES

Graduate Division, College of Letters and Science, Program in Asian-American Studies, Los Angeles, CA 90095

AWARDS MA.

Students: 21 full-time (14 women); includes 8 minority (1 African American, 7 Asian Americans or Pacific Islanders), 2 international. 30 applicants, 50% accepted, 11 enrolled. In 2001, 13 degrees awarded.
Degree requirements: For master's, one foreign language.
Entrance requirements: For master's, minimum GPA of 3.0, sample of written work. *Application deadline:* For fall admission, 12/15. *Application fee:* $60. Electronic applications accepted.
Expenses: Tuition, nonresident: full-time $10,244. Required fees: $3,609. Full-time tuition and fees vary according to program.
Financial support: In 2001–02, 3 research assistantships, 15 teaching assistantships were awarded. Fellowships Financial award application deadline: 3/1.
Dr. Min Zhou, Chair, 310-825-2974.
Application contact: Departmental Office, 310-825-2974, *E-mail:* tulisan@ucla.edu.

ASIAN STUDIES

■ BRIGHAM YOUNG UNIVERSITY

The David M. Kennedy Center for International and Area Studies, Provo, UT 84602-1001

AWARDS American studies (MA); ancient Near Eastern studies (MA); Asian studies (MA); international development (MA); international relations (MA).

Faculty: 21 full-time (2 women), 2 part-time/adjunct (0 women).
Students: 16 full-time (8 women), 13 part-time (9 women); includes 1 minority (Hispanic American), 4 international. Average age 25. 62 applicants, 31% accepted. In 2001, 17 degrees awarded.
Degree requirements: For master's, one foreign language, thesis.
Entrance requirements: For master's, GRE General Test, minimum GPA of 3.55 in last 60 hours. *Application deadline:* For fall admission, 2/1. *Application fee:* $50. Electronic applications accepted.
Expenses: Tuition: Full-time $3,860; part-time $214 per hour.
Financial support: In 2001–02, 18 research assistantships (averaging $3,500 per year), 2 teaching assistantships (averaging $3,500 per year) were awarded. Fellowships with full tuition reimbursements, career-related internships or fieldwork and tuition waivers (full) also available. Financial award application deadline: 2/1.
Faculty research: Comparative education, education for development, comparative economics. *Total annual research expenditures:* $100,000.
Dr. Donald B. Holsinger, Director, 801-422-3378, *Fax:* 801-378-8748, *E-mail:* donald_holsinger@byu.edu.
Application contact: Dr. Phillip J. Bryson, Director of Graduate Studies, Associate Director, 801-422-7402, *Fax:* 801-378-8748, *E-mail:* phillip_bryson@byu.edu.

■ CALIFORNIA INSTITUTE OF INTEGRAL STUDIES

Graduate Programs, School of Consciousness and Transformation, San Francisco, CA 94103

AWARDS Cultural anthropology and social transformation (MA); East-West psychology (MA, PhD); philosophy and religion (MA, PhD), including Asian and comparative studies, philosophy, cosmology, and consciousness, women's spirituality; social and cultural anthropology (PhD); transformative learning and change (PhD). Part-time and evening/

weekend programs available.
Postbaccalaureate distance learning degree programs offered (minimal on-campus study).

Faculty: 20 full-time (9 women), 72 part-time/adjunct (35 women).
Students: 60 full-time, 143 part-time. 157 applicants, 78% accepted, 85 enrolled. In 2001, 58 master's, 21 doctorates awarded. Terminal master's awarded for partial completion of doctoral program.
Degree requirements: For master's, comprehensive exam; for doctorate, thesis/dissertation, comprehensive exam.
Entrance requirements: For master's, TOEFL, minimum GPA of 3.0; for doctorate, TOEFL, master's degree. *Application deadline:* For fall admission, 3/15 (priority date); for spring admission, 10/15 (priority date). Applications are processed on a rolling basis. *Application fee:* $65.
Expenses: Tuition: Full-time $10,890; part-time $605 per unit. Tuition and fees vary according to degree level.
Financial support: Career-related internships or fieldwork, Federal Work-Study, institutionally sponsored loans, and scholarships/grants available. Support available to part-time students. Financial award application deadline: 6/15; financial award applicants required to submit FAFSA.
Faculty research: Altered states of consciousness, dreams, cosmology.
Daniel Deslaurier, Director, 415-575-6260, *Fax:* 415-575-1264, *E-mail:* danield@ciis.edu.
Application contact: Gregory E. Canada, Director of Admissions, 415-575-6155, *Fax:* 415-575-1268, *E-mail:* gregc@ciis.edu. *Web site:* http://www.ciis.edu/

Find an in-depth description at www.petersons.com/gradchannel.

■ CALIFORNIA STATE UNIVERSITY, LONG BEACH

Graduate Studies, College of Liberal Arts, Department of Asian and Asian American Studies, Long Beach, CA 90840

AWARDS Asian American studies (Certificate); Asian studies (MA). Part-time programs available.

Faculty: 24 full-time (7 women), 4 part-time/adjunct (2 women).
Students: 4 full-time (2 women), 10 part-time (8 women); includes 5 minority (all Asian Americans or Pacific Islanders), 3 international. Average age 41. 16 applicants, 56% accepted. In 2001, 2 degrees awarded.
Degree requirements: For master's, one foreign language.
Application deadline: For fall admission, 8/1; for spring admission, 12/1. Applications are processed on a rolling basis. *Application fee:* $55. Electronic applications accepted.
Financial support: Federal Work-Study, institutionally sponsored loans, and scholarships/grants available. Financial award application deadline: 3/2.
Faculty research: South Asia, China, Japan, Southeast Asia, Asian-American in the U.S.
Dr. Cassandra Kao, Chair, 562-985-7530, *Fax:* 562-985-1535, *E-mail:* ckao@csulb.edu.
Application contact: Information Contact, 562-985-7530, *Fax:* 562-985-1535.

■ COLUMBIA UNIVERSITY

Graduate School of Arts and Sciences, Division of Humanities, Department of East Asian Languages and Cultures, New York, NY 10027

AWARDS East Asian languages and cultures (M Phil, MA, PhD); Oriental studies (M Phil, MA, PhD).

Faculty: 17 full-time, 17 part-time/adjunct.
Students: 68 full-time (39 women), 5 part-time (3 women); includes 9 minority (all Asian Americans or Pacific Islanders), 15 international. Average age 32. 162 applicants, 31% accepted. In 2001, 11 master's, 7 doctorates awarded.
Degree requirements: For master's, one foreign language, thesis, comprehensive exam; for doctorate, 2 foreign languages, thesis/dissertation.
Entrance requirements: For master's and doctorate, GRE General Test, TOEFL. *Application deadline:* For fall admission, 1/3; for spring admission, 11/30. *Application fee:* $65.
Expenses: Tuition: Full-time $27,528. Required fees: $1,638.
Financial support: Fellowships, teaching assistantships, institutionally sponsored loans available. Support available to part-time students. Financial award application deadline: 1/5; financial award applicants required to submit FAFSA.
David Wang, Chair, 212-854-5027, *Fax:* 212-678-8629.

■ COLUMBIA UNIVERSITY

Graduate School of Arts and Sciences, Program in East Asian Regional Studies, New York, NY 10027

AWARDS MA.

Degree requirements: For master's, 2 foreign languages.
Entrance requirements: For master's, GRE General Test. *Application deadline:* For fall admission, 5/1.
Expenses: Tuition: Full-time $27,528. Required fees: $1,638.
Dr. Madeleine Zelin, Adviser, 212-854-2591, *Fax:* 212-749-1497, *E-mail:* mhz1@columbia.edu.

■ COLUMBIA UNIVERSITY

Graduate School of Arts and Sciences, Program in Liberal Studies, New York, NY 10027

AWARDS American studies (MA); East Asian studies (MA); human rights studies (MA); Islamic culture studies (MA); Jewish studies (MA); medieval studies (MA); modern European studies (MA); South Asian studies (MA). Part-time and evening/weekend programs available.

Faculty: 5 part-time/adjunct (2 women).
Students: 7 full-time (2 women), 75 part-time (51 women); includes 5 minority (1 African American, 3 Asian Americans or Pacific Islanders, 1 Hispanic American), 8 international. Average age 41. 39 applicants, 77% accepted. In 2001, 20 degrees awarded.
Degree requirements: For master's, thesis.
Application deadline: For fall admission, 4/1; for spring admission, 11/1. *Application fee:* $65.
Expenses: Tuition: Full-time $27,528. Required fees: $1,638.
Steve Laymon, Assistant Dean, 212-854-4932, *Fax:* 212-854-4912.
Application contact: Director of Admissions, 212-854-3331.

Find an in-depth description at www.petersons.com/gradchannel.

■ COLUMBIA UNIVERSITY

School of International and Public Affairs, East Asian Institute, New York, NY 10027

AWARDS Asian studies (Certificate). Students must be enrolled in a separate graduate degree program at Columbia University.

Entrance requirements: For degree, proficiency in East Asian language. *Application deadline:* For fall admission, 1/5 (priority date); for spring admission, 10/15 (priority date). *Application fee:* $75. Electronic applications accepted.
Financial support: Application deadline: 1/15.
Dr. Madeleine Zelin, Director, 212-854-2591, *Fax:* 212-749-1497, *E-mail:* mhz1@columbia.edu.
Application contact: Robert Garris, Associate Director, 212-854-6216, *Fax:* 212-854-3010, *E-mail:* sipa_admission@columbia.edu.

■ COLUMBIA UNIVERSITY

School of International and Public Affairs, Southern Asian Institute, New York, NY 10027

AWARDS Certificate. Students must be enrolled in a separate graduate degree program at Columbia University.

Students: 1.
Application deadline: For fall admission, 1/5 (priority date); for spring admission, 10/15

Columbia University (continued)
(priority date). *Application fee:* $75. Electronic applications accepted.
Financial support: Application deadline: 1/15.
Dr. Giauri Viswanathan, Director, 212-854-3616, *Fax:* 212-854-6987, *E-mail:* southasia@columbia.edu.
Application contact: Robert Garris, Associate Director, 212-854-6216, *Fax:* 212-854-3010, *E-mail:* sipa_admission@columbia.edu. *Web site:* http://www.columbia.edu/cu/sipa/REGIONAL/SAi

■ CORNELL UNIVERSITY

Graduate School, Graduate Fields of Arts and Sciences, Field of Asian Studies, Ithaca, NY 14853-0001

AWARDS East Asian studies (MA); South Asian studies (MA); Southeast Asian studies (MA).

Faculty: 52 full-time.
Students: 10 full-time (7 women), 8 international. 76 applicants, 58% accepted. In 2001, 7 degrees awarded.
Degree requirements: For master's, one foreign language, thesis.
Entrance requirements: For master's, GRE General Test, TOEFL, 3 letters of recommendation. *Application deadline:* Applications are processed on a rolling basis. *Application fee:* $65. Electronic applications accepted.
Expenses: Tuition: Full-time $25,970. Required fees: $50.
Financial support: In 2001–02, 6 students received support, including 3 fellowships with full tuition reimbursements available, 3 teaching assistantships with full tuition reimbursements available; research assistantships with full tuition reimbursements available, institutionally sponsored loans, scholarships/grants, tuition waivers (full and partial), and unspecified assistantships also available. Financial award applicants required to submit FAFSA.
Faculty research: East Asian studies, South Asian studies, Southeast Asian studies.
Application contact: Graduate Field Assistant, 607-255-9099, *E-mail:* asian@cornell.edu. *Web site:* http://www.gradschool.cornell.edu/grad/fields_1/asian-st.html

■ CORNELL UNIVERSITY

Graduate School, Graduate Fields of Arts and Sciences, Field of East Asian Literature, Ithaca, NY 14853-0001

AWARDS Asian religions (MA, PhD); Chinese philology (MA, PhD); classical Chinese literature (MA, PhD); classical Japanese literature (MA, PhD); Korean literature (MA, PhD); modern Chinese literature (MA, PhD); modern Japanese literature (MA, PhD).

Faculty: 12 full-time.
Students: 21 full-time (13 women); includes 2 minority (both Asian Americans or Pacific Islanders), 13 international. 44 applicants, 18% accepted. In 2001, 4 master's, 1 doctorate awarded.
Degree requirements: For master's and doctorate, 2 foreign languages, thesis/dissertation, teaching experience.
Entrance requirements: For master's, GRE General Test, TOEFL, 3 years of study in Chinese, Japanese, Korean, or Vietnamese; for doctorate, GRE General Test, TOEFL, 3 years of study in Chinese, Japanese, Korean, or Vietnamese. *Application deadline:* For fall admission, 2/15. *Application fee:* $65. Electronic applications accepted.
Expenses: Tuition: Full-time $25,970. Required fees: $50.
Financial support: In 2001–02, 19 students received support, including 14 fellowships with full tuition reimbursements available, 5 teaching assistantships with full tuition reimbursements available; research assistantships with full tuition reimbursements available, institutionally sponsored loans, scholarships/grants, tuition waivers (full and partial), and unspecified assistantships also available. Financial award applicants required to submit FAFSA.
Faculty research: Vietnamese literature; Chinese literature, drama, and film; Japanese theater and literature; popular culture in East Asia; Korean literature.
Application contact: Graduate Field Assistant, 607-255-9099, *E-mail:* east_asian_lit@cornell.edu. *Web site:* http://www.gradschool.cornell.edu/grad/fields_1/ea-lit.html

■ DUKE UNIVERSITY

Graduate School, Department of East Asian Studies, Durham, NC 27708-0586

AWARDS AM, Certificate. Part-time programs available.

Faculty: 30 full-time, 1 part-time/adjunct.
Students: 5 full-time (4 women); includes 1 minority (Asian American or Pacific Islander), 3 international. 8 applicants, 63% accepted, 1 enrolled.
Entrance requirements: For master's, GRE General Test. *Application deadline:* For fall admission, 12/31; for spring admission, 11/1. *Application fee:* $75.
Expenses: Tuition: Full-time $24,600.
Financial support: Application deadline: 12/31.
Nan Lin, Director, 919-684-2604, *Fax:* 919-681-6247, *E-mail:* paula@duke.edu. *Web site:* http://www.duke.edu/APSI/home.html/

■ FLORIDA STATE UNIVERSITY

Graduate Studies, College of Social Sciences, Program in Asian Studies, Tallahassee, FL 32306

AWARDS MA. Part-time programs available.

Students: 2 full-time (both women), 2 part-time, 2 international. Average age 28. 7 applicants, 71% accepted, 2 enrolled. In 2001, 1 degree awarded.
Degree requirements: For master's, one foreign language, comprehensive exam. *Median time to degree:* Master's–2 years full-time.
Entrance requirements: For master's, GRE General Test, minimum GPA of 3.0. *Application deadline:* For fall admission, 6/15; for spring admission, 10/15. Applications are processed on a rolling basis. *Application fee:* $20.
Expenses: Tuition, state resident: part-time $163 per credit hour. Tuition, nonresident: part-time $570 per credit hour. Tuition and fees vary according to program.
Financial support: In 2001–02, fellowships with full tuition reimbursements (averaging $10,000 per year), 1 research assistantship with full tuition reimbursement (averaging $5,000 per year) were awarded. Federal Work-Study and institutionally sponsored loans also available. Financial award application deadline: 3/15; financial award applicants required to submit FAFSA.
Faculty research: Art history of the Orient, Asian history and politics.
Dr. Burton Atkins, Director, 850-644-7327, *Fax:* 850-645-4981, *E-mail:* batkins@garnet.acns.fsu.edu.
Application contact: Patty Lollis, Program Assistant, 850-644-4418, *Fax:* 850-645-4981, *E-mail:* plollis@mailer.fsu.edu. *Web site:* http://www.fsu.edu/~asian/

■ THE GEORGE WASHINGTON UNIVERSITY

Elliott School of International Affairs, Program in Asian Studies, Washington, DC 20052

AWARDS MA, JD/MA, LL M/MA, MBA/MA, MPH/MA. Part-time and evening/weekend programs available.

Students: 18 full-time (13 women), 4 part-time (2 women); includes 5 minority (all Asian Americans or Pacific Islanders), 8 international. Average age 26. 50 applicants, 86% accepted. In 2001, 5 degrees awarded.
Degree requirements: For master's, one foreign language.
Entrance requirements: For master's, GRE General Test, TOEFL, minimum B average in undergraduate course work. *Application deadline:* For fall admission, 2/1. *Application fee:* $55. Electronic applications accepted.
Expenses: Tuition: Part-time $810 per credit. Required fees: $1 per credit.
Financial support: Fellowships with tuition reimbursements, research assistantships with tuition reimbursements, career-related internships or fieldwork, Federal Work-Study, institutionally sponsored loans, and tuition waivers (full) available. Financial award application deadline: 1/15;

financial award applicants required to submit FAFSA.
Faculty research: Sino-Soviet studies, Japanese-U.S. relations, Chinese foreign policy, economic development in China. Dr. Mike Mochizuki, Director, 202-994-4186.
Application contact: Jeff V. Miles, Director of Graduate Admissions, 202-994-7050, *Fax:* 202-994-9537, *E-mail:* esiagrad@gwu.edu. *Web site:* http://www.gwu.edu/~elliott/academicprograms/ma/as/

Find an in-depth description at www.petersons.com/gradchannel.

■ HARVARD UNIVERSITY

Graduate School of Arts and Sciences, Committee on History and East Asian Languages, Cambridge, MA 02138

AWARDS PhD.

Degree requirements: For doctorate, 3 foreign languages, thesis/dissertation, 2 seminar reports, general oral exam.
Entrance requirements: For doctorate, GRE General Test, TOEFL.
Expenses: Tuition: Full-time $23,370. Required fees: $816. Full-time tuition and fees vary according to program and student level.

■ HARVARD UNIVERSITY

Graduate School of Arts and Sciences, Committee on Inner Asian and Altaic Studies, Cambridge, MA 02138

AWARDS PhD.

Degree requirements: For doctorate, 2 foreign languages, thesis/dissertation, oral general exam.
Entrance requirements: For doctorate, GRE General Test, TOEFL, proficiency in a related foreign language.
Expenses: Tuition: Full-time $23,370. Required fees: $816. Full-time tuition and fees vary according to program and student level.

■ HARVARD UNIVERSITY

Graduate School of Arts and Sciences, Committee on Regional Studies–East Asia, Cambridge, MA 02138

AWARDS Chinese studies (AM); Japanese studies (AM); Korean studies (AM); Mongolian studies (AM); Vietnamese studies (AM).

Degree requirements: For master's, one foreign language.
Entrance requirements: For master's, GRE General Test, TOEFL.
Expenses: Tuition: Full-time $23,370. Required fees: $816. Full-time tuition and fees vary according to program and student level.

■ HARVARD UNIVERSITY

Graduate School of Arts and Sciences, Department of Sanskrit and Indian Studies, Cambridge, MA 02138

AWARDS Indian philosophy (AM, PhD); Pali (AM, PhD); Sanskrit (AM, PhD); Tibetan (AM, PhD); Urdu (AM, PhD). Terminal master's awarded for partial completion of doctoral program.

Degree requirements: For master's, 3 foreign languages; for doctorate, 3 foreign languages, thesis/dissertation.
Entrance requirements: For master's, GRE General Test, TOEFL; for doctorate, GRE General Test, TOEFL, proficiency in French and German.
Expenses: Tuition: Full-time $23,370. Required fees: $816. Full-time tuition and fees vary according to program and student level.

■ INDIANA UNIVERSITY BLOOMINGTON

Graduate School, College of Arts and Sciences, Department of Central Eurasian Studies, Bloomington, IN 47405

AWARDS MA, PhD. PhD offered through the University Graduate School.

Faculty: 10 full-time (0 women).
Students: 14 full-time (5 women), 16 part-time (3 women); includes 1 minority (Asian American or Pacific Islander), 7 international. Average age 33. Terminal master's awarded for partial completion of doctoral program.
Degree requirements: For master's, one foreign language, thesis; for doctorate, 2 foreign languages, thesis/dissertation, qualifying exams.
Entrance requirements: For master's, TOEFL, minimum GPA of 3.0, 2 years of a foreign language; for doctorate, TOEFL, minimum GPA of 3.5, 1 research language. *Application deadline:* For fall admission, 1/15 (priority date); for spring admission, 9/1 (priority date). Applications are processed on a rolling basis. *Application fee:* $45 ($55 for international students). Electronic applications accepted.
Expenses: Tuition, state resident: full-time $4,720; part-time $197 per credit. Tuition, nonresident: full-time $13,748; part-time $573 per credit. Required fees: $642.
Financial support: In 2001–02, 2 fellowships with full tuition reimbursements (averaging $7,500 per year), 1 research assistantship with full tuition reimbursement (averaging $7,000 per year), 3 teaching assistantships with full tuition reimbursements (averaging $4,300 per year) were awarded. Federal Work-Study also available. Financial award application deadline: 2/16.
Faculty research: Central Asia, Hungarian civilization, Tibetan civilization, Turkish studies, Mongolian philology.
Toivo Raun, Chair, 812-855-2233, *Fax:* 812-855-7500, *E-mail:* ceus@indiana.edu. *Web site:* http://www.indiana.edu/~ceus/

■ INDIANA UNIVERSITY BLOOMINGTON

Graduate School, College of Arts and Sciences, Department of East Asian Languages and Cultures, Bloomington, IN 47405

AWARDS Chinese language and literature (MA, PhD); East Asian studies (MA); Japanese language and literature (MA, PhD). PhD offered through the University Graduate School. Part-time programs available.

Faculty: 12 full-time (5 women).
Students: 2 full-time (0 women), 1 international. Average age 28. 60 applicants, 37% accepted. In 2001, 1 degree awarded.
Degree requirements: For master's and doctorate, 2 foreign languages, thesis/dissertation.
Entrance requirements: For master's and doctorate, TOEFL. *Application deadline:* For fall admission, 1/15. Applications are processed on a rolling basis. *Application fee:* $45 ($55 for international students). Electronic applications accepted.
Expenses: Tuition, state resident: full-time $4,720; part-time $197 per credit. Tuition, nonresident: full-time $13,748; part-time $573 per credit. Required fees: $642.
Financial support: Fellowships, teaching assistantships, Federal Work-Study and tuition waivers (full) available. Financial award application deadline: 3/1.
Faculty research: Postwar/postmodern Japanese fiction, modern Chinese film and literature, classical Chinese literature and philosophy, Chinese and Japanese linguistics and pedagogy, East Asian politics.
Dr. Richard Rubinger, Chair, 812-855-1992, *Fax:* 812-855-6402, *E-mail:* rubinge@indiana.edu.
Application contact: Edith Sarra, Director of Graduate Studies, 812-855-1992, *Fax:* 812-855-6402, *E-mail:* esarra@indiana.edu. *Web site:* http://www.indiana.edu/~ealc/home.html

■ JOHNS HOPKINS UNIVERSITY

Paul H. Nitze School of Advanced International Studies, Washington, DC 20036

AWARDS Emerging markets (Certificate); interdisciplinary studies (MA, PhD), including African studies, American foreign policy (MA), Asian studies, Canadian studies, conflict resolution and mediation (MA), environmental policy and resource management (MA), European studies, international business (MA), international development (MA), international economics (MA), international relations (MA), Latin American studies, Middle Eastern studies (MA), military and defense studies (MA), Russian area and East

Johns Hopkins University (continued)
European studies (MA), social change and development (MA); international public policy (MIPP). MBA/MA offered jointly with the University of Pennsylvania–Wharton School and INSEAD in France.

Faculty: 44 full-time (13 women), 113 part-time/adjunct (29 women).
Students: 567 full-time (275 women), 17 part-time (8 women); includes 71 minority (14 African Americans, 46 Asian Americans or Pacific Islanders, 10 Hispanic Americans, 1 Native American). Average age 27. 1,288 applicants, 35% accepted. In 2001, 294 master's, 13 doctorates, 34 other advanced degrees awarded. Terminal master's awarded for partial completion of doctoral program.
Degree requirements: For master's, one foreign language, comprehensive exam; for doctorate, 2 foreign languages, thesis/dissertation.
Entrance requirements: For master's, GMAT or GRE General Test or TOEFL, previous course work in economics, foreign language; for doctorate, GRE General Test or TOEFL; for Certificate, TOEFL. *Application deadline:* For fall admission, 1/15. *Application fee:* $75. Electronic applications accepted.
Expenses: Contact institution.
Financial support: In 2001–02, 431 fellowships (averaging $5,500 per year) were awarded; career-related internships or fieldwork and Federal Work-Study also available. Financial award application deadline: 2/1; financial award applicants required to submit FAFSA.
Faculty research: Comparative politics, regional studies, language and linguistics. Dr. Jessica Einhorn, Dean, 202-663-5624, *Fax:* 202-663-5621.
Application contact: Bonnie Wilson, Associate Dean of Student Affairs, 202-663-5700, *Fax:* 202-663-7788, *E-mail:* admissions.sais@jhu.edu. *Web site:* http://www.sais-jhu.edu/

Find an in-depth description at www.petersons.com/gradchannel.

■ OHIO UNIVERSITY

Graduate Studies, Center for International Studies, Program in Southeast Asian Studies, Athens, OH 45701-2979

AWARDS MA.

Faculty: 37 full-time (10 women), 9 part-time/adjunct (4 women).
Students: 25 full-time (16 women), 2 part-time (1 woman); includes 1 minority (Asian American or Pacific Islander), 17 international. Average age 26. 23 applicants, 78% accepted. In 2001, 4 degrees awarded.
Degree requirements: For master's, one foreign language, thesis optional.
Entrance requirements: For master's, TOEFL, minimum GPA of 3.0. *Application deadline:* For fall admission, 3/1 (priority date). *Application fee:* $30.
Expenses: Tuition, state resident: full-time $6,585. Tuition, nonresident: full-time $12,254.
Financial support: In 2001–02, 10 fellowships with full tuition reimbursements (averaging $11,000 per year), 12 research assistantships with full tuition reimbursements (averaging $9,000 per year), 2 teaching assistantships with full tuition reimbursements (averaging $9,000 per year) were awarded. Federal Work-Study, institutionally sponsored loans, and tuition waivers (full) also available. Financial award application deadline: 1/15.
Faculty research: Indonesian and Malaysian: political, history, literature, media, Islam, and environmental problems. Dr. Drew McDaniel, Director, 740-593-1840, *Fax:* 740-593-1837, *E-mail:* seas@www.cats.ohio.edu.
Application contact: Joan Kraynanski, Administrative Assistant, 740-593-1840, *Fax:* 740-593-1837, *E-mail:* kraynans@ohio.edu. *Web site:* http://www.ohiou.edu/internationalstudies/

■ PRINCETON UNIVERSITY

Graduate School, Department of East Asian Studies, Princeton, NJ 08544-1019

AWARDS Chinese and Japanese art and archaeology (PhD); East Asian civilizations (PhD); East Asian studies (PhD).

Degree requirements: For doctorate, 2 foreign languages, thesis/dissertation.
Entrance requirements: For doctorate, GRE General Test, TOEFL, fluency in Japanese and/or Chinese.
Faculty research: Modern and classical Japanese literature, premodern Chinese and Japanese history, Chinese narrative and poetry.

■ ST. JOHN'S COLLEGE

Graduate Institute in Liberal Education, Program in Eastern Classics, Santa Fe, NM 87505-4599

AWARDS MA. Evening/weekend programs available.

Faculty: 10 full-time (3 women).
Students: 18 full-time (8 women). 40 applicants, 60% accepted, 18 enrolled. In 2001, 10 degrees awarded. *Median time to degree:* Master's–1 year full-time.
Application deadline: For fall admission, 4/15 (priority date). Applications are processed on a rolling basis. *Application fee:* $0.
Expenses: Contact institution.
Financial support: Scholarships/grants available. Support available to part-time students. Financial award application deadline: 5/1; financial award applicants required to submit FAFSA.
Application contact: Jean-Paul Ruch, Assistant Director of Graduate Admissions, 505-984-6083, *Fax:* 505-984-6003, *E-mail:* giadmiss@mail.sjcsf.edu.

■ ST. JOHN'S UNIVERSITY

St. John's College of Liberal Arts and Sciences, Institute of Asian Studies, Jamaica, NY 11439

AWARDS Asian and African cultural studies (Adv C); Asian studies (Adv C); Chinese studies (MA, Adv C); East Asian culture studies (Adv C); East Asian studies (MA). Part-time and evening/weekend programs available.

Faculty: 1 (woman) full-time, 5 part-time/adjunct (4 women).
Students: 4 full-time (3 women), 9 part-time (7 women); includes 6 minority (5 Asian Americans or Pacific Islanders, 1 Hispanic American), 6 international. Average age 34. 11 applicants, 4 enrolled. In 2001, 4 degrees awarded.
Degree requirements: For master's, one foreign language, comprehensive exam.
Entrance requirements: For master's, 18 hours in the field, minimum GPA of 3.0. *Application deadline:* Applications are processed on a rolling basis. *Application fee:* $40.
Expenses: Tuition: Full-time $14,520; part-time $605 per credit. Required fees: $150; $75 per term. Tuition and fees vary according to class time, course load, degree level, campus/location, program and student level.
Financial support: Research assistantships with full tuition reimbursements, scholarships/grants available. Support available to part-time students. Financial award application deadline: 3/1; financial award applicants required to submit FAFSA.
Faculty research: East Asian philosophy and religion, Chinese language and literature, Japanese language, modern Japan, Chinese art and history. Dr. John Lin, Director, 718-990-6582, *E-mail:* linj@stjohns.edu.
Application contact: Matthew Whelan, Director, Office of Admission, 718-990-2000, *Fax:* 718-990-2096, *E-mail:* admissions@stjohns.edu. *Web site:* http://www.stjohns.edu/

■ SAN DIEGO STATE UNIVERSITY

Graduate and Research Affairs, College of Arts and Letters, Center for Asian Studies, San Diego, CA 92182

AWARDS MA.

Degree requirements: For master's, one foreign language.
Entrance requirements: For master's, GRE General Test, TOEFL.
Faculty research: Language acquisition process, social organization of Asia, economic development.

■ SETON HALL UNIVERSITY

College of Arts and Sciences, Department of Asian Studies, South Orange, NJ 07079-2697

AWARDS MA. Part-time and evening/weekend programs available.

Degree requirements: For master's, thesis optional.
Entrance requirements: For master's, minimum B average.
Expenses: Tuition: Full-time $10,818; part-time $601 per credit. Required fees: $610; $185 per term. Tuition and fees vary according to course load, program and student's religious affiliation.
Faculty research: Modern Chinese history, contemporary Chinese politics, ancient Chinese history, Hinduism, Asian business.

■ STANFORD UNIVERSITY

School of Humanities and Sciences, Center for East Asian Studies, Stanford, CA 94305-9991

AWARDS AM.

Students: 20 full-time (10 women), 3 part-time; includes 5 minority (4 Asian Americans or Pacific Islanders, 1 Native American), 6 international. Average age 25. 55 applicants, 56% accepted. In 2001, 14 degrees awarded.
Degree requirements: For master's, one foreign language, thesis.
Entrance requirements: For master's, GRE General Test, TOEFL. *Application deadline:* For fall admission, 1/4. *Application fee:* $65 ($80 for international students). Electronic applications accepted.
Financial support: Research assistantships available.
Jean Oi, Director, 650-725-1418, *Fax:* 650-725-0597, *E-mail:* joi@stanford.edu.
Application contact: Director of Graduate Admissions, 650-723-3362. *Web site:* http://www.stanford.edu/dept/ceas/

■ THE UNIVERSITY OF ARIZONA

Graduate College, College of Humanities, Department of East Asian Studies, Tucson, AZ 85721

AWARDS MA, PhD. Part-time programs available.

Faculty: 14 full-time (4 women), 1 (woman) part-time/adjunct.
Students: 28 full-time (17 women), 13 part-time (8 women); includes 2 minority (both Asian Americans or Pacific Islanders), 30 international. Average age 36. 31 applicants, 52% accepted, 6 enrolled. In 2001, 6 master's, 2 doctorates awarded. Terminal master's awarded for partial completion of doctoral program.
Degree requirements: For master's, one foreign language; for doctorate, 2 foreign languages.
Entrance requirements: For master's, GRE General Test, TOEFL, minimum GPA of 3.5; for doctorate, GRE General Test, TOEFL. *Application deadline:* For fall admission, 8/1. Applications are processed on a rolling basis. *Application fee:* $45.
Expenses: Tuition, state resident: full-time $2,490; part-time $436 per unit. Tuition, nonresident: full-time $10,300; part-time $436 per unit. Full-time tuition and fees vary according to degree level and program.
Financial support: Fellowships, teaching assistantships available.
Faculty research: Chinese history, Chinese/Japanese linguistics, Chinese/Japanese literature, Chinese/Japanese religion.
Dr. Timothy J Vance, Head, 520-621-5534, *Fax:* 520-621-1149, *E-mail:* vancet@u.arizona.edu.
Application contact: Janet Kania, Administrative Associate, 520-621-5452, *Fax:* 520-621-1149, *E-mail:* kaniaj@u.arizona.edu.

■ UNIVERSITY OF CALIFORNIA, BERKELEY

Graduate Division, College of Letters and Science, Department of South and Southeast Asian Studies, Berkeley, CA 94720-1500

AWARDS Hindi-Urdu (MA, PhD); Malay-Indonesian (MA, PhD); Sanskrit (MA, PhD); South Asian civilization (MA); Tamil (MA, PhD).

Faculty: 6 full-time (3 women), 14 part-time/adjunct (10 women).
Students: 28 full-time (14 women); includes 2 minority (1 Asian American or Pacific Islander, 1 Hispanic American), 7 international. 24 applicants, 50% accepted, 6 enrolled. In 2001, 6 master's, 2 doctorates awarded. Terminal master's awarded for partial completion of doctoral program.
Degree requirements: For master's, 2 foreign languages, thesis; for doctorate, 2 foreign languages, thesis/dissertation, oral qualifying exam.
Entrance requirements: For master's and doctorate, GRE General Test, minimum GPA of 3.0. *Application deadline:* For fall admission, 12/7. *Application fee:* $40. Electronic applications accepted.
Expenses: Tuition, nonresident: full-time $10,704. Required fees: $4,349.
Financial support: Fellowships, research assistantships, teaching assistantships available. Financial award application deadline: 12/7.
Vasudha Dalmia, Chair, 510-642-3582.
Application contact: Lee Amazonas, Student Affairs Officer, 510-642-4219. *Web site:* http://ls.berkeley.edu/dept/sseas/

■ UNIVERSITY OF CALIFORNIA, BERKELEY

Graduate Division, Group in Asian Studies, Berkeley, CA 94720-1500

AWARDS Asian studies (PhD); East Asian studies (MA); Northeast Asian studies (MA); South Asian studies (MA); Southeast Asian studies (MA).

Degree requirements: For master's, one foreign language; for doctorate, 2 foreign languages, thesis/dissertation, qualifying exam.
Entrance requirements: For master's and doctorate, GRE General Test, minimum GPA of 3.0.
Expenses: Tuition, nonresident: full-time $10,704. Required fees: $4,349. *Web site:* http://www.socrates.berkeley.edu:4258/

■ UNIVERSITY OF CALIFORNIA, BERKELEY

Graduate Division, Group in Buddhist Studies, Berkeley, CA 94720-1500

AWARDS PhD.

Faculty: 9 full-time (3 women).
Students: In 2001, 3 degrees awarded.
Degree requirements: For doctorate, 4 foreign languages, thesis/dissertation, dissertation defense, qualifying exam.
Entrance requirements: For doctorate, GRE General Test, MA in Japanese, Chinese, or Sanskrit; minimum GPA of 3.0. *Application deadline:* For fall admission, 12/7. *Application fee:* $60. Electronic applications accepted.
Expenses: Tuition, nonresident: full-time $10,704. Required fees: $4,349.
Financial support: Application deadline: 12/7.
Padmanadh Jaini, Chair Emeritus.
Application contact: Lee Amazonas, Student Affairs Officer, 510-642-4219.

■ UNIVERSITY OF CALIFORNIA, BERKELEY

Graduate Division, Haas School of Business and Group in Asian Studies, Concurrent MBA/MA Program with Asian Studies, Berkeley, CA 94720-1500

AWARDS MBA/MA.

Students: 1 full-time (0 women). Average age 28. 8 applicants, 25% accepted. *Application deadline:* For fall admission, 12/15. *Application fee:* $125.
Expenses: Tuition, nonresident: full-time $10,704. Required fees: $4,349.
Financial support: In 2001–02, 1 student received support, including 1 fellowship (averaging $2,500 per year); research assistantships with partial tuition reimbursements available, teaching assistantships with partial tuition reimbursements available, career-related internships or fieldwork and scholarships/grants also available. Financial award

University of California, Berkeley (continued)
application deadline: 3/2; financial award applicants required to submit FAFSA.
David Downes, Director, MBA Program, 510-642-1405, *Fax:* 510-643-6659, *E-mail:* mbaadms@haas.berkeley.edu.
Application contact: MBA Admissions, 510-642-1405, *Fax:* 510-643-6659, *E-mail:* mbaadms@haas.berkley.edu. *Web site:* http://www.socrates.berkeley.edu:4258/

■ UNIVERSITY OF CALIFORNIA, IRVINE

Office of Research and Graduate Studies, School of Humanities, Department of East Asian Languages and Literatures, Irvine, CA 92697

AWARDS Chinese (MA, PhD); East Asian cultures (MA, PhD); Japanese (MA, PhD).

Faculty: 10.
Students: 9 full-time (5 women); includes 4 minority (all Asian Americans or Pacific Islanders), 2 international. 17 applicants, 47% accepted, 3 enrolled.
Degree requirements: For doctorate, 2 foreign languages, thesis/dissertation.
Entrance requirements: For doctorate, GRE General Test, minimum GPA of 3.0. *Application deadline:* For fall and spring admission, 1/15 (priority date); for winter admission, 10/15 (priority date). *Application fee:* $60. Electronic applications accepted.
Expenses: Tuition, nonresident: full-time $10,704. Required fees: $8,396. Tuition and fees vary according to course load, program and student level.
Financial support: Fellowships with tuition reimbursements, research assistantships, teaching assistantships with partial tuition reimbursements, institutionally sponsored loans and tuition waivers (full and partial) available. Financial award application deadline: 3/2; financial award applicants required to submit FAFSA.
Faculty research: Chinese, Japanese, and Korean literature and culture; language and textual analysis; historical, social, and cultural dimensions of literary study.
Steven Carter, Chair, 949-824-2802.
Application contact: Indi McCarthy, Graduate Staff Contact, 949-824-1601, *Fax:* 949-824-3248, *E-mail:* imccarth@uci.edu. *Web site:* http://www.hnet.uci.edu/eastasian/

■ UNIVERSITY OF CALIFORNIA, LOS ANGELES

Graduate Division, College of Letters and Science, Department of East Asian Languages and Cultures, Los Angeles, CA 90095

AWARDS MA, PhD.

Faculty: 15.
Students: 57 full-time (37 women); includes 25 minority (1 African American, 24 Asian Americans or Pacific Islanders), 15 international. 73 applicants, 16% accepted, 6 enrolled. In 2001, 8 master's, 7 doctorates awarded.
Degree requirements: For master's, one foreign language; for doctorate, 2 foreign languages, thesis/dissertation, oral and written qualifying exams.
Entrance requirements: For master's, GRE General Test, TOEFL, minimum GPA of 3.0, sample of written work; for doctorate, GRE General Test, TOEFL, minimum undergraduate GPA of 3.0, sample of research writing or thesis in English. *Application deadline:* For fall admission, 12/15. *Application fee:* $60. Electronic applications accepted.
Expenses: Tuition, nonresident: full-time $10,244. Required fees: $3,609. Full-time tuition and fees vary according to program.
Financial support: In 2001–02, 53 students received support, including 31 fellowships, 22 research assistantships, 48 teaching assistantships; Federal Work-Study, institutionally sponsored loans, and tuition waivers (full and partial) also available. Financial award application deadline: 3/1.
Dr. Robert E. Buswell, Chair, 310-206-8235.
Application contact: Departmental Office, 310-206-8235, *E-mail:* beard@humnet.ucla.edu.

■ UNIVERSITY OF CALIFORNIA, LOS ANGELES

Graduate Division, Interdepartmental Program in East Asian Studies, Los Angeles, CA 90095

AWARDS MA.

Students: 6 full-time (5 women); includes 2 minority (both Asian Americans or Pacific Islanders). 9 applicants, 78% accepted, 6 enrolled.
Entrance requirements: For master's, GRE General Test. *Application deadline:* For fall admission, 12/15. *Application fee:* $60.
Expenses: Tuition, nonresident: full-time $10,244. Required fees: $3,609. Full-time tuition and fees vary according to program.
Financial support: Application deadline: 3/1.
Dr. Richard E. Strassberg, Director, 310-206-2806.

■ UNIVERSITY OF CALIFORNIA, SANTA BARBARA

Graduate Division, College of Letters and Sciences, Division of Humanities and Fine Arts, Department of East Asian Languages and Cultural Studies, Santa Barbara, CA 93106

AWARDS MA.

Degree requirements: For master's, one foreign language, thesis or alternative.
Entrance requirements: For master's, GRE, TOEFL.
Faculty research: Language and literature in Chinese and Japanese. *Web site:* http://www.eastasian.ucsb.edu/

■ UNIVERSITY OF CHICAGO

Division of the Humanities, Department of East Asian Languages and Civilizations, Chicago, IL 60637-1513

AWARDS AM, PhD.

Students: 46. 78 applicants, 62% accepted. Terminal master's awarded for partial completion of doctoral program.
Degree requirements: For master's, one foreign language, thesis; for doctorate, 2 foreign languages, thesis/dissertation.
Entrance requirements: For master's and doctorate, GRE General Test, TOEFL. *Application deadline:* For fall admission, 12/28. *Application fee:* $55.
Expenses: Tuition: Full-time $16,548.
Financial support: Fellowships, Federal Work-Study available. Financial award application deadline: 12/28; financial award applicants required to submit FAFSA.
Dr. Donald Harper, Chair, 773-702-1255.

■ UNIVERSITY OF CHICAGO

Division of the Humanities, Department of South Asian Languages and Civilizations, Chicago, IL 60637-1513

AWARDS South Asian languages and civilizations (AM, PhD), including Bengali (PhD), Hindi (PhD), Sanskrit (PhD), Tamil (PhD), Urdu (PhD).

Students: 39. 19 applicants, 58% accepted. Terminal master's awarded for partial completion of doctoral program.
Degree requirements: For master's, one foreign language, thesis; for doctorate, 2 foreign languages, thesis/dissertation.
Entrance requirements: For master's and doctorate, GRE General Test, TOEFL. *Application deadline:* For fall admission, 12/28. *Application fee:* $55.
Expenses: Tuition: Full-time $16,548.
Financial support: Fellowships, Federal Work-Study available. Financial award application deadline: 12/28; financial award applicants required to submit FAFSA.
Dr. Dipesh Chakrabarby, Chair, 773-702-8373.

■ UNIVERSITY OF HAWAII AT MANOA

Graduate Division, School of Hawaiian, Asian and Pacific Studies, Program in Asian Studies, Honolulu, HI 96822

AWARDS MA, JD/MA, MLI Sc/MA.

Faculty: 104 full-time (29 women), 4 part-time/adjunct (0 women).
Students: 89 full-time (31 women), 20 part-time (11 women); includes 26 Asian Americans or Pacific Islanders, 2 Hispanic Americans, 2 Native Americans. Average

age 31. 73 applicants, 36% accepted, 7 enrolled. In 2001, 4 master's awarded.
Degree requirements: For master's, one foreign language, thesis optional. *Median time to degree:* Master's–2 years full-time.
Entrance requirements: For master's, GRE General Test. *Application deadline:* For fall admission, 3/1; for spring admission, 9/1. Applications are processed on a rolling basis. *Application fee:* $25 ($50 for international students).
Expenses: Tuition, state resident: full-time $2,160; part-time $1,980 per year. Tuition, nonresident: full-time $5,190; part-time $4,829 per year.
Financial support: In 2001–02, 16 students received support, including 2 teaching assistantships (averaging $12,786 per year); fellowships, research assistantships, career-related internships or fieldwork, Federal Work-Study, and tuition waivers (full) also available. Financial award application deadline: 4/1.
Faculty research: Development, urban studies, regional history, arts, and ethnic identity in Asia. *Total annual research expenditures:* $750,000.
Dr. Ricardo D. Trimillos, Graduate Field Chairperson, 808-956-5752, *Fax:* 808-956-2682, *E-mail:* rtrimil@hawaii.edu.

■ UNIVERSITY OF ILLINOIS AT URBANA–CHAMPAIGN

Graduate College, College of Liberal Arts and Sciences, Department of East Asian Languages and Cultures, Champaign, IL 61820

AWARDS AM, PhD.

Faculty: 14 full-time, 3 part-time/adjunct.
Students: 36 full-time (24 women), 25 international. 43 applicants, 30% accepted. In 2001, 13 degrees awarded.
Degree requirements: For master's, one foreign language; for doctorate, thesis/dissertation.
Entrance requirements: For master's, GRE General Test, TOEFL, minimum GPA of 3.0. *Application deadline:* For fall admission, 2/15; for spring admission, 11/1. *Application fee:* $40 ($50 for international students). Electronic applications accepted.
Expenses: Tuition, state resident: part-time $3,227 per degree program. Tuition, nonresident: part-time $7,169 per degree program. Tuition and fees vary according to program.
Financial support: In 2001–02, 3 fellowships, 3 research assistantships, 29 teaching assistantships were awarded. Tuition waivers (full and partial) also available. Financial award application deadline: 2/15.
Jerome L. Packard, Head, 217-244-9077, *Fax:* 217-244-4010.
Application contact: Jean Poole, Administrative Secretary, 217-333-7057, *Fax:* 217-244-4010, *E-mail:* j-poole1@uiuc.edu. *Web site:* http://www.ealc.uiuc.edu/

■ THE UNIVERSITY OF IOWA

Graduate College, College of Liberal Arts and Sciences, Program in Asian Civilizations, Iowa City, IA 52242-1316

AWARDS MA.

Faculty: 9 full-time.
Students: 9 full-time (7 women), 3 part-time (1 woman); includes 1 minority (Asian American or Pacific Islander), 10 international. 17 applicants, 59% accepted, 3 enrolled. In 2001, 6 degrees awarded.
Degree requirements: For master's, exam, thesis optional.
Entrance requirements: For master's, GRE General Test, TOEFL. *Application deadline:* For fall admission, 4/15; for spring admission, 10/1. *Application fee:* $30 ($50 for international students). Electronic applications accepted.
Expenses: Tuition, state resident: full-time $3,702; part-time $206 per semester hour. Tuition, nonresident: full-time $11,924; part-time $206 per semester hour. Required fees: $101 per semester. Tuition and fees vary according to course load and program.
Financial support: In 2001–02, 2 fellowships, 1 research assistantship, 10 teaching assistantships were awarded. Financial award application deadline: 2/1; financial award applicants required to submit FAFSA.
Philip Lutgendorf, Chair, 319-335-2151, *Fax:* 319-353-2207.

■ UNIVERSITY OF KANSAS

Graduate School, College of Liberal Arts and Sciences, Department of East Asian Languages and Cultures, Lawrence, KS 66045

AWARDS MA. Part-time programs available.

Faculty: 7.
Students: 3 full-time (1 woman), 4 part-time (2 women). Average age 32. 1 applicant, 0% accepted. In 2001, 2 degrees awarded.
Degree requirements: For master's, 2 foreign languages, thesis.
Entrance requirements: For master's, GRE, TOEFL. *Application deadline:* Applications are processed on a rolling basis. *Application fee:* $35. Electronic applications accepted.
Expenses: Tuition, state resident: full-time $2,722; part-time $113 per credit. Tuition, nonresident: full-time $8,586; part-time $358 per credit. Required fees: $551; $46 per credit. Tuition and fees vary according to campus/location, program and reciprocity agreements.
Financial support: In 2001–02, 15 teaching assistantships with full and partial tuition reimbursements (averaging $8,548 per year) were awarded.
Faculty research: Gender relations in literature, ancient Chinese law, prosody in Chinese.
Keith McMahon, Chair and Graduate Director, 785-864-3100, *E-mail:* kmcmahon@ku.edu.
Application contact: Graduate Secretary, 785-864-3100, *Fax:* 785-864-4298, *E-mail:* ealc.ku.edu. *Web site:* http://www.ku.edu/~ealc/ealc.html

■ UNIVERSITY OF MICHIGAN

Horace H. Rackham School of Graduate Studies, College of Literature, Science, and the Arts, Center for Chinese Studies, Ann Arbor, MI 48109

AWARDS AM, MBA/AM.

Degree requirements: For master's, one foreign language, thesis.
Entrance requirements: For master's, GRE General Test, TOEFL. *Web site:* http://www.umich.edu/~iinet/ccs/index.html

■ UNIVERSITY OF MICHIGAN

Horace H. Rackham School of Graduate Studies, College of Literature, Science, and the Arts, Center for Japanese Studies, Ann Arbor, MI 48109

AWARDS AM, JD/AM, MBA/AM.

Degree requirements: For master's, one foreign language, thesis or alternative.
Entrance requirements: For master's, GRE General Test. *Web site:* http://www.umich.edu/~iinet/cjs

■ UNIVERSITY OF MICHIGAN

Horace H. Rackham School of Graduate Studies, College of Literature, Science, and the Arts, Center for South Asian Studies, Ann Arbor, MI 48109

AWARDS AM, MBA/AM. Part-time programs available.

Faculty: 36 full-time (12 women).
Students: 6 full-time (5 women); includes 3 minority (all Asian Americans or Pacific Islanders). Average age 25. 7 applicants, 86% accepted, 4 enrolled. In 2001, 1 degree awarded.
Degree requirements: For master's, one foreign language, thesis. *Median time to degree:* Master's–2 years full-time.
Entrance requirements: For master's, GRE General Test. *Application deadline:* For fall admission, 1/15 (priority date). Applications are processed on a rolling basis. *Application fee:* $55.
Financial support: In 2001–02, 7 fellowships with full tuition reimbursements (averaging $11,000 per year) were awarded; career-related internships or fieldwork, Federal Work-Study, institutionally sponsored loans, and scholarships/grants also available. Financial award application deadline: 2/1; financial award applicants required to submit FAFSA.

University of Michigan (continued)

Faculty research: Real behavior and education, film and cinema, language, musicology, ethnology.
Ashutosh Varshney, Director, 734-764-0352, *Fax:* 734-936-0996, *E-mail:* varshney@umich.edu.
Application contact: Zoe Stevens, CSAS Admissions, 734-764-0352, *Fax:* 734-936-0996, *E-mail:* csseas@umich.edu. *Web site:* http://www.umich.edu/~iinet/csseas/

■ UNIVERSITY OF MICHIGAN

Horace H. Rackham School of Graduate Studies, College of Literature, Science, and the Arts, Center for Southeast Asian Studies, Ann Arbor, MI 48109

AWARDS AM, MBA/AM. Part-time programs available.

Faculty: 24 full-time (10 women), 1 part-time/adjunct (0 women).
Students: 3 full-time (1 woman), 8 part-time (3 women); includes 4 minority (all Asian Americans or Pacific Islanders). Average age 25. 7 applicants, 86% accepted, 1 enrolled. In 2001, 4 degrees awarded.
Degree requirements: For master's, one foreign language, thesis. *Median time to degree:* Master's–4 years full-time.
Entrance requirements: For master's, GRE General Test. *Application deadline:* For fall admission, 1/15 (priority date). Applications are processed on a rolling basis. *Application fee:* $55. Electronic applications accepted.
Financial support: In 2001–02, 8 fellowships with full tuition reimbursements (averaging $11,000 per year) were awarded; career-related internships or fieldwork, Federal Work-Study, institutionally sponsored loans, and scholarships/grants also available. Financial award application deadline: 2/1; financial award applicants required to submit FAFSA.
Faculty research: Real behavior and education, film and cinema, language, musicology, ethnology.
Judith Becker, Director, 734-764-0352, *Fax:* 734-936-0996, *E-mail:* beckerj@umich.edu.
Application contact: Zoe Stevens, CSEAS Admissions, 734-764-1352, *Fax:* 734-936-0996, *E-mail:* csseas@umich.edu. *Web site:* http://www.umich.edu/~innet/csseas/cseos/

■ UNIVERSITY OF MICHIGAN

Horace H. Rackham School of Graduate Studies, College of Literature, Science, and the Arts, Department of Asian Languages and Cultures, Ann Arbor, MI 48109

AWARDS MA, PhD.

Faculty: 11 full-time (4 women), 7 part-time/adjunct (0 women).
Students: 32 full-time (13 women); includes 7 minority (all Asian Americans or Pacific Islanders), 1 international. Average age 30. 88 applicants, 9% accepted. In 2001, 5 master's, 3 doctorates awarded. Terminal master's awarded for partial completion of doctoral program.
Degree requirements: For master's, variable foreign language requirement, thesis; for doctorate, one foreign language, thesis/dissertation, oral defense of dissertation, preliminary exam.
Entrance requirements: For master's and doctorate, GRE General Test, TOEFL. *Application deadline:* For fall admission, 1/1. *Application fee:* $55. Electronic applications accepted.
Financial support: In 2001–02, 3 fellowships with full tuition reimbursements (averaging $16,500 per year), 15 teaching assistantships with full tuition reimbursements (averaging $16,500 per year) were awarded. Research assistantships, Federal Work-Study also available. Support available to part-time students. Financial award application deadline: 1/1; financial award applicants required to submit FAFSA.
Faculty research: Literature, linguistics, religion, philosophy, music, cinema.
Dr. Donald S. Lopez, Chair, 734-764-8286, *Fax:* 734-647-0157, *E-mail:* alcgradinfo@umich.edu.
Application contact: Cornelius Wright, Graduate Student Services Assistant, 734-936-3915, *Fax:* 734-647-0157, *E-mail:* cornw@umich.edu. *Web site:* http://www.lsa.umich.edu/asian/

■ UNIVERSITY OF MINNESOTA, TWIN CITIES CAMPUS

Graduate School, College of Liberal Arts, Program in East Asian Studies, Minneapolis, MN 55455-0213

AWARDS MA. Part-time programs available.

Faculty: 15 full-time.
Students: 2 full-time (both women), (both international). 5 applicants, 40% accepted, 0 enrolled.
Degree requirements: For master's, one foreign language, thesis or alternative. *Median time to degree:* Master's–3 years full-time.
Entrance requirements: For master's, GRE, TOEFL. *Application deadline:* Applications are processed on a rolling basis. *Application fee:* $40 ($50 for international students).
Expenses: Tuition, state resident: full-time $2,932; part-time $489 per credit. Tuition, nonresident: full-time $5,758; part-time $960 per credit. Part-time tuition and fees vary according to course load, program and reciprocity agreements.
Dr. Evelyn Davidheiser, Associate Director, 612-624-9007, *Fax:* 612-626-2242, *E-mail:* igs@umn.edu.
Application contact: Adviser, 612-624-8543, *Fax:* 612-626-2242, *E-mail:* aspiis@tc.umn.edu.

■ UNIVERSITY OF OREGON

Graduate School, College of Arts and Sciences, Program in Asian Studies, Eugene, OR 97403

AWARDS MA. Part-time programs available.

Students: 8 full-time (all women), 1 part-time; includes 2 minority (both Asian Americans or Pacific Islanders), 4 international. 24 applicants, 38% accepted. In 2001, 7 degrees awarded.
Degree requirements: For master's, one foreign language, thesis or alternative.
Entrance requirements: For master's, GRE General Test, TOEFL. *Application deadline:* For fall admission, 2/15; for winter admission, 9/15. *Application fee:* $50.
Expenses: Tuition, state resident: full-time $4,968; part-time $501 per credit hour. Tuition, nonresident: full-time $8,400; part-time $691 per credit hour.
Financial support: In 2001–02, 10 teaching assistantships were awarded; fellowships, Federal Work-Study also available. Financial award application deadline: 2/15.
Faculty research: East and Southeast Asia, Pacific Islands.
Bryna Goodman, Director, 541-346-5082, *Fax:* 541-346-0802.
Application contact: Chingling Reed, Coordinator, 541-346-5052, *Fax:* 541-346-0802. *Web site:* http://darkwing.uoregon.edu/~ast/

■ UNIVERSITY OF PENNSYLVANIA

School of Arts and Sciences, Graduate Group in Asian and Middle Eastern Studies, Philadelphia, PA 19104

AWARDS AM, PhD, JD/AM, JD/PhD. Part-time programs available. Terminal master's awarded for partial completion of doctoral program.

Degree requirements: For master's, thesis or alternative; for doctorate, thesis/dissertation.
Entrance requirements: For master's and doctorate, GRE General Test, TOEFL.
Expenses: Tuition: Part-time $12,875 per semester.

■ UNIVERSITY OF PENNSYLVANIA

School of Arts and Sciences, Graduate Group in South Asian Regional Studies, Philadelphia, PA 19104

AWARDS AM, PhD. Terminal master's awarded for partial completion of doctoral program.

Degree requirements: For master's, one foreign language, thesis, written exam; for doctorate, 3 foreign languages, thesis/dissertation, written exam.

Entrance requirements: For master's, GRE General Test; for doctorate, TOEFL.
Expenses: Tuition: Part-time $12,875 per semester.
Faculty research: South Asian linguistics, literature, and history; economic history.

■ UNIVERSITY OF PITTSBURGH

Faculty of Arts and Sciences, Department of East Asian Languages and Literatures, Pittsburgh, PA 15260

AWARDS East Asian studies (MA). Part-time programs available.

Faculty: 7 full-time (2 women), 4 part-time/adjunct (3 women).
Students: 6 full-time (1 woman), 1 (woman) part-time; includes 1 minority (Asian American or Pacific Islander). Average age 28. 13 applicants, 54% accepted, 2 enrolled. In 2001, 3 degrees awarded.
Degree requirements: For master's, one foreign language, thesis, oral comprehensive exam, comprehensive exam. *Median time to degree:* Master's–2 years full-time.
Entrance requirements: For master's, GRE General Test, TOEFL, 2 years of Chinese or Japanese, minimum QPA of 3.0. *Application deadline:* For fall admission, 1/15. *Application fee:* $40. Electronic applications accepted.
Expenses: Tuition, state resident: full-time $9,410; part-time $385 per credit. Tuition, nonresident: full-time $19,376; part-time $797 per credit. Required fees: $480; $90 per term. Tuition and fees vary according to program.
Financial support: In 2001–02, 6 students received support, including 1 fellowship with tuition reimbursement available (averaging $11,980 per year); scholarships/grants, tuition waivers (partial), and unspecified assistantships also available. Financial award application deadline: 1/30.
Faculty research: Chinese literature and poetry; Japanese literature, film, and theater; Chinese society and culture; East Asian foreign policy, security studies, and economic history; Japanese performing arts and fine arts.
Dr. Hiroshi Nara, Chairman, 412-624-5568, *Fax:* 412-624-3458, *E-mail:* hnara@pitt.edu.
Application contact: Paula Locante, Administrator, 412-624-5569, *Fax:* 412-624-3458, *E-mail:* plocante@pitt.edu. *Web site:* http://www.pitt.edu/~deall/

■ UNIVERSITY OF SAN FRANCISCO

College of Arts and Sciences, Program in Asia Pacific Studies, San Francisco, CA 94117-1080

AWARDS MA. Part-time and evening/weekend programs available.

Faculty: 4 full-time (2 women), 8 part-time/adjunct (5 women).
Students: 21 full-time (9 women), 1 (woman) part-time; includes 7 minority (2 African Americans, 5 Asian Americans or Pacific Islanders), 2 international. Average age 35. 23 applicants, 100% accepted, 11 enrolled. In 2001, 6 degrees awarded.
Degree requirements: For master's, one foreign language, thesis.
Entrance requirements: For master's, minimum GPA of 3.0. *Application deadline:* Applications are processed on a rolling basis. *Application fee:* $55 ($65 for international students).
Expenses: Tuition: Full-time $14,400; part-time $800 per unit. Tuition and fees vary according to degree level, campus/location and program.
Financial support: In 2001–02, 12 students received support. Career-related internships or fieldwork, Federal Work-Study, and institutionally sponsored loans available. Financial award application deadline: 3/2; financial award applicants required to submit FAFSA.
Faculty research: History of Christianity in China, U.S.-China policy, East Asian economies and political systems, sociolinguistic aspects of Japanese.
Dr. Shalondra Sharma, Director, 415-422-6452, *Fax:* 415-422-2291.

Find an in-depth description at www.petersons.com/gradchannel.

■ UNIVERSITY OF SOUTHERN CALIFORNIA

Graduate School, College of Letters, Arts and Sciences, Department of East Asian Languages and Cultures, Program in East Asian Languages and Cultures, Los Angeles, CA 90089

AWARDS MA, PhD.

Degree requirements: For doctorate, thesis/dissertation.
Entrance requirements: For master's and doctorate, GRE General Test.
Expenses: Tuition: Full-time $25,060; part-time $844 per unit. Required fees: $473.

■ UNIVERSITY OF SOUTHERN CALIFORNIA

Graduate School, College of Letters, Arts and Sciences, Department of East Asian Languages and Cultures, Program in East Asian Studies, Los Angeles, CA 90089

AWARDS MA, MBA/MA.

Entrance requirements: For master's, GRE General Test.
Expenses: Tuition: Full-time $25,060; part-time $844 per unit. Required fees: $473.

■ THE UNIVERSITY OF TEXAS AT AUSTIN

Graduate School, College of Liberal Arts, Center for Asian Studies, Austin, TX 78712-1111

AWARDS MA, MBA/MA, MP Aff/MA. Part-time programs available.

Students: 21 applicants, 52% accepted. In 2001, 10 degrees awarded.
Degree requirements: For master's, one foreign language, thesis.
Entrance requirements: For master's, GRE General Test. *Application deadline:* For fall admission, 2/1 (priority date); for spring admission, 10/1. Applications are processed on a rolling basis. *Application fee:* $50 ($75 for international students). Electronic applications accepted.
Expenses: Tuition, state resident: full-time $3,159. Tuition, nonresident: full-time $6,957. Tuition and fees vary according to program.
Financial support: In 2001–02, 5 fellowships with tuition reimbursements, 3 teaching assistantships with tuition reimbursements (averaging $11,000 per year) were awarded. Scholarships/grants also available. Financial award application deadline: 2/1.
Kathryn Hansen, Director, 512-471-5811, *Fax:* 512-471-4469.
Application contact: Anne Alexander, Graduate Coordinator, 512-471-5811, *Fax:* 512-471-4469, *E-mail:* cervuli@mail.utexas.edu. *Web site:* http://www.asnic.utexas.edu/asnic/cas/index.htm

■ THE UNIVERSITY OF TEXAS AT AUSTIN

Graduate School, College of Liberal Arts, Department of Asian Studies, Austin, TX 78712-1111

AWARDS Asian cultures and languages (MA, PhD). Part-time programs available.

Students: 24 applicants, 58% accepted. In 2001, 3 degrees awarded.
Degree requirements: For master's, thesis; for doctorate, 3 foreign languages, thesis/dissertation.
Entrance requirements: For master's and doctorate, GRE General Test. *Application deadline:* For fall admission, 2/1 (priority date); for spring admission, 10/1. Applications are processed on a rolling basis. *Application fee:* $50 ($75 for international students). Electronic applications accepted.
Expenses: Tuition, state resident: full-time $3,159. Tuition, nonresident: full-time $6,957. Tuition and fees vary according to program.
Financial support: In 2001–02, 8 fellowships with tuition reimbursements, 4 teaching assistantships with tuition reimbursements (averaging $11,000 per year) were awarded. Scholarships/grants also available. Financial award application deadline: 2/1.

The University of Texas at Austin (continued)
Faculty research: Modern Taiwanese fiction, modern Japanese literature, religious studies in South Asia during classical period.
J. Patrick Olivelle, Chairman, 512-471-5811, *Fax:* 512-471-4469.
Application contact: Anne Alexander, Graduate Coordinator, 512-471-5811, *Fax:* 512-471-4469, *E-mail:* ansgrads@uts.cc.utexas.edu. *Web site:* http://www.asnic.utexas.edu/asmic/index.html

■ UNIVERSITY OF VIRGINIA

College and Graduate School of Arts and Sciences, Division of Asian and Middle Eastern Languages and Cultures, Charlottesville, VA 22903

AWARDS MA, MBA/MA.

Faculty: 18 full-time (11 women), 2 part-time/adjunct (1 woman).
Students: 1 (woman) full-time, 1 (woman) part-time; includes 1 minority (Native American). Average age 41. 9 applicants, 56% accepted, 1 enrolled. In 2001, 2 degrees awarded.
Entrance requirements: For master's, GRE General Test. *Application deadline:* For fall admission, 7/15; for spring admission, 12/1. Applications are processed on a rolling basis. *Application fee:* $40. Electronic applications accepted.
Expenses: Tuition, state resident: full-time $3,988. Tuition, nonresident: full-time $17,078. Required fees: $1,190.
Financial support: Application deadline: 2/1.
Robert Hueckstedt, Chairman, 434-982-2304, *Fax:* 434-924-6977.
Application contact: Duane J. Osheim, Associate Dean for Graduate Programs, 434-924-7184, *Fax:* 434-924-3084, *E-mail:* grad-a-s@virginia.edu. *Web site:* http://www.virginia.edu/~amelc/

■ UNIVERSITY OF WASHINGTON

Graduate School, College of Arts and Sciences, Henry M. Jackson School of International Studies, China Studies Program, Seattle, WA 98195

AWARDS MAIS.

Faculty: 29 full-time (12 women).
Students: 28 full-time (18 women); includes 3 minority (1 African American, 2 Asian Americans or Pacific Islanders), 9 international. Average age 28. 36 applicants, 83% accepted. In 2001, 10 degrees awarded.
Degree requirements: For master's, one foreign language, thesis optional.
Entrance requirements: For master's, GRE General Test, TOEFL, minimum GPA of 3.0. *Application deadline:* For fall admission, 1/15 (priority date). *Application fee:* $45. Electronic applications accepted.
Expenses: Tuition, state resident: full-time $5,539. Tuition, nonresident: full-time $14,376. Required fees: $390. Tuition and fees vary according to course load and program.
Financial support: In 2001–02, 1 teaching assistantship was awarded; fellowships, research assistantships, career-related internships or fieldwork, Federal Work-Study, and institutionally sponsored loans also available. Financial award application deadline: 1/15; financial award applicants required to submit FAFSA.
Prof. David M. Bachman, Chair, 206-685-1945.
Application contact: 206-543-6001, *Fax:* 206-616-3170, *E-mail:* jsisinfo@u.washington.edu. *Web site:* http://jsis.artsci.washington.edu/

■ UNIVERSITY OF WASHINGTON

Graduate School, College of Arts and Sciences, Henry M. Jackson School of International Studies, Japan Studies Program, Seattle, WA 98195

AWARDS MAIS.

Faculty: 20 full-time (10 women).
Students: 12 full-time (7 women); includes 2 minority (both Asian Americans or Pacific Islanders), 2 international. Average age 27. 20 applicants, 70% accepted. In 2001, 1 degree awarded.
Degree requirements: For master's, one foreign language.
Entrance requirements: For master's, GRE General Test, TOEFL, minimum GPA of 3.0. *Application deadline:* For fall admission, 1/15 (priority date). *Application fee:* $45. Electronic applications accepted.
Expenses: Tuition, state resident: full-time $5,539. Tuition, nonresident: full-time $14,376. Required fees: $390. Tuition and fees vary according to course load and program.
Financial support: In 2001–02, 4 research assistantships with full tuition reimbursements were awarded; fellowships, teaching assistantships, career-related internships or fieldwork, Federal Work-Study, and institutionally sponsored loans also available. Financial award application deadline: 1/15; financial award applicants required to submit FAFSA.
Prof. Marie Anchordoguy, Chair, 206-543-1693.
Application contact: 206-543-6001, *Fax:* 206-616-3170, *E-mail:* jsisinfo@u.washington.edu. *Web site:* http://jsis.artsci.washington.edu/

■ UNIVERSITY OF WASHINGTON

Graduate School, College of Arts and Sciences, Henry M. Jackson School of International Studies, Korea Studies Program, Seattle, WA 98195

AWARDS MAIS.

Faculty: 5 full-time (2 women).
Students: 11 full-time (3 women); includes 3 minority (all Asian Americans or Pacific Islanders), 5 international. Average age 30. 16 applicants, 94% accepted. In 2001, 2 degrees awarded.
Degree requirements: For master's, one foreign language.
Entrance requirements: For master's, GRE General Test, TOEFL, minimum GPA of 3.0. *Application deadline:* For fall admission, 1/15 (priority date). *Application fee:* $45. Electronic applications accepted.
Expenses: Tuition, state resident: full-time $5,539. Tuition, nonresident: full-time $14,376. Required fees: $390. Tuition and fees vary according to course load and program.
Financial support: In 2001–02, 2 fellowships with tuition reimbursements were awarded; research assistantships, career-related internships or fieldwork, Federal Work-Study, institutionally sponsored loans, and summer language study awards also available. Financial award application deadline: 1/15; financial award applicants required to submit FAFSA.
Prof. Clark W. Sorsensen, Chair, 206-543-1696, *E-mail:* sangok@u.washington.edu.
Application contact: 206-543-6001, *Fax:* 206-616-3170, *E-mail:* jsisinfo@u.washington.edu. *Web site:* http://jsis.artsci.washington.edu/

■ UNIVERSITY OF WASHINGTON

Graduate School, College of Arts and Sciences, Henry M. Jackson School of International Studies, Russian, East European and Central Asian Studies Program, Seattle, WA 98195

AWARDS Central Asian studies (MAIS); East European studies (MAIS); Russian studies (MAIS).

Faculty: 46 full-time (20 women).
Students: 37 full-time (20 women); includes 1 minority (African American), 4 international. Average age 29. 43 applicants, 93% accepted. In 2001, 8 degrees awarded.
Degree requirements: For master's, one foreign language, thesis.
Entrance requirements: For master's, GRE General Test, TOEFL, 2 years of relevant language, minimum GPA of 3.0. *Application deadline:* For fall admission, 1/15 (priority date). *Application fee:* $45. Electronic applications accepted.
Expenses: Tuition, state resident: full-time $5,539. Tuition, nonresident: full-time $14,376. Required fees: $390. Tuition and fees vary according to course load and program.
Financial support: In 2001–02, 5 fellowships with tuition reimbursements were awarded; research assistantships, teaching assistantships, career-related internships or fieldwork, Federal Work-Study, institutionally sponsored loans, and summer language study awards also available. Financial award application deadline: 1/15.
Prof. Stephen E. Hanson, Chair, 206-543-9460, *Fax:* 206-685-0668, *E-mail:* shanson@u.washington.edu.

Application contact: 206-543-6001, *Fax:* 206-616-3170, *E-mail:* jsisinfo@u.washington.edu. *Web site:* http://jsis.artsci.washington.edu/

■ UNIVERSITY OF WASHINGTON

Graduate School, College of Arts and Sciences, Henry M. Jackson School of International Studies, South Asian Studies Program, Seattle, WA 98195

AWARDS MAIS.

Degree requirements: For master's, one foreign language.
Entrance requirements: For master's, GRE General Test, TOEFL, minimum GPA of 3.0. Electronic applications accepted.
Expenses: Tuition, state resident: full-time $5,539. Tuition, nonresident: full-time $14,376. Required fees: $390. Tuition and fees vary according to course load and program. *Web site:* http://jsis.artsci.washington.edu/

■ UNIVERSITY OF WISCONSIN–MADISON

Graduate School, College of Letters and Science, Center for Southeast Asian Studies, Madison, WI 53706

AWARDS MA. Part-time programs available.

Degree requirements: For master's, one foreign language.
Electronic applications accepted.
Expenses: Tuition, state resident: full-time $7,361; part-time $399 per credit. Tuition, nonresident: full-time $20,499; part-time $1,282 per credit. Required fees: $34 per credit. Full-time tuition and fees vary according to course load, program, reciprocity agreements and student level.
Faculty research: Economic development, censorship, political change, pedagogical developments in Indonesia, Philippine historical demography, environment photography. *Web site:* http://www.wisc.edu/ctrseasia/

■ UNIVERSITY OF WISCONSIN–MADISON

Graduate School, College of Letters and Science, Department of Languages and Cultures of Asia, Madison, WI 53706-1380

AWARDS MA, PhD. Part-time programs available. Terminal master's awarded for partial completion of doctoral program.

Degree requirements: For master's, one foreign language, thesis or alternative; for doctorate, 2 foreign languages, thesis/dissertation.
Entrance requirements: For master's, minimum GPA of 3.0; for doctorate, minimum GPA of 3.25, master's degree. Electronic applications accepted.
Expenses: Tuition, state resident: full-time $7,361; part-time $399 per credit. Tuition, nonresident: full-time $20,499; part-time $1,282 per credit. Required fees: $34 per credit. Full-time tuition and fees vary according to course load, program, reciprocity agreements and student level.
Faculty research: Literature, folklore, religion. *Web site:* http://polyglot.lss.wisc.edu/langasia/

■ WASHINGTON UNIVERSITY IN ST. LOUIS

Graduate School of Arts and Sciences, Department of Asian and Near Eastern Languages and Literatures, St. Louis, MO 63130-4899

AWARDS Asian language (MA); Asian studies (MA); Chinese (PhD); comparative literature (MA, PhD); Japanese (PhD). Part-time programs available.

Students: 24 full-time (12 women), 1 (woman) part-time; includes 2 minority (both Asian Americans or Pacific Islanders), 13 international. 48 applicants, 50% accepted. In 2001, 10 master's, 4 doctorates awarded. Terminal master's awarded for partial completion of doctoral program.
Degree requirements: For master's, thesis optional; for doctorate, thesis/dissertation.
Entrance requirements: For master's and doctorate, GRE General Test. *Application deadline:* For fall admission, 1/15 (priority date). Applications are processed on a rolling basis. *Application fee:* $35. Electronic applications accepted.
Expenses: Tuition: Full-time $26,900.
Financial support: Teaching assistantships, Federal Work-Study, institutionally sponsored loans, and tuition waivers (full and partial) available. Support available to part-time students. Financial award application deadline: 1/15.
Dr. Beata Grant, Chairperson, 314-935-5156. *Web site:* http://artsci.wustl.edu/~smbenjam/anell/html

■ WASHINGTON UNIVERSITY IN ST. LOUIS

Graduate School of Arts and Sciences, Program in East Asian Studies, St. Louis, MO 63130-4899

AWARDS Art history (PhD); Chinese (MA); Chinese and comparative literature (PhD); East Asian studies (MA); history (PhD); Japanese (MA); Japanese and comparative literature (PhD). PhD offered through specific departments. Part-time programs available.

Students: 15 full-time (8 women), 1 (woman) part-time; includes 1 minority (Asian American or Pacific Islander), 7 international. 24 applicants, 67% accepted. In 2001, 3 degrees awarded.
Entrance requirements: For master's and doctorate, GRE General Test. *Application deadline:* For fall admission, 1/15 (priority date). Applications are processed on a rolling basis. *Application fee:* $35. Electronic applications accepted.
Expenses: Tuition: Full-time $26,900.
Financial support: Fellowships, research assistantships, teaching assistantships available. Financial award application deadline: 1/15.
Dr. Rebecca Copeland, Chairperson, 314-935-4448. *Web site:* http://artsci.wustl.edu/~eas/

■ WEST VIRGINIA UNIVERSITY

Eberly College of Arts and Sciences, Department of History, Morgantown, WV 26506

AWARDS African history (MA, PhD); African-American history (MA, PhD); American history (MA, PhD); Appalachian/regional history (MA, PhD); East Asian history (MA, PhD); European history (MA, PhD); history of science and technology (MA, PhD); Latin American history (MA). Part-time programs available.

Faculty: 19 full-time (4 women), 2 part-time/adjunct (1 woman).
Students: 35 full-time (13 women), 29 part-time (10 women); includes 5 minority (2 African Americans, 1 Asian American or Pacific Islander, 1 Hispanic American, 1 Native American), 5 international. Average age 34. 86 applicants, 44% accepted. In 2001, 4 master's, 1 doctorate awarded.
Degree requirements: For master's, one foreign language; for doctorate, one foreign language, comprehensive exam, dissertation defense.
Entrance requirements: For master's, GRE General Test, TOEFL, minimum GPA of 3.0; for doctorate, GRE General Test, TOEFL, MA or equivalent. *Application deadline:* For spring admission, 11/1. Applications are processed on a rolling basis. *Application fee:* $45.
Expenses: Tuition, state resident: full-time $2,791. Tuition, nonresident: full-time $8,659. Required fees: $1,002. Tuition and fees vary according to program.
Financial support: In 2001–02, 43 students received support, including 2 research assistantships, 23 teaching assistantships; fellowships, career-related internships or fieldwork, Federal Work-Study, institutionally sponsored loans, tuition waivers (full and partial), and graduate administrative assistantships also available. Financial award application deadline: 2/1; financial award applicants required to submit FAFSA.
Faculty research: U.S., Appalachia, modern Europe, Africa, science and technology.
Dr. Robert M. Maxon, Chair, 304-293-2421 Ext. 5223, *Fax:* 304-293-3616, *E-mail:* robert.maxon@mail.wvu.edu.
Application contact: Dr. Robert E. Blobaum, Director of Graduate Studies, 304-293-2421 Ext. 5241, *Fax:* 304-293-3616, *E-mail:* robert.blobaum@mail.wvu.edu. *Web site:* http://www.as.wvu.edu/history/

■ **YALE UNIVERSITY**

Graduate School of Arts and Sciences, Program in East Asian Studies, New Haven, CT 06520

AWARDS MA.

Degree requirements: For master's, one foreign language.
Entrance requirements: For master's, GRE General Test.

CANADIAN STUDIES

■ **JOHNS HOPKINS UNIVERSITY**

Paul H. Nitze School of Advanced International Studies, Washington, DC 20036

AWARDS Emerging markets (Certificate); interdisciplinary studies (MA, PhD), including African studies, American foreign policy (MA), Asian studies, Canadian studies, conflict resolution and mediation (MA), environmental policy and resource management (MA), European studies, international business (MA), international development (MA), international economics (MA), international relations (MA), Latin American studies, Middle Eastern studies (MA), military and defense studies (MA), Russian area and East European studies (MA), social change and development (MA); international public policy (MIPP). MBA/MA offered jointly with the University of Pennsylvania–Wharton School and INSEAD in France.

Faculty: 44 full-time (13 women), 113 part-time/adjunct (29 women).
Students: 567 full-time (275 women), 17 part-time (8 women); includes 71 minority (14 African Americans, 46 Asian Americans or Pacific Islanders, 10 Hispanic Americans, 1 Native American). Average age 27. 1,288 applicants, 35% accepted. In 2001, 294 master's, 13 doctorates, 34 other advanced degrees awarded. Terminal master's awarded for partial completion of doctoral program.
Degree requirements: For master's, one foreign language, comprehensive exam; for doctorate, 2 foreign languages, thesis/dissertation.
Entrance requirements: For master's, GMAT or GRE General Test or TOEFL, previous course work in economics, foreign language; for doctorate, GRE General Test or TOEFL; for Certificate, TOEFL. *Application deadline:* For fall admission, 1/15. *Application fee:* $75. Electronic applications accepted.
Expenses: Contact institution.
Financial support: In 2001–02, 431 fellowships (averaging $5,500 per year) were awarded; career-related internships or fieldwork and Federal Work-Study also available. Financial award application deadline: 2/1; financial award applicants required to submit FAFSA.
Faculty research: Comparative politics, regional studies, language and linguistics.
Dr. Jessica Einhorn, Dean, 202-663-5624, *Fax:* 202-663-5621.
Application contact: Bonnie Wilson, Associate Dean of Student Affairs, 202-663-5700, *Fax:* 202-663-7788, *E-mail:* admissions.sais@jhu.edu. *Web site:* http://www.sais-jhu.edu/

Find an in-depth description at www.petersons.com/gradchannel.

CULTURAL STUDIES

■ **CLAREMONT GRADUATE UNIVERSITY**

Graduate Programs, Center for the Humanities, Department of Cultural Studies, Claremont, CA 91711-6160

AWARDS MA, PhD. Part-time programs available.

Faculty: 2 full-time (1 woman), 2 part-time/adjunct (1 woman).
Students: 32 full-time (24 women), 11 part-time (6 women); includes 18 minority (5 African Americans, 5 Asian Americans or Pacific Islanders, 8 Hispanic Americans), 2 international. Average age 35. In 2001, 4 master's, 1 doctorate awarded.
Degree requirements: For master's, one foreign language, thesis; for doctorate, 2 foreign languages, thesis/dissertation, comprehensive exam.
Entrance requirements: For master's and doctorate, GRE General Test. *Application deadline:* For fall admission, 2/15 (priority date). Applications are processed on a rolling basis. *Application fee:* $50. Electronic applications accepted.
Expenses: Tuition: Full-time $22,984; part-time $1,000 per unit. Required fees: $160; $80 per semester.
Financial support: Fellowships, research assistantships, career-related internships or fieldwork, Federal Work-Study, and institutionally sponsored loans available. Support available to part-time students. Financial award application deadline: 2/15; financial award applicants required to submit FAFSA.
Elazar Barkan, Chair, 909-607-1271, *Fax:* 909-621-8609, *E-mail:* elazar.barkan@cgu.edu.
Application contact: Holly Domingo, Department Secretary, 909-621-8002, *Fax:* 909-607-1221, *E-mail:* cultural@cgu.edu. *Web site:* http://www.cgu.edu/hum/cul/index.html

■ **CORNELL UNIVERSITY**

Graduate School, Graduate Fields of Arts and Sciences, Field of English Language and Literature, Ithaca, NY 14853-0001

AWARDS African-American literature (PhD); American literature after 1865 (PhD); American literature to 1865 (PhD); American studies (PhD); colonial and postcolonial literature (PhD); creative writing (MFA); cultural studies (PhD); dramatic literature (PhD); English poetry (PhD); English Renaissance to 1660 (PhD); lesbian, bisexual, and gay literature studies (PhD); literary criticism and theory (PhD); nineteenth century (PhD); Old and Middle English (PhD); prose fiction (PhD); Restoration and eighteenth century (PhD); twentieth century (PhD); women's literature (PhD).

Faculty: 50 full-time.
Students: 101 full-time (55 women); includes 34 minority (8 African Americans, 9 Asian Americans or Pacific Islanders, 11 Hispanic Americans, 6 Native Americans), 17 international. 614 applicants, 7% accepted. In 2001, 21 master's, 8 doctorates awarded. Terminal master's awarded for partial completion of doctoral program.
Degree requirements: For master's, one foreign language, thesis; for doctorate, one foreign language, thesis/dissertation, teaching experience.
Entrance requirements: For master's, GRE General Test, TOEFL, 3 letters of recommendation, creative writing sample; for doctorate, GRE General Test, GRE Subject Test (English), TOEFL, 3 letters of recommendation, critical writing sample. *Application deadline:* For fall admission, 1/10. *Application fee:* $65. Electronic applications accepted.
Expenses: Tuition: Full-time $25,970. Required fees: $50.
Financial support: In 2001–02, 90 students received support, including 47 fellowships with full tuition reimbursements available, 43 teaching assistantships with full tuition reimbursements available; research assistantships with full tuition reimbursements available, institutionally sponsored loans, scholarships/grants, tuition waivers (full and partial), and unspecified assistantships also available. Financial award applicants required to submit FAFSA.
Faculty research: English and American literature, women's writing ethnic and post-colonial literature.
Application contact: Graduate Field Assistant, 607-255-7989, *E-mail:* english_grad@cornell.edu. *Web site:* http://www.gradschool.cornell.edu/grad/fields_1/english.html

■ **GEORGE MASON UNIVERSITY**

College of Arts and Sciences, Program in Cultural Studies, Fairfax, VA 22030-4444

AWARDS PhD.

Faculty: 2 full-time (0 women).
Students: 4 full-time (0 women), 40 part-time (29 women); includes 6 minority (2 African Americans, 2 Asian Americans or Pacific Islanders, 2 Hispanic Americans), 5 international. Average age 39. 35 applicants, 54% accepted, 9 enrolled.

Degree requirements: For doctorate, one foreign language, thesis/dissertation, foreign language exams, comprehensive exam.
Entrance requirements: For doctorate, GRE General Test, TOEFL, sample of written work, MA or simultaneous application to related MA program at George Mason University. *Application deadline:* For fall admission, 1/15. *Application fee:* $30. Electronic applications accepted.
Expenses: Tuition, state resident: full-time $3,168; part-time $132 per credit hour. Tuition, nonresident: full-time $11,280; part-time $470 per credit hour. Required fees: $1,416; $59 per credit hour.
Financial support: Fellowships, research assistantships, teaching assistantships, tuition remissions available. Support available to part-time students. Financial award application deadline: 1/15; financial award applicants required to submit FAFSA.
Roger N. Lancaster, Chairman, 703-993-2851, *Fax:* 703-993-2852, *E-mail:* cultural@gmu.edu. *Web site:* http://www.gmu.edu/departments/cultural/

Find an in-depth description at www.petersons.com/gradchannel.

■ GRADUATE THEOLOGICAL UNION

Graduate Programs, Berkeley, CA 94709-1212

AWARDS Arts and religion (MA, Th D); biblical languages (MA); biblical studies (Old and New Testament) (MA, PhD, Th D); Buddhist studies (MA); Christian spirituality (MA); cultural and historical studies (MA, PhD); ethics and social theory (PhD); historical studies (MA, PhD, Th D); history of art and religion (PhD); homiletics (MA, PhD, Th D); interdisciplinary studies (PhD, Th D); Jewish studies (MA, PhD, Certificate); liturgical studies (MA, PhD, Th D); Near Eastern religions (PhD); religion and psychology (MA, PhD); religion and society (MA); systematic and philosophical theology (MA, PhD, Th D);). MA/M Div offered jointly with individual denominations.

Faculty: 80 full-time (29 women), 14 part-time/adjunct (3 women).
Students: 308 full-time (154 women), 39 part-time (13 women); includes 48 minority (9 African Americans, 28 Asian Americans or Pacific Islanders, 9 Hispanic Americans, 2 Native Americans), 60 international. Average age 42. 193 applicants, 65% accepted, 76 enrolled. In 2001, 28 master's, 20 doctorates awarded. Terminal master's awarded for partial completion of doctoral program.
Degree requirements: For master's, one foreign language, thesis/dissertation; for doctorate, one foreign language, thesis/dissertation, comprehensive exam.
Entrance requirements: For master's, GRE General Test, TOEFL; for doctorate, GRE General Test, TOEFL, MA or M Div degree. *Application deadline:* For fall admission, 12/15; for winter admission, 2/15; for spring admission, 9/30. *Application fee:* $40. Electronic applications accepted.
Expenses: Tuition: Full-time $16,000. Tuition and fees vary according to degree level.
Financial support: In 2001–02, 160 students received support, including 15 fellowships (averaging $19,000 per year), 22 research assistantships (averaging $4,000 per year); teaching assistantships, Federal Work-Study, scholarships/grants, and tuition waivers (full and partial) also available. Support available to part-time students. Financial award application deadline: 2/1; financial award applicants required to submit FAFSA.
Dr. Eldon G. Ernst, Interim Dean, 510-649-2440, *Fax:* 510-649-1417, *E-mail:* eernst@gtu.edu.
Application contact: Dr. Kathleen Kook, Assistant Dean for Admissions, 800-826-4488, *Fax:* 510-649-1730, *E-mail:* gtuadm@gtu.edu. *Web site:* http://www.gtu.edu/

■ SIMMONS COLLEGE

Graduate School, College of Arts and Sciences and Professional Studies, Program in Gender/Cultural Studies, Boston, MA 02115

AWARDS MA. Part-time programs available.

Faculty: 17 full-time (13 women).
Students: 9 full-time (all women), 22 part-time (all women). Average age 26. 27 applicants, 78% accepted. In 2001, 6 degrees awarded.
Degree requirements: For master's, project, thesis, internship, or fieldwork, thesis optional.
Application deadline: Applications are processed on a rolling basis. *Application fee:* $35. Electronic applications accepted.
Financial support: In 2001–02, teaching assistantships (averaging $3,400 per year); research assistantships, Federal Work-Study, institutionally sponsored loans, and scholarships/grants also available. Support available to part-time students. Financial award application deadline: 3/1; financial award applicants required to submit FAFSA.
Dr. Jyoti Puri, Director, 617-521-2593, *E-mail:* jyoti.puri@simmons.edu.
Application contact: Bryan E. Moody, Director, Graduate Enrollment Management and Admission, 617-521-2910, *Fax:* 617-521-3058, *E-mail:* gsa@simmons.edu. *Web site:* http://www.simmons.edu/

■ SONOMA STATE UNIVERSITY

School of Education, Department of Reading, Language, and Culture, Rohnert Park, CA 94928-3609

AWARDS Culture (MA); language (MA); reading (MA). Part-time and evening/weekend programs available.

Faculty: 3 full-time (2 women), 6 part-time/adjunct (4 women).
Students: 1 (woman) full-time, 27 part-time (all women); includes 3 minority (1 Asian American or Pacific Islander, 2 Hispanic Americans). Average age 40. 3 applicants, 67% accepted, 2 enrolled. In 2001, 9 degrees awarded.
Degree requirements: For master's, thesis or alternative.
Entrance requirements: For master's, GRE General Test, minimum GPA of 2.5. *Application fee:* $55.
Expenses: Tuition, nonresident: full-time $4,428; part-time $246 per unit. Required fees: $2,084; $727 per semester.
Financial support: Application deadline: 3/2.
Dr. Paul Crowley, Advocate, 707-664-2556, *E-mail:* paul.crowley@sonoma.edu.

■ SOUTHERN ILLINOIS UNIVERSITY CARBONDALE

Graduate School, College of Liberal Arts, Department of Foreign Languages and Literatures, Carbondale, IL 62901-6806

AWARDS MA. Part-time programs available.

Faculty: 18 full-time (5 women), 1 (woman) part-time/adjunct.
Students: 16 full-time (9 women), 2 part-time (both women); includes 6 minority (1 African American, 1 Asian American or Pacific Islander, 4 Hispanic Americans), 7 international. Average age 24. 15 applicants, 80% accepted. In 2001, 9 degrees awarded.
Degree requirements: For master's, one foreign language, thesis.
Entrance requirements: For master's, TOEFL, minimum GPA of 2.7. *Application deadline:* Applications are processed on a rolling basis. *Application fee:* $0.
Expenses: Tuition, state resident: full-time $3,794; part-time $154 per hour. Tuition, nonresident: full-time $6,566; part-time $308 per hour. Required fees: $277 per hour.
Financial support: In 2001–02, 9 students received support; fellowships with full tuition reimbursements available, research assistantships with full tuition reimbursements available, teaching assistantships with full tuition reimbursements available, career-related internships or fieldwork, Federal Work-Study, institutionally sponsored loans, scholarships/grants, and tuition waivers (full) available. Support available to part-time students. Financial award application deadline: 5/15.
Faculty research: Bibliography, historical linguistics, language pedagogy, philology, commercial facets.
Dr. Frederick Betz, Chairperson, 618-453-5435.

Find an in-depth description at www.petersons.com/gradchannel.

■ STONY BROOK UNIVERSITY, STATE UNIVERSITY OF NEW YORK

School of Professional Development and Continuing Studies, Stony Brook, NY 11794

AWARDS Art and philosophy (Certificate); biology 7-12 (MAT); chemistry-grade 7-12 (MAT); coaching (Certificate); computer integrated engineering (Certificate); cultural studies (Certificate); earth science-grade 7-12 (MAT); educational computing (Certificate); English-grade 7-12 (MAT); environmental/ occupational health and safety (Certificate); French-grade 7-12 (MAT); German-grade 7-12 (MAT); human resource management (Certificate); industrial management (Certificate); information systems management (Certificate); Italian-grade 7-12 (MAT); liberal studies (MA); liberal studies online (MA); Long Island regional studies (Certificate); oceanic science (Certificate); operation research (Certificate); physics-grade 7-12 (MAT); Russian-grade 7-12 (MAT); school administration and supervision (Certificate); school district administration (Certificate); social science and the professions (MPS), including labor management, public affairs, waste management; social studies 7-12 (MAT); waste management (Certificate); women's studies (Certificate). Part-time and evening/weekend programs available. Postbaccalaureate distance learning degree programs offered.

Faculty: 1 full-time, 101 part-time/ adjunct.
Students: 240 full-time (133 women), 1,307 part-time (868 women); includes 101 minority (43 African Americans, 13 Asian Americans or Pacific Islanders, 43 Hispanic Americans, 2 Native Americans), 9 international. Average age 28. In 2001, 478 master's, 157 other advanced degrees awarded.
Degree requirements: For master's, one foreign language, thesis or alternative. *Application deadline:* Applications are processed on a rolling basis. *Application fee:* $50.
Expenses: Tuition, state resident: full-time $5,100; part-time $213 per credit. Tuition, nonresident: full-time $8,416; part-time $351 per credit. Required fees: $496.
Financial support: In 2001–02, 1 fellowship, 7 teaching assistantships were awarded. Research assistantships, career-related internships or fieldwork also available. Support available to part-time students.
Dr. Paul J. Edelson, Dean, 631-632-7052, *Fax:* 631-632-9046, *E-mail:* paul.edelson@sunysb.edu.
Application contact: Sandra Romansky, Director of Admissions and Advisement, 631-632-7050, *Fax:* 631-632-9046, *E-mail:* sandra.romansky@sunysb.edu. *Web site:* http://www.sunysb.edu/spd/

■ TRINITY INTERNATIONAL UNIVERSITY

Trinity Evangelical Divinity School, Deerfield, IL 60015-1284

AWARDS Biblical studies (Certificate); biblical, historical and theological studies (M Div); bioethics for the chaplaincy (D Min); children's ministries (MA); Christian thought (MA), including church history, counseling psychology, educational ministries; church history (Th M); counseling ministries (MA); cultural studies (M Div); educational leadership (M Div); educational studies (PhD); evangelism (MA); general studies (MAR); intercultural studies (PhD); interdisciplinary studies (M Div); leadership and management (D Min); missiology (D Min); missions (M Div, MA); missions and evangelism (Th M); New Testament (MA, Th M); Old Testament (MA, Th M); pastoral and general church ministries (M Div); pastoral care (D Min); pastoral counseling (Th M); pastoral ministry (D Min); practical theology (Th M); preaching (D Min); systematics (Th M); theological studies (PhD); urban ministry (MAR); youth ministries (MA). Part-time programs available. Postbaccalaureate distance learning degree programs offered (minimal on-campus study).

Entrance requirements: For M Div, GRE, MAT, minimum GPA of 2.5; for master's, GRE, MAT, cumulative undergraduate GPA of 3.0 or higher. Electronic applications accepted.
Expenses: Contact institution. *Web site:* http://www.tiu.edu/

■ UNIVERSITY OF CALIFORNIA, DAVIS

Graduate Studies, Graduate Group in Cultural Studies, Davis, CA 95616

AWARDS MA, PhD.

Faculty: 66 full-time (42 women).
Students: 15 full-time (11 women); includes 5 minority (2 African Americans, 1 Asian American or Pacific Islander, 2 Hispanic Americans), 2 international. Average age 34. 50 applicants, 28% accepted, 6 enrolled.
Entrance requirements: For doctorate, GRE. *Application deadline:* For fall admission, 1/15 (priority date). *Application fee:* $60. Electronic applications accepted.
Expenses: Tuition, state resident: full-time $4,831. Tuition, nonresident: full-time $15,725.
Financial support: In 2001–02, 12 students received support, including 3 fellowships with full and partial tuition reimbursements available (averaging $10,612 per year), 1 research assistantship with full and partial tuition reimbursement available (averaging $5,485 per year), 10 teaching assistantships with partial tuition reimbursements available (averaging $14,145 per year). Financial award application deadline: 1/15; financial award applicants required to submit FAFSA.
Kent Ono, Chair, 530-752-4901, *E-mail:* kaono@ucdavis.edu.
Application contact: Stella Mancillas, Administrative Assistant, 530-454-2201, *E-mail:* schmancillas@ucdavis.edu. *Web site:* http://cougar.ucdavis.edu/gpcs/

■ UNIVERSITY OF CHICAGO

Division of the Humanities, Committee on History of Culture, Chicago, IL 60637-1513

AWARDS History of culture (AM, PhD); Jewish history and culture (AM, PhD).

Students: 33. 10 applicants, 60% accepted.
Degree requirements: For doctorate, 2 foreign languages, thesis/dissertation.
Entrance requirements: For master's and doctorate, GRE General Test. *Application deadline:* For fall admission, 1/5. *Application fee:* $55.
Expenses: Tuition: Full-time $16,548.
Financial support: Fellowships, Federal Work-Study and tuition waivers (full and partial) available. Financial award application deadline: 12/28; financial award applicants required to submit FAFSA.
Dr. Robert Nelson, Chair, 773-702-0250.

■ UNIVERSITY OF MINNESOTA, TWIN CITIES CAMPUS

Graduate School, College of Liberal Arts, Department of Cultural Studies and Comparative Literature, Program in Comparative Studies in Discourse and Society, Minneapolis, MN 55455-0213

AWARDS MA, PhD.

Faculty: 24 full-time (10 women).
Students: 41 full-time (17 women); includes 3 minority (2 African Americans, 1 Hispanic American), 7 international. 48 applicants, 10% accepted. In 2001, 4 master's, 7 doctorates awarded. Terminal master's awarded for partial completion of doctoral program.
Degree requirements: For master's, one foreign language; for doctorate, 2 foreign languages, thesis/dissertation.
Entrance requirements: For doctorate, GRE General Test, sample of written work. *Application deadline:* For fall admission, 1/4. *Application fee:* $40 ($50 for international students).
Expenses: Tuition, state resident: full-time $2,932; part-time $489 per credit. Tuition, nonresident: full-time $5,758; part-time $960 per credit. Part-time tuition and fees vary according to course load, program and reciprocity agreements.
Financial support: In 2001–02, 30 students received support, including 28 teaching assistantships with full tuition reimbursements available (averaging $11,500 per year); fellowships with full tuition reimbursements available, research assistantships with full tuition reimbursements available, Federal Work-Study,

institutionally sponsored loans, tuition waivers (full and partial), and tuition fellowships also available. Financial award application deadline: 1/4.
Faculty research: Cultural theory; music; architecture, space, and urbanism; body and gender; film and popular culture.
Robert Brown, Director, 612-624-8878, *Fax:* 612-626-0228, *E-mail:* complit@tc.umn.edu.
Application contact: Kate Porter, Executive Secretary, 612-624-7896, *Fax:* 612-626-0228, *E-mail:* porte003@umn.edu. *Web site:* http://csds.cla.umn.edu/

Find an in-depth description at www.petersons.com/gradchannel.

■ UNIVERSITY OF PITTSBURGH

Faculty of Arts and Sciences, Department of English, Pittsburgh, PA 15260

AWARDS Cultural and critical studies (PhD); English (MA); writing (MFA). Part-time programs available.

Faculty: 51 full-time (22 women).
Students: 130 full-time (85 women), 41 part-time (28 women); includes 20 minority (8 African Americans, 4 Asian Americans or Pacific Islanders, 8 Hispanic Americans). 333 applicants, 21% accepted, 43 enrolled. In 2001, 29 master's, 7 doctorates awarded.
Degree requirements: For master's, one foreign language, registration; for doctorate, 2 foreign languages, thesis/dissertation, comprehensive exam, registration.
Entrance requirements: For master's and doctorate, GRE General Test, TOEFL, writing sample. *Application deadline:* For fall admission, 1/8. *Application fee:* $40.
Expenses: Tuition, state resident: full-time $9,410; part-time $385 per credit. Tuition, nonresident: full-time $19,376; part-time $797 per credit. Required fees: $480; $90 per term. Tuition and fees vary according to program.
Financial support: In 2001–02, 91 students received support, including 6 fellowships with full tuition reimbursements available (averaging $13,500 per year), 8 research assistantships with full and partial tuition reimbursements available (averaging $9,400 per year), 77 teaching assistantships with full tuition reimbursements available (averaging $11,500 per year); Federal Work-Study, tuition waivers (full and partial), and unspecified assistantships also available. Financial award application deadline: 1/8.
Faculty research: Cultural studies, literary history and theory, film, composition.
Dr. David Bartholomae, Chairman, 412-624-6509, *Fax:* 412-624-6639, *E-mail:* barth@pitt.edu.
Application contact: Connie Arelt, Graduate Administrator, 412-624-6549, *Fax:* 412-624-6639, *E-mail:* car100@pitt.edu. *Web site:* http://www.pitt.edu/~englweb/

■ THE UNIVERSITY OF TEXAS AT SAN ANTONIO

College of Education and Human Development, Division of Bicultural-Bilingual Studies, San Antonio, TX 78249-0617

AWARDS Bicultural studies (MA); bicultural-bilingual studies (MA); culture and languages (PhD); teaching English as a second language (MA).

Faculty: 6 full-time (2 women), 1 part-time/adjunct (0 women).
Students: 21 full-time (15 women), 80 part-time (61 women); includes 72 minority (1 Asian American or Pacific Islander, 71 Hispanic Americans), 10 international. Average age 36. 48 applicants, 79% accepted, 30 enrolled. In 2001, 44 degrees awarded.
Degree requirements: For master's, one foreign language, comprehensive exam, registration; for doctorate, one foreign language, thesis/dissertation, comprehensive exam, registration.
Entrance requirements: For master's, GRE General Test. *Application deadline:* For fall admission, 7/1. Applications are processed on a rolling basis. *Application fee:* $25.
Expenses: Tuition, state resident: full-time $2,268; part-time $126 per credit hour. Tuition, nonresident: full-time $6,066; part-time $337 per credit hour. Required fees: $781. Tuition and fees vary according to course load.
Financial support: Career-related internships or fieldwork and Federal Work-Study available. Support available to part-time students.
Faculty research: Spanish-English bilingualism, cultural transmission in bilingual communities, literacy in bilingual settings, content-based ESL, second language acquisition in classroom contexts. *Total annual research expenditures:* $229,149.
Dr. Robert D. Milk, Director, 210-458-4426.

■ UNIVERSITY OF THE SACRED HEART

Graduate Programs, Department of Communication, Program in Contemporary Culture and Means, San Juan, PR 00914-0383

AWARDS MA.

Faculty: 6 full-time (4 women), 4 part-time/adjunct (2 women).
Degree requirements: For master's, thesis.
Application deadline: For fall admission, 5/15. *Application fee:* $25.
Expenses: Tuition: Full-time $2,880; part-time $160 per credit. Required fees: $200 per term.
Financial support: Application deadline: 6/30.

■ VALPARAISO UNIVERSITY

Graduate Division, Program in U.S. Culture, Valparaiso, IN 46383-6493

AWARDS MALS.

Students: 1 full-time (0 women), 1 international. Average age 25.
Entrance requirements: For master's, minimum GPA of 3.0. *Application fee:* $30. Electronic applications accepted.
Expenses: Tuition: Full-time $5,400; part-time $300 per credit.
Financial support: Institutionally sponsored loans available. Financial award applicants required to submit FAFSA.
Dot Nuechterlein, Program Coordinator, Graduate/Continuing Education, 219-464-5313, *E-mail:* dot.nuechterlein@valpo.edu.

■ WHEATON COLLEGE

Graduate School, Department of Missions/Intercultural Studies, Wheaton, IL 60187-5593

AWARDS Intercultural studies/teaching English as a second language (MA); missions/intercultural studies (MA); teaching English as a second language (Certificate). Part-time programs available.

Faculty: 5 full-time (2 women), 4 part-time/adjunct (2 women).
Students: 72. 84 applicants, 83% accepted, 47 enrolled. In 2001, 29 degrees awarded.
Degree requirements: For master's, thesis or alternative.
Entrance requirements: For master's, GRE General Test, MAT. *Application deadline:* For fall admission, 3/1 (priority date); for spring admission, 11/1. Applications are processed on a rolling basis. *Application fee:* $30.
Expenses: Tuition: Part-time $410 per hour.
Financial support: Career-related internships or fieldwork, scholarships/grants, and unspecified assistantships available. Financial award application deadline: 6/1; financial award applicants required to submit FAFSA.
Dr. Scott Moreau, Chair, 630-752-5949.
Application contact: Julie A. Huebner, Director of Graduate Admissions, 630-752-5195, *Fax:* 630-752-5935, *E-mail:* gradadm@wheaton.edu. *Web site:* http://www.wheaton.edu/missions/

EAST EUROPEAN AND RUSSIAN STUDIES

■ BOSTON COLLEGE

Graduate School of Arts and Sciences, Department of Slavic and Eastern Languages, Program in Slavic Studies, Chestnut Hill, MA 02467-3800

AWARDS MA, MBA/MA.

Boston College (continued)
Degree requirements: For master's, 3 foreign languages, thesis or alternative, comprehensive exam.
Application deadline: For fall admission, 2/1. *Application fee:* $50.
Expenses: Tuition: Full-time $17,664; part-time $8,832 per semester.
Financial support: Application deadline: 3/1. *Web site:* http://fmwww.bc.edu/SL/SL.html

■ COLUMBIA UNIVERSITY

Graduate School of Arts and Sciences, Program in Russian, Eurasian and East European Regional Studies, New York, NY 10027

AWARDS MA. Part-time programs available.

Expenses: Tuition: Full-time $27,528. Required fees: $1,638.
Dr. Mark L. von Hagen, Adviser, 212-854-6216, *Fax:* 212-854-3010, *E-mail:* sipa_admission@columbia.edu.

■ COLUMBIA UNIVERSITY

School of International and Public Affairs, Harriman Institute, New York, NY 10027

AWARDS Certificate. Students must be enrolled in a separate graduate degree program at Columbia University. Part-time programs available.

Degree requirements: For Certificate, one foreign language, thesis.
Entrance requirements: For degree, minimum 2 years of Russian. *Application deadline:* For fall admission, 1/5 (priority date); for spring admission, 10/15 (priority date). *Application fee:* $75. Electronic applications accepted.
Financial support: Fellowships, career-related internships or fieldwork and Federal Work-Study available. Financial award application deadline: 1/15.
Dr. Mark L. von Hagen, Director, 212-854-6216, *Fax:* 212-854-3010, *E-mail:* sipa_admission@columbia.edu.
Application contact: Robert Garris, Associate Director, 212-854-4623, *Fax:* 212-854-3010, *E-mail:* sipa_admission@columbia.edu. *Web site:* http://www.columbia.edu/cu/sipa/REGINALl/HI/home.html

■ COLUMBIA UNIVERSITY

School of International and Public Affairs, Institute on East Central Europe, New York, NY 10027

AWARDS Certificate. Students must be enrolled in a separate graduate degree program at Columbia University.

Faculty: 10 full-time, 10 part-time/adjunct.
Application deadline: For fall admission, 1/5 (priority date); for spring admission, 10/15 (priority date). *Application fee:* $75. Electronic applications accepted.
Financial support: In 2001–02, 1 research assistantship was awarded; fellowships, career-related internships or fieldwork and Federal Work-Study also available. Financial award application deadline: 1/15.
Faculty research: Ethnic politics, modern East Central European history, post-Communist economic and political transitions, East Central European language and literature.
Dr. John Micgiel, Director, 212-854-4618, *Fax:* 212-854-8577, *E-mail:* jsm6@columbia.edu.
Application contact: Robert Garris, Associate Director, 212-854-6216, *Fax:* 212-854-3010, *E-mail:* sipa_admission@columbia.edu.

■ FLORIDA STATE UNIVERSITY

Graduate Studies, College of Social Sciences, Program in Russian and East European Studies, Tallahassee, FL 32306

AWARDS MA. Part-time programs available.

Students: 4 full-time (2 women), 4 part-time; includes 1 minority (Asian American or Pacific Islander). Average age 26. 12 applicants, 83% accepted, 4 enrolled. In 2001, 7 degrees awarded.
Degree requirements: For master's, one foreign language, comprehensive exam. *Median time to degree:* Master's–1.5 years full-time, 2 years part-time.
Entrance requirements: For master's, GRE General Test, minimum GPA of 3.0. *Application deadline:* For fall admission, 6/15; for spring admission, 10/15. Applications are processed on a rolling basis. *Application fee:* $20.
Expenses: Tuition, state resident: part-time $163 per credit hour. Tuition, nonresident: part-time $570 per credit hour. Tuition and fees vary according to program.
Financial support: In 2001–02, 2 research assistantships with full tuition reimbursements (averaging $5,000 per year) were awarded; fellowships, career-related internships or fieldwork, Federal Work-Study, and institutionally sponsored loans also available. Financial award application deadline: 3/15; financial award applicants required to submit FAFSA.
Dr. Ljubisa Adamovich, Director, 850-644-7097, *Fax:* 850-645-4981, *E-mail:* ladamovi@garnet.acns.fsu.edu.
Application contact: Patty Lollis, Program Assistant, 850-644-4418, *Fax:* 850-645-4981, *E-mail:* plollis@mailer.fsu.edu. *Web site:* http://www.fsu.edu/~russia/

■ GEORGETOWN UNIVERSITY

Graduate School of Arts and Sciences, Program in Russian and East European Studies, Washington, DC 20057

AWARDS MA, MA/PhD.

Degree requirements: For master's, one foreign language, comprehensive exam.
Entrance requirements: For master's, GRE General Test, TOEFL.
Faculty research: East-West trade.

■ THE GEORGE WASHINGTON UNIVERSITY

Elliott School of International Affairs, Program in Russian and East European Studies, Washington, DC 20052

AWARDS MA, JD/MA, LL M/MA, MBA/MA. Part-time and evening/weekend programs available.

Students: 7 full-time (3 women), 4 part-time (2 women). Average age 29. 30 applicants, 87% accepted. In 2001, 5 degrees awarded.
Degree requirements: For master's, one foreign language.
Entrance requirements: For master's, GRE General Test, TOEFL, 2 years of college-level Russian language course work or equivalent. *Application deadline:* For fall admission, 2/1. *Application fee:* $55. Electronic applications accepted.
Expenses: Tuition: Part-time $810 per credit. Required fees: $1 per credit.
Financial support: Fellowships with tuition reimbursements, research assistantships with tuition reimbursements, career-related internships or fieldwork, Federal Work-Study, institutionally sponsored loans, and tuition waivers (full) available. Financial award application deadline: 1/15; financial award applicants required to submit FAFSA.
Faculty research: Russian politics, history, and literature; Central/East European politics and history; economics and issues in Central/Eastern Europe and the former Soviet Union.
Dr. James Goldgeier, Director, 202-994-7099.
Application contact: Jeff V. Miles, Director of Graduate Admissions, 202-994-7050, *Fax:* 202-994-9537, *E-mail:* esiagrad@gwu.edu. *Web site:* http://www.gwu.edu/~elliott/

Find an in-depth description at www.petersons.com/gradchannel.

■ HARVARD UNIVERSITY

Graduate School of Arts and Sciences, Committee on Regional Studies-Russia, Eastern Europe, and Central Asia, Cambridge, MA 02138

AWARDS AM.

Degree requirements: For master's, one foreign language.
Entrance requirements: For master's, GRE General Test, TOEFL.
Expenses: Tuition: Full-time $23,370. Required fees: $816. Full-time tuition and fees vary according to program and student level.

Faculty research: Strategic policy, ethnography and demography of U.S.S.R., non-Russian nationality language training.

■ INDIANA UNIVERSITY BLOOMINGTON

Graduate School, College of Arts and Sciences, Russian and East European Institute, Bloomington, IN 47405

AWARDS East European studies (Certificate); Russian and East European studies (MA); Russian area studies (Certificate). Part-time programs available.

Students: 18 full-time (6 women), 1 part-time; includes 1 minority (Hispanic American), 2 international. Average age 30. In 2001, 4 degrees awarded.
Degree requirements: For master's, one foreign language; for Certificate, one foreign language.
Entrance requirements: For master's, GRE General Test, TOEFL, minimum 2 years of college Russian (Russian area studies); for Certificate, GRE General Test. *Application deadline:* For fall admission, 1/15 (priority date); for spring admission, 9/1 (priority date). Applications are processed on a rolling basis. *Application fee:* $45 ($55 for international students).
Expenses: Tuition, state resident: full-time $4,720; part-time $197 per credit. Tuition, nonresident: full-time $13,748; part-time $573 per credit. Required fees: $642.
Financial support: In 2001–02, 3 research assistantships with full tuition reimbursements (averaging $9,500 per year) were awarded; fellowships, teaching assistantships, career-related internships or fieldwork, Federal Work-Study, and institutionally sponsored loans also available. Financial award application deadline: 2/15; financial award applicants required to submit FAFSA.
Faculty research: Political and economic transition of former Soviet Union and Eastern Europe, Russian and Soviet history, Slavic literature and linguistics, education and mass media of former Soviet Union and Eastern Europe.
David Ransel, Director, 812-855-7309, *Fax:* 812-855-6411, *E-mail:* ransel@indiana.edu.
Application contact: Laura L. Rasbach, Administrative Secretary, 812-855-7309, *Fax:* 812-855-6411, *E-mail:* reei@ucs.indiana.edu. *Web site:* http://www.indiana.edu/~reeiweb/

■ JOHNS HOPKINS UNIVERSITY

Paul H. Nitze School of Advanced International Studies, Washington, DC 20036

AWARDS Emerging markets (Certificate); interdisciplinary studies (MA, PhD), including African studies, American foreign policy (MA), Asian studies, Canadian studies, conflict resolution and mediation (MA), environmental policy and resource management (MA), European studies, international business (MA), international development (MA), international economics (MA), international relations (MA), Latin American studies, Middle Eastern studies (MA), military and defense studies (MA), Russian area and East European studies (MA), social change and development (MA); international public policy (MIPP). MBA/MA offered jointly with the University of Pennsylvania–Wharton School and INSEAD in France.

Faculty: 44 full-time (13 women), 113 part-time/adjunct (29 women).
Students: 567 full-time (275 women), 17 part-time (8 women); includes 71 minority (14 African Americans, 46 Asian Americans or Pacific Islanders, 10 Hispanic Americans, 1 Native American). Average age 27. 1,288 applicants, 35% accepted. In 2001, 294 master's, 13 doctorates, 34 other advanced degrees awarded. Terminal master's awarded for partial completion of doctoral program.
Degree requirements: For master's, one foreign language, comprehensive exam; for doctorate, 2 foreign languages, thesis/dissertation.
Entrance requirements: For master's, GMAT or GRE General Test or TOEFL, previous course work in economics, foreign language; for doctorate, GRE General Test or TOEFL; for Certificate, TOEFL. *Application deadline:* For fall admission, 1/15. *Application fee:* $75. Electronic applications accepted.
Expenses: Contact institution.
Financial support: In 2001–02, 431 fellowships (averaging $5,500 per year) were awarded; career-related internships or fieldwork and Federal Work-Study also available. Financial award application deadline: 2/1; financial award applicants required to submit FAFSA.
Faculty research: Comparative politics, regional studies, language and linguistics.
Dr. Jessica Einhorn, Dean, 202-663-5624, *Fax:* 202-663-5621.
Application contact: Bonnie Wilson, Associate Dean of Student Affairs, 202-663-5700, *Fax:* 202-663-7788, *E-mail:* admissions.sais@jhu.edu. *Web site:* http://www.sais-jhu.edu/

Find an in-depth description at www.petersons.com/gradchannel.

■ LA SALLE UNIVERSITY

School of Arts and Sciences, Central and Eastern European Studies Program, Philadelphia, PA 19141-1199

AWARDS MA. Part-time and evening/weekend programs available.

Faculty: 7 full-time (1 woman), 5 part-time/adjunct (1 woman).
Students: 2 full-time (1 woman), 16 part-time (8 women); includes 1 minority (African American), 5 international. Average age 31. 9 applicants, 89% accepted, 8 enrolled. In 2001, 5 degrees awarded.
Degree requirements: For master's, one foreign language, thesis or alternative.
Entrance requirements: For master's, MAT, TOEFL. *Application deadline:* Applications are processed on a rolling basis. *Application fee:* $30.
Expenses: Contact institution.
Financial support: Career-related internships or fieldwork, Federal Work-Study, and scholarships/grants available.
Faculty research: Ukrainian culture, Russian studies, business in Central and Eastern European countries.
Dr. Berhhardt G. Blumenthal, Director, 215-951-7201, *E-mail:* blumenth@lasalle.edu.

■ THE OHIO STATE UNIVERSITY

Graduate School, College of Humanities, Department of History, Columbus, OH 43210

AWARDS History (MA, PhD); Latin American studies (Certificate); Russian area studies (Certificate).

Degree requirements: For master's, thesis optional; for doctorate, variable foreign language requirement, thesis/dissertation.
Entrance requirements: For master's and doctorate, GRE General Test.

■ THE OHIO STATE UNIVERSITY

Graduate School, College of Humanities, Department of Slavic and East European Languages and Literatures, Columbus, OH 43210

AWARDS Russian area studies (Certificate); Slavic and East European languages and literatures (MA, PhD).

Degree requirements: For master's, variable foreign language requirement, thesis optional; for doctorate, variable foreign language requirement, thesis/dissertation.
Entrance requirements: For master's and doctorate, GRE General Test, TOEFL.
Faculty research: Polish literature.

■ THE OHIO STATE UNIVERSITY

Graduate School, College of Social and Behavioral Sciences, Department of Political Science, Columbus, OH 43210

AWARDS Latin American studies (Certificate); political science (MA, PhD); Russian area studies (Certificate).

Degree requirements: For master's, thesis optional; for doctorate, thesis/dissertation.
Entrance requirements: For master's and doctorate, GRE General Test, TOEFL.
Faculty research: American, comparative, and international politics; political theory.

■ THE OHIO STATE UNIVERSITY

Graduate School, Program in Slavic and East European Studies, Columbus, OH 43210

AWARDS MA.

Degree requirements: For master's, thesis optional.
Entrance requirements: For master's, GRE General Test, TOEFL.

■ STANFORD UNIVERSITY

School of Humanities and Sciences, Center for Russian and East European Studies, Stanford, CA 94305-9991

AWARDS AM.

Students: 6 full-time (4 women), 2 international. Average age 29. 7 applicants, 57% accepted. In 2001, 5 degrees awarded.
Degree requirements: For master's, one foreign language.
Entrance requirements: For master's, GRE General Test, TOEFL. *Application deadline:* For fall admission, 1/1. *Application fee:* $65 ($80 for international students). Electronic applications accepted.
Nancy Kollman, Director, 650-723-9475, *Fax:* 650-725-0597, *E-mail:* kollmann@leland.stanford.edu.
Application contact: Graduate Program Administrator, 650-723-3568. *Web site:* http://www.stanford.edu/dept/crees/

■ UNIVERSITY OF CONNECTICUT

Graduate School, College of Liberal Arts and Sciences, Field of Slavic and East European Studies, Storrs, CT 06269

AWARDS MA.

Entrance requirements: For master's, GRE General Test.

■ UNIVERSITY OF ILLINOIS AT CHICAGO

Graduate College, College of Liberal Arts and Sciences, Department of Slavic and Baltic Languages and Literatures, Chicago, IL 60607-7128

AWARDS Slavic languages and literatures (PhD); Slavic studies (MA). Evening/weekend programs available.

Faculty: 9 full-time (5 women).
Students: 12 full-time (9 women), 11 part-time (6 women), 8 international. Average age 34. 11 applicants, 73% accepted, 5 enrolled. In 2001, 1 degree awarded. Terminal master's awarded for partial completion of doctoral program.
Degree requirements: For doctorate, one foreign language, thesis/dissertation.
Entrance requirements: For master's and doctorate, GRE General Test, TOEFL, minimum GPA of 4.0 on a 5.0 scale. *Application deadline:* For fall admission, 6/1; for spring admission, 11/1. *Application fee:* $40 ($50 for international students). Electronic applications accepted.
Expenses: Tuition, state resident: full-time $3,060. Tuition, nonresident: full-time $6,688.
Financial support: In 2001–02, 13 students received support; fellowships with full tuition reimbursements available, research assistantships with full tuition reimbursements available, teaching assistantships with full tuition reimbursements available, institutionally sponsored loans and tuition waivers (full) available. Financial award application deadline: 3/1; financial award applicants required to submit FAFSA.
Sona Hoisington, Head, 312-996-4412, *E-mail:* sonahoi@uic.edu.
Application contact: Biljana Sljivic-Simsic, Director of Graduate Studies.

■ UNIVERSITY OF ILLINOIS AT URBANA–CHAMPAIGN

Graduate College, College of Liberal Arts and Sciences, Russian and East European Studies Center, Champaign, IL 61820

AWARDS AM.

Students: 7 full-time (3 women), 1 international. 6 applicants, 50% accepted. In 2001, 1 degree awarded.
Application deadline: Applications are processed on a rolling basis. *Application fee:* $40 ($50 for international students). Electronic applications accepted.
Expenses: Tuition, state resident: part-time $3,227 per degree program. Tuition, nonresident: part-time $7,169 per degree program. Tuition and fees vary according to program.
Financial support: In 2001–02, 3 fellowships, 1 research assistantship, 2 teaching assistantships were awarded. Financial award application deadline: 2/15.
Mark Steinberg, Director, 217-333-1244, *Fax:* 217-333-1582, *E-mail:* steinb@uiuc.edu.
Application contact: Diane P. Merridith, Administrative Assistant, 217-244-4719, *Fax:* 217-333-1582, *E-mail:* diannem@uiuc.edu. *Web site:* http://www.uiuc.edu/unit/reec/

■ UNIVERSITY OF KANSAS

Graduate School, College of Liberal Arts and Sciences, Department of Russian and East European Studies, Lawrence, KS 66045

AWARDS MA. Part-time programs available.

Faculty: 10.
Students: 14 full-time (1 woman), 3 part-time (1 woman); includes 1 minority (Hispanic American). Average age 34. 17 applicants, 65% accepted, 3 enrolled. In 2001, 12 degrees awarded.
Degree requirements: For master's, one foreign language, comprehensive exam, interdisciplinary capstone seminar.
Entrance requirements: For master's, GRE General Test, TOEFL. *Application deadline:* Applications are processed on a rolling basis. *Application fee:* $35.
Expenses: Tuition, state resident: full-time $2,722; part-time $113 per credit. Tuition, nonresident: full-time $8,586; part-time $358 per credit. Required fees: $551; $46 per credit. Tuition and fees vary according to campus/location, program and reciprocity agreements.
Financial support: Fellowships, teaching assistantships with partial tuition reimbursements available.
Faculty research: Transitional studies, modern Russian history and philosophy, Ukrainian and Russian domestic and foreign policies.
Maria Carlson, Director, 785-864-4236, *Fax:* 785-864-3800, *E-mail:* crees@ku.edu.
Application contact: Bruce Berglund, Graduate Advisor, 785-864-4236, *E-mail:* berglund@ku.edu. *Web site:* http://www.ku.edu/~crees/

■ UNIVERSITY OF MICHIGAN

Horace H. Rackham School of Graduate Studies, College of Literature, Science, and the Arts, Interdepartmental Program in Russian and East European Studies, Ann Arbor, MI 48109

AWARDS AM, Certificate, JD/AM, MBA/AM, MLA/AM, MPP/AM, MS/AM. Part-time programs available.

Faculty: 64.
Students: 15 full-time (6 women); includes 2 minority (both Asian Americans or Pacific Islanders).
Degree requirements: For master's, one foreign language, thesis.
Entrance requirements: For master's, GRE General Test. *Application deadline:* For fall admission, 2/1. *Application fee:* $55. Electronic applications accepted.
Financial support: In 2001–02, 10 fellowships with tuition reimbursements (averaging $11,000 per year), 3 teaching assistantships with tuition reimbursements (averaging $8,000 per year) were awarded. Research and travel grants also available. Financial award application deadline: 2/1.
Dr. Katherine Verdery, Director, 734-764-0351, *Fax:* 734-763-4765, *E-mail:* crees@umich.edu.
Application contact: Lynda Norton, Student Services Associate, 734-764-0351, *Fax:* 734-763-4765, *E-mail:* crees@umich.edu. *Web site:* http://www.umich.edu/~iinet/crees

■ UNIVERSITY OF MINNESOTA, TWIN CITIES CAMPUS

Graduate School, College of Liberal Arts, Program in Russian Area Studies, Minneapolis, MN 55455-0213

AWARDS MA. Part-time programs available.

Faculty: 13 full-time.

Students: In 2001, 7 degrees awarded.
Degree requirements: For master's, one foreign language, thesis or alternative. *Median time to degree:* Master's–3 years full-time, 5 years part-time.
Entrance requirements: For master's, GRE, TOEFL. *Application deadline:* Applications are processed on a rolling basis. *Application fee:* $40 ($50 for international students).
Expenses: Tuition, state resident: full-time $2,932; part-time $489 per credit. Tuition, nonresident: full-time $5,758; part-time $960 per credit. Part-time tuition and fees vary according to course load, program and reciprocity agreements.
Dr. Evelyn Davidheiser, Associate Director, 612-624-9007, *Fax:* 612-626-2242, *E-mail:* igs@umn.edu.
Application contact: Adviser, 612-624-8543, *Fax:* 612-626-2242, *E-mail:* aspiis@tc.umn.edu.

■ THE UNIVERSITY OF NORTH CAROLINA AT CHAPEL HILL

Graduate School, Curriculum in Russian and East European Studies, Chapel Hill, NC 27599

AWARDS MA. Part-time programs available.

Degree requirements: For master's, one foreign language, thesis.
Entrance requirements: For master's, GRE, TOEFL. Electronic applications accepted.
Expenses: Tuition, state resident: full-time $2,864. Tuition, nonresident: full-time $12,030.
Faculty research: Language, area studies, social sciences, sciences, professional schools. *Web site:* http://www.unc.edu/depts/slavic/

■ THE UNIVERSITY OF TEXAS AT AUSTIN

Graduate School, Program in Russian, East European and Eurasian Studies, Austin, TX 78712-1111

AWARDS MA, JD/MA, MBA/MA, MP Aff/MA. Part-time programs available.

Degree requirements: For master's, one foreign language.
Entrance requirements: For master's, GRE General Test, 3 years of formal language training or equivalent, minimum GPA of 3.0. Electronic applications accepted.
Expenses: Tuition, state resident: full-time $3,159. Tuition, nonresident: full-time $6,957. Tuition and fees vary according to program.
Faculty research: East European gypsies, elite transformation and democracy in Eastern Europe, elite partisanship as an intervening variable in Russian politics, post-Soviet youth in Russia. *Web site:* http://reenic.utexas.edu/reenic/CPSEES/online.html

■ UNIVERSITY OF WASHINGTON

Graduate School, College of Arts and Sciences, Henry M. Jackson School of International Studies, Russian, East European and Central Asian Studies Program, Seattle, WA 98195

AWARDS Central Asian studies (MAIS); East European studies (MAIS); Russian studies (MAIS).

Faculty: 46 full-time (20 women).
Students: 37 full-time (20 women); includes 1 minority (African American), 4 international. Average age 29. 43 applicants, 93% accepted. In 2001, 8 degrees awarded.
Degree requirements: For master's, one foreign language, thesis.
Entrance requirements: For master's, GRE General Test, TOEFL, 2 years of relevant language, minimum GPA of 3.0. *Application deadline:* For fall admission, 1/15 (priority date). *Application fee:* $45. Electronic applications accepted.
Expenses: Tuition, state resident: full-time $5,539. Tuition, nonresident: full-time $14,376. Required fees: $390. Tuition and fees vary according to course load and program.
Financial support: In 2001–02, 5 fellowships with tuition reimbursements were awarded; research assistantships, teaching assistantships, career-related internships or fieldwork, Federal Work-Study, institutionally sponsored loans, and summer language study awards also available. Financial award application deadline: 1/15.
Prof. Stephen E. Hanson, Chair, 206-543-9460, *Fax:* 206-685-0668, *E-mail:* shanson@u.washington.edu.
Application contact: 206-543-6001, *Fax:* 206-616-3170, *E-mail:* jsisinfo@u.washington.edu. *Web site:* http://jsis.artsci.washington.edu/

■ YALE UNIVERSITY

Graduate School of Arts and Sciences, Program in Russian and East European Studies, New Haven, CT 06520

AWARDS MA.

Degree requirements: For master's, 2 foreign languages.
Entrance requirements: For master's, GRE General Test.

ETHNIC STUDIES

■ CORNELL UNIVERSITY

Graduate School, Graduate Fields of Arts and Sciences, Field of Sociology, Ithaca, NY 14853-0001

AWARDS Economy and society (MA, PhD); gender and life course (MA, PhD); organizations (MA, PhD); political sociology/social movements (MA, PhD); racial and ethnic relations (MA, PhD); social networks (MA, PhD); social psychology (MA, PhD); social stratification (MA, PhD).

Faculty: 19 full-time.
Students: 33 full-time (17 women); includes 3 minority (1 African American, 1 Asian American or Pacific Islander, 1 Hispanic American), 17 international. 126 applicants, 13% accepted. In 2001, 2 master's, 3 doctorates awarded. Terminal master's awarded for partial completion of doctoral program.
Degree requirements: For master's, thesis; for doctorate, thesis/dissertation, 1 year of teaching experience.
Entrance requirements: For master's and doctorate, GRE General Test, TOEFL. *Application deadline:* For fall admission, 1/15. *Application fee:* $65. Electronic applications accepted.
Expenses: Tuition: Full-time $25,970. Required fees: $50.
Financial support: In 2001–02, 32 students received support, including 13 fellowships with full tuition reimbursements available, 10 research assistantships with full tuition reimbursements available, 9 teaching assistantships with full tuition reimbursements available; institutionally sponsored loans, scholarships/grants, tuition waivers (full and partial), and unspecified assistantships also available. Financial award applicants required to submit FAFSA.
Faculty research: Comparative societal analysis, work and family, simulations, social class and mobility, racial segregation and inequality.
Application contact: Graduate Field Assistant, 607-255-4266, *Fax:* 607-255-8473, *E-mail:* sociology@cornell.edu. *Web site:* http://www.gradschool.cornell.edu/grad/fields_1/socio.html

■ SAN FRANCISCO STATE UNIVERSITY

Graduate Division, College of Ethnic Studies, San Francisco, CA 94132-1722

AWARDS MA. Part-time programs available.

Entrance requirements: For master's, minimum GPA of 2.5 in last 60 units.

■ UNIVERSITY OF CALIFORNIA, BERKELEY

Graduate Division, Group in Ethnic Studies, Berkeley, CA 94720-1500

AWARDS PhD.

Faculty: 17 full-time (10 women).
Students: 64 full-time (40 women); includes 53 minority (2 African Americans, 20 Asian Americans or Pacific Islanders, 26 Hispanic Americans, 5 Native Americans), 3 international. 82 applicants, 26% accepted, 11 enrolled. In 2001, 4 degrees awarded.
Degree requirements: For doctorate, one foreign language, thesis/dissertation,

University of California, Berkeley (continued)
qualifying exam. *Median time to degree:* Doctorate–6 years full-time.
Entrance requirements: For doctorate, GRE General Test, minimum GPA of 3.0. *Application deadline:* For fall admission, 12/15. *Application fee:* $60.
Expenses: Tuition, nonresident: full-time $10,704. Required fees: $4,349.
Financial support: In 2001–02, 24 fellowships with full tuition reimbursements (averaging $14,000 per year), 76 teaching assistantships with partial tuition reimbursements (averaging $14,000 per year) were awarded. Research assistantships with partial tuition reimbursements Financial award application deadline: 12/15.
Faculty research: Gender and race, Asian American visual art, racial theory and politics, Chicana/o literature and visual arts, history of Native North Americans.
Jose David Saldivar, Chair, 510-643-5000, *Fax:* 510-642-6456, *E-mail:* saldivar@uclink4.berkeley.edu.
Application contact: Jahleezah Eskew, Student Affairs Officer, 510-642-6643, *Fax:* 510-642-6456, *E-mail:* jahleeza@uclink.berkeley.edu. *Web site:* http://socrates.berkeley.edu/~ethnicst/

■ UNIVERSITY OF CALIFORNIA, SAN DIEGO

Graduate Studies and Research, Department of Ethnic Studies, La Jolla, CA 92093

AWARDS PhD.

Students: 24 (18 women). 56 applicants, 25% accepted, 7 enrolled.
Application deadline: For fall admission, 7/18. *Application fee:* $40. Electronic applications accepted.
Expenses: Tuition, nonresident: full-time $10,434. Required fees: $4,883.
Yen Espirtu, Chair.
Application contact: Graduate Coordinator, 858-534-3276.

FOLKLORE

■ THE GEORGE WASHINGTON UNIVERSITY

Columbian College of Arts and Sciences, Department of American Studies, Concentration in Folklife, Washington, DC 20052

AWARDS MA.

Students: Average age 33. 5 applicants, 80% accepted.
Degree requirements: For master's, thesis or alternative, comprehensive exam.
Entrance requirements: For master's, GRE General Test, minimum GPA of 3.0. *Application fee:* $55.
Expenses: Tuition: Part-time $810 per credit. Required fees: $1 per credit.
Financial support: Fellowships, teaching assistantships available. Financial award application deadline: 2/1.
Dr. John Vlach, Chair. *Web site:* http://www.gwu.edu/~gradinfo/

■ INDIANA UNIVERSITY BLOOMINGTON

Graduate School, College of Arts and Sciences, Department of Folklore and Ethnomusicology, Bloomington, IN 47405

AWARDS Folklore (MA, PhD), including ethnomusicology.

Faculty: 20 full-time (11 women), 8 part-time/adjunct (3 women).
Students: 52 full-time (35 women), 74 part-time (44 women); includes 13 minority (6 African Americans, 2 Asian Americans or Pacific Islanders, 5 Hispanic Americans), 23 international. Average age 32. In 2001, 10 master's, 10 doctorates awarded.
Degree requirements: For master's, one foreign language; for doctorate, 2 foreign languages, thesis/dissertation, qualifying exams.
Entrance requirements: For master's and doctorate, GRE General Test, TOEFL, minimum GPA of 3.0. *Application deadline:* For fall admission, 1/15. *Application fee:* $45 ($55 for international students).
Expenses: Tuition, state resident: full-time $4,720; part-time $197 per credit. Tuition, nonresident: full-time $13,748; part-time $573 per credit. Required fees: $642.
Financial support: In 2001–02, research assistantships (averaging $6,930 per year), teaching assistantships (averaging $6,930 per year) were awarded. Fellowships, Federal Work-Study also available.
Dr. John H. McDowell, Chair, 812-855-1027, *Fax:* 812-855-4003, *E-mail:* folkethn@indiana.edu.
Application contact: Susan Harris, Admissions Recorder, 812-855-1027, *Fax:* 812-855-4003, *E-mail:* folkethn@indiana.edu. *Web site:* http://www.indiana.edu/~folklore/

■ UNIVERSITY OF CALIFORNIA, BERKELEY

Graduate Division, Group in Folklore, Berkeley, CA 94720-1500

AWARDS MA.

Entrance requirements: For master's, GRE General Test, minimum GPA of 3.0.
Expenses: Tuition, nonresident: full-time $10,704. Required fees: $4,349.

■ UNIVERSITY OF LOUISIANA AT LAFAYETTE

Graduate School, College of Liberal Arts, Department of English, Lafayette, LA 70504

AWARDS British and American literature (MA), including creative writing, folklore, rhetoric; creative writing (PhD); literature (PhD); rhetoric (PhD). Part-time programs available.

Faculty: 24 full-time (7 women).
Students: 67 full-time (41 women), 37 part-time (29 women); includes 10 minority (5 African Americans, 2 Asian Americans or Pacific Islanders, 1 Hispanic American, 2 Native Americans), 3 international. 45 applicants, 73% accepted, 22 enrolled. In 2001, 10 master's, 10 doctorates awarded. Terminal master's awarded for partial completion of doctoral program.
Degree requirements: For master's, one foreign language, thesis or alternative; for doctorate, 2 foreign languages, thesis/dissertation.
Entrance requirements: For master's, GRE General Test, minimum GPA of 2.75; for doctorate, GRE General Test, minimum GPA of 3.0. *Application deadline:* For fall admission, 5/15. *Application fee:* $20 ($30 for international students).
Expenses: Tuition, state resident: full-time $2,317; part-time $79 per credit. Tuition, nonresident: full-time $8,882; part-time $369 per credit. International tuition: $9,018 full-time.
Financial support: In 2001–02, 22 fellowships with full tuition reimbursements (averaging $12,432 per year), 8 research assistantships with full tuition reimbursements (averaging $5,500 per year), 39 teaching assistantships with full tuition reimbursements (averaging $10,000 per year) were awarded. Federal Work-Study also available. Financial award application deadline: 5/1.
Faculty research: Composition theory, Southern literature, medieval literature.
Dr. Darrell Bourque, Head, 337-482-6906.
Application contact: Dr. M. Marcia Gaudet, Graduate Coordinator, 337-482-5505.

■ THE UNIVERSITY OF NORTH CAROLINA AT CHAPEL HILL

Graduate School, College of Arts and Sciences, Curriculum in Folklore, Chapel Hill, NC 27599

AWARDS MA.

Faculty: 20 full-time.
Students: 12 full-time (9 women), 2 part-time (both women); includes 3 minority (2 African Americans, 1 Hispanic American). 26 applicants, 35% accepted. In 2001, 5 degrees awarded.
Degree requirements: For master's, one foreign language, thesis, comprehensive exam.

Entrance requirements: For master's, GRE General Test, minimum GPA of 3.0, writing sample. *Application deadline:* For fall admission, 1/1 (priority date). Applications are processed on a rolling basis. *Application fee:* $55. Electronic applications accepted.
Expenses: Tuition, state resident: full-time $2,864. Tuition, nonresident: full-time $12,030.
Financial support: In 2001–02, 2 fellowships with full tuition reimbursements, 5 research assistantships with full tuition reimbursements were awarded. Unspecified assistantships also available. Financial award application deadline: 3/1.
Faculty research: Public folklore, politics of culture, folklore and feminist theory, belief and health systems, Southern culture.
Dr. Glenn Hinson, Chairman, 919-962-4065, *Fax:* 919-962-3520, *E-mail:* ghinson@unc.edu. *Web site:* http://www.unc.edu/depts/folklore/

■ UNIVERSITY OF OREGON

Graduate School, College of Arts and Sciences, Folklore Program, Eugene, OR 97403

AWARDS Independent study: folklore (MA, MS). Part-time programs available.

Students: 7 full-time (5 women), 2 part-time (1 woman). 5 applicants, 80% accepted. In 2001, 5 degrees awarded.
Degree requirements: For master's, one foreign language.
Entrance requirements: For master's, GRE General Test, TOEFL, minimum GPA of 3.0. *Application deadline:* For fall admission, 2/15. *Application fee:* $50.
Expenses: Tuition, state resident: full-time $4,968; part-time $501 per credit hour. Tuition, nonresident: full-time $8,400; part-time $691 per credit hour.
Financial support: In 2001–02, 6 teaching assistantships were awarded; career-related internships or fieldwork and Federal Work-Study also available.
Faculty research: American folklore, East European folklore, film and folklore, folk religion and belief, ballad.
Sharon Sherman, Director, 541-346-3911, *Fax:* 541-346-5026, *E-mail:* srs@oregon.uoregon.edu.
Application contact: Wendy Anderson, Admissions Contact, 541-346-1505. *Web site:* http://darkwing.uoregon.edu/~flr/

■ UNIVERSITY OF PENNSYLVANIA

School of Arts and Sciences, Graduate Group in Folklore and Folklife, Philadelphia, PA 19104

AWARDS AM, PhD. Part-time programs available. Terminal master's awarded for partial completion of doctoral program.

Degree requirements: For master's, one foreign language, thesis or alternative; for doctorate, 2 foreign languages, thesis/dissertation.
Entrance requirements: For master's and doctorate, GRE General Test.
Expenses: Tuition: Part-time $12,875 per semester.
Faculty research: Material culture, narrative and poetics of language, alternative health systems, public display of events.
Web site: http://www.sas.upenn.edu/folklore/

■ THE UNIVERSITY OF TEXAS AT AUSTIN

Graduate School, College of Liberal Arts, Department of Anthropology, Program in Folklore and Public Culture, Austin, TX 78712-1111

AWARDS MA, PhD. Part-time programs available. Terminal master's awarded for partial completion of doctoral program.

Degree requirements: For master's, one foreign language, thesis, report; for doctorate, one foreign language, thesis/dissertation.
Entrance requirements: For master's and doctorate, GRE General Test. Electronic applications accepted.
Expenses: Tuition, state resident: full-time $3,159. Tuition, nonresident: full-time $6,957. Tuition and fees vary according to program.
Faculty research: Expressive culture, gender, genre, folklores and culture of British Isles, ethnography of speaking.

■ UTAH STATE UNIVERSITY

School of Graduate Studies, College of Humanities, Arts and Social Sciences, Department of English and Department of History, Program in American Studies, Logan, UT 84322

AWARDS Folklore (MA, MS). Part-time and evening/weekend programs available.

Faculty: 12 full-time (5 women).
Students: 5 full-time (3 women), 26 part-time (17 women); includes 1 minority (Native American), 2 international. Average age 32. 17 applicants, 94% accepted. In 2001, 7 degrees awarded.
Degree requirements: For master's, thesis or alternative.
Entrance requirements: For master's, GRE General Test or MAT, TOEFL, minimum GPA of 3.0. *Application deadline:* For fall admission, 2/15 (priority date); for spring admission, 10/15. *Application fee:* $40.
Expenses: Tuition, state resident: full-time $1,693. Tuition, nonresident: full-time $4,233. Required fees: $501. Tuition and fees vary according to program.
Financial support: In 2001–02, teaching assistantships with partial tuition reimbursements (averaging $7,200 per year); fellowships with partial tuition reimbursements, career-related internships or fieldwork, Federal Work-Study, institutionally sponsored loans, and tuition waivers (partial) also available. Financial award application deadline: 2/15.
Faculty research: Folklore and folklife, American culture, regional studies, material culture, Jewish folklore, Native American folklore.
Barre Toelken, Graduate Adviser, 435-797-2737, *Fax:* 435-797-3797, *E-mail:* btoelken@english.usu.edu.
Application contact: Dr. Keith A. Grant-Davie, Director of Graduate Studies, 435-797-2733, *Fax:* 435-797-3797, *E-mail:* dept@english.usu.edu. *Web site:* http://english.usu.edu/dept/

■ WESTERN KENTUCKY UNIVERSITY

Graduate Studies, Potter College of Arts, Humanities and Social Sciences, Department of Modern Languages and Intercultural Studies, Programs in Folk Studies, Bowling Green, KY 42101-3576

AWARDS Folk studies (MA); historic preservation (MA).

Faculty: 14 full-time (10 women).
Students: In 2001, 10 degrees awarded.
Degree requirements: For master's, written exam, thesis optional.
Entrance requirements: For master's, GRE General Test, minimum GPA of 3.0. *Application deadline:* For fall admission, 7/1 (priority date); for spring admission, 11/1. Applications are processed on a rolling basis. *Application fee:* $30.
Expenses: Tuition, area resident: Part-time $167 per credit. Tuition, state resident: full-time $2,490. Tuition, nonresident: full-time $6,660; part-time $399 per credit. Required fees: $554. Part-time tuition and fees vary according to campus/location and reciprocity agreements.
Financial support: Research assistantships with partial tuition reimbursements, career-related internships or fieldwork, Federal Work-Study, institutionally sponsored loans, tuition waivers (partial), unspecified assistantships, and service awards available. Support available to part-time students. Financial award application deadline: 4/1; financial award applicants required to submit FAFSA.
Faculty research: Public folklore, folklore and education, vernacular belief, music and culture, historic presentation.
Dr. Erica Brady, Director, 270-745-5898, *Fax:* 270-745-6859, *E-mail:* erica.brady@wku.edu.

GENDER STUDIES

■ CORNELL UNIVERSITY

Graduate School, Graduate Fields of Arts and Sciences, Field of Sociology, Ithaca, NY 14853-0001

AWARDS Economy and society (MA, PhD); gender and life course (MA, PhD); organizations (MA, PhD); political sociology/social movements (MA, PhD); racial and ethnic relations (MA, PhD); social networks (MA, PhD); social psychology (MA, PhD); social stratification (MA, PhD).

Faculty: 19 full-time.
Students: 33 full-time (17 women); includes 3 minority (1 African American, 1 Asian American or Pacific Islander, 1 Hispanic American), 17 international. 126 applicants, 13% accepted. In 2001, 2 master's, 3 doctorates awarded. Terminal master's awarded for partial completion of doctoral program.
Degree requirements: For master's, thesis; for doctorate, thesis/dissertation, 1 year of teaching experience.
Entrance requirements: For master's and doctorate, GRE General Test, TOEFL. *Application deadline:* For fall admission, 1/15. *Application fee:* $65. Electronic applications accepted.
Expenses: Tuition: Full-time $25,970. Required fees: $50.
Financial support: In 2001–02, 32 students received support, including 13 fellowships with full tuition reimbursements available, 10 research assistantships with full tuition reimbursements available, 9 teaching assistantships with full tuition reimbursements available; institutionally sponsored loans, scholarships/grants, tuition waivers (full and partial), and unspecified assistantships also available. Financial award applicants required to submit FAFSA.
Faculty research: Comparative societal analysis, work and family, simulations, social class and mobility, racial segregation and inequality.
Application contact: Graduate Field Assistant, 607-255-4266, *Fax:* 607-255-8473, *E-mail:* sociology@cornell.edu. *Web site:* http://www.gradschool.cornell.edu/grad/fields_1/socio.html

■ HARVARD UNIVERSITY

Graduate School of Education, Area of Human Development and Psychology, Cambridge, MA 02138

AWARDS Gender studies (Ed M); human development and psychology (Ed M, Ed D, CAS); individualized program (Ed M); language and literacy (Ed M, Ed D, CAS); mind brain and education (Ed M); risk and prevention (Ed M, CAS). Part-time programs available.

Faculty: 13 full-time (7 women), 33 part-time/adjunct (12 women).
Students: 243 full-time (204 women), 37 part-time (31 women); includes 59 minority (21 African Americans, 16 Asian Americans or Pacific Islanders, 18 Hispanic Americans, 4 Native Americans), 35 international. Average age 32. 162 applicants, 21% accepted. In 2001, 118 master's, 18 doctorates, 2 other advanced degrees awarded. Terminal master's awarded for partial completion of doctoral program.
Degree requirements: For doctorate, thesis/dissertation.
Entrance requirements: For master's, GRE General Test or MAT, TOEFL, TWE; for doctorate and CAS, GRE General Test, TOEFL, TWE. *Application deadline:* For fall admission, 1/2. *Application fee:* $65.
Financial support: In 2001–02, 146 students received support, including 22 fellowships (averaging $19,708 per year), 5 research assistantships, 106 teaching assistantships (averaging $3,733 per year); career-related internships or fieldwork, Federal Work-Study, and scholarships/grants also available. Support available to part-time students. Financial award application deadline: 2/3; financial award applicants required to submit FAFSA.
Faculty research: Educational technologies; reading, writing, and language; risk and prevention of developmental and educational problems; bilingualism and multicultural education; gender difference in development.
Dr. Robert L. Selman, Chair, 617-495-3414.
Application contact: Roland A. Hence, Director of Admissions, 617-495-3414, *Fax:* 617-496-3577, *E-mail:* gseadmissions@harvard.edu. *Web site:* http://gse.harvard.edu/

■ NORTHWESTERN UNIVERSITY

The Graduate School, Program in Gender Studies, Evanston, IL 60208

AWARDS PhD/Certificate.

Faculty: 6 full-time (all women), 8 part-time/adjunct (5 women).
Students: 60 full-time (50 women); includes 13 minority (3 African Americans, 7 Asian Americans or Pacific Islanders, 3 Hispanic Americans). Average age 28. *Application fee:* $50 ($55 for international students).
Expenses: Tuition: Full-time $26,526.
Financial support: In 2001–02, 1 research assistantship with full tuition reimbursement, 2 teaching assistantships with full tuition reimbursements were awarded. Scholarships/grants also available.
Faculty research: Anthropology, gender in Victorian period, autobiography, performance ethnographies, Slavic literature, women in the law.
Prof. Micaela di Leonardo, Director, 847-491-5871, *Fax:* 847-467-4957, *E-mail:* L-DI@northwestern.edu.
Application contact: Kristine Thompson, Program Assistant, 847-491-5871, *Fax:* 847-467-4957, *E-mail:* gender@northwestern.edu. *Web site:* http://www.genderstudies.northwestern.edu/

■ RUTGERS, THE STATE UNIVERSITY OF NEW JERSEY, NEW BRUNSWICK

Graduate School, Program in Women's Studies, New Brunswick, NJ 08901-1281

AWARDS Women's and gender studies (MA); women's studies (MA). Part-time programs available.

Degree requirements: For master's, thesis or alternative.
Entrance requirements: For master's, GRE General Test.
Faculty research: Feminist theory, gender and sexuality, global and cultural studies, women in history, literature, and politics.
Web site: http://womens-studies.rutgers.edu/

■ SIMMONS COLLEGE

Graduate School, College of Arts and Sciences and Professional Studies, Program in Gender/Cultural Studies, Boston, MA 02115

AWARDS MA. Part-time programs available.

Faculty: 17 full-time (13 women).
Students: 9 full-time (all women), 22 part-time (all women). Average age 26. 27 applicants, 78% accepted. In 2001, 6 degrees awarded.
Degree requirements: For master's, project, thesis, internship, or fieldwork, thesis optional.
Application deadline: Applications are processed on a rolling basis. *Application fee:* $35. Electronic applications accepted.
Financial support: In 2001–02, teaching assistantships (averaging $3,400 per year); research assistantships, Federal Work-Study, institutionally sponsored loans, and scholarships/grants also available. Support available to part-time students. Financial award application deadline: 3/1; financial award applicants required to submit FAFSA.
Dr. Jyoti Puri, Director, 617-521-2593, *E-mail:* jyoti.puri@simmons.edu.
Application contact: Bryan E. Moody, Director, Graduate Enrollment Management and Admission, 617-521-2910, *Fax:* 617-521-3058, *E-mail:* gsa@simmons.edu. *Web site:* http://www.simmons.edu/

■ UNIVERSITY OF CENTRAL FLORIDA

College of Arts and Sciences, Department of Sociology, Orlando, FL 32816

AWARDS Applied sociology (MA); domestic violence (Certificate); gender studies

(Certificate); Mayan studies (Certificate). Part-time and evening/weekend programs available.

Faculty: 25 full-time (12 women), 3 part-time/adjunct (2 women).
Students: 12 full-time (10 women), 40 part-time (33 women); includes 5 minority (3 African Americans, 2 Hispanic Americans). Average age 33. 34 applicants, 82% accepted, 22 enrolled. In 2001, 6 degrees awarded.
Degree requirements: For master's, comprehensive written exam or thesis.
Entrance requirements: For master's, GRE General Test, TOEFL, minimum GPA of 3.0 in last 60 hours. *Application deadline:* For fall admission, 7/15; for spring admission, 12/1. *Application fee:* $20. Electronic applications accepted.
Expenses: Tuition, state resident: part-time $162 per hour. Tuition, nonresident: part-time $569 per hour.
Financial support: In 2001–02, 5 fellowships with partial tuition reimbursements (averaging $2,500 per year), 15 research assistantships with partial tuition reimbursements (averaging $1,990 per year), 22 teaching assistantships with partial tuition reimbursements (averaging $2,681 per year) were awarded. Career-related internships or fieldwork, Federal Work-Study, institutionally sponsored loans, tuition waivers (partial), and unspecified assistantships also available. Financial award application deadline: 3/1; financial award applicants required to submit FAFSA.
Faculty research: Religious subcultures, attitudes toward abortion, population, sport research, stratification.
Dr. Jay Corzine, Chair, 407-823-2227, *Fax:* 407-823-5156, *E-mail:* hcorzine@mail.ucf.edu. *Web site:* http://www.ucf.edu/

■ UNIVERSITY OF MISSOURI–ST. LOUIS

Graduate School, College of Arts and Sciences, Institute of Women's and Gender Studies, St. Louis, MO 63121-4499

AWARDS Certificate.

Faculty: 38.
Students: 1 (woman) full-time, 1 (woman) part-time.
Application deadline: For fall admission, 7/1 (priority date); for spring admission, 12/1 (priority date). Applications are processed on a rolling basis. *Application fee:* $25 ($40 for international students). Electronic applications accepted.
Expenses: Tuition, state resident: part-time $231 per credit hour. Tuition, nonresident: part-time $621 per credit hour.
Financial support: In 2001–02, 1 research assistantship with full tuition reimbursement (averaging $10,000 per year) was awarded
Jeanne Sevelius, Interim Director, 314-516-5581, *Fax:* 314-516-5268, *E-mail:* iwgs@umsl.edu.
Application contact: Graduate Admissions, 314-516-5458, *Fax:* 314-516-5310, *E-mail:* gradadm@umsl.edu. *Web site:* http://www.umsl.edu/divisions/artscience/iwgs/iwgs.html

HISPANIC STUDIES

■ BROWN UNIVERSITY

Graduate School, Department of Hispanic Studies, Providence, RI 02912

AWARDS AM, PhD.

Degree requirements: For master's, one foreign language, thesis; for doctorate, 2 foreign languages, thesis/dissertation, preliminary exam.

■ CALIFORNIA STATE UNIVERSITY, LOS ANGELES

Graduate Studies, College of Natural and Social Sciences, Department of Chicano Studies, Los Angeles, CA 90032-8530

AWARDS Mexican-American studies (MA). Part-time and evening/weekend programs available.

Faculty: 5 full-time, 1 part-time/adjunct.
Students: 5 full-time (4 women), 14 part-time (7 women); includes 18 minority (all Hispanic Americans). In 2001, 2 degrees awarded.
Degree requirements: For master's, one foreign language.
Entrance requirements: For master's, TOEFL, undergraduate major in Mexican-American studies or related area, 12 units in Chicano studies. *Application deadline:* For fall admission, 6/30; for spring admission, 2/1. Applications are processed on a rolling basis. *Application fee:* $55.
Expenses: Tuition, nonresident: part-time $164 per unit.
Financial support: Career-related internships or fieldwork and Federal Work-Study available. Support available to part-time students. Financial award application deadline: 3/1.
Faculty research: U.S.-Mexican relations, Chicano literature, community organization among Chicanos and Hispanics, Spanish language in the American Southwest.
Lionel MacDonado, Acting Chair, 323-343-2190.

■ CALIFORNIA STATE UNIVERSITY, NORTHRIDGE

Graduate Studies, College of Humanities, Department of Chicano Studies, Northridge, CA 91330

AWARDS MA.

Faculty: 22 full-time, 32 part-time/adjunct.
Students: 6 full-time (4 women), 17 part-time (9 women); includes 21 minority (all Hispanic Americans), 1 international. Average age 31. 13 applicants, 69% accepted, 4 enrolled. In 2001, 1 degree awarded.
Entrance requirements: For master's, TOEFL. *Application deadline:* For fall admission, 11/30. *Application fee:* $55.
Expenses: Tuition, nonresident: part-time $631 per semester. Required fees: $246 per unit.
Financial support: Application deadline: 3/1.
Dr. Gerald Resendez, Chair, 818-677-2734.

■ CONNECTICUT COLLEGE

Graduate School, Department of Hispanic Studies, New London, CT 06320-4196

AWARDS MA. Part-time programs available.

Degree requirements: For master's, one foreign language, thesis or alternative.
Entrance requirements: For master's, interview.

■ NEW MEXICO HIGHLANDS UNIVERSITY

Graduate Studies, College of Arts and Sciences, Program in Southwest Studies, Las Vegas, NM 87701

AWARDS Anthropology (MA); Hispanic language and literature (MA); history and political science (MA). Program is interdisciplinary. Part-time programs available.

Faculty: 16 full-time (5 women).
Students: 6 full-time (4 women), 15 part-time (9 women); includes 10 minority (all Hispanic Americans). Average age 39. In 2001, 3 degrees awarded.
Degree requirements: For master's, thesis or alternative.
Entrance requirements: For master's, minimum undergraduate GPA of 3.0. *Application deadline:* For fall admission, 8/1 (priority date). Applications are processed on a rolling basis. *Application fee:* $15.
Expenses: Tuition, state resident: full-time $2,238. Tuition, nonresident: full-time $9,366.
Financial support: Research assistantships with full and partial tuition reimbursements, Federal Work-Study available. Financial award application deadline: 3/1.
Dr. Tomas Salazar, Dean, 505-454-3080, *Fax:* 505-454-3389, *E-mail:* salazar_t@nmhu.edu.
Application contact: Dr. Linda LaGrange, Associate Dean of Graduate Studies, 505-454-3266, *Fax:* 505-454-3558, *E-mail:* lagrange_l@nmhu.edu.

■ PONTIFICAL CATHOLIC UNIVERSITY OF PUERTO RICO

College of Arts and Humanities, Department of Hispanic Studies, Ponce, PR 00717-0777

AWARDS Divinity (MA); hispanic studies (MA); history (MA). Part-time and evening/weekend programs available.

Faculty: 8 full-time (4 women).
Students: 21 full-time (6 women), 19 part-time (13 women); all minorities (all Hispanic Americans). Average age 30. 15 applicants, 93% accepted, 13 enrolled. In 2001, 2 degrees awarded.
Entrance requirements: For master's, GRE, 2 recommendation letters, interview, minimum GPA of 2.0. *Application deadline:* For fall admission, 3/15 (priority date); for spring admission, 11/15 (priority date). Applications are processed on a rolling basis. *Application fee:* $25.
Expenses: Tuition: Full-time $2,880; part-time $160 per credit. Required fees: $360. Tuition and fees vary according to degree level and program.
Financial support: Federal Work-Study, institutionally sponsored loans, and tuition waivers (partial) available. Support available to part-time students. Financial award application deadline: 7/15.
Jaime Martel, Chairperson, 787-841-2000 Ext. 1085.
Application contact: Ana O. Bonilla, Director of Admissions, 787-841-2000 Ext. 1000, *Fax:* 787-840-4295.

■ SAN JOSE STATE UNIVERSITY

Graduate Studies, College of Social Work, Department of Mexican-American Studies, San Jose, CA 95192-0001

AWARDS MA.

Students: 8 full-time (4 women), 9 part-time (3 women); includes 16 minority (15 Hispanic Americans, 1 Native American). Average age 30. 10 applicants, 60% accepted.
Application deadline: For fall admission, 6/29; for spring admission, 11/30. Applications are processed on a rolling basis. *Application fee:* $59. Electronic applications accepted.
Expenses: Tuition, nonresident: part-time $246 per unit. Required fees: $678 per semester. Tuition and fees vary according to course load.
Financial support: Application deadline: 5/31.
Dr. Lou Holscher, Chair, 408-924-5760, *Fax:* 408-924-5700.
Application contact: R. C. Jiminez, Graduate Coordinator, 408-924-5310.

■ STONY BROOK UNIVERSITY, STATE UNIVERSITY OF NEW YORK

Graduate School, College of Arts and Sciences, Department of Hispanic Languages and Literature, Stony Brook, NY 11794

AWARDS MA, DA, PhD. Evening/weekend programs available.

Faculty: 10 full-time (5 women), 1 (woman) part-time/adjunct.
Students: 19 full-time (14 women), 18 part-time (13 women); includes 10 minority (all Hispanic Americans), 15 international. Average age 27. 17 applicants, 76% accepted. In 2001, 3 master's, 4 doctorates awarded.
Degree requirements: For master's, one foreign language, thesis or alternative; for doctorate, 2 foreign languages, thesis/dissertation.
Entrance requirements: For master's, GRE General Test, TOEFL, BA in Spanish; for doctorate, GRE General Test, TOEFL, MA in Spanish. *Application deadline:* For fall admission, 1/15. *Application fee:* $50.
Expenses: Contact institution.
Financial support: In 2001–02, 21 teaching assistantships were awarded; fellowships, research assistantships, tuition waivers and unspecified assistantships also available.
Faculty research: Spanish language and literature. *Total annual research expenditures:* $3,080.
Dr. Roman de la Campa, Chair, 631-632-6959.
Application contact: Dr. Antonio Vera-Leon, Director, 631-632-6935, *Fax:* 631-632-9724, *E-mail:* averaleon@notes.cc.sunysb.edu. *Web site:* http://www.sunysb.edu/hispanic/

Find an in-depth description at www.petersons.com/gradchannel.

■ UNIVERSITY OF CALIFORNIA, LOS ANGELES

Graduate Division, College of Letters and Science, Department of Spanish and Portuguese, Program in Hispanic Languages and Literature, Los Angeles, CA 90095

AWARDS PhD.

Students: 37 full-time (18 women); includes 16 minority (1 Asian American or Pacific Islander, 15 Hispanic Americans), 9 international. 16 applicants, 44% accepted, 5 enrolled. In 2001, 3 degrees awarded.
Degree requirements: For doctorate, 2 foreign languages.
Entrance requirements: For doctorate, GRE General Test, minimum undergraduate GPA of 3.0, sample of written work (recommended). *Application deadline:* For fall admission, 12/31. *Application fee:* $60. Electronic applications accepted.
Expenses: Tuition, nonresident: full-time $10,244. Required fees: $3,609. Full-time tuition and fees vary according to program.
Financial support: In 2001–02, 15 fellowships, 8 research assistantships, 44 teaching assistantships were awarded.
Application contact: Departmental Office, 310-825-1036, *E-mail:* peinado@humnet.ucla.edu.

■ UNIVERSITY OF CALIFORNIA, SANTA BARBARA

Graduate Division, College of Letters and Sciences, Division of Humanities and Fine Arts, Department of Spanish and Portuguese, Santa Barbara, CA 93106

AWARDS Hispanic languages and literature (PhD); Portuguese (MA); Spanish (MA).

Degree requirements: For master's, one foreign language, thesis or alternative; for doctorate, one foreign language, thesis/dissertation.
Entrance requirements: For master's, GRE, TOEFL; for doctorate, GRE, TOEFL, 2 samples of written work.

■ UNIVERSITY OF ILLINOIS AT CHICAGO

Graduate College, College of Liberal Arts and Sciences, Department of Spanish and French, Program in Latin American and Latino Studies, Chicago, IL 60607-7128

AWARDS MA, PhD.

Faculty: 24 full-time (14 women).
Students: 18 full-time (8 women), 26 part-time (18 women); includes 26 minority (2 African Americans, 1 Asian American or Pacific Islander, 23 Hispanic Americans), 10 international. Average age 33. 34 applicants, 38% accepted, 10 enrolled. In 2001, 9 degrees awarded.
Degree requirements: For master's, one foreign language.
Entrance requirements: For master's, GRE General Test, TOEFL, minimum GPA of 3.75 on a 5.0 scale, undergraduate major in Spanish. *Application deadline:* For fall admission, 6/1; for spring admission, 11/1. Applications are processed on a rolling basis. *Application fee:* $40 ($50 for international students). Electronic applications accepted.
Expenses: Tuition, state resident: full-time $3,060. Tuition, nonresident: full-time $6,688.
Financial support: In 2001–02, 24 students received support; fellowships with full tuition reimbursements available, research assistantships with full tuition reimbursements available, teaching assistantships with full tuition reimbursements available, Federal Work-Study and tuition waivers (full) available. Financial

award application deadline: 3/1; financial award applicants required to submit FAFSA.
Leda Schiavo, Director of Graduate Studies, 312-996-0125.

■ **UNIVERSITY OF PITTSBURGH**

Faculty of Arts and Sciences, Department of Hispanic Languages and Literatures, Pittsburgh, PA 15260

AWARDS MA, PhD. Part-time programs available.

Faculty: 9 full-time (3 women), 4 part-time/adjunct (2 women).
Students: 41 full-time (22 women), 6 part-time (5 women); includes 5 minority (1 African American, 1 Asian American or Pacific Islander, 3 Hispanic Americans), 36 international. Average age 34. 53 applicants, 53% accepted, 16 enrolled. In 2001, 7 master's, 5 doctorates awarded. Terminal master's awarded for partial completion of doctoral program.
Degree requirements: For master's, thesis or alternative, seminar paper, comprehensive exam; for doctorate, one foreign language, thesis/dissertation, comprehensive exam. *Median time to degree:* Master's–2 years full-time, 4 years part-time; doctorate–6 years full-time, 8 years part-time.
Entrance requirements: For master's and doctorate, TOEFL. *Application deadline:* For fall admission, 1/15 (priority date); for spring admission, 11/2 (priority date). *Application fee:* $40. Electronic applications accepted.
Expenses: Tuition, state resident: full-time $9,410; part-time $385 per credit. Tuition, nonresident: full-time $19,376; part-time $797 per credit. Required fees: $480; $90 per term. Tuition and fees vary according to program.
Financial support: In 2001–02, 38 students received support, including 5 fellowships (averaging $14,500 per year), 30 teaching assistantships with partial tuition reimbursements available (averaging $12,000 per year); tuition waivers (partial) also available. Financial award application deadline: 1/15.
Faculty research: Latin American literature and culture, Luso-Brazilian literature and culture, peninsular literature and culture, Hispanic linguistics, methodology and applied linguistics.
Dr. John R. Beverley, Chairman, 412-624-5225, *Fax:* 412-624-8505, *E-mail:* brq@pitt.edu.
Application contact: Dr. Susan Berk-Seligson, Graduate Director, 412-624-5245, *Fax:* 412-624-8505, *E-mail:* sberksel+@pitt.edu. *Web site:* http://www.pitt.edu/~hispan/

■ **UNIVERSITY OF PUERTO RICO, MAYAGÜEZ CAMPUS**

Graduate Studies, College of Arts and Sciences, Department of Hispanic Studies, Mayagüez, PR 00681-9000

AWARDS MA. Part-time programs available.

Degree requirements: For master's, thesis, comprehensive exam.
Faculty research: Spanish literature, Hispanic-American literature, Puerto Rican literature, stylistics, linguistics.

■ **UNIVERSITY OF PUERTO RICO, RÍO PIEDRAS**

College of Humanities, Department of Hispanic Studies, San Juan, PR 00931

AWARDS MA, PhD. Part-time and evening/weekend programs available.

Faculty: 25.
Students: 70 full-time (49 women), 90 part-time (64 women); includes 159 minority (all Hispanic Americans), 1 international. 41 applicants, 63% accepted. In 2001, 2 master's, 4 doctorates awarded.
Degree requirements: For master's and doctorate, one foreign language, thesis/dissertation, comprehensive exam.
Entrance requirements: For master's, interview, minimum GPA of 3.0; for doctorate, interview, master's degree, minimum GPA of 3.0. *Application deadline:* For fall admission, 2/1. *Application fee:* $17.
Expenses: Students that provide official evidence of private medicine insurance or service are exempt of the payment of $529 per academic year.
Financial support: Fellowships, research assistantships, teaching assistantships, Federal Work-Study, institutionally sponsored loans, and tuition waivers (partial) available. Financial award application deadline: 5/31.
Faculty research: Poetry of Luis Palés Matos, short stories in Puerto Rico, language in the social process, "Decima Popular", Anglicism.
Dr. Carmen I. Pérez-Marín, Coordinator, 787-764-0000 Ext. 2486, *Fax:* 787-763-5899.
Application contact: Dr. Luis Felipe Díaz, Coordinator.

■ **UNIVERSITY OF WASHINGTON**

Graduate School, College of Arts and Sciences, Department of Romance Languages and Literature, Division of Spanish and Portuguese Studies, Seattle, WA 98195

AWARDS Hispanic literacy and cultural studies (MA).

Degree requirements: For master's, 2 foreign languages.
Entrance requirements: For master's, GRE General Test, TOEFL, TSE, minimum GPA of 3.0. Electronic applications accepted.
Expenses: Tuition, state resident: full-time $5,539. Tuition, nonresident: full-time $14,376. Required fees: $390. Tuition and fees vary according to course load and program. *Web site:* http://depts.washington.edu/spanport/

HOLOCAUST STUDIES

■ **CLARK UNIVERSITY**

Graduate School, Department of History, Program in Holocaust History, Worcester, MA 01610-1477

AWARDS PhD.

Degree requirements: For doctorate, thesis/dissertation.
Entrance requirements: For doctorate, TOEFL. *Application fee:* $40.
Expenses: Tuition: Full-time $24,400; part-time $763 per credit. Required fees: $10.
Financial support: In 2001–02, fellowships with full and partial tuition reimbursements (averaging $10,250 per year), research assistantships with full and partial tuition reimbursements (averaging $10,250 per year), teaching assistantships with full and partial tuition reimbursements (averaging $10,250 per year) were awarded. Tuition waivers (partial) also available.
Faculty research: Jewish persecution, children and survivors, Germany's role in the holocaust.
Deborah Dwork, Professor, 508-421-3745.
Application contact: Susan Levitin, Program Officer, 508-421-3745. *Web site:* http://www2.clarku.edu/newsite/graduatefolder/programs/index.shtml

■ **THE RICHARD STOCKTON COLLEGE OF NEW JERSEY**

Graduate Programs, Program in Holocaust and Genocide Studies, Pomona, NJ 08240-0195

AWARDS MA.

Faculty research: Women and the Holocaust, survivor perspectives, liberty and persecution. *Web site:* http://www2.stockton.edu/academics/

Find an in-depth description at www.petersons.com/gradchannel.

JEWISH STUDIES

■ **BALTIMORE HEBREW UNIVERSITY**

Peggy Meyerhoff Pearlstone School of Graduate Studies, Program in Jewish Education, Baltimore, MD 21215-3996

AWARDS MAJE. Part-time programs available.

Faculty: 8 full-time (2 women), 3 part-time/adjunct (2 women).

Baltimore Hebrew University (continued)
Students: 2 full-time (both women), 11 part-time (all women). Average age 30. 7 applicants, 86% accepted, 3 enrolled. In 2001, 5 degrees awarded.
Degree requirements: For master's, one foreign language, thesis or alternative.
Entrance requirements: For master's, minimum GPA of 3.0. *Application deadline:* For fall admission, 7/15; for spring admission, 11/15. Applications are processed on a rolling basis. *Application fee:* $35.
Expenses: Tuition: Part-time $900 per course.
Financial support: Fellowships with partial tuition reimbursements, career-related internships or fieldwork, scholarships/grants, and tuition waivers (partial) available. Support available to part-time students. Financial award application deadline: 9/15; financial award applicants required to submit FAFSA.
Dr. Hana Bor, Director, 410-578-6903, *Fax:* 410-578-6940, *E-mail:* bor@bhu.edu.
Application contact: Essie Keyser, Director of Admissions, 410-578-6967, *Fax:* 410-578-6940, *E-mail:* keyser@bhu.edu.

■ BALTIMORE HEBREW UNIVERSITY

Peggy Meyerhoff Pearlstone School of Graduate Studies, Program in Jewish Studies, Baltimore, MD 21215-3996

AWARDS MA, PhD. Part-time programs available.

Faculty: 8 full-time (2 women), 3 part-time/adjunct (2 women).
Students: 3 full-time (all women), 20 part-time (13 women). 6 applicants, 83% accepted, 2 enrolled. In 2001, 10 master's awarded. Terminal master's awarded for partial completion of doctoral program.
Degree requirements: For master's, one foreign language, thesis or alternative, comprehensive exam (for some programs); for doctorate, 3 foreign languages, thesis/dissertation, comprehensive exam.
Entrance requirements: For master's, minimum GPA of 3.0; for doctorate, GRE, minimum GPA of 3.5, master's thesis or equivalent. *Application deadline:* For fall admission, 7/15; for spring admission, 11/15. Applications are processed on a rolling basis. *Application fee:* $35.
Expenses: Tuition: Part-time $900 per course.
Financial support: In 2001–02, 5 students received support; fellowships with partial tuition reimbursements available, scholarships/grants and tuition waivers (partial) available. Support available to part-time students. Financial award application deadline: 9/15.
Application contact: Essie Keyser, Director of Admissions, 410-578-6967, *Fax:* 410-578-6940, *E-mail:* keyser@bhu.edu.

■ BRANDEIS UNIVERSITY

Graduate School of Arts and Sciences, Benjamin S. Hornstein Program in Jewish Communal Service, Waltham, MA 02454-9110

AWARDS MA, MAMM, MA/MA, MBA/MA. Part-time programs available.

Faculty: 7 full-time (3 women), 4 part-time/adjunct (1 woman).
Students: 33 full-time (25 women), 2 part-time (1 woman). Average age 25. 36 applicants, 61% accepted. In 2001, 19 degrees awarded.
Degree requirements: For master's, one foreign language.
Entrance requirements: For master's, GRE General Test, interview, sample of written work, resumé, 3 letters of recommendation. *Application deadline:* For fall admission, 3/15 (priority date). Applications are processed on a rolling basis. *Application fee:* $60. Electronic applications accepted.
Expenses: Tuition: Full-time $27,392. Required fees: $35.
Financial support: In 2001–02, 29 students received support, including 12 fellowships with partial tuition reimbursements available (averaging $1,200 per year); research assistantships, career-related internships or fieldwork, institutionally sponsored loans, scholarships/grants, and tuition waivers (partial) also available. Financial award application deadline: 3/15; financial award applicants required to submit CSS PROFILE or FAFSA.
Faculty research: Leadership, informal education, demography, Jewish identity, Israel-Diaspora relations.
Dr. Susan L. Shevitz, Director, 781-736-2990, *Fax:* 781-736-2070, *E-mail:* hornstein@brandeis.edu.
Application contact: Natalie Greene, Program Administrator, 781-736-2990, *Fax:* 781-736-2070, *E-mail:* hornstein@brandeis.edu. *Web site:* http://www.brandeis.edu/jcs/index.html

■ BRANDEIS UNIVERSITY

Graduate School of Arts and Sciences, Department of Near Eastern and Judaic Studies, Waltham, MA 02454-9110

AWARDS Near Eastern and Judaic studies (MA, PhD); Near Eastern and Judaic studies and sociology (PhD); Near Eastern and Judaic studies and women's studies (MA); Near Eastern and Judiac studies and sociology (MA); teaching of Hebrew (MA). Part-time programs available.

Faculty: 27 full-time (13 women), 11 part-time/adjunct (4 women).
Students: 66 full-time (34 women), 2 part-time (1 woman); includes 3 minority (1 African American, 1 Asian American or Pacific Islander, 1 Hispanic American), 14 international. Average age 33. 70 applicants, 80% accepted. In 2001, 9 master's, 5 doctorates awarded. Terminal master's awarded for partial completion of doctoral program.
Degree requirements: For master's, one foreign language, thesis (for some programs), comprehensive exam; for doctorate, 3 foreign languages, thesis/dissertation, comprehensive exam. *Median time to degree:* Master's–2 years full-time; doctorate–6.5 years full-time.
Entrance requirements: For master's, GRE General Test (suggested), resumé, letters of recommendation; for doctorate, GRE General Test (suggested). *Application deadline:* For fall admission, 1/15. Applications are processed on a rolling basis. *Application fee:* $60. Electronic applications accepted.
Expenses: Tuition: Full-time $27,392. Required fees: $35.
Financial support: In 2001–02, 25 students received support, including 4 fellowships with full and partial tuition reimbursements available (averaging $13,000 per year); research assistantships with full and partial tuition reimbursements available, teaching assistantships with full and partial tuition reimbursements available, Federal Work-Study, institutionally sponsored loans, scholarships/grants, and tuition waivers (full and partial) also available. Support available to part-time students. Financial award application deadline: 4/15; financial award applicants required to submit CSS PROFILE or FAFSA.
Faculty research: Ancient Near East and Bible, philosophy, history, Hebrew literature, modern Middle East.
Dr. Marc Z. Brettler, Chair, 781-736-2968, *Fax:* 781-736-2070, *E-mail:* brettler@brandeis.edu.
Application contact: Dr. David Wright, Graduate Adviser, 781-736-2957, *Fax:* 781-736-2070, *E-mail:* wright@brandeis.edu. *Web site:* http://www.brandeis.edu/departments/nejs/index.html

■ BROOKLYN COLLEGE OF THE CITY UNIVERSITY OF NEW YORK

Division of Graduate Studies, Department of Judaic Studies, Brooklyn, NY 11210-2889

AWARDS MA. Part-time and evening/weekend programs available.

Students: In 2001, 1 degree awarded.
Degree requirements: For master's, 2 foreign languages.
Entrance requirements: For master's, TOEFL, 18 upper-level credits in Judaic studies, interview. *Application deadline:* For fall admission, 3/1; for spring admission, 11/1. *Application fee:* $40.
Expenses: Tuition, state resident: full-time $4,350; part-time $185 per credit. Tuition, nonresident: full-time $7,600; part-time $320 per credit.
Financial support: Fellowships, Federal Work-Study, institutionally sponsored loans, and scholarships/grants available.

Support available to part-time students. Financial award application deadline: 5/1; financial award applicants required to submit FAFSA.
Faculty research: Biblical studies, Talmud and Midrash, modern Jewish history and thought.
Dr. Sara Reguer, Chairperson, 718-951-5229, *Fax:* 718-951-4703.
Application contact: Dr. Herbert Druks, Deputy Chairman, Graduate Studies, 718-951-5229, *Fax:* 718-951-4703.

■ BROWN UNIVERSITY

Graduate School, Department of Religious Studies, Program in Judaic Studies, Providence, RI 02912

AWARDS AM, PhD.

Degree requirements: For master's, one foreign language, thesis; for doctorate, 2 foreign languages, thesis/dissertation.
Entrance requirements: For master's, GRE General Test, proficiency in Hebrew; for doctorate, GRE General Test, proficiency in Hebrew and Aramaic.

■ CHICAGO THEOLOGICAL SEMINARY

Graduate and Professional Programs, Chicago, IL 60637-1507

AWARDS Clinical pastoral education (D Min); Jewish-Christian studies (PhD); pastoral care (PhD); pastoral counseling (D Min); preaching (D Min); spiritual leadership (D Min); theology (M Div, MA); theology and the human sciences (PhD), including theology and society, theology and the personality sciences. Part-time programs available.

Faculty: 9 full-time (1 woman), 11 part-time/adjunct (2 women).
Students: 99 full-time (43 women), 105 part-time (60 women); includes 47 minority (44 African Americans, 3 Asian Americans or Pacific Islanders), 33 international. Average age 41.
Degree requirements: For M Div, thesis; for doctorate, 2 foreign languages, thesis/dissertation.
Entrance requirements: For master's, TOEFL; for doctorate, GRE General Test, TOEFL. *Application deadline:* For fall admission, 5/1; for winter admission, 11/1. Applications are processed on a rolling basis. *Application fee:* $50.
Expenses: Tuition: Full-time $7,960; part-time $995 per course. Required fees: $120; $60 per semester. One-time fee: $125 full-time. Tuition and fees vary according to degree level and program.
Financial support: Fellowships, institutionally sponsored loans and scholarships/grants available. Support available to part-time students. Financial award application deadline: 4/1; financial award applicants required to submit FAFSA.
Faculty research: Asian prostitution, globalization of educational styles, early Church community, health in African-American communities, abuse in seminarians' backgrounds. *Total annual research expenditures:* $150,000.
Dr. Dow Edgerton, Dean, 773-752-5757, *Fax:* 773-752-5925, *E-mail:* dedgerton@ctschicago.edu.
Application contact: Rev. Alison Buttrick Patton, Director of Admissions, Recruitment and Financial Aid, 773-752-5757 Ext. 229, *Fax:* 773-752-1903, *E-mail:* apatton@ctschicago.edu. *Web site:* http://www.ctschicago.edu/

■ COLUMBIA UNIVERSITY

Graduate School of Arts and Sciences, Division of Humanities, Program in Jewish Studies, New York, NY 10027

AWARDS M Phil, MA, PhD.

Students: 1 applicant, 0% accepted.
Entrance requirements: For master's and doctorate, GRE General Test, TOEFL. *Application deadline:* For fall admission, 1/3; for spring admission, 11/30. *Application fee:* $60.
Expenses: Tuition: Full-time $27,528. Required fees: $1,638.
Financial support: Available to part-time students. Application deadline: 1/5;
Faculty research: Jewish history, culture, and institutions; Hebrew, Yiddish, and Jewish languages and literatures; history of Jewish philosophy and religion.
Yosef Yerushalmi, Chair, 212-854-2581, *Fax:* 212-854-2590.

■ COLUMBIA UNIVERSITY

Graduate School of Arts and Sciences, Interdepartmental Committee on Yiddish Studies, New York, NY 10027

AWARDS MA. Applicants must apply for admission to one of the participating departments: Germanic Languages, History, Middle East Languages and Cultures, Religion.

Entrance requirements: For master's, high degree of proficiency in Yiddish.
Expenses: Tuition: Full-time $27,528. Required fees: $1,638.
Application contact: Robert Furno, Assistant Dean for Admissions, 212-854-4737, *Fax:* 212-854-2863, *E-mail:* jc12@columbia.edu.

■ COLUMBIA UNIVERSITY

Graduate School of Arts and Sciences, Program in Liberal Studies, New York, NY 10027

AWARDS American studies (MA); East Asian studies (MA); human rights studies (MA); Islamic culture studies (MA); Jewish studies (MA); medieval studies (MA); modern European studies (MA); South Asian studies (MA). Part-time and evening/weekend programs available.

Faculty: 5 part-time/adjunct (2 women).
Students: 7 full-time (2 women), 75 part-time (51 women); includes 5 minority (1 African American, 3 Asian Americans or Pacific Islanders, 1 Hispanic American), 8 international. Average age 41. 39 applicants, 77% accepted. In 2001, 20 degrees awarded.
Degree requirements: For master's, thesis.
Application deadline: For fall admission, 4/1; for spring admission, 11/1. *Application fee:* $65.
Expenses: Tuition: Full-time $27,528. Required fees: $1,638.
Steve Laymon, Assistant Dean, 212-854-4932, *Fax:* 212-854-4912.
Application contact: Director of Admissions, 212-854-3331.

Find an in-depth description at www.petersons.com/gradchannel.

■ CORNELL UNIVERSITY

Graduate School, Graduate Fields of Arts and Sciences, Field of Near Eastern Studies, Ithaca, NY 14853-0001

AWARDS Ancient Near Eastern studies (MA, PhD); Arabic and Islamic studies (MA, PhD); biblical studies (MA, PhD); Hebrew and Judaic studies (MA, PhD).

Faculty: 7 full-time.
Students: 13 applicants. In 2001, 1 degree awarded. Terminal master's awarded for partial completion of doctoral program.
Degree requirements: For master's, one foreign language, thesis; for doctorate, 2 foreign languages, thesis/dissertation.
Entrance requirements: For master's and doctorate, GRE General Test, TOEFL, 2 years of 1 Near Eastern language, 3 letters of recommendation. *Application deadline:* For fall admission, 2/1. *Application fee:* $65. Electronic applications accepted.
Expenses: Tuition: Full-time $25,970. Required fees: $50.
Financial support: Fellowships with full tuition reimbursements, research assistantships with full tuition reimbursements, teaching assistantships with full tuition reimbursements, institutionally sponsored loans, scholarships/grants, tuition waivers (full and partial), and unspecified assistantships available. Financial award applicants required to submit FAFSA.
Faculty research: Hebrew and Judaic studies (including Bible), early Christianity, Arabic and Islamic studies, modern Middle East.
Application contact: Graduate Field Assistant, 607-255-1329, *E-mail:* neareastern@cornell.edu. *Web site:* http://www.gradschool.cornell.edu/grad/fields_1/ne-st.html

■ EMORY UNIVERSITY

Graduate School of Arts and Sciences, Program in Jewish Studies, Atlanta, GA 30322-1100

AWARDS MA.

Emory University (continued)
Faculty: 14 full-time (3 women).
Students: 7 full-time (5 women), 1 international. 15 applicants, 27% accepted, 4 enrolled. In 2001, 5 degrees awarded.
Degree requirements: For master's, thesis, registration.
Entrance requirements: For master's, GRE General Test, TOEFL, 2 years of course work in Hebrew or equivalent. *Application deadline:* For fall admission, 1/20. *Application fee:* $50. Electronic applications accepted.
Expenses: Tuition: Full-time $24,770. Required fees: $100. Tuition and fees vary according to program and student level.
Financial support: Scholarships/grants available. Financial award application deadline: 1/20.
Dr. Deborah Lipstadt, Director, 404-727-2298.
Application contact: Dr. Benjamin Hary, Director of Graduate Studies, 404-727-2298, *E-mail:* bhary@emory.edu.

■ GRADUATE THEOLOGICAL UNION

Graduate Programs, Berkeley, CA 94709-1212

AWARDS Arts and religion (MA, Th D); biblical languages (MA); biblical studies (Old and New Testament) (MA, PhD, Th D); Buddhist studies (MA); Christian spirituality (MA); cultural and historical studies (MA, PhD); ethics and social theory (PhD); historical studies (MA, PhD, Th D); history of art and religion (PhD); homiletics (MA, PhD, Th D); interdisciplinary studies (PhD, Th D); Jewish studies (MA, PhD, Certificate); liturgical studies (MA, PhD, Th D); Near Eastern religions (PhD); religion and psychology (MA, PhD); religion and society (MA); systematic and philosophical theology (MA, PhD, Th D);). MA/M Div offered jointly with individual denominations.

Faculty: 80 full-time (29 women), 14 part-time/adjunct (3 women).
Students: 308 full-time (154 women), 39 part-time (13 women); includes 48 minority (9 African Americans, 28 Asian Americans or Pacific Islanders, 9 Hispanic Americans, 2 Native Americans), 60 international. Average age 42. 193 applicants, 65% accepted, 76 enrolled. In 2001, 28 master's, 20 doctorates awarded. Terminal master's awarded for partial completion of doctoral program.
Degree requirements: For master's, one foreign language, thesis/dissertation; for doctorate, one foreign language, thesis/dissertation, comprehensive exam.
Entrance requirements: For master's, GRE General Test, TOEFL; for doctorate, GRE General Test, TOEFL, MA or M Div degree. *Application deadline:* For fall admission, 12/15; for winter admission, 2/15; for spring admission, 9/30. *Application fee:* $40. Electronic applications accepted.
Expenses: Tuition: Full-time $16,000. Tuition and fees vary according to degree level.
Financial support: In 2001–02, 160 students received support, including 15 fellowships (averaging $19,000 per year), 22 research assistantships (averaging $4,000 per year); teaching assistantships, Federal Work-Study, scholarships/grants, and tuition waivers (full and partial) also available. Support available to part-time students. Financial award application deadline: 2/1; financial award applicants required to submit FAFSA.
Dr. Eldon G. Ernst, Interim Dean, 510-649-2440, *Fax:* 510-649-1417, *E-mail:* eernst@gtu.edu.
Application contact: Dr. Kathleen Kook, Assistant Dean for Admissions, 800-826-4488, *Fax:* 510-649-1730, *E-mail:* gtuadm@gtu.edu. *Web site:* http://www.gtu.edu/

■ GRATZ COLLEGE

Graduate Programs, Program in Jewish Studies, Melrose Park, PA 19027

AWARDS Classical studies (MA); Jewish studies (MA); modern studies (MA). Part-time programs available.

Faculty: 7 full-time (3 women), 11 part-time/adjunct (7 women).
Students: 2 full-time, 14 part-time. In 2001, 5 degrees awarded.
Degree requirements: For master's, one foreign language, comprehensive exam.
Application deadline: Applications are processed on a rolling basis. *Application fee:* $50.
Expenses: Tuition: Full-time $9,950; part-time $466 per credit.
Financial support: Fellowships, Federal Work-Study and unspecified assistantships available. Support available to part-time students. Financial award application deadline: 4/15; financial award applicants required to submit FAFSA.
Dr. Joseph Davis, Coordinator, 215-635-7300 Ext. 142, *Fax:* 215-635-7320, *E-mail:* jdavis@gratz.edu.
Application contact: Adena E. Johnston, Director of Admissions, 215-635-7300 Ext. 140, *Fax:* 215-635-7320, *E-mail:* admissions@gratz.edu.

■ HARVARD UNIVERSITY

Graduate School of Arts and Sciences, Department of Near Eastern Languages and Civilizations, Cambridge, MA 02138

AWARDS Akkadian and Sumerian (AM, PhD); Arabic (AM, PhD); Armenian (AM, PhD); biblical history (AM, PhD); Hebrew (AM, PhD); Indo-Muslim culture (AM, PhD); Iranian (AM, PhD); Jewish history and literature (AM, PhD); Persian (AM, PhD); Semitic philology (AM, PhD); Syro-Palestinian archaeology (AM, PhD); Turkish (AM, PhD).

Degree requirements: For doctorate, variable foreign language requirement, thesis/dissertation, general exams.
Entrance requirements: For master's, GRE General Test, TOEFL; for doctorate, GRE General Test, TOEFL, proficiency in a Near Eastern language.
Expenses: Tuition: Full-time $23,370. Required fees: $816. Full-time tuition and fees vary according to program and student level.

■ HEBREW COLLEGE

Program in Jewish Studies, Newton Centre, MA 02459

AWARDS Jewish cantorial arts (Certificate); Jewish communal and clinical social work (Certificate); Jewish music (Certificate); Jewish studies (MA); management of Jewish philanthropic and community organizations (Certificate). Part-time and evening/weekend programs available. Postbaccalaureate distance learning degree programs offered.

Faculty: 6 full-time (1 woman), 19 part-time/adjunct (7 women).
Students: Average age 30. 20 applicants, 100% accepted, 19 enrolled.
Degree requirements: For master's, one foreign language.
Application deadline: For fall admission, 5/31 (priority date). Applications are processed on a rolling basis. *Application fee:* $40.
Expenses: Tuition: Part-time $550 per credit.
Financial support: Fellowships, teaching assistantships, tuition waivers (partial) available. Support available to part-time students. Financial award application deadline: 4/15.
Dr. Barry Mesch, Provost, 617-559-8600, *Fax:* 617-559-8601, *E-mail:* bmesch@hebrewcollege.edu.
Application contact: Melissa Roiter, Assistant to Dean of Students, 617-559-8610, *Fax:* 617-559-8601, *E-mail:* admissions@hebrewcollege.edu. *Web site:* http://www.hebrewcollege.edu/online/

■ HEBREW UNION COLLEGE–JEWISH INSTITUTE OF RELIGION

Edgar F. Magnin School of Graduate Studies, Los Angeles, CA 90007-3796

AWARDS MAJS, DHL, DHS. Part-time programs available.

Students: 4 full-time (all women), 2 part-time (both women). Average age 45. 3 applicants, 100% accepted, 2 enrolled. Terminal master's awarded for partial completion of doctoral program.
Degree requirements: For master's and doctorate, one foreign language, thesis/dissertation, Hebrew.
Entrance requirements: For master's, GRE General Test, Hebrew Language Test, interview, minimum undergraduate GPA of 3.0; for doctorate, GRE General Test, Hebrew Language Test, interview,

minimum graduate GPA of 3.0. *Application deadline:* For fall admission, 3/1. Applications are processed on a rolling basis. *Application fee:* $55.
Expenses: Tuition: Full-time $8,500; part-time $355 per unit. Required fees: $373.
Financial support: In 2001–02, 2 students received support, including teaching assistantships (averaging $12,000 per year); fellowships, career-related internships or fieldwork, scholarships/grants, and unspecified assistantships also available. Financial award application deadline: 3/15; financial award applicants required to submit FAFSA.
Dr. Reuven Firestone, Director, 213-749-3424, *Fax:* 213-747-6128, *E-mail:* rfirestone@huc.edu.
Application contact: Lisa Kaplan, Director of Admissions and Recruitment, 213-749-3424, *Fax:* 213-747-6128, *E-mail:* lkaplan@huc.edu.

■ HEBREW UNION COLLEGE–JEWISH INSTITUTE OF RELIGION

School of Graduate Studies, Program in Judaic Studies, New York, NY 10012-1186

AWARDS MAJS. Part-time programs available.

Faculty: 12 full-time (5 women), 23 part-time/adjunct (10 women).
Students: 2 full-time (1 woman), 2 part-time (both women). Average age 40. 3 applicants, 100% accepted.
Degree requirements: For master's, one foreign language, thesis.
Entrance requirements: For master's, GRE, minimum 1 year of college-level Hebrew. *Application deadline:* For fall admission, 12/15 (priority date); for winter admission, 3/15 (priority date); for spring admission, 6/15 (priority date). Applications are processed on a rolling basis. *Application fee:* $35.
Expenses: Tuition: Full-time $8,500; part-time $355 per credit hour. Required fees: $3,000. Part-time tuition and fees vary according to course load, degree level and program.
Financial support: Applicants required to submit FAFSA.
Faculty research: Philosophy and theology, Bible, Hebrew, history and Rabbinics.
Dr. Carol Ochs, Coordinator, School of Graduate Studies, 212-674-5300 Ext. 267, *Fax:* 212-388-1720.

■ HEBREW UNION COLLEGE–JEWISH INSTITUTE OF RELIGION

Rabbinic School, Cincinnati, OH 45220-2488

AWARDS MAHL.

Faculty: 18 full-time (2 women), 7 part-time/adjunct (3 women).
Students: 58 full-time (24 women); includes 1 minority (Hispanic American). Average age 30. 73 applicants, 71% accepted.
Degree requirements: For first-professional, one foreign language, thesis.
Entrance requirements: GRE, interview, psychological test, passing Hebrew competency exam. *Application deadline:* For fall admission, 11/1 (priority date); for spring admission, 12/18. *Application fee:* $75.
Expenses: Tuition: Full-time $8,500; part-time $355 per credit hour.
Financial support: In 2001–02, 42 students received support, including 1 teaching assistantship (averaging $2,000 per year); career-related internships or fieldwork, institutionally sponsored loans, and scholarships/grants also available. Financial award application deadline: 6/1; financial award applicants required to submit FAFSA.
Faculty research: Comprehensive Aramaic lexicon, four-volume history (German Jews and modern times).
Rabbi Kenneth E. Ehrlich, Dean, 513-221-1875 Ext. 227, *Fax:* 513-221-0321, *E-mail:* kehrlich@huc.edu.
Application contact: Rabbi Roxanne J. Schneider, Dean of Admissions, 513-221-1875, *Fax:* 513-221-5372, *E-mail:* rschneider@huc.edu. *Web site:* http://www.huc.edu/

■ HEBREW UNION COLLEGE–JEWISH INSTITUTE OF RELIGION

School of Graduate Studies, Cincinnati, OH 45220-2488

AWARDS Bible and the ancient Near East (M Phil, MA, PhD); Hebrew letters (DHL); history of biblical interpretation (M Phil, MA, PhD); Jewish and Christian studies in the Greco-Roman period (M Phil, PhD); Jewish and cognate studies (M Phil); Judaic and cognate studies (MA, PhD); modern Jewish history (M Phil, MA, PhD); philosophy and Jewish religious thought (M Phil, MA, PhD); rabbinics (M Phil, MA, PhD).

Faculty: 17 full-time (2 women), 1 part-time/adjunct (0 women).
Students: 65 full-time (16 women), 1 part-time; includes 2 minority (1 African American, 1 Asian American or Pacific Islander), 8 international. Average age 35. 22 applicants, 64% accepted, 6 enrolled. In 2001, 5 master's, 3 doctorates awarded. Terminal master's awarded for partial completion of doctoral program.
Degree requirements: For master's, one foreign language, thesis optional; for doctorate, 3 foreign languages, thesis/dissertation.
Entrance requirements: For master's and doctorate, GRE General Test, TSE, knowledge of Hebrew. *Application deadline:* For fall admission, 2/15. *Application fee:* $35.
Expenses: Tuition: Full-time $8,500; part-time $355 per credit hour.
Financial support: In 2001–02, 30 students received support, including 20 fellowships with full and partial tuition reimbursements available (averaging $6,000 per year), 4 teaching assistantships with full and partial tuition reimbursements available (averaging $2,000 per year); institutionally sponsored loans, scholarships/grants, and tuition waivers (full and partial) also available. Financial award application deadline: 2/15; financial award applicants required to submit FAFSA.
Faculty research: Aramaic lexicon translations, German-Jewish history, neo-Babylonian texts.
Dr. Adam Kamesar, Director of School of Graduate Studies, 513-221-1875, *Fax:* 513-221-0321, *E-mail:* akamesar@huc.edu. *Web site:* http://www.huc.edu/

■ JEWISH THEOLOGICAL SEMINARY OF AMERICA

Graduate School, New York, NY 10027-4649

AWARDS Ancient Judaism (MA, DHL, PhD); Bible (MA, DHL, PhD); Jewish education (PhD); Jewish history (MA, DHL, PhD); Jewish literature (MA, DHL, PhD); Jewish philosophy (MA, DHL, PhD); liturgy (DHL, PhD); medieval Jewish studies (MA, DHL, PhD); Midrash (MA, DHL, PhD); modern Jewish studies (MA, DHL, PhD); Talmud and rabbinics (MA, DHL, PhD). Part-time programs available. Terminal master's awarded for partial completion of doctoral program.

Degree requirements: For master's, one foreign language, comprehensive exam; for doctorate, 3 foreign languages, thesis/dissertation, comprehensive exam.
Entrance requirements: For master's and doctorate, GRE or MAT.
Expenses: Tuition: Full-time $17,680; part-time $620 per credit. Required fees: $4,180. One-time fee: $2,310 part-time.
Faculty research: Talmud database. *Web site:* http://www.jtsa.edu

Find an in-depth description at www.petersons.com/gradchannel.

■ JEWISH THEOLOGICAL SEMINARY OF AMERICA

William Davidson Graduate School of Jewish Education, New York, NY 10027-4649

AWARDS Jewish education (MA, Ed D, PhD). Offered in conjunction with Rabbinical School; H. L. Miller Cantorial School and College of Jewish Music; Teacher's College, Columbia University; and Union Theological Seminary. Part-time programs available.

Expenses: Tuition: Full-time $17,680; part-time $620 per credit. Required fees: $4,180. One-time fee: $2,310 part-time.

Find an in-depth description at www.petersons.com/gradchannel.

■ JEWISH UNIVERSITY OF AMERICA

Graduate School, Graduate Research Division, Skokie, IL 60077-3248

AWARDS Bible (MHL, DHL); Hebrew (MHL, DHL); history (MHL, DHL); Jewish studies (MHL, DHL); philosophy (MHL, DHL); rabbinics (MHL, DHL). Part-time programs available.

Degree requirements: For MHL, thesis optional; for doctorate, one foreign language, thesis/dissertation.
Entrance requirements: For MHL and doctorate, interview.

■ LAURA AND ALVIN SIEGAL COLLEGE OF JUDAIC STUDIES

Graduate Programs, Program in Religious Education, Beachwood, OH 44122-7116

AWARDS MAJS. Part-time and evening/weekend programs available. Postbaccalaureate distance learning degree programs offered (minimal on-campus study).

Faculty: 13 full-time (4 women), 22 part-time/adjunct (17 women).
Students: 8 full-time (6 women), 105 part-time (81 women). Average age 37. 25 applicants, 88% accepted. In 2001, 2 degrees awarded.
Degree requirements: For master's, one foreign language, thesis.
Entrance requirements: For master's, interview. *Application deadline:* For fall admission, 9/1 (priority date); for spring admission, 1/5 (priority date). Applications are processed on a rolling basis. *Application fee:* $50.
Expenses: Tuition: Full-time $4,050; part-time $225 per credit. Required fees: $25; $25 per year. Tuition and fees vary according to course load and program.
Financial support: In 2001–02, 1 student received support, including fellowships with partial tuition reimbursements available (averaging $4,050 per year); career-related internships or fieldwork and scholarships/grants also available. Support available to part-time students.
Dr. Sylvia F. Abrams, Dean, 216-464-4050 Ext. 114, *Fax:* 216-464-5827, *E-mail:* sfabrams@siegalcollege.edu.
Application contact: Linda L. Rosen, Director of Student Services, 216-464-4050 Ext. 101, *Fax:* 216-464-5827, *E-mail:* lrosen@siegalcollege.edu.

■ NEW YORK UNIVERSITY

Graduate School of Arts and Science, Skirball Department of Hebrew and Judaic Studies, New York, NY 10012-1019

AWARDS Hebrew and Judaic studies (MA, PhD); Hebrew and Judaic studies/history (PhD); Hebrew and Judaic studies/museum studies (MA). Part-time programs available.

Faculty: 12 full-time (4 women), 11 part-time/adjunct.
Students: 41 full-time (22 women), 22 part-time (8 women); includes 1 minority (African American), 10 international. Average age 29. 39 applicants, 36% accepted, 9 enrolled. In 2001, 2 master's, 3 doctorates awarded. Terminal master's awarded for partial completion of doctoral program.
Degree requirements: For master's, 2 foreign languages, comprehensive exam; for doctorate, 4 foreign languages, thesis/dissertation, comprehensive exam.
Entrance requirements: For master's, GRE General Test, TOEFL, minimum 2 years of undergraduate course work in Hebrew; for doctorate, GRE General Test, TOEFL. *Application deadline:* For fall admission, 1/4 (priority date). *Application fee:* $60.
Expenses: Tuition: Full-time $19,536; part-time $814 per credit. Required fees: $1,330; $38 per credit. Tuition and fees vary according to course load and program.
Financial support: Fellowships with tuition reimbursements, teaching assistantships with tuition reimbursements, Federal Work-Study and institutionally sponsored loans available. Financial award application deadline: 1/4; financial award applicants required to submit FAFSA.
Faculty research: Post-biblical and Talmudic literature and history, mysticism, Bible and ancient Near East, medieval and modern Jewish history, medieval and modern Jewish philosophy.
Lawrence Schiffman, Chairman, 212-998-8980.
Application contact: David Engel, Director of Graduate Studies, 212-998-8980, *Fax:* 212-995-4178, *E-mail:* gsas.admissions@nyu.edu. *Web site:* http://www.nyu.edu/gsas/dept/hebrew/

■ SETON HALL UNIVERSITY

College of Arts and Sciences, Department of Jewish-Christian Studies, South Orange, NJ 07079-2697

AWARDS MA. Part-time and evening/weekend programs available.

Degree requirements: For master's, one foreign language, thesis or alternative.
Expenses: Tuition: Full-time $10,818; part-time $601 per credit. Required fees: $610; $185 per term. Tuition and fees vary according to course load, program and student's religious affiliation.
Faculty research: Jewish-Christian issues, biblical studies.

■ SPERTUS INSTITUTE OF JEWISH STUDIES

Judaica Studies Graduate Programs Institute of Advanced Judaica, Program in Jewish Studies, Chicago, IL 60605-1901

AWARDS MAJS, MSJE, MSJS, DJS, DSJS. Part-time and evening/weekend programs available. Postbaccalaureate distance learning degree programs offered (minimal on-campus study).

Faculty: 6 part-time/adjunct (2 women).
Students: 15 applicants, 93% accepted. In 2001, 14 degrees awarded.
Degree requirements: For master's, one foreign language, thesis (for some programs); for doctorate, one foreign language, thesis/dissertation.
Entrance requirements: For master's, interview, BAJS (MAJS); for doctorate, MAJS. *Application deadline:* Applications are processed on a rolling basis. *Application fee:* $50.
Expenses: Tuition: Part-time $200 per quarter hour. Tuition and fees vary according to degree level and program.
Financial support: In 2001–02, 85 students received support. Scholarships/grants available. Support available to part-time students. Financial award applicants required to submit FAFSA.
Dr. Dean Bell, Dean, 312-922-9012, *Fax:* 312-922-6406, *E-mail:* college@spertus.edu.
Application contact: Lisa Burnstein, Director of Student Services, 312-922-9012, *Fax:* 312-922-6406, *E-mail:* lisa@spertus.edu.

■ TOURO COLLEGE

School of Jewish Studies, New York, NY 10010

AWARDS MA. Part-time programs available.

Degree requirements: For master's, one foreign language, thesis.
Entrance requirements: For master's, previous course work in Jewish studies, proficiency in Hebrew.
Faculty research: Medieval and modern Jewish history, Jewish philosophy, holocaust studies, Jewish education.

■ UNIVERSITY OF CALIFORNIA, SAN DIEGO

Graduate Studies and Research, Department of History, La Jolla, CA 92093

AWARDS History (MA, PhD); Judaic studies (MA); science studies (PhD).

Faculty: 31.
Students: 60 (29 women). 118 applicants, 36% accepted, 12 enrolled. In 2001, 7 master's, 7 doctorates awarded.
Degree requirements: For doctorate, thesis/dissertation.
Entrance requirements: For master's and doctorate, GRE General Test. *Application deadline:* For fall admission, 1/16. *Application fee:* $40. Electronic applications accepted.
Expenses: Tuition, nonresident: full-time $10,434. Required fees: $4,883.
Financial support: Fellowships, career-related internships or fieldwork available.
Eric Van Young, Chair.

Application contact: Graduate Coordinator, 858-534-3614.

■ UNIVERSITY OF CHICAGO

Division of the Humanities, Committee on History of Culture, Chicago, IL 60637-1513

AWARDS History of culture (AM, PhD); Jewish history and culture (AM, PhD).

Students: 33. 10 applicants, 60% accepted.
Degree requirements: For doctorate, 2 foreign languages, thesis/dissertation.
Entrance requirements: For master's and doctorate, GRE General Test. *Application deadline:* For fall admission, 1/5. *Application fee:* $55.
Expenses: Tuition: Full-time $16,548.
Financial support: Fellowships, Federal Work-Study and tuition waivers (full and partial) available. Financial award application deadline: 12/28; financial award applicants required to submit FAFSA.
Dr. Robert Nelson, Chair, 773-702-0250.

■ UNIVERSITY OF CHICAGO

Division of the Humanities, Committee on Jewish Studies, Chicago, IL 60637-1513

AWARDS AM.

Students: 7. 7 applicants, 100% accepted.
Degree requirements: For master's, one foreign language.
Entrance requirements: For master's, GRE General Test. *Application deadline:* For fall admission, 12/28. *Application fee:* $55.
Expenses: Tuition: Full-time $16,548.
Financial support: Fellowships available. Financial award application deadline: 12/28; financial award applicants required to submit FAFSA.
Michael Fishbane, Chair, 773-702-8234.

■ UNIVERSITY OF DENVER

Graduate Studies, Faculty of Arts and Humanities/Social Sciences, Center for Judaic Studies, Denver, CO 80208

AWARDS Judaic studies (MA). Part-time programs available.

Faculty: 2 full-time (1 woman).
Degree requirements: For master's, one foreign language, thesis or alternative, proficiency in Hebrew.
Entrance requirements: For master's, GRE, TOEFL, minimum GPA of 3.0. *Application deadline:* Applications are processed on a rolling basis. *Application fee:* $45.
Expenses: Tuition: Full-time $21,456.
Financial support: Scholarships/grants available. Support available to part-time students. Financial award application deadline: 3/1; financial award applicants required to submit FAFSA.
Faculty research: Jewish history, Hebrew, Bible, Islam, Jewish-Christian relations, American Jewish history.
Dr. Nancy Reichman, Director, 303-871-3020.
Application contact: Dr. Thyria Wilson, Chair, 303-871-3012. *Web site:* http://phoebe.cair.du.edu/cjs/

■ UNIVERSITY OF JUDAISM

Graduate School, Bel Air, CA 90077-1599

AWARDS MA, MA Ed, MARS, MBA, MS. Part-time and evening/weekend programs available.

Entrance requirements: For master's, interview, minimum undergraduate GPA of 3.0.

■ THE UNIVERSITY OF MONTANA–MISSOULA

Graduate School, School of Fine Arts, Department of Art, Missoula, MT 59812-0002

AWARDS Fine arts (MA, MFA), including art history (MA), art, studio (MA), ceramics (MFA), integrated arts and education (MA), media arts (MFA), painting and drawing (MFA), photography (MFA), print making (MFA), sculpture (MFA).

Faculty: 12 full-time (6 women).
Degree requirements: For master's, thesis exhibit.
Entrance requirements: For master's, GRE General Test, portfolio. *Application deadline:* For fall admission, 2/15; for spring admission, 11/1. Applications are processed on a rolling basis. *Application fee:* $45.
Expenses: Tuition, state resident: full-time $2,482; part-time $1,700 per year. Tuition, nonresident: full-time $7,372; part-time $5,000 per year. Required fees: $1,900. Tuition and fees vary according to degree level.
Financial support: In 2001–02, 3 teaching assistantships with full tuition reimbursements (averaging $8,665 per year) were awarded; Federal Work-Study and unspecified assistantships also available. Financial award application deadline: 3/1; financial award applicants required to submit FAFSA.
James Bailey, Chair, 406-243-5663, *Fax:* 406-243-4968, *E-mail:* jbailey@selway.umt.edu.
Application contact: Stephen Connell, Head, 406-243-5704. *Web site:* http://www.umt.edu/art/

■ UNIVERSITY OF WISCONSIN–MADISON

Graduate School, College of Letters and Science, Department of Hebrew and Semitic Studies, Madison, WI 53706-1380

AWARDS MA, PhD. Terminal master's awarded for partial completion of doctoral program.

Degree requirements: For master's, 2 foreign languages; for doctorate, thesis/dissertation.
Entrance requirements: For master's and doctorate, GRE. Electronic applications accepted.
Expenses: Tuition, state resident: full-time $7,361; part-time $399 per credit. Tuition, nonresident: full-time $20,499; part-time $1,282 per credit. Required fees: $34 per credit. Full-time tuition and fees vary according to course load, program, reciprocity agreements and student level.
Faculty research: Biblical language and literature, Northwest Semitic languages. *Web site:* http://www.polyglot.lss.wisc.edu/hebrew/

■ UNIVERSITY OF WISCONSIN–MILWAUKEE

Graduate School, College of Letters and Sciences, Program in Foreign Language and Literature, Milwaukee, WI 53201-0413

AWARDS Classics and Hebrew studies (MAFLL); comparative literature (MAFLL); French and Italian (MAFLL); German (MAFLL); Slavic studies (MAFLL); Spanish (MAFLL). Part-time programs available.

Faculty: 16 full-time (5 women).
Students: 7 full-time (6 women), 21 part-time (17 women); includes 4 minority (3 African Americans, 1 Asian American or Pacific Islander), 7 international. 27 applicants, 67% accepted. In 2001, 7 degrees awarded.
Degree requirements: For master's, 2 foreign languages, thesis or alternative. *Application deadline:* For fall admission, 1/1 (priority date); for spring admission, 9/1. Applications are processed on a rolling basis. *Application fee:* $45 ($75 for international students).
Expenses: Tuition, state resident: full-time $6,180; part-time $535 per credit. Tuition, nonresident: full-time $19,482; part-time $1,366 per credit. Tuition and fees vary according to course load, program and reciprocity agreements.
Financial support: In 2001–02, 1 fellowship, 15 teaching assistantships were awarded. Research assistantships, career-related internships or fieldwork and unspecified assistantships also available. Support available to part-time students. Financial award application deadline: 4/15.
Charles Ward, Representative, 414-229-5378, *Fax:* 414-229-2741, *E-mail:* caward@uwm.edu. *Web site:* http://www.uwm.edu/dept/dept/FLL/

■ WASHINGTON UNIVERSITY IN ST. LOUIS

Graduate School of Arts and Sciences, Department of History, Program in Jewish Studies, St. Louis, MO 63130-4899

AWARDS MA.

Washington University in St. Louis (continued)

Degree requirements: For master's, one foreign language, thesis (for some programs).
Entrance requirements: For master's, GRE General Test. *Application deadline:* For fall admission, 1/15 (priority date). Applications are processed on a rolling basis. *Application fee:* $35. Electronic applications accepted.
Expenses: Tuition: Full-time $26,900.
Financial support: Application deadline: 1/15.
Dr. Hillel Kieval, Chairperson, 314-935-5461. *Web site:* http://artsci.wustl.edu/~jewishne/

■ YESHIVA UNIVERSITY

Bernard Revel Graduate School of Jewish Studies, New York, NY 10033-3201

AWARDS MA, PhD. Part-time programs available.

Faculty: 9 full-time (0 women), 6 part-time/adjunct (1 woman).
Students: 34 full-time (11 women), 79 part-time (35 women). Average age 27. In 2001, 6 master's awarded. Terminal master's awarded for partial completion of doctoral program.
Degree requirements: For master's, comprehensive exam; for doctorate, 2 foreign languages, thesis/dissertation, comprehensive exam. *Median time to degree:* Doctorate–2.5 years part-time.
Entrance requirements: For master's and doctorate, GRE General Test (recommended), reading knowledge of Hebrew, minimum GPA of 3.0. *Application deadline:* Applications are processed on a rolling basis. *Application fee:* $25.
Financial support: In 2001–02, 45 fellowships with full and partial tuition reimbursements (averaging $4,840 per year) were awarded; institutionally sponsored loans, scholarships/grants, and tuition waivers (full and partial) also available. Support available to part-time students. Financial award application deadline: 3/1.
Faculty research: Bible, Jewish history, Jewish philosophy and mysticism, Talmud, Semitic languages.
Dr. Arthur Hyman, Dean, 212-960-5253, *Fax:* 212-960-5245, *E-mail:* ahyman@ymail.yu.edu.
Application contact: Sheniagia Alise Warren, Executive Secretary, 212-960-5254, *Fax:* 212-960-5245, *E-mail:* swarren@ymail.yu.edu.

LATIN AMERICAN STUDIES

■ AMERICAN UNIVERSITY

College of Arts and Sciences, Department of Language and Foreign Studies, Program in Spanish: Latin American Studies, Washington, DC 20016-8001

AWARDS Spanish: Latin American studies (MA); translation (Certificate). Part-time and evening/weekend programs available.

Students: 15 full-time (10 women), 21 part-time (20 women); includes 12 minority (5 African Americans, 3 Asian Americans or Pacific Islanders, 4 Hispanic Americans), 2 international. In 2001, 8 degrees awarded.
Degree requirements: For master's, one foreign language, thesis or alternative, comprehensive exam.
Entrance requirements: For master's, bachelor's degree in language or equivalent, essay in Spanish. *Application deadline:* For fall admission, 2/1; for spring admission, 10/1. *Application fee:* $50.
Expenses: Tuition: Full-time $14,274; part-time $793 per credit. Required fees: $290. Tuition and fees vary according to program.
Financial support: Fellowships with full and partial tuition reimbursements, career-related internships or fieldwork, Federal Work-Study, and institutionally sponsored loans available. Financial award application deadline: 2/1.
Faculty research: Latin American culture, literature, and history; computer-aided instruction.
Dr. Consuelo Hernandez, Graduate Adviser, 202-885-2345, *Fax:* 202-885-1076, *E-mail:* chdez@american.edu.

Find an in-depth description at www.petersons.com/gradchannel.

■ ARIZONA STATE UNIVERSITY

Graduate College, College of Liberal Arts and Sciences, Department of History, Tempe, AZ 85287

AWARDS Asian history (MA, PhD); British history (MA, PhD); European history (MA, PhD); Latin American studies (MA, PhD); public history (MA); U.S. history (PhD); U.S. western history (MA).

Degree requirements: For master's, thesis or alternative; for doctorate, 2 foreign languages, thesis/dissertation.
Entrance requirements: For master's and doctorate, GRE.
Faculty research: International relations, women's history, social and cultural history.

■ BROWN UNIVERSITY

Graduate School, Center for Portuguese and Brazilian Studies, Providence, RI 02912

AWARDS Brazilian studies (AM); Luso-Brazilian studies (PhD); Portuguese studies and bilingual education (AM).

Degree requirements: For doctorate, thesis/dissertation.

■ CALIFORNIA STATE UNIVERSITY, LOS ANGELES

Graduate Studies, College of Natural and Social Sciences, Program in Latin American Studies, Los Angeles, CA 90032-8530

AWARDS MA. Part-time and evening/weekend programs available.

Faculty: 2 part-time/adjunct.
Students: 12 full-time (8 women), 26 part-time (16 women); includes 34 minority (1 Asian American or Pacific Islander, 33 Hispanic Americans), 1 international. In 2001, 8 degrees awarded.
Degree requirements: For master's, one foreign language, thesis, comprehensive exam.
Entrance requirements: For master's, TOEFL, minimum GPA of 2.5. *Application deadline:* For fall admission, 6/30; for spring admission, 2/1. Applications are processed on a rolling basis. *Application fee:* $55.
Expenses: Tuition, nonresident: part-time $164 per unit.
Financial support: Federal Work-Study available. Support available to part-time students. Financial award application deadline: 3/1.
Faculty research: Central America, Cuba, Third World development, labor history, redemocratization.
Dr. Marjorie Bray, Coordinator, 323-343-2180.

■ CENTRO DE ESTUDIOS AVANZADOS DE PUERTO RICO Y EL CARIBE

Graduate Program in Puerto Rican and Caribbean Studies, Old San Juan, PR 00902-3970

AWARDS MA, PhD. Part-time and evening/weekend programs available.

Degree requirements: For master's, thesis, comprehensive exam; for doctorate, 2 foreign languages, thesis/dissertation, comprehensive exam.
Entrance requirements: For master's and doctorate, interview.
Faculty research: Literature, history, art, folklore, and culture of Puerto Rico and Caribbean countries. *Web site:* http://www.prtc.net/~centro

■ COLUMBIA UNIVERSITY

School of International and Public Affairs, Institute of Latin American and Iberian Studies, New York, NY 10027

AWARDS Certificate. Students must be enrolled in a separate graduate degree program at Columbia University.

Faculty: 47 full-time, 17 part-time/adjunct.
Students: 2.
Application deadline: For fall admission, 1/5 (priority date); for spring admission, 10/15 (priority date). *Application fee:* $75. Electronic applications accepted.
Financial support: Application deadline: 1/15.
Faculty research: Rights vs. efficiency in a globalized era, citizenship and governance in Latin America and Western Europe.
Dr. Douglas Chalmers, Director, 212-854-4643, *Fax:* 212-854-4607, *E-mail:* chalmers@columbia.edu.
Application contact: Robert Garris, Associate Director, 212-854-6216, *Fax:* 212-854-3010, *E-mail:* sipa_admission@columbia.edu. *Web site:* http://www.columbia.edu/cu/ilais/

■ DUKE UNIVERSITY

Graduate School, Council on Latin American Studies, Durham, NC 27708-0586

AWARDS Certificate.

Faculty: 30 full-time, 15 part-time/adjunct.
Application deadline: For fall admission, 12/31. *Application fee:* $75.
Expenses: Tuition: Full-time $24,600.
Financial support: Fellowships, scholarships/grants available. Financial award application deadline: 12/31.
Faculty research: Political economy of development, social transformations in Central America, Colonial literature, history and fiscal policies, comparative Spanish-American literature and poetry.
John French, Director, 919-681-3980.

■ DUKE UNIVERSITY

Graduate School, Department of History, Durham, NC 27708-0586

AWARDS History (PhD); Latin American studies (PhD).

Faculty: 41 full-time, 13 part-time/adjunct.
Students: 81 full-time (40 women); includes 18 minority (11 African Americans, 2 Asian Americans or Pacific Islanders, 3 Hispanic Americans, 2 Native Americans), 17 international. 157 applicants, 27% accepted, 15 enrolled. In 2001, 16 doctorates awarded.
Degree requirements: For doctorate, 2 foreign languages, thesis/dissertation.
Entrance requirements: For doctorate, GRE General Test. *Application deadline:* For fall admission, 12/31. *Application fee:* $75.
Expenses: Tuition: Full-time $24,600.
Financial support: Fellowships, research assistantships, teaching assistantships, Federal Work-Study available. Financial award application deadline: 12/31.
Ron Witt, Director of Graduate Studies, 919-681-5746, *Fax:* 919-681-7670, *E-mail:* huppert@duke.edu. *Web site:* http://www.history.aas.duke.edu/hist./grd.html

■ FLORIDA INTERNATIONAL UNIVERSITY

College of Arts and Sciences, Department of Latin American Studies, Miami, FL 33199

AWARDS Latin American and Caribbean studies (MA).

Faculty: 1 full-time (0 women).
Students: 19 full-time (10 women), 21 part-time (14 women); includes 23 minority (4 African Americans, 19 Hispanic Americans), 8 international. Average age 26. 18 applicants, 100% accepted, 9 enrolled. In 2001, 5 degrees awarded.
Degree requirements: For master's, one foreign language, thesis.
Entrance requirements: For master's, GRE General Test, TOEFL. *Application fee:* $20.
Expenses: Tuition, state resident: full-time $2,916; part-time $162 per credit hour. Tuition, nonresident: full-time $10,245; part-time $569 per credit hour. Required fees: $168 per term.
Financial support: Application deadline: 4/1.
Dr. Eduardo Gamarra, Graduate Director, 305-348-3188, *Fax:* 305-348-3593, *E-mail:* gamarra@fiu.edu.

■ GEORGETOWN UNIVERSITY

Graduate School of Arts and Sciences, Center for Latin American Studies, Washington, DC 20057-1026

AWARDS MA, MA/PhD.

Degree requirements: For master's, one foreign language, comprehensive exam.
Entrance requirements: For master's, GRE General Test, TOEFL, minimum B average. *Web site:* http://sfswww.georgetown.edu/sfs/program/clas

■ THE GEORGE WASHINGTON UNIVERSITY

Elliott School of International Affairs, Program in Latin American Studies, Washington, DC 20052

AWARDS MA, JD/MA, LL M/MA, MBA/MA. Part-time and evening/weekend programs available.

Students: 9 full-time (5 women), 5 part-time (4 women); includes 5 minority (1 African American, 2 Asian Americans or Pacific Islanders, 2 Hispanic Americans), 1 international. Average age 27. 37 applicants, 89% accepted. In 2001, 5 degrees awarded.
Degree requirements: For master's, one foreign language.
Entrance requirements: For master's, GRE General Test, TOEFL, minimum B average in undergraduate course work. *Application deadline:* For fall admission, 2/1. *Application fee:* $55. Electronic applications accepted.
Expenses: Tuition: Part-time $810 per credit. Required fees: $1 per credit.
Financial support: Fellowships with tuition reimbursements, research assistantships with tuition reimbursements, career-related internships or fieldwork, Federal Work-Study, institutionally sponsored loans, and tuition waivers (full) available. Financial award application deadline: 1/15; financial award applicants required to submit FAFSA.
Faculty research: Democracy and change in Andean nations, rural economic development, peasant cooperatives and political change.
Dr. James Ferrer, Director, 202-994-5205.
Application contact: Jeff V. Miles, Director of Graduate Admissions, 202-994-7050, *Fax:* 202-994-9537, *E-mail:* esiagrad@gwu.edu. *Web site:* http://www.gwu.edu/~elliott/

Find an in-depth description at www.petersons.com/gradchannel.

■ INDIANA UNIVERSITY BLOOMINGTON

Graduate School, College of Arts and Sciences, Center for Latin American and Caribbean Studies, Bloomington, IN 47405

AWARDS MA, MBA/MA, MLS/MA, MPA/MA. Students working on a PhD in other departments may qualify for a PhD certificate or minor in Latin American and Caribbean Studies. Part-time programs available.

Students: 4 full-time (2 women); includes 2 minority (both Hispanic Americans), 1 international. Average age 27. In 2001, 3 degrees awarded.
Degree requirements: For master's, one foreign language.
Entrance requirements: For master's, GRE General Test, TOEFL. *Application deadline:* For fall admission, 1/15 (priority date); for spring admission, 9/1 (priority date). Applications are processed on a rolling basis. *Application fee:* $45 ($55 for international students).
Expenses: Tuition, state resident: full-time $4,720; part-time $197 per credit. Tuition, nonresident: full-time $13,748; part-time $573 per credit. Required fees: $642.
Financial support: In 2001–02, research assistantships with tuition reimbursements (averaging $7,500 per year), 3 teaching assistantships with tuition reimbursements (averaging $10,000 per year) were awarded. Career-related internships or

Indiana University Bloomington (continued)
fieldwork, Federal Work-Study, institutionally sponsored loans, scholarships/grants, and unspecified assistantships also available. Financial award application deadline: 7/15; financial award applicants required to submit FAFSA.
Dr. Jeffrey Gould, Director, 812-855-9097, *Fax:* 812-855-5345, *E-mail:* gouldj@indiana.edu.
Application contact: Valerie Savage, Secretary, 812-855-9097, *Fax:* 812-855-5345, *E-mail:* vsavage@indiana.edu. *Web site:* http://www.indiana.edu/~clas/

■ JOHNS HOPKINS UNIVERSITY

Paul H. Nitze School of Advanced International Studies, Washington, DC 20036

AWARDS Emerging markets (Certificate); interdisciplinary studies (MA, PhD), including African studies, American foreign policy (MA), Asian studies, Canadian studies, conflict resolution and mediation (MA), environmental policy and resource management (MA), European studies, international business (MA), international development (MA), international economics (MA), international relations (MA), Latin American studies, Middle Eastern studies (MA), military and defense studies (MA), Russian area and East European studies (MA), social change and development (MA); international public policy (MIPP). MBA/MA offered jointly with the University of Pennsylvania–Wharton School and INSEAD in France.

Faculty: 44 full-time (13 women), 113 part-time/adjunct (29 women).
Students: 567 full-time (275 women), 17 part-time (8 women); includes 71 minority (14 African Americans, 46 Asian Americans or Pacific Islanders, 10 Hispanic Americans, 1 Native American). Average age 27. 1,288 applicants, 35% accepted. In 2001, 294 master's, 13 doctorates, 34 other advanced degrees awarded. Terminal master's awarded for partial completion of doctoral program.
Degree requirements: For master's, one foreign language, comprehensive exam; for doctorate, 2 foreign languages, thesis/dissertation.
Entrance requirements: For master's, GMAT or GRE General Test or TOEFL, previous course work in economics, foreign language; for doctorate, GRE General Test or TOEFL; for Certificate, TOEFL. *Application deadline:* For fall admission, 1/15. *Application fee:* $75. Electronic applications accepted.
Expenses: Contact institution.
Financial support: In 2001–02, 431 fellowships (averaging $5,500 per year) were awarded; career-related internships or fieldwork and Federal Work-Study also available. Financial award application deadline: 2/1; financial award applicants required to submit FAFSA.
Faculty research: Comparative politics, regional studies, language and linguistics.
Dr. Jessica Einhorn, Dean, 202-663-5624, *Fax:* 202-663-5621.
Application contact: Bonnie Wilson, Associate Dean of Student Affairs, 202-663-5700, *Fax:* 202-663-7788, *E-mail:* admissions.sais@jhu.edu. *Web site:* http://www.sais-jhu.edu/

Find an in-depth description at www.petersons.com/gradchannel.

■ LA SALLE UNIVERSITY

School of Arts and Sciences, Program in Bilingual/Bicultural Studies (Spanish), Philadelphia, PA 19141-1199

AWARDS MA. Part-time and evening/weekend programs available.

Faculty: 5 full-time (1 woman), 5 part-time/adjunct (1 woman).
Students: 3 full-time (1 woman), 32 part-time (25 women); includes 17 minority (7 African Americans, 10 Hispanic Americans). Average age 35. 13 applicants, 69% accepted, 4 enrolled. In 2001, 20 degrees awarded.
Degree requirements: For master's, one foreign language, thesis or alternative, project.
Entrance requirements: For master's, GRE or MAT. *Application deadline:* Applications are processed on a rolling basis. *Application fee:* $30.
Expenses: Contact institution.
Financial support: Scholarships/grants and tuition waivers (partial) available. Support available to part-time students. Financial award application deadline: 5/16.
Faculty research: Puerto Rican literature, cross-cultural communication, English as a second language methodology, Spanish language.
Dr. Luis Gomez, Acting Director, 215-951-1209.

■ NEW YORK UNIVERSITY

Graduate School of Arts and Science, Center for Latin American and Caribbean Studies, New York, NY 10012-1019

AWARDS Latin American and Caribbean studies (MA); Latin American and Caribbean studies/journalism (MA); Latin American and Caribbean studies/museum studies (MA). Part-time programs available.

Faculty: 2 full-time (0 women), 5 part-time/adjunct.
Students: 19 full-time (15 women), 15 part-time (11 women); includes 10 minority (1 African American, 2 Asian Americans or Pacific Islanders, 7 Hispanic Americans), 5 international. Average age 34. 63 applicants, 83% accepted, 14 enrolled. In 2001, 19 degrees awarded.
Degree requirements: For master's, one foreign language, thesis or alternative, major project.
Entrance requirements: For master's, GRE General Test, TOEFL, knowledge of Portuguese or Spanish. *Application deadline:* For fall admission, 1/4 (priority date); for spring admission, 11/1. *Application fee:* $60.
Expenses: Tuition: Full-time $19,536; part-time $814 per credit. Required fees: $1,330; $38 per credit. Tuition and fees vary according to course load and program.
Financial support: Fellowships with tuition reimbursements, teaching assistantships with tuition reimbursements, Federal Work-Study, institutionally sponsored loans, and unspecified assistantships available. Financial award application deadline: 1/4; financial award applicants required to submit FAFSA.
Faculty research: Latin American politics; Caribbean societies; Andean history; political economy of cultural policies.
George Yudice, Director, 212-998-8686, *Fax:* 212-995-4163, *E-mail:* clacs.info@nyu.edu. *Web site:* http://www.nyu.edu/gsas/dept/latin/

■ THE OHIO STATE UNIVERSITY

Graduate School, College of Humanities, Department of History, Columbus, OH 43210

AWARDS History (MA, PhD); Latin American studies (Certificate); Russian area studies (Certificate).

Degree requirements: For master's, thesis optional; for doctorate, variable foreign language requirement, thesis/dissertation.
Entrance requirements: For master's and doctorate, GRE General Test.

■ THE OHIO STATE UNIVERSITY

Graduate School, College of Social and Behavioral Sciences, Department of Political Science, Columbus, OH 43210

AWARDS Latin American studies (Certificate); political science (MA, PhD); Russian area studies (Certificate).

Degree requirements: For master's, thesis optional; for doctorate, thesis/dissertation.
Entrance requirements: For master's and doctorate, GRE General Test, TOEFL.
Faculty research: American, comparative, and international politics; political theory.

■ OHIO UNIVERSITY

Graduate Studies, Center for International Studies, Program in Latin American Studies, Athens, OH 45701-2979

AWARDS MA.

Faculty: 24 full-time (5 women).
Students: 30 full-time (14 women), 1 part-time; includes 6 minority (1 African American, 5 Hispanic Americans), 17 international. 23 applicants, 87% accepted.

Degree requirements: For master's, one foreign language, thesis optional.
Entrance requirements: For master's, TOEFL, minimum GPA of 3.0. *Application deadline:* For fall admission, 3/1 (priority date). Applications are processed on a rolling basis. *Application fee:* $30.
Expenses: Tuition, state resident: full-time $6,585. Tuition, nonresident: full-time $12,254.
Financial support: In 2001–02, 26 students received support, including 2 research assistantships with full tuition reimbursements available (averaging $9,430 per year), 2 teaching assistantships with full tuition reimbursements available (averaging $9,430 per year); Federal Work-Study, institutionally sponsored loans, and graduate scholarships/stipends also available. Financial award application deadline: 1/15.
Faculty research: Central America, Ecuador, Brazil, transnational migration, microfinance.
Dr. Thomas Walker, Director, 740-593-1835, *Fax:* 740-593-1837, *E-mail:* walker@ohiou.edu.
Application contact: Joan Kraynanski, Administrative Assistant, 740-593-1840, *Fax:* 740-593-1837, *E-mail:* kraynans@ohio.edu. *Web site:* http://www.ohiou.edu/~intsdept/internationalstudies1

■ PRINCETON UNIVERSITY

Graduate School, Program in Latin American Studies, Princeton, NJ 08544-1019

AWARDS PhD. Offered through the Departments of Anthropology, Art and Archaeology, History, Politics, and Romance Languages.

Degree requirements: For doctorate, thesis/dissertation.
Entrance requirements: For doctorate, GRE General Test, sample of written work.

■ SAN DIEGO STATE UNIVERSITY

Graduate and Research Affairs, College of Arts and Letters, Center for Latin American Studies, San Diego, CA 92182

AWARDS MA, MBA/MA.

Degree requirements: For master's, 2 foreign languages, thesis or alternative.
Entrance requirements: For master's, GRE General Test, TOEFL.
Faculty research: Latin American politics and economics. *Web site:* http://www.rohan.sdsu.edu/dept/latamweb/

■ SOUTHERN METHODIST UNIVERSITY

Dedman College, Program in Latin American Studies, Dallas, TX 75275

AWARDS MA. Part-time programs available.

Degree requirements: For master's, one foreign language, thesis optional.
Entrance requirements: For master's, GRE General Test, minimum GPA of 3.0. *Application deadline:* For fall admission, 6/30; for spring admission, 11/30. *Application fee:* $50.
Expenses: Tuition: Part-time $285 per credit hour.
Financial support: Applicants required to submit FAFSA.
Faculty research: Journalism, Spanish Civil War, Spanish painters, U.S. and Mexico studies.
Dr. James Hollifield, Director, 214-768-1414.

■ STANFORD UNIVERSITY

School of Humanities and Sciences, Center for Latin American Studies, Stanford, CA 94305-9991

AWARDS AM.

Students: 12 full-time (7 women); includes 3 minority (2 Hispanic Americans, 1 Native American), 2 international. Average age 28. 28 applicants, 57% accepted. In 2001, 14 degrees awarded.
Degree requirements: For master's, one foreign language, thesis or alternative, research paper or comprehensive written exam.
Entrance requirements: For master's, GRE General Test, TOEFL. *Application deadline:* For fall admission, 1/5. *Application fee:* $65 ($80 for international students). Electronic applications accepted.
Terry L. Karl, Director, 650-725-2012, *Fax:* 650-725-9255, *E-mail:* tkarl@stanford.edu.
Application contact: Graduate Program Administrator, 650-723-4444. *Web site:* http://www.stanford.edu/group/las/

■ STATE UNIVERSITY OF NEW YORK AT ALBANY

College of Arts and Sciences, Department of Latin American and Caribbean Studies, Albany, NY 12222-0001

AWARDS MA, Certificate. Part-time and evening/weekend programs available.

Students: 11 full-time (9 women), 2 part-time (both women); includes 8 minority (2 African Americans, 6 Hispanic Americans), 2 international. Average age 33. 7 applicants, 86% accepted. In 2001, 1 degree awarded.
Degree requirements: For master's, thesis.
Entrance requirements: For master's, ability to read and write Spanish. *Application deadline:* For fall admission, 5/1; for spring admission, 11/1. *Application fee:* $50.
Expenses: Tuition, state resident: full-time $2,550; part-time $213 per credit. Tuition, nonresident: full-time $4,208; part-time $351 per credit. Required fees: $470; $470 per year.
Financial support: Fellowships, research assistantships, teaching assistantships available. Financial award application deadline: 3/15.
Faculty research: Meso-American anthropology, Latin American women's studies, Latinos in the U.S.
Liliana Goldin, Chair, 518-442-4890.

■ TULANE UNIVERSITY

Graduate School, Roger Thayer Stone Center for Latin American Studies, New Orleans, LA 70118-5669

AWARDS MA, PhD, MBA/MA, MCL/MA. Terminal master's awarded for partial completion of doctoral program.

Degree requirements: For master's, one foreign language, thesis optional; for doctorate, 2 foreign languages, thesis/dissertation.
Entrance requirements: For master's, GRE General Test, TSE, minimum B average in undergraduate course work; for doctorate, GRE General Test, TSE.
Expenses: Tuition: Full-time $24,675. Required fees: $2,210.

Find an in-depth description at www.petersons.com/gradchannel.

■ THE UNIVERSITY OF ALABAMA

Graduate School, College of Arts and Sciences, Program in Latin American Studies, Tuscaloosa, AL 35487

AWARDS MA, Certificate. Part-time programs available.

Faculty: 1 (woman) full-time.
Students: 2 full-time (both women); both minorities (both Native Americans). Average age 50. 1 applicant, 0% accepted.
Degree requirements: For master's, one foreign language, thesis optional.
Entrance requirements: For master's, GRE General Test, TOEFL. *Application deadline:* For fall admission, 7/1. Applications are processed on a rolling basis. *Application fee:* $25. Electronic applications accepted.
Expenses: Tuition, state resident: full-time $3,292; part-time $183 per credit hour. Tuition, nonresident: full-time $8,912; part-time $495 per credit hour. Tuition and fees vary according to course load, campus/location and program.
Financial support: In 2001–02, 2 research assistantships with full tuition reimbursements (averaging $8,102 per year) were awarded; career-related internships or fieldwork and institutionally sponsored loans also available. Financial award application deadline: 3/15.
Faculty research: Mexico, Central America, Andean nations, U.S.-Latin American relations, Yucatan.
Dr. Connie Janiga-Perkins, Director, 205-348-1857.

■ THE UNIVERSITY OF ARIZONA

Graduate College, College of Social and Behavioral Sciences, Program in Latin American Studies, Tucson, AZ 85721

AWARDS MA. Part-time programs available.

Faculty: 35.
Students: 32 full-time (25 women), 2 part-time (1 woman); includes 6 minority (1 Asian American or Pacific Islander, 5 Hispanic Americans), 2 international. Average age 29. 39 applicants, 74% accepted, 17 enrolled. In 2001, 9 degrees awarded.
Degree requirements: For master's, 2 foreign languages, thesis optional.
Entrance requirements: For master's, GRE, TOEFL, minimum GPA of 3.0. *Application deadline:* For fall admission, 5/1. Applications are processed on a rolling basis. *Application fee:* $45.
Expenses: Tuition, state resident: full-time $2,490; part-time $436 per unit. Tuition, nonresident: full-time $10,300; part-time $436 per unit. Full-time tuition and fees vary according to degree level and program.
Financial support: Fellowships, research assistantships, teaching assistantships, Federal Work-Study, institutionally sponsored loans, scholarships/grants, and tuition waivers (full and partial) available. Financial award application deadline: 5/1.
Faculty research: Agriculture economics development, U.S. policy in Central America, Argentine economics and social history, U.S.-Mexico border history, Latin American culture.
Dr. Dana Liverman, Director, 520-622-4002.
Application contact: Dr. Raul P. Saba, Graduate Adviser, 520-622-4002, *Fax:* 520-622-0177.

■ UNIVERSITY OF CALIFORNIA, BERKELEY

Graduate Division, Group in Latin American Studies, Berkeley, CA 94720-1500

AWARDS MA, PhD, MJ/MA.

Faculty: 14 full-time.
Students: 19 full-time (10 women); includes 6 African Americans, 5 international. Average age 25. 41 applicants, 37% accepted, 7 enrolled. In 2001, 1 degree awarded.
Degree requirements: For master's, 2 foreign languages; for doctorate, 2 foreign languages, thesis/dissertation, qualifying exam.
Entrance requirements: For master's, GRE General Test, TOEFL, minimum GPA of 3.0, reading knowledge of Spanish or Portuguese; for doctorate, GRE General Test, TOEFL, minimum GPA of 3.0, master's degree or equivalent graduate study. *Application deadline:* For fall admission, 12/15. *Application fee:* $60. Electronic applications accepted.
Expenses: Tuition, nonresident: full-time $10,704. Required fees: $4,349.
Financial support: In 2001–02, 4 students received support, including 3 fellowships (averaging $12,000 per year), teaching assistantships with tuition reimbursements available (averaging $28,000 per year). Financial award application deadline: 12/15.
Faculty research: Rural development, border communities, political economy, geography, history.
Margaret Chowning, Chair, *E-mail:* chowning@socrates.berkeley.edu.
Application contact: Katie Dustin, Graduate Assistant for Admission, 510-642-4466, *Fax:* 510-642-9850, *E-mail:* lasgrad@uclink.berkeley.edu. *Web site:* http://www.ias.berkeley.edu/iastp/las/grad/lasgrad.html/

■ UNIVERSITY OF CALIFORNIA, LOS ANGELES

Graduate Division, College of Letters and Science, Program in Latin American Studies, Los Angeles, CA 90095

AWARDS MA, M Ed/MA, MA/MA, MBA/MA, MLIS/MA, MPH/MA.

Students: 52 full-time (33 women); includes 27 minority (2 Asian Americans or Pacific Islanders, 25 Hispanic Americans), 6 international. 50 applicants, 78% accepted, 22 enrolled. In 2001, 17 degrees awarded.
Degree requirements: For master's, 2 foreign languages, comprehensive exam.
Entrance requirements: For master's, GRE General Test, minimum GPA of 3.0. *Application deadline:* For fall admission, 12/15. *Application fee:* $60. Electronic applications accepted.
Expenses: Tuition, nonresident: full-time $10,244. Required fees: $3,609. Full-time tuition and fees vary according to program.
Financial support: In 2001–02, 21 students received support, including 14 fellowships, 4 research assistantships, 2 teaching assistantships; Federal Work-Study, institutionally sponsored loans, scholarships/grants, and tuition waivers (full and partial) also available. Financial award application deadline: 3/1.
Dr. Susanna B. Hecht, Chair, 310-825-6571.
Application contact: Departmental Office, 310-206-6571, *E-mail:* cramirez@isop.ucla.edu.

■ UNIVERSITY OF CALIFORNIA, SAN DIEGO

Graduate Studies and Research, Department of Political Science, Latin American Studies Program, La Jolla, CA 92093

AWARDS MA.

Students: 10 (5 women). 45 applicants, 58% accepted, 4 enrolled. In 2001, 5 degrees awarded.
Entrance requirements: For master's, GRE General Test, GRE Subject Test. *Application deadline:* For fall admission, 1/18. *Application fee:* $40. Electronic applications accepted.
Expenses: Tuition, nonresident: full-time $10,434. Required fees: $4,883.
Leon Zamosc, Director, 858-822-4376.
Application contact: Graduate Coordinator, 858-534-7967.

■ UNIVERSITY OF CALIFORNIA, SANTA BARBARA

Graduate Division, College of Letters and Sciences, Division of Humanities and Fine Arts, Department of Spanish and Portuguese, Santa Barbara, CA 93106

AWARDS Hispanic languages and literature (PhD); Portuguese (MA); Spanish (MA).

Degree requirements: For master's, one foreign language, thesis or alternative; for doctorate, one foreign language, thesis/dissertation.
Entrance requirements: For master's, GRE, TOEFL; for doctorate, GRE, TOEFL, 2 samples of written work.

■ UNIVERSITY OF CALIFORNIA, SANTA BARBARA

Graduate Division, College of Letters and Sciences, Division of Humanities and Fine Arts, Program in Latin American and Iberian Studies, Santa Barbara, CA 93106

AWARDS MA.

Degree requirements: For master's, one foreign language, thesis or alternative, comprehensive exam.
Entrance requirements: For master's, GRE, TOEFL, 2 samples of written work.

■ UNIVERSITY OF CENTRAL FLORIDA

College of Arts and Sciences, Department of Sociology, Orlando, FL 32816

AWARDS Applied sociology (MA); domestic violence (Certificate); gender studies (Certificate); Mayan studies (Certificate). Part-time and evening/weekend programs available.

Faculty: 25 full-time (12 women), 3 part-time/adjunct (2 women).
Students: 12 full-time (10 women), 40 part-time (33 women); includes 5 minority (3 African Americans, 2 Hispanic Americans). Average age 33. 34 applicants, 82% accepted, 22 enrolled. In 2001, 6 degrees awarded.
Degree requirements: For master's, comprehensive written exam or thesis.

Entrance requirements: For master's, GRE General Test, TOEFL, minimum GPA of 3.0 in last 60 hours. *Application deadline:* For fall admission, 7/15; for spring admission, 12/1. *Application fee:* $20. Electronic applications accepted.
Expenses: Tuition, state resident: part-time $162 per hour. Tuition, nonresident: part-time $569 per hour.
Financial support: In 2001–02, 5 fellowships with partial tuition reimbursements (averaging $2,500 per year), 15 research assistantships with partial tuition reimbursements (averaging $1,990 per year), 22 teaching assistantships with partial tuition reimbursements (averaging $2,681 per year) were awarded. Career-related internships or fieldwork, Federal Work-Study, institutionally sponsored loans, tuition waivers (partial), and unspecified assistantships also available. Financial award application deadline: 3/1; financial award applicants required to submit FAFSA.
Faculty research: Religious subcultures, attitudes toward abortion, population, sport research, stratification.
Dr. Jay Corzine, Chair, 407-823-2227, *Fax:* 407-823-5156, *E-mail:* hcorzine@mail.ucf.edu. *Web site:* http://www.ucf.edu/

■ UNIVERSITY OF CHICAGO

Division of Social Sciences and Division of the Humanities, Latin American and Caribbean Studies Program, Chicago, IL 60637-1513

AWARDS AM, MBA/AM.

Students: 3.
Degree requirements: For master's, one foreign language, thesis.
Entrance requirements: For master's, GRE General Test, TOEFL. *Application deadline:* For fall admission, 12/28. *Application fee:* $55. Electronic applications accepted.
Expenses: Tuition: Full-time $16,548.
Financial support: Federal Work-Study and institutionally sponsored loans available. Financial award application deadline: 12/28.
Prof. Thomas Cummins, Director, 773-702-9741.
Application contact: Office of the Dean of Students, 773-702-8415.

■ UNIVERSITY OF CONNECTICUT

Graduate School, College of Liberal Arts and Sciences, Field of Latin American Studies, Storrs, CT 06269

AWARDS MA.

Entrance requirements: For master's, GRE General Test.

■ UNIVERSITY OF FLORIDA

Graduate School, College of Liberal Arts and Sciences, Center for Latin American Studies, Gainesville, FL 32611

AWARDS MA, MAT, Certificate, JD/MA. Part-time programs available.

Degree requirements: For master's, variable foreign language requirement, thesis.
Entrance requirements: For master's, GRE General Test, minimum GPA of 3.0. Electronic applications accepted.
Expenses: Tuition, state resident: part-time $164 per hour. Tuition, nonresident: part-time $571 per hour. Tuition and fees vary according to course level and program.
Faculty research: Tropical conservation and development; ethnicity in the Americas, Brazil, and Cuba; North American Free Trade Agreement. *Web site:* http://www.latam.ufl.edu/

■ UNIVERSITY OF ILLINOIS AT URBANA–CHAMPAIGN

Graduate College, College of Liberal Arts and Sciences, Center for Latin American and Caribbean Studies, Champaign, IL 61820

AWARDS AM.

Students: 7 full-time (4 women), 2 international. 12 applicants, 33% accepted. In 2001, 1 degree awarded.
Entrance requirements: For master's, GRE, minimum GPA of 3.0. *Application deadline:* For fall admission, 1/4. Applications are processed on a rolling basis. *Application fee:* $40 ($50 for international students). Electronic applications accepted.
Expenses: Tuition, state resident: part-time $3,227 per degree program. Tuition, nonresident: part-time $7,169 per degree program. Tuition and fees vary according to program.
Financial support: In 2001–02, 1 fellowship, 2 teaching assistantships were awarded. Research assistantships Financial award application deadline: 2/15.
Norman Whitten, Director, 217-333-3182, *Fax:* 217-244-7333.
Application contact: Nan Volinsky, Academic Programs and Outreach Coordinator, 217-333-8419, *Fax:* 217-244-7333. *Web site:* http://www.uiuc.edu/unit/lat/

■ UNIVERSITY OF KANSAS

Graduate School, College of Liberal Arts and Sciences, Department of Latin American Studies, Lawrence, KS 66045

AWARDS MA.

Faculty: 6.
Students: 15 full-time (9 women), 8 part-time (7 women); includes 3 minority (2 African Americans, 1 Hispanic American), 4 international. Average age 29. 13 applicants, 85% accepted, 5 enrolled. In 2001, 11 degrees awarded.
Degree requirements: For master's, 2 foreign languages, thesis optional.
Entrance requirements: For master's, GRE, TOEFL. *Application fee:* $35.
Expenses: Tuition, state resident: full-time $2,722; part-time $113 per credit. Tuition, nonresident: full-time $8,586; part-time $358 per credit. Required fees: $551; $46 per credit. Tuition and fees vary according to campus/location, program and reciprocity agreements.
Financial support: In 2001–02, 1 research assistantship with partial tuition reimbursement, 2 teaching assistantships with full and partial tuition reimbursements (averaging $8,420 per year) were awarded.
Faculty research: Democracy, international trade, ethnicity, literature, politics.
Elizabeth Kuznesof, Chair, 785-864-9433, *Fax:* 785-864-3800.
Application contact: Adriana Natali-Sommerville, Program Assistant, 785-864-4213, *Fax:* 785-864-3800, *E-mail:* adriana@ku.edu. *Web site:* http://www.ku.edu/~latamst/

■ UNIVERSITY OF NEW MEXICO

Graduate School, College of Arts and Sciences, Committee on Latin American Studies, Albuquerque, NM 87131-2039

AWARDS MA, PhD, JD/MA, MBA/MA, MCRP/MA, MSN/MA.

Students: 43 full-time (21 women), 22 part-time (11 women); includes 21 minority (1 African American, 19 Hispanic Americans, 1 Native American), 4 international. Average age 32. 60 applicants, 77% accepted, 21 enrolled. In 2001, 20 degrees awarded.
Degree requirements: For master's, one foreign language; for doctorate, 2 foreign languages, thesis/dissertation.
Entrance requirements: For master's and doctorate, GRE General Test. *Application deadline:* For fall admission, 2/1 (priority date); for spring admission, 11/10. *Application fee:* $40.
Expenses: Tuition, state resident: full-time $2,771; part-time $115 per credit hour. Tuition, nonresident: full-time $11,207; part-time $467 per credit hour. Required fees: $570; $24 per credit hour. Part-time tuition and fees vary according to course load and program.
Financial support: In 2001–02, 48 students received support; fellowships, research assistantships, teaching assistantships, health care benefits available. Financial award application deadline: 3/1; financial award applicants required to submit FAFSA.
Dr. William Stanley, Interim Director, 505-277-2961, *Fax:* 505-277-5989, *E-mail:* wstanley@unm.edu.

University of New Mexico (continued)
Application contact: Joan Swanson, Program Advisement Coordinator, 505-277-7044, *Fax:* 505-277-5989, *E-mail:* jswanson@unm.edu. *Web site:* http://www.unm.edu/~laiinfo/

■ THE UNIVERSITY OF NORTH CAROLINA AT CHAPEL HILL

Graduate School, College of Arts and Sciences, Department of Political Science, Chapel Hill, NC 27599

AWARDS Latin American studies (Certificate); political science (MA, PhD); trans-Atlantic studies (MA).

Faculty: 37 full-time.
Students: 94 full-time (44 women); includes 14 minority (7 African Americans, 2 Asian Americans or Pacific Islanders, 5 Hispanic Americans), 6 international. 185 applicants, 21% accepted. In 2001, 11 master's, 7 doctorates awarded.
Degree requirements: For master's, comprehensive exam; for doctorate, one foreign language, thesis/dissertation, comprehensive exam.
Entrance requirements: For master's and doctorate, GRE General Test, minimum GPA of 3.0 recommended. *Application deadline:* For fall admission, 1/1 (priority date). Applications are processed on a rolling basis. *Application fee:* $55. Electronic applications accepted.
Expenses: Tuition, state resident: full-time $2,864. Tuition, nonresident: full-time $12,030.
Financial support: In 2001–02, 17 research assistantships with full tuition reimbursements (averaging $11,000 per year), 29 teaching assistantships with full tuition reimbursements (averaging $11,000 per year) were awarded. Fellowships, unspecified assistantships also available. Financial award application deadline: 3/1; financial award applicants required to submit FAFSA.
Dr. Jonathan Hartlyn, Chair, 919-962-3041, *Fax:* 919-962-0432, *E-mail:* hartlyn@email.unc.edu.
Application contact: Coordinator of Graduate Studies, 919-962-0437, *Fax:* 919-962-0432. *Web site:* http://www.unc.edu/depts/polisci/

■ UNIVERSITY OF NOTRE DAME

Graduate School, College of Arts and Letters, Division of Humanities, Department of Romance Languages and Literatures, Program in Iberian and Latin American Studies, Notre Dame, IN 46556

AWARDS MA. Part-time programs available.

Faculty: 10 full-time (5 women).
Students: 8 full-time (all women); includes 2 minority (both Hispanic Americans), 4 international. 14 applicants, 71% accepted, 5 enrolled. In 2001, 3 degrees awarded.
Degree requirements: For master's, 2 foreign languages, comprehensive exam.
Entrance requirements: For master's, GRE General Test, TOEFL, bachelor's degree in Spanish. *Application deadline:* For fall admission, 2/1 (priority date). Applications are processed on a rolling basis. *Application fee:* $50. Electronic applications accepted.
Expenses: Tuition: Full-time $24,220; part-time $1,346 per credit hour. Required fees: $155.
Financial support: Teaching assistantships, tuition waivers (full) available. Financial award application deadline: 2/1.
Faculty research: Colonial novel, Mexican Revolution, Cervantes, Spanish American theater, modern Spanish literature.
Application contact: Dr. Terrence J. Akai, Director of Graduate Admissions, 574-631-7706, *Fax:* 574-631-4183, *E-mail:* gradad@nd.edu. *Web site:* http://www.nd.edu/~romlang/

■ UNIVERSITY OF PITTSBURGH

Faculty of Arts and Sciences, Center for Latin American Studies, Pittsburgh, PA 15260

AWARDS Certificate. Students must be enrolled in a separate degree granting program to attain the Certificate.

Faculty: 122 full-time (31 women), 16 part-time/adjunct (7 women).
Students: 150 full-time (89 women), 18 part-time (11 women); includes 15 minority (6 African Americans, 9 Hispanic Americans), 89 international. In 2001, 19 degrees awarded.
Degree requirements: For Certificate, one foreign language.
Application deadline: Applications are processed on a rolling basis.
Expenses: Tuition, state resident: full-time $9,410; part-time $385 per credit. Tuition, nonresident: full-time $19,376; part-time $797 per credit. Required fees: $480; $90 per term. Tuition and fees vary according to program.
Financial support: In 2001–02, 32 students received support, including 16 fellowships; career-related internships or fieldwork, scholarships/grants, tuition waivers (full and partial), and unspecified assistantships also available. Support available to part-time students. Financial award application deadline: 2/28.
Faculty research: Latin American archaeology; Latin American economic and political restructuring; Latin American social and public policy.
Kathleen M. DeWalt, Director, 412-648-7391, *Fax:* 412-648-2199, *E-mail:* kmdewalt@ucis.pitt.edu.
Application contact: Shirley A. Kregar, Associate Director for Academic Affairs, 412-648-7396, *Fax:* 412-648-2199, *E-mail:* kregar@ucis.pitt.edu. *Web site:* http://www.ucis.pitt.edu/clas/

■ UNIVERSITY OF PITTSBURGH

Graduate School of Public Health, Department of Health Services Administration, Program in Behavioral and Community Health Services, Pittsburgh, PA 15260

AWARDS Behavioral and community health services (MHPE, MPH); Latin American studies (Certificate); non-profit organization (Certificate); public health/aging (Certificate). Part-time programs available.

Faculty: 18 full-time (12 women), 12 part-time/adjunct (5 women).
Students: 22 full-time (15 women), 19 part-time (17 women); includes 16 minority (7 African Americans, 6 Asian Americans or Pacific Islanders, 3 Hispanic Americans), 11 international. Average age 30. 60 applicants, 83% accepted. In 2001, 9 degrees awarded.
Degree requirements: For master's, thesis.
Entrance requirements: For master's, GRE General Test, TOEFL, GMAT or MCAT, bachelor's degree in public health or related field. *Application deadline:* For fall admission, 5/1; for spring admission, 10/1. Applications are processed on a rolling basis. *Application fee:* $50 ($60 for international students).
Expenses: Tuition, state resident: full-time $9,410; part-time $385 per credit. Tuition, nonresident: full-time $19,376; part-time $797 per credit. Required fees: $480; $90 per term. Tuition and fees vary according to program.
Financial support: In 2001–02, 10 students received support, including 3 research assistantships with tuition reimbursements available (averaging $9,780 per year); career-related internships or fieldwork, Federal Work-Study, institutionally sponsored loans, and unspecified assistantships also available. Support available to part-time students. Financial award applicants required to submit FAFSA.
Faculty research: Public health and aging, maternal and child health, substance abuse, privatization of health service. *Total annual research expenditures:* $2.1 million.
Prof. Karen S. Peterson, Assistant Professor and Program Coordinator, 412-624-4756, *Fax:* 412-624-5510, *E-mail:* pskph@pitt.edu.
Application contact: Dan Bach, Program Administrator, 412-624-3107, *Fax:* 412-624-5510, *E-mail:* paudb5@pitt.edu.

Find an in-depth description at www.petersons.com/gradchannel.

■ THE UNIVERSITY OF TEXAS AT AUSTIN

Graduate School, College of Liberal Arts, Center for Latin American Studies, Austin, TX 78712-1111

AWARDS MA, PhD, JD/MA, MBA/MA, MP Aff/MA, MSCRP/MA.

Students: 84 (40 women); includes 20 minority (3 African Americans, 2 Asian Americans or Pacific Islanders, 15 Hispanic Americans) 13 international. In 2001, 32 master's, 2 doctorates awarded.
Entrance requirements: For master's and doctorate, GRE General Test. *Application fee:* $50 ($75 for international students).
Expenses: Tuition, state resident: full-time $3,159. Tuition, nonresident: full-time $6,957. Tuition and fees vary according to program.
Financial support: Fellowships available. Financial award application deadline: 2/1.
Dr. Nicolas Shumway, Director, 512-471-5551.
Application contact: Henry A. Selby, Graduate Adviser, 512-471-5551.

■ UNIVERSITY OF WISCONSIN–MADISON

Graduate School, College of Letters and Science, Latin American, Caribbean and Iberian Studies Program, Madison, WI 53706-1380

AWARDS MA.

Degree requirements: For master's, 2 foreign languages, thesis.
Entrance requirements: For master's, minimum GPA of 3.0. Electronic applications accepted.
Expenses: Tuition, state resident: full-time $7,361; part-time $399 per credit. Tuition, nonresident: full-time $20,499; part-time $1,282 per credit. Required fees: $34 per credit. Full-time tuition and fees vary according to course load, program, reciprocity agreements and student level.
Faculty research: Development, gender, social movements, cultural studies, history.
Web site: http://polyglot.lss.wisc.edu/lacis/

■ VANDERBILT UNIVERSITY

Graduate School, Program in Latin American Studies, Nashville, TN 37240-1001

AWARDS MA, MBA/MA.

Faculty: 24 full-time (5 women).
Students: 11 full-time (5 women). Average age 26. 12 applicants, 92% accepted. In 2001, 3 degrees awarded.
Degree requirements: For master's, 2 foreign languages, thesis or alternative.
Entrance requirements: For master's, GRE General Test. *Application deadline:* For fall admission, 1/15. *Application fee:* $40. Electronic applications accepted.
Expenses: Tuition: Full-time $28,350.
Financial support: In 2001–02, 7 students received support, including 5 teaching assistantships with full tuition reimbursements available (averaging $9,700 per year); Federal Work-Study and institutionally sponsored loans also available. Financial award application deadline: 1/15.
Faculty research: Latin American and Iberian studies, anthropology, history, Spanish and Portuguese, social and political science.
Jane Gilmer Landers, Director, 615-322-2527, *Fax:* 615-322-2305.
Application contact: Norma G. Antillon, Secretary, 615-322-2527, *Fax:* 615-322-2305, *E-mail:* norma.g.antillon@vanderbilt.edu. *Web site:* http://www.vanderbilt.edu/AnS/LAS/

■ WEST VIRGINIA UNIVERSITY

Eberly College of Arts and Sciences, Department of History, Morgantown, WV 26506

AWARDS African history (MA, PhD); African-American history (MA, PhD); American history (MA, PhD); Appalachian/regional history (MA, PhD); East Asian history (MA, PhD); European history (MA, PhD); history of science and technology (MA, PhD); Latin American history (MA). Part-time programs available.

Faculty: 19 full-time (4 women), 2 part-time/adjunct (1 woman).
Students: 35 full-time (13 women), 29 part-time (10 women); includes 5 minority (2 African Americans, 1 Asian American or Pacific Islander, 1 Hispanic American, 1 Native American), 5 international. Average age 34. 86 applicants, 44% accepted. In 2001, 4 master's, 1 doctorate awarded.
Degree requirements: For master's, one foreign language; for doctorate, one foreign language, comprehensive exam, dissertation defense.
Entrance requirements: For master's, GRE General Test, TOEFL, minimum GPA of 3.0; for doctorate, GRE General Test, TOEFL, MA or equivalent. *Application deadline:* For spring admission, 11/1. Applications are processed on a rolling basis. *Application fee:* $45.
Expenses: Tuition, state resident: full-time $2,791. Tuition, nonresident: full-time $8,659. Required fees: $1,002. Tuition and fees vary according to program.
Financial support: In 2001–02, 43 students received support, including 2 research assistantships, 23 teaching assistantships; fellowships, career-related internships or fieldwork, Federal Work-Study, institutionally sponsored loans, tuition waivers (full and partial), and graduate administrative assistantships also available. Financial award application deadline: 2/1; financial award applicants required to submit FAFSA.
Faculty research: U.S., Appalachia, modern Europe, Africa, science and technology.
Dr. Robert M. Maxon, Chair, 304-293-2421 Ext. 5223, *Fax:* 304-293-3616, *E-mail:* robert.maxon@mail.wvu.edu.
Application contact: Dr. Robert E. Blobaum, Director of Graduate Studies, 304-293-2421 Ext. 5241, *Fax:* 304-293-3616, *E-mail:* robert.blobaum@mail.wvu.edu. *Web site:* http://www.as.wvu.edu/history/

NATIVE AMERICAN STUDIES

■ MONTANA STATE UNIVERSITY–BOZEMAN

College of Graduate Studies, College of Letters and Science, Center for Native American Studies, Bozeman, MT 59717

AWARDS MA.

Students: 5 full-time (2 women), 4 part-time (all women); includes 6 minority (all Native Americans). Average age 41. 3 applicants, 100% accepted, 2 enrolled. *Application deadline:* Applications are processed on a rolling basis. *Application fee:* $50. Electronic applications accepted.
Expenses: Tuition, state resident: full-time $3,894; part-time $198 per credit. Tuition, nonresident: full-time $10,661; part-time $480 per credit. International tuition: $10,811 full-time. Tuition and fees vary according to course load and program.
Financial support: Application deadline: 3/1.
Total annual research expenditures: $62,993.
Dr. Wayne Stein, Director, 406-994-3881, *E-mail:* inaws@montana.edu.

■ THE UNIVERSITY OF ARIZONA

Graduate College, Graduate Interdisciplinary Programs, Graduate Interdisciplinary Program in American Indian Studies, Tucson, AZ 85721

AWARDS MA, PhD, JD/MA. Part-time programs available.

Faculty: 10 full-time (6 women), 16 part-time/adjunct (7 women).
Students: 48 full-time (34 women), 9 part-time (7 women); includes 37 minority (4 Hispanic Americans, 33 Native Americans), 1 international. Average age 36. 54 applicants, 69% accepted, 23 enrolled. In 2001, 12 master's, 1 doctorate awarded.
Degree requirements: For master's, thesis optional; for doctorate, one foreign language, thesis/dissertation, comprehensive exam, registration. *Median time to degree:* Master's–2 years full-time, 3 years part-time; doctorate–5 years full-time, 7 years part-time.
Entrance requirements: For master's, TOEFL, minimum GPA of 3.0; for doctorate, GRE, minimum GPA of 3.0. *Application deadline:* For fall admission, 2/1. Applications are processed on a rolling basis. *Application fee:* $45.
Expenses: Tuition, state resident: full-time $2,490; part-time $436 per unit. Tuition, nonresident: full-time $10,300; part-time $436 per unit. Full-time tuition and fees vary according to degree level and program.
Financial support: Fellowships, research assistantships, teaching assistantships,

The University of Arizona (continued)
institutionally sponsored loans, scholarships/grants, tuition waivers (partial), and unspecified assistantships available. Support available to part-time students. Financial award application deadline: 2/15.
Faculty research: Indian policy, Indian societies, religion, language and literature, treaties.
Dr. Jay Stauss, Director, 520-621-7108, *Fax:* 520-621-7952, *E-mail:* jstauss@u.arizona.edu.
Application contact: Shelly Lowe, Secretary, 520-621-7108, *Fax:* 520-621-7952, *E-mail:* idp@ccit.arizona.edu. *Web site:* http://w3.arizona.edu/~aisp/index.html/

■ UNIVERSITY OF CALIFORNIA, DAVIS

Graduate Studies, Program in Native American Studies, Davis, CA 95616

AWARDS MA, PhD.

Faculty: 8 full-time (3 women), 1 (woman) part-time/adjunct.
Students: 19 full-time (13 women); includes 9 minority (all Native Americans). Average age 37. 26 applicants, 54% accepted, 8 enrolled. In 2001, 3 degrees awarded.
Degree requirements: For doctorate, thesis/dissertation.
Entrance requirements: For doctorate, GRE. *Application fee:* $60.
Expenses: Tuition, state resident: full-time $4,831. Tuition, nonresident: full-time $15,725.
Financial support: In 2001–02, 16 students received support, including 7 fellowships with full and partial tuition reimbursements available (averaging $4,125 per year), 4 research assistantships with full tuition reimbursements available (averaging $16,456 per year), 8 teaching assistantships with partial tuition reimbursements available (averaging $16,157 per year); tuition waivers (full and partial) also available. Financial award application deadline: 1/15; financial award applicants required to submit FAFSA.
Victor Montejo, Chair, 530-752-6128, *E-mail:* vmontejo@ucdavis.edu.
Application contact: Gladys Bell, Administrative Assistant, 530-752-7874, *Fax:* 530-752-7097, *E-mail:* gmbell@ucdavis.edu. *Web site:* http://www.cougar.ucdavis.edu/nas/home.html

■ UNIVERSITY OF CALIFORNIA, LOS ANGELES

Graduate Division, College of Letters and Science, Program in American Indian Studies, Los Angeles, CA 90095

AWARDS MA, JD/MA.

Students: 22 full-time (13 women); includes 17 minority (3 Hispanic Americans, 14 Native Americans). 26 applicants, 50% accepted, 8 enrolled. In 2001, 7 degrees awarded.
Degree requirements: For master's, comprehensive exam or thesis.
Entrance requirements: For master's, GRE General Test (recommended), minimum GPA of 3.0, sample of written work. *Application deadline:* For fall admission, 12/15. *Application fee:* $60. Electronic applications accepted.
Expenses: Tuition, nonresident: full-time $10,244. Required fees: $3,609. Full-time tuition and fees vary according to program.
Financial support: In 2001–02, 6 research assistantships, 7 teaching assistantships were awarded. Fellowships, Federal Work-Study, institutionally sponsored loans, and tuition waivers (full and partial) also available. Financial award application deadline: 3/1.
Dr. Paul Kroskrity, Chair, 310-825-7315.
Application contact: Departmental Office, 310-825-7315, *E-mail:* aisc@ucla.edu.

■ UNIVERSITY OF KANSAS

Graduate School, College of Liberal Arts and Sciences, Department of Indigenous Nations Studies, Lawrence, KS 66045

AWARDS MA.

Faculty: 1.
Students: 9 full-time (6 women), 4 part-time (2 women); includes 7 minority (all Native Americans), 1 international. Average age 38. 9 applicants, 89% accepted, 7 enrolled. In 2001, 4 degrees awarded.
Entrance requirements: For master's, TOEFL, GRE, resumé, writing sample. *Application deadline:* For fall admission, 12/15 (priority date). Applications are processed on a rolling basis. *Application fee:* $35. Electronic applications accepted.
Expenses: Tuition, state resident: full-time $2,722; part-time $113 per credit. Tuition, nonresident: full-time $8,586; part-time $358 per credit. Required fees: $551; $46 per credit. Tuition and fees vary according to campus/location, program and reciprocity agreements.
Donald Fixico, Director, 785-864-2660, *Fax:* 785-864-0370.
Application contact: Sharon O'Brien, Graduate Director, 785-864-9057, *Fax:* 785-864-0370, *E-mail:* insp@ku.edu. *Web site:* http://www.ku.edu/~insp/

NEAR AND MIDDLE EASTERN STUDIES

■ BRANDEIS UNIVERSITY

Graduate School of Arts and Sciences, Department of Near Eastern and Judaic Studies, Waltham, MA 02454-9110

AWARDS Near Eastern and Judaic studies (MA, PhD); Near Eastern and Judaic studies and sociology (PhD); Near Eastern and Judaic studies and women's studies (MA); Near Eastern and Judiac studies and sociology (MA); teaching of Hebrew (MA). Part-time programs available.

Faculty: 27 full-time (13 women), 11 part-time/adjunct (4 women).
Students: 66 full-time (34 women), 2 part-time (1 woman); includes 3 minority (1 African American, 1 Asian American or Pacific Islander, 1 Hispanic American), 14 international. Average age 33. 70 applicants, 80% accepted. In 2001, 9 master's, 5 doctorates awarded. Terminal master's awarded for partial completion of doctoral program.
Degree requirements: For master's, one foreign language, thesis (for some programs), comprehensive exam; for doctorate, 3 foreign languages, thesis/dissertation, comprehensive exam. *Median time to degree:* Master's–2 years full-time; doctorate–6.5 years full-time.
Entrance requirements: For master's, GRE General Test (suggested), resumé, letters of recommendation; for doctorate, GRE General Test (suggested). *Application deadline:* For fall admission, 1/15. Applications are processed on a rolling basis. *Application fee:* $60. Electronic applications accepted.
Expenses: Tuition: Full-time $27,392. Required fees: $35.
Financial support: In 2001–02, 25 students received support, including 4 fellowships with full and partial tuition reimbursements available (averaging $13,000 per year); research assistantships with full and partial tuition reimbursements available, teaching assistantships with full and partial tuition reimbursements available, Federal Work-Study, institutionally sponsored loans, scholarships/grants, and tuition waivers (full and partial) also available. Support available to part-time students. Financial award application deadline: 4/15; financial award applicants required to submit CSS PROFILE or FAFSA.
Faculty research: Ancient Near East and Bible, philosophy, history, Hebrew literature, modern Middle East.
Dr. Marc Z. Brettler, Chair, 781-736-2968, *Fax:* 781-736-2070, *E-mail:* brettler@brandeis.edu.
Application contact: Dr. David Wright, Graduate Adviser, 781-736-2957, *Fax:* 781-736-2070, *E-mail:* wright@brandeis.edu.

Web site: http://www.brandeis.edu/departments/nejs/index.html

■ BRIGHAM YOUNG UNIVERSITY

The David M. Kennedy Center for International and Area Studies, Provo, UT 84602-1001

AWARDS American studies (MA); ancient Near Eastern studies (MA); Asian studies (MA); international development (MA); international relations (MA).

Faculty: 21 full-time (2 women), 2 part-time/adjunct (0 women).
Students: 16 full-time (8 women), 13 part-time (9 women); includes 1 minority (Hispanic American), 4 international. Average age 25. 62 applicants, 31% accepted. In 2001, 17 degrees awarded.
Degree requirements: For master's, one foreign language, thesis.
Entrance requirements: For master's, GRE General Test, minimum GPA of 3.55 in last 60 hours. *Application deadline:* For fall admission, 2/1. *Application fee:* $50. Electronic applications accepted.
Expenses: Tuition: Full-time $3,860; part-time $214 per hour.
Financial support: In 2001–02, 18 research assistantships (averaging $3,500 per year), 2 teaching assistantships (averaging $3,500 per year) were awarded. Fellowships with full tuition reimbursements, career-related internships or fieldwork and tuition waivers (full) also available. Financial award application deadline: 2/1.
Faculty research: Comparative education, education for development, comparative economics. *Total annual research expenditures:* $100,000.
Dr. Donald B. Holsinger, Director, 801-422-3378, *Fax:* 801-378-8748, *E-mail:* donald_holsinger@byu.edu.
Application contact: Dr. Phillip J. Bryson, Director of Graduate Studies, Associate Director, 801-422-7402, *Fax:* 801-378-8748, *E-mail:* phillip_bryson@byu.edu.

■ COLUMBIA UNIVERSITY

Graduate School of Arts and Sciences, Division of Humanities, Department of Middle East Languages and Cultures, New York, NY 10027

AWARDS Hebrew language and literature (M Phil, MA, PhD); Middle Eastern languages and cultures (M Phil, MA, PhD). Part-time programs available.

Faculty: 22 full-time, 11 part-time/adjunct.
Students: 52 full-time (25 women), 4 part-time (3 women); includes 4 minority (3 Asian Americans or Pacific Islanders, 1 Hispanic American), 12 international. Average age 35. 42 applicants, 48% accepted. In 2001, 2 master's, 5 doctorates awarded.
Degree requirements: For master's, thesis, oral and written exams; for doctorate, 3 foreign languages, thesis/dissertation.
Entrance requirements: For master's and doctorate, GRE General Test, TOEFL. *Application deadline:* For fall admission, 1/3; for spring admission, 11/30. *Application fee:* $65.
Expenses: Tuition: Full-time $27,528. Required fees: $1,638.
Financial support: Fellowships, teaching assistantships, Federal Work-Study and institutionally sponsored loans available. Support available to part-time students. Financial award application deadline: 1/5; financial award applicants required to submit FAFSA.
Faculty research: Indo-Iranian, Turkish, central Asian, and Armenian studies; Arabic and ancient Semitics.
Hamid Dabashi, Chair, 212-854-7524, *Fax:* 212-854-5517.

■ COLUMBIA UNIVERSITY

Graduate School of Arts and Sciences, Program in Liberal Studies, New York, NY 10027

AWARDS American studies (MA); East Asian studies (MA); human rights studies (MA); Islamic culture studies (MA); Jewish studies (MA); medieval studies (MA); modern European studies (MA); South Asian studies (MA). Part-time and evening/weekend programs available.

Faculty: 5 part-time/adjunct (2 women).
Students: 7 full-time (2 women), 75 part-time (51 women); includes 5 minority (1 African American, 3 Asian Americans or Pacific Islanders, 1 Hispanic American), 8 international. Average age 41. 39 applicants, 77% accepted. In 2001, 20 degrees awarded.
Degree requirements: For master's, thesis.
Application deadline: For fall admission, 4/1; for spring admission, 11/1. *Application fee:* $65.
Expenses: Tuition: Full-time $27,528. Required fees: $1,638.
Steve Laymon, Assistant Dean, 212-854-4932, *Fax:* 212-854-4912.
Application contact: Director of Admissions, 212-854-3331.

Find an in-depth description at www.petersons.com/gradchannel.

■ COLUMBIA UNIVERSITY

School of International and Public Affairs, Middle East Institute, New York, NY 10027

AWARDS Certificate. Students must be enrolled in a separate graduate degree program at Columbia University.

Application deadline: For fall admission, 1/5 (priority date); for spring admission, 10/15 (priority date). *Application fee:* $75. Electronic applications accepted.
Financial support: Application deadline: 1/5.
Dr. Gary Sick, Director, 212-854-2584, *Fax:* 212-854-1413, *E-mail:* ggs2@columbia.edu.
Application contact: Robert Garris, Associate Director, 212-854-6216, *Fax:* 212-854-3010, *E-mail:* sipa_admission@columbia.edu.

■ CORNELL UNIVERSITY

Graduate School, Graduate Fields of Arts and Sciences, Field of Near Eastern Studies, Ithaca, NY 14853-0001

AWARDS Ancient Near Eastern studies (MA, PhD); Arabic and Islamic studies (MA, PhD); biblical studies (MA, PhD); Hebrew and Judaic studies (MA, PhD).

Faculty: 7 full-time.
Students: 13 applicants. In 2001, 1 degree awarded. Terminal master's awarded for partial completion of doctoral program.
Degree requirements: For master's, one foreign language, thesis; for doctorate, 2 foreign languages, thesis/dissertation.
Entrance requirements: For master's and doctorate, GRE General Test, TOEFL, 2 years of 1 Near Eastern language, 3 letters of recommendation. *Application deadline:* For fall admission, 2/1. *Application fee:* $65. Electronic applications accepted.
Expenses: Tuition: Full-time $25,970. Required fees: $50.
Financial support: Fellowships with full tuition reimbursements, research assistantships with full tuition reimbursements, teaching assistantships with full tuition reimbursements, institutionally sponsored loans, scholarships/grants, tuition waivers (full and partial), and unspecified assistantships available. Financial award applicants required to submit FAFSA.
Faculty research: Hebrew and Judaic studies (including Bible), early Christianity, Arabic and Islamic studies, modern Middle East.
Application contact: Graduate Field Assistant, 607-255-1329, *E-mail:* neareastern@cornell.edu. *Web site:* http://www.gradschool.cornell.edu/grad/fields_1/ne-st.html

■ GEORGETOWN UNIVERSITY

Graduate School of Arts and Sciences, Arab Studies Program, Washington, DC 20057

AWARDS MA, Certificate, MA/PhD.

Degree requirements: For master's, one foreign language, comprehensive exam, proficiency in Arabic.
Entrance requirements: For master's, GRE, TOEFL, minimum GPA of 3.0.
Faculty research: Contemporary Arab world.

■ GRATZ COLLEGE

Graduate Programs, Program in Israel Studies, Melrose Park, PA 19027

AWARDS Certificate. Part-time and evening/weekend programs available.

Faculty: 8 full-time (4 women), 11 part-time/adjunct (7 women).
Degree requirements: For Certificate, one foreign language.
Application deadline: Applications are processed on a rolling basis. *Application fee:* $50.
Expenses: Tuition: Full-time $9,950; part-time $466 per credit.
Financial support: Federal Work-Study and unspecified assistantships available. Support available to part-time students. Financial award application deadline: 4/15; financial award applicants required to submit FAFSA.
Dr. Jerome Kutnick, Dean for Academic Affairs, 215-635-7300 Ext. 137, *Fax:* 215-635-7320, *E-mail:* jkutnick@gratz.edu.
Application contact: Adena E. Johnston, Director of Admissions, 215-635-7300 Ext. 140, *Fax:* 215-635-7320, *E-mail:* admissions@gratz.edu.

■ HARVARD UNIVERSITY

Graduate School of Arts and Sciences, Committee on Middle Eastern Studies, Cambridge, MA 02138

AWARDS Anthropology and Middle Eastern studies (PhD); economics and Middle Eastern studies (PhD); fine arts and Middle Eastern studies (PhD); history and Middle Eastern studies (PhD); regional studies–Middle East (AM). Terminal master's awarded for partial completion of doctoral program.

Degree requirements: For master's, one foreign language; for doctorate, 2 foreign languages, thesis/dissertation.
Entrance requirements: For master's, GRE General Test, TOEFL; for doctorate, GRE General Test, TOEFL, 1 year of course work in Middle Eastern regional studies, proficiency in a related language.
Expenses: Tuition: Full-time $23,370. Required fees: $816. Full-time tuition and fees vary according to program and student level.

■ HARVARD UNIVERSITY

Graduate School of Arts and Sciences, Department of Near Eastern Languages and Civilizations, Cambridge, MA 02138

AWARDS Akkadian and Sumerian (AM, PhD); Arabic (AM, PhD); Armenian (AM, PhD); biblical history (AM, PhD); Hebrew (AM, PhD); Indo-Muslim culture (AM, PhD); Iranian (AM, PhD); Jewish history and literature (AM, PhD); Persian (AM, PhD); Semitic philology (AM, PhD); Syro-Palestinian archaeology (AM, PhD); Turkish (AM, PhD).

Degree requirements: For doctorate, variable foreign language requirement, thesis/dissertation, general exams.
Entrance requirements: For master's, GRE General Test, TOEFL; for doctorate, GRE General Test, TOEFL, proficiency in a Near Eastern language.
Expenses: Tuition: Full-time $23,370. Required fees: $816. Full-time tuition and fees vary according to program and student level.

■ HEBREW UNION COLLEGE–JEWISH INSTITUTE OF RELIGION

School of Graduate Studies, Cincinnati, OH 45220-2488

AWARDS Bible and the ancient Near East (M Phil, MA, PhD); Hebrew letters (DHL); history of biblical interpretation (M Phil, MA, PhD); Jewish and Christian studies in the Greco-Roman period (M Phil, PhD); Jewish and cognate studies (M Phil); Judaic and cognate studies (MA, PhD); modern Jewish history (M Phil, MA, PhD); philosophy and Jewish religious thought (M Phil, MA, PhD); rabbinics (M Phil, MA, PhD).

Faculty: 17 full-time (2 women), 1 part-time/adjunct (0 women).
Students: 65 full-time (16 women), 1 part-time; includes 2 minority (1 African American, 1 Asian American or Pacific Islander), 8 international. Average age 35. 22 applicants, 64% accepted, 6 enrolled. In 2001, 5 master's, 3 doctorates awarded. Terminal master's awarded for partial completion of doctoral program.
Degree requirements: For master's, one foreign language, thesis optional; for doctorate, 3 foreign languages, thesis/dissertation.
Entrance requirements: For master's and doctorate, GRE General Test, TSE, knowledge of Hebrew. *Application deadline:* For fall admission, 2/15. *Application fee:* $35.
Expenses: Tuition: Full-time $8,500; part-time $355 per credit hour.
Financial support: In 2001–02, 30 students received support, including 20 fellowships with full and partial tuition reimbursements available (averaging $6,000 per year), 4 teaching assistantships with full and partial tuition reimbursements available (averaging $2,000 per year); institutionally sponsored loans, scholarships/grants, and tuition waivers (full and partial) also available. Financial award application deadline: 2/15; financial award applicants required to submit FAFSA.
Faculty research: Aramaic lexicon translations, German-Jewish history, neo-Babylonian texts.
Dr. Adam Kamesar, Director of School of Graduate Studies, 513-221-1875, *Fax:* 513-221-0321, *E-mail:* akamesar@huc.edu. *Web site:* http://www.huc.edu/

■ JOHNS HOPKINS UNIVERSITY

Paul H. Nitze School of Advanced International Studies, Washington, DC 20036

AWARDS Emerging markets (Certificate); interdisciplinary studies (MA, PhD), including African studies, American foreign policy (MA), Asian studies, Canadian studies, conflict resolution and mediation (MA), environmental policy and resource management (MA), European studies, international business (MA), international development (MA), international economics (MA), international relations (MA), Latin American studies, Middle Eastern studies (MA), military and defense studies (MA), Russian area and East European studies (MA), social change and development (MA); international public policy (MIPP). MBA/MA offered jointly with the University of Pennsylvania–Wharton School and INSEAD in France.

Faculty: 44 full-time (13 women), 113 part-time/adjunct (29 women).
Students: 567 full-time (275 women), 17 part-time (8 women); includes 71 minority (14 African Americans, 46 Asian Americans or Pacific Islanders, 10 Hispanic Americans, 1 Native American). Average age 27. 1,288 applicants, 35% accepted. In 2001, 294 master's, 13 doctorates, 34 other advanced degrees awarded. Terminal master's awarded for partial completion of doctoral program.
Degree requirements: For master's, one foreign language, comprehensive exam; for doctorate, 2 foreign languages, thesis/dissertation.
Entrance requirements: For master's, GMAT or GRE General Test or TOEFL, previous course work in economics, foreign language; for doctorate, GRE General Test or TOEFL; for Certificate, TOEFL. *Application deadline:* For fall admission, 1/15. *Application fee:* $75. Electronic applications accepted.
Expenses: Contact institution.
Financial support: In 2001–02, 431 fellowships (averaging $5,500 per year) were awarded; career-related internships or fieldwork and Federal Work-Study also available. Financial award application deadline: 2/1; financial award applicants required to submit FAFSA.
Faculty research: Comparative politics, regional studies, language and linguistics.
Dr. Jessica Einhorn, Dean, 202-663-5624, *Fax:* 202-663-5621.
Application contact: Bonnie Wilson, Associate Dean of Student Affairs, 202-663-5700, *Fax:* 202-663-7788, *E-mail:* admissions.sais@jhu.edu. *Web site:* http://www.sais-jhu.edu/

Find an in-depth description at www.petersons.com/gradchannel.

■ JOHNS HOPKINS UNIVERSITY

Zanvyl Krieger School of Arts and Sciences, Department of Near Eastern Studies, Baltimore, MD 21218-2699

AWARDS MA, PhD.

Faculty: 6 full-time (1 woman).
Students: 32 full-time (17 women), 1 (woman) part-time; includes 2 minority (1 African American, 1 Asian American or Pacific Islander), 8 international. Average age 29. 37 applicants, 11% accepted, 4 enrolled. In 2001, 4 master's, 2 doctorates awarded. Terminal master's awarded for partial completion of doctoral program.
Degree requirements: For master's, one foreign language; for doctorate, 2 foreign languages, thesis/dissertation, registration.
Entrance requirements: For master's and doctorate, GRE General Test. *Application deadline:* For fall admission, 1/15. *Application fee:* $55. Electronic applications accepted.
Expenses: Tuition: Full-time $27,390.
Financial support: In 2001–02, 3 fellowships, 13 research assistantships, 5 teaching assistantships were awarded. Career-related internships or fieldwork and Federal Work-Study also available. Financial award application deadline: 4/15; financial award applicants required to submit FAFSA.
Faculty research: Egyptology, Assyriology, Northwest Semitic languages, Hebrew Bible. *Total annual research expenditures:* $54,745.
Dr. Betsy Bryan, Chair, 410-516-7499, *Fax:* 410-516-5218, *E-mail:* vwild@jhu.edu.
Application contact: Vonnie Wild, Administrative Assistant, 410-516-7499, *Fax:* 410-516-5218, *E-mail:* vwild@jhu.edy. *Web site:* http://www.jhu.edu/~neareast/

■ NEW YORK UNIVERSITY

Graduate School of Arts and Science, Hagop Kevorkian Center for Near Eastern Studies, Department of Middle Eastern Studies, New York, NY 10012-1019

AWARDS Middle Eastern studies (MA, PhD); Middle Eastern studies/history (PhD). Part-time programs available.

Faculty: 17 full-time (6 women), 3 part-time/adjunct.
Students: 32 full-time (15 women), 2 part-time; includes 2 minority (1 Asian American or Pacific Islander, 1 Hispanic American), 7 international. Average age 29. 43 applicants, 21% accepted, 5 enrolled. In 2001, 2 master's, 6 doctorates awarded. Terminal master's awarded for partial completion of doctoral program.
Degree requirements: For master's, 2 foreign languages, thesis; for doctorate, 4 foreign languages, thesis/dissertation, comprehensive exam.
Entrance requirements: For master's and doctorate, GRE General Test, TOEFL. *Application deadline:* For fall admission, 1/4. *Application fee:* $60.
Expenses: Tuition: Full-time $19,536; part-time $814 per credit. Required fees: $1,330; $38 per credit. Tuition and fees vary according to course load and program.
Financial support: Fellowships with tuition reimbursements, teaching assistantships with tuition reimbursements, Federal Work-Study and institutionally sponsored loans available. Financial award application deadline: 1/4; financial award applicants required to submit FAFSA.
Faculty research: Middle Eastern history, Arabic/Persian/Turkish language and literature, cultures and societies of Middle East, Islamic studies.
Zachary Lockman, Chairman, 212-998-8880, *Fax:* 212-995-4144, *E-mail:* kevorkian.center@nyu.edu.
Application contact: Khaled Fahmy, Director of Graduate Studies, 212-998-8880, *Fax:* 212-995-4689, *E-mail:* mideast.studies@nyu.edu. *Web site:* http://www.nyu.edu/gsas/dept/mideast/

■ NEW YORK UNIVERSITY

Graduate School of Arts and Science, Hagop Kevorkian Center for Near Eastern Studies, Program in Near Eastern Studies, New York, NY 10012-1019

AWARDS Near Eastern studies (MA); Near Eastern studies/journalism (MA); Near Eastern studies/museum studies (MA). Part-time programs available.

Faculty: 2 full-time (0 women).
Students: 21 full-time (20 women), 10 part-time (4 women); includes 4 minority (1 African American, 2 Asian Americans or Pacific Islanders, 1 Hispanic American), 7 international. Average age 24. 32 applicants, 72% accepted, 12 enrolled. In 2001, 8 degrees awarded.
Degree requirements: For master's, one foreign language, thesis.
Entrance requirements: For master's, GRE General Test, TOEFL. *Application deadline:* For fall admission, 1/4. *Application fee:* $60.
Expenses: Tuition: Full-time $19,536; part-time $814 per credit. Required fees: $1,330; $38 per credit. Tuition and fees vary according to course load and program.
Financial support: Fellowships with tuition reimbursements, teaching assistantships with tuition reimbursements, Federal Work-Study and institutionally sponsored loans available. Financial award application deadline: 1/4; financial award applicants required to submit FAFSA.
Faculty research: Politics, political economy, anthropology, history and culture of the Middle East.
Timothy Mitchell, Chair, 212-998-8877, *Fax:* 212-995-4144, *E-mail:* kevorkian.center@nyu.edu.
Application contact: Information Contact, 212-998-8877, *Fax:* 212-995-4144, *E-mail:* kevorkian.center@nyu.edu. *Web site:* http://www.nyu.edu/gsas/program/neareast/

■ PRINCETON UNIVERSITY

Graduate School, Department of Near Eastern Studies, Interdisciplinary Program in Modern Near Eastern Studies, Princeton, NJ 08544-1019

AWARDS MA.

Degree requirements: For master's, one foreign language, thesis.
Entrance requirements: For master's, GRE General Test.

■ PRINCETON UNIVERSITY

Graduate School, Department of Near Eastern Studies, Program in Ancient Near Eastern Studies, Princeton, NJ 08544-1019

AWARDS PhD.

Degree requirements: For doctorate, 2 foreign languages, thesis/dissertation.
Entrance requirements: For doctorate, GRE General Test.

■ PRINCETON UNIVERSITY

Graduate School, Department of Near Eastern Studies, Program in Islamic Studies, Princeton, NJ 08544-1019

AWARDS PhD.

Degree requirements: For doctorate, 2 foreign languages, thesis/dissertation.
Entrance requirements: For doctorate, GRE General Test.

■ THE UNIVERSITY OF ARIZONA

Graduate College, College of Social and Behavioral Sciences, Department of Near Eastern Studies, Tucson, AZ 85721

AWARDS MA, PhD. Part-time and evening/weekend programs available.

Faculty: 10.
Students: 14 full-time (9 women), 15 part-time (11 women); includes 3 minority (1 Asian American or Pacific Islander, 1 Hispanic American, 1 Native American), 3 international. Average age 36. 26 applicants, 54% accepted, 6 enrolled. In 2001, 3 master's, 5 doctorates awarded. Terminal master's awarded for partial completion of doctoral program.
Degree requirements: For master's, one foreign language; for doctorate, 3 foreign languages, thesis/dissertation.
Entrance requirements: For master's, GRE, TOEFL; for doctorate, GRE General Test, TOEFL. *Application fee:* $45.
Expenses: Tuition, state resident: full-time $2,490; part-time $436 per unit. Tuition, nonresident: full-time $10,300; part-time $436 per unit. Full-time tuition and fees vary according to degree level and program.
Financial support: Fellowships, research assistantships, teaching assistantships,

The University of Arizona (continued)
Federal Work-Study, institutionally sponsored loans, and tuition waivers (full) available. Support available to part-time students.
Dr. Michael E Bonine, Head, 520-626-9140, *Fax:* 520-621-2333, *E-mail:* bonine@u.arizona.edu.
Application contact: Sylvia R Gourdin, Graduate Coordinator, 520-621-8013, *Fax:* 520-621-2333, *E-mail:* sgourdin@u.arizona.edu. *Web site:* http://3fp.arizona.edu/neareast/

■ UNIVERSITY OF CALIFORNIA, BERKELEY

Graduate Division, College of Letters and Science, Department of Near Eastern Studies, Program in Near Eastern Religions, Berkeley, CA 94720-1500

AWARDS PhD.

Degree requirements: For doctorate, 2 foreign languages, thesis/dissertation, qualifying exam.
Entrance requirements: For doctorate, GRE General Test, MA or equivalent in Near Eastern studies or related field; minimum GPA of 3.0.
Expenses: Tuition, nonresident: full-time $10,704. Required fees: $4,349.

■ UNIVERSITY OF CALIFORNIA, BERKELEY

Graduate Division, College of Letters and Science, Department of Near Eastern Studies, Program in Near Eastern Studies, Berkeley, CA 94720-1500

AWARDS MA, PhD, C Phil.

Degree requirements: For doctorate, 2 foreign languages, thesis/dissertation, qualifying exam.
Entrance requirements: For master's and doctorate, GRE General Test, minimum GPA of 3.0.
Expenses: Tuition, nonresident: full-time $10,704. Required fees: $4,349.

■ UNIVERSITY OF CALIFORNIA, LOS ANGELES

Graduate Division, College of Letters and Science, Department of Near Eastern Languages and Cultures, Los Angeles, CA 90095

AWARDS MA, PhD.

Students: 28 full-time (9 women); includes 1 minority (Hispanic American), 4 international. 53 applicants, 23% accepted, 4 enrolled. In 2001, 6 master's, 1 doctorate awarded.
Degree requirements: For master's, one foreign language, comprehensive exam; for doctorate, 2 foreign languages, thesis/dissertation, oral and written qualifying exams.
Entrance requirements: For master's and doctorate, GRE General Test, TOEFL, minimum GPA of 3.25, sample of written work recommended. *Application deadline:* For fall admission, 12/30. *Application fee:* $60. Electronic applications accepted.
Expenses: Tuition, nonresident: full-time $10,244. Required fees: $3,609. Full-time tuition and fees vary according to program.
Financial support: In 2001–02, 14 research assistantships, 18 teaching assistantships were awarded. Fellowships, Federal Work-Study, institutionally sponsored loans, scholarships/grants, and tuition waivers (full and partial) also available. Financial award application deadline: 3/1.
Dr. William Schniedewind, Chair, 310-825-4165.
Application contact: Departmental Office, 310-825-4165, *E-mail:* nreast@humnet.ucla.edu.

■ UNIVERSITY OF CALIFORNIA, LOS ANGELES

Graduate Division, College of Letters and Science, Program in Indo-European Studies, Los Angeles, CA 90095

AWARDS PhD.

Students: 9 full-time (1 woman); includes 1 minority (Hispanic American), 2 international. 7 applicants, 43% accepted, 2 enrolled.
Degree requirements: For doctorate, 2 foreign languages, thesis/dissertation, oral and written qualifying exams.
Entrance requirements: For doctorate, minimum undergraduate GPA of 3.0, writing sample. *Application deadline:* For fall admission, 1/15. *Application fee:* $60. Electronic applications accepted.
Expenses: Tuition, nonresident: full-time $10,244. Required fees: $3,609. Full-time tuition and fees vary according to program.
Financial support: In 2001–02, 5 fellowships, 8 research assistantships, 7 teaching assistantships were awarded. Federal Work-Study, institutionally sponsored loans, and tuition waivers (full and partial) also available. Financial award application deadline: 3/1.
Dr. Brent Vine, Chair, 310-825-3480.
Application contact: Departmental Office, 310-825-3480, *E-mail:* gray@humnet.ucla.edu.

■ UNIVERSITY OF CALIFORNIA, LOS ANGELES

Graduate Division, College of Letters and Science, Program in Islamic Studies, Los Angeles, CA 90095

AWARDS MA, PhD, MPH/MA.

Students: 15 full-time (7 women); includes 1 minority (African American). In 2001, 2 master's, 2 doctorates awarded.
Degree requirements: For master's, one foreign language, comprehensive exam; for doctorate, 2 foreign languages, thesis/dissertation, oral and written qualifying exams.
Entrance requirements: For master's, GRE General Test, minimum GPA of 3.0; for doctorate, GRE General Test, minimum undergraduate GPA of 3.0. *Application deadline:* For fall admission, 12/15. *Application fee:* $60. Electronic applications accepted.
Expenses: Tuition, nonresident: full-time $10,244. Required fees: $3,609. Full-time tuition and fees vary according to program.
Financial support: In 2001–02, 6 fellowships, 15 research assistantships, 9 teaching assistantships were awarded. Federal Work-Study, institutionally sponsored loans, scholarships/grants, and tuition waivers (full and partial) also available. Financial award application deadline: 3/1.
Dr. Irene Bierman, Chair, 310-825-1181.
Application contact: Departmental Office, 310-825-1181.

■ UNIVERSITY OF CHICAGO

Division of Social Sciences and Division of the Humanities, Middle Eastern Studies Program, Chicago, IL 60637-1513

AWARDS AM, MBA/AM.

Students: 9.
Degree requirements: For master's, one foreign language, thesis.
Entrance requirements: For master's, GRE General Test, TOEFL. *Application deadline:* For fall admission, 12/28. *Application fee:* $55. Electronic applications accepted.
Expenses: Tuition: Full-time $16,548.
Financial support: Federal Work-Study and institutionally sponsored loans available. Financial award application deadline: 12/28.
Prof. John Woods, Director, 773-702-8296.
Application contact: Office of the Dean of Students, 773-702-8415.

■ UNIVERSITY OF CHICAGO

Division of the Humanities, Department of Near Eastern Languages and Civilizations, Chicago, IL 60637-1513

AWARDS AM, PhD.

Faculty: 52.
Students: 131. 95 applicants, 62% accepted. Terminal master's awarded for partial completion of doctoral program.
Degree requirements: For master's, one foreign language, thesis, comprehensive exam; for doctorate, 2 foreign languages, thesis/dissertation, comprehensive exam.
Entrance requirements: For master's and doctorate, GRE General Test, TOEFL. *Application deadline:* For fall admission, 12/28. *Application fee:* $55.

Expenses: Tuition: Full-time $16,548.
Financial support: Fellowships, Federal Work-Study available. Financial award application deadline: 12/28; financial award applicants required to submit FAFSA.
Dr. Fred M. Donner, Chair, 773-702-9512.

■ UNIVERSITY OF MICHIGAN

Horace H. Rackham School of Graduate Studies, College of Literature, Science, and the Arts, Department of Near Eastern Studies, Ann Arbor, MI 48109

AWARDS Ancient Israel/Hebrew Bible (AM, PhD); Arabic (AM, PhD); Armenian (AM, PhD); early Christian studies (AM, PhD); Hebrew (AM, PhD); Islamic studies (AM, PhD); Mesopotamian and ancient Near Eastern studies (AM, PhD); Persian (AM, PhD); teaching of Arabic as a foreign Language (AM); Turkish (AM, PhD). Part-time programs available. Terminal master's awarded for partial completion of doctoral program.

Degree requirements: For master's, 2 foreign languages; for doctorate, 4 foreign languages.
Entrance requirements: For master's, GRE General Test, TOEFL; for doctorate, GRE General Test, TOEFL, master's degree.
Faculty research: Middle and Near Eastern literatures, languages, cultures from ancient times to the present. *Web site:* http://www.umich.edu/~neareast/

■ UNIVERSITY OF MICHIGAN

Horace H. Rackham School of Graduate Studies, Interdepartmental Program in Modern Middle Eastern and North African Studies, Ann Arbor, MI 48109

AWARDS AM, JD/AM, MBA/AM, MPH/AM.

Degree requirements: For master's, one foreign language, thesis or alternative.
Entrance requirements: For master's, GRE General Test. *Web site:* http://www.umich.edu/~iinet/cmenas/

■ UNIVERSITY OF PENNSYLVANIA

School of Arts and Sciences, Graduate Group in Asian and Middle Eastern Studies, Philadelphia, PA 19104

AWARDS AM, PhD, JD/AM, JD/PhD. Part-time programs available. Terminal master's awarded for partial completion of doctoral program.

Degree requirements: For master's, thesis or alternative; for doctorate, thesis/dissertation.
Entrance requirements: For master's and doctorate, GRE General Test, TOEFL.
Expenses: Tuition: Part-time $12,875 per semester.

■ THE UNIVERSITY OF TEXAS AT AUSTIN

Graduate School, College of Liberal Arts, Center for Middle Eastern Studies, Austin, TX 78712-1111

AWARDS MA, JD/MA, MBA/MA, MLIS/MA, MP Aff/MA.

Faculty: 28 full-time (10 women), 39 part-time/adjunct (16 women).
Students: 33 full-time (17 women), 7 part-time (2 women); includes 2 minority (1 African American, 1 Asian American or Pacific Islander), 2 international. In 2001, 16 degrees awarded.
Degree requirements: For master's, one foreign language, thesis optional.
Entrance requirements: For master's, GRE General Test. *Application deadline:* For fall admission, 2/1 (priority date); for spring admission, 10/1. *Application fee:* $50 ($75 for international students). Electronic applications accepted.
Expenses: Tuition, state resident: full-time $3,159. Tuition, nonresident: full-time $6,957. Tuition and fees vary according to program.
Financial support: In 2001–02, 23 students received support, including 14 fellowships with full tuition reimbursements available (averaging $6,000 per year), 5 research assistantships (averaging $2,500 per year), 4 teaching assistantships with partial tuition reimbursements available (averaging $9,200 per year); career-related internships or fieldwork, Federal Work-Study, institutionally sponsored loans, and unspecified assistantships also available. Financial award application deadline: 2/1; financial award applicants required to submit FAFSA. *Total annual research expenditures:* $100,000.
Dr. Abraham Marcus, Director, 512-475-7229, *Fax:* 512-471-7834, *E-mail:* cmes@menic.utexas.edu.
Application contact: Diane Watts, Graduate Coordinator, 512-471-3881, *Fax:* 512-471-7834, *E-mail:* cmes@menic.utexas.edu. *Web site:* http://menic.utexas.edu/menic/cmes/

■ THE UNIVERSITY OF TEXAS AT AUSTIN

Graduate School, College of Liberal Arts, Department of Middle Eastern Languages and Cultures, Austin, TX 78712-1111

AWARDS Arabic studies (MA, PhD); Hebrew studies (MA, PhD); Persian studies (MA, PhD).

Entrance requirements: For master's and doctorate, GRE General Test. *Application fee:* $50 ($75 for international students).
Expenses: Tuition, state resident: full-time $3,159. Tuition, nonresident: full-time $6,957. Tuition and fees vary according to program.
Harold Liebowitz, Chair, 512-471-1365.
Application contact: Avraham Zilkha, Graduate Adviser, 512-471-1365.

■ UNIVERSITY OF UTAH

Graduate School, College of Humanities, Program in Middle East Studies, Salt Lake City, UT 84112-1107

AWARDS MA, PhD.

Students: 14 full-time (4 women), 12 part-time (6 women); includes 2 minority (both Asian Americans or Pacific Islanders), 4 international. Average age 33. 23 applicants, 48% accepted. In 2001, 3 degrees awarded.
Degree requirements: For master's, 2 foreign languages, thesis optional; for doctorate, 3 foreign languages, thesis/dissertation.
Entrance requirements: For master's, GRE General Test, TOEFL, minimum GPA of 3.2; for doctorate, GRE General Test, TOEFL, MA in Middle East studies or equivalent, minimum GPA of 3.2. *Application deadline:* For fall admission, 1/15; for spring admission, 9/15. *Application fee:* $40 ($60 for international students). Electronic applications accepted.
Expenses: Tuition, state resident: part-time $320 per semester hour. Tuition, nonresident: part-time $1,135 per semester hour. Required fees: $143 per semester hour. Tuition and fees vary according to course load, degree level and program.
Financial support: Fellowships with full tuition reimbursements, teaching assistantships with full tuition reimbursements, Federal Work-Study and unspecified assistantships available. Financial award application deadline: 1/15.
Faculty research: Arabic literature and linguistics, Islamic studies, Middle East history, political science, Judaic studies.
Dr. Ibrahim A. Karawan, Director, 801-581-6181, *Fax:* 801-581-6183, *E-mail:* ibrahim.karawan@poli-sci.utah.edu.
Application contact: Bernard W. Weiss, Director of Graduate Studies, 801-581-5401, *Fax:* 801-581-6183, *E-mail:* bgw34@qwest.net. *Web site:* http://www.hum.utah.edu/

■ UNIVERSITY OF VIRGINIA

College and Graduate School of Arts and Sciences, Division of Asian and Middle Eastern Languages and Cultures, Charlottesville, VA 22903

AWARDS MA, MBA/MA.

Faculty: 18 full-time (11 women), 2 part-time/adjunct (1 woman).
Students: 1 (woman) full-time, 1 (woman) part-time; includes 1 minority (Native American). Average age 41. 9 applicants, 56% accepted, 1 enrolled. In 2001, 2 degrees awarded.

University of Virginia (continued)
Entrance requirements: For master's, GRE General Test. *Application deadline:* For fall admission, 7/15; for spring admission, 12/1. Applications are processed on a rolling basis. *Application fee:* $40. Electronic applications accepted.
Expenses: Tuition, state resident: full-time $3,988. Tuition, nonresident: full-time $17,078. Required fees: $1,190.
Financial support: Application deadline: 2/1.
Robert Hueckstedt, Chairman, 434-982-2304, *Fax:* 434-924-6977.
Application contact: Duane J. Osheim, Associate Dean for Graduate Programs, 434-924-7184, *Fax:* 434-924-3084, *E-mail:* grad-a-s@virginia.edu. *Web site:* http://www.virginia.edu/~amelc/

■ UNIVERSITY OF WASHINGTON

Graduate School, College of Arts and Sciences, Department of Near Eastern Languages and Civilization, Seattle, WA 98195

AWARDS MA.

Degree requirements: For master's, 2 foreign languages.
Entrance requirements: For master's, GRE, TOEFL, minimum GPA of 3.0. Electronic applications accepted.
Expenses: Tuition, state resident: full-time $5,539. Tuition, nonresident: full-time $14,376. Required fees: $390. Tuition and fees vary according to course load and program.
Faculty research: Arabic, Hebrew, Persian, and Turkish literature; Islamic civilization and religion; Central Asian Turkic language and literature; Hebrew Bible and ancient Near East; ancient Christianity. *Web site:* http://www.depts.washington.edu/nelc/

■ UNIVERSITY OF WASHINGTON

Graduate School, College of Arts and Sciences, Henry M. Jackson School of International Studies, Middle Eastern Studies Program, Seattle, WA 98195

AWARDS MAIS.

Faculty: 36 full-time (8 women).
Students: 10 full-time (3 women); includes 1 minority (Hispanic American), 3 international. Average age 32. 15 applicants, 87% accepted. In 2001, 5 degrees awarded.
Degree requirements: For master's, one foreign language, thesis optional.
Entrance requirements: For master's, GRE General Test, TOEFL, minimum GPA of 3.0. *Application deadline:* For fall admission, 1/15 (priority date). *Application fee:* $45. Electronic applications accepted.
Expenses: Tuition, state resident: full-time $5,539. Tuition, nonresident: full-time $14,376. Required fees: $390. Tuition and fees vary according to course load and program.
Financial support: In 2001–02, 1 fellowship was awarded; research assistantships, teaching assistantships, career-related internships or fieldwork, Federal Work-Study, institutionally sponsored loans, and summer language study awards also available. Financial award application deadline: 1/15; financial award applicants required to submit FAFSA.
Ellis Goldberg, Chair.
Application contact: 206-543-6001, *Fax:* 206-616-3170, *E-mail:* jsisinfo@u.washington.edu. *Web site:* http://jsis.artsci.washington.edu/

■ UNIVERSITY OF WASHINGTON

Graduate School, Interdisciplinary Program in Near and Middle Eastern Studies, Seattle, WA 98195

AWARDS PhD.

Degree requirements: For doctorate, 3 foreign languages, thesis/dissertation.
Entrance requirements: For doctorate, GRE General Test, TOEFL, minimum GPA of 3.0. Electronic applications accepted.
Expenses: Tuition, state resident: full-time $5,539. Tuition, nonresident: full-time $14,376. Required fees: $390. Tuition and fees vary according to course load and program. *Web site:* http://www.grad.washington.edu/inter/nme.htm

■ WASHINGTON UNIVERSITY IN ST. LOUIS

Graduate School of Arts and Sciences, Department of History, Program in Islamic and Near Eastern Studies, St. Louis, MO 63130-4899

AWARDS MA.

Students: 6 full-time (4 women); includes 1 minority (Asian American or Pacific Islander), 3 international. 8 applicants, 88% accepted. In 2001, 2 degrees awarded.
Degree requirements: For master's, one foreign language, thesis (for some programs).
Entrance requirements: For master's, GRE General Test. *Application deadline:* For fall admission, 1/15 (priority date). Applications are processed on a rolling basis. *Application fee:* $35. Electronic applications accepted.
Expenses: Tuition: Full-time $26,900.
Financial support: Application deadline: 1/15.
Dr. Fatemeh Keshavarz, Director, 314-935-5166. *Web site:* http://artsci.wustl.edu/~sandrew/csisc.html

■ WAYNE STATE UNIVERSITY

Graduate School, College of Liberal Arts, Department of Near Eastern and Asian Studies, Detroit, MI 48202

AWARDS Language learning (MA); Near Eastern studies (MA).

Faculty: 2 full-time.
Students: 2. 3 applicants, 0% accepted.
Degree requirements: For master's, one foreign language.
Entrance requirements: For master's, GRE General Test. *Application deadline:* For fall admission, 7/1. *Application fee:* $20 ($30 for international students). Electronic applications accepted.
Expenses: Tuition, state resident: full-time $3,764. Tuition and fees vary according to degree level and program.
Financial support: In 2001–02, 1 teaching assistantship was awarded
Faculty research: Modern Middle East history, Arabic studies, linguistics, Islamic studies, Judaic studies.
Dr. Aleya Rouchdy, Chairperson, 313-577-3015, *Fax:* 313-577-3266.

NORTHERN STUDIES

■ UNIVERSITY OF ALASKA FAIRBANKS

Graduate School, College of Liberal Arts, Department of Northern Studies, Fairbanks, AK 99775-7480

AWARDS MA, PhD.

Faculty: 1 (woman) full-time.
Students: 17 full-time (9 women), 14 part-time (10 women); includes 3 minority (1 African American, 2 Native Americans), 4 international. Average age 40. 13 applicants, 77% accepted, 8 enrolled. In 2001, 4 degrees awarded.
Degree requirements: For master's, thesis or alternative, comprehensive exam; for doctorate, one foreign language, thesis/dissertation, comprehensive exam.
Entrance requirements: For master's and doctorate, GRE General Test, TOEFL. *Application deadline:* For fall admission, 4/1; for spring admission, 11/1. Applications are processed on a rolling basis. *Application fee:* $35. Electronic applications accepted.
Expenses: Tuition, state resident: full-time $4,272; part-time $178 per credit. Tuition, nonresident: full-time $8,328; part-time $347 per credit. Required fees: $960; $60 per term. Part-time tuition and fees vary according to course load.
Financial support: In 2001–02, fellowships (averaging $10,000 per year); research assistantships, teaching assistantships, career-related internships or fieldwork, Federal Work-Study, and scholarships/grants also available.
Faculty research: Canadian history, environmental history, Native Alaskan history and art, fetal alcohol syndrome.
Dr. Judith Kleinfeld, Director, 907-474-5266.

WESTERN EUROPEAN STUDIES

■ BOSTON COLLEGE

Graduate School of Arts and Sciences, Department of History, Chestnut Hill, MA 02467-3800

AWARDS European national studies (MA); history (MA, PhD); medieval studies (MA).

Students: 21 full-time (9 women), 69 part-time (24 women); includes 5 minority (3 African Americans, 2 Hispanic Americans), 8 international. 121 applicants, 37% accepted. In 2001, 7 master's, 10 doctorates awarded. Terminal master's awarded for partial completion of doctoral program.
Degree requirements: For master's, one foreign language, comprehensive exam; for doctorate, 2 foreign languages, thesis/dissertation, comprehensive exam.
Entrance requirements: For master's and doctorate, GRE General Test, sample of written work. *Application deadline:* For fall admission, 2/1. *Application fee:* $50.
Expenses: Tuition: Full-time $17,664; part-time $8,832 per semester.
Financial support: Fellowships, research assistantships, teaching assistantships, Federal Work-Study and scholarships/grants available. Support available to part-time students. Financial award application deadline: 3/1; financial award applicants required to submit FAFSA.
Faculty research: Modern and early modern European, U.S., Russian, and Soviet history; European and U.S. intellectual history.
Dr. Peter Weiler, Chairperson, 617-552-3781, *E-mail:* peter.weiler@bc.edu.
Application contact: Dr. Robin Fleming, Director of Graduate Studies, 617-552-3781, *E-mail:* robin.fleming@bc.edu. *Web site:* http://www.bc.edu/bc_org/avp/cas/his/history.html

■ BROWN UNIVERSITY

Graduate School, Center for Portuguese and Brazilian Studies, Providence, RI 02912

AWARDS Brazilian studies (AM); Luso-Brazilian studies (PhD); Portuguese studies and bilingual education (AM).

Degree requirements: For doctorate, thesis/dissertation.

■ THE CATHOLIC UNIVERSITY OF AMERICA

School of Arts and Sciences, Program in Irish Studies, Washington, DC 20064

AWARDS MA. Part-time programs available.

Students: 3 full-time (1 woman), 2 part-time (both women). Average age 31. 6 applicants, 83% accepted, 1 enrolled. In 2001, 5 degrees awarded.
Degree requirements: For master's, one foreign language, comprehensive exam.
Entrance requirements: For master's, GRE General Test. *Application deadline:* For fall admission, 8/1 (priority date); for spring admission, 12/1. Applications are processed on a rolling basis. *Application fee:* $55. Electronic applications accepted.
Expenses: Tuition: Full-time $20,050; part-time $770 per credit. Required fees: $430 per term. Tuition and fees vary according to program.
Financial support: Career-related internships or fieldwork and tuition waivers (partial) available. Support available to part-time students. Financial award application deadline: 2/1.
Faculty research: Eighteenth- and nineteenth-century Irish literature, contemporary Irish literature, Irish language, Irish politics, Irish American history.
Christina Mahony, Acting Director, 202-319-5488.

■ CLAREMONT GRADUATE UNIVERSITY

Graduate Programs, Center for the Humanities, Department of History, Claremont, CA 91711-6160

AWARDS American studies (MA, PhD); European studies (MA, PhD); history (MA, PhD).

Faculty: 2 full-time (1 woman), 2 part-time/adjunct (both women).
Students: 55 full-time (32 women), 24 part-time (9 women); includes 17 minority (3 African Americans, 4 Asian Americans or Pacific Islanders, 10 Hispanic Americans), 3 international. Average age 37. In 2001, 11 master's, 5 doctorates awarded.
Degree requirements: For master's, 2 foreign languages, thesis/dissertation; for doctorate, 2 foreign languages, thesis/dissertation, comprehensive exam.
Entrance requirements: For master's and doctorate, GRE General Test. *Application deadline:* For fall admission, 2/15 (priority date). Applications are processed on a rolling basis. *Application fee:* $50. Electronic applications accepted.
Expenses: Tuition: Full-time $22,984; part-time $1,000 per unit. Required fees: $160; $80 per semester.
Financial support: Fellowships, research assistantships, Federal Work-Study and institutionally sponsored loans available. Support available to part-time students. Financial award application deadline: 2/15; financial award applicants required to submit FAFSA.
Faculty research: Intellectual and social history, cultural studies, gender studies, Western history, Chicano history.
Janet Farrell Brodie, Chair, 909-621-8172, *Fax:* 909-621-8609.
Application contact: Elisabeth Flores Griffith, Secretary, 909-621-8172, *Fax:* 909-621-8390, *E-mail:* history@cgu.edu. *Web site:* http://www.cgu.edu/hum/his/index.html

■ COLUMBIA UNIVERSITY

Graduate School of Arts and Sciences, Program in Liberal Studies, New York, NY 10027

AWARDS American studies (MA); East Asian studies (MA); human rights studies (MA); Islamic culture studies (MA); Jewish studies (MA); medieval studies (MA); modern European studies (MA); South Asian studies (MA). Part-time and evening/weekend programs available.

Faculty: 5 part-time/adjunct (2 women).
Students: 7 full-time (2 women), 75 part-time (51 women); includes 5 minority (1 African American, 3 Asian Americans or Pacific Islanders, 1 Hispanic American), 8 international. Average age 41. 39 applicants, 77% accepted. In 2001, 20 degrees awarded.
Degree requirements: For master's, thesis.
Application deadline: For fall admission, 4/1; for spring admission, 11/1. *Application fee:* $65.
Expenses: Tuition: Full-time $27,528. Required fees: $1,638.
Steve Laymon, Assistant Dean, 212-854-4932, *Fax:* 212-854-4912.
Application contact: Director of Admissions, 212-854-3331.

Find an in-depth description at www.petersons.com/gradchannel.

■ COLUMBIA UNIVERSITY

School of International and Public Affairs, Institute for the Study of Europe, New York, NY 10027

AWARDS Certificate. Students must be enrolled in a separate graduate degree program at Columbia University.

Application deadline: For fall admission, 1/5 (priority date); for spring admission, 10/15 (priority date). *Application fee:* $75. Electronic applications accepted.
Financial support: Application deadline: 1/15.
Dr. John Micgiel, Director, 212-854-4618, *Fax:* 212-854-8577, *E-mail:* jsm6@columbia.edu.
Application contact: Robert Garris, Associate Director, 212-854-6216, *Fax:* 212-854-3010, *E-mail:* sipa_admission@columbia.edu. *Web site:* http://www.columbia.edu/cu/sipa/REGIONAL/WE/iwe.html

■ COLUMBIA UNIVERSITY

School of International and Public Affairs, Institute of Latin American and Iberian Studies, New York, NY 10027

AWARDS Certificate. Students must be enrolled in a separate graduate degree program at Columbia University.

Columbia University (continued)
Faculty: 47 full-time, 17 part-time/adjunct.
Students: 2.
Application deadline: For fall admission, 1/5 (priority date); for spring admission, 10/15 (priority date). *Application fee:* $75. Electronic applications accepted.
Financial support: Application deadline: 1/15.
Faculty research: Rights vs. efficiency in a globalized era, citizenship and governance in Latin America and Western Europe.
Dr. Douglas Chalmers, Director, 212-854-4643, *Fax:* 212-854-4607, *E-mail:* chalmers@columbia.edu.
Application contact: Robert Garris, Associate Director, 212-854-6216, *Fax:* 212-854-3010, *E-mail:* sipa_admission@columbia.edu. *Web site:* http://www.columbia.edu/cu/ilais/

■ EAST CAROLINA UNIVERSITY

Graduate School, College of Arts and Sciences, Department of History, Greenville, NC 27858-4353

AWARDS American history (MA, MA Ed); European history (MA, MA Ed); maritime history (MA). Part-time and evening/weekend programs available.

Faculty: 22 full-time (3 women).
Students: 32 full-time (9 women), 40 part-time (13 women); includes 4 minority (1 African American, 2 Asian Americans or Pacific Islanders, 1 Native American), 1 international. Average age 31. 36 applicants, 69% accepted. In 2001, 17 degrees awarded.
Degree requirements: For master's, one foreign language, thesis, comprehensive exam.
Entrance requirements: For master's, GRE General Test, GRE Subject Test, MAT (MA Ed), TOEFL. *Application deadline:* For fall admission, 6/1 (priority date); for spring admission, 10/15. Applications are processed on a rolling basis. *Application fee:* $45.
Expenses: Tuition, state resident: full-time $2,636. Tuition, nonresident: full-time $11,365.
Financial support: Fellowships, research assistantships with partial tuition reimbursements, teaching assistantships with partial tuition reimbursements, Federal Work-Study available. Support available to part-time students. Financial award application deadline: 6/1.
Dr. Michael Palmer, Chairperson, 252-328-6155, *Fax:* 252-328-6774, *E-mail:* palmerm@mail.ecu.edu.
Application contact: Dr. Carl Swanson, Director of Graduate Studies, 252-328-6485, *E-mail:* swansonc@mail.ecu.edu.

■ GEORGETOWN UNIVERSITY

Graduate School of Arts and Sciences, BMW Center for German and European Studies, Washington, DC 20057

AWARDS MA, MA/PhD.

Degree requirements: For master's, 2 foreign languages, comprehensive exam.
Entrance requirements: For master's, GRE General Test, TOEFL. *Web site:* http://www.georgetown.edu/sfs/cges

Find an in-depth description at www.petersons.com/gradchannel.

■ THE GEORGE WASHINGTON UNIVERSITY

Elliott School of International Affairs, Program in European and Eurasian Studies, Washington, DC 20052

AWARDS MA, JD/MA, MBA/MA. Part-time and evening/weekend programs available.

Students: 1 (woman) full-time. Average age 25. 29 applicants, 83% accepted.
Degree requirements: For master's, one foreign language.
Entrance requirements: For master's, GRE General Test, TOEFL, minimum B average. *Application deadline:* For fall admission, 2/1. *Application fee:* $55. Electronic applications accepted.
Expenses: Tuition: Part-time $810 per credit. Required fees: $1 per credit.
Financial support: Fellowships with tuition reimbursements, research assistantships with tuition reimbursements, career-related internships or fieldwork, Federal Work-Study, and institutionally sponsored loans available. Financial award application deadline: 1/15; financial award applicants required to submit FAFSA.
Faculty research: NATO, European economics, European history, European Union.
Dr. James Goldgeier, Director, 202-994-7099.
Application contact: Jeff V. Miles, Director of Graduate Admissions, 202-994-7050, *Fax:* 202-994-9537, *E-mail:* esiagrad@gwu.edu. *Web site:* http://www.gwu.edu/~elliott/academicprograms/ma/ees/

Find an in-depth description at www.petersons.com/gradchannel.

■ INDIANA UNIVERSITY BLOOMINGTON

Graduate School, College of Arts and Sciences, Department of West European Studies, Bloomington, IN 47405

AWARDS MA, PhD, Certificate.

Faculty: 5 full-time (0 women).
Students: 3 full-time (1 woman), 2 part-time (1 woman); includes 2 minority (1 African American, 1 Hispanic American). Average age 30. In 2001, 4 degrees awarded.
Degree requirements: For master's, 2 foreign languages, thesis; for doctorate, thesis/dissertation; for Certificate, 2 foreign languages.
Entrance requirements: For master's, GRE General Test, TOEFL; for doctorate, TOEFL. *Application deadline:* For fall admission, 1/15 (priority date); for spring admission, 9/1 (priority date). Applications are processed on a rolling basis. *Application fee:* $45 ($55 for international students).
Expenses: Tuition, state resident: full-time $4,720; part-time $197 per credit. Tuition, nonresident: full-time $13,748; part-time $573 per credit. Required fees: $642.
Financial support: In 2001–02, 3 fellowships with full tuition reimbursements (averaging $10,000 per year), 2 research assistantships with full tuition reimbursements (averaging $9,859 per year), 4 teaching assistantships with partial tuition reimbursements (averaging $7,200 per year) were awarded.
Faculty research: European integration, economics of Europe, European union, European culture and identity, expansion of European union.
Dr. Peter Bondanella, Chairman, 812-855-3280, *Fax:* 812-855-7695, *E-mail:* bondanel@indiana.edu.
Application contact: Amanda Ciccarelli, Associate Director, 812-855-3280, *Fax:* 812-855-7695, *E-mail:* weur@indiana.edu. *Web site:* http://www.indiana.edu/~weur/

■ JOHNS HOPKINS UNIVERSITY

Paul H. Nitze School of Advanced International Studies, Washington, DC 20036

AWARDS Emerging markets (Certificate); interdisciplinary studies (MA, PhD), including African studies, American foreign policy (MA), Asian studies, Canadian studies, conflict resolution and mediation (MA), environmental policy and resource management (MA), European studies, international business (MA), international development (MA), international economics (MA), international relations (MA), Latin American studies, Middle Eastern studies (MA), military and defense studies (MA), Russian area and East European studies (MA), social change and development (MA); international public policy (MIPP). MBA/MA offered jointly with the University of Pennsylvania–Wharton School and INSEAD in France.

Faculty: 44 full-time (13 women), 113 part-time/adjunct (29 women).
Students: 567 full-time (275 women), 17 part-time (8 women); includes 71 minority (14 African Americans, 46 Asian Americans or Pacific Islanders, 10 Hispanic Americans, 1 Native American). Average age 27. 1,288 applicants, 35% accepted. In 2001, 294 master's, 13 doctorates, 34 other advanced degrees awarded. Terminal

master's awarded for partial completion of doctoral program.

Degree requirements: For master's, one foreign language, comprehensive exam; for doctorate, 2 foreign languages, thesis/dissertation.
Entrance requirements: For master's, GMAT or GRE General Test or TOEFL, previous course work in economics, foreign language; for doctorate, GRE General Test or TOEFL; for Certificate, TOEFL. *Application deadline:* For fall admission, 1/15. *Application fee:* $75. Electronic applications accepted.
Expenses: Contact institution.
Financial support: In 2001–02, 431 fellowships (averaging $5,500 per year) were awarded; career-related internships or fieldwork and Federal Work-Study also available. Financial award application deadline: 2/1; financial award applicants required to submit FAFSA.
Faculty research: Comparative politics, regional studies, language and linguistics.
Dr. Jessica Einhorn, Dean, 202-663-5624, *Fax:* 202-663-5621.
Application contact: Bonnie Wilson, Associate Dean of Student Affairs, 202-663-5700, *Fax:* 202-663-7788, *E-mail:* admissions.sais@jhu.edu. *Web site:* http://www.sais-jhu.edu/

Find an in-depth description at www.petersons.com/gradchannel.

■ NEW YORK UNIVERSITY

Graduate School of Arts and Science, Center for European Studies, New York, NY 10012-1019

AWARDS MA.

Faculty: 4 full-time (0 women).
Students: 9 full-time (6 women), 1 part-time; includes 3 minority (1 Asian American or Pacific Islander, 1 Hispanic American, 1 Native American), 3 international. Average age 24. 27 applicants, 78% accepted, 4 enrolled. In 2001, 4 degrees awarded.
Entrance requirements: For master's, GRE General Test, TOEFL. *Application deadline:* For fall admission, 1/4 (priority date). *Application fee:* $60.
Expenses: Tuition: Full-time $19,536; part-time $814 per credit. Required fees: $1,330; $38 per credit. Tuition and fees vary according to course load and program.
Financial support: Fellowships with tuition reimbursements, teaching assistantships with tuition reimbursements, career-related internships or fieldwork, Federal Work-Study, and institutionally sponsored loans available. Financial award application deadline: 1/4; financial award applicants required to submit FAFSA.
Faculty research: Xenophobia, migration, and identity politics in Europe; European Union and political economy; Central Eastern Europe.
Martin Schain, Director, 212-998-3838, *Fax:* 212-995-4188, *E-mail:* gsas.admissions@nyu.edu.
Application contact: Jan Gross, Associate Chair, 212-998-3838, *Fax:* 212-995-4188. *Web site:* http://www.nyu.edu/gsas/dept/europe/

■ UNIVERSITY OF CALIFORNIA, SANTA BARBARA

Graduate Division, College of Letters and Sciences, Division of Humanities and Fine Arts, Program in Latin American and Iberian Studies, Santa Barbara, CA 93106

AWARDS MA.

Degree requirements: For master's, one foreign language, thesis or alternative, comprehensive exam.
Entrance requirements: For master's, GRE, TOEFL, 2 samples of written work.

■ UNIVERSITY OF CONNECTICUT

Graduate School, College of Liberal Arts and Sciences, Field of Western European Studies, Storrs, CT 06269

AWARDS MA.

Entrance requirements: For master's, GRE General Test.

■ UNIVERSITY OF NEVADA, RENO

Graduate School, College of Arts and Science, Interdisciplinary Program in Basque Studies, Reno, NV 89557

AWARDS PhD.

Faculty: 3.
Students: 3 full-time (2 women), 1 (woman) part-time, 1 international. Average age 38.
Degree requirements: For doctorate, thesis/dissertation.
Entrance requirements: For doctorate, TOEFL, master's degree in related field, minimum GPA of 3.0. *Application deadline:* For fall admission, 3/1 (priority date); for spring admission, 11/1. Applications are processed on a rolling basis. *Application fee:* $40.
Expenses: Tuition, state resident: full-time $2,067; part-time $108 per credit. Tuition, nonresident: full-time $9,282; part-time $109 per credit. Required fees: $57 per semester. Tuition and fees vary according to course load.
Financial support: In 2001–02, 3 research assistantships were awarded; teaching assistantships available. Financial award application deadline: 3/1.
Faculty research: Ethnic groups, Basque society, migration studies, symbolic anthropology, terrorism.
Linda White, Graduate Program Director, 775-784-4854, *E-mail:* linda@unr.edu.

■ WASHINGTON UNIVERSITY IN ST. LOUIS

Graduate School of Arts and Sciences, European Studies Program, St. Louis, MO 63130-4899

AWARDS MA. Part-time programs available.

Students: 1 (woman) full-time, 1 international. 7 applicants, 86% accepted. In 2001, 3 degrees awarded.
Entrance requirements: For master's, GRE General Test. *Application deadline:* For fall admission, 1/15 (priority date). Applications are processed on a rolling basis. *Application fee:* $35. Electronic applications accepted.
Expenses: Tuition: Full-time $26,900.
Financial support: Research assistantships, Federal Work-Study, institutionally sponsored loans, and tuition waivers (full and partial) available. Support available to part-time students. Financial award application deadline: 1/15.
Dr. Paul Michael Lutzeler, Chairman, 314-935-4784. *Web site:* http://artsci.wustl.edu/~europe/

WOMEN'S STUDIES

■ BRANDEIS UNIVERSITY

Graduate School of Arts and Sciences, Joint Degree Programs in Women's Studies, Waltham, MA 02454-9110

AWARDS Anthropology and women's studies (MA); English and women's studies (MA); music and women's studies (MA); Near Eastern and Judaic studies and women's studies (MA); sociology and women's studies (MA).

Faculty: 54 full-time (46 women), 9 part-time/adjunct (6 women).
Students: 35 full-time (32 women). Average age 25. 38 applicants, 26% accepted. In 2001, 15 degrees awarded.
Degree requirements: For master's, thesis (for some programs).
Entrance requirements: For master's, GRE, sample of written work, resumé. *Application deadline:* For fall admission, 1/15. *Application fee:* $60. Electronic applications accepted.
Expenses: Tuition: Full-time $27,392. Required fees: $35.
Financial support: In 2001–02, 3 students received support; fellowships, research assistantships, teaching assistantships, scholarships/grants and tuition waivers (full and partial) available. Support available to part-time students. Financial award application deadline: 4/15; financial award applicants required to submit CSS PROFILE or FAFSA.
Shulamit Reinharz, Director, 781-736-2637, *Fax:* 781-736-3044, *E-mail:* reinharz@brandeis.edu.

Brandeis University (continued)
Application contact: Rachel Richer, Coordinator, 781-736-3042, *Fax:* 781-736-3044, *E-mail:* wstudies@binah.cc.brandeis.edu. *Web site:* http://www.brandeis.edu/mns/main.html

■ CALIFORNIA INSTITUTE OF INTEGRAL STUDIES

Graduate Programs, School of Consciousness and Transformation, San Francisco, CA 94103

AWARDS Cultural anthropology and social transformation (MA); East-West psychology (MA, PhD); philosophy and religion (MA, PhD), including Asian and comparative studies, philosophy, cosmology, and consciousness, women's spirituality; social and cultural anthropology (PhD); transformative learning and change (PhD). Part-time and evening/weekend programs available. Postbaccalaureate distance learning degree programs offered (minimal on-campus study).

Faculty: 20 full-time (9 women), 72 part-time/adjunct (35 women).
Students: 60 full-time, 143 part-time. 157 applicants, 78% accepted, 85 enrolled. In 2001, 58 master's, 21 doctorates awarded. Terminal master's awarded for partial completion of doctoral program.
Degree requirements: For master's, comprehensive exam; for doctorate, thesis/dissertation, comprehensive exam.
Entrance requirements: For master's, TOEFL, minimum GPA of 3.0; for doctorate, TOEFL, master's degree. *Application deadline:* For fall admission, 3/15 (priority date); for spring admission, 10/15 (priority date). Applications are processed on a rolling basis. *Application fee:* $65.
Expenses: Tuition: Full-time $10,890; part-time $605 per unit. Tuition and fees vary according to degree level.
Financial support: Career-related internships or fieldwork, Federal Work-Study, institutionally sponsored loans, and scholarships/grants available. Support available to part-time students. Financial award application deadline: 6/15; financial award applicants required to submit FAFSA.
Faculty research: Altered states of consciousness, dreams, cosmology.
Daniel Deslaurier, Director, 415-575-6260, *Fax:* 415-575-1264, *E-mail:* danield@ciis.edu.
Application contact: Gregory E. Canada, Director of Admissions, 415-575-6155, *Fax:* 415-575-1268, *E-mail:* gregc@ciis.edu. *Web site:* http://www.ciis.edu/

Find an in-depth description at www.petersons.com/gradchannel.

■ CLAREMONT GRADUATE UNIVERSITY

Graduate Programs, Independent Programs, Program in Applied Women's Studies, Claremont, CA 91711-6160

AWARDS MA.

Students: 9 full-time (all women), 4 part-time (all women); includes 2 minority (both Asian Americans or Pacific Islanders), 1 international. Average age 33. In 2001, 4 degrees awarded.
Degree requirements: For master's, internship.
Entrance requirements: For master's, GRE General Test. *Application deadline:* For fall admission, 2/15 (priority date). Applications are processed on a rolling basis. *Application fee:* $50. Electronic applications accepted.
Expenses: Tuition: Full-time $22,984; part-time $1,000 per unit. Required fees: $160; $80 per semester.
Financial support: Fellowships, career-related internships or fieldwork and Federal Work-Study available. Support available to part-time students. Financial award application deadline: 2/15; financial award applicants required to submit FAFSA.
Jean Schroedel, Chair, 909-621-8696, *Fax:* 909-621-8390, *E-mail:* jean.schroedel@cgu.edu.
Application contact: Michelle Johnson, Program Coordinator, 909-607-8305, *Fax:* 909-621-8390, *E-mail:* michelle.johnson@cgu.edu. *Web site:* http://www.cgu.edu/interdis/aws/index.html

■ CLAREMONT GRADUATE UNIVERSITY

Graduate Programs, School of Religion, Claremont, CA 91711-6160

AWARDS Hebrew Bible (MA, PhD); history of Christianity (MA, PhD); New Testament (MA, PhD); philosophy of religion and theology (MA, PhD); theology, ethics and culture (MA, PhD); women's studies in religion (MA, PhD). MA/PhD (philosophy of religion and theology) offered in cooperation with the Department of Philosophy. Part-time programs available.

Faculty: 4 full-time (2 women), 3 part-time/adjunct (2 women).
Students: 117 full-time (20 women), 33 part-time (12 women); includes 34 minority (9 African Americans, 18 Asian Americans or Pacific Islanders, 7 Hispanic Americans), 33 international. Average age 38. In 2001, 7 master's, 6 doctorates awarded. Terminal master's awarded for partial completion of doctoral program.
Degree requirements: For master's, one foreign language, thesis, comprehensive exam (for some programs); for doctorate, 2 foreign languages, thesis/dissertation, comprehensive exam.
Entrance requirements: For master's and doctorate, GRE General Test. *Application deadline:* For fall admission, 2/15 (priority date). Applications are processed on a rolling basis. *Application fee:* $50. Electronic applications accepted.
Expenses: Tuition: Full-time $22,984; part-time $1,000 per unit. Required fees: $160; $80 per semester.
Financial support: Fellowships, research assistantships, teaching assistantships, Federal Work-Study and institutionally sponsored loans available. Support available to part-time students. Financial award application deadline: 2/15; financial award applicants required to submit FAFSA.
Karen Jo Torjesen, Dean, 909-621-8085, *Fax:* 909-607-9587, *E-mail:* karen.torjesen@cgu.edu.
Application contact: Jackie Huntzinger, Secretary, 909-621-8085, *Fax:* 909-607-9587, *E-mail:* religion@cgu.edu. *Web site:* http://religion.cgu.edu/

■ CLARK ATLANTA UNIVERSITY

School of Arts and Sciences, Department of Africana Women's Studies, Atlanta, GA 30314

AWARDS MA, DA.

Degree requirements: For master's, one foreign language, thesis; for doctorate, 2 foreign languages, thesis/dissertation.
Entrance requirements: For master's, GRE General Test, minimum GPA of 2.5; for doctorate, GRE General Test, minimum graduate GPA of 3.0.
Faculty research: Concerns of women of African descent globally.

■ CLARK UNIVERSITY

Graduate School, Women's Studies Program, Worcester, MA 01610-1477

AWARDS PhD.

Students: 13 full-time (all women); includes 1 minority (Native American), 6 international. Average age 37. 39 applicants, 18% accepted, 3 enrolled.
Degree requirements: For doctorate, thesis/dissertation.
Entrance requirements: For doctorate, TOEFL. *Application deadline:* For fall admission, 2/15. Applications are processed on a rolling basis. *Application fee:* $40.
Expenses: Tuition: Full-time $24,400; part-time $763 per credit. Required fees: $10.
Financial support: In 2001–02, fellowships with full tuition reimbursements (averaging $10,250 per year), research assistantships with full tuition reimbursements (averaging $10,250 per year), 5 teaching assistantships with full tuition reimbursements (averaging $10,250 per year) were awarded. Tuition waivers (full) also available.
Faculty research: Gender, environment, and development; women, work, and entrepreneurship; women in post-colonial societies; women in politics; women and militarization.

Dr. Cynthia Enloe, Director, 508-793-7358.
Application contact: Joanne Ljungberg, Assistant Director, 508-793-7358, *Fax:* 508-793-8896, *E-mail:* womenstudy@clarku.edu. *Web site:* http://www2.clarku.edu/newsite/graduatefolder/index.shtml

■ DEPAUL UNIVERSITY

College of Liberal Arts and Sciences, Program in Women's Studies, Chicago, IL 60604-2287

AWARDS Certificate. Part-time and evening/weekend programs available.

Faculty: 3 full-time (all women), 3 part-time/adjunct (all women).
Students: Average age 55. 1 applicant, 100% accepted. In 2001, 1 degree awarded.
Application deadline: Applications are processed on a rolling basis. *Application fee:* $25.
Expenses: Tuition: Part-time $362 per credit hour. Tuition and fees vary according to program.
Financial support: Tuition waivers (partial) available.
Faculty research: Feminist ethics, feminist pedagogy, women's literature, race and gender, gender and communication.
Dr. Elizabeth A. Kelly, Director, 773-325-1979, *Fax:* 773-325-4761, *E-mail:* bkelly@depaul.edu.
Application contact: Susan Gartner, Administrative Assistant, 773-325-4500, *Fax:* 773-325-4761, *E-mail:* sgartner@depaul.edu.

■ DREW UNIVERSITY

Caspersen School of Graduate Studies, Women's Studies Program, Madison, NJ 07940-1493

AWARDS MA.

Students: 4 full-time (all women), 1 (woman) part-time; includes 3 minority (1 African American, 1 Asian American or Pacific Islander, 1 Hispanic American), 2 international. Average age 33.
Degree requirements: For master's, one foreign language, thesis.
Entrance requirements: For master's, GRE General Test, TOEFL, TWE. *Application deadline:* For fall admission, 2/1. *Application fee:* $35.
Expenses: Tuition: Full-time $23,238; part-time $1,291 per credit. Required fees: $690; $690 per year. One-time fee: $125. Tuition and fees vary according to program.
Financial support: Career-related internships or fieldwork, Federal Work-Study, scholarships/grants, and tuition waivers (full and partial) available. Support available to part-time students. Financial award application deadline: 2/15; financial award applicants required to submit FAFSA.
Faculty research: Feminist theory, feminist literature, gender analysis, social theory and religion.
Dr. Wendy Kolmar, Director, 973-408-3632, *Fax:* 973-408-3040, *E-mail:* wkolmar@drew.edu.
Application contact: Carla J. Osit, Director of Graduate Admissions, 973-408-3110, *Fax:* 973-408-3242, *E-mail:* gradm@drew.edu. *Web site:* http://www.drew.edu/

■ DUKE UNIVERSITY

Graduate School, Women's Studies Program, Durham, NC 27708-0586

AWARDS Certificate.

Faculty: 8 full-time, 1 part-time/adjunct.
Application deadline: For fall admission, 12/31. *Application fee:* $75.
Expenses: Tuition: Full-time $24,600.
Financial support: Application deadline: 12/31.
Faculty research: History of women's studies, feminist pedagogy, higher education, women's health, race/class/gender and sexual orientation.
Robyn Wiegman, Director, 919-684-5683, *Fax:* 919-684-4652, *E-mail:* wstprog@duke.edu. *Web site:* http://www.duke.edu/womstud/

■ EASTERN MICHIGAN UNIVERSITY

Graduate School, College of Arts and Sciences, Program in Women's Studies, Ypsilanti, MI 48197

AWARDS MLS.

Students: 8 full-time, 15 part-time; includes 3 minority (1 African American, 1 Hispanic American, 1 Native American), 3 international. In 2001, 6 degrees awarded.
Degree requirements: For master's, thesis optional.
Entrance requirements: For master's, TOEFL. *Application deadline:* For fall admission, 5/15; for spring admission, 3/15. Applications are processed on a rolling basis. *Application fee:* $30.
Expenses: Tuition, state resident: part-time $285 per credit hour. Tuition, nonresident: part-time $510 per credit hour.
Financial support: Application deadline: 3/15.
Dr. Margo Duley, Coordinator, 734-487-1177.

■ EMORY UNIVERSITY

Graduate School of Arts and Sciences, Department of Spanish, Atlanta, GA 30322-1100

AWARDS Comparative literature (Certificate); Spanish (PhD); women's studies (Certificate).

Faculty: 8 full-time (4 women).
Students: 22 full-time (13 women); includes 5 minority (all Hispanic Americans), 4 international. 22 applicants, 27% accepted, 6 enrolled. In 2001, 2 degrees awarded.
Degree requirements: For doctorate, 2 foreign languages, thesis/dissertation, comprehensive exam, registration.
Entrance requirements: For doctorate, GRE General Test, TOEFL. *Application deadline:* For fall admission, 1/20 (priority date). *Application fee:* $50. Electronic applications accepted.
Expenses: Tuition: Full-time $24,770. Required fees: $100. Tuition and fees vary according to program and student level.
Financial support: Fellowships, teaching assistantships, institutionally sponsored loans, scholarships/grants, and tuition waivers (full) available. Financial award application deadline: 1/20.
Faculty research: Spanish literature, Spanish-American literature, literary theory, criticism, cultural studies, feminism.
Dr. Hazel Gold, Chair, 404-727-6434.
Application contact: Dr. Karen Stolley, Director of Graduate Studies, 404-727-6434, *E-mail:* kstolle@emory.edu.

■ EMORY UNIVERSITY

Graduate School of Arts and Sciences, Program in Women's Studies, Atlanta, GA 30322-1100

AWARDS PhD.

Faculty: 9 full-time (all women), 60 part-time/adjunct (50 women).
Students: 38 full-time (37 women); includes 9 minority (8 African Americans, 1 Hispanic American), 2 international. Average age 30. 66 applicants, 11% accepted, 6 enrolled. In 2001, 10 doctorates awarded.
Degree requirements: For doctorate, thesis/dissertation, comprehensive exam, registration.
Entrance requirements: For doctorate, GRE General Test, TOEFL, writing sample. *Application deadline:* For fall admission, 1/20 (priority date). *Application fee:* $50.
Expenses: Tuition: Full-time $24,770. Required fees: $100. Tuition and fees vary according to program and student level.
Financial support: In 2001–02, 28 fellowships were awarded; research assistantships, teaching assistantships, scholarships/grants also available. Financial award application deadline: 1/20.
Faculty research: Feminist theory, women's literature, African-American literature, gender in cross-cultural perspective, public policy and globalization.
Dr. Francis Smith-Foster, Director, 404-727-0096, *Fax:* 404-727-4659.
Application contact: Lee Ann Lloyd, Graduate Admissions Secretary, 404-727-6317, *Fax:* 404-727-4659, *E-mail:* lloyd@emory.edu. *Web site:* http://www.emory.edu/womens_studies/

Find an in-depth description at www.petersons.com/gradchannel.

■ FAIRLEIGH DICKINSON UNIVERSITY, COLLEGE AT FLORHAM

Maxwell Becton College of Arts and Sciences, Department of English, Communications and Philosophy, Program in Creative Writing, Madison, NJ 07940-1099

AWARDS MFA.

Application deadline: Applications are processed on a rolling basis. *Application fee:* $40.
Expenses: Tuition: Full-time $11,484; part-time $638 per credit. Required fees: $420. One-time fee: $97 part-time.
Dr. Geoffrey Weinman, Chairperson, Department of English, Communications and Philosophy, 973-443-8712, *Fax:* 973-443-8713, *E-mail:* weinman@fdu.edu.

■ FLORIDA ATLANTIC UNIVERSITY

Dorothy F. Schmidt College of Arts and Letters, Women's Studies Center, Boca Raton, FL 33431-0991

AWARDS MA, Certificate.

Faculty: 4 full-time (all women), 1 (woman) part-time/adjunct.
Students: 5 full-time (all women), 5 part-time (all women); includes 4 minority (1 African American, 2 Asian Americans or Pacific Islanders, 1 Hispanic American). Average age 35. 9 applicants, 56% accepted, 5 enrolled. In 2001, 3 degrees awarded.
Degree requirements: For master's, thesis or alternative, comprehensive exam.
Entrance requirements: For master's, GRE General Test, minimum GPA of 3.0. *Application deadline:* Applications are processed on a rolling basis. *Application fee:* $20.
Expenses: Tuition, state resident: full-time $3,098; part-time $172 per credit. Tuition, nonresident: full-time $10,427; part-time $579 per credit.
Financial support: In 2001–02, 8 students received support, including 4 fellowships with full and partial tuition reimbursements available (averaging $750 per year), 4 teaching assistantships with full and partial tuition reimbursements available (averaging $6,012 per year); career-related internships or fieldwork, Federal Work-Study, institutionally sponsored loans, scholarships/grants, and unspecified assistantships also available. Support available to part-time students.
Faculty research: Women and science/technology, feminist theory, violence against women, women and international development, feminist medical anthropology.
Dr. Mary M. Cameron, Chair, 561-297-3865, *Fax:* 561-297-2127, *E-mail:* mcameron@fau.edu.
Application contact: Dr. Jane Caputi, Associate Professor, 954-297-3865, *Fax:* 561-297-2127, *E-mail:* jcaputi@fau.edu. *Web site:* http://www.fau.edu/divdept/womenstd/women.htm

■ THE GEORGE WASHINGTON UNIVERSITY

Columbian College of Arts and Sciences, Department of Women's Studies, Washington, DC 20052

AWARDS Public policy (MA, PhD); women's studies (MA). Part-time and evening/weekend programs available.

Faculty: 8 full-time (all women), 2 part-time/adjunct (both women).
Students: 12 full-time (all women), 11 part-time (all women); includes 2 minority (1 Asian American or Pacific Islander, 1 Hispanic American), 2 international. Average age 25. 38 applicants, 97% accepted. In 2001, 13 degrees awarded.
Degree requirements: For master's, thesis or alternative, comprehensive exam.
Entrance requirements: For master's, GRE General Test, minimum GPA of 3.0. *Application deadline:* For fall admission, 5/1; for spring admission, 10/1. *Application fee:* $55.
Expenses: Tuition: Part-time $810 per credit. Required fees: $1 per credit.
Financial support: In 2001–02, 2 fellowships with tuition reimbursements (averaging $5,000 per year), 2 teaching assistantships with tuition reimbursements (averaging $4,400 per year) were awarded. Federal Work-Study and institutionally sponsored loans also available. Financial award application deadline: 2/1.
Dr. Diane Bell, Director, 202-994-6942. *Web site:* http://www.gwu.edu/~gradinfo/

■ THE GEORGE WASHINGTON UNIVERSITY

Columbian College of Arts and Sciences, Interdisciplinary Programs in Public Policy, Program in Public Policy-Women's Studies, Washington, DC 20052

AWARDS MA.

Students: 4 full-time (all women), 3 part-time (all women); includes 1 minority (Hispanic American). Average age 24. 14 applicants, 93% accepted. In 2001, 3 degrees awarded.
Degree requirements: For master's, comprehensive exam.
Entrance requirements: For master's, GRE General Test, minimum GPA of 3.0. *Application fee:* $55.
Expenses: Tuition: Part-time $810 per credit. Required fees: $1 per credit.
Financial support: In 2001–02, 4 students received support, including 2 fellowships, 2 teaching assistantships Financial award application deadline: 2/1.
Dr. Joseph J. Cordes, Director, Interdisciplinary Programs in Public Policy, 202-994-8500. *Web site:* http://www.gwu.edu/~gradinfo/

■ GEORGIA STATE UNIVERSITY

College of Arts and Sciences, Women's Studies Institute, Atlanta, GA 30303-3083

AWARDS MA. Part-time and evening/weekend programs available.

Degree requirements: For master's, one foreign language, thesis, exam.
Entrance requirements: For master's, GRE General Test, TOEFL. Electronic applications accepted.
Faculty research: Violence against women, women's health, global women's movements, African-American women's history, feminist ethics, women and performance. *Web site:* http://www.gsu.edu/~wwwwsi/

Find an in-depth description at www.petersons.com/gradchannel.

■ GRADUATE SCHOOL AND UNIVERSITY CENTER OF THE CITY UNIVERSITY OF NEW YORK

Graduate Studies, Interdisciplinary Studies, New York, NY 10016-4039

AWARDS Language in social context (PhD); medieval studies (PhD); public policy (MA, PhD); urban studies (MA, PhD); women's studies (MA, PhD). Terminal master's awarded for partial completion of doctoral program.

Degree requirements: For master's, thesis/dissertation; for doctorate, thesis/dissertation, comprehensive exam.
Entrance requirements: For master's and doctorate, GRE General Test. *Application deadline:* For fall admission, 2/1. *Application fee:* $40.
Expenses: Tuition, state resident: part-time $245 per credit. Tuition, nonresident: part-time $425 per credit. Required fees: $72 per semester.
Financial support: Application deadline: 2/1.

■ MINNESOTA STATE UNIVERSITY, MANKATO

College of Graduate Studies, College of Social and Behavioral Sciences, Department of Women's Studies, Mankato, MN 56001

AWARDS MS. Part-time programs available.

Faculty: 3 full-time (all women).
Students: 8 full-time (all women), 5 part-time (all women). Average age 28. In 2001, 7 degrees awarded.
Degree requirements: For master's, thesis or alternative, comprehensive exam.
Entrance requirements: For master's, minimum GPA of 3.0 during previous 2

years. *Application deadline:* For fall admission, 7/9 (priority date); for spring admission, 11/27. Applications are processed on a rolling basis. *Application fee:* $20.
Expenses: Tuition, state resident: full-time $3,253; part-time $157 per credit. Tuition, nonresident: full-time $4,893; part-time $248 per credit. Required fees: $24 per credit. Tuition and fees vary according to reciprocity agreements.
Financial support: Research assistantships, teaching assistantships with full tuition reimbursements, career-related internships or fieldwork, Federal Work-Study, and institutionally sponsored loans available. Support available to part-time students. Financial award application deadline: 3/15; financial award applicants required to submit FAFSA.
Dr. Carol Perkins, Chairperson, 507-389-2077.
Application contact: Joni Roberts, Admissions Coordinator, 507-389-5244, *Fax:* 507-389-5974, *E-mail:* grad@mankato.msus.edu.

■ NEW COLLEGE OF CALIFORNIA

School of Humanities, Division of Humanities, San Francisco, CA 94102-5206

AWARDS Culture, ecology, and sustainable community (MA); humanities and leadership (MA); media studies (MA); poetics (MA, MFA), including poetics (MA), poetics and writing (MFA); psychology (MA); women's spirituality (MA); writing and consciousness (MA). Part-time and evening/weekend programs available.

Degree requirements: For master's, thesis.

■ NEW COLLEGE OF CALIFORNIA

School of Psychology, San Francisco, CA 94102-5206

AWARDS Feminist clinical psychology (MA); social-clinical psychology (MA). Evening/weekend programs available.

Faculty: 6 full-time (3 women), 10 part-time/adjunct (7 women).
Students: 43 full-time (32 women). Average age 28. 60 applicants, 77% accepted, 40 enrolled.
Degree requirements: For master's, 3 trimesters of fieldwork.
Entrance requirements: For master's, letters of recommendation. *Application deadline:* For fall admission, 4/1 (priority date). Applications are processed on a rolling basis. *Application fee:* $50 ($75 for international students).
Expenses: Contact institution.
Financial support: In 2001–02, 4 students received support, including 2 teaching assistantships (averaging $900 per year); career-related internships or fieldwork and Federal Work-Study also available. Financial award application deadline: 7/15; financial award applicants required to submit FAFSA.
Faculty research: AIDS and therapy, dynamics of unemployment, self-psychology, sexuality and gender issues, multicultural therapy.
Dr. Ali Chavoshian, Dean, 415-437-3435.
Application contact: Carmen Gonzalez, Admissions Director, 415-437-3421. *Web site:* http://www.newcollege.edu/psychology/

■ THE OHIO STATE UNIVERSITY

Graduate School, College of Humanities, Department of Women's Studies, Columbus, OH 43210

AWARDS MA.

Degree requirements: For master's, thesis optional.

■ ROOSEVELT UNIVERSITY

Graduate Division, College of Arts and Sciences, School of Liberal Studies, Program in Women's Studies, Chicago, IL 60605-1394

AWARDS MA. Part-time and evening/weekend programs available.

Degree requirements: For master's, thesis.
Entrance requirements: For master's, minimum GPA of 2.7. *Application deadline:* For fall admission, 6/1 (priority date). Applications are processed on a rolling basis. *Application fee:* $25 ($35 for international students).
Expenses: Tuition: Full-time $9,090; part-time $505 per credit hour. Required fees: $100 per term.
Financial support: Application deadline: 2/15.
Faculty research: Feminist economics; philosophy of feminism; race, class, and gender; women and art; women's history.
Ann Brigham, Head, 312-341-3725, *Fax:* 312-341-3680.
Application contact: Joanne Canyon-Heller, Coordinator of Graduate Admissions, 312-281-3250, *Fax:* 312-341-3523, *E-mail:* applyru@roosevelt.edu.

■ RUTGERS, THE STATE UNIVERSITY OF NEW JERSEY, NEW BRUNSWICK

Graduate School, Program in Political Science, New Brunswick, NJ 08901-1281

AWARDS American political institutions (PhD); comparative politics (PhD); international relations (PhD); political economy (PhD); political theory (PhD); public law (PhD); women and politics (PhD).

Degree requirements: For doctorate, one foreign language, thesis/dissertation.
Entrance requirements: For doctorate, GRE General Test. *Web site:* http://policsci.rutgers.edu/

■ RUTGERS, THE STATE UNIVERSITY OF NEW JERSEY, NEW BRUNSWICK

Graduate School, Program in Women's Studies, New Brunswick, NJ 08901-1281

AWARDS Women's and gender studies (MA); women's studies (MA). Part-time programs available.

Degree requirements: For master's, thesis or alternative.
Entrance requirements: For master's, GRE General Test.
Faculty research: Feminist theory, gender and sexuality, global and cultural studies, women in history, literature, and politics. *Web site:* http://womens-studies.rutgers.edu/

■ SAN DIEGO STATE UNIVERSITY

Graduate and Research Affairs, College of Arts and Letters, Department of Women's Studies, San Diego, CA 92182

AWARDS MA.

Entrance requirements: For master's, GRE General Test, TOEFL.

■ SAN FRANCISCO STATE UNIVERSITY

Graduate Division, College of Humanities, Department of Women's Studies, San Francisco, CA 94132-1722

AWARDS MA. Part-time and evening/weekend programs available.

Degree requirements: For master's, thesis or alternative.
Entrance requirements: For master's, BA in women's studies or 9-12 upper-level units in women's studies; minimum GPA of 3.0 in last 60 units.
Faculty research: Multiculturalism and feminist perspectives, anthropological research of women's struggle for economic independence in the Third World.

■ SARAH LAWRENCE COLLEGE

Graduate Studies, Program in Women's History, Bronxville, NY 10708

AWARDS MA.

Degree requirements: For master's, thesis.
Entrance requirements: For master's, previous course work in history, minimum B average in undergraduate coursework.

Find an in-depth description at www.petersons.com/gradchannel.

■ SOUTHEASTERN BAPTIST THEOLOGICAL SEMINARY

Graduate and Professional Programs, Wake Forest, NC 27588-1889

AWARDS Advanced biblical studies (M Div); Christian education (M Div, MACE); Christian ethics (PhD); Christian ministry (M Div); Christian planting (M Div); church music (MACM); counseling (MACO); evangelism (PhD); language (M Div); ministry (D Min); New Testament (PhD); Old Testament (PhD); philosophy (PhD); theology (Th M, PhD); women's studies (M Div).

Degree requirements: For M Div, supervised ministry; for master's, thesis (for some programs), oral exam; for doctorate, thesis/dissertation, fieldwork.
Entrance requirements: For master's, Cooperative English Test, minimum GPA of 2.0, M Div or equivalent (Th M); for doctorate, GRE General Test or MAT, Cooperative English Test, M Div or equivalent, 3 years of professional experience.

■ SOUTHERN CONNECTICUT STATE UNIVERSITY

School of Graduate Studies, School of Arts and Sciences, Program in Women's Studies, New Haven, CT 06515-1355

AWARDS MA. Part-time and evening/weekend programs available.

Students: 3 full-time (all women), 5 part-time (all women). 11 applicants, 36% accepted.
Degree requirements: For master's, thesis or alternative.
Entrance requirements: For master's, interview. *Application deadline:* Applications are processed on a rolling basis. *Application fee:* $40.
Financial support: Application deadline: 4/15.
Dr. Virginia Metaxas, Co-Coordinator, 203-392-6717, *Fax:* 203-392-6723, *E-mail:* metaxas@southernct.edu.
Application contact: June Dunn, Graduate Contact, 203-392-6133, *Fax:* 203-392-6723, *E-mail:* womenstudies@southernct.edu. *Web site:* http://www.southernct.edu/

■ STATE UNIVERSITY OF NEW YORK AT ALBANY

College of Arts and Sciences, Department of Women's Studies, Albany, NY 12222-0001

AWARDS MA.

Students: 13 full-time (12 women), 5 part-time (all women); includes 2 minority (1 African American, 1 Asian American or Pacific Islander), 1 international. Average age 33. 13 applicants, 77% accepted. In 2001, 5 degrees awarded.
Application fee: $50.
Expenses: Tuition, state resident: full-time $2,550; part-time $213 per credit. Tuition, nonresident: full-time $4,208; part-time $351 per credit. Required fees: $470; $470 per year.
Judith Barlow, Chair, 518-442-4220.

■ STONY BROOK UNIVERSITY, STATE UNIVERSITY OF NEW YORK

School of Professional Development and Continuing Studies, Stony Brook, NY 11794

AWARDS Art and philosophy (Certificate); biology 7-12 (MAT); chemistry-grade 7-12 (MAT); coaching (Certificate); computer integrated engineering (Certificate); cultural studies (Certificate); earth science-grade 7-12 (MAT); educational computing (Certificate); English-grade 7-12 (MAT); environmental/occupational health and safety (Certificate); French-grade 7-12 (MAT); German-grade 7-12 (MAT); human resource management (Certificate); industrial management (Certificate); information systems management (Certificate); Italian-grade 7-12 (MAT); liberal studies (MA); liberal studies online (MA); Long Island regional studies (Certificate); oceanic science (Certificate); operation research (Certificate); physics-grade 7-12 (MAT); Russian-grade 7-12 (MAT); school administration and supervision (Certificate); school district administration (Certificate); social science and the professions (MPS), including labor management, public affairs, waste management; social studies 7-12 (MAT); waste management (Certificate); women's studies (Certificate). Part-time and evening/weekend programs available. Postbaccalaureate distance learning degree programs offered.

Faculty: 1 full-time, 101 part-time/adjunct.
Students: 240 full-time (133 women), 1,307 part-time (868 women); includes 101 minority (43 African Americans, 13 Asian Americans or Pacific Islanders, 43 Hispanic Americans, 2 Native Americans), 9 international. Average age 28. In 2001, 478 master's, 157 other advanced degrees awarded.
Degree requirements: For master's, one foreign language, thesis or alternative.
Application deadline: Applications are processed on a rolling basis. *Application fee:* $50.
Expenses: Tuition, state resident: full-time $5,100; part-time $213 per credit. Tuition, nonresident: full-time $8,416; part-time $351 per credit. Required fees: $496.
Financial support: In 2001–02, 1 fellowship, 7 teaching assistantships were awarded. Research assistantships, career-related internships or fieldwork also available. Support available to part-time students.
Dr. Paul J. Edelson, Dean, 631-632-7052, *Fax:* 631-632-9046, *E-mail:* paul.edelson@sunysb.edu.
Application contact: Sandra Romansky, Director of Admissions and Advisement, 631-632-7050, *Fax:* 631-632-9046, *E-mail:* sandra.romansky@sunysb.edu. *Web site:* http://www.sunysb.edu/spd/

■ SYRACUSE UNIVERSITY

Graduate School, College of Arts and Sciences, Program in Women's Studies, Syracuse, NY 13244-0003

AWARDS CAS.

Expenses: Tuition: Full-time $15,528; part-time $647 per credit. Required fees: $420; $38 per term. Tuition and fees vary according to program.

■ TEXAS WOMAN'S UNIVERSITY

Graduate Studies and Research, College of Arts and Sciences, Department of Sociology and Social Work, Program in Women's Studies, Denton, TX 76201

AWARDS MA.

Faculty: 2 full-time (both women).
Students: 6 full-time (all women), 9 part-time (all women); includes 3 minority (2 African Americans, 1 Hispanic American). Average age 33. In 2001, 2 degrees awarded.
Degree requirements: For master's, thesis.
Entrance requirements: For master's, 2 letters of reference. *Application deadline:* For fall admission, 8/1 (priority date); for spring admission, 11/1 (priority date). Applications are processed on a rolling basis. *Application fee:* $30. Electronic applications accepted.
Expenses: Tuition, state resident: part-time $90 per semester hour. Tuition, nonresident: part-time $303 per semester hour. Required fees: $24 per credit hour. $79 per semester.
Financial support: In 2001–02, 3 teaching assistantships (averaging $7,245 per year) were awarded; career-related internships or fieldwork, Federal Work-Study, and scholarships/grants also available. Financial award application deadline: 4/1.
Faculty research: Feminist theory, women of color, feminist pedagogy, women and religion, feminist ethics.
Dr. Claire L. Sahlin, Director, 940-898-2119, *Fax:* 940-898-2101, *E-mail:* csahlin@twu.edu. *Web site:* http://www.twu.edu/as/ws/

■ TOWSON UNIVERSITY

Graduate School, Program in Women's Studies, Towson, MD 21252-0001

AWARDS MS.

Students: 10.

Degree requirements: For master's, thesis optional.
Application deadline: Applications are processed on a rolling basis. *Application fee:* $40. Electronic applications accepted.
Expenses: Tuition, state resident: part-time $211 per credit. Tuition, nonresident: part-time $435 per credit. Required fees: $52 per credit.
Financial support: Application deadline: 4/1.
Dr. Esther Wangari, Director, 410-704-2580, *Fax:* 410-704-3469, *E-mail:* ewangari@towson.edu.
Application contact: 410-704-2501, *Fax:* 410-704-4675, *E-mail:* grads@towson.edu.

■ UNITED THEOLOGICAL SEMINARY OF THE TWIN CITIES

Graduate and Professional Programs, Program in Religion, Theology and Women's Studies, New Brighton, MN 55112-2598

AWARDS Religion and theology (MA); theology and the arts (MA); women's studies (MA), including ministry, religion, theology.

Expenses: Tuition: Full-time $8,340.
Application contact: Sandy Casney, Direction of Admissions, 651-633-4311.

■ THE UNIVERSITY OF ALABAMA

Graduate School, College of Arts and Sciences, Department of Women's Studies, Tuscaloosa, AL 35487

AWARDS MA. Part-time programs available.

Faculty: 3 full-time (all women).
Students: 9 full-time (all women); includes 1 minority (Asian American or Pacific Islander), 2 international. Average age 30. 11 applicants, 73% accepted, 5 enrolled. In 2001, 3 degrees awarded.
Degree requirements: For master's, thesis, comprehensive exam.
Entrance requirements: For master's, GRE General Test, TOEFL. *Application deadline:* For fall admission, 7/6 (priority date). Applications are processed on a rolling basis. *Application fee:* $25.
Expenses: Tuition, state resident: full-time $3,292; part-time $183 per credit hour. Tuition, nonresident: full-time $8,912; part-time $495 per credit hour. Tuition and fees vary according to course load, campus/location and program.
Financial support: In 2001–02, 7 students received support, including research assistantships with full tuition reimbursements available (averaging $8,120 per year), teaching assistantships with full tuition reimbursements available (averaging $8,120 per year); career-related internships or fieldwork and Federal Work-Study also available. Financial award application deadline: 2/15.
Faculty research: Feminist theory, Southern women, issues of oppression, comparative religions, women and work.
Dr. Carol J. Pierman, Chairperson, 205-348-5782, *E-mail:* cpierman@tenhoor.as.ua.edu. *Web site:* http://www.as.ua.edu/ws/

■ THE UNIVERSITY OF ARIZONA

Graduate College, College of Social and Behavioral Sciences, Department of Women's Studies, Tucson, AZ 85721

AWARDS MA. Part-time programs available.

Faculty: 14 full-time (all women).
Students: 14 full-time (all women), 4 part-time (all women); includes 3 minority (1 Asian American or Pacific Islander, 1 Hispanic American, 1 Native American). Average age 31. 14 applicants, 71% accepted, 7 enrolled. In 2001, 6 degrees awarded.
Degree requirements: For master's, thesis/project. *Median time to degree:* Master's–2 years full-time.
Entrance requirements: For master's, GRE, TOEFL. *Application deadline:* For fall admission, 1/15. *Application fee:* $45. Electronic applications accepted.
Expenses: Tuition, state resident: full-time $2,490; part-time $436 per unit. Tuition, nonresident: full-time $10,300; part-time $436 per unit. Full-time tuition and fees vary according to degree level and program.
Financial support: In 2001–02, 12 students received support, including 3 fellowships with full tuition reimbursements available (averaging $5,000 per year), 7 research assistantships with full tuition reimbursements available (averaging $6,145 per year), 6 teaching assistantships with full tuition reimbursements available (averaging $6,145 per year); career-related internships or fieldwork, scholarships/grants, health care benefits, tuition waivers (full and partial), and unspecified assistantships also available. Financial award application deadline: 1/15.
Faculty research: Gender race and border studies, sexuality and the body, gender health and science, cultural representation and theory, public policy and social movements. *Total annual research expenditures:* $1.7 million.
Dr. Elizabeth Lapovsky Kennedy, Head, 520-621-7338, *Fax:* 520-621-1533.
Application contact: Dr. Julia Balen, Graduate Adviser, 520-621-7338, *Fax:* 520-6211533, *E-mail:* jbalen@u.arizona.edu. *Web site:* http://w3.arizona.edu/~ws/

■ UNIVERSITY OF CALIFORNIA, LOS ANGELES

Graduate Division, College of Letters and Science, Program in Women's Studies, Los Angeles, CA 90095

AWARDS MS, PhD.

Students: 8 full-time (all women); includes 1 minority (Hispanic American). 37 applicants, 24% accepted, 4 enrolled.
Application deadline: For fall admission, 12/15. *Application fee:* $60. Electronic applications accepted.
Expenses: Tuition, nonresident: full-time $10,244. Required fees: $3,609. Full-time tuition and fees vary according to program.
Financial support: In 2001–02, 1 research assistantship, 5 teaching assistantships were awarded.
Dr. Christine Littleton, Chair, 310-206-8101.

■ UNIVERSITY OF CINCINNATI

Division of Research and Advanced Studies, McMicken College of Arts and Sciences, Center for Women's Studies, Cincinnati, OH 45221

AWARDS MA, Certificate, JD/MA. Part-time programs available.

Faculty: 3 full-time (all women).
Students: 22 full-time (all women), 1 (woman) part-time; includes 6 minority (4 African Americans, 1 Asian American or Pacific Islander, 1 Hispanic American), 1 international. Average age 23. 32 applicants, 31% accepted. In 2001, 7 degrees awarded.
Degree requirements: For master's, paper/project. *Median time to degree:* Master's–2 years full-time.
Entrance requirements: For master's, GRE General Test, TOEFL. *Application deadline:* For fall admission, 2/1. *Application fee:* $30. Electronic applications accepted.
Expenses: Tuition, state resident: part-time $2,698 per quarter. Tuition, nonresident: part-time $4,977 per quarter.
Financial support: In 2001–02, 16 students received support, including 2 fellowships with full tuition reimbursements available (averaging $11,500 per year), 3 research assistantships with full tuition reimbursements available (averaging $9,649 per year), 6 teaching assistantships with full tuition reimbursements available (averaging $9,649 per year); career-related internships or fieldwork, Federal Work-Study, institutionally sponsored loans, scholarships/grants, tuition waivers (partial), and unspecified assistantships also available. Financial award application deadline: 2/1.
Faculty research: American women writers, gender and international relations, gender and immigration.
Dr. Anne S. Runyan, Director, 513-556-6652, *Fax:* 513-556-6771.
Application contact: Dr. Lisa M. Hogeland, Acting Director of Graduate Studies, 513-556-6776, *Fax:* 513-556-6771, *E-mail:* lisa.hogeland@uc.edu. *Web site:* http://www.artscienc.edu/womens_studies/

■ THE UNIVERSITY OF IOWA

Graduate College, College of Liberal Arts and Sciences, Department of Women's Studies, Iowa City, IA 52242-1316

AWARDS PhD.

Faculty: 3 full-time.
Students: 11 full-time (all women), 4 part-time (all women); includes 1 minority (Native American), 6 international. 30 applicants, 20% accepted, 3 enrolled.
Degree requirements: For doctorate, thesis/dissertation, comprehensive exam.
Entrance requirements: For doctorate, GRE General Test, TOEFL, minimum GPA of 3.0. *Application deadline:* For fall admission, 2/1. *Application fee:* $30 ($50 for international students). Electronic applications accepted.
Expenses: Tuition, state resident: full-time $3,702; part-time $206 per semester hour. Tuition, nonresident: full-time $11,924; part-time $206 per semester hour. Required fees: $101 per semester. Tuition and fees vary according to course load and program.
Financial support: In 2001–02, 1 fellowship, 4 research assistantships, 9 teaching assistantships were awarded. Financial award applicants required to submit FAFSA.
Ellen Lewin, Chair, 319-335-0322, *Fax:* 319-335-0314.

■ UNIVERSITY OF MARYLAND, COLLEGE PARK

Graduate Studies and Research, College of Arts and Humanities, Program in Women's Studies, College Park, MD 20742

AWARDS MA, PhD.

Faculty: 8 full-time (all women), 1 (woman) part-time/adjunct.
Students: 10 full-time (all women), 1 (woman) part-time; includes 2 minority (1 African American, 1 Asian American or Pacific Islander), 3 international. 58 applicants, 16% accepted, 6 enrolled.
Degree requirements: For master's, thesis or alternative; for doctorate, one foreign language, thesis/dissertation or alternative.
Entrance requirements: For master's, GRE General Test. *Application deadline:* For fall admission, 2/1. *Application fee:* $50 ($70 for international students).
Expenses: Tuition, state resident: part-time $289 per credit hour. Tuition, nonresident: part-time $448 per credit hour. One-time fee: $436 part-time. Full-time tuition and fees vary according to course load, campus/location and program.
Financial support: In 2001–02, 4 fellowships (averaging $11,785 per year), 12 teaching assistantships with tuition reimbursements (averaging $10,471 per year) were awarded. Research assistantships, career-related internships or fieldwork, Federal Work-Study, and scholarships/grants also available. Support available to part-time students.
Faculty research: Gender roles, national and global diversity, sexuality. *Total annual research expenditures:* $119,575.
Dr. Claire Moses, Chair, 301-405-6877, *E-mail:* cm45@umail.umd.edu.
Application contact: Trudy Lindsey, Director, Graduate Admissions and Records, 301-405-6991, *Fax:* 301-314-9305, *E-mail:* grschool@deans.umd.edu.

■ UNIVERSITY OF MASSACHUSETTS BOSTON

Office of Graduate Studies and Research, Division of Continuing Education, Program in Women in Politics and Government, Boston, MA 02125-3393

AWARDS Certificate. Part-time and evening/weekend programs available.

Degree requirements: For Certificate, practicum, final project.
Entrance requirements: For degree, interview, minimum GPA of 2.75.

■ UNIVERSITY OF MICHIGAN

Horace H. Rackham School of Graduate Studies, College of Literature, Science, and the Arts, Women's Studies Program, Ann Arbor, MI 48109

AWARDS English and women's studies (PhD); history and women's studies (PhD); psychology and women's studies (PhD); women's studies (Certificate).

Faculty: 60 part-time/adjunct (all women).
Students: 31 full-time (all women); includes 6 minority (1 African American, 2 Asian Americans or Pacific Islanders, 2 Hispanic Americans, 1 Native American), 2 international. Average age 24. 91 applicants, 8% accepted. In 2001, 1 doctorate, 8 other advanced degrees awarded.
Degree requirements: For doctorate, variable foreign language requirement, thesis/dissertation.
Entrance requirements: For doctorate, GRE General Test, previous undergraduate course work in women's studies. *Application deadline:* For fall admission, 12/15. *Application fee:* $55.
Financial support: In 2001–02, 3 fellowships with full tuition reimbursements (averaging $14,500 per year), 25 teaching assistantships with full and partial tuition reimbursements (averaging $12,984 per year) were awarded.
Faculty research: Women and psychology, work and gender, gender issues, English literature, women and science.
Pamela Trotman Reid, Director, 734-763-2047, *Fax:* 734-647-4943, *E-mail:* pamreid@umich.edu.
Application contact: Bonnie Miller, Graduate Secretary, 734-763-2047, *Fax:* 734-647-4943, *E-mail:* bonniemj@umich.edu. *Web site:* http://www.lsa.umich.edu/women/

■ UNIVERSITY OF MISSOURI–ST. LOUIS

Graduate School, College of Arts and Sciences, Institute of Women's and Gender Studies, St. Louis, MO 63121-4499

AWARDS Certificate.

Faculty: 38.
Students: 1 (woman) full-time, 1 (woman) part-time.
Application deadline: For fall admission, 7/1 (priority date); for spring admission, 12/1 (priority date). Applications are processed on a rolling basis. *Application fee:* $25 ($40 for international students). Electronic applications accepted.
Expenses: Tuition, state resident: part-time $231 per credit hour. Tuition, nonresident: part-time $621 per credit hour.
Financial support: In 2001–02, 1 research assistantship with full tuition reimbursement (averaging $10,000 per year) was awarded
Jeanne Sevelius, Interim Director, 314-516-5581, *Fax:* 314-516-5268, *E-mail:* iwgs@umsl.edu.
Application contact: Graduate Admissions, 314-516-5458, *Fax:* 314-516-5310, *E-mail:* gradadm@umsl.edu. *Web site:* http://www.umsl.edu/divisions/artscience/iwgs/iwgs.html

■ THE UNIVERSITY OF NORTH CAROLINA AT GREENSBORO

Graduate School, College of Arts and Sciences, Department of English, Program in English, Greensboro, NC 27412-5001

AWARDS English (M Ed, MA, PhD); technical writing (Certificate); women's studies (Certificate).

Faculty: 28 full-time (13 women), 2 part-time/adjunct (0 women).
Students: 36 full-time (25 women), 71 part-time (49 women); includes 13 minority (10 African Americans, 1 Hispanic American, 2 Native Americans), 2 international. 87 applicants, 45% accepted, 29 enrolled. In 2001, 15 master's, 12 doctorates awarded.
Degree requirements: For master's, thesis or alternative, comprehensive exam; for doctorate, variable foreign language requirement, thesis/dissertation, preliminary exam.
Entrance requirements: For master's, GRE General Test, GRE Subject Test, TOEFL, minimum GPA of 3.0; for doctorate, GRE General Test, GRE Subject Test, TOEFL, critical writing sample, minimum GPA of 3.0. *Application deadline:* For fall admission, 1/20 (priority

date); for spring admission, 11/1. *Application fee:* $35.
Expenses: Tuition, state resident: part-time $344 per course. Tuition, nonresident: part-time $2,457 per course.
Financial support: Fellowships, research assistantships, teaching assistantships available.
Dr. Robert Langenfeld, Director of Graduate Studies, 336-334-5446, *E-mail:* lagenfeld@uncg.edu.
Application contact: Dr. James Lynch, Director of Graduate Recruitment and Information Services, 336-334-4881, *Fax:* 336-334-4424. *Web site:* http://www.uncg.edu/eng/

■ UNIVERSITY OF NORTHERN IOWA

Graduate College, Program in Women's Studies, Cedar Falls, IA 50614

AWARDS MA.

Students: 4 full-time (all women), 1 (woman) part-time, 1 international. 10 applicants, 100% accepted. In 2001, 4 degrees awarded.
Application fee: $20 ($50 for international students).
Expenses: Tuition, state resident: full-time $3,704; part-time $206 per credit hour. Tuition, nonresident: full-time $9,122; part-time $501 per credit hour. Required fees: $324; $108 per semester. Part-time tuition and fees vary according to course load.
Financial support: Application deadline: 3/1.
Dr. Phyllis L. Baker, Director, 319-273-2109, *Fax:* 319-273-3053, *E-mail:* phyllis.baker@uni.edu. *Web site:* http://fp.uni.edu/womenstudies/

■ UNIVERSITY OF PITTSBURGH

Faculty of Arts and Sciences, Program in Women's Studies, Pittsburgh, PA 15260

AWARDS Certificate.

Faculty: 36 full-time (33 women).
Students: 52 full-time; includes 14 minority (2 African Americans, 6 Asian Americans or Pacific Islanders, 6 Hispanic Americans). 50 applicants.
Application fee: $40.
Expenses: Tuition, state resident: full-time $9,410; part-time $385 per credit. Tuition, nonresident: full-time $19,376; part-time $797 per credit. Required fees: $480; $90 per term. Tuition and fees vary according to program.
Financial support: In 2001–02, 2 teaching assistantships with full tuition reimbursements (averaging $11,520 per year) were awarded
Faculty research: Feminist theory; feminist ethics; gender, economic restructuring and resistance; gender and poverty; women and development.
Carol Stabile, Director, 412-624-6485, *Fax:* 412-624-6492, *E-mail:* wstudies@pitt.edu. *Web site:* http://www.pitt.edu/wstudies

■ UNIVERSITY OF SOUTH CAROLINA

The Graduate School, College of Liberal Arts, Program of Women's Studies, Columbia, SC 29208

AWARDS Certificate. Part-time programs available.

Faculty: 2 full-time (both women), 79 part-time/adjunct (69 women).
Students: 3 full-time (all women), 27 part-time (26 women); includes 3 minority (1 African American, 1 Asian American or Pacific Islander, 1 Native American). Average age 30. 8 applicants, 100% accepted. In 2001, 7 degrees awarded.
Entrance requirements: For degree, GRE General Test or MAT. *Application deadline:* For fall admission, 8/1 (priority date); for spring admission, 12/1 (priority date). Applications are processed on a rolling basis. *Application fee:* $40. Electronic applications accepted.
Expenses: Tuition, state resident: full-time $4,434. Tuition, nonresident: full-time $9,854. Tuition and fees vary according to program.
Financial support: In 2001–02, 5 students received support, including 4 research assistantships with full tuition reimbursements available (averaging $9,000 per year). Financial award application deadline: 4/1.
Faculty research: Health; pedagogy; intersection of race, class, gender; public policy; politics of culture and representations.
Dr. Lynn Weber, Director, 803-777-4007, *Fax:* 803-777-9114, *E-mail:* weberl@sc.edu.
Application contact: Dr. Wanda A. Hendricks, Graduate Director, 803-777-4007, *Fax:* 803-777-9114, *E-mail:* hendricw@gwm.sc.edu. *Web site:* http://www.cla.sc.edu/WOST/index.html

■ UNIVERSITY OF SOUTH FLORIDA

College of Graduate Studies, College of Arts and Sciences, Department of Women's Studies, Tampa, FL 33620-9951

AWARDS MA. Part-time programs available.

Faculty: 9 full-time (all women).
Students: 7 full-time (all women), 3 part-time (all women); includes 3 minority (2 Asian Americans or Pacific Islanders, 1 Hispanic American). 12 applicants, 75% accepted, 5 enrolled. In 2001, 1 degree awarded.
Degree requirements: For master's, thesis or internship.
Entrance requirements: For master's, GRE General Test, writing sample. *Application deadline:* For fall admission, 6/1; for spring admission, 10/15. Applications are processed on a rolling basis. *Application fee:* $20.
Expenses: Tuition, state resident: part-time $166 per credit hour. Tuition, nonresident: part-time $573 per credit hour. Required fees: $17 per term.
Financial support: In 2001–02, 2 teaching assistantships with partial tuition reimbursements were awarded; research assistantships with partial tuition reimbursements *Total annual research expenditures:* $6,649.
Ofelia Schutte, Chairperson, 813-974-0982, *Fax:* 813-974-0336.
Application contact: Carolyn DiPalma, Graduate Director, 813-974-0979, *Fax:* 813-974-0336, *E-mail:* cdipalma@luna.cas.usf.edu. *Web site:* http://www.cas.usf.edu/womens_studies/index/html

■ UNIVERSITY OF WASHINGTON

Graduate School, College of Arts and Sciences, Department of Women Studies, Seattle, WA 98195

AWARDS MA, PhD. Terminal master's awarded for partial completion of doctoral program.

Degree requirements: For master's, thesis; for doctorate, one foreign language, thesis/dissertation, exam.
Entrance requirements: For master's, GRE General Test, TOEFL; for doctorate, GRE General Test, TOEFL, TSE. Electronic applications accepted.
Expenses: Tuition, state resident: full-time $5,539. Tuition, nonresident: full-time $14,376. Required fees: $390. Tuition and fees vary according to course load and program.
Faculty research: Women's history in U.S. and China; Native American ethnography and identity; women, science, and technology; political economy of development, feminism and nationalism.
Web site: http://www.depts.washington.edu/webwomen/

Conflict Resolution and Mediation

CONFLICT RESOLUTION AND MEDIATION/PEACE STUDIES

■ AMERICAN UNIVERSITY

School of International Service, Washington, DC 20016-8001

AWARDS Comparative and regional studies (MA); development management (MS); environmental policy (MA); international communication (MA); international development (MA); international development management (Certificate); international economic policy (MA); international economic relations (Certificate); international peace and conflict resolution (MA); international politics (MA); international relations (PhD); U.S. foreign policy (MA). Part-time and evening/weekend programs available.

Faculty: 59 full-time (21 women), 35 part-time/adjunct (11 women).
Students: 347 full-time (214 women), 300 part-time (176 women); includes 87 minority (30 African Americans, 20 Asian Americans or Pacific Islanders, 35 Hispanic Americans, 2 Native Americans), 152 international. Average age 27. 1,254 applicants, 74% accepted, 215 enrolled. In 2001, 193 master's, 1 doctorate awarded. Terminal master's awarded for partial completion of doctoral program.
Degree requirements: For master's, one foreign language, thesis or alternative, comprehensive exam; for doctorate, one foreign language, thesis/dissertation, comprehensive exam.
Entrance requirements: For master's, GRE General Test, TOEFL, 24 credits in related social sciences, minimum of 3.3; 2 letter of recommendations; for doctorate, GRE General Test, TOEFL, 2 letters of recommendations; 24 credits in related social sciences. *Application deadline:* For fall admission, 1/15 (priority date); for spring admission, 10/1 (priority date). Applications are processed on a rolling basis. *Application fee:* $50.
Expenses: Tuition: Full-time $14,274; part-time $793 per credit. Required fees: $290. Tuition and fees vary according to program.
Financial support: In 2001–02, 13 fellowships with tuition reimbursements, 62 research assistantships with tuition reimbursements were awarded. Teaching assistantships, career-related internships or fieldwork, Federal Work-Study, and institutionally sponsored loans also available. Financial award application deadline: 1/15.
Faculty research: International intellectual property, international environmental issues, international law and legal order, international telecommunications/technology, international sustainable development.
Dr. Louis W. Goodman, Dean, 202-885-1600, *Fax:* 202-885-2494.
Application contact: Christopher Derickson, Director of Graduate Admissions and Financial Aid, 202-885-1599, *Fax:* 202-885-2494.

■ ANTIOCH UNIVERSITY MCGREGOR

Graduate Programs, Program of Conflict Resolution, Yellow Springs, OH 45387-1609

AWARDS MA. Part-time and evening/weekend programs available. Postbaccalaureate distance learning degree programs offered (minimal on-campus study).

Faculty: 2 full-time (both women), 14 part-time/adjunct (8 women).
Students: 32 applicants, 97% accepted, 30 enrolled. In 2001, 29 degrees awarded.
Degree requirements: For master's, thesis or alternative.
Application deadline: For fall admission, 8/15. Applications are processed on a rolling basis. *Application fee:* $50. Electronic applications accepted.
Expenses: Contact institution.
Financial support: Federal Work-Study available. Financial award application deadline: 7/1; financial award applicants required to submit FAFSA.
Dr. Katherine Hale, Director, 937-769-1868, *Fax:* 937-769-1807.
Application contact: Karen E. Crist, Enrollment Services Officer, 937-769-1818, *Fax:* 937-769-1804, *E-mail:* kcrist@mcgregor.edu. *Web site:* http://www.mcgregor.edu

■ ARCADIA UNIVERSITY

Graduate Studies, Program in International Peace and Conflict Management, Glenside, PA 19038-3295

AWARDS MAIPCR. Part-time and evening/weekend programs available.

Students: 17 full-time (13 women), 3 part-time (2 women); includes 2 minority (1 African American, 1 Asian American or Pacific Islander), 5 international.
Degree requirements: For master's, one foreign language.
Entrance requirements: For master's, GRE, TOEFL. *Application deadline:* For fall admission, 4/1 (priority date). *Application fee:* $50.
Expenses: Contact institution.
Dr. Warren Haffar, Director, 215-572-4094, *Fax:* 215-572-4049, *E-mail:* harrar@arcadia.edu.
Application contact: 215-572-2910, *Fax:* 215-572-4049, *E-mail:* admiss@arcadia.edu.

■ ASSOCIATED MENNONITE BIBLICAL SEMINARY

Graduate and Professional Programs, Elkhart, IN 46517-1999

AWARDS Christian formation (MA); divinity (M Div); mission and evangelism (MA); peace studies (MA); theological studies (MA, Certificate). Part-time programs available.

Faculty: 11 full-time (2 women), 20 part-time/adjunct (6 women).
Students: 56 full-time (29 women), 106 part-time (63 women); includes 8 minority (3 African Americans, 1 Asian American or Pacific Islander, 3 Hispanic Americans, 1 Native American), 22 international. Average age 36. 44 applicants, 57% accepted. In 2001, 12 first professional degrees, 20 master's, 1 other advanced degree awarded.
Degree requirements: For master's, thesis optional.
Application deadline: For fall admission, 5/1 (priority date). Applications are processed on a rolling basis. *Application fee:* $30.
Expenses: Tuition: Part-time $270 per credit hour. Required fees: $7 per semester.
Financial support: Career-related internships or fieldwork and scholarships/grants available. Support available to part-time students. Financial award application deadline: 5/1; financial award applicants required to submit FAFSA.
Faculty research: Biblical studies, theology, church history, church leadership.
J. Nelson Kraybill, President, 574-295-3726, *Fax:* 574-295-0092.
Application contact: Randall C. Miller, Director of Admissions, 574-295-3726, *Fax:* 574-295-0092, *E-mail:* admissions@ambs.edu. *Web site:* http://www.ambs.edu/

■ BETHANY THEOLOGICAL SEMINARY

Graduate and Professional Programs, Richmond, IN 47374-4019

AWARDS Biblical studies (MA Th); ministry studies (M Div); peace studies (M Div, MA Th); theological studies (MA Th, CATS). Part-time programs available.

Degree requirements: For master's, thesis. *Web site:* http://www.brethren.org/bethany/

■ CALIFORNIA STATE UNIVERSITY, DOMINGUEZ HILLS

College of Arts and Sciences, Program in Behavioral Science, Carson, CA 90747-0001

AWARDS Applied behavioral science (MA); gerontology (MA); negotiation and conflict resolution (MA, Certificate). Part-time and evening/weekend programs available.

Faculty: 18 full-time, 10 part-time/adjunct.
Students: 35 full-time (30 women), 70 part-time (53 women); includes 73 minority (58 African Americans, 6 Asian Americans or Pacific Islanders, 8 Hispanic Americans, 1 Native American), 1 international. Average age 40. 149 applicants, 83% accepted, 27 enrolled. In 2001, 80 degrees awarded.
Degree requirements: For master's, thesis or alternative.
Entrance requirements: For master's, minimum GPA of 3.0. *Application deadline:* For fall admission, 6/1. *Application fee:* $55.
Expenses: Tuition, nonresident: full-time $1,508; part-time $438 per semester. Required fees: $442; $246 per unit. $227 per semester.
A. Elba Frickel, Administrative Coordinator, 310-243-3435, *E-mail:* efrickel@dhvx20.csudh.edu.

■ CHAMINADE UNIVERSITY OF HONOLULU

Graduate Programs, Program in Education, Honolulu, HI 96816-1578

AWARDS Social science via peace education (M Ed). Part-time and evening/weekend programs available. Postbaccalaureate distance learning degree programs offered (minimal on-campus study).

Faculty: 9 full-time (8 women), 29 part-time/adjunct (23 women).
Students: 347 full-time (255 women), 23 part-time (19 women). Average age 35. 230 applicants, 78% accepted. In 2001, 40 degrees awarded.
Degree requirements: For master's, thesis or alternative.
Entrance requirements: For master's, PRAXIS I, TOEFL, minimum GPA of 2.75. *Application deadline:* For fall admission, 9/15 (priority date); for winter admission, 12/15 (priority date); for spring admission, 3/1 (priority date). Applications are processed on a rolling basis. *Application fee:* $50.
Financial support: In 2001–02, 70 students received support. Career-related internships or fieldwork, Federal Work-Study, institutionally sponsored loans, scholarships/grants, and tuition waivers (partial) available. Support available to part-time students. Financial award application deadline: 3/1; financial award applicants required to submit FAFSA.
Faculty research: Peace and curriculum education.
Dr. Michael Fassiotto, Director, 808-739-4674, *Fax:* 808-739-4607, *E-mail:* mfassiot@chaminade.edu.
Application contact: 808-739-4652; *Fax:* 808-739-4607.

■ COLUMBIA COLLEGE

Graduate Programs, Department of Human Relations, Columbia, SC 29203-5998

AWARDS Human behavior and conflict management (MA); interpersonal relations/conflict management (Certificate); organizational behavior/conflict management (Certificate). Part-time and evening/weekend programs available. Postbaccalaureate distance learning degree programs offered (minimal on-campus study).

Faculty: 2 full-time (both women), 3 part-time/adjunct (1 woman).
Students: 4 full-time (3 women), 20 part-time (16 women); includes 13 minority (all African Americans). Average age 41. 12 applicants, 58% accepted, 0 enrolled. In 2001, 15 degrees awarded.
Degree requirements: For master's, thesis, practicum.
Entrance requirements: For master's, GRE or MAT. *Application deadline:* For fall admission, 8/22 (priority date); for winter admission, 1/8 (priority date). Applications are processed on a rolling basis. *Application fee:* $50. Electronic applications accepted.
Expenses: Contact institution.
Financial support: Available to part-time students. Application deadline: 7/1;
Faculty research: "Envisioning and the Resolution of Conflict," environmental conflict resolution, crisis negotiation.
Dr. Elaine Ferraro, Chair, 803-786-3635, *Fax:* 803-786-3790, *E-mail:* eferraro@colacoll.edu.
Application contact: Carol Williams, Graduate Director of Recruitment and Admissions, 803-786-3191, *Fax:* 803-786-3184, *E-mail:* cwms@colucoll.edu. *Web site:* http://www.colacoll.edu/conflres/conres.htm

■ CORNELL UNIVERSITY

Graduate School, Graduate Fields of Architecture, Art and Planning, Field of Regional Science, Ithaca, NY 14853-0001

AWARDS Environmental studies (MA, MS, PhD); international spatial problems (MA, MS, PhD); location theory (MA, MS, PhD); multiregional economic analysis (MA, MS, PhD); peace science (MA, MS, PhD); planning methods (MA, MS, PhD); urban and regional economics (MA, MS, PhD).

Faculty: 15 full-time.
Students: 10 full-time (3 women), 8 international. 3 applicants, 100% accepted. In 2001, 2 master's, 2 doctorates awarded. Terminal master's awarded for partial completion of doctoral program.
Degree requirements: For master's and doctorate, thesis/dissertation.
Entrance requirements: For master's, GRE General Test (native English speakers only), TOEFL, 2 letters of recommendation; for doctorate, GRE General Test, TOEFL, 2 letters of recommendation. *Application deadline:* For fall admission, 1/15 (priority date). *Application fee:* $65. Electronic applications accepted.
Expenses: Tuition: Full-time $25,970. Required fees: $50.
Financial support: In 2001–02, 3 students received support, including 2 research assistantships with full tuition reimbursements available, 1 teaching assistantship with full tuition reimbursement available; fellowships with full tuition reimbursements available, institutionally sponsored loans, scholarships/grants, tuition waivers (full and partial), and unspecified assistantships also available. Financial award applicants required to submit FAFSA.
Faculty research: Urban and regional growth, spatial economics, formation of spatial patterns by socioeconomic systems, non-linear dynamics and complex systems, environmental-economic systems.
Application contact: Graduate Field Assistant, 607-255-6848, *Fax:* 607-255-1971, *E-mail:* regsci@cornell.edu. *Web site:* http://www.gradschool.cornell.edu/grad/fields_1/reg-sci.html

■ DALLAS BAPTIST UNIVERSITY

College of Business, Organizational Management Program, Dallas, TX 75211-9299

AWARDS Conflict resolution management (MA); general management (MA); health care management (MA); human resource management (MA). Part-time and evening/weekend programs available. Postbaccalaureate distance learning degree programs offered (no on-campus study).

Faculty: 14 full-time (5 women), 31 part-time/adjunct (10 women).
Students: 152 (105 women). 83 applicants, 69% accepted, 27 enrolled. In 2001, 45 degrees awarded.
Entrance requirements: For master's, TOEFL, minimum GPA of 3.0. *Application deadline:* Applications are processed on a rolling basis. *Application fee:* $25. Electronic applications accepted.
Expenses: Tuition: Full-time $6,030; part-time $335 per credit.
Financial support: Federal Work-Study, institutionally sponsored loans, scholarships/grants, and tuition waivers (full and partial) available. Support available to part-time students.
Faculty research: Organizational behavior, conflict personalities.
Connie Throne, Director of Organizational Management Program, 214-333-5280, *Fax:* 214-333-5579, *E-mail:* graduate@dbu.edu.

Dallas Baptist University (continued)
Application contact: Sarah R. Brancaccio, Director of Graduate Programs, 214-333-5243, *Fax:* 214-333-5579, *E-mail:* graduate@dbu.edu. *Web site:* http://www.dbu.edu

■ DUQUESNE UNIVERSITY

Graduate School of Liberal Arts, Graduate Center for Social and Public Policy, Pittsburgh, PA 15282-1750

AWARDS Conflict resolution and peace studies (Certificate); social and public policy (MA). Programs are a collaboration between the Departments of Political Science and Sociology. Part-time and evening/weekend programs available.

Faculty: 15 full-time (3 women), 1 (woman) part-time/adjunct.
Students: 35 full-time (16 women), 17 part-time (6 women); includes 2 minority (1 African American, 1 Hispanic American), 26 international. Average age 31. 52 applicants, 58% accepted, 18 enrolled. In 2001, 13 degrees awarded.
Degree requirements: For master's, thesis.
Entrance requirements: For master's, GRE General Test, TOEFL. *Application deadline:* For fall admission, 4/30 (priority date); for spring admission, 10/31 (priority date). Applications are processed on a rolling basis. *Application fee:* $50.
Expenses: Tuition: Part-time $566 per credit. Required fees: $56 per credit. Part-time tuition and fees vary according to degree level and program.
Financial support: In 2001–02, 20 students received support, including 12 research assistantships with full and partial tuition reimbursements available (averaging $9,000 per year), 4 teaching assistantships with full and partial tuition reimbursements available (averaging $9,000 per year); career-related internships or fieldwork, institutionally sponsored loans, scholarships/grants, and tuition waivers (full and partial) also available. Support available to part-time students. Financial award application deadline: 5/1.
Faculty research: Program evaluation, environmental policy, criminal justice policy, health care policy. *Total annual research expenditures:* $30,000.
Dr. Michael Irwin, Head, 412-396-6488, *Fax:* 412-396-5197, *E-mail:* socialpolicy@duq.edu. *Web site:* http://www.liberalarts.duq.edu/sociology/

■ EASTERN MENNONITE UNIVERSITY

Program in Conflict Transformation, Harrisonburg, VA 22802-2462

AWARDS MA. Part-time programs available.

Faculty: 6 full-time (3 women), 1 part-time/adjunct (0 women).
Students: 35 full-time (19 women), 27 part-time (18 women); includes 3 minority (1 African American, 2 Hispanic Americans), 26 international. Average age 38. 52 applicants, 94% accepted, 28 enrolled. In 2001, 13 degrees awarded.
Degree requirements: For master's, fieldwork, final seminar.
Entrance requirements: For master's, minimum 2.75 undergraduate GPA. *Application deadline:* For fall admission, 3/1 (priority date). Applications are processed on a rolling basis. *Application fee:* $25.
Expenses: Contact institution.
Financial support: In 2001–02, 28 students received support. Federal Work-Study, scholarships/grants, and unspecified assistantships available. Support available to part-time students. Financial award application deadline: 6/30; financial award applicants required to submit FAFSA.
Faculty research: Restorative justice, victims in serious crime, trauma healing, ritual in conflict transformation, peacebuilding.
Dr. Vernon E. Jantzi, Director, 540-432-4490, *Fax:* 540-432-4449, *E-mail:* jantziv@emu.edu.
Application contact: Don A. Yoder, Director of Admissions, 540-432-4257, *Fax:* 540-432-4444, *E-mail:* yoderda@emu.edu. *Web site:* http://www.emu.edu/

■ FRESNO PACIFIC UNIVERSITY

Graduate School, Program in Conflict Management and Peacemaking, Fresno, CA 93702-4709

AWARDS MA. Part-time and evening/weekend programs available.

Faculty: 3 full-time (0 women).
Students: Average age 42. 2 applicants, 50% accepted, 0 enrolled. In 2001, 2 degrees awarded.
Degree requirements: For master's, thesis, registration. *Median time to degree:* Master's–2 years full-time, 4 years part-time.
Entrance requirements: For master's, GMAT, MAT, GRE, interview, 2 writing samples. *Application deadline:* Applications are processed on a rolling basis. *Application fee:* $90. Electronic applications accepted.
Expenses: Tuition: Full-time $5,760; part-time $320 per unit. Tuition and fees vary according to course level and program.
Financial support: In 2001–02, 4 students received support. Career-related internships or fieldwork, scholarships/grants, and tuition waivers (full and partial) available. Support available to part-time students. Financial award applicants required to submit FAFSA.
Dr. Dalton Reimer, Director, 559-453-2055, *Fax:* 559-453-2001, *E-mail:* dreimer@fresno.edu.
Application contact: Edith D. Thiessen, Director of Graduate Admissions, 559-453-2256, *Fax:* 559-453-2001, *E-mail:* edthiess@fresno.edu.

■ GEORGE MASON UNIVERSITY

Institute for Conflict Analysis and Resolution, Fairfax, VA 22030-4444

AWARDS MS, PhD. Part-time programs available.

Faculty: 11 full-time (3 women), 8 part-time/adjunct (5 women).
Students: 55 full-time (40 women), 75 part-time (44 women); includes 18 minority (12 African Americans, 3 Asian Americans or Pacific Islanders, 3 Hispanic Americans), 33 international. Average age 36. 190 applicants, 37% accepted, 40 enrolled. In 2001, 16 master's, 4 doctorates awarded.
Degree requirements: For master's, thesis optional; for doctorate, one foreign language.
Entrance requirements: For master's, GRE General Test, minimum GPA of 3.0 in last 60 hours; for doctorate, GRE General Test, sample of written work. *Application deadline:* For fall admission, 3/1; for spring admission, 11/1. *Application fee:* $35. Electronic applications accepted.
Expenses: Tuition, state resident: full-time $3,168; part-time $132 per credit hour. Tuition, nonresident: full-time $11,280; part-time $470 per credit hour. Required fees: $1,416; $59 per credit hour.
Financial support: Fellowships, research assistantships, teaching assistantships, career-related internships or fieldwork available. Support available to part-time students. Financial award application deadline: 3/1; financial award applicants required to submit FAFSA.
Faculty research: Preventive diplomacy, conflict/dispute resolution, peace/security, political violence, international terrorism. *Total annual research expenditures:* $90,000.
Dr. Sara Cobb, Director, 703-993-1300, *Fax:* 703-993-1302, *E-mail:* icarinfo@gmu.edu. *Web site:* http://www.gmu.edu/departments/ICAR/

Find an in-depth description at www.petersons.com/gradchannel.

■ GEORGE MASON UNIVERSITY

School of Public Policy, Program in Peace Operations, Fairfax, VA 22030-4444

AWARDS MAIS.

Degree requirements: For master's, thesis or alternative.
Entrance requirements: For master's, minimum GPA of 3.0 in last 60 hours.
Expenses: Tuition, state resident: full-time $3,168; part-time $132 per credit hour. Tuition, nonresident: full-time $11,280; part-time $470 per credit hour. Required fees: $1,416; $59 per credit hour.

■ JOHN F. KENNEDY UNIVERSITY

Graduate School of Professional Psychology, Program in Conflict Resolution, Orinda, CA 94563-2603

AWARDS Certificate.

Expenses: Tuition: Full-time $9,396; part-time $348 per unit. Required fees: $9 per quarter. Tuition and fees vary according to degree level and program.

■ JOHNS HOPKINS UNIVERSITY

Paul H. Nitze School of Advanced International Studies, Washington, DC 20036

AWARDS Emerging markets (Certificate); interdisciplinary studies (MA, PhD), including African studies, American foreign policy (MA), Asian studies, Canadian studies, conflict resolution and mediation (MA), environmental policy and resource management (MA), European studies, international business (MA), international development (MA), international economics (MA), international relations (MA), Latin American studies, Middle Eastern studies (MA), military and defense studies (MA), Russian area and East European studies (MA), social change and development (MA); international public policy (MIPP). MBA/MA offered jointly with the University of Pennsylvania–Wharton School and INSEAD in France.

Faculty: 44 full-time (13 women), 113 part-time/adjunct (29 women).
Students: 567 full-time (275 women), 17 part-time (8 women); includes 71 minority (14 African Americans, 46 Asian Americans or Pacific Islanders, 10 Hispanic Americans, 1 Native American). Average age 27. 1,288 applicants, 35% accepted. In 2001, 294 master's, 13 doctorates, 34 other advanced degrees awarded. Terminal master's awarded for partial completion of doctoral program.
Degree requirements: For master's, one foreign language, comprehensive exam; for doctorate, 2 foreign languages, thesis/dissertation.
Entrance requirements: For master's, GMAT or GRE General Test or TOEFL, previous course work in economics, foreign language; for doctorate, GRE General Test or TOEFL; for Certificate, TOEFL. *Application deadline:* For fall admission, 1/15. *Application fee:* $75. Electronic applications accepted.
Expenses: Contact institution.
Financial support: In 2001–02, 431 fellowships (averaging $5,500 per year) were awarded; career-related internships or fieldwork and Federal Work-Study also available. Financial award application deadline: 2/1; financial award applicants required to submit FAFSA.
Faculty research: Comparative politics, regional studies, language and linguistics. Dr. Jessica Einhorn, Dean, 202-663-5624, *Fax:* 202-663-5621.
Application contact: Bonnie Wilson, Associate Dean of Student Affairs, 202-663-5700, *Fax:* 202-663-7788, *E-mail:* admissions.sais@jhu.edu. *Web site:* http://www.sais-jhu.edu/

Find an in-depth description at www.petersons.com/gradchannel.

■ JONES INTERNATIONAL UNIVERSITY

Graduate School of Business and e-Learning, Englewood, CO 80112

AWARDS Business communication (MA, MBA); electric commerce (MBA); entrepreneurship (MBA); global enterprise management (MBA); health care management (MBA); information technology management (MBA); negotiation and conflict management (MBA); project management (MBA). Program offered through the Internet only. Postbaccalaureate distance learning degree programs offered (no on-campus study).

Degree requirements: For master's, one foreign language.
Expenses: Tuition: Part-time $925 per course. *Web site:* http://www.jonesinternational.edu/

Find an in-depth description at www.petersons.com/gradchannel.

■ KENNESAW STATE UNIVERSITY

College of Humanities and Social Sciences, Program in Conflict Management, Kennesaw, GA 30144-5591

AWARDS MSCM.

Faculty: 2 full-time (both women).
Students: 44 full-time (31 women); includes 15 minority (12 African Americans, 3 Hispanic Americans). Average age 34. 30 applicants, 87% accepted, 14 enrolled.
Entrance requirements: For master's, GMAT, GRE, LSAT. *Application deadline:* For fall admission, 7/7 (priority date); for spring admission, 10/20. Applications are processed on a rolling basis. *Application fee:* $20. Electronic applications accepted.
Expenses: Tuition, state resident: part-time $97 per credit hour. Tuition, nonresident: part-time $387 per credit hour. Required fees: $178 per semester. Ansley Barton, Director, 770-423-6299, *Fax:* 770-423-6312, *E-mail:* abarton@kennesaw.edu/.
Application contact: Karen Ohlsson, Assistant Director, 770-423-6299, *Fax:* 770-423-6312, *E-mail:* kohlsson@kennesaw.edu. *Web site:* http://www.kennesaw.edu/

■ LESLEY UNIVERSITY

Graduate School of Arts and Social Sciences, Program in Intercultural Relations, Cambridge, MA 02138-2790

AWARDS Development project administration (MA); individually designed (MA); intercultural conflict resolution (MA); intercultural health and human services (MA); intercultural relations (CAGS); intercultural training and consulting (MA); international education exchange (MA); international student advising (MA); managing culturally diverse human resources (MA); multicultural education (MA). Part-time and evening/weekend programs available.

Faculty: 3 full-time (2 women), 3 part-time/adjunct (all women).
Students: Average age 30. 35 applicants, 94% accepted, 4 enrolled. In 2001, 9 degrees awarded.
Degree requirements: For master's, one foreign language; for CAGS, one foreign language, thesis. *Median time to degree:* Master's–2 years part-time.
Entrance requirements: For master's, TOEFL, interview; for CAGS, interview, master's degree. *Application deadline:* Applications are processed on a rolling basis. *Application fee:* $50.
Expenses: Tuition: Part-time $330 per credit. Required fees: $15 per term. Part-time tuition and fees vary according to campus/location and program.
Financial support: In 2001–02, 8 students received support; research assistantships, teaching assistantships, career-related internships or fieldwork, Federal Work-Study, scholarships/grants, and unspecified assistantships available. Support available to part-time students. Financial award application deadline: 4/1; financial award applicants required to submit FAFSA.
Faculty research: Sociolinguistics, cross-cultural feminist theory, immigration and diaspora, intercultural business training. Sylvia R. Cowan, Coordinator, 617-349-8978, *E-mail:* scowan@mail.lesley.edu.
Application contact: Hugh Norwood, Dean of Admissions and Enrollment Planning, 800-999-1959, *Fax:* 617-349-8366, *E-mail:* hnorwood@mail.lesley.edu.

■ MONTCLAIR STATE UNIVERSITY

The School of Graduate, Professional and Continuing Education, College of Humanities and Social Sciences, Department of Legal Studies, Upper Montclair, NJ 07043-1624

AWARDS Dispute resolution (MA); law office management and technology (MA); legal studies (MA); paralegal (Certificate). Part-time and evening/weekend programs available.

Entrance requirements: For master's, GRE General Test, minimum undergraduate GPA of 2.75. Electronic applications accepted.

■ NOVA SOUTHEASTERN UNIVERSITY

Graduate School of Humanities and Social Sciences, Department of Conflict Analysis and Resolution, Fort Lauderdale, FL 33314-7721

AWARDS MS, PhD, Certificate, JD/MS. Part-time and evening/weekend programs available. Postbaccalaureate distance learning degree programs offered (minimal on-campus study).

Faculty: 7 full-time (5 women), 3 part-time/adjunct (2 women).
Students: 135 (91 women). Average age 38. 48 applicants, 40% accepted. In 2001, 11 degrees awarded.
Degree requirements: For master's, thesis optional; for doctorate, thesis/dissertation, qualifying exam.
Entrance requirements: For master's, TOEFL, interview, minimum GPA of 2.5, sample of academic/professional work; for doctorate, TOEFL, minimum GPA of 3.0, interview. *Application deadline:* For fall admission, 7/1 (priority date); for winter admission, 11/1 (priority date); for spring admission, 3/1. Applications are processed on a rolling basis. *Application fee:* $50.
Expenses: Tuition: Full-time $7,380; part-time $432 per credit. Required fees: $200. Tuition and fees vary according to campus/location and program.
Financial support: In 2001–02, 94 students received support; research assistantships with tuition reimbursements available, teaching assistantships, career-related internships or fieldwork, Federal Work-Study, institutionally sponsored loans, scholarships/grants, and unspecified assistantships available. Support available to part-time students. Financial award application deadline: 4/1; financial award applicants required to submit CSS PROFILE.
Faculty research: International conflict, environmental disputes, violence prevention, communication and conflict, facilitation.
Application contact: Yolanda Hankerson, Graduate Admissions Office, 954-262-3000, *Fax:* 954-262-3968, *E-mail:* hankerso@nova.edu. *Web site:* http://www.nova.edu/shss/dcar/

■ PEPPERDINE UNIVERSITY

School of Law, Program in Dispute Resolution, Malibu, CA 90263-0002

AWARDS MDR.

Students: 2 full-time (1 woman), 34 part-time (16 women); includes 6 minority (1 African American, 2 Asian Americans or Pacific Islanders, 3 Hispanic Americans), 2 international. Average age 47. 10 applicants, 70% accepted. In 2001, 32 degrees awarded.
Degree requirements: For master's, thesis.
Entrance requirements: For master's, GRE General Test or LSAT. *Application deadline:* For fall admission, 6/15 (priority date); for spring admission, 3/15. Applications are processed on a rolling basis. *Application fee:* $50.
Expenses: Tuition: Full-time $15,700; part-time $785 per unit. Tuition and fees vary according to degree level and program.
Financial support: Career-related internships or fieldwork, Federal Work-Study, institutionally sponsored loans, and scholarships/grants available. Support available to part-time students. Financial award application deadline: 4/1; financial award applicants required to submit FAFSA.
Dr. L. Randolph Lowry, Director, Institute for Dispute Resolution, 310-506-4655, *Fax:* 310-506-4266.
Application contact: Shellee Warnes, Assistant Director, Academic Programs, 310-506-4655, *Fax:* 310-506-4266. *Web site:* http://www.pepperdine.edu/

■ ST. EDWARD'S UNIVERSITY

College of Professional and Graduate Studies, Program in Human Services, Austin, TX 78704-6489

AWARDS Conflict resolution (Certificate); human services (MA), including administration, conflict resolution, human resource management, sports management; sports management (Certificate). Part-time and evening/weekend programs available.

Faculty: 4 full-time (1 woman), 12 part-time/adjunct (6 women).
Students: 12 full-time (11 women), 90 part-time (71 women); includes 28 minority (9 African Americans, 5 Asian Americans or Pacific Islanders, 13 Hispanic Americans, 1 Native American), 3 international. Average age 36. 22 applicants, 86% accepted, 16 enrolled. In 2001, 43 degrees awarded.
Degree requirements: For master's, minimum 24 resident hours.
Entrance requirements: For master's, GRE General Test, TOEFL, minimum GPA of 3.0 in last 60 hours or 2.75 overall. *Application deadline:* For fall admission, 8/1; for spring admission, 12/1. Applications are processed on a rolling basis. *Application fee:* $30 ($50 for international students). Electronic applications accepted.
Expenses: Tuition: Full-time $7,974; part-time $443 per credit hour.
Financial support: In 2001–02, 56 students received support. Career-related internships or fieldwork, institutionally sponsored loans, and scholarships/grants available. Support available to part-time students. Financial award application deadline: 4/15; financial award applicants required to submit FAFSA.
Dr. James A. Johnson, Dean, 512-416-5827, *Fax:* 512-448-8492, *E-mail:* jamesj@admin.stedwards.edu.
Application contact: Bridget Sowinski, Graduate Admissions Coordinator, 512-428-1061, *Fax:* 512-428-1032, *E-mail:* bridgets@admin.stewards.edu. *Web site:* http://www.stedwards.edu/

■ UNIVERSITY OF BALTIMORE

Graduate School, College of Liberal Arts, Center for Negotiations and Conflict Management, Baltimore, MD 21201-5779

AWARDS MS. Part-time and evening/weekend programs available.

Faculty: 1 full-time (0 women), 7 part-time/adjunct (0 women).
Students: 13 full-time (12 women), 75 part-time (47 women); includes 47 minority (all African Americans). Average age 31. 54 applicants, 89% accepted. In 2001, 5 degrees awarded.
Degree requirements: For master's, internship, thesis optional.
Entrance requirements: For master's, minimum GPA of 3.0. *Application deadline:* For fall admission, 7/15; for spring admission, 12/15. *Application fee:* $30. Electronic applications accepted.
Expenses: Tuition, state resident: full-time $5,508; part-time $306 per credit. Tuition, nonresident: full-time $8,352; part-time $464 per credit. Required fees: $37 per credit. $60 per semester. Tuition and fees vary according to course load and degree level.
Financial support: In 2001–02, 1 research assistantship with full and partial tuition reimbursement was awarded. Financial award application deadline: 4/1; financial award applicants required to submit FAFSA.
Faculty research: Communication and conflict, conflict management systems theory.
Dr. Donald Mulcahey, Head, 410-837-5320, *E-mail:* dmulcahey@ubmail.ubalt.edu.
Application contact: Jeffrey Zavrotny, Assistant Director of Admissions, 410-837-4777, *Fax:* 410-837-4793, *E-mail:* jzavrotny@ubalt.edu.

■ UNIVERSITY OF MASSACHUSETTS BOSTON

Office of Graduate Studies and Research, College of Public and Community Service, Program in Dispute Resolution, Boston, MA 02125-3393

AWARDS MA, Certificate. MA program accepts applications for fall admission only; Certificate program accepts applications for spring admission only.

Degree requirements: For master's, practicum, final project.
Entrance requirements: For master's, MAT or GRE, minimum GPA of 2.75; for Certificate, minimum GPA of 2.75.

Faculty research: Mediation and negotiation, justice and conflict, cross-cultural mediation, environmental fairness, dispute resolution theory and ethics.

■ UNIVERSITY OF MISSOURI–COLUMBIA

Graduate School and School of Law, Program in Dispute Resolution, Columbia, MO 65211

AWARDS LL M.

Students: 11 full-time (6 women), 8 part-time (6 women); includes 1 minority (Hispanic American), 7 international. In 2001, 10 degrees awarded.
Application deadline: For fall admission, 1/1 (priority date). *Application fee:* $25 ($50 for international students).
Expenses: Tuition, state resident: part-time $179 per credit hour. Tuition, nonresident: part-time $539 per credit hour. Required fees: $122 per semester. Tuition and fees vary according to program.
Financial support: Research assistantships, teaching assistantships, institutionally sponsored loans available.
Dr. John Lande, Director, 573-882-3914, *E-mail:* landej@missouri.edu. *Web site:* http://mail.law.missouri.edu/~llmdr/

■ UNIVERSITY OF MISSOURI–ST. LOUIS

Graduate School, College of Arts and Sciences, Department of Sociology, St. Louis, MO 63121-4499

AWARDS Advanced social perspective (MA); community conflict intervention (MA); program design and evaluation research (MA); social policy planning and administration (MA). Part-time and evening/weekend programs available.

Faculty: 5.
Students: 4 full-time (2 women), 6 part-time (4 women); includes 2 minority (1 African American, 1 Native American), 1 international. In 2001, 5 degrees awarded.
Degree requirements: For master's, thesis optional.
Entrance requirements: For master's, GRE General Test. *Application deadline:* For fall admission, 7/1 (priority date); for spring admission, 12/1 (priority date). Applications are processed on a rolling basis. *Application fee:* $25 ($40 for international students). Electronic applications accepted.
Expenses: Tuition, state resident: part-time $231 per credit hour. Tuition, nonresident: part-time $621 per credit hour.
Financial support: In 2001–02, 3 students received support, including 3 teaching assistantships with full and partial tuition reimbursements available (averaging $10,333 per year); research assistantships, career-related internships or fieldwork also available. Support available to part-time students.
Faculty research: Homeless populations, theory, social deviance, conflict resolution, Japan, Republic of South Africa, social change in East Germany. *Total annual research expenditures:* $30,040.
Dr. George McCall, Director of Graduate Studies, 314-516-6366, *Fax:* 314-516-5310.
Application contact: Jean Smith, Graduate Admissions, 314-516-6928, *Fax:* 314-516-5310, *E-mail:* gradadm@umsl.edu. *Web site:* http://www.umsl.edu/divisions/artscience/sociology/

■ UNIVERSITY OF NOTRE DAME

Graduate School, College of Arts and Letters, Division of Social Science, Joan B. Kroc Institute for International Peace Studies, Notre Dame, IN 46556

AWARDS MA.

Faculty: 38 full-time (11 women).
Students: 22 full-time (13 women); includes 4 minority (2 African Americans, 2 Asian Americans or Pacific Islanders), 16 international. Average age 25. 154 applicants, 14% accepted, 19 enrolled. In 2001, 20 degrees awarded.
Degree requirements: For master's, one foreign language, comprehensive exam. *Median time to degree:* Master's–1.1 years full-time.
Entrance requirements: For master's, GRE General Test, TOEFL. *Application deadline:* For fall admission, 1/5. *Application fee:* $50. Electronic applications accepted.
Expenses: Tuition: Full-time $24,220; part-time $1,346 per credit hour. Required fees: $155.
Financial support: In 2001–02, 22 students received support, including 22 fellowships with full tuition reimbursements available (averaging $11,000 per year); career-related internships or fieldwork, scholarships/grants, health care benefits, and tuition waivers (full) also available. Financial award application deadline: 1/5.
Faculty research: The role of international norms and institutions in peacemaking; the impact of religious, philosophical, and cultural influences on peace; the dynamics of intergroup conflict and conflict transformation; the promotion of social, economic, and environmental justice.
Dr. Robert C. Johansen, Director of Graduate Studies, 574-631-6970, *Fax:* 574-631-6973, *E-mail:* kroc-admissions@nd.edu.
Application contact: Rosemarie Green, Admissions Coordinator, 574-631-8535, *Fax:* 574-631-6973, *E-mail:* green.2@nd.edu. *Web site:* http://www.nd.edu/~krocinst/

■ WAYNE STATE UNIVERSITY

Graduate School, College of Urban, Labor and Metropolitan Affairs, Interdisciplinary Program in Dispute Resolution, Detroit, MI 48202

AWARDS MADR, Certificate, JD/MADR.

Faculty: 1 full-time.
Students: 31. In 2001, 8 master's, 1 other advanced degree awarded.
Entrance requirements: For master's, GMAT, GRE General Test, or LSAT. *Application deadline:* For fall admission, 7/1. *Application fee:* $20 ($30 for international students). Electronic applications accepted.
Expenses: Tuition, state resident: full-time $3,764. Tuition and fees vary according to degree level and program.
Faculty research: Cultural diversity, social/human conflict, negotiation/arbitration, conflict resolution, intervention policies of major powers and small states.
Loraleigh Keashley, Director, 313-577-3221, *Fax:* 313-577-8800, *E-mail:* loraleigh.keashley@wayne.edu.

Criminology and Forensics

CRIMINAL JUSTICE AND CRIMINOLOGY

■ ALBANY STATE UNIVERSITY

College of Arts and Sciences, Department of Criminal Justice, Albany, GA 31705-2717

AWARDS Criminal justice (MS). Part-time programs available.

Degree requirements: For master's, comprehensive exam.
Entrance requirements: For master's, GRE General Test, minimum GPA of 2.5. Electronic applications accepted.
Faculty research: Criminal alcoholic program, prevention of juvenile delinquency, police selection, constitutional issues.

■ ALBANY STATE UNIVERSITY

College of Arts and Sciences, Department of History, Political Science and Public Administration, Albany, GA 31705-2717

AWARDS Community and economic development (MPA); criminal justice (MPA); fiscal management (MPA); general management (MPA); health administration and policy (MPA); human resources management (MPA); public policy (MPA); water resource management and policy (MPA). Part-time programs available.

Degree requirements: For master's, thesis, comprehensive exam.
Entrance requirements: For master's, GRE General Test, minimum GPA of 2.5. Electronic applications accepted.
Faculty research: Transportation, urban affairs, political economy.

■ AMERICAN INTERNATIONAL COLLEGE

School of Continuing Education and Graduate Studies, School of Psychology and Education, Department of Criminal Justice Studies, Springfield, MA 01109-3189

AWARDS MS.

Degree requirements: For master's, thesis optional.
Entrance requirements: For master's, minimum B average in undergraduate course work.

■ AMERICAN MILITARY UNIVERSITY

Graduate School of Military Studies, Manassas, VA 20110

AWARDS Air warfare (MA Military Studies); American revolution studies (MA Military Studies); business administration (MBA); civil war studies (MA Military Studies); criminal justice (MA); defense management (MA Military Studies); emergency and disaster management (MA); intelligence (MA Strategic Intelligence); land warfare (MA Military Studies); management (MA); national security studies (MA); naval warfare (MA Military Studies); political science (MA); public administration (MA); public health (MA); security management (MA); space studies (MA Military Studies); special operations (MA Military Studies); transportation management (MA); unconventional warfare (MA Military Studies). Program offered via distance learning only. Part-time and evening/weekend programs available. Postbaccalaureate distance learning degree programs offered (no on-campus study).

Faculty: 2 full-time (1 woman), 100 part-time/adjunct (8 women).
Students: Average age 35. 830 applicants, 100% accepted, 550 enrolled. In 2001, 87 degrees awarded. Terminal master's awarded for partial completion of doctoral program.
Entrance requirements: For master's, bachelor's degree or equivalent, minimum GPA of 2.7 in last 60 hours. *Application deadline:* For fall admission, 9/1 (priority date); for winter admission, 1/1; for spring admission, 5/1 (priority date). Applications are processed on a rolling basis. Electronic applications accepted.
Expenses: Tuition: Part-time $750 per course.
Faculty research: Military history, criminal justice, management performance, national security.
Dr. Michael J. Hillyard, Provost, 703-330-5398 Ext. 862, *Fax:* 703-330-5109, *E-mail:* mhillyard@amunet.edu.
Application contact: Cathi Bauer, Office of Student Services, 703-330-5398 Ext. 894, *Fax:* 703-330-5109, *E-mail:* info@amunet.edu. *Web site:* http://www.amunet.edu/

■ AMERICAN UNIVERSITY

School of Public Affairs, Department of Justice, Law and Society, Washington, DC 20016-8001

AWARDS Justice, law and society (MS); sociology/justice (PhD). Part-time and evening/weekend programs available.

Faculty: 18 full-time (8 women), 20 part-time/adjunct (8 women).
Students: 30 full-time (24 women), 30 part-time (23 women); includes 10 minority (5 African Americans, 1 Asian American or Pacific Islander, 4 Hispanic Americans). Average age 26. 92 applicants, 82% accepted, 23 enrolled. In 2001, 21 master's, 1 doctorate awarded. Terminal master's awarded for partial completion of doctoral program.
Degree requirements: For master's, comprehensive exam; for doctorate, one foreign language, thesis/dissertation, comprehensive exam.
Entrance requirements: For master's and doctorate, GRE General Test. *Application deadline:* For fall admission, 2/1; for spring admission, 10/1. *Application fee:* $50.
Expenses: Tuition: Full-time $14,274; part-time $793 per credit. Required fees: $290. Tuition and fees vary according to program.
Financial support: Fellowships, research assistantships, teaching assistantships, career-related internships or fieldwork, Federal Work-Study, institutionally sponsored loans, and tuition waivers (full and partial) available. Financial award application deadline: 2/1.
Faculty research: Mental health, court management.
Dr. Robert P. Johnson, Chair, 202-885-2951, *Fax:* 202-885-2907.
Application contact: Linda Spicer, Academic Counselor, 202-885-6465, *Fax:* 202-885-2907.

■ ANDREW JACKSON UNIVERSITY

School of Civil Sciences, Program in Criminal Justice, Birmingham, AL 35209

AWARDS MS. Part-time and evening/weekend programs available. Postbaccalaureate distance learning degree programs offered (no on-campus study).

Faculty: 12 part-time/adjunct.
Application deadline: Applications are processed on a rolling basis. *Application fee:* $75. Electronic applications accepted.
Expenses: Tuition: Part-time $475 per course.
Application contact: Bell N. Woods, Director of Admissions, 205-871-9288, *Fax:* 205-871-9294, *E-mail:* bnw@aju.edu.

■ ANNA MARIA COLLEGE

Graduate Division, Program in Criminal Justice, Paxton, MA 01612

AWARDS MA. Part-time and evening/weekend programs available.

Faculty: 2 full-time (1 woman), 16 part-time/adjunct (3 women).
Students: 49 full-time (11 women), 56 part-time (18 women); includes 6 minority (5 African Americans, 1 Hispanic American). Average age 36. In 2001, 116 degrees awarded.
Degree requirements: For master's, capstone project.
Entrance requirements: For master's, bachelor's degree in related field, minimum GPA of 2.7. *Application deadline:* For fall admission, 3/1 (priority date); for spring admission, 11/1 (priority date). Applications are processed on a rolling basis. *Application fee:* $30. Electronic applications accepted.
Expenses: Tuition: Part-time $900 per course.
Financial support: Institutionally sponsored loans available. Financial award applicants required to submit FAFSA.
Patricia Gavin, Director, 508-849-3377, *Fax:* 508-849-3343, *E-mail:* pgavin@annamaria.edu.
Application contact: Eva Eaton, Director of Admissions for Graduate Programs and the Department of Professional Studies, 508-849-3488, *Fax:* 508-849-3362, *E-mail:* eveaton@annamaria.edu. *Web site:* http://www.annamaria.edu/

■ ARIZONA STATE UNIVERSITY WEST

College of Human Services, Program in Administration of Justice, Phoenix, AZ 85069-7100

AWARDS Criminal justice (MA). Part-time and evening/weekend programs available.

Faculty: 4 full-time (3 women), 2 part-time/adjunct (0 women).
Students: 11 full-time (7 women), 18 part-time (12 women); includes 6 minority (1 African American, 2 Asian Americans or Pacific Islanders, 2 Hispanic Americans, 1 Native American). Average age 32. 28 applicants, 71% accepted, 15 enrolled.
Entrance requirements: For master's, GRE or MAT. *Application deadline:* For fall admission, 4/15. *Application fee:* $45.
Expenses: Tuition, state resident: full-time $2,412; part-time $126 per credit hour. Tuition, nonresident: full-time $10,352; part-time $428 per credit hour. Tuition and fees vary according to program.
Financial support: Scholarships/grants available.
Dr. Charles Katz, Director, 602-543-6618, *Fax:* 602-543-6658, *E-mail:* ckatz@asu.edu.
Application contact: Susan Chism, Administrative Assistant, 602-543-6266, *Fax:* 602-543-6612, *E-mail:* susan.chism@asu.edu.

■ ARMSTRONG ATLANTIC STATE UNIVERSITY

School of Graduate Studies, Program in Criminal Justice, Savannah, GA 31419-1997

AWARDS MS.

Entrance requirements: For master's, GRE General Test or MAT, minimum GPA of 2.5. *Web site:* http://www.cjsocpols.armstrong.edu/

■ AUBURN UNIVERSITY MONTGOMERY

School of Sciences, Department of Justice and Public Safety, Montgomery, AL 36124-4023

AWARDS MSJPS. Part-time and evening/weekend programs available.

Students: 13 full-time (7 women), 35 part-time (25 women); includes 15 minority (13 African Americans, 1 Asian American or Pacific Islander, 1 Hispanic American). Average age 32. In 2001, 34 degrees awarded.
Degree requirements: For master's, thesis optional.
Entrance requirements: For master's, GRE General Test or MAT. *Application deadline:* Applications are processed on a rolling basis. *Application fee:* $25. Electronic applications accepted.
Expenses: Tuition, state resident: full-time $3,072; part-time $128 per credit hour. Tuition, nonresident: full-time $9,216; part-time $384 per credit hour.
Financial support: Career-related internships or fieldwork and scholarships/grants available. Support available to part-time students. Financial award application deadline: 3/1; financial award applicants required to submit FAFSA.
Faculty research: Law enforcement, corrections, juvenile justice.
Dr. Robert J. Van Der Velde, Head, 334-244-3694, *E-mail:* rvanderv@strudel.aum.edu.

■ BOISE STATE UNIVERSITY

Graduate College, College of Social Science and Public Affairs, Program in Criminal Justice Administration, Boise, ID 83725-0399

AWARDS MA.

Degree requirements: For master's, thesis.
Entrance requirements: For master's, minimum GPA of 3.0. Electronic applications accepted.

■ BOSTON UNIVERSITY

Metropolitan College, Program in Criminal Justice, Boston, MA 02215

AWARDS MCJ. Part-time and evening/weekend programs available.

Faculty: 1 full-time (0 women), 7 part-time/adjunct (1 woman).
Students: 6 full-time (4 women), 33 part-time (10 women); includes 4 minority (3 African Americans, 1 Hispanic American), 4 international. Average age 35. 40 applicants, 75% accepted. In 2001, 13 degrees awarded.
Degree requirements: For master's, thesis.
Application deadline: For fall admission, 7/15 (priority date); for spring admission, 1/15. Applications are processed on a rolling basis. *Application fee:* $60.
Expenses: Tuition: Full-time $25,872; part-time $340 per credit. Required fees: $40 per semester. Part-time tuition and fees vary according to class time, course level and program.
Financial support: In 2001–02, 1 student received support, including 1 research assistantship; career-related internships or fieldwork, Federal Work-Study, institutionally sponsored loans, and tuition waivers (partial) also available. Support available to part-time students. Financial award application deadline: 6/15.
Faculty research: Criminal justice administration and planning, criminology, police corrections, collective violence, juvenile issues.
Application contact: Prof. Daniel P. LeClair, Director, 617-353-3025, *Fax:* 617-353-6328. *Web site:* http://bu.edu.met/cj

■ BOWLING GREEN STATE UNIVERSITY

Graduate College, College of Arts and Sciences, Department of Sociology, Bowling Green, OH 43403

AWARDS Criminology/deviant behavior (MA, PhD); demography and population studies (MA, PhD); family studies (MA, PhD); social psychology (MA, PhD). Part-time programs available.

Faculty: 17.
Students: 32 full-time (22 women), 12 part-time (8 women); includes 3 minority (2 African Americans, 1 Hispanic American), 6 international. Average age 28. 53 applicants, 53% accepted, 12 enrolled. In 2001, 7 master's, 4 doctorates awarded.
Degree requirements: For master's, thesis or alternative; for doctorate, thesis/dissertation, comprehensive exam.
Entrance requirements: For master's and doctorate, GRE General Test, TOEFL. *Application deadline:* For fall admission, 2/15. *Application fee:* $30. Electronic applications accepted.
Expenses: Tuition, state resident: full-time $7,376; part-time $342 per credit hour. Tuition, nonresident: full-time $13,628; part-time $640 per credit hour.
Financial support: In 2001–02, 26 research assistantships with full tuition reimbursements (averaging $9,134 per year), 6 teaching assistantships with full tuition reimbursements (averaging $11,000 per year) were awarded. Career-related

Bowling Green State University (continued)

internships or fieldwork, Federal Work-Study, institutionally sponsored loans, and unspecified assistantships also available. Financial award applicants required to submit FAFSA.

Faculty research: Applied demography, criminology and deviance, family studies, population studies, social psychology.

Dr. Gary Lee, Chair, 419-372-2294.

Application contact: Dr. Steve Cernkovich, Graduate Coordinator, 419-372-2743.

■ BOWLING GREEN STATE UNIVERSITY

Graduate College, College of Health and Human Services, Program in Criminal Justice, Bowling Green, OH 43403

AWARDS MSCJ. Part-time and evening/weekend programs available.

Faculty: 5.

Students: 6 full-time (3 women); includes 2 minority (both African Americans). 7 applicants, 100% accepted, 4 enrolled.

Degree requirements: For master's, thesis or alternative.

Entrance requirements: For master's, GRE General Test, TOEFL.

Expenses: Tuition, state resident: full-time $7,376; part-time $342 per credit hour. Tuition, nonresident: full-time $13,628; part-time $640 per credit hour.

Financial support: In 2001–02, 2 research assistantships (averaging $7,300 per year) were awarded; unspecified assistantships also available.

Dr. Steven Lab, Head, 419-372-2326.

Application contact: Dr. Michael Buerger, Graduate Coordinator, 419-372-8905.

■ CALIFORNIA STATE UNIVERSITY, FRESNO

Division of Graduate Studies, College of Social Sciences, Department of Criminology, Fresno, CA 93740-8027

AWARDS MS. Part-time and evening/weekend programs available.

Faculty: 14 full-time (4 women).

Students: 15 full-time (8 women), 24 part-time (13 women); includes 17 minority (2 African Americans, 2 Asian Americans or Pacific Islanders, 13 Hispanic Americans), 2 international. Average age 31. 23 applicants, 83% accepted, 10 enrolled. In 2001, 17 degrees awarded.

Degree requirements: For master's, thesis or alternative. *Median time to degree:* Master's–2.5 years full-time, 3.5 years part-time.

Entrance requirements: For master's, GRE General Test, TOEFL, minimum GPA of 3.0. *Application deadline:* For fall admission, 8/1 (priority date); for spring admission, 12/1. Applications are processed on a rolling basis. *Application fee:* $55. Electronic applications accepted.

Expenses: Tuition, nonresident: part-time $246 per unit. Required fees: $605 per semester. Tuition and fees vary according to course load.

Financial support: Career-related internships or fieldwork, Federal Work-Study, scholarships/grants, and unspecified assistantships available. Support available to part-time students. Financial award application deadline: 3/1; financial award applicants required to submit FAFSA.

Faculty research: Substance abuse, gangs vs. law enforcement, needs of female offenders, battered women, crime victims.

Prof. Harvey Wallace, Chair, 559-278-2305, *Fax:* 559-278-7265, *E-mail:* harvey_wallace@csufresno.edu.

Application contact: Dr. Thomas Dull, Graduate Program Coordinator, 559-278-2305, *Fax:* 559-278-7265, *E-mail:* thomas_dull@csufresno.edu.

■ CALIFORNIA STATE UNIVERSITY, LONG BEACH

Graduate Studies, College of Health and Human Services, Department of Criminal Justice, Long Beach, CA 90840

AWARDS MS. Part-time programs available.

Students: 19 full-time (8 women), 40 part-time (30 women); includes 26 minority (5 African Americans, 8 Asian Americans or Pacific Islanders, 12 Hispanic Americans, 1 Native American), 3 international. Average age 29. 54 applicants, 57% accepted. In 2001, 5 degrees awarded.

Degree requirements: For master's, comprehensive course or thesis.

Entrance requirements: For master's, minimum GPA of 3.0. *Application deadline:* For fall admission, 8/1; for spring admission, 12/1. Applications are processed on a rolling basis. *Application fee:* $55. Electronic applications accepted.

Financial support: Federal Work-Study, institutionally sponsored loans, and scholarships/grants available. Financial award application deadline: 3/2.

Dr. Ronald Vogel, Chair, 562-985-4738, *Fax:* 562-985-8086, *E-mail:* rvogel@csulb.edu.

Application contact: Dr. Elizabeth Deschenes, Graduate Adviser, 562-985-8567, *Fax:* 562-985-8086, *E-mail:* libby@csulb.edu.

■ CALIFORNIA STATE UNIVERSITY, LOS ANGELES

Graduate Studies, College of Health and Human Services, Department of Criminal Justice, Major in Criminalistics, Los Angeles, CA 90032-8530

AWARDS MS.

Students: 11 full-time (8 women), 15 part-time (8 women); includes 7 minority (5 Asian Americans or Pacific Islanders, 2 Hispanic Americans). In 2001, 4 degrees awarded.

Degree requirements: For master's, thesis.

Entrance requirements: For master's, TOEFL, minimum GPA of 2.75. *Application deadline:* For fall admission, 6/30; for spring admission, 2/1. Applications are processed on a rolling basis. *Application fee:* $55.

Expenses: Tuition, nonresident: part-time $164 per unit.

Financial support: Application deadline: 3/1.

Dr. Debbie Baskin, Acting Chair, Department of Criminal Justice, 323-343-4610.

■ CALIFORNIA STATE UNIVERSITY, LOS ANGELES

Graduate Studies, College of Health and Human Services, Department of Criminal Justice, Major in Criminal Justice, Los Angeles, CA 90032-8530

AWARDS MS.

Students: 13 full-time (12 women), 25 part-time (14 women); includes 22 minority (4 African Americans, 3 Asian Americans or Pacific Islanders, 14 Hispanic Americans, 1 Native American). In 2001, 11 degrees awarded.

Degree requirements: For master's, thesis.

Entrance requirements: For master's, TOEFL, minimum GPA of 2.75. *Application deadline:* For fall admission, 6/30; for spring admission, 2/1. Applications are processed on a rolling basis. *Application fee:* $55.

Expenses: Tuition, nonresident: part-time $164 per unit.

Financial support: Application deadline: 3/1.

Dr. Debbie Baskin, Acting Chair, Department of Criminal Justice, 323-343-4610.

■ CALIFORNIA STATE UNIVERSITY, SACRAMENTO

Graduate Studies, College of Health and Human Services, Division of Criminal Justice, Sacramento, CA 95819-6048

AWARDS MS. Part-time programs available.

Students: 28 full-time (14 women), 47 part-time (19 women); includes 19 minority (5 African Americans, 3 Asian Americans or Pacific Islanders, 10 Hispanic Americans, 1 Native American), 1 international.

Degree requirements: For master's, thesis or alternative, writing proficiency exam.

Entrance requirements: For master's, TOEFL, BA in criminal justice or equivalent, minimum GPA of 2.5 during previous 2 years. *Application deadline:* For fall admission, 4/15; for spring admission, 11/1. *Application fee:* $55.

Expenses: Tuition, state resident: full-time $1,965; part-time $668 per semester. Tuition, nonresident: part-time $246 per unit.
Financial support: Career-related internships or fieldwork and Federal Work-Study available. Support available to part-time students. Financial award application deadline: 3/1.
Dr. William Vizzard, Chair, 916-278-6487.
Application contact: Dr. Thomas Phelps, Coordinator, 916-278-7048.

■ CALIFORNIA STATE UNIVERSITY, SAN BERNARDINO

Graduate Studies, College of Social and Behavioral Sciences, Department of Criminal Justice, San Bernardino, CA 92407-2397

AWARDS MA. Part-time programs available.

Faculty: 7 full-time (2 women), 2 part-time/adjunct (0 women).
Students: 19 full-time (14 women), 15 part-time (12 women); includes 19 minority (7 African Americans, 3 Asian Americans or Pacific Islanders, 9 Hispanic Americans), 3 international. Average age 27. 25 applicants, 80% accepted. In 2001, 1 degree awarded.
Degree requirements: For master's, comprehensive exam or thesis.
Entrance requirements: For master's, GRE General Test, minimum GPA of 3.0. *Application deadline:* For fall admission, 9/1 (priority date). Applications are processed on a rolling basis. *Application fee:* $55.
Expenses: Tuition, nonresident: full-time $4,428. Required fees: $1,733.
Financial support: Research assistantships, career-related internships or fieldwork, Federal Work-Study, and institutionally sponsored loans available. Support available to part-time students.
Faculty research: Crime seriousness, fear of crime, victimization, corrections management, crime correlates.
Dr. Larry Gaines, Chair, 909-880-5506, *Fax:* 909-880-7025, *E-mail:* lgaines@csusb.edu.

■ CALIFORNIA STATE UNIVERSITY, STANISLAUS

Graduate Programs, College of Arts, Letters, and Sciences, Department of Criminal Justice, Turlock, CA 95382

AWARDS MA.

Students: 15 (10 women); includes 7 minority (1 African American, 6 Hispanic Americans). 27 applicants, 100% accepted.
Degree requirements: For master's, thesis optional.
Entrance requirements: For master's, minimum GPA of 3.0, references, research paper.
Expenses: Tuition, nonresident: part-time $246 per unit. Required fees: $1,919. Tuition and fees vary according to campus/location and program.
Financial support: Application deadline: 3/2.
Dr. Paul O'Brien, Chair, 209-677-3498.
Application contact: Dr. Peter Nelligan, Director, 209-667-3408.

■ CENTRAL CONNECTICUT STATE UNIVERSITY

School of Graduate Studies, School of Arts and Sciences, Department of Criminology and Criminal Justice, New Britain, CT 06050-4010

AWARDS Criminal justice (MS).

Faculty: 9 full-time (4 women), 3 part-time/adjunct (1 woman).
Students: 5 full-time (4 women), 29 part-time (18 women); includes 9 minority (5 African Americans, 1 Asian American or Pacific Islander, 2 Hispanic Americans, 1 Native American). Average age 33. 15 applicants, 93% accepted. In 2001, 7 degrees awarded.
Entrance requirements: For master's, TOEFL, minimum GPA of 3.0. *Application deadline:* For fall admission, 8/10 (priority date); for spring admission, 12/10. Applications are processed on a rolling basis. *Application fee:* $40.
Expenses: Tuition, state resident: full-time $2,772; part-time $245 per credit. Tuition, nonresident: full-time $7,726; part-time $245 per credit. Required fees: $2,102. Tuition and fees vary according to course level and degree level.
Financial support: Application deadline: 3/15.
Dr. Susan Pease, Chair, 860-832-3005.
Application contact: Dr. Stephen Cox, Coordinator.

■ CENTRAL MICHIGAN UNIVERSITY

College of Graduate Studies, College of Humanities and Social and Behavioral Sciences, Department of Sociology, Anthropology and Social Work, Mount Pleasant, MI 48859

AWARDS Social and criminal justice (MA); sociology (MA).

Degree requirements: For master's, thesis or alternative.
Entrance requirements: For master's, 20 hours in sociology, minimum GPA of 3.0.
Expenses: Tuition, state resident: part-time $182 per unit. Tuition, nonresident: part-time $182 per unit. Required fees: $208 per semester. Part-time tuition and fees vary according to course load.
Faculty research: Sociological theory, race concept, environmental justice, cultural anthropology.

■ CENTRAL MISSOURI STATE UNIVERSITY

School of Graduate Studies, College of Applied Sciences and Technology, Department of Safety Science Technology, Warrensburg, MO 64093

AWARDS Human services/public services (Ed S); industrial hygiene (MS); industrial safety management (MS); occupational safety management (MS); public services administration (MS); safety management (MS); secondary education/safety education (MSE); security (MS); transportation safety (MS). Part-time programs available.

Faculty: 7 full-time (2 women), 3 part-time/adjunct (0 women).
Students: 7 full-time (4 women), 39 part-time (15 women); includes 5 minority (4 Hispanic Americans, 1 Native American). Average age 37. 20 applicants, 75% accepted. In 2001, 40 degrees awarded.
Degree requirements: For master's, comprehensive exam (MS), comprehensive exam or thesis (MSE).
Entrance requirements: For master's, GRE General Test, minimum GPA of 2.5, 15 hours in related area (MS); minimum GPA of 2.75, teaching certificate (MSE); for Ed S, master's degree in related field. *Application deadline:* Applications are processed on a rolling basis. *Application fee:* $25 ($50 for international students).
Expenses: Tuition, area resident: Full-time $4,200; part-time $175 per credit hour. Tuition, nonresident: full-time $8,352; part-time $348 per credit hour.
Financial support: In 2001–02, 2 research assistantships with full and partial tuition reimbursements (averaging $8,000 per year), 9 teaching assistantships (averaging $4,000 per year) were awarded. Federal Work-Study, scholarships/grants, unspecified assistantships, and administrative and laboratory assistantships also available. Support available to part-time students. Financial award application deadline: 3/1; financial award applicants required to submit FAFSA.
Faculty research: Hazard assessment, crisis and disaster, ergonomics, fire science, safety management. *Total annual research expenditures:* $2,000.
Larry Womble, Interim Chair, 660-543-8764, *Fax:* 660-543-8142, *E-mail:* womble@cmsu1.cmsu.edu. *Web site:* http://www.cmsu.edu/

■ CENTRAL MISSOURI STATE UNIVERSITY

School of Graduate Studies, College of Education and Human Services, Department of Criminal Justice, Warrensburg, MO 64093

AWARDS Criminal justice (MS), including administration of justice, administration/corrections, administrative/juvenile justices, corrections; human services-public services (Ed S). Part-time programs available.

Central Missouri State University (continued)

Faculty: 13 full-time (2 women), 1 part-time/adjunct (0 women).
Students: 16 full-time (9 women), 90 part-time (35 women); includes 6 minority (4 African Americans, 2 Hispanic Americans), 1 international. Average age 32. 45 applicants, 84% accepted. In 2001, 14 degrees awarded.
Degree requirements: For master's, thesis or comprehensive exam; for Ed S, thesis.
Entrance requirements: For master's, GRE General Test, minimum GPA of 2.75, 15 hours in criminal justice; for Ed S, master's degree in related field, minimum GPA of 3.25. *Application deadline:* Applications are processed on a rolling basis. *Application fee:* $25 ($50 for international students).
Expenses: Tuition, area resident: Full-time $4,200; part-time $175 per credit hour. Tuition, nonresident: full-time $8,352; part-time $348 per credit hour.
Financial support: In 2001–02, 1 research assistantship with partial tuition reimbursement (averaging $5,440 per year), 7 teaching assistantships with partial tuition reimbursements (averaging $4,125 per year) were awarded. Federal Work-Study, scholarships/grants, unspecified assistantships, and 2 administrative assistantships also available. Support available to part-time students. Financial award application deadline: 3/1; financial award applicants required to submit FAFSA.
Faculty research: Arson, capital punishments, electronic monitoring, terrorism, juvenile justice.
Dr. Richard N. Holden, Chair, 660-543-4950, *Fax:* 660-543-8306, *E-mail:* holden@cmsu1.cmsu.edu. *Web site:* http://www.cmsu.edu/

■ CHAMINADE UNIVERSITY OF HONOLULU

Graduate Programs, Program in Criminal Justice Administration, Honolulu, HI 96816-1578

AWARDS MSCJA. Part-time and evening/weekend programs available.

Faculty: 3 full-time (1 woman), 14 part-time/adjunct (5 women).
Students: 37 full-time (11 women), 19 part-time (7 women); includes 31 minority (7 African Americans, 12 Asian Americans or Pacific Islanders, 4 Hispanic Americans, 8 Native Americans), 3 international. Average age 30. 20 applicants, 80% accepted. In 2001, 18 degrees awarded.
Degree requirements: For master's, thesis optional.
Entrance requirements: For master's, GRE, TOEFL, minimum undergraduate GPA of 3.0. *Application deadline:* For fall admission, 9/1 (priority date). Applications are processed on a rolling basis. *Application fee:* $50. Electronic applications accepted.
Financial support: In 2001–02, 16 students received support. Career-related internships or fieldwork available. Financial award application deadline: 3/1.
Faculty research: Penology, juvenile delinquency, multicultural and ethnic diversity in criminology, law enforcement administration and training.
Dr. Dorothy M. Goldsborough, Director, 808-735-4703, *Fax:* 808-739-4614, *E-mail:* dgoldsbo@chaminade.edu.

Find an in-depth description at www.petersons.com/gradchannel.

■ CHARLESTON SOUTHERN UNIVERSITY

Program in Criminal Justice, Charleston, SC 29423-8087

AWARDS MSCJ. Part-time and evening/weekend programs available.

Faculty: 4 full-time (3 women), 2 part-time/adjunct (0 women).
Students: 4 full-time (3 women), 24 part-time (15 women); includes 8 minority (all African Americans), 3 international. 23 applicants, 52% accepted, 12 enrolled. In 2001, 2 degrees awarded.
Degree requirements: For master's, thesis optional.
Entrance requirements: For master's, GRE or MAT, bachelor's degree in criminal justice. *Application fee:* $25.
Expenses: Tuition: Full-time $6,184; part-time $200 per credit hour. Part-time tuition and fees vary according to program.
Financial support: Research assistantships, institutionally sponsored loans available. Financial award application deadline: 4/15; financial award applicants required to submit FAFSA.
Faculty research: Law enforcement, corrections, legal issues.
Dr. Beth McConnell, Chair, 843-863-7131, *E-mail:* bmcconne@csuniv.edu.
Application contact: Heather Brooks, Graduate School Coordinator, 843-863-7534, *Fax:* 843-863-7070, *E-mail:* hbrooks@csuniv.edu.

■ CHICAGO STATE UNIVERSITY

Graduate Studies, College of Arts and Sciences, Department of Criminal Justice, Chicago, IL 60628

AWARDS MS. Part-time and evening/weekend programs available.

Faculty: 3 full-time (0 women).
Students: 17 full-time (8 women), 44 part-time (21 women). 20 applicants, 50% accepted.
Entrance requirements: For master's, minimum GPA of 2.75. *Application deadline:* For fall admission, 7/1; for spring admission, 11/10. Applications are processed on a rolling basis. *Application fee:* $25.
Financial support: Research assistantships, career-related internships or fieldwork, Federal Work-Study, scholarships/grants, and tuition waivers (full) available.
Faculty research: Gang crime.
Dr. Mark Cooper, Chairperson, 773-995-2108, *Fax:* 773-995-3819, *E-mail:* ce-davis@csu.edu.
Application contact: Graduate Studies Office, 773-995-2404.

■ CLARK ATLANTA UNIVERSITY

School of Arts and Sciences, Department of Criminal Justice, Atlanta, GA 30314

AWARDS MA. Part-time programs available.

Degree requirements: For master's, one foreign language, thesis.
Entrance requirements: For master's, GRE General Test, minimum GPA of 2.5.
Faculty research: Race and crime, black ex-offenders in the labor market.

■ COLORADO TECHNICAL UNIVERSITY DENVER CAMPUS

Program in Computer Science, Greenwood Village, CO 80111

AWARDS Computer systems security (MSCS); software engineering (MSCS); software project management (MSCS). Part-time and evening/weekend programs available.

Faculty: 4 full-time (2 women), 4 part-time/adjunct (2 women).
Students: 24 full-time (4 women), 2 part-time (1 woman); includes 9 minority (3 African Americans, 6 Asian Americans or Pacific Islanders). Average age 34. 6 applicants, 83% accepted, 5 enrolled. In 2001, 10 master's awarded.
Degree requirements: For master's, thesis or alternative. *Median time to degree:* Master's–2 years full-time, 3 years part-time.
Entrance requirements: For master's, minimum undergraduate GPA of 3.0, resume. *Application deadline:* For fall admission, 10/2; for winter admission, 1/3; for spring admission, 4/3. Applications are processed on a rolling basis. *Application fee:* $100.
Expenses: Tuition: Full-time $6,960; part-time $290 per credit. Required fees: $40 per quarter. One-time fee: $100. Tuition and fees vary according to course load and degree level.
Financial support: Federal Work-Study and scholarships/grants available. Support available to part-time students. Financial award applicants required to submit FAFSA.
Dr. Jack Klag, Dean of Computer Science, 719-590-6850, *Fax:* 719-598-3740, *E-mail:* jklag@coloradotech.edu.
Application contact: Suzanne Hyman, Director of Admissions, 303-694-6600, *Fax:* 303-694-6673, *E-mail:* shyman@coloradotech.edu. *Web site:* http://www.coloradotech.edu/

■ COLUMBIA COLLEGE

Program in Criminal Justice, Columbia, MO 65216-0002

AWARDS MSCJ. Part-time and evening/weekend programs available.

Faculty: 1 full-time (0 women), 3 part-time/adjunct (1 woman).
Students: 35 full-time (19 women); includes 7 minority (5 African Americans, 2 Native Americans). Average age 34. 7 applicants, 100% accepted. In 2001, 7 degrees awarded.
Degree requirements: For master's, final exams, culminating experience (intensive writing seminar). *Median time to degree:* Master's–2 years full-time.
Entrance requirements: For master's, bachelor's degree in criminal justice, minimum GPA of 3.0. *Application deadline:* For fall admission, 8/1 (priority date); for spring admission, 12/15 (priority date). Applications are processed on a rolling basis. *Application fee:* $25 ($50 for international students).
Expenses: Tuition: Full-time $2,985; part-time $199 per credit hour. Full-time tuition and fees vary according to campus/location.
Financial support: Career-related internships or fieldwork, institutionally sponsored loans, and scholarships/grants available. Support available to part-time students. Financial award applicants required to submit FAFSA.
Faculty research: Organized crime, policing in America.
Dr. Michael Lyman, Chairman, 573-875-7472, *Fax:* 573-875-7209, *E-mail:* mlyman@email.ccis.edu.
Application contact: Regina Morin, Director of Admissions, 573-875-7354, *Fax:* 573-875-7506, *E-mail:* rmmorin@email.ccis.edu. *Web site:* http://www.ccis.edu/academics/graduate/mscj

■ CONCORDIA UNIVERSITY

College of Graduate and Continuing Studies, School of Human Services, St. Paul, MN 55104-5494

AWARDS Community education (MA Ed); criminal justice (MAHS); early childhood education (MA Ed); family studies (MAHS); leadership (MAHS); parish education (MA Ed); school-age care (MA Ed); youth development (MA Ed). Evening/weekend programs available. Postbaccalaureate distance learning degree programs offered (minimal on-campus study).

Faculty: 8 full-time (3 women), 98 part-time/adjunct (51 women).
Students: 161 full-time (136 women); includes 24 minority (20 African Americans, 2 Asian Americans or Pacific Islanders, 2 Hispanic Americans). Average age 34. 50 applicants, 90% accepted. In 2001, 18 degrees awarded.
Degree requirements: For master's, thesis or alternative, final project.
Entrance requirements: For master's, leadership portfolio, minimum GPA of 2.75. *Application deadline:* Applications are processed on a rolling basis. *Application fee:* $50. Electronic applications accepted.
Expenses: Tuition: Part-time $300 per semester hour. Tuition and fees vary according to program.
Financial support: Federal Work-Study available. Support available to part-time students. Financial award application deadline: 4/6.
James Ollhoff, Associate Dean, 651-603-6148, *E-mail:* ollhoff@csp.edu.
Application contact: Gail Ann Wells, Marketing Coordinator, 651-603-6186, *Fax:* 651-603-6144, *E-mail:* wells@csp.edu. *Web site:* http://www.cshs.csp.edu/

■ COPPIN STATE COLLEGE

Division of Graduate Studies, Division of Arts and Sciences, Department of Criminal Justice and Law Enforcement, Baltimore, MD 21216-3698

AWARDS Criminal justice (MS). Part-time and evening/weekend programs available.

Faculty: 6 full-time (1 woman), 2 part-time/adjunct (1 woman).
Students: 8 full-time (7 women), 44 part-time (26 women); includes 49 minority (all African Americans), 2 international. 35 applicants, 83% accepted. In 2001, 18 degrees awarded.
Degree requirements: For master's, thesis.
Entrance requirements: For master's, GRE, minimum GPA of 3.0. *Application deadline:* For fall admission, 7/15 (priority date); for spring admission, 12/15 (priority date). Applications are processed on a rolling basis. *Application fee:* $25.
Expenses: Tuition, state resident: full-time $3,576; part-time $149 per credit. Tuition, nonresident: full-time $6,360; part-time $265 per credit. Required fees: $589; $589 per year.
Financial support: Federal Work-Study, institutionally sponsored loans, and scholarships/grants available. Support available to part-time students. Financial award application deadline: 4/1; financial award applicants required to submit FAFSA.
Dr. Concetta Culliver, Chair, 410-951-3044, *E-mail:* cculliver@coppin.edu.
Application contact: Vell Lyles, Associate Vice President for Enrollment Management, 410-951-3575, *E-mail:* vlyles@coppin.edu.

■ DELTA STATE UNIVERSITY

Graduate Programs, College of Arts and Sciences, Department of Social Sciences, Program in Criminal Justice, Cleveland, MS 38733-0001

AWARDS MSCJ. Part-time programs available.

Degree requirements: For master's, thesis or alternative.
Application deadline: For fall admission, 8/1 (priority date); for spring admission, 12/1 (priority date). Applications are processed on a rolling basis. *Application fee:* $0.
Expenses: Tuition, state resident: full-time $3,100; part-time $144 per hour. Tuition, nonresident: full-time $7,174; part-time $382 per hour.
Financial support: Research assistantships, career-related internships or fieldwork, Federal Work-Study, and institutionally sponsored loans available. Support available to part-time students. Financial award application deadline: 6/1.

■ DRURY UNIVERSITY

Program in Criminology/Criminal Justice, Springfield, MO 65802-3791

AWARDS Criminal justice (MS); criminology (MA). Part-time and evening/weekend programs available.

Students: Average age 33.
Degree requirements: For master's, thesis (for some programs).
Entrance requirements: For master's, GMAT or MAT. *Application deadline:* For fall admission, 8/26 (priority date); for spring admission, 1/15 (priority date). Applications are processed on a rolling basis. *Application fee:* $25. Electronic applications accepted.
Expenses: Contact institution.
Financial support: Application deadline: 10/15;
Faculty research: Gangs, fear of crime, social justice, social change and law, drug laws in Iran.
Dr. Victor Agruso, Graduate Director, 417-873-7306, *Fax:* 417-873-7529, *E-mail:* vagruso@lib.drury.edu.
Application contact: Dr. Jane Bufkin, Director, 417-873-6948, *Fax:* 417-873-7529, *E-mail:* grad@drury.edu. *Web site:* http://www.drury.edu/info/academic/depart/MAcrim.html

■ EAST CAROLINA UNIVERSITY

Graduate School, School of Social Work and Criminal Justice Studies, Department of Criminal Justice Studies, Greenville, NC 27858-4353

AWARDS MA.

Students: 12 full-time (7 women), 18 part-time (8 women); includes 11 minority (10 African Americans, 1 Hispanic American). Average age 31. 25 applicants, 68% accepted.
Degree requirements: For master's, comprehensive exam.
Application deadline: For fall admission, 1/15 (priority date). *Application fee:* $45.
Expenses: Tuition, state resident: full-time $2,636. Tuition, nonresident: full-time $11,365.
Financial support: Application deadline: 6/1.

East Carolina University (continued)
Dr. Mary Jackson, Director of Graduate Studies, 252-328-1448, *Fax:* 252-328-4196, *E-mail:* jacksonm@mail.ecu.edu.

■ EAST CENTRAL UNIVERSITY

Graduate School, Department of Human Resources, Ada, OK 74820-6899

AWARDS Administration (MSHR); counseling (MSHR); criminal justice (MSHR); rehabilitation counseling (MSHR). Part-time and evening/weekend programs available.

Degree requirements: For master's, thesis optional.
Entrance requirements: For master's, GRE General Test, MAT, minimum GPA of 2.5.
Expenses: Tuition, state resident: part-time $96 per credit hour. Tuition, nonresident: part-time $225 per credit hour. Full-time tuition and fees vary according to course load.

■ EASTERN KENTUCKY UNIVERSITY

The Graduate School, College of Justice and Safety, Criminal Justice Program, Richmond, KY 40475-3102

AWARDS Corrections and juvenile services (MS); criminal justice (MS); criminal justice education (MS); loss prevention administration (MS); police studies (MS). Part-time programs available.

Faculty: 17 full-time (3 women).
Students: 53 full-time (27 women), 6 part-time (3 women); includes 8 minority (6 African Americans, 2 Hispanic Americans), 2 international. 93 applicants, 60% accepted. In 2001, 25 degrees awarded.
Degree requirements: For master's, thesis optional.
Entrance requirements: For master's, GRE General Test, minimum GPA of 3.0. *Application fee:* $0.
Expenses: Tuition, state resident: full-time $1,468; part-time $165 per credit hour. Tuition, nonresident: full-time $4,034; part-time $450 per credit hour.
Financial support: Research assistantships, teaching assistantships, career-related internships or fieldwork and Federal Work-Study available. Support available to part-time students. *Total annual research expenditures:* $37.5 million.
Dr. Victor E. Kappeler, Professor, 859-622-1980, *E-mail:* brenda.kelley@eku.edu. *Web site:* http://www.eku.edu/

■ EASTERN MICHIGAN UNIVERSITY

Graduate School, College of Arts and Sciences, Department of Sociology, Anthropology and Criminology, Program in Criminology and Criminal Justice, Ypsilanti, MI 48197

AWARDS MA. Evening/weekend programs available.

Degree requirements: For master's, thesis optional.
Entrance requirements: For master's, TOEFL. *Application deadline:* For fall admission, 5/15; for spring admission, 3/15. Applications are processed on a rolling basis. *Application fee:* $30.
Expenses: Tuition, state resident: part-time $285 per credit hour. Tuition, nonresident: part-time $510 per credit hour.
Financial support: Fellowships, teaching assistantships available. Support available to part-time students. Financial award application deadline: 3/15; financial award applicants required to submit FAFSA.
Dr. Paul Leighton, Coordinator, 734-487-0012.

■ EAST TENNESSEE STATE UNIVERSITY

School of Graduate Studies, College of Arts and Sciences, Department of Criminal Justice and Criminology, Johnson City, TN 37614

AWARDS MA. Part-time and evening/weekend programs available.

Faculty: 7 full-time (3 women).
Students: 21 full-time (11 women), 13 part-time (7 women); includes 4 minority (all African Americans). Average age 28. In 2001, 6 degrees awarded.
Degree requirements: For master's, thesis or alternative.
Entrance requirements: For master's, GRE General Test, TOEFL, minimum GPA of 3.0. *Application deadline:* For fall admission, 7/15 (priority date); for spring admission, 11/1. Applications are processed on a rolling basis. *Application fee:* $25 ($35 for international students).
Expenses: Tuition, state resident: part-time $181 per hour. Tuition, nonresident: part-time $270 per hour. Required fees: $220 per term.
Financial support: In 2001–02, 6 research assistantships with full tuition reimbursements were awarded; teaching assistantships with full tuition reimbursements, career-related internships or fieldwork, Federal Work-Study, and institutionally sponsored loans also available. Financial award application deadline: 4/1.
Faculty research: Death penalty, white-collar crime, research methods, criminological theory.
Dr. John Whitehead, Chair, 423-439-5346, *Fax:* 423-439-4660, *E-mail:* whitehej@etsu.edu. *Web site:* http://www.etsu.edu/

■ FERRIS STATE UNIVERSITY

College of Education and Human Services, School of Criminal Justice, Big Rapids, MI 49307

AWARDS MS. Part-time programs available.

Faculty: 5 full-time (2 women).
Students: 27 full-time (15 women), 43 part-time (10 women); includes 16 minority (12 African Americans, 1 Asian American or Pacific Islander, 1 Hispanic American, 2 Native Americans), 3 international. Average age 26. In 2001, 15 degrees awarded.
Degree requirements: For master's, thesis optional.
Entrance requirements: For master's, bachelor's degree in criminal justice or related field, minimum GPA of 3.0. *Application deadline:* For fall admission, 8/23 (priority date); for winter admission, 12/10 (priority date). Applications are processed on a rolling basis. *Application fee:* $30. Electronic applications accepted.
Expenses: Tuition, state resident: full-time $2,335; part-time $196 per credit hour. Tuition, nonresident: full-time $4,945; part-time $414 per credit hour. Required fees: $200 per semester.
Financial support: In 2001–02, 4 students received support, including research assistantships (averaging $3,960 per year); career-related internships or fieldwork also available.
Faculty research: Policy enactment, health and safety issues, criminological theory, juvenile justice, policy techniques, job satisfaction.
Dr. Frank Crowe, Acting Director, 231-591-2840, *Fax:* 231-591-3792, *E-mail:* crowef@ferris.edu.
Application contact: Dr. Nancy L. Hogan, Assistant Professor, 231-591-2664, *Fax:* 231-591-3792, *E-mail:* nancy_hogan@ferris.edu. *Web site:* http://www.ferris.edu/

■ FITCHBURG STATE COLLEGE

Division of Graduate and Continuing Education, Program in Criminal Justice, Fitchburg, MA 01420-2697

AWARDS MS. Part-time and evening/weekend programs available.

Students: In 2001, 1 degree awarded.
Entrance requirements: For master's, GRE General Test or MAT. *Application deadline:* Applications are processed on a rolling basis. *Application fee:* $10.
Expenses: Tuition, state resident: part-time $150 per credit. Required fees: $7 per credit. $65 per term. Tuition and fees vary according to course load.
Financial support: In 2001–02, research assistantships with partial tuition reimbursements (averaging $5,500 per year), teaching assistantships with partial tuition reimbursements (averaging $5,500 per year) were awarded. Federal Work-Study and unspecified assistantships also available. Support available to part-time students. Financial award application

deadline: 3/1; financial award applicants required to submit FAFSA.
Dr. Paul Weizer, Chair, 978-665-3272, *Fax:* 978-665-3658, *E-mail:* gce@fsc.edu.
Application contact: Director of Admissions, 978-665-3144, *Fax:* 978-665-4540, *E-mail:* admissions@fsc.edu. *Web site:* http://www.fsc.edu/

■ FLORIDA ATLANTIC UNIVERSITY

College of Architecture, Urban and Public Affairs, Department of Criminology and Criminal Justice, Boca Raton, FL 33431-0991

AWARDS MJPM. Part-time and evening/weekend programs available. Postbaccalaureate distance learning degree programs offered.

Faculty: 6 full-time (3 women), 1 part-time/adjunct (0 women).
Students: 3 full-time (all women), 12 part-time (7 women); includes 3 minority (2 African Americans, 1 Hispanic American), 1 international. Average age 33. 12 applicants, 42% accepted, 3 enrolled. In 2001, 6 degrees awarded.
Degree requirements: For master's, thesis optional.
Entrance requirements: For master's, GRE General Test, TOEFL, minimum GPA of 3.0, previous undergraduate course work in statistics and criminology. *Application deadline:* For fall admission, 4/1 (priority date); for spring admission, 10/15 (priority date). Applications are processed on a rolling basis. *Application fee:* $20. Electronic applications accepted.
Expenses: Tuition, state resident: full-time $3,098; part-time $172 per credit. Tuition, nonresident: full-time $10,427; part-time $579 per credit.
Financial support: In 2001–02, 1 research assistantship with partial tuition reimbursement (averaging $7,500 per year) was awarded; institutionally sponsored loans, scholarships/grants, and unspecified assistantships also available. Financial award application deadline: 4/1.
Faculty research: Restorative, justice corrections, logic modeling, criminal justice management, crime causation.
Dr. Dave Kalinich, Chair, 561-297-3240, *E-mail:* kalinich@fau.edu.
Application contact: Jeanne Stinchcomts, Coordinator of Academic Programs, 954-762-5662, *E-mail:* stinchc@fau.edu. *Web site:* http://www.fau.edu/divdept/cupa/depts/cj.htm

■ FLORIDA GULF COAST UNIVERSITY

College of Public and Social Services, Program in Public Administration, Fort Myers, FL 33965-6565

AWARDS Criminal justice (MPA); environmental policy (MPA); general public administration (MPA); management (MPA).

Faculty: 16 full-time (9 women), 7 part-time/adjunct (1 woman).
Students: 7 full-time (4 women), 58 part-time (31 women); includes 5 minority (2 African Americans, 2 Hispanic Americans, 1 Native American), 1 international. Average age 38. 18 applicants, 83% accepted, 10 enrolled. In 2001, 18 degrees awarded.
Entrance requirements: For master's, GRE General Test, MAT, minimum GPA of 3.0. *Application deadline:* Applications are processed on a rolling basis. *Application fee:* $20. Electronic applications accepted.
Expenses: Tuition, state resident: part-time $164 per credit hour. Tuition, nonresident: part-time $571 per credit hour. Required fees: $36 per semester.
Financial support: In 2001–02, 5 research assistantships were awarded; career-related internships or fieldwork and tuition waivers (full and partial) also available. Support available to part-time students.
Faculty research: Personnel, public policy, public finance. *Total annual research expenditures:* $45,500.
Roberta Walsh, Chair, 239-590-7841, *Fax:* 239-590-7846, *E-mail:* rwalsh@fgcu.edu.
Application contact: Roger Green, Information Contact, 239-590-7838, *Fax:* 239-590-7846.

■ FLORIDA INTERNATIONAL UNIVERSITY

College of Health and Urban Affairs, School of Policy and Management, Department of Criminal Justice, Miami, FL 33199

AWARDS MS. Part-time and evening/weekend programs available.

Faculty: 12 full-time (4 women).
Students: 25 full-time (13 women), 55 part-time (27 women); includes 58 minority (21 African Americans, 1 Asian American or Pacific Islander, 36 Hispanic Americans). Average age 34. 54 applicants, 48% accepted, 18 enrolled. In 2001, 32 degrees awarded.
Degree requirements: For master's, thesis optional.
Entrance requirements: For master's, GRE General Test, TOEFL, minimum GPA of 3.0. *Application deadline:* For fall admission, 4/1 (priority date); for spring admission, 10/1. Applications are processed on a rolling basis. *Application fee:* $20.
Expenses: Tuition, state resident: full-time $2,916; part-time $162 per credit hour. Tuition, nonresident: full-time $10,245; part-time $569 per credit hour. Required fees: $168 per term.
Dr. Terry Buss, Director, School of Policy and Management, 305-348-2653, *Fax:* 305-348-5848, *E-mail:* busst@fiu.edu.

■ FLORIDA METROPOLITAN UNIVERSITY–BRANDON CAMPUS

Program in Criminal Justice, Tampa, FL 33619

AWARDS MS.

■ FLORIDA METROPOLITAN UNIVERSITY–PINELLAS CAMPUS

Program in Criminal Justice, Clearwater, FL 33759

AWARDS MS.

■ FLORIDA STATE UNIVERSITY

Graduate Studies, School of Criminology and Criminal Justice, Tallahassee, FL 32306

AWARDS MA, MSC, PhD, MPA/MSC. Part-time and evening/weekend programs available. Postbaccalaureate distance learning degree programs offered (no on-campus study).

Faculty: 12 full-time (1 woman).
Students: 77 full-time (44 women). Average age 30. 103 applicants, 50% accepted. In 2001, 17 master's, 1 doctorate awarded.
Degree requirements: For master's, thesis optional; for doctorate, thesis/dissertation.
Entrance requirements: For master's and doctorate, GRE General Test. *Application deadline:* For fall admission, 1/1 (priority date); for spring admission, 10/1. *Application fee:* $20. Electronic applications accepted.
Expenses: Tuition, state resident: part-time $163 per credit hour. Tuition, nonresident: part-time $570 per credit hour. Tuition and fees vary according to program.
Financial support: In 2001–02, 1 fellowship, 9 research assistantships with full tuition reimbursements (averaging $5,500 per year), 6 teaching assistantships with full tuition reimbursements (averaging $8,250 per year) were awarded. Career-related internships or fieldwork, Federal Work-Study, and institutionally sponsored loans also available. Support available to part-time students. Financial award application deadline: 2/1; financial award applicants required to submit FAFSA.
Faculty research: Criminological theory, criminal justice administration and planning, criminal justice evaluation, law and social control.
Daniel Maier-Katkin, Dean, 850-644-1298, *Fax:* 850-644-9614.
Application contact: Brenda McCarthy, Graduate Coordinator, 850-644-7657, *Fax:* 850-644-7364, *E-mail:* bmccarth@mailer.fsu.edu. *Web site:* http://www.criminology.fsu.edu/

■ FORDHAM UNIVERSITY

Graduate School of Arts and Sciences, Department of Sociology, New York, NY 10458

AWARDS Criminology (MA); sociology (MA, PhD), including demography, ethnic minorities, sociology of religions. Part-time and evening/weekend programs available.

Faculty: 21 full-time (11 women).

Fordham University (continued)
Students: 14 full-time (10 women), 19 part-time (7 women); includes 8 minority (4 African Americans, 1 Asian American or Pacific Islander, 3 Hispanic Americans), 6 international. 35 applicants, 60% accepted. In 2001, 4 master's, 3 doctorates awarded. Terminal master's awarded for partial completion of doctoral program.
Degree requirements: For master's, one foreign language, comprehensive exam; for doctorate, 2 foreign languages, thesis/dissertation, comprehensive exam.
Entrance requirements: For master's and doctorate, GRE General Test. *Application deadline:* For fall admission, 1/15 (priority date); for spring admission, 12/1. *Application fee:* $65. Electronic applications accepted.
Expenses: Tuition: Part-time $720 per credit. Required fees: $135 per semester.
Financial support: In 2001–02, 13 students received support, including fellowships with tuition reimbursements available (averaging $15,000 per year), 1 research assistantship with tuition reimbursement available (averaging $12,000 per year), teaching assistantships with tuition reimbursements available (averaging $14,000 per year); career-related internships or fieldwork, Federal Work-Study, institutionally sponsored loans, tuition waivers (full and partial), and unspecified assistantships also available. Financial award application deadline: 1/16.
Dr. Orlando Rodriguez, Chair, 718-817-3853, *Fax:* 718-817-3846, *E-mail:* orodriguez@fordham.edu.
Application contact: Dr. Craig W. Pilant, Assistant Dean, 718-817-4420, *Fax:* 718-817-3566, *E-mail:* pilant@fordham.edu. *Web site:* http://www.fordham.edu/gsas/

■ THE GEORGE WASHINGTON UNIVERSITY

Columbian College of Arts and Sciences, Department of Forensic Sciences, Program in Criminal Justice, Washington, DC 20052

AWARDS Crime and commerce (MA); criminal justice (MA); security management (MA).

Students: 1 full-time (0 women), 1 part-time. Average age 33. 9 applicants, 78% accepted. In 2001, 2 degrees awarded.
Degree requirements: For master's, comprehensive exam.
Entrance requirements: For master's, GRE General Test, minimum GPA of 3.0. *Application deadline:* For fall admission, 5/1. *Application fee:* $55.
Expenses: Tuition: Part-time $810 per credit. Required fees: $1 per credit.
Financial support: Application deadline: 2/1.
Dr. David Rowley, Chair, Department of Forensic Sciences, 202-994-7319. *Web site:* http://www.gwu.edu/~gradinfo/

■ GEORGIA STATE UNIVERSITY

College of Health and Human Sciences, Department of Criminal Justice, Atlanta, GA 30303-3083

AWARDS MS. Part-time and evening/weekend programs available.

Degree requirements: For master's, thesis or alternative.
Entrance requirements: For master's, GRE General Test, TOEFL. Electronic applications accepted.
Faculty research: Violence against women, social support and adolescent crime, agencies and assault victims, minority trust of police, active offender crime and minority status. *Web site:* http://www.cjgsu.net/

■ GRADUATE SCHOOL AND UNIVERSITY CENTER OF THE CITY UNIVERSITY OF NEW YORK

Graduate Studies, Program in Criminal Justice, New York, NY 10016-4039

AWARDS PhD.

Faculty: 28 full-time (6 women).
Students: 64 full-time (39 women), 37 part-time (15 women); includes 13 minority (7 African Americans, 2 Asian Americans or Pacific Islanders, 4 Hispanic Americans), 7 international. Average age 40. 59 applicants, 51% accepted, 21 enrolled.
Degree requirements: For doctorate, one foreign language, thesis/dissertation.
Entrance requirements: For doctorate, GRE General Test. *Application deadline:* For fall admission, 4/15. *Application fee:* $40.
Expenses: Tuition, state resident: part-time $245 per credit. Tuition, nonresident: part-time $425 per credit. Required fees: $72 per semester.
Financial support: In 2001–02, 13 students received support, including 7 fellowships; research assistantships, teaching assistantships, career-related internships or fieldwork, Federal Work-Study, institutionally sponsored loans, and tuition waivers (full and partial) also available. Financial award application deadline: 2/1; financial award applicants required to submit FAFSA.
Dr. Todd Clear, Executive Officer, 212-237-8470, *Fax:* 212-237-8940, *E-mail:* tclear@jjay.cuny.edu.

■ GRAMBLING STATE UNIVERSITY

Division of Graduate Studies, College of Liberal Arts, Program in Criminal Justice, Grambling, LA 71245

AWARDS MS. Part-time and evening/weekend programs available.

Entrance requirements: For master's, GRE General Test, minimum GPA of 2.5.
Faculty research: Corrections, terrorism, delinquency, complex organizations, postmodern theory. *Web site:* http://www.gram.edu/

■ GRAND VALLEY STATE UNIVERSITY

Social Science Division, School of Criminal Justice, Allendale, MI 49401-9403

AWARDS MS, MS/MA. Part-time and evening/weekend programs available. Postbaccalaureate distance learning degree programs offered (no on-campus study).

Faculty: 10 full-time (2 women).
Students: 6 full-time (all women), 22 part-time (11 women); includes 4 minority (2 African Americans, 1 Hispanic American, 1 Native American). Average age 36. 26 applicants, 88% accepted, 18 enrolled. In 2001, 2 degrees awarded.
Degree requirements: For master's, thesis or alternative.
Entrance requirements: For master's, GRE or MAT, minimum GPA of 3.0, 4-5 years of professional experience. *Application deadline:* For fall admission, 7/30 (priority date); for winter admission, 12/10 (priority date); for spring admission, 4/10 (priority date). *Application fee:* $20.
Expenses: Tuition, state resident: part-time $202 per credit hour. Tuition, nonresident: part-time $437 per credit hour.
Financial support: In 2001–02, research assistantships with full tuition reimbursements (averaging $4,000 per year); career-related internships or fieldwork, Federal Work-Study, and scholarships/grants also available. Financial award application deadline: 5/1.
Faculty research: Community policing, privatization of public services, correctional administration, juvenile justice issues/gangs, women's issues.
Dr. James Houston, Director, 616-336-7131, *Fax:* 616-336-7155, *E-mail:* houstonj@gvsu.edu.
Application contact: Dr. John Hewitt, Professor, 616-336-7145, *Fax:* 616-336-7155, *E-mail:* hewittj@gvsu.edu. *Web site:* http://www4.gvsu.edu/cj/

■ ILLINOIS STATE UNIVERSITY

Graduate School, College of Applied Science and Technology, Department of Criminal Justice Sciences, Normal, IL 61790-2200

AWARDS MA, MS.

Faculty: 10 full-time (4 women).
Students: 14 full-time (8 women), 21 part-time (12 women); includes 2 minority (both African Americans), 3 international. 12 applicants, 100% accepted. In 2001, 10 degrees awarded.
Degree requirements: For master's, thesis or alternative.

Entrance requirements: For master's, GRE General Test, minimum GPA of 2.6 in last 60 hours. *Application deadline:* Applications are processed on a rolling basis. *Application fee:* $30.
Expenses: Tuition, state resident: full-time $2,691; part-time $112 per credit hour. Tuition, nonresident: full-time $5,880; part-time $245 per credit hour. Required fees: $1,146; $48 per credit hour.
Financial support: In 2001–02, 11 research assistantships (averaging $6,975 per year) were awarded; teaching assistantships, career-related internships or fieldwork, tuition waivers (full and partial), and unspecified assistantships also available. Financial award application deadline: 4/1.
Faculty research: Program support regional alternative school. *Total annual research expenditures:* $44,303.
Dr. Thomas Ellsworth, Chairperson, 309-438-7626. *Web site:* http://www.ilstu.edu/depts/cjs/

■ INDIANA STATE UNIVERSITY

School of Graduate Studies, College of Arts and Sciences, Department of Criminology, Terre Haute, IN 47809-1401

AWARDS MA, MS. Part-time programs available.

Degree requirements: For master's, thesis.
Entrance requirements: For master's, minimum GPA of 2.75. Electronic applications accepted.
Faculty research: Violent crime, rape attitudes, classification of offenders, substance abuse, domestic violence.

■ INDIANA UNIVERSITY BLOOMINGTON

Graduate School, College of Arts and Sciences, Department of Criminal Justice, Bloomington, IN 47405

AWARDS Cross-cultural studies of crime and justice (MA, PhD); justice systems and processes (MA, PhD); law and society (MA, PhD); nature of crime (MA, PhD). Part-time programs available.

Faculty: 14 full-time (4 women).
Students: 22 full-time (9 women), 7 part-time (5 women); includes 2 minority (1 African American, 1 Native American), 2 international. Average age 29. In 2001, 5 degrees awarded. Terminal master's awarded for partial completion of doctoral program.
Degree requirements: For master's, thesis optional; for doctorate, thesis/dissertation, foreign language or research practicum.
Entrance requirements: For master's and doctorate, GRE General Test, TOEFL. *Application deadline:* For fall admission, 1/15. *Application fee:* $45 ($55 for international students). Electronic applications accepted.
Expenses: Contact institution.
Financial support: In 2001–02, 1 fellowship with full tuition reimbursement (averaging $13,000 per year), 19 teaching assistantships with full tuition reimbursements (averaging $9,100 per year) were awarded. Financial award application deadline: 1/15.
Edmund McGarrell, Chairperson, 812-855-9880, *E-mail:* mcgarrel@indiana.edu.
Application contact: Judy Kelley, Administrative Assistant, 812-855-9880, *Fax:* 812-855-5522, *E-mail:* kelleyj@indiana.edu. *Web site:* http://www.indiana.edu/~crimjust/

■ INDIANA UNIVERSITY NORTHWEST

School of Public and Environmental Affairs, Gary, IN 46408-1197

AWARDS Criminal justice (MPA); health services administration (MPA); human services administration (MPA); management of public affairs (MPA); non-profit management (NPMC); public management (PMC). Part-time programs available.

Faculty: 2 full-time (1 woman).
Students: 11 full-time (9 women), 88 part-time (58 women); includes 55 minority (45 African Americans, 10 Hispanic Americans). Average age 38. In 2001, 25 master's, 13 other advanced degrees awarded.
Entrance requirements: For master's, GRE General Test. *Application deadline:* For fall admission, 8/15 (priority date). Applications are processed on a rolling basis. *Application fee:* $25.
Expenses: Tuition, state resident: full-time $3,827. Tuition, nonresident: full-time $8,567. Required fees: $416.
Financial support: Career-related internships or fieldwork, Federal Work-Study, and tuition waivers (partial) available. Support available to part-time students. Financial award application deadline: 3/1.
Faculty research: Employment in income security policies, evidence in criminal justice, equal employment law, social welfare policy and welfare reform, public finance in developing countries.
Joseph M. Pellicciotti, Director, 219-980-6695, *Fax:* 219-980-6737, *E-mail:* jpelli@iunhaw1.iun.indiana.edu.
Application contact: Suzanne Green, Recorder, 219-980-6695, *Fax:* 219-980-6737, *E-mail:* sgreen@iunhaw1.iun.indiana.edu.

■ INDIANA UNIVERSITY OF PENNSYLVANIA

Graduate School and Research, College of Humanities and Social Sciences, Department of Criminology, Doctoral Program in Criminology, Indiana, PA 15705-1087

AWARDS PhD. Part-time programs available.

Students: 34 full-time (12 women), 3 part-time (2 women); includes 3 minority (2 African Americans, 1 Asian American or Pacific Islander), 3 international. Average age 32. 16 applicants, 50% accepted. In 2001, 5 degrees awarded.
Degree requirements: For doctorate, one foreign language, thesis/dissertation, comprehensive exam.
Entrance requirements: For doctorate, TOEFL, GRE, letters of recommendation (3), writing sample, interview. *Application deadline:* For fall admission, 7/1 (priority date); for spring admission, 11/1. Applications are processed on a rolling basis. *Application fee:* $30.
Expenses: Tuition, state resident: full-time $4,600; part-time $256 per credit hour. Tuition, nonresident: full-time $7,554; part-time $420 per credit hour. Required fees: $800. Part-time tuition and fees vary according to course load.
Financial support: In 2001–02, 2 fellowships (averaging $5,000 per year), 11 research assistantships with full and partial tuition reimbursements (averaging $6,170 per year), 4 teaching assistantships with partial tuition reimbursements (averaging $17,001 per year) were awarded. Federal Work-Study also available. Support available to part-time students. Financial award application deadline: 3/15; financial award applicants required to submit FAFSA.
Dr. Randy Martin, Graduate Coordinator, 724-357-5608, *E-mail:* rmartin@iup.edu.

■ INDIANA UNIVERSITY OF PENNSYLVANIA

Graduate School and Research, College of Humanities and Social Sciences, Department of Criminology, Master's Program in Criminology, Indiana, PA 15705-1087

AWARDS MA. Part-time and evening/weekend programs available.

Students: 38 full-time (19 women), 34 part-time (17 women); includes 10 minority (9 African Americans, 1 Hispanic American), 1 international. Average age 27. 77 applicants, 81% accepted. In 2001, 41 degrees awarded.
Degree requirements: For master's, thesis optional.
Entrance requirements: For master's, TOEFL, letters of recommendation (2). *Application deadline:* For fall admission, 7/1 (priority date); for spring admission, 11/1. Applications are processed on a rolling basis. *Application fee:* $30.

Indiana University of Pennsylvania (continued)

Expenses: Tuition, state resident: full-time $4,600; part-time $256 per credit hour. Tuition, nonresident: full-time $7,554; part-time $420 per credit hour. Required fees: $800. Part-time tuition and fees vary according to course load.
Financial support: In 2001–02, 1 fellowship (averaging $500 per year), 14 research assistantships with full and partial tuition reimbursements (averaging $5,040 per year) were awarded. Federal Work-Study also available. Support available to part-time students. Financial award application deadline: 3/15; financial award applicants required to submit FAFSA.
Dr. David Myers, Graduate Coordinator, 724-357-5611, *E-mail:* david@iup.edu.

■ INTER AMERICAN UNIVERSITY OF PUERTO RICO, METROPOLITAN CAMPUS

Graduate Programs, Division of Behavioral Science and Allied Professions, Program in Criminal Justice, San Juan, PR 00919-1293

AWARDS MA.

Degree requirements: For master's, comprehensive exam.
Entrance requirements: For master's, GRE or PAEG, interview. Electronic applications accepted.

■ IONA COLLEGE

School of Arts and Science, Program in Criminal Justice, New Rochelle, NY 10801-1890

AWARDS MS. Part-time and evening/weekend programs available.

Faculty: 7 full-time (1 woman).
Students: Average age 31. In 2001, 12 degrees awarded.
Degree requirements: For master's, thesis.
Application deadline: Applications are processed on a rolling basis. *Application fee:* $25.
Expenses: Tuition: Part-time $525 per credit.
Financial support: Unspecified assistantships available.
Dr. Robert Mealia, Chair, 914-633-2747, *E-mail:* rmealia@iona.edu.
Application contact: Alyce Ware, Associate Director of Graduate Recruitment, 914-633-2420, *Fax:* 914-633-2023, *E-mail:* aware@iona.edu. *Web site:* http://www.iona.edu/

■ JACKSON STATE UNIVERSITY

Graduate School, School of Liberal Arts, Center for Urban Affairs/Criminology and Justice Services, Jackson, MS 39217

AWARDS Criminology and justice service (MA). Part-time and evening/weekend programs available.

Degree requirements: For master's, thesis optional.
Entrance requirements: For master's, GRE General Test, TOEFL.

■ JACKSONVILLE STATE UNIVERSITY

College of Graduate Studies and Continuing Education, College of Arts and Sciences, Department of Criminal Justice, Jacksonville, AL 36265-1602

AWARDS MS. Part-time and evening/weekend programs available.

Degree requirements: For master's, thesis optional.
Entrance requirements: For master's, GRE General Test or MAT.

■ JOHN JAY COLLEGE OF CRIMINAL JUSTICE OF THE CITY UNIVERSITY OF NEW YORK

Graduate Studies, Programs in Criminal Justice, New York, NY 10019-1093

AWARDS Criminal justice (MA, PhD); criminology and deviance (PhD); forensic psychology (PhD); forensic science (PhD); law and philosophy (PhD); organizational behavior (PhD); public policy (PhD). Part-time and evening/weekend programs available.

Students: 33 full-time (20 women), 165 part-time (86 women); includes 68 minority (36 African Americans, 11 Asian Americans or Pacific Islanders, 21 Hispanic Americans). 150 applicants, 80% accepted. In 2001, 58 degrees awarded. Terminal master's awarded for partial completion of doctoral program.
Degree requirements: For master's, thesis or alternative; for doctorate, one foreign language, thesis/dissertation.
Entrance requirements: For master's, GRE General Test, TOEFL, minimum B average; for doctorate, GRE General Test, TOEFL. *Application deadline:* For fall admission, 6/30 (priority date); for spring admission, 12/1. Applications are processed on a rolling basis. *Application fee:* $40.
Expenses: Tuition, state resident: full-time $4,350; part-time $185 per credit. Tuition, nonresident: full-time $7,600; part-time $285 per credit. Required fees: $80; $40 per semester. Tuition and fees vary according to degree level.
Financial support: Career-related internships or fieldwork, Federal Work-Study, institutionally sponsored loans, and scholarships/grants available. Support available to part-time students. Financial award applicants required to submit FAFSA.
Dr. Andrew Karmen, Co-Director, 212-237-8695, *E-mail:* akarmen@jjay.cuny.edu.
Application contact: Shirley Rodriguez-Melendez, Admissions Assistant, 212-237-8863, *Fax:* 212-237-8777, *E-mail:* srodrigu@jjay.cuny.edu.

Find an in-depth description at www.petersons.com/gradchannel.

■ KENT STATE UNIVERSITY

College of Arts and Sciences, Department of Justice Studies, Kent, OH 44242-0001

AWARDS MA.

Degree requirements: For master's, thesis optional.
Entrance requirements: For master's, GRE General Test or MAT, minimum GPA of 2.75. Electronic applications accepted.

■ LAMAR UNIVERSITY

College of Graduate Studies, College of Arts and Sciences, Department of Sociology, Social Work, and Criminal Justice, Beaumont, TX 77710

AWARDS Applied criminology (MS). Part-time programs available.

Faculty: 5 full-time (2 women).
Students: 8 full-time (4 women), 5 part-time (3 women); includes 3 African Americans. Average age 32. 13 applicants, 69% accepted. In 2001, 7 degrees awarded.
Degree requirements: For master's, thesis or alternative, applied projects.
Entrance requirements: For master's, GRE General Test, TOEFL. *Application deadline:* For fall admission, 8/1 (priority date); for spring admission, 12/1 (priority date). Applications are processed on a rolling basis. *Application fee:* $25 ($50 for international students).
Expenses: Tuition, state resident: full-time $1,114. Tuition, nonresident: full-time $3,670.
Financial support: In 2001–02, 9 students received support, including 3 fellowships with partial tuition reimbursements available (averaging $1,000 per year); career-related internships or fieldwork, Federal Work-Study, and scholarships/grants also available. Support available to part-time students. Financial award application deadline: 4/1; financial award applicants required to submit FAFSA.
Faculty research: Corrections, planning and evaluations, juveniles, terrorism, Mexican criminal justice.
Dr. James J. Love, Chair, 409-880-8538, *Fax:* 409-880-2324.
Application contact: Dr. J. Rick Altemose, Graduate Program Director, 409-880-8549, *Fax:* 409-880-2324, *E-mail:* altemosejr@hal.lamar.edu.

■ LEWIS UNIVERSITY

College of Arts and Sciences, Program in Criminal/Social Justice, Romeoville, IL 60446

AWARDS Crinimal/social justice (MS); public safety (MPSA). Part-time and evening/weekend programs available.

Faculty: 4 full-time (1 woman), 11 part-time/adjunct (3 women).
Students: 26 full-time (10 women), 141 part-time (37 women); includes 46 minority (29 African Americans, 1 Asian American or Pacific Islander, 15 Hispanic Americans, 1 Native American), 1 international. Average age 37. In 2001, 63 degrees awarded. *Median time to degree:* Master's–2 years full-time, 3 years part-time.
Entrance requirements: For master's, bachelor's degree or a minimum of 12 related hours in criminal/social justice, 2 letters of recommendation. *Application deadline:* For fall admission, 9/1; for spring admission, 1/1. Applications are processed on a rolling basis. *Application fee:* $35.
Expenses: Tuition: Part-time $425. Tuition and fees vary according to program.
Financial support: In 2001–02, 28 students received support, including 5 research assistantships with full tuition reimbursements available (averaging $6,780 per year); career-related internships or fieldwork, scholarships/grants, and unspecified assistantships also available. Support available to part-time students. Financial award application deadline: 4/1; financial award applicants required to submit FAFSA.
Faculty research: Community policing, management, terrorism, biological warfare, drugs.
Dr. Edward Shannon, Chair of Criminal/Social Justice Department, 815-836-0500 Ext. 5949, *Fax:* 815-836-5870, *E-mail:* shannoed@lewisu.edu.
Application contact: Gayle Mikel, Coordinator, 815-835-0500 Ext. 5686, *Fax:* 815-836-5870. *Web site:* http://www.lewisu.edu/academics/grad.htm/

■ LINCOLN UNIVERSITY

Graduate School, College of Liberal Arts, Science, and Agriculture, Division of Social and Behavioral Sciences, Jefferson City, MO 65102

AWARDS History (MA); sociology (MA); sociology/criminal justice (MA). Part-time and evening/weekend programs available.

Faculty: 10 part-time/adjunct (1 woman).
Students: 2 full-time (1 woman), 21 part-time (15 women); includes 7 minority (all African Americans), 2 international. Average age 36. 3 applicants, 100% accepted, 3 enrolled. In 2001, 12 degrees awarded.
Degree requirements: For master's, thesis or alternative.
Entrance requirements: For master's, GRE General Test or MAT, minimum GPA of 2.75 in major, 2.5 overall. *Application deadline:* For fall admission, 7/1; for spring admission, 12/1. *Application fee:* $17.
Expenses: Tuition, state resident: part-time $136 per credit hour. Tuition, nonresident: part-time $272 per credit hour. Required fees: $50 per term.
Financial support: Fellowships available.
Faculty research: Rural black elderly, international politics, convict labor, blacks in higher education.
Dr. Antonio Holland, Head, 573-681-5145.

■ LONG ISLAND UNIVERSITY, BRENTWOOD CAMPUS

School of Public Service, Brentwood, NY 11717

AWARDS Criminal justice (MS); health administration (MPA); public administration (MPA). Part-time and evening/weekend programs available.

Students: Average age 39.
Application deadline: Applications are processed on a rolling basis. *Application fee:* $0.
Expenses: Tuition: Part-time $572 per credit. Part-time tuition and fees vary according to program.
Financial support: Scholarships/grants and unspecified assistantships available. Support available to part-time students.
Dr. Robert Sanatore, Head, 516-299-3017.

■ LONG ISLAND UNIVERSITY, C.W. POST CAMPUS

College of Management, School of Public Service, Department of Criminal Justice and Security Administration, Brookville, NY 11548-1300

AWARDS Fraud examination (MS); security administration (MS). Part-time and evening/weekend programs available.

Faculty: 5 full-time (1 woman), 11 part-time/adjunct (1 woman).
Students: 18 full-time (12 women), 38 part-time (19 women). Average age 28. 18 applicants, 94% accepted, 13 enrolled. In 2001, 35 degrees awarded.
Degree requirements: For master's, thesis.
Entrance requirements: For master's, minimum GPA of 3.0, background in criminal justice. *Application deadline:* For fall admission, 8/15; for spring admission, 12/15. Applications are processed on a rolling basis. *Application fee:* $30. Electronic applications accepted.
Expenses: Tuition: Full-time $10,296; part-time $572 per credit. Required fees: $380; $190 per semester.
Financial support: In 2001–02, 1 student received support, including research assistantships (averaging $6,000 per year); career-related internships or fieldwork, Federal Work-Study, institutionally sponsored loans, and unspecified assistantships also available. Support available to part-time students. Financial award application deadline: 5/15; financial award applicants required to submit CSS PROFILE or FAFSA.
Faculty research: Crime statistics, terrorism, women and law, policing.
Dr. Harvey Kushner, Chairperson, 516-299-2467, *Fax:* 516-299-2587, *E-mail:* hkushner@liu.edu.
Application contact: Laura Tojo, Advisor, 516-299-2986, *E-mail:* laura.tojo@liu.edu. *Web site:* http://www.liu.edu/com/

■ LONGWOOD UNIVERSITY

Graduate Programs, Department of Sociology, Farmville, VA 23909-1800

AWARDS Criminal justice (MS). Part-time and evening/weekend programs available.

Degree requirements: For master's, thesis (for some programs), comprehensive exam.
Entrance requirements: For master's, minimum GPA of 2.5.

■ LOYOLA UNIVERSITY CHICAGO

Graduate School, Department of Criminal Justice, Chicago, IL 60611-2196

AWARDS MA. Part-time and evening/weekend programs available.

Faculty: 8 full-time (1 woman), 2 part-time/adjunct (0 women).
Students: 16 full-time (11 women), 17 part-time (12 women); includes 7 minority (3 African Americans, 4 Hispanic Americans). Average age 25. 29 applicants, 93% accepted. In 2001, 6 degrees awarded.
Degree requirements: For master's, thesis or alternative, field practicum, comprehensive exam.
Entrance requirements: For master's, minimum GPA of 3.0. *Application deadline:* For fall admission, 6/15 (priority date); for spring admission, 1/5. Applications are processed on a rolling basis. *Application fee:* $40.
Expenses: Tuition: Part-time $529 per credit hour.
Financial support: In 2001–02, 2 students received support, including 2 research assistantships; career-related internships or fieldwork, scholarships/grants, and tuition waivers (full and partial) also available. Financial award application deadline: 2/1; financial award applicants required to submit FAFSA.
Faculty research: Crime and delinquency causation, effectiveness and efficiency of criminal justice system. *Total annual research expenditures:* $200,000.
Dr. Gad Bensinger, Director, 312-915-7568, *Fax:* 312-915-7650, *E-mail:* gbensin@luc.edu.

■ LOYOLA UNIVERSITY NEW ORLEANS

College of Arts and Sciences, Program in Criminal Justice, New Orleans, LA 70118-6195

AWARDS MCJ.

Faculty: 5 full-time (2 women), 2 part-time/adjunct (1 woman).
Students: 21 full-time (6 women), 4 part-time (2 women); includes 14 minority (13 African Americans, 1 Hispanic American). Average age 34. 10 applicants, 100% accepted, 10 enrolled.
Degree requirements: For master's, research and practicum.
Entrance requirements: For master's, GRE, TOEFL, MAT, resumé, interview, 3 letters of recommendation. *Application deadline:* Applications are processed on a rolling basis. *Application fee:* $20. Electronic applications accepted.
Expenses: Tuition: Part-time $764 per hour. Required fees: $122 per semester. Tuition and fees vary according to degree level and program.
Dr. William E. Thornton, Director, 504-865-3323, *Fax:* 504-865-3883, *E-mail:* thornton@loyno.edu.
Application contact: David Aplin, Assistant to the Director, 504-865-3323, *Fax:* 504-865-3883, *E-mail:* crimjust@loyno.edu. *Web site:* http://www.loyno.edu/

■ LYNN UNIVERSITY

School of Graduate Studies, Program in Criminal Justice Administration, Boca Raton, FL 33431-5598

AWARDS MS. Part-time and evening/weekend programs available.

Degree requirements: For master's, project.
Entrance requirements: For master's, MAT, TOEFL, sample of written work. Electronic applications accepted. *Web site:* http://www.lynn.edu

■ MADONNA UNIVERSITY

School of Business, Livonia, MI 48150-1173

AWARDS Business administration (MBA); international business (MSBA); leadership studies (MSBA); leadership studies in criminal justice (MSBA); quality and operations management (MSBA). Part-time and evening/weekend programs available. Postbaccalaureate distance learning degree programs offered (minimal on-campus study).

Faculty: 8 full-time (2 women), 13 part-time/adjunct (2 women).
Students: 115 full-time (15 women), 369 part-time (293 women). 92 applicants, 98% accepted. In 2001, 113 degrees awarded.
Degree requirements: For master's, thesis (for some programs), foreign language proficiency (international business).
Entrance requirements: For master's, GMAT, GRE General Test, minimum GPA of 3.0. *Application deadline:* For fall admission, 8/1 (priority date); for winter admission, 12/1 (priority date); for spring admission, 4/1 (priority date). Applications are processed on a rolling basis. *Application fee:* $0 ($25 for international students). Electronic applications accepted.
Expenses: Tuition: Part-time $325 per credit hour.
Financial support: Career-related internships or fieldwork, institutionally sponsored loans, and scholarships/grants available. Support available to part-time students.
Faculty research: Management, women in management, future studies.
Dr. Stuart Arends, Dean of Business School, 734-432-5366, *Fax:* 734-432-5364, *E-mail:* arends@smtp.munet.edu.
Application contact: Sandra Kellums, Coordinator of Graduate Admissions, 734-432-5667, *Fax:* 734-432-5862, *E-mail:* kellums@smtp.munet.edu. *Web site:* http://ww3.munet.edu/gradstdy

■ MARSHALL UNIVERSITY

Graduate College, College of Liberal Arts, Department of Criminal Justice, Huntington, WV 25755

AWARDS MS. Evening/weekend programs available.

Faculty: 4 full-time (2 women).
Students: 15 full-time (4 women), 16 part-time (9 women). In 2001, 4 degrees awarded.
Degree requirements: For master's, thesis optional.
Entrance requirements: For master's, GRE General Test.
Expenses: Tuition, state resident: part-time $147 per credit. Tuition, nonresident: part-time $468 per credit. Tuition and fees vary according to campus/location and reciprocity agreements.
Dr. Margaret Phipps Brown, Chairperson, 304-696-3086, *E-mail:* brownmp@marshall.edu.
Application contact: Ken O'Neal, Assistant Vice President, Adult Student Services, 304-746-2500 Ext. 1907, *Fax:* 304-746-1902, *E-mail:* oneal@marshall.edu.

■ MARYWOOD UNIVERSITY

Graduate School of Arts and Sciences, Department of Public Administration, Scranton, PA 18509-1598

AWARDS Criminal justice (MS); health services administration (MHSA); public administration (MPA). Part-time and evening/weekend programs available.

Faculty: 3 full-time (2 women), 8 part-time/adjunct (0 women).
Students: 16 full-time (9 women), 44 part-time (26 women); includes 2 minority (both African Americans). Average age 35. 23 applicants, 96% accepted. In 2001, 26 degrees awarded.
Degree requirements: For master's, thesis or alternative, internship/practicum.
Entrance requirements: For master's, TOEFL. *Application deadline:* For fall admission, 4/15; for spring admission, 11/15 (priority date). Applications are processed on a rolling basis. *Application fee:* $20. Electronic applications accepted.
Financial support: Research assistantships, career-related internships or fieldwork, scholarships/grants, and tuition waivers (partial) available. Support available to part-time students. Financial award application deadline: 2/15; financial award applicants required to submit FAFSA.
Faculty research: Long-term care management, nonprofit sector, volunteerism, Alzheimer's disease, gerontology.
Dr. Alice McDonnell, Chairperson, 570-348-6284.
Application contact: Deborah M. Flynn, Coordinator of Admissions, 570-340-6002, *Fax:* 570-961-4745, *E-mail:* gsas_adm@ac.marywood.edu.

■ MERCYHURST COLLEGE

Graduate Program, Program in Administration of Justice, Erie, PA 16546

AWARDS Administration of justice (MS); applied intelligence (MS). Part-time and evening/weekend programs available.

Faculty: 1 full-time (0 women), 8 part-time/adjunct (0 women).
Students: 38 full-time (18 women), 4 part-time; includes 2 minority (1 African American, 1 Hispanic American), 1 international. Average age 28. 16 applicants, 88% accepted. In 2001, 16 degrees awarded.
Degree requirements: For master's, thesis optional.
Entrance requirements: For master's, GRE General Test, MAT, or minimum GPA of 3.0. *Application deadline:* For fall admission, 8/1 (priority date); for spring admission, 1/1. Applications are processed on a rolling basis. *Application fee:* $35. Electronic applications accepted.
Financial support: In 2001–02, 4 fellowships with tuition reimbursements were awarded; research assistantships with tuition reimbursements, career-related internships or fieldwork, institutionally sponsored loans, scholarships/grants, and unspecified assistantships also available. Support available to part-time students. Financial award application deadline: 5/15.
Faculty research: Research methods, criminal justice administration, juvenile justice.
Dr. Frank E. Hagan, Director, 814-824-2265, *Fax:* 814-824-2438.
Application contact: Mary Ellen Dahlkemper, Director, Office of Adult and Graduate Programs, 814-824-2294, *Fax:*

814-824-2055, *E-mail:* medahlk@mercyhurst.edu.

■ METROPOLITAN STATE UNIVERSITY

College of Management, St. Paul, MN 55106-5000

AWARDS Finance (MBA); human resource management (MBA); information management (MMIS); international business (MBA); law enforcement (MPNA); management information systems (MBA); marketing (MBA); nonprofit management (MPNA); organizational studies (MBA); public administration (MPNA); purchasing management (MBA); systems management (MMIS). Part-time and evening/weekend programs available.

Degree requirements: For master's, computer language (MMIS), thesis optional.
Entrance requirements: For master's, GMAT (MBA), resumé.
Faculty research: Yugoslav economic system, workers' cooperatives, participative management and job enrichment, global business systems. *Web site:* http://www.metrostate.edu/

■ MICHIGAN STATE UNIVERSITY

Graduate School, College of Social Science, School of Criminal Justice, East Lansing, MI 48824

AWARDS Cricimal justice-urban studies (MS); criminal justice (MS, PhD). Part-time programs available. Postbaccalaureate distance learning degree programs offered.

Faculty: 18.
Students: 56 full-time (32 women), 66 part-time (25 women); includes 25 minority (14 African Americans, 1 Asian American or Pacific Islander, 7 Hispanic Americans, 3 Native Americans), 17 international. Average age 29. 158 applicants, 33% accepted. In 2001, 38 master's, 4 doctorates awarded.
Degree requirements: For master's, thesis optional.
Entrance requirements: For master's, GRE General Test or MAT, minimum GPA of 3.2. *Application deadline:* For fall admission, 2/1; for spring admission, 9/1. Applications are processed on a rolling basis. *Application fee:* $30 ($40 for international students). Electronic applications accepted.
Expenses: Tuition, state resident: part-time $244 per credit hour. Tuition, nonresident: part-time $494 per credit hour. Required fees: $268 per semester. Tuition and fees vary according to course load, degree level and program.
Financial support: In 2001–02, 10 fellowships (averaging $2,662 per year), 25 research assistantships with tuition reimbursements (averaging $11,005 per year), 14 teaching assistantships with tuition reimbursements (averaging $10,716 per year) were awarded. Career-related internships or fieldwork and Federal Work-Study also available. Support available to part-time students. Financial award application deadline: 4/15; financial award applicants required to submit FAFSA.
Faculty research: Community policing, women in policing, community-based correction, research utilization. *Total annual research expenditures:* $666,584.
Dr. Edmund McGarrell, Director, 517-355-2197, *Fax:* 517-432-1787.
Application contact: Information Contact, 517-355-2193. *Web site:* http://www.ssc.msu.edu/~cj/

Find an in-depth description at www.petersons.com/gradchannel.

■ MIDDLE TENNESSEE STATE UNIVERSITY

College of Graduate Studies, College of Education and Behavioral Science, Department of Criminal Justice Administration, Murfreesboro, TN 37132

AWARDS MCJ. Part-time programs available.

Faculty: 3 full-time (1 woman).
Students: 2 full-time (both women), 45 part-time (30 women); includes 19 minority (15 African Americans, 3 Hispanic Americans, 1 Native American). Average age 30. 41 applicants, 100% accepted. In 2001, 8 degrees awarded.
Degree requirements: For master's, one foreign language, thesis, comprehensive exam.
Entrance requirements: For master's, GRE or MAT. *Application deadline:* For fall admission, 8/1 (priority date). Applications are processed on a rolling basis. *Application fee:* $25. Electronic applications accepted.
Expenses: Tuition, state resident: full-time $1,716; part-time $191 per hour. Tuition, nonresident: full-time $4,952; part-time $461 per hour. Required fees: $14 per hour. $58 per semester.
Financial support: Career-related internships or fieldwork and institutionally sponsored loans available. Support available to part-time students. Financial award application deadline: 5/1; financial award applicants required to submit FAFSA.
Dr. Frank Lee, Chair, 615-898-2630, *Fax:* 615-898-5614, *E-mail:* flee@mtsu.edu.

■ MINOT STATE UNIVERSITY

Graduate School, Program in Criminal Justice, Minot, ND 58707-0002

AWARDS MS.

Degree requirements: For master's, thesis or alternative.
Entrance requirements: For master's, bachelor's degree minor in criminal justice or related field; minimum GPA of 3.0 or GRE General Test.
Faculty research: Sentencing, white-collar/organizational crime, juveniles, gender issues, policy analysis.

■ MISSISSIPPI COLLEGE

Graduate School, College of Arts and Sciences, Department of History and Political Science, Clinton, MS 39058

AWARDS Administration of justice (MSS); history (M Ed, MA, MSS); political science (MSS); social sciences (M Ed, MSS); sociology (MSS).

Degree requirements: For master's, one foreign language, thesis (for some programs), comprehensive exam.
Entrance requirements: For master's, GRE or NTE, minimum GPA of 2.5.

■ MISSISSIPPI VALLEY STATE UNIVERSITY

Department of Criminal Justice and Social Work, Itta Bena, MS 38941-1400

AWARDS Criminal justice (MS). Part-time and evening/weekend programs available.

Degree requirements: For master's, thesis optional.
Entrance requirements: For master's, minimum GPA of 2.5. Electronic applications accepted.
Faculty research: Police in the criminal justice system, the United States and international terrorism.

■ MONMOUTH UNIVERSITY

Graduate School, Department of Criminal Justice, West Long Branch, NJ 07764-1898

AWARDS Criminal justice administration (MA, Certificate). Part-time and evening/weekend programs available.

Faculty: 4 full-time (0 women).
Students: 6 full-time (3 women), 28 part-time (9 women); includes 4 minority (2 African Americans, 2 Hispanic Americans), 2 international. Average age 28. 32 applicants, 78% accepted, 12 enrolled. In 2001, 9 degrees awarded.
Degree requirements: For master's, thesis optional.
Entrance requirements: For master's, minimum GPA of 3.0 in major, 2.5 overall. *Application deadline:* For fall admission, 8/15 (priority date); for spring admission, 12/15 (priority date). Applications are processed on a rolling basis. *Application fee:* $35. Electronic applications accepted.
Expenses: Tuition: Full-time $9,900; part-time $549 per credit. Required fees: $568.
Financial support: In 2001–02, 29 students received support, including 29 fellowships (averaging $1,161 per year), 2 research assistantships (averaging $3,606 per year); career-related internships or fieldwork, scholarships/grants, tuition waivers (full and partial), and unspecified assistantships also available. Support available to part-time students. Financial award application deadline: 3/1; financial award applicants required to submit FAFSA.
Faculty research: Violent crimes, criminal pathology.

Monmouth University (continued)
Dr. Gregory Coram, Director, 732-571-3448, *Fax:* 732-263-5148, *E-mail:* coram@monmouth.edu.
Application contact: Kevin Roane, Director, Office of Graduate Admissions, 732-571-3452, *Fax:* 732-263-5123, *E-mail:* gradadm@monmouth.edu. *Web site:* http://www.monmouth.edu/~cj/crimjust.htm

Find an in-depth description at www.petersons.com/gradchannel.

■ MOREHEAD STATE UNIVERSITY

Graduate Programs, Caudill College of Humanities, Department of Sociology, Social Work and Criminology, Morehead, KY 40351

AWARDS Criminology (MA); general sociology (MA); gerontology (MA). Part-time and evening/weekend programs available.

Faculty: 12 full-time (4 women).
Students: 7 full-time (5 women), 11 part-time (10 women), 2 international. Average age 25. 10 applicants, 60% accepted. In 2001, 2 degrees awarded.
Degree requirements: For master's, final comprehensive exam, thesis optional.
Entrance requirements: For master's, GRE General Test, TOFEL, minimum GPA of 3.0 in sociology, 2.5 overall; 18 hours in sociology. *Application deadline:* For fall admission, 8/1 (priority date); for spring admission, 12/1 (priority date). Applications are processed on a rolling basis. *Application fee:* $0.
Expenses: Tuition, state resident: part-time $176 per hour. Tuition, nonresident: full-time $1,584; part-time $472 per hour. International tuition: $4,247 full-time.
Financial support: In 2001–02, 5 teaching assistantships (averaging $5,000 per year) were awarded; career-related internships or fieldwork and Federal Work-Study also available. Financial award application deadline: 4/1; financial award applicants required to submit FAFSA.
Faculty research: Death and dying; aging, drinking, and drugs; economic development; adult children of alcoholics.
Dr. Edward Reeves, Chair, 606-783-2546, *Fax:* 606-783-5027, *E-mail:* e.reeves@moreheadstate.edu.
Application contact: Betty R. Cowsert, Graduate Admissions/Records Manager, 606-783-2039, *Fax:* 606-783-5061, *E-mail:* b.cowsert@moreheadstate.edu. *Web site:* http://www.moreheadstate.edu/

■ MOUNTAIN STATE UNIVERSITY

Graduate Studies, Program in Criminal Justice Administration, Beckley, WV 25802-9003

AWARDS MS.

Degree requirements: For master's, thesis, comprehensive exam.
Entrance requirements: For master's, GRE. Electronic applications accepted.
Expenses: Tuition: Part-time $210 per credit hour. Part-time tuition and fees vary according to program.

■ NATIONAL UNIVERSITY

Academic Affairs, School of Business and Technology, Department of Public Policy and Administration, La Jolla, CA 92037-1011

AWARDS Criminal justice (MCJ, MPA); forensic science (MFS); health care administration (MBA, MHCA); human resource management (MA); human resources administration (MBA); public administration (MBA, MPA). Part-time and evening/weekend programs available. Postbaccalaureate distance learning degree programs offered (minimal on-campus study).

Faculty: 9 full-time (2 women), 173 part-time/adjunct (43 women).
Students: 463 full-time (269 women), 169 part-time (79 women); includes 237 minority (97 African Americans, 45 Asian Americans or Pacific Islanders, 90 Hispanic Americans, 5 Native Americans), 37 international. Average age 34. 204 applicants, 100% accepted. In 2001, 281 degrees awarded.
Entrance requirements: For master's, interview, minimum GPA of 2.5. *Application deadline:* Applications are processed on a rolling basis. *Application fee:* $60 ($100 for international students).
Expenses: Tuition: Part-time $221 per quarter hour.
Financial support: Institutionally sponsored loans, scholarships/grants, and tuition waivers (full and partial) available. Support available to part-time students. Financial award application deadline: 5/1; financial award applicants required to submit FAFSA.
Dr. Thomas Green, Chair, 858-642-8439, *Fax:* 858-642-8716, *E-mail:* tgreen@nu.edu.
Application contact: Nancy Rohland, Director of Enrollment Management, 858-642-8180, *Fax:* 858-642-8710, *E-mail:* advisor@nu.edu. *Web site:* http://www.nu.edu/

■ NEW JERSEY CITY UNIVERSITY

Graduate Studies, College of Professional Studies, Department of Criminal Justice, Jersey City, NJ 07305-1597

AWARDS MS. Evening/weekend programs available.

Faculty: 4 full-time (1 woman).
Students: 4 full-time (3 women), 55 part-time (31 women); includes 28 minority (14 African Americans, 2 Asian Americans or Pacific Islanders, 12 Hispanic Americans). Average age 30. 37 applicants, 81% accepted. In 2001, 9 degrees awarded.
Degree requirements: For master's, thesis or alternative.
Entrance requirements: For master's, GRE General Test or MAT, TOEFL. *Application deadline:* For fall admission, 8/1 (priority date); for spring admission, 12/1. Applications are processed on a rolling basis. *Application fee:* $0.
Expenses: Tuition, state resident: full-time $5,062. Tuition, nonresident: full-time $8,663.
Dr. Bodham Yaworsky, Chairperson, 201-200-3492.

■ NEW MEXICO STATE UNIVERSITY

Graduate School, College of Arts and Sciences, Department of Criminal Justice, Las Cruces, NM 88003-8001

AWARDS MCJ. Part-time and evening/weekend programs available. Postbaccalaureate distance learning degree programs offered (no on-campus study).

Faculty: 7 full-time (2 women).
Students: 18 full-time (12 women), 23 part-time (18 women); includes 21 minority (2 African Americans, 16 Hispanic Americans, 3 Native Americans), 1 international. Average age 29. 15 applicants, 87% accepted, 10 enrolled. In 2001, 15 degrees awarded.
Degree requirements: For master's, thesis (for some programs), oral and written exams.
Entrance requirements: For master's, minimum GPA of 3.0. *Application deadline:* For fall admission, 3/15 (priority date); for spring admission, 11/1 (priority date). Applications are processed on a rolling basis. *Application fee:* $15 ($35 for international students). Electronic applications accepted.
Expenses: Tuition, state resident: full-time $3,234; part-time $135 per credit. Tuition, nonresident: full-time $9,420; part-time $428 per credit. Required fees: $858.
Financial support: In 2001–02, 9 teaching assistantships with partial tuition reimbursements were awarded; fellowships with partial tuition reimbursements, research assistantships with partial tuition reimbursements, career-related internships or fieldwork also available. Financial award application deadline: 3/1.
Faculty research: Juvenile justice, jails and prison administration, courts and legal decision making, victim studies, policy and evaluation research.
Dr. Peter P. Gregware, Head, 505-646-3316, *Fax:* 505-646-2827, *E-mail:* pgregwar@nmsu.edu.
Application contact: Dr. Jim Maupin, Graduate Coordinator, 505-646-3195, *Fax:* 505-646-2827, *E-mail:* jmaupin@nmsu.edu. *Web site:* http://www.nmsu.edu/~crimjust/

■ NIAGARA UNIVERSITY

Graduate Division of Arts and Sciences, Department of Criminal Justice, Niagara Falls, Niagara University, NY 14109

AWARDS Criminal justice administration (MS).

Faculty: 4 full-time (1 woman).
Students: 7 full-time (5 women), 18 part-time (7 women); includes 1 minority (African American), 6 international. In 2001, 8 degrees awarded.
Application deadline: For fall admission, 8/1. Applications are processed on a rolling basis. *Application fee:* $30.
Expenses: Tuition: Part-time $350 per credit. Full-time tuition and fees vary according to program.
Financial support: Fellowships, career-related internships or fieldwork and Federal Work-Study available. Support available to part-time students.
Dr. Harry Dammer, Chairman, 716-286-8095, *Fax:* 716-286-8061, *E-mail:* hrdammer@niagara.edu.

■ NORTH CAROLINA CENTRAL UNIVERSITY

Division of Academic Affairs, College of Arts and Sciences, Department of Criminal Justice, Durham, NC 27707-3129

AWARDS MS. Part-time and evening/weekend programs available.

Faculty: 5 full-time (0 women), 2 part-time/adjunct (0 women).
Students: 21 full-time (18 women), 24 part-time (16 women); includes 39 minority (38 African Americans, 1 Hispanic American). Average age 31. 16 applicants, 94% accepted. In 2001, 3 degrees awarded.
Degree requirements: For master's, one foreign language, thesis or alternative, comprehensive exam.
Entrance requirements: For master's, minimum GPA of 3.0 in major, 2.5 overall. *Application deadline:* For fall admission, 8/1. *Application fee:* $30.
Expenses: Tuition, state resident: full-time $1,424. Tuition, nonresident: full-time $9,492. Required fees: $1,054.
Financial support: Career-related internships or fieldwork, Federal Work-Study, and institutionally sponsored loans available. Support available to part-time students. Financial award application deadline: 5/1.
Dr. George P. Wilson, Chairman, 919-530-7089, *Fax:* 919-560-5195, *E-mail:* gwilson@wpa.ncu.edu.
Application contact: Dr. Bernice D. Johnson, Dean, College of Arts and Sciences, 919-560-6368, *Fax:* 919-560-5361, *E-mail:* bjohnson@wpo.nccu.edu.

■ NORTH DAKOTA STATE UNIVERSITY

The Graduate School, College of Arts, Humanities and Social Sciences, Program in Sociology and Anthropology, Fargo, ND 58105

AWARDS Criminal justice (PhD); social science (MA, MS). Part-time programs available.

Faculty: 11 full-time (3 women), 2 part-time/adjunct (1 woman).
Students: 16 full-time (14 women), 11 part-time (7 women); includes 2 minority (both African Americans), 1 international. Average age 27. 11 applicants, 82% accepted. In 2001, 3 degrees awarded.
Degree requirements: For master's, thesis.
Entrance requirements: For master's, TOEFL, background courses in sociology, minimum GPA of 3.0. *Application deadline:* For fall admission, 4/1 (priority date). Applications are processed on a rolling basis. *Application fee:* $35.
Expenses: Tuition, state resident: part-time $124 per credit. Tuition, nonresident: part-time $325 per credit. Required fees: $22 per credit. Tuition and fees vary according to reciprocity agreements.
Financial support: In 2001–02, 4 research assistantships with full tuition reimbursements (averaging $6,156 per year), 7 teaching assistantships with full tuition reimbursements (averaging $3,078 per year) were awarded. Fellowships, career-related internships or fieldwork, Federal Work-Study, institutionally sponsored loans, and tuition waivers (full) also available. Support available to part-time students. Financial award application deadline: 4/15.
Faculty research: Criminal justice, medical sociology, demography, ethnology, archaeology. *Total annual research expenditures:* $206,000.
Dr. Gary A. Goreham, Chair, 701-231-7637, *Fax:* 701-231-1047, *E-mail:* gary.goreham@ndsu.nodak.edu. *Web site:* http://www.ndsu.nodak.edu/sociology/

■ NORTHEASTERN STATE UNIVERSITY

Graduate College, College of Behavioral and Social Sciences, Program in Criminal Justice, Tahlequah, OK 74464-2399

AWARDS MS. Part-time and evening/weekend programs available.

Students: 14 full-time (5 women), 18 part-time (8 women); includes 10 minority (3 African Americans, 1 Hispanic American, 6 Native Americans). In 2001, 9 degrees awarded.
Degree requirements: For master's, oral exam, thesis optional.
Entrance requirements: For master's, minimum GPA of 2.5. *Application deadline:* For fall admission, 6/1 (priority date). Applications are processed on a rolling basis. *Application fee:* $0.
Expenses: Tuition, area resident: Part-time $87 per credit hour. Tuition, state resident: part-time $206 per credit hour.
Financial support: Teaching assistantships, Federal Work-Study available. Financial award application deadline: 3/1.
Dr. Greg Combs, Assistant Dean/Coordinator, 918-456-5511 Ext. 3619, *Fax:* 918-458-2390, *E-mail:* combsgn@cherokee.nsuok.edu.

■ NORTHEASTERN UNIVERSITY

College of Criminal Justice, Boston, MA 02115-5096

AWARDS MS. Part-time and evening/weekend programs available.

Faculty: 14 full-time (5 women), 5 part-time/adjunct (1 woman).
Students: 35 full-time (23 women), 10 part-time (4 women); includes 3 minority (2 African Americans, 1 Asian American or Pacific Islander), 2 international. Average age 26. 110 applicants, 64% accepted. In 2001, 35 degrees awarded.
Degree requirements: For master's, thesis optional.
Entrance requirements: For master's, GRE General Test or LSAT. *Application deadline:* For fall admission, 6/1; for winter admission, 11/1; for spring admission, 2/1. Applications are processed on a rolling basis. *Application fee:* $50.
Expenses: Tuition: Part-time $535 per credit hour. Required fees: $56. Tuition and fees vary according to program.
Financial support: In 2001–02, 1 fellowship with tuition reimbursement (averaging $10,500 per year), 12 teaching assistantships with tuition reimbursements (averaging $10,800 per year) were awarded. Research assistantships with partial tuition reimbursements, career-related internships or fieldwork, Federal Work-Study, institutionally sponsored loans, and minority fellowships also available. Support available to part-time students. Financial award application deadline: 3/31; financial award applicants required to submit FAFSA.
Faculty research: Juvenile justice, victimology, serial and mass murder, private security, criminology corrections. *Total annual research expenditures:* $715,451.
Jack McDevitt, Director, 617-373-2813, *Fax:* 617-373-8723.
Application contact: Laurie A. Mastone, Assistant to the Director, 617-373-2813, *Fax:* 617-373-8723, *E-mail:* l.mastone@neu.edu.

Find an in-depth description at www.petersons.com/gradchannel.

■ NORTHERN ARIZONA UNIVERSITY

Graduate College, College of Social and Behavioral Sciences, Department of Criminal Justice, Flagstaff, AZ 86011

AWARDS Criminal justice (MS); criminal justice policy and planning (Certificate).

Faculty: 12.
Students: 19 full-time (11 women), 9 part-time (6 women); includes 10 minority (1 African American, 1 Asian American or Pacific Islander, 6 Hispanic Americans, 2 Native Americans). Average age 30. 14 applicants, 57% accepted, 6 enrolled. In 2001, 1 degree awarded.
Degree requirements: For master's, thesis.
Application deadline: For fall admission, 3/15 (priority date). Applications are processed on a rolling basis. *Application fee:* $45.
Expenses: Tuition, state resident: full-time $2,488. Tuition, nonresident: full-time $10,354.
Financial support: In 2001–02, 1 research assistantship, 7 teaching assistantships were awarded. Financial award application deadline: 3/15.
Dr. Marianne Neilson, Graduate Coordinator, *E-mail:* master.cj@nau.edu. *Web site:* http://www.nau.edu/jerimj-p

■ NORTHERN MICHIGAN UNIVERSITY

College of Graduate Studies, College of Professional Studies, Department of Criminal Justice, Marquette, MI 49855-5301

AWARDS MS. Part-time and evening/weekend programs available.

Faculty: 2 full-time (both women), 2 part-time/adjunct (1 woman).
Students: 7 full-time (4 women).
Entrance requirements: For master's, minimum GPA of 3.0. *Application fee:* $25.
Expenses: Tuition, state resident: full-time $158. Tuition, nonresident: full-time $260. Tuition and fees vary according to course load.
Financial support: Teaching assistantships, Federal Work-Study, institutionally sponsored loans, scholarships/grants, and unspecified assistantships available. Support available to part-time students.
Dr. Paul Lang, Head, 906-227-2660, *Fax:* 906-227-1754.

■ OKLAHOMA CITY UNIVERSITY

Petree College of Arts and Sciences, Division of Social Sciences, Oklahoma City, OK 73106-1402

AWARDS Criminal justice administration (MCJA). Part-time and evening/weekend programs available.

Degree requirements: For master's, thesis optional.
Entrance requirements: For master's, minimum GPA of 3.0.
Expenses: Contact institution.
Faculty research: Victims, police, corrections, security, women and crime. *Web site:* http://www.okcu.edu/

■ OKLAHOMA STATE UNIVERSITY

Graduate College, College of Arts and Sciences, Department of Sociology, Stillwater, OK 74078

AWARDS Corrections (MS); sociology (MS, PhD).

Faculty: 14 full-time (3 women), 4 part-time/adjunct (3 women).
Students: 14 full-time (6 women), 17 part-time (10 women); includes 7 minority (3 African Americans, 1 Hispanic American, 3 Native Americans), 3 international. Average age 33. 12 applicants, 92% accepted. In 2001, 2 master's, 1 doctorate awarded.
Degree requirements: For master's, thesis; for doctorate, 2 foreign languages, thesis/dissertation.
Entrance requirements: For master's and doctorate, GRE General Test, TOEFL. *Application deadline:* For fall admission, 7/1 (priority date). *Application fee:* $25.
Expenses: Tuition, state resident: part-time $92 per credit hour. Tuition, nonresident: part-time $297 per credit hour. Required fees: $21 per credit hour. $14 per semester. One-time fee: $20. Tuition and fees vary according to course load.
Financial support: In 2001–02, 23 students received support, including 16 research assistantships (averaging $13,087 per year), 6 teaching assistantships (averaging $8,862 per year); career-related internships or fieldwork, Federal Work-Study, and tuition waivers (partial) also available. Support available to part-time students. Financial award application deadline: 3/1.
Faculty research: Criminology/correction/legal issues; race, ethnicity, and gender in American society; environmental conflict and population problems; international comparative research; social change and social movement in American culture.
Dr. Charles K. Edgley, Head, 405-744-6104, *E-mail:* edgley@okstate.edu.

■ THE PENNSYLVANIA STATE UNIVERSITY UNIVERSITY PARK CAMPUS

Graduate School, College of Liberal Arts, Department of Sociology, Program in Crime, Law, and Justice, State College, University Park, PA 16802-1503

AWARDS MA, PhD.

Students: 17 full-time (11 women), 5 part-time (4 women). In 2001, 4 master's, 1 doctorate awarded.
Entrance requirements: For master's and doctorate, GRE General Test. *Application fee:* $45.
Expenses: Tuition, state resident: full-time $7,882; part-time $333 per credit. Tuition, nonresident: full-time $16,142; part-time $673 per credit. Required fees: $124 per semester.
D. Wayne Osgood, Graduate Officer, 814-865-6222.
Application contact: Dr. Roy Austin, Director, 814-863-0078.

■ PONTIFICAL CATHOLIC UNIVERSITY OF PUERTO RICO

Institute of Graduate Studies in Behavioral Science and Community Affairs, Ponce, PR 00717-0777

AWARDS Clinical psychology (MS); clinical social work (MSW); criminology (MA); industrial psychology (MS); psychology (PhD); public administration (MA). Part-time and evening/weekend programs available.

Faculty: 10 full-time (7 women), 17 part-time/adjunct (12 women).
Students: 86 full-time (56 women), 394 part-time (266 women); all minorities (all Hispanic Americans). 141 applicants, 83% accepted, 104 enrolled. In 2001, 35 degrees awarded.
Entrance requirements: For master's, GRE, 2 recommendation letters, interview, minimum GPA of 2.75. *Application deadline:* For fall admission, 4/30 (priority date). Applications are processed on a rolling basis. *Application fee:* $50. Electronic applications accepted.
Expenses: Tuition: Full-time $2,880; part-time $160 per credit. Required fees: $360. Tuition and fees vary according to degree level and program.
Financial support: Federal Work-Study and tuition waivers (partial) available. Support available to part-time students. Financial award application deadline: 7/15.
Dr. Nilde Cordoline, Director, 787-841-2000 Ext. 1024.
Application contact: Ana O. Bonilla, Director of Admissions, 787-841-2000 Ext. 1000, *Fax:* 787-840-4295. *Web site:* http://www.pucpr.edu/

■ PORTLAND STATE UNIVERSITY

Graduate Studies, College of Urban and Public Affairs, School of Government, Division of Administration of Justice, Portland, OR 97207-0751

AWARDS MS, PhD. Part-time programs available.

Faculty: 5 full-time (1 woman), 2 part-time/adjunct (0 women).
Students: 6 full-time (4 women), 4 part-time (2 women); includes 2 minority (1

Asian American or Pacific Islander, 1 Hispanic American), 2 international. Average age 28. 7 applicants, 71% accepted. In 2001, 1 degree awarded.
Degree requirements: For master's, thesis; for doctorate, thesis/dissertation, residency, comprehensive exam.
Entrance requirements: For master's, GRE, TOEFL, interview, minimum GPA of 3.0 in upper-division course work or 2.75 overall; for doctorate, GRE General Test. *Application deadline:* For fall admission, 3/15 (priority date). *Application fee:* $50.
Financial support: Fellowships, research assistantships, teaching assistantships, career-related internships or fieldwork, Federal Work-Study, and institutionally sponsored loans available. Support available to part-time students. Financial award application deadline: 3/1; financial award applicants required to submit FAFSA.
Faculty research: History of criminal justice, mental health issues, international terrorism, offender assessment, domestic violence. *Total annual research expenditures:* $3,009.
Dr. Gary Perlstein, Chair, 503-725-4014, *Fax:* 503-725-5199, *E-mail:* gary@upa.pdx.edu.
Application contact: Laura Winnen, Office Coordinator, 503-725-4014, *Fax:* 503-725-5199, *E-mail:* laura@upa.pdx.edu. *Web site:* http://www.upa.pdx.edu/aj/

■ RADFORD UNIVERSITY

Graduate College, College of Arts and Sciences, Department of Criminal Justice, Radford, VA 24142

AWARDS MA, MS. Part-time programs available. Postbaccalaureate distance learning degree programs offered (minimal on-campus study).

Faculty: 8 full-time (3 women).
Students: 13 full-time (4 women), 32 part-time (19 women); includes 1 minority (Hispanic American), 1 international. Average age 30. 20 applicants, 70% accepted, 6 enrolled. In 2001, 14 degrees awarded.
Degree requirements: For master's, thesis (for some programs), comprehensive exam.
Application deadline: For fall admission, 2/1 (priority date); for spring admission, 10/1. Applications are processed on a rolling basis. *Application fee:* $25.
Expenses: Tuition, state resident: full-time $2,564; part-time $167 per credit hour. Tuition, nonresident: full-time $6,314; part-time $323 per credit hour. Required fees: $1,440.
Financial support: In 2001–02, 21 students received support, including 12 research assistantships (averaging $4,456 per year); fellowships with tuition reimbursements available, teaching assistantships with tuition reimbursements available, career-related internships or fieldwork, Federal Work-Study, institutionally sponsored loans, and scholarships/grants also available. Financial award application deadline: 2/1; financial award applicants required to submit FAFSA.
Dr. Isaac Van Patten, Chair, 540-831-6148, *Fax:* 540-831-6075, *E-mail:* ivanpatt@radford.edu. *Web site:* http://www.radford.edu/

■ ROSEMONT COLLEGE

Graduate School, Accelerated Program in Management, Rosemont, PA 19010-1699

AWARDS Arts/culture/project management (MS); criminal justice (MS); not for profit (MS); training and leadership (MS). Part-time and evening/weekend programs available.

Students: 54 (36 women). Average age 33. 25 applicants, 80% accepted. In 2001, 11 degrees awarded.
Degree requirements: For master's, thesis or alternative.
Entrance requirements: For master's, GRE or MAT. *Application deadline:* Applications are processed on a rolling basis. *Application fee:* $50.
Expenses: Contact institution.
Financial support: Applicants required to submit FAFSA.
Laurie Keenan McGarvey, Assistant Dean, 610-527-0200 Ext. 2380, *Fax:* 610-520-4337, *E-mail:* lmcgarvey@rosemont.edu. *Web site:* http://www.rosemont.edu/root/cont_studies/cs_mba.html

■ RUTGERS, THE STATE UNIVERSITY OF NEW JERSEY, CAMDEN

Graduate School, Program in Criminal Justice, Camden, NJ 08102-1401

AWARDS MA.

■ RUTGERS, THE STATE UNIVERSITY OF NEW JERSEY, NEWARK

Graduate School, Program in Criminal Justice, Newark, NJ 07102

AWARDS PhD.

■ RUTGERS, THE STATE UNIVERSITY OF NEW JERSEY, NEWARK

Graduate School, School of Criminal Justice, Newark, NJ 07102

AWARDS MA, PhD. Part-time and evening/weekend programs available. Terminal master's awarded for partial completion of doctoral program.

Degree requirements: For master's, thesis optional; for doctorate, thesis/dissertation.
Entrance requirements: For master's and doctorate, GRE General Test, minimum GPA of 3.0. Electronic applications accepted.
Faculty research: Delinquency crime and criminal justice system, delinquency prevention and treatment, crime prevention, policing. *Web site:* http://rutgers.newark.rutgers.edu/rscj/

■ ST. AMBROSE UNIVERSITY

College of Human Services, Program in Criminal Justice, Davenport, IA 52803-2898

AWARDS Criminal justice (MCJ); juvenile justice (MCJ). Part-time and evening/weekend programs available.

Faculty: 4 full-time (1 woman).
Students: 9 full-time (4 women), 8 part-time (4 women); includes 1 minority (African American). Average age 32. 16 applicants, 100% accepted, 11 enrolled. In 2001, 10 degrees awarded.
Degree requirements: For master's, thesis (for some programs), practicum or project. *Median time to degree:* Master's–2 years full-time, 4 years part-time.
Entrance requirements: For master's, Two years of work experience, two letters of recommendation, personal interview. *Application deadline:* For fall admission, 8/15 (priority date); for spring admission, 11/1. Applications are processed on a rolling basis. *Application fee:* $25. Electronic applications accepted.
Financial support: In 2001–02, 9 students received support, including 2 teaching assistantships with partial tuition reimbursements available (averaging $4,000 per year); career-related internships or fieldwork and unspecified assistantships also available. Support available to part-time students. Financial award application deadline: 3/15; financial award applicants required to submit FAFSA.
Faculty research: Community policing.
Melissa Burek, Head, 563-333-6096, *Fax:* 563-333-6243, *E-mail:* mburek@sau.edu. *Web site:* http://www.sau.edu/

■ ST. CLOUD STATE UNIVERSITY

School of Graduate Studies, College of Social Sciences, Department of Criminal Justice, Program in Public Safety Executive Leadership, St. Cloud, MN 56301-4498

AWARDS MS.

Degree requirements: For master's, thesis or alternative.
Entrance requirements: For master's, GRE General Test, minimum GPA of 2.75. *Application deadline:* Applications are processed on a rolling basis. *Application fee:* $35.
Expenses: Tuition, state resident: part-time $156 per credit. Tuition, nonresident: part-time $244 per credit. Required fees: $20 per credit.
Financial support: Federal Work-Study and unspecified assistantships available. Financial award application deadline: 3/1.
John Campbell, Coordinator, 320-255-2985.

■ SAINT JOSEPH'S UNIVERSITY

College of Arts and Sciences, Program in Criminal Justice, Philadelphia, PA 19131-1395

AWARDS MS. Evening/weekend programs available.

Degree requirements: For master's, thesis.
Entrance requirements: For master's, TOEFL, GRE General Test or minimum GPA of 3.0.
Expenses: Tuition: Part-time $550 per credit. Tuition and fees vary according to program.

■ SAINT MARY'S UNIVERSITY OF MINNESOTA

Graduate School, Program in Resource Analysis, Winona, MN 55987-1399

AWARDS Business (MS); criminal justice (MS); natural resources (MS); public administration (MS).

■ ST. MARY'S UNIVERSITY OF SAN ANTONIO

Graduate School, Department of Criminal Justice and Criminology, San Antonio, TX 78228-8507

AWARDS Justice administration (MJA).

Faculty: 3 full-time (0 women).
Students: 1 (woman) full-time, 8 part-time (3 women); includes 8 minority (1 African American, 7 Hispanic Americans). In 2001, 8 degrees awarded.
Entrance requirements: For master's, GRE General Test. *Application deadline:* Applications are processed on a rolling basis. *Application fee:* $15. Electronic applications accepted.
Expenses: Tuition: Full-time $8,190; part-time $455 per credit hour. Required fees: $375.
Financial support: Application deadline: 2/15.
Dr. Armando Abney, Graduate Program Director, 210-436-3519.

■ ST. THOMAS UNIVERSITY

School of Graduate Studies, Department of Professional Management, Specialization in Justice Administration, Miami, FL 33054-6459

AWARDS MSM, Certificate.

Degree requirements: For master's, comprehensive exam.
Entrance requirements: For master's, TOEFL, interview, minimum GPA of 3.0 or GMAT.

■ SALVE REGINA UNIVERSITY

Graduate School, Program in Administration of Justice, Newport, RI 02840-4192

AWARDS MS. Part-time and evening/weekend programs available.

Faculty: 2 full-time (1 woman), 3 part-time/adjunct (0 women).
Students: 6 full-time (4 women), 24 part-time (3 women). Average age 31. 19 applicants, 74% accepted, 2 enrolled. In 2001, 14 degrees awarded.
Degree requirements: For master's, thesis optional. *Median time to degree:* Master's–2 years full-time, 2.5 years part-time.
Entrance requirements: For master's, GMAT, GRE General Test, or MAT. *Application deadline:* Applications are processed on a rolling basis. *Application fee:* $50. Electronic applications accepted.
Expenses: Tuition: Full-time $5,400; part-time $300 per credit. Required fees: $330; $40 per term. Tuition and fees vary according to degree level.
Financial support: Career-related internships or fieldwork and Federal Work-Study available. Support available to part-time students. Financial award application deadline: 3/1.
Dr. Thomas Svogun, Director, 401-341-3176, *Fax:* 401-341-2973, *E-mail:* svogunt@salve.edu.
Application contact: Karen E. Johnson, Graduate Admissions Counselor, 401-341-2153, *Fax:* 401-341-2973, *E-mail:* graduate_studies@salve.edu. *Web site:* http://www.salve.edu/programs_grad/index.html

■ SAM HOUSTON STATE UNIVERSITY

College of Criminal Justice, Huntsville, TX 77341

AWARDS MA, MS, PhD.

Students: 61 full-time (28 women), 84 part-time (41 women); includes 19 minority (8 African Americans, 1 Asian American or Pacific Islander, 8 Hispanic Americans, 2 Native Americans), 22 international. Average age 33. In 2001, 16 master's, 4 doctorates awarded.
Degree requirements: For master's, thesis (for some programs); for doctorate, thesis/dissertation, comprehensive exam.
Entrance requirements: For master's, GRE General Test; for doctorate, GRE General Test, master's degree. *Application deadline:* For fall admission, 8/1; for spring admission, 12/1. Applications are processed on a rolling basis. *Application fee:* $20.
Expenses: Tuition, area resident: Part-time $69 per credit. Tuition, state resident: full-time $1,380; part-time $69 per credit. Tuition, nonresident: full-time $5,600; part-time $280 per credit. Required fees: $748. Tuition and fees vary according to course load.
Financial support: Fellowships, research assistantships, teaching assistantships, career-related internships or fieldwork, Federal Work-Study, institutionally sponsored loans, and unspecified assistantships available. Support available to part-time students. Financial award application deadline: 5/31; financial award applicants required to submit FAFSA.
Faculty research: Police information systems, juvenile gangs, prison health services, public opinion on gun control. *Total annual research expenditures:* $86,362.
Dr. Richard Ward, Dean, 936-294-1632.
Application contact: Joann Davis, Administrative Assistant to Graduate Programs, 936-294-1647, *Fax:* 936-294-1653. *Web site:* http://www.shsu.edu.cjcenter/

Find an in-depth description at www.petersons.com/gradchannel.

■ SAN DIEGO STATE UNIVERSITY

Graduate and Research Affairs, College of Professional Studies and Fine Arts, School of Public Administration and Urban Studies, Program in Criminal Justice Administration, San Diego, CA 92182

AWARDS MPA. Part-time programs available.

Entrance requirements: For master's, GRE General Test, TOEFL.

■ SAN DIEGO STATE UNIVERSITY

Graduate and Research Affairs, College of Professional Studies and Fine Arts, School of Public Administration and Urban Studies, Program in Criminal Justice and Criminology, San Diego, CA 92182

AWARDS MS.

Entrance requirements: For master's, GRE General Test, TOEFL.

■ SAN JOSE STATE UNIVERSITY

Graduate Studies, College of Applied Arts and Sciences, Department of Administration of Justice, San Jose, CA 95192-0001

AWARDS MS. Part-time programs available.

Faculty: 6 full-time (2 women).
Students: 11 full-time (4 women), 24 part-time (14 women); includes 12 minority (3 African Americans, 4 Asian Americans or Pacific Islanders, 4 Hispanic Americans, 1 Native American). Average age 31. 39 applicants, 74% accepted. In 2001, 13 degrees awarded.
Degree requirements: For master's, thesis or alternative.
Entrance requirements: For master's, TOEFL, minimum GPA of 3.0. *Application deadline:* For fall admission, 6/29; for spring admission, 11/30. Applications are

processed on a rolling basis. *Application fee:* $59. Electronic applications accepted.
Expenses: Tuition, nonresident: part-time $246 per unit. Required fees: $678 per semester. Tuition and fees vary according to course load.
Financial support: Career-related internships or fieldwork and institutionally sponsored loans available. Support available to part-time students. Financial award application deadline: 7/1; financial award applicants required to submit FAFSA.
Faculty research: Employee stress, interagency cooperation, prison industries, application of death penalty sentences, sucrose ingestion and delinquency.
Inger Sagatun-Edwards, Chair, 408-924-2940, *Fax:* 408-924-2953.

■ SAN JOSE STATE UNIVERSITY

Graduate Studies, College of Social Sciences, Department of Sociology, San Jose, CA 95192-0001

AWARDS Criminology (MA); sociology (MA). Part-time and evening/weekend programs available.

Faculty: 19 full-time (0 women), 6 part-time/adjunct (3 women).
Students: 16 full-time (13 women), 28 part-time (22 women); includes 21 minority (4 African Americans, 6 Asian Americans or Pacific Islanders, 11 Hispanic Americans), 2 international. Average age 31. 29 applicants, 76% accepted. In 2001, 6 degrees awarded.
Degree requirements: For master's, comprehensive exams or thesis.
Entrance requirements: For master's, GRE Subject Test, minimum GPA of 3.0. *Application deadline:* For fall admission, 6/29; for spring admission, 11/30. Applications are processed on a rolling basis. *Application fee:* $59. Electronic applications accepted.
Expenses: Tuition, nonresident: part-time $246 per unit. Required fees: $678 per semester. Tuition and fees vary according to course load.
Financial support: In 2001–02, 1 teaching assistantship was awarded; career-related internships or fieldwork, Federal Work-Study, and institutionally sponsored loans also available. Financial award application deadline: 3/1; financial award applicants required to submit FAFSA.
Faculty research: Theory construction, sexuality, sociology of the media, social causes of stress, social change.
Dr. Carol Ray, Chair, 408-924-5320, *Fax:* 408-924-5322.
Application contact: Yoko Baba, Graduate Coordinator, 408-924-5334.

■ SETON HALL UNIVERSITY

College of Arts and Sciences, Center for Public Service, Department of Criminal Justice, South Orange, NJ 07079-2697

AWARDS MPA. Part-time and evening/weekend programs available.

Degree requirements: For master's, research project.
Entrance requirements: For master's, GMAT, GRE General Test, or LSAT.
Expenses: Tuition: Full-time $10,818; part-time $601 per credit. Required fees: $610; $185 per term. Tuition and fees vary according to course load, program and student's religious affiliation.

■ SHIPPENSBURG UNIVERSITY OF PENNSYLVANIA

School of Graduate Studies and Research, College of Education and Human Services, Department of Criminal Justice, Shippensburg, PA 17257-2299

AWARDS Administration of justice (MS). Part-time and evening/weekend programs available.

Faculty: 4 full-time (0 women).
Students: 14 full-time (9 women), 74 part-time (28 women); includes 11 minority (9 African Americans, 2 Asian Americans or Pacific Islanders). Average age 30. 84 applicants, 76% accepted, 50 enrolled. In 2001, 25 degrees awarded.
Degree requirements: For master's, thesis optional. *Median time to degree:* Master's–1.08 years full-time, 1.92 years part-time.
Entrance requirements: For master's, GRE, MAT, or minimum GPA of 2.75; previous course work in criminal justice or related field. *Application deadline:* Applications are processed on a rolling basis. *Application fee:* $30. Electronic applications accepted.
Expenses: Tuition, state resident: full-time $4,600; part-time $256 per credit hour. Tuition, nonresident: full-time $7,554; part-time $420 per credit hour. Required fees: $290; $145 per semester.
Financial support: In 2001–02, 11 research assistantships with full tuition reimbursements were awarded; career-related internships or fieldwork and unspecified assistantships also available. Support available to part-time students. Financial award application deadline: 3/1; financial award applicants required to submit FAFSA.
Dr. Robert Freeman, Chairperson, 77-477-1558, *E-mail:* rmfree@ship.edu.
Application contact: Renee Payne, Associate Dean of Graduate Admissions, 717-477-1231, *Fax:* 717-477-4016, *E-mail:* rmpayn@ship.edu. *Web site:* http://www.ship.edu/%7ecrimjust/

■ SOUTHEAST MISSOURI STATE UNIVERSITY

School of Graduate Studies and Research, Department of Criminal Justice, Cape Girardeau, MO 63701-4799

AWARDS MS.

Students: 6 applicants, 83% accepted. In 2001, 1 degree awarded.
Entrance requirements: For master's, minimum GPA of 2.5.
Expenses: Tuition, state resident: full-time $1,242; part-time $138 per hour. Tuition, nonresident: full-time $2,268; part-time $252 per hour.
Dr. John Wade, Chairperson, 573-651-2685, *E-mail:* jwade@semo.edu.
Application contact: Marsha L. Arant, Senior Administrative Assistant, 573-651-2192, *Fax:* 573-651-2001, *E-mail:* marant@semo.edu.

■ SOUTHEAST MISSOURI STATE UNIVERSITY

School of Graduate Studies and Research, Program in Administration, Cape Girardeau, MO 63701-4799

AWARDS Athletic administration (MSA); criminal justice administration (MSA); health fitness administration (MSA); human services administration (MSA); public administration (MSA). Part-time and evening/weekend programs available.

Students: 24 full-time (12 women), 50 part-time (21 women); includes 14 minority (10 African Americans, 1 Asian American or Pacific Islander, 1 Hispanic American, 2 Native Americans), 1 international. Average age 31. 46 applicants, 96% accepted. In 2001, 19 degrees awarded.
Degree requirements: For master's, thesis or alternative.
Entrance requirements: For master's, minimum GPA of 2.5. *Application deadline:* For fall admission, 4/1 (priority date); for spring admission, 11/21. Applications are processed on a rolling basis. *Application fee:* $20 ($100 for international students).
Expenses: Tuition, state resident: full-time $1,242; part-time $138 per hour. Tuition, nonresident: full-time $2,268; part-time $252 per hour.
Financial support: In 2001–02, 7 research assistantships with full tuition reimbursements (averaging $6,100 per year) were awarded; teaching assistantships with full tuition reimbursements, career-related internships or fieldwork also available.
Application contact: Marsha L. Arant, Office of Graduate Studies, 573-651-2192, *Fax:* 573-651-2001, *E-mail:* marant@semovm.semo.edu.

■ SOUTHERN ILLINOIS UNIVERSITY CARBONDALE

Graduate School, College of Liberal Arts, Administration of Justice Program, Carbondale, IL 62901-6806

AWARDS MA.

Faculty: 10 full-time (3 women).
Students: 20 full-time (13 women), 12 part-time (9 women); includes 6 minority (4 African Americans, 2 Hispanic Americans), 5 international. 13 applicants, 46% accepted. In 2001, 9 degrees awarded.
Degree requirements: For master's, thesis optional.
Entrance requirements: For master's, GRE General Test, TOEFL, minimum GPA of 2.7. *Application deadline:* Applications are processed on a rolling basis. *Application fee:* $20.
Expenses: Tuition, state resident: full-time $3,794; part-time $154 per hour. Tuition, nonresident: full-time $6,566; part-time $308 per hour. Required fees: $277 per hour.
Financial support: In 2001–02, 18 students received support, including 2 fellowships with full tuition reimbursements available, 5 research assistantships with full tuition reimbursements available, 13 teaching assistantships with full tuition reimbursements available; career-related internships or fieldwork, Federal Work-Study, and institutionally sponsored loans also available. Support available to part-time students.
Faculty research: Corrections, criminology, law enforcement, crime prevention, victims of crime. *Total annual research expenditures:* $300,000.
Thomas C. Castellano, Chair, 618-453-5701, *Fax:* 618-453-6377, *E-mail:* tcastell@siu.edu.
Application contact: Phyllis Hunziker, Graduate Secretary, 618-453-5701, *Fax:* 618-453-6377, *E-mail:* crimjust@siu.edu. *Web site:* http://www.siu.edu/~ajsiuc/

Find an in-depth description at www.petersons.com/gradchannel.

■ SOUTHWEST TEXAS STATE UNIVERSITY

Graduate School, College of Applied Arts, Department of Criminal Justice, San Marcos, TX 78666

AWARDS MSCJ. Part-time and evening/weekend programs available.

Faculty: 6 full-time (2 women).
Students: 7 full-time (4 women), 25 part-time (15 women); includes 16 minority (6 African Americans, 1 Asian American or Pacific Islander, 9 Hispanic Americans). Average age 33. 26 applicants, 73% accepted, 9 enrolled. In 2001, 16 degrees awarded.
Degree requirements: For master's, comprehensive exam.
Entrance requirements: For master's, GRE General Test, TOEFL, minimum GPA of 2.75 in last 60 hours. *Application deadline:* For fall admission, 6/15 (priority date); for spring admission, 10/15 (priority date). Applications are processed on a rolling basis. *Application fee:* $40 ($90 for international students).
Expenses: Tuition, state resident: full-time $1,512; part-time $84 per credit hour. Tuition, nonresident: full-time $5,310; part-time $295 per credit hour. Required fees: $864; $29 per credit hour. $195 per term. Full-time tuition and fees vary according to course load.
Financial support: In 2001–02, 6 teaching assistantships (averaging $8,720 per year) were awarded; research assistantships, Federal Work-Study and institutionally sponsored loans also available. Support available to part-time students. Financial award application deadline: 4/1; financial award applicants required to submit FAFSA.
Faculty research: Workplace violence, ethics, psychological profiling, tactical law enforcement, comparative justice systems.
Dr. Quint C. Thurman, Chair, 512-245-2174, *Fax:* 512-245-8063, *E-mail:* qt10@swt.edu.
Application contact: Dr. Joy Pollock, Advisor, 512-245-7706, *Fax:* 512-245-8063, *E-mail:* jp12@swt.edu. *Web site:* http://www.swt.edu/acad_depts/criminaljustice/crime.html

■ SOUTHWEST TEXAS STATE UNIVERSITY

Graduate School, Interdisciplinary Studies Program in Criminal Justice, San Marcos, TX 78666

AWARDS MSIS. Part-time and evening/weekend programs available.

Degree requirements: For master's, comprehensive exam.
Application deadline: For fall admission, 6/15 (priority date); for spring admission, 10/15 (priority date). Applications are processed on a rolling basis. *Application fee:* $40 ($90 for international students).
Expenses: Tuition, state resident: full-time $1,512; part-time $84 per credit hour. Tuition, nonresident: full-time $5,310; part-time $295 per credit hour. Required fees: $864; $29 per credit hour. $195 per term. Full-time tuition and fees vary according to course load.
Financial support: Application deadline: 4/1.
Dr. Joy Pollock, Advisor, 512-245-7706, *Fax:* 512-245-8063, *E-mail:* jp12@swt.edu.

■ STATE UNIVERSITY OF NEW YORK AT ALBANY

School of Criminal Justice, Albany, NY 12222-0001

AWARDS MA, PhD, MSW/MA. Part-time and evening/weekend programs available.

Students: 93 full-time (52 women), 63 part-time (38 women); includes 18 minority (11 African Americans, 2 Asian Americans or Pacific Islanders, 4 Hispanic Americans, 1 Native American), 21 international. Average age 32. 111 applicants, 63% accepted. In 2001, 36 master's, 6 doctorates awarded.
Degree requirements: For doctorate, thesis/dissertation.
Entrance requirements: For master's and doctorate, GRE General Test. *Application deadline:* For fall admission, 7/1. *Application fee:* $50.
Expenses: Tuition, state resident: full-time $2,550; part-time $213 per credit. Tuition, nonresident: full-time $4,208; part-time $351 per credit. Required fees: $470; $470 per year.
Financial support: Fellowships, research assistantships, teaching assistantships, career-related internships or fieldwork, Federal Work-Study, and institutionally sponsored loans available. Financial award application deadline: 4/1.
Faculty research: Causes of delinquency, comparative policing, world crime data, correctional policy, family violence.
James Acker, Dean, 518-442-5214.

■ STATE UNIVERSITY OF NEW YORK COLLEGE AT BUFFALO

Graduate Studies and Research, Faculty of Applied Science and Education, Department of Criminal Justice, Buffalo, NY 14222-1095

AWARDS MS. Part-time and evening/weekend programs available.

Faculty: 7 full-time (1 woman), 2 part-time/adjunct (0 women).
Students: 19 full-time (11 women), 10 part-time (6 women); includes 10 minority (8 African Americans, 1 Asian American or Pacific Islander, 1 Hispanic American), 2 international. Average age 28. 36 applicants, 69% accepted. In 2001, 2 degrees awarded.
Degree requirements: For master's, project.
Entrance requirements: For master's, minimum GPA of 3.0. *Application deadline:* For fall admission, 5/1 (priority date); for spring admission, 10/1 (priority date). Applications are processed on a rolling basis. *Application fee:* $50.
Expenses: Tuition, state resident: full-time $5,100; part-time $226 per credit hour. Tuition, nonresident: full-time $8,416; part-time $351 per credit hour.
Financial support: In 2001–02, 1 fellowship with tuition reimbursement, 2 research assistantships with partial tuition reimbursements were awarded. Federal Work-Study and unspecified assistantships also available. Support available to part-time students. Financial award application deadline: 3/1.
Dr. John Song, Chairperson, 716-878-4517, *Fax:* 716-878-3240, *E-mail:* songjh@buffalostate.edu.

■ SUFFOLK UNIVERSITY

College of Arts and Sciences, Department of Criminal Justice, Boston, MA 02108-2770

AWARDS JD/MS. Part-time programs available.

Faculty: 6 full-time (2 women), 7 part-time/adjunct (2 women).
Students: 18 full-time (14 women), 60 part-time (39 women); includes 16 minority (12 African Americans, 4 Hispanic Americans), 1 international. Average age 29. 58 applicants, 91% accepted, 24 enrolled.
Application deadline: For fall admission, 6/15 (priority date); for spring admission, 11/15 (priority date). Applications are processed on a rolling basis. *Application fee:* $35.
Expenses: Contact institution.
Financial support: In 2001–02, 47 students received support; fellowships with partial tuition reimbursements available, career-related internships or fieldwork, Federal Work-Study, and institutionally sponsored loans available. Support available to part-time students. Financial award application deadline: 3/15; financial award applicants required to submit FAFSA.
Faculty research: Probation and parole, restorative justice, domestic violence, substance abuse, criminal justice policy.
Dr. Donald R. Morton, Director, 617-305-1990, *Fax:* 617-720-0490, *E-mail:* dmorton@suffolk.edu.
Application contact: Judith Reynolds, Director of Graduate Admissions, 617-573-8302, *Fax:* 617-523-0116, *E-mail:* grad.admission@suffolk.edu. *Web site:* http://www.cas.suffolk.edu/sociology/ejms/home.html

■ SUL ROSS STATE UNIVERSITY

School of Professional Studies, Department of Criminal Justice, Alpine, TX 79832

AWARDS MS.

Faculty: 2 full-time (0 women), 1 part-time/adjunct (0 women).
Students: 1 full-time (0 women), 19 part-time (4 women); includes 7 minority (all Hispanic Americans). Average age 38.
Entrance requirements: For master's, GRE General Test, minimum GPA of 2.5 in last 60 hours of undergraduate work. *Application deadline:* Applications are processed on a rolling basis. *Application fee:* $0 ($50 for international students).
Expenses: Tuition, state resident: part-time $64 per semester hour. Tuition, nonresident: part-time $275 per semester hour. Required fees: $71; $32 per semester hour.
Financial support: Application deadline: 5/1.
Raymond Kessler, Chair, 915-837-8166.

■ TARLETON STATE UNIVERSITY

College of Graduate Studies, College of Sciences and Technology, Department of Social Work, Sociology, and Criminal Justice, Stephenville, TX 76402

AWARDS MCJ.

Degree requirements: For master's, thesis optional.
Entrance requirements: For master's, GRE General Test.

■ TEMPLE UNIVERSITY

Graduate School, College of Liberal Arts, Department of Criminal Justice, Philadelphia, PA 19122-6096

AWARDS MA, PhD. Part-time programs available. Terminal master's awarded for partial completion of doctoral program.

Degree requirements: For master's, thesis optional; for doctorate, thesis/dissertation, qualifying exams.
Entrance requirements: For master's, GRE General Test, minimum GPA of 3.0 during previous 2 years, 2.8 overall; for doctorate, GRE General Test, TOEFL. Electronic applications accepted.
Expenses: Tuition, state resident: full-time $8,487; part-time $369 per credit hour. Tuition, nonresident: full-time $12,282; part-time $534 per credit hour. Required fees: $350. Tuition and fees vary according to course load, program and reciprocity agreements.
Faculty research: Criminal justice policy formulation, courts, correctional alternatives, community crime prevention, juvenile justice. *Web site:* http://www.cjgrad.temple.edu/

■ TENNESSEE STATE UNIVERSITY

Graduate School, College of Arts and Sciences, Department of Criminal Justice, Nashville, TN 37209-1561

AWARDS MCJ.

Faculty: 4 full-time (1 woman).
Students: 5 full-time (4 women), 21 part-time (15 women); includes 12 minority (11 African Americans, 1 Asian American or Pacific Islander). Average age 29. 29 applicants, 72% accepted. In 2001, 8 degrees awarded.
Degree requirements: For master's, thesis.
Entrance requirements: For master's, Cooperative English Test, GRE General Test, minimum GPA of 2.5. *Application deadline:* Applications are processed on a rolling basis. *Application fee:* $15.
Expenses: Tuition, state resident: full-time $3,884; part-time $247 per hour. Tuition, nonresident: full-time $10,356; part-time $517 per hour.
Financial support: In 2001–02, 1 teaching assistantship (averaging $2,962 per year) was awarded; unspecified assistantships also available. Financial award application deadline: 5/1.
Dr. Bruce Mallard, Head, 615-963-5588.

■ TEXAS A&M INTERNATIONAL UNIVERSITY

Division of Graduate Studies, College of Arts and Humanities, Department of Social Sciences, Laredo, TX 78041-1900

AWARDS Criminal justice (MSCJ); history (MA); political science (MA); public administration (MPAD).

Students: 9 full-time (5 women), 59 part-time (21 women); includes 57 minority (2 Asian Americans or Pacific Islanders, 55 Hispanic Americans), 1 international. In 2001, 12 degrees awarded.
Degree requirements: For master's, thesis (for some programs).
Entrance requirements: For master's, GRE General Test. *Application deadline:* For fall admission, 7/15 (priority date); for spring admission, 11/12. Applications are processed on a rolling basis. *Application fee:* $0.
Expenses: Tuition, state resident: full-time $1,536; part-time $64 per credit. Tuition, nonresident: full-time $6,600; part-time $275 per credit. Required fees: $594; $9 per credit. $33 per term. One-time fee: $10 part-time.
Financial support: Application deadline: 11/1.
Dr. Nasser Momayezi, Interim Dean, 956-326-2460, *Fax:* 956-326-2459, *E-mail:* nmomayezi@tamiu.edu.
Application contact: Veronica Gonzalez, Director of Enrollment Management and School Relations, 956-326-2270, *Fax:* 956-326-2269, *E-mail:* enroll@tamiu.edu.

■ TIFFIN UNIVERSITY

Master of Criminal Justice Program, Tiffin, OH 44883-2161

AWARDS MCJ. Part-time and evening/weekend programs available. Postbaccalaureate distance learning degree programs offered.

Faculty: 7 full-time (1 woman), 6 part-time/adjunct (0 women).
Students: 60 full-time (33 women), 6 part-time (all women); includes 29 African Americans. Average age 29. 94 applicants, 78% accepted. In 2001, 48 degrees awarded.
Entrance requirements: For master's, minimum undergraduate GPA of 2.5. *Application deadline:* For fall admission, 8/10 (priority date); for spring admission, 1/5 (priority date). Applications are processed on a rolling basis. *Application fee:* $50. Electronic applications accepted.
Expenses: Tuition: Full-time $8,400; part-time $525 per credit hour. Tuition and fees vary according to course load.

Tiffin University (continued)

Financial support: In 2001–02, 34 students received support. Available to part-time students. Application deadline: 7/31.

Dr. Shawn P. Daly, Dean of the School of Graduate Studies, 419-448-3404, *Fax:* 419-443-5002, *E-mail:* sdaly@tiffin.edu.

Application contact: Richard A. Geyer, Director of Graduate Admissions, 800-968-6446 Ext. 3310, *Fax:* 419-443-5002, *E-mail:* geyerra@tiffin.edu. *Web site:* http://www.tiffin.edu

■ TROY STATE UNIVERSITY

Graduate School, College of Arts and Sciences and University College, Program in Criminal Justice, Troy, AL 36082

AWARDS Administration of criminal justice (MS); corrections (MS); police administration (MS). Part-time and evening/weekend programs available.

Degree requirements: For master's, thesis, comprehensive exam.

Entrance requirements: For master's, GRE General Test, MAT, minimum GPA of 2.5. Electronic applications accepted.

Web site: http://www.troyst.edu/

■ UNIVERSIDAD DEL TURABO

Graduate Programs, Programs in Public Affairs, Program in Criminal Justice Studies, Turabo, PR 00778-3030

AWARDS MPA.

Entrance requirements: For master's, GRE, PAEG, interview.

■ THE UNIVERSITY OF ALABAMA

Graduate School, College of Arts and Sciences, Department of Criminal Justice, Tuscaloosa, AL 35487

AWARDS MSCJ. Part-time programs available.

Faculty: 6 full-time (1 woman).

Students: 18 full-time (12 women), 18 part-time (6 women); includes 10 minority (all African Americans). Average age 30. 16 applicants, 81% accepted, 7 enrolled. In 2001, 28 degrees awarded.

Degree requirements: For master's, thesis optional.

Entrance requirements: For master's, MAT or GRE. *Application deadline:* For fall admission, 4/1 (priority date). Applications are processed on a rolling basis. *Application fee:* $25. Electronic applications accepted.

Expenses: Tuition, state resident: full-time $3,292; part-time $183 per credit hour. Tuition, nonresident: full-time $8,912; part-time $495 per credit hour. Tuition and fees vary according to course load, campus/location and program.

Financial support: In 2001–02, 10 students received support, including 5 research assistantships, 4 teaching assistantships; fellowships Financial award application deadline: 3/14.

Faculty research: Domestic violence, stress of victims, prisonization, private security, court administration.

Dr. David C. Weaver, Interim Chairman, 205-348-5047, *Fax:* 205-348-7178.

Application contact: Dr. Ida M. Johnson, Director of Graduate Studies, 205-348-7795, *Fax:* 205-348-8090, *E-mail:* ijohnson@bama.ua.edu.

■ THE UNIVERSITY OF ALABAMA AT BIRMINGHAM

Graduate School, School of Social and Behavioral Sciences, Department of Justice Sciences, Birmingham, AL 35294

AWARDS Criminal justice (MSCJ); forensic science (MSFS). Evening/weekend programs available.

Students: 39 full-time (29 women), 1 (woman) part-time; includes 6 minority (4 African Americans, 2 Hispanic Americans), 1 international. 204 applicants, 34% accepted. In 2001, 19 degrees awarded.

Degree requirements: For master's, thesis or alternative.

Entrance requirements: For master's, GRE General Test or MAT. *Application deadline:* Applications are processed on a rolling basis. *Application fee:* $35 ($60 for international students). Electronic applications accepted.

Expenses: Tuition, state resident: full-time $3,058. Tuition, nonresident: full-time $5,746. Tuition and fees vary according to course load, degree level and program.

Financial support: Career-related internships or fieldwork available.

Dr. Brent L. Smith, Chair, 205-934-2069, *E-mail:* blsmith@uab.edu. *Web site:* http://www.sbs.uab.edu/crim.htm/

■ UNIVERSITY OF ALASKA FAIRBANKS

Graduate School, College of Liberal Arts, Department of Justice, Fairbanks, AK 99775-7480

AWARDS Administration of justice (MA).

Degree requirements: For master's, comprehensive exam.

Entrance requirements: For master's, GRE General Test, TOEFL.

Expenses: Tuition, state resident: full-time $4,272; part-time $178 per credit. Tuition, nonresident: full-time $8,328; part-time $347 per credit. Required fees: $960; $60 per term. Part-time tuition and fees vary according to course load.

■ UNIVERSITY OF ARKANSAS AT LITTLE ROCK

Graduate School, College of Professional Studies, Department of Criminal Justice, Little Rock, AR 72204-1099

AWARDS MA. Part-time and evening/weekend programs available.

Degree requirements: For master's, thesis defense or written comprehensive exam.

Entrance requirements: For master's, GRE General Test or MAT, interview, minimum GPA of 2.75.

Expenses: Tuition, state resident: full-time $3,006; part-time $107 per credit. Tuition, nonresident: full-time $6,012; part-time $357 per credit. Required fees: $22 per credit. Tuition and fees vary according to program.

Faculty research: Dissemination and analysis of behavioral science knowledge, leadership and managerial skills, philosophy of individual rights and humane treatment.

■ UNIVERSITY OF BALTIMORE

Graduate School, College of Liberal Arts, Program in Criminal Justice, Baltimore, MD 21201-5779

AWARDS MS, JD/MS. Part-time and evening/weekend programs available.

Faculty: 5 full-time (1 woman), 7 part-time/adjunct (1 woman).

Students: 23 full-time (16 women), 47 part-time (33 women); includes 35 minority (34 African Americans, 1 Asian American or Pacific Islander). Average age 30. 51 applicants, 82% accepted. In 2001, 23 degrees awarded.

Degree requirements: For master's, thesis or alternative.

Entrance requirements: For master's, interview, minimum GPA of 2.8. *Application deadline:* For fall admission, 7/15 (priority date); for spring admission, 12/15. Applications are processed on a rolling basis. *Application fee:* $30. Electronic applications accepted.

Expenses: Tuition, state resident: full-time $5,508; part-time $306 per credit. Tuition, nonresident: full-time $8,352; part-time $464 per credit. Required fees: $37 per credit. $60 per semester. Tuition and fees vary according to course load and degree level.

Financial support: In 2001–02, 8 research assistantships were awarded; fellowships, career-related internships or fieldwork and Federal Work-Study also available. Support available to part-time students. Financial award application deadline: 4/1; financial award applicants required to submit FAFSA.

Faculty research: Drugs and violence, police and community policing, women and crime, victimization, correction in

community. *Total annual research expenditures:* $218,765.
Dr. Cynthia Smith, Director, 410-837-6087, *E-mail:* cjsmith@ubalt.edu.
Application contact: Jeffrey Zavrotny, Assistant Director of Admissions, 410-837-4777, *Fax:* 410-837-4793, *E-mail:* jzavrotny@ubalt.edu.

Find an in-depth description at www.petersons.com/gradchannel.

■ UNIVERSITY OF CALIFORNIA, IRVINE

Office of Research and Graduate Studies, School of Social Ecology, Department of Criminology, Law and Society, Irvine, CA 92697

AWARDS Criminology, law and society (PhD).

Faculty: 15.
Students: 29 full-time (15 women); includes 6 minority (1 African American, 1 Asian American or Pacific Islander, 3 Hispanic Americans, 1 Native American). 36 applicants, 39% accepted, 7 enrolled. In 2001, 1 degree awarded.
Degree requirements: For doctorate, thesis/dissertation, research project.
Entrance requirements: For doctorate, GRE General Test. *Application deadline:* For fall and spring admission, 1/15 (priority date); for winter admission, 10/15 (priority date). *Application fee:* $60. Electronic applications accepted.
Expenses: Tuition, nonresident: full-time $10,704. Required fees: $8,396. Tuition and fees vary according to course load, program and student level.
Financial support: Fellowships, research assistantships, teaching assistantships, institutionally sponsored loans and tuition waivers (full and partial) available. Financial award application deadline: 3/2; financial award applicants required to submit FAFSA.
Faculty research: White-collar and corporate crime; immigration, the poor, homelessness, and governmental regulation; sentencing, community corrections, and diversion; mathematical and scientific evidence in jury trials; legal and criminological theory development.
Valerie Jenness, Chair, 949-824-5575.
Application contact: Jeanne Haynes, Academic Counselor, 949-824-5917, *Fax:* 949-824-2056, *E-mail:* jhaynes@uci.edu. *Web site:* http://www.socecol.uci.edu/~socecol/

■ UNIVERSITY OF CENTRAL FLORIDA

College of Health and Public Affairs, Department of Criminal Justice, Orlando, FL 32816

AWARDS Crime analysis (Certificate); criminal justice (MS). Part-time and evening/weekend programs available.

Faculty: 30 full-time (9 women), 28 part-time/adjunct (6 women).
Students: 90 full-time (44 women), 141 part-time (69 women); includes 51 minority (31 African Americans, 3 Asian Americans or Pacific Islanders, 16 Hispanic Americans, 1 Native American). Average age 33. 79 applicants, 85% accepted, 54 enrolled. In 2001, 54 degrees awarded.
Degree requirements: For master's, thesis or alternative.
Entrance requirements: For master's, TOEFL, GRE General Test, minimum GPA of 3.0. *Application deadline:* For fall admission, 7/15; for spring admission, 4/15. *Application fee:* $20. Electronic applications accepted.
Expenses: Tuition, state resident: part-time $162 per hour. Tuition, nonresident: part-time $569 per hour.
Financial support: In 2001–02, 13 fellowships with partial tuition reimbursements (averaging $2,692 per year), 38 research assistantships with partial tuition reimbursements (averaging $2,132 per year) were awarded. Teaching assistantships with partial tuition reimbursements, career-related internships or fieldwork, Federal Work-Study, institutionally sponsored loans, tuition waivers (partial), and unspecified assistantships also available. Financial award application deadline: 3/1; financial award applicants required to submit FAFSA.
Dr. B. J. McCarthy, Chair, 407-823-5929, *E-mail:* mccarthy@pegasus.cc.ucf.edu.
Application contact: Dr. Kenneth Reynolds, Coordinator, 407-823-2603, *Fax:* 407-823-5360, *E-mail:* kreynold@pegasus.cc.ucf.edu. *Web site:* http://www.ucf.edu/

■ UNIVERSITY OF CENTRAL OKLAHOMA

College of Graduate Studies and Research, College of Liberal Arts, Department of Sociology, Edmond, OK 73034-5209

AWARDS Criminal justice management and administration (MA). Part-time programs available.

Faculty research: Gender issues, violent offenders. *Web site:* http://www.libarts.ucok.edu/dept/sociology/

■ UNIVERSITY OF CINCINNATI

Division of Research and Advanced Studies, College of Education, Division of Criminal Justice, Cincinnati, OH 45221

AWARDS MS, PhD. Part-time programs available. Postbaccalaureate distance learning degree programs offered (no on-campus study).

Faculty: 7 full-time.
Students: 81 full-time (52 women), 55 part-time (26 women); includes 29 minority (20 African Americans, 5 Asian Americans or Pacific Islanders, 4 Hispanic Americans), 2 international. 91 applicants, 42% accepted. In 2001, 25 master's, 2 doctorates awarded.
Degree requirements: For master's, thesis or alternative; for doctorate, thesis/dissertation.
Entrance requirements: For master's, GRE or MAT, minimum GPA of 3.0; for doctorate, minimum GPA of 3.5. *Application deadline:* For fall admission, 2/1. *Application fee:* $30. Electronic applications accepted.
Expenses: Tuition, state resident: part-time $2,698 per quarter. Tuition, nonresident: part-time $4,977 per quarter.
Financial support: Fellowships, tuition waivers (partial) and unspecified assistantships available. Support available to part-time students. Financial award application deadline: 5/1. *Total annual research expenditures:* $903,893.
Dr. Edward J. Latessa, Head, 513-556-5836, *Fax:* 513-556-3303, *E-mail:* edward.latessa@uc.edu.
Application contact: James Frank, Director, Graduate Programs, 513-556-5832, *Fax:* 513-556-3303, *E-mail:* james.frank@uc.edu. *Web site:* http://www.education.uc.edu/programs/

■ UNIVERSITY OF COLORADO AT COLORADO SPRINGS

Graduate School of Public Affairs, Colorado Springs, CO 80933-7150

AWARDS Criminal justice (MCJ); public administration (MPA). Part-time and evening/weekend programs available.

Faculty: 4 full-time (1 woman), 7 part-time/adjunct (3 women).
Students: 34 full-time (23 women), 39 part-time (20 women); includes 11 minority (3 Asian Americans or Pacific Islanders, 6 Hispanic Americans, 2 Native Americans). Average age 37. 8 applicants, 100% accepted. In 2001, 22 degrees awarded.
Degree requirements: For master's, internship (if no experience).
Entrance requirements: For master's, GRE General Test, minimum GPA of 3.0. *Application deadline:* For fall admission, 6/1 (priority date); for spring admission, 11/1. Applications are processed on a rolling basis. *Application fee:* $60 ($75 for international students).
Expenses: Contact institution.
Financial support: Career-related internships or fieldwork and Federal Work-Study available. Support available to part-time students.
Faculty research: Organizational effectiveness, public administration, human resources management, social policy, nonprofit management.

University of Colorado at Colorado Springs (continued)
Dr. Kathleen Beatty, Dean, 719-262-4103, *Fax:* 719-262-4183, *E-mail:* kbeatty@carbon.cudenver.edu.
Application contact: Mary Lou Kartis, Program Assistant, 719-262-4182, *Fax:* 719-262-4183, *E-mail:* mkartis@uccs.edu.
Web site: http://www.carbon.cudenver.edu/public/gspa/

■ UNIVERSITY OF COLORADO AT DENVER

Graduate School of Public Affairs, Program in Criminal Justice, Denver, CO 80217-3364

AWARDS MCJ. Part-time and evening/weekend programs available.

Faculty: 3 full-time (1 woman).
Students: 10 full-time (7 women), 62 part-time (42 women); includes 14 minority (5 African Americans, 2 Asian Americans or Pacific Islanders, 5 Hispanic Americans, 2 Native Americans), 2 international. Average age 25. 52 applicants, 85% accepted, 18 enrolled. In 2001, 18 degrees awarded.
Degree requirements: For master's, thesis optional.
Entrance requirements: For master's, GRE General Test, minimum GPA of 3.0. *Application deadline:* For fall admission, 6/1 (priority date); for spring admission, 11/1. Applications are processed on a rolling basis. *Application fee:* $50 ($60 for international students).
Expenses: Tuition, state resident: full-time $3,284; part-time $198 per credit hour. Tuition, nonresident: full-time $13,380; part-time $802 per credit hour. Required fees: $444; $222 per semester.
Financial support: In 2001–02, 6 fellowships were awarded; research assistantships, teaching assistantships, career-related internships or fieldwork, Federal Work-Study, and institutionally sponsored loans also available. Support available to part-time students. Financial award application deadline: 4/1.
Mark R. Pogrebin, Director, 303-556-5995, *Fax:* 303-556-5971.
Application contact: Antoinette Sandoval, Student Service Specialist, 303-556-5970, *Fax:* 303-556-5971, *E-mail:* asandoval@castle.cudenver.edu.

Find an in-depth description at www.petersons.com/gradchannel.

■ UNIVERSITY OF DELAWARE

College of Arts and Science, Department of Sociology and Criminal Justice, Newark, DE 19716

AWARDS Criminology (MA, PhD); sociology (MA, PhD).

Faculty: 29 full-time (13 women).
Students: 31 full-time (18 women), 2 part-time (both women); includes 6 minority (2 African Americans, 1 Asian American or Pacific Islander, 3 Hispanic Americans), 1 international. Average age 26. 44 applicants, 34% accepted, 5 enrolled. In 2001, 4 master's, 2 doctorates awarded.
Degree requirements: For master's, thesis/dissertation; for doctorate, thesis/dissertation, comprehensive exam.
Entrance requirements: For master's and doctorate, GRE, TOEFL, letters of recommendation (3). *Application deadline:* For fall admission, 2/1. *Application fee:* $50. Electronic applications accepted.
Expenses: Tuition, state resident: full-time $4,770; part-time $265 per credit. Tuition, nonresident: full-time $13,860; part-time $770 per credit. Required fees: $414.
Financial support: In 2001–02, 25 students received support, including 3 fellowships with full tuition reimbursements available (averaging $10,100 per year), 11 research assistantships with full tuition reimbursements available (averaging $10,450 per year), 14 teaching assistantships with full tuition reimbursements available (averaging $10,450 per year). Financial award application deadline: 2/1.
Faculty research: Sex and gender, criminology/deviance, theory, methods, collective behavior. *Total annual research expenditures:* $2.7 million.
Dr. Joel Best, Chairman, 302-831-2581, *Fax:* 302-831-2607, *E-mail:* joelbest@udel.edu.
Application contact: Dr. Ronet Bachman, Director of Graduate Studies, 302-831-2581, *Fax:* 302-831-2607, *E-mail:* ronet@udel.edu. *Web site:* http://www.udel.edu/soc/homepage.htm

■ UNIVERSITY OF DETROIT MERCY

College of Liberal Arts and Education, Department of Criminal Justice and Human Services, Program in Criminal Justice Studies, Detroit, MI 48219-0900

AWARDS MA. Part-time and evening/weekend programs available.

Faculty: 3 full-time (0 women).
Students: 6 full-time (2 women), 13 part-time (9 women); includes 13 minority (all African Americans). Average age 34. In 2001, 9 degrees awarded.
Degree requirements: For master's, thesis or alternative.
Entrance requirements: For master's, minimum GPA of 2.75. *Application deadline:* For fall admission, 8/1. *Application fee:* $30 ($50 for international students).
Expenses: Tuition: Full-time $10,620; part-time $590 per credit hour. Required fees: $400. Tuition and fees vary according to program.
Financial support: Career-related internships or fieldwork available.
Faculty research: Socialization and social control, law and correction practices.

■ UNIVERSITY OF DETROIT MERCY

College of Liberal Arts and Education, Department of Criminal Justice and Human Services, Program in Security Administration, Detroit, MI 48219-0900

AWARDS MS. Part-time and evening/weekend programs available.

Faculty: 3 full-time (0 women).
Students: 2 full-time (both women), 13 part-time (6 women); includes 10 minority (all African Americans). In 2001, 3 degrees awarded.
Degree requirements: For master's, thesis or alternative.
Entrance requirements: For master's, minimum GPA of 2.75. *Application deadline:* For fall admission, 8/1. *Application fee:* $30 ($50 for international students).
Expenses: Tuition: Full-time $10,620; part-time $590 per credit hour. Required fees: $400. Tuition and fees vary according to program.
Financial support: Career-related internships or fieldwork and Federal Work-Study available.
Faculty research: Physical information and personnel security.

■ UNIVERSITY OF GREAT FALLS

Graduate Studies Division, Program in Criminal Justice Administration, Great Falls, MT 59405

AWARDS MCJ. Part-time and evening/weekend programs available.

Faculty: 3 full-time (1 woman), 2 part-time/adjunct (1 woman).
Students: 3 full-time (1 woman), 7 part-time (2 women); includes 2 minority (both Native Americans). Average age 35. 20 applicants, 100% accepted. In 2001, 7 degrees awarded. *Median time to degree:* Master's–1 year full-time, 1.5 years part-time.
Entrance requirements: For master's, GRE General Test or MAT. *Application deadline:* For fall admission, 8/15 (priority date); for winter admission, 11/15 (priority date); for spring admission, 12/15 (priority date). Applications are processed on a rolling basis. *Application fee:* $35.
Expenses: Tuition: Part-time $440 per credit. One-time fee: $35 full-time.
Financial support: Research assistantships, career-related internships or fieldwork, Federal Work-Study, and scholarships/grants available. Support available to part-time students. Financial award application deadline: 3/1. *Total annual research expenditures:* $100,000.
Dr. Deborah J. Kottel, Dean, 406-791-5339, *Fax:* 406-793-5990, *E-mail:* dkottel@ugf.edu.

■ UNIVERSITY OF ILLINOIS AT CHICAGO

Graduate College, College of Liberal Arts and Sciences, Department of Criminal Justice, Chicago, IL 60607-7128

AWARDS MA. Evening/weekend programs available.

Faculty: 12 full-time (3 women).
Students: 16 full-time (11 women), 30 part-time (19 women); includes 14 minority (6 African Americans, 1 Asian American or Pacific Islander, 7 Hispanic Americans), 2 international. Average age 30. 59 applicants, 44% accepted, 16 enrolled. In 2001, 7 degrees awarded.
Degree requirements: For master's, thesis.
Entrance requirements: For master's, GRE General Test, TOEFL, minimum GPA of 4.0 on a 5.0 scale. *Application deadline:* For fall admission, 6/1; for spring admission, 11/1. Applications are processed on a rolling basis. *Application fee:* $40 ($50 for international students). Electronic applications accepted.
Expenses: Tuition, state resident: full-time $3,060. Tuition, nonresident: full-time $6,688.
Financial support: In 2001–02, 21 students received support; fellowships with full tuition reimbursements available, research assistantships with full tuition reimbursements available, teaching assistantships with full tuition reimbursements available, career-related internships or fieldwork, Federal Work-Study, institutionally sponsored loans, and tuition waivers (full) available. Financial award application deadline: 3/1; financial award applicants required to submit FAFSA.
Faculty research: Sentencing probation, police and court use of scientific evidence, community mediation and conflict resolution.
Joseph Peterson, Director of Graduate Studies, 312-413-0439.
Application contact: Director of Graduate Studies, 312-996-6679.

Find an in-depth description at www.petersons.com/gradchannel.

■ UNIVERSITY OF LOUISIANA AT MONROE

Graduate Studies and Research, College of Liberal Arts, Department of Criminal Justice, Social Work, and Sociology, Program in Criminal Justice, Monroe, LA 71209-0001

AWARDS MA. Part-time and evening/weekend programs available.

Degree requirements: For master's, thesis optional.
Entrance requirements: For master's, GRE General Test.

■ UNIVERSITY OF LOUISVILLE

Graduate School, College of Arts and Sciences, Department of Justice Administration, Louisville, KY 40292-0001

AWARDS MS.

Students: 21 full-time (12 women), 62 part-time (33 women); includes 14 minority (11 African Americans, 2 Asian Americans or Pacific Islanders, 1 Native American). Average age 33. In 2001, 14 degrees awarded.
Entrance requirements: For master's, GRE General Test. *Application deadline:* For fall admission, 7/1 (priority date). *Application fee:* $25. Electronic applications accepted.
Expenses: Tuition, state resident: full-time $4,134. Tuition, nonresident: full-time $11,486.
Financial support: In 2001–02, 3 research assistantships (averaging $10,000 per year) were awarded
Dr. Deborah G. Wilson, Chair, 502-852-6570, *Fax:* 502-852-0065, *E-mail:* dgwilson@louisville.edu.

■ UNIVERSITY OF MARYLAND, COLLEGE PARK

Graduate Studies and Research, College of Behavioral and Social Sciences, Department of Criminology and Criminal Justice, College Park, MD 20742

AWARDS MA, PhD, JD/MA. Part-time and evening/weekend programs available.

Faculty: 32 full-time (18 women), 10 part-time/adjunct (3 women).
Students: 63 full-time (44 women), 44 part-time (22 women); includes 19 minority (12 African Americans, 2 Asian Americans or Pacific Islanders, 5 Hispanic Americans), 4 international. 162 applicants, 44% accepted, 35 enrolled. In 2001, 16 master's, 9 doctorates awarded. Terminal master's awarded for partial completion of doctoral program.
Degree requirements: For master's, thesis optional; for doctorate, variable foreign language requirement, thesis/dissertation, comprehensive exam.
Entrance requirements: For master's, GRE General Test, minimum GPA of 3.0; for doctorate, GRE General Test. *Application deadline:* For fall admission, 8/1; for spring admission, 12/1. Applications are processed on a rolling basis. *Application fee:* $50 ($70 for international students). Electronic applications accepted.
Expenses: Tuition, state resident: part-time $289 per credit hour. Tuition, nonresident: part-time $448 per credit hour. One-time fee: $436 part-time. Full-time tuition and fees vary according to course load, campus/location and program.
Financial support: In 2001–02, 6 fellowships with full tuition reimbursements (averaging $10,985 per year), 4 research assistantships with tuition reimbursements (averaging $13,915 per year), 44 teaching assistantships with tuition reimbursements (averaging $12,416 per year) were awarded. Federal Work-Study and scholarships/grants also available. Support available to part-time students. Financial award applicants required to submit FAFSA.
Faculty research: Theory, law enforcement.
Dr. Charles Wellford, Chairman, 301-405-4701, *Fax:* 301-405-4733.
Application contact: Trudy Lindsey, Director, Graduate Admissions and Records, 301-405-6991, *Fax:* 301-314-9305, *E-mail:* grschool@deans.umd.edu.

■ UNIVERSITY OF MASSACHUSETTS LOWELL

Graduate School, College of Arts and Sciences, Department of Criminal Justice, Lowell, MA 01854-2881

AWARDS MA. Part-time and evening/weekend programs available.

Degree requirements: For master's, thesis optional.
Entrance requirements: For master's, GRE General Test or MAT. Electronic applications accepted.
Faculty research: Family violence, criminal justice management, corrections, policing, delinquency.

■ THE UNIVERSITY OF MEMPHIS

Graduate School, College of Arts and Sciences, School of Urban Affairs and Public Policy, Department of Criminology and Criminal Justice, Memphis, TN 38152

AWARDS MA. Part-time programs available.

Faculty: 7 full-time (3 women), 5 part-time/adjunct (0 women).
Students: 9 full-time (6 women), 2 part-time (both women); includes 2 minority (both African Americans), 1 international. Average age 30. 23 applicants, 43% accepted. In 2001, 7 degrees awarded.
Degree requirements: For master's, thesis optional.
Entrance requirements: For master's, GRE General Test or MAT, minimum GPA of 3.0. *Application deadline:* For fall admission, 5/1; for spring admission, 11/1. *Application fee:* $25 ($50 for international students).
Expenses: Tuition, state resident: full-time $2,026. Tuition, nonresident: full-time $4,528.
Financial support: In 2001–02, 9 research assistantships were awarded; teaching assistantships, career-related internships or fieldwork, institutionally sponsored loans, and tuition waivers (partial) also available.
Faculty research: Death penalty, violence, domestic violence, sexual assault, gambling. *Total annual research expenditures:* $500,000.

The University of Memphis (continued)
Prof. W. Richard Janikowski, Chairman, 901-678-2737, *Fax:* 901-678-5279, *E-mail:* wrjaniko@memphis.edu.
Application contact: Dr. Margaret Vandiver, Coordinator of Graduate Studies, 901-678-2737, *Fax:* 901-678-5279, *E-mail:* vandiver@memphis.edu. *Web site:* http://www.people.memphis.edu/~cjustice/cjus.htm

■ UNIVERSITY OF MISSOURI–KANSAS CITY

College of Arts and Sciences, Department of Sociology, Program in Criminal Justice and Criminology, Kansas City, MO 64110-2499

AWARDS MS. Part-time and evening/weekend programs available.

Faculty: 6 full-time (2 women).
Students: 6 full-time (3 women), 10 part-time (all women); includes 3 minority (1 African American, 1 Hispanic American, 1 Native American). Average age 32. 14 applicants, 57% accepted. In 2001, 30 degrees awarded.
Degree requirements: For master's, thesis optional.
Entrance requirements: For master's, GRE, minimum GPA of 3.0 in major, 2.6 overall. *Application deadline:* For fall admission, 4/1; for spring admission, 11/1. *Application fee:* $25.
Expenses: Tuition, state resident: part-time $233 per credit hour. Tuition, nonresident: part-time $623 per credit hour. Tuition and fees vary according to course load.
Financial support: In 2001–02, 7 teaching assistantships (averaging $7,600 per year) were awarded; career-related internships or fieldwork, Federal Work-Study, institutionally sponsored loans, and tuition waivers (partial) also available. Support available to part-time students. Financial award application deadline: 6/15.
Faculty research: Homicide, death penalty, crimes by elderly, drug abuse, community corrections.
Application contact: Dr. Wayne L. Lucas, Graduate Adviser, 816-235-1598, *Fax:* 816-235-1117, *E-mail:* lucasw@umkc.edu.

■ UNIVERSITY OF MISSOURI–ST. LOUIS

Graduate School, College of Arts and Sciences, Department of Criminology and Criminal Justice, St. Louis, MO 63121-4499

AWARDS MA, PhD.

Faculty: 12.
Students: 17 full-time (12 women), 41 part-time (20 women); includes 9 minority (7 African Americans, 1 Asian American or Pacific Islander, 1 Hispanic American), 3 international. In 2001, 11 master's, 3 doctorates awarded.
Degree requirements: For master's, thesis (for some programs); for doctorate, thesis/dissertation.
Entrance requirements: For doctorate, GRE General Test, sample of written work. *Application deadline:* For fall admission, 4/1. Applications are processed on a rolling basis. *Application fee:* $25 ($40 for international students). Electronic applications accepted.
Expenses: Tuition, state resident: part-time $231 per credit hour. Tuition, nonresident: part-time $621 per credit hour.
Financial support: In 2001–02, 1 fellowship with full tuition reimbursement (averaging $14,000 per year), 11 research assistantships with full and partial tuition reimbursements (averaging $9,989 per year), 6 teaching assistantships with full and partial tuition reimbursements (averaging $10,000 per year) were awarded. Career-related internships or fieldwork also available.
Faculty research: Crime control, criminological theory, juvenile delinquency, violence, drugs. *Total annual research expenditures:* $479,762.
Dr. Bruce Jacobs, Director of Graduate Studies, 314-516-5031, *Fax:* 314-516-5048, *E-mail:* jacobsb@msx.umsl.edu.
Application contact: Graduate Admissions, 314-516-5458, *Fax:* 314-516-5310, *E-mail:* gradadm@umsl.edu.

■ THE UNIVERSITY OF MONTANA–MISSOULA

Graduate School, College of Arts and Sciences, Department of Sociology, Missoula, MT 59812-0002

AWARDS Criminology (MA); rural and environmental change (MA).

Faculty: 11 full-time (3 women).
Students: 15 full-time (11 women), 2 part-time (both women); includes 1 minority (Native American). 17 applicants, 88% accepted, 9 enrolled. In 2001, 4 degrees awarded.
Entrance requirements: For master's, GRE General Test. *Application deadline:* For fall admission, 3/15 (priority date). *Application fee:* $45.
Expenses: Tuition, state resident: full-time $2,482; part-time $1,700 per year. Tuition, nonresident: full-time $7,372; part-time $5,000 per year. Required fees: $1,900. Tuition and fees vary according to degree level.
Financial support: In 2001–02, 5 teaching assistantships with full tuition reimbursements (averaging $8,665 per year) were awarded; research assistantships, career-related internships or fieldwork, Federal Work-Study, and unspecified assistantships also available. Financial award application deadline: 3/1; financial award applicants required to submit FAFSA.
Faculty research: Housing, homelessness, hunger, infant mortality, work safety. *Total annual research expenditures:* $191,297.
Dr. Jill Belsky, Chair, 406-243-5281, *Fax:* 406-243-5951, *E-mail:* belsky@selway.umt.edu.
Application contact: Dr. Daniel P. Doyle, Graduate Coordinator, 406-243-2855, *Fax:* 406-243-5951, *E-mail:* ddoyle@selway.umt.edu. *Web site:* http://www.umt.edu/sociology/

■ UNIVERSITY OF NEBRASKA AT OMAHA

Graduate Studies and Research, College of Public Affairs and Community Service, Department of Criminal Justice, Omaha, NE 68182

AWARDS MA, MS, PhD. Part-time and evening/weekend programs available.

Faculty: 17 full-time (8 women).
Students: 26 full-time (13 women), 31 part-time (25 women); includes 5 minority (2 African Americans, 2 Hispanic Americans, 1 Native American), 1 international. Average age 28. 52 applicants, 73% accepted, 16 enrolled. In 2001, 8 master's, 3 doctorates awarded. Terminal master's awarded for partial completion of doctoral program.
Degree requirements: For master's, thesis (for some programs), comprehensive exam; for doctorate, thesis/dissertation, comprehensive exam.
Entrance requirements: For master's, GRE General Test or MAT, previous course work in criminal justice, statistics, and research methods; minimum GPA of 3.0; for doctorate, GRE General Test. *Application deadline:* For fall admission, 7/1 (priority date); for spring admission, 12/1 (priority date). Applications are processed on a rolling basis. *Application fee:* $35. Electronic applications accepted.
Expenses: Tuition, state resident: part-time $116 per credit hour. Tuition, nonresident: part-time $291 per credit hour. Required fees: $13 per credit hour. $4 per semester. One-time fee: $52 part-time.
Financial support: In 2001–02, 23 students received support, including 16 research assistantships; teaching assistantships, career-related internships or fieldwork, Federal Work-Study, institutionally sponsored loans, scholarships/grants, tuition waivers (partial), and unspecified assistantships also available. Support available to part-time students. Financial award application deadline: 3/1; financial award applicants required to submit FAFSA.
Dr. Robert Meier, Chairperson, 402-554-2610.

■ UNIVERSITY OF NEVADA, LAS VEGAS

Graduate College, Greenspun College of Urban Affairs, Department of Criminal Justice, Las Vegas, NV 89154-9900

AWARDS MA. Part-time programs available.

Faculty: 7 full-time (0 women).
Students: 5 full-time (2 women), 8 part-time (4 women); includes 1 minority (Asian American or Pacific Islander), 1 international. 18 applicants, 56% accepted, 8 enrolled. In 2001, 2 degrees awarded.
Degree requirements: For master's, thesis (for some programs), comprehensive exam (for some programs).
Entrance requirements: For master's, minimum GPA of 3.0 during previous 2 years, 2.75 overall. *Application deadline:* For fall admission, 6/15. *Application fee:* $40 ($55 for international students).
Expenses: Tuition, state resident: full-time $1,926; part-time $107 per credit. Tuition, nonresident: full-time $9,376; part-time $220 per credit. Tuition and fees vary according to course load.
Financial support: In 2001–02, 5 teaching assistantships with partial tuition reimbursements (averaging $10,000 per year) were awarded; research assistantships Financial award application deadline: 3/1.
Dr. Richard McCorkle, Chair, 702-895-3731.
Application contact: Graduate College Admissions Evaluator, 702-895-3320, *Fax:* 702-895-4180, *E-mail:* gradcollege@ccmail.nevada.edu. *Web site:* http://www.unlv.edu/Colleges/Urban/Criminal_Justice/ma/

■ UNIVERSITY OF NEW HAVEN

Graduate School, School of Public Safety and Professional Studies, Program in Criminal Justice, West Haven, CT 06516-1916

AWARDS Correctional counseling (MS); criminal justice management (MS); security management (MS). Part-time and evening/weekend programs available.

Students: 17 full-time (7 women), 58 part-time (32 women); includes 19 minority (12 African Americans, 6 Hispanic Americans, 1 Native American), 4 international. In 2001, 22 degrees awarded.
Degree requirements: For master's, thesis or alternative.
Application deadline: Applications are processed on a rolling basis. *Application fee:* $50.
Expenses: Tuition: Full-time $12,015; part-time $445 per credit hour. Required fees: $30. One-time fee: $100 full-time.
Financial support: Career-related internships or fieldwork and Federal Work-Study available. Support available to part-time students. Financial award application deadline: 5/1.
William Norton, Coordinator, 203-932-7374.

■ UNIVERSITY OF NEW HAVEN

Graduate School, School of Public Safety and Professional Studies, Program in Forensic Science, West Haven, CT 06516-1916

AWARDS Advanced investigation (MS); criminalistics (MS); forensic science (MS). Part-time and evening/weekend programs available.

Students: 55 full-time (41 women), 32 part-time (12 women); includes 7 minority (2 African Americans, 2 Asian Americans or Pacific Islanders, 3 Hispanic Americans), 1 international. In 2001, 44 degrees awarded.
Degree requirements: For master's, thesis or alternative.
Entrance requirements: For master's, GRE Subject Test. *Application deadline:* Applications are processed on a rolling basis. *Application fee:* $50.
Expenses: Tuition: Full-time $12,015; part-time $445 per credit hour. Required fees: $30. One-time fee: $100 full-time.
Financial support: Career-related internships or fieldwork and Federal Work-Study available. Support available to part-time students. Financial award application deadline: 5/1; financial award applicants required to submit FAFSA.
Dr. Howard Harris, Coordinator, 203-932-7116.

■ UNIVERSITY OF NORTH ALABAMA

College of Arts and Sciences, Department of Social Work/Criminal Justice, Florence, AL 35632-0001

AWARDS Criminal justice (MSCJ). Part-time and evening/weekend programs available.

Faculty: 3 part-time/adjunct (0 women).
Students: 8 full-time (7 women), 15 part-time (10 women); includes 5 minority (3 African Americans, 2 Native Americans). Average age 30. In 2001, 9 degrees awarded.
Entrance requirements: For master's, GRE General Test, MAT. *Application deadline:* For fall admission, 7/1 (priority date); for spring admission, 12/1. Applications are processed on a rolling basis. *Application fee:* $25.
Expenses: Tuition, state resident: full-time $2,214; part-time $123 per credit hour. Tuition, nonresident: full-time $4,428; part-time $246 per credit hour. Required fees: $176; $7 per credit hour.
Application contact: Dr. Sue Wilson, Dean of Enrollment Management, 256-765-4316.

■ THE UNIVERSITY OF NORTH CAROLINA AT CHARLOTTE

Graduate School, College of Arts and Sciences, Department of Criminal Justice, Charlotte, NC 28223-0001

AWARDS MS. Part-time and evening/weekend programs available.

Faculty: 8 full-time (5 women).
Students: 8 full-time (4 women), 34 part-time (22 women); includes 6 minority (5 African Americans, 1 Asian American or Pacific Islander), 1 international. Average age 29. 31 applicants, 55% accepted, 7 enrolled. In 2001, 6 degrees awarded.
Degree requirements: For master's, thesis or comprehensive exam.
Entrance requirements: For master's, GRE General Test or MAT, minimum GPA of 3.0 in undergraduate major, 2.75 overall. *Application deadline:* For fall admission, 7/15; for spring admission, 11/15. Applications are processed on a rolling basis. *Application fee:* $35. Electronic applications accepted.
Expenses: Tuition, state resident: full-time $1,483; part-time $371 per year. Tuition, nonresident: full-time $9,850; part-time $2,463 per year. Required fees: $1,043; $277 per year. Tuition and fees vary according to course load.
Financial support: In 2001–02, 4 teaching assistantships were awarded; research assistantships, career-related internships or fieldwork, Federal Work-Study, institutionally sponsored loans, scholarships/grants, and unspecified assistantships also available. Support available to part-time students. Financial award application deadline: 4/1; financial award applicants required to submit FAFSA.
Faculty research: Criminological, legal, and penological theory; victimology, violence and international and domestic victims; court processing and the legal system; policing and police issues; criminal justice policy.
Dr. Bruce A. Arrigo, Chair, 704-687-2262, *Fax:* 704-687-3091, *E-mail:* barrigo@email.uncc.edu.
Application contact: Kathy Barringer, Director of Graduate Admissions, 704-687-3366, *Fax:* 704-687-3279, *E-mail:* gradadm@email.uncc.edu. *Web site:* http://www.uncc.edu/gradmiss/

■ UNIVERSITY OF NORTH FLORIDA

College of Arts and Sciences, Department of Sociology, Anthropology and Criminal Justice, Jacksonville, FL 32224-2645

AWARDS Criminal justice (MSCJ). Part-time and evening/weekend programs available.

Faculty: 22 full-time (6 women).
Students: 5 full-time (2 women), 22 part-time (15 women); includes 8 minority (5 African Americans, 2 Asian Americans or Pacific Islanders, 1 Native American).

University of North Florida (continued)
Average age 33. 20 applicants, 25% accepted, 3 enrolled. In 2001, 5 degrees awarded.
Degree requirements: For master's, thesis optional.
Entrance requirements: For master's, TOEFL, GRE General Test or minimum GPA of 3.0 in last 60 hours. *Application deadline:* For fall admission, 7/6 (priority date); for winter admission, 11/2 (priority date); for spring admission, 3/10 (priority date). Applications are processed on a rolling basis. *Application fee:* $20. Electronic applications accepted.
Expenses: Tuition, state resident: full-time $2,411; part-time $134 per credit hour. Tuition, nonresident: full-time $9,391; part-time $522 per credit hour. Required fees: $670; $37 per credit hour.
Financial support: In 2001–02, 14 students received support. Career-related internships or fieldwork, Federal Work-Study, and tuition waivers (partial) available. Support available to part-time students. Financial award application deadline: 4/1; financial award applicants required to submit FAFSA.
Faculty research: Women/crime, juvenile justice, minorities/crime, prison privatization; drug courts. *Total annual research expenditures:* $328,643.
Dr. R. Scott Frey, Chair, 904-620-1643, *E-mail:* rsfrey@unf.edu.
Application contact: Dr. Michael Hallett, Coordinator, 904-620-1644, *E-mail:* mhallett@unf.edu.

■ UNIVERSITY OF PITTSBURGH

Graduate School of Public and International Affairs, Doctoral Program in Public and International Affairs, Pittsburgh, PA 15260

AWARDS Development studies (PhD); foreign and security policy (PhD); international political economy (PhD); public administration (PhD); public policy (PhD). Part-time programs available.

Faculty: 32 full-time (8 women), 12 part-time/adjunct (9 women).
Students: 60 full-time (17 women), 12 part-time (4 women); includes 4 minority (2 African Americans, 1 Asian American or Pacific Islander, 1 Hispanic American), 45 international. Average age 30. 81 applicants, 41% accepted, 14 enrolled. In 2001, 3 degrees awarded.
Degree requirements: For doctorate, thesis/dissertation.
Application deadline: For fall admission, 3/1 (priority date). Applications are processed on a rolling basis. *Application fee:* $40. Electronic applications accepted.
Expenses: Tuition, state resident: full-time $9,410; part-time $385 per credit. Tuition, nonresident: full-time $19,376; part-time $797 per credit. Required fees: $480; $90 per term. Tuition and fees vary according to program.
Financial support: In 2001–02, 15 students received support, including 12 fellowships (averaging $21,500 per year), 1 research assistantship (averaging $21,500 per year), 5 teaching assistantships (averaging $7,700 per year); career-related internships or fieldwork, scholarships/grants, unspecified assistantships, and graduate student assistantships also available. Financial award application deadline: 2/1.
Faculty research: International political economy, international development, public administration, public policy, foreign policy, international security policy.
Dr. William F. Matlack, Doctoral Program Coordinator, 412-648-7604, *E-mail:* wfm@birch.gspia.pitt.edu.
Application contact: Elizabeth Barthen-Braunsdorf, Assistant Director of Admissions, 412-648-7643, *Fax:* 412-648-7641, *E-mail:* barthen@bitch.gspia.pitt.edu. *Web site:* http://www.gspia.pitt.edu/

Find an in-depth description at www.petersons.com/gradchannel.

■ UNIVERSITY OF PITTSBURGH

Graduate School of Public and International Affairs, Executive Programs in Public Policy and Management, Pittsburgh, PA 15260

AWARDS Criminal justice (MPPM); development planning (MPPM); environmental management and policy (MPPM); international development (MPPM); international political economy (MPPM); international security studies (MPPM); management of non profit organizations (MPPM); metropolitan management and regional development (MPPM); personnel and labor relations (MPPM); policy analysis and evaluation (MPPM). Part-time programs available.

Faculty: 32 full-time (8 women), 12 part-time/adjunct (9 women).
Students: 7 full-time (4 women), 51 part-time (27 women); includes 8 minority (all African Americans), 3 international. Average age 38. 34 applicants, 79% accepted, 18 enrolled. In 2001, 24 degrees awarded.
Degree requirements: For master's, thesis optional.
Application deadline: For fall admission, 3/1 (priority date); for spring admission, 10/1 (priority date). Applications are processed on a rolling basis. *Application fee:* $40.
Expenses: Tuition, state resident: full-time $9,410; part-time $385 per credit. Tuition, nonresident: full-time $19,376; part-time $797 per credit. Required fees: $480; $90 per term. Tuition and fees vary according to program.
Financial support: Institutionally sponsored loans and scholarships/grants available. Support available to part-time students. Financial award application deadline: 2/1.
Faculty research: Executive training and technical assistance for U.S. and international clients. *Total annual research expenditures:* $101,000.
Michele Garrity, Director, Executive Education, 412-648-7610, *Fax:* 412-648-2605, *E-mail:* garrity@birch.gspia.pitt.edu.
Application contact: Maureen O'Malley, Admissions Counselor, 412-648-7646, *Fax:* 412-648-7641, *E-mail:* pronobis@birch.gspia.pitt.edu. *Web site:* http://www.gspia.pitt.edu/

Find an in-depth description at www.petersons.com/gradchannel.

■ UNIVERSITY OF SOUTH CAROLINA

The Graduate School, College of Criminal Justice, Columbia, SC 29208

AWARDS MCJ, JD/MCJ. Part-time and evening/weekend programs available. Postbaccalaureate distance learning degree programs offered.

Degree requirements: For master's, thesis or alternative.
Entrance requirements: For master's, GRE or MAT. Electronic applications accepted.
Expenses: Tuition, state resident: full-time $4,434. Tuition, nonresident: full-time $9,854. Tuition and fees vary according to program.
Faculty research: Juvenile delinquency, substance abuse, policy development, minority issues, civil liability, law enforcement services.

■ UNIVERSITY OF SOUTHERN MISSISSIPPI

Graduate School, College of Liberal Arts, Department of Criminal Justice, Hattiesburg, MS 39406

AWARDS Administration of justice (PhD); corrections (MA, MS); juvenile justice (MA, MS); law enforcement (MA, MS). Part-time programs available.

Faculty: 7 full-time (0 women), 2 part-time/adjunct (0 women).
Students: 30 full-time (14 women), 16 part-time (7 women); includes 3 minority (all African Americans). Average age 28. 53 applicants, 62% accepted. In 2001, 14 degrees awarded.
Degree requirements: For master's, comprehensive exam.
Entrance requirements: For master's, GRE General Test, minimum GPA of 2.75 in last 2 years, 3.0 in field of study.
Application deadline: For fall admission, 8/6 (priority date). Applications are processed on a rolling basis. *Application fee:* $0 ($25 for international students).
Expenses: Tuition, state resident: full-time $3,416; part-time $190 per credit hour. Tuition, nonresident: full-time $7,932; part-time $441 per credit hour.
Financial support: In 2001–02, 2 research assistantships with full tuition reimbursements (averaging $5,000 per year) were

awarded; teaching assistantships with full and partial tuition reimbursements, career-related internships or fieldwork, Federal Work-Study, and institutionally sponsored loans also available. Financial award application deadline: 3/15.
Faculty research: Crime in the family, police training models, humanities and criminal justice.
Dr. Stephen Mallory, Chair, 601-266-4509, *Fax:* 601-266-4391.

■ UNIVERSITY OF SOUTH FLORIDA

College of Graduate Studies, College of Arts and Sciences, Department of Criminology, Tampa, FL 33620-9951

AWARDS MA, PhD.

Faculty: 18 full-time (4 women).
Students: 26 full-time (17 women), 20 part-time (13 women); includes 7 minority (4 African Americans, 3 Hispanic Americans), 3 international. Average age 30. 46 applicants, 57% accepted, 15 enrolled. In 2001, 12 degrees awarded.
Degree requirements: For master's, thesis optional; for doctorate, thesis/dissertation.
Entrance requirements: For master's, GRE General Test, minimum GPA of 3.0 in last 60 hours; for doctorate, GRE General Test, minimum GPA of 3.0. *Application deadline:* For fall admission, 2/1; for spring admission, 9/30. *Application fee:* $20. Electronic applications accepted.
Expenses: Tuition, state resident: part-time $166 per credit hour. Tuition, nonresident: part-time $573 per credit hour. Required fees: $17 per term.
Financial support: Fellowships with partial tuition reimbursements, research assistantships with partial tuition reimbursements, teaching assistantships with partial tuition reimbursements, Federal Work-Study and institutionally sponsored loans available. Support available to part-time students. Financial award applicants required to submit FAFSA.
Faculty research: Criminal theory, drug abuse, violence, policing, gangs. *Total annual research expenditures:* $72,466.
William R. Blount, Chairperson, 813-974-9704, *Fax:* 813-974-2803, *E-mail:* blount@luna.cas.usf.edu.
Application contact: Michael Lynch, Graduate Coordinator, 813-974-8148, *Fax:* 813-974-2803, *E-mail:* mlynch@luna.cas.usf.edu. *Web site:* http://www.cas.usf.edu/criminology/index.html

■ THE UNIVERSITY OF TENNESSEE

Graduate School, College of Arts and Sciences, Department of Sociology, Knoxville, TN 37996

AWARDS Criminology (MA, PhD); energy, environment, and resource policy (MA, PhD); political economy (MA, PhD). Part-time programs available.

Faculty: 15 full-time (2 women), 1 (woman) part-time/adjunct.
Students: 22 full-time (14 women), 26 part-time (11 women); includes 7 minority (6 African Americans, 1 Asian American or Pacific Islander), 4 international. 30 applicants, 63% accepted. In 2001, 3 degrees awarded.
Degree requirements: For master's, thesis or alternative; for doctorate, thesis/dissertation.
Entrance requirements: For master's, GRE General Test, TOEFL, minimum GPA of 3.0; for doctorate, GRE General Test, TOEFL, minimum GPA of 3.5. *Application deadline:* For fall admission, 2/1 (priority date). Applications are processed on a rolling basis. *Application fee:* $35. Electronic applications accepted.
Expenses: Tuition, state resident: full-time $4,280; part-time $233 per hour. Tuition, nonresident: full-time $12,066; part-time $666 per hour. Tuition and fees vary according to program.
Financial support: In 2001–02, 1 fellowship, 2 research assistantships, 20 teaching assistantships were awarded. Federal Work-Study, institutionally sponsored loans, and unspecified assistantships also available. Financial award application deadline: 2/1; financial award applicants required to submit FAFSA.
Dr. Suzanne Kurth, Head, 865-974-6021, *Fax:* 865-974-7013, *E-mail:* skurth@utk.edu.
Application contact: Dr. T. C. Hood, Graduate Representative, 865-974-7032, *E-mail:* tomhood@utk.edu.

■ THE UNIVERSITY OF TENNESSEE AT CHATTANOOGA

Graduate Division, College of Health and Human Services, Program in Criminal Justice, Chattanooga, TN 37403-2598

AWARDS MSCJ. Part-time and evening/weekend programs available.

Faculty: 4 full-time (1 woman).
Students: 12 full-time (8 women), 34 part-time (20 women); includes 6 minority (5 African Americans, 1 Asian American or Pacific Islander). Average age 31. 21 applicants, 100% accepted, 13 enrolled. In 2001, 13 degrees awarded.
Degree requirements: For master's, qualifying exams.
Entrance requirements: For master's, GRE General Test or LSAT, MAT. *Application deadline:* For fall admission, 8/1 (priority date); for spring admission, 12/1 (priority date). Applications are processed on a rolling basis. *Application fee:* $25.
Expenses: Tuition, state resident: full-time $3,752; part-time $228 per hour. Tuition, nonresident: full-time $10,282; part-time $565 per hour.
Financial support: Fellowships, research assistantships, Federal Work-Study and institutionally sponsored loans available. Support available to part-time students. Financial award application deadline: 4/1; financial award applicants required to submit FAFSA.
Dr. Helen M. Eigenberg, Head, 423-425-4135, *Fax:* 423-425-2228, *E-mail:* helen-eigenberg@utc.edu.
Application contact: Dr. Deborah E. Arfken, Dean of Graduate Studies, 865-425-1740, *Fax:* 865-425-5223, *E-mail:* deborah-arfken@utc.edu. *Web site:* http://www.utc.edu/

■ THE UNIVERSITY OF TEXAS AT ARLINGTON

Graduate School, College of Liberal Arts, Department of Criminology and Criminal Justice, Arlington, TX 76019

AWARDS MA. Part-time and evening/weekend programs available.

Faculty: 4 full-time (0 women).
Students: 6 full-time (4 women), 31 part-time (19 women); includes 11 minority (4 African Americans, 1 Asian American or Pacific Islander, 6 Hispanic Americans), 1 international. 16 applicants, 100% accepted, 10 enrolled. In 2001, 9 degrees awarded.
Degree requirements: For master's, thesis or alternative.
Entrance requirements: For master's, GRE General Test, minimum GPA of 3.0 in last 60 hours of undergraduate course work. *Application deadline:* For fall admission, 6/16. Applications are processed on a rolling basis. *Application fee:* $25 ($50 for international students).
Expenses: Tuition, area resident: Full-time $2,268. Tuition, nonresident: full-time $6,264. Required fees: $839. Tuition and fees vary according to course load.
Financial support: In 2001–02, fellowships (averaging $1,000 per year), 1 research assistantship, 1 teaching assistantship were awarded. Career-related internships or fieldwork also available. Financial award application deadline: 6/1; financial award applicants required to submit FAFSA.
Dr. Robert L. Bing, Chair, 817-272-3318, *Fax:* 817-272-5673, *E-mail:* rbing@uta.edu.
Application contact: Dr. Alejandro del Carmen, Graduate Adviser, 817-272-3318, *Fax:* 817-272-5673, *E-mail:* adelcarmen@uta.edu.

■ THE UNIVERSITY OF TEXAS AT SAN ANTONIO

College of Public Policy, Department of Criminal Justice, San Antonio, TX 78249-0617

AWARDS Justice policy (MS).

Faculty: 3 full-time (1 woman), 1 part-time/adjunct (0 women).

The University of Texas at San Antonio (continued)

Students: 1 (woman) full-time, 9 part-time (1 woman); includes 3 minority (1 African American, 2 Hispanic Americans). Average age 32. 8 applicants, 38% accepted, 2 enrolled.
Degree requirements: For master's, thesis optional.
Entrance requirements: For master's, GRE General Test, minimum GPA of 3.0 on last 60 hours. *Application deadline:* For fall admission, 7/1. Applications are processed on a rolling basis. *Application fee:* $25.
Expenses: Tuition, state resident: full-time $2,268; part-time $126 per credit hour. Tuition, nonresident: full-time $6,066; part-time $337 per credit hour. Required fees: $781. Tuition and fees vary according to course load.
Financial support: Research assistantships, career-related internships or fieldwork and Federal Work-Study available. *Total annual research expenditures:* $1,684.
Dr. Patricia Harris, Chair, 210-458-2535.

■ THE UNIVERSITY OF TEXAS AT TYLER

Graduate Studies, College of Arts and Sciences, Department of Social Sciences, Tyler, TX 75799-0001

AWARDS Criminal justice (MAIS, MS); economics (MAIS); political science (MA, MAIS, MAT); public administration (MPA); sociology (MAIS, MAT, MS). Part-time and evening/weekend programs available. Postbaccalaureate distance learning degree programs offered.

Faculty: 14 full-time (1 woman).
Students: 13 full-time (9 women), 54 part-time (34 women); includes 16 minority (14 African Americans, 1 Hispanic American, 1 Native American), 1 international. Average age 35. 8 applicants, 100% accepted, 8 enrolled. In 2001, 10 degrees awarded.
Degree requirements: For master's, thesis (for some programs), comprehensive exam.
Entrance requirements: For master's, GRE General Test, minimum GPA of 3.0. *Application deadline:* Applications are processed on a rolling basis. *Application fee:* $0.
Expenses: Tuition, state resident: part-time $44 per credit hour. Tuition, nonresident: part-time $262 per credit hour. Required fees: $58 per credit hour. $76 per semester.
Financial support: Teaching assistantships, career-related internships or fieldwork, Federal Work-Study, and scholarships/grants available. Support available to part-time students. Financial award application deadline: 7/1; financial award applicants required to submit FAFSA.
Faculty research: Urban segregation, minority business, violent crime, gender discrimination, Third World agriculture production.
Dr. Barbara L. Hart, Chair, 903-566-7426, *Fax:* 903-565-5537, *E-mail:* bhart@mail.uttyl.edu.
Application contact: Carol A. Hodge, Office of Graduate Studies, 903-566-5642, *Fax:* 903-566-7068, *E-mail:* chodge@mail.uttly.edu.

■ THE UNIVERSITY OF TEXAS OF THE PERMIAN BASIN

Graduate School, College of Arts and Sciences, Department of Behavioral Science, Program in Criminal Justice Administration, Odessa, TX 79762-0001

AWARDS MS. Part-time and evening/weekend programs available.

Degree requirements: For master's, thesis.
Entrance requirements: For master's, GRE General Test.
Expenses: Tuition, state resident: full-time $1,746. Tuition, nonresident: full-time $5,292. Required fees: $523. Tuition and fees vary according to course load.

■ THE UNIVERSITY OF TEXAS–PAN AMERICAN

College of Social and Behavioral Sciences, Department of Criminal Justice, Edinburg, TX 78539-2999

AWARDS MS. Part-time and evening/weekend programs available. Postbaccalaureate distance learning degree programs offered (minimal on-campus study).

Faculty: 6 full-time (1 woman).
Students: 4 full-time (2 women), 14 part-time (3 women); includes 11 minority (all Hispanic Americans). Average age 29. 2 applicants, 100% accepted, 2 enrolled. In 2001, 9 degrees awarded.
Degree requirements: For master's, applied project or thesis, thesis optional. *Median time to degree:* Master's–2 years part-time.
Entrance requirements: For master's, minimum GPA of 2.75. *Application deadline:* For fall admission, 5/30 (priority date). Applications are processed on a rolling basis. *Application fee:* $0.
Expenses: Tuition, state resident: part-time $212 per semester hour. Tuition, nonresident: part-time $367 per semester hour.
Financial support: In 2001–02, 2 teaching assistantships (averaging $7,008 per year) were awarded; institutionally sponsored loans also available. Support available to part-time students. Financial award application deadline: 4/15; financial award applicants required to submit CSS PROFILE or FAFSA.
Faculty research: Comparative criminal justice systems, death penalty, community policing, Hispanic women.
Dr. Daniel Dearth, Chair, 956-381-3566, *Fax:* 956-381-2490, *E-mail:* dkd@panam.edu.
Application contact: Dr. Mark L. Dantzker, Graduate Director, 956-381-2967, *Fax:* 956-381-2490, *E-mail:* mldantz@panam.edu.

■ UNIVERSITY OF WISCONSIN–MILWAUKEE

Graduate School, School of Social Welfare, Program in Criminal Justice, Milwaukee, WI 53201-0413

AWARDS MS. Part-time programs available.

Faculty: 7 full-time (1 woman).
Students: 14 full-time (11 women), 11 part-time (9 women); includes 6 minority (4 African Americans, 2 Hispanic Americans). 17 applicants, 59% accepted. In 2001, 11 degrees awarded.
Degree requirements: For master's, thesis or alternative.
Entrance requirements: For master's, GRE General Test, MAT. *Application deadline:* For fall admission, 1/1 (priority date); for spring admission, 9/1. Applications are processed on a rolling basis. *Application fee:* $45 ($75 for international students).
Expenses: Tuition, state resident: full-time $6,180; part-time $535 per credit. Tuition, nonresident: full-time $19,482; part-time $1,366 per credit. Tuition and fees vary according to course load, program and reciprocity agreements.
Financial support: In 2001–02, 1 fellowship, 2 teaching assistantships were awarded. Research assistantships, career-related internships or fieldwork and unspecified assistantships also available. Support available to part-time students. Financial award application deadline: 4/15.
Melissa Barlow, Representative, 414-229-2392, *Fax:* 414-229-5311, *E-mail:* mhbarlow@uwm.edu. *Web site:* http://www.uwm.edu/Dept/CJ/

■ UNIVERSITY OF WISCONSIN–PLATTEVILLE

School of Graduate Studies, Distance Learning Center, Online Program in Criminal Justice, Platteville, WI 53818-3099

AWARDS MS. Postbaccalaureate distance learning degree programs offered (no on-campus study).

Degree requirements: For master's, thesis or alternative.
Electronic applications accepted.
Expenses: Tuition, state resident: full-time $4,564; part-time $224 per credit. Tuition, nonresident: full-time $14,388; part-time $769 per credit. Part-time tuition and fees vary according to course load.

■ UTICA COLLEGE

Program in Economic Crime Management, Utica, NY 13502-4892

AWARDS MS. Postbaccalaureate distance learning degree programs offered (minimal on-campus study).

■ VALDOSTA STATE UNIVERSITY

Graduate School, College of Arts and Sciences, Department of Sociology and Criminal Justice, Program in Criminal Justice, Valdosta, GA 31698

AWARDS MS. Part-time and evening/weekend programs available.

Faculty: 4 full-time (1 woman).
Students: 13 full-time (11 women), 10 part-time (9 women); includes 2 minority (both African Americans). Average age 27. 17 applicants, 82% accepted. In 2001, 16 degrees awarded.
Degree requirements: For master's, thesis or alternative, comprehensive written and/or oral exams.
Entrance requirements: For master's, GRE General Test, minimum GPA of 2.5. *Application deadline:* For fall admission, 7/1; for spring admission, 11/15. Applications are processed on a rolling basis. *Application fee:* $20. Electronic applications accepted.
Expenses: Tuition, state resident: full-time $1,746; part-time $97 per hour. Tuition, nonresident: full-time $6,966; part-time $387 per hour. Required fees: $594; $297 per semester.
Financial support: In 2001–02, 2 research assistantships with full tuition reimbursements (averaging $2,452 per year) were awarded; institutionally sponsored loans, scholarships/grants, and unspecified assistantships also available. Support available to part-time students. Financial award application deadline: 7/1; financial award applicants required to submit FAFSA.
Dr. Deborah Robinson, Area Chair, 229-333-5943, *Fax:* 229-333-5492, *E-mail:* dmrobins@valdosta.edu.

■ VILLANOVA UNIVERSITY

Graduate School of Liberal Arts and Sciences, Department of Criminal Justice Administration, Villanova, PA 19085-1699

AWARDS MS. Evening/weekend programs available.

Students: 9 full-time (3 women), 11 part-time (5 women); includes 5 minority (3 African Americans, 2 Hispanic Americans). Average age 27. 18 applicants, 61% accepted. In 2001, 4 degrees awarded.
Degree requirements: For master's, comprehensive exam.
Entrance requirements: For master's, GRE General Test, minimum GPA of 3.0. *Application deadline:* For fall admission, 8/1 (priority date); for spring admission, 12/1. *Application fee:* $40.
Expenses: Tuition: Part-time $340 per credit. One-time fee: $115 full-time. Tuition and fees vary according to program.
Financial support: Career-related internships or fieldwork and Federal Work-Study available. Financial award application deadline: 2/1; financial award applicants required to submit FAFSA.
Dr. Craig Wheeland, Director. *Web site:* http://www.gradcj.villanova.edu/

■ VIRGINIA COMMONWEALTH UNIVERSITY

School of Graduate Studies, College of Humanities and Sciences, Department of Criminal Justice, Richmond, VA 23284-9005

AWARDS Criminal justice (MS, CCJA); forensic science (MS). Part-time and evening/weekend programs available.

Students: 42 full-time, 63 part-time; includes 11 minority (9 African Americans, 2 Hispanic Americans). 226 applicants, 18% accepted. In 2001, 26 master's, 16 other advanced degrees awarded.
Degree requirements: For master's, thesis or comprehensive exam, thesis optional.
Entrance requirements: For master's, GRE General Test, minimum GPA of 2.7. *Application deadline:* For fall admission, 4/1; for spring admission, 11/1. Applications are processed on a rolling basis. *Application fee:* $30.
Expenses: Tuition, state resident: full-time $4,276; part-time $238 per credit. Tuition, nonresident: full-time $12,672; part-time $704 per credit. Required fees: $1,167; $43 per credit.
Financial support: Federal Work-Study, institutionally sponsored loans, and tuition waivers (full and partial) available. Support available to part-time students. Financial award application deadline: 3/1.
Dr. Jay S. Albanese, Chair, 804-828-1050, *Fax:* 804-828-1253, *E-mail:* jsalbane@vcu.edu.
Application contact: Dr. James L. Hague, Graduate Program Director, 804-828-1050, *Fax:* 804-828-1253, *E-mail:* hague@vcu.edu. *Web site:* http://www.has.vcu.edu/crj/

■ WASHINGTON STATE UNIVERSITY

Graduate School, College of Liberal Arts, Department of Political Science, Program in Criminal Justice, Pullman, WA 99164

AWARDS MA.

Faculty: 5 full-time (1 woman).
Students: 12 full-time (7 women), 7 part-time (2 women); includes 1 minority (Hispanic American), 1 international. Average age 25. 29 applicants, 45% accepted. In 2001, 14 degrees awarded.
Degree requirements: For master's, oral exam.
Entrance requirements: For master's, GRE General Test, minimum GPA of 3.0. *Application deadline:* For fall admission, 2/1; for spring admission, 11/1. *Application fee:* $35. Electronic applications accepted.
Expenses: Tuition, state resident: full-time $6,088; part-time $304 per semester. Tuition, nonresident: full-time $14,918; part-time $746 per semester. Tuition and fees vary according to program.
Financial support: In 2001–02, 4 research assistantships with full and partial tuition reimbursements, 8 teaching assistantships with full and partial tuition reimbursements were awarded. Career-related internships or fieldwork, Federal Work-Study, institutionally sponsored loans, tuition waivers (partial), and teaching associateships also available. Financial award application deadline: 2/1; financial award applicants required to submit FAFSA.
Faculty research: Community policing, community justice, corrections policy, crime prevention policy, criminal justice management, gender. *Total annual research expenditures:* $55,561.
Dr. Faithe Lutze, Director, 509-335-2272, *Fax:* 509-335-7990, *E-mail:* lutze@wsu.edu.
Application contact: Diane Berger, Graduate Secretary, 509-335-2545, *Fax:* 509-335-7990, *E-mail:* bergerd@wsu.edu. *Web site:* http://www.libarts.wsu.edu/polisci/

■ WASHINGTON STATE UNIVERSITY SPOKANE

Graduate Programs, Program in Criminal Justice, Spokane, WA 99201-3899

AWARDS MA.

■ WAYNE STATE UNIVERSITY

Graduate School, College of Liberal Arts, Department of Criminal Justice, Detroit, MI 48202

AWARDS MS.

Faculty: 6 full-time.
Students: 22. 17 applicants, 47% accepted, 7 enrolled. In 2001, 6 degrees awarded.
Degree requirements: For master's, essay.
Entrance requirements: For master's, GRE General Test, GRE Subject Test, minimum GPA of 3.0. *Application deadline:* For fall admission, 7/1. *Application fee:* $20 ($30 for international students).
Expenses: Tuition, state resident: full-time $3,764. Tuition and fees vary according to degree level and program.
Financial support: In 2001–02, 1 teaching assistantship was awarded
Faculty research: Social deviance; corrections; juvenile justice; women and crime; law, politics and crime.

Wayne State University (continued)
Marvin Zalman, Interim Chairperson, 313-577-2705, *E-mail:* marvin.zalman@wayne.edu.
Application contact: Dr. Olga Tsoudis, Graduate Director, 313-577-0975, *Fax:* 313-577-9977, *E-mail:* tsoudis@wayne.edu.

■ WAYNE STATE UNIVERSITY

Graduate School, College of Liberal Arts, Department of Political Science, Program in Public Administration, Detroit, MI 48202

AWARDS Criminal justice (MPA); public administration (MPA). Evening/weekend programs available.

Students: 24. In 2001, 3 degrees awarded.
Entrance requirements: For master's, GRE General Test. *Application deadline:* For fall admission, 7/1. Applications are processed on a rolling basis. *Application fee:* $20 ($30 for international students). Electronic applications accepted.
Expenses: Tuition, state resident: full-time $3,764. Tuition and fees vary according to degree level and program.
Faculty research: Urban politics, urban education, state administration.
John Strate, Director, 313-577-2668, *E-mail:* jstrate@wayne.edu.

■ WEBSTER UNIVERSITY

School of Business and Technology, Department of Business, St. Louis, MO 63119-3194

AWARDS Business (MA, MBA); computer resources and information management (MA, MBA); computer science/distributed systems (MS); environmental management (MS); finance (MA, MBA); health care management (MA); health services management (MA, MBA); human resources development (MA, MBA); human resources management (MA); international business (MA, MBA); management (MA, MBA); marketing (MA, MBA); procurement and acquisitions management (MA, MBA); public administration (MA); real estate management (MA, MBA); security management (MA, MBA); space systems management (MA, MBA, MS); telecommunications management (MA, MBA).

Students: 1,415 full-time (661 women), 3,483 part-time (1,566 women); includes 1,604 minority (1,183 African Americans, 166 Asian Americans or Pacific Islanders, 220 Hispanic Americans, 35 Native Americans), 606 international. Average age 33. In 2001, 1439 degrees awarded. *Application deadline:* Applications are processed on a rolling basis. *Application fee:* $25 ($50 for international students).
Expenses: Tuition: Full-time $7,164; part-time $398 per credit hour.
Financial support: Federal Work-Study available. Support available to part-time students. Financial award application deadline: 4/1; financial award applicants required to submit FAFSA.
Steve Hinson, Chair, 314-968-7017, *Fax:* 314-968-7077.
Application contact: Denise Harrell, Associate Director of Graduate and Evening Student Admissions, 314-968-6983, *Fax:* 314-968-7116, *E-mail:* gadmit@webster.edu.

■ WEST CHESTER UNIVERSITY OF PENNSYLVANIA

Graduate Studies, School of Business and Public Affairs, Department of Criminal Justice, West Chester, PA 19383

AWARDS MS. Part-time and evening/weekend programs available.

Faculty: 3.
Students: 11 full-time (3 women), 34 part-time (11 women); includes 4 minority (3 African Americans, 1 Asian American or Pacific Islander). Average age 30. 17 applicants, 94% accepted. In 2001, 18 degrees awarded.
Degree requirements: For master's, thesis optional.
Entrance requirements: For master's, MAT, interview, minimum GPA of 3.0. *Application deadline:* For fall admission, 4/15 (priority date); for spring admission, 10/15. Applications are processed on a rolling basis. *Application fee:* $25.
Expenses: Tuition, state resident: full-time $4,600; part-time $256 per credit. Tuition, nonresident: full-time $7,554; part-time $420 per credit. Required fees: $44 per credit.
Financial support: In 2001–02, 1 research assistantship with full tuition reimbursement (averaging $5,000 per year) was awarded; unspecified assistantships also available. Support available to part-time students. Financial award application deadline: 2/15; financial award applicants required to submit FAFSA.
Faculty research: Criminal law, criminal procedure, constitutional interpretation.
Dr. Jana Nestlerode, Chair, 610-436-2647.
Application contact: Dr. Mary P. Brewster, Graduate Coordinator, 610-436-2630, *E-mail:* mbrewster@wcupa.edu.

■ WESTERN CONNECTICUT STATE UNIVERSITY

Division of Graduate Studies, Ancell School of Business and Public Administration, Program in Justice Administration, Danbury, CT 06810-6885

AWARDS MS. Part-time and evening/weekend programs available.

Faculty: 4 full-time (1 woman).
Students: 1 full-time (0 women), 12 part-time (3 women). Average age 36. In 2001, 4 degrees awarded.
Degree requirements: For master's, comprehensive exam or research project.
Entrance requirements: For master's, GMAT, GRE, LSAT, or MAT. *Application deadline:* For fall admission, 8/1 (priority date). Applications are processed on a rolling basis. *Application fee:* $40.
Expenses: Tuition, state resident: full-time $2,772; part-time $215 per credit hour. Tuition, nonresident: full-time $7,726. Required fees: $30 per term.
Financial support: Fellowships, career-related internships or fieldwork available. Support available to part-time students. Financial award application deadline: 5/1; financial award applicants required to submit FAFSA.
Dr. Michael Foley, Associate Professor, 203-837-8597.
Application contact: Chris Shankle, Associate Director of Graduate Admissions, 203-837-8244, *Fax:* 203-837-8338, *E-mail:* shanklec@wcsu.edu. *Web site:* http://www.wcsu.edu/JLA/MSJA

■ WESTERN ILLINOIS UNIVERSITY

School of Graduate Studies, College of Education and Human Services, Department of Law Enforcement and Justice Administration, Macomb, IL 61455-1390

AWARDS Law enforcement and justice administration (MA); Police Executive Certification (Certificate). Part-time programs available.

Faculty: 15 full-time (2 women), 6 part-time/adjunct (1 woman).
Students: 26 full-time (11 women), 94 part-time (28 women); includes 11 minority (6 African Americans, 1 Asian American or Pacific Islander, 4 Hispanic Americans). Average age 32. 56 applicants, 86% accepted. In 2001, 20 master's, 7 other advanced degrees awarded.
Degree requirements: For master's, thesis or alternative.
Entrance requirements: For master's, minimum GPA of 3.0. *Application deadline:* Applications are processed on a rolling basis. *Application fee:* $0 ($25 for international students). Electronic applications accepted.
Expenses: Tuition, state resident: part-time $108 per credit hour. Tuition, nonresident: part-time $216 per credit hour. Required fees: $33 per credit hour.
Financial support: In 2001–02, 8 students received support, including 8 research assistantships with full tuition reimbursements available (averaging $5,720 per year). Financial award applicants required to submit FAFSA.
Faculty research: Law enforcement executive institute, media resource center, law enforcement programming, victim assistance.
Col. Steve Reinhart, Chairperson, 309-298-1038.
Application contact: Dr. Barbara Baily, Director of Graduate Studies, 309-298-1806, *Fax:* 309-298-2345, *E-mail:* grad-office@wiu.edu. *Web site:* http://www.wiu.edu/

■ WESTERN NEW ENGLAND COLLEGE

School of Business, Program in Criminal Justice Administration, Springfield, MA 01119-2654

AWARDS MSCJA.

Students: 51 applicants, 71% accepted. In 2001, 304 degrees awarded.
Application deadline: Applications are processed on a rolling basis. *Application fee:* $30.
Expenses: Tuition: Part-time $429 per credit. Required fees: $9 per credit. $20 per semester.
Financial support: Application deadline: 4/1.
Dr. Larry F. Field, Head.
Application contact: Douglas Kenyon, Administrative Director, Off-Campus Programs, 781-933-1595, *E-mail:* dkenyon@wnec.edu.

■ WESTERN OREGON UNIVERSITY

Graduate Programs, College of Liberal Arts and Sciences, Division of Social Science, Monmouth, OR 97361-1394

AWARDS Correctional administration (MA, MS). Part-time and evening/weekend programs available.

Faculty: 3 full-time (1 woman), 8 part-time/adjunct (3 women).
Students: 7 full-time (3 women), 4 part-time (1 woman); includes 1 minority (Native American). Average age 35. In 2001, 3 degrees awarded.
Degree requirements: For master's, written exams, thesis optional.
Entrance requirements: For master's, minimum GPA of 3.0. *Application deadline:* Applications are processed on a rolling basis. *Application fee:* $50.
Financial support: In 2001–02, 2 teaching assistantships with full tuition reimbursements (averaging $676 per year) were awarded; research assistantships with full tuition reimbursements, career-related internships or fieldwork, Federal Work-Study, and tuition waivers (full and partial) also available. Support available to part-time students. Financial award application deadline: 3/1; financial award applicants required to submit FAFSA.
Faculty research: Prison to community transition of adult felons, community justice, restorative justice, parole and probation.
Dr. Stephen Gibbons, Coordinator, 503-838-8317, *Fax:* 503-838-8034, *E-mail:* gibbons@wou.edu.
Application contact: Alison Marshall, Director of Admissions, 503-838-8211, *Fax:* 503-838-8067, *E-mail:* marshaa@wou.edu.

■ WESTFIELD STATE COLLEGE

Division of Graduate Studies and Continuing Education, Department of Criminal Justice, Westfield, MA 01086

AWARDS MS. Part-time and evening/weekend programs available.

Faculty: 4 full-time (2 women).
Students: 5 full-time (2 women), 50 part-time (15 women); includes 7 minority (4 African Americans, 3 Hispanic Americans). Average age 30. In 2001, 19 degrees awarded.
Degree requirements: For master's, thesis (for some programs), comprehensive exam.
Entrance requirements: For master's, GRE General Test or MAT, minimum undergraduate GPA of 2.7. *Application deadline:* Applications are processed on a rolling basis. *Application fee:* $30.
Expenses: Tuition, state resident: part-time $155 per credit. Tuition, nonresident: part-time $165 per credit.
Financial support: In 2001–02, 1 research assistantship with tuition reimbursement (averaging $1,600 per year) was awarded; career-related internships or fieldwork, Federal Work-Study, and tuition waivers (full and partial) also available. Support available to part-time students. Financial award application deadline: 4/1; financial award applicants required to submit CSS PROFILE.
Dr. Kimberly Tobin, Director, 413-572-5309 Ext. 5634.
Application contact: Russ Leary, Admissions Clerk, 413-572-8022, *Fax:* 413-572-5227, *E-mail:* rleary@wisdom.wsc.mass.edu.

■ WEST TEXAS A&M UNIVERSITY

College of Education and Social Sciences, Department of History and Political Science, Program in Criminal Justice, Canyon, TX 79016-0001

AWARDS MA. Part-time and evening/weekend programs available.

Faculty: 4 full-time (1 woman).
Students: 5 full-time (3 women), 12 part-time (5 women); includes 5 minority (1 African American, 3 Hispanic Americans, 1 Native American). 14 applicants, 71% accepted. In 2001, 3 degrees awarded.
Degree requirements: For master's, thesis optional. *Median time to degree:* Master's–3 years full-time, 6 years part-time.
Entrance requirements: For master's, GRE General Test. *Application deadline:* Applications are processed on a rolling basis. *Application fee:* $25 ($75 for international students). Electronic applications accepted.
Expenses: Tuition, state resident: part-time $120 per hour. Tuition, nonresident: part-time $253 per hour.
Financial support: In 2001–02, research assistantships with partial tuition reimbursements (averaging $6,500 per year), teaching assistantships with partial tuition reimbursements (averaging $6,700 per year) were awarded. Career-related internships or fieldwork and scholarships/grants also available. Support available to part-time students. Financial award applicants required to submit CSS PROFILE or FAFSA.
Application contact: Susan Coleman, Graduate Adviser, 806-651-2434, *Fax:* 806-651-2601, *E-mail:* scoleman@mail.wtamu.edu.

■ WICHITA STATE UNIVERSITY

Graduate School, Fairmount College of Liberal Arts and Sciences, School of Community Affairs, Wichita, KS 67260

AWARDS Criminal justice (MA); gerontology (MA). Part-time programs available.

Faculty: 10 full-time (4 women), 2 part-time/adjunct (1 woman).
Students: 23 full-time (15 women), 44 part-time (26 women); includes 5 minority (2 African Americans, 1 Asian American or Pacific Islander, 2 Hispanic Americans), 1 international. Average age 35. 20 applicants, 60% accepted, 12 enrolled. In 2001, 25 degrees awarded.
Application deadline: For spring admission, 1/1. Applications are processed on a rolling basis. *Application fee:* $25 ($40 for international students). Electronic applications accepted.
Expenses: Tuition, state resident: full-time $1,888; part-time $105 per credit. Tuition, nonresident: full-time $6,129; part-time $341 per credit. Required fees: $345; $19 per credit. $17 per semester. Tuition and fees vary according to course load and program.
Financial support: In 2001–02, 8 research assistantships (averaging $1,941 per year), 8 teaching assistantships with full tuition reimbursements (averaging $4,879 per year) were awarded. Career-related internships or fieldwork, Federal Work-Study, institutionally sponsored loans, and unspecified assistantships also available. Financial award application deadline: 4/1; financial award applicants required to submit FAFSA.
Dr. Paul Cromwell, Director, 316-978-7200, *Fax:* 316-978-3626, *E-mail:* paul.cromwell@wichita.edu.

■ WIDENER UNIVERSITY

College of Arts and Sciences, Program in Criminal Justice, Chester, PA 19013-5792

AWARDS MA, Psy D/MA. Part-time and evening/weekend programs available.

Degree requirements: For master's, project.
Entrance requirements: For master's, interview, minimum undergraduate GPA of 3.0.
Expenses: Contact institution.

Widener University (continued)
Faculty research: Criminal law and procedure, corrections, domestic violence.

■ WILMINGTON COLLEGE

Division of Behavioral Science, New Castle, DE 19720-6491

AWARDS Community counseling (MS); criminal justice studies (MS); student affairs and college counseling (MS). Part-time and evening/weekend programs available.

Faculty: 6 full-time (2 women), 35 part-time/adjunct (15 women).
Students: 9 full-time (6 women), 79 part-time (64 women); includes 21 minority (19 African Americans, 2 Hispanic Americans). In 2001, 25 degrees awarded. *Median time to degree:* Master's–3 years full-time, 4 years part-time.
Application deadline: For fall admission, 4/15. *Application fee:* $25.
Expenses: Tuition: Full-time $4,788; part-time $266 per credit. Required fees: $50; $25 per semester. Tuition and fees vary according to course level, course load, degree level, campus/location and program.
Financial support: Applicants required to submit FAFSA.
James Wilson, Chair, 302-328-9401 Ext. 154, *Fax:* 302-328-5164, *E-mail:* jwils@wilmcoll.edu.
Application contact: Michael Lee, Director of Admissions and Financial Aid, 302-328-9407 Ext. 102, *Fax:* 302-328-5164, *E-mail:* inquire@wilmcoll.edu.

■ WRIGHT STATE UNIVERSITY

School of Graduate Studies, College of Liberal Arts, Program in Applied Behavioral Science, Dayton, OH 45435

AWARDS Criminal justice and social problems (MA); international and comparative politics (MA).

Students: 18 full-time (12 women), 14 part-time (11 women); includes 6 minority (5 African Americans, 1 Hispanic American). Average age 32. 20 applicants, 95% accepted. In 2001, 17 degrees awarded.
Degree requirements: For master's, thesis optional.
Entrance requirements: For master's, TOEFL. *Application fee:* $25.
Expenses: Tuition, state resident: full-time $7,161; part-time $225 per quarter hour. Tuition, nonresident: full-time $12,324; part-time $385 per quarter hour. Tuition and fees vary according to course load, degree level and program.
Financial support: Fellowships, research assistantships, unspecified assistantships available. Support available to part-time students. Financial award applicants required to submit FAFSA.
Faculty research: Training and development, criminal justice and social problems, community systems, human factors, industrial/organizational psychology.
Dr. David M. Orenstein, Director, 937-775-2667, *Fax:* 937-775-4228, *E-mail:* david.orenstein@wright.edu.

■ XAVIER UNIVERSITY

College of Social Sciences, Department of Criminal Justice, Cincinnati, OH 45207

AWARDS MS. Part-time and evening/weekend programs available.

Faculty: 2 full-time (0 women).
Students: 4 full-time (all women), 28 part-time (15 women); includes 7 minority (all African Americans). Average age 31. 30 applicants, 60% accepted. In 2001, 16 degrees awarded.
Degree requirements: For master's, thesis or alternative, comprehensive exam. *Median time to degree:* Master's–2 years full-time, 3 years part-time.
Entrance requirements: For master's, minimum GPA of 2.5. *Application deadline:* For fall admission, 8/15 (priority date). Applications are processed on a rolling basis. *Application fee:* $35. Electronic applications accepted.
Expenses: Tuition: Part-time $450 per hour.
Financial support: In 2001–02, 18 students received support, including 1 teaching assistantship (averaging $1,500 per year); career-related internships or fieldwork and scholarships/grants also available. Support available to part-time students.
Faculty research: Standardized curriculum for correctional officers, morality of capital punishment in the U.S., risk assessment classification of juvenile offenders, school violence.
Dr. John Richardson, Chairman, 513-745-1071, *Fax:* 513-745-3220, *E-mail:* richardj@xu.edu.
Application contact: John Cooper, Director of Graduate Services, 513-745-3357, *Fax:* 513-745-1048, *E-mail:* xugrad@xu.edu. *Web site:* http://www.xu.edu/MS_CJ/index.htm

■ YOUNGSTOWN STATE UNIVERSITY

Graduate School, College of Health and Human Services, Department of Criminal Justice, Youngstown, OH 44555-0001

AWARDS MS. Part-time and evening/weekend programs available.

Degree requirements: For master's, thesis optional.
Entrance requirements: For master's, TOEFL, minimum GPA of 2.7.
Faculty research: Police human resource allocation, police administration, computerized test development, criminal law.

FORENSIC SCIENCES

■ ARGOSY UNIVERSITY-CHICAGO

Illinois School of Professional Psychology, Chicago, IL 60603

AWARDS Clinical psychology (MA, Psy D), including child and adolescent psychology (Psy D), ethnic and racial psychology (Psy D), family psychology (Psy D), forensic psychology (Psy D), health psychology (Psy D), maltreatment and trauma (Psy D), psychoanalytic psychotherapy (Psy D), psychology and spirituality (Psy D); clinical respecialization (Certificate); health sciences (MA); professional counseling (MA). Part-time programs available.

Faculty: 28 full-time (15 women), 58 part-time/adjunct (35 women).
Students: 403 full-time (304 women), 155 part-time (120 women); includes 115 minority (64 African Americans, 28 Asian Americans or Pacific Islanders, 23 Hispanic Americans). Average age 39. 374 applicants, 67% accepted. In 2001, 58 master's, 92 doctorates, 43 other advanced degrees awarded. Terminal master's awarded for partial completion of doctoral program.
Degree requirements: For master's, comprehensive exam; for doctorate, thesis/dissertation, internship, research project, clinical competency exam, comprehensive exam.
Entrance requirements: For doctorate, minimum GPA of 3.25. *Application deadline:* For fall admission, 5/15; for winter admission, 10/15. *Application fee:* $55. Electronic applications accepted.
Expenses: Tuition: Part-time $332 per credit hour. Required fees: $75 per year. $35 per term.
Financial support: In 2001–02, 200 students received support, including 25 fellowships with partial tuition reimbursements available (averaging $2,000 per year), 150 teaching assistantships with partial tuition reimbursements available (averaging $600 per year); research assistantships with partial tuition reimbursements available, career-related internships or fieldwork, Federal Work-Study, scholarships/grants, tuition waivers (partial), and unspecified assistantships also available. Support available to part-time students. Financial award application deadline: 5/29; financial award applicants required to submit FAFSA.
Faculty research: Personality disorders, meditation-based stress reduction, cross-cultural mothers and daughters, theory process and schizophrenia, development of clinical competencies. *Total annual research expenditures:* $30,000.
Dr. David Harpool, President, 312-279-3902, *Fax:* 312-201-1907, *E-mail:* dharpool@argosyu.edu.

Application contact: Ashley Delaney, Director of Admissions, 312-279-3906, *Fax:* 312-201-1907, *E-mail:* adelaney@argosyu.edu. *Web site:* http://www.argosy.edu/

■ FITCHBURG STATE COLLEGE

Division of Graduate and Continuing Education, Programs in Counseling, Fitchburg, MA 01420-2697

AWARDS Adolescent and family therapy (Certificate); child protective services (Certificate); elementary school guidance counseling (MS); forensic case work (Certificate); mental health counseling (MS); school guidance counselor (Certificate); secondary school guidance counseling (MS). Part-time and evening/weekend programs available.

Students: 30 full-time (24 women), 52 part-time (48 women); includes 4 minority (1 African American, 1 Asian American or Pacific Islander, 2 Hispanic Americans), 3 international. In 2001, 27 degrees awarded.
Entrance requirements: For master's, GRE General Test or MAT, interview, previous course work in psychology; for Certificate, master's degree. *Application deadline:* Applications are processed on a rolling basis. *Application fee:* $10.
Expenses: Tuition, state resident: part-time $150 per credit. Required fees: $7 per credit. $65 per term. Tuition and fees vary according to course load.
Financial support: In 2001–02, research assistantships with partial tuition reimbursements (averaging $5,500 per year), teaching assistantships with partial tuition reimbursements (averaging $5,500 per year) were awarded. Federal Work-Study and unspecified assistantships also available. Support available to part-time students. Financial award application deadline: 3/1; financial award applicants required to submit FAFSA.
Dr. Richard Spencer, Co-Chair, 978-665-3349, *Fax:* 978-665-3658, *E-mail:* gce@fsc.edu.
Application contact: Director of Admissions, 978-665-3144, *Fax:* 978-665-4540, *E-mail:* admissions@fsc.edu. *Web site:* http://www.fsc.edu/

■ FLORIDA INTERNATIONAL UNIVERSITY

College of Arts and Sciences, Department of Chemistry, Miami, FL 33199

AWARDS Chemistry (MS, PhD); forensic science (MS). Part-time and evening/weekend programs available.

Faculty: 19 full-time (3 women).
Students: 44 full-time (23 women), 17 part-time (7 women); includes 29 minority (8 African Americans, 2 Asian Americans or Pacific Islanders, 19 Hispanic Americans), 17 international. Average age 31. 96 applicants, 33% accepted, 16 enrolled. In 2001, 7 degrees awarded.
Degree requirements: For master's and doctorate, thesis/dissertation.
Entrance requirements: For master's and doctorate, GRE General Test, TOEFL. *Application deadline:* For fall admission, 4/1 (priority date); for spring admission, 10/1. Applications are processed on a rolling basis. *Application fee:* $20.
Expenses: Tuition, state resident: full-time $2,916; part-time $162 per credit hour. Tuition, nonresident: full-time $10,245; part-time $569 per credit hour. Required fees: $168 per term.
Financial support: Research assistantships, teaching assistantships, Federal Work-Study, institutionally sponsored loans, and tuition waivers (full and partial) available. Support available to part-time students. Financial award application deadline: 4/1.
Faculty research: Organic synthesis and reaction catalysis, environmental chemistry, molecular beam studies, organic geochemistry, bioinorganic and organometallic chemistry.
Dr. Gary Hoffman, Chairperson, 305-348-2606, *Fax:* 305-348-3772, *E-mail:* hoffmang@fui.edu.

■ THE GEORGE WASHINGTON UNIVERSITY

Columbian College of Arts and Sciences, Department of Forensic Sciences, Washington, DC 20052

AWARDS Chemical toxicology (MS); criminal justice (MA), including crime and commerce, criminal justice, security management; forensic molecular biology (MFS); forensic sciences (MFS, MSFS). Part-time and evening/weekend programs available.

Faculty: 6 full-time (1 woman), 13 part-time/adjunct (4 women).
Students: 164 full-time (127 women), 80 part-time (48 women); includes 27 minority (11 African Americans, 13 Asian Americans or Pacific Islanders, 3 Hispanic Americans), 4 international. Average age 26. 329 applicants, 58% accepted. In 2001, 94 degrees awarded.
Degree requirements: For master's, comprehensive exam.
Entrance requirements: For master's, GRE General Test, minimum GPA of 3.0. *Application deadline:* For fall admission, 5/1. *Application fee:* $55.
Expenses: Tuition: Part-time $810 per credit. Required fees: $1 per credit.
Financial support: In 2001–02, 5 students received support. Federal Work-Study available. Financial award application deadline: 2/1.
Dr. David Rowley, Chair, 202-994-7319. *Web site:* http://www.gwu.edu/~gradinfo/

■ JOHN JAY COLLEGE OF CRIMINAL JUSTICE OF THE CITY UNIVERSITY OF NEW YORK

Graduate Studies, Program in Forensic Science, New York, NY 10019-1093

AWARDS Forensic science (MS). Part-time and evening/weekend programs available.

Students: 2 full-time (1 woman), 72 part-time (40 women); includes 14 minority (1 African American, 11 Asian Americans or Pacific Islanders, 2 Hispanic Americans). 150 applicants, 27% accepted, 24 enrolled. In 2001, 7 degrees awarded. Terminal master's awarded for partial completion of doctoral program.
Degree requirements: For master's, thesis.
Entrance requirements: For master's, GRE, TOEFL, minimum B average. *Application deadline:* For fall admission, 6/30 (priority date); for spring admission, 12/1. Applications are processed on a rolling basis. *Application fee:* $40.
Expenses: Tuition, state resident: full-time $4,350; part-time $185 per credit. Tuition, nonresident: full-time $7,600; part-time $285 per credit. Required fees: $80; $40 per semester. Tuition and fees vary according to degree level.
Financial support: Career-related internships or fieldwork, Federal Work-Study, institutionally sponsored loans, scholarships/grants, and unspecified assistantships available. Support available to part-time students. Financial award applicants required to submit FAFSA.
Dr. Peter DeForest, Director, 212-237-8945.
Application contact: Shirley Rodriguez-Melendez, Admissions Assistant, 212-237-8863, *Fax:* 212-237-8777, *E-mail:* srodrigu@jjay.cuny.edu.

■ JOHN JAY COLLEGE OF CRIMINAL JUSTICE OF THE CITY UNIVERSITY OF NEW YORK

Graduate Studies, Programs in Criminal Justice, New York, NY 10019-1093

AWARDS Criminal justice (MA, PhD); criminology and deviance (PhD); forensic psychology (PhD); forensic science (PhD); law and philosophy (PhD); organizational behavior (PhD); public policy (PhD). Part-time and evening/weekend programs available.

Students: 33 full-time (20 women), 165 part-time (86 women); includes 68 minority (36 African Americans, 11 Asian Americans or Pacific Islanders, 21 Hispanic Americans). 150 applicants, 80% accepted. In 2001, 58 degrees awarded. Terminal master's awarded for partial completion of doctoral program.
Degree requirements: For master's, thesis or alternative; for doctorate, one foreign language, thesis/dissertation.

John Jay College of Criminal Justice of the City University of New York (continued)

Entrance requirements: For master's, GRE General Test, TOEFL, minimum B average; for doctorate, GRE General Test, TOEFL. *Application deadline:* For fall admission, 6/30 (priority date); for spring admission, 12/1. Applications are processed on a rolling basis. *Application fee:* $40.
Expenses: Tuition, state resident: full-time $4,350; part-time $185 per credit. Tuition, nonresident: full-time $7,600; part-time $285 per credit. Required fees: $80; $40 per semester. Tuition and fees vary according to degree level.
Financial support: Career-related internships or fieldwork, Federal Work-Study, institutionally sponsored loans, and scholarships/grants available. Support available to part-time students. Financial award applicants required to submit FAFSA.
Dr. Andrew Karmen, Co-Director, 212-237-8695, *E-mail:* akarmen@jjay.cuny.edu.
Application contact: Shirley Rodriguez-Melendez, Admissions Assistant, 212-237-8863, *Fax:* 212-237-8777, *E-mail:* srodrigu@jjay.cuny.edu.

Find an in-depth description at www.petersons.com/gradchannel.

■ MARSHALL UNIVERSITY

Joan C. Edwards School of Medicine and Graduate College, Forensic Science Program, Huntington, WV 25755-9310

AWARDS MS.

Faculty: 4 full-time (2 women), 7 part-time/adjunct (2 women).
Students: 27 full-time (18 women). Average age 23. 200 applicants, 8% accepted. In 2001, 15 degrees awarded.
Degree requirements: For master's, thesis optional. *Median time to degree:* Master's–2 years full-time.
Entrance requirements: For master's, GRE General Test, 1 year of course work in biology, physics, chemistry, and organic chemistry with associated labs. *Application deadline:* For spring admission, 5/1. *Application fee:* $30 ($40 for international students).
Expenses: Tuition, state resident: part-time $147 per credit. Tuition, nonresident: part-time $468 per credit. Tuition and fees vary according to campus/location and reciprocity agreements.
Financial support: In 2001–02, 6 students received support. Career-related internships or fieldwork, Federal Work-Study, institutionally sponsored loans, and unspecified assistantships available. Support available to part-time students. Financial award application deadline: 5/1; financial award applicants required to submit FAFSA.
Faculty research: DNA polymorphisms, STR analysis of DNA for human identification, drug analysis/forensic analytical chemistry.
Dr. Terry W. Fenger, Director, 304-690-4373, *Fax:* 304-690-4360, *E-mail:* fenger@marshall.edu.
Application contact: Marlene P. Gruetter, Senior Administrative Assistant, 304-696-7326, *Fax:* 304-696-7171, *E-mail:* gruettem@marshall.edu. *Web site:* http://www.forensics@marshall.edu/

■ NATIONAL UNIVERSITY

Academic Affairs, School of Business and Technology, Department of Public Policy and Administration, La Jolla, CA 92037-1011

AWARDS Criminal justice (MCJ, MPA); forensic science (MFS); health care administration (MBA, MHCA); human resource management (MA); human resources administration (MBA); public administration (MBA, MPA). Part-time and evening/weekend programs available. Postbaccalaureate distance learning degree programs offered (minimal on-campus study).

Faculty: 9 full-time (2 women), 173 part-time/adjunct (43 women).
Students: 463 full-time (269 women), 169 part-time (79 women); includes 237 minority (97 African Americans, 45 Asian Americans or Pacific Islanders, 90 Hispanic Americans, 5 Native Americans), 37 international. Average age 34. 204 applicants, 100% accepted. In 2001, 281 degrees awarded.
Entrance requirements: For master's, interview, minimum GPA of 2.5. *Application deadline:* Applications are processed on a rolling basis. *Application fee:* $60 ($100 for international students).
Expenses: Tuition: Part-time $221 per quarter hour.
Financial support: Institutionally sponsored loans, scholarships/grants, and tuition waivers (full and partial) available. Support available to part-time students. Financial award application deadline: 5/1; financial award applicants required to submit FAFSA.
Dr. Thomas Green, Chair, 858-642-8439, *Fax:* 858-642-8716, *E-mail:* tgreen@nu.edu.
Application contact: Nancy Rohland, Director of Enrollment Management, 858-642-8180, *Fax:* 858-642-8710, *E-mail:* advisor@nu.edu. *Web site:* http://www.nu.edu/

■ PACE UNIVERSITY

Dyson College of Arts and Sciences, Program in Forensic Science, New York, NY 10038

AWARDS MS.

Entrance requirements: For master's, TOEFL. Electronic applications accepted.
Expenses: Tuition: Part-time $545 per credit.

Find an in-depth description at www.petersons.com/gradchannel.

■ STATE UNIVERSITY OF NEW YORK AT ALBANY

College of Arts and Sciences, Department of Biological Sciences, Albany, NY 12222-0001

AWARDS Biodiversity, conservation, and policy (MS); ecology, evolution, and behavior (MS, PhD); forensic molecular biology (MS); molecular, cellular, developmental, and neural biology (MS, PhD). Evening/weekend programs available.

Students: 52 full-time (29 women); includes 4 minority (3 African Americans, 1 Asian American or Pacific Islander), 14 international. Average age 28. 90 applicants, 43% accepted. In 2001, 8 master's, 5 doctorates awarded.
Degree requirements: For master's, one foreign language; for doctorate, one foreign language, thesis/dissertation.
Entrance requirements: For master's and doctorate, GRE General Test. *Application deadline:* For fall admission, 8/1; for spring admission, 11/1. *Application fee:* $50.
Expenses: Tuition, state resident: full-time $2,550; part-time $213 per credit. Tuition, nonresident: full-time $4,208; part-time $351 per credit. Required fees: $470; $470 per year.
Financial support: Fellowships, research assistantships, teaching assistantships, unspecified assistantships and minority assistantships available. Financial award application deadline: 5/1.
Faculty research: Interferon, neural development, RNA self-splicing, behavioral ecology, DNA repair enzymes.
Dr. David Shub, Chair, 518-442-4300.

Find an in-depth description at www.petersons.com/gradchannel.

■ THE UNIVERSITY OF ALABAMA AT BIRMINGHAM

Graduate School, School of Social and Behavioral Sciences, Department of Justice Sciences, Birmingham, AL 35294

AWARDS Criminal justice (MSCJ); forensic science (MSFS). Evening/weekend programs available.

Students: 39 full-time (29 women), 1 (woman) part-time; includes 6 minority (4 African Americans, 2 Hispanic Americans), 1 international. 204 applicants, 34% accepted. In 2001, 19 degrees awarded.
Degree requirements: For master's, thesis or alternative.
Entrance requirements: For master's, GRE General Test or MAT. *Application deadline:* Applications are processed on a rolling basis. *Application fee:* $35 ($60 for international students). Electronic applications accepted.
Expenses: Tuition, state resident: full-time $3,058. Tuition, nonresident: full-time $5,746. Tuition and fees vary according to course load, degree level and program.

Financial support: Career-related internships or fieldwork available.
Dr. Brent L. Smith, Chair, 205-934-2069, *E-mail:* blsmith@uab.edu. *Web site:* http://www.sbs.uab.edu/crim.htm/

■ UNIVERSITY OF CENTRAL FLORIDA

College of Health and Public Affairs, Department of Criminal Justice, Orlando, FL 32816

AWARDS Crime analysis (Certificate); criminal justice (MS). Part-time and evening/weekend programs available.

Faculty: 30 full-time (9 women), 28 part-time/adjunct (6 women).
Students: 90 full-time (44 women), 141 part-time (69 women); includes 51 minority (31 African Americans, 3 Asian Americans or Pacific Islanders, 16 Hispanic Americans, 1 Native American). Average age 33. 79 applicants, 85% accepted, 54 enrolled. In 2001, 54 degrees awarded.
Degree requirements: For master's, thesis or alternative.
Entrance requirements: For master's, TOEFL, GRE General Test, minimum GPA of 3.0. *Application deadline:* For fall admission, 7/15; for spring admission, 4/15. *Application fee:* $20. Electronic applications accepted.
Expenses: Tuition, state resident: part-time $162 per hour. Tuition, nonresident: part-time $569 per hour.
Financial support: In 2001–02, 13 fellowships with partial tuition reimbursements (averaging $2,692 per year), 38 research assistantships with partial tuition reimbursements (averaging $2,132 per year) were awarded. Teaching assistantships with partial tuition reimbursements, career-related internships or fieldwork, Federal Work-Study, institutionally sponsored loans, tuition waivers (partial), and unspecified assistantships also available. Financial award application deadline: 3/1; financial award applicants required to submit FAFSA.
Dr. B. J. McCarthy, Chair, 407-823-5929, *E-mail:* mccarthy@pegasus.cc.ucf.edu.
Application contact: Dr. Kenneth Reynolds, Coordinator, 407-823-2603, *Fax:* 407-823-5360, *E-mail:* kreynold@pegasus.cc.ucf.edu. *Web site:* http://www.ucf.edu/

■ UNIVERSITY OF ILLINOIS AT CHICAGO

College of Pharmacy and Graduate College, Research & Graduate Studies, College of Pharmacy, Program in Forensic Science, Chicago, IL 60607-7128

AWARDS MS.

Students: 12 full-time (9 women), 11 part-time (6 women); includes 5 minority (3 African Americans, 2 Asian Americans or Pacific Islanders). Average age 25. 95 applicants, 24% accepted, 14 enrolled. In 2001, 16 degrees awarded.
Degree requirements: For master's, thesis.
Entrance requirements: For master's, GRE General Test, TOEFL. *Application deadline:* For fall admission, 6/1; for spring admission, 11/1. *Application fee:* $40 ($50 for international students).
Expenses: Tuition, state resident: full-time $3,060. Tuition, nonresident: full-time $6,688.
Financial support: In 2001–02, 7 students received support; fellowships with full tuition reimbursements available, research assistantships with full tuition reimbursements available, teaching assistantships with full tuition reimbursements available, career-related internships or fieldwork, Federal Work-Study, institutionally sponsored loans, and tuition waivers (full) available. Financial award application deadline: 2/1; financial award applicants required to submit FAFSA.
Faculty research: Interpretation of physical evidence, utilization of physical evidence, analytical toxicology of controlled substances, automated fingerprint systems, dye and ink characterizations.
Robert Gaensslen, Director of Graduate Studies, 312-996-0888, *E-mail:* reg@uic.edu.

■ UNIVERSITY OF NEW HAVEN

Graduate School, School of Public Safety and Professional Studies, Program in Forensic Science, West Haven, CT 06516-1916

AWARDS Advanced investigation (MS); criminalistics (MS); forensic science (MS). Part-time and evening/weekend programs available.

Students: 55 full-time (41 women), 32 part-time (12 women); includes 7 minority (2 African Americans, 2 Asian Americans or Pacific Islanders, 3 Hispanic Americans), 1 international. In 2001, 44 degrees awarded.
Degree requirements: For master's, thesis or alternative.
Entrance requirements: For master's, GRE Subject Test. *Application deadline:* Applications are processed on a rolling basis. *Application fee:* $50.
Expenses: Tuition: Full-time $12,015; part-time $445 per credit hour. Required fees: $30. One-time fee: $100 full-time.
Financial support: Career-related internships or fieldwork and Federal Work-Study available. Support available to part-time students. Financial award application deadline: 5/1; financial award applicants required to submit FAFSA.
Dr. Howard Harris, Coordinator, 203-932-7116.

■ UNIVERSITY OF NORTH TEXAS HEALTH SCIENCE CENTER AT FORT WORTH

Graduate School of Biomedical Sciences, Fort Worth, TX 76107-2699

AWARDS Anatomy and cell biology (MS, PhD); biochemistry and molecular biology (MS, PhD); biomedical sciences (MS, PhD); biotechnology (MS); forensic genetics (MS); integrative physiology (MS, PhD); medical science (MS); microbiology and immunology (MS, PhD); pharmacology (MS, PhD); science education (MS).

Faculty: 68 full-time (11 women), 7 part-time/adjunct (0 women).
Students: 101 full-time (61 women), 35 part-time (19 women); includes 36 minority (13 African Americans, 7 Asian Americans or Pacific Islanders, 16 Hispanic Americans), 32 international. Average age 29. 90 applicants, 84% accepted, 42 enrolled. In 2001, 11 master's, 13 doctorates awarded. Terminal master's awarded for partial completion of doctoral program.
Degree requirements: For master's and doctorate, thesis/dissertation.
Entrance requirements: For master's and doctorate, GRE General Test, TOEFL. *Application deadline:* For fall admission, 5/1; for spring admission, 11/1. Applications are processed on a rolling basis. *Application fee:* $25 ($50 for international students).
Expenses: Tuition, state resident: full-time $6,550; part-time $858 per year. Tuition, nonresident: full-time $19,650; part-time $3,633 per year. Required fees: $1,300; $473 per year. Tuition and fees vary according to program.
Financial support: In 2001–02, 80 research assistantships (averaging $16,000 per year) were awarded; fellowships, teaching assistantships, career-related internships or fieldwork, Federal Work-Study, institutionally sponsored loans, scholarships/grants, and traineeships also available. Support available to part-time students. Financial award application deadline: 4/1; financial award applicants required to submit FAFSA.
Faculty research: Alzheimer's disease, aging, eye diseases, cancer, cardiovascular disease. *Total annual research expenditures:* $10.1 million.
Dr. Thomas Yorio, Dean, 817-735-2560, *Fax:* 817-735-0243, *E-mail:* yoriot@hsc.unt.edu.
Application contact: Carla Lee, Director of Graduate Admissions and Services, 817-735-2560, *Fax:* 817-735-0243, *E-mail:* gsbs@hsc.unt.edu. *Web site:* http://www.hsc.unt.edu/

Find an in-depth description at www.petersons.com/gradchannel.

■ VIRGINIA COMMONWEALTH UNIVERSITY

School of Graduate Studies, College of Humanities and Sciences, Department of Criminal Justice, Richmond, VA 23284-9005

AWARDS Criminal justice (MS, CCJA); forensic science (MS). Part-time and evening/weekend programs available.

Students: 42 full-time, 63 part-time; includes 11 minority (9 African Americans, 2 Hispanic Americans). 226 applicants, 18% accepted. In 2001, 26 master's, 16 other advanced degrees awarded.
Degree requirements: For master's, thesis or comprehensive exam, thesis optional.
Entrance requirements: For master's, GRE General Test, minimum GPA of 2.7. *Application deadline:* For fall admission, 4/1; for spring admission, 11/1. Applications are processed on a rolling basis. *Application fee:* $30.
Expenses: Tuition, state resident: full-time $4,276; part-time $238 per credit. Tuition, nonresident: full-time $12,672; part-time $704 per credit. Required fees: $1,167; $43 per credit.
Financial support: Federal Work-Study, institutionally sponsored loans, and tuition waivers (full and partial) available. Support available to part-time students. Financial award application deadline: 3/1.
Dr. Jay S. Albanese, Chair, 804-828-1050, *Fax:* 804-828-1253, *E-mail:* jsalbane@vcu.edu.
Application contact: Dr. James L. Hague, Graduate Program Director, 804-828-1050, *Fax:* 804-828-1253, *E-mail:* hague@vcu.edu. *Web site:* http://www.has.vcu.edu/crj/

Economics

AGRICULTURAL ECONOMICS AND AGRIBUSINESS

■ ALABAMA AGRICULTURAL AND MECHANICAL UNIVERSITY

School of Graduate Studies, School of Agricultural and Environmental Sciences, Department of Agribusiness, Huntsville, AL 35811

AWARDS MS. Part-time programs available.

Faculty: 5 full-time (0 women).
Students: In 2001, 5 degrees awarded.
Degree requirements: For master's, thesis (for some programs).
Entrance requirements: For master's, GRE General Test. *Application deadline:* For fall admission, 5/1 (priority date). Applications are processed on a rolling basis. *Application fee:* $15 ($20 for international students).
Expenses: Tuition, state resident: full-time $1,380. Tuition, nonresident: full-time $2,500.
Financial support: In 2001–02, fellowships with tuition reimbursements (averaging $15,000 per year), research assistantships with tuition reimbursements (averaging $10,000 per year) were awarded. Financial award application deadline: 4/1.
Faculty research: Farm economics.
Dr. Willie J. Cheatham, Chair, 256-851-5410.

■ ALCORN STATE UNIVERSITY

School of Graduate Studies, School of Agriculture and Applied Science, Alcorn State, MS 39096-7500

AWARDS Agricultural economics (MS Ag); agronomy (MS Ag); animal science (MS Ag).

Faculty: 11 full-time (2 women).
Degree requirements: For master's, thesis optional.
Application deadline: For fall admission, 7/15 (priority date); for spring admission, 11/25. Applications are processed on a rolling basis. *Application fee:* $0 ($10 for international students).
Expenses: Tuition, state resident: full-time $6,418; part-time $924 per credit. Tuition, nonresident: full-time $12,497; part-time $1,656 per credit.
Financial support: Career-related internships or fieldwork available. Support available to part-time students.
Faculty research: Aquatic systems, dairy herd improvement, fruit production, alternative farming practices.
Napoleon Moses, Dean, 601-877-6137, *Fax:* 601-877-6219.

■ ARIZONA STATE UNIVERSITY EAST

Morrison School of Agribusiness and Resource Management, Mesa, AZ 85212

AWARDS Agribusiness (MS); environmental resources (MS). Part-time and evening/weekend programs available.

Faculty: 17 full-time (1 woman), 1 part-time/adjunct (0 women).
Students: 30 full-time (19 women), 38 part-time (17 women); includes 4 minority (all Hispanic Americans), 17 international. Average age 32. 64 applicants, 59% accepted, 1 enrolled. In 2001, 18 degrees awarded.
Degree requirements: For master's, thesis, oral defense. *Median time to degree:* Master's–2 years full-time, 2.75 years part-time.
Entrance requirements: For master's, GMAT, GRE General Test, MAT, TOEFL, minimum GPA of 3.0, 3 letters of recommendation, resumé. *Application deadline:* Applications are processed on a rolling basis. *Application fee:* $45. Electronic applications accepted.
Expenses: Tuition, state resident: full-time $2,412; part-time $126 per credit hour. Tuition, nonresident: full-time $10,278; part-time $428 per credit hour. Required fees: $26. Tuition and fees vary according to course load.
Financial support: In 2001–02, 30 students received support, including 18 research assistantships with partial tuition reimbursements available (averaging $4,202 per year), 3 teaching assistantships with partial tuition reimbursements available (averaging $4,202 per year); fellowships, career-related internships or fieldwork, Federal Work-Study, institutionally sponsored loans, scholarships/grants, and tuition waivers (full and partial) also available. Support available to part-time students. Financial award application deadline: 3/1; financial award applicants required to submit CSS PROFILE or FAFSA.
Faculty research: Agribusiness marketing, management and financial structuring. *Total annual research expenditures:* $1.2 million.
Dr. Raymond Marquardt, Dean, 480-727-1585, *Fax:* 480-727-1961, *E-mail:* ray.marquardt@asu.edu. *Web site:* http://www.agbiz.asu.edu/

■ AUBURN UNIVERSITY

Graduate School, College of Agriculture, Department of Agricultural Economics and Rural Sociology, Auburn University, AL 36849

AWARDS M Ag, MS, PhD. Part-time programs available.

Faculty: 22 full-time (1 woman).
Students: 18 full-time (6 women), 17 part-time (10 women); includes 4 minority (all African Americans), 11 international. 19

applicants, 84% accepted. In 2001, 9 master's, 1 doctorate awarded.
Degree requirements: For master's, thesis (for some programs); for doctorate, thesis/dissertation.
Entrance requirements: For master's and doctorate, GRE General Test. *Application deadline:* For fall admission, 7/7; for spring admission, 11/24. Applications are processed on a rolling basis. *Application fee:* $25 ($50 for international students). Electronic applications accepted.
Financial support: Research assistantships, teaching assistantships, Federal Work-Study available. Support available to part-time students. Financial award application deadline: 3/15.
Faculty research: Farm management, agricultural marketing, production economics, resource economics, agricultural finance.
Dr. John L. Adrian, Chair, 334-844-4800.
Application contact: Dr. John F. Pritchett, Dean of the Graduate School, 334-844-4700, *E-mail:* hatchlb@mail.auburn.edu. *Web site:* http://www.ag.auburn.edu/dept/aec/aec.html

■ CALIFORNIA POLYTECHNIC STATE UNIVERSITY, SAN LUIS OBISPO

Orfalea College of Business, San Luis Obispo, CA 93407

AWARDS Agribusiness management (MBA); architectural management (MBA); engineering management (MBA/MS); industrial technology (MA), including industrial and technical studies.

Faculty: 60 full-time (13 women).
Students: 99 full-time (29 women), 16 part-time (4 women); includes 18 minority (11 Asian Americans or Pacific Islanders, 7 Hispanic Americans). 123 applicants, 73% accepted, 65 enrolled. In 2001, 43 degrees awarded.
Entrance requirements: For master's, GMAT. *Application deadline:* For fall admission, 7/1. Applications are processed on a rolling basis. *Application fee:* $55.
Expenses: Tuition, nonresident: part-time $164 per unit. One-time fee: $2,153 part-time.
Financial support: Career-related internships or fieldwork, Federal Work-Study, and institutionally sponsored loans available. Support available to part-time students. Financial award application deadline: 3/2; financial award applicants required to submit FAFSA.
Faculty research: Management of high-tech firms, Pacific Rim, capital market structures, economics of environmental policy, marketing of services.
Dr. Terry Swartz, Dean, 805-756-2705, *Fax:* 805-756-5452.
Application contact: Dr. Earl Keller, Director, Graduate Programs, 805-756-2588, *Fax:* 805-756-0110, *E-mail:* eckeller@calpoly.edu. *Web site:* http://www.cob.calpoly.edu/

■ CLEMSON UNIVERSITY

Graduate School, College of Agriculture, Forestry and Life Sciences, Department of Agriculture and Applied Economics, Program in Agricultural and Applied Economics, Clemson, SC 29634

AWARDS MS.

Students: 16 full-time (6 women), 4 part-time (1 woman); includes 2 minority (1 African American, 1 Asian American or Pacific Islander), 10 international. Average age 24. 21 applicants, 95% accepted, 4 enrolled. In 2001, 4 degrees awarded.
Degree requirements: For master's, thesis optional.
Entrance requirements: For master's, GRE General Test, TOEFL, minimum GPA of 3.0. *Application deadline:* For fall admission, 5/1; for spring admission, 10/1. Applications are processed on a rolling basis. *Application fee:* $40.
Expenses: Tuition, state resident: full-time $5,310. Tuition, nonresident: full-time $11,284.
Financial support: Application deadline: 3/1.
Dr. Michael D. Hammig, Chair, 864-656-5771, *Fax:* 864-656-5776, *E-mail:* mhammig@clemson.edu.
Application contact: Janice Thacker, Staff Assistant for Graduate Programs, 864-656-6536, *Fax:* 864-656-5776, *E-mail:* jthckr@clemson.edu.

■ COLORADO STATE UNIVERSITY

Graduate School, College of Agricultural Sciences, Department of Agricultural and Resource Economics, Fort Collins, CO 80523-0015

AWARDS M Agr, MS, PhD.

Faculty: 17 full-time (4 women).
Students: 23 full-time (7 women), 15 part-time (7 women); includes 3 minority (1 African American, 1 Asian American or Pacific Islander, 1 Hispanic American), 15 international. Average age 31. 32 applicants, 88% accepted, 8 enrolled. In 2001, 3 master's, 3 doctorates awarded.
Degree requirements: For master's, thesis; for doctorate, thesis/dissertation, exams.
Entrance requirements: For master's and doctorate, GRE General Test, TOEFL, minimum GPA of 3.0. *Application deadline:* For fall admission, 2/1 (priority date); for spring admission, 11/1 (priority date). Applications are processed on a rolling basis. *Application fee:* $30. Electronic applications accepted.
Expenses: Tuition, state resident: full-time $2,880; part-time $160 per credit. Tuition, nonresident: full-time $11,412; part-time $634 per credit. Required fees: $750; $34 per credit.
Financial support: In 2001–02, 14 students received support, including 1 fellowship (averaging $3,000 per year), 11 research assistantships with full tuition reimbursements available (averaging $11,565 per year), 2 teaching assistantships with full tuition reimbursements available (averaging $11,565 per year); career-related internships or fieldwork and traineeships also available. Financial award application deadline: 2/15.
Faculty research: Agricultural production economics, marketing and agribusiness economics, international development, natural resource economics, environmental economics. *Total annual research expenditures:* $291,020.
S. Lee Gray, Chair, 970-491-6325, *Fax:* 970-491-2067, *E-mail:* lgray@agsci.colostate.edu.
Application contact: Paul C. Huszar, Graduate Coordinator, 970-491-6955, *Fax:* 970-491-2067, *E-mail:* phuszar@agsci.colostate.edu. *Web site:* http://www.agsci.colostate.edu/

■ CORNELL UNIVERSITY

Graduate School, Graduate Fields of Agriculture and Life Sciences, Field of Agricultural Economics, Ithaca, NY 14853-0001

AWARDS Agricultural economics (MPS, MS, PhD), including agricultural finance, applied econometrics and quantitative analysis, economics of development, farm management and production economics (MPS, MS), food management and production economics (PhD), marketing and food distribution, public policy analysis; environmental economics (MPS, MS); environmental management (MPS); resource economics (MPS, MS, PhD), including environmental economics (PhD), resource economics (PhD).

Faculty: 39 full-time.
Students: 62 full-time (26 women); includes 2 minority (1 African American, 1 Asian American or Pacific Islander), 36 international. 216 applicants, 29% accepted. In 2001, 14 master's, 4 doctorates awarded. Terminal master's awarded for partial completion of doctoral program.
Degree requirements: For master's, thesis (MS); for doctorate, thesis/dissertation.
Entrance requirements: For master's and doctorate, GRE General Test, TOEFL, 2 letters of recommendation. *Application deadline:* For fall admission, 1/15. *Application fee:* $65. Electronic applications accepted.
Expenses: Tuition: Full-time $25,970. Required fees: $50.
Financial support: In 2001–02, 46 students received support, including 9 fellowships with full tuition reimbursements available, 26 research assistantships with full tuition reimbursements available, 11

Cornell University (continued)
teaching assistantships with full tuition reimbursements available; institutionally sponsored loans, scholarships/grants, tuition waivers (full and partial), and unspecified assistantships also available. Financial award applicants required to submit FAFSA.
Faculty research: Production economics, international economic development and trade, farm management and finance, resource and environmental economics, agricultural marketing and policy.
Application contact: Graduate Field Assistant, 607-255-8048, *E-mail:* aegrad@cornell.edu. *Web site:* http://www.gradschool.cornell.edu/grad/fields_1/ag-econ.html

■ CORNELL UNIVERSITY

Graduate School, Graduate Fields of Agriculture and Life Sciences, Field of International Agriculture and Rural Development, Ithaca, NY 14853-0001

AWARDS International agriculture and development (MPS).

Faculty: 46 full-time.
Students: 13 full-time (4 women); includes 3 minority (1 Asian American or Pacific Islander, 2 Hispanic Americans), 7 international. 23 applicants, 87% accepted. In 2001, 6 degrees awarded.
Degree requirements: For master's, project paper.
Entrance requirements: For master's, GRE General Test (recommended), TOEFL, 2 years of development experience, 2 letters of recommendation. *Application deadline:* For fall admission, 3/1. *Application fee:* $65. Electronic applications accepted.
Expenses: Tuition: Full-time $25,970. Required fees: $50.
Financial support: In 2001–02, 3 research assistantships with full tuition reimbursements were awarded; fellowships with full tuition reimbursements, teaching assistantships with full tuition reimbursements, institutionally sponsored loans, scholarships/grants, tuition waivers (full and partial), and unspecified assistantships also available. Financial award applicants required to submit FAFSA.
Application contact: Graduate Field Assistant, 607-255-3037, *E-mail:* mpsiard@cornell.edu. *Web site:* http://www.gradschool.cornell.edu/grad/fields_1/iard.html

■ ILLINOIS STATE UNIVERSITY

Graduate School, College of Applied Science and Technology, Department of Agriculture, Normal, IL 61790-2200

AWARDS Agribusiness (MS).

Faculty: 9 full-time (0 women).
Students: 21 full-time (6 women), 8 part-time (2 women); includes 1 minority (Hispanic American), 23 international. 22 applicants, 100% accepted. In 2001, 2 degrees awarded.
Degree requirements: For master's, thesis optional.
Entrance requirements: For master's, GRE General Test, minimum GPA of 3.0 in last 60 hours. *Application deadline:* Applications are processed on a rolling basis. *Application fee:* $30.
Expenses: Tuition, state resident: full-time $2,691; part-time $112 per credit hour. Tuition, nonresident: full-time $5,880; part-time $245 per credit hour. Required fees: $1,146; $48 per credit hour.
Financial support: In 2001–02, 17 research assistantships (averaging $5,572 per year) were awarded; teaching assistantships, tuition waivers (full) and unspecified assistantships also available. Financial award application deadline: 4/1.
Faculty research: Animal waste management, hog management, solid/liquid separation-aeration system for swine slurry. *Total annual research expenditures:* $951,370.
Dr. J. R. Winter, Chairperson, 309-438-5654. *Web site:* http://www.cast.ilstu.edu/agr/agrhome.htm

■ IOWA STATE UNIVERSITY OF SCIENCE AND TECHNOLOGY

Graduate College, College of Liberal Arts and Sciences, Department of Economics and College of Agriculture, Program in Agricultural Economics, Ames, IA 50011

AWARDS MS, PhD.

Students: 11 full-time (2 women), 8 part-time (4 women), 12 international. In 2001, 5 degrees awarded.
Degree requirements: For master's, thesis or alternative; for doctorate, thesis/dissertation. *Median time to degree:* Doctorate–6.2 years full-time.
Entrance requirements: For master's and doctorate, GRE General Test, TOEFL or IELTS. *Application deadline:* For fall admission, 2/1 (priority date). Applications are processed on a rolling basis. *Application fee:* $20 ($50 for international students). Electronic applications accepted.
Expenses: Tuition, state resident: full-time $1,851. Tuition, nonresident: full-time $5,449. Tuition and fees vary according to program.
Financial support: In 2001–02, 9 research assistantships with partial tuition reimbursements (averaging $15,000 per year), 3 teaching assistantships with partial tuition reimbursements (averaging $13,686 per year) were awarded. Fellowships, scholarships/grants, health care benefits, and unspecified assistantships also available.

■ KANSAS STATE UNIVERSITY

Graduate School, College of Agriculture, Department of Agricultural Economics, Manhattan, KS 66506

AWARDS MAB, MS, PhD. Part-time programs available. Postbaccalaureate distance learning degree programs offered (minimal on-campus study).

Faculty: 30 full-time (1 woman).
Students: 129 full-time (37 women); includes 6 minority (2 African Americans, 3 Hispanic Americans, 1 Native American), 26 international. Average age 27. 23 applicants, 96% accepted, 15 enrolled. In 2001, 8 degrees awarded. Terminal master's awarded for partial completion of doctoral program.
Degree requirements: For master's, thesis or alternative, oral exam; for doctorate, thesis/dissertation, preliminary exams.
Entrance requirements: For master's and doctorate, GRE General Test, TOEFL. *Application deadline:* For fall admission, 2/1 (priority date); for spring admission, 10/1. Applications are processed on a rolling basis. *Application fee:* $0 ($25 for international students). Electronic applications accepted.
Expenses: Tuition, state resident: part-time $113 per credit hour. Tuition, nonresident: part-time $358 per credit hour.
Financial support: In 2001–02, 82 research assistantships (averaging $11,000 per year), 4 teaching assistantships with partial tuition reimbursements (averaging $4,500 per year) were awarded. Federal Work-Study, institutionally sponsored loans, and scholarships/grants also available. Support available to part-time students. Financial award application deadline: 3/1; financial award applicants required to submit FAFSA.
Faculty research: Finance, farm management, agribusiness, international development, natural resources. *Total annual research expenditures:* $800,000.
Daniel Bernardo, Head, 785-532-6702, *Fax:* 785-532-6925, *E-mail:* dbernar@agecon.ksu.edu.
Application contact: Dr. Allen Featherstone, Graduate Program Director, 785-532-4441, *Fax:* 785-532-6925, *E-mail:* afeather@agecon.ksu.edu. *Web site:* http://www.agecon.ksu.edu/

■ LOUISIANA STATE UNIVERSITY AND AGRICULTURAL AND MECHANICAL COLLEGE

Graduate School, College of Agriculture, Department of Agricultural Economics and Agribusiness, Baton Rouge, LA 70803

AWARDS MS, PhD.

Faculty: 14 full-time (0 women).
Students: 23 full-time (4 women), 5 part-time (1 woman); includes 3 minority (all

African Americans), 21 international. Average age 31. 25 applicants, 44% accepted, 8 enrolled. In 2001, 5 master's, 3 doctorates awarded.
Degree requirements: For master's, thesis (for some programs); for doctorate, thesis/dissertation.
Entrance requirements: For master's and doctorate, GRE General Test, minimum GPA of 3.0. *Application deadline:* For fall admission, 1/25 (priority date). Applications are processed on a rolling basis. *Application fee:* $25.
Expenses: Tuition, state resident: full-time $2,551. Tuition, nonresident: full-time $5,551. Required fees: $854. Part-time tuition and fees vary according to course load.
Financial support: In 2001–02, 1 fellowship (averaging $14,333 per year), 14 research assistantships with partial tuition reimbursements (averaging $11,948 per year) were awarded. Teaching assistantships with partial tuition reimbursements Financial award applicants required to submit FAFSA.
Faculty research: Farm management/ product economy, resource/environmental economy, agribusiness management, agriculture marketing, international trade/ policy. *Total annual research expenditures:* $3,000.
Dr. Gail L. Cramer, Head, 225-578-3282, *Fax:* 225-578-2716, *E-mail:* gcramer@ agctr.lsu.edu.
Application contact: Dr. Hector Zapata, Graduate Coordinator, 225-578-2766, *Fax:* 225-578-2716, *E-mail:* hzapata@ agctr.lsu.edu. *Web site:* http:// www.agecon.lsu.edu

■ MICHIGAN STATE UNIVERSITY

Graduate School, College of Agriculture and Natural Resources, Department of Agricultural Economics, East Lansing, MI 48824

AWARDS MS, PhD.

Faculty: 42 full-time (10 women), 3 part-time/adjunct (1 woman).
Students: 44 full-time (18 women), 24 part-time (11 women); includes 4 minority (3 African Americans, 1 Asian American or Pacific Islander), 41 international. Average age 31. 121 applicants, 33% accepted, 15 enrolled. In 2001, 8 master's, 4 doctorates awarded. Terminal master's awarded for partial completion of doctoral program.
Degree requirements: For master's, thesis (for some programs); for doctorate, thesis/dissertation, comprehensive exam, registration.
Entrance requirements: For master's and doctorate, GRE General Test, TOEFL. *Application deadline:* For fall admission, 12/31 (priority date); for spring admission, 9/30 (priority date). Applications are processed on a rolling basis. *Application fee:* $30 ($40 for international students). Electronic applications accepted.
Expenses: Tuition, state resident: part-time $244 per credit hour. Tuition, nonresident: part-time $494 per credit hour. Required fees: $268 per semester. Tuition and fees vary according to course load, degree level and program.
Financial support: In 2001–02, 10 fellowships with tuition reimbursements (averaging $2,000 per year), 50 research assistantships with tuition reimbursements (averaging $11,642 per year), 9 teaching assistantships with tuition reimbursements (averaging $11,191 per year) were awarded. Career-related internships or fieldwork, Federal Work-Study, institutionally sponsored loans, tuition waivers (partial), and supplementary fellowships also available. Financial award application deadline: 12/31; financial award applicants required to submit FAFSA.
Faculty research: Agribusiness strategy and management, agribusiness markets and price analysis, environment and resource economics, finance and production economics, international agriculture development. *Total annual research expenditures:* $7.2 million.
Dr. Larry Hamm, Chairperson, 517-355-4563, *Fax:* 517-432-1800, *E-mail:* aecgrad@msu.edu.
Application contact: Dr. Eric Crawford, Associate Chairperson, 517-353-6644, *Fax:* 517-432-1800, *E-mail:* aecgrad@msu.edu. *Web site:* http://www.aec.msu.edu/agecon/

■ MISSISSIPPI STATE UNIVERSITY

College of Agriculture and Life Sciences, Department of Agricultural Economics, Mississippi State, MS 39762

AWARDS Agribusiness management (MABM); applied economics (PhD). Part-time programs available.

Faculty: 16 full-time (1 woman), 3 part-time/adjunct (0 women).
Students: 16 full-time (4 women), 8 part-time (1 woman); includes 1 minority (Hispanic American), 7 international. Average age 29. 31 applicants, 90% accepted, 3 enrolled. In 2001, 17 master's, 3 doctorates awarded.
Degree requirements: For master's, thesis (for some programs), comprehensive oral or written exam, thesis defense; for doctorate, thesis/dissertation, qualifying written exam, research exam.
Entrance requirements: For master's, GRE, TOEFL, GMAT, minimum GPA of 3.0; for doctorate, GRE, TOEFL, minimum GPA of 3.0. *Application deadline:* For fall admission, 7/1; for spring admission, 11/1. Applications are processed on a rolling basis. *Application fee:* $25 for international students. Electronic applications accepted.
Expenses: Tuition, state resident: full-time $3,586; part-time $150 per credit hour. Tuition, nonresident: full-time $8,128; part-time $339 per credit hour. Tuition and fees vary according to course load and campus/location.
Financial support: In 2001–02, 7 research assistantships with full tuition reimbursements (averaging $7,200 per year), 2 teaching assistantships with full tuition reimbursements (averaging $9,600 per year) were awarded. Career-related internships or fieldwork, Federal Work-Study, institutionally sponsored loans, and unspecified assistantships also available. Financial award application deadline: 4/1; financial award applicants required to submit FAFSA.
Faculty research: Production economics, policy, resource economics, international trade, agribusiness management. *Total annual research expenditures:* $1.4 million.
Dr. Cary W. Herndon, Interim Department Head, 662-325-2752, *Fax:* 662-325-8777, *E-mail:* office@agecon.msstate.edu.
Application contact: Jerry B. Inmon, Director of Admissions, 662-325-2224, *Fax:* 662-325-7360, *E-mail:* admit@ admissions.msstate.edu. *Web site:* http:// www.msstate.edu/

■ MONTANA STATE UNIVERSITY–BOZEMAN

College of Graduate Studies, College of Agriculture, Department of Agricultural Economics and Economics, Bozeman, MT 59717

AWARDS Applied economics (MS). Part-time programs available.

Students: 4 full-time (0 women), 7 part-time (3 women), 5 international. Average age 25. 9 applicants, 100% accepted, 3 enrolled. In 2001, 1 degree awarded.
Degree requirements: For master's, thesis.
Entrance requirements: For master's, GRE General Test, TOEFL, minimum GPA of 3.0. *Application deadline:* For fall admission, 1/15; for spring admission, 6/15. Applications are processed on a rolling basis. *Application fee:* $50. Electronic applications accepted.
Expenses: Tuition, state resident: full-time $3,894; part-time $198 per credit. Tuition, nonresident: full-time $10,661; part-time $480 per credit. International tuition: $10,811 full-time. Tuition and fees vary according to course load and program.
Financial support: In 2001–02, 11 students received support, including 3 fellowships (averaging $6,000 per year), 6 research assistantships (averaging $10,800 per year), 3 teaching assistantships (averaging $9,000 per year); career-related internships or fieldwork and unspecified assistantships also available. Financial award application deadline: 3/1; financial award applicants required to submit FAFSA.
Faculty research: Economic theory, applied microeconomics, resource economics, farm and ranch management, agriculture in global context. *Total annual research expenditures:* $1 million.

Montana State University–Bozeman (continued)
Dr. Myles Watts, Head, 406-994-3703, *Fax:* 406-994-4838, *E-mail:* zae7022@montana.edu. *Web site:* http://www.montana.edu/wwwae/homepage/graduate.html

■ NEW MEXICO STATE UNIVERSITY

Graduate School, College of Agriculture and Home Economics, Department of Agricultural Economics and Agricultural Business, Las Cruces, NM 88003-8001

AWARDS Agricultural economics (MS); economics (MA). Part-time programs available.

Faculty: 11 full-time (3 women).
Students: 11 full-time (4 women), 6 part-time (3 women); includes 3 minority (1 Asian American or Pacific Islander, 2 Hispanic Americans), 4 international. Average age 29. 9 applicants, 100% accepted, 5 enrolled. In 2001, 2 degrees awarded.
Degree requirements: For master's, thesis (for some programs).
Entrance requirements: For master's, previous course work in intermediate microeconomics, intermediate macroeconomics, college-level calculus, statistics. *Application deadline:* For fall admission, 7/1 (priority date); for spring admission, 11/1 (priority date). Applications are processed on a rolling basis. *Application fee:* $15 ($35 for international students). Electronic applications accepted.
Expenses: Tuition, state resident: full-time $3,234; part-time $135 per credit. Tuition, nonresident: full-time $9,420; part-time $428 per credit. Required fees: $858.
Financial support: In 2001–02, 7 research assistantships, 6 teaching assistantships were awarded. Career-related internships or fieldwork also available. Financial award application deadline: 3/1.
Faculty research: Natural resource policy, rural development policy and issues, agribusiness and marketing, international marketing and trade, agricultural risk management.
Dr. Lowell Catlett, Interim Head, 505-646-3215, *Fax:* 505-646-3808, *E-mail:* lcatlett@nmsu.edu.
Application contact: Dr. James D. Libbon, Professor, 505-646-2915, *Fax:* 505-646-3808, *E-mail:* jlibbin@nmsu.edu. *Web site:* http://www.nmsu.edu/~agecon/

■ NORTH CAROLINA AGRICULTURAL AND TECHNICAL STATE UNIVERSITY

Graduate School, School of Agriculture and Environmental and Allied Sciences, Department of Agribusiness, Applied Economics, and Agriscience Education, Greensboro, NC 27411

AWARDS Agricultural economics (MS); agricultural education (MS). Part-time and evening/weekend programs available.

Degree requirements: For master's, thesis or alternative, qualifying exam, comprehensive exam.
Entrance requirements: For master's, GRE General Test, minimum GPA of 3.0.
Faculty research: Aid for small farmers, agricultural technology resources, labor force mobility, agrology.

■ NORTH CAROLINA STATE UNIVERSITY

Graduate School, College of Agriculture and Life Sciences, Program in Agricultural Economics, Raleigh, NC 27695

AWARDS M Econ, MS, PhD. Part-time programs available.

Students: 1 full-time (0 women), 1 part-time; includes 1 minority (African American). Average age 38. 5 applicants, 0% accepted. Terminal master's awarded for partial completion of doctoral program.
Degree requirements: For master's, thesis (for some programs); for doctorate, thesis/dissertation.
Entrance requirements: For master's and doctorate, GRE General Test (financial award applicants), TOEFL. *Application deadline:* For fall admission, 3/15 (priority date). Applications are processed on a rolling basis. *Application fee:* $45.
Expenses: Tuition, state resident: full-time $1,748. Tuition, nonresident: full-time $6,904.
Financial support: Fellowships, research assistantships, teaching assistantships available. Financial award application deadline: 3/1.
Faculty research: Resource economics, international economics, labor economics, econometrics, environmental economics. *Total annual research expenditures:* $4.9 million.
Dr. James E. Easley, Director of Graduate Programs, 919-515-4617, *Fax:* 919-515-9367, *E-mail:* jim_easley@ncsu.edu. *Web site:* http://www.ag-econ.ncsu.edu

■ NORTH DAKOTA STATE UNIVERSITY

The Graduate School, College of Agriculture, Department of Agribusiness and Applied Economics, Fargo, ND 58105

AWARDS MS.

Faculty: 15 full-time (0 women).
Students: 12 full-time (4 women); includes 1 minority (African American), 2 international. Average age 24. 10 applicants, 50% accepted. In 2001, 3 degrees awarded.
Degree requirements: For master's, thesis or alternative.
Entrance requirements: For master's, GRE, TOEFL. *Application deadline:* For fall admission, 4/1 (priority date). Applications are processed on a rolling basis. *Application fee:* $35.
Expenses: Tuition, state resident: part-time $124 per credit. Tuition, nonresident: part-time $325 per credit. Required fees: $22 per credit. Tuition and fees vary according to reciprocity agreements.
Financial support: In 2001–02, 5 research assistantships with tuition reimbursements (averaging $13,200 per year) were awarded; Federal Work-Study and institutionally sponsored loans also available. Financial award application deadline: 4/15.
Faculty research: Agribusiness, transportation, marketing. *Total annual research expenditures:* $500,000.
Dr. David K. Lambert, Chair, 701-231-7444, *Fax:* 701-231-7400.
Application contact: Dr. Steven D. Shultz, Assistant Professor, 701-231-8935, *Fax:* 701-231-7400, *E-mail:* sshultz@ndsuext.nodak.edu. *Web site:* http://www.ext.nodak.edu/agecon/

■ NORTHWEST MISSOURI STATE UNIVERSITY

Graduate School, Melvin and Valorie Booth College of Business and Professional Studies, Program in Agricultural Economics, Maryville, MO 64468-6001

AWARDS MBA.

Degree requirements: For master's, comprehensive exam.
Entrance requirements: For master's, GMAT, TOEFL, minimum GPA of 2.5. *Application deadline:* For fall admission, 7/1; for spring admission, 12/1. Applications are processed on a rolling basis. *Application fee:* $0 ($50 for international students).
Expenses: Tuition, state resident: full-time $2,777; part-time $154 per hour. Tuition, nonresident: full-time $4,626; part-time $257 per hour. Tuition and fees vary according to course level and course load.
Financial support: Application deadline: 3/1.
Dr. Arley Larson, Chairperson, 660-562-1161.

Application contact: Dr. Frances Shipley, Dean of Graduate School, 660-562-1145, *Fax:* 660-562-0000, *E-mail:* gradsch@mail.nwmissouri.edu.

■ THE OHIO STATE UNIVERSITY

Graduate School, College of Food, Agricultural, and Environmental Sciences, Department of Agricultural, Environmental, and Development Economics, Columbus, OH 43210

AWARDS Agricultural economics and rural sociology (MS, PhD).

Degree requirements: For master's, thesis optional; for doctorate, thesis/dissertation.
Entrance requirements: For master's and doctorate, GMAT or GRE General Test.

■ OKLAHOMA STATE UNIVERSITY

Graduate College, College of Agricultural Sciences and Natural Resources, Department of Agricultural Economics, Stillwater, OK 74078

AWARDS M Ag, MS, PhD.

Faculty: 32 full-time (7 women), 1 part-time/adjunct (0 women).
Students: 26 full-time (6 women), 25 part-time (9 women); includes 1 minority (Hispanic American), 31 international. Average age 32. 43 applicants, 81% accepted. In 2001, 7 master's, 9 doctorates awarded.
Degree requirements: For master's, thesis or report; for doctorate, one foreign language, thesis/dissertation.
Entrance requirements: For master's and doctorate, TOEFL. *Application deadline:* For fall admission, 7/1 (priority date). *Application fee:* $25.
Expenses: Tuition, state resident: part-time $92 per credit hour. Tuition, nonresident: part-time $297 per credit hour. Required fees: $21 per credit hour. $14 per semester. One-time fee: $20. Tuition and fees vary according to course load.
Financial support: In 2001–02, 22 research assistantships (averaging $14,239 per year), 6 teaching assistantships (averaging $12,900 per year) were awarded. Career-related internships or fieldwork, Federal Work-Study, and tuition waivers (partial) also available. Support available to part-time students. Financial award application deadline: 3/1; financial award applicants required to submit FAFSA.
Faculty research: Marketing and agribusiness, production and farm management, policy and natural resources, community and rural development, international trade and development.
Dr. James Trapp, Head, 405-744-6157, *Fax:* 405-744-8210, *E-mail:* jntrapp@okstate.edu.

■ OREGON STATE UNIVERSITY

Graduate School, College of Agricultural Sciences and College of Forestry, Department of Agricultural and Resource Economics, Corvallis, OR 97331

AWARDS Agricultural and resource economics (M Agr, MAIS, MS, PhD); economics (MS, PhD). MS and PhD (economics) offered through the University Graduate Faculty of Economics. Part-time programs available.

Faculty: 10 full-time (1 woman), 1 (woman) part-time/adjunct.
Students: 24 full-time (8 women), 2 part-time (1 woman), 13 international. Average age 29. In 2001, 3 degrees awarded. Terminal master's awarded for partial completion of doctoral program.
Degree requirements: For master's, thesis (for some programs); for doctorate, thesis/dissertation.
Entrance requirements: For master's and doctorate, GRE General Test, TOEFL, minimum GPA of 3.0 in last 90 hours. *Application deadline:* For fall admission, 3/1. Applications are processed on a rolling basis. *Application fee:* $50.
Expenses: Tuition, area resident: Full-time $15,933. Tuition, state resident: full-time $28,937.
Financial support: Fellowships, research assistantships, teaching assistantships, career-related internships or fieldwork, Federal Work-Study, and institutionally sponsored loans available. Support available to part-time students. Financial award application deadline: 2/1.
Faculty research: Marine economics, environmental economics, effects of global climate change on agriculture, efficiency of agricultural markets, analysis of aquaculture development.
Dr. William G. Boggess, Head, 541-737-1395, *Fax:* 541-737-1441, *E-mail:* bill.boggess@orst.edu.
Application contact: Kathy Carpenter, Administrative Assistant, 541-737-1398, *Fax:* 541-737-1441, *E-mail:* kathy.carpenter@orst.edu. *Web site:* http://www.orst.edu/Dept/ag_resrc_econ/

■ THE PENNSYLVANIA STATE UNIVERSITY UNIVERSITY PARK CAMPUS

Graduate School, College of Agricultural Sciences, Department of Agricultural Economics and Rural Sociology, Program in Agricultural, Environmental and Regional Economics, State College, University Park, PA 16802-1503

AWARDS M Agr, MS, PhD.

Students: 27 full-time (13 women), 13 part-time (5 women). In 2001, 7 master's, 3 doctorates awarded.
Entrance requirements: For master's, GRE General Test; for doctorate, GRE General Test, GRE Subject Test (economics). *Application fee:* $45.
Expenses: Tuition, state resident: full-time $7,882; part-time $333 per credit. Tuition, nonresident: full-time $16,142; part-time $673 per credit. Required fees: $124 per semester.
Dr. David Abler, Chair, 814-863-8630.

■ PRAIRIE VIEW A&M UNIVERSITY

Graduate School, College of Agriculture and Human Sciences, Prairie View, TX 77446-0188

AWARDS Agricultural economics (MS); animal sciences (MS); interdisciplinary human sciences (MS); marriage and family therapy (MS); soil science (MS).

Faculty: 15 full-time (5 women), 1 part-time/adjunct (0 women).
Students: 45 full-time (28 women), 28 part-time (21 women); includes 63 minority (61 African Americans, 2 Asian Americans or Pacific Islanders), 6 international. Average age 35. 15 applicants, 100% accepted. In 2001, 20 degrees awarded.
Entrance requirements: For master's, GRE General Test. *Application deadline:* For fall admission, 10/2 (priority date); for spring admission, 2/19. Applications are processed on a rolling basis. *Application fee:* $25.
Expenses: Tuition, state resident: full-time $864; part-time $48 per credit hour. Tuition, nonresident: full-time $4,716; part-time $262 per credit hour. Required fees: $1,324; $59 per credit hour. $131 per term.
Financial support: In 2001–02, 10 research assistantships with tuition reimbursements (averaging $13,500 per year) were awarded; career-related internships or fieldwork, Federal Work-Study, and institutionally sponsored loans also available. Financial award application deadline: 4/1. *Total annual research expenditures:* $3 million.
Dr. Elizabeth Noel, Dean, 936-857-2996, *Fax:* 936-857-2998.

■ RUTGERS, THE STATE UNIVERSITY OF NEW JERSEY, NEW BRUNSWICK

Graduate School, Program in Agricultural Economics, New Brunswick, NJ 08901-1281

AWARDS MS. Part-time programs available.

Degree requirements: For master's, thesis or alternative.
Entrance requirements: For master's, GRE General Test.
Faculty research: Agricultural production and marketing, rural economic development, natural resources. *Web site:* http://www.cook.rutgers.edu/~agecon/grad.htm

■ SAM HOUSTON STATE UNIVERSITY

College of Education and Applied Science, Department of Agricultural Sciences, Huntsville, TX 77341

AWARDS Agricultural business (MS); agricultural education (M Ed); agricultural mechanization (MS); agriculture (MS); vocational education (M Ed, MS). Part-time and evening/weekend programs available.

Students: 12 full-time (6 women), 11 part-time (5 women), 1 international. Average age 26. In 2001, 7 degrees awarded.
Degree requirements: For master's, thesis optional.
Entrance requirements: For master's, GRE General Test, minimum GPA of 2.5. *Application deadline:* For fall admission, 8/1; for spring admission, 12/1. *Application fee:* $20.
Expenses: Tuition, area resident: Part-time $69 per credit. Tuition, state resident: full-time $1,380; part-time $69 per credit. Tuition, nonresident: full-time $5,600; part-time $280 per credit. Required fees: $748. Tuition and fees vary according to course load.
Financial support: Teaching assistantships, career-related internships or fieldwork available. Financial award application deadline: 5/31; financial award applicants required to submit FAFSA.
Faculty research: Legumes in pastures, fire ant control, plasma cholesterol in swine, obesity/lean in swine, water management. *Total annual research expenditures:* $80,000.
Dr. Robert A. Lane, Chair, 936-294-1225, *Fax:* 936-294-1232, *E-mail:* agr_ral@shsu.edu. *Web site:* http://www.shsu.edu/~agr_www/

■ SOUTH CAROLINA STATE UNIVERSITY

School of Graduate Studies, School of Business, Department of Agribusiness and Economics, Orangeburg, SC 29117-0001

AWARDS Agribusiness (MS). Part-time and evening/weekend programs available.

Degree requirements: For master's, departmental qualifying exam, thesis optional.
Entrance requirements: For master's, GMAT or GRE, minimum GPA of 2.8.
Faculty research: Small farm income and profitability, agricultural credit, aquaculture, low-input sustainable agriculture, rural development. *Web site:* http://www.scsu.edu

■ SOUTHERN ILLINOIS UNIVERSITY CARBONDALE

Graduate School, College of Agriculture, Department of Agribusiness Economics, Carbondale, IL 62901-6806

AWARDS MS, MBA/MS. Part-time programs available.

Faculty: 6 full-time (0 women).
Students: 12 full-time (9 women), 6 part-time (5 women), 6 international. 21 applicants, 48% accepted. In 2001, 4 degrees awarded.
Degree requirements: For master's, thesis.
Entrance requirements: For master's, TOEFL, minimum GPA of 2.7. *Application deadline:* For fall admission, 7/1 (priority date). Applications are processed on a rolling basis. *Application fee:* $0.
Expenses: Tuition, state resident: full-time $3,794; part-time $154 per hour. Tuition, nonresident: full-time $6,566; part-time $308 per hour. Required fees: $277 per hour.
Financial support: In 2001–02, 14 students received support, including 12 research assistantships with tuition reimbursements available, 5 teaching assistantships with tuition reimbursements available; fellowships with tuition reimbursements available, Federal Work-Study, institutionally sponsored loans, and tuition waivers (full) also available. Support available to part-time students. Financial award application deadline: 3/15.
Faculty research: Agricultural finance and credit, agribusiness management, resource use, rural area economic development, marketing and price analysis.
Steven Kraft, Chairperson, 618-453-2421, *E-mail:* sekraft@siu.edu.
Application contact: Lisa David, Administrative Clerk, 618-453-2421, *Fax:* 618-453-1708, *E-mail:* ldavid@siu.edu.

Find an in-depth description at www.petersons.com/gradchannel.

■ TEXAS A&M UNIVERSITY

College of Agriculture and Life Sciences, Department of Agricultural Economics, College Station, TX 77843

AWARDS MAB, MS, PhD. Part-time programs available.

Faculty: 64 full-time (3 women), 1 part-time/adjunct (0 women).
Students: 121 full-time (41 women), 4 part-time (2 women); includes 2 minority (1 Asian American or Pacific Islander, 1 Hispanic American), 64 international. Average age 29. 87 applicants, 84% accepted. In 2001, 29 master's, 3 doctorates awarded. Terminal master's awarded for partial completion of doctoral program.
Degree requirements: For master's, thesis (for some programs), comprehensive exam (for some programs), registration; for doctorate, thesis/dissertation, comprehensive exam, registration.
Entrance requirements: For master's and doctorate, GRE General Test, TOEFL. *Application deadline:* For fall admission, 3/1; for spring admission, 8/1. Applications are processed on a rolling basis. *Application fee:* $50 ($75 for international students). Electronic applications accepted.
Expenses: Tuition, state resident: full-time $11,872. Tuition, nonresident: full-time $17,892.
Financial support: In 2001–02, 55 students received support, including 3 fellowships, 28 research assistantships, 15 teaching assistantships; career-related internships or fieldwork, Federal Work-Study, institutionally sponsored loans, and unspecified assistantships also available. Financial award application deadline: 3/1; financial award applicants required to submit FAFSA.
Faculty research: Production economics, agricultural finance, resources, marketing and policy, agribusiness. *Total annual research expenditures:* $2.5 million.
A. Gene Nelson, Head, 979-845-2116, *Fax:* 979-862-1563.
Application contact: Vicki L. Heard, Graduate Admissions Supervisor, 979-845-5222, *Fax:* 979-862-1563, *E-mail:* vheard@tamu.edu. *Web site:* http://agecon.tamu.edu/

■ TEXAS A&M UNIVERSITY–KINGSVILLE

College of Graduate Studies, College of Agriculture and Home Economics, Program in Agribusiness, Kingsville, TX 78363

AWARDS MS.

Students: 5 full-time (2 women), 2 part-time, 6 international. Average age 25. In 2001, 2 degrees awarded.
Degree requirements: For master's, thesis or alternative, comprehensive exam.
Entrance requirements: For master's, GRE General Test, TOEFL, minimum GPA of 3.0. *Application deadline:* For fall admission, 6/1; for spring admission, 11/15. Applications are processed on a rolling basis. *Application fee:* $15 ($25 for international students).
Expenses: Tuition, state resident: part-time $42 per hour. Tuition, nonresident: part-time $253 per hour. Required fees: $56 per hour. One-time fee: $46 part-time. Tuition and fees vary according to program.
Financial support: Application deadline: 5/15.

■ TEXAS TECH UNIVERSITY

Graduate School, College of Agricultural Sciences and Natural Resources, Department of Agricultural and Applied Economics, Lubbock, TX 79409

AWARDS MS, PhD, JD/MS. Part-time programs available.

Faculty: 8 full-time (0 women).
Students: 17 full-time (3 women), 4 part-time (1 woman); includes 1 minority (Hispanic American), 9 international. Average age 28. 14 applicants, 57% accepted, 5 enrolled. In 2001, 4 degrees awarded.
Degree requirements: For master's, thesis or alternative; for doctorate, thesis/dissertation.
Entrance requirements: For master's and doctorate, GRE General Test. *Application deadline:* Applications are processed on a rolling basis. *Application fee:* $25 ($50 for international students). Electronic applications accepted.
Expenses: Tuition, state resident: full-time $1,926; part-time $107 per credit hour. Tuition, nonresident: full-time $5,724; part-time $318 per credit hour. Required fees: $779; $737 per year. Tuition and fees vary according to course level, course load and program.
Financial support: In 2001–02, 15 students received support, including 14 research assistantships with partial tuition reimbursements available (averaging $9,748 per year), 5 teaching assistantships with partial tuition reimbursements available (averaging $10,170 per year); fellowships, Federal Work-Study and institutionally sponsored loans also available. Support available to part-time students. Financial award application deadline: 5/1; financial award applicants required to submit FAFSA.
Faculty research: Economics of the U.S. cotton and textile industries, natural resource management in semi-arid climates, commodity policy analysis, international trade in agricultural products, agribusiness analysis. *Total annual research expenditures:* $384,465.
Dr. Don E. Ethridge, Chair, 806-742-2821, *Fax:* 806-742-1099.
Application contact: Graduate Adviser, 806-742-2821, *Fax:* 806-742-1099. *Web site:* http://www.aeco.ttu.edu/

■ TEXAS TECH UNIVERSITY

Graduate School, Jerry S. Rawls College of Business Administration, Programs in Business Administration, Lubbock, TX 79409

AWARDS Agricultural business (MBA); e-business (MBA); entrepreneurial family studies (MBA); entrepreneurial skills (MBA); finance (MBA); general business (MBA); global entrepreneurship (MBA); high performance management (MBA); international business (MBA); management information systems (MBA), including systems, technology, telecom and network management; marketing (MBA). Part-time and evening/weekend programs available.

Students: 138 full-time (38 women), 25 part-time (10 women); includes 14 minority (3 African Americans, 2 Asian Americans or Pacific Islanders, 8 Hispanic Americans, 1 Native American), 23 international. Average age 25. 201 applicants, 49% accepted, 55 enrolled. In 2001, 82 degrees awarded.
Degree requirements: For master's, capstone course.
Entrance requirements: For master's, GMAT, holistic review of academic credentials. *Application deadline:* For fall admission, 3/1 (priority date); for spring admission, 9/1 (priority date). Applications are processed on a rolling basis. *Application fee:* $25 ($50 for international students). Electronic applications accepted.
Expenses: Tuition, state resident: full-time $1,926; part-time $107 per credit hour. Tuition, nonresident: full-time $5,724; part-time $318 per credit hour. Required fees: $779; $737 per year. Tuition and fees vary according to course level, course load and program.
Financial support: In 2001–02, 10 research assistantships (averaging $5,500 per year) were awarded; teaching assistantships, career-related internships or fieldwork, Federal Work-Study, scholarships/grants, health care benefits, and unspecified assistantships also available. Support available to part-time students. Financial award applicants required to submit FAFSA.
Dr. W. Jay Conover, Director, 806-742-1546, *Fax:* 806-742-3958, *E-mail:* conover@ba.ttu.edu.
Application contact: Janet L. Hubbert, Director, Graduate Services Center, 806-742-3184, *Fax:* 806-742-3958, *E-mail:* bagrad@ba.ttu.edu. *Web site:* http://grad.ba.ttu.edu/

■ TUSKEGEE UNIVERSITY

Graduate Programs, College of Agricultural, Environmental and Natural Sciences, Department of Agricultural Sciences, Program in Agricultural and Resource Economics, Tuskegee, AL 36088

AWARDS MS.

Faculty: 13 full-time (1 woman), 2 part-time/adjunct (1 woman).
Students: 3 full-time (all women), 3 part-time (2 women); all minorities (all African Americans). Average age 29.
Degree requirements: For master's, thesis.
Entrance requirements: For master's, GRE General Test. *Application deadline:* For fall admission, 7/15. Applications are processed on a rolling basis. *Application fee:* $25 ($35 for international students).
Expenses: Tuition: Full-time $5,163; part-time $612 per credit hour.
Financial support: Application deadline: 4/15.
Dr. P. K. Biswas, Head, Department of Agricultural Sciences, 334-727-8632.

■ THE UNIVERSITY OF ARIZONA

Graduate College, College of Agriculture and Life Sciences, Department of Agricultural and Resource Economics, Tucson, AZ 85721

AWARDS MS.

Faculty: 20.
Students: 24 full-time (13 women); includes 1 minority (African American), 18 international. Average age 30. 45 applicants, 33% accepted, 9 enrolled. In 2001, 9 degrees awarded.
Degree requirements: For master's, thesis or alternative.
Entrance requirements: For master's, GRE General Test, TOEFL. *Application deadline:* For fall admission, 2/1. Applications are processed on a rolling basis. *Application fee:* $45.
Expenses: Tuition, state resident: full-time $2,490; part-time $436 per unit. Tuition, nonresident: full-time $10,300; part-time $436 per unit. Full-time tuition and fees vary according to degree level and program.
Financial support: Research assistantships, teaching assistantships, institutionally sponsored loans and tuition waivers (partial) available. Financial award application deadline: 3/1.
Faculty research: Natural resources, international development trade, production and marketing, agricultural policy, rural development.
Dr. Alan Ker, Head, 520-621-6242, *Fax:* 520-621-6250, *E-mail:* aker@ag.arizona.edu.
Application contact: Nancy Smith, Coordinator, 520-621-2421, *Fax:* 520-621-6250, *E-mail:* nansmith@ag.arizona.edu.

■ UNIVERSITY OF ARKANSAS

Graduate School, Dale Bumpers College of Agricultural, Food and Life Sciences, Department of Agricultural Economics, Fayetteville, AR 72701-1201

AWARDS MS.

Students: 24 full-time (6 women), 6 part-time (3 women); includes 5 minority (all African Americans), 12 international. 24 applicants, 96% accepted. In 2001, 7 degrees awarded.
Degree requirements: For master's, thesis optional.
Application fee: $40 ($50 for international students).
Expenses: Tuition, state resident: full-time $3,553; part-time $197 per credit. Tuition, nonresident: full-time $8,411; part-time $467 per credit. Required fees: $42 per credit. Tuition and fees vary according to course load and program.

University of Arkansas (continued)
Financial support: In 2001–02, 13 research assistantships, 2 teaching assistantships were awarded. Career-related internships or fieldwork and Federal Work-Study also available. Support available to part-time students. Financial award application deadline: 4/1; financial award applicants required to submit FAFSA.
Dr. Mark Cochran, Chair, 479-575-2256.
Application contact: Bruce Dixon, Adviser of Studies, 479-575-2256, *E-mail:* aminden@comp.uark.edu.

■ UNIVERSITY OF CALIFORNIA, BERKELEY

Graduate Division, College of Natural Resources, Department of Agricultural and Resource Economics and Policy, Berkeley, CA 94720-1500

AWARDS PhD.

Degree requirements: For doctorate, thesis/dissertation, qualifying exam.
Entrance requirements: For doctorate, GRE General Test, minimum GPA of 3.0.
Expenses: Tuition, nonresident: full-time $10,704. Required fees: $4,349.
Faculty research: Agricultural economics and policy, environmental and resource economics and policy, international agricultural development and trade. *Web site:* http://are.berkeley.edu/

■ UNIVERSITY OF CALIFORNIA, DAVIS

Graduate Studies, Program in Agricultural and Resource Economics, Davis, CA 95616

AWARDS MS, PhD, MBA/MS. Part-time programs available.

Faculty: 36 full-time (4 women).
Students: 71 full-time (39 women); includes 10 minority (6 Asian Americans or Pacific Islanders, 4 Hispanic Americans), 39 international. Average age 29. 144 applicants, 40% accepted, 24 enrolled. In 2001, 7 master's, 11 doctorates awarded. Terminal master's awarded for partial completion of doctoral program.
Degree requirements: For master's, thesis optional; for doctorate, thesis/dissertation.
Entrance requirements: For master's, GRE General Test, minimum GPA of 3.0; for doctorate, GRE General Test, minimum GPA of 3.25. *Application deadline:* Applications are processed on a rolling basis. *Application fee:* $60. Electronic applications accepted.
Expenses: Tuition, state resident: full-time $4,831. Tuition, nonresident: full-time $15,725.
Financial support: In 2001–02, 62 students received support, including 29 fellowships with full and partial tuition reimbursements available (averaging $5,379 per year), 17 teaching assistantships with partial tuition reimbursements available (averaging $14,140 per year); research assistantships with full and partial tuition reimbursements available, career-related internships or fieldwork, Federal Work-Study, institutionally sponsored loans, and tuition waivers (partial) also available. Financial award application deadline: 1/15; financial award applicants required to submit FAFSA.
Faculty research: Applied microeconomics, international trade, development, econometrics, environmental economics. *Total annual research expenditures:* $2 million.
James Chalfont, Chair, 530-752-9028, *E-mail:* jim@primal.ucdavis.edu.
Application contact: Kris Carpenter, Graduate Program Assistant, 530-752-6185, *E-mail:* kris@primal.ucdavis.edu. *Web site:* http://www.agecon.ucdavis.edu/

■ UNIVERSITY OF CONNECTICUT

Graduate School, College of Agriculture and Natural Resources, Field of Agricultural and Resource Economics, Storrs, CT 06269

AWARDS MS, PhD.

Degree requirements: For doctorate, thesis/dissertation.
Entrance requirements: For master's and doctorate, GRE General Test, TOEFL.
Faculty research: Food marketing, international agricultural development.

■ UNIVERSITY OF DELAWARE

College of Agriculture and Natural Resources, Department of Food and Resource Economics, Newark, DE 19716

AWARDS Agricultural economics (MS); statistics (MS). Part-time programs available.

Faculty: 12 full-time (2 women).
Students: 18 full-time (7 women); includes 2 minority (1 African American, 1 Asian American or Pacific Islander), 11 international. Average age 25. 39 applicants, 36% accepted, 8 enrolled. In 2001, 8 degrees awarded.
Degree requirements: For master's, thesis.
Entrance requirements: For master's, GRE General Test, TOEFL, letters of recommendation (3). *Application deadline:* For fall admission, 2/1 (priority date); for spring admission, 12/1. *Application fee:* $50. Electronic applications accepted.
Expenses: Tuition, state resident: full-time $4,770; part-time $265 per credit. Tuition, nonresident: full-time $13,860; part-time $770 per credit. Required fees: $414.
Financial support: In 2001–02, 14 students received support, including 9 research assistantships with full tuition reimbursements available (averaging $11,000 per year), 3 teaching assistantships with full tuition reimbursements available (averaging $10,000 per year); fellowships, scholarships/grants, tuition waivers (full), and unspecified assistantships also available. Financial award application deadline: 3/1.
Faculty research: Experimental economics, environmental and resource economics, land use, law and economics. *Total annual research expenditures:* $1.1 million.
Dr. Thomas W. Ilvento, Chairman, 302-831-6773, *Fax:* 302-831-6243, *E-mail:* ilvento@udel.edu.
Application contact: Vicki Lynn Taylor, Office Coordinator, 302-831-2511, *Fax:* 302-831-6243, *E-mail:* vtaylor@udel.edu. *Web site:* http://ag.udel.edu/departments/frec.html

■ UNIVERSITY OF FLORIDA

Graduate School, College of Agricultural and Life Sciences, Department of Food and Resource Economics, Gainesville, FL 32611

AWARDS Agribusiness (MAB); food and resource economics (M Ag, MS, PhD).

Degree requirements: For master's, thesis optional; for doctorate, thesis/dissertation.
Entrance requirements: For master's and doctorate, GRE General Test, TOEFL, minimum GPA of 3.0. Electronic applications accepted.
Expenses: Tuition, state resident: part-time $164 per hour. Tuition, nonresident: part-time $571 per hour. Tuition and fees vary according to course level and program.
Faculty research: Agribusiness management, production, environmental economics, international trade, economic development. *Web site:* http://www.fred.ifas.ufl.edu/

■ UNIVERSITY OF GEORGIA

Graduate School, College of Agricultural and Environmental Sciences, Department of Agricultural and Applied Economics, Athens, GA 30602

AWARDS Agricultural economics (MAE, MS, PhD); environmental economics (MS).

Faculty: 22 full-time (1 woman).
Students: 31 full-time (9 women), 8 part-time (3 women); includes 4 minority (all African Americans), 20 international. 81 applicants, 21% accepted. In 2001, 12 master's awarded.
Degree requirements: For master's, thesis (MS); for doctorate, thesis/dissertation.
Entrance requirements: For master's and doctorate, GRE General Test. *Application deadline:* For fall admission, 7/1 (priority date); for spring admission, 11/15. *Application fee:* $30. Electronic applications accepted.
Expenses: Tuition, state resident: full-time $2,376; part-time $132 per credit hour. Tuition, nonresident: full-time $9,504; part-time $528 per credit hour. Required fees: $236 per semester.

Financial support: Fellowships, research assistantships, teaching assistantships, career-related internships or fieldwork and unspecified assistantships available.
Dr. Fred C. White, Head, 706-542-0764, *Fax:* 706-542-0739, *E-mail:* fwhite@agecon.uga.edu.
Application contact: Dr. James E. Epperson, Contact, 706-542-0766, *Fax:* 706-542-0739, *E-mail:* jepperson@agecon.uga.edu. *Web site:* http://www.agecon.uga.edu/

Find an in-depth description at www.petersons.com/gradchannel.

■ UNIVERSITY OF HAWAII AT MANOA

Graduate Division, College of Tropical Agriculture and Human Resources, Department of Natural Resources and Environmental Management, Honolulu, HI 96822

AWARDS MS, PhD. Part-time programs available.

Faculty: 12 full-time (2 women), 5 part-time/adjunct (0 women).
Students: 11 full-time (1 woman), 2 part-time (1 woman). Average age 34. 18 applicants, 83% accepted. In 2001, 1 degree awarded. Terminal master's awarded for partial completion of doctoral program.
Degree requirements: For master's, thesis or alternative; for doctorate, thesis/dissertation.
Entrance requirements: For master's and doctorate, GRE, TOEFL, minimum GPA of 3.0 in last 4 semesters. *Application deadline:* For fall admission, 3/1; for spring admission, 9/1. Applications are processed on a rolling basis. *Application fee:* $25 ($50 for international students).
Expenses: Tuition, state resident: full-time $2,160; part-time $1,980 per year. Tuition, nonresident: full-time $5,190; part-time $4,829 per year.
Financial support: In 2001–02, 9 students received support, including 1 research assistantship (averaging $15,558 per year), 3 teaching assistantships (averaging $13,830 per year); fellowships, career-related internships or fieldwork and tuition waivers (full and partial) also available.
Faculty research: Bioeconomics, natural resource management.
Dr. Samir El-Swarfy, Chairperson, 808-956-7039, *Fax:* 808-956-2811.

■ UNIVERSITY OF IDAHO

College of Graduate Studies, College of Agriculture, Department of Agricultural Economics, Moscow, ID 83844-2282

AWARDS MS.

Faculty: 12 full-time (0 women).
Students: 8 full-time (5 women); includes 2 minority (both Hispanic Americans), 2 international. 10 applicants, 80% accepted. In 2001, 4 degrees awarded.
Entrance requirements: For master's, minimum GPA of 2.8. *Application deadline:* For fall admission, 8/1; for spring admission, 12/15. *Application fee:* $35 ($45 for international students).
Expenses: Tuition, state resident: full-time $1,613. Tuition, nonresident: full-time $3,000.
Financial support: In 2001–02, 7 research assistantships (averaging $10,482 per year), 3 teaching assistantships (averaging $10,896 per year) were awarded. Financial award application deadline: 2/15.
Dr. Larry Van Tassell, Head, 208-885-7869, *Fax:* 208-885-5759. *Web site:* http://www.uidaho.edu/ag/agecon/

Find an in-depth description at www.petersons.com/gradchannel.

■ UNIVERSITY OF ILLINOIS AT URBANA–CHAMPAIGN

Graduate College, College of Agricultural, Consumer and Environmental Sciences, Department of Agricultural and Consumer Economics, Champaign, IL 61820

AWARDS MS, PhD.

Faculty: 41 full-time (13 women), 1 part-time/adjunct (0 women).
Students: 80 full-time (34 women); includes 4 minority (all African Americans), 61 international. 107 applicants, 23% accepted. In 2001, 8 master's, 15 doctorates awarded.
Degree requirements: For master's and doctorate, thesis/dissertation.
Entrance requirements: For master's, minimum GPA of 3.0. *Application deadline:* Applications are processed on a rolling basis. *Application fee:* $40 ($50 for international students). Electronic applications accepted.
Expenses: Tuition, state resident: part-time $3,227 per degree program. Tuition, nonresident: part-time $7,169 per degree program. Tuition and fees vary according to program.
Financial support: In 2001–02, 6 fellowships, 48 research assistantships, 12 teaching assistantships were awarded. Tuition waivers (full and partial) also available. Financial award application deadline: 2/15.
Darrel L. Good, Interim Head, 217-333-8859, *Fax:* 217-333-5538, *E-mail:* d-good@uiuc.edu.
Application contact: Linda Foste, Secretary, 217-333-1830, *Fax:* 217-333-5538, *E-mail:* l-foste@uiuc.edu. *Web site:* http://w3.ag.uiuc.edu/ACE/welcome/

■ UNIVERSITY OF KENTUCKY

Graduate School, Graduate School Programs from the College of Agriculture, Department of Agricultural Economics, Lexington, KY 40546-0276

AWARDS MS, PhD.

Faculty: 21 full-time (2 women).
Students: 40 full-time (15 women), 4 part-time (1 woman); includes 3 minority (2 African Americans, 1 Asian American or Pacific Islander), 27 international. 43 applicants, 74% accepted. In 2001, 8 master's, 2 doctorates awarded.
Degree requirements: For master's, thesis optional; for doctorate, thesis/dissertation, comprehensive exam.
Entrance requirements: For master's, GRE General Test, minimum undergraduate GPA of 2.5; for doctorate, GRE General Test, minimum graduate GPA of 3.0. *Application deadline:* For fall admission, 7/19. Applications are processed on a rolling basis. *Application fee:* $30 ($35 for international students).
Expenses: Tuition, state resident: full-time $4,075; part-time $213 per credit hour. Tuition, nonresident: full-time $11,295; part-time $614 per credit hour.
Financial support: In 2001–02, 3 fellowships, 23 research assistantships, 1 teaching assistantship were awarded. Federal Work-Study and institutionally sponsored loans also available. Support available to part-time students.
Faculty research: Food and agricultural marketing, agricultural and food policy, natural resources and environment, rural economic development.
Dr. Michael R. Reed, Director of Graduate Studies, 859-257-7259, *E-mail:* mrreed@pop.uky.edu.
Application contact: Dr. Jeannine Blackwell, Associate Dean, 859-257-4905, *Fax:* 859-323-1928.

■ UNIVERSITY OF MAINE

Graduate School, College of Natural Sciences, Forestry, and Agriculture, Department of Resource Economics and Policy, Orono, ME 04469

AWARDS Resource economics and policy (MS); resource utilization (MS). Part-time programs available.

Faculty: 12 full-time (1 woman), 2 part-time/adjunct (0 women).
Students: 13 full-time (9 women), 3 part-time (2 women); includes 1 minority (Asian American or Pacific Islander), 5 international. Average age 26. 26 applicants, 85% accepted, 6 enrolled. In 2001, 6 degrees awarded.
Degree requirements: For master's, thesis (for some programs).
Entrance requirements: For master's, GRE General Test, TOEFL. *Application deadline:* For fall admission, 2/1 (priority

University of Maine (continued)
date). Applications are processed on a rolling basis. *Application fee:* $50. Electronic applications accepted.
Expenses: Tuition, state resident: full-time $3,780; part-time $210 per credit hour. Tuition, nonresident: full-time $10,782; part-time $599 per credit hour. Required fees: $9.50 per credit hour. $32 per semester. Tuition and fees vary according to reciprocity agreements.
Financial support: In 2001–02, 10 research assistantships with tuition reimbursements (averaging $14,000 per year), 3 teaching assistantships with tuition reimbursements (averaging $10,190 per year) were awarded. Career-related internships or fieldwork, Federal Work-Study, institutionally sponsored loans, scholarships/grants, and tuition waivers (full and partial) also available. Support available to part-time students. Financial award application deadline: 3/1.
Faculty research: International trade, agricultural marketing, nonmarketing valuation, livestock health economics.
Dr. George Criner, Chair, 207-581-3150, *Fax:* 207-581-4278.
Application contact: Scott G. Delcourt, Director of the Graduate School, 207-581-3218, *Fax:* 207-581-3232, *E-mail:* graduate@maine.edu. *Web site:* http://www.umaine.edu/graduate/

■ UNIVERSITY OF MARYLAND, COLLEGE PARK

Graduate Studies and Research, College of Agriculture and Natural Resources, Department of Agricultural and Resource Economics, College Park, MD 20742

AWARDS Agriculture economics (MS, PhD); resource economics (MS, PhD). Part-time and evening/weekend programs available.

Faculty: 24 full-time (4 women), 1 (woman) part-time/adjunct.
Students: 34 full-time (13 women), 25 part-time (9 women), 38 international. 126 applicants, 19% accepted, 14 enrolled. In 2001, 6 master's, 11 doctorates awarded.
Entrance requirements: For master's, GRE General Test, minimum GPA of 3.0, previous course work in microeconomics and calculus; for doctorate, GRE General Test. *Application deadline:* For fall admission, 7/1; for spring admission, 12/1. Applications are processed on a rolling basis. *Application fee:* $50 ($70 for international students). Electronic applications accepted.
Expenses: Tuition, state resident: part-time $289 per credit hour. Tuition, nonresident: part-time $448 per credit hour. One-time fee: $436 part-time. Full-time tuition and fees vary according to course load, campus/location and program.
Financial support: In 2001–02, 3 fellowships with full tuition reimbursements (averaging $20,581 per year), 32 research assistantships with tuition reimbursements (averaging $18,391 per year), 1 teaching assistantship with tuition reimbursement (averaging $9,500 per year) were awarded. Federal Work-Study and scholarships/grants also available. Support available to part-time students. Financial award applicants required to submit FAFSA.
Faculty research: Agricultural development, international trade, agricultural marketing, econometrics, farm management and production economics.
Dr. Bruce Gardner, Chairman, 301-405-1290, *Fax:* 301-314-9091.
Application contact: Trudy Lindsey, Director, Graduate Admissions and Records, 301-405-6991, *Fax:* 301-314-9305, *E-mail:* grschool@deans.umd.edu.

■ UNIVERSITY OF MASSACHUSETTS AMHERST

Graduate School, College of Food and Natural Resources, Department of Resource Economics, Amherst, MA 01003

AWARDS MS, PhD. Part-time programs available.

Faculty: 12 full-time (1 woman).
Students: 14 full-time (6 women), 8 part-time (4 women), 11 international. Average age 26. 37 applicants, 35% accepted. In 2001, 3 master's, 3 doctorates awarded. Terminal master's awarded for partial completion of doctoral program.
Degree requirements: For master's, thesis or alternative; for doctorate, thesis/dissertation.
Entrance requirements: For master's and doctorate, GRE General Test. *Application deadline:* For fall admission, 2/1 (priority date). Applications are processed on a rolling basis. *Application fee:* $40 ($50 for international students).
Expenses: Tuition, state resident: full-time $1,980; part-time $110 per credit. Tuition, nonresident: full-time $7,456; part-time $414 per credit. Required fees: $4,112. One-time fee: $115 full-time.
Financial support: In 2001–02, 18 research assistantships with full tuition reimbursements (averaging $6,969 per year), 9 teaching assistantships with full tuition reimbursements (averaging $8,551 per year) were awarded. Fellowships with full tuition reimbursements, career-related internships or fieldwork, Federal Work-Study, scholarships/grants, traineeships, and unspecified assistantships also available. Support available to part-time students. Financial award application deadline: 2/1.
Dr. P. Geoffrey Allen, Director, 413-545-2491, *Fax:* 413-545-5853, *E-mail:* allen@resecon.umass.edu.

■ UNIVERSITY OF MINNESOTA, TWIN CITIES CAMPUS

Graduate School, College of Agricultural, Food, and Environmental Sciences, Department of Applied Economics, Minneapolis, MN 55455-0213

AWARDS Agricultural and applied economics (MS, PhD).

Faculty: 39 full-time (8 women).
Students: 70 full-time (31 women), 43 international. 71 applicants, 75% accepted, 17 enrolled. In 2001, 7 master's, 6 doctorates awarded.
Degree requirements: For master's and doctorate, thesis/dissertation. *Median time to degree:* Master's–2.3 years full-time; doctorate–4.3 years full-time.
Entrance requirements: For master's and doctorate, GRE, TOEFL, minimum GPA of 3.0. *Application deadline:* For fall admission, 6/15; for spring admission, 10/15. Applications are processed on a rolling basis. *Application fee:* $50 ($55 for international students). Electronic applications accepted.
Expenses: Tuition, state resident: full-time $2,932; part-time $489 per credit. Tuition, nonresident: full-time $5,758; part-time $960 per credit. Part-time tuition and fees vary according to course load, program and reciprocity agreements.
Financial support: In 2001–02, 52 students received support, including 6 fellowships with full tuition reimbursements available (averaging $19,850 per year), 40 research assistantships with full tuition reimbursements available (averaging $17,612 per year), 6 teaching assistantships with full tuition reimbursements available (averaging $17,612 per year); tuition waivers (full and partial) and stipends also available. Financial award application deadline: 12/31.
Faculty research: Consumptions and marketing economics, development economics, trade and policy, production and managerial economics, regional and community economics. *Total annual research expenditures:* $450,000.
Dr. Vernon R. Eidman, Head, 612-625-0231, *Fax:* 612-625-6245, *E-mail:* veidman@dept.agecon.umn.edu.
Application contact: Dr. Glenn D. Pederson, Director of Graduate Studies, 612-625-7028, *Fax:* 612-625-6245, *E-mail:* dgs@dept.agecon.umn.edu. *Web site:* http://www.apecon.agri.umn.edu/

■ UNIVERSITY OF MISSOURI–COLUMBIA

Graduate School, College of Agriculture, Food and Natural Resources, Department of Agricultural Economics, Columbia, MO 65211

AWARDS MS, PhD.

Faculty: 26 full-time (3 women), 2 part-time/adjunct (1 woman).

Students: 22 full-time (9 women), 24 part-time (4 women); includes 2 minority (both African Americans), 26 international. 19 applicants, 58% accepted. In 2001, 10 master's, 8 doctorates awarded.
Degree requirements: For doctorate, thesis/dissertation.
Entrance requirements: For master's and doctorate, GRE General Test, minimum GPA of 3.0. *Application deadline:* For fall admission, 4/1 (priority date). Applications are processed on a rolling basis. *Application fee:* $25 ($50 for international students).
Expenses: Tuition, state resident: part-time $179 per credit hour. Tuition, nonresident: part-time $539 per credit hour. Required fees: $122 per semester. Tuition and fees vary according to program.
Financial support: Research assistantships, teaching assistantships, institutionally sponsored loans available.
Dr. Thomas Johnson, Director of Graduate Studies, 573-882-2157, *E-mail:* johnsontg@missouri.edu.
Application contact: Dr. Tony Prato, Chair, 573-882-0147, *E-mail:* pratoa@missouri.edu. *Web site:* http://www.ssu.missouri.edu/agecon/

■ UNIVERSITY OF NEBRASKA–LINCOLN

Graduate College, College of Agricultural Sciences and Natural Resources, Department of Agricultural Economics, Lincoln, NE 68588

AWARDS MS, PhD.

Faculty: 24.
Students: 18 (6 women) 13 international. Average age 35. 29 applicants, 28% accepted, 6 enrolled. In 2001, 1 master's, 4 doctorates awarded.
Degree requirements: For master's, thesis optional; for doctorate, thesis/dissertation, comprehensive exam.
Entrance requirements: For master's and doctorate, GRE General Test, TOEFL. *Application deadline:* For fall admission, 3/1 (priority date). Applications are processed on a rolling basis. *Application fee:* $35. Electronic applications accepted.
Expenses: Tuition, state resident: full-time $2,412; part-time $134 per credit. Tuition, nonresident: full-time $6,223; part-time $346 per credit. Tuition and fees vary according to course load.
Financial support: In 2001–02, 9 research assistantships were awarded; fellowships, teaching assistantships, Federal Work-Study, health care benefits, and unspecified assistantships also available. Support available to part-time students. Financial award application deadline: 2/15.
Faculty research: Marketing and agribusiness, production economics, resource law, international trade and development, rural policy and revitalization.
Dr. Jeffrey Royer, Head, 402-472-3401, *Fax:* 402-472-3460. *Web site:* http://agecon.unl.edu/

■ UNIVERSITY OF NEVADA, RENO

Graduate School, College of Agriculture, Biotechnology and Natural Resources, Department of Resource and Applied Economics, Reno, NV 89557

AWARDS Resource and applied economics (MS).

Faculty: 3.
Students: 9 full-time (2 women), 2 part-time, 2 international. Average age 32. In 2001, 8 degrees awarded.
Degree requirements: For master's, thesis optional.
Entrance requirements: For master's, GRE, TOEFL, minimum GPA of 2.75. *Application deadline:* For fall admission, 3/1 (priority date). Applications are processed on a rolling basis. *Application fee:* $40.
Expenses: Tuition, state resident: full-time $2,067; part-time $108 per credit. Tuition, nonresident: full-time $9,282; part-time $109 per credit. Required fees: $57 per semester. Tuition and fees vary according to course load.
Financial support: In 2001–02, 12 research assistantships were awarded. Financial award application deadline: 3/1.
Dr. Casey VanKooten, Graduate Program Director, 775-784-4411.
Application contact: Dr. Jeff Englin, Director of Graduate Studies, 775-784-4411, *E-mail:* englin@scs.unr.edu.

■ UNIVERSITY OF PUERTO RICO, MAYAGÜEZ CAMPUS

Graduate Studies, College of Agricultural Sciences, Department of Agricultural Economics, Mayagüez, PR 00681-9000

AWARDS MS. Part-time programs available.

Degree requirements: For master's, thesis, comprehensive exam.
Faculty research: Farm management, agricultural development, agrimarketing, natural resource economics.

■ UNIVERSITY OF RHODE ISLAND

Graduate School, College of the Environment and Life Sciences, Department of Environmental and Natural Resource Economics, Kingston, RI 02881

AWARDS Resource economics and marine resources (MS, PhD).

Students: In 2001, 15 master's, 1 doctorate awarded.
Degree requirements: For master's, thesis optional; for doctorate, thesis/dissertation.
Entrance requirements: For master's and doctorate, GRE General Test, TOEFL. *Application deadline:* For fall admission, 4/15 (priority date). Applications are processed on a rolling basis.
Expenses: Tuition, state resident: full-time $3,756; part-time $209 per credit. Tuition, nonresident: full-time $10,774; part-time $599 per credit. Required fees: $1,586; $76 per credit. One-time fee: $60 full-time.
Dr. James Anderson, Chairperson.
Application contact: Dr. Tim Tyrrell, Graduate Admissions Committee, 401-874-2472, *Fax:* 401-782-4766, *E-mail:* renri@uriacc.uri.edu.

Find an in-depth description at www.petersons.com/gradchannel.

■ THE UNIVERSITY OF TENNESSEE

Graduate School, College of Agricultural Sciences and Natural Resources, Department of Agricultural Economics, Knoxville, TN 37996

AWARDS Agribusiness (MS); agricultural economics (MS); rural sociology (MS).

Faculty: 16 full-time (1 woman).
Students: 16 full-time (9 women), 2 part-time (1 woman); includes 3 minority (2 African Americans, 1 Hispanic American), 2 international. 16 applicants, 75% accepted. In 2001, 10 degrees awarded.
Degree requirements: For master's, thesis or alternative.
Entrance requirements: For master's, GRE General Test, TOEFL, minimum GPA of 2.7. *Application deadline:* For fall admission, 2/1 (priority date). Applications are processed on a rolling basis. *Application fee:* $35. Electronic applications accepted.
Expenses: Tuition, state resident: full-time $4,280; part-time $233 per hour. Tuition, nonresident: full-time $12,066; part-time $666 per hour. Tuition and fees vary according to program.
Financial support: In 2001–02, 14 research assistantships were awarded; fellowships, teaching assistantships, career-related internships or fieldwork, Federal Work-Study, and institutionally sponsored loans also available. Financial award application deadline: 2/1; financial award applicants required to submit FAFSA.
Dr. Dan McLemore, Head, 865-974-7231, *Fax:* 865-974-7484, *E-mail:* dmclemore@utk.edu.
Application contact: Dr. John Brooker, Graduate Representative, *E-mail:* jbrooker@utk.edu.

■ UNIVERSITY OF VERMONT

Graduate College, College of Agriculture and Life Sciences, Department of Community Development and Applied Economics, Burlington, VT 05405

AWARDS M Ext Ed, MS.

University of Vermont (continued)
Degree requirements: For master's, thesis.
Entrance requirements: For master's, GRE General Test, TOEFL.
Expenses: Tuition, state resident: part-time $335 per credit. Tuition, nonresident: part-time $838 per credit.
Faculty research: Agricultural production and marketing.

■ UNIVERSITY OF WISCONSIN–MADISON

Graduate School, College of Agricultural and Life Sciences, Department of Agricultural and Applied Economics, Madison, WI 53706-1380

AWARDS MA, MS, PhD. Part-time programs available.

Faculty: 20 full-time (1 woman), 2 part-time/adjunct (0 women).
Students: 43 full-time (23 women); includes 1 minority (Asian American or Pacific Islander), 27 international. Average age 25. 71 applicants, 70% accepted, 12 enrolled. In 2001, 9 master's, 1 doctorate awarded.
Degree requirements: For doctorate, thesis/dissertation, preliminary exams. *Median time to degree:* Master's–2 years full-time; doctorate–5.5 years full-time.
Entrance requirements: For master's and doctorate, GRE General Test, TOEFL. *Application deadline:* For fall admission, 2/1 (priority date). *Application fee:* $45. Electronic applications accepted.
Expenses: Tuition, state resident: full-time $7,361; part-time $399 per credit. Tuition, nonresident: full-time $20,499; part-time $1,282 per credit. Required fees: $34 per credit. Full-time tuition and fees vary according to course load, program, reciprocity agreements and student level.
Financial support: In 2001–02, 34 students received support, including 23 fellowships with full tuition reimbursements available (averaging $15,000 per year), 32 research assistantships with full tuition reimbursements available (averaging $16,350 per year); career-related internships or fieldwork, Federal Work-Study, and unspecified assistantships also available. Support available to part-time students. Financial award application deadline: 1/5.
Faculty research: Environmental and resource economics, international development, state and local economics, food systems, markets and trade. *Total annual research expenditures:* $1.3 million.
Richard C. Bishop, Chair, 608-262-8966, *Fax:* 608-262-4376.
Application contact: Barbara Forrest, Academic Programs Coordinator, 608-262-9489, *Fax:* 608-262-4376, *E-mail:* admissions@aae.wisc.edu. *Web site:* http://www.aae.wisc.edu/

■ UNIVERSITY OF WISCONSIN–MADISON

Graduate School, School of Business, Program in Agribusiness, Madison, WI 53706-1380

AWARDS MBA.

Students: 7 full-time (1 woman), 2 international. 6 applicants, 67% accepted, 3 enrolled. In 2001, 1 degree awarded.
Entrance requirements: For master's, GMAT, TOEFL. *Application deadline:* For fall admission, 4/15. Applications are processed on a rolling basis. *Application fee:* $45. Electronic applications accepted.
Expenses: Tuition, state resident: full-time $7,361; part-time $399 per credit. Tuition, nonresident: full-time $20,499; part-time $1,282 per credit. Required fees: $34 per credit. Full-time tuition and fees vary according to course load, program, reciprocity agreements and student level.
Financial support: In 2001–02, fellowships (averaging $10,000 per year), 5 research assistantships with full tuition reimbursements (averaging $9,200 per year) were awarded. Teaching assistantships, career-related internships or fieldwork, Federal Work-Study, institutionally sponsored loans, scholarships/grants, and unspecified assistantships also available. Financial award application deadline: 2/15; financial award applicants required to submit FAFSA.
Dr. Don Hausch, Director, 608-262-3535, *Fax:* 608-265-4195.
Application contact: Cory Lathbury, Admissions, 608-262-4000, *Fax:* 608-265-4195, *E-mail:* uwmadmba@bus.wisc.edu. *Web site:* http://www.bus.wisc.edu/

■ UNIVERSITY OF WYOMING

Graduate School, College of Agriculture, Department of Agricultural and Applied Economics, Laramie, WY 82071

AWARDS MS. Part-time programs available.

Faculty: 11 full-time (0 women).
Students: 9 full-time (5 women), 2 part-time (both women), 1 international. Average age 25. 14 applicants, 29% accepted. In 2001, 13 degrees awarded.
Degree requirements: For master's, thesis (for some programs).
Entrance requirements: For master's, GRE General Test, minimum GPA of 3.0. *Application deadline:* For fall admission, 8/1 (priority date); for spring admission, 10/1 (priority date). Applications are processed on a rolling basis. *Application fee:* $40. Electronic applications accepted.
Expenses: Tuition, state resident: full-time $2,895; part-time $161 per credit hour. Tuition, nonresident: full-time $8,367; part-time $465 per credit hour. Required fees: $491; $10 per credit hour. $2 per credit hour. Tuition and fees vary according to course load and program.
Financial support: In 2001–02, 5 research assistantships with tuition reimbursements (averaging $8,667 per year) were awarded; career-related internships or fieldwork, Federal Work-Study, and institutionally sponsored loans also available. Financial award application deadline: 3/1; financial award applicants required to submit FAFSA.
Faculty research: Farm management, agricultural markets, water economics, community development, agricultural business. *Total annual research expenditures:* $107,000.
Edward B. Bradley, Head, 307-766-2386, *Fax:* 307-766-5544, *E-mail:* bradley@uwyo.edu. *Web site:* http://www.uwyo.edu/ag/agecon/pageone.htm

■ VIRGINIA POLYTECHNIC INSTITUTE AND STATE UNIVERSITY

Graduate School, College of Agriculture and Life Sciences, Department of Agricultural and Applied Economics, Blacksburg, VA 24061

AWARDS Agribusiness (MS); agricultural economics (MS); applied economics (MS); developmental and international economics (PhD); econometrics (PhD); macro and micro economics (PhD); markets and industrial organizations (PhD); public and regional/urban economics (PhD); resource and environmental economics (PhD).

Faculty: 27 full-time (3 women).
Students: 36 full-time (13 women), 13 international. Average age 25. 68 applicants, 25% accepted, 10 enrolled. In 2001, 7 master's, 3 doctorates awarded. Terminal master's awarded for partial completion of doctoral program.
Degree requirements: For master's, thesis (for some programs); for doctorate, thesis/dissertation, dissertation defense, qualifying exams.
Entrance requirements: For master's and doctorate, GRE General Test, TOEFL. *Application deadline:* For winter admission, 2/1 (priority date). Applications are processed on a rolling basis. *Application fee:* $45. Electronic applications accepted.
Expenses: Tuition, state resident: part-time $241 per hour. Tuition, nonresident: part-time $406 per hour. Tuition and fees vary according to program.
Financial support: In 2001–02, 32 students received support, including 10 research assistantships with full tuition reimbursements available (averaging $16,000 per year), 4 teaching assistantships with full tuition reimbursements available (averaging $16,000 per year). Financial award application deadline: 2/15.
Faculty research: Rural development. *Total annual research expenditures:* $1.5 million.

Dr. David Orden, Graduate Program Chairman, 540-231-7559, *Fax:* 540-231-3318, *E-mail:* orden@vt.edu.
Application contact: Marilyn Echols, Graduate Program Administrator, 540-231-6846, *Fax:* 540-231-7417, *E-mail:* squid@vt.edu. *Web site:* http://www.aaec.vt.edu/

■ WASHINGTON STATE UNIVERSITY

Graduate School, College of Agriculture and Home Economics, Department of Agricultural Economics, Pullman, WA 99164

AWARDS Agribusiness (MA); agricultural economics (MA, PhD).

Faculty: 17 full-time (2 women), 1 part-time/adjunct (0 women).
Students: 28 full-time (10 women), 1 (woman) part-time; includes 7 minority (all Asian Americans or Pacific Islanders), 8 international. Average age 25. 39 applicants, 7 enrolled. In 2001, 4 master's, 4 doctorates awarded. Terminal master's awarded for partial completion of doctoral program.
Degree requirements: For master's, thesis, oral exam; for doctorate, thesis/dissertation, oral exam, written exam, qualifying exams.
Entrance requirements: For master's and doctorate, GRE General Test (international applicants), minimum GPA of 3.0. *Application deadline:* For fall admission, 3/1 (priority date). Applications are processed on a rolling basis. *Application fee:* $35. Electronic applications accepted.
Expenses: Tuition, state resident: full-time $6,088; part-time $304 per semester. Tuition, nonresident: full-time $14,918; part-time $746 per semester. Tuition and fees vary according to program.
Financial support: In 2001–02, 2 fellowships (averaging $3,000 per year), 29 research assistantships with full and partial tuition reimbursements (averaging $11,200 per year), 3 teaching assistantships with full and partial tuition reimbursements (averaging $11,200 per year) were awarded. Career-related internships or fieldwork, Federal Work-Study, institutionally sponsored loans, tuition waivers (partial), and teaching associateships also available. Financial award application deadline: 4/1; financial award applicants required to submit FAFSA.
Faculty research: Marketing, natural resources, production economics. *Total annual research expenditures:* $523,577.
Dr. C. Richard Shumway, Chair, 509-335-5555. *Web site:* http://www.agecon.wsu.edu/

■ WEST TEXAS A&M UNIVERSITY

College of Agriculture, Nursing, and Natural Sciences, Division of Agriculture, Emphasis in Agricultural Business and Economics, Canyon, TX 79016-0001

AWARDS MS. Part-time programs available.

Faculty: 1 full-time (0 women), 3 part-time/adjunct (0 women).
Students: 4 full-time (3 women), 4 part-time (2 women), 2 international. Average age 34. 8 applicants, 8 enrolled. In 2001, 5 degrees awarded.
Degree requirements: For master's, thesis optional. *Median time to degree:* Master's–3 years full-time, 6 years part-time.
Entrance requirements: For master's, GRE General Test. *Application deadline:* Applications are processed on a rolling basis. *Application fee:* $25 ($75 for international students). Electronic applications accepted.
Expenses: Tuition, state resident: part-time $120 per hour. Tuition, nonresident: part-time $253 per hour.
Financial support: In 2001–02, research assistantships (averaging $6,500 per year), 1 teaching assistantship (averaging $6,750 per year) were awarded. Federal Work-Study, institutionally sponsored loans, and scholarships/grants also available. Support available to part-time students. Financial award applicants required to submit FAFSA.
Application contact: Dr. W. Arden Colette, Graduate Adviser, 806-651-2555, *Fax:* 806-651-2938, *E-mail:* acolette@mail.wtamu.edu.

■ WEST VIRGINIA UNIVERSITY

Davis College of Agriculture, Forestry and Consumer Sciences, Division of Resource Management, Program in Agricultural and Resource Economics, Morgantown, WV 26506

AWARDS MS. Part-time programs available.

Students: 14 full-time (6 women), 3 part-time (all women), 5 international. Average age 30. 50 applicants, 60% accepted. In 2001, 2 degrees awarded.
Degree requirements: For master's, thesis optional.
Entrance requirements: For master's, GRE General Test, TOEFL, minimum GPA of 2.5, 1 calculus course. *Application deadline:* Applications are processed on a rolling basis. *Application fee:* $45.
Expenses: Tuition, state resident: full-time $2,791. Tuition, nonresident: full-time $8,659. Required fees: $1,002. Tuition and fees vary according to program.
Financial support: In 2001–02, 9 research assistantships, 1 teaching assistantship were awarded. Federal Work-Study, institutionally sponsored loans, and tuition waivers (full and partial) also available. Financial award application deadline: 2/1; financial award applicants required to submit FAFSA.
Faculty research: Agricultural production and marketing, rural development, mineral and energy economics, economic development.
Dr. Gerard E. D'Souza, Graduate Coordinator, 304-293-6253 Ext. 4471, *Fax:* 304-293-3752, *E-mail:* gerard.d'souza@mail.wvu.edu. *Web site:* http://www.caf.wvu.edu/resm/are/index.html

APPLIED ECONOMICS

■ AMERICAN UNIVERSITY

College of Arts and Sciences, Department of Economics, Washington, DC 20016-8001

AWARDS Applied economics (Certificate); development banking (MA); economics (MA, PhD); financial economics for public policy (MA). Part-time and evening/weekend programs available.

Faculty: 20 full-time (6 women), 5 part-time/adjunct (1 woman).
Students: 54 full-time (22 women), 99 part-time (37 women); includes 18 minority (10 African Americans, 5 Asian Americans or Pacific Islanders, 3 Hispanic Americans), 82 international. Average age 30. 338 applicants, 60% accepted, 38 enrolled. In 2001, 19 master's, 7 doctorates awarded. Terminal master's awarded for partial completion of doctoral program.
Degree requirements: For master's, comprehensive exam; for doctorate, thesis/dissertation, comprehensive exam.
Entrance requirements: For master's, TOEFL; for doctorate, GRE General Test, TOEFL. *Application deadline:* For spring admission, 10/1. Applications are processed on a rolling basis. *Application fee:* $50.
Expenses: Tuition: Full-time $14,274; part-time $793 per credit. Required fees: $290. Tuition and fees vary according to program.
Financial support: Fellowships with full tuition reimbursements, research assistantships, teaching assistantships with full tuition reimbursements, career-related internships or fieldwork, Federal Work-Study, institutionally sponsored loans, and tuition waivers (full and partial) available. Financial award application deadline: 2/1.
Faculty research: Political economy, development, labor, gender.
Larry Sawers, Adviser, 202-885-3766, *Fax:* 202-885-3790.
Application contact: Dr. Mieke Meurs, Ph.D. Adviser, 202-885-3376, *Fax:* 202-885-3790, *E-mail:* mmeurs@american.edu. *Web site:* http://www.american.edu/academic.depts/cas/econ/

■ CLEMSON UNIVERSITY

Graduate School, College of Agriculture, Forestry and Life Sciences, Department of Agriculture and Applied Economics, Program in Agricultural and Applied Economics, Clemson, SC 29634

AWARDS MS.

Students: 16 full-time (6 women), 4 part-time (1 woman); includes 2 minority (1 African American, 1 Asian American or Pacific Islander), 10 international. Average age 24. 21 applicants, 95% accepted, 4 enrolled. In 2001, 4 degrees awarded.
Degree requirements: For master's, thesis optional.
Entrance requirements: For master's, GRE General Test, TOEFL, minimum GPA of 3.0. *Application deadline:* For fall admission, 5/1; for spring admission, 10/1. Applications are processed on a rolling basis. *Application fee:* $40.
Expenses: Tuition, state resident: full-time $5,310. Tuition, nonresident: full-time $11,284.
Financial support: Application deadline: 3/1.
Dr. Michael D. Hammig, Chair, 864-656-5771, *Fax:* 864-656-5776, *E-mail:* mhammig@clemson.edu.
Application contact: Janice Thacker, Staff Assistant for Graduate Programs, 864-656-6536, *Fax:* 864-656-5776, *E-mail:* jthckr@clemson.edu.

■ CLEMSON UNIVERSITY

Graduate School, College of Agriculture, Forestry and Life Sciences, Department of Agriculture and Applied Economics and Department of Economics, Program in Applied Economics, Clemson, SC 29634

AWARDS PhD.

Students: 45 full-time (12 women), 8 part-time (1 woman); includes 3 minority (all African Americans), 32 international. Average age 26. 65 applicants, 77% accepted, 13 enrolled. In 2001, 4 degrees awarded.
Degree requirements: For doctorate, thesis/dissertation.
Entrance requirements: For doctorate, GRE General Test, TOEFL, minimum GPA of 3.0, MS. *Application deadline:* For fall admission, 5/1; for spring admission, 10/1. Applications are processed on a rolling basis. *Application fee:* $40.
Expenses: Tuition, state resident: full-time $5,310. Tuition, nonresident: full-time $11,284.
Financial support: Research assistantships, teaching assistantships available. Financial award application deadline: 3/1; financial award applicants required to submit FAFSA.
Faculty research: Policy production, marketing, natural resources, regional development, industrial organization.
Application contact: Janice Thacker, Staff Assistant for Graduate Programs, 864-656-6536, *Fax:* 864-656-5776, *E-mail:* jthckr@clemson.edu.

■ CLEMSON UNIVERSITY

Graduate School, College of Business and Behavioral Science, Department of Economics, Clemson, SC 29634

AWARDS Applied economics (PhD); economics (MA).

Students: 69 full-time (20 women), 9 part-time (1 woman); includes 4 minority (3 African Americans, 1 Hispanic American), 44 international. Average age 23. 112 applicants, 78% accepted, 28 enrolled. In 2001, 5 master's, 4 doctorates awarded.
Degree requirements: For doctorate, thesis/dissertation.
Entrance requirements: For master's and doctorate, GRE General Test, TOEFL. *Application deadline:* For fall admission, 6/1. *Application fee:* $40.
Expenses: Tuition, state resident: full-time $5,310. Tuition, nonresident: full-time $11,284.
Financial support: Fellowships, research assistantships, teaching assistantships available. Financial award applicants required to submit FAFSA.
Faculty research: Applied price theory, financial economics, industrial economics, labor economics, monetary economics.
Dr. William Dougan, Chair, 864-656-3481, *Fax:* 864-656-4192, *E-mail:* douganw@clemson.edu.
Application contact: Dr. C. M. Lindsay, Director of Graduate Programs, 864-656-3955, *Fax:* 864-656-4192, *E-mail:* lindsay@clemson.edu. *Web site:* http://hubcap.clemson.edu:80/economics/

Find an in-depth description at www.petersons.com/gradchannel.

■ CORNELL UNIVERSITY

Graduate School, Graduate Fields of Arts and Sciences, Field of Economics, Ithaca, NY 14853-0001

AWARDS Applied economics (PhD); econometrics and economic statistics (PhD); economic development and planning (PhD); economic theory (PhD); industrial organization and control (PhD); international economics (PhD); labor economics (PhD); monetary and macroeconomics (PhD); public finance (PhD).

Faculty: 55 full-time.
Students: 112 full-time (41 women); includes 8 minority (1 African American, 4 Asian Americans or Pacific Islanders, 2 Hispanic Americans, 1 Native American), 85 international. 581 applicants, 18% accepted. In 2001, 10 doctorates awarded.
Degree requirements: For doctorate, thesis/dissertation.
Entrance requirements: For doctorate, GRE General Test, TOEFL, 3 letters of recommendation. *Application deadline:* For fall admission, 1/15. *Application fee:* $65. Electronic applications accepted.
Expenses: Tuition: Full-time $25,970. Required fees: $50.
Financial support: In 2001–02, 88 students received support, including 22 fellowships with full tuition reimbursements available, 21 research assistantships with full tuition reimbursements available, 45 teaching assistantships with full tuition reimbursements available; institutionally sponsored loans, scholarships/grants, tuition waivers (full and partial), and unspecified assistantships also available. Financial award applicants required to submit FAFSA.
Faculty research: Learning and games, monetary theory, political economy, transfer payments, time series and nonparametics.
Application contact: Graduate Field Assistant, 607-255-4893, *E-mail:* econ_phd@cornell.edu. *Web site:* http://www.gradschool.cornell.edu/grad/fields_1/econ.html

■ EASTERN MICHIGAN UNIVERSITY

Graduate School, College of Arts and Sciences, Department of Economics, Ypsilanti, MI 48197

AWARDS Applied economics (MA); development, trade and planning (MA); economics (MA). Evening/weekend programs available.

Faculty: 11 full-time (1 woman).
Students: 18 full-time (8 women), 19 part-time (7 women); includes 23 minority (2 African Americans, 20 Asian Americans or Pacific Islanders, 1 Hispanic American). 67 applicants, 34% accepted. In 2001, 6 degrees awarded.
Degree requirements: For master's, thesis or alternative.
Entrance requirements: For master's, TOEFL. *Application deadline:* For fall admission, 5/15; for spring admission, 3/15. Applications are processed on a rolling basis. *Application fee:* $30.
Expenses: Tuition, state resident: part-time $285 per credit hour. Tuition, nonresident: part-time $510 per credit hour.
Financial support: Fellowships, teaching assistantships available. Support available to part-time students. Financial award application deadline: 3/15; financial award applicants required to submit FAFSA.
Dr. Raouf S. Hanna, Head, 734-487-3395.
Application contact: Dr. James Thornton, Coordinator, 734-487-3395.

■ MISSISSIPPI STATE UNIVERSITY

College of Agriculture and Life Sciences, Department of Agricultural Economics, Mississippi State, MS 39762

AWARDS Agribusiness management (MABM); applied economics (PhD). Part-time programs available.

Faculty: 16 full-time (1 woman), 3 part-time/adjunct (0 women).
Students: 16 full-time (4 women), 8 part-time (1 woman); includes 1 minority (Hispanic American), 7 international. Average age 29. 31 applicants, 90% accepted, 3 enrolled. In 2001, 17 master's, 3 doctorates awarded.
Degree requirements: For master's, thesis (for some programs), comprehensive oral or written exam, thesis defense; for doctorate, thesis/dissertation, qualifying written exam, research exam.
Entrance requirements: For master's, GRE, TOEFL, GMAT, minimum GPA of 3.0; for doctorate, GRE, TOEFL, minimum GPA of 3.0. *Application deadline:* For fall admission, 7/1; for spring admission, 11/1. Applications are processed on a rolling basis. *Application fee:* $25 for international students. Electronic applications accepted.
Expenses: Tuition, state resident: full-time $3,586; part-time $150 per credit hour. Tuition, nonresident: full-time $8,128; part-time $339 per credit hour. Tuition and fees vary according to course load and campus/location.
Financial support: In 2001–02, 7 research assistantships with full tuition reimbursements (averaging $7,200 per year), 2 teaching assistantships with full tuition reimbursements (averaging $9,600 per year) were awarded. Career-related internships or fieldwork, Federal Work-Study, institutionally sponsored loans, and unspecified assistantships also available. Financial award application deadline: 4/1; financial award applicants required to submit FAFSA.
Faculty research: Production economics, policy, resource economics, international trade, agribusiness management. *Total annual research expenditures:* $1.4 million.
Dr. Cary W. Herndon, Interim Department Head, 662-325-2752, *Fax:* 662-325-8777, *E-mail:* office@agecon.msstate.edu.
Application contact: Jerry B. Inmon, Director of Admissions, 662-325-2224, *Fax:* 662-325-7360, *E-mail:* admit@admissions.msstate.edu. *Web site:* http://www.msstate.edu/

■ MISSISSIPPI STATE UNIVERSITY

College of Business and Industry, Department of Finance and Economics, Mississippi State, MS 39762

AWARDS Applied economics (PhD); economics (MA); finance (MSBA). Part-time programs available.

Faculty: 18 full-time (2 women).
Students: 318 full-time (81 women), 22 part-time (9 women); includes 53 minority (51 African Americans, 1 Hispanic American, 1 Native American). 40 applicants, 75% accepted, 10 enrolled. In 2001, 9 master's awarded. Terminal master's awarded for partial completion of doctoral program.
Degree requirements: For master's, thesis optional; for doctorate, thesis/dissertation, comprehensive exam, registration. *Median time to degree:* Master's–1.5 years full-time; doctorate–5 years full-time.
Entrance requirements: For master's and doctorate, GMAT, GRE. *Application deadline:* For fall admission, 7/1; for spring admission, 11/1. Applications are processed on a rolling basis. *Application fee:* $25 for international students.
Expenses: Tuition, state resident: full-time $3,586; part-time $150 per credit hour. Tuition, nonresident: full-time $8,128; part-time $339 per credit hour. Tuition and fees vary according to course load and campus/location.
Financial support: In 2001–02, 6 research assistantships with tuition reimbursements (averaging $8,500 per year), 6 teaching assistantships with tuition reimbursements (averaging $10,200 per year) were awarded. Federal Work-Study, scholarships/grants, health care benefits, and unspecified assistantships also available. Financial award applicants required to submit FAFSA.
Faculty research: Economics development, mergers, event studies, economic education, bank performance, risk management.
Dr. Paul W. Grimes, Head, 662-325-2341, *Fax:* 662-325-1977, *E-mail:* pwg1@ra.msstate.edu.
Application contact: Jerry B. Inmon, Director of Admissions, 662-325-2224, *Fax:* 662-325-7360, *E-mail:* admit@admissions.msstate.edu. *Web site:* http://www.msstate.edu/dept/finecon

■ MONTANA STATE UNIVERSITY–BOZEMAN

College of Graduate Studies, College of Agriculture, Department of Agricultural Economics and Economics, Bozeman, MT 59717

AWARDS Applied economics (MS). Part-time programs available.

Students: 4 full-time (0 women), 7 part-time (3 women), 5 international. Average age 25. 9 applicants, 100% accepted, 3 enrolled. In 2001, 1 degree awarded.
Degree requirements: For master's, thesis.
Entrance requirements: For master's, GRE General Test, TOEFL, minimum GPA of 3.0. *Application deadline:* For fall admission, 1/15; for spring admission, 6/15. Applications are processed on a rolling basis. *Application fee:* $50. Electronic applications accepted.
Expenses: Tuition, state resident: full-time $3,894; part-time $198 per credit. Tuition, nonresident: full-time $10,661; part-time $480 per credit. International tuition: $10,811 full-time. Tuition and fees vary according to course load and program.
Financial support: In 2001–02, 11 students received support, including 3 fellowships (averaging $6,000 per year), 6 research assistantships (averaging $10,800 per year), 3 teaching assistantships (averaging $9,000 per year); career-related internships or fieldwork and unspecified assistantships also available. Financial award application deadline: 3/1; financial award applicants required to submit FAFSA.
Faculty research: Economic theory, applied microeconomics, resource economics, farm and ranch management, agriculture in global context. *Total annual research expenditures:* $1 million.
Dr. Myles Watts, Head, 406-994-3703, *Fax:* 406-994-4838, *E-mail:* zae7022@montana.edu. *Web site:* http://www.montana.edu/wwwae/homepage/graduate.html

■ NORTH CAROLINA AGRICULTURAL AND TECHNICAL STATE UNIVERSITY

Graduate School, School of Agriculture and Environmental and Allied Sciences, Department of Agribusiness, Applied Economics, and Agriscience Education, Greensboro, NC 27411

AWARDS Agricultural economics (MS); agricultural education (MS). Part-time and evening/weekend programs available.

Degree requirements: For master's, thesis or alternative, qualifying exam, comprehensive exam.
Entrance requirements: For master's, GRE General Test, minimum GPA of 3.0.
Faculty research: Aid for small farmers, agricultural technology resources, labor force mobility, agrology.

■ PORTLAND STATE UNIVERSITY

Graduate Studies, College of Liberal Arts and Sciences, Department of Economics, Portland, OR 97207-0751

AWARDS Applied economics (MA, MS); economics (PhD); general economics (MA, MS). Part-time programs available.

Portland State University (continued)
Faculty: 9 full-time (2 women), 6 part-time/adjunct (1 woman).
Students: 6 full-time (3 women), 7 part-time (5 women); includes 1 minority (Asian American or Pacific Islander), 7 international. Average age 31. 8 applicants, 88% accepted. In 2001, 9 degrees awarded.
Degree requirements: For master's, thesis optional; for doctorate, one foreign language, thesis/dissertation.
Entrance requirements: For master's, TOEFL, minimum GPA of 3.0 in upper-division course work or 2.75 overall, previous course work in calculus. *Application deadline:* For fall admission, 4/1; for spring admission, 11/1. Applications are processed on a rolling basis. *Application fee:* $50.
Financial support: In 2001–02, 1 research assistantship with full tuition reimbursement (averaging $2,434 per year) was awarded; teaching assistantships, career-related internships or fieldwork, Federal Work-Study, and institutionally sponsored loans also available. Support available to part-time students. Financial award application deadline: 3/1; financial award applicants required to submit FAFSA.
Faculty research: NAFTA, economies of transition, economics of Eastern Europe, artificial intelligence, comparative economic systems. *Total annual research expenditures:* $35,995.
Dr. John Walker, Head, 503-725-3934, *Fax:* 503-725-3945, *E-mail:* walkers@pdx.edu.
Application contact: Rita Spears, Office Coordinator, 503-725-3915, *Fax:* 503-725-3945, *E-mail:* rita@ch2.ch.pdx.edu. *Web site:* http://www.econ.pdx.edu/

■ ROOSEVELT UNIVERSITY

Graduate Division, College of Arts and Sciences, School of Policy Studies, Program in Economics, Chicago, IL 60605-1394

AWARDS Applied economics (MA); economics (MA). Part-time and evening/weekend programs available.

Faculty: 6 full-time (1 woman), 7 part-time/adjunct (0 women).
Students: Average age 28. In 2001, 12 degrees awarded.
Degree requirements: For master's, thesis or alternative.
Entrance requirements: For master's, minimum GPA of 2.7. *Application deadline:* For fall admission, 6/1 (priority date). Applications are processed on a rolling basis. *Application fee:* $25 ($35 for international students).
Expenses: Tuition: Full-time $9,090; part-time $505 per credit hour. Required fees: $100 per term.
Financial support: In 2001–02, 4 students received support, including 1 teaching assistantship; career-related internships or fieldwork, Federal Work-Study, scholarships/grants, and tuition waivers (full and partial) also available. Financial award application deadline: 2/15.
Faculty research: Labor, gender issues, international trade and development, entrepreneurship, political economy and money. *Total annual research expenditures:* $5,000.
Graduate Adviser, 312-341-3767.
Application contact: Joanne Canyon-Heller, Coordinator of Graduate Admissions, 312-281-3250, *Fax:* 312-341-3523, *E-mail:* applyru@roosevelt.edu.

■ ST. CLOUD STATE UNIVERSITY

School of Graduate Studies, College of Social Sciences, Program in Economics, St. Cloud, MN 56301-4498

AWARDS Applied economics (MS).

Faculty: 16 full-time (2 women), 1 part-time/adjunct (0 women).
Students: 3 full-time (0 women), 2 part-time; includes 2 minority (1 African American, 1 Asian American or Pacific Islander). 14 applicants, 14% accepted. In 2001, 4 degrees awarded.
Degree requirements: For master's, thesis or alternative.
Entrance requirements: For master's, GRE General Test, minimum GPA of 2.75. *Application deadline:* Applications are processed on a rolling basis. *Application fee:* $35.
Expenses: Tuition, state resident: part-time $156 per credit. Tuition, nonresident: part-time $244 per credit. Required fees: $20 per credit.
Financial support: Unspecified assistantships available.
Dr. Mary Edwards, Coordinator, 320-255-2968, *E-mail:* 100002@stcloudstate.edu.
Application contact: Lindalou Krueger, Graduate Studies Office, 320-255-2113, *Fax:* 320-654-5371, *E-mail:* lekrueger@stcloudstate.edu.

■ SAN JOSE STATE UNIVERSITY

Graduate Studies, College of Social Sciences, Department of Economics, San Jose, CA 95192-0001

AWARDS Applied economics (MA); economics (MA). Part-time programs available.

Faculty: 15 full-time (6 women), 5 part-time/adjunct (0 women).
Students: 15 full-time (8 women), 14 part-time (3 women); includes 17 minority (12 Asian Americans or Pacific Islanders, 5 Hispanic Americans), 4 international. Average age 30. 46 applicants, 65% accepted. In 2001, 22 degrees awarded.
Degree requirements: For master's, thesis optional.
Entrance requirements: For master's, GRE, minimum GPA of 3.0. *Application deadline:* For fall admission, 6/29; for spring admission, 11/30. Applications are processed on a rolling basis. *Application fee:* $59. Electronic applications accepted.
Expenses: Tuition, nonresident: part-time $246 per unit. Required fees: $678 per semester. Tuition and fees vary according to course load.
Financial support: In 2001–02, 2 teaching assistantships were awarded. Financial award applicants required to submit FAFSA.
Lydia Ortega, Chair, 408-924-5400, *Fax:* 408-924-5406.
Application contact: Dr. Thayer Watkins, Director, 408-924-5420.

■ SOUTHERN METHODIST UNIVERSITY

Dedman College, Department of Economics, Dallas, TX 75275

AWARDS Applied economics (MA); economics (MA, PhD). Part-time and evening/weekend programs available.

Faculty: 16 full-time (3 women).
Students: 53 full-time (18 women), 16 part-time (4 women); includes 18 minority (2 African Americans, 14 Asian Americans or Pacific Islanders, 2 Hispanic Americans), 37 international. Average age 28. 322 applicants, 39% accepted, 25 enrolled. In 2001, 17 master's, 2 doctorates awarded. Terminal master's awarded for partial completion of doctoral program.
Degree requirements: For master's, oral qualifying exam, thesis optional; for doctorate, thesis/dissertation, written exams.
Entrance requirements: For master's, GRE General Test or GMAT, 12 hours in economics, minimum GPA of 3.0, previous course work in calculus, 3 hours calculus and statistics; for doctorate, GRE General Test, minimum GPA of 3.0, previous course work in calculus, 12 hours economics, 1 year of previous coursework in calculus and statistics. *Application deadline:* For fall admission, 2/1 (priority date); for spring admission, 11/30 (priority date). Applications are processed on a rolling basis. *Application fee:* $50.
Expenses: Tuition: Part-time $285 per credit hour.
Financial support: In 2001–02, 18 students received support, including 2 research assistantships with full tuition reimbursements available (averaging $10,000 per year), 16 teaching assistantships with full tuition reimbursements available (averaging $10,200 per year); tuition waivers (partial) also available. Financial award applicants required to submit FAFSA.
Faculty research: Economic theory, game theory, econometrics, international trade, labor.
Dr. Nathan Balke, Interim Chair, 214-768-2693.
Application contact: Information Contact, 214-768-2693.

■ STATE UNIVERSITY OF NEW YORK COLLEGE AT BUFFALO

Graduate Studies and Research, Faculty of Natural and Social Sciences, Department of Economics and Finance, Buffalo, NY 14222-1095

AWARDS Applied economics (MA).

Faculty: 10 full-time (1 woman).
Students: 3 full-time (1 woman), 10 part-time (2 women); includes 3 minority (1 African American, 1 Asian American or Pacific Islander, 1 Hispanic American). Average age 33. 11 applicants, 73% accepted.
Application deadline: For fall admission, 5/1 (priority date); for spring admission, 10/1 (priority date). Applications are processed on a rolling basis. *Application fee:* $50.
Expenses: Tuition, state resident: full-time $5,100; part-time $226 per credit hour. Tuition, nonresident: full-time $8,416; part-time $351 per credit hour.
Financial support: Application deadline: 3/1.
Dr. Douglas Koritz, Chairperson, 716-878-6640, *E-mail:* koritzdg@buffalostate.edu.

■ TEXAS TECH UNIVERSITY

Graduate School, College of Agricultural Sciences and Natural Resources, Department of Agricultural and Applied Economics, Lubbock, TX 79409

AWARDS MS, PhD, JD/MS. Part-time programs available.

Faculty: 8 full-time (0 women).
Students: 17 full-time (3 women), 4 part-time (1 woman); includes 1 minority (Hispanic American), 9 international. Average age 28. 14 applicants, 57% accepted, 5 enrolled. In 2001, 4 degrees awarded.
Degree requirements: For master's, thesis or alternative; for doctorate, thesis/dissertation.
Entrance requirements: For master's and doctorate, GRE General Test. *Application deadline:* Applications are processed on a rolling basis. *Application fee:* $25 ($50 for international students). Electronic applications accepted.
Expenses: Tuition, state resident: full-time $1,926; part-time $107 per credit hour. Tuition, nonresident: full-time $5,724; part-time $318 per credit hour. Required fees: $779; $737 per year. Tuition and fees vary according to course level, course load and program.
Financial support: In 2001–02, 15 students received support, including 14 research assistantships with partial tuition reimbursements available (averaging $9,748 per year), 5 teaching assistantships with partial tuition reimbursements available (averaging $10,170 per year); fellowships, Federal Work-Study and institutionally sponsored loans also available. Support available to part-time students. Financial award application deadline: 5/1; financial award applicants required to submit FAFSA.
Faculty research: Economics of the U.S. cotton and textile industries, natural resource management in semi-arid climates, commodity policy analysis, international trade in agricultural products, agribusiness analysis. *Total annual research expenditures:* $384,465.
Dr. Don E. Ethridge, Chair, 806-742-2821, *Fax:* 806-742-1099.
Application contact: Graduate Adviser, 806-742-2821, *Fax:* 806-742-1099. *Web site:* http://www.aeco.ttu.edu/

■ UNIVERSITY OF CALIFORNIA, SANTA CRUZ

Division of Graduate Studies, Division of Social Sciences, Program in Applied Economics, Santa Cruz, CA 95064

AWARDS MS.

Faculty: 19 full-time.
Students: 19 full-time (6 women); includes 1 minority (Hispanic American), 3 international. 42 applicants, 76% accepted. In 2001, 15 degrees awarded.
Degree requirements: For master's, thesis or alternative. *Median time to degree:* Master's–11 years full-time.
Entrance requirements: For master's, GRE General Test, GRE Subject Test. *Application deadline:* For fall admission, 2/1. *Application fee:* $40.
Expenses: Tuition: Full-time $19,857.
Financial support: Research assistantships, teaching assistantships, career-related internships or fieldwork, Federal Work-Study, and institutionally sponsored loans available. Financial award application deadline: 2/1.
Faculty research: Economic decision-making skills for the design and operation of complex institutional systems.
Michael Hutchison, Chairperson, 831-459-4981.
Application contact: Cristina Intintoli, Graduate Admissions, 831-459-2301, *E-mail:* cmintint@cats.ucsc.edu. *Web site:* http://www.ucsc.edu/

■ UNIVERSITY OF GEORGIA

Graduate School, College of Agricultural and Environmental Sciences, Department of Agricultural and Applied Economics, Athens, GA 30602

AWARDS Agricultural economics (MAE, MS, PhD); environmental economics (MS).

Faculty: 22 full-time (1 woman).
Students: 31 full-time (9 women), 8 part-time (3 women); includes 4 minority (all African Americans), 20 international. 81 applicants, 21% accepted. In 2001, 12 master's awarded.
Degree requirements: For master's, thesis (MS); for doctorate, thesis/dissertation.
Entrance requirements: For master's and doctorate, GRE General Test. *Application deadline:* For fall admission, 7/1 (priority date); for spring admission, 11/15. *Application fee:* $30. Electronic applications accepted.
Expenses: Tuition, state resident: full-time $2,376; part-time $132 per credit hour. Tuition, nonresident: full-time $9,504; part-time $528 per credit hour. Required fees: $236 per semester.
Financial support: Fellowships, research assistantships, teaching assistantships, career-related internships or fieldwork and unspecified assistantships available.
Dr. Fred C. White, Head, 706-542-0764, *Fax:* 706-542-0739, *E-mail:* fwhite@agecon.uga.edu.
Application contact: Dr. James E. Epperson, Contact, 706-542-0766, *Fax:* 706-542-0739, *E-mail:* jepperson@agecon.uga.edu. *Web site:* http://www.agecon.uga.edu/

Find an in-depth description at www.petersons.com/gradchannel.

■ UNIVERSITY OF MICHIGAN

Horace H. Rackham School of Graduate Studies, College of Literature, Science, and the Arts, Department of Economics, Program in Applied Economics, Ann Arbor, MI 48109

AWARDS AM.

Faculty: 57.
Students: 49 full-time (17 women); includes 4 minority (1 African American, 3 Asian Americans or Pacific Islanders), 34 international. 82 applicants, 60% accepted. In 2001, 31 degrees awarded.
Entrance requirements: For master's, GRE General Test. *Application deadline:* For fall admission, 2/5. *Application fee:* $55.
George Johnson, Director, 734-763-5316, *Fax:* 734-764-2769, *E-mail:* gjohnson@umich.edu.
Application contact: Larue Cochran, Student Services Assistant, 734-763-5316, *Fax:* 734-764-2769, *E-mail:* larue@umich.edu. *Web site:* http://www.lsa.econ.umich.edu/

■ UNIVERSITY OF MINNESOTA, TWIN CITIES CAMPUS

Graduate School, College of Agricultural, Food, and Environmental Sciences, Department of Applied Economics, Minneapolis, MN 55455-0213

AWARDS Agricultural and applied economics (MS, PhD).

Faculty: 39 full-time (8 women).
Students: 70 full-time (31 women), 43 international. 71 applicants, 75% accepted,

University of Minnesota, Twin Cities Campus (continued)
17 enrolled. In 2001, 7 master's, 6 doctorates awarded.
Degree requirements: For master's and doctorate, thesis/dissertation. *Median time to degree:* Master's–2.3 years full-time; doctorate–4.3 years full-time.
Entrance requirements: For master's and doctorate, GRE, TOEFL, minimum GPA of 3.0. *Application deadline:* For fall admission, 6/15; for spring admission, 10/15. Applications are processed on a rolling basis. *Application fee:* $50 ($55 for international students). Electronic applications accepted.
Expenses: Tuition, state resident: full-time $2,932; part-time $489 per credit. Tuition, nonresident: full-time $5,758; part-time $960 per credit. Part-time tuition and fees vary according to course load, program and reciprocity agreements.
Financial support: In 2001–02, 52 students received support, including 6 fellowships with full tuition reimbursements available (averaging $19,850 per year), 40 research assistantships with full tuition reimbursements available (averaging $17,612 per year), 6 teaching assistantships with full tuition reimbursements available (averaging $17,612 per year); tuition waivers (full and partial) and stipends also available. Financial award application deadline: 12/31.
Faculty research: Consumptions and marketing economics, development economics, trade and policy, production and managerial economics, regional and community economics. *Total annual research expenditures:* $450,000.
Dr. Vernon R. Eidman, Head, 612-625-0231, *Fax:* 612-625-6245, *E-mail:* veidman@dept.agecon.umn.edu.
Application contact: Dr. Glenn D. Pederson, Director of Graduate Studies, 612-625-7028, *Fax:* 612-625-6245, *E-mail:* dgs@dept.agecon.umn.edu. *Web site:* http://www.apecon.agri.umn.edu/

■ UNIVERSITY OF NEVADA, RENO

Graduate School, College of Agriculture, Biotechnology and Natural Resources, Department of Resource and Applied Economics, Reno, NV 89557
AWARDS Resource and applied economics (MS).
Faculty: 3.
Students: 9 full-time (2 women), 2 part-time, 2 international. Average age 32. In 2001, 8 degrees awarded.
Degree requirements: For master's, thesis optional.
Entrance requirements: For master's, GRE, TOEFL, minimum GPA of 2.75. *Application deadline:* For fall admission, 3/1 (priority date). Applications are processed on a rolling basis. *Application fee:* $40.
Expenses: Tuition, state resident: full-time $2,067; part-time $108 per credit. Tuition, nonresident: full-time $9,282; part-time $109 per credit. Required fees: $57 per semester. Tuition and fees vary according to course load.
Financial support: In 2001–02, 12 research assistantships were awarded. Financial award application deadline: 3/1.
Dr. Casey VanKooten, Graduate Program Director, 775-784-4411.
Application contact: Dr. Jeff Englin, Director of Graduate Studies, 775-784-4411, *E-mail:* englin@scs.unr.edu.

■ THE UNIVERSITY OF NORTH CAROLINA AT GREENSBORO

Graduate School, Joseph M. Bryan School of Business and Economics, Department of Economics, Greensboro, NC 27412-5001
AWARDS Applied economics (MA).
Faculty: 10 full-time (0 women).
Students: 17 full-time (5 women), 7 part-time (5 women); includes 3 African Americans, 8 international. 35 applicants, 51% accepted, 14 enrolled. In 2001, 8 degrees awarded.
Degree requirements: For master's, thesis or alternative.
Entrance requirements: For master's, GMAT, GRE General Test, TOEFL. *Application deadline:* For fall admission, 3/1 (priority date); for spring admission, 11/1. Applications are processed on a rolling basis. *Application fee:* $35.
Expenses: Tuition, state resident: part-time $344 per course. Tuition, nonresident: part-time $2,457 per course.
Financial support: In 2001–02, 15 students received support; fellowships, research assistantships available.
Faculty research: South East economic index.
Dr. Stuart Allen, Head, 336-334-5463, *Fax:* 336-334-4089, *E-mail:* stuart_allen@uncg.edu.
Application contact: Dr. James Lynch, Director of Graduate Recruitment and Information Services, 336-334-4881, *Fax:* 336-334-4424. *Web site:* http://www.uncg.edu/bae/eco/

■ UNIVERSITY OF NORTH TEXAS

Robert B. Toulouse School of Graduate Studies, School of Community Service, Institute of Applied Economics, Denton, TX 76203
AWARDS MS. Part-time programs available.
Faculty: 3 full-time (0 women), 1 part-time/adjunct (0 women).
Students: 16. Average age 29. In 2001, 5 degrees awarded.
Degree requirements: For master's, thesis (for some programs), comprehensive exam.
Entrance requirements: For master's, GRE General Test, minimum B average in last 60 hours. *Application deadline:* For fall admission, 7/17. *Application fee:* $25 ($50 for international students).
Expenses: Tuition, state resident: part-time $186 per hour. Tuition, nonresident: part-time $319 per hour. Required fees: $88; $21 per hour.
Financial support: Research assistantships, career-related internships or fieldwork, Federal Work-Study, and tuition waivers (partial) available.
Faculty research: Labor market information, economic evaluation, local economic analysis, teaching evaluation.
Dr. Bernard L. Weinstein, Director, 940-565-3437.
Application contact: Dr. Harold Gross, Graduate Adviser, 940-565-3437.

■ THE UNIVERSITY OF TEXAS AT DALLAS

School of Social Sciences, Program in Applied Economics, Richardson, TX 75083-0688
AWARDS Applied economics (MS). Part-time and evening/weekend programs available.
Faculty: 8 full-time (1 woman).
Students: 13 full-time (6 women), 13 part-time (6 women); includes 5 minority (3 African Americans, 2 Asian Americans or Pacific Islanders), 6 international. Average age 30. 22 applicants, 82% accepted. In 2001, 10 degrees awarded.
Degree requirements: For master's, internship.
Entrance requirements: For master's, GRE General Test, TOEFL, minimum GPA of 3.0 in upper-level course work in field. *Application deadline:* For fall admission, 7/15; for spring admission, 11/15. Applications are processed on a rolling basis. *Application fee:* $25 ($75 for international students). Electronic applications accepted.
Expenses: Tuition, state resident: full-time $1,440; part-time $84 per credit. Tuition, nonresident: full-time $5,310; part-time $295 per credit. Required fees: $1,835; $87 per credit. $138 per term.
Financial support: In 2001–02, 3 research assistantships with tuition reimbursements (averaging $5,225 per year), 4 teaching assistantships with tuition reimbursements (averaging $5,150 per year) were awarded. Fellowships, career-related internships or fieldwork, Federal Work-Study, institutionally sponsored loans, and scholarships/grants also available. Support available to part-time students. Financial award application deadline: 4/30; financial award applicants required to submit FAFSA.
Faculty research: Economic base of distressed counties, analysis of nonprofits and their for-profit counterparts.
Application contact: Coordinator, 972-883-2720, *Fax:* 972-883-2735, *E-mail:* ss-grad-info@utdallas.edu. *Web site:* http://www.utdallas.edu/dept/socsci/msae.htm

Find an in-depth description at www.petersons.com/gradchannel.

■ UNIVERSITY OF VERMONT

Graduate College, College of Agriculture and Life Sciences, Department of Community Development and Applied Economics, Burlington, VT 05405

AWARDS M Ext Ed, MS.

Degree requirements: For master's, thesis.
Entrance requirements: For master's, GRE General Test, TOEFL.
Expenses: Tuition, state resident: part-time $335 per credit. Tuition, nonresident: part-time $838 per credit.
Faculty research: Agricultural production and marketing.

■ UNIVERSITY OF WISCONSIN–MADISON

Graduate School, College of Agricultural and Life Sciences, Department of Agricultural and Applied Economics, Madison, WI 53706-1380

AWARDS MA, MS, PhD. Part-time programs available.

Faculty: 20 full-time (1 woman), 2 part-time/adjunct (0 women).
Students: 43 full-time (23 women); includes 1 minority (Asian American or Pacific Islander), 27 international. Average age 25. 71 applicants, 70% accepted, 12 enrolled. In 2001, 9 master's, 1 doctorate awarded.
Degree requirements: For doctorate, thesis/dissertation, preliminary exams. *Median time to degree:* Master's–2 years full-time; doctorate–5.5 years full-time.
Entrance requirements: For master's and doctorate, GRE General Test, TOEFL. *Application deadline:* For fall admission, 2/1 (priority date). *Application fee:* $45. Electronic applications accepted.
Expenses: Tuition, state resident: full-time $7,361; part-time $399 per credit. Tuition, nonresident: full-time $20,499; part-time $1,282 per credit. Required fees: $34 per credit. Full-time tuition and fees vary according to course load, program, reciprocity agreements and student level.
Financial support: In 2001–02, 34 students received support, including 23 fellowships with full tuition reimbursements available (averaging $15,000 per year), 32 research assistantships with full tuition reimbursements available (averaging $16,350 per year); career-related internships or fieldwork, Federal Work-Study, and unspecified assistantships also available. Support available to part-time students. Financial award application deadline: 1/5.
Faculty research: Environmental and resource economics, international development, state and local economics, food systems, markets and trade. *Total annual research expenditures:* $1.3 million.
Richard C. Bishop, Chair, 608-262-8966, *Fax:* 608-262-4376.
Application contact: Barbara Forrest, Academic Programs Coordinator, 608-262-9489, *Fax:* 608-262-4376, *E-mail:* admissions@aae.wisc.edu. *Web site:* http://www.aae.wisc.edu/

■ UNIVERSITY OF WYOMING

Graduate School, College of Agriculture, Department of Agricultural and Applied Economics, Laramie, WY 82071

AWARDS MS. Part-time programs available.

Faculty: 11 full-time (0 women).
Students: 9 full-time (5 women), 2 part-time (both women), 1 international. Average age 25. 14 applicants, 29% accepted. In 2001, 13 degrees awarded.
Degree requirements: For master's, thesis (for some programs).
Entrance requirements: For master's, GRE General Test, minimum GPA of 3.0. *Application deadline:* For fall admission, 8/1 (priority date); for spring admission, 10/1 (priority date). Applications are processed on a rolling basis. *Application fee:* $40. Electronic applications accepted.
Expenses: Tuition, state resident: full-time $2,895; part-time $161 per credit hour. Tuition, nonresident: full-time $8,367; part-time $465 per credit hour. Required fees: $491; $10 per credit hour. $2 per credit hour. Tuition and fees vary according to course load and program.
Financial support: In 2001–02, 5 research assistantships with tuition reimbursements (averaging $8,667 per year) were awarded; career-related internships or fieldwork, Federal Work-Study, and institutionally sponsored loans also available. Financial award application deadline: 3/1; financial award applicants required to submit FAFSA.
Faculty research: Farm management, agricultural markets, water economics, community development, agricultural business. *Total annual research expenditures:* $107,000.
Edward B. Bradley, Head, 307-766-2386, *Fax:* 307-766-5544, *E-mail:* bradley@uwyo.edu. *Web site:* http://www.uwyo.edu/ag/agecon/pageone.htm

■ UTAH STATE UNIVERSITY

School of Graduate Studies, College of Business and College of Agriculture, Department of Economics, Logan, UT 84322

AWARDS Applied economics (MS); economics (MA, MS, PhD).

Faculty: 22 full-time (2 women).
Students: 25 full-time (11 women), 4 part-time (1 woman), 19 international. Average age 31. 61 applicants, 84% accepted. In 2001, 6 master's, 4 doctorates awarded. Terminal master's awarded for partial completion of doctoral program.
Degree requirements: For master's, thesis (for some programs); for doctorate, thesis/dissertation, comprehensive exam.
Entrance requirements: For master's and doctorate, GRE General Test, TOEFL, minimum GPA of 3.0. *Application deadline:* For fall admission, 1/15 (priority date); for spring admission, 10/15. Applications are processed on a rolling basis. *Application fee:* $40.
Expenses: Tuition, state resident: full-time $1,693. Tuition, nonresident: full-time $4,233. Required fees: $501. Tuition and fees vary according to program.
Financial support: In 2001–02, 3 fellowships with partial tuition reimbursements (averaging $12,000 per year), 14 research assistantships with partial tuition reimbursements (averaging $9,000 per year), 4 teaching assistantships with partial tuition reimbursements (averaging $9,000 per year) were awarded. Career-related internships or fieldwork, Federal Work-Study, institutionally sponsored loans, and tuition waivers (partial) also available. Financial award application deadline: 3/1.
Faculty research: Resource economics, economic theory, international trade, industrial organization, development. *Total annual research expenditures:* $250,000.
Keith R. Criddle, Head, 435-797-2310, *Fax:* 435-797-2701, *E-mail:* econinfo@econ.usu.edu.
Application contact: Amanda Litchford, Graduate Student Secretary, 435-797-2290, *Fax:* 435-797-2701, *E-mail:* econinfo@econ.usu.edu. *Web site:* http://www.econ.usu.edu/

■ VIRGINIA POLYTECHNIC INSTITUTE AND STATE UNIVERSITY

Graduate School, College of Agriculture and Life Sciences, Department of Agricultural and Applied Economics, Blacksburg, VA 24061

AWARDS Agribusiness (MS); agricultural economics (MS); applied economics (MS); developmental and international economics (PhD); econometrics (PhD); macro and micro economics (PhD); markets and industrial organizations (PhD); public and regional/urban economics (PhD); resource and environmental economics (PhD).

Faculty: 27 full-time (3 women).
Students: 36 full-time (13 women), 13 international. Average age 25. 68 applicants, 25% accepted, 10 enrolled. In 2001, 7 master's, 3 doctorates awarded. Terminal master's awarded for partial completion of doctoral program.
Degree requirements: For master's, thesis (for some programs); for doctorate, thesis/dissertation, dissertation defense, qualifying exams.
Entrance requirements: For master's and doctorate, GRE General Test, TOEFL. *Application deadline:* For winter admission,

Virginia Polytechnic Institute and State University (continued)
2/1 (priority date). Applications are processed on a rolling basis. *Application fee:* $45. Electronic applications accepted.
Expenses: Tuition, state resident: part-time $241 per hour. Tuition, nonresident: part-time $406 per hour. Tuition and fees vary according to program.
Financial support: In 2001–02, 32 students received support, including 10 research assistantships with full tuition reimbursements available (averaging $16,000 per year), 4 teaching assistantships with full tuition reimbursements available (averaging $16,000 per year). Financial award application deadline: 2/15.
Faculty research: Rural development. *Total annual research expenditures:* $1.5 million.
Dr. David Orden, Graduate Program Chairman, 540-231-7559, *Fax:* 540-231-3318, *E-mail:* orden@vt.edu.
Application contact: Marilyn Echols, Graduate Program Administrator, 540-231-6846, *Fax:* 540-231-7417, *E-mail:* squid@vt.edu. *Web site:* http://www.aaec.vt.edu/

■ WESTERN MICHIGAN UNIVERSITY

Graduate College, College of Arts and Sciences, Department of Economics, Kalamazoo, MI 49008-5202

AWARDS Applied economics (PhD); economics (MA).

Faculty: 18 full-time (3 women).
Students: 52 full-time (19 women), 5 part-time (1 woman); includes 1 minority (African American), 49 international. 131 applicants, 31% accepted, 19 enrolled. In 2001, 13 degrees awarded.
Degree requirements: For master's, thesis, oral or written exams; for doctorate, thesis/dissertation, oral exam, internship.
Entrance requirements: For doctorate, GRE General Test. *Application deadline:* For fall admission, 2/15 (priority date). Applications are processed on a rolling basis. *Application fee:* $25.
Expenses: Tuition, state resident: part-time $186 per credit hour. Tuition, nonresident: part-time $442 per credit hour. Required fees: $602. One-time fee: $132 part-time. Tuition and fees vary according to course load.
Financial support: Fellowships, research assistantships, teaching assistantships, Federal Work-Study available. Financial award application deadline: 2/15; financial award applicants required to submit FAFSA.
Dr. Bassam Harik, Chairperson, 616-387-5535.
Application contact: Admissions and Orientation, 616-387-2000, *Fax:* 616-387-2355.

■ WRIGHT STATE UNIVERSITY

School of Graduate Studies, Raj Soin College of Business, Department of Economics, Dayton, OH 45435

AWARDS Business economics (MBA); social and applied economics (MS).

Students: 10 full-time (5 women), 7 part-time (3 women). Average age 30. 31 applicants, 87% accepted. In 2001, 9 degrees awarded.
Entrance requirements: For master's, GRE General Test, TOEFL. *Application fee:* $25.
Expenses: Tuition, state resident: full-time $7,161; part-time $225 per quarter hour. Tuition, nonresident: full-time $12,324; part-time $385 per quarter hour. Tuition and fees vary according to course load, degree level and program.
Financial support: Fellowships, research assistantships, teaching assistantships, career-related internships or fieldwork and unspecified assistantships available. Support available to part-time students. Financial award applicants required to submit FAFSA.
Dr. James A. Swaney, Chair, 937-775-3070, *Fax:* 937-775-2441, *E-mail:* james.swaney@wright.edu.
Application contact: Dr. Len Kloft, Director, 937-775-2322, *Fax:* 937-775-2441, *E-mail:* leonard.kloft@wright.edu.

ECONOMICS

■ ALABAMA AGRICULTURAL AND MECHANICAL UNIVERSITY

School of Graduate Studies, School of Business, Department of Economics and Finance, Huntsville, AL 35811

AWARDS MS. Evening/weekend programs available.

Faculty: 5 full-time (0 women).
Students: Average age 24. In 2001, 3 degrees awarded.
Degree requirements: For master's, comprehensive exam.
Entrance requirements: For master's, GRE General Test, TOEFL, minimum undergraduate GPA of 2.5. *Application deadline:* For fall admission, 5/1. Applications are processed on a rolling basis. *Application fee:* $15 ($20 for international students).
Expenses: Tuition, state resident: full-time $1,380. Tuition, nonresident: full-time $2,500.
Financial support: In 2001–02, 1 teaching assistantship with tuition reimbursement (averaging $9,000 per year) was awarded; career-related internships or fieldwork also available. Financial award application deadline: 4/1.
Faculty research: Energy, banking, financial management, agricultural economics, sports economics.
Dr. Eric Rahimian, Chair, 256-851-5294, *Fax:* 256-851-5874.

■ ALBANY STATE UNIVERSITY

College of Arts and Sciences, Department of History, Political Science and Public Administration, Albany, GA 31705-2717

AWARDS Community and economic development (MPA); criminal justice (MPA); fiscal management (MPA); general management (MPA); health administration and policy (MPA); human resources management (MPA); public policy (MPA); water resource management and policy (MPA). Part-time programs available.

Degree requirements: For master's, thesis, comprehensive exam.
Entrance requirements: For master's, GRE General Test, minimum GPA of 2.5. Electronic applications accepted.
Faculty research: Transportation, urban affairs, political economy.

■ AMERICAN UNIVERSITY

College of Arts and Sciences, Department of Economics, Program in Economics, Washington, DC 20016-8001

AWARDS MA, PhD. Part-time and evening/weekend programs available.

Students: 43 full-time (20 women), 87 part-time (33 women); includes 15 minority (9 African Americans, 5 Asian Americans or Pacific Islanders, 1 Hispanic American), 69 international. Average age 31. In 2001, 10 master's, 7 doctorates awarded. Terminal master's awarded for partial completion of doctoral program.
Degree requirements: For master's, comprehensive exam; for doctorate, thesis/dissertation, comprehensive exam.
Entrance requirements: For master's, TOEFL; for doctorate, GRE General Test, TOEFL. *Application deadline:* For fall admission, 2/1 (priority date); for spring admission, 10/1. Applications are processed on a rolling basis. *Application fee:* $50.
Expenses: Tuition: Full-time $14,274; part-time $793 per credit. Required fees: $290. Tuition and fees vary according to program.
Financial support: Fellowships, teaching assistantships, career-related internships or fieldwork, Federal Work-Study, institutionally sponsored loans, and tuition waivers (full and partial) available. Financial award application deadline: 2/1.
Faculty research: Macroeconomic policy, international finance, economic development, political economy.
Application contact: Dr. Mieke Meurs, Ph.D. Adviser, 202-885-3376, *Fax:* 202-885-3790, *E-mail:* mmeurs@american.edu. *Web site:* http://www.american.edu/academic.depts/cas/econ/

Find an in-depth description at www.petersons.com/gradchannel.

■ AMERICAN UNIVERSITY

College of Arts and Sciences, Department of Economics, Program in Financial Economics for Public Policy, Washington, DC 20016-8001

AWARDS MA. Part-time and evening/weekend programs available.

Students: 6 full-time (1 woman), 3 part-time, 6 international. Average age 26. In 2001, 3 degrees awarded.
Degree requirements: For master's, comprehensive exam.
Entrance requirements: For master's, TOEFL. *Application deadline:* For fall admission, 2/1 (priority date); for spring admission, 10/1. Applications are processed on a rolling basis. *Application fee:* $50.
Expenses: Tuition: Full-time $14,274; part-time $793 per credit. Required fees: $290. Tuition and fees vary according to program.
Financial support: Career-related internships or fieldwork, Federal Work-Study, and institutionally sponsored loans available. Financial award application deadline: 2/1.
Application contact: Dr. Mieke Meurs, Ph.D. Adviser, 202-885-3376, *Fax:* 202-885-3790, *E-mail:* mmeurs@american.edu. *Web site:* http://www.american.edu/academic.depts/cas/econ/

Find an in-depth description at www.petersons.com/gradchannel.

■ ARIZONA STATE UNIVERSITY

Graduate College, College of Business, Department of Economics, Tempe, AZ 85287

AWARDS MS, PhD, JD/MS.

Degree requirements: For master's, thesis or alternative; for doctorate, thesis/dissertation.
Entrance requirements: For master's and doctorate, GRE.
Faculty research: Income policies, imperfect capital markets and lifecycle consumption, full employment as a labor-market and policy concept.

■ AUBURN UNIVERSITY

Graduate School, College of Business, Department of Economics, Auburn University, AL 36849

AWARDS MS, PhD. Part-time programs available.

Faculty: 15 full-time (0 women).
Students: 9 full-time (3 women), 9 part-time (3 women); includes 2 minority (1 African American, 1 Asian American or Pacific Islander), 3 international. 6 applicants, 67% accepted. In 2001, 11 master's, 5 doctorates awarded.
Degree requirements: For master's and doctorate, thesis/dissertation.
Entrance requirements: For master's and doctorate, GMAT, GRE General Test, TOEFL. *Application deadline:* For fall admission, 7/7; for spring admission, 11/24. Applications are processed on a rolling basis. *Application fee:* $25 ($50 for international students). Electronic applications accepted.
Financial support: Teaching assistantships, career-related internships or fieldwork and Federal Work-Study available. Support available to part-time students. Financial award application deadline: 3/15.
Dr. James E. Long, Interim Head, 334-844-4910.
Application contact: Dr. John F. Pritchett, Dean of the Graduate School, 334-844-4700, *E-mail:* hatchlb@mail.auburn.edu. *Web site:* http://www.auburn.edu/business/economics/auburn.html

■ BAYLOR UNIVERSITY

Graduate School, Hankamer School of Business, Department of Economics, Waco, TX 76798

AWARDS Economics (MS Eco); international economics (MA, MS).

Students: 8 full-time (5 women), 1 (woman) part-time, 6 international. In 2001, 5 degrees awarded.
Entrance requirements: For master's, GMAT or GRE General Test, minimum GPA of 3.0 in economics, 2.7 overall. *Application deadline:* For fall admission, 8/1; for spring admission, 12/1. Applications are processed on a rolling basis. *Application fee:* $25.
Expenses: Tuition: Part-time $379 per semester hour. Required fees: $42 per semester hour. $101 per semester. Tuition and fees vary according to program.
Financial support: Research assistantships, Federal Work-Study and institutionally sponsored loans available. Financial award application deadline: 4/1.
Faculty research: Econometrics, international economics, private enterprise, comparative economic systems.
Dr. Steve Green, Chair, 254-710-2263, *Fax:* 254-710-3265, *E-mail:* steve_green@baylor.edu.
Application contact: Suzanne Keener, Administrative Assistant, 254-710-3588, *Fax:* 254-710-3870, *E-mail:* graduate_school@baylor.edu. *Web site:* http://www.baylor.edu/eco/default.asp

■ BENTLEY COLLEGE

The Elkin B. McCallum Graduate School of Business, Part-Time MBA Program, Waltham, MA 02452-4705

AWARDS Accountancy (MBA); advanced accountancy (MBA); business administration (Advanced Certificate); business communication (MBA); business data analysis (MBA, Certificate); business economics (MBA); business ethics (MBA, Certificate); e-business (MBA, Certificate); entrepreneurial studies (MBA); finance (MBA); international business (MBA); management (MBA); management information systems (MBA); management of technology (MBA); marketing (MBA); operations management (MBA); taxation (MBA). Part-time and evening/weekend programs available.

Faculty: 243 full-time (82 women), 179 part-time/adjunct (79 women).
Students: Average age 30. In 2001, 290 degrees awarded.
Entrance requirements: For master's, GMAT, TOEFL; for other advanced degree, MBA (Advanced Certificate). *Application deadline:* For fall admission, 6/1 (priority date); for spring admission, 11/1. Applications are processed on a rolling basis. *Application fee:* $50. Electronic applications accepted.
Expenses: Tuition: Full-time $18,640; part-time $777 per credit. Required fees: $100.
Financial support: In 2001–02, 182 students received support, including 32 research assistantships; career-related internships or fieldwork, Federal Work-Study, and unspecified assistantships also available. Support available to part-time students. Financial award application deadline: 4/15; financial award applicants required to submit CSS PROFILE or FAFSA.
Faculty research: Information technology for high-performance teams, electronic commerce, mergers and acquisitions, workforce diversity, accounting profession.
Dr. Judith B. Kamm, Director, 781-891-3433, *Fax:* 781-891-2464.
Application contact: Paul Vaccaro, Director of Graduate Admissions, 781-891-2108, *Fax:* 781-891-2464, *E-mail:* pvaccaro@bentley.edu.

Find an in-depth description at www.petersons.com/gradchannel.

■ BERNARD M. BARUCH COLLEGE OF THE CITY UNIVERSITY OF NEW YORK

Zicklin School of Business, Department of Economics and Finance, Program in Economics, New York, NY 10010-5585

AWARDS MBA. Part-time and evening/weekend programs available.

Faculty: 19 full-time (2 women), 1 part-time/adjunct (0 women).
Students: 1 full-time (0 women), 4 part-time. 11 applicants, 45% accepted, 1 enrolled.
Entrance requirements: For master's, GMAT, TOEFL, TWE. *Application deadline:* For fall admission, 4/30; for spring admission, 10/31. *Application fee:* $40.
Expenses: Tuition, state resident: full-time $4,350; part-time $185 per credit. Tuition, nonresident: full-time $7,600; part-time $320 per credit. Tuition and fees vary according to program.

Bernard M. Baruch College of the City University of New York (continued)
Financial support: Fellowships, research assistantships, career-related internships or fieldwork and Federal Work-Study available. Financial award application deadline: 5/1; financial award applicants required to submit FAFSA.
Application contact: Frances Murphy, Office of Graduate Admissions, 646-312-1300, *Fax:* 646-312-1301, *E-mail:* zicklingradadmissions@baruch.cuny.edu.

■ BOSTON COLLEGE

Graduate School of Arts and Sciences, Department of Economics, Chestnut Hill, MA 02467-3800

AWARDS MA, PhD.

Students: 31 full-time (12 women), 33 part-time (19 women), 50 international. 294 applicants, 16% accepted. In 2001, 15 master's, 11 doctorates awarded.
Degree requirements: For doctorate, thesis/dissertation, comprehensive exam.
Entrance requirements: For doctorate, GRE General Test, GRE Subject Test. *Application deadline:* For fall admission, 2/1. *Application fee:* $50.
Expenses: Tuition: Full-time $17,664; part-time $8,832 per semester.
Financial support: Fellowships, research assistantships, teaching assistantships, Federal Work-Study, scholarships/grants, and tuition waivers (full) available. Support available to part-time students. Financial award application deadline: 3/1; financial award applicants required to submit FAFSA.
Faculty research: Econometrics, international economics, public sector economics, monetary economics, urban economics.
Dr. Peter Ireland, Chairperson, 617-552-3683, *E-mail:* peter.ireland@bc.edu.
Application contact: Dr. Frank Gollop, Graduate Program Director, 617-552-3683, *E-mail:* frank.gollop@bc.edu. *Web site:* http://fmwww.bc.edu/EC/EC.html

■ BOSTON UNIVERSITY

Graduate School of Arts and Sciences, Department of Economics, Boston, MA 02215

AWARDS Economic policy (MAEP); economics (MA, PhD); political economy (MAPE).

Students: 114 full-time (41 women), 3 part-time (1 woman); includes 1 minority (Hispanic American), 97 international. Average age 28. 730 applicants, 22% accepted, 43 enrolled. In 2001, 45 master's, 12 doctorates awarded. Terminal master's awarded for partial completion of doctoral program.
Degree requirements: For master's, one foreign language, comprehensive exam, registration; for doctorate, one foreign language, thesis/dissertation, qualifying exam, comprehensive exam, registration.
Entrance requirements: For master's, GRE General Test, TOEFL, previous course work in intermediate economics and calculus, 3 letters of recommendation; for doctorate, GRE General Test, TOEFL, strong quantitative and theory background, 3 letters of recommendation. *Application deadline:* For fall admission, 6/1. *Application fee:* $60.
Expenses: Tuition: Full-time $25,872; part-time $340 per credit. Required fees: $40 per semester. Part-time tuition and fees vary according to class time, course level and program.
Financial support: In 2001–02, 55 students received support, including 2 fellowships with full tuition reimbursements available (averaging $14,000 per year), 17 research assistantships with full and partial tuition reimbursements available (averaging $13,500 per year), 21 teaching assistantships with full tuition reimbursements available (averaging $13,500 per year); Federal Work-Study and scholarships/grants also available. Support available to part-time students. Financial award application deadline: 1/15; financial award applicants required to submit FAFSA.
Laurence Kotlikoff, Chairman, 617-353-4002, *Fax:* 617-353-4449, *E-mail:* kotlikof@bu.edu.
Application contact: Sylvia A. Holmes, Graduate Program Administrator, 617-353-4454, *Fax:* 617-353-4449, *E-mail:* sholmes@bu.edu. *Web site:* http://www.bu.edu/econ/

■ BOSTON UNIVERSITY

Metropolitan College, Program in Administrative Studies, Boston, MA 02215

AWARDS Electronic commerce (MSAS); financial economics (MSAS); innovation and technology (MSAS); multinational commerce (MSAS). Part-time and evening/weekend programs available.

Faculty: 7 full-time (2 women), 25 part-time/adjunct (5 women).
Students: 105 full-time (39 women), 204 part-time (85 women); includes 32 minority (6 African Americans, 17 Asian Americans or Pacific Islanders, 8 Hispanic Americans, 1 Native American), 122 international. Average age 31.
Degree requirements: For master's, thesis optional.
Entrance requirements: For master's, TOEFL, 1 year of work experience. *Application deadline:* Applications are processed on a rolling basis. *Application fee:* $60.
Expenses: Tuition: Full-time $25,872; part-time $340 per credit. Required fees: $40 per semester. Part-time tuition and fees vary according to class time, course level and program.
Financial support: In 2001–02, 10 students received support; research assistantships, career-related internships or fieldwork and Federal Work-Study available.
Faculty research: International business, innovative process.
Dr. Kip Becker, Chairman, *E-mail:* adminsc@bu.edu.
Application contact: Department of Administrative Sciences, 617-353-3016, *Fax:* 617-353-6840, *E-mail:* adminsc@bu.edu. *Web site:* http://www.bu.edu/met/programs

Find an in-depth description at www.petersons.com/gradchannel.

■ BOWLING GREEN STATE UNIVERSITY

Graduate College, College of Business Administration, Department of Economics, Bowling Green, OH 43403

AWARDS MA. Part-time programs available.

Faculty: 10.
Students: 15 full-time (6 women), 1 (woman) part-time; includes 2 minority (both Hispanic Americans), 13 international. Average age 25. 53 applicants, 68% accepted, 9 enrolled. In 2001, 7 degrees awarded.
Degree requirements: For master's, thesis or alternative.
Entrance requirements: For master's, GRE General Test, TOEFL, minimum GPA of 3.0. *Application fee:* $30.
Expenses: Tuition, state resident: full-time $7,376; part-time $342 per credit hour. Tuition, nonresident: full-time $13,628; part-time $640 per credit hour.
Financial support: In 2001–02, 8 research assistantships with full tuition reimbursements (averaging $5,088 per year) were awarded; teaching assistantships with full tuition reimbursements, career-related internships or fieldwork, institutionally sponsored loans, and unspecified assistantships also available. Financial award applicants required to submit FAFSA.
Faculty research: Labor economics, monetary economics, economic education, mathematical economics.
Dr. John Hoag, Chair, 419-372-8231.
Application contact: Dr. Peter VanderHart, Graduate Coordinator, 419-372-8070.

■ BRANDEIS UNIVERSITY

Graduate School of International Economics and Finance, Waltham, MA 02454-9110

AWARDS Finance (MSF); international business (MBAi); international economics and finance (MA, PhD). Part-time and evening/weekend programs available.

Faculty: 25 full-time (4 women), 10 part-time/adjunct (0 women).
Students: 165 full-time (63 women), 57 part-time (14 women). Average age 28. 450 applicants, 50% accepted, 114 enrolled. In 2001, 58 master's, 1 doctorate awarded.

Terminal master's awarded for partial completion of doctoral program.
Degree requirements: For master's, one foreign language; for doctorate, thesis/dissertation.
Entrance requirements: For master's, GMAT or GRE General Test (MA), GMAT (MBAi), TOEFL; for doctorate, GRE General Test, GRE Subject Test, TOEFL. *Application deadline:* For fall admission, 2/15 (priority date). *Application fee:* $50. Electronic applications accepted.
Expenses: Tuition: Full-time $27,392. Required fees: $35.
Financial support: In 2001–02, 166 students received support, including research assistantships (averaging $4,000 per year), teaching assistantships (averaging $4,000 per year); career-related internships or fieldwork, Federal Work-Study, institutionally sponsored loans, scholarships/grants, and unspecified assistantships also available. Financial award application deadline: 2/15; financial award applicants required to submit FAFSA.
Faculty research: International finance and business, trade policy, macroeconomics, Asian economic issues, developmental economics.
Dr. Peter Petri, Dean, 781-736-4817, *Fax:* 781-736-2267, *E-mail:* ppetri@brandeis.edu.
Application contact: Geraldine F. Koch, Assistant Dean for Admission, 781-736-2252, *Fax:* 781-736-2263, *E-mail:* admission@lemberg.brandeis.edu. *Web site:* http://www.brandeis.edu/global

Find an in-depth description at www.petersons.com/gradchannel.

■ BROOKLYN COLLEGE OF THE CITY UNIVERSITY OF NEW YORK

Division of Graduate Studies, Department of Economics, Brooklyn, NY 11210-2889

AWARDS Accounting (MA); economics (MA); economics and computer and information science (MPS). Part-time and evening/weekend programs available.

Students: 7 full-time (1 woman), 38 part-time (20 women); includes 26 minority (17 African Americans, 7 Asian Americans or Pacific Islanders, 2 Hispanic Americans), 8 international. 62 applicants, 31% accepted. In 2001, 12 degrees awarded.
Degree requirements: For master's, thesis or alternative.
Entrance requirements: For master's, TOEFL. *Application deadline:* For fall admission, 3/1 (priority date); for spring admission, 11/1 (priority date). Applications are processed on a rolling basis. *Application fee:* $40.
Expenses: Tuition, state resident: full-time $4,350; part-time $185 per credit. Tuition, nonresident: full-time $7,600; part-time $320 per credit.
Financial support: In 2001–02, 3 fellowships were awarded; career-related internships or fieldwork, Federal Work-Study, institutionally sponsored loans, and scholarships/grants also available. Support available to part-time students. Financial award application deadline: 5/1; financial award applicants required to submit FAFSA.
Faculty research: Econometrics, environmental economics, microeconomics, macroeconomics, taxation.
Dr. Antony Arcadi, Chairperson, 718-951-5317.
Application contact: Dr. Gary Testa, Graduate Deputy Chairperson, 718-951-5548, *Fax:* 718-951-4867.

■ BROWN UNIVERSITY

Graduate School, Department of Economics, Providence, RI 02912

AWARDS AM, PhD. Terminal master's awarded for partial completion of doctoral program.

Degree requirements: For master's, core exam; for doctorate, thesis/dissertation.
Entrance requirements: For master's and doctorate, GRE General Test.

■ CALIFORNIA INSTITUTE OF TECHNOLOGY

Division of the Humanities and Social Sciences, Social Science Program, Specialization in Economics, Pasadena, CA 91125-0001

AWARDS PhD.

Faculty: 22 full-time (1 woman), 1 part-time/adjunct (0 women).
Degree requirements: For doctorate, thesis/dissertation.
Entrance requirements: For doctorate, GRE General Test. *Application deadline:* For fall admission, 1/15. *Application fee:* $0. Electronic applications accepted.
Financial support: Fellowships, research assistantships, teaching assistantships, Federal Work-Study and institutionally sponsored loans available.
Faculty research: Finance, design of incentive schemes, learning, economic history, decision theory, public policy.
Application contact: Laurel Auchampaugh, Graduate Secretary, 626-395-4206, *Fax:* 626-405-9841, *E-mail:* gradsec@hss.caltech.edu. *Web site:* http://www.hss.caltech.edu/Ph.D_html

■ CALIFORNIA STATE POLYTECHNIC UNIVERSITY, POMONA

Academic Affairs, College of Letters, Arts, and Social Sciences, Program in Economics, Pomona, CA 91768-2557

AWARDS MS. Part-time programs available.

Students: 15 full-time (5 women), 15 part-time (4 women); includes 12 minority (1 African American, 3 Asian Americans or Pacific Islanders, 8 Hispanic Americans), 5 international. Average age 31. 25 applicants, 60% accepted. In 2001, 12 degrees awarded.
Degree requirements: For master's, thesis or alternative.
Entrance requirements: For master's, GRE General Test. *Application deadline:* For fall admission, 5/1 (priority date); for winter admission, 10/15 (priority date); for spring admission, 1/20 (priority date). Applications are processed on a rolling basis. *Application fee:* $55. Electronic applications accepted.
Expenses: Tuition, nonresident: part-time $164 per unit. Required fees: $1,850.
Financial support: In 2001–02, 9 students received support. Federal Work-Study and institutionally sponsored loans available. Support available to part-time students. Financial award application deadline: 3/2; financial award applicants required to submit FAFSA.
Dr. Franklin Ho, Coordinator, 909-869-3854, *E-mail:* fho@csupomona.edu. *Web site:* http://www.csupomona.edu/~ec/

■ CALIFORNIA STATE UNIVERSITY, FULLERTON

Graduate Studies, College of Business and Economics, Department of Economics, Fullerton, CA 92834-9480

AWARDS Business economics (MBA); economics (MA). Part-time and evening/weekend programs available.

Faculty: 30 full-time (6 women), 12 part-time/adjunct.
Students: 9 full-time (1 woman), 16 part-time (6 women); includes 6 minority (4 Asian Americans or Pacific Islanders, 2 Hispanic Americans), 7 international. Average age 31. 27 applicants, 48% accepted, 10 enrolled. In 2001, 4 degrees awarded.
Degree requirements: For master's, thesis.
Entrance requirements: For master's, GMAT, GRE General Test. *Application fee:* $55.
Expenses: Tuition, nonresident: part-time $246 per unit. Required fees: $964.
Financial support: Teaching assistantships, Federal Work-Study, institutionally sponsored loans, and scholarships/grants available. Support available to part-time students. Financial award application deadline: 3/1.
Faculty research: Environmental and natural resource issues. *Total annual research expenditures:* $61,000.
Dr. David Wong, Chair, 714-278-2228.
Application contact: Dr. Jane Hall, Adviser, 714-278-2236.

■ CALIFORNIA STATE UNIVERSITY, HAYWARD

Academic Programs and Graduate Studies, School of Business and Economics, Department of Economics, Hayward, CA 94542-3000

AWARDS MA, MBA. Part-time and evening/weekend programs available.

Students: 6 full-time (1 woman), 26 part-time (11 women); includes 6 minority (3 African Americans, 3 Asian Americans or Pacific Islanders), 18 international. 31 applicants, 42% accepted. In 2001, 11 degrees awarded.
Degree requirements: For master's, project or thesis.
Entrance requirements: For master's, minimum GPA of 2.75 during previous 2 years. *Application deadline:* For fall admission, 6/15; for winter admission, 10/27; for spring admission, 1/5. Applications are processed on a rolling basis. *Application fee:* $55. Electronic applications accepted.
Expenses: Tuition, nonresident: part-time $164 per unit. Required fees: $405 per semester.
Financial support: Career-related internships or fieldwork, Federal Work-Study, and institutionally sponsored loans available. Support available to part-time students. Financial award application deadline: 3/1.
Dr. Charles Baird, Chair, 510-885-3265.
Application contact: Dr. Donna L. Wiley, Director of Graduate Programs, 510-885-3964.

■ CALIFORNIA STATE UNIVERSITY, LONG BEACH

Graduate Studies, College of Liberal Arts, Department of Economics, Long Beach, CA 90840

AWARDS MA. Part-time programs available.

Faculty: 10 full-time (3 women).
Students: 8 full-time (2 women), 12 part-time (9 women); includes 2 minority (both African Americans), 9 international. Average age 31. 31 applicants, 48% accepted. In 2001, 3 degrees awarded.
Degree requirements: For master's, comprehensive exam or thesis.
Entrance requirements: For master's, GRE General Test, GRE Subject Test, minimum GPA of 3.0. *Application deadline:* For fall admission, 8/1; for spring admission, 12/1. Applications are processed on a rolling basis. *Application fee:* $55. Electronic applications accepted.
Financial support: Federal Work-Study, institutionally sponsored loans, and scholarships/grants available. Financial award application deadline: 3/2.
Faculty research: Trade and development, economic forecasting, resource economics.
Dr. Joseph P. Magaddino, Chair, 562-985-5061, *Fax:* 562-985-5804, *E-mail:* jmagaddi@csulb.edu.
Application contact: Dr. Dennis Muraoka, Graduate Coordinator, 562-985-5078, *Fax:* 562-985-5804.

■ CALIFORNIA STATE UNIVERSITY, LOS ANGELES

Graduate Studies, College of Business and Economics, Department of Economics and Statistics, Los Angeles, CA 90032-8530

AWARDS Analytical quantitative economics (MA); business economics (MA, MBA, MS); economics (MA). Part-time and evening/weekend programs available.

Faculty: 10 full-time, 13 part-time/adjunct.
Students: 18 full-time (6 women), 29 part-time (11 women); includes 21 minority (4 African Americans, 9 Asian Americans or Pacific Islanders, 8 Hispanic Americans), 15 international. In 2001, 3 degrees awarded.
Degree requirements: For master's, comprehensive exam or thesis.
Entrance requirements: For master's, GMAT, TOEFL, minimum GPA of 2.5 during previous 2 years. *Application deadline:* For fall admission, 6/30; for spring admission, 11/30. Applications are processed on a rolling basis. *Application fee:* $55.
Expenses: Tuition, nonresident: part-time $164 per unit.
Financial support: Career-related internships or fieldwork and Federal Work-Study available. Support available to part-time students. Financial award application deadline: 3/1.
Dr. Kon Lai, Chair, 323-343-2930.

■ CARNEGIE MELLON UNIVERSITY

Graduate School of Industrial Administration, Program in Economics, Pittsburgh, PA 15213-3891

AWARDS MS, PhD.

Degree requirements: For doctorate, thesis/dissertation.
Entrance requirements: For master's, GMAT; for doctorate, GMAT, GRE General Test.
Faculty research: Research allocation under asymmetric information, monetary theory, estimation of rational expectations models. *Web site:* http://www.gsia.cmu.edu/

■ CARNEGIE MELLON UNIVERSITY

Graduate School of Industrial Administration, Program in Political Economy, Pittsburgh, PA 15213-3891

AWARDS PhD.

Degree requirements: For doctorate, thesis/dissertation. *Web site:* http://www.gsia.cmu.edu/

■ CASE WESTERN RESERVE UNIVERSITY

Weatherhead School of Management, Department of Economics, Cleveland, OH 44106

AWARDS MBA. Part-time and evening/weekend programs available.

Faculty: 12 full-time (2 women), 4 part-time/adjunct (1 woman).
Students: In 2001, 2 degrees awarded.
Entrance requirements: For master's, GMAT. *Application deadline:* For fall admission, 4/15 (priority date). Applications are processed on a rolling basis. *Application fee:* $50.
Financial support: Career-related internships or fieldwork, Federal Work-Study, institutionally sponsored loans, and tuition waivers (full and partial) available. Financial award application deadline: 5/1.
Faculty research: Public finance and public choice, direct foreign investment, employment relationships, technical and institutional change, regional economics.
James B. Rebitzeir, Chairman, 216-368-4110, *Fax:* 216-368-5039, *E-mail:* jbr@po.cwru.edu.
Application contact: Christine L. Gill, Director of Marketing and Admissions, 216-368-3845, *Fax:* 216-368-4776, *E-mail:* clg3@po.cwru.edu.

■ THE CATHOLIC UNIVERSITY OF AMERICA

School of Arts and Sciences, Department of Business and Economics, Program in Economics, Washington, DC 20064

AWARDS MA, JD/MA. Part-time and evening/weekend programs available.

Students: 1 full-time (0 women), 4 part-time (1 woman); includes 1 minority (African American), 2 international. Average age 40. 3 applicants, 100% accepted, 1 enrolled. In 2001, 1 master's awarded.
Degree requirements: For master's, comprehensive exam.
Entrance requirements: For master's, GRE General Test, TOEFL. *Application deadline:* For fall admission, 8/1 (priority date); for spring admission, 12/1. Applications are processed on a rolling basis. *Application fee:* $55. Electronic applications accepted.
Expenses: Tuition: Full-time $20,050; part-time $770 per credit. Required fees: $430 per term. Tuition and fees vary according to program.
Financial support: Teaching assistantships, career-related internships or fieldwork, Federal Work-Study, institutionally sponsored loans, scholarships/grants, and tuition waivers (full and partial) available. Support available to part-time students. Financial award application deadline: 2/1.

Faculty research: Oligopoly theory, economic growth, social growth, economic efficiency, quantitative analysis.
Dr. Kevin F Forbes, Chair, Department of Business and Economics, 202-319-5236, *Fax:* 202-319-4426.

■ THE CATHOLIC UNIVERSITY OF AMERICA

School of Arts and Sciences, Department of Business and Economics, Program in International Political Economics, Washington, DC 20064

AWARDS MA. Part-time and evening/weekend programs available.

Students: 2 applicants, 50% accepted, 0 enrolled.
Degree requirements: For master's, comprehensive exam.
Entrance requirements: For master's, GRE General Test, TOEFL. *Application deadline:* For fall admission, 8/1 (priority date); for spring admission, 12/1. Applications are processed on a rolling basis. *Application fee:* $55. Electronic applications accepted.
Expenses: Tuition: Full-time $20,050; part-time $770 per credit. Required fees: $430 per term. Tuition and fees vary according to program.
Financial support: Teaching assistantships, career-related internships or fieldwork, Federal Work-Study, institutionally sponsored loans, and tuition waivers (full and partial) available. Support available to part-time students. Financial award application deadline: 2/1.
Faculty research: Role of the U.S. in the world economy.
Dr. Kevin F Forbes, Chair, Department of Business and Economics, 202-319-5236, *Fax:* 202-319-4426.

■ CENTRAL MICHIGAN UNIVERSITY

College of Graduate Studies, College of Business Administration, Department of Economics, Mount Pleasant, MI 48859

AWARDS MA.

Degree requirements: For master's, thesis or alternative.
Expenses: Tuition, state resident: part-time $182 per unit. Tuition, nonresident: part-time $182 per unit. Required fees: $208 per semester. Part-time tuition and fees vary according to course load.
Faculty research: International trade, public choice/labor, economic development.

■ CENTRAL MISSOURI STATE UNIVERSITY

School of Graduate Studies, Harmon College of Business Administration, Department of Economics and Finance, Warrensburg, MO 64093

AWARDS Economics (MA). Part-time programs available.

Faculty: 7 full-time (2 women).
Students: 4 full-time (1 woman), 3 part-time; includes 1 minority (Asian American or Pacific Islander), 5 international. Average age 26. In 2001, 2 degrees awarded.
Degree requirements: For master's, thesis or alternative, research paper, comprehensive exam.
Entrance requirements: For master's, GRE General Test, TOEFL, minimum GPA of 2.5, 15 hours in economics. *Application deadline:* Applications are processed on a rolling basis. *Application fee:* $25 ($50 for international students).
Expenses: Tuition, area resident: Full-time $4,200; part-time $175 per credit hour. Tuition, nonresident: full-time $8,352; part-time $348 per credit hour.
Financial support: In 2001–02, 4 research assistantships with full and partial tuition reimbursements (averaging $6,813 per year), 1 teaching assistantship with full tuition reimbursement (averaging $8,000 per year) were awarded. Federal Work-Study, scholarships/grants, unspecified assistantships, and administrative assistantships also available. Support available to part-time students. Financial award application deadline: 3/1; financial award applicants required to submit FAFSA.
Faculty research: Environmental economics, economic education.
Dr. Paul H. Engelmann, Chair, 660-543-4246, *Fax:* 660-543-8465, *E-mail:* engelmann@cmsu1.cmsu.edu. *Web site:* http://www.cmsu.edu/

■ CITY COLLEGE OF THE CITY UNIVERSITY OF NEW YORK

Graduate School, College of Liberal Arts and Science, Division of Social Science, Department of Economics, New York, NY 10031-9198

AWARDS MA. Part-time programs available.

Students: 17. In 2001, 6 degrees awarded.
Degree requirements: For master's, proficiency in a foreign language or advanced statistics.
Entrance requirements: For master's, TOEFL. *Application deadline:* For fall admission, 5/1; for spring admission, 12/1. *Application fee:* $40.
Expenses: Tuition, state resident: part-time $185 per credit. Tuition, nonresident: part-time $320 per credit. Required fees: $43 per term.
Financial support: Fellowships, Federal Work-Study and tuition waivers (full and partial) available. Support available to part-time students. Financial award application deadline: 5/1.
Faculty research: International economics, health, banking.
Stanley Friedlander, Chairman, 212-650-5403.
Application contact: Benjamin J. Klebaner, Adviser, 212-650-6718.

■ CLAREMONT GRADUATE UNIVERSITY

Graduate Programs, School of Politics and Economics, Department of Economics, Claremont, CA 91711-6160

AWARDS Business and financial economics (MA, PhD); economics (PhD); international economic policy and management (MA, PhD); political economy and public policy (MA, PhD). Part-time programs available.

Faculty: 5 full-time (0 women), 2 part-time/adjunct (0 women).
Students: 64 full-time (18 women), 21 part-time (7 women); includes 6 minority (1 African American, 1 Asian American or Pacific Islander, 4 Hispanic Americans), 62 international. Average age 33. In 2001, 11 master's, 8 doctorates awarded.
Degree requirements: For doctorate, 2 foreign languages, thesis/dissertation, comprehensive exam.
Entrance requirements: For master's and doctorate, GRE General Test. *Application deadline:* For fall admission, 2/15 (priority date). Applications are processed on a rolling basis. *Application fee:* $50. Electronic applications accepted.
Expenses: Tuition: Full-time $22,984; part-time $1,000 per unit. Required fees: $160; $80 per semester.
Financial support: Fellowships, research assistantships, teaching assistantships, Federal Work-Study and institutionally sponsored loans available. Support available to part-time students. Financial award application deadline: 2/15; financial award applicants required to submit FAFSA.
Faculty research: International and financial economics, law and economics, regulation, public choice economics.
Thomas Borcherding, Chair, 909-621-8074, *Fax:* 909-621-8545, *E-mail:* thomas.borcherding@cgu.edu.
Application contact: Lynda Marquez, Program Secretary, 909-621-8074, *Fax:* 909-621-8460, *E-mail:* econ@cgu.edu. *Web site:* http://spe.cgu.edu/econ/index.html

Find an in-depth description at www.petersons.com/gradchannel.

■ CLAREMONT GRADUATE UNIVERSITY

Graduate Programs, School of Politics and Economics, Department of Politics and Policy, Claremont, CA 91711-6160

AWARDS International political economy (MAIPE); international studies (MAIS); political science (PhD); politics (MAP); politics, economics, and business (MAPEB); public policy (MAPP). Part-time programs available.

Faculty: 9 full-time (2 women), 2 part-time/adjunct (1 woman).
Students: 158 full-time (62 women), 43 part-time (19 women); includes 42 minority (19 African Americans, 6 Asian Americans or Pacific Islanders, 17 Hispanic Americans), 40 international. Average age 34. In 2001, 25 master's, 9 doctorates awarded. Terminal master's awarded for partial completion of doctoral program.
Degree requirements: For master's, thesis; for doctorate, one foreign language, thesis/dissertation.
Entrance requirements: For master's and doctorate, GRE General Test. *Application deadline:* For fall admission, 2/15 (priority date). Applications are processed on a rolling basis. *Application fee:* $50. Electronic applications accepted.
Expenses: Tuition: Full-time $22,984; part-time $1,000 per unit. Required fees: $160; $80 per semester.
Financial support: Fellowships, research assistantships, teaching assistantships, career-related internships or fieldwork, Federal Work-Study, and institutionally sponsored loans available. Support available to part-time students. Financial award application deadline: 2/15; financial award applicants required to submit FAFSA.
Faculty research: Environmental policy, international debt, global democratization, Third World development, public sector discrimination.
Yi Fens, Chair, 909-621-8171, *Fax:* 909-621-8390, *E-mail:* yi.fens@cgu.edu.
Application contact: Gwen Williams, Program Administrator, 909-621-8179, *Fax:* 909-621-8545, *E-mail:* gwen.williams@cgu.edu. *Web site:* http://spe.cgu.edu/politics/index.html

Find an in-depth description at www.petersons.com/gradchannel.

■ CLARK ATLANTA UNIVERSITY

School of Arts and Sciences, Department of Economics, Atlanta, GA 30314

AWARDS MA. Part-time programs available.

Degree requirements: For master's, one foreign language, thesis.
Entrance requirements: For master's, GRE General Test, minimum GPA of 2.5.
Faculty research: Minority energy demand.

■ CLARK UNIVERSITY

Graduate School, Department of Economics, Worcester, MA 01610-1477

AWARDS PhD.

Faculty: 10 full-time (2 women), 3 part-time/adjunct (2 women).
Students: 23 full-time (12 women), 2 part-time (both women), 23 international. Average age 28. 107 applicants, 23% accepted, 4 enrolled. In 2001, 4 doctorates awarded.
Degree requirements: For doctorate, thesis/dissertation.
Entrance requirements: For doctorate, GRE General Test, TOEFL. *Application deadline:* For fall admission, 2/15 (priority date). Applications are processed on a rolling basis. *Application fee:* $40.
Expenses: Tuition: Full-time $24,400; part-time $763 per credit. Required fees: $10.
Financial support: In 2001–02, fellowships with full and partial tuition reimbursements (averaging $10,250 per year), 5 research assistantships with full and partial tuition reimbursements (averaging $10,250 per year), 10 teaching assistantships with full and partial tuition reimbursements (averaging $10,250 per year) were awarded. Career-related internships or fieldwork, institutionally sponsored loans, and tuition waivers (full and partial) also available.
Faculty research: Public finance, economic development, industrial organization, international finance and trade. *Total annual research expenditures:* $286,465.
Dr. Maurice Weinrobe, Chair, 508-793-7226.
Application contact: Cindy Rice, Department Secretary, 508-793-7226, *Fax:* 508-793-8849, *E-mail:* crice@clarku.edu. *Web site:* http://www2.clarku.edu/newsite/graduatefolder/programs/index.shtml

■ CLEMSON UNIVERSITY

Graduate School, College of Business and Behavioral Science, Department of Economics, Clemson, SC 29634

AWARDS Applied economics (PhD); economics (MA).

Students: 69 full-time (20 women), 9 part-time (1 woman); includes 4 minority (3 African Americans, 1 Hispanic American), 44 international. Average age 23. 112 applicants, 78% accepted, 28 enrolled. In 2001, 5 master's, 4 doctorates awarded.
Degree requirements: For doctorate, thesis/dissertation.
Entrance requirements: For master's and doctorate, GRE General Test, TOEFL. *Application deadline:* For fall admission, 6/1. *Application fee:* $40.
Expenses: Tuition, state resident: full-time $5,310. Tuition, nonresident: full-time $11,284.
Financial support: Fellowships, research assistantships, teaching assistantships available. Financial award applicants required to submit FAFSA.
Faculty research: Applied price theory, financial economics, industrial economics, labor economics, monetary economics.
Dr. William Dougan, Chair, 864-656-3481, *Fax:* 864-656-4192, *E-mail:* douganw@clemson.edu.
Application contact: Dr. C. M. Lindsay, Director of Graduate Programs, 864-656-3955, *Fax:* 864-656-4192, *E-mail:* lindsay@clemson.edu. *Web site:* http://hubcap.clemson.edu:80/economics/

Find an in-depth description at www.petersons.com/gradchannel.

■ CLEVELAND STATE UNIVERSITY

College of Graduate Studies, College of Arts and Sciences, Department of Economics, Cleveland, OH 44115

AWARDS MA. Part-time and evening/weekend programs available.

Faculty: 7 full-time (0 women).
Students: 2 full-time (1 woman), 4 part-time, 2 international. Average age 28. 40 applicants, 70% accepted. In 2001, 6 degrees awarded.
Entrance requirements: For master's, TOEFL, minimum GPA of 2.75. *Application deadline:* For fall admission, 8/20 (priority date). Applications are processed on a rolling basis. *Application fee:* $30. Electronic applications accepted.
Expenses: Tuition, state resident: full-time $6,838; part-time $263 per credit hour. Tuition, nonresident: full-time $13,526; part-time $520 per credit hour.
Financial support: In 2001–02, 2 students received support, including 2 research assistantships with full tuition reimbursements available (averaging $4,360 per year); Federal Work-Study and tuition waivers (full) also available.
Faculty research: Urban economics, energy, environment, economics of law, organization theory.
Dr. Vijay K. Mathur, Chairperson, 216-687-4526, *Fax:* 216-687-9206, *E-mail:* v.mathur@csuohio.edu.
Application contact: Dr. Allan J. Taub, Director of Graduate Program, 216-687-4528, *Fax:* 216-687-9206, *E-mail:* a.taub@csuohio.edu. *Web site:* http://www.asic.csuohio.edu/econ/

■ COLORADO STATE UNIVERSITY

Graduate School, College of Liberal Arts, Department of Economics, Fort Collins, CO 80523-0015

AWARDS MA, PhD. Part-time programs available.

Faculty: 16 full-time (3 women), 6 part-time/adjunct (1 woman).

Students: 36 full-time (13 women), 29 part-time (7 women); includes 3 minority (all Hispanic Americans), 32 international. Average age 31. 76 applicants, 72% accepted, 21 enrolled. In 2001, 5 master's, 1 doctorate awarded. Terminal master's awarded for partial completion of doctoral program.
Degree requirements: For master's, thesis optional; for doctorate, thesis/dissertation.
Entrance requirements: For master's and doctorate, GRE General Test, TOEFL, minimum GPA of 3.0. *Application deadline:* For fall admission, 2/1 (priority date). Applications are processed on a rolling basis. *Application fee:* $30. Electronic applications accepted.
Expenses: Tuition, state resident: full-time $2,880; part-time $160 per credit. Tuition, nonresident: full-time $11,412; part-time $634 per credit. Required fees: $750; $34 per credit.
Financial support: In 2001–02, 7 fellowships (averaging $7,000 per year), 13 teaching assistantships with full tuition reimbursements (averaging $11,000 per year) were awarded. Research assistantships, career-related internships or fieldwork, Federal Work-Study, institutionally sponsored loans, and traineeships also available. Financial award application deadline: 3/1.
Faculty research: Capitalism and the state, gender and income distribution, financial system reforms, multinationals, natural hazards. *Total annual research expenditures:* $41,000.
Dr. Ronnie J. Phillips, Chair, 970-491-6556, *Fax:* 970-491-2925, *E-mail:* ronnie.phillips@colostate.edu.
Application contact: Barbara Alldredge, Program Assistant, 970-491-6566, *Fax:* 970-491-2925, *E-mail:* barbara.alldredge@colostate.edu. *Web site:* http://www.colostate.edu/Depts/Econ/

■ COLUMBIA UNIVERSITY

Graduate School of Arts and Sciences, Division of Social Sciences, Department of Economics, New York, NY 10027

AWARDS M Phil, MA, PhD, JD/MA, JD/PhD.

Faculty: 36 full-time, 1 part-time/adjunct.
Students: 118 full-time (38 women), 5 part-time (2 women). Average age 29. 715 applicants, 10% accepted. In 2001, 16 master's, 15 doctorates awarded.
Degree requirements: For master's, thesis or alternative; for doctorate, thesis/dissertation.
Entrance requirements: For master's and doctorate, GRE General Test, GRE Subject Test, TOEFL, previous course work in mathematics. *Application deadline:* For fall admission, 1/3; for spring admission, 11/30. *Application fee:* $65.
Expenses: Tuition: Full-time $27,528. Required fees: $1,638.
Financial support: Fellowships, teaching assistantships, Federal Work-Study and institutionally sponsored loans available. Support available to part-time students. Financial award application deadline: 1/5; financial award applicants required to submit FAFSA.
Faculty research: International trade.
Donald Davis, Chair, 212-854-3682, *Fax:* 212-854-8059.

■ COLUMBIA UNIVERSITY

Graduate School of Business, Doctoral Program in Business, New York, NY 10027

AWARDS Business (PhD), including accounting, decision, risk, and operations, finance and economics, management, management science/operations management, marketing.

Faculty: 127 full-time (19 women), 80 part-time/adjunct (14 women).
Students: 100 full-time (34 women); includes 7 minority (2 African Americans, 5 Asian Americans or Pacific Islanders), 73 international. Average age 30. 653 applicants, 6% accepted, 19 enrolled. In 2001, 16 degrees awarded.
Degree requirements: For doctorate, thesis/dissertation, major field exam, research paper, oral exam.
Entrance requirements: For doctorate, GMAT or GRE, TOEFL, 2 letters of reference, resumé. *Application deadline:* For fall admission, 2/1. *Application fee:* $60.
Expenses: Contact institution.
Financial support: In 2001–02, 78 students received support, including 77 fellowships with full tuition reimbursements available (averaging $18,000 per year); research assistantships, teaching assistantships, institutionally sponsored loans also available. Financial award application deadline: 2/1.
Elizabeth Elam, Administrative Director, 212-854-2836, *Fax:* 212-932-2359, *E-mail:* phdinfo@claven.gsb.columbia.edu. *Web site:* http://www.gsb.columbia.edu/doctoral/

■ COLUMBIA UNIVERSITY

Graduate School of Business, MBA Program, New York, NY 10027

AWARDS Accounting (MBA); decision, risk, and operations (MBA); entrepreneurship (MBA); finance and economics (MBA); human resource management (MBA); international business (MBA); management (MBA); marketing (MBA); media, entertainment and communications (MBA); real estate (MBA); social enterprise (MBA).

Faculty: 127 full-time (19 women), 80 part-time/adjunct (14 women).
Students: 1,225 full-time (447 women); includes 237 minority (82 African Americans, 118 Asian Americans or Pacific Islanders, 34 Hispanic Americans, 3 Native Americans), 325 international. Average age 27. 5,277 applicants, 13% accepted, 488 enrolled. In 2001, 714 degrees awarded. *Median time to degree:* Master's–1.5 years full-time.
Entrance requirements: For master's, GMAT, TOEFL, minimum 2 years of work experience, 2 letters of reference. *Application deadline:* For fall admission, 4/20; for spring admission, 10/1. Applications are processed on a rolling basis. *Application fee:* $150. Electronic applications accepted.
Expenses: Tuition: Full-time $27,528. Required fees: $1,638.
Financial support: Fellowships, career-related internships or fieldwork, Federal Work-Study, institutionally sponsored loans, and scholarships/grants available. Financial award application deadline: 2/1; financial award applicants required to submit FAFSA.
Prof. Safwan Masri, Vice Dean of Students and the MBA Program, 212-854-8716, *Fax:* 212-932-0545, *E-mail:* smm1@columbia.edu.
Application contact: Linda B. Meehan, Assistant Dean and Executive Director of Admissions and Financial Aid, 212-854-1961, *Fax:* 212-662-6754, *E-mail:* apply@claven.gsb.columbia.edu. *Web site:* http://www.gsb.columbia.edu/

■ CONVERSE COLLEGE

Department of Education, Program in Liberal Arts, Spartanburg, SC 29302-0006

AWARDS Economics (MLA); English (MLA); history (MLA); political science (MLA); sociology (MLA).

Degree requirements: For master's, capstone paper.
Entrance requirements: For master's, NTE, minimum GPA of 2.75.
Expenses: Tuition: Part-time $225 per credit hour. One-time fee: $20 part-time.

■ CORNELL UNIVERSITY

Graduate School, Graduate Field of Management, Ithaca, NY 14853-0001

AWARDS Accounting (PhD); behavioral decision theory (PhD); finance (PhD); managerial economics (PhD); marketing (PhD); organizational behavior (PhD); production and operations management (PhD).

Faculty: 46 full-time.
Students: 33 full-time (15 women); includes 4 minority (2 African Americans, 1 Asian American or Pacific Islander, 1 Native American), 21 international. 455 applicants, 5% accepted. In 2001, 6 doctorates awarded.
Degree requirements: For doctorate, thesis/dissertation.
Entrance requirements: For doctorate, GMAT or GRE General Test, TOEFL. *Application deadline:* For fall admission, 1/3 (priority date). *Application fee:* $65. Electronic applications accepted.
Expenses: Contact institution.

Cornell University (continued)
Financial support: In 2001–02, 29 students received support, including 4 fellowships with full tuition reimbursements available, 25 research assistantships with full tuition reimbursements available; teaching assistantships with full tuition reimbursements available, institutionally sponsored loans, scholarships/grants, tuition waivers (full and partial), and unspecified assistantships also available. Financial award applicants required to submit FAFSA.
Faculty research: Operations and manufacturing.
Application contact: Graduate Field Assistant, 607-255-3669, *E-mail:* js_phd.cornell.edu. *Web site:* http://www.gradschool.cornell.edu/grad/fields_1/manage.html

■ CORNELL UNIVERSITY

Graduate School, Graduate Fields of Arts and Sciences, Field of Economics, Ithaca, NY 14853-0001

AWARDS Applied economics (PhD); econometrics and economic statistics (PhD); economic development and planning (PhD); economic theory (PhD); industrial organization and control (PhD); international economics (PhD); labor economics (PhD); monetary and macroeconomics (PhD); public finance (PhD).

Faculty: 55 full-time.
Students: 112 full-time (41 women); includes 8 minority (1 African American, 4 Asian Americans or Pacific Islanders, 2 Hispanic Americans, 1 Native American), 85 international. 581 applicants, 18% accepted. In 2001, 10 doctorates awarded.
Degree requirements: For doctorate, thesis/dissertation.
Entrance requirements: For doctorate, GRE General Test, TOEFL, 3 letters of recommendation. *Application deadline:* For fall admission, 1/15. *Application fee:* $65. Electronic applications accepted.
Expenses: Tuition: Full-time $25,970. Required fees: $50.
Financial support: In 2001–02, 88 students received support, including 22 fellowships with full tuition reimbursements available, 21 research assistantships with full tuition reimbursements available, 45 teaching assistantships with full tuition reimbursements available; institutionally sponsored loans, scholarships/grants, tuition waivers (full and partial), and unspecified assistantships also available. Financial award applicants required to submit FAFSA.
Faculty research: Learning and games, monetary theory, political economy, transfer payments, time series and nonparametics.
Application contact: Graduate Field Assistant, 607-255-4893, *E-mail:* econ_phd@cornell.edu. *Web site:* http://www.gradschool.cornell.edu/grad/fields_1/econ.html

■ DEPAUL UNIVERSITY

Charles H. Kellstadt Graduate School of Business and College of Liberal Arts and Sciences, Department of Economics, Chicago, IL 60604-2287

AWARDS Business economics (MBA); economics (MA); international business (MBA).

Faculty: 21 full-time (4 women), 8 part-time/adjunct (2 women).
Students: 18 full-time (9 women), 16 part-time (2 women); includes 7 minority (2 African Americans, 2 Asian Americans or Pacific Islanders, 3 Hispanic Americans), 4 international. Average age 29. 23 applicants, 83% accepted. In 2001, 7 degrees awarded.
Entrance requirements: For master's, GMAT (MBA), TOEFL. *Application deadline:* For fall admission, 7/1; for winter admission, 10/1; for spring admission, 2/1. Applications are processed on a rolling basis. *Application fee:* $40. Electronic applications accepted.
Expenses: Tuition: Part-time $362 per credit hour. Tuition and fees vary according to program.
Financial support: In 2001–02, 3 research assistantships with partial tuition reimbursements (averaging $9,999 per year) were awarded. Support available to part-time students.
Dr. Michael S. Miller, Chairperson, 312-362-8477, *Fax:* 312-362-5452.
Application contact: Marion Blackmon, Director of Graduate Admissions, 773-362-8880, *Fax:* 773-325-7311, *E-mail:* mblackmo@wppost.depaul.edu. *Web site:* http://condor.depaul.edu/~dpuecon/

■ DREXEL UNIVERSITY

Graduate School, College of Business and Administration, Program in Business Administration, Philadelphia, PA 19104-2875

AWARDS Business administration (MBA, PhD, APC), including accounting (MBA, PhD), decision sciences (PhD), economics (MBA, PhD), finance (MBA, PhD), legal studies (MBA), management (MBA), marketing (MBA, PhD), organizational sciences (PhD), quantitative methods (MBA), strategic management (PhD). Part-time and evening/weekend programs available. Postbaccalaureate distance learning degree programs offered (minimal on-campus study).

Faculty: 88 full-time (19 women), 11 part-time/adjunct (2 women).
Students: 273 full-time (117 women), 438 part-time (171 women); includes 73 minority (23 African Americans, 41 Asian Americans or Pacific Islanders, 8 Hispanic Americans, 1 Native American), 184 international. Average age 30. 510 applicants, 62% accepted, 131 enrolled. In 2001, 263 master's, 8 doctorates, 1 other advanced degree awarded. Terminal master's awarded for partial completion of doctoral program.
Entrance requirements: For master's, GMAT, TOEFL, minimum GPA of 2.75; for doctorate, GMAT, TOEFL. *Application deadline:* For fall admission, 8/21; for spring admission, 3/5. Applications are processed on a rolling basis. *Application fee:* $50. Electronic applications accepted.
Expenses: Tuition: Full-time $20,088; part-time $558 per credit. Required fees: $78 per term. One-time fee: $200. Tuition and fees vary according to course load, degree level and program.
Financial support: Research assistantships, teaching assistantships, career-related internships or fieldwork and unspecified assistantships available. Financial award application deadline: 2/1.
Faculty research: Decision support systems, individual and group behavior, operations research, techniques and strategy.
Dr. Thomas Wieckowski, Director of Master's Programs in Business, 215-895-1791, *Fax:* 215-895-1012.
Application contact: Director of Graduate Admissions, 215-895-6700, *Fax:* 215-895-5939, *E-mail:* enroll@drexel.edu.

Find an in-depth description at www.petersons.com/gradchannel.

■ DUKE UNIVERSITY

Graduate School, Department of Economics, Durham, NC 27708-0586

AWARDS AM, PhD, JD/AM.

Faculty: 29 full-time, 8 part-time/adjunct.
Students: 100 full-time (29 women); includes 4 minority (1 African American, 2 Asian Americans or Pacific Islanders, 1 Hispanic American), 61 international. 427 applicants, 22% accepted, 32 enrolled. In 2001, 19 master's, 5 doctorates awarded. Terminal master's awarded for partial completion of doctoral program.
Degree requirements: For doctorate, thesis/dissertation.
Entrance requirements: For master's and doctorate, GRE General Test. *Application deadline:* For fall admission, 12/31. *Application fee:* $75.
Expenses: Tuition: Full-time $24,600.
Financial support: Fellowships, research assistantships, teaching assistantships, Federal Work-Study available. Financial award application deadline: 12/31.
Tim Bollerslev, Director of Graduate Studies, 919-660-1847, *Fax:* 919-684-8974, *E-mail:* dgs@econ.duke.edu. *Web site:* http://www.econ.duke.edu/

■ EAST CAROLINA UNIVERSITY

Graduate School, College of Arts and Sciences, Department of Economics, Greenville, NC 27858-4353

AWARDS Applied resource economics (MS). Part-time programs available.

Faculty: 9 full-time (1 woman).

Students: 20 full-time (6 women), 2 part-time (1 woman); includes 1 minority (Asian American or Pacific Islander), 5 international. Average age 25. 29 applicants, 69% accepted. In 2001, 13 degrees awarded.
Degree requirements: For master's, one foreign language, comprehensive exam.
Entrance requirements: For master's, GRE General Test, TOEFL. *Application deadline:* For fall admission, 6/1 (priority date). Applications are processed on a rolling basis. *Application fee:* $45.
Expenses: Tuition, state resident: full-time $2,636. Tuition, nonresident: full-time $11,365.
Financial support: Research assistantships with partial tuition reimbursements, teaching assistantships with partial tuition reimbursements available. Financial award application deadline: 6/1.
Dr. John Bishop, Director of Graduate Studies, 252-328-6756, *Fax:* 252-328-6743, *E-mail:* bishopj@mail.ecu.edu.
Application contact: Dr. Paul D. Tschetter, Senior Associate Dean of the Graduate School, 252-328-6012, *Fax:* 252-328-6071, *E-mail:* gradschool@mail.ecu.edu.

■ EASTERN ILLINOIS UNIVERSITY

Graduate School, College of Sciences, Department of Economics, Charleston, IL 61920-3099

AWARDS MA.

■ EASTERN MICHIGAN UNIVERSITY

Graduate School, College of Arts and Sciences, Department of Economics, Ypsilanti, MI 48197

AWARDS Applied economics (MA); development, trade and planning (MA); economics (MA). Evening/weekend programs available.

Faculty: 11 full-time (1 woman).
Students: 18 full-time (8 women), 19 part-time (7 women); includes 23 minority (2 African Americans, 20 Asian Americans or Pacific Islanders, 1 Hispanic American). 67 applicants, 34% accepted. In 2001, 6 degrees awarded.
Degree requirements: For master's, thesis or alternative.
Entrance requirements: For master's, TOEFL. *Application deadline:* For fall admission, 5/15; for spring admission, 3/15. Applications are processed on a rolling basis. *Application fee:* $30.
Expenses: Tuition, state resident: part-time $285 per credit hour. Tuition, nonresident: part-time $510 per credit hour.
Financial support: Fellowships, teaching assistantships available. Support available to part-time students. Financial award application deadline: 3/15; financial award applicants required to submit FAFSA.
Dr. Raouf S. Hanna, Head, 734-487-3395.
Application contact: Dr. James Thornton, Coordinator, 734-487-3395.

■ EASTERN UNIVERSITY

Graduate Business Programs, St. Davids, PA 19087-3696

AWARDS Business administration (MBA), including accounting, economics, finance, management, marketing; economic development (MBA, MS); nonprofit management (MBA, MS). Part-time and evening/weekend programs available.

Degree requirements: For master's, thesis (for some programs).
Entrance requirements: For master's, GMAT (MBA), minimum GPA of 2.5.
Expenses: Contact institution.
Faculty research: Micro-level economic development, China welfare and economic development, macroethics, micro- and macro-level economic development in transitional economics, organizational effectiveness. *Web site:* http://www.eastern.edu/academic/undg/depts/business/index.html

Find an in-depth description at www.petersons.com/gradchannel.

■ EAST TENNESSEE STATE UNIVERSITY

School of Graduate Studies, College of Business, Department of Economics, Finance, and Urban Studies, Johnson City, TN 37614

AWARDS City management (MCM); community development (MPM); general administration (MPM); municipal service management (MPM); urban and regional economic development (MPM); urban and regional planning (MPM).

Faculty: 1 full-time (0 women).
Students: 15 full-time (6 women), 14 part-time (9 women); includes 4 minority (all African Americans), 2 international. Average age 35. In 2001, 10 degrees awarded.
Degree requirements: For master's, internship, oral defense of thesis, research report.
Entrance requirements: For master's, GRE General Test, TOEFL, minimum GPA of 3.0. *Application deadline:* For fall admission, 7/1 (priority date); for spring admission, 12/1. Applications are processed on a rolling basis. *Application fee:* $25 ($35 for international students).
Expenses: Tuition, state resident: part-time $181 per hour. Tuition, nonresident: part-time $270 per hour. Required fees: $220 per term.
Financial support: Research assistantships with full tuition reimbursements available.
Dr. Jafar Alavi, Chair, 423-439-4455, *Fax:* 423-439-5383, *E-mail:* drjalavi@etsu.edu.
Application contact: Dr. Lon Felker, Director, 423-439-6631, *Fax:* 423-439-5383, *E-mail:* felker@etsu.edu. *Web site:* http://www.etsu.edu/

■ EMORY UNIVERSITY

Graduate School of Arts and Sciences, Department of Economics, Atlanta, GA 30322-1100

AWARDS PhD.

Faculty: 14 full-time (1 woman), 3 part-time/adjunct (2 women).
Students: 34 full-time (17 women); includes 6 minority (2 African Americans, 2 Asian Americans or Pacific Islanders, 2 Hispanic Americans), 13 international. 140 applicants, 8% accepted, 6 enrolled. In 2001, 1 degree awarded.
Degree requirements: For doctorate, thesis/dissertation, registration.
Entrance requirements: For doctorate, GRE General Test, TOEFL. *Application deadline:* For fall admission, 1/20 (priority date). *Application fee:* $50. Electronic applications accepted.
Expenses: Tuition: Full-time $24,770. Required fees: $100. Tuition and fees vary according to program and student level.
Financial support: In 2001–02, 24 fellowships were awarded; research assistantships, teaching assistantships, scholarships/grants and tuition waivers (full and partial) also available. Financial award application deadline: 1/20.
Faculty research: Applied microeconomics, econometrics, public choice, macroeconomics, law and economics.
Dr. Hashem Dezhbakhsh, Chair, 404-727-6648, *Fax:* 404-727-4639, *E-mail:* paranso@emory.edu.
Application contact: Dr. Robert Chirinko, Director of Graduate Studies, 404-727-6645, *E-mail:* rchirin@emory.edu. *Web site:* http://emory.edu/COLLEGE/ECON/

■ EMPORIA STATE UNIVERSITY

School of Graduate Studies, College of Liberal Arts and Sciences, Department of Mathematics, Computer Science and Economics, Emporia, KS 66801-5087

AWARDS Mathematics (MS).

Faculty: 13 full-time (2 women).
Students: 1 full-time (0 women), 4 part-time (3 women). 2 applicants, 0% accepted. In 2001, 1 degree awarded.
Degree requirements: For master's, comprehensive exam or thesis.
Entrance requirements: For master's, TOEFL. *Application deadline:* For fall admission, 8/15 (priority date). Applications are processed on a rolling basis. *Application fee:* $30 ($75 for international students). Electronic applications accepted.
Expenses: Tuition, state resident: full-time $2,632; part-time $119 per credit hour. Tuition, nonresident: full-time $6,734; part-time $290 per credit hour.
Financial support: In 2001–02, 1 teaching assistantship with full tuition reimbursement (averaging $5,273 per year) was

Emporia State University (continued)
awarded; fellowships, research assistantships, career-related internships or fieldwork, Federal Work-Study, institutionally sponsored loans, health care benefits, and unspecified assistantships also available. Financial award application deadline: 3/15; financial award applicants required to submit FAFSA.
Dr. Larry Scott, Chair, 620-341-5281, *Fax:* 620-341-6055, *E-mail:* scottlar@emporia.edu.
Application contact: Dr. Joe Yanik, Graduate Coordinator, 620-341-5639, *E-mail:* yanikjoe@emporia.edu. *Web site:* http://www.emporia.edu/math-cs/home.htm

■ FLORIDA ATLANTIC UNIVERSITY

College of Business, Department of Economics, Boca Raton, FL 33431-0991

AWARDS MS, MST. Part-time programs available.

Faculty: 11 full-time (3 women).
Students: 8 full-time (1 woman), 6 part-time (2 women); includes 2 minority (both Hispanic Americans), 5 international. Average age 34. 29 applicants, 62% accepted, 5 enrolled. In 2001, 2 degrees awarded.
Degree requirements: For master's, thesis optional.
Entrance requirements: For master's, GMAT or GRE, minimum GPA of 3.0 or GMAT (minimum score of 450 required) or GRE General Test. *Application deadline:* For fall admission, 6/15 (priority date); for spring admission, 10/15 (priority date). Applications are processed on a rolling basis. *Application fee:* $20.
Expenses: Tuition, state resident: full-time $3,098; part-time $172 per credit. Tuition, nonresident: full-time $10,427; part-time $579 per credit.
Financial support: In 2001–02, 5 students received support, including 4 teaching assistantships with tuition reimbursements available (averaging $6,000 per year); tuition waivers (partial) and unspecified assistantships also available. Financial award application deadline: 3/1.
Faculty research: International trade and finance, decision making, monetary conditions, economic fluctuations and growth.
Dr. Charles Register, Chair, 561-297-3220, *Fax:* 561-297-2542, *E-mail:* cregister@fau.edu. *Web site:* http://www.collegeofbusiness.fau.edu/ecn/econhome.htm

■ FLORIDA INTERNATIONAL UNIVERSITY

College of Arts and Sciences, Department of Economics, Miami, FL 33199

AWARDS MA, PhD. Part-time and evening/weekend programs available.

Faculty: 18 full-time (3 women).
Students: 21 full-time (8 women), 7 part-time (3 women); includes 6 minority (1 African American, 5 Hispanic Americans), 20 international. Average age 31. 51 applicants, 47% accepted, 10 enrolled. In 2001, 6 master's, 2 doctorates awarded.
Degree requirements: For master's, thesis or alternative; for doctorate, thesis/dissertation.
Entrance requirements: For master's, TOEFL, GRE General Test or minimum GPA of 3.0; for doctorate, GRE General Test, TOEFL. *Application deadline:* For fall admission, 4/1 (priority date); for spring admission, 10/1. Applications are processed on a rolling basis. *Application fee:* $20.
Expenses: Tuition, state resident: full-time $2,916; part-time $162 per credit hour. Tuition, nonresident: full-time $10,245; part-time $569 per credit hour. Required fees: $168 per term.
Financial support: In 2001–02, 2 fellowships, 4 research assistantships, 1 teaching assistantship were awarded. Career-related internships or fieldwork, Federal Work-Study, and tuition waivers (partial) also available. Financial award application deadline: 4/1.
Faculty research: Economic development, international economics, urban/regional economics, Latin American economics.
Dr. Panagis S. Liossatos, Chairperson, 305-348-2317, *Fax:* 305-348-1524, *E-mail:* liossato@fiu.edu.

■ FLORIDA STATE UNIVERSITY

Graduate Studies, College of Social Sciences, Department of Economics, Tallahassee, FL 32306

AWARDS MS, PhD, JD/MS. Part-time programs available.

Faculty: 28 full-time (2 women), 4 part-time/adjunct (0 women).
Students: 43 full-time (12 women), 7 part-time (2 women); includes 2 minority (1 African American, 1 Asian American or Pacific Islander), 17 international. Average age 28. 126 applicants, 87% accepted, 21 enrolled. In 2001, 13 master's, 3 doctorates awarded. Terminal master's awarded for partial completion of doctoral program.
Degree requirements: For master's, thesis or alternative; for doctorate, thesis/dissertation, 4 comprehensive exams, 4 workshops, comprehensive exam. *Median time to degree:* Master's–1.75 years full-time, 2 years part-time; doctorate–5 years full-time, 7 years part-time.
Entrance requirements: For master's, GRE General Test, TOEFL, minimum GPA of 3.0, minimum GPA of 3.4 on gradute work, at least one course each in statistics and calculus; for doctorate, GRE General Test, TOEFL, minimum graduate GPA of 3.4, at least one course in statistics and two in calculus. *Application deadline:* For fall admission, 7/13 (priority date); for spring admission, 11/12 (priority date). Applications are processed on a rolling basis. *Application fee:* $20. Electronic applications accepted.
Expenses: Tuition, state resident: part-time $163 per credit hour. Tuition, nonresident: part-time $570 per credit hour. Tuition and fees vary according to program.
Financial support: In 2001–02, 31 students received support, including 5 fellowships with full tuition reimbursements available (averaging $17,000 per year), 5 research assistantships with full tuition reimbursements available (averaging $13,250 per year), 20 teaching assistantships with full tuition reimbursements available (averaging $13,250 per year); career-related internships or fieldwork and Federal Work-Study also available. Financial award application deadline: 1/31; financial award applicants required to submit FAFSA.
Faculty research: Applied econometrics, financial economics, international economics, public economics, labor economics. *Total annual research expenditures:* $55,701.
Dr. James H. Cobbe, Chairman, 850-644-5001, *Fax:* 850-644-4535, *E-mail:* jcobbe@coss.fsu.edu.
Application contact: Dr. Thomas W. Zuehlke, Graduate Director, 850-644-7206, *Fax:* 850-644-7072, *E-mail:* tzeuhlke@coss.fsu.edu. *Web site:* http://www.fsu.edu/~economic/

■ FORDHAM UNIVERSITY

Graduate School of Arts and Sciences, Department of Economics, New York, NY 10458

AWARDS Economics (MA, PhD), including economic development, economics of public policy, financial economics, industrial organization, international economics, monetary economics. Part-time and evening/weekend programs available.

Faculty: 21 full-time (2 women), 1 part-time/adjunct (0 women).
Students: 22 full-time (7 women), 44 part-time (10 women); includes 14 minority (6 African Americans, 5 Asian Americans or Pacific Islanders, 3 Hispanic Americans), 20 international. Average age 31. 179 applicants, 35% accepted. In 2001, 18 master's, 3 doctorates awarded. Terminal master's awarded for partial completion of doctoral program.
Degree requirements: For master's, comprehensive exam; for doctorate, thesis/dissertation, comprehensive exam.
Entrance requirements: For master's and doctorate, GRE General Test. *Application deadline:* For fall admission, 1/15 (priority date); for spring admission, 12/1. *Application fee:* $65. Electronic applications accepted.
Expenses: Tuition: Part-time $720 per credit. Required fees: $135 per semester.
Financial support: In 2001–02, 26 students received support, including fellowships with tuition reimbursements available (averaging $15,000 per year),

research assistantships with tuition reimbursements available (averaging $12,000 per year), 1 teaching assistantship with tuition reimbursement available (averaging $14,000 per year); career-related internships or fieldwork, institutionally sponsored loans, tuition waivers (full and partial), and unspecified assistantships also available. Financial award application deadline: 1/16.
Faculty research: Developmental economics, law and economics.
Dr. Henry Schwalbenberg, Chair, 718-817-4048, *Fax:* 718-817-3518, *E-mail:* schwalbenberg@fordham.edu.
Application contact: Dr. Craig W. Pilant, Assistant Dean, 718-817-4420, *Fax:* 718-817-3566, *E-mail:* pilant@fordham.edu.
Web site: http://www.fordham.edu/gsas/

■ FORDHAM UNIVERSITY

Graduate School of Arts and Sciences, Program in International Political Economy and Development, New York, NY 10458

AWARDS MA, CIF. Part-time and evening/weekend programs available.

Faculty: 16.
Students: 28 full-time (16 women), 22 part-time (12 women); includes 2 minority (1 Asian American or Pacific Islander, 1 Hispanic American), 21 international. 118 applicants, 75% accepted. In 2001, 19 degrees awarded.
Degree requirements: For master's, comprehensive exam.
Entrance requirements: For master's, GRE General Test. *Application deadline:* For fall admission, 1/15 (priority date); for spring admission, 12/1. *Application fee:* $65. Electronic applications accepted.
Expenses: Tuition: Part-time $720 per credit. Required fees: $135 per semester.
Financial support: In 2001–02, 10 students received support, including 1 fellowship with tuition reimbursement available (averaging $15,000 per year), research assistantships with tuition reimbursements available (averaging $12,000 per year); career-related internships or fieldwork, institutionally sponsored loans, tuition waivers (full and partial), and unspecified assistantships also available. Financial award application deadline: 1/16.
Faculty research: International economics, development economics, comparative international politics, demography, emerging markets.
Dr. Henry Schwalbenberg, Chair, 718-817-4048, *Fax:* 718-817-3518, *E-mail:* schwalbenberg@fordham.edu.
Application contact: Dr. Craig W. Pilant, Assistant Dean, 718-817-4420, *Fax:* 718-817-3566, *E-mail:* pilant@fordham.edu.
Web site: http://www.fordham.edu/gsas/

■ GEORGE MASON UNIVERSITY

College of Arts and Sciences, Department of Economics, Fairfax, VA 22030-4444

AWARDS MA, PhD.

Faculty: 25 full-time (3 women), 15 part-time/adjunct (3 women).
Students: 50 full-time (11 women), 81 part-time (20 women); includes 11 minority (8 Asian Americans or Pacific Islanders, 3 Hispanic Americans), 39 international. Average age 32. 186 applicants, 39% accepted, 29 enrolled. In 2001, 21 master's, 15 doctorates awarded.
Degree requirements: For master's, 2 comprehensive exams, thesis optional; for doctorate, thesis/dissertation, 2 preliminary exams, field exams.
Entrance requirements: For master's, GRE General Test, GRE Subject Test (economics), previous introductory and intermediate course work in macro and microeconomics, previous undergraduate course work in calculus; for doctorate, GRE General Test, GRE Subject Test (economics), previous course work in analytic geometry, 1 year of course work in statistics, previous introductory and intermediate course work in macro and microeconomics. *Application deadline:* For fall admission, 5/1; for spring admission, 11/1. *Application fee:* $30. Electronic applications accepted.
Expenses: Tuition, state resident: full-time $3,168; part-time $132 per credit hour. Tuition, nonresident: full-time $11,280; part-time $470 per credit hour. Required fees: $1,416; $59 per credit hour.
Financial support: Fellowships, research assistantships, teaching assistantships available. Support available to part-time students. Financial award application deadline: 3/1; financial award applicants required to submit FAFSA.
Dr. Richard Wagner, Graduate Director, 703-993-1135, *Fax:* 703-993-1133, *E-mail:* econgrad@gmu.edu. *Web site:* http://www.gmu.edu/departments/economics/gradstuf.html

Find an in-depth description at www.petersons.com/gradchannel.

■ GEORGETOWN UNIVERSITY

Graduate School of Arts and Sciences, Department of Economics, Washington, DC 20057

AWARDS PhD, MA/PhD, MS/MA.

Degree requirements: For doctorate, thesis/dissertation, comprehensive exam.
Entrance requirements: For doctorate, GRE General Test, TOEFL.
Faculty research: International economics, economic development.

■ THE GEORGE WASHINGTON UNIVERSITY

Columbian College of Arts and Sciences, Department of Economics, Washington, DC 20052

AWARDS MA, PhD. Part-time and evening/weekend programs available.

Faculty: 23 full-time (4 women), 6 part-time/adjunct (1 woman).
Students: 21 full-time (11 women), 77 part-time (27 women); includes 12 minority (4 African Americans, 5 Asian Americans or Pacific Islanders, 2 Hispanic Americans, 1 Native American), 56 international. Average age 32. 220 applicants, 70% accepted. In 2001, 12 master's, 2 doctorates awarded. Terminal master's awarded for partial completion of doctoral program.
Degree requirements: For master's, thesis or alternative, comprehensive exam; for doctorate, thesis/dissertation, general exam.
Entrance requirements: For master's and doctorate, GRE General Test, minimum GPA of 3.0. *Application fee:* $55.
Expenses: Tuition: Part-time $810 per credit. Required fees: $1 per credit.
Financial support: In 2001–02, 18 students received support, including 16 fellowships with tuition reimbursements available (averaging $8,000 per year), 14 teaching assistantships with tuition reimbursements available (averaging $4,700 per year); Federal Work-Study also available. Financial award application deadline: 2/1.
Dr. Harry Watson, Chair, 202-994-6685.
Web site: http://www.gwu.edu/~gradinfo/

■ GEORGIA INSTITUTE OF TECHNOLOGY

Graduate Studies and Research, Ivan Allen College of Policy and International Affairs, School of Economics, Atlanta, GA 30332-0001

AWARDS MS.

Degree requirements: For master's, thesis.
Entrance requirements: For master's, GRE, TOEFL.
Faculty research: Land use patterns in developing countries, office automation and productivity, dynamic modeling of financial markets. *Web site:* http://www.econ.gatech.edu/

■ GEORGIA STATE UNIVERSITY

Andrew Young School of Policy Studies, Department of Economics, Atlanta, GA 30303-3083

AWARDS MA, PhD. MA offered through the College of Arts and Sciences. Part-time and evening/weekend programs available. Terminal master's awarded for partial completion of doctoral program.

Georgia State University (continued)
Degree requirements: For doctorate, thesis/dissertation.
Entrance requirements: For master's, GRE General Test, GRE Subject Test (MA), GMAT (MS, MBA); for doctorate, GMAT or GRE General Test.
Faculty research: Tax policy, economic growth and development, environmental economics, urban and regional economics, economics of science.

■ GOLDEN GATE UNIVERSITY

School of Business, San Francisco, CA 94105-2968

AWARDS Accounting (M Ac, MBA); business administration (EMBA, DBA); economics (MS); finance (MBA, MS); financial planning (Certificate); human resource management (MS); human resources management (Certificate); information systems (MBA); international business (MBA); management (MBA); marketing (MBA, MS); operations management (MBA); public relations (MS, Certificate); telecommunications (MBA). Part-time and evening/weekend programs available.

Degree requirements: For doctorate, thesis/dissertation.
Entrance requirements: For master's, GMAT (MBA), TOEFL, minimum GPA of 2.5 (MS). *Web site:* http://www.ggu.edu/schools/business/home.html

■ GRADUATE SCHOOL AND UNIVERSITY CENTER OF THE CITY UNIVERSITY OF NEW YORK

Graduate Studies, Program in Economics, New York, NY 10016-4039

AWARDS PhD.

Faculty: 53 full-time (10 women).
Students: 82 full-time (30 women), 3 part-time; includes 8 minority (1 African American, 5 Asian Americans or Pacific Islanders, 2 Hispanic Americans), 57 international. Average age 33. 168 applicants, 86% accepted, 17 enrolled. In 2001, 6 degrees awarded.
Degree requirements: For doctorate, thesis/dissertation.
Entrance requirements: For doctorate, GRE General Test. *Application deadline:* For fall admission, 4/15. *Application fee:* $40.
Expenses: Tuition, state resident: part-time $245 per credit. Tuition, nonresident: part-time $425 per credit. Required fees: $72 per semester.
Financial support: In 2001–02, 28 students received support, including 17 fellowships, 3 teaching assistantships; research assistantships, career-related internships or fieldwork, Federal Work-Study, institutionally sponsored loans, and tuition waivers (full and partial) also available. Financial award application deadline: 2/1; financial award applicants required to submit FAFSA.
Dr. Thom Thurston, Executive Officer, 212-817-8256, *Fax:* 212-817-1514, *E-mail:* tthurston@gc.cuny.edu.

■ HARVARD UNIVERSITY

Graduate School of Arts and Sciences, Committee on Business Economics, Cambridge, MA 02138

AWARDS AM, PhD.

Degree requirements: For doctorate, thesis/dissertation.
Entrance requirements: For master's, GRE General Test, TOEFL; for doctorate, GMAT or GRE General Test, TOEFL.
Expenses: Tuition: Full-time $23,370. Required fees: $816. Full-time tuition and fees vary according to program and student level.

■ HARVARD UNIVERSITY

Graduate School of Arts and Sciences, Department of Economics, Cambridge, MA 02138

AWARDS AM, PhD.

Degree requirements: For doctorate, thesis/dissertation, oral exam.
Entrance requirements: For master's, GRE General Test, TOEFL; for doctorate, GRE General Test, GRE Subject Test, TOEFL.
Expenses: Tuition: Full-time $23,370. Required fees: $816. Full-time tuition and fees vary according to program and student level.
Faculty research: Industrial organization, macromonetary issues, international economics.

■ HOWARD UNIVERSITY

Graduate School of Arts and Sciences, Department of Economics, Washington, DC 20059-0002

AWARDS MA, PhD. Part-time programs available.

Degree requirements: For master's, thesis, comprehensive exam; for doctorate, one foreign language, thesis/dissertation, comprehensive exam.
Entrance requirements: For master's, GRE General Test, minimum GPA of 3.0; for doctorate, GRE General Test, master's degree in economics or related field, minimum GPA of 3.0.

■ HUNTER COLLEGE OF THE CITY UNIVERSITY OF NEW YORK

Graduate School, School of Arts and Sciences, Department of Economics, New York, NY 10021-5085

AWARDS MA. Part-time and evening/weekend programs available.

Faculty: 18 full-time (5 women), 24 part-time/adjunct (7 women).
Students: 6 full-time (1 woman), 32 part-time (15 women); includes 17 minority (6 African Americans, 6 Asian Americans or Pacific Islanders, 5 Hispanic Americans), 4 international. Average age 31. 16 applicants, 44% accepted, 6 enrolled. In 2001, 6 degrees awarded.
Degree requirements: For master's, thesis or alternative, research paper or thesis. *Median time to degree:* Master's–3 years part-time.
Entrance requirements: For master's, GMAT or GRE General Test, TOEFL, minimum GPA of 3.0. *Application deadline:* For fall admission, 4/28; for spring admission, 11/21. *Application fee:* $40.
Expenses: Tuition, state resident: full-time $2,175; part-time $185 per credit. Tuition, nonresident: full-time $3,800; part-time $320 per credit.
Financial support: Fellowships, research assistantships, teaching assistantships, career-related internships or fieldwork, Federal Work-Study, institutionally sponsored loans, and tuition waivers (partial) available. Support available to part-time students.
Faculty research: Earnings of immigrants and minority groups, taxation and the regional economy.
Dr. Marjorie P. Honig, Chairperson, 212-772-5400, *Fax:* 212-772-5398.
Application contact: Randall Filer, Professor of Economics, *Fax:* 212-772-5398, *E-mail:* grad.econadvisor@hunter.cuny.edu. *Web site:* http://www.econ.hunter.cuny.edu/

■ ILLINOIS STATE UNIVERSITY

Graduate School, College of Arts and Sciences, Department of Economics, Normal, IL 61790-2200

AWARDS MA, MS.

Faculty: 13 full-time (0 women).
Students: 18 full-time (8 women), 4 part-time (3 women), 13 international. 29 applicants, 83% accepted. In 2001, 9 degrees awarded.
Degree requirements: For master's, thesis or alternative.
Entrance requirements: For master's, GRE General Test, minimum GPA of 2.6 in last 60 hours. *Application deadline:* Applications are processed on a rolling basis. *Application fee:* $30.
Expenses: Tuition, state resident: full-time $2,691; part-time $112 per credit hour. Tuition, nonresident: full-time $5,880; part-time $245 per credit hour. Required fees: $1,146; $48 per credit hour.
Financial support: In 2001–02, 17 research assistantships (averaging $6,763 per year) were awarded; teaching assistantships, tuition waivers (full) and unspecified assistantships also available. Financial award application deadline: 4/1.
Faculty research: Peace Corps Fellows Programs: community and economic development, professional practice in applied community development. *Total annual research expenditures:* $175,563.

Dr. David Ramsey, Chairperson, 309-438-8625. *Web site:* http://www.econ.ilstu.edu/

■ INDIANA STATE UNIVERSITY

School of Graduate Studies, College of Arts and Sciences, Department of Economics, Terre Haute, IN 47809-1401

AWARDS MA, MS.

Degree requirements: For master's, thesis or alternative.
Faculty research: Financial markets, international economics, labor markets, microeconomics.

■ INDIANA UNIVERSITY BLOOMINGTON

Graduate School, College of Arts and Sciences, Department of Economics, Bloomington, IN 47405

AWARDS MA, MAT, PhD. PhD offered through the University Graduate School.

Faculty: 16 full-time (1 woman).
Students: 55 full-time (16 women), 39 part-time (12 women); includes 1 minority (Native American), 68 international. Average age 29. In 2001, 17 master's, 8 doctorates awarded. Terminal master's awarded for partial completion of doctoral program.
Degree requirements: For master's, one foreign language, thesis optional; for doctorate, one foreign language, thesis/dissertation, field exams, comprehensive exam.
Entrance requirements: For master's and doctorate, GRE General Test, TOEFL, minimum 3 intermediate-level mathematics courses. *Application deadline:* For fall admission, 1/15 (priority date). Applications are processed on a rolling basis. *Application fee:* $45 ($55 for international students).
Expenses: Tuition, state resident: full-time $4,720; part-time $197 per credit. Tuition, nonresident: full-time $13,748; part-time $573 per credit. Required fees: $642.
Financial support: In 2001–02, 51 students received support, including 5 fellowships with full tuition reimbursements available (averaging $10,700 per year), 2 research assistantships with full tuition reimbursements available (averaging $17,700 per year), 44 teaching assistantships with full tuition reimbursements available (averaging $10,350 per year); institutionally sponsored loans also available. Financial award application deadline: 1/15.
Faculty research: Games, experiments and organization, transition economics, growth and development, macroeconomics, econometrics.
Dr. Robert A. Becker, Chair, 812-855-1021, *E-mail:* becker@indiana.edu.
Application contact: Chris Cunningham, Graduate Services Assistant, 812-855-8453, *Fax:* 812-855-3736, *E-mail:* rcunning@indiana.edu. *Web site:* http://www.indiana.edu/~econweb/

■ INDIANA UNIVERSITY–PURDUE UNIVERSITY INDIANAPOLIS

School of Liberal Arts, Department of Economics, Indianapolis, IN 46202-2896

AWARDS MA, MA/MA.

Students: 13 full-time (9 women), 9 part-time (2 women), 15 international. Average age 28. In 2001, 8 degrees awarded.
Entrance requirements: For master's, GRE. *Application deadline:* For fall admission, 3/1 (priority date). *Application fee:* $45 ($55 for international students).
Expenses: Tuition, state resident: full-time $4,480; part-time $187 per credit. Tuition, nonresident: full-time $12,926; part-time $539 per credit. Required fees: $177.
Financial support: Fellowships with partial tuition reimbursements, research assistantships with partial tuition reimbursements available.
Dr. Robert Sandy, Chair, 317-274-2176.
Application contact: Jeannette Rowe, Senior Administrative Secretary, 317-274-4756, *Fax:* 317-274-0097, *E-mail:* jrowe@iupui.edu. *Web site:* http://www.iupui.edu/~econ/

■ INDIANA UNIVERSITY SOUTHEAST

School of Business, New Albany, IN 47150-6405

AWARDS Accounting (Certificate); business administration (MBA); economics (Certificate); finance (Certificate); general business (Certificate); information and operations management (Certificate); management and marketing (Certificate); strategic finance (MS).

Students: 9 full-time (5 women), 226 part-time (73 women); includes 18 minority (10 African Americans, 4 Asian Americans or Pacific Islanders, 4 Hispanic Americans), 2 international. Average age 31. In 2001, 32 degrees awarded.
Application fee: $30.
Expenses: Tuition, state resident: full-time $3,644; part-time $152 per credit. Tuition, nonresident: full-time $8,311; part-time $346 per credit. Required fees: $386; $386 per year.
Dr. Uric Dufrene, Dean, 812-941-2325. *Web site:* http://www.business.ius.edu

■ IOWA STATE UNIVERSITY OF SCIENCE AND TECHNOLOGY

Graduate College, College of Liberal Arts and Sciences, Department of Economics, Ames, IA 50011

AWARDS Agricultural economics (MS, PhD); economics (MS, PhD).

Faculty: 53 full-time, 2 part-time/adjunct.
Students: 59 full-time (14 women), 39 part-time (14 women); includes 1 minority (Asian American or Pacific Islander), 74 international. 651 applicants, 20% accepted, 22 enrolled. In 2001, 12 master's, 11 doctorates awarded.
Degree requirements: For master's, thesis or alternative; for doctorate, thesis/dissertation. *Median time to degree:* Master's–2 years full-time; doctorate–6.2 years full-time.
Entrance requirements: For master's and doctorate, GRE General Test, TOEFL or IELTS. *Application deadline:* For fall admission, 2/1 (priority date). Applications are processed on a rolling basis. *Application fee:* $20 ($50 for international students). Electronic applications accepted.
Expenses: Tuition, state resident: full-time $1,851. Tuition, nonresident: full-time $5,449. Tuition and fees vary according to program.
Financial support: In 2001–02, 40 research assistantships with partial tuition reimbursements (averaging $13,103 per year), 28 teaching assistantships with partial tuition reimbursements (averaging $13,715 per year) were awarded. Fellowships, scholarships/grants, health care benefits, and unspecified assistantships also available.
Dr. J. Arne Hallam, Chair, 515-294-2701, *Fax:* 515-294-7755, *E-mail:* grad@econ.iastate.edu. *Web site:* http://www.econ.iastate.edu/

■ JOHNS HOPKINS UNIVERSITY

Paul H. Nitze School of Advanced International Studies, Washington, DC 20036

AWARDS Emerging markets (Certificate); interdisciplinary studies (MA, PhD), including African studies, American foreign policy (MA), Asian studies, Canadian studies, conflict resolution and mediation (MA), environmental policy and resource management (MA), European studies, international business (MA), international development (MA), international economics (MA), international relations (MA), Latin American studies, Middle Eastern studies (MA), military and defense studies (MA), Russian area and East European studies (MA), social change and development (MA); international public policy (MIPP). MBA/MA offered jointly with the University of Pennsylvania–Wharton School and INSEAD in France.

Faculty: 44 full-time (13 women), 113 part-time/adjunct (29 women).
Students: 567 full-time (275 women), 17 part-time (8 women); includes 71 minority (14 African Americans, 46 Asian Americans or Pacific Islanders, 10 Hispanic Americans, 1 Native American). Average age 27. 1,288 applicants, 35% accepted. In 2001, 294 master's, 13 doctorates, 34 other advanced degrees awarded. Terminal master's awarded for partial completion of doctoral program.
Degree requirements: For master's, one foreign language, comprehensive exam; for

Johns Hopkins University (continued)
doctorate, 2 foreign languages, thesis/dissertation.
Entrance requirements: For master's, GMAT or GRE General Test or TOEFL, previous course work in economics, foreign language; for doctorate, GRE General Test or TOEFL; for Certificate, TOEFL. *Application deadline:* For fall admission, 1/15. *Application fee:* $75. Electronic applications accepted.
Expenses: Contact institution.
Financial support: In 2001–02, 431 fellowships (averaging $5,500 per year) were awarded; career-related internships or fieldwork and Federal Work-Study also available. Financial award application deadline: 2/1; financial award applicants required to submit FAFSA.
Faculty research: Comparative politics, regional studies, language and linguistics.
Dr. Jessica Einhorn, Dean, 202-663-5624, *Fax:* 202-663-5621.
Application contact: Bonnie Wilson, Associate Dean of Student Affairs, 202-663-5700, *Fax:* 202-663-7788, *E-mail:* admissions.sais@jhu.edu. *Web site:* http://www.sais-jhu.edu/

Find an in-depth description at www.petersons.com/gradchannel.

■ JOHNS HOPKINS UNIVERSITY

Zanvyl Krieger School of Arts and Sciences, Department of Economics, Baltimore, MD 21218-2699

AWARDS PhD.

Faculty: 13 full-time (1 woman).
Students: 67 full-time (23 women), 52 international. Average age 25. 377 applicants, 14% accepted, 24 enrolled. In 2001, 11 doctorates awarded.
Degree requirements: For doctorate, thesis/dissertation, comprehensive exam, registration.
Entrance requirements: For doctorate, GRE General Test, TOEFL. *Application deadline:* For fall admission, 1/1 (priority date). Applications are processed on a rolling basis. *Application fee:* $55. Electronic applications accepted.
Expenses: Tuition: Full-time $27,390.
Financial support: In 2001–02, 5 research assistantships, 31 teaching assistantships were awarded. Fellowships, Federal Work-Study, institutionally sponsored loans, and tuition waivers (full and partial) also available. Financial award application deadline: 4/15; financial award applicants required to submit FAFSA.
Faculty research: General economic theory, econometrics and mathematical economics, trade and development, game theory, urban economics. *Total annual research expenditures:* $310,664.
Dr. Louis Maccini, Chair, 410-516-7607, *Fax:* 410-516-7600.
Application contact: Julia Ross, Admissions Secretary, 410-516-7601, *Fax:* 410-516-7600, *E-mail:* econ@jhu.edu. *Web site:* http://www.econ.jhu.edu/

■ KANSAS STATE UNIVERSITY

Graduate School, College of Arts and Sciences, Department of Economics, Manhattan, KS 66506

AWARDS MA, PhD. Part-time programs available.

Faculty: 14 full-time (1 woman).
Students: 45 full-time (11 women); includes 3 minority (1 African American, 2 Hispanic Americans), 31 international. 21 applicants, 100% accepted, 8 enrolled. In 2001, 6 master's, 7 doctorates awarded. Terminal master's awarded for partial completion of doctoral program.
Degree requirements: For master's, thesis optional; for doctorate, thesis/dissertation, comprehensive exam.
Entrance requirements: For master's, minimum GPA of 3.0; previous course work in microeconomics, macroeconomics, calculus and statistics; for doctorate, previous course work in microeconomics, macroeconomics, and calculus. *Application deadline:* For fall admission, 2/1 (priority date); for spring admission, 10/1. Applications are processed on a rolling basis. *Application fee:* $0 ($25 for international students). Electronic applications accepted.
Expenses: Tuition, state resident: part-time $113 per credit hour. Tuition, nonresident: part-time $358 per credit hour.
Financial support: In 2001–02, 4 research assistantships (averaging $9,000 per year), 21 teaching assistantships (averaging $9,000 per year) were awarded. Fellowships, career-related internships or fieldwork, institutionally sponsored loans, and scholarships/grants also available. Support available to part-time students. Financial award application deadline: 3/1; financial award applicants required to submit FAFSA.
Faculty research: Labor economics, money, industrial organization, international development, econometrics. *Total annual research expenditures:* $51,622.
Dr. James Ragan, Head, 785-532-7357, *Fax:* 785-532-6919, *E-mail:* jfrjr@ksu.edu.
Application contact: Dr. Yang-Ming Chang, Information Contact, 785-532-4573, *Fax:* 785-532-6919, *E-mail:* ymchang@ksu.edu. *Web site:* http://www.ksu.edu/economics/

■ KENT STATE UNIVERSITY

Graduate School of Management, Master's Program in Economics, Kent, OH 44242-0001

AWARDS MA. Part-time programs available.

Faculty: 10 full-time (4 women).
Students: 10 full-time (7 women), 9 international. Average age 25. 25 applicants, 16% accepted. In 2001, 7 degrees awarded.
Entrance requirements: For master's, GMAT or GRE General Test, minimum GPA of 2.75. *Application deadline:* For fall admission, 4/1 (priority date); for spring admission, 12/15. Applications are processed on a rolling basis. *Application fee:* $30. Electronic applications accepted.
Financial support: In 2001–02, 10 students received support, including 10 research assistantships with full tuition reimbursements available (averaging $4,875 per year); Federal Work-Study also available. Financial award application deadline: 4/1; financial award applicants required to submit FAFSA.
Faculty research: Macro- and microeconomic theory, labor economics, international economics, quantitative methods.
Dr. Richard J. Kent, Chair, 330-672-2366, *Fax:* 330-672-9808, *E-mail:* rkent@bsa3.kent.edu.
Application contact: Louise M. Ditchey, Director, 330-672-2282, *Fax:* 330-672-7303, *E-mail:* gradbus@bsa3.kent.edu.

■ LEHIGH UNIVERSITY

College of Business and Economics, Department of Economics, Bethlehem, PA 18015-3094

AWARDS MS, PhD. Part-time and evening/weekend programs available.

Faculty: 15 full-time (3 women).
Students: 24 full-time (9 women), 2 part-time (1 woman); includes 16 minority (15 African Americans, 1 Asian American or Pacific Islander), 10 international. Average age 29. 33 applicants, 79% accepted, 12 enrolled. In 2001, 6 master's, 2 doctorates awarded. Terminal master's awarded for partial completion of doctoral program.
Degree requirements: For master's, thesis optional; for doctorate, thesis/dissertation, proposal defense, comprehensive exam.
Entrance requirements: For master's and doctorate, GMAT or GRE, TOEFL. *Application deadline:* For fall admission, 7/15; for spring admission, 12/1. Applications are processed on a rolling basis. *Application fee:* $50. Electronic applications accepted.
Expenses: Tuition: Part-time $468 per credit hour. Required fees: $200; $100 per semester. Tuition and fees vary according to program.
Financial support: In 2001–02, 2 fellowships with tuition reimbursements, 1 research assistantship with tuition reimbursement, 11 teaching assistantships with tuition reimbursements were awarded. Tuition waivers (full and partial) also available. Financial award application deadline: 1/15.
Faculty research: Public finance, investments, applied econometrics, labor economics.
Dr. Thomas J. Hyclak, Chairperson, 610-758-3425, *Fax:* 610-758-6549, *E-mail:* tjh7@lehigh.edu.
Application contact: Dr. James Dearden, Chair, Doctoral Committee, 610-758-5129, *Fax:* 610-758-6549, *E-mail:* jad8@

lehigh.edu. *Web site:* http://www.lehigh.edu/~incbe/incbe.html

■ LONG ISLAND UNIVERSITY, BROOKLYN CAMPUS

Richard L. Conolly College of Liberal Arts and Sciences, Department of Economics, Brooklyn, NY 11201-8423

AWARDS MA. Part-time and evening/weekend programs available.

Degree requirements: For master's, thesis or alternative.
Electronic applications accepted.

■ LOUISIANA STATE UNIVERSITY AND AGRICULTURAL AND MECHANICAL COLLEGE

Graduate School, E.J. Ourso College of Business Administration, Department of Economics, Baton Rouge, LA 70803

AWARDS MS, PhD.

Faculty: 13 full-time (1 woman).
Students: 20 full-time (7 women), 6 part-time (3 women), 16 international. Average age 31. 85 applicants, 19% accepted, 9 enrolled. In 2001, 2 degrees awarded. Terminal master's awarded for partial completion of doctoral program.
Degree requirements: For doctorate, thesis/dissertation.
Entrance requirements: For master's and doctorate, GRE General Test, minimum GPA of 3.0. *Application deadline:* For fall admission, 1/25 (priority date). Applications are processed on a rolling basis. *Application fee:* $25.
Expenses: Tuition, state resident: full-time $2,551. Tuition, nonresident: full-time $5,551. Required fees: $854. Part-time tuition and fees vary according to course load.
Financial support: In 2001–02, 11 research assistantships with partial tuition reimbursements (averaging $12,521 per year), 5 teaching assistantships with partial tuition reimbursements (averaging $11,850 per year) were awarded. Fellowships, Federal Work-Study and unspecified assistantships also available. Financial award application deadline: 6/15; financial award applicants required to submit FAFSA.
Faculty research: Natural resource economics and the environment, monetary theory, labor economics, microeconomic theory, international trade. *Total annual research expenditures:* $151,207.
Dr. R. Carter Hill, Chair, 225-578-3799, *Fax:* 225-578-3807, *E-mail:* eohill@lsu.edu.
Application contact: Dr. Robert Newman, Graduate Director, 225-578-5211, *Fax:* 225-578-3807, *E-mail:* eonewm@lsu.edu. *Web site:* http://www.bus.lsu.edu/economics/

■ LOUISIANA TECH UNIVERSITY

Graduate School, College of Administration and Business, Department of Finance and Economics, Ruston, LA 71272

AWARDS Business economics (MBA, DBA); finance (MBA, DBA). Part-time programs available.

Degree requirements: For doctorate, thesis/dissertation.
Entrance requirements: For master's and doctorate, GMAT.

■ LOYOLA COLLEGE IN MARYLAND

Graduate Programs, The Joseph A. Sellinger S.J. School of Business and Management, Programs in Business Administration, Baltimore, MD 21210-2699

AWARDS Decision sciences (MBA); economics (MBA); finance (MBA); international business (MIB); marketing/management (MBA). Part-time and evening/weekend programs available.

Students: 77 full-time (22 women), 669 part-time (260 women). In 2001, 269 degrees awarded.
Entrance requirements: For master's, GMAT, TOEFL. *Application deadline:* For fall admission, 8/20 (priority date); for spring admission, 11/20 (priority date). *Application fee:* $50.
Expenses: Tuition: Part-time $244 per unit. Tuition and fees vary according to degree level, program and student level.
Financial support: Applicants required to submit FAFSA.
John White, Director, 410-617-2308, *E-mail:* jwhite@loyola.edu.

■ MARQUETTE UNIVERSITY

Graduate School, College of Business Administration, Department of Economics, Milwaukee, WI 53201-1881

AWARDS Business economics (MSAE); financial economics (MSAE); international economics (MSAE); public policy economics (MSAE). Part-time and evening/weekend programs available.

Faculty: 14 full-time (1 woman), 1 part-time/adjunct (0 women).
Students: 17 full-time (7 women), 11 part-time (2 women); includes 1 minority (African American), 8 international. Average age 25. 35 applicants, 46% accepted. In 2001, 4 degrees awarded.
Degree requirements: For master's, thesis or alternative, essay, comprehensive exam.
Entrance requirements: For master's, GMAT or GRE General Test, TOEFL. *Application fee:* $40.
Expenses: Tuition: Full-time $10,170; part-time $445 per credit hour. Tuition and fees vary according to course load.
Financial support: In 2001–02, 6 teaching assistantships were awarded; research assistantships, Federal Work-Study, institutionally sponsored loans, scholarships/grants, and tuition waivers (full and partial) also available. Support available to part-time students. Financial award application deadline: 2/15.
Faculty research: Monetary and fiscal policy in open economy, housing and regional migration, political economy of taxation and state/local government. *Total annual research expenditures:* $110,000.
Dr. Brian Brush, Chairman, 414-288-7377, *Fax:* 414-288-5757.

■ MASSACHUSETTS INSTITUTE OF TECHNOLOGY

School of Humanities, Arts and Social Sciences, Department of Economics, Cambridge, MA 02139-4307

AWARDS MA, PhD.

Faculty: 31 full-time (4 women).
Students: 132 full-time (43 women); includes 13 minority (2 African Americans, 11 Asian Americans or Pacific Islanders), 56 international. Average age 27. 586 applicants, 8% accepted. In 2001, 20 degrees awarded. Terminal master's awarded for partial completion of doctoral program.
Degree requirements: For master's and doctorate, thesis/dissertation.
Entrance requirements: For master's and doctorate, GRE General Test, TOEFL. *Application deadline:* For fall admission, 1/15. *Application fee:* $60.
Expenses: Tuition: Full-time $26,960. Full-time tuition and fees vary according to program.
Financial support: In 2001–02, 60 fellowships, 9 research assistantships, 31 teaching assistantships were awarded. Institutionally sponsored loans also available. Financial award application deadline: 1/15.
Olivier Blanchard, Head, 617-253-8891.
Application contact: Katherine Swan, Graduate Program Administrator, 617-253-8787, *Fax:* 617-253-1330. *Web site:* http://web.mit.edu/economics/www

■ MIAMI UNIVERSITY

Graduate School, Richard T. Farmer School of Business Administration, Department of Economics, Oxford, OH 45056

AWARDS MA. Part-time programs available.

Faculty: 12 full-time (1 woman), 4 part-time/adjunct (0 women).
Students: 16 full-time (7 women); includes 1 minority (African American), 3 international. 57 applicants, 88% accepted, 14 enrolled. In 2001, 6 degrees awarded.
Degree requirements: For master's, thesis or alternative, final exam.
Entrance requirements: For master's, GMAT, minimum undergraduate GPA of 3.0 during previous 2 years or 2.75 overall.

Miami University (continued)
Application deadline: For fall admission, 3/1 (priority date). Applications are processed on a rolling basis. *Application fee:* $35.
Expenses: Tuition, state resident: full-time $7,155; part-time $295 per semester hour. Tuition, nonresident: full-time $14,829; part-time $615 per semester hour. Tuition and fees vary according to degree level and campus/location.
Financial support: In 2001–02, 10 fellowships (averaging $4,391 per year) were awarded; research assistantships, teaching assistantships, Federal Work-Study and tuition waivers (full) also available. Financial award application deadline: 3/1.
Dr. Prosper Raynold, Director of Graduate Studies, 513-529-2836, *Fax:* 513-529-6992, *E-mail:* miamieco@muohio.edu. *Web site:* http://www.sba.muohio.edu/home/GraduatePages/GraduateMAECON.htm

■ MICHIGAN STATE UNIVERSITY

Graduate School, College of Social Science, Department of Economics, East Lansing, MI 48824

AWARDS MA, PhD.

Faculty: 36.
Students: 75 full-time (25 women), 31 part-time (6 women); includes 6 minority (1 African American, 2 Asian Americans or Pacific Islanders, 3 Hispanic Americans), 85 international. Average age 30. 368 applicants, 20% accepted. In 2001, 12 master's, 12 doctorates awarded.
Degree requirements: For doctorate, thesis/dissertation.
Entrance requirements: For master's, GRE General Test; for doctorate, GRE General Test, minimum GPA of 3.4. *Application deadline:* For fall admission, 2/1. Applications are processed on a rolling basis. *Application fee:* $30 ($40 for international students).
Expenses: Tuition, state resident: part-time $244 per credit hour. Tuition, nonresident: part-time $494 per credit hour. Required fees: $268 per semester. Tuition and fees vary according to course load, degree level and program.
Financial support: In 2001–02, 29 fellowships (averaging $2,813 per year), 3 research assistantships with tuition reimbursements (averaging $13,731 per year), 31 teaching assistantships with tuition reimbursements (averaging $11,173 per year) were awarded. Financial award applicants required to submit FAFSA.
Faculty research: Applied and theoretical economics. *Total annual research expenditures:* $311,236.
Dr. Rowena Pecchenino, Chairperson, 517-355-7583, *Fax:* 517-432-1068. *Web site:* http://www.msu.edu/nec/

■ MIDDLE TENNESSEE STATE UNIVERSITY

College of Graduate Studies, College of Business, Department of Economics and Finance, Murfreesboro, TN 37132

AWARDS Economics (MA, DA); industrial relations (MA).

Faculty: 19 full-time (2 women).
Students: 8 full-time (1 woman), 36 part-time (15 women); includes 24 minority (8 African Americans, 14 Asian Americans or Pacific Islanders, 1 Hispanic American, 1 Native American). Average age 31. 17 applicants, 100% accepted. In 2001, 4 master's, 1 doctorate awarded.
Degree requirements: For master's, thesis optional; for doctorate, thesis/dissertation, comprehensive exam.
Entrance requirements: For master's and doctorate, GRE or MAT. *Application deadline:* For fall admission, 8/1 (priority date). Applications are processed on a rolling basis. *Application fee:* $25. Electronic applications accepted.
Expenses: Tuition, state resident: full-time $1,716; part-time $191 per hour. Tuition, nonresident: full-time $4,952; part-time $461 per hour. Required fees: $14 per hour. $58 per semester.
Financial support: In 2001–02, 12 teaching assistantships were awarded; institutionally sponsored loans also available. Support available to part-time students. Financial award application deadline: 5/1; financial award applicants required to submit FAFSA. *Total annual research expenditures:* $7,558.
Dr. John Lee, Chair, 615-898-2520, *Fax:* 615-898-5596, *E-mail:* jlee@mtsu.edu.

■ MISSISSIPPI STATE UNIVERSITY

College of Business and Industry, Department of Finance and Economics, Mississippi State, MS 39762

AWARDS Applied economics (PhD); economics (MA); finance (MSBA). Part-time programs available.

Faculty: 18 full-time (2 women).
Students: 318 full-time (81 women), 22 part-time (9 women); includes 53 minority (51 African Americans, 1 Hispanic American, 1 Native American). 40 applicants, 75% accepted, 10 enrolled. In 2001, 9 master's awarded. Terminal master's awarded for partial completion of doctoral program.
Degree requirements: For master's, thesis optional; for doctorate, thesis/dissertation, comprehensive exam, registration. *Median time to degree:* Master's–1.5 years full-time; doctorate–5 years full-time.
Entrance requirements: For master's and doctorate, GMAT, GRE. *Application deadline:* For fall admission, 7/1; for spring admission, 11/1. Applications are processed on a rolling basis. *Application fee:* $25 for international students.
Expenses: Tuition, state resident: full-time $3,586; part-time $150 per credit hour. Tuition, nonresident: full-time $8,128; part-time $339 per credit hour. Tuition and fees vary according to course load and campus/location.
Financial support: In 2001–02, 6 research assistantships with tuition reimbursements (averaging $8,500 per year), 6 teaching assistantships with tuition reimbursements (averaging $10,200 per year) were awarded. Federal Work-Study, scholarships/grants, health care benefits, and unspecified assistantships also available. Financial award applicants required to submit FAFSA.
Faculty research: Economics development, mergers, event studies, economic education, bank performance, risk management.
Dr. Paul W. Grimes, Head, 662-325-2341, *Fax:* 662-325-1977, *E-mail:* pwg1@ra.msstate.edu.
Application contact: Jerry B. Inmon, Director of Admissions, 662-325-2224, *Fax:* 662-325-7360, *E-mail:* admit@admissions.msstate.edu. *Web site:* http://www.msstate.edu/dept/finecon

■ MONTCLAIR STATE UNIVERSITY

The School of Graduate, Professional and Continuing Education, College of Humanities and Social Sciences, Programs in Social Science, Program in Economics, Upper Montclair, NJ 07043-1624

AWARDS MA.

Degree requirements: For master's, comprehensive exam.
Entrance requirements: For master's, GRE General Test. Electronic applications accepted.

■ MONTCLAIR STATE UNIVERSITY

The School of Graduate, Professional and Continuing Education, School of Business, Department of Economics and Finance, Upper Montclair, NJ 07043-1624

AWARDS Economics (MA); social science (MA). Part-time and evening/weekend programs available.

Degree requirements: For master's, comprehensive exam.
Entrance requirements: For master's, GRE General Test. Electronic applications accepted.

■ MONTCLAIR STATE UNIVERSITY

The School of Graduate, Professional and Continuing Education, School of Business, Program in Business Administration, Concentration in Business Economics, Upper Montclair, NJ 07043-1624

AWARDS MBA. Part-time and evening/weekend programs available.

Entrance requirements: For master's, GMAT. Electronic applications accepted.

■ MORGAN STATE UNIVERSITY

School of Graduate Studies, College of Liberal Arts, Department of Economics, Baltimore, MD 21251

AWARDS MA.

Students: 6 (2 women); includes 2 minority (both African Americans) 4 international.
Degree requirements: For master's, comprehensive exam.
Entrance requirements: For master's, GRE. *Application deadline:* For fall admission, 2/1; for spring admission, 10/1. Applications are processed on a rolling basis. *Application fee:* $0.
Expenses: Tuition, state resident: part-time $193 per credit. Tuition, nonresident: part-time $364 per credit. Required fees: $40 per credit.
Financial support: Application deadline: 4/1.
Dr. Tekie Fessehatzion, Chair, 443-885-3662, *E-mail:* tfessehatzion@moac.morgan.edu.
Application contact: Dr. James E. Waller, Admissions and Programs Officer, 443-885-3185, *Fax:* 443-319-3837, *E-mail:* jwaller@moac.morgan.edu.

■ MURRAY STATE UNIVERSITY

College of Business and Public Affairs, Department of Economics, Murray, KY 42071-0009

AWARDS MS. Part-time programs available.

Students: 15 full-time (6 women), 2 part-time, 14 international. 6 applicants, 100% accepted. In 2001, 2 degrees awarded.
Entrance requirements: For master's, GRE General Test or GMAT, TOEFL. *Application deadline:* Applications are processed on a rolling basis. *Application fee:* $25.
Expenses: Tuition, state resident: full-time $1,440; part-time $169 per hour. Tuition, nonresident: full-time $4,004; part-time $450 per hour.
Financial support: Research assistantships, teaching assistantships available. Financial award application deadline: 4/1.
Mary Tripp Reed, Graduate Coordinator, 270-762-3932, *Fax:* 270-762-5478, *E-mail:* marytripp.reed@murraystate.edu.

■ NEW MEXICO STATE UNIVERSITY

Graduate School, College of Agriculture and Home Economics, Department of Agricultural Economics and Agricultural Business, Las Cruces, NM 88003-8001

AWARDS Agricultural economics (MS); economics (MA). Part-time programs available.

Faculty: 11 full-time (3 women).
Students: 11 full-time (4 women), 6 part-time (3 women); includes 3 minority (1 Asian American or Pacific Islander, 2 Hispanic Americans), 4 international. Average age 29. 9 applicants, 100% accepted, 5 enrolled. In 2001, 2 degrees awarded.
Degree requirements: For master's, thesis (for some programs).
Entrance requirements: For master's, previous course work in intermediate microeconomics, intermediate macroeconomics, college-level calculus, statistics. *Application deadline:* For fall admission, 7/1 (priority date); for spring admission, 11/1 (priority date). Applications are processed on a rolling basis. *Application fee:* $15 ($35 for international students). Electronic applications accepted.
Expenses: Tuition, state resident: full-time $3,234; part-time $135 per credit. Tuition, nonresident: full-time $9,420; part-time $428 per credit. Required fees: $858.
Financial support: In 2001–02, 7 research assistantships, 6 teaching assistantships were awarded. Career-related internships or fieldwork also available. Financial award application deadline: 3/1.
Faculty research: Natural resource policy, rural development policy and issues, agribusiness and marketing, international marketing and trade, agricultural risk management.
Dr. Lowell Catlett, Interim Head, 505-646-3215, *Fax:* 505-646-3808, *E-mail:* lcatlett@nmsu.edu.
Application contact: Dr. James D. Libbon, Professor, 505-646-2915, *Fax:* 505-646-3808, *E-mail:* jlibbin@nmsu.edu. *Web site:* http://www.nmsu.edu/~agecon/

■ NEW MEXICO STATE UNIVERSITY

Graduate School, College of Business Administration and Economics, Department of Economics and International Business, Las Cruces, NM 88003-8001

AWARDS Economics (MA, MBA, MS); experimental statistics (MS). Part-time programs available.

Faculty: 20 full-time (4 women), 3 part-time/adjunct (1 woman).
Students: 21 full-time (12 women), 5 part-time (3 women); includes 3 minority (all Hispanic Americans), 11 international. Average age 29. 9 applicants, 89% accepted, 5 enrolled. In 2001, 10 degrees awarded.
Degree requirements: For master's, thesis or alternative.
Entrance requirements: For master's, GMAT, TOEFL, minimum GPA of 3.0. *Application deadline:* For fall admission, 7/1 (priority date); for spring admission, 11/1. Applications are processed on a rolling basis. *Application fee:* $15 ($35 for international students). Electronic applications accepted.
Expenses: Tuition, state resident: full-time $3,234; part-time $135 per credit. Tuition, nonresident: full-time $9,420; part-time $428 per credit. Required fees: $858.
Financial support: In 2001–02, 3 research assistantships, 11 teaching assistantships were awarded. Career-related internships or fieldwork and Federal Work-Study also available. Support available to part-time students. Financial award application deadline: 3/1.
Faculty research: Public utilities, environment, border demographics, linear models, biological sampling.
Dr. Michael Ellis, Head, 505-646-2113, *Fax:* 505-646-1915, *E-mail:* mellis@nmsu.edu.
Application contact: Dr. Anthony Popp, Graduate Adviser, 505-646-5198, *Fax:* 505-646-1915, *E-mail:* apopp@nmsu.edu. *Web site:* http://cbae.nmsu.edu/Departments/Economics/economics.html

■ NEW SCHOOL UNIVERSITY

Graduate Faculty of Political and Social Science, Department of Economics, New York, NY 10011-8603

AWARDS MA, DS Sc, PhD. Part-time and evening/weekend programs available.

Students: 96 full-time (25 women), 16 part-time (1 woman); includes 19 minority (7 African Americans, 5 Asian Americans or Pacific Islanders, 7 Hispanic Americans), 59 international. Average age 38. 129 applicants, 84% accepted. In 2001, 8 master's, 5 doctorates awarded. Terminal master's awarded for partial completion of doctoral program.
Degree requirements: For master's, exam; for doctorate, one foreign language, thesis/dissertation, qualifying exam.
Entrance requirements: For master's, GRE General Test; for doctorate, GRE General Test, MA. *Application deadline:* For fall admission, 1/15 (priority date). Applications are processed on a rolling basis. *Application fee:* $40.
Expenses: Tuition: Full-time $18,720; part-time $1,040 per credit. Required fees: $450; $115 per term. Tuition and fees vary according to program.
Financial support: In 2001–02, 46 students received support, including 9 fellowships with full and partial tuition reimbursements available (averaging $3,200 per year), 15 research assistantships

New School University (continued)
with full and partial tuition reimbursements available (averaging $7,500 per year), 12 teaching assistantships with full and partial tuition reimbursements available (averaging $2,700 per year); career-related internships or fieldwork, Federal Work-Study, scholarships/grants, and tuition waivers (full and partial) also available. Financial award application deadline: 1/15; financial award applicants required to submit FAFSA.
Faculty research: Heterodox, institutionalist, history of economic thought, post-Keynesian, global political economy and finance.
Dr. Duncan Foley, Chair, 212-229-5717.
Application contact: Emanuel Lomax, Director of Admissions, 800-523-5411, *Fax:* 212-989-7102, *E-mail:* gfadmit@newschool.edu. *Web site:* http://www.newschool.edu/

Find an in-depth description at www.petersons.com/gradchannel.

■ NEW YORK UNIVERSITY

Graduate School of Arts and Science, Department of Economics, New York, NY 10012-1019

AWARDS Applied economic analysis (Advanced Certificate); economics (MA, PhD). Part-time and evening/weekend programs available.

Faculty: 35 full-time (2 women), 29 part-time/adjunct.
Students: 205 full-time (72 women), 78 part-time (30 women); includes 26 minority (2 African Americans, 18 Asian Americans or Pacific Islanders, 6 Hispanic Americans), 196 international. Average age 26. 895 applicants, 23% accepted, 81 enrolled. In 2001, 56 master's, 21 doctorates awarded. Terminal master's awarded for partial completion of doctoral program.
Degree requirements: For master's, thesis; for doctorate, one foreign language, thesis/dissertation, 4 qualifying exams.
Entrance requirements: For master's and doctorate, GRE General Test, TOEFL; for Advanced Certificate, master's degree. *Application deadline:* For fall admission, 1/4 (priority date). *Application fee:* $60.
Expenses: Tuition: Full-time $19,536; part-time $814 per credit. Required fees: $1,330; $38 per credit. Tuition and fees vary according to course load and program.
Financial support: Fellowships with tuition reimbursements, research assistantships with tuition reimbursements, teaching assistantships with tuition reimbursements, Federal Work-Study and institutionally sponsored loans available. Financial award application deadline: 1/4; financial award applicants required to submit FAFSA.
Faculty research: Economic theory, experimental economics, growth and development, macroeconomics and finance, international trade and international finance.
Douglas Gale, Chair, 212-998-8900.
Application contact: Debraj Ray, Director of Graduate Studies, 212-998-8900, *Fax:* 212-995-4186, *E-mail:* gsas.admissions@nyu.edu. *Web site:* http://www.econ.nyu.edu/

■ NEW YORK UNIVERSITY

Leonard N. Stern School of Business, Economics Department, New York, NY 10012-1019

AWARDS MBA, PhD, APC.

Degree requirements: For doctorate, thesis/dissertation.
Entrance requirements: For master's, GMAT, TOEFL; for doctorate, GMAT. Electronic applications accepted.
Expenses: Tuition: Full-time $19,536; part-time $814 per credit. Required fees: $1,330; $38 per credit. Tuition and fees vary according to course load and program.
Faculty research: Macroeconomics and macroeconomic policy, applied microeconomics and regulatory policy, international financial markets, international trade and business, monetary economics and monetary policy.

■ NORTH CAROLINA STATE UNIVERSITY

Graduate School, College of Management, Program in Economics, Raleigh, NC 27695

AWARDS M Econ, MA, PhD. Part-time programs available.

Faculty: 54 full-time (2 women).
Students: 95 full-time (34 women), 29 part-time (6 women); includes 10 minority (3 African Americans, 4 Asian Americans or Pacific Islanders, 3 Hispanic Americans), 62 international. Average age 31. 201 applicants, 33% accepted. In 2001, 12 master's, 7 doctorates awarded. Terminal master's awarded for partial completion of doctoral program.
Degree requirements: For master's, thesis (for some programs); for doctorate, thesis/dissertation.
Entrance requirements: For master's and doctorate, GRE General Test (recommended), TOEFL. *Application deadline:* For fall admission, 4/1 (priority date); for spring admission, 9/15. Applications are processed on a rolling basis. *Application fee:* $45.
Expenses: Tuition, state resident: full-time $1,748. Tuition, nonresident: full-time $6,904.
Financial support: In 2001–02, 3 fellowships (averaging $7,621 per year), 22 research assistantships (averaging $5,356 per year), 31 teaching assistantships (averaging $5,301 per year) were awarded. Financial award application deadline: 3/10.
Faculty research: Endogenous growth modeling, generalized methods of moments estimation, integration and trade, agricultural policy, path dependence and network externalities.
Dr. Stephen E. Margolis, Head, 919-515-3274, *Fax:* 919-515-7873, *E-mail:* steve_margolis@ncsu.edu.
Application contact: Dr. James E. Easley, Director of Graduate Programs, 919-515-4617, *Fax:* 919-515-9367, *E-mail:* jim_easley@ncsu.edu. *Web site:* http://www.mgt.ncsu.edu/facdep/econ/econo.html

■ NORTHEASTERN UNIVERSITY

College of Arts and Sciences, Department of Economics, Boston, MA 02115-5096

AWARDS MA. Part-time and evening/weekend programs available.

Faculty: 14 full-time (2 women), 5 part-time/adjunct (1 woman).
Students: 25 full-time (7 women), 6 part-time (1 woman); includes 1 minority (Hispanic American), 20 international. Average age 29. In 2001, 17 master's awarded.
Degree requirements: For master's, comprehensive exam.
Entrance requirements: For master's, GRE, TOEFL. *Application deadline:* For fall admission, 7/31; for spring admission, 10/31. Applications are processed on a rolling basis. *Application fee:* $50.
Expenses: Tuition: Part-time $535 per credit hour. Required fees: $56. Tuition and fees vary according to program.
Financial support: In 2001–02, 4 teaching assistantships (averaging $13,550 per year) were awarded; Federal Work-Study, institutionally sponsored loans, tuition waivers (full and partial), and unspecified assistantships also available. Financial award application deadline: 3/15; financial award applicants required to submit FAFSA.
Faculty research: U.S. labor markets, political economy, growth theory, airline deregulation and macroeconomics of OECD. *Total annual research expenditures:* $200,000.
Dr. Steven Morrison, Chair, 617-373-2872, *Fax:* 617-373-3640, *E-mail:* econ@lynx.neu.edu.
Application contact: Dr. Daryl A. Hellman, Graduate Coordinator, 617-373-2871, *Fax:* 617-373-3640, *E-mail:* econ@lynx.neu.edu. *Web site:* http://www.dac.neu.edu/economics/

Find an in-depth description at www.petersons.com/gradchannel.

■ NORTHERN ILLINOIS UNIVERSITY

Graduate School, College of Liberal Arts and Sciences, Department of Economics, De Kalb, IL 60115-2854

AWARDS MA, PhD. Part-time programs available.

Faculty: 14 full-time (3 women).
Students: 26 full-time (10 women), 9 part-time (2 women); includes 3 minority (2 Asian Americans or Pacific Islanders, 1 Hispanic American), 24 international. Average age 33. 73 applicants, 92% accepted, 13 enrolled. In 2001, 8 master's, 4 doctorates awarded. Terminal master's awarded for partial completion of doctoral program.
Degree requirements: For master's, thesis or alternative, comprehensive exam; for doctorate, thesis/dissertation, candidacy exam, dissertation defense, research seminar.
Entrance requirements: For master's, GRE General Test, TOEFL, minimum GPA of 2.75; for doctorate, GRE General Test, TOEFL, minimum GPA of 2.75 (undergraduate), 3.2 (graduate). *Application deadline:* For fall admission, 6/1; for spring admission, 11/1. Applications are processed on a rolling basis. *Application fee:* $30.
Expenses: Tuition, state resident: full-time $5,124; part-time $148 per credit hour. Tuition, nonresident: full-time $8,666; part-time $295 per credit hour. Required fees: $51 per term.
Financial support: In 2001–02, 10 research assistantships with full tuition reimbursements, 13 teaching assistantships with full tuition reimbursements were awarded. Fellowships with full tuition reimbursements, career-related internships or fieldwork, Federal Work-Study, tuition waivers (full), and unspecified assistantships also available. Support available to part-time students.
Dr. Eliakim Katz, Chair, 815-753-6970, *Fax:* 815-753-6302.
Application contact: Dr. George Slotsve, Director, Graduate Studies, 815-753-6966.

■ NORTHWESTERN UNIVERSITY

The Graduate School, Judd A. and Marjorie Weinberg College of Arts and Sciences, Department of Economics, Evanston, IL 60208

AWARDS MA, PhD, JD/PhD. Admissions and degrees offered through The Graduate School.

Faculty: 33 full-time (3 women), 3 part-time/adjunct (1 woman).
Students: 98 full-time. 524 applicants, 17% accepted. In 2001, 17 master's, 21 doctorates awarded. Terminal master's awarded for partial completion of doctoral program.
Degree requirements: For doctorate, thesis/dissertation, preliminary written exam. *Median time to degree:* Master's–1 year full-time; doctorate–5 years full-time.
Entrance requirements: For doctorate, GRE General Test, TOEFL. *Application deadline:* For fall admission, 8/30. *Application fee:* $50 ($55 for international students).
Expenses: Tuition: Full-time $26,526.
Financial support: In 2001–02, 73 students received support, including 12 fellowships with full tuition reimbursements available (averaging $11,700 per year), 18 research assistantships with partial tuition reimbursements available (averaging $12,465 per year), 38 teaching assistantships with full tuition reimbursements available (averaging $12,465 per year); career-related internships or fieldwork, Federal Work-Study, institutionally sponsored loans, and tuition waivers (full and partial) also available. Financial award application deadline: 12/31; financial award applicants required to submit FAFSA.
Faculty research: Organization of industry, behavior of labor markets, effects of monetary policy, theory of markets. *Total annual research expenditures:* $68,670.
Martin Eichenbaum, Chair, 847-491-8232, *Fax:* 847-491-7001, *E-mail:* eich@northwestern.edu.
Application contact: Mercedes Thomas, Secretary, 847-491-5694, *Fax:* 847-491-7001, *E-mail:* m-thomas@northwestern.edu. *Web site:* http://www.econ.northwestern.edu/

■ NORTHWESTERN UNIVERSITY

The Graduate School, Kellogg School of Management, Program in Managerial Economics and Strategy, Evanston, IL 60208

AWARDS PhD. Admissions and degree offered through The Graduate School.

Faculty: 47 full-time (6 women).
Students: 23 full-time (3 women); includes 1 minority (Asian American or Pacific Islander), 17 international. Average age 27. 62 applicants, 21% accepted, 4 enrolled. In 2001, 1 degree awarded.
Degree requirements: For doctorate, thesis/dissertation, comprehensive exam, registration.
Entrance requirements: For doctorate, GMAT or GRE General Test, TOEFL. *Application deadline:* For fall admission, 12/31. *Application fee:* $60 ($75 for international students). Electronic applications accepted.
Expenses: Tuition: Full-time $26,526.
Financial support: In 2001–02, 17 students received support; fellowships with full tuition reimbursements available, research assistantships with full tuition reimbursements available, teaching assistantships with full tuition reimbursements available, career-related internships or fieldwork, institutionally sponsored loans, scholarships/grants, and health care benefits available. Financial award application deadline: 12/31; financial award applicants required to submit FAFSA.
Faculty research: Competitive strategy and organization, managerial economics, decision sciences, game theory, operations management.
Shane Greenstein, Co-Director, 847-491-3465, *Fax:* 847-467-1777, *E-mail:* kellogg-phd@northwestern.edu.
Application contact: Susan Jackman, Admission Contact, 847-491-2832, *Fax:* 847-467-6717, *E-mail:* s-jackman@northwestern.edu. *Web site:* http://www.kellogg.northwestern.edu/academic/deptprog/

■ THE OHIO STATE UNIVERSITY

Graduate School, College of Social and Behavioral Sciences, Department of Economics, Columbus, OH 43210

AWARDS MA, PhD.

Degree requirements: For doctorate, thesis/dissertation.
Entrance requirements: For master's and doctorate, GRE General Test.

■ OHIO UNIVERSITY

Graduate Studies, College of Arts and Sciences, Department of Economics, Athens, OH 45701-2979

AWARDS MA.

Faculty: 15 full-time (3 women).
Students: 28 full-time (8 women), 6 part-time; includes 1 minority (African American), 28 international. 69 applicants, 87% accepted, 11 enrolled. In 2001, 7 degrees awarded.
Degree requirements: For master's, thesis or alternative.
Application fee: $30.
Expenses: Tuition, state resident: full-time $6,585. Tuition, nonresident: full-time $12,254.
Financial support: In 2001–02, 15 research assistantships were awarded; Federal Work-Study and institutionally sponsored loans also available. Financial award application deadline: 3/15.
Dr. Jan Palmer, Chair, 740-593-2040.
Application contact: Dr. K. Doroodian, Graduate Chair, 740-593-2046.

■ OKLAHOMA STATE UNIVERSITY

Graduate College, College of Business Administration, Department of Economics and Legal Studies in Business, Stillwater, OK 74078

AWARDS MS, PhD.

Faculty: 19 full-time (1 woman), 1 part-time/adjunct (0 women).
Students: 29 full-time (9 women), 19 part-time (4 women); includes 3 minority (1 African American, 1 Asian American or Pacific Islander, 1 Native American), 23 international. Average age 32. 52 applicants, 60% accepted. In 2001, 4 master's, 11 doctorates awarded.
Degree requirements: For doctorate, thesis/dissertation.
Entrance requirements: For master's and doctorate, GRE General Test, TOEFL. *Application deadline:* For fall admission, 7/1 (priority date). *Application fee:* $25.
Expenses: Tuition, state resident: part-time $92 per credit hour. Tuition,

Oklahoma State University (continued)
nonresident: part-time $297 per credit hour. Required fees: $21 per credit hour. $14 per semester. One-time fee: $20. Tuition and fees vary according to course load.
Financial support: In 2001–02, 11 research assistantships (averaging $10,580 per year), 19 teaching assistantships (averaging $5,823 per year) were awarded. Career-related internships or fieldwork, Federal Work-Study, and tuition waivers (partial) also available. Support available to part-time students. Financial award application deadline: 3/1.
Faculty research: Economics and legal studies in business regional economic modeling/econometrics, urban/regional economics, monetary economics, international trade/finance/development, environmental economics.
Dr. Keith Willett, Head, 405-744-5195, *E-mail:* kwillet@okstate.edu.

■ OLD DOMINION UNIVERSITY

College of Business and Public Administration, Program in Economics, Norfolk, VA 23529

AWARDS MA. Part-time and evening/weekend programs available.

Faculty: 12 full-time (3 women).
Students: 18 full-time (5 women), 11 part-time (7 women); includes 4 minority (3 African Americans, 1 Asian American or Pacific Islander), 20 international. Average age 27. 47 applicants, 91% accepted. In 2001, 7 degrees awarded.
Degree requirements: For master's, thesis optional.
Entrance requirements: For master's, GMAT or GRE General Test, minimum GPA of 2.5. *Application deadline:* For fall admission, 7/1; for spring admission, 10/1. Applications are processed on a rolling basis. *Application fee:* $30. Electronic applications accepted.
Expenses: Tuition, state resident: part-time $202 per credit. Tuition, nonresident: part-time $534 per credit. Required fees: $76 per semester.
Financial support: In 2001–02, 9 students received support, including 1 fellowship with tuition reimbursement available (averaging $8,914 per year), 3 research assistantships with tuition reimbursements available (averaging $4,625 per year); teaching assistantships, career-related internships or fieldwork, scholarships/grants, and tuition waivers (partial) also available. Support available to part-time students. Financial award application deadline: 2/15; financial award applicants required to submit FAFSA.
Faculty research: International economics, transportation, monetary economics, immigration, econometrics. *Total annual research expenditures:* $10,053.
Dr. Vinod Agarwal, Graduate Program Director, 757-683-3526, *Fax:* 757-638-5639, *E-mail:* econgpd@odu.edu. *Web site:* http://www.odu-cbpa.org/mecon.htm

■ OREGON STATE UNIVERSITY

Graduate School, College of Agricultural Sciences and College of Forestry, Department of Agricultural and Resource Economics, Corvallis, OR 97331

AWARDS Agricultural and resource economics (M Agr, MAIS, MS, PhD); economics (MS, PhD). MS and PhD (economics) offered through the University Graduate Faculty of Economics. Part-time programs available.

Faculty: 10 full-time (1 woman), 1 (woman) part-time/adjunct.
Students: 24 full-time (8 women), 2 part-time (1 woman), 13 international. Average age 29. In 2001, 3 degrees awarded. Terminal master's awarded for partial completion of doctoral program.
Degree requirements: For master's, thesis (for some programs); for doctorate, thesis/dissertation.
Entrance requirements: For master's and doctorate, GRE General Test, TOEFL, minimum GPA of 3.0 in last 90 hours. *Application deadline:* For fall admission, 3/1. Applications are processed on a rolling basis. *Application fee:* $50.
Expenses: Tuition, area resident: Full-time $15,933. Tuition, state resident: full-time $28,937.
Financial support: Fellowships, research assistantships, teaching assistantships, career-related internships or fieldwork, Federal Work-Study, and institutionally sponsored loans available. Support available to part-time students. Financial award application deadline: 2/1.
Faculty research: Marine economics, environmental economics, effects of global climate change on agriculture, efficiency of agricultural markets, analysis of aquaculture development.
Dr. William G. Boggess, Head, 541-737-1395, *Fax:* 541-737-1441, *E-mail:* bill.boggess@orst.edu.
Application contact: Kathy Carpenter, Administrative Assistant, 541-737-1398, *Fax:* 541-737-1441, *E-mail:* kathy.carpenter@orst.edu. *Web site:* http://www.orst.edu/Dept/ag_resrc_econ/

■ OREGON STATE UNIVERSITY

Graduate School, College of Forestry, Department of Forest Resources, Corvallis, OR 97331

AWARDS Economics (MS, PhD); forest resources (MAIS, MF, MS, PhD). MS and PhD (economics) offered through the University Graduate Faculty of Economics. Part-time programs available.

Faculty: 19 full-time (4 women).
Students: 31 full-time (14 women); includes 1 minority (Hispanic American), 6 international. Average age 30. In 2001, 9 master's, 2 doctorates awarded. Terminal master's awarded for partial completion of doctoral program.
Degree requirements: For master's, thesis (for some programs); for doctorate, thesis/dissertation.
Entrance requirements: For master's and doctorate, GRE General Test, TOEFL, minimum GPA of 3.0 in last 90 hours. *Application deadline:* For fall admission, 2/1 (priority date). Applications are processed on a rolling basis. *Application fee:* $50.
Expenses: Tuition, area resident: Full-time $15,933. Tuition, state resident: full-time $28,937.
Financial support: Fellowships, research assistantships, teaching assistantships, career-related internships or fieldwork, Federal Work-Study, and institutionally sponsored loans available. Support available to part-time students. Financial award application deadline: 2/1.
Faculty research: Geographic information systems, long-term productivity, recreation, silviculture, biometrics, policy.
Dr. John D. Walstad, Head, 541-737-3607, *Fax:* 541-737-3049, *E-mail:* john.walstad@orst.edu.
Application contact: Marty Roberts, Coordinator, 541-737-1485, *Fax:* 541-737-3049, *E-mail:* roberts@for.orst.edu. *Web site:* http://www.cof.orst.edu/cof/fr/

■ OREGON STATE UNIVERSITY

Graduate School, College of Liberal Arts, Department of Economics, Corvallis, OR 97331

AWARDS MA, MS, PhD. Part-time programs available.

Faculty: 10 full-time (3 women).
Students: 18 full-time (6 women), 2 part-time (both women), 19 international. Average age 29. In 2001, 5 master's, 1 doctorate awarded. Terminal master's awarded for partial completion of doctoral program.
Degree requirements: For master's, thesis or alternative; for doctorate, thesis/dissertation.
Entrance requirements: For master's and doctorate, GRE General Test, TOEFL, minimum GPA of 3.0 in last 90 hours. *Application deadline:* For fall admission, 3/1 (priority date). Applications are processed on a rolling basis. *Application fee:* $50.
Expenses: Tuition, area resident: Full-time $15,933. Tuition, state resident: full-time $28,937.
Financial support: Research assistantships, teaching assistantships, career-related internships or fieldwork, Federal Work-Study, and institutionally sponsored loans available. Support available to part-time students. Financial award application deadline: 3/1.
Faculty research: Applied microeconomics, applied econometrics.

Dr. Victor J. Tremblay, Chair, 541-737-1471, *Fax:* 541-737-5917, *E-mail:* v.tremblay@orst.edu.
Application contact: B. Starr McMullen, Graduate Director, 541-737-1480, *Fax:* 541-737-5917, *E-mail:* mcmullen@orst.edu.

■ PACE UNIVERSITY

Lubin School of Business, Program in Business Economics, New York, NY 10038

AWARDS Corporate economic planning (MBA); economics (MS); financial economics (MBA); international economics (MBA). Part-time and evening/weekend programs available.

Faculty: 17 full-time, 9 part-time/adjunct.
Students: 14 full-time (9 women), 21 part-time (8 women); includes 5 minority (3 African Americans, 1 Asian American or Pacific Islander, 1 Hispanic American), 4 international. Average age 30. In 2001, 9 degrees awarded.
Entrance requirements: For master's, GMAT. *Application deadline:* For fall admission, 7/31 (priority date); for spring admission, 11/30. Applications are processed on a rolling basis. *Application fee:* $65. Electronic applications accepted.
Expenses: Tuition: Part-time $545 per credit.
Financial support: Research assistantships, career-related internships or fieldwork and Federal Work-Study available. Support available to part-time students. Financial award applicants required to submit FAFSA.
Dr. Richard Lynn, Chairperson, 212-346-1817.
Application contact: Joanna Broda, Director of Admissions, 212-346-1652, *Fax:* 212-346-1585, *E-mail:* gradnyc@pace.edu. *Web site:* http://www.pace.edu/

■ PACE UNIVERSITY, WHITE PLAINS CAMPUS

Lubin School of Business, Program in Business Economics, White Plains, NY 10603

AWARDS Corporate economic planning (MBA); economics (MS); financial economics (MBA); international economics (MBA). Part-time and evening/weekend programs available.

Faculty: 5 full-time, 3 part-time/adjunct.
Entrance requirements: For master's, GMAT. *Application deadline:* For fall admission, 8/1 (priority date); for spring admission, 12/1 (priority date). Applications are processed on a rolling basis. *Application fee:* $65. Electronic applications accepted.
Expenses: Tuition: Part-time $545 per credit.
Financial support: Research assistantships, career-related internships or fieldwork and Federal Work-Study available. Support available to part-time students. Financial award applicants required to submit FAFSA.
Dr. Edmond Mantell, Chairperson, 914-422-4165.
Application contact: Joanna Broda, Director of Admissions, 914-422-4283, *Fax:* 914-422-4287, *E-mail:* gradwp@pace.edu. *Web site:* http://www.pace.edu/

■ THE PENNSYLVANIA STATE UNIVERSITY UNIVERSITY PARK CAMPUS

Graduate School, College of Liberal Arts, Department of Economics, State College, University Park, PA 16802-1503

AWARDS MA, PhD.

Students: 58 full-time (17 women), 3 part-time. In 2001, 11 master's, 3 doctorates awarded.
Entrance requirements: For master's and doctorate, GRE General Test, TOEFL, minimum GPA of 3.0. *Application fee:* $45.
Expenses: Tuition, state resident: full-time $7,882; part-time $333 per credit. Tuition, nonresident: full-time $16,142; part-time $673 per credit. Required fees: $124 per semester.
Financial support: Application deadline: 2/15.
Dr. Robert C. Marshall, Head, 814-865-1458.
Application contact: Dr. N. Edward Coulson, Graduate Officer, 814-865-1458.

■ PORTLAND STATE UNIVERSITY

Graduate Studies, College of Engineering and Computer Science, Systems Science Program, Portland, OR 97207-0751

AWARDS Systems science/anthropology (PhD); systems science/business administration (PhD); systems science/civil engineering (PhD); systems science/economics (PhD); systems science/engineering management (PhD); systems science/general (PhD); systems science/mathematical sciences (PhD); systems science/mechanical engineering (PhD); systems science/psychology (PhD); systems science/sociology (PhD).

Faculty: 4 full-time (0 women).
Students: 47 full-time (19 women), 32 part-time (10 women); includes 9 minority (4 Asian Americans or Pacific Islanders, 3 Hispanic Americans, 2 Native Americans), 15 international. Average age 36. 52 applicants, 38% accepted. In 2001, 8 degrees awarded.
Degree requirements: For doctorate, variable foreign language requirement, thesis/dissertation.
Entrance requirements: For doctorate, GMAT, GRE General Test, TOEFL, minimum undergraduate GPA of 3.0. *Application deadline:* For fall admission, 2/1; for spring admission, 11/1. *Application fee:* $50.
Financial support: In 2001–02, 1 research assistantship with full tuition reimbursement (averaging $6,839 per year) was awarded; teaching assistantships with full tuition reimbursements, career-related internships or fieldwork, Federal Work-Study, and institutionally sponsored loans also available. Support available to part-time students. Financial award application deadline: 3/1; financial award applicants required to submit FAFSA.
Faculty research: Systems theory and methodology, artificial intelligence neural networks, information theory, nonlinear dynamics/chaos, modeling and simulation. *Total annual research expenditures:* $106,413.
Dr. Nancy Perrin, Director, 503-725-4960, *E-mail:* perrinn@pdx.edu.
Application contact: Dawn Kuenle, Coordinator, 503-725-4960, *E-mail:* dawn@sysc.pdx.edu. *Web site:* http://www.sysc.pdx.edu/

■ PORTLAND STATE UNIVERSITY

Graduate Studies, College of Liberal Arts and Sciences, Department of Economics, Portland, OR 97207-0751

AWARDS Applied economics (MA, MS); economics (PhD); general economics (MA, MS). Part-time programs available.

Faculty: 9 full-time (2 women), 6 part-time/adjunct (1 woman).
Students: 6 full-time (3 women), 7 part-time (5 women); includes 1 minority (Asian American or Pacific Islander), 7 international. Average age 31. 8 applicants, 88% accepted. In 2001, 9 degrees awarded.
Degree requirements: For master's, thesis optional; for doctorate, one foreign language, thesis/dissertation.
Entrance requirements: For master's, TOEFL, minimum GPA of 3.0 in upper-division course work or 2.75 overall, previous course work in calculus. *Application deadline:* For fall admission, 4/1; for spring admission, 11/1. Applications are processed on a rolling basis. *Application fee:* $50.
Financial support: In 2001–02, 1 research assistantship with full tuition reimbursement (averaging $2,434 per year) was awarded; teaching assistantships, career-related internships or fieldwork, Federal Work-Study, and institutionally sponsored loans also available. Support available to part-time students. Financial award application deadline: 3/1; financial award applicants required to submit FAFSA.
Faculty research: NAFTA, economies of transition, economics of Eastern Europe, artificial intelligence, comparative economic systems. *Total annual research expenditures:* $35,995.
Dr. John Walker, Head, 503-725-3934, *Fax:* 503-725-3945, *E-mail:* walkers@pdx.edu.

Portland State University (continued)
Application contact: Rita Spears, Office Coordinator, 503-725-3915, *Fax:* 503-725-3945, *E-mail:* rita@ch2.ch.pdx.edu. *Web site:* http://www.econ.pdx.edu/

■ PRINCETON UNIVERSITY

Graduate School, Department of Economics, Princeton, NJ 08544-1019

AWARDS Economics (PhD); economics and demography (PhD).

Degree requirements: For doctorate, thesis/dissertation.
Entrance requirements: For doctorate, GRE General Test, GRE Subject Test (recommended), working knowledge of multivariate calculus and matrix algebra.

■ PRINCETON UNIVERSITY

Graduate School, Program in Population Studies and Department of Economics, Concentration in Economics and Demography, Princeton, NJ 08544-1019

AWARDS PhD.

Degree requirements: For doctorate, thesis/dissertation.
Entrance requirements: For doctorate, GRE General Test.

■ PURDUE UNIVERSITY

Graduate School, Krannert Graduate School of Management, Department of Economics, West Lafayette, IN 47907

AWARDS MS, PhD.

Faculty: 23 full-time (2 women).
Students: 43 full-time (14 women), 9 part-time (3 women); includes 2 minority (both Asian Americans or Pacific Islanders), 45 international. Average age 29. 443 applicants, 5% accepted. In 2001, 11 master's, 8 doctorates awarded.
Degree requirements: For doctorate, thesis/dissertation.
Entrance requirements: For doctorate, GRE General Test, TOEFL. *Application deadline:* For fall admission, 2/15. *Application fee:* $30. Electronic applications accepted.
Expenses: Tuition, state resident: full-time $4,164; part-time $149 per credit hour. Tuition, nonresident: full-time $13,872; part-time $458 per credit hour. Tuition and fees vary according to campus/location and program.
Financial support: In 2001–02, 14 fellowships with partial tuition reimbursements (averaging $13,800 per year), 18 research assistantships with partial tuition reimbursements (averaging $13,800 per year), 14 teaching assistantships with partial tuition reimbursements (averaging $13,800 per year) were awarded. Support available to part-time students. Financial award application deadline: 2/15; financial award applicants required to submit FAFSA.
Faculty research: Experimental economics, monetary economics, transportation, industrial organization.
Dr. John M. Barron, Director of Doctoral Programs and Research, 765-494-4451, *Fax:* 765-494-1526.
Application contact: Kelly Felty, Assistant Director of Administration for Doctoral Programs, 765-494-4375, *Fax:* 765-494-1526, *E-mail:* feltyk@mgmt.purdue.edu. *Web site:* http://www2.mgmt.purdue.edu/Ph.D./

■ QUINNIPIAC UNIVERSITY

Lender School of Business, Program in Business Administration, Hamden, CT 06518-1940

AWARDS Accounting (MBA); computer information systems (MBA); economics (MBA); finance (MBA); health management (MBA); international business (MBA); management (MBA); marketing (MBA). Part-time and evening/weekend programs available.

Faculty: 20 full-time (4 women).
Students: 37 full-time (12 women), 137 part-time (60 women); includes 8 minority (1 African American, 3 Asian Americans or Pacific Islanders, 4 Hispanic Americans), 9 international. Average age 29. 70 applicants, 77% accepted, 44 enrolled. In 2001, 58 degrees awarded.
Degree requirements: For master's, thesis optional. *Median time to degree:* Master's–1.5 years full-time, 3 years part-time.
Entrance requirements: For master's, GMAT, minimum GPA of 2.5. *Application deadline:* For fall admission, 7/30 (priority date); for spring admission, 12/15 (priority date). Applications are processed on a rolling basis. *Application fee:* $45. Electronic applications accepted.
Expenses: Tuition: Part-time $450 per credit hour. Required fees: $25 per term.
Financial support: In 2001–02, 5 research assistantships with tuition reimbursements were awarded; career-related internships or fieldwork also available. Support available to part-time students. Financial award application deadline: 4/15; financial award applicants required to submit FAFSA.
Faculty research: Taxation, labor relations, financial institutions, consumer satisfaction, international capital market efficiency.
Dr. Mark Thompson, Director, 203-582-8914, *Fax:* 203-582-8664, *E-mail:* mark.thompson@quinnipiac.edu.
Application contact: Louise Howe, Associate Director of Graduate Admissions and Financial Aid, 800-462-1944, *Fax:* 203-582-3443, *E-mail:* graduate@quinnipiac.edu. *Web site:* http://www.quinnipiac.edu/

Find an in-depth description at www.petersons.com/gradchannel.

■ RENSSELAER POLYTECHNIC INSTITUTE

Graduate School, School of Humanities and Social Sciences, Department of Economics, Program in Economics, Troy, NY 12180-3590

AWARDS MS. Part-time programs available.

Faculty: 7 full-time (1 woman).
Students: 1 full-time (0 women). 12 applicants, 67% accepted. In 2001, 1 degree awarded.
Degree requirements: For master's, thesis.
Entrance requirements: For master's, GRE General Test, TOEFL. *Application deadline:* For fall admission, 1/15 (priority date). Applications are processed on a rolling basis. *Application fee:* $45. Electronic applications accepted.
Expenses: Tuition: Full-time $26,400; part-time $1,320 per credit hour. Required fees: $1,437.
Financial support: Application deadline: 2/1.
Faculty research: Economic development, cost-benefit analysis, productivity and technological change.
Dr. John M. Gowdy, Director, 518-276-8094, *Fax:* 518-276-2235, *E-mail:* gowdyj@rpi.edu.
Application contact: Kathy M. Keenan, Administrative Secretary, 518-276-8088, *Fax:* 518-276-2235, *E-mail:* keenak@rpi.edu. *Web site:* http://www.rpi.edu/dept/economics/

Find an in-depth description at www.petersons.com/gradchannel.

■ RENSSELAER POLYTECHNIC INSTITUTE

Graduate School, School of Humanities and Social Sciences, Program in Ecological Economics, Values, and Policy, Troy, NY 12180-3590

AWARDS MS. Part-time programs available.

Faculty: 5 full-time (1 woman).
Students: 3 full-time (1 woman), 6 part-time (3 women), 2 international. Average age 26. 11 applicants, 100% accepted, 5 enrolled.
Entrance requirements: For master's, TOEFL, GRE General Test. *Application deadline:* For fall admission, 1/15 (priority date). Applications are processed on a rolling basis. *Application fee:* $45. Electronic applications accepted.
Expenses: Tuition: Full-time $26,400; part-time $1,320 per credit hour. Required fees: $1,437.
Financial support: Fellowships, research assistantships, teaching assistantships available. Financial award application deadline: 2/1.
Faculty research: Environmental politics and policy, environmentalism, political economy, third world politics,

environmental health. *Total annual research expenditures:* $25,000.
Dr. Steve Breyman, Director, 518-276-8515, *Fax:* 518-276-2659, *E-mail:* breyms@rpi.edu.

Find an in-depth description at www.petersons.com/gradchannel.

■ RICE UNIVERSITY

Graduate Programs, School of Social Sciences, Department of Economics, Houston, TX 77251-1892

AWARDS MA, PhD.

Faculty: 17 full-time.
Students: 34 full-time (10 women), 25 international. Average age 24. 89 applicants, 11% accepted. In 2001, 2 master's, 8 doctorates awarded.
Degree requirements: For master's and doctorate, thesis/dissertation.
Entrance requirements: For master's and doctorate, GRE General Test, TOEFL, minimum GPA of 3.0. *Application deadline:* For fall admission, 2/1. *Application fee:* $25.
Expenses: Tuition: Full-time $17,300. Required fees: $250.
Financial support: In 2001–02, 21 fellowships with full tuition reimbursements (averaging $12,000 per year), 7 teaching assistantships with full tuition reimbursements (averaging $10,000 per year) were awarded. Research assistantships Financial award application deadline: 2/1.
Faculty research: Income distribution and small-scale industry in less developed countries, international commodity markets, microeconomic foundations, urban development, optimal taxation.
Dr. Peter Hartley, Chair, 713-348-4875, *Fax:* 713-348-5278, *E-mail:* hartley@rice.edu.
Application contact: Margie Robertson, Office Assistant, 713-348-2289, *Fax:* 713-348-5278, *E-mail:* mroberts@rice.edu.

■ ROOSEVELT UNIVERSITY

Graduate Division, College of Arts and Sciences, School of Policy Studies, Program in Economics, Chicago, IL 60605-1394

AWARDS Applied economics (MA); economics (MA). Part-time and evening/weekend programs available.

Faculty: 6 full-time (1 woman), 7 part-time/adjunct (0 women).
Students: Average age 28. In 2001, 12 degrees awarded.
Degree requirements: For master's, thesis or alternative.
Entrance requirements: For master's, minimum GPA of 2.7. *Application deadline:* For fall admission, 6/1 (priority date). Applications are processed on a rolling basis. *Application fee:* $25 ($35 for international students).
Expenses: Tuition: Full-time $9,090; part-time $505 per credit hour. Required fees: $100 per term.
Financial support: In 2001–02, 4 students received support, including 1 teaching assistantship; career-related internships or fieldwork, Federal Work-Study, scholarships/grants, and tuition waivers (full and partial) also available. Financial award application deadline: 2/15.
Faculty research: Labor, gender issues, international trade and development, entrepreneurship, political economy and money. *Total annual research expenditures:* $5,000.
Graduate Adviser, 312-341-3767.
Application contact: Joanne Canyon-Heller, Coordinator of Graduate Admissions, 312-281-3250, *Fax:* 312-341-3523, *E-mail:* applyru@roosevelt.edu.

■ RUTGERS, THE STATE UNIVERSITY OF NEW JERSEY, NEWARK

Rutgers Business School: Graduate Programs-Newark/New Brunswick, Department of Finance and Economics, Newark, NJ 07102

AWARDS MBA.

Entrance requirements: For master's, GMAT, TOEFL. *Web site:* http://business.rutgers.edu/

■ RUTGERS, THE STATE UNIVERSITY OF NEW JERSEY, NEW BRUNSWICK

Graduate School, Program in Economics, New Brunswick, NJ 08901-1281

AWARDS MA, PhD. Terminal master's awarded for partial completion of doctoral program.

Degree requirements: For master's, thesis or alternative; for doctorate, thesis/dissertation.
Entrance requirements: For master's, GRE General Test, GRE Subject Test (recommended), TOEFL; for doctorate, GRE General Test, GRE Subject Test (recommended).
Faculty research: Economic theory, econometrics, labor, economic history. *Web site:* http://economics.rutgers.edu/

■ ST. CLOUD STATE UNIVERSITY

School of Graduate Studies, College of Social Sciences, Program in Economics, St. Cloud, MN 56301-4498

AWARDS Applied economics (MS).

Faculty: 16 full-time (2 women), 1 part-time/adjunct (0 women).
Students: 3 full-time (0 women), 2 part-time; includes 2 minority (1 African American, 1 Asian American or Pacific Islander). 14 applicants, 14% accepted. In 2001, 4 degrees awarded.
Degree requirements: For master's, thesis or alternative.
Entrance requirements: For master's, GRE General Test, minimum GPA of 2.75. *Application deadline:* Applications are processed on a rolling basis. *Application fee:* $35.
Expenses: Tuition, state resident: part-time $156 per credit. Tuition, nonresident: part-time $244 per credit. Required fees: $20 per credit.
Financial support: Unspecified assistantships available.
Dr. Mary Edwards, Coordinator, 320-255-2968, *E-mail:* 100002@stcloudstate.edu.
Application contact: Lindalou Krueger, Graduate Studies Office, 320-255-2113, *Fax:* 320-654-5371, *E-mail:* lekrueger@stcloudstate.edu.

■ ST. JOHN'S UNIVERSITY

The Peter J. Tobin College of Business, Department of Economics and Finance, Program in Economics, Jamaica, NY 11439

AWARDS MBA, Adv C. Part-time and evening/weekend programs available.

Students: Average age 30. 2 applicants, 100% accepted, 0 enrolled. In 2001, 4 degrees awarded.
Degree requirements: For master's, thesis optional.
Entrance requirements: For master's, GMAT, minimum GPA of 3.0. *Application deadline:* Applications are processed on a rolling basis. *Application fee:* $40.
Expenses: Tuition: Full-time $14,520; part-time $605 per credit. Required fees: $150; $75 per term. Tuition and fees vary according to class time, course load, degree level, campus/location, program and student level.
Financial support: Research assistantships, scholarships/grants available. Support available to part-time students. Financial award application deadline: 3/1; financial award applicants required to submit FAFSA.
Application contact: Nicole T. Bryan, Assistant Dean, 718-990-2599, *Fax:* 718-990-5242, *E-mail:* admissions@stjohns.edu. *Web site:* http://www.stjohns.edu/

■ SAINT LOUIS UNIVERSITY

John Cook School of Business, Department of Economics, St. Louis, MO 63103-2097

AWARDS MA. Part-time programs available.

Students: Average age 35. 4 applicants, 75% accepted, 0 enrolled. In 2001, 1 master's awarded.
Degree requirements: For master's, comprehensive exam.
Entrance requirements: For master's, GMAT, GRE General Test. *Application deadline:* For fall admission, 7/1; for spring admission, 11/1. Applications are processed on a rolling basis. *Application fee:* $40.
Expenses: Tuition: Part-time $630 per credit hour.

Saint Louis University (continued)
Financial support: In 2001–02, 2 students received support. Federal Work-Study available. Support available to part-time students. Financial award application deadline: 4/1; financial award applicants required to submit FAFSA.
Faculty research: GMM estimation, R and D expenditures and trade, health and labor supply decision, international economics and purchasing power parity.
Dr. Muhammad Q. Islam, Chairperson, 314-977-3822, *Fax:* 314-977-1478, *E-mail:* islampq@slu.edu.
Application contact: Dr. Marcia Buresch, Associate Dean of the Graduate School, 314-977-2240, *Fax:* 314-977-3943, *E-mail:* bureschm@slu.edu.

■ ST. MARY'S UNIVERSITY OF SAN ANTONIO

Graduate School, Department of Economics, San Antonio, TX 78228-8507

AWARDS Financial economics (MA); political economy (MA). Part-time and evening/weekend programs available.

Faculty: 3 full-time (0 women), 1 (woman) part-time/adjunct.
Students: Average age 26.
Entrance requirements: For master's, GRE General Test. *Application deadline:* Applications are processed on a rolling basis. *Application fee:* $15. Electronic applications accepted.
Expenses: Tuition: Full-time $8,190; part-time $455 per credit hour. Required fees: $375.
Financial support: Teaching assistantships, career-related internships or fieldwork and Federal Work-Study available. Financial award application deadline: 2/15; financial award applicants required to submit FAFSA.
Faculty research: Forensic economics, offshore assembly, international trade, small business research, Mexico-U.S. relations.
Dr. Gary Scott, Graduate Program Director, 210-436-3142.

■ SAN DIEGO STATE UNIVERSITY

Graduate and Research Affairs, College of Arts and Letters, Department of Economics, San Diego, CA 92182

AWARDS MA.

Entrance requirements: For master's, GRE General Test, TOEFL.
Faculty research: Financing public education, demand for alternative fuel vehicles, economics of the Gold Rush, interdependence of equity and economic efficiency, economics of welfare, work and marriage.

■ SAN FRANCISCO STATE UNIVERSITY

Graduate Division, College of Behavioral and Social Sciences, Department of Economics, San Francisco, CA 94132-1722

AWARDS MA. Part-time and evening/weekend programs available.

Entrance requirements: For master's, minimum GPA of 3.0.

■ SAN JOSE STATE UNIVERSITY

Graduate Studies, College of Social Sciences, Department of Economics, San Jose, CA 95192-0001

AWARDS Applied economics (MA); economics (MA). Part-time programs available.

Faculty: 15 full-time (6 women), 5 part-time/adjunct (0 women).
Students: 15 full-time (8 women), 14 part-time (3 women); includes 17 minority (12 Asian Americans or Pacific Islanders, 5 Hispanic Americans), 4 international. Average age 30. 46 applicants, 65% accepted. In 2001, 22 degrees awarded.
Degree requirements: For master's, thesis optional.
Entrance requirements: For master's, GRE, minimum GPA of 3.0. *Application deadline:* For fall admission, 6/29; for spring admission, 11/30. Applications are processed on a rolling basis. *Application fee:* $59. Electronic applications accepted.
Expenses: Tuition, nonresident: part-time $246 per unit. Required fees: $678 per semester. Tuition and fees vary according to course load.
Financial support: In 2001–02, 2 teaching assistantships were awarded. Financial award applicants required to submit FAFSA.
Lydia Ortega, Chair, 408-924-5400, *Fax:* 408-924-5406.
Application contact: Dr. Thayer Watkins, Director, 408-924-5420.

■ SEATTLE PACIFIC UNIVERSITY

Graduate School, School of Business and Economics, Seattle, WA 98119-1997

AWARDS MBA, MS. Part-time and evening/weekend programs available.

Students: 120 (48 women); includes 19 minority (1 African American, 15 Asian Americans or Pacific Islanders, 2 Hispanic Americans, 1 Native American) 25 international. In 2001, 39 degrees awarded.
Entrance requirements: For master's, GMAT, minimum AACSB index of 1060. *Application deadline:* For fall admission, 8/1 (priority date); for winter admission, 11/1; for spring admission, 2/1. Applications are processed on a rolling basis.
Expenses: Contact institution.
Financial support: In 2001–02, 5 students received support, including 2 research assistantships; career-related internships or fieldwork also available. Financial award applicants required to submit FAFSA.
Gary Karns, Graduate Director, 206-281-2753, *Fax:* 206-281-2733.
Application contact: Debbie Wysomierski, Assistant Graduate Director, 206-281-2753, *Fax:* 206-281-2733, *E-mail:* mba@spu.edu. *Web site:* http://www.spu.edu/sbe

■ SOUTH DAKOTA STATE UNIVERSITY

Graduate School, College of Agriculture and Biological Sciences, Department of Economics, Brookings, SD 57007

AWARDS MS.

Degree requirements: For master's, thesis, oral and written exams.
Entrance requirements: For master's, TOEFL, minimum GPA of 2.75.
Faculty research: Sustainable agriculture, land rent and prices, rural finance, grain and livestock marketing, agricultural policy.

■ SOUTHERN ILLINOIS UNIVERSITY CARBONDALE

Graduate School, College of Liberal Arts, Department of Economics, Carbondale, IL 62901-6806

AWARDS MA, MS, PhD.

Faculty: 9 full-time (0 women).
Students: 30 full-time (12 women), 10 part-time (2 women); includes 5 minority (2 African Americans, 3 Asian Americans or Pacific Islanders), 29 international. 44 applicants, 32% accepted. In 2001, 2 master's, 2 doctorates awarded.
Degree requirements: For master's and doctorate, thesis/dissertation.
Entrance requirements: For master's, GRE General Test, TOEFL, minimum GPA of 2.7; for doctorate, GRE General Test, TOEFL, minimum GPA of 3.25. *Application deadline:* Applications are processed on a rolling basis. *Application fee:* $20.
Expenses: Tuition, state resident: full-time $3,794; part-time $154 per hour. Tuition, nonresident: full-time $6,566; part-time $308 per hour. Required fees: $277 per hour.
Financial support: In 2001–02, 23 students received support, including 2 fellowships with full tuition reimbursements available, 2 research assistantships with full tuition reimbursements available, 17 teaching assistantships with full tuition reimbursements available; Federal Work-Study, institutionally sponsored loans, and tuition waivers (full) also available. Support available to part-time students.
Faculty research: Advanced economic theory, applied microeconomics, economic development, finance, international economics, monetary theory and policy.

Dr. Richard Grabowski, Chairperson, 618-453-2713. *Web site:* http://www.siu.edu/~econ/

Find an in-depth description at www.petersons.com/gradchannel.

■ SOUTHERN ILLINOIS UNIVERSITY EDWARDSVILLE

Graduate Studies and Research, School of Business, Department of Economics and Finance, Edwardsville, IL 62026-0001

AWARDS MA, MS. Part-time programs available.

Students: 21 full-time (6 women), 12 part-time (4 women); includes 1 minority (Hispanic American), 22 international. Average age 33. 34 applicants, 85% accepted, 13 enrolled. In 2001, 17 degrees awarded.
Degree requirements: For master's, final exam. *Median time to degree:* Master's–2.5 years full-time, 4.5 years part-time.
Entrance requirements: For master's, GMAT, TOEFL, minimum GPA of 3.5 in field. *Application deadline:* For fall admission, 7/20; for spring admission, 12/7. *Application fee:* $25.
Expenses: Tuition, state resident: full-time $2,712; part-time $113 per credit hour. Tuition, nonresident: full-time $5,424; part-time $226 per credit hour. Required fees: $250; $125 per term. Tuition and fees vary according to course load, campus/location and reciprocity agreements.
Financial support: In 2001–02, 1 fellowship with full tuition reimbursement, 9 research assistantships with full tuition reimbursements were awarded. Teaching assistantships with full tuition reimbursements, career-related internships or fieldwork, Federal Work-Study, institutionally sponsored loans, traineeships, and unspecified assistantships also available. Support available to part-time students. Financial award application deadline: 3/1; financial award applicants required to submit FAFSA.
Dr. Rik Hafer, Chairperson, 618-650-2542, *E-mail:* rhafer@siue.edu.
Application contact: Dr. Don Elliot, Graduate Program Director, 618-650-2542, *E-mail:* delliot@siue.edu.

■ SOUTHERN METHODIST UNIVERSITY

Dedman College, Department of Economics, Dallas, TX 75275

AWARDS Applied economics (MA); economics (MA, PhD). Part-time and evening/weekend programs available.

Faculty: 16 full-time (3 women).
Students: 53 full-time (18 women), 16 part-time (4 women); includes 18 minority (2 African Americans, 14 Asian Americans or Pacific Islanders, 2 Hispanic Americans), 37 international. Average age 28. 322 applicants, 39% accepted, 25 enrolled. In 2001, 17 master's, 2 doctorates awarded. Terminal master's awarded for partial completion of doctoral program.
Degree requirements: For master's, oral qualifying exam, thesis optional; for doctorate, thesis/dissertation, written exams.
Entrance requirements: For master's, GRE General Test or GMAT, 12 hours in economics, minimum GPA of 3.0, previous course work in calculus, 3 hours calculus and statistics; for doctorate, GRE General Test, minimum GPA of 3.0, previous course work in calculus, 12 hours economics, 1 year of previous coursework in calculus and statistics. *Application deadline:* For fall admission, 2/1 (priority date); for spring admission, 11/30 (priority date). Applications are processed on a rolling basis. *Application fee:* $50.
Expenses: Tuition: Part-time $285 per credit hour.
Financial support: In 2001–02, 18 students received support, including 2 research assistantships with full tuition reimbursements available (averaging $10,000 per year), 16 teaching assistantships with full tuition reimbursements available (averaging $10,200 per year); tuition waivers (partial) also available. Financial award applicants required to submit FAFSA.
Faculty research: Economic theory, game theory, econometrics, international trade, labor.
Dr. Nathan Balke, Interim Chair, 214-768-2693.
Application contact: Information Contact, 214-768-2693.

■ SOUTHERN NEW HAMPSHIRE UNIVERSITY

School of Community Economic Development, Manchester, NH 03106-1045

AWARDS MS, PhD. Part-time and evening/weekend programs available.

Faculty: 4 full-time (1 woman), 13 part-time/adjunct (7 women).
Students: 20 full-time (9 women), 74 part-time (37 women), 30 international. Average age 30. In 2001, 45 degrees awarded.
Degree requirements: For master's, thesis or alternative, community project.
Entrance requirements: For master's, 2 years of work experience, minimum GPA of 2.5. *Application deadline:* Applications are processed on a rolling basis. *Application fee:* $20.
Expenses: Tuition: Full-time $11,340; part-time $1,260 per course. One-time fee: $540 full-time. Full-time tuition and fees vary according to course load, degree level and program.
Financial support: In 2001–02, 1 research assistantship was awarded; Federal Work-Study also available. Support available to part-time students.
Dr. Michael Swack, Director, *E-mail:* mswack@minerva.snhc.edu.
Application contact: Patricia Gerard, Assistant Dean, Academic Services, School of Business, 603-644-3102, *Fax:* 603-644-3144, *E-mail:* p.gerard@snhu.edu.

Find an in-depth description at www.petersons.com/gradchannel.

■ STANFORD UNIVERSITY

School of Humanities and Sciences, Department of Economics, Stanford, CA 94305-9991

AWARDS PhD.

Faculty: 40 full-time (4 women).
Students: 114 full-time (43 women), 30 part-time (5 women); includes 14 minority (1 African American, 11 Asian Americans or Pacific Islanders, 2 Hispanic Americans), 90 international. Average age 27. 501 applicants, 10% accepted. In 2001, 22 doctorates awarded.
Degree requirements: For doctorate, thesis/dissertation, oral exam.
Entrance requirements: For doctorate, GRE General Test, TOEFL. *Application deadline:* For fall admission, 1/5. *Application fee:* $65 ($80 for international students). Electronic applications accepted.
Financial support: Teaching assistantships available.
Gavin Wright, Chair, 650-723-3837, *Fax:* 650-725-5702, *E-mail:* write@stanford.edu.
Application contact: Graduate Administrator, 650-723-3977. *Web site:* http://www-econ.stanford.edu

■ STATE UNIVERSITY OF NEW YORK AT ALBANY

College of Arts and Sciences, Department of Economics, Albany, NY 12222-0001

AWARDS MA, PhD, Certificate. Part-time and evening/weekend programs available.

Students: 53 full-time (21 women), 17 part-time (6 women); includes 3 minority (2 African Americans, 1 Asian American or Pacific Islander), 55 international. Average age 29. 145 applicants, 42% accepted. In 2001, 17 master's, 1 doctorate awarded. Terminal master's awarded for partial completion of doctoral program.
Degree requirements: For doctorate, one foreign language, thesis/dissertation.
Entrance requirements: For master's, TOEFL; for doctorate, GRE General Test, GRE Subject Test, TOEFL. *Application deadline:* For fall admission, 8/1. Applications are processed on a rolling basis. *Application fee:* $50.
Expenses: Tuition, state resident: full-time $2,550; part-time $213 per credit. Tuition, nonresident: full-time $4,208; part-time $351 per credit. Required fees: $470; $470 per year.
Financial support: Fellowships, research assistantships, teaching assistantships, career-related internships or fieldwork,

State University of New York at Albany (continued)
institutionally sponsored loans, and lectureships available. Financial award application deadline: 2/15.
Faculty research: Expectations of inflation and interest rates, diffusion of new technology, labor markets in developing countries, government deficits and international exchange markets.
Dr. Michael Sattinger, Chair, 518-442-4735.

■ STATE UNIVERSITY OF NEW YORK AT BINGHAMTON

Graduate School, School of Arts and Sciences, Department of Economics, Binghamton, NY 13902-6000

AWARDS Economics (MA, PhD); economics and finance (MA, PhD).

Faculty: 23 full-time (4 women), 4 part-time/adjunct (0 women).
Students: 43 full-time (19 women), 7 part-time (2 women); includes 7 minority (2 African Americans, 3 Asian Americans or Pacific Islanders, 2 Hispanic Americans), 33 international. Average age 29. 203 applicants, 21% accepted, 17 enrolled. In 2001, 13 master's, 4 doctorates awarded. Terminal master's awarded for partial completion of doctoral program.
Degree requirements: For doctorate, thesis/dissertation.
Entrance requirements: For master's and doctorate, GRE General Test, TOEFL. *Application deadline:* For fall admission, 8/15 (priority date); for spring admission, 11/1. Applications are processed on a rolling basis. Electronic applications accepted.
Expenses: Tuition, state resident: full-time $5,100; part-time $213 per credit. Tuition, nonresident: full-time $8,416; part-time $351 per credit. Required fees: $811.
Financial support: In 2001–02, 27 students received support, including 5 fellowships with full tuition reimbursements available (averaging $5,849 per year), 23 teaching assistantships with full tuition reimbursements available (averaging $7,716 per year); research assistantships, Federal Work-Study, institutionally sponsored loans, scholarships/grants, tuition waivers (full and partial), and unspecified assistantships also available. Financial award application deadline: 2/15.
Dr. Edward Kokkelenberg, Chairperson, 607-777-2573.

■ STATE UNIVERSITY OF NEW YORK COLLEGE AT BUFFALO

Graduate Studies and Research, Faculty of Natural and Social Sciences, Department of Economics and Finance, Buffalo, NY 14222-1095

AWARDS Applied economics (MA).

Faculty: 10 full-time (1 woman).
Students: 3 full-time (1 woman), 10 part-time (2 women); includes 3 minority (1 African American, 1 Asian American or Pacific Islander, 1 Hispanic American). Average age 33. 11 applicants, 73% accepted.
Application deadline: For fall admission, 5/1 (priority date); for spring admission, 10/1 (priority date). Applications are processed on a rolling basis. *Application fee:* $50.
Expenses: Tuition, state resident: full-time $5,100; part-time $226 per credit hour. Tuition, nonresident: full-time $8,416; part-time $351 per credit hour.
Financial support: Application deadline: 3/1.
Dr. Douglas Koritz, Chairperson, 716-878-6640, *E-mail:* koritzdg@buffalostate.edu.

■ STONY BROOK UNIVERSITY, STATE UNIVERSITY OF NEW YORK

Graduate School, College of Arts and Sciences, Department of Economics, Stony Brook, NY 11794

AWARDS MA, PhD.

Faculty: 13 full-time (1 woman), 6 part-time/adjunct (0 women).
Students: 25 full-time (11 women), 27 part-time (10 women); includes 2 minority (both Asian Americans or Pacific Islanders), 45 international. 96 applicants, 35% accepted. In 2001, 3 master's, 6 doctorates awarded.
Degree requirements: For doctorate, thesis/dissertation, comprehensive exam.
Entrance requirements: For master's and doctorate, GRE General Test, TOEFL. *Application deadline:* For fall admission, 1/15. *Application fee:* $50.
Expenses: Tuition, state resident: full-time $5,100; part-time $213 per credit. Tuition, nonresident: full-time $8,416; part-time $351 per credit. Required fees: $496.
Financial support: In 2001–02, 1 research assistantship, 28 teaching assistantships were awarded.
Faculty research: Economic theory, game theory, econometrics, macroeconomics, applied microeconomics. *Total annual research expenditures:* $151,053.
Dr. William Dawes, Chairperson, 631-632-7530.
Application contact: Dr. Mark Montgomery, Director, 631-632-7530, *E-mail:* mmontgomery@datalab2.sbs.sunysb.edu. *Web site:* http://walras.economics.sunysb.edu/

Find an in-depth description at www.petersons.com/gradchannel.

■ SUFFOLK UNIVERSITY

College of Arts and Sciences, Department of Economics, Boston, MA 02108-2770

AWARDS Economic policy (MSEP); international economics (MSIE). Part-time and evening/weekend programs available.

Faculty: 8 full-time (3 women).
Students: 3 full-time (1 woman), 14 part-time (4 women), 5 international. Average age 24. 23 applicants, 74% accepted, 8 enrolled. In 2001, 4 degrees awarded.
Entrance requirements: For master's, GRE General Test or GMAT. *Application deadline:* For fall admission, 6/15 (priority date); for spring admission, 11/15 (priority date). Applications are processed on a rolling basis. *Application fee:* $35.
Expenses: Contact institution.
Financial support: In 2001–02, 6 students received support, including 1 fellowship with full and partial tuition reimbursement available (averaging $3,450 per year); career-related internships or fieldwork, Federal Work-Study, and institutionally sponsored loans also available. Support available to part-time students. Financial award application deadline: 3/15; financial award applicants required to submit FAFSA.
Faculty research: International trade, international finance, economic forecasting, country risk analysis, econometrics.
Dr. David Tuerch, Director, 617-573-8670, *Fax:* 617-720-4272, *E-mail:* dtuerch@suffolk.edu.
Application contact: Judith Reynolds, Director of Graduate Admissions, 617-573-8302, *Fax:* 617-523-0116, *E-mail:* grad.admission@suffolk.edu. *Web site:* http://www.suffolk.edu/cas/economics

■ SYRACUSE UNIVERSITY

Graduate School, Maxwell School of Citizenship and Public Affairs, Department of Economics, Syracuse, NY 13244-0003

AWARDS MA, PhD, JD/MA.

Faculty: 21 full-time (3 women), 4 part-time/adjunct (0 women).
Students: 56 full-time (25 women), 7 part-time (3 women); includes 2 minority (1 African American, 1 Hispanic American), 37 international. Average age 29. 189 applicants, 13% accepted, 14 enrolled. In 2001, 14 master's, 5 doctorates awarded.
Degree requirements: For doctorate, thesis/dissertation, comprehensive exam. *Median time to degree:* Master's–2 years full-time; doctorate–5 years full-time.
Entrance requirements: For master's and doctorate, GRE General Test, TOEFL. *Application deadline:* Applications are processed on a rolling basis. *Application fee:* $50.
Expenses: Tuition: Full-time $15,528; part-time $647 per credit. Required fees: $420; $38 per term. Tuition and fees vary according to program.
Financial support: In 2001–02, 40 students received support, including 2 fellowships (averaging $12,000 per year), 14 research assistantships (averaging $10,600 per year), 21 teaching assistantships (averaging $10,600 per year); Federal Work-Study and tuition waivers (partial) also available.

Faculty research: International economics, labor economics, public finance, urban economics.
Thomas Kniesner, Chair, 315-443-3612.
Application contact: Dr. Donald Dutkowsky, Graduate Director, 315-443-1918.

Find an in-depth description at www.petersons.com/gradchannel.

■ TEACHERS COLLEGE COLUMBIA UNIVERSITY

Graduate Faculty of Education, Department of International and Transcultural Studies, Program in Economics and Education, New York, NY 10027-6696

AWARDS Ed M, MA, Ed D, PhD.

Degree requirements: For doctorate, variable foreign language requirement, thesis/dissertation.
Entrance requirements: For master's and doctorate, GRE.
Expenses: Tuition: Full-time $19,080; part-time $780 per unit. Required fees: $170 per semester.
Faculty research: Education and economic growth, efficiency in education, training in education, labor and education policy, economic status of immigrant groups.

■ TEMPLE UNIVERSITY

Graduate School, Fox School of Business and Management, Doctoral Programs in Business, Philadelphia, PA 19122-6096

AWARDS Accounting (PhD); economics (PhD); finance (PhD); general and strategic management (PhD); healthcare management (PhD); human resource administration (PhD); international business administration (PhD); management information systems (PhD); management science/operations research (PhD); marketing (PhD); risk, insurance, and health-care management (PhD); statistics (PhD); tourism (PhD).

Students: 140; includes 18 minority (5 African Americans, 11 Asian Americans or Pacific Islanders, 2 Hispanic Americans), 81 international. Average age 31. 771 applicants, 63% accepted.
Entrance requirements: For doctorate, GRE General Test, TOEFL, minimum GPA of 3.0. *Application deadline:* For fall admission, 1/15. Applications are processed on a rolling basis. *Application fee:* $40.
Natale Butto, Director of Graduate Admissions, 215-204-7678, *Fax:* 215-204-8300, *E-mail:* butto@sbm.temple.edu. *Web site:* http://www.sbm.temple.edu/

Find an in-depth description at www.petersons.com/gradchannel.

■ TEMPLE UNIVERSITY

Graduate School, Fox School of Business and Management, MA Programs, Philadelphia, PA 19122-6096

AWARDS Economics (MA).

Students: 7 full-time (3 women), 6 part-time (3 women); includes 2 minority (1 Asian American or Pacific Islander, 1 Hispanic American), 3 international. Average age 29. 31 applicants, 90% accepted. In 2001, 11 degrees awarded.
Entrance requirements: For master's, GRE and TOEFL, minimum GPA of 3.0. *Application deadline:* For fall admission, 4/15; for spring admission, 9/30. *Application fee:* $40.
Expenses: Tuition, state resident: full-time $8,487; part-time $369 per credit hour. Tuition, nonresident: full-time $12,282; part-time $534 per credit hour. Required fees: $350. Tuition and fees vary according to course load, program and reciprocity agreements.
Natale Butto, Director of Graduate Admissions, 215-204-7678, *Fax:* 215-204-8300, *E-mail:* butto@sbm.temple.edu.

■ TEMPLE UNIVERSITY

Graduate School, Fox School of Business and Management, Masters Programs in Business, Philadelphia, PA 19122-6096

AWARDS Accounting (MBA, MS); actuarial science (MS); business administration (EMBA, MBA); e-business (MBA, MS); economics (MA, MBA); finance (MBA, MS); general and strategic management (MBA); healthcare financial management (MS); healthcare management (MBA); human resource administration (MBA, MS); international business administration (IMBA); management information systems (MBA, MS); management science/operations management (MS); management science/operations research (MBA); marketing (MBA, MS); risk management and insurance (MBA); statistics (MBA, MS). EMBA offered in Philadelphia, PA, or Tokyo, Japan.

Students: Average age 31.
Entrance requirements: For master's, GMAT, TOEFL, minimum GPA of 3.0. *Application deadline:* For fall admission, 4/15; for spring admission, 9/30. Applications are processed on a rolling basis. *Application fee:* $40. Electronic applications accepted.
Natale Butto, Director of Graduate Admissions, 215-204-7678, *Fax:* 215-204-8300, *E-mail:* butto@sbm.temple.edu.

Find an in-depth description at www.petersons.com/gradchannel.

■ TEMPLE UNIVERSITY

Graduate School, Fox School of Business and Management, MBA Programs, Philadelphia, PA 19122-6096

AWARDS Accounting (MBA); business administration (MBA); e-business (MBA); economics (MBA); finance (MBA); general and strategic management (MBA); healthcare management (MBA); human resource administration (MBA); international business (IMBA); management information systems (MBA); management science/operations management (MBA); marketing (MBA); Philadelphia (EMBA); risk management and insurance (MBA); statistics (MBA); Tokyo (EMBA).

Students: 243 full-time (79 women), 552 part-time (225 women); includes 94 minority (42 African Americans, 41 Asian Americans or Pacific Islanders, 10 Hispanic Americans, 1 Native American), 140 international. Average age 31. 348 applicants, 66% accepted. In 2001, 328 degrees awarded.
Entrance requirements: For master's, GMAT and TOEFL, minimum GPA of 3.0. *Application deadline:* For fall admission, 4/15; for spring admission, 9/30. *Application fee:* $40.
Natale Butto, Director of Graduate Admissions, 215-204-7678, *Fax:* 215-204-8300, *E-mail:* butto@sbm.temple.edu.

■ TEMPLE UNIVERSITY

Graduate School, Fox School of Business and Management, PhD Programs, Philadelphia, PA 19122-6096

AWARDS Accounting (PhD); economics (PhD); finance (PhD); general and strategic management (PhD); healthcare management (PhD); human resource administration (PhD); international business administration (PhD); management information systems (PhD); management science/operations research (PhD); marketing (PhD); risk, insurance, and healthcare (PhD); statistics (PhD); tourism (PhD).

Students: 140; includes 18 minority (5 African Americans, 11 Asian Americans or Pacific Islanders, 2 Hispanic Americans), 81 international. Average age 31. 771 applicants, 63% accepted. In 2001, 411 degrees awarded.
Entrance requirements: For doctorate, GRE and TOEFL, minimum GPA of 3.0. *Application deadline:* For fall admission, 1/15. *Application fee:* $40.
Natale Butto, Director of Graduate Admissions, 215-204-7678, *Fax:* 215-204-8300, *E-mail:* butto@sbm.temple.edu.

■ TEXAS A&M UNIVERSITY

College of Liberal Arts, Department of Economics, College Station, TX 77843

AWARDS MS, PhD. Part-time programs available.

Faculty: 29 full-time (2 women), 6 part-time/adjunct (2 women).
Students: 86 full-time (13 women), 11 part-time (1 woman); includes 13 minority (1 African American, 9 Asian Americans or Pacific Islanders, 3 Hispanic Americans), 64 international. Average age 31. 199 applicants, 40% accepted, 27 enrolled. In 2001, 6 master's, 9 doctorates awarded. Terminal master's awarded for partial completion of doctoral program.
Degree requirements: For master's, thesis optional; for doctorate, thesis/dissertation, comprehensive exam.
Entrance requirements: For master's and doctorate, GRE General Test, TOEFL. *Application deadline:* For fall admission, 3/1 (priority date); for winter admission, 8/1 (priority date); for spring admission, 11/1 (priority date). Applications are processed on a rolling basis. *Application fee:* $50 ($75 for international students). Electronic applications accepted.
Expenses: Tuition, state resident: full-time $11,872. Tuition, nonresident: full-time $17,892.
Financial support: In 2001–02, 47 students received support, including 4 fellowships (averaging $14,850 per year), 29 research assistantships (averaging $12,380 per year), 13 teaching assistantships (averaging $10,062 per year); scholarships/grants, health care benefits, unspecified assistantships, and out of state tuition waiver also available. Financial award application deadline: 2/1; financial award applicants required to submit FAFSA.
Faculty research: Tax policy, state tax, labor, international economics, macroeconomics. *Total annual research expenditures:* $111,138.
Dr. Leonardo Avernheimer, Head, 979-845-7358, *Fax:* 979-847-8757, *E-mail:* leonardo@econ.tamu.edu.
Application contact: Christi Essix, Graduate Admissions Supervisor, 979-845-7376, *Fax:* 979-847-8557, *E-mail:* christi@econ.tamu.edu. *Web site:* http://econweb.tamu.edu/

■ TEXAS A&M UNIVERSITY–COMMERCE

Graduate School, College of Business and Technology, Department of Economics and Finance, Commerce, TX 75429-3011

AWARDS Economics (MA, MS). Part-time programs available.

Faculty: 3 full-time (0 women), 1 part-time/adjunct (0 women).
Students: 2 full-time (1 woman), 5 part-time (2 women); includes 1 minority (Hispanic American), 3 international. Average age 36. 3 applicants, 100% accepted. In 2001, 2 degrees awarded.
Degree requirements: For master's, thesis (for some programs), comprehensive exam.
Entrance requirements: For master's, GMAT or GRE General Test. *Application deadline:* For fall admission, 6/1 (priority date); for spring admission, 11/1 (priority date). Applications are processed on a rolling basis. *Application fee:* $0 ($25 for international students). Electronic applications accepted.
Expenses: Tuition, state resident: full-time $2,221. International tuition: $7,285 full-time.
Financial support: In 2001–02, research assistantships (averaging $7,875 per year), teaching assistantships (averaging $7,875 per year) were awarded. Federal Work-Study, institutionally sponsored loans, and scholarships/grants also available. Financial award application deadline: 5/1; financial award applicants required to submit FAFSA.
Faculty research: Economic activity, forensic economics, volatility and finance, international economics.
Stephen L. Avard, Interim Head, 903-886-5681, *E-mail:* steve_avard@tamu-commerce.edu.
Application contact: Tammi Higginbotham, Graduate Admissions Adviser, 843-886-5167, *Fax:* 843-886-5165, *E-mail:* tammi_higginbotham@tamu-commerce.edu.

■ TEXAS CHRISTIAN UNIVERSITY

AddRan College of Humanities and Social Sciences, Department of Economics, Fort Worth, TX 76129-0002

AWARDS MA. Part-time and evening/weekend programs available.

Degree requirements: For master's, one foreign language, thesis optional.
Entrance requirements: For master's, GRE General Test, TOEFL. *Application deadline:* For fall admission, 3/1; for spring admission, 12/1. *Application fee:* $0.
Expenses: Tuition: Full-time $8,190; part-time $455 per credit hour. Required fees: $1,760.
Financial support: Application deadline: 3/1.
Dr. Edward McNertney, Chairperson, 817-257-7230.
Application contact: Dr. Mike Butler, Associate Dean, AddRan College of Humanities and Social Sciences, *E-mail:* m.butler@tcu.edu. *Web site:* http://www.graduate.tcu.edu/

■ TEXAS TECH UNIVERSITY

Graduate School, College of Arts and Sciences, Department of Economics and Geography, Lubbock, TX 79409

AWARDS Economics (MA, PhD). Part-time programs available.

Faculty: 11 full-time (2 women), 3 part-time/adjunct (0 women).
Students: 23 full-time (7 women), 3 part-time (1 woman), 18 international. Average age 30. 22 applicants, 77% accepted, 9 enrolled. In 2001, 7 master's, 3 doctorates awarded.
Degree requirements: For master's, thesis (for some programs); for doctorate, thesis/dissertation.
Entrance requirements: For master's and doctorate, GRE General Test. *Application deadline:* Applications are processed on a rolling basis. *Application fee:* $25 ($50 for international students). Electronic applications accepted.
Expenses: Tuition, state resident: full-time $1,926; part-time $107 per credit hour. Tuition, nonresident: full-time $5,724; part-time $318 per credit hour. Required fees: $779; $737 per year. Tuition and fees vary according to course level, course load and program.
Financial support: In 2001–02, 4 research assistantships with partial tuition reimbursements (averaging $9,525 per year), 16 teaching assistantships with partial tuition reimbursements (averaging $10,276 per year) were awarded. Fellowships, Federal Work-Study and institutionally sponsored loans also available. Support available to part-time students. Financial award application deadline: 5/1; financial award applicants required to submit FAFSA.
Faculty research: Guide to Keynes' aggregate supply/demand, consumption of farm output (1800 to 1840).
Dr. Joseph King, Chair, 806-742-2201, *Fax:* 806-742-1137.
Application contact: Graduate Adviser, 806-742-2201. *Web site:* http://www.ttu.edu/~ecogeog/

■ TRINITY COLLEGE

Graduate Programs, Department of Economics, Hartford, CT 06106-3100

AWARDS MA. Part-time and evening/weekend programs available.

Faculty: 3 full-time (0 women), 2 part-time/adjunct (0 women).
Students: Average age 38. In 2001, 6 degrees awarded.
Degree requirements: For master's, qualifying exam, thesis optional.
Entrance requirements: For master's, minimum GPA of 3.0. *Application deadline:* For fall admission, 4/1; for spring admission, 11/1. *Application fee:* $50.
Expenses: Tuition: Part-time $900 per course. Required fees: $25 per term.
Financial support: In 2001–02, 3 students received support; fellowships, tuition waivers (full) available. Support available to part-time students. Financial award application deadline: 4/1.
Dr. William Butos, Graduate Adviser, 860-297-2448.

■ TUFTS UNIVERSITY

Division of Graduate and Continuing Studies and Research, Graduate School of Arts and Sciences, Department of Economics, Medford, MA 02155

AWARDS MA.

Faculty: 15 full-time, 7 part-time/adjunct.
Students: 41 (25 women); includes 3 minority (2 African Americans, 1 Asian American or Pacific Islander) 29 international. 85 applicants, 74% accepted. In 2001, 11 degrees awarded.
Entrance requirements: For master's, GRE General Test, TOEFL. *Application deadline:* For fall admission, 2/15. Applications are processed on a rolling basis. *Application fee:* $50. Electronic applications accepted.
Expenses: Tuition: Full-time $26,853. Full-time tuition and fees vary according to program.
Financial support: Teaching assistantships with full and partial tuition reimbursements, Federal Work-Study, scholarships/grants, and tuition waivers (partial) available. Support available to part-time students. Financial award application deadline: 2/15; financial award applicants required to submit FAFSA.
David Garman, Chair, 617-627-3560, *Fax:* 617-627-3917.
Application contact: George Norman, Information Contact, 617-627-3560, *Fax:* 617-627-3917. *Web site:* http://ase.tufts.edu/econ

■ TULANE UNIVERSITY

Graduate School, Department of Economics, New Orleans, LA 70118-5669

AWARDS MA, PhD.

Degree requirements: For master's, thesis or alternative; for doctorate, one foreign language, thesis/dissertation.
Entrance requirements: For master's, GRE General Test, TSE, minimum B average in undergraduate course work; for doctorate, GRE General Test, TSE.
Expenses: Tuition: Full-time $24,675. Required fees: $2,210.
Faculty research: Economic development, public finance, labor economics, international and regional economics, industrial organization.

■ UNIVERSITY AT BUFFALO, THE STATE UNIVERSITY OF NEW YORK

Graduate School, College of Arts and Sciences, Department of Economics, Buffalo, NY 14260

AWARDS Economics (MA, PhD); financial economics (Certificate); health services (Certificate); information and Internet economics (Certificate); international economics (Certificate); law and regulation (Certificate); urban and regional economics (Certificate).

Faculty: 16 full-time (0 women), 1 part-time/adjunct (0 women).
Students: 96 full-time (31 women), 18 part-time (6 women); includes 10 minority (3 African Americans, 5 Asian Americans or Pacific Islanders, 1 Hispanic American, 1 Native American), 76 international. Average age 27. 361 applicants, 37% accepted, 72 enrolled. In 2001, 48 master's, 2 doctorates, 6 other advanced degrees awarded. Terminal master's awarded for partial completion of doctoral program.
Degree requirements: For master's, theory exam, thesis optional; for doctorate, thesis/dissertation, field and theory exams.
Entrance requirements: For master's and doctorate, GRE General Test, TOEFL; for Certificate, TOEFL, master's degree/MA. *Application deadline:* For fall admission, 2/1 (priority date); for spring admission, 10/20 (priority date). Applications are processed on a rolling basis. *Application fee:* $35. Electronic applications accepted.
Expenses: Tuition, state resident: full-time $6,118. Tuition, nonresident: full-time $9,434.
Financial support: In 2001–02, 1 fellowship with full tuition reimbursement (averaging $14,000 per year), 15 research assistantships with full tuition reimbursements (averaging $8,400 per year), 5 teaching assistantships with full tuition reimbursements (averaging $8,400 per year) were awarded. Federal Work-Study and unspecified assistantships also available. Financial award application deadline: 2/1; financial award applicants required to submit FAFSA.
Faculty research: International economics, econometrics, applied economics, urban and regional economics, financial economics.
Dr. Isaac Ehrlich, Chair, 716-645-2121, *Fax:* 716-645-2127.
Application contact: Dr. Nagesh Revankar, Director of Graduate Studies, 716-645-2121, *Fax:* 716-645-2127, *E-mail:* ecorevan@acsu.buffalo.edu. *Web site:* http://www.economics.buffalo.edu/

■ THE UNIVERSITY OF AKRON

Graduate School, Buchtel College of Arts and Sciences, Department of Economics, Akron, OH 44325-0001

AWARDS Economics (MA); labor and industrial relations (MA). Part-time programs available.

Faculty: 10 full-time (0 women), 3 part-time/adjunct (2 women).
Students: 14 full-time (7 women), 2 part-time; includes 2 minority (1 African American, 1 Hispanic American), 8 international. Average age 27. 21 applicants, 81% accepted, 2 enrolled. In 2001, 7 degrees awarded.
Degree requirements: For master's, thesis optional.
Entrance requirements: For master's, minimum GPA of 2.75. *Application deadline:* For fall admission, 3/1. Applications are processed on a rolling basis. *Application fee:* $40 ($50 for international students).
Expenses: Tuition, state resident: full-time $6,562; part-time $219 per credit. Tuition, nonresident: full-time $9,027; part-time $383 per credit. Required fees: $272; $11 per credit. Tuition and fees vary according to course load.
Financial support: In 2001–02, 11 teaching assistantships with full tuition reimbursement were awarded; research assistantships with full tuition reimbursements, institutionally sponsored loans and tuition waivers (full) also available. Financial award application deadline: 4/1.
Faculty research: Urban capital stock estimates, technology transfer, determinants of research and development spending, forecasting models.
Dr. Michael Nelson, Chair, 330-972-7937, *E-mail:* nelson2@uakron.edu.
Application contact: Dr. Gary Garofalo, Director of Graduate Studies, 330-972-7974, *E-mail:* ggarofalo@uakron.edu. *Web site:* http://www.uakron.edu/econ/

■ THE UNIVERSITY OF ALABAMA

Graduate School, The Manderson Graduate School of Business, Economics, Finance and Legal Studies Department, Tuscaloosa, AL 35487

AWARDS Banking and finance (MA, MSC, PhD); economics (MA, MSC, PhD).

Faculty: 24 full-time (1 woman), 1 part-time/adjunct (0 women).
Students: 44 full-time (7 women), 4 part-time (2 women); includes 1 minority (African American), 16 international. Average age 27. 98 applicants, 32% accepted, 26 enrolled. In 2001, 24 master's, 7 doctorates awarded. Terminal master's awarded for partial completion of doctoral program.
Degree requirements: For master's, comprehensive exam (MA), thesis (MSC); for doctorate, thesis/dissertation, comprehensive exam.
Entrance requirements: For master's, GMAT, TOEFL, minimum GPA of 3.0; for doctorate, TOEFL, minimum GPA of 3.0. *Application deadline:* For fall admission, 7/1; for spring admission, 11/1. Applications are processed on a rolling basis. *Application fee:* $25. Electronic applications accepted.
Expenses: Tuition, state resident: full-time $3,292; part-time $183 per credit hour. Tuition, nonresident: full-time $8,912; part-time $495 per credit hour. Tuition and fees vary according to course load, campus/location and program.
Financial support: In 2001–02, 3 fellowships with full tuition reimbursements (averaging $4,000 per year), 14 research

The University of Alabama (continued)
assistantships with full and partial tuition reimbursements (averaging $8,833 per year), 20 teaching assistantships with full and partial tuition reimbursements (averaging $8,833 per year) were awarded. Federal Work-Study and institutionally sponsored loans also available. Financial award application deadline: 6/15.
Faculty research: Taxation, futures market, monetary theory and policy, income distribution.
Dr. Billy Helms, Head, 205-348-7842, *Fax:* 205-348-0590, *E-mail:* bhelms@cba.ua.edu.
Application contact: Debra Wheatley, Secretary, 205-348-6683, *Fax:* 205-348-0590, *E-mail:* dwheatle@cba.ua.edu. *Web site:* http://www.cba.ua.edu/

■ UNIVERSITY OF ALASKA FAIRBANKS

Graduate School, School of Management, Department of Economics, Fairbanks, AK 99775-7480

AWARDS Resource economics (MS).

Faculty: 6 full-time (0 women).
Students: 7 full-time (5 women), 3 part-time (2 women), 2 international. Average age 29. 11 applicants, 73% accepted, 6 enrolled. In 2001, 2 degrees awarded.
Degree requirements: For master's, thesis, comprehensive exam.
Entrance requirements: For master's, GRE General Test, TOEFL. *Application deadline:* For fall admission, 4/1; for spring admission, 11/1. Applications are processed on a rolling basis. *Application fee:* $35.
Expenses: Tuition, state resident: full-time $4,272; part-time $178 per credit. Tuition, nonresident: full-time $8,328; part-time $347 per credit. Required fees: $960; $60 per term. Part-time tuition and fees vary according to course load.
Financial support: In 2001–02, fellowships with tuition reimbursements (averaging $10,000 per year); research assistantships with tuition reimbursements, teaching assistantships with tuition reimbursements, career-related internships or fieldwork, Federal Work-Study, and scholarships/grants also available.
Faculty research: Statistics; resource and agriculture economics; oil, gas, and energy.
Dr. Mike Pippenger, Head, 907-474-6530.
Application contact: Dr. Mark Herrman, Graduate Director, 907-474-7116, *Fax:* 907-474-5219.

■ THE UNIVERSITY OF ARIZONA

Graduate College, College of Business and Public Administration, Eller Graduate School of Management, Department of Economics, Tucson, AZ 85721

AWARDS MA, PhD, JD/MA, JD/PhD.

Faculty: 36 full-time (3 women).
Students: 35 full-time (10 women), 6 part-time (2 women); includes 4 minority (1 African American, 1 Asian American or Pacific Islander, 2 Hispanic Americans), 23 international. Average age 29. 141 applicants, 27% accepted, 8 enrolled. In 2001, 9 master's, 3 doctorates awarded. Terminal master's awarded for partial completion of doctoral program.
Degree requirements: For doctorate, thesis/dissertation.
Entrance requirements: For master's and doctorate, GRE General Test, TOEFL, minimum GPA of 3.0. *Application deadline:* For fall admission, 2/1 (priority date). Applications are processed on a rolling basis. *Application fee:* $45.
Expenses: Tuition, state resident: full-time $2,490; part-time $436 per unit. Tuition, nonresident: full-time $10,300; part-time $436 per unit. Full-time tuition and fees vary according to degree level and program.
Financial support: Fellowships, research assistantships with tuition reimbursements, teaching assistantships with tuition reimbursements, Federal Work-Study, scholarships/grants, and tuition waivers (partial) available. Financial award application deadline: 2/1.
Faculty research: Applied microeconomics, experimental economics, economic history, microeconomic theory, property rights.
Dr. Mark A Walker, Head, 520-621-2821.
Application contact: Pamela L Schloss, Graduate Coordinator, 520-621-2455, *Fax:* 520-621-8450, *E-mail:* pschloss@eller.arizona.edu. *Web site:* http://w3.arizona.edu/~econ

■ UNIVERSITY OF ARKANSAS

Graduate School, Sam M. Walton College of Business Administration, Department of Economics, Fayetteville, AR 72701-1201

AWARDS MA, PhD.

Students: 14 full-time (7 women), 1 part-time, 12 international. 11 applicants, 82% accepted. In 2001, 6 master's, 1 doctorate awarded.
Degree requirements: For doctorate, variable foreign language requirement, thesis/dissertation.
Entrance requirements: For master's and doctorate, GMAT or GRE General Test. *Application fee:* $40 ($50 for international students).
Expenses: Tuition, state resident: full-time $3,553; part-time $197 per credit. Tuition, nonresident: full-time $8,411; part-time $467 per credit. Required fees: $42 per credit. Tuition and fees vary according to course load and program.
Financial support: Research assistantships, career-related internships or fieldwork and Federal Work-Study available. Support available to part-time students. Financial award application deadline: 4/1; financial award applicants required to submit FAFSA.
Dr. Joseph Ziegler, Chair, 479-575-3266.
Application contact: Gary Ferrier, Graduate Coordinator, *E-mail:* gferrier@comp.uark.edu.

■ UNIVERSITY OF CALIFORNIA, BERKELEY

Graduate Division, College of Letters and Science, Department of Economics, Berkeley, CA 94720-1500

AWARDS PhD, JD/MA.

Degree requirements: For doctorate, thesis/dissertation, field exams, oral qualifying exam.
Entrance requirements: For doctorate, GRE General Test, TOEFL, minimum GPA of 3.0.
Expenses: Tuition, nonresident: full-time $10,704. Required fees: $4,349. *Web site:* http://emlab.berkeley.edu/econ/index.html

■ UNIVERSITY OF CALIFORNIA, DAVIS

Graduate Studies, Program in Economics, Davis, CA 95616

AWARDS MA, PhD.

Faculty: 26 full-time (4 women).
Students: 65 full-time (26 women); includes 3 minority (2 Asian Americans or Pacific Islanders, 1 Hispanic American), 33 international. Average age 30. 151 applicants, 60% accepted, 29 enrolled. In 2001, 20 master's, 6 doctorates awarded. Terminal master's awarded for partial completion of doctoral program.
Degree requirements: For master's, thesis optional; for doctorate, thesis/dissertation.
Entrance requirements: For master's, GRE General Test, minimum GPA of 3.0; for doctorate, GRE General Test, minimum GPA of 3.25. *Application deadline:* For fall admission, 1/15 (priority date). Applications are processed on a rolling basis. *Application fee:* $60. Electronic applications accepted.
Expenses: Tuition, state resident: full-time $4,831. Tuition, nonresident: full-time $15,725.
Financial support: In 2001–02, 46 students received support, including 22 fellowships with full and partial tuition reimbursements available (averaging $6,352 per year), 8 research assistantships with full and partial tuition reimbursements available (averaging $10,971 per year), 31 teaching assistantships with partial tuition reimbursements available (averaging $13,917 per year); career-related internships or fieldwork, institutionally sponsored loans, scholarships/grants, and tuition waivers (full and partial) also available. Financial

award application deadline: 1/15; financial award applicants required to submit FAFSA.
Faculty research: Applied microeconomics, macroeconomics, international studies, economic theory, economic history.
Kevin D. Hoover, Graduate Chair, 530-752-2129, *E-mail:* kdhoover@ucdavis.edu.
Application contact: Marilyn Dexter, Graduate Program Staff, 530-752-0743, *Fax:* 530-952-9382, *E-mail:* mldexter@ucdavis.edu. *Web site:* http://www.econ.ucdavis.edu/graduate/grad.html

■ UNIVERSITY OF CALIFORNIA, IRVINE

Office of Research and Graduate Studies, School of Social Sciences, Department of Economics, Irvine, CA 92697

AWARDS Economics (MA, PhD); public choice (MA, PhD); transportation economics (MA, PhD).

Faculty: 21.
Students: 44 full-time (12 women), 1 part-time; includes 10 minority (all Asian Americans or Pacific Islanders), 19 international. 151 applicants, 36% accepted, 11 enrolled. In 2001, 2 degrees awarded.
Degree requirements: For doctorate, one foreign language, thesis/dissertation.
Entrance requirements: For master's, minimum GPA of 3.0; for doctorate, GRE General Test. *Application deadline:* For fall and spring admission, 1/15 (priority date); for winter admission, 10/15 (priority date). Applications are processed on a rolling basis. *Application fee:* $40. Electronic applications accepted.
Expenses: Tuition, nonresident: full-time $10,704. Required fees: $8,396. Tuition and fees vary according to course load, program and student level.
Financial support: Fellowships, research assistantships, teaching assistantships, institutionally sponsored loans and tuition waivers (full and partial) available. Financial award application deadline: 3/2; financial award applicants required to submit FAFSA.
Faculty research: Public choice, econometrics, transportation economics, urban economics, applied microeconomics.
Michelle Garfinkel, Chair, 949-824-3190.
Application contact: Ivonne Maldonado, Graduate Counselor, 949-824-7352, *Fax:* 949-824-3548, *E-mail:* immaldon@uci.edu. *Web site:* http://www.socsci.uci.edu/econ/econ.html

■ UNIVERSITY OF CALIFORNIA, LOS ANGELES

Graduate Division, College of Letters and Science, Department of Economics, Los Angeles, CA 90095

AWARDS MA, PhD.

Students: 129 full-time (34 women); includes 3 minority (all Asian Americans or Pacific Islanders), 97 international. 477 applicants, 37% accepted, 33 enrolled. In 2001, 21 master's, 21 doctorates awarded.
Degree requirements: For doctorate, thesis/dissertation, oral and written qualifying exams.
Entrance requirements: For master's, GRE General Test, minimum GPA of 3.0; for doctorate, GRE General Test, minimum undergraduate GPA of 3.0. *Application deadline:* For fall admission, 12/15. *Application fee:* $60. Electronic applications accepted.
Expenses: Tuition, nonresident: full-time $10,244. Required fees: $3,609. Full-time tuition and fees vary according to program.
Financial support: In 2001–02, 64 fellowships, 59 research assistantships, 96 teaching assistantships were awarded. Federal Work-Study, institutionally sponsored loans, scholarships/grants, and tuition waivers (full and partial) also available. Financial award application deadline: 3/1.
Dr. Duncan Thomas, Chair, 310-206-1413.
Application contact: Departmental Office, 310-206-1413, *E-mail:* iclarke@econ.ucla.edu.

■ UNIVERSITY OF CALIFORNIA, RIVERSIDE

Graduate Division, Department of Economics, Riverside, CA 92521-0102

AWARDS MA, PhD.

Faculty: 20 full-time (3 women).
Students: 50 full-time (22 women); includes 6 minority (1 African American, 4 Asian Americans or Pacific Islanders, 1 Hispanic American), 31 international. Average age 30. 197 applicants, 16% accepted, 7 enrolled. In 2001, 3 master's, 6 doctorates awarded. Terminal master's awarded for partial completion of doctoral program.
Degree requirements: For master's, comprehensive exam; for doctorate, thesis/dissertation, qualifying exams. *Median time to degree:* Master's–2.3 years full-time; doctorate–6 years full-time.
Entrance requirements: For master's and doctorate, GRE General Test, TOEFL, minimum GPA of 3.2. *Application deadline:* For fall admission, 5/1; for winter admission, 9/1; for spring admission, 12/1. Applications are processed on a rolling basis. *Application fee:* $40. Electronic applications accepted.
Expenses: Tuition, state resident: full-time $5,001. Tuition, nonresident: full-time $15,897.
Financial support: In 2001–02, 10 fellowships with partial tuition reimbursements (averaging $12,000 per year), 1 teaching assistantship with partial tuition reimbursement (averaging $14,000 per year) were awarded. Research assistantships, career-related internships or fieldwork, institutionally sponsored loans, and tuition waivers (full and partial) also available. Financial award application deadline: 2/1; financial award applicants required to submit FAFSA.
Faculty research: Political economy and international development; resource and environment; econometrics; labor economics; microeconomics; macroeconomics; money, credit, and business cycles.
Dr. Stephen Cullenberg, Chair, 909-787-5037, *Fax:* 909-787-5685, *E-mail:* econgrad@pop.ucr.edu.
Application contact: Karina Wyckstandt, Graduate Program Assistant, 909-787-5037 Ext. 1474, *Fax:* 909-787-5685, *E-mail:* econgrad@ucr.edu. *Web site:* http://www.ucr.edu/CHSS/depts/econ/EconGradInfo.html

■ UNIVERSITY OF CALIFORNIA, SAN DIEGO

Graduate Studies and Research, Department of Economics, La Jolla, CA 92093

AWARDS Economics (PhD); economics and international affairs (PhD).

Faculty: 29.
Students: 73 (17 women). 345 applicants, 29% accepted, 25 enrolled. In 2001, 11 doctorates awarded.
Degree requirements: For doctorate, thesis/dissertation.
Entrance requirements: For doctorate, GRE General Test. *Application deadline:* For fall admission, 1/18. *Application fee:* $40. Electronic applications accepted.
Expenses: Tuition, nonresident: full-time $10,434. Required fees: $4,883.
Financial support: Application deadline: 2/1.
Faculty research: Microfoundations of macroeconomics, econometric model specification and testing, industrial organization.
James Hamilton, Chair.
Application contact: Applications Coordinator, 858-534-1867.

■ UNIVERSITY OF CALIFORNIA, SAN DIEGO

Graduate Studies and Research, Graduate School of International Relations and Pacific Studies, La Jolla, CA 92093-0520

AWARDS Economics and international affairs (PhD); Pacific international affairs (MPIA); political science and international affairs (PhD). Part-time programs available.

Faculty: 24 full-time (3 women), 31 part-time/adjunct (12 women).
Students: 204 full-time (105 women); includes 44 minority (31 Asian Americans or Pacific Islanders, 13 Hispanic Americans), 86 international. Average age 27. 384 applicants, 61% accepted. In 2001, 87 master's, 1 doctorate awarded.

University of California, San Diego (continued)

Degree requirements: For master's, one foreign language; for doctorate, thesis/dissertation. *Median time to degree:* Master's–2 years full-time, 3 years part-time.

Entrance requirements: For master's, GMAT or GRE General Test, TOEFL; for doctorate, GRE General Test, TOEFL. *Application deadline:* For fall admission, 2/15 (priority date). Applications are processed on a rolling basis. *Application fee:* $40. Electronic applications accepted.

Expenses: Tuition, nonresident: full-time $10,434. Required fees: $4,883.

Financial support: In 2001–02, 120 students received support, including 20 fellowships with full and partial tuition reimbursements available (averaging $6,387 per year), 11 research assistantships with partial tuition reimbursements available, 65 teaching assistantships with partial tuition reimbursements available; career-related internships or fieldwork, institutionally sponsored loans, and tuition waivers (full and partial) also available. Support available to part-time students. Financial award application deadline: 3/2; financial award applicants required to submit FAFSA.

Faculty research: Pacific Rim as system and placement in global relations; studies in international economics, management and finance; analysis patterns of policy making in countries of the Pacific.

Peter Cowhey, Dean, 858-534-1946, *Fax:* 858-534-3939.

Application contact: Jori J. Cincotta, Director of Admissions, 858-534-5914, *Fax:* 858-534-1135, *E-mail:* irps-apply@ucsd.edu. *Web site:* http://www-irps.ucsd.edu/

Find an in-depth description at www.petersons.com/gradchannel.

■ UNIVERSITY OF CALIFORNIA, SANTA BARBARA

Graduate Division, College of Letters and Sciences, Division of Social Science, Department of Economics, Santa Barbara, CA 93106

AWARDS MA, PhD. Terminal master's awarded for partial completion of doctoral program.

Degree requirements: For master's, written exam; for doctorate, thesis/dissertation.

Entrance requirements: For master's and doctorate, GRE General Test, TOEFL. Electronic applications accepted. *Web site:* http://www.econ.ucsb.edu/

■ UNIVERSITY OF CALIFORNIA, SANTA CRUZ

Division of Graduate Studies, Division of Social Sciences, Program in International Economics, Santa Cruz, CA 95064

AWARDS PhD.

Faculty: 19 full-time.

Students: 40 full-time (16 women); includes 5 minority (all Asian Americans or Pacific Islanders), 26 international. 84 applicants, 32% accepted. In 2001, 8 doctorates awarded.

Degree requirements: For doctorate, one foreign language, thesis/dissertation, 2 field exams, major research paper. *Median time to degree:* Doctorate–2 years full-time.

Entrance requirements: For doctorate, GRE General Test. *Application deadline:* For fall admission, 2/1. *Application fee:* $40.

Expenses: Tuition: Full-time $19,857.

Financial support: Research assistantships, teaching assistantships, career-related internships or fieldwork, Federal Work-Study, institutionally sponsored loans, and tuition waivers (partial) available. Financial award application deadline: 2/1.

Faculty research: Current and emerging issues in taxation, industrial policy, environmental regulation, market structure.

Michael Hutchison, Chairperson, 831-459-4981.

Application contact: Cristina Intintoli, Graduate Assistant, 831-459-2219, *E-mail:* cmintint@cats.ucsc.edu. *Web site:* http://www.ucsc.edu/

■ UNIVERSITY OF CENTRAL FLORIDA

College of Business Administration, Department of Economics, Orlando, FL 32816

AWARDS MAAE. Part-time and evening/weekend programs available.

Faculty: 27 full-time (7 women), 3 part-time/adjunct (0 women).

Students: 7 full-time (3 women), 15 part-time (6 women); includes 3 minority (2 Asian Americans or Pacific Islanders, 1 Hispanic American), 2 international. Average age 32. 21 applicants, 43% accepted, 6 enrolled. In 2001, 10 degrees awarded.

Degree requirements: For master's, thesis or alternative, comprehensive exam.

Entrance requirements: For master's, GMAT, TOEFL, minimum GPA of 3.0 in last 60 hours. *Application deadline:* For fall admission, 6/15 (priority date); for spring admission, 11/1 (priority date). *Application fee:* $20. Electronic applications accepted.

Expenses: Tuition, state resident: part-time $162 per hour. Tuition, nonresident: part-time $569 per hour.

Financial support: In 2001–02, 1 fellowship with partial tuition reimbursement (averaging $7,500 per year), 19 research assistantships with partial tuition reimbursements (averaging $2,681 per year) were awarded. Teaching assistantships with partial tuition reimbursements, career-related internships or fieldwork, Federal Work-Study, institutionally sponsored loans, tuition waivers (partial), and unspecified assistantships also available. Financial award application deadline: 3/1; financial award applicants required to submit FAFSA.

Dr. Djehane A. Hosni, Interim Chair, 407-823-2069, *E-mail:* djehane@bus.ucf.edu.

Application contact: Dr. Robert L. Ford, Assistant Dean, 407-823-2385, *Fax:* 407-823-6206, *E-mail:* robert.ford@bus.ucf.edu. *Web site:* http://www.ucf.edu/

■ UNIVERSITY OF CHICAGO

Division of Social Sciences, Department of Economics, Chicago, IL 60637-1513

AWARDS PhD.

Students: 180.

Degree requirements: For doctorate, one foreign language, thesis/dissertation, written exams in 2 fields.

Entrance requirements: For doctorate, GRE General Test, TOEFL. *Application deadline:* For fall admission, 12/28. *Application fee:* $100. Electronic applications accepted.

Expenses: Tuition: Full-time $16,548.

Financial support: Fellowships, research assistantships, teaching assistantships, Federal Work-Study and institutionally sponsored loans available. Financial award application deadline: 12/28.

Prof. Lars Hansen, Chair, 773-702-8254.

Application contact: Office of the Dean of Students, 773-702-8415.

■ UNIVERSITY OF CINCINNATI

Division of Research and Advanced Studies, McMicken College of Arts and Sciences, Department of Economics, Program in Applied Economics, Cincinnati, OH 45221

AWARDS MA. Part-time and evening/weekend programs available.

Faculty: 13 full-time (2 women).

Students: 17 full-time (6 women), 11 part-time (7 women); includes 2 minority (both Asian Americans or Pacific Islanders), 15 international. 46 applicants, 48% accepted, 10 enrolled. In 2001, 5 degrees awarded.

Degree requirements: For master's, thesis.

Entrance requirements: For master's, GRE General Test or GMAT, TOEFL. *Application deadline:* For fall admission, 4/1 (priority date). Applications are processed on a rolling basis. *Application fee:* $30. Electronic applications accepted.

Expenses: Tuition, state resident: part-time $2,698 per quarter. Tuition, nonresident: part-time $4,977 per quarter.

Financial support: Fellowships with full tuition reimbursements, research assistantships with full tuition reimbursements,

teaching assistantships with full tuition reimbursements, career-related internships or fieldwork, scholarships/grants, tuition waivers (partial), and unspecified assistantships available. Financial award application deadline: 4/1.
Application contact: Dr. Nicholas Williams, Graduate Program Director, 513-556-2600, *Fax:* 513-556-2669, *E-mail:* nicholas.williams@uc.edu. *Web site:* http://ucaswww.mcm.uc.edu/

■ UNIVERSITY OF COLORADO AT BOULDER

Graduate School, College of Arts and Sciences, Department of Economics, Boulder, CO 80309

AWARDS MA, PhD.

Faculty: 26 full-time (4 women).
Students: 74 full-time (29 women), 20 part-time (11 women); includes 5 minority (3 Asian Americans or Pacific Islanders, 2 Hispanic Americans), 51 international. Average age 29. 139 applicants, 38% accepted. In 2001, 20 master's, 7 doctorates awarded. Terminal master's awarded for partial completion of doctoral program.
Degree requirements: For master's, thesis or alternative, comprehensive exam; for doctorate, thesis/dissertation, preliminary exam, comprehensive exam.
Entrance requirements: For master's, GRE General Test, TOEFL, minimum undergraduate GPA of 2.75; for doctorate, GRE General Test, TOEFL. *Application deadline:* For fall admission, 2/1 (priority date). Applications are processed on a rolling basis. *Application fee:* $50 ($60 for international students).
Expenses: Tuition, state resident: full-time $3,474. Tuition, nonresident: full-time $16,624.
Financial support: In 2001–02, 13 fellowships with full tuition reimbursements (averaging $2,367 per year), 3 research assistantships with full tuition reimbursements (averaging $15,709 per year), 23 teaching assistantships with full tuition reimbursements (averaging $16,043 per year) were awarded. Tuition waivers (full) also available. Financial award application deadline: 2/1; financial award applicants required to submit FAFSA.
Faculty research: International, public economics, econometrics, natural resources environmental, labor economics. *Total annual research expenditures:* $123,515.
Keith E. Maskus, Chair, 303-492-6394, *Fax:* 303-492-8960.
Application contact: Georgiana Esquibel, Graduate Assistant, 303-492-6396, *Fax:* 303-492-8960, *E-mail:* georgiana.esquibel@colorado.edu. *Web site:* http://www.colorado.edu/economics

■ UNIVERSITY OF COLORADO AT DENVER

Graduate School, College of Liberal Arts and Sciences, Program in Economics, Denver, CO 80217-3364

AWARDS MA. Part-time and evening/weekend programs available.

Faculty: 12 full-time (4 women).
Students: 30 full-time (9 women), 20 part-time (8 women); includes 4 minority (2 African Americans, 1 Asian American or Pacific Islander, 1 Hispanic American), 35 international. Average age 28. 39 applicants, 67% accepted, 13 enrolled. In 2001, 21 degrees awarded.
Degree requirements: For master's, thesis or alternative.
Entrance requirements: For master's, GRE General Test, 16 hours of course work in economics. *Application deadline:* For fall admission, 6/1; for spring admission, 11/1. Applications are processed on a rolling basis. *Application fee:* $50 ($60 for international students). Electronic applications accepted.
Expenses: Tuition, state resident: full-time $3,284; part-time $198 per credit hour. Tuition, nonresident: full-time $13,380; part-time $802 per credit hour. Required fees: $444; $222 per semester.
Financial support: Research assistantships, teaching assistantships, Federal Work-Study available. Financial award application deadline: 3/1; financial award applicants required to submit FAFSA. *Total annual research expenditures:* $178,330.
Naci Mocan, Chair, 303-556-8540, *Fax:* 303-556-3547, *E-mail:* nmocan@carbon.cudenver.edu.
Application contact: Lynn Ferguson, Program Assistant, 303-556-4413, *Fax:* 303-556-3547, *E-mail:* tferguson@carbon.cudenver.edu. *Web site:* http://www.cudenver.edu/public/economics/degrees.htm

■ UNIVERSITY OF CONNECTICUT

Graduate School, College of Liberal Arts and Sciences, Field of Economics, Storrs, CT 06269

AWARDS MA, PhD.

Degree requirements: For doctorate, thesis/dissertation.
Entrance requirements: For master's and doctorate, GRE General Test, GRE Subject Test, TOEFL.

Find an in-depth description at www.petersons.com/gradchannel.

■ UNIVERSITY OF DELAWARE

College of Business and Economics, Department of Economics, Newark, DE 19716

AWARDS Economics (MA, MS, PhD); economics for educators (MA). Part-time and evening/weekend programs available.

Faculty: 25 full-time (2 women).
Students: 63 full-time (20 women), 1 part-time; includes 1 minority (African American), 36 international. Average age 29. 109 applicants, 57% accepted, 25 enrolled. In 2001, 14 master's, 4 doctorates awarded.
Degree requirements: For master's, thesis (for some programs), mathematics review exam, research project, comprehensive exam; for doctorate, thesis/dissertation, comprehensive exam. *Median time to degree:* Master's–2 years full-time.
Entrance requirements: For master's, GMAT or GRE General Test, TOEFL, minimum GPA of 2.5; for doctorate, GRE General Test, TOEFL, minimum GPA of 3.5 in graduate economics course work. *Application deadline:* For fall admission, 5/1. *Application fee:* $50. Electronic applications accepted.
Expenses: Tuition, state resident: full-time $4,770; part-time $265 per credit. Tuition, nonresident: full-time $13,860; part-time $770 per credit. Required fees: $414.
Financial support: In 2001–02, 41 students received support, including 2 fellowships with full tuition reimbursements available (averaging $10,440 per year), 8 research assistantships with full and partial tuition reimbursements available (averaging $5,070 per year), 22 teaching assistantships with full and partial tuition reimbursements available (averaging $10,440 per year); career-related internships or fieldwork, scholarships/grants, and tuition waivers (full and partial) also available. Financial award application deadline: 2/15.
Faculty research: Applied quantitative economics, industrial organization, benefit-cost analysis, resource economics, monetary economics. *Total annual research expenditures:* $176,980.
Saul D. Hoffman, Chairman, 302-831-2565, *Fax:* 302-831-6968.
Application contact: Dr. Kenneth Lewis, Associate Chairman, 302-831-1912, *Fax:* 302-831-6968, *E-mail:* lewisk@udel.edu. *Web site:* http://www.udel.edu/catalog/current/be/econ/grad.html

■ UNIVERSITY OF DENVER

Graduate Studies, Faculty of Arts and Humanities/Social Sciences, Department of Economics, Denver, CO 80208

AWARDS MA. Part-time programs available.

Faculty: 7 full-time (2 women).
Students: 10 (2 women); includes 2 minority (both African Americans) 3 international. 34 applicants, 68% accepted. In 2001, 2 degrees awarded.
Degree requirements: For master's, thesis.
Entrance requirements: For master's, GRE, TOEFL. *Application deadline:* For fall admission, 6/1 (priority date). Applications are processed on a rolling basis. *Application fee:* $45.
Expenses: Tuition: Full-time $21,456.

University of Denver (continued)
Financial support: In 2001–02, 2 teaching assistantships with full and partial tuition reimbursements (averaging $6,597 per year) were awarded; career-related internships or fieldwork, Federal Work-Study, and scholarships/grants also available. Support available to part-time students. Financial award application deadline: 3/1; financial award applicants required to submit FAFSA.
Dr. Tracy Mott, Chairperson, 303-871-2569.
Application contact: Information Contact, 303-871-2685. *Web site:* http://www.du.edu/econ/

■ UNIVERSITY OF FLORIDA

Graduate School, Warrington College of Business Administration, Department of Economics, Gainesville, FL 32611

AWARDS MA, MS, PhD. Terminal master's awarded for partial completion of doctoral program.

Degree requirements: For master's, thesis optional; for doctorate, thesis/dissertation.
Electronic applications accepted.
Expenses: Tuition, state resident: part-time $164 per hour. Tuition, nonresident: part-time $571 per hour. Tuition and fees vary according to course level and program.
Faculty research: Econometrics, international economics, industrial organization, public finance, microeconomic theory. *Web site:* http://www.cba.ufl.edu/eco/

■ UNIVERSITY OF GEORGIA

Graduate School, Terry College of Business, Department of Economics, Athens, GA 30602

AWARDS MA, PhD.

Faculty: 17 full-time (1 woman).
Students: 20 full-time (5 women), 3 part-time; includes 1 minority (African American), 10 international. 59 applicants, 15% accepted. In 2001, 1 master's, 5 doctorates awarded.
Degree requirements: For master's and doctorate, thesis/dissertation.
Entrance requirements: For master's and doctorate, GRE General Test. *Application deadline:* For fall admission, 7/1 (priority date); for spring admission, 11/15. *Application fee:* $30. Electronic applications accepted.
Expenses: Tuition, state resident: full-time $2,376; part-time $132 per credit hour. Tuition, nonresident: full-time $9,504; part-time $528 per credit hour. Required fees: $236 per semester.
Financial support: Fellowships, research assistantships, teaching assistantships available.
Dr. Charles C. DeLorme, Interim Head, 706-542-3682, *Fax:* 706-542-3376, *E-mail:* delorme@terry.uga.edu.
Application contact: Dr. William D. Lastrapes, Graduate Coordinator, 706-542-3569, *Fax:* 706-542-3376, *E-mail:* last@terry.uga.edu. *Web site:* http://www.terry.uga.edu/economics/

■ UNIVERSITY OF HAWAII AT MANOA

Graduate Division, College of Arts and Sciences, College of Social Sciences, Department of Economics, Honolulu, HI 96822

AWARDS MA, PhD.

Faculty: 19 full-time (3 women), 8 part-time/adjunct (1 woman).
Students: 57 full-time (22 women), 10 part-time (4 women); includes 12 Asian Americans or Pacific Islanders. Average age 31. 43 applicants, 79% accepted, 23 enrolled. In 2001, 30 master's, 3 doctorates awarded. Terminal master's awarded for partial completion of doctoral program.
Degree requirements: For master's, thesis optional; for doctorate, thesis/dissertation. *Median time to degree:* Master's–2 years full-time.
Entrance requirements: For master's and doctorate, GRE General Test, TOEFL. *Application deadline:* For fall admission, 3/1; for spring admission, 9/1. *Application fee:* $25 ($50 for international students).
Expenses: Tuition, state resident: full-time $2,160; part-time $1,980 per year. Tuition, nonresident: full-time $5,190; part-time $4,829 per year.
Financial support: In 2001–02, 3 research assistantships (averaging $16,652 per year), 8 teaching assistantships (averaging $13,976 per year) were awarded.
Faculty research: Trade, development, demography, labor, resource economics.
Dr. Sumner LeCroix, Chair, 808-956-8496, *Fax:* 808-956-4347.
Application contact: Chung Lee, Graduate Chair, 808-956-8427, *Fax:* 808-956-4347, *E-mail:* lchung@hawaii.edu.

■ UNIVERSITY OF HOUSTON

College of Liberal Arts and Social Sciences, Department of Economics, Houston, TX 77204

AWARDS MA, PhD. Part-time programs available.

Faculty: 14 full-time (2 women).
Students: 37 full-time (21 women), 9 part-time (2 women); includes 5 minority (2 African Americans, 2 Asian Americans or Pacific Islanders, 1 Hispanic American), 29 international. Average age 30. 72 applicants, 42% accepted. In 2001, 4 master's, 1 doctorate awarded. Terminal master's awarded for partial completion of doctoral program.
Degree requirements: For doctorate, thesis/dissertation.
Entrance requirements: For master's, GRE General Test, minimum GPA of 3.0; for doctorate, GRE General Test, master's degree, minimum GPA of 3.0. *Application deadline:* For fall admission, 5/2. *Application fee:* $0 ($75 for international students).
Expenses: Tuition, state resident: full-time $1,512. Tuition, nonresident: full-time $5,310. Required fees: $1,308. Tuition and fees vary according to program.
Financial support: Research assistantships, institutionally sponsored loans available. Financial award application deadline: 2/1.
Faculty research: Econometrics, labor economics, international economics, public finance. *Total annual research expenditures:* $223,471.
Dr. John Antel, Chairperson, 713-743-3800, *Fax:* 713-743-3798.
Application contact: Dr. David Papell, Graduate Director, 713-743-3800, *Fax:* 713-743-3798. *Web site:* http://www.uh.edu/academics/SOS/econ/

■ UNIVERSITY OF IDAHO

College of Graduate Studies, College of Business and Economics, Department of Economics, Moscow, ID 83844-2282

AWARDS MS.

Faculty: 6 full-time (0 women), 1 part-time/adjunct (0 women).
Students: 2 full-time (1 woman), 3 part-time (1 woman), 4 international. 19 applicants, 63% accepted. In 2001, 3 degrees awarded.
Degree requirements: For master's, comprehensive exam.
Entrance requirements: For master's, GMAT, GRE, TOEFL, minimum GPA of 2.8. *Application deadline:* For fall admission, 8/1; for spring admission, 12/15. *Application fee:* $35 ($45 for international students).
Expenses: Tuition, state resident: full-time $1,613. Tuition, nonresident: full-time $3,000.
Financial support: Application deadline: 2/15.

Find an in-depth description at www.petersons.com/gradchannel.

■ UNIVERSITY OF ILLINOIS AT CHICAGO

Graduate College, College of Business Administration, Department of Economics, Chicago, IL 60607-7128

AWARDS Economics (MA, PhD); public policy analysis (PhD).

Faculty: 19 full-time (3 women).
Students: 56 full-time (29 women), 19 part-time (5 women); includes 10 minority (4 African Americans, 3 Asian Americans or Pacific Islanders, 3 Hispanic Americans), 34 international. Average age 31. 163 applicants, 22% accepted, 18

enrolled. In 2001, 10 master's, 7 doctorates awarded. Terminal master's awarded for partial completion of doctoral program.
Degree requirements: For master's, comprehensive exam; for doctorate, thesis/dissertation.
Entrance requirements: For master's and doctorate, GRE General Test, TOEFL, minimum GPA of 3.75 on a 5.0 scale. *Application deadline:* For fall admission, 6/1. *Application fee:* $40 ($50 for international students). Electronic applications accepted.
Expenses: Tuition, state resident: full-time $3,060. Tuition, nonresident: full-time $6,688.
Financial support: In 2001–02, 42 students received support; fellowships with full tuition reimbursements available, research assistantships with full tuition reimbursements available, teaching assistantships with full tuition reimbursements available, career-related internships or fieldwork, Federal Work-Study, and tuition waivers (full) available. Financial award application deadline: 3/1; financial award applicants required to submit FAFSA.
Faculty research: International, labor, and urban economics.
Paul Pieper, Director of Graduate Studies, 312-996-5314, *E-mail:* pjpieper@uic.edu.
Application contact: Lynn Lacey, Graduate Secretary, 312-996-2684.

■ UNIVERSITY OF ILLINOIS AT CHICAGO

Graduate College, College of Business Administration, Graduate Professional Development Programs (CBA), Chicago, IL 60607-7128

AWARDS Business administration (MBA); business economics (PhD); finance (PhD); human resource management (PhD); management information systems (PhD); marketing (PhD). Part-time programs available.

Students: 94 full-time (35 women), 287 part-time (109 women); includes 81 minority (24 African Americans, 35 Asian Americans or Pacific Islanders, 19 Hispanic Americans, 3 Native Americans), 65 international. Average age 29. 505 applicants, 57% accepted. In 2001, 226 degrees awarded.
Entrance requirements: For master's, GMAT, TOEFL, minimum GPA of 3.75 on a 5.0 scale; for doctorate, GMAT, TOEFL. *Application fee:* $40 ($50 for international students).
Expenses: Tuition, state resident: full-time $3,060. Tuition, nonresident: full-time $6,688.
Financial support: In 2001–02, 15 students received support; fellowships, research assistantships, teaching assistantships, career-related internships or fieldwork, Federal Work-Study, institutionally sponsored loans, and tuition waivers (full) available. Support available to part-time students. Financial award application deadline: 2/15.
Assistant Director, 312-996-4573.
Application contact: Ann G. Rosi, Information Contact, 312-996-4751, *E-mail:* agrois@uic.edu.

■ UNIVERSITY OF ILLINOIS AT SPRINGFIELD

Graduate Programs, College of Business and Management, Economics Department, Springfield, IL 62703-5404

AWARDS MA. Part-time and evening/weekend programs available.

Faculty: 2 full-time (0 women), 1 part-time/adjunct (0 women).
Students: Average age 38. In 2001, 3 degrees awarded.
Degree requirements: For master's, thesis or alternative.
Application deadline: Applications are processed on a rolling basis. *Application fee:* $0.
Expenses: Tuition, state resident: full-time $2,680. Tuition, nonresident: full-time $8,064. Required fees: $626. One-time fee: $626.
Financial support: Research assistantships with full and partial tuition reimbursements, career-related internships or fieldwork, Federal Work-Study, scholarships/grants, tuition waivers (partial), and unspecified assistantships available. Support available to part-time students. Financial award application deadline: 6/1; financial award applicants required to submit FAFSA.
Dr. Paul McDevitt, Chairperson, 217-206-6534.

■ UNIVERSITY OF ILLINOIS AT URBANA–CHAMPAIGN

Graduate College, College of Commerce and Business Administration, Department of Economics, Champaign, IL 61820

AWARDS MS, PhD.

Faculty: 30 full-time, 5 part-time/adjunct.
Students: 183 full-time (59 women); includes 4 minority (1 African American, 2 Asian Americans or Pacific Islanders, 1 Native American), 161 international. 117 applicants, 40% accepted. In 2001, 49 master's, 22 doctorates awarded. Terminal master's awarded for partial completion of doctoral program.
Degree requirements: For doctorate, thesis/dissertation.
Entrance requirements: For master's, GRE General Test, minimum GPA of 3.0; for doctorate, GRE General Test, minimum GPA of 3.3. *Application deadline:* Applications are processed on a rolling basis. *Application fee:* $40 ($50 for international students). Electronic applications accepted.
Expenses: Tuition, state resident: part-time $3,227 per degree program. Tuition, nonresident: part-time $7,169 per degree program. Tuition and fees vary according to program.
Financial support: In 2001–02, 6 fellowships, 12 research assistantships, 54 teaching assistantships were awarded. Financial award application deadline: 2/15.
Dr. Richard J. Arnould, Head, 217-333-0120, *Fax:* 217-244-6678, *E-mail:* rarnould@uiuc.edu.
Application contact: Dr. Judy Carl, Staff Secretary, 217-333-0120, *Fax:* 217-244-6678, *E-mail:* j-carl@uiuc.edu. *Web site:* http://www.cba.uiuc.edu/college/econ/intro/econ.html

Find an in-depth description at www.petersons.com/gradchannel.

■ THE UNIVERSITY OF IOWA

Graduate College, Henry B. Tippie College of Business, Department of Economics, Iowa City, IA 52242-1316

AWARDS PhD.

Faculty: 23 full-time (3 women), 5 part-time/adjunct (2 women).
Students: 39 full-time (12 women), 1 part-time; includes 1 minority (Native American), 27 international. Average age 29. 333 applicants, 9% accepted. In 2001, 6 doctorates awarded.
Degree requirements: For doctorate, thesis/dissertation, thesis defense, comprehensive exam. *Median time to degree:* Doctorate–5 years full-time.
Entrance requirements: For doctorate, GRE General Test, TOEFL. *Application deadline:* For fall admission, 2/15 (priority date). Applications are processed on a rolling basis. *Application fee:* $30 ($50 for international students). Electronic applications accepted.
Expenses: Tuition, state resident: full-time $3,702; part-time $206 per semester hour. Tuition, nonresident: full-time $11,924; part-time $206 per semester hour. Required fees: $101 per semester. Tuition and fees vary according to course load and program.
Financial support: In 2001–02, 6 fellowships with full and partial tuition reimbursements (averaging $16,500 per year), 1 research assistantship with partial tuition reimbursement (averaging $16,500 per year), 32 teaching assistantships with partial tuition reimbursements (averaging $15,000 per year) were awarded. Health care benefits also available.
Faculty research: Macroeconomics, econometrics, labor economics, industrial organization, applied microeconomics. *Total annual research expenditures:* $452,314.
Prof. Stephen Williamson, Chair, 319-335-0829, *Fax:* 319-335-1956, *E-mail:* stephen-williamson@uiowa.edu.
Application contact: Renea L. Jay, Graduate Secretary, 319-335-0830, *Fax:* 319-335-1956, *E-mail:* econphd@uiowa.edu. *Web site:* http://www.biz.uiowa.edu/econ/index.html

■ UNIVERSITY OF KANSAS

Graduate School, College of Liberal Arts and Sciences, Department of Economics, Lawrence, KS 66045

AWARDS MA, PhD, JD/MA. Part-time programs available.

Faculty: 18.
Students: 42 full-time (16 women), 11 part-time; includes 2 minority (both Hispanic Americans), 41 international. Average age 30. 48 applicants, 29% accepted, 8 enrolled. In 2001, 6 master's, 2 doctorates awarded.
Degree requirements: For master's, thesis or alternative; for doctorate, thesis/dissertation.
Entrance requirements: For master's, TOEFL, TSE; for doctorate, TOEFL, TSE, GRE. *Application deadline:* For fall admission, 7/1 (priority date); for spring admission, 12/1 (priority date). Applications are processed on a rolling basis. *Application fee:* $35. Electronic applications accepted.
Expenses: Tuition, state resident: full-time $2,722; part-time $113 per credit. Tuition, nonresident: full-time $8,586; part-time $358 per credit. Required fees: $551; $46 per credit. Tuition and fees vary according to campus/location, program and reciprocity agreements.
Financial support: In 2001–02, 23 teaching assistantships with full and partial tuition reimbursements (averaging $10,005 per year) were awarded; fellowships, institutionally sponsored loans also available. Financial award application deadline: 2/15.
Faculty research: Economic history, financial economy, applied macroeconomics, econometrics, industrial organization.
Joseph Sicilian, Chair, 785-864-3501, *Fax:* 785-864-5270, *E-mail:* jsicilian@bschool.wpo.ukans.edu.
Application contact: Gautam Bhattacharyya, Graduate Director, 785-864-2869, *Fax:* 785-864-5270, *E-mail:* gbhattacharya@ku.edu. *Web site:* http://www.econ.ku.edu/

■ UNIVERSITY OF KENTUCKY

Graduate School, Graduate School Programs from the College of Business and Economics, Program in Economics, Lexington, KY 40506-0032

AWARDS MS, PhD.

Faculty: 22 full-time (2 women).
Students: 26 full-time (11 women), 8 part-time (2 women); includes 1 minority (African American), 21 international. 85 applicants, 81% accepted. In 2001, 4 master's, 5 doctorates awarded.
Degree requirements: For master's, comprehensive exam; for doctorate, thesis/dissertation, comprehensive exam.
Entrance requirements: For master's, GMAT, minimum undergraduate GPA of 2.5; for doctorate, GMAT, minimum graduate GPA of 3.0. *Application deadline:* For fall admission, 7/19. Applications are processed on a rolling basis. *Application fee:* $30 ($35 for international students).
Expenses: Tuition, state resident: full-time $4,075; part-time $213 per credit hour. Tuition, nonresident: full-time $11,295; part-time $614 per credit hour.
Financial support: In 2001–02, 4 fellowships, 1 research assistantship, 17 teaching assistantships were awarded. Federal Work-Study, institutionally sponsored loans, and unspecified assistantships also available. Support available to part-time students.
Faculty research: Public economics, international economics and economic development, labor economics, environmental economics, industrial economics.
Dr. John Garen, Director of Graduate Studies, 859-257-3581, *Fax:* 859-323-1920, *E-mail:* jgaren@pop.uky.edu.
Application contact: Dr. Jeannine Blackwell, Associate Dean, 859-257-4905, *Fax:* 859-323-1928.

■ UNIVERSITY OF MAINE

Graduate School, College of Liberal Arts and Sciences, Department of Economics, Orono, ME 04469

AWARDS Economics (MA); financial economics (MA). Part-time programs available.

Faculty: 9 full-time (1 woman).
Students: 10 full-time (4 women), 7 international. Average age 26. 21 applicants, 86% accepted, 5 enrolled. In 2001, 3 degrees awarded.
Degree requirements: For master's, thesis optional.
Entrance requirements: For master's, GRE General Test, TOEFL. *Application deadline:* For fall admission, 2/1 (priority date). Applications are processed on a rolling basis. *Application fee:* $50. Electronic applications accepted.
Expenses: Tuition, state resident: full-time $3,780; part-time $210 per credit hour. Tuition, nonresident: full-time $10,782; part-time $599 per credit hour. Required fees: $9.50 per credit hour. $32 per semester. Tuition and fees vary according to reciprocity agreements.
Financial support: In 2001–02, 3 teaching assistantships with tuition reimbursements (averaging $9,010 per year) were awarded; career-related internships or fieldwork, Federal Work-Study, institutionally sponsored loans, and tuition waivers (full and partial) also available. Support available to part-time students. Financial award application deadline: 3/1.
Faculty research: Health and marine resource economics, alternative political economy.
Dr. David Wihry, Chair, 207-581-1850, *Fax:* 207-581-1953.
Application contact: Scott G. Delcourt, Director of the Graduate School, 207-581-3218, *Fax:* 207-581-3232, *E-mail:* graduate@maine.edu. *Web site:* http://www.umaine.edu/graduate/

■ UNIVERSITY OF MARYLAND, BALTIMORE COUNTY

Graduate School, Department of Economics, Program in Economic Policy Analysis, Baltimore, MD 21250-5398

AWARDS MA. Part-time and evening/weekend programs available.

Entrance requirements: For master's, GRE General Test.

■ UNIVERSITY OF MARYLAND, COLLEGE PARK

Graduate Studies and Research, College of Behavioral and Social Sciences, Department of Economics, College Park, MD 20742

AWARDS MA, PhD. Part-time and evening/weekend programs available.

Faculty: 69 full-time (20 women), 12 part-time/adjunct (5 women).
Students: 131 full-time (48 women), 39 part-time (13 women); includes 10 minority (4 African Americans, 3 Asian Americans or Pacific Islanders, 3 Hispanic Americans), 122 international. 527 applicants, 16% accepted, 32 enrolled. In 2001, 20 master's, 15 doctorates awarded. Terminal master's awarded for partial completion of doctoral program.
Degree requirements: For master's, variable foreign language requirement, thesis or alternative; for doctorate, variable foreign language requirement, thesis/dissertation, exams.
Entrance requirements: For master's, GRE General Test, minimum GPA of 3.0, previous course work in calculus and mathematics; for doctorate, GRE General Test, calculus background. *Application deadline:* For fall admission, 7/1. Applications are processed on a rolling basis. *Application fee:* $50 ($70 for international students). Electronic applications accepted.
Expenses: Tuition, state resident: part-time $289 per credit hour. Tuition, nonresident: part-time $448 per credit hour. One-time fee: $436 part-time. Full-time tuition and fees vary according to course load, campus/location and program.
Financial support: In 2001–02, 3 fellowships with full tuition reimbursements (averaging $10,296 per year), 1 research assistantship with tuition reimbursement (averaging $12,150 per year), 95 teaching assistantships with tuition reimbursements (averaging $11,512 per year) were awarded. Federal Work-Study and scholarships/grants also available. Support available to part-time students. Financial award applicants required to submit FAFSA.
Faculty research: Econometrics, comparative, and international economics.

Dr. Mahlon Straszheim, Chairman, 301-405-3266, *Fax:* 301-405-3542.
Application contact: Trudy Lindsey, Director, Graduate Admissions and Records, 301-405-6991, *Fax:* 301-314-9305, *E-mail:* grschool@deans.umd.edu.

■ UNIVERSITY OF MASSACHUSETTS AMHERST

Graduate School, College of Social and Behavioral Sciences, Department of Economics, Amherst, MA 01003

AWARDS MA, PhD. Part-time programs available.

Faculty: 25 full-time (6 women).
Students: 27 full-time (8 women), 58 part-time (27 women); includes 8 minority (1 African American, 3 Asian Americans or Pacific Islanders, 4 Hispanic Americans), 42 international. Average age 32. 197 applicants, 12% accepted. In 2001, 5 master's, 10 doctorates awarded. Terminal master's awarded for partial completion of doctoral program.
Degree requirements: For doctorate, thesis/dissertation.
Entrance requirements: For master's and doctorate, GRE General Test. *Application deadline:* For fall admission, 1/15 (priority date). Applications are processed on a rolling basis. *Application fee:* $40 ($50 for international students).
Expenses: Tuition, state resident: full-time $1,980; part-time $110 per credit. Tuition, nonresident: full-time $7,456; part-time $414 per credit. Required fees: $4,112. One-time fee: $115 full-time.
Financial support: In 2001–02, 2 fellowships with full tuition reimbursements (averaging $7,074 per year), 27 research assistantships with full tuition reimbursements (averaging $6,029 per year), 51 teaching assistantships with full tuition reimbursements (averaging $9,137 per year) were awarded. Career-related internships or fieldwork, Federal Work-Study, scholarships/grants, traineeships, and unspecified assistantships also available. Support available to part-time students. Financial award application deadline: 1/15.
Dr. Diane Flaherty, Chair, 413-545-3815, *Fax:* 413-545-2921, *E-mail:* gibson@econs.umass.edu.

■ UNIVERSITY OF MASSACHUSETTS LOWELL

Graduate School, College of Arts and Sciences, Department of Regional Economic and Social Development, Lowell, MA 01854-2881

AWARDS MS.

Entrance requirements: For master's, GRE. Electronic applications accepted.

■ THE UNIVERSITY OF MEMPHIS

Graduate School, Fogelman College of Business and Economics, Economics Area, Memphis, TN 38152

AWARDS MA, PhD. Part-time programs available.

Faculty: 16 full-time (3 women).
Students: 7 full-time (4 women), 3 part-time (2 women), 6 international. Average age 29. 60 applicants, 25% accepted. In 2001, 2 degrees awarded.
Degree requirements: For master's, thesis or alternative, comprehensive exam; for doctorate, thesis/dissertation, comprehensive exam.
Entrance requirements: For master's, GMAT or GRE General Test, previous course work in statistics, intermediate micro and macro theory; for doctorate, GMAT, interview, minimum GPA of 3.4. *Application deadline:* For fall admission, 8/1; for spring admission, 12/1. *Application fee:* $25 ($50 for international students).
Expenses: Tuition, state resident: full-time $2,026. Tuition, nonresident: full-time $4,528.
Financial support: In 2001–02, 8 research assistantships with full tuition reimbursements were awarded; teaching assistantships, scholarships/grants also available. Financial award application deadline: 3/1.
Faculty research: Tax research, medical economics, law and economics, labor economics, U.S. and Japanese economic relations.
Dr. Julia A. Heath, Chair, 901-678-2785, *Fax:* 901-678-8397, *E-mail:* jheath@cc.memphis.edu.
Application contact: Dr. Coy A. Jones, Interim Associate Dean for Academic Programs, 901-678-4649, *Fax:* 901-678-4705, *E-mail:* fcbegp@memphis.edu. *Web site:* http://economics.memphis.edu/schedule.htm

■ THE UNIVERSITY OF MEMPHIS

Graduate School, Fogelman College of Business and Economics, Management Department, Memphis, TN 38152

AWARDS Accounting (MBA, PhD); economics (MBA, PhD); executive business administration (MBA); finance (PhD); finance, insurance, and real estate (MBA, MS); international business administration (MBA); management (MBA, MS, PhD); management information systems (MBA, MS); management information systems and decision sciences (PhD); management science (MBA); marketing (MBA, MS, PhD); real estate development (MS).

Faculty: 95 full-time (18 women), 35 part-time/adjunct (11 women).
Students: 343 full-time (150 women), 302 part-time (114 women); includes 89 minority (67 African Americans, 18 Asian Americans or Pacific Islanders, 3 Hispanic Americans, 1 Native American), 176 international. Average age 29. 522 applicants, 66% accepted. In 2001, 123 master's, 1 doctorate awarded.
Degree requirements: For master's, comprehensive exam; for doctorate, thesis/dissertation, comprehensive exam.
Entrance requirements: For master's, GMAT, essay, resumé; for doctorate, GMAT, interview, minimum GPA of 3.4. *Application deadline:* For fall admission, 8/1; for spring admission, 12/1. *Application fee:* $25 ($50 for international students).
Expenses: Tuition, state resident: full-time $2,026. Tuition, nonresident: full-time $4,528.
Financial support: In 2001–02, 191 students received support, including 81 research assistantships with full tuition reimbursements available, 54 teaching assistantships; career-related internships or fieldwork, scholarships/grants, and unspecified assistantships also available. Financial award application deadline: 3/1.
Faculty research: Government contracts and tax policy, medical economics, interest rates and monetary policy, mergers, econometrics.
Application contact: Dr. Coy A. Jones, Interim Associate Dean for Academic Programs, 901-678-4649, *Fax:* 901-678-4705, *E-mail:* fcbegp@memphis.edu. *Web site:* http://business.memphis.edu/

■ UNIVERSITY OF MIAMI

Graduate School, School of Business Administration, Department of Economics, Coral Gables, FL 33124

AWARDS Economic development (MA, PhD); financial economics (PhD); human resource economics (MA, PhD); international economics (MA, PhD). PhD students admitted every two years in the fall semester.

Faculty: 14 full-time (3 women).
Students: 13 full-time (4 women); includes 10 minority (2 African Americans, 8 Asian Americans or Pacific Islanders). Average age 28. 89 applicants, 11% accepted. In 2001, 5 degrees awarded. Terminal master's awarded for partial completion of doctoral program.
Degree requirements: For master's, comprehensive exam; for doctorate, thesis/dissertation, comprehensive exam.
Entrance requirements: For master's and doctorate, GRE General Test, TOEFL, minimum GPA of 3.0. *Application deadline:* For fall admission, 3/1. *Application fee:* $50.
Expenses: Tuition: Part-time $960 per credit hour. Required fees: $85 per semester. Tuition and fees vary according to program.
Financial support: In 2001–02, 13 students received support, including 1 fellowship with full tuition reimbursement available (averaging $17,000 per year), 9 research assistantships with full tuition reimbursements available (averaging $12,000 per year), 3 teaching assistantships with full tuition reimbursements available (averaging $3,500 per year); tuition waivers (partial) and unspecified assistantships also

University of Miami (continued)
available. Financial award application deadline: 3/1.
Faculty research: Monetary economics, international economics/trade, financial economics, applied microeconomics, development. *Total annual research expenditures:* $363,406.
Dr. Michael Connolly, Chairman, 305-284-4898, *Fax:* 305-284-2985, *E-mail:* mconnolly@miami.edu.
Application contact: Dr. David L. Kelly, Director of Graduate Programs in Economics, 305-284-3725, *Fax:* 305-284-2985, *E-mail:* dkelly@miami.edu. *Web site:* http://www.bus.miami.edu/~eco/

■ UNIVERSITY OF MICHIGAN

Horace H. Rackham School of Graduate Studies, College of Literature, Science, and the Arts, Department of Economics, Ann Arbor, MI 48109

AWARDS Applied economics (AM); economics (AM, PhD); social work and economics (PhD).

Faculty: 49 full-time (6 women).
Students: 131 full-time (37 women); includes 9 minority (3 African Americans, 3 Asian Americans or Pacific Islanders, 1 Hispanic American, 2 Native Americans), 66 international. 594 applicants, 20% accepted. In 2001, 18 master's, 11 doctorates awarded. Terminal master's awarded for partial completion of doctoral program.
Degree requirements: For doctorate, oral defense of dissertation, preliminary exam. *Median time to degree:* Master's–2 years full-time; doctorate–6 years full-time.
Entrance requirements: For master's and doctorate, GRE General Test. *Application deadline:* For fall admission, 12/31. *Application fee:* $55. Electronic applications accepted.
Financial support: In 2001–02, 113 students received support, including 38 fellowships with tuition reimbursements available (averaging $15,000 per year), 16 research assistantships with tuition reimbursements available (averaging $12,000 per year), 59 teaching assistantships with tuition reimbursements available (averaging $12,000 per year); career-related internships or fieldwork also available. Financial award application deadline: 12/31.
Faculty research: Economic and econometrical analysis, industrial organization, international trade, public finance, transition, health, labor, population standard, macro.
Prof. Gary Solon, Chair, 734-763-3836, *Fax:* 734-764-2769, *E-mail:* gsolon@umich.edu.
Application contact: Prof. Linda Tesar, Director of Graduate Studies, 734-763-2254, *Fax:* 734-764-2769, *E-mail:* econ.graduate.admissions@umich.edu. *Web site:* http://www.econ.lsa.umich.edu/

■ UNIVERSITY OF MINNESOTA, TWIN CITIES CAMPUS

Graduate School, College of Liberal Arts, Department of Economics, Minneapolis, MN 55455-0213

AWARDS PhD.

Faculty: 28 full-time (4 women), 11 part-time/adjunct (1 woman).
Students: 114 full-time (27 women); includes 1 minority (Asian American or Pacific Islander), 96 international. 428 applicants, 17% accepted, 22 enrolled. In 2001, 17 degrees awarded.
Degree requirements: For doctorate, thesis/dissertation, preliminary exams.
Entrance requirements: For doctorate, GRE General Test, TOEFL. *Application deadline:* For fall admission, 1/15 (priority date). *Application fee:* $50 ($55 for international students).
Expenses: Tuition, state resident: full-time $2,932; part-time $489 per credit. Tuition, nonresident: full-time $5,758; part-time $960 per credit. Part-time tuition and fees vary according to course load, program and reciprocity agreements.
Financial support: In 2001–02, 80 students received support, including fellowships with full tuition reimbursements available (averaging $6,045 per year), research assistantships with full tuition reimbursements available (averaging $12,400 per year), teaching assistantships with full tuition reimbursements available (averaging $11,269 per year). Financial award application deadline: 12/31.
Faculty research: Econometrics, macro- and monetary economics, mathematical economics, industrial organization. *Total annual research expenditures:* $559,700.
Edward Foster, Chairman, 612-625-6353, *Fax:* 612-624-0209.
Application contact: Andrew McLennan, Director of Graduate Studies, 612-625-6833, *Fax:* 612-624-0209, *E-mail:* econdgs@econ.umn.edu. *Web site:* http://www.econ.umn.edu/

■ UNIVERSITY OF MISSISSIPPI

Graduate School, School of Business Administration, Oxford, University, MS 38677

AWARDS Business administration (MBA); economics (MA, PhD); systems management (MS).

Faculty: 59.
Students: 132 full-time (46 women), 26 part-time (6 women); includes 13 minority (8 African Americans, 3 Asian Americans or Pacific Islanders, 1 Hispanic American, 1 Native American), 55 international. In 2001, 57 master's, 3 doctorates awarded.
Degree requirements: For doctorate, thesis/dissertation.
Entrance requirements: For master's, GMAT, TOEFL, minimum GPA of 3.0; for doctorate, GMAT, TOEFL. *Application deadline:* For fall admission, 8/1. Applications are processed on a rolling basis. *Application fee:* $0 ($25 for international students).
Expenses: Tuition, state resident: full-time $3,626; part-time $202 per hour. Tuition, nonresident: full-time $8,172; part-time $454 per hour.
Financial support: Fellowships, career-related internships or fieldwork, tuition waivers (full), and unspecified assistantships available. Financial award application deadline: 3/1.
Dr. N. Keith Womer, Dean, 662-915-5820, *Fax:* 662-915-5821, *E-mail:* kwomer@olemiss.edu. *Web site:* http://www.bus.olemiss.edu

■ UNIVERSITY OF MISSOURI–COLUMBIA

Graduate School, College of Arts and Sciences, Department of Economics, Columbia, MO 65211

AWARDS MA, PhD, JD/MA.

Faculty: 18 full-time (1 woman), 1 (woman) part-time/adjunct.
Students: 41 full-time (13 women), 15 part-time (3 women), 48 international. 28 applicants, 36% accepted. In 2001, 10 master's, 11 doctorates awarded. Terminal master's awarded for partial completion of doctoral program.
Degree requirements: For doctorate, thesis/dissertation.
Entrance requirements: For master's and doctorate, GRE General Test, minimum GPA of 3.0. *Application deadline:* For fall admission, 1/15 (priority date); for winter admission, 11/1 (priority date); for spring admission, 3/1 (priority date). *Application fee:* $25 ($50 for international students).
Expenses: Tuition, state resident: part-time $179 per credit hour. Tuition, nonresident: part-time $539 per credit hour. Required fees: $122 per semester. Tuition and fees vary according to program.
Financial support: Research assistantships, teaching assistantships, institutionally sponsored loans available.
Dr. Ronald Ratti, Director of Graduate Studies, 573-882-7989, *E-mail:* rattir@missouri.edu. *Web site:* http://web.missouri.edu/~econwww/graduate_program.html

■ UNIVERSITY OF MISSOURI–KANSAS CITY

College of Arts and Sciences, Department of Economics, Kansas City, MO 64110-2499

AWARDS MA, PhD. PhD offered through the School of Graduate Studies. Part-time and evening/weekend programs available.

Faculty: 11 full-time (2 women), 1 part-time/adjunct (0 women).
Students: 15 full-time (5 women), 20 part-time (8 women); includes 9 minority (6

African Americans, 3 Hispanic Americans), 12 international. Average age 29. 75 applicants, 20% accepted. In 2001, 10 degrees awarded.
Degree requirements: For doctorate, thesis/dissertation.
Entrance requirements: For master's, GRE or minimum undergraduate GPA of 2.5; for doctorate, GRE, master's degree in economics or equivalent. *Application deadline:* For fall admission, 3/15. Applications are processed on a rolling basis. *Application fee:* $25.
Expenses: Tuition, state resident: part-time $233 per credit hour. Tuition, nonresident: part-time $623 per credit hour. Tuition and fees vary according to course load.
Financial support: In 2001–02, 10 students received support, including 2 fellowships with tuition reimbursements available (averaging $14,000 per year), 3 research assistantships with tuition reimbursements available (averaging $10,000 per year), 5 teaching assistantships with tuition reimbursements available (averaging $9,000 per year); career-related internships or fieldwork, Federal Work-Study, institutionally sponsored loans, and tuition waivers (full and partial) also available. Support available to part-time students.
Faculty research: International trade, general theory, institutions/utilities, forensic economics, human resources. *Total annual research expenditures:* $600,000.
Dr. John Ward, Chairperson, 816-235-1314, *Fax:* 816-235-2836, *E-mail:* wardjo@umkc.edu.
Application contact: James Sturgeon, Graduate Adviser, 816-235-2837, *Fax:* 816-238-2836, *E-mail:* sturgeonj@umkc.edu. *Web site:* http://iml.umkc.edu/econ/

■ UNIVERSITY OF MISSOURI–ST. LOUIS

Graduate School, College of Arts and Sciences, Department of Economics, St. Louis, MO 63121-4499

AWARDS General economics (MA), including business economics; managerial economics (Certificate). Part-time and evening/weekend programs available.

Faculty: 13.
Students: 14 full-time (3 women), 4 part-time (1 woman), 12 international. In 2001, 8 degrees awarded.
Entrance requirements: For master's, GRE General Test. *Application deadline:* For fall admission, 7/1 (priority date); for spring admission, 12/1 (priority date). Applications are processed on a rolling basis. *Application fee:* $25 ($40 for international students). Electronic applications accepted.
Expenses: Tuition, state resident: part-time $231 per credit hour. Tuition, nonresident: part-time $621 per credit hour.
Financial support: In 2001–02, 1 fellowship with full tuition reimbursement (averaging $12,000 per year), 4 research assistantships with full and partial tuition reimbursements (averaging $6,750 per year), 1 teaching assistantship with full and partial tuition reimbursement (averaging $10,000 per year) were awarded.
Faculty research: Health economics, public policy analysis, econometrics, public choice, telecommunications and forensic economics; institutional economics. *Total annual research expenditures:* $147,579.
Dr. Sharon Levin, Director of Graduate Studies, 314-516-5351, *Fax:* 314-516-5562, *E-mail:* slevin@umsl.edu.
Application contact: Graduate Admissions, 314-516-5458, *Fax:* 314-516-5310, *E-mail:* gradadm@umsl.edu. *Web site:* http://www.umsl.edu/divisions/artscience/economics/

■ THE UNIVERSITY OF MONTANA–MISSOULA

Graduate School, College of Arts and Sciences, Department of Economics, Missoula, MT 59812-0002

AWARDS MA.

Faculty: 11 full-time (1 woman).
Students: 4 full-time (0 women), 3 part-time; includes 1 minority (African American), 2 international. Average age 24. 6 applicants, 83% accepted, 2 enrolled. In 2001, 2 degrees awarded.
Degree requirements: For master's, thesis.
Entrance requirements: For master's, GRE General Test. *Application deadline:* Applications are processed on a rolling basis. *Application fee:* $45.
Expenses: Tuition, state resident: full-time $2,482; part-time $1,700 per year. Tuition, nonresident: full-time $7,372; part-time $5,000 per year. Required fees: $1,900. Tuition and fees vary according to degree level.
Financial support: In 2001–02, 4 teaching assistantships with full tuition reimbursements (averaging $8,665 per year) were awarded; career-related internships or fieldwork, Federal Work-Study, and unspecified assistantships also available. Financial award application deadline: 3/1; financial award applicants required to submit FAFSA.
Faculty research: Resource economics, public policy, environmental economics, economic development, regional economics. *Total annual research expenditures:* $74,019.
Dr. Thomas Power, Chair, 406-243-2925.
Application contact: Dr. Doug Dalenberg, Coordinator, 406-243-4406, *E-mail:* ecdrd@selway.umt.edu. *Web site:* http://www.cas.umt.edu/econ/

■ UNIVERSITY OF NEBRASKA AT OMAHA

Graduate Studies and Research, College of Business Administration, Department of Economics, Omaha, NE 68182

AWARDS MA, MS. Part-time and evening/weekend programs available.

Faculty: 9 full-time (2 women).
Students: 11 full-time (4 women), 12 part-time (3 women), 12 international. Average age 34. 39 applicants, 69% accepted, 10 enrolled. In 2001, 14 degrees awarded.
Degree requirements: For master's, thesis (for some programs), comprehensive exam.
Entrance requirements: For master's, minimum GPA of 3.0. *Application deadline:* For fall admission, 7/1 (priority date); for spring admission, 12/1 (priority date). Applications are processed on a rolling basis. *Application fee:* $35. Electronic applications accepted.
Expenses: Tuition, state resident: part-time $116 per credit hour. Tuition, nonresident: part-time $291 per credit hour. Required fees: $13 per credit hour. $4 per semester. One-time fee: $52 part-time.
Financial support: In 2001–02, 14 students received support; research assistantships, Federal Work-Study, institutionally sponsored loans, scholarships/grants, and unspecified assistantships available. Support available to part-time students. Financial award application deadline: 3/1; financial award applicants required to submit FAFSA.
Faculty research: Labor, economics of science, international development, monetary economics, econometrics.
Dr. Kim Sosin, Chair, 402-554-2570.
Application contact: Dr. Donald Baum, Graduate Chair, 402-554-2570.

■ UNIVERSITY OF NEBRASKA–LINCOLN

Graduate College, College of Business Administration, Department of Economics, Lincoln, NE 68588

AWARDS MA, PhD, JD/MA.

Faculty: 19.
Students: 18 (7 women); includes 1 minority (Asian American or Pacific Islander) 10 international. Average age 33. 104 applicants, 7% accepted, 3 enrolled. In 2001, 6 master's, 3 doctorates awarded.
Degree requirements: For master's, thesis optional; for doctorate, thesis/dissertation, comprehensive exam.
Entrance requirements: For master's and doctorate, GRE General Test, GRE Subject Test, TOEFL. *Application deadline:* For fall admission, 3/1 (priority date). Applications are processed on a rolling basis. *Application fee:* $35. Electronic applications accepted.

University of Nebraska–Lincoln (continued)
Expenses: Tuition, state resident: full-time $2,412; part-time $134 per credit. Tuition, nonresident: full-time $6,223; part-time $346 per credit. Tuition and fees vary according to course load.
Financial support: In 2001–02, 1 fellowship, 3 research assistantships, 3 teaching assistantships were awarded. Federal Work-Study and health care benefits also available. Support available to part-time students. Financial award application deadline: 2/15.
Faculty research: Applied microeconomics, economic education, international trade and finance, public finance, regional and institutional economics.
Dr. James Schmidt, Chair, 402-472-2319. *Web site:* http://www.cba.unl.edu/dept/economics/

■ UNIVERSITY OF NEVADA, LAS VEGAS

Graduate College, College of Business, Department of Economics, Las Vegas, NV 89154-9900

AWARDS MA. Part-time and evening/weekend programs available.

Faculty: 16 full-time (1 woman).
Students: 3 full-time (0 women), 11 part-time (3 women); includes 2 minority (1 African American, 1 Hispanic American). 7 applicants, 86% accepted, 4 enrolled. In 2001, 4 degrees awarded.
Degree requirements: For master's, thesis.
Entrance requirements: For master's, GRE General Test or GMAT, minimum GPA of 3.0. *Application deadline:* For fall admission, 6/15; for spring admission, 11/15. *Application fee:* $40 ($55 for international students).
Expenses: Tuition, state resident: full-time $1,926; part-time $107 per credit. Tuition, nonresident: full-time $9,376; part-time $220 per credit. Tuition and fees vary according to course load.
Financial support: In 2001–02, 2 research assistantships with partial tuition reimbursements (averaging $10,000 per year), 1 teaching assistantship with partial tuition reimbursement (averaging $10,000 per year) were awarded. Financial award application deadline: 3/1.
Dr. Steve Miller, Chair, 702-895-3194.
Application contact: Graduate College Admissions Evaluator, 702-895-3320, *Fax:* 702-895-4180, *E-mail:* gradcollege@ccmail.nevada.edu. *Web site:* http://www.unlv.edu/colleges/business/economics/

■ UNIVERSITY OF NEVADA, RENO

Graduate School, College of Business Administration, Department of Economics, Reno, NV 89557

AWARDS MA, MS.

Faculty: 15.
Students: 18 full-time (4 women), 5 part-time (2 women); includes 4 minority (3 Asian Americans or Pacific Islanders, 1 Native American), 4 international. Average age 31. In 2001, 4 degrees awarded.
Degree requirements: For master's, thesis.
Entrance requirements: For master's, GMAT, TOEFL, minimum GPA of 2.75. *Application deadline:* For fall admission, 3/1 (priority date); for spring admission, 11/1. Applications are processed on a rolling basis. *Application fee:* $40.
Expenses: Tuition, state resident: full-time $2,067; part-time $108 per credit. Tuition, nonresident: full-time $9,282; part-time $109 per credit. Required fees: $57 per semester. Tuition and fees vary according to course load.
Financial support: In 2001–02, 4 research assistantships, 1 teaching assistantship were awarded. Federal Work-Study and institutionally sponsored loans also available. Financial award application deadline: 3/1.
Faculty research: Applied microeconomics, public finance, development, labor.
Dr. Shufenz Song, Graduate Program Director, 775-784-6850.

■ UNIVERSITY OF NEW HAMPSHIRE

Graduate School, Whittemore School of Business and Economics, Department of Economics, Durham, NH 03824

AWARDS MA, PhD. Part-time programs available.

Faculty: 14 full-time.
Students: 18 full-time (5 women), 2 part-time, 12 international. Average age 35. 68 applicants, 57% accepted, 8 enrolled. In 2001, 4 master's, 1 doctorate awarded. Terminal master's awarded for partial completion of doctoral program.
Degree requirements: For master's, thesis or alternative; for doctorate, one foreign language, thesis/dissertation.
Entrance requirements: For master's and doctorate, GRE General Test. *Application deadline:* For fall admission, 4/1 (priority date). Applications are processed on a rolling basis. *Application fee:* $50. Electronic applications accepted.
Expenses: Tuition, state resident: full-time $6,300; part-time $350 per credit. Tuition, nonresident: full-time $15,720; part-time $643 per credit. Required fees: $560; $280 per term. One-time fee: $15 part-time. Tuition and fees vary according to course load.
Financial support: In 2001–02, 13 teaching assistantships were awarded; fellowships, research assistantships, career-related internships or fieldwork, Federal Work-Study, scholarships/grants, and tuition waivers (full and partial) also available. Support available to part-time students. Financial award application deadline: 2/15.
Faculty research: Labor economics, international development, econometrics, finance, political economy.
Dr. James Wilbe, Head, 603-862-1367, *E-mail:* tornsten.schmidt@unh.edu.
Application contact: Dr. Karen Conway, Coordinator, 603-862-3347, *E-mail:* bte@cisunix.unh.edu. *Web site:* http://orbit.unh.edu/econ/

Find an in-depth description at www.petersons.com/gradchannel.

■ UNIVERSITY OF NEW MEXICO

Graduate School, College of Arts and Sciences, Department of Economics, Albuquerque, NM 87131-2039

AWARDS MA, PhD. Part-time programs available.

Faculty: 13 full-time (4 women), 3 part-time/adjunct (1 woman).
Students: 27 full-time (13 women), 11 part-time (4 women); includes 6 minority (1 Asian American or Pacific Islander, 4 Hispanic Americans, 1 Native American), 9 international. Average age 35. 59 applicants, 83% accepted, 7 enrolled. In 2001, 3 master's, 4 doctorates awarded. Terminal master's awarded for partial completion of doctoral program.
Degree requirements: For master's, thesis optional; for doctorate, thesis/dissertation.
Entrance requirements: For master's and doctorate, GRE General Test. *Application deadline:* For fall admission, 7/12; for spring admission, 11/9. *Application fee:* $40.
Expenses: Tuition, state resident: full-time $2,771; part-time $115 per credit hour. Tuition, nonresident: full-time $11,207; part-time $467 per credit hour. Required fees: $570; $24 per credit hour. Part-time tuition and fees vary according to course load and program.
Financial support: In 2001–02, 18 students received support, including 4 research assistantships with full tuition reimbursements available (averaging $11,000 per year), 6 teaching assistantships with partial tuition reimbursements available (averaging $6,000 per year); health care benefits and unspecified assistantships also available. Financial award application deadline: 3/1; financial award applicants required to submit FAFSA.
Faculty research: Applied microeconomics, labor, public finance, resource, environmental economics, experimental economics, international/

development economics. *Total annual research expenditures:* $289,043.
Dr. Richard Santos, Chair, 505-277-2107, *Fax:* 505-277-9445, *E-mail:* santos@unm.edu.
Application contact: Lourdes McKenna, Administrator II, 505-277-5304, *Fax:* 505-277-9445, *E-mail:* lourdes@unm.edu. *Web site:* http://www.unm.edu/~econ/

■ UNIVERSITY OF NEW ORLEANS

Graduate School, College of Business Administration, Department of Economics and Finance, Program in Financial Economics, New Orleans, LA 70148

AWARDS PhD.

Faculty: 9 full-time (1 woman), 2 part-time/adjunct (0 women).
Students: 27 full-time (7 women), 4 part-time (1 woman); includes 1 minority (Asian American or Pacific Islander), 22 international. Average age 31. 67 applicants, 30% accepted, 7 enrolled. In 2001, 3 degrees awarded.
Degree requirements: For doctorate, one foreign language, thesis/dissertation, general exams, comprehensive exam.
Entrance requirements: For doctorate, GRE General Test, minimum GPA of 3.0. *Application deadline:* For fall admission, 7/1 (priority date); for spring admission, 11/15 (priority date). Applications are processed on a rolling basis. *Application fee:* $20. Electronic applications accepted.
Expenses: Tuition, state resident: full-time $2,748; part-time $435 per credit. Tuition, nonresident: full-time $9,792; part-time $1,773 per credit.
Financial support: Fellowships, research assistantships, teaching assistantships, Federal Work-Study available. Financial award application deadline: 4/15; financial award applicants required to submit FAFSA.
Faculty research: Urban and regional economics, economic development, monetary theory and policy, international finance.
Application contact: Dr. Atsuyuki Naka, Graduate Coordinator, 504-280-6896, *Fax:* 504-280-6397, *E-mail:* anaka@uo.edu.

■ THE UNIVERSITY OF NORTH CAROLINA AT CHAPEL HILL

Graduate School, College of Arts and Sciences, Department of Economics, Chapel Hill, NC 27599

AWARDS MS, PhD.

Faculty: 31 full-time (4 women).
Students: 77 full-time (24 women), 1 (woman) part-time; includes 26 minority (3 African Americans, 20 Asian Americans or Pacific Islanders, 3 Hispanic Americans). Average age 25. 303 applicants, 18% accepted, 18 enrolled. In 2001, 5 master's, 8 doctorates awarded. Terminal master's awarded for partial completion of doctoral program.
Degree requirements: For master's, thesis or alternative, comprehensive exam, registration; for doctorate, thesis/dissertation, comprehensive exam, registration. *Median time to degree:* Master's–3 years full-time; doctorate–7 years full-time.
Entrance requirements: For master's, GRE General Test, minimum GPA of 3.0; for doctorate, GRE General Test, minimum GPA of 3.5. *Application deadline:* For fall admission, 1/1 (priority date). *Application fee:* $55. Electronic applications accepted.
Expenses: Tuition, state resident: full-time $2,864. Tuition, nonresident: full-time $12,030.
Financial support: In 2001–02, 4 fellowships with full tuition reimbursements (averaging $12,000 per year), 10 research assistantships with full tuition reimbursements (averaging $12,000 per year), 38 teaching assistantships with full tuition reimbursements (averaging $11,250 per year) were awarded. Scholarships/grants, health care benefits, and unspecified assistantships also available. Financial award application deadline: 1/1.
Faculty research: Health economics, micro theory/IO, labor economics, economic history, financial econometrics.
Dr. John S. Akin, Chairman, 919-966-2385, *Fax:* 919-966-4986, *E-mail:* john_akin@unc.edu.
Application contact: Dr. Helen V. Tauchen, Director of Graduate Studies, 919-966-2384, *Fax:* 919-966-4986, *E-mail:* tauchen@unc.edu. *Web site:* http://www.unc.edu/depts/econ/

■ THE UNIVERSITY OF NORTH CAROLINA AT CHARLOTTE

Graduate School, Belk College of Business Administration, Department of Economics, Charlotte, NC 28223-0001

AWARDS MS. Part-time and evening/weekend programs available.

Faculty: 15 full-time (3 women), 1 part-time/adjunct (0 women).
Students: 10 full-time (3 women), 6 part-time (1 woman); includes 1 minority (African American), 7 international. Average age 27. 17 applicants, 94% accepted, 9 enrolled. In 2001, 6 degrees awarded.
Degree requirements: For master's, thesis or project.
Entrance requirements: For master's, GRE General Test, minimum undergraduate GPA of 3.0 in major, 2.8 overall. *Application deadline:* For fall admission, 7/15; for spring admission, 11/15. Applications are processed on a rolling basis. *Application fee:* $35. Electronic applications accepted.
Expenses: Tuition, state resident: full-time $1,483; part-time $371 per year. Tuition, nonresident: full-time $9,850; part-time $2,463 per year. Required fees: $1,043; $277 per year. Tuition and fees vary according to course load.
Financial support: In 2001–02, 3 teaching assistantships were awarded; fellowships, research assistantships, career-related internships or fieldwork, Federal Work-Study, institutionally sponsored loans, scholarships/grants, and unspecified assistantships also available. Support available to part-time students. Financial award application deadline: 4/1; financial award applicants required to submit FAFSA.
Dr. John M. Gandar, Chair, 704-687-2185, *Fax:* 704-687-6442, *E-mail:* jmgandar@email.uncc.edu.
Application contact: Kathy Barringer, Director of Graduate Admissions, 704-687-3366, *Fax:* 704-687-3279, *E-mail:* gradadm@email.uncc.edu. *Web site:* http://www.uncc.edu/gradmiss/

■ THE UNIVERSITY OF NORTH CAROLINA AT GREENSBORO

Graduate School, Joseph M. Bryan School of Business and Economics, Department of Economics, Greensboro, NC 27412-5001

AWARDS Applied economics (MA).

Faculty: 10 full-time (0 women).
Students: 17 full-time (5 women), 7 part-time (5 women); includes 3 African Americans, 8 international. 35 applicants, 51% accepted, 14 enrolled. In 2001, 8 degrees awarded.
Degree requirements: For master's, thesis or alternative.
Entrance requirements: For master's, GMAT, GRE General Test, TOEFL. *Application deadline:* For fall admission, 3/1 (priority date); for spring admission, 11/1. Applications are processed on a rolling basis. *Application fee:* $35.
Expenses: Tuition, state resident: part-time $344 per course. Tuition, nonresident: part-time $2,457 per course.
Financial support: In 2001–02, 15 students received support; fellowships, research assistantships available.
Faculty research: South East economic index.
Dr. Stuart Allen, Head, 336-334-5463, *Fax:* 336-334-4089, *E-mail:* stuart_allen@uncg.edu.
Application contact: Dr. James Lynch, Director of Graduate Recruitment and Information Services, 336-334-4881, *Fax:* 336-334-4424. *Web site:* http://www.uncg.edu/bae/eco/

■ UNIVERSITY OF NORTH TEXAS

Robert B. Toulouse School of Graduate Studies, College of Arts and Sciences, Department of Economics, Denton, TX 76203

AWARDS Economic research (MS); economics (MA); labor and industrial relations (MS). Part-time programs available.

University of North Texas (continued)
Faculty: 14 full-time (3 women), 3 part-time/adjunct (1 woman).
Students: 36 full-time (13 women), 15 part-time (5 women); includes 7 minority (1 African American, 1 Asian American or Pacific Islander, 5 Hispanic Americans), 25 international. Average age 24. In 2001, 21 degrees awarded.
Degree requirements: For master's, thesis (for some programs), comprehensive exam.
Entrance requirements: For master's, GMAT, GRE General Test, minimum B average in last 60 hours. *Application deadline:* For fall admission, 7/17. *Application fee:* $25 ($50 for international students).
Expenses: Tuition, state resident: part-time $186 per hour. Tuition, nonresident: part-time $319 per hour. Required fees: $88; $21 per hour.
Financial support: Fellowships, research assistantships, teaching assistantships, career-related internships or fieldwork, Federal Work-Study, and institutionally sponsored loans available. Support available to part-time students. Financial award application deadline: 4/1.
Faculty research: Health economics, resource economics, international trade and development, monetary theory and policy, public finance.
Dr. Steven L. Cobb, Chair, 940-565-2573, *Fax:* 940-565-4426, *E-mail:* cobb@econ.unt.edu.
Application contact: Dr. Michael McPherson, Graduate Adviser, 940-565-2573, *Fax:* 940-565-4426, *E-mail:* michael@po6.cas.unt.edu.

■ UNIVERSITY OF NOTRE DAME

Graduate School, College of Arts and Letters, Division of Social Science, Department of Economics, Notre Dame, IN 46556

AWARDS MA, PhD.

Faculty: 23 full-time (3 women), 1 (woman) part-time/adjunct.
Students: 45 full-time (16 women), 1 part-time; includes 7 minority (3 African Americans, 1 Asian American or Pacific Islander, 3 Hispanic Americans), 20 international. 206 applicants, 11% accepted, 11 enrolled. In 2001, 4 master's, 5 doctorates awarded. Terminal master's awarded for partial completion of doctoral program.
Degree requirements: For master's, thesis optional; for doctorate, thesis/dissertation, comprehensive exam. *Median time to degree:* Doctorate–7.1 years full-time.
Entrance requirements: For master's and doctorate, GRE General Test, TOEFL. *Application deadline:* For fall admission, 2/1 (priority date). Applications are processed on a rolling basis. *Application fee:* $50. Electronic applications accepted.
Expenses: Tuition: Full-time $24,220; part-time $1,346 per credit hour. Required fees: $155.
Financial support: In 2001–02, 42 students received support, including 7 fellowships with full tuition reimbursements available (averaging $16,000 per year), 3 research assistantships with full tuition reimbursements available (averaging $11,400 per year), 23 teaching assistantships with full tuition reimbursements available (averaging $11,400 per year); career-related internships or fieldwork and tuition waivers (full) also available. Financial award application deadline: 2/1.
Faculty research: Development and international labor, political economy, macroeconomics, microeconomics, econometrics and methodology. *Total annual research expenditures:* $327,000.
Dr. Kali P. Rath, Director of Graduate Studies, 574-631-6335, *Fax:* 574-631-8809.
Application contact: Dr. Terrence J. Akai, Director of Graduate Admissions, 574-631-7706, *Fax:* 574-631-4183, *E-mail:* gradad@nd.edu. *Web site:* http://www.nd.edu/~economic/

■ UNIVERSITY OF OKLAHOMA

Graduate College, College of Arts and Sciences, Department of Economics, Norman, OK 73019-0390

AWARDS MA, PhD.

Faculty: 15 full-time (3 women).
Students: 46 full-time (12 women), 116 part-time (19 women); includes 46 minority (13 African Americans, 28 Asian Americans or Pacific Islanders, 4 Hispanic Americans, 1 Native American), 21 international. 67 applicants, 88% accepted, 28 enrolled. In 2001, 45 master's, 2 doctorates awarded. Terminal master's awarded for partial completion of doctoral program.
Degree requirements: For doctorate, 2 foreign languages, thesis/dissertation, general exams.
Entrance requirements: For master's, GRE General Test, TOEFL, minimum GPA of 3.0 in last 60 hours; for doctorate, GRE General Test, TOEFL. *Application deadline:* For fall admission, 4/1; for spring admission, 9/1. Applications are processed on a rolling basis. *Application fee:* $25 ($50 for international students).
Expenses: Tuition, state resident: full-time $2,208; part-time $92 per credit hour. Tuition, nonresident: part-time $297 per credit hour. Tuition and fees vary according to course level, course load and program.
Financial support: In 2001–02, 1 fellowship (averaging $6,000 per year), 4 research assistantships with partial tuition reimbursements (averaging $15,495 per year), 19 teaching assistantships with partial tuition reimbursements (averaging $12,101 per year) were awarded. Tuition waivers (partial) and unspecified assistantships also available. Financial award applicants required to submit FAFSA.
Faculty research: Macro-economics, micro-economics, international development. *Total annual research expenditures:* $55,625.
Dr. Timothy Dunne, Chair, 405-325-5900, *Fax:* 405-325-5842, *E-mail:* tdunne@ou.edu.
Application contact: Lin Goldsten, Graduate Liaison, 405-325-2861, *Fax:* 405-325-5842, *E-mail:* lin_goldsten@ou.edu.

■ UNIVERSITY OF OREGON

Graduate School, College of Arts and Sciences, Department of Economics, Eugene, OR 97403

AWARDS MA, MS, PhD.

Faculty: 14 full-time (2 women), 2 part-time/adjunct (0 women).
Students: 45 full-time (13 women), 6 part-time, 21 international. 44 applicants, 70% accepted. In 2001, 22 master's, 5 doctorates awarded. Terminal master's awarded for partial completion of doctoral program.
Degree requirements: For master's, thesis or alternative; for doctorate, thesis/dissertation, qualifying exam.
Entrance requirements: For master's, GRE General Test, TOEFL, SPEAK or TSE, minimum GPA of 3.0; for doctorate, GRE General Test, TOEFL, minimum GPA of 3.0. *Application deadline:* For fall admission, 7/15; for winter admission, 10/15; for spring admission, 1/15. *Application fee:* $50.
Expenses: Tuition, state resident: full-time $4,968; part-time $501 per credit hour. Tuition, nonresident: full-time $8,400; part-time $691 per credit hour.
Financial support: In 2001–02, 24 teaching assistantships were awarded. Financial award application deadline: 3/15.
Faculty research: Labor economics, macroeconomics, international economics, industrial organization, public finance.
Van Kolpin, Head, 541-346-4661.
Application contact: Georgette Winther, Admissions Contact, 541-346-1261, *Fax:* 541-346-1243, *E-mail:* gwinther@oregon.uoregon.edu. *Web site:* http://economics.uoregon.edu/

■ UNIVERSITY OF PENNSYLVANIA

School of Arts and Sciences, Graduate Group in Economics, Philadelphia, PA 19104

AWARDS AM, PhD, JD/AM, JD/PhD.

Degree requirements: For doctorate, thesis/dissertation.
Entrance requirements: For doctorate, GRE General Test, TOEFL.
Expenses: Tuition: Part-time $12,875 per semester.

Faculty research: Economic theory, econometrics, international economics, monetary/macroeconomics, applied microeconomics, empirical microeconomics.

■ UNIVERSITY OF PITTSBURGH

Faculty of Arts and Sciences, Department of Economics, Pittsburgh, PA 15260

AWARDS MA, PhD. Part-time programs available.

Faculty: 20 full-time (3 women), 2 part-time/adjunct (both women).
Students: 40 full-time (11 women), 2 part-time (1 woman). Average age 28. 385 applicants, 7% accepted, 11 enrolled. In 2001, 4 master's, 2 doctorates awarded. Terminal master's awarded for partial completion of doctoral program.
Degree requirements: For master's, thesis optional; for doctorate, thesis/dissertation, 2nd year papers, overview, dissertation. *Median time to degree:* Master's–2 years full-time; doctorate–5 years full-time.
Entrance requirements: For doctorate, GRE, TOEFL. *Application deadline:* For fall admission, 2/1 (priority date). Applications are processed on a rolling basis. *Application fee:* $40.
Expenses: Tuition, state resident: full-time $9,410; part-time $385 per credit. Tuition, nonresident: full-time $19,376; part-time $797 per credit. Required fees: $480; $90 per term. Tuition and fees vary according to program.
Financial support: In 2001–02, 7 fellowships with full tuition reimbursements (averaging $12,465 per year), 4 research assistantships with full tuition reimbursements (averaging $12,465 per year), 27 teaching assistantships with full tuition reimbursements (averaging $11,980 per year) were awarded. Career-related internships or fieldwork, Federal Work-Study, institutionally sponsored loans, scholarships/grants, traineeships, health care benefits, tuition waivers (full and partial), and unspecified assistantships also available. Support available to part-time students. Financial award application deadline: 2/1; financial award applicants required to submit FAFSA.
Faculty research: Game theory, experimental economics, regional economics, labor, international trade. *Total annual research expenditures:* $504,870.
Dr. Jean-Françedil;ois Richard, Department Chair, 412-648-2821, *Fax:* 412-648-1793, *E-mail:* fantin@pitt.edu.
Application contact: Terri Waters, Administrative/Graduate Secretary, 412-648-1399, *Fax:* 412-648-1793, *E-mail:* tmw40@pitt.edu. *Web site:* http://www.pitt.edu/~econdept/

■ UNIVERSITY OF PITTSBURGH

Graduate School of Public and International Affairs, Division of International Development, Pittsburgh, PA 15260

AWARDS Development planning and environmental sustainability (MPIA); governmental organizations and civil society (MPIA). Part-time programs available.

Faculty: 32 full-time (8 women), 12 part-time/adjunct (9 women).
Students: 56 full-time (39 women), 8 part-time (7 women); includes 12 minority (7 African Americans, 4 Asian Americans or Pacific Islanders, 1 Hispanic American), 21 international. Average age 26. 114 applicants, 82% accepted, 35 enrolled. In 2001, 27 degrees awarded.
Degree requirements: For master's, internship, thesis optional.
Application deadline: For fall admission, 3/1 (priority date); for spring admission, 10/1 (priority date). Applications are processed on a rolling basis. *Application fee:* $40. Electronic applications accepted.
Expenses: Tuition, state resident: full-time $9,410; part-time $385 per credit. Tuition, nonresident: full-time $19,376; part-time $797 per credit. Required fees: $480; $90 per term. Tuition and fees vary according to program.
Financial support: In 2001–02, 15 students received support, including 3 fellowships (averaging $20,260 per year), 3 research assistantships; career-related internships or fieldwork, scholarships/grants, tuition waivers (full and partial), and unspecified assistantships also available. Financial award application deadline: 2/1.
Faculty research: Project/program evaluation, population and environment, international development, development economics, civil society.
Dr. Paul J. Nelson, Director, International Development Division, 412-648-7645, *Fax:* 412-648-2605, *E-mail:* pjnelson@birch.gspia.pitt.edu.
Application contact: Maureen O'Malley, Admissions Counselor, 412-648-7646, *Fax:* 412-648-7641, *E-mail:* pronobis@birch.gspia.pitt.edu. *Web site:* http://www.gspia.pitt.edu/

■ UNIVERSITY OF PITTSBURGH

Graduate School of Public and International Affairs, Doctoral Program in Public and International Affairs, Pittsburgh, PA 15260

AWARDS Development studies (PhD); foreign and security policy (PhD); international political economy (PhD); public administration (PhD); public policy (PhD). Part-time programs available.

Faculty: 32 full-time (8 women), 12 part-time/adjunct (9 women).
Students: 60 full-time (17 women), 12 part-time (4 women); includes 4 minority (2 African Americans, 1 Asian American or Pacific Islander, 1 Hispanic American), 45 international. Average age 30. 81 applicants, 41% accepted, 14 enrolled. In 2001, 3 degrees awarded.
Degree requirements: For doctorate, thesis/dissertation.
Application deadline: For fall admission, 3/1 (priority date). Applications are processed on a rolling basis. *Application fee:* $40. Electronic applications accepted.
Expenses: Tuition, state resident: full-time $9,410; part-time $385 per credit. Tuition, nonresident: full-time $19,376; part-time $797 per credit. Required fees: $480; $90 per term. Tuition and fees vary according to program.
Financial support: In 2001–02, 15 students received support, including 12 fellowships (averaging $21,500 per year), 1 research assistantship (averaging $21,500 per year), 5 teaching assistantships (averaging $7,700 per year); career-related internships or fieldwork, scholarships/grants, unspecified assistantships, and graduate student assistantships also available. Financial award application deadline: 2/1.
Faculty research: International political economy, international development, public administration, public policy, foreign policy, international security policy.
Dr. William F. Matlack, Doctoral Program Coordinator, 412-648-7604, *E-mail:* wfm@birch.gspia.pitt.edu.
Application contact: Elizabeth Barthen-Braunsdorf, Assistant Director of Admissions, 412-648-7643, *Fax:* 412-648-7641, *E-mail:* barthen@bitch.gspia.pitt.edu. *Web site:* http://www.gspia.pitt.edu/

Find an in-depth description at www.petersons.com/gradchannel.

■ UNIVERSITY OF PITTSBURGH

Graduate School of Public and International Affairs, International Affairs Division, Program in Global Political Economy, Pittsburgh, PA 15260

AWARDS MPIA, JD/MPIA, MBA/MPIA, MPA/MPIA, MPH/MPIA, MSIS/MPIA, MSW/MPIA. Part-time and evening/weekend programs available.

Faculty: 32 full-time (8 women), 12 part-time/adjunct (9 women).
Students: 93 full-time (54 women), 12 part-time (7 women); includes 11 minority (7 African Americans, 1 Asian American or Pacific Islander, 3 Hispanic Americans), 28 international. Average age 23. 88 applicants, 78% accepted, 31 enrolled.
Degree requirements: For master's, internship, thesis optional.
Application deadline: For fall admission, 3/1 (priority date); for spring admission, 10/1 (priority date). Applications are processed on a rolling basis. *Application fee:* $40. Electronic applications accepted.
Expenses: Tuition, state resident: full-time $9,410; part-time $385 per credit. Tuition, nonresident: full-time $19,376; part-time

University of Pittsburgh (continued)
$797 per credit. Required fees: $480; $90 per term. Tuition and fees vary according to program.
Financial support: In 2001–02, 44 students received support, including 9 fellowships (averaging $14,240 per year); career-related internships or fieldwork, scholarships/grants, tuition waivers (full and partial), unspecified assistantships, and graduate student assistantships also available. Financial award application deadline: 2/1.
Faculty research: Political economy, international security/defense/intelligence, transnational crime, international trade, international finance, terrorism.
Application contact: Elizabeth Barthen-Braunsdorf, Assistant Director of Admissions, 412-648-7643, *Fax:* 412-648-7641, *E-mail:* barthen@bitch.gspia.pitt.edu. *Web site:* http://www.gspia.pitt.edu/

■ UNIVERSITY OF PUERTO RICO, RÍO PIEDRAS

College of Social Sciences, Department of Economics, San Juan, PR 00931

AWARDS MA. Part-time and evening/weekend programs available.

Faculty: 6.
Students: 20 full-time (7 women), 32 part-time (13 women); all minorities (all Hispanic Americans). 13 applicants, 100% accepted. In 2001, 5 degrees awarded.
Degree requirements: For master's, thesis, comprehensive exam.
Entrance requirements: For master's, GRE, PAEG, interview, minimum GPA of 3.0. *Application deadline:* For fall admission, 2/1. *Application fee:* $17.
Expenses: Students that provide official evidence of private medicine insurance or service are exempt of the payment of $529 per academic year.
Financial support: Fellowships, research assistantships, teaching assistantships, Federal Work-Study, institutionally sponsored loans, and tuition waivers (partial) available. Financial award application deadline: 5/31.
Faculty research: Minimum wages in Puerto Rico; financial market in Puerto Rico; labor economics; economical impact of the University of Puerto Rico, Río Piedras campus.
Dr. Eileen Y. Segarra-Alméstica, Coordinator, 787-764-0000 Ext. 7405.
Application contact: Iris Gadrean, Administrative Officer, 787-764-0000 Ext. 4167.

■ UNIVERSITY OF RHODE ISLAND

Graduate School, College of the Environment and Life Sciences, Department of Environmental and Natural Resource Economics, Kingston, RI 02881

AWARDS Resource economics and marine resources (MS, PhD).

Students: In 2001, 15 master's, 1 doctorate awarded.
Degree requirements: For master's, thesis optional; for doctorate, thesis/dissertation.
Entrance requirements: For master's and doctorate, GRE General Test, TOEFL. *Application deadline:* For fall admission, 4/15 (priority date). Applications are processed on a rolling basis.
Expenses: Tuition, state resident: full-time $3,756; part-time $209 per credit. Tuition, nonresident: full-time $10,774; part-time $599 per credit. Required fees: $1,586; $76 per credit. One-time fee: $60 full-time.
Dr. James Anderson, Chairperson.
Application contact: Dr. Tim Tyrrell, Graduate Admissions Committee, 401-874-2472, *Fax:* 401-782-4766, *E-mail:* renri@uriacc.uri.edu.

Find an in-depth description at www.petersons.com/gradchannel.

■ UNIVERSITY OF ROCHESTER

The College, Arts and Sciences, Department of Economics, Rochester, NY 14627-0250

AWARDS MA, PhD.

Faculty: 17.
Students: 83 full-time (20 women), 80 international. 739 applicants, 10% accepted, 22 enrolled. In 2001, 10 master's, 16 doctorates awarded.
Degree requirements: For doctorate, thesis/dissertation, qualifying exam.
Entrance requirements: For doctorate, GRE General Test, GRE Subject Test (strongly recommended), TOEFL. *Application deadline:* For fall admission, 2/1 (priority date). *Application fee:* $25.
Expenses: Tuition: Part-time $755 per credit hour.
Financial support: Fellowships, research assistantships, teaching assistantships, tuition waivers (full and partial) available. Financial award application deadline: 2/1.
Ronald Jones, Chair, 585-275-2688.
Application contact: Rosemary Dow, Graduate Program Secretary, 585-275-8625.

■ UNIVERSITY OF SAN FRANCISCO

College of Arts and Sciences, Department of Economics, San Francisco, CA 94117-1080

AWARDS MA. Part-time and evening/weekend programs available.

Faculty: 9 full-time (1 woman), 1 part-time/adjunct (0 women).
Students: 23 full-time (18 women), 2 part-time (both women); includes 5 minority (1 African American, 4 Asian Americans or Pacific Islanders), 17 international. Average age 27. 36 applicants, 94% accepted, 9 enrolled. In 2001, 10 degrees awarded.
Degree requirements: For master's, thesis or alternative, comprehensive exam.
Entrance requirements: For master's, GRE General Test (recommended), TOEFL, BA in economics (preferred). *Application deadline:* For fall admission, 7/15 (priority date); for spring admission, 12/15. Applications are processed on a rolling basis. *Application fee:* $55 ($65 for international students).
Expenses: Tuition: Full-time $14,400; part-time $800 per unit. Tuition and fees vary according to degree level, campus/location and program.
Financial support: In 2001–02, 14 students received support; fellowships, teaching assistantships, career-related internships or fieldwork available. Financial award application deadline: 3/2; financial award applicants required to submit FAFSA.
Faculty research: Economic development, forecasting and planning, labor markets, Pacific Rim, financial markets.
John M. Veitch, Chair, 415-422-6271, *Fax:* 415-422-2772, *E-mail:* veitchj@usfca.edu.

■ UNIVERSITY OF SOUTH CAROLINA

The Graduate School, The Darla Moore School of Business, Department of Economics, Columbia, SC 29208

AWARDS MA, PhD, JD/MA.

Faculty: 17 full-time (3 women).
Students: 15 full-time (4 women), 5 part-time (2 women); includes 1 minority (African American), 9 international. Average age 30.
Degree requirements: For master's, thesis, comprehensive exam (for some programs); for doctorate, thesis/dissertation, qualifying exam, comprehensive exam, registration.
Entrance requirements: For master's, GMAT or GRE General Test, TOEFL, minimum GPA of 3.0; for doctorate, GRE General Test, TOEFL. *Application deadline:* For fall admission, 2/1. Applications are processed on a rolling basis. *Application fee:* $35. Electronic applications accepted.
Expenses: Tuition, state resident: full-time $4,434. Tuition, nonresident: full-time $9,854. Tuition and fees vary according to program.
Financial support: In 2001–02, 9 research assistantships with partial tuition reimbursements (averaging $13,500 per year), 2 teaching assistantships with partial tuition reimbursements (averaging $11,500 per year) were awarded. Fellowships, Federal Work-Study, institutionally

sponsored loans, and unspecified assistantships also available. Financial award application deadline: 2/1.
Faculty research: Monetary theory, labor economics, international economics, industrial organization.
Dr. Ron Wilder, Chairperson, 803-777-6955, *Fax:* 803-777-6876, *E-mail:* ronwilder@darla.badm.sc.edu.
Application contact: Dr. McKinley L. Blackburn, Academic Director, 803-777-4931, *Fax:* 803-777-3176, *E-mail:* blackbrn@moore.sc.edu. *Web site:* http://mooreschool.sc.edu/

■ UNIVERSITY OF SOUTHERN CALIFORNIA

Graduate School, College of Letters, Arts and Sciences, Department of Economics, Program in Economic Development Programming, Los Angeles, CA 90089

AWARDS MA.

Entrance requirements: For master's, GRE General Test.
Expenses: Tuition: Full-time $25,060; part-time $844 per unit. Required fees: $473.

■ UNIVERSITY OF SOUTHERN CALIFORNIA

Graduate School, College of Letters, Arts and Sciences, Department of Economics, Program in Economics, Los Angeles, CA 90089

AWARDS MA, PhD, JD/MA, M Pl/MA. Terminal master's awarded for partial completion of doctoral program.

Degree requirements: For master's, thesis optional; for doctorate, thesis/dissertation.
Entrance requirements: For master's and doctorate, GRE General Test.
Expenses: Tuition: Full-time $25,060; part-time $844 per unit. Required fees: $473.
Faculty research: Economics organization and law, economic development, econometrics, theory, dynamic.

■ UNIVERSITY OF SOUTHERN CALIFORNIA

Graduate School, College of Letters, Arts and Sciences, Department of Political Economy and Public Policy, Los Angeles, CA 90089

AWARDS PhD.

Degree requirements: For doctorate, thesis/dissertation.
Entrance requirements: For doctorate, GRE General Test.
Expenses: Tuition: Full-time $25,060; part-time $844 per unit. Required fees: $473.

■ UNIVERSITY OF SOUTHERN MISSISSIPPI

Graduate School, College of International and Continuing Education, Department of Economic Development, Hattiesburg, MS 39406

AWARDS Economic development (MS); international development (PhD). Part-time programs available.

Faculty: 4 full-time (0 women), 1 part-time/adjunct (0 women).
Students: 15 full-time (8 women), 8 part-time (2 women); includes 5 minority (3 African Americans, 1 Asian American or Pacific Islander, 1 Hispanic American). 10 applicants, 80% accepted. In 2001, 7 degrees awarded.
Degree requirements: For master's, internships, thesis optional; for doctorate, thesis/dissertation.
Entrance requirements: For master's and doctorate, GMAT, GRE General Test. *Application deadline:* For fall admission, 8/1; for spring admission, 1/3. *Application fee:* $40. Electronic applications accepted.
Expenses: Tuition, state resident: full-time $3,416; part-time $190 per credit hour. Tuition, nonresident: full-time $7,932; part-time $441 per credit hour.
Financial support: In 2001–02, 11 students received support, including 7 research assistantships with full tuition reimbursements available (averaging $4,000 per year), 1 teaching assistantship with full tuition reimbursement available (averaging $4,000 per year). Financial award application deadline: 3/1.
Faculty research: Economic development, international studies, geography.
Dr. David Kolzow, Chair, 601-266-6519, *Fax:* 601-266-6219.

■ UNIVERSITY OF SOUTH FLORIDA

College of Graduate Studies, College of Business Administration, Department of Economics, Tampa, FL 33620-9951

AWARDS MA. Part-time and evening/weekend programs available.

Faculty: 19 full-time (3 women).
Students: 9 full-time (2 women), 13 part-time (5 women); includes 3 minority (2 African Americans, 1 Hispanic American), 4 international. Average age 30. 25 applicants, 60% accepted, 9 enrolled. In 2001, 7 degrees awarded.
Degree requirements: For master's, comprehensive exam.
Entrance requirements: For master's, GMAT or GRE General Test. *Application deadline:* For fall admission, 7/1; for spring admission, 11/1. Applications are processed on a rolling basis. *Application fee:* $20.
Expenses: Tuition, state resident: part-time $166 per credit hour. Tuition, nonresident: part-time $573 per credit hour. Required fees: $17 per term.
Financial support: Fellowships, research assistantships, teaching assistantships, Federal Work-Study, institutionally sponsored loans, and unspecified assistantships available. Financial award applicants required to submit FAFSA. *Total annual research expenditures:* $39,351.
Joseph DeSalvo, Chairperson, 813-974-4252, *Fax:* 813-974-6510, *E-mail:* jdesalvo@coba.usf.edu.
Application contact: Dr. Brad Kamp, Coordinator, 813-974-6549, *Fax:* 813-974-6510, *E-mail:* bkamp@coba.usf.edu. *Web site:* http://www.coba.usf.edu/

■ THE UNIVERSITY OF TENNESSEE

Graduate School, College of Arts and Sciences, Department of Sociology, Knoxville, TN 37996

AWARDS Criminology (MA, PhD); energy, environment, and resource policy (MA, PhD); political economy (MA, PhD). Part-time programs available.

Faculty: 15 full-time (2 women), 1 (woman) part-time/adjunct.
Students: 22 full-time (14 women), 26 part-time (11 women); includes 7 minority (6 African Americans, 1 Asian American or Pacific Islander), 4 international. 30 applicants, 63% accepted. In 2001, 3 degrees awarded.
Degree requirements: For master's, thesis or alternative; for doctorate, thesis/dissertation.
Entrance requirements: For master's, GRE General Test, TOEFL, minimum GPA of 3.0; for doctorate, GRE General Test, TOEFL, minimum GPA of 3.5. *Application deadline:* For fall admission, 2/1 (priority date). Applications are processed on a rolling basis. *Application fee:* $35. Electronic applications accepted.
Expenses: Tuition, state resident: full-time $4,280; part-time $233 per hour. Tuition, nonresident: full-time $12,066; part-time $666 per hour. Tuition and fees vary according to program.
Financial support: In 2001–02, 1 fellowship, 2 research assistantships, 20 teaching assistantships were awarded. Federal Work-Study, institutionally sponsored loans, and unspecified assistantships also available. Financial award application deadline: 2/1; financial award applicants required to submit FAFSA.
Dr. Suzanne Kurth, Head, 865-974-6021, *Fax:* 865-974-7013, *E-mail:* skurth@utk.edu.
Application contact: Dr. T. C. Hood, Graduate Representative, 865-974-7032, *E-mail:* tomhood@utk.edu.

■ THE UNIVERSITY OF TENNESSEE

Graduate School, College of Business Administration, Department of Economics, Knoxville, TN 37996

AWARDS MA, PhD.

Faculty: 22 full-time (4 women).
Students: 25 full-time (13 women), 11 part-time (4 women); includes 2 minority (1 Asian American or Pacific Islander, 1 Hispanic American), 9 international. 110 applicants, 49% accepted. In 2001, 5 master's, 8 doctorates awarded.
Degree requirements: For master's, thesis or alternative; for doctorate, thesis/dissertation.
Entrance requirements: For master's and doctorate, GRE General Test or GMAT, TOEFL, minimum GPA of 2.7. *Application deadline:* For fall admission, 2/1 (priority date). Applications are processed on a rolling basis. *Application fee:* $35. Electronic applications accepted.
Expenses: Tuition, state resident: full-time $4,280; part-time $233 per hour. Tuition, nonresident: full-time $12,066; part-time $666 per hour. Tuition and fees vary according to program.
Financial support: In 2001–02, 3 research assistantships, 15 teaching assistantships were awarded. Fellowships, career-related internships or fieldwork, Federal Work-Study, institutionally sponsored loans, and unspecified assistantships also available. Financial award application deadline: 2/1; financial award applicants required to submit FAFSA.
Dr. Matthew Murray, Head, 865-974-1697, *Fax:* 865-974-4601, *E-mail:* mmurray1@utk.edu.
Application contact: Dr. Sidney Carroll, Graduate Representative, 865-974-1690, *E-mail:* scarrol3@utk.edu.

■ THE UNIVERSITY OF TENNESSEE AT CHATTANOOGA

Graduate Division, College of Business Administration, Program in Business Administration, Chattanooga, TN 37403-2598

AWARDS Business administration (MBA); economics (MBA); finance (MBA); marketing (MBA); operations/production (MBA); organizational management (MBA). Part-time and evening/weekend programs available.

Students: 65 full-time (35 women), 251 part-time (100 women); includes 49 minority (24 African Americans, 15 Asian Americans or Pacific Islanders, 10 Hispanic Americans), 13 international. Average age 28. 151 applicants, 85% accepted, 87 enrolled. In 2001, 167 degrees awarded.
Entrance requirements: For master's, GMAT. *Application deadline:* For fall admission, 8/1 (priority date); for spring admission, 12/1 (priority date). Applications are processed on a rolling basis. *Application fee:* $25.
Expenses: Tuition, state resident: full-time $3,752; part-time $228 per hour. Tuition, nonresident: full-time $10,282; part-time $565 per hour.
Financial support: Fellowships, research assistantships, Federal Work-Study and institutionally sponsored loans available. Support available to part-time students. Financial award application deadline: 4/1; financial award applicants required to submit FAFSA.
Kimberly Gee, Executive Director, 423-425-4210, *Fax:* 423-425-5255, *E-mail:* kimberly-gee@utc.edu.
Application contact: Dr. Deborah E. Arfken, Dean of Graduate Studies, 865-425-1740, *Fax:* 865-425-5223, *E-mail:* deborah-arfken@utc.edu. *Web site:* http://www.utc.edu/

■ THE UNIVERSITY OF TEXAS AT ARLINGTON

Graduate School, College of Business Administration, Department of Economics, Arlington, TX 76019

AWARDS MA, PhD. Part-time and evening/weekend programs available.

Faculty: 7 full-time (0 women).
Students: 14 full-time (6 women), 8 part-time (1 woman); includes 4 minority (1 African American, 1 Asian American or Pacific Islander, 2 Hispanic Americans), 12 international. 8 applicants, 88% accepted, 5 enrolled. In 2001, 2 degrees awarded. Terminal master's awarded for partial completion of doctoral program.
Degree requirements: For master's, thesis optional.
Entrance requirements: For master's, GMAT or GRE General Test. *Application deadline:* For fall admission, 6/15. Applications are processed on a rolling basis. *Application fee:* $25 ($50 for international students).
Expenses: Tuition, area resident: Full-time $2,268. Tuition, nonresident: full-time $6,264. Required fees: $839. Tuition and fees vary according to course load.
Financial support: In 2001–02, 1 fellowship (averaging $1,000 per year), 14 teaching assistantships (averaging $10,000 per year) were awarded. Research assistantships, career-related internships or fieldwork, scholarships/grants, and unspecified assistantships also available. Support available to part-time students. Financial award application deadline: 6/1; financial award applicants required to submit FAFSA.
Dr. Daniel Himarios, Dean, 817-272-3061, *Fax:* 817-272-2073, *E-mail:* himarios@uta.edu.
Application contact: Dr. Paul M. Hayashi, Graduate Adviser, 817-272-3257, *Fax:* 817-272-3145, *E-mail:* hayashi@uta.edu.

■ THE UNIVERSITY OF TEXAS AT AUSTIN

Graduate School, College of Liberal Arts, Department of Economics, Austin, TX 78712-1111

AWARDS MA, MS Econ, PhD. Part-time programs available.

Faculty: 29 full-time.
Students: 116 (35 women); includes 6 minority (1 African American, 3 Asian Americans or Pacific Islanders, 2 Hispanic Americans) 59 international.
Degree requirements: For master's, thesis/dissertation; for doctorate, thesis/dissertation, comprehensive exam.
Entrance requirements: For master's and doctorate, GRE General Test, TOEFL, minimum GPA of 3.5 (based on upper-division undergraduate and graduate course work). *Application deadline:* For fall admission, 2/1. *Application fee:* $50 ($75 for international students). Electronic applications accepted.
Expenses: Tuition, state resident: full-time $3,159. Tuition, nonresident: full-time $6,957. Tuition and fees vary according to program.
Financial support: Fellowships, research assistantships, teaching assistantships, assistant instructorships available. Financial award application deadline: 2/1.
Faculty research: Industrial organization, game theory, monetary economics, labor economics, public economics.
Dr. Stephen G. Bronars, Chair, 512-475-8529.
Application contact: Vivian Goldman-Leffler, Graduate Coordinator, 512-475-8510.

■ THE UNIVERSITY OF TEXAS AT DALLAS

School of Social Sciences, Program in Political Economy, Richardson, TX 75083-0688

AWARDS PhD. Part-time and evening/weekend programs available.

Faculty: 18 full-time (4 women), 1 (woman) part-time/adjunct.
Students: 23 full-time (9 women), 41 part-time (12 women); includes 19 minority (9 African Americans, 6 Asian Americans or Pacific Islanders, 3 Hispanic Americans, 1 Native American), 10 international. Average age 40. 39 applicants, 59% accepted. In 2001, 9 degrees awarded.
Degree requirements: For doctorate, thesis/dissertation.
Entrance requirements: For doctorate, GRE General Test, TOEFL, minimum GPA of 3.0 in upper-level course work in field. *Application deadline:* For fall admission, 7/15; for spring admission, 11/15.

Applications are processed on a rolling basis. *Application fee:* $25 ($75 for international students). Electronic applications accepted.
Expenses: Tuition, state resident: full-time $1,440; part-time $84 per credit. Tuition, nonresident: full-time $5,310; part-time $295 per credit. Required fees: $1,835; $87 per credit. $138 per term.
Financial support: In 2001–02, 6 research assistantships with tuition reimbursements (averaging $4,863 per year), 18 teaching assistantships with tuition reimbursements (averaging $5,208 per year) were awarded. Fellowships, career-related internships or fieldwork, Federal Work-Study, institutionally sponsored loans, and scholarships/grants also available. Support available to part-time students. Financial award application deadline: 4/30; financial award applicants required to submit FAFSA.
Faculty research: New leadership development, gender and leadership, globalization and leadership opportunities in democracy. *Web site:* http://www.utdallas.edu/dept/socsci/poec.htm

■ THE UNIVERSITY OF TEXAS AT EL PASO

Graduate School, College of Business Administration, Department of Economics and Finance, El Paso, TX 79968-0001

AWARDS MS. Part-time and evening/weekend programs available.

Students: 22 (4 women); includes 11 minority (1 Asian American or Pacific Islander, 10 Hispanic Americans) 6 international. Average age 34. 1 applicant, 100% accepted. In 2001, 1 degree awarded.
Degree requirements: For master's, thesis optional.
Entrance requirements: For master's, GMAT, TOEFL, minimum GPA of 2.7. *Application deadline:* For fall admission, 7/1 (priority date); for spring admission, 11/1 (priority date). Applications are processed on a rolling basis. *Application fee:* $15 ($65 for international students). Electronic applications accepted.
Expenses: Tuition, state resident: full-time $2,450. Tuition, nonresident: full-time $6,000.
Financial support: In 2001–02, research assistantships with partial tuition reimbursements (averaging $18,750 per year), teaching assistantships with partial tuition reimbursements (averaging $15,000 per year) were awarded. Federal Work-Study and institutionally sponsored loans also available. Support available to part-time students. Financial award application deadline: 3/15; financial award applicants required to submit FAFSA.
Dr. Timothy Roth, Chairperson, 915-747-5245, *Fax:* 915-747-6282, *E-mail:* troth@miners.utep.edu.
Application contact: Dr. Charles H. Ambler, Director, Graduate Student Services, 915-747-5491, *Fax:* 915-747-5778, *E-mail:* sjordan@utep.edu.

■ THE UNIVERSITY OF TEXAS AT SAN ANTONIO

College of Business, Department of Economics, San Antonio, TX 78249-0617

AWARDS Business economics (MBA); economics (MA).

Faculty: 6 full-time (1 woman), 3 part-time/adjunct (0 women).
Students: 5 full-time (1 woman), 6 part-time (1 woman); includes 2 minority (1 Asian American or Pacific Islander, 1 Hispanic American), 1 international. Average age 32. 11 applicants, 82% accepted, 6 enrolled. In 2001, 2 degrees awarded.
Degree requirements: For master's, thesis optional.
Entrance requirements: For master's, GMAT, minimum GPA of 3.0.
Expenses: Tuition, state resident: full-time $2,268; part-time $126 per credit hour. Tuition, nonresident: full-time $6,066; part-time $337 per credit hour. Required fees: $781. Tuition and fees vary according to course load.
Dr. Don Lien, Interim Chair, 210-458-7312.

■ THE UNIVERSITY OF TEXAS AT TYLER

Graduate Studies, College of Arts and Sciences, Department of Social Sciences, Tyler, TX 75799-0001

AWARDS Criminal justice (MAIS, MS); economics (MAIS); political science (MA, MAIS, MAT); public administration (MPA); sociology (MAIS, MAT, MS). Part-time and evening/weekend programs available. Postbaccalaureate distance learning degree programs offered.

Faculty: 14 full-time (1 woman).
Students: 13 full-time (9 women), 54 part-time (34 women); includes 16 minority (14 African Americans, 1 Hispanic American, 1 Native American), 1 international. Average age 35. 8 applicants, 100% accepted, 8 enrolled. In 2001, 10 degrees awarded.
Degree requirements: For master's, thesis (for some programs), comprehensive exam.
Entrance requirements: For master's, GRE General Test, minimum GPA of 3.0. *Application deadline:* Applications are processed on a rolling basis. *Application fee:* $0.
Expenses: Tuition, state resident: part-time $44 per credit hour. Tuition, nonresident: part-time $262 per credit hour. Required fees: $58 per credit hour. $76 per semester.
Financial support: Teaching assistantships, career-related internships or fieldwork, Federal Work-Study, and scholarships/grants available. Support available to part-time students. Financial award application deadline: 7/1; financial award applicants required to submit FAFSA.
Faculty research: Urban segregation, minority business, violent crime, gender discrimination, Third World agriculture production.
Dr. Barbara L. Hart, Chair, 903-566-7426, *Fax:* 903-565-5537, *E-mail:* bhart@mail.uttyl.edu.
Application contact: Carol A. Hodge, Office of Graduate Studies, 903-566-5642, *Fax:* 903-566-7068, *E-mail:* chodge@mail.uttly.edu.

■ UNIVERSITY OF TOLEDO

Graduate School, College of Arts and Sciences, Department of Economics, Toledo, OH 43606-3398

AWARDS MA, MAE.

Faculty: 5.
Students: 18 full-time (8 women), 2 part-time; includes 3 minority (1 African American, 2 Asian Americans or Pacific Islanders), 15 international. Average age 27. 75 applicants, 23% accepted. In 2001, 9 degrees awarded.
Degree requirements: For master's, paper or thesis.
Entrance requirements: For master's, GRE General Test, minimum GPA of 2.75. *Application deadline:* For fall admission, 8/1 (priority date). *Application fee:* $30. Electronic applications accepted.
Expenses: Tuition, state resident: full-time $7,278; part-time $303 per hour. Tuition, nonresident: full-time $15,731; part-time $699 per hour. Required fees: $43 per hour.
Financial support: Research assistantships, teaching assistantships, career-related internships or fieldwork, Federal Work-Study, institutionally sponsored loans, and tuition waivers (full) available. Support available to part-time students. Financial award application deadline: 4/1; financial award applicants required to submit FAFSA.
Faculty research: Economic development.
Dr. Micheal Dowd, Chair, 419-530-2572, *Fax:* 419-530-7844.
Application contact: Dr. David Black, Information Contact, 419-530-4153. *Web site:* http://www.econ.utoledo.edu/

■ UNIVERSITY OF TOLEDO

Graduate School, College of Business Administration, Department of Finance and Business Economics, Toledo, OH 43606-3398

AWARDS MBA. Evening/weekend programs available.

Faculty: 5 full-time (2 women).
Students: 27 full-time (3 women), 27 part-time (5 women); includes 5 minority (3 African Americans, 1 Asian American or Pacific Islander, 1 Hispanic American), 18 international. Average age 28. 43

University of Toledo (continued)
applicants, 81% accepted, 19 enrolled. In 2001, 20 degrees awarded.
Degree requirements: For master's, thesis or alternative.
Entrance requirements: For master's, GMAT, TOEFL. *Application deadline:* For fall admission, 8/1 (priority date). Applications are processed on a rolling basis. *Application fee:* $30.
Expenses: Tuition, state resident: full-time $7,278; part-time $303 per hour. Tuition, nonresident: full-time $15,731; part-time $699 per hour. Required fees: $43 per hour.
Financial support: In 2001–02, 8 research assistantships were awarded; career-related internships or fieldwork, Federal Work-Study, institutionally sponsored loans, scholarships/grants, tuition waivers (full), and administrative assistantships also available. Support available to part-time students. Financial award application deadline: 4/1; financial award applicants required to submit FAFSA.
Faculty research: Financial management, banking, international finance, investments.
Dr. Andrew Solocha, Chair, 419-530-2464.
Application contact: Dr. Gary Moore, MBA Director, 419-530-2564, *Fax:* 419-530-7260, *E-mail:* mba@!uft01.utoledo.edu. *Web site:* http://www.utoledo.edu/mba/

■ UNIVERSITY OF UTAH

Graduate School, College of Social and Behavioral Science, Department of Economics, Salt Lake City, UT 84112-1107

AWARDS M Phil, M Stat, MA, MS, PhD. Part-time programs available.

Faculty: 16 full-time (2 women), 4 part-time/adjunct (2 women).
Students: 42 full-time (16 women), 34 part-time (9 women); includes 17 minority (1 African American, 15 Asian Americans or Pacific Islanders, 1 Hispanic American), 14 international. Average age 32. 105 applicants, 56% accepted. In 2001, 9 master's, 3 doctorates awarded. Terminal master's awarded for partial completion of doctoral program.
Degree requirements: For master's, thesis or alternative, exam, oral presentation, research project, comprehensive exam; for doctorate, thesis/dissertation.
Entrance requirements: For master's, GRE General Test, TOEFL, previous undergraduate course work in economics; for doctorate, GRE General Test, GRE Subject Test, TOEFL, minimum GPA of 3.0, previous course work in calculus and statistics. *Application deadline:* For fall admission, 7/1. *Application fee:* $40 ($60 for international students).
Expenses: Tuition, state resident: part-time $320 per semester hour. Tuition, nonresident: part-time $1,135 per semester hour. Required fees: $143 per semester hour. Tuition and fees vary according to course load, degree level and program.
Financial support: Fellowships, research assistantships, teaching assistantships, career-related internships or fieldwork, Federal Work-Study, and institutionally sponsored loans available.
Faculty research: History of economic thought, political economy, monetary economy, labor.
E. K. Hunt, Chair, 801-581-7481, *Fax:* 801-585-5649, *E-mail:* hunt@econ.sbs.utah.edu.
Application contact: Dr. Carrie Mayne, Advisor, 801-581-7481, *E-mail:* mayne@econ.sbs.utah.edu.

■ UNIVERSITY OF VIRGINIA

College and Graduate School of Arts and Sciences, Department of Economics, Charlottesville, VA 22903

AWARDS MA, PhD, JD/MA.

Faculty: 30 full-time (2 women), 20 part-time/adjunct (5 women).
Students: 89 full-time (23 women); includes 1 minority (Asian American or Pacific Islander), 49 international. Average age 27. 329 applicants, 80% accepted, 34 enrolled. In 2001, 27 master's, 6 doctorates awarded.
Degree requirements: For master's and doctorate, thesis/dissertation, exam.
Entrance requirements: For master's and doctorate, GRE General Test. *Application deadline:* For fall admission, 7/15; for spring admission, 12/1. Applications are processed on a rolling basis. *Application fee:* $40. Electronic applications accepted.
Expenses: Tuition, state resident: full-time $3,988. Tuition, nonresident: full-time $17,078. Required fees: $1,190.
Financial support: Fellowships, research assistantships, teaching assistantships, tuition waivers (full and partial) available. Financial award application deadline: 2/1; financial award applicants required to submit FAFSA.
Faculty research: Macroeconomics, public economics, labor, industrial organization, economic history.
David E. Mills, Chairman, 434-924-3177, *Fax:* 434-982-2904, *E-mail:* econ-dgs@virginia.edu.
Application contact: Duane J. Osheim, Associate Dean for Graduate Programs, 434-924-7184, *Fax:* 434-924-3084, *E-mail:* grad-a-s@virginia.edu. *Web site:* http://www.virginia.edu/%7Eecon/

■ UNIVERSITY OF WASHINGTON

Graduate School, College of Arts and Sciences, Department of Economics, Seattle, WA 98195

AWARDS MA, PhD.

Faculty: 27 full-time (5 women), 4 part-time/adjunct (1 woman).
Students: 77 full-time (22 women), 11 part-time (4 women); includes 4 minority (3 Asian Americans or Pacific Islanders, 1 Hispanic American), 61 international. Average age 29. 266 applicants, 23% accepted, 14 enrolled. In 2001, 12 master's, 17 doctorates awarded. Terminal master's awarded for partial completion of doctoral program.
Degree requirements: For master's, internship; for doctorate, thesis/dissertation, comprehensive exam, registration. *Median time to degree:* Master's–2 years full-time; doctorate–7 years full-time.
Entrance requirements: For master's and doctorate, GRE General Test, TOEFL, minimum GPA of 3.0. *Application deadline:* For fall admission, 2/1. *Application fee:* $50. Electronic applications accepted.
Expenses: Tuition, state resident: full-time $5,539. Tuition, nonresident: full-time $14,376. Required fees: $390. Tuition and fees vary according to course load and program.
Financial support: In 2001–02, 61 students received support, including 15 fellowships with full tuition reimbursements available (averaging $11,340 per year), 13 research assistantships with full tuition reimbursements available (averaging $11,340 per year), 46 teaching assistantships with full tuition reimbursements available (averaging $12,159 per year); career-related internships or fieldwork, Federal Work-Study, institutionally sponsored loans, scholarships/grants, traineeships, health care benefits, and unspecified assistantships also available. Financial award application deadline: 2/1; financial award applicants required to submit FAFSA.
Faculty research: Microeconomic theory; macroeconomic theory; econometrics; natural resource economics; international, development, and industrial organization. *Total annual research expenditures:* $371,230.
Neil Bruce, Chair, 206-543-5874, *Fax:* 206-685-7477, *E-mail:* brucen@u.washington.edu.
Application contact: Jacques Lawarree, Graduate Adviser, 206-543-5632, *Fax:* 206-685-7477, *E-mail:* econadv@u.washington.edu. *Web site:* http://www.econ.washington.edu/

■ UNIVERSITY OF WISCONSIN–MADISON

Graduate School, College of Letters and Science, Department of Economics, Madison, WI 53706-1380

AWARDS PhD.

Degree requirements: For doctorate, thesis/dissertation.
Entrance requirements: For doctorate, GRE General Test, 3 semesters of course work in calculus, 1 semester of course work in algebra and mathematics/statistics. Electronic applications accepted.
Expenses: Tuition, state resident: full-time $7,361; part-time $399 per credit. Tuition, nonresident: full-time $20,499; part-time $1,282 per credit. Required fees: $34 per credit. Full-time tuition and fees vary

according to course load, program, reciprocity agreements and student level. *Web site:* http://www.ssc.wisc.edu/econ/grad/

■ UNIVERSITY OF WISCONSIN–MILWAUKEE

Graduate School, College of Letters and Sciences, Department of Economics, Milwaukee, WI 53201-0413

AWARDS MA, PhD.

Faculty: 18 full-time (4 women).
Students: 41 full-time (15 women), 12 part-time (2 women); includes 5 minority (1 African American, 4 Asian Americans or Pacific Islanders), 32 international. 78 applicants, 73% accepted. In 2001, 11 master's, 3 doctorates awarded.
Degree requirements: For doctorate, thesis/dissertation.
Entrance requirements: For master's, GRE General Test; for doctorate, GRE General Test, GRE Subject Test. *Application deadline:* For fall admission, 1/1 (priority date); for spring admission, 9/1. Applications are processed on a rolling basis. *Application fee:* $45 ($75 for international students).
Expenses: Tuition, state resident: full-time $6,180; part-time $535 per credit. Tuition, nonresident: full-time $19,482; part-time $1,366 per credit. Tuition and fees vary according to course load, program and reciprocity agreements.
Financial support: In 2001–02, 2 fellowships, 22 teaching assistantships were awarded. Research assistantships, career-related internships or fieldwork and unspecified assistantships also available. Support available to part-time students. Financial award application deadline: 4/15.
M. Bahmani-Oskooee, Representative, 414-229-4812, *Fax:* 414-229-3860, *E-mail:* bahmani@uwm.edu. *Web site:* http://www.uwm.edu/dept/economics/

■ UNIVERSITY OF WYOMING

Graduate School, College of Business, Department of Economics and Finance, Program in Economics, Laramie, WY 82071

AWARDS MS, PhD. Part-time programs available.

Faculty: 13.
Students: 29 full-time (9 women), 3 part-time (2 women), 11 international. 17 applicants, 100% accepted. In 2001, 1 master's, 5 doctorates awarded.
Degree requirements: For doctorate, thesis/dissertation.
Entrance requirements: For master's and doctorate, GRE General Test, minimum GPA of 3.0. *Application deadline:* For fall admission, 3/1; for spring admission, 10/1. Applications are processed on a rolling basis. *Application fee:* $40.
Expenses: Tuition, state resident: full-time $2,895; part-time $161 per credit hour. Tuition, nonresident: full-time $8,367; part-time $465 per credit hour. Required fees: $491; $10 per credit hour. $2 per credit hour. Tuition and fees vary according to course load and program.
Financial support: In 2001–02, 2 research assistantships, 12 teaching assistantships were awarded. Financial award application deadline: 3/1.
Faculty research: Resource and environmental economics, industrial organization, regulation.
Application contact: Delilah I. Axlund, Information Contact, 307-766-6813, *Fax:* 307-766-5090, *E-mail:* daxlund@uwyo.edu.

■ UTAH STATE UNIVERSITY

School of Graduate Studies, College of Business and College of Agriculture, Department of Economics, Logan, UT 84322

AWARDS Applied economics (MS); economics (MA, MS, PhD).

Faculty: 22 full-time (2 women).
Students: 25 full-time (11 women), 4 part-time (1 woman), 19 international. Average age 31. 61 applicants, 84% accepted. In 2001, 6 master's, 4 doctorates awarded. Terminal master's awarded for partial completion of doctoral program.
Degree requirements: For master's, thesis (for some programs); for doctorate, thesis/dissertation, comprehensive exam.
Entrance requirements: For master's and doctorate, GRE General Test, TOEFL, minimum GPA of 3.0. *Application deadline:* For fall admission, 1/15 (priority date); for spring admission, 10/15. Applications are processed on a rolling basis. *Application fee:* $40.
Expenses: Tuition, state resident: full-time $1,693. Tuition, nonresident: full-time $4,233. Required fees: $501. Tuition and fees vary according to program.
Financial support: In 2001–02, 3 fellowships with partial tuition reimbursements (averaging $12,000 per year), 14 research assistantships with partial tuition reimbursements (averaging $9,000 per year), 4 teaching assistantships with partial tuition reimbursements (averaging $9,000 per year) were awarded. Career-related internships or fieldwork, Federal Work-Study, institutionally sponsored loans, and tuition waivers (partial) also available. Financial award application deadline: 3/1.
Faculty research: Resource economics, economic theory, international trade, industrial organization, development. *Total annual research expenditures:* $250,000.
Keith R. Criddle, Head, 435-797-2310, *Fax:* 435-797-2701, *E-mail:* econinfo@econ.usu.edu.
Application contact: Amanda Litchford, Graduate Student Secretary, 435-797-2290, *Fax:* 435-797-2701, *E-mail:* econinfo@econ.usu.edu. *Web site:* http://www.econ.usu.edu/

■ VANDERBILT UNIVERSITY

Graduate School, Department of Economics, Nashville, TN 37240-1001

AWARDS MA, MAT, PhD.

Faculty: 31 full-time (6 women), 2 part-time/adjunct (0 women).
Students: 45 full-time (13 women); includes 1 minority (Asian American or Pacific Islander), 38 international. Average age 32. 187 applicants, 96% accepted. In 2001, 31 master's, 7 doctorates awarded.
Degree requirements: For master's, thesis or alternative; for doctorate, thesis/dissertation, final and qualifying exams.
Entrance requirements: For master's and doctorate, GRE General Test, GRE Subject Test (recommended). *Application deadline:* For fall admission, 1/15; for spring admission, 11/1. Applications are processed on a rolling basis. *Application fee:* $40. Electronic applications accepted.
Expenses: Tuition: Full-time $28,350.
Financial support: In 2001–02, 29 students received support, including 8 fellowships with full tuition reimbursements available (averaging $11,700 per year), 19 teaching assistantships with full tuition reimbursements available (averaging $11,700 per year); Federal Work-Study and institutionally sponsored loans also available. Financial award application deadline: 1/15.
Faculty research: Economic theory, applied fields, developmental economics, environmental economics, health economics and policy. *Total annual research expenditures:* $295,558.
Jeremy Atack, Chair, 615-322-2871, *Fax:* 615-343-8495, *E-mail:* jeremy.atack@vanderbilt.edu.
Application contact: Andrew F. Daughety, Director of Graduate Studies, 615-322-2871, *Fax:* 615-343-8495, *E-mail:* andrew.f.daughety@vanderbilt.edu. *Web site:* http://www.vanderbilt.edu/Econ/Econtop.html

■ VIRGINIA COMMONWEALTH UNIVERSITY

School of Graduate Studies, School of Business, Program in Economics, Richmond, VA 23284-9005

AWARDS MA, MS.

Students: 11 (4 women); includes 1 minority (Asian American or Pacific Islander). 24 applicants, 67% accepted. In 2001, 5 degrees awarded.
Degree requirements: For master's, thesis optional.
Entrance requirements: For master's, GRE General Test. *Application deadline:* For fall admission, 7/15; for spring admission, 3/15. Applications are processed on a rolling basis. *Application fee:* $30.
Expenses: Tuition, state resident: full-time $4,276; part-time $238 per credit. Tuition, nonresident: full-time $12,672; part-time $704 per credit. Required fees: $1,167; $43 per credit.

Virginia Commonwealth University (continued)

Financial support: Fellowships, research assistantships, teaching assistantships, Federal Work-Study, institutionally sponsored loans, and tuition waivers (full and partial) available. Financial award application deadline: 3/15.

Dr. Edward L. Millner, Chair, 804-828-1717, *Fax:* 804-828-1719, *E-mail:* emiller@saturn.vcu.edu.

Application contact: Tracy Green, Graduate Program Director, 804-828-1741, *Fax:* 804-828-7174, *E-mail:* tsgreen@vcu.edu. *Web site:* http://www.vcu.edu/busweb/gsib/

■ VIRGINIA POLYTECHNIC INSTITUTE AND STATE UNIVERSITY

Graduate School, College of Agriculture and Life Sciences, Department of Agricultural and Applied Economics, Blacksburg, VA 24061

AWARDS Agribusiness (MS); agricultural economics (MS); applied economics (MS); developmental and international economics (PhD); econometrics (PhD); macro and micro economics (PhD); markets and industrial organizations (PhD); public and regional/urban economics (PhD); resource and environmental economics (PhD).

Faculty: 27 full-time (3 women).

Students: 36 full-time (13 women), 13 international. Average age 25. 68 applicants, 25% accepted, 10 enrolled. In 2001, 7 master's, 3 doctorates awarded. Terminal master's awarded for partial completion of doctoral program.

Degree requirements: For master's, thesis (for some programs); for doctorate, thesis/dissertation, dissertation defense, qualifying exams.

Entrance requirements: For master's and doctorate, GRE General Test, TOEFL. *Application deadline:* For winter admission, 2/1 (priority date). Applications are processed on a rolling basis. *Application fee:* $45. Electronic applications accepted.

Expenses: Tuition, state resident: part-time $241 per hour. Tuition, nonresident: part-time $406 per hour. Tuition and fees vary according to program.

Financial support: In 2001–02, 32 students received support, including 10 research assistantships with full tuition reimbursements available (averaging $16,000 per year), 4 teaching assistantships with full tuition reimbursements available (averaging $16,000 per year). Financial award application deadline: 2/15.

Faculty research: Rural development. *Total annual research expenditures:* $1.5 million.

Dr. David Orden, Graduate Program Chairman, 540-231-7559, *Fax:* 540-231-3318, *E-mail:* orden@vt.edu.

Application contact: Marilyn Echols, Graduate Program Administrator, 540-231-6846, *Fax:* 540-231-7417, *E-mail:* squid@vt.edu. *Web site:* http://www.aaec.vt.edu/

■ VIRGINIA POLYTECHNIC INSTITUTE AND STATE UNIVERSITY

Graduate School, College of Arts and Sciences, Department of Economics, Blacksburg, VA 24061

AWARDS MA, PhD.

Students: 35 full-time (14 women); includes 29 minority (27 Asian Americans or Pacific Islanders, 2 Hispanic Americans). 97 applicants, 27% accepted, 9 enrolled. In 2001, 11 master's, 1 doctorate awarded.

Entrance requirements: For master's and doctorate, GRE, TOEFL. *Application deadline:* For fall admission, 12/1 (priority date). Applications are processed on a rolling basis. *Application fee:* $45. Electronic applications accepted.

Expenses: Tuition, state resident: part-time $241 per hour. Tuition, nonresident: part-time $406 per hour. Tuition and fees vary according to program.

Financial support: In 2001–02, 14 teaching assistantships with full tuition reimbursements (averaging $12,000 per year) were awarded; fellowships, unspecified assistantships also available. Financial award application deadline: 4/1.

Dr. Aris Spanos, Head, 540-231-5689, *Fax:* 540-231-5097, *E-mail:* aris@vt.edu.

■ VIRGINIA STATE UNIVERSITY

School of Graduate Studies, Research, and Outreach, School of Business, Department of Economics and Finance, Petersburg, VA 23806-0001

AWARDS MA.

Faculty: 4 full-time (0 women).

Students: In 2001, 2 degrees awarded.

Degree requirements: For master's, thesis optional.

Entrance requirements: For master's, GRE General Test. *Application deadline:* For fall admission, 8/15. Applications are processed on a rolling basis. *Application fee:* $25.

Expenses: Tuition, area resident: Full-time $2,446; part-time $113 per credit hour. Tuition, state resident: full-time $8,814; part-time $420 per credit hour. Required fees: $1,724; $31 per credit hour.

Financial support: Application deadline: 5/1.

Dr. Maxwell Eseonu, Chair, 804-524-5930, *Fax:* 804-524-5541, *E-mail:* meseonu@vsu.edu.

Application contact: Dr. Wayne F. Virag, Dean, Graduate Studies, Research, and Outreach, 804-524-5985, *Fax:* 804-524-5104, *E-mail:* wvirag@vsu.edu.

■ WALSH COLLEGE OF ACCOUNTANCY AND BUSINESS ADMINISTRATION

Graduate Programs, Program in Economics, Troy, MI 48007-7006

AWARDS MAE.

Faculty: 3 full-time (0 women), 18 part-time/adjunct (1 woman).

Students: 2 full-time (1 woman), 33 part-time (10 women); includes 4 minority (2 African Americans, 2 Hispanic Americans). 16 applicants, 100% accepted. *Application deadline:* For fall admission, 8/24 (priority date); for winter admission, 1/1 (priority date); for spring admission, 4/1 (priority date). *Application fee:* $25.

Expenses: Tuition: Part-time $318 per credit hour. Required fees: $110 per term.

Financial support: Application deadline: 6/30.

Harry Veryser, Chairman, Economics and Finance Department, 248-823-1265 Ext. 265, *Fax:* 248-689-0920, *E-mail:* hveryser@walshcollege.edu.

Application contact: Karen Mahaffy, Director of Admissions and Academic Advising, 248-823-1610, *Fax:* 248-689-0938, *E-mail:* kmahaffy@walshcollegegr.edu.

■ WASHINGTON STATE UNIVERSITY

Graduate School, College of Business and Economics, Department of Economics, Pullman, WA 99164

AWARDS Economics (MA, PhD); international business economics (Certificate).

Faculty: 16 full-time (1 woman).

Students: 25 full-time (3 women), 3 part-time, 17 international. Average age 30. 287 applicants, 11% accepted. In 2001, 4 master's, 4 doctorates awarded.

Degree requirements: For master's, oral exam, thesis optional; for doctorate, thesis/dissertation, oral exam, written exam, field exams.

Entrance requirements: For master's, GRE General Test, minimum GPA of 3.0; for doctorate, GRE General Test or GMAT, TOEFL, minimum GPA of 3.0. *Application deadline:* For fall admission, 3/1 (priority date). Applications are processed on a rolling basis. *Application fee:* $35.

Expenses: Tuition, state resident: full-time $6,088; part-time $304 per semester. Tuition, nonresident: full-time $14,918; part-time $746 per semester. Tuition and fees vary according to program.

Financial support: In 2001–02, 1 research assistantship, 21 teaching assistantships were awarded. Career-related internships or fieldwork, Federal Work-Study, institutionally sponsored loans, tuition waivers (partial), and teaching associateships also available. Financial award application deadline: 4/1; financial award applicants required to submit FAFSA.

Faculty research: Economic theory and quantitative methods, applied microeconomics. *Total annual research expenditures:* $80,141.
Dr. Duane Leigh, Chair, 509-335-6651.
Application contact: Maggie Kettwig, Graduate Coordinator, 509-335-1667, *Fax:* 509-335-4362, *E-mail:* econdept@mail.wsu.edu. *Web site:* http://www.wsu.edu/~econdept/grad%20frame.htm

■ WASHINGTON UNIVERSITY IN ST. LOUIS

Graduate School of Arts and Sciences, Department of Economics, St. Louis, MO 63130-4899

AWARDS MA, PhD, JD/MA, JD/PhD. Part-time programs available.

Students: 53 full-time (19 women), 1 part-time; includes 1 minority (African American), 25 international. 358 applicants, 8% accepted. In 2001, 12 master's, 6 doctorates awarded. Terminal master's awarded for partial completion of doctoral program.
Degree requirements: For master's, thesis or alternative; for doctorate, one foreign language, thesis/dissertation.
Entrance requirements: For master's and doctorate, GRE General Test, GRE Subject Test. *Application deadline:* For fall admission, 1/15 (priority date). Applications are processed on a rolling basis. *Application fee:* $35. Electronic applications accepted.
Expenses: Tuition: Full-time $26,900.
Financial support: Fellowships, research assistantships, teaching assistantships, Federal Work-Study, institutionally sponsored loans, and tuition waivers (full and partial) available. Support available to part-time students. Financial award application deadline: 1/15.
Dr. Steven Fazzari, Chairman, 314-935-5632. *Web site:* http://wuecon.wustl.edu/econdept/main.html

■ WAYNE STATE UNIVERSITY

Graduate School, College of Liberal Arts, Department of Economics, Detroit, MI 48202

AWARDS MA, PhD, JD/MA.

Faculty: 11 full-time.
Students: 64. Average age 28. 67 applicants, 39% accepted, 15 enrolled. In 2001, 16 master's, 2 doctorates awarded.
Degree requirements: For master's, thesis optional; for doctorate, thesis/dissertation.
Entrance requirements: For master's, TOEFL, minimum GPA of 3.0; for doctorate, GRE, TOEFL, minimum GPA of 3.0. *Application deadline:* For fall admission, 7/1. Applications are processed on a rolling basis. *Application fee:* $20 ($30 for international students). Electronic applications accepted.
Expenses: Tuition, state resident: full-time $3,764. Tuition and fees vary according to degree level and program.
Financial support: In 2001–02, 4 fellowships, 20 teaching assistantships were awarded. Institutionally sponsored loans and tuition waivers (full and partial) also available. Support available to part-time students. Financial award application deadline: 3/1.
Faculty research: Health care, international economics, macroeconomics, urban and labor issues, econometrics.
Jay Levin, Chairperson, 313-577-3345, *Fax:* 313-577-0149, *E-mail:* jlevin@econ.wayne.edu.
Application contact: Allen Goodman, Director, 313-577-3235, *E-mail:* allen.goodman@wayne.edu. *Web site:* http://www.econ.wayne.edu/

■ WAYNE STATE UNIVERSITY

Graduate School, College of Urban, Labor and Metropolitan Affairs, Interdisciplinary Program in Economic Development, Detroit, MI 48202

AWARDS Certificate.

Students: 2. Average age 26.
Application deadline: For fall admission, 7/1. *Application fee:* $20 ($30 for international students). Electronic applications accepted.
Expenses: Tuition, state resident: full-time $3,764. Tuition and fees vary according to degree level and program.
Robin Boyle, Associate Dean, 313-577-8711, *Fax:* 313-577-8800, *E-mail:* r.boyle@wayne.edu.
Application contact: Linda Johnson, Academic Services Officer, 313-577-0175, *Fax:* 313-577-8800.

■ WEST CHESTER UNIVERSITY OF PENNSYLVANIA

Graduate Studies, School of Business and Public Affairs, Program in Business Administration, West Chester, PA 19383

AWARDS Economics/finance (MBA); executive business administration (MBA); general business (MBA); management (MBA); technology and electronic commerce (MBA). Part-time and evening/weekend programs available.

Students: 5 full-time (all women), 174 part-time (58 women); includes 19 minority (8 African Americans, 9 Asian Americans or Pacific Islanders, 2 Hispanic Americans), 10 international. Average age 37. 74 applicants, 68% accepted. In 2001, 76 degrees awarded.
Degree requirements: For master's, thesis optional.
Entrance requirements: For master's, GMAT, interview, minimum GPA of 3.0. *Application deadline:* For fall admission, 4/15 (priority date); for spring admission, 10/15. Applications are processed on a rolling basis. *Application fee:* $25.
Expenses: Tuition, state resident: full-time $4,600; part-time $256 per credit. Tuition, nonresident: full-time $7,554; part-time $420 per credit. Required fees: $44 per credit.
Financial support: In 2001–02, 1 research assistantship with full tuition reimbursement (averaging $5,000 per year) was awarded; unspecified assistantships also available. Support available to part-time students. Financial award application deadline: 2/15; financial award applicants required to submit FAFSA.
Dr. Randall LaSalle, Director, 610-436-2608, *E-mail:* rlasalle@wcupa.edu.

■ WESTERN ILLINOIS UNIVERSITY

School of Graduate Studies, College of Business and Technology, Department of Economics, Macomb, IL 61455-1390

AWARDS MA. Part-time programs available.

Faculty: 9 full-time (1 woman).
Students: 27 full-time (9 women), 4 part-time (2 women); includes 4 minority (2 African Americans, 2 Asian Americans or Pacific Islanders), 16 international. Average age 28. 44 applicants, 52% accepted. In 2001, 13 degrees awarded.
Degree requirements: For master's, thesis or alternative.
Application deadline: Applications are processed on a rolling basis. *Application fee:* $0 ($25 for international students). Electronic applications accepted.
Expenses: Tuition, state resident: part-time $108 per credit hour. Tuition, nonresident: part-time $216 per credit hour. Required fees: $33 per credit hour.
Financial support: In 2001–02, 12 students received support, including 12 research assistantships with full tuition reimbursements available (averaging $5,720 per year). Financial award applicants required to submit FAFSA.
Faculty research: Economic systems, environmental economics.
Dr. Warren Jones, Chairperson, 309-298-1153.
Application contact: Dr. Barbara Baily, Director of Graduate Studies, 309-298-1806, *Fax:* 309-298-2345, *E-mail:* grad-office@wiu.edu. *Web site:* http://www.wiu.edu/

■ WESTERN MICHIGAN UNIVERSITY

Graduate College, College of Arts and Sciences, Department of Economics, Kalamazoo, MI 49008-5202

AWARDS Applied economics (PhD); economics (MA).

Faculty: 18 full-time (3 women).
Students: 52 full-time (19 women), 5 part-time (1 woman); includes 1 minority (African American), 49 international. 131

Western Michigan University (continued)
applicants, 31% accepted, 19 enrolled. In 2001, 13 degrees awarded.
Degree requirements: For master's, thesis, oral or written exams; for doctorate, thesis/dissertation, oral exam, internship.
Entrance requirements: For doctorate, GRE General Test. *Application deadline:* For fall admission, 2/15 (priority date). Applications are processed on a rolling basis. *Application fee:* $25.
Expenses: Tuition, state resident: part-time $186 per credit hour. Tuition, nonresident: part-time $442 per credit hour. Required fees: $602. One-time fee: $132 part-time. Tuition and fees vary according to course load.
Financial support: Fellowships, research assistantships, teaching assistantships, Federal Work-Study available. Financial award application deadline: 2/15; financial award applicants required to submit FAFSA.
Dr. Bassam Harik, Chairperson, 616-387-5535.
Application contact: Admissions and Orientation, 616-387-2000, *Fax:* 616-387-2355.

■ WEST TEXAS A&M UNIVERSITY

T. Boone Pickens College of Business, Department of Accounting, Economics, and Finance, Program in Finance and Economics, Canyon, TX 79016-0001

AWARDS MS. Part-time and evening/weekend programs available. Postbaccalaureate distance learning degree programs offered (minimal on-campus study).

Faculty: 8 full-time (3 women), 2 part-time/adjunct (1 woman).
Students: 4 full-time (0 women), 12 part-time (2 women); includes 3 minority (1 Asian American or Pacific Islander, 2 Hispanic Americans), 4 international. Average age 34. 12 applicants, 12 enrolled. In 2001, 4 degrees awarded.
Degree requirements: For master's, thesis optional. *Median time to degree:* Master's–3 years full-time, 6 years part-time.
Entrance requirements: For master's, GMAT. *Application deadline:* Applications are processed on a rolling basis. *Application fee:* $25 ($75 for international students). Electronic applications accepted.
Expenses: Tuition, state resident: part-time $120 per hour. Tuition, nonresident: part-time $253 per hour.
Financial support: In 2001–02, research assistantships (averaging $6,500 per year), 1 teaching assistantship with partial tuition reimbursement (averaging $6,700 per year) were awarded. Federal Work-Study, institutionally sponsored loans, and tuition waivers (partial) also available. Support available to part-time students. Financial award applicants required to submit CSS PROFILE or FAFSA.
Application contact: Dr. Neil Terry, Graduate Adviser, 806-651-2512, *Fax:* 806-651-2927, *E-mail:* nterry@mail.wtamu.edu.

■ WEST VIRGINIA UNIVERSITY

College of Business and Economics, Department of Economics and Finance, Morgantown, WV 26506

AWARDS Business analysis (MA); econometrics (PhD); industrial economics (PhD); international economics (PhD); labor economics (PhD); mathematical economics (MA, PhD); monetary economics (PhD); public finance (PhD); public policy (MA); regional and urban economics (PhD); statistics and economics (MA).

Faculty: 22 full-time (2 women), 1 part-time/adjunct (0 women).
Students: 43 full-time (14 women), 4 part-time (1 woman); includes 2 minority (both Asian Americans or Pacific Islanders), 34 international. Average age 29. 81 applicants, 73% accepted. In 2001, 6 master's, 5 doctorates awarded. Terminal master's awarded for partial completion of doctoral program.
Degree requirements: For master's, thesis optional; for doctorate, thesis/dissertation, comprehensive exam.
Entrance requirements: For master's and doctorate, GRE General Test, TOEFL, minimum GPA of 3.0. *Application deadline:* For fall admission, 6/30; for spring admission, 11/15. Applications are processed on a rolling basis. *Application fee:* $45.
Expenses: Tuition, state resident: full-time $2,791. Tuition, nonresident: full-time $8,659. Required fees: $1,002. Tuition and fees vary according to program.
Financial support: In 2001–02, 29 research assistantships, 5 teaching assistantships were awarded. Federal Work-Study, institutionally sponsored loans, and tuition waivers (full and partial) also available. Financial award application deadline: 2/1; financial award applicants required to submit FAFSA.
Faculty research: Labor supply, pensions, international trade, regional economics.
Dr. William S. Trumbull, Chair, 304-293-7860, *Fax:* 304-293-2233, *E-mail:* william.trumbull@mail.wvu.edu.
Application contact: Dr. Paul J. Speaker, Director, 304-293-7810, *Fax:* 304-293-5652, *E-mail:* paul.speaker@mail.wvu.edu. *Web site:* http://www.be.wvu.edu/people/division.econfina/index.htm

■ WRIGHT STATE UNIVERSITY

School of Graduate Studies, Raj Soin College of Business, Department of Economics, Dayton, OH 45435

AWARDS Business economics (MBA); social and applied economics (MS).

Students: 10 full-time (5 women), 7 part-time (3 women). Average age 30. 31 applicants, 87% accepted. In 2001, 9 degrees awarded.
Entrance requirements: For master's, GRE General Test, TOEFL. *Application fee:* $25.
Expenses: Tuition, state resident: full-time $7,161; part-time $225 per quarter hour. Tuition, nonresident: full-time $12,324; part-time $385 per quarter hour. Tuition and fees vary according to course load, degree level and program.
Financial support: Fellowships, research assistantships, teaching assistantships, career-related internships or fieldwork and unspecified assistantships available. Support available to part-time students. Financial award applicants required to submit FAFSA.
Dr. James A. Swaney, Chair, 937-775-3070, *Fax:* 937-775-2441, *E-mail:* james.swaney@wright.edu.
Application contact: Dr. Len Kloft, Director, 937-775-2322, *Fax:* 937-775-2441, *E-mail:* leonard.kloft@wright.edu.

■ YALE UNIVERSITY

Graduate School of Arts and Sciences, Department of Economics, New Haven, CT 06520

AWARDS Economics (PhD); international and development economics (MA).

Degree requirements: For doctorate, thesis/dissertation.
Entrance requirements: For master's, GRE General Test; for doctorate, GRE General Test, GRE Subject Test.
Faculty research: Economic history of Western Europe, environmental economics, economic growth and development.

■ YOUNGSTOWN STATE UNIVERSITY

Graduate School, College of Arts and Sciences, Department of Economics, Youngstown, OH 44555-0001

AWARDS MA. Part-time programs available.

Degree requirements: For master's, thesis optional.
Entrance requirements: For master's, TOEFL, minimum GPA of 2.7, 21 hours in economics.
Faculty research: Forecasting, applied econometrics, labor economics, applied macroeconomics, industrial organization.

MINERAL ECONOMICS

■ COLORADO SCHOOL OF MINES

Graduate School, Division of Economics and Business, Golden, CO 80401-1887

AWARDS Engineering and technology management (MS); mineral economics (MS, PhD). Part-time programs available.

Faculty: 13 full-time (2 women), 13 part-time/adjunct (5 women).
Students: 58 full-time (11 women), 27 part-time (5 women); includes 6 minority (2 African Americans, 2 Asian Americans or Pacific Islanders, 2 Hispanic Americans), 37 international. 114 applicants, 94% accepted, 30 enrolled. In 2001, 31 master's, 2 doctorates awarded.
Degree requirements: For doctorate, thesis/dissertation, comprehensive exam. *Median time to degree:* Master's–2 years full-time; doctorate–4 years full-time.
Entrance requirements: For master's and doctorate, GRE General Test. *Application deadline:* For fall admission, 12/1 (priority date); for spring admission, 5/1 (priority date). Applications are processed on a rolling basis. *Application fee:* $40. Electronic applications accepted.
Expenses: Tuition, state resident: full-time $4,940; part-time $246 per credit. Tuition, nonresident: full-time $16,070; part-time $803 per credit. Required fees: $341 per semester.
Financial support: In 2001–02, 32 students received support, including 5 fellowships (averaging $6,471 per year), 4 research assistantships (averaging $7,793 per year), 31 teaching assistantships (averaging $5,232 per year); unspecified assistantships also available. Support available to part-time students. Financial award applicants required to submit FAFSA.
Faculty research: International trade, resource and environmental economics, energy economics, operations research. *Total annual research expenditures:* $45,408.
Dr. Roderick G. Eggert, Head, 303-273-3981, *Fax:* 303-273-3416, *E-mail:* reggert@mines.edu.
Application contact: Kathleen A. Feighny, Administrative Faculty, 303-273-3979, *Fax:* 303-273-3416, *E-mail:* kfeighny@mines.edu. *Web site:* http://www.mines.edu/academic/econbus/

■ MICHIGAN TECHNOLOGICAL UNIVERSITY

Graduate School, School of Business and Economics, Program in Mineral Economics, Houghton, MI 49931-1295

AWARDS MS. Part-time programs available.

Degree requirements: For master's, thesis.
Entrance requirements: For master's, GMAT, TOEFL, bachelor's degree in business, economics, engineering, or science. Electronic applications accepted.
Faculty research: Natural resources and environmental economics, project evaluation methods, metal markets, mineral demands. *Web site:* http://www.sbea.mtu.edu/school/index.html

Find an in-depth description at www.petersons.com/gradchannel.

■ MONTANA TECH OF THE UNIVERSITY OF MONTANA

Graduate School, Geoscience Program, Butte, MT 59701-8997

AWARDS Geochemistry (MS); geological engineering (MS); geology (MS); geophysical engineering (MS); hydrogeological engineering (MS); hydrogeology (MS); mineral economics (MS). Part-time programs available.

Faculty: 8 full-time (1 woman).
Students: 12 full-time (5 women), 5 part-time (3 women); includes 1 minority (Hispanic American). 13 applicants, 62% accepted, 6 enrolled. In 2001, 7 degrees awarded.
Degree requirements: For master's, thesis (for some programs), registration.
Entrance requirements: For master's, GRE General Test, TOEFL, minimum GPA of 3.0. *Application deadline:* For fall admission, 4/1 (priority date); for spring admission, 10/1 (priority date). Applications are processed on a rolling basis. *Application fee:* $30.
Expenses: Tuition, state resident: full-time $3,717; part-time $196 per credit. Tuition, nonresident: full-time $11,770; part-time $324 per credit.
Financial support: In 2001–02, 13 students received support, including 4 research assistantships with partial tuition reimbursements available (averaging $8,600 per year), 7 teaching assistantships with partial tuition reimbursements available (averaging $5,343 per year); career-related internships or fieldwork, institutionally sponsored loans, and tuition waivers (full and partial) also available. Financial award application deadline: 4/1; financial award applicants required to submit FAFSA.
Faculty research: Water resource development, seismic processing, petroleum reservoir characterization, environmental geochemistry, molecular modeling, magmatic and hydrothermal ore deposits. *Total annual research expenditures:* $293,854.
Dr. Diane Wolfgram, Department Head, 406-496-4353, *Fax:* 406-496-4260, *E-mail:* dwolfgram@mtech.edu.
Application contact: Cindy Dunstan, Administrator, Graduate School, 406-496-4304, *Fax:* 406-496-4334, *E-mail:* cdunstan@mtech.edu. *Web site:* http://www.mtech.edu/

■ THE UNIVERSITY OF TEXAS AT AUSTIN

Graduate School, College of Engineering, Department of Petroleum and Geosystems Engineering, Program in Energy and Mineral Resources, Austin, TX 78712-1111

AWARDS MA, MS.

Faculty: 2 full-time (0 women).
Students: 13 full-time (3 women), 12 international. Average age 30. 7 applicants, 43% accepted.
Degree requirements: For master's, thesis, seminar.
Entrance requirements: For master's, GRE General Test, TOEFL. *Application deadline:* For fall admission, 4/30 (priority date). Applications are processed on a rolling basis. *Application fee:* $50 ($75 for international students). Electronic applications accepted.
Expenses: Tuition, state resident: full-time $3,159. Tuition, nonresident: full-time $6,957. Tuition and fees vary according to program.
Dr. Willem C. J. vanRensburg, Graduate Adviser, 512-471-3248, *Fax:* 512-471-9605, *E-mail:* willem_vanrensburg@pe.utexas.edu.
Application contact: Julia Casarez, Graduate Coordinator, 512-471-3247, *Fax:* 512-471-9605, *E-mail:* julia_casarez@mail.utexas.edu. *Web site:* http://www.pe.utexas.edu/dept/academic.emr/

Family and Consumer Sciences

FAMILY AND CONSUMER SCIENCES-GENERAL

■ ALABAMA AGRICULTURAL AND MECHANICAL UNIVERSITY

School of Graduate Studies, School of Agricultural and Environmental Sciences, Department of Family and Consumer Sciences, Huntsville, AL 35811

AWARDS Family and consumer sciences (MS); food science (MS, PhD). Part-time and evening/weekend programs available.

Faculty: 5 full-time (4 women).
Students: 4 full-time (all women), 12 part-time (all women); includes 11 minority (all African Americans), 2 international. In 2001, 7 master's, 1 doctorate awarded.
Degree requirements: For master's, thesis optional; for doctorate, one foreign language, thesis/dissertation.
Entrance requirements: For master's, GRE General Test; for doctorate, GRE General Test, MS. *Application deadline:* For fall admission, 5/1. *Application fee:* $15 ($20 for international students).
Expenses: Tuition, state resident: full-time $1,380. Tuition, nonresident: full-time $2,500.
Financial support: In 2001–02, 2 research assistantships with tuition reimbursements (averaging $9,000 per year), teaching assistantships with tuition reimbursements (averaging $9,000 per year) were awarded. Career-related internships or fieldwork, Federal Work-Study, and traineeships also available. Financial award application deadline: 4/1.
Faculty research: Food biotechnology, nutrition, food microbiology, food engineering, food chemistry.
Dr. Bernice Richardson, Chair, 256-851-5455, *Fax:* 256-851-5433.

■ APPALACHIAN STATE UNIVERSITY

Cratis D. Williams Graduate School, College of Fine and Applied Arts, Department of Family and Consumer Sciences, Boone, NC 28608

AWARDS Child development (MA); family and consumer science (MA). Part-time programs available.

Faculty: 5 full-time (4 women).
Students: 19 full-time (16 women), 3 part-time (all women); includes 1 minority (Native American). 21 applicants, 90% accepted, 8 enrolled. In 2001, 7 degrees awarded.
Degree requirements: For master's, thesis or alternative, comprehensive exam.
Entrance requirements: For master's, GRE General Test. *Application deadline:* For fall admission, 7/1 (priority date); for spring admission, 11/1. *Application fee:* $35.
Expenses: Tuition, state resident: full-time $1,286. Tuition, nonresident: full-time $9,354. Required fees: $1,116.
Financial support: In 2001–02, 3 research assistantships (averaging $6,250 per year), 4 teaching assistantships (averaging $6,250 per year) were awarded. Fellowships, career-related internships or fieldwork, scholarships/grants, and unspecified assistantships also available. Support available to part-time students. Financial award application deadline: 7/1; financial award applicants required to submit FAFSA.
Faculty research: Food antioxidants, preschool curriculum, children with special needs, family child care, FCS curriculum content. *Total annual research expenditures:* $138,358.
Dr. Sammie Garner, Chairperson, 828-262-2661, *E-mail:* garnersg@appstate.edu.
Application contact: Dr. Cindy McGaha, Graduate Director, 828-262-2698.

■ BALL STATE UNIVERSITY

Graduate School, College of Applied Science and Technology, Department of Family and Consumer Sciences, Muncie, IN 47306-1099

AWARDS MA, MAE, MS.

Faculty: 22.
Students: 21 full-time (19 women), 24 part-time (22 women). Average age 26. 37 applicants, 78% accepted. In 2001, 21 degrees awarded.
Entrance requirements: For master's, resumé. *Application fee:* $25 ($35 for international students).
Expenses: Tuition, state resident: full-time $4,068; part-time $2,542. Tuition, nonresident: full-time $10,944; part-time $6,462. Required fees: $1,000; $500 per term.
Financial support: In 2001–02, 11 teaching assistantships with full tuition reimbursements (averaging $6,930 per year) were awarded; research assistantships with full tuition reimbursements, career-related internships or fieldwork also available. Financial award application deadline: 3/1.
Faculty research: Maternal and infant nutrition, nutrition education.
Dr. Alice Spangler, Head, 765-285-5932, *Fax:* 765-285-2314, *E-mail:* aspangler@bsu.edu. *Web site:* http://www.bsu.edu/fcs/

■ BOWLING GREEN STATE UNIVERSITY

Graduate College, College of Education and Human Development, School of Family and Consumer Sciences, Bowling Green, OH 43403

AWARDS Food and nutrition (MFCS); human development and family studies (MFCS). Part-time programs available.

Faculty: 24.
Students: 14 full-time (all women), 8 part-time (7 women), 3 international. Average age 26. 14 applicants, 57% accepted, 7 enrolled. In 2001, 6 degrees awarded.
Degree requirements: For master's, thesis.
Entrance requirements: For master's, GRE General Test, TOEFL, minimum GPA of 3.0. *Application deadline:* For fall admission, 2/15. *Application fee:* $30.
Expenses: Tuition, state resident: full-time $7,376; part-time $342 per credit hour. Tuition, nonresident: full-time $13,628; part-time $640 per credit hour.
Financial support: In 2001–02, 12 research assistantships with full tuition reimbursements (averaging $4,486 per year), 2 teaching assistantships with full tuition reimbursements (averaging $5,475 per year) were awarded. Career-related internships or fieldwork and unspecified assistantships also available. Financial award applicants required to submit FAFSA.
Faculty research: Public health, wellness, social issues and policies, ethnic foods, nutrition and aging.
Dr. Joe Williford, Acting Chair, 419-372-7823.
Application contact: Dr. Rebecca Pebocik, Graduate Coordinator, 419-372-6920.

■ CALIFORNIA STATE UNIVERSITY, FRESNO

Division of Graduate Studies, College of Agricultural Sciences and Technology, Department of Child, Family and Consumer Sciences, Fresno, CA 93740-8027

AWARDS Family and consumer sciences (MS). Part-time and evening/weekend programs available.

Faculty: 8.
Students: 3 full-time (all women), 3 part-time (all women); includes 2 minority (1 African American, 1 Hispanic American). Average age 31. 3 applicants, 33% accepted, 1 enrolled. In 2001, 2 degrees awarded.
Degree requirements: For master's, thesis (for some programs), registration.

Median time to degree: Master's–2.5 years full-time, 3.5 years part-time.
Entrance requirements: For master's, GRE General Test, TOEFL, minimum GPA of 3.0 in last 60 hours. *Application deadline:* For fall admission, 6/1 (priority date); for spring admission, 11/1. Applications are processed on a rolling basis. *Application fee:* $55. Electronic applications accepted.
Expenses: Tuition, nonresident: part-time $246 per unit. Required fees: $605 per semester. Tuition and fees vary according to course load.
Financial support: Fellowships, career-related internships or fieldwork, Federal Work-Study, institutionally sponsored loans, and scholarships/grants available. Support available to part-time students. Financial award application deadline: 3/1; financial award applicants required to submit FAFSA.
Faculty research: Student exchange program, ecofashion, low-impact processing of apparel, organic cotton and natural dyes.
Nina J. Dilbeck, Chair, 559-278-2283, *Fax:* 559-278-7824, *E-mail:* nina_dilbeck@csufresno.edu.
Application contact: Dr. Carolyn Jackson, Coordinator, 559-278-2283, *E-mail:* carolyn_jackson@csufresno.edu.

■ CALIFORNIA STATE UNIVERSITY, LONG BEACH

Graduate Studies, College of Health and Human Services, Department of Family and Consumer Sciences, Long Beach, CA 90840

AWARDS Home economics (MA); nutritional sciences (MS). Part-time and evening/weekend programs available.

Faculty: 25 full-time (20 women).
Students: 7 full-time (all women), 16 part-time (14 women); includes 4 minority (1 African American, 1 Asian American or Pacific Islander, 2 Hispanic Americans), 2 international. Average age 33. 9 applicants, 67% accepted. In 2001, 3 degrees awarded.
Degree requirements: For master's, comprehensive exam or thesis.
Entrance requirements: For master's, minimum GPA of 3.0. *Application deadline:* For fall admission, 8/1; for spring admission, 12/1. Applications are processed on a rolling basis. *Application fee:* $55. Electronic applications accepted.
Financial support: Federal Work-Study, institutionally sponsored loans, and scholarships/grants available. Financial award application deadline: 3/2.
Faculty research: Premarital relationships, adolescent pregnancy prevention, premarital therapy, minerals and blood pressure, child nutrition.
Dr. Sue Stanley, Chair, 562-985-4484, *Fax:* 562-985-4414, *E-mail:* stanleym@csulb.edu.
Application contact: Dr. Mary Jacob, Graduate Coordinator, 562-985-4516, *Fax:* 562-985-4414, *E-mail:* mjacob@csulb.edu.

■ CALIFORNIA STATE UNIVERSITY, LOS ANGELES

Graduate Studies, College of Health and Human Services, Department of Child and Family Studies, Major in Home Economics, Los Angeles, CA 90032-8530

AWARDS MA.

Degree requirements: For master's, project, or thesis.
Entrance requirements: For master's, TOEFL. *Application deadline:* For fall admission, 6/30; for spring admission, 2/1. Applications are processed on a rolling basis. *Application fee:* $55.
Expenses: Tuition, nonresident: part-time $164 per unit.
Financial support: Application deadline: 3/1.
Dr. Jeffrey Gilger, Co-Chair, Department of Child and Family Studies, 323-343-4590.

■ CENTRAL MICHIGAN UNIVERSITY

College of Graduate Studies, College of Education and Human Services, Department of Human Environmental Studies, Mount Pleasant, MI 48859

AWARDS Human development and family studies (MA); nutrition and dietetics (MS).

Degree requirements: For master's, thesis or alternative.
Entrance requirements: For master's, GRE (MA), minimum GPA of 3.0 in last 60 hours, 15 credits in human development and family studies or related area (MA).
Expenses: Tuition, state resident: part-time $182 per unit. Tuition, nonresident: part-time $182 per unit. Required fees: $208 per semester. Part-time tuition and fees vary according to course load.
Faculty research: Human growth and development, family studies and human sexuality, nutritional food science/food services, apparel and textile retailing, computer-aided design for apparel and interior design.

■ CENTRAL WASHINGTON UNIVERSITY

Graduate Studies and Research, College of Education and Professional Studies, Department of Family and Consumer Sciences, Ellensburg, WA 98926-7463

AWARDS Apparel design (MS); family and consumer sciences education (MS); family studies (MS); nutrition (MS). Part-time programs available.

Faculty: 8 full-time (5 women).
Students: 5 full-time (4 women), 6 part-time (all women); includes 1 minority (African American), 1 international. 1 applicant, 100% accepted, 1 enrolled. In 2001, 4 degrees awarded.
Degree requirements: For master's, thesis or alternative.
Entrance requirements: For master's, GRE General Test (nutrition), minimum GPA of 3.0. *Application deadline:* For fall admission, 4/1 (priority date); for winter admission, 10/1; for spring admission, 1/1. Applications are processed on a rolling basis. *Application fee:* $35.
Expenses: Tuition, state resident: full-time $4,848; part-time $162 per credit. Tuition, nonresident: full-time $14,772; part-time $492 per credit. Required fees: $324.
Financial support: In 2001–02, 3 teaching assistantships with partial tuition reimbursements (averaging $7,120 per year) were awarded; research assistantships, Federal Work-Study also available. Financial award application deadline: 3/1; financial award applicants required to submit FAFSA.
Dr. Jan Bowers, Chair, 509-963-2766.
Application contact: Barbara Sisko, Office Assistant, Graduate Studies and Research, 509-963-3103, *Fax:* 509-963-1799, *E-mail:* masters@cwu.edu. *Web site:* http://www.cwu.edu/

■ COLLEGE OF THE ATLANTIC

Program in Human Ecology, Bar Harbor, ME 04609-1198

AWARDS M Phil.

Electronic applications accepted.
Expenses: Tuition: Full-time $14,844. Required fees: $270.
Faculty research: Human ecology, evolutionary biology, fine arts, history, anthropology. *Web site:* http://www.coa.edu/

■ CORNELL UNIVERSITY

Graduate School, Graduate Fields of Human Ecology, Ithaca, NY 14853-0001

AWARDS MA, MHA, MPS, MS, PhD.

Faculty: 89 full-time.
Students: 120 full-time (83 women); includes 28 minority (13 African Americans, 10 Asian Americans or Pacific Islanders, 5 Hispanic Americans), 42 international. 233 applicants, 41% accepted. In 2001, 26 master's, 6 doctorates awarded. Terminal master's awarded for partial completion of doctoral program.
Degree requirements: For doctorate, thesis/dissertation.
Entrance requirements: For master's and doctorate, GRE General Test, TOEFL. *Application fee:* $65. Electronic applications accepted.
Expenses: Contact institution.
Financial support: In 2001–02, 91 students received support, including 23

Cornell University (continued)
fellowships with full tuition reimbursements available, 15 research assistantships with full tuition reimbursements available, 53 teaching assistantships with full tuition reimbursements available; institutionally sponsored loans, scholarships/grants, tuition waivers (full and partial), and unspecified assistantships also available. Financial award applicants required to submit FAFSA.
Dr. Patsy Brannon, Dean.
Application contact: Graduate School Application Requests, Caldwell Hall, 607-255-5816. *Web site:* http://www.gradschool.cornell.edu/

■ EAST CAROLINA UNIVERSITY

Graduate School, School of Human Environmental Sciences, Greenville, NC 27858-4353

AWARDS MS. Part-time programs available.

Faculty: 17 full-time (12 women).
Students: 53 full-time (45 women), 32 part-time (all women); includes 12 minority (9 African Americans, 3 Asian Americans or Pacific Islanders), 2 international. Average age 29. 78 applicants, 47% accepted. In 2001, 29 degrees awarded.
Degree requirements: For master's, comprehensive exam.
Entrance requirements: For master's, GRE or MAT, TOEFL. *Application deadline:* Applications are processed on a rolling basis. *Application fee:* $45.
Expenses: Tuition, state resident: full-time $2,636. Tuition, nonresident: full-time $11,365.
Financial support: Fellowships, research assistantships, teaching assistantships, career-related internships or fieldwork and Federal Work-Study available. Support available to part-time students. Financial award application deadline: 6/1.
Dr. Karla Hughes, Dean, 252-328-6891, *Fax:* 252-328-4276.
Application contact: Dr. Paul D. Tschetter, Senior Associate Dean of the Graduate School, 252-328-6012, *Fax:* 252-328-6071, *E-mail:* gradschool@mail.ecu.edu.

■ EASTERN ILLINOIS UNIVERSITY

Graduate School, Lumpkin College of Business and Applied Sciences, School of Family and Consumer Sciences, Charleston, IL 61920-3099

AWARDS Dietetics (MS); home economics (MS). Part-time programs available.

Degree requirements: For master's, comprehensive exam.

■ EASTERN MICHIGAN UNIVERSITY

Graduate School, College of Health and Human Services, Department of Human, Environmental, and Consumer Resources, Ypsilanti, MI 48197

AWARDS MS. Part-time and evening/weekend programs available.

Faculty: 11 full-time (7 women).
Students: 24 full-time, 38 part-time. In 2001, 4 degrees awarded.
Entrance requirements: For master's, TOEFL. *Application deadline:* For fall admission, 5/15; for spring admission, 3/15. Applications are processed on a rolling basis. *Application fee:* $30.
Expenses: Tuition, state resident: part-time $285 per credit hour. Tuition, nonresident: part-time $510 per credit hour.
Financial support: Fellowships, teaching assistantships, Federal Work-Study available. Support available to part-time students. Financial award application deadline: 3/15; financial award applicants required to submit FAFSA.
Dr. George Liepa, Head, 734-487-1217.
Application contact: Coordinator of Advising, 734-487-2490.

■ FLORIDA STATE UNIVERSITY

Graduate Studies, College of Human Sciences, Tallahassee, FL 32306

AWARDS MS, PhD. Part-time programs available.

Faculty: 41 full-time (29 women).
Students: 120 full-time (83 women), 45 part-time (34 women); includes 37 minority (28 African Americans, 2 Asian Americans or Pacific Islanders, 7 Hispanic Americans), 20 international. 187 applicants, 53% accepted, 53 enrolled. In 2001, 39 master's, 12 doctorates awarded.
Degree requirements: For master's, thesis optional; for doctorate, thesis/dissertation.
Entrance requirements: For master's and doctorate, GRE General Test, minimum GPA of 3.0. *Application deadline:* Applications are processed on a rolling basis. *Application fee:* $20. Electronic applications accepted.
Expenses: Tuition, state resident: part-time $163 per credit hour. Tuition, nonresident: part-time $570 per credit hour. Tuition and fees vary according to program.
Financial support: In 2001–02, 85 students received support, including 3 fellowships with partial tuition reimbursements available (averaging $10,000 per year), 26 research assistantships with partial tuition reimbursements available (averaging $8,000 per year), 56 teaching assistantships with partial tuition reimbursements available (averaging $8,000 per year); career-related internships or fieldwork, Federal Work-Study, institutionally sponsored loans, scholarships/grants, and unspecified assistantships also available. Financial award applicants required to submit FAFSA.
Faculty research: Child and adolescent development, merchandising, accessible housing, culturally diverse classrooms, motor behavior.
Dr. Penny A. Ralston, Dean, 850-644-1281, *Fax:* 850-644-0700, *E-mail:* pralston@mailer.fsu.edu.
Application contact: Marcia Ann Williams, Coordinator of Academic Support Services, 850-644-7221, *Fax:* 850-644-0700, *E-mail:* mwilliam@mailer.fsu.edu. *Web site:* http://www.chs.fsu.edu/

Find an in-depth description at www.petersons.com/gradchannel.

■ ILLINOIS STATE UNIVERSITY

Graduate School, College of Applied Science and Technology, Department of Family and Consumer Sciences, Normal, IL 61790-2200

AWARDS MA, MS.

Faculty: 9 full-time (8 women), 1 (woman) part-time/adjunct.
Students: 24 full-time (all women), 23 part-time (22 women); includes 3 minority (2 African Americans, 1 Hispanic American), 2 international. 18 applicants, 94% accepted. In 2001, 20 degrees awarded.
Degree requirements: For master's, thesis or alternative.
Entrance requirements: For master's, GRE General Test, minimum GPA of 2.8 in last 60 hours. *Application deadline:* Applications are processed on a rolling basis. *Application fee:* $30.
Expenses: Tuition, state resident: full-time $2,691; part-time $112 per credit hour. Tuition, nonresident: full-time $5,880; part-time $245 per credit hour. Required fees: $1,146; $48 per credit hour.
Financial support: In 2001–02, 9 research assistantships (averaging $5,638 per year), 13 teaching assistantships (averaging $4,440 per year) were awarded. Tuition waivers (full) and unspecified assistantships also available. Financial award application deadline: 4/1.
Faculty research: Editing journal teaching of marriage and family, a journey of the old and young: Hope Meadows, prenatal WIC clients to increase breastfeeding. *Total annual research expenditures:* $59,986.
Dr. Susan Winchip, Acting Chairperson, 309-438-2517. *Web site:* http://www.cast.ilstu.edu/fcs/cast.shtml

■ INDIANA STATE UNIVERSITY

School of Graduate Studies, College of Arts and Sciences, Department of Family and Consumer Sciences, Terre Haute, IN 47809-1401

AWARDS Child and family relations (MS); clothing and textiles (MS); dietetics (MS);

home management (MS); nutrition and foods (MS). Part-time programs available.

Electronic applications accepted.

■ IOWA STATE UNIVERSITY OF SCIENCE AND TECHNOLOGY

Graduate College, College of Family and Consumer Sciences, Ames, IA 50011

AWARDS M Ed, MFCS, MS, PhD. Part-time programs available.

Faculty: 87 full-time, 4 part-time/adjunct.
Students: 83 full-time (63 women), 98 part-time (79 women); includes 15 minority (3 African Americans, 5 Asian Americans or Pacific Islanders, 6 Hispanic Americans, 1 Native American), 52 international. 203 applicants, 28% accepted, 34 enrolled. In 2001, 32 master's, 24 doctorates awarded.
Degree requirements: For doctorate, thesis/dissertation.
Application fee: $20 ($50 for international students). Electronic applications accepted.
Expenses: Tuition, state resident: full-time $1,851. Tuition, nonresident: full-time $5,449. Tuition and fees vary according to program.
Financial support: In 2001–02, 60 research assistantships with partial tuition reimbursements (averaging $13,714 per year), 21 teaching assistantships with partial tuition reimbursements (averaging $11,483 per year) were awarded. Fellowships, Federal Work-Study, scholarships/grants, health care benefits, and unspecified assistantships also available. Support available to part-time students.
Dr. Carol B. Meeks, Dean, 515-294-5980, *Fax:* 515-294-6775, *E-mail:* cbmeeks@iastate.edu. *Web site:* http://www.fcs.iastate.edu/

■ KANSAS STATE UNIVERSITY

Graduate School, College of Human Ecology, Manhattan, KS 66506

AWARDS MS, PhD. Part-time programs available. Postbaccalaureate distance learning degree programs offered.

Faculty: 55 full-time (37 women).
Students: 193 full-time (142 women), 119 part-time (85 women); includes 32 minority (19 African Americans, 4 Asian Americans or Pacific Islanders, 7 Hispanic Americans, 2 Native Americans), 79 international. 197 applicants, 66% accepted, 79 enrolled. In 2001, 46 master's, 13 doctorates awarded.
Degree requirements: For master's, residency; for doctorate, thesis/dissertation, residency.
Application deadline: For fall admission, 2/1 (priority date); for spring admission, 10/1. *Application fee:* $0 ($25 for international students). Electronic applications accepted.
Expenses: Tuition, state resident: part-time $113 per credit hour. Tuition, nonresident: part-time $358 per credit hour.
Financial support: In 2001–02, 1 fellowship with partial tuition reimbursement, 99 research assistantships with partial tuition reimbursements (averaging $9,000 per year), 30 teaching assistantships with partial tuition reimbursements (averaging $9,000 per year) were awarded. Career-related internships or fieldwork, Federal Work-Study, institutionally sponsored loans, scholarships/grants, and tuition waivers (full) also available. Support available to part-time students. Financial award application deadline: 3/1; financial award applicants required to submit FAFSA.
Faculty research: Apparels and textiles, good service and hospitality management, life span human development, family life education and consultation, manage and family therapy. *Total annual research expenditures:* $7.6 million.
Dr. Carol Kellett, Dean, 785-532-5500, *Fax:* 785-532-5504, *E-mail:* heinfo@ksu.edu.
Application contact: Carol W. Shanklin, Graduate Program Director, 785-532-2206, *Fax:* 785-532-5522, *E-mail:* shanklin@humec.ksu.edu. *Web site:* http://www.ksu.edu/humec/

■ KENT STATE UNIVERSITY

College of Fine and Professional Arts, School of Family and Consumer Studies, Kent, OH 44242-0001

AWARDS Child and family relations (MA); nutrition (MS).

Degree requirements: For master's, thesis (for some programs).
Entrance requirements: For master's, minimum GPA of 2.75. Electronic applications accepted.

■ LAMAR UNIVERSITY

College of Graduate Studies, College of Education and Human Development, Department of Family and Consumer Sciences, Beaumont, TX 77710

AWARDS MS. Part-time and evening/weekend programs available.

Faculty: 4 full-time (all women).
Students: 8 full-time (all women), 8 part-time (all women); includes 2 minority (1 African American, 1 Asian American or Pacific Islander). Average age 35. 5 applicants, 100% accepted. In 2001, 7 degrees awarded.
Degree requirements: For master's, thesis optional.
Entrance requirements: For master's, GRE General Test, TOEFL. *Application deadline:* For fall admission, 8/1; for spring admission, 12/1. Applications are processed on a rolling basis. *Application fee:* $25 ($50 for international students).
Expenses: Tuition, state resident: full-time $1,114. Tuition, nonresident: full-time $3,670.
Financial support: In 2001–02, 3 students received support, including 1 teaching assistantship; fellowships, research assistantships, career-related internships or fieldwork, Federal Work-Study, and institutionally sponsored loans also available. Support available to part-time students. Financial award application deadline: 4/1.
Faculty research: Maternal and infant nutrition, eating disorders, sports nutrition, human sexuality, family violence.
Dr. Connie Ruiz, Interim Chair, 409-880-8663, *Fax:* 409-880-8666.
Application contact: Sandy Drane, Coordinator of Graduate Admissions, 409-880-8356, *Fax:* 409-880-8414, *E-mail:* gradmissions@hal.lamar.edu.

■ LOUISIANA STATE UNIVERSITY AND AGRICULTURAL AND MECHANICAL COLLEGE

Graduate School, College of Agriculture, School of Human Ecology, Baton Rouge, LA 70803

AWARDS MS, PhD. Part-time programs available.

Faculty: 20 full-time (15 women).
Students: 25 full-time (20 women), 14 part-time (10 women); includes 4 minority (2 African Americans, 1 Asian American or Pacific Islander, 1 Hispanic American), 9 international. Average age 31. 17 applicants, 59% accepted, 6 enrolled. In 2001, 3 degrees awarded.
Degree requirements: For master's and doctorate, thesis/dissertation.
Entrance requirements: For master's and doctorate, GRE General Test, minimum GPA of 3.0. *Application deadline:* For fall admission, 1/25 (priority date). Applications are processed on a rolling basis.
Application fee: $25.
Expenses: Tuition, state resident: full-time $2,551. Tuition, nonresident: full-time $5,551. Required fees: $854. Part-time tuition and fees vary according to course load.
Financial support: In 2001–02, 1 fellowship (averaging $13,000 per year), 10 research assistantships with partial tuition reimbursements (averaging $12,696 per year), 9 teaching assistantships with partial tuition reimbursements (averaging $9,689 per year) were awarded. Career-related internships or fieldwork, Federal Work-Study, institutionally sponsored loans, and unspecified assistantships also available. Support available to part-time students. Financial award application deadline: 4/15; financial award applicants required to submit FAFSA.
Faculty research: Family policy, nutritional health, aging, human resource management, fiber science and textile

Louisiana State University and Agricultural and Mechanical College (continued)

properties. *Total annual research expenditures:* $40,704.
Dr. Roy Martin, Director, 225-578-2282, *Fax:* 225-578-2697, *E-mail:* rjmartin@lsu.edu.
Application contact: Dr. David C. Blouin, Associate Dean, 225-578-8303, *Fax:* 225-578-2526, *E-mail:* dblouin@lsu.edu. *Web site:* http://sun.huec.lsu.edu

■ LOUISIANA TECH UNIVERSITY

Graduate School, College of Applied and Natural Sciences, School for Human Ecology, Ruston, LA 71272

AWARDS Dietetics (MS); human ecology (MS). Part-time programs available.

Degree requirements: For master's, thesis or alternative, Registered Dietician Exam eligibility.
Entrance requirements: For master's, GRE General Test.

■ MARSHALL UNIVERSITY

Graduate College, College of Education and Human Services, Division of Human Development and Allied Technology, Department of Family and Consumer Sciences, Huntington, WV 25755

AWARDS MA.

Faculty: 2 full-time (both women).
Students: 6 full-time (all women), 7 part-time (all women); includes 1 minority (African American), 1 international. In 2001, 2 degrees awarded.
Degree requirements: For master's, comprehensive assessment, thesis optional.
Expenses: Tuition, state resident: part-time $147 per credit. Tuition, nonresident: part-time $468 per credit. Tuition and fees vary according to campus/location and reciprocity agreements.
Application contact: Ken O'Neal, Assistant Vice President, Adult Student Services, 304-746-2500 Ext. 1907, *Fax:* 304-746-1902, *E-mail:* oneal@marshall.edu.

■ MICHIGAN STATE UNIVERSITY

Graduate School, College of Human Ecology, East Lansing, MI 48824

AWARDS MA, MS, PhD. Part-time and evening/weekend programs available. Postbaccalaureate distance learning degree programs offered.

Faculty: 54.
Students: 115 full-time (89 women), 134 part-time (109 women); includes 40 minority (25 African Americans, 9 Asian Americans or Pacific Islanders, 6 Hispanic Americans), 75 international. Average age 34. 173 applicants, 36% accepted. In 2001, 50 master's, 10 doctorates awarded. Terminal master's awarded for partial completion of doctoral program.
Degree requirements: For master's, thesis optional; for doctorate, thesis/dissertation.
Entrance requirements: For master's, GRE General Test, minimum GPA of 3.0 in last 2 years of undergraduate course work; for doctorate, GRE General Test. *Application deadline:* Applications are processed on a rolling basis. *Application fee:* $30 ($40 for international students). Electronic applications accepted.
Expenses: Tuition, state resident: part-time $244 per credit hour. Tuition, nonresident: part-time $494 per credit hour. Required fees: $268 per semester. Tuition and fees vary according to course load, degree level and program.
Financial support: In 2001–02, 109 fellowships (averaging $3,600 per year), 32 research assistantships (averaging $11,393 per year), 21 teaching assistantships with tuition reimbursements (averaging $10,730 per year) were awarded. Career-related internships or fieldwork and Federal Work-Study also available. Support available to part-time students. Financial award applicants required to submit FAFSA.
Faculty research: Children, youth, and family in communities; community and biochemical nutrition; food modification; cancer; international retailing. *Total annual research expenditures:* $1.7 million.
Dr. Julia R. Miller, Dean, 517-355-7714, *Fax:* 517-353-9426, *E-mail:* jrmiller@msu.edu. *Web site:* http://www.he.msu.edu/

■ MONTCLAIR STATE UNIVERSITY

The School of Graduate, Professional and Continuing Education, College of Education and Human Services, Department of Human Ecology, Upper Montclair, NJ 07043-1624

AWARDS Family life education (MA); family relations/child development (MA); home economics education (MA); home management/consumer economics (MA); nutrition education (MA). Part-time and evening/weekend programs available.

Degree requirements: For master's, thesis or alternative, comprehensive exam.
Entrance requirements: For master's, GRE General Test. Electronic applications accepted. *Web site:* http://www.montclair.edu

■ NEW MEXICO STATE UNIVERSITY

Graduate School, College of Agriculture and Home Economics, Department of Family and Consumer Sciences, Las Cruces, NM 88003-8001

AWARDS MS. Part-time programs available.

Faculty: 14 full-time (10 women).
Students: 29 full-time (25 women), 18 part-time (14 women); includes 20 minority (1 Asian American or Pacific Islander, 17 Hispanic Americans, 2 Native Americans), 3 international. Average age 31. In 2001, 14 degrees awarded.
Degree requirements: For master's, thesis (for some programs), internship. *Application deadline:* For fall admission, 7/1 (priority date); for spring admission, 11/1. Applications are processed on a rolling basis. *Application fee:* $15 ($35 for international students). Electronic applications accepted.
Expenses: Tuition, state resident: full-time $3,234; part-time $135 per credit. Tuition, nonresident: full-time $9,420; part-time $428 per credit. Required fees: $858.
Financial support: In 2001–02, 3 research assistantships, 7 teaching assistantships were awarded. Career-related internships or fieldwork and Federal Work-Study also available. Support available to part-time students. Financial award application deadline: 3/1.
Faculty research: Work, stress, and family functioning; youth at risk; nutrient bioavailability; food product analysis; social/psychological aspects of clothing.
Dr. Ann Vail, Head, 505-646-3936, *Fax:* 505-646-1889, *E-mail:* avail@nmsu.edu. *Web site:* http://www.cahe.nmsu.edu/CAHE/ACP/homecon.html

■ NORTH CAROLINA CENTRAL UNIVERSITY

Division of Academic Affairs, College of Arts and Sciences, Department of Human Sciences, Durham, NC 27707-3129

AWARDS MS. Part-time and evening/weekend programs available.

Faculty: 8 full-time (6 women), 8 part-time/adjunct (all women).
Students: 15 full-time (14 women), 42 part-time (39 women); includes 44 minority (43 African Americans, 1 Hispanic American). Average age 34. 24 applicants, 96% accepted. In 2001, 22 degrees awarded.
Degree requirements: For master's, one foreign language, thesis, comprehensive exam.
Entrance requirements: For master's, minimum GPA of 3.0 in major, 2.5 overall. *Application deadline:* For fall admission, 8/1. *Application fee:* $30.
Expenses: Tuition, state resident: full-time $1,424. Tuition, nonresident: full-time $9,492. Required fees: $1,054.
Financial support: Teaching assistantships, Federal Work-Study and institutionally sponsored loans available. Support available to part-time students. Financial award application deadline: 5/1.
Faculty research: Nutrition, textiles, early childhood, consumer sciences.
Dr. Deborah O. Parker, Chairperson, 919-560-5257, *Fax:* 919-530-7983, *E-mail:* dparker@wpo.nccu.edu.

Application contact: Dr. Bernice D. Johnson, Dean, College of Arts and Sciences, 919-560-6368, *Fax:* 919-560-5361, *E-mail:* bjohnson@wpo.nccu.edu.

■ NORTH DAKOTA STATE UNIVERSITY

The Graduate School, College of Human Development and Education, School of Education, Program in Family and Consumer Sciences Education, Fargo, ND 58105

AWARDS M Ed, MS. Part-time programs available.

Faculty: 1 (woman) part-time/adjunct.
Students: Average age 40.
Degree requirements: For master's, thesis or alternative.
Entrance requirements: For master's, MAT, TOEFL. *Application deadline:* Applications are processed on a rolling basis. *Application fee:* $35.
Expenses: Tuition, state resident: part-time $124 per credit. Tuition, nonresident: part-time $325 per credit. Required fees: $22 per credit. Tuition and fees vary according to reciprocity agreements.
Financial support: Teaching assistantships, career-related internships or fieldwork and institutionally sponsored loans available. Financial award application deadline: 4/15.
Faculty research: Needs of beginning teachers, learning styles and achievement, school-level variables and curriculum change.

■ THE OHIO STATE UNIVERSITY

Graduate School, College of Human Ecology, Columbus, OH 43210

AWARDS M Ed, MS, PhD. Part-time programs available.

Degree requirements: For master's, thesis optional; for doctorate, thesis/dissertation.
Entrance requirements: For master's and doctorate, GRE General Test.

■ OHIO UNIVERSITY

Graduate Studies, College of Health and Human Services, School of Human and Consumer Sciences, Athens, OH 45701-2979

AWARDS Child development and family life (MSHCS); food and nutrition (MSHCS).

Faculty: 13 full-time (9 women), 5 part-time/adjunct (all women).
Students: 6 full-time (all women), 9 part-time (all women); includes 1 minority (African American), 6 international. Average age 26. 17 applicants, 65% accepted, 6 enrolled. In 2001, 21 degrees awarded.
Degree requirements: For master's, thesis.
Entrance requirements: For master's, GRE. *Application deadline:* For fall admission, 8/30 (priority date). Applications are processed on a rolling basis. *Application fee:* $30.
Expenses: Tuition, state resident: full-time $6,585. Tuition, nonresident: full-time $12,254.
Financial support: In 2001–02, 6 teaching assistantships were awarded; career-related internships or fieldwork, Federal Work-Study, and institutionally sponsored loans also available. Financial award application deadline: 3/15.
Faculty research: Diversity, developmentally appropriate activities, death and dying, gerontology, sexuality education.
Dr. V. Ann Paulins, Director, 740-593-2880, *Fax:* 740-593-0289, *E-mail:* paulins@ohio.edu. *Web site:* http://www.cats.ohiou.edu/humanandconsumer/school.html

■ OKLAHOMA STATE UNIVERSITY

Graduate College, College of Human Environmental Sciences, Stillwater, OK 74078

AWARDS MS, PhD.

Faculty: 47 full-time (34 women), 3 part-time/adjunct (2 women).
Students: 95 full-time (71 women), 109 part-time (90 women); includes 22 minority (9 African Americans, 3 Asian Americans or Pacific Islanders, 10 Native Americans), 48 international. Average age 32. 96 applicants, 92% accepted. In 2001, 27 master's, 8 doctorates awarded.
Degree requirements: For master's and doctorate, thesis/dissertation.
Entrance requirements: For master's and doctorate, TOEFL. *Application deadline:* For fall admission, 7/1 (priority date). *Application fee:* $25.
Expenses: Tuition, state resident: part-time $92 per credit hour. Tuition, nonresident: part-time $297 per credit hour. Required fees: $21 per credit hour. $14 per semester. One-time fee: $20. Tuition and fees vary according to course load.
Financial support: In 2001–02, 83 students received support, including 58 research assistantships (averaging $8,770 per year), 15 teaching assistantships (averaging $7,332 per year); career-related internships or fieldwork, Federal Work-Study, and tuition waivers (partial) also available. Support available to part-time students. Financial award application deadline: 3/1.
Dr. Patricia Knaub, Dean, 405-744-5053.

■ OREGON STATE UNIVERSITY

Graduate School, College of Home Economics, Corvallis, OR 97331

AWARDS MA, MAIS, MS, Ed D, PhD. Part-time programs available. Terminal master's awarded for partial completion of doctoral program.

Degree requirements: For doctorate, thesis/dissertation.
Entrance requirements: For master's and doctorate, TOEFL, minimum GPA of 3.0 in last 90 hours.
Expenses: Tuition, area resident: Full-time $15,933. Tuition, state resident: full-time $28,937.
Faculty research: Human development, family relations, nutrition, merchandising management, housing.

■ OREGON STATE UNIVERSITY

Graduate School, School of Education, Program in Family and Consumer Sciences, Corvallis, OR 97331

AWARDS MAT, MS. Part-time programs available.

Degree requirements: For master's, thesis (for some programs).
Entrance requirements: For master's, NTE, California Basic Educational Skills Test, TOEFL, minimum GPA of 3.0 in last 90 hours. *Application deadline:* For fall admission, 1/15. *Application fee:* $50.
Expenses: Tuition, area resident: Full-time $15,933. Tuition, state resident: full-time $28,937.
Financial support: Fellowships, career-related internships or fieldwork, Federal Work-Study, and institutionally sponsored loans available. Support available to part-time students. Financial award application deadline: 2/1.
Faculty research: Economy of time and methods.
Dr. Chris L. Ward, Coordinator, 541-737-1080, *E-mail:* southers@orst.edu.

■ PRAIRIE VIEW A&M UNIVERSITY

Graduate School, College of Agriculture and Human Sciences, Prairie View, TX 77446-0188

AWARDS Agricultural economics (MS); animal sciences (MS); interdisciplinary human sciences (MS); marriage and family therapy (MS); soil science (MS).

Faculty: 15 full-time (5 women), 1 part-time/adjunct (0 women).
Students: 45 full-time (28 women), 28 part-time (21 women); includes 63 minority (61 African Americans, 2 Asian Americans or Pacific Islanders), 6 international. Average age 35. 15 applicants, 100% accepted. In 2001, 20 degrees awarded.
Entrance requirements: For master's, GRE General Test. *Application deadline:*

Prairie View A&M University (continued)
For fall admission, 10/2 (priority date); for spring admission, 2/19. Applications are processed on a rolling basis. *Application fee:* $25.
Expenses: Tuition, state resident: full-time $864; part-time $48 per credit hour. Tuition, nonresident: full-time $4,716; part-time $262 per credit hour. Required fees: $1,324; $59 per credit hour. $131 per term.
Financial support: In 2001–02, 10 research assistantships with tuition reimbursements (averaging $13,500 per year) were awarded; career-related internships or fieldwork, Federal Work-Study, and institutionally sponsored loans also available. Financial award application deadline: 4/1. *Total annual research expenditures:* $3 million.
Dr. Elizabeth Noel, Dean, 936-857-2996, *Fax:* 936-857-2998.

■ PURDUE UNIVERSITY

Graduate School, School of Consumer and Family Sciences, West Lafayette, IN 47907

AWARDS MS, PhD. Part-time programs available.

Faculty: 70.
Students: 115 full-time (90 women), 53 part-time (37 women); includes 14 minority (7 African Americans, 5 Asian Americans or Pacific Islanders, 2 Hispanic Americans), 74 international. Average age 30. 234 applicants, 47% accepted. In 2001, 33 master's, 17 doctorates awarded.
Degree requirements: For doctorate, thesis/dissertation.
Entrance requirements: For master's and doctorate, TOEFL. *Application fee:* $30. Electronic applications accepted.
Expenses: Tuition, state resident: full-time $4,164; part-time $149 per credit hour. Tuition, nonresident: full-time $13,872; part-time $458 per credit hour. Tuition and fees vary according to campus/location and program.
Financial support: Fellowships, research assistantships, teaching assistantships, career-related internships or fieldwork available. Support available to part-time students. Financial award applicants required to submit FAFSA.
Dr. Dennis A. Savaiano, Dean, 765-494-8210.

■ QUEENS COLLEGE OF THE CITY UNIVERSITY OF NEW YORK

Division of Graduate Studies, Mathematics and Natural Sciences Division, Department of Family, Nutrition and Exercise Sciences, Flushing, NY 11367-1597

AWARDS Home economics (MS Ed); physical education and exercise sciences (MS Ed). Part-time and evening/weekend programs available.

Faculty: 11 full-time (6 women).
Students: 77 applicants, 90% accepted. In 2001, 81 degrees awarded.
Degree requirements: For master's, research project.
Entrance requirements: For master's, TOEFL, minimum GPA of 3.0. *Application deadline:* For fall admission, 4/1; for spring admission, 11/1. Applications are processed on a rolling basis. *Application fee:* $40.
Expenses: Tuition, state resident: full-time $2,175; part-time $185 per credit. Tuition, nonresident: full-time $3,800; part-time $320 per credit. Required fees: $114; $57 per semester. Tuition and fees vary according to course load.
Financial support: Career-related internships or fieldwork, Federal Work-Study, institutionally sponsored loans, tuition waivers (partial), and adjunct lectureships available. Support available to part-time students. Financial award application deadline: 4/1; financial award applicants required to submit FAFSA.
Faculty research: Exercise and environmental physiology, interdisciplinary approaches to school curricula using outdoor education, program development in cardiac rehabilitation and adult fitness, nutrition education.
Dr. Michael Toner, Chairperson, 718-997-4150, *E-mail:* michael_toner@qc.edu.
Application contact: Mario Caruso, Director of Graduate Admissions, 718-997-5200, *Fax:* 718-997-5193, *E-mail:* graduate_admissions@qc.edu.

■ SAM HOUSTON STATE UNIVERSITY

College of Education and Applied Science, Department of Family and Consumer Sciences, Huntsville, TX 77341

AWARDS Home economics (MA). Part-time and evening/weekend programs available.

Students: 3 full-time (all women), 2 part-time (both women). Average age 40.
Entrance requirements: For master's, GRE General Test, minimum GPA of 2.5. *Application deadline:* For fall admission, 8/1; for spring admission, 12/1. *Application fee:* $20.
Expenses: Tuition, area resident: Part-time $69 per credit. Tuition, state resident: full-time $1,380; part-time $69 per credit. Tuition, nonresident: full-time $5,600; part-time $280 per credit. Required fees: $748. Tuition and fees vary according to course load.
Financial support: Teaching assistantships available. Financial award application deadline: 5/31; financial award applicants required to submit FAFSA.
Faculty research: Occupational home economics, family issues, textile chemistry, housing and design.
Dr. Janis White, Acting Chair, 936-294-1242. *Web site:* http://www.shsu.edu/~hec_www/

■ SAN FRANCISCO STATE UNIVERSITY

Graduate Division, College of Health and Human Services, Department of Consumer and Family Studies/ Dietetics, San Francisco, CA 94132-1722

AWARDS Home economics (MA). Part-time programs available.

Entrance requirements: For master's, essay test, bachelor's degree with minimum GPA of 3.0 in home economics or 30 units in home economics.
Faculty research: Nutritional status and osteoporosis, nutritional status and diabetes, housing and the maturing population, CAD applied to space planning and clothing effects of color in near environment.

■ SOUTH DAKOTA STATE UNIVERSITY

Graduate School, College of Family and Consumer Sciences, Brookings, SD 57007

AWARDS MS.

Degree requirements: For master's, thesis, oral exam.
Entrance requirements: For master's, TOEFL.
Faculty research: Resource management, community development and vitality, work and family, life span and family development, nutritional wellness.

■ SOUTHEAST MISSOURI STATE UNIVERSITY

School of Graduate Studies and Research, Department of Human Environmental Studies, Cape Girardeau, MO 63701-4799

AWARDS MA. Part-time programs available.

Faculty: 9 full-time (8 women).
Students: 12 full-time (11 women), 23 part-time (22 women); includes 5 minority (all African Americans). Average age 33. 31 applicants, 100% accepted. In 2001, 5 degrees awarded.
Degree requirements: For master's, thesis or alternative.
Entrance requirements: For master's, minimum GPA of 2.5. *Application deadline:* For fall admission, 8/1 (priority date); for spring admission, 11/21. Applications are processed on a rolling basis. *Application fee:* $20 ($100 for international students).
Expenses: Tuition, state resident: full-time $1,242; part-time $138 per hour. Tuition, nonresident: full-time $2,268; part-time $252 per hour.
Financial support: In 2001–02, 1 research assistantship with full tuition reimbursement (averaging $6,100 per year), 7 teaching assistantships with full tuition reimbursements (averaging $6,100 per year) were awarded.

Dr. Paula King, Chairperson, 573-651-2312, *E-mail:* pking@semo.edu.
Application contact: Marsha L. Arant, Office of Graduate Studies, 573-651-2192, *Fax:* 573-651-2001, *E-mail:* marant@semovm.semo.edu.

■ STEPHEN F. AUSTIN STATE UNIVERSITY

Graduate School, College of Education, Department of Human Sciences, Nacogdoches, TX 75962

AWARDS MS.

Faculty: 12 full-time (all women).
Students: 11 full-time (9 women), 8 part-time (all women); includes 2 minority (1 African American, 1 Asian American or Pacific Islander). Average age 30. 12 applicants, 100% accepted. In 2001, 5 degrees awarded.
Degree requirements: For master's, thesis or alternative, comprehensive exam.
Entrance requirements: For master's, GRE General Test, TOEFL. *Application deadline:* For fall admission, 8/1 (priority date); for spring admission, 12/1. Applications are processed on a rolling basis. *Application fee:* $0 ($50 for international students).
Expenses: Tuition, state resident: full-time $1,008; part-time $42 per credit. Tuition, nonresident: full-time $6,072; part-time $253 per credit. Required fees: $1,248; $52 per credit. Tuition and fees vary according to course load.
Financial support: In 2001–02, 1 research assistantship (averaging $6,633 per year) was awarded; teaching assistantships, career-related internships or fieldwork and Federal Work-Study also available. Support available to part-time students. Financial award application deadline: 3/1.
Faculty research: Consumer economics, nutrition education, clothing and textiles, family, interior design.
Dr. Gloria Durr, Chair, 936-468-4502.

■ TEXAS A&M UNIVERSITY–KINGSVILLE

College of Graduate Studies, College of Agriculture and Home Economics, Department of Human Sciences, Kingsville, TX 78363

AWARDS MS. Part-time and evening/weekend programs available.

Faculty: 2 full-time (both women), 1 (woman) part-time/adjunct.
Students: 8 full-time (all women), 17 part-time (16 women); includes 7 minority (1 African American, 6 Hispanic Americans). Average age 31. In 2001, 2 degrees awarded.
Degree requirements: For master's, thesis or alternative, comprehensive exam.
Entrance requirements: For master's, GRE General Test, TOEFL, minimum GPA of 3.0. *Application deadline:* For fall admission, 6/1 (priority date); for spring admission, 11/15. Applications are processed on a rolling basis. *Application fee:* $15 ($25 for international students).
Expenses: Tuition, state resident: part-time $42 per hour. Tuition, nonresident: part-time $253 per hour. Required fees: $56 per hour. One-time fee: $46 part-time. Tuition and fees vary according to program.
Financial support: Fellowships available. Support available to part-time students. Financial award application deadline: 5/15.
Faculty research: Mexican-American families, abuse in families, nontraditional students. *Total annual research expenditures:* $70,000.
Dr. Janice Van Buren, Chair, 361-593-2211.

■ TEXAS SOUTHERN UNIVERSITY

Graduate School, College of Liberal Arts and Behavioral Sciences, Department of Human Services and Consumer Sciences, Houston, TX 77004-4584

AWARDS Human services and consumer sciences (MS), including child development, comprehensive human services and consumer sciences, foods and nutrition. Part-time and evening/weekend programs available.

Faculty: 3 full-time (all women), 1 (woman) part-time/adjunct.
Students: 3 full-time (all women), 22 part-time (18 women); includes 22 minority (21 African Americans, 1 Asian American or Pacific Islander), 3 international. 6 applicants, 100% accepted. In 2001, 10 degrees awarded.
Degree requirements: For master's, thesis (for some programs), comprehensive exam.
Entrance requirements: For master's, GRE General Test, TOEFL, minimum GPA of 2.5. *Application deadline:* For fall admission, 7/15 (priority date). Applications are processed on a rolling basis. *Application fee:* $35 ($75 for international students).
Expenses: Tuition, state resident: full-time $1,188. Tuition, nonresident: full-time $4,644. Required fees: $900. Tuition and fees vary according to degree level.
Financial support: In 2001–02, 1 research assistantship was awarded; teaching assistantships, career-related internships or fieldwork and institutionally sponsored loans also available. Financial award application deadline: 5/1.
Faculty research: Food radiation/food for space travel, adolescent parenting, gerontology/grandparenting. *Total annual research expenditures:* $185,000.
Dr. Shirley R. Nealy, Chair, 713-313-7638, *Fax:* 713-313-7228, *E-mail:* nealy_sr@tsu.edu.

■ TEXAS TECH UNIVERSITY

Graduate School, College of Human Sciences, Lubbock, TX 79409

AWARDS MS, PhD. Part-time programs available. Postbaccalaureate distance learning degree programs offered (minimal on-campus study).

Faculty: 49 full-time (29 women), 4 part-time/adjunct (all women).
Students: 124 full-time (90 women), 63 part-time (42 women); includes 17 minority (9 African Americans, 1 Asian American or Pacific Islander, 7 Hispanic Americans), 46 international. Average age 32. 102 applicants, 65% accepted, 31 enrolled. In 2001, 35 master's, 9 doctorates awarded.
Degree requirements: For doctorate, thesis/dissertation.
Entrance requirements: For master's, GRE; for doctorate, GRE General Test. *Application deadline:* Applications are processed on a rolling basis. *Application fee:* $25 ($50 for international students). Electronic applications accepted.
Expenses: Contact institution.
Financial support: In 2001–02, 132 students received support, including 56 research assistantships with partial tuition reimbursements available (averaging $10,045 per year), 48 teaching assistantships with partial tuition reimbursements available (averaging $9,707 per year); career-related internships or fieldwork, Federal Work-Study, institutionally sponsored loans, and scholarships/grants also available. Support available to part-time students. Financial award application deadline: 5/1; financial award applicants required to submit FAFSA.
Faculty research: Adolescent drug abuse, trace elements in nutrition (selenium, molybdenum, zinc, and chromium), adolescent development, resiliency, retirement planning. *Total annual research expenditures:* $658,669.
Linda Hoover, Interim Dean, 806-742-3031, *Fax:* 806-742-1849.
Application contact: Dr. Steven M. Harris, Associate Dean, 806-742-3031, *Fax:* 806-742-1849, *E-mail:* sharris@HS.ttu.edu. *Web site:* http://www.hs.ttu.edu/

■ THE UNIVERSITY OF AKRON

Graduate School, College of Fine and Applied Arts, School of Family and Consumer Sciences, Akron, OH 44325-0001

AWARDS Child development (MA); child life (MA); clothing, textiles and interiors (MA); family development (MA); food science (MA); nutrition and dietetics (MS). Part-time and evening/weekend programs available.

Faculty: 15 full-time (13 women), 27 part-time/adjunct (19 women).
Students: 16 full-time (15 women), 21 part-time (19 women); includes 1 minority (African American), 4 international. Average age 35. 21 applicants, 86% accepted, 7 enrolled. In 2001, 8 degrees awarded.

The University of Akron (continued)
Degree requirements: For master's, thesis or alternative.
Entrance requirements: For master's, GRE General Test, minimum GPA of 2.75. *Application deadline:* For fall admission, 8/15. Applications are processed on a rolling basis. *Application fee:* $40 ($50 for international students).
Expenses: Tuition, state resident: full-time $6,562; part-time $219 per credit. Tuition, nonresident: full-time $9,027; part-time $383 per credit. Required fees: $272; $11 per credit. Tuition and fees vary according to course load.
Financial support: In 2001–02, 15 students received support, including 3 research assistantships with full tuition reimbursements available, 13 teaching assistantships with full tuition reimbursements available; career-related internships or fieldwork, Federal Work-Study, institutionally sponsored loans, tuition waivers (full), and unspecified assistantships also available. Financial award application deadline: 3/1.
Faculty research: Effects of divorce on children, community support for singles, children and money, nutrition and disease, effects of early marriage.
Dr. Virginia Gunn, Acting Director, 330-972-7729, *E-mail:* vgunn@uakron.edu. *Web site:* http://www.uakron.edu/hefe/hefepage.html

■ THE UNIVERSITY OF ALABAMA

Graduate School, College of Human Environmental Sciences, Tuscaloosa, AL 35487

AWARDS MA, MSHES, PhD. Part-time and evening/weekend programs available. Postbaccalaureate distance learning degree programs offered (no on-campus study).

Faculty: 37 full-time (23 women), 3 part-time/adjunct (all women).
Students: 75 full-time (54 women), 62 part-time (47 women); includes 24 minority (20 African Americans, 3 Hispanic Americans, 1 Native American), 3 international. Average age 30. 127 applicants, 75% accepted, 76 enrolled. In 2001, 80 master's, 4 doctorates awarded.
Degree requirements: For doctorate, thesis/dissertation.
Entrance requirements: For master's and doctorate, GRE General Test or MAT, minimum GPA of 3.0. *Application deadline:* For fall admission, 7/6. Applications are processed on a rolling basis. *Application fee:* $25.
Expenses: Tuition, state resident: full-time $3,292; part-time $183 per credit hour. Tuition, nonresident: full-time $8,912; part-time $495 per credit hour. Tuition and fees vary according to course load, campus/location and program.
Financial support: In 2001–02, 1 fellowship with tuition reimbursement (averaging $10,000 per year), 10 research assistantships with full tuition reimbursements (averaging $8,100 per year), 11 teaching assistantships with full tuition reimbursements (averaging $8,100 per year) were awarded. Career-related internships or fieldwork, Federal Work-Study, institutionally sponsored loans, and scholarships/grants also available.
Dr. Judy L. Bonner, Dean and Acting Head, 205-348-6250, *Fax:* 205-348-3789, *E-mail:* jbonne@ches.ua.edu. *Web site:* http://www.ches.ua.edu/

■ THE UNIVERSITY OF ARIZONA

Graduate College, College of Agriculture and Life Sciences, School of Family and Consumer Sciences, Tucson, AZ 85721

AWARDS MS, PhD. Part-time programs available.

Faculty: 28.
Students: 33 full-time (26 women), 7 part-time (6 women); includes 5 minority (1 Asian American or Pacific Islander, 4 Hispanic Americans), 9 international. Average age 34. 21 applicants, 71% accepted, 13 enrolled. In 2001, 6 master's, 3 doctorates awarded.
Entrance requirements: For master's, GRE General Test, TOEFL, minimum GPA of 3.0; for doctorate, GRE General Test, TOEFL. *Application deadline:* Applications are processed on a rolling basis. *Application fee:* $45.
Expenses: Tuition, state resident: full-time $2,490; part-time $436 per unit. Tuition, nonresident: full-time $10,300; part-time $436 per unit. Full-time tuition and fees vary according to degree level and program.
Financial support: Fellowships, research assistantships, teaching assistantships, career-related internships or fieldwork, Federal Work-Study, institutionally sponsored loans, and tuition waivers (full) available. Financial award application deadline: 3/1.
Dr. Soyeon Shim, Director, 520-621-7147, *Fax:* 520-621-9445, *E-mail:* shim@ag.arizona.edu.
Application contact: Mary Miller, Administrative Associate, 520-621-7147, *Fax:* 520-621-9445, *E-mail:* mamiller@ag.arizona.edu. *Web site:* http://ag.arizona.edu/fcs

■ UNIVERSITY OF ARKANSAS

Graduate School, Dale Bumpers College of Agricultural, Food and Life Sciences, School of Human Environmental Sciences, Fayetteville, AR 72701-1201

AWARDS MS.

Students: 19 full-time (16 women), 28 part-time (20 women); includes 9 minority (7 African Americans, 1 Hispanic American, 1 Native American), 3 international. 25 applicants, 96% accepted. In 2001, 6 degrees awarded.
Degree requirements: For master's, thesis (for some programs), comprehensive exam.
Application fee: $40 ($50 for international students).
Expenses: Tuition, state resident: full-time $3,553; part-time $197 per credit. Tuition, nonresident: full-time $8,411; part-time $467 per credit. Required fees: $42 per credit. Tuition and fees vary according to course load and program.
Financial support: In 2001–02, 1 fellowship, 3 research assistantships, 6 teaching assistantships were awarded. Federal Work-Study also available. Support available to part-time students. Financial award application deadline: 4/1; financial award applicants required to submit FAFSA.
Dr. Mary Warnock, Interim Chair, 479-575-4305.

■ UNIVERSITY OF CENTRAL ARKANSAS

Graduate School, College of Health and Applied Sciences, Department of Family and Consumer Sciences, Conway, AR 72035-0001

AWARDS MS.

Faculty: 1.
Students: 7 full-time (6 women), 17 part-time (16 women); includes 1 minority (African American). In 2001, 12 degrees awarded.
Degree requirements: For master's, thesis optional.
Entrance requirements: For master's, GRE General Test, minimum GPA of 2.7. *Application deadline:* For fall admission, 3/1 (priority date); for spring admission, 10/1. Applications are processed on a rolling basis. *Application fee:* $25 ($40 for international students).
Expenses: Contact institution.
Financial support: In 2001–02, 17 students received support, including 3 research assistantships (averaging $5,700 per year); career-related internships or fieldwork, scholarships/grants, and unspecified assistantships also available. Support available to part-time students. Financial award application deadline: 2/15. *Total annual research expenditures:* $11,590.
Dr. Mary Harlan, Chairperson, 501-450-5950, *Fax:* 501-450-5958, *E-mail:* maryh@mail.uca.edu.
Application contact: Nancy Gage, Co-Admissions Secretary, 501-450-3124, *Fax:* 501-450-5066, *E-mail:* nancyg@ecom.uca.edu. *Web site:* http://www.uca.edu/chas/diet.html

■ UNIVERSITY OF CENTRAL OKLAHOMA

College of Graduate Studies and Research, College of Education, Department of Human Environmental Sciences, Edmond, OK 73034-5209

AWARDS Family and child studies (MS); family and consumer science education (MS); interior design (MS); nutrition-food management (MS). Part-time programs available.

Faculty research: Dietetics and food science. *Web site:* http://www.ucok.edu/graduate/human.htm/

■ UNIVERSITY OF GEORGIA

Graduate School, College of Family and Consumer Sciences, Athens, GA 30602

AWARDS MFCS, MS, PhD.

Faculty: 56 full-time (33 women).
Students: 99 full-time (72 women), 22 part-time (17 women); includes 15 minority (9 African Americans, 2 Asian Americans or Pacific Islanders, 4 Hispanic Americans), 38 international. 157 applicants, 33% accepted. In 2001, 20 master's, 17 doctorates awarded.
Degree requirements: For doctorate, thesis/dissertation.
Entrance requirements: For master's and doctorate, GRE General Test. *Application deadline:* For fall admission, 7/1 (priority date); for spring admission, 11/15. *Application fee:* $30. Electronic applications accepted.
Expenses: Tuition, state resident: full-time $2,376; part-time $132 per credit hour. Tuition, nonresident: full-time $9,504; part-time $528 per credit hour. Required fees: $236 per semester.
Financial support: Fellowships, research assistantships, teaching assistantships, unspecified assistantships available.
Dr. Sharon Y. Nickols, Dean, 706-542-4860, *Fax:* 706-542-4862, *E-mail:* snickols@fcs.uga.edu. *Web site:* http://www.fcs.uga.edu/

■ UNIVERSITY OF IDAHO

College of Graduate Studies, College of Agriculture, School of Family and Consumer Sciences, Moscow, ID 83844-3183

AWARDS Home economics (MS).

Faculty: 8 full-time (all women).
Students: 9 full-time (8 women), 7 part-time (all women); includes 1 minority (Asian American or Pacific Islander), 1 international. 14 applicants, 50% accepted. In 2001, 4 degrees awarded.
Degree requirements: For master's, thesis.
Entrance requirements: For master's, minimum GPA of 2.8. *Application deadline:* For fall admission, 8/1; for spring admission, 12/15. *Application fee:* $35 ($45 for international students).
Expenses: Tuition, state resident: full-time $1,613. Tuition, nonresident: full-time $3,000.
Financial support: In 2001–02, 1 research assistantship (averaging $10,007 per year), 6 teaching assistantships (averaging $6,905 per year) were awarded. Financial award application deadline: 2/15. *Total annual research expenditures:* $112,795.
Dr. Linda Kirk Fox, Director, 208-885-6546, *Fax:* 208-885-5751. *Web site:* http://www.uidaho.edu/fcs/

Find an in-depth description at www.petersons.com/gradchannel.

■ UNIVERSITY OF KENTUCKY

Graduate School, College of Human Environmental Sciences, Lexington, KY 40506-0032

AWARDS MAIDM, MS, MSFAM, MSIDM, PhD.

Faculty: 46 full-time (36 women).
Students: 49 full-time (41 women), 14 part-time (12 women); includes 8 minority (7 African Americans, 1 Native American), 3 international. 55 applicants, 53% accepted. In 2001, 25 degrees awarded.
Degree requirements: For master's, thesis optional.
Entrance requirements: For master's, GRE General Test, minimum undergraduate GPA of 2.5. *Application deadline:* Applications are processed on a rolling basis. *Application fee:* $30 ($35 for international students).
Expenses: Tuition, state resident: full-time $4,075; part-time $213 per credit hour. Tuition, nonresident: full-time $11,295; part-time $614 per credit hour.
Financial support: In 2001–02, 2 fellowships, 10 research assistantships, 17 teaching assistantships were awarded. Federal Work-Study, institutionally sponsored loans, and unspecified assistantships also available. Support available to part-time students.
Dr. Retia Scott Walker, Dean, 859-257-2878.
Application contact: Dr. Jeannine Blackwell, Associate Dean, 859-257-4905, *Fax:* 859-323-1928.

■ UNIVERSITY OF LOUISIANA AT LAFAYETTE

Graduate School, College of Applied Life Sciences, School of Human Resources, Lafayette, LA 70504

AWARDS MS. Part-time programs available.

Faculty: 9 full-time (3 women).
Students: 5 full-time (3 women), 17 part-time (15 women); includes 1 minority (African American). 14 applicants, 57% accepted, 6 enrolled. In 2001, 4 degrees awarded.
Degree requirements: For master's, thesis or alternative.
Entrance requirements: For master's, GRE General Test, minimum GPA of 2.75. *Application deadline:* For fall admission, 5/15. *Application fee:* $20 ($30 for international students).
Expenses: Tuition, state resident: full-time $2,317; part-time $79 per credit. Tuition, nonresident: full-time $8,882; part-time $369 per credit. International tuition: $9,018 full-time.
Financial support: In 2001–02, 5 research assistantships with full tuition reimbursements (averaging $5,500 per year) were awarded; fellowships, teaching assistantships, Federal Work-Study also available. Financial award application deadline: 5/1.
Faculty research: Nutrition education, crawfish use and nutrients.
Dr. Rachel Fournet, Interim Director, 337-482-5724.
Application contact: Dr. David Yarborough, Graduate Coordinator, 337-482-5709.

■ UNIVERSITY OF MINNESOTA, TWIN CITIES CAMPUS

Graduate School, College of Human Ecology, Minneapolis, MN 55455-0213

AWARDS MA, MFA, MS, MSW, PhD, MSW/MPH, MSW/MPP. Part-time and evening/weekend programs available. Postbaccalaureate distance learning degree programs offered.

Degree requirements: For doctorate, thesis/dissertation.
Entrance requirements: For master's, minimum GPA of 3.0; for doctorate, GRE, minimum GPA of 3.0.
Expenses: Tuition, state resident: full-time $2,932; part-time $489 per credit. Tuition, nonresident: full-time $5,758; part-time $960 per credit. Part-time tuition and fees vary according to course load, program and reciprocity agreements.

■ UNIVERSITY OF MISSOURI–COLUMBIA

Graduate School, College of Human Environmental Science, Columbia, MO 65211

AWARDS MA, MS, PhD. Part-time programs available.

Faculty: 40 full-time (24 women), 2 part-time/adjunct (both women).
Students: 45 full-time (34 women), 32 part-time (21 women); includes 5 minority (4 African Americans, 1 Hispanic American), 18 international. 93 applicants, 44% accepted. In 2001, 28 master's, 10 doctorates awarded.
Degree requirements: For doctorate, thesis/dissertation.
Entrance requirements: For master's, GRE General Test, minimum GPA of 3.0; for doctorate, GRE General Test, TOEFL, minimum GPA of 3.0. *Application deadline:* Applications are processed on a rolling basis. *Application fee:* $25 ($50 for international students).

University of Missouri–Columbia (continued)

Expenses: Tuition, state resident: part-time $179 per credit hour. Tuition, nonresident: part-time $539 per credit hour. Required fees: $122 per semester. Tuition and fees vary according to program.

Financial support: Fellowships, research assistantships, teaching assistantships, institutionally sponsored loans available.

Dr. Bea Smith, Dean, 573-882-6227, *E-mail:* beasmith@missouri.edu. *Web site:* http://web.missouri.edu/~hes/

■ UNIVERSITY OF NEBRASKA–LINCOLN

Graduate College, College of Human Resources and Family Sciences, Interdepartmental Area of Human Resources and Family Sciences, Lincoln, NE 68588

AWARDS MS, PhD. Postbaccalaureate distance learning degree programs offered.

Students: 40 (38 women); includes 5 minority (3 African Americans, 2 Asian Americans or Pacific Islanders) 4 international. Average age 39. 9 applicants, 33% accepted, 1 enrolled. In 2001, 3 degrees awarded.

Degree requirements: For master's, thesis optional; for doctorate, thesis/dissertation, comprehensive exam.

Entrance requirements: For master's, GRE General Test, TOEFL; for doctorate, GRE General Test, TOEFL, writing sample. *Application deadline:* For fall admission, 3/1 (priority date). Applications are processed on a rolling basis. *Application fee:* $35. Electronic applications accepted.

Expenses: Tuition, state resident: full-time $2,412; part-time $134 per credit. Tuition, nonresident: full-time $6,223; part-time $346 per credit. Tuition and fees vary according to course load.

Financial support: In 2001–02, 3 research assistantships, 1 teaching assistantship were awarded. Fellowships, Federal Work-Study, health care benefits, and unspecified assistantships also available. Financial award application deadline: 2/15.

Dr. Lisa Crockett, Graduate Committee Chair, 402-472-2913, *E-mail:* agri030@unlvm.unl.edu.

■ THE UNIVERSITY OF NORTH CAROLINA AT GREENSBORO

Graduate School, School of Human Environmental Sciences, Greensboro, NC 27412-5001

AWARDS M Ed, MS, MSW, PhD.

Faculty: 42 full-time (30 women), 2 part-time/adjunct (0 women).

Students: 126 full-time (111 women), 64 part-time (55 women); includes 43 minority (38 African Americans, 2 Asian Americans or Pacific Islanders, 2 Hispanic Americans, 1 Native American), 29 international. 229 applicants, 52% accepted, 80 enrolled. In 2001, 56 master's, 7 doctorates awarded.

Degree requirements: For master's, thesis (for some programs); for doctorate, thesis/dissertation.

Entrance requirements: For master's and doctorate, GRE General Test, TOEFL. *Application fee:* $35.

Expenses: Tuition, state resident: part-time $344 per course. Tuition, nonresident: part-time $2,457 per course.

Financial support: In 2001–02, 6 fellowships with full tuition reimbursements (averaging $6,333 per year), 74 research assistantships with full tuition reimbursements (averaging $7,072 per year), 8 teaching assistantships with full tuition reimbursements (averaging $6,672 per year) were awarded. Unspecified assistantships also available.

Faculty research: Impact of phosphate removal, protective clothing for pesticide workers, adolescent mothers, cancer prevention, immuno-stimulant effects.

Laura S. Sims, Dean, 336-334-5980, *Fax:* 336-334-5089, *E-mail:* laura_sims@uncg.edu.

Application contact: Dr. James Lynch, Director of Graduate Recruitment and Information Services, 336-334-4881, *Fax:* 336-334-4424. *Web site:* http://www.uncg.edu/hes/

■ UNIVERSITY OF NORTH FLORIDA

College of Health, Department of Public Health, Jacksonville, FL 32224-2645

AWARDS Addictions counseling (MSH); aging studies (Certificate); community health (MPH); employee health services (MSH); health administration (MHA); health care administration (MSH); human ecology and nutrition (MSH); human performance (MSH). Part-time and evening/weekend programs available.

Faculty: 19 full-time (14 women).

Students: 59 full-time (45 women), 60 part-time (40 women); includes 34 minority (19 African Americans, 6 Asian Americans or Pacific Islanders, 7 Hispanic Americans, 2 Native Americans), 1 international. Average age 31. 128 applicants, 49% accepted, 31 enrolled. In 2001, 42 degrees awarded.

Degree requirements: For master's, thesis optional.

Entrance requirements: For master's, GMAT (MHA), GRE General Test (MSH), TOEFL. *Application deadline:* For fall admission, 7/6 (priority date); for winter admission, 11/2 (priority date); for spring admission, 3/10 (priority date). Applications are processed on a rolling basis. *Application fee:* $20. Electronic applications accepted.

Expenses: Tuition, state resident: full-time $2,411; part-time $134 per credit hour. Tuition, nonresident: full-time $9,391; part-time $522 per credit hour. Required fees: $670; $37 per credit hour.

Financial support: In 2001–02, 54 students received support, including 1 research assistantship (averaging $4,205 per year); career-related internships or fieldwork, Federal Work-Study, scholarships/grants, and tuition waivers (partial) also available. Support available to part-time students. Financial award application deadline: 4/1; financial award applicants required to submit FAFSA.

Faculty research: Lower extremity biomechanics; alcohol, tobacco, and other drug use prevention; turnover among health professionals; aging; psychosocial aspects of disabilities. *Total annual research expenditures:* $850,234.

Dr. Jeanne Patterson, Chair, 904-620-2840, *E-mail:* jpatters@unf.edu.

Application contact: Rachel Broderick, Director of Advising, 904-620-2812, *E-mail:* rbroderi@unf.edu.

■ UNIVERSITY OF PUERTO RICO, RÍO PIEDRAS

College of Education, Program in Family Ecology and Nutrition, San Juan, PR 00931

AWARDS M Ed. Part-time programs available.

Students: 3 full-time (all women), 18 part-time (all women); all minorities (all Hispanic Americans). Average age 29. 22 applicants, 55% accepted.

Degree requirements: For master's, thesis.

Entrance requirements: For master's, PAEG, minimum GPA of 3.0. *Application deadline:* For fall admission, 2/1. *Application fee:* $17.

Expenses: Students that provide official evidence of private medicine insurance or service are exempt of the payment of $529 per academic year.

Financial support: Fellowships, research assistantships, teaching assistantships, career-related internships or fieldwork, Federal Work-Study, institutionally sponsored loans, and tuition waivers (partial) available. Financial award application deadline: 5/31.

Dr. Nayda Neris, Coordinator, 787-764-0000 Ext. 2607, *Fax:* 787-764-0000 Ext. 2374.

Application contact: Juanita Rodríguez-Colón, Director of Graduate Education, 787-764-0000 Ext. 4368, *Fax:* 787-763-4130.

■ UNIVERSITY OF SOUTHERN MISSISSIPPI

Graduate School, College of Health and Human Sciences, School of Family and Consumer Sciences, Hattiesburg, MS 39406

AWARDS Early intervention (MS); family and consumer studies (MS); human nutrition

(MS); institution management (MS); marriage and family therapy (MS); nutrition and food systems (PhD). Part-time programs available.

Faculty: 19 full-time (15 women), 3 part-time/adjunct (all women).
Students: 48 full-time (39 women), 30 part-time (29 women); includes 19 minority (14 African Americans, 3 Asian Americans or Pacific Islanders, 2 Hispanic Americans). Average age 32. 63 applicants, 54% accepted. In 2001, 26 master's, 4 doctorates awarded.
Degree requirements: For master's, thesis optional; for doctorate, one foreign language, thesis/dissertation.
Entrance requirements: For master's, GRE General Test, minimum GPA of 2.75; for doctorate, GRE General Test, minimum GPA of 3.5. *Application deadline:* For fall admission, 8/9 (priority date). Applications are processed on a rolling basis. *Application fee:* $0 ($25 for international students). Electronic applications accepted.
Expenses: Tuition, state resident: full-time $3,416; part-time $190 per credit hour. Tuition, nonresident: full-time $7,932; part-time $441 per credit hour.
Financial support: In 2001–02, 21 students received support, including research assistantships with full tuition reimbursements available (averaging $3,500 per year), teaching assistantships with full tuition reimbursements available (averaging $3,500 per year); fellowships, career-related internships or fieldwork, Federal Work-Study, institutionally sponsored loans, scholarships/grants, and unspecified assistantships also available. Financial award application deadline: 3/15.
Faculty research: School food service, teen pregnancy, diet and cholesterol metabolism.
Dr. Patricia Sims, Director, 601-266-4679, *Fax:* 601-266-4680.
Application contact: Dr. Kathy Yadrick, Graduate Coordinator, 601-266-4479, *Fax:* 601-266-4680, *E-mail:* kathy.yadrick@usm.edu. *Web site:* http://hhs.usm.edu/fcs

■ THE UNIVERSITY OF TENNESSEE

Graduate School, College of Human Ecology, Program in Human Ecology, Knoxville, TN 37996

AWARDS Child and family studies (PhD); community health (PhD); human resource development (PhD); nutrition science (PhD); retailing and consumer sciences (PhD); textile science (PhD).

Students: 62 full-time (42 women), 44 part-time (34 women); includes 12 minority (11 African Americans, 1 Asian American or Pacific Islander), 20 international. 39 applicants, 44% accepted. In 2001, 22 degrees awarded.
Degree requirements: For doctorate, thesis/dissertation.
Entrance requirements: For doctorate, GRE General Test, TOEFL, minimum GPA of 2.7. *Application deadline:* For fall admission, 2/1 (priority date). Applications are processed on a rolling basis. *Application fee:* $35. Electronic applications accepted.
Expenses: Tuition, state resident: full-time $4,280; part-time $233 per hour. Tuition, nonresident: full-time $12,066; part-time $666 per hour. Tuition and fees vary according to program.
Financial support: Fellowships, research assistantships, teaching assistantships, Federal Work-Study, institutionally sponsored loans, and unspecified assistantships available. Financial award application deadline: 2/1; financial award applicants required to submit FAFSA.
Dr. Billie J. Collier, Interim Head, 865-974-5224, *E-mail:* bcollier@utk.edu.

Find an in-depth description at www.petersons.com/gradchannel.

■ THE UNIVERSITY OF TENNESSEE AT MARTIN

Graduate Studies, College of Agriculture and Applied Sciences, Department of Family and Consumer Sciences, Martin, TN 38238-1000

AWARDS Child development and family relations (MSFCS); food science and nutrition (MSFCS). Part-time programs available.

Faculty: 7.
Students: 21 (19 women). 18 applicants, 100% accepted, 11 enrolled. In 2001, 11 degrees awarded.
Degree requirements: For master's, thesis optional.
Entrance requirements: For master's, GRE General Test, minimum GPA of 2.5. *Application deadline:* For fall admission, 7/1 (priority date). Applications are processed on a rolling basis. *Application fee:* $25 ($50 for international students).
Expenses: Tuition, area resident: Full-time $3,796; part-time $213 per hour. Tuition, nonresident: full-time $10,326; part-time $576 per hour.
Financial support: In 2001–02, 1 research assistantship with full tuition reimbursement (averaging $6,888 per year) was awarded; fellowships, teaching assistantships, scholarships/grants, tuition waivers (partial), and unspecified assistantships also available. Financial award application deadline: 3/1.
Faculty research: Children with developmental disabilities, regional food product development and marketing, parent education.
Dr. Lisa LeBleu, Coordinator, 731-587-7116, *E-mail:* llebleu@utm.edu.

■ THE UNIVERSITY OF TEXAS AT AUSTIN

Graduate School, College of Natural Sciences, Department of Human Ecology, Austin, TX 78712-1111

AWARDS Child development and family relations (MA, PhD); nutritional sciences (MA, PhD), including nutrition (MA), nutritional sciences (PhD).

Degree requirements: For master's and doctorate, thesis/dissertation.
Entrance requirements: For master's and doctorate, GRE General Test. Electronic applications accepted.
Expenses: Tuition, state resident: full-time $3,159. Tuition, nonresident: full-time $6,957. Tuition and fees vary according to program.

■ UNIVERSITY OF WISCONSIN–MADISON

Graduate School, School of Human Ecology, Madison, WI 53706-1380

AWARDS Consumer behavior and family economics (MS, PhD); continuing and vocational education (MS, PhD); design studies (MS); design studies (PhD); family and consumer journalism (MS, PhD); human development and family studies (MS, PhD).

Faculty: 39 full-time (28 women), 1 (woman) part-time/adjunct.
Students: 70 full-time (59 women), 30 part-time (22 women). Average age 36. 88 applicants, 28% accepted, 23 enrolled. In 2001, 17 master's, 12 doctorates awarded.
Degree requirements: For doctorate, thesis/dissertation.
Entrance requirements: For master's and doctorate, GRE General Test. *Application deadline:* For fall admission, 2/15 (priority date). Applications are processed on a rolling basis. *Application fee:* $45. Electronic applications accepted.
Expenses: Tuition, state resident: full-time $7,361; part-time $399 per credit. Tuition, nonresident: full-time $20,499; part-time $1,282 per credit. Required fees: $34 per credit. Full-time tuition and fees vary according to course load, program, reciprocity agreements and student level.
Financial support: In 2001–02, 1 fellowship with full tuition reimbursement, 4 research assistantships with full tuition reimbursements, 24 teaching assistantships with full tuition reimbursements were awarded. Scholarships/grants, health care benefits, and unspecified assistantships also available.
Robin A. Douthitt, Dean, 608-262-4847.
Application contact: Anthony Johnson, Assistant Dean, 608-262-2608, *Fax:* 608-265-3616, *E-mail:* sketheri@facstaff.wisc.edu. *Web site:* http://sohe.wisc.edu

■ UNIVERSITY OF WISCONSIN–STEVENS POINT

College of Professional Studies, School of Health Promotion and Human Development, Program in Human and Community Resources, Stevens Point, WI 54481-3897

AWARDS MS. Part-time programs available.

Faculty: 11 full-time (6 women).
Students: In 2001, 13 degrees awarded.
Degree requirements: For master's, thesis or alternative.
Entrance requirements: For master's, minimum GPA of 2.75. *Application deadline:* For fall admission, 5/1 (priority date). Applications are processed on a rolling basis. *Application fee:* $45.
Expenses: Tuition, state resident: full-time $4,020; part-time $223 per credit. Tuition, nonresident: full-time $13,844; part-time $769 per credit. Required fees: $487; $54 per credit.
Financial support: Research assistantships, teaching assistantships, Federal Work-Study available. Support available to part-time students. Financial award application deadline: 5/1; financial award applicants required to submit FAFSA.
John Munson, Associate Dean, School of Health Promotion and Human Development, 715-346-2830, *Fax:* 715-346-3751.

■ UNIVERSITY OF WISCONSIN–STOUT

Graduate School, College of Human Development, Program in Home Economics, Menomonie, WI 54751

AWARDS MS. Part-time programs available.

Students: 7 full-time (6 women), 14 part-time (all women), 3 international. 14 applicants, 93% accepted, 10 enrolled. In 2001, 10 degrees awarded.
Degree requirements: For master's, thesis.
Application deadline: Applications are processed on a rolling basis. *Application fee:* $45.
Expenses: Tuition, state resident: full-time $4,915. Tuition, nonresident: full-time $12,553.
Financial support: In 2001–02, 1 research assistantship was awarded; teaching assistantships, Federal Work-Study and tuition waivers (full and partial) also available. Support available to part-time students. Financial award application deadline: 4/1; financial award applicants required to submit FAFSA.
Dr. Karen Zimmerman, Director, 715-232-2530, *E-mail:* zimmermank@uwstout.edu.
Application contact: Dr. Christine Clements, Chair, 715-232-2567, *Fax:* 715-232-2588, *E-mail:* clementsc@uwstout.edu.

■ UTAH STATE UNIVERSITY

School of Graduate Studies, College of Family Life, Department of Human Environments, Logan, UT 84322

AWARDS MS. Part-time programs available. Postbaccalaureate distance learning degree programs offered.

Faculty: 11 full-time (10 women), 3 part-time/adjunct (1 woman).
Students: 5 full-time (all women), 15 part-time (10 women), 1 international. Average age 33. 20 applicants, 85% accepted. In 2001, 16 degrees awarded.
Degree requirements: For master's, thesis (for some programs).
Entrance requirements: For master's, GRE General Test, MAT, TOEFL, minimum GPA of 3.0. *Application deadline:* For fall admission, 6/15 (priority date); for spring admission, 10/15. Applications are processed on a rolling basis. *Application fee:* $40.
Expenses: Tuition, state resident: full-time $1,693. Tuition, nonresident: full-time $4,233. Required fees: $501. Tuition and fees vary according to program.
Financial support: In 2001–02, 9 research assistantships with partial tuition reimbursements (averaging $6,000 per year), 2 teaching assistantships with partial tuition reimbursements (averaging $7,000 per year) were awarded. Fellowships, career-related internships or fieldwork, Federal Work-Study, and institutionally sponsored loans also available.
Faculty research: Consumer bankruptcy, consumption and saving analysis, retirement planning, effective distance education, enzymatic analysis of textiles. *Total annual research expenditures:* $130,000.
Gong-Soog Hong, Head, 435-797-1570, *Fax:* 435-797-3845, *E-mail:* shong78@cc.usu.edu.
Application contact: Tom Peterson, Information Contact, 435-797-1556, *Fax:* 435-797-3845, *E-mail:* tom@cc.usu.edu. *Web site:* http://www.usu.edu/~famlife/humenv/index.html

■ WESTERN MICHIGAN UNIVERSITY

Graduate College, College of Education, Department of Family and Consumer Sciences, Program in Family and Consumer Sciences, Kalamazoo, MI 49008-5202

AWARDS MA.

Faculty: 18 full-time (15 women).
Students: 18 full-time (17 women), 32 part-time (30 women); includes 8 minority (6 African Americans, 2 Hispanic Americans). 19 applicants, 79% accepted, 14 enrolled. In 2001, 12 degrees awarded.
Application deadline: For fall admission, 2/15 (priority date). Applications are processed on a rolling basis. *Application fee:* $25.
Expenses: Tuition, state resident: part-time $186 per credit hour. Tuition, nonresident: part-time $442 per credit hour. Required fees: $602. One-time fee: $132 part-time. Tuition and fees vary according to course load.
Financial support: Fellowships, research assistantships, teaching assistantships, career-related internships or fieldwork and Federal Work-Study available. Financial award application deadline: 2/15; financial award applicants required to submit FAFSA.
Faculty research: Use of computers in custom designing of personal patterns for the handicapped.
Application contact: Admissions and Orientation, 616-387-2000, *Fax:* 616-387-2355.

CHILD AND FAMILY STUDIES

■ ANTIOCH UNIVERSITY SANTA BARBARA

Psychology Program, Santa Barbara, CA 93101-1581

AWARDS Family and child studies (MA); professional development and career counseling (MA). Part-time and evening/weekend programs available.

Faculty: 14 full-time (8 women), 43 part-time/adjunct (29 women).
Students: 13 full-time, 8 part-time. In 2001, 12 degrees awarded.
Entrance requirements: For master's, TOEFL. *Application deadline:* For fall admission, 8/5 (priority date); for winter admission, 11/11 (priority date). Applications are processed on a rolling basis. *Application fee:* $60.
Expenses: Tuition: Part-time $375 per unit. Required fees: $426 per year. $10 per quarter. Tuition and fees vary according to class time and program.
Financial support: Federal Work-Study available. Support available to part-time students. Financial award application deadline: 8/5; financial award applicants required to submit FAFSA.
Dr. Catherine Radecki-Bush, Chair, 805-962-8179 Ext. 229, *Fax:* 805-962-4786, *E-mail:* cradecki-bush@antiochsb.edu.
Application contact: Carol Flores, Admissions Director, 805-962-8179 Ext. 113, *Fax:* 805-962-4786, *E-mail:* cflores@antiochsb.edu. *Web site:* http://www.antiochsb.edu/

■ ARIZONA STATE UNIVERSITY

Graduate College, College of Liberal Arts and Sciences, Department of Family Resources and Human Development, Program in Family Science, Tempe, AZ 85287

AWARDS PhD.

Degree requirements: For doctorate, thesis/dissertation.
Entrance requirements: For doctorate, GRE.
Faculty research: Marriage and family therapy, child development, marital interaction, parent-child relationships, sexuality.

■ AUBURN UNIVERSITY

Graduate School, College of Human Sciences, Department of Human Development and Family Studies, Auburn University, AL 36849

AWARDS MS, PhD. Part-time programs available.

Faculty: 14 full-time (7 women).
Students: 26 full-time (20 women), 20 part-time (12 women); includes 7 minority (6 African Americans, 1 Native American), 2 international. 77 applicants, 57% accepted. In 2001, 11 master's, 5 doctorates awarded.
Degree requirements: For master's, thesis (MS), oral exam; for doctorate, thesis/dissertation.
Entrance requirements: For master's, GRE General Test; for doctorate, GRE General Test, master's degree. *Application deadline:* For fall admission, 7/7; for spring admission, 11/24. Applications are processed on a rolling basis. *Application fee:* $25 ($50 for international students).
Financial support: Research assistantships, teaching assistantships, Federal Work-Study available. Support available to part-time students. Financial award application deadline: 3/15.
Faculty research: Family influences on personality and social development, parent-child relations, infancy, day care, parent education.
Dr. Marilyn Bradbard, Head, 334-844-4151, *E-mail:* mbradbar@humsci.auburn.edu.
Application contact: Dr. John F. Pritchett, Dean of the Graduate School, 334-844-4700, *E-mail:* hatchlb@mail.auburn.edu. *Web site:* http://www.humsci.auburn.edu/fcd/

■ BANK STREET COLLEGE OF EDUCATION

Graduate School, Program in Child Life, New York, NY 10025-1120

AWARDS).

Degree requirements: For master's, thesis.
Application deadline: For fall admission, 3/1 (priority date); for spring admission, 11/1 (priority date). Applications are processed on a rolling basis.
Expenses: Tuition: Part-time $690 per credit. One-time fee: $250 full-time.
Financial support: Career-related internships or fieldwork, Federal Work-Study, scholarships/grants, and unspecified assistantships available. Support available to part-time students. Financial award application deadline: 4/15; financial award applicants required to submit FAFSA.
Dr. Adine Usher, Director, 212-875-4473, *Fax:* 212-875-4753.
Application contact: Ann K. Morgan, Director of Graduate Admissions, 212-875-4404, *Fax:* 212-875-4678, *E-mail:* gradcourses@bankstreet.edu. *Web site:* http://www.bankstreet.edu/

■ BOWLING GREEN STATE UNIVERSITY

Graduate College, College of Arts and Sciences, Department of Sociology, Bowling Green, OH 43403

AWARDS Criminology/deviant behavior (MA, PhD); demography and population studies (MA, PhD); family studies (MA, PhD); social psychology (MA, PhD). Part-time programs available.

Faculty: 17.
Students: 32 full-time (22 women), 12 part-time (8 women); includes 3 minority (2 African Americans, 1 Hispanic American), 6 international. Average age 28. 53 applicants, 53% accepted, 12 enrolled. In 2001, 7 master's, 4 doctorates awarded.
Degree requirements: For master's, thesis or alternative; for doctorate, thesis/dissertation, comprehensive exam.
Entrance requirements: For master's and doctorate, GRE General Test, TOEFL. *Application deadline:* For fall admission, 2/15. *Application fee:* $30. Electronic applications accepted.
Expenses: Tuition, state resident: full-time $7,376; part-time $342 per credit hour. Tuition, nonresident: full-time $13,628; part-time $640 per credit hour.
Financial support: In 2001–02, 26 research assistantships with full tuition reimbursements (averaging $9,134 per year), 6 teaching assistantships with full tuition reimbursements (averaging $11,000 per year) were awarded. Career-related internships or fieldwork, Federal Work-Study, institutionally sponsored loans, and unspecified assistantships also available. Financial award applicants required to submit FAFSA.
Faculty research: Applied demography, criminology and deviance, family studies, population studies, social psychology.
Dr. Gary Lee, Chair, 419-372-2294.
Application contact: Dr. Steve Cernkovich, Graduate Coordinator, 419-372-2743.

■ BOWLING GREEN STATE UNIVERSITY

Graduate College, College of Education and Human Development, School of Family and Consumer Sciences, Bowling Green, OH 43403

AWARDS Food and nutrition (MFCS); human development and family studies (MFCS). Part-time programs available.

Faculty: 24.
Students: 14 full-time (all women), 8 part-time (7 women), 3 international. Average age 26. 14 applicants, 57% accepted, 7 enrolled. In 2001, 6 degrees awarded.
Degree requirements: For master's, thesis.
Entrance requirements: For master's, GRE General Test, TOEFL, minimum GPA of 3.0. *Application deadline:* For fall admission, 2/15. *Application fee:* $30.
Expenses: Tuition, state resident: full-time $7,376; part-time $342 per credit hour. Tuition, nonresident: full-time $13,628; part-time $640 per credit hour.
Financial support: In 2001–02, 12 research assistantships with full tuition reimbursements (averaging $4,486 per year), 2 teaching assistantships with full tuition reimbursements (averaging $5,475 per year) were awarded. Career-related internships or fieldwork and unspecified assistantships also available. Financial award applicants required to submit FAFSA.
Faculty research: Public health, wellness, social issues and policies, ethnic foods, nutrition and aging.
Dr. Joe Williford, Acting Chair, 419-372-7823.
Application contact: Dr. Rebecca Pebocik, Graduate Coordinator, 419-372-6920.

■ BRANDEIS UNIVERSITY

The Heller School for Social Policy and Management, Program in Management and Social Policy, Waltham, MA 02454-9110

AWARDS Child, youth, and family services (MBA, MM); elder and disabled services (MBA, MM); health care administration (MBA, MM); human services (MBA, MM). Part-time and evening/weekend programs available.

Faculty: 44 full-time (17 women), 16 part-time/adjunct (6 women).
Students: 45 full-time (32 women), 31 part-time (19 women). Average age 28. 72 applicants, 75% accepted. In 2001, 45 degrees awarded.
Degree requirements: For master's, team consulting project.
Entrance requirements: For master's, GRE General Test or GMAT (MM), GMAT (MBA). *Application deadline:* For fall admission, 6/1 (priority date); for winter admission, 11/1 (priority date); for spring admission, 2/15. Applications are processed on a rolling basis. *Application fee:* $50. Electronic applications accepted.
Expenses: Tuition: Full-time $27,392. Required fees: $35.
Financial support: Fellowships, institutionally sponsored loans, scholarships/grants, and tuition waivers (partial) available. Financial award application deadline: 2/15; financial award applicants required to submit CSS PROFILE or FAFSA.

Brandeis University (continued)
Faculty research: Health care, child and family, elder and disabled services, general human services.
Barry Friedman, Director, 781-736-3783, *E-mail:* hfriedman@brandeis.edu.
Application contact: Lisa Hamlin Sherry, Assistant Director for Admissions and Financial Aid, 781-736-3835, *Fax:* 781-736-3881, *E-mail:* sherry@brandeis.edu.
Web site: http://heller.brandeis.edu

Find an in-depth description at www.petersons.com/gradchannel.

■ BRIGHAM YOUNG UNIVERSITY

Graduate Studies, College of Family, Home, and Social Sciences, Marriage, Family and Human Development Department, Provo, UT 84602-1001

AWARDS MS, PhD.

Faculty: 26 full-time (6 women).
Students: 31 full-time (24 women); includes 4 minority (1 Asian American or Pacific Islander, 1 Hispanic American, 2 Native Americans), 3 international. Average age 30. 29 applicants, 52% accepted, 13 enrolled. In 2001, 2 master's, 2 doctorates awarded.
Degree requirements: For master's, thesis, publishable paper; for doctorate, thesis/dissertation, comprehensive exam, registration. *Median time to degree:* Master's–3 years full-time; doctorate–6 years full-time.
Entrance requirements: For master's and doctorate, GRE General Test, GRE Writing Assessment, minimum GPA of 3.0 in last 60 hours. *Application deadline:* For fall admission, 1/10. *Application fee:* $50. Electronic applications accepted.
Expenses: Tuition: Full-time $3,860; part-time $214 per hour.
Financial support: In 2001–02, 27 students received support, including 19 research assistantships with partial tuition reimbursements available (averaging $5,096 per year), 8 teaching assistantships with partial tuition reimbursements available (averaging $5,096 per year); fellowships, career-related internships or fieldwork and tuition waivers (partial) also available. Financial award application deadline: 1/10.
Faculty research: Early childhood education, family process, family life education.
Dr. Craig H. Hart, Chair, 801-422-2069.
Application contact: Shauna Pitts, MFHD and Graduate Secretary, School of Family Life, 801-422-2060, *E-mail:* shauna_pitts@byu.edu. *Web site:* http://fhss.byu.edu/mfhd/main.htm

■ CALIFORNIA STATE UNIVERSITY, LOS ANGELES

Graduate Studies, College of Health and Human Services, Department of Child and Family Studies, Program in Child Development, Los Angeles, CA 90032-8530

AWARDS MA. Part-time and evening/weekend programs available.

Students: 30 full-time (29 women), 73 part-time (66 women); includes 81 minority (9 African Americans, 12 Asian Americans or Pacific Islanders, 60 Hispanic Americans), 5 international. In 2001, 5 degrees awarded.
Degree requirements: For master's, project, or thesis.
Entrance requirements: For master's, TOEFL, bachelor's degree in child development or related field. *Application deadline:* For fall admission, 6/30; for spring admission, 2/1. Applications are processed on a rolling basis. *Application fee:* $55.
Expenses: Tuition, nonresident: part-time $164 per unit.
Financial support: Career-related internships or fieldwork and Federal Work-Study available. Support available to part-time students. Financial award application deadline: 3/1.
Faculty research: Parenting, infancy, family life.
Dr. Jeffrey Gilger, Co-Chair, Department of Child and Family Studies, 323-343-4590.

■ CENTRAL MICHIGAN UNIVERSITY

College of Graduate Studies, College of Education and Human Services, Department of Human Environmental Studies, Mount Pleasant, MI 48859

AWARDS Human development and family studies (MA); nutrition and dietetics (MS).

Degree requirements: For master's, thesis or alternative.
Entrance requirements: For master's, GRE (MA), minimum GPA of 3.0 in last 60 hours, 15 credits in human development and family studies or related area (MA).
Expenses: Tuition, state resident: part-time $182 per unit. Tuition, nonresident: part-time $182 per unit. Required fees: $208 per semester. Part-time tuition and fees vary according to course load.
Faculty research: Human growth and development, family studies and human sexuality, nutritional food science/food services, apparel and textile retailing, computer-aided design for apparel and interior design.

■ CENTRAL WASHINGTON UNIVERSITY

Graduate Studies and Research, College of Education and Professional Studies, Department of Family and Consumer Sciences, Ellensburg, WA 98926-7463

AWARDS Apparel design (MS); family and consumer sciences education (MS); family studies (MS); nutrition (MS). Part-time programs available.

Faculty: 8 full-time (5 women).
Students: 5 full-time (4 women), 6 part-time (all women); includes 1 minority (African American), 1 international. 1 applicant, 100% accepted, 1 enrolled. In 2001, 4 degrees awarded.
Degree requirements: For master's, thesis or alternative.
Entrance requirements: For master's, GRE General Test (nutrition), minimum GPA of 3.0. *Application deadline:* For fall admission, 4/1 (priority date); for winter admission, 10/1; for spring admission, 1/1. Applications are processed on a rolling basis. *Application fee:* $35.
Expenses: Tuition, state resident: full-time $4,848; part-time $162 per credit. Tuition, nonresident: full-time $14,772; part-time $492 per credit. Required fees: $324.
Financial support: In 2001–02, 3 teaching assistantships with partial tuition reimbursements (averaging $7,120 per year) were awarded; research assistantships, Federal Work-Study also available. Financial award application deadline: 3/1; financial award applicants required to submit FAFSA.
Dr. Jan Bowers, Chair, 509-963-2766.
Application contact: Barbara Sisko, Office Assistant, Graduate Studies and Research, 509-963-3103, *Fax:* 509-963-1799, *E-mail:* masters@cwu.edu. *Web site:* http://www.cwu.edu/

■ COLLEGE OF MOUNT SAINT VINCENT

Program in Allied Health Studies, Riverdale, NY 10471-1093

AWARDS Allied health studies (MS), including child and family health, counseling, health care management, health care systems and policies; counseling (Certificate); health care management (Certificate); health care systems and policies (Certificate). Part-time and evening/weekend programs available.

Faculty: 7 full-time (4 women), 4 part-time/adjunct (1 woman).
Students: 7 full-time (all women), 43 part-time (35 women); includes 33 minority (19 African Americans, 1 Asian American or Pacific Islander, 13 Hispanic Americans). Average age 36. In 2001, 14 master's, 2 other advanced degrees awarded.
Degree requirements: For master's, thesis or alternative, project, 250 hours of field work. *Median time to degree:*

Master's–2 years part-time; Certificate–1 year part-time.
Entrance requirements: For master's and Certificate, interview, writing sample. *Application deadline:* For fall admission, 8/1 (priority date); for winter admission, 11/1 (priority date); for spring admission, 1/1 (priority date). Applications are processed on a rolling basis. *Application fee:* $50.
Expenses: Tuition: Part-time $496 per credit.
Financial support: Career-related internships or fieldwork available. Support available to part-time students. Financial award applicants required to submit FAFSA.
Faculty research: Work and family stress and health outcomes, siblings, women's health issues, children's stress, international health, legal issues.
Dr. Rita Scher Dytell, Director, 718-405-3788, *Fax:* 718-405-3734, *E-mail:* rdytell@cmsv.edu.
Application contact: Director of Transfer and Graduate Admissions, 718-405-3267, *Fax:* 718-549-7945, *E-mail:* admissns@cmsv.edu. *Web site:* http://www.cmsv.edu/

■ COLORADO STATE UNIVERSITY

Graduate School, College of Applied Human Sciences, Department of Human Development and Family Studies, Fort Collins, CO 80523-0015

AWARDS MS. Part-time programs available.

Faculty: 12 full-time (6 women), 2 part-time/adjunct (1 woman).
Students: 23 full-time (21 women), 10 part-time (9 women); includes 5 minority (1 African American, 3 Hispanic Americans, 1 Native American), 2 international. Average age 29. 49 applicants, 47% accepted, 15 enrolled. In 2001, 7 degrees awarded.
Degree requirements: For master's, thesis.
Entrance requirements: For master's, GRE General Test, TOEFL, minimum GPA of 3.0; previous course work in human development, family studies, and statistics. *Application deadline:* For fall admission, 1/15 (priority date). *Application fee:* $30. Electronic applications accepted.
Expenses: Tuition, state resident: full-time $2,880; part-time $160 per credit. Tuition, nonresident: full-time $11,412; part-time $634 per credit. Required fees: $750; $34 per credit.
Financial support: In 2001–02, 1 fellowship, 4 research assistantships, 13 teaching assistantships were awarded. Career-related internships or fieldwork, Federal Work-Study, institutionally sponsored loans, and traineeships also available. Support available to part-time students. Financial award application deadline: 1/15.
Faculty research: Development of self in the social context, risk factors in development, grief and loss, intergeneration relationships. *Total annual research expenditures:* $625,000.
Dr. Clifton E. Barber, Head, 970-491-3581, *Fax:* 970-491-7975.
Application contact: Dr. Karen C. Barrett, Graduate Coordinator, 970-491-7382, *Fax:* 970-491-7975, *E-mail:* barrett@cahs.colostate.edu. *Web site:* http://www.cahs.colostate.edu/Depts/HDFS/

■ CONCORDIA UNIVERSITY

College of Graduate and Continuing Studies, School of Human Services, St. Paul, MN 55104-5494

AWARDS Community education (MA Ed); criminal justice (MAHS); early childhood education (MA Ed); family studies (MAHS); leadership (MAHS); parish education (MA Ed); school-age care (MA Ed); youth development (MA Ed). Evening/weekend programs available. Postbaccalaureate distance learning degree programs offered (minimal on-campus study).

Faculty: 8 full-time (3 women), 98 part-time/adjunct (51 women).
Students: 161 full-time (136 women); includes 24 minority (20 African Americans, 2 Asian Americans or Pacific Islanders, 2 Hispanic Americans). Average age 34. 50 applicants, 90% accepted. In 2001, 18 degrees awarded.
Degree requirements: For master's, thesis or alternative, final project.
Entrance requirements: For master's, leadership portfolio, minimum GPA of 2.75. *Application deadline:* Applications are processed on a rolling basis. *Application fee:* $50. Electronic applications accepted.
Expenses: Tuition: Part-time $300 per semester hour. Tuition and fees vary according to program.
Financial support: Federal Work-Study available. Support available to part-time students. Financial award application deadline: 4/6.
James Ollhoff, Associate Dean, 651-603-6148, *E-mail:* ollhoff@csp.edu.
Application contact: Gail Ann Wells, Marketing Coordinator, 651-603-6186, *Fax:* 651-603-6144, *E-mail:* wells@csp.edu. *Web site:* http://www.cshs.csp.edu/

■ CONCORDIA UNIVERSITY

Graduate Programs in Education, Program in Family Life, Seward, NE 68434-1599

AWARDS MS. Part-time and evening/weekend programs available.

Faculty: 8 full-time (3 women), 2 part-time/adjunct (1 woman).
Students: 22 applicants, 100% accepted. In 2001, 9 degrees awarded.
Degree requirements: For master's, thesis or alternative.
Entrance requirements: For master's, GRE, MAT, or NTE, minimum GPA of 3.0, BS in education or equivalent. *Application deadline:* For fall admission, 8/1 (priority date); for spring admission, 12/1. Applications are processed on a rolling basis. *Application fee:* $15.
Expenses: Tuition: Part-time $155 per credit hour.
Financial support: Federal Work-Study and institutionally sponsored loans available. Support available to part-time students. Financial award applicants required to submit FAFSA.
Dr. Shirley Bergman, Coordinator, 402-643-7432.

■ CONCORDIA UNIVERSITY WISCONSIN

School of Graduate Studies, Education Department, Program in Family Studies, Mequon, WI 53097-2402

AWARDS MS Ed.

Degree requirements: For master's, thesis or alternative, comprehensive exam.
Entrance requirements: For master's, TOEFL, minimum GPA of 3.0.

■ CORNELL UNIVERSITY

Graduate School, Graduate Fields of Human Ecology, Field of Human Development, Ithaca, NY 14853-0001

AWARDS Developmental psychology (PhD), including cognitive development, developmental psychopathology, ecology of human development, sociology and personality development; human development and family studies (PhD), including ecology of human development, family studies and the life course.

Faculty: 33 full-time.
Students: 33 full-time (23 women); includes 7 minority (4 African Americans, 1 Asian American or Pacific Islander, 2 Hispanic Americans), 6 international. 70 applicants, 16% accepted. In 2001, 6 doctorates awarded.
Degree requirements: For doctorate, thesis/dissertation, predoctoral research project, teaching experience.
Entrance requirements: For doctorate, GRE General Test, TOEFL, 2 letters of recommendation. *Application deadline:* For fall admission, 1/15. *Application fee:* $65. Electronic applications accepted.
Expenses: Tuition: Full-time $25,970. Required fees: $50.
Financial support: In 2001–02, 33 students received support, including 7 fellowships with full tuition reimbursements available, 10 research assistantships with full tuition reimbursements available, 16 teaching assistantships with full tuition reimbursements available; institutionally sponsored loans, scholarships/grants, tuition waivers (full and partial), and unspecified assistantships also available. Financial award applicants required to submit FAFSA.
Faculty research: Cognitive development, developmental psychopathology, ecology of human development, family studies and the life course, social and personality development.

Cornell University (continued)

Application contact: Graduate Field Assistant, 607-255-3181, *Fax:* 607-255-9856, *E-mail:* hdfs@cornell.edu. *Web site:* http://www.gradschool.cornell.edu/grad/fields_1/hdfs.html

■ EAST CAROLINA UNIVERSITY

Graduate School, School of Human Environmental Sciences, Department of Child Development and Family Relations, Greenville, NC 27858-4353

AWARDS Child development and family relations (MS); marriage and family therapy (MS). Part-time programs available.

Faculty: 7 full-time (3 women).
Students: 42 full-time (36 women), 14 part-time (all women); includes 9 minority (8 African Americans, 1 Asian American or Pacific Islander). Average age 29. 59 applicants, 47% accepted. In 2001, 24 degrees awarded.
Degree requirements: For master's, thesis optional.
Application deadline: For fall admission, 1/15; for spring admission, 10/15. Applications are processed on a rolling basis. *Application fee:* $45.
Expenses: Tuition, state resident: full-time $2,636. Tuition, nonresident: full-time $11,365.
Financial support: Career-related internships or fieldwork and Federal Work-Study available. Support available to part-time students. Financial award application deadline: 6/1.
Faculty research: Child care quality, mental health delivery systems for children, family violence.
Dr. Mel Markowski, Chairperson, 252-328-1333, *E-mail:* markowskie@mail.ecu.edu.

■ FITCHBURG STATE COLLEGE

Division of Graduate and Continuing Education, Programs in Counseling, Fitchburg, MA 01420-2697

AWARDS Adolescent and family therapy (Certificate); child protective services (Certificate); elementary school guidance counseling (MS); forensic case work (Certificate); mental health counseling (MS); school guidance counselor (Certificate); secondary school guidance counseling (MS). Part-time and evening/weekend programs available.

Students: 30 full-time (24 women), 52 part-time (48 women); includes 4 minority (1 African American, 1 Asian American or Pacific Islander, 2 Hispanic Americans), 3 international. In 2001, 27 degrees awarded.
Entrance requirements: For master's, GRE General Test or MAT, interview, previous course work in psychology; for Certificate, master's degree. *Application deadline:* Applications are processed on a rolling basis. *Application fee:* $10.
Expenses: Tuition, state resident: part-time $150 per credit. Required fees: $7 per credit. $65 per term. Tuition and fees vary according to course load.
Financial support: In 2001–02, research assistantships with partial tuition reimbursements (averaging $5,500 per year), teaching assistantships with partial tuition reimbursements (averaging $5,500 per year) were awarded. Federal Work-Study and unspecified assistantships also available. Support available to part-time students. Financial award application deadline: 3/1; financial award applicants required to submit FAFSA.
Dr. Richard Spencer, Co-Chair, 978-665-3349, *Fax:* 978-665-3658, *E-mail:* gce@fsc.edu.
Application contact: Director of Admissions, 978-665-3144, *Fax:* 978-665-4540, *E-mail:* admissions@fsc.edu. *Web site:* http://www.fsc.edu/

■ FLORIDA STATE UNIVERSITY

Graduate Studies, College of Human Sciences, Department of Family and Child Sciences, Tallahassee, FL 32306

AWARDS Child development (MS, PhD); family and consumer sciences education (MS, PhD); family relations (MS, PhD). Part-time programs available.

Faculty: 13 full-time (9 women).
Students: 22 full-time (18 women), 21 part-time (20 women); includes 16 minority (14 African Americans, 1 Asian American or Pacific Islander, 1 Hispanic American), 2 international. Average age 32. 22 applicants, 59% accepted, 9 enrolled. In 2001, 10 master's, 4 doctorates awarded.
Degree requirements: For master's, thesis optional; for doctorate, thesis/dissertation.
Entrance requirements: For master's and doctorate, GRE General Test, minimum GPA of 3.0. *Application fee:* $20. Electronic applications accepted.
Expenses: Tuition, state resident: part-time $163 per credit hour. Tuition, nonresident: part-time $570 per credit hour. Tuition and fees vary according to program.
Financial support: In 2001–02, 31 students received support, including 1 fellowship (averaging $10,000 per year), 14 research assistantships with partial tuition reimbursements available (averaging $5,000 per year), 16 teaching assistantships with partial tuition reimbursements available (averaging $5,000 per year); career-related internships or fieldwork, Federal Work-Study, institutionally sponsored loans, scholarships/grants, and unspecified assistantships also available. Financial award applicants required to submit FAFSA.
Faculty research: Addictions, family therapy, sexuality, parent-child relations, adolescent development.
Dr. Jay Schvaneveldt, Chair, 850-644-3217, *Fax:* 850-644-3439, *E-mail:* cwalersc@mailer.fsu.edu.
Application contact: Lynn LaCombe, Program Assistant, 850-644-3217, *Fax:* 850-644-3439, *E-mail:* llacomb@mailer.fsu.edu. *Web site:* http://www.chs.fsu.edu/dfcs/

Find an in-depth description at www.petersons.com/gradchannel.

■ INDIANA STATE UNIVERSITY

School of Graduate Studies, College of Arts and Sciences, Department of Family and Consumer Sciences, Terre Haute, IN 47809-1401

AWARDS Child and family relations (MS); clothing and textiles (MS); dietetics (MS); home management (MS); nutrition and foods (MS). Part-time programs available.

Electronic applications accepted.

■ IOWA STATE UNIVERSITY OF SCIENCE AND TECHNOLOGY

Graduate College, College of Family and Consumer Sciences, Department of Human Development and Family Studies, Ames, IA 50011

AWARDS Human development and family studies (MFCS, MS, PhD); marriage and family therapy (PhD).

Faculty: 33 full-time, 3 part-time/adjunct.
Students: 35 full-time (27 women), 67 part-time (51 women); includes 8 minority (1 African American, 2 Asian Americans or Pacific Islanders, 5 Hispanic Americans), 16 international. 42 applicants, 64% accepted, 14 enrolled. In 2001, 10 master's, 15 doctorates awarded.
Degree requirements: For master's and doctorate, thesis/dissertation. *Median time to degree:* Master's–2.4 years full-time; doctorate–5.9 years full-time.
Entrance requirements: For master's and doctorate, GRE General Test, TOEFL or IELTS. *Application deadline:* For fall admission, 1/15 (priority date). *Application fee:* $20 ($50 for international students). Electronic applications accepted.
Expenses: Tuition, state resident: full-time $1,851. Tuition, nonresident: full-time $5,449. Tuition and fees vary according to program.
Financial support: In 2001–02, 25 research assistantships with partial tuition reimbursements (averaging $12,175 per year), 17 teaching assistantships with partial tuition reimbursements (averaging $11,439 per year) were awarded. Fellowships, scholarships/grants also available.
Faculty research: Child development, early childhood education, family resource management and housing, life span studies.
Dr. Maurice M. MacDonald, Chair, 515-294-6316, *Fax:* 515-294-2502, *E-mail:* hdfs-grad-adm@iastate.edu.

Application contact: Dr. Dee Draper, Director of Graduate Education, 515-294-6321, *Fax:* 515-294-2502, *E-mail:* hdfs-grad-adm@iastate.edu. *Web site:* http://www.fcs.iastate.edu/hdfs/grad/default.htm/

■ IOWA STATE UNIVERSITY OF SCIENCE AND TECHNOLOGY

Graduate College, Interdisciplinary Programs, Program in Family and Consumer Sciences, Ames, IA 50011

AWARDS MFCS.

Students: 1 (woman) full-time, 9 part-time (all women); includes 1 minority (Native American). 7 applicants, 71% accepted, 4 enrolled. In 2001, 7 degrees awarded.
Degree requirements: For master's, thesis or alternative. *Median time to degree:* Master's–3.7 years full-time.
Entrance requirements: For master's, GRE General Test, TOEFL or IELTS. *Application deadline:* For fall admission, 3/1; for spring admission, 10/1. *Application fee:* $20 ($50 for international students). Electronic applications accepted.
Expenses: Tuition, state resident: full-time $1,851. Tuition, nonresident: full-time $5,449. Tuition and fees vary according to program.
Financial support: In 2001–02, 1 research assistantship with partial tuition reimbursement (averaging $11,312 per year), 2 teaching assistantships with partial tuition reimbursements (averaging $11,312 per year) were awarded. Scholarships/grants, health care benefits, and unspecified assistantships also available.
Dr. Mary Winter, Supervisory Committee Chair, 515-294-5982, *E-mail:* mfcsinfo@iastate.edu. *Web site:* http://www.fcs.iastate.edu/

■ KANSAS STATE UNIVERSITY

Graduate School, College of Human Ecology, School of Family Studies and Human Services, Manhattan, KS 66506

AWARDS Family studies and human services (MS); human ecology (PhD). Part-time programs available.

Faculty: 24 full-time (14 women).
Students: 69 full-time (58 women), 109 part-time (76 women); includes 22 minority (14 African Americans, 2 Asian Americans or Pacific Islanders, 4 Hispanic Americans, 2 Native Americans), 3 international. 88 applicants, 82% accepted, 48 enrolled. In 2001, 26 degrees awarded.
Degree requirements: For master's, thesis or alternative, oral exam, residency; for doctorate, thesis/dissertation, preliminary exam, residency.
Entrance requirements: For master's, GRE, TOEFL, minimum GPA of 3.0 in last 2 years of undergraduate study; for doctorate, GRE, TOEFL, minimum GPA of 3.5 in master's program. *Application deadline:* For fall admission, 2/1 (priority date); for spring admission, 10/1 (priority date). Applications are processed on a rolling basis. *Application fee:* $0 ($25 for international students).
Expenses: Tuition, state resident: part-time $113 per credit hour. Tuition, nonresident: part-time $358 per credit hour.
Financial support: In 2001–02, 15 research assistantships with partial tuition reimbursements (averaging $8,000 per year), 22 teaching assistantships with partial tuition reimbursements (averaging $8,000 per year) were awarded. Federal Work-Study, institutionally sponsored loans, scholarships/grants, and unspecified assistantships also available. Support available to part-time students. Financial award application deadline: 3/1; financial award applicants required to submit FAFSA.
Faculty research: Military families, neurogenic communication and swallowing disorders, child language and early literacy, communicative competence of people who use AAC systems, assessment of financial attitudes and financial risk tolerance. *Total annual research expenditures:* $2.8 million.
Dr. William Meredith, Department Head, 785-532-5510, *Fax:* 785-532-5505, *E-mail:* fshs@ksu.edu.
Application contact: Information Contact, 785-532-5510, *Fax:* 785-532-5505, *E-mail:* fshs@ksu.edu. *Web site:* http://www.ksu.edu/humec/fshs/

■ KENT STATE UNIVERSITY

College of Fine and Professional Arts, School of Family and Consumer Studies, Kent, OH 44242-0001

AWARDS Child and family relations (MA); nutrition (MS).

Degree requirements: For master's, thesis (for some programs).
Entrance requirements: For master's, minimum GPA of 2.75. Electronic applications accepted.

■ LOMA LINDA UNIVERSITY

Graduate School, Department of Counseling and Family Science, Program in Family Studies, Loma Linda, CA 92350

AWARDS MA, Certificate, MA/Certificate. Part-time programs available.

Faculty: 10 full-time (6 women), 5 part-time/adjunct (3 women).
Students: 66 full-time (50 women), 10 part-time (5 women).
Degree requirements: For master's, thesis optional.
Entrance requirements: For master's, GRE General Test. *Application fee:* $40.
Expenses: Tuition: Part-time $420 per unit.
Financial support: Federal Work-Study, tuition waivers (partial), and unspecified assistantships available.
Dr. Mary Moline, Coordinator, 909-824-4547, *Fax:* 909-824-4859.

■ MIAMI UNIVERSITY

Graduate School, School of Education and Allied Professions, Program in Social Work, Oxford, OH 45056

AWARDS Child and family studies (MS). Part-time programs available.

Faculty: 4 full-time (2 women), 1 (woman) part-time/adjunct.
Students: 15 full-time (11 women), 5 part-time (4 women); includes 6 minority (5 African Americans, 1 Asian American or Pacific Islander). 16 applicants, 100% accepted, 8 enrolled. In 2001, 1 degree awarded.
Degree requirements: For master's, thesis or alternative, final exam.
Entrance requirements: For master's, MAT, minimum undergraduate GPA of 3.0 during previous 2 years or 2.75 overall. *Application deadline:* For fall admission, 3/1 (priority date); for spring admission, 12/1. Applications are processed on a rolling basis. *Application fee:* $35.
Expenses: Tuition, state resident: full-time $7,155; part-time $295 per semester hour. Tuition, nonresident: full-time $14,829; part-time $615 per semester hour. Tuition and fees vary according to degree level and campus/location.
Financial support: In 2001–02, 4 fellowships (averaging $8,695 per year) were awarded; research assistantships, teaching assistantships, career-related internships or fieldwork, Federal Work-Study, and tuition waivers (full) also available. Financial award application deadline: 3/1.
Dr. Susan Cross Lipnickey, Chair, 513-529-2323. *Web site:* http://www.muohio.edu/~fswcwis/msreg.html

■ MICHIGAN STATE UNIVERSITY

Graduate School, College of Human Ecology, Department of Family and Child Ecology, East Lansing, MI 48824

AWARDS Child development (MA); community service-urban studies (MS); community services (MS); family and child ecology (PhD); family consumer sciences education (MA); family ecology (PhD); family economics and management (MA); family studies (MA); home economics education (MA); marriage and family therapy (MA). Part-time and evening/weekend programs available. Postbaccalaureate distance learning degree programs offered.

Faculty: 26.
Students: 56 full-time (50 women), 75 part-time (67 women); includes 28 minority (20 African Americans, 2 Asian Americans or Pacific Islanders, 6 Hispanic Americans), 21 international. Average age 35. 80 applicants, 61% accepted. In 2001, 39 master's, 9 doctorates awarded.
Degree requirements: For master's, thesis optional; for doctorate, thesis/dissertation.
Entrance requirements: For master's, GRE General Test, minimum GPA of 3.0

Michigan State University (continued)
in last 2 years of undergraduate course work; for doctorate, GRE General Test. *Application deadline:* Applications are processed on a rolling basis. *Application fee:* $30 ($40 for international students). Electronic applications accepted.
Expenses: Tuition, state resident: part-time $244 per credit hour. Tuition, nonresident: part-time $494 per credit hour. Required fees: $268 per semester. Tuition and fees vary according to course load, degree level and program.
Financial support: In 2001–02, 35 fellowships with tuition reimbursements (averaging $2,480 per year), 8 research assistantships with tuition reimbursements (averaging $10,944 per year), 14 teaching assistantships with tuition reimbursements (averaging $10,845 per year) were awarded. Financial award applicants required to submit FAFSA.
Faculty research: Early childhood education, family dynamics, family utilization, parenting. *Total annual research expenditures:* $357,600.
Dr. Anne Soderman, Chairperson, 517-432-2953, *E-mail:* fce@msu.edu. *Web site:* http://www.he.msu.edu/fce.html/

■ MIDDLE TENNESSEE STATE UNIVERSITY

College of Graduate Studies, College of Education and Behavioral Science, Department of Human Sciences, Murfreesboro, TN 37132

AWARDS Child development and family studies (MS); nutrition and food science (MS). Part-time programs available.

Faculty: 8 full-time (all women).
Students: 1 (woman) full-time, 26 part-time (all women); includes 2 minority (1 African American, 1 Hispanic American). Average age 29. 7 applicants, 100% accepted.
Degree requirements: For master's, thesis, comprehensive exam.
Entrance requirements: For master's, GRE or MAT. *Application deadline:* For fall admission, 8/1 (priority date). Applications are processed on a rolling basis. *Application fee:* $25. Electronic applications accepted.
Expenses: Tuition, state resident: full-time $1,716; part-time $191 per hour. Tuition, nonresident: full-time $4,952; part-time $461 per hour. Required fees: $14 per hour. $58 per semester.
Financial support: In 2001–02, 4 teaching assistantships were awarded. Financial award application deadline: 5/1.
Faculty research: Courtship relationships, feminist methodology and epistemology in family studies, school uniforms, body fat in elderly, asynchronous distance education.
Dr. Dellmar Walker, Interim Chair, 615-898-2884.

■ MONTCLAIR STATE UNIVERSITY

The School of Graduate, Professional and Continuing Education, College of Education and Human Services, Department of Human Ecology, Upper Montclair, NJ 07043-1624

AWARDS Family life education (MA); family relations/child development (MA); home economics education (MA); home management/consumer economics (MA); nutrition education (MA). Part-time and evening/weekend programs available.

Degree requirements: For master's, thesis or alternative, comprehensive exam.
Entrance requirements: For master's, GRE General Test. Electronic applications accepted. *Web site:* http://www.montclair.edu

■ NORTH DAKOTA STATE UNIVERSITY

The Graduate School, College of Human Development and Education, Department of Child Development and Family Science, Fargo, ND 58105

AWARDS Child development and family science (MS); gerontology (PhD). Part-time programs available.

Faculty: 9 full-time (4 women).
Students: 20 full-time (16 women), 17 part-time (16 women); includes 1 minority (African American). 13 applicants, 46% accepted. In 2001, 4 degrees awarded.
Degree requirements: For master's, thesis or alternative.
Entrance requirements: For master's, TOEFL. *Application deadline:* For fall admission, 2/1; for spring admission, 10/1. *Application fee:* $35.
Expenses: Tuition, state resident: part-time $124 per credit. Tuition, nonresident: part-time $325 per credit. Required fees: $22 per credit. Tuition and fees vary according to reciprocity agreements.
Financial support: In 2001–02, 17 teaching assistantships (averaging $3,000 per year) were awarded; research assistantships, career-related internships or fieldwork, Federal Work-Study, institutionally sponsored loans, and tuition waivers (full) also available. Financial award application deadline: 4/1.
Faculty research: Family therapy, gerontology, resilience, parenting, adolescent development. *Total annual research expenditures:* $46,057.
Dr. James Deal, Chair, 701-231-7568, *Fax:* 701-231-9645, *E-mail:* jim_deal@ndsu.nodak.edu.
Application contact: Barb Morin Koehler, Administrative Assistant, 701-231-8628, *Fax:* 701-231-9645, *E-mail:* barb_morin_koehler@ndsu.nodak.edu. *Web site:* http://www.ndsu.nodak.edu/ndsu/ideal/cdfs/

■ NORTHERN ILLINOIS UNIVERSITY

Graduate School, College of Health and Human Sciences, School of Family, Consumer and Nutrition Sciences, Program in Applied Family and Child Studies, De Kalb, IL 60115-2854

AWARDS MS. Part-time programs available.

Faculty: 12 full-time (10 women), 1 (woman) part-time/adjunct.
Students: 10 full-time (all women), 15 part-time (14 women); includes 2 minority (1 African American, 1 Hispanic American). Average age 29. 36 applicants, 94% accepted, 20 enrolled. In 2001, 20 degrees awarded.
Degree requirements: For master's, internship, thesis optional.
Entrance requirements: For master's, GRE General Test, TOEFL, minimum GPA of 2.75, 9 hours in family and child studies. *Application deadline:* For fall admission, 1/15; for spring admission, 11/1. Applications are processed on a rolling basis. *Application fee:* $30.
Expenses: Tuition, state resident: full-time $5,124; part-time $148 per credit hour. Tuition, nonresident: full-time $8,666; part-time $295 per credit hour. Required fees: $51 per term.
Financial support: Fellowships with full tuition reimbursements, research assistantships with full tuition reimbursements, teaching assistantships with full tuition reimbursements, career-related internships or fieldwork, Federal Work-Study, tuition waivers (full), and unspecified assistantships available. Support available to part-time students.

■ NOVA SOUTHEASTERN UNIVERSITY

Fischler Graduate School of Education and Human Services, Programs in Child, Youth and Family Studies, Fort Lauderdale, FL 33314-7721

AWARDS Child and youth care administration (MS); child and youth studies (Ed D); early childhood education administration (MS); family support studies (MS); substance abuse counseling and education (MS). Evening/weekend programs available. Postbaccalaureate distance learning degree programs offered.

Students: 508 (388 women). In 2001, 21 master's, 86 doctorates awarded.
Degree requirements: For master's and doctorate, thesis/dissertation, practicum.
Entrance requirements: For master's, work experience in field. *Application deadline:* Applications are processed on a rolling basis. *Application fee:* $50.
Expenses: Contact institution.

Financial support: Career-related internships or fieldwork and Federal Work-Study available. Support available to part-time students.
Dr. Cleveland Clark, Director, 954-262-8601, *Fax:* 954-262-3912, *E-mail:* clarkc@nova.edu.
Application contact: Dr. Marcia Skapp, Director of Student Services, 800-986-8550 Ext. 8302, *Fax:* 954-262-3907, *E-mail:* skapp@nova.edu. *Web site:* http://www.fgse.nova.edu/cyfs.htm

■ THE OHIO STATE UNIVERSITY

Graduate School, College of Human Ecology, Department of Human Development and Family Science, Columbus, OH 43210

AWARDS Family and consumer sciences education (M Ed, MS, PhD); family relations and human development (MS, PhD).

Degree requirements: For master's, thesis optional; for doctorate, thesis/dissertation.
Entrance requirements: For master's and doctorate, GRE General Test.

■ OHIO UNIVERSITY

Graduate Studies, College of Health and Human Services, School of Human and Consumer Sciences, Athens, OH 45701-2979

AWARDS Child development and family life (MSHCS); food and nutrition (MSHCS).

Faculty: 13 full-time (9 women), 5 part-time/adjunct (all women).
Students: 6 full-time (all women), 9 part-time (all women); includes 1 minority (African American), 6 international. Average age 26. 17 applicants, 65% accepted, 6 enrolled. In 2001, 21 degrees awarded.
Degree requirements: For master's, thesis.
Entrance requirements: For master's, GRE. *Application deadline:* For fall admission, 8/30 (priority date). Applications are processed on a rolling basis. *Application fee:* $30.
Expenses: Tuition, state resident: full-time $6,585. Tuition, nonresident: full-time $12,254.
Financial support: In 2001–02, 6 teaching assistantships were awarded; career-related internships or fieldwork, Federal Work-Study, and institutionally sponsored loans also available. Financial award application deadline: 3/15.
Faculty research: Diversity, developmentally appropriate activities, death and dying, gerontology, sexuality education.
Dr. V. Ann Paulins, Director, 740-593-2880, *Fax:* 740-593-0289, *E-mail:* paulins@ohio.edu. *Web site:* http://www.cats.ohiou.edu/humanandconsumer/school.html

■ OKLAHOMA STATE UNIVERSITY

Graduate College, College of Human Environmental Sciences, Department of Family Relations and Child Development, Stillwater, OK 74078

AWARDS Family relations and child development (MS, PhD).

Faculty: 14 full-time (11 women), 3 part-time/adjunct (2 women).
Students: 21 full-time (18 women), 50 part-time (45 women); includes 6 minority (3 African Americans, 3 Native Americans), 1 international. Average age 34. 27 applicants, 96% accepted. In 2001, 10 degrees awarded.
Degree requirements: For master's and doctorate, thesis/dissertation.
Entrance requirements: For master's, GRE, TOEFL; for doctorate, GRE. *Application deadline:* For fall admission, 7/1 (priority date). *Application fee:* $25.
Expenses: Tuition, state resident: part-time $92 per credit hour. Tuition, nonresident: part-time $297 per credit hour. Required fees: $21 per credit hour. $14 per semester. One-time fee: $20. Tuition and fees vary according to course load.
Financial support: In 2001–02, 28 students received support, including 17 research assistantships (averaging $8,169 per year), 1 teaching assistantship (averaging $6,609 per year); career-related internships or fieldwork, Federal Work-Study, and tuition waivers (partial) also available. Support available to part-time students. Financial award application deadline: 3/1.
Faculty research: Family Relations and Child Development, consequences of adolescent parenting, family stress and coping, impacts of sexual abuse on families, children's social cognition and self-competence, gerontology and health care.
Dr. Kathleen Briggs, Interim Head, 405-744-5057.

■ OKLAHOMA STATE UNIVERSITY

Graduate College, College of Human Environmental Sciences, Program in Human Environmental Sciences, Stillwater, OK 74078

AWARDS Design, housing, and merchandising (PhD); family relations and child development (PhD); hotel and restaurant administration (PhD); nutritional sciences (PhD).

Faculty: 1 (woman) full-time.
Students: 23 full-time (14 women), 21 part-time (15 women); includes 7 minority (4 African Americans, 2 Asian Americans or Pacific Islanders, 1 Native American), 12 international. Average age 38. 14 applicants, 100% accepted. In 2001, 6 degrees awarded.
Degree requirements: For doctorate, thesis/dissertation.
Entrance requirements: For doctorate, TOEFL. *Application deadline:* For fall admission, 7/1 (priority date). *Application fee:* $25.
Expenses: Tuition, state resident: part-time $92 per credit hour. Tuition, nonresident: part-time $297 per credit hour. Required fees: $21 per credit hour. $14 per semester. One-time fee: $20. Tuition and fees vary according to course load.
Financial support: Research assistantships, teaching assistantships, career-related internships or fieldwork, Federal Work-Study, and tuition waivers (partial) available. Support available to part-time students. Financial award application deadline: 3/1.

■ OREGON STATE UNIVERSITY

Graduate School, College of Home Economics, Department of Human Development and Family Sciences, Corvallis, OR 97331

AWARDS Gerontology (MAIS); human development and family studies (MS, PhD).

Faculty: 19 full-time (18 women).
Students: 21 full-time (20 women), 7 part-time (all women); includes 4 minority (3 Asian Americans or Pacific Islanders, 1 Hispanic American), 7 international. Average age 36. In 2001, 3 master's, 4 doctorates awarded.
Degree requirements: For doctorate, thesis/dissertation.
Entrance requirements: For master's and doctorate, GRE, TOEFL, minimum GPA of 3.0 in last 90 hours. *Application deadline:* Applications are processed on a rolling basis. *Application fee:* $50.
Expenses: Tuition, area resident: Full-time $15,933. Tuition, state resident: full-time $28,937.
Financial support: Research assistantships, teaching assistantships, career-related internships or fieldwork, Federal Work-Study, and institutionally sponsored loans available. Support available to part-time students. Financial award application deadline: 2/1.
Dr. Alan Acock, Head, 541-737-4992, *Fax:* 541-737-1076, *E-mail:* alan.acock@orst.edu.

■ THE PENNSYLVANIA STATE UNIVERSITY UNIVERSITY PARK CAMPUS

Graduate School, College of Health and Human Development, Department of Human Development and Family Studies, State College, University Park, PA 16802-1503

AWARDS MS, PhD.

Students: 57 full-time (46 women), 4 part-time (3 women). In 2001, 11 master's, 15 doctorates awarded.

The Pennsylvania State University University Park Campus (continued)
Entrance requirements: For master's and doctorate, GRE General Test. *Application fee:* $45.
Expenses: Tuition, state resident: full-time $7,882; part-time $333 per credit. Tuition, nonresident: full-time $16,142; part-time $673 per credit. Required fees: $124 per semester.
Dr. Leann Birch, Head, 814-863-0241.
Application contact: Dr. Lisa J. Crockett, Chair, 814-863-8000.

Find an in-depth description at www.petersons.com/gradchannel.

■ PURDUE UNIVERSITY

Graduate School, School of Consumer and Family Sciences, Department of Child Development and Family Studies, West Lafayette, IN 47907

AWARDS Developmental studies (MS, PhD); family studies (MS, PhD); marriage and family therapy (MS, PhD). Part-time programs available.

Faculty: 19 full-time (14 women).
Students: 46 full-time (37 women), 20 part-time (15 women); includes 6 minority (3 African Americans, 1 Asian American or Pacific Islander, 2 Hispanic Americans), 11 international. Average age 29. 82 applicants, 48% accepted. In 2001, 13 master's, 10 doctorates awarded. Terminal master's awarded for partial completion of doctoral program.
Degree requirements: For master's and doctorate, thesis/dissertation.
Entrance requirements: For master's and doctorate, GRE General Test, TWE. *Application deadline:* For fall admission, 1/10. *Application fee:* $30. Electronic applications accepted.
Expenses: Tuition, state resident: full-time $4,164; part-time $149 per credit hour. Tuition, nonresident: full-time $13,872; part-time $458 per credit hour. Tuition and fees vary according to campus/location and program.
Financial support: In 2001–02, 50 students received support, including 1 fellowship with full tuition reimbursement available (averaging $13,299 per year), 26 research assistantships with full tuition reimbursements available (averaging $9,900 per year), 26 teaching assistantships with full tuition reimbursements available (averaging $9,900 per year); career-related internships or fieldwork also available. Support available to part-time students. Financial award application deadline: 1/15; financial award applicants required to submit FAFSA.
Faculty research: Inclusion of children with special needs, families as learning environments, relationships in child care, work-family relations, AIDS prevention.
Dr. D. R. Powell, Head, 765-494-9511.
Application contact: Becky Harshman, Graduate Secretary, 765-494-2965, *Fax:* 765-494-0503, *E-mail:* harshman@cfs.purdue.edu. *Web site:* http://www.cfs.purdue.edu/cdfs/

■ ROBERTS WESLEYAN COLLEGE

Division of Social Work and Social Sciences, Rochester, NY 14624-1997

AWARDS Child and family services (MSW); physical and mental health services (MSW).

Entrance requirements: For master's, minimum GPA of 2.75.
Faculty research: Religion and social work, family studies, values and ethics.

Find an in-depth description at www.petersons.com/gradchannel.

■ SAGE GRADUATE SCHOOL

Graduate School, Division of Psychology, Program in Community Psychology, Troy, NY 12180-4115

AWARDS Chemical dependence (MA); child care and children's services (MA); community counseling (MA); community health (MA); general psychology (MA); visual art therapy (MA).

Students: 10 full-time (9 women), 46 part-time (39 women); includes 2 minority (both African Americans). Average age 32. 20 applicants, 100% accepted, 14 enrolled. In 2001, 15 degrees awarded.
Degree requirements: For master's, thesis or alternative.
Entrance requirements: For master's, minimum GPA of 2.75. *Application deadline:* Applications are processed on a rolling basis. *Application fee:* $40.
Expenses: Tuition: Full-time $7,600. Required fees: $100.
Financial support: Application deadline: 3/1.
Dr. Pat O'Connor, Director, 518-244-2221, *E-mail:* oconnp@sage.edu.
Application contact: Melissa M. Robertson, Associate Director of Admissions, 518-244-6878, *Fax:* 518-244-6880, *E-mail:* sgsadm@sage.edu.

■ ST. CLOUD STATE UNIVERSITY

School of Graduate Studies, College of Education, Department of Child and Family Studies, St. Cloud, MN 56301-4498

AWARDS MS.

Faculty: 5 full-time (4 women), 4 part-time/adjunct (3 women).
Students: 5 full-time (4 women), 26 part-time (25 women). 17 applicants, 94% accepted. In 2001, 5 degrees awarded.
Degree requirements: For master's, thesis or alternative.
Entrance requirements: For master's, GRE General Test, minimum GPA of 2.75. *Application deadline:* Applications are processed on a rolling basis. *Application fee:* $35.
Expenses: Tuition, state resident: part-time $156 per credit. Tuition, nonresident: part-time $244 per credit. Required fees: $20 per credit.
Financial support: Federal Work-Study and unspecified assistantships available. Financial award application deadline: 3/1.
Dr. Robin Hasslen, Chair, 320-255-2132, *E-mail:* gpalm@stcloudstate.edu.
Application contact: Lindalou Krueger, Graduate Studies Office, 320-255-2113, *Fax:* 320-654-5371, *E-mail:* lekrueger@stcloudstate.edu.

■ SAINT JOSEPH COLLEGE

Graduate Division, Department of Counseling, West Hartford, CT 06117-2700

AWARDS Community counseling (MA), including child welfare, pastoral counseling; spirituality (Certificate). Part-time and evening/weekend programs available.

Faculty: 3 full-time (1 woman), 3 part-time/adjunct (2 women).
Students: 11 full-time (all women), 69 part-time (62 women); includes 7 minority (6 African Americans, 1 Hispanic American). Average age 33. In 2001, 24 degrees awarded.
Degree requirements: For master's, thesis optional.
Entrance requirements: For master's, GRE or MAT. *Application deadline:* Applications are processed on a rolling basis. *Application fee:* $25.
Expenses: Tuition: Part-time $475 per credit hour.
Financial support: In 2001–02, 2 research assistantships with full tuition reimbursements were awarded; tuition waivers (partial) and unspecified assistantships also available. Financial award application deadline: 7/15; financial award applicants required to submit FAFSA.
Dr. Richard W. Halstead, Chair, 860-231-5213, *E-mail:* rhalstead@sjc.edu. *Web site:* http://www.sjc.edu/

■ SAN JOSE STATE UNIVERSITY

Graduate Studies, College of Education, Child Development Program, San Jose, CA 95192-0001

AWARDS MA.

Students: 2 full-time (both women), 17 part-time (16 women); includes 6 minority (1 African American, 3 Asian Americans or Pacific Islanders, 2 Hispanic Americans), 1 international. Average age 33. 17 applicants, 41% accepted. In 2001, 2 degrees awarded.
Application deadline: For fall admission, 6/29; for spring admission, 11/30. Applications are processed on a rolling basis. *Application fee:* $59. Electronic applications accepted.
Expenses: Tuition, nonresident: part-time $246 per unit. Required fees: $678 per semester. Tuition and fees vary according to course load.

Financial support: Applicants required to submit FAFSA.
Dr. Chungsoon Kim, Chair, 408-924-3718, *Fax:* 408-924-3758.

■ SOUTH CAROLINA STATE UNIVERSITY

School of Graduate Studies, School of Applied Professional Sciences, Department of Family and Consumer Sciences, Orangeburg, SC 29117-0001

AWARDS Individual and family development (MS); nutritional sciences (MS). Part-time and evening/weekend programs available.

Degree requirements: For master's, departmental qualifying exam, thesis optional.
Entrance requirements: For master's, GRE, MAT, or NTE, minimum GPA of 2.7.
Faculty research: Societal competence, relationship of parent-child interaction to adult, quality of well-being of rural elders.

■ SOUTHWEST TEXAS STATE UNIVERSITY

Graduate School, College of Applied Arts, Department of Family and Consumer Science, Program in Family and Child Studies, San Marcos, TX 78666

AWARDS MS.

Faculty: 4 full-time (all women), 1 (woman) part-time/adjunct.
Students: 3 full-time (all women), 9 part-time (8 women); includes 7 minority (3 African Americans, 4 Hispanic Americans). Average age 30. 10 applicants, 80% accepted, 6 enrolled.
Degree requirements: For master's, thesis (for some programs).
Entrance requirements: For master's, GRE General Test, minimum GPA of 2.75 in last 60 hours. *Application deadline:* For fall admission, 6/15 (priority date); for spring admission, 10/15. Applications are processed on a rolling basis. *Application fee:* $40 ($90 for international students).
Expenses: Tuition, state resident: full-time $1,512; part-time $84 per credit hour. Tuition, nonresident: full-time $5,310; part-time $295 per credit hour. Required fees: $864; $29 per credit hour. $195 per term. Full-time tuition and fees vary according to course load.
Dr. Sue Williams, Graduate Advisor, 512-245-2415, *Fax:* 512-245-3829.

■ STANFORD UNIVERSITY

School of Education, Program in Psychological Studies in Education, Stanford, CA 94305-9991

AWARDS Child and adolescent development (PhD); counseling psychology (PhD); educational psychology (PhD).

Degree requirements: For doctorate, thesis/dissertation.
Entrance requirements: For doctorate, GRE General Test. *Application deadline:* For fall admission, 1/2. *Application fee:* $65 ($80 for international students). Electronic applications accepted.
Application contact: Graduate Admissions Office, 650-723-4794.

■ SYRACUSE UNIVERSITY

Graduate School, College of Human Services and Health Professions, Department of Child and Family Studies, Syracuse, NY 13244-0003

AWARDS MA, MS, PhD.

Faculty: 4 full-time (2 women), 1 part-time/adjunct (0 women).
Students: 36 full-time (31 women), 2 part-time (both women); includes 14 minority (7 African Americans, 7 Asian Americans or Pacific Islanders). Average age 34. 20 applicants, 75% accepted.
Degree requirements: For master's, comprehensive exam (for some programs); for doctorate, thesis/dissertation.
Entrance requirements: For master's and doctorate, GRE General Test. *Application deadline:* For fall admission, 5/15; for spring admission, 11/1. *Application fee:* $50. Electronic applications accepted.
Expenses: Tuition: Full-time $15,528; part-time $647 per credit. Required fees: $420; $38 per term. Tuition and fees vary according to program.
Financial support: Fellowships, research assistantships, teaching assistantships, Federal Work-Study and tuition waivers (partial) available.
Dr. Norma Burgess, Chair, 315-443-2757.
Application contact: Dr. Alan Taylor, Graduate Program Director, 315-443-1639.

■ TENNESSEE STATE UNIVERSITY

Graduate School, School of Agriculture and Family Services, Nashville, TN 37209-1561

AWARDS MS. Part-time and evening/weekend programs available.

Faculty: 8 full-time (5 women), 5 part-time/adjunct (1 woman).
Students: 5 full-time (3 women), 15 part-time (8 women); includes 17 minority (16 African Americans, 1 Hispanic American). Average age 35. 10 applicants, 60% accepted. In 2001, 5 degrees awarded.
Degree requirements: For master's, thesis.
Entrance requirements: For master's, GRE General Test, GRE Subject Test, MAT. *Application deadline:* Applications are processed on a rolling basis. *Application fee:* $15. Electronic applications accepted.
Expenses: Tuition, state resident: full-time $3,884; part-time $247 per hour. Tuition, nonresident: full-time $10,356; part-time $517 per hour.
Financial support: In 2001–02, 2 research assistantships (averaging $5,924 per year), 1 teaching assistantship (averaging $2,962 per year) were awarded.
Faculty research: Small farm economics, ornamental horticulture, beef cattle production, rural elderly.
Dr. Troy Wakefield, Dean, 615-963-7620, *E-mail:* twakefield@picard.tnstate.edu.

■ TEXAS TECH UNIVERSITY

Graduate School, College of Human Sciences, Department of Human Development and Family Studies, Lubbock, TX 79409

AWARDS Human development and family studies (MS, PhD); marriage and family therapy (MS, PhD).

Faculty: 21 full-time (12 women), 3 part-time/adjunct (all women).
Students: 49 full-time (38 women), 25 part-time (18 women); includes 11 minority (6 African Americans, 5 Hispanic Americans), 15 international. Average age 32. 49 applicants, 61% accepted, 15 enrolled. In 2001, 5 master's, 6 doctorates awarded.
Degree requirements: For master's and doctorate, thesis/dissertation.
Entrance requirements: For master's and doctorate, GRE General Test. *Application deadline:* Applications are processed on a rolling basis. *Application fee:* $25 ($50 for international students). Electronic applications accepted.
Expenses: Tuition, state resident: full-time $1,926; part-time $107 per credit hour. Tuition, nonresident: full-time $5,724; part-time $318 per credit hour. Required fees: $779; $737 per year. Tuition and fees vary according to course level, course load and program.
Financial support: In 2001–02, 57 students received support, including 26 research assistantships with partial tuition reimbursements available (averaging $11,313 per year), 24 teaching assistantships with partial tuition reimbursements available (averaging $11,641 per year); fellowships with tuition reimbursements available, career-related internships or fieldwork, Federal Work-Study, institutionally sponsored loans, and scholarships/grants also available. Support available to part-time students. Financial award application deadline: 5/1; financial award applicants required to submit FAFSA.
Faculty research: Parenting, marital and premarital relationships, adolescent drug abuse, early childhood, life span. *Total annual research expenditures:* $190,567.
Dr. Dean M. Busby, Chair, 806-742-3000, *Fax:* 806-742-0285, *E-mail:* dbusby@hs.ttu.edu.
Application contact: Graduate Adviser, 806-742-3000, *Fax:* 806-742-1849. *Web site:* http://www.hs.ttu.edu/HDFS/default.htm

■ TEXAS WOMAN'S UNIVERSITY

Graduate Studies and Research, College of Professional Education, Department of Family Sciences, Denton, TX 76201

AWARDS Child development (MS, PhD); counseling and development (MS); early childhood education (M Ed, MA, MS); family studies (MS, PhD); family therapy (MS, PhD). Part-time and evening/weekend programs available.

Faculty: 15 full-time (11 women), 3 part-time/adjunct (2 women).
Students: 42 full-time (36 women), 213 part-time (189 women); includes 41 minority (25 African Americans, 1 Asian American or Pacific Islander, 14 Hispanic Americans, 1 Native American), 12 international. Average age 39. 40 applicants, 88% accepted. In 2001, 28 master's, 8 doctorates awarded. Terminal master's awarded for partial completion of doctoral program.
Degree requirements: For doctorate, thesis/dissertation.
Application deadline: For fall admission, 1/7 (priority date); for spring admission, 8/31 (priority date). Applications are processed on a rolling basis. *Application fee:* $30.
Expenses: Tuition, state resident: part-time $90 per semester hour. Tuition, nonresident: part-time $303 per semester hour. Required fees: $24 per credit hour. $79 per semester.
Financial support: In 2001–02, 52 students received support, including 2 research assistantships, 5 teaching assistantships; career-related internships or fieldwork, institutionally sponsored loans, scholarships/grants, tuition waivers (partial), and graders also available. Support available to part-time students. Financial award application deadline: 2/1.
Faculty research: Parenting/parent education, family therapy counseling, early development, education, distance education.
Dr. Linda Ladd, Chair, 940-898-2685, *Fax:* 940-898-2676, *E-mail:* lladd@twu.edu. *Web site:* http://www.twu.edu/cope/famsci/

■ TUFTS UNIVERSITY

Division of Graduate and Continuing Studies and Research, Graduate School of Arts and Sciences, Department of Child Development, Medford, MA 02155

AWARDS Applied developmental psychology (PhD); child development (MA, CAGS); early childhood education (MAT). Part-time programs available.

Faculty: 10 full-time, 12 part-time/adjunct.
Students: 111 (99 women); includes 15 minority (6 African Americans, 6 Asian Americans or Pacific Islanders, 2 Hispanic Americans, 1 Native American) 10 international. 141 applicants, 75% accepted. In 2001, 36 master's, 1 doctorate awarded.
Degree requirements: For master's, thesis (for some programs); for doctorate, thesis/dissertation.
Entrance requirements: For master's and doctorate, GRE General Test, TOEFL. *Application deadline:* For fall admission, 1/15. Applications are processed on a rolling basis. *Application fee:* $50. Electronic applications accepted.
Expenses: Tuition: Full-time $26,853. Full-time tuition and fees vary according to program.
Financial support: Research assistantships with full and partial tuition reimbursements, teaching assistantships with full and partial tuition reimbursements, career-related internships or fieldwork, Federal Work-Study, scholarships/grants, and tuition waivers (partial) available. Support available to part-time students. Financial award application deadline: 2/15; financial award applicants required to submit FAFSA.
Ann Easterbrooks, Head, 617-627-3355, *Fax:* 617-627-3503, *E-mail:* sbarry@emerald.tufts.edu.
Application contact: Fred Rothbaum, Information Contact, 617-627-3355, *Fax:* 617-627-3503, *E-mail:* sbarry@emerald.tufts.edu. *Web site:* http://ase.tufts.edu/eped/

■ THE UNIVERSITY OF AKRON

Graduate School, College of Fine and Applied Arts, School of Family and Consumer Sciences, Program in Child Development, Akron, OH 44325-0001

AWARDS MA.

Students: 2 full-time (both women), 7 part-time (5 women). Average age 36. 2 applicants, 100% accepted, 1 enrolled. In 2001, 1 degree awarded.
Degree requirements: For master's, project or thesis.
Entrance requirements: For master's, GRE General Test, minimum GPA of 2.75. *Application deadline:* For fall admission, 8/15. Applications are processed on a rolling basis. *Application fee:* $40 ($50 for international students).
Expenses: Tuition, state resident: full-time $6,562; part-time $219 per credit. Tuition, nonresident: full-time $9,027; part-time $383 per credit. Required fees: $272; $11 per credit. Tuition and fees vary according to course load.
Financial support: Application deadline: 3/1.
Dr. Susan M. Witt, Assistant Professor, 330-972-7723, *E-mail:* susan8@uakron.edu.
Application contact: Dr. Virginia Gunn, Acting Director, 330-972-7729, *E-mail:* vgunn@uakron.edu.

■ THE UNIVERSITY OF AKRON

Graduate School, College of Fine and Applied Arts, School of Family and Consumer Sciences, Program in Child Life, Akron, OH 44325-0001

AWARDS MA.

Students: 2 full-time (both women), 3 part-time (all women). Average age 28. 4 applicants, 100% accepted, 1 enrolled.
Degree requirements: For master's, project or thesis.
Entrance requirements: For master's, GRE General Test, minimum GPA of 2.75. *Application deadline:* For fall admission, 8/15. Applications are processed on a rolling basis. *Application fee:* $40 ($50 for international students).
Expenses: Tuition, state resident: full-time $6,562; part-time $219 per credit. Tuition, nonresident: full-time $9,027; part-time $383 per credit. Required fees: $272; $11 per credit. Tuition and fees vary according to course load.
Financial support: Application deadline: 3/1.
Dr. Jeanne Thibo Karns, Assistant Professor, 330-972-8040, *E-mail:* jtkarns@uakron.edu.
Application contact: Dr. Virginia Gunn, Acting Director, 330-972-7729, *E-mail:* vgunn@uakron.edu.

■ THE UNIVERSITY OF AKRON

Graduate School, College of Fine and Applied Arts, School of Family and Consumer Sciences, Program in Family Development, Akron, OH 44325-0001

AWARDS MA.

Students: Average age 43. 2 applicants, 100% accepted, 1 enrolled. In 2001, 3 degrees awarded.
Degree requirements: For master's, project or thesis.
Entrance requirements: For master's, GRE General Test, minimum GPA of 2.75. *Application deadline:* For fall admission, 8/15. Applications are processed on a rolling basis. *Application fee:* $40 ($50 for international students).
Expenses: Tuition, state resident: full-time $6,562; part-time $219 per credit. Tuition, nonresident: full-time $9,027; part-time $383 per credit. Required fees: $272; $11 per credit. Tuition and fees vary according to course load.
Financial support: Application deadline: 3/1.
Dr. David D. Witt, Professor, 330-972-6044, *E-mail:* dwitt@uakron.edu.
Application contact: Dr. Virginia Gunn, Acting Director, 330-972-7729, *E-mail:* vgunn@uakron.edu.

■ THE UNIVERSITY OF ALABAMA

Graduate School, College of Human Environmental Sciences, Department of Human Development and Family Studies, Tuscaloosa, AL 35487

AWARDS MSHES.

Faculty: 8 full-time (5 women).
Students: 11 full-time (9 women), 9 part-time (all women); includes 3 minority (2 African Americans, 1 Hispanic American). Average age 29. 2 applicants, 50% accepted, 1 enrolled. In 2001, 6 degrees awarded.
Degree requirements: For master's, thesis (for some programs).
Entrance requirements: For master's, GRE General Test or MAT, minimum GPA of 3.0. *Application deadline:* For fall admission, 7/6. Applications are processed on a rolling basis. *Application fee:* $25.
Expenses: Tuition, state resident: full-time $3,292; part-time $183 per credit hour. Tuition, nonresident: full-time $8,912; part-time $495 per credit hour. Tuition and fees vary according to course load, campus/location and program.
Financial support: In 2001–02, 7 research assistantships with full tuition reimbursements (averaging $8,100 per year), 3 teaching assistantships with full tuition reimbursements (averaging $8,100 per year) were awarded. Career-related internships or fieldwork, Federal Work-Study, and scholarships/grants also available. Financial award application deadline: 3/15.
Faculty research: Parent/child relationships, psychosocial care of hospitalized children, family care to elders, moral judgment development, family strengths and adolescent wildness.
Dr. Stephen J. Thoma, Chair and Professor, 205-348-8146, *Fax:* 205-348-3789, *E-mail:* sthoma@ches.ua.edu. *Web site:* http://www.ches.ua.edu/

■ THE UNIVERSITY OF ARIZONA

Graduate College, College of Agriculture and Life Sciences, School of Family and Consumer Sciences, Division of Family Studies and Human Development, Tucson, AZ 85721

AWARDS Family and consumer sciences (MS); family studies and human development (PhD). Terminal master's awarded for partial completion of doctoral program.

Entrance requirements: For master's and doctorate, GRE General Test, TOEFL, minimum undergraduate GPA of 3.0.
Expenses: Tuition, state resident: full-time $2,490; part-time $436 per unit. Tuition, nonresident: full-time $10,300; part-time $436 per unit. Full-time tuition and fees vary according to degree level and program. *Web site:* http://ag.arizona.edu/fcs/fshd

■ UNIVERSITY OF CALIFORNIA, DAVIS

Graduate Studies, Graduate Group in Child Development, Davis, CA 95616

AWARDS MS.

Faculty: 19 full-time (10 women), 1 part-time/adjunct (0 women).
Students: 18 full-time (15 women); includes 2 minority (1 African American, 1 Native American), 3 international. Average age 30. 16 applicants, 56% accepted, 4 enrolled. In 2001, 6 degrees awarded.
Degree requirements: For master's, thesis optional.
Entrance requirements: For master's, GRE General Test, minimum GPA of 3.0. *Application deadline:* For fall admission, 4/1. *Application fee:* $60. Electronic applications accepted.
Expenses: Tuition, state resident: full-time $4,831. Tuition, nonresident: full-time $15,725.
Financial support: In 2001–02, 17 students received support, including 10 fellowships with full and partial tuition reimbursements available (averaging $2,342 per year), 3 research assistantships with full and partial tuition reimbursements available (averaging $6,141 per year), 8 teaching assistantships with partial tuition reimbursements available (averaging $14,145 per year); Federal Work-Study, institutionally sponsored loans, scholarships/grants, traineeships, and tuition waivers (full and partial) also available. Financial award application deadline: 1/15; financial award applicants required to submit FAFSA.
Faculty research: Cognitive development, socio-emotional development, early childhood.
Lawrence Harper, Graduate Chair, 530-752-3624, *Fax:* 530-752-5660, *E-mail:* lharper@ucdavis.edu.
Application contact: Judy Erwin, Graduate Assistant, 530-752-1926, *Fax:* 530-752-5660, *E-mail:* gjerwin@ucdavis.edu. *Web site:* http://hcd.ucdavis.edu/

■ UNIVERSITY OF CONNECTICUT

Graduate School, School of Family Studies, Field of Family Studies, Storrs, CT 06269

AWARDS PhD.

Degree requirements: For doctorate, thesis/dissertation.
Entrance requirements: For doctorate, GRE General Test, MAT, TOEFL.

■ UNIVERSITY OF CONNECTICUT

Graduate School, School of Family Studies, Field of Human Development and Family Relations, Storrs, CT 06269

AWARDS MA, PhD.

Degree requirements: For doctorate, thesis/dissertation.
Entrance requirements: For master's, GRE General Test, TOEFL.

■ UNIVERSITY OF DELAWARE

College of Human Services, Education and Public Policy, Department of Individual and Family Studies, Newark, DE 19716

AWARDS Family studies (PhD); individual and family studies (MS). Part-time programs available.

Faculty: 23 full-time (16 women).
Students: 27 full-time (22 women), 12 part-time (11 women); includes 8 minority (7 African Americans, 1 Hispanic American), 4 international. Average age 34. 14 applicants, 64% accepted, 8 enrolled. In 2001, 10 master's, 1 doctorate awarded. Terminal master's awarded for partial completion of doctoral program.
Degree requirements: For master's, thesis or alternative; for doctorate, thesis/dissertation.
Entrance requirements: For master's and doctorate, GRE General Test, TOEFL, letters of recommendation (3). *Application deadline:* For fall admission, 2/1. *Application fee:* $50. Electronic applications accepted.
Expenses: Tuition, state resident: full-time $4,770; part-time $265 per credit. Tuition, nonresident: full-time $13,860; part-time $770 per credit. Required fees: $414.
Financial support: In 2001–02, 20 students received support, including 1 fellowship with full tuition reimbursement available (averaging $11,000 per year), 16 research assistantships with full tuition reimbursements available (averaging $11,000 per year), 3 teaching assistantships with full tuition reimbursements available (averaging $11,000 per year); career-related internships or fieldwork and institutionally sponsored loans also available. Financial award application deadline: 2/1.
Faculty research: Early childhood inclusive education, relationships, family risk and resilience, disability issues, program development and evaluation.
Dr. Michael Ferrari, Interim Chair, 302-831-8566, *Fax:* 302-831-8776, *E-mail:* mferrari@udel.edu.
Application contact: Dr. Penny Deiner, Graduate Coordinator, 302-831-6932, *Fax:* 302-831-8776, *E-mail:* pennyd@udel.edu. *Web site:* http://www.udel.edu/ifst/

■ UNIVERSITY OF DENVER

College of Education, Denver, CO 80208

AWARDS Counseling psychology (MA, PhD); curriculum and instruction (MA, PhD), including curriculum leadership; educational psychology (MA, PhD, Ed S), including child and family studies (MA, PhD), quantitative research methods (MA, PhD), school psychology (PhD, Ed S); higher education and adult studies (MA, PhD); school administration (PhD). Part-time and evening/weekend

University of Denver (continued)
programs available. Postbaccalaureate distance learning degree programs offered (no on-campus study).
Faculty: 25 full-time (16 women), 1 (woman) part-time/adjunct.
Students: 392 (312 women); includes 47 minority (10 African Americans, 11 Asian Americans or Pacific Islanders, 23 Hispanic Americans, 3 Native Americans) 12 international. Average age 31. 352 applicants, 68% accepted. In 2001, 71 master's, 27 doctorates awarded.
Degree requirements: For master's, comprehensive exam; for doctorate, 2 foreign languages, thesis/dissertation, comprehensive exam.
Entrance requirements: For master's and doctorate, GRE General Test, TSE. *Application deadline:* For fall admission, 1/1. Applications are processed on a rolling basis. *Application fee:* $45. Electronic applications accepted.
Expenses: Tuition: Full-time $21,456.
Financial support: In 2001–02, 92 students received support, including 7 fellowships with full and partial tuition reimbursements available, 1 research assistantship with full and partial tuition reimbursement available (averaging $7,785 per year), 19 teaching assistantships with full and partial tuition reimbursements available (averaging $7,677 per year); career-related internships or fieldwork, Federal Work-Study, institutionally sponsored loans, and scholarships/grants also available. Support available to part-time students. Financial award application deadline: 3/1; financial award applicants required to submit FAFSA.
Faculty research: Parkinson's disease, personnel training, development and assessments, gifted education, sexual functioning, service learning. *Total annual research expenditures:* $369,539.
Dr. Virginia Maloney, Dean, 303-871-3828.
Application contact: Linda McCarthy, Contact, 303-871-2509. *Web site:* http://www.du.edu/education/

■ UNIVERSITY OF GEORGIA

Graduate School, College of Family and Consumer Sciences, Department of Child and Family Development, Athens, GA 30602

AWARDS MFCS, MS, PhD.

Faculty: 18 full-time (10 women).
Students: 39 full-time (33 women), 15 part-time (11 women); includes 11 minority (7 African Americans, 4 Hispanic Americans), 4 international. 64 applicants, 30% accepted. In 2001, 2 master's, 8 doctorates awarded.
Degree requirements: For master's, thesis (MS); for doctorate, thesis/dissertation.
Entrance requirements: For master's and doctorate, GRE General Test. *Application deadline:* For fall admission, 7/1 (priority date); for spring admission, 11/15. *Application fee:* $30. Electronic applications accepted.
Expenses: Tuition, state resident: full-time $2,376; part-time $132 per credit hour. Tuition, nonresident: full-time $9,504; part-time $528 per credit hour. Required fees: $236 per semester.
Financial support: Fellowships, research assistantships, teaching assistantships, unspecified assistantships available.
Dr. David Wright, Head, 706-542-4844, *Fax:* 706-542-4389, *E-mail:* dwright@fcs.uga.edu.
Application contact: Dr. Lynda Walters, Graduate Coordinator, 706-542-4859, *Fax:* 706-542-4389, *E-mail:* lwalters@fcs.uga.edu. *Web site:* http://www.fcs.uga.edu/cfd/

■ UNIVERSITY OF GREAT FALLS

Graduate Studies Division, Program in Human Services, Great Falls, MT 59405

AWARDS Chemical dependent services (MHSA); family services (MHSA). Part-time and evening/weekend programs available. Postbaccalaureate distance learning degree programs offered (minimal on-campus study).

Faculty: 6 full-time (3 women), 10 part-time/adjunct (6 women).
Students: 6 full-time (4 women), 6 part-time (5 women); includes 4 minority (all Native Americans). Average age 41. 20 applicants, 100% accepted. In 2001, 6 degrees awarded. *Median time to degree:* Master's–1 year full-time, 1.5 years part-time.
Entrance requirements: For master's, GRE General Test or MAT. *Application deadline:* For fall admission, 8/15 (priority date); for winter admission, 11/15 (priority date); for spring admission, 12/15 (priority date). Applications are processed on a rolling basis. *Application fee:* $35.
Expenses: Tuition: Part-time $440 per credit. One-time fee: $35 full-time.
Financial support: In 2001–02, 2 research assistantships were awarded; fellowships, career-related internships or fieldwork, Federal Work-Study, and institutionally sponsored loans also available. Support available to part-time students. Financial award application deadline: 3/1.
Dr. Deborah J. Kottel, Dean, 406-791-5339, *Fax:* 406-793-5990, *E-mail:* dkottel@ugf.edu.

■ UNIVERSITY OF ILLINOIS AT SPRINGFIELD

Graduate Programs, College of Education and Human Services, Program in Human Services, Springfield, IL 62703-5404

AWARDS Alcoholism and substance abuse (MA); child and family studies (MA); gerontology (MA); social services administration (MA).

Faculty: 7 full-time (3 women), 10 part-time/adjunct (7 women).
Students: 44 full-time (32 women), 109 part-time (79 women); includes 32 minority (29 African Americans, 1 Asian American or Pacific Islander, 1 Hispanic American, 1 Native American), 2 international. Average age 37. 55 applicants, 85% accepted, 38 enrolled. In 2001, 16 degrees awarded.
Expenses: Tuition, state resident: full-time $2,680. Tuition, nonresident: full-time $8,064. Required fees: $626. One-time fee: $626.
Financial support: In 2001–02, 71 students received support, including 9 research assistantships (averaging $6,300 per year)
Rachell Anderson, Director, 217-206-7335.

■ UNIVERSITY OF KENTUCKY

Graduate School, College of Human Environmental Sciences, Program in Family Studies, Human Development, and Resource Management, Lexington, KY 40506-0032

AWARDS MSFAM, PhD.

Faculty: 23 full-time (16 women).
Students: 35 full-time (30 women), 11 part-time (10 women); includes 6 African Americans, 1 Native American. 39 applicants, 51% accepted. In 2001, 13 degrees awarded.
Degree requirements: For master's, thesis optional.
Entrance requirements: For master's, GRE General Test, minimum undergraduate GPA of 2.5. *Application deadline:* For fall admission, 2/15; for spring admission, 8/15. *Application fee:* $30 ($35 for international students).
Expenses: Tuition, state resident: full-time $4,075; part-time $213 per credit hour. Tuition, nonresident: full-time $11,295; part-time $614 per credit hour.
Financial support: In 2001–02, 2 fellowships, 10 research assistantships, 13 teaching assistantships were awarded. Unspecified assistantships also available.
Faculty research: Early childhood education, family therapy, family resource management and consumer studies, human development.
Dr. Stephan Wilson, Chair, 859-257-8900, *Fax:* 859-257-4095, *E-mail:* swilson@uky.edu.
Application contact: Dr. Jeannine Blackwell, Associate Dean, 859-257-4905, *Fax:* 859-323-1928.

■ UNIVERSITY OF LA VERNE

School of Education and Organizational Leadership, Department of Education, Program in Child Development/Child Life, La Verne, CA 91750-4443

AWARDS Child development (MS); child life (MS). Part-time programs available.

Faculty: 17 full-time (12 women), 56 part-time/adjunct (35 women).
Students: 8 full-time (all women), 17 part-time (all women); includes 12 minority (2 African Americans, 5 Asian Americans or Pacific Islanders, 5 Hispanic Americans), 1 international. Average age 33. In 2001, 9 degrees awarded.
Entrance requirements: For master's, TOEFL, minimum GPA of 2.5. *Application deadline:* Applications are processed on a rolling basis. *Application fee:* $40.
Expenses: Tuition: Full-time $4,410; part-time $245 per unit. Required fees: $60. Tuition and fees vary according to course load, degree level, campus/location and program.
Financial support: In 2001–02, 18 students received support, including 2 research assistantships (averaging $510 per year); fellowships, teaching assistantships, institutionally sponsored loans and scholarships/grants also available. Financial award application deadline: 3/2; financial award applicants required to submit FAFSA.
Dr. Barbara Nicoll, Chairperson, 909-593-3511 Ext. 4632, *Fax:* 909-392-2710, *E-mail:* nicollb@ulv.edu.
Application contact: Jo Nell Baker, Director, Graduate Admissions and Academic Services, 909-593-3511 Ext. 4504, *Fax:* 909-392-2761, *E-mail:* bakerj@ulv.edu. *Web site:* http://www.ulv.edu/education/

■ UNIVERSITY OF MARYLAND, COLLEGE PARK

Graduate Studies and Research, College of Health and Human Performance, Department of Family Studies, College Park, MD 20742

AWARDS Family studies (MS, PhD); marriage and family therapy (MS). Part-time and evening/weekend programs available.

Faculty: 11 full-time (7 women), 11 part-time/adjunct (7 women).
Students: 31 full-time (25 women), 13 part-time (12 women); includes 12 minority (7 African Americans, 1 Asian American or Pacific Islander, 4 Hispanic Americans), 1 international. 68 applicants, 59% accepted, 21 enrolled. In 2001, 16 master's, 1 doctorate awarded.
Degree requirements: For master's, thesis or alternative.
Entrance requirements: For master's and doctorate, GRE General Test, minimum GPA of 3.0. *Application deadline:* For fall admission, 2/1; for spring admission, 11/15. Applications are processed on a rolling basis. *Application fee:* $50 ($70 for international students). Electronic applications accepted.
Expenses: Tuition, state resident: part-time $289 per credit hour. Tuition, nonresident: part-time $448 per credit hour. One-time fee: $436 part-time. Full-time tuition and fees vary according to course load, campus/location and program.
Financial support: In 2001–02, 12 fellowships with full tuition reimbursements (averaging $11,158 per year), 3 research assistantships with tuition reimbursements (averaging $10,153 per year), 9 teaching assistantships with tuition reimbursements (averaging $8,768 per year) were awarded. Career-related internships or fieldwork, Federal Work-Study, and scholarships/grants also available. Support available to part-time students. Financial award applicants required to submit FAFSA.
Faculty research: Family life quality.
Dr. Sally Koblinsky, Chairman, 301-405-4009, *Fax:* 301-314-9161.
Application contact: Trudy Lindsey, Director, Graduate Admissions and Records, 301-405-6991, *Fax:* 301-314-9305, *E-mail:* grschool@deans.umd.edu.

Find an in-depth description at www.petersons.com/gradchannel.

■ UNIVERSITY OF MINNESOTA, TWIN CITIES CAMPUS

Graduate School, College of Human Ecology, Department of Family Social Science, Minneapolis, MN 55455-0213

AWARDS MA, PhD.

Degree requirements: For master's and doctorate, thesis/dissertation.
Entrance requirements: For master's and doctorate, GRE General Test, TOEFL, minimum undergraduate GPA of 3.0.
Expenses: Tuition, state resident: full-time $2,932; part-time $489 per credit. Tuition, nonresident: full-time $5,758; part-time $960 per credit. Part-time tuition and fees vary according to course load, program and reciprocity agreements.
Faculty research: Aging, economic consequences of divorce, farm family loss, Alzheimer's disease and ambiguous loss, adoptive family relationships.

■ UNIVERSITY OF MISSOURI–COLUMBIA

Graduate School, College of Human Environmental Science, Department of Human Development and Family Studies, Columbia, MO 65211

AWARDS MA, MS, PhD.

Faculty: 13 full-time (10 women).
Students: 22 full-time (20 women), 11 part-time (10 women); includes 3 minority (all African Americans), 5 international. 3 applicants, 33% accepted. In 2001, 17 degrees awarded.
Entrance requirements: For master's, GRE General Test, minimum GPA of 3.0. *Application deadline:* For fall admission, 2/1 (priority date); for winter admission, 11/15 (priority date). Applications are processed on a rolling basis. *Application fee:* $25 ($50 for international students).
Expenses: Tuition, state resident: part-time $179 per credit hour. Tuition, nonresident: part-time $539 per credit hour. Required fees: $122 per semester. Tuition and fees vary according to program.
Financial support: Research assistantships, teaching assistantships, institutionally sponsored loans available.
Dr. Marilyn Coleman, Director of Graduate Studies, 573-882-4360, *E-mail:* colemanma@missouri.edu. *Web site:* http://web.missouri.edu/~hdfswww/

■ UNIVERSITY OF NEBRASKA–LINCOLN

Graduate College, College of Human Resources and Family Sciences, Department of Family and Consumer Science, Lincoln, NE 68588

AWARDS Family and consumer sciences (MS); human resources and family sciences (PhD). Postbaccalaureate distance learning degree programs offered.

Faculty: 28.
Students: 25 (20 women); includes 2 minority (1 African American, 1 Hispanic American) 2 international. Average age 32. 19 applicants, 53% accepted, 6 enrolled. In 2001, 5 degrees awarded.
Degree requirements: For master's, thesis optional.
Entrance requirements: For master's, GRE General Test, TOEFL. *Application deadline:* For fall admission, 2/1; for spring admission, 10/1. *Application fee:* $35. Electronic applications accepted.
Expenses: Tuition, state resident: full-time $2,412; part-time $134 per credit. Tuition, nonresident: full-time $6,223; part-time $346 per credit. Tuition and fees vary according to course load.
Financial support: In 2001–02, 1 fellowship, 5 research assistantships, 2 teaching assistantships were awarded. Federal Work-Study, health care benefits, and unspecified assistantships also available. Financial award application deadline: 2/15.
Faculty research: Marriage and family therapy, child development/early childhood education, family financial management.
Dr. Julie Johnson, Interim Chair, 402-472-2957. *Web site:* http://www.chrfs.unl.edu/FCS.htm/

■ UNIVERSITY OF NEVADA, RENO

Graduate School, College of Human and Community Sciences, Department of Human Development and Family Studies, Reno, NV 89557

AWARDS MS.

Faculty: 10.
Students: 9 full-time (all women), 8 part-time (all women); includes 2 minority (1 Hispanic American, 1 Native American), 1 international. Average age 36. In 2001, 3 degrees awarded.
Degree requirements: For master's, thesis.

University of Nevada, Reno (continued)
Entrance requirements: For master's, TOEFL, GRE General Test, minimum GPA of 3.0. *Application deadline:* For fall admission, 3/1; for spring admission, 10/1. *Application fee:* $40.
Expenses: Tuition, state resident: full-time $2,067; part-time $108 per credit. Tuition, nonresident: full-time $9,282; part-time $109 per credit. Required fees: $57 per semester. Tuition and fees vary according to course load.
Financial support: In 2001–02, 10 research assistantships, 2 teaching assistantships were awarded. Financial award application deadline: 3/1.
Colleen I. Murray, Graduate Program Director, 775-784-6490, *E-mail:* cimurray@scs.unr.edu.

■ UNIVERSITY OF NEW HAMPSHIRE

Graduate School, School of Health and Human Services, Department of Family Studies, Durham, NH 03824

AWARDS Family studies (MS); marriage and family therapy (MS). Part-time programs available.

Faculty: 8 full-time.
Students: 16 full-time (13 women), 11 part-time (10 women); includes 2 minority (1 Asian American or Pacific Islander, 1 Hispanic American), 2 international. Average age 30. 12 applicants, 83% accepted, 6 enrolled.
Degree requirements: For master's, thesis or alternative.
Entrance requirements: For master's, GRE General Test. *Application deadline:* For fall admission, 4/1 (priority date); for winter admission, 12/1. Applications are processed on a rolling basis. *Application fee:* $50. Electronic applications accepted.
Expenses: Tuition, state resident: full-time $6,300; part-time $350 per credit. Tuition, nonresident: full-time $15,720; part-time $643 per credit. Required fees: $560; $280 per term. One-time fee: $15 part-time. Tuition and fees vary according to course load.
Financial support: In 2001–02, 7 teaching assistantships were awarded; fellowships, research assistantships, career-related internships or fieldwork, Federal Work-Study, scholarships/grants, and tuition waivers (full and partial) also available. Support available to part-time students. Financial award application deadline: 2/15.
Dr. Kristine Baber, Chairperson, 603-862-2160, *E-mail:* dkmbaber@cisunix.unh.edu.
Application contact: Dr. Larry Hansen, Coordinator, 603-862-2146, *E-mail:* ljhansen@cisunix.unh.edu. *Web site:* http://www.unh.edu/family-studies/

■ UNIVERSITY OF NEW MEXICO

Graduate School, College of Education, Department of Individual, Family and Community Education, Program in Family Studies, Albuquerque, NM 87131-2039

AWARDS MA, PhD. Part-time programs available.

Faculty: 7 full-time (5 women), 1 (woman) part-time/adjunct.
Students: 10 full-time (9 women), 19 part-time (17 women); includes 11 minority (10 Hispanic Americans, 1 Native American). Average age 41. 5 applicants, 60% accepted, 3 enrolled. In 2001, 7 master's, 2 doctorates awarded. Terminal master's awarded for partial completion of doctoral program.
Degree requirements: For doctorate, thesis/dissertation.
Entrance requirements: For master's, GRE General Test, 18 hours in behavioral science; for doctorate, GRE General Test. *Application deadline:* For fall admission, 3/15; for spring admission, 10/15. *Application fee:* $40.
Expenses: Tuition, state resident: full-time $2,771; part-time $115 per credit hour. Tuition, nonresident: full-time $11,207; part-time $467 per credit hour. Required fees: $570; $24 per credit hour. Part-time tuition and fees vary according to course load and program.
Financial support: In 2001–02, 14 students received support, including 2 teaching assistantships with full tuition reimbursements available (averaging $11,000 per year); health care benefits also available. Financial award application deadline: 3/1; financial award applicants required to submit FAFSA.
Faculty research: Home, community, school relations; multicultural issues; parent-child interactions; adolescent development; fathering.
Application contact: 505-277-4535, *Fax:* 505-277-8361, *E-mail:* currie@unm.edu.

■ THE UNIVERSITY OF NORTH CAROLINA AT CHARLOTTE

Graduate School, College of Education, Department of Counseling, Special Education and Child Development, Charlotte, NC 28223-0001

AWARDS Child and family studies (M Ed); community and school counseling (MA); counseling (PhD); special education (M Ed, PhD). Part-time and evening/weekend programs available. Postbaccalaureate distance learning degree programs offered (no on-campus study).

Faculty: 25 full-time (18 women), 9 part-time/adjunct (all women).
Students: 83 full-time (70 women), 119 part-time (108 women); includes 33 minority (31 African Americans, 1 Asian American or Pacific Islander, 1 Native American), 2 international. Average age 33. 164 applicants, 69% accepted, 91 enrolled. In 2001, 63 degrees awarded.
Application deadline: For fall admission, 7/15; for spring admission, 11/15. Applications are processed on a rolling basis. *Application fee:* $35. Electronic applications accepted.
Expenses: Tuition, state resident: full-time $1,483; part-time $371 per year. Tuition, nonresident: full-time $9,850; part-time $2,463 per year. Required fees: $1,043; $277 per year. Tuition and fees vary according to course load.
Financial support: In 2001–02, 6 fellowships (averaging $2,792 per year), 9 research assistantships, 3 teaching assistantships were awarded. Career-related internships or fieldwork, Federal Work-Study, institutionally sponsored loans, scholarships/grants, and unspecified assistantships also available. Support available to part-time students. Financial award application deadline: 4/1; financial award applicants required to submit FAFSA.
Dr. Richard B. White, Chair, 704-687-2531, *Fax:* 704-687-2916, *E-mail:* rbwhite@email.uncc.edu.
Application contact: Kathy Barringer, Director of Graduate Admissions, 704-687-3366, *Fax:* 704-687-3279, *E-mail:* gradadm@email.uncc.edu.

■ THE UNIVERSITY OF NORTH CAROLINA AT GREENSBORO

Graduate School, School of Human Environmental Sciences, Department of Human Development and Family Studies, Greensboro, NC 27412-5001

AWARDS Human development and family studies (M Ed, MS, PhD).

Faculty: 14 full-time (11 women), 1 part-time/adjunct (0 women).
Students: 20 full-time (15 women), 26 part-time (25 women); includes 11 minority (10 African Americans, 1 Native American), 4 international. 35 applicants, 46% accepted, 14 enrolled. In 2001, 10 master's, 3 doctorates awarded.
Degree requirements: For master's, one foreign language; for doctorate, one foreign language, thesis/dissertation.
Entrance requirements: For master's and doctorate, GRE General Test, TOEFL. *Application deadline:* For fall admission, 3/15. *Application fee:* $35.
Expenses: Contact institution.
Financial support: In 2001–02, 3 fellowships with full tuition reimbursements (averaging $4,666 per year), 29 research assistantships with full tuition reimbursements (averaging $9,767 per year), 4 teaching assistantships with full tuition reimbursements (averaging $8,000 per year) were awarded. Career-related internships or fieldwork, Federal Work-Study, scholarships/grants, traineeships, and unspecified assistantships also available. Support available to part-time students.

Faculty research: Adolescent mothers, multihandicapped, older adults.
Dr. David Demo, Chair, 336-334-5307, *Fax:* 336-334-5076, *E-mail:* dhdemo@office.uncg.edu.
Application contact: Dr. James Lynch, Director of Graduate Recruitment and Information Services, 336-334-4881, *Fax:* 336-334-4424. *Web site:* http://www.uncg.edu/hdf/

■ UNIVERSITY OF NORTH TEXAS

Robert B. Toulouse School of Graduate Studies, College of Education, Department of Counseling, Development and Higher Education, Program in Development and Family Studies, Denton, TX 76203

AWARDS MS. Evening/weekend programs available.

Students: 27.
Degree requirements: For master's, thesis optional.
Entrance requirements: For master's, GRE General Test. *Application deadline:* For fall admission, 7/17. *Application fee:* $25 ($50 for international students).
Expenses: Tuition, state resident: part-time $186 per hour. Tuition, nonresident: part-time $319 per hour. Required fees: $88; $21 per hour.
Financial support: Teaching assistantships, career-related internships or fieldwork, Federal Work-Study, and institutionally sponsored loans available. Financial award application deadline: 4/1.
Application contact: Arminta Jacobson, Adviser, 940-565-2910.

■ UNIVERSITY OF PITTSBURGH

School of Education, Department of Psychology in Education, Program in Child Development, Pittsburgh, PA 15260

AWARDS MS. Part-time and evening/weekend programs available.

Students: 12 full-time (11 women), 26 part-time (22 women); includes 6 minority (5 African Americans, 1 Asian American or Pacific Islander), 2 international. 29 applicants, 100% accepted, 26 enrolled. In 2001, 11 degrees awarded.
Degree requirements: For master's, thesis.
Entrance requirements: For master's, TOEFL. *Application deadline:* For fall admission, 2/1. *Application fee:* $40. Electronic applications accepted.
Expenses: Tuition, state resident: full-time $9,410; part-time $385 per credit. Tuition, nonresident: full-time $19,376; part-time $797 per credit. Required fees: $480; $90 per term. Tuition and fees vary according to program.
Financial support: Tuition waivers (partial) available. Support available to part-time students. Financial award applicants required to submit FAFSA.
Application contact: Jackie Harden, Manager, 412-648-2230, *Fax:* 412-648-1899, *E-mail:* soeinfo@pitt.edu. *Web site:* http://www.education.pitt.edu/programs/childdev/

■ UNIVERSITY OF RHODE ISLAND

Graduate School, College of Human Science and Services, Department of Human Development, Counseling, and Family Studies, Kingston, RI 02881

AWARDS Guidance and counseling (MS); marriage and family therapy (MS). Evening/weekend programs available.

Entrance requirements: For master's, GRE or MAT. *Application deadline:* For fall admission, 4/15 (priority date); for spring admission, 11/15. Applications are processed on a rolling basis. *Application fee:* $35.
Expenses: Tuition, state resident: full-time $3,756; part-time $209 per credit. Tuition, nonresident: full-time $10,774; part-time $599 per credit. Required fees: $1,586; $76 per credit. One-time fee: $60 full-time.
Financial support: Career-related internships or fieldwork available.
Dr. Barbara Newman, Chair, 401-874-2440.

■ UNIVERSITY OF SOUTHERN MISSISSIPPI

Graduate School, College of Health and Human Sciences, School of Family and Consumer Sciences, Hattiesburg, MS 39406

AWARDS Early intervention (MS); family and consumer studies (MS); human nutrition (MS); institution management (MS); marriage and family therapy (MS); nutrition and food systems (PhD). Part-time programs available.

Faculty: 19 full-time (15 women), 3 part-time/adjunct (all women).
Students: 48 full-time (39 women), 30 part-time (29 women); includes 19 minority (14 African Americans, 3 Asian Americans or Pacific Islanders, 2 Hispanic Americans). Average age 32. 63 applicants, 54% accepted. In 2001, 26 master's, 4 doctorates awarded.
Degree requirements: For master's, thesis optional; for doctorate, one foreign language, thesis/dissertation.
Entrance requirements: For master's, GRE General Test, minimum GPA of 2.75; for doctorate, GRE General Test, minimum GPA of 3.5. *Application deadline:* For fall admission, 8/9 (priority date). Applications are processed on a rolling basis. *Application fee:* $0 ($25 for international students). Electronic applications accepted.
Expenses: Tuition, state resident: full-time $3,416; part-time $190 per credit hour. Tuition, nonresident: full-time $7,932; part-time $441 per credit hour.
Financial support: In 2001–02, 21 students received support, including research assistantships with full tuition reimbursements available (averaging $3,500 per year), teaching assistantships with full tuition reimbursements available (averaging $3,500 per year); fellowships, career-related internships or fieldwork, Federal Work-Study, institutionally sponsored loans, scholarships/grants, and unspecified assistantships also available. Financial award application deadline: 3/15.
Faculty research: School food service, teen pregnancy, diet and cholesterol metabolism.
Dr. Patricia Sims, Director, 601-266-4679, *Fax:* 601-266-4680.
Application contact: Dr. Kathy Yadrick, Graduate Coordinator, 601-266-4479, *Fax:* 601-266-4680, *E-mail:* kathy.yadrick@usm.edu. *Web site:* http://hhs.usm.edu/fcs

■ THE UNIVERSITY OF TENNESSEE

Graduate School, College of Human Ecology, Department of Child and Family Studies, Knoxville, TN 37996

AWARDS Child and family studies (MS); early childhood education (MS). Part-time programs available.

Faculty: 13 full-time (11 women).
Students: 33 full-time (32 women), 9 part-time (7 women), 3 international. 29 applicants, 83% accepted. In 2001, 26 degrees awarded.
Degree requirements: For master's, thesis or alternative.
Entrance requirements: For master's, GRE General Test, TOEFL, minimum GPA of 2.7. *Application deadline:* For fall admission, 2/1 (priority date). Applications are processed on a rolling basis. *Application fee:* $35. Electronic applications accepted.
Expenses: Tuition, state resident: full-time $4,280; part-time $233 per hour. Tuition, nonresident: full-time $12,066; part-time $666 per hour. Tuition and fees vary according to program.
Financial support: In 2001–02, 1 fellowship, 23 teaching assistantships were awarded. Research assistantships, Federal Work-Study, institutionally sponsored loans, and unspecified assistantships also available. Financial award application deadline: 2/1; financial award applicants required to submit FAFSA.
Dr. Gary Peterson, Head, 865-974-0748, *Fax:* 865-974-2617.

Find an in-depth description at www.petersons.com/gradchannel.

■ THE UNIVERSITY OF TENNESSEE

Graduate School, College of Human Ecology, Program in Human Ecology, Knoxville, TN 37996

AWARDS Child and family studies (PhD); community health (PhD); human resource

The University of Tennessee (continued)
development (PhD); nutrition science (PhD); retailing and consumer sciences (PhD); textile science (PhD).
Students: 62 full-time (42 women), 44 part-time (34 women); includes 12 minority (11 African Americans, 1 Asian American or Pacific Islander), 20 international. 39 applicants, 44% accepted. In 2001, 22 degrees awarded.
Degree requirements: For doctorate, thesis/dissertation.
Entrance requirements: For doctorate, GRE General Test, TOEFL, minimum GPA of 2.7. *Application deadline:* For fall admission, 2/1 (priority date). Applications are processed on a rolling basis. *Application fee:* $35. Electronic applications accepted.
Expenses: Tuition, state resident: full-time $4,280; part-time $233 per hour. Tuition, nonresident: full-time $12,066; part-time $666 per hour. Tuition and fees vary according to program.
Financial support: Fellowships, research assistantships, teaching assistantships, Federal Work-Study, institutionally sponsored loans, and unspecified assistantships available. Financial award application deadline: 2/1; financial award applicants required to submit FAFSA.
Dr. Billie J. Collier, Interim Head, 865-974-5224, *E-mail:* bcollier@utk.edu.

Find an in-depth description at www.petersons.com/gradchannel.

■ THE UNIVERSITY OF TENNESSEE AT MARTIN

Graduate Studies, College of Agriculture and Applied Sciences, Department of Family and Consumer Sciences, Martin, TN 38238-1000

AWARDS Child development and family relations (MSFCS); food science and nutrition (MSFCS). Part-time programs available.

Faculty: 7.
Students: 21 (19 women). 18 applicants, 100% accepted, 11 enrolled. In 2001, 11 degrees awarded.
Degree requirements: For master's, thesis optional.
Entrance requirements: For master's, GRE General Test, minimum GPA of 2.5. *Application deadline:* For fall admission, 7/1 (priority date). Applications are processed on a rolling basis. *Application fee:* $25 ($50 for international students).
Expenses: Tuition, area resident: Full-time $3,796; part-time $213 per hour. Tuition, nonresident: full-time $10,326; part-time $576 per hour.
Financial support: In 2001–02, 1 research assistantship with full tuition reimbursement (averaging $6,888 per year) was awarded; fellowships, teaching assistantships, scholarships/grants, tuition waivers (partial), and unspecified assistantships also available. Financial award application deadline: 3/1.
Faculty research: Children with developmental disabilities, regional food product development and marketing, parent education.
Dr. Lisa LeBleu, Coordinator, 731-587-7116, *E-mail:* llebleu@utm.edu.

■ THE UNIVERSITY OF TEXAS AT AUSTIN

Graduate School, College of Natural Sciences, Department of Human Ecology, Program in Human Development and Family Sciences, Austin, TX 78712-1111

AWARDS MA, PhD.

Faculty: 11 full-time (7 women).
Students: 29 full-time (24 women); includes 5 minority (1 African American, 4 Asian Americans or Pacific Islanders), 4 international. Average age 25. 32 applicants, 25% accepted, 8 enrolled. In 2001, 4 doctorates awarded.
Degree requirements: For master's and doctorate, thesis/dissertation.
Entrance requirements: For master's and doctorate, GRE General Test. *Application deadline:* For fall admission, 2/1 (priority date). *Application fee:* $50 ($75 for international students). Electronic applications accepted.
Expenses: Tuition, state resident: full-time $3,159. Tuition, nonresident: full-time $6,957. Tuition and fees vary according to program.
Financial support: In 2001–02, 23 students received support, including 4 fellowships with full tuition reimbursements available, 6 research assistantships, 16 teaching assistantships with partial tuition reimbursements available; career-related internships or fieldwork, Federal Work-Study, institutionally sponsored loans, and scholarships/grants also available. Financial award application deadline: 2/1.
Faculty research: Marriage and family relationships, parenting, impact of television on children, courtship, family policy.
Nancy Hazen-Swan, Graduate Adviser, 512-471-1261, *Fax:* 512-471-5630.
Application contact: Elsa Villanueva, Graduate Coordinator II, 512-471-0337, *Fax:* 512-471-5844, *E-mail:* hegrad@uts.cc.utexas.edu. *Web site:* http://www.utexas.edu/depts/he

■ THE UNIVERSITY OF TEXAS AT DALLAS

School of Human Development, Program in Human Development and Early Childhood Disorders, Richardson, TX 75083-0688

AWARDS MS. Part-time and evening/weekend programs available.

Faculty: 11 full-time (7 women), 4 part-time/adjunct (2 women).
Students: 17 full-time (15 women), 11 part-time (10 women); includes 5 minority (1 African American, 1 Asian American or Pacific Islander, 3 Hispanic Americans), 4 international. Average age 26. 17 applicants, 47% accepted. In 2001, 6 degrees awarded.
Degree requirements: For master's, directed project or internship.
Entrance requirements: For master's, GRE General Test, TOEFL, minimum GPA of 3.0 in upper-level course work. *Application deadline:* For fall admission, 7/15; for spring admission, 11/15. Applications are processed on a rolling basis. *Application fee:* $25 ($75 for international students). Electronic applications accepted.
Expenses: Tuition, state resident: full-time $1,440; part-time $84 per credit. Tuition, nonresident: full-time $5,310; part-time $295 per credit. Required fees: $1,835; $87 per credit. $138 per term.
Financial support: In 2001–02, 4 research assistantships with tuition reimbursements (averaging $5,850 per year), 4 teaching assistantships with tuition reimbursements (averaging $4,428 per year) were awarded. Fellowships, Federal Work-Study also available. Support available to part-time students. Financial award application deadline: 4/30; financial award applicants required to submit FAFSA.
Faculty research: Social competence in normal and hyperactive youth, preschool number development, social-emotional development, family and peer relationships.
Dr. Margaret Tresch Owen, Associate Dean and College Master, 972-883-0000, *Fax:* 972-883-2491, *E-mail:* mowen@utdallas.edu.
Application contact: Dr. Robert D. Stillman, Head, 972-883-3106, *Fax:* 972-883-3022, *E-mail:* stillman@utdallas.edu. *Web site:* http://www.utdallas.edu/dept/hd/

■ UNIVERSITY OF UTAH

Graduate School, College of Social and Behavioral Science, Department of Family and Consumer Studies, Salt Lake City, UT 84112-1107

AWARDS MS.

Faculty: 14 full-time (8 women), 7 part-time/adjunct (0 women).
Students: 8 full-time (all women), 3 part-time (all women); includes 1 minority (Asian American or Pacific Islander), 2 international. Average age 34. 13 applicants, 54% accepted. In 2001, 3 degrees awarded.
Degree requirements: For master's, thesis optional.
Entrance requirements: For master's, GRE General Test, TOEFL. *Application deadline:* For fall admission, 3/1. *Application fee:* $40 ($60 for international students).
Expenses: Tuition, state resident: part-time $320 per semester hour. Tuition, nonresident: part-time $1,135 per semester hour. Required fees: $143 per semester hour. Tuition and fees vary according to course load, degree level and program.

Financial support: In 2001–02, 8 students received support, including 3 research assistantships with full tuition reimbursements available (averaging $9,000 per year), 5 teaching assistantships with full tuition reimbursements available (averaging $9,000 per year). Financial award application deadline: 3/1.
Faculty research: Social, physical and economic contexts of families and communities. *Total annual research expenditures:* $70,143.
Cathleen D. Zick, Chair, 801-581-7712, *Fax:* 801-581-5156, *E-mail:* zick@fcs.utah.edu.
Application contact: Shauna Wright, Advisor, 801-581-4431, *E-mail:* shauna.wright@fcs.utah.edu.

■ UNIVERSITY OF VERMONT

Graduate College, College of Agriculture and Life Sciences, Department of Nutrition and Food Sciences, Burlington, VT 05405

AWARDS Family and consumer sciences (MAT); nutritional sciences (MS).

Degree requirements: For master's, thesis.
Entrance requirements: For master's, GRE General Test, TOEFL.
Expenses: Tuition, state resident: part-time $335 per credit. Tuition, nonresident: part-time $838 per credit.

■ UNIVERSITY OF WISCONSIN–MADISON

Graduate School, School of Human Ecology, Program in Human Development and Family Studies, Madison, WI 53706-1380

AWARDS MS, PhD.

Faculty: 12 full-time (8 women), 4 part-time/adjunct (1 woman).
Students: 40 full-time (34 women), 4 part-time (all women); includes 6 minority (3 Asian Americans or Pacific Islanders, 3 Hispanic Americans), 10 international. Average age 32. 48 applicants, 48% accepted, 7 enrolled. In 2001, 3 master's, 4 doctorates awarded.
Degree requirements: For master's and doctorate, thesis/dissertation.
Entrance requirements: For master's and doctorate, GRE General Test, TOEFL. *Application deadline:* For fall admission, 1/15 (priority date). Applications are processed on a rolling basis. *Application fee:* $45. Electronic applications accepted.
Expenses: Tuition, state resident: full-time $7,361; part-time $399 per credit. Tuition, nonresident: full-time $20,499; part-time $1,282 per credit. Required fees: $34 per credit. Full-time tuition and fees vary according to course load, program, reciprocity agreements and student level.
Financial support: In 2001–02, 17 students received support, including 1 fellowship with full tuition reimbursement available, 2 research assistantships with full tuition reimbursements available, 14 teaching assistantships with full tuition reimbursements available; institutionally sponsored loans, scholarships/grants, and unspecified assistantships also available. Financial award application deadline: 1/15.
Faculty research: Human development, adolescence, adulthood, prevention, intervention, marital relationships, infancy, family policy, life span, poverty.
William Aquilino, Chair, 608-263-2381, *Fax:* 608-265-1172.
Application contact: Jane A. Weier, Program Assistant, 608-263-2381, *Fax:* 608-265-1172, *E-mail:* jaweier@facstaff.wisc.edu. *Web site:* http://sohe.wisc.edu/cfs/

■ UTAH STATE UNIVERSITY

School of Graduate Studies, College of Family Life, Department of Family and Human Development, Logan, UT 84322

AWARDS Family and human development (MFHD, MS); marriage and family therapy (MS). Part-time programs available.

Faculty: 13 full-time (7 women).
Students: 21 full-time (14 women), 20 part-time (15 women); includes 2 minority (both Hispanic Americans), 2 international. 40 applicants, 25% accepted. In 2001, 9 degrees awarded.
Degree requirements: For master's, thesis, registration.
Entrance requirements: For master's, GRE General Test or MAT, TOEFL, minimum GPA of 3.0. *Application deadline:* For fall admission, 1/15 (priority date). Applications are processed on a rolling basis. *Application fee:* $40.
Expenses: Tuition, state resident: full-time $1,693. Tuition, nonresident: full-time $4,233. Required fees: $501. Tuition and fees vary according to program.
Financial support: In 2001–02, 23 students received support, including 2 fellowships (averaging $500 per year), 3 research assistantships with partial tuition reimbursements available (averaging $6,933 per year), 18 teaching assistantships with partial tuition reimbursements available (averaging $4,400 per year); Federal Work-Study, institutionally sponsored loans, scholarships/grants, and tuition waivers (full and partial) also available. Financial award application deadline: 3/1.
Faculty research: Parent-infant attachment, marriage and family relations, intergenerational relationships, adolescent problem behavior, child and adolescent development. *Total annual research expenditures:* $983,720.
Shelley K. Lindauer, Interim Head, 435-797-1501, *Fax:* 435-797-3845, *E-mail:* lindauer@cc.usu.edu.
Application contact: Randall M. Jones, Graduate Coordinator, 435-797-1553, *Fax:* 435-797-3845, *E-mail:* rjones@cc.usu.edu. *Web site:* http://www.usu.edu/fhd/

■ UTAH STATE UNIVERSITY

School of Graduate Studies, College of Family Life, Program in Family Life, Logan, UT 84322

AWARDS PhD.

Faculty: 14 full-time (6 women).
Students: 11 full-time (4 women), 3 part-time (2 women), 3 international. 10 applicants, 90% accepted. In 2001, 3 degrees awarded.
Degree requirements: For doctorate, thesis/dissertation.
Entrance requirements: For doctorate, GRE General Test, TOEFL, minimum GPA of 3.0. *Application deadline:* For fall admission, 1/15 (priority date); for spring admission, 10/15 (priority date). Applications are processed on a rolling basis. *Application fee:* $40.
Expenses: Tuition, state resident: full-time $1,693. Tuition, nonresident: full-time $4,233. Required fees: $501. Tuition and fees vary according to program.
Financial support: In 2001–02, 7 students received support, including 3 fellowships with partial tuition reimbursements available (averaging $12,000 per year), 3 research assistantships with partial tuition reimbursements available (averaging $10,000 per year), 1 teaching assistantship with partial tuition reimbursement available (averaging $6,000 per year); Federal Work-Study also available. Financial award application deadline: 3/1.
Faculty research: Parent-infant attachment, adolescent pregnancy, marriage and family relations, intergenerational relationships, child and adolescent development. *Total annual research expenditures:* $780,000.
Application contact: Randall M. Jones, Graduate Coordinator, 435-797-1553, *Fax:* 435-797-3845, *E-mail:* rjones@cc.usu.edu. *Web site:* http://www.usu.edu/~famlife/fhd/

■ VIRGINIA POLYTECHNIC INSTITUTE AND STATE UNIVERSITY

Graduate School, College of Human Resources and Education, Department of Human Development, Doctoral Program in Child Development, Blacksburg, VA 24061

AWARDS PhD. Part-time programs available.

Faculty: 5 full-time (3 women).
Students: 7 full-time (6 women), 2 part-time (both women); includes 2 minority (1 African American, 1 Asian American or Pacific Islander). Average age 28. 8 applicants, 88% accepted, 3 enrolled. In 2001, 2 degrees awarded.
Degree requirements: For doctorate, dissertation option, thesis/dissertation optional.
Entrance requirements: For doctorate, GRE General Test, TOEFL, minimum GPA of 3.5. *Application deadline:* For fall admission, 1/2 (priority date). *Application fee:* $45. Electronic applications accepted.

Virginia Polytechnic Institute and State University (continued)
Expenses: Tuition, state resident: part-time $241 per hour. Tuition, nonresident: part-time $406 per hour. Tuition and fees vary according to program.
Financial support: Unspecified assistantships available. Support available to part-time students. Financial award application deadline: 3/1; financial award applicants required to submit FAFSA.
Faculty research: Using Reggio Emilia approach in the contexts of social, political, and cultural context of the U.S; playfulness as a personality trait; self-esteem, identity, and playfulness in children's play; influence of family system on children's development; constructive approach to teaching middle childhood.
Application contact: Katharine Ann Surface, Administrative and Program Specialist III, 540-231-6149, *Fax:* 540-231-7012, *E-mail:* ksurface@vt.edu. *Web site:* http://www.chre.vt.edu/hd/hd.html

■ VIRGINIA POLYTECHNIC INSTITUTE AND STATE UNIVERSITY

Graduate School, College of Human Resources and Education, Department of Human Development, Doctoral Program in Family Studies, Blacksburg, VA 24061

AWARDS PhD. Part-time programs available.

Faculty: 7 full-time (5 women).
Students: 5 full-time (4 women), 2 part-time (both women); includes 2 minority (1 African American, 1 Asian American or Pacific Islander). Average age 40. 5 applicants, 100% accepted, 2 enrolled. In 2001, 1 degree awarded.
Degree requirements: For doctorate, thesis/dissertation optional.
Entrance requirements: For doctorate, GRE General Test, TOEFL, minimum GPA of 3.5. *Application deadline:* For fall admission, 12/1 (priority date). *Application fee:* $45. Electronic applications accepted.
Expenses: Tuition, state resident: part-time $241 per hour. Tuition, nonresident: part-time $406 per hour. Tuition and fees vary according to program.
Financial support: In 2001–02, 1 teaching assistantship (averaging $8,336 per year) was awarded; unspecified assistantships also available. Support available to part-time students. Financial award application deadline: 3/1; financial award applicants required to submit FAFSA.
Faculty research: Community-based programs, sustainability research, child and youth program effectiveness analysis. *Total annual research expenditures:* $350,000.
Application contact: Katharine Ann Surface, Administrative and Program Specialist III, 540-231-6149, *Fax:* 540-231-7012, *E-mail:* ksurface@vt.edu. *Web site:* http://www.chre.vt.edu/hd/hd.html

■ VIRGINIA POLYTECHNIC INSTITUTE AND STATE UNIVERSITY

Graduate School, College of Human Resources and Education, Department of Human Development, Master's Program in Child Development, Blacksburg, VA 24061

AWARDS MS. Part-time programs available.

Faculty: 5 full-time (3 women).
Students: 5 full-time (all women). 6 applicants, 67% accepted, 2 enrolled. In 2001, 2 degrees awarded.
Degree requirements: For master's, thesis optional.
Entrance requirements: For master's, GRE General Test, TOEFL, minimum GPA of 3.0. *Application deadline:* For fall admission, 1/2 (priority date). *Application fee:* $45. Electronic applications accepted.
Expenses: Tuition, state resident: part-time $241 per hour. Tuition, nonresident: part-time $406 per hour. Tuition and fees vary according to program.
Financial support: Unspecified assistantships available. Support available to part-time students. Financial award application deadline: 3/1.
Faculty research: Using Reggio Emilia approach in the contexts of social, political, and cultural contexts of the U.S; playfulness as a personality trait; self-esteem, identity, and playfulness in children's play; influence of family system on children's development; constructive approach to teaching middle childhood.
Application contact: Katharine Ann Surface, Administrative and Program Specialist III, 540-231-6149, *Fax:* 540-231-7012, *E-mail:* ksurface@vt.edu. *Web site:* http://www.chre.vt.edu/HD/hd.html

■ VIRGINIA POLYTECHNIC INSTITUTE AND STATE UNIVERSITY

Graduate School, College of Human Resources and Education, Department of Human Development, Master's Program in Family Studies, Blacksburg, VA 24061

AWARDS MS. Part-time programs available.

Faculty: 7 full-time (5 women).
Students: 7 full-time (6 women); includes 1 minority (African American). Average age 24. 10 applicants, 60% accepted, 5 enrolled. In 2001, 1 degree awarded.
Degree requirements: For master's, thesis optional.
Entrance requirements: For master's, GRE General Test, TOEFL, minimum GPA of 3.0. *Application deadline:* For fall admission, 1/2 (priority date). *Application fee:* $45. Electronic applications accepted.
Expenses: Tuition, state resident: part-time $241 per hour. Tuition, nonresident: part-time $406 per hour. Tuition and fees vary according to program.
Financial support: Unspecified assistantships available. Support available to part-time students. Financial award application deadline: 3/1.
Faculty research: Drug policy, family policy, domestic violence. *Total annual research expenditures:* $350,000.
Application contact: Katharine Ann Surface, Administrative and Program Specialist III, 540-231-6149, *Fax:* 540-231-7012, *E-mail:* ksurface@vt.edu. *Web site:* http://www.chre.vt.edu/hd.hd.html

■ WAYNE STATE UNIVERSITY

Graduate School, Interdisciplinary Program in Infant Mental Health, Detroit, MI 48202

AWARDS Certificate.

Students: In 2001, 5 degrees awarded.
Degree requirements: For Certificate, completion of master's degree.
Entrance requirements: For degree, concurrent admission to a master's or doctoral program, or master's degree. *Application deadline:* For fall admission, 7/1. *Application fee:* $20 ($30 for international students). Electronic applications accepted.
Expenses: Tuition, state resident: full-time $3,764. Tuition and fees vary according to degree level and program.
Financial support: Career-related internships or fieldwork, institutionally sponsored loans, scholarships/grants, and tuition waivers (partial) available.
Faculty research: Infant mental health treatment, early intervention, child abuse and neglect.
Rita Casey, Director, 313-872-2408, *Fax:* 313-875-0947.
Application contact: Debbie Weatherston, Education Director, 313-872-1790.

■ WEST VIRGINIA UNIVERSITY

Davis College of Agriculture, Forestry and Consumer Sciences, Division of Family and Consumer Sciences, Morgantown, WV 26506

AWARDS MSFCS. Part-time programs available.

Faculty: 15 full-time (12 women), 5 part-time/adjunct (all women).
Students: 11 full-time (all women), 10 part-time (9 women); includes 1 minority (Asian American or Pacific Islander), 1 international. Average age 27. 8 applicants, 100% accepted. In 2001, 16 degrees awarded.
Degree requirements: For master's, thesis or alternative, research project.
Entrance requirements: For master's, GRE General Test, TOEFL, minimum GPA of 2.75. *Application deadline:* For fall admission, 5/1; for spring admission, 10/1. Applications are processed on a rolling basis. *Application fee:* $45.
Expenses: Tuition, state resident: full-time $2,791. Tuition, nonresident: full-time

$8,659. Required fees: $1,002. Tuition and fees vary according to program.
Financial support: In 2001–02, 8 students received support, including 4 research assistantships, 4 teaching assistantships; Federal Work-Study, institutionally sponsored loans, tuition waivers (full and partial), and unspecified assistantships also available. Financial award application deadline: 2/1; financial award applicants required to submit FAFSA.
Faculty research: Nutrition epidemiology, energy metabolism, dietary methodology, infant development, family development.
Dr. Jan Yeager, Chair, 304-293-2769, *Fax:* 304-293-2750, *E-mail:* jan.yeager@mail.wvu.edu. *Web site:* http://www.caf.wvu.edu/fcs

■ WHEELOCK COLLEGE

Graduate School, Program in Birth to Three: Development and Intervention, Boston, MA 02215

AWARDS MS.

Faculty: 1 (woman) full-time.
Students: 1 (woman) full-time, 9 part-time (all women). Average age 25. 7 applicants, 86% accepted, 4 enrolled. In 2001, 3 degrees awarded.
Entrance requirements: For master's, interview. *Application deadline:* For fall admission, 7/1 (priority date). Applications are processed on a rolling basis. *Application fee:* $35 ($40 for international students). Electronic applications accepted.
Expenses: Tuition: Full-time $21,600; part-time $600 per credit.
Financial support: Career-related internships or fieldwork, Federal Work-Study, institutionally sponsored loans, scholarships/grants, and unspecified assistantships available. Support available to part-time students. Financial award application deadline: 4/1; financial award applicants required to submit FAFSA.
Faculty research: Cross-cultural perspectives on families, cultural influences on parenting and early development, parental beliefs about learning and early development, the development of professional identity in infant/toddler educators.
Catherine Finn, Coordinator, 617-879-2160, *Fax:* 617-232-7127, *E-mail:* cfinn@wheelock.edu.
Application contact: Deborah A. Sheehan, Director of Graduate Admissions and Student Financial Planning, 617-879-2178, *Fax:* 617-232-7127, *E-mail:* dsheehan@wheelock.edu.

■ WHEELOCK COLLEGE

Graduate School, Program in Child Development and Early Childhood Education, Boston, MA 02215

AWARDS MS. Part-time and evening/weekend programs available. Postbaccalaureate distance learning degree programs offered (minimal on-campus study).

Faculty: 4 full-time (all women), 4 part-time/adjunct (all women).
Students: 6 full-time (4 women), 100 part-time (all women); includes 1 minority (Asian American or Pacific Islander), 1 international. 5 applicants, 80% accepted, 1 enrolled. In 2001, 94 degrees awarded.
Application deadline: For fall admission, 7/1 (priority date); for spring admission, 11/1 (priority date). Applications are processed on a rolling basis. *Application fee:* $35 ($40 for international students). Electronic applications accepted.
Expenses: Tuition: Full-time $21,600; part-time $600 per credit.
Financial support: Career-related internships or fieldwork, Federal Work-Study, institutionally sponsored loans, scholarships/grants, and unspecified assistantships available. Support available to part-time students. Financial award application deadline: 4/1; financial award applicants required to submit FAFSA.
Faculty research: Cultural influences on early development and parenting, design of learning environments for young children.
Dr. Eleanor Chasdi, Coordinator, 617-879-2162, *Fax:* 617-232-7127, *E-mail:* echasdi@wheelock.edu.
Application contact: Deborah A. Sheehan, Director of Graduate Admissions and Student Financial Planning, 617-879-2178, *Fax:* 617-232-7127, *E-mail:* dsheehan@wheelock.edu.

■ WHEELOCK COLLEGE

Graduate School, Program in Family Studies, Boston, MA 02215

AWARDS Family studies (CAGS); family support and parent education (MS); family, culture, and society (MS).

Students: 4 full-time (3 women), 10 part-time (all women); includes 2 minority (1 African American, 1 Hispanic American). Average age 25. 5 applicants, 80% accepted, 3 enrolled. In 2001, 11 degrees awarded.
Degree requirements: For CAGS, thesis.
Entrance requirements: For degree, interview. *Application deadline:* For fall admission, 7/1 (priority date); for spring admission, 11/1 (priority date). Applications are processed on a rolling basis. *Application fee:* $35 ($40 for international students). Electronic applications accepted.
Expenses: Tuition: Full-time $21,600; part-time $600 per credit.
Financial support: Career-related internships or fieldwork, Federal Work-Study, institutionally sponsored loans, scholarships/grants, and unspecified assistantships available. Support available to part-time students. Financial award application deadline: 4/1; financial award applicants required to submit FAFSA.
Faculty research: Cross-cultural studies of parenting, media literacy, psychological effects of violence.
Dr. Stefi Rubin, Co-Coordinator, 617-879-2155, *E-mail:* srubin@wheelock.edu.
Application contact: Deborah A. Sheehan, Director of Graduate Admissions and Student Financial Planning, 617-879-2178, *Fax:* 617-232-7127, *E-mail:* dsheehan@wheelock.edu.

CLOTHING AND TEXTILES

■ AUBURN UNIVERSITY

Graduate School, College of Human Sciences, Department of Consumer Affairs, Auburn University, AL 36849

AWARDS Apparel and textiles (MS). Part-time programs available.

Faculty: 15 full-time (12 women).
Students: 7 full-time (all women), 1 part-time; includes 1 minority (African American), 3 international. 15 applicants, 47% accepted. In 2001, 6 degrees awarded.
Degree requirements: For master's, thesis (for some programs).
Entrance requirements: For master's, GRE General Test. *Application deadline:* For fall admission, 7/7; for spring admission, 11/24. Applications are processed on a rolling basis. *Application fee:* $25 ($50 for international students). Electronic applications accepted.
Financial support: Fellowships, research assistantships, teaching assistantships, career-related internships or fieldwork and Federal Work-Study available. Support available to part-time students. Financial award application deadline: 3/15.
Faculty research: Merchandising, consumer behavior, international marketing of textiles and apparel, apparel product development. *Total annual research expenditures:* $875,000.
Dr. Carol L. Warfield, Head, 334-844-4084, *E-mail:* cwarfiel@humsci.auburn.edu.
Application contact: Dr. John F. Pritchett, Dean of the Graduate School, 334-844-4700, *E-mail:* hatchlb@mail.auburn.edu. *Web site:* http://www.humsci.auburn.edu/conaff.html

■ CORNELL UNIVERSITY

Graduate School, Graduate Fields of Human Ecology, Field of Textiles, Ithaca, NY 14853-0001

AWARDS Apparel design (MA, MPS); fiber science (MS, PhD); polymer science (MS, PhD); textile science (MS, PhD).

Faculty: 12 full-time.
Students: 13 full-time (7 women), 12 international. 29 applicants, 34% accepted. In 2001, 4 degrees awarded.
Degree requirements: For master's, thesis (MA, MS), project paper (MPS); for doctorate, thesis/dissertation.
Entrance requirements: For master's, GRE General Test, TOEFL, 2 letters of recommendation, portfolio (functional apparel design); for doctorate, GRE

Cornell University (continued)
General Test, TOEFL, 2 letters of recommendation. *Application deadline:* For fall admission, 3/1. *Application fee:* $65. Electronic applications accepted.
Expenses: Tuition: Full-time $25,970. Required fees: $50.
Financial support: In 2001–02, 12 students received support, including 2 fellowships with full tuition reimbursements available, 2 research assistantships with full tuition reimbursements available, 8 teaching assistantships with full tuition reimbursements available; institutionally sponsored loans, scholarships/grants, tuition waivers (full and partial), and unspecified assistantships also available. Financial award applicants required to submit FAFSA.
Faculty research: High performance fibers and composites; surface chemistry of fibers; geosynthetics; mechanics of fibrous assemblies/ biopolymers; biological tissue engineering, detergency, protective clothing.
Application contact: Graduate Field Assistant, 607-255-8065, *E-mail:* textiles_grad@cornell.edu. *Web site:* http://www.gradschool.cornell.edu/grad/fields_1/textiles.html

■ FASHION INSTITUTE OF TECHNOLOGY

Division of Graduate Studies, Programs in Museum Studies, New York, NY 10001-5992

AWARDS Museum studies: applied arts (MA); museum studies: costume and textiles (MA).

Faculty: 2 full-time (both women), 12 part-time/adjunct (10 women).
Students: 22 full-time (all women), 10 part-time (all women); includes 4 minority (1 African American, 2 Asian Americans or Pacific Islanders, 1 Hispanic American), 6 international. Average age 30. 52 applicants, 62% accepted. In 2001, 12 degrees awarded.
Degree requirements: For master's, one foreign language, thesis, internship.
Entrance requirements: For master's, GRE General Test or GRE Subject Test, TOEFL, previous course work in art history and chemistry, 4 semesters of a foreign language. *Application deadline:* For fall admission, 2/15 (priority date). *Application fee:* $25.
Expenses: Tuition, area resident: Full-time $4,654; part-time $228 per credit. Tuition, nonresident: full-time $10,396; part-time $486 per credit. Required fees: $270.

Find an in-depth description at www.petersons.com/gradchannel.

■ FLORIDA STATE UNIVERSITY

Graduate Studies, College of Human Sciences, Department of Textiles and Consumer Sciences, Tallahassee, FL 32306

AWARDS MS, PhD. Part-time programs available.

Faculty: 10 full-time (9 women).
Students: 20 full-time (all women), 6 part-time (4 women); includes 5 minority (2 African Americans, 1 Asian American or Pacific Islander, 2 Hispanic Americans), 8 international. 35 applicants, 57% accepted, 8 enrolled. In 2001, 7 master's, 2 doctorates awarded.
Degree requirements: For master's, thesis optional; for doctorate, thesis/dissertation.
Entrance requirements: For master's and doctorate, GRE General Test, minimum GPA of 3.0. *Application deadline:* For fall admission, 2/1 (priority date); for spring admission, 11/1. Applications are processed on a rolling basis. *Application fee:* $20. Electronic applications accepted.
Expenses: Tuition, state resident: part-time $163 per credit hour. Tuition, nonresident: part-time $570 per credit hour. Tuition and fees vary according to program.
Financial support: In 2001–02, 12 students received support, including 1 fellowship with partial tuition reimbursement available (averaging $10,000 per year), 2 research assistantships with partial tuition reimbursements available (averaging $8,000 per year), 9 teaching assistantships with partial tuition reimbursements available (averaging $8,000 per year); career-related internships or fieldwork, Federal Work-Study, institutionally sponsored loans, scholarships/grants, and unspecified assistantships also available. Financial award application deadline: 3/1; financial award applicants required to submit FAFSA.
Faculty research: Soft goods retailing, small business strategies, textile product performance, consumer behavior, accessible housing. *Total annual research expenditures:* $67,689.
Dr. Rinn Cloud, Chair, 850-644-2498, *Fax:* 850-644-0700, *E-mail:* rcloud@garnet.acns.fsu.edu.
Application contact: Dr. Jeanne Heitmeyer, Graduate Coordinator, 850-644-2498, *Fax:* 850-644-0700, *E-mail:* jheitmey@mailer.fsu.edu.

Find an in-depth description at www.petersons.com/gradchannel.

■ INDIANA STATE UNIVERSITY

School of Graduate Studies, College of Arts and Sciences, Department of Family and Consumer Sciences, Terre Haute, IN 47809-1401

AWARDS Child and family relations (MS); clothing and textiles (MS); dietetics (MS); home management (MS); nutrition and foods (MS). Part-time programs available.

Electronic applications accepted.

■ INDIANA UNIVERSITY BLOOMINGTON

Graduate School, College of Arts and Sciences, Department of Apparel Merchandising and Interior Design, Bloomington, IN 47405

AWARDS Apparel studies (MS); interior design (MS).

Faculty: 3 full-time (2 women).
Students: 2 full-time (both women), 1 (woman) part-time, 2 international. Average age 30. In 2001, 2 degrees awarded.
Degree requirements: For master's, thesis or alternative.
Entrance requirements: For master's, GRE, TOEFL. *Application deadline:* For fall admission, 1/15 (priority date); for spring admission, 9/1 (priority date). Applications are processed on a rolling basis. *Application fee:* $45 ($55 for international students).
Expenses: Tuition, state resident: full-time $4,720; part-time $197 per credit. Tuition, nonresident: full-time $13,748; part-time $573 per credit. Required fees: $642.
Financial support: Teaching assistantships, career-related internships or fieldwork available. Support available to part-time students. Financial award application deadline: 4/1.
Faculty research: Eighteenth-century French design, appearance and behavior, apparel marketing, costume collection management, design processes.
Kathleen Rowold, Chair, 812-855-5497, *E-mail:* rowold@indiana.edu.
Application contact: Tammie Stikeleather, Secretary, 812-855-5497, *Fax:* 812-855-4869, *E-mail:* stikelea@ucs.indiana.edu. *Web site:* http://www.fa.indiana.edu/~amid/

■ IOWA STATE UNIVERSITY OF SCIENCE AND TECHNOLOGY

Graduate College, College of Family and Consumer Sciences, Department of Apparel, Education Studies, and Hospitality Management, Ames, IA 50011

AWARDS Family and consumer science education and studies (M Ed); family and consumer sciences education and studies (MS, PhD); foodservice and lodging management (MFCS, MS, PhD); textiles and clothing (MFCS, MS, PhD).

Faculty: 25 full-time.
Students: 22 full-time (15 women), 32 part-time (28 women). 71 applicants, 18% accepted, 0 enrolled. In 2001, 7 master's, 5 doctorates awarded.
Degree requirements: For doctorate, thesis/dissertation.
Entrance requirements: For master's and doctorate, GRE General Test, TOEFL or

IELTS. *Application fee:* $20 ($50 for international students).
Expenses: Tuition, state resident: full-time $1,851. Tuition, nonresident: full-time $5,449. Tuition and fees vary according to program.
Financial support: In 2001–02, 8 research assistantships (averaging $12,645 per year), 4 teaching assistantships (averaging $12,104 per year) were awarded.
Dr. Mary B. Gregoire, Chair, 515-294-7474, *Fax:* 515-294-6364, *E-mail:* texclo@iastate.edu.

■ IOWA STATE UNIVERSITY OF SCIENCE AND TECHNOLOGY

Graduate College, College of Family and Consumer Sciences, Department of Textiles and Clothing, Ames, IA 50011

AWARDS MFCS, MS, PhD.

Students: 9 full-time (all women), 10 part-time (all women); includes 2 minority (1 African American, 1 Asian American or Pacific Islander), 10 international. 41 applicants, 22% accepted, 4 enrolled. In 2001, 6 master's, 4 doctorates awarded.
Degree requirements: For master's and doctorate, thesis/dissertation. *Median time to degree:* Master's–1.8 years full-time; doctorate–5.5 years full-time.
Entrance requirements: For master's and doctorate, GRE General Test, TOEFL or IELTS. *Application deadline:* For fall admission, 3/1 (priority date). Applications are processed on a rolling basis. *Application fee:* $20 ($50 for international students). Electronic applications accepted.
Expenses: Tuition, state resident: full-time $1,851. Tuition, nonresident: full-time $5,449. Tuition and fees vary according to program.
Financial support: In 2001–02, 2 research assistantships with partial tuition reimbursements (averaging $12,104 per year), 2 teaching assistantships with partial tuition reimbursements (averaging $12,104 per year) were awarded. Scholarships/grants also available.
Dr. Mary Littrell, Director of Graduate Education, 515-294-5284, *E-mail:* mlittel@iastate.edu. *Web site:* http://www.tc.iastate.edu/

■ KANSAS STATE UNIVERSITY

Graduate School, College of Human Ecology, Department of Apparel, Textiles, and Interior Design, Manhattan, KS 66506

AWARDS Apparel and textiles (MS); human ecology (PhD).

Faculty: 12 full-time (11 women).
Students: 13 full-time (9 women), 1 part-time, 8 international. Average age 25. 31 applicants, 42% accepted, 5 enrolled. In 2001, 3 degrees awarded.
Degree requirements: For master's, residency, thesis optional; for doctorate, thesis/dissertation, preliminary exams, residency.
Entrance requirements: For master's, GRE General Test, TOEFL, minimum undergraduate GPA of 3.0; for doctorate, GRE General Test, TOEFL, minimum graduate GPA of 3.5. *Application deadline:* For fall admission, 2/15 (priority date); for spring admission, 10/1. Applications are processed on a rolling basis. *Application fee:* $0 ($25 for international students). Electronic applications accepted.
Expenses: Tuition, state resident: part-time $113 per credit hour. Tuition, nonresident: part-time $358 per credit hour.
Financial support: In 2001–02, 1 fellowship, 8 research assistantships with partial tuition reimbursements (averaging $8,000 per year), 2 teaching assistantships with full tuition reimbursements (averaging $8,000 per year) were awarded. Career-related internships or fieldwork, Federal Work-Study, institutionally sponsored loans, and scholarships/grants also available. Support available to part-time students. Financial award application deadline: 3/1; financial award applicants required to submit FAFSA.
Faculty research: Thermal properties, textile chemistry, economic issues in textiles, apparel marketing and consumer behavior, textile dyeing and finishing. *Total annual research expenditures:* $160,000.
Dr. Gwendolyn O'Neal, Dean, 785-532-6993, *Fax:* 785-532-3796, *E-mail:* oneal@humec.ksu.edu.
Application contact: Gina Jackson, Office Specialist, 785-532-6993, *Fax:* 785-532-3796, *E-mail:* jackson@humec.ksu.edu. *Web site:* http://www.ksu.edu/humec/atid/

■ MICHIGAN STATE UNIVERSITY

Graduate School, College of Human Ecology, Department of Human Environment and Design, East Lansing, MI 48824

AWARDS Apparel and textiles (MA); clothing and textiles (MA); human design and management (PhD); interior design and facilities management (MA); interior design and human environment (MA); merchandising management (MS).

Faculty: 13.
Students: 14 full-time (12 women), 18 part-time (13 women); includes 1 minority (Asian American or Pacific Islander), 20 international. Average age 33. 32 applicants, 13% accepted. In 2001, 1 degree awarded.
Degree requirements: For master's, oral exam, thesis optional; for doctorate, thesis/dissertation.
Entrance requirements: For master's, GRE General Test, minimum GPA of 3.0 in last 2 years of undergraduate course work; for doctorate, GRE General Test. *Application deadline:* For fall admission, 11/15. Applications are processed on a rolling basis. *Application fee:* $30 ($40 for international students). Electronic applications accepted.
Expenses: Tuition, state resident: part-time $244 per credit hour. Tuition, nonresident: part-time $494 per credit hour. Required fees: $268 per semester. Tuition and fees vary according to course load, degree level and program.
Financial support: In 2001–02, 14 fellowships (averaging $1,503 per year), 2 research assistantships with tuition reimbursements (averaging $11,160 per year), 7 teaching assistantships with tuition reimbursements (averaging $10,499 per year) were awarded. Career-related internships or fieldwork also available. Financial award applicants required to submit FAFSA.
Faculty research: Apparel production, clothing decisions, tourist-related small business, performance standards. *Total annual research expenditures:* $146,827.
Dr. Dana Stewart, Chairperson, 517-355-7712, *Fax:* 517-432-1058, *E-mail:* infohed@msu.edu. *Web site:* http://www.msu.edu/~hed/

■ NORTH CAROLINA STATE UNIVERSITY

Graduate School, College of Management, Program in Management, Raleigh, NC 27695

AWARDS Biotechnology (MS); computer science (MS); engineering (MS); forest resources management (MS); general business (MS); management information systems (MS); operations research (MS); statistics (MS); telecommunications systems engineering (MS); textile management (MS); total quality management (MS). Part-time programs available.

Faculty: 14 full-time (6 women), 3 part-time/adjunct (0 women).
Students: 60 full-time (18 women), 138 part-time (47 women); includes 27 minority (12 African Americans, 13 Asian Americans or Pacific Islanders, 2 Hispanic Americans), 17 international. Average age 32. 225 applicants, 44% accepted. In 2001, 67 degrees awarded.
Entrance requirements: For master's, GMAT or GRE, TOEFL, minimum undergraduate GPA of 3.0. *Application deadline:* For fall admission, 6/25; for spring admission, 11/25. Applications are processed on a rolling basis. *Application fee:* $45.
Expenses: Tuition, state resident: full-time $1,748. Tuition, nonresident: full-time $6,904.
Financial support: In 2001–02, fellowships (averaging $3,551 per year), 32 teaching assistantships (averaging $3,027 per year) were awarded. Research assistantships Financial award application deadline: 3/1.

North Carolina State University (continued)
Faculty research: Manufacturing strategy, information systems, technology commercialization, managing research and development, historical stock returns. *Total annual research expenditures:* $69,089.
Dr. Stephen G. Allen, Head, 919-515-5584, *Fax:* 919-515-5073, *E-mail:* steve_allen@ncsu.edu. *Web site:* http://www.mgt.ncsu.edu/facdep/bizmgmt/bizman.html

■ THE OHIO STATE UNIVERSITY

Graduate School, College of Human Ecology, Program in Textiles and Clothing, Columbus, OH 43210

AWARDS MS, PhD.

Degree requirements: For master's, thesis optional; for doctorate, thesis/dissertation.
Entrance requirements: For master's and doctorate, GRE General Test.

■ OKLAHOMA STATE UNIVERSITY

Graduate College, College of Human Environmental Sciences, Department of Design, Housing and Merchandising, Stillwater, OK 74078

AWARDS MS, PhD.

Faculty: 12 full-time (9 women).
Students: 8 full-time (all women), 12 part-time (9 women); includes 3 minority (1 African American, 2 Native Americans), 7 international. Average age 35. 14 applicants, 64% accepted. In 2001, 5 master's, 2 doctorates awarded.
Degree requirements: For master's and doctorate, thesis/dissertation.
Entrance requirements: For master's, GRE, TOEFL; for doctorate, GRE. *Application deadline:* For fall admission, 7/1 (priority date). *Application fee:* $25.
Expenses: Tuition, state resident: part-time $92 per credit hour. Tuition, nonresident: part-time $297 per credit hour. Required fees: $21 per credit hour. $14 per semester. One-time fee: $20. Tuition and fees vary according to course load.
Financial support: In 2001–02, 13 students received support, including 7 research assistantships (averaging $10,673 per year), 4 teaching assistantships (averaging $13,218 per year); career-related internships or fieldwork, Federal Work-Study, and tuition waivers (partial) also available. Support available to part-time students. Financial award application deadline: 3/1.
Faculty research: Environmental sciences design, housing & merchandising, creativity and physical environment; product development, production and evaluation; experimental learning and critical thinking, technology strategies and assessment, customer expectation and satisfaction.
Dr. Donna Branson, Head, 405-744-5049.

■ OKLAHOMA STATE UNIVERSITY

Graduate College, College of Human Environmental Sciences, Program in Human Environmental Sciences, Stillwater, OK 74078

AWARDS Design, housing, and merchandising (PhD); family relations and child development (PhD); hotel and restaurant administration (PhD); nutritional sciences (PhD).

Faculty: 1 (woman) full-time.
Students: 23 full-time (14 women), 21 part-time (15 women); includes 7 minority (4 African Americans, 2 Asian Americans or Pacific Islanders, 1 Native American), 12 international. Average age 38. 14 applicants, 100% accepted. In 2001, 6 degrees awarded.
Degree requirements: For doctorate, thesis/dissertation.
Entrance requirements: For doctorate, TOEFL. *Application deadline:* For fall admission, 7/1 (priority date). *Application fee:* $25.
Expenses: Tuition, state resident: part-time $92 per credit hour. Tuition, nonresident: part-time $297 per credit hour. Required fees: $21 per credit hour. $14 per semester. One-time fee: $20. Tuition and fees vary according to course load.
Financial support: Research assistantships, teaching assistantships, career-related internships or fieldwork, Federal Work-Study, and tuition waivers (partial) available. Support available to part-time students. Financial award application deadline: 3/1.

■ OREGON STATE UNIVERSITY

Graduate School, College of Home Economics, Department of Apparel, Interiors, Housing, and Merchandising, Corvallis, OR 97331

AWARDS MA, MAIS, MS, PhD.

Faculty: 6 full-time (all women).
Students: 8 full-time (all women), 5 part-time (all women), 6 international. Average age 39. In 2001, 1 master's, 2 doctorates awarded. Terminal master's awarded for partial completion of doctoral program.
Degree requirements: For master's, thesis or alternative; for doctorate, thesis/dissertation.
Entrance requirements: For master's and doctorate, GRE General Test, TOEFL, minimum GPA of 3.0 in last 90 hours. *Application deadline:* For fall admission, 2/1 (priority date). *Application fee:* $50.
Expenses: Tuition, area resident: Full-time $15,933. Tuition, state resident: full-time $28,937.
Financial support: Research assistantships, teaching assistantships, career-related internships or fieldwork, Federal Work-Study, and institutionally sponsored loans available. Support available to part-time students. Financial award application deadline: 2/1.
Dr. Cheryl W. Jordan, Interim Head, 541-737-0987, *Fax:* 541-737-0993, *E-mail:* jordanc@orst.edu.
Application contact: Dr. Elaine Pedersen, Chair, Graduate Committee, 541-737-0984, *Fax:* 541-737-0993.

■ PHILADELPHIA UNIVERSITY

School of Textiles and Materials Science, Program in Fashion-Apparel Studies, Philadelphia, PA 19144-5497

AWARDS MS. Part-time programs available.

Faculty: 12 full-time (2 women), 3 part-time/adjunct (1 woman).
Students: 9 full-time (3 women), 2 part-time (both women); includes 1 minority (African American), 9 international. 32 applicants, 59% accepted, 1 enrolled.
Entrance requirements: For master's, GRE, or GMAT, minimum GPA of 2.80. *Application deadline:* Applications are processed on a rolling basis. *Application fee:* $35. Electronic applications accepted.
Expenses: Tuition: Part-time $517 per credit.
Financial support: In 2001–02, research assistantships with full tuition reimbursements (averaging $2,000 per year); career-related internships or fieldwork, Federal Work-Study, and unspecified assistantships also available. Financial award applicants required to submit FAFSA.
Mel Wiener, Director, 215-951-2979, *Fax:* 215-951-2651, *E-mail:* wienerm@philau.edu.
Application contact: William H. Firman, Director of Graduate Admissions, 215-951-2943, *Fax:* 215-951-2907, *E-mail:* gradadm@philau.edu. *Web site:* http://www.philau.edu/

■ PURDUE UNIVERSITY

Graduate School, School of Consumer and Family Sciences, Department of Consumer Sciences and Retailing, West Lafayette, IN 47907

AWARDS Consumer behavior (MS, PhD); family and consumer economics (MS, PhD); retail management (MS, PhD); textile science (MS, PhD). Part-time programs available.

Faculty: 11.
Students: 20 full-time (14 women), 20 part-time (12 women); includes 5 minority (1 African American, 4 Asian Americans or Pacific Islanders), 32 international. Average age 30. 48 applicants, 46% accepted. In 2001, 2 master's, 2 doctorates awarded.
Degree requirements: For master's and doctorate, thesis/dissertation.
Entrance requirements: For master's and doctorate, GMAT or GRE General Test, TOEFL. *Application fee:* $30. Electronic applications accepted.
Expenses: Tuition, state resident: full-time $4,164; part-time $149 per credit hour. Tuition, nonresident: full-time $13,872;

part-time $458 per credit hour. Tuition and fees vary according to campus/location and program.
Financial support: Fellowships, research assistantships, teaching assistantships, career-related internships or fieldwork available. Support available to part-time students. Financial award applicants required to submit FAFSA.
Faculty research: Family financial resources, retail management and patronage, chemical analysis of textile dyes and finishes.
R. A. Feinberg, Head, 765-494-8296, *Fax:* 765-494-0869.
Application contact: Jean M. Navarre, Graduate Admissions Coordinator, 765-494-8356, *Fax:* 765-494-0869, *E-mail:* jnavarre@purdue.edu. *Web site:* http://www.cfs.purdue.edu/conscirt/

■ SYRACUSE UNIVERSITY

Graduate School, College of Visual and Performing Arts, Department of Fashion and Design Technologies, Syracuse, NY 13244-0003

AWARDS Fashion design (MA); textile design (MS). Part-time programs available.

Faculty: 6 full-time (4 women), 2 part-time/adjunct (0 women).
Students: 6 full-time (5 women), 4 part-time (all women); includes 2 minority (both Hispanic Americans), 4 international. Average age 40. 5 applicants, 60% accepted. In 2001, 3 degrees awarded.
Entrance requirements: For master's, GRE General Test. *Application deadline:* For spring admission, 3/1 (priority date). Applications are processed on a rolling basis. *Application fee:* $50. Electronic applications accepted.
Expenses: Tuition: Full-time $15,528; part-time $647 per credit. Required fees: $420; $38 per term. Tuition and fees vary according to program.
Financial support: In 2001–02, 6 students received support, including fellowships with full tuition reimbursements available (averaging $13,000 per year), 2 research assistantships with full and partial tuition reimbursements available (averaging $8,610 per year), 4 teaching assistantships with full and partial tuition reimbursements available (averaging $8,610 per year); Federal Work-Study and tuition waivers (partial) also available.
Karen Bakke, Chair, 315-443-4644, *E-mail:* kmbakke@syr.edu.
Application contact: Janith Wright, Information Contact, 315-443-2180, *E-mail:* jswright@syr.edu.

■ THE UNIVERSITY OF AKRON

Graduate School, College of Fine and Applied Arts, School of Family and Consumer Sciences, Program in Clothing, Textiles and Interiors, Akron, OH 44325-0001

AWARDS MA.

Students: 4 full-time (all women), 2 part-time (both women), 1 international. Average age 39. 5 applicants, 80% accepted.
Degree requirements: For master's, thesis or project.
Entrance requirements: For master's, GRE General Test, minimum GPA of 2.75. *Application deadline:* For fall admission, 8/15. Applications are processed on a rolling basis. *Application fee:* $40 ($50 for international students).
Expenses: Tuition, state resident: full-time $6,562; part-time $219 per credit. Tuition, nonresident: full-time $9,027; part-time $383 per credit. Required fees: $272; $11 per credit. Tuition and fees vary according to course load.
Financial support: Application deadline: 3/1.

■ THE UNIVERSITY OF ALABAMA

Graduate School, College of Human Environmental Sciences, Department of Clothing, Textiles, and Interior Design, Tuscaloosa, AL 35487

AWARDS MSHES.

Faculty: 10 full-time (8 women), 1 (woman) part-time/adjunct.
Students: 3 full-time (all women), 1 (woman) part-time; includes 1 minority (African American). Average age 26. 5 applicants, 40% accepted, 2 enrolled. In 2001, 1 degree awarded.
Degree requirements: For master's, thesis.
Entrance requirements: For master's, GRE General Test or MAT, minimum GPA of 3.0. *Application deadline:* For fall admission, 7/6. Applications are processed on a rolling basis. *Application fee:* $25.
Expenses: Tuition, state resident: full-time $3,292; part-time $183 per credit hour. Tuition, nonresident: full-time $8,912; part-time $495 per credit hour. Tuition and fees vary according to course load, campus/location and program.
Financial support: In 2001–02, 1 research assistantship with full tuition reimbursement (averaging $8,100 per year), 2 teaching assistantships with full tuition reimbursements (averaging $8,100 per year) were awarded. Fellowships, career-related internships or fieldwork, Federal Work-Study, and scholarships/grants also available. Financial award application deadline: 3/15.
Dr. Carolyn Callis, Head and Associate Professor, 205-348-6176, *Fax:* 205-348-3789, *E-mail:* ccallis@ches.ua.edu. *Web site:* http://www.ches.ua.edu/

■ UNIVERSITY OF CALIFORNIA, DAVIS

Graduate Studies, Graduate Group in Textiles, Davis, CA 95616

AWARDS MS. Part-time programs available.

Faculty: 13 full-time (6 women).
Students: 6 full-time (all women), 3 international. Average age 28. 14 applicants, 79% accepted, 2 enrolled. In 2001, 2 degrees awarded.
Degree requirements: For master's, thesis optional.
Entrance requirements: For master's, GRE General Test, minimum GPA of 3.0. *Application deadline:* For fall admission, 4/1. *Application fee:* $60. Electronic applications accepted.
Expenses: Tuition, state resident: full-time $4,831. Tuition, nonresident: full-time $15,725.
Financial support: In 2001–02, 4 students received support, including 3 fellowships with full and partial tuition reimbursements available (averaging $1,048 per year), 3 research assistantships with full and partial tuition reimbursements available (averaging $9,142 per year), 2 teaching assistantships with partial tuition reimbursements available (averaging $10,608 per year); career-related internships or fieldwork, Federal Work-Study, institutionally sponsored loans, scholarships/grants, and tuition waivers (partial) also available. Financial award application deadline: 1/15; financial award applicants required to submit FAFSA.
Faculty research: Fiber science, social psychology, consumer psychology, chemical and physical properties of fibrous and polymeric materials.
Ning Pan, Chair, 530-752-6232, *Fax:* 530-752-7584, *E-mail:* npan@ucdavis.edu.
Application contact: Sandy Brito, Graduate Staff, 530-752-6650, *Fax:* 530-752-7584, *E-mail:* slbrito@ucdavis.edu. *Web site:* http://textiles.ucdavis.edu/

■ UNIVERSITY OF GEORGIA

Graduate School, College of Family and Consumer Sciences, Department of Textiles, Merchandising, and Interiors, Athens, GA 30602

AWARDS MS, PhD.

Faculty: 13 full-time (7 women).
Students: 15 full-time (5 women), 1 (woman) part-time; includes 1 minority (African American), 11 international. 24 applicants, 42% accepted. In 2001, 6 master's, 3 doctorates awarded.
Degree requirements: For master's and doctorate, thesis/dissertation.
Entrance requirements: For master's and doctorate, GRE General Test. *Application deadline:* For fall admission, 7/1 (priority date); for spring admission, 11/15. *Application fee:* $30. Electronic applications accepted.
Expenses: Tuition, state resident: full-time $2,376; part-time $132 per credit hour. Tuition, nonresident: full-time $9,504; part-time $528 per credit hour. Required fees: $236 per semester.
Financial support: Fellowships, research assistantships, teaching assistantships, unspecified assistantships available.

University of Georgia (continued)
Dr. Ian R. Hardin, Head and Graduate Coordinator, 706-542-0357, *Fax:* 706-542-0410, *E-mail:* ihardin@fcs.uga.edu. *Web site:* http://www.fcs.uga.edu/tmi/

■ UNIVERSITY OF KENTUCKY

Graduate School, College of Human Environmental Sciences, Program in Human Environment: Interior Design, Merchandising, and Textiles, Lexington, KY 40506-0032

AWARDS MAIDM, MSIDM.

Faculty: 9 full-time (all women).
Students: 7 full-time (6 women), 2 part-time (1 woman), 2 international. 8 applicants, 50% accepted. In 2001, 3 degrees awarded.
Degree requirements: For master's, thesis optional.
Entrance requirements: For master's, GRE General Test, minimum undergraduate GPA of 2.5. *Application deadline:* For fall admission, 7/19. *Application fee:* $30 ($35 for international students).
Expenses: Tuition, state resident: full-time $4,075; part-time $213 per credit hour. Tuition, nonresident: full-time $11,295; part-time $614 per credit hour.
Financial support: In 2001–02, 1 research assistantship, 6 teaching assistantships were awarded. Unspecified assistantships also available.
Faculty research: Interior design, apparel merchandising, textile evaluation, creativity in design, social-psychological aspects of dress and interiors.
Dr. Kim Spillman-Miller, Director of Graduate Studies, 859-257-7779, *Fax:* 859-257-1278, *E-mail:* kmilller@pop.uky.edu.
Application contact: Dr. Jeannine Blackwell, Associate Dean, 859-257-4905, *Fax:* 859-323-1928.

■ UNIVERSITY OF MISSOURI–COLUMBIA

Graduate School, College of Human Environmental Science, Department of Textiles and Apparel Management, Columbia, MO 65211

AWARDS MA, MS.

Faculty: 5 full-time (all women).
Students: 4 full-time (3 women), 3 part-time (all women), 4 international. 1 applicant, 0% accepted. In 2001, 2 degrees awarded.
Entrance requirements: For master's, GRE General Test, minimum GPA of 3.0. *Application deadline:* For fall admission, 2/1 (priority date); for winter admission, 6/1 (priority date); for spring admission, 10/1 (priority date). Applications are processed on a rolling basis. *Application fee:* $25 ($50 for international students).
Expenses: Tuition, state resident: part-time $179 per credit hour. Tuition, nonresident: part-time $539 per credit hour. Required fees: $122 per semester. Tuition and fees vary according to program.
Financial support: Research assistantships, teaching assistantships, institutionally sponsored loans available.
Dr. Pam Norum, Director of Graduate Studies, 573-882-2934, *E-mail:* norump@missouri.edu. *Web site:* http://web.missouri.edu/~tam/

■ UNIVERSITY OF NEBRASKA–LINCOLN

Graduate College, College of Human Resources and Family Sciences, Department of Textiles, Clothing and Design, Lincoln, NE 68588

AWARDS Human resources and family sciences (PhD); textiles, clothing, and design (MA, MS). Part-time programs available. Postbaccalaureate distance learning degree programs offered (minimal on-campus study).

Faculty: 9.
Students: 14 (all women). Average age 29. 15 applicants, 47% accepted, 1 enrolled. In 2001, 2 degrees awarded.
Degree requirements: For master's, thesis optional.
Entrance requirements: For master's, GRE General Test, TOEFL. *Application deadline:* For fall admission, 3/1 (priority date). Applications are processed on a rolling basis. *Application fee:* $35. Electronic applications accepted.
Expenses: Tuition, state resident: full-time $2,412; part-time $134 per credit. Tuition, nonresident: full-time $6,223; part-time $346 per credit. Tuition and fees vary according to course load.
Financial support: In 2001–02, 4 research assistantships, 2 teaching assistantships were awarded. Fellowships, Federal Work-Study, health care benefits, and unspecified assistantships also available. Financial award application deadline: 2/15.
Faculty research: Merchandising, textile science, fiber arts, textile history, quilt studies.
Dr. Carol Thayer, Acting Chair, 402-472-2911. *Web site:* http://textiles.unl.edu/

■ UNIVERSITY OF NORTH TEXAS

Robert B. Toulouse School of Graduate Studies, School of Merchandising and Hospitality Management, Denton, TX 76203

AWARDS Hotel/restaurant management (MS); merchandising and fabric analytics (MS). Part-time programs available.

Faculty: 21.
Students: 27. In 2001, 5 degrees awarded.
Degree requirements: For master's, thesis or alternative, comprehensive exam.
Entrance requirements: For master's, GRE General Test, minimum GPA of 2.8, previous course work in major area. *Application deadline:* For fall admission, 7/17. *Application fee:* $25 ($50 for international students).
Expenses: Tuition, state resident: part-time $186 per hour. Tuition, nonresident: part-time $319 per hour. Required fees: $88; $21 per hour.
Financial support: Fellowships, research assistantships, teaching assistantships, career-related internships or fieldwork, Federal Work-Study, and institutionally sponsored loans available. Financial award application deadline: 4/1.
Faculty research: Employee imaging, western wear, diversity in the workplace, leadership development, quality assessment.
Dr. Judith C. Forney, Interim Dean, 940-565-2436, *Fax:* 940-565-4348, *E-mail:* forney@smhm.cmm.unt.edu.
Application contact: Dr. Richard Tas, Graduate Adviser, 940-565-2436, *Fax:* 940-565-4348, *E-mail:* tas@smhm.cmm.unt.edu.

■ UNIVERSITY OF RHODE ISLAND

Graduate School, College of Human Science and Services, Department of Textiles, Fashion Merchandising and Design, Kingston, RI 02881

AWARDS MS.

Students: In 2001, 6 degrees awarded.
Entrance requirements: For master's, GRE. *Application deadline:* For fall admission, 4/15 (priority date); for spring admission, 11/15. Applications are processed on a rolling basis. *Application fee:* $35.
Expenses: Tuition, state resident: full-time $3,756; part-time $209 per credit. Tuition, nonresident: full-time $10,774; part-time $599 per credit. Required fees: $1,586; $76 per credit. One-time fee: $60 full-time.
Dr. Martin Bide, Chair, 401-874-4574.

■ THE UNIVERSITY OF TENNESSEE

Graduate School, College of Human Ecology, Program in Human Ecology, Knoxville, TN 37996

AWARDS Child and family studies (PhD); community health (PhD); human resource development (PhD); nutrition science (PhD); retailing and consumer sciences (PhD); textile science (PhD).

Students: 62 full-time (42 women), 44 part-time (34 women); includes 12 minority (11 African Americans, 1 Asian American or Pacific Islander), 20 international. 39 applicants, 44% accepted. In 2001, 22 degrees awarded.
Degree requirements: For doctorate, thesis/dissertation.
Entrance requirements: For doctorate, GRE General Test, TOEFL, minimum GPA of 2.7. *Application deadline:* For fall admission, 2/1 (priority date). Applications are processed on a rolling basis. *Application fee:* $35. Electronic applications accepted.

Expenses: Tuition, state resident: full-time $4,280; part-time $233 per hour. Tuition, nonresident: full-time $12,066; part-time $666 per hour. Tuition and fees vary according to program.
Financial support: Fellowships, research assistantships, teaching assistantships, Federal Work-Study, institutionally sponsored loans, and unspecified assistantships available. Financial award application deadline: 2/1; financial award applicants required to submit FAFSA.
Dr. Billie J. Collier, Interim Head, 865-974-5224, *E-mail:* bcollier@utk.edu.

Find an in-depth description at www.petersons.com/gradchannel.

■ VIRGINIA POLYTECHNIC INSTITUTE AND STATE UNIVERSITY

Graduate School, College of Human Resources and Education, Department of Near Environments, Blacksburg, VA 24061

AWARDS Apparel business and economics (MS, PhD); apparel product design and analysis (MS, PhD); apparel quality analysis (MS, PhD); consumer studies (MS, PhD); family financial management (MS, PhD); household equipment (MS, PhD); housing (MS, PhD); interior design (MS, PhD); resource management (MS, PhD). Part-time programs available.

Faculty: 15 full-time (11 women).
Students: 32 full-time (31 women), 3 part-time; includes 2 minority (both African Americans), 14 international. Average age 24. 31 applicants, 32% accepted. In 2001, 7 master's, 8 doctorates awarded.
Degree requirements: For master's and doctorate, thesis/dissertation.
Entrance requirements: For master's and doctorate, GRE General Test, TOEFL. *Application deadline:* For fall admission, 12/1 (priority date). Applications are processed on a rolling basis. *Application fee:* $45.
Expenses: Tuition, state resident: part-time $241 per hour. Tuition, nonresident: part-time $406 per hour. Tuition and fees vary according to program.
Financial support: In 2001–02, 6 teaching assistantships with full tuition reimbursements (averaging $7,186 per year) were awarded; research assistantships with full tuition reimbursements, career-related internships or fieldwork, tuition waivers (full and partial), and unspecified assistantships also available. Financial award application deadline: 4/1.
Faculty research: Housing for elderly, affordable housing, household time use, phosphate laundry study, economic well-living.
Dr. LuAnn Gaskill, Head, 540-231-6164, *E-mail:* lagaskill@vt.edu.

■ WASHINGTON STATE UNIVERSITY

Graduate School, College of Agriculture and Home Economics, Department of Apparel, Merchandising and Interior Design, Pullman, WA 99164

AWARDS Apparel, merchandising and textiles (MA); interior design (MA).

Faculty: 6 full-time (4 women).
Students: 5 full-time (all women), 1 (woman) part-time; includes 2 minority (1 Asian American or Pacific Islander, 1 Hispanic American), 1 international. Average age 22. 24 applicants, 58% accepted. In 2001, 2 degrees awarded.
Degree requirements: For master's, thesis, oral exam.
Entrance requirements: For master's, TOEFL, minimum GPA of 3.0, 3 writing samples. *Application deadline:* For fall admission, 3/1 (priority date). Applications are processed on a rolling basis. *Application fee:* $35. Electronic applications accepted.
Expenses: Tuition, state resident: full-time $6,088; part-time $304 per semester. Tuition, nonresident: full-time $14,918; part-time $746 per semester. Tuition and fees vary according to program.
Financial support: In 2001–02, 5 students received support, including 4 teaching assistantships with full and partial tuition reimbursements available; research assistantships with full and partial tuition reimbursements available, career-related internships or fieldwork, Federal Work-Study, institutionally sponsored loans, and scholarships/grants also available. Financial award application deadline: 4/1; financial award applicants required to submit FAFSA.
Faculty research: Product development, design theory, cultural diversity, computer design accessibility. *Total annual research expenditures:* $48,961.
Dr. Carol J. Salusso, Chair, 509-335-7949, *Fax:* 509-355-7299, *E-mail:* amid@wsu.edu.
Application contact: Aviva M. Suchow, Office Assistant, 509-335-3823, *Fax:* 509-335-7299, *E-mail:* suchow@wsu.edu. *Web site:* http://amid.wsu.edu/

CONSUMER ECONOMICS

■ COLORADO STATE UNIVERSITY

Graduate School, College of Applied Human Sciences, Department of Design and Merchandising, Fort Collins, CO 80523-0015

AWARDS Apparel and merchandising (MS); interior design (MS). Part-time programs available.

Faculty: 15 full-time (12 women).
Students: 10 full-time (8 women), 15 part-time (14 women); includes 4 minority (1 African American, 1 Asian American or Pacific Islander, 1 Hispanic American, 1 Native American), 2 international. Average age 33. 33 applicants, 55% accepted, 7 enrolled. In 2001, 3 degrees awarded.
Degree requirements: For master's, thesis.
Entrance requirements: For master's, GRE General Test, TOEFL, minimum GPA of 3.0. *Application deadline:* For fall admission, 1/15 (priority date). Applications are processed on a rolling basis. *Application fee:* $30. Electronic applications accepted.
Expenses: Tuition, state resident: full-time $2,880; part-time $160 per credit. Tuition, nonresident: full-time $11,412; part-time $634 per credit. Required fees: $750; $34 per credit.
Financial support: In 2001–02, 2 research assistantships, 3 teaching assistantships were awarded. Fellowships, career-related internships or fieldwork, Federal Work-Study, institutionally sponsored loans, and traineeships also available. Support available to part-time students. Financial award application deadline: 1/15; financial award applicants required to submit FAFSA.
Faculty research: Consumer and textile end use, apparel design, consumer behavior and technology, interior design.
Dr. Kevin Oltjenbruns, Head, 970-491-5811, *Fax:* 470-491-7859, *E-mail:* oltjenbrun@cahs.colostate.edu.
Application contact: Jen Ogle, Graduate Coordinator, 970-491-3794, *Fax:* 970-491-4855, *E-mail:* ogle@cahs.colostate.edu. *Web site:* http://www.cahs.colostate.edu/

■ CORNELL UNIVERSITY

Graduate School, Graduate Fields of Human Ecology, Field of Policy Analysis and Management, Ithaca, NY 14853-0001

AWARDS Consumer policy evaluation (PhD); family and social welfare policy (PhD); health administration (MHA); health management policy (PhD).

Faculty: 33 full-time.
Students: 52 full-time (36 women); includes 19 minority (9 African Americans, 7 Asian Americans or Pacific Islanders, 3 Hispanic Americans), 12 international. 88 applicants, 52% accepted.
Degree requirements: For master's, thesis.
Entrance requirements: For doctorate, GRE General Test, 2 letters of recommendation. *Application deadline:* For fall admission, 2/1. *Application fee:* $65. Electronic applications accepted.
Expenses: Tuition: Full-time $25,970. Required fees: $50.
Financial support: In 2001–02, 31 students received support, including 13 fellowships with full and partial tuition reimbursements available, 3 research assistantships with full and partial tuition

Cornell University (continued)
reimbursements available, 15 teaching assistantships with full and partial tuition reimbursements available; institutionally sponsored loans, scholarships/grants, tuition waivers (full and partial), and unspecified assistantships also available. Financial award applicants required to submit FAFSA.
Faculty research: Health policy analysis and management, family and social welfare policy analysis and management, policy planning and evaluation, mixed methods research, applied research methods.
Application contact: Graduate Field Assistant, 607-255-7772, *Fax:* 607-255-4071, *E-mail:* PhDprogram-pam_phd@cornell.edu. *Web site:* http://www.gradschool.cornell.edu/grad/fields_1/pam.html

■ FLORIDA STATE UNIVERSITY

Graduate Studies, College of Human Sciences, Department of Family and Child Sciences, Tallahassee, FL 32306

AWARDS Child development (MS, PhD); family and consumer sciences education (MS, PhD); family relations (MS, PhD). Part-time programs available.

Faculty: 13 full-time (9 women).
Students: 22 full-time (18 women), 21 part-time (20 women); includes 16 minority (14 African Americans, 1 Asian American or Pacific Islander, 1 Hispanic American), 2 international. Average age 32. 22 applicants, 59% accepted, 9 enrolled. In 2001, 10 master's, 4 doctorates awarded.
Degree requirements: For master's, thesis optional; for doctorate, thesis/dissertation.
Entrance requirements: For master's and doctorate, GRE General Test, minimum GPA of 3.0. *Application fee:* $20. Electronic applications accepted.
Expenses: Tuition, state resident: part-time $163 per credit hour. Tuition, nonresident: part-time $570 per credit hour. Tuition and fees vary according to program.
Financial support: In 2001–02, 31 students received support, including 1 fellowship (averaging $10,000 per year), 14 research assistantships with partial tuition reimbursements available (averaging $5,000 per year), 16 teaching assistantships with partial tuition reimbursements available (averaging $5,000 per year); career-related internships or fieldwork, Federal Work-Study, institutionally sponsored loans, scholarships/grants, and unspecified assistantships also available. Financial award applicants required to submit FAFSA.
Faculty research: Addictions, family therapy, sexuality, parent-child relations, adolescent development.
Dr. Jay Schvaneveldt, Chair, 850-644-3217, *Fax:* 850-644-3439, *E-mail:* cwalersc@mailer.fsu.edu.
Application contact: Lynn LaCombe, Program Assistant, 850-644-3217, *Fax:* 850-644-3439, *E-mail:* llacomb@mailer.fsu.edu. *Web site:* http://www.chs.fsu.edu/dfcs/

Find an in-depth description at www.petersons.com/gradchannel.

■ FLORIDA STATE UNIVERSITY

Graduate Studies, College of Human Sciences, Department of Textiles and Consumer Sciences, Tallahassee, FL 32306

AWARDS MS, PhD. Part-time programs available.

Faculty: 10 full-time (9 women).
Students: 20 full-time (all women), 6 part-time (4 women); includes 5 minority (2 African Americans, 1 Asian American or Pacific Islander, 2 Hispanic Americans), 8 international. 35 applicants, 57% accepted, 8 enrolled. In 2001, 7 master's, 2 doctorates awarded.
Degree requirements: For master's, thesis optional; for doctorate, thesis/dissertation.
Entrance requirements: For master's and doctorate, GRE General Test, minimum GPA of 3.0. *Application deadline:* For fall admission, 2/1 (priority date); for spring admission, 11/1. Applications are processed on a rolling basis. *Application fee:* $20. Electronic applications accepted.
Expenses: Tuition, state resident: part-time $163 per credit hour. Tuition, nonresident: part-time $570 per credit hour. Tuition and fees vary according to program.
Financial support: In 2001–02, 12 students received support, including 1 fellowship with partial tuition reimbursement available (averaging $10,000 per year), 2 research assistantships with partial tuition reimbursements available (averaging $8,000 per year), 9 teaching assistantships with partial tuition reimbursements available (averaging $8,000 per year); career-related internships or fieldwork, Federal Work-Study, institutionally sponsored loans, scholarships/grants, and unspecified assistantships also available. Financial award application deadline: 3/1; financial award applicants required to submit FAFSA.
Faculty research: Soft goods retailing, small business strategies, textile product performance, consumer behavior, accessible housing. *Total annual research expenditures:* $67,689.
Dr. Rinn Cloud, Chair, 850-644-2498, *Fax:* 850-644-0700, *E-mail:* rcloud@garnet.acns.fsu.edu.
Application contact: Dr. Jeanne Heitmeyer, Graduate Coordinator, 850-644-2498, *Fax:* 850-644-0700, *E-mail:* jheitmey@mailer.fsu.edu.

Find an in-depth description at www.petersons.com/gradchannel.

■ IOWA STATE UNIVERSITY OF SCIENCE AND TECHNOLOGY

Graduate College, College of Family and Consumer Sciences, Department of Apparel, Education Studies, and Hospitality Management, Ames, IA 50011

AWARDS Family and consumer science education and studies (M Ed); family and consumer sciences education and studies (MS, PhD); foodservice and lodging management (MFCS, MS, PhD); textiles and clothing (MFCS, MS, PhD).

Faculty: 25 full-time.
Students: 22 full-time (15 women), 32 part-time (28 women). 71 applicants, 18% accepted, 0 enrolled. In 2001, 7 master's, 5 doctorates awarded.
Degree requirements: For doctorate, thesis/dissertation.
Entrance requirements: For master's and doctorate, GRE General Test, TOEFL or IELTS. *Application fee:* $20 ($50 for international students).
Expenses: Tuition, state resident: full-time $1,851. Tuition, nonresident: full-time $5,449. Tuition and fees vary according to program.
Financial support: In 2001–02, 8 research assistantships (averaging $12,645 per year), 4 teaching assistantships (averaging $12,104 per year) were awarded.
Dr. Mary B. Gregoire, Chair, 515-294-7474, *Fax:* 515-294-6364, *E-mail:* texclo@iastate.edu.

■ IOWA STATE UNIVERSITY OF SCIENCE AND TECHNOLOGY

Graduate College, College of Family and Consumer Sciences, Program in Family and Consumer Sciences Education and Studies, Ames, IA 50011

AWARDS M Ed, MS, PhD.

Students: 3 full-time (2 women), 15 part-time (14 women); includes 2 minority (both African Americans), 4 international. 9 applicants, 33% accepted, 1 enrolled. In 2001, 1 degree awarded.
Degree requirements: For master's, thesis (for some programs); for doctorate, thesis/dissertation. *Median time to degree:* Doctorate–3.7 years full-time.
Entrance requirements: For master's and doctorate, GRE General Test, TOEFL or IELTS, resumé. *Application deadline:* For fall admission, 1/15 (priority date); for spring admission, 9/15. *Application fee:* $20 ($50 for international students). Electronic applications accepted.
Expenses: Tuition, state resident: full-time $1,851. Tuition, nonresident: full-time $5,449. Tuition and fees vary according to program.
Financial support: In 2001–02, 2 research assistantships with partial tuition reimbursements (averaging $11,913 per

year), 1 teaching assistantship with partial tuition reimbursement (averaging $10,168 per year) were awarded. Scholarships/grants also available.
Dr. Cheryl O. Ptausafus, Director of Graduate Education, 515-294-7474, *E-mail:* feeds@iastate.edu. *Web site:* http://www.iastate.edu/~fceds/

■ IOWA STATE UNIVERSITY OF SCIENCE AND TECHNOLOGY

Graduate College, Interdisciplinary Programs, Program in Family and Consumer Sciences, Ames, IA 50011

AWARDS MFCS.

Students: 1 (woman) full-time, 9 part-time (all women); includes 1 minority (Native American). 7 applicants, 71% accepted, 4 enrolled. In 2001, 7 degrees awarded.
Degree requirements: For master's, thesis or alternative. *Median time to degree:* Master's–3.7 years full-time.
Entrance requirements: For master's, GRE General Test, TOEFL or IELTS. *Application deadline:* For fall admission, 3/1; for spring admission, 10/1. *Application fee:* $20 ($50 for international students). Electronic applications accepted.
Expenses: Tuition, state resident: full-time $1,851. Tuition, nonresident: full-time $5,449. Tuition and fees vary according to program.
Financial support: In 2001–02, 1 research assistantship with partial tuition reimbursement (averaging $11,312 per year), 2 teaching assistantships with partial tuition reimbursements (averaging $11,312 per year) were awarded. Scholarships/grants, health care benefits, and unspecified assistantships also available.
Dr. Mary Winter, Supervisory Committee Chair, 515-294-5982, *E-mail:* mfcsinfo@iastate.edu. *Web site:* http://www.fcs.iastate.edu/

■ MICHIGAN STATE UNIVERSITY

Graduate School, College of Human Ecology, Department of Family and Child Ecology, East Lansing, MI 48824

AWARDS Child development (MA); community service-urban studies (MS); community services (MS); family and child ecology (PhD); family consumer sciences education (MA); family ecology (PhD); family economics and management (MA); family studies (MA); home economics education (MA); marriage and family therapy (MA). Part-time and evening/weekend programs available. Postbaccalaureate distance learning degree programs offered.

Faculty: 26.
Students: 56 full-time (50 women), 75 part-time (67 women); includes 28 minority (20 African Americans, 2 Asian Americans or Pacific Islanders, 6 Hispanic Americans), 21 international. Average age 35. 80 applicants, 61% accepted. In 2001, 39 master's, 9 doctorates awarded.
Degree requirements: For master's, thesis optional; for doctorate, thesis/dissertation.
Entrance requirements: For master's, GRE General Test, minimum GPA of 3.0 in last 2 years of undergraduate course work; for doctorate, GRE General Test. *Application deadline:* Applications are processed on a rolling basis. *Application fee:* $30 ($40 for international students). Electronic applications accepted.
Expenses: Tuition, state resident: part-time $244 per credit hour. Tuition, nonresident: part-time $494 per credit hour. Required fees: $268 per semester. Tuition and fees vary according to course load, degree level and program.
Financial support: In 2001–02, 35 fellowships with tuition reimbursements (averaging $2,480 per year), 8 research assistantships with tuition reimbursements (averaging $10,944 per year), 14 teaching assistantships with tuition reimbursements (averaging $10,845 per year) were awarded. Financial award applicants required to submit FAFSA.
Faculty research: Early childhood education, family dynamics, family utilization, parenting. *Total annual research expenditures:* $357,600.
Dr. Anne Soderman, Chairperson, 517-432-2953, *E-mail:* fce@msu.edu. *Web site:* http://www.he.msu.edu/fce.html/

■ MINNESOTA STATE UNIVERSITY, MANKATO

College of Graduate Studies, College of Allied Health and Nursing, Department of Family Consumer Science and Interior Design, Mankato, MN 56001

AWARDS MS, MT.

Faculty: 6 full-time (5 women).
Students: 5 full-time (3 women), 5 part-time (4 women). Average age 34. In 2001, 1 degree awarded.
Degree requirements: For master's, one foreign language, thesis or alternative, comprehensive exam.
Entrance requirements: For master's, GRE General Test, minimum GPA of 3.0 during previous 2 years. *Application deadline:* For fall admission, 7/9 (priority date); for spring admission, 11/27. Applications are processed on a rolling basis. *Application fee:* $20.
Expenses: Tuition, state resident: full-time $3,253; part-time $157 per credit. Tuition, nonresident: full-time $4,893; part-time $248 per credit. Required fees: $24 per credit. Tuition and fees vary according to reciprocity agreements.
Financial support: Research assistantships with full tuition reimbursements, teaching assistantships with full tuition reimbursements, career-related internships or fieldwork, Federal Work-Study, and institutionally sponsored loans available. Support available to part-time students. Financial award application deadline: 3/15.
Faculty research: Family consumer science education, factors affecting success in teaching.
Dr. Lois Hughes, Head, 507-389-5924.
Application contact: Joni Roberts, Admissions Coordinator, 507-389-5244, *Fax:* 507-389-5974, *E-mail:* grad@mankato.msus.edu. *Web site:* http://www.mankato.msus.edu/dept/fcs/

■ MONTCLAIR STATE UNIVERSITY

The School of Graduate, Professional and Continuing Education, College of Education and Human Services, Department of Human Ecology, Upper Montclair, NJ 07043-1624

AWARDS Family life education (MA); family relations/child development (MA); home economics education (MA); home management/consumer economics (MA); nutrition education (MA). Part-time and evening/weekend programs available.

Degree requirements: For master's, thesis or alternative, comprehensive exam.
Entrance requirements: For master's, GRE General Test. Electronic applications accepted. *Web site:* http://www.montclair.edu

■ THE OHIO STATE UNIVERSITY

Graduate School, College of Human Ecology, Program in Family Resource Management, Columbus, OH 43210

AWARDS MS, PhD.

Degree requirements: For master's, thesis optional; for doctorate, thesis/dissertation.
Entrance requirements: For master's and doctorate, GRE General Test.

■ PURDUE UNIVERSITY

Graduate School, School of Consumer and Family Sciences, Department of Consumer Sciences and Retailing, West Lafayette, IN 47907

AWARDS Consumer behavior (MS, PhD); family and consumer economics (MS, PhD); retail management (MS, PhD); textile science (MS, PhD). Part-time programs available.

Faculty: 11.
Students: 20 full-time (14 women), 20 part-time (12 women); includes 5 minority (1 African American, 4 Asian Americans or Pacific Islanders), 32 international. Average age 30. 48 applicants, 46% accepted. In 2001, 2 master's, 2 doctorates awarded.
Degree requirements: For master's and doctorate, thesis/dissertation.
Entrance requirements: For master's and doctorate, GMAT or GRE General Test, TOEFL. *Application fee:* $30. Electronic applications accepted.
Expenses: Tuition, state resident: full-time $4,164; part-time $149 per credit hour. Tuition, nonresident: full-time $13,872;

Purdue University (continued)
part-time $458 per credit hour. Tuition and fees vary according to campus/location and program.
Financial support: Fellowships, research assistantships, teaching assistantships, career-related internships or fieldwork available. Support available to part-time students. Financial award applicants required to submit FAFSA.
Faculty research: Family financial resources, retail management and patronage, chemical analysis of textile dyes and finishes.
R. A. Feinberg, Head, 765-494-8296, *Fax:* 765-494-0869.
Application contact: Jean M. Navarre, Graduate Admissions Coordinator, 765-494-8356, *Fax:* 765-494-0869, *E-mail:* jnavarre@purdue.edu. *Web site:* http://www.cfs.purdue.edu/conscirt/

■ SYRACUSE UNIVERSITY

Graduate School, College of Visual and Performing Arts, Department of Consumer Studies, Syracuse, NY 13244-0003

AWARDS MA, MS.

Faculty: 1 (woman) full-time.
Students: 1 (woman) full-time. Average age 37.
Entrance requirements: For master's, GRE General Test. *Application deadline:* For spring admission, 3/1 (priority date). Applications are processed on a rolling basis. *Application fee:* $50. Electronic applications accepted.
Expenses: Tuition: Full-time $15,528; part-time $647 per credit. Required fees: $420; $38 per term. Tuition and fees vary according to program.
Financial support: Fellowships, research assistantships, teaching assistantships, Federal Work-Study and tuition waivers (partial) available.
Dr. Linda Cushman, Chair, 315-443-4635, *E-mail:* lmcushma@syr.edu.
Application contact: Sarah Dayton, Information Contact, 315-443-9631.

■ TEXAS TECH UNIVERSITY

Graduate School, College of Human Sciences, Department of Merchandising, Environmental Design, and Consumer Economics, Program in Environmental Design and Consumer Economics, Lubbock, TX 79409

AWARDS PhD. Part-time programs available.

Faculty: 12 full-time (7 women).
Students: 6 full-time (3 women), 3 part-time; includes 2 minority (both African Americans), 3 international. Average age 37. 6 applicants, 67% accepted, 2 enrolled. In 2001, 1 degree awarded.
Degree requirements: For doctorate, thesis/dissertation.
Entrance requirements: For doctorate, GRE General Test, GMAT. *Application deadline:* Applications are processed on a rolling basis. *Application fee:* $25 ($50 for international students).
Expenses: Tuition, state resident: full-time $1,926; part-time $107 per credit hour. Tuition, nonresident: full-time $5,724; part-time $318 per credit hour. Required fees: $779; $737 per year. Tuition and fees vary according to course level, course load and program.
Financial support: Fellowships, research assistantships, teaching assistantships, career-related internships or fieldwork, Federal Work-Study, and institutionally sponsored loans available. Support available to part-time students. Financial award application deadline: 5/1; financial award applicants required to submit FAFSA.
Faculty research: Environmental design; surface design, purchase, and consumption of leather products; multicultural housing environments and behavior correlations.
Application contact: Dr. Steven M. Harris, Associate Dean, 806-742-3031, *Fax:* 806-742-1849, *E-mail:* sharris@HS.ttu.edu.

■ THE UNIVERSITY OF ALABAMA

Graduate School, College of Human Environmental Sciences, Department of Consumer Sciences, Tuscaloosa, AL 35487

AWARDS MSHES.

Faculty: 5 full-time (2 women), 1 (woman) part-time/adjunct.
Students: 1 applicant, 0% accepted. In 2001, 2 degrees awarded.
Degree requirements: For master's, thesis.
Entrance requirements: For master's, GRE General Test or MAT, minimum GPA of 3.0. *Application deadline:* For fall admission, 7/6. Applications are processed on a rolling basis. *Application fee:* $25.
Expenses: Tuition, state resident: full-time $3,292; part-time $183 per credit hour. Tuition, nonresident: full-time $8,912; part-time $495 per credit hour. Tuition and fees vary according to course load, campus/location and program.
Financial support: In 2001–02, 1 research assistantship with tuition reimbursement (averaging $8,100 per year), 1 teaching assistantship with tuition reimbursement (averaging $8,100 per year) were awarded. Career-related internships or fieldwork also available. Financial award application deadline: 3/15.
Faculty research: Time allocation, energy consumption, food consumption patterns, expenditures patterns.
Dr. Milla D. Boschung, Head and Assistant Dean, 205-348-8722, *Fax:* 205-348-1786, *E-mail:* mboschun@ches.ua.edu. *Web site:* http://www.ches.ua.edu/

■ THE UNIVERSITY OF ARIZONA

Graduate College, College of Agriculture and Life Sciences, School of Family and Consumer Sciences, Division of Family Studies and Human Development, Tucson, AZ 85721

AWARDS Family and consumer sciences (MS); family studies and human development (PhD). Terminal master's awarded for partial completion of doctoral program.

Entrance requirements: For master's and doctorate, GRE General Test, TOEFL, minimum undergraduate GPA of 3.0.
Expenses: Tuition, state resident: full-time $2,490; part-time $436 per unit. Tuition, nonresident: full-time $10,300; part-time $436 per unit. Full-time tuition and fees vary according to degree level and program. *Web site:* http://ag.arizona.edu/fcs/fshd

■ THE UNIVERSITY OF ARIZONA

Graduate College, College of Agriculture and Life Sciences, School of Family and Consumer Sciences, Division of Retailing and Consumer Sciences, Tucson, AZ 85721

AWARDS MS, PhD.

Entrance requirements: For master's and doctorate, GRE General Test, TOEFL, minimum GPA of 3.0.
Expenses: Tuition, state resident: full-time $2,490; part-time $436 per unit. Tuition, nonresident: full-time $10,300; part-time $436 per unit. Full-time tuition and fees vary according to degree level and program. *Web site:* http://ag.arizona.edu/fcs/rcsc

■ UNIVERSITY OF GEORGIA

Graduate School, College of Family and Consumer Sciences, Department of Housing and Consumer Economics, Athens, GA 30602

AWARDS MS, PhD.

Faculty: 11 full-time (8 women).
Students: 16 full-time (11 women), 3 part-time (2 women); includes 3 minority (1 African American, 2 Asian Americans or Pacific Islanders), 12 international. 23 applicants, 30% accepted. In 2001, 1 master's awarded.
Degree requirements: For master's and doctorate, thesis/dissertation.
Entrance requirements: For master's and doctorate, GRE General Test, TOEFL. *Application deadline:* For fall admission, 7/1 (priority date); for spring admission, 11/15. *Application fee:* $30. Electronic applications accepted.
Expenses: Tuition, state resident: full-time $2,376; part-time $132 per credit hour. Tuition, nonresident: full-time $9,504; part-time $528 per credit hour. Required fees: $236 per semester.

Financial support: Fellowships, research assistantships, teaching assistantships, unspecified assistantships available.
Dr. Brenda J. Cude, Head, 706-542-4856, *Fax:* 706-583-0313, *E-mail:* bcude@fcs.uga.edu.
Application contact: Dr. Teresa Maudlin, Graduate Coordinator, 706-542-4854, *Fax:* 706-583-0313, *E-mail:* tmaudlin@fcs.uga.edu. *Web site:* http://www.fcs.uga.edu/hce/

■ UNIVERSITY OF ILLINOIS AT URBANA–CHAMPAIGN

Graduate College, College of Agricultural, Consumer and Environmental Sciences, Department of Agricultural and Consumer Economics, Champaign, IL 61820

AWARDS MS, PhD.

Faculty: 41 full-time (13 women), 1 part-time/adjunct (0 women).
Students: 80 full-time (34 women); includes 4 minority (all African Americans), 61 international. 107 applicants, 23% accepted. In 2001, 8 master's, 15 doctorates awarded.
Degree requirements: For master's and doctorate, thesis/dissertation.
Entrance requirements: For master's, minimum GPA of 3.0. *Application deadline:* Applications are processed on a rolling basis. *Application fee:* $40 ($50 for international students). Electronic applications accepted.
Expenses: Tuition, state resident: part-time $3,227 per degree program. Tuition, nonresident: part-time $7,169 per degree program. Tuition and fees vary according to program.
Financial support: In 2001–02, 6 fellowships, 48 research assistantships, 12 teaching assistantships were awarded. Tuition waivers (full and partial) also available. Financial award application deadline: 2/15.
Darrel L. Good, Interim Head, 217-333-8859, *Fax:* 217-333-5538, *E-mail:* d-good@uiuc.edu.
Application contact: Linda Foste, Secretary, 217-333-1830, *Fax:* 217-333-5538, *E-mail:* l-foste@uiuc.edu. *Web site:* http://w3.ag.uiuc.edu/ACE/welcome/

■ THE UNIVERSITY OF MEMPHIS

Graduate School, College of Education, Department of Consumer Science and Education, Memphis, TN 38152

AWARDS Clinical nutrition (MS); consumer science and education (MS). Part-time programs available.

Faculty: 6 full-time (all women), 4 part-time/adjunct (all women).
Students: 16 full-time (all women), 12 part-time (all women); includes 8 minority (all African Americans). Average age 28. 21 applicants, 76% accepted. In 2001, 6 degrees awarded.
Degree requirements: For master's, thesis (for some programs), comprehensive exam.
Entrance requirements: For master's, GRE General Test or MAT. *Application deadline:* For fall admission, 8/1; for spring admission, 2/15. *Application fee:* $25 ($50 for international students).
Expenses: Tuition, state resident: full-time $2,026. Tuition, nonresident: full-time $4,528.
Financial support: In 2001–02, 15 students received support, including 13 research assistantships with tuition reimbursements available, 1 teaching assistantship with tuition reimbursement available; career-related internships or fieldwork and scholarships/grants also available.
Faculty research: State vocation education services, marketing education, clinical nutrition outcomes. *Total annual research expenditures:* $272,700.
Dr. Dixie R. Crase, Chair and Coordinator of Graduate Studies, 901-678-2301, *Fax:* 901-678-5324, *E-mail:* drcrase@memphis.edu.
Application contact: Dr. Linda Clemens, Director, Clinical Nutrition, 901-678-3108, *Fax:* 901-678-5324, *E-mail:* lhclemns@memphis.edu.

■ UNIVERSITY OF MISSOURI–COLUMBIA

Graduate School, College of Human Environmental Science, Department of Consumer and Family Economics, Columbia, MO 65211

AWARDS MS.

Faculty: 6 full-time (2 women), 1 (woman) part-time/adjunct.
Students: 5 full-time (4 women), 4 part-time (3 women), 4 international. 2 applicants, 50% accepted. In 2001, 1 degree awarded.
Entrance requirements: For master's, GRE General Test, minimum GPA of 3.0. *Application deadline:* Applications are processed on a rolling basis. *Application fee:* $25 ($50 for international students).
Expenses: Tuition, state resident: part-time $179 per credit hour. Tuition, nonresident: part-time $539 per credit hour. Required fees: $122 per semester. Tuition and fees vary according to program.
Financial support: Research assistantships, teaching assistantships, institutionally sponsored loans available.
Dr. Robert Weagley, Director of Graduate Studies, 573-882-9651, *E-mail:* weagleyr@missouri.edu. *Web site:* http://web.missouri.edu/~cfewww/

■ UNIVERSITY OF NEBRASKA–LINCOLN

Graduate College, College of Human Resources and Family Sciences, Department of Family and Consumer Science, Lincoln, NE 68588

AWARDS Family and consumer sciences (MS); human resources and family sciences (PhD). Postbaccalaureate distance learning degree programs offered.

Faculty: 28.
Students: 25 (20 women); includes 2 minority (1 African American, 1 Hispanic American) 2 international. Average age 32. 19 applicants, 53% accepted, 6 enrolled. In 2001, 5 degrees awarded.
Degree requirements: For master's, thesis optional.
Entrance requirements: For master's, GRE General Test, TOEFL. *Application deadline:* For fall admission, 2/1; for spring admission, 10/1. *Application fee:* $35. Electronic applications accepted.
Expenses: Tuition, state resident: full-time $2,412; part-time $134 per credit. Tuition, nonresident: full-time $6,223; part-time $346 per credit. Tuition and fees vary according to course load.
Financial support: In 2001–02, 1 fellowship, 5 research assistantships, 2 teaching assistantships were awarded. Federal Work-Study, health care benefits, and unspecified assistantships also available. Financial award application deadline: 2/15.
Faculty research: Marriage and family therapy, child development/early childhood education, family financial management.
Dr. Julie Johnson, Interim Chair, 402-472-2957. *Web site:* http://www.chrfs.unl.edu/FCS.htm/

■ THE UNIVERSITY OF TENNESSEE

Graduate School, College of Human Ecology, Program in Human Ecology, Knoxville, TN 37996

AWARDS Child and family studies (PhD); community health (PhD); human resource development (PhD); nutrition science (PhD); retailing and consumer sciences (PhD); textile science (PhD).

Students: 62 full-time (42 women), 44 part-time (34 women); includes 12 minority (11 African Americans, 1 Asian American or Pacific Islander), 20 international. 39 applicants, 44% accepted. In 2001, 22 degrees awarded.
Degree requirements: For doctorate, thesis/dissertation.
Entrance requirements: For doctorate, GRE General Test, TOEFL, minimum GPA of 2.7. *Application deadline:* For fall admission, 2/1 (priority date). Applications are processed on a rolling basis. *Application fee:* $35. Electronic applications accepted.
Expenses: Tuition, state resident: full-time $4,280; part-time $233 per hour. Tuition, nonresident: full-time $12,066; part-time

The University of Tennessee (continued)
$666 per hour. Tuition and fees vary according to program.
Financial support: Fellowships, research assistantships, teaching assistantships, Federal Work-Study, institutionally sponsored loans, and unspecified assistantships available. Financial award application deadline: 2/1; financial award applicants required to submit FAFSA.
Dr. Billie J. Collier, Interim Head, 865-974-5224, *E-mail:* bcollier@utk.edu.

Find an in-depth description at www.petersons.com/gradchannel.

■ UNIVERSITY OF UTAH

Graduate School, College of Social and Behavioral Science, Department of Family and Consumer Studies, Salt Lake City, UT 84112-1107

AWARDS MS.

Faculty: 14 full-time (8 women), 7 part-time/adjunct (0 women).
Students: 8 full-time (all women), 3 part-time (all women); includes 1 minority (Asian American or Pacific Islander), 2 international. Average age 34. 13 applicants, 54% accepted. In 2001, 3 degrees awarded.
Degree requirements: For master's, thesis optional.
Entrance requirements: For master's, GRE General Test, TOEFL. *Application deadline:* For fall admission, 3/1. *Application fee:* $40 ($60 for international students).
Expenses: Tuition, state resident: part-time $320 per semester hour. Tuition, nonresident: part-time $1,135 per semester hour. Required fees: $143 per semester hour. Tuition and fees vary according to course load, degree level and program.
Financial support: In 2001–02, 8 students received support, including 3 research assistantships with full tuition reimbursements available (averaging $9,000 per year), 5 teaching assistantships with full tuition reimbursements available (averaging $9,000 per year). Financial award application deadline: 3/1.
Faculty research: Social, physical and economic contexts of families and communities. *Total annual research expenditures:* $70,143.
Cathleen D. Zick, Chair, 801-581-7712, *Fax:* 801-581-5156, *E-mail:* zick@fcs.utah.edu.
Application contact: Shauna Wright, Advisor, 801-581-4431, *E-mail:* shauna.wright@fcs.utah.edu.

■ UNIVERSITY OF VERMONT

Graduate College, College of Agriculture and Life Sciences, Department of Nutrition and Food Sciences, Burlington, VT 05405

AWARDS Family and consumer sciences (MAT); nutritional sciences (MS).

Degree requirements: For master's, thesis.
Entrance requirements: For master's, GRE General Test, TOEFL.
Expenses: Tuition, state resident: part-time $335 per credit. Tuition, nonresident: part-time $838 per credit.

■ UNIVERSITY OF WISCONSIN–MADISON

Graduate School, School of Human Ecology, Program in Consumer Behavior and Family Economics, Madison, WI 53706-1380

AWARDS MS, PhD.

Faculty: 11 full-time (10 women).
Students: 5 full-time (2 women), 2 part-time (both women). Average age 31. 48 applicants, 48% accepted, 7 enrolled. In 2001, 2 degrees awarded.
Degree requirements: For master's and doctorate, thesis/dissertation.
Entrance requirements: For master's, GRE General Test. *Application deadline:* For fall admission, 2/15 (priority date). Applications are processed on a rolling basis. *Application fee:* $45. Electronic applications accepted.
Expenses: Tuition, state resident: full-time $7,361; part-time $399 per credit. Tuition, nonresident: full-time $20,499; part-time $1,282 per credit. Required fees: $34 per credit. Full-time tuition and fees vary according to course load, program, reciprocity agreements and student level.
Financial support: In 2001–02, 2 research assistantships with full tuition reimbursements, 4 teaching assistantships with full tuition reimbursements were awarded. Fellowships, institutionally sponsored loans, scholarships/grants, and unspecified assistantships also available.
Faculty research: Economic well-being of elderly, finance, financial planning, health care policy, retailing.
Cynthia Jasper, Chair, 608-263-5675, *Fax:* 608-262-5335.
Application contact: Karen C. Holden, Professor, 608-263-1802, *E-mail:* holden@lafollette.wisc.edu.

■ UNIVERSITY OF WYOMING

Graduate School, College of Agriculture, Department of Family and Consumer Sciences, Laramie, WY 82071

AWARDS MS. Part-time programs available.

Faculty: 11 full-time (6 women).
Students: 5 full-time (3 women), 8 part-time (7 women). 2 applicants, 100% accepted. In 2001, 3 degrees awarded.
Degree requirements: For master's, thesis.
Entrance requirements: For master's, GRE General Test, minimum GPA of 3.0. *Application deadline:* For fall admission, 6/1 (priority date); for spring admission, 10/1 (priority date). Applications are processed on a rolling basis. *Application fee:* $40. Electronic applications accepted.
Expenses: Tuition, state resident: full-time $2,895; part-time $161 per credit hour. Tuition, nonresident: full-time $8,367; part-time $465 per credit hour. Required fees: $491; $10 per credit hour. $2 per credit hour. Tuition and fees vary according to course load and program.
Financial support: In 2001–02, 5 research assistantships with full tuition reimbursements (averaging $8,667 per year), 3 teaching assistantships with full tuition reimbursements (averaging $8,667 per year) were awarded. Career-related internships or fieldwork, Federal Work-Study, institutionally sponsored loans, and scholarships/grants also available. Financial award application deadline: 3/1; financial award applicants required to submit FAFSA.
Faculty research: Physical and chemical characteristics of wool, rural retailing, family stress and coping, ethics in research conducted with young children, food product development.
Dr. Bernita Quoss, Head, 307-766-4145, *Fax:* 307-766-5686, *E-mail:* bquoss@uwyo.edu.

■ VIRGINIA POLYTECHNIC INSTITUTE AND STATE UNIVERSITY

Graduate School, College of Human Resources and Education, Department of Near Environments, Blacksburg, VA 24061

AWARDS Apparel business and economics (MS, PhD); apparel product design and analysis (MS, PhD); apparel quality analysis (MS, PhD); consumer studies (MS, PhD); family financial management (MS, PhD); household equipment (MS, PhD); housing (MS, PhD); interior design (MS, PhD); resource management (MS, PhD). Part-time programs available.

Faculty: 15 full-time (11 women).
Students: 32 full-time (31 women), 3 part-time; includes 2 minority (both African Americans), 14 international. Average age 24. 31 applicants, 32% accepted. In 2001, 7 master's, 8 doctorates awarded.
Degree requirements: For master's and doctorate, thesis/dissertation.
Entrance requirements: For master's and doctorate, GRE General Test, TOEFL. *Application deadline:* For fall admission, 12/1 (priority date). Applications are processed on a rolling basis. *Application fee:* $45.
Expenses: Tuition, state resident: part-time $241 per hour. Tuition, nonresident: part-time $406 per hour. Tuition and fees vary according to program.
Financial support: In 2001–02, 6 teaching assistantships with full tuition reimbursements (averaging $7,186 per year) were awarded; research assistantships with full tuition reimbursements, career-related

internships or fieldwork, tuition waivers (full and partial), and unspecified assistantships also available. Financial award application deadline: 4/1.
Faculty research: Housing for elderly, affordable housing, household time use, phosphate laundry study, economic well-living.
Dr. LuAnn Gaskill, Head, 540-231-6164, *E-mail:* lagaskill@vt.edu.

GERONTOLOGY

■ ABILENE CHRISTIAN UNIVERSITY

Graduate School, College of Arts and Sciences, Department of Sociology and Social Work, Program in Gerontology, Abilene, TX 79699-9100

AWARDS MS.

Faculty: 7 part-time/adjunct (0 women).
Students: 4 full-time (3 women), 4 part-time (3 women); includes 1 minority (African American), 1 international. 5 applicants, 100% accepted, 4 enrolled. In 2001, 3 degrees awarded.
Degree requirements: For master's, comprehensive exam.
Entrance requirements: For master's, GRE General Test or MAT. *Application deadline:* For fall admission, 4/1 (priority date); for spring admission, 11/1. Applications are processed on a rolling basis. *Application fee:* $25 ($45 for international students).
Expenses: Tuition: Full-time $8,904; part-time $371 per hour. Required fees: $520; $17 per hour.
Financial support: Career-related internships or fieldwork and Federal Work-Study available. Support available to part-time students. Financial award application deadline: 4/1.
C. D. Pruett, Director of the Center for Aging, 915-674-2350, *Fax:* 915-674-6804, *E-mail:* pruettc@acu.edu.
Application contact: Dr. Roger Gee, Graduate Dean, 915-674-2122, *Fax:* 915-674-2123, *E-mail:* gradinfo@education.acu.edu.

■ ADLER SCHOOL OF PROFESSIONAL PSYCHOLOGY

Programs in Psychology, Chicago, IL 60601-7203

AWARDS Art therapy (Certificate); clinical hypnosis (Certificate); clinical psychology (Psy D); counseling psychology (MACP); counseling psychology/art therapy (MACAT); gerontology (MAGP, Certificate); marriage and family counseling (MAMFC); marriage and family therapy (Certificate); organizational psychology (MAO); substance abuse counseling (MASAC, Certificate). Part-time and evening/weekend programs available.

Faculty: 19 full-time (9 women), 48 part-time/adjunct (21 women).
Students: 124 full-time (78 women), 284 part-time (208 women); includes 77 minority (43 African Americans, 20 Asian Americans or Pacific Islanders, 13 Hispanic Americans, 1 Native American), 8 international. Average age 39. 253 applicants, 59% accepted, 121 enrolled. In 2001, 101 master's, 29 doctorates, 5 other advanced degrees awarded. Terminal master's awarded for partial completion of doctoral program.
Degree requirements: For master's, thesis or alternative, oral exam, practicum; for doctorate, thesis/dissertation, clinical exam, internship, oral exam, practicum, written qualifying exam.
Entrance requirements: For master's, 12 semester hours in psychology, minimum GPA of 3.0; for doctorate, 18 semester hours in psychology, minimum GPA of 3.25; for Certificate, appropriate master's or doctoral degree. *Application deadline:* For fall admission, 1/1 (priority date). Applications are processed on a rolling basis. *Application fee:* $50.
Expenses: Tuition: Full-time $13,680; part-time $380 per credit. Required fees: $100; $15 per credit.
Financial support: In 2001–02, 180 students received support. Career-related internships or fieldwork, Federal Work-Study, scholarships/grants, and tuition waivers (full and partial) available. Support available to part-time students. Financial award application deadline: 5/15; financial award applicants required to submit FAFSA.
Dr. Frank Gruba-McCallister, Dean of Academic Affairs, 312-201-5900, *Fax:* 312-201-5917.
Application contact: Erene Soliman, Admissions Counselor, 312-201-5900, *Fax:* 312-201-5917.

Find an in-depth description at www.petersons.com/gradchannel.

■ APPALACHIAN STATE UNIVERSITY

Cratis D. Williams Graduate School, College of Arts and Sciences, Department of Sociology, Program in Gerontology, Boone, NC 28608

AWARDS MA. Part-time programs available.

Faculty: 12 full-time (3 women).
Students: 7 full-time (6 women). 6 applicants, 100% accepted, 4 enrolled. In 2001, 5 degrees awarded.
Degree requirements: For master's, thesis optional.
Entrance requirements: For master's, GRE General Test. *Application deadline:* For fall admission, 7/1; for spring admission, 11/1. Applications are processed on a rolling basis. *Application fee:* $35.
Expenses: Tuition, state resident: full-time $1,286. Tuition, nonresident: full-time $9,354. Required fees: $1,116.
Financial support: In 2001–02, 3 research assistantships (averaging $6,250 per year), 1 teaching assistantship (averaging $6,250 per year) were awarded. Fellowships, career-related internships or fieldwork and unspecified assistantships also available. Support available to part-time students. Financial award application deadline: 7/1; financial award applicants required to submit FAFSA.
Faculty research: Caregiving, housing, substance abuse, health care delivery, elder abuse and neglect.
Dr. Edwin Rosenberg, Director, 828-262-6146, *E-mail:* rosenberge@appstate.edu.

■ ARIZONA STATE UNIVERSITY

Graduate College, Interdisciplinary Program in Gerontology, Tempe, AZ 85287

AWARDS Certificate.

Faculty research: Psychology, sociology, biology, and policy of aging.

■ BALL STATE UNIVERSITY

Graduate School, College of Applied Science and Technology, Interdepartmental Program in Wellness Management, Muncie, IN 47306-1099

AWARDS Applied gerontology (MA); wellness management (MS).

Faculty: 2.
Students: 23 full-time (21 women), 9 part-time (5 women); includes 1 African American, 2 Hispanic Americans. Average age 30. 23 applicants, 83% accepted. In 2001, 28 degrees awarded.
Entrance requirements: For master's, GRE General Test, interview. *Application fee:* $25 ($35 for international students).
Expenses: Tuition, state resident: full-time $4,068; part-time $2,542. Tuition, nonresident: full-time $10,944; part-time $6,462. Required fees: $1,000; $500 per term.
Financial support: In 2001–02, 28 teaching assistantships (averaging $6,498 per year) were awarded; research assistantships with full tuition reimbursements, career-related internships or fieldwork also available. Financial award application deadline: 3/1.
Dr. David Gobble, Director, Institute for Wellness, 765-285-8259, *Fax:* 765-285-8237, *E-mail:* dgobble@bsu.edu. *Web site:* http://www.bsu.edu/wellness/

■ BAYLOR UNIVERSITY

Graduate School, College of Arts and Sciences, School of Social Work, Program in Clinical Gerontology, Waco, TX 76798

AWARDS MCG.

Students: 1 full-time (0 women), 1 (woman) part-time. In 2001, 4 degrees awarded.

Baylor University (continued)
Entrance requirements: For master's, GRE General Test. *Application deadline:* For fall admission, 8/1. Applications are processed on a rolling basis. *Application fee:* $25.
Expenses: Tuition: Part-time $379 per semester hour. Required fees: $42 per semester hour. $101 per semester. Tuition and fees vary according to program.
Dr. Ben E. Dickerson, Director of Graduate Studies, 254-710-3701, *Fax:* 254-710-1175, *E-mail:* ben_dickerson@baylor.edu.
Application contact: Suzanne Keener, Administrative Assistant, 254-710-3588, *Fax:* 254-710-3870, *E-mail:* graduate_school@baylor.edu. *Web site:* http://www.baylor.edu/~Graduate_School/Grad_Catalog/Geront.html#clinical

■ BAYLOR UNIVERSITY

Graduate School, College of Arts and Sciences, School of Social Work, Program in Gerontology, Waco, TX 76798

AWARDS MSG.

Students: 17 full-time (10 women), 2 part-time; includes 7 minority (5 African Americans, 1 Asian American or Pacific Islander, 1 Hispanic American), 2 international. In 2001, 8 degrees awarded.
Entrance requirements: For master's, GRE General Test. *Application deadline:* For fall admission, 8/1. Applications are processed on a rolling basis. *Application fee:* $25.
Expenses: Tuition: Part-time $379 per semester hour. Required fees: $42 per semester hour. $101 per semester. Tuition and fees vary according to program.
Dr. Ben E. Dickerson, Director of Graduate Studies, 254-710-3701, *Fax:* 254-710-1175, *E-mail:* ben_dickerson@baylor.edu.
Application contact: Suzanne Keener, Administrative Assistant, 254-710-3588, *Fax:* 254-710-3870, *E-mail:* graduate_school@baylor.edu. *Web site:* http://www.baylor.edu/~Gerontology/

■ CALIFORNIA STATE UNIVERSITY, DOMINGUEZ HILLS

College of Arts and Sciences, Program in Behavioral Science, Carson, CA 90747-0001

AWARDS Applied behavioral science (MA); gerontology (MA); negotiation and conflict resolution (MA, Certificate). Part-time and evening/weekend programs available.

Faculty: 18 full-time, 10 part-time/adjunct.
Students: 35 full-time (30 women), 70 part-time (53 women); includes 73 minority (58 African Americans, 6 Asian Americans or Pacific Islanders, 8 Hispanic Americans, 1 Native American), 1 international. Average age 40. 149 applicants, 83% accepted, 27 enrolled. In 2001, 80 degrees awarded.
Degree requirements: For master's, thesis or alternative.
Entrance requirements: For master's, minimum GPA of 3.0. *Application deadline:* For fall admission, 6/1. *Application fee:* $55.
Expenses: Tuition, nonresident: full-time $1,508; part-time $438 per semester. Required fees: $442; $246 per unit. $227 per semester.
A. Elba Frickel, Administrative Coordinator, 310-243-3435, *E-mail:* efrickel@dhvx20.csudh.edu.

■ CALIFORNIA STATE UNIVERSITY, FULLERTON

Graduate Studies, College of Humanities and Social Sciences, Program in Gerontology, Fullerton, CA 92834-9480

AWARDS MS.

Students: 7 full-time (6 women), 9 part-time (all women); includes 9 minority (5 Asian Americans or Pacific Islanders, 3 Hispanic Americans, 1 Native American). 21 applicants, 100% accepted, 16 enrolled.
Expenses: Tuition, nonresident: part-time $246 per unit. Required fees: $964.
Dr. Eric Solberg, Coordinator, 714-278-7057.

■ CALIFORNIA STATE UNIVERSITY, LONG BEACH

Graduate Studies, College of Health and Human Services, Program in Gerontology, Long Beach, CA 90840

AWARDS MS. Part-time programs available.

Students: 5 full-time (4 women), 7 part-time (all women); includes 4 minority (1 African American, 3 Hispanic Americans), 1 international. Average age 32. 9 applicants, 56% accepted. In 2001, 2 degrees awarded.
Degree requirements: For master's, thesis optional.
Application deadline: For fall admission, 8/1; for spring admission, 12/1. Applications are processed on a rolling basis. *Application fee:* $55. Electronic applications accepted.
Financial support: Federal Work-Study, institutionally sponsored loans, and scholarships/grants available. Financial award application deadline: 3/2.
Dr. Barbara White, Director, 562-985-1582, *Fax:* 562-985-4414, *E-mail:* bwhite@csulb.edu.

■ CASE WESTERN RESERVE UNIVERSITY

School of Graduate Studies, Department of Communication Sciences, Cleveland, OH 44106

AWARDS Gerontology (Certificate); speech-language pathology (MA, PhD). Terminal master's awarded for partial completion of doctoral program.

Degree requirements: For master's, thesis optional; for doctorate, thesis/dissertation.
Entrance requirements: For master's and doctorate, GRE General Test, TOEFL.
Faculty research: Traumatic brain injury, phonological disorders, child language disorders, communication problems in the aged and Alzheimer's patients, cleft palate, voice disorders. *Web site:* http://www.cwru.edu/CWRU/artsci/cosi/cosi.html

■ CENTRAL MISSOURI STATE UNIVERSITY

School of Graduate Studies, College of Education and Human Services, Department of Sociology, Warrensburg, MO 64093

AWARDS Social gerontology (MS); sociology (MA). Part-time programs available.

Faculty: 11 full-time (6 women).
Students: 10 full-time (7 women), 35 part-time (30 women); includes 6 minority (all African Americans), 2 international. Average age 34. 22 applicants, 95% accepted. In 2001, 16 degrees awarded.
Degree requirements: For master's, comprehensive exam.
Entrance requirements: For master's, minimum GPA of 2.5. *Application deadline:* Applications are processed on a rolling basis. *Application fee:* $25 ($50 for international students).
Expenses: Tuition, area resident: Full-time $4,200; part-time $175 per credit hour. Tuition, nonresident: full-time $8,352; part-time $348 per credit hour.
Financial support: In 2001–02, 6 research assistantships with full and partial tuition reimbursements (averaging $6,063 per year), 1 teaching assistantship with partial tuition reimbursement (averaging $2,650 per year) were awarded. Federal Work-Study, scholarships/grants, unspecified assistantships, and administrative assistantship also available. Support available to part-time students. Financial award application deadline: 3/1; financial award applicants required to submit FAFSA.
Faculty research: Political economy of health and aging, sociology of suicide, sociology of religion, sociology of natural resources and the environment, Lithuanian American ethnic identity.
Dr. J. Mark Wehrle, Chair, 660-543-4407, *Fax:* 660-543-8215, *E-mail:* wehrle@cmsu1.cmsu.edu. *Web site:* http://wwwcmsu.edu/

■ THE COLLEGE OF NEW ROCHELLE

Graduate School, Division of Human Services, Program in Gerontology, New Rochelle, NY 10805-2308

AWARDS MS, Certificate. Part-time and evening/weekend programs available.

Degree requirements: For master's, fieldwork, internship.
Entrance requirements: For master's, interview, minimum GPA of 3.0, sample of written work.

■ COLLEGE OF NOTRE DAME OF MARYLAND

Graduate Studies, Program in Studies in Aging, Baltimore, MD 21210-2476

AWARDS MA.

Students: Average age 35.
Entrance requirements: For master's, minimum GPA of 3.0. *Application deadline:* For fall admission, 8/15 (priority date); for winter admission, 12/15; for spring admission, 1/15. Applications are processed on a rolling basis. *Application fee:* $25. Electronic applications accepted.
Expenses: Tuition: Part-time $320 per credit. Required fees: $30 per course. Full-time tuition and fees vary according to reciprocity agreements and student's religious affiliation.
Financial support: Career-related internships or fieldwork and institutionally sponsored loans available. Financial award application deadline: 6/30; financial award applicants required to submit FAFSA.
Joanne Gladden, Head, 410-532-5316, *Fax:* 410-532-5333.
Application contact: Kathy Nikolaidis, Graduate Admissions Secretary, 410-532-5317, *Fax:* 410-532-5333, *E-mail:* gradadm@ndm.edu.

■ CONCORDIA UNIVERSITY

Graduate Studies, Program in Gerontology, River Forest, IL 60305-1499

AWARDS MA, CAS. Part-time and evening/weekend programs available.

Degree requirements: For master's, thesis, comprehensive exam; for CAS, thesis, final project.
Entrance requirements: For master's, minimum GPA of 2.9; for CAS, master's degree.

■ EASTERN ILLINOIS UNIVERSITY

Graduate School, Lumpkin College of Business and Applied Sciences, Program in Gerontology, Charleston, IL 61920-3099

AWARDS MA.

■ EAST TENNESSEE STATE UNIVERSITY

School of Graduate Studies, College of Public and Allied Health, Department of Public Health, Johnson City, TN 37614

AWARDS Community health (MPH); gerontology (Certificate); health care management (Certificate); public health (MPH); public health administration (MPH). Part-time programs available.

Faculty: 9 full-time (4 women).
Students: 20 full-time (12 women), 13 part-time (11 women); includes 4 minority (2 African Americans, 2 Asian Americans or Pacific Islanders), 9 international. Average age 36. In 2001, 18 degrees awarded.
Degree requirements: For master's, thesis optional.
Entrance requirements: For master's, GRE General Test, TOEFL, 2 years of community health experience. *Application deadline:* For fall admission, 7/15 (priority date). Applications are processed on a rolling basis. *Application fee:* $25 ($35 for international students).
Expenses: Tuition, state resident: part-time $181 per hour. Tuition, nonresident: part-time $270 per hour. Required fees: $220 per term.
Financial support: Research assistantships with full tuition reimbursements, teaching assistantships with full tuition reimbursements, career-related internships or fieldwork, institutionally sponsored loans, and tuition waivers (full) available.
Dr. Joanne W. Shields, Chair, 423-439-4332, *Fax:* 423-439-6491, *E-mail:* shields@etsu.edu. *Web site:* http://www.etsu.edu/

■ FLORIDA STATE UNIVERSITY

Graduate Studies, College of Social Sciences, Program in Aging Studies, Tallahassee, FL 32306

AWARDS MS.

Application fee: $20.
Expenses: Tuition, state resident: part-time $163 per credit hour. Tuition, nonresident: part-time $570 per credit hour. Tuition and fees vary according to program.
Dr. Melissa Hardy, Head, 850-644-2831, *Fax:* 850-644-2304, *E-mail:* mhardy@garnet.acns.fsu.edu.
Application contact: Susan Lampman, 850-644-3520, *Fax:* 850-644-2304, *E-mail:* slampman@mailer.fsu.edu.

■ GANNON UNIVERSITY

School of Graduate Studies, College of Humanities, Business, and Education, School of Humanities, Program in Gerontology, Erie, PA 16541-0001

AWARDS Certificate. Part-time and evening/weekend programs available.

Entrance requirements: For degree, interview. *Web site:* http://www.gannon.edu/

■ GEORGE MASON UNIVERSITY

College of Arts and Sciences, Interdisciplinary Studies Program, Fairfax, VA 22030-4444

AWARDS Interdisciplinary studies (MAIS), including archaeology, gerontology, regional economic development and technology, video-based production; liberal studies (MAIS). Part-time and evening/weekend programs available.

Faculty: 4 full-time (0 women), 5 part-time/adjunct (4 women).
Students: 8 full-time (6 women), 61 part-time (38 women); includes 13 minority (6 African Americans, 4 Asian Americans or Pacific Islanders, 3 Hispanic Americans), 7 international. Average age 36. 33 applicants, 61% accepted, 10 enrolled. In 2001, 17 degrees awarded.
Degree requirements: For master's, thesis optional.
Entrance requirements: For master's, GRE, GMAT, or MAT, interview, minimum GPA of 3.0 in last 60 hours. *Application deadline:* For fall admission, 5/1 (priority date); for spring admission, 11/1. Applications are processed on a rolling basis. *Application fee:* $30. Electronic applications accepted.
Expenses: Tuition, state resident: full-time $3,168; part-time $132 per credit hour. Tuition, nonresident: full-time $11,280; part-time $470 per credit hour. Required fees: $1,416; $59 per credit hour.
Financial support: Fellowships, teaching assistantships, career-related internships or fieldwork, Federal Work-Study, and institutionally sponsored loans available. Support available to part-time students. Financial award application deadline: 3/1; financial award applicants required to submit FAFSA.
Catherine A. McCormick, Coordinator, 703-993-8762, *Fax:* 703-993-8871, *E-mail:* emccorm1@gmu.edu.
Application contact: Dr. Johannes D. Bergmann, Information Contact, 703-993-8762, *E-mail:* mais@gmu.edu. *Web site:* http://cas.gmu.edu/mais/

■ HOFSTRA UNIVERSITY

School of Education and Allied Human Services, Department of Counseling, Research, Special Education and Rehabilitation, Program in Gerontology, Hempstead, NY 11549

AWARDS MS, CAS. Part-time and evening/weekend programs available.

Faculty: 13 full-time (5 women), 22 part-time/adjunct (12 women).
Students: 3 full-time (2 women), 20 part-time (17 women). Average age 42. In 2001, 3 master's, 1 other advanced degree awarded.
Degree requirements: For master's, comprehensive exam or essay.
Entrance requirements: For master's, interview, minimum GPA of 2.5; for CAS, letters of recommendation (3), interview, minimum GPA of 2.5. *Application deadline:* Applications are processed on a rolling basis. *Application fee:* $40 ($75 for international students).
Expenses: Tuition: Full-time $12,408. Tuition and fees vary according to course load and program.

Hofstra University (continued)
Financial support: In 2001–02, 10 students received support, including 10 fellowships; career-related internships or fieldwork, institutionally sponsored loans, and scholarships/grants also available. Support available to part-time students. Financial award application deadline: 6/30; financial award applicants required to submit FAFSA.
Dr. Ruth F. Gold, Coordinator, 516-463-5785, *Fax:* 516-463-6503, *E-mail:* cprrfg@hofstra.edu.
Application contact: Mary Beth Carey, Vice President of Enrollment Services, *Fax:* 516-560-7660, *E-mail:* hofstra@hofstra.edu.

■ KIRKSVILLE COLLEGE OF OSTEOPATHIC MEDICINE

School of Health Management, Kirksville, MO 63501

AWARDS Geriatric health management (MGH); health administration (MHA); medical office management (Certificate); public health (MPH). Part-time and evening/weekend programs available. Postbaccalaureate distance learning degree programs offered (no on-campus study).

Faculty: 3 full-time (0 women), 16 part-time/adjunct (4 women).
Students: Average age 30. 12 applicants, 83% accepted.
Degree requirements: For master's, capstone project.
Entrance requirements: For master's, DAT, GMAT, GRE, LSAT or MCAT, minimum GPA of 2.0. *Application deadline:* For fall admission, 7/31 (priority date); for winter admission, 10/30 (priority date); for spring admission, 2/5 (priority date). *Application fee:* $50.
Expenses: Tuition: Full-time $24,950. Required fees: $690.
Financial support: Application deadline: 6/1.
Dr. D. Kent Mulford, Dean, 660-626-2820, *Fax:* 660-626-2826, *E-mail:* shm@shm-kcom.edu.
Application contact: Lori A. Haxton, Assistant Dean for Student Affairs/Director of Admissions, 660-626-2237, *Fax:* 660-626-2969, *E-mail:* admissions@kcom.edu. *Web site:* http://www.shm-kcom.edu/

■ LINDENWOOD UNIVERSITY

Graduate Programs, Programs in Individualized Education, St. Charles, MO 63301-1695

AWARDS Administration (MSA); business administration (MBA); corporate communication (MS); counseling psychology (MA); gerontology (MA); health management (MS); human resource management (MS); human service agency management (MS); management (MSA); marketing (MSA); mass communication (MS). Part-time and evening/weekend programs available.

Faculty: 11 full-time (6 women), 23 part-time/adjunct (6 women).
Students: 515 full-time (340 women), 266 part-time (232 women); includes 117 minority (107 African Americans, 1 Asian American or Pacific Islander, 5 Hispanic Americans, 4 Native Americans), 11 international. Average age 35. In 2001, 298 degrees awarded.
Degree requirements: For master's, thesis. *Median time to degree:* Master's–1.25 years full-time.
Entrance requirements: For master's, interview, minimum GPA of 3.0. *Application deadline:* For fall admission, 6/30 (priority date); for spring admission, 12/1. Applications are processed on a rolling basis. *Application fee:* $25.
Expenses: Tuition: Full-time $10,800; part-time $300 per hour. Tuition and fees vary according to course load and program.
Financial support: Career-related internships or fieldwork, institutionally sponsored loans, tuition waivers (partial), and unspecified assistantships available. Financial award application deadline: 6/30.
Dan Kemper, Director, 636-916-9125, *E-mail:* dkemper@lindenwood.edu.
Application contact: John Guffey, Dean of Admissions, 636-949-4934, *Fax:* 636-949-4910, *E-mail:* jguffey@lindenwood.edu.

■ LONG ISLAND UNIVERSITY, C.W. POST CAMPUS

College of Management, School of Public Service, Department of Health Care and Public Administration, Brookville, NY 11548-1300

AWARDS Gerontology (Certificate); health care administration (MPA); health care administration/gerontology (MPA); public administration (MPA). Part-time and evening/weekend programs available.

Faculty: 10 full-time (5 women), 14 part-time/adjunct (4 women).
Students: 22 full-time (13 women), 136 part-time (100 women). 55 applicants, 85% accepted, 35 enrolled. In 2001, 42 degrees awarded.
Degree requirements: For master's, thesis.
Entrance requirements: For master's, GMAT, minimum GPA of 2.5; for Certificate, minimum GPA of 2.5. *Application deadline:* For fall admission, 8/15; for spring admission, 12/15. Applications are processed on a rolling basis. *Application fee:* $30. Electronic applications accepted.
Expenses: Tuition: Full-time $10,296; part-time $572 per credit. Required fees: $380; $190 per semester.
Financial support: In 2001–02, 10 students received support, including 3 research assistantships with partial tuition reimbursements available; Federal Work-Study and unspecified assistantships also available. Support available to part-time students. Financial award application deadline: 5/15; financial award applicants required to submit CSS PROFILE or FAFSA.
Faculty research: Critical issues in sexuality, social work in religious communities, gerontological social work.
Dr. Matthew C. Cordaro, Chairperson, 516-299-3920, *E-mail:* mcordaro@liu.edu.
Application contact: Barbara Bavlsik, Advisor, 516-299-2770, *E-mail:* barbara.bavlsik@liu.edu. *Web site:* http://www.liu.edu/com/

■ LONG ISLAND UNIVERSITY, SOUTHAMPTON COLLEGE

Gerontology Division, Southampton, NY 11968-4198

AWARDS MPS, AC. Part-time programs available. Postbaccalaureate distance learning degree programs offered (minimal on-campus study).

Degree requirements: For master's, thesis, fieldwork; for AC, fieldwork.
Faculty research: Baby boomers and the aging process, retirement planning for the twenty-first century.

■ LYNN UNIVERSITY

School of Graduate Studies, Department of Gerontology and Health Services, Boca Raton, FL 33431-5598

AWARDS Aging studies (Certificate); biomechanical trauma (MS); health care administration (MS, Certificate), including nursing home administrator licensure (MS). Part-time and evening/weekend programs available.

Degree requirements: For master's, internship, comprehensive exam (health care administration), thesis (biomechanical trauma).
Entrance requirements: For master's, MAT, minimum undergraduate GPA of 3.0. Electronic applications accepted.
Faculty research: Alzheimer's disease, therapeutic programming, physician training in geriatrics, case management, long term care administration. *Web site:* http://www.lynn.edu

■ MARYLHURST UNIVERSITY

Master of Arts in Interdisciplinary Studies, Marylhurst, OR 97036-0261

AWARDS Gerontology (MA); liberal arts (MA); organizational communications (MA); spiritual traditions (MA). Part-time and evening/weekend programs available.

Faculty: 1 (woman) full-time, 5 part-time/adjunct (3 women).
Students: 5 full-time (4 women), 44 part-time (36 women). Average age 42. In 2001, 11 degrees awarded.

Degree requirements: For master's, thesis. *Median time to degree:* Master's–3 years part-time.
Entrance requirements: For master's, MAT. *Application deadline:* Applications are processed on a rolling basis. *Application fee:* $40 ($55 for international students).
Expenses: Tuition: Full-time $8,235; part-time $305 per credit. Required fees: $195; $40 per quarter. Tuition and fees vary according to course load.
Financial support: In 2001–02, 25 students received support. Federal Work-Study and scholarships/grants available. Support available to part-time students. Financial award applicants required to submit FAFSA.
Faculty research: World religions, spirituality and literature, gerontology, philosophy, humanities.
Dr. Debrah B. Bokowski, Chair, 503-636-8141 Ext. 3338, *Fax:* 503-697-5597, *E-mail:* dbokowski@marylhurst.edu. *Web site:* http://www.marylhurst.edu/

■ MIAMI UNIVERSITY

Graduate School, College of Arts and Sciences, Department of Sociology and Anthropology, Program in Gerontology, Oxford, OH 45056

AWARDS MGS.

Students: 13 full-time (11 women), 2 part-time (1 woman); includes 1 minority (African American), 2 international. 14 applicants, 100% accepted, 7 enrolled. In 2001, 8 degrees awarded.
Degree requirements: For master's, final exam.
Entrance requirements: For master's, GRE General Test, minimum undergraduate GPA of 3.0 during previous 2 years or 2.75 overall. *Application deadline:* For fall admission, 3/1 (priority date); for spring admission, 12/1. Applications are processed on a rolling basis. *Application fee:* $35.
Expenses: Tuition, state resident: full-time $7,155; part-time $295 per semester hour. Tuition, nonresident: full-time $14,829; part-time $615 per semester hour. Tuition and fees vary according to degree level and campus/location.
Financial support: In 2001–02, 12 fellowships (averaging $8,821 per year) were awarded; research assistantships, teaching assistantships, career-related internships or fieldwork, Federal Work-Study, and tuition waivers (full) also available. Financial award application deadline: 3/1.
Dr. Lisa Groger, Director of Graduate Studies, 513-529-2914. *Web site:* http://www.muohio.edu/~scripps/mgs-welc.htm

■ MINNESOTA STATE UNIVERSITY, MANKATO

College of Graduate Studies, College of Social and Behavioral Sciences, Program in Gerontology, Mankato, MN 56001

AWARDS MS.

Faculty: 1 (woman) full-time.
Students: 5 full-time (all women), 7 part-time (5 women). Average age 32. In 2001, 4 degrees awarded.
Degree requirements: For master's, thesis, comprehensive exam.
Entrance requirements: For master's, minimum GPA of 3.0 during previous 2 years. *Application deadline:* For fall admission, 7/9 (priority date); for spring admission, 11/27. Applications are processed on a rolling basis. *Application fee:* $20.
Expenses: Tuition, state resident: full-time $3,253; part-time $157 per credit. Tuition, nonresident: full-time $4,893; part-time $248 per credit. Required fees: $24 per credit. Tuition and fees vary according to reciprocity agreements.
Financial support: Application deadline: 3/15.
Dr. K. Elliott, Chairperson, 507-389-1563.
Application contact: Joni Roberts, Admissions Coordinator, 507-389-5244, *Fax:* 507-389-5974, *E-mail:* grad@mankato.msus.edu.

■ MOREHEAD STATE UNIVERSITY

Graduate Programs, Caudill College of Humanities, Department of Sociology, Social Work and Criminology, Morehead, KY 40351

AWARDS Criminology (MA); general sociology (MA); gerontology (MA). Part-time and evening/weekend programs available.

Faculty: 12 full-time (4 women).
Students: 7 full-time (5 women), 11 part-time (10 women), 2 international. Average age 25. 10 applicants, 60% accepted. In 2001, 2 degrees awarded.
Degree requirements: For master's, final comprehensive exam, thesis optional.
Entrance requirements: For master's, GRE General Test, TOFEL, minimum GPA of 3.0 in sociology, 2.5 overall; 18 hours in sociology. *Application deadline:* For fall admission, 8/1 (priority date); for spring admission, 12/1 (priority date). Applications are processed on a rolling basis. *Application fee:* $0.
Expenses: Tuition, state resident: part-time $176 per hour. Tuition, nonresident: full-time $1,584; part-time $472 per hour. International tuition: $4,247 full-time.
Financial support: In 2001–02, 5 teaching assistantships (averaging $5,000 per year) were awarded; career-related internships or fieldwork and Federal Work-Study also available. Financial award application deadline: 4/1; financial award applicants required to submit FAFSA.
Faculty research: Death and dying; aging, drinking, and drugs; economic development; adult children of alcoholics.
Dr. Edward Reeves, Chair, 606-783-2546, *Fax:* 606-783-5027, *E-mail:* e.reeves@moreheadstate.edu.
Application contact: Betty R. Cowsert, Graduate Admissions/Records Manager, 606-783-2039, *Fax:* 606-783-5061, *E-mail:* b.cowsert@moreheadstate.edu. *Web site:* http://www.moreheadstate.edu/

■ MOUNTAIN STATE UNIVERSITY

Graduate Studies, School of Health Sciences, Beckley, WV 25802-9003

AWARDS Administration (MHS); administration/education (MSN); classroom teaching (MHS); clinical teaching (MHS); community/rural medicine (MHS); diagnostic ultrasound (MHS); emergency medicine (MHS); family medicine (MHS); family nurse practitioner (MSN); geriatric medicine (MHS); special topics (MHS).

Degree requirements: For master's, thesis, comprehensive exam.
Entrance requirements: For master's, GRE. Electronic applications accepted.
Expenses: Tuition: Part-time $210 per credit hour. Part-time tuition and fees vary according to program.

■ MOUNT MARY COLLEGE

Graduate Programs, Program in Gerontology, Milwaukee, WI 53222-4597

AWARDS MA. Part-time programs available.

Faculty: 1 (woman) full-time, 1 (woman) part-time/adjunct.
Students: 4 applicants, 100% accepted, 4 enrolled.
Degree requirements: For master's, thesis or alternative, internship. *Median time to degree:* Master's–3.5 years part-time.
Entrance requirements: For master's, TOEFL, minimum GPA of 2.75. *Application deadline:* For fall admission, 8/25 (priority date); for winter admission, 1/15 (priority date); for spring admission, 6/15 (priority date). Applications are processed on a rolling basis. *Application fee:* $35 ($110 for international students).
Expenses: Tuition: Full-time $7,254; part-time $403 per credit. Required fees: $160; $35 per semester.
Financial support: In 2001–02, 6 students received support. Career-related internships or fieldwork, Federal Work-Study, and unspecified assistantships available. Support available to part-time students.
Dr. Krista Moore, Director, 414-256-4810 Ext. 312, *Fax:* 414-256-1224, *E-mail:* moorek@mtmary.edu. *Web site:* http://www.mtmary.edu/graduate.htm

■ NAROPA UNIVERSITY

Graduate Programs, Program in Gerontology, Boulder, CO 80302-6697

AWARDS MA.

Faculty: 1 full-time (0 women), 11 part-time/adjunct (8 women).
Students: 10 full-time (8 women), 3 part-time (2 women); includes 2 minority (1 African American, 1 Asian American or Pacific Islander). Average age 39. 9 applicants, 100% accepted, 7 enrolled. In 2001, 6 degrees awarded.

Naropa University (continued)
Degree requirements: For master's, thesis, internship.
Entrance requirements: For master's, interview. *Application deadline:* For fall admission, 2/1 (priority date); for spring admission, 11/1 (priority date). Applications are processed on a rolling basis. *Application fee:* $50 ($0 for international students). Electronic applications accepted.
Expenses: Tuition: Full-time $10,766; part-time $489 per credit. Required fees: $560; $280 per semester. Tuition and fees vary according to course load and campus/location.
Financial support: In 2001–02, 1 student received support. Career-related internships or fieldwork, Federal Work-Study, scholarships/grants, health care benefits, and tuition waivers (partial) available. Support available to part-time students. Financial award application deadline: 3/1; financial award applicants required to submit FAFSA.
Dr. Robert Atchley, Chair, 303-245-4823.
Application contact: Donna McIntyre, Assistant Director of Admissions, 303-546-3555, *Fax:* 303-546-3583, *E-mail:* donna@naropa.edu. *Web site:* http://www.naropa.edu/gerontology/index.html/

Find an in-depth description at www.petersons.com/gradchannel.

■ NATIONAL-LOUIS UNIVERSITY

College of Arts and Sciences, Division of Health and Human Services, Chicago, IL 60603

AWARDS Addictions counseling (MS, Certificate); addictions treatment (Certificate); career counseling and development studies (Certificate); community wellness and prevention (MS, Certificate); counseling (MS, Certificate); eating disorders counseling (Certificate); employee assistance programs (MS, Certificate); gerontology administration (Certificate); gerontology counseling (MS, Certificate); human services administration (MS, Certificate); long-term care administration (Certificate). Part-time programs available.

Degree requirements: For master's and Certificate, internship.
Entrance requirements: For master's and Certificate, GRE, MAT, or Watson-Glaser Critical Thinking Appraisal, interview, minimum GPA of 3.0.
Expenses: Tuition: Full-time $13,830; part-time $461 per credit hour.
Faculty research: Religion and aging, drug abuse prevention, hunger, homelessness, multicultural diversity.

■ NEW YORK MEDICAL COLLEGE

School of Public Health, Program in Gerontology, Valhalla, NY 10595-1691

AWARDS MPH, CGS. Part-time and evening/weekend programs available.

Entrance requirements: For master's, 2-3 years health-related experience desirable.

■ NORTH DAKOTA STATE UNIVERSITY

The Graduate School, College of Human Development and Education, Department of Child Development and Family Science, Fargo, ND 58105

AWARDS Child development and family science (MS); gerontology (PhD). Part-time programs available.

Faculty: 9 full-time (4 women).
Students: 20 full-time (16 women), 17 part-time (16 women); includes 1 minority (African American). 13 applicants, 46% accepted. In 2001, 4 degrees awarded.
Degree requirements: For master's, thesis or alternative.
Entrance requirements: For master's, TOEFL. *Application deadline:* For fall admission, 2/1; for spring admission, 10/1. *Application fee:* $35.
Expenses: Tuition, state resident: part-time $124 per credit. Tuition, nonresident: part-time $325 per credit. Required fees: $22 per credit. Tuition and fees vary according to reciprocity agreements.
Financial support: In 2001–02, 17 teaching assistantships (averaging $3,000 per year) were awarded; research assistantships, career-related internships or fieldwork, Federal Work-Study, institutionally sponsored loans, and tuition waivers (full) also available. Financial award application deadline: 4/1.
Faculty research: Family therapy, gerontology, resilience, parenting, adolescent development. *Total annual research expenditures:* $46,057.
Dr. James Deal, Chair, 701-231-7568, *Fax:* 701-231-9645, *E-mail:* jim_deal@ndsu.nodak.edu.
Application contact: Barb Morin Koehler, Administrative Assistant, 701-231-8628, *Fax:* 701-231-9645, *E-mail:* barb_morin_koehler@ndsu.nodak.edu. *Web site:* http://www.ndsu.nodak.edu/ndsu/ideal/cdfs/

■ NORTHEASTERN ILLINOIS UNIVERSITY

Graduate College, College of Arts and Sciences, Department of Psychology, Program in Gerontology, Chicago, IL 60625-4699

AWARDS MA. Part-time and evening/weekend programs available.

Faculty: 13 full-time (9 women), 6 part-time/adjunct (5 women).
Students: Average age 44. 5 applicants, 100% accepted. In 2001, 2 degrees awarded.
Degree requirements: For master's, paper and project or thesis, practicum.
Entrance requirements: For master's, 15 hours in social sciences (3 hours in gerontology), 1 course in research methods or statistics, minimum GPA of 2.75. *Application deadline:* For fall admission, 4/1 (priority date); for spring admission, 8/15. Applications are processed on a rolling basis. *Application fee:* $25.
Expenses: Tuition, area resident: Full-time $2,882; part-time $107 per semester hour. Tuition, nonresident: part-time $320 per semester hour. International tuition: $8,646 full-time. Required fees: $20 per semester hour.
Financial support: In 2001–02, 12 students received support, including 2 research assistantships with full tuition reimbursements available (averaging $6,600 per year); career-related internships or fieldwork, Federal Work-Study, institutionally sponsored loans, and tuition waivers (full and partial) also available. Support available to part-time students. Financial award applicants required to submit FAFSA.
Faculty research: Later life development, cultural diversity, humanities and aging, elder abuse, AIDS and aging, computer training.
Dr. Margaret Condon, Coordinator, 773-442-5838, *Fax:* 773-442-4900, *E-mail:* m-condon@neiu.edu.
Application contact: Dr. Mohan K. Sood, Dean of the Graduate College, 773-442-6010, *Fax:* 773-442-6020, *E-mail:* m-sood@neiu.edu.

■ NOTRE DAME DE NAMUR UNIVERSITY

Graduate School, School of Sciences, Department of Counseling and Psychology/Gerontology, Program in Gerontology, Belmont, CA 94002-1997

AWARDS MA, Certificate.

Expenses: Tuition: Full-time $9,450; part-time $525 per unit. Required fees: $35 per term.
Denise Hughes, Director, 650-508-3723, *E-mail:* dhughes@ndnu.edu.
Application contact: Barbara Sterner, Assistant Director of Graduate Admissions, 650-508-3527, *Fax:* 650-508-3662, *E-mail:* grad.admit@ndnu.edu.

■ OREGON STATE UNIVERSITY

Graduate School, College of Home Economics, Department of Human Development and Family Sciences, Program in Gerontology, Corvallis, OR 97331

AWARDS MAIS.

Degree requirements: For master's, thesis optional.
Entrance requirements: For master's, GRE, TOEFL, minimum GPA of 3.0 in last 90 hours. *Application deadline:* For fall admission, 1/15. *Application fee:* $50.
Expenses: Tuition, area resident: Full-time $15,933. Tuition, state resident: full-time $28,937.
Financial support: Research assistantships, teaching assistantships, career-related

internships or fieldwork, Federal Work-Study, and institutionally sponsored loans available. Support available to part-time students. Financial award application deadline: 2/1.
Faculty research: Aging/families, social/psychological aspects of aging, osteoporosis, nutrition, disease and aging.
Dr. Karen Hooker, Director, 541-737-4336, *Fax:* 541-737-1076, *E-mail:* hookerk@orst.edu. *Web site:* http://www.orst.edu/DEPT/hafs/index/html

■ PORTLAND STATE UNIVERSITY

Graduate Studies, College of Urban and Public Affairs, School of Urban Studies and Planning, Division of Urban Studies, Program in Gerontology, Portland, OR 97207-0751

AWARDS Certificate. Part-time programs available.

Application deadline: For fall admission, 2/1. *Application fee:* $50.
Financial support: Fellowships, research assistantships, teaching assistantships, career-related internships or fieldwork, Federal Work-Study, and institutionally sponsored loans available. Support available to part-time students. Financial award application deadline: 3/1; financial award applicants required to submit FAFSA. *Total annual research expenditures:* $317,470.
Dr. Elizabeth Kutza, Director, 503-725-3952, *Fax:* 503-725-5199, *E-mail:* beth@upa.pdx.edu.

■ ROOSEVELT UNIVERSITY

Graduate Division, College of Arts and Sciences, School of Policy Studies, Department of Sociology, Program in Sociology-Gerontology, Chicago, IL 60605-1394

AWARDS MA. Part-time and evening/weekend programs available.

Degree requirements: For master's, thesis or alternative, comprehensive exam. *Application deadline:* For fall admission, 6/1 (priority date). Applications are processed on a rolling basis. *Application fee:* $25 ($35 for international students).
Expenses: Tuition: Full-time $9,090; part-time $505 per credit hour. Required fees: $100 per term.
Financial support: Teaching assistantships available. Financial award application deadline: 2/15.
Application contact: Joanne Canyon-Heller, Coordinator of Graduate Admissions, 312-281-3250, *Fax:* 312-341-3523, *E-mail:* applyru@roosevelt.edu.

■ SAGE GRADUATE SCHOOL

Graduate School, Division of Management, Communications and Legal Studies, Program in Health Services Administration, Troy, NY 12180-4115

AWARDS Gerontology (MS); health education (MS); management (MS); nutrition and dietetics (MS). Part-time and evening/weekend programs available.

Students: 7 full-time (4 women), 35 part-time (28 women); includes 2 minority (1 African American, 1 Asian American or Pacific Islander). Average age 34. 8 applicants, 100% accepted, 7 enrolled. In 2001, 22 degrees awarded.
Entrance requirements: For master's, minimum GPA of 2.75. *Application fee:* $40.
Expenses: Tuition: Full-time $7,600. Required fees: $100.
Financial support: Career-related internships or fieldwork available. Support available to part-time students. Financial award application deadline: 3/1; financial award applicants required to submit FAFSA.
Application contact: Melissa M. Robertson, Associate Director of Admissions, 518-244-6878, *Fax:* 518-244-6880, *E-mail:* sgsadm@sage.edu. *Web site:* http://www.sage.edu/

■ SAGE GRADUATE SCHOOL

Graduate School, Division of Management, Communications and Legal Studies, Program in Public Administration, Troy, NY 12180-4115

AWARDS Communications (MS); gerontology (MS); human services administration (MS); nutrition and dietetics (MS); public management (MS). Part-time and evening/weekend programs available.

Students: 5 full-time (4 women), 21 part-time (16 women). Average age 31. 9 applicants, 100% accepted, 8 enrolled. In 2001, 12 degrees awarded.
Entrance requirements: For master's, minimum GPA of 2.75. *Application fee:* $40.
Expenses: Tuition: Full-time $7,600. Required fees: $100.
Financial support: Career-related internships or fieldwork available. Support available to part-time students. Financial award application deadline: 3/1; financial award applicants required to submit FAFSA. 518-292-1770.
Application contact: Melissa M. Robertson, Associate Director of Admissions, 518-244-6878, *Fax:* 518-244-6880, *E-mail:* sgsadm@sage.edu. *Web site:* http://www.sage.edu/

■ ST. CLOUD STATE UNIVERSITY

School of Graduate Studies, College of Social Sciences, Program in Gerontology, St. Cloud, MN 56301-4498

AWARDS MS.

Faculty: 9 full-time (5 women), 1 part-time/adjunct (0 women).
Students: 5 full-time (3 women), 5 part-time (4 women); includes 2 minority (both Asian Americans or Pacific Islanders). 5 applicants, 100% accepted. In 2001, 4 degrees awarded.
Degree requirements: For master's, thesis or alternative.
Entrance requirements: For master's, GRE General Test, minimum GPA of 2.75. *Application deadline:* Applications are processed on a rolling basis. *Application fee:* $35.
Expenses: Tuition, state resident: part-time $156 per credit. Tuition, nonresident: part-time $244 per credit. Required fees: $20 per credit.
Financial support: Federal Work-Study and unspecified assistantships available. Financial award application deadline: 3/1.
Dr. Phyllis Greenberg, Coordinator, 320-255-3947.
Application contact: Lindalou Krueger, Graduate Studies Office, 320-255-2113, *Fax:* 320-654-5371, *E-mail:* lekrueger@stcloudstate.edu.

■ SAINT JOSEPH COLLEGE

Graduate Division, Department of Gerontology, West Hartford, CT 06117-2700

AWARDS Human development/gerontology (MA, Certificate). Part-time and evening/weekend programs available.

Faculty: 1 (woman) full-time, 3 part-time/adjunct (2 women).
Students: 2 full-time (both women), 31 part-time (30 women), 1 international. Average age 33. In 2001, 11 degrees awarded.
Degree requirements: For master's, thesis or alternative. *Median time to degree:* Master's–2 years full-time, 3 years part-time.
Entrance requirements: For master's, GRE or MAT. *Application deadline:* For fall admission, 9/2 (priority date); for spring admission, 1/20 (priority date). Applications are processed on a rolling basis. *Application fee:* $25.
Expenses: Tuition: Part-time $475 per credit hour.
Financial support: In 2001–02, 8 students received support, including 8 fellowships with partial tuition reimbursements available (averaging $1,000 per year), 2 research assistantships with full tuition reimbursements available; tuition waivers (full) and unspecified assistantships also available. Financial award application deadline: 7/15; financial award applicants required to submit FAFSA.
Faculty research: Education, aging, public health.
Dr. Mary Alice Wolf, Chair, 860-231-5325, *Fax:* 860-233-5695, *E-mail:* mawolf@sjc.edu.

■ SAINT JOSEPH'S UNIVERSITY

College of Arts and Sciences, Program in Gerontological Services, Philadelphia, PA 19131-1395

AWARDS MS. Evening/weekend programs available.

Entrance requirements: For master's, TOEFL.
Expenses: Tuition: Part-time $550 per credit. Tuition and fees vary according to program.

■ SAN FRANCISCO STATE UNIVERSITY

Graduate Division, College of Health and Human Services, Gerontology Program, San Francisco, CA 94132-1722

AWARDS Ethnogerontology (MA); healthy aging (MA); life-long learning (MA); long-term care administration (MA). Part-time programs available.

Degree requirements: For master's, special study or thesis.
Entrance requirements: For master's, minimum GPA of 2.5 in last 60 units.
Faculty research: Older adult education.

■ SAN JOSE STATE UNIVERSITY

Graduate Studies, College of Applied Arts and Sciences, Department of Health Science, San Jose, CA 95192-0001

AWARDS Gerontology (MS); health administration (Certificate); health science (MA); public health (MPH).

Faculty: 5 full-time (1 woman), 2 part-time/adjunct (1 woman).
Students: 47 full-time (36 women), 56 part-time (50 women); includes 35 minority (6 African Americans, 19 Asian Americans or Pacific Islanders, 10 Hispanic Americans), 3 international. Average age 36. 104 applicants, 45% accepted. In 2001, 42 degrees awarded.
Entrance requirements: For master's, GRE General Test, minimum B average. *Application deadline:* For fall admission, 6/29; for spring admission, 11/30. Applications are processed on a rolling basis. *Application fee:* $59. Electronic applications accepted.
Expenses: Tuition, nonresident: part-time $246 per unit. Required fees: $678 per semester. Tuition and fees vary according to course load.
Financial support: In 2001–02, 4 fellowships were awarded; career-related internships or fieldwork, Federal Work-Study, institutionally sponsored loans, and tuition waivers (partial) also available. Support available to part-time students. Financial award applicants required to submit FAFSA.
Faculty research: Behavioral science in occupational and health care settings, epidemiology in health care settings.
Kathleen Roe, Chair, 408-924-2970, *Fax:* 408-924-2979.

■ STATE UNIVERSITY OF WEST GEORGIA

Graduate School, College of Arts and Sciences, Department of Sociology, Anthropology, and Criminology, Program of Gerontology, Carrollton, GA 30118

AWARDS MA. Part-time programs available.

Faculty: 14 full-time (7 women).
Students: 4 full-time (3 women), 11 part-time (10 women); includes 4 minority (all African Americans). Average age 37. 1 applicant, 100% accepted, 1 enrolled. In 2001, 9 degrees awarded.
Degree requirements: For master's, one foreign language, thesis (for some programs), comprehensive exam (for some programs), registration.
Entrance requirements: For master's, GRE, references, intellectual biography, minimum GPA of 2.5. *Application deadline:* For fall admission, 8/2 (priority date); for spring admission, 12/20. *Application fee:* $20. Electronic applications accepted.
Expenses: Tuition, state resident: full-time $232; part-time $97 per credit hour. Tuition, nonresident: full-time $928; part-time $387 per credit hour. Required fees: $536; $14 per credit. $100 per semester.
Financial support: In 2001–02, 3 research assistantships with full tuition reimbursements (averaging $2,000 per year) were awarded; career-related internships or fieldwork, scholarships/grants, and unspecified assistantships also available.
Faculty research: Direct services, administrative, research, policy/planning. *Total annual research expenditures:* $15,000.
Application contact: Dr. Jack O. Jenkins, Dean, Graduate School, 770-836-6419, *Fax:* 770-836-2301, *E-mail:* jjenkins@westga.edu.

■ TEXAS A&M UNIVERSITY–KINGSVILLE

College of Graduate Studies, College of Arts and Sciences, Department of Psychology and Sociology, Kingsville, TX 78363

AWARDS Gerontology (MS); psychology (MA, MS); sociology (MA, MS). Part-time and evening/weekend programs available.

Faculty: 8 full-time (2 women).
Students: 23 full-time (19 women), 40 part-time (33 women); includes 41 minority (3 African Americans, 1 Asian American or Pacific Islander, 37 Hispanic Americans), 2 international. Average age 35. In 2001, 18 degrees awarded.
Degree requirements: For master's, thesis or alternative, comprehensive exam.
Entrance requirements: For master's, GRE General Test, TOEFL, minimum GPA of 2.5. *Application deadline:* For fall admission, 6/1; for spring admission, 11/15. Applications are processed on a rolling basis. *Application fee:* $15 ($25 for international students).
Expenses: Tuition, state resident: part-time $42 per hour. Tuition, nonresident: part-time $253 per hour. Required fees: $56 per hour. One-time fee: $46 part-time. Tuition and fees vary according to program.
Financial support: Federal Work-Study and institutionally sponsored loans available. Support available to part-time students. Financial award application deadline: 5/15.
Faculty research: Hispanic female voting behavior, attitudes toward criminal justice, immigration of aged into south Texas, folk medicine. *Total annual research expenditures:* $50,000.
Dr. Dorothy Pace, Graduate Coordinator, 361-593-2701, *Fax:* 361-593-3107.

■ TOWSON UNIVERSITY

Graduate School, Program in Applied Gerontology, Towson, MD 21252-0001

AWARDS MS.

Application deadline: Applications are processed on a rolling basis. *Application fee:* $40. Electronic applications accepted.
Expenses: Tuition, state resident: part-time $211 per credit. Tuition, nonresident: part-time $435 per credit. Required fees: $52 per credit.
Financial support: Application deadline: 4/1.
Donna I. Wagner, Director, 410-704-4643, *E-mail:* dwagner@towson.edu.
Application contact: 410-704-2501, *Fax:* 410-704-4675, *E-mail:* grads@towson.edu.

■ THE UNIVERSITY OF ARIZONA

Graduate College, Graduate Interdisciplinary Programs, Graduate Interdisciplinary Program in Gerontological Studies, Tucson, AZ 85721

AWARDS MS, Certificate. Part-time programs available.

Faculty: 16.
Students: 8 full-time (7 women), 7 part-time (6 women); includes 2 minority (1 Hispanic American, 1 Native American), 1 international. Average age 41. 10 applicants, 80% accepted, 2 enrolled. In 2001, 10 degrees awarded.
Degree requirements: For master's, thesis; for Certificate, practicum.
Entrance requirements: For master's, GRE, TOEFL; for Certificate, TOEFL, minimum B average. *Application deadline:* For fall admission, 3/31; for spring admission, 10/31. *Application fee:* $45.
Expenses: Tuition, state resident: full-time $2,490; part-time $436 per unit. Tuition, nonresident: full-time $10,300; part-time $436 per unit. Full-time tuition and fees vary according to degree level and program.

Financial support: In 2001–02, 4 students received support; fellowships, scholarships/grants available.
Faculty research: Osteoporosis, Alzheimer's disease, cognition and aging, aging and communication, elder abuse.
Dr. Elizabeth Glisky, Acting Head, 520-626-5804, *Fax:* 520-626-5801.
Application contact: Mick Beyers, Program Coordinator, 520-626-5804, *Fax:* 520-626-5801, *E-mail:* geron@u.arizona.edu. *Web site:* http://grad.admin.arizona.edu/idps/gero/gero.html

■ UNIVERSITY OF ARKANSAS AT LITTLE ROCK

Graduate School, College of Professional Studies, School of Social Work, Program in Gerontology, Little Rock, AR 72204-1099

AWARDS Applied gerontology (CG); gerontology (MA).

Degree requirements: For master's, fieldwork or written thesis and oral defense.
Entrance requirements: For master's, GRE General Test or MAT, minimum GPA of 2.7.
Expenses: Tuition, state resident: full-time $3,006; part-time $107 per credit. Tuition, nonresident: full-time $6,012; part-time $357 per credit. Required fees: $22 per credit. Tuition and fees vary according to program.

■ UNIVERSITY OF CENTRAL FLORIDA

College of Health and Public Affairs, School of Social Work, Orlando, FL 32816

AWARDS Gerontology (Certificate); non-profit management (Certificate); social work (MSW). Part-time and evening/weekend programs available.

Faculty: 15 full-time (10 women), 19 part-time/adjunct (12 women).
Students: 143 full-time (124 women), 69 part-time (65 women); includes 60 minority (27 African Americans, 3 Asian Americans or Pacific Islanders, 29 Hispanic Americans, 1 Native American), 2 international. Average age 32. 171 applicants, 90% accepted, 105 enrolled. In 2001, 73 degrees awarded.
Degree requirements: For master's, thesis or alternative, field education.
Entrance requirements: For master's, TOEFL, resumé. *Application deadline:* For fall admission, 3/1. *Application fee:* $20. Electronic applications accepted.
Expenses: Tuition, state resident: part-time $162 per hour. Tuition, nonresident: part-time $569 per hour.
Financial support: In 2001–02, 17 fellowships with partial tuition reimbursements (averaging $3,000 per year), 18 research assistantships with partial tuition reimbursements (averaging $1,752 per year), 16 teaching assistantships with partial tuition reimbursements (averaging $1,667 per year) were awarded. Career-related internships or fieldwork, Federal Work-Study, institutionally sponsored loans, and unspecified assistantships also available. Financial award application deadline: 3/1; financial award applicants required to submit FAFSA.
Dr. Mary Van Hook, Director, 407-823-2114, *E-mail:* mvanhook@pegasus.cc.ucf.edu.
Application contact: Dr. Ken Kazmerski, Coordinator, 407-823-2114, *Fax:* 407-823-5697, *E-mail:* kenkaz@aol.com. *Web site:* http://www.ucf.edu/

■ UNIVERSITY OF CENTRAL OKLAHOMA

College of Graduate Studies and Research, College of Education, Department of Occupational and Technical Education, Program in Adult Education, Edmond, OK 73034-5209

AWARDS Community services (M Ed); gerontology (M Ed). Part-time programs available.

Entrance requirements: For master's, GRE General Test.

■ UNIVERSITY OF ILLINOIS AT SPRINGFIELD

Graduate Programs, College of Education and Human Services, Program in Human Services, Springfield, IL 62703-5404

AWARDS Alcoholism and substance abuse (MA); child and family studies (MA); gerontology (MA); social services administration (MA).

Faculty: 7 full-time (3 women), 10 part-time/adjunct (7 women).
Students: 44 full-time (32 women), 109 part-time (79 women); includes 32 minority (29 African Americans, 1 Asian American or Pacific Islander, 1 Hispanic American, 1 Native American), 2 international. Average age 37. 55 applicants, 85% accepted, 38 enrolled. In 2001, 16 degrees awarded.
Expenses: Tuition, state resident: full-time $2,680. Tuition, nonresident: full-time $8,064. Required fees: $626. One-time fee: $626.
Financial support: In 2001–02, 71 students received support, including 9 research assistantships (averaging $6,300 per year)
Rachell Anderson, Director, 217-206-7335.

■ UNIVERSITY OF KANSAS

Graduate School, College of Liberal Arts and Sciences, Program in Gerontology, Lawrence, KS 66045

AWARDS MA, PhD.

Students: 2 full-time (both women), 1 (woman) part-time, 1 international. Average age 27. 9 applicants, 0% accepted. In 2001, 1 degree awarded.
Degree requirements: For doctorate, thesis/dissertation.
Entrance requirements: For master's and doctorate, GRE, TOEFL. *Application deadline:* For fall admission, 2/15. *Application fee:* $35.
Expenses: Tuition, state resident: full-time $2,722; part-time $113 per credit. Tuition, nonresident: full-time $8,586; part-time $358 per credit. Required fees: $551; $46 per credit. Tuition and fees vary according to campus/location, program and reciprocity agreements.
Financial support: In 2001–02, 12 research assistantships with partial tuition reimbursements (averaging $10,029 per year) were awarded
Rhonda J. V. Montgomery, Center Director, 785-864-4130, *Fax:* 785-864-2666, *E-mail:* gerontology@ku.edu.
Application contact: Mary Lee Hummert, Graduate Advisor, 785-864-4130, *E-mail:* gerontology@ku.edu. *Web site:* http://www.ku.edu/~kugeron/

■ UNIVERSITY OF KENTUCKY

Graduate School, Program in Gerontology, Lexington, KY 40506-0032

AWARDS PhD.

Faculty: 7 full-time (5 women).
Students: 26 full-time (21 women), 7 part-time (6 women); includes 6 minority (5 African Americans, 1 Asian American or Pacific Islander). 17 applicants, 47% accepted.
Degree requirements: For doctorate, thesis/dissertation, comprehensive exam. *Application deadline:* For fall admission, 7/19. *Application fee:* $30 ($35 for international students).
Expenses: Tuition, state resident: full-time $4,075; part-time $213 per credit hour. Tuition, nonresident: full-time $11,295; part-time $614 per credit hour.
Financial support: In 2001–02, 14 fellowships, 10 research assistantships, 2 teaching assistantships were awarded.
Dr. John Watkins, Director, 859-323-6040 Ext. 328, *E-mail:* geg173@pop.uky.edu.
Application contact: Dr. Jeannine Blackwell, Associate Dean, 859-257-4905, *Fax:* 859-323-1928.

■ UNIVERSITY OF LA VERNE

School of Public Affairs and Health Administration, Department of Health Services Management and Gerontology, Graduate Program in Gerontology, La Verne, CA 91750-4443

AWARDS Business administration (MS); counseling (MS); gerontology administration (MS); health services management (MS); public administration (MS). Part-time programs available.

University of La Verne (continued)
Faculty: 3 full-time (2 women), 5 part-time/adjunct (all women).
Students: 1 (woman) full-time, 20 part-time (15 women); includes 8 minority (7 African Americans, 1 Asian American or Pacific Islander), 2 international. Average age 50. In 2001, 9 degrees awarded.
Entrance requirements: For master's, minimum GPA of 3.0. *Application deadline:* Applications are processed on a rolling basis. *Application fee:* $40.
Expenses: Tuition: Full-time $4,410; part-time $245 per unit. Required fees: $60. Tuition and fees vary according to course load, degree level, campus/location and program.
Financial support: In 2001–02, 8 students received support. Institutionally sponsored loans available. Financial award application deadline: 3/2; financial award applicants required to submit FAFSA.
Application contact: Jo Nell Baker, Director, Graduate Admissions and Academic Services, 909-593-3511 Ext. 4504, *Fax:* 909-392-2761, *E-mail:* bakerj@ulv.edu. *Web site:* http://www.ulv.edu/gerontology/

■ UNIVERSITY OF LOUISIANA AT MONROE

Graduate Studies and Research, College of Liberal Arts, Department of Criminal Justice, Social Work, and Sociology, Program in Gerontological Studies, Monroe, LA 71209-0001

AWARDS CGS. Part-time and evening/weekend programs available.

Entrance requirements: For degree, GRE General Test.

■ UNIVERSITY OF LOUISIANA AT MONROE

Graduate Studies and Research, College of Liberal Arts, Department of Criminal Justice, Social Work, and Sociology, Program in Gerontology, Monroe, LA 71209-0001

AWARDS MA.

Degree requirements: For master's, thesis optional.
Entrance requirements: For master's, GRE General Test, minimum GPA of 2.75, 3.0 in last 60 credits.

■ UNIVERSITY OF MARYLAND, BALTIMORE COUNTY

Graduate School, Department of Sociology and Anthropology, Baltimore, MD 21250-5398

AWARDS Applied sociology (MA, Certificate); medical sociology (MA). Part-time and evening/weekend programs available.

Degree requirements: For master's, thesis.
Entrance requirements: For master's, GRE General Test, GRE Subject Test, TOEFL, minimum GPA of 3.0.
Faculty research: Sociology of aging, gerontology, social stratification, medical sociology. *Web site:* http://www.umbc.edu/sociology/

Find an in-depth description at www.petersons.com/gradchannel.

■ UNIVERSITY OF MARYLAND, BALTIMORE COUNTY

Graduate School, Interdisciplinary Program in Gerontology, Baltimore, MD 21250-5398

AWARDS Biomedical and biobehavioral aspects of aging (PhD); epidemiology of aging (PhD); law and social policy of aging (PhD); social and behavioral aspects of aging (PhD).

Degree requirements: For doctorate, thesis/dissertation.
Entrance requirements: For doctorate, GRE General Test.

Find an in-depth description at www.petersons.com/gradchannel.

■ UNIVERSITY OF MASSACHUSETTS BOSTON

Office of Graduate Studies and Research, College of Public and Community Service, Program in Gerontology, Boston, MA 02125-3393

AWARDS PhD. Part-time programs available.

Degree requirements: For doctorate, thesis/dissertation, comprehensive exam.
Entrance requirements: For doctorate, GRE General Test, minimum GPA of 3.0 required.
Faculty research: Aging with a chronic disability, pension policy and social security system, elderly minorities, health services research, living arrangements, family relations, and well-being of older persons, especially minorities.

Find an in-depth description at www.petersons.com/gradchannel.

■ UNIVERSITY OF MISSOURI–ST. LOUIS

Graduate School, Program in Gerontology, St. Louis, MO 63121-4499

AWARDS Gerontological social work (Certificate); gerontology (MS, Certificate). Part-time and evening/weekend programs available.

Faculty: 11.
Students: 2 full-time (both women), 7 part-time (5 women); includes 2 minority (1 African American, 1 Asian American or Pacific Islander). In 2001, 8 degrees awarded.
Application deadline: For fall admission, 7/1 (priority date); for spring admission, 12/1 (priority date). Applications are processed on a rolling basis. *Application fee:* $25 ($40 for international students). Electronic applications accepted.
Expenses: Tuition, state resident: part-time $231 per credit hour. Tuition, nonresident: part-time $621 per credit hour.
Financial support: In 2001–02, 1 research assistantship with full tuition reimbursement (averaging $15,000 per year) was awarded; career-related internships or fieldwork and Federal Work-Study also available.
Faculty research: Health care policy, social support and stress, retirement policy health behavior, ethnic differences in aging. *Total annual research expenditures:* $896,161.
Dr. Robert Calsyn, Director, 314-516-5421.
Application contact: Jeff Headtke, Graduate Admissions, 314-516-6928, *Fax:* 314-516-5310, *E-mail:* gradadm@umsl.edu.

■ UNIVERSITY OF NEBRASKA AT OMAHA

Graduate Studies and Research, College of Education, Department of Counseling, Omaha, NE 68182

AWARDS Community counseling (MA, MS); counseling gerontology (MA, MS); school counseling-elementary (MA, MS); school counseling-secondary (MA, MS); student affairs practice in higher education (MA, MS). Part-time and evening/weekend programs available.

Faculty: 4 full-time (2 women).
Students: 39 full-time (32 women), 134 part-time (114 women); includes 19 minority (10 African Americans, 3 Asian Americans or Pacific Islanders, 6 Hispanic Americans), 1 international. Average age 32. 40 applicants, 65% accepted, 25 enrolled. In 2001, 41 degrees awarded.
Degree requirements: For master's, thesis (for some programs), comprehensive exam.
Entrance requirements: For master's, GRE General Test, MAT, or department test, interview, minimum GPA of 3.0. *Application deadline:* For fall admission, 3/1; for spring admission, 10/1. Applications are processed on a rolling basis. *Application fee:* $35. Electronic applications accepted.
Expenses: Tuition, state resident: part-time $116 per credit hour. Tuition, nonresident: part-time $291 per credit hour. Required fees: $13 per credit hour. $4 per semester. One-time fee: $52 part-time.
Financial support: In 2001–02, 74 students received support, including 2 research assistantships; fellowships, Federal Work-Study, institutionally sponsored loans, scholarships/grants, tuition waivers (partial), and unspecified assistantships also available. Support available to part-time students. Financial award application

deadline: 3/1; financial award applicants required to submit FAFSA.
Dr. Jeanette Seaberry, Chairperson, 402-554-2727.

■ UNIVERSITY OF NEBRASKA AT OMAHA

Graduate Studies and Research, College of Public Affairs and Community Service, Department of Gerontology, Omaha, NE 68182

AWARDS MA, Certificate. Part-time and evening/weekend programs available.

Faculty: 5 full-time (1 woman).
Students: Average age 36. 5 applicants, 60% accepted, 3 enrolled.
Degree requirements: For master's, thesis, comprehensive exam.
Entrance requirements: For master's, GRE General Test, MAT, minimum GPA of 3.0. *Application deadline:* For fall admission, 7/1 (priority date); for spring admission, 12/1 (priority date). Applications are processed on a rolling basis. *Application fee:* $35. Electronic applications accepted.
Expenses: Tuition, state resident: part-time $116 per credit hour. Tuition, nonresident: part-time $291 per credit hour. Required fees: $13 per credit hour. $4 per semester. One-time fee: $52 part-time.
Financial support: In 2001–02, 3 students received support; fellowships, career-related internships or fieldwork, Federal Work-Study, institutionally sponsored loans, scholarships/grants, and tuition waivers (partial) available. Support available to part-time students. Financial award application deadline: 3/1.
Dr. James Thorson, Chairperson, 402-554-2272.

■ UNIVERSITY OF NEW ORLEANS

Graduate School, College of Education, Department of Health and Physical Education, New Orleans, LA 70148

AWARDS Adapted physical education (MA); exercise physiology (MA); gerontology (Certificate); health and physical education (Certificate); physical education (M Ed); science, pedagogy and coaching sport management (MA). Evening/weekend programs available.

Faculty: 8 full-time (4 women).
Students: 11 full-time (7 women), 33 part-time (26 women); includes 14 minority (12 African Americans, 2 Hispanic Americans). Average age 31. 15 applicants, 40% accepted, 2 enrolled. In 2001, 20 degrees awarded.
Entrance requirements: For master's, GRE General Test. *Application deadline:* For fall admission, 7/1 (priority date); for spring admission, 11/15 (priority date). Applications are processed on a rolling basis. *Application fee:* $20. Electronic applications accepted.
Expenses: Tuition, state resident: full-time $2,748; part-time $435 per credit. Tuition, nonresident: full-time $9,792; part-time $1,773 per credit.
Financial support: Teaching assistantships, scholarships/grants and tuition waivers (partial) available. Financial award applicants required to submit FAFSA.
Faculty research: Motor control, health science, biomechanics.
Dr. Barbara Warren, Chairperson, 504-280-6412, *Fax:* 504-280-6018, *E-mail:* blwarren@uno.edu.
Application contact: Dr. Peter Anderson, Graduate Coordinator, 504-280-7061, *Fax:* 504-280-6018, *E-mail:* panderso@uno.edu.

■ THE UNIVERSITY OF NORTH CAROLINA AT CHARLOTTE

Graduate School, College of Arts and Sciences, Program in Gerontology, Charlotte, NC 28223-0001

AWARDS MA.

Students: 2 full-time (1 woman), 20 part-time (all women); includes 4 minority (all African Americans). Average age 33. 8 applicants, 100% accepted, 4 enrolled. In 2001, 4 degrees awarded.
Degree requirements: For master's, thesis optional.
Entrance requirements: For master's, GRE. *Application deadline:* For fall admission, 7/15; for spring admission, 11/15. Applications are processed on a rolling basis. *Application fee:* $35. Electronic applications accepted.
Expenses: Tuition, state resident: full-time $1,483; part-time $371 per year. Tuition, nonresident: full-time $9,850; part-time $2,463 per year. Required fees: $1,043; $277 per year. Tuition and fees vary according to course load.
Financial support: Fellowships, research assistantships, teaching assistantships, career-related internships or fieldwork, Federal Work-Study, institutionally sponsored loans, scholarships/grants, and unspecified assistantships available. Support available to part-time students. Financial award application deadline: 4/1; financial award applicants required to submit FAFSA.
Faculty research: Rural older adults, person-centered dementia care, formal and informal systems of care, health care issues: gay, lesbian, and African American aging.
Dr. Dena Shenk, Director, 704-687-4349, *Fax:* 704-687-4347, *E-mail:* dshenk@email.uncc.edu.
Application contact: Kathy Barringer, Director of Graduate Admissions, 704-687-3366, *Fax:* 704-687-3279, *E-mail:* gradadm@email.uncc.edu. *Web site:* http://www.uncc.edu/gradmiss/

■ THE UNIVERSITY OF NORTH CAROLINA AT GREENSBORO

Graduate School, Program in Interdisciplinary Studies, Greensboro, NC 27412-5001

AWARDS Genetic counseling (MS); gerontology (MS). Part-time programs available.

Faculty: 1 (woman) full-time, 1 (woman) part-time/adjunct.
Students: 19 full-time (18 women), 14 part-time (all women); includes 4 minority (2 African Americans, 1 Asian American or Pacific Islander, 1 Hispanic American), 1 international. 107 applicants, 29% accepted.
Degree requirements: For master's, thesis or alternative, comprehensive exam.
Entrance requirements: For master's, GRE or MAT, TOEFL. *Application deadline:* Applications are processed on a rolling basis. *Application fee:* $35.
Expenses: Tuition, state resident: part-time $344 per course. Tuition, nonresident: part-time $2,457 per course.
Financial support: In 2001–02, 2 students received support; fellowships available.
Dr. James Lynch, Director of Graduate Recruitment and Information Services, 336-334-4881, *Fax:* 336-334-4424.

■ UNIVERSITY OF NORTHERN COLORADO

Graduate School, College of Health and Human Sciences, Department of Human Services, Gerontology Program, Greeley, CO 80639

AWARDS MA.

Students: 6 full-time (all women), 2 part-time (1 woman); includes 1 minority (Asian American or Pacific Islander), 1 international. Average age 34. 3 applicants, 100% accepted. In 2001, 7 degrees awarded.
Degree requirements: For master's, comprehensive exam.
Application deadline: Applications are processed on a rolling basis. *Application fee:* $35.
Expenses: Tuition, state resident: full-time $2,549; part-time $546 per credit hour. Tuition, nonresident: full-time $10,459; part-time $581 per credit hour. Required fees: $631; $85 per year. Part-time tuition and fees vary according to course load.
Financial support: In 2001–02, 5 students received support, including 4 fellowships (averaging $649 per year), 1 research assistantship (averaging $4,431 per year); teaching assistantships, unspecified assistantships also available. Financial award application deadline: 3/1.
Dr. Marcia Carter, Assistant Dean, 970-351-2403.

■ UNIVERSITY OF NORTH FLORIDA

College of Health, Department of Public Health, Jacksonville, FL 32224-2645

AWARDS Addictions counseling (MSH); aging studies (Certificate); community health (MPH); employee health services (MSH); health administration (MHA); health care administration (MSH); human ecology and nutrition (MSH); human performance (MSH). Part-time and evening/weekend programs available.

Faculty: 19 full-time (14 women).
Students: 59 full-time (45 women), 60 part-time (40 women); includes 34 minority (19 African Americans, 6 Asian Americans or Pacific Islanders, 7 Hispanic Americans, 2 Native Americans), 1 international. Average age 31. 128 applicants, 49% accepted, 31 enrolled. In 2001, 42 degrees awarded.
Degree requirements: For master's, thesis optional.
Entrance requirements: For master's, GMAT (MHA), GRE General Test (MSH), TOEFL. *Application deadline:* For fall admission, 7/6 (priority date); for winter admission, 11/2 (priority date); for spring admission, 3/10 (priority date). Applications are processed on a rolling basis. *Application fee:* $20. Electronic applications accepted.
Expenses: Tuition, state resident: full-time $2,411; part-time $134 per credit hour. Tuition, nonresident: full-time $9,391; part-time $522 per credit hour. Required fees: $670; $37 per credit hour.
Financial support: In 2001–02, 54 students received support, including 1 research assistantship (averaging $4,205 per year); career-related internships or fieldwork, Federal Work-Study, scholarships/grants, and tuition waivers (partial) also available. Support available to part-time students. Financial award application deadline: 4/1; financial award applicants required to submit FAFSA.
Faculty research: Lower extremity biomechanics; alcohol, tobacco, and other drug use prevention; turnover among health professionals; aging; psychosocial aspects of disabilities. *Total annual research expenditures:* $850,234.
Dr. Jeanne Patterson, Chair, 904-620-2840, *E-mail:* jpatters@unf.edu.
Application contact: Rachel Broderick, Director of Advising, 904-620-2812, *E-mail:* rbroderi@unf.edu.

■ UNIVERSITY OF NORTH TEXAS

Robert B. Toulouse School of Graduate Studies, School of Community Service, Department of Applied Gerontology, Denton, TX 76203

AWARDS Administration of aging organizations (MA, MS); administration of retirement facilities (MA, MS); aging (MA, MS, Certificate). Part-time programs available.

Faculty: 6 full-time (3 women), 5 part-time/adjunct (4 women).
Students: 15. Average age 35. In 2001, 18 degrees awarded.
Degree requirements: For master's, thesis, internship.
Entrance requirements: For master's, GRE General Test. *Application deadline:* For fall admission, 7/17; for spring admission, 12/1. Applications are processed on a rolling basis. *Application fee:* $25 ($50 for international students).
Expenses: Tuition, state resident: part-time $186 per hour. Tuition, nonresident: part-time $319 per hour. Required fees: $88; $21 per hour.
Financial support: Research assistantships, career-related internships or fieldwork, Federal Work-Study, institutionally sponsored loans, and scholarships/grants available. Financial award application deadline: 6/1.
Faculty research: Minority aging, housing for the elderly, aging and developmental disability.
Dr. Richard A. Lusky, Chair, 940-565-2765, *Fax:* 940-565-4370, *E-mail:* lusky@scs.unt.edu.

■ UNIVERSITY OF PITTSBURGH

Graduate School of Public Health, Department of Health Services Administration, Program in Behavioral and Community Health Services, Pittsburgh, PA 15260

AWARDS Behavioral and community health services (MHPE, MPH); Latin American studies (Certificate); non-profit organization (Certificate); public health/aging (Certificate). Part-time programs available.

Faculty: 18 full-time (12 women), 12 part-time/adjunct (5 women).
Students: 22 full-time (15 women), 19 part-time (17 women); includes 16 minority (7 African Americans, 6 Asian Americans or Pacific Islanders, 3 Hispanic Americans), 11 international. Average age 30. 60 applicants, 83% accepted. In 2001, 9 degrees awarded.
Degree requirements: For master's, thesis.
Entrance requirements: For master's, GRE General Test, TOEFL, GMAT or MCAT, bachelor's degree in public health or related field. *Application deadline:* For fall admission, 5/1; for spring admission, 10/1. Applications are processed on a rolling basis. *Application fee:* $50 ($60 for international students).
Expenses: Tuition, state resident: full-time $9,410; part-time $385 per credit. Tuition, nonresident: full-time $19,376; part-time $797 per credit. Required fees: $480; $90 per term. Tuition and fees vary according to program.
Financial support: In 2001–02, 10 students received support, including 3 research assistantships with tuition reimbursements available (averaging $9,780 per year); career-related internships or fieldwork, Federal Work-Study, institutionally sponsored loans, and unspecified assistantships also available. Support available to part-time students. Financial award applicants required to submit FAFSA.
Faculty research: Public health and aging, maternal and child health, substance abuse, privatization of health service. *Total annual research expenditures:* $2.1 million.
Prof. Karen S. Peterson, Assistant Professor and Program Coordinator, 412-624-4756, *Fax:* 412-624-5510, *E-mail:* pskph@pitt.edu.
Application contact: Dan Bach, Program Administrator, 412-624-3107, *Fax:* 412-624-5510, *E-mail:* paudb5@pitt.edu.

Find an in-depth description at www.petersons.com/gradchannel.

■ UNIVERSITY OF PITTSBURGH

School of Social Work, Program in Social Work, Pittsburgh, PA 15260

AWARDS Gerontology (Certificate); social work (MSW, PhD). Part-time programs available. Postbaccalaureate distance learning degree programs offered (no on-campus study).

Faculty: 20 full-time (11 women), 32 part-time/adjunct (23 women).
Students: 350 full-time (300 women), 228 part-time (189 women); includes 83 minority (81 African Americans, 1 Hispanic American, 1 Native American), 19 international. Average age 31. 415 applicants, 54% accepted, 218 enrolled. In 2001, 171 master's, 4 doctorates awarded.
Degree requirements: For master's, practicum; for doctorate, thesis/dissertation, comprehensive exam, registration. *Median time to degree:* Master's–2 years full-time, 3.75 years part-time; doctorate–4 years full-time, 8 years part-time.
Entrance requirements: For master's, minimum QPA of 3.0, previous course work in descriptive statistics and human biology; for doctorate, MSW or related degree, previous course work in statistics. *Application deadline:* For fall admission, 3/31. Applications are processed on a rolling basis. *Application fee:* $40.
Expenses: Tuition, state resident: full-time $9,410; part-time $385 per credit. Tuition, nonresident: full-time $19,376; part-time $797 per credit. Required fees: $480; $90 per term. Tuition and fees vary according to program.
Financial support: In 2001–02, 79 students received support, including 2 research assistantships with full tuition reimbursements available (averaging $9,780 per year), 3 teaching assistantships with full tuition reimbursements available (averaging $11,980 per year); career-related internships or fieldwork, institutionally sponsored loans, scholarships/grants, traineeships, and

unspecified assistantships also available. Financial award application deadline: 6/1; financial award applicants required to submit FAFSA.
Faculty research: Child abuse and neglect, poverty race relations and community empowerment, family preservation, welfare reform, mental health services research. *Total annual research expenditures:* $4 million.
Application contact: Dr. Grady H. Roberts, Associate Dean of Admissions, 412-624-6346, *Fax:* 412-624-6323. *Web site:* http://www.pitt.edu/~pittssw/

■ UNIVERSITY OF PUERTO RICO, MEDICAL SCIENCES CAMPUS

Graduate School of Public Health, Department of Human Development, Program in Gerontology, San Juan, PR 00936-5067

AWARDS MPH, Certificate. Part-time and evening/weekend programs available.

Entrance requirements: For master's, GRE, previous course work in social sciences, biology, psychology, and algebra. *Web site:* http://www.rcm.upr.edu/

■ UNIVERSITY OF SOUTH ALABAMA

Graduate School, College of Arts and Sciences, Program in Gerontology, Mobile, AL 36688-0002

AWARDS Certificate. Part-time programs available.

Students: 1 applicant, 100% accepted.
Entrance requirements: For degree, GRE General Test. *Application deadline:* For fall admission, 9/1 (priority date). Applications are processed on a rolling basis. *Application fee:* $25.
Expenses: Tuition, state resident: full-time $3,048. Tuition, nonresident: full-time $6,096. Required fees: $320.
Financial support: Application deadline: 4/1.
Dr. Roma Hanks, Chair, 334-460-6347.

■ UNIVERSITY OF SOUTH CAROLINA

The Graduate School, Program in Gerontology, Columbia, SC 29208

AWARDS Certificate. Part-time programs available.

Students: 11 full-time (9 women). Average age 39. 11 applicants, 100% accepted. In 2001, 11 degrees awarded.
Degree requirements: For Certificate, practicum.
Application fee: $35. Electronic applications accepted.
Expenses: Tuition, state resident: full-time $4,434. Tuition, nonresident: full-time $9,854. Tuition and fees vary according to program.
Dr. Gerald L. Euster, Graduate Director, 803-777-0139, *Fax:* 803-777-3498, *E-mail:* gerald.euster@sc.edu.
Application contact: Geraldine B. Washington, Administrative Assistant, 803-777-4221, *Fax:* 803-576-5501, *E-mail:* geraldinew@gwm.sc.edu.

■ UNIVERSITY OF SOUTHERN CALIFORNIA

Graduate School, Leonard Davis School of Gerontology, Los Angeles, CA 90089

AWARDS MS, PhD, Certificate, DDS/MS, JD/MS, M Pl/MS, MAJCS/MS, MBA/MS, MHA/MS, MPA/MS, MSW/MS. Part-time programs available. Postbaccalaureate distance learning degree programs offered.

Faculty: 15 full-time (5 women), 29 part-time/adjunct (10 women).
Students: 59 full-time (46 women), 25 part-time (18 women); includes 21 minority (3 African Americans, 16 Asian Americans or Pacific Islanders, 2 Hispanic Americans), 9 international. Average age 29. 70 applicants, 70% accepted, 32 enrolled. In 2001, 14 master's, 2 doctorates awarded.
Degree requirements: For doctorate, thesis/dissertation.
Entrance requirements: For master's and doctorate, GRE General Test. *Application deadline:* For fall admission, 2/1 (priority date); for spring admission, 10/1 (priority date). Applications are processed on a rolling basis. *Application fee:* $65 ($75 for international students).
Expenses: Tuition: Full-time $25,060; part-time $844 per unit. Required fees: $473.
Financial support: In 2001–02, fellowships with partial tuition reimbursements (averaging $18,000 per year), research assistantships with full tuition reimbursements (averaging $3,111 per year), teaching assistantships with full tuition reimbursements (averaging $3,111 per year) were awarded. Career-related internships or fieldwork, Federal Work-Study, institutionally sponsored loans, and scholarships/grants also available. Financial award application deadline: 2/15; financial award applicants required to submit FAFSA.
Faculty research: Cognition in aging, biodemographic of aging, health outcomes research, families and intergenerational relatives, care-giving of elderly.
Dr. Elizabeth Zelinski, Dean, 213-740-4918, *E-mail:* zelinski@usc.edu.
Application contact: Steve Arbuckle, Public Communications Manager, 213-821-5452, *Fax:* 213-740-0792, *E-mail:* arbuckle@usc.edu. *Web site:* http://www.usc.edu/gero

Find an in-depth description at www.petersons.com/gradchannel.

■ UNIVERSITY OF SOUTH FLORIDA

College of Graduate Studies, College of Arts and Sciences, Department of Gerontology, Tampa, FL 33620-9951

AWARDS MA. Part-time and evening/weekend programs available.

Faculty: 8 full-time (4 women).
Students: 22 full-time (17 women), 18 part-time (16 women); includes 3 minority (2 Asian Americans or Pacific Islanders, 1 Hispanic American), 5 international. Average age 37. 32 applicants, 38% accepted, 6 enrolled. In 2001, 3 master's awarded.
Entrance requirements: For master's, GRE General Test, minimum GPA of 3.0 in last 60 hours. *Application fee:* $20. Electronic applications accepted.
Expenses: Tuition, state resident: part-time $166 per credit hour. Tuition, nonresident: part-time $573 per credit hour. Required fees: $17 per term.
Financial support: Fellowships with partial tuition reimbursements, research assistantships, career-related internships or fieldwork, Federal Work-Study, and institutionally sponsored loans available. Support available to part-time students. Financial award applicants required to submit FAFSA.
Faculty research: Minorities, caregiving, guardianship, Alzheimer's disease, cognitive aging. *Total annual research expenditures:* $71,667.
William E. Haley, Chairperson, 813-974-2414, *Fax:* 813-974-9754, *E-mail:* whaley@chuma1.cas.usf.edu.
Application contact: John F. Skinner, Director, 813-974-9753, *Fax:* 813-974-9754, *E-mail:* jskinner@chuma.cas.usf.edu. *Web site:* http://www.cas.usf.edu/gerontology/index.html

■ THE UNIVERSITY OF TENNESSEE

Graduate School, College of Human Ecology, Department of Health and Safety Sciences, Program in Public Health, Knoxville, TN 37996

AWARDS Community health education (MPH); gerontology (MPH); health planning/administration (MPH).

Students: 27 full-time (22 women), 23 part-time (21 women); includes 8 minority (4 African Americans, 4 Asian Americans or Pacific Islanders). 48 applicants, 54% accepted. In 2001, 17 degrees awarded.
Degree requirements: For master's, thesis optional.
Entrance requirements: For master's, TOEFL, minimum GPA of 2.7. *Application deadline:* For fall admission, 2/1 (priority date). Applications are processed on a rolling basis. *Application fee:* $35. Electronic applications accepted.
Expenses: Tuition, state resident: full-time $4,280; part-time $233 per hour. Tuition, nonresident: full-time $12,066; part-time

The University of Tennessee (continued)
$666 per hour. Tuition and fees vary according to program.
Financial support: Application deadline: 2/1.
Dr. Charles B. Hamilton, Graduate Representative, 865-974-6674, *E-mail:* cbhamilton@utk.edu.

■ UNIVERSITY OF UTAH

Graduate School, College of Nursing, Gerontology Center, Salt Lake City, UT 84112-1107

AWARDS MS, Certificate. Part-time programs available.

Students: 4 full-time (all women), 8 part-time (7 women). Average age 36. 14 applicants, 71% accepted. In 2001, 8 degrees awarded.
Degree requirements: For master's, thesis optional.
Entrance requirements: For master's, GRE General Test, TOEFL. *Application deadline:* For fall admission, 3/1. Applications are processed on a rolling basis. *Application fee:* $20.
Expenses: Tuition, state resident: part-time $320 per semester hour. Tuition, nonresident: part-time $1,135 per semester hour. Required fees: $143 per semester hour. Tuition and fees vary according to course load, degree level and program.
Financial support: In 2001–02, 1 student received support, including 1 teaching assistantship; fellowships, research assistantships, scholarships/grants also available. Financial award application deadline: 9/15.
Faculty research: Spousal bereavement, family caregiving, healthy promotion and self-care, environmental issues, geriatric care management.
Dr. Dale A. Lund, Director, 801-581-8198, *Fax:* 801-581-4642, *E-mail:* dale@nurfac.nurs.utah.edu.
Application contact: Sara Taber, Graduate Coordinator, 801-581-8198, *Fax:* 801-581-4642, *E-mail:* sara.taber@nurs.utah.edu. *Web site:* http://www.nurs.utah.edu/gerontology

■ VIRGINIA COMMONWEALTH UNIVERSITY

School of Graduate Studies, School of Allied Health Professions, Department of Gerontology, Richmond, VA 23284-9005

AWARDS Aging studies (CAS); gerontology (MS).

Students: 7 full-time, 20 part-time; includes 5 minority (4 African Americans, 1 Asian American or Pacific Islander). 18 applicants, 89% accepted. In 2001, 11 degrees awarded.
Entrance requirements: For master's, GRE General Test or MAT. *Application fee:* $30.
Expenses: Tuition, state resident: full-time $4,276; part-time $238 per credit. Tuition, nonresident: full-time $12,672; part-time $704 per credit. Required fees: $1,167; $43 per credit.
Financial support: Career-related internships or fieldwork available.
Faculty research: Alzheimer's disease, age-related alcoholism and suicide, pain perception, curriculum development and evaluation in gerontology/geriatrics.
Dr. Iris A. Parham, Chair, 804-828-1565, *Fax:* 804-828-5259, *E-mail:* iaparham@gems.vcu.edu. *Web site:* http://views.vcu.edu/views/sahp/gerontology/

■ VIRGINIA POLYTECHNIC INSTITUTE AND STATE UNIVERSITY

Graduate School, College of Human Resources and Education, Department of Human Development, Doctoral Program in Adult Development and Aging, Blacksburg, VA 24061

AWARDS PhD. Part-time programs available.

Faculty: 4 full-time (all women).
Students: 1 (woman) full-time, 4 part-time (all women). Average age 35. 3 applicants, 67% accepted, 0 enrolled. In 2001, 1 degree awarded.
Degree requirements: For doctorate, thesis/dissertation optional.
Entrance requirements: For doctorate, GRE General Test, TOEFL, minimum GPA of 3.5. *Application deadline:* For fall admission, 1/2 (priority date). *Application fee:* $45. Electronic applications accepted.
Expenses: Tuition, state resident: part-time $241 per hour. Tuition, nonresident: part-time $406 per hour. Tuition and fees vary according to program.
Financial support: Unspecified assistantships available. Support available to part-time students. Financial award application deadline: 3/1; financial award applicants required to submit FAFSA.
Faculty research: Research on healthcare, friendship, and dementia; research of older families in rural communities; agricultural experimental study of osteoporosis; study of Alzheimer's and evaluation of public guardianship; study of Virginia-area Agencies on Aging for medical disease fraud. *Total annual research expenditures:* $180,000.
Application contact: Katharine Ann Surface, Administrative and Program Specialist III, 540-231-6149, *Fax:* 540-231-7012, *E-mail:* ksurface@vt.edu. *Web site:* http://www.chre.vt.edu/hd/hd.html

■ VIRGINIA POLYTECHNIC INSTITUTE AND STATE UNIVERSITY

Graduate School, College of Human Resources and Education, Department of Human Development, Master's Program in Adult Development and Aging, Blacksburg, VA 24061

AWARDS MS. Part-time programs available.

Faculty: 6 full-time (all women).
Students: 6 full-time (all women). Average age 26. 6 applicants, 83% accepted, 4 enrolled.
Degree requirements: For master's, thesis optional.
Entrance requirements: For master's, GRE General Test, TOEFL, minimum GPA of 3.0. *Application deadline:* For fall admission, 1/2 (priority date). *Application fee:* $45. Electronic applications accepted.
Expenses: Tuition, state resident: part-time $241 per hour. Tuition, nonresident: part-time $406 per hour. Tuition and fees vary according to program.
Financial support: Unspecified assistantships available. Support available to part-time students. Financial award application deadline: 3/1.
Faculty research: Research of healthcare, friendship, and dementia; research of older families in rural communities; agricultural experimental study of osteoporosis; study of Alzheimer's and evaluation of public guardianship; study of Virginia-area Agencies on Aging for medical disease fraud. *Total annual research expenditures:* $180,000.
Application contact: Katharine Ann Surface, Administrative and Program Specialist III, 540-231-6149, *Fax:* 540-231-7012, *E-mail:* ksurface@vt.edu. *Web site:* http://www.chre.vt.edu/HD/hd.html

■ WASHINGTON STATE UNIVERSITY SPOKANE

Graduate Programs, Program in Aging, Spokane, WA 99201-3899

AWARDS Certificate.

■ WAYNE STATE UNIVERSITY

Graduate School, Interdisciplinary Program in Gerontology, Detroit, MI 48202

AWARDS Certificate.

Students: In 2001, 4 degrees awarded. *Application deadline:* For fall admission, 7/1. *Application fee:* $20 ($30 for international students). Electronic applications accepted.
Expenses: Tuition, state resident: full-time $3,764. Tuition and fees vary according to degree level and program.
Financial support: In 2001–02, 15 research assistantships were awarded
Faculty research: Aging and health, cognitive and neuroscience, aging and disability, minority aging, human factors and aging.

Dr. Peter Lichtenburg, Interim Director, 313-577-2297, *Fax:* 313-875-0127, *E-mail:* p.lichtenberg@wayne.edu.
Application contact: Jenny Mendez, Education Director, 313-875-3722, *E-mail:* jmendez@wayne.edu.

■ WEBSTER UNIVERSITY

College of Arts and Sciences, Department of Behavioral and Social Sciences, Program in Gerontology, St. Louis, MO 63119-3194

AWARDS MA.

Students: 5 full-time (all women), 15 part-time (all women); includes 9 minority (all African Americans), 1 international. Average age 41. In 2001, 4 degrees awarded. *Application deadline:* Applications are processed on a rolling basis. *Application fee:* $25 ($50 for international students).
Expenses: Tuition: Full-time $7,164; part-time $398 per credit hour.
Financial support: Federal Work-Study available. Support available to part-time students. Financial award application deadline: 4/1; financial award applicants required to submit FAFSA.
Linda Wolf, Head, 314-968-7062.
Application contact: Denise Harrell, Associate Director of Graduate and Evening Student Admissions, 314-968-6983, *Fax:* 314-968-7116, *E-mail:* gadmit@webster.edu.

■ WEST CHESTER UNIVERSITY OF PENNSYLVANIA

Graduate Studies, College of Arts and Sciences, Department of Anthropology and Sociology, West Chester, PA 19383

AWARDS Gerontology (Certificate); long term care (MSA). Part-time and evening/weekend programs available.

Faculty: 1.
Students: 2 full-time (both women), 3 part-time (all women); includes 1 minority (African American). Average age 43. 4 applicants, 75% accepted. In 2001, 3 degrees awarded.
Degree requirements: For master's, comprehensive exam.
Entrance requirements: For master's, MAT, GRE, or GMAT, interview. *Application deadline:* For fall admission, 4/15 (priority date); for spring admission, 10/15. Applications are processed on a rolling basis. *Application fee:* $25.
Expenses: Tuition, state resident: full-time $4,600; part-time $256 per credit. Tuition, nonresident: full-time $7,554; part-time $420 per credit. Required fees: $44 per credit.
Financial support: In 2001–02, research assistantships with full tuition reimbursements (averaging $5,000 per year); unspecified assistantships also available. Support available to part-time students. Financial award application deadline: 2/15; financial award applicants required to submit FAFSA.
Faculty research: West African communities in the U.S., life long learning-distance education, comparative religions.
Dr. Anthony Zumpetta, Chair, 610-436-2556.
Application contact: Dr. Douglas McConatha, Graduate Coordinator, 610-436-3125, *E-mail:* dmcconatha@wcupa.edu.

■ WEST CHESTER UNIVERSITY OF PENNSYLVANIA

Graduate Studies, School of Health Sciences, Department of Health, West Chester, PA 19383

AWARDS Environmental health (MS); gerontology (MS); health services (MSA); public health (MS); school health (M Ed). Part-time and evening/weekend programs available.

Faculty: 7.
Students: 15 full-time (11 women), 37 part-time (28 women); includes 6 minority (4 African Americans, 1 Asian American or Pacific Islander, 1 Native American). Average age 33. 36 applicants, 78% accepted. In 2001, 20 degrees awarded.
Degree requirements: For master's, thesis (for some programs), comprehensive exam.
Entrance requirements: For master's, GRE. *Application deadline:* For fall admission, 4/15 (priority date); for spring admission, 10/15. Applications are processed on a rolling basis. *Application fee:* $25.
Expenses: Tuition, state resident: full-time $4,600; part-time $256 per credit. Tuition, nonresident: full-time $7,554; part-time $420 per credit. Required fees: $44 per credit.
Financial support: In 2001–02, 2 research assistantships with full tuition reimbursements (averaging $5,000 per year) were awarded; unspecified assistantships also available. Support available to part-time students. Financial award application deadline: 2/15; financial award applicants required to submit FAFSA.
Faculty research: HIV/AIDS education, teacher preparation, water quality.
Dr. Roger Mustalish, Chair, 610-436-2931.
Application contact: Dr. Lyn Carson, Graduate Coordinator, 610-436-2138, *E-mail:* lcarson@wcupa.edu.

■ WESTERN KENTUCKY UNIVERSITY

Graduate Studies, School of Health and Human Services, Department of Public Health, Bowling Green, KY 42101-3576

AWARDS Environmental health (MS); gerontology (MS); healthcare administration (MHA); public health (MPH); public health education (MA Ed, MPH). Part-time and evening/weekend programs available.

Faculty: 18 full-time (8 women), 1 part-time/adjunct (0 women).
Students: In 2001, 16 degrees awarded.
Degree requirements: For master's, thesis or alternative, comprehensive exam.
Entrance requirements: For master's, GRE General Test, minimum GPA of 2.75. *Application deadline:* For fall admission, 7/1 (priority date); for spring admission, 11/1. Applications are processed on a rolling basis. *Application fee:* $30.
Expenses: Tuition, area resident: Part-time $167 per credit. Tuition, state resident: full-time $2,490. Tuition, nonresident: full-time $6,660; part-time $399 per credit. Required fees: $554. Part-time tuition and fees vary according to campus/location and reciprocity agreements.
Financial support: Research assistantships, career-related internships or fieldwork, Federal Work-Study, institutionally sponsored loans, tuition waivers (partial), unspecified assistantships, and service awards available. Support available to part-time students. Financial award application deadline: 4/1; financial award applicants required to submit FAFSA.
Faculty research: Health education training, driver traffic safety, community readiness, occupational injuries, local health departments.
Dr. Wayne Higgins, Head, 270-745-4797, *Fax:* 270-745-4437, *E-mail:* wayne.higgins@wku.edu.

■ WICHITA STATE UNIVERSITY

Graduate School, Fairmount College of Liberal Arts and Sciences, School of Community Affairs, Wichita, KS 67260

AWARDS Criminal justice (MA); gerontology (MA). Part-time programs available.

Faculty: 10 full-time (4 women), 2 part-time/adjunct (1 woman).
Students: 23 full-time (15 women), 44 part-time (26 women); includes 5 minority (2 African Americans, 1 Asian American or Pacific Islander, 2 Hispanic Americans), 1 international. Average age 35. 20 applicants, 60% accepted, 12 enrolled. In 2001, 25 degrees awarded.
Application deadline: For spring admission, 1/1. Applications are processed on a rolling basis. *Application fee:* $25 ($40 for international students). Electronic applications accepted.
Expenses: Tuition, state resident: full-time $1,888; part-time $105 per credit. Tuition, nonresident: full-time $6,129; part-time $341 per credit. Required fees: $345; $19 per credit. $17 per semester. Tuition and fees vary according to course load and program.
Financial support: In 2001–02, 8 research assistantships (averaging $1,941 per year), 8 teaching assistantships with full tuition reimbursements (averaging $4,879 per year) were awarded. Career-related internships or fieldwork, Federal Work-Study,

Wichita State University (continued)
institutionally sponsored loans, and unspecified assistantships also available. Financial award application deadline: 4/1; financial award applicants required to submit FAFSA.
Dr. Paul Cromwell, Director, 316-978-7200, *Fax:* 316-978-3626, *E-mail:* paul.cromwell@wichita.edu.

■ WILMINGTON COLLEGE

Division of Nursing, New Castle, DE 19720-6491

AWARDS Adult nurse practitioner (MSN); family nurse practitioner (MSN); gerontology (MSN); leadership (MSN); nursing (MSN). Part-time programs available.

Faculty: 8 full-time (all women), 15 part-time/adjunct (12 women).
Students: 82 full-time (72 women), 49 part-time (45 women); includes 21 minority (18 African Americans, 2 Hispanic Americans, 1 Native American), 1 international. In 2001, 41 degrees awarded.
Degree requirements: For master's, thesis. *Median time to degree:* Master's–2.25 years full-time, 3 years part-time.
Entrance requirements: For master's, BSN, RN license, interview, letters of recommendation (3). *Application deadline:* For fall admission, 3/31 (priority date). Applications are processed on a rolling basis. *Application fee:* $25.
Expenses: Tuition: Full-time $4,788; part-time $266 per credit. Required fees: $50; $25 per semester. Tuition and fees vary according to course level, course load, degree level, campus/location and program.
Financial support: In 2001–02, 28 fellowships with tuition reimbursements (averaging $2,200 per year) were awarded; traineeships also available. Financial award applicants required to submit FAFSA.
Faculty research: Outcomes assessment, student writing ability.
Mary Letitia Gallagher, Chair, 302-328-9401 Ext. 161, *Fax:* 302-328-7081, *E-mail:* tgall@wilmcoll.edu.
Application contact: Michael Lee, Director of Admissions and Financial Aid, 302-328-9407 Ext. 102, *Fax:* 302-328-5164, *E-mail:* inquire@wilmcoll.edu.

Geography

GEOGRAPHIC INFORMATION SYSTEMS

■ BOSTON UNIVERSITY

Graduate School of Arts and Sciences, Program in Energy and Environmental Studies, Boston, MA 02215

AWARDS Energy and environmental analysis (MA); environmental remote sensing and geographic information systems (MA); international relations and enivronmental policy (MA).

Students: 10 full-time (7 women), 3 part-time (2 women); includes 1 minority (Hispanic American), 1 international. Average age 26. 110 applicants, 58% accepted, 20 enrolled.
Degree requirements: For master's, one foreign language, comprehensive exam, registration, research paper.
Entrance requirements: For master's, GRE General Test, TOEFL, 2 letters of recommendation. *Application deadline:* For fall admission, 7/1; for spring admission, 11/15. *Application fee:* $60.
Expenses: Tuition: Full-time $25,872; part-time $340 per credit. Required fees: $40 per semester. Part-time tuition and fees vary according to class time, course level and program.
Financial support: In 2001–02, 8 students received support, including 3 research assistantships; fellowships, career-related internships or fieldwork and Federal Work-Study also available. Support available to part-time students. Financial award application deadline: 1/15; financial award applicants required to submit FAFSA.
Cutler J. Cleveland, Director, 617-353-7552, *Fax:* 617-353-5986, *E-mail:* cutler@bu.edu.
Application contact: Alpana Roy, Administrative Assistant, 617-353-3083, *Fax:* 617-353-5986, *E-mail:* alpana@bu.edu. *Web site:* http://www.bu.edu//CEES/

■ CLARK UNIVERSITY

Graduate School, Department of International Development, Community, and Environment, Program in Geographic Information Science for Development and Environment, Worcester, MA 01610-1477

AWARDS MA.

Students: 16 full-time (3 women), 1 part-time; includes 1 minority (Asian American or Pacific Islander), 5 international. Average age 29. 35 applicants, 91% accepted, 10 enrolled. In 2001, 10 degrees awarded.
Degree requirements: For master's, thesis.
Application deadline: For fall admission, 2/1. *Application fee:* $40.
Expenses: Tuition: Full-time $24,400; part-time $763 per credit. Required fees: $10.
Financial support: In 2001–02, research assistantships with full and partial tuition reimbursements (averaging $9,250 per year), teaching assistantships with full and partial tuition reimbursements (averaging $9,250 per year) were awarded. Fellowships, tuition waivers (full and partial) also available. *Total annual research expenditures:* $34,654.
Dr. William F. Fisher, Director, *Fax:* 508-793-8820, *E-mail:* wfisher@clarku.edu.
Application contact: Liz Owens, IDCE Graduate Admissions, 508-793-7201, *Fax:* 508-793-8820, *E-mail:* idce@clarku.edu. *Web site:* http://www2.clarku.edu/newsite/graduatefolder/index.shtml

■ GEORGE MASON UNIVERSITY

College of Arts and Sciences, Department of Geography and Earth Science, Fairfax, VA 22030-4444

AWARDS Geography and cartographic sciences (MS).

Faculty: 8 full-time (3 women), 6 part-time/adjunct (1 woman).
Students: 9 full-time (5 women), 37 part-time (15 women); includes 1 minority (Hispanic American), 1 international. Average age 34. 24 applicants, 79% accepted, 10 enrolled. In 2001, 15 degrees awarded.
Degree requirements: For master's, thesis optional.
Entrance requirements: For master's, GRE General Test, minimum GPA of 3.0 in last 60 hours; BS or BA in geography, cartography, or related field. *Application deadline:* For fall admission, 5/1; for spring admission, 11/1. *Application fee:* $30. Electronic applications accepted.
Expenses: Tuition, state resident: full-time $3,168; part-time $132 per credit hour. Tuition, nonresident: full-time $11,280; part-time $470 per credit hour. Required fees: $1,416; $59 per credit hour.
Financial support: Research assistantships, teaching assistantships available. Support available to part-time students. Financial award application deadline: 3/1; financial award applicants required to submit FAFSA.
David Wong, Graduate Coordinator, 703-993-1215, *E-mail:* dwong2@gmu.edu. *Web site:* http://geog.gmu.edu/default.html

■ HUNTER COLLEGE OF THE CITY UNIVERSITY OF NEW YORK

Graduate School, School of Arts and Sciences, Department of Geography, New York, NY 10021-5085

AWARDS Analytical geography (MA); earth system science (MA); environmental and social issues (MA); geographic information science (Certificate); geographic information systems (MA); teaching earth science (MA). Part-time and evening/weekend programs available.

Faculty: 15 full-time (7 women), 23 part-time/adjunct (10 women).
Students: 1 (woman) full-time, 32 part-time (17 women); includes 4 minority (1 African American, 1 Asian American or Pacific Islander, 2 Hispanic Americans), 2 international. Average age 35. 18 applicants, 72% accepted. In 2001, 8 degrees awarded.
Degree requirements: For master's, comprehensive exam or thesis.
Entrance requirements: For master's, GRE General Test, TOEFL, minimum B average in major, B- overall; 18 credits in geography; for Certificate, TOEFL. *Application deadline:* For fall admission, 3/24; for spring admission, 11/7. Applications are processed on a rolling basis. *Application fee:* $40.
Expenses: Tuition, state resident: full-time $2,175; part-time $185 per credit. Tuition, nonresident: full-time $3,800; part-time $320 per credit.
Financial support: In 2001–02, 1 fellowship (averaging $3,000 per year), 2 research assistantships (averaging $10,000 per year), 10 teaching assistantships (averaging $6,000 per year) were awarded. Career-related internships or fieldwork, Federal Work-Study, institutionally sponsored loans, and unspecified assistantships also available. Financial award application deadline: 3/1.
Faculty research: Urban geography, economic geography, geographic information science, demographic methods, climate change.
Prof. Charles A. Heatwole, Chair, 212-772-5265, *Fax:* 212-772-5268, *E-mail:* cah@geo.hunter.cuny.edu.
Application contact: Prof. Marianna Pavlovskaya, Graduate Adviser, 212-772-5320, *Fax:* 212-772-5268, *E-mail:* mpavlov@geo.hunter.cuny.edu. *Web site:* http://geo.hunter.cuny.edu/

■ NORTH CAROLINA STATE UNIVERSITY

Graduate School, College of Natural Resources, Department of Parks, Recreation and Tourism Management, Raleigh, NC 27695

AWARDS Geographic information systems (MS); maintenance management (MRRA, MS); recreation planning (MRRA, MS); recreation resources administration/public administration (MRRA); recreation/park management (MRRA, MS); sports management (MRRA, MS); travel and tourism management (MS).

Faculty: 14 full-time (4 women), 7 part-time/adjunct (1 woman).
Students: 40 full-time (22 women), 21 part-time (14 women); includes 5 minority (1 African American, 1 Asian American or Pacific Islander, 2 Hispanic Americans, 1 Native American). Average age 29. 36 applicants, 75% accepted. In 2001, 22 degrees awarded.
Degree requirements: For master's, thesis (for some programs).
Entrance requirements: For master's, GRE General Test, TOEFL. *Application deadline:* For fall admission, 6/25; for spring admission, 11/25. *Application fee:* $45.
Expenses: Tuition, state resident: full-time $1,748. Tuition, nonresident: full-time $6,904.
Financial support: In 2001–02, 1 fellowship (averaging $5,331 per year), 13 research assistantships (averaging $4,268 per year), 4 teaching assistantships (averaging $4,213 per year) were awarded. Career-related internships or fieldwork and institutionally sponsored loans also available. Financial award application deadline: 4/1.
Faculty research: Tourism policy and development, spatial information systems, natural resource recreation management, recreational sports management. *Total annual research expenditures:* $3.2 million.
Dr. Phillip S. Rea, Head, 919-515-3675, *Fax:* 919-515-3687, *E-mail:* phil_rea@ncsu.edu.
Application contact: Dr. Beth E. Wilson, Director of Graduate Programs, 919-515-3665, *Fax:* 919-515-3687, *E-mail:* beth_wilson@ncsu.edu. *Web site:* http://www.cfr.ncsu.edu/prtm

■ NORTHERN ARIZONA UNIVERSITY

Graduate College, College of Ecosystem Science and Management, Department of Geography and Public Planning, Flagstaff, AZ 86011

AWARDS Geographic information systems (Certificate); rural geography (MA).

Faculty: 9 full-time (4 women), 5 part-time/adjunct (0 women).
Students: 13 full-time (6 women), 13 part-time (8 women); includes 3 minority (1 Hispanic American, 2 Native Americans). Average age 32. 12 applicants, 75% accepted, 8 enrolled. In 2001, 5 degrees awarded.
Degree requirements: For master's, thesis.
Entrance requirements: For master's, GRE General Test. *Application deadline:* For fall admission, 2/15 (priority date); for spring admission, 10/15. Applications are processed on a rolling basis. *Application fee:* $45.
Expenses: Tuition, state resident: full-time $2,488. Tuition, nonresident: full-time $10,354.
Financial support: In 2001–02, 9 research assistantships were awarded
Dr. Robert Clark, Chair, 928-523-1321.
Application contact: Dr. Alan Lew, Graduate Coordinator, 928-523-2650, *E-mail:* geog@nau.edu. *Web site:* http://www.for.nau.edu/geography

■ SAINT MARY'S UNIVERSITY OF MINNESOTA

Graduate School, Program in Resource Analysis, Winona, MN 55987-1399

AWARDS Business (MS); criminal justice (MS); natural resources (MS); public administration (MS).

■ SOUTHWEST TEXAS STATE UNIVERSITY

Graduate School, College of Liberal Arts, Department of Geography, Program in Cartography/Geographic Information Systems, San Marcos, TX 78666

AWARDS MAG. Part-time and evening/weekend programs available.

Students: 6 full-time (4 women), 18 part-time (6 women); includes 1 minority (African American), 3 international. Average age 33. 10 applicants, 30% accepted, 3 enrolled. In 2001, 8 degrees awarded.
Degree requirements: For master's, internship or thesis.
Entrance requirements: For master's, GRE General Test, TOEFL, minimum GPA of 3.00 in last 60 hours. *Application deadline:* For fall admission, 6/15 (priority date); for spring admission, 10/15 (priority date). Applications are processed on a rolling basis. *Application fee:* $40 ($90 for international students).
Expenses: Tuition, state resident: full-time $1,512; part-time $84 per credit hour. Tuition, nonresident: full-time $5,310; part-time $295 per credit hour. Required fees: $864; $29 per credit hour. $195 per term. Full-time tuition and fees vary according to course load.
Financial support: Research assistantships, teaching assistantships, career-related internships or fieldwork, Federal Work-Study, institutionally sponsored loans, and scholarships/grants available. Support available to part-time students. Financial award application deadline: 4/1; financial award applicants required to submit FAFSA.
Dr. Fred Shelley, Graduate Adviser, 512-245-8704, *Fax:* 512-245-8353, *E-mail:* fs03@swt.edu. *Web site:* http://www.geo.swt.edu/

■ STATE UNIVERSITY OF NEW YORK AT ALBANY

College of Arts and Sciences, Department of Geography and Planning, Program in Geography, Albany, NY 12222-0001

AWARDS Geographic information systems and spatial analysis (Certificate); geography (MA). Evening/weekend programs available.

Degree requirements: For master's, thesis or alternative.
Application deadline: For fall admission, 8/1; for spring admission, 11/1. *Application fee:* $50.
Expenses: Tuition, state resident: full-time $2,550; part-time $213 per credit. Tuition, nonresident: full-time $4,208; part-time $351 per credit. Required fees: $470; $470 per year.
Financial support: Fellowships, teaching assistantships, Federal Work-Study and institutionally sponsored loans available. Financial award application deadline: 6/1.
Faculty research: Remote sensing, cultural/social geography, urban geography.

■ UNIVERSITY AT BUFFALO, THE STATE UNIVERSITY OF NEW YORK

Graduate School, College of Arts and Sciences, Department of Geography, Buffalo, NY 14260

AWARDS Geographic information science (Certificate); geography (MA, PhD). Part-time programs available.

Faculty: 16 full-time (4 women), 1 (woman) part-time/adjunct.
Students: 71 full-time (21 women), 57 part-time (15 women); includes 14 minority (5 African Americans, 4 Asian Americans or Pacific Islanders, 3 Hispanic Americans, 2 Native Americans), 47 international. Average age 25. 108 applicants, 60% accepted, 32 enrolled. In 2001, 19 master's, 8 doctorates awarded.
Degree requirements: For master's, project; for doctorate, thesis/dissertation; for Certificate, portfolio.
Entrance requirements: For master's, GRE General Test, TOEFL, minimum GPA of 3.0; for doctorate, TOEFL, GRE General Test, minimum GPA of 3.0.
Application deadline: For fall admission, 2/1 (priority date); for spring admission, 10/1. Applications are processed on a rolling basis. *Application fee:* $35. Electronic applications accepted.
Expenses: Tuition, state resident: full-time $6,118. Tuition, nonresident: full-time $9,434.
Financial support: In 2001–02, 28 students received support, including 9 fellowships with full tuition reimbursements available (averaging $14,000 per year), 10 teaching assistantships with full tuition reimbursements available (averaging $8,400 per year); career-related internships or fieldwork, Federal Work-Study, institutionally sponsored loans, traineeships, health care benefits, tuition waivers (partial), and unspecified assistantships also available. Financial award application deadline: 2/1; financial award applicants required to submit FAFSA.
Faculty research: International business and world trade, geographic information systems and cartography, transportation, urban and regional analysis, physical and environmental geography. *Total annual research expenditures:* $915,000.
Dr. Hugh W. Calkins, Chairman, 716-645-2722 Ext. 15, *Fax:* 716-645-2329, *E-mail:* calkins@geog.buffalo.edu.
Application contact: Joseph Murray, Graduate Secretary, 716-645-2722 Ext. 13, *Fax:* 716-645-2329, *E-mail:* jlm@buffalo.edu. *Web site:* http://www.geog.buffalo.edu/

■ UNIVERSITY OF MINNESOTA, TWIN CITIES CAMPUS

Graduate School, College of Liberal Arts, Department of Geography, Program in Geographic Information Science, Minneapolis, MN 55455-0213

AWARDS MGIS. Part-time programs available.

Faculty: 13 full-time (1 woman), 2 part-time/adjunct (0 women).
Students: 38 full-time (15 women), 22 part-time (3 women); includes 2 minority (both Asian Americans or Pacific Islanders), 10 international. 55 applicants, 51% accepted, 21 enrolled. In 2001, 6 degrees awarded.
Degree requirements: For master's, major project.
Entrance requirements: For master's, TOEFL, minimum GPA of 3.0; previous course work in advanced algebra, statistics, and computer programming. *Application deadline:* For fall admission, 3/30; for spring admission, 9/1. Applications are processed on a rolling basis. *Application fee:* $50 ($55 for international students).
Expenses: Tuition, state resident: full-time $2,932; part-time $489 per credit. Tuition, nonresident: full-time $5,758; part-time $960 per credit. Part-time tuition and fees vary according to course load, program and reciprocity agreements.
Financial support: In 2001–02, 10 students received support, including 9 research assistantships with full and partial tuition reimbursements available, 1 teaching assistantship with full and partial tuition reimbursement available
Faculty research: Building better communities (law and justice), accuracy assessment.
Robert B. McMaster, Director of Graduate Studies, 612-625-9883, *Fax:* 612-624-1044, *E-mail:* mcmaster@atlas.socsci.umn.edu.
Application contact: Susanna A. McMaster, Associate Program Director, 612-624-1498, *Fax:* 612-624-1044, *E-mail:* smcmaster@geog.umn.edu. *Web site:* http://www.geog.umn.edu/graduate/mgis/

■ THE UNIVERSITY OF MONTANA–MISSOULA

Graduate School, College of Arts and Sciences, Department of Geography, Missoula, MT 59812-0002

AWARDS Geography (MA), including cartography and GIS, rural town and regional planning.

Faculty: 8 full-time (1 woman).
Students: 13 full-time (4 women), 17 part-time (10 women), 1 international. 18 applicants, 94% accepted, 11 enrolled. In 2001, 2 degrees awarded.
Entrance requirements: For master's, GRE General Test. *Application deadline:* For fall admission, 4/30 (priority date). *Application fee:* $45.
Expenses: Tuition, state resident: full-time $2,482; part-time $1,700 per year. Tuition, nonresident: full-time $7,372; part-time $5,000 per year. Required fees: $1,900. Tuition and fees vary according to degree level.
Financial support: In 2001–02, 7 teaching assistantships with full tuition reimbursements (averaging $8,665 per year) were awarded; Federal Work-Study and unspecified assistantships also available. Financial award application deadline: 3/1; financial award applicants required to submit FAFSA. *Total annual research expenditures:* $44,000.
Dr. Jeffrey Gritzner, Chair, 406-243-5626, *E-mail:* jag@selway.umt.edu. *Web site:* http://www.umt.edu/geograph/

■ UNIVERSITY OF PITTSBURGH

Faculty of Arts and Sciences, Department of Geology and Planetary Science, Pittsburgh, PA 15260

AWARDS Geographical information systems (PM Sc); geology and planetary science (MS, PhD). Part-time programs available.

Faculty: 11 full-time (2 women), 2 part-time/adjunct (0 women).
Students: 22 full-time (13 women), 5 part-time (1 woman), 1 international. Average age 31. 41 applicants, 32% accepted, 11 enrolled. In 2001, 4 master's, 1 doctorate awarded.
Degree requirements: For master's, thesis, oral thesis defense; for doctorate, thesis/dissertation, oral dissertation defense.
Entrance requirements: For master's and doctorate, GRE General Test, TOEFL. *Application deadline:* For fall admission, 8/1 (priority date); for winter admission, 12/1 (priority date); for spring admission, 4/1 (priority date). Applications are processed on a rolling basis. *Application fee:* $40. Electronic applications accepted.
Expenses: Tuition, state resident: full-time $9,410; part-time $385 per credit. Tuition, nonresident: full-time $19,376; part-time $797 per credit. Required fees: $480; $90 per term. Tuition and fees vary according to program.

Financial support: In 2001–02, 19 students received support, including 3 fellowships with tuition reimbursements available (averaging $14,500 per year), 7 research assistantships with tuition reimbursements available (averaging $10,400 per year), 11 teaching assistantships with tuition reimbursements available (averaging $11,752 per year); career-related internships or fieldwork, Federal Work-Study, institutionally sponsored loans, scholarships/grants, and tuition waivers (full and partial) also available. Support available to part-time students. Financial award application deadline: 2/1; financial award applicants required to submit FAFSA.
Faculty research: Geographical information systems, hydrology, low temperature geochemistry, radiogenic isotopes, volcanology. *Total annual research expenditures:* $574,116.
Dr. William Harbert, Chair, 412-624-8783, *Fax:* 412-624-3914, *E-mail:* harbert@pitt.edu.
Application contact: Dr. Brian Stewart, Graduate Adviser, 412-624-8883, *Fax:* 412-624-3914, *E-mail:* bstewart@pitt.edu. *Web site:* http://www.geology.pitt.edu/

■ THE UNIVERSITY OF TEXAS AT DALLAS

School of Social Sciences, Program in Geographic Information Sciences, Richardson, TX 75083-0688

AWARDS MS. Part-time and evening/weekend programs available.

Faculty: 1 full-time (0 women), 1 part-time/adjunct (0 women).
Students: 5 full-time (3 women), 18 part-time (6 women); includes 5 minority (all African Americans), 4 international. Average age 32. 21 applicants, 62% accepted. In 2001, 11 degrees awarded.
Degree requirements: For master's, internship.
Entrance requirements: For master's, GRE General Test, TOEFL, minimum GPA of 3.0 in upper-level coursework in field. *Application deadline:* For fall admission, 7/15; for spring admission, 11/15. Applications are processed on a rolling basis. *Application fee:* $25 ($75 for international students). Electronic applications accepted.
Expenses: Tuition, state resident: full-time $1,440; part-time $84 per credit. Tuition, nonresident: full-time $5,310; part-time $295 per credit. Required fees: $1,835; $87 per credit. $138 per term.
Financial support: In 2001–02, 1 research assistantship (averaging $5,000 per year), 2 teaching assistantships with tuition reimbursements (averaging $5,000 per year) were awarded. Fellowships, career-related internships or fieldwork, Federal Work-Study, institutionally sponsored loans, and scholarships/grants also available. Support available to part-time students. Financial award application deadline: 4/30; financial award applicants required to submit FAFSA.
Faculty research: Neighborhood evaluation using GIS.
Application contact: Dr. Ronald Briggs, Coordinator, 972-883-2720, *Fax:* 972-883-2735, *E-mail:* briggs@utdallas.edu. *Web site:* http://www.bruton.utdallas.edu/educ/

Find an in-depth description at www.petersons.com/gradchannel.

■ UNIVERSITY OF WISCONSIN–MADISON

Graduate School, College of Letters and Science, Department of Geography, Madison, WI 53706-1380

AWARDS Cartography and geographic information systems (MS); geographic information systems (Certificate); geography (MS, PhD). Part-time programs available.

Faculty: 18 full-time (3 women).
Students: 77 full-time (20 women), 22 part-time (10 women); includes 4 minority (1 African American, 1 Asian American or Pacific Islander, 2 Hispanic Americans), 10 international. 108 applicants, 55% accepted. In 2001, 8 master's, 2 doctorates awarded.
Degree requirements: For master's and doctorate, thesis/dissertation; for Certificate, internship.
Entrance requirements: For master's and doctorate, GRE General Test, minimum GPA of 3.25. *Application deadline:* For fall admission, 12/15 (priority date). Applications are processed on a rolling basis. *Application fee:* $45. Electronic applications accepted.
Expenses: Tuition, state resident: full-time $7,361; part-time $399 per credit. Tuition, nonresident: full-time $20,499; part-time $1,282 per credit. Required fees: $34 per credit. Full-time tuition and fees vary according to course load, program, reciprocity agreements and student level.
Financial support: In 2001–02, 57 students received support, including 9 fellowships with full tuition reimbursements available (averaging $15,000 per year), 2 research assistantships with full tuition reimbursements available, 22 teaching assistantships with full tuition reimbursements available (averaging $8,436 per year); career-related internships or fieldwork, Federal Work-Study, and unspecified assistantships also available. Financial award application deadline: 12/15.
Faculty research: Physical geography, urban/historical geography, people-environment, history of cartography, GIS.
James E. Burt, Chair, 608-262-2138, *Fax:* 608-265-3991, *E-mail:* jburt@geography.wisc.edu.
Application contact: Roxanne Moermond, Graduate Student Coordinator, 608-262-3861, *Fax:* 608-265-3991, *E-mail:* gradschool@geography.wisc.edu. *Web site:* http://www.geography.wisc.edu/

■ WEST VIRGINIA UNIVERSITY

Eberly College of Arts and Sciences, Department of Geology and Geography, Program in Geography, Morgantown, WV 26506

AWARDS Energy and environmental resources (MA); geographic information systems (PhD); geography-regional development (PhD); GIS/cartographic analysis (MA); regional development and urban planning (MA). Part-time programs available.

Students: 10 full-time (3 women), 3 part-time (1 woman), 3 international. Average age 27. 30 applicants, 33% accepted. In 2001, 14 degrees awarded.
Degree requirements: For master's, thesis, oral and written exams.
Entrance requirements: For master's, GRE General Test, TOEFL, minimum GPA of 2.75. *Application deadline:* For fall admission, 3/15 (priority date). Applications are processed on a rolling basis. *Application fee:* $45.
Expenses: Tuition, state resident: full-time $2,791. Tuition, nonresident: full-time $8,659. Required fees: $1,002. Tuition and fees vary according to program.
Financial support: In 2001–02, 4 research assistantships, 4 teaching assistantships were awarded. Career-related internships or fieldwork, Federal Work-Study, institutionally sponsored loans, and tuition waivers (full and partial) also available. Financial award application deadline: 2/1; financial award applicants required to submit FAFSA.
Faculty research: Resources, regional development, planning, geographic information systems, gender geography.
Dr. Kenneth Martis, Associate Chair, 304-293-5603 Ext. 4350, *Fax:* 304-293-6522, *E-mail:* ken.martis@mail.wvu.edu.
Application contact: Dr. Timothy Warner, Associate Professor, 304-293-5603 Ext. 4328, *Fax:* 304-293-6522, *E-mail:* tim.warner@mail.wvu.edu. *Web site:* http://www.geo.wvu.edu/programs/geography.html

GEOGRAPHY

■ APPALACHIAN STATE UNIVERSITY

Cratis D. Williams Graduate School, College of Arts and Sciences, Department of Geography and Planning, Boone, NC 28608

AWARDS Geography (MA); social sciences (MA).

Faculty: 9 full-time (1 woman).
Students: 13 full-time (6 women), 1 (woman) part-time, 1 international. Average age 26. 8 applicants, 88% accepted, 4 enrolled. In 2001, 9 degrees awarded.

Appalachian State University (continued)
Degree requirements: For master's, one foreign language, thesis or alternative, comprehensive exam.
Entrance requirements: For master's, GRE General Test. *Application deadline:* For fall admission, 7/1; for spring admission, 11/1. Applications are processed on a rolling basis. *Application fee:* $35.
Expenses: Tuition, state resident: full-time $1,286. Tuition, nonresident: full-time $9,354. Required fees: $1,116.
Financial support: In 2001–02, 12 research assistantships (averaging $6,250 per year), 2 teaching assistantships (averaging $6,250 per year) were awarded. Fellowships, career-related internships or fieldwork, scholarships/grants, and unspecified assistantships also available. Support available to part-time students. Financial award application deadline: 7/1; financial award applicants required to submit FAFSA.
Faculty research: Global change, climatology, production cartography, geographic information systems, North Carolina geography, Latin America. *Total annual research expenditures:* $92,327.
Dr. Michael Mayfield, Chairperson, 828-262-3000, *Fax:* 828-262-3067, *E-mail:* mayfldmw@appstate.edu.
Application contact: Dr. Peter Soule, Graduate Program Director, 828-262-3000, *E-mail:* soulep@appstate.edu.

■ ARIZONA STATE UNIVERSITY

Graduate College, College of Liberal Arts and Sciences, Department of Geography, Tempe, AZ 85287

AWARDS MA, PhD.

Degree requirements: For master's and doctorate, thesis/dissertation.
Entrance requirements: For master's and doctorate, GRE.
Faculty research: Physical geography, climatology, geomorphology, spatial land use, urban geography.

■ AUBURN UNIVERSITY

Graduate School, College of Sciences and Mathematics, Department of Geology and Geography, Auburn University, AL 36849

AWARDS MS. Part-time programs available.

Faculty: 11 full-time (1 woman).
Students: 9 full-time (2 women), 10 part-time (3 women), 2 international. 12 applicants, 83% accepted. In 2001, 2 degrees awarded.
Degree requirements: For master's, computer language or GIS, field camp.
Entrance requirements: For master's, GRE General Test. *Application deadline:* For fall admission, 7/7; for spring admission, 11/24. Applications are processed on a rolling basis. *Application fee:* $25 ($50 for international students). Electronic applications accepted.
Financial support: Research assistantships, teaching assistantships, Federal Work-Study available. Support available to part-time students. Financial award application deadline: 3/15.
Faculty research: Empirical magma dynamics and melt migration, ore mineralogy, role of terrestrial plant biomass in deposition, metamorphic petrology and isotope geochemistry, reef development, crinoid taphology.
Dr. Robert B. Cook, Head, 334-844-4282.
Application contact: Dr. John F. Pritchett, Dean of the Graduate School, 334-844-4700, *E-mail:* hatchlb@mail.auburn.edu. *Web site:* http://www.auburn.edu/academic/science_math/geology/docs

■ BOSTON UNIVERSITY

Graduate School of Arts and Sciences, Department of Geography, Boston, MA 02215

AWARDS MA, PhD.

Students: 41 full-time (14 women), 3 part-time (2 women), 30 international. Average age 31. 41 applicants, 17% accepted, 6 enrolled. In 2001, 1 master's, 6 doctorates awarded. Terminal master's awarded for partial completion of doctoral program.
Degree requirements: For master's, one foreign language, thesis, thesis or final written exam; for doctorate, one foreign language, thesis/dissertation, colloquium presentation, qualifying exam.
Entrance requirements: For master's, GRE General Test, GRE Subject Test, TOEFL, 3 letters of recommendation; for doctorate, GRE General Test, GRE Subject Test. TOEFL, 3 letters of recommendation. *Application deadline:* For fall admission, 7/1; for spring admission, 11/15. *Application fee:* $60.
Expenses: Tuition: Full-time $25,872; part-time $340 per credit. Required fees: $40 per semester. Part-time tuition and fees vary according to class time, course level and program.
Financial support: In 2001–02, 2 fellowships with full tuition reimbursements (averaging $14,000 per year), 34 research assistantships with full tuition reimbursements (averaging $13,500 per year), 8 teaching assistantships with full tuition reimbursements (averaging $13,500 per year) were awarded. Federal Work-Study and unspecified assistantships also available. Support available to part-time students. Financial award application deadline: 1/15; financial award applicants required to submit FAFSA. *Total annual research expenditures:* $1.2 million.
Curtis Woodcock, Chairman, 617-353-5746, *Fax:* 617-353-8399, *E-mail:* curtis@bu.edu.
Application contact: Nathan Giarnese, Academic Research Coordinator, 617-353-2526, *Fax:* 617-353-8399, *E-mail:* giarnese@bu.edu. *Web site:* http://geography.bu.edu/

■ BRIGHAM YOUNG UNIVERSITY

Graduate Studies, College of Family, Home, and Social Sciences, Department of Geography, Provo, UT 84602-1001

AWARDS MS. Part-time programs available.

Faculty: 10 full-time (0 women).
Students: 8 full-time (3 women), 8 part-time (3 women). Average age 29. 13 applicants, 62% accepted, 5 enrolled. In 2001, 5 degrees awarded.
Degree requirements: For master's, thesis. *Median time to degree:* Master's–2.8 years full-time, 5 years part-time.
Entrance requirements: For master's, GRE General Test, minimum GPA of 3.0 in last 60 hours. *Application deadline:* For fall admission, 2/15. *Application fee:* $50. Electronic applications accepted.
Expenses: Tuition: Full-time $3,860; part-time $214 per hour.
Financial support: In 2001–02, 15 students received support, including 2 research assistantships with partial tuition reimbursements available (averaging $7,500 per year), 3 teaching assistantships with partial tuition reimbursements available (averaging $7,500 per year); career-related internships or fieldwork, institutionally sponsored loans, scholarships/grants, and tuition waivers (partial) also available. Financial award application deadline: 2/15.
Faculty research: Cultural geography, physical geography, populations, geographic information systems, planning. *Total annual research expenditures:* $100,000.
Dr. J. Matthew Shumway, Chair, 801-422-3851, *Fax:* 801-378-5110, *E-mail:* jms7@email.byu.edu.
Application contact: Dr. Samuel M. Otterstrom, Coordinator, 801-422-7751, *Fax:* 801-378-5110, *E-mail:* samuel_otterstrom@byu.edu. *Web site:* http://geog.byu.edu

■ CALIFORNIA STATE UNIVERSITY, CHICO

Graduate School, College of Behavioral and Social Sciences, Department of Geography and Planning, Program in Geography, Chico, CA 95929-0722

AWARDS MA.

Students: 13 applicants, 92% accepted, 9 enrolled. In 2001, 9 degrees awarded.
Degree requirements: For master's, thesis or alternative, oral exam.
Entrance requirements: For master's, GRE General Test. *Application deadline:* For fall admission, 4/1; for spring admission, 10/1. Applications are processed on a rolling basis. *Application fee:* $55. Electronic applications accepted.
Expenses: Tuition, state resident: full-time $2,148. Tuition, nonresident: full-time $6,576.
Graduate Coordinator.

Application contact: Dr. Paul Melcon, Graduate Coordinator, 530-898-6871.

■ CALIFORNIA STATE UNIVERSITY, FULLERTON

Graduate Studies, College of Humanities and Social Sciences, Department of Geography, Fullerton, CA 92834-9480

AWARDS MA.

Faculty: 8 full-time (1 woman), 11 part-time/adjunct.
Students: 6 full-time (3 women), 8 part-time (4 women); includes 1 minority (Hispanic American), 1 international. Average age 36. 12 applicants, 67% accepted, 3 enrolled. In 2001, 12 degrees awarded.
Degree requirements: For master's, comprehensive exam or thesis.
Entrance requirements: For master's, minimum GPA of 3.0, 18 undergraduate credits in field. *Application fee:* $55.
Expenses: Tuition, nonresident: part-time $246 per unit. Required fees: $964.
Financial support: Teaching assistantships, career-related internships or fieldwork, Federal Work-Study, institutionally sponsored loans, and scholarships/grants available. Support available to part-time students. Financial award application deadline: 3/1.
Faculty research: Human geography, physical geography.
Dr. William Lloyd, Chair, 714-278-3161.

■ CALIFORNIA STATE UNIVERSITY, HAYWARD

Academic Programs and Graduate Studies, School of Arts, Letters, and Social Sciences, Department of Geography and Environmental Studies, Hayward, CA 94542-3000

AWARDS Geography (MA). Part-time programs available.

Students: 2 full-time (both women), 12 part-time (6 women); includes 3 minority (1 African American, 1 Asian American or Pacific Islander, 1 Hispanic American). 6 applicants, 50% accepted. In 2001, 6 degrees awarded.
Entrance requirements: For master's, minimum GPA of 3.0 in field. *Application deadline:* For fall admission, 6/15; for winter admission, 10/27; for spring admission, 1/5. Applications are processed on a rolling basis. *Application fee:* $55. Electronic applications accepted.
Expenses: Tuition, nonresident: part-time $164 per unit. Required fees: $405 per semester.
Financial support: Fellowships, teaching assistantships, career-related internships or fieldwork, Federal Work-Study, institutionally sponsored loans, and scholarships/grants available. Support available to part-time students. Financial award application deadline: 3/1.
Application contact: Jennifer Cason, Graduate Program Coordinator/Operations Analyst, 510-885-3286, *Fax:* 510-885-4777, *E-mail:* jcason@csuhayward.edu.

■ CALIFORNIA STATE UNIVERSITY, LONG BEACH

Graduate Studies, College of Liberal Arts, Department of Geography, Long Beach, CA 90840

AWARDS MA. Part-time programs available.

Faculty: 7 full-time (3 women).
Students: 5 full-time (1 woman), 19 part-time (11 women); includes 5 minority (2 Asian Americans or Pacific Islanders, 2 Hispanic Americans, 1 Native American), 1 international. Average age 33. 11 applicants, 82% accepted. In 2001, 6 degrees awarded.
Degree requirements: For master's, thesis.
Application deadline: For fall admission, 8/1; for spring admission, 12/1. Applications are processed on a rolling basis. *Application fee:* $55. Electronic applications accepted.
Financial support: Career-related internships or fieldwork, Federal Work-Study, institutionally sponsored loans, and scholarships/grants available. Financial award application deadline: 3/2.
Faculty research: Demography, geographic information systems, world landforms and societies.
Dr. Joel Splansky, Chair, 562-985-4977, *Fax:* 562-985-8993, *E-mail:* splansky@csulb.edu.
Application contact: Information Contact, 562-985-4977, *Fax:* 562-985-8993.

■ CALIFORNIA STATE UNIVERSITY, LOS ANGELES

Graduate Studies, College of Natural and Social Sciences, Department of Geography and Urban Analysis, Los Angeles, CA 90032-8530

AWARDS Geography (MA). Part-time and evening/weekend programs available.

Faculty: 8 full-time, 8 part-time/adjunct.
Students: 10 full-time (3 women), 17 part-time (7 women); includes 12 minority (5 Asian Americans or Pacific Islanders, 7 Hispanic Americans), 1 international. In 2001, 4 degrees awarded.
Degree requirements: For master's, one foreign language.
Entrance requirements: For master's, TOEFL. *Application deadline:* For fall admission, 6/30; for spring admission, 2/1. Applications are processed on a rolling basis. *Application fee:* $55.
Expenses: Tuition, nonresident: part-time $164 per unit.
Financial support: Career-related internships or fieldwork and Federal Work-Study available. Support available to part-time students. Financial award application deadline: 3/1.
Faculty research: Technique focus–air photography, cartography, locational analysis.
Dr. Killian Ying, Chair, 323-343-2220.

■ CALIFORNIA STATE UNIVERSITY, NORTHRIDGE

Graduate Studies, College of Social and Behavioral Sciences, Department of Geography, Northridge, CA 91330

AWARDS MA. Part-time programs available.

Faculty: 19 full-time, 9 part-time/adjunct.
Students: 8 full-time (5 women), 11 part-time (4 women); includes 4 minority (1 Asian American or Pacific Islander, 2 Hispanic Americans, 1 Native American). Average age 35. 18 applicants, 67% accepted, 4 enrolled. In 2001, 4 degrees awarded.
Degree requirements: For master's, one foreign language, thesis.
Entrance requirements: For master's, TOEFL, GRE General Test or minimum GPA of 3.0. *Application deadline:* For fall admission, 11/30. *Application fee:* $55.
Expenses: Tuition, nonresident: part-time $631 per semester. Required fees: $246 per unit.
Financial support: Teaching assistantships available. Financial award application deadline: 3/1.
Dr. I-Shou Wang, Chair, 818-677-3532.
Application contact: Robert Gohstand, Graduate Coordinator, 818-677-3532.

■ CALIFORNIA UNIVERSITY OF PENNSYLVANIA

School of Graduate Studies, School of Liberal Arts, Program in Geography and Earth Sciences, California, PA 15419-1394

AWARDS Earth science (MS); geography (M Ed, MA). Part-time and evening/weekend programs available.

Faculty: 1 full-time (0 women), 3 part-time/adjunct (1 woman).
Students: 22 full-time (9 women), 12 part-time (4 women); includes 4 minority (3 African Americans, 1 Hispanic American).
Degree requirements: For master's, thesis optional.
Entrance requirements: For master's, MAT, TOEFL, minimum GPA of 2.5, teaching certificate (M Ed). *Application deadline:* Applications are processed on a rolling basis. *Application fee:* $25.
Expenses: Tuition, state resident: full-time $4,600. Tuition, nonresident: full-time $7,554.
Financial support: Tuition waivers (full) and unspecified assistantships available.

California University of Pennsylvania (continued)
Dr. Chad Kauffman, Coordinator, 724-938-4130, *E-mail:* moses@cup.edu. *Web site:* http://www.cup.edu/graduate

■ CENTRAL CONNECTICUT STATE UNIVERSITY

School of Graduate Studies, School of Arts and Sciences, Department of Geography, New Britain, CT 06050-4010

AWARDS MS. Part-time and evening/weekend programs available.

Faculty: 9 full-time (2 women), 4 part-time/adjunct (0 women).
Students: 4 full-time (3 women), 9 part-time (1 woman); includes 2 minority (1 African American, 1 Hispanic American). Average age 32. 8 applicants, 100% accepted. In 2001, 2 degrees awarded.
Degree requirements: For master's, thesis or alternative, comprehensive exam or special project.
Entrance requirements: For master's, TOEFL, minimum GPA of 2.7. *Application deadline:* For fall admission, 8/10 (priority date); for spring admission, 12/10. Applications are processed on a rolling basis. *Application fee:* $40.
Expenses: Tuition, state resident: full-time $2,772; part-time $245 per credit. Tuition, nonresident: full-time $7,726; part-time $245 per credit. Required fees: $2,102. Tuition and fees vary according to course level and degree level.
Financial support: In 2001–02, 2 research assistantships (averaging $4,800 per year) were awarded; career-related internships or fieldwork and Federal Work-Study also available. Financial award application deadline: 3/15; financial award applicants required to submit FAFSA.
Faculty research: Regional planning, environmental protection, tourism, computer mapping and geographic information systems.
Dr. Brian Sommers, Chair, 860-832-2785.

■ CHICAGO STATE UNIVERSITY

Graduate Studies, College of Arts and Sciences, Department of Geography, Chicago, IL 60628

AWARDS MA.

Faculty: 4 full-time (0 women).
Students: 18 (4 women); includes 14 minority (12 African Americans, 1 Asian American or Pacific Islander, 1 Hispanic American) 3 international.
Entrance requirements: For master's, minimum GPA of 2.75. *Application deadline:* For fall admission, 7/1; for spring admission, 11/10. *Application fee:* $25.
Financial support: Research assistantships available.
Dr. Mark Bouman, Chairperson, 773-995-2186, *Fax:* 773-995-2030, *E-mail:* bouman@csu.edu.
Application contact: Anika Miller, Graduate Studies Office, 773-995-2404, *E-mail:* g-studies1@csu.edu.

■ CLARK UNIVERSITY

Graduate School, Department of Geography, Worcester, MA 01610-1477

AWARDS PhD.

Faculty: 15 full-time (4 women).
Students: 57 full-time (28 women); includes 1 minority (African American), 32 international. Average age 33. 89 applicants, 25% accepted, 11 enrolled. In 2001, 14 doctorates awarded.
Degree requirements: For doctorate, thesis/dissertation.
Entrance requirements: For doctorate, GRE General Test, TOEFL. *Application deadline:* For fall admission, 2/15 (priority date). Applications are processed on a rolling basis. *Application fee:* $40.
Expenses: Tuition: Full-time $24,400; part-time $763 per credit. Required fees: $10.
Financial support: In 2001–02, 3 fellowships with full tuition reimbursements (averaging $12,000 per year), 14 research assistantships with full tuition reimbursements (averaging $12,000 per year), 14 teaching assistantships with full tuition reimbursements (averaging $12,000 per year) were awarded. Career-related internships or fieldwork and tuition waivers (full) also available.
Faculty research: Global environmental change, geographic information systems, natural and technological hazards, water resources, urbanization. *Total annual research expenditures:* $2 million.
Dr. Susan Hanson, Director, 508-793-7336.
Application contact: Madeline Grinkis, Admissions Secretary, 508-793-7337, *Fax:* 508-793-8881, *E-mail:* geography@clarku.edu. *Web site:* http://www2.clarku.edu/newsite/graduatefolder/programs/index.shtml

■ EAST CAROLINA UNIVERSITY

Graduate School, College of Arts and Sciences, Department of Geography, Greenville, NC 27858-4353

AWARDS MA. Part-time and evening/weekend programs available.

Faculty: 8 full-time (0 women).
Students: 11 full-time (6 women), 9 part-time (2 women); includes 2 minority (1 African American, 1 Asian American or Pacific Islander), 2 international. Average age 26. 9 applicants, 78% accepted.
Degree requirements: For master's, one foreign language, comprehensive exam.
Entrance requirements: For master's, GRE General Test, TOEFL. *Application deadline:* For fall admission, 6/1 (priority date); for spring admission, 10/15. Applications are processed on a rolling basis. *Application fee:* $45.
Expenses: Tuition, state resident: full-time $2,636. Tuition, nonresident: full-time $11,365.
Financial support: Research assistantships with partial tuition reimbursements, teaching assistantships with partial tuition reimbursements, Federal Work-Study available. Support available to part-time students. Financial award application deadline: 6/1.
Dr. Ron Mitchelson, Chairperson, 252-328-6230, *Fax:* 252-328-6054, *E-mail:* mitchelsonr@mail.ecu.edu.
Application contact: Dr. Scott Lecce, Director of Graduate Studies, 252-328-1047, *Fax:* 252-328-6054, *E-mail:* lecces@mail.ecu.edu. *Web site:* http://www.ecu.edu/academics/schdept/geog/geog.html

■ EASTERN MICHIGAN UNIVERSITY

Graduate School, College of Arts and Sciences, Department of Geography and Geology, Program in Geography, Ypsilanti, MI 48197

AWARDS MA, MS. Evening/weekend programs available.

Degree requirements: For master's, thesis optional.
Entrance requirements: For master's, TOEFL. *Application deadline:* For fall admission, 5/15; for spring admission, 3/15. Applications are processed on a rolling basis. *Application fee:* $30.
Expenses: Tuition, state resident: part-time $285 per credit hour. Tuition, nonresident: part-time $510 per credit hour.
Financial support: Fellowships, teaching assistantships available. Support available to part-time students. Financial award application deadline: 3/15; financial award applicants required to submit FAFSA.
Dr. Robert Ward, Coordinator, 734-487-3140.

■ FLORIDA ATLANTIC UNIVERSITY

Charles E. Schmidt College of Science, Department of Geography and Geology, Program in Geography, Boca Raton, FL 33431-0991

AWARDS MA, MAT. Part-time programs available.

Faculty: 9 full-time (2 women).
Students: 11 full-time (6 women), 10 part-time (5 women); includes 3 minority (all Hispanic Americans), 5 international. Average age 31. 11 applicants, 82% accepted, 7 enrolled. In 2001, 6 degrees awarded.
Degree requirements: For master's, thesis (for some programs).
Entrance requirements: For master's, GRE General Test, minimum GPA of 3.0. *Application deadline:* For fall admission, 6/1 (priority date); for spring admission, 10/15. Applications are processed on a rolling

basis. *Application fee:* $20. Electronic applications accepted.
Expenses: Tuition, state resident: full-time $3,098; part-time $172 per credit. Tuition, nonresident: full-time $10,427; part-time $579 per credit.
Financial support: In 2001–02, 12 students received support, including 3 research assistantships with partial tuition reimbursements available (averaging $9,100 per year), 2 teaching assistantships with partial tuition reimbursements available (averaging $9,100 per year); career-related internships or fieldwork, Federal Work-Study, institutionally sponsored loans, and unspecified assistantships also available. Financial award application deadline: 4/15.
Faculty research: Remote sensoring/digital images, location-allocation modeling, analysis of less-developed countries, historical settlement patterns, urban form, geographic information systems. *Total annual research expenditures:* $298,136.
Application contact: Dr. David Warburton, Graduate Coordinator, 561-297-3250, *Fax:* 561-297-2745, *E-mail:* warburto@fau.edu. *Web site:* http://www.geoggeol.fau.edu/

■ FLORIDA STATE UNIVERSITY

Graduate Studies, College of Social Sciences, Department of Geography, Tallahassee, FL 32306

AWARDS MA, MS, PhD. Part-time programs available.

Faculty: 12 full-time (1 woman), 4 part-time/adjunct (0 women).
Students: 18 full-time (7 women), 10 part-time (3 women); includes 14 minority (2 African Americans, 9 Asian Americans or Pacific Islanders, 2 Hispanic Americans, 1 Native American), 5 international. Average age 30. 19 applicants, 74% accepted, 7 enrolled. In 2001, 6 master's, 1 doctorate awarded.
Degree requirements: For master's, thesis (for some programs); for doctorate, thesis/dissertation.
Entrance requirements: For master's and doctorate, GRE General Test, minimum GPA of 3.0. *Application deadline:* For fall admission, 2/1 (priority date); for spring admission, 11/1. Applications are processed on a rolling basis. *Application fee:* $20.
Expenses: Tuition, state resident: part-time $163 per credit hour. Tuition, nonresident: part-time $570 per credit hour. Tuition and fees vary according to program.
Financial support: In 2001–02, 12 students received support, including 6 research assistantships with full tuition reimbursements available (averaging $11,500 per year), 6 teaching assistantships with full tuition reimbursements available (averaging $11,500 per year); fellowships, career-related internships or fieldwork, Federal Work-Study, institutionally sponsored loans, and scholarships/grants also available. Financial award application deadline: 2/1; financial award applicants required to submit FAFSA.
Faculty research: Public policy, natural hazards, global power relations, migration, environmental politics. *Total annual research expenditures:* $385,000.
Dr. Barney Warf, Chair, 850-644-8371, *Fax:* 850-644-5913, *E-mail:* bwarf@coss.fsu.edu.
Application contact: Dr. Jonathan Leib, Graduate Director, 850-644-8378, *Fax:* 850-644-5193, *E-mail:* jleib@coss.fsu.edu. *Web site:* http://www.fsu.edu/~geog/

■ GEORGE MASON UNIVERSITY

College of Arts and Sciences, Department of Geography and Earth Science, Fairfax, VA 22030-4444

AWARDS Geography and cartographic sciences (MS).

Faculty: 8 full-time (3 women), 6 part-time/adjunct (1 woman).
Students: 9 full-time (5 women), 37 part-time (15 women); includes 1 minority (Hispanic American), 1 international. Average age 34. 24 applicants, 79% accepted, 10 enrolled. In 2001, 15 degrees awarded.
Degree requirements: For master's, thesis optional.
Entrance requirements: For master's, GRE General Test, minimum GPA of 3.0 in last 60 hours; BS or BA in geography, cartography, or related field. *Application deadline:* For fall admission, 5/1; for spring admission, 11/1. *Application fee:* $30. Electronic applications accepted.
Expenses: Tuition, state resident: full-time $3,168; part-time $132 per credit hour. Tuition, nonresident: full-time $11,280; part-time $470 per credit hour. Required fees: $1,416; $59 per credit hour.
Financial support: Research assistantships, teaching assistantships available. Support available to part-time students. Financial award application deadline: 3/1; financial award applicants required to submit FAFSA.
David Wong, Graduate Coordinator, 703-993-1215, *E-mail:* dwong2@gmu.edu. *Web site:* http://geog.gmu.edu/default.html

■ THE GEORGE WASHINGTON UNIVERSITY

Columbian College of Arts and Sciences, Department of Geography and Regional Science, Washington, DC 20052

AWARDS MA.

Faculty: 6 full-time (3 women).
Students: 4 full-time (2 women), 2 part-time (both women). Average age 26. 8 applicants, 100% accepted. In 2001, 5 degrees awarded.
Degree requirements: For master's, thesis or alternative, comprehensive exam.
Entrance requirements: For master's, GRE General Test, BA in geography or related field, minimum GPA of 3.0. *Application deadline:* For fall admission, 5/1. *Application fee:* $55.
Expenses: Tuition: Part-time $810 per credit. Required fees: $1 per credit.
Financial support: In 2001–02, 2 fellowships with tuition reimbursements (averaging $4,400 per year), 2 teaching assistantships with tuition reimbursements (averaging $4,400 per year) were awarded. Federal Work-Study and institutionally sponsored loans also available. Financial award application deadline: 2/1.
Dr. Dorn McGrath, Chair, 202-994-6185. *Web site:* http://www.gwu.edu/~gradinfo/

■ GEORGIA STATE UNIVERSITY

College of Arts and Sciences, Department of Anthropology and Geography, Program in Geography, Atlanta, GA 30303-3083

AWARDS MA. Part-time and evening/weekend programs available.

Degree requirements: For master's, one foreign language, thesis or alternative, exam.
Entrance requirements: For master's, GRE General Test, TOEFL. Electronic applications accepted. *Web site:* http://monarch.gsu.edu/

Find an in-depth description at www.petersons.com/gradchannel.

■ HUNTER COLLEGE OF THE CITY UNIVERSITY OF NEW YORK

Graduate School, School of Arts and Sciences, Department of Geography, New York, NY 10021-5085

AWARDS Analytical geography (MA); earth system science (MA); environmental and social issues (MA); geographic information science (Certificate); geographic information systems (MA); teaching earth science (MA). Part-time and evening/weekend programs available.

Faculty: 15 full-time (7 women), 23 part-time/adjunct (10 women).
Students: 1 (woman) full-time, 32 part-time (17 women); includes 4 minority (1 African American, 1 Asian American or Pacific Islander, 2 Hispanic Americans), 2 international. Average age 35. 18 applicants, 72% accepted. In 2001, 8 degrees awarded.
Degree requirements: For master's, comprehensive exam or thesis.
Entrance requirements: For master's, GRE General Test, TOEFL, minimum B average in major, B- overall; 18 credits in geography; for Certificate, TOEFL. *Application deadline:* For fall admission, 3/24; for spring admission, 11/7. Applications are processed on a rolling basis. *Application fee:* $40.
Expenses: Tuition, state resident: full-time $2,175; part-time $185 per credit. Tuition, nonresident: full-time $3,800; part-time $320 per credit.

Hunter College of the City University of New York (continued)

Financial support: In 2001–02, 1 fellowship (averaging $3,000 per year), 2 research assistantships (averaging $10,000 per year), 10 teaching assistantships (averaging $6,000 per year) were awarded. Career-related internships or fieldwork, Federal Work-Study, institutionally sponsored loans, and unspecified assistantships also available. Financial award application deadline: 3/1.
Faculty research: Urban geography, economic geography, geographic information science, demographic methods, climate change.
Prof. Charles A. Heatwole, Chair, 212-772-5265, *Fax:* 212-772-5268, *E-mail:* cah@geo.hunter.cuny.edu.
Application contact: Prof. Marianna Pavlovskaya, Graduate Adviser, 212-772-5320, *Fax:* 212-772-5268, *E-mail:* mpavlov@geo.hunter.cuny.edu. *Web site:* http://geo.hunter.cuny.edu/

■ INDIANA STATE UNIVERSITY

School of Graduate Studies, College of Arts and Sciences, Department of Geography, Geology and Anthropology, Terre Haute, IN 47809-1401

AWARDS Earth sciences (MS); economic geography (PhD); geography (MA); physical geography (PhD).

Degree requirements: For doctorate, thesis/dissertation.
Entrance requirements: For doctorate, GRE General Test, departmental qualifying exam. Electronic applications accepted.

Find an in-depth description at www.petersons.com/gradchannel.

■ INDIANA UNIVERSITY BLOOMINGTON

Graduate School, College of Arts and Sciences, Department of Geography, Bloomington, IN 47405

AWARDS MA, MAT, PhD. PhD offered through the University Graduate School.

Faculty: 11 full-time (3 women).
Students: 15 full-time (6 women), 10 part-time (4 women); includes 1 minority (Hispanic American), 5 international. Average age 31. In 2001, 3 master's, 5 doctorates awarded.
Degree requirements: For master's, thesis or alternative; for doctorate, thesis/dissertation.
Entrance requirements: For master's and doctorate, GRE General Test, TOEFL. *Application deadline:* For fall admission, 1/15 (priority date); for spring admission, 9/1 (priority date). Applications are processed on a rolling basis. *Application fee:* $45 ($55 for international students). Electronic applications accepted.
Expenses: Tuition, state resident: full-time $4,720; part-time $197 per credit. Tuition, nonresident: full-time $13,748; part-time $573 per credit. Required fees: $642.
Financial support: In 2001–02, 15 students received support, including 1 research assistantship with full tuition reimbursement available (averaging $10,130 per year), 14 teaching assistantships with full tuition reimbursements available (averaging $10,130 per year); fellowships, Federal Work-Study and institutionally sponsored loans also available. Financial award application deadline: 2/15; financial award applicants required to submit FAFSA.
Faculty research: Synoptic climatology, urban and regional modeling, regional development, hydrology and statistical climatology, migration.
Dr. Daniel C. Knudsen, Chair, 812-855-6303, *Fax:* 812-855-1661, *E-mail:* knudsen@indiana.edu.
Application contact: Susan White, Graduate Secretary, 812-855-6303, *Fax:* 812-855-1661, *E-mail:* suswhite@indiana.edu. *Web site:* http://www.indiana.edu/~geog/

■ INDIANA UNIVERSITY OF PENNSYLVANIA

Graduate School and Research, College of Humanities and Social Sciences, Department of Geography and Regional Planning, Program in Geography, Indiana, PA 15705-1087

AWARDS MA, MS. Part-time programs available.

Faculty: 9 full-time (1 woman).
Students: 16 full-time (8 women), 4 part-time (2 women), 6 international. Average age 30. 17 applicants, 76% accepted. In 2001, 9 degrees awarded.
Degree requirements: For master's, thesis optional.
Entrance requirements: For master's, TOEFL, GRE, letters of recommendation (2). *Application deadline:* For fall admission, 7/1 (priority date); for spring admission, 11/1. Applications are processed on a rolling basis. *Application fee:* $30.
Expenses: Tuition, state resident: full-time $4,600; part-time $256 per credit hour. Tuition, nonresident: full-time $7,554; part-time $420 per credit hour. Required fees: $800. Part-time tuition and fees vary according to course load.
Financial support: In 2001–02, 8 research assistantships with full and partial tuition reimbursements (averaging $5,240 per year) were awarded; Federal Work-Study also available. Support available to part-time students. Financial award application deadline: 3/15; financial award applicants required to submit FAFSA.
Dr. John Benhart, Graduate Coordinator, 724-357-7652, *E-mail:* jbenhart@iup.edu.

■ JOHNS HOPKINS UNIVERSITY

G. W. C. Whiting School of Engineering, Department of Geography and Environmental Engineering, Baltimore, MD 21218-2699

AWARDS MA, MS, MSE, PhD.

Faculty: 15 full-time (3 women), 4 part-time/adjunct (0 women).
Students: 71 full-time (32 women); includes 8 minority (3 African Americans, 3 Asian Americans or Pacific Islanders, 2 Hispanic Americans), 24 international. Average age 29. 202 applicants, 33% accepted, 23 enrolled. In 2001, 17 master's, 2 doctorates awarded. Terminal master's awarded for partial completion of doctoral program.
Degree requirements: For master's, thesis (for some programs), one year full-time residency; for doctorate, thesis/dissertation, oral exam.
Entrance requirements: For master's and doctorate, GRE General Test, TOEFL. *Application deadline:* For fall admission, 1/15 (priority date). Applications are processed on a rolling basis. *Application fee:* $0. Electronic applications accepted.
Expenses: Tuition: Full-time $27,390.
Financial support: In 2001–02, 70 students received support, including 14 fellowships with full tuition reimbursements available (averaging $18,000 per year), 25 research assistantships with full tuition reimbursements available (averaging $17,400 per year), 5 teaching assistantships with full tuition reimbursements available (averaging $19,680 per year); Federal Work-Study, institutionally sponsored loans, scholarships/grants, tuition waivers (partial), and unspecified assistantships also available. Financial award application deadline: 2/1.
Faculty research: Environmental engineering; environmental chemistry; water resources engineering; systems analysis and economics for public decision making; geomorphology, hydrology and ecology. *Total annual research expenditures:* $1.9 million.
Dr. Marc B. Parlange, Chair, 410-516-6537, *Fax:* 410-516-8996, *E-mail:* mbparlange@jhu.edu.
Application contact: Dr. Edward J. Bouwer, Admissions Coordinator, 410-516-6042, *Fax:* 410-516-8996, *E-mail:* dogee@jhu.edu. *Web site:* http://www.jhu.edu/~dogee/

■ KANSAS STATE UNIVERSITY

Graduate School, College of Arts and Sciences, Department of Geography, Manhattan, KS 66506

AWARDS MA, PhD.

Faculty: 13 full-time (2 women).
Students: 16 full-time (5 women), 9 part-time (4 women); includes 1 minority (Asian American or Pacific Islander), 6 international. 12 applicants, 83% accepted,

8 enrolled. In 2001, 4 master's, 3 doctorates awarded.
Degree requirements: For master's, oral exam, thesis optional; for doctorate, one foreign language, thesis/dissertation.
Entrance requirements: For doctorate, GRE General Test. *Application deadline:* For fall admission, 2/1 (priority date); for spring admission, 10/1 (priority date). Applications are processed on a rolling basis. *Application fee:* $0 ($25 for international students). Electronic applications accepted.
Expenses: Tuition, state resident: part-time $113 per credit hour. Tuition, nonresident: part-time $358 per credit hour.
Financial support: In 2001–02, 3 research assistantships with partial tuition reimbursements (averaging $9,000 per year), 13 teaching assistantships with full tuition reimbursements (averaging $8,210 per year) were awarded. Federal Work-Study, institutionally sponsored loans, and scholarships/grants also available. Support available to part-time students. Financial award application deadline: 3/1; financial award applicants required to submit FAFSA.
Faculty research: Human/environment relationships in Great Plains and America West, remote sensing of land cover change, migration issues and population geography, cultural geography, human dimensions of global change. *Total annual research expenditures:* $269,390.
John A. Harrington, Head, 785-532-3405, *Fax:* 785-532-7310, *E-mail:* jharrin@ksu.edu.
Application contact: David Kromm, Graduate Program Director, 785-532-3408, *Fax:* 785-532-7310, *E-mail:* krommgeo@ksu.edu. *Web site:* http://www.ksu.edu/geograpy

■ KENT STATE UNIVERSITY

College of Arts and Sciences, Department of Geography, Kent, OH 44242-0001

AWARDS MA, PhD.

Degree requirements: For master's, thesis optional; for doctorate, one foreign language, thesis/dissertation.
Entrance requirements: For master's, minimum GPA of 2.75; for doctorate, minimum GPA of 3.0. Electronic applications accepted.

■ LOUISIANA STATE UNIVERSITY AND AGRICULTURAL AND MECHANICAL COLLEGE

Graduate School, College of Arts and Sciences, Department of Geography and Anthropology, Baton Rouge, LA 70803

AWARDS Anthropology (MA); geography (MA, MS, PhD). Part-time programs available.

Faculty: 25 full-time (8 women).
Students: 56 full-time (30 women), 34 part-time (16 women); includes 7 minority (3 African Americans, 1 Asian American or Pacific Islander, 2 Hispanic Americans, 1 Native American), 8 international. Average age 33. 71 applicants, 45% accepted, 14 enrolled. In 2001, 17 master's, 12 doctorates awarded. Terminal master's awarded for partial completion of doctoral program.
Degree requirements: For master's, 2 foreign languages, thesis (for some programs); for doctorate, 2 foreign languages, thesis/dissertation.
Entrance requirements: For master's and doctorate, GRE General Test, minimum GPA of 3.0. *Application deadline:* For fall admission, 1/25 (priority date). Applications are processed on a rolling basis. *Application fee:* $25.
Expenses: Tuition, state resident: full-time $2,551. Tuition, nonresident: full-time $5,551. Required fees: $854. Part-time tuition and fees vary according to course load.
Financial support: In 2001–02, 6 fellowships with full tuition reimbursements (averaging $14,222 per year), 9 research assistantships with partial tuition reimbursements (averaging $12,318 per year), 22 teaching assistantships with partial tuition reimbursements (averaging $10,274 per year) were awarded. Career-related internships or fieldwork and unspecified assistantships also available. Financial award application deadline: 3/1; financial award applicants required to submit FAFSA. *Total annual research expenditures:* $754,753.
Dr. Craig Colten, Chair, 225-578-6094, *Fax:* 225-578-4420, *E-mail:* ccolten@lsu.edu. *Web site:* http://www.ga.lsu.edu/ga/

■ MARSHALL UNIVERSITY

Graduate College, College of Liberal Arts, Department of Geography, Huntington, WV 25755

AWARDS MA, MS.

Faculty: 1 (woman) full-time, 1 part-time/adjunct (0 women).
Students: 12 full-time (2 women), 4 part-time (1 woman); includes 1 minority (African American), 1 international. In 2001, 6 degrees awarded.
Degree requirements: For master's, thesis optional.
Expenses: Tuition, state resident: part-time $147 per credit. Tuition, nonresident: part-time $468 per credit. Tuition and fees vary according to campus/location and reciprocity agreements.
Larry Jarrett, Chairperson, 304-696-2886, *E-mail:* jarrettl@marshall.edu.
Application contact: Ken O'Neal, Assistant Vice President, Adult Student Services, 304-746-2500 Ext. 1907, *Fax:* 304-746-1902, *E-mail:* oneal@marshall.edu.

■ MIAMI UNIVERSITY

Graduate School, College of Arts and Sciences, Department of Geography, Oxford, OH 45056

AWARDS MA. Part-time programs available.

Faculty: 2 full-time (0 women), 5 part-time/adjunct (1 woman).
Students: 18 full-time (4 women), 1 part-time; includes 1 minority (African American), 9 international. 18 applicants, 94% accepted, 6 enrolled. In 2001, 6 degrees awarded.
Degree requirements: For master's, thesis (for some programs), final exam.
Entrance requirements: For master's, minimum undergraduate GPA of 3.0 during previous 2 years or 2.75 overall. *Application deadline:* For fall admission, 3/1 (priority date); for spring admission, 12/1. Applications are processed on a rolling basis. *Application fee:* $35.
Expenses: Tuition, state resident: full-time $7,155; part-time $295 per semester hour. Tuition, nonresident: full-time $14,829; part-time $615 per semester hour. Tuition and fees vary according to degree level and campus/location.
Financial support: In 2001–02, fellowships (averaging $11,000 per year), teaching assistantships (averaging $11,786 per year) were awarded. Research assistantships, career-related internships or fieldwork, Federal Work-Study, and tuition waivers (full) also available. Financial award application deadline: 3/1.
Dr. James Rubenstein, Chair, 513-529-5010, *Fax:* 513-529-1948, *E-mail:* geograd@muohio.edu.
Application contact: Dr. Ian L. Yeboah, Director of Graduate Studies, *E-mail:* geograd@muohio.edu. *Web site:* http://www.muohio.edu/geography

■ MICHIGAN STATE UNIVERSITY

Graduate School, College of Social Science, Department of Geography, East Lansing, MI 48824

AWARDS Geography (MA, MS, PhD); geography-urban studies (MA); urban and regional planning (MURP); urban planning (MUP). Part-time programs available.

Faculty: 30 full-time (9 women).
Students: 37 full-time (14 women), 22 part-time (10 women); includes 9 minority (4 African Americans, 2 Asian Americans or Pacific Islanders, 3 Hispanic Americans), 17 international. Average age 29. 122 applicants, 34% accepted. In 2001, 11 master's, 2 doctorates awarded.
Degree requirements: For master's and doctorate, thesis/dissertation.
Entrance requirements: For master's, GRE General Test, TOEFL, minimum GPA of 3.4; for doctorate, GRE General Test, TOEFL, minimum GPA of 3.6. *Application deadline:* For fall admission, 2/1. Applications are processed on a rolling basis. *Application fee:* $30 ($40 for international students).

Michigan State University (continued)
Expenses: Tuition, state resident: part-time $244 per credit hour. Tuition, nonresident: part-time $494 per credit hour. Required fees: $268 per semester. Tuition and fees vary according to course load, degree level and program.
Financial support: In 2001–02, 24 fellowships (averaging $2,641 per year), 14 research assistantships with tuition reimbursements (averaging $11,518 per year), 16 teaching assistantships with tuition reimbursements (averaging $10,789 per year) were awarded. Career-related internships or fieldwork, Federal Work-Study, and institutionally sponsored loans also available. Support available to part-time students. Financial award application deadline: 2/1; financial award applicants required to submit FAFSA.
Faculty research: Geomorphology, remote sensing, regional geographic information systems, climatology. *Total annual research expenditures:* $2.4 million.
Dr. Richard Groop, Chairperson, 517-355-4649, *Fax:* 517-432-1671, *E-mail:* geo@msu.edu.
Application contact: Graduate Admissions Office, 517-355-4649, *Fax:* 517-432-1671. *Web site:* http://www.geo.msu.edu/

■ MINNESOTA STATE UNIVERSITY, MANKATO

College of Graduate Studies, College of Social and Behavioral Sciences, Department of Geography, Mankato, MN 56001

AWARDS MA, MS, MT. Part-time programs available.

Faculty: 7 full-time (2 women).
Students: 7 full-time (4 women), 8 part-time (2 women). Average age 30. In 2001, 2 degrees awarded.
Degree requirements: For master's, one foreign language, comprehensive exam.
Entrance requirements: For master's, minimum GPA of 3.0 during previous 2 years. *Application deadline:* For fall admission, 7/9 (priority date); for spring admission, 11/27. Applications are processed on a rolling basis. *Application fee:* $20.
Expenses: Tuition, state resident: full-time $3,253; part-time $157 per credit. Tuition, nonresident: full-time $4,893; part-time $248 per credit. Required fees: $24 per credit. Tuition and fees vary according to reciprocity agreements.
Financial support: Research assistantships, teaching assistantships with full tuition reimbursements, career-related internships or fieldwork, Federal Work-Study, and institutionally sponsored loans available. Support available to part-time students. Financial award application deadline: 3/15; financial award applicants required to submit FAFSA.
Dr. Jose Lopez, Head, 507-389-1890, *Fax:* 507-389-2980.
Application contact: Joni Roberts, Admissions Coordinator, 507-389-5244, *Fax:* 507-389-5974, *E-mail:* grad@mankato.msus.edu.

■ NEW MEXICO STATE UNIVERSITY

Graduate School, College of Arts and Sciences, Department of Geography, Las Cruces, NM 88003-8001

AWARDS MAG. Part-time programs available.

Faculty: 5 full-time (0 women).
Students: 12 full-time (6 women), 3 part-time (1 woman). Average age 35. 9 applicants, 100% accepted, 5 enrolled. In 2001, 7 degrees awarded.
Degree requirements: For master's, thesis or alternative.
Entrance requirements: For master's, GRE General Test, previous course work in geography, map use, and physical geography. *Application deadline:* For fall admission, 7/1 (priority date); for spring admission, 11/1. Applications are processed on a rolling basis. *Application fee:* $15 ($35 for international students). Electronic applications accepted.
Expenses: Tuition, state resident: full-time $3,234; part-time $135 per credit. Tuition, nonresident: full-time $9,420; part-time $428 per credit. Required fees: $858.
Financial support: In 2001–02, 1 research assistantship, 5 teaching assistantships were awarded. Career-related internships or fieldwork also available. Financial award application deadline: 3/1.
Faculty research: Landscape ecology, land use, geomorphology, Latin America and the U.S.-Mexico border, geographic information systems.
Dr. Michael DeMers, Head, 505-646-3509, *Fax:* 505-646-7430, *E-mail:* mdemers@nmsu.edu.
Application contact: Dr. Robert Czerniak, Professor, 505-646-3509, *Fax:* 505-646-7430, *E-mail:* rczernia@nmsu.edu.

■ NORTHEASTERN ILLINOIS UNIVERSITY

Graduate College, College of Arts and Sciences, Department of Geography, Environmental Studies and Economics, Program in Geography and Environmental Studies, Chicago, IL 60625-4699

AWARDS MA. Part-time and evening/weekend programs available.

Faculty: 6 full-time (0 women), 3 part-time/adjunct (2 women).
Students: 2 full-time (1 woman), 23 part-time (12 women); includes 3 minority (all Hispanic Americans). Average age 34. 11 applicants, 73% accepted. In 2001, 14 degrees awarded.
Degree requirements: For master's, thesis optional.
Entrance requirements: For master's, undergraduate minor in geography or environmental studies, minimum GPA of 2.75. *Application deadline:* For fall admission, 4/1 (priority date); for spring admission, 8/15. Applications are processed on a rolling basis. *Application fee:* $25.
Expenses: Tuition, area resident: Full-time $2,882; part-time $107 per semester hour. Tuition, nonresident: part-time $320 per semester hour. International tuition: $8,646 full-time. Required fees: $20 per semester hour.
Financial support: In 2001–02, 3 research assistantships with full tuition reimbursements (averaging $6,600 per year) were awarded; career-related internships or fieldwork, Federal Work-Study, institutionally sponsored loans, and tuition waivers (full and partial) also available. Support available to part-time students. Financial award applicants required to submit FAFSA.
Faculty research: Segregation and urbanization of minority groups in the Chicago area, scale dependence and parameterization in nonpoint source pollution modeling, ecological land classification and mapping, ecosystem restoration, soil-vegetation relationships.
Dr. E. Howenstine, Graduate Adviser, 773-442-5647, *Fax:* 773-442-4900, *E-mail:* e-howenstine@neiu.edu.
Application contact: Dr. Mohan K. Sood, Dean of the Graduate College, 773-442-6010, *Fax:* 773-442-6020, *E-mail:* m-sood@neiu.edu.

■ NORTHERN ARIZONA UNIVERSITY

Graduate College, College of Ecosystem Science and Management, Department of Geography and Public Planning, Flagstaff, AZ 86011

AWARDS Geographic information systems (Certificate); rural geography (MA).

Faculty: 9 full-time (4 women), 5 part-time/adjunct (0 women).
Students: 13 full-time (6 women), 13 part-time (8 women); includes 3 minority (1 Hispanic American, 2 Native Americans). Average age 32. 12 applicants, 75% accepted, 8 enrolled. In 2001, 5 degrees awarded.
Degree requirements: For master's, thesis.
Entrance requirements: For master's, GRE General Test. *Application deadline:* For fall admission, 2/15 (priority date); for spring admission, 10/15. Applications are processed on a rolling basis. *Application fee:* $45.
Expenses: Tuition, state resident: full-time $2,488. Tuition, nonresident: full-time $10,354.
Financial support: In 2001–02, 9 research assistantships were awarded
Dr. Robert Clark, Chair, 928-523-1321.
Application contact: Dr. Alan Lew, Graduate Coordinator, 928-523-2650, *E-mail:* geog@nau.edu. *Web site:* http://www.for.nau.edu/geography

■ NORTHERN ILLINOIS UNIVERSITY

Graduate School, College of Liberal Arts and Sciences, Department of Geography, De Kalb, IL 60115-2854

AWARDS MS. Part-time programs available.

Faculty: 9 full-time (2 women).
Students: 10 full-time (4 women), 10 part-time (3 women); includes 1 minority (Asian American or Pacific Islander), 2 international. Average age 32. 14 applicants, 79% accepted, 4 enrolled. In 2001, 6 degrees awarded.
Degree requirements: For master's, research seminar, thesis optional.
Entrance requirements: For master's, GRE General Test, TOEFL, minimum GPA of 2.75. *Application deadline:* For fall admission, 2/1 (priority date); for spring admission, 10/1 (priority date). Applications are processed on a rolling basis. *Application fee:* $30.
Expenses: Tuition, state resident: full-time $5,124; part-time $148 per credit hour. Tuition, nonresident: full-time $8,666; part-time $295 per credit hour. Required fees: $51 per term.
Financial support: In 2001–02, 3 research assistantships with full tuition reimbursements, 8 teaching assistantships with full tuition reimbursements were awarded. Fellowships with full tuition reimbursements, career-related internships or fieldwork, Federal Work-Study, tuition waivers (full), and unspecified assistantships also available. Support available to part-time students.
Dr. Andrew Krmenec, Chair, 815-753-6826, *Fax:* 815-753-6872.
Application contact: Dr. David Changnon, Acting Coordinator of Graduate Studies, 815-753-6842.

■ THE OHIO STATE UNIVERSITY

Graduate School, College of Social and Behavioral Sciences, Department of Geography, Columbus, OH 43210

AWARDS Atmospheric sciences (MS, PhD); geography (MA, PhD).

Degree requirements: For doctorate, variable foreign language requirement, thesis/dissertation.
Entrance requirements: For master's and doctorate, GRE General Test, TOEFL.

■ OHIO UNIVERSITY

Graduate Studies, College of Arts and Sciences, Department of Geography, Athens, OH 45701-2979

AWARDS MA. Part-time programs available.

Faculty: 11 full-time (3 women), 1 (woman) part-time/adjunct.
Students: 22 full-time (13 women), 6 part-time (3 women), 4 international. Average age 24. 21 applicants, 86% accepted, 13 enrolled. In 2001, 9 degrees awarded.
Degree requirements: For master's, thesis. *Median time to degree:* Master's–2 years full-time, 4 years part-time.
Entrance requirements: For master's, GRE General Test, minimum GPA of 3.0. *Application deadline:* For spring admission, 3/1 (priority date). *Application fee:* $30. Electronic applications accepted.
Expenses: Tuition, state resident: full-time $6,585. Tuition, nonresident: full-time $12,254.
Financial support: In 2001–02, 18 students received support, including 3 research assistantships (averaging $8,000 per year), 11 teaching assistantships (averaging $7,500 per year); Federal Work-Study, institutionally sponsored loans, and tuition waivers (full) also available. Financial award application deadline: 3/1.
Faculty research: Environmental geography, cartography and geographic information systems, remote sensing, area studies, regional/urban planning. *Total annual research expenditures:* $53,000.
Nancy R. Bain, Chair, 740-593-1140, *Fax:* 740-593-1139, *E-mail:* bainn@ohiou.edu.
Application contact: Ronald H. Isaac, Graduate Chair, 740-593-1145, *Fax:* 740-593-1139, *E-mail:* isaacr@ohiou.edu. *Web site:* http://www-as.phy.ohio.edu/department/geography/

■ OKLAHOMA STATE UNIVERSITY

Graduate College, College of Arts and Sciences, Department of Geography, Stillwater, OK 74078

AWARDS MS.

Faculty: 13 full-time (1 woman), 3 part-time/adjunct (0 women).
Students: 13 full-time (3 women), 19 part-time (6 women); includes 5 minority (1 Hispanic American, 4 Native Americans), 5 international. Average age 31. 16 applicants, 94% accepted. In 2001, 8 degrees awarded.
Degree requirements: For master's, thesis or alternative.
Entrance requirements: For master's, GRE, TOEFL, minimum GPA of 3.0. *Application deadline:* For fall admission, 7/1 (priority date). *Application fee:* $25.
Expenses: Tuition, state resident: part-time $92 per credit hour. Tuition, nonresident: part-time $297 per credit hour. Required fees: $21 per credit hour. $14 per semester. One-time fee: $20. Tuition and fees vary according to course load.
Financial support: In 2001–02, 16 students received support, including 13 research assistantships (averaging $15,208 per year), 8 teaching assistantships (averaging $12,120 per year); career-related internships or fieldwork, Federal Work-Study, and tuition waivers (partial) also available. Support available to part-time students. Financial award application deadline: 3/1.
Faculty research: Cultural ecology, resource management, historical/cultural geography, central Asia, geographic information systems.
Dr. Dale R. Lightfoot, Head, 405-744-6250.

■ OREGON STATE UNIVERSITY

Graduate School, College of Science, Department of Geosciences, Program in Geography, Corvallis, OR 97331

AWARDS MA, MAIS, MS, PhD. Part-time programs available.

Students: 36 full-time (18 women), 4 part-time (1 woman); includes 3 minority (1 African American, 1 Asian American or Pacific Islander, 1 Hispanic American), 3 international. Average age 33. In 2001, 11 master's, 2 doctorates awarded. Terminal master's awarded for partial completion of doctoral program.
Degree requirements: For master's, variable foreign language requirement, thesis optional; for doctorate, one foreign language, thesis/dissertation.
Entrance requirements: For master's and doctorate, GRE General Test, GRE Subject Test, TOEFL, minimum GPA of 3.0 in last 90 hours. *Application deadline:* For fall admission, 2/1. Applications are processed on a rolling basis. *Application fee:* $50.
Expenses: Tuition, area resident: Full-time $15,933. Tuition, state resident: full-time $28,937.
Financial support: Fellowships, research assistantships, teaching assistantships, Federal Work-Study and institutionally sponsored loans available. Support available to part-time students. Financial award application deadline: 2/1.
Faculty research: Resources, physical geography, cartography, remote sensing.
Philip L. Jackson, Director, 541-737-1203, *Fax:* 541-737-1200.
Application contact: Joanne VanGeest, Graduate Admissions Coordinator, 541-737-1204, *Fax:* 541-737-1200, *E-mail:* vangeesj@geo.orst.edu.

■ THE PENNSYLVANIA STATE UNIVERSITY UNIVERSITY PARK CAMPUS

Graduate School, College of Earth and Mineral Sciences, Department of Geography, State College, University Park, PA 16802-1503

AWARDS MS, PhD.

Students: 57 full-time (21 women), 11 part-time (5 women). In 2001, 12 master's, 4 doctorates awarded.
Entrance requirements: For master's and doctorate, GRE General Test. *Application fee:* $45.
Expenses: Tuition, state resident: full-time $7,882; part-time $333 per credit. Tuition,

The Pennsylvania State University University Park Campus (continued)
nonresident: full-time $16,142; part-time $673 per credit. Required fees: $124 per semester.
Dr. Roger Downs, Head, 814-865-3433.

■ PORTLAND STATE UNIVERSITY

Graduate Studies, College of Liberal Arts and Sciences, Department of Geography, Portland, OR 97207-0751

AWARDS MA, MS, PhD. Part-time programs available.

Faculty: 9 full-time (3 women), 1 part-time/adjunct (0 women).
Students: 20 full-time (7 women), 15 part-time (4 women); includes 1 minority (Hispanic American), 1 international. Average age 33. 19 applicants, 63% accepted. In 2001, 5 degrees awarded.
Degree requirements: For master's, variable foreign language requirement, thesis (for some programs).
Entrance requirements: For master's, GRE General Test, TOEFL, minimum GPA of 3.0 in upper-division course work or 2.75 overall. *Application deadline:* For fall admission, 4/1. Applications are processed on a rolling basis. *Application fee:* $50.
Financial support: In 2001–02, 8 research assistantships with full tuition reimbursements (averaging $4,679 per year), 7 teaching assistantships with full tuition reimbursements (averaging $4,356 per year) were awarded. Career-related internships or fieldwork, Federal Work-Study, and institutionally sponsored loans also available. Support available to part-time students. Financial award application deadline: 3/1; financial award applicants required to submit FAFSA.
Faculty research: Geographic information systems, natural lands, Latin American subsistence farming, climatic change, urban perspectives. *Total annual research expenditures:* $121,880.
Dr. Teresa Bulman, Head, 503-725-3916, *Fax:* 503-725-3166.
Application contact: Carolyn Perry, Coordinator, 503-725-3916, *Fax:* 503-725-3166, *E-mail:* carolyn@geog.pdx.edu. *Web site:* http://geog.pdx.edu/

■ RUTGERS, THE STATE UNIVERSITY OF NEW JERSEY, NEW BRUNSWICK

Graduate School, Program in Geography, New Brunswick, NJ 08901-1281

AWARDS MA, MS, PhD. Terminal master's awarded for partial completion of doctoral program.

Degree requirements: For master's, thesis or alternative; for doctorate, thesis/dissertation.
Entrance requirements: For master's and doctorate, GRE General Test.
Faculty research: Urban and social theory, environmental hazards, climate, developing world. *Web site:* http://geography.rutgers.edu/

■ ST. CLOUD STATE UNIVERSITY

School of Graduate Studies, College of Social Sciences, Department of Geography, St. Cloud, MN 56301-4498

AWARDS MS.

Faculty: 9 full-time (1 woman).
Students: 7 full-time (2 women), 13 part-time (4 women); includes 2 minority (both Asian Americans or Pacific Islanders). 11 applicants, 18% accepted. In 2001, 4 degrees awarded.
Degree requirements: For master's, thesis or alternative.
Entrance requirements: For master's, GRE General Test, minimum GPA of 2.75. *Application deadline:* Applications are processed on a rolling basis. *Application fee:* $35.
Expenses: Tuition, state resident: part-time $156 per credit. Tuition, nonresident: part-time $244 per credit. Required fees: $20 per credit.
Financial support: Federal Work-Study and unspecified assistantships available. Financial award application deadline: 3/1.
Dr. Lewis Wixon, Chairperson, 320-255-3160, *Fax:* 320-654-5198.
Application contact: Lindalou Krueger, Graduate Studies Office, 320-255-2113, *Fax:* 320-654-5371, *E-mail:* lekrueger@stcloudstate.edu.

■ SALEM STATE COLLEGE

Graduate School, Department of Geography, Salem, MA 01970-5353

AWARDS Geo-information science (MS); geography (MA).

Degree requirements: For master's, thesis optional.
Entrance requirements: For master's, GRE General Test or MAT. *Application deadline:* Applications are processed on a rolling basis. *Application fee:* $25.
William L. Hamilton, Associate Professor, 978-542-6228, *Fax:* 978-542-6269, *E-mail:* wolf@dgl.salem.mass.edu.

■ SAN DIEGO STATE UNIVERSITY

Graduate and Research Affairs, College of Arts and Letters, Department of Geography, San Diego, CA 92182

AWARDS MA, PhD.

Degree requirements: For master's and doctorate, thesis/dissertation.
Entrance requirements: For master's, GRE General Test, TOEFL, bachelor's degree in related field.
Faculty research: Physical geography, human geography, biogeography, environmental resources, geographic analysis.

■ SAN FRANCISCO STATE UNIVERSITY

Graduate Division, College of Behavioral and Social Sciences, Department of Geography and Human Environmental Studies, San Francisco, CA 94132-1722

AWARDS Geography (MA), including environmental planning, resource management. Part-time programs available.

Degree requirements: For master's, thesis, exam.
Entrance requirements: For master's, minimum GPA of 2.5 in last 60 units.
Faculty research: Geomorphology, remote sensing, GIS, biogeography.

■ SAN JOSE STATE UNIVERSITY

Graduate Studies, College of Social Sciences, Department of Geography, San Jose, CA 95192-0001

AWARDS MA.

Students: 5 full-time (2 women), 9 part-time (3 women); includes 3 minority (2 Asian Americans or Pacific Islanders, 1 Hispanic American). Average age 36. 15 applicants, 60% accepted. In 2001, 4 degrees awarded.
Entrance requirements: For master's, minimum GPA of 3.0. *Application deadline:* For fall admission, 6/29; for spring admission, 11/30. Applications are processed on a rolling basis. *Application fee:* $59. Electronic applications accepted.
Expenses: Tuition, nonresident: part-time $246 per unit. Required fees: $678 per semester. Tuition and fees vary according to course load.
Financial support: Applicants required to submit FAFSA.
Dr. David Helgren, Chair, 408-924-5475, *Fax:* 408-924-5477.

■ SOUTH DAKOTA STATE UNIVERSITY

Graduate School, College of Arts and Science, Department of Geography, Brookings, SD 57007

AWARDS MS.

Degree requirements: For master's, thesis, oral exam.
Entrance requirements: For master's, TOEFL, minimum GPA of 2.75.
Faculty research: Contemporary agriculture and rural land use, geography of Indian casino gambling, geography of illegal drug trade, geography of crop circles.

■ SOUTHERN ILLINOIS UNIVERSITY CARBONDALE

Graduate School, College of Liberal Arts, Department of Geography, Carbondale, IL 62901-6806

AWARDS MS, PhD.

Faculty: 7 full-time (1 woman), 1 part-time/adjunct (0 women).
Students: 16 full-time (5 women), 12 part-time (4 women); includes 1 minority (African American), 9 international. Average age 27. 15 applicants, 60% accepted. In 2001, 9 master's, 1 doctorate awarded.
Degree requirements: For master's and doctorate, thesis/dissertation.
Entrance requirements: For master's, TOEFL, minimum GPA of 2.7; for doctorate, TOEFL, minimum GPA of 3.25. *Application deadline:* Applications are processed on a rolling basis. *Application fee:* $20.
Expenses: Tuition, state resident: full-time $3,794; part-time $154 per hour. Tuition, nonresident: full-time $6,566; part-time $308 per hour. Required fees: $277 per hour.
Financial support: In 2001–02, 21 students received support, including 6 research assistantships with full tuition reimbursements available, 11 teaching assistantships with full tuition reimbursements available; fellowships with full tuition reimbursements available, career-related internships or fieldwork, Federal Work-Study, institutionally sponsored loans, and tuition waivers (full) also available. Support available to part-time students. Financial award application deadline: 4/1.
Faculty research: Natural resources management emphasizing water resources and environmental quality of air, water, and land systems.
Dr. Christopher Lant, Chairperson, 618-536-3375, *Fax:* 618-453-2671, *E-mail:* clant@siu.edu.
Application contact: Graduate Program Director, 618-536-3375.

Find an in-depth description at www.petersons.com/gradchannel.

■ SOUTHERN ILLINOIS UNIVERSITY EDWARDSVILLE

Graduate Studies and Research, College of Arts and Sciences, Department of Geographical Studies, Edwardsville, IL 62026-0001

AWARDS Geography (MA, MS). Part-time programs available.

Students: 14 full-time (6 women), 17 part-time (7 women); includes 1 minority (Hispanic American), 1 international. Average age 33. 18 applicants, 78% accepted, 9 enrolled. In 2001, 7 degrees awarded.
Degree requirements: For master's, thesis or alternative, final exam. *Median time to degree:* Master's–2.5 years full-time, 4 years part-time.
Entrance requirements: For master's, GRE, TOEFL. *Application deadline:* For fall admission, 7/20; for spring admission, 12/7. *Application fee:* $25.
Expenses: Tuition, state resident: full-time $2,712; part-time $113 per credit hour. Tuition, nonresident: full-time $5,424; part-time $226 per credit hour. Required fees: $250; $125 per term. Tuition and fees vary according to course load, campus/location and reciprocity agreements.
Financial support: Fellowships with full tuition reimbursements, research assistantships with full tuition reimbursements, teaching assistantships with full tuition reimbursements, career-related internships or fieldwork, Federal Work-Study, institutionally sponsored loans, and unspecified assistantships available. Support available to part-time students. Financial award application deadline: 3/1.
Dr. Wendy Shaw, Chair, 618-650-2090, *E-mail:* wshaw@siue.edu.

■ SOUTHWEST TEXAS STATE UNIVERSITY

Graduate School, College of Liberal Arts, Department of Geography, Program in Environmental Geography and Geography Education, San Marcos, TX 78666

AWARDS Environmental geography (PhD); geography education (PhD). Part-time programs available.

Students: 22 full-time (14 women), 8 part-time (3 women); includes 2 minority (both Asian Americans or Pacific Islanders), 1 international. Average age 36. In 2001, 3 degrees awarded.
Degree requirements: For doctorate, thesis/dissertation.
Entrance requirements: For doctorate, GRE General Test, TOEFL, minimum GPA of 3.5, master's degree in geography, demonstrate scholarly research. *Application deadline:* For fall admission, 6/15 (priority date); for spring admission, 10/15 (priority date). Applications are processed on a rolling basis. *Application fee:* $40 ($90 for international students).
Expenses: Tuition, state resident: full-time $1,512; part-time $84 per credit hour. Tuition, nonresident: full-time $5,310; part-time $295 per credit hour. Required fees: $864; $29 per credit hour. $195 per term. Full-time tuition and fees vary according to course load.
Financial support: Career-related internships or fieldwork, Federal Work-Study, and institutionally sponsored loans available. Support available to part-time students. Financial award application deadline: 4/1; financial award applicants required to submit FAFSA.
Dr. Fred Shelley, Graduate Adviser, 512-245-8704, *Fax:* 512-245-8353, *E-mail:* fs03@swt.edu.

■ SOUTHWEST TEXAS STATE UNIVERSITY

Graduate School, College of Liberal Arts, Department of Geography, Program in Geography, San Marcos, TX 78666

AWARDS Applied geography (MAG). Part-time and evening/weekend programs available.

Students: 23 full-time (13 women), 13 part-time (6 women); includes 1 minority (Asian American or Pacific Islander), 1 international. Average age 31. 28 applicants, 71% accepted, 15 enrolled. In 2001, 3 degrees awarded.
Degree requirements: For master's, internship or thesis.
Entrance requirements: For master's, GRE General Test, TOEFL, minimum GPA of 3.00 in last 60 hours. *Application deadline:* For fall admission, 6/15 (priority date); for spring admission, 10/15 (priority date). Applications are processed on a rolling basis. *Application fee:* $40 ($90 for international students).
Expenses: Tuition, state resident: full-time $1,512; part-time $84 per credit hour. Tuition, nonresident: full-time $5,310; part-time $295 per credit hour. Required fees: $864; $29 per credit hour. $195 per term. Full-time tuition and fees vary according to course load.
Financial support: Research assistantships, teaching assistantships, career-related internships or fieldwork, Federal Work-Study, and institutionally sponsored loans available. Support available to part-time students. Financial award application deadline: 4/1; financial award applicants required to submit FAFSA.
Faculty research: Applied cartography and geographic information systems, physical and environmental studies, land/area development and management.
Dr. Fred Shelley, Graduate Adviser, 512-245-8704, *Fax:* 512-245-8353, *E-mail:* fs03@swt.edu. *Web site:* http://www.geo.swt.edu/

■ SOUTHWEST TEXAS STATE UNIVERSITY

Graduate School, College of Liberal Arts, Department of Geography, Program in Land/Area Studies, San Marcos, TX 78666

AWARDS MAG. Part-time and evening/weekend programs available.

Students: 9 full-time (5 women), 3 part-time (2 women); includes 1 minority (Hispanic American). Average age 31. 6 applicants, 67% accepted, 3 enrolled.
Degree requirements: For master's, internship or thesis.
Entrance requirements: For master's, GRE General Test, TOEFL, minimum GPA of 3.00 in last 60 hours. *Application deadline:* For fall admission, 6/15 (priority date); for spring admission, 10/15 (priority

Southwest Texas State University (continued)

date). Applications are processed on a rolling basis. *Application fee:* $40 ($90 for international students).
Expenses: Tuition, state resident: full-time $1,512; part-time $84 per credit hour. Tuition, nonresident: full-time $5,310; part-time $295 per credit hour. Required fees: $864; $29 per credit hour. $195 per term. Full-time tuition and fees vary according to course load.
Financial support: Research assistantships, teaching assistantships, career-related internships or fieldwork, Federal Work-Study, institutionally sponsored loans, and scholarships/grants available. Support available to part-time students. Financial award application deadline: 4/1; financial award applicants required to submit FAFSA.
Dr. Fred Shelley, Graduate Adviser, 512-245-8704, *Fax:* 512-245-8353, *E-mail:* fs03@swt.edu. *Web site:* http://www.geo.swt.edu/

■ STATE UNIVERSITY OF NEW YORK AT ALBANY

College of Arts and Sciences, Department of Geography and Planning, Program in Geography, Albany, NY 12222-0001

AWARDS Geographic information systems and spatial analysis (Certificate); geography (MA). Evening/weekend programs available.

Degree requirements: For master's, thesis or alternative.
Application deadline: For fall admission, 8/1; for spring admission, 11/1. *Application fee:* $50.
Expenses: Tuition, state resident: full-time $2,550; part-time $213 per credit. Tuition, nonresident: full-time $4,208; part-time $351 per credit. Required fees: $470; $470 per year.
Financial support: Fellowships, teaching assistantships, Federal Work-Study and institutionally sponsored loans available. Financial award application deadline: 6/1.
Faculty research: Remote sensing, cultural/social geography, urban geography.

■ STATE UNIVERSITY OF NEW YORK AT BINGHAMTON

Graduate School, School of Arts and Sciences, Department of Geography, Binghamton, NY 13902-6000

AWARDS MA.

Faculty: 7 full-time (2 women), 1 part-time/adjunct (0 women).
Students: 19 full-time (9 women), 3 part-time (1 woman); includes 4 minority (2 African Americans, 2 Asian Americans or Pacific Islanders), 4 international. Average age 27. 19 applicants, 68% accepted, 7 enrolled. In 2001, 10 degrees awarded.
Degree requirements: For master's, one foreign language, thesis (for some programs), oral and written exams.
Entrance requirements: For master's, GRE General Test, GRE Subject Test, TOEFL. *Application deadline:* For fall admission, 4/15 (priority date); for spring admission, 11/1. Applications are processed on a rolling basis. Electronic applications accepted.
Expenses: Tuition, state resident: full-time $5,100; part-time $213 per credit. Tuition, nonresident: full-time $8,416; part-time $351 per credit. Required fees: $811.
Financial support: In 2001–02, 18 students received support, including 1 fellowship with full tuition reimbursement available (averaging $7,828 per year), 17 teaching assistantships with full tuition reimbursements available (averaging $6,523 per year); research assistantships with full tuition reimbursements available, career-related internships or fieldwork, Federal Work-Study, institutionally sponsored loans, tuition waivers (full and partial), and unspecified assistantships also available. Support available to part-time students. Financial award application deadline: 2/15.
Dr. Shin-Yi Hsu, Chairperson, 607-777-2755.

■ SYRACUSE UNIVERSITY

Graduate School, Maxwell School of Citizenship and Public Affairs, Department of Geography, Syracuse, NY 13244-0003

AWARDS MA, PhD.

Faculty: 16 full-time (4 women), 1 part-time/adjunct (0 women).
Students: 28 full-time (14 women), 1 (woman) part-time, 6 international. Average age 30. 76 applicants, 46% accepted, 14 enrolled. In 2001, 4 master's, 1 doctorate awarded.
Degree requirements: For master's, thesis or alternative; for doctorate, thesis/dissertation.
Entrance requirements: For master's and doctorate, GRE General Test. *Application deadline:* For fall admission, 2/1 (priority date). Applications are processed on a rolling basis. *Application fee:* $50.
Expenses: Tuition: Full-time $15,528; part-time $647 per credit. Required fees: $420; $38 per term. Tuition and fees vary according to program.
Financial support: In 2001–02, 23 students received support, including 3 fellowships with partial tuition reimbursements available (averaging $12,313 per year), 4 research assistantships with partial tuition reimbursements available (averaging $10,600 per year), 11 teaching assistantships with full tuition reimbursements available (averaging $10,600 per year); career-related internships or fieldwork, Federal Work-Study, and tuition waivers (partial) also available.
John Western, Chair, 315-443-2607.
Application contact: Donald Mitchell, Graduate Director, 315-443-3679.
Find an in-depth description at www.petersons.com/gradchannel.

■ TEMPLE UNIVERSITY

Graduate School, College of Liberal Arts, Department of Geography/Urban Studies, Philadelphia, PA 19122-6096

AWARDS Geography (MA); urban studies (MA).

Degree requirements: For master's, thesis or alternative, comprehensive exam.
Entrance requirements: For master's, GRE General Test, minimum GPA of 3.0 during previous 2 years, 2.8 overall. Electronic applications accepted.
Expenses: Tuition, state resident: full-time $8,487; part-time $369 per credit hour. Tuition, nonresident: full-time $12,282; part-time $534 per credit hour. Required fees: $350. Tuition and fees vary according to course load, program and reciprocity agreements.
Faculty research: Environmental issues, urban political economy, poverty and unemployment, neighborhood development, African and Asian urbanization, housing, computer cartography. *Web site:* http://www.temple.edu/GUS/

■ TEXAS A&M UNIVERSITY

College of Geosciences, Department of Geography, College Station, TX 77843

AWARDS MS, PhD. Part-time programs available.

Faculty: 22.
Students: 38 (17 women). Average age 34.
Degree requirements: For master's, thesis optional; for doctorate, thesis/dissertation.
Entrance requirements: For master's and doctorate, GRE General Test, TOEFL. *Application deadline:* For fall admission, 3/1 (priority date); for spring admission, 10/1. Applications are processed on a rolling basis. *Application fee:* $50 ($75 for international students). Electronic applications accepted.
Expenses: Tuition, state resident: full-time $11,872. Tuition, nonresident: full-time $17,892.
Financial support: Fellowships, research assistantships, teaching assistantships, career-related internships or fieldwork, Federal Work-Study, and institutionally sponsored loans available. Financial award application deadline: 3/1; financial award applicants required to submit FAFSA.
Faculty research: Geomorphology, historical geography, urban-economic geography, geographic education and technology, human-environment interaction.
Dr. Jonathan D. Phillips, Head, 979-845-7141, *Fax:* 979-862-4487, *E-mail:* phillips@geog.tamu.edu.

Application contact: Daniel J. Sui, Graduate Advisor, 979-845-7154, *Fax:* 979-862-4487, *E-mail:* d-sui@tamu.edu. *Web site:* http://geog.tamu.edu/

■ TOWSON UNIVERSITY

Graduate School, Program in Geography and Environmental Planning, Towson, MD 21252-0001

AWARDS MA. Part-time and evening/weekend programs available.

Faculty: 9 full-time (1 woman), 2 part-time/adjunct (0 women).
Students: 33. In 2001, 4 degrees awarded.
Degree requirements: For master's, one foreign language, exam, thesis optional.
Entrance requirements: For master's, 18 credits in geography, minimum GPA of 3.0 in geography. *Application deadline:* Applications are processed on a rolling basis. *Application fee:* $40. Electronic applications accepted.
Expenses: Tuition, state resident: part-time $211 per credit. Tuition, nonresident: part-time $435 per credit. Required fees: $52 per credit.
Financial support: Federal Work-Study and unspecified assistantships available. Financial award application deadline: 4/1; financial award applicants required to submit FAFSA.
Faculty research: Geographic information systems, historical planning, regional planning.
Dr. Kent Barnes, Director, 410-704-3462, *Fax:* 410-704-3880, *E-mail:* kbarnes@towson.edu.
Application contact: 410-704-2501, *Fax:* 410-704-4675, *E-mail:* grads@towson.edu.

■ UNIVERSITY AT BUFFALO, THE STATE UNIVERSITY OF NEW YORK

Graduate School, College of Arts and Sciences, Department of Geography, Buffalo, NY 14260

AWARDS Geographic information science (Certificate); geography (MA, PhD). Part-time programs available.

Faculty: 16 full-time (4 women), 1 (woman) part-time/adjunct.
Students: 71 full-time (21 women), 57 part-time (15 women); includes 14 minority (5 African Americans, 4 Asian Americans or Pacific Islanders, 3 Hispanic Americans, 2 Native Americans), 47 international. Average age 25. 108 applicants, 60% accepted, 32 enrolled. In 2001, 19 master's, 8 doctorates awarded.
Degree requirements: For master's, project; for doctorate, thesis/dissertation; for Certificate, portfolio.
Entrance requirements: For master's, GRE General Test, TOEFL, minimum GPA of 3.0; for doctorate, TOEFL, GRE General Test, minimum GPA of 3.0. *Application deadline:* For fall admission, 2/1 (priority date); for spring admission, 10/1. Applications are processed on a rolling basis. *Application fee:* $35. Electronic applications accepted.
Expenses: Tuition, state resident: full-time $6,118. Tuition, nonresident: full-time $9,434.
Financial support: In 2001–02, 28 students received support, including 9 fellowships with full tuition reimbursements available (averaging $14,000 per year), 10 teaching assistantships with full tuition reimbursements available (averaging $8,400 per year); career-related internships or fieldwork, Federal Work-Study, institutionally sponsored loans, traineeships, health care benefits, tuition waivers (partial), and unspecified assistantships also available. Financial award application deadline: 2/1; financial award applicants required to submit FAFSA.
Faculty research: International business and world trade, geographic information systems and cartography, transportation, urban and regional analysis, physical and environmental geography. *Total annual research expenditures:* $915,000.
Dr. Hugh W. Calkins, Chairman, 716-645-2722 Ext. 15, *Fax:* 716-645-2329, *E-mail:* calkins@geog.buffalo.edu.
Application contact: Joseph Murray, Graduate Secretary, 716-645-2722 Ext. 13, *Fax:* 716-645-2329, *E-mail:* jlm@buffalo.edu. *Web site:* http://www.geog.buffalo.edu/

■ THE UNIVERSITY OF AKRON

Graduate School, Buchtel College of Arts and Sciences, Department of Geography and Planning, Akron, OH 44325-0001

AWARDS Geography (MS); urban planning (MA, PhD). Part-time and evening/weekend programs available.

Faculty: 11 full-time (1 woman), 9 part-time/adjunct (1 woman).
Students: 13 full-time (6 women), 9 part-time (3 women); includes 3 minority (1 African American, 2 Hispanic Americans), 4 international. Average age 30. 16 applicants, 81% accepted, 8 enrolled. In 2001, 9 degrees awarded.
Degree requirements: For master's, thesis (for some programs).
Entrance requirements: For master's, minimum GPA of 2.75. *Application deadline:* For fall admission, 8/15. Applications are processed on a rolling basis. *Application fee:* $40 ($50 for international students).
Expenses: Tuition, state resident: full-time $6,562; part-time $219 per credit. Tuition, nonresident: full-time $9,027; part-time $383 per credit. Required fees: $272; $11 per credit. Tuition and fees vary according to course load.
Financial support: In 2001–02, 1 research assistantship with full tuition reimbursement, 34 teaching assistantships with full tuition reimbursements were awarded. Fellowships with full tuition reimbursements, career-related internships or fieldwork, Federal Work-Study, institutionally sponsored loans, scholarships/grants, tuition waivers (full), and unspecified assistantships also available.
Faculty research: Planning, Asian urbanization, culture.
Dr. Robert Kent, Chair, 330-972-8003, *E-mail:* rkent@uakron.edu.
Application contact: Dr. Vern Harnapp, Director of Graduate Studies, 330-972-7623, *E-mail:* vharnapp@uakron.edu. *Web site:* http://www.uakron.edu/geography/

■ THE UNIVERSITY OF ALABAMA

Graduate School, College of Arts and Sciences, Department of Geography, Tuscaloosa, AL 35487

AWARDS MS. Part-time programs available.

Faculty: 8 full-time (0 women).
Students: 19 full-time (4 women), 4 part-time (1 woman); includes 1 minority (African American), 3 international. Average age 25. 17 applicants, 65% accepted, 8 enrolled. In 2001, 6 degrees awarded.
Degree requirements: For master's, thesis optional.
Entrance requirements: For master's, GRE General Test, minimum GPA of 3.0 in last 60 hours. *Application deadline:* For fall admission, 7/6. Applications are processed on a rolling basis. *Application fee:* $25. Electronic applications accepted.
Expenses: Tuition, state resident: full-time $3,292; part-time $183 per credit hour. Tuition, nonresident: full-time $8,912; part-time $495 per credit hour. Tuition and fees vary according to course load, campus/location and program.
Financial support: In 2001–02, 20 students received support, including fellowships with tuition reimbursements available (averaging $12,500 per year), 4 research assistantships with full tuition reimbursements available (averaging $8,433 per year), 6 teaching assistantships with full tuition reimbursements available (averaging $8,433 per year); career-related internships or fieldwork, Federal Work-Study, and institutionally sponsored loans also available. Financial award application deadline: 7/14.
Faculty research: Land use, regional and urban planning, geographic information systems, forest ecology, environmental management. *Total annual research expenditures:* $711,000.
Gerald Webster, Chair, 205-348-1532, *Fax:* 205-348-2278, *E-mail:* gwebster@bama.ua.edu.
Application contact: David Shankman, Graduate Adviser, 205-348-5047, *Fax:* 205-348-2278. *Web site:* http://www.as.ua.edu/geography/

■ THE UNIVERSITY OF ARIZONA

Graduate College, College of Social and Behavioral Sciences, Department of Geography and Regional Development, Tucson, AZ 85721

AWARDS Geography (MA, PhD). Part-time programs available.

Faculty: 29.
Students: 44 full-time (24 women), 9 part-time (5 women); includes 3 minority (1 African American, 2 Hispanic Americans), 8 international. Average age 32. 53 applicants, 55% accepted, 10 enrolled. In 2001, 8 master's, 5 doctorates awarded. Terminal master's awarded for partial completion of doctoral program.
Degree requirements: For master's, thesis or additional course work; for doctorate, variable foreign language requirement, thesis/dissertation.
Entrance requirements: For master's, GRE, TOEFL, minimum GPA of 3.0; for doctorate, GRE General Test, TOEFL, minimum GPA of 3.0. *Application deadline:* For fall admission, 2/1. *Application fee:* $45.
Expenses: Tuition, state resident: full-time $2,490; part-time $436 per unit. Tuition, nonresident: full-time $10,300; part-time $436 per unit. Full-time tuition and fees vary according to degree level and program.
Financial support: Fellowships, research assistantships, teaching assistantships, career-related internships or fieldwork and scholarships/grants available. Financial award application deadline: 2/1.
Faculty research: Population, Latin America, Anglo America, the former Soviet Union, Middle East.
Dr. Sallie Marston, Head, 520-621-1652.
Application contact: Linda Koski, Coordinator, 520-621-1652, *Fax:* 520-621-2889, *E-mail:* lkoski@email.arizona.edu.

■ UNIVERSITY OF ARKANSAS

Graduate School, J. William Fulbright College of Arts and Sciences, Department of Geosciences, Program in Geography, Fayetteville, AR 72701-1201

AWARDS MA.

Students: 11 full-time (5 women), 7 part-time (2 women); includes 2 minority (both Native Americans), 4 international. 9 applicants, 100% accepted. In 2001, 8 degrees awarded.
Degree requirements: For master's, thesis.
Application fee: $40 ($50 for international students).
Expenses: Tuition, state resident: full-time $3,553; part-time $197 per credit. Tuition, nonresident: full-time $8,411; part-time $467 per credit. Required fees: $42 per credit. Tuition and fees vary according to course load and program.
Financial support: Research assistantships, teaching assistantships, career-related internships or fieldwork and Federal Work-Study available. Support available to part-time students. Financial award application deadline: 4/1; financial award applicants required to submit FAFSA.
David Stahle, Chair, 479-575-3355.

■ UNIVERSITY OF ARKANSAS

Graduate School, J. William Fulbright College of Arts and Sciences, Interdisciplinary Program in Environmental Dynamics, Fayetteville, AR 72701-1201

AWARDS PhD.

Students: 17 full-time (4 women), 9 part-time (4 women); includes 1 minority (Asian American or Pacific Islander), 5 international. 10 applicants, 90% accepted. In 2001, 1 degree awarded.
Degree requirements: For doctorate, thesis/dissertation.
Application fee: $40 ($50 for international students).
Expenses: Tuition, state resident: full-time $3,553; part-time $197 per credit. Tuition, nonresident: full-time $8,411; part-time $467 per credit. Required fees: $42 per credit. Tuition and fees vary according to course load and program.
Financial support: Teaching assistantships available. Financial award application deadline: 4/1.
Allen McCartney, Head, 479-575-2508, *E-mail:* endy@comp.uark.edu.

■ UNIVERSITY OF CALIFORNIA, BERKELEY

Graduate Division, College of Letters and Science, Department of Geography, Berkeley, CA 94720-1500

AWARDS PhD.

Students: 51 full-time (23 women); includes 4 minority (1 African American, 3 Asian Americans or Pacific Islanders), 3 international. 59 applicants, 24% accepted, 8 enrolled. In 2001, 5 doctorates awarded.
Degree requirements: For doctorate, thesis/dissertation, qualifying exam.
Entrance requirements: For doctorate, GRE General Test, minimum GPA of 3.0. *Application deadline:* For fall admission, 12/15. *Application fee:* $60. Electronic applications accepted.
Expenses: Tuition, nonresident: full-time $10,704. Required fees: $4,349.
Financial support: Fellowships, research assistantships, teaching assistantships available. Financial award application deadline: 12/15.
Dr. Michael Johns, Chair, 510-643-8226.
Application contact: Carol Page, Graduate Assistant for Admission, 510-642-3904, *Fax:* 510-642-3370.

■ UNIVERSITY OF CALIFORNIA, DAVIS

Graduate Studies, Graduate Group in Geography, Davis, CA 95616

AWARDS MA, PhD.

Faculty: 50 full-time (17 women).
Students: 33 full-time (14 women); includes 3 minority (1 Asian American or Pacific Islander, 2 Hispanic Americans), 1 international. Average age 34. 32 applicants, 78% accepted, 15 enrolled. In 2001, 3 master's, 2 doctorates awarded. Terminal master's awarded for partial completion of doctoral program.
Degree requirements: For master's, thesis optional; for doctorate, thesis/dissertation.
Entrance requirements: For master's, GRE General Test, minimum GPA of 3.0; for doctorate, GRE General Test, master's degree, minimum GPA of 3.0. *Application deadline:* For fall admission, 1/15. Applications are processed on a rolling basis. *Application fee:* $60. Electronic applications accepted.
Expenses: Tuition, state resident: full-time $4,831. Tuition, nonresident: full-time $15,725.
Financial support: In 2001–02, 25 students received support, including 18 fellowships with full and partial tuition reimbursements available (averaging $3,750 per year), 11 research assistantships with full and partial tuition reimbursements available (averaging $6,192 per year), 6 teaching assistantships with partial tuition reimbursements available (averaging $11,775 per year); Federal Work-Study, institutionally sponsored loans, scholarships/grants, and tuition waivers (full and partial) also available. Financial award application deadline: 1/15; financial award applicants required to submit FAFSA.
Faculty research: Cultural agrosystems, mountain society habitat and South Asia.
Deborah Elliott-Fisk, Graduate Group Chair, 530-752-8559, *E-mail:* dlelliottfisk@ucdavis.edu.
Application contact: Levada McDowell, Graduate Assistant, 530-752-4119, *Fax:* 530-752-1392, *E-mail:* lmmcdowell@ucdavis.edu. *Web site:* http://ggg.ucdavis.edu/

■ UNIVERSITY OF CALIFORNIA, LOS ANGELES

Graduate Division, College of Letters and Science, Department of Geography, Los Angeles, CA 90095

AWARDS MA, PhD.

Students: 53 full-time (25 women); includes 3 minority (2 Asian Americans or Pacific Islanders, 1 Hispanic American), 13 international. 64 applicants, 48% accepted, 11 enrolled. In 2001, 6 master's, 4 doctorates awarded.

Degree requirements: For master's, thesis; for doctorate, thesis/dissertation, oral and written qualifying exams.
Entrance requirements: For master's, GRE General Test, minimum GPA of 3.0; for doctorate, GRE General Test, minimum undergraduate GPA of 3.0, sample of research writing or thesis. *Application deadline:* For fall admission, 12/15. *Application fee:* $60. Electronic applications accepted.
Expenses: Tuition, nonresident: full-time $10,244. Required fees: $3,609. Full-time tuition and fees vary according to program.
Financial support: In 2001–02, 50 students received support, including 33 fellowships, 26 research assistantships, 41 teaching assistantships; Federal Work-Study, institutionally sponsored loans, scholarships/grants, and tuition waivers (full and partial) also available. Financial award application deadline: 3/1.
Faculty research: Culture, technology, and the environment; spatial demography; industrial restructuring; people and the environment.
Dr. John A. Agnew, Chair, 310-825-1071.
Application contact: Departmental Office, 310-825-1071, *E-mail:* jcorbett@geog.ucla.edu.

■ UNIVERSITY OF CALIFORNIA, SANTA BARBARA

Graduate Division, College of Letters and Sciences, Division of Mathematics, Life, and Physical Sciences, Department of Geography, Santa Barbara, CA 93106

AWARDS MA, PhD.

Degree requirements: For master's, thesis or alternative; for doctorate, thesis/dissertation.
Entrance requirements: For master's and doctorate, GRE General Test, TOEFL. Electronic applications accepted.
Faculty research: Human spatial behavior, urban and regional modeling, resource and environmental management, hydrology, climatology, earth system science. *Web site:* http://www.geog.ucsb.edu/

■ UNIVERSITY OF CINCINNATI

Division of Research and Advanced Studies, McMicken College of Arts and Sciences, Department of Geography, Cincinnati, OH 45221

AWARDS MA, PhD.

Faculty: 10 full-time (2 women).
Students: 27 full-time (14 women), 15 part-time (9 women). 31 applicants, 58% accepted, 10 enrolled. In 2001, 1 master's, 4 doctorates awarded. Terminal master's awarded for partial completion of doctoral program.
Degree requirements: For master's, thesis optional; for doctorate, one foreign language, thesis/dissertation, comprehensive exam, registration. *Median time to degree:* Master's–2.3 years full-time; doctorate–6.8 years full-time.
Entrance requirements: For master's and doctorate, GRE General Test. *Application deadline:* For fall admission, 7/1 (priority date). *Application fee:* $30. Electronic applications accepted.
Expenses: Tuition, state resident: part-time $2,698 per quarter. Tuition, nonresident: part-time $4,977 per quarter.
Financial support: In 2001–02, 11 research assistantships with full tuition reimbursements (averaging $10,692 per year), 14 teaching assistantships with full tuition reimbursements (averaging $10,692 per year) were awarded. Tuition waivers (partial) and unspecified assistantships also available. Financial award application deadline: 5/1.
Faculty research: Urban-economics, GIS, physical-environmental. *Total annual research expenditures:* $631,657.
Dr. Howard Stafford, Head, 513-556-3426, *Fax:* 513-556-3370, *E-mail:* howard.stafford@uc.edu.
Application contact: Roger Selya, Graduate Program Director, 513-556-3423, *Fax:* 513-556-3370, *E-mail:* selyarm@uc.edu. *Web site:* http://www.geography.uc.edu/

■ UNIVERSITY OF COLORADO AT BOULDER

Graduate School, College of Arts and Sciences, Department of Geography, Boulder, CO 80309

AWARDS MA, PhD. Part-time programs available.

Faculty: 23 full-time (5 women).
Students: 58 full-time (25 women), 17 part-time (10 women); includes 4 minority (1 African American, 2 Hispanic Americans, 1 Native American), 11 international. Average age 32. 54 applicants, 56% accepted. In 2001, 5 master's, 6 doctorates awarded. Terminal master's awarded for partial completion of doctoral program.
Degree requirements: For master's, thesis; for doctorate, one foreign language, thesis/dissertation, comprehensive exam.
Entrance requirements: For master's and doctorate, GRE General Test. *Application deadline:* For fall admission, 1/15 (priority date). *Application fee:* $50 ($60 for international students).
Expenses: Tuition, state resident: full-time $3,474. Tuition, nonresident: full-time $16,624.
Financial support: In 2001–02, 9 fellowships (averaging $1,602 per year), 4 research assistantships with tuition reimbursements (averaging $15,974 per year), 32 teaching assistantships with tuition reimbursements (averaging $17,553 per year) were awarded. Financial award application deadline: 1/15.
Faculty research: Physical, human, environmental society relations, technical, GIS and cartography. *Total annual research expenditures:* $7.2 million.
Gary Gaile, Chair, 303-492-8310, *Fax:* 303-492-7501, *E-mail:* gary.gaile@colorado.edu.
Application contact: Karen Weingarten, Graduate Secretary, 303-492-8311, *Fax:* 303-492-7501, *E-mail:* weingart@spot.colorado.edu. *Web site:* http://www.colorado.edu/geography/

■ UNIVERSITY OF CONNECTICUT

Graduate School, College of Liberal Arts and Sciences, Field of Geography, Storrs, CT 06269

AWARDS MS, PhD.

Entrance requirements: For master's, GRE General Test, TOEFL.

■ UNIVERSITY OF DELAWARE

College of Arts and Science, Department of Geography, Newark, DE 19716

AWARDS Climatology (PhD); geography (MA, MS).

Faculty: 11 full-time (3 women).
Students: 26 full-time (14 women), 3 part-time (all women); includes 4 minority (1 African American, 2 Asian Americans or Pacific Islanders, 1 Native American). Average age 25. 21 applicants, 57% accepted, 8 enrolled. In 2001, 5 degrees awarded.
Degree requirements: For master's and doctorate, thesis/dissertation.
Entrance requirements: For master's and doctorate, GRE General Test. *Application deadline:* For fall admission, 2/1. *Application fee:* $50. Electronic applications accepted.
Expenses: Tuition, state resident: full-time $4,770; part-time $265 per credit. Tuition, nonresident: full-time $13,860; part-time $770 per credit. Required fees: $414.
Financial support: In 2001–02, 14 students received support, including 3 fellowships with full tuition reimbursements available (averaging $11,400 per year), 6 research assistantships with full tuition reimbursements available (averaging $11,400 per year), 10 teaching assistantships with full tuition reimbursements available (averaging $11,400 per year); tuition waivers (full) also available. Financial award application deadline: 2/1.
Faculty research: Urban, human and cultural geography; geographic education; geographic methods. *Total annual research expenditures:* $450,000.
Dr. Daniel J. Leathers, Chairman, 302-831-8764, *Fax:* 302-831-6654, *E-mail:* leathers@udel.edu.
Application contact: Janice Spry, Assistant to the Chair, 302-831-8998, *Fax:* 302-831-6654, *E-mail:* jspry@udel.edu. *Web site:* http://www.udel.edu/geography/geog.html

■ UNIVERSITY OF DENVER

Graduate Studies, Faculty of Natural Sciences, Mathematics and Engineering, Department of Geography, Denver, CO 80208

AWARDS MA, PhD. Part-time programs available.

Faculty: 8 full-time (1 woman).
Students: 29 (17 women). 61 applicants, 64% accepted. In 2001, 3 master's, 2 doctorates awarded. Terminal master's awarded for partial completion of doctoral program.
Degree requirements: For master's, thesis or alternative; for doctorate, one foreign language, thesis/dissertation.
Entrance requirements: For master's, GRE General Test, TOEFL, TSE; for doctorate, GRE General Test, TOEFL, TSE, MA. *Application deadline:* Applications are processed on a rolling basis. *Application fee:* $45.
Expenses: Tuition: Full-time $21,456.
Financial support: In 2001–02, 1 fellowship with full and partial tuition reimbursement, 8 teaching assistantships with full and partial tuition reimbursements (averaging $8,514 per year) were awarded. Research assistantships with full and partial tuition reimbursements, career-related internships or fieldwork, Federal Work-Study, institutionally sponsored loans, and scholarships/grants also available. Support available to part-time students. Financial award application deadline: 3/1; financial award applicants required to submit FAFSA.
Faculty research: Transportation and land use, fluvial geography and water resources, climatology, geographic information systems, biogeography. *Total annual research expenditures:* $42,936.
Dr. David Longbrake, Chairman, 303-871-2659.
Application contact: Dr. Michael Keables, Graduate Director, 303-871-2653. *Web site:* http://www.du.edu/~mkeables/geog.html

■ UNIVERSITY OF FLORIDA

Graduate School, College of Liberal Arts and Sciences, Department of Geography, Gainesville, FL 32611

AWARDS MA, MAT, MS, MST, PhD.

Degree requirements: For master's, variable foreign language requirement, thesis (for some programs); for doctorate, variable foreign language requirement, thesis/dissertation.
Entrance requirements: For master's and doctorate, GRE General Test, minimum GPA of 3.0. Electronic applications accepted.
Expenses: Tuition, state resident: part-time $164 per hour. Tuition, nonresident: part-time $571 per hour. Tuition and fees vary according to course level and program.
Faculty research: Economic development, physical geography, hydrology, climatology, tropical agriculture. *Web site:* http://www.geog.ufl.edu/

■ UNIVERSITY OF GEORGIA

Graduate School, College of Arts and Sciences, Department of Geography, Athens, GA 30602

AWARDS MA, MS, PhD.

Faculty: 22 full-time (5 women).
Students: 50 full-time (19 women), 8 part-time, 17 international. 87 applicants, 54% accepted. In 2001, 8 master's, 6 doctorates awarded.
Degree requirements: For master's and doctorate, one foreign language, thesis/dissertation.
Entrance requirements: For master's and doctorate, GRE General Test. *Application deadline:* For fall admission, 7/1 (priority date); for spring admission, 11/15. *Application fee:* $30. Electronic applications accepted.
Expenses: Tuition, state resident: full-time $2,376; part-time $132 per credit hour. Tuition, nonresident: full-time $9,504; part-time $528 per credit hour. Required fees: $236 per semester.
Financial support: Fellowships, research assistantships, teaching assistantships, unspecified assistantships available.
Dr. Vernon Meentemeyer, Head, 706-542-2856, *Fax:* 706-542-2388, *E-mail:* vmeente@uga.edu.
Application contact: Dr. C. P. Lo, Graduate Coordinator, 706-542-2330, *Fax:* 706-542-2388, *E-mail:* chpanglo@uga.edu. *Web site:* http://www.ggy.uga.edu/

■ UNIVERSITY OF HAWAII AT MANOA

Graduate Division, College of Arts and Sciences, College of Social Sciences, Department of Geography, Honolulu, HI 96822

AWARDS MA, PhD. Part-time programs available.

Faculty: 20 full-time (5 women), 5 part-time/adjunct (0 women).
Students: 60 full-time (30 women), 15 part-time (8 women); includes 20 Asian Americans or Pacific Islanders, 4 Hispanic Americans, 1 Native American. Average age 35. 86 applicants, 27% accepted, 6 enrolled. In 2001, 8 master's, 6 doctorates awarded.
Degree requirements: For master's, thesis; for doctorate, one foreign language, thesis/dissertation. *Median time to degree:* Master's–2 years full-time.
Entrance requirements: For master's, GRE; for doctorate, GRE, sample of written work. *Application deadline:* For fall admission, 3/1. Applications are processed on a rolling basis. *Application fee:* $25 ($50 for international students).
Expenses: Tuition, state resident: full-time $2,160; part-time $1,980 per year. Tuition, nonresident: full-time $5,190; part-time $4,829 per year.
Financial support: In 2001–02, 20 students received support, including 9 research assistantships (averaging $16,590 per year), 12 teaching assistantships (averaging $13,664 per year); career-related internships or fieldwork, Federal Work-Study, institutionally sponsored loans, and tuition waivers (full) also available. Financial award application deadline: 3/1.
Faculty research: Physical geography, human geography, methodology. *Total annual research expenditures:* $3.7 million.
Dr. Lyndon Wester, Chairperson, 808-956-8465.
Application contact: Ross Sutherland, Graduate Chair, 808-956-3524, *Fax:* 808-956-3512, *E-mail:* sutherla@hawaii.edu.

■ UNIVERSITY OF IDAHO

College of Graduate Studies, College of Mines and Earth Resources, Department of Geography, Moscow, ID 83844-2282

AWARDS Geography (MS, PhD); geography education (MAT).

Faculty: 8 full-time (2 women), 2 part-time/adjunct (0 women).
Students: 12 full-time (4 women), 12 part-time (1 woman), 3 international. 27 applicants, 52% accepted. In 2001, 2 master's, 1 doctorate awarded.
Degree requirements: For doctorate, one foreign language, thesis/dissertation.
Entrance requirements: For master's, minimum GPA of 2.8; for doctorate, minimum undergraduate GPA of 2.8, graduate GPA of 3.0. *Application deadline:* For fall admission, 8/1; for spring admission, 12/15. *Application fee:* $35 ($45 for international students).
Expenses: Tuition, state resident: full-time $1,613. Tuition, nonresident: full-time $3,000.
Financial support: In 2001–02, 1 research assistantship, 9 teaching assistantships were awarded. Financial award application deadline: 2/15.
Dr. Harley E. Johansen, Head, 208-885-6216. *Web site:* http://www.mines.uidaho.edu/geography/
Find an in-depth description at www.petersons.com/gradchannel.

■ UNIVERSITY OF ILLINOIS AT CHICAGO

Graduate College, College of Liberal Arts and Sciences, Department of Anthropology, Program in Environmental and Urban Geography, Chicago, IL 60607-7128

AWARDS Environmental studies (MA); urban geography (MA).

Faculty: 9 full-time (0 women).
Students: 2 full-time (1 woman), 4 part-time (1 woman), 1 international. Average

age 27. 8 applicants, 75% accepted, 4 enrolled. In 2001, 14 degrees awarded.
Degree requirements: For master's, thesis.
Entrance requirements: For master's, GRE General Test, TOEFL, minimum GPA of 3.75 on a 5.0 scale. *Application deadline:* For fall admission, 6/1; for spring admission, 11/1. Applications are processed on a rolling basis. *Application fee:* $40 ($50 for international students). Electronic applications accepted.
Expenses: Tuition, state resident: full-time $3,060. Tuition, nonresident: full-time $6,688.
Financial support: In 2001–02, 4 students received support; fellowships with full tuition reimbursements available, research assistantships with full tuition reimbursements available, teaching assistantships with full tuition reimbursements available, Federal Work-Study and tuition waivers (full) available. Financial award application deadline: 3/1; financial award applicants required to submit FAFSA.
Application contact: Jim Phillips, Director of Graduate Studies, 312-413-3582, *E-mail:* jphillip@uic.edu.

■ UNIVERSITY OF ILLINOIS AT URBANA–CHAMPAIGN

Graduate College, College of Liberal Arts and Sciences, Department of Geography, Champaign, IL 61820

AWARDS AM, MS, PhD.

Faculty: 13 full-time (2 women), 1 part-time/adjunct (0 women).
Students: 31 full-time (16 women); includes 3 minority (1 African American, 2 Asian Americans or Pacific Islanders), 12 international. Average age 27. 61 applicants, 15% accepted. In 2001, 4 degrees awarded.
Degree requirements: For master's and doctorate, thesis/dissertation.
Entrance requirements: For master's, minimum GPA of 3.0. *Application deadline:* For fall admission, 2/15 (priority date); for spring admission, 12/15. Applications are processed on a rolling basis. *Application fee:* $40 ($50 for international students).
Expenses: Tuition, state resident: part-time $3,227 per degree program. Tuition, nonresident: part-time $7,169 per degree program. Tuition and fees vary according to program.
Financial support: In 2001–02, 28 students received support, including 5 fellowships, 9 research assistantships, 16 teaching assistantships; career-related internships or fieldwork, institutionally sponsored loans, and tuition waivers (full and partial) also available. Financial award application deadline: 2/15. *Total annual research expenditures:* $250,000.
Bruce L. Rhoads, Head, 217-333-1880, *Fax:* 217-244-1785, *E-mail:* b-rhoads@uiuc.edu.
Application contact: Barbara Bonnell, Officer, 217-244-3486, *Fax:* 217-244-1785, *E-mail:* bbonnell@uiuc.edu. *Web site:* http://www.staff.uiuc.edu/~j-domier/index.html

■ THE UNIVERSITY OF IOWA

Graduate College, College of Liberal Arts and Sciences, Department of Geography, Iowa City, IA 52242-1316

AWARDS MA, PhD.

Faculty: 13 full-time, 2 part-time/adjunct.
Students: 13 full-time (6 women), 26 part-time (11 women); includes 5 minority (1 African American, 1 Hispanic American, 3 Native Americans), 15 international. 44 applicants, 41% accepted, 7 enrolled. In 2001, 2 master's, 2 doctorates awarded.
Degree requirements: For master's, exam, thesis optional; for doctorate, thesis/dissertation, comprehensive exam.
Entrance requirements: For master's, GRE General Test, TOEFL; for doctorate, GRE General Test, TOEFL, minimum GPA of 3.0. *Application deadline:* For fall admission, 2/1. *Application fee:* $30 ($50 for international students). Electronic applications accepted.
Expenses: Tuition, state resident: full-time $3,702; part-time $206 per semester hour. Tuition, nonresident: full-time $11,924; part-time $206 per semester hour. Required fees: $101 per semester. Tuition and fees vary according to course load and program.
Financial support: In 2001–02, 3 fellowships, 10 research assistantships, 15 teaching assistantships were awarded. Financial award applicants required to submit FAFSA.
Mark Armstrong, Chair, 319-335-0151, *Fax:* 319-335-2725.

■ UNIVERSITY OF KANSAS

Graduate School, College of Liberal Arts and Sciences, Department of Geography, Lawrence, KS 66045

AWARDS MA, PhD.

Faculty: 16.
Students: 38 full-time (9 women), 32 part-time (10 women); includes 3 minority (1 African American, 1 Asian American or Pacific Islander, 1 Native American), 12 international. Average age 32. 26 applicants, 27% accepted, 7 enrolled. In 2001, 11 master's, 3 doctorates awarded.
Degree requirements: For master's, thesis or alternative; for doctorate, one foreign language, thesis/dissertation.
Entrance requirements: For master's and doctorate, GRE General Test, TOEFL. *Application deadline:* For fall admission, 2/1 (priority date); for spring admission, 11/1. Applications are processed on a rolling basis. *Application fee:* $35.
Expenses: Tuition, state resident: full-time $2,722; part-time $113 per credit. Tuition, nonresident: full-time $8,586; part-time $358 per credit. Required fees: $551; $46 per credit. Tuition and fees vary according to campus/location, program and reciprocity agreements.
Financial support: In 2001–02, 5 fellowships (averaging $7,000 per year), 1 research assistantship with partial tuition reimbursement, 17 teaching assistantships with full and partial tuition reimbursements (averaging $10,165 per year) were awarded.
Robert McColl, Chair, 785-864-5143, *Fax:* 785-864-5378, *E-mail:* mccoll@ku.edu.
Application contact: Terry Slocum, Graduate Director, 785-864-5143, *Fax:* 785-864-5378, *E-mail:* t-slocum@ku.edu. *Web site:* http://www.geog.ku.edu/

■ UNIVERSITY OF KENTUCKY

Graduate School, Graduate School Programs from the College of Arts and Sciences, Program in Geography, Lexington, KY 40506-0032

AWARDS MA, PhD.

Faculty: 25 full-time (5 women).
Students: 43 full-time (20 women), 8 part-time (4 women), 8 international. 38 applicants, 55% accepted. In 2001, 4 master's, 5 doctorates awarded.
Degree requirements: For master's, thesis optional; for doctorate, one foreign language, thesis/dissertation, comprehensive exam.
Entrance requirements: For master's, GRE General Test, minimum undergraduate GPA of 2.5; for doctorate, GRE General Test, minimum graduate GPA of 3.0. *Application deadline:* For fall admission, 7/19. Applications are processed on a rolling basis. *Application fee:* $30 ($35 for international students).
Expenses: Tuition, state resident: full-time $4,075; part-time $213 per credit hour. Tuition, nonresident: full-time $11,295; part-time $614 per credit hour.
Financial support: In 2001–02, 6 fellowships, 8 research assistantships, 16 teaching assistantships were awarded. Federal Work-Study, institutionally sponsored loans, and unspecified assistantships also available. Support available to part-time students.
Faculty research: Cultural, industrial, medical, political, social, population, and transportation geography; geographic analysis; Third World (especially Southeast Asia theory); Eastern Europe.
Dr. Richard Schein, Director of Graduate Studies, 859-257-2119, *Fax:* 859-323-1969, *E-mail:* shein@pop.uky.edu.
Application contact: Dr. Jeannine Blackwell, Associate Dean, 859-257-4905, *Fax:* 859-323-1928.

■ UNIVERSITY OF LOUISIANA AT LAFAYETTE

Graduate School, College of Liberal Arts, Department of History and Geography, Lafayette, LA 70504

AWARDS MA. Part-time programs available.

University of Louisiana at Lafayette (continued)
Faculty: 15 full-time (4 women).
Students: 10 full-time (5 women), 8 part-time (1 woman); includes 2 minority (1 African American, 1 Hispanic American). 13 applicants, 77% accepted, 6 enrolled. In 2001, 10 degrees awarded.
Degree requirements: For master's, one foreign language, thesis or alternative.
Entrance requirements: For master's, GRE General Test, minimum GPA of 2.75. *Application deadline:* For fall admission, 5/15. *Application fee:* $20 ($30 for international students).
Expenses: Tuition, state resident: full-time $2,317; part-time $79 per credit. Tuition, nonresident: full-time $8,882; part-time $369 per credit. International tuition: $9,018 full-time.
Financial support: In 2001–02, 1 fellowship with full tuition reimbursement (averaging $12,000 per year), 6 research assistantships with full tuition reimbursements (averaging $5,500 per year) were awarded. Federal Work-Study also available. Financial award application deadline: 5/1.
Dr. Vaughan Baker, Head, 337-482-6900.
Application contact: Dr. Chester Rzadkiewicz, Graduate Coordinator, 337-482-5415.

■ UNIVERSITY OF MARYLAND, COLLEGE PARK

Graduate Studies and Research, College of Behavioral and Social Sciences, Department of Geography, College Park, MD 20742

AWARDS MA, PhD, MA/MLS. Part-time and evening/weekend programs available.

Faculty: 49 full-time (17 women), 5 part-time/adjunct (3 women).
Students: 47 full-time (27 women), 34 part-time (12 women); includes 13 minority (7 African Americans, 2 Asian Americans or Pacific Islanders, 4 Hispanic Americans), 7 international. 96 applicants, 48% accepted, 32 enrolled. In 2001, 12 master's, 1 doctorate awarded. Terminal master's awarded for partial completion of doctoral program.
Degree requirements: For master's, thesis, oral exam; for doctorate, thesis/dissertation.
Entrance requirements: For master's, GRE General Test, minimum GPA of 3.0; for doctorate, GRE General Test. *Application deadline:* For fall admission, 2/1. Applications are processed on a rolling basis. *Application fee:* $50 ($70 for international students). Electronic applications accepted.
Expenses: Tuition, state resident: part-time $289 per credit hour. Tuition, nonresident: part-time $448 per credit hour. One-time fee: $436 part-time. Full-time tuition and fees vary according to course load, campus/location and program.
Financial support: In 2001–02, 8 fellowships with full tuition reimbursements (averaging $9,055 per year), 18 research assistantships with tuition reimbursements (averaging $13,255 per year), 20 teaching assistantships with tuition reimbursements (averaging $12,040 per year) were awarded. Federal Work-Study and scholarships/grants also available. Support available to part-time students. Financial award applicants required to submit FAFSA.
Faculty research: Cartography and automated mapping, environmental systems analysis, metropolitan analysis and planning, historical and human geography, coastal geomorphology.
Dr. John Townsend, Chairman, 301-405-4050, *Fax:* 301-314-9299.
Application contact: Trudy Lindsey, Director, Graduate Admissions and Records, 301-405-6991, *Fax:* 301-314-9305, *E-mail:* grschool@deans.umd.edu.

■ UNIVERSITY OF MASSACHUSETTS AMHERST

Graduate School, College of Natural Sciences and Mathematics, Department of Geosciences, Program in Geography, Amherst, MA 01003

AWARDS MS. Part-time programs available.

Students: 9 full-time (4 women), 12 part-time (4 women); includes 1 minority (Asian American or Pacific Islander), 1 international. Average age 31. 21 applicants, 48% accepted. In 2001, 9 degrees awarded.
Degree requirements: For master's, thesis optional.
Entrance requirements: For master's, GRE General Test. *Application deadline:* For fall admission, 2/1 (priority date); for spring admission, 10/1. Applications are processed on a rolling basis. *Application fee:* $40 ($50 for international students).
Expenses: Tuition, state resident: full-time $1,980; part-time $110 per credit. Tuition, nonresident: full-time $7,456; part-time $414 per credit. Required fees: $4,112. One-time fee: $115 full-time.
Financial support: Fellowships with full tuition reimbursements, research assistantships with full tuition reimbursements, teaching assistantships with full tuition reimbursements, career-related internships or fieldwork, Federal Work-Study, scholarships/grants, traineeships, and unspecified assistantships available. Support available to part-time students. Financial award application deadline: 2/1.
Dr. Richard Wilkie, Director, 413-545-5933, *Fax:* 413-545-1200, *E-mail:* rwilkie@geo.umass.edu.

■ THE UNIVERSITY OF MEMPHIS

Graduate School, College of Arts and Sciences, Department of Geography and Planning, Program in Geography, Memphis, TN 38152

AWARDS MA, MS. Part-time programs available.

Faculty: 7 full-time (1 woman), 4 part-time/adjunct (2 women).
Students: 24 full-time (9 women), 22 part-time (7 women); includes 11 minority (9 African Americans, 2 Hispanic Americans), 4 international. Average age 31. 11 applicants, 73% accepted, 7 enrolled. In 2001, 3 degrees awarded.
Degree requirements: For master's, comprehensive exam.
Entrance requirements: For master's, GRE General Test. *Application deadline:* For fall admission, 5/1; for spring admission, 11/1. Applications are processed on a rolling basis. *Application fee:* $25 ($50 for international students).
Expenses: Tuition, state resident: full-time $2,026. Tuition, nonresident: full-time $4,528.
Financial support: Research assistantships, teaching assistantships, career-related internships or fieldwork, Federal Work-Study, and institutionally sponsored loans available.
Faculty research: Geographic information systems, remote sensing, historical and cultural geography, physical geography,. *Total annual research expenditures:* $10,000.
Dr. Roy B. Van Arsdale, Chair, 901-678-2386, *Fax:* 901-678-4467, *E-mail:* rvanrsdl@memphis.edu.
Application contact: Dr. Thad Wasklewicz, Coordinator of Graduate Studies, 901-678-4452, *Fax:* 901-678-4467, *E-mail:* twsklwcz@memphis.edu.

■ UNIVERSITY OF MINNESOTA, TWIN CITIES CAMPUS

Graduate School, College of Liberal Arts, Department of Geography, Program in Geography, Minneapolis, MN 55455-0213

AWARDS MA, PhD.

Faculty: 23 full-time (7 women), 4 part-time/adjunct (0 women).
Students: 60 full-time (30 women), 4 part-time (2 women); includes 5 minority (2 African Americans, 1 Asian American or Pacific Islander, 2 Hispanic Americans), 21 international. 81 applicants, 38% accepted, 11 enrolled. In 2001, 6 master's, 5 doctorates awarded.
Degree requirements: For master's, thesis or 3 papers; for doctorate, thesis/dissertation. *Median time to degree:* Master's–2 years full-time; doctorate–4 years full-time.
Entrance requirements: For master's and doctorate, GRE General Test, TOEFL, minimum GPA of 3.5. *Application deadline:*

For fall admission, 1/1. *Application fee:* $50 ($55 for international students).
Expenses: Tuition, state resident: full-time $2,932; part-time $489 per credit. Tuition, nonresident: full-time $5,758; part-time $960 per credit. Part-time tuition and fees vary according to course load, program and reciprocity agreements.
Financial support: In 2001–02, 52 students received support, including 11 fellowships with full and partial tuition reimbursements available (averaging $14,000 per year), 12 research assistantships with full and partial tuition reimbursements available (averaging $10,920 per year), 29 teaching assistantships with full and partial tuition reimbursements available (averaging $10,920 per year); career-related internships or fieldwork, Federal Work-Study, institutionally sponsored loans, scholarships/grants, traineeships, health care benefits, tuition waivers (full and partial), and unspecified assistantships also available. Support available to part-time students. Financial award application deadline: 1/1.
Faculty research: Space, place, and the environment, biogeography/forest dynamics, international labor migration, political economy of development/globalization, historical urban geography. *Total annual research expenditures:* $1.2 million.
Robert B. McMaster, Director of Graduate Studies, 612-625-9883, *Fax:* 612-624-1044, *E-mail:* mcmaster@socsci.umn.edu.
Application contact: Bonnie L. Williams, Graduate Secretary, 612-625-6080, *Fax:* 612-624-1044, *E-mail:* willi046@tc.umn.edu. *Web site:* http://www.geog.umn.edu/

■ UNIVERSITY OF MISSOURI–COLUMBIA

Graduate School, College of Arts and Sciences, Department of Geography, Columbia, MO 65211

AWARDS MA.

Faculty: 8 full-time (1 woman).
Students: 12 full-time (4 women), 7 part-time (4 women); includes 1 minority (Hispanic American). 9 applicants, 33% accepted. In 2001, 3 degrees awarded.
Entrance requirements: For master's, GRE General Test, minimum GPA of 3.0. *Application deadline:* For fall admission, 2/15 (priority date); for winter admission, 10/1 (priority date); for spring admission, 4/1 (priority date). Applications are processed on a rolling basis. *Application fee:* $25 ($50 for international students).
Expenses: Tuition, state resident: part-time $179 per credit hour. Tuition, nonresident: part-time $539 per credit hour. Required fees: $122 per semester. Tuition and fees vary according to program.
Financial support: Research assistantships, teaching assistantships, institutionally sponsored loans available.
Dr. Edward Kinman, Director of Graduate Studies, 573-882-8808, *E-mail:* kinmane@missouri.edu. *Web site:* http://www.geog.missouri.edu/

■ THE UNIVERSITY OF MONTANA–MISSOULA

Graduate School, College of Arts and Sciences, Department of Geography, Missoula, MT 59812-0002

AWARDS Geography (MA), including cartography and GIS, rural town and regional planning.

Faculty: 8 full-time (1 woman).
Students: 13 full-time (4 women), 17 part-time (10 women), 1 international. 18 applicants, 94% accepted, 11 enrolled. In 2001, 2 degrees awarded.
Entrance requirements: For master's, GRE General Test. *Application deadline:* For fall admission, 4/30 (priority date). *Application fee:* $45.
Expenses: Tuition, state resident: full-time $2,482; part-time $1,700 per year. Tuition, nonresident: full-time $7,372; part-time $5,000 per year. Required fees: $1,900. Tuition and fees vary according to degree level.
Financial support: In 2001–02, 7 teaching assistantships with full tuition reimbursements (averaging $8,665 per year) were awarded; Federal Work-Study and unspecified assistantships also available. Financial award application deadline: 3/1; financial award applicants required to submit FAFSA. *Total annual research expenditures:* $44,000.
Dr. Jeffrey Gritzner, Chair, 406-243-5626, *E-mail:* jag@selway.umt.edu. *Web site:* http://www.umt.edu/geograph/

■ UNIVERSITY OF NEBRASKA AT OMAHA

Graduate Studies and Research, College of Arts and Sciences, Department of Geography and Geology, Omaha, NE 68182

AWARDS Geographic information science (Certificate); geography (MA). Part-time programs available.

Faculty: 11 full-time (1 woman).
Students: 9 full-time (5 women), 21 part-time (9 women); includes 1 minority (Native American), 3 international. Average age 36. 28 applicants, 86% accepted, 19 enrolled. In 2001, 2 degrees awarded.
Degree requirements: For master's, thesis (for some programs), comprehensive exam.
Entrance requirements: For master's, GRE, minimum GPA of 3.0. *Application deadline:* For fall admission, 7/1 (priority date); for spring admission, 12/1 (priority date). Applications are processed on a rolling basis. *Application fee:* $35. Electronic applications accepted.
Expenses: Tuition, state resident: part-time $116 per credit hour. Tuition, nonresident: part-time $291 per credit hour. Required fees: $13 per credit hour. $4 per semester. One-time fee: $52 part-time.
Financial support: In 2001–02, 17 students received support; fellowships, research assistantships, teaching assistantships, Federal Work-Study, institutionally sponsored loans, scholarships/grants, tuition waivers (partial), and unspecified assistantships available. Support available to part-time students. Financial award application deadline: 3/1; financial award applicants required to submit FAFSA.
Dr. George Engelman, Chairperson, 402-554-2662.

■ UNIVERSITY OF NEBRASKA–LINCOLN

Graduate College, College of Arts and Sciences, Department of Anthropology and Geography, Program in Geography, Lincoln, NE 68588

AWARDS MA, PhD.

Faculty: 8.
Students: 38 (9 women); includes 2 minority (1 Asian American or Pacific Islander, 1 Hispanic American) 10 international. Average age 31. 25 applicants, 44% accepted, 7 enrolled. In 2001, 9 master's, 3 doctorates awarded.
Degree requirements: For master's, thesis optional; for doctorate, thesis/dissertation, comprehensive exam.
Entrance requirements: For master's and doctorate, GRE General Test, TOEFL. *Application deadline:* For fall admission, 4/15; for spring admission, 10/15. *Application fee:* $35. Electronic applications accepted.
Expenses: Tuition, state resident: full-time $2,412; part-time $134 per credit. Tuition, nonresident: full-time $6,223; part-time $346 per credit. Tuition and fees vary according to course load.
Financial support: In 2001–02, 1 fellowship, 12 research assistantships, 6 teaching assistantships were awarded. Federal Work-Study, health care benefits, and unspecified assistantships also available. Support available to part-time students. Financial award application deadline: 1/15.
Faculty research: Climatology, historical-cultural geography, geographic information systems/cartography/remote sensing, human geography, Great Plains studies.
Application contact: Dr. Stephen Lavin, Graduate Committee Chair, 402-472-2865. *Web site:* http://www.unl.edu/unlgeog/home.htm

■ UNIVERSITY OF NEVADA, RENO

Graduate School, College of Arts and Science, Department of Geography, Reno, NV 89557

AWARDS MS.

Faculty: 9.

University of Nevada, Reno (continued)
Students: 8 full-time (2 women), 11 part-time (5 women), 1 international. Average age 33. In 2001, 1 degree awarded.
Degree requirements: For master's, thesis.
Entrance requirements: For master's, GRE General Test, TOEFL, minimum GPA of 3.0. *Application deadline:* For fall admission, 3/1 (priority date). Applications are processed on a rolling basis. *Application fee:* $40.
Expenses: Tuition, state resident: full-time $2,067; part-time $108 per credit. Tuition, nonresident: full-time $9,282; part-time $109 per credit. Required fees: $57 per semester. Tuition and fees vary according to course load.
Financial support: In 2001–02, 6 teaching assistantships were awarded; research assistantships available. Financial award application deadline: 3/1.
Faculty research: Natural resources, education, climatology, biogeography, ethnic/cultural geography.
Dr. Franco Biondi, Graduate Program Director, 775-784-6921. *Web site:* http://www.geography.unr.edu/

■ UNIVERSITY OF NEW MEXICO

Graduate School, College of Arts and Sciences, Department of Geography, Albuquerque, NM 87131-2039

AWARDS MS. Part-time programs available.

Faculty: 4 full-time (0 women), 7 part-time/adjunct (1 woman).
Students: 7 full-time (1 woman), 10 part-time (4 women); includes 1 minority (Hispanic American). Average age 37. 5 applicants, 80% accepted, 1 enrolled. In 2001, 10 degrees awarded.
Degree requirements: For master's, thesis optional.
Entrance requirements: For master's, GRE. *Application deadline:* For fall admission, 4/15 (priority date); for spring admission, 11/30. *Application fee:* $40.
Expenses: Tuition, state resident: full-time $2,771; part-time $115 per credit hour. Tuition, nonresident: full-time $11,207; part-time $467 per credit hour. Required fees: $570; $24 per credit hour. Part-time tuition and fees vary according to course load and program.
Financial support: In 2001–02, 8 students received support. Federal Work-Study, institutionally sponsored loans, scholarships/grants, traineeships, health care benefits, tuition waivers (partial), and unspecified assistantships available. Support available to part-time students. Financial award application deadline: 3/1; financial award applicants required to submit FAFSA.
Faculty research: Geographic information systems, water resources, economic development, remote sensing, biogeography, climatology. *Total annual research expenditures:* $290,951.
Dr. Bradley Thomas Cullen, Acting Chair, 505-277-3643, *Fax:* 505-277-3614, *E-mail:* bcullen@unm.edu.
Application contact: Jazmin K. Knight, Administrator I, 505-277-5041, *Fax:* 505-277-1626, *E-mail:* jkknight@unm.edu. *Web site:* http://www.unm.edu/~geog/

■ UNIVERSITY OF NEW ORLEANS

Graduate School, College of Liberal Arts, Department of Geography, New Orleans, LA 70148

AWARDS MA.

Faculty: 1 full-time (0 women).
Students: 8 full-time (5 women), 17 part-time (10 women); includes 2 minority (1 African American, 1 Asian American or Pacific Islander). Average age 37. 7 applicants, 43% accepted, 3 enrolled. In 2001, 1 degree awarded.
Entrance requirements: For master's, GRE General Test. *Application deadline:* For fall admission, 7/1 (priority date); for spring admission, 11/15 (priority date). Applications are processed on a rolling basis. *Application fee:* $20. Electronic applications accepted.
Expenses: Tuition, state resident: full-time $2,748; part-time $435 per credit. Tuition, nonresident: full-time $9,792; part-time $1,773 per credit.
Financial support: Applicants required to submit FAFSA.
Dr. Peter Yaukey, Graduate Coordinator, 504-280-7133, *E-mail:* pyaukey@uno.edu.
Application contact: Dr. Mahtab Lodhi, Graduate Coordinator, 504-280-6329, *E-mail:* mlodhi@uno.edu.

■ THE UNIVERSITY OF NORTH CAROLINA AT CHAPEL HILL

Graduate School, College of Arts and Sciences, Department of Geography, Chapel Hill, NC 27599

AWARDS MA, PhD.

Faculty: 18 full-time (4 women), 1 part-time/adjunct (0 women).
Students: 31 full-time (12 women), 7 part-time (5 women); includes 7 minority (2 African Americans, 5 Asian Americans or Pacific Islanders). Average age 25. 51 applicants, 25% accepted, 11 enrolled. In 2001, 4 master's, 6 doctorates awarded.
Degree requirements: For master's, one foreign language, thesis, comprehensive exam; for doctorate, 2 foreign languages, thesis/dissertation, comprehensive exam.
Entrance requirements: For master's and doctorate, GRE General Test, minimum GPA of 3.0. *Application deadline:* For fall admission, 1/1 (priority date). Applications are processed on a rolling basis. *Application fee:* $55.
Expenses: Tuition, state resident: full-time $2,864. Tuition, nonresident: full-time $12,030.
Financial support: In 2001–02, 2 fellowships with full tuition reimbursements (averaging $12,000 per year), 6 research assistantships with full tuition reimbursements (averaging $14,000 per year), 9 teaching assistantships with full tuition reimbursements (averaging $12,000 per year) were awarded. Traineeships, health care benefits, and unspecified assistantships also available. Financial award application deadline: 3/1.
Faculty research: Geographic information systems, climatology, hydrology, population research, Latino immigration. *Total annual research expenditures:* $300,000.
Dr. Larry E Band, Chairman, 919-962-3921, *Fax:* 919-962-1537, *E-mail:* lband@email.unc.edu.
Application contact: Dr. Thomas M. Whitmore, Director, Graduate Program, 919-962-3916, *Fax:* 919-962-1537, *E-mail:* whitmore@email.unc.edu.

■ THE UNIVERSITY OF NORTH CAROLINA AT CHARLOTTE

Graduate School, College of Arts and Sciences, Department of Geography and Earth Sciences, Charlotte, NC 28223-0001

AWARDS Earth sciences (MS); geography (MA). Part-time and evening/weekend programs available.

Faculty: 16 full-time (2 women), 4 part-time/adjunct (1 woman).
Students: 22 full-time (6 women), 39 part-time (12 women); includes 3 minority (2 African Americans, 1 Asian American or Pacific Islander). Average age 30. 9 applicants, 89% accepted, 7 enrolled. In 2001, 13 degrees awarded.
Degree requirements: For master's, project.
Entrance requirements: For master's, GRE General Test or MAT, Doppelt Math Reasoning Test, minimum GPA of 3.0 in undergraduate major, 2.75 overall. *Application deadline:* For fall admission, 7/15; for spring admission, 11/15. Applications are processed on a rolling basis. *Application fee:* $35. Electronic applications accepted.
Expenses: Tuition, state resident: full-time $1,483; part-time $371 per year. Tuition, nonresident: full-time $9,850; part-time $2,463 per year. Required fees: $1,043; $277 per year. Tuition and fees vary according to course load.
Financial support: In 2001–02, 4 fellowships (averaging $1,633 per year), 9 research assistantships, 12 teaching assistantships were awarded. Career-related internships or fieldwork, Federal Work-Study, institutionally sponsored loans, scholarships/grants, and unspecified assistantships also available. Support available to part-time students. Financial award application deadline: 4/1; financial award applicants required to submit FAFSA.

Faculty research: Location analysis; applications of GIS technology; community planning and development; regional economic modeling; retail geography.
Dr. Owen J. Furuseth, Chair, 704-687-2293, *Fax:* 704-687-3182, *E-mail:* ojifuruse@email.uncc.edu.
Application contact: Kathy Barringer, Director of Graduate Admissions, 704-687-3366, *Fax:* 704-687-3279, *E-mail:* gradadm@email.uncc.edu. *Web site:* http://www.uncc.edu/gradmiss/

■ THE UNIVERSITY OF NORTH CAROLINA AT GREENSBORO

Graduate School, College of Arts and Sciences, Department of Geography, Greensboro, NC 27412-5001

AWARDS MA.

Faculty: 9 full-time (1 woman).
Students: 10 full-time (3 women), 20 part-time (8 women); includes 5 minority (4 African Americans, 1 Hispanic American). 14 applicants, 86% accepted, 12 enrolled. In 2001, 7 degrees awarded.
Degree requirements: For master's, thesis or alternative, comprehensive exam.
Entrance requirements: For master's, GRE General Test, TOEFL. *Application deadline:* For fall admission, 6/15; for spring admission, 3/15. *Application fee:* $35.
Expenses: Tuition, state resident: part-time $344 per course. Tuition, nonresident: part-time $2,457 per course.
Financial support: In 2001–02, 10 research assistantships with full tuition reimbursements (averaging $4,065 per year) were awarded; teaching assistantships with full tuition reimbursements, career-related internships or fieldwork, Federal Work-Study, scholarships/grants, and traineeships also available. Support available to part-time students.
Dr. D. Gordon Bennett, Head, 336-334-5338, *Fax:* 336-334-5864, *E-mail:* dgbennet@uncg.edu.
Application contact: Dr. James Lynch, Director of Graduate Recruitment and Information Services, 336-334-4881, *Fax:* 336-334-4424. *Web site:* http://www.uncg.edu/geo/

■ UNIVERSITY OF NORTH DAKOTA

Graduate School, College of Arts and Sciences, Department of Geography, Grand Forks, ND 58202

AWARDS MA, MS. Part-time programs available.

Faculty: 5 full-time (0 women).
Students: 1 full-time (0 women), 13 part-time (2 women). 7 applicants, 86% accepted, 4 enrolled. In 2001, 6 degrees awarded.
Degree requirements: For master's, thesis or alternative, comprehensive exam.
Entrance requirements: For master's, TOEFL, minimum GPA of 3.0. *Application deadline:* For fall admission, 3/1 (priority date). Applications are processed on a rolling basis. *Application fee:* $30.
Expenses: Tuition, state resident: full-time $3,298. Tuition, nonresident: full-time $7,998.
Financial support: In 2001–02, 9 students received support, including 6 teaching assistantships with full tuition reimbursements available (averaging $8,775 per year); fellowships, research assistantships, Federal Work-Study, institutionally sponsored loans, scholarships/grants, tuition waivers (full and partial), and unspecified assistantships also available. Support available to part-time students. Financial award application deadline: 3/15; financial award applicants required to submit FAFSA.
Faculty research: Regional and urban development, environmental geography, geographic education, geographic techniques.
Dr. Mohammad Hemmasi, Chairperson, 701-777-4592, *Fax:* 701-777-6195, *E-mail:* mohammad_hemmasi@und.nodak.edu. *Web site:* http://www.und.edu/dept/grad/depts/geography/

■ UNIVERSITY OF NORTHERN IOWA

Graduate College, College of Social and Behavioral Sciences, Department of Geography, Cedar Falls, IA 50614

AWARDS MA. Part-time programs available.

Students: 8 full-time (2 women), 6 part-time, 2 international. 12 applicants, 100% accepted. In 2001, 2 degrees awarded.
Degree requirements: For master's, thesis.
Application deadline: For fall admission, 8/1 (priority date). Applications are processed on a rolling basis. *Application fee:* $20 ($50 for international students).
Expenses: Tuition, state resident: full-time $3,704; part-time $206 per credit hour. Tuition, nonresident: full-time $9,122; part-time $501 per credit hour. Required fees: $324; $108 per semester. Part-time tuition and fees vary according to course load.
Financial support: Career-related internships or fieldwork, Federal Work-Study, scholarships/grants, and tuition waivers (full and partial) available. Support available to part-time students. Financial award application deadline: 3/1.
Dr. Philip W. Suckling, Head, 319-273-2772, *Fax:* 319-273-7103, *E-mail:* philip.suckling@uni.edu. *Web site:* http://www.uni.edu/geography/

■ UNIVERSITY OF NORTH TEXAS

Robert B. Toulouse School of Graduate Studies, College of Arts and Sciences, Department of Geography, Denton, TX 76203

AWARDS MS.

Faculty: 9 full-time (1 woman), 2 part-time/adjunct (1 woman).
Students: 14 full-time (8 women), 9 part-time (3 women); includes 3 minority (2 Hispanic Americans, 1 Native American), 5 international. In 2001, 11 degrees awarded.
Entrance requirements: For master's, GRE General Test. *Application fee:* $25 ($50 for international students).
Expenses: Tuition, state resident: part-time $186 per hour. Tuition, nonresident: part-time $319 per hour. Required fees: $88; $21 per hour.
Dr. C. Reid Ferring, Chair, 940-565-2091, *Fax:* 940-369-7550.
Application contact: Dr. Donald Lyons, Graduate Adviser, 940-565-2091, *Fax:* 940-369-7550, *E-mail:* dlyons@unt.edu.

■ UNIVERSITY OF OKLAHOMA

Graduate College, College of Geosciences, Department of Geography, Norman, OK 73019-0390

AWARDS MA, PhD. Part-time programs available.

Faculty: 8 full-time (0 women), 1 (woman) part-time/adjunct.
Students: 18 full-time (8 women), 16 part-time (5 women); includes 1 minority (Native American), 6 international. 3 applicants, 100% accepted, 2 enrolled. In 2001, 3 master's, 3 doctorates awarded.
Degree requirements: For master's, thesis, oral and written exams; for doctorate, one foreign language, thesis/dissertation, general exams.
Entrance requirements: For master's, TOEFL, minimum GPA of 3.0, writing sample; for doctorate, TOEFL. *Application deadline:* For fall admission, 2/1; for spring admission, 12/1. Applications are processed on a rolling basis. *Application fee:* $25 ($50 for international students).
Expenses: Tuition, state resident: full-time $2,208; part-time $92 per credit hour. Tuition, nonresident: part-time $297 per credit hour. Tuition and fees vary according to course level, course load and program.
Financial support: In 2001–02, 6 fellowships (averaging $5,000 per year), 6 research assistantships with partial tuition reimbursements (averaging $10,960 per year), 12 teaching assistantships with partial tuition reimbursements (averaging $13,445 per year) were awarded. Federal Work-Study and tuition waivers (partial) also available. Financial award application deadline: 2/1; financial award applicants required to submit FAFSA.
Faculty research: Cultural geography, economic geography, physical geography,

University of Oklahoma (continued)
geotechniques. *Total annual research expenditures:* $391,299.
Bret Wallach, Chairperson, 405-325-5325, *Fax:* 405-325-3148, *E-mail:* bwallach@ou.edu.
Application contact: Dr. Sally Gros, Graduate Liaison, 405-325-9193, *Fax:* 405-325-6090, *E-mail:* sgros@ou.edu.

■ UNIVERSITY OF OREGON

Graduate School, College of Arts and Sciences, Department of Geography, Eugene, OR 97403

AWARDS MA, MS, PhD.

Faculty: 12 full-time (5 women).
Students: 28 full-time (15 women), 8 part-time (4 women); includes 5 minority (2 Hispanic Americans, 3 Native Americans), 1 international. 36 applicants, 25% accepted. In 2001, 5 master's, 1 doctorate awarded.
Degree requirements: For master's and doctorate, one foreign language, thesis/dissertation.
Entrance requirements: For master's and doctorate, GRE General Test, TOEFL, minimum GPA of 3.0. *Application deadline:* For fall admission, 1/15. *Application fee:* $50.
Expenses: Tuition, state resident: full-time $4,968; part-time $501 per credit hour. Tuition, nonresident: full-time $8,400; part-time $691 per credit hour.
Financial support: In 2001–02, 30 teaching assistantships were awarded; career-related internships or fieldwork and Federal Work-Study also available. Financial award application deadline: 1/15.
Faculty research: Place-name research, past climates, Quaternary environments, plant diffusions, population redistributions.
Cathy Whitlock, Head, 541-346-4555.
Application contact: Mary Milo, Admissions Contact, 541-346-4555, *E-mail:* uogeog@darkwing.uoregon.edu. *Web site:* http://geography.uoregon.edu/

■ UNIVERSITY OF SOUTH CAROLINA

The Graduate School, College of Liberal Arts, Department of Geography, Columbia, SC 29208

AWARDS Geography (MA, MS, PhD); geography education (IMA). IMA and MAT offered in cooperation with the College of Education. Part-time programs available.

Faculty: 20 full-time (4 women), 2 part-time/adjunct (0 women).
Students: 48 full-time (16 women), 17 part-time (5 women); includes 4 minority (1 African American, 1 Asian American or Pacific Islander, 2 Hispanic Americans), 12 international. Average age 27. 84 applicants, 52% accepted, 21 enrolled. In 2001, 6 master's, 5 doctorates awarded.
Degree requirements: For master's, thesis (for some programs), comprehensive exam, registration; for doctorate, thesis/dissertation, comprehensive exam, registration. *Median time to degree:* Master's–2 years full-time; doctorate–4 years full-time.
Entrance requirements: For master's, GRE General Test; for doctorate, GRE General Test, master's degree. *Application deadline:* For fall admission, 2/15 (priority date); for spring admission, 11/1 (priority date). Applications are processed on a rolling basis. *Application fee:* $35. Electronic applications accepted.
Expenses: Tuition, state resident: full-time $4,434. Tuition, nonresident: full-time $9,854. Tuition and fees vary according to program.
Financial support: In 2001–02, 42 students received support, including 3 fellowships (averaging $9,000 per year), 25 research assistantships (averaging $9,500 per year), 13 teaching assistantships (averaging $9,500 per year); career-related internships or fieldwork, Federal Work-Study, scholarships/grants, traineeships, tuition waivers (full), and unspecified assistantships also available. Financial award application deadline: 2/15.
Faculty research: Geographic information processing; economic, cultural, physical, and environmental geography. *Total annual research expenditures:* $917,949.
Dr. David J. Cowen, Chair, 803-777-5234, *Fax:* 803-777-4972, *E-mail:* cowend@gwm.sc.edu.
Application contact: Dr. John F. Jakubs, Director of Graduate Studies, 803-777-6604, *Fax:* 803-777-4972, *E-mail:* jjakubs@sc.edu. *Web site:* http://www.cla.sc.edu/GEOG/index.html

■ UNIVERSITY OF SOUTHERN CALIFORNIA

Graduate School, College of Letters, Arts and Sciences, Department of Geography, Los Angeles, CA 90089

AWARDS MA, MS, PhD. Postbaccalaureate distance learning degree programs offered.

Degree requirements: For master's and doctorate, thesis/dissertation.
Entrance requirements: For master's and doctorate, GRE General Test.
Expenses: Tuition: Full-time $25,060; part-time $844 per unit. Required fees: $473.
Faculty research: Landscape dynamics, geomorphology, geographic information science, urban geography and nature-society relations.

■ UNIVERSITY OF SOUTHERN MISSISSIPPI

Graduate School, College of International and Continuing Education, Department of Geography, Hattiesburg, MS 39406

AWARDS MS. Part-time programs available.

Faculty: 6 full-time (0 women).
Students: 7 full-time (1 woman), 7 part-time (4 women). Average age 31. 6 applicants, 100% accepted. In 2001, 5 degrees awarded.
Degree requirements: For master's, thesis or alternative, internships.
Entrance requirements: For master's, GMAT, GRE General Test, minimum GPA of 3.0. *Application deadline:* For fall admission, 3/15; for spring admission, 1/3. Applications are processed on a rolling basis. *Application fee:* $0 ($25 for international students). Electronic applications accepted.
Expenses: Tuition, state resident: full-time $3,416; part-time $190 per credit hour. Tuition, nonresident: full-time $7,932; part-time $441 per credit hour.
Financial support: Fellowships, teaching assistantships, career-related internships or fieldwork, Federal Work-Study, and institutionally sponsored loans available. Financial award application deadline: 3/15.
Faculty research: City and regional planning, geographic techniques, physical geography, human geography.
Dr. Clifton Dixon, Chair, 601-266-4729, *E-mail:* c.dixon@usm.edu.
Application contact: Ken Panton, Graduate Coordinator, 601-266-6519.

■ UNIVERSITY OF SOUTH FLORIDA

College of Graduate Studies, College of Arts and Sciences, Department of Geography, Tampa, FL 33620-9951

AWARDS MA. Part-time and evening/weekend programs available.

Faculty: 15 full-time (3 women).
Students: 10 full-time (7 women), 10 part-time (4 women). Average age 31. 13 applicants, 54% accepted, 5 enrolled. In 2001, 2 degrees awarded.
Degree requirements: For master's, thesis, written exam.
Entrance requirements: For master's, GRE General Test, minimum GPA of 3.0 in last 60 hours. *Application deadline:* For fall admission, 6/1; for spring admission, 10/15. *Application fee:* $20.
Expenses: Tuition, state resident: part-time $166 per credit hour. Tuition, nonresident: part-time $573 per credit hour. Required fees: $17 per term.
Financial support: Fellowships, research assistantships with partial tuition reimbursements, teaching assistantships with partial tuition reimbursements, career-related internships or fieldwork, Federal Work-Study, and institutionally sponsored loans available. Support available to part-time students. Financial award applicants required to submit FAFSA.
Faculty research: Natural hazards, geographic information systems models, soil contamination, urban geography and social theory,. *Total annual research expenditures:* $243,479.

Dr. Graham A. Tobin, Chairperson, 813-974-4932, *Fax:* 813-974-4808, *E-mail:* gtobin@chuma1.cas.usf.edu.
Application contact: Dr. Martin Bosman, Graduate Coordinator, 813-974-4808, *Fax:* 813-974-4808, *E-mail:* mbosman@chuma1.cas.usf.edu. *Web site:* http://www.cas.usf.edu/geography/index.html

■ THE UNIVERSITY OF TENNESSEE

Graduate School, College of Arts and Sciences, Department of Geography, Knoxville, TN 37996

AWARDS MS, PhD.

Faculty: 12 full-time (3 women).
Students: 39 full-time (14 women), 9 part-time (3 women); includes 1 minority (Hispanic American), 3 international. 28 applicants, 64% accepted. In 2001, 1 master's, 4 doctorates awarded.
Degree requirements: For master's, thesis or alternative; for doctorate, thesis/dissertation.
Entrance requirements: For master's and doctorate, GRE General Test, TOEFL, minimum GPA of 2.7. *Application deadline:* For fall admission, 2/1 (priority date). Applications are processed on a rolling basis. *Application fee:* $35. Electronic applications accepted.
Expenses: Tuition, state resident: full-time $4,280; part-time $233 per hour. Tuition, nonresident: full-time $12,066; part-time $666 per hour. Tuition and fees vary according to program.
Financial support: In 2001–02, 14 research assistantships, 24 teaching assistantships were awarded. Fellowships, Federal Work-Study, institutionally sponsored loans, and unspecified assistantships also available. Financial award application deadline: 2/1; financial award applicants required to submit FAFSA.
Dr. Bruce Ralston, Head, 865-974-2418, *Fax:* 865-974-6025, *E-mail:* bralston@utk.edu.
Application contact: Dr. Charles Aiken, Graduate Representative, *E-mail:* csaiken@utk.edu.

■ THE UNIVERSITY OF TEXAS AT AUSTIN

Graduate School, College of Liberal Arts, Department of Geography, Austin, TX 78712-1111

AWARDS MA, PhD, MSCRP/PhD.

Faculty: 17 full-time (4 women).
Students: 44 full-time (21 women); includes 7 minority (3 Asian Americans or Pacific Islanders, 4 Hispanic Americans), 1 international. Average age 34. 66 applicants, 44% accepted. In 2001, 4 master's, 3 doctorates awarded.
Degree requirements: For master's, thesis or alternative; for doctorate, thesis/dissertation.
Entrance requirements: For master's and doctorate, GRE General Test. *Application deadline:* For fall admission, 2/1. *Application fee:* $50 ($75 for international students). Electronic applications accepted.
Expenses: Tuition, state resident: full-time $3,159. Tuition, nonresident: full-time $6,957. Tuition and fees vary according to program.
Financial support: In 2001–02, 22 students received support, including 2 fellowships with partial tuition reimbursements available (averaging $12,000 per year), 2 research assistantships with partial tuition reimbursements available (averaging $11,000 per year), 16 teaching assistantships with partial tuition reimbursements available (averaging $10,000 per year); career-related internships or fieldwork also available. Financial award application deadline: 2/1.
Faculty research: Cultural and historical geography, environmental and physical geography, human-environment interactions, electronic technology and hypermedia, international area studies.
Dr. Gregory W. Knapp, Chairman, 512-232-1588, *E-mail:* utgeog@uts.cc.utexas.edu.
Application contact: William E. Doolittle, Graduate Adviser, 512-471-5116, *E-mail:* dolitl@mail.utexas.edu. *Web site:* http://www.utexas.edu/depts/grg/main.html

■ THE UNIVERSITY OF TEXAS AT SAN ANTONIO

College of Liberal and Fine Arts, Department of Political Science and Geography, San Antonio, TX 78249-0617

AWARDS Political science (MA). Part-time and evening/weekend programs available.

Faculty: 15 full-time (2 women).
Students: 9 full-time (5 women), 20 part-time (13 women); includes 15 minority (1 Asian American or Pacific Islander, 14 Hispanic Americans), 1 international. Average age 33. 21 applicants, 90% accepted, 14 enrolled. In 2001, 1 degree awarded.
Degree requirements: For master's, thesis optional. *Median time to degree:* Master's–3 years full-time.
Entrance requirements: For master's, GRE General Test. *Application deadline:* For fall admission, 7/1 (priority date); for spring admission, 11/1. Applications are processed on a rolling basis. *Application fee:* $25 ($50 for international students). Electronic applications accepted.
Expenses: Tuition, state resident: full-time $2,268; part-time $126 per credit hour. Tuition, nonresident: full-time $6,066; part-time $337 per credit hour. Required fees: $781. Tuition and fees vary according to course load.
Financial support: In 2001–02, 1 research assistantship was awarded; career-related internships or fieldwork, Federal Work-Study, scholarships/grants, and readers/graders also available.
Dr. Richard Gambitta, Department Chair, 210-458-5883, *Fax:* 210-458-4629, *E-mail:* mluna@utsa.edu.
Application contact: Elsie Clay, Administrative Assistant I, 210-458-4627, *Fax:* 210-458-4629, *E-mail:* eclay@utsa.edu.

■ UNIVERSITY OF TOLEDO

Graduate School, College of Arts and Sciences, Department of Geography and Planning, Toledo, OH 43606-3398

AWARDS Geography (MA); planning (MA). Part-time programs available.

Faculty: 7.
Students: 24 full-time (9 women), 6 part-time (5 women); includes 5 minority (4 African Americans, 1 Native American), 4 international. Average age 30. 20 applicants, 60% accepted. In 2001, 11 degrees awarded.
Degree requirements: For master's, thesis.
Entrance requirements: For master's, GRE General Test. *Application deadline:* For fall admission, 3/15 (priority date). Applications are processed on a rolling basis. *Application fee:* $30. Electronic applications accepted.
Expenses: Tuition, state resident: full-time $7,278; part-time $303 per hour. Tuition, nonresident: full-time $15,731; part-time $699 per hour. Required fees: $43 per hour.
Financial support: In 2001–02, 4 research assistantships, 10 teaching assistantships were awarded. Career-related internships or fieldwork, institutionally sponsored loans, and tuition waivers (full) also available. Support available to part-time students. Financial award application deadline: 4/1.
Dr. Samuel Aryeetey-Attoh, Chair, 419-530-4709, *Fax:* 419-530-7919, *E-mail:* sattoh@utnet.utoledo.edu.
Application contact: Dr. Peter Lindquist, Graduate Advisor, 419-530-2545, *Fax:* 419-530-7919, *E-mail:* plindqu@uoft02.utoledo.edu.

■ UNIVERSITY OF UTAH

Graduate School, College of Social and Behavioral Science, Department of Geography, Salt Lake City, UT 84112-1107

AWARDS MA, MS, PhD. Part-time programs available.

Faculty: 10 full-time (1 woman).
Students: 21 full-time (7 women), 28 part-time (13 women); includes 5 minority (all Asian Americans or Pacific Islanders), 5 international. Average age 33. 54 applicants, 46% accepted. In 2001, 11 master's, 2 doctorates awarded.

University of Utah (continued)
Degree requirements: For master's, thesis or alternative; for doctorate, one foreign language, thesis/dissertation.
Entrance requirements: For master's and doctorate, GRE General Test, TOEFL. *Application deadline:* For fall admission, 7/1. *Application fee:* $40 ($60 for international students).
Expenses: Tuition, state resident: part-time $320 per semester hour. Tuition, nonresident: part-time $1,135 per semester hour. Required fees: $143 per semester hour. Tuition and fees vary according to course load, degree level and program.
Financial support: Fellowships, research assistantships, career-related internships or fieldwork available.
Faculty research: Quaternary studies, urban economic studies, natural resources analysis, remote sensing.
Dr. Tom Kontuly, Director of Graduate Studies, 801-581-8218.
Application contact: Spike Hampson, Advisor, 801-585-5698, *E-mail:* hampson@geog.utah.edu.

■ UNIVERSITY OF VERMONT

Graduate College, College of Arts and Sciences, Department of Geography, Burlington, VT 05405

AWARDS MA, MAT.

Degree requirements: For master's, thesis.
Entrance requirements: For master's, GRE General Test, TOEFL.
Expenses: Tuition, state resident: part-time $335 per credit. Tuition, nonresident: part-time $838 per credit.
Faculty research: Historical geography, cartography, remote sensing.

■ UNIVERSITY OF WASHINGTON

Graduate School, College of Arts and Sciences, Department of Geography, Seattle, WA 98195

AWARDS MA, PhD.

Faculty: 18 full-time (7 women).
Students: 61 full-time (36 women); includes 17 minority (1 African American, 11 Asian Americans or Pacific Islanders, 4 Hispanic Americans, 1 Native American), 15 international. Average age 26. 95 applicants, 33% accepted, 17 enrolled. In 2001, 9 master's, 5 doctorates awarded.
Degree requirements: For master's and doctorate, thesis/dissertation. *Median time to degree:* Master's–2.8 years full-time; doctorate–5.5 years full-time.
Entrance requirements: For master's and doctorate, GRE General Test, TOEFL. *Application deadline:* For fall admission, 1/15 (priority date). Applications are processed on a rolling basis. *Application fee:* $50. Electronic applications accepted.
Expenses: Tuition, state resident: full-time $5,539. Tuition, nonresident: full-time $14,376. Required fees: $390. Tuition and fees vary according to course load and program.
Financial support: In 2001–02, 4 fellowships with full tuition reimbursements (averaging $10,250 per year), 9 research assistantships with full tuition reimbursements (averaging $12,725 per year), 17 teaching assistantships with full tuition reimbursements (averaging $11,256 per year) were awarded. Career-related internships or fieldwork, Federal Work-Study, institutionally sponsored loans, scholarships/grants, and tuition waivers (partial) also available. Financial award application deadline: 1/15; financial award applicants required to submit FAFSA.
Faculty research: Globalization and social theory, nature and society, regional economic development, urban patterns and processes, geographic information systems.
J. W. Harrington, Chair, 206-616-3821, *Fax:* 206-543-3313, *E-mail:* jwh@u.washington.edu.
Application contact: Richard Roth, Assistant to the Chair, 206-543-3246, *Fax:* 206-543-3313, *E-mail:* rroth@u.washington.edu. *Web site:* http://depts.u.washington.edu/geog/

■ UNIVERSITY OF WISCONSIN–MADISON

Graduate School, College of Letters and Science, Department of Geography, Madison, WI 53706-1380

AWARDS Cartography and geographic information systems (MS); geographic information systems (Certificate); geography (MS, PhD). Part-time programs available.

Faculty: 18 full-time (3 women).
Students: 77 full-time (20 women), 22 part-time (10 women); includes 4 minority (1 African American, 1 Asian American or Pacific Islander, 2 Hispanic Americans), 10 international. 108 applicants, 55% accepted. In 2001, 8 master's, 2 doctorates awarded.
Degree requirements: For master's and doctorate, thesis/dissertation; for Certificate, internship.
Entrance requirements: For master's and doctorate, GRE General Test, minimum GPA of 3.25. *Application deadline:* For fall admission, 12/15 (priority date). Applications are processed on a rolling basis. *Application fee:* $45. Electronic applications accepted.
Expenses: Tuition, state resident: full-time $7,361; part-time $399 per credit. Tuition, nonresident: full-time $20,499; part-time $1,282 per credit. Required fees: $34 per credit. Full-time tuition and fees vary according to course load, program, reciprocity agreements and student level.
Financial support: In 2001–02, 57 students received support, including 9 fellowships with full tuition reimbursements available (averaging $15,000 per year), 2 research assistantships with full tuition reimbursements available, 22 teaching assistantships with full tuition reimbursements available (averaging $8,436 per year); career-related internships or fieldwork, Federal Work-Study, and unspecified assistantships also available. Financial award application deadline: 12/15.
Faculty research: Physical geography, urban/historical geography, people-environment, history of cartography, GIS.
James E. Burt, Chair, 608-262-2138, *Fax:* 608-265-3991, *E-mail:* jburt@geography.wisc.edu.
Application contact: Roxanne Moermond, Graduate Student Coordinator, 608-262-3861, *Fax:* 608-265-3991, *E-mail:* gradschool@geography.wisc.edu. *Web site:* http://www.geography.wisc.edu/

■ UNIVERSITY OF WISCONSIN–MILWAUKEE

Graduate School, College of Letters and Sciences, Department of Geography, Milwaukee, WI 53201-0413

AWARDS MA, MS, MLIS/MA.

Faculty: 11 full-time (4 women).
Students: 14 full-time (7 women), 16 part-time (4 women); includes 4 minority (1 African American, 1 Asian American or Pacific Islander, 2 Hispanic Americans), 9 international. 15 applicants, 60% accepted. In 2001, 3 degrees awarded.
Degree requirements: For master's, thesis.
Application deadline: For fall admission, 1/1 (priority date); for spring admission, 9/1. Applications are processed on a rolling basis. *Application fee:* $45 ($75 for international students).
Expenses: Tuition, state resident: full-time $6,180; part-time $535 per credit. Tuition, nonresident: full-time $19,482; part-time $1,366 per credit. Tuition and fees vary according to course load, program and reciprocity agreements.
Financial support: In 2001–02, 2 fellowships, 1 research assistantship, 8 teaching assistantships were awarded. Career-related internships or fieldwork and unspecified assistantships also available. Support available to part-time students. Financial award application deadline: 4/15.
Judith Kenny, Representative, 414-229-4866, *Fax:* 414-229-3981, *E-mail:* jkenny@uwm.edu. *Web site:* http://uwm.edu/dept/geography

■ UNIVERSITY OF WYOMING

Graduate School, College of Arts and Sciences, Department of Geography and Recreation, Laramie, WY 82071

AWARDS Geography (MA, MP, MST); geography/water resources (MA); rural planning and natural resources (MP), including community and regional planning and natural resources. Postbaccalaureate distance learning degree programs offered (minimal on-campus study).

Faculty: 8 full-time (1 woman), 1 part-time/adjunct (0 women).
Students: 11 full-time (3 women), 14 part-time (9 women); includes 1 minority (Hispanic American), 1 international. 17 applicants, 71% accepted. In 2001, 8 degrees awarded.
Degree requirements: For master's, thesis or alternative.
Entrance requirements: For master's, GRE General Test, minimum GPA of 3.0. *Application deadline:* For fall admission, 2/15. Applications are processed on a rolling basis. *Application fee:* $40.
Expenses: Tuition, state resident: full-time $2,895; part-time $161 per credit hour. Tuition, nonresident: full-time $8,367; part-time $465 per credit hour. Required fees: $491; $10 per credit hour. $2 per credit hour. Tuition and fees vary according to course load and program.
Financial support: In 2001–02, 2 research assistantships with full and partial tuition reimbursements (averaging $8,797 per year), 5 teaching assistantships with full tuition reimbursements (averaging $8,797 per year) were awarded. Career-related internships or fieldwork and Federal Work-Study also available. Financial award application deadline: 3/1.
Faculty research: Landscape ecology, landscape change, public land management, rural and small town planning. *Total annual research expenditures:* $347,000.
Dr. John Allen, Head, 307-766-3311.

■ UTAH STATE UNIVERSITY

School of Graduate Studies, College of Natural Resources, Department of Geography and Earth Resources, Logan, UT 84322

AWARDS Geography (MA, MS).

Faculty: 10 full-time (2 women), 4 part-time/adjunct (2 women).
Students: 6 full-time (2 women), 14 part-time (5 women), 3 international. Average age 32. 7 applicants, 43% accepted. In 2001, 5 degrees awarded.
Degree requirements: For master's, thesis (for some programs), comprehensive exam.
Entrance requirements: For master's, GRE General Test, TOEFL, minimum GPA of 3.0. *Application deadline:* For fall admission, 6/15 (priority date); for spring admission, 10/15. Applications are processed on a rolling basis. *Application fee:* $40.
Expenses: Tuition, state resident: full-time $1,693. Tuition, nonresident: full-time $4,233. Required fees: $501. Tuition and fees vary according to program.
Financial support: In 2001–02, 14 research assistantships with partial tuition reimbursements (averaging $11,000 per year), 1 teaching assistantship (averaging $10,000 per year) were awarded. Fellowships with partial tuition reimbursements, career-related internships or fieldwork, Federal Work-Study, and tuition waivers (full and partial) also available.
Faculty research: Remote sensing, geographic information systems/ geographic and environmental education, fluvial geomorphology, climatology, rural development. *Total annual research expenditures:* $1.4 million.
Ted J. Alsop, Interim Head, 435-797-1790, *Fax:* 435-797-4048, *E-mail:* tjalsop@cc.usu.edu.
Application contact: Dr. Derrick J. Thom, Information Contact, 435-797-1292, *Fax:* 435-797-4048, *E-mail:* djthom@cc.usu.edu. *Web site:* http://www.nr.usu.edu/Geography-Department/GER.html

■ VIRGINIA POLYTECHNIC INSTITUTE AND STATE UNIVERSITY

Graduate School, College of Arts and Sciences, Department of Geography, Blacksburg, VA 24061

AWARDS MS.

Faculty: 8 full-time (1 woman), 1 (woman) part-time/adjunct.
Students: 16 full-time (7 women); includes 2 minority (1 African American, 1 Native American). Average age 25. 15 applicants, 80% accepted. In 2001, 8 degrees awarded.
Degree requirements: For master's, thesis optional.
Entrance requirements: For master's, TOEFL. *Application deadline:* For fall admission, 12/1 (priority date). Applications are processed on a rolling basis. *Application fee:* $45. Electronic applications accepted.
Expenses: Tuition, state resident: part-time $241 per hour. Tuition, nonresident: part-time $406 per hour. Tuition and fees vary according to program.
Financial support: In 2001–02, 6 research assistantships with full tuition reimbursements (averaging $9,954 per year), 9 teaching assistantships with full tuition reimbursements (averaging $9,954 per year) were awarded. Career-related internships or fieldwork, institutionally sponsored loans, tuition waivers (full and partial), and unspecified assistantships also available. Financial award application deadline: 4/1.
Faculty research: Third World development, geographical information systems, remote sensing, critical geopolitics, medical geography.
Dr. James B. Campbell, Head, 540-231-6886, *Fax:* 540-231-2089, *E-mail:* jayhawk@vt.edu.
Application contact: Dr. Bonham C. Richardson, Director, 540-231-5514, *Fax:* 540-231-2089, *E-mail:* borichar@vt.edu. *Web site:* http://www.geog.vt.edu/

■ WAYNE STATE UNIVERSITY

Graduate School, College of Urban, Labor and Metropolitan Affairs, Department of Geography and Urban Planning, Program in Geography, Detroit, MI 48202

AWARDS MA.

Students: 2. In 2001, 2 degrees awarded.
Entrance requirements: For master's, GRE General Test. *Application deadline:* For fall admission, 7/1. *Application fee:* $20 ($30 for international students). Electronic applications accepted.
Expenses: Tuition, state resident: full-time $3,764. Tuition and fees vary according to degree level and program.
Avis Vidal, Acting Chairperson, Department of Geography and Urban Planning, 313-577-2701, *Fax:* 313-577-0022, *E-mail:* r.boyle@wayne.edu.

■ WEST CHESTER UNIVERSITY OF PENNSYLVANIA

Graduate Studies, School of Business and Public Affairs, Department of Geography and Planning, West Chester, PA 19383

AWARDS Geography (MA); regional planning (MSA). Part-time and evening/weekend programs available.

Faculty: 5.
Students: 6 full-time (1 woman), 11 part-time (7 women); includes 1 minority (African American). Average age 32. 13 applicants, 92% accepted. In 2001, 6 degrees awarded.
Degree requirements: For master's, thesis optional.
Entrance requirements: For master's, GRE General Test, interview, minimum GPA of 3.0, resumé. *Application deadline:* For fall admission, 4/15 (priority date); for spring admission, 10/15. Applications are processed on a rolling basis. *Application fee:* $25.
Expenses: Tuition, state resident: full-time $4,600; part-time $256 per credit. Tuition, nonresident: full-time $7,554; part-time $420 per credit. Required fees: $44 per credit.
Financial support: In 2001–02, 1 research assistantship with full tuition reimbursement (averaging $5,000 per year) was awarded; unspecified assistantships also available. Support available to part-time students. Financial award application deadline: 2/15; financial award applicants required to submit FAFSA.
Faculty research: Environmental education, land use/suburban planning, landscapes of Catalunya.
Dr. Arlene Rengert, Chair and Graduate Coordinator, 610-436-2343.
Application contact: Dr. Joan Welch, Regional Planning, Concentration Adviser, 610-436-2940, *E-mail:* jwelch@wcupa.edu.

■ WESTERN ILLINOIS UNIVERSITY

School of Graduate Studies, College of Arts and Sciences, Department of Geography, Macomb, IL 61455-1390

AWARDS Community development (Certificate); geography (MA). Part-time programs available.

Faculty: 8 full-time (0 women).
Students: 7 full-time (2 women), 5 part-time (2 women), 2 international. Average age 34. 9 applicants, 78% accepted. In 2001, 5 master's, 5 other advanced degrees awarded.
Degree requirements: For master's, thesis or alternative.
Application deadline: Applications are processed on a rolling basis. *Application fee:* $0 ($25 for international students). Electronic applications accepted.
Expenses: Tuition, state resident: part-time $108 per credit hour. Tuition, nonresident: part-time $216 per credit hour. Required fees: $33 per credit hour.
Financial support: In 2001–02, 6 students received support, including 6 research assistantships with full tuition reimbursements available (averaging $5,720 per year). Financial award applicants required to submit FAFSA.
Faculty research: 911 rural mapping, geographic information systems, social geography.
Dr. Lawrence T. Lewis, Chairperson, 309-298-1648.
Application contact: Dr. Barbara Baily, Director of Graduate Studies, 309-298-1806, *Fax:* 309-298-2345, *E-mail:* gradoffice@wiu.edu. *Web site:* http://www.wiu.edu/

■ WESTERN KENTUCKY UNIVERSITY

Graduate Studies, Ogden College of Science, and Engineering, Department of Geography and Geology, Bowling Green, KY 42101-3576

AWARDS MS.

Faculty: 9 full-time (2 women).
Students: In 2001, 8 degrees awarded.
Degree requirements: For master's, thesis or alternative, comprehensive exam.
Entrance requirements: For master's, GRE General Test, minimum GPA of 2.75. *Application deadline:* For fall admission, 7/1 (priority date); for spring admission, 11/1. Applications are processed on a rolling basis. *Application fee:* $30.
Expenses: Tuition, area resident: Part-time $167 per credit. Tuition, state resident: full-time $2,490. Tuition, nonresident: full-time $6,660; part-time $399 per credit. Required fees: $554. Part-time tuition and fees vary according to campus/location and reciprocity agreements.
Financial support: Research assistantships with partial tuition reimbursements, teaching assistantships, Federal Work-Study, institutionally sponsored loans, unspecified assistantships, and service awards available. Support available to part-time students. Financial award application deadline: 4/1; financial award applicants required to submit FAFSA.
Faculty research: Hydroclimatology, electronic data sets, groundwater, sinkhole liquification potential, meteorological analysis. *Total annual research expenditures:* $597,300.
Dr. David Keeling, Head, 270-745-4555.
Web site: http://www.wku.edu/www/geoweb/

■ WESTERN MICHIGAN UNIVERSITY

Graduate College, College of Arts and Sciences, Department of Geography, Kalamazoo, MI 49008-5202

AWARDS MA.

Faculty: 10 full-time (2 women).
Students: 13 full-time (7 women), 10 part-time (7 women), 3 international. 12 applicants, 83% accepted, 4 enrolled. In 2001, 2 degrees awarded.
Degree requirements: For master's, thesis, internship.
Application deadline: For fall admission, 2/15 (priority date). Applications are processed on a rolling basis. *Application fee:* $25.
Expenses: Tuition, state resident: part-time $186 per credit hour. Tuition, nonresident: part-time $442 per credit hour. Required fees: $602. One-time fee: $132 part-time. Tuition and fees vary according to course load.
Financial support: Fellowships, research assistantships, teaching assistantships, Federal Work-Study available. Financial award application deadline: 2/15; financial award applicants required to submit FAFSA.
Dr. David Dickason, Chairperson, 616-387-3410.
Application contact: Admissions and Orientation, 616-387-2000, *Fax:* 616-387-2355.

■ WESTERN WASHINGTON UNIVERSITY

Graduate School, Huxley College of Environmental Studies, Department of Environmental Studies, Bellingham, WA 98225-5996

AWARDS Geography (MS). Part-time programs available.

Degree requirements: For master's, thesis.
Entrance requirements: For master's, GRE General Test, TOEFL, minimum GPA of 3.0 in last 60 semester hours or last 90 quarter hours.

■ WEST VIRGINIA UNIVERSITY

Eberly College of Arts and Sciences, Department of Geology and Geography, Program in Geography, Morgantown, WV 26506

AWARDS Energy and environmental resources (MA); geographic information systems (PhD); geography-regional development (PhD); GIS/cartographic analysis (MA); regional development and urban planning (MA). Part-time programs available.

Students: 10 full-time (3 women), 3 part-time (1 woman), 3 international. Average age 27. 30 applicants, 33% accepted. In 2001, 14 degrees awarded.
Degree requirements: For master's, thesis, oral and written exams.
Entrance requirements: For master's, GRE General Test, TOEFL, minimum GPA of 2.75. *Application deadline:* For fall admission, 3/15 (priority date). Applications are processed on a rolling basis. *Application fee:* $45.
Expenses: Tuition, state resident: full-time $2,791. Tuition, nonresident: full-time $8,659. Required fees: $1,002. Tuition and fees vary according to program.
Financial support: In 2001–02, 4 research assistantships, 4 teaching assistantships were awarded. Career-related internships or fieldwork, Federal Work-Study, institutionally sponsored loans, and tuition waivers (full and partial) also available. Financial award application deadline: 2/1; financial award applicants required to submit FAFSA.
Faculty research: Resources, regional development, planning, geographic information systems, gender geography.
Dr. Kenneth Martis, Associate Chair, 304-293-5603 Ext. 4350, *Fax:* 304-293-6522, *E-mail:* ken.martis@mail.wvu.edu.
Application contact: Dr. Timothy Warner, Associate Professor, 304-293-5603 Ext. 4328, *Fax:* 304-293-6522, *E-mail:* tim.warner@mail.wvu.edu. *Web site:* http://www.geo.wvu.edu/programs/geography.html

Military and Defense Studies

MILITARY AND DEFENSE STUDIES

■ AMERICAN MILITARY UNIVERSITY

Graduate School of Military Studies, Manassas, VA 20110

AWARDS Air warfare (MA Military Studies); American revolution studies (MA Military Studies); business administration (MBA); civil war studies (MA Military Studies); criminal justice (MA); defense management (MA Military Studies); emergency and disaster management (MA); intelligence (MA Strategic Intelligence); land warfare (MA Military Studies); management (MA); national security studies (MA); naval warfare (MA Military Studies); political science (MA); public administration (MA); public health (MA); security management (MA); space studies (MA Military Studies); special operations (MA Military Studies); transportation management (MA); unconventional warfare (MA Military Studies). Program offered via distance learning only. Part-time and evening/weekend programs available. Postbaccalaureate distance learning degree programs offered (no on-campus study).

Faculty: 2 full-time (1 woman), 100 part-time/adjunct (8 women).
Students: Average age 35. 830 applicants, 100% accepted, 550 enrolled. In 2001, 87 degrees awarded. Terminal master's awarded for partial completion of doctoral program.
Entrance requirements: For master's, bachelor's degree or equivalent, minimum GPA of 2.7 in last 60 hours. *Application deadline:* For fall admission, 9/1 (priority date); for winter admission, 1/1; for spring admission, 5/1 (priority date). Applications are processed on a rolling basis. Electronic applications accepted.
Expenses: Tuition: Part-time $750 per course.
Faculty research: Military history, criminal justice, management performance, national security.
Dr. Michael J. Hillyard, Provost, 703-330-5398 Ext. 862, *Fax:* 703-330-5109, *E-mail:* mhillyard@amunet.edu.
Application contact: Cathi Bauer, Office of Student Services, 703-330-5398 Ext. 894, *Fax:* 703-330-5109, *E-mail:* info@amunet.edu. *Web site:* http://www.amunet.edu/

■ CALIFORNIA STATE UNIVERSITY, SAN BERNARDINO

Graduate Studies, College of Social and Behavioral Sciences, National Security Studies Program, San Bernardino, CA 92407-2397

AWARDS MA. Part-time and evening/weekend programs available.

Faculty: 13 full-time (0 women).
Students: 25 full-time (4 women), 12 part-time (4 women); includes 12 minority (4 African Americans, 2 Asian Americans or Pacific Islanders, 6 Hispanic Americans), 2 international. Average age 32. 15 applicants, 67% accepted. In 2001, 8 degrees awarded.
Degree requirements: For master's, comprehensive exam.
Entrance requirements: For master's, minimum GPA of 2.5. *Application deadline:* Applications are processed on a rolling basis. *Application fee:* $55.
Expenses: Tuition, nonresident: full-time $4,428. Required fees: $1,733.
Financial support: Career-related internships or fieldwork, Federal Work-Study, institutionally sponsored loans, and unspecified assistantships available. Support available to part-time students.
Faculty research: Strategy, arms control, defense policy, terrorism, U.S. foreign policy, operations analysis.
Dr. Mark Clark, Director, 909-880-5534, *Fax:* 909-880-7018, *E-mail:* mtclark@csusb.edu.

■ FLORIDA STATE UNIVERSITY

Graduate Studies, College of Education, Department of Educational Leadership and Policy Studies, Tallahassee, FL 32306

AWARDS Adult education (MS, Ed D, PhD, Ed S); comprehensive vocational education (PhD, Ed S); educational administration/leadership (MS, Ed D, PhD, Ed S), including educational administration/leadership, policy planning and analysis; foundations of education (MS, PhD, Ed S), including history and philosophy of education, international and intercultural education, social science and education (Ed S); higher education (MS, Ed D, PhD, Ed S), including higher education, institutional research; social science and education (PhD);). Part-time and evening/weekend programs available.

Faculty: 9 full-time (2 women), 1 part-time/adjunct (0 women).
Students: 81 full-time (53 women), 104 part-time (71 women); includes 44 minority (33 African Americans, 2 Asian Americans or Pacific Islanders, 7 Hispanic Americans, 2 Native Americans), 9 international. 145 applicants, 30% accepted. In 2001, 8 master's, 10 doctorates, 2 other advanced degrees awarded. Terminal master's awarded for partial completion of doctoral program.
Degree requirements: For master's and Ed S, thesis optional; for doctorate, thesis/dissertation, comprehensive exam.
Entrance requirements: For master's, doctorate, and Ed S, GRE General Test, minimum GPA of 3.0. *Application deadline:* For fall admission, 7/1 (priority date); for spring admission, 11/1. Applications are processed on a rolling basis. *Application fee:* $20. Electronic applications accepted.
Expenses: Tuition, state resident: part-time $163 per credit hour. Tuition, nonresident: part-time $570 per credit hour. Tuition and fees vary according to program.
Financial support: Fellowships, research assistantships, teaching assistantships, career-related internships or fieldwork available. Financial award applicants required to submit FAFSA.
Dr. Carolyn Herrington, Chair, 850-644-4594, *Fax:* 850-644-6401.
Application contact: Program Assistant, 850-644-4594, *Fax:* 850-644-6401. *Web site:* http://fsu.edu/~coe/

■ GEORGETOWN UNIVERSITY

Graduate School of Arts and Sciences, Department of National Security Studies, Washington, DC 20057

AWARDS MA, MA/PhD.

Entrance requirements: For master's, GRE, TOEFL.

Find an in-depth description at www.petersons.com/gradchannel.

■ THE GEORGE WASHINGTON UNIVERSITY

Elliott School of International Affairs, Program in Security Policy Studies, Washington, DC 20052

AWARDS MA, JD/MA. Part-time and evening/weekend programs available.

Students: 44 full-time (17 women), 17 part-time (11 women); includes 9 minority (2 African Americans, 7 Hispanic Americans), 2 international. Average age 26. 108 applicants, 79% accepted. In 2001, 18 degrees awarded.
Degree requirements: For master's, one foreign language.
Entrance requirements: For master's, GRE General Test, TOEFL, minimum B average. *Application deadline:* For fall admission, 2/1. *Application fee:* $55. Electronic applications accepted.

The George Washington University (continued)
Expenses: Tuition: Part-time $810 per credit. Required fees: $1 per credit.
Financial support: Fellowships with tuition reimbursements, research assistantships with tuition reimbursements, career-related internships or fieldwork, Federal Work-Study, institutionally sponsored loans, and tuition waivers (full) available. Financial award application deadline: 1/15; financial award applicants required to submit FAFSA.
Faculty research: U.S. arms transfer policies, military balance in the Third World, U.S. foreign policy, technology and security policy.
Dr. Gordon Adams, Director, 202-994-7003.
Application contact: Jeff V. Miles, Director of Graduate Admissions, 202-994-7050, *Fax:* 202-994-9537, *E-mail:* esiagrad@gwu.edu. *Web site:* http://www.gwu.edu/~elliott/

■ HAWAI'I PACIFIC UNIVERSITY

Division of Arts and Sciences, Honolulu, HI 96813-2785

AWARDS Diplomacy and military studies (MA); political science (MA).

Faculty: 2 full-time (0 women), 3 part-time/adjunct (1 woman).
Students: 66. Average age 30. 34 applicants, 91% accepted, 18 enrolled. In 2001, 1 degree awarded.
Degree requirements: For master's, thesis.
Application deadline: Applications are processed on a rolling basis. *Application fee:* $50. Electronic applications accepted.
Expenses: Tuition: Full-time $7,380; part-time $410 per credit.
Financial support: Career-related internships or fieldwork, Federal Work-Study, and unspecified assistantships available. Support available to part-time students. Financial award application deadline: 3/1; financial award applicants required to submit FAFSA.
Dr. Leslie Correa, Associate Vice President and Dean, 808-549-9340, *Fax:* 808-544-9306, *E-mail:* lcorrea@hpu.edu.
Application contact: Jose Rosal, Admissions Coordinator, 808-544-1135, *Fax:* 800-544-0280, *E-mail:* gradservctr@hpu.edu. *Web site:* http://www.hpu.edu/

Find an in-depth description at www.petersons.com/gradchannel.

■ JOHNS HOPKINS UNIVERSITY

Paul H. Nitze School of Advanced International Studies, Washington, DC 20036

AWARDS Emerging markets (Certificate); interdisciplinary studies (MA, PhD), including African studies, American foreign policy (MA), Asian studies, Canadian studies, conflict resolution and mediation (MA), environmental policy and resource management (MA), European studies, international business (MA), international development (MA), international economics (MA), international relations (MA), Latin American studies, Middle Eastern studies (MA), military and defense studies (MA), Russian area and East European studies (MA), social change and development (MA); international public policy (MIPP). MBA/MA offered jointly with the University of Pennsylvania–Wharton School and INSEAD in France.

Faculty: 44 full-time (13 women), 113 part-time/adjunct (29 women).
Students: 567 full-time (275 women), 17 part-time (8 women); includes 71 minority (14 African Americans, 46 Asian Americans or Pacific Islanders, 10 Hispanic Americans, 1 Native American). Average age 27. 1,288 applicants, 35% accepted. In 2001, 294 master's, 13 doctorates, 34 other advanced degrees awarded. Terminal master's awarded for partial completion of doctoral program.
Degree requirements: For master's, one foreign language, comprehensive exam; for doctorate, 2 foreign languages, thesis/dissertation.
Entrance requirements: For master's, GMAT or GRE General Test or TOEFL, previous course work in economics, foreign language; for doctorate, GRE General Test or TOEFL; for Certificate, TOEFL. *Application deadline:* For fall admission, 1/15. *Application fee:* $75. Electronic applications accepted.
Expenses: Contact institution.
Financial support: In 2001–02, 431 fellowships (averaging $5,500 per year) were awarded; career-related internships or fieldwork and Federal Work-Study also available. Financial award application deadline: 2/1; financial award applicants required to submit FAFSA.
Faculty research: Comparative politics, regional studies, language and linguistics.
Dr. Jessica Einhorn, Dean, 202-663-5624, *Fax:* 202-663-5621.
Application contact: Bonnie Wilson, Associate Dean of Student Affairs, 202-663-5700, *Fax:* 202-663-7788, *E-mail:* admissions.sais@jhu.edu. *Web site:* http://www.sais-jhu.edu/

Find an in-depth description at www.petersons.com/gradchannel.

■ JOINT MILITARY INTELLIGENCE COLLEGE

School of Intelligence Studies, Washington, DC 20340-5100

AWARDS MSSI, Certificate. Open only to federal government employees. Part-time and evening/weekend programs available.

Degree requirements: For master's, thesis.
Entrance requirements: For master's, MAT, authorized nomination.
Faculty research: Law and intelligence, intelligence and higher education, low-intensity conflict, intelligence information systems.

■ THE JUDGE ADVOCATE GENERAL'S SCHOOL, U.S. ARMY

Graduate Programs, Charlottesville, VA 22903-1781

AWARDS Military law (LL M). Only active duty military lawyers attend this school.

Degree requirements: For master's, thesis optional.
Entrance requirements: For master's, active duty military lawyer.
Faculty research: Criminal law, administrative and civil law, contract law, international law, legal research and writing.

■ MERCYHURST COLLEGE

Graduate Program, Program in Administration of Justice, Erie, PA 16546

AWARDS Administration of justice (MS); applied intelligence (MS). Part-time and evening/weekend programs available.

Faculty: 1 full-time (0 women), 8 part-time/adjunct (0 women).
Students: 38 full-time (18 women), 4 part-time; includes 2 minority (1 African American, 1 Hispanic American), 1 international. Average age 28. 16 applicants, 88% accepted. In 2001, 16 degrees awarded.
Degree requirements: For master's, thesis optional.
Entrance requirements: For master's, GRE General Test, MAT, or minimum GPA of 3.0. *Application deadline:* For fall admission, 8/1 (priority date); for spring admission, 1/1. Applications are processed on a rolling basis. *Application fee:* $35. Electronic applications accepted.
Financial support: In 2001–02, 4 fellowships with tuition reimbursements were awarded; research assistantships with tuition reimbursements, career-related internships or fieldwork, institutionally sponsored loans, scholarships/grants, and unspecified assistantships also available. Support available to part-time students. Financial award application deadline: 5/15.
Faculty research: Research methods, criminal justice administration, juvenile justice.
Dr. Frank E. Hagan, Director, 814-824-2265, *Fax:* 814-824-2438.
Application contact: Mary Ellen Dahlkemper, Director, Office of Adult and Graduate Programs, 814-824-2294, *Fax:* 814-824-2055, *E-mail:* medahlk@mercyhurst.edu.

■ NATIONAL DEFENSE UNIVERSITY

Industrial College of the Armed Forces, Washington, DC 20319-5066

AWARDS National resource strategy (MS). Open only to Department of Defense employees and specific federal agencies.

Faculty: 85 full-time.
Students: 299 full-time. In 2001, 299 degrees awarded. *Median time to degree:* Master's–1 year full-time.
Maj. Gen. Harold Mashburn, Commandant.

■ NATIONAL DEFENSE UNIVERSITY

National War College, Washington, DC 20319-5066

AWARDS National security strategy (MS). Open only to Department of Defense employees and specific federal agencies.

Faculty: 60 full-time.
Students: 195 full-time. In 2001, 189 degrees awarded. *Median time to degree:* Master's–1 year full-time.
Maj. Reginal Clemmons, Commandant.
Application contact: Col. David H. McIntyre, Dean of Faculty and Academic Programs.

■ NAVAL POSTGRADUATE SCHOOL

Graduate Programs, Department of National Security Affairs, Monterey, CA 93943

AWARDS MA. Program only open to commissioned officers of the United States and friendly nations and selected United States federal civilian employees. Part-time programs available.

Degree requirements: For master's, thesis.

■ NAVAL POSTGRADUATE SCHOOL

Graduate Programs, Program in Command, Control, Communications, Computers and Intelligence, Monterey, CA 93943

AWARDS MS. Program only open to commissioned officers of the United States and friendly nations and selected United States federal civilian employees. Part-time programs available.

Degree requirements: For master's, thesis.

■ NAVAL POSTGRADUATE SCHOOL

Graduate Programs, Program in Information Warfare and Electronic Warfare Systems Technology, Monterey, CA 93943

AWARDS MS. Program only open to commissioned officers of the United States and friendly nations and selected United States federal civilian employees. Part-time programs available.

Degree requirements: For master's, thesis.

■ NAVAL POSTGRADUATE SCHOOL

Graduate Programs, Program in Modeling Virtual Environments and Simulations, Monterey, CA 93943

AWARDS MS, PhD. Program only open to commissioned officers of the United States and friendly nations and selected United States federal civilian employees. Part-time programs available.

Degree requirements: For master's, thesis; for doctorate, one foreign language, thesis/dissertation.

■ NAVAL POSTGRADUATE SCHOOL

Graduate Programs, Program in Undersea Warfare, Monterey, CA 93943

AWARDS MS. Program only open to commissioned officers of the United States and friendly nations and selected United States federal civilian employees. Part-time programs available.

Degree requirements: For master's, thesis.

■ NAVAL POSTGRADUATE SCHOOL

Graduate Programs, Programs in Special Operations, Monterey, CA 93943

AWARDS MS. Program only open to commissioned officers of the United States and friendly nations and selected United States federal civilian employees. Part-time programs available.

Degree requirements: For master's, thesis.

■ NAVAL WAR COLLEGE

Program in National Security and Strategic Studies, Newport, RI 02841-1207

AWARDS MA. Program open only to full-time military personnel. *Web site:* http://www.nwc.navy.mil/

■ NORWICH UNIVERSITY

Military Graduate Program, Northfield, VT 05663

AWARDS Diplomacy and military science (MA). Part-time and evening/weekend programs available. Postbaccalaureate distance learning degree programs offered (minimal on-campus study).

Degree requirements: For master's, thesis optional.
Entrance requirements: For master's, GRE. Electronic applications accepted.

■ SCHOOL OF ADVANCED AIRPOWER STUDIES

Program in Airpower Art and Science, Maxwell AFB, AL 36112-6424

AWARDS MA. Available to active duty military officers only.

Degree requirements: For master's, thesis, minimum GPA of 3.0, comprehensive exam.
Entrance requirements: For master's, less than 16 years total of active commissioned service; master's degree or undergraduate degree with a minimum GPA of 2.75.

■ SOUTHWEST MISSOURI STATE UNIVERSITY

Graduate College, College of Humanities and Public Affairs, Department of Defense and Strategic Studies, Springfield, MO 65804-0094

AWARDS MS. Part-time and evening/weekend programs available.

Faculty: 2 full-time (0 women), 16 part-time/adjunct (3 women).
Students: 30 full-time (4 women), 4 part-time; includes 4 minority (2 Asian Americans or Pacific Islanders, 2 Hispanic Americans), 4 international. Average age 27. In 2001, 20 degrees awarded.
Degree requirements: For master's, thesis or alternative, comprehensive exam.
Entrance requirements: For master's, GRE General Test, minimum GPA of 2.75. *Application deadline:* For fall admission, 8/5 (priority date); for spring admission, 12/20 (priority date). Applications are processed on a rolling basis. *Application fee:* $25. Electronic applications accepted.
Expenses: Tuition, state resident: full-time $2,286; part-time $127 per credit. Tuition, nonresident: full-time $4,572; part-time $254 per credit. Required fees: $151 per semester. Tuition and fees vary according to course level and program.
Financial support: In 2001–02, 9 research assistantships with full tuition reimbursements (averaging $6,150 per year) were awarded; career-related internships or fieldwork, Federal Work-Study, institutionally sponsored loans, scholarships/grants, tuition waivers (partial), and unspecified assistantships also available. Financial award application deadline: 3/31.

Southwest Missouri State University (continued)

Faculty research: Arms control, U.S.-Soviet military balance, Strategic Defense Initiative, geopolitics, strategy.

Dr. William R. Van Cleave, Head, 417-836-4137, *Fax:* 417-836-6667, *E-mail:* wiv914f@smsu.edu.

Application contact: Valerie Murphy, Administrative Assistant, 417-836-4137, *Fax:* 417-836-6667, *E-mail:* vam979t@smsu.edu. *Web site:* http://www.smsu.edu/contrib/dss/index.html

Find an in-depth description at www.petersons.com/gradchannel.

■ UNITED STATES ARMY COMMAND AND GENERAL STAFF COLLEGE

Graduate Program, Fort Leavenworth, KS 66027-1352

AWARDS Military art and science (MMAS). Only career military officers are selected to attend United States Army Command and General Staff College.

■ UNIVERSITY OF PITTSBURGH

Graduate School of Public and International Affairs, International Affairs Division, Program in Security and Intelligence Studies, Pittsburgh, PA 15260

AWARDS MPIA, JD/MPIA, MBA/MPIA, MPA/MPIA, MPH/MPIA, MSIS/MPIA, MSW/MPIA. Part-time and evening/weekend programs available.

Faculty: 32 full-time (8 women), 12 part-time/adjunct (9 women).

Students: 93 full-time (54 women), 12 part-time (7 women); includes 11 minority (7 African Americans, 1 Asian American or Pacific Islander, 3 Hispanic Americans), 28 international. Average age 23. 64 applicants, 88% accepted, 24 enrolled.

Degree requirements: For master's, internship, thesis optional.

Entrance requirements: For master's, TOEFL. *Application deadline:* For fall admission, 3/1 (priority date); for spring admission, 10/1 (priority date). Applications are processed on a rolling basis. *Application fee:* $40. Electronic applications accepted.

Expenses: Tuition, state resident: full-time $9,410; part-time $385 per credit. Tuition, nonresident: full-time $19,376; part-time $797 per credit. Required fees: $480; $90 per term. Tuition and fees vary according to program.

Financial support: In 2001–02, 44 students received support, including 9 fellowships (averaging $14,240 per year); career-related internships or fieldwork, institutionally sponsored loans, scholarships/grants, tuition waivers (full and partial), and unspecified assistantships also available. Financial award application deadline: 2/1.

Faculty research: Political economy, international security/defense/intelligence, transnational crime, international trade, international finance, terrorism.

Application contact: Elizabeth Barthen-Braunsdorf, Assistant Director of Admissions, 412-648-7643, *Fax:* 412-648-7641, *E-mail:* barthen@bitch.gspia.pitt.edu.

Political Science and International Affairs

INTERNATIONAL AFFAIRS

■ ALLIANT INTERNATIONAL UNIVERSITY

College of Arts and Sciences, San Francisco, CA 94109

AWARDS International relations (MA).

Students: 21.

Expenses: Tuition: Part-time $397 per credit hour. Tuition and fees vary according to degree level, campus/location and program.

Dr. Ramona Kunard, Dean, 858-635-4505, *Fax:* 858-635-4843, *E-mail:* rkunard@alliant.edu.

Application contact: Patricia J. Mullen, Vice President, Enrollment and Student Services, 800-457-1273 Ext. 303, *Fax:* 415-931-8322, *E-mail:* admissions@alliant.edu. *Web site:* http://www.alliant.edu/

■ AMERICAN UNIVERSITY

College of Arts and Sciences, Department of Sociology, International Training and Education Program, Washington, DC 20016-8001

AWARDS MA. Part-time and evening/weekend programs available.

Faculty: 9 full-time (4 women), 7 part-time/adjunct (4 women).

Students: 9 full-time (8 women), 28 part-time (24 women); includes 6 minority (3 African Americans, 3 Hispanic Americans), 2 international. 20 applicants, 75% accepted, 15 enrolled. In 2001, 10 degrees awarded.

Degree requirements: For master's, thesis optional.

Entrance requirements: For master's, GRE (financial merit award applicants), TOEFL, minimum GPA of 3.0. *Application deadline:* For fall admission, 2/1 (priority date); for spring admission, 10/1. Applications are processed on a rolling basis. *Application fee:* $50.

Expenses: Tuition: Full-time $14,274; part-time $793 per credit. Required fees: $290. Tuition and fees vary according to program.

Financial support: In 2001–02, 10 students received support, including 2 research assistantships with full tuition reimbursements available (averaging $10,000 per year); career-related internships or fieldwork, Federal Work-Study, and institutionally sponsored loans also available. Support available to part-time students. Financial award application deadline: 2/1; financial award applicants required to submit FAFSA.

Faculty research: Education sector analysis, global and multicultural education, grassroots development, gender studies, international training.

Dr. Wendy Bokhorst-Heng, Director, 202-885-3723, *E-mail:* itep@american.edu. *Web site:* http://www.american.edu/academic.depts/cas/sociology/itep/

■ AMERICAN UNIVERSITY

School of International Service, Washington, DC 20016-8001

AWARDS Comparative and regional studies (MA); development management (MS); environmental policy (MA); international communication (MA); international development (MA); international development management (Certificate); international economic policy (MA); international economic relations (Certificate); international peace and conflict resolution (MA); international politics (MA); international relations (PhD); U.S. foreign policy (MA). Part-time and evening/weekend programs available.

Faculty: 59 full-time (21 women), 35 part-time/adjunct (11 women).

Students: 347 full-time (214 women), 300 part-time (176 women); includes 87 minority (30 African Americans, 20 Asian Americans or Pacific Islanders, 35 Hispanic Americans, 2 Native Americans), 152 international. Average age 27. 1,254 applicants, 74% accepted, 215 enrolled. In 2001, 193 master's, 1 doctorate awarded. Terminal master's awarded for partial completion of doctoral program.

Degree requirements: For master's, one foreign language, thesis or alternative, comprehensive exam; for doctorate, one

foreign language, thesis/dissertation, comprehensive exam.
Entrance requirements: For master's, GRE General Test, TOEFL, 24 credits in related social sciences, minimum of 3.3; 2 letter of recommendations; for doctorate, GRE General Test, TOEFL, 2 letters of recommendations; 24 credits in related social sciences. *Application deadline:* For fall admission, 1/15 (priority date); for spring admission, 10/1 (priority date). Applications are processed on a rolling basis. *Application fee:* $50.
Expenses: Tuition: Full-time $14,274; part-time $793 per credit. Required fees: $290. Tuition and fees vary according to program.
Financial support: In 2001–02, 13 fellowships with tuition reimbursements, 62 research assistantships with tuition reimbursements were awarded. Teaching assistantships, career-related internships or fieldwork, Federal Work-Study, and institutionally sponsored loans also available. Financial award application deadline: 1/15.
Faculty research: International intellectual property, international environmental issues, international law and legal order, international telecommunications/technology, international sustainable development.
Dr. Louis W. Goodman, Dean, 202-885-1600, *Fax:* 202-885-2494.
Application contact: Christopher Derickson, Director of Graduate Admissions and Financial Aid, 202-885-1599, *Fax:* 202-885-2494.

■ ANGELO STATE UNIVERSITY

Graduate School, College of Liberal and Fine Arts, Department of Government, San Angelo, TX 76909

AWARDS International studies (MA); public administration (MPA). Part-time and evening/weekend programs available.

Faculty: 6 full-time (0 women).
Students: 5 full-time (2 women), 9 part-time (6 women); includes 4 minority (all Hispanic Americans), 1 international. Average age 35. 17 applicants, 53% accepted, 6 enrolled. In 2001, 6 degrees awarded.
Degree requirements: For master's, thesis optional.
Entrance requirements: For master's, GRE General Test, minimum GPA of 2.5. *Application deadline:* For fall admission, 8/7 (priority date); for spring admission, 1/2. Applications are processed on a rolling basis. *Application fee:* $25 ($50 for international students).
Expenses: Tuition, area resident: Full-time $960; part-time $40 per credit hour. Tuition, nonresident: full-time $6,120; part-time $255 per credit hour. Required fees: $1,336; $56 per credit hour.
Financial support: In 2001–02, 2 students received support, including 2 fellowships with full and partial tuition reimbursements available; teaching assistantships, Federal Work-Study and tuition waivers (partial) also available. Support available to part-time students. Financial award application deadline: 8/1.
Dr. Edward C. Olson, Head, 915-942-2005.
Application contact: Dr. Jack Barbour, Graduate Advisor, 915-942-2262, *E-mail:* jack.barbour@angelo.edu. *Web site:* http://www.angelo.edu/dept/government/

■ BAYLOR UNIVERSITY

Graduate School, College of Arts and Sciences, Department of Political Science, Program in International Studies, Waco, TX 76798

AWARDS MA.

Students: 3 full-time (2 women); includes 1 minority (Hispanic American), 1 international. In 2001, 4 degrees awarded.
Degree requirements: For master's, one foreign language, thesis optional.
Entrance requirements: For master's, GRE General Test. *Application deadline:* Applications are processed on a rolling basis. *Application fee:* $25.
Expenses: Tuition: Part-time $379 per semester hour. Required fees: $42 per semester hour. $101 per semester. Tuition and fees vary according to program.
Financial support: Research assistantships, career-related internships or fieldwork, Federal Work-Study, and institutionally sponsored loans available. Financial award application deadline: 3/1.
Application contact: Suzanne Keener, Administrative Assistant, 254-710-3588, *Fax:* 254-710-3870, *E-mail:* graduate_school@baylor.edu.

■ BAYLOR UNIVERSITY

Graduate School, Hankamer School of Business, Department of Economics, Waco, TX 76798

AWARDS Economics (MS Eco); international economics (MA, MS).

Students: 8 full-time (5 women), 1 (woman) part-time, 6 international. In 2001, 5 degrees awarded.
Entrance requirements: For master's, GMAT or GRE General Test, minimum GPA of 3.0 in economics, 2.7 overall. *Application deadline:* For fall admission, 8/1; for spring admission, 12/1. Applications are processed on a rolling basis. *Application fee:* $25.
Expenses: Tuition: Part-time $379 per semester hour. Required fees: $42 per semester hour. $101 per semester. Tuition and fees vary according to program.
Financial support: Research assistantships, Federal Work-Study and institutionally sponsored loans available. Financial award application deadline: 4/1.
Faculty research: Econometrics, international economics, private enterprise, comparative economic systems.
Dr. Steve Green, Chair, 254-710-2263, *Fax:* 254-710-3265, *E-mail:* steve_green@baylor.edu.
Application contact: Suzanne Keener, Administrative Assistant, 254-710-3588, *Fax:* 254-710-3870, *E-mail:* graduate_school@baylor.edu. *Web site:* http://www.baylor.edu/eco/default.asp

■ BOSTON UNIVERSITY

Graduate School of Arts and Sciences, Department of International Relations, Boston, MA 02215

AWARDS African studies (Certificate); international relations (MA); international relations and environmental policy management (MA); international relations and international communication (MA).

Students: 65 full-time (30 women), 11 part-time (5 women); includes 4 minority (1 Asian American or Pacific Islander, 3 Hispanic Americans), 25 international. Average age 28. 299 applicants, 61% accepted, 42 enrolled. In 2001, 27 degrees awarded.
Degree requirements: For master's, one foreign language, thesis, comprehensive exam, registration.
Entrance requirements: For master's, GRE General Test, TOEFL, 3 letters of recommendation; for Certificate, GRE General Test, TOEFL. *Application deadline:* For fall admission, 4/15; for spring admission, 10/15. *Application fee:* $60.
Expenses: Tuition: Full-time $25,872; part-time $340 per credit. Required fees: $40 per semester. Part-time tuition and fees vary according to class time, course level and program.
Financial support: In 2001–02, 25 students received support. Federal Work-Study, scholarships/grants, and unspecified assistantships available. Support available to part-time students. Financial award application deadline: 1/15; financial award applicants required to submit FAFSA.
Dr. Erik Goldstein, Chairman, 617-353-9280, *Fax:* 617-353-9290, *E-mail:* goldstee@bu.edu.
Application contact: David E. Clark, Graduate Program Administrator, 617-353-9349, *Fax:* 617-353-9290, *E-mail:* ir@bu.edu. *Web site:* http://www.bu.edu/IR/

■ BRANDEIS UNIVERSITY

Graduate School of International Economics and Finance, Waltham, MA 02454-9110

AWARDS Finance (MSF); international business (MBAi); international economics and finance (MA, PhD). Part-time and evening/weekend programs available.

Faculty: 25 full-time (4 women), 10 part-time/adjunct (0 women).
Students: 165 full-time (63 women), 57 part-time (14 women). Average age 28. 450 applicants, 50% accepted, 114 enrolled. In 2001, 58 master's, 1 doctorate awarded.

Brandeis University (continued)
Terminal master's awarded for partial completion of doctoral program.
Degree requirements: For master's, one foreign language; for doctorate, thesis/dissertation.
Entrance requirements: For master's, GMAT or GRE General Test (MA), GMAT (MBAi), TOEFL; for doctorate, GRE General Test, GRE Subject Test, TOEFL. *Application deadline:* For fall admission, 2/15 (priority date). *Application fee:* $50. Electronic applications accepted.
Expenses: Tuition: Full-time $27,392. Required fees: $35.
Financial support: In 2001–02, 166 students received support, including research assistantships (averaging $4,000 per year), teaching assistantships (averaging $4,000 per year); career-related internships or fieldwork, Federal Work-Study, institutionally sponsored loans, scholarships/grants, and unspecified assistantships also available. Financial award application deadline: 2/15; financial award applicants required to submit FAFSA.
Faculty research: International finance and business, trade policy, macroeconomics, Asian economic issues, developmental economics.
Dr. Peter Petri, Dean, 781-736-4817, *Fax:* 781-736-2267, *E-mail:* ppetri@brandeis.edu.
Application contact: Geraldine F. Koch, Assistant Dean for Admission, 781-736-2252, *Fax:* 781-736-2263, *E-mail:* admission@lemberg.brandeis.edu. *Web site:* http://www.brandeis.edu/global
Find an in-depth description at www.petersons.com/gradchannel.

■ BRIGHAM YOUNG UNIVERSITY

The David M. Kennedy Center for International and Area Studies, Provo, UT 84602-1001

AWARDS American studies (MA); ancient Near Eastern studies (MA); Asian studies (MA); international development (MA); international relations (MA).

Faculty: 21 full-time (2 women), 2 part-time/adjunct (0 women).
Students: 16 full-time (8 women), 13 part-time (9 women); includes 1 minority (Hispanic American), 4 international. Average age 25. 62 applicants, 31% accepted. In 2001, 17 degrees awarded.
Degree requirements: For master's, one foreign language, thesis.
Entrance requirements: For master's, GRE General Test, minimum GPA of 3.55 in last 60 hours. *Application deadline:* For fall admission, 2/1. *Application fee:* $50. Electronic applications accepted.
Expenses: Tuition: Full-time $3,860; part-time $214 per hour.
Financial support: In 2001–02, 18 research assistantships (averaging $3,500 per year), 2 teaching assistantships (averaging $3,500 per year) were awarded. Fellowships with full tuition reimbursements, career-related internships or fieldwork and tuition waivers (full) also available. Financial award application deadline: 2/1.
Faculty research: Comparative education, education for development, comparative economics. *Total annual research expenditures:* $100,000.
Dr. Donald B. Holsinger, Director, 801-422-3378, *Fax:* 801-378-8748, *E-mail:* donald_holsinger@byu.edu.
Application contact: Dr. Phillip J. Bryson, Director of Graduate Studies, Associate Director, 801-422-7402, *Fax:* 801-378-8748, *E-mail:* phillip_bryson@byu.edu.

■ CALIFORNIA STATE UNIVERSITY, FRESNO

Division of Graduate Studies, College of Social Sciences, Department of Political Science, Program in International Relations, Fresno, CA 93740-8027

AWARDS MA. Part-time and evening/weekend programs available.

Faculty: 6 full-time (1 woman).
Students: 8 full-time (3 women), 8 part-time (3 women); includes 4 minority (1 African American, 3 Hispanic Americans), 6 international. Average age 31. 15 applicants, 67% accepted, 5 enrolled. In 2001, 3 degrees awarded.
Degree requirements: For master's, one foreign language, thesis or alternative. *Median time to degree:* Master's–2.5 years full-time, 3.5 years part-time.
Entrance requirements: For master's, GRE General Test, TOEFL, minimum GPA of 3.0. *Application deadline:* For fall admission, 8/1 (priority date); for spring admission, 12/1. Applications are processed on a rolling basis. *Application fee:* $55. Electronic applications accepted.
Expenses: Tuition, nonresident: part-time $246 per unit. Required fees: $605 per semester. Tuition and fees vary according to course load.
Financial support: Career-related internships or fieldwork, Federal Work-Study, scholarships/grants, and unspecified assistantships available. Support available to part-time students. Financial award application deadline: 3/1; financial award applicants required to submit FAFSA.
Dr. Alfred Evans, Graduate Program Coordinator, 559-278-2888, *Fax:* 559-278-6931, *E-mail:* alfred_evans@csufresno.edu.

■ CALIFORNIA STATE UNIVERSITY, SACRAMENTO

Graduate Studies, College of Social Sciences and Interdisciplinary Studies, International Affairs Graduate Program, Sacramento, CA 95819-6048

AWARDS MA. Part-time programs available.

Students: 8 full-time (5 women), 9 part-time (3 women); includes 3 minority (1 Asian American or Pacific Islander, 2 Hispanic Americans), 2 international.
Degree requirements: For master's, one foreign language, thesis or alternative, writing proficiency exam.
Entrance requirements: For master's, GRE General Test, TOEFL, appropriate bachelor's degree, minimum GPA of 3.0 during previous 2 years. *Application deadline:* For fall admission, 4/15; for spring admission, 11/1. *Application fee:* $55.
Expenses: Tuition, state resident: full-time $1,965; part-time $668 per semester. Tuition, nonresident: part-time $246 per unit.
Financial support: Teaching assistantships, career-related internships or fieldwork and Federal Work-Study available. Support available to part-time students. Financial award application deadline: 3/1.
Dr. Bahman Fozouni, Head, 916-278-6202.

■ CALIFORNIA STATE UNIVERSITY, STANISLAUS

Graduate Programs, College of Arts, Letters, and Sciences, Department of History, Turlock, CA 95382

AWARDS History (MA); international relations (MA); secondary school history teaching (MA). Part-time programs available.

Students: 18 (3 women); includes 2 minority (1 Asian American or Pacific Islander, 1 Hispanic American). 5 applicants, 80% accepted. In 2001, 5 degrees awarded.
Degree requirements: For master's, one foreign language, thesis or alternative.
Entrance requirements: For master's, GRE General Test, GRE Subject Test, minimum undergraduate GPA of 3.0. *Application fee:* $55. Electronic applications accepted.
Expenses: Tuition, nonresident: part-time $246 per unit. Required fees: $1,919. Tuition and fees vary according to campus/location and program.
Financial support: In 2001–02, 2 fellowships (averaging $2,500 per year) were awarded; Federal Work-Study also available. Financial award application deadline: 3/2; financial award applicants required to submit FAFSA.
Faculty research: American and modern European history.
Dr. Sam Regalado, Chair, 209-667-3238.
Application contact: Dr. Nancy J. Taniguchi, Graduate Director, 209-667-3238, *E-mail:* nancy@athena.csustan.edu.

■ THE CATHOLIC UNIVERSITY OF AMERICA

School of Arts and Sciences, Department of Business and Economics, Program in International Political Economics, Washington, DC 20064

AWARDS MA. Part-time and evening/weekend programs available.

Students: 2 applicants, 50% accepted, 0 enrolled.
Degree requirements: For master's, comprehensive exam.
Entrance requirements: For master's, GRE General Test, TOEFL. *Application deadline:* For fall admission, 8/1 (priority date); for spring admission, 12/1. Applications are processed on a rolling basis. *Application fee:* $55. Electronic applications accepted.
Expenses: Tuition: Full-time $20,050; part-time $770 per credit. Required fees: $430 per term. Tuition and fees vary according to program.
Financial support: Teaching assistantships, career-related internships or fieldwork, Federal Work-Study, institutionally sponsored loans, and tuition waivers (full and partial) available. Support available to part-time students. Financial award application deadline: 2/1.
Faculty research: Role of the U.S. in the world economy.
Dr. Kevin F Forbes, Chair, Department of Business and Economics, 202-319-5236, *Fax:* 202-319-4426.

■ THE CATHOLIC UNIVERSITY OF AMERICA

School of Arts and Sciences, Department of Politics, Program in International Affairs, Washington, DC 20064

AWARDS MA. Part-time programs available.

Students: 1 (woman) full-time, 18 part-time (5 women); includes 2 minority (1 African American, 1 Hispanic American). Average age 33. 25 applicants, 76% accepted, 8 enrolled. In 2001, 14 degrees awarded.
Degree requirements: For master's, one foreign language, thesis or alternative, comprehensive exam.
Entrance requirements: For master's, GRE General Test, TOEFL. *Application deadline:* For fall admission, 8/1 (priority date); for spring admission, 12/1. Applications are processed on a rolling basis. *Application fee:* $55. Electronic applications accepted.
Expenses: Tuition: Full-time $20,050; part-time $770 per credit. Required fees: $430 per term. Tuition and fees vary according to program.
Financial support: Career-related internships or fieldwork, Federal Work-Study, institutionally sponsored loans, and tuition waivers (full and partial) available. Support available to part-time students. Financial award application deadline: 2/1.
Faculty research: International relations, area studies.
Dr. David Walsh, Director, 202-319-5128, *Fax:* 202-319-6289, *E-mail:* walshd@cua.edu.
Application contact: Helen Foggo, Office Manager, 202-319-5128.

■ CENTRAL CONNECTICUT STATE UNIVERSITY

School of Graduate Studies, Program in Interdisciplinary Area Studies, New Britain, CT 06050-4010

AWARDS International studies (MS); social science (MS). Part-time and evening/weekend programs available.

Students: 4 full-time (3 women), 23 part-time (12 women); includes 2 minority (1 African American, 1 Hispanic American). Average age 35. 1 applicant, 0% accepted. In 2001, 5 degrees awarded.
Degree requirements: For master's, thesis or alternative, comprehensive exam or special project.
Entrance requirements: For master's, TOEFL, minimum GPA of 2.7. *Application deadline:* For fall admission, 8/10 (priority date); for spring admission, 12/10. Applications are processed on a rolling basis. *Application fee:* $40.
Expenses: Tuition, state resident: full-time $2,772; part-time $245 per credit. Tuition, nonresident: full-time $7,726; part-time $245 per credit. Required fees: $2,102. Tuition and fees vary according to course level and degree level.
Financial support: In 2001–02, research assistantships (averaging $4,800 per year), teaching assistantships (averaging $4,800 per year) were awarded. Federal Work-Study also available. Financial award application deadline: 3/15; financial award applicants required to submit FAFSA.
Dr. Timothy Rickard, Coordinator, 860-832-2921.

■ CENTRAL CONNECTICUT STATE UNIVERSITY

School of Graduate Studies, School of Arts and Sciences, Department of International Studies, New Britain, CT 06050-4010

AWARDS MA. Part-time and evening/weekend programs available.

Students: 2 full-time (both women), 12 part-time (5 women); includes 6 minority (3 African Americans, 1 Asian American or Pacific Islander, 2 Hispanic Americans). Average age 38. 8 applicants, 63% accepted. In 2001, 2 degrees awarded.
Entrance requirements: For master's, TOEFL, minimum GPA of 2.7.
Expenses: Tuition, state resident: full-time $2,772; part-time $245 per credit. Tuition, nonresident: full-time $7,726; part-time $245 per credit. Required fees: $2,102. Tuition and fees vary according to course level and degree level.
Financial support: Application deadline: 3/15.
Dr. Timothy Rickard, Coordinator, 860-832-2921.

■ CENTRAL MICHIGAN UNIVERSITY

College of Extended Learning, Program in Administration, Mount Pleasant, MI 48859

AWARDS General administration (MSA); health services administration (MSA, Certificate); hospitality and tourism (MSA, Certificate); human resources administration (MSA, Certificate); information resource management (MSA, Certificate); international administration (MSA, Certificate); leadership (MSA, Certificate); public administration (MSA, Certificate); software engineering administration (MSA, Certificate). Part-time and evening/weekend programs available. Postbaccalaureate distance learning degree programs offered (no on-campus study).

Faculty: 1,800 part-time/adjunct (0 women).
Students: Average age 38.
Entrance requirements: For master's, minimum GPA of 2.7 in major. *Application fee:* $50.
Financial support: Available to part-time students. Applicants required to submit FAFSA.
Dr. Terry Rawls, Director, 989-774-6525.
Application contact: 800-950-1144 Ext. 1205, *Fax:* 989-774-2461, *E-mail:* celinfo@mail.cel.cmich.edu. *Web site:* http://www.cel.cmich.edu/

■ CITY COLLEGE OF THE CITY UNIVERSITY OF NEW YORK

Graduate School, College of Liberal Arts and Science, Division of Social Science, Program in International Relations, New York, NY 10031-9198

AWARDS MA. Part-time programs available.

Students: 75. In 2001, 8 degrees awarded.
Degree requirements: For master's, one foreign language, thesis.
Entrance requirements: For master's, TOEFL. *Application deadline:* For fall admission, 5/1; for spring admission, 12/1. *Application fee:* $40.
Expenses: Tuition, state resident: part-time $185 per credit. Tuition, nonresident: part-time $320 per credit. Required fees: $43 per term.
Financial support: Fellowships, research assistantships, teaching assistantships, career-related internships or fieldwork available.
Faculty research: International finance, international economics, European diplomatic history, area studies, international politics and diplomacy.

City College of the City University of New York (continued)

Prof. Jacqueline Braveboy-Wagner, Director, 212-650-5846.

■ CLAREMONT GRADUATE UNIVERSITY

Graduate Programs, School of Politics and Economics, Department of Politics and Policy, Claremont, CA 91711-6160

AWARDS International political economy (MAIPE); international studies (MAIS); political science (PhD); politics (MAP); politics, economics, and business (MAPEB); public policy (MAPP). Part-time programs available.

Faculty: 9 full-time (2 women), 2 part-time/adjunct (1 woman).
Students: 158 full-time (62 women), 43 part-time (19 women); includes 42 minority (19 African Americans, 6 Asian Americans or Pacific Islanders, 17 Hispanic Americans), 40 international. Average age 34. In 2001, 25 master's, 9 doctorates awarded. Terminal master's awarded for partial completion of doctoral program.
Degree requirements: For master's, thesis; for doctorate, one foreign language, thesis/dissertation.
Entrance requirements: For master's and doctorate, GRE General Test. *Application deadline:* For fall admission, 2/15 (priority date). Applications are processed on a rolling basis. *Application fee:* $50. Electronic applications accepted.
Expenses: Tuition: Full-time $22,984; part-time $1,000 per unit. Required fees: $160; $80 per semester.
Financial support: Fellowships, research assistantships, teaching assistantships, career-related internships or fieldwork, Federal Work-Study, and institutionally sponsored loans available. Support available to part-time students. Financial award application deadline: 2/15; financial award applicants required to submit FAFSA.
Faculty research: Environmental policy, international debt, global democratization, Third World development, public sector discrimination.
Yi Fens, Chair, 909-621-8171, *Fax:* 909-621-8390, *E-mail:* yi.fens@cgu.edu.
Application contact: Gwen Williams, Program Administrator, 909-621-8179, *Fax:* 909-621-8545, *E-mail:* gwen.williams@cgu.edu. *Web site:* http://spe.cgu.edu/politics/index.html

Find an in-depth description at www.petersons.com/gradchannel.

■ CLARK ATLANTA UNIVERSITY

School of International Affairs and Development, Atlanta, GA 30314

AWARDS International affairs and development (PhD); international business and development (MA); international development administration (MA); international development education and planning (MA); international relations (MA); regional studies (MA).

Degree requirements: For master's, one foreign language, thesis; for doctorate, 2 foreign languages, thesis/dissertation.
Entrance requirements: For master's, GRE General Test, minimum GPA of 2.5; for doctorate, GRE General Test, minimum graduate GPA of 3.0.

■ COLUMBIA UNIVERSITY

School of International and Public Affairs, Program in International Affairs, New York, NY 10027

AWARDS MIA, JD/MIA, MBA/MIA, MIA/MS, MPH/MIA, MSJ/MIA. Part-time programs available.

Students: 623 full-time (332 women), 75 part-time (45 women). Average age 27. 1,600 applicants, 34% accepted. In 2001, 383 degrees awarded.
Degree requirements: For master's, one foreign language.
Entrance requirements: For master's, GRE General Test (recommended), TOEFL. *Application deadline:* For fall admission, 1/5 (priority date); for spring admission, 10/15. *Application fee:* $75. Electronic applications accepted.
Financial support: In 2001–02, 455 students received support, including 173 fellowships with full and partial tuition reimbursements available (averaging $4,000 per year), 14 teaching assistantships with full and partial tuition reimbursements available (averaging $6,000 per year); research assistantships, career-related internships or fieldwork, Federal Work-Study, and institutionally sponsored loans also available. Financial award application deadline: 1/5; financial award applicants required to submit FAFSA.
Dr. Anthony Marx, Director, 212-854-6216, *Fax:* 212-854-3010, *E-mail:* sipa_admission@columbia.edu.
Application contact: Robert Garris, Associate Director, 212-854-6216, *Fax:* 212-854-3010, *E-mail:* sipa_admission@columbia.edu.

Find an in-depth description at www.petersons.com/gradchannel.

■ CORNELL UNIVERSITY

Graduate School, Graduate Fields of Arts and Sciences, Field of Government, Ithaca, NY 14853-0001

AWARDS American politics (PhD); comparative politics (PhD); international relations (PhD); political thought (PhD).

Faculty: 41 full-time.
Students: 69 full-time (31 women); includes 8 minority (2 African Americans, 4 Asian Americans or Pacific Islanders, 2 Hispanic Americans), 36 international. 283 applicants, 10% accepted. In 2001, 8 doctorates awarded.
Degree requirements: For doctorate, thesis/dissertation.
Entrance requirements: For doctorate, GRE General Test, TOEFL, sample of written work, 3 letters of recommendation. *Application deadline:* For fall admission, 1/15. *Application fee:* $65. Electronic applications accepted.
Expenses: Tuition: Full-time $25,970. Required fees: $50.
Financial support: In 2001–02, 62 students received support, including 28 fellowships with full tuition reimbursements available, 1 research assistantship with full tuition reimbursement available, 33 teaching assistantships with full tuition reimbursements available; institutionally sponsored loans, scholarships/grants, tuition waivers (full and partial), and unspecified assistantships also available. Financial award applicants required to submit FAFSA.
Faculty research: Political theory, American politics, comparative politics, international relations, methodology.
Application contact: Graduate Field Assistant, 607-255-3567, *E-mail:* cu_govt@cornell.edu. *Web site:* http://www.gradschool.cornell.edu/grad/fields_1/govt.html

■ CREIGHTON UNIVERSITY

Graduate School, College of Arts and Sciences, Program in International Relations, Omaha, NE 68178-0001

AWARDS MA.

Faculty: 13 full-time.
Students: 3 full-time (0 women), 11 part-time (5 women), 3 international. In 2001, 3 degrees awarded.
Degree requirements: For master's, one foreign language, thesis.
Entrance requirements: For master's, GRE General Test, TOEFL. *Application deadline:* For fall admission, 3/1. Applications are processed on a rolling basis. *Application fee:* $40.
Dr. Terry Clark, Chair, 402-280-2884, *E-mail:* tclark@creighton.edu.
Application contact: Dr. Barbara J. Braden, Dean, Graduate School, 402-280-2870, *Fax:* 402-280-5762, *E-mail:* bbraden@creighton.edu.

■ DEPAUL UNIVERSITY

College of Liberal Arts and Sciences, Program in International Studies, Chicago, IL 60604-2287

AWARDS MA, MA/MS. Evening/weekend programs available.

Faculty: 16 full-time (6 women).
Students: 6 full-time (4 women), 10 part-time (9 women); includes 2 minority (1 Asian American or Pacific Islander, 1 Hispanic American), 4 international. Average age 25. 25 applicants, 76% accepted. In 2001, 6 degrees awarded.

Degree requirements: For master's, one foreign language, thesis. *Median time to degree:* Master's–3 years full-time.
Entrance requirements: For master's, previous course work in microeconomics, macroeconomics, or equivalent; competence in a second language. *Application deadline:* For fall admission, 3/1 (priority date). Applications are processed on a rolling basis. *Application fee:* $25.
Expenses: Tuition: Part-time $362 per credit hour. Tuition and fees vary according to program.
Financial support: In 2001–02, 9 students received support; fellowships with partial tuition reimbursements available, career-related internships or fieldwork, institutionally sponsored loans, scholarships/grants, and tuition waivers (partial) available. Support available to part-time students. Financial award application deadline: 4/1.
Faculty research: International political economy, global culture, human rights, law, international organization.
Michael McIntyre, Director, 773-325-7877, *Fax:* 773-325-7556, *E-mail:* mmcintyr@depaul.edu.
Application contact: Dr. Gil Gott, Director of Graduate Studies, 773-325-4548, *Fax:* 773-325-7556, *E-mail:* ggott@depaul.edu. *Web site:* http://condor.depaul.edu/~intstuds/

■ DEPAUL UNIVERSITY

College of Liberal Arts and Sciences, Programs in Public Services, Program in International Public Service Management, Chicago, IL 60604-2287

AWARDS MA/MS.

Faculty: 11 full-time (5 women), 18 part-time/adjunct (9 women).
Students: 4 full-time (3 women), 5 part-time (3 women); includes 4 minority (1 African American, 2 Asian Americans or Pacific Islanders, 1 Hispanic American), 1 international. 4 applicants, 100% accepted.
Degree requirements: One foreign language.
Application deadline: For fall admission, 7/1 (priority date); for winter admission, 10/1 (priority date); for spring admission, 2/1 (priority date). Applications are processed on a rolling basis. *Application fee:* $25. Electronic applications accepted.
Expenses: Tuition: Part-time $362 per credit hour. Tuition and fees vary according to program.
Financial support: In 2001–02, 2 research assistantships (averaging $6,000 per year) were awarded; career-related internships or fieldwork, Federal Work-Study, and scholarships/grants also available. Support available to part-time students. Financial award application deadline: 7/1.
Faculty research: Government financing, transportation, leadership, health care, empowerment zones. *Total annual research expenditures:* $20,000.
Dr. J. Patrick Murphy, Director, 312-362-8441, *Fax:* 312-362-5506, *E-mail:* jpmurphy@depaul.edu.
Application contact: 312-362-8441, *Fax:* 312-362-5506, *E-mail:* pubserv@depaul.edu. *Web site:* http://www.depaul.edu/~pubserv/

■ EAST CAROLINA UNIVERSITY

Graduate School, College of Arts and Sciences, Program in International Studies, Greenville, NC 27858-4353

AWARDS MA. Part-time programs available.

Students: 14 full-time (9 women), 11 part-time (5 women); includes 6 minority (1 African American, 4 Hispanic Americans, 1 Native American), 2 international. Average age 27. 13 applicants, 69% accepted. In 2001, 12 degrees awarded.
Degree requirements: For master's, comprehensive exam.
Entrance requirements: For master's, GRE General Test, TOEFL. *Application deadline:* Applications are processed on a rolling basis. *Application fee:* $45.
Expenses: Tuition, state resident: full-time $2,636. Tuition, nonresident: full-time $11,365.
Financial support: Research assistantships with partial tuition reimbursements available. Financial award application deadline: 6/1.
Lester Zeager, Director of Graduate Studies, 252-328-6408, *E-mail:* zeager1@mail.ecu.edu.
Application contact: Dr. Paul D. Tschetter, Senior Associate Dean of the Graduate School, 252-328-6012, *Fax:* 252-328-6071, *E-mail:* gradschool@mail.ecu.edu.

■ FAIRLEIGH DICKINSON UNIVERSITY, METROPOLITAN CAMPUS

University College: Arts, Sciences, and Professional Studies, School of History, Political, and International Studies, Program in International Studies, Teaneck, NJ 07666-1914

AWARDS MA.

Students: 2 full-time (1 woman), 1 part-time, 2 international. Average age 41. 2 applicants, 100% accepted, 0 enrolled. In 2001, 1 degree awarded.
Application deadline: Applications are processed on a rolling basis. *Application fee:* $40.
Expenses: Tuition: Full-time $11,484; part-time $638 per credit. Required fees: $420; $97.
Dr. Faramarz Fatemi, Director, School of History, Political, and International Studies, 201-692-2272, *Fax:* 201-692-9096, *E-mail:* fatemi@fdu.edu.

■ FLORIDA INTERNATIONAL UNIVERSITY

College of Arts and Sciences, Department of International Relations, Miami, FL 33199

AWARDS International relations (PhD); international studies (MA). Part-time and evening/weekend programs available.

Faculty: 17 full-time (4 women).
Students: 24 full-time (8 women), 21 part-time (9 women); includes 12 minority (5 African Americans, 7 Hispanic Americans), 17 international. Average age 35. 83 applicants, 45% accepted, 10 enrolled. In 2001, 5 master's, 2 doctorates awarded.
Degree requirements: For master's, one foreign language, thesis optional; for doctorate, one foreign language, thesis/dissertation.
Entrance requirements: For master's, GRE General Test, TOEFL; for doctorate, GRE General Test, TOEFL, minimum GPA of 3.2. *Application deadline:* For fall admission, 4/1 (priority date); for spring admission, 10/1. Applications are processed on a rolling basis. *Application fee:* $20.
Expenses: Tuition, state resident: full-time $2,916; part-time $162 per credit hour. Tuition, nonresident: full-time $10,245; part-time $569 per credit hour. Required fees: $168 per term.
Financial support: In 2001–02, 3 research assistantships were awarded; Federal Work-Study, institutionally sponsored loans, and tuition waivers (partial) also available. Support available to part-time students. Financial award application deadline: 4/1.
Faculty research: Democratization processes in Russia and the Ukraine.
Dr. Roderich Neumann, Chairperson, 305-348-2556, *Fax:* 305-348-2197, *E-mail:* neumannr@fiu.edu.

■ FLORIDA STATE UNIVERSITY

Graduate Studies, College of Social Sciences, Program in International Affairs, Tallahassee, FL 32306

AWARDS MA, MS, JD/MA, JD/MS. Part-time programs available.

Students: 20 full-time (11 women), 25 part-time (17 women); includes 16 minority (6 African Americans, 3 Asian Americans or Pacific Islanders, 6 Hispanic Americans, 1 Native American), 7 international. Average age 25. 83 applicants, 86% accepted, 25 enrolled. In 2001, 25 degrees awarded.
Degree requirements: For master's, one foreign language, comprehensive exam. *Median time to degree:* Master's–1.5 years full-time, 2 years part-time.
Entrance requirements: For master's, GRE General Test, minimum GPA of 3.0. *Application deadline:* For fall admission,

Florida State University (continued)
6/15; for spring admission, 10/15. Applications are processed on a rolling basis. *Application fee:* $20.
Expenses: Tuition, state resident: part-time $163 per credit hour. Tuition, nonresident: part-time $570 per credit hour. Tuition and fees vary according to program.
Financial support: In 2001–02, fellowships with full tuition reimbursements (averaging $10,000 per year), 5 research assistantships with full tuition reimbursements (averaging $5,000 per year) were awarded. Career-related internships or fieldwork, Federal Work-Study, and institutionally sponsored loans also available. Financial award application deadline: 3/15; financial award applicants required to submit FAFSA.
Dr. Burton Atkins, Director, 850-644-7327, *Fax:* 850-645-4981, *E-mail:* batkins@garnet.acns.fsu.edu.
Application contact: Patty Lollis, Program Assistant, 850-644-4418, *Fax:* 850-645-4981, *E-mail:* plollis@mailer.fsu.edu. *Web site:* http://www.fsu.edu/~inaprog/

■ GEORGE MASON UNIVERSITY

School of Public Policy, Program in International Commerce and Policy, Fairfax, VA 22030-4444

AWARDS MA.

Degree requirements: For master's, thesis or alternative.
Entrance requirements: For master's, minimum GPA of 3.0 in last 60 hours. Electronic applications accepted.
Expenses: Tuition, state resident: full-time $3,168; part-time $132 per credit hour. Tuition, nonresident: full-time $11,280; part-time $470 per credit hour. Required fees: $1,416; $59 per credit hour. *Web site:* http://www.gmu.edu/departments/t-mait/program/mait-p.htm

■ GEORGETOWN UNIVERSITY

Graduate School of Arts and Sciences, BMW Center for German and European Studies, Washington, DC 20057

AWARDS MA, MA/PhD.

Degree requirements: For master's, 2 foreign languages, comprehensive exam.
Entrance requirements: For master's, GRE General Test, TOEFL. *Web site:* http://www.georgetown.edu/sfs/cges

Find an in-depth description at www.petersons.com/gradchannel.

■ GEORGETOWN UNIVERSITY

Graduate School of Arts and Sciences, Department of Government, Washington, DC 20057

AWARDS American government (MA, PhD); comparative government (PhD); international relations (PhD); political theory (PhD). Terminal master's awarded for partial completion of doctoral program.

Degree requirements: For master's, one foreign language, comprehensive exam; for doctorate, one foreign language, thesis/dissertation, comprehensive exam.
Entrance requirements: For master's, GRE General Test, TOEFL, minimum B average; for doctorate, GRE General Test, TOEFL, MA.
Faculty research: Western Europe, Latin America, the Middle East, political theory, international relations and law, methodology, American politics and institutions.

■ GEORGETOWN UNIVERSITY

Graduate School of Arts and Sciences, Edmund A. Walsh School of Foreign Service, Washington, DC 20057

AWARDS MS, JD/MS, MBA/MS, MS/MA.

Degree requirements: For master's, one foreign language, comprehensive exam.
Entrance requirements: For master's, GRE General Test, TOEFL, 3 semesters of undergraduate course work in economics.
Faculty research: International business diplomacy, political risk analysis, foreign policy decision making, intercultural perspectives on contemporary issues.

Find an in-depth description at www.petersons.com/gradchannel.

■ THE GEORGE WASHINGTON UNIVERSITY

Elliott School of International Affairs, Program in International Affairs, Washington, DC 20052

AWARDS MA, JD/MA, LL M/MA, MBA/MA. Part-time and evening/weekend programs available.

Students: 187 full-time (119 women), 57 part-time (35 women); includes 41 minority (8 African Americans, 14 Asian Americans or Pacific Islanders, 18 Hispanic Americans, 1 Native American), 34 international. Average age 25. 507 applicants, 76% accepted. In 2001, 91 degrees awarded.
Degree requirements: For master's, one foreign language.
Entrance requirements: For master's, GRE General Test, TOEFL, minimum B average. *Application deadline:* For fall admission, 2/1. *Application fee:* $55. Electronic applications accepted.
Expenses: Tuition: Part-time $810 per credit. Required fees: $1 per credit.
Financial support: Fellowships with tuition reimbursements, research assistantships with tuition reimbursements, career-related internships or fieldwork, Federal Work-Study, institutionally sponsored loans, and tuition waivers (full) available. Financial award application deadline: 1/15; financial award applicants required to submit FAFSA.
Faculty research: Area studies, international economics, national security policy studies, international economic development, Sino-Soviet studies.
Dr. Karl Inderfurth, Director, 202-994-2619.
Application contact: Jeff V. Miles, Director of Graduate Admissions, 202-994-7050, *Fax:* 202-994-9537, *E-mail:* esiagrad@gwu.edu. *Web site:* http://www.gwu.edu/~elliott/

Find an in-depth description at www.petersons.com/gradchannel.

■ THE GEORGE WASHINGTON UNIVERSITY

Elliott School of International Affairs, Program in International Policy and Practice, Washington, DC 20052

AWARDS MIS. Part-time and evening/weekend programs available.

Students: 21 full-time (10 women), 12 part-time (5 women); includes 2 minority (1 African American, 1 Hispanic American), 19 international. Average age 39. 106 applicants, 63% accepted. In 2001, 17 degrees awarded.
Degree requirements: For master's, one foreign language.
Entrance requirements: For master's, GRE General Test, TOEFL, advanced degree or 8 years experience plus BA. *Application deadline:* For fall admission, 5/15; for spring admission, 11/15. *Application fee:* $55. Electronic applications accepted.
Expenses: Tuition: Part-time $810 per credit. Required fees: $1 per credit.
Financial support: Fellowships with tuition reimbursements, research assistantships with tuition reimbursements, career-related internships or fieldwork, Federal Work-Study, and institutionally sponsored loans available. Financial award application deadline: 1/15; financial award applicants required to submit FAFSA.
Dr. Kristin Lord, Director, 202-994-0562.
Application contact: Jeff V. Miles, Director of Graduate Admissions, 202-994-7050, *Fax:* 202-994-9537, *E-mail:* esiagrad@gwu.edu. *Web site:* http://www.gwu.edu/~elliott/

■ GEORGIA INSTITUTE OF TECHNOLOGY

Graduate Studies and Research, Ivan Allen College of Policy and International Affairs, Sam Nunn School of International Affairs, Atlanta, GA 30332-0001

AWARDS MS Int A.

Degree requirements: For master's, one foreign language.
Entrance requirements: For master's, TOEFL. Electronic applications accepted.

Faculty research: International political economy, international security, Asian and European studies.

Find an in-depth description at www.petersons.com/gradchannel.

■ HARVARD UNIVERSITY

Graduate School of Arts and Sciences, Department of Government, Cambridge, MA 02138

AWARDS Political science (AM, PhD), including American politics, comparative politics, international relations, political thought, quantitative methods.

Degree requirements: For doctorate, one foreign language, thesis/dissertation, general exams.
Entrance requirements: For master's and doctorate, GRE General Test, TOEFL.
Expenses: Tuition: Full-time $23,370. Required fees: $816. Full-time tuition and fees vary according to program and student level.

■ JOHNS HOPKINS UNIVERSITY

Paul H. Nitze School of Advanced International Studies, Washington, DC 20036

AWARDS Emerging markets (Certificate); interdisciplinary studies (MA, PhD), including African studies, American foreign policy (MA), Asian studies, Canadian studies, conflict resolution and mediation (MA), environmental policy and resource management (MA), European studies, international business (MA), international development (MA), international economics (MA), international relations (MA), Latin American studies, Middle Eastern studies (MA), military and defense studies (MA), Russian area and East European studies (MA), social change and development (MA); international public policy (MIPP). MBA/MA offered jointly with the University of Pennsylvania–Wharton School and INSEAD in France.

Faculty: 44 full-time (13 women), 113 part-time/adjunct (29 women).
Students: 567 full-time (275 women), 17 part-time (8 women); includes 71 minority (14 African Americans, 46 Asian Americans or Pacific Islanders, 10 Hispanic Americans, 1 Native American). Average age 27. 1,288 applicants, 35% accepted. In 2001, 294 master's, 13 doctorates, 34 other advanced degrees awarded. Terminal master's awarded for partial completion of doctoral program.
Degree requirements: For master's, one foreign language, comprehensive exam; for doctorate, 2 foreign languages, thesis/dissertation.
Entrance requirements: For master's, GMAT or GRE General Test or TOEFL, previous course work in economics, foreign language; for doctorate, GRE General Test or TOEFL; for Certificate, TOEFL. *Application deadline:* For fall admission, 1/15. *Application fee:* $75. Electronic applications accepted.
Expenses: Contact institution.
Financial support: In 2001–02, 431 fellowships (averaging $5,500 per year) were awarded; career-related internships or fieldwork and Federal Work-Study also available. Financial award application deadline: 2/1; financial award applicants required to submit FAFSA.
Faculty research: Comparative politics, regional studies, language and linguistics.
Dr. Jessica Einhorn, Dean, 202-663-5624, *Fax:* 202-663-5621.
Application contact: Bonnie Wilson, Associate Dean of Student Affairs, 202-663-5700, *Fax:* 202-663-7788, *E-mail:* admissions.sais@jhu.edu. *Web site:* http://www.sais-jhu.edu/

Find an in-depth description at www.petersons.com/gradchannel.

■ KANSAS STATE UNIVERSITY

Graduate School, College of Arts and Sciences, Department of Political Science, Program in Political Science, Manhattan, KS 66506

AWARDS International relations (MA). Part-time programs available.

Students: 15 full-time (6 women), 11 part-time (6 women); includes 4 minority (2 African Americans, 1 Asian American or Pacific Islander, 1 Native American), 11 international. Average age 33. In 2001, 2 degrees awarded.
Degree requirements: For master's, thesis or alternative.
Entrance requirements: For master's, GRE (recommended), TOEFL, minimum GPA of 3.0. *Application deadline:* For fall admission, 2/1 (priority date); for spring admission, 10/1. Applications are processed on a rolling basis. *Application fee:* $0 ($25 for international students).
Expenses: Tuition, state resident: part-time $113 per credit hour. Tuition, nonresident: part-time $358 per credit hour.
Financial support: Fellowships, research assistantships, teaching assistantships, institutionally sponsored loans and scholarships/grants available. Support available to part-time students. Financial award application deadline: 3/1; financial award applicants required to submit FAFSA. *Total annual research expenditures:* $16,958.
Application contact: Scott Tollefson, Graduate Program Director, 785-532-0449, *Fax:* 785-532-2339, *E-mail:* tollef@ksu.edu. *Web site:* http://www.ksu.edu/polsci/

■ KENT STATE UNIVERSITY

College of Arts and Sciences, Department of Political Science, Kent, OH 44242-0001

AWARDS American politics (MA, PhD); comparative politics (MA); international politics (PhD); international relations (MA); political theory (MA, PhD); public administration (MPA).

Degree requirements: For master's, thesis optional; for doctorate, 2 foreign languages, thesis/dissertation.
Entrance requirements: For master's, GRE General Test, TOEFL, minimum GPA of 2.75; for doctorate, GRE General Test, TOEFL, minimum GPA of 3.0. Electronic applications accepted.

■ LESLEY UNIVERSITY

Graduate School of Arts and Social Sciences, Program in Intercultural Relations, Cambridge, MA 02138-2790

AWARDS Development project administration (MA); individually designed (MA); intercultural conflict resolution (MA); intercultural health and human services (MA); intercultural relations (CAGS); intercultural training and consulting (MA); international education exchange (MA); international student advising (MA); managing culturally diverse human resources (MA); multicultural education (MA). Part-time and evening/weekend programs available.

Faculty: 3 full-time (2 women), 3 part-time/adjunct (all women).
Students: Average age 30. 35 applicants, 94% accepted, 4 enrolled. In 2001, 9 degrees awarded.
Degree requirements: For master's, one foreign language; for CAGS, one foreign language, thesis. *Median time to degree:* Master's–2 years part-time.
Entrance requirements: For master's, TOEFL, interview; for CAGS, interview, master's degree. *Application deadline:* Applications are processed on a rolling basis. *Application fee:* $50.
Expenses: Tuition: Part-time $330 per credit. Required fees: $15 per term. Part-time tuition and fees vary according to campus/location and program.
Financial support: In 2001–02, 8 students received support; research assistantships, teaching assistantships, career-related internships or fieldwork, Federal Work-Study, scholarships/grants, and unspecified assistantships available. Support available to part-time students. Financial award application deadline: 4/1; financial award applicants required to submit FAFSA.
Faculty research: Sociolinguistics, cross-cultural feminist theory, immigration and diaspora, intercultural business training.
Sylvia R. Cowan, Coordinator, 617-349-8978, *E-mail:* scowan@mail.lesley.edu.
Application contact: Hugh Norwood, Dean of Admissions and Enrollment Planning, 800-999-1959, *Fax:* 617-349-8366, *E-mail:* hnorwood@mail.lesley.edu.

■ LONG ISLAND UNIVERSITY, BROOKLYN CAMPUS

Richard L. Conolly College of Liberal Arts and Sciences, Program in Social Science, Brooklyn, NY 11201-8423

AWARDS History (MS); United Nations studies (Certificate). Part-time and evening/weekend programs available.

Electronic applications accepted.

■ LONG ISLAND UNIVERSITY, C.W. POST CAMPUS

College of Liberal Arts and Sciences, Department of Political Science/International Studies, Brookville, NY 11548-1300

AWARDS Political science/international studies (MA); social studies secondary education (MS). Part-time and evening/weekend programs available.

Faculty: 7 full-time (1 woman), 6 part-time/adjunct (2 women).
Students: 4 full-time (3 women), 9 part-time (6 women). Average age 23. 33 applicants, 91% accepted, 19 enrolled. In 2001, 12 degrees awarded.
Degree requirements: For master's, thesis or alternative, comprehensive exam.
Entrance requirements: For master's, GRE. *Application deadline:* For fall admission, 9/1 (priority date); for winter admission, 12/15 (priority date); for spring admission, 1/20 (priority date). Applications are processed on a rolling basis. *Application fee:* $30. Electronic applications accepted.
Expenses: Tuition: Full-time $10,296; part-time $572 per credit. Required fees: $380; $190 per semester.
Financial support: In 2001–02, 2 research assistantships were awarded; career-related internships or fieldwork and Federal Work-Study also available. Support available to part-time students. Financial award application deadline: 5/15; financial award applicants required to submit CSS PROFILE or FAFSA.
Faculty research: International relations, middle eastern politics, political philosophy.
Dr. Roger Goldstein, Chairman, 516-299-2407, *Fax:* 516-299-4140.
Application contact: Dr. Michael Soupios, Graduate Adviser, 516-299-3026. *Web site:* http://www.liu.edu/postlas/

■ LOYOLA UNIVERSITY CHICAGO

Graduate School, Department of Political Science, Chicago, IL 60611-2196

AWARDS American politics and policy (MA, PhD); international studies (MA, PhD); political theory and philosophy (MA, PhD). Part-time and evening/weekend programs available.

Faculty: 18 full-time (2 women).
Students: 42 full-time (18 women), 8 part-time (4 women); includes 6 minority (2 African Americans, 4 Hispanic Americans), 2 international. Average age 25. 66 applicants, 79% accepted. In 2001, 8 master's, 3 doctorates awarded.
Degree requirements: For master's, thesis or alternative; for doctorate, variable foreign language requirement, thesis/dissertation, comprehensive exam.
Entrance requirements: For master's and doctorate, GRE General Test. *Application deadline:* For fall admission, 8/1 (priority date); for spring admission, 12/1 (priority date). Applications are processed on a rolling basis. *Application fee:* $40. Electronic applications accepted.
Expenses: Tuition: Part-time $529 per credit hour.
Financial support: In 2001–02, 22 students received support, including 14 fellowships with full tuition reimbursements available (averaging $9,000 per year), 14 research assistantships with full tuition reimbursements available (averaging $9,000 per year); Federal Work-Study, institutionally sponsored loans, scholarships/grants, tuition waivers (partial), and unspecified assistantships also available. Financial award application deadline: 2/1; financial award applicants required to submit FAFSA.
Faculty research: American parties and elections, state and local politics, American political institutions, international political economy, modern and contemporary political thought.
Dr. John P. Pelissero, Chair, 773-508-3066, *Fax:* 773-508-3131, *E-mail:* jpeliss@luc.edu.
Application contact: Dr. Claudio Katz, Director of Graduate Programs, 773-508-3068, *Fax:* 773-508-3131, *E-mail:* ckatz@luc.edu. *Web site:* http://www.luc.edu/grad/polisci/

■ MARQUETTE UNIVERSITY

Graduate School, College of Arts and Sciences, Department of Political Science, Milwaukee, WI 53201-1881

AWARDS International affairs (MA), including comparative politics, international political economy, international politics; political science (MA), including American politics, comparative politics, international politics, political philosophy. Part-time programs available.

Faculty: 13 full-time (1 woman), 1 part-time/adjunct (0 women).
Students: 5 full-time (2 women), 3 part-time (1 woman); includes 1 minority (African American). Average age 27. 9 applicants, 89% accepted. In 2001, 2 degrees awarded.
Degree requirements: For master's, thesis optional.
Entrance requirements: For master's, GRE General Test, TOEFL. *Application fee:* $40.
Expenses: Tuition: Full-time $10,170; part-time $445 per credit hour. Tuition and fees vary according to course load.
Financial support: In 2001–02, 5 research assistantships were awarded; Federal Work-Study, institutionally sponsored loans, scholarships/grants, and tuition waivers (full and partial) also available. Support available to part-time students. Financial award application deadline: 2/15.
Faculty research: Public opinion and electoral behavior, public policy analysis, Congress and the Presidency, judicial behavior, political system transitions. *Total annual research expenditures:* $228,488.
Dr. H. Richard Friman, Chairman, 414-288-6842, *Fax:* 414-288-3360.
Application contact: Dr. Barrett McCormick, Director of Graduate Studies, 414-288-6842, *Fax:* 414-288-3360.

■ MONTEREY INSTITUTE OF INTERNATIONAL STUDIES

Graduate School of International Policy Studies, Program in Commercial Diplomacy, Monterey, CA 93940-2691

AWARDS MA.

Students: 35 full-time (13 women), 2 part-time (1 woman); includes 2 minority (both Hispanic Americans), 18 international. Average age 28. 21 applicants, 95% accepted, 14 enrolled. In 2001, 19 degrees awarded.
Degree requirements: For master's, one foreign language.
Entrance requirements: For master's, TOEFL, minimum GPA of 3.0, proficiency in a foreign language. *Application deadline:* For fall admission, 3/15 (priority date); for spring admission, 10/1 (priority date). Applications are processed on a rolling basis. *Application fee:* $50. Electronic applications accepted.
Expenses: Tuition: Full-time $19,988; part-time $840 per unit. Required fees: $50. Part-time tuition and fees vary according to course load and reciprocity agreements.
Dr. William Monning, Head, 831-647-6426, *E-mail:* bill.monning@miis.edu.
Application contact: 831-647-4123, *Fax:* 831-647-6405, *E-mail:* admit@miis.edu.

■ MONTEREY INSTITUTE OF INTERNATIONAL STUDIES

Graduate School of International Policy Studies, Program in International Environmental Policy, Monterey, CA 93940-2691

AWARDS International environmental policy (MA).

Students: 39 full-time (23 women), 3 part-time (1 woman); includes 7 minority (1 African American, 3 Asian Americans or Pacific Islanders, 3 Hispanic Americans), 13 international. Average age 28. 34

applicants, 97% accepted, 14 enrolled. In 2001, 24 degrees awarded.
Degree requirements: For master's, one foreign language.
Entrance requirements: For master's, TOEFL, minimum GPA of 3.0, proficiency in a foreign language. *Application deadline:* For fall admission, 3/15 (priority date); for spring admission, 10/1 (priority date). Applications are processed on a rolling basis. *Application fee:* $50. Electronic applications accepted.
Expenses: Tuition: Full-time $19,988; part-time $840 per unit. Required fees: $50. Part-time tuition and fees vary according to course load and reciprocity agreements.
Financial support: Applicants required to submit FAFSA.
Dr. Jackson Davis, Head, 831-647-3564, *Fax:* 831-647-4199.
Application contact: 831-647-4123, *Fax:* 831-647-6405, *E-mail:* admit@miis.edu.

Find an in-depth description at www.petersons.com/gradchannel.

■ MONTEREY INSTITUTE OF INTERNATIONAL STUDIES

Graduate School of International Policy Studies, Program in International Policy Studies, Monterey, CA 93940-2691

AWARDS MA.

Students: 144 full-time (90 women), 8 part-time (4 women); includes 14 minority (4 African Americans, 5 Asian Americans or Pacific Islanders, 5 Hispanic Americans), 48 international. Average age 28. 185 applicants, 96% accepted, 72 enrolled. In 2001, 73 degrees awarded.
Degree requirements: For master's, one foreign language.
Entrance requirements: For master's, TOEFL, minimum GPA of 3.0, proficiency in a foreign language. *Application deadline:* For fall admission, 3/15 (priority date); for spring admission, 10/1 (priority date). Applications are processed on a rolling basis. *Application fee:* $50. Electronic applications accepted.
Expenses: Tuition: Full-time $19,988; part-time $840 per unit. Required fees: $50. Part-time tuition and fees vary according to course load and reciprocity agreements.
Financial support: In 2001–02, 82 students received support. Application deadline: 3/15.
Dr. Leslie Eliason, Head, 831-647-4159, *Fax:* 831-647-4199.
Application contact: 831-647-4123, *Fax:* 831-647-6405, *E-mail:* admit@miis.edu.

Find an in-depth description at www.petersons.com/gradchannel.

■ MONTEREY INSTITUTE OF INTERNATIONAL STUDIES

Graduate School of International Policy Studies, Program in International Public Administration, Monterey, CA 93940-2691

AWARDS International management (MPA).

Students: 29 full-time (21 women), 1 (woman) part-time. Average age 28. 14 applicants, 93% accepted, 9 enrolled. In 2001, 19 degrees awarded.
Degree requirements: For master's, one foreign language.
Entrance requirements: For master's, TOEFL, minimum GPA of 3.0, proficiency in a foreign language. *Application deadline:* For fall admission, 3/15 (priority date); for spring admission, 10/1 (priority date). Applications are processed on a rolling basis. *Application fee:* $50. Electronic applications accepted.
Expenses: Tuition: Full-time $19,988; part-time $840 per unit. Required fees: $50. Part-time tuition and fees vary according to course load and reciprocity agreements.
Financial support: In 2001–02, 11 students received support. Career-related internships or fieldwork, Federal Work-Study, and institutionally sponsored loans available. Support available to part-time students. Financial award application deadline: 3/15; financial award applicants required to submit FAFSA.
Application contact: 831-647-4123, *Fax:* 831-647-6405, *E-mail:* admit@miis.edu.

Find an in-depth description at www.petersons.com/gradchannel.

■ MORGAN STATE UNIVERSITY

School of Graduate Studies, College of Liberal Arts, Department of Political Science and International Studies, Baltimore, MD 21251

AWARDS International studies (MA). Part-time and evening/weekend programs available.

Students: 10 (6 women); includes 5 minority (all African Americans) 5 international.
Degree requirements: For master's, one foreign language, thesis, comprehensive exam.
Entrance requirements: For master's, GRE. *Application deadline:* For fall admission, 2/1; for spring admission, 10/1. Applications are processed on a rolling basis. *Application fee:* $0.
Expenses: Tuition, state resident: part-time $193 per credit. Tuition, nonresident: part-time $364 per credit. Required fees: $40 per credit.
Financial support: Application deadline: 4/1.
Dr. Max Hilaire, Chair, 443-885-3277, *Fax:* 443-319-3837, *E-mail:* gmetaferia@moac.morgan.edu.
Application contact: Dr. James E. Waller, Admissions and Programs Officer, 443-885-3185, *Fax:* 443-319-3837, *E-mail:* jwaller@moac.morgan.edu.

■ NEW SCHOOL UNIVERSITY

New School, Program in International Affairs, New York, NY 10011-8603

AWARDS Global management, trade, and finance (MA, MS); international development (MA, MS); international media and communication (MA, MS); international politics and diplomacy (MA, MS); service, civic, and non-profit management (MA, MS).

Students: 22 full-time (17 women), 23 part-time (12 women); includes 11 minority (5 African Americans, 1 Asian American or Pacific Islander, 5 Hispanic Americans), 8 international. 73 applicants, 93% accepted, 45 enrolled.
Application fee: $40.
Financial support: In 2001–02, 31 students received support. Tuition waivers (partial) available. Financial award application deadline: 5/1; financial award applicants required to submit FAFSA.
Dr. Michael Cohen, Head, *E-mail:* cohenm2@newschool.edu.
Application contact: Gerianne Brusati, Associate Dean, Admissions and Student Services, 212-229-5630, *Fax:* 212-989-3887, *E-mail:* nsadmissions@newschool.edu. *Web site:* http://www.nus.newschool.edu/04h_interaff.htm

Find an in-depth description at www.petersons.com/gradchannel.

■ NEW YORK UNIVERSITY

Graduate School of Arts and Science, Department of Politics, New York, NY 10012-1019

AWARDS French studies and politics (PhD); international politics and international business (MA); politics (MA, PhD); politics (Near Eastern studies) (PhD). Part-time programs available.

Faculty: 30 full-time (4 women), 24 part-time/adjunct.
Students: 73 full-time (36 women), 37 part-time (20 women); includes 12 minority (3 African Americans, 5 Asian Americans or Pacific Islanders, 4 Hispanic Americans), 47 international. Average age 27. 316 applicants, 27% accepted, 27 enrolled. In 2001, 17 master's, 6 doctorates awarded. Terminal master's awarded for partial completion of doctoral program.
Degree requirements: For master's, one foreign language, thesis or alternative; for doctorate, 2 foreign languages, thesis/dissertation, comprehensive exam.
Entrance requirements: For master's, GRE General Test, TOEFL; for doctorate, GRE General Test, TOEFL, master's degree in political science, minimum GPA of 2.5. *Application deadline:* For fall admission, 1/4 (priority date). *Application fee:* $60.

New York University (continued)
Expenses: Tuition: Full-time $19,536; part-time $814 per credit. Required fees: $1,330; $38 per credit. Tuition and fees vary according to course load and program.
Financial support: Fellowships with tuition reimbursements, teaching assistantships with tuition reimbursements, career-related internships or fieldwork, Federal Work-Study, and institutionally sponsored loans available. Financial award application deadline: 1/4; financial award applicants required to submit FAFSA.
Faculty research: Comparative politics, democratic theory and practice, rational choice, political economy; international relations.
Anna Harvey, Chair, 212-998-8500.
Application contact: Steven Brams, Director of Graduate Studies, 212-998-8500, *Fax:* 212-995-4184, *E-mail:* politics.program@nyu.edu. *Web site:* http://www.nyu.edu/gsas/dept/politics/

■ NEW YORK UNIVERSITY

Robert F. Wagner Graduate School of Public Service, Program in Public Administration, New York, NY 10012-1019

AWARDS Public administration (PhD); public and nonprofit management and policy (MPA, Advanced Certificate), including developmental administration (Advanced Certificate), financial management and public finance, human resources management (Advanced Certificate), international administration (Advanced Certificate), management for public and nonprofit organizations, public policy analysis, quantitative analysis and computer applications (Advanced Certificate), urban public policy (Advanced Certificate). Part-time and evening/weekend programs available.

Faculty: 15 full-time (6 women), 56 part-time/adjunct (28 women).
Students: 248 full-time (176 women), 226 part-time (168 women); includes 137 minority (61 African Americans, 43 Asian Americans or Pacific Islanders, 33 Hispanic Americans), 78 international. Average age 27. 614 applicants, 76% accepted, 185 enrolled. In 2001, 137 master's, 6 doctorates awarded.
Degree requirements: For master's, thesis or alternative, capstone/end event; for doctorate, one foreign language, thesis/dissertation.
Entrance requirements: For master's, minimum undergraduate GPA of 3.0; for doctorate, GMAT or GRE General Test, minimum GPA of 3.5. *Application deadline:* For fall admission, 7/15; for spring admission, 1/1. Applications are processed on a rolling basis. *Application fee:* $50.
Expenses: Tuition: Full-time $19,536; part-time $814 per credit. Required fees: $1,330; $38 per credit. Tuition and fees vary according to course load and program.
Financial support: In 2001–02, 217 students received support, including 203 fellowships (averaging $5,257 per year), 14 research assistantships with partial tuition reimbursements available (averaging $7,580 per year); career-related internships or fieldwork, Federal Work-Study, institutionally sponsored loans, scholarships/grants, and tuition waivers (full and partial) also available. Support available to part-time students. Financial award application deadline: 2/15; financial award applicants required to submit FAFSA.
Application contact: James Short, Director, Admissions and Financial Aid, 212-998-7414, *Fax:* 212-995-4164, *E-mail:* wagner.admissions@nyu.edu. *Web site:* http://www.nyu.edu.wagner/

Find an in-depth description at www.petersons.com/gradchannel.

■ NORTH CAROLINA STATE UNIVERSITY

Graduate School, College of Humanities and Social Sciences, Department of Political Science and Public Administration, Program in International Studies, Raleigh, NC 27695

AWARDS MAIS.

Faculty: 29 full-time (5 women), 1 part-time/adjunct (0 women).
Students: 15 full-time (7 women), 7 part-time (3 women); includes 3 minority (2 African Americans, 1 Asian American or Pacific Islander), 1 international. Average age 30. 22 applicants, 55% accepted. In 2001, 12 degrees awarded.
Entrance requirements: For master's, GRE General Test, minimum GPA of 3.0 during previous 2 years. *Application deadline:* For fall admission, 6/25; for spring admission, 11/25. *Application fee:* $45.
Expenses: Tuition, state resident: full-time $1,748. Tuition, nonresident: full-time $6,904.
Financial support: In 2001–02, 1 fellowship (averaging $1,504 per year), 4 teaching assistantships (averaging $3,024 per year) were awarded.
Faculty research: Global environmental policy and climate change, drug policy and the Carribbean, U.S. national security politics, local responses to globalization.
Dr. Marvin S. Soroos, Director of Graduate Programs, 919-515-3755, *Fax:* 919-515-7333, *E-mail:* soroos@social.chass.ncsu.edu.
Application contact: Clifford E Griffin, Director of Graduate Programs, 919-515-3755, *Fax:* 919-515-7333. *Web site:* http://www2.ncsu.edu/ncsu/chass/intstu/grad.html

■ NORTHEASTERN UNIVERSITY

College of Arts and Sciences, Department of Political Science, Boston, MA 02115-5096

AWARDS American government and politics (MA); comparative government and politics (MA); international relations (MA); political theory (MA); public administration (MPA), including development administration, health administration and policy, management information systems, state and local government; public and international affairs (PhD). Part-time and evening/weekend programs available.

Faculty: 18 full-time (2 women), 10 part-time/adjunct (1 woman).
Students: 54 full-time (26 women), 27 part-time (17 women); includes 11 minority (3 African Americans, 2 Asian Americans or Pacific Islanders, 6 Hispanic Americans), 15 international. Average age 30. 133 applicants, 66% accepted. In 2001, 33 degrees awarded.
Degree requirements: For master's, thesis optional.
Entrance requirements: For master's, GRE General Test, TOEFL. *Application deadline:* Applications are processed on a rolling basis. *Application fee:* $50.
Expenses: Tuition: Part-time $535 per credit hour. Required fees: $56. Tuition and fees vary according to program.
Financial support: In 2001–02, 12 teaching assistantships with tuition reimbursements (averaging $12,000 per year) were awarded; research assistantships with tuition reimbursements, career-related internships or fieldwork, Federal Work-Study, tuition waivers (full and partial), and unspecified assistantships also available. Support available to part-time students. Financial award applicants required to submit FAFSA.
Faculty research: Presidency, public opinion, Congress, democratization, national identity.
Dr. Denis Sullivan, Chair, 617-373-2796, *Fax:* 617-373-5311, *E-mail:* gradpolisci@neu.edu.
Application contact: Mary Churchill, Administrative Assistant for Graduate Programs, 617-373-4404, *Fax:* 617-373-5311, *E-mail:* gradpolisci@neu.edu. *Web site:* http://www.casdn.neu.edu/~poliscil/

Find an in-depth description at www.petersons.com/gradchannel.

■ NORTHWESTERN UNIVERSITY

The Graduate School, Center for International and Comparative Studies, Evanston, IL 60208

AWARDS Certificate.

Application fee: $50 ($55 for international students).
Expenses: Tuition: Full-time $26,526.
Kenneth W. Abbott, Director, 847-467-2770, *Fax:* 847-467-1996, *E-mail:*

k-abbott@northwestern.edu. *Web site:* http://www.nwu.edu/cics/

■ OHIO UNIVERSITY

Graduate Studies, Center for International Studies, Program in Communications and Development Studies, Athens, OH 45701-2979

AWARDS MA.

Faculty: 13 full-time (5 women), 4 part-time/adjunct (2 women).
Students: 19 full-time (8 women), 2 part-time (both women). Average age 24. 42 applicants, 90% accepted.
Degree requirements: For master's, one foreign language, thesis optional.
Entrance requirements: For master's, GRE, TOEFL (for foreign language area studies), minimum GPA of 3.0. *Application deadline:* For fall admission, 3/1 (priority date). *Application fee:* $30.
Expenses: Tuition, state resident: full-time $6,585. Tuition, nonresident: full-time $12,254.
Financial support: In 2001–02, 13 students received support, including 6 research assistantships with full tuition reimbursements available (averaging $9,400 per year); Federal Work-Study, institutionally sponsored loans, and tuition waivers (full) also available. Financial award application deadline: 1/15.
Faculty research: National development processes, public relations and participatory research, audio and video production, health communication, urban development.
Dr. David Mould, Director, 740-593-1833, *Fax:* 740-593-1837, *E-mail:* commdev@ohio.edu.
Application contact: Joan Kraynanski, Administrative Assistant, 740-593-1840, *Fax:* 740-593-1837, *E-mail:* kraynans@ohio.edu. *Web site:* http://www.ohiou.edu/~intsdept/

■ OKLAHOMA CITY UNIVERSITY

Petree College of Arts and Sciences, Program in Liberal Arts, Oklahoma City, OK 73106-1402

AWARDS Art (MLA); international studies (MLA); leadership management (MLA); literature (MLA); philosophy (MLA); writing (MLA). Part-time and evening/weekend programs available.

Degree requirements: For master's, thesis optional.
Entrance requirements: For master's, minimum GPA of 3.0. *Web site:* http://www.okcu.edu/

■ OKLAHOMA STATE UNIVERSITY

Graduate College, Program in International Studies, Stillwater, OK 74078

AWARDS MS.

Students: 20 full-time (7 women), 10 part-time (5 women); includes 6 minority (2 African Americans, 2 Hispanic Americans, 2 Native Americans), 11 international. Average age 30. 27 applicants, 96% accepted. In 2001, 4 degrees awarded.
Expenses: Tuition, state resident: part-time $92 per credit hour. Tuition, nonresident: part-time $297 per credit hour. Required fees: $21 per credit hour. $14 per semester. One-time fee: $20. Tuition and fees vary according to course load.
Financial support: In 2001–02, 1 research assistantship (averaging $480 per year) was awarded
James G. Hromas, Dean of University Extension International and Economic Development, 405-744-6606.

■ OLD DOMINION UNIVERSITY

College of Arts and Letters, Programs in International Studies, Norfolk, VA 23529

AWARDS MA, PhD. Part-time programs available.

Faculty: 4 full-time (2 women).
Students: 34 full-time (14 women), 38 part-time (11 women); includes 9 minority (6 African Americans, 1 Asian American or Pacific Islander, 2 Hispanic Americans), 16 international. Average age 34. 51 applicants, 86% accepted. In 2001, 10 master's, 5 doctorates awarded.
Degree requirements: For master's, one foreign language, comprehensive exam; for doctorate, one foreign language, thesis/dissertation, comprehensive exam.
Entrance requirements: For master's and doctorate, GRE General Test, TOEFL, sample of written work. *Application deadline:* For fall admission, 3/15. *Application fee:* $30. Electronic applications accepted.
Expenses: Tuition, state resident: part-time $202 per credit. Tuition, nonresident: part-time $534 per credit. Required fees: $76 per semester.
Financial support: In 2001–02, 50 students received support, including 12 research assistantships with tuition reimbursements available (averaging $10,000 per year), 4 teaching assistantships with tuition reimbursements available (averaging $10,200 per year); fellowships, career-related internships or fieldwork, institutionally sponsored loans, scholarships/grants, and tuition waivers (partial) also available. Support available to part-time students. Financial award application deadline: 3/1; financial award applicants required to submit FAFSA.
Faculty research: U.S. foreign policy, international relations, world health, transatlantic and transpacific relations, transnational issues. *Total annual research expenditures:* $53,456.
Dr. Kurt Taylor Gaubatz, Graduate Program Director, 757-683-5700, *Fax:* 757-683-5701, *E-mail:* isgpd@odu.edu. *Web site:* http://www.odu.edu/al/gpis/gpis.html

■ PRINCETON UNIVERSITY

Graduate School, Woodrow Wilson School of Public and International Affairs, Princeton, NJ 08544-1019

AWARDS MPA, MPA-URP, MPP, PhD, JD/MPA.

Degree requirements: For master's, internship; for doctorate, one foreign language, thesis/dissertation.
Entrance requirements: For master's, GRE General Test, original policy memo; for doctorate, GRE General Test.

■ RUTGERS, THE STATE UNIVERSITY OF NEW JERSEY, CAMDEN

Graduate School, Department of Public Policy and Administration, Camden, NJ 08102-1401

AWARDS Health care management and policy (MPA); international public service and development (MPA); public management (MPA). Part-time and evening/weekend programs available.

Degree requirements: For master's, oral presentation, directed study.
Entrance requirements: For master's, GRE General Test or GMAT or LSAT. Electronic applications accepted.
Faculty research: Nonprofit management, county and municipal administration, health and human services, government communication, administrative law, educational finance.

■ RUTGERS, THE STATE UNIVERSITY OF NEW JERSEY, NEWARK

Graduate School, Center for Global Change and Governance, Newark, NJ 07102

AWARDS Global studies (MA); international studies (MS). Part-time and evening/weekend programs available.

Degree requirements: For master's, one foreign language, thesis optional.
Entrance requirements: For master's, GRE General Test, minimum B average. Electronic applications accepted.
Faculty research: International organizations, diplomacy, world history, international political economy, global environment. *Web site:* http://newark.rutgers.edu/~cgcg/home.html

■ RUTGERS, THE STATE UNIVERSITY OF NEW JERSEY, NEWARK

Graduate School, Department of Global Affairs, Newark, NJ 07102

AWARDS PhD.

■ RUTGERS, THE STATE UNIVERSITY OF NEW JERSEY, NEWARK

Graduate School, Department of Political Science, Newark, NJ 07102

AWARDS American political system (MA); international relations (MA). Part-time and evening/weekend programs available.

Degree requirements: For master's, thesis optional.
Entrance requirements: For master's, GRE, minimum undergraduate B average. Electronic applications accepted.
Faculty research: Policymaking and policy evaluation in the United States; government and politics in Europe, Middle East, Asia, Africa, and Latin America.

■ RUTGERS, THE STATE UNIVERSITY OF NEW JERSEY, NEW BRUNSWICK

Graduate School, Program in Political Science, New Brunswick, NJ 08901-1281

AWARDS American political institutions (PhD); comparative politics (PhD); international relations (PhD); political economy (PhD); political theory (PhD); public law (PhD); women and politics (PhD).

Degree requirements: For doctorate, one foreign language, thesis/dissertation.
Entrance requirements: For doctorate, GRE General Test. *Web site:* http://policsci.rutgers.edu/

■ ST. JOHN FISHER COLLEGE

Office of Academic Affairs, International Studies Program, Rochester, NY 14618-3597

AWARDS MS. Part-time and evening/weekend programs available.

Faculty: 3 full-time (0 women), 2 part-time/adjunct (0 women).
Students: 2 full-time (0 women), 12 part-time (7 women); includes 2 minority (1 African American, 1 Hispanic American). Average age 33. 8 applicants, 75% accepted. In 2001, 2 degrees awarded.
Degree requirements: For master's, project. *Median time to degree:* Master's–2 years full-time, 6 years part-time.
Entrance requirements: For master's, minimum GPA of 3.0. *Application deadline:* For fall admission, 8/1; for spring admission, 11/15. *Application fee:* $30.
Expenses: Tuition: Part-time $465 per credit hour.
Financial support: Federal Work-Study and scholarships/grants available. Financial award application deadline: 2/15; financial award applicants required to submit FAFSA.
Dr. Zhiyue Bo, Graduate Director, 585-385-8197, *E-mail:* bo@sjfc.edu.
Application contact: Scott Kelly, Director, Graduate Admissions, 585-385-8161, *Fax:* 585-385-8344, *E-mail:* kelly@sjfc.edu.

■ ST. MARY'S UNIVERSITY OF SAN ANTONIO

Graduate School, Department of Political Science, Interdisciplinary Program in International Relations, San Antonio, TX 78228-8507

AWARDS International relations (MA), including inter-American studies, international conflict resolution, international economics, security policy. Part-time programs available. Postbaccalaureate distance learning degree programs offered (no on-campus study).

Faculty: 14 full-time (3 women), 2 part-time/adjunct (0 women).
Students: 21 full-time (10 women), 73 part-time (24 women); includes 43 minority (9 African Americans, 3 Asian Americans or Pacific Islanders, 31 Hispanic Americans), 1 international. In 2001, 28 degrees awarded.
Degree requirements: For master's, one foreign language, comprehensive exam.
Entrance requirements: For master's, GRE General Test. *Application deadline:* Applications are processed on a rolling basis. *Application fee:* $15. Electronic applications accepted.
Expenses: Tuition: Full-time $8,190; part-time $455 per credit hour. Required fees: $375.
Financial support: Fellowships, career-related internships or fieldwork, institutionally sponsored loans, and tuition waivers (full) available. Financial award application deadline: 2/15; financial award applicants required to submit FAFSA.
Faculty research: Eastern Europe, Soviet Union, Balkans, modern Asia, Latin America.
Dr. Larry Hufford, Graduate Program Director, *E-mail:* polarry@stmarytx.edu.

■ SALVE REGINA UNIVERSITY

Graduate School, Program in International Relations, Newport, RI 02840-4192

AWARDS MA. Part-time and evening/weekend programs available. Postbaccalaureate distance learning degree programs offered (minimal on-campus study).

Faculty: 1 full-time (0 women), 7 part-time/adjunct (3 women).
Students: 3 full-time (2 women), 35 part-time (7 women); includes 1 minority (Asian American or Pacific Islander). Average age 38. 40 applicants, 48% accepted, 4 enrolled. In 2001, 20 degrees awarded.
Median time to degree: Master's–2 years full-time, 2.5 years part-time.
Entrance requirements: For master's, GMAT, GRE General Test, or MAT. *Application deadline:* Applications are processed on a rolling basis. *Application fee:* $50. Electronic applications accepted.
Expenses: Tuition: Full-time $5,400; part-time $300 per credit. Required fees: $330; $40 per term. Tuition and fees vary according to degree level.
Financial support: Career-related internships or fieldwork and Federal Work-Study available. Support available to part-time students. Financial award application deadline: 3/1.
Dr. Theresa I. Madonna, Acting Director, 401-341-2222, *Fax:* 401-341-2917, *E-mail:* maddonat@salve.edu.
Application contact: Karen E. Johnson, Graduate Admissions Counselor, 401-341-2153, *Fax:* 401-341-2973, *E-mail:* graduate_studies@salve.edu. *Web site:* http://www.salve.edu/programs_grad/index.html

■ SAN FRANCISCO STATE UNIVERSITY

Graduate Division, College of Behavioral and Social Sciences, Department of International Relations, San Francisco, CA 94132-1722

AWARDS MA.

Degree requirements: For master's, one foreign language, thesis.
Entrance requirements: For master's, GRE, TOEFL, minimum undergraduate GPA of 3.25 in last 60 units.

■ SCHOOL FOR INTERNATIONAL TRAINING

Graduate Programs, Master's Programs in Intercultural Service, Leadership, and Management, Brattleboro, VT 05302-0676

AWARDS Conflict transformation intercultural service, leadership and management (MA); intercultural relations (MA); international education (MA); non-governmental organization leadership and management (Postgraduate Diploma); organizational management (MS); sustainable development (MA).

Faculty: 11 full-time (8 women), 10 part-time/adjunct (3 women).
Students: 94 full-time (71 women). Average age 30. In 2001, 81 degrees awarded.
Degree requirements: For master's, one foreign language, thesis.
Entrance requirements: For master's, TOEFL. *Application deadline:* Applications are processed on a rolling basis. *Application fee:* $45.
Financial support: Career-related internships or fieldwork, Federal Work-Study, institutionally sponsored loans, and scholarships/grants available. Financial award applicants required to submit FAFSA.

Faculty research: Intercultural communication, conflict resolution, advising and training, world issues, international business.
Jeff Unsicker, Dean, 802-257-7751 Ext. 3332.
Application contact: Marshall Brewer, Admissions Counselor, 802-258-3265, *Fax:* 802-258-3500. *Web site:* http://www.sit.edu/

■ SETON HALL UNIVERSITY

School of Diplomacy and International Relations, South Orange, NJ 07079-2697

AWARDS MA, JD/MA, MBA/MA, MPA/MA, MSIB/MA. Part-time and evening/weekend programs available.

Faculty: 4 full-time (1 woman), 14 part-time/adjunct (4 women).
Students: 80 full-time (48 women), 45 part-time (26 women); includes 34 minority (23 African Americans, 10 Asian Americans or Pacific Islanders, 1 Hispanic American), 21 international. Average age 26. 93 applicants, 85% accepted. In 2001, 12 degrees awarded.
Degree requirements: For master's, thesis. *Median time to degree:* Master's–2 years full-time, 4 years part-time.
Entrance requirements: For master's, GMAT, GRE, MAT, or LSAT; TOEFL, minimum GPA of 3.0. *Application deadline:* For fall admission, 6/1 (priority date); for winter admission, 10/1 (priority date); for spring admission, 2/1 (priority date). Applications are processed on a rolling basis. *Application fee:* $50.
Expenses: Tuition: Full-time $10,818; part-time $601 per credit. Required fees: $610; $185 per term. Tuition and fees vary according to course load, program and student's religious affiliation.
Financial support: In 2001–02, 10 students received support, including 3 research assistantships with full and partial tuition reimbursements available (averaging $4,500 per year), 2 teaching assistantships (averaging $3,000 per year); career-related internships or fieldwork, Federal Work-Study, and unspecified assistantships also available. Support available to part-time students. Financial award application deadline: 4/15; financial award applicants required to submit FAFSA.
Faculty research: International law, united nations, migration and refugees, Africa, Eastern Europe. *Total annual research expenditures:* $102,000.
Clay Constantinou, Dean, 973-275-2515, *Fax:* 973-275-2519, *E-mail:* constacl@shu.edu.
Application contact: David P. Giovanella, Director of Graduate Admissions, 973-275-2515, *Fax:* 973-275-2519, *E-mail:* diplomat@shu.edu. *Web site:* http://diplomacy.shu.edu/

Find an in-depth description at www.petersons.com/gradchannel.

■ SOUTHWEST MISSOURI STATE UNIVERSITY

Graduate College, College of Humanities and Public Affairs, Department of Political Science, Program in International Affairs and Administration, Springfield, MO 65804-0094

AWARDS MIAA.

Faculty: 16 full-time (1 woman).
Students: 13 full-time (4 women), 5 part-time (2 women), 11 international. In 2001, 2 degrees awarded.
Application deadline: For fall admission, 8/5 (priority date); for spring admission, 12/20 (priority date). Applications are processed on a rolling basis. *Application fee:* $25. Electronic applications accepted.
Expenses: Tuition, state resident: full-time $2,286; part-time $127 per credit. Tuition, nonresident: full-time $4,572; part-time $254 per credit. Required fees: $151 per semester. Tuition and fees vary according to course level and program.
Financial support: In 2001–02, research assistantships (averaging $6,150 per year), teaching assistantships (averaging $6,150 per year) were awarded. Federal Work-Study, scholarships/grants, and unspecified assistantships also available. Support available to part-time students. Financial award application deadline: 3/31.
Application contact: Dr. Dennis V. Hickey, Graduate Director, 417-836-5926, *Fax:* 417-836-8472, *E-mail:* dvh804f@smsu.edu.

■ SOUTHWEST TEXAS STATE UNIVERSITY

Graduate School, Program in International Studies, San Marcos, TX 78666

AWARDS MA.

Students: 2 full-time (1 woman), 5 part-time (2 women); includes 1 minority (Hispanic American), 1 international. Average age 32. 8 applicants, 100% accepted, 7 enrolled.
Degree requirements: For master's, comprehensive exam.
Application deadline: For fall admission, 6/15 (priority date); for spring admission, 10/15 (priority date). Applications are processed on a rolling basis. *Application fee:* $40 ($90 for international students).
Expenses: Tuition, state resident: full-time $1,512; part-time $84 per credit hour. Tuition, nonresident: full-time $5,310; part-time $295 per credit hour. Required fees: $864; $29 per credit hour. $195 per term. Full-time tuition and fees vary according to course load.
Financial support: Application deadline: 4/1.
Dr. Dennis Dunn, Head, 512-245-2107, *E-mail:* dd05@swt.edu.

■ STANFORD UNIVERSITY

School of Humanities and Sciences, Program in International Policy Studies, Stanford, CA 94305-9991

AWARDS AM.

Students: 44 full-time (20 women), 1 part-time; includes 7 minority (1 African American, 4 Asian Americans or Pacific Islanders, 2 Hispanic Americans), 25 international. Average age 26. 107 applicants, 36% accepted. In 2001, 28 degrees awarded.
Degree requirements: For master's, thesis optional.
Entrance requirements: For master's, GRE General Test, TOEFL. *Application deadline:* For fall admission, 1/5. *Application fee:* $65 ($80 for international students). Electronic applications accepted.
Judith L. Goldstein, Co-Director, 650-723-4547, *Fax:* 650-723-3010, *E-mail:* judy@leland.stanford.edu.
Application contact: Graduate Administrator, 650-723-4547, *Fax:* 650-723-3010, *E-mail:* kp.ask@forsythe.stanford.edu. *Web site:* http://www.stanford.edu/dept/IR/

■ SYRACUSE UNIVERSITY

Graduate School, Maxwell School of Citizenship and Public Affairs, Program in International Relations, Syracuse, NY 13244-0003

AWARDS MA, JD/MA.

Faculty: 41.
Students: 124 full-time (74 women), 12 part-time (9 women); includes 16 minority (4 African Americans, 7 Asian Americans or Pacific Islanders, 4 Hispanic Americans, 1 Native American), 61 international. Average age 27. 310 applicants, 61% accepted, 62 enrolled. In 2001, 56 degrees awarded.
Degree requirements: For master's, thesis or alternative.
Entrance requirements: For master's, GRE General Test. *Application deadline:* For fall admission, 1/15 (priority date); for spring admission, 11/15 (priority date). Applications are processed on a rolling basis. *Application fee:* $50. Electronic applications accepted.
Expenses: Tuition: Full-time $15,528; part-time $647 per credit. Required fees: $420; $38 per term. Tuition and fees vary according to program.
Financial support: In 2001–02, 57 students received support, including teaching assistantships with partial tuition reimbursements available (averaging $10,600 per year); fellowships, research assistantships, Federal Work-Study and tuition waivers (partial) also available.
Matthew Bonham, Chair, 315-443-3827.
Application contact: Terrence Guay, Information Contact, 315-443-9346.

Find an in-depth description at www.petersons.com/gradchannel.

■ TEXAS A&M UNIVERSITY

George Bush School of Government and Public Service, Program in International Affairs, College Station, TX 77843

AWARDS MA. Program begins Fall 2002.

Application deadline: For fall admission, 1/31 (priority date). *Application fee:* $50 ($75 for international students).
Expenses: Tuition, state resident: full-time $11,872. Tuition, nonresident: full-time $17,892.
Financial support: Application deadline: 2/1.
Charles Hermann, Head, 979-458-2276.
Application contact: Information Contact, 979-458-2276. *Web site:* http://bush.tamu.edu/programs/

■ TROY STATE UNIVERSITY

Graduate School, College of Arts and Sciences and University College, Program in International Relations, Troy, AL 36082

AWARDS MS. Offered only through the University College. Part-time and evening/weekend programs available.

Degree requirements: For master's, thesis, comprehensive exam.
Entrance requirements: For master's, GRE General Test, MAT, minimum GPA of 2.5. Electronic applications accepted.
Web site: http://www.troyst.edu/

■ TUFTS UNIVERSITY

Fletcher School of Law and Diplomacy, Medford, MA 02155

AWARDS MA, MAHA, MALD, PhD, DVM/MA, JD/MALD, MALD/MA, MALD/MBA, MALD/MS, MALD/MSJ, MD/MALD. Postbaccalaureate distance learning degree programs offered (minimal on-campus study).

Faculty: 29 full-time (5 women), 40 part-time/adjunct (11 women).
Students: 427 full-time (224 women); includes 45 minority (14 African Americans, 24 Asian Americans or Pacific Islanders, 7 Hispanic Americans), 210 international. Average age 28. 1,158 applicants, 41% accepted, 158 enrolled. In 2001, 192 master's, 11 doctorates awarded. Terminal master's awarded for partial completion of doctoral program.
Degree requirements: For master's, one foreign language, thesis; for doctorate, one foreign language, thesis/dissertation, dissertation defense, comprehensive exam. *Median time to degree:* Master's–2 years full-time; doctorate–5 years full-time.
Entrance requirements: For master's, GMAT or GRE General Test, TOEFL; for doctorate, GRE General Test, TOEFL, appropriate master's degree, research proposal. *Application deadline:* For fall admission, 1/15; for spring admission, 10/15. *Application fee:* $50. Electronic applications accepted.
Expenses: Contact institution.
Financial support: In 2001–02, 221 students received support, including 221 fellowships (averaging $7,000 per year); research assistantships, teaching assistantships, career-related internships or fieldwork, Federal Work-Study, institutionally sponsored loans, and scholarships/grants also available. Financial award application deadline: 1/15; financial award applicants required to submit FAFSA.
Faculty research: Negotiation and conflict resolution, international organizations, international business and economic law, security studies, development economics, complex humanitarian issues.
Stephen W. Bosworth, Dean, 617-627-3050, *Fax:* 617-627-3712.
Application contact: Laurie A. Hurley, Director of Admissions and Financial Aid, 617-627-3040, *Fax:* 617-627-3712, *E-mail:* fletcheradmissions@tufts.edu. *Web site:* http://www.fletcher.tufts.edu

Find an in-depth description at www.petersons.com/gradchannel.

■ UNIVERSITY OF CALIFORNIA, BERKELEY

Graduate Division, Group in International and Area Studies, Berkeley, CA 94720-1500

AWARDS International and area studies (MA). Program open only to currently matriculated University of California, Berkeley graduate students.

Students: 2 full-time (0 women).
Application deadline: For fall admission, 2/15.
Expenses: Tuition, nonresident: full-time $10,704. Required fees: $4,349.
Ariadne Prater, Chair, 510-642-4466, *Fax:* 510-642-9850, *E-mail:* iastp@uclink.berkeley.edu.

■ UNIVERSITY OF CALIFORNIA, BERKELEY

Graduate Division, Haas School of Business and Group in International and Area Studies, Concurrent MBA/MIAS Program in International and Area Studies, Berkeley, CA 94720-1500

AWARDS MBA/MIAS.

Application deadline: For fall admission, 3/31. *Application fee:* $125.
Expenses: Tuition, nonresident: full-time $10,704. Required fees: $4,349.
Financial support: Fellowships with full tuition reimbursements, research assistantships, teaching assistantships with partial tuition reimbursements, career-related internships or fieldwork and scholarships/grants available. Support available to part-time students. Financial award application deadline: 3/2; financial award applicants required to submit FAFSA.
David Downes, Director, MBA Program, 510-642-1405, *Fax:* 510-643-6659, *E-mail:* downes@haas.berkeley.edu.
Application contact: MBA Admissions Office, 510-642-1405, *Fax:* 510-643-6659, *E-mail:* mbaadms@haas.berkeley.edu. *Web site:* http://www.haas.berkeley.edu/

■ UNIVERSITY OF CALIFORNIA, SAN DIEGO

Graduate Studies and Research, Department of Economics, La Jolla, CA 92093

AWARDS Economics (PhD); economics and international affairs (PhD).

Faculty: 29.
Students: 73 (17 women). 345 applicants, 29% accepted, 25 enrolled. In 2001, 11 doctorates awarded.
Degree requirements: For doctorate, thesis/dissertation.
Entrance requirements: For doctorate, GRE General Test. *Application deadline:* For fall admission, 1/18. *Application fee:* $40. Electronic applications accepted.
Expenses: Tuition, nonresident: full-time $10,434. Required fees: $4,883.
Financial support: Application deadline: 2/1.
Faculty research: Microfoundations of macroeconomics, econometric model specification and testing, industrial organization.
James Hamilton, Chair.
Application contact: Applications Coordinator, 858-534-1867.

■ UNIVERSITY OF CALIFORNIA, SAN DIEGO

Graduate Studies and Research, Department of Political Science, La Jolla, CA 92093

AWARDS Latin American studies (MA); political science (PhD); political science and international affairs (PhD).

Faculty: 24.
Students: 68 (22 women). 167 applicants, 23% accepted, 19 enrolled. In 2001, 1 master's, 6 doctorates awarded.
Entrance requirements: For master's and doctorate, GRE General Test. *Application deadline:* For fall admission, 1/5. *Application fee:* $40. Electronic applications accepted.
Expenses: Tuition, nonresident: full-time $10,434. Required fees: $4,883.
David Lake, Chair.
Application contact: Christine Vaz, Graduate Coordinator, 619-534-3015.

■ UNIVERSITY OF CALIFORNIA, SAN DIEGO

Graduate Studies and Research, Graduate School of International Relations and Pacific Studies, La Jolla, CA 92093-0520

AWARDS Economics and international affairs (PhD); Pacific international affairs (MPIA);

political science and international affairs (PhD). Part-time programs available.

Faculty: 24 full-time (3 women), 31 part-time/adjunct (12 women).
Students: 204 full-time (105 women); includes 44 minority (31 Asian Americans or Pacific Islanders, 13 Hispanic Americans), 86 international. Average age 27. 384 applicants, 61% accepted. In 2001, 87 master's, 1 doctorate awarded.
Degree requirements: For master's, one foreign language; for doctorate, thesis/dissertation. *Median time to degree:* Master's–2 years full-time, 3 years part-time.
Entrance requirements: For master's, GMAT or GRE General Test, TOEFL; for doctorate, GRE General Test, TOEFL. *Application deadline:* For fall admission, 2/15 (priority date). Applications are processed on a rolling basis. *Application fee:* $40. Electronic applications accepted.
Expenses: Tuition, nonresident: full-time $10,434. Required fees: $4,883.
Financial support: In 2001–02, 120 students received support, including 20 fellowships with full and partial tuition reimbursements available (averaging $6,387 per year), 11 research assistantships with partial tuition reimbursements available, 65 teaching assistantships with partial tuition reimbursements available; career-related internships or fieldwork, institutionally sponsored loans, and tuition waivers (full and partial) also available. Support available to part-time students. Financial award application deadline: 3/2; financial award applicants required to submit FAFSA.
Faculty research: Pacific Rim as system and placement in global relations; studies in international economics, management and finance; analysis patterns of policy making in countries of the Pacific.
Peter Cowhey, Dean, 858-534-1946, *Fax:* 858-534-3939.
Application contact: Jori J. Cincotta, Director of Admissions, 858-534-5914, *Fax:* 858-534-1135, *E-mail:* irps-apply@ucsd.edu. *Web site:* http://www-irps.ucsd.edu/

Find an in-depth description at www.petersons.com/gradchannel.

■ UNIVERSITY OF CALIFORNIA, SANTA CRUZ

Division of Graduate Studies, Division of Social Sciences, Program in International Economics, Santa Cruz, CA 95064

AWARDS PhD.

Faculty: 19 full-time.
Students: 40 full-time (16 women); includes 5 minority (all Asian Americans or Pacific Islanders), 26 international. 84 applicants, 32% accepted. In 2001, 8 doctorates awarded.
Degree requirements: For doctorate, one foreign language, thesis/dissertation, 2 field exams, major research paper. *Median time to degree:* Doctorate–2 years full-time.
Entrance requirements: For doctorate, GRE General Test. *Application deadline:* For fall admission, 2/1. *Application fee:* $40.
Expenses: Tuition: Full-time $19,857.
Financial support: Research assistantships, teaching assistantships, career-related internships or fieldwork, Federal Work-Study, institutionally sponsored loans, and tuition waivers (partial) available. Financial award application deadline: 2/1.
Faculty research: Current and emerging issues in taxation, industrial policy, environmental regulation, market structure.
Michael Hutchison, Chairperson, 831-459-4981.
Application contact: Cristina Intintoli, Graduate Assistant, 831-459-2219, *E-mail:* cmintint@cats.ucsc.edu. *Web site:* http://www.ucsc.edu/

■ UNIVERSITY OF CENTRAL OKLAHOMA

College of Graduate Studies and Research, College of Liberal Arts, Department of Political Science, Program in International Affairs, Edmond, OK 73034-5209

AWARDS MA. Part-time programs available.

Faculty research: Korean and Japanese politics.

■ UNIVERSITY OF CHICAGO

Division of Social Sciences, Committee on International Relations, Chicago, IL 60637-1513

AWARDS AM, MBA/AM.

Students: 53.
Degree requirements: For master's, one foreign language, thesis.
Entrance requirements: For master's, GRE General Test, TOEFL. *Application deadline:* For fall admission, 12/28. *Application fee:* $55. Electronic applications accepted.
Expenses: Tuition: Full-time $16,548.
Financial support: Federal Work-Study and institutionally sponsored loans available. Financial award application deadline: 12/28.
Prof. Dali Yang, Chair, 773-702-8073.
Application contact: Office of the Dean of Students, 773-702-8415.

■ UNIVERSITY OF COLORADO AT BOULDER

Graduate School, College of Arts and Sciences, Department of Political Science, Boulder, CO 80309

AWARDS International affairs (MA); political science (MA, PhD); public policy analysis (MA).

Faculty: 26 full-time (5 women).
Students: 51 full-time (18 women), 14 part-time (6 women); includes 7 minority (1 African American, 2 Asian Americans or Pacific Islanders, 4 Hispanic Americans), 8 international. Average age 29. 51 applicants, 61% accepted. In 2001, 9 master's, 6 doctorates awarded. Terminal master's awarded for partial completion of doctoral program.
Degree requirements: For master's, thesis, comprehensive exam; for doctorate, one foreign language, thesis/dissertation.
Entrance requirements: For master's, GRE General Test, minimum undergraduate GPA of 3.0; for doctorate, GRE General Test, minimum GPA of 3.5 (undergraduate), 3.0 (graduate). *Application deadline:* For fall admission, 1/15 (priority date). *Application fee:* $50 ($60 for international students).
Expenses: Tuition, state resident: full-time $3,474. Tuition, nonresident: full-time $16,624.
Financial support: In 2001–02, 12 fellowships (averaging $2,836 per year), 3 research assistantships (averaging $17,735 per year), 32 teaching assistantships (averaging $17,902 per year) were awarded. Federal Work-Study also available. Financial award application deadline: 1/15.
Faculty research: American government and politics, comparative politics, international relations, public policy, law and politics. *Total annual research expenditures:* $985,125.
J. Samuel Fitch, Chair, 303-492-8601, *Fax:* 303-492-0978, *E-mail:* fitchs@colorado.edu.
Application contact: Mary Gregory, Graduate Program Assistant, 303-492-7872, *Fax:* 303-492-0978, *E-mail:* mary.gregory@colorado.edu. *Web site:* http://socsci.colorado.edu/POLSCI/

■ UNIVERSITY OF CONNECTICUT

Graduate School, College of Liberal Arts and Sciences, Department of International Studies, Storrs, CT 06269

AWARDS MA, MA/MBA.

Entrance requirements: For master's, GRE General Test.

■ UNIVERSITY OF CONNECTICUT

Graduate School, College of Liberal Arts and Sciences, Field of International Studies, Storrs, CT 06269

AWARDS MA.

Entrance requirements: For master's, GRE General Test.

■ UNIVERSITY OF DELAWARE

College of Arts and Science, Department of Political Science and International Relations, Newark, DE 19716

AWARDS International relations (MA); political science (MA, PhD).

Faculty: 25 full-time (6 women).
Students: 32 full-time (12 women), 3 part-time; includes 4 minority (2 African Americans, 1 Hispanic American, 1 Native American), 13 international. Average age 29. 62 applicants, 29% accepted, 10 enrolled. In 2001, 8 master's, 2 doctorates awarded. Terminal master's awarded for partial completion of doctoral program.
Degree requirements: For master's, one foreign language; for doctorate, one foreign language, thesis/dissertation. *Median time to degree:* Master's–2 years full-time; doctorate–7 years full-time.
Entrance requirements: For master's and doctorate, GRE General Test, TOEFL, minimum GPA of 3.2 in major, 3.0 overall. *Application deadline:* For fall admission, 7/1 (priority date). *Application fee:* $50. Electronic applications accepted.
Expenses: Tuition, state resident: full-time $4,770; part-time $265 per credit. Tuition, nonresident: full-time $13,860; part-time $770 per credit. Required fees: $414.
Financial support: In 2001–02, 23 students received support, including 1 fellowship with full tuition reimbursement available (averaging $10,800 per year), 1 research assistantship with full tuition reimbursement available (averaging $11,000 per year), 14 teaching assistantships with full tuition reimbursements available (averaging $10,600 per year); career-related internships or fieldwork, Federal Work-Study, institutionally sponsored loans, scholarships/grants, and tuition waivers (full and partial) also available. Financial award application deadline: 2/1.
Faculty research: Human rights and humanitarian interventions, ethnic conflict, international migration, health policy, environmental and disaster policy, complexity theory, public law.
Dr. Joseph Pika, Acting Chairperson, 302-831-2355, *Fax:* 302-831-4452, *E-mail:* jpika@udel.edu.
Application contact: William H. Meyer, Director of Graduate Studies, 302-831-2355, *Fax:* 302-831-4452, *E-mail:* whmeyer@udel.edu. *Web site:* http://www.udel.edu/catalog/current/as/psc/grad.html#overview

■ UNIVERSITY OF DENVER

Graduate School of International Studies, Denver, CO 80208

AWARDS MA, MIM, PhD, JD/MA, MSW/MA. Part-time and evening/weekend programs available.

Faculty: 21 full-time (4 women), 1 part-time/adjunct (0 women).
Students: 209 (112 women); includes 22 minority (7 African Americans, 4 Asian Americans or Pacific Islanders, 11 Hispanic Americans) 48 international. Average age 27. 470 applicants, 73% accepted. In 2001, 99 master's, 9 doctorates awarded.
Degree requirements: For master's and doctorate, one foreign language, thesis/dissertation.
Entrance requirements: For master's and doctorate, GMAT, GRE General Test, LSAT, TOEFL. *Application deadline:* For fall admission, 2/15 (priority date); for spring admission, 1/15. *Application fee:* $50 ($45 for international students).
Expenses: Tuition: Full-time $21,456.
Financial support: In 2001–02, 116 students received support, including 3 fellowships with full and partial tuition reimbursements available, 1 research assistantship with full and partial tuition reimbursement available (averaging $6,003 per year), 2 teaching assistantships with full and partial tuition reimbursements available (averaging $9,518 per year); career-related internships or fieldwork, Federal Work-Study, institutionally sponsored loans, and research and teaching internships, language/dissertation/travel grants also available. Support available to part-time students. Financial award application deadline: 2/15; financial award applicants required to submit FAFSA.
Faculty research: International politics and economics, international technology analysis and management, human rights and international security, economic-social and political development. *Total annual research expenditures:* $443,581.
Dr. Tom Farer, Dean, 303-871-2539.
Application contact: Andrew Burns, Director of Admissions and Student Affairs, 303-871-2544, *Fax:* 303-871-2456, *E-mail:* gsisadm@du.edu. *Web site:* http://www.du.edu/gsis/

■ UNIVERSITY OF FLORIDA

Graduate School, College of Liberal Arts and Sciences, Department of Political Science, Program in International Relations, Gainesville, FL 32611

AWARDS MA, MAT, PhD. Part-time programs available. Terminal master's awarded for partial completion of doctoral program.

Degree requirements: For master's, variable foreign language requirement, thesis or alternative; for doctorate, variable foreign language requirement, thesis/dissertation.
Entrance requirements: For master's and doctorate, GRE General Test, minimum GPA of 3.0. Electronic applications accepted.
Expenses: Tuition, state resident: part-time $164 per hour. Tuition, nonresident: part-time $571 per hour. Tuition and fees vary according to course level and program.
Faculty research: American and comparative foreign policy, North-South relations, international political economy. *Web site:* http://www.clas.ufl.edu/polisci/grad.html

■ UNIVERSITY OF KANSAS

Graduate School, College of Liberal Arts and Sciences, Division of Government, Program in International Studies, Lawrence, KS 66045

AWARDS MA.

Students: 5 full-time (4 women), 4 part-time (1 woman). Average age 29. 4 applicants, 75% accepted, 2 enrolled.
Entrance requirements: For master's, GRE. *Application fee:* $35.
Expenses: Tuition, state resident: full-time $2,722; part-time $113 per credit. Tuition, nonresident: full-time $8,586; part-time $358 per credit. Required fees: $551; $46 per credit. Tuition and fees vary according to campus/location, program and reciprocity agreements.
Paul Schumaker, Chair, 785-864-3523, *Fax:* 785-864-5700, *E-mail:* pauljohn@ku.edu.
Application contact: Deborah Gerner, Professor, 785-864-3523, *Fax:* 785-864-5700, *E-mail:* mais@ku.edu. *Web site:* http://www.ku.edu/~mais

■ UNIVERSITY OF KENTUCKY

Patterson School of Diplomacy and International Commerce, Lexington, KY 40506-0032

AWARDS MA.

Faculty: 6 full-time (0 women).
Students: 49 full-time (23 women), 5 part-time (4 women); includes 1 minority (Asian American or Pacific Islander), 8 international. 58 applicants, 67% accepted. In 2001, 24 degrees awarded.
Degree requirements: For master's, one foreign language, comprehensive exam.
Entrance requirements: For master's, GRE General Test, minimum undergraduate GPA of 3.0. *Application deadline:* For fall admission, 2/1. *Application fee:* $30 ($35 for international students).
Expenses: Tuition, state resident: full-time $4,075; part-time $213 per credit hour. Tuition, nonresident: full-time $11,295; part-time $614 per credit hour.
Financial support: In 2001–02, 7 fellowships, 2 research assistantships, 4 teaching assistantships were awarded. Federal Work-Study, institutionally sponsored loans, and unspecified assistantships also available.
Faculty research: International relations, foreign and defense policy, cross-cultural negotiation, international science and technology, diplomacy. *Total annual research expenditures:* $26,000.
Dr. John D. Stempel, Director of Graduate Studies, 859-257-4666, *Fax:* 859-257-4676, *E-mail:* psdstem@ukcc.uky.edu.

Application contact: Dr. Jeannine Blackwell, Associate Dean, 859-257-4905, *Fax:* 859-323-1928.

Find an in-depth description at www.petersons.com/gradchannel.

■ UNIVERSITY OF MIAMI

Graduate School, School of International Studies, Coral Gables, FL 33124

AWARDS MA, PhD. Part-time programs available.

Faculty: 18 full-time (2 women), 6 part-time/adjunct (3 women).
Students: 92 full-time (55 women), 24 part-time (12 women); includes 34 minority (6 African Americans, 28 Hispanic Americans), 33 international. Average age 34. 115 applicants, 80% accepted, 40 enrolled. In 2001, 20 master's, 5 doctorates awarded.
Degree requirements: For master's, one foreign language, comprehensive exam; for doctorate, 2 foreign languages, thesis/dissertation, comprehensive exam.
Entrance requirements: For master's, GRE General Test, TOEFL, minimum GPA of 3.0; for doctorate, GRE General Test, TOEFL. *Application deadline:* For fall admission, 5/15 (priority date); for spring admission, 11/15. Applications are processed on a rolling basis. *Application fee:* $50.
Expenses: Tuition: Part-time $960 per credit hour. Required fees: $85 per semester. Tuition and fees vary according to program.
Financial support: In 2001–02, fellowships with tuition reimbursements (averaging $17,000 per year), research assistantships with tuition reimbursements (averaging $11,000 per year), teaching assistantships with tuition reimbursements (averaging $11,000 per year) were awarded. Federal Work-Study, institutionally sponsored loans, and tuition waivers (partial) also available. Support available to part-time students. Financial award application deadline: 2/1.
Faculty research: Latin American studies, international economics, international security and conflict, comparative development, international health policy.
Application contact: Steven Ralph, Coordinator of Student Services, 305-284-3117, *Fax:* 305-284-4406, *E-mail:* sisdmissions@miami.edu. *Web site:* http://www.miami.edu/sis/

■ UNIVERSITY OF MISSOURI–ST. LOUIS

Graduate School, College of Arts and Sciences, Center for International Studies, St. Louis, MO 63121-4499

AWARDS Certificate.

Application deadline: For fall admission, 7/1 (priority date); for spring admission, 11/1 (priority date). Applications are processed on a rolling basis. *Application fee:* $25 ($40 for international students). Electronic applications accepted.
Expenses: Tuition, state resident: part-time $231 per credit hour. Tuition, nonresident: part-time $621 per credit hour.
Financial support: In 2001–02, 4 research assistantships with full tuition reimbursements (averaging $6,750 per year) were awarded *Total annual research expenditures:* $197,200.
Dr. Joel N. Glassman, Director, 314-516-5755.
Application contact: Jeff Headtke, Graduate Admissions, 314-516-6928, *Fax:* 314-516-5310, *E-mail:* gradadm@umsl.edu.

■ UNIVERSITY OF NEW ORLEANS

Graduate School, College of Liberal Arts, Department of Political Science, New Orleans, LA 70148

AWARDS International relations (MA); political science (MA, PhD). Evening/weekend programs available.

Faculty: 5 full-time (1 woman).
Students: 25 full-time (8 women), 21 part-time (10 women); includes 8 minority (5 African Americans, 1 Asian American or Pacific Islander, 2 Hispanic Americans), 7 international. Average age 31. 36 applicants, 44% accepted, 9 enrolled. In 2001, 3 master's, 4 doctorates awarded.
Degree requirements: For master's, one foreign language, thesis or alternative; for doctorate, one foreign language, thesis/dissertation.
Entrance requirements: For master's, GRE General Test; for doctorate, GRE General Test, GRE Subject Test. *Application deadline:* For fall admission, 7/1 (priority date); for spring admission, 11/15 (priority date). Applications are processed on a rolling basis. *Application fee:* $20. Electronic applications accepted.
Expenses: Tuition, state resident: full-time $2,748; part-time $435 per credit. Tuition, nonresident: full-time $9,792; part-time $1,773 per credit.
Financial support: Fellowships, research assistantships, teaching assistantships, institutionally sponsored loans available. Financial award application deadline: 3/15; financial award applicants required to submit FAFSA.
Faculty research: Judicial politics, public policy, voting rights, Southern politics, presidential-congressional relations.
Dr. Charles Hadley, Chair, 504-280-6456, *Fax:* 504-280-6468, *E-mail:* chandley@uno.edu.
Application contact: Dr. Richard Engstrom, Graduate Coordinator, 504-280-6671, *Fax:* 504-280-6468, *E-mail:* rengstro@uno.edu.

■ UNIVERSITY OF OKLAHOMA

Graduate College, College of Arts and Sciences, School of International and Area Studies, Norman, OK 73019-0390

AWARDS International studies (MA), including global affairs, global management. Part-time programs available.

Faculty: 3 full-time (1 woman), 1 part-time/adjunct (0 women).
Students: 7 full-time (4 women), 4 part-time (all women); includes 2 minority (1 Asian American or Pacific Islander, 1 Native American), 2 international. 5 applicants, 100% accepted, 0 enrolled. In 2001, 15 degrees awarded.
Degree requirements: For master's, one foreign language, thesis optional.
Entrance requirements: For master's, GMAT or GRE, TOEFL. *Application deadline:* For fall admission, 10/15; for winter admission, 2/15. Applications are processed on a rolling basis. *Application fee:* $25 ($50 for international students).
Expenses: Tuition, state resident: full-time $2,208; part-time $92 per credit hour. Tuition, nonresident: part-time $297 per credit hour. Tuition and fees vary according to course level, course load and program.
Financial support: In 2001–02, 2 students received support, including 2 teaching assistantships with partial tuition reimbursements available (averaging $11,080 per year); traineeships, tuition waivers (partial), and unspecified assistantships also available. Financial award applicants required to submit FAFSA.
Faculty research: Comparative politics, international economics, security studies, cultural studies. *Total annual research expenditures:* $20,000.
Dr. Robert Cox, Director, 405-325-1584, *Fax:* 405-325-7402, *E-mail:* rhcox@ou.edu. *Web site:* http://www.ou.edu/ipc/

■ UNIVERSITY OF OREGON

Graduate School, College of Arts and Sciences, Program in International Studies, Eugene, OR 97403

AWARDS MA. Part-time programs available.

Faculty: 2 full-time (1 woman).
Students: 26 full-time (21 women), 6 part-time (5 women); includes 6 minority (2 African Americans, 1 Hispanic American, 3 Native Americans), 17 international. 41 applicants, 51% accepted. In 2001, 19 degrees awarded.
Degree requirements: For master's, one foreign language, thesis, internship.
Entrance requirements: For master's, TOEFL, minimum GPA of 3.0. *Application deadline:* For fall admission, 2/1. *Application fee:* $50.
Expenses: Tuition, state resident: full-time $4,968; part-time $501 per credit hour. Tuition, nonresident: full-time $8,400; part-time $691 per credit hour.
Financial support: In 2001–02, 9 teaching assistantships were awarded; career-related

University of Oregon (continued)
internships or fieldwork and Federal Work-Study also available. Financial award application deadline: 2/1.
Faculty research: International development studies; environmental studies; cross-cultural communications; planning, public policy, and management; several world regions.
Linda Fuller, Director, 541-346-5051.
Application contact: Chingling Reed, Graduate Secretary, 541-346-5052, *Fax:* 541-346-0802. *Web site:* http://darkwing.uoregon.edu/~isp/

■ UNIVERSITY OF PENNSYLVANIA

Fels Center of Government, Philadelphia, PA 19104

AWARDS MGA. Part-time and evening/weekend programs available.

Degree requirements: For master's, thesis (for some programs).
Entrance requirements: For master's, GRE, TOEFL.
Expenses: Tuition: Part-time $12,875 per semester. *Web site:* http://dolphin.upenn.edu/~gsfa/admin/admin.htm

Find an in-depth description at www.petersons.com/gradchannel.

■ UNIVERSITY OF PITTSBURGH

Graduate School of Public and International Affairs, Doctoral Program in Public and International Affairs, Pittsburgh, PA 15260

AWARDS Development studies (PhD); foreign and security policy (PhD); international political economy (PhD); public administration (PhD); public policy (PhD). Part-time programs available.

Faculty: 32 full-time (8 women), 12 part-time/adjunct (9 women).
Students: 60 full-time (17 women), 12 part-time (4 women); includes 4 minority (2 African Americans, 1 Asian American or Pacific Islander, 1 Hispanic American), 45 international. Average age 30. 81 applicants, 41% accepted, 14 enrolled. In 2001, 3 degrees awarded.
Degree requirements: For doctorate, thesis/dissertation.
Application deadline: For fall admission, 3/1 (priority date). Applications are processed on a rolling basis. *Application fee:* $40. Electronic applications accepted.
Expenses: Tuition, state resident: full-time $9,410; part-time $385 per credit. Tuition, nonresident: full-time $19,376; part-time $797 per credit. Required fees: $480; $90 per term. Tuition and fees vary according to program.
Financial support: In 2001–02, 15 students received support, including 12 fellowships (averaging $21,500 per year), 1 research assistantship (averaging $21,500 per year), 5 teaching assistantships (averaging $7,700 per year); career-related internships or fieldwork, scholarships/grants, unspecified assistantships, and graduate student assistantships also available. Financial award application deadline: 2/1.
Faculty research: International political economy, international development, public administration, public policy, foreign policy, international security policy.
Dr. William F. Matlack, Doctoral Program Coordinator, 412-648-7604, *E-mail:* wfm@birch.gspia.pitt.edu.
Application contact: Elizabeth Barthen-Braunsdorf, Assistant Director of Admissions, 412-648-7643, *Fax:* 412-648-7641, *E-mail:* barthen@bitch.gspia.pitt.edu. *Web site:* http://www.gspia.pitt.edu/

Find an in-depth description at www.petersons.com/gradchannel.

■ UNIVERSITY OF PITTSBURGH

Graduate School of Public and International Affairs, International Affairs Division, Pittsburgh, PA 15260

AWARDS Global political economy (MPIA); security and intelligence studies (MPIA). Part-time and evening/weekend programs available.

Faculty: 32 full-time (8 women), 12 part-time/adjunct (9 women).
Students: 93 full-time (54 women), 12 part-time (7 women); includes 11 minority (7 African Americans, 1 Asian American or Pacific Islander, 3 Hispanic Americans), 28 international. Average age 23. 166 applicants, 79% accepted, 55 enrolled. In 2001, 52 degrees awarded.
Degree requirements: For master's, internship, thesis optional.
Application deadline: For fall admission, 3/1 (priority date); for spring admission, 10/1 (priority date). Applications are processed on a rolling basis. *Application fee:* $40. Electronic applications accepted.
Expenses: Tuition, state resident: full-time $9,410; part-time $385 per credit. Tuition, nonresident: full-time $19,376; part-time $797 per credit. Required fees: $480; $90 per term. Tuition and fees vary according to program.
Financial support: In 2001–02, 44 students received support, including 9 fellowships (averaging $14,240 per year); career-related internships or fieldwork, scholarships/grants, tuition waivers (full and partial), and unspecified assistantships also available. Financial award application deadline: 2/1.
Faculty research: Political economy, international security, transnational crime, international trade, international finance, terrorism.
Dr. Martin Staniland, Director, International Affairs Division, 412-648-7656, *Fax:* 412-648-2605, *E-mail:* mstan@birch.gspia.pitt.edu.
Application contact: Elizabeth Barthen-Braunsdorf, Assistant Director of Admissions, 412-648-7643, *Fax:* 412-648-7641, *E-mail:* barthen@bitch.gspia.pitt.edu. *Web site:* http://www.gspia.pitt.edu/

Find an in-depth description at www.petersons.com/gradchannel.

■ UNIVERSITY OF RHODE ISLAND

Graduate School, College of Arts and Sciences, Department of Political Science, Kingston, RI 02881

AWARDS International development studies (Certificate); political science (MA), including American government, American politics, comparative government, international relations, public policy; public policy and administration (MPA).

Students: In 2001, 6 degrees awarded.
Application deadline: For fall admission, 4/15 (priority date). Applications are processed on a rolling basis. *Application fee:* $35.
Expenses: Tuition, state resident: full-time $3,756; part-time $209 per credit. Tuition, nonresident: full-time $10,774; part-time $599 per credit. Required fees: $1,586; $76 per credit. One-time fee: $60 full-time.
Dr. Maureen F. Moakley, Chairperson, 401-874-2183.

■ UNIVERSITY OF SAN DIEGO

College of Arts and Sciences, Department of Political Science, San Diego, CA 92110-2492

AWARDS International relations (MA). Part-time and evening/weekend programs available.

Faculty: 9 full-time (5 women), 12 part-time/adjunct (3 women).
Students: 8 full-time (5 women), 20 part-time (10 women); includes 9 minority (7 Asian Americans or Pacific Islanders, 2 Hispanic Americans), 2 international. Average age 28. 39 applicants, 69% accepted. In 2001, 7 degrees awarded.
Degree requirements: For master's, one foreign language, comprehensive exam.
Entrance requirements: For master's, GRE, TOEFL, TWE, minimum GPA of 3.0 in major, 2.75 overall. *Application deadline:* For fall admission, 5/1 (priority date); for spring admission, 11/15. Applications are processed on a rolling basis. *Application fee:* $45. Electronic applications accepted.
Financial support: In 2001–02, 8 fellowships (averaging $1,000 per year) were awarded; Federal Work-Study, institutionally sponsored loans, and unspecified assistantships also available. Support available to part-time students. Financial award application deadline: 5/1; financial award applicants required to submit FAFSA.
Faculty research: Soviet politics, Latin American politics, China, Canada, international organizations.
Dr. Vidya Nadkarni, Graduate Program Director, 619-260-4482, *Fax:* 619-260-6840, *E-mail:* nadkarni@sandiego.edu.

Application contact: Mary Jane Tiernan, Director of Graduate Admissions, 619-260-4524, *Fax:* 619-260-4158, *E-mail:* grads@sandiego.edu.

■ UNIVERSITY OF SOUTH CAROLINA

The Graduate School, College of Liberal Arts, Department of Government and International Studies, Program in International Studies, Columbia, SC 29208

AWARDS MA, PhD. Part-time programs available. Terminal master's awarded for partial completion of doctoral program.

Degree requirements: For master's, one foreign language, thesis; for doctorate, 2 foreign languages, thesis/dissertation.
Entrance requirements: For master's, GRE General Test, TOEFL, minimum GPA of 3.3; for doctorate, GRE General Test, TOEFL, minimum GPA of 3.5. Electronic applications accepted.
Expenses: Tuition, state resident: full-time $4,434. Tuition, nonresident: full-time $9,854. Tuition and fees vary according to program.
Faculty research: International relations, international organization, foreign policy, comparative politics. *Web site:* http://www.cla.sc.edu/gint/

■ UNIVERSITY OF SOUTHERN CALIFORNIA

Graduate School, College of Letters, Arts and Sciences, School of International Relations, Los Angeles, CA 90089

AWARDS MA, PhD, JD/MA. Part-time programs available. Terminal master's awarded for partial completion of doctoral program.

Degree requirements: For master's, one foreign language, substantive paper, thesis optional; for doctorate, one foreign language, thesis/dissertation, substantive paper, written/oral exams.
Entrance requirements: For master's and doctorate, GRE General Test.
Expenses: Tuition: Full-time $25,060; part-time $844 per unit. Required fees: $473.
Faculty research: International environmental agreements and regimes, Middle East regional and domestic political economies, negotiation and conflict among states on economic issues.

■ UNIVERSITY OF THE PACIFIC

Graduate School, School of International Studies, Program in Intercultural Relations, Stockton, CA 95211-0197

AWARDS MA.

Application fee: $50.
Expenses: Tuition: Full-time $21,150; part-time $661 per unit. Required fees: $375.
Dr. Margee Ensign, Dean, School of International Studies, 209-946-2650, *E-mail:* mensign@uop.edu.

■ UNIVERSITY OF THE PACIFIC

McGeorge School of Law, Sacramento, CA 95817

AWARDS Government and public policy (LL M); international waters resources law (LL M, JSD); law (JD); transnational business practice (LL M). Part-time and evening/weekend programs available.

Faculty: 39 full-time (12 women), 31 part-time/adjunct (7 women).
Students: 609 full-time (316 women), 313 part-time (158 women); includes 168 minority (34 African Americans, 93 Asian Americans or Pacific Islanders, 27 Hispanic Americans, 14 Native Americans). Average age 24. 1,592 applicants, 73% accepted, 386 enrolled. In 2001, 261 first professional degrees, 19 master's awarded.
Degree requirements: For master's, thesis (for some programs); for doctorate, thesis/dissertation. *Median time to degree:* JD–3 years full-time; master's–1 year full-time.
Entrance requirements: For JD, LSAT; for master's, JD; for doctorate, LL M. *Application deadline:* For fall admission, 5/1 (priority date). Applications are processed on a rolling basis. *Application fee:* $40. Electronic applications accepted.
Expenses: Contact institution.
Financial support: In 2001–02, 528 students received support, including 9 fellowships, 20 research assistantships (averaging $6,485 per year); career-related internships or fieldwork, Federal Work-Study, institutionally sponsored loans, and scholarships/grants also available. Support available to part-time students. Financial award applicants required to submit FAFSA.
Faculty research: Taxation and business, family and juvenile law, governmental affairs, environmental law, intellectual property law.
Elizabeth Rindscopf Parker, Dean, 916-739-7151, *E-mail:* elizabeth@uop.edu.
Application contact: 916-739-7105, *Fax:* 916-739-7134, *E-mail:* admissionsmcgeorge@uop.edu. *Web site:* http://www.mcgeorge.edu/

■ UNIVERSITY OF VIRGINIA

College and Graduate School of Arts and Sciences, Department of Government and Foreign Affairs, Program in Foreign Affairs, Charlottesville, VA 22903

AWARDS MA, PhD, JD/MA, MBA/MA.

Faculty: 36 full-time (5 women), 11 part-time/adjunct (3 women).
Students: 41 full-time (14 women), 4 part-time (2 women); includes 6 minority (4 African Americans, 1 Asian American or Pacific Islander, 1 Hispanic American), 5 international. Average age 31. 50 applicants, 44% accepted, 9 enrolled. In 2001, 10 master's, 3 doctorates awarded.
Degree requirements: For master's, one foreign language, thesis; for doctorate, variable foreign language requirement, thesis/dissertation.
Entrance requirements: For master's and doctorate, GRE General Test, GRE Subject Test. *Application deadline:* For fall admission, 7/15; for spring admission, 12/1. Applications are processed on a rolling basis. *Application fee:* $40. Electronic applications accepted.
Expenses: Tuition, state resident: full-time $3,988. Tuition, nonresident: full-time $17,078. Required fees: $1,190.
Financial support: Application deadline: 2/1.
Application contact: Duane J. Osheim, Associate Dean for Graduate Programs, 434-924-7184, *Fax:* 434-924-3084, *E-mail:* grad-a-s@virginia.edu.

■ UNIVERSITY OF WASHINGTON

Graduate School, College of Arts and Sciences, Henry M. Jackson School of International Studies, Seattle, WA 98195

AWARDS China studies (MAIS); comparative religion (MAIS); international studies (MAIS); Japan studies (MAIS); Korea studies (MAIS); Middle Eastern studies (MAIS); Russian, East European and Central Asian studies (MAIS), including Central Asian studies, East European studies, Russian studies; South Asian studies (MAIS).

Students: 158 full-time (87 women); includes 18 minority (4 African Americans, 12 Asian Americans or Pacific Islanders, 1 Hispanic American, 1 Native American), 33 international. Average age 28. 235 applicants, 72% accepted. In 2001, 46 degrees awarded.
Entrance requirements: For master's, GRE General Test, TOEFL, minimum GPA of 3.0. *Application deadline:* For fall admission, 1/15 (priority date). *Application fee:* $50. Electronic applications accepted.
Expenses: Tuition, state resident: full-time $5,539. Tuition, nonresident: full-time $14,376. Required fees: $390. Tuition and fees vary according to course load and program.
Financial support: Fellowships with tuition reimbursements, research assistantships with full tuition reimbursements, teaching assistantships with full tuition reimbursements, career-related internships or fieldwork, Federal Work-Study, institutionally sponsored loans, and summer language study awards available. Financial award application deadline: 1/15; financial award applicants required to submit FAFSA.

University of Washington (continued)
Prof. Anand A Yang, Director, 206-5434373.
Application contact: 206-543-6001, *Fax:* 206-616-3170, *E-mail:* jsisinfo@u.washington.edu. *Web site:* http://jsis.artsci.washington.edu/

Find an in-depth description at www.petersons.com/gradchannel.

■ UNIVERSITY OF WYOMING

Graduate School, College of Arts and Sciences, Program in International Studies, Laramie, WY 82071

AWARDS MA. Part-time programs available.

Faculty: 24 part-time/adjunct (7 women).
Students: 16 full-time (11 women), 4 part-time (1 woman), 10 international. Average age 31. 14 applicants, 71% accepted. In 2001, 3 degrees awarded.
Degree requirements: For master's, thesis or alternative.
Entrance requirements: For master's, GRE General Test, minimum GPA of 3.0. *Application deadline:* For fall admission, 3/1 (priority date); for spring admission, 8/1 (priority date). Applications are processed on a rolling basis. *Application fee:* $40. Electronic applications accepted.
Expenses: Tuition, state resident: full-time $2,895; part-time $161 per credit hour. Tuition, nonresident: full-time $8,367; part-time $465 per credit hour. Required fees: $491; $10 per credit hour. $2 per credit hour. Tuition and fees vary according to course load and program.
Financial support: In 2001–02, 5 teaching assistantships with full and partial tuition reimbursements (averaging $8,667 per year) were awarded. Financial award application deadline: 3/1.
Faculty research: International political economy, comparative social institutions, foreign policy, economic development.
Dr. Garth M. Massey, Director, 307-766-3423, *Fax:* 307-766-3812, *E-mail:* gmmassey@uwyo.edu.
Application contact: Gale M.V. Bandsma, Office Assistant, Sr., 307-766-3423, *Fax:* 307-766-3812, *E-mail:* intstudy.grad@uwyo.edu. *Web site:* http://www.uwyo.edu/IntStudy/inst.htm

■ VIRGINIA POLYTECHNIC INSTITUTE AND STATE UNIVERSITY

Graduate School, College of Architecture and Urban Studies, Department of Urban Affairs and Planning, Program in Public and International Affairs, Blacksburg, VA 24061

AWARDS MPIA. Part-time programs available.

Degree requirements: For master's, thesis or alternative.
Entrance requirements: For master's, TOEFL.
Expenses: Tuition, state resident: part-time $241 per hour. Tuition, nonresident: part-time $406 per hour. Tuition and fees vary according to program.
Faculty research: Economic development, health policy, disadvantaged regions, program evaluation, comparative social policy.

Find an in-depth description at www.petersons.com/gradchannel.

■ WEBSTER UNIVERSITY

College of Arts and Sciences, Department of History, Politics and Law, Program in International Relations, St. Louis, MO 63119-3194

AWARDS MA. Part-time and evening/weekend programs available.

Students: 42 full-time (25 women), 71 part-time (25 women); includes 17 minority (8 African Americans, 2 Asian Americans or Pacific Islanders, 7 Hispanic Americans), 38 international. Average age 31. In 2001, 34 degrees awarded.
Degree requirements: For master's, thesis optional.
Application deadline: Applications are processed on a rolling basis. *Application fee:* $25 ($50 for international students).
Expenses: Tuition: Full-time $7,164; part-time $398 per credit hour.
Financial support: Career-related internships or fieldwork and Federal Work-Study available. Support available to part-time students. Financial award application deadline: 4/1; financial award applicants required to submit FAFSA.
Faculty research: International organizations, international political economy, politics of development, environmental law, Latin American law, public policy and human rights.
Kelly Kate Pease, Head, 314-968-7083, *Fax:* 314-968-7403.
Application contact: Denise Harrell, Associate Director of Graduate and Evening Student Admissions, 314-968-6983, *Fax:* 314-968-7116, *E-mail:* gadmit@webster.edu. *Web site:* http://www.webster.edu/depts/artsci/hpl/hpl.html

■ WEST VIRGINIA UNIVERSITY

Eberly College of Arts and Sciences, Department of Political Science, Morgantown, WV 26506

AWARDS American public policy and politics (MA); international and comparative public policy and U.S. politics (MA); political science (PhD); public policy analysis (PhD).

Faculty: 17 full-time (2 women), 4 part-time/adjunct (2 women).
Students: 30 full-time (8 women), 10 part-time (4 women); includes 1 minority (African American), 7 international. Average age 31. 45 applicants, 47% accepted. In 2001, 8 master's, 1 doctorate awarded. Terminal master's awarded for partial completion of doctoral program.
Degree requirements: For master's, thesis optional; for doctorate, thesis/dissertation, comprehensive exam.
Entrance requirements: For master's and doctorate, GRE General Test, TOEFL, minimum GPA of 2.75. *Application deadline:* For fall admission, 4/1 (priority date). Applications are processed on a rolling basis. *Application fee:* $45.
Expenses: Tuition, state resident: full-time $2,791. Tuition, nonresident: full-time $8,659. Required fees: $1,002. Tuition and fees vary according to program.
Financial support: In 2001–02, 14 students received support, including 4 research assistantships, 14 teaching assistantships; career-related internships or fieldwork, Federal Work-Study, institutionally sponsored loans, tuition waivers (full and partial), and unspecified assistantships also available. Financial award application deadline: 2/1; financial award applicants required to submit FAFSA.
Faculty research: Public policy, research methods, foreign policy analysis, judicial politics, environmental and energy policy.
Dr. Allan S. Hammock, Chair, 304-293-3198 Ext. 5273, *Fax:* 304-293-8644, *E-mail:* allan.hammock@mail.wvu.edu.
Application contact: Dr. Jeff Worsham, Director, Graduate Studies, 304-293-3811 Ext. 5277, *Fax:* 304-293-8644, *E-mail:* jeff.worsham@mail.wvu.edu. *Web site:* http://www.polsci.wvu.edu/

■ YALE UNIVERSITY

Graduate School of Arts and Sciences, Department of Economics, Program in International and Development Economics, New Haven, CT 06520

AWARDS MA.

Entrance requirements: For master's, GRE General Test.

■ YALE UNIVERSITY

Graduate School of Arts and Sciences, Graduate Program in International Relations, New Haven, CT 06520

AWARDS MA, JD/MA, MBA/MA, MES/MA, MF/MA, MPH/MA.

Students: 50 full-time (27 women). Average age 25. 214 applicants, 25% accepted. In 2001, 37 degrees awarded.
Degree requirements: For master's, one foreign language. *Median time to degree:* Master's–2 years full-time.
Entrance requirements: For master's, GRE General Test, TOEFL, previous course work in microeconomics and macroeconomics, professional experience preferable. *Application deadline:* For fall admission, 1/2. *Application fee:* $65. Electronic applications accepted.
Financial support: In 2001–02, 29 students received support, including 29 fellowships with full and partial tuition

reimbursements available (averaging $10,000 per year); institutionally sponsored loans and tuition waivers (full and partial) also available. Financial award application deadline: 1/2.
Faculty research: Agrarian studies, international security studies, UN studies, international human rights, international economic development.
Cheryl Doss, Director of Graduate Studies, 203-432-3418, *Fax:* 203-432-9886, *E-mail:* international.relations@yale.edu.
Application contact: Cheryl Morrison, Registrar, 203-432-3418, *Fax:* 203-432-9886, *E-mail:* international.relations@yale.edu. *Web site:* http://www.yale.edu/ycias/ia/ia3.htm

Find an in-depth description at www.petersons.com/gradchannel.

INTERNATIONAL DEVELOPMENT

■ AMERICAN UNIVERSITY

School of International Service, Washington, DC 20016-8001

AWARDS Comparative and regional studies (MA); development management (MS); environmental policy (MA); international communication (MA); international development (MA); international development management (Certificate); international economic policy (MA); international economic relations (Certificate); international peace and conflict resolution (MA); international politics (MA); international relations (PhD); U.S. foreign policy (MA). Part-time and evening/weekend programs available.

Faculty: 59 full-time (21 women), 35 part-time/adjunct (11 women).
Students: 347 full-time (214 women), 300 part-time (176 women); includes 87 minority (30 African Americans, 20 Asian Americans or Pacific Islanders, 35 Hispanic Americans, 2 Native Americans), 152 international. Average age 27. 1,254 applicants, 74% accepted, 215 enrolled. In 2001, 193 master's, 1 doctorate awarded. Terminal master's awarded for partial completion of doctoral program.
Degree requirements: For master's, one foreign language, thesis or alternative, comprehensive exam; for doctorate, one foreign language, thesis/dissertation, comprehensive exam.
Entrance requirements: For master's, GRE General Test, TOEFL, 24 credits in related social sciences, minimum of 3.3; 2 letter of recommendations; for doctorate, GRE General Test, TOEFL, 2 letters of recommendations; 24 credits in related social sciences. *Application deadline:* For fall admission, 1/15 (priority date); for spring admission, 10/1 (priority date). Applications are processed on a rolling basis. *Application fee:* $50.
Expenses: Tuition: Full-time $14,274; part-time $793 per credit. Required fees: $290. Tuition and fees vary according to program.
Financial support: In 2001–02, 13 fellowships with tuition reimbursements, 62 research assistantships with tuition reimbursements were awarded. Teaching assistantships, career-related internships or fieldwork, Federal Work-Study, and institutionally sponsored loans also available. Financial award application deadline: 1/15.
Faculty research: International intellectual property, international environmental issues, international law and legal order, international telecommunications/technology, international sustainable development.
Dr. Louis W. Goodman, Dean, 202-885-1600, *Fax:* 202-885-2494.
Application contact: Christopher Derickson, Director of Graduate Admissions and Financial Aid, 202-885-1599, *Fax:* 202-885-2494.

■ ANDREWS UNIVERSITY

School of Graduate Studies, Program in International Development, Berrien Springs, MI 49104

AWARDS MSA. Postbaccalaureate distance learning degree programs offered.

Entrance requirements: For master's, GRE General Test. *Application fee:* $40.
Expenses: Tuition: Full-time $12,600; part-time $525 per semester. Required fees: $268. Tuition and fees vary according to degree level.
Dr. Øysteim S. LaBianca, Director, 616-471-3968.
Application contact: Carolyn Hurst, Supervisor of Graduate Admission, 800-253-2874, *Fax:* 616-471-3228, *E-mail:* enroll@andrews.edu. *Web site:* http://www.idp.andrews.edu/graduate.html

■ BRANDEIS UNIVERSITY

The Heller School for Social Policy and Management, Program in Sustainable International Development, Waltham, MA 02454-9110

AWARDS MA.

Faculty: 5 full-time (1 woman), 7 part-time/adjunct (3 women).
Students: 39 full-time (14 women), 28 international. Average age 30. 461 applicants, 53% accepted, 60 enrolled. In 2001, 14 degrees awarded.
Degree requirements: For master's, 2nd-year fieldwork or internship.
Entrance requirements: For master's, TOEFL. *Application deadline:* For fall admission, 6/1. Applications are processed on a rolling basis. *Application fee:* $50 ($0 for international students). Electronic applications accepted.
Expenses: Tuition: Full-time $27,392. Required fees: $35.
Financial support: In 2001–02, 2 fellowships with full and partial tuition reimbursements (averaging $10,000 per year) were awarded; scholarships/grants and tuition waivers (full and partial) also available.
Faculty research: Water resource management, human rights, biosphere management, rural development, public policy and governance.
Dr. Laurence R. Simon, Director, 781-736-2770, *Fax:* 781-736-2774, *E-mail:* sid@brandeis.edu.
Application contact: Fiona Figueiredo, Admissions Officer, 781-736-2763, *Fax:* 781-736-2774, *E-mail:* fif@brandeis.edu. *Web site:* http://heller.brandeis.edu/sid

Find an in-depth description at www.petersons.com/gradchannel.

■ BRIGHAM YOUNG UNIVERSITY

The David M. Kennedy Center for International and Area Studies, Provo, UT 84602-1001

AWARDS American studies (MA); ancient Near Eastern studies (MA); Asian studies (MA); international development (MA); international relations (MA).

Faculty: 21 full-time (2 women), 2 part-time/adjunct (0 women).
Students: 16 full-time (8 women), 13 part-time (9 women); includes 1 minority (Hispanic American), 4 international. Average age 25. 62 applicants, 31% accepted. In 2001, 17 degrees awarded.
Degree requirements: For master's, one foreign language, thesis.
Entrance requirements: For master's, GRE General Test, minimum GPA of 3.55 in last 60 hours. *Application deadline:* For fall admission, 2/1. *Application fee:* $50. Electronic applications accepted.
Expenses: Tuition: Full-time $3,860; part-time $214 per hour.
Financial support: In 2001–02, 18 research assistantships (averaging $3,500 per year), 2 teaching assistantships (averaging $3,500 per year) were awarded. Fellowships with full tuition reimbursements, career-related internships or fieldwork and tuition waivers (full) also available. Financial award application deadline: 2/1.
Faculty research: Comparative education, education for development, comparative economics. *Total annual research expenditures:* $100,000.
Dr. Donald B. Holsinger, Director, 801-422-3378, *Fax:* 801-378-8748, *E-mail:* donald_holsinger@byu.edu.
Application contact: Dr. Phillip J. Bryson, Director of Graduate Studies, Associate Director, 801-422-7402, *Fax:* 801-378-8748, *E-mail:* phillip_bryson@byu.edu.

■ CLARK ATLANTA UNIVERSITY

School of International Affairs and Development, Atlanta, GA 30314

AWARDS International affairs and development (PhD); international business and

Clark Atlanta University (continued)
development (MA); international development administration (MA); international development education and planning (MA); international relations (MA); regional studies (MA).
Degree requirements: For master's, one foreign language, thesis; for doctorate, 2 foreign languages, thesis/dissertation.
Entrance requirements: For master's, GRE General Test, minimum GPA of 2.5; for doctorate, GRE General Test, minimum graduate GPA of 3.0.

■ CLARK UNIVERSITY

Graduate School, Department of International Development, Community, and Environment, Program in International Development and Social Change, Worcester, MA 01610-1477

AWARDS MA.

Students: 46 full-time (24 women), 3 part-time, 13 international. Average age 30. 94 applicants, 63% accepted, 29 enrolled. In 2001, 14 degrees awarded.
Degree requirements: For master's, thesis.
Application deadline: For fall admission, 2/1. *Application fee:* $40.
Expenses: Tuition: Full-time $24,400; part-time $763 per credit. Required fees: $10.
Financial support: In 2001–02, research assistantships with full and partial tuition reimbursements (averaging $9,250 per year), teaching assistantships with full and partial tuition reimbursements (averaging $9,250 per year) were awarded. Tuition waivers (full and partial) also available.
Dr. William F. Fisher, Director, *Fax:* 508-793-8820, *E-mail:* wfisher@clarku.edu.
Application contact: Liz Owens, IDCE Graduate Admissions, 508-793-7201, *Fax:* 508-793-8820, *E-mail:* idce@clarku.edu. *Web site:* http://www2.clarku.edu/newsite/graduatefolder/index.shtml

■ CORNELL UNIVERSITY

Graduate School, Graduate Fields of Arts and Sciences, Field of International Development, Ithaca, NY 14853-0001

AWARDS Development policy (MPS); international nutrition (MPS); international planning (MPS); international population (MPS); science and technology policy (MPS).

Faculty: 48 full-time.
Students: 24 full-time (15 women); includes 6 minority (2 African Americans, 2 Asian Americans or Pacific Islanders, 2 Hispanic Americans), 18 international. 34 applicants, 68% accepted. In 2001, 4 degrees awarded.
Degree requirements: For master's, project paper.
Entrance requirements: For master's, GRE General Test (recommended), TOEFL, 2 academic recommendations, 2 years of development experience. *Application deadline:* Applications are processed on a rolling basis. *Application fee:* $65. Electronic applications accepted.
Expenses: Tuition: Full-time $25,970. Required fees: $50.
Financial support: In 2001–02, 14 students received support, including 11 fellowships with full tuition reimbursements available, 1 research assistantship with full tuition reimbursement available, 2 teaching assistantships with full tuition reimbursements available; institutionally sponsored loans, scholarships/grants, tuition waivers (full and partial), and unspecified assistantships also available. Financial award applicants required to submit FAFSA.
Faculty research: Development policy, international nutrition, international planning, science and technology policy, international population.
Application contact: Graduate Field Assistant, 607-255-3037, *E-mail:* mpsid@cornell.edu. *Web site:* http://www.gradschool.cornell.edu/grad/fields_1/int-dev.html

■ DUKE UNIVERSITY

Graduate School, Center for International Development, Durham, NC 27708-0237

AWARDS MA.

Faculty: 10 full-time (2 women), 14 part-time/adjunct (4 women).
Students: 40; includes 1 minority (Asian American or Pacific Islander), 38 international. Average age 34. In 2001, 14 degrees awarded.
Degree requirements: For master's, internship, project. *Median time to degree:* Master's–2 years full-time.
Entrance requirements: For master's, TOEFL, minimum 3 years of professional experience in a development-related field. *Application deadline:* For fall admission, 12/31 (priority date); for spring admission, 10/1. Applications are processed on a rolling basis. *Application fee:* $75. Electronic applications accepted.
Expenses: Contact institution.
Financial support: In 2001–02, 1 fellowship with partial tuition reimbursement (averaging $24,000 per year) was awarded; scholarships/grants and tuition waivers (full and partial) also available. Financial award application deadline: 12/31.
Faculty research: Privatization and structural adjustment, public finance, economic development, environmental policy, sustainable development.
Dr. Francis Lethem, Director of Graduate Studies, 919-613-7333, *Fax:* 919-684-2861.
Application contact: Stephanie Alt Lamm, Coordinator, 919-613-7356, *Fax:* 919-684-2861, *E-mail:* dcid@pps.duke.edu. *Web site:* http://www.pubpol.duke.edu/dcid/

■ FORDHAM UNIVERSITY

Graduate School of Arts and Sciences, Program in International Political Economy and Development, New York, NY 10458

AWARDS MA, CIF. Part-time and evening/weekend programs available.

Faculty: 16.
Students: 28 full-time (16 women), 22 part-time (12 women); includes 2 minority (1 Asian American or Pacific Islander, 1 Hispanic American), 21 international. 118 applicants, 75% accepted. In 2001, 19 degrees awarded.
Degree requirements: For master's, comprehensive exam.
Entrance requirements: For master's, GRE General Test. *Application deadline:* For fall admission, 1/15 (priority date); for spring admission, 12/1. *Application fee:* $65. Electronic applications accepted.
Expenses: Tuition: Part-time $720 per credit. Required fees: $135 per semester.
Financial support: In 2001–02, 10 students received support, including 1 fellowship with tuition reimbursement available (averaging $15,000 per year), research assistantships with tuition reimbursements available (averaging $12,000 per year); career-related internships or fieldwork, institutionally sponsored loans, tuition waivers (full and partial), and unspecified assistantships also available. Financial award application deadline: 1/16.
Faculty research: International economics, development economics, comparative international politics, demography, emerging markets.
Dr. Henry Schwalbenberg, Chair, 718-817-4048, *Fax:* 718-817-3518, *E-mail:* schwalbenberg@fordham.edu.
Application contact: Dr. Craig W. Pilant, Assistant Dean, 718-817-4420, *Fax:* 718-817-3566, *E-mail:* pilant@fordham.edu. *Web site:* http://www.fordham.edu/gsas/

■ THE GEORGE WASHINGTON UNIVERSITY

Elliott School of International Affairs, Program in International Development Studies, Washington, DC 20052

AWARDS MA, JD/MA, MPH/MA.

Students: 36 full-time (28 women), 18 part-time (14 women); includes 8 minority (3 African Americans, 2 Asian Americans or Pacific Islanders, 3 Hispanic Americans), 5 international. Average age 27. 128 applicants, 69% accepted. In 2001, 18 degrees awarded.
Degree requirements: For master's, one foreign language.
Entrance requirements: For master's, GRE General Test, TOEFL, minimum B average. *Application deadline:* For fall admission, 2/1. *Application fee:* $55. Electronic applications accepted.
Expenses: Tuition: Part-time $810 per credit. Required fees: $1 per credit.

Financial support: Fellowships with tuition reimbursements, research assistantships with tuition reimbursements, career-related internships or fieldwork, Federal Work-Study, and institutionally sponsored loans available. Financial award application deadline: 1/15; financial award applicants required to submit FAFSA.
Faculty research: Development, anthropology, health and development, political science, education.
Dr. David Gow, Director, 202-994-4318.
Application contact: Jeff V. Miles, Director of Graduate Admissions, 202-994-7050, *Fax:* 202-994-9537, *E-mail:* esiagrad@gwu.edu. *Web site:* http://www.gwu.edu/~elliott/

Find an in-depth description at www.petersons.com/gradchannel.

■ HARVARD UNIVERSITY

John F. Kennedy School of Government, Program in Public Administration and International Development, Cambridge, MA 02138

AWARDS MPAID.

Students: 91 full-time (41 women); includes 7 minority (5 Asian Americans or Pacific Islanders, 2 Hispanic Americans), 64 international. Average age 26. 321 applicants, 38% accepted, 91 enrolled.
Entrance requirements: For master's, GMAT or GRE General Test, TOEFL. *Application deadline:* For fall admission, 1/4. *Application fee:* $80.
Expenses: Tuition: Full-time $23,370. Required fees: $816. Full-time tuition and fees vary according to program and student level.
Financial support: Career-related internships or fieldwork, Federal Work-Study, institutionally sponsored loans, scholarships/grants, and health care benefits available. Financial award applicants required to submit CSS PROFILE or FAFSA.
Carol Finney, Director, 617-495-7799.
Application contact: International Program Office, 617-495-1155.

■ HOPE INTERNATIONAL UNIVERSITY

School of Graduate Studies, Program in Business Administration, Fullerton, CA 92831-3138

AWARDS International development (MBA, MSM); nonprofit management (MBA). Part-time programs available.

Degree requirements: For master's, thesis (for some programs), project.
Entrance requirements: For master's, minimum GPA of 3.0. Electronic applications accepted. *Web site:* http://www.hiu.edu

■ JOHNS HOPKINS UNIVERSITY

Paul H. Nitze School of Advanced International Studies, Washington, DC 20036

AWARDS Emerging markets (Certificate); interdisciplinary studies (MA, PhD), including African studies, American foreign policy (MA), Asian studies, Canadian studies, conflict resolution and mediation (MA), environmental policy and resource management (MA), European studies, international business (MA), international development (MA), international economics (MA), international relations (MA), Latin American studies, Middle Eastern studies (MA), military and defense studies (MA), Russian area and East European studies (MA), social change and development (MA); international public policy (MIPP). MBA/MA offered jointly with the University of Pennsylvania–Wharton School and INSEAD in France.

Faculty: 44 full-time (13 women), 113 part-time/adjunct (29 women).
Students: 567 full-time (275 women), 17 part-time (8 women); includes 71 minority (14 African Americans, 46 Asian Americans or Pacific Islanders, 10 Hispanic Americans, 1 Native American). Average age 27. 1,288 applicants, 35% accepted. In 2001, 294 master's, 13 doctorates, 34 other advanced degrees awarded. Terminal master's awarded for partial completion of doctoral program.
Degree requirements: For master's, one foreign language, comprehensive exam; for doctorate, 2 foreign languages, thesis/dissertation.
Entrance requirements: For master's, GMAT or GRE General Test or TOEFL, previous course work in economics, foreign language; for doctorate, GRE General Test or TOEFL; for Certificate, TOEFL. *Application deadline:* For fall admission, 1/15. *Application fee:* $75. Electronic applications accepted.
Expenses: Contact institution.
Financial support: In 2001–02, 431 fellowships (averaging $5,500 per year) were awarded; career-related internships or fieldwork and Federal Work-Study also available. Financial award application deadline: 2/1; financial award applicants required to submit FAFSA.
Faculty research: Comparative politics, regional studies, language and linguistics.
Dr. Jessica Einhorn, Dean, 202-663-5624, *Fax:* 202-663-5621.
Application contact: Bonnie Wilson, Associate Dean of Student Affairs, 202-663-5700, *Fax:* 202-663-7788, *E-mail:* admissions.sais@jhu.edu. *Web site:* http://www.sais-jhu.edu/

Find an in-depth description at www.petersons.com/gradchannel.

■ NEW SCHOOL UNIVERSITY

New School, Program in International Affairs, New York, NY 10011-8603

AWARDS Global management, trade, and finance (MA, MS); international development (MA, MS); international media and communication (MA, MS); international politics and diplomacy (MA, MS); service, civic, and non-profit management (MA, MS).

Students: 22 full-time (17 women), 23 part-time (12 women); includes 11 minority (5 African Americans, 1 Asian American or Pacific Islander, 5 Hispanic Americans), 8 international. 73 applicants, 93% accepted, 45 enrolled.
Application fee: $40.
Financial support: In 2001–02, 31 students received support. Tuition waivers (partial) available. Financial award application deadline: 5/1; financial award applicants required to submit FAFSA.
Dr. Michael Cohen, Head, *E-mail:* cohenm2@newschool.edu.
Application contact: Gerianne Brusati, Associate Dean, Admissions and Student Services, 212-229-5630, *Fax:* 212-989-3887, *E-mail:* nsadmissions@newschool.edu. *Web site:* http://www.nus.newschool.edu/04h_interaff.htm

Find an in-depth description at www.petersons.com/gradchannel.

■ OHIO UNIVERSITY

Graduate Studies, Center for International Studies, Program in Development Studies, Athens, OH 45701-2979

AWARDS MA.

Students: 35 full-time (21 women), 1 (woman) part-time, 31 international. 101 applicants, 59% accepted. In 2001, 17 degrees awarded.
Degree requirements: For master's, one foreign language, thesis optional.
Entrance requirements: For master's, GRE, TOEFL (for foreign language area studies), minimum GPA of 3.0. *Application deadline:* For fall admission, 3/1 (priority date). *Application fee:* $30.
Expenses: Tuition, state resident: full-time $6,585. Tuition, nonresident: full-time $12,254.
Financial support: In 2001–02, 25 students received support, including 6 research assistantships with full tuition reimbursements available (averaging $9,430 per year); career-related internships or fieldwork, Federal Work-Study, institutionally sponsored loans, and tuition waivers (full) also available. Financial award application deadline: 1/15.
Faculty research: Problems and issues in social, economic, political, health and environmental development.
Dr. Ann Tickamyer, Director, 740-593-1832, *Fax:* 740-593-1837.
Application contact: Joan Kraynanski, Administrative Assistant, 740-593-1840,

Ohio University (continued)
Fax: 740-593-1837, *E-mail:* kraynans@ohio.edu. *Web site:* http://www.ohiou.edu/~intsdept/international studies/

■ OLD DOMINION UNIVERSITY

College of Engineering and Technology, Program in Global Engineering, Norfolk, VA 23529

AWARDS ME.

Faculty: 6 full-time (0 women), 3 part-time/adjunct (1 woman).
Students: 12 full-time (4 women); includes 3 minority (all Asian Americans or Pacific Islanders). Average age 26.
Degree requirements: For master's, thesis.
Application deadline: For fall admission, 4/15; for spring admission, 10/15.
Expenses: Tuition, state resident: part-time $202 per credit. Tuition, nonresident: part-time $534 per credit. Required fees: $76 per semester.
Faculty research: Project management.
Dr. Ralph Rogers, Graduate Program Director, 757-683-4938, *Fax:* 757-683-5640, *E-mail:* globaleng@odu.edu. *Web site:* http://www.odu.edu/engr/coet/globalengineering/

■ RUTGERS, THE STATE UNIVERSITY OF NEW JERSEY, CAMDEN

Graduate School, Department of Public Policy and Administration, Camden, NJ 08102-1401

AWARDS Health care management and policy (MPA); international public service and development (MPA); public management (MPA). Part-time and evening/weekend programs available.

Degree requirements: For master's, oral presentation, directed study.
Entrance requirements: For master's, GRE General Test or GMAT or LSAT. Electronic applications accepted.
Faculty research: Nonprofit management, county and municipal administration, health and human services, government communication, administrative law, educational finance.

■ TUFTS UNIVERSITY

Fletcher School of Law and Diplomacy, Medford, MA 02155

AWARDS MA, MAHA, MALD, PhD, DVM/MA, JD/MALD, MALD/MA, MALD/MBA, MALD/MS, MALD/MSJ, MD/MALD. Postbaccalaureate distance learning degree programs offered (minimal on-campus study).

Faculty: 29 full-time (5 women), 40 part-time/adjunct (11 women).
Students: 427 full-time (224 women); includes 45 minority (14 African Americans, 24 Asian Americans or Pacific Islanders, 7 Hispanic Americans), 210 international. Average age 28. 1,158 applicants, 41% accepted, 158 enrolled. In 2001, 192 master's, 11 doctorates awarded. Terminal master's awarded for partial completion of doctoral program.
Degree requirements: For master's, one foreign language, thesis; for doctorate, one foreign language, thesis/dissertation, dissertation defense, comprehensive exam. *Median time to degree:* Master's–2 years full-time; doctorate–5 years full-time.
Entrance requirements: For master's, GMAT or GRE General Test, TOEFL; for doctorate, GRE General Test, TOEFL, appropriate master's degree, research proposal. *Application deadline:* For fall admission, 1/15; for spring admission, 10/15. *Application fee:* $50. Electronic applications accepted.
Expenses: Contact institution.
Financial support: In 2001–02, 221 students received support, including 221 fellowships (averaging $7,000 per year); research assistantships, teaching assistantships, career-related internships or fieldwork, Federal Work-Study, institutionally sponsored loans, and scholarships/grants also available. Financial award application deadline: 1/15; financial award applicants required to submit FAFSA.
Faculty research: Negotiation and conflict resolution, international organizations, international business and economic law, security studies, development economics, complex humanitarian issues.
Stephen W. Bosworth, Dean, 617-627-3050, *Fax:* 617-627-3712.
Application contact: Laurie A. Hurley, Director of Admissions and Financial Aid, 617-627-3040, *Fax:* 617-627-3712, *E-mail:* fletcheradmissions@tufts.edu. *Web site:* http://www.fletcher.tufts.edu

Find an in-depth description at www.petersons.com/gradchannel.

■ TULANE UNIVERSITY

Graduate School, Program in Applied Development, New Orleans, LA 70118-5669

AWARDS MA, PhD.

Entrance requirements: For master's, GRE General Test, TSE, minimum B average in undergraduate course work.
Expenses: Tuition: Full-time $24,675. Required fees: $2,210.
Faculty research: Third World development.

■ UNIVERSITY OF FLORIDA

Graduate School, College of Liberal Arts and Sciences, Department of Political Science, Gainesville, FL 32611

AWARDS International development policy (MA); international relations (MA, MAT, PhD); political campaigning (MA, Certificate); political science (MA, MAT, PhD); public affairs (MA, Certificate). Part-time programs available. Terminal master's awarded for partial completion of doctoral program.

Degree requirements: For master's, variable foreign language requirement, thesis or alternative; for doctorate, variable foreign language requirement, thesis/dissertation.
Entrance requirements: For master's and doctorate, GRE General Test, minimum GPA of 3.0. Electronic applications accepted.
Expenses: Tuition, state resident: part-time $164 per hour. Tuition, nonresident: part-time $571 per hour. Tuition and fees vary according to course level and program.
Faculty research: U.S. political development, religion and politics, environmental politics and policy, developing societies, international relations. *Web site:* http://clas.ufl.edu/polisci/

■ UNIVERSITY OF PITTSBURGH

Graduate School of Public and International Affairs, Executive Programs in Public Policy and Management, Pittsburgh, PA 15260

AWARDS Criminal justice (MPPM); development planning (MPPM); environmental management and policy (MPPM); international development (MPPM); international political economy (MPPM); international security studies (MPPM); management of non profit organizations (MPPM); metropolitan management and regional development (MPPM); personnel and labor relations (MPPM); policy analysis and evaluation (MPPM). Part-time programs available.

Faculty: 32 full-time (8 women), 12 part-time/adjunct (9 women).
Students: 7 full-time (4 women), 51 part-time (27 women); includes 8 minority (all African Americans), 3 international. Average age 38. 34 applicants, 79% accepted, 18 enrolled. In 2001, 24 degrees awarded.
Degree requirements: For master's, thesis optional.
Application deadline: For fall admission, 3/1 (priority date); for spring admission, 10/1 (priority date). Applications are processed on a rolling basis. *Application fee:* $40.
Expenses: Tuition, state resident: full-time $9,410; part-time $385 per credit. Tuition, nonresident: full-time $19,376; part-time $797 per credit. Required fees: $480; $90 per term. Tuition and fees vary according to program.
Financial support: Institutionally sponsored loans and scholarships/grants available. Support available to part-time students. Financial award application deadline: 2/1.
Faculty research: Executive training and technical assistance for U.S. and international clients. *Total annual research expenditures:* $101,000.

Michele Garrity, Director, Executive Education, 412-648-7610, *Fax:* 412-648-2605, *E-mail:* garrity@birch.gspia.pitt.edu.
Application contact: Maureen O'Malley, Admissions Counselor, 412-648-7646, *Fax:* 412-648-7641, *E-mail:* pronobis@birch.gspia.pitt.edu. *Web site:* http://www.gspia.pitt.edu/

Find an in-depth description at www.petersons.com/gradchannel.

■ UNIVERSITY OF RHODE ISLAND

Graduate School, College of Arts and Sciences, Department of Political Science, Kingston, RI 02881

AWARDS International development studies (Certificate); political science (MA), including American government, American politics, comparative government, international relations, public policy; public policy and administration (MPA).

Students: In 2001, 6 degrees awarded. *Application deadline:* For fall admission, 4/15 (priority date). Applications are processed on a rolling basis. *Application fee:* $35.
Expenses: Tuition, state resident: full-time $3,756; part-time $209 per credit. Tuition, nonresident: full-time $10,774; part-time $599 per credit. Required fees: $1,586; $76 per credit. One-time fee: $60 full-time.
Dr. Maureen F. Moakley, Chairperson, 401-874-2183.

POLITICAL SCIENCE

■ AMERICAN MILITARY UNIVERSITY

Graduate School of Military Studies, Manassas, VA 20110

AWARDS Air warfare (MA Military Studies); American revolution studies (MA Military Studies); business administration (MBA); civil war studies (MA Military Studies); criminal justice (MA); defense management (MA Military Studies); emergency and disaster management (MA); intelligence (MA Strategic Intelligence); land warfare (MA Military Studies); management (MA); national security studies (MA); naval warfare (MA Military Studies); political science (MA); public administration (MA); public health (MA); security management (MA); space studies (MA Military Studies); special operations (MA Military Studies); transportation management (MA); unconventional warfare (MA Military Studies). Program offered via distance learning only. Part-time and evening/weekend programs available.
Postbaccalaureate distance learning degree programs offered (no on-campus study).

Faculty: 2 full-time (1 woman), 100 part-time/adjunct (8 women).
Students: Average age 35. 830 applicants, 100% accepted, 550 enrolled. In 2001, 87 degrees awarded. Terminal master's awarded for partial completion of doctoral program.
Entrance requirements: For master's, bachelor's degree or equivalent, minimum GPA of 2.7 in last 60 hours. *Application deadline:* For fall admission, 9/1 (priority date); for winter admission, 1/1; for spring admission, 5/1 (priority date). Applications are processed on a rolling basis. Electronic applications accepted.
Expenses: Tuition: Part-time $750 per course.
Faculty research: Military history, criminal justice, management performance, national security.
Dr. Michael J. Hillyard, Provost, 703-330-5398 Ext. 862, *Fax:* 703-330-5109, *E-mail:* mhillyard@amunet.edu.
Application contact: Cathi Bauer, Office of Student Services, 703-330-5398 Ext. 894, *Fax:* 703-330-5109, *E-mail:* info@amunet.edu. *Web site:* http://www.amunet.edu/

■ AMERICAN UNIVERSITY

School of Public Affairs, Department of Government, Washington, DC 20016-8001

AWARDS Political science (MA, PhD), including American politics (MA), comparative politics (MA). Part-time and evening/weekend programs available.

Faculty: 25 full-time (14 women), 39 part-time/adjunct (13 women).
Students: 26 full-time (9 women), 32 part-time (14 women); includes 7 minority (4 African Americans, 1 Asian American or Pacific Islander, 2 Hispanic Americans), 9 international. Average age 27. 88 applicants, 65% accepted, 22 enrolled. In 2001, 19 master's, 4 doctorates awarded. Terminal master's awarded for partial completion of doctoral program.
Degree requirements: For master's, comprehensive exam; for doctorate, thesis/dissertation, comprehensive exam.
Entrance requirements: For master's, GRE General Test (financial award applicants); for doctorate, GRE General Test. *Application deadline:* For fall admission, 2/1; for spring admission, 10/1. *Application fee:* $50.
Expenses: Tuition: Full-time $14,274; part-time $793 per credit. Required fees: $290. Tuition and fees vary according to program.
Financial support: Fellowships, research assistantships, teaching assistantships, career-related internships or fieldwork and institutionally sponsored loans available. Financial award application deadline: 2/1.
Faculty research: Political leadership, interest groups, politics of regulation, public law, political behavior.
Dr. Gregg Ivers, Chair, 202-885-6237, *Fax:* 202-885-2967.
Application contact: Robert Briggs, Academic Counselor, 202-885-6204, *Fax:* 202-885-2967. *Web site:* http://www.american.edu/academic.depts/spa/academic.htm#grad.progs/

■ AMERICAN UNIVERSITY

School of Public Affairs, Department of Public Administration, Program in Public Administration, Washington, DC 20016-8001

AWARDS MPA, PhD, Certificate. Part-time and evening/weekend programs available.

Students: 99 full-time (75 women), 74 part-time (43 women); includes 46 minority (36 African Americans, 6 Asian Americans or Pacific Islanders, 4 Hispanic Americans), 26 international. Average age 33. In 2001, 59 master's, 1 doctorate awarded.
Degree requirements: For doctorate, thesis/dissertation.
Entrance requirements: For doctorate, GRE General Test. *Application deadline:* For fall admission, 2/1; for spring admission, 10/1. *Application fee:* $50.
Expenses: Tuition: Full-time $14,274; part-time $793 per credit. Required fees: $290. Tuition and fees vary according to program.
Financial support: Fellowships, teaching assistantships, career-related internships or fieldwork, Federal Work-Study, and institutionally sponsored loans available. Financial award application deadline: 2/1.
Application contact: Brenda Manley, Academic Counselor, 202-885-6202, *Fax:* 202-885-2355, *E-mail:* bmanley@american.edu.

Find an in-depth description at www.petersons.com/gradchannel.

■ APPALACHIAN STATE UNIVERSITY

Cratis D. Williams Graduate School, College of Arts and Sciences, Department of Political Science, Program in Political Science, Boone, NC 28608

AWARDS MA.

Faculty: 16 full-time (3 women).
Students: 19 full-time (10 women). In 2001, 2 degrees awarded.
Degree requirements: For master's, one foreign language, comprehensive exam.
Entrance requirements: For master's, GRE General Test. *Application deadline:* For fall admission, 7/1; for spring admission, 11/1. *Application fee:* $35.
Expenses: Tuition, state resident: full-time $1,286. Tuition, nonresident: full-time $9,354. Required fees: $1,116.
Financial support: In 2001–02, research assistantships (averaging $6,250 per year), teaching assistantships (averaging $6,250 per year) were awarded. Scholarships/grants and unspecified assistantships also available. Financial award application

Appalachian State University (continued)
deadline: 7/1; financial award applicants required to submit FAFSA.
Faculty research: Campaign finance, emerging democracies, bureaucratic politics, judicial behavior, administration of justice.
Dr. Ron Stidham, Graduate Advisor, 828-262-6039, *E-mail:* stidhamr@appstate.edu.

■ ARIZONA STATE UNIVERSITY

Graduate College, College of Liberal Arts and Sciences, Department of Political Science, Tempe, AZ 85287

AWARDS MA, PhD.

Degree requirements: For master's, thesis or alternative; for doctorate, thesis/dissertation.
Entrance requirements: For master's and doctorate, GRE.
Faculty research: Humanism and politics, interaction between administrative agencies and the federal courts in public policy-making, international crisis behavior of democracies and dictatorships.

■ ARKANSAS STATE UNIVERSITY

Graduate School, College of Arts and Sciences, Department of Political Science, Jonesboro, State University, AR 72467

AWARDS Political science (MA, SCCT); public administration (MPA). Part-time programs available.

Faculty: 9 full-time (2 women).
Students: 9 full-time (7 women), 8 part-time (6 women); includes 6 minority (5 African Americans, 1 Hispanic American), 1 international. Average age 27. In 2001, 14 master's, 1 other advanced degree awarded.
Degree requirements: For master's, thesis or alternative, comprehensive exam.
Entrance requirements: For master's, GRE General Test or MAT, appropriate bachelor's degree; for SCCT, GRE General Test or MAT, interview, master's degree. *Application deadline:* For fall admission, 7/1 (priority date); for spring admission, 11/15 (priority date). Applications are processed on a rolling basis. *Application fee:* $15 ($25 for international students). Electronic applications accepted.
Expenses: Tuition, state resident: full-time $3,384; part-time $141 per hour. Tuition, nonresident: full-time $8,520; part-time $355 per hour. Required fees: $742; $28 per hour. $25 per semester. One-time fee: $15 full-time. Tuition and fees vary according to degree level.
Financial support: Fellowships, teaching assistantships, career-related internships or fieldwork, Federal Work-Study, and scholarships/grants available. Support available to part-time students. Financial award application deadline: 7/1; financial award applicants required to submit FAFSA.
Dr. Jane Gates, Chair, 870-972-3048, *Fax:* 870-972-2720, *E-mail:* jgates@astate.edu. *Web site:* http://www.cas.astate.edu/posc/

■ AUBURN UNIVERSITY

Graduate School, College of Liberal Arts, Department of Political Science, Auburn University, AL 36849

AWARDS Public administration (MPA, PhD). Part-time programs available.

Faculty: 20 full-time (5 women).
Students: 23 full-time (11 women), 48 part-time (28 women); includes 14 minority (11 African Americans, 3 Hispanic Americans), 3 international. 52 applicants, 48% accepted. In 2001, 10 master's, 2 doctorates awarded.
Degree requirements: For doctorate, thesis/dissertation.
Entrance requirements: For master's, GRE General Test, minimum GPA of 3.0 in political science, 2.5 overall; for doctorate, GRE General Test. *Application deadline:* For fall admission, 7/7; for spring admission, 11/24. Applications are processed on a rolling basis. *Application fee:* $25 ($50 for international students). Electronic applications accepted.
Financial support: Fellowships, research assistantships, teaching assistantships, career-related internships or fieldwork and Federal Work-Study available. Support available to part-time students. Financial award application deadline: 3/15.
Faculty research: Policy evaluation, political economy, privatization, participation, election administration. *Total annual research expenditures:* $200,000.
Dr. Paul M. Johnson, Chair, 334-844-5370.
Application contact: Dr. John F. Pritchett, Dean of the Graduate School, 334-844-4700, *E-mail:* hatchlb@mail.auburn.edu. *Web site:* http://www.auburn.edu/academic/liberal_arts/poli_sci/

■ AUBURN UNIVERSITY MONTGOMERY

School of Sciences, Department of Political Science, Montgomery, AL 36124-4023

AWARDS MPS. Part-time and evening/weekend programs available.

Students: 1 full-time (0 women), 9 part-time (4 women); includes 3 minority (2 African Americans, 1 Hispanic American). Average age 33. In 2001, 5 degrees awarded.
Degree requirements: For master's, comprehensive exam.
Entrance requirements: For master's, GRE General Test or MAT. *Application deadline:* Applications are processed on a rolling basis. *Application fee:* $25. Electronic applications accepted.
Expenses: Tuition, state resident: full-time $3,072; part-time $128 per credit hour. Tuition, nonresident: full-time $9,216; part-time $384 per credit hour.
Financial support: Career-related internships or fieldwork and scholarships/grants available. Support available to part-time students. Financial award application deadline: 3/1; financial award applicants required to submit FAFSA.
Dr. Thomas Vocino, Head, 334-244-3696, *E-mail:* vocino@strudel.aum.edu.

■ AUGUSTA STATE UNIVERSITY

Graduate Studies, College of Arts and Sciences, Department of Political Science, Augusta, GA 30904-2200

AWARDS MPA. Part-time and evening/weekend programs available.

Faculty: 4 full-time (2 women), 1 part-time/adjunct (0 women).
Students: 1 (woman) full-time, 20 part-time (12 women); includes 7 minority (4 African Americans, 1 Asian American or Pacific Islander, 2 Hispanic Americans). 11 applicants, 64% accepted, 6 enrolled. In 2001, 3 degrees awarded.
Degree requirements: For master's, thesis, comprehensive exam.
Entrance requirements: For master's, GRE General Test. *Application deadline:* For fall admission, 7/16 (priority date). Applications are processed on a rolling basis. *Application fee:* $20. Electronic applications accepted.
Expenses: Tuition, area resident: Full-time $2,320; part-time $97 per credit hour. Required fees: $175.
Financial support: In 2001–02, 1 student received support. Federal Work-Study and institutionally sponsored loans available. Financial award application deadline: 4/15; financial award applicants required to submit FAFSA.
Faculty research: Political behavior, administrative law, political participation, human resources administration.
Dr. Chris Bourdouvalis, Acting Chair, 706-737-1710, *Fax:* 706-667-4116, *E-mail:* cbourdou@aug.edu.
Application contact: Dr. Gwen Wood, MPA Director, 706-667-4424, *Fax:* 706-667-4116, *E-mail:* gwood@aug.edu. *Web site:* http://www.aug.edu/political_science/

■ BALL STATE UNIVERSITY

Graduate School, College of Sciences and Humanities, Department of Political Science, Department of Political Science, Muncie, IN 47306-1099

AWARDS MA.

Faculty: 13.
Students: 9 full-time (3 women), 5 part-time (3 women). Average age 27. 7 applicants, 100% accepted. In 2001, 5 degrees awarded.

Application fee: $25 ($35 for international students).
Expenses: Tuition, state resident: full-time $4,068; part-time $2,542. Tuition, nonresident: full-time $10,944; part-time $6,462. Required fees: $1,000; $500 per term.
Financial support: Teaching assistantships with full tuition reimbursements, career-related internships or fieldwork available. Financial award application deadline: 3/1.
Faculty research: Survey research, public policy.
Dr. Joseph Losco, Director, 765-285-8780, *Fax:* 765-285-5345. *Web site:* http://www.bsu.edu/poli-sci/

■ BAYLOR UNIVERSITY

Graduate School, College of Arts and Sciences, Department of Political Science, Waco, TX 76798

AWARDS International relations (MA); political science (MA); public policy and administration (MPPA).

Students: 12 full-time (7 women); includes 2 minority (both Hispanic Americans), 2 international. In 2001, 7 degrees awarded.
Entrance requirements: For master's, GRE General Test. *Application deadline:* Applications are processed on a rolling basis. *Application fee:* $25.
Expenses: Tuition: Part-time $379 per semester hour. Required fees: $42 per semester hour. $101 per semester. Tuition and fees vary according to program.
Financial support: Research assistantships, career-related internships or fieldwork, Federal Work-Study, and institutionally sponsored loans available. Financial award application deadline: 3/1.
Dr. Janet Adamski, Director of Graduate Studies, 254-710-3161, *Fax:* 254-710-3122, *E-mail:* janet_adamski@baylor.edu.
Application contact: Suzanne Keener, Administrative Assistant, 254-710-3588, *Fax:* 254-710-3870, *E-mail:* graduate_school@baylor.edu. *Web site:* http://www.baylor.edu/~Political_Science/welcome.html

■ BAYLOR UNIVERSITY

Graduate School, J. M. Dawson Institute of Church-State Studies, Waco, TX 76798

AWARDS MA, PhD.

Students: 24 full-time (4 women), 1 (woman) part-time; includes 1 minority (Asian American or Pacific Islander), 3 international. In 2001, 3 master's, 3 doctorates awarded.
Degree requirements: For master's, thesis, oral exam; for doctorate, one foreign language, thesis/dissertation, preliminary exams.
Entrance requirements: For master's, GRE General Test, minimum GPA of 3.0 in major, 2.7 overall; for doctorate, GRE General Test, MA or equivalent. *Application deadline:* For fall admission, 3/1. Applications are processed on a rolling basis. *Application fee:* $25.
Expenses: Tuition: Part-time $379 per semester hour. Required fees: $42 per semester hour. $101 per semester. Tuition and fees vary according to program.
Financial support: Fellowships, research assistantships, teaching assistantships, Federal Work-Study and institutionally sponsored loans available. Financial award application deadline: 3/1.
Faculty research: Religion and politics, religion and public education, religious freedom and international politics, First Amendment jurisprudence.
Dr. Derek H. Davis, Director, 254-710-1510, *Fax:* 254-710-1571, *E-mail:* derek_davis@baylor.edu.
Application contact: Suzanne Keener, Administrative Assistant, 254-710-3588, *Fax:* 254-710-3870, *E-mail:* graduate_school@baylor.edu. *Web site:* http://www.baylor.edu/~Graduate_School/Grad_Catalog/Church-StateStudies.htm.#PhD

■ BOSTON COLLEGE

Graduate School of Arts and Sciences, Department of Political Science, Chestnut Hill, MA 02467-3800

AWARDS MA, PhD.

Students: 21 full-time (4 women), 36 part-time (7 women); includes 3 minority (1 African American, 1 Asian American or Pacific Islander, 1 Native American), 18 international. 115 applicants, 35% accepted. In 2001, 7 master's, 2 doctorates awarded. Terminal master's awarded for partial completion of doctoral program.
Degree requirements: For master's, thesis or alternative; for doctorate, one foreign language, thesis/dissertation.
Entrance requirements: For master's and doctorate, GRE General Test. *Application deadline:* For fall admission, 2/1. *Application fee:* $50.
Expenses: Tuition: Full-time $17,664; part-time $8,832 per semester.
Financial support: Fellowships, research assistantships, teaching assistantships, Federal Work-Study and scholarships/grants available. Support available to part-time students. Financial award application deadline: 3/1; financial award applicants required to submit FAFSA.
Faculty research: Political theory, American politics, international politics.
Dr. Kay Schlozman, Chairperson, 617-552-4160.
Application contact: Dr. Susan Shell, Graduate Program Director, 617-552-4168, *E-mail:* susan.shell@bc.edu. *Web site:* http://www.bc.edu/bc_org/avp/cas/polsc/

■ BOSTON UNIVERSITY

Graduate School of Arts and Sciences, Department of Political Science, Boston, MA 02215

AWARDS MA, PhD.

Students: 35 full-time (17 women), 10 part-time (2 women); includes 5 minority (1 African American, 1 Asian American or Pacific Islander, 3 Hispanic Americans), 22 international. Average age 33. 105 applicants, 34% accepted, 13 enrolled. In 2001, 3 master's, 8 doctorates awarded. Terminal master's awarded for partial completion of doctoral program.
Degree requirements: For master's, one foreign language, registration; for doctorate, 2 foreign languages, thesis/dissertation, qualifying exam.
Entrance requirements: For master's and doctorate, GRE General Test, TOEFL, 3 letters of recommendation. *Application deadline:* For fall admission, 4/1; for spring admission, 10/15. *Application fee:* $60.
Expenses: Tuition: Full-time $25,872; part-time $340 per credit. Required fees: $40 per semester. Part-time tuition and fees vary according to class time, course level and program.
Financial support: In 2001–02, 20 students received support, including 1 fellowship (averaging $14,000 per year), 9 teaching assistantships with full tuition reimbursements available (averaging $12,500 per year); career-related internships or fieldwork, Federal Work-Study, and stipends also available. Support available to part-time students. Financial award application deadline: 1/15; financial award applicants required to submit FAFSA.
David Mayers, Chairman, 617-353-2540, *Fax:* 617-353-5508, *E-mail:* dmayers@bu.edu.
Application contact: Linda Simons, Senior Program Coordinator, 617-353-2541, *Fax:* 617-353-5508, *E-mail:* pograd@bu.edu. *Web site:* http://www.bu.edu/polisci

■ BOWLING GREEN STATE UNIVERSITY

Graduate College, College of Arts and Sciences, Department of Political Science, Program in Political Science, Bowling Green, OH 43403

AWARDS MA/MA.

Students: 1 full-time (0 women). Average age 29. 3 applicants, 67% accepted, 0 enrolled.
Degree requirements: One foreign language.
Application fee: $30. Electronic applications accepted.
Expenses: Tuition, state resident: full-time $7,376; part-time $342 per credit hour. Tuition, nonresident: full-time $13,628; part-time $640 per credit hour.
Financial support: Research assistantships with full tuition reimbursements, teaching assistantships with full tuition reimbursements, Federal Work-Study and unspecified assistantships available. Financial award applicants required to submit FAFSA.

■ BRANDEIS UNIVERSITY

Graduate School of Arts and Sciences, Department of Politics, Waltham, MA 02454-9110

AWARDS MA, PhD. Part-time programs available.

Faculty: 12 full-time (2 women).
Students: 38 full-time (18 women), 1 part-time; includes 2 African Americans. Average age 33. 29 applicants, 24% accepted. In 2001, 5 master's, 3 doctorates awarded. Terminal master's awarded for partial completion of doctoral program.
Degree requirements: For master's, thesis; for doctorate, one foreign language, thesis/dissertation, comprehensive exam.
Entrance requirements: For master's and doctorate, GRE General Test, sample of written work, resumé, 3 letters of recommendation. *Application deadline:* For fall admission, 2/1. *Application fee:* $60. Electronic applications accepted.
Expenses: Tuition: Full-time $27,392. Required fees: $35.
Financial support: In 2001–02, 16 students received support, including 12 fellowships with full and partial tuition reimbursements available (averaging $13,000 per year); teaching assistantships, scholarships/grants, health care benefits, tuition waivers (full), and unspecified assistantships also available. Financial award application deadline: 2/1; financial award applicants required to submit CSS PROFILE or FAFSA.
Faculty research: American institutions, international law and foreign policy, political theory, comparative politics, European politics.
Jytte Klausen, Graduate Director, 781-736-2750, *Fax:* 781-736-2777, *E-mail:* klausen@brandeis.edu.
Application contact: Linda Boothroyd, Information Contact, 781-736-2750, *Fax:* 781-736-2777, *E-mail:* lindab@brandeis.edu. *Web site:* http://www.brandeis.edu/departments/politics/graduate.html

■ BROOKLYN COLLEGE OF THE CITY UNIVERSITY OF NEW YORK

Division of Graduate Studies, Department of Political Science, Brooklyn, NY 11210-2889

AWARDS Political science (MA, PhD); political science, urban policy and administration (MA). Part-time and evening/weekend programs available.

Students: 8 full-time (2 women), 110 part-time (65 women); includes 77 minority (63 African Americans, 5 Asian Americans or Pacific Islanders, 9 Hispanic Americans), 5 international. 36 applicants, 69% accepted. In 2001, 42 degrees awarded.
Degree requirements: For master's, thesis or alternative.
Application deadline: For fall admission, 3/1; for spring admission, 11/1. *Application fee:* $40.
Expenses: Tuition, state resident: full-time $4,350; part-time $185 per credit. Tuition, nonresident: full-time $7,600; part-time $320 per credit.
Financial support: Fellowships, career-related internships or fieldwork, Federal Work-Study, and tuition waivers (full and partial) available. Support available to part-time students. Financial award application deadline: 5/1; financial award applicants required to submit FAFSA.
Faculty research: Ethics and politics, politics of criminal justice, Western Europe, international law and politics, labor politics.
Dr. Vincent Fuccillo, Chairperson, 718-951-5306.
Application contact: Dr. Patricia Ruffin, Graduate Deputy, 718-951-5058.

■ BROWN UNIVERSITY

Graduate School, Department of Political Science, Providence, RI 02912

AWARDS AM, PhD.

Degree requirements: For master's, thesis, oral exam; for doctorate, thesis/dissertation.
Entrance requirements: For master's and doctorate, GRE General Test.

■ CALIFORNIA INSTITUTE OF TECHNOLOGY

Division of the Humanities and Social Sciences, Social Science Program, Specialization in Political Science, Pasadena, CA 91125-0001

AWARDS PhD.

Faculty: 23 full-time (1 woman), 1 part-time/adjunct (0 women).
Degree requirements: For doctorate, thesis/dissertation.
Entrance requirements: For doctorate, GRE General Test. *Application deadline:* For fall admission, 1/15. *Application fee:* $0. Electronic applications accepted.
Financial support: Fellowships, research assistantships, teaching assistantships, Federal Work-Study and institutionally sponsored loans available.
Faculty research: Social choice, Congress and electoral behavior, constitutional design, theoretical political science.
Application contact: Laurel Auchampaugh, Graduate Secretary, 626-395-4206, *Fax:* 626-405-9841, *E-mail:* gradsec@hss.caltech.edu. *Web site:* http://www.hss.caltech.edu/Ph.D_html

■ CALIFORNIA STATE UNIVERSITY, CHICO

Graduate School, College of Behavioral and Social Sciences, Department of Political Science, Program in Political Science, Chico, CA 95929-0722

AWARDS MA.

Students: 15 applicants, 80% accepted, 10 enrolled. In 2001, 4 degrees awarded.
Degree requirements: For master's, thesis or alternative, oral exam.
Application deadline: For fall admission, 4/1; for spring admission, 10/1. Applications are processed on a rolling basis. *Application fee:* $55. Electronic applications accepted.
Expenses: Tuition, state resident: full-time $2,148. Tuition, nonresident: full-time $6,576.
Financial support: Career-related internships or fieldwork available.
Dr. Diana Dwyer, Graduate Coordinator, 530-898-5734.

■ CALIFORNIA STATE UNIVERSITY, FULLERTON

Graduate Studies, College of Humanities and Social Sciences, Division of Political Science and Criminal Justice, Fullerton, CA 92834-9480

AWARDS Political science (MA); public administration (MPA). Part-time programs available.

Faculty: 17 full-time (4 women), 15 part-time/adjunct.
Students: 37 full-time (20 women), 84 part-time (36 women); includes 45 minority (6 African Americans, 12 Asian Americans or Pacific Islanders, 27 Hispanic Americans), 5 international. Average age 31. 88 applicants, 65% accepted, 32 enrolled. In 2001, 31 degrees awarded.
Degree requirements: For master's, project or thesis.
Entrance requirements: For master's, minimum GPA of 2.5 in last 60 units, 12 units in social sciences. *Application fee:* $55.
Expenses: Tuition, nonresident: part-time $246 per unit. Required fees: $964.
Financial support: Career-related internships or fieldwork, Federal Work-Study, institutionally sponsored loans, and scholarships/grants available. Support available to part-time students. Financial award application deadline: 3/1.
Faculty research: Emergency management plans.
Dr. Alan Saltzstein, Chair, 714-278-3521.

■ CALIFORNIA STATE UNIVERSITY, LONG BEACH

Graduate Studies, College of Liberal Arts, Department of Political Science, Long Beach, CA 90840

AWARDS MA. Part-time programs available.

Faculty: 8 full-time (1 woman).
Students: 12 full-time (6 women), 11 part-time (6 women); includes 9 minority (3 Asian Americans or Pacific Islanders, 6 Hispanic Americans), 3 international. Average age 33. 23 applicants, 52% accepted. In 2001, 9 degrees awarded.
Degree requirements: For master's, one foreign language.
Entrance requirements: For master's, GRE General Test, minimum GPA of 3.0 in field. *Application deadline:* For fall admission, 8/1; for spring admission, 12/1. Applications are processed on a rolling basis. *Application fee:* $55. Electronic applications accepted.
Financial support: In 2001–02, 6 students received support; teaching assistantships, Federal Work-Study, institutionally sponsored loans, and scholarships/grants available. Financial award application deadline: 3/2.
Faculty research: Social welfare policy, international political economy, Marxism, voting behavior.
Dr. Charles Noble, Chair, 562-985-4704, *Fax:* 562-985-4979, *E-mail:* cnoble@csulb.edu.
Application contact: Dr. Gerry Riposa, Graduate Advisor, 562-985-4705, *Fax:* 562-985-4979, *E-mail:* griposa@csulb.edu.

■ CALIFORNIA STATE UNIVERSITY, LOS ANGELES

Graduate Studies, College of Natural and Social Sciences, Department of Political Science, Major in Political Science, Los Angeles, CA 90032-8530

AWARDS MA.

Students: 6 full-time (2 women), 19 part-time (11 women); includes 12 minority (2 African Americans, 1 Asian American or Pacific Islander, 8 Hispanic Americans, 1 Native American), 6 international. In 2001, 3 degrees awarded.
Degree requirements: For master's, comprehensive exam or thesis.
Entrance requirements: For master's, TOEFL, minimum GPA of 3.0 in last 90 units. *Application deadline:* For fall admission, 6/30; for spring admission, 2/1. Applications are processed on a rolling basis. *Application fee:* $55.
Expenses: Tuition, nonresident: part-time $164 per unit.
Financial support: Application deadline: 3/1.
Faculty research: American government and politics, public policy, legal systems, international politics and economic relations.
Dr. Ted Anagnoson, Chair, Department of Political Science, 323-343-2230.

■ CALIFORNIA STATE UNIVERSITY, NORTHRIDGE

Graduate Studies, College of Social and Behavioral Sciences, Department of Political Science, Northridge, CA 91330

AWARDS Political science (MA); public administration (MPA).

Faculty: 16 full-time, 10 part-time/adjunct.
Students: 4 full-time (2 women), 18 part-time (8 women); includes 4 minority (1 African American, 3 Hispanic Americans), 1 international. Average age 33. 100 applicants, 77% accepted, 4 enrolled. In 2001, 67 degrees awarded.
Entrance requirements: For master's, TOEFL. *Application deadline:* For fall admission, 11/30. *Application fee:* $55.
Expenses: Tuition, nonresident: part-time $631 per semester. Required fees: $246 per unit.
Financial support: Application deadline: 3/1.
Dr. Matthew A. Cahn, Interim Department Chair, 818-677-3488.

■ CALIFORNIA STATE UNIVERSITY, SACRAMENTO

Graduate Studies, College of Social Sciences and Interdisciplinary Studies, Department of Government, Sacramento, CA 95819-6048

AWARDS MA. Part-time programs available.

Students: 14 full-time (7 women), 22 part-time (7 women); includes 8 minority (5 African Americans, 3 Asian Americans or Pacific Islanders), 1 international.
Degree requirements: For master's, thesis or alternative, writing proficiency exam.
Entrance requirements: For master's, GRE General Test, TOEFL, minimum GPA of 3.0 during previous 2 years. *Application deadline:* For fall admission, 4/15; for spring admission, 11/1. *Application fee:* $55.
Expenses: Tuition, state resident: full-time $1,965; part-time $668 per semester. Tuition, nonresident: part-time $246 per unit.
Financial support: Career-related internships or fieldwork and Federal Work-Study available. Support available to part-time students. Financial award application deadline: 3/1.
Dr. Mignon Gregg, Chair, 916-278-6202.
Application contact: Dr. Ken Debow, Graduate Coordinator, 916-278-6673.

■ CASE WESTERN RESERVE UNIVERSITY

School of Graduate Studies, Department of Political Science, Cleveland, OH 44106

AWARDS MA, PhD. Part-time programs available. Terminal master's awarded for partial completion of doctoral program.

Degree requirements: For doctorate, thesis/dissertation.
Entrance requirements: For master's, GRE General Test, TOEFL, 18 hours in political science; for doctorate, GRE General Test, GRE Subject Test (political science), TOEFL, master's degree in political science.
Faculty research: American cultural politics and policy, Western and Eastern European governments, African politics in international affairs, American legislative and presidential politics, women and politics, Southern politics.

■ THE CATHOLIC UNIVERSITY OF AMERICA

School of Arts and Sciences, Department of Politics, Washington, DC 20064

AWARDS American government (MA, PhD); congressional studies (MA); international affairs (MA); international political economics (MA); political theory (MA, PhD); world politics (MA, PhD). Part-time programs available.

Faculty: 15 full-time (2 women), 4 part-time/adjunct (0 women).
Students: 17 full-time (5 women), 83 part-time (23 women); includes 9 minority (3 African Americans, 1 Asian American or Pacific Islander, 4 Hispanic Americans, 1 Native American), 9 international. Average age 34. 69 applicants, 81% accepted, 30 enrolled. In 2001, 32 master's, 4 doctorates awarded.
Degree requirements: For master's, one foreign language, thesis or alternative, comprehensive exam; for doctorate, 2 foreign languages, thesis/dissertation, comprehensive exam.
Entrance requirements: For master's, GRE General Test, TOEFL; for doctorate, GRE General Test. *Application deadline:* For fall admission, 8/1 (priority date); for spring admission, 12/1. Applications are processed on a rolling basis. *Application fee:* $55. Electronic applications accepted.
Expenses: Tuition: Full-time $20,050; part-time $770 per credit. Required fees: $430 per term. Tuition and fees vary according to program.
Financial support: In 2001–02, 51 students received support; teaching assistantships, career-related internships or fieldwork, Federal Work-Study, institutionally sponsored loans, and tuition waivers (full and partial) available. Support available to part-time students. Financial award application deadline: 2/1.

The Catholic University of America (continued)

Faculty research: Political philosophy, American political institutions and processes, political economy, national security.

Dr. Stephen Schneck, Director, 202-319-5128, *Fax:* 202-319-6289.

Application contact: Helen Foggo, Office Manager, 202-319-5128.

■ CENTRAL MICHIGAN UNIVERSITY

College of Graduate Studies, College of Humanities and Social and Behavioral Sciences, Department of Political Science, Program in Political Science, Mount Pleasant, MI 48859

AWARDS MA.

Degree requirements: For master's, thesis or alternative.

Entrance requirements: For master's, GRE.

Expenses: Tuition, state resident: part-time $182 per unit. Tuition, nonresident: part-time $182 per unit. Required fees: $208 per semester. Part-time tuition and fees vary according to course load.

■ CLAREMONT GRADUATE UNIVERSITY

Graduate Programs, School of Politics and Economics, Department of Politics and Policy, Claremont, CA 91711-6160

AWARDS International political economy (MAIPE); international studies (MAIS); political science (PhD); politics (MAP); politics, economics, and business (MAPEB); public policy (MAPP). Part-time programs available.

Faculty: 9 full-time (2 women), 2 part-time/adjunct (1 woman).

Students: 158 full-time (62 women), 43 part-time (19 women); includes 42 minority (19 African Americans, 6 Asian Americans or Pacific Islanders, 17 Hispanic Americans), 40 international. Average age 34. In 2001, 25 master's, 9 doctorates awarded. Terminal master's awarded for partial completion of doctoral program.

Degree requirements: For master's, thesis; for doctorate, one foreign language, thesis/dissertation.

Entrance requirements: For master's and doctorate, GRE General Test. *Application deadline:* For fall admission, 2/15 (priority date). Applications are processed on a rolling basis. *Application fee:* $50. Electronic applications accepted.

Expenses: Tuition: Full-time $22,984; part-time $1,000 per unit. Required fees: $160; $80 per semester.

Financial support: Fellowships, research assistantships, teaching assistantships, career-related internships or fieldwork, Federal Work-Study, and institutionally sponsored loans available. Support available to part-time students. Financial award application deadline: 2/15; financial award applicants required to submit FAFSA.

Faculty research: Environmental policy, international debt, global democratization, Third World development, public sector discrimination.

Yi Fens, Chair, 909-621-8171, *Fax:* 909-621-8390, *E-mail:* yi.fens@cgu.edu.

Application contact: Gwen Williams, Program Administrator, 909-621-8179, *Fax:* 909-621-8545, *E-mail:* gwen.williams@cgu.edu. *Web site:* http://spe.cgu.edu/politics/index.html

Find an in-depth description at www.petersons.com/gradchannel.

■ CLARK ATLANTA UNIVERSITY

School of Arts and Sciences, Department of Political Science, Atlanta, GA 30314

AWARDS MA, PhD. Part-time programs available. Terminal master's awarded for partial completion of doctoral program.

Degree requirements: For master's, one foreign language, thesis; for doctorate, 2 foreign languages, thesis/dissertation.

Entrance requirements: For master's, GRE General Test, minimum GPA of 2.5; for doctorate, GRE General Test, minimum graduate GPA of 3.0.

Faculty research: Public policy and education, rural politics, women and state economic programs, reconstruction after war in Africa, environmental policies.

■ THE COLLEGE OF SAINT ROSE

Graduate Studies, School of Arts and Humanities, History/Political Science Program, Albany, NY 12203-1419

AWARDS MA. Part-time and evening/weekend programs available.

Faculty: 10 full-time (5 women).

Students: 1 full-time (0 women), 18 part-time (7 women); includes 1 minority (Hispanic American). Average age 36. 12 applicants, 100% accepted, 4 enrolled. In 2001, 3 degrees awarded.

Degree requirements: For master's, thesis or alternative, comprehensive exam.

Entrance requirements: For master's, minimum undergraduate GPA of 3.0. *Application deadline:* For fall admission, 7/15 (priority date); for spring admission, 12/1 (priority date). Applications are processed on a rolling basis. *Application fee:* $30.

Expenses: Tuition: Full-time $8,712. Required fees: $190.

Financial support: Research assistantships, career-related internships or fieldwork and tuition waivers (partial) available. Support available to part-time students. Financial award application deadline: 3/1.

Dr. Keith Haynes, Head, 518-454-5203.

Application contact: 518-454-5136, *Fax:* 518-458-5479, *E-mail:* ace@mail.strose.edu.

■ COLORADO STATE UNIVERSITY

Graduate School, College of Liberal Arts, Department of Political Science, Fort Collins, CO 80523-0015

AWARDS Environmental politics and policy (PhD); political science (MA, PhD). Part-time programs available.

Faculty: 16 full-time (4 women).

Students: 9 full-time (5 women), 21 part-time (7 women). Average age 32. 22 applicants, 68% accepted, 5 enrolled. In 2001, 2 master's, 2 doctorates awarded.

Degree requirements: For master's, thesis (for some programs), comprehensive exam; for doctorate, thesis/dissertation, comprehensive exam.

Entrance requirements: For master's, GRE General Test, TOEFL, minimum GPA of 3.0; for doctorate, GRE General Test, TOEFL, MA, minimum GPA of 3.0. *Application deadline:* For fall admission, 2/15; for spring admission, 10/15. Applications are processed on a rolling basis. *Application fee:* $30. Electronic applications accepted.

Expenses: Tuition, state resident: full-time $2,880; part-time $160 per credit. Tuition, nonresident: full-time $11,412; part-time $634 per credit. Required fees: $750; $34 per credit.

Financial support: In 2001–02, 12 students received support, including 1 fellowship (averaging $4,500 per year), 11 teaching assistantships with full tuition reimbursements available (averaging $9,720 per year); research assistantships, career-related internships or fieldwork, Federal Work-Study, institutionally sponsored loans, and traineeships also available. Financial award application deadline: 2/15; financial award applicants required to submit FAFSA.

Faculty research: Environmental politics and policy, international relations, politics of developing nations, state and local politics and administration, political behavior.

Dr. Wayne Peak, Chair, 970-491-5156, *Fax:* 970-491-2490, *E-mail:* wayne.peak@colostate.edu.

Application contact: Dr. Dimitris Stevis, Coordinator, 970-491-6082, *Fax:* 970-491-2490, *E-mail:* dimitris@lamar.colostate.edu. *Web site:* http://www.colostate.edu/Depts/PoliSci/grad2.html

■ COLUMBIA UNIVERSITY

Graduate School of Arts and Sciences, Division of Social Sciences, Department of Political Science, New York, NY 10027

AWARDS M Phil, MA, PhD, JD/MA, JD/PhD.

Faculty: 44 full-time, 10 part-time/adjunct.
Students: 190 full-time (78 women), 23 part-time (9 women). Average age 32. 555 applicants, 25% accepted. In 2001, 32 master's, 29 doctorates awarded.
Degree requirements: For master's, one foreign language; for doctorate, 2 foreign languages, thesis/dissertation.
Entrance requirements: For master's and doctorate, GRE General Test, TOEFL. *Application deadline:* For fall admission, 1/3; for spring admission, 11/30. *Application fee:* $65.
Expenses: Tuition: Full-time $27,528. Required fees: $1,638.
Financial support: Fellowships, teaching assistantships, Federal Work-Study and institutionally sponsored loans available. Support available to part-time students. Financial award application deadline: 1/5; financial award applicants required to submit FAFSA.
Faculty research: Comparative politics, American government, international relations.
Robert Shapiro, Chair, 212-854-3944, *Fax:* 212-222-0598.

■ CONVERSE COLLEGE

Department of Education, Program in Liberal Arts, Spartanburg, SC 29302-0006

AWARDS Economics (MLA); English (MLA); history (MLA); political science (MLA); sociology (MLA).

Degree requirements: For master's, capstone paper.
Entrance requirements: For master's, NTE, minimum GPA of 2.75.
Expenses: Tuition: Part-time $225 per credit hour. One-time fee: $20 part-time.

■ CORNELL UNIVERSITY

Graduate School, Graduate Fields of Arts and Sciences, Field of Government, Ithaca, NY 14853-0001

AWARDS American politics (PhD); comparative politics (PhD); international relations (PhD); political thought (PhD).

Faculty: 41 full-time.
Students: 69 full-time (31 women); includes 8 minority (2 African Americans, 4 Asian Americans or Pacific Islanders, 2 Hispanic Americans), 36 international. 283 applicants, 10% accepted. In 2001, 8 doctorates awarded.
Degree requirements: For doctorate, thesis/dissertation.
Entrance requirements: For doctorate, GRE General Test, TOEFL, sample of written work, 3 letters of recommendation. *Application deadline:* For fall admission, 1/15. *Application fee:* $65. Electronic applications accepted.
Expenses: Tuition: Full-time $25,970. Required fees: $50.
Financial support: In 2001–02, 62 students received support, including 28 fellowships with full tuition reimbursements available, 1 research assistantship with full tuition reimbursement available, 33 teaching assistantships with full tuition reimbursements available; institutionally sponsored loans, scholarships/grants, tuition waivers (full and partial), and unspecified assistantships also available. Financial award applicants required to submit FAFSA.
Faculty research: Political theory, American politics, comparative politics, international relations, methodology.
Application contact: Graduate Field Assistant, 607-255-3567, *E-mail:* cu_govt@cornell.edu. *Web site:* http://www.gradschool.cornell.edu/grad/fields_1/govt.html

■ DUKE UNIVERSITY

Graduate School, Department of Political Science, Durham, NC 27708-0586

AWARDS AM, PhD, JD/AM, JD/PhD.

Faculty: 35 full-time, 8 part-time/adjunct.
Students: 94 full-time (33 women); includes 10 minority (5 African Americans, 3 Asian Americans or Pacific Islanders, 2 Hispanic Americans), 24 international. 294 applicants, 19% accepted, 19 enrolled. In 2001, 12 master's, 3 doctorates awarded. Terminal master's awarded for partial completion of doctoral program.
Degree requirements: For doctorate, 2 foreign languages, thesis/dissertation.
Entrance requirements: For master's and doctorate, GRE General Test. *Application deadline:* For fall admission, 12/31. *Application fee:* $75.
Expenses: Tuition: Full-time $24,600.
Financial support: Fellowships, research assistantships, teaching assistantships, Federal Work-Study available. Financial award application deadline: 12/31.
Rom Coles, Director of Graduate Studies, 919-660-4327, *Fax:* 919-660-4330, *E-mail:* cghgross@duke.edu. *Web site:* http://www.poli.duke.edu/

■ EAST CAROLINA UNIVERSITY

Graduate School, College of Arts and Sciences, Department of Political Science, Greenville, NC 27858-4353

AWARDS Public administration (MPA). Part-time and evening/weekend programs available.

Faculty: 4 full-time (1 woman).
Students: 16 full-time (9 women), 30 part-time (14 women); includes 8 minority (7 African Americans, 1 Hispanic American), 3 international. Average age 31. 22 applicants, 68% accepted. In 2001, 12 degrees awarded.
Degree requirements: For master's, one foreign language, comprehensive exam.
Entrance requirements: For master's, GRE General Test, TOEFL. *Application deadline:* For fall admission, 6/1 (priority date); for spring admission, 10/15. Applications are processed on a rolling basis. *Application fee:* $45.
Expenses: Tuition, state resident: full-time $2,636. Tuition, nonresident: full-time $11,365.
Financial support: Research assistantships with partial tuition reimbursements, teaching assistantships with partial tuition reimbursements, Federal Work-Study available. Support available to part-time students. Financial award application deadline: 6/1.
Dr. Carmine Scavo, Director of Graduate Studies, 252-328-6030, *Fax:* 252-328-4134, *E-mail:* scavo@mail.ecu.edu.
Application contact: Dr. Paul D. Tschetter, Senior Associate Dean of the Graduate School, 252-328-6012, *Fax:* 252-328-6071, *E-mail:* gradschool@mail.ecu.edu.

■ EASTERN ILLINOIS UNIVERSITY

Graduate School, College of Sciences, Department of Political Science, Charleston, IL 61920-3099

AWARDS MA.

■ EASTERN KENTUCKY UNIVERSITY

The Graduate School, College of Arts and Sciences, Department of Government, Program in Political Science, Richmond, KY 40475-3102

AWARDS MA.

Students: 18.
Entrance requirements: For master's, GRE General Test, minimum GPA of 2.5. *Application fee:* $0.
Expenses: Tuition, state resident: full-time $1,468; part-time $165 per credit hour. Tuition, nonresident: full-time $4,034; part-time $450 per credit hour.
Dr. Richard Vance, Chair, Department of Government, 859-622-5931.

■ EAST STROUDSBURG UNIVERSITY OF PENNSYLVANIA

Graduate School, School of Arts and Sciences, Department of Political Science, East Stroudsburg, PA 18301-2999

AWARDS Political science (M Ed, MA). Part-time and evening/weekend programs available.

Faculty: 4 full-time (0 women).
Students: 10 full-time (3 women), 5 part-time (3 women); includes 2 minority (1 African American, 1 Hispanic American), 3 international. Average age 28. In 2001, 2 degrees awarded.
Degree requirements: For master's, variable foreign language requirement, thesis or alternative, comprehensive exam.

East Stroudsburg University of Pennsylvania (continued)

Application deadline: For fall admission, 7/31 (priority date); for spring admission, 11/30. Applications are processed on a rolling basis. *Application fee:* $25.
Expenses: Tuition, state resident: full-time $4,600; part-time $256 per credit. Tuition, nonresident: full-time $7,554; part-time $420 per credit. Required fees: $806; $45 per credit.
Financial support: In 2001–02, 8 research assistantships with full tuition reimbursements (averaging $2,500 per year) were awarded; Federal Work-Study and institutionally sponsored loans also available. Financial award application deadline: 3/1; financial award applicants required to submit FAFSA.
Merlyn J. Clarke, Graduate Coordinator, 570-422-3286, *Fax:* 570-422-3506, *E-mail:* mclarke@po-box.esu.edu. *Web site:* http://www.esu.edu/pols/

■ EMORY UNIVERSITY

Graduate School of Arts and Sciences, Department of Political Science, Atlanta, GA 30322-1100

AWARDS PhD.

Faculty: 27 full-time (6 women).
Students: 60 full-time (35 women); includes 12 minority (7 African Americans, 5 Asian Americans or Pacific Islanders), 4 international. 69 applicants, 17% accepted, 10 enrolled. In 2001, 3 doctorates awarded.
Degree requirements: For doctorate, thesis/dissertation, comprehensive exam, registration.
Entrance requirements: For doctorate, GRE General Test, TOEFL, minimum GPA of 3.0. *Application deadline:* For fall admission, 1/20. *Application fee:* $50. Electronic applications accepted.
Expenses: Tuition: Full-time $24,770. Required fees: $100. Tuition and fees vary according to program and student level.
Financial support: In 2001–02, 36 fellowships were awarded; research assistantships, teaching assistantships, career-related internships or fieldwork, scholarships/grants, and tuition waivers (partial) also available. Financial award application deadline: 1/20.
Faculty research: American national political institutions, post-Soviet politics, comparative politics, international politics, judicial politics.
Dr. Thomas Walker, Chair, 404-727-6572.
Application contact: Dr. Dan Reiter, Director of Graduate Studies, 404-727-0111, *E-mail:* dreiter@emory.edu. *Web site:* http://www.cc.emory.edu/POLS/index.html

■ FAIRLEIGH DICKINSON UNIVERSITY, METROPOLITAN CAMPUS

University College: Arts, Sciences, and Professional Studies, School of History, Political, and International Studies, Program in Political Science, Teaneck, NJ 07666-1914

AWARDS MA.

Students: 2 full-time (1 woman), 4 part-time (2 women); includes 1 minority (African American), 2 international. Average age 31. 6 applicants, 83% accepted, 2 enrolled. In 2001, 2 degrees awarded.
Application deadline: Applications are processed on a rolling basis. *Application fee:* $40.
Expenses: Tuition: Full-time $11,484; part-time $638 per credit. Required fees: $420; $97.
Dr. Faramarz Fatemi, Director, School of History, Political, and International Studies, 201-692-2272, *Fax:* 201-692-9096, *E-mail:* fatemi@fdu.edu.

■ FAYETTEVILLE STATE UNIVERSITY

Graduate School, Department of Geography, History and Political Science, Fayetteville, NC 28301-4298

AWARDS History (MA); political science (MA). Part-time and evening/weekend programs available.

Faculty: 9 full-time (2 women).
Students: 7 full-time (3 women), 6 part-time (3 women); includes 7 minority (6 African Americans, 1 Asian American or Pacific Islander). Average age 37. In 2001, 6 degrees awarded.
Degree requirements: For master's, internship.
Entrance requirements: For master's, GRE General Test. *Application deadline:* For fall admission, 8/1; for spring admission, 12/15. Applications are processed on a rolling basis. *Application fee:* $25.
Expenses: Tuition, state resident: full-time $810; part-time $426 per year. Tuition, nonresident: full-time $4,445; part-time $2,223 per year. Tuition and fees vary according to course load.
Dr. K. Boakye-Sarpong, Chairperson, 910-672-1137, *E-mail:* ksarpong@uncfsu.edu.

■ FLORIDA ATLANTIC UNIVERSITY

Dorothy F. Schmidt College of Arts and Letters, Department of Political Science, Boca Raton, FL 33431-0991

AWARDS MA, MAT. Part-time programs available.

Faculty: 6 full-time (2 women).
Students: 5 full-time (4 women), 13 part-time (4 women); includes 2 minority (1 African American, 1 Hispanic American), 1 international. Average age 37. 18 applicants, 83% accepted, 11 enrolled. In 2001, 5 degrees awarded.
Degree requirements: For master's, one foreign language, thesis or alternative.
Entrance requirements: For master's, GRE General Test, minimum GPA of 3.0 during last 60 hours. *Application deadline:* For fall admission, 6/2; for spring admission, 10/20. Applications are processed on a rolling basis. *Application fee:* $20. Electronic applications accepted.
Expenses: Tuition, state resident: full-time $3,098; part-time $172 per credit. Tuition, nonresident: full-time $10,427; part-time $579 per credit.
Financial support: In 2001–02, 6 students received support, including 3 teaching assistantships with partial tuition reimbursements available (averaging $7,195 per year); research assistantships, career-related internships or fieldwork, Federal Work-Study, and institutionally sponsored loans also available. Support available to part-time students. Financial award application deadline: 4/16.
Faculty research: Public policy, comparative policy affecting women, Congress, international system, urban policy.
Dr. Anita Pritchard, Chair, 561-297-3212, *Fax:* 561-297-2997, *E-mail:* pritchar@fau.edu.
Application contact: Dr. Jeffrey S. Morton, Director of Graduate Studies, 561-297-3216, *Fax:* 561-297-2997, *E-mail:* jmorton@fau.edu. *Web site:* http://www.fau.edu/polsci/index.htm

■ FLORIDA INTERNATIONAL UNIVERSITY

College of Arts and Sciences, Department of Political Science, Miami, FL 33199

AWARDS MS, PhD. Part-time and evening/weekend programs available.

Faculty: 18 full-time (6 women).
Students: 16 full-time (10 women), 10 part-time (1 woman); includes 11 minority (1 African American, 1 Asian American or Pacific Islander, 9 Hispanic Americans), 4 international. Average age 32. 18 applicants, 50% accepted, 4 enrolled. In 2001, 1 degree awarded.
Degree requirements: For master's, one foreign language, thesis, research project; for doctorate, one foreign language, thesis/dissertation.
Entrance requirements: For master's, GRE General Test, TOEFL, minimum GPA of 3.2; for doctorate, GRE General Test, TOEFL, minimum GPA of 3.2 (undergraduate), 3.25 (graduate). *Application deadline:* For fall admission, 5/1 (priority date); for spring admission, 10/1. Applications are processed on a rolling basis. *Application fee:* $20.
Expenses: Tuition, state resident: full-time $2,916; part-time $162 per credit hour. Tuition, nonresident: full-time $10,245;

part-time $569 per credit hour. Required fees: $168 per term.
Financial support: Application deadline: 4/1.
Dr. Nicol Rae, Chairperson, 305-348-2226, *Fax:* 305-348-3765, *E-mail:* raen@fiu.edu.

■ FLORIDA STATE UNIVERSITY

Graduate Studies, College of Social Sciences, Department of Political Science, Tallahassee, FL 32306

AWARDS MA, MS, PhD. Part-time programs available.

Faculty: 20 full-time (2 women).
Students: 25 full-time (6 women), 28 part-time (10 women); includes 3 minority (1 African American, 1 Asian American or Pacific Islander, 1 Hispanic American), 10 international. 69 applicants, 83% accepted, 14 enrolled. In 2001, 8 master's, 2 doctorates awarded. Terminal master's awarded for partial completion of doctoral program.
Degree requirements: For master's, thesis optional; for doctorate, thesis/dissertation.
Entrance requirements: For master's, GRE General Test, minimum GPA of 3.0; for doctorate, GRE General Test, minimum GPA of 3.5. *Application deadline:* For fall admission, 2/1 (priority date). *Application fee:* $20. Electronic applications accepted.
Expenses: Tuition, state resident: part-time $163 per credit hour. Tuition, nonresident: part-time $570 per credit hour. Tuition and fees vary according to program.
Financial support: In 2001–02, 21 students received support, including fellowships (averaging $15,000 per year), 12 research assistantships with full tuition reimbursements available (averaging $12,000 per year), 6 teaching assistantships with full tuition reimbursements available (averaging $12,000 per year); Federal Work-Study and institutionally sponsored loans also available. Financial award application deadline: 2/1; financial award applicants required to submit FAFSA.
Faculty research: American government, international relations, comparative government, public policy.
Dr. Charles Barrilleaux, Director of Graduate Studies, 850-644-5727, *Fax:* 850-644-1367, *E-mail:* cbarrile@garnet.acns.fsu.edu.
Application contact: Mary Schneider, Academic Coordinator, 850-644-7305, *Fax:* 850-644-1367, *E-mail:* mschneid@garnet.acns.fsu.edu. *Web site:* http://www.fsu.edu/~polisci/

■ FORDHAM UNIVERSITY

Graduate School of Arts and Sciences, Department of Political Science, New York, NY 10458

AWARDS Political science (MA), including American politics, comparative politics, international politics, political philosophy. Part-time and evening/weekend programs available.

Faculty: 20 full-time (5 women).
Students: 14 full-time (5 women), 25 part-time (8 women); includes 2 minority (1 African American, 1 Hispanic American), 4 international. 52 applicants, 54% accepted. In 2001, 6 master's awarded.
Degree requirements: For master's, comprehensive exam.
Entrance requirements: For master's, GRE General Test. *Application deadline:* For fall admission, 1/15 (priority date); for spring admission, 12/1. *Application fee:* $65. Electronic applications accepted.
Expenses: Tuition: Part-time $720 per credit. Required fees: $135 per semester.
Financial support: In 2001–02, 23 students received support, including 1 fellowship with tuition reimbursement available (averaging $15,000 per year), research assistantships with tuition reimbursements available (averaging $12,000 per year), 9 teaching assistantships with tuition reimbursements available (averaging $14,000 per year); institutionally sponsored loans, tuition waivers (full and partial), and unspecified assistantships also available. Financial award application deadline: 1/16.
Dr. Richard Fleisher, Chair, 718-817-3950, *Fax:* 718-817-3972, *E-mail:* fleisher@fordham.edu.
Application contact: Dr. Craig W. Pilant, Assistant Dean, 718-817-4420, *Fax:* 718-817-3566, *E-mail:* pilant@fordham.edu. *Web site:* http://www.fordham.edu/gsas/

■ GEORGETOWN UNIVERSITY

Graduate School of Arts and Sciences, Department of Government, Washington, DC 20057

AWARDS American government (MA, PhD); comparative government (PhD); international relations (PhD); political theory (PhD). Terminal master's awarded for partial completion of doctoral program.

Degree requirements: For master's, one foreign language, comprehensive exam; for doctorate, one foreign language, thesis/dissertation, comprehensive exam.
Entrance requirements: For master's, GRE General Test, TOEFL, minimum B average; for doctorate, GRE General Test, TOEFL, MA.
Faculty research: Western Europe, Latin America, the Middle East, political theory, international relations and law, methodology, American politics and institutions.

■ THE GEORGE WASHINGTON UNIVERSITY

Columbian College of Arts and Sciences, Department of Political Science, Washington, DC 20052

AWARDS MA, PhD. Part-time and evening/weekend programs available.

Faculty: 28 full-time (8 women), 11 part-time/adjunct (1 woman).
Students: 23 full-time (8 women), 50 part-time (20 women); includes 3 minority (all Asian Americans or Pacific Islanders), 10 international. Average age 33. 175 applicants, 50% accepted. In 2001, 5 master's, 4 doctorates awarded. Terminal master's awarded for partial completion of doctoral program.
Degree requirements: For master's, one foreign language, thesis or alternative, comprehensive exam; for doctorate, 2 foreign languages, thesis/dissertation, general exam.
Entrance requirements: For master's and doctorate, GRE General Test, minimum GPA of 3.0. *Application fee:* $55.
Expenses: Tuition: Part-time $810 per credit. Required fees: $1 per credit.
Financial support: In 2001–02, 23 students received support, including 20 fellowships with tuition reimbursements available (averaging $7,000 per year), 19 teaching assistantships with tuition reimbursements available (averaging $3,900 per year); Federal Work-Study also available. Financial award application deadline: 2/1.
Dr. Jeff Henig, Chair, 202-994-6290. *Web site:* http://www.gwu.edu/~gradinfo/

■ THE GEORGE WASHINGTON UNIVERSITY

Columbian College of Arts and Sciences, Graduate School of Political Management, Washington, DC 20052

AWARDS MA.

Students: 79 full-time (42 women), 86 part-time (44 women); includes 15 minority (7 African Americans, 2 Asian Americans or Pacific Islanders, 6 Hispanic Americans), 13 international. Average age 26. 125 applicants, 89% accepted. In 2001, 54 degrees awarded.
Degree requirements: For master's, thesis optional.
Entrance requirements: For master's, GRE General Test, minimum GPA of 3.0. *Application fee:* $55.
Expenses: Tuition: Part-time $810 per credit. Required fees: $1 per credit.
Financial support: Research assistantships, career-related internships or fieldwork and scholarships/grants available. Financial award application deadline: 2/1.
Dr. Christopher Arterton, Dean, 202-994-5843, *Fax:* 202-994-5806.
Application contact: Admissions Office, 202-994-6000. *Web site:* http://www.gwu.edu/~gradinfo/

■ THE GEORGE WASHINGTON UNIVERSITY

Columbian College of Arts and Sciences, Program in Legislative Affairs, Washington, DC 20052

AWARDS MA. Part-time and evening/weekend programs available.

The George Washington University (continued)

Students: 6 full-time (3 women), 22 part-time (11 women); includes 3 minority (1 African American, 1 Asian American or Pacific Islander, 1 Hispanic American). Average age 27. 26 applicants, 96% accepted. In 2001, 12 degrees awarded.
Degree requirements: For master's, comprehensive exam.
Entrance requirements: For master's, GRE General Test, minimum GPA of 3.0. *Application fee:* $55.
Expenses: Tuition: Part-time $810 per credit. Required fees: $1 per credit.
Financial support: Application deadline: 2/1.
Dennis W. Johnson, Director, 202-994-5765, *Fax:* 202-994-7743. *Web site:* http://www.gwu.edu/~gradinfo/

■ THE GEORGE WASHINGTON UNIVERSITY

Elliott School of International Affairs, Program in Security Policy Studies, Washington, DC 20052

AWARDS MA, JD/MA. Part-time and evening/weekend programs available.

Students: 44 full-time (17 women), 17 part-time (11 women); includes 9 minority (2 African Americans, 7 Hispanic Americans), 2 international. Average age 26. 108 applicants, 79% accepted. In 2001, 18 degrees awarded.
Degree requirements: For master's, one foreign language.
Entrance requirements: For master's, GRE General Test, TOEFL, minimum B average. *Application deadline:* For fall admission, 2/1. *Application fee:* $55. Electronic applications accepted.
Expenses: Tuition: Part-time $810 per credit. Required fees: $1 per credit.
Financial support: Fellowships with tuition reimbursements, research assistantships with tuition reimbursements, career-related internships or fieldwork, Federal Work-Study, institutionally sponsored loans, and tuition waivers (full) available. Financial award application deadline: 1/15; financial award applicants required to submit FAFSA.
Faculty research: U.S. arms transfer policies, military balance in the Third World, U.S. foreign policy, technology and security policy.
Dr. Gordon Adams, Director, 202-994-7003.
Application contact: Jeff V. Miles, Director of Graduate Admissions, 202-994-7050, *Fax:* 202-994-9537, *E-mail:* esiagrad@gwu.edu. *Web site:* http://www.gwu.edu/~elliott/

■ GEORGIA SOUTHERN UNIVERSITY

Jack N. Averitt College of Graduate Studies, College of Liberal Arts and Social Sciences, Department of Political Science, Program in Political Science, Statesboro, GA 30460

AWARDS MA. Part-time and evening/weekend programs available.

Students: 1 (woman) full-time. Average age 22. 1 applicant, 100% accepted, 1 enrolled. In 2001, 3 degrees awarded.
Degree requirements: For master's, one foreign language, thesis, oral defense of thesis.
Entrance requirements: For master's, GRE General Test, minimum GPA of 3.0, undergraduate major in political science. *Application deadline:* For fall admission, 7/1 (priority date); for spring admission, 11/15 (priority date). Applications are processed on a rolling basis. *Application fee:* $0. Electronic applications accepted.
Expenses: Tuition, state resident: full-time $1,746; part-time $97 per credit hour. Tuition, nonresident: full-time $6,966; part-time $387 per credit hour. Required fees: $294 per semester.
Financial support: Career-related internships or fieldwork and Federal Work-Study available. Support available to part-time students. Financial award application deadline: 4/15; financial award applicants required to submit FAFSA.
Faculty research: Gender and politics, technology in the classroom, media and politics, international relations and politics, politics and public opinion.
Dr. Barry J. Balleck, Coordinator, 912-871-1398, *Fax:* 912-681-5348, *E-mail:* bballeck@gasou.edu.
Application contact: Dr. John R. Diebolt, Associate Graduate Dean, 912-681-5384, *Fax:* 912-681-0740, *E-mail:* gradschool@gasou.edu.

■ GEORGIA STATE UNIVERSITY

College of Arts and Sciences, Department of Political Science, Atlanta, GA 30303-3083

AWARDS MA, PhD. Part-time and evening/weekend programs available.

Degree requirements: For master's, thesis or alternative, exam; for doctorate, one foreign language, thesis/dissertation, exam.
Entrance requirements: For master's and doctorate, GRE General Test, TOEFL. Electronic applications accepted.
Faculty research: International politics, American politics, comparative politics, public administration, international political economy. *Web site:* http://www.gsu.edu/~wwwpol/

Find an in-depth description at www.petersons.com/gradchannel.

■ GOVERNORS STATE UNIVERSITY

College of Arts and Sciences, Division of Liberal Arts, Program in Political and Justice Studies, University Park, IL 60466-0975

AWARDS MA. Part-time and evening/weekend programs available.

Faculty: 3 full-time (2 women).
Students: 68 (34 women). Average age 32. In 2001, 19 degrees awarded.
Degree requirements: For master's, thesis or alternative.
Entrance requirements: For master's, bachelor's degree in related field. *Application deadline:* For fall admission, 7/15 (priority date); for spring admission, 11/10. Applications are processed on a rolling basis. *Application fee:* $0.
Expenses: Tuition, state resident: part-time $111 per hour. Tuition, nonresident: part-time $333 per hour.
Financial support: Research assistantships, Federal Work-Study, institutionally sponsored loans, and scholarships/grants available. Support available to part-time students. Financial award application deadline: 5/1.
Dr. Joyce Kennedy, Chairperson, Division of Liberal Arts, 708-534-4010.

■ GRADUATE SCHOOL AND UNIVERSITY CENTER OF THE CITY UNIVERSITY OF NEW YORK

Graduate Studies, Program in Political Science, New York, NY 10016-4039

AWARDS MA, PhD.

Faculty: 56 full-time (10 women).
Students: 114 full-time (52 women), 39 part-time (15 women); includes 30 minority (13 African Americans, 5 Asian Americans or Pacific Islanders, 12 Hispanic Americans), 26 international. Average age 37. 68 applicants, 60% accepted, 14 enrolled. In 2001, 7 master's, 4 doctorates awarded. Terminal master's awarded for partial completion of doctoral program.
Degree requirements: For master's and doctorate, one foreign language, thesis/dissertation.
Entrance requirements: For master's and doctorate, GRE General Test. *Application deadline:* For fall admission, 4/15. *Application fee:* $40.
Expenses: Tuition, state resident: part-time $245 per credit. Tuition, nonresident: part-time $425 per credit. Required fees: $72 per semester.
Financial support: In 2001–02, 84 students received support, including 55 fellowships, 1 research assistantship, 3 teaching assistantships; career-related internships or fieldwork, Federal Work-Study, institutionally sponsored loans, and tuition waivers (full and partial) also available. Financial award application deadline:

2/1; financial award applicants required to submit FAFSA.
Dr. W. Ofuatey-Kodjoe, Executive Officer, 212-817-8670, *Fax:* 212-817-1532, *E-mail:* wofuatey-kodjoe@gc.cuny.edu.

■ HARVARD UNIVERSITY

Graduate School of Arts and Sciences, Committee on Political Economy and Government, Cambridge, MA 02138

AWARDS PhD.

Entrance requirements: For doctorate, GRE General Test or GMAT, TOEFL.
Expenses: Tuition: Full-time $23,370. Required fees: $816. Full-time tuition and fees vary according to program and student level.

■ HARVARD UNIVERSITY

Graduate School of Arts and Sciences, Department of Government, Cambridge, MA 02138

AWARDS Political science (AM, PhD), including American politics, comparative politics, international relations, political thought, quantitative methods.

Degree requirements: For doctorate, one foreign language, thesis/dissertation, general exams.
Entrance requirements: For master's and doctorate, GRE General Test, TOEFL.
Expenses: Tuition: Full-time $23,370. Required fees: $816. Full-time tuition and fees vary according to program and student level.

■ HARVARD UNIVERSITY

John F. Kennedy School of Government, Cambridge, MA 02138

AWARDS MPA, MPAID, MPP, MPPUP, PhD, JD/MPP, MBA/MPP, MD/MPP.

Faculty: 70.
Students: 558 full-time (236 women); includes 105 minority (34 African Americans, 36 Asian Americans or Pacific Islanders, 30 Hispanic Americans, 5 Native Americans), 229 international. Average age 31. 1,886 applicants, 44% accepted, 558 enrolled.
Degree requirements: For doctorate, thesis/dissertation.
Entrance requirements: For master's and doctorate, GMAT or GRE General Test, TOEFL. *Application fee:* $80. Electronic applications accepted.
Expenses: Tuition: Full-time $23,370. Required fees: $816. Full-time tuition and fees vary according to program and student level.
Financial support: Fellowships, research assistantships, teaching assistantships, career-related internships or fieldwork, Federal Work-Study, institutionally sponsored loans, and scholarships/grants available. Support available to part-time students. Financial award applicants required to submit CSS PROFILE or FAFSA.
Dr. Joseph Nye, Dean.
Application contact: Office of Admissions, 617-495-1155, *E-mail:* ksg_admissions@harvard.edu. *Web site:* http://www.ksg.harvard.edu/

Find an in-depth description at www.petersons.com/gradchannel.

■ HAWAI'I PACIFIC UNIVERSITY

Division of Arts and Sciences, Honolulu, HI 96813-2785

AWARDS Diplomacy and military studies (MA); political science (MA).

Faculty: 2 full-time (0 women), 3 part-time/adjunct (1 woman).
Students: 66. Average age 30. 34 applicants, 91% accepted, 18 enrolled. In 2001, 1 degree awarded.
Degree requirements: For master's, thesis.
Application deadline: Applications are processed on a rolling basis. *Application fee:* $50. Electronic applications accepted.
Expenses: Tuition: Full-time $7,380; part-time $410 per credit.
Financial support: Career-related internships or fieldwork, Federal Work-Study, and unspecified assistantships available. Support available to part-time students. Financial award application deadline: 3/1; financial award applicants required to submit FAFSA.
Dr. Leslie Correa, Associate Vice President and Dean, 808-549-9340, *Fax:* 808-544-9306, *E-mail:* lcorrea@hpu.edu.
Application contact: Jose Rosal, Admissions Coordinator, 808-544-1135, *Fax:* 800-544-0280, *E-mail:* gradservctr@hpu.edu. *Web site:* http://www.hpu.edu/

Find an in-depth description at www.petersons.com/gradchannel.

■ HOWARD UNIVERSITY

Graduate School of Arts and Sciences, Department of Political Science, Program in Political Science, Washington, DC 20059-0002

AWARDS MA, PhD.

Degree requirements: For master's, comprehensive exam.
Entrance requirements: For master's, GRE General Test, minimum GPA of 3.0; for doctorate, GRE General Test, minimum GPA of 2.8.

■ IDAHO STATE UNIVERSITY

Office of Graduate Studies, College of Arts and Sciences, Department of Political Science, Pocatello, ID 83209

AWARDS Political science (MA, DA); public administration (MPA). Part-time programs available.

Faculty: 9 full-time (1 woman).
Students: 22 full-time (11 women), 24 part-time (10 women); includes 2 minority (1 African American, 1 Hispanic American), 3 international. Average age 39. In 2001, 3 doctorates awarded.
Degree requirements: For master's, thesis optional; for doctorate, thesis/dissertation.
Entrance requirements: For master's and doctorate, GRE General Test. *Application deadline:* For fall admission, 7/1; for spring admission, 12/1. Applications are processed on a rolling basis. *Application fee:* $35.
Expenses: Tuition, area resident: Full-time $3,432. Tuition, state resident: part-time $172 per credit. Tuition, nonresident: full-time $10,196; part-time $262 per credit. International tuition: $9,672 full-time. Part-time tuition and fees vary according to course load, program and reciprocity agreements.
Financial support: In 2001–02, 8 students received support, including 6 fellowships with full and partial tuition reimbursements available (averaging $11,352 per year), 4 teaching assistantships with full and partial tuition reimbursements available (averaging $7,722 per year); career-related internships or fieldwork and Federal Work-Study also available. Support available to part-time students. Financial award application deadline: 1/31.
Faculty research: International affairs, environmental policy, decision making, Constitution, executive/legislative relations.
Dr. Richard Henry Foster, Chairman, 208-282-2211. *Web site:* http://www.isu.edu/departments/polsci/

Find an in-depth description at www.petersons.com/gradchannel.

■ ILLINOIS STATE UNIVERSITY

Graduate School, College of Arts and Sciences, Department of Politics and Government, Normal, IL 61790-2200

AWARDS MA, MS.

Faculty: 18 full-time (4 women).
Students: 30 full-time (12 women), 34 part-time (15 women); includes 13 minority (7 African Americans, 4 Asian Americans or Pacific Islanders, 2 Hispanic Americans), 5 international. 32 applicants, 78% accepted. In 2001, 14 degrees awarded.
Degree requirements: For master's, thesis or alternative.
Entrance requirements: For master's, GRE General Test, minimum GPA of 3.0 in last 60 hours, 15 hours of political science course work. *Application deadline:* Applications are processed on a rolling basis. *Application fee:* $30.
Expenses: Tuition, state resident: full-time $2,691; part-time $112 per credit hour. Tuition, nonresident: full-time $5,880; part-time $245 per credit hour. Required fees: $1,146; $48 per credit hour.
Financial support: In 2001–02, 29 research assistantships (averaging $7,044

Illinois State University (continued)
per year), 1 teaching assistantship (averaging $6,255 per year) were awarded. Tuition waivers (full) and unspecified assistantships also available. Financial award application deadline: 4/1. *Total annual research expenditures:* $52,792.
Dr. Jamal Nassar, Chairperson, 309-438-8638. *Web site:* http://www.politicsandgovernment.ilstu.edu/

■ INDIANA STATE UNIVERSITY

School of Graduate Studies, College of Arts and Sciences, Department of Political Science, Terre Haute, IN 47809-1401

AWARDS Political science (MA, MS); public administration (MPA), including comparative and international administration, human resources and organizational development, national administration, state/local administration.

Electronic applications accepted.

■ INDIANA UNIVERSITY BLOOMINGTON

Graduate School, College of Arts and Sciences, Department of Political Science, Bloomington, IN 47405

AWARDS MA, PhD. PhD offered through the University Graduate School.

Faculty: 27 full-time (6 women).
Students: 41 full-time (13 women), 39 part-time (9 women); includes 6 minority (5 African Americans, 1 Hispanic American), 19 international. Average age 28. In 2001, 6 master's, 8 doctorates awarded. Terminal master's awarded for partial completion of doctoral program.
Degree requirements: For master's, one foreign language, thesis; for doctorate, 2 foreign languages, thesis/dissertation.
Entrance requirements: For master's and doctorate, GRE, TOEFL, sample of written work. *Application deadline:* For fall admission, 1/15 (priority date); for spring admission, 9/1 (priority date). Applications are processed on a rolling basis. *Application fee:* $45 ($55 for international students). Electronic applications accepted.
Expenses: Tuition, state resident: full-time $4,720; part-time $197 per credit. Tuition, nonresident: full-time $13,748; part-time $573 per credit. Required fees: $642.
Financial support: In 2001–02, 43 students received support, including 4 fellowships (averaging $15,000 per year), 30 teaching assistantships (averaging $11,000 per year); research assistantships, Federal Work-Study, institutionally sponsored loans, tuition waivers, and unspecified assistantships also available. Financial award application deadline: 1/15.
Faculty research: American politics, comparative politics, theory and methodology, international relations, political philosophy.
Robert Huckfeldt, Chair, 812-855-6308, *Fax:* 812-855-2027, *E-mail:* huckfeld@indiana.edu.
Application contact: Sharon LaRoche, Graduate Secretary, 812-855-1208, *Fax:* 812-855-2027, *E-mail:* laroches@indiana.edu. *Web site:* http://www.indiana.edu/~iupolsci/

■ INDIANA UNIVERSITY OF PENNSYLVANIA

Graduate School and Research, College of Humanities and Social Sciences, Department of Political Science, Indiana, PA 15705-1087

AWARDS Public affairs (MA). Part-time programs available.

Faculty: 5 full-time (0 women).
Students: 13 full-time (5 women), 2 part-time; includes 3 minority (1 African American, 1 Asian American or Pacific Islander, 1 Hispanic American), 2 international. Average age 27. 11 applicants, 55% accepted. In 2001, 8 degrees awarded.
Degree requirements: For master's, thesis optional.
Entrance requirements: For master's, TOEFL, GRE, letters of recommendation (2). *Application deadline:* For fall admission, 7/1 (priority date); for spring admission, 11/1. Applications are processed on a rolling basis. *Application fee:* $30.
Expenses: Tuition, state resident: full-time $4,600; part-time $256 per credit hour. Tuition, nonresident: full-time $7,554; part-time $420 per credit hour. Required fees: $800. Part-time tuition and fees vary according to course load.
Financial support: In 2001–02, 6 research assistantships with full and partial tuition reimbursements (averaging $4,840 per year) were awarded; Federal Work-Study also available. Support available to part-time students. Financial award application deadline: 3/15; financial award applicants required to submit FAFSA.
Dr. David Chambers, Chairperson, 724-357-2776, *E-mail:* chambers@iup.edu.
Application contact: Information Contact, 724-357-2290.

■ IOWA STATE UNIVERSITY OF SCIENCE AND TECHNOLOGY

Graduate College, College of Liberal Arts and Sciences, Department of Political Science, Ames, IA 50011

AWARDS Political science (MA); public administration (MPA).

Faculty: 17 full-time, 2 part-time/adjunct.
Students: 20 full-time (12 women), 21 part-time (9 women); includes 3 minority (2 African Americans, 1 Asian American or Pacific Islander), 11 international. 35 applicants, 54% accepted, 14 enrolled. In 2001, 7 degrees awarded.
Degree requirements: For master's, thesis (for some programs). *Median time to degree:* Master's–3.2 years full-time.
Entrance requirements: For master's, GRE General Test or GMAT, TOEFL or IELTS. *Application deadline:* For fall admission, 3/1 (priority date); for spring admission, 10/1. Applications are processed on a rolling basis. *Application fee:* $20 ($50 for international students). Electronic applications accepted.
Expenses: Tuition, state resident: full-time $1,851. Tuition, nonresident: full-time $5,449. Tuition and fees vary according to program.
Financial support: In 2001–02, 11 research assistantships with partial tuition reimbursements (averaging $11,099 per year), 7 teaching assistantships with partial tuition reimbursements (averaging $10,846 per year) were awarded. Fellowships, scholarships/grants, health care benefits, and unspecified assistantships also available.
Dr. James M. McCormick, Chair, 515-294-7256, *Fax:* 515-294-1003, *E-mail:* polsc@iastate.edu.
Application contact: Barb Marvick, Head, 515-294-3764, *E-mail:* polsci@iastate.edu. *Web site:* http://www.iastate.edu/~polsci/

■ JACKSON STATE UNIVERSITY

Graduate School, School of Liberal Arts, Department of Political Science, Jackson, MS 39217

AWARDS MA. Part-time and evening/weekend programs available.

Degree requirements: For master's, thesis or alternative, comprehensive exam.
Entrance requirements: For master's, GRE General Test, TOEFL.

■ JACKSONVILLE STATE UNIVERSITY

College of Graduate Studies and Continuing Education, College of Arts and Sciences, Department of Political Science, Jacksonville, AL 36265-1602

AWARDS MA.

Degree requirements: For master's, thesis optional.
Entrance requirements: For master's, GRE General Test or MAT.

■ JOHNS HOPKINS UNIVERSITY

Zanvyl Krieger School of Arts and Sciences, Department of Political Science, Baltimore, MD 21218-2699

AWARDS PhD.

Faculty: 18 full-time (3 women).
Students: 63 full-time (28 women); includes 4 minority (2 Asian Americans or Pacific Islanders, 2 Hispanic Americans), 24 international. Average age 24. 187 applicants, 16% accepted, 16 enrolled. In 2001, 8 doctorates awarded.

Degree requirements: For doctorate, one foreign language, thesis/dissertation, registration.
Entrance requirements: For doctorate, GRE General Test. *Application deadline:* For fall admission, 1/15. *Application fee:* $55. Electronic applications accepted.
Expenses: Tuition: Full-time $27,390.
Financial support: In 2001–02, 54 students received support, including 1 research assistantship, 21 teaching assistantships; fellowships, Federal Work-Study, institutionally sponsored loans, and tuition waivers (full and partial) also available. Financial award application deadline: 4/15; financial award applicants required to submit FAFSA.
Faculty research: American politics, comparative politics, international relations, political theory, urban politics. *Total annual research expenditures:* $1,861.
Dr. William Connolly, Chair, 410-516-7535, *Fax:* 410-516-5515.
Application contact: Barbara Hall, Graduate Admissions Committee, 410-516-7540, *Fax:* 410-516-5515, *E-mail:* political.science@jhu.edu. *Web site:* http://www.jhu.edu/~polysci/

■ KANSAS STATE UNIVERSITY

Graduate School, College of Arts and Sciences, Department of Political Science, Program in Political Science, Manhattan, KS 66506

AWARDS International relations (MA). Part-time programs available.

Students: 15 full-time (6 women), 11 part-time (6 women); includes 4 minority (2 African Americans, 1 Asian American or Pacific Islander, 1 Native American), 11 international. Average age 33. In 2001, 2 degrees awarded.
Degree requirements: For master's, thesis or alternative.
Entrance requirements: For master's, GRE (recommended), TOEFL, minimum GPA of 3.0. *Application deadline:* For fall admission, 2/1 (priority date); for spring admission, 10/1. Applications are processed on a rolling basis. *Application fee:* $0 ($25 for international students).
Expenses: Tuition, state resident: part-time $113 per credit hour. Tuition, nonresident: part-time $358 per credit hour.
Financial support: Fellowships, research assistantships, teaching assistantships, institutionally sponsored loans and scholarships/grants available. Support available to part-time students. Financial award application deadline: 3/1; financial award applicants required to submit FAFSA. *Total annual research expenditures:* $16,958.
Application contact: Scott Tollefson, Graduate Program Director, 785-532-0449, *Fax:* 785-532-2339, *E-mail:* tollef@ksu.edu. *Web site:* http://www.ksu.edu/polsci/

■ KENT STATE UNIVERSITY

College of Arts and Sciences, Department of Political Science, Kent, OH 44242-0001

AWARDS American politics (MA, PhD); comparative politics (MA); international politics (PhD); international relations (MA); political theory (MA, PhD); public administration (MPA).

Degree requirements: For master's, thesis optional; for doctorate, 2 foreign languages, thesis/dissertation.
Entrance requirements: For master's, GRE General Test, TOEFL, minimum GPA of 2.75; for doctorate, GRE General Test, TOEFL, minimum GPA of 3.0. Electronic applications accepted.

■ LAMAR UNIVERSITY

College of Graduate Studies, College of Arts and Sciences, Department of Political Science, Beaumont, TX 77710

AWARDS Public administration (MPA). Part-time programs available.

Faculty: 8 full-time (1 woman).
Students: 2 full-time (1 woman), 9 part-time (3 women); includes 4 minority (3 African Americans, 1 Hispanic American), 1 international. Average age 35. 16 applicants, 100% accepted. In 2001, 3 degrees awarded.
Degree requirements: For master's, practicum.
Entrance requirements: For master's, GRE General Test, TOEFL. *Application deadline:* For fall admission, 8/1; for spring admission, 12/1. Applications are processed on a rolling basis. *Application fee:* $25 ($50 for international students).
Expenses: Tuition, state resident: full-time $1,114. Tuition, nonresident: full-time $3,670.
Financial support: In 2001–02, 1 teaching assistantship (averaging $2,000 per year) was awarded; fellowships, research assistantships, career-related internships or fieldwork, Federal Work-Study, and institutionally sponsored loans also available. Financial award application deadline: 4/1.
Faculty research: Political activities of administrators, impact of race on voting behavior, term limitations, Latin American policy, judicial process.
Dr. Glenn Utter, Chair, 409-880-8526, *Fax:* 409-880-8710.
Application contact: Dr. Bert Dubose, Director, 409-880-8529, *Fax:* 409-880-8710, *E-mail:* dubose@hal.lamar.edu.

■ LEHIGH UNIVERSITY

College of Arts and Sciences, Department of Political Science, Bethlehem, PA 18015-3094

AWARDS MA. Part-time programs available.

Faculty: 7 full-time (2 women).
Students: 13 full-time (9 women), 2 part-time (1 woman). Average age 24. 7 applicants, 86% accepted, 6 enrolled. In 2001, 6 degrees awarded.
Degree requirements: For master's, thesis optional. *Median time to degree:* Master's–1.5 years full-time, 6 years part-time.
Entrance requirements: For master's, GRE General Test, TOEFL. *Application deadline:* For fall admission, 7/15; for spring admission, 12/1. Applications are processed on a rolling basis. *Application fee:* $50.
Expenses: Tuition: Part-time $468 per credit hour. Required fees: $200; $100 per semester. Tuition and fees vary according to program.
Financial support: In 2001–02, 11 students received support, including 2 teaching assistantships with partial tuition reimbursements available (averaging $11,650 per year); fellowships, research assistantships, career-related internships or fieldwork and tuition waivers (partial) also available. Financial award application deadline: 1/15.
Faculty research: American politics and institutions.
Dr. Frank L. Davis, Chairman, 610-758-5987, *Fax:* 610-758-3348, *E-mail:* fld1@lehigh.edu.
Application contact: Dr. Hannah Stewart-Gambino, Director, Graduate Studies, 610-758-3342, *Fax:* 610-758-3348, *E-mail:* hws1@lehigh.edu. *Web site:* http://www.lehigh.edu/~ingov/graduat.html

Find an in-depth description at www.petersons.com/gradchannel.

■ LONG ISLAND UNIVERSITY, BROOKLYN CAMPUS

Richard L. Conolly College of Liberal Arts and Sciences, Department of Political Science, Brooklyn, NY 11201-8423

AWARDS MA. Part-time and evening/weekend programs available.

Degree requirements: For master's, thesis or alternative.
Electronic applications accepted.

■ LONG ISLAND UNIVERSITY, C.W. POST CAMPUS

College of Liberal Arts and Sciences, Department of Political Science/International Studies, Brookville, NY 11548-1300

AWARDS Political science/international studies (MA); social studies secondary education (MS). Part-time and evening/weekend programs available.

Faculty: 7 full-time (1 woman), 6 part-time/adjunct (2 women).
Students: 4 full-time (3 women), 9 part-time (6 women). Average age 23. 33

Long Island University, C.W. Post Campus (continued)

applicants, 91% accepted, 19 enrolled. In 2001, 12 degrees awarded.
Degree requirements: For master's, thesis or alternative, comprehensive exam.
Entrance requirements: For master's, GRE. *Application deadline:* For fall admission, 9/1 (priority date); for winter admission, 12/15 (priority date); for spring admission, 1/20 (priority date). Applications are processed on a rolling basis. *Application fee:* $30. Electronic applications accepted.
Expenses: Tuition: Full-time $10,296; part-time $572 per credit. Required fees: $380; $190 per semester.
Financial support: In 2001–02, 2 research assistantships were awarded; career-related internships or fieldwork and Federal Work-Study also available. Support available to part-time students. Financial award application deadline: 5/15; financial award applicants required to submit CSS PROFILE or FAFSA.
Faculty research: International relations, middle eastern politics, political philosophy.
Dr. Roger Goldstein, Chairman, 516-299-2407, *Fax:* 516-299-4140.
Application contact: Dr. Michael Soupios, Graduate Adviser, 516-299-3026. *Web site:* http://www.liu.edu/postlas/

■ LOUISIANA STATE UNIVERSITY AND AGRICULTURAL AND MECHANICAL COLLEGE

Graduate School, College of Arts and Sciences, Department of Political Science, Baton Rouge, LA 70803

AWARDS MA, PhD.

Faculty: 20 full-time (4 women), 1 part-time/adjunct (0 women).
Students: 21 full-time (6 women), 17 part-time (5 women); includes 1 minority (African American), 1 international. Average age 30. 24 applicants, 58% accepted, 8 enrolled. In 2001, 5 master's, 5 doctorates awarded. Terminal master's awarded for partial completion of doctoral program.
Degree requirements: For master's, thesis or alternative; for doctorate, one foreign language, thesis/dissertation.
Entrance requirements: For master's and doctorate, GRE General Test, minimum GPA of 3.0. *Application deadline:* For fall admission, 2/15 (priority date); for spring admission, 10/15. *Application fee:* $25.
Expenses: Tuition, state resident: full-time $2,551. Tuition, nonresident: full-time $5,551. Required fees: $854. Part-time tuition and fees vary according to course load.
Financial support: In 2001–02, 2 fellowships (averaging $14,166 per year), 1 research assistantship with partial tuition reimbursement (averaging $12,000 per year), 13 teaching assistantships with partial tuition reimbursements (averaging $11,904 per year) were awarded. Federal Work-Study, institutionally sponsored loans, tuition waivers (full), and unspecified assistantships also available. Financial award application deadline: 3/1; financial award applicants required to submit FAFSA.
Faculty research: American government and policy, political theory, international relations and comparative politics. *Total annual research expenditures:* $106,621.
Dr. Wayne Parent, Chair, 225-578-2535, *Fax:* 225-578-2540, *E-mail:* popare@lsu.edu.
Application contact: Dr. James Garand, Director of Graduate Studies, 225-578-2548, *Fax:* 225-578-2540, *E-mail:* pogara@lsu.edu. *Web site:* http://www.artsci.lsu.edu/poli/

■ LOYOLA UNIVERSITY CHICAGO

Graduate School, Department of Political Science, Chicago, IL 60611-2196

AWARDS American politics and policy (MA, PhD); international studies (MA, PhD); political theory and philosophy (MA, PhD). Part-time and evening/weekend programs available.

Faculty: 18 full-time (2 women).
Students: 42 full-time (18 women), 8 part-time (4 women); includes 6 minority (2 African Americans, 4 Hispanic Americans), 2 international. Average age 25. 66 applicants, 79% accepted. In 2001, 8 master's, 3 doctorates awarded.
Degree requirements: For master's, thesis or alternative; for doctorate, variable foreign language requirement, thesis/dissertation, comprehensive exam.
Entrance requirements: For master's and doctorate, GRE General Test. *Application deadline:* For fall admission, 8/1 (priority date); for spring admission, 12/1 (priority date). Applications are processed on a rolling basis. *Application fee:* $40. Electronic applications accepted.
Expenses: Tuition: Part-time $529 per credit hour.
Financial support: In 2001–02, 22 students received support, including 14 fellowships with full tuition reimbursements available (averaging $9,000 per year), 14 research assistantships with full tuition reimbursements available (averaging $9,000 per year); Federal Work-Study, institutionally sponsored loans, scholarships/grants, tuition waivers (partial), and unspecified assistantships also available. Financial award application deadline: 2/1; financial award applicants required to submit FAFSA.
Faculty research: American parties and elections, state and local politics, American political institutions, international political economy, modern and contemporary political thought.
Dr. John P. Pelissero, Chair, 773-508-3066, *Fax:* 773-508-3131, *E-mail:* jpeliss@luc.edu.
Application contact: Dr. Claudio Katz, Director of Graduate Programs, 773-508-3068, *Fax:* 773-508-3131, *E-mail:* ckatz@luc.edu. *Web site:* http://www.luc.edu/grad/polisci/

■ MARQUETTE UNIVERSITY

Graduate School, College of Arts and Sciences, Department of Political Science, Milwaukee, WI 53201-1881

AWARDS International affairs (MA), including comparative politics, international political economy, international politics; political science (MA), including American politics, comparative politics, international politics, political philosophy. Part-time programs available.

Faculty: 13 full-time (1 woman), 1 part-time/adjunct (0 women).
Students: 5 full-time (2 women), 3 part-time (1 woman); includes 1 minority (African American). Average age 27. 9 applicants, 89% accepted. In 2001, 2 degrees awarded.
Degree requirements: For master's, thesis optional.
Entrance requirements: For master's, GRE General Test, TOEFL. *Application fee:* $40.
Expenses: Tuition: Full-time $10,170; part-time $445 per credit hour. Tuition and fees vary according to course load.
Financial support: In 2001–02, 5 research assistantships were awarded; Federal Work-Study, institutionally sponsored loans, scholarships/grants, and tuition waivers (full and partial) also available. Support available to part-time students. Financial award application deadline: 2/15.
Faculty research: Public opinion and electoral behavior, public policy analysis, Congress and the Presidency, judicial behavior, political system transitions. *Total annual research expenditures:* $228,488.
Dr. H. Richard Friman, Chairman, 414-288-6842, *Fax:* 414-288-3360.
Application contact: Dr. Barrett McCormick, Director of Graduate Studies, 414-288-6842, *Fax:* 414-288-3360.

■ MARSHALL UNIVERSITY

Graduate College, College of Liberal Arts, Department of Political Science, Huntington, WV 25755

AWARDS MA.

Faculty: 6 full-time (2 women).
Students: 9 full-time (4 women), 6 part-time (2 women). In 2001, 7 degrees awarded.
Degree requirements: For master's, thesis optional.
Entrance requirements: For master's, GRE General Test.
Expenses: Tuition, state resident: part-time $147 per credit. Tuition, nonresident: part-time $468 per credit. Tuition and fees

vary according to campus/location and reciprocity agreements.
Dr. Simon D. Perry, Chairperson, 304-696-2767, *Fax:* 304-696-3245.
Application contact: Ken O'Neal, Assistant Vice President, Adult Student Services, 304-746-2500 Ext. 1907, *Fax:* 304-746-1902, *E-mail:* oneal@marshall.edu.

■ MASSACHUSETTS INSTITUTE OF TECHNOLOGY

School of Humanities, Arts and Social Sciences, Department of Political Science, Cambridge, MA 02139-4307

AWARDS SM, PhD.

Faculty: 23 full-time (5 women), 3 part-time/adjunct (all women).
Students: 82 full-time (36 women); includes 7 minority (5 Asian Americans or Pacific Islanders, 1 Hispanic American, 1 Native American), 27 international. 244 applicants, 16% accepted, 10 enrolled. In 2001, 10 master's, 16 doctorates awarded. Terminal master's awarded for partial completion of doctoral program.
Degree requirements: For master's, thesis; for doctorate, one foreign language, thesis/dissertation.
Entrance requirements: For master's and doctorate, GRE General Test, TOEFL. *Application deadline:* For fall admission, 1/8. *Application fee:* $60.
Expenses: Tuition: Full-time $26,960. Full-time tuition and fees vary according to program.
Financial support: In 2001–02, 80 students received support, including 9 fellowships with full tuition reimbursements available (averaging $16,200 per year), 31 research assistantships with full tuition reimbursements available (averaging $16,200 per year), 18 teaching assistantships with full tuition reimbursements available (averaging $16,200 per year); Federal Work-Study, institutionally sponsored loans, and partial tuition fellowships also available. Financial award application deadline: 1/16; financial award applicants required to submit FAFSA.
Faculty research: American history, comparative history, models and methods, political philosophy, security studies.
Joshua Cohen, Head, 617-253-5237, *Fax:* 617-258-8546, *E-mail:* jcohen@mit.edu.
Application contact: Monica Wolf, Graduate Administrator, 617-253-8336, *Fax:* 617-258-6164, *E-mail:* mwolf@mit.edu. *Web site:* http://web.mit.edu/polisci/www/

■ MIAMI UNIVERSITY

Graduate School, College of Arts and Sciences, Department of Political Science, Oxford, OH 45056

AWARDS MA, MAT, PhD.

Faculty: 11 full-time (2 women), 8 part-time/adjunct (3 women).
Students: 25 full-time (9 women); includes 1 minority (Hispanic American), 7 international. 29 applicants, 66% accepted, 8 enrolled. In 2001, 8 master's, 3 doctorates awarded.
Degree requirements: For master's, thesis (for some programs), final exam; for doctorate, thesis/dissertation, final exams, comprehensive exam.
Entrance requirements: For master's, GRE, minimum undergraduate GPA of 3.0 during previous 2 years or 2.75 overall; for doctorate, GRE, minimum undergraduate GPA of 2.75, 3.0 graduate. *Application deadline:* For fall admission, 2/1. *Application fee:* $35.
Expenses: Tuition, state resident: full-time $7,155; part-time $295 per semester hour. Tuition, nonresident: full-time $14,829; part-time $615 per semester hour. Tuition and fees vary according to degree level and campus/location.
Financial support: In 2001–02, 17 fellowships (averaging $9,134 per year), 6 teaching assistantships (averaging $11,337 per year) were awarded. Research assistantships, Federal Work-Study and tuition waivers (full) also available. Financial award application deadline: 3/1.
Dr. Ryan Barilleaux, Chair, 513-529-2010, *E-mail:* political@muohio.edu.
Application contact: Dr. John Rothgeb, Director of Graduate Studies, *E-mail:* political@muohio.edu. *Web site:* http://www.muohio.edu/politicalscience/index2.htmlx

■ MICHIGAN STATE UNIVERSITY

Graduate School, College of Social Science, Department of Political Science, East Lansing, MI 48824

AWARDS Political science (MA, PhD); political science-urban studies (PhD); public administration (MPA); public administration-urban studies (MPA). Part-time and evening/weekend programs available.

Faculty: 31.
Students: 61 full-time (28 women), 14 part-time (5 women); includes 8 minority (5 African Americans, 2 Asian Americans or Pacific Islanders, 1 Native American), 21 international. Average age 28. 162 applicants, 43% accepted. In 2001, 15 master's, 6 doctorates awarded. Terminal master's awarded for partial completion of doctoral program.
Degree requirements: For doctorate, thesis/dissertation.
Entrance requirements: For master's, GRE General Test, TOEFL, minimum GPA of 3.0; for doctorate, GRE General Test, TOEFL. *Application deadline:* Applications are processed on a rolling basis. *Application fee:* $30 ($40 for international students). Electronic applications accepted.
Expenses: Tuition, state resident: part-time $244 per credit hour. Tuition, nonresident: part-time $494 per credit hour. Required fees: $268 per semester. Tuition and fees vary according to course load, degree level and program.
Financial support: In 2001–02, 28 fellowships with tuition reimbursements (averaging $2,564 per year), 15 research assistantships with tuition reimbursements (averaging $10,970 per year), 24 teaching assistantships with tuition reimbursements (averaging $11,174 per year) were awarded. Career-related internships or fieldwork and Federal Work-Study also available. Financial award application deadline: 2/15; financial award applicants required to submit FAFSA.
Faculty research: American politics, positive theory, political thought, comparative politics, public policy analysis. *Total annual research expenditures:* $891,802.
Dr. Richard Hula, Chair, 517-355-6590, *Fax:* 517-432-1091.
Application contact: Director, PhD Program, 517-355-6590, *Fax:* 517-432-1091. *Web site:* http://www.polisci.msu.edu/

■ MIDWESTERN STATE UNIVERSITY

Graduate Studies, College of Liberal Arts, Program in Political Science, Wichita Falls, TX 76308

AWARDS MA.

Faculty: 4 full-time (0 women).
Students: 3 full-time (1 woman), 13 part-time (5 women); includes 2 minority (1 African American, 1 Hispanic American), 1 international. Average age 32. 4 applicants, 100% accepted. In 2001, 2 degrees awarded.
Degree requirements: For master's, one foreign language.
Entrance requirements: For master's, GRE General Test, MAT, TOEFL. *Application deadline:* For fall admission, 8/7; for spring admission, 12/15. *Application fee:* $0 ($50 for international students).
Expenses: Tuition, state resident: full-time $936. Tuition, nonresident: full-time $4,734. Required fees: $1,280. One-time fee: $190. Tuition and fees vary according to course load.
Financial support: In 2001–02, 2 teaching assistantships with partial tuition reimbursements were awarded; career-related internships or fieldwork, Federal Work-Study, institutionally sponsored loans, and tuition waivers (partial) also available. Support available to part-time students.
Dr. Samuel E. Watson, Program Chair, 940-397-4746, *Fax:* 940-397-4865.
Application contact: Dr. Ernest Dover, Graduate Coordinator, Political Science, 940-397-4750, *Fax:* 940-397-4865. *Web site:* http://www.mwsu.edu/

■ MINNESOTA STATE UNIVERSITY, MANKATO

College of Graduate Studies, College of Social and Behavioral Sciences, Department of Political Science, Program in Political Science, Mankato, MN 56001

AWARDS MA, MS, MT.

Students: 9 full-time (3 women), 6 part-time (2 women). Average age 33. In 2001, 2 degrees awarded.
Degree requirements: For master's, one foreign language, thesis or alternative, comprehensive exam.
Entrance requirements: For master's, minimum GPA of 3.0 during previous 2 years. *Application deadline:* For fall admission, 7/9 (priority date); for spring admission, 11/27. Applications are processed on a rolling basis. *Application fee:* $20.
Expenses: Tuition, state resident: full-time $3,253; part-time $157 per credit. Tuition, nonresident: full-time $4,893; part-time $248 per credit. Required fees: $24 per credit. Tuition and fees vary according to reciprocity agreements.
Financial support: Research assistantships with full tuition reimbursements, teaching assistantships with full tuition reimbursements available. Financial award application deadline: 3/15; financial award applicants required to submit FAFSA.
Dr. John Parham, Coordinator, 507-389-6939.
Application contact: Joni Roberts, Admissions Coordinator, 507-389-5244, *Fax:* 507-389-5974, *E-mail:* grad@mankato.msus.edu.

■ MISSISSIPPI COLLEGE

Graduate School, College of Arts and Sciences, Department of History and Political Science, Clinton, MS 39058

AWARDS Administration of justice (MSS); history (M Ed, MA, MSS); political science (MSS); social sciences (M Ed, MSS); sociology (MSS).

Degree requirements: For master's, one foreign language, thesis (for some programs), comprehensive exam.
Entrance requirements: For master's, GRE or NTE, minimum GPA of 2.5.

■ MISSISSIPPI STATE UNIVERSITY

College of Arts and Sciences, Department of Political Science, Mississippi State, MS 39762

AWARDS Political science (MA); public policy and administration (MPPA, PhD). Evening/weekend programs available.

Faculty: 12 full-time (1 woman).
Students: 29 full-time (12 women), 38 part-time (16 women); includes 26 minority (25 African Americans, 1 Hispanic American), 1 international. Average age 33. 55 applicants, 93% accepted, 17 enrolled. In 2001, 15 master's, 2 doctorates awarded.
Degree requirements: For master's, comprehensive oral or written exam; for doctorate, thesis/dissertation, comprehensive oral and written exam. *Median time to degree:* Master's–2 years full-time, 3 years part-time; doctorate–5 years full-time, 7 years part-time.
Entrance requirements: For master's, TOEFL, minimum GPA of 3.0; for doctorate, GRE General Test, TOEFL, minimum graduate GPA of 3.35. *Application deadline:* For fall admission, 8/1 (priority date); for spring admission, 12/1 (priority date). Applications are processed on a rolling basis. *Application fee:* $25 for international students.
Expenses: Tuition, state resident: full-time $3,586; part-time $150 per credit hour. Tuition, nonresident: full-time $8,128; part-time $339 per credit hour. Tuition and fees vary according to course load and campus/location.
Financial support: In 2001–02, 16 students received support, including 4 research assistantships with full tuition reimbursements available (averaging $6,600 per year), 6 teaching assistantships with full tuition reimbursements available (averaging $10,125 per year); Federal Work-Study, institutionally sponsored loans, and unspecified assistantships also available. Financial award application deadline: 4/15.
Faculty research: American politics, international relations, state and local government, comparative government , public administration. *Total annual research expenditures:* $10,000.
Dr. Douglas G. Feig, Head, 662-325-2711, *Fax:* 662-325-2716, *E-mail:* ejc1@ps.msstate.edu.
Application contact: Jerry B. Inmon, Director of Admissions, 662-325-2224, *Fax:* 662-325-7360, *E-mail:* admit@admissions.msstate.edu. *Web site:* http://www.msstate.edu/dept/politicalscience/

■ NEW MEXICO HIGHLANDS UNIVERSITY

Graduate Studies, College of Arts and Sciences, Program in Southwest Studies, Las Vegas, NM 87701

AWARDS Anthropology (MA); Hispanic language and literature (MA); history and political science (MA). Program is interdisciplinary. Part-time programs available.

Faculty: 16 full-time (5 women).
Students: 6 full-time (4 women), 15 part-time (9 women); includes 10 minority (all Hispanic Americans). Average age 39. In 2001, 3 degrees awarded.
Degree requirements: For master's, thesis or alternative.
Entrance requirements: For master's, minimum undergraduate GPA of 3.0. *Application deadline:* For fall admission, 8/1 (priority date). Applications are processed on a rolling basis. *Application fee:* $15.
Expenses: Tuition, state resident: full-time $2,238. Tuition, nonresident: full-time $9,366.
Financial support: Research assistantships with full and partial tuition reimbursements, Federal Work-Study available. Financial award application deadline: 3/1.
Dr. Tomas Salazar, Dean, 505-454-3080, *Fax:* 505-454-3389, *E-mail:* salazar_t@nmhu.edu.
Application contact: Dr. Linda LaGrange, Associate Dean of Graduate Studies, 505-454-3266, *Fax:* 505-454-3558, *E-mail:* lagrange_l@nmhu.edu.

■ NEW MEXICO STATE UNIVERSITY

Graduate School, College of Arts and Sciences, Department of Government, Las Cruces, NM 88003-8001

AWARDS MA, MPA. Part-time and evening/weekend programs available.

Faculty: 8 full-time (2 women).
Students: 13 full-time (9 women), 12 part-time (7 women); includes 5 minority (all Hispanic Americans), 1 international. Average age 35. 14 applicants, 93% accepted, 9 enrolled. In 2001, 9 degrees awarded.
Degree requirements: For master's, thesis optional.
Entrance requirements: For master's, GRE, writing sample. *Application deadline:* Applications are processed on a rolling basis. *Application fee:* $15 ($35 for international students). Electronic applications accepted.
Expenses: Tuition, state resident: full-time $3,234; part-time $135 per credit. Tuition, nonresident: full-time $9,420; part-time $428 per credit. Required fees: $858.
Financial support: In 2001–02, 13 teaching assistantships with tuition reimbursements were awarded; fellowships with tuition reimbursements, research assistantships, career-related internships or fieldwork, Federal Work-Study, and scholarships/grants also available. Support available to part-time students. Financial award application deadline: 3/1.
Faculty research: U.S./Mexico border studies, public administration and policy, international relations, women and politics, Latin America.
Dr. William Taggart, Head, 505-646-4935, *Fax:* 505-646-2052, *E-mail:* govt002@nmsu.edu. *Web site:* http://www.nmsu.edu/~govdept/

■ NEW SCHOOL UNIVERSITY

Graduate Faculty of Political and Social Science, Department of Political Science, New York, NY 10011-8603

AWARDS MA, DS Sc, PhD. Part-time and evening/weekend programs available.

Students: 130 full-time (63 women), 17 part-time (7 women); includes 25 minority

(6 African Americans, 5 Asian Americans or Pacific Islanders, 13 Hispanic Americans, 1 Native American), 58 international. Average age 34. 115 applicants, 86% accepted. In 2001, 16 master's, 5 doctorates awarded. Terminal master's awarded for partial completion of doctoral program.
Degree requirements: For master's, exam or major paper; for doctorate, one foreign language, thesis/dissertation, qualifying exam.
Entrance requirements: For master's, GRE General Test; for doctorate, GRE General Test, MA. *Application deadline:* For fall admission, 1/15 (priority date). Applications are processed on a rolling basis. *Application fee:* $40.
Expenses: Tuition: Full-time $18,720; part-time $1,040 per credit. Required fees: $450; $115 per term. Tuition and fees vary according to program.
Financial support: In 2001–02, 69 students received support, including 13 fellowships with full and partial tuition reimbursements available (averaging $2,100 per year), 14 research assistantships with full and partial tuition reimbursements available (averaging $3,000 per year), 8 teaching assistantships with full and partial tuition reimbursements available (averaging $2,000 per year); career-related internships or fieldwork, Federal Work-Study, scholarships/grants, and tuition waivers (full and partial) also available. Financial award application deadline: 1/15; financial award applicants required to submit FAFSA.
Faculty research: Democratic transitions and institution; race, class and gender; immigration and incorporation.
Dr. David Plotke, Chair, 212-229-5748.
Application contact: Emanuel Lomax, Director of Admissions, 800-523-5411, *Fax:* 212-989-7102, *E-mail:* gfadmit@newschool.edu. *Web site:* http://www.newschool.edu/

Find an in-depth description at www.petersons.com/gradchannel.

■ NEW SCHOOL UNIVERSITY

New School, Program in International Affairs, New York, NY 10011-8603

AWARDS Global management, trade, and finance (MA, MS); international development (MA, MS); international media and communication (MA, MS); international politics and diplomacy (MA, MS); service, civic, and non-profit management (MA, MS).

Students: 22 full-time (17 women), 23 part-time (12 women); includes 11 minority (5 African Americans, 1 Asian American or Pacific Islander, 5 Hispanic Americans), 8 international. 73 applicants, 93% accepted, 45 enrolled.
Application fee: $40.
Financial support: In 2001–02, 31 students received support. Tuition waivers (partial) available. Financial award application deadline: 5/1; financial award applicants required to submit FAFSA.
Dr. Michael Cohen, Head, *E-mail:* cohenm2@newschool.edu.
Application contact: Gerianne Brusati, Associate Dean, Admissions and Student Services, 212-229-5630, *Fax:* 212-989-3887, *E-mail:* nsadmissions@newschool.edu. *Web site:* http://www.nus.newschool.edu/04h_interaff.htm

Find an in-depth description at www.petersons.com/gradchannel.

■ NEW YORK UNIVERSITY

Graduate School of Arts and Science, Department of Politics, New York, NY 10012-1019

AWARDS French studies and politics (PhD); international politics and international business (MA); politics (MA, PhD); politics (Near Eastern studies) (PhD). Part-time programs available.

Faculty: 30 full-time (4 women), 24 part-time/adjunct.
Students: 73 full-time (36 women), 37 part-time (20 women); includes 12 minority (3 African Americans, 5 Asian Americans or Pacific Islanders, 4 Hispanic Americans), 47 international. Average age 27. 316 applicants, 27% accepted, 27 enrolled. In 2001, 17 master's, 6 doctorates awarded. Terminal master's awarded for partial completion of doctoral program.
Degree requirements: For master's, one foreign language, thesis or alternative; for doctorate, 2 foreign languages, thesis/dissertation, comprehensive exam.
Entrance requirements: For master's, GRE General Test, TOEFL; for doctorate, GRE General Test, TOEFL, master's degree in political science, minimum GPA of 2.5. *Application deadline:* For fall admission, 1/4 (priority date). *Application fee:* $60.
Expenses: Tuition: Full-time $19,536; part-time $814 per credit. Required fees: $1,330; $38 per credit. Tuition and fees vary according to course load and program.
Financial support: Fellowships with tuition reimbursements, teaching assistantships with tuition reimbursements, career-related internships or fieldwork, Federal Work-Study, and institutionally sponsored loans available. Financial award application deadline: 1/4; financial award applicants required to submit FAFSA.
Faculty research: Comparative politics, democratic theory and practice, rational choice, political economy; international relations.
Anna Harvey, Chair, 212-998-8500.
Application contact: Steven Brams, Director of Graduate Studies, 212-998-8500, *Fax:* 212-995-4184, *E-mail:* politics.program@nyu.edu. *Web site:* http://www.nyu.edu/gsas/dept/politics/

■ NORTH DAKOTA STATE UNIVERSITY

The Graduate School, College of Arts, Humanities and Social Sciences, Program in Political Science, Fargo, ND 58105

AWARDS MA, MS. Part-time programs available.

Faculty: 4 full-time (1 woman), 1 part-time/adjunct (0 women).
Students: 3 full-time (1 woman), 1 part-time; includes 1 minority (Hispanic American), 1 international. Average age 35.
Degree requirements: For master's, one foreign language, thesis or alternative.
Entrance requirements: For master's, GRE General Test, TOEFL. *Application deadline:* For spring admission, 4/1 (priority date). Applications are processed on a rolling basis. *Application fee:* $35.
Expenses: Tuition, state resident: part-time $124 per credit. Tuition, nonresident: part-time $325 per credit. Required fees: $22 per credit. Tuition and fees vary according to reciprocity agreements.
Financial support: In 2001–02, 2 research assistantships with tuition reimbursements (averaging $3,000 per year), 1 teaching assistantship with tuition reimbursement (averaging $5,600 per year) were awarded. Career-related internships or fieldwork and institutionally sponsored loans also available. Financial award application deadline: 4/15.
Faculty research: Political behavior, international relations, comparative politics, constitutional law.
Dr. Paul E. Nelson, Chair, 701-231-7705, *Fax:* 701-231-7784, *E-mail:* paul.nelson.1@ndsu.nodak.edu. *Web site:* http://www.ndsu.nodak.edu/political_science/home.html/

■ NORTHEASTERN ILLINOIS UNIVERSITY

Graduate College, College of Arts and Sciences, Department of Political Science, Program in Political Science, Chicago, IL 60625-4699

AWARDS MA. Part-time and evening/weekend programs available.

Faculty: 9 full-time (2 women), 4 part-time/adjunct (3 women).
Students: 7 full-time (3 women), 8 part-time (4 women); includes 6 minority (5 African Americans, 1 Hispanic American). Average age 36. 9 applicants, 100% accepted. In 2001, 4 degrees awarded.
Degree requirements: For master's, thesis optional.
Entrance requirements: For master's, minimum GPA of 2.75. *Application deadline:* For fall admission, 4/1 (priority date); for spring admission, 8/15. Applications are processed on a rolling basis. *Application fee:* $25.
Expenses: Tuition, area resident: Full-time $2,882; part-time $107 per semester hour.

Northeastern Illinois University (continued)

Tuition, nonresident: part-time $320 per semester hour. International tuition: $8,646 full-time. Required fees: $20 per semester hour.

Financial support: In 2001–02, 13 students received support, including 3 research assistantships with full tuition reimbursements available (averaging $6,600 per year); career-related internships or fieldwork, Federal Work-Study, institutionally sponsored loans, and tuition waivers (full and partial) also available. Support available to part-time students. Financial award applicants required to submit FAFSA.

Faculty research: Chinese politics, Latin American democratization, Jewish feminism, administration and delegation.

Dr. Kusol Varophas, Graduate Adviser, 773-442-5662, *Fax:* 773-442-4900, *E-mail:* k-varaphas@neiu.edu.

Application contact: Dr. Mohan K. Sood, Dean of the Graduate College, 773-442-6010, *Fax:* 773-442-6020, *E-mail:* m-sood@neiu.edu.

■ NORTHEASTERN UNIVERSITY

College of Arts and Sciences, Department of Political Science, Boston, MA 02115-5096

AWARDS American government and politics (MA); comparative government and politics (MA); international relations (MA); political theory (MA); public administration (MPA), including development administration, health administration and policy, management information systems, state and local government; public and international affairs (PhD). Part-time and evening/weekend programs available.

Faculty: 18 full-time (2 women), 10 part-time/adjunct (1 woman).

Students: 54 full-time (26 women), 27 part-time (17 women); includes 11 minority (3 African Americans, 2 Asian Americans or Pacific Islanders, 6 Hispanic Americans), 15 international. Average age 30. 133 applicants, 66% accepted. In 2001, 33 degrees awarded.

Degree requirements: For master's, thesis optional.

Entrance requirements: For master's, GRE General Test, TOEFL. *Application deadline:* Applications are processed on a rolling basis. *Application fee:* $50.

Expenses: Tuition: Part-time $535 per credit hour. Required fees: $56. Tuition and fees vary according to program.

Financial support: In 2001–02, 12 teaching assistantships with tuition reimbursements (averaging $12,000 per year) were awarded; research assistantships with tuition reimbursements, career-related internships or fieldwork, Federal Work-Study, tuition waivers (full and partial), and unspecified assistantships also available. Support available to part-time students. Financial award applicants required to submit FAFSA.

Faculty research: Presidency, public opinion, Congress, democratization, national identity.

Dr. Denis Sullivan, Chair, 617-373-2796, *Fax:* 617-373-5311, *E-mail:* gradpolisci@neu.edu.

Application contact: Mary Churchill, Administrative Assistant for Graduate Programs, 617-373-4404, *Fax:* 617-373-5311, *E-mail:* gradpolisci@neu.edu. *Web site:* http://www.casdn.neu.edu/~polisci/

Find an in-depth description at www.petersons.com/gradchannel.

■ NORTHERN ARIZONA UNIVERSITY

Graduate College, College of Social and Behavioral Sciences, Department of Political Science, Program in Political Science, Flagstaff, AZ 86011

AWARDS Political science (MA, PhD); public management (Certificate); public policy (PhD).

Students: 33 full-time (20 women), 22 part-time (10 women); includes 19 minority (6 African Americans, 1 Asian American or Pacific Islander, 9 Hispanic Americans, 3 Native Americans), 5 international. Average age 35. 31 applicants, 61% accepted, 10 enrolled. In 2001, 2 master's, 2 doctorates awarded.

Degree requirements: For master's, thesis optional; for doctorate, one foreign language, thesis/dissertation.

Entrance requirements: For doctorate, GRE General Test. *Application deadline:* For fall admission, 2/15 (priority date). Applications are processed on a rolling basis. *Application fee:* $45.

Expenses: Tuition, state resident: full-time $2,488. Tuition, nonresident: full-time $10,354.

Financial support: In 2001–02, 15 research assistantships, 2 teaching assistantships were awarded. Tuition waivers (full and partial) also available.

Application contact: Susan Bemus, Secretary, 928-523-6979, *E-mail:* political.science@nau.edu. *Web site:* http://www.nau.edu/~pos/

■ NORTHERN ILLINOIS UNIVERSITY

Graduate School, College of Liberal Arts and Sciences, Department of Political Science, Program in Political Science, De Kalb, IL 60115-2854

AWARDS MA, PhD. Part-time and evening/weekend programs available.

Faculty: 23 full-time (6 women), 5 part-time/adjunct (0 women).

Students: 44 full-time (18 women), 41 part-time (15 women); includes 7 minority (4 African Americans, 3 Asian Americans or Pacific Islanders), 28 international. 33 applicants, 79% accepted, 14 enrolled. In 2001, 8 master's, 1 doctorate awarded. Terminal master's awarded for partial completion of doctoral program.

Degree requirements: For master's, thesis or alternative, comprehensive exam; for doctorate, variable foreign language requirement, thesis/dissertation, candidacy exam, dissertation defense.

Entrance requirements: For master's, GRE General Test, TOEFL, minimum GPA of 2.75; for doctorate, GRE General Test, TOEFL, minimum undergraduate GPA of 2.75, 3.2 graduate. *Application deadline:* For fall admission, 3/1 (priority date); for spring admission, 11/1. Applications are processed on a rolling basis. *Application fee:* $30.

Expenses: Tuition, state resident: full-time $5,124; part-time $148 per credit hour. Tuition, nonresident: full-time $8,666; part-time $295 per credit hour. Required fees: $51 per term.

Financial support: Fellowships with full tuition reimbursements, research assistantships with full tuition reimbursements, teaching assistantships with full tuition reimbursements, career-related internships or fieldwork, Federal Work-Study, tuition waivers (full), and unspecified assistantships available. Support available to part-time students.

Application contact: Dr. James Schubert, Director, Graduate Studies, 815-753-7054.

■ NORTHWESTERN UNIVERSITY

The Graduate School, Judd A. and Marjorie Weinberg College of Arts and Sciences, Department of Political Science, Evanston, IL 60208

AWARDS MA, PhD, JD/PhD. Admissions and degrees offered through The Graduate School.

Faculty: 32 full-time (9 women).

Students: 78 full-time (43 women); includes 5 African Americans, 1 Asian American or Pacific Islander, 2 Hispanic Americans, 39 international. Average age 28. 145 applicants, 48% accepted. In 2001, 6 master's, 2 doctorates awarded. Terminal master's awarded for partial completion of doctoral program.

Degree requirements: For master's, thesis or alternative; for doctorate, thesis/dissertation, qualifying exams. *Median time to degree:* Master's–4 years full-time; doctorate–3 years full-time.

Entrance requirements: For master's and doctorate, GRE General Test, TOEFL, sample of written work. *Application deadline:* For fall admission, 8/30. *Application fee:* $50 ($55 for international students).

Expenses: Tuition: Full-time $26,526.

Financial support: In 2001–02, 7 fellowships with full tuition reimbursements (averaging $16,080 per year), 1 research assistantship with partial tuition reimbursement (averaging $16,080 per year), 18 teaching assistantships with full tuition reimbursements (averaging $16,080 per

year) were awarded. Career-related internships or fieldwork, Federal Work-Study, institutionally sponsored loans, and scholarships/grants also available. Financial award application deadline: 12/31; financial award applicants required to submit FAFSA.
Faculty research: Formal theory/formal political economy, political economy of development/state-business relations, labor market institutions and welfare policy, public opinion and political behavior, feminist political theory.
Susan Herbst, Chair, 847-467-3207, *Fax:* 847-491-8985, *E-mail:* s-herbst@northwestern.edu.
Application contact: Carla Lowe, Graduate Program Assistant, 847-491-7452, *Fax:* 847-491-8985, *E-mail:* political-science@northwestern.edu. *Web site:* http://www.polisci.northwestern.edu/

■ THE OHIO STATE UNIVERSITY

Graduate School, College of Social and Behavioral Sciences, Department of Political Science, Columbus, OH 43210

AWARDS Latin American studies (Certificate); political science (MA, PhD); Russian area studies (Certificate).

Degree requirements: For master's, thesis optional; for doctorate, thesis/dissertation.
Entrance requirements: For master's and doctorate, GRE General Test, TOEFL.
Faculty research: American, comparative, and international politics; political theory.

■ OHIO UNIVERSITY

Graduate Studies, College of Arts and Sciences, Department of Political Science, Athens, OH 45701-2979

AWARDS Political science (MA); public administration (MPA). Part-time programs available.

Faculty: 24 full-time (8 women).
Students: 33 full-time (12 women), 24 part-time (15 women); includes 4 minority (2 African Americans, 1 Asian American or Pacific Islander, 1 Native American), 21 international. 113 applicants, 91% accepted, 58 enrolled. In 2001, 14 degrees awarded.
Degree requirements: For master's, thesis or alternative, comprehensive exam.
Entrance requirements: For master's, GRE General Test, minimum GPA of 3.0. *Application deadline:* For fall admission, 3/1 (priority date). Applications are processed on a rolling basis. *Application fee:* $30. Electronic applications accepted.
Expenses: Tuition, state resident: full-time $6,585. Tuition, nonresident: full-time $12,254.
Financial support: In 2001–02, 30 students received support, including 10 research assistantships with full tuition reimbursements available (averaging $8,000 per year), 6 teaching assistantships with full tuition reimbursements available (averaging $8,000 per year); career-related internships or fieldwork, Federal Work-Study, institutionally sponsored loans, and tuition waivers (full and partial) also available. Financial award application deadline: 3/15.
Faculty research: International relations, Latin American politics, public policy, economic development, political theory.
Dr. Michael Mumper, Chair, 740-593-4372, *Fax:* 740-593-0394, *E-mail:* mumper@ohio.edu.
Application contact: Dr. Ronald Hunt, Graduate Director, 740-593-4368, *Fax:* 740-593-0394, *E-mail:* huntr@ohiou.edu. *Web site:* http://www.ohiou.edu/pols

■ OKLAHOMA STATE UNIVERSITY

Graduate College, College of Arts and Sciences, Department of Political Science, Stillwater, OK 74078

AWARDS Fire protection and safety (MS); political science (MA).

Faculty: 17 full-time (2 women), 4 part-time/adjunct (0 women).
Students: 15 full-time (6 women), 34 part-time (5 women); includes 7 minority (3 African Americans, 4 Native Americans), 5 international. Average age 34. 21 applicants, 95% accepted. In 2001, 10 degrees awarded.
Entrance requirements: For master's, GRE (MA), TOEFL. *Application deadline:* For fall admission, 6/1 (priority date). *Application fee:* $25.
Expenses: Tuition, state resident: part-time $92 per credit hour. Tuition, nonresident: part-time $297 per credit hour. Required fees: $21 per credit hour. $14 per semester. One-time fee: $20. Tuition and fees vary according to course load.
Financial support: In 2001–02, 14 students received support, including 4 research assistantships (averaging $10,763 per year), 12 teaching assistantships (averaging $8,713 per year); Federal Work-Study and tuition waivers (partial) also available. Support available to part-time students. Financial award application deadline: 3/1.
Faculty research: Fire and emergency management, environmental dispute resolution, voting and elections, women and politics, urban politics.
Dr. David L Nixon, Head, 405-744-5569, *Fax:* 405-744-6534, *E-mail:* mhirlin@okstate.edu.

■ THE PENNSYLVANIA STATE UNIVERSITY UNIVERSITY PARK CAMPUS

Graduate School, College of Liberal Arts, Department of Political Science, State College, University Park, PA 16802-1503

AWARDS MA, PhD.

Students: 30 full-time (12 women), 4 part-time (2 women). In 2001, 3 master's, 6 doctorates awarded.
Entrance requirements: For master's and doctorate, GRE General Test. *Application fee:* $45.
Expenses: Tuition, state resident: full-time $7,882; part-time $333 per credit. Tuition, nonresident: full-time $16,142; part-time $673 per credit. Required fees: $124 per semester.
Dr. Frank Baugmgartner, Head, 814-863-1595.

■ PORTLAND STATE UNIVERSITY

Graduate Studies, College of Urban and Public Affairs, School of Government, Division of Political Science, Portland, OR 97207-0751

AWARDS MA, MAT, MS, MST, PhD. Part-time programs available.

Faculty: 9 full-time (2 women), 4 part-time/adjunct (1 woman).
Students: 8 full-time (1 woman), 4 part-time (3 women), 4 international. Average age 31. 14 applicants, 43% accepted. In 2001, 4 degrees awarded.
Degree requirements: For master's, variable foreign language requirement, thesis; for doctorate, thesis/dissertation, residency, comprehensive exam.
Entrance requirements: For master's, GRE General Test or MAT, TOEFL, minimum GPA of 3.0; for doctorate, GRE General Test. *Application deadline:* For fall admission, 4/1 (priority date); for spring admission, 11/1. Applications are processed on a rolling basis. *Application fee:* $50.
Financial support: In 2001–02, 6 research assistantships with full tuition reimbursements (averaging $3,386 per year) were awarded; teaching assistantships, career-related internships or fieldwork, Federal Work-Study, and institutionally sponsored loans also available. Support available to part-time students. Financial award application deadline: 3/1; financial award applicants required to submit FAFSA.
Faculty research: Congress, presidency, political reform, international environment, hate speech.
Dr. John Damis, Chair, 503-725-3921, *Fax:* 503-725-8444, *E-mail:* damisj@pdx.edu. *Web site:* http://www.upa.pdx.edu/POLISCI/

■ PRINCETON UNIVERSITY

Graduate School, Department of Politics, Princeton, NJ 08544-1019

AWARDS Political philosophy (PhD); politics (PhD).

Degree requirements: For doctorate, variable foreign language requirement, thesis/dissertation.
Entrance requirements: For doctorate, GRE General Test, GRE Subject Test, sample of written work.

■ PURDUE UNIVERSITY

Graduate School, School of Liberal Arts, Department of Political Science, West Lafayette, IN 47907

AWARDS MA, PhD. Part-time and evening/weekend programs available.

Faculty: 25 full-time (7 women), 1 part-time/adjunct (0 women).
Students: 51 full-time (25 women), 18 part-time (8 women). Average age 30. 98 applicants, 49% accepted. In 2001, 8 master's, 7 doctorates awarded. Terminal master's awarded for partial completion of doctoral program.
Degree requirements: For doctorate, 2 foreign languages, thesis/dissertation.
Entrance requirements: For master's and doctorate, GRE General Test, TOEFL, minimum GPA of 3.0. *Application deadline:* For fall admission, 7/15 (priority date); for spring admission, 11/30. Applications are processed on a rolling basis. *Application fee:* $30. Electronic applications accepted.
Expenses: Tuition, state resident: full-time $4,164; part-time $149 per credit hour. Tuition, nonresident: full-time $13,872; part-time $458 per credit hour. Tuition and fees vary according to campus/location and program.
Financial support: In 2001–02, 7 fellowships, 3 research assistantships, 36 teaching assistantships were awarded. Career-related internships or fieldwork also available. Support available to part-time students. Financial award application deadline: 2/1; financial award applicants required to submit FAFSA.
Faculty research: American politics, comparative politics, political theory, public policy/public administration, international relations. *Total annual research expenditures:* $88,500.
Dr. W. R. Shaffer, Head, 765-494-4162, *E-mail:* shaffer@polsci.purdue.edu.
Application contact: Glenda Gutwein, Graduate Secretary, 765-494-4163, *Fax:* 765-494-0833, *E-mail:* gutwein@polsci.purdue.edu. *Web site:* http://www.polsci.purdue.edu/

■ PURDUE UNIVERSITY CALUMET

Graduate School, School of Liberal Arts and Sciences, Department of History and Political Science, Hammond, IN 46323-2094

AWARDS MA.

Entrance requirements: For master's, GRE, TOEFL.

■ RICE UNIVERSITY

Graduate Programs, School of Social Sciences, Department of Political Science, Houston, TX 77251-1892

AWARDS MA, PhD.

Faculty: 16 full-time (3 women).
Students: 25 full-time (14 women); includes 6 minority (1 African American, 1 Asian American or Pacific Islander, 3 Hispanic Americans, 1 Native American), 4 international. Average age 26. 48 applicants, 27% accepted, 8 enrolled. In 2001, 4 master's, 4 doctorates awarded. Terminal master's awarded for partial completion of doctoral program.
Degree requirements: For master's, thesis optional; for doctorate, thesis/dissertation, comprehensive exam. *Median time to degree:* Master's–2 years full-time; doctorate–6 years full-time.
Entrance requirements: For doctorate, GRE General Test, TOEFL. *Application deadline:* For fall admission, 2/1 (priority date). *Application fee:* $25. Electronic applications accepted.
Expenses: Tuition: Full-time $17,300. Required fees: $250.
Financial support: In 2001–02, 22 students received support, including 13 fellowships with full tuition reimbursements available (averaging $12,500 per year), 6 research assistantships with full tuition reimbursements available (averaging $13,500 per year), 2 teaching assistantships with full tuition reimbursements available (averaging $13,300 per year); Federal Work-Study and scholarships/grants also available. Financial award application deadline: 2/1; financial award applicants required to submit FAFSA.
Faculty research: Comparative government in Western Europe, Latin America and the former Soviet Union, international relations, Congress and public policy in American government, minority politics. *Total annual research expenditures:* $445,729.
Dr. T. Clifton Morgan, Chairman, 713-348-4842, *Fax:* 713-348-5273, *E-mail:* poli@rice.edu.
Application contact: Ann S. Mikus, Information Contact, 713-348-4842, *Fax:* 713-348-5273, *E-mail:* poli@rice.edu. *Web site:* http://www.ruf.rice.edu/~poli/

■ ROOSEVELT UNIVERSITY

Graduate Division, College of Arts and Sciences, School of Policy Studies, Program in Political Science, Chicago, IL 60605-1394

AWARDS MA. Part-time and evening/weekend programs available.

Faculty: 4 full-time (0 women), 4 part-time/adjunct (0 women).
Students: 8 full-time (3 women), 15 part-time (8 women); includes 14 minority (13 African Americans, 1 Asian American or Pacific Islander), 2 international. In 2001, 22 degrees awarded.
Degree requirements: For master's, thesis or alternative.
Entrance requirements: For master's, minimum GPA of 2.7. *Application deadline:* For fall admission, 6/1 (priority date). Applications are processed on a rolling basis. *Application fee:* $25 ($35 for international students).
Expenses: Tuition: Full-time $9,090; part-time $505 per credit hour. Required fees: $100 per term.
Financial support: Application deadline: 2/15.
Faculty research: Metropolitan social movements, American politics, comparative politics, political theory.
Application contact: Joanne Canyon-Heller, Coordinator of Graduate Admissions, 312-281-3250, *Fax:* 312-341-3523, *E-mail:* applyru@roosevelt.edu.

■ RUTGERS, THE STATE UNIVERSITY OF NEW JERSEY, NEWARK

Graduate School, Department of Political Science, Newark, NJ 07102

AWARDS American political system (MA); international relations (MA). Part-time and evening/weekend programs available.

Degree requirements: For master's, thesis optional.
Entrance requirements: For master's, GRE, minimum undergraduate B average. Electronic applications accepted.
Faculty research: Policymaking and policy evaluation in the United States; government and politics in Europe, Middle East, Asia, Africa, and Latin America.

■ RUTGERS, THE STATE UNIVERSITY OF NEW JERSEY, NEW BRUNSWICK

Graduate School, Eagleton Institute of Politics, New Brunswick, NJ 08901-1281

AWARDS MS, JD/MS. Part-time programs available.

Entrance requirements: For master's, GRE General Test or LSAT.
Faculty research: Legislative process, public finance, public opinion, campaigning, public policy.

■ RUTGERS, THE STATE UNIVERSITY OF NEW JERSEY, NEW BRUNSWICK

Graduate School, Program in Political Science, New Brunswick, NJ 08901-1281

AWARDS American political institutions (PhD); comparative politics (PhD); international relations (PhD); political economy (PhD); political theory (PhD); public law (PhD); women and politics (PhD).

Degree requirements: For doctorate, one foreign language, thesis/dissertation.
Entrance requirements: For doctorate, GRE General Test. *Web site:* http://policsci.rutgers.edu/

■ ST. JOHN'S UNIVERSITY

St. John's College of Liberal Arts and Sciences, Department of Government and Politics, Program in Government and Politics, Jamaica, NY 11439

AWARDS MA, JD/MA. Part-time and evening/weekend programs available.

Faculty: 10 full-time (4 women), 8 part-time/adjunct (2 women).
Students: 23 full-time (10 women), 87 part-time (41 women); includes 26 minority (21 African Americans, 5 Hispanic Americans), 16 international. Average age 30. 82 applicants, 77% accepted, 40 enrolled. In 2001, 29 degrees awarded.
Degree requirements: For master's, thesis optional.
Entrance requirements: For master's, minimum GPA of 3.0. *Application deadline:* Applications are processed on a rolling basis. *Application fee:* $40.
Expenses: Tuition: Full-time $14,520; part-time $605 per credit. Required fees: $150; $75 per term. Tuition and fees vary according to class time, course load, degree level, campus/location, program and student level.
Financial support: Research assistantships, scholarships/grants available. Support available to part-time students. Financial award application deadline: 3/1; financial award applicants required to submit FAFSA.
Application contact: Matthew Whelan, Director, Office of Admission, 718-990-2000, *Fax:* 718-990-2096, *E-mail:* admissions@stjohns.edu. *Web site:* http://www.stjohns.edu/

■ ST. JOHN'S UNIVERSITY

St. John's College of Liberal Arts and Sciences, Department of Government and Politics and Division of Library and Information Science, Program in Government Information Specialist, Jamaica, NY 11439

AWARDS MA/MLS. Part-time and evening/weekend programs available.

Students: Average age 36. 1 applicant, 100% accepted, 0 enrolled.
Application deadline: Applications are processed on a rolling basis. *Application fee:* $40.
Expenses: Tuition: Full-time $14,520; part-time $605 per credit. Required fees: $150; $75 per term. Tuition and fees vary according to class time, course load, degree level, campus/location, program and student level.
Financial support: Research assistantships, career-related internships or fieldwork and scholarships/grants available. Support available to part-time students. Financial award application deadline: 3/1; financial award applicants required to submit FAFSA.
Application contact: Matthew Whelan, Director, Office of Admission, 718-990-2000, *Fax:* 718-990-2096, *E-mail:* admissions@stjohns.edu. *Web site:* http://www.stjohns.edu/

■ ST. MARY'S UNIVERSITY OF SAN ANTONIO

Graduate School, Department of Political Science, San Antonio, TX 78228-8507

AWARDS Political communications and applied science (MA); political science (MA). Part-time programs available.

Faculty: 32 full-time (5 women), 4 part-time/adjunct (0 women).
Students: 42 full-time (23 women), 93 part-time (34 women); includes 69 minority (10 African Americans, 59 Hispanic Americans), 1 international. Average age 32. In 2001, 1 degree awarded.
Entrance requirements: For master's, GRE General Test. *Application deadline:* Applications are processed on a rolling basis. *Application fee:* $15. Electronic applications accepted.
Expenses: Tuition: Full-time $8,190; part-time $455 per credit hour. Required fees: $375.
Financial support: Fellowships, research assistantships, career-related internships or fieldwork, Federal Work-Study, and institutionally sponsored loans available. Financial award application deadline: 2/15; financial award applicants required to submit FAFSA.
Faculty research: Voting rights, natural resources and urban policy, comparative politics and international relations.
Dr. Sonia R. Garcia, Graduate Program Director.

■ SAM HOUSTON STATE UNIVERSITY

College of Arts and Sciences, Department of Political Science, Huntsville, TX 77341

AWARDS MA. Evening/weekend programs available.

Students: 4 full-time (1 woman), 2 part-time (1 woman); includes 1 minority (African American), 3 international. Average age 34. In 2001, 1 degree awarded.
Degree requirements: For master's, thesis or alternative.
Entrance requirements: For master's, GRE General Test, TOEFL. *Application deadline:* For fall admission, 8/1; for spring admission, 12/1. Applications are processed on a rolling basis. *Application fee:* $20.
Expenses: Tuition, area resident: Part-time $69 per credit. Tuition, state resident: full-time $1,380; part-time $69 per credit. Tuition, nonresident: full-time $5,600; part-time $280 per credit. Required fees: $748. Tuition and fees vary according to course load.
Financial support: Research assistantships, teaching assistantships, career-related internships or fieldwork and institutionally sponsored loans available. Support available to part-time students. Financial award application deadline: 5/31; financial award applicants required to submit FAFSA.
Faculty research: Gender politics, child-care policy, rural politics, Canadian intergovernmental relations, wildlife conservation policy.
Dr. Robert H. Biles, Chair, 936-294-1457.
Application contact: Dr. John Holcombe, Graduate Adviser, 936-294-1467.

■ SAN DIEGO STATE UNIVERSITY

Graduate and Research Affairs, College of Arts and Letters, Department of Political Science, San Diego, CA 92182

AWARDS MA.

Degree requirements: For master's, thesis.
Entrance requirements: For master's, GRE General Test, TOEFL, minimum GPA of 3.0.

■ SAN FRANCISCO STATE UNIVERSITY

Graduate Division, College of Behavioral and Social Sciences, Department of Political Science, San Francisco, CA 94132-1722

AWARDS MA.

Entrance requirements: For master's, TOEFL, minimum GPA of 3.0.
Faculty research: American politics—institutions and electoral, comparative politics—development and West European, history, theology, and American political theory.

■ SONOMA STATE UNIVERSITY

School of Social Sciences, Department of Political Science, Rohnert Park, CA 94928-3609

AWARDS Political science (MA); public administration (MPA). Part-time and evening/weekend programs available.

Faculty: 6 full-time (2 women), 7 part-time/adjunct (2 women).
Students: 4 full-time (3 women), 25 part-time (14 women); includes 5 minority (2 African Americans, 3 Hispanic Americans), 1 international. Average age 38. 13 applicants, 77% accepted, 10 enrolled. In 2001, 9 degrees awarded.
Degree requirements: For master's, thesis or alternative.
Entrance requirements: For master's, GRE General Test, minimum GPA of 3.0. *Application deadline:* For fall admission, 11/30; for spring admission, 8/31. *Application fee:* $55.
Expenses: Tuition, nonresident: full-time $4,428; part-time $246 per unit. Required fees: $2,084; $727 per semester.
Financial support: Career-related internships or fieldwork available. Financial award application deadline: 3/2.
Faculty research: Cross-disciplinary viewpoint in public administration, public policy implementation and evaluation.
Dr. Andrew Merrifield, Coordinator, 707-664-2179, *E-mail:* andrew.merrifield@sonoma.edu.

■ SOUTHERN CONNECTICUT STATE UNIVERSITY

School of Graduate Studies, School of Arts and Sciences, Department of Political Science, New Haven, CT 06515-1355

AWARDS MS. Part-time and evening/weekend programs available.

Faculty: 7 full-time (1 woman).
Students: 20 applicants, 35% accepted. In 2001, 7 degrees awarded.
Degree requirements: For master's, thesis or alternative.
Entrance requirements: For master's, interview. *Application deadline:* For fall admission, 7/15 (priority date). Applications are processed on a rolling basis. *Application fee:* $40.
Financial support: Application deadline: 4/15.
Dr. David Walsh, Chairperson, 203-392-5665, *Fax:* 203-392-5670, *E-mail:* walsh@southernct.edu.
Application contact: Dr. John Critzer, Graduate Coordinator, 203-392-5665, *Fax:* 203-392-5670, *E-mail:* critzer@southernct.edu. *Web site:* http://www.southernct.edu/

■ SOUTHERN ILLINOIS UNIVERSITY CARBONDALE

Graduate School, College of Liberal Arts, Department of Political Science, Program in Political Science, Carbondale, IL 62901-6806

AWARDS MA, PhD, JD/PhD. Part-time programs available.

Faculty: 17 full-time (1 woman), 2 part-time/adjunct (0 women).
Students: 17 full-time (6 women), 19 part-time (4 women); includes 2 minority (both Asian Americans or Pacific Islanders), 10 international. 30 applicants, 27% accepted. In 2001, 4 master's, 2 doctorates awarded.
Degree requirements: For doctorate, thesis/dissertation.
Entrance requirements: For master's, GRE General Test, TOEFL, minimum GPA of 2.7; for doctorate, GRE General Test, TOEFL, minimum GPA of 3.5. *Application deadline:* Applications are processed on a rolling basis. *Application fee:* $20.
Expenses: Tuition, state resident: full-time $3,794; part-time $154 per hour. Tuition, nonresident: full-time $6,566; part-time $308 per hour. Required fees: $277 per hour.
Financial support: In 2001–02, 16 students received support, including 3 fellowships with full tuition reimbursements available, 5 research assistantships with full tuition reimbursements available, 10 teaching assistantships with full tuition reimbursements available; career-related internships or fieldwork, Federal Work-Study, institutionally sponsored loans, and tuition waivers (full) also available. Support available to part-time students. Financial award application deadline: 2/1.
Faculty research: Public law, international relations, comparative government, American government.
Application contact: William S. Turley, Graduate Director, 618-536-2371.

Find an in-depth description at www.petersons.com/gradchannel.

■ SOUTHERN UNIVERSITY AND AGRICULTURAL AND MECHANICAL COLLEGE

Graduate School, School of Public Policy and Urban Affairs, Department of Political Science, Baton Rouge, LA 70813

AWARDS Social sciences (MA).

Students: Average age 25.
Degree requirements: For master's, thesis.
Entrance requirements: For master's, GMAT or GRE General Test, TOEFL, minimum GPA of 3.0. *Application deadline:* For fall admission, 6/1 (priority date); for spring admission, 11/1. Applications are processed on a rolling basis. *Application fee:* $25.
Expenses: Tuition, state resident: full-time $1,323. Tuition, nonresident: full-time $2,583. International tuition: $2,613 full-time. Tuition and fees vary according to program.
Financial support: In 2001–02, research assistantships (averaging $7,000 per year), teaching assistantships (averaging $7,000 per year) were awarded. Financial award application deadline: 4/15; financial award applicants required to submit FAFSA.
Faculty research: Redistricting, comparative studies, environmental politics, political geography, mayoral elections.
Dr. William Arp, Chairman, 225-771-3210, *Fax:* 225-771-3105, *E-mail:* warp333@aol.com.

■ SOUTHWEST TEXAS STATE UNIVERSITY

Graduate School, College of Liberal Arts, Department of Political Science, Program in Political Science, San Marcos, TX 78666

AWARDS Political science (MA); political science education (M Ed). Part-time and evening/weekend programs available.

Students: 10 full-time (6 women), 17 part-time (9 women); includes 6 minority (1 African American, 4 Hispanic Americans, 1 Native American), 5 international. Average age 30. 19 applicants, 95% accepted, 7 enrolled. In 2001, 16 degrees awarded.
Degree requirements: For master's, thesis (for some programs), comprehensive exam.
Entrance requirements: For master's, GRE General Test, TOEFL, minimum GPA of 2.85 in last 60 hours. *Application deadline:* For fall admission, 6/15 (priority date); for spring admission, 10/15 (priority date). Applications are processed on a rolling basis. *Application fee:* $40 ($90 for international students).
Expenses: Tuition, state resident: full-time $1,512; part-time $84 per credit hour. Tuition, nonresident: full-time $5,310; part-time $295 per credit hour. Required fees: $864; $29 per credit hour. $195 per term. Full-time tuition and fees vary according to course load.
Financial support: Teaching assistantships, career-related internships or fieldwork, Federal Work-Study, and institutionally sponsored loans available. Support available to part-time students. Financial award application deadline: 4/1; financial award applicants required to submit FAFSA.
Faculty research: Religion in American public life, international humanitarian and refugee policy, judicial biography and history, citizenship and ethics, business and government policy making.
Dr. Ed Mihalkanin, Graduate Adviser, 512-245-3365, *Fax:* 512-245-7815, *E-mail:* rg06@swt.edu. *Web site:* http://www.swt.edu/

■ SOUTHWEST TEXAS STATE UNIVERSITY

Graduate School, Interdisciplinary Studies in Political Science, San Marcos, TX 78666

AWARDS MAIS.

Degree requirements: For master's, comprehensive exam.
Application deadline: For fall admission, 6/15 (priority date); for spring admission, 10/15 (priority date). Applications are processed on a rolling basis. *Application fee:* $40 ($90 for international students).
Expenses: Tuition, state resident: full-time $1,512; part-time $84 per credit hour. Tuition, nonresident: full-time $5,310; part-time $295 per credit hour. Required fees: $864; $29 per credit hour. $195 per term. Full-time tuition and fees vary according to course load.
Financial support: Application deadline: 4/1.
Dr. Cynthia Opheim, Head, 512-245-2143, *Fax:* 512-245-7815, *E-mail:* co01@swt.edu.

■ STANFORD UNIVERSITY

School of Humanities and Sciences, Department of Political Science, Stanford, CA 94305-9991

AWARDS AM, PhD.

Faculty: 32 full-time (10 women).
Students: 80 full-time (31 women), 21 part-time (8 women); includes 19 minority (5 African Americans, 9 Asian Americans or Pacific Islanders, 5 Hispanic Americans), 35 international. Average age 28. 287 applicants, 13% accepted. In 2001, 8 master's, 16 doctorates awarded. Terminal master's awarded for partial completion of doctoral program.
Degree requirements: For doctorate, one foreign language, thesis/dissertation, oral exam.
Entrance requirements: For master's and doctorate, GRE General Test, TOEFL, TSE. *Application deadline:* For fall admission, 1/4. *Application fee:* $65 ($80 for international students). Electronic applications accepted.
Barry R. Weingast, Chair, 650-723-1806, *Fax:* 650-723-1808, *E-mail:* weingast@stanford.edu.
Application contact: Graduate Administrator, 650-725-1318, *Fax:* 650-723-1808. *Web site:* http://www.stanford.edu/group/polisci/

■ STATE UNIVERSITY OF NEW YORK AT ALBANY

Nelson A. Rockefeller College of Public Affairs and Policy, Department of Political Science, Albany, NY 12222-0001

AWARDS MA, PhD. Evening/weekend programs available.

Students: 42 full-time (17 women), 44 part-time (17 women); includes 7 minority (3 African Americans, 4 Hispanic Americans), 15 international. Average age 32. 60 applicants, 72% accepted. In 2001, 14 master's, 1 doctorate awarded.
Degree requirements: For doctorate, one foreign language, thesis/dissertation.
Entrance requirements: For doctorate, GRE General Test. *Application deadline:* For fall admission, 7/1; for spring admission, 11/1. *Application fee:* $50.
Expenses: Tuition, state resident: full-time $2,550; part-time $213 per credit. Tuition, nonresident: full-time $4,208; part-time $351 per credit. Required fees: $470; $470 per year.
Financial support: Fellowships available. Financial award application deadline: 2/1.
Dr. Bruce Miroff, Chair, 518-442-5255.

■ STATE UNIVERSITY OF NEW YORK AT BINGHAMTON

Graduate School, School of Arts and Sciences, Department of Political Science, Binghamton, NY 13902-6000

AWARDS Political science (MA, PhD); public policy (MA, PhD).

Faculty: 11 full-time (2 women), 1 part-time/adjunct (0 women).
Students: 24 full-time (13 women), 11 part-time (4 women); includes 7 minority (5 African Americans, 2 Hispanic Americans), 12 international. Average age 31. 44 applicants, 36% accepted, 3 enrolled. In 2001, 2 master's, 3 doctorates awarded. Terminal master's awarded for partial completion of doctoral program.
Degree requirements: For master's, thesis or alternative, written exam; for doctorate, 2 foreign languages, thesis/dissertation, written exam.
Entrance requirements: For master's and doctorate, GRE General Test, GRE Subject Test, TOEFL. *Application deadline:* For fall admission, 4/15 (priority date); for spring admission, 11/1. Applications are processed on a rolling basis. Electronic applications accepted.
Expenses: Tuition, state resident: full-time $5,100; part-time $213 per credit. Tuition, nonresident: full-time $8,416; part-time $351 per credit. Required fees: $811.
Financial support: In 2001–02, 24 students received support, including 6 fellowships with full tuition reimbursements available (averaging $10,547 per year), 3 research assistantships with full tuition reimbursements available (averaging $6,147 per year), 15 teaching assistantships with full tuition reimbursements available (averaging $9,167 per year); career-related internships or fieldwork, Federal Work-Study, institutionally sponsored loans, tuition waivers (full and partial), and unspecified assistantships also available. Support available to part-time students. Financial award application deadline: 2/15.
Dr. Michael McDonald, Chairperson, 607-777-2252.

■ STONY BROOK UNIVERSITY, STATE UNIVERSITY OF NEW YORK

Graduate School, College of Arts and Sciences, Department of Political Science, Stony Brook, NY 11794

AWARDS Public policy (MAPP). Evening/weekend programs available.

Faculty: 15 full-time (2 women), 2 part-time/adjunct (0 women).
Students: 43 full-time (17 women), 25 part-time (13 women); includes 13 minority (8 African Americans, 5 Hispanic Americans), 15 international. Average age 27. 64 applicants, 55% accepted. In 2001, 16 master's, 5 doctorates awarded.
Degree requirements: For doctorate, thesis/dissertation.
Entrance requirements: For master's and doctorate, GRE General Test. *Application deadline:* For fall admission, 1/15. *Application fee:* $50.
Expenses: Tuition, state resident: full-time $5,100; part-time $213 per credit. Tuition, nonresident: full-time $8,416; part-time $351 per credit. Required fees: $496.
Financial support: In 2001–02, 1 fellowship, 28 teaching assistantships were awarded. *Total annual research expenditures:* $563,656.
Dr. Mark Schneider, Chair, 631-632-7640.
Application contact: Dr. Paul Teske, Director, 631-632-7634, *Fax:* 631-632-7132, *E-mail:* pteske@datalab2.sbs.sunysb.edu. *Web site:* http://www.sunysb.edu/polsci/

Find an in-depth description at www.petersons.com/gradchannel.

■ SUFFOLK UNIVERSITY

College of Arts and Sciences, Department of Government, Boston, MA 02108-2770

AWARDS Political science (MS). Part-time and evening/weekend programs available.

Faculty: 9 full-time (5 women), 4 part-time/adjunct (1 woman).
Students: 11 full-time (7 women), 13 part-time (6 women); includes 1 minority (Hispanic American), 5 international. Average age 26. 35 applicants, 63% accepted, 12 enrolled. In 2001, 4 degrees awarded.
Degree requirements: For master's, thesis optional.
Entrance requirements: For master's, GRE General Test or MAT. *Application deadline:* For fall admission, 6/15 (priority date); for spring admission, 11/15 (priority date). Applications are processed on a rolling basis. *Application fee:* $35.
Expenses: Contact institution.
Financial support: In 2001–02, 15 students received support, including 3 fellowships with full and partial tuition reimbursements available (averaging $5,400 per year); career-related internships or fieldwork, Federal Work-Study, and

Suffolk University (continued)
institutionally sponsored loans also available. Support available to part-time students. Financial award application deadline: 3/15; financial award applicants required to submit FAFSA.
Faculty research: Political parties, women in politics, Canadian politics, public policy, legislative policies.
Agnes S. Bain, Chair, 617-573-8126, *Fax:* 617-367-4623, *E-mail:* abain@suffolk.edu.
Application contact: Judith Reynolds, Director of Graduate Admissions, 617-573-8302, *Fax:* 617-523-0116, *E-mail:* grad.admission@suffolk.edu. *Web site:* http://www.cas.suffolk.edu/government/grad.html

■ SUL ROSS STATE UNIVERSITY

School of Arts and Sciences, Department of Behavioral and Social Sciences, Program in Political Science, Alpine, TX 79832

AWARDS MA. Part-time and evening/weekend programs available.

Faculty: 4 full-time (1 woman).
Students: 8 full-time (3 women), 11 part-time (4 women); includes 8 minority (1 African American, 7 Hispanic Americans). Average age 32. In 2001, 2 degrees awarded.
Degree requirements: For master's, thesis optional.
Entrance requirements: For master's, GRE General Test, minimum undergraduate GPA of 2.5 in last 60 hours. *Application deadline:* Applications are processed on a rolling basis. *Application fee:* $0 ($50 for international students).
Expenses: Tuition, state resident: part-time $64 per semester hour. Tuition, nonresident: part-time $275 per semester hour. Required fees: $71; $32 per semester hour.
Financial support: Research assistantships, teaching assistantships, career-related internships or fieldwork, Federal Work-Study, and institutionally sponsored loans available. Support available to part-time students. Financial award application deadline: 5/1; financial award applicants required to submit FAFSA.
Faculty research: Local government, state government, borderland studies, British studies.
Dr. Jimmy Case, Chairman, Department of Behavioral and Social Sciences, 915-837-8161, *Fax:* 915-837-8046.

■ SYRACUSE UNIVERSITY

Graduate School, Maxwell School of Citizenship and Public Affairs, Department of Political Science, Syracuse, NY 13244-0003

AWARDS MA, PhD, JD/MA.

Faculty: 26 full-time (6 women).
Students: 61 full-time (29 women), 5 part-time (2 women); includes 11 minority (6 African Americans, 3 Asian Americans or Pacific Islanders, 2 Hispanic Americans), 18 international. Average age 31. 119 applicants, 22% accepted, 10 enrolled. In 2001, 3 master's, 4 doctorates awarded.
Degree requirements: For doctorate, thesis/dissertation. *Median time to degree:* Master's–2 years full-time, 5 years part-time; doctorate–6.2 years full-time.
Entrance requirements: For master's and doctorate, GRE General Test. *Application deadline:* For fall admission, 2/1 (priority date). Applications are processed on a rolling basis. *Application fee:* $50.
Expenses: Tuition: Full-time $15,528; part-time $647 per credit. Required fees: $420; $38 per term. Tuition and fees vary according to program.
Financial support: In 2001–02, 35 students received support, including 6 fellowships with full tuition reimbursements available (averaging $10,500 per year), 23 teaching assistantships with full tuition reimbursements available (averaging $10,600 per year); Federal Work-Study and tuition waivers (partial) also available.
Jeffrey Stonecash, Chair, 315-443-2416.
Application contact: Mehrzad Boroujerdi, Graduate Director, 315-443-5877.

Find an in-depth description at www.petersons.com/gradchannel.

■ TARLETON STATE UNIVERSITY

College of Graduate Studies, College of Sciences and Technology, Department of Social Sciences, Stephenville, TX 76402

AWARDS History (MA); political science (MA). Part-time and evening/weekend programs available. Postbaccalaureate distance learning degree programs offered (minimal on-campus study).

Degree requirements: For master's, variable foreign language requirement, comprehensive exam.
Entrance requirements: For master's, GRE General Test.

■ TEACHERS COLLEGE COLUMBIA UNIVERSITY

Graduate Faculty of Education, Department of Human Development, Program in Politics and Education, New York, NY 10027-6696

AWARDS Ed M, MA, Ed D, PhD.

Degree requirements: For doctorate, thesis/dissertation.
Expenses: Tuition: Full-time $19,080; part-time $780 per unit. Required fees: $170 per semester.
Faculty research: Urban and social programs in education.

■ TEMPLE UNIVERSITY

Graduate School, College of Liberal Arts, Department of Political Science, Philadelphia, PA 19122-6096

AWARDS MA, PhD. Part-time programs available. Terminal master's awarded for partial completion of doctoral program.

Degree requirements: For master's, comprehensive exam; for doctorate, thesis/dissertation, preliminary and oral exams.
Entrance requirements: For master's, GRE General Test, minimum GPA of 3.3 in major, 3.0 overall; for doctorate, GRE General Test, minimum GPA of 3.4 in major, 3.2 overall. Electronic applications accepted.
Expenses: Tuition, state resident: full-time $8,487; part-time $369 per credit hour. Tuition, nonresident: full-time $12,282; part-time $534 per credit hour. Required fees: $350. Tuition and fees vary according to course load, program and reciprocity agreements.
Faculty research: American politics, international politics, comparative politics, political theory, urban politics, public policy. *Web site:* http://www.temple.edu/polsci/

■ TEXAS A&M INTERNATIONAL UNIVERSITY

Division of Graduate Studies, College of Arts and Humanities, Department of Social Sciences, Laredo, TX 78041-1900

AWARDS Criminal justice (MSCJ); history (MA); political science (MA); public administration (MPAD).

Students: 9 full-time (5 women), 59 part-time (21 women); includes 57 minority (2 Asian Americans or Pacific Islanders, 55 Hispanic Americans), 1 international. In 2001, 12 degrees awarded.
Degree requirements: For master's, thesis (for some programs).
Entrance requirements: For master's, GRE General Test. *Application deadline:* For fall admission, 7/15 (priority date); for spring admission, 11/12. Applications are processed on a rolling basis. *Application fee:* $0.
Expenses: Tuition, state resident: full-time $1,536; part-time $64 per credit. Tuition, nonresident: full-time $6,600; part-time $275 per credit. Required fees: $594; $9 per credit. $33 per term. One-time fee: $10 part-time.
Financial support: Application deadline: 11/1.
Dr. Nasser Momayezi, Interim Dean, 956-326-2460, *Fax:* 956-326-2459, *E-mail:* nmomayezi@tamiu.edu.
Application contact: Veronica Gonzalez, Director of Enrollment Management and School Relations, 956-326-2270, *Fax:* 956-326-2269, *E-mail:* enroll@tamiu.edu.

■ TEXAS A&M UNIVERSITY

College of Liberal Arts, Department of Political Science, College Station, TX 77843

AWARDS MA, PhD.

Faculty: 36 full-time (10 women).
Students: 33 full-time (14 women), 14 part-time (4 women); includes 2 minority (both Hispanic Americans), 9 international. Average age 30. 35 applicants, 54% accepted. In 2001, 3 master's, 7 doctorates awarded.
Degree requirements: For master's, thesis optional; for doctorate, thesis/dissertation, comprehensive exam.
Entrance requirements: For master's and doctorate, GRE General Test, TOEFL, minimum GPA of 3.4. *Application deadline:* For fall admission, 2/1 (priority date). *Application fee:* $50 ($75 for international students). Electronic applications accepted.
Expenses: Tuition, state resident: full-time $11,872. Tuition, nonresident: full-time $17,892.
Financial support: In 2001–02, 3 fellowships (averaging $3,000 per year), 36 research assistantships (averaging $15,000 per year) were awarded. Institutionally sponsored loans and assistant lecturer positions also available. Financial award application deadline: 2/1; financial award applicants required to submit FAFSA.
Faculty research: American politics, international relations, comparative politics, political theory, public policy. *Total annual research expenditures:* $100,000.
Dr. Patricia A. Hurley, Interim Head, 979-845-2511, *Fax:* 979-847-8924, *E-mail:* pat_hurley@polisci.tamu.edu.
Application contact: Dr. Cary J. Nederman, Graduate Advisor, 979-845-4845, *Fax:* 979-845-4845, *E-mail:* nederman@polisci.tamu.edu. *Web site:* http://www-polisci.tamu.edu

■ TEXAS A&M UNIVERSITY–KINGSVILLE

College of Graduate Studies, College of Arts and Sciences, Program in History and Political Science, Kingsville, TX 78363

AWARDS MA, MS. Part-time and evening/weekend programs available.

Faculty: 8 full-time (0 women), 1 part-time/adjunct (0 women).
Students: 3 full-time (2 women), 14 part-time (7 women); includes 9 minority (1 African American, 8 Hispanic Americans), 1 international. Average age 38. In 2001, 6 degrees awarded.
Degree requirements: For master's, thesis or alternative, comprehensive exam.
Entrance requirements: For master's, GRE General Test, TOEFL. *Application deadline:* For fall admission, 6/1; for spring admission, 11/15. Applications are processed on a rolling basis. *Application fee:* $15 ($25 for international students).
Expenses: Tuition, state resident: part-time $42 per hour. Tuition, nonresident: part-time $253 per hour. Required fees: $56 per hour. One-time fee: $46 part-time. Tuition and fees vary according to program.
Financial support: Application deadline: 5/15.
Dr. Sonny Davis, Coordinator, 361-593-3601.

■ TEXAS TECH UNIVERSITY

Graduate School, College of Arts and Sciences, Department of Political Science, Lubbock, TX 79409

AWARDS Political science (MA, PhD); public administration (MPA). Part-time programs available.

Faculty: 10 full-time (2 women), 1 part-time/adjunct (0 women).
Students: 45 full-time (20 women), 14 part-time (5 women); includes 9 minority (1 African American, 8 Hispanic Americans), 7 international. Average age 34. 49 applicants, 61% accepted, 13 enrolled. In 2001, 25 master's, 2 doctorates awarded.
Degree requirements: For master's, thesis or alternative; for doctorate, thesis/dissertation.
Entrance requirements: For master's and doctorate, GRE General Test. *Application deadline:* Applications are processed on a rolling basis. *Application fee:* $25 ($50 for international students). Electronic applications accepted.
Expenses: Tuition, state resident: full-time $1,926; part-time $107 per credit hour. Tuition, nonresident: full-time $5,724; part-time $318 per credit hour. Required fees: $779; $737 per year. Tuition and fees vary according to course level, course load and program.
Financial support: In 2001–02, 46 students received support, including 2 research assistantships with partial tuition reimbursements available (averaging $9,056 per year), 20 teaching assistantships with partial tuition reimbursements available (averaging $9,248 per year); Federal Work-Study and institutionally sponsored loans also available. Support available to part-time students. Financial award application deadline: 5/1; financial award applicants required to submit FAFSA.
Faculty research: State politics, American institutions and behavior, Asian politics, international and comparative political economy, public organizations. *Total annual research expenditures:* $40,400.
Dr. Philip H. Marshall, Chair, 806-742-3121, *Fax:* 806-742-0850.
Application contact: Graduate Adviser, 806-742-3121, *Fax:* 806-742-0850. *Web site:* http://www.ttu.edu/~polisci/

■ TEXAS WOMAN'S UNIVERSITY

Graduate Studies and Research, College of Arts and Sciences, Department of History and Government, Denton, TX 76201

AWARDS Government (MA); history (MA). Part-time and evening/weekend programs available.

Faculty: 6 full-time (2 women), 2 part-time/adjunct (1 woman).
Students: 7 full-time (all women), 16 part-time (all women); includes 5 minority (all African Americans). Average age 36. 3 applicants, 100% accepted. In 2001, 5 degrees awarded.
Degree requirements: For master's, thesis. *Median time to degree:* Master's–2 years full-time, 3 years part-time.
Entrance requirements: For master's, minimum GPA of 3.3. *Application deadline:* Applications are processed on a rolling basis. *Application fee:* $30.
Expenses: Tuition, state resident: part-time $90 per semester hour. Tuition, nonresident: part-time $303 per semester hour. Required fees: $24 per credit hour. $79 per semester.
Financial support: In 2001–02, 4 research assistantships (averaging $3,000 per year), 2 teaching assistantships (averaging $6,300 per year) were awarded. Career-related internships or fieldwork, Federal Work-Study, and institutionally sponsored loans also available. Support available to part-time students. Financial award application deadline: 4/1.
Faculty research: American constitutionalism, 19th century American history, legislative politics, Roman republic, Japanese constitutionalism.
Dr. Jim R. Alexander, Chair, 940-898-2133, *Fax:* 940-898-2130, *E-mail:* d_alexander@twu.edu.
Application contact: Dr. Paul Travis, Professor, 940-898-2133, *Fax:* 940-898-2130, *E-mail:* ptravis@twu.edu. *Web site:* http://www.twu.edu/as/histgov/

■ TROY STATE UNIVERSITY DOTHAN

Graduate School, College of Arts and Sciences, Department of History and Political Sciences, Dothan, AL 36304-0368

AWARDS MS. Part-time and evening/weekend programs available.

Faculty: 21 full-time (7 women), 2 part-time/adjunct (0 women).
Students: Average age 33. 24 applicants, 63% accepted, 3 enrolled.
Degree requirements: For master's, comprehensive exam.
Entrance requirements: For master's, GRE General Test, MAT, minimum GPA of 2.5. *Application deadline:* For fall admission, 7/20; for spring admission, 12/1. Applications are processed on a rolling basis. *Application fee:* $20.

Troy State University Dothan (continued)
Expenses: Tuition, state resident: part-time $138 per credit hour. Tuition, nonresident: part-time $276 per credit hour. Required fees: $64 per semester.
Dr. Priscilla McArthur, Head, 334-983-6556 Ext. 384.
Application contact: Reta Cordell, Director of Admissions and Records, 334-983-6556 Ext. 228, *Fax:* 334-983-6322, *E-mail:* rcordell@tsud.edu.

■ TULANE UNIVERSITY

Graduate School, Department of Political Science, New Orleans, LA 70118-5669

AWARDS MA, PhD.

Degree requirements: For master's, one foreign language, seminar, thesis optional; for doctorate, 2 foreign languages, thesis/dissertation.
Entrance requirements: For master's, GRE General Test, TSE, minimum B average in undergraduate course work; for doctorate, GRE General Test, TSE.
Expenses: Tuition: Full-time $24,675. Required fees: $2,210.

■ UNIVERSITY AT BUFFALO, THE STATE UNIVERSITY OF NEW YORK

Graduate School, College of Arts and Sciences, Department of Political Science, Buffalo, NY 14260

AWARDS MA, PhD.

Faculty: 15 full-time (3 women), 1 part-time/adjunct (0 women).
Students: 24 full-time (9 women), 9 part-time (2 women); includes 2 minority (both Asian Americans or Pacific Islanders), 13 international. Average age 28. 34 applicants, 56% accepted, 7 enrolled. In 2001, 7 master's, 4 doctorates awarded. Terminal master's awarded for partial completion of doctoral program.
Degree requirements: For master's, thesis or alternative, paper, project; for doctorate, thesis/dissertation, comprehensive exam.
Entrance requirements: For master's, GRE General Test, TOEFL, minimum GPA of 3.0; for doctorate, GRE General Test, TOEFL, minimum GPA of 3.3. *Application deadline:* For fall admission, 2/1; for spring admission, 11/1. Applications are processed on a rolling basis. *Application fee:* $35. Electronic applications accepted.
Expenses: Tuition, state resident: full-time $6,118. Tuition, nonresident: full-time $9,434.
Financial support: In 2001–02, 11 students received support, including 3 fellowships with full tuition reimbursements available (averaging $14,800 per year), 11 teaching assistantships with full tuition reimbursements available (averaging $8,400 per year); research assistantships, career-related internships or fieldwork, Federal Work-Study, tuition waivers (partial), and unspecified assistantships also available. Financial award application deadline: 2/1; financial award applicants required to submit FAFSA.
Faculty research: American politics, public law, comparative politics, international politics. *Total annual research expenditures:* $35,000.
Dr. Frank C. Zagare, Chairman, 716-645-2251 Ext. 522, *Fax:* 716-645-2166, *E-mail:* fczagare@acsu.buffalo.edu.
Application contact: Margaret M. Kasprzyk, Graduate Program Secretary, 716-645-2251 Ext. 518, *Fax:* 716-645-2166, *E-mail:* pscmmk@acsu.buffalo.edu. *Web site:* http://wings.buffalo.edu/pol-sci/

■ THE UNIVERSITY OF AKRON

Graduate School, Buchtel College of Arts and Sciences, Department of Political Science, Akron, OH 44325-0001

AWARDS Applied politics (MA); political science (MA). Part-time programs available.

Faculty: 13 full-time (4 women), 6 part-time/adjunct (4 women).
Students: 17 full-time (10 women), 5 part-time (2 women); includes 4 minority (3 African Americans, 1 Hispanic American), 5 international. Average age 31. 32 applicants, 91% accepted, 19 enrolled. In 2001, 12 degrees awarded.
Degree requirements: For master's, essay, seminars (political science); portfolio (applied politics).
Entrance requirements: For master's, minimum GPA of 2.75. *Application deadline:* For fall admission, 8/15. Applications are processed on a rolling basis. *Application fee:* $40 ($50 for international students).
Expenses: Tuition, state resident: full-time $6,562; part-time $219 per credit. Tuition, nonresident: full-time $9,027; part-time $383 per credit. Required fees: $272; $11 per credit. Tuition and fees vary according to course load.
Financial support: In 2001–02, 18 teaching assistantships with full tuition reimbursements were awarded; research assistantships with full tuition reimbursements, tuition waivers (full) also available. Financial award application deadline: 3/1.
Faculty research: Public policy, public opinion, applied election politics, international relations, comparative politics.
Dr. David Louscher, Chair, 330-972-6291, *E-mail:* dlouscher@uakron.edu.
Application contact: Dr. Bill Lyons, Graduate Adviser, 330-972-5855, *E-mail:* wtlyons@uakron.edu. *Web site:* http://www.uakron.edu/artsci/

■ THE UNIVERSITY OF ALABAMA

Graduate School, College of Arts and Sciences, Department of Political Science, Tuscaloosa, AL 35487

AWARDS Political science (MA, MPA, PhD); public administration (MPA, DPA). Part-time programs available.

Faculty: 14 full-time (4 women), 1 (woman) part-time/adjunct.
Students: 37 full-time (9 women), 44 part-time (14 women); includes 13 minority (9 African Americans, 2 Asian Americans or Pacific Islanders, 1 Hispanic American, 1 Native American), 2 international. Average age 37. 44 applicants, 30% accepted, 10 enrolled. In 2001, 7 master's, 8 doctorates awarded. Terminal master's awarded for partial completion of doctoral program.
Degree requirements: For master's, thesis optional; for doctorate, one foreign language, thesis/dissertation.
Entrance requirements: For master's and doctorate, GRE General Test, MAT, minimum GPA of 3.0. *Application deadline:* For fall admission, 7/6; for spring admission, 11/1. Applications are processed on a rolling basis. *Application fee:* $25.
Expenses: Tuition, state resident: full-time $3,292; part-time $183 per credit hour. Tuition, nonresident: full-time $8,912; part-time $495 per credit hour. Tuition and fees vary according to course load, campus/location and program.
Financial support: In 2001–02, 13 teaching assistantships with full tuition reimbursements (averaging $8,147 per year) were awarded; career-related internships or fieldwork and Federal Work-Study also available. Financial award application deadline: 2/1.
Faculty research: American politics, comparative politics, international relations, state government. *Total annual research expenditures:* $22,898.
Dr. David J. Lanoue, Chairperson, 205-348-5980, *Fax:* 205-348-5248.
Application contact: Dr. Don Snow, Graduate Studies Committee, 205-348-5980, *Fax:* 205-348-5248, *E-mail:* dsnow@tenhoor.as.ua.edu.

■ THE UNIVERSITY OF ARIZONA

Graduate College, College of Social and Behavioral Sciences, Department of Political Science, Tucson, AZ 85721

AWARDS MA, PhD.

Faculty: 33.
Students: 38 full-time (13 women), 7 part-time (3 women); includes 6 minority (1 African American, 1 Asian American or Pacific Islander, 3 Hispanic Americans, 1 Native American), 8 international. Average age 31. 57 applicants, 18% accepted, 9 enrolled. In 2001, 2 master's, 2 doctorates awarded.
Entrance requirements: For master's and doctorate, GRE General Test, GRE

Subject Test, TOEFL, TSE. *Application deadline:* For fall admission, 2/1. *Application fee:* $45.
Expenses: Tuition, state resident: full-time $2,490; part-time $436 per unit. Tuition, nonresident: full-time $10,300; part-time $436 per unit. Full-time tuition and fees vary according to degree level and program.
Financial support: In 2001–02, 28 students received support; fellowships, research assistantships, teaching assistantships, institutionally sponsored loans, scholarships/grants, health care benefits, tuition waivers (partial), and unspecified assistantships available.
Faculty research: Voting behavior, political participation, Soviet domestic and Sino-Soviet relations, presidential leadership and congressional behavior.
Dr. William Mishler, Head, 520-621-1093, *Fax:* 520-621-5051.
Application contact: Victoria Healey, Coordinator, 520-621-7600, *Fax:* 520-621-5051, *E-mail:* vhealey@u.arizona.edu. *Web site:* http://w3.arizona.edu/~polisci

■ UNIVERSITY OF ARKANSAS

Graduate School, J. William Fulbright College of Arts and Sciences, Department of Political Science, Program in Political Science, Fayetteville, AR 72701-1201

AWARDS MA.

Students: 14 full-time (9 women), 1 part-time, 3 international. 12 applicants, 100% accepted. In 2001, 13 degrees awarded.
Degree requirements: For master's, thesis or alternative.
Entrance requirements: For master's, GRE or MAT. *Application fee:* $40 ($50 for international students).
Expenses: Tuition, state resident: full-time $3,553; part-time $197 per credit. Tuition, nonresident: full-time $8,411; part-time $467 per credit. Required fees: $42 per credit. Tuition and fees vary according to course load and program.
Financial support: Teaching assistantships, career-related internships or fieldwork and Federal Work-Study available. Support available to part-time students. Financial award application deadline: 4/1; financial award applicants required to submit FAFSA.
Margaret Reid, Director, 479-575-3356, *E-mail:* mreid@comp.uark.edu.

■ UNIVERSITY OF CALIFORNIA, BERKELEY

Graduate Division, College of Letters and Science, Department of Political Science, Berkeley, CA 94720-1500

AWARDS PhD.

Faculty: 44 full-time (7 women), 1 (woman) part-time/adjunct.
Students: 153 full-time (58 women); includes 12 minority (3 African Americans, 6 Asian Americans or Pacific Islanders, 3 Hispanic Americans), 18 international. 411 applicants, 17% accepted, 29 enrolled. In 2001, 27 doctorates awarded.
Degree requirements: For doctorate, thesis/dissertation, oral qualifying exams.
Entrance requirements: For doctorate, GRE General Test, minimum GPA of 3.0. *Application deadline:* For fall admission, 12/15. *Application fee:* $60. Electronic applications accepted.
Expenses: Tuition, nonresident: full-time $10,704. Required fees: $4,349.
Financial support: Fellowships, research assistantships, teaching assistantships available.
Dr. Judith E. Gruber, Chair, 510-642-6326.
Application contact: Jane Stahlhut, Graduate Office Admissions Assistant, 510-643-4408, *Fax:* 510-642-9515, *E-mail:* janes@socrates.berkeley.edu. *Web site:* http://www.polisci.berkeley.edu/polisci/

■ UNIVERSITY OF CALIFORNIA, DAVIS

Graduate Studies, Program in Political Science, Davis, CA 95616

AWARDS MA, PhD.

Faculty: 22 full-time (5 women).
Students: 38 full-time (14 women); includes 2 Asian Americans or Pacific Islanders. Average age 31. 41 applicants, 44% accepted, 9 enrolled. In 2001, 4 master's, 4 doctorates awarded. Terminal master's awarded for partial completion of doctoral program.
Degree requirements: For master's and doctorate, thesis/dissertation.
Entrance requirements: For master's and doctorate, GRE General Test, minimum GPA of 3.0, sample of written work. *Application deadline:* For fall admission, 1/15. *Application fee:* $60. Electronic applications accepted.
Expenses: Tuition, state resident: full-time $4,831. Tuition, nonresident: full-time $15,725.
Financial support: In 2001–02, 33 students received support, including 9 fellowships with full and partial tuition reimbursements available (averaging $6,091 per year), 8 research assistantships with full and partial tuition reimbursements available (averaging $8,403 per year), 16 teaching assistantships with partial tuition reimbursements available (averaging $14,145 per year); Federal Work-Study, institutionally sponsored loans, scholarships/grants, and tuition waivers (full and partial) also available. Financial award application deadline: 1/15; financial award applicants required to submit FAFSA.
Faculty research: American government and politics, political theory, comparative politics, international relations, public law.
Walter Stone, Chair, 530-752-0976, *E-mail:* wstone@ucdavis.edu.
Application contact: Cindy Koga, Administrative Assistant, 530-752-2183, *Fax:* 530-752-8666, *E-mail:* cclpga@ucdavis.edu. *Web site:* http://ps.ucdavis.edu/

■ UNIVERSITY OF CALIFORNIA, IRVINE

Office of Research and Graduate Studies, School of Social Sciences, Department of Political Science, Irvine, CA 92697

AWARDS Political psychology (PhD); political sciences (PhD); public choice (PhD).

Faculty: 20.
Students: 42 full-time (17 women), 2 part-time (1 woman); includes 5 minority (1 Asian American or Pacific Islander, 4 Hispanic Americans), 1 international. 68 applicants, 25% accepted, 9 enrolled. In 2001, 3 degrees awarded.
Degree requirements: For doctorate, one foreign language, thesis/dissertation.
Entrance requirements: For doctorate, GRE General Test. *Application deadline:* For fall and spring admission, 1/15 (priority date); for winter admission, 10/15 (priority date). Applications are processed on a rolling basis. *Application fee:* $60. Electronic applications accepted.
Expenses: Tuition, nonresident: full-time $10,704. Required fees: $8,396. Tuition and fees vary according to course load, program and student level.
Financial support: Fellowships, research assistantships, teaching assistantships, institutionally sponsored loans and tuition waivers (full and partial) available. Financial award application deadline: 3/2; financial award applicants required to submit FAFSA.
Faculty research: Political psychology, political behavior, political economy, international relations, public choice.
Mark Petracca, Chair, 949-824-5175.
Application contact: Ivonne Maldonado, Graduate Counselor, 949-824-7352, *Fax:* 949-824-3548, *E-mail:* immaldon@uci.edu. *Web site:* http://www.socsci.uci.edu/pol/pol.html

■ UNIVERSITY OF CALIFORNIA, LOS ANGELES

Graduate Division, College of Letters and Science, Department of Political Science, Los Angeles, CA 90095

AWARDS MA, PhD.

Students: 115 full-time (37 women); includes 22 minority (5 African Americans, 13 Asian Americans or Pacific Islanders, 4 Hispanic Americans), 24 international. 235 applicants, 29% accepted, 15 enrolled. In 2001, 14 master's, 23 doctorates awarded.
Degree requirements: For master's, qualifying exams; for doctorate, one foreign language, thesis/dissertation, oral and written qualifying exams.
Entrance requirements: For master's, GRE General Test, minimum GPA of 3.0,

University of California, Los Angeles (continued)

sample of written work; for doctorate, GRE General Test, minimum undergraduate GPA of 3.0, sample of written work. *Application deadline:* For fall admission, 12/15. *Application fee:* $60. Electronic applications accepted.
Expenses: Tuition, nonresident: full-time $10,244. Required fees: $3,609. Full-time tuition and fees vary according to program.
Financial support: In 2001–02, 93 fellowships, 120 research assistantships, 114 teaching assistantships were awarded. Federal Work-Study, institutionally sponsored loans, scholarships/grants, and tuition waivers (full and partial) also available. Financial award application deadline: 3/1.
Dr. Michael Lofchie, Chair, 310-825-3372.
Application contact: Departmental Office, 310-825-3862, *E-mail:* escobedo@polisci.ucla.edu.

■ UNIVERSITY OF CALIFORNIA, RIVERSIDE

Graduate Division, Department of Political Science, Riverside, CA 92521-0102

AWARDS MA, PhD. Part-time programs available.

Faculty: 9 full-time (1 woman).
Students: 33 full-time (16 women); includes 7 minority (3 Asian Americans or Pacific Islanders, 3 Hispanic Americans, 1 Native American), 2 international. Average age 34. 35 applicants, 54% accepted, 9 enrolled. In 2001, 4 doctorates awarded. Terminal master's awarded for partial completion of doctoral program.
Degree requirements: For master's, comprehensive exams or thesis; for doctorate, variable foreign language requirement, thesis/dissertation, qualifying exams. *Median time to degree:* Master's–2.67 years full-time; doctorate–6 years full-time.
Entrance requirements: For master's and doctorate, GRE General Test, TOEFL, minimum GPA of 3.2. *Application deadline:* For fall admission, 5/1; for winter admission, 9/1; for spring admission, 12/1. Applications are processed on a rolling basis. *Application fee:* $40. Electronic applications accepted.
Expenses: Tuition, state resident: full-time $5,001. Tuition, nonresident: full-time $15,897.
Financial support: In 2001–02, 4 fellowships, 82 teaching assistantships with full and partial tuition reimbursements were awarded. Career-related internships or fieldwork also available. Financial award application deadline: 12/1; financial award applicants required to submit FAFSA.
Faculty research: American politics, mass political behavior, comparative politics, international relations, political theory.
Dr. Max Neiman, Graduate Adviser, 909-787-4693, *Fax:* 909-787-3933, *E-mail:* max.neiman@ucr.edu.
Application contact: Le Dina Joy, Graduate Program Assistant, 909-787-5597, *Fax:* 909-787-3933, *E-mail:* politics@ucr.edu. *Web site:* http://www.politicalscience.ucr.edu/

■ UNIVERSITY OF CALIFORNIA, SAN DIEGO

Graduate Studies and Research, Department of Political Science, La Jolla, CA 92093

AWARDS Latin American studies (MA); political science (PhD); political science and international affairs (PhD).

Faculty: 24.
Students: 68 (22 women). 167 applicants, 23% accepted, 19 enrolled. In 2001, 1 master's, 6 doctorates awarded.
Entrance requirements: For master's and doctorate, GRE General Test. *Application deadline:* For fall admission, 1/5. *Application fee:* $40. Electronic applications accepted.
Expenses: Tuition, nonresident: full-time $10,434. Required fees: $4,883.
David Lake, Chair.
Application contact: Christine Vaz, Graduate Coordinator, 619-534-3015.

■ UNIVERSITY OF CALIFORNIA, SAN DIEGO

Graduate Studies and Research, Graduate School of International Relations and Pacific Studies, La Jolla, CA 92093-0520

AWARDS Economics and international affairs (PhD); Pacific international affairs (MPIA); political science and international affairs (PhD). Part-time programs available.

Faculty: 24 full-time (3 women), 31 part-time/adjunct (12 women).
Students: 204 full-time (105 women); includes 44 minority (31 Asian Americans or Pacific Islanders, 13 Hispanic Americans), 86 international. Average age 27. 384 applicants, 61% accepted. In 2001, 87 master's, 1 doctorate awarded.
Degree requirements: For master's, one foreign language; for doctorate, thesis/dissertation. *Median time to degree:* Master's–2 years full-time, 3 years part-time.
Entrance requirements: For master's, GMAT or GRE General Test, TOEFL; for doctorate, GRE General Test, TOEFL. *Application deadline:* For fall admission, 2/15 (priority date). Applications are processed on a rolling basis. *Application fee:* $40. Electronic applications accepted.
Expenses: Tuition, nonresident: full-time $10,434. Required fees: $4,883.
Financial support: In 2001–02, 120 students received support, including 20 fellowships with full and partial tuition reimbursements available (averaging $6,387 per year), 11 research assistantships with partial tuition reimbursements available, 65 teaching assistantships with partial tuition reimbursements available; career-related internships or fieldwork, institutionally sponsored loans, and tuition waivers (full and partial) also available. Support available to part-time students. Financial award application deadline: 3/2; financial award applicants required to submit FAFSA.
Faculty research: Pacific Rim as system and placement in global relations; studies in international economics, management and finance; analysis patterns of policy making in countries of the Pacific.
Peter Cowhey, Dean, 858-534-1946, *Fax:* 858-534-3939.
Application contact: Jori J. Cincotta, Director of Admissions, 858-534-5914, *Fax:* 858-534-1135, *E-mail:* irps-apply@ucsd.edu. *Web site:* http://www-irps.ucsd.edu/

Find an in-depth description at www.petersons.com/gradchannel.

■ UNIVERSITY OF CALIFORNIA, SANTA BARBARA

Graduate Division, College of Letters and Sciences, Division of Social Science, Department of Political Science, Santa Barbara, CA 93106

AWARDS MA, PhD.

Degree requirements: For master's, thesis or alternative; for doctorate, variable foreign language requirement, thesis/dissertation.
Entrance requirements: For master's and doctorate, GRE General Test, TOEFL, sample of written work.

■ UNIVERSITY OF CALIFORNIA, SANTA CRUZ

Division of Graduate Studies, Division of Social Sciences, Politics Department, Santa Cruz, CA 95064

AWARDS PhD.

Faculty: 15 full-time.
Students: 13 full-time (6 women); includes 3 minority (2 Hispanic Americans, 1 Native American), 4 international. 35 applicants, 49% accepted.
Expenses: Tuition: Full-time $19,857.
Michael E. Urban, Chair, 831-459-5220.
Web site: http://www.politics.ucsc.edu/

■ UNIVERSITY OF CENTRAL FLORIDA

College of Arts and Sciences, Department of Political Science, Orlando, FL 32816

AWARDS MA. Part-time and evening/weekend programs available.

Faculty: 15 full-time (4 women), 4 part-time/adjunct (1 woman).

Students: 13 full-time (5 women), 16 part-time (8 women); includes 6 minority (3 African Americans, 1 Asian American or Pacific Islander, 2 Hispanic Americans), 3 international. Average age 31. 19 applicants, 95% accepted, 12 enrolled. In 2001, 7 degrees awarded.
Degree requirements: For master's, thesis, comprehensive exam.
Entrance requirements: For master's, GRE General Test, TOEFL, minimum GPA of 3.0 in last 60 hours. *Application deadline:* For fall admission, 7/15; for spring admission, 12/1. *Application fee:* $20. Electronic applications accepted.
Expenses: Tuition, state resident: part-time $162 per hour. Tuition, nonresident: part-time $569 per hour.
Financial support: In 2001–02, 4 fellowships with partial tuition reimbursements (averaging $2,500 per year), 12 research assistantships with partial tuition reimbursements (averaging $3,020 per year), 1 teaching assistantship with partial tuition reimbursement (averaging $5,500 per year) were awarded. Career-related internships or fieldwork, Federal Work-Study, institutionally sponsored loans, tuition waivers (partial), and unspecified assistantships also available. Financial award application deadline: 3/1; financial award applicants required to submit FAFSA.
Faculty research: Environment, presidential campaigning, term limits for elected officials.
Dr. R. L. Bledsoe, Chair, 407-823-2608, *Fax:* 407-823-0051, *E-mail:* rbledsoe@ucf1vm.cc.ucf.edu.
Application contact: Dr. Dwight Kiel, Coordinator, 407-823-2608, *Fax:* 407-823-0051, *E-mail:* kield@pegasus.cc.ucf.edu. *Web site:* http://www.ucf.edu/

■ UNIVERSITY OF CENTRAL OKLAHOMA

College of Graduate Studies and Research, College of Liberal Arts, Department of Political Science, Program in Political Science, Edmond, OK 73034-5209

AWARDS MA. Part-time programs available.

Faculty research: U. S. Congress.

■ UNIVERSITY OF CHICAGO

Division of Social Sciences, Department of Political Science, Chicago, IL 60637-1513

AWARDS PhD.

Students: 139.
Degree requirements: For doctorate, one foreign language, thesis/dissertation, exam, qualifying paper.
Entrance requirements: For doctorate, GRE General Test, TOEFL. *Application deadline:* For fall admission, 12/28. *Application fee:* $55. Electronic applications accepted.
Expenses: Tuition: Full-time $16,548.
Financial support: Fellowships, research assistantships, teaching assistantships, Federal Work-Study and institutionally sponsored loans available. Financial award application deadline: 12/28.
Faculty research: Political philosophy, international political economy, strategic studies, public policy and race relations, comparative politics (China, Middle East, Soviet Union, Africa, India, Japan).
Prof. Alexander Wendt, Chair, 773-702-3042.
Application contact: Office of the Dean of Students, 773-702-8415.

■ UNIVERSITY OF CINCINNATI

Division of Research and Advanced Studies, McMicken College of Arts and Sciences, Department of Political Science, Cincinnati, OH 45221

AWARDS MA, PhD.

Degree requirements: For master's, thesis (for some programs); for doctorate, thesis/dissertation.
Entrance requirements: For master's and doctorate, GRE General Test, GRE Subject Test, TOEFL. *Application deadline:* For fall admission, 2/1. *Application fee:* $30. Electronic applications accepted.
Expenses: Tuition, state resident: part-time $2,698 per quarter. Tuition, nonresident: part-time $4,977 per quarter.
Financial support: Fellowships, tuition waivers (partial) and unspecified assistantships available. Financial award application deadline: 5/1.
Dr. James Stever, Head, 513-556-3305, *Fax:* 513-556-2314, *E-mail:* james.stever@uc.edu.
Application contact: Dr. Richard Harknett, Graduate Program Director, 513-556-3314, *Fax:* 513-556-2314, *E-mail:* richard.harknett@uc.edu. *Web site:* http://ucaswww.mcm.uc.edu/

■ UNIVERSITY OF COLORADO AT BOULDER

Graduate School, College of Arts and Sciences, Department of Political Science, Boulder, CO 80309

AWARDS International affairs (MA); political science (MA, PhD); public policy analysis (MA).

Faculty: 26 full-time (5 women).
Students: 51 full-time (18 women), 14 part-time (6 women); includes 7 minority (1 African American, 2 Asian Americans or Pacific Islanders, 4 Hispanic Americans), 8 international. Average age 29. 51 applicants, 61% accepted. In 2001, 9 master's, 6 doctorates awarded. Terminal master's awarded for partial completion of doctoral program.
Degree requirements: For master's, thesis, comprehensive exam; for doctorate, one foreign language, thesis/dissertation.
Entrance requirements: For master's, GRE General Test, minimum undergraduate GPA of 3.0; for doctorate, GRE General Test, minimum GPA of 3.5 (undergraduate), 3.0 (graduate). *Application deadline:* For fall admission, 1/15 (priority date). *Application fee:* $50 ($60 for international students).
Expenses: Tuition, state resident: full-time $3,474. Tuition, nonresident: full-time $16,624.
Financial support: In 2001–02, 12 fellowships (averaging $2,836 per year), 3 research assistantships (averaging $17,735 per year), 32 teaching assistantships (averaging $17,902 per year) were awarded. Federal Work-Study also available. Financial award application deadline: 1/15.
Faculty research: American government and politics, comparative politics, international relations, public policy, law and politics. *Total annual research expenditures:* $985,125.
J. Samuel Fitch, Chair, 303-492-8601, *Fax:* 303-492-0978, *E-mail:* fitchs@colorado.edu.
Application contact: Mary Gregory, Graduate Program Assistant, 303-492-7872, *Fax:* 303-492-0978, *E-mail:* mary.gregory@colorado.edu. *Web site:* http://socsci.colorado.edu/POLSCI/

■ UNIVERSITY OF COLORADO AT DENVER

Graduate School, College of Liberal Arts and Sciences, Program in Political Science, Denver, CO 80217-3364

AWARDS MA. Part-time and evening/weekend programs available.

Faculty: 11 full-time (3 women).
Students: 13 full-time (6 women), 31 part-time (15 women); includes 13 minority (4 African Americans, 1 Asian American or Pacific Islander, 7 Hispanic Americans, 1 Native American), 3 international. Average age 28. 15 applicants, 80% accepted, 9 enrolled. In 2001, 6 degrees awarded.
Degree requirements: For master's, thesis or alternative.
Entrance requirements: For master's, GRE, 18 hours in political science. *Application deadline:* For fall admission, 6/1; for spring admission, 11/1. Applications are processed on a rolling basis. *Application fee:* $50 ($60 for international students). Electronic applications accepted.
Expenses: Tuition, state resident: full-time $3,284; part-time $198 per credit hour. Tuition, nonresident: full-time $13,380; part-time $802 per credit hour. Required fees: $444; $222 per semester.
Financial support: Research assistantships, teaching assistantships, Federal Work-Study available. Financial award application deadline: 3/1; financial award applicants required to submit FAFSA.

University of Colorado at Denver (continued)

Glenn Morris, Chair, 303-556-6243, *Fax:* 303-556-6041, *E-mail:* gmorris@carbon.cudenver.edu.

Application contact: Jana Smilanich, Program Assistant, 303-556-3556, *Fax:* 303-556-6041, *E-mail:* jsmilani@carbon.cudenver.edu. *Web site:* http://www.cudenver.edu/psrp/psrp.html

■ UNIVERSITY OF CONNECTICUT

Graduate School, College of Liberal Arts and Sciences, Department of Political Science, Field of Political Science, Storrs, CT 06269

AWARDS MA, PhD.

Degree requirements: For doctorate, 2 foreign languages, thesis/dissertation.
Entrance requirements: For master's and doctorate, GRE General Test.

■ UNIVERSITY OF DALLAS

Braniff Graduate School of Liberal Arts, Institute of Philosophic Studies, Doctoral Program in Politics, Irving, TX 75062-4736

AWARDS PhD.

Faculty: 3 full-time (0 women).
Students: 12 (3 women). Average age 31. 5 applicants, 80% accepted. In 2001, 4 degrees awarded.
Degree requirements: For doctorate, 2 foreign languages, thesis/dissertation.
Entrance requirements: For doctorate, GRE General Test. *Application deadline:* For fall admission, 2/15 (priority date); for spring admission, 11/15. Applications are processed on a rolling basis. *Application fee:* $40.
Expenses: Tuition: Full-time $3,807; part-time $423 per credit.
Financial support: Research assistantships, tuition remissions available. Financial award application deadline: 2/15.
Faculty research: Classical, medieval, and modern political philosophy; American political thought and institutions; politics and literature.
Dr. Leo Paul de Alvarez, Chair, 972-721-5344, *Fax:* 972-721-4007, *E-mail:* alvarez@udallas.edu.
Application contact: Graduate Coordinator, 972-721-5106, *Fax:* 972-721-5280, *E-mail:* graduate@acad.udallas.edu. *Web site:* http://www.udallas.edu/bgs/politics.html/

■ UNIVERSITY OF DALLAS

Braniff Graduate School of Liberal Arts, Master's Program in Politics, Irving, TX 75062-4736

AWARDS M Pol, MA. Part-time programs available.

Faculty: 3 full-time (0 women).
Students: 5 (1 woman). Average age 31. 15 applicants, 53% accepted. In 2001, 8 degrees awarded.
Degree requirements: For master's, one foreign language, thesis, comprehensive exam.
Entrance requirements: For master's, GRE General Test. *Application deadline:* For fall admission, 2/15 (priority date); for spring admission, 11/15. Applications are processed on a rolling basis. *Application fee:* $40.
Expenses: Tuition: Full-time $3,807; part-time $423 per credit.
Financial support: Scholarships/grants, tuition waivers, and tuition remissions available. Financial award application deadline: 2/15.
Faculty research: Classical, medieval, and modern political philosophy; American political thought and institutions; politics and literature.
Dr. Leo Paul de Alvarez, Chair, 972-721-5344, *Fax:* 972-721-4007, *E-mail:* alvarez@udallas.edu.
Application contact: Graduate Coordinator, 972-721-5106, *Fax:* 972-721-5280, *E-mail:* graduate@acad.udallas.edu. *Web site:* http://www.udallas.edu/bgs/politicsmas.html/

■ UNIVERSITY OF DELAWARE

College of Arts and Science, Department of Political Science and International Relations, Newark, DE 19716

AWARDS International relations (MA); political science (MA, PhD).

Faculty: 25 full-time (6 women).
Students: 32 full-time (12 women), 3 part-time; includes 4 minority (2 African Americans, 1 Hispanic American, 1 Native American), 13 international. Average age 29. 62 applicants, 29% accepted, 10 enrolled. In 2001, 8 master's, 2 doctorates awarded. Terminal master's awarded for partial completion of doctoral program.
Degree requirements: For master's, one foreign language; for doctorate, one foreign language, thesis/dissertation. *Median time to degree:* Master's–2 years full-time; doctorate–7 years full-time.
Entrance requirements: For master's and doctorate, GRE General Test, TOEFL, minimum GPA of 3.2 in major, 3.0 overall. *Application deadline:* For fall admission, 7/1 (priority date). *Application fee:* $50. Electronic applications accepted.
Expenses: Tuition, state resident: full-time $4,770; part-time $265 per credit. Tuition, nonresident: full-time $13,860; part-time $770 per credit. Required fees: $414.
Financial support: In 2001–02, 23 students received support, including 1 fellowship with full tuition reimbursement available (averaging $10,800 per year), 1 research assistantship with full tuition reimbursement available (averaging $11,000 per year), 14 teaching assistantships with full tuition reimbursements available (averaging $10,600 per year); career-related internships or fieldwork, Federal Work-Study, institutionally sponsored loans, scholarships/grants, and tuition waivers (full and partial) also available. Financial award application deadline: 2/1.
Faculty research: Human rights and humanitarian interventions, ethnic conflict, international migration, health policy, environmental and disaster policy, complexity theory, public law.
Dr. Joseph Pika, Acting Chairperson, 302-831-2355, *Fax:* 302-831-4452, *E-mail:* jpika@udel.edu.
Application contact: William H. Meyer, Director of Graduate Studies, 302-831-2355, *Fax:* 302-831-4452, *E-mail:* whmeyer@udel.edu. *Web site:* http://www.udel.edu/catalog/current/as/psc/grad.html#overview

■ UNIVERSITY OF FLORIDA

Graduate School, College of Liberal Arts and Sciences, Department of Political Science, Gainesville, FL 32611

AWARDS International development policy (MA); international relations (MA, MAT, PhD); political campaigning (MA, Certificate); political science (MA, MAT, PhD); public affairs (MA, Certificate). Part-time programs available. Terminal master's awarded for partial completion of doctoral program.

Degree requirements: For master's, variable foreign language requirement, thesis or alternative; for doctorate, variable foreign language requirement, thesis/dissertation.
Entrance requirements: For master's and doctorate, GRE General Test, minimum GPA of 3.0. Electronic applications accepted.
Expenses: Tuition, state resident: part-time $164 per hour. Tuition, nonresident: part-time $571 per hour. Tuition and fees vary according to course level and program.
Faculty research: U.S. political development, religion and politics, environmental politics and policy, developing societies, international relations. *Web site:* http://clas.ufl.edu/polisci/

■ UNIVERSITY OF GEORGIA

Graduate School, College of Arts and Sciences, Department of Political Science, Program in Political Science, Athens, GA 30602

AWARDS MA, PhD.

Faculty: 32 full-time (4 women).
Students: 31 full-time (10 women), 10 part-time (5 women); includes 2 minority (both Asian Americans or Pacific Islanders), 11 international. 100 applicants, 25% accepted. In 2001, 6 master's, 7 doctorates awarded.

Degree requirements: For master's and doctorate, one foreign language, thesis/dissertation.
Entrance requirements: For master's and doctorate, GRE General Test. *Application deadline:* For fall admission, 7/1 (priority date); for spring admission, 11/15. *Application fee:* $30. Electronic applications accepted.
Expenses: Tuition, state resident: full-time $2,376; part-time $132 per credit hour. Tuition, nonresident: full-time $9,504; part-time $528 per credit hour. Required fees: $236 per semester.
Financial support: Fellowships, research assistantships, teaching assistantships, unspecified assistantships available.
Application contact: Dr. Arnold P. Fleischmann, Graduate Coordinator, 706-542-2994, *Fax:* 706-542-4421, *E-mail:* arnie@uga.edu. *Web site:* http://www.uga.edu/~pol-sci/

■ UNIVERSITY OF HAWAII AT MANOA

Graduate Division, College of Arts and Sciences, College of Social Sciences, Department of Political Science, Honolulu, HI 96822

AWARDS MA, PhD.

Faculty: 26 full-time (6 women), 3 part-time/adjunct (0 women).
Students: 76 full-time (35 women), 42 part-time (21 women); includes 4 African Americans, 28 Asian Americans or Pacific Islanders, 2 Hispanic Americans. Average age 33. 82 applicants, 78% accepted. In 2001, 16 master's, 16 doctorates awarded. Terminal master's awarded for partial completion of doctoral program.
Degree requirements: For master's, thesis optional; for doctorate, thesis/dissertation.
Entrance requirements: For master's and doctorate, GRE. *Application deadline:* For fall admission, 2/1. *Application fee:* $25 ($50 for international students).
Expenses: Tuition, state resident: full-time $2,160; part-time $1,980 per year. Tuition, nonresident: full-time $5,190; part-time $4,829 per year.
Financial support: In 2001–02, 2 research assistantships (averaging $16,284 per year), 7 teaching assistantships (averaging $13,996 per year) were awarded. Career-related internships or fieldwork, Federal Work-Study, and institutionally sponsored loans also available. Support available to part-time students. Financial award application deadline: 3/1.
Faculty research: Asia/Pacific, political economy, human rights, futures, postmodernism.
Dr. Sankeran Krishna, Chair, 808-956-8357.
Application contact: Dr. Jon Goldberg-Hiller, Graduate Field Chairperson, 808-956-8630, *Fax:* 808-956-6877, *E-mail:* hiller@hawaii.edu.

■ UNIVERSITY OF HOUSTON

College of Liberal Arts and Social Sciences, Department of Political Science, Houston, TX 77204

AWARDS MA, PhD. Part-time and evening/weekend programs available.

Faculty: 16 full-time (2 women), 4 part-time/adjunct (0 women).
Students: 39 full-time (13 women), 65 part-time (24 women); includes 24 minority (3 African Americans, 11 Asian Americans or Pacific Islanders, 9 Hispanic Americans, 1 Native American), 6 international. Average age 33. In 2001, 8 master's, 5 doctorates awarded.
Degree requirements: For doctorate, thesis/dissertation.
Entrance requirements: For master's and doctorate, GRE General Test, minimum GPA of 3.0. *Application deadline:* For fall admission, 4/1; for spring admission, 10/1. Applications are processed on a rolling basis. *Application fee:* $0.
Expenses: Tuition, state resident: full-time $1,512. Tuition, nonresident: full-time $5,310. Required fees: $1,308. Tuition and fees vary according to program.
Financial support: In 2001–02, 3 research assistantships with tuition reimbursements, 19 teaching assistantships with tuition reimbursements (averaging $11,500 per year) were awarded. Institutionally sponsored loans also available. Support available to part-time students.
Faculty research: American politics, political theory, judicial process, public policy, comparative politics.
Dr. Kent Tedin, Chairman, 713-743-3890.
Application contact: Director of Graduate Studies, 713-743-3890, *E-mail:* polsgrad@bayou.uh.edu. *Web site:* http://www.uh.edu/

■ UNIVERSITY OF IDAHO

College of Graduate Studies, College of Letters and Science, Department of Political Science, Program in Political Science, Moscow, ID 83844-2282

AWARDS MA, PhD.

Students: 4 full-time (2 women), 7 part-time (2 women), 4 international. In 2001, 2 doctorates awarded.
Degree requirements: For doctorate, thesis/dissertation.
Entrance requirements: For master's, minimum GPA of 2.8; for doctorate, minimum undergraduate GPA of 2.8, 3.0 graduate. *Application deadline:* For fall admission, 8/1; for spring admission, 12/15. *Application fee:* $35 ($45 for international students).
Expenses: Tuition, state resident: full-time $1,613. Tuition, nonresident: full-time $3,000.
Financial support: Application deadline: 2/15.
Dr. Donald W. Crowley, Chair, Department of Political Science, 208-885-7290.

■ UNIVERSITY OF ILLINOIS AT CHICAGO

Graduate College, College of Liberal Arts and Sciences, Department of Political Science, Chicago, IL 60607-7128

AWARDS Political science (MA); public policy analysis (PhD). Part-time programs available.

Faculty: 19 full-time (3 women).
Students: 15 full-time (6 women), 35 part-time (14 women); includes 13 minority (5 African Americans, 2 Asian Americans or Pacific Islanders, 5 Hispanic Americans, 1 Native American), 8 international. Average age 34. 38 applicants, 50% accepted, 12 enrolled. In 2001, 5 master's, 5 doctorates awarded.
Degree requirements: For master's, thesis or comprehensive exam.
Entrance requirements: For master's, GRE General Test, TOEFL, minimum GPA of 4.0 on a 5.0 scale. *Application deadline:* For fall admission, 6/1; for spring admission, 11/1. Applications are processed on a rolling basis. *Application fee:* $40 ($50 for international students). Electronic applications accepted.
Expenses: Tuition, state resident: full-time $3,060. Tuition, nonresident: full-time $6,688.
Financial support: In 2001–02, 17 students received support; fellowships with full tuition reimbursements available, research assistantships with full tuition reimbursements available, teaching assistantships with full tuition reimbursements available, Federal Work-Study, institutionally sponsored loans, and tuition waivers (full) available. Financial award application deadline: 3/15; financial award applicants required to submit FAFSA.
Faculty research: Policy analysis/national urban politics and policy, electoral behavior.
Barry Rundquist, Acting Chair, 312-413-2190, *E-mail:* barryr@uic.edu.
Application contact: Thomas Carsey, Director of Graduate Studies, 312-996-8660.

■ UNIVERSITY OF ILLINOIS AT SPRINGFIELD

Graduate Programs, College of Public Affairs and Administration, Program in Political Studies, Springfield, IL 62703-5404

AWARDS MA. Part-time and evening/weekend programs available.

Faculty: 7 full-time (1 woman), 9 part-time/adjunct (3 women).
Students: 15 full-time (9 women), 53 part-time (20 women); includes 9 African Americans, 1 Hispanic American, 1 Native American. Average age 32. 33 applicants, 97% accepted, 29 enrolled. In 2001, 11 degrees awarded.
Degree requirements: For master's, thesis or alternative.

University of Illinois at Springfield (continued)
Application deadline: Applications are processed on a rolling basis. *Application fee:* $0.
Expenses: Tuition, state resident: full-time $2,680. Tuition, nonresident: full-time $8,064. Required fees: $626. One-time fee: $626.
Financial support: In 2001–02, 46 students received support, including 7 research assistantships with full and partial tuition reimbursements available (averaging $6,300 per year); career-related internships or fieldwork, Federal Work-Study, scholarships/grants, and unspecified assistantships also available. Support available to part-time students. Financial award application deadline: 6/1; financial award applicants required to submit FAFSA.
Faculty research: Democratization and quality of life.
Calvin Moulw, Chair, 217-206-6646.

■ UNIVERSITY OF ILLINOIS AT URBANA–CHAMPAIGN

Graduate College, College of Liberal Arts and Sciences, Department of Political Science, Champaign, IL 61820

AWARDS AM, PhD.

Faculty: 25 full-time, 3 part-time/adjunct.
Students: 36 full-time (13 women); includes 5 minority (4 African Americans, 1 Asian American or Pacific Islander), 6 international. 107 applicants, 7% accepted. In 2001, 4 master's, 1 doctorate awarded.
Degree requirements: For doctorate, thesis/dissertation.
Entrance requirements: For master's, GRE General Test, minimum GPA of 3.0; for doctorate, GRE. *Application deadline:* Applications are processed on a rolling basis. *Application fee:* $40 ($50 for international students). Electronic applications accepted.
Expenses: Tuition, state resident: part-time $3,227 per degree program. Tuition, nonresident: part-time $7,169 per degree program. Tuition and fees vary according to program.
Financial support: In 2001–02, 3 fellowships, 11 research assistantships, 20 teaching assistantships were awarded. Financial award application deadline: 2/15.
Peter Nardulli, Head, 217-333-3880, *Fax:* 217-244-5712, *E-mail:* nardulli@uiuc.edu.
Application contact: Julie Elliott, Staff Secretary, 217-333-2575, *Fax:* 217-244-5712, *E-mail:* jelliott@uiuc.edu. *Web site:* http://www.pol.uiuc.edu/

■ THE UNIVERSITY OF IOWA

Graduate College, College of Liberal Arts and Sciences, Department of Political Science, Iowa City, IA 52242-1316

AWARDS MA, PhD, JD/PhD.

Faculty: 24 full-time, 2 part-time/adjunct.
Students: 27 full-time (6 women), 15 part-time (5 women); includes 1 minority (Hispanic American), 6 international. 48 applicants, 42% accepted, 8 enrolled. In 2001, 13 master's, 2 doctorates awarded.
Degree requirements: For master's, exam, thesis optional; for doctorate, thesis/dissertation, comprehensive exam.
Entrance requirements: For master's, GRE General Test, TOEFL; for doctorate, GRE General Test, TOEFL, minimum GPA of 3.0. *Application deadline:* Applications are processed on a rolling basis. *Application fee:* $30 ($50 for international students). Electronic applications accepted.
Expenses: Tuition, state resident: full-time $3,702; part-time $206 per semester hour. Tuition, nonresident: full-time $11,924; part-time $206 per semester hour. Required fees: $101 per semester. Tuition and fees vary according to course load and program.
Financial support: In 2001–02, 5 fellowships, 4 research assistantships, 23 teaching assistantships were awarded. Financial award application deadline: 2/15; financial award applicants required to submit FAFSA.
William Reisinger, Chair, 319-335-2358, *Fax:* 319-335-3400.

■ UNIVERSITY OF KANSAS

Graduate School, College of Liberal Arts and Sciences, Division of Government, Program in Political Science, Lawrence, KS 66045

AWARDS MA, PhD.

Faculty: 33.
Students: 35 full-time (11 women), 14 part-time (4 women); includes 4 minority (1 African American, 2 Asian Americans or Pacific Islanders, 1 Hispanic American), 17 international. Average age 30. 34 applicants, 53% accepted, 10 enrolled. In 2001, 6 master's, 1 doctorate awarded.
Degree requirements: For master's, thesis or alternative; for doctorate, thesis/dissertation.
Entrance requirements: For master's, GRE General Test, TOEFL, TSE; for doctorate, GRE General Test, GRE Subject Test, TOEFL, TSE. *Application deadline:* For fall admission, 1/10. *Application fee:* $35.
Expenses: Tuition, state resident: full-time $2,722; part-time $113 per credit. Tuition, nonresident: full-time $8,586; part-time $358 per credit. Required fees: $551; $46 per credit. Tuition and fees vary according to campus/location, program and reciprocity agreements.
Financial support: In 2001–02, 10 fellowships (averaging $4,000 per year), 5 research assistantships with partial tuition reimbursements (averaging $8,840 per year), 14 teaching assistantships with full and partial tuition reimbursements (averaging $9,449 per year) were awarded.
Faculty research: Interest groups, democratization, quantitative approaches, public administration.
Paul Schumaker, Chair, 785-864-3523, *Fax:* 785-864-5700, *E-mail:* pauljohn@ku.edu.
Application contact: Paul Johnson, Graduate Director, 785-864-3523, *Fax:* 785-864-5700, *E-mail:* pauljohn@ku.edu. *Web site:* http://www.ku.edu/~kups/

■ UNIVERSITY OF KENTUCKY

Graduate School, Graduate School Programs from the College of Arts and Sciences, Program in Political Science, Lexington, KY 40506-0032

AWARDS MA, PhD.

Faculty: 29 full-time (5 women).
Students: 9 full-time (7 women), 28 part-time (1 woman); includes 1 minority (African American), 9 international. 46 applicants, 50% accepted. In 2001, 3 master's, 4 doctorates awarded.
Degree requirements: For master's, thesis optional; for doctorate, thesis/dissertation, comprehensive exam.
Entrance requirements: For master's, GRE General Test, minimum undergraduate GPA of 2.5; for doctorate, GRE General Test, minimum graduate GPA of 3.0. *Application deadline:* For fall admission, 7/19. Applications are processed on a rolling basis. *Application fee:* $30 ($35 for international students).
Expenses: Tuition, state resident: full-time $4,075; part-time $213 per credit hour. Tuition, nonresident: full-time $11,295; part-time $614 per credit hour.
Financial support: In 2001–02, 2 fellowships, 2 research assistantships, 12 teaching assistantships were awarded. Federal Work-Study, institutionally sponsored loans, and unspecified assistantships also available. Support available to part-time students. Financial award application deadline: 2/1.
Faculty research: International political economy, critical policy studies, regional conflict and integration, race and American politics, media studies. *Total annual research expenditures:* $25,000.
Dr. Stuart Kaufman, Director of Graduate Studies, 859-257-7040, *Fax:* 859-257-7034, *E-mail:* sjkauf00@pop.uky.edu.
Application contact: Dr. Jeannine Blackwell, Associate Dean, 859-257-4905, *Fax:* 859-323-1928.

■ UNIVERSITY OF LOUISVILLE

Graduate School, College of Arts and Sciences, Department of Political Science, Louisville, KY 40292-0001

AWARDS MA.

Students: 14 full-time (7 women), 12 part-time (5 women); includes 3 minority (2 African Americans, 1 Asian American or Pacific Islander). Average age 30. In 2001, 12 degrees awarded.

Entrance requirements: For master's, GRE General Test. *Application deadline:* For fall admission, 8/1; for spring admission, 12/1. Applications are processed on a rolling basis. *Application fee:* $25.
Expenses: Tuition, state resident: full-time $4,134. Tuition, nonresident: full-time $11,486.
Financial support: In 2001–02, 2 research assistantships with full tuition reimbursements (averaging $10,000 per year) were awarded
Dr. Charles E. Ziegler, Chair, 502-852-6831, *Fax:* 502-852-7923, *E-mail:* cezieg01@athena.louisville.edu.

■ UNIVERSITY OF MARYLAND, COLLEGE PARK

Graduate Studies and Research, College of Behavioral and Social Sciences, Department of Government and Politics, College Park, MD 20742

AWARDS American politics (MA, PhD); comparative politics (MA, PhD); international relations (MA, PhD); political economy (MA, PhD); political theory (MA, PhD). Part-time and evening/weekend programs available.

Faculty: 55 full-time (15 women), 6 part-time/adjunct (2 women).
Students: 96 full-time (43 women), 39 part-time (21 women); includes 25 minority (16 African Americans, 2 Asian Americans or Pacific Islanders, 7 Hispanic Americans), 26 international. 235 applicants, 26% accepted, 28 enrolled. In 2001, 23 master's, 17 doctorates awarded. Terminal master's awarded for partial completion of doctoral program.
Degree requirements: For master's, comprehensive field exam, thesis optional; for doctorate, thesis/dissertation, written exams in 2 fields.
Entrance requirements: For master's and doctorate, GRE General Test, minimum GPA of 3.5, writing sample. *Application deadline:* For fall admission, 2/1. Applications are processed on a rolling basis. *Application fee:* $50 ($70 for international students). Electronic applications accepted.
Expenses: Tuition, state resident: part-time $289 per credit hour. Tuition, nonresident: part-time $448 per credit hour. One-time fee: $436 part-time. Full-time tuition and fees vary according to course load, campus/location and program.
Financial support: In 2001–02, 13 fellowships with full tuition reimbursements (averaging $12,612 per year), 1 research assistantship with tuition reimbursement (averaging $12,475 per year), 70 teaching assistantships with tuition reimbursements (averaging $11,923 per year) were awarded. Career-related internships or fieldwork, Federal Work-Study, scholarships/grants, and unspecified assistantships also available. Support available to part-time students. Financial award applicants required to submit FAFSA.
Faculty research: International development/conflict, international security, post-communist society, public service.
Dr. Jonathan Wilkenfeld, Chairman, 301-405-4160, *Fax:* 301-314-9690.
Application contact: Trudy Lindsey, Director, Graduate Admissions and Records, 301-405-6991, *Fax:* 301-314-9305, *E-mail:* grschool@deans.umd.edu.

■ UNIVERSITY OF MASSACHUSETTS AMHERST

Graduate School, College of Social and Behavioral Sciences, Department of Political Science, Amherst, MA 01003

AWARDS MA, PhD. Part-time programs available.

Faculty: 29 full-time (6 women).
Students: 34 full-time (14 women), 36 part-time (16 women); includes 8 minority (2 African Americans, 1 Asian American or Pacific Islander, 5 Hispanic Americans), 13 international. Average age 31. 109 applicants, 40% accepted. In 2001, 10 master's, 4 doctorates awarded. Terminal master's awarded for partial completion of doctoral program.
Degree requirements: For master's, thesis or alternative; for doctorate, one foreign language, thesis/dissertation.
Entrance requirements: For master's and doctorate, GRE General Test. *Application deadline:* For fall admission, 2/1. Applications are processed on a rolling basis. *Application fee:* $40 ($50 for international students).
Expenses: Tuition, state resident: full-time $1,980; part-time $110 per credit. Tuition, nonresident: full-time $7,456; part-time $414 per credit. Required fees: $4,112. One-time fee: $115 full-time.
Financial support: In 2001–02, 15 fellowships with full tuition reimbursements (averaging $6,826 per year), 33 research assistantships with full tuition reimbursements (averaging $6,795 per year), 36 teaching assistantships with full tuition reimbursements (averaging $9,087 per year) were awarded. Career-related internships or fieldwork, Federal Work-Study, scholarships/grants, traineeships, and unspecified assistantships also available. Support available to part-time students. Financial award application deadline: 2/1.
Dr. Jerome Mileur, Chair, 413-545-2438, *Fax:* 413-545-3349, *E-mail:* jmileur@polsci.umass.edu.

■ UNIVERSITY OF MASSACHUSETTS BOSTON

Office of Graduate Studies and Research, Division of Continuing Education, Program in Women in Politics and Government, Boston, MA 02125-3393

AWARDS Certificate. Part-time and evening/weekend programs available.

Degree requirements: For Certificate, practicum, final project.
Entrance requirements: For degree, interview, minimum GPA of 2.75.

■ THE UNIVERSITY OF MEMPHIS

Graduate School, College of Arts and Sciences, Department of Political Science, Memphis, TN 38152

AWARDS MA.

Faculty: 8 full-time (1 woman).
Students: 7 full-time (2 women), 3 international. Average age 29. 8 applicants, 63% accepted. In 2001, 6 degrees awarded.
Degree requirements: For master's, thesis or alternative, internship, comprehensive exam.
Entrance requirements: For master's, GRE General Test or GMAT, minimum GPA of 3.0. *Application deadline:* For fall admission, 8/1; for spring admission, 12/1. Applications are processed on a rolling basis. *Application fee:* $25 ($50 for international students).
Expenses: Tuition, state resident: full-time $2,026. Tuition, nonresident: full-time $4,528.
Financial support: Research assistantships available.
Faculty research: Political philosophy, comparative judicial studies, conflict studies, legislative studies, foreign policy. *Total annual research expenditures:* $6,000.
T. David Mason, Coordinator, 901-678-4879, *Fax:* 901-678-2483, *E-mail:* tdmason@memphis.edu.
Application contact: James R. Carruth, Coordinator of Graduate Studies, 901-678-3360, *Fax:* 901-678-2981, *E-mail:* jrcarrth@memphis.edu.

■ UNIVERSITY OF MIAMI

Graduate School, School of Business Administration, Department of Political Science, Coral Gables, FL 33124

AWARDS MPA, MPA/MPH. Part-time and evening/weekend programs available.

Faculty: 10 full-time (2 women), 4 part-time/adjunct (2 women).
Students: 7 full-time (5 women), 14 part-time (10 women); includes 14 minority (5 African Americans, 2 Asian Americans or Pacific Islanders, 7 Hispanic Americans). 26 applicants, 46% accepted. In 2001, 7 degrees awarded.
Degree requirements: For master's, thesis optional.

University of Miami (continued)
Entrance requirements: For master's, GRE General Test, TOEFL. *Application deadline:* For fall admission, 6/30 (priority date); for spring admission, 10/31. Applications are processed on a rolling basis. *Application fee:* $50.
Expenses: Tuition: Part-time $960 per credit hour. Required fees: $85 per semester. Tuition and fees vary according to program.
Financial support: In 2001–02, 6 research assistantships were awarded; career-related internships or fieldwork and Federal Work-Study also available. Financial award application deadline: 3/1.
Dr. June F. Dreyer, Chairperson, 305-284-2401, *Fax:* 305-284-3636. *Web site:* http://www.miami.edu/political-science

■ UNIVERSITY OF MICHIGAN

Horace H. Rackham School of Graduate Studies, College of Literature, Science, and the Arts, Department of Political Science, Ann Arbor, MI 48109

AWARDS Political science (AM, PhD); social work and political science (PhD).

Faculty: 42 full-time (12 women), 9 part-time/adjunct (3 women).
Students: 94 full-time (51 women); includes 24 minority (17 African Americans, 7 Hispanic Americans), 30 international. Average age 25. 226 applicants, 16% accepted. In 2001, 6 master's, 18 doctorates awarded. Terminal master's awarded for partial completion of doctoral program.
Degree requirements: For master's, thesis, none; for doctorate, thesis/dissertation, oral defense of dissertation, preliminary exam, comprehensive exam, registration. *Median time to degree:* Master's–2 years full-time; doctorate–9 years full-time.
Entrance requirements: For master's and doctorate, GRE General Test. *Application deadline:* For fall admission, 1/5. *Application fee:* $55. Electronic applications accepted.
Financial support: In 2001–02, 43 fellowships with full tuition reimbursements (averaging $14,000 per year), 8 research assistantships with full tuition reimbursements (averaging $14,000 per year), 35 teaching assistantships with full tuition reimbursements (averaging $14,000 per year) were awarded. Career-related internships or fieldwork also available. Financial award application deadline: 1/5.
Faculty research: Political theory, American politics, world politics, comparative politics.
Daniel H. Levine, Chair, 734-764-6313, *Fax:* 734-764-3522.
Application contact: Michelle L. Spornhauer, Student Services Assistant, 734-763-2226, *Fax:* 734-764-3522, *E-mail:* migalita@umich.edu. *Web site:* http://polisci.lsa.umich.edu/

■ UNIVERSITY OF MINNESOTA, TWIN CITIES CAMPUS

Graduate School, College of Liberal Arts, Department of Political Science, Minneapolis, MN 55455-0213

AWARDS MA, PhD. Part-time programs available.

Faculty: 29 full-time (6 women), 4 part-time/adjunct (2 women).
Students: 77 full-time (38 women), 5 part-time (2 women). Average age 25. 196 applicants, 20% accepted. In 2001, 1 master's, 11 doctorates awarded. Terminal master's awarded for partial completion of doctoral program.
Degree requirements: For doctorate, thesis/dissertation, one foreign language or statistics.
Entrance requirements: For master's and doctorate, GRE. *Application fee:* $50 ($55 for international students). Electronic applications accepted.
Expenses: Tuition, state resident: full-time $2,932; part-time $489 per credit. Tuition, nonresident: full-time $5,758; part-time $960 per credit. Part-time tuition and fees vary according to course load, program and reciprocity agreements.
Financial support: In 2001–02, 54 students received support, including 9 fellowships with full tuition reimbursements available (averaging $15,000 per year), 13 research assistantships with full tuition reimbursements available (averaging $15,000 per year), 27 teaching assistantships with full tuition reimbursements available (averaging $15,000 per year); career-related internships or fieldwork also available. Financial award application deadline: 1/1.
Faculty research: Political psychology, political economy, social policy, legislative studies, history of political thought. *Total annual research expenditures:* $1.1 million.
John Freeman, Chair, 612-624-4144, *Fax:* 612-626-7599.
Application contact: Judith Mitchell, Assistant to Director of Graduate Studies, 612-624-4144, *Fax:* 612-626-7599, *E-mail:* office@polisci.umn.edu. *Web site:* http://www.polisci.umn.edu/

■ UNIVERSITY OF MISSISSIPPI

Graduate School, College of Liberal Arts, Department of Political Science, Oxford, University, MS 38677

AWARDS MA, PhD.

Faculty: 12.
Students: 11 full-time (3 women), 3 part-time (1 woman); includes 1 minority (African American), 3 international. In 2001, 3 master's, 1 doctorate awarded.
Degree requirements: For doctorate, thesis/dissertation.
Entrance requirements: For master's, GRE General Test, TOEFL, minimum GPA of 3.0; for doctorate, GRE General Test, TOEFL. *Application deadline:* For fall admission, 8/1. Applications are processed on a rolling basis. *Application fee:* $0 ($25 for international students).
Expenses: Tuition, state resident: full-time $3,626; part-time $202 per hour. Tuition, nonresident: full-time $8,172; part-time $454 per hour.
Financial support: Application deadline: 3/1.
Dr. Robert B. Albritton, Chairman, 662-915-7401, *Fax:* 662-915-7808, *E-mail:* ralbritt@olemiss.edu.

■ UNIVERSITY OF MISSOURI–COLUMBIA

Graduate School, College of Arts and Sciences, Department of Political Science, Columbia, MO 65211

AWARDS MA, PhD.

Faculty: 23 full-time (6 women).
Students: 31 full-time (9 women), 27 part-time (4 women); includes 8 minority (5 African Americans, 1 Asian American or Pacific Islander, 1 Hispanic American, 1 Native American), 22 international. 35 applicants, 54% accepted. In 2001, 5 master's, 8 doctorates awarded. Terminal master's awarded for partial completion of doctoral program.
Degree requirements: For doctorate, one foreign language, thesis/dissertation.
Entrance requirements: For master's and doctorate, GRE General Test, minimum GPA of 3.0. *Application deadline:* For fall admission, 2/15 (priority date). Applications are processed on a rolling basis. *Application fee:* $25 ($50 for international students).
Expenses: Tuition, state resident: part-time $179 per credit hour. Tuition, nonresident: part-time $539 per credit hour. Required fees: $122 per semester. Tuition and fees vary according to program.
Financial support: Fellowships, research assistantships, teaching assistantships, institutionally sponsored loans available.
Dr. Catherine Holland, Director of Graduate Studies, 573-882-7681, *E-mail:* hollandc@missouri.edu. *Web site:* http://web.missouri.edu/~polswww/

■ UNIVERSITY OF MISSOURI–KANSAS CITY

College of Arts and Sciences, Department of Political Science, Kansas City, MO 64110-2499

AWARDS MA, PhD. PhD offered through the School of Graduate Studies. Part-time and evening/weekend programs available.

Faculty: 6 full-time (1 woman), 5 part-time/adjunct (1 woman).
Students: 3 full-time (1 woman), 10 part-time (7 women); includes 1 minority (African American), 1 international. Average age 33. In 2001, 3 degrees awarded. Terminal master's awarded for partial completion of doctoral program.

Degree requirements: For master's, thesis optional; for doctorate, thesis/dissertation.
Entrance requirements: For master's, GRE, minimum GPA of 3.0, previous course work in political science; for doctorate, GRE, minimum GPA of 3.0, MA in political science or related area, writing sample. *Application deadline:* For fall admission, 4/1 (priority date). Applications are processed on a rolling basis. *Application fee:* $25.
Expenses: Tuition, state resident: part-time $233 per credit hour. Tuition, nonresident: part-time $623 per credit hour. Tuition and fees vary according to course load.
Financial support: In 2001–02, 5 students received support, including 2 research assistantships with partial tuition reimbursements available (averaging $7,600 per year); career-related internships or fieldwork and institutionally sponsored loans also available. Financial award application deadline: 5/1.
Faculty research: Gender and politics, Chinese politics, social security, voting behavior, social capital. *Total annual research expenditures:* $6,500.
Dr. Dale A. Neuman, Chair, 816-235-2787, *Fax:* 816-235-5594.
Application contact: Dr. Robert Evanson, MA Adviser, 816-235-5217, *Fax:* 816-235-5594. *Web site:* http://www.umkc.edu/

■ UNIVERSITY OF MISSOURI–ST. LOUIS

Graduate School, College of Arts and Sciences, Department of Political Science, St. Louis, MO 63121-4499

AWARDS American politics (MA); comparative politics (MA); international politics (MA); political process and behavior (MA); political science (PhD); public administration and public policy (MA); urban and regional politics (MA). Part-time and evening/weekend programs available.

Faculty: 23.
Students: 12 full-time (4 women), 37 part-time (19 women); includes 7 minority (2 African Americans, 1 Asian American or Pacific Islander, 2 Hispanic Americans, 2 Native Americans), 6 international. In 2001, 4 master's, 2 doctorates awarded. Terminal master's awarded for partial completion of doctoral program.
Degree requirements: For master's, thesis optional; for doctorate, thesis/dissertation.
Entrance requirements: For master's, GRE General Test; for doctorate, GRE General Test, GRE Subject Test. *Application deadline:* For fall admission, 2/15 (priority date); for spring admission, 10/15 (priority date). Applications are processed on a rolling basis. *Application fee:* $25 ($40 for international students). Electronic applications accepted.
Expenses: Tuition, state resident: part-time $231 per credit hour. Tuition, nonresident: part-time $621 per credit hour.
Financial support: In 2001–02, 10 research assistantships with full and partial tuition reimbursements (averaging $10,000 per year), 5 teaching assistantships with full and partial tuition reimbursements (averaging $10,000 per year) were awarded. Fellowships, career-related internships or fieldwork also available. Support available to part-time students. Financial award application deadline: 3/15.
Faculty research: Public policy, urban politics and administration, international politics, American government, comparative politics. *Total annual research expenditures:* $18,540.
Dr. Edwardo Silva, Director of Graduate Studies, 314-516-5522, *Fax:* 314-516-5268, *E-mail:* lstein@umsl.edu.
Application contact: Jeff Headtke, Graduate Admissions, 314-516-6928, *Fax:* 314-516-5310, *E-mail:* gradadm@umsl.edu. *Web site:* http://www.umsl.edu/divisions/artscience/polisci/pshome/

■ THE UNIVERSITY OF MONTANA–MISSOULA

Graduate School, College of Arts and Sciences, Department of Political Science, Program in Political Science, Missoula, MT 59812-0002

AWARDS MA.

Students: 9 full-time (4 women), 5 part-time (3 women), 2 international. 8 applicants, 100% accepted, 6 enrolled. In 2001, 3 degrees awarded.
Degree requirements: For master's, thesis.
Entrance requirements: For master's, GRE General Test. *Application deadline:* For fall admission, 4/1 (priority date). Applications are processed on a rolling basis. *Application fee:* $45.
Expenses: Tuition, state resident: full-time $2,482; part-time $1,700 per year. Tuition, nonresident: full-time $7,372; part-time $5,000 per year. Required fees: $1,900. Tuition and fees vary according to degree level.
Financial support: In 2001–02, teaching assistantships with full tuition reimbursements (averaging $8,063 per year); career-related internships or fieldwork, Federal Work-Study, and institutionally sponsored loans also available. Financial award application deadline: 3/1; financial award applicants required to submit FAFSA.
Application contact: Dr. Forest Grieves, Graduate Coordinator, 406-243-5202, *Fax:* 406-243-4076, *E-mail:* fgrieves@selway.umt.edu. *Web site:* http://www.umt.edu/polisci/

■ UNIVERSITY OF NEBRASKA AT OMAHA

Graduate Studies and Research, College of Arts and Sciences, Department of Political Science, Omaha, NE 68182

AWARDS MS. Part-time programs available.

Faculty: 9 full-time (2 women).
Students: 3 full-time (1 woman), 5 part-time (3 women); includes 2 minority (1 African American, 1 Asian American or Pacific Islander). Average age 32. 9 applicants, 89% accepted, 4 enrolled. In 2001, 2 degrees awarded.
Degree requirements: For master's, thesis (for some programs), comprehensive exam.
Entrance requirements: For master's, minimum GPA of 3.0. *Application deadline:* For fall admission, 7/1 (priority date); for spring admission, 12/1 (priority date). Applications are processed on a rolling basis. *Application fee:* $35. Electronic applications accepted.
Expenses: Tuition, state resident: part-time $116 per credit hour. Tuition, nonresident: part-time $291 per credit hour. Required fees: $13 per credit hour. $4 per semester. One-time fee: $52 part-time.
Financial support: In 2001–02, 4 students received support. Federal Work-Study, scholarships/grants, and unspecified assistantships available. Financial award application deadline: 3/1.
Dr. James Johnson, Chairperson, 402-554-2624.

■ UNIVERSITY OF NEBRASKA–LINCOLN

Graduate College, College of Arts and Sciences, Department of Political Science, Lincoln, NE 68588

AWARDS MA, PhD, JD/MA.

Faculty: 19.
Students: 30 (9 women); includes 1 minority (Asian American or Pacific Islander) 4 international. Average age 32. 21 applicants, 67% accepted, 8 enrolled. In 2001, 4 master's, 1 doctorate awarded.
Degree requirements: For master's, thesis optional; for doctorate, variable foreign language requirement, thesis/dissertation, comprehensive exam.
Entrance requirements: For master's and doctorate, GRE General Test, TOEFL, writing sample. *Application deadline:* For fall admission, 2/1 (priority date). Applications are processed on a rolling basis. *Application fee:* $35. Electronic applications accepted.
Expenses: Tuition, state resident: full-time $2,412; part-time $134 per credit. Tuition, nonresident: full-time $6,223; part-time $346 per credit. Tuition and fees vary according to course load.
Financial support: In 2001–02, 3 fellowships, 2 research assistantships, 5 teaching assistantships were awarded. Federal

University of Nebraska–Lincoln (continued)

Work-Study, health care benefits, and unspecified assistantships also available. Support available to part-time students. Financial award application deadline: 2/15.

Faculty research: Public policy; comparative politics; international relations; political theory, behavior, and methodology; American politics.

Dr. John Comer, Chair, 402-472-2343. *Web site:* http://www.unl.edu/polisci/home.html/

■ UNIVERSITY OF NEVADA, LAS VEGAS

Graduate College, College of Liberal Arts, Department of Political Science, Las Vegas, NV 89154-9900

AWARDS MA. Part-time programs available.

Faculty: 18 full-time (2 women).
Students: 5 full-time (2 women), 12 part-time (4 women); includes 5 minority (3 African Americans, 1 Asian American or Pacific Islander, 1 Hispanic American), 1 international. 10 applicants, 70% accepted, 5 enrolled. In 2001, 4 degrees awarded.
Degree requirements: For master's, thesis (for some programs), comprehensive or oral exam, comprehensive exam (for some programs).
Entrance requirements: For master's, GRE General Test, minimum GPA of 3.0. *Application deadline:* For fall admission, 6/15; for spring admission, 11/1. Applications are processed on a rolling basis. *Application fee:* $40 ($55 for international students).
Expenses: Tuition, state resident: full-time $1,926; part-time $107 per credit. Tuition, nonresident: full-time $9,376; part-time $220 per credit. Tuition and fees vary according to course load.
Financial support: In 2001–02, 1 research assistantship with partial tuition reimbursement (averaging $10,000 per year), 7 teaching assistantships with partial tuition reimbursements (averaging $10,000 per year) were awarded. Financial award application deadline: 3/1.
Dr. Ted Jelen, Chair, 702-895-3307.
Application contact: Graduate College Admissions Evaluator, 702-895-3320, *Fax:* 702-895-4180, *E-mail:* gradcollege@ccmail.nevada.edu. *Web site:* http://www.unlv.edu/Colleges/Liberal_Arts/Political_Science/

■ UNIVERSITY OF NEVADA, RENO

Graduate School, College of Arts and Science, Department of Political Science, Program in Political Science, Reno, NV 89557

AWARDS MA, PhD. Part-time and evening/weekend programs available.

Faculty: 15.
Students: 24 full-time (12 women), 20 part-time (9 women); includes 4 minority (all Hispanic Americans), 2 international. Average age 42. In 2001, 3 master's, 1 doctorate awarded. Terminal master's awarded for partial completion of doctoral program.
Degree requirements: For master's, oral exam/thesis or professional paper; for doctorate, thesis/dissertation, 2 field exams, oral exam.
Entrance requirements: For master's, GRE General Test, TOEFL, minimum GPA of 2.75; for doctorate, GRE General Test, TOEFL, minimum GPA of 3.0. *Application deadline:* For fall admission, 3/1 (priority date). Applications are processed on a rolling basis. *Application fee:* $40.
Expenses: Tuition, state resident: full-time $2,067; part-time $108 per credit. Tuition, nonresident: full-time $9,282; part-time $109 per credit. Required fees: $57 per semester. Tuition and fees vary according to course load.
Financial support: Research assistantships, teaching assistantships, Federal Work-Study, institutionally sponsored loans, tuition waivers (full), and unspecified assistantships available. Financial award application deadline: 3/1.

■ UNIVERSITY OF NEW HAMPSHIRE

Graduate School, College of Liberal Arts, Department of Political Science, Program in Political Science, Durham, NH 03824

AWARDS MA. Part-time programs available.

Faculty: 13 full-time.
Students: 1 full-time (0 women), 4 part-time (2 women). Average age 28. 6 applicants, 100% accepted, 2 enrolled. In 2001, 2 degrees awarded.
Degree requirements: For master's, thesis.
Entrance requirements: For master's, GRE General Test. *Application deadline:* For fall admission, 4/1 (priority date); for winter admission, 12/1. Applications are processed on a rolling basis. *Application fee:* $50. Electronic applications accepted.
Expenses: Tuition, state resident: full-time $6,300; part-time $350 per credit. Tuition, nonresident: full-time $15,720; part-time $643 per credit. Required fees: $560; $280 per term. One-time fee: $15 part-time. Tuition and fees vary according to course load.
Financial support: In 2001–02, 1 teaching assistantship was awarded; fellowships, research assistantships, career-related internships or fieldwork, Federal Work-Study, scholarships/grants, and tuition waivers (full and partial) also available. Support available to part-time students. Financial award application deadline: 2/15.
Application contact: Dr. Cliff Wirth, Coordinator, 603-862-1749, *E-mail:* cjwirth@cisunix.unh.edu.

■ UNIVERSITY OF NEW MEXICO

Graduate School, College of Arts and Sciences, Department of Political Science, Albuquerque, NM 87131-2039

AWARDS MA, PhD.

Faculty: 12 full-time (3 women), 10 part-time/adjunct (4 women).
Students: 18 full-time (10 women), 5 part-time (1 woman); includes 4 minority (all Hispanic Americans), 3 international. Average age 34. 25 applicants, 64% accepted, 6 enrolled. Terminal master's awarded for partial completion of doctoral program.
Degree requirements: For master's, thesis optional; for doctorate, one foreign language, thesis/dissertation, comprehensive exam.
Entrance requirements: For master's, GRE General Test, minimum GPA of 3.5 in upper-division political science course work; for doctorate, GRE General Test. *Application deadline:* For fall admission, 2/1 (priority date). *Application fee:* $40.
Expenses: Tuition, state resident: full-time $2,771; part-time $115 per credit hour. Tuition, nonresident: full-time $11,207; part-time $467 per credit hour. Required fees: $570; $24 per credit hour. Part-time tuition and fees vary according to course load and program.
Financial support: In 2001–02, 16 students received support, including 12 teaching assistantships with full tuition reimbursements available (averaging $11,972 per year); scholarships/grants and health care benefits also available. Financial award application deadline: 3/1; financial award applicants required to submit FAFSA.
Faculty research: Latin American politics, American politics, comparative politics, public policy, international relations, methodology, political theory. *Total annual research expenditures:* $19,390.
Dr. Kenneth M. Roberts, Chair, 505-277-5104, *Fax:* 505-277-2821, *E-mail:* kenrob@unm.edu.
Application contact: Joann M. Buehler, Administrative Assistant II, 505-277-5104, *Fax:* 505-288-2921, *E-mail:* joannb@unm.edu. *Web site:* http://polsci.unm.edu/

■ UNIVERSITY OF NEW ORLEANS

Graduate School, College of Liberal Arts, Department of Political Science, New Orleans, LA 70148

AWARDS International relations (MA); political science (MA, PhD). Evening/weekend programs available.

Faculty: 5 full-time (1 woman).
Students: 25 full-time (8 women), 21 part-time (10 women); includes 8 minority (5 African Americans, 1 Asian American or Pacific Islander, 2 Hispanic Americans), 7 international. Average age 31. 36 applicants, 44% accepted, 9 enrolled. In 2001, 3 master's, 4 doctorates awarded.

Degree requirements: For master's, one foreign language, thesis or alternative; for doctorate, one foreign language, thesis/dissertation.
Entrance requirements: For master's, GRE General Test; for doctorate, GRE General Test, GRE Subject Test. *Application deadline:* For fall admission, 7/1 (priority date); for spring admission, 11/15 (priority date). Applications are processed on a rolling basis. *Application fee:* $20. Electronic applications accepted.
Expenses: Tuition, state resident: full-time $2,748; part-time $435 per credit. Tuition, nonresident: full-time $9,792; part-time $1,773 per credit.
Financial support: Fellowships, research assistantships, teaching assistantships, institutionally sponsored loans available. Financial award application deadline: 3/15; financial award applicants required to submit FAFSA.
Faculty research: Judicial politics, public policy, voting rights, Southern politics, presidential-congressional relations.
Dr. Charles Hadley, Chair, 504-280-6456, *Fax:* 504-280-6468, *E-mail:* chandley@uno.edu.
Application contact: Dr. Richard Engstrom, Graduate Coordinator, 504-280-6671, *Fax:* 504-280-6468, *E-mail:* rengstro@uno.edu.

■ THE UNIVERSITY OF NORTH CAROLINA AT CHAPEL HILL

Graduate School, College of Arts and Sciences, Department of Political Science, Political Science Program, Chapel Hill, NC 27599

AWARDS MA, PhD.

Degree requirements: For master's, thesis, comprehensive exam; for doctorate, one foreign language, thesis/dissertation, comprehensive exam.
Entrance requirements: For master's and doctorate, GRE General Test, GRE Subject Test, minimum GPA of 3.0.
Expenses: Tuition, state resident: full-time $2,864. Tuition, nonresident: full-time $12,030.

■ THE UNIVERSITY OF NORTH CAROLINA AT GREENSBORO

Graduate School, College of Arts and Sciences, Department of Political Science, Program in Political Science, Greensboro, NC 27412-5001

AWARDS MA.

Faculty: 8 full-time (2 women), 1 part-time/adjunct (0 women).
Students: 1 full-time (0 women), 1 international. 1 applicant, 0% accepted.
Degree requirements: For master's, thesis, comprehensive exam.
Entrance requirements: For master's, GRE General Test, TOEFL. *Application deadline:* For fall admission, 6/15; for spring admission, 10/15. Applications are processed on a rolling basis. *Application fee:* $35.
Expenses: Tuition, state resident: part-time $344 per course. Tuition, nonresident: part-time $2,457 per course.
Financial support: In 2001–02, 1 student received support; research assistantships with partial tuition reimbursements available, teaching assistantships with full tuition reimbursements available, career-related internships or fieldwork, Federal Work-Study, scholarships/grants, and traineeships available. Support available to part-time students.
Dr. Charles Prysby, Head, 336-334-5989, *Fax:* 336-334-4315, *E-mail:* prysby@uncg.edu.
Application contact: Dr. James Lynch, Director of Graduate Recruitment and Information Services, 336-334-4881, *Fax:* 336-334-4424. *Web site:* http://www.uncg.edu/psc/

■ UNIVERSITY OF NORTHERN IOWA

Graduate College, College of Social and Behavioral Sciences, Department of Political Science, Cedar Falls, IA 50614

AWARDS MA. Part-time and evening/weekend programs available.

Students: 4 full-time (1 woman), 2 part-time (1 woman); includes 1 minority (African American). 1 applicant, 100% accepted. In 2001, 3 degrees awarded.
Degree requirements: For master's, one foreign language, thesis or alternative.
Entrance requirements: For master's, GRE. *Application deadline:* For fall admission, 8/1 (priority date). Applications are processed on a rolling basis. *Application fee:* $20 ($50 for international students).
Expenses: Tuition, state resident: full-time $3,704; part-time $206 per credit hour. Tuition, nonresident: full-time $9,122; part-time $501 per credit hour. Required fees: $324; $108 per semester. Part-time tuition and fees vary according to course load.
Financial support: Career-related internships or fieldwork, Federal Work-Study, and tuition waivers (full and partial) available. Support available to part-time students. Financial award application deadline: 3/1.
Dr. Thomas W. Rice, Head, 319-273-2039, *Fax:* 319-273-7103, *E-mail:* tom.rice@uni.edu. *Web site:* http://fp.uni.edu/polisci/

■ UNIVERSITY OF NORTH TEXAS

Robert B. Toulouse School of Graduate Studies, College of Arts and Sciences, Department of Political Science, Denton, TX 76203

AWARDS MA, MS, PhD. Evening/weekend programs available.

Faculty: 20 full-time (3 women).
Students: 31 full-time (12 women), 26 part-time (8 women); includes 10 minority (3 African Americans, 1 Asian American or Pacific Islander, 5 Hispanic Americans, 1 Native American), 10 international. Average age 30. In 2001, 1 master's, 4 doctorates awarded.
Degree requirements: For master's, thesis (for some programs), comprehensive exam; for doctorate, 2 foreign languages, thesis/dissertation, comprehensive exam.
Entrance requirements: For master's and doctorate, GRE General Test. *Application deadline:* For fall admission, 7/17. *Application fee:* $25 ($50 for international students).
Expenses: Tuition, state resident: part-time $186 per hour. Tuition, nonresident: part-time $319 per hour. Required fees: $88; $21 per hour.
Financial support: Fellowships, teaching assistantships, career-related internships or fieldwork, Federal Work-Study, and institutionally sponsored loans available.
Faculty research: Political parties, international conflict, judicial politics, comparative politics, public policy.
Dr. Harold Clarke, Chair, 940-565-2276, *Fax:* 940-565-4818, *E-mail:* hclarke@unt.edu.
Application contact: Dr. James Meernik, Graduate Adviser, 940-545-2276, *Fax:* 940-565-4818, *E-mail:* fa09@um.acs.unt.edu.

■ UNIVERSITY OF NOTRE DAME

Graduate School, College of Arts and Letters, Division of Social Science, Department of Political Science, Notre Dame, IN 46556

AWARDS PhD.

Faculty: 38 full-time (11 women), 13 part-time/adjunct (2 women).
Students: 64 full-time (28 women), 1 (woman) part-time; includes 9 minority (1 Asian American or Pacific Islander, 8 Hispanic Americans), 28 international. 223 applicants, 11% accepted, 13 enrolled. In 2001, 6 doctorates awarded.
Degree requirements: For doctorate, one foreign language, thesis/dissertation, comprehensive exam. *Median time to degree:* Doctorate–6.3 years full-time.
Entrance requirements: For doctorate, GRE General Test, TOEFL. *Application deadline:* For fall admission, 1/10 (priority date). *Application fee:* $50. Electronic applications accepted.
Expenses: Tuition: Full-time $24,220; part-time $1,346 per credit hour. Required fees: $155.
Financial support: In 2001–02, 57 students received support, including 23 fellowships with full tuition reimbursements available (averaging $16,000 per year), 4 research assistantships with full tuition reimbursements available (averaging $11,400 per year), 25 teaching assistantships with full tuition reimbursements available (averaging $11,400 per

University of Notre Dame (continued)
year); career-related internships or fieldwork and tuition waivers (full) also available. Financial award application deadline: 2/1.
Faculty research: American government, comparative politics, international relations, political theory. *Total annual research expenditures:* $254,000.
Dr. Andrew C. Gould, Director of Graduate Studies, 574-631-7674, *Fax:* 574-631-4405, *E-mail:* govtgrad@nd.edu.
Application contact: Dr. Terrence J. Akai, Director of Graduate Admissions, 574-631-7706, *Fax:* 574-631-4183, *E-mail:* gradad@nd.edu. *Web site:* http://www.nd.edu/~governme/

■ UNIVERSITY OF OKLAHOMA

Graduate College, College of Arts and Sciences, Department of Political Science, Program in Political Science, Norman, OK 73019-0390

AWARDS MA, PhD. Part-time programs available.

Students: 17 full-time (8 women), 22 part-time (7 women); includes 2 minority (1 African American, 1 Native American), 2 international. 14 applicants, 57% accepted, 4 enrolled. In 2001, 9 master's, 7 doctorates awarded.
Degree requirements: For master's, thesis or alternative; for doctorate, thesis/dissertation, language or quantitative techniques.
Entrance requirements: For master's, TOEFL; for doctorate, GRE General Test, TOEFL. *Application deadline:* For fall admission, 6/15; for spring admission, 10/15. *Application fee:* $25 ($50 for international students).
Expenses: Tuition, state resident: full-time $2,208; part-time $92 per credit hour. Tuition, nonresident: part-time $297 per credit hour. Tuition and fees vary according to course level, course load and program.
Financial support: In 2001–02, 11 students received support, including 1 fellowship (averaging $5,000 per year); research assistantships with partial tuition reimbursements available, teaching assistantships with partial tuition reimbursements available, Federal Work-Study, scholarships/grants, and tuition waivers (partial) also available.
Faculty research: Religion and politics, international terrorism, public opinion, media coverage and economic conditions, citizen's roles in local government decision making.
Application contact: Greg Russell, Director of Graduate Studies, 405-325-5517, *Fax:* 405-325-0718, *E-mail:* grussell@ou.edu.

■ UNIVERSITY OF OREGON

Graduate School, College of Arts and Sciences, Department of Political Science, Eugene, OR 97403

AWARDS MA, MS, PhD.

Faculty: 15 full-time (6 women), 2 part-time/adjunct (0 women).
Students: 27 full-time (10 women), 4 part-time (2 women); includes 1 minority (Asian American or Pacific Islander), 8 international. 54 applicants, 50% accepted. In 2001, 4 master's, 2 doctorates awarded. Terminal master's awarded for partial completion of doctoral program.
Degree requirements: For master's, thesis or alternative; for doctorate, thesis/dissertation.
Entrance requirements: For master's and doctorate, GRE General Test, TOEFL, minimum GPA of 3.0. *Application deadline:* For fall admission, 2/15. *Application fee:* $50.
Expenses: Tuition, state resident: full-time $4,968; part-time $501 per credit hour. Tuition, nonresident: full-time $8,400; part-time $691 per credit hour.
Financial support: In 2001–02, 25 teaching assistantships were awarded; career-related internships or fieldwork also available. Financial award application deadline: 3/1.
Faculty research: Public policy, public choice, comparative politics, political economy, international relations.
Pete Suttmeier, Head, 541-346-4864, *Fax:* 541-346-4860.
Application contact: Brian Bergstrom, Admissions Contact, 541-346-1326, *Fax:* 541-346-4860. *Web site:* http://darkwing.uoregon.edu/~polisci/

■ UNIVERSITY OF PENNSYLVANIA

Fels Center of Government, Philadelphia, PA 19104

AWARDS MGA. Part-time and evening/weekend programs available.

Degree requirements: For master's, thesis (for some programs).
Entrance requirements: For master's, GRE, TOEFL.
Expenses: Tuition: Part-time $12,875 per semester. *Web site:* http://dolphin.upenn.edu/~gsfa/admin/admin.htm

Find an in-depth description at www.petersons.com/gradchannel.

■ UNIVERSITY OF PENNSYLVANIA

School of Arts and Sciences, Graduate Group in Political Science, Philadelphia, PA 19104

AWARDS AM, PhD, MGA/AM. Terminal master's awarded for partial completion of doctoral program.

Degree requirements: For doctorate, one foreign language, thesis/dissertation.
Entrance requirements: For master's and doctorate, GRE General Test, TOEFL.
Expenses: Tuition: Part-time $12,875 per semester.

■ UNIVERSITY OF PITTSBURGH

Faculty of Arts and Sciences, Department of Political Science, Pittsburgh, PA 15260

AWARDS MA, PhD. Part-time programs available.

Faculty: 22 full-time (3 women), 3 part-time/adjunct (0 women).
Students: 43 full-time (12 women), 6 part-time; includes 13 minority (6 Asian Americans or Pacific Islanders, 7 Hispanic Americans), 15 international. 70 applicants, 46% accepted, 11 enrolled. In 2001, 4 master's, 6 doctorates awarded. Terminal master's awarded for partial completion of doctoral program.
Degree requirements: For master's, comprehensive exam, registration; for doctorate, thesis/dissertation, comprehensive exam, registration.
Entrance requirements: For master's and doctorate, GRE General Test, TOEFL, minimum QPA of 3.0. *Application deadline:* For fall admission, 4/15. Applications are processed on a rolling basis. *Application fee:* $40. Electronic applications accepted.
Expenses: Tuition, state resident: full-time $9,410; part-time $385 per credit. Tuition, nonresident: full-time $19,376; part-time $797 per credit. Required fees: $480; $90 per term. Tuition and fees vary according to program.
Financial support: In 2001–02, 35 students received support, including 10 fellowships with tuition reimbursements available, 4 research assistantships with tuition reimbursements available (averaging $19,980 per year), 20 teaching assistantships with tuition reimbursements available; tuition waivers (partial) also available. Financial award application deadline: 1/1.
Dr. Barry Ames, Chairman, 412-648-7290, *Fax:* 412-648-7277, *E-mail:* barrya@pitt.edu.
Application contact: Frederick Whelan, Director of Graduate Students, 412-648-7264, *Fax:* 412-648-7277, *E-mail:* fwhelan@pitt.edu. *Web site:* http://www.pitt.edu/~polisci/home.html

■ UNIVERSITY OF PITTSBURGH

Graduate School of Public and International Affairs, Executive Programs in Public Policy and Management, Pittsburgh, PA 15260

AWARDS Criminal justice (MPPM); development planning (MPPM); environmental management and policy (MPPM); international development (MPPM); international political economy (MPPM); international security studies (MPPM);

management of non profit organizations (MPPM); metropolitan management and regional development (MPPM); personnel and labor relations (MPPM); policy analysis and evaluation (MPPM). Part-time programs available.

Faculty: 32 full-time (8 women), 12 part-time/adjunct (9 women).
Students: 7 full-time (4 women), 51 part-time (27 women); includes 8 minority (all African Americans), 3 international. Average age 38. 34 applicants, 79% accepted, 18 enrolled. In 2001, 24 degrees awarded.
Degree requirements: For master's, thesis optional.
Application deadline: For fall admission, 3/1 (priority date); for spring admission, 10/1 (priority date). Applications are processed on a rolling basis. *Application fee:* $40.
Expenses: Tuition, state resident: full-time $9,410; part-time $385 per credit. Tuition, nonresident: full-time $19,376; part-time $797 per credit. Required fees: $480; $90 per term. Tuition and fees vary according to program.
Financial support: Institutionally sponsored loans and scholarships/grants available. Support available to part-time students. Financial award application deadline: 2/1.
Faculty research: Executive training and technical assistance for U.S. and international clients. *Total annual research expenditures:* $101,000.
Michele Garrity, Director, Executive Education, 412-648-7610, *Fax:* 412-648-2605, *E-mail:* garrity@birch.gspia.pitt.edu.
Application contact: Maureen O'Malley, Admissions Counselor, 412-648-7646, *Fax:* 412-648-7641, *E-mail:* pronobis@birch.gspia.pitt.edu. *Web site:* http://www.gspia.pitt.edu/

Find an in-depth description at www.petersons.com/gradchannel.

■ UNIVERSITY OF PITTSBURGH

Graduate School of Public and International Affairs, International Affairs Division, Program in Global Political Economy, Pittsburgh, PA 15260

AWARDS MPIA, JD/MPIA, MBA/MPIA, MPA/MPIA, MPH/MPIA, MSIS/MPIA, MSW/MPIA. Part-time and evening/weekend programs available.

Faculty: 32 full-time (8 women), 12 part-time/adjunct (9 women).
Students: 93 full-time (54 women), 12 part-time (7 women); includes 11 minority (7 African Americans, 1 Asian American or Pacific Islander, 3 Hispanic Americans), 28 international. Average age 23. 88 applicants, 78% accepted, 31 enrolled.
Degree requirements: For master's, internship, thesis optional.
Application deadline: For fall admission, 3/1 (priority date); for spring admission, 10/1 (priority date). Applications are processed on a rolling basis. *Application fee:* $40. Electronic applications accepted.
Expenses: Tuition, state resident: full-time $9,410; part-time $385 per credit. Tuition, nonresident: full-time $19,376; part-time $797 per credit. Required fees: $480; $90 per term. Tuition and fees vary according to program.
Financial support: In 2001–02, 44 students received support, including 9 fellowships (averaging $14,240 per year); career-related internships or fieldwork, scholarships/grants, tuition waivers (full and partial), unspecified assistantships, and graduate student assistantships also available. Financial award application deadline: 2/1.
Faculty research: Political economy, international security/defense/intelligence, transnational crime, international trade, international finance, terrorism.
Application contact: Elizabeth Barthen-Braunsdorf, Assistant Director of Admissions, 412-648-7643, *Fax:* 412-648-7641, *E-mail:* barthen@bitch.gspia.pitt.edu. *Web site:* http://www.gspia.pitt.edu/

■ UNIVERSITY OF RHODE ISLAND

Graduate School, College of Arts and Sciences, Department of Political Science, Kingston, RI 02881

AWARDS International development studies (Certificate); political science (MA), including American government, American politics, comparative government, international relations, public policy; public policy and administration (MPA).

Students: In 2001, 6 degrees awarded.
Application deadline: For fall admission, 4/15 (priority date). Applications are processed on a rolling basis. *Application fee:* $35.
Expenses: Tuition, state resident: full-time $3,756; part-time $209 per credit. Tuition, nonresident: full-time $10,774; part-time $599 per credit. Required fees: $1,586; $76 per credit. One-time fee: $60 full-time.
Dr. Maureen F. Moakley, Chairperson, 401-874-2183.

■ UNIVERSITY OF ROCHESTER

The College, Arts and Sciences, Department of Political Science, Rochester, NY 14627-0250

AWARDS MA, PhD, MPH/MS, MS/PhD.

Faculty: 21.
Students: 29 full-time (9 women), 2 part-time, 15 international. 146 applicants, 13% accepted, 9 enrolled. In 2001, 10 master's, 5 doctorates awarded. Terminal master's awarded for partial completion of doctoral program.
Degree requirements: For doctorate, thesis/dissertation, qualifying exam.
Entrance requirements: For master's, GRE General Test; for doctorate, GRE General Test, TOEFL. *Application deadline:* For fall admission, 2/1 (priority date). *Application fee:* $25.
Expenses: Tuition: Part-time $755 per credit hour.
Financial support: Fellowships, research assistantships, teaching assistantships, institutionally sponsored loans, scholarships/grants, and tuition waivers (full and partial) available. Financial award application deadline: 2/1.
Gerald Gamm, Chair, 585-275-5403.
Application contact: Pamm Ferguson, Graduate Program Secretary, 585-275-5403.

■ UNIVERSITY OF SOUTH CAROLINA

The Graduate School, College of Liberal Arts, Department of Government and International Studies, Program in Political Science, Columbia, SC 29208

AWARDS MA, PhD. Part-time programs available. Terminal master's awarded for partial completion of doctoral program.

Degree requirements: For master's, one foreign language, thesis; for doctorate, 2 foreign languages, thesis/dissertation.
Entrance requirements: For master's, GRE General Test, minimum GPA of 3.5; for doctorate, GRE General Test, TOEFL, minimum GPA of 3.5. Electronic applications accepted.
Expenses: Tuition, state resident: full-time $4,434. Tuition, nonresident: full-time $9,854. Tuition and fees vary according to program.
Faculty research: American government and politics, comparative politics, political theory, international politics, public administration and policy. *Web site:* http://www.cla.sc.edu/gint/

■ THE UNIVERSITY OF SOUTH DAKOTA

Graduate School, College of Arts and Sciences, Department of Political Science, Vermillion, SD 57069-2390

AWARDS Political science (MA); public administration (MPA).

Faculty: 8 full-time (0 women), 1 part-time/adjunct (0 women).
Students: 33. 34 applicants, 56% accepted. In 2001, 24 degrees awarded.
Degree requirements: For master's, thesis (for some programs).
Entrance requirements: For master's, GRE or LSAT for MPA. *Application deadline:* Applications are processed on a rolling basis. *Application fee:* $35.
Expenses: Tuition, state resident: full-time $1,700; part-time $95 per credit hour. Tuition, nonresident: full-time $5,027; part-time $279 per credit hour. Required fees: $1,062; $59 per credit hour.

The University of South Dakota (continued)

Financial support: Research assistantships, teaching assistantships, Federal Work-Study available. Support available to part-time students. Financial award applicants required to submit FAFSA.
Dr. William Richardson, Chair, 605-677-5242.
Application contact: David Aaronson, Graduate Student Advisor. *Web site:* http://www.usd.edu/polsci/

■ UNIVERSITY OF SOUTHERN CALIFORNIA

Graduate School, College of Letters, Arts and Sciences, Department of Political Science, Los Angeles, CA 90089

AWARDS MA, PhD. Terminal master's awarded for partial completion of doctoral program.

Degree requirements: For master's, exam; for doctorate, one foreign language, thesis/dissertation.
Entrance requirements: For master's and doctorate, GRE General Test.
Expenses: Tuition: Full-time $25,060; part-time $844 per unit. Required fees: $473.
Faculty research: Public law, urban politics, political communication, Pacific Rim studies, environmental politics.

■ UNIVERSITY OF SOUTHERN MISSISSIPPI

Graduate School, College of Liberal Arts, Department of Political Science, Hattiesburg, MS 39406

AWARDS MA, MS. Part-time programs available.

Faculty: 10 full-time (2 women), 1 part-time/adjunct (0 women).
Students: 22 full-time (9 women), 3 part-time (1 woman); includes 8 minority (all African Americans). Average age 32. 25 applicants, 76% accepted. In 2001, 5 degrees awarded.
Degree requirements: For master's, one foreign language, thesis (for some programs).
Entrance requirements: For master's, GRE General Test, minimum GPA of 2.75 in last 2 years, 3.0 in field of study. *Application deadline:* For fall admission, 8/6 (priority date). Applications are processed on a rolling basis. *Application fee:* $0 ($25 for international students).
Expenses: Tuition, state resident: full-time $3,416; part-time $190 per credit hour. Tuition, nonresident: full-time $7,932; part-time $441 per credit hour.
Financial support: Research assistantships with full and partial tuition reimbursements, career-related internships or fieldwork available. Financial award application deadline: 3/15.
Faculty research: American politics, international politics, political theory, comparative politics, public law.
Dr. Allen McBride, Chair, 601-266-4310.

■ UNIVERSITY OF SOUTH FLORIDA

College of Graduate Studies, College of Arts and Sciences, Department of Political Science, Tampa, FL 33620-9951

AWARDS MA. Part-time and evening/weekend programs available.

Faculty: 30 full-time (6 women).
Students: 14 full-time (6 women), 13 part-time (9 women); includes 6 minority (1 African American, 3 Asian Americans or Pacific Islanders, 2 Hispanic Americans), 2 international. Average age 32. In 2001, 2 degrees awarded.
Degree requirements: For master's, thesis.
Entrance requirements: For master's, GRE General Test, minimum GPA of 3.0 in last 60 hours. *Application deadline:* For fall admission, 6/1; for spring admission, 10/15. Applications are processed on a rolling basis. *Application fee:* $20. Electronic applications accepted.
Expenses: Tuition, state resident: part-time $166 per credit hour. Tuition, nonresident: part-time $573 per credit hour. Required fees: $17 per term.
Financial support: Fellowships with full and partial tuition reimbursements, research assistantships with full and partial tuition reimbursements, Federal Work-Study and institutionally sponsored loans available. Support available to part-time students. Financial award applicants required to submit FAFSA.
Dr. Mohsen Milani, Chairperson, 813-974-2384, *Fax:* 813-974-0832, *E-mail:* milani@chuma1.cas.usf.edu.
Application contact: Dr. Stephen Tauber, Graduate Coordinator, 813-974-0781, *Fax:* 813-974-0832, *E-mail:* stauber@chuma1.cas.usf.edu. *Web site:* http://www.cas.usf.edu/ps/index.html

■ THE UNIVERSITY OF TENNESSEE

Graduate School, College of Arts and Sciences, Department of Political Science, Program in Political Science, Knoxville, TN 37996

AWARDS MA, PhD. Part-time programs available.

Students: 28 full-time (13 women), 15 part-time (9 women); includes 1 minority (African American), 7 international. 36 applicants, 72% accepted. In 2001, 1 master's, 3 doctorates awarded.
Degree requirements: For master's, thesis or alternative; for doctorate, one foreign language, thesis/dissertation.
Entrance requirements: For master's and doctorate, GRE General Test, TOEFL, minimum GPA of 2.7. *Application deadline:* For fall admission, 2/1 (priority date). Applications are processed on a rolling basis. *Application fee:* $35. Electronic applications accepted.
Expenses: Tuition, state resident: full-time $4,280; part-time $233 per hour. Tuition, nonresident: full-time $12,066; part-time $666 per hour. Tuition and fees vary according to program.
Financial support: Application deadline: 2/1.
Dr. Yang Zhong, Graduate Representative, *E-mail:* yzhong@utk.edu.

■ THE UNIVERSITY OF TENNESSEE

Graduate School, College of Arts and Sciences, Department of Sociology, Knoxville, TN 37996

AWARDS Criminology (MA, PhD); energy, environment, and resource policy (MA, PhD); political economy (MA, PhD). Part-time programs available.

Faculty: 15 full-time (2 women), 1 (woman) part-time/adjunct.
Students: 22 full-time (14 women), 26 part-time (11 women); includes 7 minority (6 African Americans, 1 Asian American or Pacific Islander), 4 international. 30 applicants, 63% accepted. In 2001, 3 degrees awarded.
Degree requirements: For master's, thesis or alternative; for doctorate, thesis/dissertation.
Entrance requirements: For master's, GRE General Test, TOEFL, minimum GPA of 3.0; for doctorate, GRE General Test, TOEFL, minimum GPA of 3.5. *Application deadline:* For fall admission, 2/1 (priority date). Applications are processed on a rolling basis. *Application fee:* $35. Electronic applications accepted.
Expenses: Tuition, state resident: full-time $4,280; part-time $233 per hour. Tuition, nonresident: full-time $12,066; part-time $666 per hour. Tuition and fees vary according to program.
Financial support: In 2001–02, 1 fellowship, 2 research assistantships, 20 teaching assistantships were awarded. Federal Work-Study, institutionally sponsored loans, and unspecified assistantships also available. Financial award application deadline: 2/1; financial award applicants required to submit FAFSA.
Dr. Suzanne Kurth, Head, 865-974-6021, *Fax:* 865-974-7013, *E-mail:* skurth@utk.edu.
Application contact: Dr. T. C. Hood, Graduate Representative, 865-974-7032, *E-mail:* tomhood@utk.edu.

■ THE UNIVERSITY OF TEXAS AT ARLINGTON

Graduate School, College of Liberal Arts, Department of Political Science, Arlington, TX 76019

AWARDS MA. Part-time and evening/weekend programs available.

Faculty: 12 full-time (5 women), 1 part-time/adjunct (0 women).
Students: 3 full-time (0 women), 19 part-time (9 women); includes 1 African American. 10 applicants, 100% accepted, 8 enrolled. In 2001, 4 degrees awarded.
Degree requirements: For master's, thesis optional.
Entrance requirements: For master's, GRE General Test, minimum GPA of 3.0 last 60 hours. *Application deadline:* For fall admission, 6/16. Applications are processed on a rolling basis. *Application fee:* $25 ($50 for international students).
Expenses: Tuition, area resident: Full-time $2,268. Tuition, nonresident: full-time $6,264. Required fees: $839. Tuition and fees vary according to course load.
Financial support: In 2001–02, 1 student received support, including teaching assistantships (averaging $8,000 per year); career-related internships or fieldwork, institutionally sponsored loans, and scholarships/grants also available. Support available to part-time students. Financial award application deadline: 6/1; financial award applicants required to submit FAFSA.
Dr. Dale Story, Chair, 817-272-2991, *Fax:* 817-272-2525, *E-mail:* story@uta.edu.
Application contact: Dr. Jill Clark, Graduate Adviser, 817-272-2991, *Fax:* 817-272-2525, *E-mail:* jclark@uta.edu.

■ THE UNIVERSITY OF TEXAS AT AUSTIN

Graduate School, College of Liberal Arts, Department of Government, Austin, TX 78712-1111

AWARDS MA, PhD.

Faculty: 39 full-time (4 women), 18 part-time/adjunct (2 women).
Students: 82 full-time (32 women), 22 part-time (7 women); includes 5 minority (2 Asian Americans or Pacific Islanders, 2 Hispanic Americans, 1 Native American), 28 international. 157 applicants, 41% accepted. In 2001, 9 master's, 10 doctorates awarded.
Degree requirements: For master's, thesis/dissertation; for doctorate, thesis/dissertation, comprehensive exam.
Entrance requirements: For master's and doctorate, GRE General Test. *Application deadline:* For fall admission, 1/1. *Application fee:* $50 ($75 for international students). Electronic applications accepted.
Expenses: Tuition, state resident: full-time $3,159. Tuition, nonresident: full-time $6,957. Tuition and fees vary according to program.
Financial support: In 2001–02, 63 students received support, including 6 fellowships with full tuition reimbursements available (averaging $15,500 per year), 4 research assistantships with partial tuition reimbursements available, 53 teaching assistantships with full tuition reimbursements available; career-related internships or fieldwork, Federal Work-Study, and institutionally sponsored loans also available. Financial award application deadline: 1/1; financial award applicants required to submit FAFSA.
Dr. John Highley, Chairman, 512-471-5121, *Fax:* 512-471-1062, *E-mail:* jhigley@mail.la.utexas.edu.
Application contact: Laura Leissner-Carlson, Graduate Coordinator I, 512-471-5121, *Fax:* 512-471-1061, *E-mail:* lcarlson@mail.la.utexas. *Web site:* http://www.la.utexas.edu/depts/gov/home.htm

■ THE UNIVERSITY OF TEXAS AT BROWNSVILLE

Graduate Studies and Sponsored Programs, College of Liberal Arts, Department of Social Sciences, Program in Government, Brownsville, TX 78520-4991

AWARDS MAIS. Part-time and evening/weekend programs available.

Degree requirements: For master's, thesis optional.
Entrance requirements: For master's, GRE General Test, TOEFL.

■ THE UNIVERSITY OF TEXAS AT EL PASO

Graduate School, College of Liberal Arts, Department of Political Science, El Paso, TX 79968-0001

AWARDS MA, MPA. Part-time and evening/weekend programs available.

Students: 69 (45 women); includes 52 minority (4 African Americans, 1 Asian American or Pacific Islander, 47 Hispanic Americans). Average age 34. 10 applicants, 100% accepted. In 2001, 12 degrees awarded.
Degree requirements: For master's, thesis (for some programs).
Entrance requirements: For master's, GMAT, GRE General Test, minimum GPA of 3.0. *Application deadline:* For fall admission, 7/1 (priority date); for spring admission, 11/1 (priority date). Applications are processed on a rolling basis. *Application fee:* $15 ($65 for international students). Electronic applications accepted.
Expenses: Tuition, state resident: full-time $2,450. Tuition, nonresident: full-time $6,000.
Financial support: In 2001–02, research assistantships with partial tuition reimbursements (averaging $18,625 per year), 10 teaching assistantships with partial tuition reimbursements (averaging $14,900 per year) were awarded. Fellowships, Federal Work-Study, institutionally sponsored loans, scholarships/grants, and tuition waivers (partial) also available. Financial award application deadline: 3/15; financial award applicants required to submit FAFSA.
Dr. Roberto Villareal, Head, 915-747-5227, *Fax:* 915-747-5400, *E-mail:* rvillarr@miners.utep.edu.
Application contact: Dr. Charles H. Ambler, Dean of the Graduate School, 915-747-5491 Ext. 7886, *Fax:* 915-747-5788, *E-mail:* cambler@miners.utep.edu.

■ THE UNIVERSITY OF TEXAS AT SAN ANTONIO

College of Liberal and Fine Arts, Department of Political Science and Geography, San Antonio, TX 78249-0617

AWARDS Political science (MA). Part-time and evening/weekend programs available.

Faculty: 15 full-time (2 women).
Students: 9 full-time (5 women), 20 part-time (13 women); includes 15 minority (1 Asian American or Pacific Islander, 14 Hispanic Americans), 1 international. Average age 33. 21 applicants, 90% accepted, 14 enrolled. In 2001, 1 degree awarded.
Degree requirements: For master's, thesis optional. *Median time to degree:* Master's–3 years full-time.
Entrance requirements: For master's, GRE General Test. *Application deadline:* For fall admission, 7/1 (priority date); for spring admission, 11/1. Applications are processed on a rolling basis. *Application fee:* $25 ($50 for international students). Electronic applications accepted.
Expenses: Tuition, state resident: full-time $2,268; part-time $126 per credit hour. Tuition, nonresident: full-time $6,066; part-time $337 per credit hour. Required fees: $781. Tuition and fees vary according to course load.
Financial support: In 2001–02, 1 research assistantship was awarded; career-related internships or fieldwork, Federal Work-Study, scholarships/grants, and readers/graders also available.
Dr. Richard Gambitta, Department Chair, 210-458-5883, *Fax:* 210-458-4629, *E-mail:* mluna@utsa.edu.
Application contact: Elsie Clay, Administrative Assistant I, 210-458-4627, *Fax:* 210-458-4629, *E-mail:* eclay@utsa.edu.

■ THE UNIVERSITY OF TEXAS AT TYLER

Graduate Studies, College of Arts and Sciences, Department of Social Sciences, Tyler, TX 75799-0001

AWARDS Criminal justice (MAIS, MS); economics (MAIS); political science (MA, MAIS, MAT); public administration (MPA); sociology (MAIS, MAT, MS). Part-time and

The University of Texas at Tyler (continued)

evening/weekend programs available. Postbaccalaureate distance learning degree programs offered.

Faculty: 14 full-time (1 woman).
Students: 13 full-time (9 women), 54 part-time (34 women); includes 16 minority (14 African Americans, 1 Hispanic American, 1 Native American), 1 international. Average age 35. 8 applicants, 100% accepted, 8 enrolled. In 2001, 10 degrees awarded.
Degree requirements: For master's, thesis (for some programs), comprehensive exam.
Entrance requirements: For master's, GRE General Test, minimum GPA of 3.0. *Application deadline:* Applications are processed on a rolling basis. *Application fee:* $0.
Expenses: Tuition, state resident: part-time $44 per credit hour. Tuition, nonresident: part-time $262 per credit hour. Required fees: $58 per credit hour. $76 per semester.
Financial support: Teaching assistantships, career-related internships or fieldwork, Federal Work-Study, and scholarships/grants available. Support available to part-time students. Financial award application deadline: 7/1; financial award applicants required to submit FAFSA.
Faculty research: Urban segregation, minority business, violent crime, gender discrimination, Third World agriculture production.
Dr. Barbara L. Hart, Chair, 903-566-7426, *Fax:* 903-565-5537, *E-mail:* bhart@mail.uttyl.edu.
Application contact: Carol A. Hodge, Office of Graduate Studies, 903-566-5642, *Fax:* 903-566-7068, *E-mail:* chodge@mail.uttly.edu.

■ UNIVERSITY OF TOLEDO

Graduate School, College of Arts and Sciences, Department of Political Science and Public Administration, Program in Political Science, Toledo, OH 43606-3398

AWARDS MA.

Students: 6 full-time (4 women), 11 part-time (5 women); includes 3 minority (all African Americans), 2 international. Average age 31. 7 applicants, 86% accepted, 4 enrolled. In 2001, 3 degrees awarded.
Degree requirements: For master's, thesis.
Entrance requirements: For master's, GRE General Test, GRE Subject Test, minimum GPA of 2.7. *Application deadline:* For fall admission, 8/1 (priority date); for spring admission, 4/1. Applications are processed on a rolling basis. *Application fee:* $30. Electronic applications accepted.
Expenses: Tuition, state resident: full-time $7,278; part-time $303 per hour. Tuition, nonresident: full-time $15,731; part-time $699 per hour. Required fees: $43 per hour.
Financial support: In 2001–02, 3 teaching assistantships were awarded. Financial award application deadline: 4/1.
Faculty research: Economic policy, development, Third World, Eastern Europe, Africa.
Dr. Richard Weisfelder, Director, 419-530-2265, *Fax:* 419-530-4199, *E-mail:* rweisfe@utnet.utoledo.edu. *Web site:* http://www.utoledo.edu/poli-sci/pshome.htmlx

■ UNIVERSITY OF UTAH

Graduate School, College of Social and Behavioral Science, Department of Political Science, Program in Political Science, Salt Lake City, UT 84112-1107

AWARDS MA, MS, PhD.

Students: 22 full-time (10 women), 16 part-time (6 women); includes 3 minority (2 Asian Americans or Pacific Islanders, 1 Native American), 7 international. Average age 30. 30 applicants, 67% accepted.
Degree requirements: For master's, one foreign language; for doctorate, variable foreign language requirement, thesis/dissertation.
Entrance requirements: For master's, GRE General Test, TOEFL, minimum GPA of 3.2; for doctorate, GRE General Test, GRE Subject Test, TOEFL. *Application deadline:* For fall admission, 7/1. *Application fee:* $40 ($60 for international students).
Expenses: Tuition, state resident: part-time $320 per semester hour. Tuition, nonresident: part-time $1,135 per semester hour. Required fees: $143 per semester hour. Tuition and fees vary according to course load, degree level and program.
Financial support: Fellowships, teaching assistantships, career-related internships or fieldwork available.
Application contact: Sherlyn Marks, Advisor, 801-585-7656, *E-mail:* sdmarks@poli-sci.utah.edu.

■ UNIVERSITY OF VERMONT

Graduate College, College of Arts and Sciences, Department of Political Science, Burlington, VT 05405

AWARDS MA.

Degree requirements: For master's, thesis.
Entrance requirements: For master's, GRE General Test, GRE Subject Test, TOEFL.
Expenses: Tuition, state resident: part-time $335 per credit. Tuition, nonresident: part-time $838 per credit.
Faculty research: Public policy, political behavior.

■ UNIVERSITY OF VIRGINIA

College and Graduate School of Arts and Sciences, Department of Government and Foreign Affairs, Program in Government, Charlottesville, VA 22903

AWARDS MA, MAT, PhD, JD/MA, MBA/MA.

Faculty: 36 full-time (5 women), 11 part-time/adjunct (3 women).
Students: 60 full-time (23 women), 6 part-time; includes 4 minority (1 African American, 1 Asian American or Pacific Islander, 2 Hispanic Americans), 17 international. Average age 28. 124 applicants, 49% accepted, 14 enrolled. In 2001, 4 master's, 6 doctorates awarded.
Degree requirements: For master's, thesis; for doctorate, variable foreign language requirement, thesis/dissertation.
Entrance requirements: For master's and doctorate, GRE General Test, GRE Subject Test. *Application deadline:* For fall admission, 7/15; for spring admission, 12/1. Applications are processed on a rolling basis. *Application fee:* $40. Electronic applications accepted.
Expenses: Tuition, state resident: full-time $3,988. Tuition, nonresident: full-time $17,078. Required fees: $1,190.
Financial support: Application deadline: 2/1.
Application contact: Duane J. Osheim, Associate Dean for Graduate Programs, 434-924-7184, *Fax:* 434-924-3084, *E-mail:* grad-a-s@virginia.edu.

■ UNIVERSITY OF WASHINGTON

Graduate School, College of Arts and Sciences, Department of Political Science, Seattle, WA 98195

AWARDS MA, PhD.

Degree requirements: For doctorate, thesis/dissertation.
Entrance requirements: For master's and doctorate, GRE General Test, TOEFL, minimum GPA of 3.0. Electronic applications accepted.
Expenses: Tuition, state resident: full-time $5,539. Tuition, nonresident: full-time $14,376. Required fees: $390. Tuition and fees vary according to course load and program.
Faculty research: American politics, comparative politics, international relations, political theory, political economy.
Web site: http://depts.washington.edu/polisci/

■ UNIVERSITY OF WISCONSIN–MADISON

Graduate School, College of Letters and Science, Department of Political Science, Madison, WI 53706-1380

AWARDS MA, PhD.

Faculty: 40 full-time (10 women).
Students: 93 full-time (31 women); includes 7 minority (2 Asian Americans or

Pacific Islanders, 5 Hispanic Americans), 8 international. 202 applicants, 27% accepted, 21 enrolled. In 2001, 14 master's, 16 doctorates awarded.
Degree requirements: For doctorate, thesis/dissertation.
Entrance requirements: For master's and doctorate, GRE General Test. *Application deadline:* For fall admission, 12/15. *Application fee:* $45. Electronic applications accepted.
Expenses: Tuition, state resident: full-time $7,361; part-time $399 per credit. Tuition, nonresident: full-time $20,499; part-time $1,282 per credit. Required fees: $34 per credit. Full-time tuition and fees vary according to course load, program, reciprocity agreements and student level.
Financial support: In 2001–02, 8 fellowships with tuition reimbursements (averaging $13,446 per year), 37 teaching assistantships with tuition reimbursements (averaging $9,244 per year) were awarded. Unspecified assistantships also available.
Faculty research: Comparative politics, American politics, international relations, political theory, political methodology. *Total annual research expenditures:* $1.7 million.
Mark Beissinger, Chair, 608-263-2414, *Fax:* 608-265-2663.
Application contact: Mary Jane Hill, Graduate Program Assistant, 608-263-1878, *Fax:* 608-265-2663, *E-mail:* admit@polisci.wisc.edu. *Web site:* http://www.polisci.wisc.edu/

■ UNIVERSITY OF WISCONSIN–MILWAUKEE

Graduate School, College of Letters and Sciences, Department of Political Science, Milwaukee, WI 53201-0413

AWARDS MA, PhD.

Faculty: 22 full-time (5 women).
Students: 10 full-time (5 women), 18 part-time (6 women); includes 2 minority (both Hispanic Americans), 5 international. 24 applicants, 63% accepted. In 2001, 4 master's, 1 doctorate awarded.
Degree requirements: For master's, thesis or alternative; for doctorate, one foreign language, thesis/dissertation.
Entrance requirements: For master's, GRE General Test, minimum GPA of 3.0. *Application deadline:* For fall admission, 1/1 (priority date); for spring admission, 9/1. Applications are processed on a rolling basis. *Application fee:* $45 ($75 for international students).
Expenses: Tuition, state resident: full-time $6,180; part-time $535 per credit. Tuition, nonresident: full-time $19,482; part-time $1,366 per credit. Tuition and fees vary according to course load, program and reciprocity agreements.
Financial support: In 2001–02, 2 fellowships, 11 teaching assistantships were awarded. Research assistantships, career-related internships or fieldwork and unspecified assistantships also available. Support available to part-time students. Financial award application deadline: 4/15.
Tom Holbrook, Representative, 414-229-4221, *Fax:* 414-229-5021, *E-mail:* homeboy@uwm.edu. *Web site:* http://www.uwm.edu/dept/polsci/

■ UNIVERSITY OF WYOMING

Graduate School, College of Arts and Sciences, Department of Political Science, Program in Political Science, Laramie, WY 82071

AWARDS MA. Part-time programs available.

Faculty: 11 full-time (0 women), 3 part-time/adjunct (0 women).
Students: 11 full-time (4 women), 2 part-time, 2 international. 4 applicants, 100% accepted.
Degree requirements: For master's, thesis or alternative.
Entrance requirements: For master's, GRE General Test, TOEFL, bachelor's degree in political science, minimum GPA of 3.0. *Application deadline:* For fall admission, 6/1 (priority date). Applications are processed on a rolling basis. *Application fee:* $40.
Expenses: Tuition, state resident: full-time $2,895; part-time $161 per credit hour. Tuition, nonresident: full-time $8,367; part-time $465 per credit hour. Required fees: $491; $10 per credit hour. $2 per credit hour. Tuition and fees vary according to course load and program.
Financial support: In 2001–02, 5 teaching assistantships with full tuition reimbursements (averaging $8,667 per year) were awarded; career-related internships or fieldwork also available. Financial award application deadline: 3/1.
Faculty research: American government, public law, judicial politics, political theory, international relations, comparative government.
Application contact: Dr. James King, Director, 307-766-6484, *Fax:* 307-766-6771, *E-mail:* jking@uwyo.edu. *Web site:* http://www.uwyo.edu/pols/

■ UTAH STATE UNIVERSITY

School of Graduate Studies, College of Humanities, Arts and Social Sciences, Department of Political Science, Logan, UT 84322

AWARDS MA, MS. Part-time programs available.

Faculty: 12 full-time (4 women), 1 (woman) part-time/adjunct.
Students: 8 full-time (3 women), 12 part-time (5 women); includes 1 minority (Hispanic American), 2 international. Average age 26. 27 applicants, 67% accepted. In 2001, 10 degrees awarded.
Degree requirements: For master's, one foreign language, thesis.
Entrance requirements: For master's, GRE General Test, TOEFL, minimum GPA of 3.0. *Application deadline:* For fall admission, 6/15 (priority date); for spring admission, 10/15. Applications are processed on a rolling basis. *Application fee:* $40.
Expenses: Tuition, state resident: full-time $1,693. Tuition, nonresident: full-time $4,233. Required fees: $501. Tuition and fees vary according to program.
Financial support: In 2001–02, 10 teaching assistantships with partial tuition reimbursements were awarded; fellowships, research assistantships, career-related internships or fieldwork, Federal Work-Study, and institutionally sponsored loans also available. Financial award application deadline: 3/15.
Faculty research: Political parties; social choice; international political economics; foreign policy; politics, markets, and public policy.
Randy T. Simmons, Head, 435-797-1306, *Fax:* 435-797-3751, *E-mail:* rsimmons@wpo.hass.usu.edu. *Web site:* http://www.usu.edu/~polisci/

■ VANDERBILT UNIVERSITY

Graduate School, Department of Political Science, Nashville, TN 37240-1001

AWARDS MA, MAT, PhD.

Faculty: 17 full-time (5 women), 1 part-time/adjunct (0 women).
Students: 30 full-time (14 women), 1 part-time; includes 2 minority (1 African American, 1 Hispanic American), 6 international. Average age 28. 43 applicants, 77% accepted. In 2001, 2 master's, 1 doctorate awarded.
Degree requirements: For master's, thesis; for doctorate, thesis/dissertation, final and qualifying exams.
Entrance requirements: For master's and doctorate, GRE General Test. *Application deadline:* For fall admission, 1/15. *Application fee:* $40. Electronic applications accepted.
Expenses: Tuition: Full-time $28,350.
Financial support: In 2001–02, 19 students received support, including 5 fellowships with full tuition reimbursements available (averaging $11,700 per year), research assistantships with full tuition reimbursements available (averaging $11,700 per year), 12 teaching assistantships with full tuition reimbursements available (averaging $11,700 per year); Federal Work-Study and institutionally sponsored loans also available. Financial award application deadline: 1/15.
Faculty research: American politics, comparative politics, international politics, political theory, political culture and life. *Total annual research expenditures:* $79,765.
Gary F. Jensen, Chair, 615-322-6222, *Fax:* 615-343-6003.
Application contact: Carol M. Swain, Director of Graduate Studies, 615-322-6222, *Fax:* 615-343-6003. *Web site:* http://www.vanderbilt.edu/psci/pscimain.htm

■ VILLANOVA UNIVERSITY

Graduate School of Liberal Arts and Sciences, Department of Political Science, Program in Political Science, Villanova, PA 19085-1699

AWARDS MA, MPA.

Students: 13 full-time (10 women), 9 part-time (3 women); includes 1 minority (Hispanic American), 2 international. Average age 26. 24 applicants, 67% accepted. In 2001, 6 degrees awarded.
Degree requirements: For master's, thesis or alternative.
Application deadline: For fall admission, 8/1 (priority date); for spring admission, 12/1. *Application fee:* $40.
Expenses: Tuition: Part-time $340 per credit. One-time fee: $115 full-time. Tuition and fees vary according to program.
Financial support: Application deadline: 4/1.
Application contact: Matthew Kerbel, Information Contact, 610-519-4553, *Fax:* 610-519-7487, *E-mail:* matthew.kerbel@villanova.edu.

Find an in-depth description at www.petersons.com/gradchannel.

■ VIRGINIA POLYTECHNIC INSTITUTE AND STATE UNIVERSITY

Graduate School, College of Arts and Sciences, Department of Political Science, Blacksburg, VA 24061

AWARDS MA.

Faculty: 18 full-time (2 women), 1 (woman) part-time/adjunct.
Students: 15 full-time (2 women), 35 part-time (14 women). 34 applicants, 62% accepted. In 2001, 4 degrees awarded.
Degree requirements: For master's, thesis.
Entrance requirements: For master's, GRE General Test, TOEFL. *Application deadline:* For fall admission, 12/1 (priority date). Applications are processed on a rolling basis. *Application fee:* $45. Electronic applications accepted.
Expenses: Tuition, state resident: part-time $241 per hour. Tuition, nonresident: part-time $406 per hour. Tuition and fees vary according to program.
Financial support: Fellowships, teaching assistantships, unspecified assistantships available. Financial award application deadline: 4/1.
Faculty research: Comparative politics, international relations, American government and politics, research methods.
Dr. Richard C. Rich, Head, 540-231-6571, *Fax:* 540-231-6078, *E-mail:* urban@vt.edu.
Application contact: Darleen M. Baker, 540-231-6572, *Fax:* 540-231-6078, *E-mail:* dgibbsba@vt.edu.

■ WASHINGTON STATE UNIVERSITY

Graduate School, College of Liberal Arts, Department of Political Science, Program in Political Science, Pullman, WA 99164

AWARDS MA, PhD.

Students: 28 full-time (14 women), 11 part-time (8 women); includes 5 minority (2 African Americans, 3 Hispanic Americans), 8 international. Average age 28. 29 applicants, 72% accepted. In 2001, 1 master's, 1 doctorate awarded. Terminal master's awarded for partial completion of doctoral program.
Degree requirements: For master's, oral exam; for doctorate, thesis/dissertation, oral exam, written exam.
Entrance requirements: For master's and doctorate, GRE General Test, minimum GPA of 3.0. *Application deadline:* For fall admission, 2/1; for spring admission, 11/1. *Application fee:* $35. Electronic applications accepted.
Expenses: Tuition, state resident: full-time $6,088; part-time $304 per semester. Tuition, nonresident: full-time $14,918; part-time $746 per semester. Tuition and fees vary according to program.
Financial support: In 2001–02, 4 research assistantships with full and partial tuition reimbursements, 12 teaching assistantships with full and partial tuition reimbursements were awarded. Financial award application deadline: 3/15; financial award applicants required to submit FAFSA.
Faculty research: Political psychology and image theory, grass roots environmental policy, federal juvenile policy. *Total annual research expenditures:* $165,000.
Dr. Faithe Lutze, Director, 509-335-2272, *Fax:* 509-335-7990, *E-mail:* lutze@wsu.edu.
Application contact: Diane Berger, Graduate Secretary, 509-335-2545, *Fax:* 509-335-7990, *E-mail:* bergerd@wsu.edu. *Web site:* http://www.libarts.wsu.edu/polisci/

■ WASHINGTON UNIVERSITY IN ST. LOUIS

Graduate School of Arts and Sciences, Department of Political Science, St. Louis, MO 63130-4899

AWARDS Political economy and public policy (MA); political science (MA, PhD). Part-time programs available.

Students: 33 full-time (12 women), 1 part-time; includes 6 minority (4 African Americans, 1 Hispanic American, 1 Native American), 8 international. 71 applicants, 21% accepted. In 2001, 3 master's, 6 doctorates awarded. Terminal master's awarded for partial completion of doctoral program.
Degree requirements: For master's, thesis or alternative; for doctorate, thesis/dissertation.
Entrance requirements: For master's and doctorate, GRE General Test. *Application deadline:* For fall admission, 1/15 (priority date). Applications are processed on a rolling basis. *Application fee:* $35. Electronic applications accepted.
Expenses: Tuition: Full-time $26,900.
Financial support: Fellowships, research assistantships, teaching assistantships, career-related internships or fieldwork, Federal Work-Study, institutionally sponsored loans, and tuition waivers (full and partial) available. Support available to part-time students. Financial award application deadline: 1/15.
Dr. Jack Knight, Chairperson, 314-935-5822. *Web site:* http://www.artsci.wustl.edu/~polisci/

■ WAYNE STATE UNIVERSITY

Graduate School, College of Liberal Arts, Department of Political Science, Program in Political Science, Detroit, MI 48202

AWARDS MA, PhD, JD/MA.

Students: 56. In 2001, 3 master's, 3 doctorates awarded.
Degree requirements: For doctorate, thesis/dissertation.
Entrance requirements: For master's, GRE General Test, minimum GPA of 2.8; for doctorate, GRE General Test. *Application deadline:* For fall admission, 7/1. *Application fee:* $20 ($30 for international students). Electronic applications accepted.
Expenses: Tuition, state resident: full-time $3,764. Tuition and fees vary according to degree level and program.
Financial support: Fellowships, research assistantships, teaching assistantships, career-related internships or fieldwork, Federal Work-Study, and institutionally sponsored loans available.
Faculty research: Policy and politics, health care policy, African-American politics, representation.

■ WESTERN ILLINOIS UNIVERSITY

School of Graduate Studies, College of Arts and Sciences, Department of Political Science, Macomb, IL 61455-1390

AWARDS MA. Part-time programs available.

Faculty: 9 full-time (2 women).
Students: 16 full-time (5 women), 3 part-time; includes 4 minority (all African Americans), 3 international. Average age 27. 17 applicants, 88% accepted. In 2001, 2 degrees awarded.
Degree requirements: For master's, thesis or alternative.
Entrance requirements: For master's, minimum GPA of 2.75. *Application deadline:* Applications are processed on a rolling basis. *Application fee:* $0 ($25 for international students). Electronic applications accepted.

Expenses: Tuition, state resident: part-time $108 per credit hour. Tuition, nonresident: part-time $216 per credit hour. Required fees: $33 per credit hour.
Financial support: In 2001–02, 14 students received support, including 14 research assistantships with full tuition reimbursements available (averaging $5,720 per year). Financial award applicants required to submit FAFSA.
Faculty research: Voting behavior.
Dr. Charles Helm, Chairperson, 309-298-1055.
Application contact: Dr. Barbara Baily, Director of Graduate Studies, 309-298-1806, *Fax:* 309-298-2345, *E-mail:* grad-office@wiu.edu. *Web site:* http://www.wiu.edu/

■ WESTERN MICHIGAN UNIVERSITY

Graduate College, College of Arts and Sciences, Department of Political Science, Program in Political Science, Kalamazoo, MI 49008-5202

AWARDS MA, PhD.

Faculty: 18 full-time (5 women).
Students: 22 full-time (7 women), 17 part-time (7 women); includes 7 minority (6 African Americans, 1 Hispanic American), 10 international. 20 applicants, 60% accepted, 6 enrolled. In 2001, 2 master's, 2 doctorates awarded.
Degree requirements: For master's, oral exams, thesis optional; for doctorate, thesis/dissertation, oral exam.
Entrance requirements: For doctorate, GRE General Test. *Application deadline:* For fall admission, 2/15 (priority date). Applications are processed on a rolling basis. *Application fee:* $25.
Expenses: Tuition, state resident: part-time $186 per credit hour. Tuition, nonresident: part-time $442 per credit hour. Required fees: $602. One-time fee: $132 part-time. Tuition and fees vary according to course load.
Financial support: Fellowships, research assistantships, teaching assistantships, Federal Work-Study available. Financial award application deadline: 2/15; financial award applicants required to submit FAFSA.
Application contact: Admissions and Orientation, 616-387-2000, *Fax:* 616-387-2355.

■ WESTERN WASHINGTON UNIVERSITY

Graduate School, College of Arts and Sciences, Department of Political Science, Bellingham, WA 98225-5996

AWARDS MA. Part-time programs available.

Degree requirements: For master's, thesis (for some programs), comprehensive exam.
Entrance requirements: For master's, GRE General Test, TOEFL, minimum GPA of 3.0 in last 60 semester hours or last 90 quarter hours.

■ WEST TEXAS A&M UNIVERSITY

College of Education and Social Sciences, Department of History and Political Science, Program in Political Science, Canyon, TX 79016-0001

AWARDS MA. Part-time and evening/weekend programs available.

Faculty: 3 full-time (0 women), 2 part-time/adjunct (0 women).
Students: 2 full-time (0 women), 6 part-time (3 women). Average age 34. 8 applicants. In 2001, 3 degrees awarded.
Degree requirements: For master's, thesis optional. *Median time to degree:* Master's–3 years full-time, 6 years part-time.
Entrance requirements: For master's, GRE General Test. *Application deadline:* Applications are processed on a rolling basis. *Application fee:* $25 ($75 for international students). Electronic applications accepted.
Expenses: Tuition, state resident: part-time $120 per hour. Tuition, nonresident: part-time $253 per hour.
Financial support: In 2001–02, research assistantships with partial tuition reimbursements (averaging $6,500 per year), teaching assistantships with partial tuition reimbursements (averaging $6,700 per year) were awarded. Career-related internships or fieldwork, Federal Work-Study, institutionally sponsored loans, and tuition waivers (partial) also available. Support available to part-time students. Financial award applicants required to submit CSS PROFILE or FAFSA.
Faculty research: American government, public administration, state and local government, international politics.
Application contact: Dr. Roy Thoman, Graduate Adviser, 806-651-2432, *Fax:* 806-651-2601, *E-mail:* rthoman@mail.wtamu.edu.

■ WEST VIRGINIA UNIVERSITY

Eberly College of Arts and Sciences, Department of Political Science, Morgantown, WV 26506

AWARDS American public policy and politics (MA); international and comparative public policy and U.S. politics (MA); political science (PhD); public policy analysis (PhD).

Faculty: 17 full-time (2 women), 4 part-time/adjunct (2 women).
Students: 30 full-time (8 women), 10 part-time (4 women); includes 1 minority (African American), 7 international. Average age 31. 45 applicants, 47% accepted. In 2001, 8 master's, 1 doctorate awarded. Terminal master's awarded for partial completion of doctoral program.
Degree requirements: For master's, thesis optional; for doctorate, thesis/dissertation, comprehensive exam.
Entrance requirements: For master's and doctorate, GRE General Test, TOEFL, minimum GPA of 2.75. *Application deadline:* For fall admission, 4/1 (priority date). Applications are processed on a rolling basis. *Application fee:* $45.
Expenses: Tuition, state resident: full-time $2,791. Tuition, nonresident: full-time $8,659. Required fees: $1,002. Tuition and fees vary according to program.
Financial support: In 2001–02, 14 students received support, including 4 research assistantships, 14 teaching assistantships; career-related internships or fieldwork, Federal Work-Study, institutionally sponsored loans, tuition waivers (full and partial), and unspecified assistantships also available. Financial award application deadline: 2/1; financial award applicants required to submit FAFSA.
Faculty research: Public policy, research methods, foreign policy analysis, judicial politics, environmental and energy policy.
Dr. Allan S. Hammock, Chair, 304-293-3198 Ext. 5273, *Fax:* 304-293-8644, *E-mail:* allan.hammock@mail.wvu.edu.
Application contact: Dr. Jeff Worsham, Director, Graduate Studies, 304-293-3811 Ext. 5277, *Fax:* 304-293-8644, *E-mail:* jeff.worsham@mail.wvu.edu. *Web site:* http://www.polsci.wvu.edu/

■ WICHITA STATE UNIVERSITY

Graduate School, Fairmount College of Liberal Arts and Sciences, Department of Political Science, Wichita, KS 67260

AWARDS MA. Part-time and evening/weekend programs available.

Faculty: 5 full-time (0 women).
Students: Average age 46. In 2001, 4 degrees awarded.
Degree requirements: For master's, internship, thesis optional.
Entrance requirements: For master's, GRE, TOEFL, minimum GPA of 3.0. *Application deadline:* For fall admission, 7/1 (priority date); for spring admission, 1/1. Applications are processed on a rolling basis. *Application fee:* $25 ($40 for international students). Electronic applications accepted.
Expenses: Tuition, state resident: full-time $1,888; part-time $105 per credit. Tuition, nonresident: full-time $6,129; part-time $341 per credit. Required fees: $345; $19 per credit. $17 per semester. Tuition and fees vary according to course load and program.
Financial support: Teaching assistantships with full tuition reimbursements, career-related internships or fieldwork, Federal Work-Study, and institutionally sponsored loans available. Support available to part-time students. Financial award application deadline: 4/1; financial award applicants required to submit FAFSA.

Wichita State University (continued)
Faculty research: Foreign intelligence, political participation of U.S. parties, Southern civil rights policy.
Dr. Kenneth Ciboski, Chairperson, 316-978-3165, *E-mail:* kenneth.ciboski@wichita.edu. *Web site:* http://www.wichita.edu/

■ YALE UNIVERSITY

Graduate School of Arts and Sciences, Department of Political Science, New Haven, CT 06520

AWARDS PhD.

Degree requirements: For doctorate, one foreign language, thesis/dissertation.
Entrance requirements: For doctorate, GRE General Test.
Faculty research: U.N. and international security.

Public, Regional, and Industrial Affairs

CITY AND REGIONAL PLANNING

■ ALABAMA AGRICULTURAL AND MECHANICAL UNIVERSITY

School of Graduate Studies, School of Agricultural and Environmental Sciences, Department of Community Planning and Urban Studies, Huntsville, AL 35811

AWARDS Urban and regional planning (MURP). Part-time and evening/weekend programs available.

Faculty: 7 full-time (2 women).
Students: 4 full-time (3 women), 9 part-time (2 women); includes 12 minority (all African Americans). In 2001, 8 degrees awarded.
Degree requirements: For master's, comprehensive exam.
Entrance requirements: For master's, GRE General Test. *Application deadline:* For fall admission, 5/1. *Application fee:* $15 ($20 for international students).
Expenses: Tuition, state resident: full-time $1,380. Tuition, nonresident: full-time $2,500.
Financial support: In 2001–02, research assistantships with full tuition reimbursements (averaging $9,000 per year); career-related internships or fieldwork also available. Support available to part-time students. Financial award application deadline: 4/1.
Faculty research: Urban and rural research, needs assessment and community trends through analysis of social indicators, fiscal impact studies, rural transportation, health care. *Total annual research expenditures:* $33,000.
Dr. Chukudi Izeogu, Chair, 256-851-5425, *Fax:* 256-851-5906.

■ ARIZONA STATE UNIVERSITY

Graduate College, College of Architecture and Environmental Design, Department of Planning, Tempe, AZ 85287

AWARDS Planning (MEP).

Entrance requirements: For master's, GRE General Test.
Faculty research: Building design, human settlements.

■ AUBURN UNIVERSITY

Graduate School, College of Architecture, Design, and Construction, Program in Community Planning, Auburn University, AL 36849

AWARDS MCP, MPA/MCP. Part-time programs available.

Faculty: 38 full-time (8 women).
Students: 10 full-time (2 women), 1 international. 15 applicants, 60% accepted. In 2001, 4 degrees awarded.
Degree requirements: For master's, oral exam, project.
Entrance requirements: For master's, GRE General Test. *Application deadline:* For fall admission, 7/7; for spring admission, 11/24. Applications are processed on a rolling basis. *Application fee:* $25 ($50 for international students). Electronic applications accepted.
Financial support: Federal Work-Study available. Support available to part-time students. Financial award application deadline: 3/15.
Dr. John J. Pittari, Chairman, 334-844-4516.
Application contact: Dr. John F. Pritchett, Dean of the Graduate School, 334-844-4700, *E-mail:* hatchlb@mail.auburn.edu. *Web site:* http://www.auburn.edu/academic/architecture/arch/cp/index.html

■ BALL STATE UNIVERSITY

Graduate School, College of Architecture and Planning, Department of Urban Planning, Muncie, IN 47306-1099

AWARDS MURP.

Faculty: 9.
Students: 14 full-time (6 women), 5 part-time (1 woman); includes 3 minority (all African Americans), 3 international. Average age 26. 16 applicants, 81% accepted. In 2001, 1 degree awarded.
Degree requirements: For master's, thesis.
Entrance requirements: For master's, writing sample. *Application fee:* $25 ($35 for international students).
Expenses: Tuition, state resident: full-time $4,068; part-time $2,542. Tuition, nonresident: full-time $10,944; part-time $6,462. Required fees: $1,000; $500 per term.
Financial support: In 2001–02, 14 teaching assistantships with full tuition reimbursements were awarded; career-related internships or fieldwork also available. Financial award application deadline: 3/1.
Faculty research: Computer-assisted land-use analysis.
Dr. J. Paul Mitchell, Chair, 765-285-1963, *Fax:* 765-285-2648, *E-mail:* pmitchell@bsu.edu.
Application contact: Dr. Francis Parker, Director, 765-285-1963, *Fax:* 765-285-2648, *E-mail:* fparker@bsu.edu. *Web site:* http://www.bsu.edu/cap/planning/planning.html/

■ BOSTON UNIVERSITY

Metropolitan College, Department of Urban Affairs and Planning, Program in City Planning, Boston, MA 02215

AWARDS MCP. Part-time and evening/weekend programs available.

Faculty: 1 full-time (0 women), 9 part-time/adjunct (1 woman).
Students: 1 full-time (0 women), 5 part-time (2 women), 1 international. Average age 32. 20 applicants, 80% accepted. In 2001, 10 degrees awarded.
Degree requirements: For master's, thesis.
Application deadline: For fall admission, 7/15 (priority date); for spring admission, 1/15. Applications are processed on a rolling basis. *Application fee:* $60.
Expenses: Tuition: Full-time $25,872; part-time $340 per credit. Required fees: $40 per semester. Part-time tuition and fees vary according to class time, course level and program.
Financial support: Research assistantships, career-related internships or fieldwork, Federal Work-Study, institutionally

sponsored loans, and tuition waivers (partial) available. Support available to part-time students. Financial award application deadline: 6/15.
Faculty research: Housing, community development and land use planning, environmental management and planning, international comparative development planning.
Application contact: Chairman, Admissions Committee, 617-353-3025. *Web site:* http://bu.edu.met/cp

■ CALIFORNIA POLYTECHNIC STATE UNIVERSITY, SAN LUIS OBISPO

College of Architecture and Environmental Design, Department of City and Regional Planning, San Luis Obispo, CA 93407

AWARDS MCRP, MCRP/MS. Evening/weekend programs available.

Faculty: 5 full-time (1 woman), 11 part-time/adjunct (4 women).
Students: 32 full-time (11 women), 3 part-time (2 women). 33 applicants, 82% accepted, 16 enrolled. In 2001, 12 degrees awarded.
Degree requirements: For master's, thesis or alternative.
Entrance requirements: For master's, GRE, minimum GPA of 3.0. *Application deadline:* For fall admission, 7/1 (priority date). Applications are processed on a rolling basis. *Application fee:* $55.
Expenses: Tuition, nonresident: part-time $164 per unit. One-time fee: $2,153 part-time.
Financial support: In 2001–02, 18 students received support, including 6 research assistantships; career-related internships or fieldwork, Federal Work-Study, institutionally sponsored loans, and unspecified assistantships also available. Support available to part-time students. Financial award application deadline: 3/2; financial award applicants required to submit FAFSA.
Faculty research: Natural hazards, housing, small town and rural planning, planning implementation, subdivision site design, transportation, geographic information systems survey research.
William J. Siembieda, Head, 805-756-1592, *Fax:* 805-756-1340, *E-mail:* wsiembie@calpoly.edu.
Application contact: Linda Day, Graduate Coordinator, 805-756-1592, *Fax:* 805-756-1340, *E-mail:* lday@calpoly.edu. *Web site:* http://www.calpoly.edu/~crp/

■ CALIFORNIA STATE POLYTECHNIC UNIVERSITY, POMONA

Academic Affairs, College of Environmental Design, Program in Urban and Regional Planning, Pomona, CA 91768-2557

AWARDS MURP. Part-time programs available.

Students: 27 full-time (11 women), 17 part-time (8 women); includes 21 minority (4 African Americans, 6 Asian Americans or Pacific Islanders, 10 Hispanic Americans, 1 Native American), 4 international. Average age 30. 39 applicants, 64% accepted. In 2001, 9 degrees awarded.
Degree requirements: For master's, thesis or alternative.
Entrance requirements: For master's, GRE General Test. *Application deadline:* For fall admission, 5/1 (priority date); for winter admission, 10/15 (priority date); for spring admission, 1/20 (priority date). Applications are processed on a rolling basis. *Application fee:* $55. Electronic applications accepted.
Expenses: Tuition, nonresident: part-time $164 per unit. Required fees: $1,850.
Financial support: Career-related internships or fieldwork, Federal Work-Study, and institutionally sponsored loans available. Support available to part-time students. Financial award application deadline: 3/2; financial award applicants required to submit FAFSA.
Dr. Felix R. Barreto, Graduate Coordinator, 909-869-2727, *Fax:* 909-869-4688, *E-mail:* fbarreto@csupomona.edu. *Web site:* http://www.csupomona.edu/~urp/

■ CALIFORNIA STATE UNIVERSITY, CHICO

Graduate School, College of Behavioral and Social Sciences, Department of Geography and Planning, Program in Rural and Town Planning, Chico, CA 95929-0722

AWARDS MRTP.

Degree requirements: For master's, thesis or alternative, oral exam.
Application deadline: For fall admission, 4/1; for spring admission, 10/1. Applications are processed on a rolling basis. *Application fee:* $55. Electronic applications accepted.
Expenses: Tuition, state resident: full-time $2,148. Tuition, nonresident: full-time $6,576.
Application contact: Dr. Jacque Chase, Graduate Coordinator, 530-898-5587.

■ THE CATHOLIC UNIVERSITY OF AMERICA

School of Architecture and Planning, Washington, DC 20064

AWARDS M Arch, M Arch Studies. Part-time programs available.

Faculty: 14 full-time (3 women), 16 part-time/adjunct (3 women).
Students: 76 full-time (37 women), 7 part-time (3 women); includes 14 minority (6 African Americans, 5 Asian Americans or Pacific Islanders, 3 Hispanic Americans), 15 international. Average age 27. 80 applicants, 51% accepted, 23 enrolled. In 2001, 45 degrees awarded.
Degree requirements: For master's, thesis.
Entrance requirements: For master's, minimum GPA of 2.7, portfolio. *Application deadline:* For fall admission, 1/22 (priority date); for spring admission, 10/15. Applications are processed on a rolling basis. *Application fee:* $55. Electronic applications accepted.
Expenses: Contact institution.
Financial support: In 2001–02, 40 teaching assistantships were awarded; Federal Work-Study, scholarships/grants, and tuition waivers (partial) also available. Financial award application deadline: 1/22; financial award applicants required to submit FAFSA.
Faculty research: Architectural history, sacred architecture, computers, technology, urban design, preservation.
Gregory K. Hunt, Dean, 202-319-5784, *Fax:* 202-238-2023, *E-mail:* huntg@cua.edu.
Application contact: Dr. Terrance Williams, Associate Dean of Graduate Studies, 202-319-5188, *Fax:* 202-319-5728.

■ CLARK UNIVERSITY

Graduate School, Department of International Development, Community, and Environment, Program in Community Development and Planning, Worcester, MA 01610-1477

AWARDS MA.

Degree requirements: For master's, thesis.
Entrance requirements: For master's, TOEFL. *Application deadline:* For fall admission, 2/1. *Application fee:* $40.
Expenses: Tuition: Full-time $24,400; part-time $763 per credit. Required fees: $10.
Financial support: In 2001–02, research assistantships with full and partial tuition reimbursements (averaging $9,250 per year), teaching assistantships with full and partial tuition reimbursements (averaging $9,250 per year) were awarded. Tuition waivers (full and partial) also available.
Dr. William F. Fisher, Director, *Fax:* 508-793-8820, *E-mail:* wfisher@clarku.edu.

Clark University (continued)
Application contact: Liz Owens, IDCE Graduate Admissions, 508-793-7201, *Fax:* 508-793-8820, *E-mail:* idce@clarku.edu.

■ CLEMSON UNIVERSITY

Graduate School, College of Architecture, Arts, and Humanities, Department of Planning and Landscape Architecture, Clemson, SC 29634

AWARDS Environmental planning (MCRP); land development planning (MCRP).

Students: 32 full-time (14 women), 12 international. Average age 24. 52 applicants, 71% accepted, 18 enrolled. In 2001, 14 degrees awarded.
Degree requirements: For master's, departmental paper or thesis.
Entrance requirements: For master's, GRE General Test, TOEFL. *Application deadline:* For fall admission, 4/15 (priority date). Applications are processed on a rolling basis. *Application fee:* $40.
Expenses: Tuition, state resident: full-time $5,310. Tuition, nonresident: full-time $11,284.
Financial support: Fellowships, research assistantships, teaching assistantships, career-related internships or fieldwork, Federal Work-Study, and scholarships/grants available. Financial award application deadline: 4/15; financial award applicants required to submit FAFSA.
Faculty research: Coastal planning, regional economic development, health care access.
Jose R. Caban, Chair, 864-656-3898, *Fax:* 864-656-1810, *E-mail:* c547196@clemson.edu.
Application contact: Dr. Terry Farris, Graduate Coordinator, 856-656-3903, *Fax:* 856-656-0204, *E-mail:* jfarris@clemson.edu. *Web site:* http://hubcap.clemson.edu/aah/pla/index.html

■ CLEVELAND STATE UNIVERSITY

College of Graduate Studies, Maxine Goodman Levin College of Urban Affairs, Program in Urban Planning, Design, and Development, Cleveland, OH 44115

AWARDS MUPDD, JD/MUPDD. Part-time and evening/weekend programs available.

Faculty: 10 full-time (4 women), 2 part-time/adjunct (0 women).
Students: 19 full-time (10 women), 26 part-time (13 women); includes 6 minority (5 African Americans, 1 Hispanic American), 3 international. Average age 30. 12 applicants, 67% accepted. In 2001, 16 degrees awarded.
Degree requirements: For master's, project or thesis, thesis optional.
Entrance requirements: For master's, GRE General Test, minimum GPA of 3.0. *Application deadline:* For fall admission, 7/15 (priority date). Applications are processed on a rolling basis. *Application fee:* $25.
Expenses: Tuition, state resident: full-time $6,838; part-time $263 per credit hour. Tuition, nonresident: full-time $13,526; part-time $520 per credit hour.
Financial support: Research assistantships, career-related internships or fieldwork, Federal Work-Study, and tuition waivers (full and partial) available. Support available to part-time students. Financial award application deadline: 3/1.
Faculty research: Community development, economic development, real estate finance and development, environmental issues.
Dr. Robert Simons, Coordinator, 216-687-5258, *Fax:* 216-687-9342, *E-mail:* roby@urban.csuohio.edu.
Application contact: Graduate Programs Coordinator, 216-523-7522, *Fax:* 216-687-5398, *E-mail:* gradprog@wolf.csuohio.edu.

■ COLUMBIA UNIVERSITY

Graduate School of Architecture, Planning, and Preservation, Program in Urban Planning, New York, NY 10027

AWARDS MS, PhD, JD/MS, M Arch/MS, MBA/MS, MIA/MS, MPH/MS, MS/MS. PhD offered through the Graduate School of Arts and Sciences.

Faculty: 4 full-time (0 women), 12 part-time/adjunct (2 women).
Students: 64 full-time (38 women). In 2001, 18 degrees awarded.
Degree requirements: For master's, thesis, registration.
Entrance requirements: For master's, GRE General Test. *Application deadline:* For fall admission, 2/15. *Application fee:* $60.
Expenses: Tuition: Full-time $27,528. Required fees: $1,638.
Financial support: Fellowships, teaching assistantships available. Financial award application deadline: 2/15.
Elliott Sclar, Director, 212-854-3513.
Application contact: Office of Admissions, 212-854-3510. *Web site:* http://www.arch.columbia.edu/up/

Find an in-depth description at www.petersons.com/gradchannel.

■ CORNELL UNIVERSITY

Graduate School, Graduate Fields of Agriculture and Life Sciences, Field of Community and Rural Development, Ithaca, NY 14853-0001

AWARDS Community development process (MPS); economic development (MPS); local government organizations and operation (MPS); program development and planning (MPS).

Faculty: 17 full-time.
Students: 13 full-time (10 women), 8 international. 28 applicants, 79% accepted. In 2001, 2 degrees awarded.
Entrance requirements: For master's, GRE General Test (recommended), TOEFL, 3 letters of recommendation. *Application deadline:* For fall admission, 5/1. *Application fee:* $65. Electronic applications accepted.
Expenses: Tuition: Full-time $25,970. Required fees: $50.
Financial support: In 2001–02, 8 students received support, including 6 fellowships with full tuition reimbursements available, 2 teaching assistantships with full tuition reimbursements available; research assistantships with full tuition reimbursements available, institutionally sponsored loans, scholarships/grants, tuition waivers (full and partial), and unspecified assistantships also available. Financial award applicants required to submit FAFSA.
Application contact: Graduate Field Assistant, 607-255-1823, *E-mail:* gradcrd@cornell.edu. *Web site:* http://www.gradschool.cornell.edu/grad/fields_1/crd.html

■ CORNELL UNIVERSITY

Graduate School, Graduate Fields of Architecture, Art and Planning, Field of City and Regional Planning, Ithaca, NY 14853-0001

AWARDS City and regional planning (MRP, PhD); historic preservation planning (MA); planning theory and systems analysis (MRP, PhD); regional science (MRP, PhD); urban and regional theory (MRP, PhD); urban planning history (MRP, PhD).

Faculty: 22 full-time.
Students: 104 full-time (60 women); includes 20 minority (1 African American, 7 Asian Americans or Pacific Islanders, 12 Hispanic Americans), 15 international. 182 applicants, 69% accepted. In 2001, 30 master's, 8 doctorates awarded.
Degree requirements: For master's, thesis (MA); for doctorate, thesis/dissertation.
Entrance requirements: For master's and doctorate, GRE General Test, TOEFL, 2 letters of recommendation. *Application deadline:* For fall admission, 1/10. *Application fee:* $65. Electronic applications accepted.
Expenses: Tuition: Full-time $25,970. Required fees: $50.
Financial support: In 2001–02, 51 students received support, including 19 fellowships with full tuition reimbursements available, 2 research assistantships with full tuition reimbursements available, 30 teaching assistantships with full tuition reimbursements available; institutionally sponsored loans, scholarships/grants, tuition waivers (full and partial), and unspecified assistantships also available. Financial award applicants required to submit FAFSA.

Faculty research: Land use planning, regional and community economic development, international development, historic preservation, urban and regional industrial structure.
Application contact: Graduate Field Assistant, 607-255-6848, *Fax:* 607-255-1971, *E-mail:* crp_admissions@cornell.edu. *Web site:* http://www.gradschool.cornell.edu/grad/fields_1/crp.html

■ CORNELL UNIVERSITY

Graduate School, Graduate Fields of Architecture, Art and Planning, Field of Regional Science, Ithaca, NY 14853-0001

AWARDS Environmental studies (MA, MS, PhD); international spatial problems (MA, MS, PhD); location theory (MA, MS, PhD); multiregional economic analysis (MA, MS, PhD); peace science (MA, MS, PhD); planning methods (MA, MS, PhD); urban and regional economics (MA, MS, PhD).

Faculty: 15 full-time.
Students: 10 full-time (3 women), 8 international. 3 applicants, 100% accepted. In 2001, 2 master's, 2 doctorates awarded. Terminal master's awarded for partial completion of doctoral program.
Degree requirements: For master's and doctorate, thesis/dissertation.
Entrance requirements: For master's, GRE General Test (native English speakers only), TOEFL, 2 letters of recommendation; for doctorate, GRE General Test, TOEFL, 2 letters of recommendation. *Application deadline:* For fall admission, 1/15 (priority date). *Application fee:* $65. Electronic applications accepted.
Expenses: Tuition: Full-time $25,970. Required fees: $50.
Financial support: In 2001–02, 3 students received support, including 2 research assistantships with full tuition reimbursements available, 1 teaching assistantship with full tuition reimbursement available; fellowships with full tuition reimbursements available, institutionally sponsored loans, scholarships/grants, tuition waivers (full and partial), and unspecified assistantships also available. Financial award applicants required to submit FAFSA.
Faculty research: Urban and regional growth, spatial economics, formation of spatial patterns by socioeconomic systems, non-linear dynamics and complex systems, environmental-economic systems.
Application contact: Graduate Field Assistant, 607-255-6848, *Fax:* 607-255-1971, *E-mail:* regsci@cornell.edu. *Web site:* http://www.gradschool.cornell.edu/grad/fields_1/reg-sci.html

■ DELTA STATE UNIVERSITY

Graduate Programs, College of Arts and Sciences, Department of Social Sciences, Program in Community Development, Cleveland, MS 38733-0001

AWARDS MSCD. Part-time programs available.

Degree requirements: For master's, thesis or alternative.
Application deadline: For fall admission, 8/1 (priority date); for spring admission, 12/1 (priority date). Applications are processed on a rolling basis. *Application fee:* $0.
Expenses: Tuition, state resident: full-time $3,100; part-time $144 per hour. Tuition, nonresident: full-time $7,174; part-time $382 per hour.
Financial support: Research assistantships, career-related internships or fieldwork, Federal Work-Study, and institutionally sponsored loans available. Support available to part-time students. Financial award application deadline: 6/1.

■ DEPAUL UNIVERSITY

College of Liberal Arts and Sciences, Programs in Public Services, Chicago, IL 60604-2287

AWARDS Financial administration management (Certificate); health administration (Certificate); health law administration (MS); metropolitan planning (Certificate); nonprofit organization management (MS); public administration (MS); public service management (MS), including association management, fundraising and philanthropy, healthcare administration, higher education administration, metropolitan planning, non-profit administration, public administration, public policy; public services (Certificate). Part-time and evening/weekend programs available.

Faculty: 11 full-time (5 women), 18 part-time/adjunct (9 women).
Students: 52 full-time (32 women), 144 part-time (96 women); includes 50 minority (34 African Americans, 3 Asian Americans or Pacific Islanders, 13 Hispanic Americans), 3 international. 90 applicants, 93% accepted. In 2001, 65 degrees awarded.
Degree requirements: For master's, thesis, thesis or practicum.
Entrance requirements: For master's, minimum GPA of 2.70. *Application deadline:* Applications are processed on a rolling basis. *Application fee:* $25. Electronic applications accepted.
Expenses: Tuition: Part-time $362 per credit hour. Tuition and fees vary according to program.
Financial support: In 2001–02, 15 students received support, including 2 research assistantships with full tuition reimbursements available (averaging $6,000 per year); career-related internships or fieldwork, Federal Work-Study, institutionally sponsored loans, scholarships/grants, and tuition waivers (partial) also available. Support available to part-time students. Financial award application deadline: 7/1; financial award applicants required to submit FAFSA.
Faculty research: Government financing, transportation, leadership, health care, empowerment zones, volunteerism and organizational behavior, non-profit organizations, dating violence. *Total annual research expenditures:* $20,000.
Dr. J. Patrick Murphy, Director, 312-362-8441, *Fax:* 312-362-5506, *E-mail:* jpmurphy@depaul.edu.
Application contact: Graduate Information, 312-362-8441, *Fax:* 312-362-5506, *E-mail:* pubserv@depaul.edu. *Web site:* http://www.depaul.edu/~pubserv/

■ EASTERN KENTUCKY UNIVERSITY

The Graduate School, College of Arts and Sciences, Department of Government, Program in General Public Administration, Richmond, KY 40475-3102

AWARDS Community development (MPA); community health administration (MPA); general public administration (MPA).

Students: 33.
Entrance requirements: For master's, GRE General Test, minimum GPA of 2.5. *Application fee:* $0.
Expenses: Tuition, state resident: full-time $1,468; part-time $165 per credit hour. Tuition, nonresident: full-time $4,034; part-time $450 per credit hour.
Dr. Richard Vance, Chair, Department of Government, 859-622-5931.

■ EASTERN WASHINGTON UNIVERSITY

Graduate School Studies, College of Business Administration and Public Administration, Department of Urban and Regional Planning, Cheney, WA 99004-2431

AWARDS MURP, MPA/MURP.

Faculty: 4 full-time (1 woman).
Students: 16 full-time (7 women), 11 part-time (4 women); includes 8 minority (2 African Americans, 1 Asian American or Pacific Islander, 1 Hispanic American, 4 Native Americans). 21 applicants, 57% accepted, 6 enrolled. In 2001, 7 degrees awarded.
Degree requirements: For master's, thesis or alternative, comprehensive exam.
Entrance requirements: For master's, minimum GPA of 3.0. *Application deadline:* For fall admission, 4/1 (priority date); for spring admission, 1/15. Applications are processed on a rolling basis. *Application fee:* $35.
Expenses: Tuition, state resident: full-time $1,586; part-time $159 per credit hour. Tuition, nonresident: full-time $4,677;

Eastern Washington University (continued)
part-time $468 per credit hour. Required fees: $222; $159 per credit. $74 per quarter.
Financial support: In 2001–02, teaching assistantships with partial tuition reimbursements (averaging $7,000 per year); career-related internships or fieldwork, Federal Work-Study, institutionally sponsored loans, scholarships/grants, health care benefits, tuition waivers (partial), and unspecified assistantships also available. Financial award application deadline: 2/1.
Dr. William Kelley, Advisor, 509-358-2226, *Fax:* 509-358-2267.

■ EAST TENNESSEE STATE UNIVERSITY

School of Graduate Studies, College of Business, Department of Economics, Finance, and Urban Studies, Johnson City, TN 37614

AWARDS City management (MCM); community development (MPM); general administration (MPM); municipal service management (MPM); urban and regional economic development (MPM); urban and regional planning (MPM).

Faculty: 1 full-time (0 women).
Students: 15 full-time (6 women), 14 part-time (9 women); includes 4 minority (all African Americans), 2 international. Average age 35. In 2001, 10 degrees awarded.
Degree requirements: For master's, internship, oral defense of thesis, research report.
Entrance requirements: For master's, GRE General Test, TOEFL, minimum GPA of 3.0. *Application deadline:* For fall admission, 7/1 (priority date); for spring admission, 12/1. Applications are processed on a rolling basis. *Application fee:* $25 ($35 for international students).
Expenses: Tuition, state resident: part-time $181 per hour. Tuition, nonresident: part-time $270 per hour. Required fees: $220 per term.
Financial support: Research assistantships with full tuition reimbursements available.
Dr. Jafar Alavi, Chair, 423-439-4455, *Fax:* 423-439-5383, *E-mail:* drjalavi@etsu.edu.
Application contact: Dr. Lon Felker, Director, 423-439-6631, *Fax:* 423-439-5383, *E-mail:* felker@etsu.edu. *Web site:* http://www.etsu.edu/

■ FLORIDA ATLANTIC UNIVERSITY

College of Architecture, Urban and Public Affairs, Department of Urban and Regional Planning, Boca Raton, FL 33431-0991

AWARDS MURP. Part-time and evening/weekend programs available.

Faculty: 6 full-time (2 women), 4 part-time/adjunct (1 woman).
Students: 19 full-time (10 women), 18 part-time (10 women); includes 13 minority (6 African Americans, 1 Asian American or Pacific Islander, 6 Hispanic Americans), 2 international. Average age 31. 24 applicants, 88% accepted, 15 enrolled. In 2001, 12 degrees awarded.
Entrance requirements: For master's, GRE General Test, TOEFL, minimum GPA of 3.0. *Application deadline:* For fall admission, 6/1 (priority date); for spring admission, 10/20 (priority date). Applications are processed on a rolling basis. *Application fee:* $20.
Expenses: Tuition, state resident: full-time $3,098; part-time $172 per credit. Tuition, nonresident: full-time $10,427; part-time $579 per credit.
Financial support: In 2001–02, 6 students received support, including 4 fellowships with full tuition reimbursements available (averaging $7,000 per year), 3 research assistantships (averaging $4,200 per year); career-related internships or fieldwork, Federal Work-Study, institutionally sponsored loans, and tuition waivers (partial) also available. Financial award application deadline: 4/1.
Faculty research: Growth management, urban design, computer applications/geographical information systems, environmental planning. *Total annual research expenditures:* $30,000.
Dr. Margaret S. Murray, Chair, 954-762-5652, *Fax:* 954-762-5673, *E-mail:* mmurray@fau.edu.
Application contact: Brenda Powers, Coordinator of Academic Programs, 954-762-5662, *E-mail:* bpowers@fau.edu. *Web site:* http://www.fau.edu/divdept/cupa/depts/urb.htm

■ FLORIDA STATE UNIVERSITY

Graduate Studies, College of Social Sciences, Department of Urban and Regional Planning, Tallahassee, FL 32306

AWARDS MSP, PhD, JD/MSP, MPA/MSP. Part-time programs available.

Faculty: 10 full-time (3 women), 8 part-time/adjunct (3 women).
Students: 56 full-time (27 women), 15 part-time (10 women); includes 16 minority (9 African Americans, 2 Asian Americans or Pacific Islanders, 5 Hispanic Americans), 10 international. Average age 26. 110 applicants, 45% accepted, 31 enrolled. In 2001, 19 master's awarded.
Degree requirements: For master's, capstone project, internship; for doctorate, thesis/dissertation. *Median time to degree:* Master's–2 years full-time, 3 years part-time; doctorate–3 years full-time, 5 years part-time.
Entrance requirements: For master's and doctorate, GRE General Test, minimum GPA of 3.0. *Application deadline:* For fall admission, 1/15 (priority date); for spring admission, 9/1. Applications are processed on a rolling basis. *Application fee:* $20. Electronic applications accepted.
Expenses: Tuition, state resident: part-time $163 per credit hour. Tuition, nonresident: part-time $570 per credit hour. Tuition and fees vary according to program.
Financial support: In 2001–02, 27 students received support, including 1 fellowship with full tuition reimbursement available (averaging $20,000 per year), 20 research assistantships with full tuition reimbursements available, 6 teaching assistantships with full tuition reimbursements available; career-related internships or fieldwork, Federal Work-Study, institutionally sponsored loans, and tuition waivers (partial) also available. Financial award application deadline: 1/15; financial award applicants required to submit FAFSA.
Faculty research: Growth management, environmental planning, developing countries, transportation, health, housing and community development. *Total annual research expenditures:* $1.2 million.
Dr. Charles E. Connerly, Chairperson, 850-644-4510, *Fax:* 850-645-4841, *E-mail:* cconnerl@coss.fsu.edu.
Application contact: Cynthia Brown, Admissions Assistant, 850-644-4510, *Fax:* 850-645-4841, *E-mail:* durp@coss.fsu.edu. *Web site:* http://www.fsu.edu/~durp/

■ GEORGE MASON UNIVERSITY

School of Public Policy, Program in Regional Economic Development and Technology, Fairfax, VA 22030-4444

AWARDS MAIS.

Degree requirements: For master's, thesis or alternative.
Entrance requirements: For master's, minimum GPA of 3.0 in last 60 hours.
Expenses: Tuition, state resident: full-time $3,168; part-time $132 per credit hour. Tuition, nonresident: full-time $11,280; part-time $470 per credit hour. Required fees: $1,416; $59 per credit hour.

■ GEORGIA INSTITUTE OF TECHNOLOGY

Graduate Studies and Research, College of Architecture, City Planning Program, Atlanta, GA 30332-0001

AWARDS MCP, M Arch/MCP, MCP/MSCE.

Degree requirements: For master's, thesis, internship.
Entrance requirements: For master's, GRE General Test, TOEFL, minimum GPA of 2.7. Electronic applications accepted.
Faculty research: Institutional conflict management and negotiation, water quality, policy analysis, demographic studies, geographic information systems.

■ HARVARD UNIVERSITY

Graduate School of Arts and Sciences, Committee on Architecture, Landscape Architecture, and Urban Planning, Cambridge, MA 02138

AWARDS Architecture (PhD); landscape architecture (PhD); urban planning (PhD).

Degree requirements: For doctorate, one foreign language, thesis/dissertation, oral exam.
Entrance requirements: For doctorate, GRE General Test, TOEFL.
Expenses: Tuition: Full-time $23,370. Required fees: $816. Full-time tuition and fees vary according to program and student level.

■ HARVARD UNIVERSITY

Graduate School of Design, Department of Urban Planning and Design, Cambridge, MA 02138

AWARDS Urban planning (MUP); urban planning and design (MAUD, MLAUD).

Faculty: 8 full-time (3 women), 28 part-time/adjunct (3 women).
Students: 79 full-time (35 women); includes 14 minority (2 African Americans, 5 Asian Americans or Pacific Islanders, 6 Hispanic Americans, 1 Native American), 29 international. Average age 27. In 2001, 43 degrees awarded.
Entrance requirements: For master's, GRE General Test, TOEFL. *Application deadline:* For fall admission, 1/25. *Application fee:* $60. Electronic applications accepted.
Expenses: Tuition: Full-time $23,370. Required fees: $816. Full-time tuition and fees vary according to program and student level.
Financial support: Fellowships, teaching assistantships, Federal Work-Study available. Support available to part-time students. Financial award application deadline: 1/1; financial award applicants required to submit FAFSA.
Alex Krieger, Chairman, 617-495-2521.
Application contact: Gail Gustafson, Director of Admissions, 617-496-1238, *Fax:* 617-495-8949, *E-mail:* ggustafson@gsd.harvard.edu.

Find an in-depth description at www.petersons.com/gradchannel.

■ HARVARD UNIVERSITY

John F. Kennedy School of Government, Program in Public Policy, Cambridge, MA 02138

AWARDS Public policy (MPP); public policy and urban planning (MPPUP).

Students: 186 full-time (91 women); includes 61 minority (19 African Americans, 21 Asian Americans or Pacific Islanders, 20 Hispanic Americans, 1 Native American), 26 international. Average age 25. 798 applicants, 33% accepted, 186 enrolled.
Entrance requirements: For master's, GMAT or GRE General Test, TOEFL. *Application deadline:* For fall admission, 1/4. *Application fee:* $80.
Expenses: Contact institution.
Financial support: Fellowships, research assistantships, teaching assistantships, career-related internships or fieldwork, Federal Work-Study, institutionally sponsored loans, scholarships/grants, and health care benefits available. Financial award application deadline: 2/8; financial award applicants required to submit CSS PROFILE or FAFSA.
Katherine Kim, Director, 617-496-8382.
Application contact: Office of Admissions, 617-495-1155.

Find an in-depth description at www.petersons.com/gradchannel.

■ HUNTER COLLEGE OF THE CITY UNIVERSITY OF NEW YORK

Graduate School, School of Arts and Sciences, Department of Urban Affairs and Planning, Program in Urban Planning, New York, NY 10021-5085

AWARDS MUP, JD/MUP. Part-time programs available.

Faculty: 9 full-time (4 women), 5 part-time/adjunct (3 women).
Students: 22 full-time (12 women), 17 part-time (8 women); includes 8 minority (5 African Americans, 1 Asian American or Pacific Islander, 2 Hispanic Americans), 2 international. Average age 27. 40 applicants, 70% accepted. In 2001, 14 degrees awarded.
Entrance requirements: For master's, TOEFL, interview, minimum 12 credits in social sciences. *Application deadline:* For fall admission, 4/14; for spring admission, 11/21. *Application fee:* $40.
Expenses: Tuition, state resident: full-time $2,175; part-time $185 per credit. Tuition, nonresident: full-time $3,800; part-time $320 per credit.
Financial support: In 2001–02, 4 fellowships with full tuition reimbursements (averaging $9,000 per year), 10 teaching assistantships (averaging $1,200 per year) were awarded. Research assistantships, career-related internships or fieldwork also available.
Faculty research: Community and economic development, transportation planning and policy, geographic information systems, housing, land use.
William J. Milczarski, Director, 212-772-5601, *Fax:* 212-772-5593, *E-mail:* wmilczar@hejira.hunter.cuny.edu. *Web site:* http://maxweber.hunter.cuny.edu/urban/

■ INDIANA UNIVERSITY–PURDUE UNIVERSITY INDIANAPOLIS

School of Public and Environmental Affairs, Graduate Program in Planning, Indianapolis, IN 46202-2896

AWARDS Environmental planning (M Pl); health planning (M Pl); planning and public policy (M Pl); urban development planning (M Pl). Part-time and evening/weekend programs available.

Students: 8 full-time (4 women), 6 part-time (3 women), 2 international. Average age 29. In 2001, 9 degrees awarded.
Entrance requirements: For master's, GRE General Test, minimum GPA of 3.0 preferred. *Application deadline:* For fall admission, 7/15 (priority date); for spring admission, 11/15. Applications are processed on a rolling basis. *Application fee:* $45 ($55 for international students).
Expenses: Tuition, state resident: full-time $4,480; part-time $187 per credit. Tuition, nonresident: full-time $12,926; part-time $539 per credit. Required fees: $177.
Financial support: In 2001–02, fellowships with full and partial tuition reimbursements (averaging $7,600 per year), 2 research assistantships with full and partial tuition reimbursements (averaging $7,600 per year) were awarded. Career-related internships or fieldwork and Federal Work-Study also available. Support available to part-time students. Financial award application deadline: 3/1.
Faculty research: Urban spatial structure, small group behavior, human migration patterns, environmental policy and decision making.
Dr. John Ottensmann, Director, 317-274-2631, *E-mail:* jottensmann@iupui.edu.
Application contact: Student Services, 317-274-4656, *Fax:* 317-274-5153, *E-mail:* infospea@iupui.edu. *Web site:* http://www.spea.iupui.edu/

■ IOWA STATE UNIVERSITY OF SCIENCE AND TECHNOLOGY

Graduate College, College of Design, Department of Community and Regional Planning, Ames, IA 50011

AWARDS Community and regional planning (MCRP); transportation (MS). Part-time programs available.

Faculty: 9.
Students: 29; includes 6 minority (4 African Americans, 2 Asian Americans or Pacific Islanders), 10 international. Average age 31. 43 applicants, 56% accepted, 10 enrolled. In 2001, 14 degrees awarded.
Degree requirements: For master's, thesis or alternative. *Median time to degree:* Master's–2.67 years full-time.
Entrance requirements: For master's, TOEFL. *Application deadline:* For fall admission, 2/1 (priority date); for spring admission, 10/1 (priority date). Applications are processed on a rolling basis.

Iowa State University of Science and Technology (continued)
Application fee: $20 ($50 for international students). Electronic applications accepted.
Expenses: Tuition, state resident: full-time $1,851. Tuition, nonresident: full-time $5,449. Tuition and fees vary according to program.
Financial support: In 2001–02, 16 students received support, including 8 research assistantships with partial tuition reimbursements available (averaging $5,427 per year), 8 teaching assistantships with partial tuition reimbursements available (averaging $5,427 per year); career-related internships or fieldwork, institutionally sponsored loans, tuition waivers (partial), and unspecified assistantships also available. Support available to part-time students. Financial award application deadline: 2/1; financial award applicants required to submit FAFSA.
Faculty research: Economic development, housing, land use, geographic information systems planning in developing nations, regional and community revitalization, transportation planning in developing countries.
Dr. Riad Mahayni, Professor and Chair, 515-294-8958, *Fax:* 515-294-4015, *E-mail:* rmahayni@iastate.edu.
Application contact: Dr. Gary A. Mattson, Associate Professor and Director of Graduate Education, 515-294-7734, *Fax:* 515-294-4015, *E-mail:* crp@iastate.edu. *Web site:* http://www.public.iastate.edu/~design/crp/crp.html

■ JACKSON STATE UNIVERSITY

Graduate School, School of Liberal Arts, Department of Urban and Regional Planning, Jackson, MS 39217

AWARDS MS.

Degree requirements: For master's, comprehensive exam.
Entrance requirements: For master's, GRE General Test, TOEFL.

■ KANSAS STATE UNIVERSITY

Graduate School, College of Architecture, Planning and Design, Department of Regional and Community Planning, Manhattan, KS 66506

AWARDS Environmental planning and management (MA); regional and community planning (MRCP). Part-time and evening/weekend programs available. Postbaccalaureate distance learning degree programs offered (minimal on-campus study).

Faculty: 20 full-time (3 women).
Students: 11 full-time (3 women), 5 part-time (3 women); includes 2 minority (1 African American, 1 Hispanic American), 8 international. 32 applicants, 75% accepted, 5 enrolled. In 2001, 4 degrees awarded.
Degree requirements: For master's, thesis, oral exam.
Entrance requirements: For master's, minimum GPA of 3.0, portfolio. *Application deadline:* For fall admission, 2/1 (priority date); for spring admission, 10/1 (priority date). Applications are processed on a rolling basis. *Application fee:* $30. Electronic applications accepted.
Expenses: Tuition, state resident: part-time $113 per credit hour. Tuition, nonresident: part-time $358 per credit hour.
Financial support: In 2001–02, 6 teaching assistantships (averaging $6,900 per year) were awarded; research assistantships, career-related internships or fieldwork, Federal Work-Study, institutionally sponsored loans, and scholarships/grants also available. Support available to part-time students. Financial award application deadline: 3/1; financial award applicants required to submit FAFSA.
Faculty research: Growth management techniques, historical trends of growth and development in Kansas, small town planning, planning and networking for increasing quality of life in Kansas, economic development trends. *Total annual research expenditures:* $89,991.
Prof. Dan Donelin, Head, 785-532-5961, *Fax:* 785-532-6722, *E-mail:* la-rcp@ksu.edu.
Application contact: Prof. C. A. Keithley, Graduate Coordinator, 785-532-5961, *Fax:* 785-532-6722, *E-mail:* la-rcp@ksu.edu. *Web site:* http://aalto.arch.ksu.edu/lar/

■ MASSACHUSETTS INSTITUTE OF TECHNOLOGY

School of Architecture and Planning, Department of Urban Studies and Planning, Cambridge, MA 02139-4307

AWARDS City planning (MCP); urban and regional planning (PhD); urban and regional studies (PhD); urban studies and planning (MS).

Faculty: 28 full-time (7 women), 13 part-time/adjunct (4 women).
Students: 174 full-time (101 women), 22 part-time (12 women); includes 37 minority (16 African Americans, 11 Asian Americans or Pacific Islanders, 10 Hispanic Americans), 67 international. 304 applicants, 43% accepted. In 2001, 53 master's, 2 doctorates awarded.
Degree requirements: For master's and doctorate, thesis/dissertation.
Entrance requirements: For master's and doctorate, GRE General Test, TOEFL. *Application deadline:* For fall admission, 1/3. *Application fee:* $60. Electronic applications accepted.
Expenses: Tuition: Full-time $26,960. Full-time tuition and fees vary according to program.
Financial support: In 2001–02, 140 students received support, including 114 fellowships with partial tuition reimbursements available (averaging $10,800 per year), 28 research assistantships with partial tuition reimbursements available (averaging $6,200 per year), 17 teaching assistantships with full tuition reimbursements available (averaging $14,500 per year); career-related internships or fieldwork, Federal Work-Study, and institutionally sponsored loans also available.
Faculty research: Urban development, urban design, social policy, urban economics, management of urban systems. *Total annual research expenditures:* $655,000.
Lawrence Vale, Head, 617-253-1933, *Fax:* 617-253-2654.
Application contact: Sandra Wellford, Graduate Admissions, 617-253-9403, *Fax:* 617-253-2654, *E-mail:* altwohig@mit.edu. *Web site:* http://sap.mit.edu/dusp/

Find an in-depth description at www.petersons.com/gradchannel.

■ MICHIGAN STATE UNIVERSITY

Graduate School, College of Social Science, Department of Geography, East Lansing, MI 48824

AWARDS Geography (MA, MS, PhD); geography-urban studies (MA); urban and regional planning (MURP); urban planning (MUP). Part-time programs available.

Faculty: 30 full-time (9 women).
Students: 37 full-time (14 women), 22 part-time (10 women); includes 9 minority (4 African Americans, 2 Asian Americans or Pacific Islanders, 3 Hispanic Americans), 17 international. Average age 29. 122 applicants, 34% accepted. In 2001, 11 master's, 2 doctorates awarded.
Degree requirements: For master's and doctorate, thesis/dissertation.
Entrance requirements: For master's, GRE General Test, TOEFL, minimum GPA of 3.4; for doctorate, GRE General Test, TOEFL, minimum GPA of 3.6. *Application deadline:* For fall admission, 2/1. Applications are processed on a rolling basis. *Application fee:* $30 ($40 for international students).
Expenses: Tuition, state resident: part-time $244 per credit hour. Tuition, nonresident: part-time $494 per credit hour. Required fees: $268 per semester. Tuition and fees vary according to course load, degree level and program.
Financial support: In 2001–02, 24 fellowships (averaging $2,641 per year), 14 research assistantships with tuition reimbursements (averaging $11,518 per year), 16 teaching assistantships with tuition reimbursements (averaging $10,789 per year) were awarded. Career-related internships or fieldwork, Federal Work-Study, and institutionally sponsored loans also available. Support available to part-time students. Financial award application deadline: 2/1; financial award applicants required to submit FAFSA.
Faculty research: Geomorphology, remote sensing, regional geographic information systems, climatology. *Total annual research expenditures:* $2.4 million.

Dr. Richard Groop, Chairperson, 517-355-4649, *Fax:* 517-432-1671, *E-mail:* geo@msu.edu.
Application contact: Graduate Admissions Office, 517-355-4649, *Fax:* 517-432-1671. *Web site:* http://www.geo.msu.edu/

■ MORGAN STATE UNIVERSITY

School of Graduate Studies, Institute of Architecture and Planning, Program in City and Regional Planning, Baltimore, MD 21251

AWARDS MCRP.

Students: 17 (7 women); includes 10 minority (all African Americans) 5 international.
Degree requirements: For master's, thesis.
Entrance requirements: For master's, TOEFL, minimum GPA of 3.0. *Application deadline:* For fall admission, 2/1; for spring admission, 10/1. Applications are processed on a rolling basis. *Application fee:* $0 ($90 for international students).
Expenses: Tuition, state resident: part-time $193 per credit. Tuition, nonresident: part-time $364 per credit. Required fees: $40 per credit.
Financial support: Fellowships, Federal Work-Study available. Financial award application deadline: 4/1.
Faculty research: Nonprofit organizations, community development, urban design, transportation, international planning.
Dr. Siddhartha Sen, Coordinator, 443-885-3208.
Application contact: Dr. James E. Waller, Admissions and Programs Officer, 443-885-3185, *Fax:* 443-319-3837, *E-mail:* jwaller@moac.morgan.edu.

Find an in-depth description at www.petersons.com/gradchannel.

■ NEW YORK UNIVERSITY

Robert F. Wagner Graduate School of Public Service, Program in Urban Planning, New York, NY 10012-1019

AWARDS Housing (Advanced Certificate); public economics (Advanced Certificate); quantitative analysis and computer applications for policy and planning (Advanced Certificate); urban planning (MUP). Part-time and evening/weekend programs available.

Faculty: 4 full-time (2 women), 7 part-time/adjunct (3 women).
Students: 50 full-time (35 women), 32 part-time (20 women); includes 20 minority (5 African Americans, 7 Asian Americans or Pacific Islanders, 8 Hispanic Americans), 4 international. Average age 27. 132 applicants, 86% accepted, 31 enrolled. In 2001, 29 degrees awarded.
Degree requirements: For master's, thesis or alternative, end event workshop.
Entrance requirements: For master's, minimum undergraduate GPA of 3.0. *Application deadline:* For fall admission, 7/15; for spring admission, 1/1. Applications are processed on a rolling basis. *Application fee:* $50.
Expenses: Tuition: Full-time $19,536; part-time $814 per credit. Required fees: $1,330; $38 per credit. Tuition and fees vary according to course load and program.
Financial support: In 2001–02, 36 students received support, including 29 fellowships (averaging $5,450 per year), 7 research assistantships with partial tuition reimbursements available (averaging $7,829 per year); career-related internships or fieldwork, Federal Work-Study, institutionally sponsored loans, scholarships/grants, and tuition waivers (full and partial) also available. Support available to part-time students. Financial award application deadline: 2/15; financial award applicants required to submit FAFSA.
Prof. Mitchell Moss, Director of the Planning Program, 212-998-7400.
Application contact: James Short, Director, Admissions and Financial Aid, 212-998-7414, *Fax:* 212-995-4164, *E-mail:* wagner.admissions@nyu.edu. *Web site:* http://www.nyu.edu/wagner

Find an in-depth description at www.petersons.com/gradchannel.

■ NORTH PARK UNIVERSITY

School of Community Development, Chicago, IL 60625-4895

AWARDS MA.

■ THE OHIO STATE UNIVERSITY

Graduate School, College of Engineering, Austin E. Knowlton School of Architecture, Program in City and Regional Planning, Columbus, OH 43210

AWARDS MCRP, PhD.

Degree requirements: For master's, thesis optional; for doctorate, thesis/dissertation.
Entrance requirements: For master's and doctorate, GRE General Test or GMAT.

Find an in-depth description at www.petersons.com/gradchannel.

■ OLD DOMINION UNIVERSITY

College of Business and Public Administration, Program in Urban Studies, Norfolk, VA 23529

AWARDS Policy analysis/program evaluation (MUS); public planning analysis (MUS); urban administration (MUS). Part-time and evening/weekend programs available.

Faculty: 7 full-time (2 women), 4 part-time/adjunct (1 woman).
Students: 5 full-time (all women), 35 part-time (23 women); includes 20 minority (19 African Americans, 1 Hispanic American). Average age 36. 23 applicants, 96% accepted. In 2001, 10 degrees awarded.
Degree requirements: For master's, internship or work experience, thesis optional.
Application deadline: For fall admission, 7/1 (priority date); for spring admission, 10/1 (priority date). Applications are processed on a rolling basis. *Application fee:* $30. Electronic applications accepted.
Expenses: Tuition, state resident: part-time $202 per credit. Tuition, nonresident: part-time $534 per credit. Required fees: $76 per semester.
Financial support: In 2001–02, 19 students received support, including 1 fellowship (averaging $8,914 per year), 1 research assistantship with tuition reimbursement available (averaging $5,555 per year); teaching assistantships, career-related internships or fieldwork and tuition waivers (partial) also available. Support available to part-time students. Financial award application deadline: 2/15; financial award applicants required to submit FAFSA.
Faculty research: Program implementation, evaluation, and design. *Total annual research expenditures:* $80,919.
Dr. Berhanu Mengistu, Graduate Program Director, 757-683-5130, *Fax:* 757-683-5639, *E-mail:* urbangpd@odu.edu. *Web site:* http://www.odu-cbpa.org/mus.htm/

■ THE PENNSYLVANIA STATE UNIVERSITY UNIVERSITY PARK CAMPUS

Graduate School, College of Agricultural Sciences, Department of Agricultural Economics and Rural Sociology, Program in Community and Economic Development, State College, University Park, PA 16802-1503

AWARDS MS.

Students: 5 full-time (3 women), 2 part-time (1 woman). In 2001, 1 master's awarded.
Application fee: $45.
Expenses: Tuition, state resident: full-time $7,882; part-time $333 per credit. Tuition, nonresident: full-time $16,142; part-time $673 per credit. Required fees: $124 per semester.
Drew Hyman, Coordinator, 814-863-8655.

■ PORTLAND STATE UNIVERSITY

Graduate Studies, College of Urban and Public Affairs, School of Urban Studies and Planning, Division of Urban Studies, Program in Urban and Regional Planning, Portland, OR 97207-0751

AWARDS Urban and regional planning (MURP); urban studies: regional science (PhD). Part-time programs available.

Students: 53 full-time (27 women), 45 part-time (18 women); includes 9 minority (1 Asian American or Pacific Islander, 8

Portland State University (continued)
Hispanic Americans), 1 international. Average age 30.
Entrance requirements: For master's, GRE General Test, TOEFL, minimum GPA of 2.75. *Application deadline:* For fall admission, 2/1. *Application fee:* $50.
Financial support: Fellowships, research assistantships, teaching assistantships, career-related internships or fieldwork, Federal Work-Study, and institutionally sponsored loans available. Support available to part-time students. Financial award application deadline: 3/1; financial award applicants required to submit FAFSA.
Faculty research: Policy planning and administration, community development, land-use and environment, transportation, urban and regional analysis. *Total annual research expenditures:* $145,786.
Application contact: Carleen Simmering, Office Coordinator, 503-725-4045, *Fax:* 503-725-5199, *E-mail:* carleen@upa.pdx.edu. *Web site:* http://www.upa.pdx.edu/usp/

■ PRATT INSTITUTE

School of Architecture, Program in City and Regional Planning, Brooklyn, NY 11205-3899

AWARDS MSCRP. Part-time and evening/weekend programs available.

Degree requirements: For master's, thesis.
Entrance requirements: For master's, TOEFL, writing sample. Electronic applications accepted.
Faculty research: Advocacy planning, community development, comprehensive physical planning, transportation planning, real estate development. *Web site:* http://www.pratt.edu/arch/gcpe/index.html

Find an in-depth description at www.petersons.com/gradchannel.

■ PRATT INSTITUTE

School of Architecture, Program in Urban Environmental Systems Management, Brooklyn, NY 11205-3899

AWARDS MSUESM. Part-time and evening/weekend programs available.

Degree requirements: For master's, thesis.
Entrance requirements: For master's, TOEFL, portfolio or writing sample. *Web site:* http://www.pratt.edu/arch/gcpe/index.html

Find an in-depth description at www.petersons.com/gradchannel.

■ PRINCETON UNIVERSITY

Graduate School, Woodrow Wilson School of Public and International Affairs, Program in Public Affairs and Urban and Regional Planning, Princeton, NJ 08544-1019

AWARDS MPA-URP, PhD.

Degree requirements: For master's, one foreign language; for doctorate, one foreign language, thesis/dissertation.
Entrance requirements: For master's, GRE General Test, original policy memo; for doctorate, GRE General Test.

■ RUTGERS, THE STATE UNIVERSITY OF NEW JERSEY, NEW BRUNSWICK

Edward J. Bloustein School of Planning and Public Policy, Department of Urban Planning and Policy Development, New Brunswick, NJ 08901-1281

AWARDS MCRP, MCRS, PhD, JD/MCRP, MBA/MCRS. Part-time and evening/weekend programs available. Terminal master's awarded for partial completion of doctoral program.

Degree requirements: For master's, thesis optional; for doctorate, thesis/dissertation.
Entrance requirements: For master's and doctorate, GRE General Test. Electronic applications accepted.
Faculty research: Land use, transportation, housing, regional economic development, urban redevelopment, developing countries.

■ SAN DIEGO STATE UNIVERSITY

Graduate and Research Affairs, College of Professional Studies and Fine Arts, School of Public Administration and Urban Studies, Program in City Planning, San Diego, CA 92182

AWARDS MCP. Part-time programs available.

Entrance requirements: For master's, GRE General Test, TOEFL.
Faculty research: Community development, housing, sustainable development, visioning.

■ SAN JOSE STATE UNIVERSITY

Graduate Studies, College of Social Work, Department of Urban and Regional Planning, San Jose, CA 95192-0001

AWARDS MUP. Part-time programs available.

Faculty: 5 full-time (0 women), 5 part-time/adjunct (2 women).
Students: 29 full-time (14 women), 37 part-time (19 women); includes 26 minority (8 African Americans, 6 Asian Americans or Pacific Islanders, 11 Hispanic Americans, 1 Native American), 7 international. Average age 34. 32 applicants, 72% accepted. In 2001, 16 degrees awarded.
Degree requirements: For master's, thesis or alternative, comprehensive exam.
Entrance requirements: For master's, GRE, minimum GPA of 3.0. *Application deadline:* For fall admission, 6/29; for spring admission, 11/30. Applications are processed on a rolling basis. *Application fee:* $59. Electronic applications accepted.
Expenses: Tuition, nonresident: part-time $246 per unit. Required fees: $678 per semester. Tuition and fees vary according to course load.
Financial support: In 2001–02, 10 teaching assistantships were awarded; career-related internships or fieldwork, Federal Work-Study, and institutionally sponsored loans also available. Financial award application deadline: 5/31; financial award applicants required to submit FAFSA.
Faculty research: Retirement communities, planning and problems, women in suburbia, influence on urban development, Taiwanese urban development issues.
Simon Dominguez, Acting Chair, 408-924-5882, *Fax:* 408-924-5872.

■ SOUTHWEST MISSOURI STATE UNIVERSITY

Graduate College, College of Natural and Applied Sciences, Department of Geography, Geology, and Planning, Springfield, MO 65804-0094

AWARDS Resource planning (MS). Part-time and evening/weekend programs available.

Faculty: 23 full-time (3 women).
Students: 9 full-time (5 women), 9 part-time (4 women), 3 international. Average age 30. In 2001, 8 degrees awarded.
Degree requirements: For master's, thesis, comprehensive exam.
Entrance requirements: For master's, GRE General Test, minimum undergraduate GPA of 3.0. *Application deadline:* For fall admission, 8/5 (priority date); for spring admission, 12/20 (priority date). Applications are processed on a rolling basis. *Application fee:* $25. Electronic applications accepted.
Expenses: Tuition, state resident: full-time $2,286; part-time $127 per credit. Tuition, nonresident: full-time $4,572; part-time $254 per credit. Required fees: $151 per semester. Tuition and fees vary according to course level and program.
Financial support: In 2001–02, research assistantships with full tuition reimbursements (averaging $6,150 per year), 8 teaching assistantships with full tuition reimbursements (averaging $6,150 per year) were awarded. Career-related internships or fieldwork, Federal Work-Study, and unspecified assistantships also available. Financial award application deadline: 3/31.

Faculty research: Water resources, small town planning, recreation and open space planning.
Dr. James Skinner, Head, 417-836-5800, *Fax:* 417-836-6934.
Application contact: Dr. Robert T. Pavlowsky, Graduate Adviser, 417-836-5800, *Fax:* 417-836-6934, *E-mail:* rtp138f@smsu.edu. *Web site:* http://www.smsu.edu/geography/index.html

■ STATE UNIVERSITY OF NEW YORK AT ALBANY

College of Arts and Sciences, Department of Geography and Planning, Program in Regional Planning, Albany, NY 12222-0001

AWARDS MRP. Part-time and evening/weekend programs available.

Degree requirements: For master's, thesis optional.
Application deadline: For fall admission, 8/1; for spring admission, 11/1. *Application fee:* $50.
Expenses: Tuition, state resident: full-time $2,550; part-time $213 per credit. Tuition, nonresident: full-time $4,208; part-time $351 per credit. Required fees: $470; $470 per year.
Financial support: Fellowships, teaching assistantships, career-related internships or fieldwork, Federal Work-Study, and institutionally sponsored loans available. Financial award application deadline: 6/1.
Faculty research: Urban planning, Third World development, political and social aspects of planning, urban housing and employment, environmental planning.
Application contact: Ray Bromley, Chair, 518-442-4770.

■ STATE UNIVERSITY OF NEW YORK COLLEGE OF ENVIRONMENTAL SCIENCE AND FORESTRY

Faculty of Environmental Studies, Syracuse, NY 13210-2779

AWARDS Environmental and community land planning (MPS, MS, PhD); environmental communication and information (MPS, MS, PhD); environmental policy and democratic processes (MPS, MS, PhD); environmental systems and risk management (MPS, MS, PhD); water and wetland resource studies (MPS, MS, PhD). Part-time programs available.

Faculty: 10 full-time (5 women), 1 (woman) part-time/adjunct.
Students: 44 full-time (29 women), 35 part-time (18 women); includes 4 minority (2 African Americans, 2 Hispanic Americans), 26 international. Average age 32. 74 applicants, 76% accepted, 21 enrolled. In 2001, 15 master's, 3 doctorates awarded.
Degree requirements: For master's, thesis (for some programs), registration; for doctorate, thesis/dissertation, comprehensive exam, registration.
Entrance requirements: For master's and doctorate, GRE General Test, minimum GPA of 3.0. *Application deadline:* For fall admission, 2/1 (priority date); for spring admission, 11/1. Applications are processed on a rolling basis. *Application fee:* $50.
Expenses: Tuition, area resident: Part-time $213 per credit hour. Tuition, state resident: full-time $5,100. Tuition, nonresident: full-time $8,416; part-time $351 per credit hour. Required fees: $250. One-time fee: $43 full-time.
Financial support: In 2001–02, 25 students received support, including 7 fellowships with full and partial tuition reimbursements available (averaging $8,817 per year), 6 research assistantships with full and partial tuition reimbursements available (averaging $9,000 per year), 12 teaching assistantships with full and partial tuition reimbursements available (averaging $8,817 per year); career-related internships or fieldwork, Federal Work-Study, institutionally sponsored loans, scholarships/grants, health care benefits, and unspecified assistantships also available. Support available to part-time students. Financial award applicants required to submit FAFSA.
Faculty research: Environmental education/communications, water resources, land resources, waste management. *Total annual research expenditures:* $186,300.
Dr. Richard Smardon, Chairperson, 315-470-6636, *Fax:* 315-470-6915, *E-mail:* rsmardon@syr.edu.
Application contact: Dr. Robert H. Frey, Dean, Instruction and Graduate Studies, 315-470-6599, *Fax:* 315-470-6978, *E-mail:* esfgrad@esf.edu. *Web site:* http://www.esf.edu/faculty/es/

■ STATE UNIVERSITY OF NEW YORK COLLEGE OF ENVIRONMENTAL SCIENCE AND FORESTRY

Faculty of Landscape Architecture, Syracuse, NY 13210-2779

AWARDS Cultural landscape studies and conservation (MLA, MS); ecological design and planning (MLA, MS); landscape and urban ecology (MLA, MS).

Faculty: 17 full-time (5 women).
Students: 35 full-time (15 women), 8 part-time (5 women); includes 1 minority (African American), 6 international. Average age 31. 43 applicants, 81% accepted, 16 enrolled. In 2001, 14 degrees awarded.
Degree requirements: For master's, thesis, comprehensive exam.
Entrance requirements: For master's, GRE General Test, minimum GPA of 3.0. *Application deadline:* For fall admission, 2/1 (priority date); for spring admission, 11/1. Applications are processed on a rolling basis. *Application fee:* $50.
Expenses: Tuition, area resident: Part-time $213 per credit hour. Tuition, state resident: full-time $5,100. Tuition, nonresident: full-time $8,416; part-time $351 per credit hour. Required fees: $250. One-time fee: $43 full-time.
Financial support: In 2001–02, 24 students received support, including 3 fellowships with full and partial tuition reimbursements available (averaging $8,817 per year), 3 research assistantships with full and partial tuition reimbursements available (averaging $9,000 per year), 8 teaching assistantships with full and partial tuition reimbursements available (averaging $8,817 per year); career-related internships or fieldwork and Federal Work-Study also available. Support available to part-time students. Financial award applicants required to submit FAFSA.
Faculty research: Site analysis and design, city and regional planning, community environments. *Total annual research expenditures:* $208,204.
Richard Hawks, Chairperson, 315-470-6544, *Fax:* 315-470-6540, *E-mail:* rshawks@esf.edu.
Application contact: Dr. Robert H. Frey, Dean, Instruction and Graduate Studies, 315-470-6599, *Fax:* 315-470-6978, *E-mail:* esfgrad@esf.edu. *Web site:* http://fla.esf.edu/

■ TEXAS A&M UNIVERSITY

College of Architecture, Department of Landscape Architecture and Urban Planning, College Station, TX 77843

AWARDS Landscape architecture (MLA); urban and regional science (PhD); urban planning (MUP).

Faculty: 35.
Students: 106 (37 women). Average age 31. Terminal master's awarded for partial completion of doctoral program.
Degree requirements: For master's, professional internship, thesis optional; for doctorate, thesis/dissertation, methods statistics seminar.
Entrance requirements: For master's, GMAT or GRE General Test, TOEFL, portfolio (MLA), minimum GPR of 3.0. *Application deadline:* For fall admission, 2/1 (priority date); for spring admission, 8/1. Applications are processed on a rolling basis. *Application fee:* $50 ($75 for international students).
Expenses: Tuition, state resident: full-time $11,872. Tuition, nonresident: full-time $17,892.
Financial support: Fellowships, research assistantships, teaching assistantships, career-related internships or fieldwork, institutionally sponsored loans, and scholarships/grants available. Financial award application deadline: 4/1; financial award applicants required to submit FAFSA.
Faculty research: Erosion control/water quality, geographic information systems/

Texas A&M University (continued)
spatial information technology, transport hazards, international sustainable development.
Dr. George O. Rogers, Head, 979-845-1019, *Fax:* 979-862-1784, *E-mail:* sewald@archone.com.
Application contact: Marie Prihoda, Graduate Office, 979-845-6582, *Fax:* 979-845-4491, *E-mail:* mprihoda@archone.tamu.edu. *Web site:* http://taz.tamu.edu/LAUP

■ TEXAS SOUTHERN UNIVERSITY

Graduate School, College of Liberal Arts and Behavioral Sciences, Department of Public Affairs, Program in City Planning, Houston, TX 77004-4584

AWARDS MCP, JD/MCP.

Faculty: 1 (woman) full-time.
Students: 2 full-time (both women); both minorities (both African Americans). In 2001, 1 degree awarded.
Degree requirements: For master's, thesis optional.
Entrance requirements: For master's, GRE General Test, TOEFL, minimum GPA of 2.5. *Application deadline:* For fall admission, 7/15 (priority date). Applications are processed on a rolling basis. *Application fee:* $35 ($75 for international students).
Expenses: Tuition, state resident: full-time $1,188. Tuition, nonresident: full-time $4,644. Required fees: $900. Tuition and fees vary according to degree level.
Financial support: Career-related internships or fieldwork, Federal Work-Study, and institutionally sponsored loans available. Financial award application deadline: 5/1.
Dr. Theophilus Herrington, Head, Department of Public Affairs, 713-313-7447, *E-mail:* herrington_tx@tsu.edu.

■ TUFTS UNIVERSITY

Division of Graduate and Continuing Studies and Research, Graduate School of Arts and Sciences, Department of Urban and Environmental Policy and Planning, Medford, MA 02155

AWARDS Community development (MA); environmental policy (MA); health and human welfare (MA); housing policy (MA); international environment/development policy (MA); public policy and citizen participation (MA). Part-time programs available.

Faculty: 7 full-time, 12 part-time/adjunct.
Students: 100 (66 women); includes 16 minority (7 African Americans, 6 Asian Americans or Pacific Islanders, 3 Hispanic Americans) 11 international. 115 applicants, 88% accepted. In 2001, 30 degrees awarded.
Degree requirements: For master's, thesis, internship.
Entrance requirements: For master's, GRE General Test, TOEFL. *Application deadline:* For fall admission, 2/15. Applications are processed on a rolling basis. *Application fee:* $50. Electronic applications accepted.
Expenses: Contact institution.
Financial support: Fellowships with full and partial tuition reimbursements, teaching assistantships with full and partial tuition reimbursements, career-related internships or fieldwork, Federal Work-Study, scholarships/grants, and tuition waivers (partial) available. Support available to part-time students. Financial award application deadline: 2/15; financial award applicants required to submit FAFSA.
Fran Jacobs, Chair, 617-627-3394, *Fax:* 617-627-3377. *Web site:* http://www.tufts.edu/as/uep/

Find an in-depth description at www.petersons.com/gradchannel.

■ UNIVERSITY AT BUFFALO, THE STATE UNIVERSITY OF NEW YORK

Graduate School, School of Architecture and Planning, Department of Urban and Regional Planning, Buffalo, NY 14260

AWARDS Planning (MUP). Part-time and evening/weekend programs available.

Faculty: 9 full-time (2 women), 1 (woman) part-time/adjunct.
Students: 66 full-time (25 women), 22 part-time (7 women); includes 16 minority (10 African Americans, 1 Asian American or Pacific Islander, 5 Hispanic Americans), 14 international. Average age 25. 99 applicants, 89% accepted, 40 enrolled. In 2001, 23 degrees awarded.
Degree requirements: For master's, thesis.
Entrance requirements: For master's, TOEFL, minimum GPA of 2.8. *Application deadline:* For fall admission, 3/1 (priority date); for spring admission, 11/1 (priority date). Applications are processed on a rolling basis. *Application fee:* $35. Electronic applications accepted.
Expenses: Tuition, state resident: full-time $6,118. Tuition, nonresident: full-time $9,434.
Financial support: In 2001–02, 10 fellowships with full and partial tuition reimbursements (averaging $8,250 per year), 14 research assistantships with full and partial tuition reimbursements (averaging $7,000 per year), 10 teaching assistantships with full and partial tuition reimbursements (averaging $3,800 per year) were awarded. Career-related internships or fieldwork, Federal Work-Study, institutionally sponsored loans, scholarships/grants, traineeships, tuition waivers (full and partial), and unspecified assistantships also available. Support available to part-time students. Financial award application deadline: 3/1; financial award applicants required to submit FAFSA.
Faculty research: International planning development, economic development, governance, information technology and geographic information systems in planning, environmental planning and policy. *Total annual research expenditures:* $418,800.
Dr. Ernest Sternberg, Chair, 716-829-2133 Ext. 110, *Fax:* 716-829-3256, *E-mail:* ezs@ap.buffalo.edu.
Application contact: Donna M. Rogalski, Secretary, 716-829-2133 Ext. 109, *Fax:* 716-829-3256, *E-mail:* dmr1@ap.buffalo.edu. *Web site:* http://www.ap.buffalo.edu/planning/

■ THE UNIVERSITY OF AKRON

Graduate School, Buchtel College of Arts and Sciences, Department of Geography and Planning, Program in Urban Planning, Akron, OH 44325-0001

AWARDS MA.

Students: 22 full-time (11 women), 1 part-time; includes 3 minority (all African Americans), 14 international. Average age 29. 22 applicants, 91% accepted, 10 enrolled. In 2001, 7 degrees awarded.
Degree requirements: For master's, thesis optional.
Application deadline: For fall admission, 8/15. Applications are processed on a rolling basis. *Application fee:* $40 ($50 for international students).
Expenses: Tuition, state resident: full-time $6,562; part-time $219 per credit. Tuition, nonresident: full-time $9,027; part-time $383 per credit. Required fees: $272; $11 per credit. Tuition and fees vary according to course load.
Dr. Richard Klosterman, Head, 330-972-8037, *E-mail:* klosterman@uakron.edu.
Application contact: Dr. Vern Harnapp, Director of Graduate Studies, 330-972-7623, *E-mail:* vharnapp@uakron.edu.

■ THE UNIVERSITY OF ARIZONA

Graduate College, Graduate Interdisciplinary Programs, Graduate Interdisciplinary Program in Planning, Tucson, AZ 85721

AWARDS MS.

Faculty: 38.
Students: 29 full-time (11 women), 1 (woman) part-time; includes 1 minority (Hispanic American), 3 international. Average age 33. 27 applicants, 85% accepted, 16 enrolled. In 2001, 2 degrees awarded.
Degree requirements: For master's, thesis or alternative.
Entrance requirements: For master's, GRE General Test, TOEFL, minimum B average. *Application fee:* $45.
Expenses: Tuition, state resident: full-time $2,490; part-time $436 per unit. Tuition,

nonresident: full-time $10,300; part-time $436 per unit. Full-time tuition and fees vary according to degree level and program.
Financial support: Research assistantships, teaching assistantships, career-related internships or fieldwork, Federal Work-Study, scholarships/grants, and tuition waivers (partial) available. Financial award application deadline: 3/15.
Faculty research: Environmental analysis, regional planning, land development, regional development, arid lands.
Dr. Barbara Beaker, Director, *E-mail:* bbeaker@u.arizona.edu.
Application contact: Sandra Sanchez, Administrative Assistant, 520-621-9597, *Fax:* 520-621-9820, *E-mail:* planning@u.arizona.edu. *Web site:* http://grad.admin.arizona.edu/idps/plng/plng.html

■ UNIVERSITY OF CALIFORNIA, BERKELEY

Graduate Division, College of Environmental Design, Department of City and Regional Planning, Berkeley, CA 94720-1500

AWARDS MCP, PhD, JD/MCP, M Arch/MCP, MCP/MPH, MCP/MS, MLA/MCP.

Degree requirements: For master's, professional project or thesis; for doctorate, thesis/dissertation, qualifying exam.
Entrance requirements: For master's and doctorate, GRE General Test, TOEFL, minimum GPA of 3.0.
Expenses: Tuition, nonresident: full-time $10,704. Required fees: $4,349.
Faculty research: Housing and project development, physical planning and design, community and economic development, geographic information systems, transportation.

Find an in-depth description at www.petersons.com/gradchannel.

■ UNIVERSITY OF CALIFORNIA, DAVIS

Graduate Studies, Graduate Group in Community Development, Davis, CA 95616

AWARDS MS.

Faculty: 34 full-time (12 women), 1 (woman) part-time/adjunct.
Students: 31 full-time (24 women); includes 7 minority (1 African American, 3 Asian Americans or Pacific Islanders, 2 Hispanic Americans, 1 Native American), 3 international. Average age 30. 43 applicants, 67% accepted, 15 enrolled. In 2001, 12 degrees awarded.
Degree requirements: For master's, thesis optional.
Entrance requirements: For master's, GRE General Test, minimum GPA of 3.0. *Application deadline:* For fall admission, 1/15. *Application fee:* $60. Electronic applications accepted.
Expenses: Tuition, state resident: full-time $4,831. Tuition, nonresident: full-time $15,725.
Financial support: In 2001–02, 23 students received support, including 8 fellowships with full and partial tuition reimbursements available (averaging $4,894 per year), 7 research assistantships with full and partial tuition reimbursements available (averaging $7,705 per year), 10 teaching assistantships with partial tuition reimbursements available (averaging $13,438 per year); Federal Work-Study, institutionally sponsored loans, scholarships/grants, and traineeships also available. Financial award application deadline: 1/15; financial award applicants required to submit FAFSA.
Faculty research: Globalization; community economic change; urban and regional development; community planning design and sustainability; race, ethnic, and gender roles; community organization and political mobilization.
Michael P. Smith, Graduate Chair, 530-752-2243, *Fax:* 530-752-5660, *E-mail:* mpsmith@ucdavis.edu.
Application contact: Judy Erwin, Graduate Assistant, 530-752-1926, *Fax:* 530-752-5660, *E-mail:* gjerwin@ucdavis.edu. *Web site:* http://hcd.ucdavis.edu/

■ UNIVERSITY OF CALIFORNIA, IRVINE

Office of Research and Graduate Studies, School of Social Ecology, Department of Urban and Regional Planning, Irvine, CA 92697

AWARDS MURP, PhD.

Faculty: 15.
Students: 37 full-time (19 women); includes 6 minority (2 Asian Americans or Pacific Islanders, 4 Hispanic Americans), 4 international. 75 applicants, 56% accepted, 14 enrolled. Terminal master's awarded for partial completion of doctoral program.
Degree requirements: For master's, thesis; for doctorate, thesis/dissertation, research project.
Entrance requirements: For master's, GRE General Test, minimum GPA of 3.0; for doctorate, GRE General Test. *Application deadline:* For fall and spring admission, 1/15 (priority date); for winter admission, 10/15 (priority date). *Application fee:* $60. Electronic applications accepted.
Expenses: Tuition, nonresident: full-time $10,704. Required fees: $8,396. Tuition and fees vary according to course load, program and student level.
Financial support: Fellowships, research assistantships, teaching assistantships, institutionally sponsored loans and tuition waivers (full and partial) available. Financial award application deadline: 3/2; financial award applicants required to submit FAFSA.
Faculty research: Community and social policy, economic development, land-use and growth management, transportation planning, environmental policy.
Scott Bollens, Chair, 949-824-3480.
Application contact: Jeanne Haynes, Academic Counselor, 949-824-5917, *Fax:* 949-824-2056, *E-mail:* jhaynes@uci.edu. *Web site:* http://www.socecol.uci.edu/~socecol/

■ UNIVERSITY OF CALIFORNIA, LOS ANGELES

Graduate Division, School of Public Policy and Social Research, Department of Urban Planning, Los Angeles, CA 90095-1656

AWARDS MA, PhD, JD/MA, MA/MA, MBA/MA.

Faculty: 19.
Students: 158 full-time (84 women); includes 67 minority (11 African Americans, 20 Asian Americans or Pacific Islanders, 35 Hispanic Americans, 1 Native American), 17 international. 265 applicants, 54% accepted, 65 enrolled. In 2001, 56 master's, 6 doctorates awarded.
Degree requirements: For master's, comprehensive exam or thesis; for doctorate, thesis/dissertation, oral and written qualifying exams.
Entrance requirements: For master's, GRE General Test (recommended), TOEFL; for doctorate, GRE General Test, TOEFL, master's degree in urban planning or related field. *Application deadline:* For fall admission, 1/5. *Application fee:* $60. Electronic applications accepted.
Expenses: Tuition, nonresident: full-time $10,244. Required fees: $3,609. Full-time tuition and fees vary according to program.
Financial support: In 2001–02, 146 students received support, including 73 fellowships, 46 research assistantships, 31 teaching assistantships; career-related internships or fieldwork, Federal Work-Study, institutionally sponsored loans, scholarships/grants, and tuition waivers (full and partial) also available. Financial award application deadline: 3/1.
Faculty research: Industrial hazards, political economy of South and Southeast Asia, historic preservation, flexible production in U.S. and Western Europe, land-use controls.
Dr. Donald Shoup, Chair, 310-825-4025.
Application contact: Departmental Office, 310-825-4025, *Fax:* 310-206-5566, *E-mail:* upinfo@sppsr.ucla.edu. *Web site:* http://www/sppsr.ucla.edu/

■ UNIVERSITY OF CINCINNATI

Division of Research and Advanced Studies, College of Design, Architecture, Art and Planning, School of Planning, Program in Community Planning, Cincinnati, OH 45221

AWARDS MCP, JD/MCP.

Students: In 2001, 12 degrees awarded.

University of Cincinnati (continued)
Degree requirements: For master's, thesis.
Entrance requirements: For master's, GRE General Test, TOEFL. *Application deadline:* For fall admission, 2/1. *Application fee:* $30.
Expenses: Tuition, state resident: part-time $2,698 per quarter. Tuition, nonresident: part-time $4,977 per quarter.
Financial support: Tuition waivers (full) and unspecified assistantships available. Financial award application deadline: 5/1.
Web site: http://www.daap.uc.edu/

■ UNIVERSITY OF COLORADO AT DENVER

College of Architecture and Planning, Urban and Regional Planning Program, Denver, CO 80217-3364

AWARDS MURP. Part-time programs available.

Faculty: 6 full-time (0 women).
Students: 57 full-time (26 women), 25 part-time (15 women); includes 10 minority (3 African Americans, 1 Asian American or Pacific Islander, 6 Hispanic Americans), 6 international. Average age 32. 64 applicants, 58% accepted, 28 enrolled. In 2001, 31 degrees awarded.
Degree requirements: For master's, thesis optional.
Entrance requirements: For master's, GRE or minimum GPA of 3.0. *Application deadline:* For fall admission, 3/15; for spring admission, 10/1. *Application fee:* $50 ($60 for international students).
Expenses: Tuition, state resident: full-time $3,284; part-time $198 per credit hour. Tuition, nonresident: full-time $13,380; part-time $802 per credit hour. Required fees: $444; $222 per semester.
Financial support: In 2001–02, 1 teaching assistantship (averaging $1,050 per year) was awarded; career-related internships or fieldwork, Federal Work-Study, institutionally sponsored loans, and scholarships/grants also available. Financial award application deadline: 3/1; financial award applicants required to submit FAFSA.
Faculty research: Physical planning, environmental planning, economic development planning.
Dwayne C. Nuzum, Chair, 303-556-3382, *Fax:* 303-556-3687.
Application contact: Heather Zertuche, Administrative Assistant 2, 303-556-3382, *Fax:* 303-556-3687, *E-mail:* a&p-grad-info@carbon.cudenver.edu. *Web site:* http://www.cudenver.edu:/public/AandP/

■ UNIVERSITY OF FLORIDA

Graduate School, College of Design, Construction and Planning, Department of Urban and Regional Planning, Gainesville, FL 32611

AWARDS MAURP, JD/MAURP.

Degree requirements: For master's, thesis/dissertation.
Entrance requirements: For master's, GRE General Test, minimum GPA of 3.0. Electronic applications accepted.
Expenses: Tuition, state resident: part-time $164 per hour. Tuition, nonresident: part-time $571 per hour. Tuition and fees vary according to course level and program.
Faculty research: Planning and information systems, urban and environmental design, community and economic development, transportation and growth management. *Web site:* http://www.dcp.ufl.edu/urp/

■ UNIVERSITY OF HAWAII AT MANOA

Graduate Division, College of Arts and Sciences, College of Social Sciences, Department of Urban and Regional Planning, Honolulu, HI 96822

AWARDS Community planning and social policy (MURP); environmental planning and management (MURP); land use and infrastructure planning (MURP); urban and regional planning in Asia and Pacific (MURP).

Faculty: 8 full-time (2 women), 23 part-time/adjunct (5 women).
Students: 33 full-time (17 women), 26 part-time (11 women); includes 20 Asian Americans or Pacific Islanders, 1 Hispanic American. Average age 31. 105 applicants, 31% accepted, 19 enrolled. In 2001, 7 degrees awarded.
Entrance requirements: For master's, GRE, TOEFL, minimum GPA of 3.0. *Application deadline:* For fall admission, 2/1; for spring admission, 9/1. *Application fee:* $25 ($50 for international students).
Expenses: Tuition, state resident: full-time $2,160; part-time $1,980 per year. Tuition, nonresident: full-time $5,190; part-time $4,829 per year.
Financial support: In 2001–02, 7 research assistantships (averaging $14,958 per year), 1 teaching assistantship (averaging $12,786 per year) were awarded. Career-related internships or fieldwork, Federal Work-Study, institutionally sponsored loans, and tuition waivers (full) also available.
Karl Kim, Chairperson, 808-956-7381, *Fax:* 808-956-6870, *E-mail:* karlk@hawaii.edu.
Application contact: Kem Lowry, Graduate Chair, 808-956-6868, *Fax:* 808-956-6870, *E-mail:* lowry@hawaii.edu.

Find an in-depth description at www.petersons.com/gradchannel.

■ UNIVERSITY OF ILLINOIS AT CHICAGO

Graduate College, College of Urban Planning and Public Affairs, Program in Urban Planning and Policy, Chicago, IL 60607-7128

AWARDS Public policy analysis (PhD); urban planning and policy (MUPP). Part-time programs available.

Faculty: 13 full-time (2 women).
Students: 92 full-time (51 women), 97 part-time (44 women); includes 54 minority (30 African Americans, 5 Asian Americans or Pacific Islanders, 19 Hispanic Americans), 20 international. Average age 32. 184 applicants, 60% accepted, 70 enrolled. In 2001, 50 master's, 5 doctorates awarded.
Degree requirements: For master's, thesis or alternative, internship; for doctorate, thesis/dissertation.
Entrance requirements: For master's and doctorate, GRE General Test, TOEFL, minimum GPA of 3.75 on a 5.0 scale, writing sample. *Application deadline:* For fall admission, 6/1; for spring admission, 11/1. Applications are processed on a rolling basis. *Application fee:* $40 ($50 for international students). Electronic applications accepted.
Expenses: Tuition, state resident: full-time $3,060. Tuition, nonresident: full-time $6,688.
Financial support: In 2001–02, 63 students received support; fellowships, research assistantships, teaching assistantships, career-related internships or fieldwork, Federal Work-Study, and tuition waivers (full) available. Financial award applicants required to submit FAFSA.
Charles Hoch, Director of Graduate Studies, 312-996-2155, *E-mail:* chashoch@uic.edu.

Find an in-depth description at www.petersons.com/gradchannel.

■ UNIVERSITY OF ILLINOIS AT URBANA–CHAMPAIGN

Graduate College, College of Fine and Applied Arts, Department of Urban and Regional Planning, Champaign, IL 61820

AWARDS Regional planning (PhD); urban and regional planning (MUP).

Faculty: 13 full-time.
Students: 72 full-time (37 women); includes 4 minority (3 African Americans, 1 Asian American or Pacific Islander), 39 international. 148 applicants, 25% accepted. In 2001, 14 master's, 2 doctorates awarded.
Degree requirements: For master's and doctorate, thesis/dissertation.
Entrance requirements: For master's, GRE, minimum GPA of 3.0. *Application deadline:* For fall admission, 2/15 (priority

date). Applications are processed on a rolling basis. *Application fee:* $40 ($50 for international students).
Expenses: Tuition, state resident: part-time $3,227 per degree program. Tuition, nonresident: part-time $7,169 per degree program. Tuition and fees vary according to program.
Financial support: In 2001–02, 8 fellowships, 33 research assistantships, 12 teaching assistantships were awarded. Career-related internships or fieldwork and tuition waivers (full and partial) also available. Financial award application deadline: 2/15.
Faculty research: Environmental impact, economic development, firmation technology, planning systems, housing, community participation.
Dr. Christopher Silver, Head, 217-244-5400, *Fax:* 217-244-1717, *E-mail:* silver@uiuc.edu.
Application contact: Jane Terry, Officer, 217-244-5401, *Fax:* 217-244-1717, *E-mail:* j-terry@uiuc.edu. *Web site:* http://www.urban.uiuc.edu/

■ THE UNIVERSITY OF IOWA

Graduate College, Program in Urban and Regional Planning, Iowa City, IA 52242-1316

AWARDS MA, MS, JD/MA, JD/MS, MA/MA, MA/MS, MHA/MA, MHA/MS, MS/MS, MSW/MA, MSW/MS.

Faculty: 9 full-time.
Students: 34 full-time (18 women), 2 part-time (1 woman); includes 3 minority (all African Americans), 6 international. 60 applicants, 48% accepted, 17 enrolled. In 2001, 17 degrees awarded.
Degree requirements: For master's, exam, thesis optional.
Entrance requirements: For master's, GRE General Test, TOEFL. *Application deadline:* Applications are processed on a rolling basis. *Application fee:* $30 ($50 for international students). Electronic applications accepted.
Expenses: Tuition, state resident: full-time $3,702; part-time $206 per semester hour. Tuition, nonresident: full-time $11,924; part-time $206 per semester hour. Required fees: $101 per semester. Tuition and fees vary according to course load and program.
Financial support: In 2001–02, 10 research assistantships, 10 teaching assistantships were awarded. Fellowships available. Financial award application deadline: 2/1; financial award applicants required to submit FAFSA.
Heather MacDonald, Chair, 319-335-0032.

■ UNIVERSITY OF KANSAS

Graduate School, School of Architecture and Urban Design, Program in Urban Planning, Lawrence, KS 66045

AWARDS MUP, JD/MUP, M Arch/MUP, MUP/MA, MUP/MPA. Part-time programs available.

Faculty: 9.
Students: 50 full-time (21 women), 12 part-time (6 women); includes 5 minority (3 African Americans, 1 Hispanic American, 1 Native American), 12 international. Average age 29. 41 applicants, 93% accepted, 18 enrolled. In 2001, 10 degrees awarded.
Degree requirements: For master's, thesis or alternative.
Entrance requirements: For master's, TOEFL. *Application deadline:* For fall admission, 1/15 (priority date). Applications are processed on a rolling basis. *Application fee:* $40. Electronic applications accepted.
Expenses: Tuition, state resident: full-time $2,722; part-time $113 per credit. Tuition, nonresident: full-time $8,586; part-time $358 per credit. Required fees: $551; $46 per credit. Tuition and fees vary according to campus/location, program and reciprocity agreements.
Financial support: In 2001–02, 9 students received support; fellowships, research assistantships with partial tuition reimbursements available, teaching assistantships with full and partial tuition reimbursements available, career-related internships or fieldwork available. Financial award application deadline: 1/15.
James M. Mayo, Chair, 785-864-4184, *Fax:* 785-864-5301. *Web site:* http://www.saud.ku.edu

■ UNIVERSITY OF LOUISVILLE

Graduate School, College of Business and Public Administration, Department of Urban and Public Affairs, Program in Public Administration, Louisville, KY 40292-0001

AWARDS Labor and public management (MPA); public policy and administration (MPA); urban and regional development (MPA).

Students: 19 full-time (15 women), 29 part-time (18 women); includes 5 minority (3 African Americans, 2 Hispanic Americans), 5 international. Average age 30. In 2001, 15 degrees awarded.
Degree requirements: For master's, practicum or thesis.
Entrance requirements: For master's, GRE General Test, minimum GPA of 3.25, resumé. *Application deadline:* For fall admission, 7/1 (priority date); for spring admission, 12/1 (priority date). Applications are processed on a rolling basis. *Application fee:* $25.
Expenses: Tuition, state resident: full-time $4,134. Tuition, nonresident: full-time $11,486.
Financial support: In 2001–02, 3 research assistantships with full tuition reimbursements (averaging $8,000 per year) were awarded
Dr. Steve Koven, Director, 502-852-6626, *Fax:* 502-852-4558, *E-mail:* sgkove01@louisville.edu. *Web site:* http://www.cbpa.louisville.edu/

Find an in-depth description at www.petersons.com/gradchannel.

■ UNIVERSITY OF LOUISVILLE

Graduate School, College of Business and Public Administration, Department of Urban and Public Affairs, Program in Urban Planning, Louisville, KY 40292-0001

AWARDS MUP.

Students: 15 full-time (3 women), 8 part-time (5 women); includes 3 minority (2 African Americans, 1 Hispanic American), 5 international. In 2001, 1 degree awarded.
Expenses: Tuition, state resident: full-time $4,134. Tuition, nonresident: full-time $11,486.
Dr. Steven C. Bourassa, Chair, 502-852-5720, *Fax:* 502-852-7672, *E-mail:* scbour01@gwise.louisville.edu.

■ UNIVERSITY OF MARYLAND, COLLEGE PARK

Graduate Studies and Research, School of Architecture, Community Planning Program, College Park, MD 20742

AWARDS MCP, M Arch/MCP. Part-time and evening/weekend programs available.

Faculty: 5 full-time (0 women), 3 part-time/adjunct (1 woman).
Students: 43 full-time (30 women), 17 part-time (15 women); includes 13 minority (11 African Americans, 2 Hispanic Americans), 4 international. 91 applicants, 60% accepted, 28 enrolled. In 2001, 18 degrees awarded.
Entrance requirements: For master's, GRE General Test, minimum GPA of 3.0, portfolio. *Application deadline:* For fall admission, 7/1; for spring admission, 12/1. Applications are processed on a rolling basis. *Application fee:* $50 ($70 for international students). Electronic applications accepted.
Expenses: Tuition, state resident: part-time $289 per credit hour. Tuition, nonresident: part-time $448 per credit hour. One-time fee: $436 part-time. Full-time tuition and fees vary according to course load, campus/location and program.
Financial support: In 2001–02, 1 research assistantship with tuition reimbursement (averaging $12,044 per year), 11 teaching assistantships with tuition reimbursements (averaging $12,073 per year) were awarded. Fellowships with tuition reimbursements, Federal Work-Study and scholarships/grants also available. Support available to part-time students. Financial award applicants required to submit FAFSA.
Faculty research: Policy analysis, urban planning, program planning and management, economic development planning.

University of Maryland, College Park (continued)

Dr. Marie Howland, Director, 301-405-6789, *Fax:* 301-314-9897.
Application contact: Trudy Lindsey, Director, Graduate Admissions and Records, 301-405-6991, *Fax:* 301-314-9305, *E-mail:* grschool@deans.umd.edu.

■ UNIVERSITY OF MASSACHUSETTS AMHERST

Graduate School, College of Food and Natural Resources, Department of Landscape Architecture and Regional Planning, Program in Landscape Architecture and Regional Planning, Amherst, MA 01003

AWARDS MLA/MRP. Part-time programs available.

Students: 8 full-time (4 women), 3 part-time (2 women), 1 international. Average age 33. 9 applicants, 78% accepted. *Application deadline:* For fall admission, 2/1 (priority date). Applications are processed on a rolling basis. *Application fee:* $40 ($50 for international students).
Expenses: Tuition, state resident: full-time $1,980; part-time $110 per credit. Tuition, nonresident: full-time $7,456; part-time $414 per credit. Required fees: $4,112. One-time fee: $115 full-time.
Financial support: Fellowships with full tuition reimbursements, research assistantships with full tuition reimbursements, teaching assistantships with full tuition reimbursements, career-related internships or fieldwork, Federal Work-Study, scholarships/grants, traineeships, and unspecified assistantships available. Support available to part-time students. Financial award application deadline: 2/1.
Dr. Robert Ryan, Director, 413-545-2266, *Fax:* 413-545-1772, *E-mail:* rlryan@larp.umass.edu.

■ UNIVERSITY OF MASSACHUSETTS AMHERST

Graduate School, College of Food and Natural Resources, Department of Landscape Architecture and Regional Planning, Program in Regional Planning, Amherst, MA 01003

AWARDS MRP, PhD, MLA/MRP. Part-time programs available.

Students: 38 full-time (18 women), 16 part-time (9 women); includes 2 minority (both African Americans), 9 international. Average age 30. 64 applicants, 64% accepted. In 2001, 12 master's, 1 doctorate awarded.
Degree requirements: For master's, thesis or alternative; for doctorate, thesis/dissertation.
Entrance requirements: For master's, GRE General Test. *Application deadline:* For fall admission, 2/1 (priority date); for spring admission, 10/1. Applications are processed on a rolling basis. *Application fee:* $40 ($50 for international students).
Expenses: Tuition, state resident: full-time $1,980; part-time $110 per credit. Tuition, nonresident: full-time $7,456; part-time $414 per credit. Required fees: $4,112. One-time fee: $115 full-time.
Financial support: Fellowships with full tuition reimbursements, research assistantships with full tuition reimbursements, teaching assistantships with full tuition reimbursements, career-related internships or fieldwork, Federal Work-Study, scholarships/grants, traineeships, and unspecified assistantships available. Support available to part-time students. Financial award application deadline: 2/1.
John Mullin, Director, 413-545-2266, *Fax:* 413-545-1772, *E-mail:* jmullin@larp.umass.edu.

■ THE UNIVERSITY OF MEMPHIS

Graduate School, College of Arts and Sciences, School of Urban Affairs and Public Policy, Division of City and Regional Planning, Memphis, TN 38152

AWARDS MCRP.

Degree requirements: For master's, thesis, comprehensive exam.
Entrance requirements: For master's, GRE General Test.
Expenses: Tuition, state resident: full-time $2,026. Tuition, nonresident: full-time $4,528.
Faculty research: Growth planning, site design, economic development. *Web site:* http://planning.memphis.edu

■ THE UNIVERSITY OF MEMPHIS

Graduate School, College of Arts and Sciences, School of Urban Affairs and Public Policy, Division of Public Administration, Memphis, TN 38152

AWARDS Health services administration (MPA); human resources administration (MPA); non-profit administration (MPA); public administration (MPA); urban management and planning (MPA). Part-time and evening/weekend programs available.

Faculty: 5 full-time (3 women), 4 part-time/adjunct (3 women).
Students: 12 full-time (8 women), 13 part-time (10 women); includes 15 minority (14 African Americans, 1 Hispanic American). Average age 33. 16 applicants, 50% accepted. In 2001, 11 degrees awarded.
Degree requirements: For master's, thesis or alternative, internship, comprehensive exam.
Entrance requirements: For master's, GRE General Test or GMAT, minimum GPA of 3.0. *Application deadline:* For fall admission, 8/1; for spring admission, 12/1. Applications are processed on a rolling basis. *Application fee:* $25 ($50 for international students).
Expenses: Tuition, state resident: full-time $2,026. Tuition, nonresident: full-time $4,528.
Financial support: In 2001–02, 3 students received support, including 1 fellowship, 2 research assistantships with full tuition reimbursements available (averaging $6,000 per year); career-related internships or fieldwork, Federal Work-Study, and scholarships/grants also available. Support available to part-time students.
Faculty research: Community building, nonprofit organization governance, human resources in local government, community collaboration, urban problems. *Total annual research expenditures:* $75,000.
Dr. Dorothy Norris-Tirrell, Director, 901-678-3360, *Fax:* 901-678-2981, *E-mail:* dnrrstrr@memphis.edu.
Application contact: Aljena Ajayi, Program Assistant, 901-678-3360, *Fax:* 901-678-2981. *Web site:* http://www.people.memphis.edu/~gapubaddm/mpa.html

■ UNIVERSITY OF MICHIGAN

Taubman College of Architecture and Urban Planning, Doctoral Program in Urban, Technological, and Environmental Planning, Ann Arbor, MI 48109

AWARDS PhD. Offered through the Horace H. Rackham School of Graduate Studies. Part-time programs available.

Degree requirements: For doctorate, thesis/dissertation, 1 interdisciplinary paper, 2 preliminary exams, oral defense of dissertation.
Entrance requirements: For doctorate, GRE General Test, TOEFL.
Expenses: Contact institution.
Faculty research: Urban and regional planning, community and economic development, transportation planning and geological information systems, environmental planning, the built environment, international development and planning. *Web site:* http://www.caup.umich.edu/urp/index.html

Find an in-depth description at www.petersons.com/gradchannel.

■ UNIVERSITY OF MICHIGAN

Taubman College of Architecture and Urban Planning, Urban and Regional Planning Program, Ann Arbor, MI 48109

AWARDS Gaming/simulation studies (Certificate); urban planning (MUP); urban, technological, and environmental planning (PhD). Offered through the Horace H. Rackham School of Graduate Studies; students in the Certificate program must either be currently enrolled in a graduate program or have earned a masters or PhD degree within the last five years.

Degree requirements: For master's, thesis or alternative; for doctorate, thesis/dissertation.
Entrance requirements: For master's and doctorate, GRE General Test, TOEFL. *Web site:* http://www.caup.umich.edu/

Find an in-depth description at www.petersons.com/gradchannel.

■ UNIVERSITY OF MINNESOTA, TWIN CITIES CAMPUS

Graduate School, Hubert H. Humphrey Institute of Public Affairs, Program in Urban and Regional Planning, Minneapolis, MN 55455-0213

AWARDS Economic development (MURP); environmental and ecological planning (MURP); housing, social planning, and community development (MURP); land use and human settlements (MURP); landscape and urban design (MURP); planning process design and implementation (MURP); transportation planning (MURP). Part-time programs available.

Degree requirements: For master's, thesis or alternative, internship or equivalent work experience.
Entrance requirements: For master's, GRE General Test, TOEFL. Electronic applications accepted.
Expenses: Tuition, state resident: full-time $2,932; part-time $489 per credit. Tuition, nonresident: full-time $5,758; part-time $960 per credit. Part-time tuition and fees vary according to course load, program and reciprocity agreements.
Faculty research: Policy planning, resource allocation planning, regulatory planning, program planning, project planning. *Web site:* http://www.hhh.umn.edu/

■ UNIVERSITY OF NEBRASKA–LINCOLN

Graduate College, College of Architecture, Department of Community and Regional Planning, Lincoln, NE 68588

AWARDS MCRP, JD/MCRP, M Arch/MCRP, MS/MCRP.

Faculty: 7.
Students: 55 (24 women); includes 7 minority (3 African Americans, 1 Asian American or Pacific Islander, 1 Hispanic American, 2 Native Americans) 7 international. Average age 29. 26 applicants, 73% accepted, 12 enrolled. In 2001, 13 degrees awarded.
Degree requirements: For master's, thesis optional.
Entrance requirements: For master's, GRE General Test, TOEFL. *Application deadline:* For fall admission, 3/1; for spring admission, 10/1. *Application fee:* $35. Electronic applications accepted.
Expenses: Tuition, state resident: full-time $2,412; part-time $134 per credit. Tuition, nonresident: full-time $6,223; part-time $346 per credit. Tuition and fees vary according to course load.
Financial support: In 2001–02, 1 fellowship, 11 research assistantships, 1 teaching assistantship were awarded. Federal Work-Study, health care benefits, and unspecified assistantships also available. Support available to part-time students. Financial award application deadline: 2/15.
Faculty research: Economic development, community development and improvement, social planning, land use planning, physical planning, environmental planning. Sharon Gaber, Graduate Committee Chair, 402-472-9280, *Fax:* 402-472-3806, *E-mail:* sgaber2@unl.edu. *Web site:* http://www.unl.edu/archcoll/crp/index.html

■ UNIVERSITY OF NEW MEXICO

Graduate School, School of Architecture and Planning, Program in Community and Regional Planning, Albuquerque, NM 87131-2039

AWARDS MCRP, MCRP/MA, MPA/MCRP. Part-time programs available.

Faculty: 5 full-time (1 woman), 3 part-time/adjunct (2 women).
Students: 28 full-time (19 women), 25 part-time (12 women); includes 22 minority (2 African Americans, 1 Asian American or Pacific Islander, 16 Hispanic Americans, 3 Native Americans). Average age 33. 32 applicants, 69% accepted, 9 enrolled. In 2001, 13 degrees awarded.
Degree requirements: For master's, thesis or alternative.
Entrance requirements: For master's, minimum GPA of 3.0. *Application deadline:* For fall admission, 2/15 (priority date); for spring admission, 10/15 (priority date). *Application fee:* $40.
Expenses: Tuition, state resident: full-time $2,771; part-time $115 per credit hour. Tuition, nonresident: full-time $11,207; part-time $467 per credit hour. Required fees: $570; $24 per credit hour. Part-time tuition and fees vary according to course load and program.
Financial support: In 2001–02, 32 students received support, including 1 research assistantship (averaging $9,600 per year); Federal Work-Study, scholarships/grants, health care benefits, tuition waivers (full), and unspecified assistantships also available. Financial award application deadline: 3/1; financial award applicants required to submit FAFSA.
Faculty research: Community development, urban and ecological design, land economics, community-based planning, environmental dispute resolution, environmental justice.
Dr. David S. Henkel, Director, 505-277-5939, *Fax:* 505-277-0076, *E-mail:* cymro@unm.edu.
Application contact: Lois A. Kennedy, Senior Academic Adviser, 505-277-4847, *Fax:* 505-277-0076, *E-mail:* loisk@unm.edu. *Web site:* http://saap.unm.edu/

■ UNIVERSITY OF NEW ORLEANS

Graduate School, College of Urban and Public Affairs, Program in Urban and Regional Planning, New Orleans, LA 70148

AWARDS MURP.

Students: 30 full-time (20 women), 16 part-time (7 women); includes 16 minority (14 African Americans, 1 Asian American or Pacific Islander, 1 Native American), 3 international. Average age 31. 41 applicants, 54% accepted, 10 enrolled. In 2001, 8 degrees awarded.
Degree requirements: For master's, thesis.
Entrance requirements: For master's, GRE General Test. *Application deadline:* For fall admission, 7/1 (priority date); for spring admission, 11/15 (priority date). Applications are processed on a rolling basis. *Application fee:* $20. Electronic applications accepted.
Expenses: Tuition, state resident: full-time $2,748; part-time $435 per credit. Tuition, nonresident: full-time $9,792; part-time $1,773 per credit.
Financial support: Research assistantships available. Financial award applicants required to submit FAFSA.
Faculty research: Urban economic development, environmental planning and analysis, social and cultural change.
Dr. Ralph Thayer, Graduate Coordinator, 504-280-6592, *E-mail:* rthayer@uno.edu.
Application contact: Information Contact, 504-280-6514, *Fax:* 504-280-6272.

■ THE UNIVERSITY OF NORTH CAROLINA AT CHAPEL HILL

Graduate School, College of Arts and Sciences, Department of City and Regional Planning, Chapel Hill, NC 27599

AWARDS City and regional planning (MRP); planning (PhD); public policy analysis (PhD). Part-time programs available.

Faculty: 15 full-time (2 women), 3 part-time/adjunct (0 women).
Students: 88 full-time (36 women), 5 part-time; includes 11 minority (7 African Americans, 2 Asian Americans or Pacific Islanders, 2 Hispanic Americans), 19 international. Average age 30. 167 applicants, 46% accepted, 42 enrolled. In 2001, 41 master's, 3 doctorates awarded.
Degree requirements: For master's, project; for doctorate, thesis/dissertation, comprehensive exam. *Median time to degree:* Master's–2 years full-time; doctorate–7 years full-time.
Entrance requirements: For master's and doctorate, GRE General Test, TOEFL. *Application deadline:* For fall admission, 1/1 (priority date). *Application fee:* $60. Electronic applications accepted.

The University of North Carolina at Chapel Hill (continued)

Expenses: Tuition, state resident: full-time $2,864. Tuition, nonresident: full-time $12,030.
Financial support: In 2001–02, 61 students received support, including 9 fellowships with full tuition reimbursements available (averaging $15,000 per year), 25 research assistantships with full tuition reimbursements available (averaging $5,500 per year), 27 teaching assistantships with full tuition reimbursements available (averaging $5,500 per year); career-related internships or fieldwork, Federal Work-Study, traineeships, unspecified assistantships, and planning agency assignments also available. Financial award application deadline: 1/1; financial award applicants required to submit FAFSA.
Faculty research: Developing areas, transportation, affordable housing, growth management, coastal zone management.
Dr. David H. Moreau, Chairman, 919-962-4756, *Fax:* 919-962-5206, *E-mail:* dmoreau@email.unc.edu.
Application contact: Carolyn Turner, Student Service Manager, 919-962-4784, *E-mail:* turnerc@unc.edu. *Web site:* http://www.unc.edu/depts/dcrpweb/

■ UNIVERSITY OF OKLAHOMA

Graduate College, College of Architecture, Division of Regional and City Planning, Norman, OK 73019-0390

AWARDS MRCP, MRCP/MLA.

Faculty: 3 full-time (1 woman).
Students: 13 full-time (4 women), 10 part-time (2 women); includes 2 minority (both Native Americans), 4 international. 24 applicants, 92% accepted, 6 enrolled. In 2001, 5 degrees awarded.
Degree requirements: For master's, thesis or alternative, portfolio, project.
Entrance requirements: For master's, GRE General Test, TOEFL, appropriate bachelor's degree, portfolio. *Application deadline:* For fall admission, 6/1 (priority date). Applications are processed on a rolling basis. *Application fee:* $25 ($50 for international students).
Expenses: Tuition, state resident: full-time $2,208; part-time $92 per credit hour. Tuition, nonresident: part-time $297 per credit hour. Tuition and fees vary according to course level, course load and program.
Financial support: In 2001–02, 10 students received support, including 2 research assistantships with partial tuition reimbursements available (averaging $9,426 per year); teaching assistantships with tuition reimbursements available, career-related internships or fieldwork, institutionally sponsored loans, scholarships/grants, tuition waivers (partial), and unspecified assistantships also available. Support available to part-time students. Financial award applicants required to submit FAFSA.
Faculty research: Transportation planning, manufactured housing, growth management, urban history. *Total annual research expenditures:* $150,000.
Richard Marshment, Director, 405-325-2399, *Fax:* 405-325-7588, *E-mail:* rcpl@ou.edu.

■ UNIVERSITY OF OREGON

Graduate School, School of Architecture and Allied Arts, Department of Planning, Public Policy, and Management, Program in Community and Regional Planning, Eugene, OR 97403

AWARDS MCRP. Part-time programs available.

Students: 53 full-time (27 women), 10 part-time (4 women); includes 3 minority (1 Asian American or Pacific Islander, 1 Hispanic American, 1 Native American), 7 international. 41 applicants, 73% accepted. In 2001, 31 degrees awarded.
Degree requirements: For master's, thesis or alternative.
Entrance requirements: For master's, TOEFL, minimum GPA of 3.0. *Application fee:* $50.
Expenses: Tuition, state resident: full-time $4,968; part-time $501 per credit hour. Tuition, nonresident: full-time $8,400; part-time $691 per credit hour.
Financial support: In 2001–02, 18 teaching assistantships were awarded; career-related internships or fieldwork also available.
Faculty research: Community economic development, tourism, families in poverty.
Application contact: Janie Boals, Graduate Secretary, 541-346-6018, *Fax:* 541-346-2040.

■ UNIVERSITY OF PENNSYLVANIA

Graduate School of Fine Arts, Department of City and Regional Planning, Philadelphia, PA 19104

AWARDS MCP, PhD, Certificate, MSE/MCP. Terminal master's awarded for partial completion of doctoral program.

Degree requirements: For doctorate, thesis/dissertation.
Entrance requirements: For master's, GRE, TOEFL; for doctorate, GRE General Test, TOEFL. Electronic applications accepted.
Expenses: Tuition: Part-time $12,875 per semester.
Faculty research: Growth management, transportation planning, urban simulation modeling, housing, development planning. *Web site:* http://www.upenn.edu/gsfa/

Find an in-depth description at www.petersons.com/gradchannel.

■ UNIVERSITY OF PENNSYLVANIA

Graduate School of Fine Arts, Program in Landscape Architecture and Regional Planning, Philadelphia, PA 19104

AWARDS Landscape architecture and regional planning (MLA); landscape studies (Certificate). Part-time programs available.

Degree requirements: For master's, thesis optional.
Entrance requirements: For master's, GRE, TOEFL, portfolio.
Expenses: Tuition: Part-time $12,875 per semester.
Faculty research: Early landscape architecture, natural distribution through landslides, urban gardens, landscape registration, watershed studies. *Web site:* http://www.upenn.edu/gsfa/

Find an in-depth description at www.petersons.com/gradchannel.

■ UNIVERSITY OF PITTSBURGH

Graduate School of Public and International Affairs, Division of Public and Urban Affairs, Program in Urban and Regional Affairs, Pittsburgh, PA 15260

AWARDS MPA, JD/MPA, MPA/MPIA, MPH/MPA, MSIS/MPA, MSW/MPA. Part-time and evening/weekend programs available.

Faculty: 32 full-time (8 women), 12 part-time/adjunct (9 women).
Students: 59 full-time (37 women), 21 part-time (15 women); includes 12 minority (all African Americans), 8 international. Average age 27. 33 applicants, 64% accepted, 8 enrolled. In 2001, 9 degrees awarded.
Degree requirements: For master's, internship, thesis optional.
Application deadline: For fall admission, 3/1 (priority date); for spring admission, 10/1 (priority date). Applications are processed on a rolling basis. *Application fee:* $40. Electronic applications accepted.
Expenses: Tuition, state resident: full-time $9,410; part-time $385 per credit. Tuition, nonresident: full-time $19,376; part-time $797 per credit. Required fees: $480; $90 per term. Tuition and fees vary according to program.
Financial support: In 2001–02, 36 students received support, including 7 fellowships (averaging $11,300 per year); career-related internships or fieldwork, scholarships/grants, tuition waivers (full and partial), and unspecified assistantships also available. Financial award application deadline: 2/1.
Faculty research: Health policy and regulations, emergency management, regional finance, non-profit management, community/regional development,

environmental policy. *Web site:* http://www.gspia.pitt.edu/

Find an in-depth description at www.petersons.com/gradchannel.

■ UNIVERSITY OF PUERTO RICO, RÍO PIEDRAS

Graduate School of Planning, San Juan, PR 00931

AWARDS MP. Part-time and evening/weekend programs available.

Faculty: 10.
Students: 47 full-time (30 women), 83 part-time (42 women); all minorities (all Hispanic Americans). Average age 27. 66 applicants, 9% accepted. In 2001, 12 degrees awarded.
Degree requirements: For master's, thesis, planning project defense.
Entrance requirements: For master's, minimum GPA of 3.0. *Application deadline:* For fall admission, 2/1. *Application fee:* $17.
Expenses: Students that provide official evidence of private medicine insurance or service are exempt of the payment of $529 per academic year.
Financial support: Fellowships, research assistantships, teaching assistantships, Federal Work-Study, institutionally sponsored loans, and tuition waivers (partial) available. Financial award application deadline: 5/31.
Faculty research: Municipalities Historic Atlas, Puerto Rico Economic Future.
Dr. Elías R. R. Gutierrez, Director, 787-764-0000 Ext. 5010, *Fax:* 787-763-5375, *E-mail:* nvega@rrpac.upr.clu.edu.
Application contact: Raquel Rodríguez, Student Affairs Officer, 787-764-0000 Ext. 3182, *Fax:* 787-763-5375.

■ UNIVERSITY OF RHODE ISLAND

Graduate School, College of the Environment and Life Sciences, Department of Community Planning and Area Development, Kingston, RI 02881

AWARDS MCP.

Students: In 2001, 6 degrees awarded.
Degree requirements: For master's, thesis or alternative, internship.
Entrance requirements: For master's, GRE General Test. *Application deadline:* For fall admission, 4/15 (priority date). Applications are processed on a rolling basis. *Application fee:* $35.
Expenses: Tuition, state resident: full-time $3,756; part-time $209 per credit. Tuition, nonresident: full-time $10,774; part-time $599 per credit. Required fees: $1,586; $76 per credit. One-time fee: $60 full-time.
Dr. Farhad Atash, Chairman, 401-874-2248.

■ UNIVERSITY OF SOUTHERN CALIFORNIA

Graduate School, School of Policy, Planning and Development, Program in Planning, Los Angeles, CA 90089

AWARDS Planning (M Pl); urban and regional planning (PhD).

Degree requirements: For doctorate, thesis/dissertation.
Entrance requirements: For master's and doctorate, GRE General Test.
Expenses: Tuition: Full-time $25,060; part-time $844 per unit. Required fees: $473.

Find an in-depth description at www.petersons.com/gradchannel.

■ UNIVERSITY OF SOUTHERN CALIFORNIA

Graduate School, School of Policy, Planning and Development, Program in Planning and Development Studies, Sacramento, CA 95814

AWARDS MPDS. Part-time and evening/weekend programs available.

Faculty: 1 full-time (0 women), 7 part-time/adjunct (1 woman).
Students: Average age 30. 1 applicant, 100% accepted, 1 enrolled.
Degree requirements: For master's, thesis optional.
Entrance requirements: For master's, GRE, GMAT, LSAT, minimum GPA of 3.0. *Application deadline:* For fall admission, 7/1 (priority date); for winter admission, 11/1 (priority date); for spring admission, 4/1 (priority date). Applications are processed on a rolling basis. *Application fee:* $55.
Expenses: Tuition: Full-time $25,060; part-time $844 per unit. Required fees: $473.
Financial support: In 2001–02, 11 students received support, including 11 fellowships with partial tuition reimbursements available (averaging $1,180 per year); career-related internships or fieldwork, Federal Work-Study, institutionally sponsored loans, scholarships/grants, health care benefits, and unspecified assistantships also available. Support available to part-time students. Financial award application deadline: 7/1.
Faculty research: Management systems, transportation planning, land use planning.
Richard Callahan, Director and Assistant Dean, 916-442-6911 Ext. 18, *Fax:* 916-444-7712, *E-mail:* rcallaha@usc.edu. *Web site:* http://www.usc.edu/schools/sppd/sacto/mpds.html

■ UNIVERSITY OF SOUTHERN CALIFORNIA

Graduate School, School of Policy, Planning and Development, Program in Planning and Development Studies, Los Angeles, CA 90089

AWARDS MPDS, DPDS.

Entrance requirements: For master's, GRE General Test.
Expenses: Tuition: Full-time $25,060; part-time $844 per unit. Required fees: $473.

Find an in-depth description at www.petersons.com/gradchannel.

■ UNIVERSITY OF SOUTHERN MAINE

Edmund S. Muskie School of Public Service, Program in Community Planning and Development, Portland, ME 04104-9300

AWARDS MCPD, Certificate, JD/MCPD. Part-time and evening/weekend programs available. Postbaccalaureate distance learning degree programs offered (minimal on-campus study).

Faculty: 4 full-time (1 woman), 5 part-time/adjunct (1 woman).
Students: 6 full-time (2 women), 17 part-time (5 women); includes 1 minority (Asian American or Pacific Islander). Average age 28. 15 applicants, 80% accepted. In 2001, 5 degrees awarded.
Degree requirements: For master's, thesis, capstone project, field experience. *Median time to degree:* Master's–2 years full-time, 4 years part-time.
Entrance requirements: For master's, GRE General Test or LSAT. *Application deadline:* For fall admission, 3/1 (priority date); for spring admission, 12/1. Applications are processed on a rolling basis. *Application fee:* $50. Electronic applications accepted.
Expenses: Tuition, state resident: part-time $200 per credit. Tuition, nonresident: part-time $560 per credit.
Financial support: In 2001–02, 5 students received support, including 1 fellowship with full tuition reimbursement available (averaging $5,000 per year), 5 research assistantships (averaging $5,000 per year); career-related internships or fieldwork, Federal Work-Study, tuition waivers (full), and unspecified assistantships also available. Financial award application deadline: 4/1; financial award applicants required to submit CSS PROFILE.
Faculty research: Sustainable communities, ego system management, economic and environmental tradeoffs.
Prof. Charles Colgan, Chair, 207-780-4008, *Fax:* 207-780-4317, *E-mail:* colgan@usm.maine.edu.
Application contact: Carlene R. Goldman, Director of Student Affairs, 207-780-4864, *Fax:* 207-780-4417, *E-mail:*

University of Southern Maine (continued)
cgold@usm.maine.edu. *Web site:* http://www.muskie.usm.maine.edu/

■ THE UNIVERSITY OF TENNESSEE

Graduate School, College of Arts and Sciences, Department of Urban and Regional Planning, Knoxville, TN 37996

AWARDS Environmental planning (MSP); land-use planning (MSP); real estate development planning (MSP); transportation planning (MSP). Part-time programs available.

Faculty: 3 full-time (0 women), 3 part-time/adjunct (2 women).
Students: 35 full-time (10 women), 17 part-time (10 women); includes 7 minority (6 African Americans, 1 Asian American or Pacific Islander), 4 international. 41 applicants, 88% accepted. In 2001, 20 degrees awarded.
Degree requirements: For master's, thesis or alternative.
Entrance requirements: For master's, GRE General Test, TOEFL, minimum GPA of 2.7. *Application deadline:* For fall admission, 2/1 (priority date). Applications are processed on a rolling basis. *Application fee:* $35. Electronic applications accepted.
Expenses: Tuition, state resident: full-time $4,280; part-time $233 per hour. Tuition, nonresident: full-time $12,066; part-time $666 per hour. Tuition and fees vary according to program.
Financial support: In 2001–02, 2 fellowships were awarded; research assistantships, teaching assistantships, career-related internships or fieldwork, Federal Work-Study, institutionally sponsored loans, and unspecified assistantships also available. Financial award application deadline: 2/1; financial award applicants required to submit FAFSA.
Dr. C. W. Minkel, Head, 865-974-5227, *Fax:* 865-974-5229, *E-mail:* cminkel@utk.edu.
Application contact: James Spencer, Graduate Representative, *E-mail:* jspence3@utk.edu.

■ THE UNIVERSITY OF TEXAS AT ARLINGTON

Graduate School, School of Urban and Public Affairs, Program in City and Regional Planning, Arlington, TX 76019

AWARDS MCRP, M Arch/MCRP.

Students: 35 full-time (14 women), 28 part-time (16 women); includes 6 minority (3 African Americans, 2 Asian Americans or Pacific Islanders, 1 Hispanic American), 17 international. 34 applicants, 100% accepted, 25 enrolled. In 2001, 11 degrees awarded.
Degree requirements: For master's, thesis or alternative.
Entrance requirements: For master's, GRE General Test. *Application deadline:* For fall admission, 6/16. *Application fee:* $25 ($50 for international students).
Expenses: Tuition, area resident: Full-time $2,268. Tuition, nonresident: full-time $6,264. Required fees: $839. Tuition and fees vary according to course load.
Financial support: Fellowships, research assistantships, career-related internships or fieldwork available. Financial award application deadline: 6/1; financial award applicants required to submit FAFSA.
Elise M. Bright, Graduate Adviser, 817-272-3338, *Fax:* 817-272-5008, *E-mail:* bright@uta.edu.

■ THE UNIVERSITY OF TEXAS AT ARLINGTON

Graduate School, School of Urban and Public Affairs, Urban and Public Affairs Division, Arlington, TX 76019

AWARDS MA, MSSW/MA. Part-time and evening/weekend programs available.

Students: 4 full-time (2 women), 15 part-time (11 women); includes 4 minority (3 African Americans, 1 Hispanic American). 10 applicants, 90% accepted, 8 enrolled.
Degree requirements: For master's, thesis or alternative, registration.
Entrance requirements: For master's, GRE General Test. *Application deadline:* For fall admission, 6/16. *Application fee:* $25 ($50 for international students).
Expenses: Tuition, area resident: Full-time $2,268. Tuition, nonresident: full-time $6,264. Required fees: $839. Tuition and fees vary according to course load.
Financial support: Fellowships, research assistantships, career-related internships or fieldwork available. Financial award application deadline: 6/1; financial award applicants required to submit FAFSA.
Dr. Edith Barrett, Graduate Adviser, 817-272-3285, *Fax:* 817-272-5008, *E-mail:* ebarrett@uta.edu.

■ THE UNIVERSITY OF TEXAS AT AUSTIN

Graduate School, School of Architecture, Program in Community and Regional Planning, Austin, TX 78712-1111

AWARDS MSCRP, PhD, JD/MSCRP, MSCRP/MA, MSCRP/PhD.

Faculty: 8 full-time (2 women), 1 (woman) part-time/adjunct.
Students: 69 full-time, 8 part-time; includes 9 minority (3 African Americans, 6 Hispanic Americans), 14 international. Average age 29. 92 applicants, 64% accepted. In 2001, 29 degrees awarded.
Degree requirements: For master's and doctorate, thesis/dissertation.
Entrance requirements: For master's and doctorate, GRE General Test. *Application deadline:* For fall admission, 2/1 (priority date). *Application fee:* $50 ($75 for international students). Electronic applications accepted.
Expenses: Tuition, state resident: full-time $3,159. Tuition, nonresident: full-time $6,957. Tuition and fees vary according to program.
Financial support: In 2001–02, 6 fellowships with partial tuition reimbursements (averaging $10,000 per year), 6 research assistantships with partial tuition reimbursements (averaging $9,000 per year), 5 teaching assistantships with partial tuition reimbursements (averaging $9,000 per year) were awarded. Career-related internships or fieldwork, institutionally sponsored loans, scholarships/grants, and tuition waivers (partial) also available. Financial award application deadline: 2/1.
Dr. Robert Patterson, Director, 512-471-1922, *Fax:* 512-471-0716. *Web site:* http://www.ar.utexas.edu/admissions/

■ UNIVERSITY OF TOLEDO

Graduate School, College of Arts and Sciences, Department of Geography and Planning, Toledo, OH 43606-3398

AWARDS Geography (MA); planning (MA). Part-time programs available.

Faculty: 7.
Students: 24 full-time (9 women), 6 part-time (5 women); includes 5 minority (4 African Americans, 1 Native American), 4 international. Average age 30. 20 applicants, 60% accepted. In 2001, 11 degrees awarded.
Degree requirements: For master's, thesis.
Entrance requirements: For master's, GRE General Test. *Application deadline:* For fall admission, 3/15 (priority date). Applications are processed on a rolling basis. *Application fee:* $30. Electronic applications accepted.
Expenses: Tuition, state resident: full-time $7,278; part-time $303 per hour. Tuition, nonresident: full-time $15,731; part-time $699 per hour. Required fees: $43 per hour.
Financial support: In 2001–02, 4 research assistantships, 10 teaching assistantships were awarded. Career-related internships or fieldwork, institutionally sponsored loans, and tuition waivers (full) also available. Support available to part-time students. Financial award application deadline: 4/1.
Dr. Samuel Aryeetey-Attoh, Chair, 419-530-4709, *Fax:* 419-530-7919, *E-mail:* sattoh@utnet.utoledo.edu.
Application contact: Dr. Peter Lindquist, Graduate Advisor, 419-530-2545, *Fax:* 419-530-7919, *E-mail:* plindqu@uoft02.utoledo.edu.

■ UNIVERSITY OF VIRGINIA

School of Architecture, Department of Urban and Environmental Planning, Charlottesville, VA 22903

AWARDS MP, JD/MP.

Faculty: 7 full-time (1 woman), 5 part-time/adjunct (1 woman).
Students: 38 full-time (25 women); includes 2 minority (both African Americans), 1 international. Average age 26. 114 applicants, 42% accepted, 17 enrolled. In 2001, 35 degrees awarded.
Entrance requirements: For master's, GRE General Test, previous course work in statistics. *Application deadline:* For fall admission, 2/1. *Application fee:* $40.
Expenses: Tuition, state resident: full-time $3,988. Tuition, nonresident: full-time $17,078. Required fees: $1,190.
Financial support: Applicants required to submit FAFSA.
Faculty research: Urban development, land use, environment, policy analysis, historic preservation.
A. Bruce Dotson, Chair, 434-924-6459, *Fax:* 434-982-2678.
Application contact: Tracey Critzer, Admissions Officer, 434-924-6442, *E-mail:* arch-admissions@virginia.edu. *Web site:* http://www.virginia.edu/arch/dept/urban.html/

Find an in-depth description at www.petersons.com/gradchannel.

■ UNIVERSITY OF WASHINGTON

Graduate School, College of Architecture and Urban Planning, Department of Urban Design and Planning, Seattle, WA 98195

AWARDS Urban design and planning (PhD); urban planning (MUP).

Degree requirements: For master's, thesis or alternative; for doctorate, thesis/dissertation.
Entrance requirements: For master's and doctorate, GRE General Test, TOEFL, minimum GPA of 3.0.
Expenses: Tuition, state resident: full-time $5,539. Tuition, nonresident: full-time $14,376. Required fees: $390. Tuition and fees vary according to course load and program.
Faculty research: Land-use and growth management, urban form and travel behavior, geographic information systems/remote sensing, historic preservation, urban ecology and environmental planning. *Web site:* http://www.caup.washington.edu/html/urbdp/

■ UNIVERSITY OF WISCONSIN–MADISON

Graduate School, College of Letters and Science and College of Agricultural and Life Sciences, Department of Urban and Regional Planning, Madison, WI 53706-1380

AWARDS MS, PhD. Part-time programs available.

Degree requirements: For master's, internship, thesis optional; for doctorate, thesis/dissertation, 3 preliminary exams.
Entrance requirements: For master's, GRE, minimum GPA of 3.0, previous course work in statistics; for doctorate, 1 year of experience, master's degree in related field. Electronic applications accepted.
Expenses: Tuition, state resident: full-time $7,361; part-time $399 per credit. Tuition, nonresident: full-time $20,499; part-time $1,282 per credit. Required fees: $34 per credit. Full-time tuition and fees vary according to course load, program, reciprocity agreements and student level.
Faculty research: Land use, environmental planning, community development, economic development planning. *Web site:* http://www.wisc.edu/urpl/

■ UNIVERSITY OF WISCONSIN–MILWAUKEE

Graduate School, School of Architecture and Urban Planning, Department of Urban Planning, Milwaukee, WI 53201-0413

AWARDS MUP, M Arch/MUP, MPA/MUP, MUP/MS. Part-time programs available.

Faculty: 6 full-time (2 women).
Students: 26 full-time (8 women), 11 part-time (6 women); includes 1 minority (Asian American or Pacific Islander), 3 international. 37 applicants, 70% accepted. In 2001, 17 degrees awarded.
Entrance requirements: For master's, GRE General Test. *Application deadline:* For fall admission, 1/1 (priority date); for spring admission, 9/1. Applications are processed on a rolling basis. *Application fee:* $45 ($75 for international students).
Expenses: Tuition, state resident: full-time $6,180; part-time $535 per credit. Tuition, nonresident: full-time $19,482; part-time $1,366 per credit. Tuition and fees vary according to course load, program and reciprocity agreements.
Financial support: In 2001–02, 5 teaching assistantships were awarded; fellowships, research assistantships, career-related internships or fieldwork and unspecified assistantships also available. Support available to part-time students. Financial award application deadline: 4/15.
Joan Simuncak, Representative, 414-229-4015, *Fax:* 414-229-6976, *E-mail:* joanarch@uwm.edu. *Web site:* http://www.uwm.edu/SARUP/planning/

■ UTAH STATE UNIVERSITY

School of Graduate Studies, College of Humanities, Arts and Social Sciences, Department of Landscape Architecture and Environmental Planning, Logan, UT 84322

AWARDS Bioregional planning (MS); landscape architecture (MLA).

Faculty: 5 full-time (1 woman), 3 part-time/adjunct (0 women).
Students: 28 full-time (14 women), 2 part-time (1 woman). 28 applicants, 64% accepted. In 2001, 9 degrees awarded.
Median time to degree: Master's–3 years full-time, 4 years part-time.
Entrance requirements: For master's, GRE General Test, TOEFL, minimum GPA of 3.0. *Application deadline:* For fall admission, 3/15 (priority date); for spring admission, 10/15. Applications are processed on a rolling basis. *Application fee:* $40.
Expenses: Tuition, state resident: full-time $1,693. Tuition, nonresident: full-time $4,233. Required fees: $501. Tuition and fees vary according to program.
Financial support: In 2001–02, research assistantships with partial tuition reimbursements (averaging $9,868 per year), 7 teaching assistantships with partial tuition reimbursements (averaging $2,750 per year) were awarded. Fellowships, career-related internships or fieldwork, Federal Work-Study, tuition waivers (partial), and unspecified assistantships also available. Financial award application deadline: 2/1.
Faculty research: Visual resource management, planning for wildlife, agricultural land preservation, watershed planning.
Karen Hanna, Department Head, 435-797-0500, *Fax:* 435-797-0503, *E-mail:* kchanna@cc.usu.edu.
Application contact: John Ellsworth, Graduate Program Coordinator, 435-797-0504, *Fax:* 435-797-0503, *E-mail:* jellsworth@hass.usu.edu. *Web site:* http://www.usu.edu/~laep/

■ VALDOSTA STATE UNIVERSITY

Graduate School, College of Arts and Sciences, Department of Political Science, Valdosta, GA 31698

AWARDS City management (MPA); public human resources (MPA); public sector (MPA). Part-time and evening/weekend programs available. Postbaccalaureate distance learning degree programs offered (no on-campus study).

Faculty: 13 full-time (2 women).
Students: 53 full-time (43 women), 53 part-time (42 women); includes 16 minority (12 African Americans, 4 Hispanic Americans). Average age 29. 48 applicants, 96% accepted. In 2001, 49 degrees awarded.
Degree requirements: For master's, comprehensive written and/or oral exams, internship.
Entrance requirements: For master's, GMAT, GRE General Test, or MAT, minimum GPA of 2.5. *Application deadline:* For fall admission, 7/1; for spring admission, 11/15. Applications are processed on a rolling basis. *Application fee:* $20.
Expenses: Tuition, state resident: full-time $1,746; part-time $97 per hour. Tuition, nonresident: full-time $6,966; part-time $387 per hour. Required fees: $594; $297 per semester.

Valdosta State University (continued)
Financial support: In 2001–02, 3 research assistantships with full tuition reimbursements (averaging $2,452 per year) were awarded; institutionally sponsored loans, scholarships/grants, and unspecified assistantships also available. Support available to part-time students. Financial award applicants required to submit FAFSA.
Faculty research: Powers of state attorneys general; health, transportation, and environmental policy; public administration theory.
Dr. James Peterson, Director, 229-333-5771.
Application contact: Dr. Nolan Argyle, Program Director, 229-293-6059, *E-mail:* nargyle@valdosta.edu.

■ VIRGINIA COMMONWEALTH UNIVERSITY

School of Graduate Studies, College of Humanities and Sciences, Department of Urban Studies and Planning, Richmond, VA 23284-9005

AWARDS Urban planning (MURP); urban revitalization (CURP). Part-time and evening/weekend programs available.

Students: 19 full-time, 20 part-time; includes 11 minority (8 African Americans, 3 Asian Americans or Pacific Islanders). 32 applicants, 78% accepted. In 2001, 18 degrees awarded.
Degree requirements: For master's, internship, thesis optional.
Entrance requirements: For master's, GRE General Test or LSAT, minimum GPA of 2.7. *Application deadline:* For fall admission, 4/15; for spring admission, 11/15. Applications are processed on a rolling basis. *Application fee:* $30.
Expenses: Tuition, state resident: full-time $4,276; part-time $238 per credit. Tuition, nonresident: full-time $12,672; part-time $704 per credit. Required fees: $1,167; $43 per credit.
Financial support: Fellowships, research assistantships, teaching assistantships, career-related internships or fieldwork and institutionally sponsored loans available. Support available to part-time students. Financial award application deadline: 3/1.
Faculty research: Census impact, outdoor recreation database, housing, racial politics.
Dr. John J. Accordino, Chair, 804-828-2489, *Fax:* 804-828-6681. *Web site:* http://www.vcu.edu/hasweb/usp/usp.html

■ VIRGINIA POLYTECHNIC INSTITUTE AND STATE UNIVERSITY

Graduate School, College of Architecture and Urban Studies, Department of Urban Affairs and Planning, Program in Urban and Regional Planning, Blacksburg, VA 24061

AWARDS MURP. Part-time programs available.

Degree requirements: For master's, practicum, thesis optional.
Entrance requirements: For master's, TOEFL.
Expenses: Tuition, state resident: part-time $241 per hour. Tuition, nonresident: part-time $406 per hour. Tuition and fees vary according to program.
Faculty research: Hazardous waste, resource management, land use, economic development.
Find an in-depth description at www.petersons.com/gradchannel.

■ WASHINGTON STATE UNIVERSITY

Graduate School, College of Sciences, Program in Environmental Science and Regional Planning, Concentration in Regional Planning, Pullman, WA 99164

AWARDS MRP.

Faculty: 4 full-time (0 women), 1 part-time/adjunct (0 women).
Students: 18 full-time (11 women), 3 part-time (2 women); includes 2 minority (both Asian Americans or Pacific Islanders), 1 international.
Degree requirements: For master's, oral exam, thesis optional.
Entrance requirements: For master's, GRE General Test, TOEFL, minimum GPA of 3.0. *Application deadline:* For fall admission, 3/1 (priority date). Applications are processed on a rolling basis. *Application fee:* $35.
Expenses: Tuition, state resident: full-time $6,088; part-time $304 per semester. Tuition, nonresident: full-time $14,918; part-time $746 per semester. Tuition and fees vary according to program.
Financial support: In 2001–02, 3 teaching assistantships with full and partial tuition reimbursements were awarded; research assistantships with full and partial tuition reimbursements, Federal Work-Study, institutionally sponsored loans, and tuition waivers (partial) also available. Financial award application deadline: 4/1; financial award applicants required to submit FAFSA.
Application contact: Coordinator, 509-335-8536, *Fax:* 509-335-7636, *E-mail:* esrp@wsu.edu. *Web site:* http://www.esrp.wsu.edu/

■ WAYNE STATE UNIVERSITY

Graduate School, College of Urban, Labor and Metropolitan Affairs, Department of Geography and Urban Planning, Program in Urban Planning, Detroit, MI 48202

AWARDS MUP. Evening/weekend programs available.

Students: 49. In 2001, 5 degrees awarded.
Degree requirements: For master's, thesis.
Application deadline: For fall admission, 7/1. *Application fee:* $20 ($30 for international students). Electronic applications accepted.
Expenses: Tuition, state resident: full-time $3,764. Tuition and fees vary according to degree level and program.

■ WEST CHESTER UNIVERSITY OF PENNSYLVANIA

Graduate Studies, School of Business and Public Affairs, Department of Geography and Planning, West Chester, PA 19383

AWARDS Geography (MA); regional planning (MSA). Part-time and evening/weekend programs available.

Faculty: 5.
Students: 6 full-time (1 woman), 11 part-time (7 women); includes 1 minority (African American). Average age 32. 13 applicants, 92% accepted. In 2001, 6 degrees awarded.
Degree requirements: For master's, thesis optional.
Entrance requirements: For master's, GRE General Test, interview, minimum GPA of 3.0, resumé. *Application deadline:* For fall admission, 4/15 (priority date); for spring admission, 10/15. Applications are processed on a rolling basis. *Application fee:* $25.
Expenses: Tuition, state resident: full-time $4,600; part-time $256 per credit. Tuition, nonresident: full-time $7,554; part-time $420 per credit. Required fees: $44 per credit.
Financial support: In 2001–02, 1 research assistantship with full tuition reimbursement (averaging $5,000 per year) was awarded; unspecified assistantships also available. Support available to part-time students. Financial award application deadline: 2/15; financial award applicants required to submit FAFSA.
Faculty research: Environmental education, land use/suburban planning, landscapes of Catalunya.
Dr. Arlene Rengert, Chair and Graduate Coordinator, 610-436-2343.
Application contact: Dr. Joan Welch, Regional Planning, Concentration Adviser, 610-436-2940, *E-mail:* jwelch@wcupa.edu.

■ WEST CHESTER UNIVERSITY OF PENNSYLVANIA

Graduate Studies, School of Business and Public Affairs, Program in Administration, West Chester, PA 19383

AWARDS Health services (MSA); human research management (MSA); individualized (MSA); leadership for women (MSA); long-term care (MSA); public administration (MSA); regional planning (MSA); sport and athletic training (MSA); training and development (MSA). Part-time and evening/weekend programs available.

Students: 11 full-time (8 women), 83 part-time (45 women); includes 9 minority (5 African Americans, 3 Asian Americans or Pacific Islanders, 1 Hispanic American), 2 international. Average age 31. 44 applicants, 57% accepted. In 2001, 38 degrees awarded.
Degree requirements: For master's, comprehensive exam.
Entrance requirements: For master's, GMAT, GRE General Test, or MAT, interview, minimum GPA of 3.0. *Application deadline:* For fall admission, 4/15 (priority date); for spring admission, 10/15. Applications are processed on a rolling basis. *Application fee:* $25.
Expenses: Tuition, state resident: full-time $4,600; part-time $256 per credit. Tuition, nonresident: full-time $7,554; part-time $420 per credit. Required fees: $44 per credit.
Financial support: In 2001–02, 2 research assistantships with full tuition reimbursements (averaging $5,000 per year) were awarded; career-related internships or fieldwork and unspecified assistantships also available. Support available to part-time students. Financial award application deadline: 2/15; financial award applicants required to submit FAFSA.
Dr. Duane Milne, Director, 610-436-2448.

■ WEST VIRGINIA UNIVERSITY

Eberly College of Arts and Sciences, Department of Geology and Geography, Program in Geography, Morgantown, WV 26506

AWARDS Energy and environmental resources (MA); geographic information systems (PhD); geography-regional development (PhD); GIS/cartographic analysis (MA); regional development and urban planning (MA). Part-time programs available.

Students: 10 full-time (3 women), 3 part-time (1 woman), 3 international. Average age 27. 30 applicants, 33% accepted. In 2001, 14 degrees awarded.
Degree requirements: For master's, thesis, oral and written exams.
Entrance requirements: For master's, GRE General Test, TOEFL, minimum GPA of 2.75. *Application deadline:* For fall admission, 3/15 (priority date). Applications are processed on a rolling basis. *Application fee:* $45.
Expenses: Tuition, state resident: full-time $2,791. Tuition, nonresident: full-time $8,659. Required fees: $1,002. Tuition and fees vary according to program.
Financial support: In 2001–02, 4 research assistantships, 4 teaching assistantships were awarded. Career-related internships or fieldwork, Federal Work-Study, institutionally sponsored loans, and tuition waivers (full and partial) also available. Financial award application deadline: 2/1; financial award applicants required to submit FAFSA.
Faculty research: Resources, regional development, planning, geographic information systems, gender geography.
Dr. Kenneth Martis, Associate Chair, 304-293-5603 Ext. 4350, *Fax:* 304-293-6522, *E-mail:* ken.martis@mail.wvu.edu.
Application contact: Dr. Timothy Warner, Associate Professor, 304-293-5603 Ext. 4328, *Fax:* 304-293-6522, *E-mail:* tim.warner@mail.wvu.edu. *Web site:* http://www.geo.wvu.edu/programs/geography.html

DISABILITY STUDIES

■ BRANDEIS UNIVERSITY

The Heller School for Social Policy and Management, Program in Management and Social Policy, Waltham, MA 02454-9110

AWARDS Child, youth, and family services (MBA, MM); elder and disabled services (MBA, MM); health care administration (MBA, MM); human services (MBA, MM). Part-time and evening/weekend programs available.

Faculty: 44 full-time (17 women), 16 part-time/adjunct (6 women).
Students: 45 full-time (32 women), 31 part-time (19 women). Average age 28. 72 applicants, 75% accepted. In 2001, 45 degrees awarded.
Degree requirements: For master's, team consulting project.
Entrance requirements: For master's, GRE General Test or GMAT (MM), GMAT (MBA). *Application deadline:* For fall admission, 6/1 (priority date); for winter admission, 11/1 (priority date); for spring admission, 2/15. Applications are processed on a rolling basis. *Application fee:* $50. Electronic applications accepted.
Expenses: Tuition: Full-time $27,392. Required fees: $35.
Financial support: Fellowships, institutionally sponsored loans, scholarships/grants, and tuition waivers (partial) available. Financial award application deadline: 2/15; financial award applicants required to submit CSS PROFILE or FAFSA.
Faculty research: Health care, child and family, elder and disabled services, general human services.
Barry Friedman, Director, 781-736-3783, *E-mail:* hfriedman@brandeis.edu.
Application contact: Lisa Hamlin Sherry, Assistant Director for Admissions and Financial Aid, 781-736-3835, *Fax:* 781-736-3881, *E-mail:* sherry@brandeis.edu. *Web site:* http://heller.brandeis.edu

Find an in-depth description at www.petersons.com/gradchannel.

■ JOHNS HOPKINS UNIVERSITY

School of Professional Studies in Business and Education, Division of Education, Department of Special Education, Baltimore, MD 21218-2699

AWARDS Autism (Certificate); discipline and positive behavior management (Certificate); inclusion (Certificate); learning disabilities (CAGS); severe disabilities (Certificate); severely and profoundly handicapped (CAGS); special education (MS, Ed D); transition planning (Certificate). Part-time and evening/weekend programs available.

Faculty: 6 full-time (4 women), 25 part-time/adjunct (21 women).
Students: 20 full-time (17 women), 194 part-time (177 women); includes 30 minority (21 African Americans, 4 Asian Americans or Pacific Islanders, 4 Hispanic Americans, 1 Native American), 1 international. Average age 34. 93 applicants, 89% accepted, 72 enrolled. In 2001, 99 master's, 1 doctorate, 15 other advanced degrees awarded.
Degree requirements: For master's, registration; for doctorate, thesis/dissertation, comprehensive exam, registration.
Entrance requirements: For master's, minimum GPA of 3.0, interview; for doctorate, GRE, MAT, interview, master's degree, minimum GPA of 3.25; for other advanced degree, master's or doctoral degree, interview. *Application deadline:* Applications are processed on a rolling basis. *Application fee:* $55. Electronic applications accepted.
Expenses: Tuition: Full-time $27,390.
Financial support: Scholarships/grants available. Support available to part-time students. Financial award application deadline: 6/1; financial award applicants required to submit FAFSA. *Total annual research expenditures:* $343,618.
Gloria Lane, Chair, 410-516- 275.
Application contact: Kumari Adams, Admissions Coordinator, 410-872-1234, *Fax:* 410-872-1251, *E-mail:* emsspsbe@jhu.edu.

■ NEW YORK MEDICAL COLLEGE

School of Public Health, Program in Developmental Disabilities, Valhalla, NY 10595-1691

AWARDS Assistive technology (CGS); early intervention (CGS).

Entrance requirements: For master's, TOEFL.

■ SUFFOLK UNIVERSITY

Sawyer School of Management, Department of Public Management, Boston, MA 02108-2770

AWARDS Disability studies (MPA); health administration (MHA, MPA); nonprofit management (MPA); public administration (CASPA); public finance and human resources (MPA); state and local government (MPA). Part-time and evening/weekend programs available.

Faculty: 8 full-time (2 women), 29 part-time/adjunct (9 women).
Students: 37 full-time (26 women), 127 part-time (86 women); includes 12 minority (9 African Americans, 1 Asian American or Pacific Islander, 2 Hispanic Americans), 12 international. Average age 34. 76 applicants, 87% accepted, 36 enrolled. In 2001, 56 degrees awarded. *Median time to degree:* Master's–1.5 years full-time, 2 years part-time.
Application deadline: For fall admission, 6/15 (priority date); for spring admission, 11/15 (priority date). Applications are processed on a rolling basis. *Application fee:* $50.
Expenses: Contact institution.
Financial support: In 2001–02, 74 students received support, including 7 fellowships with full and partial tuition reimbursements available (averaging $3,300 per year); career-related internships or fieldwork and Federal Work-Study also available. Support available to part-time students. Financial award application deadline: 3/15; financial award applicants required to submit FAFSA.
Faculty research: Local government, health care, federal policy, mental health, HIV/AIDS. *Total annual research expenditures:* $200,000.
Dr. Rick Beineke, Chair, 617-573-8062, *E-mail:* rbeineck@sufffolk.edu.
Application contact: Judith Reynolds, Director of Graduate Admissions, 617-573-8302, *Fax:* 617-523-0116, *E-mail:* grad.admission@suffolk.edu. *Web site:* http://209.240.148.229/pad_main.htm

■ UNIVERSITY OF ILLINOIS AT CHICAGO

Graduate College, College of Associated Health Professions, Department of Disability, Disability Studies, and Human Development, Chicago, IL 60607-7128

AWARDS Disability and human development (MS); disability studies (PhD). Part-time programs available.

Faculty: 12 full-time (2 women), 6 part-time/adjunct (4 women).
Students: 11 full-time (8 women), 28 part-time (25 women); includes 8 minority (4 African Americans, 3 Asian Americans or Pacific Islanders, 1 Hispanic American), 7 international. Average age 34. 35 applicants, 51% accepted, 14 enrolled. In 2001, 6 degrees awarded.
Degree requirements: For master's, thesis optional; for doctorate, thesis/dissertation.
Entrance requirements: For master's and doctorate, GRE General Test, TOEFL. *Application deadline:* For fall admission, 3/1 (priority date). Applications are processed on a rolling basis. *Application fee:* $40 ($50 for international students). Electronic applications accepted.
Expenses: Tuition, state resident: full-time $3,060. Tuition, nonresident: full-time $6,688.
Financial support: In 2001–02, 17 students received support; fellowships with full tuition reimbursements available, research assistantships with full tuition reimbursements available, teaching assistantships with full tuition reimbursements available, career-related internships or fieldwork, Federal Work-Study, and institutionally sponsored loans available. Financial award application deadline: 3/1; financial award applicants required to submit FAFSA.
Faculty research: Emerging trends in disability, demography and financial structure of disability services, aging and disability, empowerment of people with disabilities, health promotion in disabilities.
Glenn Fujiura, Head, 312-413-1977, *Fax:* 312-413-1630, *E-mail:* gfujiura@uic.edu.
Application contact: Dr. Tamar Heller, Director of Graduate Studies, 312-413-1537, *Fax:* 312-413-1630, *E-mail:* theller@uic.edu. *Web site:* http://www.uic.edu/depts/idhd

INDUSTRIAL AND LABOR RELATIONS

■ BERNARD M. BARUCH COLLEGE OF THE CITY UNIVERSITY OF NEW YORK

Zicklin School of Business, Program in Industrial and Labor Relations, New York, NY 10010-5585

AWARDS MS. Part-time and evening/weekend programs available.

Students: In 2001, 19 degrees awarded.
Entrance requirements: For master's, GMAT or GRE, TOEFL, TWE.
Expenses: Contact institution.
Financial support: Application deadline: 5/1.
Richard Kopelman, Head, 646-312-3629, *E-mail:* richard_kopelman@baruch.cuny.edu.
Application contact: Executive MSILR Program, 646-312-3146, *Fax:* 646-312-3147, *E-mail:* msilr@baruch.cuny.edu.

■ CASE WESTERN RESERVE UNIVERSITY

Weatherhead School of Management, Department of Marketing and Policy Studies, Division of Labor and Human Resource Policy, Cleveland, OH 44106

AWARDS MBA, PhD. Part-time and evening/weekend programs available.

Faculty: 4 full-time (1 woman).
Students: 9 full-time (6 women), 10 part-time (7 women). Average age 28. In 2001, 7 master's, 1 doctorate awarded.
Degree requirements: For doctorate, thesis/dissertation.
Entrance requirements: For master's and doctorate, GMAT. *Application deadline:* For fall admission, 4/15 (priority date). Applications are processed on a rolling basis. *Application fee:* $50.
Financial support: Career-related internships or fieldwork, Federal Work-Study, institutionally sponsored loans, and tuition waivers (full and partial) available. Financial award application deadline: 5/1.
Faculty research: Strategic human resource management, negotiations and conflict management, human resources in high performance organizations, international human resources management, union management relations and collective bargaining.
Paul F. Gerhart, Head, 216-368-2045, *E-mail:* pfg2@po.cwru.edu.
Application contact: Christine L. Gill, Director of Marketing and Admissions, 216-368-3845, *Fax:* 216-368-4776, *E-mail:* clg3@po.cwru.edu.

■ CLEVELAND STATE UNIVERSITY

College of Graduate Studies, James J. Nance College of Business Administration, Program in Labor Relations and Human Resources, Cleveland, OH 44115

AWARDS MLRHR. Part-time programs available.

Faculty: 13 full-time (4 women).
Students: 5 full-time (4 women), 44 part-time (34 women); includes 8 minority (7 African Americans, 1 Hispanic American). Average age 31. 29 applicants, 86% accepted. In 2001, 26 degrees awarded.
Entrance requirements: For master's, GMAT or GRE. *Application deadline:* For fall admission, 7/15; for spring admission, 12/15. Applications are processed on a rolling basis. *Application fee:* $30. Electronic applications accepted.
Expenses: Tuition, state resident: full-time $6,838; part-time $263 per credit hour. Tuition, nonresident: full-time $13,526; part-time $520 per credit hour.
Financial support: Research assistantships, career-related internships or fieldwork, tuition waivers (full), and unspecified assistantships available. Financial award applicants required to submit FAFSA.
Dr. Ronald L. Coccari, Chairperson, 216-687-4754, *Fax:* 216-687-9354, *E-mail:* r.coccari@csuohio.edu. *Web site:* http://www.csuohio.edu/mlr/

■ CORNELL UNIVERSITY

Graduate School, Graduate Fields of Industrial and Labor Relations, Ithaca, NY 14853-0001

AWARDS Collective bargaining, labor law and labor history (MILR, MPS, MS, PhD); economic and social statistics (MILR, MPS, MS, PhD); human resource studies (MILR, MPS, MS, PhD); international and comparative labor (MILR, MPS, MS, PhD); labor economics (MILR, MPS, MS, PhD); organizational behavior (MILR, MPS, MS, PhD).

Faculty: 46 full-time.
Students: 145 full-time (89 women); includes 26 minority (11 African Americans, 10 Asian Americans or Pacific Islanders, 5 Hispanic Americans), 41 international. 202 applicants, 40% accepted. In 2001, 61 master's, 7 doctorates awarded.
Degree requirements: For master's, thesis(MS); for doctorate, thesis/dissertation, teaching experience.
Entrance requirements: For master's and doctorate, GMAT or GRE General Test, GRE writing assessment for non-native speakers of English, TOEFL, 2 academic recommendations. *Application deadline:* For fall admission, 2/15. *Application fee:* $65. Electronic applications accepted.
Expenses: Contact institution.
Financial support: In 2001–02, 81 students received support, including 25 fellowships with full tuition reimbursements available, 28 research assistantships with full tuition reimbursements available, 28 teaching assistantships with full tuition reimbursements available; institutionally sponsored loans, scholarships/grants, tuition waivers (full and partial), and unspecified assistantships also available. Financial award applicants required to submit FAFSA.
Application contact: Graduate Field Assistant, 607-255-1522, *E-mail:* ilrgrad@cornell.edu. *Web site:* http://www.gradschool.cornell.edu/grad/fields_1/ilr.html

Find an in-depth description at www.petersons.com/gradchannel.

■ GEORGIA STATE UNIVERSITY

J. Mack Robinson College of Business, W. T. Beebe Institute of Personnel and Employee Relations, Atlanta, GA 30303-3083

AWARDS MBA, MS, PhD. Part-time and evening/weekend programs available. Terminal master's awarded for partial completion of doctoral program.

Degree requirements: For doctorate, thesis/dissertation.
Entrance requirements: For master's and doctorate, GMAT, TOEFL.

■ INDIANA UNIVERSITY OF PENNSYLVANIA

Graduate School and Research, College of Health and Human Services, Department of Industrial and Labor Relations, Indiana, PA 15705-1087

AWARDS MA. Part-time and evening/weekend programs available.

Faculty: 5 full-time (1 woman).
Students: 28 full-time (12 women), 22 part-time (8 women); includes 4 minority (3 African Americans, 1 Asian American or Pacific Islander), 2 international. Average age 31. 42 applicants, 81% accepted. In 2001, 26 degrees awarded.
Degree requirements: For master's, thesis optional.
Entrance requirements: For master's, TOEFL, letters of recommendation (2). *Application deadline:* For fall admission, 7/1 (priority date); for spring admission, 11/1. Applications are processed on a rolling basis. *Application fee:* $30.
Expenses: Tuition, state resident: full-time $4,600; part-time $256 per credit hour. Tuition, nonresident: full-time $7,554; part-time $420 per credit hour. Required fees: $800. Part-time tuition and fees vary according to course load.
Financial support: In 2001–02, 2 fellowships (averaging $500 per year), 15 research assistantships with full and partial tuition reimbursements (averaging $5,660 per year) were awarded. Career-related internships or fieldwork and Federal Work-Study also available. Support available to part-time students. Financial award application deadline: 3/15; financial award applicants required to submit FAFSA.
Faculty research: Conflict resolution, labor-management cooperation, unemployment compensation, public sector labor relations, employee discipline.
Dr. James F. Byers, Chairperson and Graduate Coordinator, 724-357-4470, *E-mail:* jbyers@iup.edu.

■ INTER AMERICAN UNIVERSITY OF PUERTO RICO, METROPOLITAN CAMPUS

Graduate Programs, Faculty of Economics and Administrative Sciences, Program in Labor Relations, San Juan, PR 00919-1293

AWARDS MA.

Degree requirements: For master's, comprehensive exam.
Entrance requirements: For master's, GRE or PAEG, interview. Electronic applications accepted.

■ INTER AMERICAN UNIVERSITY OF PUERTO RICO, SAN GERMÁN CAMPUS

Graduate Programs, Department of Business Administration, Program in Business Administration, San Germán, PR 00683-5008

AWARDS Accounting (MBA); finance (MBA); human resources (MBA); industrial relations (MBA); marketing (MBA); quality organizational design (MBA). Part-time programs available.

Faculty: 6 full-time (1 woman), 14 part-time/adjunct (5 women).
Students: 68 full-time (43 women), 218 part-time (135 women). In 2001, 100 degrees awarded.
Degree requirements: For master's, comprehensive exam.
Entrance requirements: For master's, minimum GPA of 3.0, GRE General Test, or PAEG. *Application deadline:* For fall admission, 4/30 (priority date); for spring admission, 11/15. Applications are processed on a rolling basis. *Application fee:* $31.
Expenses: Tuition: Part-time $165 per credit. Required fees: $390; $195 per semester. Tuition and fees vary according to degree level and program.
Financial support: Teaching assistantships available.
Application contact: Dr. Waldemar Velez, Director of Graduate Program Center, 787-892-4300 Ext. 7358, *Fax:* 787-892-6350, *E-mail:* wvelez@sg.inter.edu.

■ IOWA STATE UNIVERSITY OF SCIENCE AND TECHNOLOGY

Graduate College, Interdisciplinary Programs, Program in Industrial Relations, Ames, IA 50011

AWARDS MS.

Students: 8 full-time (all women), 15 part-time (11 women); includes 1 minority (African American), 8 international. 17 applicants, 47% accepted, 6 enrolled. In 2001, 3 degrees awarded.
Degree requirements: For master's, thesis or alternative. *Median time to degree:* Master's–1.9 years full-time.
Entrance requirements: For master's, GMAT or GRE, TOEFL or IELTS. *Application deadline:* For fall admission, 3/12; for spring admission, 11/1. *Application fee:* $20 ($50 for international students). Electronic applications accepted.
Expenses: Tuition, state resident: full-time $1,851. Tuition, nonresident: full-time $5,449. Tuition and fees vary according to program.
Financial support: In 2001–02, 6 research assistantships with partial tuition reimbursements (averaging $10,518 per year) were awarded; teaching assistantships, scholarships/grants, health care benefits, and unspecified assistantships also available.
Dr. Peter F. Orazem, Supervisory Committee Chair, 515-294-2701, *E-mail:* pfo@iastate.edu. *Web site:* http://www.econ/iastate.edu/industrialrelations/ircenter.html

■ LOYOLA UNIVERSITY CHICAGO

Graduate School, Institute of Human Resources and Industrial Relations, Chicago, IL 60611-2196

AWARDS MSHR, MSIR, JD/MSIR, MSHR/MSOD, MSHR/MSTD, MSIR/MSOD, MSIR/MSTD. Part-time programs available.

Faculty: 8 full-time, 10 part-time/adjunct.
Students: 31 full-time (23 women), 119 part-time (87 women); includes 34 minority (19 African Americans, 10 Asian Americans or Pacific Islanders, 5 Hispanic Americans), 7 international. Average age 29. 58 applicants, 88% accepted. In 2001, 54 degrees awarded.
Entrance requirements: For master's, GMAT or GRE General Test. *Application deadline:* Applications are processed on a rolling basis. *Application fee:* $40.
Expenses: Contact institution.
Financial support: In 2001–02, 3 research assistantships were awarded; career-related internships or fieldwork and Federal Work-Study also available. Support available to part-time students. Financial award applicants required to submit FAFSA.
Faculty research: Human resource management, labor relations, global human resource management, organizational development, compensation.
Dr. Homer H. Johnson, Director, 312-915-6595, *Fax:* 312-915-6231, *E-mail:* hjohnso@wpo.it.luc.edu.
Application contact: Dr. Fran Daly, Associate Director, 312-915-6595, *Fax:* 312-915-6231, *E-mail:* fdaly@luc.edu.

Find an in-depth description at www.petersons.com/gradchannel.

■ LOYOLA UNIVERSITY CHICAGO

Graduate School, Program in Training and Development, Chicago, IL 60611-2196

AWARDS MSTD, MSHR/MSTD, MSIR/MSTD, MSOD/MSTD.

Students: 7 full-time (all women), 30 part-time (22 women); includes 5 minority (2 African Americans, 1 Asian American or Pacific Islander, 2 Hispanic Americans). In 2001, 9 degrees awarded.
Entrance requirements: For master's, GMAT or GRE General Test. *Application deadline:* Applications are processed on a rolling basis. *Application fee:* $40.
Expenses: Contact institution.
Financial support: Career-related internships or fieldwork, Federal Work-Study, and institutionally sponsored loans available. Support available to part-time students. Financial award applicants required to submit FAFSA.
Faculty research: Global employee development, teams.
Dr. Homer H. Johnson, Director, 312-915-6595, *Fax:* 312-915-6231, *E-mail:* hjohnso@wpo.it.luc.edu.

■ MICHIGAN STATE UNIVERSITY

Graduate School, College of Social Science, School of Labor and Industrial Relations, East Lansing, MI 48824

AWARDS Industrial relations and human resources (PhD); labor relations and human resources (MLRHR); labor relations and human resources-urban studies (MLRHR). Part-time and evening/weekend programs available.

Faculty: 12 full-time (4 women).
Students: 123 (71 women); includes 24 minority (14 African Americans, 7 Asian Americans or Pacific Islanders, 3 Hispanic Americans) 22 international. Average age 28. 125 applicants, 67% accepted, 41 enrolled. In 2001, 74 master's, 6 doctorates awarded. Terminal master's awarded for partial completion of doctoral program.
Degree requirements: For master's, thesis optional.
Entrance requirements: For master's, GMAT or GRE (preferred), minimum GPA of 3.0; for doctorate, GMAT or GRE (preferred). *Application deadline:* Applications are processed on a rolling basis. *Application fee:* $30 ($40 for international students). Electronic applications accepted.
Expenses: Tuition, state resident: part-time $244 per credit hour. Tuition, nonresident: part-time $494 per credit hour. Required fees: $268 per semester. Tuition and fees vary according to course load, degree level and program.
Financial support: In 2001–02, 58 students received support, including 37 fellowships (averaging $800 per year), 16 research assistantships with tuition reimbursements available (averaging $5,800 per year); career-related internships or fieldwork, institutionally sponsored loans, scholarships/grants, and unspecified assistantships also available. Financial award applicants required to submit FAFSA.
Faculty research: Human resource management, international/comparative employment systems, work/life balance, discrimination and diversity, high performance work systems. *Total annual research expenditures:* $234,303.
Prof. Theodore Curry, Director, 517-355-1801, *Fax:* 517-355-7656.
Application contact: Annette Bacon, Graduate Program Administrator, 517-355-3285, *Fax:* 517-355-7656, *E-mail:* graduate@lir.msu.edu. *Web site:* http://www.lir.msu.edu/

Find an in-depth description at www.petersons.com/gradchannel.

■ MIDDLE TENNESSEE STATE UNIVERSITY

College of Graduate Studies, College of Business, Department of Economics and Finance, Murfreesboro, TN 37132

AWARDS Economics (MA, DA); industrial relations (MA).

Faculty: 19 full-time (2 women).
Students: 8 full-time (1 woman), 36 part-time (15 women); includes 24 minority (8 African Americans, 14 Asian Americans or Pacific Islanders, 1 Hispanic American, 1 Native American). Average age 31. 17 applicants, 100% accepted. In 2001, 4 master's, 1 doctorate awarded.
Degree requirements: For master's, thesis optional; for doctorate, thesis/dissertation, comprehensive exam.
Entrance requirements: For master's and doctorate, GRE or MAT. *Application deadline:* For fall admission, 8/1 (priority date). Applications are processed on a rolling basis. *Application fee:* $25. Electronic applications accepted.
Expenses: Tuition, state resident: full-time $1,716; part-time $191 per hour. Tuition, nonresident: full-time $4,952; part-time $461 per hour. Required fees: $14 per hour. $58 per semester.
Financial support: In 2001–02, 12 teaching assistantships were awarded; institutionally sponsored loans also available. Support available to part-time students. Financial award application deadline: 5/1; financial award applicants

required to submit FAFSA. *Total annual research expenditures:* $7,558.
Dr. John Lee, Chair, 615-898-2520, *Fax:* 615-898-5596, *E-mail:* jlee@mtsu.edu.

■ NEW YORK INSTITUTE OF TECHNOLOGY

Graduate Division, School of Management, Program in Human Resources Management and Labor Relations, Old Westbury, AA 11568-8000

AWARDS Human resources administration (Advanced Certificate); human resources management and labor relations (MS); labor relations (Advanced Certificate). Part-time and evening/weekend programs available.

Students: 21 full-time (16 women), 78 part-time (55 women); includes 17 minority (11 African Americans, 2 Asian Americans or Pacific Islanders, 4 Hispanic Americans), 13 international. Average age 33. 50 applicants, 76% accepted, 19 enrolled. In 2001, 36 degrees awarded.
Degree requirements: For master's, thesis optional.
Entrance requirements: For master's,. *Application deadline:* For fall admission, 7/1 (priority date); for spring admission, 12/1 (priority date). Applications are processed on a rolling basis. *Application fee:* $50. Electronic applications accepted.
Expenses: Tuition: Part-time $545 per credit. Tuition and fees vary according to course load, degree level, program and student level.
Financial support: In 2001–02, 2 research assistantships were awarded; fellowships, career-related internships or fieldwork, institutionally sponsored loans, and tuition waivers (full and partial) also available. Support available to part-time students. Financial award applicants required to submit FAFSA.
Faculty research: Ethics in industrial relations, employee relations, public sector labor relations, benefits.
Dr. Richard Dibble, Chair, 516-686-7722.
Application contact: Jacquelyn Nealon, Dean of Admissions and Financial Aid, 516-686-7925, *Fax:* 516-686-7613, *E-mail:* jnealon@nyit.edu.

■ THE OHIO STATE UNIVERSITY

Graduate School, Max M. Fisher College of Business, Program in Labor and Human Resources, Columbus, OH 43210

AWARDS MLHR, PhD.

Degree requirements: For master's, thesis optional; for doctorate, thesis/dissertation.
Entrance requirements: For master's and doctorate, GRE General Test.

■ THE PENNSYLVANIA STATE UNIVERSITY UNIVERSITY PARK CAMPUS

Graduate School, College of Liberal Arts, Department of Labor Studies and Industrial Relations, State College, University Park, PA 16802-1503

AWARDS Industrial relations and human resources (MS).

Students: 12 full-time (8 women). In 2001, 4 degrees awarded.
Entrance requirements: For master's, GRE General Test. *Application fee:* $45.
Expenses: Tuition, state resident: full-time $7,882; part-time $333 per credit. Tuition, nonresident: full-time $16,142; part-time $673 per credit. Required fees: $124 per semester.
Dr. Mark Wardell, Head, 814-865-5425.

■ RUTGERS, THE STATE UNIVERSITY OF NEW JERSEY, NEW BRUNSWICK

Graduate School, Program in Industrial Relations and Human Resources, New Brunswick, NJ 08901-1281

AWARDS MS, PhD.

Faculty: 29 full-time (8 women).
Students: 8 full-time (2 women), 3 part-time (2 women); includes 1 minority (Asian American or Pacific Islander), 8 international. Average age 29. 30 applicants, 10% accepted. In 2001, 1 master's, 4 doctorates awarded.
Degree requirements: For master's and doctorate, thesis/dissertation, comprehensive exam. *Median time to degree:* Master's–3 years full-time; doctorate–6 years full-time.
Entrance requirements: For master's and doctorate, GMAT, GRE. *Application deadline:* For fall admission, 2/1 (priority date). *Application fee:* $50. Electronic applications accepted.
Financial support: In 2001–02, 11 students received support, including 3 research assistantships with full tuition reimbursements available (averaging $15,000 per year), 6 teaching assistantships with full tuition reimbursements available (averaging $15,000 per year); Federal Work-Study, institutionally sponsored loans, scholarships/grants, health care benefits, tuition waivers (full and partial), and unspecified assistantships also available. Financial award application deadline: 3/1.
Faculty research: Strategic human resource management, international human resource management, labor economics, collective bargaining, teams and diversity.
Dr. Susan E. Jackson, Director, 732-445-5447, *E-mail:* sjacksox@rci.rutgers.edu. *Web site:* http://www-rci.rutgers.edu/~smlr

Find an in-depth description at www.petersons.com/gradchannel.

■ RUTGERS, THE STATE UNIVERSITY OF NEW JERSEY, NEW BRUNSWICK

School of Management and Labor Relations, Program in Labor and Employment Relations, New Brunswick, NJ 08901-1281

AWARDS MLER. Part-time and evening/weekend programs available.

Degree requirements: For master's, thesis optional.
Entrance requirements: For master's, GRE General Test. Electronic applications accepted.
Faculty research: Labor history, women and work, labor education, comparative labor movements. *Web site:* http://www.smlr.rutgers.edu/

■ STATE UNIVERSITY OF NEW YORK EMPIRE STATE COLLEGE

Graduate Studies, Program in Labor and Policy Studies, Saratoga Springs, NY 12866-4391

AWARDS MA. Part-time and evening/weekend programs available. Postbaccalaureate distance learning degree programs offered (minimal on-campus study).

Faculty: 1 full-time (0 women), 3 part-time/adjunct (0 women).
Students: 3 full-time (2 women), 35 part-time (19 women); includes 5 minority (4 African Americans, 1 Hispanic American), 1 international. Average age 43. 28 applicants, 93% accepted. In 2001, 12 degrees awarded.
Degree requirements: For master's, thesis, exam.
Application deadline: For fall admission, 7/1 (priority date); for spring admission, 12/1 (priority date). Applications are processed on a rolling basis. *Application fee:* $50.
Expenses: Tuition, state resident: part-time $218 per credit hour. Tuition, nonresident: part-time $336 per credit hour. Tuition and fees vary according to program.
Financial support: In 2001–02, 1 fellowship with partial tuition reimbursement (averaging $1,700 per year) was awarded; career-related internships or fieldwork and Federal Work-Study also available. Support available to part-time students. Financial award application deadline: 7/1; financial award applicants required to submit FAFSA.
Faculty research: Work and technology, collective bargaining, labor law, human resources management, trade union governance.
Dr. Roger Keeran, Chair, 212-647-7800, *Fax:* 212-647-7829, *E-mail:* roger.keeran@esc.edu.
Application contact: Cammie Baker Clancy, Assistant Director, 518-587-2100 Ext. 393, *Fax:* 518-587-9760, *E-mail:*

State University of New York Empire State College (continued)
cammie.baker-clancy@esc.edu. *Web site:* http://www.esc.edu/grad/

■ STONY BROOK UNIVERSITY, STATE UNIVERSITY OF NEW YORK

School of Professional Development and Continuing Studies, Stony Brook, NY 11794

AWARDS Art and philosophy (Certificate); biology 7-12 (MAT); chemistry-grade 7-12 (MAT); coaching (Certificate); computer integrated engineering (Certificate); cultural studies (Certificate); earth science-grade 7-12 (MAT); educational computing (Certificate); English-grade 7-12 (MAT); environmental/occupational health and safety (Certificate); French-grade 7-12 (MAT); German-grade 7-12 (MAT); human resource management (Certificate); industrial management (Certificate); information systems management (Certificate); Italian-grade 7-12 (MAT); liberal studies (MA); liberal studies online (MA); Long Island regional studies (Certificate); oceanic science (Certificate); operation research (Certificate); physics-grade 7-12 (MAT); Russian-grade 7-12 (MAT); school administration and supervision (Certificate); school district administration (Certificate); social science and the professions (MPS), including labor management, public affairs, waste management; social studies 7-12 (MAT); waste management (Certificate); women's studies (Certificate). Part-time and evening/weekend programs available. Postbaccalaureate distance learning degree programs offered.

Faculty: 1 full-time, 101 part-time/adjunct.
Students: 240 full-time (133 women), 1,307 part-time (868 women); includes 101 minority (43 African Americans, 13 Asian Americans or Pacific Islanders, 43 Hispanic Americans, 2 Native Americans), 9 international. Average age 28. In 2001, 478 master's, 157 other advanced degrees awarded.
Degree requirements: For master's, one foreign language, thesis or alternative.
Application deadline: Applications are processed on a rolling basis. *Application fee:* $50.
Expenses: Tuition, state resident: full-time $5,100; part-time $213 per credit. Tuition, nonresident: full-time $8,416; part-time $351 per credit. Required fees: $496.
Financial support: In 2001–02, 1 fellowship, 7 teaching assistantships were awarded. Research assistantships, career-related internships or fieldwork also available. Support available to part-time students.
Dr. Paul J. Edelson, Dean, 631-632-7052, *Fax:* 631-632-9046, *E-mail:* paul.edelson@sunysb.edu.
Application contact: Sandra Romansky, Director of Admissions and Advisement, 631-632-7050, *Fax:* 631-632-9046, *E-mail:* sandra.romansky@sunysb.edu. *Web site:* http://www.sunysb.edu/spd/

■ THE UNIVERSITY OF AKRON

Graduate School, Buchtel College of Arts and Sciences, Department of Economics, Akron, OH 44325-0001

AWARDS Economics (MA); labor and industrial relations (MA). Part-time programs available.

Faculty: 10 full-time (0 women), 3 part-time/adjunct (2 women).
Students: 14 full-time (7 women), 2 part-time; includes 2 minority (1 African American, 1 Hispanic American), 8 international. Average age 27. 21 applicants, 81% accepted, 2 enrolled. In 2001, 7 degrees awarded.
Degree requirements: For master's, thesis optional.
Entrance requirements: For master's, minimum GPA of 2.75. *Application deadline:* For fall admission, 3/1. Applications are processed on a rolling basis. *Application fee:* $40 ($50 for international students).
Expenses: Tuition, state resident: full-time $6,562; part-time $219 per credit. Tuition, nonresident: full-time $9,027; part-time $383 per credit. Required fees: $272; $11 per credit. Tuition and fees vary according to course load.
Financial support: In 2001–02, 11 teaching assistantships with full tuition reimbursements were awarded; research assistantships with full tuition reimbursements, institutionally sponsored loans and tuition waivers (full) also available. Financial award application deadline: 4/1.
Faculty research: Urban capital stock estimates, technology transfer, determinants of research and development spending, forecasting models.
Dr. Michael Nelson, Chair, 330-972-7937, *E-mail:* nelson2@uakron.edu.
Application contact: Dr. Gary Garofalo, Director of Graduate Studies, 330-972-7974, *E-mail:* ggarofalo@uakron.edu. *Web site:* http://www.uakron.edu/econ/

■ UNIVERSITY OF CALIFORNIA, BERKELEY

Graduate Division, Haas School of Business, Doctoral Program in Business, Berkeley, CA 94720-1500

AWARDS Accounting (PhD); business and public policy (PhD); finance (PhD); marketing (PhD); organizational behavior and industrial relations (PhD); real estate (PhD).

Students: 81 full-time (23 women); includes 6 minority (all Asian Americans or Pacific Islanders), 43 international. Average age 26. 467 applicants, 8% accepted, 16 enrolled. In 2001, 12 degrees awarded.
Degree requirements: For doctorate, thesis/dissertation, oral exam, written preliminary exams, comprehensive exam. *Median time to degree:* Doctorate–4.5 years full-time.
Entrance requirements: For doctorate, GMAT or GRE, TOEFL, minimum GPA of 3.0. *Application deadline:* For fall admission, 2/1. *Application fee:* $40. Electronic applications accepted.
Expenses: Tuition, nonresident: full-time $10,704. Required fees: $4,349.
Financial support: In 2001–02, 72 students received support, including fellowships with full and partial tuition reimbursements available (averaging $16,000 per year), research assistantships with full and partial tuition reimbursements available (averaging $15,000 per year), teaching assistantships with full and partial tuition reimbursements available (averaging $15,000 per year); career-related internships or fieldwork, Federal Work-Study, scholarships/grants, health care benefits, tuition waivers (full), and unspecified assistantships also available. Financial award application deadline: 2/1; financial award applicants required to submit FAFSA.
Dr. David C. Mowery, Director, 510-642-1409, *Fax:* 510-643-1420, *E-mail:* phdadms@haas.berkeley.edu.
Application contact: Dr. Jan Price Greenough, Associate Director, 510-642-1409, *Fax:* 510-643-1420, *E-mail:* phdadms@haas.berkeley.edu.

■ UNIVERSITY OF CINCINNATI

Division of Research and Advanced Studies, McMicken College of Arts and Sciences, Department of Economics, Program in Labor and Employment Relations, Cincinnati, OH 45221

AWARDS MALER. Part-time and evening/weekend programs available.

Faculty: 3 full-time (0 women).
Students: 12 full-time (7 women), 23 part-time (15 women); includes 5 minority (2 African Americans, 3 Hispanic Americans), 1 international. 47 applicants, 68% accepted, 28 enrolled. In 2001, 12 degrees awarded.
Degree requirements: For master's, thesis or alternative.
Application deadline: For fall admission, 2/1 (priority date). Applications are processed on a rolling basis. *Application fee:* $30. Electronic applications accepted.
Expenses: Tuition, state resident: part-time $2,698 per quarter. Tuition, nonresident: part-time $4,977 per quarter.
Financial support: Research assistantships with full tuition reimbursements, teaching assistantships with full tuition reimbursements, career-related internships or fieldwork, tuition waivers (partial), and unspecified assistantships available. Financial award application deadline: 3/1.
Application contact: Howard Leftwich, Coordinator, 513-556-2600, *Fax:* 513-556-2669, *E-mail:* howard.leftwich@uc.edu. *Web site:* http://ucaswww.mcm.uc.edu/

■ UNIVERSITY OF ILLINOIS AT URBANA–CHAMPAIGN

Graduate College, Institute of Labor and Industrial Relations, Program in Labor and Industrial Relations, Champaign, IL 61820

AWARDS MHRIR, PhD. Part-time programs available.

Students: 1 (woman) full-time. Terminal master's awarded for partial completion of doctoral program.
Degree requirements: For doctorate, thesis/dissertation.
Entrance requirements: For master's, GRE General Test, minimum GPA of 3.0; for doctorate, GRE General Test, research experience. *Application fee:* $40 ($50 for international students). Electronic applications accepted.
Expenses: Tuition, state resident: part-time $3,227 per degree program. Tuition, nonresident: part-time $7,169 per degree program. Tuition and fees vary according to program.
Financial support: Fellowships, research assistantships, teaching assistantships, career-related internships or fieldwork, Federal Work-Study, scholarships/grants, and tuition waivers (full) available. Support available to part-time students. Financial award application deadline: 2/1.
Application contact: Elizabeth Barker, Staff Associate, 217-333-2381, *Fax:* 217-244-9290, *E-mail:* e-barker@uiuc.edu. *Web site:* http://www.ilir.uiuc.edu/

■ UNIVERSITY OF LOUISVILLE

Graduate School, College of Business and Public Administration, Department of Urban and Public Affairs, Program in Public Administration, Louisville, KY 40292-0001

AWARDS Labor and public management (MPA); public policy and administration (MPA); urban and regional development (MPA).

Students: 19 full-time (15 women), 29 part-time (18 women); includes 5 minority (3 African Americans, 2 Hispanic Americans), 5 international. Average age 30. In 2001, 15 degrees awarded.
Degree requirements: For master's, practicum or thesis.
Entrance requirements: For master's, GRE General Test, minimum GPA of 3.25, resumé. *Application deadline:* For fall admission, 7/1 (priority date); for spring admission, 12/1 (priority date). Applications are processed on a rolling basis. *Application fee:* $25.
Expenses: Tuition, state resident: full-time $4,134. Tuition, nonresident: full-time $11,486.
Financial support: In 2001–02, 3 research assistantships with full tuition reimbursements (averaging $8,000 per year) were awarded
Dr. Steve Koven, Director, 502-852-6626, *Fax:* 502-852-4558, *E-mail:* sgkove01@louisville.edu. *Web site:* http://www.cbpa.louisville.edu/

Find an in-depth description at www.petersons.com/gradchannel.

■ UNIVERSITY OF MASSACHUSETTS AMHERST

Graduate School, College of Social and Behavioral Sciences, Department of Labor Studies, Amherst, MA 01003

AWARDS MS. Part-time programs available.

Faculty: 4 full-time (1 woman).
Students: 26 full-time (11 women), 50 part-time (14 women); includes 14 minority (2 African Americans, 5 Asian Americans or Pacific Islanders, 6 Hispanic Americans, 1 Native American), 3 international. Average age 28. 31 applicants, 77% accepted. In 2001, 24 degrees awarded.
Entrance requirements: For master's, GRE General Test. *Application deadline:* For fall admission, 2/1 (priority date); for spring admission, 10/1. Applications are processed on a rolling basis. *Application fee:* $40 ($50 for international students).
Expenses: Tuition, state resident: full-time $1,980; part-time $110 per credit. Tuition, nonresident: full-time $7,456; part-time $414 per credit. Required fees: $4,112. One-time fee: $115 full-time.
Financial support: In 2001–02, 1 fellowship with full tuition reimbursement (averaging $10,500 per year), 14 research assistantships with full tuition reimbursements (averaging $5,257 per year), 18 teaching assistantships with full tuition reimbursements (averaging $4,641 per year) were awarded. Career-related internships or fieldwork, Federal Work-Study, scholarships/grants, traineeships, and unspecified assistantships also available. Support available to part-time students. Financial award application deadline: 2/1.
Dr. Thomas Juravich, Director, 413-545-1215, *Fax:* 413-545-0110, *E-mail:* juravich@lrrc.umass.edu.

■ UNIVERSITY OF MINNESOTA, TWIN CITIES CAMPUS

Carlson School of Management, Program in Human Resources and Industrial Relations, Minneapolis, MN 55455-0213

AWARDS MA, PhD. Part-time and evening/weekend programs available.

Faculty: 16 full-time (2 women), 6 part-time/adjunct (3 women).
Students: 148 full-time (107 women), 88 part-time (73 women); includes 20 minority (10 African Americans, 6 Asian Americans or Pacific Islanders, 3 Hispanic Americans, 1 Native American), 32 international. Average age 25. 203 applicants, 70% accepted. In 2001, 80 master's, 3 doctorates awarded. Terminal master's awarded for partial completion of doctoral program.
Degree requirements: For master's, thesis optional; for doctorate, thesis/dissertation.
Entrance requirements: For master's, GMAT or GRE General Test; for doctorate, GRE General Test. *Application deadline:* For fall admission, 6/15; for spring admission, 10/15. Applications are processed on a rolling basis. *Application fee:* $50 ($55 for international students).
Expenses: Contact institution.
Financial support: In 2001–02, 50 students received support, including 26 fellowships with partial tuition reimbursements available (averaging $6,000 per year), 12 research assistantships with full and partial tuition reimbursements available (averaging $7,500 per year), 2 teaching assistantships with full tuition reimbursements available (averaging $10,000 per year); career-related internships or fieldwork, Federal Work-Study, institutionally sponsored loans, and tuition waivers (full and partial) also available. Support available to part-time students. Financial award application deadline: 2/1.
Faculty research: Staffing, training, and development; compensation and benefits; organization theory; collective bargaining. *Total annual research expenditures:* $200,000.
Avner Ben-Ner, Chair, 612-624-2500, *Fax:* 612-624-8360.
Application contact: Lyn Birkholz, Principal Secretary, 612-624-5704, *Fax:* 612-624-8360, *E-mail:* mbirkholz@csom.umn.edu. *Web site:* http://www.irc.csom.umn.edu/

Find an in-depth description at www.petersons.com/gradchannel.

■ UNIVERSITY OF NEW HAVEN

Graduate School, School of Business, Program in Industrial Relations, West Haven, CT 06516-1916

AWARDS MS.

Students: 1 (woman) full-time, 16 part-time (10 women); includes 2 minority (both African Americans), 1 international. In 2001, 9 degrees awarded.
Degree requirements: For master's, thesis or alternative.
Application deadline: Applications are processed on a rolling basis. *Application fee:* $50.
Expenses: Tuition: Full-time $12,015; part-time $445 per credit hour. Required fees: $30. One-time fee: $100 full-time.
Financial support: Federal Work-Study available. Support available to part-time students. Financial award application deadline: 5/1; financial award applicants required to submit FAFSA.
Charles Coleman, Coordinator, 203-932-7375.

■ UNIVERSITY OF NEW HAVEN

Graduate School, School of Business, Program in Public Administration, West Haven, CT 06516-1916

AWARDS Health care management (MPA); personnel and labor relations (MPA). Part-time and evening/weekend programs available.

Students: 26 full-time (7 women), 23 part-time (12 women); includes 6 minority (2 African Americans, 4 Hispanic Americans), 22 international. In 2001, 16 degrees awarded.
Degree requirements: For master's, thesis or alternative.
Application deadline: Applications are processed on a rolling basis. *Application fee:* $50.
Expenses: Tuition: Full-time $12,015; part-time $445 per credit hour. Required fees: $30. One-time fee: $100 full-time.
Financial support: Federal Work-Study available. Support available to part-time students. Financial award application deadline: 5/1; financial award applicants required to submit FAFSA.
Charles Coleman, Chairman, 203-932-7375.

■ UNIVERSITY OF NORTH TEXAS

Robert B. Toulouse School of Graduate Studies, College of Arts and Sciences, Department of Economics, Denton, TX 76203

AWARDS Economic research (MS); economics (MA); labor and industrial relations (MS). Part-time programs available.

Faculty: 14 full-time (3 women), 3 part-time/adjunct (1 woman).
Students: 36 full-time (13 women), 15 part-time (5 women); includes 7 minority (1 African American, 1 Asian American or Pacific Islander, 5 Hispanic Americans), 25 international. Average age 24. In 2001, 21 degrees awarded.
Degree requirements: For master's, thesis (for some programs), comprehensive exam.
Entrance requirements: For master's, GMAT, GRE General Test, minimum B average in last 60 hours. *Application deadline:* For fall admission, 7/17. *Application fee:* $25 ($50 for international students).
Expenses: Tuition, state resident: part-time $186 per hour. Tuition, nonresident: part-time $319 per hour. Required fees: $88; $21 per hour.
Financial support: Fellowships, research assistantships, teaching assistantships, career-related internships or fieldwork, Federal Work-Study, and institutionally sponsored loans available. Support available to part-time students. Financial award application deadline: 4/1.
Faculty research: Health economics, resource economics, international trade and development, monetary theory and policy, public finance.
Dr. Steven L. Cobb, Chair, 940-565-2573, *Fax:* 940-565-4426, *E-mail:* cobb@econ.unt.edu.
Application contact: Dr. Michael McPherson, Graduate Adviser, 940-565-2573, *Fax:* 940-565-4426, *E-mail:* michael@po6.cas.unt.edu.

■ UNIVERSITY OF NORTH TEXAS

Robert B. Toulouse School of Graduate Studies, College of Business Administration, Department of Management, Denton, TX 76203

AWARDS Administrative management (MBA); management (MBA); organization theory and policy (PhD); personnel and industrial relations (MBA, PhD); production/operations management (MBA, PhD).

Faculty: 20 full-time (8 women), 9 part-time/adjunct (5 women).
Students: 79. In 2001, 31 degrees awarded.
Degree requirements: For doctorate, thesis/dissertation.
Entrance requirements: For master's, GMAT, TOEFL, relevant work experience; for doctorate, GMAT or GRE General Test, TOEFL, relevant work experience. *Application deadline:* For fall admission, 7/17. *Application fee:* $25 ($50 for international students).
Expenses: Tuition, state resident: part-time $186 per hour. Tuition, nonresident: part-time $319 per hour. Required fees: $88; $21 per hour.
Financial support: Fellowships, teaching assistantships, Federal Work-Study available. Financial award application deadline: 4/1.
Dr. J. Lynn Johnson, Chair, 940-565-3140, *Fax:* 940-565-4394, *E-mail:* johnsonl@cobat.unt.edu.

■ UNIVERSITY OF RHODE ISLAND

Graduate School, Labor Research Center, Kingston, RI 02881

AWARDS Labor and industrial relations (MS). Part-time and evening/weekend programs available.

Students: Average age 32. In 2001, 4 degrees awarded.
Degree requirements: For master's, core exams.
Entrance requirements: For master's, GMAT, GRE, or MAT. *Application deadline:* For fall admission, 4/15 (priority date); for spring admission, 11/15. Applications are processed on a rolling basis. *Application fee:* $35.
Expenses: Tuition, state resident: full-time $3,756; part-time $209 per credit. Tuition, nonresident: full-time $10,774; part-time $599 per credit. Required fees: $1,586; $76 per credit. One-time fee: $60 full-time.
Financial support: Fellowships, research assistantships, teaching assistantships, career-related internships or fieldwork, Federal Work-Study, institutionally sponsored loans, and tuition waivers (full and partial) available. Support available to part-time students.
Dr. Terry Thomason, Director, 401-874-2239.

■ UNIVERSITY OF WISCONSIN–MADISON

Graduate School, College of Letters and Science, Industrial Relations Research Institute, Madison, WI 53706-1380

AWARDS MA, MS, PhD. Part-time programs available.

Degree requirements: For master's, thesis or alternative; for doctorate, variable foreign language requirement, thesis/dissertation.
Entrance requirements: For master's, GRE General Test, GRE writing assessment, minimum GPA of 3.0, 1 course each in economics and statistics; for doctorate, GRE General Test, GRE writing assessment, master's degree in related field. Electronic applications accepted.
Expenses: Tuition, state resident: full-time $7,361; part-time $399 per credit. Tuition, nonresident: full-time $20,499; part-time $1,282 per credit. Required fees: $34 per credit. Full-time tuition and fees vary according to course load, program, reciprocity agreements and student level.
Faculty research: Comparative industrial relations, unions and economic competitiveness, dispute resolution in the public sector, merit pay practices. *Web site:* http://polyglot.lss.wisc.edu/irri/irri.html

■ UNIVERSITY OF WISCONSIN–MILWAUKEE

Graduate School, College of Letters and Sciences, Program in Human Resources and Labor Relations, Milwaukee, WI 53201-0413

AWARDS MHRLR. Part-time programs available.

Faculty: 21 full-time (7 women).
Students: 8 full-time (all women), 37 part-time (25 women); includes 7 minority (4 African Americans, 3 Hispanic Americans), 3 international. 34 applicants, 71% accepted. In 2001, 16 degrees awarded.
Entrance requirements: For master's, GMAT or GRE General Test. *Application deadline:* For fall admission, 1/1 (priority date); for spring admission, 9/1. Applications are processed on a rolling basis. *Application fee:* $45 ($75 for international students).
Expenses: Tuition, state resident: full-time $6,180; part-time $535 per credit. Tuition, nonresident: full-time $19,482; part-time $1,366 per credit. Tuition and fees vary according to course load, program and reciprocity agreements.
Financial support: Fellowships, research assistantships, teaching assistantships,

career-related internships or fieldwork available. Support available to part-time students. Financial award application deadline: 4/15.
Susan M. Donohue, Representative, 414-299-4009, *Fax:* 414-229-5915, *E-mail:* suedono@uwm.edu. *Web site:* http://www.uwm.edu/dept/MHRLR/

■ VIRGINIA COMMONWEALTH UNIVERSITY

School of Graduate Studies, School of Business, Program in Human Resources Management and Industrial Relations, Richmond, VA 23284-9005

AWARDS MS.

Entrance requirements: For master's, GMAT. *Application deadline:* Applications are processed on a rolling basis. *Application fee:* $30.
Expenses: Tuition, state resident: full-time $4,276; part-time $238 per credit. Tuition, nonresident: full-time $12,672; part-time $704 per credit. Required fees: $1,167; $43 per credit.
Financial support: Fellowships, research assistantships, teaching assistantships, Federal Work-Study, institutionally sponsored loans, and tuition waivers (full and partial) available. Financial award application deadline: 3/15.
Dr. George R. Gray, Chair, 804-828-1732, *Fax:* 804-828-1600.
Application contact: Tracy Green, Graduate Program Director, 804-828-1741, *Fax:* 804-828-7174, *E-mail:* tsgreen@vcu.edu. *Web site:* http://www.vcu.edu/busweb/gsib/

■ WAYNE STATE UNIVERSITY

Graduate School, College of Urban, Labor and Metropolitan Affairs, Interdisciplinary Program in Industrial Relations, Detroit, MI 48202

AWARDS MAIR. Part-time and evening/weekend programs available.

Students: 33. 16 applicants, 38% accepted, 4 enrolled. In 2001, 20 degrees awarded.
Degree requirements: For master's, thesis optional.
Entrance requirements: For master's, GMAT, GRE. *Application deadline:* For fall admission, 7/1. *Application fee:* $20 ($30 for international students). Electronic applications accepted.
Expenses: Tuition, state resident: full-time $3,764. Tuition and fees vary according to degree level and program.
Financial support: In 2001–02, 2 students received support. Career-related internships or fieldwork, institutionally sponsored loans, and scholarships/grants available. Support available to part-time students.
Faculty research: Two-tier wage system, affirmative action practices in higher education.
Michael Belzer, Director, 313-577-4380, *Fax:* 313-577-9969.

■ WEST VIRGINIA UNIVERSITY

College of Business and Economics, Department of Management, Industrial Relations and Marketing, Program in Industrial Relations, Morgantown, WV 26506

AWARDS MS. Part-time programs available.

Students: 41 full-time (25 women), 7 part-time (4 women); includes 3 minority (2 African Americans, 1 Asian American or Pacific Islander), 9 international. Average age 26. 64 applicants, 59% accepted. In 2001, 46 degrees awarded.
Entrance requirements: For master's, GMAT, TOEFL, minimum GPA of 3.0. *Application deadline:* For fall admission, 6/30 (priority date); for spring admission, 11/15. Applications are processed on a rolling basis. *Application fee:* $45.
Expenses: Tuition, state resident: full-time $2,791. Tuition, nonresident: full-time $8,659. Required fees: $1,002. Tuition and fees vary according to program.
Financial support: In 2001–02, 1 research assistantship, 4 teaching assistantships were awarded. Career-related internships or fieldwork, Federal Work-Study, institutionally sponsored loans, tuition waivers (full and partial), and graduate administrative assistantships also available. Financial award application deadline: 2/1; financial award applicants required to submit FAFSA.
Faculty research: Compensation and benefits, quality of work life, participative management, grievance handling, arbitration.
Dr. Dieter Schaupp, Coordinator, 304-293-7941, *Fax:* 304-293-8905, *E-mail:* dietrich.schaupp@mail.wvu.edu.
Application contact: Dr. Paul J. Speaker, Director, 304-293-7810, *Fax:* 304-293-5652, *E-mail:* paul.speaker@mail.wvu.edu. *Web site:* http://www.wvu.edu/~colbe/

PHILANTHROPIC STUDIES

■ INDIANA UNIVERSITY–PURDUE UNIVERSITY INDIANAPOLIS

Center on Philanthropy, Indianapolis, IN 46202

AWARDS Nonprofit management (MPA); philanthropic studies (MA). Part-time and evening/weekend programs available. Postbaccalaureate distance learning degree programs offered (minimal on-campus study).

Students: 18 full-time (16 women), 17 part-time (15 women); includes 7 minority (2 African Americans, 1 Asian American or Pacific Islander, 4 Hispanic Americans), 2 international. Average age 32. In 2001, 13 degrees awarded.
Degree requirements: For master's, thesis optional.
Entrance requirements: For master's, GRE General Test or equivalent, minimum undergraduate GPA of 3.0. *Application fee:* $45 ($55 for international students).
Expenses: Tuition, state resident: full-time $4,480; part-time $187 per credit. Tuition, nonresident: full-time $12,926; part-time $539 per credit. Required fees: $177.
Financial support: In 2001–02, 17 students received support, including 2 fellowships with full and partial tuition reimbursements available (averaging $13,000 per year), 16 research assistantships with full and partial tuition reimbursements available (averaging $7,500 per year); career-related internships or fieldwork, Federal Work-Study, institutionally sponsored loans, and scholarships/grants also available. Financial award applicants required to submit FAFSA.
Faculty research: Management of nonprofit organizations, transmitting the philanthropic tradition.
Dr. Eugene Tempel, Executive Director, 317-274-4200.
Application contact: Melissa Grider, Assistant Director for Student Services, 317-274-4200, *Fax:* 317-684-8900. *Web site:* http://www.philanthropy.iupui.edu/

■ SAINT MARY'S UNIVERSITY OF MINNESOTA

Graduate School, Program in Philanthropy and Development, Winona, MN 55987-1399

AWARDS MA. Part-time programs available.

Degree requirements: For master's, project or thesis.
Entrance requirements: For master's, minimum GPA of 2.75.
Expenses: Tuition: Full-time $4,230; part-time $235 per credit. One-time fee: $220. Tuition and fees vary according to degree level and program.

■ SUFFOLK UNIVERSITY

Sawyer School of Management, Visionaries Institute of Suffolk University, Boston, MA 02108-2770

AWARDS Philanthropy and media (M Ph M).

Students: 20 full-time (14 women), 8 part-time (7 women); includes 3 minority (1 African American, 1 Asian American or Pacific Islander, 1 Hispanic American). Average age 36. 42 applicants, 98% accepted, 31 enrolled. In 2001, 3 degrees awarded.
Degree requirements: For master's, final project.
Application deadline: For fall admission, 6/15; for spring admission, 11/15 (priority date). Applications are processed on a rolling basis. *Application fee:* $50.

Suffolk University (continued)
Financial support: In 2001–02, 17 students received support, including 5 fellowships (averaging $4,120 per year). Financial award application deadline: 3/15; financial award applicants required to submit FAFSA.
Dr. Michael Lavin, Director, 413-229-0350, *Fax:* 413-229-9970, *E-mail:* institute@visionaries.org.
Application contact: Judith Reynolds, Director of Graduate Admissions, 617-573-8302, *Fax:* 617-523-0116, *E-mail:* grad.admission@suffolk.edu. *Web site:* http://www.visionaries.org/institute/

PUBLIC POLICY AND ADMINISTRATION

■ ALBANY STATE UNIVERSITY

College of Arts and Sciences, Department of History, Political Science and Public Administration, Albany, GA 31705-2717

AWARDS Community and economic development (MPA); criminal justice (MPA); fiscal management (MPA); general management (MPA); health administration and policy (MPA); human resources management (MPA); public policy (MPA); water resource management and policy (MPA). Part-time programs available.

Degree requirements: For master's, thesis, comprehensive exam.
Entrance requirements: For master's, GRE General Test, minimum GPA of 2.5. Electronic applications accepted.
Faculty research: Transportation, urban affairs, political economy.

■ ALFRED UNIVERSITY

Graduate School, Program in Community Services Administration, Alfred, NY 14802-1205

AWARDS MPS. Part-time programs available.

Students: 6 full-time (1 woman), 11 part-time (9 women). Average age 28. 20 applicants, 70% accepted. In 2001, 11 degrees awarded.
Degree requirements: For master's, comprehensive exam.
Entrance requirements: For master's, TOEFL. *Application deadline:* Applications are processed on a rolling basis. *Application fee:* $50. Electronic applications accepted.
Expenses: Tuition: Full-time $23,554. Required fees: $698. One-time fee: $116 part-time. Full-time tuition and fees vary according to program.
Financial support: Research assistantships, tuition waivers (partial) and unspecified assistantships available. Financial award applicants required to submit FAFSA.
Faculty research: Local development, public policy, health care, aging, criminal justice.
Dr. Robert Heineman, Director, 607-871-2866.
Application contact: Cathleen R. Johnson, Coordinator of Graduate Admissions, 607-871-2141, *Fax:* 607-871-2198, *E-mail:* johnsonc@alfred.edu. *Web site:* http://www.alfred.edu/

■ AMERICAN INTERNATIONAL COLLEGE

School of Continuing Education and Graduate Studies, Program in Public Administration, Springfield, MA 01109-3189

AWARDS MPA. Part-time and evening/weekend programs available.

Degree requirements: For master's, oral exam, practicum.

■ AMERICAN MILITARY UNIVERSITY

Graduate School of Military Studies, Manassas, VA 20110

AWARDS Air warfare (MA Military Studies); American revolution studies (MA Military Studies); business administration (MBA); civil war studies (MA Military Studies); criminal justice (MA); defense management (MA Military Studies); emergency and disaster management (MA); intelligence (MA Strategic Intelligence); land warfare (MA Military Studies); management (MA); national security studies (MA); naval warfare (MA Military Studies); political science (MA); public administration (MA); public health (MA); security management (MA); space studies (MA Military Studies); special operations (MA Military Studies); transportation management (MA); unconventional warfare (MA Military Studies). Program offered via distance learning only. Part-time and evening/weekend programs available. Postbaccalaureate distance learning degree programs offered (no on-campus study).

Faculty: 2 full-time (1 woman), 100 part-time/adjunct (8 women).
Students: Average age 35. 830 applicants, 100% accepted, 550 enrolled. In 2001, 87 degrees awarded. Terminal master's awarded for partial completion of doctoral program.
Entrance requirements: For master's, bachelor's degree or equivalent, minimum GPA of 2.7 in last 60 hours. *Application deadline:* For fall admission, 9/1 (priority date); for winter admission, 1/1; for spring admission, 5/1 (priority date). Applications are processed on a rolling basis. Electronic applications accepted.
Expenses: Tuition: Part-time $750 per course.
Faculty research: Military history, criminal justice, management performance, national security.
Dr. Michael J. Hillyard, Provost, 703-330-5398 Ext. 862, *Fax:* 703-330-5109, *E-mail:* mhillyard@amunet.edu.
Application contact: Cathi Bauer, Office of Student Services, 703-330-5398 Ext. 894, *Fax:* 703-330-5109, *E-mail:* info@amunet.edu. *Web site:* http://www.amunet.edu/

■ AMERICAN UNIVERSITY

College of Arts and Sciences, Department of Economics, Program in Financial Economics for Public Policy, Washington, DC 20016-8001

AWARDS MA. Part-time and evening/weekend programs available.

Students: 6 full-time (1 woman), 3 part-time, 6 international. Average age 26. In 2001, 3 degrees awarded.
Degree requirements: For master's, comprehensive exam.
Entrance requirements: For master's, TOEFL. *Application deadline:* For fall admission, 2/1 (priority date); for spring admission, 10/1. Applications are processed on a rolling basis. *Application fee:* $50.
Expenses: Tuition: Full-time $14,274; part-time $793 per credit. Required fees: $290. Tuition and fees vary according to program.
Financial support: Career-related internships or fieldwork, Federal Work-Study, and institutionally sponsored loans available. Financial award application deadline: 2/1.
Application contact: Dr. Mieke Meurs, Ph.D. Adviser, 202-885-3376, *Fax:* 202-885-3790, *E-mail:* mmeurs@american.edu. *Web site:* http://www.american.edu/academic.depts/cas/econ/

Find an in-depth description at www.petersons.com/gradchannel.

■ AMERICAN UNIVERSITY

School of Public Affairs, Department of Public Administration, Program in Public Policy, Washington, DC 20016-8001

AWARDS MPP.

Students: 42 full-time (25 women), 32 part-time (22 women); includes 18 minority (12 African Americans, 4 Asian Americans or Pacific Islanders, 2 Hispanic Americans), 4 international. Average age 27. In 2001, 21 degrees awarded.
Application deadline: For fall admission, 2/1; for spring admission, 10/1. *Application fee:* $50.
Expenses: Tuition: Full-time $14,274; part-time $793 per credit. Required fees: $290. Tuition and fees vary according to program.
Financial support: Application deadline: 2/1.

■ ANDREW JACKSON UNIVERSITY

School of Civil Sciences, Program in Public Administration, Birmingham, AL 35209

AWARDS MPA. Part-time and evening/weekend programs available. Postbaccalaureate distance learning degree programs offered (no on-campus study).

Faculty: 12 part-time/adjunct.
Application deadline: Applications are processed on a rolling basis. *Application fee:* $75. Electronic applications accepted.
Expenses: Tuition: Part-time $475 per course.
Application contact: Bell N. Woods, Director of Admissions, 205-871-9288, *Fax:* 205-871-9294, *E-mail:* bnw@aju.edu.

■ ANGELO STATE UNIVERSITY

Graduate School, College of Liberal and Fine Arts, Department of Government, San Angelo, TX 76909

AWARDS International studies (MA); public administration (MPA). Part-time and evening/weekend programs available.

Faculty: 6 full-time (0 women).
Students: 5 full-time (2 women), 9 part-time (6 women); includes 4 minority (all Hispanic Americans), 1 international. Average age 35. 17 applicants, 53% accepted, 6 enrolled. In 2001, 6 degrees awarded.
Degree requirements: For master's, thesis optional.
Entrance requirements: For master's, GRE General Test, minimum GPA of 2.5. *Application deadline:* For fall admission, 8/7 (priority date); for spring admission, 1/2. Applications are processed on a rolling basis. *Application fee:* $25 ($50 for international students).
Expenses: Tuition, area resident: Full-time $960; part-time $40 per credit hour. Tuition, nonresident: full-time $6,120; part-time $255 per credit hour. Required fees: $1,336; $56 per credit hour.
Financial support: In 2001–02, 2 students received support, including 2 fellowships with full and partial tuition reimbursements available; teaching assistantships, Federal Work-Study and tuition waivers (partial) also available. Support available to part-time students. Financial award application deadline: 8/1.
Dr. Edward C. Olson, Head, 915-942-2005.
Application contact: Dr. Jack Barbour, Graduate Advisor, 915-942-2262, *E-mail:* jack.barbour@angelo.edu. *Web site:* http://www.angelo.edu/dept/government/

■ ANNA MARIA COLLEGE

Graduate Division, Program in Emergency Response Planning, Paxton, MA 01612

AWARDS MS. Part-time and evening/weekend programs available.

Faculty: 1 full-time (0 women), 2 part-time/adjunct (0 women).
Students: 3 full-time (2 women), 10 part-time (4 women). Average age 40.
Degree requirements: For master's, thesis.
Application deadline: For fall admission, 3/1 (priority date); for spring admission, 11/1 (priority date). Applications are processed on a rolling basis. *Application fee:* $30. Electronic applications accepted.
Expenses: Tuition: Part-time $900 per course.
Financial support: Institutionally sponsored loans available. Financial award applicants required to submit FAFSA.
Dr. Paul Erickson, Director, 508-849-3432, *E-mail:* perickson@annamaria.edu.
Application contact: Eva Eaton, Director of Admissions for Graduate Programs and the Department of Professional Studies, 508-849-3488, *Fax:* 508-849-3362, *E-mail:* eveaton@annamaria.edu. *Web site:* http://www.annamaria.edu/

■ APPALACHIAN STATE UNIVERSITY

Cratis D. Williams Graduate School, College of Arts and Sciences, Department of Political Science, Program in Public Administration, Boone, NC 28608

AWARDS MPA.

Faculty: 16 full-time (3 women).
Students: 25 full-time (11 women), 21 part-time (10 women); includes 6 minority (all African Americans), 2 international. In 2001, 14 degrees awarded.
Degree requirements: For master's, one foreign language, comprehensive exam.
Entrance requirements: For master's, GRE General Test. *Application deadline:* For fall admission, 7/1; for spring admission, 11/1. *Application fee:* $35.
Expenses: Tuition, state resident: full-time $1,286. Tuition, nonresident: full-time $9,354. Required fees: $1,116.
Financial support: In 2001–02, research assistantships (averaging $6,250 per year), teaching assistantships (averaging $6,250 per year) were awarded. Career-related internships or fieldwork, scholarships/grants, and unspecified assistantships also available. Support available to part-time students. Financial award application deadline: 7/11; financial award applicants required to submit FAFSA.
Faculty research: Campaign finance, emerging democracies, bureaucratic politics, judicial behavior, administration of justice.
Dr. Marvin Hoffman, Coordinator, 828-262-3075.

■ ARIZONA STATE UNIVERSITY

Graduate College, College of Public Programs, School for Public Affairs, Tempe, AZ 85287

AWARDS MPA, DPA.

Degree requirements: For doctorate, thesis/dissertation.
Entrance requirements: For master's, GRE.
Faculty research: Public administration, public policy, personnel and labor relations administration.

■ ARIZONA STATE UNIVERSITY

Graduate College, Interdisciplinary Program in Public Administration, Tempe, AZ 85287

AWARDS DPA.

Degree requirements: For doctorate, thesis/dissertation.

■ ARKANSAS STATE UNIVERSITY

Graduate School, College of Arts and Sciences, Department of Political Science, Jonesboro, State University, AR 72467

AWARDS Political science (MA, SCCT); public administration (MPA). Part-time programs available.

Faculty: 9 full-time (2 women).
Students: 9 full-time (7 women), 8 part-time (6 women); includes 6 minority (5 African Americans, 1 Hispanic American), 1 international. Average age 27. In 2001, 14 master's, 1 other advanced degree awarded.
Degree requirements: For master's, thesis or alternative, comprehensive exam.
Entrance requirements: For master's, GRE General Test or MAT, appropriate bachelor's degree; for SCCT, GRE General Test or MAT, interview, master's degree. *Application deadline:* For fall admission, 7/1 (priority date); for spring admission, 11/15 (priority date). Applications are processed on a rolling basis. *Application fee:* $15 ($25 for international students). Electronic applications accepted.
Expenses: Tuition, state resident: full-time $3,384; part-time $141 per hour. Tuition, nonresident: full-time $8,520; part-time $355 per hour. Required fees: $742; $28 per hour. $25 per semester. One-time fee: $15 full-time. Tuition and fees vary according to degree level.
Financial support: Fellowships, teaching assistantships, career-related internships or fieldwork, Federal Work-Study, and scholarships/grants available. Support available to part-time students. Financial award application deadline: 7/1; financial award applicants required to submit FAFSA.
Dr. Jane Gates, Chair, 870-972-3048, *Fax:* 870-972-2720, *E-mail:* jgates@astate.edu. *Web site:* http://www.cas.astate.edu/posc/

■ AUBURN UNIVERSITY

Graduate School, College of Liberal Arts, Department of Political Science, Program in Public Administration, Auburn University, AL 36849

AWARDS MPA, PhD, MPA/MCP. Part-time programs available.

Faculty: 20 full-time (5 women).
Students: 23 full-time (11 women), 47 part-time (28 women); includes 14 minority (11 African Americans, 3 Hispanic Americans), 3 international. 52 applicants, 48% accepted. In 2001, 5 master's, 2 doctorates awarded.
Degree requirements: For master's, internship or research project; for doctorate, thesis/dissertation.
Entrance requirements: For master's, GRE General Test, sample of written work; for doctorate, GRE General Test. *Application deadline:* For fall admission, 7/7; for spring admission, 11/24. Applications are processed on a rolling basis. *Application fee:* $25 ($50 for international students). Electronic applications accepted.
Financial support: Fellowships, research assistantships, teaching assistantships, career-related internships or fieldwork and Federal Work-Study available. Support available to part-time students. Financial award application deadline: 3/15.
Faculty research: Privatization studies, policy evolution, water resources, election administration.
Dr. Keenan Grenell, Head, 334-844-5371.
Application contact: Dr. John F. Pritchett, Dean of the Graduate School, 334-844-4700, *E-mail:* hatchlb@mail.auburn.edu.

■ AUBURN UNIVERSITY MONTGOMERY

School of Sciences, Department of Public Administration and Political Science, Montgomery, AL 36124-4023

AWARDS MPA, PhD. Part-time and evening/weekend programs available.

Students: 45 full-time (18 women), 84 part-time (60 women); includes 52 minority (45 African Americans, 2 Asian Americans or Pacific Islanders, 4 Hispanic Americans, 1 Native American). Average age 35. In 2001, 27 degrees awarded.
Degree requirements: For master's, comprehensive exam; for doctorate, thesis/dissertation.
Entrance requirements: For master's, GRE General Test or MAT; for doctorate, GRE General Test. *Application deadline:* Applications are processed on a rolling basis. *Application fee:* $25. Electronic applications accepted.
Expenses: Tuition, state resident: full-time $3,072; part-time $128 per credit hour. Tuition, nonresident: full-time $9,216; part-time $384 per credit hour.
Financial support: In 2001–02, 1 research assistantship was awarded; career-related internships or fieldwork and scholarships/grants also available. Support available to part-time students. Financial award application deadline: 3/1; financial award applicants required to submit FAFSA.
Dr. Thomas Vocino, Head, 334-244-3696, *E-mail:* vocino@strudel.aum.edu.

■ AUDREY COHEN COLLEGE

Program in Public Administration, New York, NY 10013

AWARDS MPA. Evening/weekend programs available.

Faculty: 13 full-time (5 women), 11 part-time/adjunct (4 women).
Students: 85 full-time (59 women), 6 part-time (4 women); includes 116 African Americans, 7 Asian Americans or Pacific Islanders, 35 Hispanic Americans. Average age 32. 122 applicants, 79% accepted, 87 enrolled. In 2001, 129 degrees awarded.
Degree requirements: For master's, thesis. *Median time to degree:* Master's–1 year full-time, 1.5 years part-time.
Entrance requirements: For master's, appropriate work experience, interview, minimum GPA of 2.7. *Application deadline:* For fall admission, 7/30 (priority date); for winter admission, 11/30 (priority date); for spring admission, 3/30 (priority date). Applications are processed on a rolling basis. *Application fee:* $45. Electronic applications accepted.
Expenses: Contact institution.
Financial support: In 2001–02, 3 fellowships with tuition reimbursements (averaging $5,700 per year) were awarded; career-related internships or fieldwork, scholarships/grants, and tuition waivers (partial) also available. Financial award application deadline: 8/15; financial award applicants required to submit FAFSA.
Faculty research: Transnational politics and culture, women and social policy, confidentiality in the human services, concepts of marginality, ethics in social policy.
Steven K. Lenhart, Director of Graduate Admissions, 212-343-1234 Ext. 2700, *Fax:* 212-343-8470, *E-mail:* slenhart@audreycohen.edu. *Web site:* http://www.audrey-cohen.edu/

■ BALL STATE UNIVERSITY

Graduate School, College of Sciences and Humanities, Department of Political Science, Program in Public Administration, Muncie, IN 47306-1099

AWARDS MPA.

Students: 10 full-time (5 women), 25 part-time (16 women); includes 6 minority (5 African Americans, 1 Hispanic American). Average age 26. 9 applicants, 100% accepted. In 2001, 9 degrees awarded.
Entrance requirements: For master's, GRE General Test. *Application fee:* $25 ($35 for international students).
Expenses: Tuition, state resident: full-time $4,068; part-time $2,542. Tuition, nonresident: full-time $10,944; part-time $6,462. Required fees: $1,000; $500 per term.
Financial support: Career-related internships or fieldwork available. Financial award application deadline: 3/1.
Faculty research: Employment training programs, personnel and labor relations, planning.
John Cranor, Director, 765-285-8800, *Fax:* 765-285-5345, *E-mail:* jcranor@bsu.edu. *Web site:* http://www.bsu.edu/poli-sci/

■ BAYLOR UNIVERSITY

Graduate School, College of Arts and Sciences, Department of Political Science, Program in Public Policy and Administration, Waco, TX 76798

AWARDS MPPA, JD/MPPA.

Students: 6 full-time (3 women); includes 1 minority (Hispanic American), 1 international. In 2001, 2 degrees awarded.
Entrance requirements: For master's, GRE General Test. *Application deadline:* Applications are processed on a rolling basis. *Application fee:* $25.
Expenses: Tuition: Part-time $379 per semester hour. Required fees: $42 per semester hour. $101 per semester. Tuition and fees vary according to program.
Financial support: Research assistantships, career-related internships or fieldwork, Federal Work-Study, and institutionally sponsored loans available. Financial award application deadline: 3/1.
Application contact: Suzanne Keener, Administrative Assistant, 254-710-3588, *Fax:* 254-710-3870, *E-mail:* graduate_school@baylor.edu.

■ BERNARD M. BARUCH COLLEGE OF THE CITY UNIVERSITY OF NEW YORK

School of Public Affairs, Program in Public Administration, New York, NY 10010-5585

AWARDS MPA. Part-time and evening/weekend programs available.

Students: 98 full-time (74 women), 236 part-time (167 women); includes 207 minority (121 African Americans, 26 Asian Americans or Pacific Islanders, 60 Hispanic Americans), 11 international. Average age 33. In 2001, 101 degrees awarded.
Degree requirements: For master's, thesis. *Median time to degree:* Master's–2 years full-time, 3 years part-time.
Entrance requirements: For master's, GMAT or GRE General Test, TOEFL. *Application deadline:* For fall admission, 7/15; for spring admission, 12/3. Applications are processed on a rolling basis. *Application fee:* $40.
Expenses: Tuition, state resident: full-time $4,350; part-time $185 per credit. Tuition, nonresident: full-time $7,600; part-time

$320 per credit. Tuition and fees vary according to program.
Financial support: In 2001–02, 19 research assistantships with tuition reimbursements (averaging $9,000 per year) were awarded; career-related internships or fieldwork and Federal Work-Study also available. Support available to part-time students. Financial award application deadline: 5/30; financial award applicants required to submit FAFSA.
Faculty research: Nonprofit administration, public policy, economic policy, health care, digital divide. *Total annual research expenditures:* $1.9 million.
Application contact: Pamela S. Ferner, Director of Admissions, 212-802-5912, *Fax:* 212-802-5928, *E-mail:* spa_admissions@baruch.cuny.edu. *Web site:* http://www.baruch.cuny.edu/spa/

Find an in-depth description at www.petersons.com/gradchannel.

■ BIRMINGHAM-SOUTHERN COLLEGE

Program in Public and Private Management, Birmingham, AL 35254

AWARDS MPPM. Part-time and evening/weekend programs available.

Faculty: 8 full-time (1 woman), 1 part-time/adjunct (0 women).
Students: 41 full-time (23 women), 34 part-time (12 women); includes 13 minority (12 African Americans, 1 Hispanic American). Average age 36. 21 applicants, 71% accepted. In 2001, 24 degrees awarded.
Degree requirements: For master's, thesis optional.
Entrance requirements: For master's, GMAT or GRE or MAT. *Application deadline:* For fall admission, 7/27; for spring admission, 12/14. Applications are processed on a rolling basis. *Application fee:* $25.
Expenses: Tuition: Full-time $11,360; part-time $1,420 per term. Required fees: $144; $18 per term.
Financial support: Scholarships/grants available. Support available to part-time students.
Dr. Cecilia McInnis-Bowers, Dean-Partner, 205-226-4985, *Fax:* 205-226-4843, *E-mail:* cmcinnis@bsc.edu.
Application contact: Patricia Redmond, Director of Admissions and Marketing, 205-226-4803, *Fax:* 205-226-4843, *E-mail:* graduate@bsc.edu. *Web site:* http://www.bsc.edu

■ BOISE STATE UNIVERSITY

Graduate College, College of Social Science and Public Affairs, Program in Public Policy and Administration, Boise, ID 83725

AWARDS Environmental and natural resources policy and administration (MPA); general public administration (MPA); state and local government policy and administration (MPA). Part-time programs available.

Degree requirements: For master's, directed research project, internship.
Entrance requirements: For master's, GRE General Test, TOEFL, minimum GPA of 3.0. Electronic applications accepted.

■ BOWIE STATE UNIVERSITY

Graduate Programs, Program in Administrative Management, Bowie, MD 20715-9465

AWARDS Business administration (M Adm Mgt); public administration (M Adm Mgt). Part-time and evening/weekend programs available.

Degree requirements: For master's, research paper, thesis optional.

■ BOWLING GREEN STATE UNIVERSITY

Graduate College, College of Arts and Sciences, Department of Political Science, Program in Public Administration, Bowling Green, OH 43403

AWARDS MPA.

Students: 21 full-time (9 women), 4 part-time (1 woman); includes 3 minority (all African Americans), 8 international. Average age 30. 23 applicants, 91% accepted, 11 enrolled. In 2001, 9 degrees awarded.
Degree requirements: For master's, thesis or alternative, comprehensive exam or thesis, experiential paper for all non-thesis students, comprehensive exam.
Entrance requirements: For master's, GRE General Test, TOEFL. *Application deadline:* For fall admission, 3/15. *Application fee:* $30. Electronic applications accepted.
Expenses: Tuition, state resident: full-time $7,376; part-time $342 per credit hour. Tuition, nonresident: full-time $13,628; part-time $640 per credit hour.
Financial support: In 2001–02, 2 research assistantships with full tuition reimbursements (averaging $5,735 per year), 10 teaching assistantships with full tuition reimbursements (averaging $6,935 per year) were awarded. Unspecified assistantships also available. Financial award applicants required to submit FAFSA.
Faculty research: Public sector labor relations, administrative law, sexual harassment and violence in the public workplace.
Application contact: Information Contact, 419-372-2831.

■ BRANDEIS UNIVERSITY

The Heller School for Social Policy and Management, Program in Social Policy, Waltham, MA 02454-9110

AWARDS PhD. Part-time programs available.

Faculty: 44 full-time (17 women), 16 part-time/adjunct (6 women).
Students: 41 full-time (26 women), 23 part-time (14 women). Average age 37. 95 applicants, 37% accepted. In 2001, 14 degrees awarded.
Degree requirements: For doctorate, thesis/dissertation, qualifying paper, 2 year residency.
Entrance requirements: For doctorate, GRE General Test or MAT. *Application deadline:* For fall admission, 12/15. *Application fee:* $50. Electronic applications accepted.
Expenses: Tuition: Full-time $27,392. Required fees: $35.
Financial support: In 2001–02, 20 fellowships with full tuition reimbursements (averaging $10,000 per year) were awarded; research assistantships, teaching assistantships, institutionally sponsored loans, scholarships/grants, traineeships, and tuition waivers (full and partial) also available. Financial award application deadline: 2/15; financial award applicants required to submit CSS PROFILE or FAFSA.
Faculty research: Health policy, child and family policy, mental health policy, disability policy, aging policy, substance abuse, work, inequality and social change. *Total annual research expenditures:* $14 million.
Jim Callahan, Director, 781-736-3800, *E-mail:* callahan@brandeis.edu.
Application contact: Lisa Hamlin Sherry, Assistant Director for Admissions and Financial Aid, 781-736-3835, *Fax:* 781-736-3881, *E-mail:* sherry@brandeis.edu. *Web site:* http://heller.brandeis.edu

Find an in-depth description at www.petersons.com/gradchannel.

■ BRIDGEWATER STATE COLLEGE

School of Graduate and Continuing Education, School of Arts and Sciences, Department of Political Science, Program in Public Administration, Bridgewater, MA 02325-0001

AWARDS MPA.

Expenses: Tuition, state resident: part-time $135 per credit. Tuition, nonresident: part-time $294 per credit. Tuition and fees vary according to class time.
Application contact: James Plotner, Assistant Dean, Graduate Admissions, 508-531-1300, *Fax:* 508-531-6162, *E-mail:* jplotner@bridgew.edu.

■ BRIGHAM YOUNG UNIVERSITY

Graduate Studies, Marriott School of Management, George W. Romney Institute of Public Management, Provo, UT 84602-1001

AWARDS MPA, JD/MPA. Part-time and evening/weekend programs available.

Brigham Young University (continued)
Entrance requirements: For master's, GMAT or GRE, TOEFL, minimum GPA of 3.0 in last 60 hours. Electronic applications accepted.
Expenses: Tuition: Full-time $3,860; part-time $214 per hour.
Faculty research: Organization theory, ethics, property taxation, role of city manager, microenterprise. *Web site:* http://marriottschool.byu.edu/mpa/

■ BROOKLYN COLLEGE OF THE CITY UNIVERSITY OF NEW YORK

Division of Graduate Studies, Department of Political Science, Program in Political Science, Urban Policy and Administration, Brooklyn, NY 11210-2889

AWARDS MA. Part-time and evening/weekend programs available.

Students: 10 applicants, 50% accepted. In 2001, 26 degrees awarded.
Degree requirements: For master's, thesis or alternative, policy paper.
Entrance requirements: For master's, TOEFL, 27 credits in political science. *Application deadline:* For fall admission, 3/1; for spring admission, 11/1. *Application fee:* $40.
Expenses: Tuition, state resident: full-time $4,350; part-time $185 per credit. Tuition, nonresident: full-time $7,600; part-time $320 per credit.
Financial support: Fellowships, career-related internships or fieldwork, Federal Work-Study, institutionally sponsored loans, scholarships/grants, and tuition waivers (full and partial) available. Support available to part-time students. Financial award application deadline: 5/1; financial award applicants required to submit FAFSA.
Dr. Joseph Wilson, Graduate Deputy, 212-966-4014, *Fax:* 212-966-4038.
Application contact: Pam Miller, Administrator, 212-966-4014, *Fax:* 212-966-4038.

■ CALIFORNIA LUTHERAN UNIVERSITY

Graduate Studies, Program in Public Policy and Administration, Thousand Oaks, CA 91360-2787

AWARDS MPPA.

Degree requirements: For master's, thesis or project, internship.
Entrance requirements: For master's, GMAT or GRE General Test, interview, minimum GPA of 3.0.
Expenses: Contact institution.

■ CALIFORNIA STATE POLYTECHNIC UNIVERSITY, POMONA

Academic Affairs, College of Letters, Arts, and Social Sciences, Program in Public Administration, Pomona, CA 91768-2557

AWARDS MPA.

Students: 6 full-time (4 women), 13 part-time (9 women); includes 9 minority (2 African Americans, 3 Asian Americans or Pacific Islanders, 4 Hispanic Americans). Average age 27. 26 applicants, 62% accepted.
Degree requirements: For master's, thesis or alternative.
Entrance requirements: For master's, GRE General Test. *Application deadline:* For fall admission, 5/1 (priority date); for winter admission, 10/15 (priority date); for spring admission, 1/20 (priority date). Applications are processed on a rolling basis. *Application fee:* $55. Electronic applications accepted.
Expenses: Tuition, nonresident: part-time $164 per unit. Required fees: $1,850.
Dr. Lisa S. Nelson, Graduate Coordinator, 909-869-4739, *E-mail:* lnelson@csupomona.edu. *Web site:* http://www.csupomona.edu/~pls/

■ CALIFORNIA STATE UNIVERSITY, BAKERSFIELD

Division of Graduate Studies and Research, School of Business and Public Administration, Program in Public Administration, Bakersfield, CA 93311-1099

AWARDS MPA.

Degree requirements: For master's, thesis or alternative.
Entrance requirements: For master's, GRE, minimum GPA of 2.75. *Web site:* http://www.csub.edu/BPA/Dept-Info/mpa.html/

■ CALIFORNIA STATE UNIVERSITY, CHICO

Graduate School, College of Behavioral and Social Sciences, Department of Political Science, Program in Public Administration, Chico, CA 95929-0722

AWARDS Health administration (MPA); public administration (MPA).

Students: 13 applicants, 85% accepted, 4 enrolled. In 2001, 9 degrees awarded.
Degree requirements: For master's, thesis or alternative, oral exam.
Application deadline: For fall admission, 4/1; for spring admission, 10/1. Applications are processed on a rolling basis. *Application fee:* $55. Electronic applications accepted.
Expenses: Tuition, state resident: full-time $2,148. Tuition, nonresident: full-time $6,576.
Financial support: Fellowships, career-related internships or fieldwork available.
Dr. Donna Kemp, Graduate Coordinator, 530-898-5734.

■ CALIFORNIA STATE UNIVERSITY, DOMINGUEZ HILLS

School of Business and Public Administration, Program in Public Administration, Carson, CA 90747-0001

AWARDS MPA. Part-time and evening/weekend programs available.

Faculty: 6 full-time (3 women), 4 part-time/adjunct (3 women).
Students: 18 full-time (11 women), 138 part-time (95 women); includes 133 minority (91 African Americans, 9 Asian Americans or Pacific Islanders, 32 Hispanic Americans, 1 Native American), 1 international. Average age 36. 90 applicants, 82% accepted, 39 enrolled. In 2001, 32 degrees awarded.
Degree requirements: For master's, thesis or alternative.
Entrance requirements: For master's, minimum GPA of 2.75. *Application deadline:* For fall admission, 6/1. *Application fee:* $55.
Expenses: Tuition, nonresident: full-time $1,508; part-time $438 per semester. Required fees: $442; $246 per unit. $227 per semester.
Faculty research: Applied public management.
Dr. Justine Bell-Waters, Coordinator, 310-243-3465, *E-mail:* jbell@soma.csudh.edu.

■ CALIFORNIA STATE UNIVERSITY, FRESNO

Division of Graduate Studies, College of Social Sciences, Department of Political Science, Program in Public Administration, Fresno, CA 93740-8027

AWARDS MPA. Part-time and evening/weekend programs available.

Faculty: 6 full-time (2 women).
Students: 11 full-time (7 women), 21 part-time (11 women); includes 13 minority (4 African Americans, 9 Hispanic Americans), 2 international. Average age 31. 14 applicants, 79% accepted, 8 enrolled. In 2001, 9 degrees awarded.
Degree requirements: For master's, thesis or alternative. *Median time to degree:* Master's–2.5 years full-time, 3.5 years part-time.
Entrance requirements: For master's, GRE General Test or GMAT, TOEFL, minimum GPA of 3.0. *Application deadline:* For fall admission, 8/1 (priority date); for spring admission, 12/1. Applications are processed on a rolling basis. *Application fee:* $55. Electronic applications accepted.

Expenses: Tuition, nonresident: part-time $246 per unit. Required fees: $605 per semester. Tuition and fees vary according to course load.
Financial support: Career-related internships or fieldwork, Federal Work-Study, scholarships/grants, and unspecified assistantships available. Support available to part-time students. Financial award application deadline: 3/1; financial award applicants required to submit FAFSA.
Dr. Marn Cha, Coordinator, 559-278-2988, *E-mail:* marn_cha@csufresno.edu.

■ CALIFORNIA STATE UNIVERSITY, FULLERTON

Graduate Studies, College of Humanities and Social Sciences, Division of Political Science and Criminal Justice, Fullerton, CA 92834-9480

AWARDS Political science (MA); public administration (MPA). Part-time programs available.

Faculty: 17 full-time (4 women), 15 part-time/adjunct.
Students: 37 full-time (20 women), 84 part-time (36 women); includes 45 minority (6 African Americans, 12 Asian Americans or Pacific Islanders, 27 Hispanic Americans), 5 international. Average age 31. 88 applicants, 65% accepted, 32 enrolled. In 2001, 31 degrees awarded.
Degree requirements: For master's, project or thesis.
Entrance requirements: For master's, minimum GPA of 2.5 in last 60 units, 12 units in social sciences. *Application fee:* $55.
Expenses: Tuition, nonresident: part-time $246 per unit. Required fees: $964.
Financial support: Career-related internships or fieldwork, Federal Work-Study, institutionally sponsored loans, and scholarships/grants available. Support available to part-time students. Financial award application deadline: 3/1.
Faculty research: Emergency management plans.
Dr. Alan Saltzstein, Chair, 714-278-3521.

■ CALIFORNIA STATE UNIVERSITY, HAYWARD

Academic Programs and Graduate Studies, School of Arts, Letters, and Social Sciences, Department of Public Administration, Hayward, CA 94542-3000

AWARDS MPA. Part-time and evening/weekend programs available.

Students: 27 full-time (17 women), 172 part-time (128 women); includes 97 minority (64 African Americans, 13 Asian Americans or Pacific Islanders, 18 Hispanic Americans, 2 Native Americans), 5 international. 96 applicants, 68% accepted. In 2001, 85 degrees awarded.
Degree requirements: For master's, comprehensive exam or thesis.
Entrance requirements: For master's, minimum GPA of 3.0. *Application deadline:* For fall admission, 6/15; for winter admission, 10/27; for spring admission, 1/5. Applications are processed on a rolling basis. *Application fee:* $55. Electronic applications accepted.
Expenses: Tuition, nonresident: part-time $164 per unit. Required fees: $405 per semester.
Financial support: Fellowships, teaching assistantships, career-related internships or fieldwork, Federal Work-Study, institutionally sponsored loans, and scholarships/grants available. Support available to part-time students. Financial award application deadline: 3/1.
Dr. Dvora Yanow, Chair, 510-885-3282.
Application contact: Jennifer Cason, Graduate Program Coordinator/Operations Analyst, 510-885-3286, *Fax:* 510-885-4777, *E-mail:* jcason@csuhayward.edu.

■ CALIFORNIA STATE UNIVERSITY, LONG BEACH

Graduate Studies, College of Health and Human Services, Center for Public Policy and Administration, Long Beach, CA 90840

AWARDS MPA, Certificate. Part-time and evening/weekend programs available.

Faculty: 8 full-time (1 woman), 26 part-time/adjunct (3 women).
Students: 62 full-time (38 women), 183 part-time (87 women); includes 124 minority (45 African Americans, 19 Asian Americans or Pacific Islanders, 57 Hispanic Americans, 3 Native Americans), 3 international. Average age 33. 132 applicants, 82% accepted. In 2001, 76 degrees awarded.
Degree requirements: For master's, comprehensive exam.
Entrance requirements: For master's, minimum GPA of 2.75. *Application deadline:* For fall admission, 8/1; for spring admission, 12/1. Applications are processed on a rolling basis. *Application fee:* $55. Electronic applications accepted.
Financial support: Fellowships, career-related internships or fieldwork, Federal Work-Study, institutionally sponsored loans, and scholarships/grants available. Financial award application deadline: 3/2.
Faculty research: Transportation access, air quality controls, coastal issues, intergovernmental relations. *Total annual research expenditures:* $48,000.
Dr. Michelle St. Germain, Director, 562-985-5383, *Fax:* 562-985-4672, *E-mail:* msaintg@csulb.edu.
Application contact: Dr. William Moore, Graduate Adviser, 562-985-5593, *Fax:* 562-985-4672, *E-mail:* wmoore2@csulb.edu.

■ CALIFORNIA STATE UNIVERSITY, LOS ANGELES

Graduate Studies, College of Natural and Social Sciences, Department of Political Science, Major in Public Administration, Los Angeles, CA 90032-8530

AWARDS MS. Part-time and evening/weekend programs available.

Students: 8 full-time (3 women), 98 part-time (59 women); includes 82 minority (18 African Americans, 13 Asian Americans or Pacific Islanders, 51 Hispanic Americans), 4 international. In 2001, 18 degrees awarded.
Degree requirements: For master's, comprehensive exam or thesis.
Entrance requirements: For master's, TOEFL, minimum GPA of 2.5. *Application deadline:* For fall admission, 6/30; for spring admission, 2/1. Applications are processed on a rolling basis. *Application fee:* $55.
Expenses: Tuition, nonresident: part-time $164 per unit.
Financial support: Career-related internships or fieldwork and Federal Work-Study available. Support available to part-time students. Financial award application deadline: 3/1.
Faculty research: Finance, state and local administration, organization and development.
Dr. Ted Anagnoson, Chair, Department of Political Science, 323-343-2230.

■ CALIFORNIA STATE UNIVERSITY, NORTHRIDGE

Graduate Studies, College of Social and Behavioral Sciences, Department of Political Science, Northridge, CA 91330

AWARDS Political science (MA); public administration (MPA).

Faculty: 16 full-time, 10 part-time/adjunct.
Students: 4 full-time (2 women), 18 part-time (8 women); includes 4 minority (1 African American, 3 Hispanic Americans), 1 international. Average age 33. 100 applicants, 77% accepted, 4 enrolled. In 2001, 67 degrees awarded.
Entrance requirements: For master's, TOEFL. *Application deadline:* For fall admission, 11/30. *Application fee:* $55.
Expenses: Tuition, nonresident: part-time $631 per semester. Required fees: $246 per unit.
Financial support: Application deadline: 3/1.
Dr. Matthew A. Cahn, Interim Department Chair, 818-677-3488.

■ CALIFORNIA STATE UNIVERSITY, NORTHRIDGE

Graduate Studies, College of Social and Behavioral Sciences, Program of Public Administration, Northridge, CA 91330

AWARDS MPA.

Students: Average age 35. 81 applicants, 83% accepted. In 2001, 60 degrees awarded.
Entrance requirements: For master's, TOEFL. *Application deadline:* For fall admission, 11/30. *Application fee:* $55.
Expenses: Tuition, nonresident: part-time $631 per semester. Required fees: $246 per unit.
Financial support: Application deadline: 3/1.
Dr. Warren Campbell, Co-Director, 818-677-3477.

■ CALIFORNIA STATE UNIVERSITY, SACRAMENTO

Graduate Studies, College of Social Sciences and Interdisciplinary Studies, Program in Public Policy and Administration, Sacramento, CA 95819-6048

AWARDS MPPA. Part-time programs available.

Students: 17 full-time (13 women), 59 part-time (29 women); includes 21 minority (7 African Americans, 2 Asian Americans or Pacific Islanders, 11 Hispanic Americans, 1 Native American).
Degree requirements: For master's, thesis or alternative, writing proficiency exam.
Entrance requirements: For master's, GRE General Test, TOEFL. *Application deadline:* For fall admission, 4/15; for spring admission, 11/1. *Application fee:* $55.
Expenses: Tuition, state resident: full-time $1,965; part-time $668 per semester. Tuition, nonresident: part-time $246 per unit.
Financial support: Career-related internships or fieldwork and Federal Work-Study available. Support available to part-time students. Financial award application deadline: 3/1.
Dr. Ted Lascher, Director, 916-278-4865.

■ CALIFORNIA STATE UNIVERSITY, SAN BERNARDINO

Graduate Studies, College of Business and Public Administration, Program in Public Administration, San Bernardino, CA 92407-2397

AWARDS MPA. Part-time and evening/weekend programs available.

Students: 81 full-time (47 women), 52 part-time (25 women); includes 59 minority (24 African Americans, 6 Asian Americans or Pacific Islanders, 26 Hispanic Americans, 3 Native Americans), 4 international. Average age 35. 59 applicants, 85% accepted. In 2001, 28 degrees awarded.
Application deadline: For fall admission, 8/31 (priority date). Applications are processed on a rolling basis. *Application fee:* $55.
Expenses: Tuition, nonresident: full-time $4,428. Required fees: $1,733.
Financial support: Career-related internships or fieldwork, Federal Work-Study, and institutionally sponsored loans available. Support available to part-time students. Financial award application deadline: 3/1.
Dr. David J. Bellis, Director, 909-880-5759, *Fax:* 909-880-7517, *E-mail:* dbellis@csusb.edu.

■ CALIFORNIA STATE UNIVERSITY, STANISLAUS

Graduate Programs, College of Arts, Letters, and Sciences, Department of Politics and Public Administration, Turlock, CA 95382

AWARDS Public administration (MPA). Part-time and evening/weekend programs available.

Students: 63 (35 women); includes 18 minority (2 African Americans, 5 Asian Americans or Pacific Islanders, 9 Hispanic Americans, 2 Native Americans). 27 applicants, 89% accepted. In 2001, 14 degrees awarded.
Degree requirements: For master's, thesis or alternative, comprehensive exam, comprehensive exam.
Entrance requirements: For master's, minimum GPA of 2.75. *Application deadline:* For fall admission, 9/9. *Application fee:* $55. Electronic applications accepted.
Expenses: Tuition, nonresident: part-time $246 per unit. Required fees: $1,919. Tuition and fees vary according to campus/location and program.
Financial support: In 2001–02, 3 fellowships (averaging $2,500 per year) were awarded; career-related internships or fieldwork and Federal Work-Study also available. Financial award application deadline: 3/2; financial award applicants required to submit FAFSA.
Faculty research: Congress, Constitution, international relations, Latin America, political theory.
Dr. J. J. Hendricks, Chair, 209-667-3388.
Application contact: Dr. April Hejha-Ekins, Director, 209-667-3388, *Fax:* 209-667-3724, *E-mail:* aheijhaekins@csustan.edu.

■ CARNEGIE MELLON UNIVERSITY

H. John Heinz III School of Public Policy and Management, Pittsburgh, PA 15213-3891

AWARDS MAM, MIS, MISM, MMM, MPM, MS, MSED, MSHCPM, PhD, JD/MS, M Div/MS. Part-time and evening/weekend programs available. Terminal master's awarded for partial completion of doctoral program.

Degree requirements: For master's, internship; for doctorate, thesis/dissertation.
Entrance requirements: For master's, GMAT or GRE (MAM, MIS, MS); for doctorate, GRE, previous course work in calculus, probability and statistics. Electronic applications accepted.
Faculty research: Policy analysis, public finance, criminal justice, labor relations, economic development. *Web site:* http://info.heinz.cmu.edu/

■ CENTRAL MICHIGAN UNIVERSITY

College of Extended Learning, Program in Administration, Mount Pleasant, MI 48859

AWARDS General administration (MSA); health services administration (MSA, Certificate); hospitality and tourism (MSA, Certificate); human resources administration (MSA, Certificate); information resource management (MSA, Certificate); international administration (MSA, Certificate); leadership (MSA, Certificate); public administration (MSA, Certificate); software engineering administration (MSA, Certificate). Part-time and evening/weekend programs available. Postbaccalaureate distance learning degree programs offered (no on-campus study).

Faculty: 1,800 part-time/adjunct (0 women).
Students: Average age 38.
Entrance requirements: For master's, minimum GPA of 2.7 in major. *Application fee:* $50.
Financial support: Available to part-time students. Applicants required to submit FAFSA.
Dr. Terry Rawls, Director, 989-774-6525.
Application contact: 800-950-1144 Ext. 1205, *Fax:* 989-774-2461, *E-mail:* celinfo@mail.cel.cmich.edu. *Web site:* http://www.cel.cmich.edu/

■ CENTRAL MICHIGAN UNIVERSITY

College of Graduate Studies, College of Humanities and Social and Behavioral Sciences, Department of Political Science, Program in Public Administration, Mount Pleasant, MI 48859

AWARDS MPA.

Degree requirements: For master's, thesis or alternative.
Entrance requirements: For master's, GRE.
Expenses: Tuition, state resident: part-time $182 per unit. Tuition, nonresident: part-time $182 per unit. Required fees: $208 per semester. Part-time tuition and fees vary according to course load.

■ CENTRAL MICHIGAN UNIVERSITY

College of Graduate Studies, Interdisciplinary Programs, Program in Administration, Mount Pleasant, MI 48859

AWARDS General administration (MSA); health service administration (MSA); hospitality and tourism administration (MSA); human resource administration (MSA); information resource administration (MSA); international administration (MSA); leadership (MSA); organizational communications (MSA); public administration (MSA); recreation and park administration (MSA); software engineering (MSA); sports administration (MSA).

Degree requirements: For master's, thesis or alternative.
Entrance requirements: For master's, minimum undergraduate GPA of 2.5.

■ CENTRAL MISSOURI STATE UNIVERSITY

School of Graduate Studies, College of Applied Sciences and Technology, Department of Safety Science Technology, Warrensburg, MO 64093

AWARDS Human services/public services (Ed S); industrial hygiene (MS); industrial safety management (MS); occupational safety management (MS); public services administration (MS); safety management (MS); secondary education/safety education (MSE); security (MS); transportation safety (MS). Part-time programs available.

Faculty: 7 full-time (2 women), 3 part-time/adjunct (0 women).
Students: 7 full-time (4 women), 39 part-time (15 women); includes 5 minority (4 Hispanic Americans, 1 Native American). Average age 37. 20 applicants, 75% accepted. In 2001, 40 degrees awarded.
Degree requirements: For master's, comprehensive exam (MS), comprehensive exam or thesis (MSE).
Entrance requirements: For master's, GRE General Test, minimum GPA of 2.5, 15 hours in related area (MS); minimum GPA of 2.75, teaching certificate (MSE); for Ed S, master's degree in related field. *Application deadline:* Applications are processed on a rolling basis. *Application fee:* $25 ($50 for international students).
Expenses: Tuition, area resident: Full-time $4,200; part-time $175 per credit hour. Tuition, nonresident: full-time $8,352; part-time $348 per credit hour.
Financial support: In 2001–02, 2 research assistantships with full and partial tuition reimbursements (averaging $8,000 per year), 9 teaching assistantships (averaging $4,000 per year) were awarded. Federal Work-Study, scholarships/grants, unspecified assistantships, and administrative and laboratory assistantships also available. Support available to part-time students. Financial award application deadline: 3/1; financial award applicants required to submit FAFSA.
Faculty research: Hazard assessment, crisis and disaster, ergonomics, fire science, safety management. *Total annual research expenditures:* $2,000.
Larry Womble, Interim Chair, 660-543-8764, *Fax:* 660-543-8142, *E-mail:* womble@cmsu1.cmsu.edu. *Web site:* http://www.cmsu.edu/

■ CHAMINADE UNIVERSITY OF HONOLULU

Graduate Programs, Program in Public Administration, Honolulu, HI 96816-1578

AWARDS MPA. Part-time and evening/weekend programs available.

Degree requirements: For master's, thesis or alternative, internship.
Entrance requirements: For master's, GRE General Test, TOEFL, minimum GPA of 3.0.
Faculty research: Law enforcement administration and training, penology, juvenile delinquency, criminology.

■ CHRISTOPHER NEWPORT UNIVERSITY

Graduate Studies, Department of Government and Public Affairs, Newport News, VA 23606-2998

AWARDS Leadership (MPSL); public safety (MPSL).

Faculty: 6 full-time (0 women).
Students: 3 full-time (2 women), 11 part-time (5 women); includes 3 minority (2 African Americans, 1 Native American). 1 applicant, 100% accepted.
Degree requirements: For master's, thesis, comprehensive exam.
Entrance requirements: For master's, GRE General Test, minimum GPA of 3.0. *Application deadline:* For fall admission, 7/1; for spring admission, 11/15. Applications are processed on a rolling basis. *Application fee:* $40. Electronic applications accepted.
Expenses: Tuition, state resident: full-time $1,782; part-time $99 per credit. Tuition, nonresident: full-time $6,138; part-time $341 per credit. Required fees: $49 per credit hour. $20 per term.
Financial support: In 2001–02, 2 research assistantships with full tuition reimbursements (averaging $2,000 per year) were awarded
Dr. Peter Carlson, Coordinator, 757-594-7874, *Fax:* 757-594-8820, *E-mail:* pcarlson@cnu.edu.
Application contact: Susan R. Chittenden, Graduate Admissions, 757-594-7359, *Fax:* 757-594-7333, *E-mail:* gradstdy@cnu.edu.

■ CITY UNIVERSITY

Graduate Division, School of Business and Management, Bellevue, WA 98005

AWARDS C++ programming (Certificate); computer systems—C++ programming (MS); computer systems—individual (MS); computer systems—web programming language (MS); computer systems-web development (MS); e-commerce (MBA, Certificate); financial management (MBA, Certificate); general management (MBA, MPA, Certificate); general management-Europe (MBA); human resource management (MBA, MPA); human resources management (Certificate); individualized study (MBA, MPA); information systems (MBA, MPA, Certificate); managerial leadership (MBA, MPA, Certificate); marketing (MBA, Certificate); organizational management-general management (MS); organizational management-human resource management (MS); organizational management-individualized study (MS); organizational management-project management (MS); personal financial planning (MBA, Certificate); project management (MBA, MPA, MS, Certificate); public administration (Certificate); web development (Certificate); web programming language (Certificate). Part-time and evening/weekend programs available. Postbaccalaureate distance learning degree programs offered (no on-campus study).

Faculty: 15 full-time (8 women), 513 part-time/adjunct (148 women).
Students: 289 full-time, 2,769 part-time; includes 819 minority (140 African Americans, 615 Asian Americans or Pacific Islanders, 49 Hispanic Americans, 15 Native Americans), 19 international. Average age 37. 786 applicants, 100% accepted, 215 enrolled. In 2001, 849 degrees awarded.
Degree requirements: For master's, thesis (for some programs).
Application deadline: Applications are processed on a rolling basis. *Application fee:* $75 ($175 for international students). Electronic applications accepted.
Expenses: Tuition: Part-time $324 per credit.
Financial support: In 2001–02, 90 students received support. Federal Work-Study available. Support available to part-time students. Financial award applicants required to submit FAFSA.
Carl Adams, Dean, 425-637-1010 Ext. 5392, *Fax:* 425-709-5363, *E-mail:* ksmith@cityu.edu.
Application contact: 800-426-5596, *Fax:* 425-709-5363, *E-mail:* info@cityu.edu. *Web site:* http://www.cityu.edu/

■ CLAREMONT GRADUATE UNIVERSITY

Graduate Programs, School of Politics and Economics, Department of Economics, Claremont, CA 91711-6160

AWARDS Business and financial economics (MA, PhD); economics (PhD); international economic policy and management (MA, PhD); political economy and public policy (MA, PhD). Part-time programs available.

Faculty: 5 full-time (0 women), 2 part-time/adjunct (0 women).
Students: 64 full-time (18 women), 21 part-time (7 women); includes 6 minority (1 African American, 1 Asian American or Pacific Islander, 4 Hispanic Americans), 62 international. Average age 33. In 2001, 11 master's, 8 doctorates awarded.
Degree requirements: For doctorate, 2 foreign languages, thesis/dissertation, comprehensive exam.
Entrance requirements: For master's and doctorate, GRE General Test. *Application deadline:* For fall admission, 2/15 (priority date). Applications are processed on a rolling basis. *Application fee:* $50. Electronic applications accepted.
Expenses: Tuition: Full-time $22,984; part-time $1,000 per unit. Required fees: $160; $80 per semester.
Financial support: Fellowships, research assistantships, teaching assistantships, Federal Work-Study and institutionally sponsored loans available. Support available to part-time students. Financial award application deadline: 2/15; financial award applicants required to submit FAFSA.
Faculty research: International and financial economics, law and economics, regulation, public choice economics.
Thomas Borcherding, Chair, 909-621-8074, *Fax:* 909-621-8545, *E-mail:* thomas.borcherding@cgu.edu.
Application contact: Lynda Marquez, Program Secretary, 909-621-8074, *Fax:* 909-621-8460, *E-mail:* econ@cgu.edu. *Web site:* http://spe.cgu.edu/econ/index.html

Find an in-depth description at www.petersons.com/gradchannel.

■ CLAREMONT GRADUATE UNIVERSITY

Graduate Programs, School of Politics and Economics, Department of Politics and Policy, Claremont, CA 91711-6160

AWARDS International political economy (MAIPE); international studies (MAIS); political science (PhD); politics (MAP); politics, economics, and business (MAPEB); public policy (MAPP). Part-time programs available.

Faculty: 9 full-time (2 women), 2 part-time/adjunct (1 woman).
Students: 158 full-time (62 women), 43 part-time (19 women); includes 42 minority (19 African Americans, 6 Asian Americans or Pacific Islanders, 17 Hispanic Americans), 40 international. Average age 34. In 2001, 25 master's, 9 doctorates awarded. Terminal master's awarded for partial completion of doctoral program.
Degree requirements: For master's, thesis; for doctorate, one foreign language, thesis/dissertation.
Entrance requirements: For master's and doctorate, GRE General Test. *Application deadline:* For fall admission, 2/15 (priority date). Applications are processed on a rolling basis. *Application fee:* $50. Electronic applications accepted.
Expenses: Tuition: Full-time $22,984; part-time $1,000 per unit. Required fees: $160; $80 per semester.
Financial support: Fellowships, research assistantships, teaching assistantships, career-related internships or fieldwork, Federal Work-Study, and institutionally sponsored loans available. Support available to part-time students. Financial award application deadline: 2/15; financial award applicants required to submit FAFSA.
Faculty research: Environmental policy, international debt, global democratization, Third World development, public sector discrimination.
Yi Fens, Chair, 909-621-8171, *Fax:* 909-621-8390, *E-mail:* yi.fens@cgu.edu.
Application contact: Gwen Williams, Program Administrator, 909-621-8179, *Fax:* 909-621-8545, *E-mail:* gwen.williams@cgu.edu. *Web site:* http://spe.cgu.edu/politics/index.html

Find an in-depth description at www.petersons.com/gradchannel.

■ CLARK ATLANTA UNIVERSITY

School of Arts and Sciences, Department of Public Administration, Atlanta, GA 30314

AWARDS MPA. Part-time programs available.

Degree requirements: For master's, one foreign language, thesis.
Entrance requirements: For master's, GRE General Test, minimum GPA of 2.5.
Faculty research: Nutrition education, Africa.

■ CLARK UNIVERSITY

Graduate School, College of Professional and Continuing Education, Program in Public Service/Public Administration, Worcester, MA 01610-1477

AWARDS Public administration (MPA, Certificate). Part-time and evening/weekend programs available.

Students: 4 full-time (3 women), 14 part-time (7 women); includes 2 minority (both Asian Americans or Pacific Islanders). Average age 33. 12 applicants, 100% accepted, 2 enrolled. In 2001, 22 degrees awarded.
Degree requirements: For master's, thesis or alternative.
Entrance requirements: For master's, GMAT or GRE General Test. *Application deadline:* For fall admission, 2/15 (priority date). Applications are processed on a rolling basis. *Application fee:* $40.
Expenses: Tuition: Full-time $24,400; part-time $763 per credit. Required fees: $10.
Financial support: Career-related internships or fieldwork available. Support available to part-time students.
Max E. Hess, Director of Graduate Studies, 508-793-7217, *Fax:* 508-793-7232.
Application contact: Julia Parent, Director of Marketing, Communications, and Admissions, 508-793-7217, *Fax:* 508-793-7232, *E-mail:* jparent@clarku.edu. *Web site:* http://copare.clarku.edu/

■ CLEMSON UNIVERSITY

Graduate School, College of Business and Behavioral Science, Department of Political Science, Clemson, SC 29634

AWARDS Public administration (MPA). Part-time and evening/weekend programs available.

Students: 1 (woman) full-time, 16 part-time (7 women); includes 3 minority (all African Americans). 16 applicants, 56% accepted, 7 enrolled. In 2001, 8 degrees awarded.
Degree requirements: For master's, internship.
Entrance requirements: For master's, GRE General Test, MAT, TOEFL. *Application deadline:* For fall admission, 7/1 (priority date); for spring admission, 11/15. Applications are processed on a rolling basis. *Application fee:* $40.
Expenses: Tuition, state resident: full-time $5,310. Tuition, nonresident: full-time $11,284.
Financial support: Research assistantships, career-related internships or fieldwork available. Financial award applicants required to submit FAFSA.
Faculty research: Public policy, total quality management, quantitative methods, public law, public personnel management.
Dr. Martin Slann, Chair, 864-656-3234, *Fax:* 864-656-0690, *E-mail:* kibbutz@clemson.edu.
Application contact: Dr. David Swindell, Graduate Coordinator, 864-656-3149, *Fax:* 864-656-0690, *E-mail:* dswinde@clemson.edu. *Web site:* http://business.clemson.edu/PoliSci/masterpa.htm

■ CLEMSON UNIVERSITY

Graduate School, Interdisciplinary Program in Policy Studies, Clemson, SC 29634

AWARDS PhD, Certificate.

Students: 2 full-time (0 women), 1 part-time. 6 applicants, 17% accepted, 1 enrolled.
Degree requirements: For doctorate, thesis/dissertation.

Entrance requirements: For doctorate, GRE General Test, TOEFL. *Application deadline:* Applications are processed on a rolling basis. *Application fee:* $40. Electronic applications accepted.
Expenses: Tuition, state resident: full-time $5,310. Tuition, nonresident: full-time $11,284.
Bruce W. Ransom, Coordinator, 864-656-1650, *E-mail:* bii@clemson.edu.

■ CLEVELAND STATE UNIVERSITY

College of Graduate Studies, Maxine Goodman Levin College of Urban Affairs, Program in Public Administration, Cleveland, OH 44115

AWARDS MPA, PhD, JD/MPA. Part-time and evening/weekend programs available.

Faculty: 15 full-time (6 women).
Students: 18 full-time (11 women), 84 part-time (55 women); includes 40 minority (37 African Americans, 3 Hispanic Americans), 2 international. Average age 34. 39 applicants, 64% accepted. In 2001, 44 degrees awarded.
Degree requirements: For master's, internship or project, thesis optional; for doctorate, thesis/dissertation, comprehensive exam, comprehensive exam, registration.
Entrance requirements: For master's, GMAT or GRE General Test, minimum GPA of 3.0; for doctorate, GRE, minimum GPA of 3.5. *Application deadline:* For fall admission, 7/15 (priority date). Applications are processed on a rolling basis. *Application fee:* $25.
Expenses: Tuition, state resident: full-time $6,838; part-time $263 per credit hour. Tuition, nonresident: full-time $13,526; part-time $520 per credit hour.
Financial support: Research assistantships, career-related internships or fieldwork, institutionally sponsored loans, and tuition waivers (full and partial) available. Financial award application deadline: 3/1.
Faculty research: Health care, public works, public management, economic development.
Application contact: Graduate Programs Coordinator, 216-523-7522, *Fax:* 216-687-5398, *E-mail:* gradprog@wolf.csuohio.edu.

■ COLLEGE OF CHARLESTON

Graduate School, School of Humanities and Social Sciences, Institute for Public Affairs and Policy Studies, Charleston, SC 29424-0001

AWARDS MPA.

Degree requirements: For master's, internship, oral and written exams, thesis optional.
Entrance requirements: For master's, GRE General Test, TOEFL, previous course work in statistics.
Expenses: Tuition, state resident: part-time $200 per hour. Tuition, nonresident: part-time $455 per hour. Required fees: $2 per hour. $15 per term. One-time fee: $45 part-time.
Faculty research: Local government, environmental policy, budgeting, ethics.
Web site: http://univchas.cofc.edu/

■ THE COLLEGE OF WILLIAM AND MARY

Faculty of Arts and Sciences, Thomas Jefferson Program in Public Policy, Williamsburg, VA 23187-8795

AWARDS MPP, JD/MPP, MBA/MPP, MS/MPP.

Faculty: 1 part-time/adjunct (0 women).
Students: 30 full-time (17 women); includes 3 minority (2 African Americans, 1 Asian American or Pacific Islander), 1 international. Average age 26. 74 applicants, 58% accepted. In 2001, 12 degrees awarded.
Entrance requirements: For master's, GRE General Test. *Application deadline:* For fall admission, 2/15 (priority date). *Application fee:* $30.
Expenses: Tuition, state resident: full-time $3,262; part-time $175 per credit hour. Tuition, nonresident: full-time $14,768; part-time $550 per credit hour. Required fees: $2,478.
Financial support: In 2001–02, 20 research assistantships (averaging $7,117 per year), 10 teaching assistantships (averaging $7,117 per year) were awarded. Career-related internships or fieldwork and Federal Work-Study also available. Financial award application deadline: 2/15; financial award applicants required to submit FAFSA.
Faculty research: Congressional behavior, social policy, administrative law, technology policy, international development. *Total annual research expenditures:* $99,628.
Dr. David Finifter, Director, 757-221-2370.
Application contact: Elaine S. McBeth, Associate Director, 757-221-2386, *Fax:* 757-221-2390, *E-mail:* mcbeth@wm.edu.

Find an in-depth description at www.petersons.com/gradchannel.

■ COLUMBIA UNIVERSITY

School of International and Public Affairs, Program in Public Policy and Administration, New York, NY 10027

AWARDS MPA, JD/MPA, MPA/MS, MPH/MPA. Part-time programs available.

Students: 193 full-time (126 women), 31 part-time (20 women); includes 58 minority (15 African Americans, 28 Asian Americans or Pacific Islanders, 14 Hispanic Americans, 1 Native American), 68 international. Average age 27. 458 applicants, 45% accepted. In 2001, 100 degrees awarded.
Entrance requirements: For master's, GRE General Test (recommended), TOEFL. *Application deadline:* For fall admission, 1/5 (priority date); for spring admission, 10/15 (priority date). *Application fee:* $75. Electronic applications accepted.
Financial support: In 2001–02, 145 students received support, including 82 fellowships with full and partial tuition reimbursements available (averaging $4,000 per year), 8 teaching assistantships with full tuition reimbursements available (averaging $6,000 per year); research assistantships, career-related internships or fieldwork, Federal Work-Study, institutionally sponsored loans, and unspecified assistantships also available. Financial award application deadline: 1/5; financial award applicants required to submit FAFSA.
Chuck Cameron, Professor, 212-854-2167, *Fax:* 212-854-8059, *E-mail:* sipa_admission@columbia.edu.
Application contact: Robert Garris, Associate Director, 212-854-6216, *Fax:* 212-854-3010, *E-mail:* sipa_admission@columbia.edu. *Web site:* http://www.columbia.edu/cu/sipa/

Find an in-depth description at www.petersons.com/gradchannel.

■ COLUMBUS STATE UNIVERSITY

Graduate Studies, College of Arts and Letters, Program in Public Administration, Columbus, GA 31907-5645

AWARDS MPA. Part-time and evening/weekend programs available.

Faculty: 8 full-time (3 women), 6 part-time/adjunct (1 woman).
Students: 65 full-time (31 women), 172 part-time (47 women); includes 64 minority (61 African Americans, 3 Hispanic Americans). Average age 37. 58 applicants, 53% accepted. In 2001, 73 degrees awarded.
Degree requirements: For master's, comprehensive exam.
Entrance requirements: For master's, GRE General Test, GMAT. *Application deadline:* For fall admission, 7/6 (priority date); for spring admission, 12/14. Applications are processed on a rolling basis. *Application fee:* $25.
Expenses: Tuition, state resident: full-time $1,166. Tuition, nonresident: full-time $7,386.
Financial support: In 2001–02, 70 students received support, including 6 research assistantships with partial tuition reimbursements available (averaging $3,000 per year); career-related internships or fieldwork, Federal Work-Study, institutionally sponsored loans, scholarships/grants, tuition waivers (full), and unspecified assistantships also available. Support available to part-time students. Financial award application deadline: 5/1; financial award applicants required to submit FAFSA.

Columbus State University (continued)
Dr. William L. Chappell, Acting Dean, 706-568-2055, *Fax:* 706-569-3123, *E-mail:* chappell_william@colstate.edu.
Application contact: Katie Thornton, Graduate Admissions Specialist, 706-568-2279, *Fax:* 706-568-2462, *E-mail:* thornton_katie@colstate.edu.

■ CONCORDIA UNIVERSITY WISCONSIN

School of Graduate Studies, MBA Program, Mequon, WI 53097-2402

AWARDS Church administration (MBA); finance (MBA); health care administration (MBA); human resource management (MBA); international business (MBA); management (MBA); management information services (MBA); managerial communications (MBA); marketing (MBA); public administration (MBA); risk management (MBA). Postbaccalaureate distance learning degree programs offered (minimal on-campus study).

Degree requirements: For master's, thesis or alternative, comprehensive exam.
Entrance requirements: For master's, TOEFL.
Expenses: Contact institution.

■ CORNELL UNIVERSITY

Graduate School, Graduate Fields of Arts and Sciences, Field of Public Affairs, Ithaca, NY 14853-0001

AWARDS Public affairs (MPA); public policy (MPA).

Faculty: 82 full-time.
Students: 60 full-time (29 women); includes 10 minority (3 African Americans, 4 Asian Americans or Pacific Islanders, 3 Hispanic Americans), 26 international. 148 applicants, 88% accepted. In 2001, 24 degrees awarded.
Degree requirements: For master's, thesis, research project, paper.
Entrance requirements: For master's, GRE General Test, TOEFL, 2 letters of recommendation. *Application deadline:* For fall admission, 3/15; for spring admission, 11/30. *Application fee:* $65. Electronic applications accepted.
Expenses: Tuition: Full-time $25,970. Required fees: $50.
Financial support: In 2001–02, 11 students received support, including 3 fellowships with full tuition reimbursements available, 8 teaching assistantships with full tuition reimbursements available; research assistantships with full tuition reimbursements available, institutionally sponsored loans, scholarships/grants, tuition waivers (full and partial), and unspecified assistantships also available. Financial award applicants required to submit FAFSA.
Application contact: Graduate Field Assistant, 607-255-8018, *Fax:* 607-255-5240, *E-mail:* cipa@cornell.edu. *Web site:* http://www.gradschool.cornell.edu/grad/fields_1/public-aff.html

Find an in-depth description at www.petersons.com/gradchannel.

■ CORNELL UNIVERSITY

Graduate School, Graduate Fields of Human Ecology, Field of Policy Analysis and Management, Ithaca, NY 14853-0001

AWARDS Consumer policy evaluation (PhD); family and social welfare policy (PhD); health administration (MHA); health management policy (PhD).

Faculty: 33 full-time.
Students: 52 full-time (36 women); includes 19 minority (9 African Americans, 7 Asian Americans or Pacific Islanders, 3 Hispanic Americans), 12 international. 88 applicants, 52% accepted.
Degree requirements: For master's, thesis.
Entrance requirements: For doctorate, GRE General Test, 2 letters of recommendation. *Application deadline:* For fall admission, 2/1. *Application fee:* $65. Electronic applications accepted.
Expenses: Tuition: Full-time $25,970. Required fees: $50.
Financial support: In 2001–02, 31 students received support, including 13 fellowships with full and partial tuition reimbursements available, 3 research assistantships with full and partial tuition reimbursements available, 15 teaching assistantships with full and partial tuition reimbursements available; institutionally sponsored loans, scholarships/grants, tuition waivers (full and partial), and unspecified assistantships also available. Financial award applicants required to submit FAFSA.
Faculty research: Health policy analysis and management, family and social welfare policy analysis and management, policy planning and evaluation, mixed methods research, applied research methods.
Application contact: Graduate Field Assistant, 607-255-7772, *Fax:* 607-255-4071, *E-mail:* PhDprogram-pam_phd@cornell.edu. *Web site:* http://www.gradschool.cornell.edu/grad/fields_1/pam.html

■ CUMBERLAND UNIVERSITY

Division of Graduate Studies, Program in Public Service Administration, Lebanon, TN 37087-3554

AWARDS MS. Part-time and evening/weekend programs available.

Faculty: 8 part-time/adjunct (2 women).
Students: 1 (woman) full-time, 79 part-time (42 women); includes 45 minority (42 African Americans, 1 Asian American or Pacific Islander, 1 Hispanic American, 1 Native American), 1 international. In 2001, 36 degrees awarded.
Entrance requirements: For master's, GMAT, GRE, or MAT. *Application fee:* $50.
Expenses: Tuition: Part-time $467 per hour. Tuition and fees vary according to program.
Financial support: In 2001–02, 40 students received support. Career-related internships or fieldwork, institutionally sponsored loans, and scholarships/grants available. Support available to part-time students. Financial award application deadline: 8/1; financial award applicants required to submit FAFSA.
Dr. C. William McKee, Executive Vice President and Undergraduate Dean, 615-444-2562 Ext. 1111, *Fax:* 615-444-2569.
Application contact: Edward Freytag, Director of Admissions, 615-444-2562 Ext. 1120, *Fax:* 615-444-2569, *E-mail:* efreytag@cumberland.edu.

■ DEPAUL UNIVERSITY

College of Liberal Arts and Sciences, Programs in Public Services, Program in International Public Service Management, Chicago, IL 60604-2287

AWARDS MA/MS.

Faculty: 11 full-time (5 women), 18 part-time/adjunct (9 women).
Students: 4 full-time (3 women), 5 part-time (3 women); includes 4 minority (1 African American, 2 Asian Americans or Pacific Islanders, 1 Hispanic American), 1 international. 4 applicants, 100% accepted.
Degree requirements: One foreign language.
Application deadline: For fall admission, 7/1 (priority date); for winter admission, 10/1 (priority date); for spring admission, 2/1 (priority date). Applications are processed on a rolling basis. *Application fee:* $25. Electronic applications accepted.
Expenses: Tuition: Part-time $362 per credit hour. Tuition and fees vary according to program.
Financial support: In 2001–02, 2 research assistantships (averaging $6,000 per year) were awarded; career-related internships or fieldwork, Federal Work-Study, and scholarships/grants also available. Support available to part-time students. Financial award application deadline: 7/1.
Faculty research: Government financing, transportation, leadership, health care, empowerment zones. *Total annual research expenditures:* $20,000.
Dr. J. Patrick Murphy, Director, 312-362-8441, *Fax:* 312-362-5506, *E-mail:* jpmurphy@depaul.edu.
Application contact: 312-362-8441, *Fax:* 312-362-5506, *E-mail:* pubserv@depaul.edu. *Web site:* http://www.depaul.edu/~pubserv/

■ DEPAUL UNIVERSITY

College of Liberal Arts and Sciences, Programs in Public Services, Program in Public Service Management, Chicago, IL 60604-2287

AWARDS Association management (MS); fundraising and philanthropy (MS); healthcare administration (MS); higher education administration (MS); metropolitan planning (MS); non-profit administration (MS); public administration (MS); public policy (MS). Part-time and evening/weekend programs available.

Faculty: 10 full-time (5 women), 13 part-time/adjunct (9 women).
Students: 43 full-time (24 women), 133 part-time (88 women); includes 45 minority (32 African Americans, 1 Asian American or Pacific Islander, 12 Hispanic Americans), 2 international. 74 applicants, 95% accepted. In 2001, 44 degrees awarded.
Degree requirements: For master's, thesis, thesis or practicum.
Entrance requirements: For master's, TOEFL, minimum GPA of 2.7 in field. *Application deadline:* For fall admission, 7/1 (priority date); for winter admission, 10/1 (priority date); for spring admission, 2/1 (priority date). Applications are processed on a rolling basis. *Application fee:* $25. Electronic applications accepted.
Expenses: Tuition: Part-time $362 per credit hour. Tuition and fees vary according to program.
Financial support: In 2001–02, research assistantships with full tuition reimbursements (averaging $5,000 per year). Financial award application deadline: 7/1.
Faculty research: Government financing transportation, leadership, health care, dating violence, volunteerism. *Total annual research expenditures:* $91,000.
Dr. J. Patrick Murphy, Head, *E-mail:* jmurphy@depaul.edu.
Application contact: Graduate Information, 312-362-8441, *Fax:* 312-362-5506. *Web site:* http://www.depaul.edu/~pubserv

■ DRAKE UNIVERSITY

College of Business and Public Administration, Des Moines, IA 50311-4516

AWARDS M Acc, MBA, MPA, JD/MBA, JD/MPA, Pharm D/MBA, Pharm D/MPA. Part-time and evening/weekend programs available.

Faculty: 21 full-time (5 women), 3 part-time/adjunct (0 women).
Students: 101 full-time, 364 part-time. Average age 29. 119 applicants, 94% accepted, 99 enrolled. In 2001, 202 degrees awarded.
Entrance requirements: For master's, GMAT. *Application deadline:* For fall admission, 7/15 (priority date); for winter admission, 12/20 (priority date); for spring admission, 12/1 (priority date). Applications are processed on a rolling basis. *Application fee:* $25. Electronic applications accepted.
Expenses: Tuition: Full-time $17,830. Required fees: $220. Full-time tuition and fees vary according to class time and program.
Financial support: In 2001–02, 1 student received support. Career-related internships or fieldwork and institutionally sponsored loans available. Support available to part-time students. Financial award application deadline: 3/1; financial award applicants required to submit FAFSA.
Faculty research: Measuring partnership interest, ethics in insurance industry, security credit regulation, management-personnel evaluation systems, e-commerce.
Dr. Antone F. Alber, Dean, College of Business and Public Administration, 515-271-2871, *Fax:* 515-271-4518, *E-mail:* joe.alber@drake.edu.
Application contact: Danette Kenne, Director of Graduate Programs, 515-271-2188, *Fax:* 515-271-4518, *E-mail:* cbpa.gradprograms@drake.edu. *Web site:* http://www.drake.edu/cbpa/grad/

■ DUKE UNIVERSITY

Graduate School, Terry Sanford Institute of Public Policy, Durham, NC 27708-0586

AWARDS MPP, JD/AM, JD/MPP, MBA/AM, MBA/MPP, MD/AM, MEM/MPP, MF/MPP.

Faculty: 35 full-time, 10 part-time/adjunct.
Students: 75 full-time (40 women); includes 11 minority (5 African Americans, 4 Asian Americans or Pacific Islanders, 1 Hispanic American, 1 Native American), 8 international. 209 applicants, 65% accepted, 40 enrolled. In 2001, 22 degrees awarded.
Entrance requirements: For master's, GRE General Test. *Application deadline:* For fall admission, 12/31 (priority date). *Application fee:* $75.
Expenses: Tuition: Full-time $24,600.
Financial support: Fellowships, research assistantships, teaching assistantships, career-related internships or fieldwork and Federal Work-Study available. Financial award application deadline: 12/31.
Bruce W. Jentleson, Director, 919-613-7325, *Fax:* 919-681-8288, *E-mail:* mpp@pps.duke.edu. *Web site:* http://www.pubpol.duke.edu/

Find an in-depth description at www.petersons.com/gradchannel.

■ DUQUESNE UNIVERSITY

Graduate School of Liberal Arts, Graduate Center for Social and Public Policy, Pittsburgh, PA 15282-1750

AWARDS Conflict resolution and peace studies (Certificate); social and public policy (MA). Programs are a collaboration between the Departments of Political Science and Sociology. Part-time and evening/weekend programs available.

Faculty: 15 full-time (3 women), 1 (woman) part-time/adjunct.
Students: 35 full-time (16 women), 17 part-time (6 women); includes 2 minority (1 African American, 1 Hispanic American), 26 international. Average age 31. 52 applicants, 58% accepted, 18 enrolled. In 2001, 13 degrees awarded.
Degree requirements: For master's, thesis.
Entrance requirements: For master's, GRE General Test, TOEFL. *Application deadline:* For fall admission, 4/30 (priority date); for spring admission, 10/31 (priority date). Applications are processed on a rolling basis. *Application fee:* $50.
Expenses: Tuition: Part-time $566 per credit. Required fees: $56 per credit. Part-time tuition and fees vary according to degree level and program.
Financial support: In 2001–02, 20 students received support, including 12 research assistantships with full and partial tuition reimbursements available (averaging $9,000 per year), 4 teaching assistantships with full and partial tuition reimbursements available (averaging $9,000 per year); career-related internships or fieldwork, institutionally sponsored loans, scholarships/grants, and tuition waivers (full and partial) also available. Support available to part-time students. Financial award application deadline: 5/1.
Faculty research: Program evaluation, environmental policy, criminal justice policy, health care policy. *Total annual research expenditures:* $30,000.
Dr. Michael Irwin, Head, 412-396-6488, *Fax:* 412-396-5197, *E-mail:* socialpolicy@duq.edu. *Web site:* http://www.liberalarts.duq.edu/sociology/

■ EAST CAROLINA UNIVERSITY

Graduate School, College of Arts and Sciences, Department of Political Science, Greenville, NC 27858-4353

AWARDS Public administration (MPA). Part-time and evening/weekend programs available.

Faculty: 4 full-time (1 woman).
Students: 16 full-time (9 women), 30 part-time (14 women); includes 8 minority (7 African Americans, 1 Hispanic American), 3 international. Average age 31. 22 applicants, 68% accepted. In 2001, 12 degrees awarded.
Degree requirements: For master's, one foreign language, comprehensive exam.
Entrance requirements: For master's, GRE General Test, TOEFL. *Application deadline:* For fall admission, 6/1 (priority date); for spring admission, 10/15. Applications are processed on a rolling basis. *Application fee:* $45.
Expenses: Tuition, state resident: full-time $2,636. Tuition, nonresident: full-time $11,365.

East Carolina University (continued)
Financial support: Research assistantships with partial tuition reimbursements, teaching assistantships with partial tuition reimbursements, Federal Work-Study available. Support available to part-time students. Financial award application deadline: 6/1.
Dr. Carmine Scavo, Director of Graduate Studies, 252-328-6030, *Fax:* 252-328-4134, *E-mail:* scavo@mail.ecu.edu.
Application contact: Dr. Paul D. Tschetter, Senior Associate Dean of the Graduate School, 252-328-6012, *Fax:* 252-328-6071, *E-mail:* gradschool@mail.ecu.edu.

■ EASTERN KENTUCKY UNIVERSITY

The Graduate School, College of Arts and Sciences, Department of Government, Program in General Public Administration, Richmond, KY 40475-3102

AWARDS Community development (MPA); community health administration (MPA); general public administration (MPA).

Students: 33.
Entrance requirements: For master's, GRE General Test, minimum GPA of 2.5. *Application fee:* $0.
Expenses: Tuition, state resident: full-time $1,468; part-time $165 per credit hour. Tuition, nonresident: full-time $4,034; part-time $450 per credit hour.
Dr. Richard Vance, Chair, Department of Government, 859-622-5931.

■ EASTERN MICHIGAN UNIVERSITY

Graduate School, College of Arts and Sciences, Department of Political Science, Program in Public Administration, Ypsilanti, MI 48197

AWARDS MPA. Evening/weekend programs available.

Entrance requirements: For master's, TOEFL. *Application deadline:* For fall admission, 5/15; for spring admission, 3/15. Applications are processed on a rolling basis. *Application fee:* $30.
Expenses: Tuition, state resident: part-time $285 per credit hour. Tuition, nonresident: part-time $510 per credit hour.
Financial support: Fellowships, teaching assistantships available. Support available to part-time students. Financial award application deadline: 3/15; financial award applicants required to submit FAFSA.
Dr. Karen Lindenberg, MPA Coordinator, 734-487-2522.

■ EASTERN WASHINGTON UNIVERSITY

Graduate School Studies, College of Business Administration and Public Administration, Program in Public Administration, Cheney, WA 99004-2431

AWARDS MPA, MBA/MPA, MPA/MSW, MPA/MURP. Part-time and evening/weekend programs available.

Faculty: 7 full-time (1 woman).
Students: 19 full-time (10 women), 32 part-time (19 women); includes 5 minority (4 Hispanic Americans, 1 Native American), 1 international. 26 applicants, 69% accepted, 10 enrolled. In 2001, 21 degrees awarded.
Degree requirements: For master's, thesis optional.
Entrance requirements: For master's, minimum GPA of 3.0. *Application deadline:* For fall admission, 4/1 (priority date); for spring admission, 1/15. Applications are processed on a rolling basis. *Application fee:* $35.
Expenses: Tuition, state resident: full-time $1,586; part-time $159 per credit hour. Tuition, nonresident: full-time $4,677; part-time $468 per credit hour. Required fees: $222; $159 per credit. $74 per quarter.
Financial support: In 2001–02, teaching assistantships with partial tuition reimbursements (averaging $7,000 per year); career-related internships or fieldwork, Federal Work-Study, institutionally sponsored loans, scholarships/grants, health care benefits, tuition waivers (partial), and unspecified assistantships also available. Support available to part-time students. Financial award application deadline: 2/1; financial award applicants required to submit FAFSA.
Dr. Larry Luton, Director, 509-358-2248, *Fax:* 509-358-2267, *E-mail:* lluton@mail.ewu.edu.

■ THE EVERGREEN STATE COLLEGE

Graduate Programs, Program in Public Administration, Olympia, WA 98505

AWARDS MPA. Part-time and evening/weekend programs available.

Degree requirements: For master's, thesis.
Entrance requirements: For master's, previous course work in microeconomics, macroeconomics, and statistics; minimum undergraduate GPA of 3.0.
Expenses: Tuition, state resident: full-time $4,848; part-time $161 per credit. Tuition, nonresident: full-time $14,769; part-time $492 per credit. Tuition and fees vary according to course load.
Faculty research: Applied policy analysis, public administration theory, gender and race in public administration; democratic governance, administration in Native American communities, emerging models of international administration. *Web site:* http://www.evergreen.edu/mpa/
Find an in-depth description at www.petersons.com/gradchannel.

■ FAIRLEIGH DICKINSON UNIVERSITY, METROPOLITAN CAMPUS

New College of General and Continuing Studies, Public Administration Institute, Program in Administrative Science, Teaneck, NJ 07666-1914

AWARDS MAS.

Students: 20 full-time (12 women), 280 part-time (133 women); includes 19 minority (11 African Americans, 2 Asian Americans or Pacific Islanders, 5 Hispanic Americans, 1 Native American), 12 international. Average age 39. 149 applicants, 100% accepted, 86 enrolled. In 2001, 96 degrees awarded.
Application deadline: Applications are processed on a rolling basis. *Application fee:* $40.
Expenses: Tuition: Full-time $11,484; part-time $638 per credit. Required fees: $420; $97.
Dr. William Roberts, Director, Public Administration Institute, 201-692-7171, *Fax:* 201-692-7179, *E-mail:* wroberts@fdu.edu.

■ FAIRLEIGH DICKINSON UNIVERSITY, METROPOLITAN CAMPUS

New College of General and Continuing Studies, Public Administration Institute, Program in Public Administration, Teaneck, NJ 07666-1914

AWARDS MPA.

Students: 14 full-time (11 women), 50 part-time (26 women); includes 19 minority (12 African Americans, 4 Asian Americans or Pacific Islanders, 3 Hispanic Americans), 4 international. Average age 37. 55 applicants, 93% accepted, 12 enrolled. In 2001, 13 degrees awarded.
Application deadline: Applications are processed on a rolling basis. *Application fee:* $40.
Expenses: Tuition: Full-time $11,484; part-time $638 per credit. Required fees: $420; $97.

■ FLORIDA ATLANTIC UNIVERSITY

College of Architecture, Urban and Public Affairs, School of Public Administration, Boca Raton, FL 33431-0991

AWARDS MNM, MPA, PhD. Part-time and evening/weekend programs available.

Faculty: 13 full-time (4 women), 14 part-time/adjunct (4 women).
Students: 28 full-time (6 women), 93 part-time (44 women); includes 33 minority (21 African Americans, 3 Asian Americans or Pacific Islanders, 8 Hispanic Americans, 1 Native American), 6 international. Average age 37. 62 applicants, 61% accepted, 35 enrolled. In 2001, 38 master's, 6 doctorates awarded.
Degree requirements: For master's, thesis optional; for doctorate, thesis/dissertation, comprehensive exam.
Entrance requirements: For master's, GRE General Test, TOEFL, minimum GPA of 3.0; for doctorate, GRE General Test, TOEFL, minimum GPA of 3.5. *Application deadline:* For fall admission, 4/1 (priority date); for spring admission, 11/1. Applications are processed on a rolling basis. *Application fee:* $20.
Expenses: Tuition, state resident: full-time $3,098; part-time $172 per credit. Tuition, nonresident: full-time $10,427; part-time $579 per credit.
Financial support: In 2001–02, 17 students received support, including 4 fellowships with full tuition reimbursements available (averaging $16,000 per year), 3 research assistantships with partial tuition reimbursements available (averaging $7,500 per year), 10 teaching assistantships with partial tuition reimbursements available (averaging $12,000 per year); career-related internships or fieldwork, Federal Work-Study, institutionally sponsored loans, and tuition waivers (partial) also available. Support available to part-time students. Financial award application deadline: 4/1.
Faculty research: Environmental growth management, public policy, aging, public finance and budgeting, public management.
Dr. Hugh T. Miller, Director, 954-762-5650, *Fax:* 954-762-5693, *E-mail:* hmiller@fau.edu.
Application contact: Anna G. Plotkin, Academic Adviser, 954-762-5662, *E-mail:* aplotkin@fau.edu. *Web site:* http://www.fau.edu/spa/

■ FLORIDA GULF COAST UNIVERSITY

College of Public and Social Services, Program in Public Administration, Fort Myers, FL 33965-6565

AWARDS Criminal justice (MPA); environmental policy (MPA); general public administration (MPA); management (MPA).

Faculty: 16 full-time (9 women), 7 part-time/adjunct (1 woman).
Students: 7 full-time (4 women), 58 part-time (31 women); includes 5 minority (2 African Americans, 2 Hispanic Americans, 1 Native American), 1 international. Average age 38. 18 applicants, 83% accepted, 10 enrolled. In 2001, 18 degrees awarded.
Entrance requirements: For master's, GRE General Test, MAT, minimum GPA of 3.0. *Application deadline:* Applications are processed on a rolling basis. *Application fee:* $20. Electronic applications accepted.
Expenses: Tuition, state resident: part-time $164 per credit hour. Tuition, nonresident: part-time $571 per credit hour. Required fees: $36 per semester.
Financial support: In 2001–02, 5 research assistantships were awarded; career-related internships or fieldwork and tuition waivers (full and partial) also available. Support available to part-time students.
Faculty research: Personnel, public policy, public finance. *Total annual research expenditures:* $45,500.
Roberta Walsh, Chair, 239-590-7841, *Fax:* 239-590-7846, *E-mail:* rwalsh@fgcu.edu.
Application contact: Roger Green, Information Contact, 239-590-7838, *Fax:* 239-590-7846.

■ FLORIDA INSTITUTE OF TECHNOLOGY

Graduate Programs, School of Extended Graduate Studies, Melbourne, FL 32901-6975

AWARDS Acquisition and contract management (MS, MSM, PMBA); aerospace engineering (MS); business administration (PMBA); computer information systems (MS); computer science (MS); ebusiness (MSM); electrical engineering (MS); engineering management (MS); health management (MS); human resource management (MSM, PMBA); human resources management (MS); information systems (MSM, PMBA); logistics management (MS, MSM); management (MS); material acquisition management (MS); mechanical engineering (MS); operations research (MS); project management (MS), including information systems, operations research; public administration (MPA); software engineering (MS); space systems (MS); space systems management (MS); systems management (MS), including information systems, operations research; transportation management (MSM). Part-time and evening/weekend programs available. Postbaccalaureate distance learning degree programs offered (no on-campus study).

Faculty: 10 full-time (2 women), 131 part-time/adjunct (15 women).
Students: 57 full-time (29 women), 1,198 part-time (455 women); includes 277 minority (183 African Americans, 38 Asian Americans or Pacific Islanders, 51 Hispanic Americans, 5 Native Americans), 16 international. Average age 37. 299 applicants, 42% accepted. In 2001, 434 degrees awarded.
Entrance requirements: For master's, minimum GPA of 3.0. *Application deadline:* Applications are processed on a rolling basis. *Application fee:* $50. Electronic applications accepted.
Expenses: Tuition: Part-time $650 per credit.
Financial support: Institutionally sponsored loans available. Financial award application deadline: 3/1; financial award applicants required to submit FAFSA.
Dr. Ronald L. Marshall, Dean, School of Extended Graduate Studies, 321-674-8880.
Application contact: Carolyn P. Farrior, Director of Graduate Admissions, 321-674-7118, *Fax:* 321-723-9468, *E-mail:* cfarrior@fit.edu. *Web site:* http://www.segs.fit.edu/

■ FLORIDA INTERNATIONAL UNIVERSITY

College of Health and Urban Affairs, School of Policy and Management, Department of Public Administration, Miami, FL 33199

AWARDS MPA, PhD. Part-time and evening/weekend programs available.

Faculty: 7 full-time (0 women).
Students: 30 full-time (18 women), 71 part-time (43 women); includes 75 minority (38 African Americans, 2 Asian Americans or Pacific Islanders, 35 Hispanic Americans), 1 international. Average age 35. 73 applicants, 48% accepted, 17 enrolled. In 2001, 43 master's, 1 doctorate awarded.
Degree requirements: For doctorate, thesis/dissertation, comprehensive exam.
Entrance requirements: For master's, GRE General Test, TOEFL, minimum GPA of 3.0; for doctorate, GRE General Test, TOEFL. *Application deadline:* For fall admission, 4/1 (priority date); for spring admission, 10/1. Applications are processed on a rolling basis. *Application fee:* $20.
Expenses: Tuition, state resident: full-time $2,916; part-time $162 per credit hour. Tuition, nonresident: full-time $10,245; part-time $569 per credit hour. Required fees: $168 per term.
Financial support: In 2001–02, 2 fellowships were awarded; career-related internships or fieldwork, Federal Work-Study, and institutionally sponsored loans also available.
Dr. Terry Buss, Director, School of Policy and Management, 305-348-2653, *Fax:* 305-348-5848, *E-mail:* busst@fiu.edu.

■ FLORIDA STATE UNIVERSITY

Graduate Studies, College of Social Sciences, Ruebin O'D. Askew School of Public Administration and Policy, Tallahassee, FL 32306

AWARDS MPA, PhD, Certificate, JD/MPA, MPA/MS, MPA/MSC, MPA/MSP, MPA/MSW. Part-time and evening/weekend programs available.

Faculty: 13 full-time (4 women), 9 part-time/adjunct (2 women).
Students: 34 full-time (19 women), 78 part-time (41 women); includes 31 minority (24 African Americans, 7 Hispanic Americans), 19 international. Average age 28. 194 applicants, 33% accepted. In 2001, 32 master's, 3 doctorates awarded.

Florida State University (continued)
Degree requirements: For master's, action report; for doctorate, thesis/dissertation. *Median time to degree:* Master's–1.5 years full-time; doctorate–3.5 years full-time.
Entrance requirements: For master's, GRE General Test or minimum GPA of 3.0; for doctorate, GRE General Test, minimum undergraduate GPA of 3.0, graduate GPA of 3.5. *Application deadline:* For fall admission, 7/14; for spring admission, 11/17. Applications are processed on a rolling basis. *Application fee:* $20. Electronic applications accepted.
Expenses: Tuition, state resident: part-time $163 per credit hour. Tuition, nonresident: part-time $570 per credit hour. Tuition and fees vary according to program.
Financial support: In 2001–02, 20 students received support, including 1 fellowship with full tuition reimbursement available (averaging $15,000 per year), 13 research assistantships with full tuition reimbursements available (averaging $10,000 per year), 6 teaching assistantships with full tuition reimbursements available (averaging $9,000 per year); career-related internships or fieldwork, Federal Work-Study, institutionally sponsored loans, scholarships/grants, and unspecified assistantships also available. Support available to part-time students. Financial award application deadline: 3/11.
Faculty research: Financial management, human resource management, policy, strategic management, organizations.
Dr. William Earle Klay, Director, 850-644-3525, *Fax:* 850-644-7617, *E-mail:* eklay@garnet.acns.fsu.edu.
Application contact: Dr. Frances S. Berry, MPA Director, 850-644-7603, *Fax:* 850-644-7617, *E-mail:* fberry@garnet.acns.fsu.edu. *Web site:* http://askew.fsu.edu/

■ FRAMINGHAM STATE COLLEGE

Graduate Programs, Program in Public Administration, Framingham, MA 01701-9101

AWARDS MA. Part-time and evening/weekend programs available.

Faculty: 2 full-time, 3 part-time/adjunct.
Students: 38 (all women). In 2001, 17 degrees awarded.
Dr. George Jarnis, Chairman, 508-626-4824 Ext. 376.
Application contact: 508-626-4550.

■ GANNON UNIVERSITY

School of Graduate Studies, College of Humanities, Business, and Education, School of Humanities, Program in Public Administration, Erie, PA 16541-0001

AWARDS MPA, Certificate. Part-time and evening/weekend programs available.

Degree requirements: For master's, thesis, internship, comprehensive exam.
Entrance requirements: For master's, GMAT, TOEFL. *Web site:* http://www.gannon.edu/

■ GEORGE MASON UNIVERSITY

College of Arts and Sciences, Department of Public and International Affairs, Fairfax, VA 22030-4444

AWARDS Public administration (MPA).

Faculty: 37 full-time (11 women), 29 part-time/adjunct (10 women).
Students: 40 full-time (28 women), 199 part-time (117 women); includes 51 minority (34 African Americans, 8 Asian Americans or Pacific Islanders, 8 Hispanic Americans, 1 Native American), 3 international. Average age 34. 193 applicants, 76% accepted, 88 enrolled. In 2001, 70 degrees awarded.
Entrance requirements: For master's, GRE General Test, minimum GPA of 3.0 in last 60 hours. *Application deadline:* For fall admission, 5/1; for spring admission, 11/1. *Application fee:* $30. Electronic applications accepted.
Expenses: Tuition, state resident: full-time $3,168; part-time $132 per credit hour. Tuition, nonresident: full-time $11,280; part-time $470 per credit hour. Required fees: $1,416; $59 per credit hour.
Financial support: Fellowships, research assistantships, teaching assistantships available. Support available to part-time students. Financial award application deadline: 3/1; financial award applicants required to submit FAFSA.
Dr. Scott Keeter, Chair, 703-993-1400, *Fax:* 703-993-1399, *E-mail:* skeeter@gmu.edu.
Application contact: Dr. Lawrence C. Walters, Information Contact, 703-993-1411, *E-mail:* mpa@gmu.edu. *Web site:* http://www.gmu.edu/departments/mpa/

■ GEORGE MASON UNIVERSITY

School of Public Policy, Program in Public Policy, Fairfax, VA 22030-4444

AWARDS MSNPS, PhD. Terminal master's awarded for partial completion of doctoral program.

Degree requirements: For master's, thesis or alternative; for doctorate, thesis/dissertation, comprehensive exam.
Entrance requirements: For master's, minimum GPA of 3.0 in last 60 hours; for doctorate, GMAT or GRE General Test, minimum GPA of 3.0 in last 60 hours, resumé, sample of written work.
Expenses: Tuition, state resident: full-time $3,168; part-time $132 per credit hour. Tuition, nonresident: full-time $11,280; part-time $470 per credit hour. Required fees: $1,416; $59 per credit hour. *Web site:* http://www.gmu.edu/departments/tipp

Find an in-depth description at www.petersons.com/gradchannel.

■ GEORGETOWN UNIVERSITY

Graduate School of Arts and Sciences, The Georgetown Public Policy Institute, Washington, DC 20057

AWARDS MPP, MBA/MPP.

Entrance requirements: For master's, GRE General Test, TOEFL, minimum B average.
Faculty research: Social policy, government, private sector.

Find an in-depth description at www.petersons.com/gradchannel.

■ THE GEORGE WASHINGTON UNIVERSITY

Columbian College of Arts and Sciences, Department of Women's Studies, Washington, DC 20052

AWARDS Public policy (MA, PhD); women's studies (MA). Part-time and evening/weekend programs available.

Faculty: 8 full-time (all women), 2 part-time/adjunct (both women).
Students: 12 full-time (all women), 11 part-time (all women); includes 2 minority (1 Asian American or Pacific Islander, 1 Hispanic American), 2 international. Average age 25. 38 applicants, 97% accepted. In 2001, 13 degrees awarded.
Degree requirements: For master's, thesis or alternative, comprehensive exam.
Entrance requirements: For master's, GRE General Test, minimum GPA of 3.0. *Application deadline:* For fall admission, 5/1; for spring admission, 10/1. *Application fee:* $55.
Expenses: Tuition: Part-time $810 per credit. Required fees: $1 per credit.
Financial support: In 2001–02, 2 fellowships with tuition reimbursements (averaging $5,000 per year), 2 teaching assistantships with tuition reimbursements (averaging $4,400 per year) were awarded. Federal Work-Study and institutionally sponsored loans also available. Financial award application deadline: 2/1.
Dr. Diane Bell, Director, 202-994-6942. *Web site:* http://www.gwu.edu/~gradinfo/

■ THE GEORGE WASHINGTON UNIVERSITY

Columbian College of Arts and Sciences, Interdisciplinary Programs in Public Policy, Program in History and Public Policy, Washington, DC 20052

AWARDS MA.

Students: 2 full-time (both women). Average age 24. 3 applicants, 67% accepted. In 2001, 2 degrees awarded.
Degree requirements: For master's, comprehensive exam.
Entrance requirements: For master's, GRE General Test, minimum GPA of 3.0. *Application fee:* $55.

Expenses: Tuition: Part-time $810 per credit. Required fees: $1 per credit.
Financial support: Application deadline: 2/1.
Dr. Ronald Spector, Chair, 202-994-6230. *Web site:* http://www.gwu.edu/~gradinfo/

■ THE GEORGE WASHINGTON UNIVERSITY

Columbian College of Arts and Sciences, Interdisciplinary Programs in Public Policy, Program in Public Policy, Washington, DC 20052

AWARDS MPP, PhD.

Faculty: 1 part-time/adjunct (0 women).
Students: 15 full-time (8 women), 41 part-time (28 women); includes 10 minority (1 African American, 8 Asian Americans or Pacific Islanders, 1 Hispanic American), 8 international. Average age 35. 57 applicants, 58% accepted. In 2001, 6 master's, 2 doctorates awarded.
Degree requirements: For doctorate, thesis/dissertation, general exam.
Entrance requirements: For doctorate, GRE General Test, interview, minimum GPA of 3.0. *Application deadline:* For fall admission, 3/15. *Application fee:* $55.
Expenses: Tuition: Part-time $810 per credit. Required fees: $1 per credit.
Financial support: In 2001–02, 3 students received support; fellowships, Federal Work-Study and institutionally sponsored loans available. Financial award application deadline: 2/1.
Application contact: Information Contact, 202-994-8500. *Web site:* http://www.gwu.edu/~pubpol/masters/

Find an in-depth description at www.petersons.com/gradchannel.

■ THE GEORGE WASHINGTON UNIVERSITY

Columbian College of Arts and Sciences, Interdisciplinary Programs in Public Policy, Program in Public Policy-Women's Studies, Washington, DC 20052

AWARDS MA.

Students: 4 full-time (all women), 3 part-time (all women); includes 1 minority (Hispanic American). Average age 24. 14 applicants, 93% accepted. In 2001, 3 degrees awarded.
Degree requirements: For master's, comprehensive exam.
Entrance requirements: For master's, GRE General Test, minimum GPA of 3.0. *Application fee:* $55.
Expenses: Tuition: Part-time $810 per credit. Required fees: $1 per credit.
Financial support: In 2001–02, 4 students received support, including 2 fellowships, 2 teaching assistantships Financial award application deadline: 2/1.
Dr. Joseph J. Cordes, Director, Interdisciplinary Programs in Public Policy, 202-994-8500. *Web site:* http://www.gwu.edu/~gradinfo/

■ THE GEORGE WASHINGTON UNIVERSITY

School of Business and Public Management, Full Time MBA Program, Department of Public Administration, Washington, DC 20052

AWARDS Budget and public finance (MPA); executive, legislative, and regulatory management (MPA); managing public organizations (MPA); managing state and local governments (MPA); policy analysis and evaluation (MPA); public administration (MBA, MPA, PhD). Part-time programs available.

Faculty: 10 full-time (5 women), 1 part-time/adjunct (0 women).
Students: 60 full-time (33 women), 65 part-time (35 women); includes 15 minority (9 African Americans, 2 Asian Americans or Pacific Islanders, 4 Hispanic Americans), 5 international. Average age 29. 122 applicants, 85% accepted. In 2001, 43 master's, 1 doctorate awarded.
Degree requirements: For doctorate, thesis/dissertation.
Entrance requirements: For master's, GRE General Test, TOEFL; for doctorate, GMAT or GRE, TOEFL. *Application deadline:* For fall admission, 4/1 (priority date); for spring admission, 10/1. Applications are processed on a rolling basis. *Application fee:* $55.
Expenses: Tuition: Part-time $810 per credit. Required fees: $1 per credit.
Financial support: In 2001–02, 9 fellowships (averaging $4,800 per year), 9 teaching assistantships (averaging $4,200 per year) were awarded. Career-related internships or fieldwork, Federal Work-Study, and institutionally sponsored loans also available. Financial award application deadline: 4/1.
Faculty research: Regulatory reform, policy and program evaluation, ethics and public management, managing not-for-profits, policy making in the White House and Congress.
Dr. Kathryn Newcomer, Chair, 202-994-3959, *E-mail:* pubadmin@gwu.edu.
Application contact: David Toomer, Director Enrollment Management, 202-994-6584, *Fax:* 202-994-6382. *Web site:* http://www.gwu.edu/~pad/

Find an in-depth description at www.petersons.com/gradchannel.

■ THE GEORGE WASHINGTON UNIVERSITY

School of Business and Public Management, Full Time MBA Program, Department of Strategic Management and Public Policy, Washington, DC 20052

AWARDS Business economics and public policy (MBA); strategic management and public policy (PhD). Part-time and evening/weekend programs available.

Faculty: 1 full-time (0 women).
Students: 5 full-time (3 women), 3 part-time; includes 1 minority (Asian American or Pacific Islander). Average age 29. 23 applicants, 39% accepted. In 2001, 9 degrees awarded.
Degree requirements: For doctorate, thesis/dissertation.
Entrance requirements: For master's, GMAT, TOEFL; for doctorate, GMAT or GRE, TOEFL. *Application deadline:* For fall admission, 4/1 (priority date); for spring admission, 10/1. Applications are processed on a rolling basis. *Application fee:* $55.
Expenses: Tuition: Part-time $810 per credit. Required fees: $1 per credit.
Financial support: Fellowships, teaching assistantships, career-related internships or fieldwork, Federal Work-Study, and institutionally sponsored loans available. Financial award application deadline: 4/1.
Dr. James Thurman, Chair, 202-994-6677.
Application contact: David Toomer, Director Enrollment Management, 202-994-6584, *Fax:* 202-994-6382. *Web site:* http://www.gwu.edu/~gradinfo/

■ GEORGIA COLLEGE & STATE UNIVERSITY

Graduate School, College of Arts and Sciences, Department of Government and Sociology, Program in Public Administration and Public Affairs, Milledgeville, GA 31061

AWARDS Public administration (MPA); public affairs (MS). Part-time and evening/weekend programs available.

Students: 18 full-time (9 women), 69 part-time (46 women); includes 37 minority (36 African Americans, 1 Asian American or Pacific Islander). Average age 34. In 2001, 46 degrees awarded.
Degree requirements: For master's, thesis optional.
Entrance requirements: For master's, GRE. *Application deadline:* For fall admission, 7/15 (priority date). Applications are processed on a rolling basis. *Application fee:* $25. Electronic applications accepted.
Expenses: Tuition, state resident: full-time $2,286. Tuition, nonresident: full-time $9,108. Required fees: $500.
Financial support: Career-related internships or fieldwork, Federal Work-Study, and unspecified assistantships available. Support available to part-time students. Financial award application deadline: 3/1; financial award applicants required to submit FAFSA.
Dr. Chris Grant, Coordinator of MPA Program, 478-445-1211.

■ GEORGIA INSTITUTE OF TECHNOLOGY

Graduate Studies and Research, Ivan Allen College of Policy and International Affairs, School of Public Policy, Atlanta, GA 30332-0001

AWARDS MS Pub P, PhD. Part-time programs available.

Degree requirements: For master's, professional paper or thesis.
Entrance requirements: For master's and doctorate, TOEFL. Electronic applications accepted.
Faculty research: National/regional science and technology policy, environmental policy, urban policy and planning, telecommunications policy.

Find an in-depth description at www.petersons.com/gradchannel.

■ GEORGIA SOUTHERN UNIVERSITY

Jack N. Averitt College of Graduate Studies, College of Liberal Arts and Social Sciences, Department of Political Science, Program in Public Administration, Statesboro, GA 30460

AWARDS MPA. Part-time programs available.

Students: 14 full-time (10 women), 37 part-time (21 women); includes 23 minority (21 African Americans, 1 Asian American or Pacific Islander, 1 Native American). Average age 33. 15 applicants, 93% accepted, 12 enrolled. In 2001, 24 degrees awarded.
Degree requirements: For master's, internship, terminal exam.
Entrance requirements: For master's, GRE General Test, minimum GPA of 2.5, resumé, undergraduate major appropriate to field. *Application deadline:* For fall admission, 7/1 (priority date); for spring admission, 11/15 (priority date). Applications are processed on a rolling basis. *Application fee:* $0. Electronic applications accepted.
Expenses: Tuition, state resident: full-time $1,746; part-time $97 per credit hour. Tuition, nonresident: full-time $6,966; part-time $387 per credit hour. Required fees: $294 per semester.
Financial support: In 2001–02, 24 students received support, including 6 research assistantships with partial tuition reimbursements available (averaging $4,900 per year); career-related internships or fieldwork and Federal Work-Study also available. Support available to part-time students. Financial award application deadline: 4/15; financial award applicants required to submit FAFSA.
Faculty research: Comparative public administration, equal employment policies, gangs, environmental policy, AIDS policy.
Application contact: Dr. John R. Diebolt, Associate Graduate Dean, 912-681-5384, *Fax:* 912-681-0740, *E-mail:* gradschool@gasou.edu.

■ GEORGIA STATE UNIVERSITY

Andrew Young School of Policy Studies, Department of Public Administration and Urban Studies, Program in Public Administration, Atlanta, GA 30303-3083

AWARDS MPA.

Entrance requirements: For master's, GMAT or GRE General Test.

■ GEORGIA STATE UNIVERSITY

Andrew Young School of Policy Studies, Department of Public Administration and Urban Studies, Program in Public Policy, Atlanta, GA 30303-3083

AWARDS PhD.

Degree requirements: For doctorate, thesis/dissertation.
Entrance requirements: For doctorate, GRE General Test.

■ GOLDEN GATE UNIVERSITY

School of Professional Programs and Undergraduate Studies, Programs in Urban and Public Affairs, Program in Public Administration, San Francisco, CA 94105-2968

AWARDS MPA, JD/MPA. Part-time and evening/weekend programs available.

Degree requirements: For master's, thesis or alternative.
Entrance requirements: For master's, GMAT (MBA), TOEFL, minimum GPA of 2.5, appropriate bachelor's degree.

■ GOVERNORS STATE UNIVERSITY

College of Business and Public Administration, Program in Public Administration, University Park, IL 60466-0975

AWARDS MPA. Part-time and evening/weekend programs available.

Faculty: 10 full-time (0 women), 2 part-time/adjunct (1 woman).
Students: 5 full-time, 128 part-time. Average age 36. In 2001, 19 degrees awarded.
Degree requirements: For master's, thesis or alternative, internship or previous work in field, comprehensive exam.
Entrance requirements: For master's, minimum GPA of 2.5. *Application deadline:* For fall admission, 7/15 (priority date); for spring admission, 11/10. Applications are processed on a rolling basis. *Application fee:* $0.
Expenses: Tuition, state resident: part-time $111 per hour. Tuition, nonresident: part-time $333 per hour.
Financial support: Fellowships, research assistantships, career-related internships or fieldwork, Federal Work-Study, institutionally sponsored loans, and tuition waivers (full and partial) available. Support available to part-time students. Financial award application deadline: 5/1.
Faculty research: State and local politics.
Dr. Carl Stover, Head, 708-534-4944, *E-mail:* c-stover@govst.edu.
Application contact: Dorothy Calvin, Adviser, 708-534-4930.

■ GRADUATE SCHOOL AND UNIVERSITY CENTER OF THE CITY UNIVERSITY OF NEW YORK

Graduate Studies, Interdisciplinary Studies, New York, NY 10016-4039

AWARDS Language in social context (PhD); medieval studies (PhD); public policy (MA, PhD); urban studies (MA, PhD); women's studies (MA, PhD). Terminal master's awarded for partial completion of doctoral program.

Degree requirements: For master's, thesis/dissertation; for doctorate, thesis/dissertation, comprehensive exam.
Entrance requirements: For master's and doctorate, GRE General Test. *Application deadline:* For fall admission, 2/1. *Application fee:* $40.
Expenses: Tuition, state resident: part-time $245 per credit. Tuition, nonresident: part-time $425 per credit. Required fees: $72 per semester.
Financial support: Application deadline: 2/1.

■ GRAMBLING STATE UNIVERSITY

Division of Graduate Studies, College of Liberal Arts, Program in Public Administration, Grambling, LA 71245

AWARDS MPA.

Entrance requirements: For master's, GRE. *Web site:* http://www.gram.edu/

■ GRAND VALLEY STATE UNIVERSITY

Social Science Division, School of Public and Nonprofit Administration, Allendale, MI 49401-9403

AWARDS MPA. Part-time and evening/weekend programs available.

Faculty: 11 full-time (4 women), 7 part-time/adjunct (3 women).
Students: 126 (80 women); includes 20 minority (12 African Americans, 4 Asian Americans or Pacific Islanders, 4 Hispanic Americans). Average age 35. 50 applicants, 90% accepted. In 2001, 30 degrees awarded.
Degree requirements: For master's, thesis optional.
Entrance requirements: For master's, minimum GPA of 3.0. *Application deadline:* For fall admission, 5/1 (priority date); for winter admission, 11/1 (priority date). Applications are processed on a rolling

basis. *Application fee:* $20. Electronic applications accepted.
Expenses: Tuition, state resident: part-time $202 per credit hour. Tuition, nonresident: part-time $437 per credit hour.
Financial support: In 2001–02, 20 students received support, including research assistantships with partial tuition reimbursements available (averaging $2,000 per year); career-related internships or fieldwork, Federal Work-Study, scholarships/grants, and unspecified assistantships also available. Financial award application deadline: 5/1.
Faculty research: Comparative urban systems; ethics and public management, local economic development, nonprofit boards and governance, public/nonprofit financial management.
Dr. Danny L. Balfour, Director, 616-771-6594, *Fax:* 616-336-7120, *E-mail:* balfourd@gvsu.edu. *Web site:* http://www.gvsu.edu/spna

■ HAMLINE UNIVERSITY

Graduate School of Public Administration and Management, St. Paul, MN 55104-1284

AWARDS Management (MAM); nonprofit management (MANM); public administration (MAPA). Part-time and evening/weekend programs available.

Faculty: 4 full-time, 25 part-time/adjunct.
Students: 80 full-time, 156 part-time. 121 applicants, 76% accepted, 66 enrolled.
Degree requirements: For master's, thesis.
Application deadline: For fall admission, 7/15 (priority date); for spring admission, 12/1 (priority date). Applications are processed on a rolling basis. *Application fee:* $30. Electronic applications accepted.
Expenses: Tuition: Full-time $6,900; part-time $1,155 per course. One-time fee: $150. Tuition and fees vary according to course load, degree level and program.
Financial support: Federal Work-Study available. Financial award applicants required to submit FAFSA.
Dr. Jane McPeak, Dean, 651-523-2900, *Fax:* 651-523-3098.
Application contact: Gwenn M. Sherburne, Assistant Director, Graduate Admission, 651-523-2900, *Fax:* 651-523-2458, *E-mail:* gradprog@gw.hamline.edu. *Web site:* http://www.hamline.edu/graduate/gpam/

■ HARVARD UNIVERSITY

Graduate School of Arts and Sciences and John F. Kennedy School of Government, Committee on Public Policy, Cambridge, MA 02138

AWARDS PhD.

Degree requirements: For doctorate, thesis/dissertation, exams.
Entrance requirements: For doctorate, GRE General Test or GMAT, TOEFL, Harvard MPP degree.
Expenses: Tuition: Full-time $23,370. Required fees: $816. Full-time tuition and fees vary according to program and student level.

■ HARVARD UNIVERSITY

John F. Kennedy School of Government, Doctoral Programs in Government, Cambridge, MA 02138

AWARDS Political economy and government (PhD); public policy (PhD).

Students: 9 full-time (6 women); includes 2 minority (both African Americans), 4 international. Average age 29. 128 applicants, 12% accepted, 9 enrolled.
Degree requirements: For doctorate, thesis/dissertation.
Entrance requirements: For doctorate, GMAT or GRE General Test, TOEFL. *Application deadline:* For fall admission, 12/14. *Application fee:* $80.
Expenses: Tuition: Full-time $23,370. Required fees: $816. Full-time tuition and fees vary according to program and student level.
Financial support: Fellowships, research assistantships, teaching assistantships, Federal Work-Study, institutionally sponsored loans, scholarships/grants, health care benefits, and unspecified assistantships available.
Louisa Van Baalen, Director, 617-495-1190.

Find an in-depth description at www.petersons.com/gradchannel.

■ HARVARD UNIVERSITY

John F. Kennedy School of Government, Lucius N. Littauer Mid-Career Program in Public Administration, Cambridge, MA 02138

AWARDS MPA.

Students: 211 full-time (75 women); includes 26 minority (12 African Americans, 4 Asian Americans or Pacific Islanders, 6 Hispanic Americans, 4 Native Americans), 95 international. Average age 40. 501 applicants, 57% accepted, 211 enrolled.
Entrance requirements: For master's, GMAT or GRE General Test, TOEFL, minimum 7 years of experience in public sector. *Application deadline:* For fall admission, 5/11. Applications are processed on a rolling basis. *Application fee:* $80. Electronic applications accepted.
Expenses: Tuition: Full-time $23,370. Required fees: $816. Full-time tuition and fees vary according to program and student level.
Financial support: Fellowships, institutionally sponsored loans, scholarships/grants, and health care benefits available. Financial award applicants required to submit CSS PROFILE or FAFSA.
Sue Williamson, Director, 617-496-1100.
Application contact: Office of Admissions, 617-495-1155.

Find an in-depth description at www.petersons.com/gradchannel.

■ HARVARD UNIVERSITY

John F. Kennedy School of Government, Program in Public Administration and International Development, Cambridge, MA 02138

AWARDS MPAID.

Students: 91 full-time (41 women); includes 7 minority (5 Asian Americans or Pacific Islanders, 2 Hispanic Americans), 64 international. Average age 26. 321 applicants, 38% accepted, 91 enrolled.
Entrance requirements: For master's, GMAT or GRE General Test, TOEFL. *Application deadline:* For fall admission, 1/4. *Application fee:* $80.
Expenses: Tuition: Full-time $23,370. Required fees: $816. Full-time tuition and fees vary according to program and student level.
Financial support: Career-related internships or fieldwork, Federal Work-Study, institutionally sponsored loans, scholarships/grants, and health care benefits available. Financial award applicants required to submit CSS PROFILE or FAFSA.
Carol Finney, Director, 617-495-7799.
Application contact: International Program Office, 617-495-1155.

■ HARVARD UNIVERSITY

John F. Kennedy School of Government, Program in Public Policy, Cambridge, MA 02138

AWARDS Public policy (MPP); public policy and urban planning (MPPUP).

Students: 186 full-time (91 women); includes 61 minority (19 African Americans, 21 Asian Americans or Pacific Islanders, 20 Hispanic Americans, 1 Native American), 26 international. Average age 25. 798 applicants, 33% accepted, 186 enrolled.
Entrance requirements: For master's, GMAT or GRE General Test, TOEFL. *Application deadline:* For fall admission, 1/4. *Application fee:* $80.
Expenses: Contact institution.
Financial support: Fellowships, research assistantships, teaching assistantships, career-related internships or fieldwork, Federal Work-Study, institutionally sponsored loans, scholarships/grants, and health care benefits available. Financial award application deadline: 2/8; financial award applicants required to submit CSS PROFILE or FAFSA.
Katherine Kim, Director, 617-496-8382.

Harvard University (continued)
Application contact: Office of Admissions, 617-495-1155.

Find an in-depth description at www.petersons.com/gradchannel.

■ HARVARD UNIVERSITY

John F. Kennedy School of Government, Two-year Program in Public Administration, Cambridge, MA 02138

AWARDS MPA.

Students: 63 full-time (22 women); includes 9 minority (1 African American, 6 Asian Americans or Pacific Islanders, 2 Hispanic Americans), 40 international. Average age 29. 135 applicants, 56% accepted, 63 enrolled.
Entrance requirements: For master's, GMAT or GRE General Test, TOEFL. *Application deadline:* For fall admission, 1/4. *Application fee:* $80.
Expenses: Tuition: Full-time $23,370. Required fees: $816. Full-time tuition and fees vary according to program and student level.
Financial support: Fellowships, teaching assistantships, career-related internships or fieldwork, Federal Work-Study, institutionally sponsored loans, scholarships/grants, and health care benefits available. Financial award application deadline: 2/8; financial award applicants required to submit CSS PROFILE or FAFSA.
Sue Williamson, Director, 617-496-1100.
Application contact: 617-495-1155.

Find an in-depth description at www.petersons.com/gradchannel.

■ HOWARD UNIVERSITY

Graduate School of Arts and Sciences, Department of Political Science, Program in Public Administration, Washington, DC 20059-0002

AWARDS MAPA. Part-time programs available.

Degree requirements: For master's, comprehensive exam.
Entrance requirements: For master's, GRE General Test, minimum GPA of 3.0.

■ HOWARD UNIVERSITY

Graduate School of Arts and Sciences, Department of Political Science, Program in Public Affairs, Washington, DC 20059-0002

AWARDS MA.

Degree requirements: For master's, one foreign language, thesis, comprehensive exam.
Entrance requirements: For master's, GRE General Test, minimum GPA of 3.0.

■ IDAHO STATE UNIVERSITY

Office of Graduate Studies, College of Arts and Sciences, Department of Political Science, Program in Public Administration, Pocatello, ID 83209

AWARDS MPA. Part-time programs available.

Degree requirements: For master's, thesis optional.
Entrance requirements: For master's, GRE General Test. *Application deadline:* For fall admission, 7/1 (priority date); for spring admission, 12/1. Applications are processed on a rolling basis. *Application fee:* $35.
Expenses: Tuition, area resident: Full-time $3,432. Tuition, state resident: part-time $172 per credit. Tuition, nonresident: full-time $10,196; part-time $262 per credit. International tuition: $9,672 full-time. Part-time tuition and fees vary according to course load, program and reciprocity agreements.
Financial support: Teaching assistantships with full and partial tuition reimbursements, career-related internships or fieldwork and Federal Work-Study available. Financial award application deadline: 1/31.
Dr. Richard Henry Foster, Chairman, Department of Political Science, 208-282-2211.

■ ILLINOIS INSTITUTE OF TECHNOLOGY

Graduate College, Armour College of Engineering and Sciences, Department of Social Sciences, Chicago, IL 60616-3793

AWARDS MPA, MPW, JD/MPA, MBA/MPA.

Faculty: 6 full-time (2 women), 6 part-time/adjunct (2 women).
Students: Average age 36. 10 applicants, 50% accepted. In 2001, 19 degrees awarded.
Degree requirements: For master's, comprehensive exam.
Entrance requirements: For master's, TOEFL, minimum undergraduate GPA of 3.0. *Application deadline:* For fall admission, 7/1; for spring admission, 11/1. Applications are processed on a rolling basis. *Application fee:* $30. Electronic applications accepted.
Expenses: Tuition: Part-time $590 per credit hour.
Financial support: Federal Work-Study, institutionally sponsored loans, and scholarships/grants available. Support available to part-time students. Financial award application deadline: 3/1; financial award applicants required to submit FAFSA.
Faculty research: Urban development politics, federal mandates, biotechnology policy, intergovernmental relations, public personnel systems.
Dr. William Grimshaw, Director, 312-567-5129, *Fax:* 312-906-5199, *E-mail:* grimshaw@iit.edu.
Application contact: Dr. Ali Cinar, Dean of Graduate College, 312-567-3637, *Fax:* 312-567-7517, *E-mail:* gradstu@iit.edu. *Web site:* http://www.armour.iit.edu/dept/soc-sci/

■ INDIANA STATE UNIVERSITY

School of Graduate Studies, College of Arts and Sciences, Department of Political Science, Terre Haute, IN 47809-1401

AWARDS Political science (MA, MS); public administration (MPA), including comparative and international administration, human resources and organizational development, national administration, state/local administration.

Electronic applications accepted.

■ INDIANA UNIVERSITY BLOOMINGTON

School of Public and Environmental Affairs, Public Affairs Programs, Bloomington, IN 47405

AWARDS Public affairs (EMPA, MPA, PhD); public policy (PhD). Part-time programs available.

Students: 219 full-time (120 women), 54 part-time (27 women); includes 22 minority (14 African Americans, 3 Asian Americans or Pacific Islanders, 3 Hispanic Americans, 2 Native Americans), 77 international. Average age 29. In 2001, 121 master's, 6 doctorates awarded. Terminal master's awarded for partial completion of doctoral program.
Degree requirements: For doctorate, thesis/dissertation.
Entrance requirements: For master's, GMAT or GRE, LSAT acceptable for joint law degrees; for doctorate, GRE General Test. *Application deadline:* For fall admission, 2/1 (priority date). Applications are processed on a rolling basis. *Application fee:* $45 ($55 for international students).
Expenses: Tuition, state resident: full-time $4,720; part-time $197 per credit. Tuition, nonresident: full-time $13,748; part-time $573 per credit. Required fees: $642.
Financial support: Fellowships, research assistantships, teaching assistantships, career-related internships or fieldwork, Federal Work-Study, institutionally sponsored loans, and minority fellowships, Peace Corps assistantships available. Financial award application deadline: 2/1; financial award applicants required to submit FAFSA.
Faculty research: Comparative and international affairs, environmental policy and resource management, policy analysis, public finance, public management, urban management, nonprofit management.

Application contact: Charles A. Johnson, Coordinator of Student Recruitment, 800-765-7755, *Fax:* 812-855-7802, *E-mail:* speainfo@indiana.edu. *Web site:* http://www.indiana.edu/~speaweb/academics/pa_index.html

Find an in-depth description at www.petersons.com/gradchannel.

■ INDIANA UNIVERSITY NORTHWEST

School of Public and Environmental Affairs, Gary, IN 46408-1197

AWARDS Criminal justice (MPA); health services administration (MPA); human services administration (MPA); management of public affairs (MPA); non-profit management (NPMC); public management (PMC). Part-time programs available.

Faculty: 2 full-time (1 woman).
Students: 11 full-time (9 women), 88 part-time (58 women); includes 55 minority (45 African Americans, 10 Hispanic Americans). Average age 38. In 2001, 25 master's, 13 other advanced degrees awarded.
Entrance requirements: For master's, GRE General Test. *Application deadline:* For fall admission, 8/15 (priority date). Applications are processed on a rolling basis. *Application fee:* $25.
Expenses: Tuition, state resident: full-time $3,827. Tuition, nonresident: full-time $8,567. Required fees: $416.
Financial support: Career-related internships or fieldwork, Federal Work-Study, and tuition waivers (partial) available. Support available to part-time students. Financial award application deadline: 3/1.
Faculty research: Employment in income security policies, evidence in criminal justice, equal employment law, social welfare policy and welfare reform, public finance in developing countries.
Joseph M. Pellicciotti, Director, 219-980-6695, *Fax:* 219-980-6737, *E-mail:* jpelli@iunhaw1.iun.indiana.edu.
Application contact: Suzanne Green, Recorder, 219-980-6695, *Fax:* 219-980-6737, *E-mail:* sgreen@iunhaw1.iun.indiana.edu.

■ INDIANA UNIVERSITY OF PENNSYLVANIA

Graduate School and Research, College of Humanities and Social Sciences, Department of Political Science, Program in Public Affairs, Indiana, PA 15705-1087

AWARDS MA. Part-time programs available.

Faculty: 5 full-time (0 women).
Students: 13 full-time (5 women), 2 part-time; includes 3 minority (1 African American, 1 Asian American or Pacific Islander, 1 Hispanic American), 2 international. Average age 27. 11 applicants, 55% accepted. In 2001, 8 degrees awarded.
Degree requirements: For master's, thesis optional.
Entrance requirements: For master's, TOEFL, GRE, letters of recommendation (2). *Application deadline:* For fall admission, 7/1 (priority date); for spring admission, 11/1. Applications are processed on a rolling basis. *Application fee:* $30.
Expenses: Tuition, state resident: full-time $4,600; part-time $256 per credit hour. Tuition, nonresident: full-time $7,554; part-time $420 per credit hour. Required fees: $800. Part-time tuition and fees vary according to course load.
Financial support: In 2001–02, 6 research assistantships with full and partial tuition reimbursements (averaging $4,840 per year) were awarded. Financial award application deadline: 3/15; financial award applicants required to submit FAFSA.
Dr. Gawdat Bahgat, Graduate Coordinator, 724-357-2489.

■ INDIANA UNIVERSITY–PURDUE UNIVERSITY FORT WAYNE

Division of Public and Environmental Affairs, Fort Wayne, IN 46805-1499

AWARDS Public affairs (MPA); public management (Certificate). Part-time programs available.

Faculty: 9 full-time (3 women).
Students: 5 full-time (3 women), 34 part-time (23 women); includes 2 minority (1 African American, 1 Hispanic American). Average age 36. 21 applicants, 76% accepted, 13 enrolled. In 2001, 7 degrees awarded.
Degree requirements: For master's, internship.
Entrance requirements: For master's, GRE or GMAT, minimum GPA of 3.0. *Application deadline:* For fall admission, 8/1 (priority date); for spring admission, 12/1. Applications are processed on a rolling basis. *Application fee:* $30.
Expenses: Tuition, state resident: full-time $2,845; part-time $158 per credit hour. Tuition, nonresident: full-time $6,323; part-time $351 per credit hour. Required fees: $9 per credit hour. Tuition and fees vary according to course load.
Financial support: Career-related internships or fieldwork, Federal Work-Study, and scholarships/grants available. Support available to part-time students. Financial award application deadline: 3/1; financial award applicants required to submit FAFSA.
Faculty research: Policy forum, urban decision making and planning, environmental policy. *Total annual research expenditures:* $36,898.
Dr. William G. Ludwin, Assistant Dean and Director, 260-481-6351, *Fax:* 260-481-6346, *E-mail:* ludwin@ipfw.edu.
Application contact: Dr. Jane A. Grant, Director of Graduate Studies, 260-481-6349, *Fax:* 260-481-6346, *E-mail:* grant@iptw.edu. *Web site:* http://www.ipfw.edu/spea/graddesc.htm

■ INDIANA UNIVERSITY–PURDUE UNIVERSITY INDIANAPOLIS

School of Public and Environmental Affairs, Graduate Program in Public Affairs, Indianapolis, IN 46202-2896

AWARDS MPA, Certificate, JD/MPA, MPA/MA, MPA/MIS, MSN/MPA. Part-time and evening/weekend programs available.

Students: 36 full-time (27 women), 270 part-time (102 women); includes 27 minority (20 African Americans, 4 Asian Americans or Pacific Islanders, 3 Hispanic Americans), 6 international. Average age 32. In 2001, 50 degrees awarded.
Entrance requirements: For master's, GRE General Test, minimum GPA of 3.0 preferred. *Application deadline:* For fall admission, 7/15 (priority date); for spring admission, 11/15. Applications are processed on a rolling basis. *Application fee:* $45 ($55 for international students).
Expenses: Tuition, state resident: full-time $4,480; part-time $187 per credit. Tuition, nonresident: full-time $12,926; part-time $539 per credit. Required fees: $177.
Financial support: In 2001–02, 3 fellowships with full and partial tuition reimbursements (averaging $7,600 per year), 9 research assistantships with full and partial tuition reimbursements (averaging $7,600 per year) were awarded. Career-related internships or fieldwork and Federal Work-Study also available. Support available to part-time students. Financial award application deadline: 3/1.
Faculty research: Workplace justice, ethics, crime and delinquency, economic development, water and air quality.
Dr. John Ottensmann, Director, 317-274-2631, *E-mail:* jottensmann@iupui.edu.
Application contact: Student Services, 317-274-4656, *Fax:* 317-274-5153, *E-mail:* infospea@iupui.edu. *Web site:* http://www.spea.iupui.edu/

Find an in-depth description at www.petersons.com/gradchannel.

■ INDIANA UNIVERSITY SOUTH BEND

School of Public and Environmental Affairs, Program in Public Affairs, South Bend, IN 46634-7111

AWARDS MPA. Part-time and evening/weekend programs available.

Faculty: 10 full-time (4 women), 1 (woman) part-time/adjunct.
Students: 6 full-time (4 women), 26 part-time (16 women); includes 6 minority (5 African Americans, 1 Hispanic American), 1 international. Average age 35. In 2001, 20 degrees awarded.
Entrance requirements: For master's, GRE General Test, minimum undergraduate GPA of 2.5. *Application deadline:* For

Indiana University South Bend (continued)
fall admission, 7/1 (priority date); for spring admission, 11/1. Applications are processed on a rolling basis. *Application fee:* $40 ($50 for international students).
Expenses: Tuition, state resident: full-time $3,664; part-time $153. Tuition, nonresident: full-time $8,929; part-time $372. Required fees: $390. Tuition and fees vary according to program.
Financial support: Fellowships, research assistantships, career-related internships or fieldwork, Federal Work-Study, and institutionally sponsored loans available. Support available to part-time students. Financial award application deadline: 3/1; financial award applicants required to submit FAFSA.
Dr. J. Paul Herr, Director, 574-237-4592, *Fax:* 574-237-6514, *E-mail:* jherr@iusb.edu. *Web site:* http://www.iusb.edu/

■ IOWA STATE UNIVERSITY OF SCIENCE AND TECHNOLOGY

Graduate College, College of Liberal Arts and Sciences, Department of Political Science, Ames, IA 50011

AWARDS Political science (MA); public administration (MPA).

Faculty: 17 full-time, 2 part-time/adjunct.
Students: 20 full-time (12 women), 21 part-time (9 women); includes 3 minority (2 African Americans, 1 Asian American or Pacific Islander), 11 international. 35 applicants, 54% accepted, 14 enrolled. In 2001, 7 degrees awarded.
Degree requirements: For master's, thesis (for some programs). *Median time to degree:* Master's–3.2 years full-time.
Entrance requirements: For master's, GRE General Test or GMAT, TOEFL or IELTS. *Application deadline:* For fall admission, 3/1 (priority date); for spring admission, 10/1. Applications are processed on a rolling basis. *Application fee:* $20 ($50 for international students). Electronic applications accepted.
Expenses: Tuition, state resident: full-time $1,851. Tuition, nonresident: full-time $5,449. Tuition and fees vary according to program.
Financial support: In 2001–02, 11 research assistantships with partial tuition reimbursements (averaging $11,099 per year), 7 teaching assistantships with partial tuition reimbursements (averaging $10,846 per year) were awarded. Fellowships, scholarships/grants, health care benefits, and unspecified assistantships also available.
Dr. James M. McCormick, Chair, 515-294-7256, *Fax:* 515-294-1003, *E-mail:* polsc@iastate.edu.
Application contact: Barb Marvick, Head, 515-294-3764, *E-mail:* polsci@iastate.edu. *Web site:* http://www.iastate.edu/~polsci/

■ JACKSON STATE UNIVERSITY

Graduate School, School of Liberal Arts, Department of Public Policy and Administration, Jackson, MS 39217

AWARDS MPPA, PhD. Evening/weekend programs available.

Degree requirements: For master's, thesis optional; for doctorate, thesis/dissertation, comprehensive exam.
Entrance requirements: For master's, GRE General Test, TOEFL; for doctorate, MAT.

■ JACKSONVILLE STATE UNIVERSITY

College of Graduate Studies and Continuing Education, Program in Interdisciplinary Studies, Program in Public Administration, Jacksonville, AL 36265-1602

AWARDS MPA.

Entrance requirements: For master's, GRE General Test or MAT.

■ JAMES MADISON UNIVERSITY

College of Graduate and Professional Programs, College of Arts and Letters, Department of Political Science, Harrisonburg, VA 22807

AWARDS Public administration (MPA). Part-time programs available.

Faculty: 2 full-time (1 woman), 1 part-time/adjunct (0 women).
Students: 8 full-time (4 women), 9 part-time (4 women); includes 1 minority (African American). Average age 29. In 2001, 12 degrees awarded.
Entrance requirements: For master's, GMAT or GRE General Test. *Application deadline:* For fall admission, 7/1 (priority date). Applications are processed on a rolling basis. *Application fee:* $55.
Expenses: Tuition, state resident: part-time $143 per credit hour. Tuition, nonresident: part-time $465 per credit hour.
Financial support: In 2001–02, 1 teaching assistantship with full tuition reimbursement (averaging $7,170 per year) was awarded; fellowships, unspecified assistantships also available. Financial award application deadline: 3/1; financial award applicants required to submit FAFSA.
Dr. Glenn P. Hastedt, Head, 540-568-6149.

■ JOHN JAY COLLEGE OF CRIMINAL JUSTICE OF THE CITY UNIVERSITY OF NEW YORK

Graduate Studies, Program in Public Administration, New York, NY 10019-1093

AWARDS MPA. MPA-Inspector General program jointly offered with Baruch College of the City University of New York. Part-time and evening/weekend programs available.

Students: 12 full-time (8 women), 227 part-time (127 women); includes 149 minority (92 African Americans, 10 Asian Americans or Pacific Islanders, 47 Hispanic Americans). 86 applicants, 70% accepted. In 2001, 58 degrees awarded.
Degree requirements: For master's, thesis or alternative.
Entrance requirements: For master's, TOEFL, minimum B average. *Application deadline:* For fall admission, 6/30 (priority date); for spring admission, 12/1. Applications are processed on a rolling basis. *Application fee:* $40.
Expenses: Tuition, state resident: full-time $4,350; part-time $185 per credit. Tuition, nonresident: full-time $7,600; part-time $285 per credit. Required fees: $80; $40 per semester. Tuition and fees vary according to degree level.
Financial support: Career-related internships or fieldwork, Federal Work-Study, institutionally sponsored loans, and scholarships/grants available. Support available to part-time students. Financial award applicants required to submit FAFSA.
Dr. Warren Benton, Co-Director, 212-237-8089, *E-mail:* nbenton@jjay.cuny.edu.
Application contact: Shirley Rodriguez-Melendez, Admissions Assistant, 212-237-8863, *Fax:* 212-237-8777, *E-mail:* srodrigu@jjay.cuny.edu.

■ JOHN JAY COLLEGE OF CRIMINAL JUSTICE OF THE CITY UNIVERSITY OF NEW YORK

Graduate Studies, Programs in Criminal Justice, New York, NY 10019-1093

AWARDS Criminal justice (MA, PhD); criminology and deviance (PhD); forensic psychology (PhD); forensic science (PhD); law and philosophy (PhD); organizational behavior (PhD); public policy (PhD). Part-time and evening/weekend programs available.

Students: 33 full-time (20 women), 165 part-time (86 women); includes 68 minority (36 African Americans, 11 Asian Americans or Pacific Islanders, 21 Hispanic Americans). 150 applicants, 80% accepted. In 2001, 58 degrees awarded. Terminal master's awarded for partial completion of doctoral program.
Degree requirements: For master's, thesis or alternative; for doctorate, one foreign language, thesis/dissertation.
Entrance requirements: For master's, GRE General Test, TOEFL, minimum B average; for doctorate, GRE General Test, TOEFL. *Application deadline:* For fall admission, 6/30 (priority date); for spring admission, 12/1. Applications are processed on a rolling basis. *Application fee:* $40.
Expenses: Tuition, state resident: full-time $4,350; part-time $185 per credit. Tuition, nonresident: full-time $7,600; part-time

$285 per credit. Required fees: $80; $40 per semester. Tuition and fees vary according to degree level.
Financial support: Career-related internships or fieldwork, Federal Work-Study, institutionally sponsored loans, and scholarships/grants available. Support available to part-time students. Financial award applicants required to submit FAFSA.
Dr. Andrew Karmen, Co-Director, 212-237-8695, *E-mail:* akarmen@jjay.cuny.edu.
Application contact: Shirley Rodriguez-Melendez, Admissions Assistant, 212-237-8863, *Fax:* 212-237-8777, *E-mail:* srodrigu@jjay.cuny.edu.

Find an in-depth description at www.petersons.com/gradchannel.

■ JOHNS HOPKINS UNIVERSITY

Zanvyl Krieger School of Arts and Sciences, Institute for Policy Studies, Baltimore, MD 21218-2699

AWARDS MA.

Faculty: 4 part-time/adjunct (2 women).
Students: 39 full-time (23 women), 1 part-time; includes 4 minority (2 African Americans, 2 Hispanic Americans), 7 international. Average age 27. 95 applicants, 57% accepted, 19 enrolled. In 2001, 22 degrees awarded.
Degree requirements: For master's, summer internship, thesis optional.
Entrance requirements: For master's, GRE General Test, TOEFL. *Application deadline:* For fall admission, 2/1. *Application fee:* $55. Electronic applications accepted.
Expenses: Tuition: Full-time $27,390.
Financial support: In 2001–02, 12 fellowships, 30 research assistantships, 5 teaching assistantships were awarded. Career-related internships or fieldwork, Federal Work-Study, and unspecified assistantships also available. Financial award application deadline: 4/15; financial award applicants required to submit FAFSA.
Faculty research: Housing, criminal justice, human capital investment, nonprofit sector, public finance and infrastructure.
Dr. Sandra J. Newman, Director, 410-516-7174, *Fax:* 410-516-8233, *E-mail:* jhuips@jhunix.hcf.jhu.edu.
Application contact: Angel Burgos, Program Coordinator, 410-516-7174, *Fax:* 410-516-8233, *E-mail:* aburgos@jhu.edu. *Web site:* http://www.jhu.edu/ips/maps/maps.html

Find an in-depth description at www.petersons.com/gradchannel.

■ KANSAS STATE UNIVERSITY

Graduate School, College of Arts and Sciences, Department of Political Science, Program in Public Administration, Manhattan, KS 66506

AWARDS MPA. Part-time programs available.

Faculty: 6 full-time (3 women).
Students: 8 full-time (3 women), 8 part-time (4 women); includes 1 minority (African American), 2 international. Average age 33. In 2001, 8 degrees awarded.
Degree requirements: For master's, thesis or alternative, comprehensive written and oral exams.
Entrance requirements: For master's, GRE (recommended), TOEFL, minimum GPA of 3.0. *Application deadline:* For fall admission, 2/1 (priority date); for spring admission, 10/1. Applications are processed on a rolling basis. *Application fee:* $0 ($25 for international students).
Expenses: Tuition, state resident: part-time $113 per credit hour. Tuition, nonresident: part-time $358 per credit hour.
Financial support: Fellowships, research assistantships, teaching assistantships, career-related internships or fieldwork, institutionally sponsored loans, and scholarships/grants available. Support available to part-time students. Financial award application deadline: 3/1; financial award applicants required to submit FAFSA.
Application contact: Prof. Krishna Tummala, Graduate Program Director, 785-532-0452, *Fax:* 785-532-2339, *E-mail:* tummala@ksu.edu. *Web site:* http://www.ksu.edu/polsci/mpa.html

■ KEAN UNIVERSITY

College of Business and Public Administration, Department of Public Administration, Union, NJ 07083

AWARDS Health services administration (MPA); public administration (MPA). Part-time programs available.

Faculty: 11 full-time (6 women), 6 part-time/adjunct.
Students: 62 full-time (33 women), 70 part-time (43 women); includes 56 minority (44 African Americans, 2 Asian Americans or Pacific Islanders, 10 Hispanic Americans), 28 international. Average age 33. 28 applicants, 79% accepted. In 2001, 38 degrees awarded.
Entrance requirements: For master's, GRE General Test. *Application deadline:* For fall admission, 6/15; for spring admission, 11/15. *Application fee:* $35.
Expenses: Tuition, state resident: full-time $7,372. Tuition, nonresident: full-time $9,004. Required fees: $1,006.
Financial support: In 2001–02, 22 research assistantships with full tuition reimbursements (averaging $2,880 per year) were awarded; career-related internships or fieldwork, institutionally sponsored loans, and unspecified assistantships also available. Financial award application deadline: 5/1.
Faculty research: Fiscal impact of New Federalism, New Jersey state and local government, computer application in public management.
Dr. Jon Erickson, Coordinator, 908-527-3022.
Application contact: Joanne Morris, Director of Graduate Admissions, 908-527-2665, *Fax:* 908-527-2286, *E-mail:* grad_adm@kean.edu.

■ KEAN UNIVERSITY

School of Natural, Applied and Health Sciences, Department of Nursing, Program in Nursing and Public Administration, Union, NJ 07083

AWARDS MSN/MPA.

Faculty: 7 full-time (all women), 7 part-time/adjunct.
Students: Average age 44.
Application deadline: For fall admission, 6/15; for spring admission, 11/15. *Application fee:* $35.
Expenses: Tuition, state resident: full-time $7,372. Tuition, nonresident: full-time $9,004. Required fees: $1,006.
Application contact: Joanne Morris, Director of Graduate Admissions, 908-527-2665, *Fax:* 908-527-2286, *E-mail:* grad_adm@turbo.kean.edu.

■ KENNESAW STATE UNIVERSITY

College of Humanities and Social Sciences, Program in Public Administration, Kennesaw, GA 30144-5591

AWARDS MPA. Part-time and evening/weekend programs available.

Faculty: 5 full-time (3 women), 2 part-time/adjunct (0 women).
Students: 8 full-time (6 women), 61 part-time (40 women); includes 18 minority (17 African Americans, 1 Asian American or Pacific Islander), 2 international. Average age 34. 37 applicants, 38% accepted, 9 enrolled. In 2001, 14 degrees awarded.
Entrance requirements: For master's, GRE General Test, minimum GPA of 2.5. *Application deadline:* For fall admission, 7/7 (priority date); for spring admission, 10/20 (priority date). Applications are processed on a rolling basis. *Application fee:* $20. Electronic applications accepted.
Expenses: Tuition, state resident: part-time $97 per credit hour. Tuition, nonresident: part-time $387 per credit hour. Required fees: $178 per semester.
Financial support: In 2001–02, 2 research assistantships with full tuition reimbursements (averaging $15,000 per year) were awarded; Federal Work-Study also available. Support available to part-time students. Financial award application deadline: 6/15; financial award applicants required to submit FAFSA.
Dr. Martha Griffith, Director, 770-423-6631, *E-mail:* mgriffith@kennesaw.edu.
Application contact: Sinem Hamitoglu, Assistant Director of Graduate Admissions, 770-420-4377, *Fax:* 770-420-4435, *E-mail:* ksugrad@kennesaw.edu. *Web site:* http://www.kennesaw.edu/

■ KENT STATE UNIVERSITY

College of Arts and Sciences, Department of Political Science, Program in Public Administration, Kent, OH 44242-0001

AWARDS MPA.

Degree requirements: For master's, public sector internship, thesis optional.
Entrance requirements: For master's, GRE General Test, TOEFL, minimum GPA of 2.75. Electronic applications accepted.

■ KENTUCKY STATE UNIVERSITY

School of Public Administration, Frankfort, KY 40601

AWARDS MPA. Part-time and evening/weekend programs available.

Degree requirements: For master's, thesis optional.
Entrance requirements: For master's, GRE General Test, TOEFL.
Faculty research: State and local program assessment. *Web site:* http://www.kysu.edu/

■ KUTZTOWN UNIVERSITY OF PENNSYLVANIA

College of Graduate Studies and Extended Learning, College of Liberal Arts and Sciences, Program in Public Administration, Kutztown, PA 19530-0730

AWARDS MPA. Part-time and evening/weekend programs available.

Faculty: 6 part-time/adjunct (2 women).
Students: 1 full-time (0 women), 24 part-time (16 women); includes 2 minority (both Hispanic Americans). Average age 33. In 2001, 8 degrees awarded.
Degree requirements: For master's, thesis.
Entrance requirements: For master's, GRE General Test, TOEFL, TSE. *Application deadline:* Applications are processed on a rolling basis. *Application fee:* $35.
Expenses: Tuition, state resident: full-time $4,600; part-time $256 per credit. Tuition, nonresident: full-time $7,554; part-time $420 per credit. Required fees: $835.
Financial support: Career-related internships or fieldwork, Federal Work-Study, and unspecified assistantships available. Financial award application deadline: 3/15; financial award applicants required to submit FAFSA.
Faculty research: Structure of code enforcement offices in smaller developing communities.
Dr. Paula Holoviak, Graduate Coordinator, 610-683-4452, *Fax:* 610-683-4603, *E-mail:* duda@kutztown.edu. *Web site:* http://www.kutztown.edu/acad/

■ LAMAR UNIVERSITY

College of Graduate Studies, College of Arts and Sciences, Department of Political Science, Beaumont, TX 77710

AWARDS Public administration (MPA). Part-time programs available.

Faculty: 8 full-time (1 woman).
Students: 2 full-time (1 woman), 9 part-time (3 women); includes 4 minority (3 African Americans, 1 Hispanic American), 1 international. Average age 35. 16 applicants, 100% accepted. In 2001, 3 degrees awarded.
Degree requirements: For master's, practicum.
Entrance requirements: For master's, GRE General Test, TOEFL. *Application deadline:* For fall admission, 8/1; for spring admission, 12/1. Applications are processed on a rolling basis. *Application fee:* $25 ($50 for international students).
Expenses: Tuition, state resident: full-time $1,114. Tuition, nonresident: full-time $3,670.
Financial support: In 2001–02, 1 teaching assistantship (averaging $2,000 per year) was awarded; fellowships, research assistantships, career-related internships or fieldwork, Federal Work-Study, and institutionally sponsored loans also available. Financial award application deadline: 4/1.
Faculty research: Political activities of administrators, impact of race on voting behavior, term limitations, Latin American policy, judicial process.
Dr. Glenn Utter, Chair, 409-880-8526, *Fax:* 409-880-8710.
Application contact: Dr. Bert Dubose, Director, 409-880-8529, *Fax:* 409-880-8710, *E-mail:* dubose@hal.lamar.edu.

■ LONG ISLAND UNIVERSITY, BRENTWOOD CAMPUS

School of Public Service, Brentwood, NY 11717

AWARDS Criminal justice (MS); health administration (MPA); public administration (MPA). Part-time and evening/weekend programs available.

Students: Average age 39.
Application deadline: Applications are processed on a rolling basis. *Application fee:* $0.
Expenses: Tuition: Part-time $572 per credit. Part-time tuition and fees vary according to program.
Financial support: Scholarships/grants and unspecified assistantships available. Support available to part-time students.
Dr. Robert Sanatore, Head, 516-299-3017.

■ LONG ISLAND UNIVERSITY, BROOKLYN CAMPUS

School of Business, Public Administration and Information Sciences, Program in Public Administration, Brooklyn, NY 11201-8423

AWARDS MPA. Part-time and evening/weekend programs available.

Entrance requirements: For master's, GMAT or GRE Subject Test. Electronic applications accepted.

■ LONG ISLAND UNIVERSITY, C.W. POST CAMPUS

College of Management, School of Public Service, Department of Health Care and Public Administration, Brookville, NY 11548-1300

AWARDS Gerontology (Certificate); health care administration (MPA); health care administration/gerontology (MPA); public administration (MPA). Part-time and evening/weekend programs available.

Faculty: 10 full-time (5 women), 14 part-time/adjunct (4 women).
Students: 22 full-time (13 women), 136 part-time (100 women). 55 applicants, 85% accepted, 35 enrolled. In 2001, 42 degrees awarded.
Degree requirements: For master's, thesis.
Entrance requirements: For master's, GMAT, minimum GPA of 2.5; for Certificate, minimum GPA of 2.5. *Application deadline:* For fall admission, 8/15; for spring admission, 12/15. Applications are processed on a rolling basis. *Application fee:* $30. Electronic applications accepted.
Expenses: Tuition: Full-time $10,296; part-time $572 per credit. Required fees: $380; $190 per semester.
Financial support: In 2001–02, 10 students received support, including 3 research assistantships with partial tuition reimbursements available; Federal Work-Study and unspecified assistantships also available. Support available to part-time students. Financial award application deadline: 5/15; financial award applicants required to submit CSS PROFILE or FAFSA.
Faculty research: Critical issues in sexuality, social work in religious communities, gerontological social work.
Dr. Matthew C. Cordaro, Chairperson, 516-299-3920, *E-mail:* mcordaro@liu.edu.
Application contact: Barbara Bavlsik, Advisor, 516-299-2770, *E-mail:* barbara.bavlsik@liu.edu. *Web site:* http://www.liu.edu/com/

■ LONG ISLAND UNIVERSITY, WESTCHESTER GRADUATE CAMPUS

Program in Health Administration, Purchase, NY 10577

AWARDS MPA.

Students: 1 (woman) full-time, 3 part-time (all women).
Expenses: Tuition: Part-time $572 per credit.
Prof. Joseph Welfeld, Coordinator, 914-251-6510, *Fax:* 914-251-5959, *E-mail:* jwelfeld@liu.edu.
Application contact: Carol A. Messar, Director of Admissions, 914-251-6510, *Fax:* 914-251-5959, *E-mail:* cmessar@liu.edu.

■ LOUISIANA STATE UNIVERSITY AND AGRICULTURAL AND MECHANICAL COLLEGE

Graduate School, E.J. Ourso College of Business Administration, Public Administration Institute, Baton Rouge, LA 70803

AWARDS MPA, JD/MPA. Part-time programs available.

Faculty: 5 full-time (1 woman).
Students: 43 full-time (29 women), 84 part-time (39 women); includes 35 minority (34 African Americans, 1 Asian American or Pacific Islander), 1 international. Average age 33. 51 applicants, 82% accepted, 33 enrolled. In 2001, 25 degrees awarded.
Degree requirements: For master's, comprehensive exam.
Entrance requirements: For master's, GRE General Test, minimum GPA of 3.0. *Application deadline:* For fall admission, 1/25 (priority date). Applications are processed on a rolling basis. *Application fee:* $25.
Expenses: Tuition, state resident: full-time $2,551. Tuition, nonresident: full-time $5,551. Required fees: $854. Part-time tuition and fees vary according to course load.
Financial support: In 2001–02, 15 students received support, including 5 research assistantships with partial tuition reimbursements available (averaging $6,440 per year); teaching assistantships with partial tuition reimbursements available, unspecified assistantships also available. Financial award applicants required to submit FAFSA.
Faculty research: Quantitative and analytical policy analysis, health care policy, financial and budget analysis. *Total annual research expenditures:* $7,363.
Dr. James A. Richardson, Director, 225-578-6745, *Fax:* 225-578-9078, *E-mail:* parich@lsu.edu. *Web site:* http://www.bus.lsu.edu/pai/

■ MARIST COLLEGE

Graduate Programs, School of Management, Program in Public Administration, Poughkeepsie, NY 12601-1387

AWARDS MPA, Certificate. Part-time and evening/weekend programs available.

Faculty: 3 full-time (0 women), 4 part-time/adjunct (2 women).
Students: 8 full-time (4 women), 236 part-time (104 women); includes 23 minority (12 African Americans, 3 Asian Americans or Pacific Islanders, 8 Hispanic Americans). Average age 29. 33 applicants, 82% accepted. In 2001, 94 degrees awarded.
Entrance requirements: For master's, GRE General Test. *Application deadline:* For fall admission, 8/1 (priority date); for spring admission, 12/15. Applications are processed on a rolling basis. *Application fee:* $30.
Expenses: Tuition: Full-time $4,320; part-time $480 per credit. Required fees: $30 per semester.
Financial support: Federal Work-Study and tuition waivers (partial) available. Support available to part-time students. Financial award application deadline: 8/15; financial award applicants required to submit FAFSA.
Faculty research: Public policy analysis, health administration.
Dr. James Kent, Director, 845-575-3343, *E-mail:* carole.richardson@marist.edu.
Application contact: Dr. John DeJoy, Acting Dean of Graduate and Continuing Education, 845-575-3530, *Fax:* 845-575-3640, *E-mail:* john.dejoy@marist.edu.

■ MARYWOOD UNIVERSITY

Graduate School of Arts and Sciences, Department of Public Administration, Program in Public Administration, Scranton, PA 18509-1598

AWARDS MPA, MPA/MSW.

Students: 13 full-time (6 women), 38 part-time (21 women); includes 2 minority (both African Americans). Average age 35. 21 applicants, 95% accepted.
Degree requirements: For master's, thesis or alternative, internship/practicum.
Entrance requirements: For master's, TOEFL. *Application deadline:* For fall admission, 4/15; for spring admission, 11/15 (priority date). Applications are processed on a rolling basis. *Application fee:* $20. Electronic applications accepted.
Financial support: Research assistantships, career-related internships or fieldwork, scholarships/grants, and tuition waivers (partial) available. Support available to part-time students. Financial award application deadline: 2/15; financial award applicants required to submit FAFSA.
Application contact: Deborah M. Flynn, Coordinator of Admissions, 570-340-6002, *Fax:* 570-961-4745, *E-mail:* gsas_adm@ac.marywood.edu.

■ METROPOLITAN STATE UNIVERSITY

College of Management, St. Paul, MN 55106-5000

AWARDS Finance (MBA); human resource management (MBA); information management (MMIS); international business (MBA); law enforcement (MPNA); management information systems (MBA); marketing (MBA); nonprofit management (MPNA); organizational studies (MBA); public administration (MPNA); purchasing management (MBA); systems management (MMIS). Part-time and evening/weekend programs available.

Degree requirements: For master's, computer language (MMIS), thesis optional.
Entrance requirements: For master's, GMAT (MBA), resumé.
Faculty research: Yugoslav economic system, workers' cooperatives, participative management and job enrichment, global business systems. *Web site:* http://www.metrostate.edu/

■ MICHIGAN STATE UNIVERSITY

Graduate School, College of Social Science, Department of Political Science, East Lansing, MI 48824

AWARDS Political science (MA, PhD); political science-urban studies (PhD); public administration (MPA); public administration-urban studies (MPA). Part-time and evening/weekend programs available.

Faculty: 31.
Students: 61 full-time (28 women), 14 part-time (5 women); includes 8 minority (5 African Americans, 2 Asian Americans or Pacific Islanders, 1 Native American), 21 international. Average age 28. 162 applicants, 43% accepted. In 2001, 15 master's, 6 doctorates awarded. Terminal master's awarded for partial completion of doctoral program.
Degree requirements: For doctorate, thesis/dissertation.
Entrance requirements: For master's, GRE General Test, TOEFL, minimum GPA of 3.0; for doctorate, GRE General Test, TOEFL. *Application deadline:* Applications are processed on a rolling basis. *Application fee:* $30 ($40 for international students). Electronic applications accepted.
Expenses: Tuition, state resident: part-time $244 per credit hour. Tuition, nonresident: part-time $494 per credit hour. Required fees: $268 per semester. Tuition and fees vary according to course load, degree level and program.
Financial support: In 2001–02, 28 fellowships with tuition reimbursements (averaging $2,564 per year), 15 research assistantships with tuition reimbursements (averaging $10,970 per year), 24 teaching assistantships with tuition reimbursements

Michigan State University (continued)
(averaging $11,174 per year) were awarded. Career-related internships or fieldwork and Federal Work-Study also available. Financial award application deadline: 2/15; financial award applicants required to submit FAFSA.
Faculty research: American politics, positive theory, political thought, comparative politics, public policy analysis. *Total annual research expenditures:* $891,802.
Dr. Richard Hula, Chair, 517-355-6590, *Fax:* 517-432-1091.
Application contact: Director, PhD Program, 517-355-6590, *Fax:* 517-432-1091. *Web site:* http://www.polisci.msu.edu/

■ MIDWESTERN STATE UNIVERSITY

Graduate Studies, College of Health and Human Services, Program in Health Services and Public Administration, Wichita Falls, TX 76308

AWARDS Health services administration (MA); public administration (MA).

Faculty: 1 full-time (0 women).
Students: 7 full-time (1 woman), 16 part-time (11 women); includes 5 minority (3 African Americans, 2 Hispanic Americans). Average age 37. In 2001, 13 degrees awarded.
Application deadline: For fall admission, 8/7; for spring admission, 12/15. *Application fee:* $0 ($50 for international students).
Expenses: Tuition, state resident: full-time $936. Tuition, nonresident: full-time $4,734. Required fees: $1,280. One-time fee: $190. Tuition and fees vary according to course load.
Application contact: Dr. Russell Porter, Chair, 940-397-4732.

■ MIDWESTERN STATE UNIVERSITY

Graduate Studies, College of Health and Human Services, Program in Public Administration, Wichita Falls, TX 76308

AWARDS Public administration (MPA).

Expenses: Tuition, state resident: full-time $936. Tuition, nonresident: full-time $4,734. Required fees: $1,280. One-time fee: $190. Tuition and fees vary according to course load. *Web site:* http://www.mwsu.edu

■ MINNESOTA STATE UNIVERSITY, MANKATO

College of Graduate Studies, College of Social and Behavioral Sciences, Department of Political Science, Dual Degree Program in Public Administration and Law, Mankato, MN 56001

AWARDS JD/MAPA.

Expenses: Tuition, state resident: full-time $3,253; part-time $157 per credit. Tuition, nonresident: full-time $4,893; part-time $248 per credit. Required fees: $24 per credit. Tuition and fees vary according to reciprocity agreements.
Dr. N. Doran Hunter, Chairperson, 507-389-6930, *Fax:* 507-389-6377.

■ MINNESOTA STATE UNIVERSITY, MANKATO

College of Graduate Studies, College of Social and Behavioral Sciences, Department of Political Science, Program in Public Administration, Mankato, MN 56001

AWARDS MAPA, MAPA/MA.

Faculty: 12 full-time (4 women).
Students: 6 full-time (3 women), 48 part-time (21 women). Average age 33. In 2001, 4 degrees awarded.
Degree requirements: For master's, one foreign language, thesis or alternative, comprehensive exam.
Entrance requirements: For master's, minimum GPA of 3.0 during previous 2 years. *Application deadline:* For fall admission, 7/9 (priority date); for spring admission, 11/27. Applications are processed on a rolling basis. *Application fee:* $20.
Expenses: Tuition, state resident: full-time $3,253; part-time $157 per credit. Tuition, nonresident: full-time $4,893; part-time $248 per credit. Required fees: $24 per credit. Tuition and fees vary according to reciprocity agreements.
Financial support: Research assistantships with full tuition reimbursements, teaching assistantships with full tuition reimbursements available. Financial award application deadline: 3/15; financial award applicants required to submit FAFSA.
Application contact: Joni Roberts, Admissions Coordinator, 507-389-5244, *Fax:* 507-389-5974, *E-mail:* grad@mankato.msus.edu.

■ MINNESOTA STATE UNIVERSITY MOORHEAD

Graduate Studies, Department of Public, Human Services, and Health Administration, Moorhead, MN 56563-0002

AWARDS MS. Part-time and evening/weekend programs available.

Faculty: 6.
Students: 19 (11 women). 9 applicants, 100% accepted. In 2001, 7 degrees awarded.
Degree requirements: For master's, final oral exam, final project paper or thesis.
Entrance requirements: For master's, GRE General Test, TOEFL, minimum GPA of 2.75. *Application deadline:* For fall admission, 5/1 (priority date); for spring admission, 11/1. Applications are processed on a rolling basis. *Application fee:* $20 ($35 for international students). Electronic applications accepted.
Expenses: Tuition, area resident: Part-time $148 per credit. Tuition, nonresident: part-time $234 per credit.
Financial support: Career-related internships or fieldwork, Federal Work-Study, and unspecified assistantships available. Financial award application deadline: 7/15; financial award applicants required to submit FAFSA.
Dr. James Danielson, Coordinator, 218-236-2825, *E-mail:* daniels@mnstate.edu. *Web site:* http://www.mnstate.edu/phsha

■ MISSISSIPPI STATE UNIVERSITY

College of Arts and Sciences, Department of Political Science, Mississippi State, MS 39762

AWARDS Political science (MA); public policy and administration (MPPA, PhD). Evening/weekend programs available.

Faculty: 12 full-time (1 woman).
Students: 29 full-time (12 women), 38 part-time (16 women); includes 26 minority (25 African Americans, 1 Hispanic American), 1 international. Average age 33. 55 applicants, 93% accepted, 17 enrolled. In 2001, 15 master's, 2 doctorates awarded.
Degree requirements: For master's, comprehensive oral or written exam; for doctorate, thesis/dissertation, comprehensive oral and written exam. *Median time to degree:* Master's–2 years full-time, 3 years part-time; doctorate–5 years full-time, 7 years part-time.
Entrance requirements: For master's, TOEFL, minimum GPA of 3.0; for doctorate, GRE General Test, TOEFL, minimum graduate GPA of 3.35. *Application deadline:* For fall admission, 8/1 (priority date); for spring admission, 12/1 (priority date). Applications are processed on a rolling basis. *Application fee:* $25 for international students.
Expenses: Tuition, state resident: full-time $3,586; part-time $150 per credit hour. Tuition, nonresident: full-time $8,128; part-time $339 per credit hour. Tuition and fees vary according to course load and campus/location.
Financial support: In 2001–02, 16 students received support, including 4 research assistantships with full tuition reimbursements available (averaging $6,600 per year), 6 teaching assistantships with full tuition reimbursements available (averaging $10,125 per year); Federal Work-Study, institutionally sponsored loans, and unspecified assistantships also available. Financial award application deadline: 4/15.
Faculty research: American politics, international relations, state and local government, comparative government , public administration. *Total annual research expenditures:* $10,000.

Dr. Douglas G. Feig, Head, 662-325-2711, *Fax:* 662-325-2716, *E-mail:* ejc1@ps.msstate.edu.
Application contact: Jerry B. Inmon, Director of Admissions, 662-325-2224, *Fax:* 662-325-7360, *E-mail:* admit@admissions.msstate.edu. *Web site:* http://www.msstate.edu/dept/politicalscience/

■ MONTANA STATE UNIVERSITY–BOZEMAN

College of Graduate Studies, College of Letters and Science, Department of Political Science, Bozeman, MT 59717

AWARDS Public administration (MPA). Part-time programs available.

Students: 1 full-time (0 women), 7 part-time (5 women); includes 1 minority (Hispanic American). Average age 38. 6 applicants, 83% accepted, 5 enrolled. In 2001, 10 degrees awarded.
Degree requirements: For master's, exam, professional paper.
Entrance requirements: For master's, GRE General Test, TOEFL, minimum GPA of 3.0. *Application deadline:* For fall admission, 6/1; for spring admission, 11/1. Applications are processed on a rolling basis. *Application fee:* $50. Electronic applications accepted.
Expenses: Tuition, state resident: full-time $3,894; part-time $198 per credit. Tuition, nonresident: full-time $10,661; part-time $480 per credit. International tuition: $10,811 full-time. Tuition and fees vary according to course load and program.
Financial support: Application deadline: 3/1;
Faculty research: International organizations, state and local government, research methods, international law, comparative public policy.
Dr. Franke Wilmer, Head, 406-994-4141, *Fax:* 406-994-6692, *E-mail:* franke@montana.edu. *Web site:* http://www.montana.edu/wwwpo/

■ MONTEREY INSTITUTE OF INTERNATIONAL STUDIES

Graduate School of International Policy Studies, Program in International Public Administration, Monterey, CA 93940-2691

AWARDS International management (MPA).

Students: 29 full-time (21 women), 1 (woman) part-time. Average age 28. 14 applicants, 93% accepted, 9 enrolled. In 2001, 19 degrees awarded.
Degree requirements: For master's, one foreign language.
Entrance requirements: For master's, TOEFL, minimum GPA of 3.0, proficiency in a foreign language. *Application deadline:* For fall admission, 3/15 (priority date); for spring admission, 10/1 (priority date). Applications are processed on a rolling basis. *Application fee:* $50. Electronic applications accepted.
Expenses: Tuition: Full-time $19,988; part-time $840 per unit. Required fees: $50. Part-time tuition and fees vary according to course load and reciprocity agreements.
Financial support: In 2001–02, 11 students received support. Career-related internships or fieldwork, Federal Work-Study, and institutionally sponsored loans available. Support available to part-time students. Financial award application deadline: 3/15; financial award applicants required to submit FAFSA.
Application contact: 831-647-4123, *Fax:* 831-647-6405, *E-mail:* admit@miis.edu.

Find an in-depth description at www.petersons.com/gradchannel.

■ MURRAY STATE UNIVERSITY

College of Business and Public Affairs, Department of Political Science and Legal Studies, Murray, KY 42071-0009

AWARDS Public affairs (MPA). Part-time programs available.

Students: 11 full-time (4 women), 32 part-time (13 women); includes 13 minority (11 African Americans, 1 Asian American or Pacific Islander, 1 Hispanic American), 1 international. 13 applicants, 100% accepted. In 2001, 14 degrees awarded.
Entrance requirements: For master's, GRE General Test, TOEFL. *Application deadline:* Applications are processed on a rolling basis. *Application fee:* $25.
Expenses: Tuition, state resident: full-time $1,440; part-time $169 per hour. Tuition, nonresident: full-time $4,004; part-time $450 per hour.
Financial support: Research assistantships, teaching assistantships, Federal Work-Study available. Financial award application deadline: 4/1.
Dr. Farouk Umar, Chairman, 270-762-2699, *Fax:* 270-762-3482, *E-mail:* farouk.umar@murraystate.edu.

■ NATIONAL UNIVERSITY

Academic Affairs, School of Business and Technology, Department of Public Policy and Administration, La Jolla, CA 92037-1011

AWARDS Criminal justice (MCJ, MPA); forensic science (MFS); health care administration (MBA, MHCA); human resource management (MA); human resources administration (MBA); public administration (MBA, MPA). Part-time and evening/weekend programs available. Postbaccalaureate distance learning degree programs offered (minimal on-campus study).

Faculty: 9 full-time (2 women), 173 part-time/adjunct (43 women).
Students: 463 full-time (269 women), 169 part-time (79 women); includes 237 minority (97 African Americans, 45 Asian Americans or Pacific Islanders, 90 Hispanic Americans, 5 Native Americans), 37 international. Average age 34. 204 applicants, 100% accepted. In 2001, 281 degrees awarded.
Entrance requirements: For master's, interview, minimum GPA of 2.5. *Application deadline:* Applications are processed on a rolling basis. *Application fee:* $60 ($100 for international students).
Expenses: Tuition: Part-time $221 per quarter hour.
Financial support: Institutionally sponsored loans, scholarships/grants, and tuition waivers (full and partial) available. Support available to part-time students. Financial award application deadline: 5/1; financial award applicants required to submit FAFSA.
Dr. Thomas Green, Chair, 858-642-8439, *Fax:* 858-642-8716, *E-mail:* tgreen@nu.edu.
Application contact: Nancy Rohland, Director of Enrollment Management, 858-642-8180, *Fax:* 858-642-8710, *E-mail:* advisor@nu.edu. *Web site:* http://www.nu.edu/

■ NEW MEXICO HIGHLANDS UNIVERSITY

Graduate Studies, College of Arts and Sciences, Program in Public Affairs, Las Vegas, NM 87701

AWARDS Administration (MA); applied sociology (MA); historical and cross-cultural perspective (MA); political and governmental processes (MA). Program is interdisciplinary.

Faculty: 16 full-time (5 women).
Students: 12 full-time (6 women), 14 part-time (6 women); includes 18 minority (4 African Americans, 2 Asian Americans or Pacific Islanders, 12 Hispanic Americans), 1 international. Average age 35. In 2001, 3 degrees awarded.
Degree requirements: For master's, thesis or alternative.
Entrance requirements: For master's, minimum undergraduate GPA of 3.0. *Application deadline:* For fall admission, 8/1 (priority date). Applications are processed on a rolling basis. *Application fee:* $15.
Expenses: Tuition, state resident: full-time $2,238. Tuition, nonresident: full-time $9,366.
Financial support: Research assistantships with full and partial tuition reimbursements, Federal Work-Study available. Financial award application deadline: 3/1.
Dr. Tomas Salazar, Dean, 505-454-3080, *Fax:* 505-454-3389, *E-mail:* salazar_t@nmhu.edu.
Application contact: Dr. Linda LaGrange, Associate Dean of Graduate Studies, 505-454-3266, *Fax:* 505-454-3558, *E-mail:* lagrange_l@nmhu.edu.

■ NEW SCHOOL UNIVERSITY

Robert J. Milano Graduate School of Management and Urban Policy, Program in Public and Urban Policy, New York, NY 10011-8603

AWARDS PhD. Part-time and evening/weekend programs available.

Students: 27 full-time (15 women), 8 part-time (3 women); includes 13 African Americans, 4 Asian Americans or Pacific Islanders, 2 Hispanic Americans, 2 international. Average age 36. 39 applicants, 38% accepted.
Degree requirements: For doctorate, thesis/dissertation, qualifying exams.
Entrance requirements: For doctorate, GRE General Test, MA in political science, urban policy or public policy. *Application deadline:* For fall admission, 4/15 (priority date). Applications are processed on a rolling basis. *Application fee:* $30.
Expenses: Tuition: Full-time $18,720; part-time $1,040 per credit. Required fees: $450; $115 per term. Tuition and fees vary according to program.
Financial support: In 2001–02, 6 fellowships (averaging $10,000 per year), 1 teaching assistantship (averaging $3,500 per year) were awarded. Research assistantships, Federal Work-Study, scholarships/grants, and tuition waivers (full and partial) also available. Support available to part-time students. Financial award application deadline: 3/1; financial award applicants required to submit FAFSA.
Dr. Robert Beauregard, Director, 212-229-5311 Ext. 1614, *Fax:* 212-229-8935.
Application contact: Mario Johnson, Director of Admissions, 212-229-5462, *Fax:* 212-229-8935, *E-mail:* mgsinfo@newschool.edu.

■ NEW YORK UNIVERSITY

Robert F. Wagner Graduate School of Public Service, Program in Public Administration, New York, NY 10012-1019

AWARDS Public administration (PhD); public and nonprofit management and policy (MPA, Advanced Certificate), including developmental administration (Advanced Certificate), financial management and public finance, human resources management (Advanced Certificate), international administration (Advanced Certificate), management for public and nonprofit organizations, public policy analysis, quantitative analysis and computer applications (Advanced Certificate), urban public policy (Advanced Certificate). Part-time and evening/weekend programs available.

Faculty: 15 full-time (6 women), 56 part-time/adjunct (28 women).
Students: 248 full-time (176 women), 226 part-time (168 women); includes 137 minority (61 African Americans, 43 Asian Americans or Pacific Islanders, 33 Hispanic Americans), 78 international. Average age 27. 614 applicants, 76% accepted, 185 enrolled. In 2001, 137 master's, 6 doctorates awarded.
Degree requirements: For master's, thesis or alternative, capstone/end event; for doctorate, one foreign language, thesis/dissertation.
Entrance requirements: For master's, minimum undergraduate GPA of 3.0; for doctorate, GMAT or GRE General Test, minimum GPA of 3.5. *Application deadline:* For fall admission, 7/15; for spring admission, 1/1. Applications are processed on a rolling basis. *Application fee:* $50.
Expenses: Tuition: Full-time $19,536; part-time $814 per credit. Required fees: $1,330; $38 per credit. Tuition and fees vary according to course load and program.
Financial support: In 2001–02, 217 students received support, including 203 fellowships (averaging $5,257 per year), 14 research assistantships with partial tuition reimbursements available (averaging $7,580 per year); career-related internships or fieldwork, Federal Work-Study, institutionally sponsored loans, scholarships/grants, and tuition waivers (full and partial) also available. Support available to part-time students. Financial award application deadline: 2/15; financial award applicants required to submit FAFSA.
Application contact: James Short, Director, Admissions and Financial Aid, 212-998-7414, *Fax:* 212-995-4164, *E-mail:* wagner.admissions@nyu.edu. *Web site:* http://www.nyu.edu.wagner/

Find an in-depth description at www.petersons.com/gradchannel.

■ NORTH CAROLINA CENTRAL UNIVERSITY

Division of Academic Affairs, College of Arts and Sciences, Public Administration Program, Durham, NC 27707-3129

AWARDS MPA. Part-time and evening/weekend programs available.

Faculty: 6 full-time (2 women), 1 part-time/adjunct (0 women).
Students: 22 full-time (14 women), 49 part-time (30 women); includes 67 minority (all African Americans). Average age 32. 20 applicants, 100% accepted. In 2001, 30 degrees awarded.
Degree requirements: For master's, one foreign language, thesis or alternative, comprehensive exam.
Entrance requirements: For master's, minimum GPA of 3.0 in major, 2.5 overall. *Application deadline:* For fall admission, 8/1. *Application fee:* $30.
Expenses: Tuition, state resident: full-time $1,424. Tuition, nonresident: full-time $9,492. Required fees: $1,054.
Financial support: Research assistantships, career-related internships or fieldwork, Federal Work-Study, and institutionally sponsored loans available. Support available to part-time students. Financial award application deadline: 5/1.
Faculty research: Racial diversity and community policing, economic development, issues in urban transportation.
Dr. Jarvis A. Hall, Interim Chairperson, 919-530-5202, *Fax:* 919-560-5195.
Application contact: Dr. Bernice D. Johnson, Dean, College of Arts and Sciences, 919-560-6368, *Fax:* 919-560-5361, *E-mail:* bjohnson@wpo.nccu.edu.

■ NORTH CAROLINA STATE UNIVERSITY

Graduate School, College of Humanities and Social Sciences, Department of Political Science and Public Administration, Program in Public Administration, Raleigh, NC 27695

AWARDS MPA, PhD.

Faculty: 8 full-time (2 women), 1 part-time/adjunct (0 women).
Students: 37 full-time (23 women), 78 part-time (36 women); includes 13 minority (12 African Americans, 1 Asian American or Pacific Islander), 6 international. Average age 33. 98 applicants, 32% accepted. In 2001, 26 master's, 1 doctorate awarded.
Entrance requirements: For master's, GRE General Test, minimum GPA of 3.0 during previous 2 years. *Application deadline:* For fall admission, 6/25; for spring admission, 11/25. *Application fee:* $45.
Expenses: Tuition, state resident: full-time $1,748. Tuition, nonresident: full-time $6,904.
Financial support: In 2001–02, 4 fellowships (averaging $2,870 per year), 3 research assistantships (averaging $5,167 per year), 14 teaching assistantships (averaging $5,168 per year) were awarded.
Faculty research: Urban management, public budgeting, public policy, human resources management, information resources.
Dr. Elizabethann O'Sullivan, Director of Graduate Programs, 919-515-5070, *Fax:* 919-515-7333, *E-mail:* elizabethann_osullivan@social.chass.ncsu.edu.

■ NORTHEASTERN UNIVERSITY

College of Arts and Sciences, Department of Political Science, Program in Public Administration, Boston, MA 02115-5096

AWARDS Development administration (MPA); health administration and policy (MPA); management information systems (MPA); state and local government (MPA). Part-time and evening/weekend programs available.

Faculty: 8 full-time (0 women), 8 part-time/adjunct (1 woman).

Students: 17 full-time (7 women), 19 part-time (12 women); includes 8 minority (2 African Americans, 1 Asian American or Pacific Islander, 5 Hispanic Americans), 3 international. Average age 32. 41 applicants, 78% accepted. In 2001, 11 degrees awarded.
Degree requirements: For master's, thesis optional.
Entrance requirements: For master's, GRE General Test, TOEFL. *Application deadline:* For fall admission, 2/15. Applications are processed on a rolling basis. *Application fee:* $50.
Expenses: Tuition: Part-time $535 per credit hour. Required fees: $56. Tuition and fees vary according to program.
Financial support: In 2001–02, 1 research assistantship with tuition reimbursement, 2 teaching assistantships with tuition reimbursements were awarded. Career-related internships or fieldwork, Federal Work-Study, tuition waivers (full and partial), and unspecified assistantships also available. Support available to part-time students. Financial award application deadline: 2/15; financial award applicants required to submit FAFSA.
Faculty research: National health care, Third World development, leadership and ethics, science and technology, budgeting.
Dr. William Kay, Graduate Coordinator, 617-373-2796, *Fax:* 617-373-5311, *E-mail:* gradpolisci@neu.edu.
Application contact: Mary Churchill, Administrative Assistant for Graduate Programs, 617-373-4404, *Fax:* 617-373-5311, *E-mail:* gradpolisci@neu.edu. *Web site:* http://www.casdn.neu.edu/~polisci/

Find an in-depth description at www.petersons.com/gradchannel.

■ NORTHEASTERN UNIVERSITY

College of Arts and Sciences, Program in Law, Policy, and Society, Boston, MA 02115-5096

AWARDS MS, PhD, JD/PhD. Part-time and evening/weekend programs available.

Faculty: 24 full-time (9 women).
Students: 30 full-time (17 women), 30 part-time (17 women); includes 3 minority (2 African Americans, 1 Hispanic American), 11 international. Average age 40. 60 applicants, 42% accepted. In 2001, 2 master's, 7 doctorates awarded.
Degree requirements: For master's, comprehensive exam; for doctorate, thesis/dissertation, comprehensive exam.
Entrance requirements: For master's, GRE General Test; for doctorate, GRE General Test or LSAT. *Application deadline:* For fall admission, 2/15. *Application fee:* $50.
Expenses: Tuition: Part-time $535 per credit hour. Required fees: $56. Tuition and fees vary according to program.
Financial support: In 2001–02, 15 fellowships with tuition reimbursements, 2 teaching assistantships with tuition reimbursements (averaging $13,000 per year) were awarded. Research assistantships with tuition reimbursements, tuition waivers (full and partial) and unspecified assistantships also available. Financial award application deadline: 2/15; financial award applicants required to submit FAFSA.
Faculty research: Policy issues in health, crime, and labor; urban studies; education; law and environmental issues; economic development, international trade and law.
Dr. Suzann Thomas-Buckle, Co-Director, 617-373-4689, *Fax:* 617-373-4691, *E-mail:* lps@neu.edu.
Application contact: Christina Braedotti, Graduate Secretary, 617-373-2891, *Fax:* 617-373-4691, *E-mail:* lps@neu.edu. *Web site:* http://www.casdn.neu.edu/~lps/

■ NORTHERN ARIZONA UNIVERSITY

Graduate College, College of Social and Behavioral Sciences, Department of Political Science, Program in Political Science, Flagstaff, AZ 86011

AWARDS Political science (MA, PhD); public management (Certificate); public policy (PhD).

Students: 33 full-time (20 women), 22 part-time (10 women); includes 19 minority (6 African Americans, 1 Asian American or Pacific Islander, 9 Hispanic Americans, 3 Native Americans), 5 international. Average age 35. 31 applicants, 61% accepted, 10 enrolled. In 2001, 2 master's, 2 doctorates awarded.
Degree requirements: For master's, thesis optional; for doctorate, one foreign language, thesis/dissertation.
Entrance requirements: For doctorate, GRE General Test. *Application deadline:* For fall admission, 2/15 (priority date). Applications are processed on a rolling basis. *Application fee:* $45.
Expenses: Tuition, state resident: full-time $2,488. Tuition, nonresident: full-time $10,354.
Financial support: In 2001–02, 15 research assistantships, 2 teaching assistantships were awarded. Tuition waivers (full and partial) also available.
Application contact: Susan Bemus, Secretary, 928-523-6979, *E-mail:* political.science@nau.edu. *Web site:* http://www.nau.edu/~pos/

■ NORTHERN ARIZONA UNIVERSITY

Graduate College, College of Social and Behavioral Sciences, Department of Political Science, Program in Public Administration, Flagstaff, AZ 86011

AWARDS MPA.

Students: 5 full-time (2 women), 13 part-time (5 women); includes 8 minority (1 African American, 2 Hispanic Americans, 5 Native Americans). Average age 32. 17 applicants, 65% accepted, 7 enrolled. In 2001, 4 degrees awarded.
Degree requirements: For master's, internship.
Application deadline: For fall admission, 2/15 (priority date). Applications are processed on a rolling basis. *Application fee:* $45.
Expenses: Tuition, state resident: full-time $2,488. Tuition, nonresident: full-time $10,354.
Financial support: Research assistantships, teaching assistantships, career-related internships or fieldwork, Federal Work-Study, and tuition waivers (full and partial) available.
Application contact: Susan Bemus, Secretary, 928-523-6979, *E-mail:* political.science@nau.edu. *Web site:* http://www.nau.edu/~pos/

■ NORTHERN ILLINOIS UNIVERSITY

Graduate School, College of Liberal Arts and Sciences, Department of Political Science, Division of Public Administration, De Kalb, IL 60115-2854

AWARDS MPA. Part-time and evening/weekend programs available.

Faculty: 6 full-time (2 women), 3 part-time/adjunct (0 women).
Students: 41 full-time (16 women), 56 part-time (19 women); includes 12 minority (7 African Americans, 2 Asian Americans or Pacific Islanders, 3 Hispanic Americans). Average age 33. 54 applicants, 44% accepted, 16 enrolled. In 2001, 33 degrees awarded.
Degree requirements: For master's, internship.
Entrance requirements: For master's, GRE General Test, TOEFL, minimum GPA of 2.75, 9 hours in social science. *Application deadline:* For fall admission, 3/1 (priority date); for spring admission, 10/1 (priority date). Applications are processed on a rolling basis. *Application fee:* $30.
Expenses: Tuition, state resident: full-time $5,124; part-time $148 per credit hour. Tuition, nonresident: full-time $8,666; part-time $295 per credit hour. Required fees: $51 per term.
Financial support: Fellowships with full tuition reimbursements, research assistantships with full tuition reimbursements, career-related internships or fieldwork, Federal Work-Study, tuition waivers (full), and unspecified assistantships available. Support available to part-time students.
Faculty research: Urban service and management, manpower public policy.
Dr. Donald Menzel, Director, 815-753-6140, *Fax:* 815-753-2539.
Application contact: Dawn Peters, Coordinator, 815-753-6149.

■ NORTHERN KENTUCKY UNIVERSITY

School of Graduate Programs, Program in Public Administration, Highland Heights, KY 41099

AWARDS MPA.

Faculty: 2 full-time (1 woman).
Students: 4 full-time (1 woman), 37 part-time (16 women); includes 3 minority (all African Americans). Average age 35. In 2001, 10 degrees awarded.
Entrance requirements: For master's, GMAT. *Application deadline:* For fall admission, 8/15 (priority date). Applications are processed on a rolling basis. *Application fee:* $25.
Expenses: Tuition, state resident: full-time $2,958; part-time $149 per credit hour. Tuition, nonresident: full-time $7,872; part-time $422 per credit hour.
Financial support: Career-related internships or fieldwork, institutionally sponsored loans, tuition waivers (full), and unspecified assistantships available. Support available to part-time students.
Dr. Dennis Sies, Director, 859-572-5324.
Application contact: Peg Griffin, Graduate Coordinator, 859-572-6364, *E-mail:* griffinp@nku.edu.

■ NORTHERN MICHIGAN UNIVERSITY

College of Graduate Studies, College of Arts and Sciences, Department of Political Science, Marquette, MI 49855-5301

AWARDS Administrative services (MA); public administration (MPA). Part-time programs available.

Faculty: 7 full-time (0 women), 2 part-time/adjunct (0 women).
Students: 33 full-time (17 women), 64 part-time (29 women); includes 17 minority (6 African Americans, 3 Asian Americans or Pacific Islanders, 8 Native Americans). In 2001, 29 degrees awarded.
Degree requirements: For master's, thesis or alternative.
Entrance requirements: For master's, minimum GPA of 3.0. *Application deadline:* For fall admission, 7/1 (priority date); for spring admission, 11/1. Applications are processed on a rolling basis. *Application fee:* $25.
Expenses: Tuition, state resident: full-time $158. Tuition, nonresident: full-time $260. Tuition and fees vary according to course load.
Financial support: Teaching assistantships, career-related internships or fieldwork, Federal Work-Study, institutionally sponsored loans, and unspecified assistantships available. Support available to part-time students. Financial award application deadline: 3/1.
Dr. Brian Cherry, Head, 906-227-1823.

■ NORTH GEORGIA COLLEGE & STATE UNIVERSITY

Graduate School, Program in Public Administration, Dahlonega, GA 30597-1001

AWARDS MPA. Part-time and evening/weekend programs available.

Faculty: 1 full-time (0 women), 2 part-time/adjunct (0 women).
Students: 8 full-time (2 women), 12 part-time (4 women). In 2001, 9 degrees awarded.
Degree requirements: For master's, thesis optional.
Entrance requirements: For master's, GMAT, GRE General Test, minimum GPA of 2.75. *Application deadline:* For fall admission, 7/1 (priority date); for spring admission, 12/1 (priority date). Applications are processed on a rolling basis. *Application fee:* $25.
Expenses: Tuition, state resident: full-time $1,160. Tuition, nonresident: full-time $4,640.
Financial support: Career-related internships or fieldwork available. Support available to part-time students. Financial award application deadline: 5/1.
Dr. Barry Friedman, Director, 706-864-1916, *Fax:* 706-864-1668, *E-mail:* bfriedman@ngcsu.edu. *Web site:* http://www.NGCSU.edu/academic/Bus_Gov/Ps_cj/mpa.htm

■ NORTHWESTERN UNIVERSITY

The Graduate School, School of Education and Social Policy, Program in Human Development and Social Policy, Evanston, IL 60208

AWARDS PhD. Admissions and degrees offered through The Graduate School.

Faculty: 12 full-time (5 women), 5 part-time/adjunct (1 woman).
Students: 32 full-time (29 women); includes 7 minority (5 African Americans, 2 Asian Americans or Pacific Islanders), 4 international. Average age 33. 60 applicants, 17% accepted, 5 enrolled. In 2001, 6 degrees awarded.
Degree requirements: For doctorate, thesis/dissertation.
Entrance requirements: For doctorate, GRE General Test, sample of written work. *Application deadline:* For fall admission, 12/31 (priority date). *Application fee:* $50 ($55 for international students). Electronic applications accepted.
Expenses: Tuition: Full-time $26,526.
Financial support: In 2001–02, 32 students received support, including 5 fellowships with full tuition reimbursements available; research assistantships with full tuition reimbursements available, teaching assistantships, career-related internships or fieldwork, Federal Work-Study, institutionally sponsored loans, and scholarships/grants also available. Financial award application deadline: 12/31; financial award applicants required to submit FAFSA.
Faculty research: Social context of development; social policy issues affecting children, adolescents, adults, and families.
Dr. Lindsay Chase-Lansdale, Program Chair, 847-491-4329.
Application contact: Mary Lou Manning, Department Assistant, 847-491-4329, *Fax:* 847-491-8999, *E-mail:* mmanning@casbah.acns.northwestern.edu. *Web site:* http://www.sesp.northwestern.edu

Find an in-depth description at www.petersons.com/gradchannel.

■ NOTRE DAME DE NAMUR UNIVERSITY

Graduate School, School of Business and Management, Department of Public Administration, Belmont, CA 94002-1997

AWARDS MPA. Part-time and evening/weekend programs available.

Faculty: 2 full-time, 10 part-time/adjunct.
Students: 2 full-time (both women), 64 part-time (45 women); includes 14 minority (2 African Americans, 7 Asian Americans or Pacific Islanders, 5 Hispanic Americans), 1 international. Average age 35. 37 applicants, 78% accepted. In 2001, 29 degrees awarded.
Entrance requirements: For master's, TOEFL, interview, minimum GPA of 2.5. *Application deadline:* For fall admission, 8/1 (priority date); for spring admission, 12/1 (priority date). Applications are processed on a rolling basis. *Application fee:* $50 ($500 for international students). Electronic applications accepted.
Expenses: Tuition: Full-time $9,450; part-time $525 per unit. Required fees: $35 per term.
Financial support: Career-related internships or fieldwork available. Support available to part-time students. Financial award applicants required to submit FAFSA.
Dr. James Kelley, Director, 650-508-3582, *E-mail:* jkelley@ndnu.edu.
Application contact: Barbara Sterner, Assistant Director of Graduate Admissions, 650-508-3527, *Fax:* 650-508-3662, *E-mail:* grad.admit@ndnu.edu.

■ NOVA SOUTHEASTERN UNIVERSITY

Wayne Huizenga Graduate School of Business and Entrepreneurship, Program in Public Administration, Fort Lauderdale, FL 33314-7721

AWARDS MPA, DPA. Part-time and evening/weekend programs available.

Students: 94 (50 women). 20 applicants, 75% accepted. In 2001, 25 master's, 3 doctorates awarded.
Degree requirements: For master's, thesis or alternative; for doctorate, thesis/dissertation, comprehensive exam.

Entrance requirements: For master's, GMAT, GRE General Test, work experience; for doctorate, GMAT or GRE, master's degree; work experience in field; previous course work in accounting, finance, and economics; computer literacy. *Application deadline:* For fall admission, 8/15 (priority date); for spring admission, 2/10. Applications are processed on a rolling basis. *Application fee:* $50.
Expenses: Tuition: Full-time $7,380; part-time $432 per credit. Required fees: $200. Tuition and fees vary according to campus/location and program.
Financial support: Career-related internships or fieldwork, Federal Work-Study, and institutionally sponsored loans available.
Dr. Jack Pinkowski, Director, 954-262-5115, *Fax:* 954-262-3822, *E-mail:* pinkowski@huizenga.nova.edu.
Application contact: Sebastian Kovacs, Marketing Manager, 954-262-5035, *Fax:* 954-262-3822, *E-mail:* kovacs@huizenga.nova.edu. *Web site:* http://www.huizenga.nova.edu/

■ OAKLAND UNIVERSITY

Graduate Study and Lifelong Learning, College of Arts and Sciences, Department of Political Science, Program in Public Administration, Rochester, MI 48309-4401

AWARDS MPA. Part-time and evening/weekend programs available.

Faculty: 13 full-time (3 women), 3 part-time/adjunct (2 women).
Students: 5 full-time (3 women), 29 part-time (18 women); includes 6 minority (4 African Americans, 1 Asian American or Pacific Islander, 1 Hispanic American). Average age 33. 13 applicants, 85% accepted. In 2001, 8 degrees awarded.
Entrance requirements: For master's, minimum GPA of 3.0 for unconditional admission. *Application deadline:* For fall admission, 7/15 (priority date); for winter admission, 12/1 (priority date); for spring admission, 3/15 (priority date). Applications are processed on a rolling basis. *Application fee:* $30. Electronic applications accepted.
Expenses: Tuition, state resident: full-time $5,904; part-time $246 per credit hour. Tuition, nonresident: full-time $12,192; part-time $508 per credit hour. Required fees: $472; $236 per term.
Financial support: Federal Work-Study, institutionally sponsored loans, and tuition waivers (full) available. Financial award application deadline: 3/1; financial award applicants required to submit FAFSA.
Dr. Michelle Piskulich, Chair, 248-370-2358.

■ THE OHIO STATE UNIVERSITY

Graduate School, College of Social and Behavioral Sciences, School of Public Policy and Management, Columbus, OH 43210

AWARDS MA, MPA, PhD, JD/MPA, MHA/MPA. Part-time programs available.

Degree requirements: For doctorate, thesis/dissertation.
Entrance requirements: For master's, GMAT or GRE General Test, TOEFL; for doctorate, GRE General Test, TOEFL.

Find an in-depth description at www.petersons.com/gradchannel.

■ OHIO UNIVERSITY

Graduate Studies, College of Arts and Sciences, Department of Political Science, Athens, OH 45701-2979

AWARDS Political science (MA); public administration (MPA). Part-time programs available.

Faculty: 24 full-time (8 women).
Students: 33 full-time (12 women), 24 part-time (15 women); includes 4 minority (2 African Americans, 1 Asian American or Pacific Islander, 1 Native American), 21 international. 113 applicants, 91% accepted, 58 enrolled. In 2001, 14 degrees awarded.
Degree requirements: For master's, thesis or alternative, comprehensive exam.
Entrance requirements: For master's, GRE General Test, minimum GPA of 3.0. *Application deadline:* For fall admission, 3/1 (priority date). Applications are processed on a rolling basis. *Application fee:* $30. Electronic applications accepted.
Expenses: Tuition, state resident: full-time $6,585. Tuition, nonresident: full-time $12,254.
Financial support: In 2001–02, 30 students received support, including 10 research assistantships with full tuition reimbursements available (averaging $8,000 per year), 6 teaching assistantships with full tuition reimbursements available (averaging $8,000 per year); career-related internships or fieldwork, Federal Work-Study, institutionally sponsored loans, and tuition waivers (full and partial) also available. Financial award application deadline: 3/15.
Faculty research: International relations, Latin American politics, public policy, economic development, political theory.
Dr. Michael Mumper, Chair, 740-593-4372, *Fax:* 740-593-0394, *E-mail:* mumper@ohio.edu.
Application contact: Dr. Ronald Hunt, Graduate Director, 740-593-4368, *Fax:* 740-593-0394, *E-mail:* huntr@ohiou.edu. *Web site:* http://www.ohiou.edu/pols

■ OKLAHOMA CITY UNIVERSITY

Meinders School of Business, Program in Business Administration, Oklahoma City, OK 73106-1402

AWARDS Arts management (MBA); finance (MBA); health administration (MBA); information systems management (MBA); integrated marketing communications (MBA); international business (MBA); management (MBA); marketing (MBA); public administration (MBA). Part-time and evening/weekend programs available.

Degree requirements: For master's, comprehensive exam.
Entrance requirements: For master's, TOEFL, minimum GPA of 2.5. *Web site:* http://www.okcu.edu/

■ OKLAHOMA STATE UNIVERSITY

Graduate College, College of Arts and Sciences, Department of Political Science, Program in Fire Protection and Safety Technology, Stillwater, OK 74078

AWARDS MS.

Faculty: 20 part-time/adjunct (19 women).
Students: Average age 36. 8 applicants, 100% accepted. In 2001, 8 degrees awarded.
Entrance requirements: For master's, TOEFL, minimum GPA of 3.0. *Application deadline:* For fall admission, 6/1 (priority date). *Application fee:* $25.
Expenses: Tuition, state resident: part-time $92 per credit hour. Tuition, nonresident: part-time $297 per credit hour. Required fees: $21 per credit hour. $14 per semester. One-time fee: $20. Tuition and fees vary according to course load.
Financial support: In 2001–02, 1 teaching assistantship (averaging $18,450 per year) was awarded. Financial award application deadline: 3/1.
Tom Woodford, Head, 405-744-5721, *E-mail:* woodfor@okstate.edu.

■ OLD DOMINION UNIVERSITY

College of Business and Public Administration, Program in Public Administration, Norfolk, VA 23529

AWARDS MPA. Part-time and evening/weekend programs available.

Faculty: 7 full-time (1 woman), 4 part-time/adjunct (1 woman).
Students: 17 full-time (13 women), 129 part-time (58 women); includes 32 minority (27 African Americans, 1 Asian American or Pacific Islander, 4 Hispanic Americans), 2 international. Average age 37. 66 applicants, 91% accepted. In 2001, 35 degrees awarded.
Degree requirements: For master's, internship, thesis optional.
Entrance requirements: For master's, GMAT or GRE General Test. *Application*

Old Dominion University (continued)
deadline: For fall admission, 7/1 (priority date); for spring admission, 10/1 (priority date). Applications are processed on a rolling basis. *Application fee:* $30. Electronic applications accepted.
Expenses: Tuition, state resident: part-time $202 per credit. Tuition, nonresident: part-time $534 per credit. Required fees: $76 per semester.
Financial support: In 2001–02, 25 students received support, including 2 research assistantships with tuition reimbursements available (averaging $5,000 per year); fellowships, teaching assistantships, career-related internships or fieldwork, scholarships/grants, and tuition waivers (partial) also available. Financial award application deadline: 2/15; financial award applicants required to submit FAFSA.
Faculty research: Environmental administration, personnel policy analysis, urban administration. *Total annual research expenditures:* $80,919.
Dr. William Leavitt, Graduate Program Director, 757-683-3961, *Fax:* 757-683-5639, *E-mail:* padmgpd@odu.edu. *Web site:* http://www.odu-cbpa.org/mpa.htm

■ PACE UNIVERSITY, WHITE PLAINS CAMPUS

Dyson College of Arts and Sciences, Department of Public Administration, White Plains, NY 10603

AWARDS Government management (MPA); health care administration (MPA); nonprofit management (MPA). Part-time and evening/weekend programs available.

Faculty: 6 full-time, 10 part-time/adjunct.
Students: 25 full-time (17 women), 63 part-time (37 women); includes 32 minority (20 African Americans, 11 Hispanic Americans, 1 Native American), 1 international. Average age 30. 53 applicants, 62% accepted, 18 enrolled. In 2001, 23 master's awarded.
Degree requirements: For master's, capstone project.
Entrance requirements: For master's, GRE General Test. *Application deadline:* For fall admission, 8/1 (priority date); for spring admission, 12/1 (priority date). Applications are processed on a rolling basis. *Application fee:* $65. Electronic applications accepted.
Expenses: Tuition: Part-time $545 per credit.
Financial support: Research assistantships, career-related internships or fieldwork, Federal Work-Study, and tuition waivers (partial) available. Support available to part-time students. Financial award applicants required to submit FAFSA.
Dr. Joseph Ryan, Chairperson, 914-422-4303.
Application contact: Joanna Broda, Director of Admissions, 914-422-4283, *Fax:* 914-422-4287, *E-mail:* gradwp@pace.edu. *Web site:* http://www.pace.edu/
Find an in-depth description at www.petersons.com/gradchannel.

■ PARK UNIVERSITY

Hauptmann School of Public Affairs, Parkville, MO 64152-3795

AWARDS Government/business relations (MPA); non-profit management (MPA); public management (MPA). Part-time and evening/weekend programs available.

Faculty: 1 full-time (0 women), 33 part-time/adjunct (12 women).
Students: 31 full-time (16 women), 45 part-time (24 women); includes 28 minority (25 African Americans, 1 Asian American or Pacific Islander, 2 Hispanic Americans). Average age 30. 25 applicants, 80% accepted, 20 enrolled. In 2001, 19 degrees awarded.
Degree requirements: For master's, thesis, oral and written exams, comprehensive exam, registration. *Median time to degree:* Master's–2 years full-time, 3 years part-time.
Entrance requirements: For master's, GRE General Test, 2.5 GPA in last 60 hours of undergraduate work, 3 letters of recommendation. *Application deadline:* For fall admission, 8/19; for spring admission, 1/13. Applications are processed on a rolling basis. *Application fee:* $50 ($100 for international students).
Financial support: In 2001–02, 30 students received support. Federal Work-Study, institutionally sponsored loans, scholarships/grants, health care benefits, and unspecified assistantships available. Support available to part-time students. Financial award application deadline: 8/1; financial award applicants required to submit FAFSA.
Faculty research: Non-profit management, public management, government/business relations.
Dr. Jerzy Hauptmann, Dean, 816-421-1125 Ext. 236, *Fax:* 816-471-1658, *E-mail:* gspa@mail.park.edu.
Application contact: Thomas E. Gee, Administrator, 816-421-1125 Ext. 236, *Fax:* 816-471-1658, *E-mail:* tgee@mail.park.edu.

■ THE PENNSYLVANIA STATE UNIVERSITY HARRISBURG CAMPUS OF THE CAPITAL COLLEGE

Graduate Center, School of Public Affairs, Program in Public Administration, Middletown, PA 17057-4898

AWARDS MPA, PhD. Evening/weekend programs available.

Students: 20 full-time (11 women), 102 part-time (47 women). Average age 33. In 2001, 34 master's, 5 doctorates awarded.
Degree requirements: For master's, thesis, fieldwork or previous experience.
Entrance requirements: For master's, GMAT or GRE General Test, minimum GPA of 3.0 during previous 2 years. *Application deadline:* For fall admission, 7/26. *Application fee:* $45.
Expenses: Tuition, state resident: full-time $7,882; part-time $333 per credit. Tuition, nonresident: full-time $14,384; part-time $600 per credit.
Financial support: Career-related internships or fieldwork available.
Faculty research: Human resources, public systems analysis.
Dr. Jack Rabin, Coordinator, 717-948-6363.

■ PEPPERDINE UNIVERSITY

School of Public Policy, Malibu, CA 90263-0002

AWARDS MPP.

Faculty: 4 full-time (0 women), 2 part-time/adjunct (0 women).
Students: 56 full-time (28 women), 1 (woman) part-time; includes 9 minority (6 African Americans, 1 Asian American or Pacific Islander, 2 Hispanic Americans), 3 international. 76 applicants, 67% accepted. In 2001, 15 degrees awarded.
Entrance requirements: For master's, GRE. *Application deadline:* For fall admission, 4/15. Applications are processed on a rolling basis. *Application fee:* $50. Electronic applications accepted.
Expenses: Tuition: Full-time $15,700; part-time $785 per unit. Tuition and fees vary according to degree level and program.
Financial support: Research assistantships, teaching assistantships, institutionally sponsored loans and scholarships/grants available. Financial award application deadline: 5/1; financial award applicants required to submit FAFSA.
Dr. James Wilburn, Dean, 310-506-7490, *Fax:* 310-506-7494.
Application contact: Melinda van Hemert, Director of Recruitment and Career Services, 310-506-7492, *Fax:* 310-506-7494.
Find an in-depth description at www.petersons.com/gradchannel.

■ PIEDMONT COLLEGE

Department of Social Sciences, Demorest, GA 30535-0010

AWARDS Public administration (MPA). Part-time and evening/weekend programs available.

Faculty: 3 full-time (1 woman), 2 part-time/adjunct (0 women).
Students: 15 (8 women); includes 3 minority (2 African Americans, 1 Hispanic American) 2 international. 7 applicants, 86% accepted, 3 enrolled. In 2001, 15 degrees awarded.
Degree requirements: For master's, capstone course, internship.

Entrance requirements: For master's, GRE General Test, MAT, minimum undergraduate GPA of 2.75. *Application deadline:* For fall admission, 7/15 (priority date); for spring admission, 12/1 (priority date). Applications are processed on a rolling basis. *Application fee:* $30.
Expenses: Tuition: Part-time $230 per hour.
Financial support: In 2001–02, 1 teaching assistantship with partial tuition reimbursement (averaging $5,000 per year) was awarded; career-related internships or fieldwork, Federal Work-Study, and institutionally sponsored loans also available. Support available to part-time students.
Dr. Kenneth E. Melichar, Chair, 706-778-3000 Ext. 1264, *Fax:* 706-776-2811, *E-mail:* kmelichar@piedmont.edu.
Application contact: Carol E. Kokesh, Director of Graduate Studies, 706-778-8500 Ext. 1181, *Fax:* 706-776-6635, *E-mail:* ckokesh@piedmont.edu. *Web site:* http://www.piedmont.edu/

■ PONTIFICAL CATHOLIC UNIVERSITY OF PUERTO RICO

Institute of Graduate Studies in Behavioral Science and Community Affairs, Ponce, PR 00717-0777

AWARDS Clinical psychology (MS); clinical social work (MSW); criminology (MA); industrial psychology (MS); psychology (PhD); public administration (MA). Part-time and evening/weekend programs available.

Faculty: 10 full-time (7 women), 17 part-time/adjunct (12 women).
Students: 86 full-time (56 women), 394 part-time (266 women); all minorities (all Hispanic Americans). 141 applicants, 83% accepted, 104 enrolled. In 2001, 35 degrees awarded.
Entrance requirements: For master's, GRE, 2 recommendation letters, interview, minimum GPA of 2.75. *Application deadline:* For fall admission, 4/30 (priority date). Applications are processed on a rolling basis. *Application fee:* $50. Electronic applications accepted.
Expenses: Tuition: Full-time $2,880; part-time $160 per credit. Required fees: $360. Tuition and fees vary according to degree level and program.
Financial support: Federal Work-Study and tuition waivers (partial) available. Support available to part-time students. Financial award application deadline: 7/15.
Dr. Nilde Cordoline, Director, 787-841-2000 Ext. 1024.
Application contact: Ana O. Bonilla, Director of Admissions, 787-841-2000 Ext. 1000, *Fax:* 787-840-4295. *Web site:* http://www.pucpr.edu/

■ PORTLAND STATE UNIVERSITY

Graduate Studies, College of Urban and Public Affairs, School of Government, Division of Public Administration, Program in Public Administration, Portland, OR 97207-0751

AWARDS MPA.

Students: 44 full-time (25 women), 92 part-time (61 women); includes 20 minority (5 African Americans, 4 Asian Americans or Pacific Islanders, 4 Hispanic Americans, 7 Native Americans), 11 international. Average age 36.
Degree requirements: For master's, internship.
Entrance requirements: For master's, TOEFL, minimum GPA of 3.0 in upper-division course work or 2.75 overall. *Application deadline:* For fall admission, 4/1; for spring admission, 11/1. Applications are processed on a rolling basis. *Application fee:* $50.
Financial support: Application deadline: 3/1.
Application contact: Betty Lewis, Coordinator, 503-725-3920, *Fax:* 503-725-8250, *E-mail:* betty@upa.pdx.edu. *Web site:* http://www.upa.pdx.edu/PA/

■ PORTLAND STATE UNIVERSITY

Graduate Studies, College of Urban and Public Affairs, School of Government, Division of Public Administration, Program in Public Administration and Policy, Portland, OR 97207-0751

AWARDS PhD. Part-time programs available.

Students: 16 full-time (8 women), 30 part-time (17 women); includes 4 minority (2 African Americans, 1 Asian American or Pacific Islander, 1 Hispanic American), 5 international. Average age 43.
Degree requirements: For doctorate, thesis/dissertation, residency, comprehensive exam.
Entrance requirements: For doctorate, GRE General Test, minimum GPA of 2.75. *Application deadline:* For fall admission, 2/1. *Application fee:* $50.
Financial support: Fellowships, research assistantships, teaching assistantships, career-related internships or fieldwork, Federal Work-Study, and institutionally sponsored loans available. Support available to part-time students. Financial award application deadline: 3/1; financial award applicants required to submit FAFSA.
Faculty research: Organizational development, aging and social policy, transportation policy.
Dr. Elizabeth Kutza, Director, 503-725-3952, *Fax:* 503-725-5199, *E-mail:* beth@upa.pdx.edu.
Application contact: Rod Johnson, Office Specialist, 503-725-4044, *Fax:* 503-725-5199, *E-mail:* johnsonro@upa.pdx.edu. *Web site:* http://www.upa.pdx.edu/

■ PRINCETON UNIVERSITY

Graduate School, Woodrow Wilson School of Public and International Affairs, Princeton, NJ 08544-1019

AWARDS MPA, MPA-URP, MPP, PhD, JD/MPA.

Degree requirements: For master's, internship; for doctorate, one foreign language, thesis/dissertation.
Entrance requirements: For master's, GRE General Test, original policy memo; for doctorate, GRE General Test.

■ RAND GRADUATE SCHOOL OF POLICY STUDIES

Program in Policy Analysis, Santa Monica, CA 90407-2138

AWARDS PhD.

Faculty: 55 part-time/adjunct (14 women).
Students: 69 full-time (21 women); includes 6 minority (1 African American, 4 Asian Americans or Pacific Islanders, 1 Hispanic American), 34 international. Average age 32. 92 applicants, 45% accepted, 20 enrolled. In 2001, 5 degrees awarded.
Degree requirements: For doctorate, thesis/dissertation, qualifying exams. *Median time to degree:* Doctorate–4.5 years full-time.
Entrance requirements: For doctorate, GMAT or GRE General Test, TOEFL. *Application deadline:* For fall admission, 2/1 (priority date). *Application fee:* $50. Electronic applications accepted.
Expenses: Tuition: Full-time $18,000.
Financial support: In 2001–02, 69 fellowships, 69 research assistantships, 10 teaching assistantships (averaging $1,500 per year) were awarded. Career-related internships or fieldwork also available.
Faculty research: Education, defense policy, health, labor and population, justice.
Dr. Robert Klitgaard, Dean, 310-393-0411 Ext. 7075, *Fax:* 310-451-6978, *E-mail:* robert_klitgaard@rgs.edu.
Application contact: Marcy F. Agmon, Assistant Dean, 310-393-0411 Ext. 6419, *Fax:* 310-451-6978, *E-mail:* agmon@rgs.edu. *Web site:* http://www.rand.org:80/fellowships/rgs/

Find an in-depth description at www.petersons.com/gradchannel.

■ REGENT UNIVERSITY

Graduate School, Robertson School of Government, Virginia Beach, VA 23464-9800

AWARDS Public administration (MA); public management (MA); public policy (MA). Part-time programs available.

Regent University (continued)
Faculty: 8 full-time (1 woman), 6 part-time/adjunct (0 women).
Students: 79 (40 women); includes 24 minority (19 African Americans, 2 Asian Americans or Pacific Islanders, 2 Hispanic Americans, 1 Native American) 3 international. Average age 32. 61 applicants, 90% accepted, 30 enrolled. In 2001, 29 degrees awarded.
Degree requirements: For master's, thesis, internship.
Entrance requirements: For master's, GRE General Test or LSAT, minimum undergraduate GPA of 2.75, sample of written work. *Application deadline:* For fall admission, 5/1 (priority date); for spring admission, 11/1 (priority date). Applications are processed on a rolling basis. *Application fee:* $40. Electronic applications accepted.
Expenses: Contact institution.
Financial support: In 2001–02, 2 students received support; research assistantships available. Financial award application deadline: 9/1; financial award applicants required to submit FAFSA.
Faculty research: Education reform, political character issues, social capital concerns, administrative ethics, biblical law and public policy.
Dr. Kathaleen Reid-Martinez, Dean, 757-226-4022, *Fax:* 757-226-4448, *E-mail:* kathrei@regent.edu.
Application contact: B. Nathaniel Smith, Acting Manager of Admissions, 800-373-5504, *Fax:* 757-226-4381, *E-mail:* admissions@regent.edu. *Web site:* http://www.regent.edu/government

■ ROOSEVELT UNIVERSITY

Graduate Division, College of Arts and Sciences, School of Policy Studies, Program in Public Administration, Chicago, IL 60605-1394

AWARDS MPA. Part-time and evening/weekend programs available.

Faculty: 6 full-time (3 women), 7 part-time/adjunct (2 women).
Students: 5 full-time (2 women), 147 part-time (100 women); includes 65 minority (54 African Americans, 2 Asian Americans or Pacific Islanders, 9 Hispanic Americans), 3 international. Average age 29. In 2001, 32 degrees awarded.
Degree requirements: For master's, thesis optional.
Entrance requirements: For master's, minimum undergraduate GPA of 3.0. *Application deadline:* For fall admission, 6/1 (priority date). Applications are processed on a rolling basis. *Application fee:* $25 ($35 for international students).
Expenses: Tuition: Full-time $9,090; part-time $505 per credit hour. Required fees: $100 per term.
Financial support: Application deadline: 2/15.
Faculty research: Health policy issues, environmental policy, local government administration.
Application contact: Joanne Canyon-Heller, Coordinator of Graduate Admissions, 312-281-3250, *Fax:* 312-341-3523, *E-mail:* applyru@roosevelt.edu.

■ RUTGERS, THE STATE UNIVERSITY OF NEW JERSEY, CAMDEN

Graduate School, Department of Public Policy and Administration, Camden, NJ 08102-1401

AWARDS Health care management and policy (MPA); international public service and development (MPA); public management (MPA). Part-time and evening/weekend programs available.

Degree requirements: For master's, oral presentation, directed study.
Entrance requirements: For master's, GRE General Test or GMAT or LSAT. Electronic applications accepted.
Faculty research: Nonprofit management, county and municipal administration, health and human services, government communication, administrative law, educational finance.

■ RUTGERS, THE STATE UNIVERSITY OF NEW JERSEY, NEWARK

Graduate School, Department of Public Administration, Newark, NJ 07102

AWARDS Health care administration (MPA); human resources administration (MPA); public administration (PhD); public management (MPA); public policy analysis (MPA); urban systems and issues (MPA). Part-time and evening/weekend programs available.

Degree requirements: For master's, thesis or alternative, comprehensive exam; for doctorate, thesis/dissertation.
Entrance requirements: For master's, GRE, minimum undergraduate B average; for doctorate, GRE, MPA, minimum B average. Electronic applications accepted.
Faculty research: Government finance, municipal and state government, public productivity. *Web site:* http://newark.rutgers.edu/pubadm/welcome.html

■ RUTGERS, THE STATE UNIVERSITY OF NEW JERSEY, NEW BRUNSWICK

Edward J. Bloustein School of Planning and Public Policy, Department of Public Policy, New Brunswick, NJ 08901-1281

AWARDS MPAP, MPP, JD/MPAP. Part-time programs available.

Entrance requirements: For master's, GRE General Test or LSAT. Electronic applications accepted.
Faculty research: Public finance, legislative process, public opinion, economics and public policy, campaigning. *Web site:* http://www.policy.rutgers.edu/dpp/

■ SAGE GRADUATE SCHOOL

Graduate School, Division of Management, Communications and Legal Studies, Program in Public Administration, Troy, NY 12180-4115

AWARDS Communications (MS); gerontology (MS); human services administration (MS); nutrition and dietetics (MS); public management (MS). Part-time and evening/weekend programs available.

Students: 5 full-time (4 women), 21 part-time (16 women). Average age 31. 9 applicants, 100% accepted, 8 enrolled. In 2001, 12 degrees awarded.
Entrance requirements: For master's, minimum GPA of 2.75. *Application fee:* $40.
Expenses: Tuition: Full-time $7,600. Required fees: $100.
Financial support: Career-related internships or fieldwork available. Support available to part-time students. Financial award application deadline: 3/1; financial award applicants required to submit FAFSA. 518-292-1770.
Application contact: Melissa M. Robertson, Associate Director of Admissions, 518-244-6878, *Fax:* 518-244-6880, *E-mail:* sgsadm@sage.edu. *Web site:* http://www.sage.edu/

■ SAGINAW VALLEY STATE UNIVERSITY

College of Arts and Behavioral Sciences, Program in Leadership in Public Administration, University Center, MI 48710

AWARDS MA. Part-time and evening/weekend programs available.

Faculty: 7 full-time (1 woman).
Students: 18 full-time (11 women), 24 part-time (15 women); includes 12 minority (9 African Americans, 2 Asian Americans or Pacific Islanders, 1 Native American), 2 international. 38 applicants, 74% accepted, 15 enrolled. In 2001, 15 degrees awarded. *Median time to degree:* Master's–2.83 years full-time, 6.56 years part-time.
Entrance requirements: For master's, TOEFL, minimum GPA of 3.0 in social sciences, 2.75 overall. *Application deadline:* Applications are processed on a rolling basis. *Application fee:* $25.
Expenses: Tuition, state resident: full-time $2,263; part-time $189 per credit. Tuition, nonresident: full-time $4,480; part-time $373 per credit. Required fees: $201; $17 per credit.
Financial support: In 2001–02, 2 fellowships with partial tuition reimbursements,

1 research assistantship with full tuition reimbursement (averaging $5,000 per year) were awarded. Federal Work-Study also available. Support available to part-time students. Financial award application deadline: 4/1; financial award applicants required to submit FAFSA.
Faculty research: Mediation and conciliation, public administration, criminal justice, fiscal administration, professional ethics.
Dr. Joni Boye-Beaman, Coordinator, 989-790-4373, *E-mail:* drw@tardis.svsu.edu.
Application contact: Barb Sageman, Director, Graduate Admissions, 989-249-1696, *Fax:* 989-790-0180, *E-mail:* gradadm@svsu.edu. *Web site:* http://www.svsu.edu/gradadm/mola/index.html

■ ST. EDWARD'S UNIVERSITY

College of Professional and Graduate Studies, Program in Human Services, Austin, TX 78704-6489

AWARDS Conflict resolution (Certificate); human services (MA), including administration, conflict resolution, human resource management, sports management; sports management (Certificate). Part-time and evening/weekend programs available.

Faculty: 4 full-time (1 woman), 12 part-time/adjunct (6 women).
Students: 12 full-time (11 women), 90 part-time (71 women); includes 28 minority (9 African Americans, 5 Asian Americans or Pacific Islanders, 13 Hispanic Americans, 1 Native American), 3 international. Average age 36. 22 applicants, 86% accepted, 16 enrolled. In 2001, 43 degrees awarded.
Degree requirements: For master's, minimum 24 resident hours.
Entrance requirements: For master's, GRE General Test, TOEFL, minimum GPA of 3.0 in last 60 hours or 2.75 overall. *Application deadline:* For fall admission, 8/1; for spring admission, 12/1. Applications are processed on a rolling basis. *Application fee:* $30 ($50 for international students). Electronic applications accepted.
Expenses: Tuition: Full-time $7,974; part-time $443 per credit hour.
Financial support: In 2001–02, 56 students received support. Career-related internships or fieldwork, institutionally sponsored loans, and scholarships/grants available. Support available to part-time students. Financial award application deadline: 4/15; financial award applicants required to submit FAFSA.
Dr. James A. Johnson, Dean, 512-416-5827, *Fax:* 512-448-8492, *E-mail:* jamesj@admin.stedwards.edu.
Application contact: Bridget Sowinski, Graduate Admissions Coordinator, 512-428-1061, *Fax:* 512-428-1032, *E-mail:* bridgets@admin.stewards.edu. *Web site:* http://www.stedwards.edu/

■ SAINT LOUIS UNIVERSITY

Graduate School, College of Public Service, Department of Public Policy Studies, St. Louis, MO 63103-2097

AWARDS Public administration (MAPA); public policy analysis (PhD); urban affairs (MAUA); urban planning and real estate development (MUPRED).

Faculty: 8 full-time (1 woman), 14 part-time/adjunct (8 women).
Students: 25 full-time (12 women), 57 part-time (30 women); includes 12 minority (all African Americans), 5 international. Average age 36. 41 applicants, 83% accepted, 23 enrolled. In 2001, 7 master's, 7 doctorates awarded.
Degree requirements: For master's, comprehensive exam; for doctorate, thesis/dissertation, preliminary exams, comprehensive exam.
Entrance requirements: For master's and doctorate, GMAT, GRE General Test, or LSAT. *Application deadline:* For fall admission, 7/1; for spring admission, 11/1. Applications are processed on a rolling basis. *Application fee:* $40.
Expenses: Tuition: Part-time $630 per credit hour.
Financial support: In 2001–02, 42 students received support, including 1 fellowship with tuition reimbursement available, 1 research assistantship with tuition reimbursement available; career-related internships or fieldwork, tuition waivers (partial), and unspecified assistantships also available. Financial award application deadline: 4/1; financial award applicants required to submit FAFSA.
Faculty research: Regional growth, community development, social capital, sustainable development, affordable housing.
Dr. Mary Domahidy, Chairperson, 314-977-3934, *Fax:* 314-977-3943, *E-mail:* domahimr@slu.edu.
Application contact: Dr. Marcia Buresch, Associate Dean of the Graduate School, 314-977-2240, *Fax:* 314-977-3943, *E-mail:* bureschm@slu.edu.

■ SAINT MARY'S UNIVERSITY OF MINNESOTA

Graduate School, Program in Resource Analysis, Winona, MN 55987-1399

AWARDS Business (MS); criminal justice (MS); natural resources (MS); public administration (MS).

■ ST. THOMAS UNIVERSITY

School of Graduate Studies, Department of Professional Management, Specialization in Public Management, Miami, FL 33054-6459

AWARDS MSM, Certificate. Part-time and evening/weekend programs available.

Degree requirements: For master's, comprehensive exam.
Entrance requirements: For master's, TOEFL, interview, minimum GPA of 3.0 or GMAT.

■ SAN DIEGO STATE UNIVERSITY

Graduate and Research Affairs, College of Professional Studies and Fine Arts, School of Public Administration and Urban Studies, Program in Public Administration, San Diego, CA 92182

AWARDS MPA.

Entrance requirements: For master's, GRE General Test, TOEFL.

■ SAN FRANCISCO STATE UNIVERSITY

Graduate Division, College of Behavioral and Social Sciences, Public Administration Program, San Francisco, CA 94132-1722

AWARDS Nonprofit administration (MPA); policy analysis (MPA); public management (MPA); urban administration (MPA).

Degree requirements: For master's, internship, project or thesis.
Entrance requirements: For master's, GRE General Test, essay exam, minimum GPA of 3.0.
Faculty research: Public and nonprofit budgeting, urban policy and politics, social service delivery for culturally diverse communities.

■ SAN JOSE STATE UNIVERSITY

Graduate Studies, College of Social Sciences, Department of Political Science, San Jose, CA 95192-0001

AWARDS Public administration (MPA). Part-time and evening/weekend programs available.

Faculty: 15 full-time (0 women), 9 part-time/adjunct (3 women).
Students: 6 full-time (4 women), 54 part-time (28 women); includes 26 minority (4 African Americans, 4 Asian Americans or Pacific Islanders, 18 Hispanic Americans). Average age 34. 45 applicants, 71% accepted. In 2001, 13 degrees awarded.
Degree requirements: For master's, thesis or alternative, comprehensive exam.
Entrance requirements: For master's, GRE Subject Test, minimum GPA of 3.0. *Application deadline:* For fall admission, 6/29; for spring admission, 11/30. Applications are processed on a rolling basis. *Application fee:* $59. Electronic applications accepted.
Expenses: Tuition, nonresident: part-time $246 per unit. Required fees: $678 per semester. Tuition and fees vary according to course load.

San Jose State University (continued)
Financial support: Career-related internships or fieldwork, Federal Work-Study, institutionally sponsored loans, scholarships/grants, and tuition waivers (partial) available. Support available to part-time students. Financial award applicants required to submit FAFSA.
Faculty research: Modern political philosophy, international relations in the Middle East, public policy, American public policy, political parties and political reform.
Dr. Terry Christensen, Chair, 408-924-5550, *Fax:* 408-924-5556.
Application contact: Dr. Mary Carroll, Graduate Coordinator, 408-924-5574.

■ SAVANNAH STATE UNIVERSITY

Program in Public Administration, Savannah, GA 31404

AWARDS MPA.

Degree requirements: For master's, major paper, oral exam.
Entrance requirements: For master's, GRE General Test, TOEFL, minimum GPA of 2.5.
Faculty research: Community development, human resources, leadership, conflict resolution. *Web site:* http://www.savstate.edu/mpa

■ SEATTLE UNIVERSITY

College of Arts and Sciences, Institute of Public Service, Program in Public Administration, Seattle, WA 98122

AWARDS MPA.

Students: 15 full-time (13 women), 63 part-time (35 women); includes 21 minority (9 African Americans, 6 Asian Americans or Pacific Islanders, 3 Hispanic Americans, 3 Native Americans), 1 international. Average age 33. 26 applicants, 85% accepted, 16 enrolled. In 2001, 43 degrees awarded.
Degree requirements: For master's, thesis or alternative.
Entrance requirements: For master's, minimum GPA of 3.0. *Application deadline:* For fall admission, 8/20 (priority date); for winter admission, 11/20; for spring admission, 2/20. Applications are processed on a rolling basis. *Application fee:* $55.
Expenses: Tuition: Full-time $7,740; part-time $430 per credit hour. Tuition and fees vary according to course load, degree level and program.
Financial support: Career-related internships or fieldwork and Federal Work-Study available. Support available to part-time students. Financial award applicants required to submit FAFSA.
Application contact: Janet Shandley, Associate Dean of Graduate Admissions, 206-296-5900, *Fax:* 206-298-5656, *E-mail:* grad_admissions@seattleu.edu.

■ SETON HALL UNIVERSITY

College of Arts and Sciences, Center for Public Service, Program in Public Service Administration and Policy, South Orange, NJ 07079-2697

AWARDS MPA. Part-time and evening/weekend programs available.

Degree requirements: For master's, research project.
Entrance requirements: For master's, GMAT, GRE General Test, or LSAT.
Expenses: Tuition: Full-time $10,818; part-time $601 per credit. Required fees: $610; $185 per term. Tuition and fees vary according to course load, program and student's religious affiliation.

Find an in-depth description at www.petersons.com/gradchannel.

■ SHENANDOAH UNIVERSITY

Byrd School of Business, Winchester, VA 22601-5195

AWARDS Business administration (MBA); health care management (Certificate); information systems and computer technology (Certificate); public management (Certificate). Part-time and evening/weekend programs available.

Faculty: 9 full-time (1 woman), 5 part-time/adjunct (0 women).
Students: 37 full-time (15 women), 26 part-time (6 women); includes 1 minority (Asian American or Pacific Islander), 23 international. Average age 32. 39 applicants, 100% accepted, 29 enrolled. In 2001, 31 master's, 14 other advanced degrees awarded.
Entrance requirements: For master's, GMAT, letters of recommendation (2). *Application deadline:* For fall admission, 3/1 (priority date). Applications are processed on a rolling basis. *Application fee:* $30. Electronic applications accepted.
Expenses: Tuition: Part-time $520 per credit hour. One-time fee: $500 full-time; $100 part-time. Tuition and fees vary according to campus/location, program and reciprocity agreements.
Financial support: In 2001–02, 31 students received support, including 12 fellowships with partial tuition reimbursements available (averaging $1,464 per year), 1 teaching assistantship with partial tuition reimbursement available (averaging $1,000 per year); career-related internships or fieldwork and unspecified assistantships also available. Support available to part-time students. Financial award application deadline: 3/15; financial award applicants required to submit FAFSA.
Faculty research: Fiscal policy, consumer expenditures, international business education, monetary policy, economic education.
Stan Harrison, Dean, 540-665-4572, *Fax:* 540-665-5437, *E-mail:* sharriso@su.edu.
Application contact: Michael Carpenter, Director of Admissions, 540-665-4581, *Fax:* 540-665-4627, *E-mail:* admit@su.edu. *Web site:* http://www.su.edu/bsb/

■ SHIPPENSBURG UNIVERSITY OF PENNSYLVANIA

School of Graduate Studies and Research, College of Arts and Sciences, Department of Political Science, Shippensburg, PA 17257-2299

AWARDS Public administration (MPA). Part-time and evening/weekend programs available.

Faculty: 6 full-time (1 woman).
Students: 9 full-time (4 women), 24 part-time (6 women); includes 8 minority (6 African Americans, 1 Asian American or Pacific Islander, 1 Native American), 1 international. Average age 34. 21 applicants, 90% accepted, 8 enrolled. In 2001, 31 degrees awarded.
Degree requirements: For master's, thesis or internship, thesis optional. *Median time to degree:* Master's–1.25 years full-time.
Entrance requirements: For master's, TOEFL, personal interview and/or GRE General Test, MAT, or minimum GPA of 2.75; 6 credits in government or political science. *Application deadline:* Applications are processed on a rolling basis. *Application fee:* $30. Electronic applications accepted.
Expenses: Tuition, state resident: full-time $4,600; part-time $256 per credit hour. Tuition, nonresident: full-time $7,554; part-time $420 per credit hour. Required fees: $290; $145 per semester.
Financial support: In 2001–02, 8 research assistantships with full tuition reimbursements were awarded; career-related internships or fieldwork and unspecified assistantships also available. Support available to part-time students. Financial award application deadline: 3/1; financial award applicants required to submit FAFSA.
Dr. Hugh E. Jones, Chairperson, 717-477-1718, *Fax:* 717-477-4030, *E-mail:* hejone@ship.edu.
Application contact: Renee Payne, Associate Dean of Graduate Admissions, 717-477-1231, *Fax:* 717-477-4016, *E-mail:* rmpayn@ship.edu. *Web site:* http://www.ship.edu/academic/artpls.html

■ SONOMA STATE UNIVERSITY

School of Social Sciences, Department of Political Science, Rohnert Park, CA 94928-3609

AWARDS Political science (MA); public administration (MPA). Part-time and evening/weekend programs available.

Faculty: 6 full-time (2 women), 7 part-time/adjunct (2 women).
Students: 4 full-time (3 women), 25 part-time (14 women); includes 5 minority (2 African Americans, 3 Hispanic Americans), 1 international. Average age 38. 13

applicants, 77% accepted, 10 enrolled. In 2001, 9 degrees awarded.
Degree requirements: For master's, thesis or alternative.
Entrance requirements: For master's, GRE General Test, minimum GPA of 3.0. *Application deadline:* For fall admission, 11/30; for spring admission, 8/31. *Application fee:* $55.
Expenses: Tuition, nonresident: full-time $4,428; part-time $246 per unit. Required fees: $2,084; $727 per semester.
Financial support: Career-related internships or fieldwork available. Financial award application deadline: 3/2.
Faculty research: Cross-disciplinary viewpoint in public administration, public policy implementation and evaluation.
Dr. Andrew Merrifield, Coordinator, 707-664-2179, *E-mail:* andrew.merrifield@sonoma.edu.

■ SOUTHEASTERN UNIVERSITY

College of Graduate Studies, Program in Government Program Management, Washington, DC 20024-2788

AWARDS MPA. Part-time and evening/weekend programs available.

Faculty: 1 (woman) full-time, 5 part-time/adjunct (3 women).
Students: 6 full-time (3 women), 36 part-time (29 women); includes 37 minority (35 African Americans, 1 Asian American or Pacific Islander, 1 Hispanic American), 4 international. Average age 36. In 2001, 2 degrees awarded.
Entrance requirements: For master's, TOEFL. *Application deadline:* Applications are processed on a rolling basis. *Application fee:* $45.
Expenses: Tuition: Full-time $7,695; part-time $285 per credit hour. One-time fee: $45.
Financial support: In 2001–02, 12 students received support. Federal Work-Study available. Support available to part-time students. Financial award application deadline: 8/21.
Dr. Ann Pharr, Head, 202-488-8162 Ext. 188.
Application contact: Information Contact, 202-265-5343, *Fax:* 202-488-8093.

■ SOUTHEAST MISSOURI STATE UNIVERSITY

School of Graduate Studies and Research, Program in Administration, Cape Girardeau, MO 63701-4799

AWARDS Athletic administration (MSA); criminal justice administration (MSA); health fitness administration (MSA); human services administration (MSA); public administration (MSA). Part-time and evening/weekend programs available.

Students: 24 full-time (12 women), 50 part-time (21 women); includes 14 minority (10 African Americans, 1 Asian American or Pacific Islander, 1 Hispanic American, 2 Native Americans), 1 international. Average age 31. 46 applicants, 96% accepted. In 2001, 19 degrees awarded.
Degree requirements: For master's, thesis or alternative.
Entrance requirements: For master's, minimum GPA of 2.5. *Application deadline:* For fall admission, 4/1 (priority date); for spring admission, 11/21. Applications are processed on a rolling basis. *Application fee:* $20 ($100 for international students).
Expenses: Tuition, state resident: full-time $1,242; part-time $138 per hour. Tuition, nonresident: full-time $2,268; part-time $252 per hour.
Financial support: In 2001–02, 7 research assistantships with full tuition reimbursements (averaging $6,100 per year) were awarded; teaching assistantships with full tuition reimbursements, career-related internships or fieldwork also available.
Application contact: Marsha L. Arant, Office of Graduate Studies, 573-651-2192, *Fax:* 573-651-2001, *E-mail:* marant@semovm.semo.edu.

■ SOUTHERN ILLINOIS UNIVERSITY CARBONDALE

Graduate School, College of Liberal Arts, Department of Political Science, Public Administration Program, Carbondale, IL 62901-6806

AWARDS MPA, JD/MPA. Part-time programs available.

Faculty: 4 full-time (0 women).
Students: 30 full-time (12 women), 44 part-time (18 women); includes 8 minority (5 African Americans, 3 Hispanic Americans), 5 international. Average age 31. 37 applicants, 51% accepted. In 2001, 6 degrees awarded.
Degree requirements: For master's, thesis or alternative.
Entrance requirements: For master's, TOEFL, minimum GPA of 2.7. *Application deadline:* Applications are processed on a rolling basis. *Application fee:* $20.
Expenses: Tuition, state resident: full-time $3,794; part-time $154 per hour. Tuition, nonresident: full-time $6,566; part-time $308 per hour. Required fees: $277 per hour.
Financial support: In 2001–02, 26 students received support, including 2 fellowships with full tuition reimbursements available, 10 teaching assistantships with full tuition reimbursements available; research assistantships with full tuition reimbursements available, career-related internships or fieldwork, Federal Work-Study, institutionally sponsored loans, and tuition waivers (full) also available. Support available to part-time students. Financial award application deadline: 2/1.
Faculty research: Natural resources and environmental management, intergovernmental relations, state mandates, rural administration, economic development policy, nonprofit management.
Keith Snavely, Director, 618-453-3179.

Find an in-depth description at www.petersons.com/gradchannel.

■ SOUTHERN ILLINOIS UNIVERSITY EDWARDSVILLE

Graduate Studies and Research, College of Arts and Sciences, Department of Public Administration, Edwardsville, IL 62026-0001

AWARDS MPA. Part-time programs available.

Students: 38 full-time (21 women), 64 part-time (42 women); includes 25 minority (20 African Americans, 2 Asian Americans or Pacific Islanders, 1 Hispanic American, 2 Native Americans), 2 international. Average age 33. 54 applicants, 91% accepted, 32 enrolled. In 2001, 24 degrees awarded.
Degree requirements: For master's, thesis or alternative, final exam. *Median time to degree:* Master's–2.5 years full-time, 4 years part-time.
Entrance requirements: For master's, TOEFL. *Application deadline:* For fall admission, 7/20; for spring admission, 12/7. *Application fee:* $25.
Expenses: Tuition, state resident: full-time $2,712; part-time $113 per credit hour. Tuition, nonresident: full-time $5,424; part-time $226 per credit hour. Required fees: $250; $125 per term. Tuition and fees vary according to course load, campus/location and reciprocity agreements.
Financial support: In 2001–02, 1 fellowship with full tuition reimbursement, 3 research assistantships with full tuition reimbursements were awarded. Teaching assistantships with full tuition reimbursements, career-related internships or fieldwork, Federal Work-Study, institutionally sponsored loans, traineeships, and unspecified assistantships also available. Support available to part-time students. Financial award application deadline: 3/1.
Dr. T. R. Carr, Chair, 618-650-3762, *E-mail:* tcarr@siue.edu.
Application contact: Dr. Drew Dolan, Graduate Director, 618-650-3762, *E-mail:* ddolan@siue.edu.

■ SOUTHERN UNIVERSITY AND AGRICULTURAL AND MECHANICAL COLLEGE

Graduate School, School of Public Policy and Urban Affairs, Department of Public Administration, Baton Rouge, LA 70813

AWARDS Public administration (MPA); public policy (PhD). Part-time and evening/weekend programs available.

Students: Average age 35.

Southern University and Agricultural and Mechanical College (continued)
Degree requirements: For master's and doctorate, thesis/dissertation.
Entrance requirements: For master's and doctorate, GRE General Test, TOEFL. *Application deadline:* For fall admission, 6/1 (priority date); for spring admission, 11/1. Applications are processed on a rolling basis. *Application fee:* $25.
Expenses: Tuition, state resident: full-time $1,323. Tuition, nonresident: full-time $2,583. International tuition: $2,613 full-time. Tuition and fees vary according to program.
Financial support: In 2001–02, research assistantships (averaging $7,000 per year); teaching assistantships, career-related internships or fieldwork and scholarships/grants also available. Financial award application deadline: 4/15; financial award applicants required to submit FAFSA.
Faculty research: Fiscal policy, public finance policy and practitioner interests; minority politics, healthcare and political economy.
Dr. James Llorens, Chair, 225-771-3104, *Fax:* 225-771-3105.

■ SOUTHWEST MISSOURI STATE UNIVERSITY

Graduate College, College of Humanities and Public Affairs, Department of Political Science, Program in Public Administration, Springfield, MO 65804-0094

AWARDS MPA. Part-time programs available.

Faculty: 16 full-time (1 woman).
Students: 12 full-time (6 women), 14 part-time (5 women); includes 1 minority (African American), 3 international. Average age 24. In 2001, 10 degrees awarded.
Degree requirements: For master's, thesis or alternative, comprehensive exam.
Entrance requirements: For master's, GRE General Test, minimum GPA of 3.0. *Application deadline:* For fall admission, 8/5 (priority date); for spring admission, 12/20. Applications are processed on a rolling basis. *Application fee:* $25.
Expenses: Tuition, state resident: full-time $2,286; part-time $127 per credit. Tuition, nonresident: full-time $4,572; part-time $254 per credit. Required fees: $151 per semester. Tuition and fees vary according to course level and program.
Financial support: In 2001–02, research assistantships with full tuition reimbursements (averaging $6,150 per year), teaching assistantships with full tuition reimbursements (averaging $6,150 per year) were awarded. Career-related internships or fieldwork, Federal Work-Study, and unspecified assistantships also available. Support available to part-time students. Financial award application deadline: 3/31; financial award applicants required to submit FAFSA.
Faculty research: Health care, global environmental problems, legislatures.
Application contact: Dr. Patrick G. Scott, Graduate Director, 417-836-5028, *Fax:* 417-836-8472, *E-mail:* pgs074f@smu.edu.

■ SOUTHWEST MISSOURI STATE UNIVERSITY

Graduate College, Program in Administrative Studies-Interdisciplinary, Springfield, MO 65804-0094

AWARDS Community analysis (MSAS); environmental management (MSAS). Postbaccalaureate distance learning degree programs offered (no on-campus study).

Faculty: 1 full-time (0 women).
Students: 5 full-time (3 women), 45 part-time (32 women); includes 4 minority (2 African Americans, 1 Asian American or Pacific Islander, 1 Native American), 1 international. In 2001, 1 degree awarded.
Degree requirements: For master's, thesis, comprehensive exam.
Entrance requirements: For master's, GRE General Test, GMAT, 3 years of work experience. *Application deadline:* For fall admission, 8/5 (priority date); for spring admission, 12/20 (priority date). Applications are processed on a rolling basis. *Application fee:* $25. Electronic applications accepted.
Expenses: Tuition, state resident: full-time $2,286; part-time $127 per credit. Tuition, nonresident: full-time $4,572; part-time $254 per credit. Required fees: $151 per semester. Tuition and fees vary according to course level and program.
Financial support: In 2001–02, 1 research assistantship with full tuition reimbursement (averaging $6,150 per year) was awarded; career-related internships or fieldwork, Federal Work-Study, institutionally sponsored loans, scholarships/grants, and unspecified assistantships also available. Support available to part-time students. Financial award application deadline: 3/31.
Application contact: John Bourhis, Coordinator, Internet-based Instruction, 417-836-6390, *Fax:* 417-836-5218, *E-mail:* jsb806@smsu.edu.

■ SOUTHWEST TEXAS STATE UNIVERSITY

Graduate School, College of Liberal Arts, Department of Political Science, Program in Public Administration, San Marcos, TX 78666

AWARDS MPA. Part-time and evening/weekend programs available.

Students: 13 full-time (7 women), 71 part-time (34 women); includes 36 minority (14 African Americans, 1 Asian American or Pacific Islander, 20 Hispanic Americans, 1 Native American), 1 international. Average age 34. 38 applicants, 89% accepted, 19 enrolled. In 2001, 18 degrees awarded.
Degree requirements: For master's, applied research project.
Entrance requirements: For master's, GRE General Test, TWE, minimum GPA of 2.75 in last 60 hours. *Application deadline:* For fall admission, 6/15 (priority date); for spring admission, 10/15 (priority date). Applications are processed on a rolling basis. *Application fee:* $40 ($90 for international students).
Expenses: Tuition, state resident: full-time $1,512; part-time $84 per credit hour. Tuition, nonresident: full-time $5,310; part-time $295 per credit hour. Required fees: $864; $29 per credit hour. $195 per term. Full-time tuition and fees vary according to course load.
Financial support: Career-related internships or fieldwork, Federal Work-Study, and institutionally sponsored loans available. Support available to part-time students. Financial award application deadline: 4/1; financial award applicants required to submit FAFSA.
Faculty research: Ethics in public management, total quality management in government, Texas state budgeting, pragmatism and public administration, minority economic development.
Dr. Patricia Shields, Director, 512-245-3256, *Fax:* 512-245-7815, *E-mail:* ps07@swt.edu. *Web site:* http://www.swt.edu/acad_depts/public_admin.html

■ STATE UNIVERSITY OF NEW YORK AT ALBANY

Nelson A. Rockefeller College of Public Affairs and Policy, Department of Public Administration and Policy, Albany, NY 12222-0001

AWARDS Administrative behavior (PhD); comparative and development administration (MPA, PhD); human resources (MPA); legislative administration (MPA); planning and policy analysis (CAS); policy analysis (MPA); program analysis and evaluation (PhD); public affairs and policy (MA); public finance (MPA, PhD); public management (MPA, PhD). Evening/weekend programs available.

Students: 133 full-time (71 women), 63 part-time (31 women); includes 29 minority (18 African Americans, 3 Asian Americans or Pacific Islanders, 8 Hispanic Americans), 44 international. Average age 31. 160 applicants, 71% accepted. In 2001, 57 master's, 4 doctorates, 7 other advanced degrees awarded.
Degree requirements: For doctorate, one foreign language, thesis/dissertation.
Entrance requirements: For doctorate, GRE General Test. *Application deadline:* For fall admission, 7/1. *Application fee:* $50.
Expenses: Tuition, state resident: full-time $2,550; part-time $213 per credit. Tuition, nonresident: full-time $4,208; part-time $351 per credit. Required fees: $470; $470 per year.
Financial support: Application deadline: 2/1.
Dr. David McCaffrey, Chair, 518-442-5258.

■ STATE UNIVERSITY OF NEW YORK AT BINGHAMTON

Graduate School, Program in Public Administration, Binghamton, NY 13902-6000

AWARDS MPA. Part-time and evening/weekend programs available.

Faculty: 2 full-time (0 women), 1 part-time/adjunct (0 women).
Students: 20 full-time (8 women), 24 part-time (16 women); includes 8 minority (3 African Americans, 1 Asian American or Pacific Islander, 3 Hispanic Americans, 1 Native American), 6 international. Average age 32. 31 applicants, 94% accepted, 23 enrolled. In 2001, 11 degrees awarded.
Entrance requirements: For master's, GRE General Test, TOEFL. *Application deadline:* For fall admission, 4/15 (priority date); for spring admission, 11/1. Applications are processed on a rolling basis. Electronic applications accepted.
Expenses: Tuition, state resident: full-time $5,100; part-time $213 per credit. Tuition, nonresident: full-time $8,416; part-time $351 per credit. Required fees: $811.
Financial support: In 2001–02, 10 students received support, including 6 teaching assistantships with full tuition reimbursements available (averaging $5,467 per year); research assistantships, career-related internships or fieldwork, Federal Work-Study, institutionally sponsored loans, and unspecified assistantships also available. Support available to part-time students. Financial award application deadline: 2/15.
Dr. Thomas Sinclair, Head, 607-777-6056.

■ STATE UNIVERSITY OF NEW YORK AT BINGHAMTON

Graduate School, School of Arts and Sciences, Department of Political Science, Binghamton, NY 13902-6000

AWARDS Political science (MA, PhD); public policy (MA, PhD).

Faculty: 11 full-time (2 women), 1 part-time/adjunct (0 women).
Students: 24 full-time (13 women), 11 part-time (4 women); includes 7 minority (5 African Americans, 2 Hispanic Americans), 12 international. Average age 31. 44 applicants, 36% accepted, 3 enrolled. In 2001, 2 master's, 3 doctorates awarded. Terminal master's awarded for partial completion of doctoral program.
Degree requirements: For master's, thesis or alternative, written exam; for doctorate, 2 foreign languages, thesis/dissertation, written exam.
Entrance requirements: For master's and doctorate, GRE General Test, GRE Subject Test, TOEFL. *Application deadline:* For fall admission, 4/15 (priority date); for spring admission, 11/1. Applications are processed on a rolling basis. Electronic applications accepted.
Expenses: Tuition, state resident: full-time $5,100; part-time $213 per credit. Tuition, nonresident: full-time $8,416; part-time $351 per credit. Required fees: $811.
Financial support: In 2001–02, 24 students received support, including 6 fellowships with full tuition reimbursements available (averaging $10,547 per year), 3 research assistantships with full tuition reimbursements available (averaging $6,147 per year), 15 teaching assistantships with full tuition reimbursements available (averaging $9,167 per year); career-related internships or fieldwork, Federal Work-Study, institutionally sponsored loans, tuition waivers (full and partial), and unspecified assistantships also available. Support available to part-time students. Financial award application deadline: 2/15.
Dr. Michael McDonald, Chairperson, 607-777-2252.

■ STATE UNIVERSITY OF NEW YORK COLLEGE AT BROCKPORT

School of Professions, Department of Public Administration, Brockport, NY 14420-2997

AWARDS MPA. Part-time and evening/weekend programs available.

Students: 18 full-time (14 women), 96 part-time (63 women); includes 19 minority (16 African Americans, 3 Hispanic Americans). 38 applicants, 76% accepted, 27 enrolled. In 2001, 53 degrees awarded.
Degree requirements: For master's, thesis or alternative.
Entrance requirements: For master's, GRE or minimum GPA of 2.75. *Application deadline:* For fall admission, 7/1; for spring admission, 10/1. *Application fee:* $50.
Expenses: Tuition, state resident: full-time $5,100; part-time $213 per credit. Tuition, nonresident: full-time $8,416; part-time $351 per credit. Required fees: $537; $23 per credit.
Financial support: Fellowships, career-related internships or fieldwork and Federal Work-Study available. Financial award application deadline: 3/15; financial award applicants required to submit FAFSA.
Faculty research: Government finance, government productivity, health policy, re-engineering in hospitals, managed care, online learning.
Dr. James Fatula, Chairperson, 585-395-2375, *Fax:* 585-395-2172, *E-mail:* jfatula@brockport.edu. *Web site:* http://www.brockport.edu/~graduate

■ STATE UNIVERSITY OF NEW YORK EMPIRE STATE COLLEGE

Graduate Studies, Program in Business and Policy Studies, Saratoga Springs, NY 12866-4391

AWARDS MA. Part-time and evening/weekend programs available. Postbaccalaureate distance learning degree programs offered (minimal on-campus study).

Faculty: 1 full-time (0 women), 8 part-time/adjunct (2 women).
Students: 3 full-time (2 women), 45 part-time (31 women); includes 7 minority (all African Americans), 1 international. Average age 41. 30 applicants, 93% accepted. In 2001, 22 degrees awarded.
Degree requirements: For master's, thesis, exam.
Entrance requirements: For master's, proficiency in statistics. *Application deadline:* For fall admission, 7/1 (priority date); for spring admission, 12/1 (priority date). Applications are processed on a rolling basis. *Application fee:* $50.
Expenses: Tuition, state resident: part-time $218 per credit hour. Tuition, nonresident: part-time $336 per credit hour. Tuition and fees vary according to program.
Financial support: In 2001–02, 1 fellowship with full tuition reimbursement (averaging $2,803 per year) was awarded; career-related internships or fieldwork and Federal Work-Study also available. Support available to part-time students. Financial award application deadline: 7/1; financial award applicants required to submit FAFSA.
Faculty research: Business history, applied business statistics, labor/management relations, American social problems and business, effect of government economic policies on business.
Dr. Joseph Angiello, Chair, 518-587-2100 Ext. 429, *Fax:* 518-587-9760, *E-mail:* joe.angiello@esc.edu.
Application contact: Cammie Baker Clancy, Assistant Director, 518-587-2100 Ext. 393, *Fax:* 518-587-9760, *E-mail:* cammie.baker-clancy@esc.edu. *Web site:* http://www.esc.edu/grad/

■ STATE UNIVERSITY OF NEW YORK EMPIRE STATE COLLEGE

Graduate Studies, Program in Social Policy, Saratoga Springs, NY 12866-4391

AWARDS MA. Part-time and evening/weekend programs available. Postbaccalaureate distance learning degree programs offered (minimal on-campus study).

Faculty: 1 full-time (0 women), 15 part-time/adjunct (8 women).
Students: 7 full-time (6 women), 96 part-time (66 women); includes 21 minority (16 African Americans, 2 Asian Americans or Pacific Islanders, 2 Hispanic Americans, 1 Native American). Average age 42. 50 applicants, 96% accepted. In 2001, 27 degrees awarded.
Degree requirements: For master's, thesis, exam.
Application deadline: For fall admission, 7/1 (priority date); for spring admission, 12/1 (priority date). Applications are processed on a rolling basis. *Application fee:* $50.

State University of New York Empire State College (continued)

Expenses: Tuition, state resident: part-time $218 per credit hour. Tuition, nonresident: part-time $336 per credit hour. Tuition and fees vary according to program.
Financial support: In 2001–02, 1 fellowship with full tuition reimbursement (averaging $2,300 per year) was awarded; career-related internships or fieldwork and Federal Work-Study also available. Support available to part-time students. Financial award application deadline: 7/1; financial award applicants required to submit FAFSA.
Faculty research: Study of culture, society and mass communications, urban culture and policy, social decision making processes.
Dr. Meredith Brown, Chair, 518-587-2100 Ext. 429, *Fax:* 518-587-9760, *E-mail:* meredith.brown@esc.edu.
Application contact: Cammie Baker Clancy, Assistant Director, 518-587-2100 Ext. 393, *Fax:* 518-587-9760, *E-mail:* cammie.baker-clancy@esc.edu. *Web site:* http://www.esc.edu/grad/

■ STATE UNIVERSITY OF WEST GEORGIA

Graduate School, College of Arts and Sciences, Department of Political Science and Planning, Program of Public Administration, Carrollton, GA 30118

AWARDS MPA. Part-time programs available.

Faculty: 8 full-time (2 women).
Students: 4 full-time (2 women), 21 part-time (9 women). Average age 26. In 2001, 4 degrees awarded.
Degree requirements: For master's, exit paper.
Entrance requirements: For master's, GRE. *Application deadline:* For fall admission, 8/1 (priority date); for spring admission, 12/1. *Application fee:* $20. Electronic applications accepted.
Expenses: Tuition, state resident: full-time $232; part-time $97 per credit hour. Tuition, nonresident: full-time $928; part-time $387 per credit hour. Required fees: $536; $14 per credit. $100 per semester.
Financial support: In 2001–02, 4 research assistantships with full tuition reimbursements (averaging $3,000 per year) were awarded. Financial award applicants required to submit FAFSA.
Faculty research: Women studies, state and local government, and animal rights.
Application contact: Dr. Jack O. Jenkins, Dean, Graduate School, 770-836-6419, *Fax:* 770-836-2301, *E-mail:* jjenkins@westga.edu. *Web site:* http://westga.edu/~polsci

■ STEPHEN F. AUSTIN STATE UNIVERSITY

Graduate School, College of Liberal Arts, Department of Political Science and Geography, Nacogdoches, TX 75962

AWARDS Public administration (MPA).

Faculty: 5 full-time (0 women).
Students: 6 full-time (2 women), 14 part-time (6 women); includes 6 minority (all African Americans). 10 applicants, 100% accepted.
Degree requirements: For master's, thesis optional.
Entrance requirements: For master's, GRE General Test, TOEFL. *Application deadline:* For fall admission, 8/1. *Application fee:* $50 for international students.
Expenses: Tuition, state resident: full-time $1,008; part-time $42 per credit. Tuition, nonresident: full-time $6,072; part-time $253 per credit. Required fees: $1,248; $52 per credit. Tuition and fees vary according to course load.
Financial support: In 2001–02, 1 research assistantship (averaging $6,633 per year) was awarded; Federal Work-Study, health care benefits, and unspecified assistantships also available. Support available to part-time students.
Dr. Richard Herzog, Director, 936-468-3903.

■ STONY BROOK UNIVERSITY, STATE UNIVERSITY OF NEW YORK

Graduate School, College of Arts and Sciences, Department of Political Science, Stony Brook, NY 11794

AWARDS Public policy (MAPP). Evening/weekend programs available.

Faculty: 15 full-time (2 women), 2 part-time/adjunct (0 women).
Students: 43 full-time (17 women), 25 part-time (13 women); includes 13 minority (8 African Americans, 5 Hispanic Americans), 15 international. Average age 27. 64 applicants, 55% accepted. In 2001, 16 master's, 5 doctorates awarded.
Degree requirements: For doctorate, thesis/dissertation.
Entrance requirements: For master's and doctorate, GRE General Test. *Application deadline:* For fall admission, 1/15. *Application fee:* $50.
Expenses: Tuition, state resident: full-time $5,100; part-time $213 per credit. Tuition, nonresident: full-time $8,416; part-time $351 per credit. Required fees: $496.
Financial support: In 2001–02, 1 fellowship, 28 teaching assistantships were awarded. *Total annual research expenditures:* $563,656.
Dr. Mark Schneider, Chair, 631-632-7640.
Application contact: Dr. Paul Teske, Director, 631-632-7634, *Fax:* 631-632-7132, *E-mail:* pteske@datalab2.sbs.sunysb.edu. *Web site:* http://www.sunysb.edu/polsci/

Find an in-depth description at www.petersons.com/gradchannel.

■ STONY BROOK UNIVERSITY, STATE UNIVERSITY OF NEW YORK

School of Professional Development and Continuing Studies, Stony Brook, NY 11794

AWARDS Art and philosophy (Certificate); biology 7-12 (MAT); chemistry-grade 7-12 (MAT); coaching (Certificate); computer integrated engineering (Certificate); cultural studies (Certificate); earth science-grade 7-12 (MAT); educational computing (Certificate); English-grade 7-12 (MAT); environmental/occupational health and safety (Certificate); French-grade 7-12 (MAT); German-grade 7-12 (MAT); human resource management (Certificate); industrial management (Certificate); information systems management (Certificate); Italian-grade 7-12 (MAT); liberal studies (MA); liberal studies online (MA); Long Island regional studies (Certificate); oceanic science (Certificate); operation research (Certificate); physics-grade 7-12 (MAT); Russian-grade 7-12 (MAT); school administration and supervision (Certificate); school district administration (Certificate); social science and the professions (MPS), including labor management, public affairs, waste management; social studies 7-12 (MAT); waste management (Certificate); women's studies (Certificate). Part-time and evening/weekend programs available. Postbaccalaureate distance learning degree programs offered.

Faculty: 1 full-time, 101 part-time/adjunct.
Students: 240 full-time (133 women), 1,307 part-time (868 women); includes 101 minority (43 African Americans, 13 Asian Americans or Pacific Islanders, 43 Hispanic Americans, 2 Native Americans), 9 international. Average age 28. In 2001, 478 master's, 157 other advanced degrees awarded.
Degree requirements: For master's, one foreign language, thesis or alternative. *Application deadline:* Applications are processed on a rolling basis. *Application fee:* $50.
Expenses: Tuition, state resident: full-time $5,100; part-time $213 per credit. Tuition, nonresident: full-time $8,416; part-time $351 per credit. Required fees: $496.
Financial support: In 2001–02, 1 fellowship, 7 teaching assistantships were awarded. Research assistantships, career-related internships or fieldwork also available. Support available to part-time students.
Dr. Paul J. Edelson, Dean, 631-632-7052, *Fax:* 631-632-9046, *E-mail:* paul.edelson@sunysb.edu.

Application contact: Sandra Romansky, Director of Admissions and Advisement, 631-632-7050, *Fax:* 631-632-9046, *E-mail:* sandra.romansky@sunysb.edu. *Web site:* http://www.sunysb.edu/spd/

■ SUFFOLK UNIVERSITY

Sawyer School of Management, Department of Public Management, Boston, MA 02108-2770

AWARDS Disability studies (MPA); health administration (MHA, MPA); nonprofit management (MPA); public administration (CASPA); public finance and human resources (MPA); state and local government (MPA). Part-time and evening/weekend programs available.

Faculty: 8 full-time (2 women), 29 part-time/adjunct (9 women).
Students: 37 full-time (26 women), 127 part-time (86 women); includes 12 minority (9 African Americans, 1 Asian American or Pacific Islander, 2 Hispanic Americans), 12 international. Average age 34. 76 applicants, 87% accepted, 36 enrolled. In 2001, 56 degrees awarded. *Median time to degree:* Master's–1.5 years full-time, 2 years part-time.
Application deadline: For fall admission, 6/15 (priority date); for spring admission, 11/15 (priority date). Applications are processed on a rolling basis. *Application fee:* $50.
Expenses: Contact institution.
Financial support: In 2001–02, 74 students received support, including 7 fellowships with full and partial tuition reimbursements available (averaging $3,300 per year); career-related internships or fieldwork and Federal Work-Study also available. Support available to part-time students. Financial award application deadline: 3/15; financial award applicants required to submit FAFSA.
Faculty research: Local government, health care, federal policy, mental health, HIV/AIDS. *Total annual research expenditures:* $200,000.
Dr. Rick Beineke, Chair, 617-573-8062, *E-mail:* rbeineck@sufffolk.edu.
Application contact: Judith Reynolds, Director of Graduate Admissions, 617-573-8302, *Fax:* 617-523-0116, *E-mail:* grad.admission@suffolk.edu. *Web site:* http://209.240.148.229/pad_main.htm

■ SUL ROSS STATE UNIVERSITY

School of Arts and Sciences, Department of Behavioral and Social Sciences, Program in Public Administration, Alpine, TX 79832

AWARDS MA. Part-time and evening/weekend programs available.

Faculty: 3 full-time (1 woman).
Students: In 2001, 4 degrees awarded.
Entrance requirements: For master's, GRE General Test, minimum GPA of 2.5 in last 60 hours of undergraduate work. *Application deadline:* Applications are processed on a rolling basis. *Application fee:* $0 ($50 for international students).
Expenses: Tuition, state resident: part-time $64 per semester hour. Tuition, nonresident: part-time $275 per semester hour. Required fees: $71; $32 per semester hour.
Financial support: Research assistantships, teaching assistantships, career-related internships or fieldwork, Federal Work-Study, and institutionally sponsored loans available. Support available to part-time students. Financial award application deadline: 5/1; financial award applicants required to submit FAFSA.
Faculty research: Local government, state government, personnel, volunteer fire departments, rural health.
Dr. Jimmy Case, Chairman, Department of Behavioral and Social Sciences, 915-837-8161, *Fax:* 915-837-8046.

■ SYRACUSE UNIVERSITY

Graduate School, Maxwell School of Citizenship and Public Affairs, Department of Public Administration, Syracuse, NY 13244-0003

AWARDS MA, MPA, PhD, JD/MPA. Part-time programs available.

Faculty: 18 full-time (2 women), 8 part-time/adjunct (2 women).
Students: 194 full-time (94 women), 53 part-time (27 women); includes 25 minority (11 African Americans, 9 Asian Americans or Pacific Islanders, 3 Hispanic Americans, 2 Native Americans), 85 international. Average age 33. 431 applicants, 68% accepted, 155 enrolled. In 2001, 146 master's, 2 doctorates awarded.
Degree requirements: For doctorate, thesis/dissertation, comprehensive exam.
Entrance requirements: For master's, GRE General Test (MPA); for doctorate, GRE General Test. *Application deadline:* For fall admission, 2/1. Applications are processed on a rolling basis. *Application fee:* $50.
Expenses: Tuition: Full-time $15,528; part-time $647 per credit. Required fees: $420; $38 per term. Tuition and fees vary according to program.
Financial support: In 2001–02, 64 students received support, including 17 research assistantships with full tuition reimbursements available (averaging $10,600 per year); fellowships, teaching assistantships, career-related internships or fieldwork, Federal Work-Study, scholarships/grants, tuition waivers (partial), and unspecified assistantships also available. Financial award application deadline: 2/1; financial award applicants required to submit FAFSA.
Jeffrey Straussman, Chair, 315-443-4000.
Application contact: Christine Omolino, Information Contact, 315-443-4000.

Find an in-depth description at www.petersons.com/gradchannel.

■ TENNESSEE STATE UNIVERSITY

Graduate School, Institute of Government, Nashville, TN 37209-1561

AWARDS Public administration (MPA, PhD). Part-time and evening/weekend programs available.

Faculty: 6 full-time (1 woman), 2 part-time/adjunct (1 woman).
Students: 16 full-time (12 women), 46 part-time (26 women); includes 30 minority (27 African Americans, 3 Asian Americans or Pacific Islanders). Average age 39. 31 applicants, 87% accepted. In 2001, 14 degrees awarded.
Degree requirements: For master's, thesis optional; for doctorate, thesis/dissertation, comprehensive exam.
Entrance requirements: For master's, GRE General Test, minimum GPA of 2.5, sample of written work; for doctorate, GRE General Test, minimum GPA of 3.25, sample of written work. *Application deadline:* Applications are processed on a rolling basis. *Application fee:* $15. Electronic applications accepted.
Expenses: Tuition, state resident: full-time $3,884; part-time $247 per hour. Tuition, nonresident: full-time $10,356; part-time $517 per hour.
Financial support: In 2001–02, 3 research assistantships (averaging $6,741 per year) were awarded. Support available to part-time students.
Faculty research: Human resource management, public policy, productivity, strategic analysis, budgeting, ethics and organization.
Dr. Ann-Marie Rizzo, Director, 615-963-7244, *Fax:* 615-963-7245, *E-mail:* arizzo@picard.tnstate.edu.
Application contact: Dr. Harry W. Fuchs, Coordinator of Graduate Studies, 615-963-7249, *Fax:* 615-963-7245, *E-mail:* hfuchs@picard.tnstate.edu.

■ TEXAS A&M INTERNATIONAL UNIVERSITY

Division of Graduate Studies, College of Arts and Humanities, Department of Social Sciences, Laredo, TX 78041-1900

AWARDS Criminal justice (MSCJ); history (MA); political science (MA); public administration (MPAD).

Students: 9 full-time (5 women), 59 part-time (21 women); includes 57 minority (2 Asian Americans or Pacific Islanders, 55 Hispanic Americans), 1 international. In 2001, 12 degrees awarded.
Degree requirements: For master's, thesis (for some programs).
Entrance requirements: For master's, GRE General Test. *Application deadline:* For fall admission, 7/15 (priority date); for spring admission, 11/12. Applications are processed on a rolling basis. *Application fee:* $0.

Texas A&M International University (continued)

Expenses: Tuition, state resident: full-time $1,536; part-time $64 per credit. Tuition, nonresident: full-time $6,600; part-time $275 per credit. Required fees: $594; $9 per credit. $33 per term. One-time fee: $10 part-time.

Financial support: Application deadline: 11/1.

Dr. Nasser Momayezi, Interim Dean, 956-326-2460, *Fax:* 956-326-2459, *E-mail:* nmomayezi@tamiu.edu.

Application contact: Veronica Gonzalez, Director of Enrollment Management and School Relations, 956-326-2270, *Fax:* 956-326-2269, *E-mail:* enroll@tamiu.edu.

■ TEXAS A&M UNIVERSITY

George Bush School of Government and Public Service, College Station, TX 77843

AWARDS MA, MPSA.

Faculty: 5 full-time (0 women), 19 part-time/adjunct (5 women).

Students: 47 full-time (22 women); includes 8 minority (3 African Americans, 1 Asian American or Pacific Islander, 4 Hispanic Americans), 3 international. Average age 24. 97 applicants, 26% accepted. In 2001, 1 degree awarded.

Degree requirements: For master's, summer internship.

Entrance requirements: For master's, GRE (preferred) or GMAT. *Application deadline:* For fall admission, 1/31 (priority date). *Application fee:* $50 ($75 for international students).

Expenses: Tuition, state resident: full-time $11,872. Tuition, nonresident: full-time $17,892.

Financial support: In 2001–02, 27 fellowships with partial tuition reimbursements (averaging $15,000 per year), 10 research assistantships with partial tuition reimbursements (averaging $11,000 per year) were awarded. Career-related internships or fieldwork, Federal Work-Study, and institutionally sponsored loans also available. Financial award application deadline: 2/1; financial award applicants required to submit FAFSA.

Faculty research: Public policy, Presidential studies, public leadership, economic policy, social policy.

Richard A. Chilcoat, Dean, 979-862-8007, *Fax:* 979-845-4155, *E-mail:* bushschool@tamu.edu.

Application contact: Reigen Smith, Recruitment/Placement Officer, 979-458-4767, *Fax:* 979-845-4155, *E-mail:* admissions@bushschool.tamu.edu. *Web site:* http://www-bushschool.tamu.edu

Find an in-depth description at www.petersons.com/gradchannel.

■ TEXAS A&M UNIVERSITY–CORPUS CHRISTI

Graduate Programs, College of Arts and Humanities, Program in Liberal Arts, Corpus Christi, TX 78412-5503

AWARDS Interdisciplinary studies (MA); public administration (MPA). Part-time and evening/weekend programs available.

Degree requirements: For master's, thesis optional.

Entrance requirements: For master's, GRE General Test. Electronic applications accepted.

■ TEXAS SOUTHERN UNIVERSITY

Graduate School, College of Liberal Arts and Behavioral Sciences, Department of Public Affairs, Program in Public Administration, Houston, TX 77004-4584

AWARDS MPA, JD/MPA.

Faculty: 6 full-time (1 woman), 1 part-time/adjunct (0 women).

Students: 18 full-time (10 women), 26 part-time (16 women); includes 43 minority (42 African Americans, 1 Asian American or Pacific Islander), 1 international. In 2001, 8 degrees awarded.

Degree requirements: For master's, thesis optional.

Entrance requirements: For master's, GRE General Test, TOEFL, minimum GPA of 2.5. *Application deadline:* For fall admission, 7/15 (priority date). Applications are processed on a rolling basis. *Application fee:* $35 ($75 for international students).

Expenses: Tuition, state resident: full-time $1,188. Tuition, nonresident: full-time $4,644. Required fees: $900. Tuition and fees vary according to degree level.

Financial support: Fellowships, teaching assistantships, career-related internships or fieldwork, Federal Work-Study, and institutionally sponsored loans available. Financial award application deadline: 5/1.

Dr. Theophilus Herrington, Head, Department of Public Affairs, 713-313-7447, *E-mail:* herrington_tx@tsu.edu.

■ TEXAS TECH UNIVERSITY

Graduate School, College of Arts and Sciences, Department of Political Science, Lubbock, TX 79409

AWARDS Political science (MA, PhD); public administration (MPA). Part-time programs available.

Faculty: 10 full-time (2 women), 1 part-time/adjunct (0 women).

Students: 45 full-time (20 women), 14 part-time (5 women); includes 9 minority (1 African American, 8 Hispanic Americans), 7 international. Average age 34. 49 applicants, 61% accepted, 13 enrolled. In 2001, 25 master's, 2 doctorates awarded.

Degree requirements: For master's, thesis or alternative; for doctorate, thesis/dissertation.

Entrance requirements: For master's and doctorate, GRE General Test. *Application deadline:* Applications are processed on a rolling basis. *Application fee:* $25 ($50 for international students). Electronic applications accepted.

Expenses: Tuition, state resident: full-time $1,926; part-time $107 per credit hour. Tuition, nonresident: full-time $5,724; part-time $318 per credit hour. Required fees: $779; $737 per year. Tuition and fees vary according to course level, course load and program.

Financial support: In 2001–02, 46 students received support, including 2 research assistantships with partial tuition reimbursements available (averaging $9,056 per year), 20 teaching assistantships with partial tuition reimbursements available (averaging $9,248 per year); Federal Work-Study and institutionally sponsored loans also available. Support available to part-time students. Financial award application deadline: 5/1; financial award applicants required to submit FAFSA.

Faculty research: State politics, American institutions and behavior, Asian politics, international and comparative political economy, public organizations. *Total annual research expenditures:* $40,400.

Dr. Philip H. Marshall, Chair, 806-742-3121, *Fax:* 806-742-0850.

Application contact: Graduate Adviser, 806-742-3121, *Fax:* 806-742-0850. *Web site:* http://www.ttu.edu/~polisci/

■ TRINITY COLLEGE

Graduate Programs, Program in Public Policy Studies, Hartford, CT 06106-3100

AWARDS MA. Part-time and evening/weekend programs available.

Faculty: 3 full-time (0 women), 1 (woman) part-time/adjunct.

Students: Average age 38. In 2001, 2 degrees awarded.

Degree requirements: For master's, departmental qualifying exam, thesis optional.

Entrance requirements: For master's, minimum GPA of 3.0. *Application deadline:* For fall admission, 4/1; for spring admission, 11/1. *Application fee:* $50.

Expenses: Tuition: Part-time $900 per course. Required fees: $25 per term.

Financial support: Fellowships, tuition waivers (full) available. Support available to part-time students. Financial award application deadline: 4/1.

Dr. Maurice Wade, Graduate Adviser, 860-297-2417.

■ TROY STATE UNIVERSITY

Graduate School, College of Arts and Sciences and University College, Program in Public Administration, Troy, AL 36082

AWARDS MS. Offered only through the University College. Part-time and evening/weekend programs available.

Degree requirements: For master's, thesis, comprehensive exam.
Entrance requirements: For master's, GRE General Test, MAT, minimum GPA of 2.5. Electronic applications accepted.
Web site: http://www.troyst.edu/

■ TUFTS UNIVERSITY

Division of Graduate and Continuing Studies and Research, Graduate School of Arts and Sciences, Department of Urban and Environmental Policy and Planning, Medford, MA 02155

AWARDS Community development (MA); environmental policy (MA); health and human welfare (MA); housing policy (MA); international environment/development policy (MA); public policy and citizen participation (MA). Part-time programs available.

Faculty: 7 full-time, 12 part-time/adjunct.
Students: 100 (66 women); includes 16 minority (7 African Americans, 6 Asian Americans or Pacific Islanders, 3 Hispanic Americans) 11 international. 115 applicants, 88% accepted. In 2001, 30 degrees awarded.
Degree requirements: For master's, thesis, internship.
Entrance requirements: For master's, GRE General Test, TOEFL. *Application deadline:* For fall admission, 2/15. Applications are processed on a rolling basis. *Application fee:* $50. Electronic applications accepted.
Expenses: Contact institution.
Financial support: Fellowships with full and partial tuition reimbursements, teaching assistantships with full and partial tuition reimbursements, career-related internships or fieldwork, Federal Work-Study, scholarships/grants, and tuition waivers (partial) available. Support available to part-time students. Financial award application deadline: 2/15; financial award applicants required to submit FAFSA.
Fran Jacobs, Chair, 617-627-3394, *Fax:* 617-627-3377. *Web site:* http://www.tufts.edu/as/uep/

Find an in-depth description at www.petersons.com/gradchannel.

■ TULANE UNIVERSITY

Graduate School, Program in Civic and Cultural Management, New Orleans, LA 70118-5669

AWARDS MA.

Entrance requirements: For master's, GRE General Test, TSE, minimum B average in undergraduate course work.
Expenses: Tuition: Full-time $24,675. Required fees: $2,210.

■ THE UNIVERSITY OF AKRON

Graduate School, Buchtel College of Arts and Sciences, Department of Public Administration and Urban Studies, Program in Public Administration, Akron, OH 44325-0001

AWARDS MPA, JD/MPA.

Students: 41 full-time (20 women), 52 part-time (24 women); includes 28 minority (26 African Americans, 1 Hispanic American, 1 Native American), 9 international. Average age 39. 39 applicants, 85% accepted, 19 enrolled. In 2001, 54 degrees awarded.
Entrance requirements: For master's, GRE, GMAT, LSAT or MAT, minimum GPA of 2.75. *Application deadline:* For fall admission, 4/15. Applications are processed on a rolling basis. *Application fee:* $40 ($50 for international students).
Expenses: Tuition, state resident: full-time $6,562; part-time $219 per credit. Tuition, nonresident: full-time $9,027; part-time $383 per credit. Required fees: $272; $11 per credit. Tuition and fees vary according to course load.
Financial support: Application deadline: 3/15.
Dr. Raymond W. Cox, Chair, Department of Public Administration and Urban Studies, 330-972-7618, *E-mail:* ngrant@uakron.edu.

■ THE UNIVERSITY OF ALABAMA

Graduate School, College of Arts and Sciences, Department of Political Science, Tuscaloosa, AL 35487

AWARDS Political science (MA, MPA, PhD); public administration (MPA, DPA). Part-time programs available.

Faculty: 14 full-time (4 women), 1 (woman) part-time/adjunct.
Students: 37 full-time (9 women), 44 part-time (14 women); includes 13 minority (9 African Americans, 2 Asian Americans or Pacific Islanders, 1 Hispanic American, 1 Native American), 2 international. Average age 37. 44 applicants, 30% accepted, 10 enrolled. In 2001, 7 master's, 8 doctorates awarded. Terminal master's awarded for partial completion of doctoral program.
Degree requirements: For master's, thesis optional; for doctorate, one foreign language, thesis/dissertation.
Entrance requirements: For master's and doctorate, GRE General Test, MAT, minimum GPA of 3.0. *Application deadline:* For fall admission, 7/6; for spring admission, 11/1. Applications are processed on a rolling basis. *Application fee:* $25.
Expenses: Tuition, state resident: full-time $3,292; part-time $183 per credit hour. Tuition, nonresident: full-time $8,912; part-time $495 per credit hour. Tuition and fees vary according to course load, campus/location and program.
Financial support: In 2001–02, 13 teaching assistantships with full tuition reimbursements (averaging $8,147 per year) were awarded; career-related internships or fieldwork and Federal Work-Study also available. Financial award application deadline: 2/1.
Faculty research: American politics, comparative politics, international relations, state government. *Total annual research expenditures:* $22,898.
Dr. David J. Lanoue, Chairperson, 205-348-5980, *Fax:* 205-348-5248.
Application contact: Dr. Don Snow, Graduate Studies Committee, 205-348-5980, *Fax:* 205-348-5248, *E-mail:* dsnow@tenhoor.as.ua.edu.

■ THE UNIVERSITY OF ALABAMA AT BIRMINGHAM

Graduate School, School of Social and Behavioral Sciences, Department of Government and Public Service, Birmingham, AL 35294

AWARDS Public administration (MPA).

Students: 13 full-time (12 women), 19 part-time (12 women); includes 15 minority (all African Americans), 1 international. 65 applicants, 54% accepted. In 2001, 18 degrees awarded.
Entrance requirements: For master's, GRE General Test or MAT. *Application deadline:* Applications are processed on a rolling basis. *Application fee:* $35 ($60 for international students). Electronic applications accepted.
Expenses: Tuition, state resident: full-time $3,058. Tuition, nonresident: full-time $5,746. Tuition and fees vary according to course load, degree level and program.
Financial support: Fellowships, career-related internships or fieldwork available.
Dr. James D. Slack, Chair, 205-934-9679, *E-mail:* jslack@uab.edu. *Web site:* http://www.sbs.uab.edu/gps.htm/

■ THE UNIVERSITY OF ALABAMA IN HUNTSVILLE

School of Graduate Studies, College of Liberal Arts, Program in Public Affairs, Huntsville, AL 35899

AWARDS MA. Part-time and evening/weekend programs available.

Faculty: 5 full-time (2 women), 2 part-time/adjunct (0 women).
Students: 6 full-time (4 women), 9 part-time (6 women); includes 6 minority (5 African Americans, 1 Hispanic American). Average age 34. 8 applicants, 100% accepted, 6 enrolled. In 2001, 6 degrees awarded.
Degree requirements: For master's, thesis or alternative, oral and written exams, comprehensive exam, registration.

The University of Alabama in Huntsville (continued)

Entrance requirements: For master's, MAT, minimum GPA of 3.0. *Application deadline:* For fall admission, 7/24 (priority date); for spring admission, 11/15 (priority date). Applications are processed on a rolling basis. *Application fee:* $35.
Expenses: Tuition, area resident: Part-time $175 per hour. Tuition, state resident: full-time $4,408. Tuition, nonresident: full-time $9,054; part-time $361 per hour.
Financial support: In 2001–02, 2 students received support, including 1 teaching assistantship with full and partial tuition reimbursement available (averaging $7,108 per year); fellowships with full and partial tuition reimbursements available, research assistantships with full and partial tuition reimbursements available, career-related internships or fieldwork, Federal Work-Study, institutionally sponsored loans, scholarships/grants, health care benefits, tuition waivers (full and partial), and unspecified assistantships also available. Support available to part-time students. Financial award application deadline: 4/1; financial award applicants required to submit FAFSA.
Faculty research: Public policy, public management professions, intergovernmental relations, international politics.
Dr. Roy Meek, Chair, 256-824-6192, *Fax:* 256-824-6949, *E-mail:* meekr@email.uah.edu. *Web site:* http://www.uah.edu/colleges/liberal/ps/

■ UNIVERSITY OF ALASKA ANCHORAGE

College of Business and Public Policy, Program in Public Administration, Anchorage, AK 99508-8060

AWARDS MPA. Part-time programs available.

Degree requirements: For master's, thesis or alternative, comprehensive exam.
Entrance requirements: For master's, GMAT or GRE General Test, TOEFL.
Faculty research: Policy analysis, policy and administration issues in the North, hypothetical government policies, public management in health care.

■ UNIVERSITY OF ALASKA SOUTHEAST

Graduate Programs, Program in Public Administration, Juneau, AK 99801

AWARDS MPA. Part-time and evening/weekend programs available. Postbaccalaureate distance learning degree programs offered (no on-campus study).

Faculty: 3 full-time (0 women), 1 part-time/adjunct (0 women).
Students: 2 full-time (1 woman), 17 part-time (9 women), 3 international. Average age 36. In 2001, 14 degrees awarded.
Degree requirements: For master's, capstone course or thesis.
Entrance requirements: For master's, minimum GPA of 3.0. *Application deadline:* Applications are processed on a rolling basis. Electronic applications accepted.
Expenses: Tuition, state resident: part-time $178 per credit hour. Tuition, nonresident: part-time $374 per credit hour. Required fees: $6 per credit hour. $100 per semester.
Financial support: Federal Work-Study, scholarships/grants, and tuition waivers (full and partial) available. Support available to part-time students. Financial award applicants required to submit FAFSA.
Faculty research: Conflict resolution, democratic governance.
Dr. Jonathan F. Anderson, Director, 907-465-6356, *Fax:* 907-465-6383, *E-mail:* jfjfa@uas.alaska.edu. *Web site:* http://www.uas.alaska.edu/uas/padmintro.html

■ THE UNIVERSITY OF ARIZONA

Graduate College, College of Business and Public Administration, School of Public Administration and Policy, Tucson, AZ 85721

AWARDS Public administration (MPA); public administration and policy (PhD).

Faculty: 10 full-time (3 women), 2 part-time/adjunct (both women).
Students: 54 full-time (28 women); includes 9 minority (2 African Americans, 2 Asian Americans or Pacific Islanders, 5 Hispanic Americans), 7 international. Average age 30. 42 applicants, 90% accepted, 19 enrolled. In 2001, 18 master's, 2 doctorates awarded.
Degree requirements: For master's, intership of 400 hours; for doctorate, thesis/dissertation, comprehensive exam, registration. *Median time to degree:* Master's–2 years full-time, 4 years part-time; doctorate–4 years full-time.
Entrance requirements: For master's, GMAT or GRE General Test, TOEFL, minimum GPA of 3.0; for doctorate, GMAT or GRE, TOEFL, minimum GPA of 3.0. *Application deadline:* For fall admission, 4/15 (priority date). Applications are processed on a rolling basis. *Application fee:* $45.
Expenses: Tuition, state resident: full-time $2,490; part-time $436 per unit. Tuition, nonresident: full-time $10,300; part-time $436 per unit. Full-time tuition and fees vary according to degree level and program.
Financial support: In 2001–02, 27 students received support, including 5 fellowships (averaging $2,000 per year), 13 teaching assistantships with partial tuition reimbursements available (averaging $4,182 per year); career-related internships or fieldwork, scholarships/grants, health care benefits, and unspecified assistantships also available. Financial award application deadline: 4/15.
Dr. Arthur L. Silvers, Associate Dean, Director, 520-621-7465, *Fax:* 520-626-5549.
Application contact: Gloria A Manzanedo, Graduate Coordinator, 520-621-7465, *Fax:* 520-621-5549. *Web site:* http://www.bpa.arizona.edu/spap/

■ UNIVERSITY OF ARKANSAS

Graduate School, Interdisciplinary Program in Public Policy, Fayetteville, AR 72701-1201

AWARDS PhD.

Students: 20 full-time (12 women), 13 part-time (8 women); includes 11 minority (7 African Americans, 1 Hispanic American, 3 Native Americans), 7 international. 16 applicants, 100% accepted.
Degree requirements: For doctorate, thesis/dissertation.
Application fee: $40 ($50 for international students).
Expenses: Tuition, state resident: full-time $3,553; part-time $197 per credit. Tuition, nonresident: full-time $8,411; part-time $467 per credit. Required fees: $42 per credit. Tuition and fees vary according to course load and program.
Financial support: In 2001–02, 5 fellowships, 2 research assistantships, 2 teaching assistantships were awarded. Financial award application deadline: 4/1; financial award applicants required to submit FAFSA.
Will Miller, Head, 479-575-3356.

■ UNIVERSITY OF ARKANSAS

Graduate School, J. William Fulbright College of Arts and Sciences, Department of Political Science, Program in Public Administration, Fayetteville, AR 72701-1201

AWARDS MPA.

Students: 12 full-time (6 women), 3 part-time (2 women), 3 international. 14 applicants, 100% accepted.
Degree requirements: For master's, thesis or alternative, comprehensive exam.
Entrance requirements: For master's, MAT. *Application fee:* $40 ($50 for international students).
Expenses: Tuition, state resident: full-time $3,553; part-time $197 per credit. Tuition, nonresident: full-time $8,411; part-time $467 per credit. Required fees: $42 per credit. Tuition and fees vary according to course load and program.
Financial support: Research assistantships, career-related internships or fieldwork and Federal Work-Study available. Support available to part-time students. Financial award application deadline: 4/1; financial award applicants required to submit FAFSA.
Margaret Reid, Director, 479-575-3356, *E-mail:* mreid@comp.uark.edu.

■ UNIVERSITY OF ARKANSAS AT LITTLE ROCK

Graduate School, College of Professional Studies, Program in Public Administration, Little Rock, AR 72204-1099

AWARDS MPA. Part-time and evening/weekend programs available.

Degree requirements: For master's, comprehensive exam.
Entrance requirements: For master's, GRE General Test or MAT, minimum GPA of 2.7.
Expenses: Tuition, state resident: full-time $3,006; part-time $107 per credit. Tuition, nonresident: full-time $6,012; part-time $357 per credit. Required fees: $22 per credit. Tuition and fees vary according to program.
Faculty research: State and local administration, nonprofit management.

■ UNIVERSITY OF BALTIMORE

Graduate School, College of Liberal Arts, Department of Government and Public Administration, Baltimore, MD 21201-5779

AWARDS MPA, DPA, JD/MPA. Part-time and evening/weekend programs available. Postbaccalaureate distance learning degree programs offered (minimal on-campus study).

Faculty: 11 full-time (2 women), 2 part-time/adjunct (0 women).
Students: 39 full-time (29 women), 160 part-time (84 women); includes 100 minority (93 African Americans, 5 Hispanic Americans, 2 Native Americans), 12 international. Average age 34. 103 applicants, 82% accepted. In 2001, 26 degrees awarded.
Degree requirements: For doctorate, final project.
Entrance requirements: For master's, interview, minimum GPA of 3.0; for doctorate, GRE, interview. *Application deadline:* For fall admission, 7/15 (priority date); for spring admission, 12/15. Applications are processed on a rolling basis. *Application fee:* $30. Electronic applications accepted.
Expenses: Contact institution.
Financial support: In 2001–02, 6 research assistantships were awarded; fellowships, career-related internships or fieldwork and Federal Work-Study also available. Support available to part-time students. Financial award application deadline: 4/1; financial award applicants required to submit FAFSA.
Faculty research: Welfare policy, public administration ethics, bureaucratic politics, public sector budgeting, program evaluation. *Total annual research expenditures:* $1.9 million.
Dr. Daniel Martin, Director, MPA Program, 410-837-6118, *E-mail:* dmartin@ubalt.edu.
Application contact: Jeffrey Zavrotny, Assistant Director of Admissions, 410-837-4777, *Fax:* 410-837-4793, *E-mail:* jzavrotny@ubalt.edu.

■ UNIVERSITY OF CALIFORNIA, BERKELEY

Graduate Division, Graduate School of Public Policy, Berkeley, CA 94720-1500

AWARDS MPP, PhD, JD/MPP, MPP/MA, MPP/MPH, MPP/MS.

Degree requirements: For doctorate, thesis/dissertation, qualifying exam.
Entrance requirements: For master's and doctorate, GRE General Test, minimum GPA of 3.0.
Expenses: Tuition, nonresident: full-time $10,704. Required fees: $4,349. *Web site:* http://socrates.berkeley.edu/~gspp/

■ UNIVERSITY OF CALIFORNIA, BERKELEY

Graduate Division, Haas School of Business, Doctoral Program in Business, Berkeley, CA 94720-1500

AWARDS Accounting (PhD); business and public policy (PhD); finance (PhD); marketing (PhD); organizational behavior and industrial relations (PhD); real estate (PhD).

Students: 81 full-time (23 women); includes 6 minority (all Asian Americans or Pacific Islanders), 43 international. Average age 26. 467 applicants, 8% accepted, 16 enrolled. In 2001, 12 degrees awarded.
Degree requirements: For doctorate, thesis/dissertation, oral exam, written preliminary exams, comprehensive exam. *Median time to degree:* Doctorate–4.5 years full-time.
Entrance requirements: For doctorate, GMAT or GRE, TOEFL, minimum GPA of 3.0. *Application deadline:* For fall admission, 2/1. *Application fee:* $40. Electronic applications accepted.
Expenses: Tuition, nonresident: full-time $10,704. Required fees: $4,349.
Financial support: In 2001–02, 72 students received support, including fellowships with full and partial tuition reimbursements available (averaging $16,000 per year), research assistantships with full and partial tuition reimbursements available (averaging $15,000 per year), teaching assistantships with full and partial tuition reimbursements available (averaging $15,000 per year); career-related internships or fieldwork, Federal Work-Study, scholarships/grants, health care benefits, tuition waivers (full), and unspecified assistantships also available. Financial award application deadline: 2/1; financial award applicants required to submit FAFSA.
Dr. David C. Mowery, Director, 510-642-1409, *Fax:* 510-643-1420, *E-mail:* phdadms@haas.berkeley.edu.
Application contact: Dr. Jan Price Greenough, Associate Director, 510-642-1409, *Fax:* 510-643-1420, *E-mail:* phdadms@haas.berkeley.edu.

■ UNIVERSITY OF CALIFORNIA, LOS ANGELES

Graduate Division, School of Public Policy and Social Research, Program in Public Policy, Los Angeles, CA 90095

AWARDS MPP.

Students: 72 full-time (49 women); includes 23 minority (6 African Americans, 10 Asian Americans or Pacific Islanders, 7 Hispanic Americans), 11 international. 201 applicants, 57% accepted, 36 enrolled. In 2001, 38 degrees awarded.
Entrance requirements: For master's, GRE General Test, TOEFL, minimum GPA of 3.0. *Application deadline:* For fall admission, 2/1. *Application fee:* $60. Electronic applications accepted.
Expenses: Tuition, nonresident: full-time $10,244. Required fees: $3,609. Full-time tuition and fees vary according to program.
Financial support: In 2001–02, 39 students received support, including 23 fellowships, 20 research assistantships, 8 teaching assistantships Financial award application deadline: 3/1.
Dr. Arlene Leibowitz, Chair, 310-206-3148.
Application contact: Departmental Office, 310-825-7667, *E-mail:* mppinfo@sppsr.ucla.edu.

■ UNIVERSITY OF CENTRAL FLORIDA

College of Health and Public Affairs, Department of Public Administration, Orlando, FL 32816

AWARDS Non-profit management (Certificate); public administration (MPA, Certificate). Part-time and evening/weekend programs available.

Faculty: 10 full-time (3 women), 8 part-time/adjunct (3 women).
Students: 32 full-time (17 women), 119 part-time (64 women); includes 33 minority (18 African Americans, 2 Asian Americans or Pacific Islanders, 13 Hispanic Americans), 3 international. Average age 33. 64 applicants, 86% accepted, 41 enrolled. In 2001, 66 degrees awarded.
Degree requirements: For master's, thesis or alternative, research report, comprehensive exam.
Entrance requirements: For master's, GRE General Test. *Application deadline:* For fall admission, 7/1; for spring admission, 12/1. *Application fee:* $20. Electronic applications accepted.
Expenses: Tuition, state resident: part-time $162 per hour. Tuition, nonresident: part-time $569 per hour.

University of Central Florida (continued)
Financial support: In 2001–02, 5 fellowships with partial tuition reimbursements (averaging $3,000 per year), 8 research assistantships with partial tuition reimbursements (averaging $3,968 per year), 4 teaching assistantships with partial tuition reimbursements (averaging $1,741 per year) were awarded. Career-related internships or fieldwork, Federal Work-Study, institutionally sponsored loans, tuition waivers (partial), and unspecified assistantships also available. Financial award application deadline: 3/1; financial award applicants required to submit FAFSA.
K. Liou, Chair, 407-823-2604, *Fax:* 407-823-5651.
Application contact: Dr. Xiao Wang, Coordinator, 407-823-2604. *Web site:* http://www.ucf.edu/

■ UNIVERSITY OF CENTRAL FLORIDA

College of Health and Public Affairs, Program in Public Affairs, Orlando, FL 32816

AWARDS PhD. Part-time and evening/weekend programs available.

Faculty: 11 full-time (3 women), 26 part-time/adjunct (8 women).
Students: 16 full-time (10 women), 35 part-time (19 women); includes 5 minority (2 African Americans, 3 Hispanic Americans). Average age 38. 47 applicants, 64% accepted, 20 enrolled.
Degree requirements: For doctorate, thesis/dissertation, candidacy and qualifying exams.
Entrance requirements: For doctorate, TOEFL, GRE General Test or minimum GPA of 3.0 during final 60 hours. *Application deadline:* For fall admission, 2/7 (priority date). *Application fee:* $20. Electronic applications accepted.
Expenses: Tuition, state resident: part-time $162 per hour. Tuition, nonresident: part-time $569 per hour.
Financial support: In 2001–02, 10 fellowships with partial tuition reimbursements (averaging $3,250 per year), 17 research assistantships with partial tuition reimbursements (averaging $4,277 per year), 19 teaching assistantships with partial tuition reimbursements (averaging $4,573 per year) were awarded. Career-related internships or fieldwork, Federal Work-Study, institutionally sponsored loans, tuition waivers (partial), and unspecified assistantships also available. Financial award application deadline: 3/1; financial award applicants required to submit FAFSA. *Web site:* http://www.ucf.edu/

■ UNIVERSITY OF CHICAGO

The Irving B. Harris Graduate School of Public Policy Studies, Chicago, IL 60637-1513

AWARDS Environmental science and policy (MS); public policy studies (AM, MPP, PhD). Part-time programs available. Terminal master's awarded for partial completion of doctoral program.

Degree requirements: For doctorate, thesis/dissertation.
Entrance requirements: For master's, GMAT or GRE General Test, TOEFL, or LSAT; for doctorate, GMAT or GRE General Test, TOEFL.
Expenses: Contact institution.
Faculty research: Family and child policy, international security, health policy, social policy. *Web site:* http://HarrisSchool.uchicago.edu/

Find an in-depth description at www.petersons.com/gradchannel.

■ UNIVERSITY OF COLORADO AT BOULDER

Graduate School, College of Arts and Sciences, Department of Political Science, Boulder, CO 80309

AWARDS International affairs (MA); political science (MA, PhD); public policy analysis (MA).

Faculty: 26 full-time (5 women).
Students: 51 full-time (18 women), 14 part-time (6 women); includes 7 minority (1 African American, 2 Asian Americans or Pacific Islanders, 4 Hispanic Americans), 8 international. Average age 29. 51 applicants, 61% accepted. In 2001, 9 master's, 6 doctorates awarded. Terminal master's awarded for partial completion of doctoral program.
Degree requirements: For master's, thesis, comprehensive exam; for doctorate, one foreign language, thesis/dissertation.
Entrance requirements: For master's, GRE General Test, minimum undergraduate GPA of 3.0; for doctorate, GRE General Test, minimum GPA of 3.5 (undergraduate), 3.0 (graduate). *Application deadline:* For fall admission, 1/15 (priority date). *Application fee:* $50 ($60 for international students).
Expenses: Tuition, state resident: full-time $3,474. Tuition, nonresident: full-time $16,624.
Financial support: In 2001–02, 12 fellowships (averaging $2,836 per year), 3 research assistantships (averaging $17,735 per year), 32 teaching assistantships (averaging $17,902 per year) were awarded. Federal Work-Study also available. Financial award application deadline: 1/15.
Faculty research: American government and politics, comparative politics, international relations, public policy, law and politics. *Total annual research expenditures:* $985,125.
J. Samuel Fitch, Chair, 303-492-8601, *Fax:* 303-492-0978, *E-mail:* fitchs@colorado.edu.
Application contact: Mary Gregory, Graduate Program Assistant, 303-492-7872, *Fax:* 303-492-0978, *E-mail:* mary.gregory@colorado.edu. *Web site:* http://socsci.colorado.edu/POLSCI/

■ UNIVERSITY OF COLORADO AT COLORADO SPRINGS

Graduate School of Public Affairs, Colorado Springs, CO 80933-7150

AWARDS Criminal justice (MCJ); public administration (MPA). Part-time and evening/weekend programs available.

Faculty: 4 full-time (1 woman), 7 part-time/adjunct (3 women).
Students: 34 full-time (23 women), 39 part-time (20 women); includes 11 minority (3 Asian Americans or Pacific Islanders, 6 Hispanic Americans, 2 Native Americans). Average age 37. 8 applicants, 100% accepted. In 2001, 22 degrees awarded.
Degree requirements: For master's, internship (if no experience).
Entrance requirements: For master's, GRE General Test, minimum GPA of 3.0. *Application deadline:* For fall admission, 6/1 (priority date); for spring admission, 11/1. Applications are processed on a rolling basis. *Application fee:* $60 ($75 for international students).
Expenses: Contact institution.
Financial support: Career-related internships or fieldwork and Federal Work-Study available. Support available to part-time students.
Faculty research: Organizational effectiveness, public administration, human resources management, social policy, nonprofit management.
Dr. Kathleen Beatty, Dean, 719-262-4103, *Fax:* 719-262-4183, *E-mail:* kbeatty@carbon.cudenver.edu.
Application contact: Mary Lou Kartis, Program Assistant, 719-262-4182, *Fax:* 719-262-4183, *E-mail:* mkartis@uccs.edu. *Web site:* http://www.carbon.cudenver.edu/public/gspa/

■ UNIVERSITY OF COLORADO AT DENVER

Graduate School of Public Affairs, Executive MPA Option, Denver, CO 80217-3364

AWARDS Exec MPA. Part-time and evening/weekend programs available. Postbaccalaureate distance learning degree programs offered.

Faculty: 11 full-time (4 women).
Students: 1 full-time (0 women), 12 part-time (4 women); includes 3 minority (1 African American, 1 Hispanic American, 1 Native American). Average age 35. 14 applicants, 86% accepted, 5 enrolled.

Degree requirements: For master's, executive research project.
Entrance requirements: For master's, 5 years of senior-level management experience, minimum GPA of 3.0 (preferred). *Application deadline:* For fall admission, 6/1 (priority date); for spring admission, 11/1. Applications are processed on a rolling basis. *Application fee:* $50 ($60 for international students).
Expenses: Tuition, state resident: full-time $3,284; part-time $198 per credit hour. Tuition, nonresident: full-time $13,380; part-time $802 per credit hour. Required fees: $444; $222 per semester.
Financial support: In 2001–02, 2 students received support; fellowships, research assistantships, teaching assistantships, career-related internships or fieldwork, Federal Work-Study, and institutionally sponsored loans available. Support available to part-time students. Financial award application deadline: 4/1.
Robert Gage, Director, 303-556-5981, *Fax:* 303-556-5971, *E-mail:* rgage@castle.cudenver.edu.
Application contact: Antoinette Sandoval, Student Service Specialist, 303-556-5970, *Fax:* 303-556-5971, *E-mail:* asandoval@castle.cudenver.edu. *Web site:* http://www.cudenver.edu/

Find an in-depth description at www.petersons.com/gradchannel.

■ UNIVERSITY OF COLORADO AT DENVER

Graduate School of Public Affairs, MPA Program in Public Administration, Denver, CO 80217-3364

AWARDS MPA. Part-time and evening/weekend programs available. Postbaccalaureate distance learning degree programs offered.

Students: 61 full-time (37 women), 146 part-time (90 women); includes 32 minority (12 African Americans, 2 Asian Americans or Pacific Islanders, 13 Hispanic Americans, 5 Native Americans), 26 international. Average age 26. 106 applicants, 85% accepted, 54 enrolled. In 2001, 65 degrees awarded.
Degree requirements: For master's, research paper.
Entrance requirements: For master's, GRE General Test or minimum GPA of 3.0. *Application deadline:* For fall admission, 6/1 (priority date); for spring admission, 11/1. Applications are processed on a rolling basis. *Application fee:* $50 ($60 for international students).
Expenses: Tuition, state resident: full-time $3,284; part-time $198 per credit hour. Tuition, nonresident: full-time $13,380; part-time $802 per credit hour. Required fees: $444; $222 per semester.
Financial support: In 2001–02, 24 fellowships with partial tuition reimbursements, 20 research assistantships with partial tuition reimbursements, 13 teaching assistantships with partial tuition reimbursements were awarded. Career-related internships or fieldwork, Federal Work-Study, and institutionally sponsored loans also available. Support available to part-time students. Financial award application deadline: 4/1.
Robert Gage, Director, 303-556-5981, *Fax:* 303-556-5971, *E-mail:* rgage@castle.cudenver.edu.
Application contact: Antoinette Sandoval, Student Service Specialist, 303-556-5970, *Fax:* 303-556-5971, *E-mail:* asandoval@castle.cudenver.edu.

Find an in-depth description at www.petersons.com/gradchannel.

■ UNIVERSITY OF COLORADO AT DENVER

Graduate School of Public Affairs, PhD Program in Public Administration, Denver, CO 80217-3364

AWARDS PhD. Part-time and evening/weekend programs available.

Students: 5 full-time (2 women), 55 part-time (30 women); includes 9 minority (3 African Americans, 3 Asian Americans or Pacific Islanders, 3 Hispanic Americans), 7 international. Average age 35. 39 applicants, 49% accepted, 11 enrolled. In 2001, 3 degrees awarded.
Degree requirements: For doctorate, thesis/dissertation, comprehensive exam.
Entrance requirements: For doctorate, GRE General Test, minimum GPA of 3.5 (preferred). *Application deadline:* For fall admission, 4/1. *Application fee:* $50 ($60 for international students).
Expenses: Tuition, state resident: full-time $3,284; part-time $198 per credit hour. Tuition, nonresident: full-time $13,380; part-time $802 per credit hour. Required fees: $444; $222 per semester.
Financial support: In 2001–02, 26 fellowships were awarded; research assistantships, teaching assistantships, career-related internships or fieldwork, Federal Work-Study, and institutionally sponsored loans also available. Support available to part-time students. Financial award application deadline: 4/1.
Allan Wallis, Director, 303-556-5991, *Fax:* 303-556-5971, *E-mail:* alan.wallis@cudenver.edu.
Application contact: Antoniette Sandoval, Student Service Specialist, 303-556-5970, *Fax:* 303-556-5971, *E-mail:* asandoval@castle.cudenver.edu.

Find an in-depth description at www.petersons.com/gradchannel.

■ UNIVERSITY OF CONNECTICUT

Graduate School, College of Liberal Arts and Sciences, Department of Political Science, Field of Public Affairs, Storrs, CT 06269

AWARDS MPA, JD/MPA, MPA/MSW.

Degree requirements: For master's, internship.
Entrance requirements: For master's, GRE General Test, TOEFL.

■ UNIVERSITY OF DAYTON

Graduate School, College of Arts and Sciences, Department of Political Science, Program in Public Administration, Dayton, OH 45469-1300

AWARDS MPA. Part-time and evening/weekend programs available.

Faculty: 5 full-time (1 woman), 6 part-time/adjunct (2 women).
Students: 12 full-time (7 women), 36 part-time (15 women); includes 5 minority (4 African Americans, 1 Asian American or Pacific Islander). Average age 30. 15 applicants, 80% accepted. In 2001, 21 degrees awarded.
Degree requirements: For master's, comprehensive exam.
Entrance requirements: For master's, GRE General Test, minimum undergraduate GPA of 2.7. *Application deadline:* For fall admission, 8/1 (priority date); for winter admission, 11/1 (priority date); for spring admission, 4/1 (priority date). Applications are processed on a rolling basis. *Application fee:* $30. Electronic applications accepted.
Expenses: Tuition: Full-time $5,436; part-time $453 per credit hour. Required fees: $50; $25 per term.
Financial support: In 2001–02, 2 research assistantships with full tuition reimbursements (averaging $8,500 per year) were awarded; career-related internships or fieldwork and unspecified assistantships also available.
Faculty research: Ethics, leadership, state government, environmental policy, privatization.
Dr. Peter B. Nelson, MPA Director, 937-229-3651, *Fax:* 937-229-3900, *E-mail:* peter.nelson@notes.udayton.edu. *Web site:* http://www.udayton.edu/~mpa

■ UNIVERSITY OF DELAWARE

College of Human Services, Education and Public Policy, School of Urban Affairs and Public Policy, Program in Public Administration, Newark, DE 19716

AWARDS MPA. Part-time and evening/weekend programs available.

Faculty: 13 full-time (3 women), 1 (woman) part-time/adjunct.
Students: 63 full-time (44 women), 30 part-time (18 women); includes 13 minority (11 African Americans, 2 Hispanic Americans), 8 international. Average age 30. 109 applicants, 42% accepted. In 2001, 29 degrees awarded.
Degree requirements: For master's, thesis or alternative, internship or thesis. *Median time to degree:* Master's–2 years full-time, 3 years part-time.

University of Delaware (continued)
Entrance requirements: For master's, GRE General Test, TOEFL. *Application deadline:* For fall admission, 2/1; for spring admission, 12/1. Applications are processed on a rolling basis. *Application fee:* $50. Electronic applications accepted.
Expenses: Tuition, state resident: full-time $4,770; part-time $265 per credit. Tuition, nonresident: full-time $13,860; part-time $770 per credit. Required fees: $414.
Financial support: In 2001–02, 45 students received support, including 3 fellowships with full tuition reimbursements available (averaging $11,000 per year), 45 research assistantships with full tuition reimbursements available (averaging $11,000 per year), 1 teaching assistantship with full tuition reimbursement available (averaging $11,000 per year); career-related internships or fieldwork, Federal Work-Study, institutionally sponsored loans, tuition waivers (full), and stipends also available. Financial award application deadline: 2/1.
Faculty research: State and local management, community development and nonprofit leadership, drug and alcohol epidemiology, fiscal and financial policy, transportation impacts and management.
Prof. Eric Jacobsen, Director, 302-831-1711, *Fax:* 302-831-3587, *E-mail:* ericj@udel.edu.
Application contact: Charlotte Karin, Information Contact, 302-831-1687, *Fax:* 302-831-3587, *E-mail:* ckarin@udel.edu. *Web site:* http://www.udel.edu/suapp/

Find an in-depth description at www.petersons.com/gradchannel.

■ UNIVERSITY OF DELAWARE

College of Human Services, Education and Public Policy, School of Urban Affairs and Public Policy, Program in Urban Affairs and Public Policy, Newark, DE 19716

AWARDS Community development and nonprofit leadership (MA); energy and environmental policy (MA); governance, planning and management (PhD); historic preservation (MA); social and urban policy (PhD); technology, environment and society (PhD). Part-time programs available.

Faculty: 15 full-time (6 women).
Students: 85 full-time (44 women), 9 part-time (4 women); includes 23 minority (18 African Americans, 1 Asian American or Pacific Islander, 2 Hispanic Americans, 2 Native Americans), 23 international. Average age 36. 83 applicants, 28% accepted. In 2001, 21 master's, 5 doctorates awarded. Terminal master's awarded for partial completion of doctoral program.
Degree requirements: For master's, thesis or alternative, analytical paper or thesis; for doctorate, thesis/dissertation. *Median time to degree:* Master's–2 years full-time, 3 years part-time.
Entrance requirements: For master's, GRE General Test, TOEFL, minimum GPA of 3.0; for doctorate, GRE General Test, TOEFL, minimum GPA of 3.5. *Application deadline:* For fall admission, 2/1; for spring admission, 12/1. Applications are processed on a rolling basis. *Application fee:* $50. Electronic applications accepted.
Expenses: Tuition, state resident: full-time $4,770; part-time $265 per credit. Tuition, nonresident: full-time $13,860; part-time $770 per credit. Required fees: $414.
Financial support: In 2001–02, 78 students received support, including 4 fellowships with full tuition reimbursements available (averaging $11,000 per year), 62 research assistantships with full tuition reimbursements available (averaging $11,000 per year), 4 teaching assistantships with full tuition reimbursements available (averaging $11,000 per year); career-related internships or fieldwork, Federal Work-Study, and tuition waivers (full) also available. Financial award application deadline: 2/1.
Faculty research: Political economy; social policy analysis; technology and society; historic preservation; urban policy.
Dr. Margaret Wilder, Director, 302-831-6294, *Fax:* 302-831-4225, *E-mail:* mwilder@udel.edu.
Application contact: Charlotte Karin, Information Contact, 302-831-1687, *Fax:* 302-831-3587, *E-mail:* ckarin@udel.edu. *Web site:* http://www.udel.edu/suapp

Find an in-depth description at www.petersons.com/gradchannel.

■ THE UNIVERSITY OF FINDLAY

Graduate Studies, MBA Program, Findlay, OH 45840-3653

AWARDS Financial management (MBA); human resource management (MBA); international management (MBA); management (MBA); marketing (MBA); public management (MBA). Part-time and evening/weekend programs available. Postbaccalaureate distance learning degree programs offered (minimal on-campus study).

Students: 473. In 2001, 131 degrees awarded.
Degree requirements: For master's, cumulative project.
Entrance requirements: For master's, GMAT, TOEFL. *Application deadline:* Applications are processed on a rolling basis. *Application fee:* $25 ($0 for international students). Electronic applications accepted.
Expenses: Contact institution.
Financial support: In 2001–02, 1 student received support, including 1 teaching assistantship with full tuition reimbursement available (averaging $6,000 per year); unspecified assistantships also available. Financial award application deadline: 4/1; financial award applicants required to submit FAFSA.
Faculty research: Health care management, operations and logistics management.
Dr. Theodore C. Alex, Dean, 419-434-4704, *Fax:* 419-434-4822.
Application contact: Dr. Ahmed I. El-Zayaty, Professor of Business, 419-434-4897, *Fax:* 419-434-4822. *Web site:* http://www.findlay.edu/

■ UNIVERSITY OF FLORIDA

Graduate School, College of Liberal Arts and Sciences, Department of Political Science, Gainesville, FL 32611

AWARDS International development policy (MA); international relations (MA, MAT, PhD); political campaigning (MA, Certificate); political science (MA, MAT, PhD); public affairs (MA, Certificate). Part-time programs available. Terminal master's awarded for partial completion of doctoral program.

Degree requirements: For master's, variable foreign language requirement, thesis or alternative; for doctorate, variable foreign language requirement, thesis/dissertation.
Entrance requirements: For master's and doctorate, GRE General Test, minimum GPA of 3.0. Electronic applications accepted.
Expenses: Tuition, state resident: part-time $164 per hour. Tuition, nonresident: part-time $571 per hour. Tuition and fees vary according to course level and program.
Faculty research: U.S. political development, religion and politics, environmental politics and policy, developing societies, international relations. *Web site:* http://clas.ufl.edu/polisci/

■ UNIVERSITY OF GEORGIA

Graduate School, College of Arts and Sciences, Department of Political Science, Program in Public Administration, Athens, GA 30602

AWARDS MPA, DPA.

Faculty: 32 full-time (4 women).
Students: 53 full-time (28 women), 46 part-time (23 women); includes 12 minority (9 African Americans, 1 Asian American or Pacific Islander, 2 Hispanic Americans), 13 international. 129 applicants, 44% accepted. In 2001, 23 master's, 2 doctorates awarded.
Degree requirements: For master's, internship; for doctorate, thesis/dissertation.
Entrance requirements: For master's and doctorate, GRE General Test. *Application deadline:* For fall admission, 7/1 (priority date); for spring admission, 11/15. *Application fee:* $30. Electronic applications accepted.
Expenses: Tuition, state resident: full-time $2,376; part-time $132 per credit hour. Tuition, nonresident: full-time $9,504;

part-time $528 per credit hour. Required fees: $236 per semester.
Financial support: Fellowships, research assistantships, teaching assistantships, unspecified assistantships available.
Application contact: Dr. Jerome S. Legge, Graduate Coordinator, 706-542-2941, *Fax:* 706-542-4421, *E-mail:* jlegge@uga.edu. *Web site:* http://www.uga.edu/~pol-sci/

■ UNIVERSITY OF GUAM

Graduate School and Research, College of Business and Public Administration, Master of Public Administration Program, Mangilao, GU 96923

AWARDS MPA.

Entrance requirements: For master's, GRE General Test, TOEFL.

■ UNIVERSITY OF HAWAII AT MANOA

Graduate Division, College of Arts and Sciences, College of Social Sciences, Program in Public Administration, Honolulu, HI 96822

AWARDS MPA, Certificate. Part-time and evening/weekend programs available.

Faculty: 7 full-time (2 women).
Students: 13 full-time (9 women), 30 part-time (12 women); includes 1 African American, 22 Asian Americans or Pacific Islanders, 2 Hispanic Americans. Average age 39. 45 applicants, 76% accepted, 18 enrolled. In 2001, 11 degrees awarded.
Degree requirements: For master's and Certificate, thesis or alternative, practicum. *Median time to degree:* Master's–1 year full-time.
Application deadline: For fall admission, 3/1 (priority date). *Application fee:* $25 ($50 for international students).
Expenses: Tuition, state resident: full-time $2,160; part-time $1,980 per year. Tuition, nonresident: full-time $5,190; part-time $4,829 per year.
Financial support: Fellowships, research assistantships, career-related internships or fieldwork, Federal Work-Study, institutionally sponsored loans, and tuition waivers (full and partial) available. Support available to part-time students.
Faculty research: Public sector finance and the budget process, collaboration between sectors, organizational problem solving and communication processes, system reform in government organizations, public policy analysis. *Total annual research expenditures:* $25,000.
Richard Pratt, Director, 808-956-8260, *Fax:* 808-956-9571, *E-mail:* pratt@hawaii.edu. *Web site:* http://www.soc.hawaii.edu/

■ UNIVERSITY OF HOUSTON–CLEAR LAKE

School of Business and Public Administration, Program in General Business, Houston, TX 77058-1098

AWARDS Administration of health services (MS); environmental management (MS); healthcare administration (MHA); human resource management (MA); public management (MA). Part-time and evening/weekend programs available.

Students: 75; includes 17 minority (5 African Americans, 8 Asian Americans or Pacific Islanders, 4 Hispanic Americans), 2 international. Average age 33. In 2001, 19 degrees awarded.
Degree requirements: For master's, thesis optional.
Entrance requirements: For master's, GMAT. *Application deadline:* For fall admission, 8/1; for spring admission, 12/1. Applications are processed on a rolling basis. *Application fee:* $30 ($70 for international students). Electronic applications accepted.
Expenses: Tuition, state resident: full-time $2,016; part-time $84 per credit hour. Tuition, nonresident: full-time $6,072; part-time $253 per credit hour. Tuition and fees vary according to course load.
Financial support: Career-related internships or fieldwork, Federal Work-Study, institutionally sponsored loans, and scholarships/grants available. Support available to part-time students. Financial award application deadline: 5/1.
Dr. Richard Allison, Chair, 281-283-3251, *E-mail:* allison@cl.uh.edu.
Application contact: Dr. Sue Neeley, Associate Professor, 281-283-3110, *E-mail:* neeley@cl.uh.edu.

■ UNIVERSITY OF IDAHO

College of Graduate Studies, College of Letters and Science, Department of Political Science, Program in Public Administration, Moscow, ID 83844-2282

AWARDS MPA.

Students: 11 full-time (6 women), 6 part-time (3 women); includes 3 minority (2 African Americans, 1 Native American). In 2001, 6 degrees awarded.
Entrance requirements: For master's, minimum GPA of 2.8. *Application deadline:* For fall admission, 8/1; for spring admission, 12/15. *Application fee:* $35 ($45 for international students).
Expenses: Tuition, state resident: full-time $1,613. Tuition, nonresident: full-time $3,000.
Financial support: Application deadline: 2/15.
Dr. Florence Heffron, Director, 208-885-6120.

■ UNIVERSITY OF ILLINOIS AT CHICAGO

Graduate College, College of Business Administration, Department of Economics, Chicago, IL 60607-7128

AWARDS Economics (MA, PhD); public policy analysis (PhD).

Faculty: 19 full-time (3 women).
Students: 56 full-time (29 women), 19 part-time (5 women); includes 10 minority (4 African Americans, 3 Asian Americans or Pacific Islanders, 3 Hispanic Americans), 34 international. Average age 31. 163 applicants, 22% accepted, 18 enrolled. In 2001, 10 master's, 7 doctorates awarded. Terminal master's awarded for partial completion of doctoral program.
Degree requirements: For master's, comprehensive exam; for doctorate, thesis/dissertation.
Entrance requirements: For master's and doctorate, GRE General Test, TOEFL, minimum GPA of 3.75 on a 5.0 scale. *Application deadline:* For fall admission, 6/1. *Application fee:* $40 ($50 for international students). Electronic applications accepted.
Expenses: Tuition, state resident: full-time $3,060. Tuition, nonresident: full-time $6,688.
Financial support: In 2001–02, 42 students received support; fellowships with full tuition reimbursements available, research assistantships with full tuition reimbursements available, teaching assistantships with full tuition reimbursements available, career-related internships or fieldwork, Federal Work-Study, and tuition waivers (full) available. Financial award application deadline: 3/1; financial award applicants required to submit FAFSA.
Faculty research: International, labor, and urban economics.
Paul Pieper, Director of Graduate Studies, 312-996-5314, *E-mail:* pjpieper@uic.edu.
Application contact: Lynn Lacey, Graduate Secretary, 312-996-2684.

■ UNIVERSITY OF ILLINOIS AT CHICAGO

Graduate College, College of Liberal Arts and Sciences, Department of Political Science, Chicago, IL 60607-7128

AWARDS Political science (MA); public policy analysis (PhD). Part-time programs available.

Faculty: 19 full-time (3 women).
Students: 15 full-time (6 women), 35 part-time (14 women); includes 13 minority (5 African Americans, 2 Asian Americans or Pacific Islanders, 5 Hispanic Americans, 1 Native American), 8 international. Average age 34. 38 applicants, 50% accepted, 12 enrolled. In 2001, 5 master's, 5 doctorates awarded.
Degree requirements: For master's, thesis or comprehensive exam.

University of Illinois at Chicago (continued)

Entrance requirements: For master's, GRE General Test, TOEFL, minimum GPA of 4.0 on a 5.0 scale. *Application deadline:* For fall admission, 6/1; for spring admission, 11/1. Applications are processed on a rolling basis. *Application fee:* $40 ($50 for international students). Electronic applications accepted.
Expenses: Tuition, state resident: full-time $3,060. Tuition, nonresident: full-time $6,688.
Financial support: In 2001–02, 17 students received support; fellowships with full tuition reimbursements available, research assistantships with full tuition reimbursements available, teaching assistantships with full tuition reimbursements available, Federal Work-Study, institutionally sponsored loans, and tuition waivers (full) available. Financial award application deadline: 3/15; financial award applicants required to submit FAFSA.
Faculty research: Policy analysis/national urban politics and policy, electoral behavior.
Barry Rundquist, Acting Chair, 312-413-2190, *E-mail:* barryr@uic.edu.
Application contact: Thomas Carsey, Director of Graduate Studies, 312-996-8660.

■ UNIVERSITY OF ILLINOIS AT CHICAGO

Graduate College, College of Urban Planning and Public Affairs, Program in Public Administration, Chicago, IL 60607-7128

AWARDS MPA, PhD. Evening/weekend programs available.

Students: 14 full-time (8 women), 60 part-time (37 women); includes 32 minority (21 African Americans, 2 Asian Americans or Pacific Islanders, 9 Hispanic Americans), 1 international. Average age 34. 71 applicants, 35% accepted, 13 enrolled. In 2001, 14 master's, 1 doctorate awarded.
Degree requirements: For master's, internship/project.
Entrance requirements: For master's, GRE General Test, TOEFL, minimum GPA of 4.0 on a 5.0 scale. *Application deadline:* For fall admission, 6/1; for spring admission, 11/1. Applications are processed on a rolling basis. *Application fee:* $40 ($50 for international students). Electronic applications accepted.
Expenses: Tuition, state resident: full-time $3,060. Tuition, nonresident: full-time $6,688.
Financial support: In 2001–02, 7 students received support; fellowships with full tuition reimbursements available, research assistantships with full tuition reimbursements available, teaching assistantships with full tuition reimbursements available, career-related internships or fieldwork, Federal Work-Study, and tuition waivers (full) available. Financial award application deadline: 3/1; financial award applicants required to submit FAFSA.
Faculty research: Public management, economic development, public personnel.
Vaughn Blankenship, Director of Graduate Studies, 312-996-3109, *E-mail:* lvaughn@uic.edu.

Find an in-depth description at www.petersons.com/gradchannel.

■ UNIVERSITY OF ILLINOIS AT CHICAGO

Graduate College, College of Urban Planning and Public Affairs, Program in Urban Planning and Policy, Chicago, IL 60607-7128

AWARDS Public policy analysis (PhD); urban planning and policy (MUPP). Part-time programs available.

Faculty: 13 full-time (2 women).
Students: 92 full-time (51 women), 97 part-time (44 women); includes 54 minority (30 African Americans, 5 Asian Americans or Pacific Islanders, 19 Hispanic Americans), 20 international. Average age 32. 184 applicants, 60% accepted, 70 enrolled. In 2001, 50 master's, 5 doctorates awarded.
Degree requirements: For master's, thesis or alternative, internship; for doctorate, thesis/dissertation.
Entrance requirements: For master's and doctorate, GRE General Test, TOEFL, minimum GPA of 3.75 on a 5.0 scale, writing sample. *Application deadline:* For fall admission, 6/1; for spring admission, 11/1. Applications are processed on a rolling basis. *Application fee:* $40 ($50 for international students). Electronic applications accepted.
Expenses: Tuition, state resident: full-time $3,060. Tuition, nonresident: full-time $6,688.
Financial support: In 2001–02, 63 students received support; fellowships, research assistantships, teaching assistantships, career-related internships or fieldwork, Federal Work-Study, and tuition waivers (full) available. Financial award applicants required to submit FAFSA.
Charles Hoch, Director of Graduate Studies, 312-996-2155, *E-mail:* chashoch@uic.edu.

Find an in-depth description at www.petersons.com/gradchannel.

■ UNIVERSITY OF ILLINOIS AT SPRINGFIELD

Graduate Programs, College of Public Affairs and Administration, Program in Public Administration, Springfield, IL 62703-5404

AWARDS MPA, DPA.

Faculty: 7 full-time (3 women), 1 part-time/adjunct (0 women).
Students: 37 full-time (22 women), 109 part-time (65 women); includes 42 minority (39 African Americans, 1 Asian American or Pacific Islander, 2 Hispanic Americans), 8 international. Average age 32. 68 applicants, 88% accepted, 38 enrolled. In 2001, 33 degrees awarded.
Degree requirements: For master's, thesis or alternative.
Entrance requirements: For master's, GRE, TOEFL. *Application deadline:* Applications are processed on a rolling basis. *Application fee:* $0.
Expenses: Tuition, state resident: full-time $2,680. Tuition, nonresident: full-time $8,064. Required fees: $626. One-time fee: $626.
Financial support: In 2001–02, 68 students received support, including 15 research assistantships with full and partial tuition reimbursements available (averaging $1,000 per year); career-related internships or fieldwork, Federal Work-Study, scholarships/grants, tuition waivers (partial), and unspecified assistantships also available. Support available to part-time students. Financial award application deadline: 6/1; financial award applicants required to submit FAFSA.
Faculty research: Human resource management, municipal bonds, organizational psychology, affirmative action, The Golden Book, distance learning technologies.

■ UNIVERSITY OF KANSAS

Graduate School, College of Liberal Arts and Sciences, Division of Government, Program in Public Administration, Lawrence, KS 66045

AWARDS MPA, JD/MPA, MUP/MPA. Part-time and evening/weekend programs available.

Faculty: 1.
Students: 18 full-time (7 women), 72 part-time (37 women); includes 12 minority (2 African Americans, 2 Asian Americans or Pacific Islanders, 7 Hispanic Americans, 1 Native American), 2 international. Average age 32. 32 applicants, 63% accepted, 19 enrolled. In 2001, 21 degrees awarded.
Entrance requirements: For master's, GRE General Test, TOEFL, TSE. *Application deadline:* For fall admission, 6/15; for spring admission, 11/15. *Application fee:* $35.
Expenses: Tuition, state resident: full-time $2,722; part-time $113 per credit. Tuition, nonresident: full-time $8,586; part-time $358 per credit. Required fees: $551; $46 per credit. Tuition and fees vary according to campus/location, program and reciprocity agreements.
Financial support: Fellowships, research assistantships, teaching assistantships, career-related internships or fieldwork and institutionally sponsored loans available.
John Nalbandian, Chair, 785-864-9096, *Fax:* 785-864-5208, *E-mail:* padept@ku.edu.

Application contact: Graduate Secretary, 785-864-5208, *Fax:* 785-864-5208, *E-mail:* padept@ku.edu. *Web site:* http://www.ku.edu/~kupa/

■ UNIVERSITY OF KENTUCKY

Graduate School, Program in Public Administration, Lexington, KY 40506-0032

AWARDS MPA, PhD, JD/MPA.

Faculty: 23 full-time (8 women).
Students: 47 full-time (26 women), 29 part-time (16 women); includes 9 minority (8 African Americans, 1 Asian American or Pacific Islander), 3 international. 77 applicants, 79% accepted. In 2001, 11 master's, 3 doctorates awarded.
Degree requirements: For master's, comprehensive exam; for doctorate, thesis/dissertation, comprehensive exam.
Entrance requirements: For master's, GMAT, GRE General Test, minimum undergraduate GPA of 2.5; for doctorate, GRE General Test, minimum graduate GPA of 3.0. *Application deadline:* For fall admission, 7/19. Applications are processed on a rolling basis. *Application fee:* $30 ($35 for international students).
Expenses: Tuition, state resident: full-time $4,075; part-time $213 per credit hour. Tuition, nonresident: full-time $11,295; part-time $614 per credit hour.
Financial support: In 2001–02, 6 fellowships, 14 research assistantships, 1 teaching assistantship were awarded. Career-related internships or fieldwork, Federal Work-Study, institutionally sponsored loans, and unspecified assistantships also available. Support available to part-time students. Financial award application deadline: 4/15.
Faculty research: Public financial management, education finance and policy, health finance and policy, welfare policy, program evaluation. *Total annual research expenditures:* $822,349.
Dr. Genia Toma, Director, 859-257-5594.
Application contact: Dr. Jeannine Blackwell, Associate Dean, 859-257-4905, *Fax:* 859-323-1928.

■ UNIVERSITY OF LA VERNE

School of Public Affairs and Health Administration, Department of Health Services Management and Gerontology, Graduate Program in Gerontology, La Verne, CA 91750-4443

AWARDS Business administration (MS); counseling (MS); gerontology administration (MS); health services management (MS); public administration (MS). Part-time programs available.

Faculty: 3 full-time (2 women), 5 part-time/adjunct (all women).
Students: 1 (woman) full-time, 20 part-time (15 women); includes 8 minority (7 African Americans, 1 Asian American or Pacific Islander), 2 international. Average age 50. In 2001, 9 degrees awarded.
Entrance requirements: For master's, minimum GPA of 3.0. *Application deadline:* Applications are processed on a rolling basis. *Application fee:* $40.
Expenses: Tuition: Full-time $4,410; part-time $245 per unit. Required fees: $60. Tuition and fees vary according to course load, degree level, campus/location and program.
Financial support: In 2001–02, 8 students received support. Institutionally sponsored loans available. Financial award application deadline: 3/2; financial award applicants required to submit FAFSA.
Application contact: Jo Nell Baker, Director, Graduate Admissions and Academic Services, 909-593-3511 Ext. 4504, *Fax:* 909-392-2761, *E-mail:* bakerj@ulv.edu. *Web site:* http://www.ulv.edu/gerontology/

■ UNIVERSITY OF LA VERNE

School of Public Affairs and Health Administration, Department of Public Administration, Doctoral Program in Public Administration, La Verne, CA 91750-4443

AWARDS DPA. Part-time programs available.

Faculty: 7 full-time (2 women), 6 part-time/adjunct (0 women).
Students: 45 full-time (23 women), 66 part-time (31 women); includes 50 minority (28 African Americans, 12 Asian Americans or Pacific Islanders, 10 Hispanic Americans), 9 international. Average age 44. In 2001, 1 degree awarded.
Degree requirements: For doctorate, thesis/dissertation.
Entrance requirements: For doctorate, 5 years work experience or 3 year internship. *Application fee:* $75.
Expenses: Tuition: Full-time $4,410; part-time $245 per unit. Required fees: $60. Tuition and fees vary according to course load, degree level, campus/location and program.
Financial support: In 2001–02, 40 students received support, including 1 fellowship (averaging $1,020 per year), 2 research assistantships (averaging $3,100 per year); institutionally sponsored loans also available. Financial award application deadline: 3/2; financial award applicants required to submit FAFSA.
Dr. Keeok Park, Chairperson, 909-593-3511, *Fax:* 909-596-5860, *E-mail:* johnsone@ulv.edu.
Application contact: Jo Nell Baker, Director, Graduate Admissions and Academic Services, 909-593-3511 Ext. 4504, *Fax:* 909-392-2761, *E-mail:* bakerj@ulv.edu. *Web site:* http://www.ulv.edu//~padm/dpa/

Find an in-depth description at www.petersons.com/gradchannel.

■ UNIVERSITY OF LA VERNE

School of Public Affairs and Health Administration, Department of Public Administration, Master's Program in Public Administration, La Verne, CA 91750-4443

AWARDS MPA. Part-time programs available.

Faculty: 7 full-time (2 women), 3 part-time/adjunct (0 women).
Students: Average age 37. In 2001, 36 degrees awarded.
Entrance requirements: For master's, minimum undergraduate GPA of 2.75. *Application deadline:* Applications are processed on a rolling basis. *Application fee:* $40.
Expenses: Tuition: Full-time $4,410; part-time $245 per unit. Required fees: $60. Tuition and fees vary according to course load, degree level, campus/location and program.
Financial support: In 2001–02, 16 students received support, including 1 research assistantship (averaging $1,575 per year); fellowships Financial award application deadline: 3/2; financial award applicants required to submit FAFSA.
Dr. Raymond Garubo, Chairperson, 909-593-3511 Ext. 4651, *Fax:* 909-596-5860, *E-mail:* garubor@ulv.edu.
Application contact: Jo Nell Baker, Director, Graduate Admissions and Academic Services, 909-593-3511 Ext. 4504, *Fax:* 909-392-2761, *E-mail:* bakerj@ulv.edu. *Web site:* http://www.ulv.edu/~padm/

Find an in-depth description at www.petersons.com/gradchannel.

■ UNIVERSITY OF LOUISVILLE

Graduate School, College of Business and Public Administration, Department of Urban and Public Affairs, Program in Public Administration, Louisville, KY 40292-0001

AWARDS Labor and public management (MPA); public policy and administration (MPA); urban and regional development (MPA).

Students: 19 full-time (15 women), 29 part-time (18 women); includes 5 minority (3 African Americans, 2 Hispanic Americans), 5 international. Average age 30. In 2001, 15 degrees awarded.
Degree requirements: For master's, practicum or thesis.
Entrance requirements: For master's, GRE General Test, minimum GPA of 3.25, resumé. *Application deadline:* For fall admission, 7/1 (priority date); for spring admission, 12/1 (priority date). Applications are processed on a rolling basis. *Application fee:* $25.
Expenses: Tuition, state resident: full-time $4,134. Tuition, nonresident: full-time $11,486.

University of Louisville (continued)
Financial support: In 2001–02, 3 research assistantships with full tuition reimbursements (averaging $8,000 per year) were awarded
Dr. Steve Koven, Director, 502-852-6626, *Fax:* 502-852-4558, *E-mail:* sgkove01@louisville.edu. *Web site:* http://www.cbpa.louisville.edu/

Find an in-depth description at www.petersons.com/gradchannel.

■ UNIVERSITY OF MAINE

Graduate School, College of Business, Public Policy and Health, Department of Public Administration, Orono, ME 04469-5754

AWARDS MPA. Part-time and evening/weekend programs available.

Students: 18 full-time (5 women), 21 part-time (10 women); includes 1 minority (Native American), 1 international. Average age 37. 20 applicants, 90% accepted, 10 enrolled. In 2001, 8 degrees awarded.
Entrance requirements: For master's, GMAT or GRE General Test, TOEFL. *Application deadline:* Applications are processed on a rolling basis. *Application fee:* $50. Electronic applications accepted.
Expenses: Tuition, state resident: full-time $3,780; part-time $210 per credit hour. Tuition, nonresident: full-time $10,782; part-time $599 per credit hour. Required fees: $9.50 per credit hour. $32 per semester. Tuition and fees vary according to reciprocity agreements.
Financial support: In 2001–02, 2 research assistantships with tuition reimbursements (averaging $9,010 per year), 3 teaching assistantships with tuition reimbursements (averaging $9,010 per year) were awarded. Career-related internships or fieldwork, Federal Work-Study, institutionally sponsored loans, tuition waivers (full and partial), and unspecified assistantships also available. Support available to part-time students. Financial award application deadline: 3/1.
Faculty research: Organization theory, personnel administration, public budgeting and finance, policy analysis, environmental policy, community policy and development.
Dr. G. Thomas Taylor, Chairperson, 207-581-1872, *Fax:* 207-581-3039.
Application contact: Scott G. Delcourt, Director of the Graduate School, 207-581-3218, *Fax:* 207-581-3232, *E-mail:* graduate@maine.edu. *Web site:* http://www.umaine.edu/graduate/

■ UNIVERSITY OF MARYLAND, BALTIMORE COUNTY

Graduate School, Department of Economics, Program in Economic Policy Analysis, Baltimore, MD 21250-5398

AWARDS MA. Part-time and evening/weekend programs available.

Entrance requirements: For master's, GRE General Test.

■ UNIVERSITY OF MARYLAND, BALTIMORE COUNTY

Graduate School, Policy Sciences Graduate Program, Baltimore, MD 21250-5398

AWARDS MPS, PhD, JD/MPS, JD/PhD, MPA/PhD. Part-time and evening/weekend programs available.

Faculty: 31 full-time (9 women), 5 part-time/adjunct (1 woman).
Students: 32 full-time (24 women), 162 part-time (94 women); includes 46 minority (34 African Americans, 11 Asian Americans or Pacific Islanders, 1 Hispanic American), 4 international. 60 applicants, 48% accepted, 15 enrolled. In 2001, 15 master's, 12 doctorates awarded. Terminal master's awarded for partial completion of doctoral program.
Degree requirements: For master's, policy analysis paper, thesis optional; for doctorate, thesis/dissertation, field qualifying exam.
Entrance requirements: For master's and doctorate, GRE General Test, TOEFL. *Application deadline:* For fall admission, 4/15 (priority date); for spring admission, 11/1 (priority date). Applications are processed on a rolling basis. *Application fee:* $45. Electronic applications accepted.
Financial support: In 2001–02, 27 students received support, including 4 fellowships with full tuition reimbursements available (averaging $15,276 per year); research assistantships with full tuition reimbursements available, teaching assistantships, career-related internships or fieldwork and Federal Work-Study also available. Support available to part-time students. Financial award applicants required to submit FAFSA.
Faculty research: Health policy, social policy, urban policy, public management, evaluation and analytical method. *Total annual research expenditures:* $3 million.
Dr. Marvin Mandell, Interim Director, 410-455-3203, *Fax:* 410-455-1172, *E-mail:* mandell@umbc.edu.
Application contact: Sally Helms, Administrator of Academic Affairs, 410-455-3202, *Fax:* 410-455-1172, *E-mail:* gradposi@umbc.edu. *Web site:* http://www.umbc.edu/posi/

Find an in-depth description at www.petersons.com/gradchannel.

■ UNIVERSITY OF MARYLAND, COLLEGE PARK

Graduate Studies and Research, Interdepartmental Programs, Joint Program in Business and Management/Public Management, College Park, MD 20742

AWARDS MBA/MPM.

Students: 7 full-time (4 women); includes 2 minority (1 African American, 1 Hispanic American). 10 applicants, 30% accepted, 3 enrolled.
Application deadline: For fall admission, 5/15. Applications are processed on a rolling basis. *Application fee:* $50 ($70 for international students). Electronic applications accepted.
Expenses: Tuition, state resident: part-time $289 per credit hour. Tuition, nonresident: part-time $448 per credit hour. One-time fee: $436 part-time. Full-time tuition and fees vary according to course load, campus/location and program.
Financial support: Fellowships, research assistantships, teaching assistantships available. Financial award applicants required to submit FAFSA.
Application contact: Trudy Lindsey, Director, Graduate Admissions and Records, 301-405-6991, *Fax:* 301-314-9305, *E-mail:* grschool@deans.umd.edu.

■ UNIVERSITY OF MARYLAND, COLLEGE PARK

Graduate Studies and Research, School of Public Affairs, Joint Program in Public Management/Law, College Park, MD 20742

AWARDS JD/MPM.

Students: 4 full-time (3 women), 2 part-time; includes 2 minority (both African Americans). 7 applicants, 57% accepted, 3 enrolled.
Application deadline: For fall admission, 5/1. Applications are processed on a rolling basis. *Application fee:* $50 ($70 for international students). Electronic applications accepted.
Expenses: Tuition, state resident: part-time $289 per credit hour. Tuition, nonresident: part-time $448 per credit hour. One-time fee: $436 part-time. Full-time tuition and fees vary according to course load, campus/location and program.
Financial support: Fellowships available. Financial award applicants required to submit FAFSA.
Dr. Terri H. Reed, Assistant Dean, 301-405-6338, *Fax:* 301-403-4675.
Application contact: Trudy Lindsey, Director, Graduate Admissions and Records, 301-405-6991, *Fax:* 301-314-9305, *E-mail:* grschool@deans.umd.edu.

Find an in-depth description at www.petersons.com/gradchannel.

■ UNIVERSITY OF MARYLAND, COLLEGE PARK

Graduate Studies and Research, School of Public Affairs, Policy Studies Program, College Park, MD 20742

AWARDS PhD.

Students: 17 full-time (3 women), 14 part-time (5 women); includes 1 minority (Asian American or Pacific Islander), 14 international. 65 applicants, 23% accepted, 10 enrolled. In 2001, 3 degrees awarded.
Degree requirements: For doctorate, thesis/dissertation, written and oral exams.
Entrance requirements: For doctorate, GRE General Test, writing sample. *Application deadline:* For fall admission, 5/1; for spring admission, 10/1. Applications are processed on a rolling basis. *Application fee:* $50 ($70 for international students). Electronic applications accepted.
Expenses: Tuition, state resident: part-time $289 per credit hour. Tuition, nonresident: part-time $448 per credit hour. One-time fee: $436 part-time. Full-time tuition and fees vary according to course load, campus/location and program.
Financial support: Fellowships available. Financial award applicants required to submit FAFSA.
Dr. Terri H. Reed, Assistant Dean, 301-405-6338, *Fax:* 301-403-4675.
Application contact: Trudy Lindsey, Director, Graduate Admissions and Records, 301-405-6991, *Fax:* 301-314-9305, *E-mail:* grschool@deans.umd.edu.

Find an in-depth description at www.petersons.com/gradchannel.

■ UNIVERSITY OF MARYLAND, COLLEGE PARK

Graduate Studies and Research, School of Public Affairs, Public Management Program, College Park, MD 20742

AWARDS MPM.

Students: 58 full-time (36 women), 12 part-time (6 women); includes 17 minority (8 African Americans, 5 Asian Americans or Pacific Islanders, 4 Hispanic Americans), 10 international. 197 applicants, 56% accepted, 39 enrolled. In 2001, 30 degrees awarded.
Degree requirements: For master's, internship.
Entrance requirements: For master's, GRE General Test, minimum GPA of 3.0. *Application deadline:* For fall admission, 5/1. Applications are processed on a rolling basis. *Application fee:* $50 ($70 for international students).
Expenses: Tuition, state resident: part-time $289 per credit hour. Tuition, nonresident: part-time $448 per credit hour. One-time fee: $436 part-time. Full-time tuition and fees vary according to course load, campus/location and program.
Financial support: Fellowships available. Financial award applicants required to submit FAFSA.
Faculty research: International security, economic policy, financial management, social policy.
Dr. Terri N. Reed, Assistant Dean, 301-405-6338, *Fax:* 301-403-4675.
Application contact: Trudy Lindsey, Director, Graduate Admissions and Records, 301-405-6991, *Fax:* 301-314-9305, *E-mail:* grschool@deans.umd.edu.

Find an in-depth description at www.petersons.com/gradchannel.

■ UNIVERSITY OF MARYLAND, COLLEGE PARK

Graduate Studies and Research, School of Public Affairs, Public Policy Program, College Park, MD 20742

AWARDS MPP.

Students: 37 full-time (21 women), 53 part-time (30 women); includes 23 minority (20 African Americans, 2 Asian Americans or Pacific Islanders, 1 Hispanic American), 9 international. 76 applicants, 39% accepted, 20 enrolled. In 2001, 9 degrees awarded.
Entrance requirements: For master's, GRE General Test, 5 years of full-time public sector work experience, resumé. *Application deadline:* For fall admission, 5/1; for spring admission, 10/31. Applications are processed on a rolling basis. *Application fee:* $50 ($70 for international students). Electronic applications accepted.
Expenses: Tuition, state resident: part-time $289 per credit hour. Tuition, nonresident: part-time $448 per credit hour. One-time fee: $436 part-time. Full-time tuition and fees vary according to course load, campus/location and program.
Financial support: Fellowships, teaching assistantships available. Financial award applicants required to submit FAFSA.
Dr. Terri H. Reed, Assistant Dean, 301-405-6338, *Fax:* 301-403-4675.
Application contact: Trudy Lindsey, Director, Graduate Admissions and Records, 301-405-6991, *Fax:* 301-314-9305, *E-mail:* grschool@deans.umd.edu.

Find an in-depth description at www.petersons.com/gradchannel.

■ UNIVERSITY OF MASSACHUSETTS AMHERST

Graduate School, College of Social and Behavioral Sciences, Department of Public Policy and Administration, Amherst, MA 01003

AWARDS MPA. Part-time programs available.

Students: 33 full-time (27 women), 15 part-time (7 women), 9 international. Average age 31. 84 applicants, 62% accepted. In 2001, 12 degrees awarded.
Entrance requirements: For master's, GRE General Test. *Application deadline:* For fall admission, 2/1 (priority date). Applications are processed on a rolling basis. *Application fee:* $40 ($50 for international students).
Expenses: Tuition, state resident: full-time $1,980; part-time $110 per credit. Tuition, nonresident: full-time $7,456; part-time $414 per credit. Required fees: $4,112. One-time fee: $115 full-time.
Financial support: Fellowships with full tuition reimbursements, research assistantships with full tuition reimbursements, teaching assistantships with full tuition reimbursements, career-related internships or fieldwork, Federal Work-Study, scholarships/grants, traineeships, and unspecified assistantships available. Support available to part-time students. Financial award application deadline: 2/1.
Dr. John Hird, Director, 413-545-3940, *Fax:* 413-545-1108, *E-mail:* jhird@pubpol.umass.edu.

■ UNIVERSITY OF MASSACHUSETTS BOSTON

Office of Graduate Studies and Research, Program in Public Affairs, Boston, MA 02125-3393

AWARDS MS. Part-time and evening/weekend programs available.

Degree requirements: For master's, final project.
Entrance requirements: For master's, GRE General Test or MAT, minimum GPA of 2.75.
Faculty research: Leadership and policy implementation, public management, disability; human services and sound policy.

■ UNIVERSITY OF MASSACHUSETTS BOSTON

Office of Graduate Studies and Research, Program in Public Policy, Boston, MA 02125-3393

AWARDS PhD. Evening/weekend programs available.

Degree requirements: For doctorate, thesis/dissertation, practicum, oral exam, comprehensive exam.
Entrance requirements: For doctorate, GRE General Test.
Faculty research: Political economy, public managerial control, healthcare policy, planning and public policy theory, economic development.

Find an in-depth description at www.petersons.com/gradchannel.

■ THE UNIVERSITY OF MEMPHIS

Graduate School, College of Arts and Sciences, School of Urban Affairs and Public Policy, Division of Public Administration, Memphis, TN 38152

AWARDS Health services administration (MPA); human resources administration (MPA); non-profit administration (MPA);

The University of Memphis (continued)
public administration (MPA); urban management and planning (MPA). Part-time and evening/weekend programs available.

Faculty: 5 full-time (3 women), 4 part-time/adjunct (3 women).
Students: 12 full-time (8 women), 13 part-time (10 women); includes 15 minority (14 African Americans, 1 Hispanic American). Average age 33. 16 applicants, 50% accepted. In 2001, 11 degrees awarded.
Degree requirements: For master's, thesis or alternative, internship, comprehensive exam.
Entrance requirements: For master's, GRE General Test or GMAT, minimum GPA of 3.0. *Application deadline:* For fall admission, 8/1; for spring admission, 12/1. Applications are processed on a rolling basis. *Application fee:* $25 ($50 for international students).
Expenses: Tuition, state resident: full-time $2,026. Tuition, nonresident: full-time $4,528.
Financial support: In 2001–02, 3 students received support, including 1 fellowship, 2 research assistantships with full tuition reimbursements available (averaging $6,000 per year); career-related internships or fieldwork, Federal Work-Study, and scholarships/grants also available. Support available to part-time students.
Faculty research: Community building, nonprofit organization governance, human resources in local government, community collaboration, urban problems. *Total annual research expenditures:* $75,000.
Dr. Dorothy Norris-Tirrell, Director, 901-678-3360, *Fax:* 901-678-2981, *E-mail:* dnrrstrr@memphis.edu.
Application contact: Aljena Ajayi, Program Assistant, 901-678-3360, *Fax:* 901-678-2981. *Web site:* http://www.people.memphis.edu/~gapubaddm/mpa.html

■ UNIVERSITY OF MICHIGAN

Horace H. Rackham School of Graduate Studies, College of Literature, Science, and the Arts, Department of Sociology, Ann Arbor, MI 48109

AWARDS Public policy and sociology (PhD); social work and sociology (PhD); sociology (PhD).

Faculty: 36 full-time (14 women), 11 part-time/adjunct (2 women).
Students: 153 full-time (102 women); includes 65 minority (32 African Americans, 11 Asian Americans or Pacific Islanders, 19 Hispanic Americans, 3 Native Americans), 18 international. 185 applicants, 30% accepted, 26 enrolled. In 2001, 17 doctorates awarded.
Degree requirements: For doctorate, thesis/dissertation, oral defense of dissertation, preliminary exam. *Median time to degree:* Doctorate–6.6 years full-time.
Entrance requirements: For doctorate, GRE General Test, letters of recommendation. *Application deadline:* For fall admission, 12/15. *Application fee:* $55. Electronic applications accepted.
Financial support: In 2001–02, 36 fellowships with tuition reimbursements (averaging $13,000 per year), 3 research assistantships with tuition reimbursements (averaging $14,000 per year), 37 teaching assistantships with tuition reimbursements (averaging $15,000 per year) were awarded. Health care benefits also available.
Faculty research: Power, history and social change; gender and sexuality; race and ethnicity; economic sociology; social demography.
Howard Kimeldorf, Chair, 734-764-5554, *Fax:* 734-763-6887, *E-mail:* hkimel@umich.edu.
Application contact: Cydne Friday, Graduate Program Office, 734-747-4428, *Fax:* 734-763-6887, *E-mail:* soc-gradprog@umich.edu. *Web site:* http://www.umich.edu/~socdept/

■ UNIVERSITY OF MICHIGAN

Horace H. Rackham School of Graduate Studies, Gerald R. Ford School of Public Policy, Ann Arbor, MI 48109

AWARDS MPA, MPP, PhD, JD/MPP, MBA/MPP, MHSA/MPP, MPH/MPP, MPP/AM, MPP/MA, MPP/MIS, MPP/MS, MPP/MUP, MSW/MPP.

Faculty: 34 full-time (13 women), 10 part-time/adjunct (1 woman).
Students: 148 full-time (80 women); includes 26 minority (12 African Americans, 7 Asian Americans or Pacific Islanders, 7 Hispanic Americans), 14 international. Average age 27. 500 applicants, 50% accepted, 80 enrolled. In 2001, 67 degrees awarded.
Degree requirements: For doctorate, thesis/dissertation, preliminary exam. *Median time to degree:* Master's–2 years full-time.
Entrance requirements: For master's and doctorate, GRE General Test. *Application deadline:* For fall admission, 1/15 (priority date). *Application fee:* $55.
Financial support: In 2001–02, 100 students received support, including 60 fellowships, 28 teaching assistantships; career-related internships or fieldwork also available. Financial award application deadline: 2/15; financial award applicants required to submit FAFSA.
Faculty research: Public policy analysis, decision making and values, institutional structure, poverty and inequality, world trade and finance.
Dr. Rebecca M. Blank, Dean, 734-764-3490, *Fax:* 734-763-9181, *E-mail:* blank@umich.edu.
Application contact: Trey Williams, Director of Student Services, 734-764-0453, *Fax:* 734-763-9181, *E-mail:* trey@umich.edu. *Web site:* http://www.fordschool.umich.edu

Find an in-depth description at www.petersons.com/gradchannel.

■ UNIVERSITY OF MICHIGAN–DEARBORN

School of Education, Division of Public Administration, Dearborn, MI 48128-1491

AWARDS MPA. Part-time and evening/weekend programs available.

Faculty: 2 full-time (0 women).
Students: 9 full-time (6 women), 82 part-time (42 women); includes 6 minority (4 African Americans, 1 Asian American or Pacific Islander, 1 Hispanic American), 1 international. Average age 35. 29 applicants, 66% accepted, 19 enrolled. In 2001, 16 degrees awarded.
Degree requirements: For master's, thesis or alternative.
Entrance requirements: For master's, GRE or minimum undergraduate GPA of 3.0. *Application deadline:* For fall admission, 8/1 (priority date); for winter admission, 12/1; for spring admission, 4/1. Applications are processed on a rolling basis. *Application fee:* $55. Electronic applications accepted.
Expenses: Tuition, state resident: part-time $300 per credit hour. Tuition, nonresident: part-time $756 per credit hour. Required fees: $90 per semester. Tuition and fees vary according to course level, course load and program.
Financial support: Career-related internships or fieldwork and Federal Work-Study available. Support available to part-time students. Financial award application deadline: 4/1; financial award applicants required to submit FAFSA.
Faculty research: Federal, state, and local agency management; independent sector management; educational administration.
Dr. Joseph Cepuran, Head, 313-436-9135, *Fax:* 313-593-9961, *E-mail:* jcepuran@umich.edu.
Application contact: Monique L. Davis, Graduate Secretary, 313-436-9135, *Fax:* 313-593-9961, *E-mail:* mpa@umd.umich.edu. *Web site:* http://www.soe.umd.umich.edu/soe/mpa.html

■ UNIVERSITY OF MICHIGAN–FLINT

Graduate Programs, Program in Public Administration, Flint, MI 48502-1950

AWARDS MPA. Part-time and evening/weekend programs available.

Faculty: 11 full-time (3 women).
Students: 6 full-time (2 women), 42 part-time (25 women). Average age 36. 10 applicants, 70% accepted. In 2001, 16 degrees awarded.
Degree requirements: For master's, thesis, internship.

Entrance requirements: For master's, minimum GPA of 3.0, 1 course each in American government, microeconomics and statistics. *Application deadline:* For fall admission, 7/15; for winter admission, 11/15; for spring admission, 3/15. *Application fee:* $55.
Expenses: Tuition, area resident: Part-time $386 per credit. Tuition, nonresident: full-time $6,950; part-time $386 per credit. Required fees: $113 per term. Full-time tuition and fees vary according to program. Part-time tuition and fees vary according to course load.
Financial support: In 2001–02, 2 fellowships were awarded; career-related internships or fieldwork, Federal Work-Study, and scholarships/grants also available. Support available to part-time students. Financial award application deadline: 4/1.
Dr. Albert Price, Director, 810-762-3470, *E-mail:* acprice@umflint.edu.
Application contact: Ann Briggs, Administrative Associate, 810-762-3171, *Fax:* 810-766-6789, *E-mail:* ahb@umich.edu.

■ UNIVERSITY OF MINNESOTA, TWIN CITIES CAMPUS

Graduate School, Hubert H. Humphrey Institute of Public Affairs, Program in Public Affairs, Minneapolis, MN 55455-0213

AWARDS MPA. Part-time and evening/weekend programs available.

Degree requirements: For master's, internship or equivalent work experience.
Entrance requirements: For master's, GRE General Test, TOEFL, 10 years of work experience. Electronic applications accepted.
Expenses: Contact institution. *Web site:* http://www.hhh.umn.edu/

Find an in-depth description at www.petersons.com/gradchannel.

■ UNIVERSITY OF MINNESOTA, TWIN CITIES CAMPUS

Graduate School, Hubert H. Humphrey Institute of Public Affairs, Program in Public Policy, Minneapolis, MN 55455-0213

AWARDS Advanced policy analysis methods (MPP); economic and community development (MPP); foreign policy (MPP); public and nonprofit leadership and management (MPP); social policy (MPP); women and public policy (MPP).

Degree requirements: For master's, internship or equivalent work experience.
Entrance requirements: For master's, GRE General Test, TOEFL.
Expenses: Tuition, state resident: full-time $2,932; part-time $489 per credit. Tuition, nonresident: full-time $5,758; part-time $960 per credit. Part-time tuition and fees vary according to course load, program and reciprocity agreements. *Web site:* http://www.hhh.umn.edu/

Find an in-depth description at www.petersons.com/gradchannel.

■ UNIVERSITY OF MISSOURI–COLUMBIA

Graduate School, Graduate School of Public Affairs, Columbia, MO 65211

AWARDS MPA.

Faculty: 8 full-time (3 women).
Students: 16 full-time (9 women), 31 part-time (16 women); includes 6 minority (4 African Americans, 2 Hispanic Americans), 1 international. In 2001, 31 degrees awarded.
Entrance requirements: For master's, GRE General Test, minimum GPA of 3.0. *Application deadline:* For fall admission, 2/15 (priority date). Applications are processed on a rolling basis. *Application fee:* $25 ($50 for international students).
Expenses: Tuition, state resident: part-time $179 per credit hour. Tuition, nonresident: part-time $539 per credit hour. Required fees: $122 per semester. Tuition and fees vary according to program.
Financial support: Fellowships, research assistantships, teaching assistantships, institutionally sponsored loans available.
Lisa Zanetti, Director of Graduate Studies, 573-884-0953, *E-mail:* zanettil@missouri.edu.

■ UNIVERSITY OF MISSOURI–KANSAS CITY

School of Business and Public Administration, L. P. Cookingham Institute of Public Affairs, Kansas City, MO 64110-2499

AWARDS MPA, PhD, LL M/MPA. PhD offered through the School of Graduate Studies. Part-time and evening/weekend programs available.

Faculty: 7 full-time (0 women), 6 part-time/adjunct (1 woman).
Students: 33 full-time (25 women), 70 part-time (49 women); includes 18 minority (16 African Americans, 2 Hispanic Americans), 7 international. Average age 34. 60 applicants, 95% accepted. In 2001, 43 degrees awarded. Terminal master's awarded for partial completion of doctoral program.
Entrance requirements: For master's, GRE General Test. *Application deadline:* For fall admission, 5/1 (priority date); for winter admission, 10/1 (priority date). Applications are processed on a rolling basis. *Application fee:* $25.
Expenses: Tuition, state resident: part-time $233 per credit hour. Tuition, nonresident: part-time $623 per credit hour. Tuition and fees vary according to course load.
Financial support: Fellowships, research assistantships, career-related internships or fieldwork, Federal Work-Study, institutionally sponsored loans, scholarships/grants, and tuition waivers (full and partial) available. Support available to part-time students. Financial award applicants required to submit FAFSA.
Faculty research: Neighborhoods, nonprofit organizations, health administration, public management, urban problems. *Total annual research expenditures:* $974,300.
Dr. Robert Herman, Director, 816-235-2338.
Application contact: 816-235-1111.

■ UNIVERSITY OF MISSOURI–ST. LOUIS

Graduate School, College of Arts and Sciences, Department of Political Science, St. Louis, MO 63121-4499

AWARDS American politics (MA); comparative politics (MA); international politics (MA); political process and behavior (MA); political science (PhD); public administration and public policy (MA); urban and regional politics (MA). Part-time and evening/weekend programs available.

Faculty: 23.
Students: 12 full-time (4 women), 37 part-time (19 women); includes 7 minority (2 African Americans, 1 Asian American or Pacific Islander, 2 Hispanic Americans, 2 Native Americans), 6 international. In 2001, 4 master's, 2 doctorates awarded. Terminal master's awarded for partial completion of doctoral program.
Degree requirements: For master's, thesis optional; for doctorate, thesis/dissertation.
Entrance requirements: For master's, GRE General Test; for doctorate, GRE General Test, GRE Subject Test. *Application deadline:* For fall admission, 2/15 (priority date); for spring admission, 10/15 (priority date). Applications are processed on a rolling basis. *Application fee:* $25 ($40 for international students). Electronic applications accepted.
Expenses: Tuition, state resident: part-time $231 per credit hour. Tuition, nonresident: part-time $621 per credit hour.
Financial support: In 2001–02, 10 research assistantships with full and partial tuition reimbursements (averaging $10,000 per year), 5 teaching assistantships with full and partial tuition reimbursements (averaging $10,000 per year) were awarded. Fellowships, career-related internships or fieldwork also available. Support available to part-time students. Financial award application deadline: 3/15.
Faculty research: Public policy, urban politics and administration, international politics, American government, comparative politics. *Total annual research expenditures:* $18,540.
Dr. Edwardo Silva, Director of Graduate Studies, 314-516-5522, *Fax:* 314-516-5268, *E-mail:* lstein@umsl.edu.

University of Missouri–St. Louis (continued)

Application contact: Jeff Headtke, Graduate Admissions, 314-516-6928, *Fax:* 314-516-5310, *E-mail:* gradadm@umsl.edu. *Web site:* http://www.umsl.edu/divisions/artscience/polisci/pshome/

■ UNIVERSITY OF MISSOURI–ST. LOUIS

Graduate School, College of Arts and Sciences, Department of Sociology, St. Louis, MO 63121-4499

AWARDS Advanced social perspective (MA); community conflict intervention (MA); program design and evaluation research (MA); social policy planning and administration (MA). Part-time and evening/weekend programs available.

Faculty: 5.
Students: 4 full-time (2 women), 6 part-time (4 women); includes 2 minority (1 African American, 1 Native American), 1 international. In 2001, 5 degrees awarded.
Degree requirements: For master's, thesis optional.
Entrance requirements: For master's, GRE General Test. *Application deadline:* For fall admission, 7/1 (priority date); for spring admission, 12/1 (priority date). Applications are processed on a rolling basis. *Application fee:* $25 ($40 for international students). Electronic applications accepted.
Expenses: Tuition, state resident: part-time $231 per credit hour. Tuition, nonresident: part-time $621 per credit hour.
Financial support: In 2001–02, 3 students received support, including 3 teaching assistantships with full and partial tuition reimbursements available (averaging $10,333 per year); research assistantships, career-related internships or fieldwork also available. Support available to part-time students.
Faculty research: Homeless populations, theory, social deviance, conflict resolution, Japan, Republic of South Africa, social change in East Germany. *Total annual research expenditures:* $30,040.
Dr. George McCall, Director of Graduate Studies, 314-516-6366, *Fax:* 314-516-5310.
Application contact: Jean Smith, Graduate Admissions, 314-516-6928, *Fax:* 314-516-5310, *E-mail:* gradadm@umsl.edu. *Web site:* http://www.umsl.edu/divisions/artscience/sociology/

■ UNIVERSITY OF MISSOURI–ST. LOUIS

Graduate School, Program in Public Policy Administration, St. Louis, MO 63121-4499

AWARDS Health policy (MPPA); nonprofit organization management (MPPA); nonprofit organization management and leadership (Certificate); public policy analysis (MPPA); public policy processes (MPPA); public sector human resources management (MPPA). Part-time and evening/weekend programs available.

Faculty: 14.
Students: 15 full-time (8 women), 68 part-time (34 women); includes 15 minority (12 African Americans, 2 Asian Americans or Pacific Islanders, 1 Hispanic American), 7 international. In 2001, 21 degrees awarded. *Application deadline:* For fall admission, 7/1 (priority date); for spring admission, 12/1 (priority date). Applications are processed on a rolling basis. *Application fee:* $25 ($40 for international students). Electronic applications accepted.
Expenses: Tuition, state resident: part-time $231 per credit hour. Tuition, nonresident: part-time $621 per credit hour.
Financial support: In 2001–02, 4 research assistantships with full tuition reimbursements (averaging $12,000 per year) were awarded; teaching assistantships with partial tuition reimbursements, career-related internships or fieldwork also available.
Faculty research: Urban policy, public finance, evaluation. *Total annual research expenditures:* $29,888.
Andrew Glassberg, Director, 314-516-5145, *Fax:* 314-516-5210.
Application contact: Jeff Headtke, Graduate Admissions, 314-516-6928, *Fax:* 314-516-5310, *E-mail:* gradadm@umsl.edu.

■ THE UNIVERSITY OF MONTANA–MISSOULA

Graduate School, College of Arts and Sciences, Department of Political Science, Program in Public Administration, Missoula, MT 59812-0002

AWARDS MPA, JD/MPA.

Students: 10 full-time (4 women), 14 part-time (7 women); includes 2 minority (1 African American, 1 Hispanic American), 1 international. 10 applicants, 100% accepted, 7 enrolled. In 2001, 7 degrees awarded.
Degree requirements: For master's, professional paper.
Entrance requirements: For master's, GRE General Test. *Application deadline:* For fall admission, 4/1 (priority date). Applications are processed on a rolling basis. *Application fee:* $45.
Expenses: Tuition, state resident: full-time $2,482; part-time $1,700 per year. Tuition, nonresident: full-time $7,372; part-time $5,000 per year. Required fees: $1,900. Tuition and fees vary according to degree level.
Financial support: In 2001–02, teaching assistantships with full tuition reimbursements (averaging $8,400 per year); career-related internships or fieldwork, Federal Work-Study, and unspecified assistantships also available. Financial award application deadline: 3/1; financial award applicants required to submit FAFSA.
Application contact: Director, 406-243-5202, *E-mail:* tompkins@selway.umt.edu. *Web site:* http://www.umt.edu/polisci/

■ UNIVERSITY OF NEBRASKA AT OMAHA

Graduate Studies and Research, College of Public Affairs and Community Service, Department of Public Administration, Omaha, NE 68182

AWARDS MPA, PhD. Part-time and evening/weekend programs available. Postbaccalaureate distance learning degree programs offered (no on-campus study).

Faculty: 15 full-time (3 women).
Students: 32 full-time (21 women), 198 part-time (115 women); includes 34 minority (23 African Americans, 4 Asian Americans or Pacific Islanders, 5 Hispanic Americans, 2 Native Americans), 11 international. Average age 35. 150 applicants, 58% accepted, 84 enrolled. In 2001, 62 master's, 1 doctorate awarded. Terminal master's awarded for partial completion of doctoral program.
Degree requirements: For master's, thesis (for some programs), comprehensive exam; for doctorate, thesis/dissertation, comprehensive exam.
Entrance requirements: For master's, minimum GPA of 3.0; for doctorate, GRE General Test, master's degree, minimum graduate GPA of 3.35, resumé. *Application deadline:* For fall admission, 7/31 (priority date); for spring admission, 11/30 (priority date). Applications are processed on a rolling basis. *Application fee:* $35. Electronic applications accepted.
Expenses: Tuition, state resident: part-time $116 per credit hour. Tuition, nonresident: part-time $291 per credit hour. Required fees: $13 per credit hour. $4 per semester. One-time fee: $52 part-time.
Financial support: In 2001–02, 96 students received support, including 8 research assistantships; career-related internships or fieldwork, Federal Work-Study, institutionally sponsored loans, scholarships/grants, tuition waivers (partial), and unspecified assistantships also available. Support available to part-time students. Financial award application deadline: 3/1.
Dr. Russell Smith, Chairperson, 402-554-2625.

■ UNIVERSITY OF NEVADA, LAS VEGAS

Graduate College, College of Liberal Arts, Program in Ethics and Policy Studies, Las Vegas, NV 89154-9900

AWARDS MA. Part-time programs available.

Faculty: 1 full-time (0 women).

Students: 5 full-time (all women), 25 part-time (19 women); includes 3 minority (1 African American, 1 Asian American or Pacific Islander, 1 Hispanic American). 11 applicants, 82% accepted, 7 enrolled. In 2001, 3 degrees awarded.
Degree requirements: For master's, thesis.
Entrance requirements: For master's, MAT, minimum GPA of 2.75. *Application deadline:* For fall admission, 6/15; for spring admission, 11/15. Applications are processed on a rolling basis. *Application fee:* $40 ($55 for international students).
Expenses: Tuition, state resident: full-time $1,926; part-time $107 per credit. Tuition, nonresident: full-time $9,376; part-time $220 per credit. Tuition and fees vary according to course load.
Financial support: In 2001–02, 1 research assistantship with partial tuition reimbursement (averaging $10,000 per year) was awarded. Financial award application deadline: 3/1.
Dr. Craig Walton, Director, 702-895-3463.
Application contact: Graduate College Admissions Evaluator, 702-895-3320, *Fax:* 702-895-4180, *E-mail:* gradcollege@ccmail.nevada.edu.

■ UNIVERSITY OF NEVADA, LAS VEGAS

Graduate College, Greenspun College of Urban Affairs, Department of Public Administration, Las Vegas, NV 89154-9900

AWARDS MPA. Part-time and evening/weekend programs available.

Faculty: 13 full-time (2 women).
Students: 7 full-time (4 women), 68 part-time (37 women); includes 22 minority (14 African Americans, 4 Asian Americans or Pacific Islanders, 3 Hispanic Americans, 1 Native American), 2 international. 34 applicants, 50% accepted, 14 enrolled. In 2001, 34 degrees awarded.
Degree requirements: For master's, professional paper.
Entrance requirements: For master's, GMAT or GRE General Test, minimum GPA of 3.0 during previous 2 years, 2.75 overall; at least one year experience; resumé. *Application deadline:* For fall admission, 6/15; for spring admission, 11/15. *Application fee:* $40 ($55 for international students).
Expenses: Tuition, state resident: full-time $1,926; part-time $107 per credit. Tuition, nonresident: full-time $9,376; part-time $220 per credit. Tuition and fees vary according to course load.
Financial support: In 2001–02, 3 research assistantships (averaging $9,617 per year), 1 teaching assistantship with partial tuition reimbursement (averaging $10,000 per year) were awarded. Career-related internships or fieldwork also available. Financial award application deadline: 3/1.
Dr. Lee Bernick, Chair, 702-895-4828.
Application contact: Graduate College Admissions Evaluator, 702-895-3320, *Fax:* 702-895-4180, *E-mail:* gradcollege@ccmail.nevada.edu. *Web site:* http://www.unlv.edu/Colleges/Urban/pubadmin/

■ UNIVERSITY OF NEVADA, RENO

Graduate School, College of Arts and Science, Department of Political Science, Program in Public Administration and Policy, Reno, NV 89557

AWARDS MPA. Part-time and evening/weekend programs available.

Faculty: 2.
Students: 11 full-time (7 women), 9 part-time (7 women); includes 2 minority (both Hispanic Americans). Average age 35. In 2001, 1 degree awarded.
Degree requirements: For master's, oral exam/thesis or professional paper.
Entrance requirements: For master's, GRE General Test, TOEFL, minimum GPA of 2.75. *Application deadline:* For fall admission, 3/1 (priority date). Applications are processed on a rolling basis. *Application fee:* $40.
Expenses: Tuition, state resident: full-time $2,067; part-time $108 per credit. Tuition, nonresident: full-time $9,282; part-time $109 per credit. Required fees: $57 per semester. Tuition and fees vary according to course load.
Financial support: Research assistantships, teaching assistantships, Federal Work-Study, institutionally sponsored loans, tuition waivers (full), and unspecified assistantships available. Financial award application deadline: 3/1.

■ UNIVERSITY OF NEW HAMPSHIRE

Graduate School, College of Liberal Arts, Department of Political Science, Program in Public Administration, Durham, NH 03824

AWARDS MPA. Part-time programs available.

Faculty: 13 full-time.
Students: 8 full-time (2 women), 13 part-time (6 women); includes 3 minority (2 Asian Americans or Pacific Islanders, 1 Hispanic American), 2 international. Average age 34. 18 applicants, 100% accepted, 11 enrolled. In 2001, 6 degrees awarded.
Entrance requirements: For master's, GMAT or GRE General Test. *Application deadline:* For fall admission, 4/1 (priority date). Applications are processed on a rolling basis. *Application fee:* $50. Electronic applications accepted.
Expenses: Tuition, state resident: full-time $6,300; part-time $350 per credit. Tuition, nonresident: full-time $15,720; part-time $643 per credit. Required fees: $560; $280 per term. One-time fee: $15 part-time. Tuition and fees vary according to course load.
Financial support: In 2001–02, 2 teaching assistantships were awarded; fellowships, research assistantships, career-related internships or fieldwork, Federal Work-Study, scholarships/grants, and tuition waivers (full and partial) also available. Support available to part-time students. Financial award application deadline: 2/15.
Application contact: Dr. Cliff Wirth, Coordinator, 603-862-1749, *E-mail:* cjwirth@cisunix.unh.edu.

■ UNIVERSITY OF NEW HAVEN

Graduate School, School of Business, Program in Public Administration, West Haven, CT 06516-1916

AWARDS Health care management (MPA); personnel and labor relations (MPA). Part-time and evening/weekend programs available.

Students: 26 full-time (7 women), 23 part-time (12 women); includes 6 minority (2 African Americans, 4 Hispanic Americans), 22 international. In 2001, 16 degrees awarded.
Degree requirements: For master's, thesis or alternative.
Application deadline: Applications are processed on a rolling basis. *Application fee:* $50.
Expenses: Tuition: Full-time $12,015; part-time $445 per credit hour. Required fees: $30. One-time fee: $100 full-time.
Financial support: Federal Work-Study available. Support available to part-time students. Financial award application deadline: 5/1; financial award applicants required to submit FAFSA.
Charles Coleman, Chairman, 203-932-7375.

■ UNIVERSITY OF NEW MEXICO

Graduate School, School of Public Administration, Albuquerque, NM 87131-2039

AWARDS MPA, JD/MPA, MPA/MCRP. Part-time and evening/weekend programs available. Postbaccalaureate distance learning degree programs offered (no on-campus study).

Faculty: 5 full-time (3 women), 3 part-time/adjunct (1 woman).
Students: 39 full-time (25 women), 115 part-time (78 women); includes 63 minority (4 African Americans, 2 Asian Americans or Pacific Islanders, 49 Hispanic Americans, 8 Native Americans), 10 international. Average age 38. 43 applicants, 88% accepted, 29 enrolled. In 2001, 39 degrees awarded.
Degree requirements: For master's, thesis or alternative, qualifying exam.
Entrance requirements: For master's, minimum GPA of 3.0. *Application deadline:* For fall admission, 7/15; for spring admission, 11/15. *Application fee:* $40.
Expenses: Tuition, state resident: full-time $2,771; part-time $115 per credit hour.

University of New Mexico (continued)
Tuition, nonresident: full-time $11,207; part-time $467 per credit hour. Required fees: $570; $24 per credit hour. Part-time tuition and fees vary according to course load and program.
Financial support: In 2001–02, 38 students received support. Health care benefits available. Financial award application deadline: 3/1; financial award applicants required to submit FAFSA.
Faculty research: Post-socialist transitions, individual reform, human resources, science and technology administration. *Total annual research expenditures:* $8,413.
Dr. Thomas Zane Reeves, Director, 505-277-3312, *Fax:* 505-277-2529, *E-mail:* tzane@unm.edu.
Application contact: Roberta Lopez, Department Administrator I, 505-277-1092, *Fax:* 505-277-2529, *E-mail:* lopez@unm.edu. *Web site:* http://www.unm.edu/~spagrad/

■ UNIVERSITY OF NEW ORLEANS

Graduate School, College of Urban and Public Affairs, Program in Public Administration and Policy, New Orleans, LA 70148

AWARDS MPA.

Faculty: 10 full-time.
Students: 4 full-time (2 women), 23 part-time (12 women). Average age 35. 15 applicants, 27% accepted, 1 enrolled. In 2001, 3 degrees awarded.
Degree requirements: For master's, thesis.
Entrance requirements: For master's, GRE General Test. *Application deadline:* For fall admission, 7/1 (priority date); for spring admission, 11/15 (priority date). Applications are processed on a rolling basis. *Application fee:* $20. Electronic applications accepted.
Expenses: Tuition, state resident: full-time $2,748; part-time $435 per credit. Tuition, nonresident: full-time $9,792; part-time $1,773 per credit.
Financial support: Research assistantships available. Financial award applicants required to submit FAFSA.
Dr. Denise Strong, Graduate Coordinator, 504-280-7103, *Fax:* 504-280-6272, *E-mail:* dstrong@uno.edu.

■ THE UNIVERSITY OF NORTH CAROLINA AT CHAPEL HILL

Graduate School, College of Arts and Sciences, Master of Public Administration Program, Chapel Hill, NC 27599

AWARDS MPA, JD/MPA, MPA/MRP, MPA/MSW.

Degree requirements: For master's, comprehensive exam.
Entrance requirements: For master's, GRE General Test, minimum GPA of 3.0. Electronic applications accepted.
Expenses: Tuition, state resident: full-time $2,864. Tuition, nonresident: full-time $12,030.
Faculty research: Local government management, nonprofit management. *Web site:* http://ncinfo.iog.unc.edu/uncmpa/

■ THE UNIVERSITY OF NORTH CAROLINA AT CHAPEL HILL

Graduate School, Department of Public Policy, Chapel Hill, NC 27599

AWARDS PhD.

Faculty: 17 full-time (2 women), 7 part-time/adjunct (2 women).
Students: 20 full-time, 6 international. Average age 35. 27 applicants, 22% accepted. In 2001, 5 degrees awarded.
Degree requirements: For doctorate, thesis/dissertation. *Median time to degree:* Doctorate–7 years full-time.
Entrance requirements: For doctorate, GRE General Test. *Application deadline:* For fall admission, 1/1 (priority date). Applications are processed on a rolling basis. *Application fee:* $55. Electronic applications accepted.
Expenses: Tuition, state resident: full-time $2,864. Tuition, nonresident: full-time $12,030.
Financial support: In 2001–02, 14 students received support, including 3 fellowships with full tuition reimbursements available (averaging $11,500 per year), 8 research assistantships with full tuition reimbursements available (averaging $11,000 per year), 2 teaching assistantships with full tuition reimbursements available (averaging $9,000 per year); career-related internships or fieldwork, Federal Work-Study, and stipends also available.
Faculty research: Environmental policy; energy policy; economic development and science and technology policy; social policy; welfare, education and low-income communities. *Total annual research expenditures:* $460,000.
Dr. Michael A. Stegman, Chairman, 919-962-6849, *Fax:* 919-962-5824, *E-mail:* stegman@email.unc.edu.
Application contact: Asta E. Crowe, Curriculum Administrator, 919-962-2788, *Fax:* 919-962-5824, *E-mail:* asta_crowe@unc.edu. *Web site:* http://www.unc.edu/depts/pubpol/

■ THE UNIVERSITY OF NORTH CAROLINA AT CHARLOTTE

Graduate School, College of Arts and Sciences, Department of Political Science, Charlotte, NC 28223-0001

AWARDS MPA. Part-time and evening/weekend programs available.

Faculty: 12 full-time (3 women), 9 part-time/adjunct (1 woman).
Students: 10 full-time (6 women), 46 part-time (22 women); includes 14 minority (13 African Americans, 1 Asian American or Pacific Islander), 1 international. Average age 30. 31 applicants, 90% accepted, 18 enrolled. In 2001, 20 degrees awarded.
Entrance requirements: For master's, GRE General Test or MAT, minimum GPA of 3.0 in undergraduate major, 2.75 overall. *Application deadline:* For fall admission, 7/15; for spring admission, 11/15. Applications are processed on a rolling basis. *Application fee:* $35. Electronic applications accepted.
Expenses: Tuition, state resident: full-time $1,483; part-time $371 per year. Tuition, nonresident: full-time $9,850; part-time $2,463 per year. Required fees: $1,043; $277 per year. Tuition and fees vary according to course load.
Financial support: In 2001–02, 6 teaching assistantships were awarded; fellowships, research assistantships, career-related internships or fieldwork, Federal Work-Study, institutionally sponsored loans, scholarships/grants, and unspecified assistantships also available. Support available to part-time students. Financial award application deadline: 4/1; financial award applicants required to submit FAFSA.
Faculty research: Representation systems and districting, environmental policy; aging policy and nonprofit management; health policy; Supreme Court decision making.
Dr. Theodore Arrington, Chair, 704-687-2571, *Fax:* 704-687-3497, *E-mail:* tarrngtn@email.uncc.edu.
Application contact: Kathy Barringer, Director of Graduate Admissions, 704-687-3366, *Fax:* 704-687-3279, *E-mail:* gradadm@email.uncc.edu. *Web site:* http://www.uncc.edu/gradmiss/

■ THE UNIVERSITY OF NORTH CAROLINA AT CHARLOTTE

Graduate School, College of Arts and Sciences, Program in Public Policy, Charlotte, NC 28223-0001

AWARDS PhD.

Students: 3 full-time (2 women), 11 part-time (6 women). Average age 42. 25 applicants, 56% accepted, 14 enrolled. *Application fee:* $35.
Expenses: Tuition, state resident: full-time $1,483; part-time $371 per year. Tuition, nonresident: full-time $9,850; part-time $2,463 per year. Required fees: $1,043; $277 per year. Tuition and fees vary according to course load.
Financial support: In 2001–02, 3 fellowships (averaging $3,500 per year) were awarded. Financial award application deadline: 4/1; financial award applicants required to submit FAFSA.
Dr. Gerald L. Ingalls, Director, 704-687-4303, *Fax:* 704-687-3228, *E-mail:* glingalls@email.uncc.edu.

Application contact: Kathy Barringer, Director of Graduate Admissions, 704-687-3366, *Fax:* 704-687-3279, *E-mail:* gradadm@email.uncc.edu.

■ THE UNIVERSITY OF NORTH CAROLINA AT GREENSBORO

Graduate School, College of Arts and Sciences, Department of Political Science, Program in Public Affairs, Greensboro, NC 27412-5001

AWARDS Nonprofit management (Certificate); public affairs (MPA).

Faculty: 8 full-time (2 women), 1 part-time/adjunct (0 women).
Students: 9 full-time (7 women), 46 part-time (30 women); includes 12 minority (all African Americans). 43 applicants, 47% accepted, 20 enrolled. In 2001, 17 degrees awarded.
Degree requirements: For master's, comprehensive exam.
Entrance requirements: For master's, GRE General Test, TOEFL, MAT if bachelor's degree is more than 3 years old. *Application deadline:* For fall admission, 3/15 (priority date); for spring admission, 11/15. Applications are processed on a rolling basis. *Application fee:* $35.
Expenses: Tuition, state resident: part-time $344 per course. Tuition, nonresident: part-time $2,457 per course.
Financial support: In 2001–02, 17 students received support; research assistantships available.
Dr. Ruth DeHoog, Director of Graduate Studies, 336-334-5989, *Fax:* 336-334-4315, *E-mail:* rhdehoog@uncg.edu.
Application contact: Dr. James Lynch, Director of Graduate Recruitment and Information Services, 336-334-4881, *Fax:* 336-334-4424. *Web site:* http://www.uncg.edu/psc/mpa/html

■ THE UNIVERSITY OF NORTH CAROLINA AT PEMBROKE

Graduate Studies, Public Management Program, Pembroke, NC 28372-1510

AWARDS MS. Part-time and evening/weekend programs available. Postbaccalaureate distance learning degree programs offered (minimal on-campus study).

Faculty: 5 full-time (1 woman).
Students: 7 full-time (4 women), 24 part-time (14 women); includes 4 minority (2 African Americans, 2 Native Americans). Average age 38. In 2001, 7 degrees awarded.
Degree requirements: For master's, thesis optional.
Entrance requirements: For master's, GMAT, GRE General Test, or MAT, minimum GPA of 3.0 in major, 2.5 overall. *Application deadline:* For fall admission, 7/15; for spring admission, 12/1. Applications are processed on a rolling basis. *Application fee:* $40.
Expenses: Tuition, state resident: full-time $1,022. Tuition, nonresident: full-time $8,292. Tuition and fees vary according to campus/location.
Financial support: Unspecified assistantships available. Support available to part-time students. Financial award application deadline: 4/15; financial award applicants required to submit FAFSA.
Dr. Nicholas Giannatasio, Director, 910-521-6637, *E-mail:* nicholas.giannatasio@uncp.edu.
Application contact: Dean of Graduate Studies, 910-521-6271, *Fax:* 910-521-6497, *E-mail:* grad@uncp.edu.

■ UNIVERSITY OF NORTH DAKOTA

Graduate School, College of Business and Public Administration, Department of Public Administration, Grand Forks, ND 58202

AWARDS MPA. Part-time programs available. Postbaccalaureate distance learning degree programs offered (minimal on-campus study).

Faculty: 3 full-time (1 woman).
Students: 3 full-time (1 woman), 37 part-time (25 women). 18 applicants, 94% accepted, 12 enrolled. In 2001, 6 degrees awarded.
Degree requirements: For master's, thesis or alternative, final exam, comprehensive exam.
Entrance requirements: For master's, GRE General Test or GMAT, TOEFL, minimum GPA of 3.0. *Application deadline:* For fall admission, 3/1 (priority date); for spring admission, 10/15 (priority date). Applications are processed on a rolling basis. *Application fee:* $30.
Expenses: Tuition, state resident: full-time $3,298. Tuition, nonresident: full-time $7,998.
Financial support: In 2001–02, 4 students received support, including 2 teaching assistantships with full tuition reimbursements available (averaging $8,775 per year); fellowships, research assistantships, Federal Work-Study, institutionally sponsored loans, scholarships/grants, and tuition waivers (full and partial) also available. Support available to part-time students. Financial award application deadline: 3/15; financial award applicants required to submit FAFSA.
Dr. Robert W. Kweit, Director, 701-777-3541, *Fax:* 701-777-5099, *E-mail:* robert_kweit@und.nodak.edu. *Web site:* http://www.und.edu/dept/grad/depts/public_admin/

■ UNIVERSITY OF NORTHERN IOWA

Graduate College, Program in Public Policy, Cedar Falls, IA 50614

AWARDS MPP. Part-time programs available.

Students: 20 full-time (12 women), 6 part-time (1 woman); includes 9 minority (7 African Americans, 1 Asian American or Pacific Islander, 1 Hispanic American), 3 international. 14 applicants, 79% accepted. In 2001, 1 degree awarded.
Application deadline: For fall admission, 3/1 (priority date). Applications are processed on a rolling basis. *Application fee:* $20 ($50 for international students).
Expenses: Tuition, state resident: full-time $3,704; part-time $206 per credit hour. Tuition, nonresident: full-time $9,122; part-time $501 per credit hour. Required fees: $324; $108 per semester. Part-time tuition and fees vary according to course load.
Financial support: Career-related internships or fieldwork, Federal Work-Study, institutionally sponsored loans, tuition waivers (full), and unspecified assistantships available. Financial award application deadline: 3/1.
Dr. Richard Allen Hays, Jr., Director, 319-273-2910, *Fax:* 319-273-7126, *E-mail:* allen.hays@uni.edu. *Web site:* http://www.uni.edu/ppolicy/

■ UNIVERSITY OF NORTH FLORIDA

College of Arts and Sciences, Department of Political Science/Public Administration, Jacksonville, FL 32224-2645

AWARDS Public administration (MPA). Part-time programs available.

Faculty: 12 full-time (2 women).
Students: 16 full-time (10 women), 46 part-time (21 women); includes 16 minority (14 African Americans, 2 Hispanic Americans). Average age 32. 31 applicants, 45% accepted, 10 enrolled. In 2001, 20 degrees awarded.
Degree requirements: For master's, thesis, internship, comprehensive exam.
Entrance requirements: For master's, TOEFL, GRE General Test or minimum GPA of 3.0 in last 60 hours. *Application deadline:* For fall admission, 7/6 (priority date); for winter admission, 11/2 (priority date); for spring admission, 3/10 (priority date). Applications are processed on a rolling basis. *Application fee:* $20. Electronic applications accepted.
Expenses: Tuition, state resident: full-time $2,411; part-time $134 per credit hour. Tuition, nonresident: full-time $9,391; part-time $522 per credit hour. Required fees: $670; $37 per credit hour.
Financial support: In 2001–02, 27 students received support. Career-related internships or fieldwork, Federal Work-Study, and tuition waivers (partial) available. Support available to part-time students. Financial award application deadline: 4/1; financial award applicants required to submit FAFSA.
Faculty research: Municipal finance and the fiscal effects of municipal enterprises, productivity enhancement and comparative public-private sector efficiency, application of the principles and tools of Total Quality

University of North Florida (continued)
Management, state and local policy and the assessment of community needs including assessment of the Ryan White Care Act. *Total annual research expenditures:* $369,546.

Dr. Henry Thomas, Chair, 904-620-2977, *E-mail:* hthomas@unf.edu.
Application contact: Dr. Patrick Plumlee, Director, 904-620-2977, *E-mail:* pplumlee@unf.edu.

■ UNIVERSITY OF NORTH TEXAS

Robert B. Toulouse School of Graduate Studies, School of Community Service, Department of Public Administration, Denton, TX 76203

AWARDS MPA. Part-time and evening/weekend programs available.

Faculty: 8 full-time (1 woman), 3 part-time/adjunct (1 woman).
Students: 39 full-time (17 women), 72 part-time (39 women); includes 24 minority (12 African Americans, 1 Asian American or Pacific Islander, 10 Hispanic Americans, 1 Native American), 4 international. Average age 26. In 2001, 30 degrees awarded.
Degree requirements: For master's, internship, thesis optional.
Entrance requirements: For master's, GMAT or GRE General Test. *Application deadline:* For fall admission, 7/17; for spring admission, 12/1. *Application fee:* $25 ($50 for international students).
Expenses: Tuition, state resident: part-time $186 per hour. Tuition, nonresident: part-time $319 per hour. Required fees: $88; $21 per hour.
Financial support: Fellowships, career-related internships or fieldwork, Federal Work-Study, institutionally sponsored loans, and tuition waivers (full and partial) available. Support available to part-time students. Financial award application deadline: 3/1; financial award applicants required to submit FAFSA.
Faculty research: Public personnel management, municipal management, government financial management, public/private cooperation, emergency administration and planning.
Dr. Robert L. Bland, Chair, 940-565-2165, *Fax:* 940-565-4466, *E-mail:* bbland@scs.cmm.unt.edu.

■ UNIVERSITY OF OKLAHOMA

Graduate College, College of Arts and Sciences, Department of Political Science, Program in Public Administration, Norman, OK 73019-0390

AWARDS MPA. Part-time and evening/weekend programs available.

Students: 33 full-time (11 women), 239 part-time (95 women); includes 70 minority (38 African Americans, 12 Asian Americans or Pacific Islanders, 9 Hispanic Americans, 11 Native Americans). 94 applicants, 90% accepted, 59 enrolled. In 2001, 96 degrees awarded.
Entrance requirements: For master's, TOEFL, minimum GPA of 3.0. *Application deadline:* For fall admission, 6/15; for spring admission, 10/15. *Application fee:* $25 ($50 for international students).
Expenses: Tuition, state resident: full-time $2,208; part-time $92 per credit hour. Tuition, nonresident: part-time $297 per credit hour. Tuition and fees vary according to course level, course load and program.
Financial support: In 2001–02, 37 students received support; research assistantships with partial tuition reimbursements available, teaching assistantships with partial tuition reimbursements available available.
Faculty research: Policy, program evaluation, budgeting, administration.
Dr. David R. Morgan, Director, 405-325-6432.
Application contact: Debbie Deering, Assistant to the Director, 405-325-6432, *Fax:* 405-325-3733, *E-mail:* ddeering@ou.edu.

■ UNIVERSITY OF OREGON

Graduate School, School of Architecture and Allied Arts, Department of Planning, Public Policy, and Management, Program in Public Policy and Management, Eugene, OR 97403

AWARDS MA, MPA, MS. Part-time and evening/weekend programs available.

Students: 25 full-time (18 women), 6 part-time (3 women); includes 3 minority (all Hispanic Americans), 4 international. 23 applicants, 91% accepted. In 2001, 12 degrees awarded.
Degree requirements: For master's, thesis.
Entrance requirements: For master's, TOEFL, minimum GPA of 3.0. *Application fee:* $50.
Expenses: Tuition, state resident: full-time $4,968; part-time $501 per credit hour. Tuition, nonresident: full-time $8,400; part-time $691 per credit hour.
Financial support: In 2001–02, 5 teaching assistantships were awarded; career-related internships or fieldwork and Federal Work-Study also available.
Faculty research: Community economic development, families in poverty, health services.
Ed Weeks, Director, 541-346-3635.
Application contact: Linda Dent, Graduate Secretary, 541-346-6018, *Fax:* 541-346-2040.

■ UNIVERSITY OF PENNSYLVANIA

Fels Center of Government, Philadelphia, PA 19104

AWARDS MGA. Part-time and evening/weekend programs available.

Degree requirements: For master's, thesis (for some programs).
Entrance requirements: For master's, GRE, TOEFL.
Expenses: Tuition: Part-time $12,875 per semester. *Web site:* http://dolphin.upenn.edu/~gsfa/admin/admin.htm

Find an in-depth description at www.petersons.com/gradchannel.

■ UNIVERSITY OF PENNSYLVANIA

Wharton School, Graduate Group in Business and Public Policy, Philadelphia, PA 19104

AWARDS Business and public policy (AM, MBA, PhD).

Faculty: 9 full-time (2 women), 1 part-time/adjunct (0 women).
Students: 33 full-time (14 women), 2 part-time. In 2001, 4 master's, 12 doctorates awarded.
Degree requirements: For doctorate, thesis/dissertation. *Median time to degree:* Master's–2.5 years full-time; doctorate–9.5 years full-time.
Entrance requirements: For doctorate, GRE General Test, TSE. *Application fee:* $160.
Expenses: Tuition: Part-time $12,875 per semester.
Financial support: In 2001–02, 10 students received support; fellowships, research assistantships, teaching assistantships available.
Faculty research: International policy, business and government, regulation, urban development and policy, transportation.
Dr. Elizabeth Bailey, Chair, 215-898-0928, *Fax:* 215-898-7635.
Application contact: Dr. Joel Waldfogel, Coordinator, 215-898-7148, *Fax:* 215-898-7635, *E-mail:* waldfogj@wharton.upenn.edu.

Find an in-depth description at www.petersons.com/gradchannel.

■ UNIVERSITY OF PITTSBURGH

Graduate School of Public and International Affairs, Division of International Development, Pittsburgh, PA 15260

AWARDS Development planning and environmental sustainability (MPIA); governmental organizations and civil society (MPIA). Part-time programs available.

Faculty: 32 full-time (8 women), 12 part-time/adjunct (9 women).

Students: 56 full-time (39 women), 8 part-time (7 women); includes 12 minority (7 African Americans, 4 Asian Americans or Pacific Islanders, 1 Hispanic American), 21 international. Average age 26. 114 applicants, 82% accepted, 35 enrolled. In 2001, 27 degrees awarded.
Degree requirements: For master's, internship, thesis optional.
Application deadline: For fall admission, 3/1 (priority date); for spring admission, 10/1 (priority date). Applications are processed on a rolling basis. *Application fee:* $40. Electronic applications accepted.
Expenses: Tuition, state resident: full-time $9,410; part-time $385 per credit. Tuition, nonresident: full-time $19,376; part-time $797 per credit. Required fees: $480; $90 per term. Tuition and fees vary according to program.
Financial support: In 2001–02, 15 students received support, including 3 fellowships (averaging $20,260 per year), 3 research assistantships; career-related internships or fieldwork, scholarships/grants, tuition waivers (full and partial), and unspecified assistantships also available. Financial award application deadline: 2/1.
Faculty research: Project/program evaluation, population and environment, international development, development economics, civil society.
Dr. Paul J. Nelson, Director, International Development Division, 412-648-7645, *Fax:* 412-648-2605, *E-mail:* pjnelson@birch.gspia.pitt.edu.
Application contact: Maureen O'Malley, Admissions Counselor, 412-648-7646, *Fax:* 412-648-7641, *E-mail:* pronobis@birch.gspia.pitt.edu. *Web site:* http://www.gspia.pitt.edu/

■ UNIVERSITY OF PITTSBURGH

Graduate School of Public and International Affairs, Division of Public and Urban Affairs, Program in Policy Research and Analysis, Pittsburgh, PA 15260

AWARDS MPA, JD/MPA, MPA/MPIA, MPH/MPA, MSIS/MPA, MSW/MPA. Part-time and evening/weekend programs available.

Faculty: 32 full-time (8 women), 12 part-time/adjunct (9 women).
Students: 59 full-time (37 women), 21 part-time (15 women); includes 12 minority (all African Americans), 8 international. Average age 27. 19 applicants, 79% accepted, 5 enrolled. In 2001, 9 degrees awarded.
Degree requirements: For master's, internship, thesis optional.
Application deadline: For fall admission, 3/1 (priority date); for spring admission, 10/1 (priority date). Applications are processed on a rolling basis. *Application fee:* $40. Electronic applications accepted.
Expenses: Tuition, state resident: full-time $9,410; part-time $385 per credit. Tuition, nonresident: full-time $19,376; part-time $797 per credit. Required fees: $480; $90 per term. Tuition and fees vary according to program.
Financial support: In 2001–02, 36 students received support, including 7 fellowships (averaging $11,300 per year); career-related internships or fieldwork, institutionally sponsored loans, scholarships/grants, tuition waivers (full and partial), and unspecified assistantships also available. Financial award application deadline: 2/1.
Faculty research: Emergency management, health policy and regulation, regional finance, non-profit management, community/regional development, environmental policy.
Application contact: Maureen O'Malley, Admissions Counselor, 412-648-7646, *Fax:* 412-648-7641, *E-mail:* pronobis@birch.gspia.pitt.edu. *Web site:* http://www.gspia.pitt.edu/

■ UNIVERSITY OF PITTSBURGH

Graduate School of Public and International Affairs, Division of Public and Urban Affairs, Program in Public and Nonprofit Management, Pittsburgh, PA 15260

AWARDS Public management and policy (MPA). Part-time and evening/weekend programs available.

Faculty: 32 full-time (8 women), 12 part-time/adjunct (9 women).
Students: 59 full-time (37 women), 21 part-time (15 women); includes 12 minority (all African Americans), 8 international. Average age 27. 58 applicants, 66% accepted, 24 enrolled. In 2001, 8 degrees awarded.
Degree requirements: For master's, internship, thesis optional.
Application deadline: For fall admission, 3/1 (priority date); for spring admission, 10/1 (priority date). Applications are processed on a rolling basis. *Application fee:* $40.
Expenses: Tuition, state resident: full-time $9,410; part-time $385 per credit. Tuition, nonresident: full-time $19,376; part-time $797 per credit. Required fees: $480; $90 per term. Tuition and fees vary according to program.
Financial support: In 2001–02, 36 students received support, including 7 fellowships (averaging $11,300 per year); research assistantships with full tuition reimbursements available, career-related internships or fieldwork, scholarships/grants, tuition waivers (full and partial), and unspecified assistantships also available. Financial award application deadline: 2/1.
Dr. Stephen Farber, Director, Public and Urban Affairs Division, 412-648-7602, *Fax:* 412-648-2605, *E-mail:* eofarb@birch.gspia.pitt.edu.
Application contact: Maureen O'Malley, Admissions Counselor, 412-648-7646, *Fax:* 412-648-7641, *E-mail:* pronobis@birch.gspia.pitt.edu. *Web site:* http://www.gspia.pitt.edu/

Find an in-depth description at www.petersons.com/gradchannel.

■ UNIVERSITY OF PITTSBURGH

Graduate School of Public and International Affairs, Doctoral Program in Public and International Affairs, Pittsburgh, PA 15260

AWARDS Development studies (PhD); foreign and security policy (PhD); international political economy (PhD); public administration (PhD); public policy (PhD). Part-time programs available.

Faculty: 32 full-time (8 women), 12 part-time/adjunct (9 women).
Students: 60 full-time (17 women), 12 part-time (4 women); includes 4 minority (2 African Americans, 1 Asian American or Pacific Islander, 1 Hispanic American), 45 international. Average age 30. 81 applicants, 41% accepted, 14 enrolled. In 2001, 3 degrees awarded.
Degree requirements: For doctorate, thesis/dissertation.
Application deadline: For fall admission, 3/1 (priority date). Applications are processed on a rolling basis. *Application fee:* $40. Electronic applications accepted.
Expenses: Tuition, state resident: full-time $9,410; part-time $385 per credit. Tuition, nonresident: full-time $19,376; part-time $797 per credit. Required fees: $480; $90 per term. Tuition and fees vary according to program.
Financial support: In 2001–02, 15 students received support, including 12 fellowships (averaging $21,500 per year), 1 research assistantship (averaging $21,500 per year), 5 teaching assistantships (averaging $7,700 per year); career-related internships or fieldwork, scholarships/grants, unspecified assistantships, and graduate student assistantships also available. Financial award application deadline: 2/1.
Faculty research: International political economy, international development, public administration, public policy, foreign policy, international security policy.
Dr. William F. Matlack, Doctoral Program Coordinator, 412-648-7604, *E-mail:* wfm@birch.gspia.pitt.edu.
Application contact: Elizabeth Barthen-Braunsdorf, Assistant Director of Admissions, 412-648-7643, *Fax:* 412-648-7641, *E-mail:* barthen@bitch.gspia.pitt.edu. *Web site:* http://www.gspia.pitt.edu/

Find an in-depth description at www.petersons.com/gradchannel.

■ UNIVERSITY OF PITTSBURGH

Graduate School of Public and International Affairs, Executive Programs in Public Policy and Management, Pittsburgh, PA 15260

AWARDS Criminal justice (MPPM); development planning (MPPM); environmental

University of Pittsburgh (continued)
management and policy (MPPM); international development (MPPM); international political economy (MPPM); international security studies (MPPM); management of non profit organizations (MPPM); metropolitan management and regional development (MPPM); personnel and labor relations (MPPM); policy analysis and evaluation (MPPM). Part-time programs available.

Faculty: 32 full-time (8 women), 12 part-time/adjunct (9 women).
Students: 7 full-time (4 women), 51 part-time (27 women); includes 8 minority (all African Americans), 3 international. Average age 38. 34 applicants, 79% accepted, 18 enrolled. In 2001, 24 degrees awarded.
Degree requirements: For master's, thesis optional.
Application deadline: For fall admission, 3/1 (priority date); for spring admission, 10/1 (priority date). Applications are processed on a rolling basis. *Application fee:* $40.
Expenses: Tuition, state resident: full-time $9,410; part-time $385 per credit. Tuition, nonresident: full-time $19,376; part-time $797 per credit. Required fees: $480; $90 per term. Tuition and fees vary according to program.
Financial support: Institutionally sponsored loans and scholarships/grants available. Support available to part-time students. Financial award application deadline: 2/1.
Faculty research: Executive training and technical assistance for U.S. and international clients. *Total annual research expenditures:* $101,000.
Michele Garrity, Director, Executive Education, 412-648-7610, *Fax:* 412-648-2605, *E-mail:* garrity@birch.gspia.pitt.edu.
Application contact: Maureen O'Malley, Admissions Counselor, 412-648-7646, *Fax:* 412-648-7641, *E-mail:* pronobis@birch.gspia.pitt.edu. *Web site:* http://www.gspia.pitt.edu/

Find an in-depth description at www.petersons.com/gradchannel.

■ UNIVERSITY OF PUERTO RICO, RÍO PIEDRAS

College of Social Sciences, School of Public Administration, San Juan, PR 00931

AWARDS MPA. Part-time and evening/weekend programs available.

Students: 53 full-time (39 women), 239 part-time (172 women); includes 291 minority (all Hispanic Americans). In 2001, 41 degrees awarded.
Degree requirements: For master's, thesis, comprehensive exam.
Entrance requirements: For master's, GRE, PAEG, interview, minimum GPA of 3.0. *Application deadline:* For fall admission, 2/1. *Application fee:* $17.
Expenses: Students that provide official evidence of private medicine insurance or service are exempt of the payment of $529 per academic year.
Financial support: Fellowships, research assistantships, teaching assistantships, Federal Work-Study, institutionally sponsored loans, and tuition waivers (partial) available. Financial award application deadline: 5/31.
Faculty research: Collective Bargaining Public Employee Syndication.
José A. Punsoda-Días, Chairperson, 787-764-0000 Ext. 2097, *Fax:* 787-763-7510.

■ UNIVERSITY OF RHODE ISLAND

Graduate School, College of Arts and Sciences, Department of Political Science, Program in Public Policy and Administration, Kingston, RI 02881

AWARDS MPA.

Students: In 2001, 24 degrees awarded.
Application deadline: For fall admission, 4/15 (priority date). Applications are processed on a rolling basis. *Application fee:* $35.
Expenses: Tuition, state resident: full-time $3,756; part-time $209 per credit. Tuition, nonresident: full-time $10,774; part-time $599 per credit. Required fees: $1,586; $76 per credit. One-time fee: $60 full-time.
Dr. Timothy Hennessey, Director, 401-874-4052.

■ UNIVERSITY OF SAN FRANCISCO

College of Professional Studies, Department of Public Management, San Francisco, CA 94117-1080

AWARDS Nonprofit administration (MNA); public administration (MPA), including health services administration, public administration. Part-time and evening/weekend programs available.

Faculty: 4 full-time (1 woman), 46 part-time/adjunct (24 women).
Students: 171 full-time (127 women); includes 57 minority (20 African Americans, 22 Asian Americans or Pacific Islanders, 13 Hispanic Americans, 2 Native Americans). Average age 36. 63 applicants, 76% accepted, 42 enrolled. In 2001, 84 degrees awarded.
Entrance requirements: For master's, minimum GPA of 3.0. *Application fee:* $55 ($65 for international students).
Expenses: Tuition: Full-time $14,400; part-time $800 per unit. Tuition and fees vary according to degree level, campus/location and program.
Financial support: In 2001–02, 97 students received support. Application deadline: 3/2;
Faculty research: Smoking and health care policy.
Dr. Ed Rimer, Chair, 415-422-2132.

■ UNIVERSITY OF SAN FRANCISCO

College of Professional Studies, Department of Public Management, Program in Public Administration, Concentration in Public Administration, San Francisco, CA 94117-1080

AWARDS MPA. Part-time and evening/weekend programs available.

Faculty: 1 full-time (0 women), 12 part-time/adjunct (6 women).
Students: 47 full-time (26 women); includes 18 minority (4 African Americans, 7 Asian Americans or Pacific Islanders, 7 Hispanic Americans). Average age 38. 21 applicants, 76% accepted, 14 enrolled. In 2001, 17 degrees awarded.
Entrance requirements: For master's, minimum GPA of 3.0. *Application fee:* $55 ($65 for international students).
Expenses: Tuition: Full-time $14,400; part-time $800 per unit. Tuition and fees vary according to degree level, campus/location and program.
Financial support: In 2001–02, 21 students received support. Application deadline: 3/2.
Application contact: 415-422-6000.

■ UNIVERSITY OF SOUTH ALABAMA

Graduate School, College of Arts and Sciences, Department of Political Science, Mobile, AL 36688-0002

AWARDS Public administration (MPA). Part-time and evening/weekend programs available.

Faculty: 9 full-time (1 woman).
Students: 20 full-time (9 women), 9 part-time (7 women); includes 7 minority (6 African Americans, 1 Native American), 4 international. 17 applicants, 88% accepted. In 2001, 16 degrees awarded.
Degree requirements: For master's, thesis optional.
Entrance requirements: For master's, GRE, minimum GPA of 3.0. *Application deadline:* For fall admission, 9/1 (priority date). Applications are processed on a rolling basis. *Application fee:* $25.
Expenses: Tuition, state resident: full-time $3,048. Tuition, nonresident: full-time $6,096. Required fees: $320.
Financial support: In 2001–02, 2 research assistantships were awarded; career-related internships or fieldwork also available. Support available to part-time students. Financial award application deadline: 4/1.
Dr. Leonard Macaluso, Interim Chair, 334-460-7161.

■ UNIVERSITY OF SOUTH CAROLINA

The Graduate School, College of Liberal Arts, Department of Government and International Studies, Program in Public Administration, Columbia, SC 29208

AWARDS MPA, JD/MPA, MSW/MPA. Part-time and evening/weekend programs available.

Degree requirements: For master's, capstone seminar.
Entrance requirements: For master's, GRE General Test, TOEFL, minimum GPA of 3.0. Electronic applications accepted.
Expenses: Tuition, state resident: full-time $4,434. Tuition, nonresident: full-time $9,854. Tuition and fees vary according to program.
Faculty research: Public policy, organizational theory, personnel administration, budgeting, finance. *Web site:* http://www.cla.sc.edu/gint/graduate/mpa.html

■ THE UNIVERSITY OF SOUTH DAKOTA

Graduate School, College of Arts and Sciences, Department of Political Science, Vermillion, SD 57069-2390

AWARDS Political science (MA); public administration (MPA).

Faculty: 8 full-time (0 women), 1 part-time/adjunct (0 women).
Students: 33. 34 applicants, 56% accepted. In 2001, 24 degrees awarded.
Degree requirements: For master's, thesis (for some programs).
Entrance requirements: For master's, GRE or LSAT for MPA. *Application deadline:* Applications are processed on a rolling basis. *Application fee:* $35.
Expenses: Tuition, state resident: full-time $1,700; part-time $95 per credit hour. Tuition, nonresident: full-time $5,027; part-time $279 per credit hour. Required fees: $1,062; $59 per credit hour.
Financial support: Research assistantships, teaching assistantships, Federal Work-Study available. Support available to part-time students. Financial award applicants required to submit FAFSA.
Dr. William Richardson, Chair, 605-677-5242.
Application contact: David Aaronson, Graduate Student Advisor. *Web site:* http://www.usd.edu/polsci/

■ UNIVERSITY OF SOUTHERN CALIFORNIA

Graduate School, College of Letters, Arts and Sciences, Department of Political Economy and Public Policy, Los Angeles, CA 90089

AWARDS PhD.

Degree requirements: For doctorate, thesis/dissertation.
Entrance requirements: For doctorate, GRE General Test.
Expenses: Tuition: Full-time $25,060; part-time $844 per unit. Required fees: $473.

■ UNIVERSITY OF SOUTHERN CALIFORNIA

Graduate School, School of Policy, Planning and Development, Program in Public Administration, Sacramento, CA 90089

AWARDS MPA. Part-time and evening/weekend programs available.

Faculty: 1 full-time (0 women), 14 part-time/adjunct (5 women).
Students: 30 full-time (21 women), 9 part-time (5 women); includes 6 minority (1 African American, 1 Asian American or Pacific Islander, 3 Hispanic Americans, 1 Native American). Average age 30. 15 applicants, 80% accepted, 9 enrolled. In 2001, 7 degrees awarded.
Degree requirements: For master's, thesis optional. *Median time to degree:* Master's–2 years full-time, 2.75 years part-time.
Entrance requirements: For master's, GRE, GMAT, minimum GPA of 3.0. *Application deadline:* For fall admission, 7/1 (priority date); for winter admission, 11/1 (priority date); for spring admission, 4/1 (priority date). Applications are processed on a rolling basis. *Application fee:* $55.
Expenses: Tuition: Full-time $25,060; part-time $844 per unit. Required fees: $473.
Financial support: In 2001–02, 28 students received support, including 28 fellowships with partial tuition reimbursements available (averaging $3,500 per year); career-related internships or fieldwork, Federal Work-Study, institutionally sponsored loans, scholarships/grants, health care benefits, and unspecified assistantships also available. Support available to part-time students. Financial award application deadline: 7/1.
Faculty research: Organizational behavior, program evaluation, international administration, California history, management systems.
Richard Callahan, Director and Assistant Dean, 916-442-6911 Ext. 18, *Fax:* 916-444-7712, *E-mail:* rcallaha@usc.edu.
Application contact: Virginia Duncan Kaser, Graduate Program Advisor, 916-442-6911 Ext. 26, *Fax:* 916-444-7712, *E-mail:* kaser@usc.edu. *Web site:* http://www.usc.edu/schools/sppd/sacto/programs.html

■ UNIVERSITY OF SOUTHERN CALIFORNIA

Graduate School, School of Policy, Planning and Development, Program in Public Administration, Los Angeles, CA 90089

AWARDS MPA, DPA, PhD, Certificate, JD/MPA, MPA/M Pl, MPA/MAJCS, MPA/MS, MPA/MSW.

Degree requirements: For doctorate, thesis/dissertation.
Entrance requirements: For master's and doctorate, GRE General Test.
Expenses: Tuition: Full-time $25,060; part-time $844 per unit. Required fees: $473.

Find an in-depth description at www.petersons.com/gradchannel.

■ UNIVERSITY OF SOUTHERN CALIFORNIA

Graduate School, School of Policy, Planning and Development, Program in Public Policy, Los Angeles, CA 90089

AWARDS MPP.

Entrance requirements: For master's, GRE General Test.
Expenses: Tuition: Full-time $25,060; part-time $844 per unit. Required fees: $473.

Find an in-depth description at www.petersons.com/gradchannel.

■ UNIVERSITY OF SOUTHERN MAINE

Edmund S. Muskie School of Public Service, Doctoral Program in Public Policy and Management, Portland, ME 04104-9300

AWARDS PhD. Part-time and evening/weekend programs available. Postbaccalaureate distance learning degree programs offered (minimal on-campus study).

Faculty: 5 full-time (2 women).
Students: 5 full-time (4 women), 17 part-time (10 women); includes 1 minority (African American). Average age 32. 25 applicants, 24% accepted.
Degree requirements: For doctorate, thesis/dissertation, comprehensive exam, registration.
Entrance requirements: For doctorate, GRE. *Application deadline:* For fall admission, 2/1 (priority date). *Application fee:* $50. Electronic applications accepted.
Expenses: Tuition, state resident: part-time $200 per credit. Tuition, nonresident: part-time $560 per credit.
Financial support: In 2001–02, 3 students received support, including 3 fellowships with partial tuition reimbursements available (averaging $5,000 per year), 3 research assistantships with partial tuition reimbursements available (averaging

University of Southern Maine (continued)
$6,000 per year); career-related internships or fieldwork, Federal Work-Study, tuition waivers (full), and unspecified assistantships also available. Financial award application deadline: 4/1.
Faculty research: Health policy, community planning and development, education policy, environmental policy.
Prof. Mark Lapping, Chair, 207-228-8180, *Fax:* 207-780-4317, *E-mail:* lapping@usm.maine.edu.
Application contact: Carlene R. Goldman, Director of Student Affairs, 207-780-4864, *Fax:* 207-780-4417, *E-mail:* cgold@usm.maine.edu. *Web site:* http://www.muskie.usm.maine.edu

■ UNIVERSITY OF SOUTHERN MAINE

Edmund S. Muskie School of Public Service, Program in Public Policy and Management, Portland, ME 04104-9300

AWARDS MPPM, JD/MPPM. Part-time and evening/weekend programs available. Postbaccalaureate distance learning degree programs offered (minimal on-campus study).

Faculty: 6 full-time (2 women), 9 part-time/adjunct (3 women).
Students: 7 full-time (4 women), 57 part-time (31 women); includes 2 minority (both African Americans). Average age 27. 30 applicants, 87% accepted, 20 enrolled. In 2001, 20 degrees awarded.
Degree requirements: For master's, thesis, capstone project, field experience.
Entrance requirements: For master's, GRE General Test or LSAT. *Application deadline:* For fall admission, 3/1 (priority date); for spring admission, 12/1. Applications are processed on a rolling basis. *Application fee:* $50. Electronic applications accepted.
Expenses: Tuition, state resident: part-time $200 per credit. Tuition, nonresident: part-time $560 per credit.
Financial support: In 2001–02, 25 students received support, including 2 fellowships with full tuition reimbursements available (averaging $5,000 per year), 4 research assistantships (averaging $5,000 per year); career-related internships or fieldwork, Federal Work-Study, scholarships/grants, and unspecified assistantships also available. Financial award application deadline: 4/1; financial award applicants required to submit CSS PROFILE.
Faculty research: Sustainable communities, juvenile justice, program management, nonprofit management. *Total annual research expenditures:* $30,000.
Prof. Dahlia Bradshaw Lynn, Chair, 207-780-4524, *Fax:* 207-780-4417, *E-mail:* dlynn@usm.maine.edu.
Application contact: Carlene R. Goldman, Director of Student Affairs, 207-780-4864, *Fax:* 207-780-4417, *E-mail:* cgold@usm.maine.edu. *Web site:* http://www.muskie.usm.maine.edu/

■ UNIVERSITY OF SOUTH FLORIDA

College of Graduate Studies, College of Arts and Sciences, Department of Public Administration, Tampa, FL 33620-9951

AWARDS MPA. Part-time and evening/weekend programs available.

Faculty: 30 full-time (6 women).
Students: 18 full-time (10 women), 50 part-time (24 women); includes 16 minority (7 African Americans, 2 Asian Americans or Pacific Islanders, 6 Hispanic Americans, 1 Native American). Average age 36. 131 applicants, 63% accepted, 55 enrolled. In 2001, 6 degrees awarded.
Entrance requirements: For master's, GRE General Test, minimum GPA of 3.0 in last 60 hours. *Application deadline:* For fall admission, 6/1; for spring admission, 10/15. *Application fee:* $20. Electronic applications accepted.
Expenses: Tuition, state resident: part-time $166 per credit hour. Tuition, nonresident: part-time $573 per credit hour. Required fees: $17 per term.
Financial support: Research assistantships with partial tuition reimbursements, Federal Work-Study and institutionally sponsored loans available. Financial award applicants required to submit FAFSA.
Faculty research: Public budgeting and financial management, policy analysis, urban management and planning, public personnel management, public organization management.
Joan E. Pynes, Director, 813-974-2510, *Fax:* 813-974-0804, *E-mail:* pynes@chuma1.cas.usf.edu.
Application contact: Ann Copeland, Program Assistant, 813-974-2510, *Fax:* 813-974-0832, *E-mail:* acopelan@luna.cas.usf.edu. *Web site:* http://www.cas.usf.edu/

■ THE UNIVERSITY OF TENNESSEE

Graduate School, College of Arts and Sciences, Department of Political Science, Program in Public Administration, Knoxville, TN 37996

AWARDS MPA, JD/MPA. Part-time programs available.

Students: 15 full-time (13 women), 8 part-time (3 women); includes 2 minority (both African Americans), 1 international. 25 applicants, 52% accepted. In 2001, 3 degrees awarded.
Degree requirements: For master's, thesis or alternative.
Entrance requirements: For master's, GRE General Test, TOEFL, minimum GPA of 2.7. *Application deadline:* For fall admission, 2/1 (priority date). Applications are processed on a rolling basis. *Application fee:* $35. Electronic applications accepted.
Expenses: Tuition, state resident: full-time $4,280; part-time $233 per hour. Tuition, nonresident: full-time $12,066; part-time $666 per hour. Tuition and fees vary according to program.
Financial support: Application deadline: 2/1.
Dr. David Folz, Graduate Representative, 865-974-0802, *E-mail:* dfolz@utk.edu.

■ THE UNIVERSITY OF TENNESSEE AT CHATTANOOGA

Graduate Division, College of Arts and Sciences, Department of Political Science, Program in Public Administration, Chattanooga, TN 37403-2598

AWARDS MPA. Part-time and evening/weekend programs available.

Faculty: 4 full-time (1 woman), 1 part-time/adjunct (0 women).
Students: 18 full-time (9 women), 16 part-time (6 women); includes 9 minority (8 African Americans, 1 Hispanic American). Average age 29. 30 applicants, 87% accepted, 17 enrolled. In 2001, 12 degrees awarded.
Degree requirements: For master's, thesis, comprehensive exam.
Entrance requirements: For master's, GRE General Test. *Application deadline:* For fall admission, 8/1 (priority date); for spring admission, 12/1 (priority date). Applications are processed on a rolling basis. *Application fee:* $25.
Expenses: Tuition, state resident: full-time $3,752; part-time $228 per hour. Tuition, nonresident: full-time $10,282; part-time $565 per hour.
Financial support: Fellowships, research assistantships available. Financial award application deadline: 4/1; financial award applicants required to submit FAFSA.
Dr. David Edwards, Coordinator, 423-425-4068, *Fax:* 423-425-2373, *E-mail:* david-edwards@utc.edu.
Application contact: Dr. Deborah E. Arfken, Dean of Graduate Studies, 865-425-1740, *Fax:* 865-425-5223, *E-mail:* deborah-arfken@utc.edu. *Web site:* http://www.utc.edu/

■ THE UNIVERSITY OF TEXAS AT ARLINGTON

Graduate School, School of Urban and Public Affairs, Program in Public Administration, Arlington, TX 76019

AWARDS MPA. Part-time and evening/weekend programs available.

Students: 9 full-time (6 women), 25 part-time (14 women); includes 13 minority (7 African Americans, 2 Asian Americans or Pacific Islanders, 4 Hispanic Americans), 1 international. 10 applicants, 100% accepted, 9 enrolled. In 2001, 10 degrees awarded.
Degree requirements: For master's, thesis or alternative.
Entrance requirements: For master's, GRE General Test. *Application deadline:*

For fall admission, 6/16. *Application fee:* $25 ($50 for international students).
Expenses: Tuition, area resident: Full-time $2,268. Tuition, nonresident: full-time $6,264. Required fees: $839. Tuition and fees vary according to course load.
Financial support: Fellowships, research assistantships, career-related internships or fieldwork available. Financial award application deadline: 6/1; financial award applicants required to submit FAFSA.
Dr. Guisette Salazar, Graduate Adviser, 817-272-3302, *Fax:* 817-272-5008, *E-mail:* salazar@uta.edu.

■ THE UNIVERSITY OF TEXAS AT ARLINGTON

Graduate School, School of Urban and Public Affairs, Program in Urban and Public Administration, Arlington, TX 76019

AWARDS PhD. Part-time and evening/weekend programs available.

Students: 6 full-time (3 women), 53 part-time (29 women); includes 16 minority (7 African Americans, 2 Asian Americans or Pacific Islanders, 6 Hispanic Americans, 1 Native American), 4 international. 13 applicants, 85% accepted, 6 enrolled. In 2001, 6 degrees awarded.
Degree requirements: For doctorate, thesis/dissertation, comprehensive exam, registration.
Entrance requirements: For doctorate, GRE General Test. *Application deadline:* For fall admission, 6/16. *Application fee:* $25 ($50 for international students).
Expenses: Tuition, area resident: Full-time $2,268. Tuition, nonresident: full-time $6,264. Required fees: $839. Tuition and fees vary according to course load.
Financial support: In 2001–02, 4 fellowships (averaging $1,000 per year), 6 research assistantships (averaging $4,500 per year) were awarded. Financial award application deadline: 6/1; financial award applicants required to submit FAFSA.
Dr. Rod Hissong, Graduate Adviser, 817-272-3350, *Fax:* 817-272-5008, *E-mail:* hissong@uta.edu.

■ THE UNIVERSITY OF TEXAS AT AUSTIN

Graduate School, Lyndon B. Johnson School of Public Affairs, Austin, TX 78712-1111

AWARDS Public affairs (MP Aff); public policy (PhD). Part-time programs available.

Faculty: 26 full-time (6 women), 15 part-time/adjunct (2 women).
Students: 236 full-time (129 women), 38 part-time (24 women); includes 52 minority (11 African Americans, 14 Asian Americans or Pacific Islanders, 26 Hispanic Americans, 1 Native American), 32 international. Average age 26. 365 applicants, 64% accepted. In 2001, 91 master's, 4 doctorates awarded.
Degree requirements: For master's, thesis, summer internship; for doctorate, thesis/dissertation.
Entrance requirements: For master's, GRE General Test; for doctorate, GRE General Test, master's degree in policy-related field. *Application deadline:* For fall admission, 1/15; for spring admission, 10/1 (priority date). Applications are processed on a rolling basis. *Application fee:* $50 ($75 for international students). Electronic applications accepted.
Expenses: Tuition, state resident: full-time $3,159. Tuition, nonresident: full-time $6,957. Tuition and fees vary according to program.
Financial support: In 2001–02, 221 students received support, including 187 fellowships with full and partial tuition reimbursements available (averaging $4,100 per year), 50 research assistantships with partial tuition reimbursements available (averaging $3,500 per year), 13 teaching assistantships with partial tuition reimbursements available (averaging $5,200 per year); career-related internships or fieldwork, institutionally sponsored loans, scholarships/grants, and tuition waivers (partial) also available. Financial award application deadline: 2/1. *Total annual research expenditures:* $11 million.
Dr. Edwin Dorn, Dean, 512-471-3200, *Fax:* 512-471-4697, *E-mail:* eddorn@mail.utexas.edu.
Application contact: Dr. Pat Wong, Graduate Adviser, 512-471-2956, *Fax:* 512-471-1835, *E-mail:* patwong@mail.utexas.edu. *Web site:* http://www.utexas.edu/lbj/

Find an in-depth description at www.petersons.com/gradchannel.

■ THE UNIVERSITY OF TEXAS AT DALLAS

School of Social Sciences, Program in Public Affairs, Richardson, TX 75083-0688

AWARDS MPA. Part-time and evening/weekend programs available.

Faculty: 22 full-time (5 women), 2 part-time/adjunct (1 woman).
Students: 14 full-time (9 women), 26 part-time (13 women); includes 10 minority (5 African Americans, 3 Asian Americans or Pacific Islanders, 2 Hispanic Americans), 6 international. Average age 37. 27 applicants, 67% accepted. In 2001, 15 degrees awarded.
Degree requirements: For master's, internship.
Entrance requirements: For master's, GRE General Test, TOEFL, minimum GPA of 3.0 in upper-level course work in field. *Application deadline:* For fall admission, 7/15; for spring admission, 11/15. Applications are processed on a rolling basis. *Application fee:* $25 ($75 for international students). Electronic applications accepted.
Expenses: Tuition, state resident: full-time $1,440; part-time $84 per credit. Tuition, nonresident: full-time $5,310; part-time $295 per credit. Required fees: $1,835; $87 per credit. $138 per term.
Financial support: In 2001–02, 3 fellowships, 1 teaching assistantship with tuition reimbursement (averaging $5,000 per year) were awarded. Research assistantships with tuition reimbursements, career-related internships or fieldwork, Federal Work-Study, institutionally sponsored loans, and scholarships/grants also available. Support available to part-time students. Financial award application deadline: 4/30; financial award applicants required to submit FAFSA.
Faculty research: Juvenile justice programs, program evaluation and outcome measurement, Hispanic American retention in educational institutions. *Web site:* http://www.utdallas.edu/dept/socsci/mpa.htm

Find an in-depth description at www.petersons.com/gradchannel.

■ THE UNIVERSITY OF TEXAS AT SAN ANTONIO

College of Public Policy, Department of Public Administration, San Antonio, TX 78249-0617

AWARDS MPA. Part-time and evening/weekend programs available.

Faculty: 6 full-time (1 woman).
Students: 7 full-time (3 women), 68 part-time (35 women); includes 37 minority (1 African American, 2 Asian Americans or Pacific Islanders, 34 Hispanic Americans). Average age 34. 30 applicants, 70% accepted, 18 enrolled. In 2001, 14 degrees awarded.
Degree requirements: For master's, thesis optional.
Entrance requirements: For master's, GMAT or GRE General Test, undergraduate course work in American government, economics, and research methods; minimum GPA of 3.0 on last 60 hours. *Application deadline:* For fall admission, 7/1. Applications are processed on a rolling basis. *Application fee:* $25.
Expenses: Tuition, state resident: full-time $2,268; part-time $126 per credit hour. Tuition, nonresident: full-time $6,066; part-time $337 per credit hour. Required fees: $781. Tuition and fees vary according to course load.
Financial support: Research assistantships, Federal Work-Study available. *Total annual research expenditures:* $1,083.
Dr. Heywood T. Sanders, Chair, 210-458-2700, *Fax:* 210-458-2535.

■ THE UNIVERSITY OF TEXAS AT TYLER

Graduate Studies, College of Arts and Sciences, Department of Social Sciences, Tyler, TX 75799-0001

AWARDS Criminal justice (MAIS, MS); economics (MAIS); political science (MA, MAIS, MAT); public administration (MPA); sociology (MAIS, MAT, MS). Part-time and evening/weekend programs available. Postbaccalaureate distance learning degree programs offered.

Faculty: 14 full-time (1 woman).
Students: 13 full-time (9 women), 54 part-time (34 women); includes 16 minority (14 African Americans, 1 Hispanic American, 1 Native American), 1 international. Average age 35. 8 applicants, 100% accepted, 8 enrolled. In 2001, 10 degrees awarded.
Degree requirements: For master's, thesis (for some programs), comprehensive exam.
Entrance requirements: For master's, GRE General Test, minimum GPA of 3.0. *Application deadline:* Applications are processed on a rolling basis. *Application fee:* $0.
Expenses: Tuition, state resident: part-time $44 per credit hour. Tuition, nonresident: part-time $262 per credit hour. Required fees: $58 per credit hour. $76 per semester.
Financial support: Teaching assistantships, career-related internships or fieldwork, Federal Work-Study, and scholarships/grants available. Support available to part-time students. Financial award application deadline: 7/1; financial award applicants required to submit FAFSA.
Faculty research: Urban segregation, minority business, violent crime, gender discrimination, Third World agriculture production.
Dr. Barbara L. Hart, Chair, 903-566-7426, *Fax:* 903-565-5537, *E-mail:* bhart@mail.uttyl.edu.
Application contact: Carol A. Hodge, Office of Graduate Studies, 903-566-5642, *Fax:* 903-566-7068, *E-mail:* chodge@mail.uttly.edu.

■ THE UNIVERSITY OF TEXAS–PAN AMERICAN

College of Social and Behavioral Sciences, Department of Political Science, Edinburg, TX 78539-2999

AWARDS Public administration (MPA). Part-time and evening/weekend programs available.

Faculty: 3 full-time (0 women).
Students: Average age 26. 10 applicants, 100% accepted, 10 enrolled. In 2001, 3 degrees awarded.
Degree requirements: For master's, thesis optional. *Median time to degree:* Master's–5 years part-time.
Entrance requirements: For master's, GRE General Test. *Application deadline:* For fall admission, 6/1 (priority date); for winter admission, 10/1 (priority date); for spring admission, 3/1 (priority date). Applications are processed on a rolling basis. *Application fee:* $0. Electronic applications accepted.
Expenses: Tuition, state resident: part-time $212 per semester hour. Tuition, nonresident: part-time $367 per semester hour.
Financial support: Career-related internships or fieldwork, Federal Work-Study, institutionally sponsored loans, scholarships/grants, and tuition waivers (partial) available. Support available to part-time students. Financial award application deadline: 6/1.
Faculty research: Immigration policy reform, agriculture food policy, social service delivery systems, community development, social welfare policy reform.
Dr. Jose R. Hinojosa, Director, 956-381-3341, *Fax:* 956-381-2386.

■ UNIVERSITY OF THE DISTRICT OF COLUMBIA

School of Business and Public Administration, Department of Management, Marketing, and Information Systems, Program in Public Administration, Washington, DC 20008-1175

AWARDS MPA. Part-time and evening/weekend programs available.

Students: 9 full-time (6 women), 25 part-time (15 women); includes 32 minority (30 African Americans, 1 Asian American or Pacific Islander, 1 Hispanic American), 1 international. Average age 28. 21 applicants, 43% accepted. In 2001, 4 degrees awarded.
Degree requirements: For master's, thesis optional.
Entrance requirements: For master's, GMAT or GRE General Test, writing proficiency exam. *Application deadline:* For fall admission, 6/15 (priority date); for spring admission, 11/1. Applications are processed on a rolling basis. *Application fee:* $20.
Expenses: Tuition, state resident: full-time $3,564; part-time $198 per credit hour. Tuition, nonresident: full-time $5,922; part-time $329 per credit hour. Required fees: $270; $135 per term.
Financial support: Career-related internships or fieldwork and Federal Work-Study available.
Faculty research: Government management, public personnel management, urban management, management information systems, public financial management.
Application contact: LaVerne Hill Flannigan, Director of Admission, 202-274-6069.

■ UNIVERSITY OF THE PACIFIC

McGeorge School of Law, Sacramento, CA 95817

AWARDS Government and public policy (LL M); international waters resources law (LL M, JSD); law (JD); transnational business practice (LL M). Part-time and evening/weekend programs available.

Faculty: 39 full-time (12 women), 31 part-time/adjunct (7 women).
Students: 609 full-time (316 women), 313 part-time (158 women); includes 168 minority (34 African Americans, 93 Asian Americans or Pacific Islanders, 27 Hispanic Americans, 14 Native Americans). Average age 24. 1,592 applicants, 73% accepted, 386 enrolled. In 2001, 261 first professional degrees, 19 master's awarded.
Degree requirements: For master's, thesis (for some programs); for doctorate, thesis/dissertation. *Median time to degree:* JD–3 years full-time; master's–1 year full-time.
Entrance requirements: For JD, LSAT; for master's, JD; for doctorate, LL M. *Application deadline:* For fall admission, 5/1 (priority date). Applications are processed on a rolling basis. *Application fee:* $40. Electronic applications accepted.
Expenses: Contact institution.
Financial support: In 2001–02, 528 students received support, including 9 fellowships, 20 research assistantships (averaging $6,485 per year); career-related internships or fieldwork, Federal Work-Study, institutionally sponsored loans, and scholarships/grants also available. Support available to part-time students. Financial award applicants required to submit FAFSA.
Faculty research: Taxation and business, family and juvenile law, governmental affairs, environmental law, intellectual property law.
Elizabeth Rindscopf Parker, Dean, 916-739-7151, *E-mail:* elizabeth@uop.edu.
Application contact: 916-739-7105, *Fax:* 916-739-7134, *E-mail:* admissionsmcgeorge@uop.edu. *Web site:* http://www.mcgeorge.edu/

■ UNIVERSITY OF THE VIRGIN ISLANDS

Graduate Programs, Program in Public Administration, Charlotte Amalie, VI 00802-9990

AWARDS MPA. Part-time and evening/weekend programs available.

Faculty: 1 full-time (0 women).
Students: Average age 38. 1 applicant, 100% accepted, 1 enrolled. In 2001, 3 degrees awarded.
Degree requirements: For master's, thesis or alternative.
Entrance requirements: For master's, GMAT, GRE, minimum GPA of 2.5. *Application deadline:* For fall admission,

4/30; for spring admission, 10/30. *Application fee:* $20.
Expenses: Tuition, area resident: Part-time $228 per credit. Tuition, nonresident: part-time $456 per credit.
Financial support: Career-related internships or fieldwork and scholarships/grants available. Financial award application deadline: 4/15.
Faculty research: Status of the Virgin Islands, comparative analysis of bureaucracies in the European community.
Dr. Dion Phillips, Chairperson, 340-693-1260, *Fax:* 340-693-1175, *E-mail:* dphilli@uvi.edu.
Application contact: Carolyn Cook, Director of Admissions and New Student Services, 340-693-1224, *Fax:* 340-693-1155, *E-mail:* ccook@uvi.edu. *Web site:* http://www.uvi.edu/

■ UNIVERSITY OF TOLEDO

Graduate School, College of Arts and Sciences, Department of Political Science and Public Administration, Program in Public Administration, Toledo, OH 43606-3398

AWARDS MPA.

Students: 16 full-time (11 women), 16 part-time (13 women); includes 9 minority (8 African Americans, 1 Hispanic American), 7 international. Average age 30. 19 applicants, 84% accepted, 6 enrolled. In 2001, 11 degrees awarded.
Degree requirements: For master's, internship.
Entrance requirements: For master's, GRE General Test, minimum GPA of 3.0. *Application deadline:* For fall admission, 8/1 (priority date). Applications are processed on a rolling basis. *Application fee:* $30. Electronic applications accepted.
Expenses: Tuition, state resident: full-time $7,278; part-time $303 per hour. Tuition, nonresident: full-time $15,731; part-time $699 per hour. Required fees: $43 per hour.
Financial support: In 2001–02, 5 teaching assistantships were awarded. Financial award application deadline: 4/1.
Faculty research: Economic development, health administration, personnel, budgeting, urban administration.
Dr. Sunday E. Ubokudom, Director, 419-530-4152, *Fax:* 419-530-4119. *Web site:* http://www.utoledo.edu/poli-sci/mpahome.html

■ UNIVERSITY OF UTAH

Graduate School, College of Social and Behavioral Science, Department of Political Science, Program in Public Administration, Salt Lake City, UT 84112-1107

AWARDS MPA, Certificate, JD/MPA, MPA/Ed D, MPA/MA, MPA/PhD.

Students: 17 full-time (8 women), 107 part-time (51 women); includes 8 minority (2 African Americans, 3 Asian Americans or Pacific Islanders, 3 Hispanic Americans), 2 international. Average age 35. 85 applicants, 72% accepted. In 2001, 28 degrees awarded.
Degree requirements: For master's, internship, thesis or research paper.
Entrance requirements: For master's, GMAT, GRE General Test, LSAT, TOEFL, minimum GPA of 3.2. *Application deadline:* For fall admission, 7/1. *Application fee:* $40 ($60 for international students).
Expenses: Tuition, state resident: part-time $320 per semester hour. Tuition, nonresident: part-time $1,135 per semester hour. Required fees: $143 per semester hour. Tuition and fees vary according to course load, degree level and program.
Financial support: Career-related internships or fieldwork available.
Application contact: Sherlyn Marks, Advisor, 801-585-7656, *E-mail:* sdmarks@poli-sci.utah.edu.

■ UNIVERSITY OF VERMONT

Graduate College, College of Arts and Sciences, Department of Public Administration, Burlington, VT 05405

AWARDS MPA.

Entrance requirements: For master's, GRE General Test, TOEFL.
Expenses: Tuition, state resident: part-time $335 per credit. Tuition, nonresident: part-time $838 per credit.

■ UNIVERSITY OF WASHINGTON

Graduate School, Daniel J. Evans School of Public Affairs, Seattle, WA 98195

AWARDS MPA, JD/MPA, MPA/MAIS, MPA/MPH, MPA/MS, MPA/MUP. Part-time and evening/weekend programs available.

Faculty: 28 full-time (8 women), 31 part-time/adjunct (13 women).
Students: 211 full-time (137 women), 65 part-time (39 women); includes 42 minority (7 African Americans, 25 Asian Americans or Pacific Islanders, 5 Hispanic Americans, 5 Native Americans), 16 international. Average age 30. 293 applicants, 76% accepted, 113 enrolled. In 2001, 82 degrees awarded.
Degree requirements: For master's, thesis, internship or cooperative experience. *Median time to degree:* Master's–2 years full-time, 3 years part-time.
Entrance requirements: For master's, GRE General Test, TOEFL, minimum GPA of 3.0. *Application deadline:* For fall admission, 2/1. *Application fee:* $45. Electronic applications accepted.
Expenses: Tuition, state resident: full-time $5,539. Tuition, nonresident: full-time $14,376. Required fees: $390. Tuition and fees vary according to course load and program.
Financial support: In 2001–02, 60 students received support, including 20 fellowships with full tuition reimbursements available (averaging $5,000 per year), 32 research assistantships with full tuition reimbursements available (averaging $11,340 per year), 5 teaching assistantships with full tuition reimbursements available (averaging $11,340 per year); career-related internships or fieldwork, Federal Work-Study, institutionally sponsored loans, and tuition waivers (full and partial) also available. Support available to part-time students. Financial award application deadline: 2/28; financial award applicants required to submit FAFSA.
Faculty research: Environmental policy, education and social policy, comparative international policy, urban and regional affairs, nonprofit management. *Total annual research expenditures:* $6.2 million.
Dr. Paul T Hill, Acting Dean, 206-616-1648, *Fax:* 206-543-1096, *E-mail:* bicycle@u.washington.edu.
Application contact: Linda Rylander Bale, Director of Admissions, 206-543-4900, *Fax:* 206-543-1096, *E-mail:* evansuw@u.washington.edu. *Web site:* http://evans.washington.edu/

Find an in-depth description at www.petersons.com/gradchannel.

■ UNIVERSITY OF WEST FLORIDA

College of Professional Studies, Division of Administrative Studies, Program in Public Administration, Pensacola, FL 32514-5750

AWARDS MPA. Part-time and evening/weekend programs available.

Students: 9 full-time (6 women), 41 part-time (25 women); includes 12 minority (7 African Americans, 3 Asian Americans or Pacific Islanders, 2 Hispanic Americans). Average age 36. 24 applicants, 58% accepted, 11 enrolled. In 2001, 18 degrees awarded.
Degree requirements: For master's, thesis or alternative.
Entrance requirements: For master's, GRE General Test, minimum GPA of 3.0. *Application deadline:* For fall admission, 6/30; for spring admission, 11/1. Applications are processed on a rolling basis. *Application fee:* $20.
Expenses: Tuition, state resident: full-time $3,995; part-time $166 per credit hour. Tuition, nonresident: full-time $13,766; part-time $574 per credit hour. Tuition and fees vary according to campus/location.
Financial support: Fellowships, research assistantships, career-related internships or fieldwork, Federal Work-Study, institutionally sponsored loans, and tuition waivers (full and partial) available. Support available to part-time students. Financial award application deadline: 4/15.
Faculty research: Law enforcement, growth management.

■ UNIVERSITY OF WISCONSIN–MADISON

Graduate School, College of Letters and Science, Public Policy and Administration Program, Robert M. La Follette School of Public Affairs, Madison, WI 53706-1380

AWARDS MPA, MPIA. Part-time programs available.

Entrance requirements: For master's, GRE General Test. Electronic applications accepted.
Expenses: Tuition, state resident: full-time $7,361; part-time $399 per credit. Tuition, nonresident: full-time $20,499; part-time $1,282 per credit. Required fees: $34 per credit. Full-time tuition and fees vary according to course load, program, reciprocity agreements and student level.
Faculty research: Social policy, personnel, economic development, tax and budget, environmental regulations. *Web site:* http://www.lafollette.wisc.edu/

Find an in-depth description at www.petersons.com/gradchannel.

■ UNIVERSITY OF WISCONSIN–MILWAUKEE

Graduate School, College of Letters and Sciences, Program in Public Administration, Milwaukee, WI 53201-0413

AWARDS MPA, MPA/MUP. Part-time programs available.

Faculty: 9 full-time (1 woman).
Students: 16 full-time (7 women), 10 part-time (4 women); includes 1 minority (African American), 1 international. 26 applicants, 65% accepted. In 2001, 8 degrees awarded.
Degree requirements: For master's, thesis or alternative.
Entrance requirements: For master's, GRE General Test, minimum GPA of 3.0. *Application deadline:* For fall admission, 1/1 (priority date); for spring admission, 9/1. Applications are processed on a rolling basis. *Application fee:* $45 ($75 for international students).
Expenses: Tuition, state resident: full-time $6,180; part-time $535 per credit. Tuition, nonresident: full-time $19,482; part-time $1,366 per credit. Tuition and fees vary according to course load, program and reciprocity agreements.
Financial support: Fellowships, research assistantships, teaching assistantships, career-related internships or fieldwork and unspecified assistantships available. Support available to part-time students. Financial award application deadline: 4/15.
Douglas Ihrke, Director, 414-229-4209, *Fax:* 414-229-5021, *E-mail:* dihrke@uwm.edu. *Web site:* http://www.uwm.edu/dept/MPA/

■ UNIVERSITY OF WISCONSIN–OSHKOSH

Graduate School, College of Letters and Science, Department of Public Affairs, Oshkosh, WI 54901

AWARDS General agency (MPA); health care (MPA). Part-time and evening/weekend programs available.

Faculty: 8 full-time (1 woman).
Students: 47; includes 5 minority (2 African Americans, 3 Asian Americans or Pacific Islanders), 1 international. Average age 42. In 2001, 26 degrees awarded.
Degree requirements: For master's, thesis or alternative.
Entrance requirements: For master's, public service-related experience, resumé, sample of written work. *Application deadline:* Applications are processed on a rolling basis. *Application fee:* $45. Electronic applications accepted.
Expenses: Tuition, state resident: full-time $2,236; part-time $250 per credit. Tuition, nonresident: full-time $7,148; part-time $795 per credit. Tuition and fees vary according to program.
Financial support: Institutionally sponsored loans, scholarships/grants, and unspecified assistantships available. Financial award application deadline: 3/15; financial award applicants required to submit FAFSA.
Faculty research: Drug policy, local government state revenues and expenditures, health care regulation.
Dr. David Jones, Chair, 920-424-3230.
Application contact: Dr. Carl Ameringer, Program Coordinator, 920-424-3230, *E-mail:* ameringc@uwosh.edu. *Web site:* http://www.uwosh.edu/mpa/

■ UNIVERSITY OF WISCONSIN–WHITEWATER

School of Graduate Studies, College of Letters and Sciences, Program in Public Administration, Whitewater, WI 53190-1790

AWARDS MPA. Part-time and evening/weekend programs available.

Students: Average age 29. 1 applicant, 100% accepted, 1 enrolled.
Application deadline: For fall admission, 7/15; for spring admission, 12/1. Electronic applications accepted.
Expenses: Tuition, state resident: full-time $4,511; part-time $251 per credit. Tuition, nonresident: full-time $14,335; part-time $797 per credit. One-time fee: $45. Tuition and fees vary according to course load and program.
Financial support: Out of state fee waiver available. Financial award application deadline: 3/15; financial award applicants required to submit FAFSA.
Dr. John Kozlowicz, Coordinator, 262-472-1120, *E-mail:* kozlowij@uww.edu.
Application contact: Sally A. Lange, School of Graduate Studies, 262-472-1006, *Fax:* 262-472-5027, *E-mail:* gradschl@uww.edu.

■ UNIVERSITY OF WYOMING

Graduate School, College of Arts and Sciences, Department of Political Science, Program in Public Administration, Laramie, WY 82071

AWARDS MPA. Part-time programs available.

Faculty: 4 full-time (0 women).
Students: 10 full-time (5 women), 30 part-time (15 women); includes 4 minority (3 Hispanic Americans, 1 Native American), 1 international. Average age 30. 17 applicants, 76% accepted. In 2001, 11 degrees awarded.
Degree requirements: For master's, thesis or alternative.
Entrance requirements: For master's, GRE General Test, TOEFL, minimum GPA of 3.0. *Application deadline:* For fall admission, 6/1 (priority date). Applications are processed on a rolling basis. *Application fee:* $40.
Expenses: Tuition, state resident: full-time $2,895; part-time $161 per credit hour. Tuition, nonresident: full-time $8,367; part-time $465 per credit hour. Required fees: $491; $10 per credit hour. $2 per credit hour. Tuition and fees vary according to course load and program.
Financial support: In 2001–02, 4 teaching assistantships with full tuition reimbursements (averaging $8,667 per year) were awarded; career-related internships or fieldwork also available. Financial award application deadline: 3/1.
Faculty research: Public policy, public ethics, administrative theory, natural resource policy.
Application contact: Dr. Robert S. Schuhmann, Director, 307-766-6484, *Fax:* 307-766-6771, *E-mail:* schuhman@uwyo.edu. *Web site:* http://uwyo.edu/pols/index.html

■ VALDOSTA STATE UNIVERSITY

Graduate School, College of Arts and Sciences, Department of Political Science, Valdosta, GA 31698

AWARDS City management (MPA); public human resources (MPA); public sector (MPA). Part-time and evening/weekend programs available. Postbaccalaureate distance learning degree programs offered (no on-campus study).

Faculty: 13 full-time (2 women).
Students: 53 full-time (43 women), 53 part-time (42 women); includes 16 minority (12 African Americans, 4 Hispanic Americans). Average age 29. 48 applicants, 96% accepted. In 2001, 49 degrees awarded.
Degree requirements: For master's, comprehensive written and/or oral exams, internship.

Entrance requirements: For master's, GMAT, GRE General Test, or MAT, minimum GPA of 2.5. *Application deadline:* For fall admission, 7/1; for spring admission, 11/15. Applications are processed on a rolling basis. *Application fee:* $20.
Expenses: Tuition, state resident: full-time $1,746; part-time $97 per hour. Tuition, nonresident: full-time $6,966; part-time $387 per hour. Required fees: $594; $297 per semester.
Financial support: In 2001–02, 3 research assistantships with full tuition reimbursements (averaging $2,452 per year) were awarded; institutionally sponsored loans, scholarships/grants, and unspecified assistantships also available. Support available to part-time students. Financial award applicants required to submit FAFSA.
Faculty research: Powers of state attorneys general; health, transportation, and environmental policy; public administration theory.
Dr. James Peterson, Director, 229-333-5771.
Application contact: Dr. Nolan Argyle, Program Director, 229-293-6059, *E-mail:* nargyle@valdosta.edu.

■ VILLANOVA UNIVERSITY

Graduate School of Liberal Arts and Sciences, Department of Political Science, Program in Public Administration, Villanova, PA 19085-1699

AWARDS MPA. Part-time and evening/weekend programs available.

Students: 6 full-time (4 women), 7 part-time (3 women); includes 1 minority (Hispanic American), 2 international. Average age 29. 9 applicants, 89% accepted. In 2001, 9 degrees awarded.
Degree requirements: For master's, comprehensive exam.
Entrance requirements: For master's, GRE General Test, minimum GPA of 3.0. *Application deadline:* For fall admission, 8/1 (priority date); for spring admission, 12/1. *Application fee:* $40.
Expenses: Tuition: Part-time $340 per credit. One-time fee: $115 full-time. Tuition and fees vary according to program.
Financial support: Career-related internships or fieldwork available. Financial award application deadline: 4/1; financial award applicants required to submit FAFSA.
Dr. Craig Wheeland, Director.
Find an in-depth description at www.petersons.com/gradchannel.

■ VIRGINIA COMMONWEALTH UNIVERSITY

School of Graduate Studies, Center for Public Policy, Richmond, VA 23284-9005

AWARDS Public policy and administration (PhD).

Students: 20 full-time, 80 part-time; includes 33 minority (29 African Americans, 4 Asian Americans or Pacific Islanders). 38 applicants, 76% accepted. In 2001, 6 degrees awarded.
Degree requirements: For doctorate, thesis/dissertation.
Entrance requirements: For doctorate, GMAT, GRE General Test, LSAT, or MAT. *Application deadline:* For fall admission, 3/15. *Application fee:* $30.
Expenses: Tuition, state resident: full-time $4,276; part-time $238 per credit. Tuition, nonresident: full-time $12,672; part-time $704 per credit. Required fees: $1,167; $43 per credit.
Financial support: Fellowships, career-related internships or fieldwork and Federal Work-Study available. Support available to part-time students. Financial award applicants required to submit FAFSA.
Dr. Robert D. Holsworth, Director, 804-828-8033, *Fax:* 804-828-6838, *E-mail:* rholswor@vcu.edu.
Application contact: Dr. Melvin I. Urofsky, Graduate Program Director, 804-828-8033, *Fax:* 804-828-6838, *E-mail:* murofsky@vcu.edu. *Web site:* http://www.vcu.edu/cppweb/

■ VIRGINIA COMMONWEALTH UNIVERSITY

School of Graduate Studies, College of Humanities and Sciences, Department of Political Science and Public Administration, Richmond, VA 23284-9005

AWARDS Political science and public administration (MPA); public management (CPM). Part-time programs available.

Students: 27 full-time, 59 part-time; includes 30 minority (25 African Americans, 3 Asian Americans or Pacific Islanders, 2 Hispanic Americans). 54 applicants, 80% accepted. In 2001, 25 degrees awarded.
Entrance requirements: For master's, GRE General Test. *Application deadline:* Applications are processed on a rolling basis. *Application fee:* $30.
Expenses: Tuition, state resident: full-time $4,276; part-time $238 per credit. Tuition, nonresident: full-time $12,672; part-time $704 per credit. Required fees: $1,167; $43 per credit.
Financial support: Fellowships, career-related internships or fieldwork, Federal Work-Study, institutionally sponsored loans, and tuition waivers (full and partial) available. Support available to part-time students. Financial award application deadline: 3/1.
Faculty research: Public human resources management, financial management, executive management, policy analysis, local government management.
Dr. Russell A. Cargo, Acting Chair, 804-828-1575, *Fax:* 804-828-7463.
Application contact: Dr. Janet S. Hutchinson, Graduate Program Director, 804-828-1046, *Fax:* 804-828-7463, *E-mail:* jhutch@vcu.edu. *Web site:* http://www.vcu.edu/hasweb/pos/

■ VIRGINIA POLYTECHNIC INSTITUTE AND STATE UNIVERSITY

Graduate School, College of Architecture and Urban Studies, Center for Public Administration and Policy, Blacksburg, VA 24061-0205

AWARDS MPA, PhD, CAGS. Part-time programs available. Terminal master's awarded for partial completion of doctoral program.

Degree requirements: For master's, thesis optional; for doctorate, thesis/dissertation.
Entrance requirements: For master's and doctorate, GRE General Test, TOEFL; for CAGS, TOEFL.
Expenses: Tuition, state resident: part-time $241 per hour. Tuition, nonresident: part-time $406 per hour. Tuition and fees vary according to program.
Faculty research: Public administration theory, strategic management, ethics, the Constitution, computer-assisted creativity. *Web site:* http://www.arch.vt.edu/CAUS/PA/PAintro.html
Find an in-depth description at www.petersons.com/gradchannel.

■ WASHINGTON STATE UNIVERSITY

Graduate School, College of Liberal Arts, Department of Political Science, Program in Public Affairs, Pullman, WA 99164

AWARDS MPA. Part-time and evening/weekend programs available.

Faculty: 9 full-time (4 women), 1 part-time/adjunct (0 women).
Students: 10 applicants, 70% accepted. In 2001, 14 degrees awarded.
Degree requirements: For master's, thesis, oral exam.
Entrance requirements: For master's, GRE General Test, minimum GPA of 3.0. *Application deadline:* For fall admission, 10/15; for spring admission, 4/15. Applications are processed on a rolling basis. *Application fee:* $35.
Expenses: Tuition, state resident: full-time $6,088; part-time $304 per semester. Tuition, nonresident: full-time $14,918;

Washington State University (continued)
part-time $746 per semester. Tuition and fees vary according to program.
Financial support: Tuition waivers (partial) available. Financial award application deadline: 3/15.
Faculty research: Public administration and gender, American institutions, congress and bureaucracy, environmental policy, comparative environmental policy.
Dr. Carolyn N. Long, Director, 360-546-9737, *Fax:* 360-546-9036, *E-mail:* long@vancouver.wsu.edu.
Application contact: Ginny Taylor, Graduate Secretary, 360-546-9640, *Fax:* 360-546-9036, *E-mail:* taylorg@vancouver.wsu.edu.

■ WASHINGTON UNIVERSITY IN ST. LOUIS

Graduate School of Arts and Sciences, Department of Political Science, Program in Political Economy and Public Policy, St. Louis, MO 63130-4899

AWARDS MA.

Students: 5 full-time (2 women); includes 1 minority (Hispanic American), 2 international. 12 applicants, 42% accepted. In 2001, 1 degree awarded.
Degree requirements: For master's, thesis or alternative.
Entrance requirements: For master's, GRE General Test. *Application deadline:* For fall admission, 1/15 (priority date). Applications are processed on a rolling basis. *Application fee:* $35. Electronic applications accepted.
Expenses: Tuition: Full-time $26,900.
Financial support: Application deadline: 1/15.
Dr. Norman Schofield, Chairperson, 314-935-4774.

■ WAYNE STATE UNIVERSITY

Graduate School, College of Liberal Arts, Department of Political Science, Program in Public Administration, Detroit, MI 48202

AWARDS Criminal justice (MPA); public administration (MPA). Evening/weekend programs available.

Students: 24. In 2001, 3 degrees awarded.
Entrance requirements: For master's, GRE General Test. *Application deadline:* For fall admission, 7/1. Applications are processed on a rolling basis. *Application fee:* $20 ($30 for international students). Electronic applications accepted.
Expenses: Tuition, state resident: full-time $3,764. Tuition and fees vary according to degree level and program.
Faculty research: Urban politics, urban education, state administration.
John Strate, Director, 313-577-2668, *E-mail:* jstrate@wayne.edu.

■ WEBSTER UNIVERSITY

School of Business and Technology, Department of Business, St. Louis, MO 63119-3194

AWARDS Business (MA, MBA); computer resources and information management (MA, MBA); computer science/distributed systems (MS); environmental management (MS); finance (MA, MBA); health care management (MA); health services management (MA, MBA); human resources development (MA, MBA); human resources management (MA); international business (MA, MBA); management (MA, MBA); marketing (MA, MBA); procurement and acquisitions management (MA, MBA); public administration (MA); real estate management (MA, MBA); security management (MA, MBA); space systems management (MA, MBA, MS); telecommunications management (MA, MBA).

Students: 1,415 full-time (661 women), 3,483 part-time (1,566 women); includes 1,604 minority (1,183 African Americans, 166 Asian Americans or Pacific Islanders, 220 Hispanic Americans, 35 Native Americans), 606 international. Average age 33. In 2001, 1439 degrees awarded.
Application deadline: Applications are processed on a rolling basis. *Application fee:* $25 ($50 for international students).
Expenses: Tuition: Full-time $7,164; part-time $398 per credit hour.
Financial support: Federal Work-Study available. Support available to part-time students. Financial award application deadline: 4/1; financial award applicants required to submit FAFSA.
Steve Hinson, Chair, 314-968-7017, *Fax:* 314-968-7077.
Application contact: Denise Harrell, Associate Director of Graduate and Evening Student Admissions, 314-968-6983, *Fax:* 314-968-7116, *E-mail:* gadmit@webster.edu.

■ WEST CHESTER UNIVERSITY OF PENNSYLVANIA

Graduate Studies, School of Business and Public Affairs, Program in Administration, West Chester, PA 19383

AWARDS Health services (MSA); human research management (MSA); individualized (MSA); leadership for women (MSA); long-term care (MSA); public administration (MSA); regional planning (MSA); sport and athletic training (MSA); training and development (MSA). Part-time and evening/weekend programs available.

Students: 11 full-time (8 women), 83 part-time (45 women); includes 9 minority (5 African Americans, 3 Asian Americans or Pacific Islanders, 1 Hispanic American), 2 international. Average age 31. 44 applicants, 57% accepted. In 2001, 38 degrees awarded.
Degree requirements: For master's, comprehensive exam.
Entrance requirements: For master's, GMAT, GRE General Test, or MAT, interview, minimum GPA of 3.0. *Application deadline:* For fall admission, 4/15 (priority date); for spring admission, 10/15. Applications are processed on a rolling basis. *Application fee:* $25.
Expenses: Tuition, state resident: full-time $4,600; part-time $256 per credit. Tuition, nonresident: full-time $7,554; part-time $420 per credit. Required fees: $44 per credit.
Financial support: In 2001–02, 2 research assistantships with full tuition reimbursements (averaging $5,000 per year) were awarded; career-related internships or fieldwork and unspecified assistantships also available. Support available to part-time students. Financial award application deadline: 2/15; financial award applicants required to submit FAFSA.
Dr. Duane Milne, Director, 610-436-2448.

■ WESTERN CAROLINA UNIVERSITY

Graduate School, College of Arts and Sciences, Program in Public Affairs, Cullowhee, NC 28723

AWARDS MPA. Part-time and evening/weekend programs available.

Faculty: 11 full-time (3 women).
Students: 14 full-time (6 women), 35 part-time (14 women); includes 7 minority (6 African Americans, 1 Asian American or Pacific Islander). 24 applicants, 67% accepted, 13 enrolled. In 2001, 17 degrees awarded.
Degree requirements: For master's, comprehensive exam.
Entrance requirements: For master's, GRE General Test. *Application deadline:* For fall admission, 5/1 (priority date); for spring admission, 10/1 (priority date). Applications are processed on a rolling basis. *Application fee:* $35.
Expenses: Tuition, state resident: full-time $1,072. Tuition, nonresident: full-time $8,704. Required fees: $1,171.
Financial support: In 2001–02, 8 students received support, including 7 research assistantships with full and partial tuition reimbursements available (averaging $3,715 per year), 1 teaching assistantship with full and partial tuition reimbursement available (averaging $6,003 per year); fellowships, Federal Work-Study, institutionally sponsored loans, and scholarships/grants also available. Financial award application deadline: 3/15; financial award applicants required to submit FAFSA.
Dr. Gordon Mercer, Program Director, 828-227-7475, *E-mail:* mercer@email.wcu.edu.
Application contact: Josie Bewsey, Assistant to the Dean, 828-227-7398, *Fax:* 828-227-7480, *E-mail:* jbewsey@email.wcu.edu. *Web site:* http://www.wcu.edu/as/politicalscience/

■ WESTERN INTERNATIONAL UNIVERSITY

Graduate Programs in Business, Program in Public Administration, Phoenix, AZ 85021-2718

AWARDS MPA. Evening/weekend programs available.

Faculty: 18 part-time/adjunct (3 women).
Students: 72 full-time (38 women). Average age 35. In 2001, 7 degrees awarded.
Degree requirements: For master's, thesis.
Entrance requirements: For master's, GMAT (strongly recommended), minimum GPA of 2.75. *Application deadline:* Applications are processed on a rolling basis. *Application fee:* $85 ($100 for international students).
Expenses: Tuition, state resident: full-time $5,130. Tuition, nonresident: full-time $5,580.
Financial support: Career-related internships or fieldwork, institutionally sponsored loans, and scholarships/grants available. Support available to part-time students. Financial award applicants required to submit FAFSA.
Dr. Rob Olding, Chair, 602-943-2311.
Application contact: Karen Janitell, Director of Enrollment, 602-943-2311 Ext. 1063, *Fax:* 602-371-8637, *E-mail:* karen_janitell@apollogrp.edu.

■ WESTERN KENTUCKY UNIVERSITY

Graduate Studies, Potter College of Arts, Humanities and Social Sciences, Department of Government, Bowling Green, KY 42101-3576

AWARDS MA Ed. Part-time and evening/weekend programs available.

Faculty: 4 full-time (2 women), 2 part-time/adjunct (both women).
Students: In 2001, 9 degrees awarded.
Degree requirements: For master's, final exam.
Entrance requirements: For master's, GRE General Test, minimum GPA of 2.75. *Application deadline:* For fall admission, 7/1 (priority date); for spring admission, 11/1. Applications are processed on a rolling basis. *Application fee:* $30.
Expenses: Tuition, area resident: Part-time $167 per credit. Tuition, state resident: full-time $2,490. Tuition, nonresident: full-time $6,660; part-time $399 per credit. Required fees: $554. Part-time tuition and fees vary according to campus/location and reciprocity agreements.
Financial support: Research assistantships with partial tuition reimbursements, career-related internships or fieldwork, Federal Work-Study, institutionally sponsored loans, tuition waivers (partial), and service awards available. Support available to part-time students. Financial award application deadline: 4/1; financial award applicants required to submit FAFSA.
Faculty research: Role of non-profits, comparative policy analysis, social welfare policy, rural administration, ethics and bureaucracy.
Dr. Saundra Ardrey, Head, 270-745-4558, *Fax:* 270-745-2945, *E-mail:* saundra.ardrey@wku.edu. *Web site:* http://www.wku.edu/Dept/Academic/AHSS/Government/govt.htm

■ WESTERN MICHIGAN UNIVERSITY

Graduate College, College of Arts and Sciences, Department of Political Science, Program in Development Administration, Kalamazoo, MI 49008-5202

AWARDS MDA.

Faculty: 19 full-time (5 women).
Students: 21 full-time (13 women), 2 part-time (both women), 20 international. 18 applicants, 67% accepted, 6 enrolled. In 2001, 10 degrees awarded.
Application deadline: For fall admission, 2/15 (priority date). Applications are processed on a rolling basis. *Application fee:* $25.
Expenses: Tuition, state resident: part-time $186 per credit hour. Tuition, nonresident: part-time $442 per credit hour. Required fees: $602. One-time fee: $132 part-time. Tuition and fees vary according to course load.
Financial support: Fellowships, research assistantships, teaching assistantships, Federal Work-Study available. Financial award application deadline: 2/15; financial award applicants required to submit FAFSA.
Application contact: Admissions and Orientation, 616-387-2000, *Fax:* 616-387-2355.

■ WESTERN MICHIGAN UNIVERSITY

Graduate College, College of Arts and Sciences, School of Public Affairs and Administration, Kalamazoo, MI 49008-5202

AWARDS MPA, DPA.

Faculty: 6 full-time (1 woman).
Students: 100 full-time (57 women), 189 part-time (100 women); includes 59 minority (50 African Americans, 5 Asian Americans or Pacific Islanders, 2 Hispanic Americans, 2 Native Americans), 2 international. 85 applicants, 85% accepted, 30 enrolled. In 2001, 81 master's, 2 doctorates awarded.
Degree requirements: For doctorate, thesis/dissertation, oral exams.
Entrance requirements: For doctorate, GRE General Test. *Application deadline:* For fall admission, 2/15 (priority date). *Application fee:* $25.
Expenses: Tuition, state resident: part-time $186 per credit hour. Tuition, nonresident: part-time $442 per credit hour. Required fees: $602. One-time fee: $132 part-time. Tuition and fees vary according to course load.
Financial support: Fellowships, research assistantships, teaching assistantships, Federal Work-Study available. Financial award application deadline: 2/15; financial award applicants required to submit FAFSA.
Dr. Robert A. Peters, Director, 616-387-8930.
Application contact: Admissions and Orientation, 616-387-2000, *Fax:* 616-387-2355.

■ WEST VIRGINIA UNIVERSITY

Eberly College of Arts and Sciences, Department of Political Science, Morgantown, WV 26506

AWARDS American public policy and politics (MA); international and comparative public policy and U.S. politics (MA); political science (PhD); public policy analysis (PhD).

Faculty: 17 full-time (2 women), 4 part-time/adjunct (2 women).
Students: 30 full-time (8 women), 10 part-time (4 women); includes 1 minority (African American), 7 international. Average age 31. 45 applicants, 47% accepted. In 2001, 8 master's, 1 doctorate awarded. Terminal master's awarded for partial completion of doctoral program.
Degree requirements: For master's, thesis optional; for doctorate, thesis/dissertation, comprehensive exam.
Entrance requirements: For master's and doctorate, GRE General Test, TOEFL, minimum GPA of 2.75. *Application deadline:* For fall admission, 4/1 (priority date). Applications are processed on a rolling basis. *Application fee:* $45.
Expenses: Tuition, state resident: full-time $2,791. Tuition, nonresident: full-time $8,659. Required fees: $1,002. Tuition and fees vary according to program.
Financial support: In 2001–02, 14 students received support, including 4 research assistantships, 14 teaching assistantships; career-related internships or fieldwork, Federal Work-Study, institutionally sponsored loans, tuition waivers (full and partial), and unspecified assistantships also available. Financial award application deadline: 2/1; financial award applicants required to submit FAFSA.
Faculty research: Public policy, research methods, foreign policy analysis, judicial politics, environmental and energy policy.
Dr. Allan S. Hammock, Chair, 304-293-3198 Ext. 5273, *Fax:* 304-293-8644, *E-mail:* allan.hammock@mail.wvu.edu.
Application contact: Dr. Jeff Worsham, Director, Graduate Studies, 304-293-3811 Ext. 5277, *Fax:* 304-293-8644, *E-mail:* jeff.worsham@mail.wvu.edu. *Web site:* http://www.polsci.wvu.edu/

■ WEST VIRGINIA UNIVERSITY

Eberly College of Arts and Sciences, School of Applied Social Science, Program in Public Administration, Morgantown, WV 26506

AWARDS MPA, JD/MPA, MSW/MPA. Part-time programs available.

Faculty: 6 full-time (1 woman).
Students: 44 full-time (23 women), 30 part-time (17 women). Average age 30. 43 applicants, 72% accepted. In 2001, 40 degrees awarded.
Degree requirements: For master's, internship.
Entrance requirements: For master's, GRE General Test, TOEFL, minimum GPA of 2.75. *Application deadline:* For fall admission, 4/1 (priority date); for spring admission, 10/15. Applications are processed on a rolling basis. *Application fee:* $45.
Expenses: Tuition, state resident: full-time $2,791. Tuition, nonresident: full-time $8,659. Required fees: $1,002. Tuition and fees vary according to program.
Financial support: In 2001–02, 14 research assistantships, 6 teaching assistantships were awarded. Career-related internships or fieldwork, Federal Work-Study, institutionally sponsored loans, tuition waivers (full and partial), and graduate administrative assistantships also available. Financial award application deadline: 2/1; financial award applicants required to submit FAFSA.
Faculty research: Public management and organization, conflict resolution, work satisfaction, health administration. *Web site:* http://www.as.wvu.edu/pubadm/

■ WICHITA STATE UNIVERSITY

Graduate School, Fairmount College of Liberal Arts and Sciences, Hugo Wall School of Urban and Public Affairs, Wichita, KS 67260

AWARDS Public administration (MPA). Part-time programs available.

Faculty: 6 full-time (1 woman).
Students: 8 full-time (7 women), 17 part-time (14 women); includes 5 minority (4 African Americans, 1 Hispanic American). Average age 36. 35 applicants, 54% accepted, 19 enrolled. In 2001, 16 degrees awarded.
Degree requirements: For master's, thesis optional.
Entrance requirements: For master's, GRE, TOEFL. *Application deadline:* For spring admission, 1/1. Applications are processed on a rolling basis. *Application fee:* $25 ($40 for international students). Electronic applications accepted.
Expenses: Tuition, state resident: full-time $1,888; part-time $105 per credit. Tuition, nonresident: full-time $6,129; part-time $341 per credit. Required fees: $345; $19 per credit. $17 per semester. Tuition and fees vary according to course load and program.
Financial support: In 2001–02, 7 research assistantships (averaging $3,454 per year), 7 teaching assistantships with full tuition reimbursements (averaging $3,722 per year) were awarded. Fellowships, career-related internships or fieldwork, Federal Work-Study, institutionally sponsored loans, and unspecified assistantships also available. Support available to part-time students. Financial award application deadline: 4/1; financial award applicants required to submit FAFSA.
Dr. H. Edward Flentje, Director, 316-978-6502, *Fax:* 316-978-3626, *E-mail:* ed.flentje@wichita.edu. *Web site:* http://www.twsuvm.uc.twsu.edu/~hwswww/

■ WIDENER UNIVERSITY

College of Arts and Sciences, Program in Public Administration, Chester, PA 19013-5792

AWARDS MPA, Psy D/MPA. Part-time and evening/weekend programs available.

Degree requirements: For master's, thesis or comprehensive exam.
Entrance requirements: For master's, minimum undergraduate GPA of 3.0. Electronic applications accepted.
Expenses: Contact institution.
Faculty research: Intergovernmental relations, nonprofit organizations, public policy, political economy, bureaucratic politics. *Web site:* http://www.science.widener.edu/ssci/gpmpa1.html

■ WILLAMETTE UNIVERSITY

George H. Atkinson Graduate School of Management, Salem, OR 97301-3931

AWARDS Business (MBA); government (MBA); not-for-profit management (MBA). Part-time programs available.

Faculty: 14 full-time (3 women), 14 part-time/adjunct (2 women).
Students: 152 full-time (56 women), 16 part-time (6 women); includes 12 minority (1 African American, 6 Asian Americans or Pacific Islanders, 4 Hispanic Americans, 1 Native American), 53 international. Average age 26. 174 applicants, 83% accepted, 83 enrolled. In 2001, 71 degrees awarded. *Median time to degree:* Master's–2 years full-time, 4 years part-time.
Entrance requirements: For master's, GMAT or GRE, TOEFL. *Application deadline:* For fall admission, 3/31 (priority date). Applications are processed on a rolling basis. *Application fee:* $50. Electronic applications accepted.
Expenses: Contact institution.
Financial support: In 2001–02, 110 students received support, including 11 research assistantships (averaging $1,200 per year); career-related internships or fieldwork, Federal Work-Study, and scholarships/grants also available. Support available to part-time students. Financial award application deadline: 7/1; financial award applicants required to submit FAFSA.
Faculty research: General management, finance, marketing, public management, international management.
Bryan Johnston, Dean, 503-370-6440, *Fax:* 503-370-3011, *E-mail:* johnstob@willamette.edu.
Application contact: Judy O'Neill, Assistant Dean and Director of Admissions, 503-370-6167, *Fax:* 503-370-3011, *E-mail:* joneill@willamette.edu. *Web site:* http://www.willamette.edu/agsm/

Find an in-depth description at www.petersons.com/gradchannel.

■ WILMINGTON COLLEGE

Division of Business, New Castle, DE 19720-6491

AWARDS Business administration (MBA); health care administration (MBA, MS); human resource management (MS); management (MS); public administration (MS); transport and logistics (MS). Part-time and evening/weekend programs available.

Faculty: 7 full-time (2 women), 75 part-time/adjunct (25 women).
Students: 179 full-time (105 women), 415 part-time (237 women); includes 111 minority (92 African Americans, 7 Asian Americans or Pacific Islanders, 9 Hispanic Americans, 3 Native Americans). In 2001, 234 degrees awarded. *Median time to degree:* Master's–2 years full-time, 3 years part-time.
Application deadline: Applications are processed on a rolling basis. *Application fee:* $25.
Expenses: Tuition: Full-time $4,788; part-time $266 per credit. Required fees: $50; $25 per semester. Tuition and fees vary according to course level, course load, degree level, campus/location and program.
Financial support: Applicants required to submit FAFSA.
Dr. Raj Parikh, Chair, 302-328-9401 Ext. 284, *Fax:* 302-328-7021, *E-mail:* rpari@wilmcoll.edu.
Application contact: Michael Lee, Director of Admissions and Financial Aid, 302-328-9407 Ext. 102, *Fax:* 302-328-5164, *E-mail:* inquire@wilmcoll.edu. *Web site:* http://www.wilmcoll.edu

■ WRIGHT STATE UNIVERSITY

School of Graduate Studies, College of Liberal Arts, Department of Urban Affairs and Geography, Dayton, OH 45435

AWARDS Urban administration (MPA).

Students: 21 full-time (14 women), 10 part-time (5 women); includes 7 minority (all African Americans), 1 international. 21 applicants, 90% accepted. In 2001, 16 degrees awarded.

Degree requirements: For master's, thesis optional.
Entrance requirements: For master's, TOEFL, interview, minimum GPA of 2.7. *Application fee:* $25.
Expenses: Tuition, state resident: full-time $7,161; part-time $225 per quarter hour. Tuition, nonresident: full-time $12,324; part-time $385 per quarter hour. Tuition and fees vary according to course load, degree level and program.
Financial support: Fellowships, unspecified assistantships available. Support available to part-time students. Financial award applicants required to submit FAFSA.
Faculty research: Strategic planning, economic development, housing and public management. *Total annual research expenditures:* $20,000.
Dr. Jack L. Dustin, Chair, 937-775-4451, *Fax:* 937-775-2422, *E-mail:* jack.dustin@wright.edu.

RURAL PLANNING AND STUDIES

■ CALIFORNIA STATE UNIVERSITY, CHICO

Graduate School, College of Behavioral and Social Sciences, Department of Geography and Planning, Program in Rural and Town Planning, Chico, CA 95929-0722

AWARDS MRTP.

Degree requirements: For master's, thesis or alternative, oral exam.
Application deadline: For fall admission, 4/1; for spring admission, 10/1. Applications are processed on a rolling basis. *Application fee:* $55. Electronic applications accepted.
Expenses: Tuition, state resident: full-time $2,148. Tuition, nonresident: full-time $6,576.
Application contact: Dr. Jacque Chase, Graduate Coordinator, 530-898-5587.

■ CORNELL UNIVERSITY

Graduate School, Graduate Fields of Agriculture and Life Sciences, Field of Community and Rural Development, Ithaca, NY 14853-0001

AWARDS Community development process (MPS); economic development (MPS); local government organizations and operation (MPS); program development and planning (MPS).

Faculty: 17 full-time.
Students: 13 full-time (10 women), 8 international. 28 applicants, 79% accepted. In 2001, 2 degrees awarded.
Entrance requirements: For master's, GRE General Test (recommended), TOEFL, 3 letters of recommendation. *Application deadline:* For fall admission, 5/1. *Application fee:* $65. Electronic applications accepted.
Expenses: Tuition: Full-time $25,970. Required fees: $50.
Financial support: In 2001–02, 8 students received support, including 6 fellowships with full tuition reimbursements available, 2 teaching assistantships with full tuition reimbursements available; research assistantships with full tuition reimbursements available, institutionally sponsored loans, scholarships/grants, tuition waivers (full and partial), and unspecified assistantships also available. Financial award applicants required to submit FAFSA.
Application contact: Graduate Field Assistant, 607-255-1823, *E-mail:* gradcrd@cornell.edu. *Web site:* http://www.gradschool.cornell.edu/grad/fields_1/crd.html

■ CORNELL UNIVERSITY

Graduate School, Graduate Fields of Agriculture and Life Sciences, Field of International Agriculture and Rural Development, Ithaca, NY 14853-0001

AWARDS International agriculture and development (MPS).

Faculty: 46 full-time.
Students: 13 full-time (4 women); includes 3 minority (1 Asian American or Pacific Islander, 2 Hispanic Americans), 7 international. 23 applicants, 87% accepted. In 2001, 6 degrees awarded.
Degree requirements: For master's, project paper.
Entrance requirements: For master's, GRE General Test (recommended), TOEFL, 2 years of development experience, 2 letters of recommendation. *Application deadline:* For fall admission, 3/1. *Application fee:* $65. Electronic applications accepted.
Expenses: Tuition: Full-time $25,970. Required fees: $50.
Financial support: In 2001–02, 3 research assistantships with full tuition reimbursements were awarded; fellowships with full tuition reimbursements, teaching assistantships with full tuition reimbursements, institutionally sponsored loans, scholarships/grants, tuition waivers (full and partial), and unspecified assistantships also available. Financial award applicants required to submit FAFSA.
Application contact: Graduate Field Assistant, 607-255-3037, *E-mail:* mpsiard@cornell.edu. *Web site:* http://www.gradschool.cornell.edu/grad/fields_1/iard.html

■ IOWA STATE UNIVERSITY OF SCIENCE AND TECHNOLOGY

Graduate College, College of Liberal Arts and Sciences, Department of History, Ames, IA 50011

AWARDS Agricultural history and rural studies (PhD); history (MA); history of technology and science (MA, PhD).

Faculty: 19 full-time.
Students: 13 full-time (6 women), 28 part-time (9 women); includes 3 minority (1 Asian American or Pacific Islander, 2 Hispanic Americans), 1 international. 12 applicants, 50% accepted, 3 enrolled. In 2001, 7 master's, 4 doctorates awarded.
Degree requirements: For master's, thesis or alternative; for doctorate, thesis/dissertation. *Median time to degree:* Master's–2.9 years full-time; doctorate–9.3 years full-time.
Entrance requirements: For master's and doctorate, GRE General Test, TOEFL or IELTS. *Application deadline:* For fall admission, 3/1 (priority date). Applications are processed on a rolling basis. *Application fee:* $20 ($50 for international students). Electronic applications accepted.
Expenses: Tuition, state resident: full-time $1,851. Tuition, nonresident: full-time $5,449. Tuition and fees vary according to program.
Financial support: In 2001–02, 1 research assistantship with partial tuition reimbursement (averaging $10,292 per year), 21 teaching assistantships with partial tuition reimbursements (averaging $11,017 per year) were awarded. Scholarships/grants, health care benefits, and unspecified assistantships also available.
Dr. George T. McJimsey, Chair, 515-294-7286, *Fax:* 515-294-6390. *Web site:* http://www.public.iastate.edu/~history/

■ STATE UNIVERSITY OF WEST GEORGIA

Graduate School, College of Arts and Sciences, Department of Political Science and Planning, Program of Rural and Small Town Planning, Carrollton, GA 30118

AWARDS MS. Part-time programs available.

Faculty: 8 full-time (2 women).
Students: 1 full-time (0 women), 2 part-time; includes 2 minority (both African Americans). Average age 43.
Degree requirements: For master's, exit paper.
Application deadline: For fall admission, 8/1 (priority date); for spring admission, 12/1. *Application fee:* $20. Electronic applications accepted.
Expenses: Tuition, state resident: full-time $232; part-time $97 per credit hour. Tuition, nonresident: full-time $928; part-time $387 per credit hour. Required fees: $536; $14 per credit. $100 per semester.
Financial support: Applicants required to submit FAFSA.
Application contact: Dr. Jack O. Jenkins, Dean, Graduate School, 770-836-6419, *Fax:* 770-836-2301, *E-mail:* jjenkins@westga.edu. *Web site:* http://westga.edu/~polsci/

■ UNIVERSITY OF ALASKA FAIRBANKS

Graduate School, College of Rural Alaska, Department of Alaska Native and Rural Development, Fairbanks, AK 99775-7480

AWARDS MS, PhD.

Faculty: 64 full-time (27 women), 35 part-time/adjunct (24 women).
Students: 7 full-time (5 women), 17 part-time (10 women); includes 19 minority (all Native Americans). Average age 46. 11 applicants, 91% accepted, 9 enrolled.
Application fee: $35.
Expenses: Tuition, state resident: full-time $4,272; part-time $178 per credit. Tuition, nonresident: full-time $8,328; part-time $347 per credit. Required fees: $960; $60 per term. Part-time tuition and fees vary according to course load.
Richard Caulfield, Head, 907-279-2700.

■ THE UNIVERSITY OF MONTANA–MISSOULA

Graduate School, College of Arts and Sciences, Department of Geography, Missoula, MT 59812-0002

AWARDS Geography (MA), including cartography and GIS, rural town and regional planning.

Faculty: 8 full-time (1 woman).
Students: 13 full-time (4 women), 17 part-time (10 women), 1 international. 18 applicants, 94% accepted, 11 enrolled. In 2001, 2 degrees awarded.
Entrance requirements: For master's, GRE General Test. *Application deadline:* For fall admission, 4/30 (priority date). *Application fee:* $45.
Expenses: Tuition, state resident: full-time $2,482; part-time $1,700 per year. Tuition, nonresident: full-time $7,372; part-time $5,000 per year. Required fees: $1,900. Tuition and fees vary according to degree level.
Financial support: In 2001–02, 7 teaching assistantships with full tuition reimbursements (averaging $8,665 per year) were awarded; Federal Work-Study and unspecified assistantships also available. Financial award application deadline: 3/1; financial award applicants required to submit FAFSA. *Total annual research expenditures:* $44,000.
Dr. Jeffrey Gritzner, Chair, 406-243-5626, *E-mail:* jag@selway.umt.edu. *Web site:* http://www.umt.edu/geograph/

■ UNIVERSITY OF WYOMING

Graduate School, College of Arts and Sciences, Department of Geography and Recreation, Program in Rural Planning and Natural Resources, Laramie, WY 82071

AWARDS Community and regional planning and natural resources (MP).

Faculty: 1 full-time (0 women), 2 part-time/adjunct (0 women).
Students: 3 full-time (1 woman), 7 part-time (6 women); includes 1 minority (Hispanic American), 1 international. 5 applicants, 60% accepted. In 2001, 1 degree awarded.
Degree requirements: For master's, thesis or alternative.
Entrance requirements: For master's, GRE General Test, minimum GPA of 3.0. *Application deadline:* For fall admission, 2/15. Applications are processed on a rolling basis. *Application fee:* $40.
Expenses: Tuition, state resident: full-time $2,895; part-time $161 per credit hour. Tuition, nonresident: full-time $8,367; part-time $465 per credit hour. Required fees: $491; $10 per credit hour. $2 per credit hour. Tuition and fees vary according to course load and program.
Financial support: Teaching assistantships, career-related internships or fieldwork and Federal Work-Study available. Financial award application deadline: 3/1. *Total annual research expenditures:* $10,400.
Dr. John Allen, Head, Department of Geography and Recreation, 307-766-3311.

SUSTAINABLE DEVELOPMENT

■ BRANDEIS UNIVERSITY

The Heller School for Social Policy and Management, Program in Sustainable International Development, Waltham, MA 02454-9110

AWARDS MA.

Faculty: 5 full-time (1 woman), 7 part-time/adjunct (3 women).
Students: 39 full-time (14 women), 28 international. Average age 30. 461 applicants, 53% accepted, 60 enrolled. In 2001, 14 degrees awarded.
Degree requirements: For master's, 2nd-year fieldwork or internship.
Entrance requirements: For master's, TOEFL. *Application deadline:* For fall admission, 6/1. Applications are processed on a rolling basis. *Application fee:* $50 ($0 for international students). Electronic applications accepted.
Expenses: Tuition: Full-time $27,392. Required fees: $35.
Financial support: In 2001–02, 2 fellowships with full and partial tuition reimbursements (averaging $10,000 per year) were awarded; scholarships/grants and tuition waivers (full and partial) also available.
Faculty research: Water resource management, human rights, biosphere management, rural development, public policy and governance.
Dr. Laurence R. Simon, Director, 781-736-2770, *Fax:* 781-736-2774, *E-mail:* sid@brandeis.edu.
Application contact: Fiona Figueiredo, Admissions Officer, 781-736-2763, *Fax:* 781-736-2774, *E-mail:* fif@brandeis.edu. *Web site:* http://heller.brandeis.edu/sid

Find an in-depth description at www.petersons.com/gradchannel.

■ CARNEGIE MELLON UNIVERSITY

H. John Heinz III School of Public Policy and Management, Program in Sustainable Economic Development, Pittsburgh, PA 15213-3891

AWARDS MIS.

Degree requirements: For master's, internship.
Entrance requirements: For master's, GMAT or GRE, previous course work in calculus and statistics. Electronic applications accepted.

■ CLARK UNIVERSITY

Graduate School, Department of International Development, Community, and Environment, Worcester, MA 01610-1477

AWARDS Community development and planning (MA); environmental science and policy (MA); geographic information science for development and environment (MA); international development and social change (MA).

Students: 71 full-time (35 women), 6 part-time; includes 2 minority (1 African American, 1 Asian American or Pacific Islander), 18 international. Average age 29. 147 applicants, 73% accepted, 49 enrolled. In 2001, 28 degrees awarded.
Degree requirements: For master's, thesis.
Entrance requirements: For master's, TOEFL. *Application deadline:* For fall admission, 2/1. *Application fee:* $40.
Expenses: Tuition: Full-time $24,400; part-time $763 per credit. Required fees: $10.
Financial support: In 2001–02, 2 research assistantships with full and partial tuition reimbursements (averaging $9,250 per year), 2 teaching assistantships with full and partial tuition reimbursements (averaging $9,250 per year) were awarded. Fellowships with full and partial tuition reimbursements, career-related internships or fieldwork, scholarships/grants, and tuition waivers (full and partial) also available.
Faculty research: Community participation, gender analysis, land-use planning, project analysis, geographic information systems. *Total annual research expenditures:* $577,496.
Dr. William F. Fisher, Director, *Fax:* 508-793-8820, *E-mail:* wfisher@clarku.edu.

Application contact: Liz Owens, IDCE Graduate Admissions, 508-793-7201, *Fax:* 508-793-8820, *E-mail:* idce@clarku.edu. *Web site:* http://www2.clarku.edu/newsite/graduatefolder/index.html

■ NEW COLLEGE OF CALIFORNIA

School of Humanities, Division of Humanities, San Francisco, CA 94102-5206

AWARDS Culture, ecology, and sustainable community (MA); humanities and leadership (MA); media studies (MA); poetics (MA, MFA), including poetics (MA), poetics and writing (MFA); psychology (MA); women's spirituality (MA); writing and consciousness (MA). Part-time and evening/weekend programs available.

Degree requirements: For master's, thesis.

■ PRESCOTT COLLEGE

Graduate Programs, Program in Environmental Studies, Prescott, AZ 86301-2990

AWARDS Agroecology (MA); ecopsychology (MA); environmental education (MA); environmental studies (MA); sustainability (MA). MA (environmental education) offered jointly with Teton Science School. Part-time programs available. Postbaccalaureate distance learning degree programs offered (minimal on-campus study).

Degree requirements: For master's, thesis, fieldwork or internship, practicum.

■ SCHOOL FOR INTERNATIONAL TRAINING

Graduate Programs, Master's Programs in Intercultural Service, Leadership, and Management, Brattleboro, VT 05302-0676

AWARDS Conflict transformation intercultural service, leadership and management (MA); intercultural relations (MA); international education (MA); non-governmental organization leadership and management (Postgraduate Diploma); organizational management (MS); sustainable development (MA).

Faculty: 11 full-time (8 women), 10 part-time/adjunct (3 women).
Students: 94 full-time (71 women). Average age 30. In 2001, 81 degrees awarded.
Degree requirements: For master's, one foreign language, thesis.
Entrance requirements: For master's, TOEFL. *Application deadline:* Applications are processed on a rolling basis. *Application fee:* $45.
Financial support: Career-related internships or fieldwork, Federal Work-Study, institutionally sponsored loans, and scholarships/grants available. Financial award applicants required to submit FAFSA.
Faculty research: Intercultural communication, conflict resolution, advising and training, world issues, international business.
Jeff Unsicker, Dean, 802-257-7751 Ext. 3332.
Application contact: Marshall Brewer, Admissions Counselor, 802-258-3265, *Fax:* 802-258-3500. *Web site:* http://www.sit.edu/

■ SLIPPERY ROCK UNIVERSITY OF PENNSYLVANIA

Graduate Studies, College of Health, Environment, and Science, Department of Parks, Recreation, and Environmental Education, Slippery Rock, PA 16057

AWARDS Environmental education (M Ed); resource management (MS); sustainable systems (MS). Part-time and evening/weekend programs available.

Faculty: 7 full-time (2 women), 1 part-time/adjunct (0 women).
Students: 29 full-time (20 women), 19 part-time (9 women); includes 2 minority (1 Asian American or Pacific Islander, 1 Native American), 2 international. Average age 28. 39 applicants, 90% accepted. In 2001, 14 degrees awarded.
Degree requirements: For master's, thesis (for some programs), comprehensive exam (for some programs).
Entrance requirements: For master's, GRE General Test, MAT, minimum GPA of 2.75. *Application deadline:* For fall admission, 7/1; for spring admission, 11/1. Applications are processed on a rolling basis. *Application fee:* $25. Electronic applications accepted.
Expenses: Tuition, state resident: full-time $4,600; part-time $256 per credit. Tuition, nonresident: full-time $7,754; part-time $420 per credit. Required fees: $67 per credit. Tuition and fees vary according to course load and program.
Financial support: In 2001–02, 20 students received support, including research assistantships with full and partial tuition reimbursements available (averaging $4,000 per year); career-related internships or fieldwork, Federal Work-Study, and scholarships/grants also available. Support available to part-time students. Financial award application deadline: 5/1; financial award applicants required to submit FAFSA.
Dr. Daniel Dziubek, Graduate Coordinator, 724-738-2958, *Fax:* 724-738-2938, *E-mail:* daniel.dziubek@sru.edu.
Application contact: Dr. Duncan M. Sargent, Director of Graduate Studies, 724-738-2051 Ext. 2116, *Fax:* 724-738-2146, *E-mail:* graduate.studies@sru.edu. *Web site:* http://www.sru.edu/depts/ehhs/pree/preehp.htm

■ UNIVERSITY OF GEORGIA

Graduate School, College of Arts and Sciences, Program in Ecology, Athens, GA 30602

AWARDS Conservation ecology and sustainable development (MS); ecology (MS, PhD).

Faculty: 33 full-time (11 women).
Students: 91 full-time (48 women), 16 part-time (7 women); includes 1 minority (Hispanic American), 13 international. 152 applicants, 16% accepted. In 2001, 14 master's, 10 doctorates awarded.
Degree requirements: For master's, thesis; for doctorate, one foreign language, thesis/dissertation.
Entrance requirements: For master's and doctorate, GRE General Test. *Application deadline:* For fall admission, 7/1 (priority date); for spring admission, 11/15. *Application fee:* $30. Electronic applications accepted.
Expenses: Tuition, state resident: full-time $2,376; part-time $132 per credit hour. Tuition, nonresident: full-time $9,504; part-time $528 per credit hour. Required fees: $236 per semester.
Financial support: Fellowships, research assistantships, teaching assistantships, unspecified assistantships available.
Dr. C. Ronald Carroll, Head, 706-542-6018, *Fax:* 706-542-4819, *E-mail:* rcarroll@uga.edu.
Application contact: Dr. William K. Fitt, Graduate Coordinator, 706-542-3328, *Fax:* 706-542-3344, *E-mail:* ecoginfo@uga.edu. *Web site:* http://www.ecology.uga.edu/

■ UNIVERSITY OF MARYLAND, COLLEGE PARK

Graduate Studies and Research, College of Life Sciences, Department of Biology, Program in Sustainable Development and Conservation Biology, College Park, MD 20742

AWARDS MS. Part-time and evening/weekend programs available.

Students: 27 full-time (22 women), 8 part-time (4 women); includes 1 minority (Hispanic American), 4 international. 72 applicants, 32% accepted, 12 enrolled. In 2001, 17 degrees awarded.
Degree requirements: For master's, internship, scholarly paper.
Entrance requirements: For master's, GRE General Test, minimum GPA of 3.0. *Application deadline:* For fall admission, 4/1; for spring admission, 12/1. Applications are processed on a rolling basis. *Application fee:* $50 ($70 for international students). Electronic applications accepted.
Expenses: Tuition, state resident: part-time $289 per credit hour. Tuition, nonresident: part-time $448 per credit hour. One-time fee: $436 part-time. Full-time tuition and fees vary according to course load, campus/location and program.

University of Maryland, College Park (continued)

Financial support: Fellowships, research assistantships, teaching assistantships available. Financial award application deadline: 2/1; financial award applicants required to submit FAFSA.
Faculty research: Biodiversity, global change, conservation.
Dr. David W. Inouye, Director, 301-405-7109, *Fax:* 301-314-9358.
Application contact: Trudy Lindsey, Director, Graduate Admissions and Records, 301-405-6991, *Fax:* 301-314-9305, *E-mail:* grschool@deans.umd.edu.

■ UNIVERSITY OF WASHINGTON

School of Law, Seattle, WA 98105-6617

AWARDS Asian law (LL M, PhD); intellectual property and technology (LL M); law (JD, LL M!T); law of sustainable international development (LL M); taxation (LL M).

Faculty: 38 full-time (18 women), 22 part-time/adjunct (8 women).
Students: 595 full-time (292 women), 59 part-time (24 women); includes 95 minority (5 African Americans, 56 Asian Americans or Pacific Islanders, 21 Hispanic Americans, 13 Native Americans), 93 international. Average age 26. 1,954 applicants, 24% accepted. In 2001, 163 first professional degrees, 83 master's awarded.
Degree requirements: For master's and doctorate, thesis/dissertation.
Entrance requirements: For JD, LSAT; for master's, TOEFL, language proficiency (LL M in Asian law). *Application deadline:* For fall admission, 1/15. *Application fee:* $50.
Expenses: Contact institution.
Financial support: In 2001–02, 326 students received support, including 8 fellowships (averaging $1,562 per year), 10 research assistantships (averaging $4,640 per year); career-related internships or fieldwork, Federal Work-Study, institutionally sponsored loans, scholarships/grants, and tuition waivers (partial) also available. Financial award application deadline: 2/28; financial award applicants required to submit FAFSA.
Faculty research: History, culture and society. *Total annual research expenditures:* $102,000.
W. H Knight, Dean, 206-685-3846, *Fax:* 206-543-5305, *E-mail:* whknight@u.washington.edu.
Application contact: Sandra Madrid, Assistant Dean, 206-543-0199, *Fax:* 206-543-5671, *E-mail:* smadrid@u.washington.edu. *Web site:* http://www.law.washington.edu/

■ UNIVERSITY OF WISCONSIN–MADISON

Graduate School, Institute for Environmental Studies, Conservation Biology and Sustainable Development Program, Madison, WI 53706-1380

AWARDS MS. Part-time programs available.

Students: 26 full-time (19 women), 8 part-time (5 women); includes 5 minority (1 African American, 4 Hispanic Americans), 1 international. 57 applicants, 42% accepted. In 2001, 6 degrees awarded.
Degree requirements: For master's, thesis optional.
Entrance requirements: For master's, GRE General Test. *Application deadline:* For fall admission, 2/1; for spring admission, 10/15. *Application fee:* $45. Electronic applications accepted.
Expenses: Tuition, state resident: full-time $7,361; part-time $399 per credit. Tuition, nonresident: full-time $20,499; part-time $1,282 per credit. Required fees: $34 per credit. Full-time tuition and fees vary according to course load, program, reciprocity agreements and student level.
Financial support: In 2001–02, 21 students received support, including 4 fellowships with full tuition reimbursements available (averaging $12,260 per year), 4 research assistantships with full tuition reimbursements available (averaging $15,075 per year), 8 teaching assistantships with full tuition reimbursements available (averaging $9,530 per year); career-related internships or fieldwork, Federal Work-Study, scholarships/grants, unspecified assistantships, and project assistantships also available. Financial award application deadline: 1/2.
Faculty research: Ornithology, forestry, sociology, rural sociology, plant ecology, wildlife conservation, resource economics, education, land use.
Stanley A. Temple, Chair, 608-263-6827, *Fax:* 608-262-2273, *E-mail:* iesgrad@mail.ies.wisc.edu.
Application contact: James E. Miller, Program Assistant, 608-262-9206, *Fax:* 608-262-2273, *E-mail:* jemiller@facstaff.wisc.edu. *Web site:* http://www.ies.wisc.edu/

■ WESTERN ILLINOIS UNIVERSITY

School of Graduate Studies, College of Arts and Sciences, Department of Geography, Macomb, IL 61455-1390

AWARDS Community development (Certificate); geography (MA). Part-time programs available.

Faculty: 8 full-time (0 women).
Students: 7 full-time (2 women), 5 part-time (2 women), 2 international. Average age 34. 9 applicants, 78% accepted. In 2001, 5 master's, 5 other advanced degrees awarded.
Degree requirements: For master's, thesis or alternative.
Application deadline: Applications are processed on a rolling basis. *Application fee:* $0 ($25 for international students). Electronic applications accepted.
Expenses: Tuition, state resident: part-time $108 per credit hour. Tuition, nonresident: part-time $216 per credit hour. Required fees: $33 per credit hour.
Financial support: In 2001–02, 6 students received support, including 6 research assistantships with full tuition reimbursements available (averaging $5,720 per year). Financial award applicants required to submit FAFSA.
Faculty research: 911 rural mapping, geographic information systems, social geography.
Dr. Lawrence T. Lewis, Chairperson, 309-298-1648.
Application contact: Dr. Barbara Baily, Director of Graduate Studies, 309-298-1806, *Fax:* 309-298-2345, *E-mail:* grad-office@wiu.edu. *Web site:* http://www.wiu.edu/

URBAN STUDIES

■ BOSTON UNIVERSITY

Metropolitan College, Department of Urban Affairs and Planning, Program in Urban Affairs, Boston, MA 02215

AWARDS MUA. Part-time and evening/weekend programs available.

Faculty: 1 full-time (0 women), 9 part-time/adjunct (1 woman).
Students: 1 (woman) full-time, 10 part-time (6 women); includes 5 minority (4 African Americans, 1 Asian American or Pacific Islander). Average age 31. 20 applicants, 80% accepted. In 2001, 1 degree awarded.
Degree requirements: For master's, thesis.
Application deadline: For fall admission, 7/15; for spring admission, 1/15. Applications are processed on a rolling basis. *Application fee:* $60.
Expenses: Tuition: Full-time $25,872; part-time $340 per credit. Required fees: $40 per semester. Part-time tuition and fees vary according to class time, course level and program.
Financial support: In 2001–02, 2 students received support, including 1 research assistantship; career-related internships or fieldwork, Federal Work-Study, institutionally sponsored loans, and tuition waivers (partial) also available. Support available to part-time students. Financial award application deadline: 6/15.
Faculty research: Housing, community development and land use planning, environmental management and planning, international comparative development planning.

Application contact: Dr. Daniel P. LeClair, Chair, 617-353-3025, *Fax:* 617-353-6328, *E-mail:* dleclair@bu.edu. *Web site:* http://bu.edu.met/ua

■ BROOKLYN COLLEGE OF THE CITY UNIVERSITY OF NEW YORK

Division of Graduate Studies, Department of Political Science, Program in Political Science, Urban Policy and Administration, Brooklyn, NY 11210-2889

AWARDS MA. Part-time and evening/weekend programs available.

Students: 10 applicants, 50% accepted. In 2001, 26 degrees awarded.
Degree requirements: For master's, thesis or alternative, policy paper.
Entrance requirements: For master's, TOEFL, 27 credits in political science. *Application deadline:* For fall admission, 3/1; for spring admission, 11/1. *Application fee:* $40.
Expenses: Tuition, state resident: full-time $4,350; part-time $185 per credit. Tuition, nonresident: full-time $7,600; part-time $320 per credit.
Financial support: Fellowships, career-related internships or fieldwork, Federal Work-Study, institutionally sponsored loans, scholarships/grants, and tuition waivers (full and partial) available. Support available to part-time students. Financial award application deadline: 5/1; financial award applicants required to submit FAFSA.
Dr. Joseph Wilson, Graduate Deputy, 212-966-4014, *Fax:* 212-966-4038.
Application contact: Pam Miller, Administrator, 212-966-4014, *Fax:* 212-966-4038.

■ CLEVELAND STATE UNIVERSITY

College of Graduate Studies, Maxine Goodman Levin College of Urban Affairs, Department of Urban Studies, Cleveland, OH 44115

AWARDS MA, MS, PhD. Part-time and evening/weekend programs available.

Students: 20 full-time (12 women), 61 part-time (35 women); includes 22 minority (18 African Americans, 4 Hispanic Americans), 9 international. Average age 38. 35 applicants, 80% accepted. In 2001, 14 degrees awarded.
Degree requirements: For master's, thesis or alternative, exit project, internship; for doctorate, thesis/dissertation, comprehensive exam, comprehensive exam, registration.
Entrance requirements: For master's, GRE General Test, minimum GPA of 3.0; for doctorate, GRE General Test, minimum GPA of 3.5. *Application deadline:* For fall admission, 7/15 (priority date). Applications are processed on a rolling basis. *Application fee:* $25.
Expenses: Tuition, state resident: full-time $6,838; part-time $263 per credit hour. Tuition, nonresident: full-time $13,526; part-time $520 per credit hour.
Financial support: Research assistantships, teaching assistantships, career-related internships or fieldwork, Federal Work-Study, and tuition waivers (partial) available. Support available to part-time students. Financial award application deadline: 3/1.
Faculty research: Environmental issues, economic development, urban and public policy, public management.
Application contact: Graduate Programs Coordinator, 216-523-7522, *Fax:* 216-687-5398, *E-mail:* gradprog@wolf.csuohio.edu.

■ EAST TENNESSEE STATE UNIVERSITY

School of Graduate Studies, College of Business, Department of Economics, Finance, and Urban Studies, Johnson City, TN 37614

AWARDS City management (MCM); community development (MPM); general administration (MPM); municipal service management (MPM); urban and regional economic development (MPM); urban and regional planning (MPM).

Faculty: 1 full-time (0 women).
Students: 15 full-time (6 women), 14 part-time (9 women); includes 4 minority (all African Americans), 2 international. Average age 35. In 2001, 10 degrees awarded.
Degree requirements: For master's, internship, oral defense of thesis, research report.
Entrance requirements: For master's, GRE General Test, TOEFL, minimum GPA of 3.0. *Application deadline:* For fall admission, 7/1 (priority date); for spring admission, 12/1. Applications are processed on a rolling basis. *Application fee:* $25 ($35 for international students).
Expenses: Tuition, state resident: part-time $181 per hour. Tuition, nonresident: part-time $270 per hour. Required fees: $220 per term.
Financial support: Research assistantships with full tuition reimbursements available.
Dr. Jafar Alavi, Chair, 423-439-4455, *Fax:* 423-439-5383, *E-mail:* drjalavi@etsu.edu.
Application contact: Dr. Lon Felker, Director, 423-439-6631, *Fax:* 423-439-5383, *E-mail:* felker@etsu.edu. *Web site:* http://www.etsu.edu/

■ GEORGIA STATE UNIVERSITY

Andrew Young School of Policy Studies, Department of Public Administration and Urban Studies, Program in Urban Policy Studies, Atlanta, GA 30303-3083

AWARDS MS.

Entrance requirements: For master's, GRE General Test or GMAT.

■ GRADUATE SCHOOL AND UNIVERSITY CENTER OF THE CITY UNIVERSITY OF NEW YORK

Graduate Studies, Interdisciplinary Studies, New York, NY 10016-4039

AWARDS Language in social context (PhD); medieval studies (PhD); public policy (MA, PhD); urban studies (MA, PhD); women's studies (MA, PhD). Terminal master's awarded for partial completion of doctoral program.

Degree requirements: For master's, thesis/dissertation; for doctorate, thesis/dissertation, comprehensive exam.
Entrance requirements: For master's and doctorate, GRE General Test. *Application deadline:* For fall admission, 2/1. *Application fee:* $40.
Expenses: Tuition, state resident: part-time $245 per credit. Tuition, nonresident: part-time $425 per credit. Required fees: $72 per semester.
Financial support: Application deadline: 2/1.

■ HUNTER COLLEGE OF THE CITY UNIVERSITY OF NEW YORK

Graduate School, School of Arts and Sciences, Department of Urban Affairs and Planning, Program in Urban Affairs, New York, NY 10021-5085

AWARDS MS. Part-time programs available.

Faculty: 9 full-time (4 women), 5 part-time/adjunct (3 women).
Students: 13 full-time (7 women), 30 part-time (23 women); includes 21 minority (18 African Americans, 3 Hispanic Americans), 2 international. Average age 31. 39 applicants, 82% accepted, 18 enrolled. In 2001, 19 degrees awarded.
Degree requirements: For master's, professional seminar, internship.
Entrance requirements: For master's, TOEFL, minimum 12 credits in social sciences. *Application deadline:* For fall admission, 3/15 (priority date); for spring admission, 11/1 (priority date). Applications are processed on a rolling basis. *Application fee:* $40.
Expenses: Tuition, state resident: full-time $2,175; part-time $185 per credit. Tuition, nonresident: full-time $3,800; part-time $320 per credit.
Financial support: Fellowships, research assistantships, teaching assistantships, career-related internships or fieldwork, Federal Work-Study, scholarships/grants, and unspecified assistantships available.
Faculty research: Women, tourism, youth, immigration, employment.
Elaine M. Walsh, Director, 212-772-5595, *Fax:* 212-772-5593, *E-mail:* ewalsh@shiva.hunter.cuny.edu.
Application contact: William Zlata, Director for Graduate Admissions, 212-772-4288, *Fax:* 212-650-3336, *E-mail:* admissions@hunter.cuny.edu.

■ LONG ISLAND UNIVERSITY, BROOKLYN CAMPUS

Richard L. Conolly College of Liberal Arts and Sciences, Department of Urban Studies, Brooklyn, NY 11201-8423

AWARDS MA. Part-time and evening/weekend programs available.

Degree requirements: For master's, thesis or alternative.
Electronic applications accepted.

■ MASSACHUSETTS INSTITUTE OF TECHNOLOGY

School of Architecture and Planning, Department of Urban Studies and Planning, Cambridge, MA 02139-4307

AWARDS City planning (MCP); urban and regional planning (PhD); urban and regional studies (PhD); urban studies and planning (MS).

Faculty: 28 full-time (7 women), 13 part-time/adjunct (4 women).
Students: 174 full-time (101 women), 22 part-time (12 women); includes 37 minority (16 African Americans, 11 Asian Americans or Pacific Islanders, 10 Hispanic Americans), 67 international. 304 applicants, 43% accepted. In 2001, 53 master's, 2 doctorates awarded.
Degree requirements: For master's and doctorate, thesis/dissertation.
Entrance requirements: For master's and doctorate, GRE General Test, TOEFL. *Application deadline:* For fall admission, 1/3. *Application fee:* $60. Electronic applications accepted.
Expenses: Tuition: Full-time $26,960. Full-time tuition and fees vary according to program.
Financial support: In 2001–02, 140 students received support, including 114 fellowships with partial tuition reimbursements available (averaging $10,800 per year), 28 research assistantships with partial tuition reimbursements available (averaging $6,200 per year), 17 teaching assistantships with full tuition reimbursements available (averaging $14,500 per year); career-related internships or fieldwork, Federal Work-Study, and institutionally sponsored loans also available.
Faculty research: Urban development, urban design, social policy, urban economics, management of urban systems. *Total annual research expenditures:* $655,000.
Lawrence Vale, Head, 617-253-1933, *Fax:* 617-253-2654.
Application contact: Sandra Wellford, Graduate Admissions, 617-253-9403, *Fax:* 617-253-2654, *E-mail:* altwohig@mit.edu. *Web site:* http://sap.mit.edu/dusp/

Find an in-depth description at www.petersons.com/gradchannel.

■ MICHIGAN STATE UNIVERSITY

Graduate School, College of Social Science, School of Criminal Justice, East Lansing, MI 48824

AWARDS Cricimal justice-urban studies (MS); criminal justice (MS, PhD). Part-time programs available. Postbaccalaureate distance learning degree programs offered.

Faculty: 18.
Students: 56 full-time (32 women), 66 part-time (25 women); includes 25 minority (14 African Americans, 1 Asian American or Pacific Islander, 7 Hispanic Americans, 3 Native Americans), 17 international. Average age 29. 158 applicants, 33% accepted. In 2001, 38 master's, 4 doctorates awarded.
Degree requirements: For master's, thesis optional.
Entrance requirements: For master's, GRE General Test or MAT, minimum GPA of 3.2. *Application deadline:* For fall admission, 2/1; for spring admission, 9/1. Applications are processed on a rolling basis. *Application fee:* $30 ($40 for international students). Electronic applications accepted.
Expenses: Tuition, state resident: part-time $244 per credit hour. Tuition, nonresident: part-time $494 per credit hour. Required fees: $268 per semester. Tuition and fees vary according to course load, degree level and program.
Financial support: In 2001–02, 10 fellowships (averaging $2,662 per year), 25 research assistantships with tuition reimbursements (averaging $11,005 per year), 14 teaching assistantships with tuition reimbursements (averaging $10,716 per year) were awarded. Career-related internships or fieldwork and Federal Work-Study also available. Support available to part-time students. Financial award application deadline: 4/15; financial award applicants required to submit FAFSA.
Faculty research: Community policing, women in policing, community-based correction, research utilization. *Total annual research expenditures:* $666,584.
Dr. Edmund McGarrell, Director, 517-355-2197, *Fax:* 517-432-1787.
Application contact: Information Contact, 517-355-2193. *Web site:* http://www.ssc.msu.edu/~cj/

Find an in-depth description at www.petersons.com/gradchannel.

■ MICHIGAN STATE UNIVERSITY

Graduate School, College of Social Science, School of Labor and Industrial Relations, East Lansing, MI 48824

AWARDS Industrial relations and human resources (PhD); labor relations and human resources (MLRHR); labor relations and human resources-urban studies (MLRHR). Part-time and evening/weekend programs available.

Faculty: 12 full-time (4 women).
Students: 123 (71 women); includes 24 minority (14 African Americans, 7 Asian Americans or Pacific Islanders, 3 Hispanic Americans) 22 international. Average age 28. 125 applicants, 67% accepted, 41 enrolled. In 2001, 74 master's, 6 doctorates awarded. Terminal master's awarded for partial completion of doctoral program.
Degree requirements: For master's, thesis optional.
Entrance requirements: For master's, GMAT or GRE (preferred), minimum GPA of 3.0; for doctorate, GMAT or GRE (preferred). *Application deadline:* Applications are processed on a rolling basis. *Application fee:* $30 ($40 for international students). Electronic applications accepted.
Expenses: Tuition, state resident: part-time $244 per credit hour. Tuition, nonresident: part-time $494 per credit hour. Required fees: $268 per semester. Tuition and fees vary according to course load, degree level and program.
Financial support: In 2001–02, 58 students received support, including 37 fellowships (averaging $800 per year), 16 research assistantships with tuition reimbursements available (averaging $5,800 per year); career-related internships or fieldwork, institutionally sponsored loans, scholarships/grants, and unspecified assistantships also available. Financial award applicants required to submit FAFSA.
Faculty research: Human resource management, international/comparative employment systems, work/life balance, discrimination and diversity, high performance work systems. *Total annual research expenditures:* $234,303.
Prof. Theodore Curry, Director, 517-355-1801, *Fax:* 517-355-7656.
Application contact: Annette Bacon, Graduate Program Administrator, 517-355-3285, *Fax:* 517-355-7656, *E-mail:* graduate@lir.msu.edu. *Web site:* http://www.lir.msu.edu/

Find an in-depth description at www.petersons.com/gradchannel.

■ MICHIGAN STATE UNIVERSITY

Urban Affairs Programs and Graduate School, Interdepartmental Graduate Programs in Urban Studies, East Lansing, MI 48824

AWARDS Administration and program evaluation-urban studies (MSW); audiology and speech sciences-urban studies (PhD); civil engineering-urban studies (MS); clinical social work-urban studies (MSW); communication-urban studies (MA); entomology-urban studies (MS, PhD); environmental engineering-urban studies (MS); forestry-urban studies (MS, PhD); geography-urban studies (MA); history-urban studies (MA, PhD); labor relations and human resources-urban studies (MLRHR); park, recreation and tourism resources-urban studies (MS, PhD); physical education and

exercise science-urban studies (MS); political science-urban studies (PhD); psychology-urban studies (PhD); public administration-urban studies (MPA); resource development-urban studies (MS, PhD); sociology-urban studies (PhD); telecommunication-urban studies (MA). Students must also be admitted to a participating academic department. Terminal master's awarded for partial completion of doctoral program.
Degree requirements: For master's, thesis (for some programs); for doctorate, thesis/dissertation.
Entrance requirements: For master's and doctorate, minimum GPA of 3.0. Electronic applications accepted.
Expenses: Tuition, state resident: part-time $244 per credit hour. Tuition, nonresident: part-time $494 per credit hour. Required fees: $268 per semester. Tuition and fees vary according to course load, degree level and program.
Faculty research: Housing/housing affordability, community and economic development, crime prevention, local public policy, poverty.

■ MINNESOTA STATE UNIVERSITY, MANKATO

College of Graduate Studies, College of Social and Behavioral Sciences, Department of Urban and Regional Studies, Mankato, MN 56001

AWARDS MA, MAPA/MA.

Faculty: 7 full-time (2 women).
Students: 10 full-time (5 women), 17 part-time (7 women). Average age 30. In 2001, 17 degrees awarded.
Degree requirements: For master's, one foreign language, thesis or alternative, comprehensive exam.
Entrance requirements: For master's, minimum GPA of 3.0 during previous 2 years. *Application deadline:* For fall admission, 7/9 (priority date); for spring admission, 11/27. Applications are processed on a rolling basis. *Application fee:* $20.
Expenses: Tuition, state resident: full-time $3,253; part-time $157 per credit. Tuition, nonresident: full-time $4,893; part-time $248 per credit. Required fees: $24 per credit. Tuition and fees vary according to reciprocity agreements.
Financial support: Fellowships with partial tuition reimbursements, research assistantships with full tuition reimbursements, teaching assistantships with full tuition reimbursements, career-related internships or fieldwork, Federal Work-Study, and institutionally sponsored loans available. Support available to part-time students. Financial award application deadline: 3/15; financial award applicants required to submit FAFSA.
Dr. Perry Wood, Chairperson, 507-389-1714.
Application contact: Joni Roberts, Admissions Coordinator, 507-389-5244, *Fax:* 507-389-5974, *E-mail:* grad@mankato.msus.edu.

■ NEW JERSEY CITY UNIVERSITY

Graduate Studies, College of Education, Programs in Urban Education, Concentration in Basics and Urban Studies, Jersey City, NJ 07305-1597

AWARDS MA.

Faculty: 2 full-time, 1 part-time/adjunct.
Students: Average age 35. In 2001, 16 degrees awarded.
Degree requirements: For master's, thesis or alternative, internship.
Entrance requirements: For master's, GRE General Test or MAT, TOEFL. *Application deadline:* For fall admission, 8/1 (priority date); for spring admission, 12/1. Applications are processed on a rolling basis. *Application fee:* $0.
Expenses: Tuition, state resident: full-time $5,062. Tuition, nonresident: full-time $8,663.
Financial support: In 2001–02, 5 fellowships, 2 teaching assistantships were awarded.
Dr. Jo Anne Juncker, Coordinator, 201-200-3321.

■ NEW JERSEY INSTITUTE OF TECHNOLOGY

Office of Graduate Studies, School of Architecture, Program in Urban System, Newark, NJ 07102

AWARDS PhD. Part-time and evening/weekend programs available.

Students: 2 full-time (1 woman), 10 part-time (6 women); includes 1 minority (Asian American or Pacific Islander), 1 international. Average age 38. 24 applicants, 58% accepted, 12 enrolled. *Application deadline:* For fall admission, 6/5 (priority date); for spring admission, 10/15. Applications are processed on a rolling basis. *Application fee:* $50. Electronic applications accepted.
Expenses: Tuition, state resident: full-time $7,812; part-time $434 per credit. Tuition, nonresident: full-time $10,746; part-time $597 per credit. Required fees: $47 per credit. $76 per semester.
Financial support: Fellowships with full and partial tuition reimbursements, research assistantships with full and partial tuition reimbursements, teaching assistantships with full and partial tuition reimbursements, career-related internships or fieldwork, Federal Work-Study, institutionally sponsored loans, and unspecified assistantships available. Financial award application deadline: 3/15.
Application contact: Kathryn Kelly, Director of Admissions, 973-596-3300, *Fax:* 973-596-3461, *E-mail:* admissions@njit.edu. *Web site:* http://www.njit.edu/

■ NEW SCHOOL UNIVERSITY

Robert J. Milano Graduate School of Management and Urban Policy, Program in Urban Policy Analysis and Management, New York, NY 10011-8603

AWARDS MS. Part-time programs available.

Students: 45 full-time (33 women), 47 part-time (35 women); includes 23 African Americans, 4 Asian Americans or Pacific Islanders, 18 Hispanic Americans, 1 international. Average age 28. 89 applicants, 93% accepted. In 2001, 22 degrees awarded.
Degree requirements: For master's, thesis.
Entrance requirements: For master's, interview. *Application deadline:* For fall admission, 8/1 (priority date); for winter admission, 1/15 (priority date). Applications are processed on a rolling basis. *Application fee:* $30.
Expenses: Tuition: Full-time $18,720; part-time $1,040 per credit. Required fees: $450; $115 per term. Tuition and fees vary according to program.
Financial support: In 2001–02, 79 students received support, including 2 research assistantships (averaging $10,000 per year), 8 teaching assistantships (averaging $3,500 per year); fellowships, career-related internships or fieldwork, Federal Work-Study, scholarships/grants, and tuition waivers (full and partial) also available. Support available to part-time students. Financial award application deadline: 3/1; financial award applicants required to submit FAFSA.
Faculty research: Community and economic development, national urban policy, social welfare policy, management of low-income housing, race and gender issues.
Dr. Alex F. Schwartz, Chair, 212-229-5434.
Application contact: Mario Johnson, Director of Admissions, 212-229-5462, *Fax:* 212-229-8935, *E-mail:* mgsinfo@newschool.edu.

■ NORFOLK STATE UNIVERSITY

School of Graduate Studies, School of Liberal Arts, Department of Sociology, Program in Urban Affairs, Norfolk, VA 23504

AWARDS MA. Part-time programs available.

Faculty: 2 full-time, 8 part-time/adjunct.
Students: 10 applicants, 80% accepted.
Degree requirements: For master's, thesis.
Entrance requirements: For master's, minimum GPA of 2.5. *Application deadline:* For fall admission, 3/1; for spring admission, 10/1. *Application fee:* $30.
Expenses: Tuition, area resident: Part-time $197 per credit. Tuition, nonresident: part-time $503 per credit.
Financial support: Fellowships with partial tuition reimbursements available.

Norfolk State University (continued)
Dr. Curtis Langley, Coordinator, 757-396-6806, *E-mail:* ctlangley@nsu.edu.

■ OLD DOMINION UNIVERSITY

College of Business and Public Administration, Doctoral Program in Urban Services/Urban Management, Norfolk, VA 23529

AWARDS PhD. Evening/weekend programs available.

Faculty: 7 full-time (2 women), 2 part-time/adjunct (1 woman).
Students: 5 full-time (2 women), 23 part-time (11 women); includes 5 minority (4 African Americans, 1 Hispanic American). Average age 42. 6 applicants, 83% accepted. In 2001, 4 degrees awarded.
Degree requirements: For doctorate, thesis/dissertation, oral and written candidacy exams.
Entrance requirements: For doctorate, GMAT, GRE General Test, master's degree, minimum graduate GPA of 3.0. *Application deadline:* For fall admission, 7/1 (priority date); for spring admission, 10/1 (priority date). Applications are processed on a rolling basis. *Application fee:* $30.
Expenses: Tuition, state resident: part-time $202 per credit. Tuition, nonresident: part-time $534 per credit. Required fees: $76 per semester.
Financial support: In 2001–02, 6 students received support, including 5 research assistantships with tuition reimbursements available (averaging $12,908 per year); fellowships, teaching assistantships, career-related internships or fieldwork, scholarships/grants, and tuition waivers (partial) also available. Support available to part-time students. Financial award application deadline: 2/15; financial award applicants required to submit FAFSA.
Faculty research: Educational needs and program development, policy analysis and administration, excellence norms for cooperative education programs. *Total annual research expenditures:* $80,919.
Dr. Berhanu Mengistu, Graduate Program Director, 757-683-5130, *Fax:* 757-683-5639, *E-mail:* urbanphd@odu.edu. *Web site:* http://www.odu-cbpa.org/usphd.htm

■ OLD DOMINION UNIVERSITY

College of Business and Public Administration, Program in Urban Studies, Norfolk, VA 23529

AWARDS Policy analysis/program evaluation (MUS); public planning analysis (MUS); urban administration (MUS). Part-time and evening/weekend programs available.

Faculty: 7 full-time (2 women), 4 part-time/adjunct (1 woman).
Students: 5 full-time (all women), 35 part-time (23 women); includes 20 minority (19 African Americans, 1 Hispanic American). Average age 36. 23 applicants, 96% accepted. In 2001, 10 degrees awarded.
Degree requirements: For master's, internship or work experience, thesis optional.
Application deadline: For fall admission, 7/1 (priority date); for spring admission, 10/1 (priority date). Applications are processed on a rolling basis. *Application fee:* $30. Electronic applications accepted.
Expenses: Tuition, state resident: part-time $202 per credit. Tuition, nonresident: part-time $534 per credit. Required fees: $76 per semester.
Financial support: In 2001–02, 19 students received support, including 1 fellowship (averaging $8,914 per year), 1 research assistantship with tuition reimbursement available (averaging $5,555 per year); teaching assistantships, career-related internships or fieldwork and tuition waivers (partial) also available. Support available to part-time students. Financial award application deadline: 2/15; financial award applicants required to submit FAFSA.
Faculty research: Program implementation, evaluation, and design. *Total annual research expenditures:* $80,919.
Dr. Berhanu Mengistu, Graduate Program Director, 757-683-5130, *Fax:* 757-683-5639, *E-mail:* urbangpd@odu.edu. *Web site:* http://www.odu-cbpa.org/mus.htm/

■ PORTLAND STATE UNIVERSITY

Graduate Studies, College of Urban and Public Affairs, School of Urban Studies and Planning, Division of Urban Studies, Program in Urban Studies, Portland, OR 97207-0751

AWARDS MUS, PhD.

Students: 29 full-time (17 women), 29 part-time (14 women); includes 2 minority (1 African American, 1 Hispanic American), 9 international. Average age 40.
Degree requirements: For doctorate, thesis/dissertation, residency, comprehensive exam.
Entrance requirements: For master's and doctorate, GRE General Test, TOEFL, minimum GPA of 2.75. *Application deadline:* For fall admission, 2/1. *Application fee:* $50.
Financial support: Application deadline: 3/1. *Total annual research expenditures:* $483,957.

■ QUEENS COLLEGE OF THE CITY UNIVERSITY OF NEW YORK

Division of Graduate Studies, Social Science Division, Department of Urban Studies, Flushing, NY 11367-1597

AWARDS MA. Part-time and evening/weekend programs available.

Faculty: 9 full-time (3 women), 13 part-time/adjunct (2 women).
Students: 5 full-time (4 women), 95 part-time (69 women). 96 applicants, 95% accepted. In 2001, 26 degrees awarded.
Degree requirements: For master's, thesis.
Entrance requirements: For master's, TOEFL, minimum GPA of 3.0. *Application deadline:* For fall admission, 4/1; for spring admission, 11/1. Applications are processed on a rolling basis. *Application fee:* $40.
Expenses: Tuition, state resident: full-time $2,175; part-time $185 per credit. Tuition, nonresident: full-time $3,800; part-time $320 per credit. Required fees: $114; $57 per semester. Tuition and fees vary according to course load.
Financial support: Career-related internships or fieldwork, Federal Work-Study, institutionally sponsored loans, and tuition waivers (partial) available. Support available to part-time students. Financial award application deadline: 4/1; financial award applicants required to submit FAFSA.
Faculty research: Housing abandonment, industrial rehabilitation of Long Island City, health facilities in Queens County.
Dr. Leonard S. Rodberg, Chairperson, 718-997-5130.
Application contact: Dr. William Muraskin, Graduate Adviser, 718-997-5130, *E-mail:* william_muraskin@qc.edu.

■ RUTGERS, THE STATE UNIVERSITY OF NEW JERSEY, NEWARK

Graduate School, Department of Public Administration, Newark, NJ 07102

AWARDS Health care administration (MPA); human resources administration (MPA); public administration (PhD); public management (MPA); public policy analysis (MPA); urban systems and issues (MPA). Part-time and evening/weekend programs available.

Degree requirements: For master's, thesis or alternative, comprehensive exam; for doctorate, thesis/dissertation.
Entrance requirements: For master's, GRE, minimum undergraduate B average; for doctorate, GRE, MPA, minimum B average. Electronic applications accepted.
Faculty research: Government finance, municipal and state government, public productivity. *Web site:* http://newark.rutgers.edu/pubadm/welcome.html

■ RUTGERS, THE STATE UNIVERSITY OF NEW JERSEY, NEWARK

Graduate School, Department of Urban Systems, Newark, NJ 07102

AWARDS PhD.

■ SAINT LOUIS UNIVERSITY

Graduate School, College of Public Service, Department of Public Policy Studies, St. Louis, MO 63103-2097

AWARDS Public administration (MAPA); public policy analysis (PhD); urban affairs

(MAUA); urban planning and real estate development (MUPRED).

Faculty: 8 full-time (1 woman), 14 part-time/adjunct (8 women).
Students: 25 full-time (12 women), 57 part-time (30 women); includes 12 minority (all African Americans), 5 international. Average age 36. 41 applicants, 83% accepted, 23 enrolled. In 2001, 7 master's, 7 doctorates awarded.
Degree requirements: For master's, comprehensive exam; for doctorate, thesis/dissertation, preliminary exams, comprehensive exam.
Entrance requirements: For master's and doctorate, GMAT, GRE General Test, or LSAT. *Application deadline:* For fall admission, 7/1; for spring admission, 11/1. Applications are processed on a rolling basis. *Application fee:* $40.
Expenses: Tuition: Part-time $630 per credit hour.
Financial support: In 2001–02, 42 students received support, including 1 fellowship with tuition reimbursement available, 1 research assistantship with tuition reimbursement available; career-related internships or fieldwork, tuition waivers (partial), and unspecified assistantships also available. Financial award application deadline: 4/1; financial award applicants required to submit FAFSA.
Faculty research: Regional growth, community development, social capital, sustainable development, affordable housing.
Dr. Mary Domahidy, Chairperson, 314-977-3934, *Fax:* 314-977-3943, *E-mail:* domahimr@slu.edu.
Application contact: Dr. Marcia Buresch, Associate Dean of the Graduate School, 314-977-2240, *Fax:* 314-977-3943, *E-mail:* bureschm@slu.edu.

■ SAVANNAH STATE UNIVERSITY

Program in Urban Studies, Savannah, GA 31404

AWARDS MS. Part-time programs available.

Degree requirements: For master's, internship, thesis optional.
Entrance requirements: For master's, GRE.
Faculty research: Transportation, political effectiveness, labor, sociology, criminal justice, waste management.

■ SOUTHERN CONNECTICUT STATE UNIVERSITY

School of Graduate Studies, School of Health and Human Services, Center for Urban Studies, New Haven, CT 06515-1355

AWARDS MS, MSW/MS. Part-time and evening/weekend programs available.

Faculty: 2 full-time, 1 part-time/adjunct.
Students: 4 full-time (3 women), 14 part-time (13 women); includes 8 minority (7 African Americans, 1 Asian American or Pacific Islander). 16 applicants, 56% accepted. In 2001, 11 degrees awarded.
Degree requirements: For master's, thesis or alternative.
Entrance requirements: For master's, interview, minimum QPA of 2.5. *Application deadline:* For fall admission, 7/15 (priority date). Applications are processed on a rolling basis. *Application fee:* $40.
Financial support: Career-related internships or fieldwork available. Financial award application deadline: 4/15; financial award applicants required to submit FAFSA.
Dr. Todd Rofuth, Coordinator, 203-392-6558, *Fax:* 203-392-6580, *E-mail:* rofuth@southernct.edu. *Web site:* http://www.southernct.edu/

■ STATE UNIVERSITY OF NEW YORK AT ALBANY

College of Arts and Sciences, Department of Sociology, Albany, NY 12222-0001

AWARDS Demography (Certificate); sociology (MA, PhD); urban policy (Certificate). Evening/weekend programs available.

Students: 46 full-time (19 women), 59 part-time (31 women); includes 13 minority (3 African Americans, 2 Asian Americans or Pacific Islanders, 8 Hispanic Americans), 13 international. Average age 31. 68 applicants, 56% accepted. In 2001, 4 master's, 7 doctorates, 1 other advanced degree awarded. Terminal master's awarded for partial completion of doctoral program.
Degree requirements: For master's, thesis; for doctorate, thesis/dissertation, 2 specialization exams, research tool.
Entrance requirements: For master's and doctorate, GRE General Test. *Application deadline:* For fall admission, 6/1 (priority date). Applications are processed on a rolling basis. *Application fee:* $50.
Expenses: Tuition, state resident: full-time $2,550; part-time $213 per credit. Tuition, nonresident: full-time $4,208; part-time $351 per credit. Required fees: $470; $470 per year.
Financial support: Fellowships, research assistantships, teaching assistantships, career-related internships or fieldwork and Federal Work-Study available. Financial award application deadline: 3/15.
Faculty research: Gender and equality, crime and deviance, aging, work and organizations.
Dr. Steve Messner, Chair, 518-442-4666.
Application contact: Richard W. Lockman, Graduate Committee Chair, 518-442-4682.

■ TEMPLE UNIVERSITY

Graduate School, College of Liberal Arts, Department of Geography/Urban Studies, Philadelphia, PA 19122-6096

AWARDS Geography (MA); urban studies (MA).

Degree requirements: For master's, thesis or alternative, comprehensive exam.
Entrance requirements: For master's, GRE General Test, minimum GPA of 3.0 during previous 2 years, 2.8 overall. Electronic applications accepted.
Expenses: Tuition, state resident: full-time $8,487; part-time $369 per credit hour. Tuition, nonresident: full-time $12,282; part-time $534 per credit hour. Required fees: $350. Tuition and fees vary according to course load, program and reciprocity agreements.
Faculty research: Environmental issues, urban political economy, poverty and unemployment, neighborhood development, African and Asian urbanization, housing, computer cartography. *Web site:* http://www.temple.edu/GUS/

■ TUFTS UNIVERSITY

Division of Graduate and Continuing Studies and Research, Graduate School of Arts and Sciences, Department of Urban and Environmental Policy and Planning, Medford, MA 02155

AWARDS Community development (MA); environmental policy (MA); health and human welfare (MA); housing policy (MA); international environment/development policy (MA); public policy and citizen participation (MA). Part-time programs available.

Faculty: 7 full-time, 12 part-time/adjunct.
Students: 100 (66 women); includes 16 minority (7 African Americans, 6 Asian Americans or Pacific Islanders, 3 Hispanic Americans) 11 international. 115 applicants, 88% accepted. In 2001, 30 degrees awarded.
Degree requirements: For master's, thesis, internship.
Entrance requirements: For master's, GRE General Test, TOEFL. *Application deadline:* For fall admission, 2/15. Applications are processed on a rolling basis. *Application fee:* $50. Electronic applications accepted.
Expenses: Contact institution.
Financial support: Fellowships with full and partial tuition reimbursements, teaching assistantships with full and partial tuition reimbursements, career-related internships or fieldwork, Federal Work-Study, scholarships/grants, and tuition waivers (partial) available. Support available to part-time students. Financial award application deadline: 2/15; financial award applicants required to submit FAFSA.

Tufts University (continued)
Fran Jacobs, Chair, 617-627-3394, *Fax:* 617-627-3377. *Web site:* http://www.tufts.edu/as/uep/

Find an in-depth description at www.petersons.com/gradchannel.

■ THE UNIVERSITY OF AKRON

Graduate School, Buchtel College of Arts and Sciences, Department of Public Administration and Urban Studies, Program in Urban Studies, Akron, OH 44325-0001

AWARDS Urban studies (MA); urban studies and public affairs (PhD).

Students: 21 full-time (13 women), 19 part-time (7 women); includes 10 minority (9 African Americans, 1 Hispanic American), 6 international. Average age 39. 23 applicants, 87% accepted, 17 enrolled. In 2001, 12 master's, 4 doctorates awarded.
Degree requirements: For master's, thesis optional; for doctorate, one foreign language, thesis/dissertation, comprehensive exam.
Entrance requirements: For master's, GRE, GMAT, LSAT, or MAT, minimum GPA of 2.75; for doctorate, GRE General Test, TOEFL, writing sample. *Application deadline:* For fall admission, 4/15. Applications are processed on a rolling basis. *Application fee:* $40 ($50 for international students).
Expenses: Tuition, state resident: full-time $6,562; part-time $219 per credit. Tuition, nonresident: full-time $9,027; part-time $383 per credit. Required fees: $272; $11 per credit. Tuition and fees vary according to course load.
Financial support: Application deadline: 3/15.
Dr. Raymond W. Cox, Chair, Department of Public Administration and Urban Studies, 330-972-7618, *E-mail:* ngrant@uakron.edu.

■ UNIVERSITY OF CENTRAL OKLAHOMA

College of Graduate Studies and Research, College of Liberal Arts, Department of Political Science, Program in Urban Affairs, Edmond, OK 73034-5209

AWARDS MA. Part-time programs available.

■ UNIVERSITY OF DELAWARE

College of Human Services, Education and Public Policy, School of Urban Affairs and Public Policy, Program in Urban Affairs and Public Policy, Newark, DE 19716

AWARDS Community development and nonprofit leadership (MA); energy and environmental policy (MA); governance, planning and management (PhD); historic preservation (MA); social and urban policy (PhD); technology, environment and society (PhD). Part-time programs available.

Faculty: 15 full-time (6 women).
Students: 85 full-time (44 women), 9 part-time (4 women); includes 23 minority (18 African Americans, 1 Asian American or Pacific Islander, 2 Hispanic Americans, 2 Native Americans), 23 international. Average age 36. 83 applicants, 28% accepted. In 2001, 21 master's, 5 doctorates awarded. Terminal master's awarded for partial completion of doctoral program.
Degree requirements: For master's, thesis or alternative, analytical paper or thesis; for doctorate, thesis/dissertation. *Median time to degree:* Master's–2 years full-time, 3 years part-time.
Entrance requirements: For master's, GRE General Test, TOEFL, minimum GPA of 3.0; for doctorate, GRE General Test, TOEFL, minimum GPA of 3.5. *Application deadline:* For fall admission, 2/1; for spring admission, 12/1. Applications are processed on a rolling basis. *Application fee:* $50. Electronic applications accepted.
Expenses: Tuition, state resident: full-time $4,770; part-time $265 per credit. Tuition, nonresident: full-time $13,860; part-time $770 per credit. Required fees: $414.
Financial support: In 2001–02, 78 students received support, including 4 fellowships with full tuition reimbursements available (averaging $11,000 per year), 62 research assistantships with full tuition reimbursements available (averaging $11,000 per year), 4 teaching assistantships with full tuition reimbursements available (averaging $11,000 per year); career-related internships or fieldwork, Federal Work-Study, and tuition waivers (full) also available. Financial award application deadline: 2/1.
Faculty research: Political economy; social policy analysis; technology and society; historic preservation; urban policy.
Dr. Margaret Wilder, Director, 302-831-6294, *Fax:* 302-831-4225, *E-mail:* mwilder@udel.edu.
Application contact: Charlotte Karin, Information Contact, 302-831-1687, *Fax:* 302-831-3587, *E-mail:* ckarin@udel.edu.
Web site: http://www.udel.edu/suapp

Find an in-depth description at www.petersons.com/gradchannel.

■ UNIVERSITY OF LOUISVILLE

Graduate School, College of Business and Public Administration, Department of Urban and Public Affairs, Program in Urban and Public Affairs, Louisville, KY 40292-0001

AWARDS PhD.

Students: 27 full-time (8 women), 11 part-time (2 women); includes 4 minority (all African Americans), 10 international. Average age 40. In 2001, 4 degrees awarded.
Degree requirements: For doctorate, thesis/dissertation.
Entrance requirements: For doctorate, GRE General Test, master's degree in appropriate field. *Application deadline:* Applications are processed on a rolling basis. *Application fee:* $25.
Expenses: Tuition, state resident: full-time $4,134. Tuition, nonresident: full-time $11,486.
Financial support: In 2001–02, 13 research assistantships with full tuition reimbursements were awarded
Dr. Steven C. Bourassa, Chair, 502-852-5720, *Fax:* 502-852-7672, *E-mail:* scbour01@gwise.louisville.edu.

Find an in-depth description at www.petersons.com/gradchannel.

■ UNIVERSITY OF NEW ORLEANS

Graduate School, College of Urban and Public Affairs, Program in Urban Studies, New Orleans, LA 70148

AWARDS MS, PhD.

Students: 30 full-time (17 women), 45 part-time (23 women); includes 20 minority (14 African Americans, 1 Asian American or Pacific Islander, 4 Hispanic Americans, 1 Native American), 4 international. Average age 39. 27 applicants, 44% accepted, 6 enrolled. In 2001, 3 master's, 4 doctorates awarded.
Degree requirements: For master's and doctorate, thesis/dissertation.
Entrance requirements: For master's, GRE General Test. *Application deadline:* For fall admission, 7/1 (priority date); for spring admission, 11/15. Applications are processed on a rolling basis. *Application fee:* $20. Electronic applications accepted.
Expenses: Tuition, state resident: full-time $2,748; part-time $435 per credit. Tuition, nonresident: full-time $9,792; part-time $1,773 per credit.
Financial support: Applicants required to submit FAFSA.
Faculty research: Urban economic development, environmental planning and analysis, social and cultural change.
Dr. Robert K. Whelan, Dean, 504-280-6592, *E-mail:* rkwhelan@uno.edu.
Application contact: Dr. Ralph Thayer, Graduate Coordinator, 504-280-6592, *E-mail:* rthayer@uno.edu.

■ UNIVERSITY OF WISCONSIN–MILWAUKEE

Graduate School, College of Letters and Sciences, Interdepartmental Program in Urban Studies, Milwaukee, WI 53201-0413

AWARDS MS, PhD, MLIS/MS.

Faculty: 25 full-time (10 women).
Students: 20 full-time (9 women), 22 part-time (16 women); includes 12 minority (10 African Americans, 2 Hispanic Americans), 2 international. 15 applicants, 53% accepted. In 2001, 3 master's, 1 doctorate awarded.

Degree requirements: For master's, thesis or alternative; for doctorate, thesis/ dissertation.
Entrance requirements: For doctorate, GRE General Test. *Application deadline:* For fall admission, 1/1 (priority date); for spring admission, 9/1. Applications are processed on a rolling basis. *Application fee:* $45 ($75 for international students).
Expenses: Tuition, state resident: full-time $6,180; part-time $535 per credit. Tuition, nonresident: full-time $19,482; part-time $1,366 per credit. Tuition and fees vary according to course load, program and reciprocity agreements.
Financial support: In 2001–02, 1 fellowship, 2 teaching assistantships were awarded. Research assistantships, career-related internships or fieldwork and unspecified assistantships also available. Support available to part-time students. Financial award application deadline: 4/15.
Margo Anderson, Representative, 414-229-4751, *Fax:* 414-229-4266, *E-mail:* margo@uwm.edu. *Web site:* http://www.uwm.edu/dept/urban_studies/

■ WRIGHT STATE UNIVERSITY

School of Graduate Studies, College of Liberal Arts, Department of Urban Affairs and Geography, Dayton, OH 45435

AWARDS Urban administration (MPA).

Students: 21 full-time (14 women), 10 part-time (5 women); includes 7 minority (all African Americans), 1 international. 21 applicants, 90% accepted. In 2001, 16 degrees awarded.
Degree requirements: For master's, thesis optional.
Entrance requirements: For master's, TOEFL, interview, minimum GPA of 2.7. *Application fee:* $25.
Expenses: Tuition, state resident: full-time $7,161; part-time $225 per quarter hour. Tuition, nonresident: full-time $12,324; part-time $385 per quarter hour. Tuition and fees vary according to course load, degree level and program.
Financial support: Fellowships, unspecified assistantships available. Support available to part-time students. Financial award applicants required to submit FAFSA.
Faculty research: Strategic planning, economic development, housing and public management. *Total annual research expenditures:* $20,000.
Dr. Jack L. Dustin, Chair, 937-775-4451, *Fax:* 937-775-2422, *E-mail:* jack.dustin@wright.edu.

Social Sciences

SOCIAL SCIENCES

■ APPALACHIAN STATE UNIVERSITY

Cratis D. Williams Graduate School, College of Arts and Sciences, Department of Geography and Planning, Boone, NC 28608

AWARDS Geography (MA); social sciences (MA).

Faculty: 9 full-time (1 woman).
Students: 13 full-time (6 women), 1 (woman) part-time, 1 international. Average age 26. 8 applicants, 88% accepted, 4 enrolled. In 2001, 9 degrees awarded.
Degree requirements: For master's, one foreign language, thesis or alternative, comprehensive exam.
Entrance requirements: For master's, GRE General Test. *Application deadline:* For fall admission, 7/1; for spring admission, 11/1. Applications are processed on a rolling basis. *Application fee:* $35.
Expenses: Tuition, state resident: full-time $1,286. Tuition, nonresident: full-time $9,354. Required fees: $1,116.
Financial support: In 2001–02, 12 research assistantships (averaging $6,250 per year), 2 teaching assistantships (averaging $6,250 per year) were awarded. Fellowships, career-related internships or fieldwork, scholarships/grants, and unspecified assistantships also available. Support available to part-time students. Financial award application deadline: 7/1; financial award applicants required to submit FAFSA.
Faculty research: Global change, climatology, production cartography, geographic information systems, North Carolina geography, Latin America. *Total annual research expenditures:* $92,327.
Dr. Michael Mayfield, Chairperson, 828-262-3000, *Fax:* 828-262-3067, *E-mail:* mayfldmw@appstate.edu.
Application contact: Dr. Peter Soule, Graduate Program Director, 828-262-3000, *E-mail:* soulep@appstate.edu.

■ APPALACHIAN STATE UNIVERSITY

Cratis D. Williams Graduate School, College of Arts and Sciences, Department of Political Science, Boone, NC 28608

AWARDS Political science (MA); public administration (MPA); social sciences (MA). Part-time programs available.

Faculty: 16 full-time (3 women).
Students: 44 full-time (21 women), 21 part-time (10 women); includes 8 minority (all African Americans), 4 international. 52 applicants, 81% accepted, 36 enrolled. In 2001, 16 degrees awarded.
Degree requirements: For master's, one foreign language, comprehensive exam.
Entrance requirements: For master's, GRE General Test. *Application deadline:* For fall admission, 7/1; for spring admission, 11/1. *Application fee:* $35.
Expenses: Tuition, state resident: full-time $1,286. Tuition, nonresident: full-time $9,354. Required fees: $1,116.
Financial support: In 2001–02, 14 research assistantships (averaging $6,000 per year), 5 teaching assistantships (averaging $6,000 per year) were awarded. Fellowships, career-related internships or fieldwork, scholarships/grants, and unspecified assistantships also available. Support available to part-time students. Financial award application deadline: 7/1; financial award applicants required to submit FAFSA.
Faculty research: Campaign finance, emerging democracies, bureaucratic politics, judicial behavior, administration of justice.
Dr. Ruth Ann Strickland, Chairperson, 828-262-3085.

■ APPALACHIAN STATE UNIVERSITY

Cratis D. Williams Graduate School, College of Arts and Sciences, Interdisciplinary Programs in Social Sciences, Boone, NC 28608

AWARDS MA. Part-time programs available.

Faculty: 5 full-time (3 women).
Students: 6 full-time (5 women), 8 part-time (6 women); includes 1 minority (African American). 16 applicants, 75% accepted, 11 enrolled. In 2001, 4 degrees awarded.
Degree requirements: For master's, thesis or alternative, comprehensive exam.
Entrance requirements: For master's, GRE General Test. *Application deadline:* For fall admission, 7/1 (priority date); for spring admission, 11/1. Applications are processed on a rolling basis. *Application fee:* $35.
Expenses: Tuition, state resident: full-time $1,286. Tuition, nonresident: full-time $9,354. Required fees: $1,116.
Financial support: In 2001–02, 1 student received support, including 1 research assistantship (averaging $6,000 per year);

Appalachian State University (continued)
fellowships, teaching assistantships, career-related internships or fieldwork, scholarships/grants, and unspecified assistantships also available. Support available to part-time students. Financial award application deadline: 7/1; financial award applicants required to submit FAFSA.
Faculty research: Media sociology, historical sociology, sociological theory.
Dr. Kenneth Muir, Director, 828-262-6388, *E-mail:* muirkb@appstate.edu.

■ ARKANSAS TECH UNIVERSITY

Graduate Studies, School of Liberal Arts, Russellville, AR 72801-2222

AWARDS Communications (MLA); English (MA); fine arts (MLA); history (MA); multimedia journalism (MA); social sciences (MLA); Spanish (MLA). Part-time and evening/weekend programs available.

Faculty: 26 full-time (6 women), 2 part-time/adjunct (1 woman).
Students: 32 (25 women); includes 3 minority (1 African American, 1 Hispanic American, 1 Native American). Average age 38. 18 applicants, 72% accepted, 13 enrolled. In 2001, 5 degrees awarded.
Degree requirements: For master's, project.
Entrance requirements: For master's, GRE General Test or MAT. *Application deadline:* For fall admission, 3/1 (priority date); for spring admission, 10/1. Applications are processed on a rolling basis. *Application fee:* $0 ($30 for international students). Electronic applications accepted.
Expenses: Tuition: Part-time $125 per hour.
Financial support: In 2001–02, 17 students received support, including 8 teaching assistantships (averaging $4,000 per year); Federal Work-Study, health care benefits, and unspecified assistantships also available. Support available to part-time students. Financial award application deadline: 4/15; financial award applicants required to submit FAFSA.
Dr. Georgena Duncan, Dean, 479-968-0266, *E-mail:* georgena.duncan@mail.atu.edu.
Application contact: Dr. Eldon G. Clary, Dean, 479-968-0398, *Fax:* 479-964-0542, *E-mail:* graduate.school@mail.atu.edu.

■ BALL STATE UNIVERSITY

Graduate School, College of Sciences and Humanities, Program in Social Sciences, Muncie, IN 47306-1099

AWARDS MA.

Students: Average age 25. 6 applicants, 33% accepted. In 2001, 3 degrees awarded. *Application fee:* $25 ($35 for international students).
Expenses: Tuition, state resident: full-time $4,068; part-time $2,542. Tuition, nonresident: full-time $10,944; part-time $6,462. Required fees: $1,000; $500 per term.
Financial support: Application deadline: 3/1.
Dr. Joan Schreiber, Coordinator, 765-285-8700, *Fax:* 765-285-5612, *E-mail:* jschreib@bsu.edu. *Web site:* http://www.bsu.edu/csh/history/

■ CALIFORNIA INSTITUTE OF TECHNOLOGY

Division of the Humanities and Social Sciences, Social Science Program, Pasadena, CA 91125-0001

AWARDS Economics (PhD); political science (PhD); social science (MS).

Faculty: 22 full-time (2 women).
Students: 21 full-time (9 women); includes 3 minority (2 Asian Americans or Pacific Islanders, 1 Hispanic American), 6 international. Average age 27. Terminal master's awarded for partial completion of doctoral program.
Degree requirements: For doctorate, thesis/dissertation.
Entrance requirements: For doctorate, GRE General Test. *Application deadline:* For fall admission, 1/1. *Application fee:* $0. Electronic applications accepted.
Financial support: Fellowships, research assistantships, teaching assistantships, Federal Work-Study, institutionally sponsored loans, and scholarships/grants available.
Faculty research: Individual and group decision making, design of political and economic institutions, experimental social science, public policy, quantitative history.
Application contact: Laurel Auchampaugh, Graduate Secretary, 626-395-4206, *Fax:* 626-405-9841, *E-mail:* gradsec@hss.caltech.edu. *Web site:* http://www.hss.caltech.edu/Ph.D_html

■ CALIFORNIA STATE UNIVERSITY, CHICO

Graduate School, College of Behavioral and Social Sciences, Social Science Program, Chico, CA 95929-0722

AWARDS MA.

Students: 11 full-time, 8 part-time; includes 5 minority (2 African Americans, 1 Asian American or Pacific Islander, 1 Hispanic American, 1 Native American). 13 applicants, 85% accepted, 9 enrolled. In 2001, 2 degrees awarded.
Degree requirements: For master's, thesis or alternative, oral exam.
Entrance requirements: For master's, GRE General Test or MAT. *Application deadline:* For fall admission, 4/1; for spring admission, 10/1. Applications are processed on a rolling basis. *Application fee:* $55. Electronic applications accepted.
Expenses: Tuition, state resident: full-time $2,148. Tuition, nonresident: full-time $6,576.
Financial support: Fellowships, teaching assistantships available.
Dr. Gwen Sheldon, Graduate Coordinator, 530-895-5204.

■ CALIFORNIA STATE UNIVERSITY, FULLERTON

Graduate Studies, College of Humanities and Social Sciences, Program in Social Sciences, Fullerton, CA 92834-9480

AWARDS MA. Part-time programs available.

Degree requirements: For master's, project or thesis.
Entrance requirements: For master's, minimum GPA of 3.0 in social sciences. *Application fee:* $55.
Expenses: Tuition, nonresident: part-time $246 per unit. Required fees: $964.
Financial support: Career-related internships or fieldwork, Federal Work-Study, institutionally sponsored loans, and scholarships/grants available. Support available to part-time students. Financial award application deadline: 3/1.
Dr. Thomas Klammer, Dean, 714-278-3256.

■ CALIFORNIA STATE UNIVERSITY, SAN BERNARDINO

Graduate Studies, College of Social and Behavioral Sciences, Program in Social Sciences, San Bernardino, CA 92407-2397

AWARDS MA.

Faculty: 6.
Students: 6 full-time (3 women), 9 part-time (4 women); includes 7 minority (4 African Americans, 3 Hispanic Americans). Average age 46. 11 applicants, 55% accepted. In 2001, 6 degrees awarded.
Degree requirements: For master's, comprehensive exam or thesis.
Entrance requirements: For master's, minimum GPA of 3.5 in major, 2.5 overall. *Application deadline:* For fall admission, 8/31 (priority date). *Application fee:* $55.
Expenses: Tuition, nonresident: full-time $4,428. Required fees: $1,733.
Financial support: Fellowships, research assistantships, teaching assistantships, career-related internships or fieldwork, Federal Work-Study, and institutionally sponsored loans available. Financial award application deadline: 5/1.
Dr. Randi Miller, Coordinator, 909-880-5546, *Fax:* 909-880-7645, *E-mail:* rmiller@csusb.edu.

■ CALIFORNIA UNIVERSITY OF PENNSYLVANIA

School of Graduate Studies, School of Liberal Arts, Department of Social Science/Criminal Justice, California, PA 15419-1394

AWARDS MA. Part-time and evening/weekend programs available.

Faculty: 4 part-time/adjunct (0 women).

Students: 5 full-time (2 women). In 2001, 11 degrees awarded.
Degree requirements: For master's, thesis optional.
Entrance requirements: For master's, MAT, TOEFL, minimum GPA of 3.0. *Application deadline:* Applications are processed on a rolling basis. *Application fee:* $25.
Expenses: Tuition, state resident: full-time $4,600. Tuition, nonresident: full-time $7,554.
Financial support: Tuition waivers (full) and unspecified assistantships available.
Dr. Lee Roy Black, Director, 724-938-4424, *E-mail:* black@cup.edu. *Web site:* http://www.cup.edu/graduate

■ CAMPBELLSVILLE UNIVERSITY

College of Arts and Sciences, Campbellsville, KY 42718-2799

AWARDS Social science (MA). Part-time programs available.

Faculty: 7 full-time (3 women), 1 part-time/adjunct (0 women).
Students: 2 full-time (1 woman), 9 part-time (8 women). 7 applicants, 100% accepted, 7 enrolled.
Entrance requirements: For master's, GRE General Test or NTE, minimum GPA of 2.9. *Application deadline:* Applications are processed on a rolling basis. *Application fee:* $25. Electronic applications accepted.
Expenses: Tuition: Full-time $5,520; part-time $345 per credit. Required fees: $90.
Financial support: In 2001–02, fellowships with full tuition reimbursements (averaging $1,500 per year); unspecified assistantships also available. Financial award applicants required to submit FAFSA.
Dr. Mary Wilgus, Head.
Application contact: Trent Argo, Director of Admissions, 270-789-5220, *Fax:* 270-789-5071, *E-mail:* targo@cambellsvil.edu. *Web site:* http://campbellsvil.edu/artsandscience/

■ CARNEGIE MELLON UNIVERSITY

College of Humanities and Social Sciences, Department of Social and Decision Sciences, Pittsburgh, PA 15213-3891

AWARDS Behavioral decision theory (PhD); organization science (PhD); social and decision science (PhD). Terminal master's awarded for partial completion of doctoral program.

Degree requirements: For doctorate, thesis/dissertation, research paper, comprehensive exam.
Entrance requirements: For doctorate, GRE General Test, TOEFL. Electronic applications accepted.
Faculty research: Organization theory, political science, sociology, technology studies. *Web site:* http://hss.cmu.edu/HTML/departments/sds/

■ CENTRAL CONNECTICUT STATE UNIVERSITY

School of Graduate Studies, Program in Interdisciplinary Area Studies, New Britain, CT 06050-4010

AWARDS International studies (MS); social science (MS). Part-time and evening/weekend programs available.

Students: 4 full-time (3 women), 23 part-time (12 women); includes 2 minority (1 African American, 1 Hispanic American). Average age 35. 1 applicant, 0% accepted. In 2001, 5 degrees awarded.
Degree requirements: For master's, thesis or alternative, comprehensive exam or special project.
Entrance requirements: For master's, TOEFL, minimum GPA of 2.7. *Application deadline:* For fall admission, 8/10 (priority date); for spring admission, 12/10. Applications are processed on a rolling basis. *Application fee:* $40.
Expenses: Tuition, state resident: full-time $2,772; part-time $245 per credit. Tuition, nonresident: full-time $7,726; part-time $245 per credit. Required fees: $2,102. Tuition and fees vary according to course level and degree level.
Financial support: In 2001–02, research assistantships (averaging $4,800 per year), teaching assistantships (averaging $4,800 per year) were awarded. Federal Work-Study also available. Financial award application deadline: 3/15; financial award applicants required to submit FAFSA.
Dr. Timothy Rickard, Coordinator, 860-832-2921.

■ COLUMBIA UNIVERSITY

Graduate School of Arts and Sciences, Program in Quantitative Methods in the Social Sciences, New York, NY 10027

AWARDS MA. Part-time programs available.

Expenses: Tuition: Full-time $27,528. Required fees: $1,638.
Peter Bearman, Adviser, 212-854-3094, *Fax:* 212-854-8925.

■ COPPIN STATE COLLEGE

Division of Graduate Studies, Division of Arts and Sciences, Department of Social Sciences, Baltimore, MD 21216-3698

AWARDS MS. Part-time and evening/weekend programs available.

Faculty: 1 full-time (0 women), 1 part-time/adjunct (0 women).
Students: 24 applicants, 71% accepted. In 2001, 4 degrees awarded.
Entrance requirements: For master's, resumé, references. *Application deadline:* For fall admission, 7/15 (priority date); for spring admission, 12/15 (priority date). Applications are processed on a rolling basis. *Application fee:* $25.
Expenses: Tuition, state resident: full-time $3,576; part-time $149 per credit. Tuition, nonresident: full-time $6,360; part-time $265 per credit. Required fees: $589; $589 per year.
Dr. John Hudgins, Chair, 410-951-3520, *E-mail:* jhudgins@coppin.edu.
Application contact: Vel Lyles, Associate Vice President, Enrollment Management, 410-951-3575, *E-mail:* vlyles@coppin.edu. *Web site:* http://www.coppin.edu/

■ EASTERN MICHIGAN UNIVERSITY

Graduate School, College of Arts and Sciences, Department of History and Philosophy, Interdisciplinary Program in Social Science, Ypsilanti, MI 48197

AWARDS MA, MLS. Evening/weekend programs available.

Entrance requirements: For master's, TOEFL. *Application deadline:* For fall admission, 5/15; for spring admission, 3/15. Applications are processed on a rolling basis. *Application fee:* $30.
Expenses: Tuition, state resident: part-time $285 per credit hour. Tuition, nonresident: part-time $510 per credit hour.
Financial support: Fellowships, teaching assistantships available. Support available to part-time students. Financial award application deadline: 3/15; financial award applicants required to submit FAFSA.
Dr. JoEllen Vinyard, Coordinator, 734-487-0053.

■ EDINBORO UNIVERSITY OF PENNSYLVANIA

Graduate Studies, School of Liberal Arts, Department of History, Edinboro, PA 16444

AWARDS Social sciences (MA). Part-time and evening/weekend programs available.

Faculty: 6 full-time (1 woman), 1 part-time/adjunct (0 women).
Students: 7 full-time (3 women), 15 part-time (8 women); includes 1 minority (African American), 2 international. Average age 34. In 2001, 3 degrees awarded.
Degree requirements: For master's, thesis or alternative, competency exam.
Entrance requirements: For master's, GRE or MAT, minimum QPA of 2.5. *Application deadline:* Applications are processed on a rolling basis. *Application fee:* $25. Electronic applications accepted.
Expenses: Tuition, state resident: full-time $4,600; part-time $256 per credit. Tuition, nonresident: full-time $7,554; part-time $420 per credit. Required fees: $68 per credit.
Financial support: In 2001–02, 4 students received support. Career-related internships or fieldwork, Federal Work-Study, institutionally sponsored loans,

Edinboro University of Pennsylvania (continued)

scholarships/grants, and unspecified assistantships available. Support available to part-time students. Financial award application deadline: 5/1; financial award applicants required to submit FAFSA.

Dr. Jerra Jenrette, Chairperson, 814-732-2575, *E-mail:* jjenrette@edinboro.edu.

Application contact: Dr. Mary Margaret Bevevino, Dean of Graduate Studies, 814-732-2856, *Fax:* 814-732-2611, *E-mail:* mbevevino@edinboro.edu.

■ FLORIDA AGRICULTURAL AND MECHANICAL UNIVERSITY

Division of Graduate Studies, Research, and Continuing Education, College of Arts and Sciences, Division of Social and Behavioral Sciences, Program in Applied Social Science, Tallahassee, FL 32307-3200

AWARDS MASS. Part-time programs available.

Degree requirements: For master's, thesis.

Entrance requirements: For master's, GRE General Test, minimum GPA of 3.0.

Faculty research: Southern history, black history, election trends, presidential history.

■ FLORIDA STATE UNIVERSITY

Graduate Studies, College of Social Sciences, Interdisciplinary Program in Social Science, Tallahassee, FL 32306

AWARDS MA, MS.

Students: 4 full-time (2 women), 28 part-time (12 women); includes 3 minority (2 African Americans, 1 Hispanic American). Average age 30. 16 applicants, 94% accepted. In 2001, 9 degrees awarded.

Entrance requirements: For master's, GRE General Test, minimum GPA of 3.0. *Application deadline:* For fall admission, 6/1. *Application fee:* $20.

Expenses: Tuition, state resident: part-time $163 per credit hour. Tuition, nonresident: part-time $570 per credit hour. Tuition and fees vary according to program.

Financial support: In 2001–02, 1 research assistantship with tuition reimbursement (averaging $11,000 per year) was awarded. Financial award applicants required to submit FAFSA.

Dr. Robert Crew, Director, 850-644-6284.

■ HENDERSON STATE UNIVERSITY

Graduate Studies, Ellis College of Arts and Sciences, Program in Social Studies, Arkadelphia, AR 71999-0001

AWARDS MLA.

Faculty: 2 full-time (0 women), 1 part-time/adjunct (0 women).

Entrance requirements: For master's, minimum GPA of 2.7, interview. *Application deadline:* For fall admission, 5/1 (priority date); for spring admission, 12/1 (priority date). *Application fee:* $0 ($30 for international students).

Expenses: Tuition, state resident: part-time $150 per credit hour. Tuition, nonresident: part-time $300 per credit hour. Required fees: $120 per semester.

Financial support: Application deadline: 7/31.

Dr. Jeddy Levar, Chair, 870-230-5240, *E-mail:* levar@hsu.edu.

■ HOLLINS UNIVERSITY

Graduate Programs, Program in Liberal Studies, Roanoke, VA 24020-1603

AWARDS Computer studies (MALS); humanities (MALS); interdisciplinary studies (MALS); liberal studies (CAS); social science (MALS). Part-time and evening/weekend programs available.

Faculty: 21 full-time (9 women), 9 part-time/adjunct (4 women).

Students: 43 full-time (35 women), 132 part-time (105 women); includes 16 minority (12 African Americans, 2 Hispanic Americans, 2 Native Americans). Average age 37. 61 applicants, 100% accepted, 54 enrolled. In 2001, 51 master's, 2 other advanced degrees awarded.

Degree requirements: For master's, thesis.

Entrance requirements: For master's, letters of recommendation, interview. *Application deadline:* For fall admission, 8/1 (priority date); for spring admission, 1/10 (priority date). Applications are processed on a rolling basis. *Application fee:* $35. Electronic applications accepted.

Expenses: Tuition: Part-time $765 per course.

Financial support: In 2001–02, 57 students received support. Available to part-time students. Application deadline: 7/15;

Faculty research: Elderly blacks, film, feminist economics, U.S. voting patterns, Wagner, diversity.

Dr. Leslie V. Willett, Dean of Graduate Studies, 540-362-7431, *Fax:* 540-362-6288, *E-mail:* lwillett@hollins.edu.

Application contact: Cathy S. Koon, Coordinator of Graduate Studies, 540-362-6575, *Fax:* 540-362-6288, *E-mail:* hugrad@hollins.edu. *Web site:* http://www.hollins.edu/

■ HUMBOLDT STATE UNIVERSITY

Graduate Studies, College of Arts, Humanities, and Social Sciences, Program in Social Science, Arcata, CA 95521-8299

AWARDS MA.

Students: 23 full-time (14 women), 5 part-time (4 women); includes 2 minority (1 African American, 1 Native American), 1 international. Average age 33. 45 applicants, 80% accepted, 27 enrolled. In 2001, 4 degrees awarded.

Degree requirements: For master's, thesis or alternative, qualifying exam.

Entrance requirements: For master's, TOEFL, minimum GPA of 2.5. *Application deadline:* Applications are processed on a rolling basis. *Application fee:* $55.

Expenses: Tuition, state resident: full-time $1,969. Tuition, nonresident: part-time $246 per unit.

Financial support: Application deadline: 3/1.

Faculty research: Geography, political science, ethnic studies, anthropology, economics.

Dr. John Meyer, Coordinator, 707-826-4497, *E-mail:* jmm7001@humboldt.edu.

■ INDIANA UNIVERSITY BLOOMINGTON

School of Law, Bloomington, IN 47405

AWARDS Comparative law (MCL); judicial science (JD); law (LL M); law and social science (PhD).

Students: 630 full-time (267 women), 62 part-time (26 women); includes 100 minority (50 African Americans, 23 Asian Americans or Pacific Islanders, 27 Hispanic Americans), 106 international. Average age 27.

Application deadline: Applications are processed on a rolling basis. *Application fee:* $45 ($55 for international students).

Expenses: Contact institution.

Alfred Aman, Dean, 812-855-8886. *Web site:* http://www.law.indiana.edu/

■ JOHNS HOPKINS UNIVERSITY

School of Public Health, Department of Health Policy and Management, Faculty of Social and Behavioral Sciences, Baltimore, MD 21205

AWARDS Genetic counseling (Sc M); health education (MHS); social and behavioral sciences (PhD, Sc D).

Students: 70.

Degree requirements: For master's, thesis (for some programs), internship, comprehensive exam (for some programs), registration; for doctorate, thesis/dissertation, 1 year full-time residency, oral and written exam, comprehensive exam, registration.

Entrance requirements: For master's and doctorate, GRE General Test, TOEFL, work experience in health-related field. *Application deadline:* For fall admission, 1/2. Applications are processed on a rolling basis. *Application fee:* $60. Electronic applications accepted.

Expenses: Tuition: Full-time $27,390.

Financial support: Federal Work-Study, institutionally sponsored loans,

scholarships/grants, and stipends available. Financial award application deadline: 4/15; financial award applicants required to submit FAFSA.
Faculty research: Health program evaluation; health education and communications, social and behavioral aspects.
Dr. Margaret Ensminger, Associate Chair, 410-955-2313, *E-mail:* mensming@jhsph.edu.
Application contact: Mary Sewell, Coordinator, 410-955-2488, *Fax:* 410-614-9152, *E-mail:* msewell@jhsph.edu.

■ LONG ISLAND UNIVERSITY, BROOKLYN CAMPUS

Richard L. Conolly College of Liberal Arts and Sciences, Program in Social Science, Brooklyn, NY 11201-8423

AWARDS History (MS); United Nations studies (Certificate). Part-time and evening/weekend programs available.

Electronic applications accepted.

■ LONG ISLAND UNIVERSITY, C.W. POST CAMPUS

College of Liberal Arts and Sciences, Department of History, Brookville, NY 11548-1300

AWARDS History (MA); social studies (MS). Part-time and evening/weekend programs available.

Faculty: 7 full-time (5 women), 5 part-time/adjunct (0 women).
Students: 5 full-time (4 women), 17 part-time (6 women). Average age 23. 33 applicants, 91% accepted, 20 enrolled. In 2001, 2 degrees awarded.
Degree requirements: For master's, thesis or alternative, comprehensive exam or thesis.
Entrance requirements: For master's, bachelor's degree in history, minimum GPA of 3.0. *Application deadline:* Applications are processed on a rolling basis. *Application fee:* $30. Electronic applications accepted.
Expenses: Tuition: Full-time $10,296; part-time $572 per credit. Required fees: $380; $190 per semester.
Financial support: Research assistantships, career-related internships or fieldwork, Federal Work-Study, and institutionally sponsored loans available. Support available to part-time students. Financial award application deadline: 5/15; financial award applicants required to submit CSS PROFILE or FAFSA.
Faculty research: American slavery, women's studies, military history.
Dr. Roger Goldstein, Chairman, 516-299-2407, *Fax:* 516-299-4140.
Application contact: Dr. Carol Bauer, Graduate Adviser, 516-299-2407. *Web site:* http://www.liu.edu/postlas/

■ LONG ISLAND UNIVERSITY, C.W. POST CAMPUS

College of Liberal Arts and Sciences, Department of Political Science/International Studies, Brookville, NY 11548-1300

AWARDS Political science/international studies (MA); social studies secondary education (MS). Part-time and evening/weekend programs available.

Faculty: 7 full-time (1 woman), 6 part-time/adjunct (2 women).
Students: 4 full-time (3 women), 9 part-time (6 women). Average age 23. 33 applicants, 91% accepted, 19 enrolled. In 2001, 12 degrees awarded.
Degree requirements: For master's, thesis or alternative, comprehensive exam.
Entrance requirements: For master's, GRE. *Application deadline:* For fall admission, 9/1 (priority date); for winter admission, 12/15 (priority date); for spring admission, 1/20 (priority date). Applications are processed on a rolling basis. *Application fee:* $30. Electronic applications accepted.
Expenses: Tuition: Full-time $10,296; part-time $572 per credit. Required fees: $380; $190 per semester.
Financial support: In 2001–02, 2 research assistantships were awarded; career-related internships or fieldwork and Federal Work-Study also available. Support available to part-time students. Financial award application deadline: 5/15; financial award applicants required to submit CSS PROFILE or FAFSA.
Faculty research: International relations, middle eastern politics, political philosophy.
Dr. Roger Goldstein, Chairman, 516-299-2407, *Fax:* 516-299-4140.
Application contact: Dr. Michael Soupios, Graduate Adviser, 516-299-3026. *Web site:* http://www.liu.edu/postlas/

■ LONG ISLAND UNIVERSITY, C.W. POST CAMPUS

School of Education, Department of Curriculum and Instruction, Brookville, NY 11548-1300

AWARDS Adolescence (MS); art education (MS); bilingual education (MS); biology education (MS); childhood (MS); early childhood (MS); early childhood/literacy (MS); early childhood/special ed (MS); earth science education (MS); English education (MS); French education (MS); Italian education (MS); literacy (MS); mathematics education (MS); music education (MS); social studies (MS); Spanish education (MS). Part-time and evening/weekend programs available.

Faculty: 12 full-time (9 women), 64 part-time/adjunct (28 women).
Students: 209 full-time (151 women), 548 part-time (436 women). 365 applicants, 91% accepted, 238 enrolled. In 2001, 233 degrees awarded.
Degree requirements: For master's, thesis, comprehensive exam or thesis, student teaching.
Entrance requirements: For master's, minimum GPA of 2.75 in major, 2.5 overall. *Application deadline:* Applications are processed on a rolling basis. *Application fee:* $30. Electronic applications accepted.
Expenses: Tuition: Full-time $10,296; part-time $572 per credit. Required fees: $380; $190 per semester.
Financial support: In 2001–02, 4 research assistantships were awarded; career-related internships or fieldwork and Federal Work-Study also available. Support available to part-time students. Financial award application deadline: 5/15; financial award applicants required to submit CSS PROFILE or FAFSA.
Faculty research: Ethics and education, teaching strategies.
Dr. Anthony De Falco, Chairperson, 516-299-2148, *Fax:* 516-299-3312, *E-mail:* defalco@pipeline.com.
Application contact: Gail Maerz, Academic Counselor, 516-299-2155, *Fax:* 516-299-3312. *Web site:* http://www.liu.edu/postedu/

■ MASSACHUSETTS INSTITUTE OF TECHNOLOGY

School of Humanities, Arts and Social Sciences, Program in Science, Technology, and Society, Cambridge, MA 02139-4307

AWARDS History and social study of science and technology (PhD).

Faculty: 15 full-time (5 women).
Students: 21 full-time (8 women); includes 4 minority (3 Asian Americans or Pacific Islanders, 1 Hispanic American), 2 international. Average age 29. 62 applicants, 8% accepted. In 2001, 5 degrees awarded.
Degree requirements: For doctorate, 2 foreign languages, thesis/dissertation.
Entrance requirements: For doctorate, GRE General Test, TOEFL. *Application deadline:* For fall admission, 1/15. *Application fee:* $60.
Expenses: Tuition: Full-time $26,960. Full-time tuition and fees vary according to program.
Financial support: In 2001–02, 21 students received support, including 17 fellowships (averaging $13,000 per year), 2 research assistantships, 6 teaching assistantships (averaging $13,000 per year); Federal Work-Study and institutionally sponsored loans also available. Financial award application deadline: 1/15.
Faculty research: Cultural studies of science and technology.
Merritt Roe Smith, Director, 617-253-2564, *Fax:* 617-258-8118, *E-mail:* roesmith@mit.edu.

Massachusetts Institute of Technology (continued)
Application contact: Le Roy Stafford, Coordinator, 617-253-4085, *Fax:* 617-258-8118, *E-mail:* stsprogram@mit.edu. *Web site:* http://web.mit.edu/sts/

■ MICHIGAN STATE UNIVERSITY

Graduate School, College of Social Science, School of Social Work, East Lansing, MI 48824

AWARDS Administration and program evaluation (MSW); administration and program evaluation-urban studies (MSW); clinical social work (MSW); clinical social work-urban studies (MSW); interdisciplinary social science/social work (PhD); organizational and community practice (MSW); program evaluation-urban studies (MSW). Postbaccalaureate distance learning degree programs offered (minimal on-campus study).

Faculty: 17 full-time (9 women).
Students: 117 full-time (100 women), 148 part-time (129 women); includes 55 minority (38 African Americans, 6 Asian Americans or Pacific Islanders, 11 Hispanic Americans), 5 international. Average age 33. 215 applicants, 74% accepted. In 2001, 69 master's, 3 doctorates awarded.
Entrance requirements: For master's, minimum GPA of 3.0. *Application deadline:* For fall admission, 1/20. Applications are processed on a rolling basis. *Application fee:* $30 ($40 for international students).
Expenses: Tuition, state resident: part-time $244 per credit hour. Tuition, nonresident: part-time $494 per credit hour. Required fees: $268 per semester. Tuition and fees vary according to course load, degree level and program.
Financial support: In 2001–02, 33 fellowships with tuition reimbursements (averaging $2,808 per year), 11 research assistantships with tuition reimbursements (averaging $10,673 per year) were awarded. Teaching assistantships with tuition reimbursements, career-related internships or fieldwork and Federal Work-Study also available. Support available to part-time students. Financial award applicants required to submit FAFSA.
Faculty research: Women at risk, juvenile offenders, infant mental health, poverty, welfare reforms. *Total annual research expenditures:* $25,497.
Dr. Gary Anderson, Director, 517-353-8616, *Fax:* 517-353-3038, *E-mail:* socialwork@ssc.msu.edu.
Application contact: Prof. Rena Harold, Coordinator of Graduate Programs, 517-353-8260. *Web site:* http://www.msu.edu/~sw/

■ MISSISSIPPI COLLEGE

Graduate School, College of Arts and Sciences, Department of History and Political Science, Program in Social Sciences, Clinton, MS 39058

AWARDS MSS.

Degree requirements: For master's, comprehensive exam.
Entrance requirements: For master's, GRE, minimum GPA of 2.5.

■ MONTCLAIR STATE UNIVERSITY

The School of Graduate, Professional and Continuing Education, College of Education and Human Services, Department of Curriculum and Teaching, Program in Teaching, Upper Montclair, NJ 07043-1624

AWARDS Art (MAT); biological science (MAT); business education (MAT); early childhood education (MAT); earth science (MAT); English (MAT); French (MAT); health and physical education (MAT); health education (MAT); home economics (MAT); industrial arts (MAT); mathematics (MAT); music (MAT); physical education (MAT); physical science (MAT); social studies (MAT); Spanish (MAT); teacher of ESL (MAT); teacher of handicapped (MAT); teaching middle school philosophy (MAT). Part-time programs available.

Degree requirements: For master's, field experience.
Entrance requirements: For master's, GRE General Test, minimum GPA of 2.67. Electronic applications accepted. *Web site:* http://www.montclair.edu/

■ MONTCLAIR STATE UNIVERSITY

The School of Graduate, Professional and Continuing Education, College of Humanities and Social Sciences, Programs in Social Science, Upper Montclair, NJ 07043-1624

AWARDS Anthropology (MA); economics (MA); history (MA). Part-time and evening/weekend programs available.

Degree requirements: For master's, comprehensive exam.
Entrance requirements: For master's, GRE General Test. Electronic applications accepted. *Web site:* http://www.montclair.edu/

■ MONTCLAIR STATE UNIVERSITY

The School of Graduate, Professional and Continuing Education, School of Business, Department of Economics and Finance, Upper Montclair, NJ 07043-1624

AWARDS Economics (MA); social science (MA). Part-time and evening/weekend programs available.

Degree requirements: For master's, comprehensive exam.
Entrance requirements: For master's, GRE General Test. Electronic applications accepted.

■ NEW SCHOOL UNIVERSITY

Graduate Faculty of Political and Social Science, New York, NY 10011-8603

AWARDS MA, MS Sc, DS Sc, PhD. Part-time and evening/weekend programs available.

Faculty: 64 full-time, 19 part-time/adjunct.
Students: 857 full-time (433 women), 184 part-time (105 women); includes 161 minority (56 African Americans, 39 Asian Americans or Pacific Islanders, 63 Hispanic Americans, 3 Native Americans), 304 international. Average age 34. 761 applicants, 87% accepted, 216 enrolled. In 2001, 101 master's, 51 doctorates awarded. Terminal master's awarded for partial completion of doctoral program.
Degree requirements: For doctorate, thesis/dissertation, qualifying exam.
Entrance requirements: For master's, GRE General Test; for doctorate, GRE General Test, MA. *Application deadline:* For fall admission, 1/15 (priority date). Applications are processed on a rolling basis. *Application fee:* $40.
Expenses: Contact institution.
Financial support: In 2001–02, 77 fellowships with full and partial tuition reimbursements (averaging $5,800 per year), 59 research assistantships with full and partial tuition reimbursements (averaging $4,700 per year), 67 teaching assistantships with full and partial tuition reimbursements (averaging $2,400 per year) were awarded. Career-related internships or fieldwork, Federal Work-Study, scholarships/grants, and tuition waivers (full and partial) also available. Financial award application deadline: 1/15; financial award applicants required to submit FAFSA.
Faculty research: Civil society and democracy, international movements of refugees, minority use of health services, memory, morality and genetics.
Dr. Kenneth Prewitt, Dean, 212-229-5777.
Application contact: Emanuel Lomax, Director of Admissions, 800-523-5411, *Fax:* 212-989-7102, *E-mail:* gfadmit@

newschool.edu. *Web site:* http://www.newschool.edu/

Find an in-depth description at www.petersons.com/gradchannel.

■ NORTH DAKOTA STATE UNIVERSITY

The Graduate School, College of Arts, Humanities and Social Sciences, Program in Sociology and Anthropology, Fargo, ND 58105

AWARDS Criminal justice (PhD); social science (MA, MS). Part-time programs available.

Faculty: 11 full-time (3 women), 2 part-time/adjunct (1 woman).
Students: 16 full-time (14 women), 11 part-time (7 women); includes 2 minority (both African Americans), 1 international. Average age 27. 11 applicants, 82% accepted. In 2001, 3 degrees awarded.
Degree requirements: For master's, thesis.
Entrance requirements: For master's, TOEFL, background courses in sociology, minimum GPA of 3.0. *Application deadline:* For fall admission, 4/1 (priority date). Applications are processed on a rolling basis. *Application fee:* $35.
Expenses: Tuition, state resident: part-time $124 per credit. Tuition, nonresident: part-time $325 per credit. Required fees: $22 per credit. Tuition and fees vary according to reciprocity agreements.
Financial support: In 2001–02, 4 research assistantships with full tuition reimbursements (averaging $6,156 per year), 7 teaching assistantships with full tuition reimbursements (averaging $3,078 per year) were awarded. Fellowships, career-related internships or fieldwork, Federal Work-Study, institutionally sponsored loans, and tuition waivers (full) also available. Support available to part-time students. Financial award application deadline: 4/15.
Faculty research: Criminal justice, medical sociology, demography, ethnology, archaeology. *Total annual research expenditures:* $206,000.
Dr. Gary A. Goreham, Chair, 701-231-7637, *Fax:* 701-231-1047, *E-mail:* gary.goreham@ndsu.nodak.edu. *Web site:* http://www.ndsu.nodak.edu/sociology/

■ NORTHWESTERN UNIVERSITY

The Graduate School, Interdepartmental Degree Programs, Program in Mathematical Methods in Social Science, Evanston, IL 60208

AWARDS MS.

Expenses: Tuition: Full-time $26,526.
Michael Wallerstein, Director, 847-491-2646, *Fax:* 847-491-4234, *E-mail:* m-wallerstein@northwestern.edu.

■ NORTHWESTERN UNIVERSITY

The Graduate School, Program in Law and Social Science, Evanston, IL 60208

AWARDS Certificate.

Faculty: 22 full-time (11 women).
Students: 4 full-time (2 women), 2 international. Average age 25. In 2001, 4 degrees awarded.
Degree requirements: For Certificate, research project. *Median time to degree:* 1 year full-time.
Application fee: $50 ($55 for international students).
Expenses: Tuition: Full-time $26,526.
Financial support: In 2001–02, 4 fellowships with full tuition reimbursements (averaging $14,000 per year) were awarded
Faculty research: Law and social science. *Total annual research expenditures:* $3 million.
Robert Nelson, Co-Director, 312-988-6532, *Fax:* 312-988-6579, *E-mail:* r-nelson@northwestern.edu. *Web site:* http://www.northwestern.edu/graduate/bulletin/index

■ OHIO UNIVERSITY

Graduate Studies, College of Arts and Sciences, Program in Social Sciences, Athens, OH 45701-2979

AWARDS MSS. Part-time programs available.

Students: 1 full-time (0 women), 30 part-time (15 women); includes 2 minority (both African Americans). Average age 29. 4 applicants, 50% accepted. In 2001, 2 degrees awarded.
Degree requirements: For master's, oral exam. *Median time to degree:* Master's–2 years full-time, 3 years part-time.
Entrance requirements: For master's, minimum GPA of 2.75. *Application fee:* $30.
Expenses: Tuition, state resident: full-time $6,585. Tuition, nonresident: full-time $12,254.
Financial support: Federal Work-Study and institutionally sponsored loans available. Financial award application deadline: 3/15.
Dr. Marvin Fletcher, Coordinator, 740-593-2969, *E-mail:* mfletcher1@ohiou.edu. *Web site:* http://www-as.phy.ohiou.edu/Departments/History/

■ OLD DOMINION UNIVERSITY

Darden College of Education, Programs in Secondary Education, Norfolk, VA 23529

AWARDS Biology (MS Ed); chemistry (MS Ed); English (MS Ed); instructional technology (MS Ed); library science (MS Ed); mathematics (MS Ed); secondary education (MS Ed); social studies (MS Ed). Part-time and evening/weekend programs available. Postbaccalaureate distance learning degree programs offered (minimal on-campus study).

Faculty: 28 full-time (11 women).
Students: 42 full-time (25 women), 127 part-time (72 women); includes 28 minority (20 African Americans, 3 Asian Americans or Pacific Islanders, 2 Hispanic Americans, 3 Native Americans). Average age 37. 44 applicants, 95% accepted. In 2001, 100 degrees awarded.
Degree requirements: For master's, candidacy exam, thesis optional. *Median time to degree:* Master's–1.5 years full-time, 3 years part-time.
Entrance requirements: For master's, GRE General Test, or MAT, PRAXIS 1 for master's with licensure, minimum GPA of 3.0, teaching certificate. *Application deadline:* Applications are processed on a rolling basis. *Application fee:* $30. Electronic applications accepted.
Expenses: Tuition, state resident: part-time $202 per credit. Tuition, nonresident: part-time $534 per credit. Required fees: $76 per semester.
Financial support: In 2001–02, 58 students received support, including 2 research assistantships with tuition reimbursements available (averaging $6,777 per year), 3 teaching assistantships with tuition reimbursements available (averaging $5,333 per year); fellowships, career-related internships or fieldwork, Federal Work-Study, institutionally sponsored loans, scholarships/grants, and tuition waivers (partial) also available. Support available to part-time students. Financial award application deadline: 2/15; financial award applicants required to submit FAFSA.
Faculty research: Mathematics retraining, writing project for teachers, geography teaching, reading.
Dr. Murray Rudisill, Graduate Program Director, 757-683-3283, *Fax:* 757-683-5862, *E-mail:* ecisgpd@odu.edu. *Web site:* http://www.odu.edu/webroots/orgs/educ/ECI/eci.nsf/pages/home

■ PITTSBURG STATE UNIVERSITY

Graduate School, College of Arts and Sciences, Department of Social Science, Pittsburg, KS 66762

AWARDS MS.

Students: 3 full-time (all women), 1 (woman) part-time.
Degree requirements: For master's, thesis or alternative.
Application fee: $0 ($40 for international students).
Expenses: Tuition, state resident: full-time $2,676; part-time $114 per credit hour. Tuition, nonresident: full-time $6,778; part-time $285 per credit hour.
Financial support: Teaching assistantships, career-related internships or fieldwork and Federal Work-Study available.
Faculty research: Kansas elections, land reclamation, Marxist humanism, Latin America.

Pittsburg State University (continued)
Dr. Michael Kelley, Chairperson, 620-235-4324.
Application contact: Marvene Darraugh, Administrative Officer, 620-235-4220, *Fax:* 620-235-4219, *E-mail:* mdarraug@pittstate.edu.

■ QUEENS COLLEGE OF THE CITY UNIVERSITY OF NEW YORK

Division of Graduate Studies, Social Science Division, Program in Social Sciences, Flushing, NY 11367-1597

AWARDS MASS. Part-time and evening/weekend programs available.

Students: 1 full-time (0 women), 15 part-time (10 women). 14 applicants, 93% accepted. In 2001, 3 degrees awarded.
Degree requirements: For master's, thesis.
Entrance requirements: For master's, TOEFL, minimum GPA of 3.0. *Application deadline:* For fall admission, 4/1; for spring admission, 11/1. Applications are processed on a rolling basis. *Application fee:* $40.
Expenses: Tuition, state resident: full-time $2,175; part-time $185 per credit. Tuition, nonresident: full-time $3,800; part-time $320 per credit. Required fees: $114; $57 per semester. Tuition and fees vary according to course load.
Financial support: Career-related internships or fieldwork, Federal Work-Study, institutionally sponsored loans, and tuition waivers (partial) available. Support available to part-time students. Financial award application deadline: 4/1; financial award applicants required to submit FAFSA.
Dr. Martin Hanlon, Graduate Adviser, 718-997-5510, *E-mail:* martin_hanlon@qc.edu.
Application contact: Mario Caruso, Director of Graduate Admissions, 718-997-5200, *Fax:* 718-997-5193, *E-mail:* graduate_admissions@qc.edu.

■ REGIS UNIVERSITY

School for Professional Studies, Program in Liberal Studies, Denver, CO 80221-1099

AWARDS Adult learning, training and development (MLS, Certificate); language and communication (MLS); licensed professional counselor (MLS); psychology (MLS); social science (MLS); technical communication (Certificate). Part-time and evening/weekend programs available. Postbaccalaureate distance learning degree programs offered (minimal on-campus study).

Students: 400. Average age 35. In 2001, 136 degrees awarded.
Degree requirements: For master's and Certificate, thesis or alternative, research project.
Entrance requirements: For master's, TOEFL, resumé; for Certificate, GMAT, TOEFL, or university-based test (international applicants), resumé. *Application deadline:* For fall admission, 7/15; for spring admission, 10/15. Applications are processed on a rolling basis. *Application fee:* $75. Electronic applications accepted.
Expenses: Contact institution.
Financial support: Federal Work-Study available. Support available to part-time students. Financial award application deadline: 3/15; financial award applicants required to submit FAFSA.
Faculty research: Independent/nonresidential graduate study: new methods and models, adult learning and the capstone experience.
Dr. David Elliot, Chair, 303-964-5315, *Fax:* 303-964-5538.
Application contact: Graduate Admissions, 800-677-9270 Ext. 4080, *Fax:* 303-964-5538, *E-mail:* masters@regis.edu. *Web site:* http://www.regis.edu/spsgraduate/

■ SAN FRANCISCO STATE UNIVERSITY

Graduate Division, College of Behavioral and Social Sciences, Social Science Program (Interdisciplinary Studies), San Francisco, CA 94132-1722

AWARDS MA.

Degree requirements: For master's, thesis, comprehensive exam.
Entrance requirements: For master's, GRE, minimum GPA of 2.5 in last 60 units.
Faculty research: American studies, sociocultural dynamics, political economy, Third World development, criminal justice.

■ SAN JOSE STATE UNIVERSITY

Graduate Studies, College of Social Sciences, Program in Social Sciences, San Jose, CA 95192-0001

AWARDS MA.

Faculty: 14 full-time (5 women), 4 part-time/adjunct (1 woman).
Students: 2 full-time (1 woman), 4 part-time (3 women); includes 1 minority (Hispanic American), 1 international. Average age 38. 9 applicants, 67% accepted. In 2001, 1 degree awarded.
Degree requirements: For master's, comprehensive exam.
Entrance requirements: For master's, minimum GPA of 3.0. *Application deadline:* For fall admission, 6/29; for spring admission, 11/30. Applications are processed on a rolling basis. *Application fee:* $59. Electronic applications accepted.
Expenses: Tuition, nonresident: part-time $246 per unit. Required fees: $678 per semester. Tuition and fees vary according to course load.
Financial support: Applicants required to submit FAFSA.
Hien Duc Do, Chair, 408-924-5740, *Fax:* 408-924-5753.

■ SOUTHERN OREGON UNIVERSITY

Graduate Office, School of Social Science, Health and Physical Education, Department of Psychology, Ashland, OR 97520

AWARDS Applied psychology (MAP); human service-organizational training and development (MA, MS); social science (MA, MS), including professional counseling, psychology. Part-time programs available.

Faculty: 10 full-time (5 women), 2 part-time/adjunct (1 woman).
Students: 37 full-time (27 women), 3 part-time (1 woman); includes 3 minority (1 Asian American or Pacific Islander, 1 Hispanic American, 1 Native American). Average age 33. 41 applicants, 39% accepted, 13 enrolled. In 2001, 6 degrees awarded.
Degree requirements: For master's, thesis, portfolio and oral defense. *Median time to degree:* Master's–2 years full-time.
Entrance requirements: For master's, GRE General Test, minimum GPA of 3.0. *Application deadline:* For fall admission, 2/15 (priority date). Applications are processed on a rolling basis. *Application fee:* $50. Electronic applications accepted.
Expenses: Tuition, state resident: full-time $5,184; part-time $192 per credit. Tuition, nonresident: full-time $9,828; part-time $364 per credit. Required fees: $927. One-time fee: $75 full-time. Full-time tuition and fees vary according to course load, program and reciprocity agreements.
Financial support: Scholarships/grants and unspecified assistantships available. Financial award applicants required to submit FAFSA.
Dr. Josie Wilson, Chair, 541-552-6946, *E-mail:* jwilson@sou.edu.
Application contact: Wri Courtney, Graduate Coordinator, 541-552-6947, *E-mail:* map@sou.edu.

■ STATE UNIVERSITY OF NEW YORK AT BINGHAMTON

Graduate School, School of Education and Human Development, Programs in Social Science, Binghamton, NY 13902-6000

AWARDS MASS, MASS/MSW. Part-time and evening/weekend programs available.

Students: 72 full-time (51 women), 55 part-time (40 women); includes 22 minority (11 African Americans, 4 Asian Americans or Pacific Islanders, 7 Hispanic Americans), 2 international. Average age 34. 79 applicants, 86% accepted, 44 enrolled. In 2001, 42 degrees awarded.
Degree requirements: For master's, thesis.
Entrance requirements: For master's, GRE General Test, TOEFL. *Application deadline:* For fall admission, 4/15 (priority

date); for spring admission, 11/1. Applications are processed on a rolling basis. Electronic applications accepted.
Expenses: Tuition, state resident: full-time $5,100; part-time $213 per credit. Tuition, nonresident: full-time $8,416; part-time $351 per credit. Required fees: $811.
Financial support: In 2001–02, 20 students received support, including 5 fellowships with full and partial tuition reimbursements available (averaging $6,870 per year), 2 research assistantships with full and partial tuition reimbursements available (averaging $4,050 per year), 13 teaching assistantships with full tuition reimbursements available (averaging $4,690 per year); career-related internships or fieldwork, Federal Work-Study, institutionally sponsored loans, and unspecified assistantships also available. Support available to part-time students. Financial award application deadline: 2/15.
Dr. Kevin Wright, Coordinator, 607-777-2245.

■ STATE UNIVERSITY OF NEW YORK COLLEGE AT FREDONIA

Graduate Studies, Interdisciplinary Program in the Social Sciences, Fredonia, NY 14063-1136

AWARDS MA, MS. Part-time and evening/weekend programs available.

Students: 5 full-time (3 women), 44 part-time (25 women); includes 2 minority (both Hispanic Americans), 1 international. 12 applicants, 100% accepted. In 2001, 5 degrees awarded.
Degree requirements: For master's, thesis optional.
Application deadline: For fall admission, 8/5. *Application fee:* $50.
Expenses: Tuition, area resident: Part-time $213 per credit hour. Tuition, state resident: full-time $3,400; part-time $351 per credit hour. Tuition, nonresident: full-time $8,300. Required fees: $825; $30 per credit hour.
Financial support: Research assistantships, teaching assistantships, career-related internships or fieldwork and tuition waivers (full and partial) available. Support available to part-time students. Financial award application deadline: 3/15.

■ STONY BROOK UNIVERSITY, STATE UNIVERSITY OF NEW YORK

School of Professional Development and Continuing Studies, Stony Brook, NY 11794

AWARDS Art and philosophy (Certificate); biology 7-12 (MAT); chemistry-grade 7-12 (MAT); coaching (Certificate); computer integrated engineering (Certificate); cultural studies (Certificate); earth science-grade 7-12 (MAT); educational computing (Certificate); English-grade 7-12 (MAT); environmental/occupational health and safety (Certificate); French-grade 7-12 (MAT); German-grade 7-12 (MAT); human resource management (Certificate); industrial management (Certificate); information systems management (Certificate); Italian-grade 7-12 (MAT); liberal studies (MA); liberal studies online (MA); Long Island regional studies (Certificate); oceanic science (Certificate); operation research (Certificate); physics-grade 7-12 (MAT); Russian-grade 7-12 (MAT); school administration and supervision (Certificate); school district administration (Certificate); social science and the professions (MPS), including labor management, public affairs, waste management; social studies 7-12 (MAT); waste management (Certificate); women's studies (Certificate). Part-time and evening/weekend programs available. Postbaccalaureate distance learning degree programs offered.

Faculty: 1 full-time, 101 part-time/adjunct.
Students: 240 full-time (133 women), 1,307 part-time (868 women); includes 101 minority (43 African Americans, 13 Asian Americans or Pacific Islanders, 43 Hispanic Americans, 2 Native Americans), 9 international. Average age 28. In 2001, 478 master's, 157 other advanced degrees awarded.
Degree requirements: For master's, one foreign language, thesis or alternative.
Application deadline: Applications are processed on a rolling basis. *Application fee:* $50.
Expenses: Tuition, state resident: full-time $5,100; part-time $213 per credit. Tuition, nonresident: full-time $8,416; part-time $351 per credit. Required fees: $496.
Financial support: In 2001–02, 1 fellowship, 7 teaching assistantships were awarded. Research assistantships, career-related internships or fieldwork also available. Support available to part-time students.
Dr. Paul J. Edelson, Dean, 631-632-7052, *Fax:* 631-632-9046, *E-mail:* paul.edelson@sunysb.edu.
Application contact: Sandra Romansky, Director of Admissions and Advisement, 631-632-7050, *Fax:* 631-632-9046, *E-mail:* sandra.romansky@sunysb.edu. *Web site:* http://www.sunysb.edu/spd/

■ SYRACUSE UNIVERSITY

Graduate School, Maxwell School of Citizenship and Public Affairs, Program in Social Sciences, Syracuse, NY 13244-0003

AWARDS MS Sc, PhD.

Students: 47 full-time (32 women), 124 part-time (40 women); includes 15 minority (6 African Americans, 1 Asian American or Pacific Islander, 6 Hispanic Americans, 2 Native Americans), 22 international. Average age 40. 29 applicants, 76% accepted. In 2001, 17 master's, 5 doctorates awarded.
Degree requirements: For doctorate, thesis/dissertation.
Entrance requirements: For master's and doctorate, GRE General Test. *Application deadline:* Applications are processed on a rolling basis. *Application fee:* $50.
Expenses: Tuition: Full-time $15,528; part-time $647 per credit. Required fees: $420; $38 per term. Tuition and fees vary according to program.
Financial support: Fellowships, research assistantships, teaching assistantships, Federal Work-Study and tuition waivers (partial) available.
Robert Bogdan, Director, 315-443-2275.

Find an in-depth description at www.petersons.com/gradchannel.

■ TEXAS A&M INTERNATIONAL UNIVERSITY

Division of Graduate Studies, College of Arts and Humanities, Department of Social Sciences, Laredo, TX 78041-1900

AWARDS Criminal justice (MSCJ); history (MA); political science (MA); public administration (MPAD).

Students: 9 full-time (5 women), 59 part-time (21 women); includes 57 minority (2 Asian Americans or Pacific Islanders, 55 Hispanic Americans), 1 international. In 2001, 12 degrees awarded.
Degree requirements: For master's, thesis (for some programs).
Entrance requirements: For master's, GRE General Test. *Application deadline:* For fall admission, 7/15 (priority date); for spring admission, 11/12. Applications are processed on a rolling basis. *Application fee:* $0.
Expenses: Tuition, state resident: full-time $1,536; part-time $64 per credit. Tuition, nonresident: full-time $6,600; part-time $275 per credit. Required fees: $594; $9 per credit. $33 per term. One-time fee: $10 part-time.
Financial support: Application deadline: 11/1.
Dr. Nasser Momayezi, Interim Dean, 956-326-2460, *Fax:* 956-326-2459, *E-mail:* nmomayezi@tamiu.edu.
Application contact: Veronica Gonzalez, Director of Enrollment Management and School Relations, 956-326-2270, *Fax:* 956-326-2269, *E-mail:* enroll@tamiu.edu.

■ TEXAS A&M UNIVERSITY–COMMERCE

Graduate School, College of Arts and Sciences, Department of History, Commerce, TX 75429-3011

AWARDS History (MA, MS); social sciences (M Ed, MS). Part-time programs available.

Faculty: 2 full-time (1 woman), 1 part-time/adjunct (0 women).
Students: 5 full-time (2 women), 29 part-time (13 women); includes 8 minority (5 African Americans, 2 Hispanic Americans, 1 Native American). Average age 36. 4

Texas A&M University–Commerce (continued)
applicants, 75% accepted. In 2001, 5 degrees awarded.
Degree requirements: For master's, thesis (for some programs), comprehensive exam.
Entrance requirements: For master's, GRE General Test. *Application deadline:* For fall admission, 6/1 (priority date); for spring admission, 11/1 (priority date). Applications are processed on a rolling basis. *Application fee:* $0 ($25 for international students). Electronic applications accepted.
Expenses: Tuition, state resident: full-time $2,221. International tuition: $7,285 full-time.
Financial support: In 2001–02, research assistantships (averaging $7,875 per year), teaching assistantships (averaging $7,875 per year) were awarded. Federal Work-Study, institutionally sponsored loans, and scholarships/grants also available. Financial award application deadline: 5/1; financial award applicants required to submit FAFSA.
Faculty research: American foreign policy, colonial America, Texas politics, medieval England.
Dr. Judy Ford, Interim Head, 903-886-5226, *Fax:* 903-468-3230, *E-mail:* judy_ford@tanu_commerce.edu.
Application contact: Tammi Higginbotham, Graduate Admissions Adviser, 843-886-5167, *Fax:* 843-886-5165, *E-mail:* tammi_higginbotham@tamu-commerce.edu. *Web site:* http://www.beta.tamu-commerce.edu/history/

■ TOWSON UNIVERSITY

Graduate School, Program in Social Science, Towson, MD 21252-0001

AWARDS MS. Part-time and evening/weekend programs available.

Application deadline: Applications are processed on a rolling basis. *Application fee:* $40. Electronic applications accepted.
Expenses: Tuition, state resident: part-time $211 per credit. Tuition, nonresident: part-time $435 per credit. Required fees: $52 per credit.
Financial support: Fellowships, teaching assistantships, career-related internships or fieldwork, Federal Work-Study, and unspecified assistantships available. Support available to part-time students. Financial award application deadline: 4/1; financial award applicants required to submit FAFSA.
Nicole Dombrowski, Director, 410-704-2907, *E-mail:* ndombrowski@towson.edu.
Application contact: 410-704-2501, *Fax:* 410-704-4675, *E-mail:* grads@towson.edu.

■ UNIVERSITY AT BUFFALO, THE STATE UNIVERSITY OF NEW YORK

Graduate School, College of Arts and Sciences, Interdisciplinary Program in Social Sciences, Buffalo, NY 14260

AWARDS MS. Part-time programs available.

Students: 12 full-time (5 women), 7 part-time (6 women); includes 2 minority (1 African American, 1 Hispanic American), 1 international. Average age 38. 7 applicants, 86% accepted. In 2001, 4 degrees awarded.
Degree requirements: For master's, research project.
Entrance requirements: For master's, GRE, TOEFL. *Application deadline:* For fall admission, 5/15 (priority date); for spring admission, 11/15. Applications are processed on a rolling basis. *Application fee:* $35. Electronic applications accepted.
Expenses: Tuition, state resident: full-time $6,118. Tuition, nonresident: full-time $9,434.
Financial support: Fellowships, Federal Work-Study and institutionally sponsored loans available. Financial award application deadline: 2/28; financial award applicants required to submit FAFSA.
Margo A. Willbern, Director, 716-645-3664 Ext. 285, *Fax:* 716-645-3640, *E-mail:* mpenman@acsu.buffalo.edu.
Application contact: Olga Iszkun, Program Secretary, 716-645-3664 Ext. 284, *Fax:* 716-645-3640, *E-mail:* iszkun@acsu.buffalo.edu. *Web site:* http://pluto.fss.buffalo.edu/programs/idp/grad/

■ UNIVERSITY OF CALIFORNIA, IRVINE

Office of Research and Graduate Studies, School of Social Sciences, Irvine, CA 92697

AWARDS MA, PhD.

Faculty: 103.
Students: 238 full-time (126 women), 4 part-time (2 women); includes 49 minority (4 African Americans, 28 Asian Americans or Pacific Islanders, 16 Hispanic Americans, 1 Native American), 45 international. Average age 32. 419 applicants, 35% accepted, 56 enrolled. In 2001, 27 master's, 20 doctorates awarded.
Degree requirements: For doctorate, one foreign language, thesis/dissertation.
Entrance requirements: For master's, minimum GPA of 3.0; for doctorate, GRE General Test. *Application deadline:* For fall and spring admission, 1/15 (priority date); for winter admission, 10/15 (priority date). Applications are processed on a rolling basis. *Application fee:* $60. Electronic applications accepted.
Expenses: Tuition, nonresident: full-time $10,704. Required fees: $8,396. Tuition and fees vary according to course load, program and student level.
Financial support: Fellowships, research assistantships, teaching assistantships, institutionally sponsored loans and tuition waivers (full and partial) available. Financial award application deadline: 3/2; financial award applicants required to submit FAFSA.
Faculty research: Mathematical modeling of perception and cognitive processes, economic analysis of transportation, impact of society's political system on its economy, exploration of authority structures and inequality in society.
William Schonfeld, Dean, 949-824-6801.
Application contact: Ivonne Maldonado, Graduate Counselor, 949-824-4074, *Fax:* 949-824-3548, *E-mail:* immaldon@uci.edu. *Web site:* http://www.socsci.uci.edu/

■ UNIVERSITY OF CALIFORNIA, SANTA CRUZ

Division of Graduate Studies, Division of Humanities, Program in the History of Consciousness, Santa Cruz, CA 95064

AWARDS PhD.

Faculty: 9 full-time.
Students: 49 full-time (37 women); includes 17 minority (3 African Americans, 8 Asian Americans or Pacific Islanders, 4 Hispanic Americans, 2 Native Americans), 3 international. 175 applicants, 14% accepted. In 2001, 5 degrees awarded.
Degree requirements: For doctorate, one foreign language, thesis/dissertation, qualifying exam. *Median time to degree:* Doctorate–8 years full-time.
Application deadline: For fall admission, 12/15. *Application fee:* $40.
Expenses: Tuition: Full-time $19,857.
Financial support: Fellowships, teaching assistantships, Federal Work-Study and institutionally sponsored loans available. Financial award application deadline: 12/15.
Faculty research: Interdisciplinary humanities and social sciences, political theory, cultural theory, feminist studies, literary theory.
Dr. Gary Lease, Chairperson, 831-459-4310, *E-mail:* rehbock@cats.ucsc.edu.
Application contact: Graduate Admissions, 831-459-2301. *Web site:* http://www.ucsc.edu/

■ UNIVERSITY OF CHICAGO

Division of Social Sciences, Committee on Social Thought, Chicago, IL 60637-1513

AWARDS PhD.

Students: 65.
Degree requirements: For doctorate, one foreign language, thesis/dissertation, exam.
Entrance requirements: For doctorate, GRE General Test, TOEFL. *Application deadline:* For fall admission, 12/28. *Application fee:* $55. Electronic applications accepted.
Expenses: Tuition: Full-time $16,548.
Financial support: Fellowships, teaching assistantships, Federal Work-Study and

institutionally sponsored loans available. Financial award application deadline: 12/28.
Prof. Robert Pippin, Chair, 773-702-8410.
Application contact: Office of the Dean of Students, 773-702-8415.

■ UNIVERSITY OF CHICAGO

Division of Social Sciences, Master of Arts Program in the Social Sciences, Chicago, IL 60637-1513

AWARDS AM. Part-time programs available.

Students: 163.
Degree requirements: For master's, thesis.
Entrance requirements: For master's, GRE General Test, TOEFL. *Application deadline:* For fall admission, 12/28. *Application fee:* $55. Electronic applications accepted.
Expenses: Tuition: Full-time $16,548.
Financial support: Fellowships, Federal Work-Study and institutionally sponsored loans available. Financial award application deadline: 12/28; financial award applicants required to submit FAFSA.
Prof. John J. MacAloon, Director, 773-702-8316.
Application contact: Office of the Dean of Students, 773-702-8415.

Find an in-depth description at www.petersons.com/gradchannel.

■ UNIVERSITY OF COLORADO AT DENVER

Graduate School, College of Liberal Arts and Sciences, Program in Social Sciences, Denver, CO 80217-3364

AWARDS MSS. Part-time and evening/weekend programs available.

Students: 4 full-time (all women), 30 part-time (20 women); includes 11 minority (2 African Americans, 2 Asian Americans or Pacific Islanders, 6 Hispanic Americans, 1 Native American), 1 international. Average age 37. 3 applicants, 100% accepted, 2 enrolled. In 2001, 9 degrees awarded.
Degree requirements: For master's, thesis or alternative.
Entrance requirements: For master's, GRE General Test, 18 hours of course work in social science. *Application deadline:* For fall admission, 5/15; for spring admission, 10/15. Applications are processed on a rolling basis. *Application fee:* $50 ($60 for international students). Electronic applications accepted.
Expenses: Tuition, state resident: full-time $3,284; part-time $198 per credit hour. Tuition, nonresident: full-time $13,380; part-time $802 per credit hour. Required fees: $444; $222 per semester.
Financial support: Research assistantships, teaching assistantships, Federal Work-Study available. Financial award application deadline: 3/1; financial award applicants required to submit FAFSA.
Mitchell Aboulafia, Director, 303-556-8558, *Fax:* 303-556-6041, *E-mail:* maboulaf@carbon.cudenver.edu.
Application contact: Jana Everett, Associate Dean, 303-556-3513, *Fax:* 303-556-4681, *E-mail:* jana.everett@cudenver.edu.

■ UNIVERSITY OF ILLINOIS AT SPRINGFIELD

Graduate Programs, College of Education and Human Services, Program in Human Services, Springfield, IL 62703-5404

AWARDS Alcoholism and substance abuse (MA); child and family studies (MA); gerontology (MA); social services administration (MA).

Faculty: 7 full-time (3 women), 10 part-time/adjunct (7 women).
Students: 44 full-time (32 women), 109 part-time (79 women); includes 32 minority (29 African Americans, 1 Asian American or Pacific Islander, 1 Hispanic American, 1 Native American), 2 international. Average age 37. 55 applicants, 85% accepted, 38 enrolled. In 2001, 16 degrees awarded.
Expenses: Tuition, state resident: full-time $2,680. Tuition, nonresident: full-time $8,064. Required fees: $626. One-time fee: $626.
Financial support: In 2001–02, 71 students received support, including 9 research assistantships (averaging $6,300 per year)
Rachell Anderson, Director, 217-206-7335.

■ UNIVERSITY OF MICHIGAN

School of Social Work, Interdepartmental Program in Social Work and Social Science, Ann Arbor, MI 48109

AWARDS PhD. Offered through the Horace H. Rackham School of Graduate Studies.

Faculty: 51 full-time (23 women), 47 part-time/adjunct (32 women).
Students: 81; includes 25 minority (12 African Americans, 7 Asian Americans or Pacific Islanders, 5 Hispanic Americans, 1 Native American), 8 international. Average age 31. 120 applicants, 6% accepted. In 2001, 9 degrees awarded.
Degree requirements: For doctorate, thesis/dissertation, oral defense of dissertation, preliminary exam.
Entrance requirements: For doctorate, GRE General Test. *Application deadline:* For fall admission, 1/2. *Application fee:* $55.
Financial support: In 2001–02, 59 students received support, including 34 fellowships with full tuition reimbursements available (averaging $15,000 per year), 19 research assistantships with full tuition reimbursements available (averaging $15,000 per year), 6 teaching assistantships with full tuition reimbursements available (averaging $18,546 per year); career-related internships or fieldwork, Federal Work-Study, scholarships/grants, traineeships, and tuition waivers (full and partial) also available. Financial award application deadline: 1/2.
Faculty research: Substance abuse, child welfare, mental health, poverty, aging. *Total annual research expenditures:* $7.1 million.
Dr. David J. Tucker, Director, 734-763-5768, *Fax:* 734-615-3192, *E-mail:* celdjt@umich.edu.
Application contact: Alfreda Onimo, Program Office, 734-763-5768, *Fax:* 734-615-3192, *E-mail:* ssw.phd.info@umich.edu. *Web site:* http://www.umich.edu/~socwk/

■ THE UNIVERSITY OF TEXAS AT TYLER

Graduate Studies, College of Arts and Sciences, Department of Social Sciences, Tyler, TX 75799-0001

AWARDS Criminal justice (MAIS, MS); economics (MAIS); political science (MA, MAIS, MAT); public administration (MPA); sociology (MAIS, MAT, MS). Part-time and evening/weekend programs available. Postbaccalaureate distance learning degree programs offered.

Faculty: 14 full-time (1 woman).
Students: 13 full-time (9 women), 54 part-time (34 women); includes 16 minority (14 African Americans, 1 Hispanic American, 1 Native American), 1 international. Average age 35. 8 applicants, 100% accepted, 8 enrolled. In 2001, 10 degrees awarded.
Degree requirements: For master's, thesis (for some programs), comprehensive exam.
Entrance requirements: For master's, GRE General Test, minimum GPA of 3.0. *Application deadline:* Applications are processed on a rolling basis. *Application fee:* $0.
Expenses: Tuition, state resident: part-time $44 per credit hour. Tuition, nonresident: part-time $262 per credit hour. Required fees: $58 per credit hour. $76 per semester.
Financial support: Teaching assistantships, career-related internships or fieldwork, Federal Work-Study, and scholarships/grants available. Support available to part-time students. Financial award application deadline: 7/1; financial award applicants required to submit FAFSA.
Faculty research: Urban segregation, minority business, violent crime, gender discrimination, Third World agriculture production.
Dr. Barbara L. Hart, Chair, 903-566-7426, *Fax:* 903-565-5537, *E-mail:* bhart@mail.uttyl.edu.
Application contact: Carol A. Hodge, Office of Graduate Studies, 903-566-5642, *Fax:* 903-566-7068, *E-mail:* chodge@mail.uttly.edu.

Sociology, Anthropology, and Archaeology

ANTHROPOLOGY

■ AMERICAN UNIVERSITY

College of Arts and Sciences, Department of Anthropology, Washington, DC 20016-8001

AWARDS Anthropology (MA, PhD); applied anthropology (MA). Part-time and evening/weekend programs available.

Faculty: 11 full-time (7 women), 3 part-time/adjunct (1 woman).
Students: 22 full-time (14 women), 35 part-time (28 women); includes 12 minority (8 African Americans, 1 Asian American or Pacific Islander, 2 Hispanic Americans, 1 Native American), 6 international. Average age 32. 59 applicants, 71% accepted, 16 enrolled. In 2001, 10 master's, 3 doctorates awarded. Terminal master's awarded for partial completion of doctoral program.
Degree requirements: For master's, thesis or alternative, comprehensive exam; for doctorate, 2 foreign languages, thesis/dissertation, comprehensive exam.
Entrance requirements: For master's and doctorate, GRE, sample of written work. *Application deadline:* For fall admission, 2/1; for spring admission, 10/1. *Application fee:* $50.
Expenses: Tuition: Full-time $14,274; part-time $793 per credit. Required fees: $290. Tuition and fees vary according to program.
Financial support: In 2001–02, 2 fellowships with full and partial tuition reimbursements, 11 teaching assistantships with full and partial tuition reimbursements were awarded. Research assistantships with full and partial tuition reimbursements, career-related internships or fieldwork, Federal Work-Study, institutionally sponsored loans, unspecified assistantships, and administrative fellowships also available. Support available to part-time students. Financial award application deadline: 1/15.
Faculty research: Poverty and race, lesbian and gay studies, class and culture, developing countries, societies and the Americas.
Dr. William Leap, Chair, 202-885-1831, *Fax:* 202-885-1837.
Application contact: Dr. Geoffrey Burkhart, Chair, Graduate Studies Committee, 202-885-1849, *Fax:* 202-885-1837.

■ ARIZONA STATE UNIVERSITY

Graduate College, College of Liberal [illegible]rts and Sciences, Department of [illegible]ology, Tempe, AZ 85287

[illegible], MA/MS.

Degree requirements: For master's, thesis or alternative; for doctorate, thesis/dissertation.
Entrance requirements: For master's and doctorate, GRE.
Faculty research: Indian religion and ritual oratory, dental and skeletal studies, ceramic and pollen analysis.

■ BALL STATE UNIVERSITY

Graduate School, College of Sciences and Humanities, Department of Anthropology, Muncie, IN 47306-1099

AWARDS MA.

Faculty: 11.
Students: 9 full-time (4 women), 6 part-time (4 women). Average age 37. 20 applicants, 90% accepted. In 2001, 4 degrees awarded.
Entrance requirements: For master's, GRE General Test, resumé. *Application fee:* $25 ($35 for international students).
Expenses: Tuition, state resident: full-time $4,068; part-time $2,542. Tuition, nonresident: full-time $10,944; part-time $6,462. Required fees: $1,000; $500 per term.
Financial support: In 2001–02, 7 teaching assistantships with full tuition reimbursements (averaging $6,896 per year) were awarded; research assistantships with full tuition reimbursements Financial award application deadline: 3/1.
Dr. Paul Wohtt, Chairman, 765-285-1575, *Fax:* 765-285-2163. *Web site:* http://www.bsu.edu/csh/anthro/

■ BETHEL COLLEGE

Center for Graduate and Continuing Studies, Department of Anthropology and Sociology, St. Paul, MN 55112-6999

AWARDS MA. Evening/weekend programs available.

Students: 13 full-time (11 women), 1 (woman) part-time.
Degree requirements: For master's, thesis.
Application deadline: Applications are processed on a rolling basis. *Application fee:* $25.
Expenses: Tuition: Part-time $325 per credit. One-time fee: $125 full-time.
Financial support: Institutionally sponsored loans and scholarships/grants available. Financial award applicants required to submit FAFSA.
Dr. Harley Schreck, Chair, 651-638-6104, *Fax:* 651-635-1464, *E-mail:* h-schreck@bethel.edu.
Application contact: Vanessa Beaudry, Graduate Admissions Advisor, 651-635-8012, *Fax:* 651-635-1464, *E-mail:* c-pritchard@bethel.edu.

■ BOSTON UNIVERSITY

Graduate School of Arts and Sciences, Department of Anthropology, Boston, MA 02215

AWARDS MA, PhD.

Students: 24 full-time (16 women), 2 part-time (both women), 7 international. Average age 32. 68 applicants, 18% accepted, 4 enrolled. In 2001, 8 master's, 2 doctorates awarded. Terminal master's awarded for partial completion of doctoral program.
Degree requirements: For master's, one foreign language, thesis or alternative, registration; for doctorate, one foreign language, thesis/dissertation, registration.
Entrance requirements: For master's and doctorate, GRE General Test, TOEFL, 2 letters of recommendation. *Application deadline:* For fall admission, 1/15. *Application fee:* $60.
Expenses: Tuition: Full-time $25,872; part-time $340 per credit. Required fees: $40 per semester. Part-time tuition and fees vary according to class time, course level and program.
Financial support: In 2001–02, 22 students received support, including 6 fellowships with full tuition reimbursements available, 5 teaching assistantships with full tuition reimbursements available (averaging $12,500 per year); Federal Work-Study and unspecified assistantships also available. Support available to part-time students. Financial award application deadline: 1/15; financial award applicants required to submit FAFSA.
Thomas Barfield, Chairman, 617-353-2195, *Fax:* 617-353-2610, *E-mail:* barfield@bu.edu.
Application contact: Janet R. O'Neil, Administrator, 617-353-2195, *E-mail:* oneil@bu.edu. *Web site:* http://www.bu.edu/ANTHROP/

■ BRANDEIS UNIVERSITY

Graduate School of Arts and Sciences, Department of Anthropology, Waltham, MA 02454-9110

AWARDS Anthropology (MA, PhD); anthropology and women's studies (MA). Part-time programs available.

Faculty: 8 full-time (3 women).
Students: Average age 34. 35 applicants, 17% accepted. In 2001, 3 master's, 2 doctorates awarded. Terminal master's awarded for partial completion of doctoral program.

Degree requirements: For master's, thesis or alternative; for doctorate, one foreign language, thesis/dissertation, general exam. *Median time to degree:* Master's–3 years full-time; doctorate–9 years full-time.
Entrance requirements: For master's and doctorate, GRE General Test (suggested), sample of written work, resumé, letters of recommendation. *Application deadline:* For fall admission, 1/15. Applications are processed on a rolling basis. *Application fee:* $60. Electronic applications accepted.
Expenses: Tuition: Full-time $27,392. Required fees: $35.
Financial support: In 2001–02, 18 students received support, including 11 fellowships with full tuition reimbursements available (averaging $10,300 per year), 15 teaching assistantships (averaging $2,300 per year); research assistantships, career-related internships or fieldwork, institutionally sponsored loans, scholarships/grants, and tuition waivers (full and partial) also available. Support available to part-time students. Financial award application deadline: 4/15; financial award applicants required to submit CSS PROFILE or FAFSA.
Faculty research: Technology and culture, comparative methods, economic anthropology, gender studies, semiotic anthropology. *Total annual research expenditures:* $75,000.
Dr. Robert Hunt, Professor and Graduate Advising Head, 781-736-2210, *Fax:* 781-736-2232, *E-mail:* anthropology@brandeis.edu. *Web site:* http://www.brandeis.edu/anthro/grad.html

■ BRIGHAM YOUNG UNIVERSITY

Graduate Studies, College of Family, Home, and Social Sciences, Department of Anthropology, Provo, UT 84602-1001

AWARDS MA.

Faculty: 10 full-time (1 woman), 1 (woman) part-time/adjunct.
Students: 7 full-time (4 women), 8 part-time (3 women); includes 4 minority (2 Asian Americans or Pacific Islanders, 1 Hispanic American, 1 Native American). Average age 24. 7 applicants, 71% accepted. In 2001, 4 degrees awarded.
Degree requirements: For master's, thesis.
Entrance requirements: For master's, GRE General Test, minimum GPA of 3.0 in last 60 hours. *Application deadline:* For fall admission, 2/1. *Application fee:* $50.
Expenses: Tuition: Full-time $3,860; part-time $214 per hour.
Financial support: In 2001–02, 7 students received support, including 5 research assistantships (averaging $2,500 per year), 4 teaching assistantships (averaging $3,200 per year); fellowships, career-related internships or fieldwork, institutionally sponsored loans, and tuition waivers (partial) also available. Financial award application deadline: 3/1; financial award applicants required to submit FAFSA.
Faculty research: Archaeology of the Southwest, Near East, and Mesoamerica; Mayan glyphs. *Total annual research expenditures:* $50,000.
Dr. Joel C. Janetski, Chair, 801-422-3058, *Fax:* 801-378-9368, *E-mail:* joel_janetski@byu.edu.
Application contact: Dr. Stephen D. Houston, Graduate Coordinator, 801-422-8966, *Fax:* 801-378-9368, *E-mail:* sdh@email.byu.edu. *Web site:* http://www.byu.edu/acd1/fhsswww/department/anthro/anthro.htm

■ BROWN UNIVERSITY

Graduate School, Department of Anthropology, Providence, RI 02912

AWARDS Anthropology (AM, PhD); old world archaeology and art (AM, PhD).

Degree requirements: For doctorate, one foreign language, thesis/dissertation, preliminary exam.

■ CALIFORNIA INSTITUTE OF INTEGRAL STUDIES

Graduate Programs, School of Consciousness and Transformation, San Francisco, CA 94103

AWARDS Cultural anthropology and social transformation (MA); East-West psychology (MA, PhD); philosophy and religion (MA, PhD), including Asian and comparative studies, philosophy, cosmology, and consciousness, women's spirituality; social and cultural anthropology (PhD); transformative learning and change (PhD). Part-time and evening/weekend programs available. Postbaccalaureate distance learning degree programs offered (minimal on-campus study).

Faculty: 20 full-time (9 women), 72 part-time/adjunct (35 women).
Students: 60 full-time, 143 part-time. 157 applicants, 78% accepted, 85 enrolled. In 2001, 58 master's, 21 doctorates awarded. Terminal master's awarded for partial completion of doctoral program.
Degree requirements: For master's, comprehensive exam; for doctorate, thesis/dissertation, comprehensive exam.
Entrance requirements: For master's, TOEFL, minimum GPA of 3.0; for doctorate, TOEFL, master's degree. *Application deadline:* For fall admission, 3/15 (priority date); for spring admission, 10/15 (priority date). Applications are processed on a rolling basis. *Application fee:* $65.
Expenses: Tuition: Full-time $10,890; part-time $605 per unit. Tuition and fees vary according to degree level.
Financial support: Career-related internships or fieldwork, Federal Work-Study, institutionally sponsored loans, and scholarships/grants available. Support available to part-time students. Financial award application deadline: 6/15; financial award applicants required to submit FAFSA.
Faculty research: Altered states of consciousness, dreams, cosmology.
Daniel Deslaurier, Director, 415-575-6260, *Fax:* 415-575-1264, *E-mail:* danield@ciis.edu.
Application contact: Gregory E. Canada, Director of Admissions, 415-575-6155, *Fax:* 415-575-1268, *E-mail:* gregc@ciis.edu. *Web site:* http://www.ciis.edu/

Find an in-depth description at www.petersons.com/gradchannel.

■ CALIFORNIA STATE UNIVERSITY, BAKERSFIELD

Division of Graduate Studies and Research, School of Humanities and Social Sciences, Program in Anthropology, Bakersfield, CA 93311-1099

AWARDS MA.

Entrance requirements: For master's, GRE.
Faculty research: Human services, social science teaching. *Web site:* http://www.csub.edu/SocAnth/MastersAnthro.html/

■ CALIFORNIA STATE UNIVERSITY, CHICO

Graduate School, College of Behavioral and Social Sciences, Department of Anthropology, Chico, CA 95929-0722

AWARDS Museum studies (MA).

Students: 10 full-time, 16 part-time; includes 3 minority (1 Asian American or Pacific Islander, 2 Hispanic Americans). 17 applicants, 47% accepted, 5 enrolled. In 2001, 6 degrees awarded.
Degree requirements: For master's, thesis or alternative, oral exam.
Entrance requirements: For master's, GRE General Test, GPA of 3.0 in last 60 semester units, letters of recommendation (2) minimum. *Application deadline:* For fall admission, 4/1. Applications are processed on a rolling basis. *Application fee:* $55. Electronic applications accepted.
Expenses: Tuition, state resident: full-time $2,148. Tuition, nonresident: full-time $6,576.
Financial support: Fellowships, career-related internships or fieldwork available.
Dr. Frank Bayham, Chair, 530-898-6192.
Application contact: Dr. Turhon Murad, Graduate Coordinator, 530-898-4300.

■ CALIFORNIA STATE UNIVERSITY, FULLERTON

Graduate Studies, College of Humanities and Social Sciences, Department of Anthropology, Fullerton, CA 92834-9480

AWARDS MA. Part-time programs available.

Faculty: 10 full-time (6 women), 10 part-time/adjunct.
Students: 24 full-time (19 women), 31 part-time (25 women); includes 13 minority (1 African American, 3 Asian Americans or Pacific Islanders, 9 Hispanic Americans), 1 international. Average age 35. 31 applicants, 74% accepted, 15 enrolled. In 2001, 25 degrees awarded.
Degree requirements: For master's, project or thesis.
Entrance requirements: For master's, minimum GPA of 2.5 in last 60 hours. *Application fee:* $55.
Expenses: Tuition, nonresident: part-time $246 per unit. Required fees: $964.
Financial support: Career-related internships or fieldwork, Federal Work-Study, institutionally sponsored loans, and scholarships/grants available. Support available to part-time students. Financial award application deadline: 3/1.
Dr. Susan Parman, Chair, 714-278-3626.

■ CALIFORNIA STATE UNIVERSITY, HAYWARD

Academic Programs and Graduate Studies, School of Arts, Letters, and Social Sciences, Department of Anthropology, Hayward, CA 94542-3000

AWARDS MA. Part-time programs available.

Students: 11 full-time (9 women), 12 part-time (5 women); includes 4 minority (2 African Americans, 1 Asian American or Pacific Islander, 1 Hispanic American), 1 international. 12 applicants, 67% accepted. In 2001, 6 degrees awarded.
Degree requirements: For master's, one foreign language, thesis, comprehensive exam.
Entrance requirements: For master's, minimum GPA of 2.5 during previous 2 years. *Application deadline:* For fall admission, 6/15; for winter admission, 10/27; for spring admission, 1/5. Applications are processed on a rolling basis. *Application fee:* $55. Electronic applications accepted.
Expenses: Tuition, nonresident: part-time $164 per unit. Required fees: $405 per semester.
Financial support: Career-related internships or fieldwork, Federal Work-Study, and institutionally sponsored loans available. Support available to part-time students. Financial award application deadline: 3/1.
Dr. Laurie Price, Chair, 510-885-3168.
Application contact: Jennifer Cason, Graduate Program Coordinator/ Operations Analyst, 510-885-3286, *Fax:* 510-885-4777, *E-mail:* jcason@csuhayward.edu.

■ CALIFORNIA STATE UNIVERSITY, LONG BEACH

Graduate Studies, College of Liberal Arts, Department of Anthropology, Long Beach, CA 90840

AWARDS MA. Part-time programs available.

Faculty: 6 full-time (1 woman), 5 part-time/adjunct (2 women).
Students: 11 full-time (4 women), 12 part-time (7 women); includes 4 minority (3 Hispanic Americans, 1 Native American), 2 international. Average age 29. 24 applicants, 54% accepted. In 2001, 1 degree awarded.
Degree requirements: For master's, one foreign language.
Application deadline: For fall admission, 8/1; for spring admission, 12/1. Applications are processed on a rolling basis. *Application fee:* $55. Electronic applications accepted.
Financial support: Research assistantships, Federal Work-Study, institutionally sponsored loans, and scholarships/grants available. Financial award application deadline: 3/2.
Faculty research: Archeology of California, Fiji, and Ireland; cultures of American Indian and Mexico.
Dr. Marcus Young Owl, Chair, 562-985-5171, *Fax:* 562-985-4379, *E-mail:* youngowl@csulb.edu.
Application contact: Dr. Pamela Bunte, Graduate Coordinator, 562-985-8179, *Fax:* 562-985-4379, *E-mail:* pbunte@csulb.edu.

■ CALIFORNIA STATE UNIVERSITY, LOS ANGELES

Graduate Studies, College of Natural and Social Sciences, Department of Anthropology, Los Angeles, CA 90032-8530

AWARDS MA. Part-time and evening/weekend programs available.

Faculty: 7 full-time, 6 part-time/adjunct.
Students: 8 full-time (7 women), 27 part-time (22 women); includes 11 minority (1 African American, 1 Asian American or Pacific Islander, 9 Hispanic Americans). In 2001, 7 degrees awarded.
Degree requirements: For master's, one foreign language.
Entrance requirements: For master's, TOEFL. *Application deadline:* For fall admission, 6/30; for spring admission, 2/1. Applications are processed on a rolling basis. *Application fee:* $55.
Expenses: Tuition, nonresident: part-time $164 per unit.
Financial support: Federal Work-Study available. Support available to part-time students. Financial award application deadline: 3/1.
Faculty research: Archaeology, folklore, petroglyphs, symbolism, medical anthropology.
Dr. Norma Klein, Chair, 323-343-2440.

■ CALIFORNIA STATE UNIVERSITY, NORTHRIDGE

Graduate Studies, College of Social and Behavioral Sciences, Department of Anthropology, Northridge, CA 91330

AWARDS MA.

Faculty: 8 full-time, 14 part-time/adjunct.
Students: 7 full-time (1 woman), 17 part-time (13 women); includes 3 minority (all Hispanic Americans), 2 international. Average age 35. 14 applicants, 93% accepted, 5 enrolled. In 2001, 9 degrees awarded.
Degree requirements: For master's, thesis or alternative.
Entrance requirements: For master's, TOEFL, GRE General Test or minimum GPA of 3.0. *Application deadline:* For fall admission, 11/30. *Application fee:* $55.
Expenses: Tuition, nonresident: part-time $631 per semester. Required fees: $246 per unit.
Financial support: Career-related internships or fieldwork, Federal Work-Study, and institutionally sponsored loans available. Financial award application deadline: 3/1.
Dr. Antonio Gilman, Chair, 818-677-3331.
Application contact: Dr. Keith Morton, Graduate Adviser, 818-677-3331.

■ CALIFORNIA STATE UNIVERSITY, SACRAMENTO

Graduate Studies, College of Social Sciences and Interdisciplinary Studies, Department of Anthropology, Sacramento, CA 95819-6048

AWARDS MA. Part-time programs available.

Students: 7 full-time (3 women), 24 part-time (15 women); includes 5 minority (3 Asian Americans or Pacific Islanders, 1 Hispanic American, 1 Native American).
Degree requirements: For master's, thesis, departmental qualifying exam, writing proficiency exam.
Entrance requirements: For master's, TOEFL, minimum GPA of 3.0 during previous 2 years. *Application deadline:* For fall admission, 4/15; for spring admission, 11/1. *Application fee:* $55.
Expenses: Tuition, state resident: full-time $1,965; part-time $668 per semester. Tuition, nonresident: part-time $246 per unit.
Financial support: Career-related internships or fieldwork and Federal Work-Study available. Support available to part-time students. Financial award application deadline: 3/1.
Dr. Jerry Johnson, Chair, 916-278-6452.
Application contact: Dr. Mark Basgall, Information Contact, 916-278-5330.

■ CASE WESTERN RESERVE UNIVERSITY

Frances Payne Bolton School of Nursing and Department of Anthropology, Nursing/Anthropology Program, Cleveland, OH 44106

AWARDS MSN/MA.

■ CASE WESTERN RESERVE UNIVERSITY

School of Graduate Studies, Department of Anthropology, Cleveland, OH 44106

AWARDS Anthropology (MA, PhD). Part-time programs available. Terminal master's awarded for partial completion of doctoral program.

Degree requirements: For master's, thesis optional; for doctorate, one foreign language, thesis/dissertation.
Entrance requirements: For master's and doctorate, GRE General Test, TOEFL.
Faculty research: Medical anthropology, psychological anthropology, cross-cultural aging, physical anthropology, international health. *Web site:* http://www.cwru.edu/CWRU/Dept/Artsci/anth/anth.html

■ THE CATHOLIC UNIVERSITY OF AMERICA

School of Arts and Sciences, Department of Anthropology, Washington, DC 20064

AWARDS MA, PhD. Part-time and evening/weekend programs available.

Faculty: 5 full-time (3 women).
Students: 4 full-time (1 woman), 26 part-time (12 women); includes 5 minority (all Hispanic Americans), 7 international. Average age 39. 13 applicants, 69% accepted, 7 enrolled. Terminal master's awarded for partial completion of doctoral program.
Degree requirements: For master's and doctorate, one foreign language, thesis/dissertation, comprehensive exam.
Entrance requirements: For master's and doctorate, GRE General Test, MAT, TOEFL. *Application deadline:* For fall admission, 8/1 (priority date); for spring admission, 12/1. Applications are processed on a rolling basis. *Application fee:* $55. Electronic applications accepted.
Expenses: Tuition: Full-time $20,050; part-time $770 per credit. Required fees: $430 per term. Tuition and fees vary according to program.
Financial support: Fellowships, research assistantships, teaching assistantships, career-related internships or fieldwork, Federal Work-Study, institutionally sponsored loans, and tuition waivers (full and partial) available. Support available to part-time students. Financial award application deadline: 2/1.
Faculty research: Medical and applied anthropology, eastern North American and South American archaeology, applied anthropology, Latin American studies, ecological anthropology.
Dr. Jon Anderson, Chair, 202-319-5080, *Fax:* 202-319-4782.

■ CITY COLLEGE OF THE CITY UNIVERSITY OF NEW YORK

Graduate School, College of Liberal Arts and Science, Division of Social Science, Department of Anthropology, New York, NY 10031-9198

AWARDS Applied urban anthropology (MA).

Students: 11.
Degree requirements: For master's, one foreign language, thesis.
Entrance requirements: For master's, TOEFL. *Application deadline:* For fall admission, 5/1; for spring admission, 12/1. *Application fee:* $40.
Expenses: Tuition, state resident: part-time $185 per credit. Tuition, nonresident: part-time $320 per credit. Required fees: $43 per term.
Financial support: Career-related internships or fieldwork, Federal Work-Study, institutionally sponsored loans, and unspecified assistantships available.
Faculty research: Education, industry and work, nutrition, aging, cultural expressions.
Dr. Carole Laderman, Chairperson, 212-650-7359.
Application contact: June Nash, Adviser, 212-650-6609.

■ CLAREMONT GRADUATE UNIVERSITY

Graduate Programs, School of Educational Studies, Claremont, CA 91711-6160

AWARDS Comparative educational studies (MA, PhD); education policy issues (MA, PhD); higher education (MA, PhD); human development (MA, PhD); linguistics and anthropology (MA, PhD); organization and administration (PhD); public school administration (MA, PhD); reading and language development (MA, PhD); teacher education (MA, PhD); teaching and learning (MA, PhD); teaching/learning process (PhD); urban education administration (MA, PhD). Part-time programs available.

Faculty: 16 full-time (8 women), 4 part-time/adjunct (3 women).
Students: 156 full-time (113 women), 250 part-time (181 women); includes 191 minority (46 African Americans, 38 Asian Americans or Pacific Islanders, 104 Hispanic Americans, 3 Native Americans), 11 international. Average age 35. In 2001, 124 master's, 31 doctorates awarded. Terminal master's awarded for partial completion of doctoral program.
Degree requirements: For master's, thesis or alternative, comprehensive exam (for some programs); for doctorate, thesis/dissertation, comprehensive exam.
Entrance requirements: For master's and doctorate, GRE General Test. *Application deadline:* For fall admission, 2/15 (priority date). Applications are processed on a rolling basis. *Application fee:* $50. Electronic applications accepted.
Expenses: Tuition: Full-time $22,984; part-time $1,000 per unit. Required fees: $160; $80 per semester.
Financial support: Fellowships, research assistantships, Federal Work-Study and institutionally sponsored loans available. Support available to part-time students. Financial award application deadline: 2/15; financial award applicants required to submit FAFSA.
Faculty research: Education administration, K–12 and higher education, multicultural education, education policy, diversity in higher education, faculty issues.
David Drew, Dean, 909-621-8075, *Fax:* 909-621-8734, *E-mail:* david.drew@cgu.edu.
Application contact: Janet Alonzo, Secretary, 909-621-8075, *Fax:* 909-621-8734, *E-mail:* educ@cgu.edu. *Web site:* http://www.cgu.edu/ces/

Find an in-depth description at www.petersons.com/gradchannel.

■ THE COLLEGE OF WILLIAM AND MARY

Faculty of Arts and Sciences, Department of Anthropology, Williamsburg, VA 23187-8795

AWARDS MA, PhD. Part-time programs available.

Faculty: 17 full-time (8 women), 1 part-time/adjunct (0 women).
Students: 18 full-time (8 women), 1 international. Average age 30. 40 applicants, 28% accepted. In 2001, 11 degrees awarded.
Degree requirements: For master's and doctorate, thesis/dissertation, fieldwork.
Entrance requirements: For master's, previous course work in anthropology or history; for doctorate, previous coursework in anthropology. *Application deadline:* For fall admission, 3/1. *Application fee:* $30.
Expenses: Tuition, state resident: full-time $3,262; part-time $175 per credit hour. Tuition, nonresident: full-time $14,768; part-time $550 per credit hour. Required fees: $2,478.
Financial support: In 2001–02, 4 research assistantships with full tuition reimbursements (averaging $8,000 per year), 5 teaching assistantships with full tuition reimbursements (averaging $8,000 per year) were awarded. Fellowships, career-related internships or fieldwork also available. Financial award applicants required to submit FAFSA.
Faculty research: Historical archaeology, comparative colonialism. *Total annual research expenditures:* $1 million.
Dr. Mary Voigt, Chair, 757-221-1055.

The College of William and Mary (continued)

Application contact: Kathleen Bragdon, Director of Graduate Studies, 757-221-1067, *E-mail:* bkbrag@wm.edu.

■ COLORADO STATE UNIVERSITY

Graduate School, College of Liberal Arts, Department of Anthropology, Fort Collins, CO 80523-0015

AWARDS MA. Part-time programs available.

Faculty: 12 full-time (7 women).
Students: 16 full-time (12 women), 14 part-time (6 women). Average age 31. 29 applicants, 66% accepted, 8 enrolled. In 2001, 5 degrees awarded.
Degree requirements: For master's, thesis optional.
Entrance requirements: For master's, GRE General Test, TOEFL, minimum GPA of 3.0. *Application deadline:* For fall admission, 2/15. Applications are processed on a rolling basis. *Application fee:* $30. Electronic applications accepted.
Expenses: Tuition, state resident: full-time $2,880; part-time $160 per credit. Tuition, nonresident: full-time $11,412; part-time $634 per credit. Required fees: $750; $34 per credit.
Financial support: In 2001–02, 7 students received support, including 5 teaching assistantships with full tuition reimbursements available (averaging $9,261 per year); fellowships, research assistantships, career-related internships or fieldwork and Federal Work-Study also available.
Faculty research: Archaeology, cultural anthropology, biological anthropology, human ecology, political economy. *Total annual research expenditures:* $80,000.
Dr. Jeffrey L. Eighmy, Chair, 970-491-5447, *Fax:* 970-491-7597, *E-mail:* eighmy@lamar.colostate.edu.
Application contact: Ann L. Magennis, Associate Professor, 970-491-5966, *Fax:* 970-491-7597, *E-mail:* magennis@lamar.colostate.edu. *Web site:* http://www.colostate.edu/Dept/Anthropology/

■ COLUMBIA UNIVERSITY

Graduate School of Arts and Sciences, Division of Social Sciences, Department of Anthropology, New York, NY 10027

AWARDS M Phil, MA, PhD, JD/MA, JD/PhD. Part-time programs available.

Faculty: 32 full-time, 3 part-time/adjunct.
Students: 152 full-time (94 women), 20 part-time (13 women). Average age 31. 256 applicants, 18% accepted. In 2001, 15 master's, 9 doctorates awarded.
Degree requirements: For master's, one foreign language; for doctorate, 2 foreign languages, thesis/dissertation.
Entrance requirements: For master's and doctorate, GRE General Test, TOEFL. *Application deadline:* For fall admission, 1/3; for spring admission, 11/30. *Application fee:* $65.
Expenses: Tuition: Full-time $27,528. Required fees: $1,638.
Financial support: Fellowships, teaching assistantships, Federal Work-Study and institutionally sponsored loans available. Support available to part-time students. Financial award application deadline: 1/5; financial award applicants required to submit FAFSA.
Faculty research: Archaeology, physical anthropology, cultural and linguistic anthropology.
Nicholas Dirks, Chair, 212-854-4552, *Fax:* 212-854-7347.

■ CORNELL UNIVERSITY

Graduate School, Graduate Fields of Arts and Sciences, Field of Anthropology, Ithaca, NY 14853-0001

AWARDS Archaeological anthropology (PhD); biological anthropology (PhD); sociocultural anthropology (PhD).

Faculty: 22 full-time.
Students: 46 full-time (28 women); includes 10 minority (3 African Americans, 3 Asian Americans or Pacific Islanders, 3 Hispanic Americans, 1 Native American), 15 international. 91 applicants, 16% accepted. In 2001, 6 doctorates awarded.
Degree requirements: For doctorate, one foreign language, thesis/dissertation, teaching experience.
Entrance requirements: For doctorate, GRE General Test, TOEFL, 3 letters of recommendation, sample of written work. *Application deadline:* For fall admission, 1/15. *Application fee:* $65. Electronic applications accepted.
Expenses: Tuition: Full-time $25,970. Required fees: $50.
Financial support: In 2001–02, 42 students received support, including 34 fellowships with full tuition reimbursements available, 8 teaching assistantships with full tuition reimbursements available; research assistantships with full tuition reimbursements available, institutionally sponsored loans, scholarships/grants, tuition waivers (full and partial), and unspecified assistantships also available. Financial award applicants required to submit FAFSA.
Faculty research: Culture: symbolism, ritual, gender, religion, ideology, media; engaged anthropology: human rights, ethnic/identity poitics, participatory action research; polical economy: complex society, nationalism, globalism, change, ethnohistory, practice theory; area studies: Asia (Southeast, Himalayas, East), Americas (South, Central, Caribbean, North), Europe; interdisiplinary and ethnic studies: Asian-American studies.
Application contact: Graduate Field Assistant, 607-255-6768, *E-mail:* bad2@cornell.edu. *Web site:* http://www.gradschool.cornell.edu/grad/fields_1/anthro.html

■ DUKE UNIVERSITY

Graduate School, Department of Biological Anthropology and Anatomy, Durham, NC 27708-0586

AWARDS Cellular and molecular biology (PhD); gross anatomy and physical anthropology (PhD), including comparative morphology of human and non-human primates, primate social behavior, vertebrate paleontology; neuroanatomy (PhD).

Faculty: 10 full-time, 1 part-time/adjunct.
Students: 25 full-time (16 women); includes 3 minority (2 African Americans, 1 Hispanic American), 1 international. 47 applicants, 26% accepted, 6 enrolled.
Degree requirements: For doctorate, one foreign language, thesis/dissertation.
Entrance requirements: For doctorate, GRE General Test. *Application deadline:* For fall admission, 12/31. *Application fee:* $75.
Expenses: Tuition: Full-time $24,600.
Financial support: Fellowships, teaching assistantships, Federal Work-Study available. Financial award application deadline: 12/31.
Carel Van Schaik, Director of Graduate Studies, 919-684-4124, *Fax:* 919-684-8034, *E-mail:* l.squires@baa.mc.duke.edu. *Web site:* http://www.baa.duke.edu/

■ DUKE UNIVERSITY

Graduate School, Department of Cultural Anthropology, Durham, NC 27708-0586

AWARDS Physical anthropology (PhD), including comparative morphology of human and non-human primates, primate social behavior; social/cultural anthropology (PhD).

Faculty: 9 full-time, 3 part-time/adjunct.
Students: 23 full-time (18 women); includes 4 minority (2 African Americans, 2 Native Americans), 7 international. In 2001, 5 doctorates awarded.
Degree requirements: For doctorate, one foreign language, thesis/dissertation.
Entrance requirements: For doctorate, GRE General Test. *Application deadline:* For fall admission, 12/31. *Application fee:* $75.
Expenses: Tuition: Full-time $24,600.
Financial support: Fellowships, research assistantships, teaching assistantships, Federal Work-Study available. Financial award application deadline: 12/31.
Charles Piot, Director of Graduate Studies, 919-684-4544, *Fax:* 919-681-8483, *E-mail:* hfrancis@duke.edu. *Web site:* http://www.aas.duke.edu/

■ EAST CAROLINA UNIVERSITY

Graduate School, College of Arts and Sciences, Department of Anthropology, Greenville, NC 27858-4353

AWARDS MA. Part-time programs available.

Faculty: 6 full-time (2 women).
Students: 16 full-time (8 women), 3 part-time (2 women); includes 3 minority (2 Asian Americans or Pacific Islanders, 1 Hispanic American). Average age 27. 17 applicants, 76% accepted. In 2001, 8 degrees awarded.
Degree requirements: For master's, one foreign language, thesis, comprehensive exam.
Entrance requirements: For master's, GRE General Test, TOEFL. *Application deadline:* For fall admission, 6/1 (priority date); for spring admission, 10/15. Applications are processed on a rolling basis. *Application fee:* $45.
Expenses: Tuition, state resident: full-time $2,636. Tuition, nonresident: full-time $11,365.
Financial support: Research assistantships with partial tuition reimbursements available. Financial award application deadline: 6/1.
Dr. Linda Wolfe, Chair and Director of Graduate Studies, 252-328-6766, *Fax:* 252-328-6759, *E-mail:* wolfel@mail.ecu.edu.
Application contact: Dr. Paul D. Tschetter, Senior Associate Dean of the Graduate School, 252-328-6012, *Fax:* 252-328-6071, *E-mail:* gradschool@mail.ecu.edu.

■ EASTERN NEW MEXICO UNIVERSITY

Graduate School, College of Liberal Arts and Sciences, Department of Anthropology and Applied Archaeology, Portales, NM 88130

AWARDS Anthropology (MA). Part-time programs available.

Faculty: 4 full-time (1 woman), 3 part-time/adjunct (1 woman).
Students: 11 full-time (5 women), 16 part-time (9 women); includes 3 minority (1 Asian American or Pacific Islander, 1 Hispanic American, 1 Native American), 1 international. Average age 32. 5 applicants, 100% accepted. In 2001, 6 degrees awarded.
Degree requirements: For master's, one foreign language, thesis, comprehensive exam.
Entrance requirements: For master's, GRE General Test, minimum GPA of 2.5. *Application deadline:* For fall admission, 8/20 (priority date). Applications are processed on a rolling basis. *Application fee:* $10. Electronic applications accepted.
Expenses: Tuition, state resident: full-time $1,740; part-time $73 per credit. Tuition, nonresident: full-time $7,296; part-time $304 per credit. Required fees: $588; $25 per credit.
Financial support: In 2001–02, 1 fellowship (averaging $7,200 per year), 11 research assistantships (averaging $7,700 per year), 1 teaching assistantship (averaging $7,700 per year) were awarded. Career-related internships or fieldwork and Federal Work-Study also available. Support available to part-time students. Financial award application deadline: 3/1.
Faculty research: Paleobotany, remote sensing, conservation archaeology, obsidian hydration.
Dr. Janet Frost, Graduate Coordinator, 505-562-2141, *E-mail:* janet.frost@enmu.edu.

■ EMORY UNIVERSITY

Graduate School of Arts and Sciences, Department of Anthropology, Atlanta, GA 30322-1100

AWARDS PhD.

Faculty: 17 full-time (9 women).
Students: 44 full-time (26 women); includes 9 minority (7 African Americans, 2 Hispanic Americans), 3 international. 99 applicants, 5% accepted, 2 enrolled. In 2001, 5 doctorates awarded.
Degree requirements: For doctorate, 5 foreign languages, thesis/dissertation, qualifying exams.
Entrance requirements: For doctorate, GRE General Test, TOEFL. *Application deadline:* For fall admission, 1/15 (priority date). *Application fee:* $50. Electronic applications accepted.
Expenses: Tuition: Full-time $24,770. Required fees: $100. Tuition and fees vary according to program and student level.
Financial support: Fellowships, teaching assistantships, scholarships/grants available. Financial award application deadline: 1/15.
Faculty research: Primate behavioral ecology, comparative human biology.
Dr. Carol Worthman, Chair, 404-727-7518.
Application contact: Dr. Patricia Whitten, Director of Graduate Studies, 404-727-7518, *Fax:* 404-727-2860, *E-mail:* antpw@emory.edu. *Web site:* http://www.emory.edu/COLLEGE/ANTHROPOLOGY/ANTGRAD.HTM/

■ FLORIDA ATLANTIC UNIVERSITY

Dorothy F. Schmidt College of Arts and Letters, Department of Anthropology, Boca Raton, FL 33431-0991

AWARDS MA, MAT. Part-time programs available.

Faculty: 6 full-time (2 women).
Students: 6 full-time (2 women), 20 part-time (14 women); includes 4 minority (1 African American, 3 Hispanic Americans), 2 international. Average age 33. 7 applicants, 71% accepted, 3 enrolled. In 2001, 3 degrees awarded.
Degree requirements: For master's, one foreign language, thesis, statistics.
Entrance requirements: For master's, GRE General Test, minimum GPA of 3.0. *Application deadline:* For fall admission, 5/1 (priority date); for spring admission, 10/15. Applications are processed on a rolling basis. *Application fee:* $20.
Expenses: Tuition, state resident: full-time $3,098; part-time $172 per credit. Tuition, nonresident: full-time $10,427; part-time $579 per credit.
Financial support: In 2001–02, 9 students received support, including 3 research assistantships with tuition reimbursements available (averaging $2,000 per year), 6 teaching assistantships with tuition reimbursements available (averaging $7,195 per year); Federal Work-Study and unspecified assistantships also available.
Faculty research: Archaeological, ethnological, ethnographical, osteological, paleoanthropological, and zoo-archaeological research.
Dr. Gerald Weiss, Chairman, 561-297-3230, *Fax:* 561-297-0084, *E-mail:* weiss@fau.edu. *Web site:* http://www.fau.edu/divdept/anthro/

■ FLORIDA STATE UNIVERSITY

Graduate Studies, College of Arts and Sciences, Department of Anthropology, Tallahassee, FL 32306

AWARDS MA, MS, PhD. Part-time programs available.

Faculty: 12 full-time (6 women), 6 part-time/adjunct (3 women).
Students: 46 full-time (24 women), 27 part-time (13 women); includes 5 minority (1 African American, 1 Asian American or Pacific Islander, 2 Hispanic Americans, 1 Native American), 3 international. Average age 29. 68 applicants, 37% accepted. In 2001, 5 master's awarded.
Degree requirements: For master's and doctorate, one foreign language, thesis/dissertation. *Median time to degree:* Master's–3 years full-time, 4 years part-time; doctorate–4 years full-time, 5 years part-time.
Entrance requirements: For master's, GRE General Test, minimum GPA of 3.0; for doctorate, GRE General Test, master's degree in anthropology. *Application deadline:* For fall admission, 1/1. *Application fee:* $20. Electronic applications accepted.
Expenses: Tuition, state resident: part-time $163 per credit hour. Tuition, nonresident: part-time $570 per credit hour. Tuition and fees vary according to program.
Financial support: In 2001–02, 27 students received support, including 1 fellowship with full tuition reimbursement available, 13 research assistantships with full tuition reimbursements available, 13 teaching assistantships with full tuition reimbursements available; career-related

Florida State University (continued)
internships or fieldwork, Federal Work-Study, institutionally sponsored loans, and unspecified assistantships also available.
Faculty research: Osteology, folklore, prehistoric and historic archaeology, paleoarchaeology, Southeastern Indians, Mesoamerica, linguistics. *Total annual research expenditures:* $500,000.
Dr. Glen H. Doran, Chairman, 850-644-8154, *Fax:* 850-644-4283, *E-mail:* gdoran@garnet.acns.fsu.edu.
Application contact: Pam Andras, Student Coordinator, 850-644-4282, *Fax:* 850-644-4283, *E-mail:* pma1305@mailer.fsu.edu. *Web site:* http://www.anthro.fsu.edu/

■ THE GEORGE WASHINGTON UNIVERSITY

Columbian College of Arts and Sciences, Department of Anthropology, Washington, DC 20052

AWARDS MA. Part-time and evening/weekend programs available.

Faculty: 6 full-time (3 women), 2 part-time/adjunct (0 women).
Students: 29 full-time (24 women), 9 part-time (7 women); includes 1 African American, 1 Asian American or Pacific Islander, 1 Hispanic American, 1 international. Average age 26. 50 applicants, 82% accepted. In 2001, 12 degrees awarded.
Degree requirements: For master's, one foreign language, thesis or alternative, comprehensive exam.
Entrance requirements: For master's, GRE General Test, minimum GPA of 3.0. *Application deadline:* For fall admission, 5/1. *Application fee:* $55.
Expenses: Tuition: Part-time $810 per credit. Required fees: $1 per credit.
Financial support: In 2001–02, 13 students received support, including 6 fellowships (averaging $4,950 per year), 5 teaching assistantships (averaging $4,400 per year); career-related internships or fieldwork and Federal Work-Study also available. Financial award application deadline: 2/1.
Dr. Alison Brooks, Director, 202-994-6079, *Fax:* 202-994-6097.
Application contact: Information Contact, 202-994-6075, *E-mail:* anth@gwu.edu. *Web site:* http://www.gwu.edu/~anth/

■ GEORGIA STATE UNIVERSITY

College of Arts and Sciences, Department of Anthropology and Geography, Program in Anthropology, Atlanta, GA 30303-3083

AWARDS MA.

Degree requirements: For master's, one foreign language, thesis or alternative, exam.
Entrance requirements: For master's, GRE General Test, TOEFL. Electronic applications accepted. *Web site:* http://monarch.gsu.edu/

Find an in-depth description at www.petersons.com/gradchannel.

■ GRADUATE SCHOOL AND UNIVERSITY CENTER OF THE CITY UNIVERSITY OF NEW YORK

Graduate Studies, Doctoral Program in Anthropology, New York, NY 10016-4039

AWARDS Anthropological linguistics (PhD); archaeology (PhD); cultural anthropology (PhD); physical anthropology (PhD).

Faculty: 39 full-time (14 women).
Students: 150 full-time (101 women), 6 part-time (4 women); includes 27 minority (9 African Americans, 8 Asian Americans or Pacific Islanders, 10 Hispanic Americans), 20 international. Average age 36. 125 applicants, 47% accepted, 29 enrolled. In 2001, 5 degrees awarded.
Degree requirements: For doctorate, one foreign language, thesis/dissertation.
Entrance requirements: For doctorate, GRE General Test. *Application deadline:* For fall admission, 1/15. *Application fee:* $40.
Expenses: Tuition, state resident: part-time $245 per credit. Tuition, nonresident: part-time $425 per credit. Required fees: $72 per semester.
Financial support: In 2001–02, 75 students received support, including 45 fellowships, 4 research assistantships; teaching assistantships, career-related internships or fieldwork, Federal Work-Study, institutionally sponsored loans, and tuition waivers (full and partial) also available. Financial award application deadline: 2/1; financial award applicants required to submit FAFSA.
Dr. Louise Lennihan, Executive Officer, 212-817-8006, *Fax:* 212-817-1501, *E-mail:* anthro@gc.cuny.edu.
Application contact: Information Contact, 212-817-8005, *Fax:* 212-817-1501, *E-mail:* anthro@gc.cuny.edu.

■ HARVARD UNIVERSITY

Graduate School of Arts and Sciences, Committee on Middle Eastern Studies, Cambridge, MA 02138

AWARDS Anthropology and Middle Eastern studies (PhD); economics and Middle Eastern studies (PhD); fine arts and Middle Eastern studies (PhD); history and Middle Eastern studies (PhD); regional studies–Middle East (AM). Terminal master's awarded for partial completion of doctoral program.

Degree requirements: For master's, one foreign language; for doctorate, 2 foreign languages, thesis/dissertation.
Entrance requirements: For master's, GRE General Test, TOEFL; for doctorate, GRE General Test, TOEFL, 1 year of course work in Middle Eastern regional studies, proficiency in a related language.
Expenses: Tuition: Full-time $23,370. Required fees: $816. Full-time tuition and fees vary according to program and student level.

■ HARVARD UNIVERSITY

Graduate School of Arts and Sciences, Department of Anthropology, Cambridge, MA 02138

AWARDS Archaeology (PhD); biological anthropology (PhD); legal anthropology (AM); medical anthropology (AM); social anthropology (AM, PhD); social change and development (AM). Terminal master's awarded for partial completion of doctoral program.

Degree requirements: For master's, 2 foreign languages, thesis (for some programs); for doctorate, 2 foreign languages, thesis/dissertation, laboratory and/or fieldwork; general, qualifying, or special exams.
Entrance requirements: For master's and doctorate, GRE General Test, TOEFL.
Expenses: Tuition: Full-time $23,370. Required fees: $816. Full-time tuition and fees vary according to program and student level.

■ HUNTER COLLEGE OF THE CITY UNIVERSITY OF NEW YORK

Graduate School, School of Arts and Sciences, Department of Anthropology, New York, NY 10021-5085

AWARDS MA. Part-time and evening/weekend programs available.

Faculty: 17 full-time (5 women), 13 part-time/adjunct (8 women).
Students: 6 full-time (5 women), 51 part-time (39 women); includes 8 minority (1 Asian American or Pacific Islander, 7 Hispanic Americans), 2 international. Average age 35. 22 applicants, 64% accepted. In 2001, 9 degrees awarded.
Degree requirements: For master's, thesis, language or statistics exam, comprehensive exam.
Entrance requirements: For master's, GRE General Test, TOEFL, minimum 9 credits in anthropology or a related field. *Application deadline:* For fall admission, 4/28; for spring admission, 11/21. *Application fee:* $40.
Expenses: Tuition, state resident: full-time $2,175; part-time $185 per credit. Tuition, nonresident: full-time $3,800; part-time $320 per credit.
Financial support: Research assistantships, tuition waivers (full and partial) available.
Faculty research: Primatology, human ecology, archeology, political anthropology, primate and human evolution.
Marc Edelman, Graduate Adviser, 212-772-5410, *Fax:* 212-772-5423, *E-mail:* medelman@shiva.hunter.cuny.edu.

Application contact: William Zlata, Director for Graduate Admissions, 212-772-4288, *Fax:* 212-650-3336, *E-mail:* admissions@hunter.cuny.edu. *Web site:* http://maxweber.hunter.cuny.edu/anthro/

■ IDAHO STATE UNIVERSITY

Office of Graduate Studies, College of Arts and Sciences, Department of Anthropology, Pocatello, ID 83209

AWARDS MA, MS. Part-time programs available.

Faculty: 3 full-time (2 women), 1 part-time/adjunct (0 women).
Students: 14 full-time (6 women), 5 part-time (3 women); includes 3 minority (all Native Americans), 1 international. Average age 38. In 2001, 2 degrees awarded.
Degree requirements: For master's, one foreign language, thesis.
Entrance requirements: For master's, GRE General Test. *Application deadline:* For fall admission, 7/1; for spring admission, 12/1. Applications are processed on a rolling basis. *Application fee:* $35.
Expenses: Tuition, area resident: Full-time $3,432. Tuition, state resident: part-time $172 per credit. Tuition, nonresident: full-time $10,196; part-time $262 per credit. International tuition: $9,672 full-time. Part-time tuition and fees vary according to course load, program and reciprocity agreements.
Financial support: In 2001–02, 7 students received support, including 4 research assistantships with full and partial tuition reimbursements available (averaging $8,316 per year), 3 teaching assistantships with full and partial tuition reimbursements available (averaging $8,117 per year); career-related internships or fieldwork, Federal Work-Study, institutionally sponsored loans, and tuition waivers (full and partial) also available. Support available to part-time students. Financial award application deadline: 3/15.
Faculty research: Native American studies: health care, language/ethnopoetics, prehistory, art, resource environmental management. *Total annual research expenditures:* $231,918.
Dr. Teri Hall, Chairman, 208-282-2629. *Web site:* http://www.isu.edu/departments/anthro/

■ INDIANA UNIVERSITY BLOOMINGTON

Graduate School, College of Arts and Sciences, Department of Anthropology, Bloomington, IN 47405

AWARDS MA, PhD. PhD offered through the University Graduate School. Part-time programs available.

Faculty: 19 full-time (7 women).
Students: 47 full-time (28 women), 63 part-time (38 women); includes 14 minority (6 African Americans, 3 Asian Americans or Pacific Islanders, 3 Hispanic Americans, 2 Native Americans), 8 international. Average age 33. In 2001, 7 master's, 1 doctorate awarded. Terminal master's awarded for partial completion of doctoral program.
Degree requirements: For master's, thesis or alternative; for doctorate, 2 foreign languages, thesis/dissertation.
Entrance requirements: For master's and doctorate, GRE General Test, TOEFL. *Application deadline:* For fall admission, 1/15 (priority date); for spring admission, 9/1 (priority date). Applications are processed on a rolling basis. *Application fee:* $45 ($55 for international students).
Expenses: Tuition, state resident: full-time $4,720; part-time $197 per credit. Tuition, nonresident: full-time $13,748; part-time $573 per credit. Required fees: $642.
Financial support: In 2001–02, 52 students received support, including 2 fellowships with tuition reimbursements available (averaging $15,000 per year), 17 teaching assistantships with tuition reimbursements available (averaging $9,000 per year); research assistantships, Federal Work-Study and institutionally sponsored loans also available. Financial award applicants required to submit FAFSA.
Faculty research: Ecologic and economic development, symbolism, arts/dance, paleoarchaeology, bioanthropology.
Dr. Robert Meier, Chair, 812-855-2555, *Fax:* 812-855-4358, *E-mail:* meier@indiana.edu.
Application contact: Debra Wilkerson, Secretary, 812-855-1041, *Fax:* 812-855-4358, *E-mail:* dwilkers@indiana.edu. *Web site:* http://www.indiana.edu/~anthro/home.html

■ IOWA STATE UNIVERSITY OF SCIENCE AND TECHNOLOGY

Graduate College, College of Liberal Arts and Sciences, Department of Anthropology, Ames, IA 50011

AWARDS MA.

Faculty: 9 full-time.
Students: 8 full-time (5 women), 2 part-time. 11 applicants, 73% accepted, 6 enrolled. In 2001, 7 degrees awarded.
Degree requirements: For master's, thesis. *Median time to degree:* Master's–2.7 years full-time.
Entrance requirements: For master's, GRE General Test, TOEFL or IELTS. *Application deadline:* For fall admission, 3/1 (priority date); for spring admission, 10/1. Applications are processed on a rolling basis. *Application fee:* $20 ($50 for international students). Electronic applications accepted.
Expenses: Tuition, state resident: full-time $1,851. Tuition, nonresident: full-time $5,449. Tuition and fees vary according to program.
Financial support: In 2001–02, 1 research assistantship with partial tuition reimbursement (averaging $11,252 per year), 6 teaching assistantships with partial tuition reimbursements (averaging $11,250 per year) were awarded. Fellowships, scholarships/grants, health care benefits, and unspecified assistantships also available.
Dr. Shu-Min Huang, Chair, 515-294-7139, *Fax:* 515-294-1708, *E-mail:* anthgrad@iastate.edu. *Web site:* http://www.publiciastate.edu/~anthr_info/anthropology/

■ JOHNS HOPKINS UNIVERSITY

Zanvyl Krieger School of Arts and Sciences, Department of Anthropology, Baltimore, MD 21218-2699

AWARDS PhD.

Faculty: 5 full-time (3 women), 1 (woman) part-time/adjunct.
Students: 21 full-time (9 women); includes 6 minority (4 African Americans, 1 Asian American or Pacific Islander, 1 Hispanic American), 7 international. Average age 26. 37 applicants, 30% accepted, 6 enrolled. In 2001, 8 degrees awarded.
Degree requirements: For doctorate, one foreign language, thesis/dissertation, registration.
Entrance requirements: For doctorate, GRE General Test. *Application deadline:* For fall admission, 1/15. *Application fee:* $55. Electronic applications accepted.
Expenses: Tuition: Full-time $27,390.
Financial support: In 2001–02, 9 teaching assistantships were awarded; fellowships, career-related internships or fieldwork, Federal Work-Study, and institutionally sponsored loans also available. Financial award application deadline: 4/15; financial award applicants required to submit FAFSA.
Faculty research: Social and cultural anthropology of complex societies, gender, politics, economic anthropology, religion. *Total annual research expenditures:* $23,644.
Dr. Gyanendra Pandey, Chair, 410-516-7274, *Fax:* 410-516-6080, *E-mail:* gpandey@jhu.edu.
Application contact: Daphne Klautky, Student Coordinator, 410-516-7271, *Fax:* 410-516-6080, *E-mail:* dklautky@jhu.edu. *Web site:* http://www.jhu.edu/~anthro/

■ KENT STATE UNIVERSITY

College of Arts and Sciences, Department of Anthropology, Kent, OH 44242-0001

AWARDS MA.

Degree requirements: For master's, thesis optional.
Entrance requirements: For master's, GRE General Test or MAT, minimum GPA of 2.75. Electronic applications accepted.

■ KENT STATE UNIVERSITY

School of Biomedical Sciences, Program in Biological Anthropology, Kent, OH 44242-0001

AWARDS PhD. Offered in cooperation with Northeastern Ohio Universities College of Medicine.

Faculty: 12 full-time (5 women).
Students: 7 full-time (2 women), 4 part-time (2 women); includes 1 minority (Native American). 11 applicants, 36% accepted. In 2001, 2 degrees awarded.
Degree requirements: For doctorate, thesis/dissertation.
Entrance requirements: For doctorate, GRE General Test. *Application deadline:* For fall admission, 6/1. Applications are processed on a rolling basis. *Application fee:* $30.
Financial support: In 2001–02, 6 students received support, including 4 teaching assistantships; fellowships, research assistantships, Federal Work-Study, scholarships/grants, and tuition waivers (full) also available. Financial award application deadline: 2/1; financial award applicants required to submit FAFSA.
Faculty research: Human evolution, paleodemography, orofacial anatomy, osteology, primate behavior.
Dr. James L. Blank, Director, School of Biomedical Sciences, 330-672-2263, *Fax:* 330-672-9391, *E-mail:* jimb@biology.kent.edu.

■ LEHIGH UNIVERSITY

College of Arts and Sciences, Department of Sociology and Anthropology, Bethlehem, PA 18015-3094

AWARDS MA. Part-time programs available.

Faculty: 7 full-time (3 women).
Students: 12 full-time (10 women), 2 part-time (1 woman); includes 1 minority (Hispanic American). 20 applicants, 75% accepted, 11 enrolled. In 2001, 4 degrees awarded.
Degree requirements: For master's, thesis optional.
Entrance requirements: For master's, GRE, TOEFL. *Application deadline:* For fall admission, 7/15; for spring admission, 12/1. Applications are processed on a rolling basis. *Application fee:* $50. Electronic applications accepted.
Expenses: Tuition: Part-time $468 per credit hour. Required fees: $200; $100 per semester. Tuition and fees vary according to program.
Financial support: In 2001–02, 4 teaching assistantships with tuition reimbursements were awarded; fellowships, career-related internships or fieldwork, Federal Work-Study, and tuition waivers (full) also available. Financial award application deadline: 1/15.
Faculty research: Juvenile delinquency, parent-child relations, urban sociology, family, alcohol studies, communication, race and class.
Dr. James R. McIntosh, Chairperson, 610-758-3809, *Fax:* 610-758-6552, *E-mail:* ijm1@lehigh.edu.
Application contact: Dr. Judith N. Lasker, Graduate Coordinator, 610-758-3811, *Fax:* 610-758-6552, *E-mail:* jnl0@lehigh.edu. *Web site:* http://www.lehigh.edu/~insan/soc-ma.htm

Find an in-depth description at www.petersons.com/gradchannel.

■ LOUISIANA STATE UNIVERSITY AND AGRICULTURAL AND MECHANICAL COLLEGE

Graduate School, College of Arts and Sciences, Department of Geography and Anthropology, Baton Rouge, LA 70803

AWARDS Anthropology (MA); geography (MA, MS, PhD). Part-time programs available.

Faculty: 25 full-time (8 women).
Students: 56 full-time (30 women), 34 part-time (16 women); includes 7 minority (3 African Americans, 1 Asian American or Pacific Islander, 2 Hispanic Americans, 1 Native American), 8 international. Average age 33. 71 applicants, 45% accepted, 14 enrolled. In 2001, 17 master's, 12 doctorates awarded. Terminal master's awarded for partial completion of doctoral program.
Degree requirements: For master's, 2 foreign languages, thesis (for some programs); for doctorate, 2 foreign languages, thesis/dissertation.
Entrance requirements: For master's and doctorate, GRE General Test, minimum GPA of 3.0. *Application deadline:* For fall admission, 1/25 (priority date). Applications are processed on a rolling basis. *Application fee:* $25.
Expenses: Tuition, state resident: full-time $2,551. Tuition, nonresident: full-time $5,551. Required fees: $854. Part-time tuition and fees vary according to course load.
Financial support: In 2001–02, 6 fellowships with full tuition reimbursements (averaging $14,222 per year), 9 research assistantships with partial tuition reimbursements (averaging $12,318 per year), 22 teaching assistantships with partial tuition reimbursements (averaging $10,274 per year) were awarded. Career-related internships or fieldwork and unspecified assistantships also available. Financial award application deadline: 3/1; financial award applicants required to submit FAFSA. *Total annual research expenditures:* $754,753.
Dr. Craig Colten, Chair, 225-578-6094, *Fax:* 225-578-4420, *E-mail:* ccolten@lsu.edu. *Web site:* http://www.ga.lsu.edu/ga/

■ MARSHALL UNIVERSITY

Graduate College, College of Liberal Arts, Department of Sociology and Anthropology, Huntington, WV 25755

AWARDS MA.

Faculty: 6 full-time (2 women), 1 (woman) part-time/adjunct.
Students: 18 full-time (14 women), 6 part-time (4 women); includes 1 minority (African American). In 2001, 8 degrees awarded.
Degree requirements: For master's, thesis optional.
Expenses: Tuition, state resident: part-time $147 per credit. Tuition, nonresident: part-time $468 per credit. Tuition and fees vary according to campus/location and reciprocity agreements.
Dr. Kenneth P. Ambrose, Chairperson, 304-696-2788, *E-mail:* ambrose@marshall.edu.
Application contact: Ken O'Neal, Assistant Vice President, Adult Student Services, 304-746-2500 Ext. 1907, *Fax:* 304-746-1902, *E-mail:* oneal@marshall.edu.

■ MICHIGAN STATE UNIVERSITY

College of Human Medicine and Graduate School, Graduate Programs in Human Medicine, East Lansing, MI 48824

AWARDS Anatomy (MS); anthropology (MA); biochemistry (MS, PhD), including biochemistry, biochemistry-environmental toxicology (PhD); epidemiology (MS); human pathology (MS, PhD); microbiology (MS, PhD); pharmacology/toxicology (MS, PhD); physiology (MS, PhD); psychology (MA); sociology (MA); surgery (MS); zoology (MS). Part-time programs available.

Students: 63 (29 women); includes 7 minority (5 Asian Americans or Pacific Islanders, 2 Hispanic Americans) 7 international. Average age 26. In 2001, 14 master's, 2 doctorates awarded.
Entrance requirements: For master's and doctorate, GRE General Test, minimum GPA of 3.0. *Application deadline:* Applications are processed on a rolling basis. *Application fee:* $30 ($40 for international students). Electronic applications accepted.
Expenses: Contact institution.
Financial support: In 2001–02, 48 research assistantships with tuition reimbursements (averaging $12,058 per year), 1 teaching assistantship with tuition reimbursement (averaging $10,944 per year) were awarded. Fellowships with tuition reimbursements, institutionally sponsored loans also available. Support available to part-time students. Financial award applicants required to submit FAFSA.
Dr. Lynne Farquhar, Director, Medical Science Training Program, 517-353-8858, *Fax:* 517-432-0148, *E-mail:* mdadmissions@msu.edu. *Web site:* http://

www.chm.msu.edu/chmhome/gradeducation/GMEWEB/

■ MICHIGAN STATE UNIVERSITY

Graduate School, College of Social Science, Department of Anthropology, East Lansing, MI 48824

AWARDS MA, PhD.

Faculty: 21.
Students: 51 full-time (32 women), 20 part-time (17 women); includes 15 minority (6 African Americans, 1 Asian American or Pacific Islander, 3 Hispanic Americans, 5 Native Americans), 4 international. Average age 31. 69 applicants, 35% accepted. In 2001, 4 master's, 6 doctorates awarded.
Degree requirements: For master's, thesis; for doctorate, variable foreign language requirement, thesis/dissertation.
Entrance requirements: For master's and doctorate, TOEFL, sample of written work. *Application deadline:* For fall admission, 1/1 (priority date). Applications are processed on a rolling basis. *Application fee:* $30 ($40 for international students). Electronic applications accepted.
Expenses: Tuition, state resident: part-time $244 per credit hour. Tuition, nonresident: part-time $494 per credit hour. Required fees: $268 per semester. Tuition and fees vary according to course load, degree level and program.
Financial support: In 2001–02, 32 fellowships (averaging $5,101 per year), 5 research assistantships with tuition reimbursements (averaging $10,541 per year), 16 teaching assistantships with tuition reimbursements (averaging $10,384 per year) were awarded. Career-related internships or fieldwork, Federal Work-Study, and institutionally sponsored loans also available. Support available to part-time students. Financial award application deadline: 1/1; financial award applicants required to submit FAFSA.
Faculty research: Latin America; Africa; Great Lakes anthropology; medical anthropology; culture, resources, and power; forensic anthropology; archaeology. *Total annual research expenditures:* $378,715.
Dr. Lynne Goldstein, Chairperson, 517-353-2950, *Fax:* 517-432-2363, *E-mail:* lynneg@pilot.msu.edu. *Web site:* http://www.ssc.msu.edu/~anp/

■ MINNESOTA STATE UNIVERSITY, MANKATO

College of Graduate Studies, College of Social and Behavioral Sciences, Program in Anthropology, Mankato, MN 56001

AWARDS MS. Part-time programs available.

Faculty: 5 full-time (1 woman).
Students: 3 full-time (1 woman), 3 part-time (all women).
Degree requirements: For master's, comprehensive exam.
Application deadline: For fall admission, 7/9 (priority date); for spring admission, 11/27. Applications are processed on a rolling basis. *Application fee:* $20.
Expenses: Tuition, state resident: full-time $3,253; part-time $157 per credit. Tuition, nonresident: full-time $4,893; part-time $248 per credit. Required fees: $24 per credit. Tuition and fees vary according to reciprocity agreements.
Financial support: Application deadline: 3/15.
Dr. Paul Brown, Head, 507-389-6613.
Application contact: College of Graduate Studies and Research, 507-389-2321, *Fax:* 507-389-5974, *E-mail:* grad@mnsu.edu.

■ MONTCLAIR STATE UNIVERSITY

The School of Graduate, Professional and Continuing Education, College of Humanities and Social Sciences, Department of Anthropology, Upper Montclair, NJ 07043-1624

AWARDS Practical anthropology (MA). Students enter program as undergraduates. Part-time and evening/weekend programs available.

Degree requirements: For master's, thesis or alternative, comprehensive exam.
Entrance requirements: For master's, GRE General Test, minimum GPA of 3.0, previous course work in social science. Electronic applications accepted.

■ MONTCLAIR STATE UNIVERSITY

The School of Graduate, Professional and Continuing Education, College of Humanities and Social Sciences, Programs in Social Science, Program in Anthropology, Upper Montclair, NJ 07043-1624

AWARDS MA. Part-time and evening/weekend programs available.

Degree requirements: For master's, comprehensive exam.
Entrance requirements: For master's, GRE General Test. Electronic applications accepted. *Web site:* http://www.montclair.edu/

■ NEW MEXICO HIGHLANDS UNIVERSITY

Graduate Studies, College of Arts and Sciences, Program in Southwest Studies, Las Vegas, NM 87701

AWARDS Anthropology (MA); Hispanic language and literature (MA); history and political science (MA). Program is interdisciplinary. Part-time programs available.

Faculty: 16 full-time (5 women).
Students: 6 full-time (4 women), 15 part-time (9 women); includes 10 minority (all Hispanic Americans). Average age 39. In 2001, 3 degrees awarded.
Degree requirements: For master's, thesis or alternative.
Entrance requirements: For master's, minimum undergraduate GPA of 3.0. *Application deadline:* For fall admission, 8/1 (priority date). Applications are processed on a rolling basis. *Application fee:* $15.
Expenses: Tuition, state resident: full-time $2,238. Tuition, nonresident: full-time $9,366.
Financial support: Research assistantships with full and partial tuition reimbursements, Federal Work-Study available. Financial award application deadline: 3/1.
Dr. Tomas Salazar, Dean, 505-454-3080, *Fax:* 505-454-3389, *E-mail:* salazar_t@nmhu.edu.
Application contact: Dr. Linda LaGrange, Associate Dean of Graduate Studies, 505-454-3266, *Fax:* 505-454-3558, *E-mail:* lagrange_l@nmhu.edu.

■ NEW MEXICO STATE UNIVERSITY

Graduate School, College of Arts and Sciences, Department of Sociology and Anthropology, Las Cruces, NM 88003-8001

AWARDS Anthropology (MA); sociology (MA). Part-time programs available.

Faculty: 15 full-time (9 women), 4 part-time/adjunct (3 women).
Students: 33 full-time (23 women), 15 part-time (12 women); includes 9 minority (8 Hispanic Americans, 1 Native American), 2 international. Average age 28. 32 applicants, 78% accepted, 15 enrolled. In 2001, 7 degrees awarded.
Degree requirements: For master's, thesis (for some programs), comprehensive exam (anthropology), comprehensive exam. *Application deadline:* For fall admission, 2/15; for spring admission, 10/15. Applications are processed on a rolling basis. *Application fee:* $15 ($35 for international students). Electronic applications accepted.
Expenses: Tuition, state resident: full-time $3,234; part-time $135 per credit. Tuition, nonresident: full-time $9,420; part-time $428 per credit. Required fees: $858.
Financial support: In 2001–02, 12 students received support, including 1 research assistantship, 12 teaching assistantships with partial tuition reimbursements available; career-related internships or fieldwork and Federal Work-Study also available. Support available to part-time students. Financial award application deadline: 3/1.
Faculty research: Native American culture and society, Latin America and border studies, prehistoric and historic archaeology, demography, medical sociology and anthropology.
Dr. Wenda Trevathan, Head, 505-646-3821, *Fax:* 505-646-3725, *E-mail:* wtrevath@nmsu.edu. *Web site:* http://www.nmsu.edu/~anthro/

■ NEW SCHOOL UNIVERSITY

Graduate Faculty of Political and Social Science, Department of Anthropology, New York, NY 10011-8603

AWARDS MA, DS Sc, PhD. Part-time and evening/weekend programs available.

Students: 76 full-time (56 women), 13 part-time (11 women); includes 22 minority (10 African Americans, 4 Asian Americans or Pacific Islanders, 8 Hispanic Americans), 19 international. Average age 35. 36 applicants, 83% accepted. In 2001, 11 master's, 6 doctorates awarded. Terminal master's awarded for partial completion of doctoral program.
Degree requirements: For master's, exam; for doctorate, one foreign language, thesis/dissertation, qualifying exam.
Entrance requirements: For master's, GRE General Test; for doctorate, GRE General Test, MA. *Application deadline:* For fall admission, 1/15 (priority date). Applications are processed on a rolling basis. *Application fee:* $40.
Expenses: Tuition: Full-time $18,720; part-time $1,040 per credit. Required fees: $450; $115 per term. Tuition and fees vary according to program.
Financial support: In 2001–02, 53 students received support, including 11 fellowships with full and partial tuition reimbursements available (averaging $3,100 per year), 3 research assistantships with full and partial tuition reimbursements available (averaging $3,300 per year), 7 teaching assistantships with full and partial tuition reimbursements available (averaging $3,600 per year); career-related internships or fieldwork, Federal Work-Study, scholarships/grants, and tuition waivers (full and partial) also available. Financial award application deadline: 1/15; financial award applicants required to submit FAFSA.
Faculty research: Critical theory; modern social and cultural systems; race, class, gender.
Dr. Judith Friedlander, Chair, 212-229-5757.
Application contact: Emanuel Lomax, Director of Admissions, 800-523-5411, *Fax:* 212-989-7102, *E-mail:* gfadmit@newschool.edu. *Web site:* http://www.newschool.edu/

Find an in-depth description at www.petersons.com/gradchannel.

■ NEW YORK UNIVERSITY

Graduate School of Arts and Science, Department of Anthropology, New York, NY 10012-1019

AWARDS Anthropology (MA, PhD), including archaeological anthropology, cultural anthropology, linguistic anthropology, physical anthropology, urban anthropology; anthropology and French studies (PhD). Part-time programs available.

Faculty: 22 full-time, 13 part-time/adjunct.
Students: 83 full-time (59 women), 11 part-time (9 women); includes 13 minority (7 Asian Americans or Pacific Islanders, 6 Hispanic Americans), 15 international. Average age 29. 225 applicants, 8% accepted, 8 enrolled. In 2001, 15 master's, 9 doctorates awarded.
Degree requirements: For master's, thesis; for doctorate, one foreign language, thesis/dissertation, comprehensive exam.
Entrance requirements: For master's, GRE General Test, TOEFL; for doctorate, GRE General Test, TOEFL, MA or equivalent. *Application deadline:* For fall admission, 1/4 (priority date). *Application fee:* $60.
Expenses: Tuition: Full-time $19,536; part-time $814 per credit. Required fees: $1,330; $38 per credit. Tuition and fees vary according to course load and program.
Financial support: Fellowships with tuition reimbursements, research assistantships with tuition reimbursements, teaching assistantships with tuition reimbursements, career-related internships or fieldwork, Federal Work-Study, and institutionally sponsored loans available. Financial award application deadline: 1/4; financial award applicants required to submit FAFSA.
Faculty research: Sociocultural anthropology, archaeology, biological anthropology, linguistic anthropology.
Fred Myers, Chairman, 212-998-8550, *E-mail:* anthropology@nyu.edu.
Application contact: Thomas Abercrombie, Director of Graduate Studies, 212-998-8550, *Fax:* 212-995-4014, *E-mail:* anthropology@nyu.edu. *Web site:* http://www.nyu.edu/gsas/dept/anthro/

■ NORTHERN ARIZONA UNIVERSITY

Graduate College, College of Social and Behavioral Sciences, Department of Anthropology, Flagstaff, AZ 86011

AWARDS Anthropology (MA); archaeology (MA).

Students: 47 full-time (23 women), 17 part-time (11 women); includes 12 minority (1 Asian American or Pacific Islander, 4 Hispanic Americans, 7 Native Americans), 3 international. Average age 32. 108 applicants, 28% accepted, 22 enrolled. In 2001, 24 degrees awarded.
Degree requirements: For master's, thesis (for some programs), internship paper.
Entrance requirements: For master's, 18 undergraduate hours in anthropology. *Application deadline:* For fall admission, 1/15. *Application fee:* $45.
Expenses: Tuition, state resident: full-time $2,488. Tuition, nonresident: full-time $10,354.
Financial support: In 2001–02, 8 research assistantships, 5 teaching assistantships were awarded. Federal Work-Study and tuition waivers (full and partial) also available. Financial award application deadline: 1/15.
Faculty research: Economic development, culture change, ethnohistory, archaeology of the Southwest, small town networks and HIV. *Total annual research expenditures:* $594,266.
Dr. Francis Smiley, Coordinator, 928-523-3180.
Application contact: Jill Dubisch, Graduate Coordinator, 928-523-6795, *E-mail:* anthropology@nau.edu. *Web site:* http://www.nau.edu/~anthro/

■ NORTHERN ILLINOIS UNIVERSITY

Graduate School, College of Liberal Arts and Sciences, Department of Anthropology, De Kalb, IL 60115-2854

AWARDS MA. Part-time programs available.

Faculty: 14 full-time (7 women), 1 part-time/adjunct (0 women).
Students: 32 full-time (18 women), 26 part-time (17 women); includes 6 minority (1 African American, 2 Asian Americans or Pacific Islanders, 3 Hispanic Americans), 6 international. Average age 30. 30 applicants, 73% accepted, 13 enrolled. In 2001, 8 degrees awarded.
Degree requirements: For master's, one foreign language, comprehensive exam.
Entrance requirements: For master's, GRE General Test, TOEFL, minimum GPA of 2.75, 15 hours in anthropology, previous course work in statistics. *Application deadline:* For fall admission, 6/1; for spring admission, 11/1. Applications are processed on a rolling basis. *Application fee:* $30.
Expenses: Tuition, state resident: full-time $5,124; part-time $148 per credit hour. Tuition, nonresident: full-time $8,666; part-time $295 per credit hour. Required fees: $51 per term.
Financial support: In 2001–02, 2 research assistantships with full tuition reimbursements, 13 teaching assistantships with full tuition reimbursements were awarded. Fellowships with full tuition reimbursements, career-related internships or fieldwork, Federal Work-Study, tuition waivers (full), and unspecified assistantships also available. Support available to part-time students.
Dr. Mark Mehrer, Chair, 815-753-0246, *Fax:* 815-753-7027.

■ NORTHWESTERN UNIVERSITY

The Graduate School, Judd A. and Marjorie Weinberg College of Arts and Sciences, Department of Anthropology, Evanston, IL 60208

AWARDS PhD, JD/PhD. Admissions and degrees offered through The Graduate School.

Faculty: 17 full-time (7 women), 4 part-time/adjunct (2 women).

Students: 32 full-time (14 women); includes 3 minority (2 African Americans, 1 Hispanic American), 3 international. Average age 28. 67 applicants, 19% accepted. In 2001, 5 doctorates awarded.
Degree requirements: For doctorate, thesis/dissertation.
Entrance requirements: For doctorate, GRE General Test, TOEFL. *Application deadline:* For fall admission, 12/31. *Application fee:* $50 ($55 for international students). Electronic applications accepted.
Expenses: Tuition: Full-time $26,526.
Financial support: In 2001–02, 16 students received support, including 5 fellowships with full tuition reimbursements available (averaging $16,080 per year), 7 teaching assistantships with full tuition reimbursements available (averaging $12,843 per year); career-related internships or fieldwork, Federal Work-Study, institutionally sponsored loans, scholarships/grants, and tuition waivers (full and partial) also available. Financial award application deadline: 12/31; financial award applicants required to submit FAFSA.
Faculty research: Archaeology of complex societies, gender, political/urban anthropology, linguistic anthropology, African studies.
Helen B. Schwartzman, Chair, 847-491-5402, *Fax:* 847-467-1778, *E-mail:* hslsjs@northwestern.edu.
Application contact: Harry E. Sanburn, Program Assistant, 847-491-4817, *Fax:* 847-467-1778, *E-mail:* h-sanburn@northwestern.edu. *Web site:* http://www.northwestern.edu/anthropology/

■ THE OHIO STATE UNIVERSITY

Graduate School, College of Social and Behavioral Sciences, Department of Anthropology, Columbus, OH 43210

AWARDS MA, PhD.

Degree requirements: For master's, thesis optional; for doctorate, one foreign language, thesis/dissertation.
Entrance requirements: For master's and doctorate, GRE General Test.

■ OREGON STATE UNIVERSITY

Graduate School, College of Liberal Arts, Department of Anthropology, Corvallis, OR 97331

AWARDS Anthropology (MAIS); applied anthropology (MA).

Faculty: 7 full-time (4 women).
Students: 25 full-time (15 women), 4 part-time (all women); includes 1 minority (Native American), 4 international. Average age 30. In 2001, 7 degrees awarded.
Degree requirements: For master's, one foreign language, thesis.
Entrance requirements: For master's, TOEFL, minimum GPA of 3.0 in last 90 hours. *Application deadline:* For fall admission, 3/1. Applications are processed on a rolling basis. *Application fee:* $50.
Expenses: Tuition, area resident: Full-time $15,933. Tuition, state resident: full-time $28,937.
Financial support: Research assistantships, teaching assistantships, career-related internships or fieldwork, Federal Work-Study, and institutionally sponsored loans available. Support available to part-time students. Financial award application deadline: 2/1.
Faculty research: Historical anthropology; first American studies; Japanese, Asian, South Pacific, and Native American cultures; business anthropology.
Dr. John A. Young, Chair, 541-737-4515, *Fax:* 541-737-3650, *E-mail:* jyoung@orst.edu.
Application contact: Loretta Wardrip, Contact, 541-737-4515, *Fax:* 541-737-6180, *E-mail:* lwardrip@orst.edu. *Web site:* http://www.orst.edu/dept/anthropology/index.html

■ THE PENNSYLVANIA STATE UNIVERSITY UNIVERSITY PARK CAMPUS

Graduate School, College of Liberal Arts, Department of Anthropology, State College, University Park, PA 16802-1503

AWARDS MA, PhD.

Students: 39 full-time (18 women), 5 part-time (1 woman). In 2001, 7 master's, 7 doctorates awarded.
Entrance requirements: For master's and doctorate, GRE General Test. *Application fee:* $45.
Expenses: Tuition, state resident: full-time $7,882; part-time $333 per credit. Tuition, nonresident: full-time $16,142; part-time $673 per credit. Required fees: $124 per semester.
Dr. Dean R. Snow, Head, 814-865-2509.

■ PORTLAND STATE UNIVERSITY

Graduate Studies, College of Engineering and Computer Science, Systems Science Program, Portland, OR 97207-0751

AWARDS Systems science/anthropology (PhD); systems science/business administration (PhD); systems science/civil engineering (PhD); systems science/economics (PhD); systems science/engineering management (PhD); systems science/general (PhD); systems science/mathematical sciences (PhD); systems science/mechanical engineering (PhD); systems science/psychology (PhD); systems science/sociology (PhD).

Faculty: 4 full-time (0 women).
Students: 47 full-time (19 women), 32 part-time (10 women); includes 9 minority (4 Asian Americans or Pacific Islanders, 3 Hispanic Americans, 2 Native Americans), 15 international. Average age 36. 52 applicants, 38% accepted. In 2001, 8 degrees awarded.
Degree requirements: For doctorate, variable foreign language requirement, thesis/dissertation.
Entrance requirements: For doctorate, GMAT, GRE General Test, TOEFL, minimum undergraduate GPA of 3.0. *Application deadline:* For fall admission, 2/1; for spring admission, 11/1. *Application fee:* $50.
Financial support: In 2001–02, 1 research assistantship with full tuition reimbursement (averaging $6,839 per year) was awarded; teaching assistantships with full tuition reimbursements, career-related internships or fieldwork, Federal Work-Study, and institutionally sponsored loans also available. Support available to part-time students. Financial award application deadline: 3/1; financial award applicants required to submit FAFSA.
Faculty research: Systems theory and methodology, artificial intelligence neural networks, information theory, nonlinear dynamics/chaos, modeling and simulation. *Total annual research expenditures:* $106,413.
Dr. Nancy Perrin, Director, 503-725-4960, *E-mail:* perrinn@pdx.edu.
Application contact: Dawn Kuenle, Coordinator, 503-725-4960, *E-mail:* dawn@sysc.pdx.edu. *Web site:* http://www.sysc.pdx.edu/

■ PORTLAND STATE UNIVERSITY

Graduate Studies, College of Liberal Arts and Sciences, Department of Anthropology, Portland, OR 97207-0751

AWARDS MA, PhD.

Faculty: 7 full-time (4 women), 1 (woman) part-time/adjunct.
Students: 10 full-time (5 women), 8 part-time (6 women); includes 1 minority (Hispanic American), 1 international. Average age 34. 14 applicants, 57% accepted. In 2001, 1 degree awarded.
Degree requirements: For master's, one foreign language, thesis; for doctorate, thesis/dissertation.
Entrance requirements: For master's, GRE General Test, TOEFL, minimum GPA of 3.25 in upper-division anthropology course work, 3.0 overall. *Application deadline:* For fall admission, 2/1; for winter admission, 9/1 (priority date); for spring admission, 11/1 (priority date). *Application fee:* $50.
Financial support: In 2001–02, 1 teaching assistantship with full tuition reimbursement (averaging $4,968 per year) was awarded; research assistantships, career-related internships or fieldwork, Federal Work-Study, and institutionally sponsored loans also available. Support available to part-time students. Financial award application deadline: 3/1; financial award applicants required to submit FAFSA.

Portland State University (continued)
Faculty research: Forensic anthropology, Northwest Coast prehistory, Native Americans, applied anthropology, urban anthropology. *Total annual research expenditures:* $35,197.
Dr. Marc Feldesman, Head, 503-725-3851, *Fax:* 503-725-3905, *E-mail:* feldesmanm@pdx.edu.
Application contact: Connie Cash, Office Specialist, 503-725-3081, *Fax:* 503-725-3905, *E-mail:* cashc@pdx.edu. *Web site:* http://www-adm.pdx.edu/user/anth/

■ PRINCETON UNIVERSITY

Graduate School, Department of Anthropology, Princeton, NJ 08544-1019

AWARDS PhD.

Degree requirements: For doctorate, variable foreign language requirement, thesis/dissertation.
Entrance requirements: For doctorate, GRE General Test, sample of written work.
Faculty research: Symbolic anthropology, social theory, gender studies, law and society, political and social anthropology.

■ PURDUE UNIVERSITY

Graduate School, School of Liberal Arts, Department of Sociology and Anthropology, West Lafayette, IN 47907

AWARDS Anthropology (MS, PhD); sociology (MS, PhD).

Faculty: 32 full-time (8 women), 1 (woman) part-time/adjunct.
Students: 67 full-time (45 women), 1 (woman) part-time; includes 9 minority (1 African American, 2 Asian Americans or Pacific Islanders, 6 Hispanic Americans), 12 international. Average age 32. 73 applicants, 52% accepted. In 2001, 7 master's, 4 doctorates awarded. Terminal master's awarded for partial completion of doctoral program.
Degree requirements: For doctorate, thesis/dissertation.
Entrance requirements: For master's and doctorate, GRE General Test, TOEFL, TWE. *Application deadline:* For fall admission, 12/31 (priority date). Applications are processed on a rolling basis. *Application fee:* $30. Electronic applications accepted.
Expenses: Tuition, state resident: full-time $4,164; part-time $149 per credit hour. Tuition, nonresident: full-time $13,872; part-time $458 per credit hour. Tuition and fees vary according to campus/location and program.
Financial support: In 2001–02, 39 students received support, including 4 fellowships, 4 research assistantships, 31 teaching assistantships; tuition waivers (full) also available. Support available to part-time students. Financial award application deadline: 2/15; financial award applicants required to submit FAFSA.
Faculty research: Communiversity survey project, risk, fear, constrained behavior, archaeological services.
Dr. C. C. Perrucci, Head, 765-494-4666, *Fax:* 765-496-1476.
Application contact: Dr. H. R. Potter, Graduate Committee Chair, 765-494-4712, *Fax:* 765-496-1476, *E-mail:* potter@sri.soc.purdue.edu. *Web site:* http://www.sla.purdue.edu/academic/grad.prog/

■ RICE UNIVERSITY

Graduate Programs, School of Social Sciences, Department of Anthropology, Houston, TX 77251-1892

AWARDS MA, PhD.

Faculty: 10 full-time (4 women).
Students: 35 full-time (19 women); includes 7 minority (1 African American, 4 Asian Americans or Pacific Islanders, 2 Hispanic Americans), 14 international. 27 applicants, 11% accepted. In 2001, 1 master's, 2 doctorates awarded. Terminal master's awarded for partial completion of doctoral program.
Degree requirements: For master's, variable foreign language requirement, thesis; for doctorate, one foreign language, thesis/dissertation.
Entrance requirements: For master's and doctorate, GRE General Test, TOEFL, minimum GPA of 3.0. *Application deadline:* For fall admission, 2/1. *Application fee:* $25.
Expenses: Tuition: Full-time $17,300. Required fees: $250.
Financial support: In 2001–02, 13 fellowships with tuition reimbursements were awarded; Federal Work-Study, institutionally sponsored loans, and scholarships/grants also available.
Faculty research: Archaeology, biological anthropology, anthropological linguistics, complex societies.
George E. Marcus, Chairman, 713-348-3382, *Fax:* 713-348-5455, *E-mail:* marcus@rice.edu.

■ RUTGERS, THE STATE UNIVERSITY OF NEW JERSEY, NEW BRUNSWICK

Graduate School, Program in Anthropology, New Brunswick, NJ 08901-1281

AWARDS MA, PhD.

Degree requirements: For master's, thesis or alternative; for doctorate, thesis/dissertation.
Entrance requirements: For master's and doctorate, GRE General Test, writing sample.
Faculty research: Human evolution, lithic technology, behavioral ecology, ethnicity, gender. *Web site:* http://anthro.rutgers.edu/

■ SAN DIEGO STATE UNIVERSITY

Graduate and Research Affairs, College of Arts and Letters, Department of Anthropology, San Diego, CA 92182

AWARDS MA.

Degree requirements: For master's, one foreign language, thesis.
Entrance requirements: For master's, GRE General Test, TOEFL.
Faculty research: Meso-American archaeology, cognitive anthropology, ethnomusicology, primate conservation, biomedical anthropology.

■ SAN FRANCISCO STATE UNIVERSITY

Graduate Division, College of Behavioral and Social Sciences, Department of Anthropology, San Francisco, CA 94132-1722

AWARDS MA.

Degree requirements: For master's, one foreign language, thesis or alternative.
Entrance requirements: For master's, minimum GPA of 2.5 in last 60 units.
Faculty research: Immigration, ethnicity, urban anthropology, Californian and Latin American archaeology.

■ SOUTHERN ILLINOIS UNIVERSITY CARBONDALE

Graduate School, College of Liberal Arts, Department of Anthropology, Carbondale, IL 62901-6806

AWARDS MA, PhD.

Faculty: 14 full-time (5 women).
Students: 42 full-time (15 women), 25 part-time (13 women); includes 4 minority (1 Asian American or Pacific Islander, 3 Hispanic Americans), 6 international. 23 applicants, 57% accepted. In 2001, 2 master's, 4 doctorates awarded.
Degree requirements: For master's and doctorate, one foreign language, thesis/dissertation.
Entrance requirements: For master's, GRE General Test, TOEFL, minimum GPA of 2.7; for doctorate, GRE General Test, TOEFL, minimum GPA of 3.25. *Application deadline:* Applications are processed on a rolling basis. *Application fee:* $20.
Expenses: Tuition, state resident: full-time $3,794; part-time $154 per hour. Tuition, nonresident: full-time $6,566; part-time $308 per hour. Required fees: $277 per hour.
Financial support: In 2001–02, 37 students received support, including 10 fellowships with full tuition reimbursements available, 10 research assistantships with full tuition reimbursements available, 16 teaching assistantships with full tuition reimbursements available; career-related

internships or fieldwork, Federal Work-Study, institutionally sponsored loans, scholarships/grants, and tuition waivers (full) also available. Support available to part-time students. Financial award application deadline: 1/15.
Faculty research: Archaeology, human variability, evolution, cultural ecology, social anthropology.
Dr. Jonathan Hill, Chairperson, 618-536-6651.
Application contact: Christi McGee, Graduate Secretary, 618-536-6651, *Fax:* 618-453-5037, *E-mail:* cmcgee@siu.edu. *Web site:* http://www.siu.edu/~anthro/

Find an in-depth description at www.petersons.com/gradchannel.

■ SOUTHERN METHODIST UNIVERSITY

Dedman College, Department of Anthropology, Dallas, TX 75275

AWARDS Anthropology (MA, PhD); archaeology (MA, PhD); medical anthropology (MA, PhD).

Faculty: 18 full-time (3 women).
Students: 16 full-time (12 women), 51 part-time (30 women); includes 2 Asian Americans or Pacific Islanders, 1 Hispanic American, 2 international. 24 applicants, 54% accepted, 13 enrolled. In 2001, 5 master's, 2 doctorates awarded. Terminal master's awarded for partial completion of doctoral program.
Degree requirements: For master's, one foreign language, thesis or alternative; for doctorate, one foreign language, thesis/dissertation, qualifying exam.
Entrance requirements: For master's and doctorate, GRE General Test, minimum GPA of 3.0. *Application deadline:* For fall admission, 2/1 (priority date); for spring admission, 11/30 (priority date). Applications are processed on a rolling basis. *Application fee:* $50.
Expenses: Tuition: Part-time $285 per credit hour.
Financial support: In 2001–02, 29 students received support, including 5 fellowships (averaging $8,500 per year), 9 research assistantships with full tuition reimbursements available (averaging $8,500 per year), 21 teaching assistantships with full tuition reimbursements available (averaging $8,500 per year); Federal Work-Study, institutionally sponsored loans, scholarships/grants, traineeships, and tuition waivers (full) also available. Financial award application deadline: 3/1; financial award applicants required to submit FAFSA.
Faculty research: Health and gender, Paleoindians, Mesoamerica, American southwest, kinship and ethnicity.
Dr. Caroline Brettell, Chair, 214-768-4254.
Application contact: Dr. Victoria Lockwood, Graduate Adviser, 214-768-4022, *E-mail:* vlockwoo@mail.smu.edu.

■ STANFORD UNIVERSITY

School of Humanities and Sciences, Department of Anthropological Sciences, Stanford, CA 94305-9991

AWARDS AM, MS, PhD.

Faculty: 7 full-time (1 woman).
Students: 10 full-time (5 women); includes 1 minority (Native American), 2 international. Average age 28. 32 applicants, 31% accepted. In 2001, 1 master's awarded. Terminal master's awarded for partial completion of doctoral program.
Degree requirements: For master's, thesis; for doctorate, one foreign language, thesis/dissertation.
Entrance requirements: For master's and doctorate, GRE General Test, TOEFL. *Application deadline:* For fall admission, 1/5. *Application fee:* $65 ($80 for international students). Electronic applications accepted.
Dr. John W. Rick, Acting Chair, 650-736-2675, *Fax:* 650-725-9996, *E-mail:* johnrick@stanford.edu.
Application contact: Mary Cahill, Student Services Coordinator, 650-723-0734, *Fax:* 650-725-9996, *E-mail:* mcahill@stanford.edu. *Web site:* http://www.stanford.edu/dept/anthsci/

■ STANFORD UNIVERSITY

School of Humanities and Sciences, Department of Cultural and Social Anthropology, Stanford, CA 94305-9991

AWARDS AM, PhD.

Faculty: 10 full-time (6 women).
Students: 10 full-time (8 women); includes 4 minority (1 African American, 2 Asian Americans or Pacific Islanders, 1 Hispanic American), 3 international. Average age 26. 127 applicants, 12% accepted. Terminal master's awarded for partial completion of doctoral program.
Degree requirements: For master's, thesis; for doctorate, one foreign language, thesis/dissertation.
Entrance requirements: For master's and doctorate, GRE General Test, TOEFL. *Application deadline:* For fall admission, 1/5. *Application fee:* $65 ($80 for international students). Electronic applications accepted.
Financial support: Teaching assistantships available.
Sylvia J. Yanigasako, Chair, 650-723-5038, *Fax:* 650-725-0605, *E-mail:* syanag@stanford.edu.
Application contact: Graduate Admissions Coordinator, 650-723-4641, *Fax:* 650-725-0605. *Web site:* http://www.stanford.edu/group/anthro/

■ STATE UNIVERSITY OF NEW YORK AT ALBANY

College of Arts and Sciences, Department of Anthropology, Albany, NY 12222-0001

AWARDS MA, PhD. Part-time and evening/weekend programs available.

Students: 36 full-time (19 women), 44 part-time (19 women); includes 8 minority (1 African American, 1 Asian American or Pacific Islander, 4 Hispanic Americans, 2 Native Americans), 10 international. Average age 33. 51 applicants, 55% accepted. In 2001, 11 master's, 6 doctorates awarded. Terminal master's awarded for partial completion of doctoral program.
Degree requirements: For master's, thesis, comprehensive exam; for doctorate, 2 foreign languages, thesis/dissertation, field exams.
Entrance requirements: For master's and doctorate, GRE. *Application deadline:* For fall admission, 4/1; for spring admission, 11/1. Applications are processed on a rolling basis. *Application fee:* $50.
Expenses: Tuition, state resident: full-time $2,550; part-time $213 per credit. Tuition, nonresident: full-time $4,208; part-time $351 per credit. Required fees: $470; $470 per year.
Financial support: Fellowships, research assistantships, teaching assistantships, career-related internships or fieldwork available. Financial award application deadline: 3/15.
Faculty research: Economic and ecological anthropology; language, culture, and cognition; symbolic and interpretive anthropology; human evolution, morphology, demography, and medical anthropology; spatial and settlement archaeology.
Dr. Robert Jarvenpa, Chair, 518-442-4700.
Application contact: 518-442-3980.

■ STATE UNIVERSITY OF NEW YORK AT BINGHAMTON

Graduate School, School of Arts and Sciences, Department of Anthropology, Binghamton, NY 13902-6000

AWARDS MA, PhD. Part-time programs available.

Faculty: 17 full-time (6 women), 4 part-time/adjunct (1 woman).
Students: 47 full-time (22 women), 66 part-time (39 women); includes 9 minority (3 African Americans, 4 Hispanic Americans, 2 Native Americans), 19 international. Average age 34. 73 applicants, 47% accepted, 9 enrolled. In 2001, 13 master's, 4 doctorates awarded. Terminal master's awarded for partial completion of doctoral program.
Degree requirements: For master's, one foreign language, thesis or alternative, written exam; for doctorate, variable foreign language requirement, thesis/dissertation, oral exam.

State University of New York at Binghamton (continued)
Entrance requirements: For master's and doctorate, GRE General Test, GRE Subject Test, TOEFL. *Application deadline:* For fall admission, 4/15 (priority date); for spring admission, 11/1. Applications are processed on a rolling basis. Electronic applications accepted.
Expenses: Tuition, state resident: full-time $5,100; part-time $213 per credit. Tuition, nonresident: full-time $8,416; part-time $351 per credit. Required fees: $811.
Financial support: In 2001–02, 41 students received support, including 7 fellowships with full tuition reimbursements available (averaging $7,788 per year), 3 research assistantships with full tuition reimbursements available (averaging $7,081 per year), 30 teaching assistantships with full tuition reimbursements available (averaging $7,230 per year); career-related internships or fieldwork, Federal Work-Study, institutionally sponsored loans, tuition waivers (full and partial), and unspecified assistantships also available. Support available to part-time students. Financial award application deadline: 2/15.
Dr. Charles Cobb, Chairperson, 607-777-2738.

■ STONY BROOK UNIVERSITY, STATE UNIVERSITY OF NEW YORK

Graduate School, College of Arts and Sciences, Department of Anthropology, Stony Brook, NY 11794

AWARDS MA, PhD.

Faculty: 12 full-time (4 women), 1 part-time/adjunct (0 women).
Students: 27 full-time (17 women), 27 part-time (14 women); includes 5 minority (1 African American, 2 Asian Americans or Pacific Islanders, 2 Hispanic Americans), 12 international. 71 applicants, 31% accepted. In 2001, 4 master's, 6 doctorates awarded.
Degree requirements: For master's, thesis, fieldwork; for doctorate, one foreign language, thesis/dissertation, fieldwork.
Entrance requirements: For master's and doctorate, GRE General Test, TOEFL. *Application deadline:* For fall admission, 1/15. *Application fee:* $50.
Expenses: Tuition, state resident: full-time $5,100; part-time $213 per credit. Tuition, nonresident: full-time $8,416; part-time $351 per credit. Required fees: $496.
Financial support: In 2001–02, 2 fellowships, 3 research assistantships, 24 teaching assistantships were awarded. Career-related internships or fieldwork also available.
Faculty research: Social and cultural anthropology, cultural history and archaeology, physical anthropology. *Total annual research expenditures:* $664,692.
Dr. Frederick Grine, Chair, 631-632-7606.
Application contact: Dr. Elizabeth Stone, Co-Director, 631-632-7606, *Fax:* 631-632-9165, *E-mail:* estone@datalab2.sbs.sunysb.edu. *Web site:* http://www.sunysb.edu/anthro/

Find an in-depth description at www.petersons.com/gradchannel.

■ SYRACUSE UNIVERSITY

Graduate School, Maxwell School of Citizenship and Public Affairs and College of Arts and Sciences, Department of Anthropology, Syracuse, NY 13244-0003

AWARDS MA, PhD.

Faculty: 13 full-time (5 women).
Students: 62 full-time (40 women), 16 part-time (9 women); includes 11 minority (4 African Americans, 4 Asian Americans or Pacific Islanders, 3 Hispanic Americans), 14 international. Average age 31. 50 applicants, 30% accepted, 11 enrolled. In 2001, 3 master's, 3 doctorates awarded.
Degree requirements: For master's, thesis or alternative; for doctorate, one foreign language, thesis/dissertation.
Entrance requirements: For master's and doctorate, GRE General Test. *Application deadline:* Applications are processed on a rolling basis. *Application fee:* $50.
Expenses: Tuition: Full-time $15,528; part-time $647 per credit. Required fees: $420; $38 per term. Tuition and fees vary according to program.
Financial support: In 2001–02, 2 fellowships with tuition reimbursements (averaging $12,313 per year), 14 teaching assistantships with full tuition reimbursements (averaging $10,600 per year) were awarded. Research assistantships, Federal Work-Study and tuition waivers (partial) also available.
Peter Castro, Chair, 315-443-1971, *Fax:* 315-443-4830, *E-mail:* ahcastro@maxwell.syr.edu.
Application contact: Christopher DeCorse, Graduate Director, 315-443-4647, *Fax:* 315-443-4830, *E-mail:* crdecoys@maxwell.syr.edu.

Find an in-depth description at www.petersons.com/gradchannel.

■ TEACHERS COLLEGE COLUMBIA UNIVERSITY

Graduate Faculty of Education, Department of International and Transcultural Studies, Program in Anthropology, New York, NY 10027-6696

AWARDS Ed M, MA, Ed D, PhD.

Degree requirements: For doctorate, variable foreign language requirement, thesis/dissertation.
Entrance requirements: For master's and doctorate, GRE General Test.
Expenses: Tuition: Full-time $19,080; part-time $780 per unit. Required fees: $170 per semester.
Faculty research: African studies, sociocultural change, education in the developing world, human development in social and cultural contexts, culture and communication theory.

■ TEMPLE UNIVERSITY

Graduate School, College of Liberal Arts, Department of Anthropology, Philadelphia, PA 19122-6096

AWARDS MA, PhD. Part-time and evening/weekend programs available. Terminal master's awarded for partial completion of doctoral program.

Degree requirements: For master's, thesis optional; for doctorate, 2 foreign languages, thesis/dissertation.
Entrance requirements: For master's and doctorate, GRE General Test, minimum GPA of 3.0. Electronic applications accepted.
Expenses: Tuition, state resident: full-time $8,487; part-time $369 per credit hour. Tuition, nonresident: full-time $12,282; part-time $534 per credit hour. Required fees: $350. Tuition and fees vary according to course load, program and reciprocity agreements.
Faculty research: Political economy, biocultural adaptation, visual anthropology, critical urban anthropology, archaeology. *Web site:* http://www.temple.edu/anthro/

■ TEXAS A&M UNIVERSITY

College of Liberal Arts, Department of Anthropology, College Station, TX 77843

AWARDS MA, PhD.

Faculty: 32.
Students: 114 (63 women). Average age 33.
Degree requirements: For doctorate, thesis/dissertation.
Entrance requirements: For master's and doctorate, GRE General Test, TOEFL. *Application fee:* $50 ($75 for international students).
Expenses: Tuition, state resident: full-time $11,872. Tuition, nonresident: full-time $17,892.
Financial support: Fellowships, research assistantships, teaching assistantships, career-related internships or fieldwork, Federal Work-Study, and institutionally sponsored loans available. Financial award application deadline: 4/1; financial award applicants required to submit FAFSA.
Faculty research: Nautical archaeology, archaeological conservation, archaeological palynology, paleoethnobotany, folklore.
Dr. David L. Carlson, Head, 979-845-5296, *Fax:* 979-845-4070.
Application contact: Karen Taylor, Assistant Advisor, 979-845-9333, *Fax:* 979-845-4070.

■ TEXAS TECH UNIVERSITY

Graduate School, College of Arts and Sciences, Department of Sociology, Anthropology and Social Work, Lubbock, TX 79409

AWARDS Anthropology (MA); sociology (MA). Part-time programs available.

Faculty: 13 full-time (3 women), 2 part-time/adjunct (1 woman).
Students: 15 full-time (9 women), 14 part-time (9 women); includes 4 minority (1 African American, 2 Asian Americans or Pacific Islanders, 1 Hispanic American), 1 international. Average age 30. 15 applicants, 47% accepted, 4 enrolled. In 2001, 9 degrees awarded.
Degree requirements: For master's, one foreign language.
Entrance requirements: For master's, GRE General Test. *Application deadline:* Applications are processed on a rolling basis. *Application fee:* $25 ($50 for international students). Electronic applications accepted.
Expenses: Tuition, state resident: full-time $1,926; part-time $107 per credit hour. Tuition, nonresident: full-time $5,724; part-time $318 per credit hour. Required fees: $779; $737 per year. Tuition and fees vary according to course level, course load and program.
Financial support: In 2001–02, 15 students received support, including 2 research assistantships with partial tuition reimbursements available (averaging $9,250 per year), 13 teaching assistantships with partial tuition reimbursements available (averaging $9,308 per year); fellowships, Federal Work-Study and institutionally sponsored loans also available. Support available to part-time students. Financial award application deadline: 5/1; financial award applicants required to submit FAFSA.
Faculty research: Minority relations, social psychology, Texas and Southwest archaeology, Latin America, Native Americans. *Total annual research expenditures:* $29,331.
Dr. Doyle Paul Johnson, Chair, 806-742-2401, *Fax:* 806-742-1088.
Application contact: Graduate Adviser, 806-742-2401, *Fax:* 806-742-1088. *Web site:* http://www.ttu.edu/sasw/

■ TULANE UNIVERSITY

Graduate School, Department of Anthropology, New Orleans, LA 70118-5669

AWARDS MA, MS, PhD. Terminal master's awarded for partial completion of doctoral program.

Degree requirements: For master's, one foreign language, thesis; for doctorate, 2 foreign languages, thesis/dissertation.
Entrance requirements: For master's, GRE General Test, TSE, minimum B average in undergraduate course work; for doctorate, GRE General Test, TSE.
Expenses: Tuition: Full-time $24,675. Required fees: $2,210.
Faculty research: Linguistics, physical anthropology, sociocultural archaeology, Mesoamerica.

■ UNIVERSITY AT BUFFALO, THE STATE UNIVERSITY OF NEW YORK

Graduate School, College of Arts and Sciences, Department of Anthropology, Buffalo, NY 14260

AWARDS MA, PhD. Part-time programs available.

Faculty: 17 full-time (5 women), 4 part-time/adjunct (2 women).
Students: 66 full-time (37 women), 13 part-time (7 women); includes 4 minority (1 African American, 1 Asian American or Pacific Islander, 2 Native Americans), 9 international. Average age 27. 91 applicants, 48% accepted, 18 enrolled. In 2001, 11 master's, 3 doctorates awarded. Terminal master's awarded for partial completion of doctoral program.
Degree requirements: For master's, project; for doctorate, one foreign language, thesis/dissertation, exam.
Entrance requirements: For master's, GRE General Test, TOEFL, minimum GPA of 3.2; for doctorate, GRE General Test, TOEFL. *Application deadline:* For fall admission, 4/1 (priority date). Applications are processed on a rolling basis. *Application fee:* $35. Electronic applications accepted.
Expenses: Tuition, state resident: full-time $6,118. Tuition, nonresident: full-time $9,434.
Financial support: In 2001–02, 23 students received support, including 7 fellowships with tuition reimbursements available, 1 research assistantship, 14 teaching assistantships with tuition reimbursements available (averaging $8,400 per year); career-related internships or fieldwork, Federal Work-Study, institutionally sponsored loans, and unspecified assistantships also available. Financial award application deadline: 2/1; financial award applicants required to submit FAFSA.
Faculty research: Old and New World archaeology, medical anthropology, primatology/human biology, cognition. *Total annual research expenditures:* $298,299.
Dr. Barbara Tedlock, Chair, 716-645-2414, *Fax:* 716-645-3808.
Application contact: Mary Anne Lang, Graduate Secretary, 716-645-2414, *Fax:* 716-645-3808, *E-mail:* mal@acsu.buffalo.edu. *Web site:* http://wings.buffalo.edu/anthropology/

■ THE UNIVERSITY OF ALABAMA

Graduate School, College of Arts and Sciences, Department of Anthropology, Tuscaloosa, AL 35487

AWARDS MA.

Faculty: 12 full-time (3 women).
Students: 14 full-time (8 women), 10 part-time (6 women); includes 1 minority (Asian American or Pacific Islander). Average age 26. 19 applicants, 58% accepted, 7 enrolled. In 2001, 8 degrees awarded.
Degree requirements: For master's, one foreign language, thesis or alternative, comprehensive exam.
Entrance requirements: For master's, GRE General Test, minimum undergraduate GPA of 3.0. *Application deadline:* For fall admission, 2/15 (priority date). *Application fee:* $25.
Expenses: Tuition, state resident: full-time $3,292; part-time $183 per credit hour. Tuition, nonresident: full-time $8,912; part-time $495 per credit hour. Tuition and fees vary according to course load, campus/location and program.
Financial support: In 2001–02, 2 fellowships with tuition reimbursements, 4 research assistantships with partial tuition reimbursements (averaging $17,208 per year), 8 teaching assistantships with tuition reimbursements were awarded. Career-related internships or fieldwork, Federal Work-Study, and institutionally sponsored loans also available. Financial award application deadline: 1/10.
Faculty research: Medical anthropology, archaeology, physical and cultural anthropology. *Total annual research expenditures:* $108,937.
Dr. Vernon J. Knight, Chairman, 205-348-5947, *E-mail:* vknight@tenhoor.as.ua.edu.
Application contact: Dr. Ian Brown, Graduate Adviser, 205-348-5947, *E-mail:* ibrown@tenhoor.as.ua.edu.

■ THE UNIVERSITY OF ALABAMA AT BIRMINGHAM

Graduate School, School of Social and Behavioral Sciences, Department of Anthropology, Birmingham, AL 35294

AWARDS MA.

Students: 1 (woman) full-time, 4 part-time (3 women).
Degree requirements: For master's, one foreign language.
Entrance requirements: For master's, GRE General Test. *Application deadline:* Applications are processed on a rolling basis. *Application fee:* $35 ($60 for international students). Electronic applications accepted.
Expenses: Tuition, state resident: full-time $3,058. Tuition, nonresident: full-time $5,746. Tuition and fees vary according to course load, degree level and program.
Financial support: Career-related internships or fieldwork, Federal Work-Study, and institutionally sponsored loans available.
Faculty research: Ethnicity, medical anthropology, primate conservation, pastoral systems, Southeastern archaeology, linguistics.
Dr. Brian C. Hesse, Chair, 205-934-3508, *Fax:* 205-934-3508, *E-mail:* bhesse@

The University of Alabama at Birmingham (continued)

uab.edu. *Web site:* http://www.sbs.uab.edu/anthro.htm/

■ UNIVERSITY OF ALASKA FAIRBANKS

Graduate School, College of Liberal Arts, Department of Anthropology, Fairbanks, AK 99775-7480

AWARDS MA, PhD. Part-time programs available.

Faculty: 10 full-time (6 women).
Students: 24 full-time (13 women), 12 part-time (5 women); includes 3 minority (all Native Americans), 4 international. Average age 35. 30 applicants, 43% accepted, 9 enrolled. In 2001, 5 master's, 1 doctorate awarded.
Degree requirements: For master's, thesis or alternative, comprehensive exam; for doctorate, one foreign language, thesis/dissertation, comprehensive exam.
Entrance requirements: For master's, GRE General Test, TOEFL, minimum GPA of 3.25, undergraduate major/minor in anthropology; for doctorate, GRE General Test, TOEFL. *Application deadline:* For fall admission, 4/1; for spring admission, 11/1. *Application fee:* $35.
Expenses: Tuition, state resident: full-time $4,272; part-time $178 per credit. Tuition, nonresident: full-time $8,328; part-time $347 per credit. Required fees: $960; $60 per term. Part-time tuition and fees vary according to course load.
Financial support: In 2001–02, fellowships with tuition reimbursements (averaging $10,000 per year); research assistantships with tuition reimbursements, teaching assistantships with tuition reimbursements, career-related internships or fieldwork, Federal Work-Study, and scholarships/grants also available. Financial award application deadline: 6/1.
Faculty research: Circumpolar archaeology and population biology, rural subsistence, late glacial and early post-glacial adaptations, Native Alaskan history and archaeology.
Dr. Peter Schweitzer, Head, 907-474-7288.
Application contact: Dr. David Smith, Graduate Program Coordinator, 907-474-7288.

■ THE UNIVERSITY OF ARIZONA

Graduate College, College of Social and Behavioral Sciences, Department of Anthropology, Tucson, AZ 85721

AWARDS MA, PhD. Part-time programs available. Terminal master's awarded for partial completion of doctoral program.

Degree requirements: For master's, thesis or alternative; for doctorate, one foreign language, thesis/dissertation.
Entrance requirements: For master's and doctorate, GRE General Test, TOEFL, minimum GPA of 3.5.
Expenses: Tuition, state resident: full-time $2,490; part-time $436 per unit. Tuition, nonresident: full-time $10,300; part-time $436 per unit. Full-time tuition and fees vary according to degree level and program.
Faculty research: Archaeology of pre-Han China, cultural ecology, health- and illness-related behavior, interaction of linguistic and social processes, human growth and development under stress.

■ UNIVERSITY OF ARKANSAS

Graduate School, J. William Fulbright College of Arts and Sciences, Department of Anthropology, Fayetteville, AR 72701-1201

AWARDS MA.

Students: 34 full-time (17 women), 13 part-time (8 women); includes 5 minority (2 African Americans, 1 Asian American or Pacific Islander, 2 Hispanic Americans), 2 international. 27 applicants, 93% accepted. In 2001, 17 degrees awarded.
Degree requirements: For master's, comprehensive exam.
Entrance requirements: For master's, GRE General Test, minimum GPA of 3.0. *Application fee:* $40 ($50 for international students).
Expenses: Tuition, state resident: full-time $3,553; part-time $197 per credit. Tuition, nonresident: full-time $8,411; part-time $467 per credit. Required fees: $42 per credit. Tuition and fees vary according to course load and program.
Financial support: In 2001–02, 1 fellowship, 24 teaching assistantships were awarded. Research assistantships, career-related internships or fieldwork and Federal Work-Study also available. Support available to part-time students. Financial award application deadline: 4/1; financial award applicants required to submit FAFSA.
Dr. Mary Jo Schneider, Chair, 479-575-2508.

■ UNIVERSITY OF ARKANSAS

Graduate School, J. William Fulbright College of Arts and Sciences, Interdisciplinary Program in Environmental Dynamics, Fayetteville, AR 72701-1201

AWARDS PhD.

Students: 17 full-time (4 women), 9 part-time (4 women); includes 1 minority (Asian American or Pacific Islander), 5 international. 10 applicants, 90% accepted. In 2001, 1 degree awarded.
Degree requirements: For doctorate, thesis/dissertation.
Application fee: $40 ($50 for international students).
Expenses: Tuition, state resident: full-time $3,553; part-time $197 per credit. Tuition, nonresident: full-time $8,411; part-time $467 per credit. Required fees: $42 per credit. Tuition and fees vary according to course load and program.
Financial support: Teaching assistantships available. Financial award application deadline: 4/1.
Allen McCartney, Head, 479-575-2508, *E-mail:* endy@comp.uark.edu.

■ UNIVERSITY OF CALIFORNIA, BERKELEY

Graduate Division, College of Letters and Science, Department of Anthropology, Program in Anthropology, Berkeley, CA 94720-1500

AWARDS PhD.

Degree requirements: For doctorate, thesis/dissertation.
Entrance requirements: For doctorate, GRE General Test, TOEFL, minimum GPA of 3.0.
Expenses: Tuition, nonresident: full-time $10,704. Required fees: $4,349.

■ UNIVERSITY OF CALIFORNIA, BERKELEY

Graduate Division, College of Letters and Science, Department of Anthropology, Program in Medical Anthropology, Berkeley, CA 94720-1500

AWARDS PhD.

Degree requirements: For doctorate, thesis/dissertation.
Entrance requirements: For doctorate, GRE General Test, TOEFL, minimum GPA of 3.0.
Expenses: Tuition, nonresident: full-time $10,704. Required fees: $4,349. *Web site:* http://ls.berkeley.edu/dept/auth/dept.html

■ UNIVERSITY OF CALIFORNIA, DAVIS

Graduate Studies, Program in Anthropology, Davis, CA 95616

AWARDS MA, PhD.

Faculty: 12 full-time (5 women), 6 part-time/adjunct (4 women).
Students: 38 full-time (22 women); includes 4 minority (1 African American, 2 Asian Americans or Pacific Islanders, 1 Hispanic American), 4 international. Average age 31. 80 applicants, 30% accepted, 11 enrolled. In 2001, 6 master's, 8 doctorates awarded. Terminal master's awarded for partial completion of doctoral program.
Degree requirements: For master's, one foreign language; for doctorate, one foreign language, thesis/dissertation.
Entrance requirements: For master's and doctorate, GRE General Test, minimum GPA of 3.0. *Application deadline:* For fall admission, 1/15. *Application fee:* $60. Electronic applications accepted.

Expenses: Tuition, state resident: full-time $4,831. Tuition, nonresident: full-time $15,725.
Financial support: In 2001–02, 38 students received support, including 21 fellowships with full and partial tuition reimbursements available (averaging $7,400 per year), 6 research assistantships with full and partial tuition reimbursements available (averaging $10,971 per year), 29 teaching assistantships with partial tuition reimbursements available (averaging $13,850 per year); career-related internships or fieldwork, Federal Work-Study, institutionally sponsored loans, and tuition waivers (full and partial) also available. Financial award application deadline: 1/15; financial award applicants required to submit FAFSA.
Faculty research: Archaeology, linguistics, biological and sociocultural anthropology.
Robert Bettinger, Graduate Chair, 530-752-0551, *Fax:* 530-752-8885, *E-mail:* rlbettinger@ucdavis.edu.
Application contact: Barbara Raney, Administrative Assistant, 530-752-8131, *Fax:* 530-752-8885, *E-mail:* bmraney@ucdavis.edu. *Web site:* http://www.anthro.ucdavis.edu/

■ UNIVERSITY OF CALIFORNIA, IRVINE

Office of Research and Graduate Studies, School of Social Sciences, Department of Anthropology, Irvine, CA 92697

AWARDS MA, PhD.

Faculty: 11.
Students: 28 full-time (22 women); includes 7 minority (3 Asian Americans or Pacific Islanders, 4 Hispanic Americans), 5 international. 36 applicants, 33% accepted, 7 enrolled. In 2001, 1 master's, 3 doctorates awarded.
Degree requirements: For doctorate, one foreign language, thesis/dissertation.
Entrance requirements: For master's, minimum GPA of 3.0; for doctorate, GRE General Test. *Application deadline:* For fall and spring admission, 1/15 (priority date); for winter admission, 10/15 (priority date). Applications are processed on a rolling basis. *Application fee:* $60. Electronic applications accepted.
Expenses: Tuition, nonresident: full-time $10,704. Required fees: $8,396. Tuition and fees vary according to course load, program and student level.
Financial support: Fellowships, research assistantships, teaching assistantships, institutionally sponsored loans and tuition waivers (full and partial) available. Financial award application deadline: 3/2; financial award applicants required to submit FAFSA.
Faculty research: Cognitive anthropology, sociology of culture, social structure, family and gender.
James Ferguson, Chair, 949-824-6179.
Application contact: Ivonne Maldonado, Graduate Counselor, 949-824-7352, *Fax:* 949-824-3548, *E-mail:* immaldon@uci.edu. *Web site:* http://www.socsci.uci.edu/anthro/anthro.html

■ UNIVERSITY OF CALIFORNIA, LOS ANGELES

Graduate Division, College of Letters and Science, Department of Anthropology, Los Angeles, CA 90095

AWARDS MA, PhD.

Students: 81 full-time (48 women); includes 14 minority (4 African Americans, 5 Asian Americans or Pacific Islanders, 3 Hispanic Americans, 2 Native Americans), 8 international. 141 applicants, 13% accepted, 7 enrolled. In 2001, 8 master's, 8 doctorates awarded. Terminal master's awarded for partial completion of doctoral program.
Degree requirements: For master's, one foreign language, thesis; for doctorate, one foreign language, thesis/dissertation, oral and written qualifying exams.
Entrance requirements: For master's, GRE General Test, minimum GPA of 3.0, sample of research writing; for doctorate, GRE General Test, minimum undergraduate GPA of 3.0, sample of research writing. *Application deadline:* For fall admission, 12/15. *Application fee:* $60. Electronic applications accepted.
Expenses: Tuition, nonresident: full-time $10,244. Required fees: $3,609. Full-time tuition and fees vary according to program.
Financial support: In 2001–02, 39 research assistantships, 64 teaching assistantships were awarded. Fellowships, Federal Work-Study, institutionally sponsored loans, scholarships/grants, and tuition waivers (full and partial) also available. Financial award application deadline: 3/1.
Dr. Douglas Hollan, Chair, 310-825-2511.
Application contact: Departmental Office, 310-825-2511, *E-mail:* awalters@anthro.ucla.edu.

■ UNIVERSITY OF CALIFORNIA, RIVERSIDE

Graduate Division, Department of Anthropology, Riverside, CA 92521-0102

AWARDS MA, MS, PhD. Part-time programs available.

Faculty: 14 full-time (3 women), 3 part-time/adjunct (2 women).
Students: 43 full-time (28 women); includes 13 minority (2 African Americans, 1 Asian American or Pacific Islander, 10 Hispanic Americans), 3 international. Average age 35. 52 applicants, 37% accepted, 12 enrolled. In 2001, 3 master's, 4 doctorates awarded. Terminal master's awarded for partial completion of doctoral program.
Degree requirements: For master's, comprehensive exams or thesis; for doctorate, one foreign language, thesis/dissertation, qualifying exams, comprehensive exam. *Median time to degree:* Master's–3 years full-time; doctorate–83 years full-time.
Entrance requirements: For master's and doctorate, GRE General Test, TOEFL, sample of written work, minimum GPA of 3.2, three letters of recommendation. *Application deadline:* For fall admission, 1/5. Applications are processed on a rolling basis. *Application fee:* $40. Electronic applications accepted.
Expenses: Tuition, state resident: full-time $5,001. Tuition, nonresident: full-time $15,897.
Financial support: In 2001–02, 8 fellowships with full and partial tuition reimbursements (averaging $8,000 per year), 3 research assistantships with partial tuition reimbursements, teaching assistantships with partial tuition reimbursements (averaging $14,000 per year) were awarded. Career-related internships or fieldwork, Federal Work-Study, institutionally sponsored loans, and tuition waivers (full and partial) also available. Financial award application deadline: 2/1; financial award applicants required to submit FAFSA.
Faculty research: Transnational processes, border communities, political and cultural ecology, Mesoamerican and Western US archaeology, applied anthropology.
Dr. Thomas C. Patterson, Chair, 909-787-5524, *Fax:* 909-787-5799, *E-mail:* thomas.patterson@ucr.edu.
Application contact: Dr. Paul Gelles, Graduate Adviser, 909-787-5394, *Fax:* 909-787-5409, *E-mail:* cultures@ucr.edu. *Web site:* http://anthropology.ucr.edu/

■ UNIVERSITY OF CALIFORNIA, SAN DIEGO

Graduate Studies and Research, Department of Anthropology, La Jolla, CA 92093

AWARDS PhD.

Faculty: 16.
Students: 44 (23 women). 91 applicants, 25% accepted, 13 enrolled. In 2001, 4 doctorates awarded.
Degree requirements: For doctorate, thesis/dissertation.
Entrance requirements: For doctorate, GRE General Test. *Application deadline:* For fall admission, 1/10. *Application fee:* $40. Electronic applications accepted.
Expenses: Tuition, nonresident: full-time $10,434. Required fees: $4,883.
Financial support: Fellowships, research assistantships, teaching assistantships available.
Guillermo Algaze, Head.
Application contact: Graduate Coordinator, 858-534-4145.

■ UNIVERSITY OF CALIFORNIA, SAN DIEGO

Graduate Studies and Research, Interdisciplinary Program in Cognitive Science, La Jolla, CA 92093

AWARDS Cognitive science/anthropology (PhD); cognitive science/communication (PhD); cognitive science/computer science and engineering (PhD); cognitive science/linguistics (PhD); cognitive science/neuroscience (PhD); cognitive science/philosophy (PhD); cognitive science/psychology (PhD); cognitive science/sociology (PhD). Admissions through affiliated departments.

Faculty: 57 full-time (12 women).
Students: 8 full-time (4 women). Average age 26. 2 applicants. In 2001, 2 degrees awarded.
Degree requirements: For doctorate, thesis/dissertation.
Entrance requirements: For doctorate, GRE General Test. *Application deadline:* Applications are processed on a rolling basis. *Application fee:* $0.
Expenses: Tuition, nonresident: full-time $10,434. Required fees: $4,883.
Faculty research: Cognition, neurobiology of cognition, artificial intelligence, neural networks, psycholinguistics.
Gary Cottrell, Director, 858-534-7141, *Fax:* 858-534-1128, *E-mail:* gcottrell@ucsd.edu.
Application contact: Graduate Coordinator, 858-534-7141, *Fax:* 858-534-1128, *E-mail:* gradinfo@cogsci.ucsd.edu. *Web site:* http://cogsci.ucsd.edu/CURRENT/Cog-interdisciplinary.html

■ UNIVERSITY OF CALIFORNIA, SAN FRANCISCO

Graduate Division, Program in Medical Anthropology, San Francisco, CA 94143

AWARDS PhD.

Students: 16 (12 women); includes 6 minority (1 African American, 3 Asian Americans or Pacific Islanders, 2 Hispanic Americans). In 2001, 4 degrees awarded.
Degree requirements: For doctorate, one foreign language, thesis/dissertation, 3 field statements.
Entrance requirements: For doctorate, GRE General Test, master's degree in anthropology or a related social or health science. *Application deadline:* For fall admission, 12/31. *Application fee:* $40.
Financial support: Application deadline: 1/10.
Faculty research: Ethnicity, gender, aging, international health, health policy.
Linda S. Mitteness, Interim Chair, 415-476-7234, *Fax:* 415-476-6715.
Application contact: Susan Reneau, Program Director, 415-476-7234.

■ UNIVERSITY OF CALIFORNIA, SANTA BARBARA

Graduate Division, College of Letters and Sciences, Division of Social Science, Department of Anthropology, Santa Barbara, CA 93106

AWARDS MA, PhD. Terminal master's awarded for partial completion of doctoral program.

Degree requirements: For master's, thesis (for some programs), comprehensive/assessment exam; for doctorate, thesis/dissertation, research paper(s) and research proposal.
Entrance requirements: For master's and doctorate, GRE General Test, TOEFL, sample of written work. Electronic applications accepted. *Web site:* http://www.anth.ucsb.edu

■ UNIVERSITY OF CALIFORNIA, SANTA CRUZ

Division of Graduate Studies, Division of Social Sciences, Program in Anthropology, Santa Cruz, CA 95064

AWARDS MA, PhD.

Faculty: 16 full-time.
Students: 44 full-time (32 women); includes 13 minority (3 African Americans, 5 Asian Americans or Pacific Islanders, 3 Hispanic Americans, 2 Native Americans), 4 international. 105 applicants, 15% accepted. In 2001, 5 master's, 3 doctorates awarded.
Degree requirements: For doctorate, thesis/dissertation, qualifying exam. *Median time to degree:* Master's–5 years full-time.
Entrance requirements: For doctorate, GRE General Test. *Application deadline:* For fall admission, 1/15. *Application fee:* $40.
Expenses: Tuition: Full-time $19,857.
Financial support: Fellowships, research assistantships, teaching assistantships, career-related internships or fieldwork, Federal Work-Study, and institutionally sponsored loans available. Financial award application deadline: 1/15.
Faculty research: Culture and power, women's roles, AIDS, folklore.
Alison Galloway, Chairperson, 831-459-3855.
Application contact: Graduate Admissions, 831-459-2301. *Web site:* http://www.ucsc.edu/

■ UNIVERSITY OF CHICAGO

Division of Social Sciences, Department of Anthropology, Chicago, IL 60637-1513

AWARDS PhD.

Students: 198.
Degree requirements: For doctorate, 2 foreign languages, thesis/dissertation, exams.
Entrance requirements: For doctorate, GRE General Test, TOEFL. *Application deadline:* For fall admission, 12/28. *Application fee:* $55. Electronic applications accepted.
Expenses: Tuition: Full-time $16,548.
Financial support: Fellowships, teaching assistantships, Federal Work-Study and institutionally sponsored loans available. Financial award application deadline: 12/28.
Prof. Susan Gal, Chair, 773-702-8551.
Application contact: Office of the Dean of Students, 773-702-8415.

■ UNIVERSITY OF CHICAGO

Division of the Humanities, Department of Linguistics, Chicago, IL 60637-1513

AWARDS Anthropology and linguistics (PhD); linguistics (AM, PhD).

Students: 56. 54 applicants, 72% accepted. Terminal master's awarded for partial completion of doctoral program.
Degree requirements: For master's, one foreign language, thesis; for doctorate, 2 foreign languages, thesis/dissertation.
Entrance requirements: For master's and doctorate, GRE General Test, TOEFL. *Application deadline:* For fall admission, 12/28. *Application fee:* $55.
Expenses: Tuition: Full-time $16,548.
Financial support: Fellowships, Federal Work-Study available. Financial award application deadline: 12/28; financial award applicants required to submit FAFSA.
Dr. Jerrold Sadock, Chair, 773-702-8522.

■ UNIVERSITY OF CINCINNATI

Division of Research and Advanced Studies, McMicken College of Arts and Sciences, Department of Anthropology, Cincinnati, OH 45221

AWARDS MA.

Faculty: 7 full-time.
Students: 5 full-time (3 women), 12 part-time (7 women), 2 international. 21 applicants, 10% accepted. In 2001, 5 degrees awarded.
Degree requirements: For master's, thesis or alternative.
Entrance requirements: For master's, GRE General Test. *Application deadline:* For fall admission, 2/1. *Application fee:* $30.
Expenses: Tuition, state resident: part-time $2,698 per quarter. Tuition, nonresident: part-time $4,977 per quarter.
Financial support: Fellowships, tuition waivers (partial) and unspecified assistantships available. Financial award application deadline: 5/1. *Total annual research expenditures:* $158,834.
Alan Sullivan, Head, 513-556-5782, *Fax:* 513-556-2778, *E-mail:* alan.sullivan@uc.edu.
Application contact: Barry Isaac, Graduate Program Director, 513-556-5780, *Fax:* 513-556-2778, *E-mail:* barry.isaac@uc.edu.

■ UNIVERSITY OF COLORADO AT BOULDER

Graduate School, College of Arts and Sciences, Department of Anthropology, Boulder, CO 80309

AWARDS MA, PhD.

Faculty: 14 full-time (5 women).
Students: 46 full-time (29 women), 17 part-time (12 women); includes 6 minority (1 Asian American or Pacific Islander, 4 Hispanic Americans, 1 Native American), 1 international. Average age 32. 20 applicants, 90% accepted. In 2001, 7 master's, 4 doctorates awarded.
Degree requirements: For master's, thesis or alternative, comprehensive exam; for doctorate, one foreign language, thesis/dissertation.
Entrance requirements: For master's, GRE General Test, minimum undergraduate GPA of 3.0; for doctorate, GRE General Test, minimum undergraduate GPA of 3.0, master's degree in Anthropology. *Application deadline:* For fall admission, 1/15. Applications are processed on a rolling basis. *Application fee:* $50 ($60 for international students). Electronic applications accepted.
Expenses: Tuition, state resident: full-time $3,474. Tuition, nonresident: full-time $16,624.
Financial support: In 2001–02, 11 fellowships (averaging $3,726 per year), 2 research assistantships (averaging $13,194 per year), 20 teaching assistantships with full tuition reimbursements (averaging $12,957 per year) were awarded. Tuition waivers (full) also available. Financial award application deadline: 1/5.
Faculty research: Archaeology of ancient Mayan, plains Indians, skeletal biology of ancient Nubians, human biology of modern people of Amazon, paleontology of early primates. *Total annual research expenditures:* $938,792.
Darna Dufour, Chair, 303-492-2547, *Fax:* 303-492-1871, *E-mail:* darna.dufour@colorado.edu.
Application contact: Linda Fry, Graduate Secretary, 303-492-7947, *Fax:* 303-492-1871, *E-mail:* linda.fry@colorado.edu. *Web site:* http://www.colorado.edu/anthropology/

■ UNIVERSITY OF COLORADO AT DENVER

Graduate School, College of Liberal Arts and Sciences, Program in Anthropology, Denver, CO 80217-3364

AWARDS MA. Part-time and evening/weekend programs available.

Faculty: 7 full-time (3 women).
Students: 7 full-time (all women), 26 part-time (16 women); includes 2 minority (1 Asian American or Pacific Islander, 1 Hispanic American), 1 international. Average age 31. 18 applicants, 83% accepted, 10 enrolled. In 2001, 11 degrees awarded.
Degree requirements: For master's, thesis or alternative.
Entrance requirements: For master's, GRE General Test, minimum 18 hours in anthropology training. *Application deadline:* For fall admission, 4/15; for spring admission, 10/15. Applications are processed on a rolling basis. *Application fee:* $50 ($60 for international students). Electronic applications accepted.
Expenses: Tuition, state resident: full-time $3,284; part-time $198 per credit hour. Tuition, nonresident: full-time $13,380; part-time $802 per credit hour. Required fees: $444; $222 per semester.
Financial support: Research assistantships, teaching assistantships, Federal Work-Study available. Financial award application deadline: 3/1; financial award applicants required to submit FAFSA. *Total annual research expenditures:* $416,744.
Tammy Stone, Chair, 303-556-3063, *Fax:* 303-556-8501, *E-mail:* tstone@carbon.cudenver.edu.
Application contact: Connie Turner, Administrative Assistant, 303-556-3554, *Fax:* 303-556-8501, *E-mail:* cturner@carbon.cudenver.edu.

■ UNIVERSITY OF CONNECTICUT

Graduate School, College of Liberal Arts and Sciences, Field of Anthropology, Storrs, CT 06269

AWARDS MA, PhD.

Degree requirements: For doctorate, thesis/dissertation.
Entrance requirements: For master's and doctorate, GRE General Test.

■ UNIVERSITY OF DENVER

Graduate Studies, Faculty of Arts and Humanities/Social Sciences, Department of Anthropology, Denver, CO 80208

AWARDS MA. Part-time programs available.

Faculty: 6 full-time (3 women).
Students: 16 (15 women) 1 international. 30 applicants, 70% accepted. In 2001, 11 degrees awarded.
Degree requirements: For master's, thesis or alternative, 1 foreign language or quantitative methods.
Entrance requirements: For master's, GRE, TOEFL. *Application deadline:* Applications are processed on a rolling basis. *Application fee:* $45.
Expenses: Tuition: Full-time $21,456.
Financial support: In 2001–02, 4 teaching assistantships with full and partial tuition reimbursements (averaging $7,533 per year) were awarded; career-related internships or fieldwork, Federal Work-Study, institutionally sponsored loans, and scholarships/grants also available. Support available to part-time students. Financial award application deadline: 2/20; financial award applicants required to submit FAFSA.
Faculty research: Gender, class, race. *Total annual research expenditures:* $22,564.
Dr. Dean Saitta, Chairperson, 303-871-2680.
Application contact: Lisa Saccomanno, Assistant to Chair, 303-871-2677. *Web site:* http://www.du.edu/anthro/

■ UNIVERSITY OF FLORIDA

Graduate School, College of Liberal Arts and Sciences, Department of Anthropology, Gainesville, FL 32611

AWARDS MA, MAT, PhD, JD/MA, JD/PhD. Part-time programs available.

Degree requirements: For master's, variable foreign language requirement, thesis optional; for doctorate, variable foreign language requirement, thesis/dissertation.
Entrance requirements: For master's and doctorate, GRE General Test, minimum GPA of 3.2. Electronic applications accepted.
Expenses: Tuition, state resident: part-time $164 per hour. Tuition, nonresident: part-time $571 per hour. Tuition and fees vary according to course level and program.
Faculty research: Social and cultural anthropology, archaeology, anthropological linguistics, physical anthropology. *Web site:* http://www.clas.ufl.edu/anthro/

■ UNIVERSITY OF GEORGIA

Graduate School, College of Arts and Sciences, Department of Anthropology, Athens, GA 30602

AWARDS MA, PhD.

Faculty: 16 full-time (4 women).
Students: 45 full-time (19 women), 6 part-time (all women); includes 1 minority (Hispanic American), 8 international. 75 applicants, 35% accepted. In 2001, 1 master's, 1 doctorate awarded.
Degree requirements: For master's and doctorate, one foreign language, thesis/dissertation.
Entrance requirements: For master's and doctorate, GRE General Test. *Application deadline:* For fall admission, 7/1 (priority date); for spring admission, 11/15. *Application fee:* $30. Electronic applications accepted.
Expenses: Tuition, state resident: full-time $2,376; part-time $132 per credit hour. Tuition, nonresident: full-time $9,504; part-time $528 per credit hour. Required fees: $236 per semester.
Financial support: Fellowships, research assistantships, teaching assistantships, unspecified assistantships available.
Dr. Michael Olien, Graduate Coordinator, 706-542-3962, *Fax:* 706-542-3998, *E-mail:* molien@uga.edu.
Application contact: Dr. David Hally, Graduate Coordinator, 706-542-1458, *Fax:* 706-542-3998, *E-mail:* dhally@uga.edu. *Web site:* http://anthro.dac.uga.edu/home.html

■ UNIVERSITY OF HAWAII AT MANOA

Graduate Division, College of Arts and Sciences, College of Social Sciences, Department of Anthropology, Honolulu, HI 96822

AWARDS MA, PhD.

Faculty: 25 full-time (9 women), 9 part-time/adjunct (3 women).
Students: 62 full-time (32 women), 18 part-time (9 women); includes 18 Asian Americans or Pacific Islanders, 1 Hispanic American. Average age 32. 43 applicants, 58% accepted. In 2001, 5 master's, 2 doctorates awarded.
Degree requirements: For master's, thesis optional; for doctorate, thesis/dissertation. *Median time to degree:* Master's–2 years full-time.
Entrance requirements: For master's and doctorate, GRE. *Application deadline:* For fall admission, 2/1. *Application fee:* $25 ($50 for international students).
Expenses: Tuition, state resident: full-time $2,160; part-time $1,980 per year. Tuition, nonresident: full-time $5,190; part-time $4,829 per year.
Financial support: In 2001–02, 32 students received support, including 3 research assistantships (averaging $15,364 per year), 8 teaching assistantships (averaging $13,577 per year); Federal Work-Study, institutionally sponsored loans, and tuition waivers (full) also available. Financial award application deadline: 3/1; financial award applicants required to submit FAFSA.
Faculty research: Evolution of social complexity, ethnopharmacology, social interaction, faunal analysis, human ecology. *Total annual research expenditures:* $202,490.
Dr. Nina Etkin, Chairperson, 808-956-8415, *Fax:* 808-956-4893.
Application contact: Dr. Terry L. Hunt, Graduate Field Chairperson, 808-956-7310, *Fax:* 808-956-9541, *E-mail:* thunt@hawaii.edu. *Web site:* http://www2.soc.hawaii.edu/

■ UNIVERSITY OF HOUSTON

College of Liberal Arts and Social Sciences, Department of Anthropology, Houston, TX 77204

AWARDS MA. Part-time and evening/weekend programs available.

Faculty: 6 full-time (4 women).
Students: 12 full-time (8 women), 15 part-time (12 women); includes 3 minority (2 African Americans, 1 Hispanic American), 1 international. Average age 35. 10 applicants, 80% accepted. In 2001, 3 degrees awarded.
Degree requirements: For master's, thesis optional.
Entrance requirements: For master's, GRE General Test, minimum GPA of 3.0. *Application deadline:* For fall admission, 7/6; for spring admission, 12/3. *Application fee:* $0 ($75 for international students).
Expenses: Tuition, state resident: full-time $1,512. Tuition, nonresident: full-time $5,310. Required fees: $1,308. Tuition and fees vary according to program.
Financial support: In 2001–02, 6 teaching assistantships (averaging $10,666 per year) were awarded; career-related internships or fieldwork and Federal Work-Study also available. Financial award application deadline: 3/30.
Faculty research: Medical anthropology, international development, archaeology, Mesoamerica, gender. *Total annual research expenditures:* $71,981.
Dr. Norris Lang, Chairperson, 713-743-3780, *Fax:* 713-743-4287, *E-mail:* nlang@uh.edu.
Application contact: Dr. Rebecca Storey, Graduate Director, 713-743-3780, *Fax:* 713-743-4287, *E-mail:* rstorey@uh.edu. *Web site:* http://firenza.uh.edu/anthropology/

■ UNIVERSITY OF IDAHO

College of Graduate Studies, College of Letters and Science, Department of Sociology and Anthropology, Program in Anthropology, Moscow, ID 83844-2282

AWARDS MA.

Faculty: 11 full-time (4 women), 2 part-time/adjunct (1 woman).
Students: 9 full-time (4 women), 11 part-time (8 women); includes 2 minority (1 Asian American or Pacific Islander, 1 Native American), 1 international. 5 applicants, 100% accepted. In 2001, 4 degrees awarded.
Degree requirements: For master's, one foreign language, thesis (for some programs).
Entrance requirements: For master's, minimum GPA of 2.8. *Application deadline:* For fall admission, 8/1; for spring admission, 12/15. *Application fee:* $35 ($45 for international students).
Expenses: Tuition, state resident: full-time $1,613. Tuition, nonresident: full-time $3,000.
Financial support: In 2001–02, 1 research assistantship (averaging $13,499 per year), 6 teaching assistantships (averaging $4,630 per year) were awarded. Financial award application deadline: 2/15.
Application contact: Dr. Don Tyler, Department Chair, 208-885-6752.

Find an in-depth description at www.petersons.com/gradchannel.

■ UNIVERSITY OF ILLINOIS AT CHICAGO

Graduate College, College of Liberal Arts and Sciences, Department of Anthropology, Chicago, IL 60607-7128

AWARDS Anthropology (MA, PhD); environmental and urban geography (MA), including environmental studies, urban geography.

Faculty: 10 full-time (2 women).
Students: 18 full-time (9 women), 21 part-time (12 women); includes 5 minority (2 African Americans, 2 Hispanic Americans, 1 Native American), 4 international. Average age 33. 41 applicants, 56% accepted, 11 enrolled. In 2001, 7 degrees awarded.
Degree requirements: For doctorate, comprehensive exam.
Entrance requirements: For master's and doctorate, TOEFL, minimum GPA of 3.75 on a 5.0 scale. *Application deadline:* For fall admission, 6/1; for spring admission, 11/1. Applications are processed on a rolling basis. *Application fee:* $40 ($50 for international students). Electronic applications accepted.
Expenses: Tuition, state resident: full-time $3,060. Tuition, nonresident: full-time $6,688.
Financial support: In 2001–02, 23 students received support; fellowships with full tuition reimbursements available, research assistantships with full tuition reimbursements available, teaching assistantships with full tuition reimbursements available, career-related internships or fieldwork, Federal Work-Study, and tuition waivers (full) available. Financial award application deadline: 3/1; financial award applicants required to submit FAFSA.
Faculty research: Archaeological, physical, and cultural anthropology.
Jim Phillips, Director of Graduate Studies, 312-413-3582, *E-mail:* jphillip@uic.edu.

■ UNIVERSITY OF ILLINOIS AT URBANA–CHAMPAIGN

Graduate College, College of Liberal Arts and Sciences, Department of Anthropology, Champaign, IL 61820

AWARDS AM, PhD.

Faculty: 23 full-time.
Students: 65 full-time (42 women); includes 5 minority (1 Asian American or Pacific Islander, 4 Hispanic Americans), 23 international. 98 applicants, 15% accepted. In 2001, 5 master's, 5 doctorates awarded. Terminal master's awarded for partial completion of doctoral program.
Degree requirements: For doctorate, variable foreign language requirement, thesis/dissertation.
Entrance requirements: For master's, GRE General Test, minimum GPA of 3.0; for doctorate, GRE General Test. *Application deadline:* For fall admission, 1/15.

Application fee: $40 ($50 for international students). Electronic applications accepted.
Expenses: Tuition, state resident: part-time $3,227 per degree program. Tuition, nonresident: part-time $7,169 per degree program. Tuition and fees vary according to program.
Financial support: In 2001–02, 14 fellowships, 9 research assistantships, 29 teaching assistantships were awarded. Career-related internships or fieldwork, Federal Work-Study, and tuition waivers (full) also available. Financial award application deadline: 1/15.
Paul Garber, Head, 217-333-3616, *Fax:* 217-244-3490, *E-mail:* p-garber@uiuc.edu.
Application contact: Ronda Rigdon, Administrative Aide, 217-244-3495, *Fax:* 217-244-3490, *E-mail:* rrigdon@uiuc.edu.
Web site: http://www.staff.uiuc.edu/~bmccall/anthro.html

■ THE UNIVERSITY OF IOWA

Graduate College, College of Liberal Arts and Sciences, Department of Anthropology, Iowa City, IA 52242-1316

AWARDS MA, PhD.

Faculty: 20 full-time, 1 part-time/adjunct.
Students: 23 full-time (15 women), 29 part-time (19 women); includes 5 minority (3 Hispanic Americans, 2 Native Americans), 4 international. 41 applicants, 37% accepted, 10 enrolled. In 2001, 3 master's, 6 doctorates awarded.
Degree requirements: For master's, exam, thesis optional; for doctorate, thesis/dissertation, comprehensive exam.
Entrance requirements: For master's, GRE General Test, TOEFL; for doctorate, GRE General Test, TOEFL, minimum GPA of 3.0. *Application deadline:* For fall admission, 2/1. *Application fee:* $30 ($50 for international students). Electronic applications accepted.
Expenses: Tuition, state resident: full-time $3,702; part-time $206 per semester hour. Tuition, nonresident: full-time $11,924; part-time $206 per semester hour. Required fees: $101 per semester. Tuition and fees vary according to course load and program.
Financial support: In 2001–02, 2 fellowships, 6 research assistantships, 23 teaching assistantships were awarded. Financial award applicants required to submit FAFSA.
Florence Babb, Chair, 319-335-3506, *Fax:* 319-335-0653.

■ UNIVERSITY OF KANSAS

Graduate School, College of Liberal Arts and Sciences, Department of Anthropology, Lawrence, KS 66045

AWARDS MA, PhD.

Faculty: 18.
Students: 27 full-time (17 women), 17 part-time (13 women); includes 2 minority (both Asian Americans or Pacific Islanders), 4 international. Average age 34. 32 applicants, 25% accepted, 7 enrolled. In 2001, 9 master's, 4 doctorates awarded.
Degree requirements: For master's, thesis; for doctorate, one foreign language, thesis/dissertation, comprehensive exam.
Entrance requirements: For master's and doctorate, TOEFL, minimum GPA of 3.2. *Application deadline:* For fall admission, 1/5. *Application fee:* $35. Electronic applications accepted.
Expenses: Tuition, state resident: full-time $2,722; part-time $113 per credit. Tuition, nonresident: full-time $8,586; part-time $358 per credit. Required fees: $551; $46 per credit. Tuition and fees vary according to campus/location, program and reciprocity agreements.
Financial support: In 2001–02, 4 research assistantships with partial tuition reimbursements (averaging $7,650 per year), 14 teaching assistantships with full and partial tuition reimbursements (averaging $9,354 per year) were awarded. Fellowships, career-related internships or fieldwork and institutionally sponsored loans also available. Financial award application deadline: 3/1; financial award applicants required to submit FAFSA.
Faculty research: Paleoecology and human adaptation, anthropological genetics, African medical systems, Native American linguistics, computer applications to archaeology.
Donald D. Stull, Chair, 785-864-4103, *Fax:* 785-864-5224, *E-mail:* stull@ku.edu.
Application contact: Jane Gibson, Graduate Coordinator, 785-864-2635, *Fax:* 785-864-5224, *E-mail:* jwgc@ku.edu. *Web site:* http://www.ku.edu/~kuanth/

■ UNIVERSITY OF KENTUCKY

Graduate School, Graduate School Programs from the College of Arts and Sciences, Program in Anthropology, Lexington, KY 40506-0032

AWARDS MA, PhD. Part-time programs available.

Faculty: 22 full-time (10 women).
Students: 47 full-time (27 women), 6 part-time (2 women); includes 4 minority (2 African Americans, 2 Hispanic Americans), 4 international. 45 applicants, 62% accepted. In 2001, 6 master's, 2 doctorates awarded.
Degree requirements: For master's, thesis optional; for doctorate, one foreign language, thesis/dissertation, comprehensive exam.
Entrance requirements: For master's, GRE General Test, minimum undergraduate GPA of 3.0; for doctorate, GRE General Test, minimum graduate GPA of 3.0. *Application deadline:* For fall admission, 2/15. Applications are processed on a rolling basis. *Application fee:* $30 ($35 for international students).
Expenses: Tuition, state resident: full-time $4,075; part-time $213 per credit hour. Tuition, nonresident: full-time $11,295; part-time $614 per credit hour.
Financial support: In 2001–02, 5 fellowships, 8 research assistantships, 19 teaching assistantships were awarded. Career-related internships or fieldwork, Federal Work-Study, and institutionally sponsored loans also available. Financial award application deadline: 3/1.
Faculty research: Applied social anthropology, developmental change, medical anthropology, culture history, ethnohistory.
Dr. Mary Anglin, Director of Graduate Studies, 859-257-1051, *E-mail:* manglin@pop.uky.edu.
Application contact: Dr. Jeannine Blackwell, Associate Dean, 859-257-4905, *Fax:* 859-323-1928.

■ UNIVERSITY OF MARYLAND, COLLEGE PARK

Graduate Studies and Research, College of Behavioral and Social Sciences, Department of Anthropology, College Park, MD 20742

AWARDS Applied anthropology (MAA). Part-time and evening/weekend programs available.

Faculty: 11 full-time (3 women), 4 part-time/adjunct (3 women).
Students: 28 full-time (22 women), 2 part-time (both women); includes 6 minority (2 African Americans, 1 Asian American or Pacific Islander, 3 Hispanic Americans), 2 international. 47 applicants, 47% accepted, 13 enrolled. In 2001, 23 degrees awarded.
Degree requirements: For master's, internship.
Entrance requirements: For master's, GRE General Test, minimum GPA of 3.0. *Application deadline:* For fall admission, 2/1. Applications are processed on a rolling basis. *Application fee:* $50 ($70 for international students). Electronic applications accepted.
Expenses: Tuition, state resident: part-time $289 per credit hour. Tuition, nonresident: part-time $448 per credit hour. One-time fee: $436 part-time. Full-time tuition and fees vary according to course load, campus/location and program.
Financial support: In 2001–02, 5 fellowships with full tuition reimbursements (averaging $10,585 per year), 10 teaching assistantships with tuition reimbursements (averaging $8,225 per year) were awarded. Research assistantships, Federal Work-Study and scholarships/grants also available. Support available to part-time students. Financial award applicants required to submit FAFSA.
Faculty research: Physical anthropology and archaeology.
Dr. Mark Leone, Chairman, 301-405-1423, *Fax:* 301-314-8305.
Application contact: Trudy Lindsey, Director, Graduate Admissions and

University of Maryland, College Park (continued)

Records, 301-405-6991, *Fax:* 301-314-9305, *E-mail:* grschool@deans.umd.edu.

■ UNIVERSITY OF MASSACHUSETTS AMHERST

Graduate School, College of Social and Behavioral Sciences, Department of Anthropology, Amherst, MA 01003

AWARDS MA, PhD. Part-time programs available.

Faculty: 15 full-time (5 women).
Students: 28 full-time (21 women), 51 part-time (36 women); includes 18 minority (8 African Americans, 1 Asian American or Pacific Islander, 6 Hispanic Americans, 3 Native Americans), 9 international. Average age 35. 95 applicants, 22% accepted. In 2001, 7 master's, 6 doctorates awarded. Terminal master's awarded for partial completion of doctoral program.
Degree requirements: For doctorate, thesis/dissertation.
Entrance requirements: For master's and doctorate, GRE General Test. *Application deadline:* For fall admission, 2/1 (priority date). Applications are processed on a rolling basis. *Application fee:* $40 ($50 for international students).
Expenses: Tuition, state resident: full-time $1,980; part-time $110 per credit. Tuition, nonresident: full-time $7,456; part-time $414 per credit. Required fees: $4,112. One-time fee: $115 full-time.
Financial support: In 2001–02, 20 fellowships with full tuition reimbursements (averaging $5,807 per year), 21 research assistantships with full tuition reimbursements (averaging $7,322 per year), 33 teaching assistantships with full tuition reimbursements (averaging $11,748 per year) were awarded. Career-related internships or fieldwork, Federal Work-Study, scholarships/grants, traineeships, and unspecified assistantships also available. Support available to part-time students. Financial award application deadline: 2/1.
Dr. Ralph Faulkingham, Head, 413-545-0028, *Fax:* 413-545-9494, *E-mail:* faulkingham@anthro.umass.edu.

■ THE UNIVERSITY OF MEMPHIS

Graduate School, College of Arts and Sciences, Department of Anthropology, Memphis, TN 38152

AWARDS MA. Part-time programs available.

Degree requirements: For master's, practicum.
Entrance requirements: For master's, GRE General Test or MAT.
Expenses: Tuition, state resident: full-time $2,026. Tuition, nonresident: full-time $4,528.
Faculty research: Archaeological investigations along Bootheel fault line, drug and alcohol abuse, housing and urban development, grassroots community development, immigrant housing and health. *Web site:* http://www.people.memphis.edu/~anthropology/

■ UNIVERSITY OF MICHIGAN

Horace H. Rackham School of Graduate Studies, College of Literature, Science, and the Arts, Department of Anthropology, Ann Arbor, MI 48109

AWARDS AM, PhD.

Faculty: 26 full-time (10 women), 24 part-time/adjunct (11 women).
Students: 113 full-time (72 women). Average age 31. 205 applicants, 36% accepted, 31 enrolled. In 2001, 9 master's, 12 doctorates awarded. Terminal master's awarded for partial completion of doctoral program.
Degree requirements: For doctorate, one foreign language, thesis/dissertation, oral defense of dissertation, preliminary exam.
Entrance requirements: For master's, GRE General Test, TOEFL; for doctorate, GRE General Test, TOEFL, master's degree. *Application deadline:* For fall admission, 1/5. Applications are processed on a rolling basis. *Application fee:* $55.
Financial support: In 2001–02, 88 students received support, including 38 fellowships with full tuition reimbursements available, 8 research assistantships with full tuition reimbursements available, 42 teaching assistantships with full tuition reimbursements available; institutionally sponsored loans, scholarships/grants, and traineeships also available. Financial award application deadline: 4/15.
Faculty research: Ancient DNA, evolutionary ecology, reproductive endocrinology, social anthropology of nation state (Botswana), primate behavioral ecology. *Total annual research expenditures:* $118,189.
Conrad P. Kottak, Chair, 734-764-7275.
Application contact: Laurie R. Marx, Graduate Student Services Associate, 734-764-7275, *Fax:* 734-763-6077, *E-mail:* lmarx@umich.edu. *Web site:* http://www.lsa.umich.edu/anthro/

■ UNIVERSITY OF MICHIGAN

Horace H. Rackham School of Graduate Studies, College of Literature, Science, and the Arts, Doctoral Program in Anthropology and History, Ann Arbor, MI 48109

AWARDS PhD.

Degree requirements: For doctorate, 2 foreign languages, thesis/dissertation, oral defense of dissertation, preliminary exam.
Entrance requirements: For doctorate, GRE General Test, TOEFL, writing sample.
Faculty research: Latin America, Near East archaeology, former Soviet Union, modern performance, religion, Chinese minorities. *Web site:* http://www.umich.edu/~idpah/

■ UNIVERSITY OF MINNESOTA, DULUTH

Graduate School, College of Liberal Arts, Department of Sociology/Anthropology, Duluth, MN 55812-2496

AWARDS MLS. Part-time programs available.

Faculty: 1 full-time (0 women), 21 part-time/adjunct (5 women).
Students: 5 full-time (all women), 11 part-time (8 women); includes 2 minority (1 African American, 1 Native American). Average age 38. 10 applicants, 80% accepted. In 2001, 4 degrees awarded.
Entrance requirements: For master's, interview, minimum GPA of 3.0. *Application deadline:* For fall admission, 7/15; for spring admission, 11/15. Applications are processed on a rolling basis. *Application fee:* $50 ($55 for international students).
Expenses: Tuition, state resident: full-time $2,932; part-time $489 per credit. Tuition, nonresident: full-time $5,758; part-time $960 per credit. Tuition and fees vary according to course load.
Financial support: Teaching assistantships with full tuition reimbursements, Federal Work-Study, institutionally sponsored loans, and scholarships/grants available. Financial award application deadline: 3/15.
Faculty research: Nature of knowledge, philosophy of science, ecology, cultural studies.
Dr. James Fetzer, Graduate Director, 218-726-7269, *Fax:* 218-726-7119, *E-mail:* jfetzer@d.umn.edu.
Application contact: Nancy Peterson, Assistant Director, 218-726-6149, *Fax:* 218-726-7119, *E-mail:* npeters3@d.umn.edu.

■ UNIVERSITY OF MINNESOTA, TWIN CITIES CAMPUS

Graduate School, College of Liberal Arts, Department of Anthropology, Minneapolis, MN 55455-0213

AWARDS MA, PhD.

Faculty: 15 full-time (5 women), 2 part-time/adjunct (1 woman).
Students: 46 full-time (29 women), 13 part-time (8 women); includes 9 minority (1 African American, 4 Asian Americans or Pacific Islanders, 2 Hispanic Americans, 2 Native Americans). Average age 31. 41 applicants, 49% accepted, 10 enrolled. In 2001, 3 degrees awarded. Terminal master's awarded for partial completion of doctoral program.
Degree requirements: For master's, thesis or alternative; for doctorate, one foreign language, thesis/dissertation. *Median time to degree:* Doctorate–10 years full-time.
Entrance requirements: For master's and doctorate, GRE, TOEFL. *Application deadline:* For fall admission, 1/5. *Application fee:* $40 ($50 for international students).
Expenses: Tuition, state resident: full-time $2,932; part-time $489 per credit. Tuition,

nonresident: full-time $5,758; part-time $960 per credit. Part-time tuition and fees vary according to course load, program and reciprocity agreements.
Financial support: In 2001–02, 42 students received support, including 3 fellowships with tuition reimbursements available (averaging $9,000 per year), 1 research assistantship with tuition reimbursement available (averaging $10,200 per year), 15 teaching assistantships with tuition reimbursements available (averaging $10,200 per year); career-related internships or fieldwork, Federal Work-Study, institutionally sponsored loans, and tuition waivers (full and partial) also available. Financial award application deadline: 1/5; financial award applicants required to submit FAFSA.
Faculty research: Psychological anthropology, gender and feminist anthropology, economic anthropology, Latin America, the Pacific, South Asia, globalization. *Total annual research expenditures:* $140,000.
Dr. John M. Ingham, Chair, 612-625-3400, *Fax:* 612-625-3095, *E-mail:* ingha001@tc.umn.edu.
Application contact: Dr. Peter S. Wells, Director of Graduate Studies, 612-624-6845, *Fax:* 612-625-3095, *E-mail:* wells001@umn.edu. *Web site:* http://cla.umn.edu/anthropology/

■ UNIVERSITY OF MISSISSIPPI

Graduate School, College of Liberal Arts, Department of Sociology and Anthropology, Oxford, University, MS 38677

AWARDS Anthropology (MA); sociology (MA, MSS).

Faculty: 11 full-time (3 women).
Students: 20 full-time (9 women), 2 part-time (1 woman); includes 3 minority (all Native Americans). In 2001, 4 degrees awarded.
Degree requirements: For master's, thesis (for some programs).
Entrance requirements: For master's, GRE General Test, TOEFL, minimum GPA of 3.0. *Application deadline:* For fall admission, 8/1. Applications are processed on a rolling basis. *Application fee:* $0 ($25 for international students).
Expenses: Tuition, state resident: full-time $3,626; part-time $202 per hour. Tuition, nonresident: full-time $8,172; part-time $454 per hour.
Financial support: Application deadline: 3/1.
Dr. Max Williams, Acting Chairman, 662-915-7288, *Fax:* 662-915-5372, *E-mail:* samax@olemiss.edu.

■ UNIVERSITY OF MISSOURI–COLUMBIA

Graduate School, College of Arts and Sciences, Department of Anthropology, Columbia, MO 65211

AWARDS MA, PhD.

Faculty: 13 full-time (5 women).
Students: 26 full-time (14 women), 26 part-time (12 women); includes 4 minority (2 Asian Americans or Pacific Islanders, 1 Hispanic American, 1 Native American), 7 international. 34 applicants, 44% accepted. In 2001, 8 master's, 4 doctorates awarded.
Degree requirements: For doctorate, one foreign language, thesis/dissertation.
Entrance requirements: For master's and doctorate, GRE General Test, minimum GPA of 3.0. *Application deadline:* For fall admission, 1/15 (priority date); for winter admission, 10/15. Applications are processed on a rolling basis. *Application fee:* $25 ($50 for international students).
Expenses: Tuition, state resident: part-time $179 per credit hour. Tuition, nonresident: part-time $539 per credit hour. Required fees: $122 per semester. Tuition and fees vary according to program.
Financial support: Research assistantships, teaching assistantships, institutionally sponsored loans available.
Dr. Deborah Pearsall, Director of Graduate Studies, 573-882-3038, *E-mail:* pearsalld@missouri.edu. *Web site:* http://web.missouri.edu/~anthwww/grad.html

■ THE UNIVERSITY OF MONTANA–MISSOULA

Graduate School, College of Arts and Sciences, Department of Anthropology, Missoula, MT 59812-0002

AWARDS Cultural heritage (MA); linguistics (MA).

Faculty: 9 full-time (2 women), 1 part-time/adjunct (0 women).
Students: 40 full-time (29 women), 13 part-time (6 women); includes 4 minority (2 Asian Americans or Pacific Islanders, 2 Native Americans), 1 international. 26 applicants, 85% accepted, 19 enrolled. In 2001, 13 degrees awarded.
Degree requirements: For master's, thesis (for some programs).
Entrance requirements: For master's, GRE General Test. *Application deadline:* For fall admission, 2/15 (priority date); for spring admission, 10/15 (priority date). *Application fee:* $45.
Expenses: Tuition, state resident: full-time $2,482; part-time $1,700 per year. Tuition, nonresident: full-time $7,372; part-time $5,000 per year. Required fees: $1,900. Tuition and fees vary according to degree level.
Financial support: In 2001–02, 10 teaching assistantships with full tuition reimbursements (averaging $8,663 per year) were awarded; research assistantships, career-related internships or fieldwork, Federal Work-Study, institutionally sponsored loans, and unspecified assistantships also available. Financial award application deadline: 3/1; financial award applicants required to submit FAFSA.
Faculty research: Historical preservation, plateau-plains archaeology and ethnohistory. *Total annual research expenditures:* $230,812.
Gregory R. Campbell, Chair, 406-243-2693, *E-mail:* greg@selway.umt.edu. *Web site:* http://www.cas.umt.edu/anthro/

■ UNIVERSITY OF NEBRASKA–LINCOLN

Graduate College, College of Arts and Sciences, Department of Anthropology and Geography, Program in Anthropology, Lincoln, NE 68588

AWARDS MA.

Faculty: 15.
Students: 18 (12 women) 1 international. Average age 27. 7 applicants, 57% accepted, 3 enrolled. In 2001, 7 degrees awarded.
Degree requirements: For master's, thesis optional.
Entrance requirements: For master's, GRE General Test, TOEFL. *Application deadline:* For fall admission, 2/1; for spring admission, 10/1. *Application fee:* $35. Electronic applications accepted.
Expenses: Tuition, state resident: full-time $2,412; part-time $134 per credit. Tuition, nonresident: full-time $6,223; part-time $346 per credit. Tuition and fees vary according to course load.
Financial support: In 2001–02, 1 fellowship, 5 teaching assistantships were awarded. Research assistantships, Federal Work-Study, health care benefits, and unspecified assistantships also available. Support available to part-time students. Financial award application deadline: 2/15.
Faculty research: Cultural, archaeologic, linguistic, and physical anthropology.
Dr. Pat Draper, Chair, 402-472-2480.
Application contact: Dr. Raymond Hames, Graduate Committee Chair, 402-472-6240. *Web site:* http://www.unl.edu/anthro/

■ UNIVERSITY OF NEVADA, LAS VEGAS

Graduate College, College of Liberal Arts, Department of Anthropology, Las Vegas, NV 89154-9900

AWARDS MA, PhD. Part-time programs available.

Faculty: 19 full-time (5 women).
Students: 19 full-time (16 women), 16 part-time (13 women); includes 4 minority (2 African Americans, 2 Hispanic Americans), 1 international. 28 applicants, 46% accepted, 8 enrolled. In 2001, 4 degrees awarded.

University of Nevada, Las Vegas (continued)

Degree requirements: For master's and doctorate, thesis/dissertation, oral exam.
Entrance requirements: For master's, minimum GPA of 3.0 in field, 2.75 overall; sample of research; for doctorate, GRE General Test, minimum GPA of 3.5 in previous graduate work, sample of research. *Application deadline:* For fall admission, 3/1 (priority date); for spring admission, 10/1. Applications are processed on a rolling basis. *Application fee:* $40 ($55 for international students).
Expenses: Tuition, state resident: full-time $1,926; part-time $107 per credit. Tuition, nonresident: full-time $9,376; part-time $220 per credit. Tuition and fees vary according to course load.
Financial support: In 2001–02, 2 research assistantships with partial tuition reimbursements (averaging $10,000 per year), 10 teaching assistantships with partial tuition reimbursements (averaging $11,000 per year) were awarded. Financial award application deadline: 3/1.
Faculty research: New World studies.
Dr. Malvin Miranda, Chair, 702-895-3590.
Application contact: Graduate College Admissions Evaluator, 702-895-3320, *Fax:* 702-895-4180, *E-mail:* gradcollege@ccmail.nevada.edu. *Web site:* http://www.unlv.edu/Colleges/Liberal_Arts/Anthropology

■ UNIVERSITY OF NEVADA, RENO

Graduate School, College of Arts and Science, Department of Anthropology, Reno, NV 89557

AWARDS MA, PhD.

Faculty: 13.
Students: 20 full-time (13 women), 6 part-time (4 women); includes 2 minority (1 Hispanic American, 1 Native American), 1 international. Average age 36. In 2001, 4 degrees awarded. Terminal master's awarded for partial completion of doctoral program.
Degree requirements: For master's and doctorate, thesis/dissertation.
Entrance requirements: For master's, GRE, TOEFL, minimum GPA of 2.75; for doctorate, GRE, TOEFL, minimum GPA of 3.0. *Application deadline:* For fall admission, 2/1 (priority date); for spring admission, 11/1. *Application fee:* $40.
Expenses: Tuition, state resident: full-time $2,067; part-time $108 per credit. Tuition, nonresident: full-time $9,282; part-time $109 per credit. Required fees: $57 per semester. Tuition and fees vary according to course load.
Financial support: In 2001–02, 3 research assistantships, 8 teaching assistantships were awarded. Federal Work-Study and institutionally sponsored loans also available. Financial award application deadline: 3/1.
Faculty research: Ethnology, linguistics, cultural/medical/religious/ethnic relations, ecological anthropology, historical anthropology.
Dr. Don Hardesty, Graduate Program Director, 775-784-6049.

■ UNIVERSITY OF NEW MEXICO

Graduate School, College of Arts and Sciences, Department of Anthropology, Albuquerque, NM 87131-2039

AWARDS MA, MS, PhD.

Faculty: 27 full-time (13 women), 2 part-time/adjunct (both women).
Students: 117 full-time (74 women), 63 part-time (40 women); includes 18 minority (2 African Americans, 2 Asian Americans or Pacific Islanders, 12 Hispanic Americans, 2 Native Americans), 11 international. Average age 34. 156 applicants, 38% accepted, 20 enrolled. In 2001, 17 master's, 10 doctorates awarded. Terminal master's awarded for partial completion of doctoral program.
Degree requirements: For master's, written exam, thesis optional; for doctorate, 2 foreign languages, thesis/dissertation, written and oral exam.
Entrance requirements: For master's and doctorate, GRE General Test. *Application deadline:* For fall admission, 1/25. *Application fee:* $40.
Expenses: Tuition, state resident: full-time $2,771; part-time $115 per credit hour. Tuition, nonresident: full-time $11,207; part-time $467 per credit hour. Required fees: $570; $24 per credit hour. Part-time tuition and fees vary according to course load and program.
Financial support: In 2001–02, 115 students received support, including 6 research assistantships with full tuition reimbursements available (averaging $11,000 per year), 16 teaching assistantships with full tuition reimbursements available (averaging $11,000 per year); career-related internships or fieldwork, Federal Work-Study, institutionally sponsored loans, scholarships/grants, traineeships, health care benefits, tuition waivers (full), and unspecified assistantships also available. Support available to part-time students. Financial award application deadline: 3/1; financial award applicants required to submit FAFSA.
Faculty research: Biological anthropology, ethnology, archaeology, human evolutionary ecology. *Total annual research expenditures:* $341,471.
Dr. Marta Weigle, Chair, 505-277-4524, *Fax:* 505-277-0874, *E-mail:* mweigle@unm.edu.
Application contact: Erika Gerety, Graduate Coordinator, 505-277-2732, *Fax:* 505-277-0874, *E-mail:* erika@unm.edu. *Web site:* http://www.unm.edu/~anthro/

■ THE UNIVERSITY OF NORTH CAROLINA AT CHAPEL HILL

Graduate School, College of Arts and Sciences, Department of Anthropology, Chapel Hill, NC 27599

AWARDS MA, PhD.

Faculty: 26 full-time (11 women), 3 part-time/adjunct (1 woman).
Students: 70 full-time (46 women), 9 part-time (5 women); includes 13 minority (5 African Americans, 5 Asian Americans or Pacific Islanders, 2 Hispanic Americans, 1 Native American). Average age 31. 118 applicants, 19% accepted, 13 enrolled. In 2001, 2 master's, 7 doctorates awarded. Terminal master's awarded for partial completion of doctoral program.
Degree requirements: For master's, variable foreign language requirement, thesis/dissertation; for doctorate, variable foreign language requirement, thesis/dissertation, comprehensive exam. *Median time to degree:* Master's–2 years full-time; doctorate–8 years full-time.
Entrance requirements: For master's and doctorate, GRE General Test, minimum GPA of 3.0. *Application deadline:* For fall admission, 1/1 (priority date). Applications are processed on a rolling basis. *Application fee:* $55. Electronic applications accepted.
Expenses: Tuition, state resident: full-time $2,864. Tuition, nonresident: full-time $12,030.
Financial support: In 2001–02, 13 fellowships with tuition reimbursements (averaging $12,000 per year), 10 research assistantships with tuition reimbursements (averaging $10,000 per year), 35 teaching assistantships with tuition reimbursements (averaging $10,000 per year) were awarded. Career-related internships or fieldwork, Federal Work-Study, scholarships/grants, traineeships, and tuition waivers (full) also available. Financial award application deadline: 3/1.
Faculty research: Social anthropology, economic anthropology, gender, medical anthropology, biological anthropology, archaeology. *Total annual research expenditures:* $135,000.
Prof. Judith B Farquhar, Chair, 919-962-1243, *Fax:* 919-962-1613, *E-mail:* farquhar@email.unc.edu.
Application contact: Suphronia J Cheek, Graduate Program Coordinator, 919-843-8977, *Fax:* 919-962-1613, *E-mail:* sjcheek@email.unc.edu. *Web site:* http://www.unc.edu/depts/anthro/

■ UNIVERSITY OF OKLAHOMA

Graduate College, College of Arts and Sciences, Department of Anthropology, Norman, OK 73019-0390

AWARDS MA, PhD.

Faculty: 16 full-time (6 women), 1 part-time/adjunct (0 women).

Students: 33 full-time (17 women), 18 part-time (8 women); includes 9 minority (2 African Americans, 3 Hispanic Americans, 4 Native Americans), 1 international. 17 applicants, 71% accepted, 9 enrolled. In 2001, 7 master's, 5 doctorates awarded. Terminal master's awarded for partial completion of doctoral program.
Degree requirements: For master's, thesis; for doctorate, thesis/dissertation, departmental qualifying exam.
Entrance requirements: For master's, GRE, TOEFL, BA with 12 hours in anthropology; for doctorate, TOEFL. *Application deadline:* For fall admission, 1/30 (priority date). Applications are processed on a rolling basis. *Application fee:* $25 ($50 for international students).
Expenses: Tuition, state resident: full-time $2,208; part-time $92 per credit hour. Tuition, nonresident: part-time $297 per credit hour. Tuition and fees vary according to course level, course load and program.
Financial support: In 2001–02, 30 students received support, including 10 research assistantships with partial tuition reimbursements available (averaging $10,141 per year), 17 teaching assistantships with partial tuition reimbursements available (averaging $9,442 per year); career-related internships or fieldwork, Federal Work-Study, and tuition waivers (partial) also available. Financial award applicants required to submit FAFSA.
Faculty research: Archaeology, sociocultural anthropology, linguistics, Native American languages, biological anthropology. *Total annual research expenditures:* $91,226.
Patricia Gilman, Interim Chair, 405-325-3261, *Fax:* 405-325-7386, *E-mail:* pgilman@ou.edu.
Application contact: Don Wyckoff, Graduate Liaison, 405-325-2179, *Fax:* 405-325-7386, *E-mail:* ktrambler@ou.edu.

■ UNIVERSITY OF OREGON

Graduate School, College of Arts and Sciences, Department of Anthropology, Eugene, OR 97403

AWARDS MA, MS, PhD.

Faculty: 13 full-time (7 women), 1 (woman) part-time/adjunct.
Students: 42 full-time (28 women), 15 part-time (8 women); includes 8 minority (1 Asian American or Pacific Islander, 2 Hispanic Americans, 5 Native Americans), 8 international. 64 applicants, 17% accepted. In 2001, 5 master's, 7 doctorates awarded. Terminal master's awarded for partial completion of doctoral program.
Degree requirements: For master's, one foreign language; for doctorate, 2 foreign languages, thesis/dissertation.
Entrance requirements: For master's and doctorate, GRE General Test, TOEFL. *Application deadline:* For fall admission, 2/1. *Application fee:* $50.
Expenses: Tuition, state resident: full-time $4,968; part-time $501 per credit hour. Tuition, nonresident: full-time $8,400; part-time $691 per credit hour.
Financial support: In 2001–02, 23 teaching assistantships were awarded; career-related internships or fieldwork and Federal Work-Study also available. Support available to part-time students. Financial award application deadline: 3/1.
Faculty research: Prehistory, primatology, cultural anthropology of Native Americans, human evolution, Africa.
Lynn Stephen, Head, 541-346-5102.
Application contact: Tiffany Brannon, Graduate Secretary, 541-346-5103. *Web site:* http://darkwing.uoregon.edu/~anthro/

■ UNIVERSITY OF PENNSYLVANIA

School of Arts and Sciences, Graduate Group in Anthropology, Philadelphia, PA 19104

AWARDS AM, MS, PhD. Terminal master's awarded for partial completion of doctoral program.

Degree requirements: For master's, thesis, final exam; for doctorate, one foreign language, thesis/dissertation, fieldwork, preliminary and final exams.
Entrance requirements: For doctorate, GRE General Test, TOEFL.
Expenses: Tuition: Part-time $12,875 per semester. *Web site:* http://www.sas.upenn.edu/anthro/Overview.html

■ UNIVERSITY OF PITTSBURGH

Faculty of Arts and Sciences, Department of Anthropology, Pittsburgh, PA 15260

AWARDS MA, PhD. Part-time programs available.

Faculty: 19 full-time (3 women), 4 part-time/adjunct (3 women).
Students: 67 full-time (42 women), 7 part-time (6 women); includes 5 minority (1 African American, 1 Asian American or Pacific Islander, 3 Hispanic Americans), 19 international. 93 applicants, 25% accepted, 11 enrolled. In 2001, 7 master's, 8 doctorates awarded.
Degree requirements: For master's, one foreign language, thesis or alternative; for doctorate, one foreign language, thesis/dissertation.
Entrance requirements: For master's and doctorate, GRE General Test, TOEFL. *Application deadline:* For fall admission, 1/15 (priority date). Applications are processed on a rolling basis. *Application fee:* $40. Electronic applications accepted.
Expenses: Tuition, state resident: full-time $9,410; part-time $385 per credit. Tuition, nonresident: full-time $19,376; part-time $797 per credit. Required fees: $480; $90 per term. Tuition and fees vary according to program.
Financial support: In 2001–02, 48 students received support, including 13 fellowships with full tuition reimbursements available (averaging $13,728 per year), 23 teaching assistantships with full tuition reimbursements available (averaging $11,980 per year); research assistantships with full tuition reimbursements available, career-related internships or fieldwork, Federal Work-Study, scholarships/grants, health care benefits, tuition waivers (full and partial), and unspecified assistantships also available. Support available to part-time students. Financial award application deadline: 1/15.
Faculty research: Conflict studies; ethnicity, nationalism, and the state; origins of complex societies; Latin American archaeology; human evolutionary biology. *Total annual research expenditures:* $312,783.
Dr. Robert D. Drennan, Chair, 412-648-7530, *Fax:* 412-648-7535, *E-mail:* drennan@pitt.edu.
Application contact: Phyllis J. Deasy, Graduate Coordinator, 412-648-7504, *Fax:* 412-648-7535, *E-mail:* pdeasy@pitt.edu. *Web site:* http://www.pitt.edu/~pittanth/

■ UNIVERSITY OF SOUTH CAROLINA

The Graduate School, College of Liberal Arts, Department of Anthropology, Columbia, SC 29208

AWARDS MA.

Degree requirements: For master's, thesis, comprehensive exam.
Entrance requirements: For master's, GRE General Test. Electronic applications accepted.
Expenses: Tuition, state resident: full-time $4,434. Tuition, nonresident: full-time $9,854. Tuition and fees vary according to program.
Faculty research: Biocultural anthropology, archaeology, cultural anthropology.

■ UNIVERSITY OF SOUTHERN CALIFORNIA

Graduate School, College of Letters, Arts and Sciences, Department of Anthropology, Program in Social Anthropology, Los Angeles, CA 90089

AWARDS PhD.

Degree requirements: For doctorate, thesis/dissertation.
Entrance requirements: For doctorate, GRE General Test.
Expenses: Tuition: Full-time $25,060; part-time $844 per unit. Required fees: $473.

■ UNIVERSITY OF SOUTHERN CALIFORNIA

Graduate School, College of Letters, Arts and Sciences, Department of Anthropology, Program in Visual Anthropology, Los Angeles, CA 90089

AWARDS MA.

Degree requirements: For master's, thesis.
Entrance requirements: For master's, GRE General Test.
Expenses: Tuition: Full-time $25,060; part-time $844 per unit. Required fees: $473.

■ UNIVERSITY OF SOUTHERN MISSISSIPPI

Graduate School, College of Liberal Arts, Department of Anthropology and Sociology, Hattiesburg, MS 39406

AWARDS Anthropology (MA). Part-time programs available.

Faculty: 11 full-time (5 women).
Students: 14 full-time (8 women), 3 part-time (1 woman). Average age 34. 19 applicants, 47% accepted. In 2001, 1 degree awarded.
Degree requirements: For master's, one foreign language, thesis.
Entrance requirements: For master's, GRE General Test, minimum GPA of 2.75 in last 2 years, 3.0 in field of study. *Application deadline:* For fall admission, 8/6 (priority date). Applications are processed on a rolling basis. *Application fee:* $0 ($25 for international students).
Expenses: Tuition, state resident: full-time $3,416; part-time $190 per credit hour. Tuition, nonresident: full-time $7,932; part-time $441 per credit hour.
Financial support: Research assistantships with tuition reimbursements, teaching assistantships with tuition reimbursements, career-related internships or fieldwork, Federal Work-Study, and tuition waivers (partial) available. Financial award application deadline: 3/15.
Faculty research: Archaeology of North America, historic archaeology, bioarchaeology, ethnography of Europe, ethnography of Africa.
Dr. H. Edwin Jackson, Chair, 601-266-4306.
Application contact: Dr. Marie Danforth, Coordinator, Program in Anthropology, 601-266-4306. *Web site:* http://www.dept.usm.edu/~antsoc/

■ UNIVERSITY OF SOUTH FLORIDA

College of Graduate Studies, College of Arts and Sciences, Department of Anthropology, Tampa, FL 33620-9951

AWARDS Applied anthropology (MA, PhD). Part-time and evening/weekend programs available.

Faculty: 17 full-time (8 women).
Students: 56 full-time (41 women), 56 part-time (44 women); includes 22 minority (7 African Americans, 5 Asian Americans or Pacific Islanders, 10 Hispanic Americans), 4 international. Average age 36. 60 applicants, 68% accepted, 31 enrolled. In 2001, 12 master's, 4 doctorates awarded.
Degree requirements: For master's and doctorate, thesis/dissertation, internship.
Entrance requirements: For master's, GRE General Test, minimum GPA of 3.2 in last 60 hours; for doctorate, GRE General Test. *Application deadline:* For fall admission, 1/5. *Application fee:* $20. Electronic applications accepted.
Expenses: Tuition, state resident: part-time $166 per credit hour. Tuition, nonresident: part-time $573 per credit hour. Required fees: $17 per term.
Financial support: In 2001–02, 2 fellowships with tuition reimbursements, 8 research assistantships with partial tuition reimbursements, 6 teaching assistantships with partial tuition reimbursements were awarded. Federal Work-Study, institutionally sponsored loans, tuition waivers (partial), and unspecified assistantships also available. Support available to part-time students. Financial award applicants required to submit FAFSA.
Faculty research: Media folklore and popular culture, population genetics, historical demography, biological anthropology, Mediterranean, archaeological science, origins of agriculture. *Total annual research expenditures:* $194,768.
Dr. Linda Whiteford, Chairperson, 813-974-2138, *Fax:* 813-974-2668, *E-mail:* lindaw@luna.cas.usf.edu.
Application contact: Dr. Susan D. Greenbaum, Graduate Director, 813-974-0777, *Fax:* 813-974-2668, *E-mail:* greenbau@chuma1.cas.usf.edu. *Web site:* http://www.cas.usf.edu/anthropology/index.html

■ THE UNIVERSITY OF TENNESSEE

Graduate School, College of Arts and Sciences, Department of Anthropology, Knoxville, TN 37996

AWARDS Archaeology (MA, PhD); biological anthropology (MA, PhD); cultural anthropology (MA, PhD); zooarchaeology (MA, PhD).

Faculty: 13 full-time (2 women).
Students: 36 full-time (28 women), 37 part-time (25 women); includes 2 minority (both Hispanic Americans). 105 applicants, 35% accepted. In 2001, 9 master's, 6 doctorates awarded.
Degree requirements: For master's, thesis; for doctorate, one foreign language, thesis/dissertation.
Entrance requirements: For master's and doctorate, GRE General Test, TOEFL, minimum GPA of 2.7. *Application deadline:* For fall admission, 1/1. *Application fee:* $35. Electronic applications accepted.
Expenses: Tuition, state resident: full-time $4,280; part-time $233 per hour. Tuition, nonresident: full-time $12,066; part-time $666 per hour. Tuition and fees vary according to program.
Financial support: In 2001–02, 7 research assistantships, 21 teaching assistantships were awarded. Fellowships, career-related internships or fieldwork, Federal Work-Study, institutionally sponsored loans, and unspecified assistantships also available. Financial award application deadline: 2/1; financial award applicants required to submit FAFSA.
Dr. Andrew Kramer, Head, 865-974-4408, *Fax:* 865-974-2686, *E-mail:* akramer@utk.edu.

■ THE UNIVERSITY OF TEXAS AT ARLINGTON

Graduate School, College of Liberal Arts, Department of Sociology and Anthropology, Program in Anthropology, Arlington, TX 76019

AWARDS MA. Part-time and evening/weekend programs available.

Students: 6 full-time (5 women), 13 part-time (9 women); includes 2 Hispanic Americans. 7 applicants, 100% accepted, 5 enrolled. In 2001, 6 degrees awarded.
Degree requirements: For master's, thesis or alternative.
Entrance requirements: For master's, GRE General Test, minimum GPA of 3.0, 3 letters of recommendation. *Application deadline:* For fall admission, 6/16. Applications are processed on a rolling basis. *Application fee:* $25 ($50 for international students).
Expenses: Tuition, area resident: Full-time $2,268. Tuition, nonresident: full-time $6,264. Required fees: $839. Tuition and fees vary according to course load.
Financial support: In 2001–02, 1 fellowship (averaging $1,000 per year), 2 teaching assistantships (averaging $8,000 per year) were awarded. Federal Work-Study and institutionally sponsored loans also available. Financial award application deadline: 6/1; financial award applicants required to submit FAFSA.
Application contact: Dr. Shelly L. Smith, Graduate Adviser, 817-272-3765, *Fax:* 817-272-3759, *E-mail:* slsmith@uta.edu.

■ THE UNIVERSITY OF TEXAS AT AUSTIN

Graduate School, College of Liberal Arts, Department of Anthropology, Austin, TX 78712-1111

AWARDS Archaeology (MA, PhD); folklore and public culture (MA, PhD); linguistic anthropology (MA, PhD); physical anthropology (MA, PhD); social anthropology (MA, PhD). Part-time programs available.

Faculty: 34 full-time (13 women), 4 part-time/adjunct (2 women).

Students: 124 full-time (80 women), 47 part-time (24 women); includes 40 minority (12 African Americans, 6 Asian Americans or Pacific Islanders, 22 Hispanic Americans), 12 international. Average age 33. 184 applicants, 22% accepted, 21 enrolled. In 2001, 15 master's, 10 doctorates awarded. Terminal master's awarded for partial completion of doctoral program.
Degree requirements: For master's, thesis; for doctorate, one foreign language, thesis/dissertation.
Entrance requirements: For master's and doctorate, GRE General Test. *Application deadline:* For fall admission, 1/15. *Application fee:* $50 ($75 for international students). Electronic applications accepted.
Expenses: Tuition, state resident: full-time $3,159. Tuition, nonresident: full-time $6,957. Tuition and fees vary according to program.
Financial support: In 2001–02, 15 fellowships with partial tuition reimbursements (averaging $10,188 per year), 36 teaching assistantships with full tuition reimbursements (averaging $21,331 per year) were awarded. Research assistantships, career-related internships or fieldwork, Federal Work-Study, institutionally sponsored loans, scholarships/grants, tuition waivers (partial), and unspecified assistantships also available. Financial award application deadline: 1/1.
Dr. James Brow, Chairman, 512-232-2183, *Fax:* 512-471-6535.
Application contact: Jennifer Jones, Graduate Coordinator, 512-471-4206, *Fax:* 512-471-6535, *E-mail:* jenjen@mail.utexas.edu. *Web site:* http://www.utexas.edu/cola/depts/anthropology/

■ THE UNIVERSITY OF TEXAS AT SAN ANTONIO

College of Liberal and Fine Arts, Department of Anthropology, San Antonio, TX 78249-0617

AWARDS MA. Part-time programs available.

Faculty: 7 full-time (2 women), 1 part-time/adjunct (0 women).
Students: 3 full-time (1 woman), 27 part-time (18 women); includes 7 minority (all Hispanic Americans). Average age 36. 7 applicants, 71% accepted, 5 enrolled. In 2001, 6 degrees awarded.
Degree requirements: For master's, one foreign language, comprehensive exam, registration.
Entrance requirements: For master's, GRE General Test, minimum GPA of 3.0 during last 60 hours, 18 hours in major field. *Application deadline:* For fall admission, 7/1; for spring admission, 12/1. Applications are processed on a rolling basis. *Application fee:* $25.
Expenses: Tuition, state resident: full-time $2,268; part-time $126 per credit hour. Tuition, nonresident: full-time $6,066; part-time $337 per credit hour. Required fees: $781. Tuition and fees vary according to course load.
Financial support: Career-related internships or fieldwork and Federal Work-Study available. Support available to part-time students.
Faculty research: Archaeology, ethnohistory, American social history, borderlands history, history of imperialism. *Total annual research expenditures:* $70,381.
Dr. Daniel J. Gelo, Chair, 210-458-4375.
Application contact: Dr. Laura Levi, Graduate Adviser, 210-458-5709.

■ UNIVERSITY OF TOLEDO

Graduate School, College of Arts and Sciences, Department of Sociology, Anthropology, and Social Work, Toledo, OH 43606-3398

AWARDS Anthropology (MAE); sociology (MA, MAE). Part-time programs available.

Faculty: 10.
Students: 14 full-time (8 women), 6 part-time (5 women); includes 2 minority (1 African American, 1 Asian American or Pacific Islander), 2 international. Average age 32. 17 applicants, 71% accepted, 5 enrolled. In 2001, 5 degrees awarded.
Degree requirements: For master's, thesis or alternative.
Application deadline: For fall admission, 8/1 (priority date). Applications are processed on a rolling basis. *Application fee:* $30. Electronic applications accepted.
Expenses: Tuition, state resident: full-time $7,278; part-time $303 per hour. Tuition, nonresident: full-time $15,731; part-time $699 per hour. Required fees: $43 per hour.
Financial support: In 2001–02, 13 teaching assistantships were awarded; research assistantships, career-related internships or fieldwork, Federal Work-Study, institutionally sponsored loans, and tuition waivers (full) also available. Support available to part-time students. Financial award application deadline: 4/1; financial award applicants required to submit FAFSA.
Faculty research: Medical and social gerontology, population, social movements, socioeconomic development, corporations and work, race and ethnicity.
Dr. Barbara Chesney, Chair, 419-530-2791, *Fax:* 419-530-8406.
Application contact: Elias T. Nigem, Graduate Director, 419-530-4662, *Fax:* 419-530-8406, *E-mail:* enigem@utnet.utoledo.edu. *Web site:* http://uac.rdp.utoledo.edu/docs/socdept/soc.htm

■ UNIVERSITY OF TULSA

Graduate School, College of Arts and Sciences, Department of Anthropology, Tulsa, OK 74104-3189

AWARDS MA.

Faculty: 6 full-time (0 women).
Students: 7 full-time (4 women), 1 part-time; includes 2 minority (both African Americans), 1 international. Average age 32. 3 applicants, 100% accepted, 3 enrolled. In 2001, 2 degrees awarded.
Degree requirements: For master's, thesis.
Entrance requirements: For master's, GRE General Test, TOEFL. *Application deadline:* Applications are processed on a rolling basis. *Application fee:* $30. Electronic applications accepted.
Expenses: Tuition: Full-time $9,540; part-time $530 per credit hour. Required fees: $80. One-time fee: $230 full-time.
Financial support: In 2001–02, 2 research assistantships with full and partial tuition reimbursements (averaging $6,000 per year), 3 teaching assistantships with full and partial tuition reimbursements (averaging $5,175 per year) were awarded. Fellowships with full and partial tuition reimbursements, career-related internships or fieldwork, Federal Work-Study, scholarships/grants, tuition waivers (partial), and unspecified assistantships also available. Support available to part-time students. Financial award application deadline: 2/1; financial award applicants required to submit FAFSA.
Faculty research: Cultural ecology, prehistory of Jordan, Oceania, archaeology of Mexico, sociolinguistics. *Total annual research expenditures:* $78,505.
Dr. George Odell, Chairperson, 918-631-3082, *E-mail:* george-odell@utulsa.edu.
Application contact: Dr. Michael Whalen, Adviser, 918-631-2370, *Fax:* 918-631-2540, *E-mail:* grad@utulsa.edu.

■ UNIVERSITY OF UTAH

Graduate School, College of Social and Behavioral Science, Department of Anthropology, Salt Lake City, UT 84112-1107

AWARDS MA, MS, PhD.

Faculty: 11 full-time (2 women), 2 part-time/adjunct (1 woman).
Students: 14 full-time (7 women), 16 part-time (9 women); includes 1 minority (Hispanic American). Average age 38. 31 applicants, 58% accepted. In 2001, 2 master's, 3 doctorates awarded.
Degree requirements: For master's, thesis or alternative; for doctorate, one foreign language, thesis/dissertation, comprehensive exam.
Entrance requirements: For master's and doctorate, GRE General Test, TOEFL. *Application deadline:* For fall admission, 7/1. *Application fee:* $40 ($60 for international students).
Expenses: Tuition, state resident: part-time $320 per semester hour. Tuition, nonresident: part-time $1,135 per semester hour. Required fees: $143 per semester hour. Tuition and fees vary according to course load, degree level and program.
Financial support: Fellowships, research assistantships, teaching assistantships, career-related internships or fieldwork available.

University of Utah (continued)
Faculty research: Evolutionary ecology, anthropological genetics, North American and Middle Eastern archaeology.
Kristen Hawkes, Chair, 801-581-6251, *Fax:* 801-581-6252, *E-mail:* hawkes@anthro.utah.edu.
Application contact: Julie Anzelmo, Advisor, 801-581-6251, *E-mail:* julie.anzelmo@anthro.utah.edu.

■ UNIVERSITY OF VIRGINIA

College and Graduate School of Arts and Sciences, Department of Anthropology, Charlottesville, VA 22903

AWARDS MA, PhD.

Faculty: 22 full-time (9 women), 4 part-time/adjunct (3 women).
Students: 44 full-time (28 women), 3 part-time (2 women); includes 4 minority (2 African Americans, 1 Asian American or Pacific Islander, 1 Hispanic American), 4 international. Average age 30. 78 applicants, 18% accepted, 9 enrolled. In 2001, 3 master's, 2 doctorates awarded.
Degree requirements: For master's and doctorate, variable foreign language requirement, thesis/dissertation.
Entrance requirements: For master's and doctorate, GRE General Test, GRE Subject Test. *Application deadline:* For fall admission, 7/15; for spring admission, 12/1. Applications are processed on a rolling basis. *Application fee:* $40. Electronic applications accepted.
Expenses: Tuition, state resident: full-time $3,988. Tuition, nonresident: full-time $17,078. Required fees: $1,190.
Financial support: Application deadline: 2/1.
Ellen L. Contini-Morava, Chairman, 434-924-7044, *Fax:* 434-924-1350.
Application contact: Duane J. Osheim, Associate Dean for Graduate Programs, 434-924-7184, *Fax:* 434-924-3084, *E-mail:* grad-a-s@virginia.edu. *Web site:* http://www.virginia.edu/artsandsciences/

■ UNIVERSITY OF WASHINGTON

Graduate School, College of Arts and Sciences, Department of Anthropology, Seattle, WA 98195

AWARDS MA, PhD.

Faculty: 31 full-time (12 women), 22 part-time/adjunct (11 women).
Students: 114 full-time (77 women); includes 11 minority (2 African Americans, 5 Asian Americans or Pacific Islanders, 2 Hispanic Americans, 2 Native Americans), 19 international. Average age 32. 110 applicants, 35% accepted, 15 enrolled. In 2001, 15 master's, 15 doctorates awarded.
Degree requirements: For master's, one foreign language, thesis (for some programs), comprehensive exam (for some programs); for doctorate, one foreign language, thesis/dissertation, comprehensive exam (for some programs).
Median time to degree: Master's–3 years full-time; doctorate–8 years full-time.
Entrance requirements: For master's and doctorate, GRE General Test, TOEFL, minimum GPA of 3.4. *Application deadline:* For fall admission, 1/15. *Application fee:* $50. Electronic applications accepted.
Expenses: Tuition, state resident: full-time $5,539. Tuition, nonresident: full-time $14,376. Required fees: $390. Tuition and fees vary according to course load and program.
Financial support: In 2001–02, 45 students received support, including 3 fellowships with full tuition reimbursements available (averaging $12,000 per year), 4 research assistantships with full tuition reimbursements available (averaging $12,400 per year), 20 teaching assistantships with full tuition reimbursements available (averaging $12,300 per year); career-related internships or fieldwork, Federal Work-Study, and institutionally sponsored loans also available. Financial award application deadline: 1/15.
Faculty research: Sociocultural anthropology, biocultural anthropology, archaeology, environmental anthropology.
Miriam Kahn, Chair, 206-543-5240.
Application contact: Graduate Program Assistant, 206-685-1562, *Fax:* 206-543-3285, *E-mail:* gradanth@u.washington.edu. *Web site:* http://www.anthro.washington.edu/

■ UNIVERSITY OF WISCONSIN–MADISON

Graduate School, College of Letters and Science, Department of Anthropology, Madison, WI 53706-1380

AWARDS MA, MS, PhD. Terminal master's awarded for partial completion of doctoral program.

Degree requirements: For master's, Qualifying Exam; for doctorate, thesis/dissertation.
Entrance requirements: For doctorate, qualifying exam. Electronic applications accepted.
Expenses: Tuition, state resident: full-time $7,361; part-time $399 per credit. Tuition, nonresident: full-time $20,499; part-time $1,282 per credit. Required fees: $34 per credit. Full-time tuition and fees vary according to course load, program, reciprocity agreements and student level.
Faculty research: Archaeology, biological, anthropology, cultural anthropology. *Web site:* http://www.wisc.edu/anthropology/

■ UNIVERSITY OF WISCONSIN–MILWAUKEE

Graduate School, College of Letters and Sciences, Department of Anthropology, Milwaukee, WI 53201-0413

AWARDS MS, PhD.

Faculty: 12 full-time (5 women).
Students: 39 full-time (20 women), 30 part-time (21 women); includes 7 minority (1 African American, 3 Asian Americans or Pacific Islanders, 3 Hispanic Americans), 3 international. 32 applicants, 84% accepted. In 2001, 9 master's, 5 doctorates awarded.
Degree requirements: For master's, thesis or alternative; for doctorate, one foreign language, thesis/dissertation, departmental qualifying exam.
Application deadline: For fall admission, 1/1 (priority date); for spring admission, 9/1. Applications are processed on a rolling basis. *Application fee:* $45 ($75 for international students).
Expenses: Tuition, state resident: full-time $6,180; part-time $535 per credit. Tuition, nonresident: full-time $19,482; part-time $1,366 per credit. Tuition and fees vary according to course load, program and reciprocity agreements.
Financial support: In 2001–02, 4 fellowships, 1 research assistantship, 14 teaching assistantships were awarded. Career-related internships or fieldwork and unspecified assistantships also available. Support available to part-time students. Financial award application deadline: 4/15.
J. Patrick Gray, Chair, 414-229-4174, *Fax:* 414-229-5848, *E-mail:* jpgray@uwm.edu. *Web site:* http://www.uwm.edu/dept/anthropology/

■ UNIVERSITY OF WYOMING

Graduate School, College of Arts and Sciences, Department of Anthropology, Laramie, WY 82071

AWARDS MA, PhD. Part-time programs available.

Faculty: 11 full-time (5 women), 7 part-time/adjunct (1 woman).
Students: 19 full-time (10 women), 21 part-time (8 women). 32 applicants, 53% accepted. In 2001, 11 degrees awarded. Terminal master's awarded for partial completion of doctoral program.
Degree requirements: For master's, one foreign language, thesis optional.
Entrance requirements: For master's and doctorate, GRE General Test, minimum GPA of 3.0. *Application deadline:* For fall admission, 3/1. *Application fee:* $40. Electronic applications accepted.
Expenses: Tuition, state resident: full-time $2,895; part-time $161 per credit hour. Tuition, nonresident: full-time $8,367; part-time $465 per credit hour. Required fees: $491; $10 per credit hour. $2 per credit hour. Tuition and fees vary according to course load and program.
Financial support: In 2001–02, 22 students received support, including research assistantships with partial tuition reimbursements available (averaging $4,333 per year); career-related internships or fieldwork, Federal Work-Study, and institutionally sponsored loans also available. Financial award application deadline: 3/1.

Faculty research: Paleo-Indian archaeology, osteology, faunal analysis, lithic analysis, hunter-gatherers. *Total annual research expenditures:* $70,000.
Audrey C. Shalinsky, Chair, 307-766-2750, *Fax:* 307-766-2473, *E-mail:* ashal@uwyo.edu.
Application contact: Robert L. Kelly, Graduate Advisor, 307-766-3135, *Fax:* 307-766-2473, *E-mail:* rlkelly@uwo.edu.

■ VANDERBILT UNIVERSITY

Graduate School, Department of Anthropology, Nashville, TN 37240-1001

AWARDS MA, PhD.

Faculty: 8 full-time (2 women).
Students: 16 full-time (6 women); includes 1 minority (Hispanic American), 2 international. Average age 27. 14 applicants, 36% accepted. In 2001, 3 degrees awarded.
Degree requirements: For master's, thesis or alternative, comprehensive exam; for doctorate, 2 foreign languages, thesis/dissertation, general, qualifying, and final exams.
Entrance requirements: For master's and doctorate, GRE General Test. *Application deadline:* For fall admission, 1/15. *Application fee:* $40. Electronic applications accepted.
Expenses: Tuition: Full-time $28,350.
Financial support: In 2001–02, 9 teaching assistantships with full tuition reimbursements (averaging $13,300 per year) were awarded; fellowships, research assistantships, career-related internships or fieldwork, Federal Work-Study, and institutionally sponsored loans also available. Financial award application deadline: 1/15.
Faculty research: Archaeology, ethnohistory and ethnography, epigraphy, conflict theory, Latin America. *Total annual research expenditures:* $18,275.
Thomas A. Gregor, Chair, 615-343-6120, *Fax:* 615-343-0230, *E-mail:* thomas.a.gregor@vanderbilt.edu.
Application contact: Arthur A. Demarest, Director of Graduate Studies, 615-343-6120, *Fax:* 615-343-0230, *E-mail:* arthur.a.demarest@vanderbilt.edu. *Web site:* http://www.vanderbilt.edu/gradschool/

■ WASHINGTON STATE UNIVERSITY

Graduate School, College of Liberal Arts, Department of Anthropology, Pullman, WA 99164

AWARDS MA, PhD.

Faculty: 14 full-time (4 women), 17 part-time/adjunct (7 women).
Students: 36 full-time (15 women), 22 part-time (11 women); includes 2 minority (1 African American, 1 Asian American or Pacific Islander), 3 international. Average age 29. 37 applicants, 62% accepted, 10 enrolled. In 2001, 12 master's, 3 doctorates awarded.
Degree requirements: For master's, one foreign language, thesis, oral exam; for doctorate, one foreign language, thesis/dissertation, qualifying exam. oral exam and written exam. *Median time to degree:* Master's–2 years full-time, 4 years part-time; doctorate–4 years full-time, 8 years part-time.
Entrance requirements: For master's and doctorate, GRE General Test, minimum GPA of 3.0. *Application deadline:* For fall admission, 1/15 (priority date); for spring admission, 10/15 (priority date). Applications are processed on a rolling basis. *Application fee:* $35. Electronic applications accepted.
Expenses: Tuition, state resident: full-time $6,088; part-time $304 per semester. Tuition, nonresident: full-time $14,918; part-time $746 per semester. Tuition and fees vary according to program.
Financial support: In 2001–02, 3 research assistantships with full and partial tuition reimbursements (averaging $11,000 per year), 20 teaching assistantships with full and partial tuition reimbursements (averaging $11,000 per year) were awarded. Fellowships, Federal Work-Study, institutionally sponsored loans, and tuition waivers (partial) also available. Financial award application deadline: 3/1; financial award applicants required to submit FAFSA.
Faculty research: Western North American archaeology and paleoenvironments, zoo archaeology, gender and culture issues, issues of globalization, cultural ecology. *Total annual research expenditures:* $120,035.
Dr. William Andrefsky, Chair, 509-335-3441, *Fax:* 509-335-3999, *E-mail:* and@wsu.edu.
Application contact: Annette Bednar, Program Coordinator, 509-335-3441, *Fax:* 509-335-3999, *E-mail:* abednar@wsu.edu. *Web site:* http://www.libarts.wsu.edu/anthro/

■ WASHINGTON UNIVERSITY IN ST. LOUIS

Graduate School of Arts and Sciences, Department of Anthropology, St. Louis, MO 63130-4899

AWARDS MA, PhD. Part-time programs available.

Students: 41 full-time (30 women); includes 3 minority (1 African American, 1 Asian American or Pacific Islander, 1 Hispanic American), 2 international. 83 applicants, 17% accepted. In 2001, 7 master's, 5 doctorates awarded. Terminal master's awarded for partial completion of doctoral program.
Degree requirements: For master's, thesis optional; for doctorate, thesis/dissertation.
Entrance requirements: For master's and doctorate, GRE General Test. *Application deadline:* For fall admission, 1/15 (priority date). Applications are processed on a rolling basis. *Application fee:* $35. Electronic applications accepted.
Expenses: Tuition: Full-time $26,900.
Financial support: Fellowships, research assistantships, teaching assistantships, career-related internships or fieldwork, Federal Work-Study, institutionally sponsored loans, and tuition waivers (full and partial) available. Support available to part-time students. Financial award application deadline: 1/15.
Dr. Richard J. Smith, Chairperson, 314-935-5252. *Web site:* http://artsci.wustl.edu/~anthro/

■ WAYNE STATE UNIVERSITY

Graduate School, College of Liberal Arts, Department of Anthropology, Detroit, MI 48202

AWARDS MA, PhD.

Faculty: 15 full-time.
Students: 66. 31 applicants, 61% accepted, 13 enrolled. In 2001, 6 master's, 1 doctorate awarded.
Degree requirements: For master's and doctorate, one foreign language, thesis/dissertation.
Application deadline: For fall admission, 7/1. *Application fee:* $20 ($30 for international students).
Expenses: Tuition, state resident: full-time $3,764. Tuition and fees vary according to degree level and program.
Financial support: In 2001–02, 5 fellowships, 2 research assistantships, 5 teaching assistantships were awarded.
Faculty research: Role of Arab women, home care of AIDS, organizational and cultural issues impact, black church.
Dr. Thomas Killion, Chairperson, 313-577-2935, *Fax:* 313-577-5958, *E-mail:* thomas.killion@wayne.edu.
Application contact: Beverly Fogelson, Graduate Director, 313-577-2935, *E-mail:* bfogelson@wayne.edu.

■ WEST CHESTER UNIVERSITY OF PENNSYLVANIA

Graduate Studies, College of Arts and Sciences, Department of Anthropology and Sociology, West Chester, PA 19383

AWARDS Gerontology (Certificate); long term care (MSA). Part-time and evening/weekend programs available.

Faculty: 1.
Students: 2 full-time (both women), 3 part-time (all women); includes 1 minority (African American). Average age 43. 4 applicants, 75% accepted. In 2001, 3 degrees awarded.
Degree requirements: For master's, comprehensive exam.

West Chester University of Pennsylvania (continued)

Entrance requirements: For master's, MAT, GRE, or GMAT, interview. *Application deadline:* For fall admission, 4/15 (priority date); for spring admission, 10/15. Applications are processed on a rolling basis. *Application fee:* $25.
Expenses: Tuition, state resident: full-time $4,600; part-time $256 per credit. Tuition, nonresident: full-time $7,554; part-time $420 per credit. Required fees: $44 per credit.
Financial support: In 2001–02, research assistantships with full tuition reimbursements (averaging $5,000 per year); unspecified assistantships also available. Support available to part-time students. Financial award application deadline: 2/15; financial award applicants required to submit FAFSA.
Faculty research: West African communities in the U.S., life long learning-distance education, comparative religions.
Dr. Anthony Zumpetta, Chair, 610-436-2556.
Application contact: Dr. Douglas McConatha, Graduate Coordinator, 610-436-3125, *E-mail:* dmcconatha@wcupa.edu.

■ WESTERN MICHIGAN UNIVERSITY

Graduate College, College of Arts and Sciences, Department of Anthropology, Kalamazoo, MI 49008-5202

AWARDS MA.

Faculty: 13 full-time (6 women).
Students: 22 full-time (12 women), 11 part-time (6 women); includes 2 minority (both Hispanic Americans), 1 international. 22 applicants, 77% accepted. In 2001, 8 degrees awarded.
Degree requirements: For master's, thesis, written exams, comprehensive exam. *Application deadline:* For fall admission, 2/15 (priority date). Applications are processed on a rolling basis. *Application fee:* $25.
Expenses: Tuition, state resident: part-time $186 per credit hour. Tuition, nonresident: part-time $442 per credit hour. Required fees: $602. One-time fee: $132 part-time. Tuition and fees vary according to course load.
Financial support: Fellowships, research assistantships, teaching assistantships, Federal Work-Study available. Financial award application deadline: 2/15; financial award applicants required to submit FAFSA.
Dr. Robert Ulin, Chairperson, 616-387-3969.
Application contact: Admissions and Orientation, 616-387-2000, *Fax:* 616-387-2355.

■ WESTERN WASHINGTON UNIVERSITY

Graduate School, College of Arts and Sciences, Department of Anthropology, Bellingham, WA 98225-5996

AWARDS MA. Part-time programs available.

Degree requirements: For master's, thesis.
Entrance requirements: For master's, GRE General Test, TOEFL, minimum GPA of 3.0 in last 60 semester hours or last 90 quarter hours.

■ WEST VIRGINIA UNIVERSITY

Eberly College of Arts and Sciences, Department of Sociology and Anthropology, Morgantown, WV 26506

AWARDS Applied social research (MA). Part-time programs available.

Faculty: 10 full-time (2 women), 5 part-time/adjunct (2 women).
Students: 10 full-time (5 women), 7 part-time (all women); includes 1 minority (African American), 1 international. Average age 27. 28 applicants, 39% accepted. In 2001, 5 degrees awarded.
Degree requirements: For master's, thesis or alternative.
Entrance requirements: For master's, GRE General Test, TOEFL, minimum GPA of 2.5. *Application deadline:* For fall admission, 3/1. *Application fee:* $45.
Expenses: Tuition, state resident: full-time $2,791. Tuition, nonresident: full-time $8,659. Required fees: $1,002. Tuition and fees vary according to program.
Financial support: In 2001–02, 10 students received support, including 8 teaching assistantships; research assistantships, Federal Work-Study, institutionally sponsored loans, and tuition waivers (full and partial) also available. Financial award application deadline: 2/1; financial award applicants required to submit FAFSA.
Faculty research: Applied sociology, research methodology, stratification, social/complex organization.
Dr. F. Carson Mencken, Chair, 304-293-5801 Ext. 1627, *Fax:* 304-293-5994, *E-mail:* carson.mencken@wvu.edu. *Web site:* http://www.as.wvu.edu/soc_a/

■ WICHITA STATE UNIVERSITY

Graduate School, Fairmount College of Liberal Arts and Sciences, Department of Anthropology, Wichita, KS 67260

AWARDS MA. Part-time programs available.

Faculty: 6 full-time (1 woman).
Students: 16 full-time (9 women), 35 part-time (23 women); includes 2 minority (both Hispanic Americans), 5 international. Average age 34. 17 applicants, 100% accepted, 10 enrolled. In 2001, 15 degrees awarded.
Degree requirements: For master's, project, thesis optional.
Entrance requirements: For master's, GRE, TOEFL, minimum GPA of 2.75 in last 60 hours, 3.0 in anthropology. *Application deadline:* For fall admission, 7/1 (priority date); for spring admission, 1/1. Applications are processed on a rolling basis. *Application fee:* $25 ($40 for international students). Electronic applications accepted.
Expenses: Tuition, state resident: full-time $1,888; part-time $105 per credit. Tuition, nonresident: full-time $6,129; part-time $341 per credit. Required fees: $345; $19 per credit. $17 per semester. Tuition and fees vary according to course load and program.
Financial support: In 2001–02, 6 teaching assistantships with full tuition reimbursements (averaging $3,417 per year) were awarded; fellowships, research assistantships, Federal Work-Study, institutionally sponsored loans, and unspecified assistantships also available. Financial award application deadline: 4/1; financial award applicants required to submit FAFSA.
Faculty research: Archaeology (plains and southwest), cross-cultural studies of aging, action anthropology, hostility and warfare, human osteology and nutrition.
Dr. Peer H. Moore-Jansen, Chairperson, 316-978-3195, *E-mail:* pmojan@wichita.edu. *Web site:* http://www.wichita.edu/

■ YALE UNIVERSITY

Graduate School of Arts and Sciences, Department of Anthropology, New Haven, CT 06520

AWARDS MA, PhD.

Degree requirements: For doctorate, thesis/dissertation.
Entrance requirements: For master's and doctorate, GRE General Test.
Faculty research: Linguistics, national identity.

ARCHAEOLOGY

■ BOSTON UNIVERSITY

Graduate School of Arts and Sciences, Department of Archaeology, Boston, MA 02215

AWARDS MA, PhD.

Students: 8 full-time (5 women), 5 part-time (4 women); includes 1 minority (Hispanic American). Average age 33. 85 applicants, 48% accepted, 4 enrolled. In 2001, 5 master's, 2 doctorates awarded. Terminal master's awarded for partial completion of doctoral program.
Degree requirements: For master's, one foreign language, thesis or alternative, 2 written exams; for doctorate, 2 foreign languages, thesis/dissertation, 3 written exams, 1 oral exam.

Entrance requirements: For master's, GRE General Test, TOEFL, 3 letters of recommendation; for doctorate, GRE General Test, TOEFL, scholarly writing sample, 3 letters of recommendation. *Application deadline:* For fall admission, 4/1. *Application fee:* $60.
Expenses: Tuition: Full-time $25,872; part-time $340 per credit. Required fees: $40 per semester. Part-time tuition and fees vary according to class time, course level and program.
Financial support: In 2001–02, 2 fellowships with full tuition reimbursements, 7 teaching assistantships with full tuition reimbursements (averaging $12,500 per year) were awarded. Research assistantships, career-related internships or fieldwork, Federal Work-Study, and unspecified assistantships also available. Support available to part-time students. Financial award application deadline: 1/15; financial award applicants required to submit FAFSA.
Julie Hansen, Chairman, 617-353-3415, *Fax:* 617-353-6800, *E-mail:* jmh@bu.edu.
Application contact: Maria H. Sousa, Sr. Program Coordinator, 617-353-3415, *Fax:* 617-353-6800, *E-mail:* mhsousa@bu.edu. *Web site:* http://www.bu.edu/ARCHAEOLOGY/

■ BROWN UNIVERSITY

Graduate School, Center for Old World Archaeology and Art, Providence, RI 02912

AWARDS AM, PhD.

Degree requirements: For doctorate, thesis/dissertation.
Entrance requirements: For master's and doctorate, GRE General Test.

■ BROWN UNIVERSITY

Graduate School, Department of Egyptology, Providence, RI 02912

AWARDS AM, PhD.

Degree requirements: For master's, one foreign language, thesis, final exam; for doctorate, 2 foreign languages, thesis/dissertation, comprehensive exam.
Entrance requirements: For master's and doctorate, GRE General Test.

■ BRYN MAWR COLLEGE

Graduate School of Arts and Sciences, Department of Classical and Near Eastern Archaeology, Bryn Mawr, PA 19010-2899

AWARDS MA, PhD. Part-time programs available.

Faculty: 4.
Students: 9 full-time (6 women), 12 part-time (9 women). 14 applicants, 21% accepted. In 2001, 5 master's, 2 doctorates awarded.
Degree requirements: For master's, 2 foreign languages, thesis; for doctorate, 3 foreign languages, thesis/dissertation.
Entrance requirements: For master's and doctorate, GRE General Test. *Application deadline:* For fall admission, 6/30; for spring admission, 1/2. *Application fee:* $25.
Expenses: Tuition: Full-time $22,260.
Financial support: In 2001–02, 17 fellowships, 2 teaching assistantships were awarded. Federal Work-Study, institutionally sponsored loans, and tuition awards also available. Support available to part-time students. Financial award application deadline: 1/2.
Dr. Stella Miller-Collett, Chairman, 610-526-5053.
Application contact: Graduate School of Arts and Sciences, 610-526-5072.

■ COLUMBIA UNIVERSITY

Graduate School of Arts and Sciences, Division of Humanities, Department of Art History and Archaeology, New York, NY 10027

AWARDS Archaeology (M Phil, MA, PhD); art history and archaeology (M Phil, MA, PhD); modern art (MA).

Faculty: 24 full-time, 12 part-time/adjunct.
Students: 217 full-time (160 women), 24 part-time (21 women); includes 21 minority (3 African Americans, 15 Asian Americans or Pacific Islanders, 3 Hispanic Americans), 24 international. Average age 35. 329 applicants, 33% accepted. In 2001, 22 master's, 20 doctorates awarded.
Degree requirements: For master's, 2 foreign languages, thesis; for doctorate, 3 foreign languages, thesis/dissertation.
Entrance requirements: For master's and doctorate, GRE General Test, TOEFL. *Application deadline:* For fall admission, 1/3. *Application fee:* $65.
Expenses: Tuition: Full-time $27,528. Required fees: $1,638.
Financial support: Fellowships, teaching assistantships, Federal Work-Study and institutionally sponsored loans available. Support available to part-time students. Financial award application deadline: 1/5; financial award applicants required to submit FAFSA.
Hilary Ballon, Chair, 212-854-4505, *Fax:* 212-854-7329.

■ CORNELL UNIVERSITY

Graduate School, Graduate Fields of Arts and Sciences, Field of Archaeology, Ithaca, NY 14853-0001

AWARDS Environmental archaeology (MA); historical archaeology (MA); Latin American archaeology (MA); medieval archaeology (MA); Mediterranean and Near Eastern archaeology (MA); Stone Age archaeology (MA).

Faculty: 14 full-time.
Students: 1 full-time (0 women). 10 applicants, 10% accepted.
Degree requirements: For master's, one foreign language, thesis.
Entrance requirements: For master's, GRE General Test, TOEFL, 3 letters of recommendation, sample of written work. *Application deadline:* For fall admission, 2/1. *Application fee:* $65. Electronic applications accepted.
Expenses: Tuition: Full-time $25,970. Required fees: $50.
Financial support: In 2001–02, 1 student received support, including 1 teaching assistantship with full tuition reimbursement available; fellowships with full tuition reimbursements available, research assistantships with full tuition reimbursements available, institutionally sponsored loans, scholarships/grants, tuition waivers (full and partial), and unspecified assistantships also available. Financial award applicants required to submit FAFSA.
Faculty research: Anatolia, Lydia, and Sardis; classical and Hellenistic Greece; science in archaeology; North American Indians; Stone Age Africa.
Application contact: Graduate Field Assistant, 607-255-3354, *E-mail:* classics@cornell.edu. *Web site:* http://www.gradschool.cornell.edu/grad/fields_1/archaeol.html

■ CORNELL UNIVERSITY

Graduate School, Graduate Fields of Arts and Sciences, Field of History of Art and Archaeology, Ithaca, NY 14853

AWARDS American art (PhD); ancient art and archaeology (PhD); baroque art (PhD); medieval art (PhD); modern art (PhD); Renaissance art (PhD); Southeast Asian art (PhD); theory and criticism (PhD).

Faculty: 13 full-time.
Students: 18 full-time (11 women); includes 5 minority (2 African Americans, 3 Asian Americans or Pacific Islanders), 5 international. 41 applicants, 15% accepted. In 2001, 2 doctorates awarded.
Degree requirements: For doctorate, one foreign language, thesis/dissertation, general exams in 3 areas.
Entrance requirements: For doctorate, GRE General Test, TOEFL, sample of written work, 3 letters of recommendation. *Application deadline:* For fall admission, 1/15. *Application fee:* $65. Electronic applications accepted.
Expenses: Tuition: Full-time $25,970. Required fees: $50.
Financial support: In 2001–02, 14 students received support, including 8 fellowships with full tuition reimbursements available, 6 teaching assistantships with full tuition reimbursements available; research assistantships with full tuition reimbursements available, institutionally sponsored loans, scholarships/grants, tuition waivers (full and partial), and unspecified assistantships also available. Financial award applicants required to submit FAFSA.
Application contact: Graduate Field Assistant, 607-255-4905, *Fax:* 607-255-0566, *E-mail:* art_history@cornell.edu. *Web*

Cornell University (continued)
site: http://www.gradschool.cornell.edu/grad/fields_1/hist-art.html

■ FLORIDA STATE UNIVERSITY

Graduate Studies, College of Arts and Sciences, Department of Classical Languages, Literature, and Civilization, Tallahassee, FL 32306

AWARDS Classical archaeology (MA); classical civilization (MA, PhD), including archaeology (PhD), literature and languages (PhD); classics (MA); Greek (MA); Greek and Latin (MA); Latin (MA). Part-time programs available.

Faculty: 10 full-time (4 women), 4 part-time/adjunct (0 women).
Students: 31 full-time (18 women), 9 part-time (5 women); includes 1 Asian American or Pacific Islander, 1 Hispanic American. Average age 26. 35 applicants, 80% accepted, 14 enrolled. In 2001, 8 master's awarded.
Degree requirements: For master's, one foreign language, thesis (for some programs), comprehensive exam (for some programs); for doctorate, 2 foreign languages, thesis/dissertation, comprehensive exam.
Entrance requirements: For master's, GRE General Test, minimum GPA of 3.0; for doctorate, GRE General Test. *Application deadline:* For fall admission, 2/15. Applications are processed on a rolling basis. *Application fee:* $20. Electronic applications accepted.
Expenses: Tuition, state resident: part-time $163 per credit hour. Tuition, nonresident: part-time $570 per credit hour. Tuition and fees vary according to program.
Financial support: In 2001–02, 31 students received support, including 1 fellowship with full tuition reimbursement available (averaging $10,000 per year), 1 research assistantship with full tuition reimbursement available (averaging $8,000 per year), 18 teaching assistantships with full tuition reimbursements available (averaging $8,000 per year); Federal Work-Study and institutionally sponsored loans also available. Support available to part-time students. Financial award application deadline: 2/1; financial award applicants required to submit FAFSA.
Faculty research: Greek and Latin literature, mythology, classical archaeology, history, Roman religion. *Total annual research expenditures:* $35,000.
Dr. W. Jeffrey Tatum, Chairman, 850-644-9231, *Fax:* 850-644-4073, *E-mail:* jtatum@mailer.fsu.edu.
Application contact: Dr. Laurel Fulkerson, Admissions Director, 850-644-0305, *Fax:* 850-644-4073, *E-mail:* lfulkers@mailer.fsu.edu. *Web site:* http://www.fsu.edu/~classics/

■ GEORGE MASON UNIVERSITY

College of Arts and Sciences, Interdisciplinary Studies Program, Fairfax, VA 22030-4444

AWARDS Interdisciplinary studies (MAIS), including archaeology, gerontology, regional economic development and technology, video-based production; liberal studies (MAIS). Part-time and evening/weekend programs available.

Faculty: 4 full-time (0 women), 5 part-time/adjunct (4 women).
Students: 8 full-time (6 women), 61 part-time (38 women); includes 13 minority (6 African Americans, 4 Asian Americans or Pacific Islanders, 3 Hispanic Americans), 7 international. Average age 36. 33 applicants, 61% accepted, 10 enrolled. In 2001, 17 degrees awarded.
Degree requirements: For master's, thesis optional.
Entrance requirements: For master's, GRE, GMAT, or MAT, interview, minimum GPA of 3.0 in last 60 hours. *Application deadline:* For fall admission, 5/1 (priority date); for spring admission, 11/1. Applications are processed on a rolling basis. *Application fee:* $30. Electronic applications accepted.
Expenses: Tuition, state resident: full-time $3,168; part-time $132 per credit hour. Tuition, nonresident: full-time $11,280; part-time $470 per credit hour. Required fees: $1,416; $59 per credit hour.
Financial support: Fellowships, teaching assistantships, career-related internships or fieldwork, Federal Work-Study, and institutionally sponsored loans available. Support available to part-time students. Financial award application deadline: 3/1; financial award applicants required to submit FAFSA.
Catherine A. McCormick, Coordinator, 703-993-8762, *Fax:* 703-993-8871, *E-mail:* emccorm1@gmu.edu.
Application contact: Dr. Johannes D. Bergmann, Information Contact, 703-993-8762, *E-mail:* mais@gmu.edu. *Web site:* http://cas.gmu.edu/mais/

■ GRADUATE SCHOOL AND UNIVERSITY CENTER OF THE CITY UNIVERSITY OF NEW YORK

Graduate Studies, Doctoral Program in Anthropology, New York, NY 10016-4039

AWARDS Anthropological linguistics (PhD); archaeology (PhD); cultural anthropology (PhD); physical anthropology (PhD).

Faculty: 39 full-time (14 women).
Students: 150 full-time (101 women), 6 part-time (4 women); includes 27 minority (9 African Americans, 8 Asian Americans or Pacific Islanders, 10 Hispanic Americans), 20 international. Average age 36. 125 applicants, 47% accepted, 29 enrolled. In 2001, 5 degrees awarded.
Degree requirements: For doctorate, one foreign language, thesis/dissertation.
Entrance requirements: For doctorate, GRE General Test. *Application deadline:* For fall admission, 1/15. *Application fee:* $40.
Expenses: Tuition, state resident: part-time $245 per credit. Tuition, nonresident: part-time $425 per credit. Required fees: $72 per semester.
Financial support: In 2001–02, 75 students received support, including 45 fellowships, 4 research assistantships; teaching assistantships, career-related internships or fieldwork, Federal Work-Study, institutionally sponsored loans, and tuition waivers (full and partial) also available. Financial award application deadline: 2/1; financial award applicants required to submit FAFSA.
Dr. Louise Lennihan, Executive Officer, 212-817-8006, *Fax:* 212-817-1501, *E-mail:* anthro@gc.cuny.edu.
Application contact: Information Contact, 212-817-8005, *Fax:* 212-817-1501, *E-mail:* anthro@gc.cuny.edu.

■ HARVARD UNIVERSITY

Graduate School of Arts and Sciences, Department of Anthropology, Cambridge, MA 02138

AWARDS Archaeology (PhD); biological anthropology (PhD); legal anthropology (AM); medical anthropology (AM); social anthropology (AM, PhD); social change and development (AM). Terminal master's awarded for partial completion of doctoral program.

Degree requirements: For master's, 2 foreign languages, thesis (for some programs); for doctorate, 2 foreign languages, thesis/dissertation, laboratory and/or fieldwork; general, qualifying, or special exams.
Entrance requirements: For master's and doctorate, GRE General Test, TOEFL.
Expenses: Tuition: Full-time $23,370. Required fees: $816. Full-time tuition and fees vary according to program and student level.

■ HARVARD UNIVERSITY

Graduate School of Arts and Sciences, Department of Near Eastern Languages and Civilizations, Cambridge, MA 02138

AWARDS Akkadian and Sumerian (AM, PhD); Arabic (AM, PhD); Armenian (AM, PhD); biblical history (AM, PhD); Hebrew (AM, PhD); Indo-Muslim culture (AM, PhD); Iranian (AM, PhD); Jewish history and literature (AM, PhD); Persian (AM, PhD); Semitic philology (AM, PhD); Syro-Palestinian archaeology (AM, PhD); Turkish (AM, PhD).

Degree requirements: For doctorate, variable foreign language requirement, thesis/dissertation, general exams.

Entrance requirements: For master's, GRE General Test, TOEFL; for doctorate, GRE General Test, TOEFL, proficiency in a Near Eastern language.
Expenses: Tuition: Full-time $23,370. Required fees: $816. Full-time tuition and fees vary according to program and student level.

■ HARVARD UNIVERSITY

Graduate School of Arts and Sciences, Department of the Classics, Cambridge, MA 02138

AWARDS Byzantine Greek (PhD); classical archaeology (AM, PhD); classical philology (AM, PhD); classical philosophy (PhD); medieval Latin (PhD).

Degree requirements: For doctorate, 4 foreign languages, thesis/dissertation, preliminary and special exams.
Entrance requirements: For master's and doctorate, GRE General Test, TOEFL.
Expenses: Tuition: Full-time $23,370. Required fees: $816. Full-time tuition and fees vary according to program and student level.

■ MICHIGAN TECHNOLOGICAL UNIVERSITY

Graduate School, College of Sciences and Arts, Department of Social Sciences, Program in Industrial Archaeology, Houghton, MI 49931-1295

AWARDS MS. Part-time programs available.

Degree requirements: For master's, thesis, fieldwork.
Entrance requirements: For master's, GRE General Test, TOEFL. Electronic applications accepted.
Faculty research: Historical archaeology, industrial archaeology, cultural resource management, historical preservation, history of technology. *Web site:* http://www.ss.mtu.edu

Find an in-depth description at www.petersons.com/gradchannel.

■ NORTHERN ARIZONA UNIVERSITY

Graduate College, College of Social and Behavioral Sciences, Department of Anthropology, Flagstaff, AZ 86011

AWARDS Anthropology (MA); archaeology (MA).

Students: 47 full-time (23 women), 17 part-time (11 women); includes 12 minority (1 Asian American or Pacific Islander, 4 Hispanic Americans, 7 Native Americans), 3 international. Average age 32. 108 applicants, 28% accepted, 22 enrolled. In 2001, 24 degrees awarded.
Degree requirements: For master's, thesis (for some programs), internship paper.
Entrance requirements: For master's, 18 undergraduate hours in anthropology. *Application deadline:* For fall admission, 1/15. *Application fee:* $45.
Expenses: Tuition, state resident: full-time $2,488. Tuition, nonresident: full-time $10,354.
Financial support: In 2001–02, 8 research assistantships, 5 teaching assistantships were awarded. Federal Work-Study and tuition waivers (full and partial) also available. Financial award application deadline: 1/15.
Faculty research: Economic development, culture change, ethnohistory, archaeology of the Southwest, small town networks and HIV. *Total annual research expenditures:* $594,266.
Dr. Francis Smiley, Coordinator, 928-523-3180.
Application contact: Jill Dubisch, Graduate Coordinator, 928-523-6795, *E-mail:* anthropology@nau.edu. *Web site:* http://www.nau.edu/~anthro/

■ PRINCETON UNIVERSITY

Graduate School, Department of Art and Archaeology, Princeton, NJ 08544-1019

AWARDS Archaeology (PhD); Chinese and Japanese art and archaeology (PhD); classical archaeology (PhD).

Degree requirements: For doctorate, 2 foreign languages, thesis/dissertation.
Entrance requirements: For doctorate, GRE General Test.

■ PRINCETON UNIVERSITY

Graduate School, Department of Classics, Program in History, Archaeology and Religions of the Ancient World, Princeton, NJ 08544-1019

AWARDS PhD. Offered through the Departments of Art and Archaeology, Classics, History, and Religion.

Degree requirements: For doctorate, 4 foreign languages, thesis/dissertation.
Entrance requirements: For doctorate, GRE General Test, sample of written work.
Faculty research: Ancient history, classical art and archaeology, Judaism, early Christianity, late antiquity.

■ PRINCETON UNIVERSITY

Graduate School, Department of East Asian Studies and Department of Art and Archaeology, Program in Chinese and Japanese Art and Archaeology, Princeton, NJ 08544-1019

AWARDS PhD.

Degree requirements: For doctorate, 2 foreign languages, thesis/dissertation, departmental exam.
Entrance requirements: For doctorate, GRE General Test, TOEFL, fluency in Japanese and/or Chinese.

■ SOUTHERN METHODIST UNIVERSITY

Dedman College, Department of Anthropology, Dallas, TX 75275

AWARDS Anthropology (MA, PhD); archaeology (MA, PhD); medical anthropology (MA, PhD).

Faculty: 18 full-time (3 women).
Students: 16 full-time (12 women), 51 part-time (30 women); includes 2 Asian Americans or Pacific Islanders, 1 Hispanic American, 2 international. 24 applicants, 54% accepted, 13 enrolled. In 2001, 5 master's, 2 doctorates awarded. Terminal master's awarded for partial completion of doctoral program.
Degree requirements: For master's, one foreign language, thesis or alternative; for doctorate, one foreign language, thesis/dissertation, qualifying exam.
Entrance requirements: For master's and doctorate, GRE General Test, minimum GPA of 3.0. *Application deadline:* For fall admission, 2/1 (priority date); for spring admission, 11/30 (priority date). Applications are processed on a rolling basis. *Application fee:* $50.
Expenses: Tuition: Part-time $285 per credit hour.
Financial support: In 2001–02, 29 students received support, including 5 fellowships (averaging $8,500 per year), 9 research assistantships with full tuition reimbursements available (averaging $8,500 per year), 21 teaching assistantships with full tuition reimbursements available (averaging $8,500 per year); Federal Work-Study, institutionally sponsored loans, scholarships/grants, traineeships, and tuition waivers (full) also available. Financial award application deadline: 3/1; financial award applicants required to submit FAFSA.
Faculty research: Health and gender, Paleoindians, Mesoamerica, American southwest, kinship and ethnicity.
Dr. Caroline Brettell, Chair, 214-768-4254.
Application contact: Dr. Victoria Lockwood, Graduate Adviser, 214-768-4022, *E-mail:* vlockwoo@mail.smu.edu.

■ TUFTS UNIVERSITY

Division of Graduate and Continuing Studies and Research, Graduate School of Arts and Sciences, Department of Classics, Medford, MA 02155

AWARDS Classical archaeology (MA); classics (MA). Part-time programs available.

Faculty: 6 full-time, 5 part-time/adjunct.
Students: 19 (10 women); includes 1 minority (Asian American or Pacific

Tufts University (continued)
Islander) 1 international. 22 applicants, 86% accepted. In 2001, 1 degree awarded.
Degree requirements: For master's, 2 foreign languages, thesis or alternative, comprehensive exam.
Entrance requirements: For master's, GRE General Test, TOEFL. *Application deadline:* For fall admission, 2/15; for spring admission, 10/15. Applications are processed on a rolling basis. *Application fee:* $50. Electronic applications accepted.
Expenses: Tuition: Full-time $26,853. Full-time tuition and fees vary according to program.
Financial support: Teaching assistantships with full and partial tuition reimbursements, Federal Work-Study, scholarships/grants, and tuition waivers (partial) available. Support available to part-time students. Financial award application deadline: 2/15; financial award applicants required to submit FAFSA.
Peter Reid, Chair, 617-627-3213. *Web site:* http://www.perseus.tufts.edu/classicsdept/

■ UNIVERSITY OF CALIFORNIA, BERKELEY

Graduate Division, College of Letters and Science, Department of Classics, Program in Classical Archaeology, Berkeley, CA 94720-1500

AWARDS MA, PhD.

Degree requirements: For master's, one foreign language, thesis; for doctorate, 2 foreign languages, thesis/dissertation, qualifying exam.
Entrance requirements: For master's and doctorate, GRE General Test, minimum GPA of 3.0.
Expenses: Tuition, nonresident: full-time $10,704. Required fees: $4,349. *Web site:* http://www.ls.berkeley.edu/Dept/Classics/dept.html

■ UNIVERSITY OF CALIFORNIA, BERKELEY

Graduate Division, Group in Ancient History and Mediterranean Archaeology, Berkeley, CA 94720-1500

AWARDS MA, PhD.

Degree requirements: For master's, one foreign language; for doctorate, 2 foreign languages, thesis/dissertation, qualifying exam.
Entrance requirements: For master's and doctorate, GRE General Test, minimum GPA of 3.0.
Expenses: Tuition, nonresident: full-time $10,704. Required fees: $4,349.

■ UNIVERSITY OF CALIFORNIA, LOS ANGELES

Graduate Division, College of Letters and Science, Program in Archaeology, Los Angeles, CA 90095

AWARDS MA, PhD.

Faculty: 25 full-time (18 women).
Students: 18 full-time (10 women); includes 3 minority (1 Asian American or Pacific Islander, 2 Hispanic Americans), 5 international. 46 applicants, 20% accepted, 5 enrolled. In 2001, 4 master's, 2 doctorates awarded.
Degree requirements: For master's, one foreign language, thesis or alternative, comprehensive core exam, paper; for doctorate, 2 foreign languages, thesis/dissertation, oral and written qualifying exams.
Entrance requirements: For master's, GRE General Test, minimum GPA of 3.0, sample of research writing; for doctorate, GRE General Test, minimum undergraduate GPA of 3.0, sample of research writing. *Application deadline:* For fall admission, 12/15. *Application fee:* $60. Electronic applications accepted.
Expenses: Tuition, nonresident: full-time $10,244. Required fees: $3,609. Full-time tuition and fees vary according to program.
Financial support: In 2001–02, 16 students received support, including 13 fellowships, 4 research assistantships, 4 teaching assistantships; Federal Work-Study, institutionally sponsored loans, and tuition waivers (full and partial) also available. Financial award application deadline: 3/1.
Dr. Sarah P. Morris, Chair, 310-825-4169.
Application contact: Departmental Office, 310-825-4169, *E-mail:* hgirey@ucla.edu.

■ UNIVERSITY OF CHICAGO

Division of the Humanities, Department of Classical Languages and Literatures, Chicago, IL 60637-1513

AWARDS Ancient philosophy (AM, PhD); classical archaeology (AM, PhD); classical languages and literatures (AM, PhD).

Students: 37. 58 applicants, 74% accepted. Terminal master's awarded for partial completion of doctoral program.
Degree requirements: For master's, one foreign language, thesis; for doctorate, 2 foreign languages, thesis/dissertation.
Entrance requirements: For master's and doctorate, GRE General Test, TOEFL. *Application deadline:* For fall admission, 12/28. *Application fee:* $55.
Expenses: Tuition: Full-time $16,548.
Financial support: Fellowships, Federal Work-Study available. Financial award application deadline: 12/28; financial award applicants required to submit FAFSA.
Dr. Shadi Barbsch, Chair, 773-702-8514.

■ UNIVERSITY OF MASSACHUSETTS BOSTON

Office of Graduate Studies and Research, College of Arts and Sciences, Faculty of Arts, Program in History, Track in Historical Archaeology, Boston, MA 02125-3393

AWARDS MA. Part-time and evening/weekend programs available.

Degree requirements: For master's, thesis, oral exams, practicum.
Entrance requirements: For master's, GRE General Test, minimum GPA of 2.75.
Faculty research: New World Colonialism, New England archeology, historical and urban archeology, archeological botany, ethnology.

■ UNIVERSITY OF MICHIGAN

Horace H. Rackham School of Graduate Studies, College of Literature, Science, and the Arts, Interdepartmental Program in Classical Art and Archaeology, Ann Arbor, MI 48109

AWARDS PhD.

Faculty: 10.
Students: 21 full-time (12 women); includes 3 minority (2 Asian Americans or Pacific Islanders, 1 Hispanic American), 1 international. Average age 28. 42 applicants, 10% accepted, 4 enrolled. In 2001, 4 degrees awarded.
Degree requirements: For doctorate, 4 foreign languages, thesis/dissertation, oral defense of dissertation, preliminary exam. *Median time to degree:* Doctorate–8 years full-time.
Entrance requirements: For doctorate, GRE General Test. *Application deadline:* For fall admission, 1/1. Applications are processed on a rolling basis. *Application fee:* $55. Electronic applications accepted.
Financial support: In 2001–02, 9 fellowships with full tuition reimbursements (averaging $13,000 per year), 2 research assistantships with full tuition reimbursements (averaging $13,000 per year), 9 teaching assistantships with full tuition reimbursements (averaging $13,000 per year) were awarded. Career-related internships or fieldwork and health care benefits also available. Financial award application deadline: 3/15.
John F. Cherry, Director, 734-764-6323, *Fax:* 734-763-8976, *E-mail:* jcherry@umich.edu.
Application contact: Debbie L. Fitch, Student Services Assistant, 734-764-6323, *Fax:* 734-763-8976, *E-mail:* ipcaa@umich.edu. *Web site:* http://www.umich.edu/~ipcaa/

■ UNIVERSITY OF MINNESOTA, TWIN CITIES CAMPUS

Graduate School, College of Liberal Arts, Department of Classical and Near Eastern Studies, Minneapolis, MN 55455-0213

AWARDS Ancient and medieval art and archaeology (MA, PhD); classics (MA, PhD); Greek (MA, PhD); Latin (MA, PhD). Part-time programs available.

Faculty: 16 full-time (4 women), 6 part-time/adjunct (1 woman).
Students: 30 full-time (17 women), 8 part-time; includes 1 minority (Asian American or Pacific Islander). Average age 29. 31 applicants, 13% accepted. In 2001, 3 master's, 1 doctorate awarded. Terminal master's awarded for partial completion of doctoral program.
Degree requirements: For master's, 2 foreign languages, thesis or alternative; for doctorate, variable foreign language requirement, thesis/dissertation.
Entrance requirements: For master's and doctorate, GRE. *Application deadline:* For fall admission, 7/15; for spring admission, 12/15. Applications are processed on a rolling basis. *Application fee:* $40 ($50 for international students).
Expenses: Tuition, state resident: full-time $2,932; part-time $489 per credit. Tuition, nonresident: full-time $5,758; part-time $960 per credit. Part-time tuition and fees vary according to course load, program and reciprocity agreements.
Financial support: In 2001–02, 26 students received support; fellowships, research assistantships, teaching assistantships, career-related internships or fieldwork, Federal Work-Study, institutionally sponsored loans, and tuition waivers (full and partial) available. Support available to part-time students. Financial award application deadline: 1/15.
Faculty research: Hellenistic literature, New Testament, late Latin, Greek and Roman archaeology, ancient languages.
William Malandra, Chairman, 612-625-8874, *Fax:* 612-624-4894, *E-mail:* malan001@maroon.tc.umn.edu.
Application contact: Nita Krevans, Director of Graduate Studies, 612-625-3422, *Fax:* 612-624-4894, *E-mail:* nkrevans@maroon.tc.umn.edu. *Web site:* http://www.cnes.cla.umn.edu/

■ UNIVERSITY OF MISSOURI–COLUMBIA

Graduate School, College of Arts and Sciences, Department of Art History and Archaeology, Columbia, MO 65211

AWARDS MA, PhD.

Faculty: 8 full-time (4 women).
Students: 10 full-time (5 women), 14 part-time (9 women), 2 international. 19 applicants, 16% accepted. Terminal master's awarded for partial completion of doctoral program.
Degree requirements: For master's and doctorate, 2 foreign languages, thesis/dissertation.
Entrance requirements: For master's and doctorate, GRE General Test, minimum GPA of 3.0. *Application deadline:* For fall admission, 2/1 (priority date). Applications are processed on a rolling basis. *Application fee:* $25 ($50 for international students).
Expenses: Tuition, state resident: part-time $179 per credit hour. Tuition, nonresident: part-time $539 per credit hour. Required fees: $122 per semester. Tuition and fees vary according to program.
Financial support: Research assistantships, teaching assistantships, institutionally sponsored loans available.
Dr. John R. Klein, Director of Graduate Studies, 573-882-9532, *E-mail:* kleinj@missouri.edu. *Web site:* http://web.missouri.edu/~ahawww/grprogram.html

■ THE UNIVERSITY OF NORTH CAROLINA AT CHAPEL HILL

Graduate School, College of Arts and Sciences, Department of Classics, Chapel Hill, NC 27599

AWARDS Classical archaeology (MA, PhD); classics (MA, PhD).

Faculty: 14 full-time (4 women), 5 part-time/adjunct (2 women).
Students: 21 full-time (7 women), 7 part-time (2 women); includes 1 minority (Hispanic American), 4 international. 66 applicants, 38% accepted, 8 enrolled. In 2001, 1 master's, 3 doctorates awarded. Terminal master's awarded for partial completion of doctoral program.
Degree requirements: For master's, one foreign language, thesis, comprehensive exam; for doctorate, 2 foreign languages, thesis/dissertation, comprehensive exam.
Entrance requirements: For master's and doctorate, GRE General Test, minimum GPA of 3.0. *Application deadline:* For fall admission, 1/1 (priority date). *Application fee:* $60. Electronic applications accepted.
Expenses: Tuition, state resident: full-time $2,864. Tuition, nonresident: full-time $12,030.
Financial support: In 2001–02, 21 students received support, including fellowships with full tuition reimbursements available (averaging $14,000 per year), 3 research assistantships with full tuition reimbursements available (averaging $10,000 per year), 15 teaching assistantships with full tuition reimbursements available (averaging $10,000 per year); Federal Work-Study, scholarships/grants, and unspecified assistantships also available. Financial award application deadline: 1/1.
Dr. William H Race, Chairman, 919-962-7662, *Fax:* 919-962-4036, *E-mail:* whrace@email.unc.edu.
Application contact: Kim S. Miles, Student Services Manager, 919-962-7192, *Fax:* 919-962-4036, *E-mail:* kmiles@email.unc.edu. *Web site:* http://www.classics.unc.edu/

■ UNIVERSITY OF PENNSYLVANIA

School of Arts and Sciences, Graduate Group in Art and Archaeology of the Mediterranean World, Philadelphia, PA 19104

AWARDS AM, PhD. Part-time programs available. Terminal master's awarded for partial completion of doctoral program.

Degree requirements: For master's, 3 foreign languages, thesis, Greek or Latin exam, German and French or Italian exam; for doctorate, 4 foreign languages, thesis/dissertation, Greek or Latin exam, 2nd ancient language exam, German and French or Italian exam.
Entrance requirements: For master's and doctorate, GRE General Test, TOEFL, knowledge of Greek or Latin and either French, German, or Italian.
Expenses: Tuition: Part-time $12,875 per semester.

■ THE UNIVERSITY OF TENNESSEE

Graduate School, College of Arts and Sciences, Department of Anthropology, Knoxville, TN 37996

AWARDS Archaeology (MA, PhD); biological anthropology (MA, PhD); cultural anthropology (MA, PhD); zooarchaeology (MA, PhD).

Faculty: 13 full-time (2 women).
Students: 36 full-time (28 women), 37 part-time (25 women); includes 2 minority (both Hispanic Americans). 105 applicants, 35% accepted. In 2001, 9 master's, 6 doctorates awarded.
Degree requirements: For master's, thesis; for doctorate, one foreign language, thesis/dissertation.
Entrance requirements: For master's and doctorate, GRE General Test, TOEFL, minimum GPA of 2.7. *Application deadline:* For fall admission, 1/1. *Application fee:* $35. Electronic applications accepted.
Expenses: Tuition, state resident: full-time $4,280; part-time $233 per hour. Tuition, nonresident: full-time $12,066; part-time $666 per hour. Tuition and fees vary according to program.
Financial support: In 2001–02, 7 research assistantships, 21 teaching assistantships were awarded. Fellowships, career-related internships or fieldwork, Federal Work-Study, institutionally sponsored loans, and unspecified assistantships also available. Financial award application deadline: 2/1; financial award applicants required to submit FAFSA.
Dr. Andrew Kramer, Head, 865-974-4408, *Fax:* 865-974-2686, *E-mail:* akramer@utk.edu.

■ THE UNIVERSITY OF TEXAS AT AUSTIN

Graduate School, College of Liberal Arts, Department of Anthropology, Austin, TX 78712-1111

AWARDS Archaeology (MA, PhD); folklore and public culture (MA, PhD); linguistic anthropology (MA, PhD); physical anthropology (MA, PhD); social anthropology (MA, PhD). Part-time programs available.

Faculty: 34 full-time (13 women), 4 part-time/adjunct (2 women).
Students: 124 full-time (80 women), 47 part-time (24 women); includes 40 minority (12 African Americans, 6 Asian Americans or Pacific Islanders, 22 Hispanic Americans), 12 international. Average age 33. 184 applicants, 22% accepted, 21 enrolled. In 2001, 15 master's, 10 doctorates awarded. Terminal master's awarded for partial completion of doctoral program.
Degree requirements: For master's, thesis; for doctorate, one foreign language, thesis/dissertation.
Entrance requirements: For master's and doctorate, GRE General Test. *Application deadline:* For fall admission, 1/15. *Application fee:* $50 ($75 for international students). Electronic applications accepted.
Expenses: Tuition, state resident: full-time $3,159. Tuition, nonresident: full-time $6,957. Tuition and fees vary according to program.
Financial support: In 2001–02, 15 fellowships with partial tuition reimbursements (averaging $10,188 per year), 36 teaching assistantships with full tuition reimbursements (averaging $21,331 per year) were awarded. Research assistantships, career-related internships or fieldwork, Federal Work-Study, institutionally sponsored loans, scholarships/grants, tuition waivers (partial), and unspecified assistantships also available. Financial award application deadline: 1/1.
Dr. James Brow, Chairman, 512-232-2183, *Fax:* 512-471-6535.
Application contact: Jennifer Jones, Graduate Coordinator, 512-471-4206, *Fax:* 512-471-6535, *E-mail:* jenjen@mail.utexas.edu. *Web site:* http://www.utexas.edu/cola/depts/anthropology/

■ UNIVERSITY OF VIRGINIA

College and Graduate School of Arts and Sciences, McIntire Department of Art, Charlottesville, VA 22903

AWARDS Art history (MA, PhD); classical art and archaeology (MA, PhD).

Faculty: 13 full-time (4 women), 1 (woman) part-time/adjunct.
Students: 29 full-time (25 women); includes 1 minority (African American), 1 international. 55 applicants, 55% accepted, 11 enrolled. In 2001, 2 master's, 1 doctorate awarded.
Degree requirements: For master's and doctorate, 2 foreign languages, thesis/dissertation, exam.
Entrance requirements: For master's and doctorate, GRE General Test. *Application deadline:* For fall admission, 1/15. *Application fee:* $40. Electronic applications accepted.
Expenses: Tuition, state resident: full-time $3,988. Tuition, nonresident: full-time $17,078. Required fees: $1,190.
Financial support: In 2001–02, 20 students received support, including 4 fellowships with full tuition reimbursements available (averaging $24,000 per year), 1 research assistantship (averaging $2,000 per year), 9 teaching assistantships with full tuition reimbursements available (averaging $6,600 per year); career-related internships or fieldwork, Federal Work-Study, health care benefits, and unspecified assistantships also available. Financial award application deadline: 12/1; financial award applicants required to submit CSS PROFILE. *Total annual research expenditures:* $75,000.
Lawrence O. Goedde, Chair, 434-924-6123, *Fax:* 434-924-3647, *E-mail:* log@virginia.edu.
Application contact: Peter Brunjes, Associate Dean, 434-924-7184, *E-mail:* grad-a-s@virginia.edu. *Web site:* http://minerva.acc.virginia.edu/~finearts/

■ WASHINGTON UNIVERSITY IN ST. LOUIS

Graduate School of Arts and Sciences, Department of Art History and Archaeology, St. Louis, MO 63130-4899

AWARDS Art history (MA, PhD); classical archaeology (MA, PhD). Part-time programs available.

Students: 20 full-time (14 women), 1 part-time; includes 1 minority (Asian American or Pacific Islander), 2 international. 21 applicants, 33% accepted. In 2001, 4 master's, 1 doctorate awarded.
Degree requirements: For doctorate, 2 foreign languages, thesis/dissertation, comprehensive exam.
Entrance requirements: For master's and doctorate, GRE General Test, sample of written work. *Application deadline:* For fall admission, 1/15 (priority date). Applications are processed on a rolling basis. *Application fee:* $35. Electronic applications accepted.
Expenses: Tuition: Full-time $26,900.
Financial support: Fellowships, teaching assistantships, career-related internships or fieldwork, Federal Work-Study, institutionally sponsored loans, and tuition waivers (full and partial) available. Support available to part-time students. Financial award application deadline: 1/15.
Dr. William Wallace, Chairperson, 314-935-5270. *Web site:* http://artsci.wustl.edu/~artarch/

Find an in-depth description at www.petersons.com/gradchannel.

■ WHEATON COLLEGE

Graduate School, Department of Biblical and Theological Studies, Program in Biblical Archaeology, Wheaton, IL 60187-5593

AWARDS MA.

Faculty: 2 full-time (0 women).
Students: 6. 14 applicants, 50% accepted, 5 enrolled. In 2001, 2 degrees awarded.
Degree requirements: For master's, thesis or alternative, semester of study in Israel.
Entrance requirements: For master's, GRE General Test or MAT. *Application deadline:* For fall admission, 3/1 (priority date); for spring admission, 11/1. Applications are processed on a rolling basis. *Application fee:* $30.
Expenses: Tuition: Part-time $410 per hour.
Financial support: Scholarships/grants available. Financial award application deadline: 6/1; financial award applicants required to submit FAFSA.
John Monson, Coordinator, 630-752-5706.
Application contact: Julie A. Huebner, Director of Graduate Admissions, 630-752-5195, *Fax:* 630-752-5935, *E-mail:* gradadm@wheaton.edu. *Web site:* http://www.wheaton.edu/gradadmiss

■ YALE UNIVERSITY

Graduate School of Arts and Sciences, Interdisciplinary Program in Archaeological Studies, New Haven, CT 06520

AWARDS MA.

Degree requirements: For master's, thesis.
Entrance requirements: For master's, GRE General Test.

DEMOGRAPHY AND POPULATION STUDIES

■ ARIZONA STATE UNIVERSITY

Graduate College, College of Liberal Arts and Sciences, Department of Sociology, Tempe, AZ 85287

AWARDS Demography and population studies (MA, PhD); sociology (MA, PhD).

Degree requirements: For master's, thesis or alternative; for doctorate, thesis/dissertation.
Entrance requirements: For master's and doctorate, GRE General Test.

Faculty research: Political sociology, marriage and family, demography and human ecology.

■ BOWLING GREEN STATE UNIVERSITY

Graduate College, College of Arts and Sciences, Department of Sociology, Bowling Green, OH 43403

AWARDS Criminology/deviant behavior (MA, PhD); demography and population studies (MA, PhD); family studies (MA, PhD); social psychology (MA, PhD). Part-time programs available.

Faculty: 17.
Students: 32 full-time (22 women), 12 part-time (8 women); includes 3 minority (2 African Americans, 1 Hispanic American), 6 international. Average age 28. 53 applicants, 53% accepted, 12 enrolled. In 2001, 7 master's, 4 doctorates awarded.
Degree requirements: For master's, thesis or alternative; for doctorate, thesis/dissertation, comprehensive exam.
Entrance requirements: For master's and doctorate, GRE General Test, TOEFL. *Application deadline:* For fall admission, 2/15. *Application fee:* $30. Electronic applications accepted.
Expenses: Tuition, state resident: full-time $7,376; part-time $342 per credit hour. Tuition, nonresident: full-time $13,628; part-time $640 per credit hour.
Financial support: In 2001–02, 26 research assistantships with full tuition reimbursements (averaging $9,134 per year), 6 teaching assistantships with full tuition reimbursements (averaging $11,000 per year) were awarded. Career-related internships or fieldwork, Federal Work-Study, institutionally sponsored loans, and unspecified assistantships also available. Financial award applicants required to submit FAFSA.
Faculty research: Applied demography, criminology and deviance, family studies, population studies, social psychology.
Dr. Gary Lee, Chair, 419-372-2294.
Application contact: Dr. Steve Cernkovich, Graduate Coordinator, 419-372-2743.

■ BROWN UNIVERSITY

Graduate School, Department of Sociology, Program in Population Studies, Providence, RI 02912

AWARDS PhD.

Degree requirements: For doctorate, thesis/dissertation, oral exam.
Entrance requirements: For doctorate, GRE General Test.

■ CORNELL UNIVERSITY

Graduate School, Graduate Fields of Agriculture and Life Sciences, Field of Development Sociology, Ithaca, NY 14853-0001

AWARDS Community and regional sociology (MPS, PhD); environmental management (MPS); population and development (MPS, PhD); rural and environmental sociology (MPS, PhD); state, economy, and society (MPS, PhD).

Faculty: 18 full-time.
Students: 41 full-time (24 women); includes 5 minority (all Hispanic Americans), 16 international. 56 applicants, 27% accepted. In 2001, 4 master's, 9 doctorates awarded.
Degree requirements: For doctorate, thesis/dissertation.
Entrance requirements: For master's and doctorate, GRE General Test, TOEFL, 3 letters of recommendation. *Application deadline:* For fall admission, 1/15. *Application fee:* $65. Electronic applications accepted.
Expenses: Tuition: Full-time $25,970. Required fees: $50.
Financial support: In 2001–02, 35 students received support, including 7 fellowships with full tuition reimbursements available, 13 research assistantships with full tuition reimbursements available, 15 teaching assistantships with full tuition reimbursements available; institutionally sponsored loans, scholarships/grants, tuition waivers (full and partial), and unspecified assistantships also available. Financial award applicants required to submit FAFSA.
Faculty research: Demography (population and development), environmental sociology, international and rural community development, political economy and ecology, sustainable agriculture.
Application contact: Graduate Field Assistant, 607-255-3092, *E-mail:* devsoc@cornell.edu. *Web site:* http://www.gradschool.cornell.edu/grad/fields_1/dev-soc.html

■ CORNELL UNIVERSITY

Graduate School, Graduate Fields of Arts and Sciences, Field of International Development, Ithaca, NY 14853-0001

AWARDS Development policy (MPS); international nutrition (MPS); international planning (MPS); international population (MPS); science and technology policy (MPS).

Faculty: 48 full-time.
Students: 24 full-time (15 women); includes 6 minority (2 African Americans, 2 Asian Americans or Pacific Islanders, 2 Hispanic Americans), 18 international. 34 applicants, 68% accepted. In 2001, 4 degrees awarded.
Degree requirements: For master's, project paper.
Entrance requirements: For master's, GRE General Test (recommended), TOEFL, 2 academic recommendations, 2 years of development experience. *Application deadline:* Applications are processed on a rolling basis. *Application fee:* $65. Electronic applications accepted.
Expenses: Tuition: Full-time $25,970. Required fees: $50.
Financial support: In 2001–02, 14 students received support, including 11 fellowships with full tuition reimbursements available, 1 research assistantship with full tuition reimbursement available, 2 teaching assistantships with full tuition reimbursements available; institutionally sponsored loans, scholarships/grants, tuition waivers (full and partial), and unspecified assistantships also available. Financial award applicants required to submit FAFSA.
Faculty research: Development policy, international nutrition, international planning, science and technology policy, international population.
Application contact: Graduate Field Assistant, 607-255-3037, *E-mail:* mpsid@cornell.edu. *Web site:* http://www.gradschool.cornell.edu/grad/fields_1/int-dev.html

■ DUKE UNIVERSITY

Graduate School, Center for Demographic Studies, Durham, NC 27708-0586

AWARDS PhD.

Degree requirements: For doctorate, thesis/dissertation.
Entrance requirements: For doctorate, GRE General Test. *Application deadline:* For fall admission, 12/31. *Application fee:* $75.
Expenses: Tuition: Full-time $24,600.
Financial support: Application deadline: 12/31.
Dr. Ken Manton, Director, 919-684-6126.

■ FLORIDA STATE UNIVERSITY

Graduate Studies, College of Social Sciences, Center for the Study of Population, Tallahassee, FL 32306

AWARDS MS, Certificate.

Faculty: 9 full-time (4 women).
Students: 4 full-time (1 woman), 1 international. Average age 25. 6 applicants, 67% accepted. In 2001, 3 degrees awarded.
Degree requirements: For master's, thesis.
Entrance requirements: For master's, GRE General Test, minimum GPA of 3.0. *Application deadline:* For fall admission, 3/15 (priority date). Applications are processed on a rolling basis. *Application fee:* $20. Electronic applications accepted.
Expenses: Tuition, state resident: part-time $163 per credit hour. Tuition, nonresident: part-time $570 per credit hour. Tuition and fees vary according to program.

Florida State University (continued)
Financial support: In 2001–02, 2 research assistantships with full tuition reimbursements (averaging $7,200 per year) were awarded; career-related internships or fieldwork, Federal Work-Study, institutionally sponsored loans, and unspecified assistantships also available. Financial award application deadline: 1/31; financial award applicants required to submit FAFSA.
Faculty research: Health, aging, migration, AIDS, gender. *Total annual research expenditures:* $681,000.
Dr. William J. Serow, Director, 850-644-1762, *Fax:* 850-644-8818, *E-mail:* wserow@garnet.acns.fsu.edu.

■ FORDHAM UNIVERSITY

Graduate School of Arts and Sciences, Department of Sociology, New York, NY 10458

AWARDS Criminology (MA); sociology (MA, PhD), including demography, ethnic minorities, sociology of religions. Part-time and evening/weekend programs available.

Faculty: 21 full-time (11 women).
Students: 14 full-time (10 women), 19 part-time (7 women); includes 8 minority (4 African Americans, 1 Asian American or Pacific Islander, 3 Hispanic Americans), 6 international. 35 applicants, 60% accepted. In 2001, 4 master's, 3 doctorates awarded. Terminal master's awarded for partial completion of doctoral program.
Degree requirements: For master's, one foreign language, comprehensive exam; for doctorate, 2 foreign languages, thesis/dissertation, comprehensive exam.
Entrance requirements: For master's and doctorate, GRE General Test. *Application deadline:* For fall admission, 1/15 (priority date); for spring admission, 12/1. *Application fee:* $65. Electronic applications accepted.
Expenses: Tuition: Part-time $720 per credit. Required fees: $135 per semester.
Financial support: In 2001–02, 13 students received support, including fellowships with tuition reimbursements available (averaging $15,000 per year), 1 research assistantship with tuition reimbursement available (averaging $12,000 per year), teaching assistantships with tuition reimbursements available (averaging $14,000 per year); career-related internships or fieldwork, Federal Work-Study, institutionally sponsored loans, tuition waivers (full and partial), and unspecified assistantships also available. Financial award application deadline: 1/16.
Dr. Orlando Rodriguez, Chair, 718-817-3853, *Fax:* 718-817-3846, *E-mail:* orodriguez@fordham.edu.
Application contact: Dr. Craig W. Pilant, Assistant Dean, 718-817-4420, *Fax:* 718-817-3566, *E-mail:* pilant@fordham.edu. *Web site:* http://www.fordham.edu/gsas/

■ GEORGETOWN UNIVERSITY

Graduate School of Arts and Sciences, Department of Demography, Washington, DC 20057

AWARDS MA.

Degree requirements: For master's, thesis or alternative, comprehensive exam.
Entrance requirements: For master's, GRE, TOEFL.
Faculty research: Social and demographic aspects of aging, determinants of human fertility behavior, demographic and economic aspects of social development, economic development and development policy.

■ HARVARD UNIVERSITY

School of Public Health, Department of Population and International Health, Boston, MA 02115-6096

AWARDS SM, DPH, SD. Part-time programs available.

Faculty: 13 full-time (4 women), 12 part-time/adjunct (6 women).
Students: 42 full-time (32 women), 1 (woman) part-time; includes 8 minority (2 African Americans, 4 Asian Americans or Pacific Islanders, 2 Hispanic Americans), 13 international. Average age 30. 100 applicants, 39% accepted, 21 enrolled. In 2001, 13 master's, 6 doctorates awarded.
Degree requirements: For master's, thesis; for doctorate, thesis/dissertation, qualifying exam.
Entrance requirements: For master's and doctorate, GRE, TOEFL. *Application deadline:* For fall admission, 12/15. *Application fee:* $60. Electronic applications accepted.
Expenses: Tuition: Full-time $23,370. Required fees: $816. Full-time tuition and fees vary according to program and student level.
Financial support: Fellowships, research assistantships, teaching assistantships, Federal Work-Study, scholarships/grants, traineeships, tuition waivers (partial), and unspecified assistantships available. Support available to part-time students. Financial award application deadline: 2/12; financial award applicants required to submit FAFSA.
Faculty research: International health policy, economics, reproductive health, ecology.
Dr. David Bloom, Acting Chair, 617-432-1232, *Fax:* 617-566-0365, *E-mail:* ajaimung@hsph.harvard.edu.
Application contact: Vincent W. James, Director of Admissions, 617-432-1031, *Fax:* 617-432-2009, *E-mail:* admisofc@hsph.harvard.edu.

■ JOHNS HOPKINS UNIVERSITY

School of Public Health, Program in Public Health, Baltimore, MD 21218-2699

AWARDS Biochemistry (MPH); biostatistics (MPH); environmental health sciences (MPH); epidemiology (MPH); health policy and management (MPH); international health (MPH); mental hygiene (MPH); molecular microbiology and immunology (MPH); population and family health sciences (MPH). Part-time and evening/weekend programs available. Postbaccalaureate distance learning degree programs offered.

Faculty: 431 full-time, 564 part-time/adjunct.
Students: 178 full-time (102 women), 189 part-time (117 women); includes 87 minority (30 African Americans, 43 Asian Americans or Pacific Islanders, 12 Hispanic Americans, 2 Native Americans), 90 international. Average age 34. 810 applicants, 58% accepted, 281 enrolled. In 2001, 258 degrees awarded.
Degree requirements: For master's, registration.
Entrance requirements: For master's, GRE General Test, TOEFL, 2 years of work related experience, course preparation in math and science. *Application deadline:* For fall admission, 12/1 (priority date). Applications are processed on a rolling basis. *Application fee:* $60. Electronic applications accepted.
Expenses: Tuition: Full-time $27,390.
Financial support: In 2001–02, 150 students received support, including 2 fellowships (averaging $17,530 per year); research assistantships, teaching assistantships, Federal Work-Study, institutionally sponsored loans, and scholarships/grants also available. Support available to part-time students. Financial award application deadline: 4/15; financial award applicants required to submit FAFSA.
Dr. Miriam Alexander, Director, 410-955-1291, *Fax:* 410-955-4749.
Application contact: Shawnise Smith, Administrator, 410-614-6876, *Fax:* 410-955-4749, *E-mail:* sfsmith@jhsph.edu. *Web site:* http://ww3.jhsph.edu

■ PRINCETON UNIVERSITY

Graduate School, Department of Economics, Princeton, NJ 08544-1019

AWARDS Economics (PhD); economics and demography (PhD).

Degree requirements: For doctorate, thesis/dissertation.
Entrance requirements: For doctorate, GRE General Test, GRE Subject Test (recommended), working knowledge of multivariate calculus and matrix algebra.

■ PRINCETON UNIVERSITY

Graduate School, Department of Sociology, Princeton, NJ 08544-1019

AWARDS Sociology (PhD); sociology and demography (PhD).

Degree requirements: For doctorate, variable foreign language requirement, thesis/dissertation.
Entrance requirements: For doctorate, GRE General Test, GRE Subject Test (recommended), sample of written work.

■ PRINCETON UNIVERSITY

Graduate School, Program in Population Studies and Department of Economics, Concentration in Economics and Demography, Princeton, NJ 08544-1019

AWARDS PhD.

Degree requirements: For doctorate, thesis/dissertation.
Entrance requirements: For doctorate, GRE General Test.

■ PRINCETON UNIVERSITY

Graduate School, Program in Population Studies and Department of Sociology, Concentration in Sociology and Demography, Princeton, NJ 08544-1019

AWARDS PhD.

Degree requirements: For doctorate, thesis/dissertation.
Entrance requirements: For doctorate, GRE General Test.

■ STATE UNIVERSITY OF NEW YORK AT ALBANY

College of Arts and Sciences, Department of Sociology, Albany, NY 12222-0001

AWARDS Demography (Certificate); sociology (MA, PhD); urban policy (Certificate). Evening/weekend programs available.

Students: 46 full-time (19 women), 59 part-time (31 women); includes 13 minority (3 African Americans, 2 Asian Americans or Pacific Islanders, 8 Hispanic Americans), 13 international. Average age 31. 68 applicants, 56% accepted. In 2001, 4 master's, 7 doctorates, 1 other advanced degree awarded. Terminal master's awarded for partial completion of doctoral program.
Degree requirements: For master's, thesis; for doctorate, thesis/dissertation, 2 specialization exams, research tool.
Entrance requirements: For master's and doctorate, GRE General Test. *Application deadline:* For fall admission, 6/1 (priority date). Applications are processed on a rolling basis. *Application fee:* $50.
Expenses: Tuition, state resident: full-time $2,550; part-time $213 per credit. Tuition, nonresident: full-time $4,208; part-time $351 per credit. Required fees: $470; $470 per year.
Financial support: Fellowships, research assistantships, teaching assistantships, career-related internships or fieldwork and Federal Work-Study available. Financial award application deadline: 3/15.
Faculty research: Gender and equality, crime and deviance, aging, work and organizations.
Dr. Steve Messner, Chair, 518-442-4666.
Application contact: Richard W. Lockman, Graduate Committee Chair, 518-442-4682.

■ TULANE UNIVERSITY

School of Public Health and Tropical Medicine, Program in Population Studies, New Orleans, LA 70118-5669

AWARDS MPH.

Degree requirements: For master's, one foreign language.
Entrance requirements: For master's, GRE General Test, TOEFL.
Expenses: Tuition: Full-time $24,675. Required fees: $2,210.

■ UNIVERSITY OF CALIFORNIA, BERKELEY

Graduate Division, Group in Demography, Berkeley, CA 94720-1500

AWARDS MA, PhD.

Students: 16 full-time (12 women), 10 international. 27 applicants, 30% accepted, 6 enrolled. In 2001, 1 degree awarded.
Degree requirements: For doctorate, thesis/dissertation, qualifying exam.
Entrance requirements: For master's and doctorate, GRE General Test, minimum GPA of 3.0. *Application deadline:* For fall admission, 2/10. *Application fee:* $60. Electronic applications accepted.
Expenses: Tuition, nonresident: full-time $10,704. Required fees: $4,349.
Financial support: Fellowships with full and partial tuition reimbursements, research assistantships with full and partial tuition reimbursements, teaching assistantships with full and partial tuition reimbursements, traineeships and unspecified assistantships available. Financial award application deadline: 1/5.
Dr. Kenneth Wachter, Chair, 510-642-9800.
Application contact: Liz Ozselcuk, Graduate Assistant for Admission, 510-642-9800, *Fax:* 510-643-8853, *E-mail:* office@demog.berkeley.edu. *Web site:* http://www.demog.berkeley.edu/

■ UNIVERSITY OF CALIFORNIA, BERKELEY

Graduate Division, Group in Sociology and Demography, Berkeley, CA 94720-1500

AWARDS PhD.

Degree requirements: For doctorate, thesis/dissertation, qualifying exam.
Entrance requirements: For doctorate, GRE General Test, minimum GPA of 3.0. *Application deadline:* For fall admission, 2/10. *Application fee:* $60.
Expenses: Tuition, nonresident: full-time $10,704. Required fees: $4,349.
Financial support: Fellowships with full and partial tuition reimbursements, research assistantships with full and partial tuition reimbursements, teaching assistantships with full and partial tuition reimbursements available. Financial award application deadline: 1/5.
Dr. Michael Hout, Chair, 510-643-6874.
Application contact: Liz Ozselcuk, Graduate Assistant for Admission, 510-642-9800, *Fax:* 510-643-8853, *E-mail:* office@demog.berkeley.edu. *Web site:* http://www.demog.berkeley.edu/

■ UNIVERSITY OF CALIFORNIA, IRVINE

Office of Research and Graduate Studies, School of Social Sciences and School of Social Ecology, Department of Demographic and Social Analysis, Irvine, CA 92697

AWARDS MA.

Students: 11 full-time (8 women); includes 5 minority (4 Asian Americans or Pacific Islanders, 1 Hispanic American), 1 international. 14 applicants, 64% accepted, 8 enrolled. In 2001, 6 degrees awarded.
Application deadline: For fall and spring admission, 1/15; for winter admission, 10/15.
Expenses: Tuition, nonresident: full-time $10,704. Required fees: $8,396. Tuition and fees vary according to course load, program and student level.
Ken Chew, Graduate Director, 949-824-6990.
Application contact: Ivonne Maldonado, Graduate Counselor, 949-824-7352, *Fax:* 949-824-3548, *E-mail:* immaldon@uci.edu.

■ UNIVERSITY OF ILLINOIS AT URBANA–CHAMPAIGN

Graduate College, College of Liberal Arts and Sciences, Department of Sociology, Champaign, IL 61820

AWARDS Demography (AM, PhD); sociology (AM, PhD).

Faculty: 15 full-time, 1 part-time/adjunct.
Students: 48 full-time (28 women); includes 5 minority (2 Asian Americans or Pacific Islanders, 3 Hispanic Americans), 30 international. 79 applicants, 15% accepted. In 2001, 1 master's, 1 doctorate awarded.
Degree requirements: For doctorate, thesis/dissertation.
Entrance requirements: For master's, GRE General Test, GRE Subject Test, minimum GPA of 3.0. *Application deadline:* For fall admission, 1/5. Applications are

University of Illinois at Urbana–Champaign (continued)
processed on a rolling basis. *Application fee:* $40 ($50 for international students). Electronic applications accepted.
Expenses: Tuition, state resident: part-time $3,227 per degree program. Tuition, nonresident: part-time $7,169 per degree program. Tuition and fees vary according to program.
Financial support: In 2001–02, 4 fellowships, 10 research assistantships, 25 teaching assistantships were awarded. Tuition waivers (full and partial) also available. Financial award application deadline: 2/15.
Andrew Pickering, Acting Head, 217-333-1950, *Fax:* 217-333-5225.
Application contact: Elizabeth Wilson, Administrative Secretary, 217-244-1808, *Fax:* 217-333-5225, *E-mail:* efleming@uiuc.edu. *Web site:* http://www.soc.uiuc.edu/

■ UNIVERSITY OF PENNSYLVANIA

School of Arts and Sciences, Graduate Group in Demography, Philadelphia, PA 19104

AWARDS AM, PhD. Terminal master's awarded for partial completion of doctoral program.

Degree requirements: For master's, thesis or alternative; for doctorate, thesis/dissertation.
Entrance requirements: For master's and doctorate, GRE General Test, TOEFL.
Expenses: Tuition: Part-time $12,875 per semester.

■ UNIVERSITY OF PUERTO RICO, MEDICAL SCIENCES CAMPUS

Graduate School of Public Health, Department of Social Sciences, Program in Demography, San Juan, PR 00936-5067

AWARDS MS. Part-time programs available.

Degree requirements: For master's, thesis.
Entrance requirements: For master's, GRE, previous course work in algebra and statistics. *Web site:* http://www.rcm.upr.edu/

■ UNIVERSITY OF SOUTHERN CALIFORNIA

Graduate School, College of Letters, Arts and Sciences, Department of Sociology, Program in Applied Demography, Los Angeles, CA 90089

AWARDS MS.

Degree requirements: For master's, thesis.
Entrance requirements: For master's, GRE General Test.
Expenses: Tuition: Full-time $25,060; part-time $844 per unit. Required fees: $473.

RURAL SOCIOLOGY

■ AUBURN UNIVERSITY

Graduate School, College of Agriculture, Department of Agricultural Economics and Rural Sociology, Auburn University, AL 36849

AWARDS M Ag, MS, PhD. Part-time programs available.

Faculty: 22 full-time (1 woman).
Students: 18 full-time (6 women), 17 part-time (10 women); includes 4 minority (all African Americans), 11 international. 19 applicants, 84% accepted. In 2001, 9 master's, 1 doctorate awarded.
Degree requirements: For master's, thesis (for some programs); for doctorate, thesis/dissertation.
Entrance requirements: For master's and doctorate, GRE General Test. *Application deadline:* For fall admission, 7/7; for spring admission, 11/24. Applications are processed on a rolling basis. *Application fee:* $25 ($50 for international students). Electronic applications accepted.
Financial support: Research assistantships, teaching assistantships, Federal Work-Study available. Support available to part-time students. Financial award application deadline: 3/15.
Faculty research: Farm management, agricultural marketing, production economics, resource economics, agricultural finance.
Dr. John L. Adrian, Chair, 334-844-4800.
Application contact: Dr. John F. Pritchett, Dean of the Graduate School, 334-844-4700, *E-mail:* hatchlb@mail.auburn.edu. *Web site:* http://www.ag.auburn.edu/dept/aec/aec.html

■ CORNELL UNIVERSITY

Graduate School, Graduate Fields of Agriculture and Life Sciences, Field of Development Sociology, Ithaca, NY 14853-0001

AWARDS Community and regional sociology (MPS, PhD); environmental management (MPS); population and development (MPS, PhD); rural and environmental sociology (MPS, PhD); state, economy, and society (MPS, PhD).

Faculty: 18 full-time.
Students: 41 full-time (24 women); includes 5 minority (all Hispanic Americans), 16 international. 56 applicants, 27% accepted. In 2001, 4 master's, 9 doctorates awarded.
Degree requirements: For doctorate, thesis/dissertation.
Entrance requirements: For master's and doctorate, GRE General Test, TOEFL, 3 letters of recommendation. *Application deadline:* For fall admission, 1/15. *Application fee:* $65. Electronic applications accepted.
Expenses: Tuition: Full-time $25,970. Required fees: $50.
Financial support: In 2001–02, 35 students received support, including 7 fellowships with full tuition reimbursements available, 13 research assistantships with full tuition reimbursements available, 15 teaching assistantships with full tuition reimbursements available; institutionally sponsored loans, scholarships/grants, tuition waivers (full and partial), and unspecified assistantships also available. Financial award applicants required to submit FAFSA.
Faculty research: Demography (population and development), environmental sociology, international and rural community development, political economy and ecology, sustainable agriculture.
Application contact: Graduate Field Assistant, 607-255-3092, *E-mail:* devsoc@cornell.edu. *Web site:* http://www.gradschool.cornell.edu/grad/fields_1/dev-soc.html

■ IOWA STATE UNIVERSITY OF SCIENCE AND TECHNOLOGY

Graduate College, College of Liberal Arts and Sciences, Department of Sociology and College of Agriculture, Program in Rural Sociology, Ames, IA 50011

AWARDS MS, PhD.

Students: 8 full-time (4 women), 6 part-time (4 women); includes 2 minority (1 African American, 1 Asian American or Pacific Islander), 7 international. 6 applicants, 83% accepted, 2 enrolled. In 2001, 1 master's, 3 doctorates awarded.
Degree requirements: For master's and doctorate, thesis/dissertation. *Median time to degree:* Master's–1.9 years full-time; doctorate–5.7 years full-time.
Entrance requirements: For master's, GRE General Test, TOEFL or IELTS; for doctorate, GRE General Test, TOEFL or IELTS, master's degree. *Application deadline:* For fall admission, 2/1 (priority date); for spring admission, 10/1. *Application fee:* $20 ($50 for international students). Electronic applications accepted.
Expenses: Tuition, state resident: full-time $1,851. Tuition, nonresident: full-time $5,449. Tuition and fees vary according to program.
Financial support: In 2001–02, 8 research assistantships with partial tuition reimbursements (averaging $15,426 per year) were awarded; teaching assistantships with partial tuition reimbursements, scholarships/grants, health care benefits, and unspecified assistantships also available.

■ NORTH CAROLINA STATE UNIVERSITY

Graduate School, College of Humanities and Social Sciences and College of Agriculture and Life Sciences, Department of Sociology and Anthropology, Raleigh, NC 27695

AWARDS Rural sociology (MS); sociology (M Soc, PhD). Part-time programs available.

Faculty: 35 full-time (11 women), 12 part-time/adjunct (1 woman).
Students: 47 full-time (34 women), 31 part-time (23 women); includes 13 minority (12 African Americans, 1 Asian American or Pacific Islander), 1 international. Average age 34. 66 applicants, 48% accepted. In 2001, 6 master's, 5 doctorates awarded.
Degree requirements: For master's, practicum (M Soc), thesis (MS); for doctorate, thesis/dissertation, comprehensive exam.
Entrance requirements: For master's and doctorate, GRE General Test, sample of written work. *Application deadline:* For fall admission, 5/1 (priority date); for spring admission, 11/1. Applications are processed on a rolling basis. *Application fee:* $45.
Expenses: Tuition, state resident: full-time $1,748. Tuition, nonresident: full-time $6,904.
Financial support: In 2001–02, 2 fellowships (averaging $5,694 per year), 14 research assistantships (averaging $5,867 per year), 23 teaching assistantships (averaging $5,607 per year) were awarded. Career-related internships or fieldwork and minority grants also available. Support available to part-time students. Financial award application deadline: 2/1.
Faculty research: Gender and racial inequality, globalization and commodity chains, biotechnology and environment, poverty and economic development, work and families. *Total annual research expenditures:* $377,502.
Dr. William B. Clifford, Head, 919-515-3180, *Fax:* 919-515-2610, *E-mail:* william_clifford@ncsu.edu.
Application contact: Dr. Jeffrey C. Leiter, Director of Graduate Programs, 919-515-9009, *Fax:* 919-515-2610, *E-mail:* gradprog@server.sasw.ncsu.edu. *Web site:* http://sasw.chass.ncsu.edu/s&a/s&ahmpg.htm

■ THE OHIO STATE UNIVERSITY

Graduate School, College of Food, Agricultural, and Environmental Sciences, Department of Agricultural, Environmental, and Development Economics, Columbus, OH 43210

AWARDS Agricultural economics and rural sociology (MS, PhD).

Degree requirements: For master's, thesis optional; for doctorate, thesis/dissertation.
Entrance requirements: For master's and doctorate, GMAT or GRE General Test.

■ THE PENNSYLVANIA STATE UNIVERSITY UNIVERSITY PARK CAMPUS

Graduate School, College of Agricultural Sciences, Department of Agricultural Economics and Rural Sociology, Program in Rural Sociology, State College, University Park, PA 16802-1503

AWARDS M Agr, MS, PhD.

Students: 16 full-time (8 women), 7 part-time (6 women).
Entrance requirements: For master's and doctorate, GRE General Test. *Application fee:* $45.
Expenses: Tuition, state resident: full-time $7,882; part-time $333 per credit. Tuition, nonresident: full-time $16,142; part-time $673 per credit. Required fees: $124 per semester.
Dr. C. Shannon Stokes, Chair, 814-863-8633.

■ SOUTH DAKOTA STATE UNIVERSITY

Graduate School, College of Agriculture and Biological Sciences, Department of Rural Sociology, Brookings, SD 57007

AWARDS MS, PhD.

Degree requirements: For master's, thesis, oral and written exams; for doctorate, thesis/dissertation, preliminary oral and written exams.
Entrance requirements: For master's and doctorate, TOEFL.
Faculty research: Demography, rural families, rural development, Native Americans, Hutterites.

■ UNIVERSITY OF MISSOURI–COLUMBIA

Graduate School, College of Agriculture, Food and Natural Resources, Department of Rural Sociology, Columbia, MO 65211

AWARDS MS, PhD. Part-time programs available.

Faculty: 8 full-time (1 woman).
Students: 15 full-time (10 women), 14 part-time (4 women); includes 6 minority (4 African Americans, 1 Hispanic American, 1 Native American), 8 international. 6 applicants, 50% accepted. In 2001, 3 degrees awarded.
Degree requirements: For doctorate, thesis/dissertation.
Entrance requirements: For master's and doctorate, GRE General Test, minimum GPA of 3.0. *Application deadline:* For fall admission, 5/15 (priority date). Applications are processed on a rolling basis. *Application fee:* $25 ($50 for international students).
Expenses: Tuition, state resident: part-time $179 per credit hour. Tuition, nonresident: part-time $539 per credit hour. Required fees: $122 per semester. Tuition and fees vary according to program.
Financial support: Research assistantships, teaching assistantships, institutionally sponsored loans available.
Dr. Jere Gilles, Director of Graduate Studies, 573-882-3791, *E-mail:* gillesj@missouri.edu. *Web site:* http://www.ssu.missouri.edu/ruralsoc/

■ THE UNIVERSITY OF MONTANA–MISSOULA

Graduate School, College of Arts and Sciences, Department of Sociology, Missoula, MT 59812-0002

AWARDS Criminology (MA); rural and environmental change (MA).

Faculty: 11 full-time (3 women).
Students: 15 full-time (11 women), 2 part-time (both women); includes 1 minority (Native American). 17 applicants, 88% accepted, 9 enrolled. In 2001, 4 degrees awarded.
Entrance requirements: For master's, GRE General Test. *Application deadline:* For fall admission, 3/15 (priority date). *Application fee:* $45.
Expenses: Tuition, state resident: full-time $2,482; part-time $1,700 per year. Tuition, nonresident: full-time $7,372; part-time $5,000 per year. Required fees: $1,900. Tuition and fees vary according to degree level.
Financial support: In 2001–02, 5 teaching assistantships with full tuition reimbursements (averaging $8,665 per year) were awarded; research assistantships, career-related internships or fieldwork, Federal Work-Study, and unspecified assistantships also available. Financial award application deadline: 3/1; financial award applicants required to submit FAFSA.
Faculty research: Housing, homelessness, hunger, infant mortality, work safety. *Total annual research expenditures:* $191,297.
Dr. Jill Belsky, Chair, 406-243-5281, *Fax:* 406-243-5951, *E-mail:* belsky@selway.umt.edu.
Application contact: Dr. Daniel P. Doyle, Graduate Coordinator, 406-243-2855, *Fax:* 406-243-5951, *E-mail:* ddoyle@selway.umt.edu. *Web site:* http://www.umt.edu/sociology/

■ THE UNIVERSITY OF TENNESSEE

Graduate School, College of Agricultural Sciences and Natural Resources, Department of Agricultural Economics, Knoxville, TN 37996

AWARDS Agribusiness (MS); agricultural economics (MS); rural sociology (MS).

Faculty: 16 full-time (1 woman).
Students: 16 full-time (9 women), 2 part-time (1 woman); includes 3 minority (2 African Americans, 1 Hispanic American), 2 international. 16 applicants, 75% accepted. In 2001, 10 degrees awarded.
Degree requirements: For master's, thesis or alternative.
Entrance requirements: For master's, GRE General Test, TOEFL, minimum GPA of 2.7. *Application deadline:* For fall admission, 2/1 (priority date). Applications are processed on a rolling basis. *Application fee:* $35. Electronic applications accepted.
Expenses: Tuition, state resident: full-time $4,280; part-time $233 per hour. Tuition, nonresident: full-time $12,066; part-time $666 per hour. Tuition and fees vary according to program.
Financial support: In 2001–02, 14 research assistantships were awarded; fellowships, teaching assistantships, career-related internships or fieldwork, Federal Work-Study, and institutionally sponsored loans also available. Financial award application deadline: 2/1; financial award applicants required to submit FAFSA.
Dr. Dan McLemore, Head, 865-974-7231, *Fax:* 865-974-7484, *E-mail:* dmclemore@utk.edu.
Application contact: Dr. John Brooker, Graduate Representative, *E-mail:* jbrooker@utk.edu.

■ UNIVERSITY OF WISCONSIN–MADISON

Graduate School, College of Letters and Science, Department of Sociology, Madison, WI 53706-1380

AWARDS Rural sociology (MS); sociology (MS, PhD). Part-time programs available.

Faculty: 56 full-time (16 women), 2 part-time/adjunct (1 woman).
Students: 175 full-time (106 women), 2 part-time (both women); includes 20 minority (8 African Americans, 2 Asian Americans or Pacific Islanders, 10 Hispanic Americans), 27 international. Average age 32. 195 applicants, 46% accepted, 25 enrolled. In 2001, 21 master's, 19 doctorates awarded. Terminal master's awarded for partial completion of doctoral program.
Degree requirements: For master's, thesis, oral exam; for doctorate, thesis/dissertation, preliminary and final oral exams, 4 seminars. *Median time to degree:* Master's–3 years full-time; doctorate–7 years full-time.
Entrance requirements: For master's and doctorate, GRE General Test, TOEFL. *Application deadline:* For fall admission, 2/1; for spring admission, 9/1. Applications are processed on a rolling basis. *Application fee:* $45. Electronic applications accepted.
Expenses: Tuition, state resident: full-time $7,361; part-time $399 per credit. Tuition, nonresident: full-time $20,499; part-time $1,282 per credit. Required fees: $34 per credit. Full-time tuition and fees vary according to course load, program, reciprocity agreements and student level.
Financial support: In 2001–02, 96 students received support, including 17 fellowships with full tuition reimbursements available (averaging $13,446 per year), 23 research assistantships with full tuition reimbursements available (averaging $13,379 per year), 30 teaching assistantships with full tuition reimbursements available (averaging $10,476 per year); Federal Work-Study, institutionally sponsored loans, traineeships, and unspecified assistantships also available. Financial award application deadline: 12/15. *Total annual research expenditures:* $796,221.
Prof. Adam Gamoran, Chair, 608-262-1498, *Fax:* 608-265-5389.
Application contact: Mary E. Powers, Graduate Admissions, 608-262-4863, *Fax:* 608-265-5389, *E-mail:* gradinfo@ssc.wisc.edu. *Web site:* http://www.ssc.wisc.edu/soc/

SOCIOLOGY

■ AMERICAN UNIVERSITY

College of Arts and Sciences, Department of Sociology, Program in Applied Sociology, Washington, DC 20016-8001

AWARDS MA.

Students: Average age 32.
Degree requirements: For master's, thesis or alternative, comprehensive exam. *Application deadline:* For fall admission, 2/1; for spring admission, 10/1. *Application fee:* $50.
Expenses: Tuition: Full-time $14,274; part-time $793 per credit. Required fees: $290. Tuition and fees vary according to program.
Financial support: Fellowships, research assistantships, teaching assistantships, career-related internships or fieldwork, Federal Work-Study, institutionally sponsored loans, and tuition waivers (full and partial) available. Support available to part-time students. Financial award application deadline: 2/1.
Application contact: Prof. Gloria A. Young, Director of Graduate Studies, Sociology, 202-885-2475, *Fax:* 202-885-2477, *E-mail:* gyoung@american.edu. *Web site:* http://www.american.edu/academic.depts/cas/sociology/sochome.htm

■ AMERICAN UNIVERSITY

College of Arts and Sciences, Department of Sociology, Program in Sociology, Washington, DC 20016-8001

AWARDS MA, PhD. Part-time and evening/weekend programs available.

Students: 18 full-time (14 women), 60 part-time (37 women); includes 24 minority (18 African Americans, 1 Asian American or Pacific Islander, 5 Hispanic Americans), 15 international. Average age 36. In 2001, 2 master's, 7 doctorates awarded. Terminal master's awarded for partial completion of doctoral program.
Degree requirements: For master's, thesis or alternative, comprehensive exam; for doctorate, one foreign language, thesis/dissertation, comprehensive exam.
Entrance requirements: For master's, GRE (recommended); for doctorate, GRE. *Application deadline:* For fall admission, 2/1 (priority date); for spring admission, 10/1. Applications are processed on a rolling basis. *Application fee:* $50.
Expenses: Tuition: Full-time $14,274; part-time $793 per credit. Required fees: $290. Tuition and fees vary according to program.
Financial support: In 2001–02, 11 students received support; fellowships, research assistantships, teaching assistantships, career-related internships or fieldwork, Federal Work-Study, institutionally sponsored loans, tuition waivers (full and partial), unspecified assistantships, and administrative fellowships available. Support available to part-time students. Financial award application deadline: 2/1.
Faculty research: Gender, policy, race and ethnic development, macro/comparative international education.
Application contact: Prof. Gloria A. Young, Director of Graduate Studies, Sociology, 202-885-2475, *Fax:* 202-885-2477, *E-mail:* gyoung@american.edu. *Web site:* http://www.american.edu/academic.depts/cas/sociology/socio.html

■ AMERICAN UNIVERSITY

School of Public Affairs, Department of Justice, Law and Society and Department of Sociology, Program in Sociology/Justice, Washington, DC 20016-8001

AWARDS PhD. Part-time and evening/weekend programs available.

Students: Average age 32.
Degree requirements: For doctorate, one foreign language, thesis/dissertation, comprehensive exam.
Entrance requirements: For doctorate, GRE General Test. *Application deadline:* For fall admission, 2/1; for spring admission, 10/1. *Application fee:* $50.
Expenses: Tuition: Full-time $14,274; part-time $793 per credit. Required fees: $290. Tuition and fees vary according to program.

Financial support: In 2001–02, 4 students received support, including 1 fellowship, 1 research assistantship, 1 teaching assistantship; career-related internships or fieldwork, Federal Work-Study, institutionally sponsored loans, and tuition waivers (full and partial) also available. Financial award application deadline: 2/1.
Faculty research: Inequality, death penalty, drug policy.
Prof. Gloria A. Young, Director of Graduate Studies, Sociology, 202-885-2475, *Fax:* 202-885-2477, *E-mail:* gyoung@american.edu.

■ ARIZONA STATE UNIVERSITY

Graduate College, College of Liberal Arts and Sciences, Department of Sociology, Tempe, AZ 85287

AWARDS Demography and population studies (MA, PhD); sociology (MA, PhD).

Degree requirements: For master's, thesis or alternative; for doctorate, thesis/dissertation.
Entrance requirements: For master's and doctorate, GRE General Test.
Faculty research: Political sociology, marriage and family, demography and human ecology.

■ ARKANSAS STATE UNIVERSITY

Graduate School, College of Arts and Sciences, Department of Criminology, Sociology, Social Work and Geography, Jonesboro, State University, AR 72467

AWARDS Sociology (MA, SCCT). Part-time programs available.

Faculty: 8 full-time (3 women).
Students: 5 full-time (all women), 10 part-time (7 women); includes 3 minority (all African Americans). Average age 31. In 2001, 8 degrees awarded.
Degree requirements: For master's, one foreign language, thesis or alternative, comprehensive exam.
Entrance requirements: For master's, GRE General Test or MAT, appropriate bachelor's degree; for SCCT, GRE General Test or MAT, interview, master's degree. *Application deadline:* For fall admission, 7/1 (priority date); for spring admission, 11/15 (priority date). Applications are processed on a rolling basis. *Application fee:* $15 ($25 for international students). Electronic applications accepted.
Expenses: Tuition, state resident: full-time $3,384; part-time $141 per hour. Tuition, nonresident: full-time $8,520; part-time $355 per hour. Required fees: $742; $28 per hour. $25 per semester. One-time fee: $15 full-time. Tuition and fees vary according to degree level.
Financial support: Teaching assistantships, career-related internships or fieldwork, Federal Work-Study, and scholarships/grants available. Support available to part-time students. Financial award application deadline: 7/1; financial award applicants required to submit FAFSA.
Dr. George Lord, Chair, 870-972-3705, *Fax:* 870-972-3694, *E-mail:* glord@astate.edu. *Web site:* http://www.cas.astate.edu/csswg/

■ AUBURN UNIVERSITY

Graduate School, Interdepartmental Programs, Program in Sociology, Auburn University, AL 36849

AWARDS MA, MS. Part-time programs available.

Students: 11 full-time (7 women), 10 part-time (8 women); includes 3 minority (2 African Americans, 1 Asian American or Pacific Islander). 12 applicants, 83% accepted. In 2001, 2 degrees awarded.
Degree requirements: For master's, computer language (MS), foreign language (MA), thesis (MA, MS).
Entrance requirements: For master's, GRE General Test. *Application deadline:* For fall admission, 7/7; for spring admission, 11/24. Applications are processed on a rolling basis. *Application fee:* $25 ($50 for international students).
Financial support: Research assistantships, teaching assistantships available. Financial award application deadline: 3/15.
Dr. Artur Wilke, Head, 334-844-5623.

■ BALL STATE UNIVERSITY

Graduate School, College of Sciences and Humanities, Department of Sociology, Muncie, IN 47306-1099

AWARDS MA.

Faculty: 8.
Students: 12 full-time (7 women), 4 part-time (3 women); includes 1 minority (Hispanic American), 1 international. Average age 29. 10 applicants, 80% accepted. In 2001, 3 degrees awarded.
Entrance requirements: For master's, GRE General Test. *Application fee:* $25 ($35 for international students).
Expenses: Tuition, state resident: full-time $4,068; part-time $2,542. Tuition, nonresident: full-time $10,944; part-time $6,462. Required fees: $1,000; $500 per term.
Financial support: In 2001–02, 10 research assistantships with full tuition reimbursements (averaging $6,202 per year) were awarded; teaching assistantships with full tuition reimbursements, career-related internships or fieldwork also available. Financial award application deadline: 3/1.
Faculty research: Retention policies for secondary education, community mental health.
Roger Wojtkiewicz, Chairman, 765-285-5978, *Fax:* 765-285-8980, *E-mail:* rwojtkiew@gw.bsu.edu.
Application contact: Dr. Ione DeOllos, Director of Graduate Programs, 765-285-5978, *Fax:* 765-285-8980. *Web site:* http://www.bsu.edu/csh/sociology/

■ BAYLOR UNIVERSITY

Graduate School, College of Arts and Sciences, Department of Sociology and Anthropology, Program in Applied Sociology, Waco, TX 76798

AWARDS PhD.

Students: 3 full-time (1 woman), 1 (woman) part-time. In 2001, 1 degree awarded.
Entrance requirements: For doctorate, GRE General Test. *Application deadline:* For fall admission, 8/1. Applications are processed on a rolling basis. *Application fee:* $25.
Expenses: Tuition: Part-time $379 per semester hour. Required fees: $42 per semester hour. $101 per semester. Tuition and fees vary according to program.
Application contact: Suzanne Keener, Administrative Assistant, 254-710-3588, *Fax:* 254-710-3870, *E-mail:* graduate_school@baylor.edu. *Web site:* http://www.baylor.edu/~Sociology/

■ BAYLOR UNIVERSITY

Graduate School, College of Arts and Sciences, Department of Sociology and Anthropology, Program in Sociology, Waco, TX 76798

AWARDS MA.

Students: 9 full-time (8 women); includes 3 minority (1 African American, 1 Asian American or Pacific Islander, 1 Hispanic American). In 2001, 5 degrees awarded.
Entrance requirements: For master's, GRE General Test. *Application deadline:* For fall admission, 8/1. Applications are processed on a rolling basis. *Application fee:* $25.
Expenses: Tuition: Part-time $379 per semester hour. Required fees: $42 per semester hour. $101 per semester. Tuition and fees vary according to program.
Application contact: Suzanne Keener, Administrative Assistant, 254-710-3588, *Fax:* 254-710-3870, *E-mail:* graduate_school@baylor.edu. *Web site:* http://www.baylor.edu/~sociology/

■ BETHEL COLLEGE

Center for Graduate and Continuing Studies, Department of Anthropology and Sociology, St. Paul, MN 55112-6999

AWARDS MA. Evening/weekend programs available.

Students: 13 full-time (11 women), 1 (woman) part-time.
Degree requirements: For master's, thesis.

Bethel College (continued)
Application deadline: Applications are processed on a rolling basis. *Application fee:* $25.
Expenses: Tuition: Part-time $325 per credit. One-time fee: $125 full-time.
Financial support: Institutionally sponsored loans and scholarships/grants available. Financial award applicants required to submit FAFSA.
Dr. Harley Schreck, Chair, 651-638-6104, *Fax:* 651-635-1464, *E-mail:* h-schreck@bethel.edu.
Application contact: Vanessa Beaudry, Graduate Admissions Advisor, 651-635-8012, *Fax:* 651-635-1464, *E-mail:* c-pritchard@bethel.edu.

■ BOSTON COLLEGE

Graduate School of Arts and Sciences, Department of Sociology, Chestnut Hill, MA 02467-3800

AWARDS MA, PhD, MBA/MA, MBA/PhD. Part-time programs available.

Students: 14 full-time (7 women), 41 part-time (28 women); includes 9 minority (6 African Americans, 1 Asian American or Pacific Islander, 2 Hispanic Americans), 8 international. 102 applicants, 39% accepted. In 2001, 8 master's, 8 doctorates awarded. Terminal master's awarded for partial completion of doctoral program.
Degree requirements: For master's, thesis optional; for doctorate, thesis/dissertation.
Application deadline: For fall admission, 2/1. *Application fee:* $50.
Expenses: Tuition: Full-time $17,664; part-time $8,832 per semester.
Financial support: Fellowships, research assistantships, teaching assistantships, Federal Work-Study available. Support available to part-time students. Financial award application deadline: 3/1; financial award applicants required to submit FAFSA.
Faculty research: Sociological theory, social economy, social psychology, political sociology, development modernization.
Dr. Stephen Pfohl, Chairperson, 617-552-4130, *E-mail:* stephen.pfohl@bc.edu.
Application contact: Dr. Eve Spangler, Graduate Program Director, 617-552-2131, *E-mail:* eve.spangler@bc.edu. *Web site:* http://infoeagle.bc.edu/bc_org/avp/cas/soc/socdept.html

■ BOSTON UNIVERSITY

Graduate School of Arts and Sciences, Department of Sociology, Boston, MA 02215

AWARDS MA, PhD.

Students: 23 full-time (16 women); includes 1 minority (Asian American or Pacific Islander), 11 international. Average age 30. 91 applicants, 21% accepted, 2 enrolled. In 2001, 2 master's, 3 doctorates ...ded. Terminal master's awarded for ...letion of doctoral program.
Degree requirements: For master's, one foreign language, thesis, comprehensive exam, registration; for doctorate, one foreign language, thesis/dissertation, critical essay, qualifying exam.
Entrance requirements: For master's, GRE General Test, TOEFL, sample of written work, 3 letters of recommendation; for doctorate, GRE General Test or MAT, TOEFL, sample of written work, 3 letters of recommendation. *Application deadline:* For fall admission, 1/15. *Application fee:* $60.
Expenses: Tuition: Full-time $25,872; part-time $340 per credit. Required fees: $40 per semester. Part-time tuition and fees vary according to class time, course level and program.
Financial support: In 2001–02, 8 students received support, including 1 fellowship (averaging $14,000 per year), 1 research assistantship, 4 teaching assistantships with full tuition reimbursements available (averaging $12,500 per year); career-related internships or fieldwork, Federal Work-Study, and scholarships/grants also available. Support available to part-time students. Financial award application deadline: 1/15; financial award applicants required to submit FAFSA.
John Stone, Chairman, 617-358-2591, *Fax:* 617-353-4837, *E-mail:* jstone2@bu.edu.
Application contact: William B. Morris, Senior Program Coordinator, 617-353-2591, *Fax:* 617-353-4837, *E-mail:* wmorris@bu.edu. *Web site:* http://www.bu.edu/sociology/

■ BOWLING GREEN STATE UNIVERSITY

Graduate College, College of Arts and Sciences, Department of Sociology, Bowling Green, OH 43403

AWARDS Criminology/deviant behavior (MA, PhD); demography and population studies (MA, PhD); family studies (MA, PhD); social psychology (MA, PhD). Part-time programs available.

Faculty: 17.
Students: 32 full-time (22 women), 12 part-time (8 women); includes 3 minority (2 African Americans, 1 Hispanic American), 6 international. Average age 28. 53 applicants, 53% accepted, 12 enrolled. In 2001, 7 master's, 4 doctorates awarded.
Degree requirements: For master's, thesis or alternative; for doctorate, thesis/dissertation, comprehensive exam.
Entrance requirements: For master's and doctorate, GRE General Test, TOEFL. *Application deadline:* For fall admission, 2/15. *Application fee:* $30. Electronic applications accepted.
Expenses: Tuition, state resident: full-time $7,376; part-time $342 per credit hour. Tuition, nonresident: full-time $13,628; part-time $640 per credit hour.
Financial support: In 2001–02, 26 research assistantships with full tuition reimbursements (averaging $9,134 per year), 6 teaching assistantships with full tuition reimbursements (averaging $11,000 per year) were awarded. Career-related internships or fieldwork, Federal Work-Study, institutionally sponsored loans, and unspecified assistantships also available. Financial award applicants required to submit FAFSA.
Faculty research: Applied demography, criminology and deviance, family studies, population studies, social psychology.
Dr. Gary Lee, Chair, 419-372-2294.
Application contact: Dr. Steve Cernkovich, Graduate Coordinator, 419-372-2743.

■ BRANDEIS UNIVERSITY

Graduate School of Arts and Sciences, Department of Sociology, Waltham, MA 02454-9110

AWARDS Near Eastern and Judaic studies and sociology (MA, PhD); social policy and sociology (PhD); sociology (MA, PhD); sociology and women's studies (MA). Part-time programs available.

Faculty: 11 full-time (5 women), 3 part-time/adjunct (2 women).
Students: 10 full-time (8 women), 25 part-time (18 women); includes 3 minority (1 African American, 1 Asian American or Pacific Islander, 1 Hispanic American). Average age 30. 80 applicants, 15% accepted. In 2001, 7 master's, 2 doctorates awarded. Terminal master's awarded for partial completion of doctoral program.
Degree requirements: For master's, thesis or alternative; for doctorate, thesis/dissertation.
Entrance requirements: For master's and doctorate, writing sample, resumé, letters of recommendation. *Application deadline:* For fall admission, 2/15. *Application fee:* $60. Electronic applications accepted.
Expenses: Tuition: Full-time $27,392. Required fees: $35.
Financial support: In 2001–02, 35 students received support, including 4 fellowships with tuition reimbursements available (averaging $13,000 per year); scholarships/grants and tuition waivers (full and partial) also available. Support available to part-time students. Financial award application deadline: 4/15; financial award applicants required to submit CSS PROFILE or FAFSA.
Faculty research: Social theory and cultural studies; feminist sociology; political sociology; sociology of medicine, health and health care; comparative social structures.
Dr. Karen V. Hansen, Chair, Graduate Committee, 781-736-2651, *E-mail:* khansen@brandeis.edu.
Application contact: Elaine Brooks, Graduate Secretary, 781-736-2631, *Fax:* 781-736-2653, *E-mail:* brooks@brandeis.edu. *Web site:* http://www.brandeis.edu/departments/sociology/

■ BRIDGEWATER STATE COLLEGE

School of Graduate and Continuing Education, School of Arts and Sciences, Department of Sociology, Bridgewater, MA 02325-0001

AWARDS MS.

Expenses: Tuition, state resident: part-time $135 per credit. Tuition, nonresident: part-time $294 per credit. Tuition and fees vary according to class time.
Application contact: James Plotner, Assistant Dean, Graduate Admissions, 508-531-1300, *Fax:* 508-531-6162, *E-mail:* jplotner@bridgew.edu.

■ BRIGHAM YOUNG UNIVERSITY

Graduate Studies, College of Family, Home, and Social Sciences, Department of Sociology, Provo, UT 84602-1001

AWARDS MS, PhD.

Faculty: 18 full-time (5 women).
Students: 16 full-time (9 women), 18 part-time (11 women); includes 1 minority (Asian American or Pacific Islander), 6 international. Average age 33. 13 applicants, 62% accepted, 8 enrolled. In 2001, 6 master's, 2 doctorates awarded. Terminal master's awarded for partial completion of doctoral program.
Degree requirements: For master's, thesis; for doctorate, thesis/dissertation, qualifying exam, comprehensive exam.
Entrance requirements: For master's and doctorate, GRE General Test, minimum GPA of 3.0 in last 60 hours, writing sample. *Application deadline:* For fall admission, 1/10. *Application fee:* $50. Electronic applications accepted.
Expenses: Tuition: Full-time $3,860; part-time $214 per hour.
Financial support: In 2001–02, 18 students received support, including 12 research assistantships with partial tuition reimbursements available (averaging $12,187 per year), 6 teaching assistantships with partial tuition reimbursements available (averaging $12,187 per year); institutionally sponsored loans also available. Financial award application deadline: 1/10.
Faculty research: Demography, race and ethnicity, gender, rural and community, international development, comparative family.
Dr. Vaughn R. A. Call, Chair, 801-422-4453, *Fax:* 801-378-4888, *E-mail:* vaughn_call@byu.edu.
Application contact: Dr. Ralph B. Brown, Graduate Coordinator, 801-422-3242, *Fax:* 801-378-4888, *E-mail:* ralph_brown@byu.edu. *Web site:* http://www.fhss.byu.edu/soc/grad/index.htm

■ BROOKLYN COLLEGE OF THE CITY UNIVERSITY OF NEW YORK

Division of Graduate Studies, Department of Sociology, Brooklyn, NY 11210-2889

AWARDS MA, PhD. Part-time and evening/weekend programs available.

Students: 1 (woman) full-time, 21 part-time (16 women); includes 13 minority (10 African Americans, 1 Asian American or Pacific Islander, 2 Hispanic Americans), 5 international. 24 applicants, 67% accepted. In 2001, 5 degrees awarded.
Degree requirements: For master's, comprehensive exam or research essay.
Entrance requirements: For master's, TOEFL, 12 upper-level credits in sociology. *Application deadline:* For fall admission, 3/1; for spring admission, 11/1. *Application fee:* $40.
Expenses: Tuition, state resident: full-time $4,350; part-time $185 per credit. Tuition, nonresident: full-time $7,600; part-time $320 per credit.
Financial support: Career-related internships or fieldwork, Federal Work-Study, institutionally sponsored loans, and scholarships/grants available. Support available to part-time students. Financial award application deadline: 5/1; financial award applicants required to submit FAFSA.
Faculty research: Urbanization, religion, family, gender, research methods.
Dr. Jerome Krase, Chairperson, 718-951-5314.
Application contact: Dr. Egon Mayer, Graduate Deputy, 718-951-5314.

■ BROWN UNIVERSITY

Graduate School, Department of Sociology, Program in Sociology, Providence, RI 02912

AWARDS AM, PhD.

Degree requirements: For master's, thesis; for doctorate, thesis/dissertation, oral exam.
Entrance requirements: For master's and doctorate, GRE General Test.

■ CALIFORNIA STATE UNIVERSITY, BAKERSFIELD

Division of Graduate Studies and Research, School of Humanities and Social Sciences, Program in Sociology, Bakersfield, CA 93311-1099

AWARDS MA. *Web site:* http://www.csub.edu/SocAnth/MastersSoc.html/

■ CALIFORNIA STATE UNIVERSITY, DOMINGUEZ HILLS

College of Arts and Sciences, Program in Sociology, Carson, CA 90747-0001

AWARDS Social research (Certificate); sociology (MA). Part-time and evening/weekend programs available.

Faculty: 15 full-time.
Students: 17 full-time (13 women), 48 part-time (37 women); includes 47 minority (31 African Americans, 3 Asian Americans or Pacific Islanders, 12 Hispanic Americans, 1 Native American). Average age 37. 35 applicants, 86% accepted, 15 enrolled. In 2001, 17 degrees awarded.
Degree requirements: For master's, thesis or alternative.
Entrance requirements: For master's and Certificate, minimum GPA of 2.85. *Application deadline:* For fall admission, 6/1. *Application fee:* $55.
Expenses: Tuition, nonresident: full-time $1,508; part-time $438 per semester. Required fees: $442; $246 per unit. $227 per semester.
Dr. Robert Christie, Chair, 310-243-3431, *E-mail:* bchistie@csudh.edu.

■ CALIFORNIA STATE UNIVERSITY, FULLERTON

Graduate Studies, College of Humanities and Social Sciences, Department of Sociology, Fullerton, CA 92834-9480

AWARDS MA. Part-time programs available.

Faculty: 19 full-time (5 women), 17 part-time/adjunct.
Students: 26 full-time (18 women), 38 part-time (30 women); includes 27 minority (3 African Americans, 7 Asian Americans or Pacific Islanders, 17 Hispanic Americans), 3 international. Average age 32. 53 applicants, 75% accepted, 26 enrolled. In 2001, 26 degrees awarded.
Degree requirements: For master's, thesis.
Entrance requirements: For master's, minimum GPA of 3.0 in sociology, 2.5 in last 60 units. *Application fee:* $55.
Expenses: Tuition, nonresident: part-time $246 per unit. Required fees: $964.
Financial support: Career-related internships or fieldwork, Federal Work-Study, institutionally sponsored loans, and scholarships/grants available. Support available to part-time students. Financial award application deadline: 3/1.
Faculty research: Gerontology, wellness clinic.
Dr. Ronald Hughes, Chair, 714-278-3531.
Application contact: Dr. Rae Newton, Adviser, 714-278-3135.

■ CALIFORNIA STATE UNIVERSITY, HAYWARD

Academic Programs and Graduate Studies, School of Arts, Letters, and Social Sciences, Department of Sociology and Social Services, Hayward, CA 94542-3000

AWARDS Sociology (MA). Part-time and evening/weekend programs available.

Students: 1 (woman) full-time, 14 part-time (9 women); includes 6 minority (2 African Americans, 2 Asian Americans or Pacific Islanders, 1 Hispanic American, 1 Native American). 24 applicants, 38% accepted. In 2001, 3 degrees awarded.
Degree requirements: For master's, project or thesis.
Entrance requirements: For master's, minimum GPA of 3.0. *Application deadline:* For fall admission, 6/15; for winter admission, 10/27; for spring admission, 1/5. Applications are processed on a rolling basis. *Application fee:* $55. Electronic applications accepted.
Expenses: Tuition, nonresident: part-time $164 per unit. Required fees: $405 per semester.
Financial support: Fellowships, teaching assistantships, career-related internships or fieldwork, Federal Work-Study, institutionally sponsored loans, and scholarships/grants available. Support available to part-time students. Financial award application deadline: 3/1.
Dr. Diane Beeson, Head, 510-885-3173.
Application contact: Jennifer Cason, Graduate Program Coordinator/ Operations Analyst, 510-885-3286, *Fax:* 510-885-4777, *E-mail:* jcason@csuhayward.edu.

■ CALIFORNIA STATE UNIVERSITY, LOS ANGELES

Graduate Studies, College of Natural and Social Sciences, Department of Sociology, Los Angeles, CA 90032-8530

AWARDS MA. Part-time and evening/weekend programs available.

Faculty: 15 full-time, 16 part-time/ adjunct.
Students: 8 full-time (5 women), 36 part-time (22 women); includes 32 minority (8 African Americans, 3 Asian Americans or Pacific Islanders, 21 Hispanic Americans), 2 international. In 2001, 6 degrees awarded.
Degree requirements: For master's, comprehensive exam or thesis.
Entrance requirements: For master's, TOEFL, minimum GPA of 2.5 in last 90 units. *Application deadline:* For fall admission, 6/30; for spring admission, 2/1. Applications are processed on a rolling basis. *Application fee:* $55.
Expenses: Tuition, nonresident: part-time $164 per unit.
Financial support: Federal Work-Study available. Support available to part-time students. Financial award application deadline: 3/1.
Faculty research: Criminal and delinquent careers, family and sex, ethnic minorities, demographic trends, human socialization and aging.
Dr. Delos K. Kelly, Chair, 323-343-2200.

■ CALIFORNIA STATE UNIVERSITY, NORTHRIDGE

Graduate Studies, College of Social and Behavioral Sciences, Department of Sociology, Northridge, CA 91330

AWARDS MA. Part-time and evening/weekend programs available.

Faculty: 23 full-time, 21 part-time/ adjunct.
Students: 8 full-time (6 women), 11 part-time (5 women); includes 5 minority (3 African Americans, 2 Hispanic Americans). Average age 33. 21 applicants, 62% accepted, 6 enrolled. In 2001, 6 degrees awarded.
Degree requirements: For master's, thesis or alternative.
Entrance requirements: For master's, TOEFL, GRE General Test or minimum GPA of 3.0. *Application deadline:* For fall admission, 11/30. *Application fee:* $55.
Expenses: Tuition, nonresident: part-time $631 per semester. Required fees: $246 per unit.
Financial support: Career-related internships or fieldwork, Federal Work-Study, and institutionally sponsored loans available. Support available to part-time students. Financial award application deadline: 3/1.
Faculty research: Crime and corrections, relationships between adult children and parents.
Dr. Jane Prather, Chair, 818-677-3591.
Application contact: Dr. E. Bogdanoff, Graduate Coordinator, 818-677-3594.

■ CALIFORNIA STATE UNIVERSITY, SACRAMENTO

Graduate Studies, College of Social Sciences and Interdisciplinary Studies, Department of Sociology, Sacramento, CA 95819-6048

AWARDS MA. Part-time programs available.

Students: 13 full-time (10 women), 24 part-time (18 women); includes 10 minority (4 African Americans, 3 Asian Americans or Pacific Islanders, 3 Hispanic Americans), 3 international.
Degree requirements: For master's, thesis or alternative, writing proficiency exam.
Entrance requirements: For master's, TOEFL, minimum GPA of 3.0 during previous 2 years. *Application deadline:* For fall admission, 4/15; for spring admission, 11/1. *Application fee:* $55.
Expenses: Tuition, state resident: full-time $1,965; part-time $668 per semester. Tuition, nonresident: part-time $246 per unit.
Financial support: Career-related internships or fieldwork and Federal Work-Study available. Support available to part-time students. Financial award application deadline: 3/1.
Dr. Judson Landis, Chair, 916-278-6522.
Application contact: Dr. Randy MacIntosh, Coordinator, 916-278-7961.

■ CALIFORNIA STATE UNIVERSITY, SAN MARCOS

College of Arts and Sciences, Program in Sociological Practice, San Marcos, CA 92096-0001

AWARDS MA.

Faculty: 12 full-time (6 women).
Students: 6 full-time (5 women), 20 part-time (16 women); includes 9 minority (1 African American, 2 Asian Americans or Pacific Islanders, 5 Hispanic Americans, 1 Native American). Average age 38. 12 applicants, 42% accepted. In 2001, 3 degrees awarded.
Degree requirements: For master's, thesis.
Entrance requirements: For master's, GRE General Test. *Application deadline:* For fall admission, 3/1 (priority date). Applications are processed on a rolling basis. *Application fee:* $55.
Expenses: Tuition, state resident: part-time $567 per semester. Tuition, nonresident: part-time $813 per semester.
Financial support: Research assistantships, teaching assistantships, career-related internships or fieldwork, Federal Work-Study, institutionally sponsored loans, scholarships/grants, traineeships, and unspecified assistantships available. Support available to part-time students.
Faculty research: Organized crime, juvenile detention, counseling services for minorities, mental-health facilities.
Richard T. Serpe, Department Chair, 760-750-4159, *Fax:* 760-750-3551, *E-mail:* rserpe@csusm.edu.
Application contact: Toni Shaffer, Administrative Coordinator, 760-750-4117, *E-mail:* tshaffer@csusm.edu.

■ CASE WESTERN RESERVE UNIVERSITY

School of Graduate Studies, Department of Sociology, Cleveland, OH 44106

AWARDS PhD. Terminal master's awarded for partial completion of doctoral program.

Degree requirements: For doctorate, thesis/dissertation.
Faculty research: Gerontology, medical sociology, sociology of aging and the life course, family sociology. *Web site:* http://socwww.cwru.edu/

■ THE CATHOLIC UNIVERSITY OF AMERICA

School of Arts and Sciences, Department of Sociology, Washington, DC 20064

AWARDS MA, PhD. Part-time and evening/weekend programs available.

Faculty: 5 full-time (1 woman).
Students: 8 full-time (4 women), 6 part-time (3 women); includes 2 minority (1 African American, 1 Asian American or Pacific Islander), 6 international. Average age 32. 12 applicants, 67% accepted, 4 enrolled. In 2001, 2 degrees awarded.
Degree requirements: For master's, comprehensive exam; for doctorate, one foreign language, thesis/dissertation, comprehensive exam.
Entrance requirements: For master's, GRE General Test, TOEFL; for doctorate, GRE General Test. *Application deadline:* For fall admission, 8/3. Applications are processed on a rolling basis. *Application fee:* $55. Electronic applications accepted.
Expenses: Tuition: Full-time $20,050; part-time $770 per credit. Required fees: $430 per term. Tuition and fees vary according to program.
Financial support: In 2001–02, 5 students received support, including 2 research assistantships, 2 teaching assistantships; career-related internships or fieldwork, Federal Work-Study, institutionally sponsored loans, and tuition waivers (full and partial) also available. Support available to part-time students. Financial award application deadline: 2/1.
Faculty research: Social movements, education, gender, religion, demography.
Dr. Che-Fu Lee, Chair, 202-319-5445, *Fax:* 202-319-4980, *E-mail:* lee@cua.edu.

■ CENTRAL MICHIGAN UNIVERSITY

College of Graduate Studies, College of Humanities and Social and Behavioral Sciences, Department of Sociology, Anthropology and Social Work, Mount Pleasant, MI 48859

AWARDS Social and criminal justice (MA); sociology (MA).

Degree requirements: For master's, thesis or alternative.
Entrance requirements: For master's, 20 hours in sociology, minimum GPA of 3.0.
Expenses: Tuition, state resident: part-time $182 per unit. Tuition, nonresident: part-time $182 per unit. Required fees: $208 per semester. Part-time tuition and fees vary according to course load.
Faculty research: Sociological theory, race concept, environmental justice, cultural anthropology.

■ CENTRAL MISSOURI STATE UNIVERSITY

School of Graduate Studies, College of Education and Human Services, Department of Sociology, Warrensburg, MO 64093

AWARDS Social gerontology (MS); sociology (MA). Part-time programs available.

Faculty: 11 full-time (6 women).
Students: 10 full-time (7 women), 35 part-time (30 women); includes 6 minority (all African Americans), 2 international. Average age 34. 22 applicants, 95% accepted. In 2001, 16 degrees awarded.
Degree requirements: For master's, comprehensive exam.
Entrance requirements: For master's, minimum GPA of 2.5. *Application deadline:* Applications are processed on a rolling basis. *Application fee:* $25 ($50 for international students).
Expenses: Tuition, area resident: Full-time $4,200; part-time $175 per credit hour. Tuition, nonresident: full-time $8,352; part-time $348 per credit hour.
Financial support: In 2001–02, 6 research assistantships with full and partial tuition reimbursements (averaging $6,063 per year), 1 teaching assistantship with partial tuition reimbursement (averaging $2,650 per year) were awarded. Federal Work-Study, scholarships/grants, unspecified assistantships, and administrative assistantship also available. Support available to part-time students. Financial award application deadline: 3/1; financial award applicants required to submit FAFSA.
Faculty research: Political economy of health and aging, sociology of suicide, sociology of religion, sociology of natural resources and the environment, Lithuanian American ethnic identity.
Dr. J. Mark Wehrle, Chair, 660-543-4407, *Fax:* 660-543-8215, *E-mail:* wehrle@cmsu1.cmsu.edu. *Web site:* http://wwwcmsu.edu/

■ CITY COLLEGE OF THE CITY UNIVERSITY OF NEW YORK

Graduate School, College of Liberal Arts and Science, Division of Social Science, Department of Sociology, New York, NY 10031-9198

AWARDS MA.

Students: 35. In 2001, 5 degrees awarded.
Degree requirements: For master's, one foreign language, thesis, comprehensive exam.
Entrance requirements: For master's, TOEFL, minimum B average in undergraduate course work. *Application deadline:* For fall admission, 5/1; for spring admission, 12/1. *Application fee:* $40.
Expenses: Tuition, state resident: part-time $185 per credit. Tuition, nonresident: part-time $320 per credit. Required fees: $43 per term.
Financial support: Fellowships available.
Faculty research: Urban sociology, criminology and deviance, race and ethnicity.
Steven Goldberg, Chairman, 212-650-5485.
Application contact: Wayne Cotton, Adviser, 212-650-5854.

■ CLARK ATLANTA UNIVERSITY

School of Arts and Sciences, Department of Sociology, Atlanta, GA 30314

AWARDS MA. Part-time programs available.

Degree requirements: For master's, one foreign language, thesis.
Entrance requirements: For master's, GRE General Test, minimum GPA of 2.5.
Faculty research: Gerontology, geriatric education.

■ CLEMSON UNIVERSITY

Graduate School, College of Business and Behavioral Science, Department of Sociology, Clemson, SC 29634

AWARDS Applied sociology (MS). Part-time programs available.

Students: 11 full-time (9 women), 3 part-time (all women); includes 2 minority (1 African American, 1 Hispanic American), 2 international. 10 applicants, 90% accepted, 4 enrolled. In 2001, 1 degree awarded.
Degree requirements: For master's, thesis.
Entrance requirements: For master's, GRE General Test, TOEFL, minimum GPA of 3.0. *Application deadline:* For fall admission, 3/15 (priority date). *Application fee:* $40.
Expenses: Tuition, state resident: full-time $5,310. Tuition, nonresident: full-time $11,284.
Financial support: Fellowships, teaching assistantships, career-related internships or fieldwork, Federal Work-Study, and institutionally sponsored loans available. Financial award application deadline: 3/15; financial award applicants required to submit FAFSA.
Faculty research: Organizational and industrial sociology, inequality, sexual abuse and police-community relations, homelessness, emotions.
Dr. Martin Slann, Chair, 864-656-3234, *Fax:* 864-656-0690, *E-mail:* kibbutz@clemson.edu.
Application contact: Dr. James Hawdon, Graduate Coordinator, 864-656-3238, *Fax:* 864-656-1252, *E-mail:* hawdonj@clemson.edu. *Web site:* http://business.clemson.edu/socio/ms-soc.htm

■ CLEVELAND STATE UNIVERSITY

College of Graduate Studies, College of Arts and Sciences, Department of Sociology, Cleveland, OH 44115

AWARDS MA. Part-time and evening/weekend programs available.

Cleveland State University (continued)
Faculty: 9 full-time (3 women).
Students: 53 full-time (47 women), 44 part-time (33 women); includes 28 minority (25 African Americans, 1 Asian American or Pacific Islander, 1 Hispanic American, 1 Native American). Average age 31. 30 applicants, 53% accepted, 12 enrolled. In 2001, 4 degrees awarded. *Median time to degree:* Master's–1.5 years full-time, 3 years part-time.
Entrance requirements: For master's, minimum GPA of 3.0, undergraduate statistics. *Application deadline:* For fall admission, 7/15; for spring admission, 12/1. Applications are processed on a rolling basis. *Application fee:* $25. Electronic applications accepted.
Expenses: Tuition, state resident: full-time $6,838; part-time $263 per credit hour. Tuition, nonresident: full-time $13,526; part-time $520 per credit hour.
Financial support: In 2001–02, 5 students received support, including 5 research assistantships with full tuition reimbursements available (averaging $9,000 per year); tuition waivers (partial) also available. Financial award application deadline: 7/15.
Faculty research: Criminology, research methods, theory, aging, methods.
Dr. Peter Meiksins, Chair, 216-687-4518, *Fax:* 216-687-9314, *E-mail:* p.meiksins@popmail.csuohio.edu.
Application contact: Dr. Sarah H. Matthews, Director, 216-687-4500, *Fax:* 216-687-9314, *E-mail:* s.matthews@csuohio.edu.

■ COLORADO STATE UNIVERSITY

Graduate School, College of Liberal Arts, Department of Sociology, Fort Collins, CO 80523-0015

AWARDS MA, PhD.

Faculty: 14 full-time (3 women), 9 part-time/adjunct (6 women).
Students: 15 full-time (10 women), 20 part-time (14 women); includes 4 minority (1 African American, 2 Asian Americans or Pacific Islanders, 1 Hispanic American), 4 international. Average age 35. 21 applicants, 57% accepted, 6 enrolled. In 2001, 1 degree awarded.
Degree requirements: For master's and doctorate, thesis/dissertation.
Entrance requirements: For master's and doctorate, GRE General Test, TOEFL, minimum GPA of 3.0. *Application deadline:* For fall admission, 2/1 (priority date). Applications are processed on a rolling basis. *Application fee:* $30. Electronic applications accepted.
Expenses: Tuition, state resident: full-time $2,880; part-time $160 per credit. Tuition, nonresident: full-time $11,412; part-time $634 per credit. Required fees: $750; $34 per credit.
Financial support: In 2001–02, 1 research assistantship with full tuition reimbursement (averaging $13,023 per year), 16 teaching assistantships with full tuition reimbursements (averaging $10,998 per year) were awarded. Fellowships, career-related internships or fieldwork, Federal Work-Study, institutionally sponsored loans, and traineeships also available. Financial award application deadline: 2/1.
Faculty research: Social policy analysis, environmental impact, criminology, community development, rural development and natural resources. *Total annual research expenditures:* $628,195.
Dr. Louis Swanson, Chairman, 970-491-6044, *Fax:* 970-491-2191.
Application contact: Helain Steele, Administrative Assistant, 970-491-6045, *E-mail:* hsteele@lamar.colostate.edu.

■ COLUMBIA UNIVERSITY

Graduate School of Arts and Sciences, Division of Social Sciences, Department of Sociology, New York, NY 10027

AWARDS M Phil, MA, PhD, JD/MA, JD/PhD.

Faculty: 24 full-time, 2 part-time/adjunct.
Students: 89 full-time (48 women), 17 part-time (10 women). Average age 33. 238 applicants, 24% accepted. In 2001, 13 master's, 4 doctorates awarded.
Degree requirements: For master's, 2 research papers; for doctorate, one foreign language, thesis/dissertation.
Entrance requirements: For master's and doctorate, GRE General Test, TOEFL. *Application deadline:* For fall admission, 1/3; for spring admission, 11/30. *Application fee:* $65.
Expenses: Tuition: Full-time $27,528. Required fees: $1,638.
Financial support: Fellowships, teaching assistantships, Federal Work-Study and institutionally sponsored loans available. Support available to part-time students. Financial award application deadline: 1/5; financial award applicants required to submit FAFSA.
Faculty research: Urban and political studies, sociology of knowledge, organizations.
Peter Bearman, Chair, 212-854-3094, *Fax:* 212-854-8925.

■ CONVERSE COLLEGE

Department of Education, Program in Liberal Arts, Spartanburg, SC 29302-0006

AWARDS Economics (MLA); English (MLA); history (MLA); political science (MLA); sociology (MLA).

Degree requirements: For master's, capstone paper.
Entrance requirements: For master's, NTE, minimum GPA of 2.75.
Expenses: Tuition: Part-time $225 per credit hour. One-time fee: $20 part-time.

■ CORNELL UNIVERSITY

Graduate School, Graduate Fields of Agriculture and Life Sciences, Field of Development Sociology, Ithaca, NY 14853-0001

AWARDS Community and regional sociology (MPS, PhD); environmental management (MPS); population and development (MPS, PhD); rural and environmental sociology (MPS, PhD); state, economy, and society (MPS, PhD).

Faculty: 18 full-time.
Students: 41 full-time (24 women); includes 5 minority (all Hispanic Americans), 16 international. 56 applicants, 27% accepted. In 2001, 4 master's, 9 doctorates awarded.
Degree requirements: For doctorate, thesis/dissertation.
Entrance requirements: For master's and doctorate, GRE General Test, TOEFL, 3 letters of recommendation. *Application deadline:* For fall admission, 1/15. *Application fee:* $65. Electronic applications accepted.
Expenses: Tuition: Full-time $25,970. Required fees: $50.
Financial support: In 2001–02, 35 students received support, including 7 fellowships with full tuition reimbursements available, 13 research assistantships with full tuition reimbursements available, 15 teaching assistantships with full tuition reimbursements available; institutionally sponsored loans, scholarships/grants, tuition waivers (full and partial), and unspecified assistantships also available. Financial award applicants required to submit FAFSA.
Faculty research: Demography (population and development), environmental sociology, international and rural community development, political economy and ecology, sustainable agriculture.
Application contact: Graduate Field Assistant, 607-255-3092, *E-mail:* devsoc@cornell.edu. *Web site:* http://www.gradschool.cornell.edu/grad/fields_1/dev-soc.html

■ CORNELL UNIVERSITY

Graduate School, Graduate Fields of Arts and Sciences, Field of Sociology, Ithaca, NY 14853-0001

AWARDS Economy and society (MA, PhD); gender and life course (MA, PhD); organizations (MA, PhD); political sociology/social movements (MA, PhD); racial and ethnic relations (MA, PhD); social networks (MA, PhD); social psychology (MA, PhD); social stratification (MA, PhD).

Faculty: 19 full-time.
Students: 33 full-time (17 women); includes 3 minority (1 African American, 1 Asian American or Pacific Islander, 1 Hispanic American), 17 international. 126 applicants, 13% accepted. In 2001, 2 master's, 3 doctorates awarded. Terminal

master's awarded for partial completion of doctoral program.
Degree requirements: For master's, thesis; for doctorate, thesis/dissertation, 1 year of teaching experience.
Entrance requirements: For master's and doctorate, GRE General Test, TOEFL. *Application deadline:* For fall admission, 1/15. *Application fee:* $65. Electronic applications accepted.
Expenses: Tuition: Full-time $25,970. Required fees: $50.
Financial support: In 2001–02, 32 students received support, including 13 fellowships with full tuition reimbursements available, 10 research assistantships with full tuition reimbursements available, 9 teaching assistantships with full tuition reimbursements available; institutionally sponsored loans, scholarships/grants, tuition waivers (full and partial), and unspecified assistantships also available. Financial award applicants required to submit FAFSA.
Faculty research: Comparative societal analysis, work and family, simulations, social class and mobility, racial segregation and inequality.
Application contact: Graduate Field Assistant, 607-255-4266, *Fax:* 607-255-8473, *E-mail:* sociology@cornell.edu. *Web site:* http://www.gradschool.cornell.edu/grad/fields_1/socio.html

■ DEPAUL UNIVERSITY

College of Liberal Arts and Sciences, Department of Sociology, Chicago, IL 60604-2287

AWARDS MA. Part-time and evening/weekend programs available.

Faculty: 17 full-time (7 women), 1 part-time/adjunct (0 women).
Students: 31 full-time (22 women), 33 part-time (25 women); includes 21 minority (15 African Americans, 6 Hispanic Americans), 1 international. Average age 28. 28 applicants, 82% accepted. In 2001, 17 degrees awarded.
Degree requirements: For master's, thesis or alternative, essay, research project. *Median time to degree:* Master's–2 years full-time, 4 years part-time.
Application deadline: Applications are processed on a rolling basis. *Application fee:* $25.
Expenses: Tuition: Part-time $362 per credit hour. Tuition and fees vary according to program.
Financial support: In 2001–02, 14 students received support, including 1 research assistantship with full tuition reimbursement available (averaging $5,000 per year); career-related internships or fieldwork, tuition waivers (full and partial), and tuition remissions also available. Financial award application deadline: 6/15.
Faculty research: Law and criminal justice, urban sociology, race and ethnicity, gender, cultural studies.
Dr. Richard T. Schaefer, Chairperson, 773-325-7823, *Fax:* 773-325-7821, *E-mail:* rschaefe@depaul.edu.
Application contact: Dr. Kenneth Fidel, Graduate Program Director, 773-325-4436, *Fax:* 773-325-7821, *E-mail:* kfidel@depaul.edu. *Web site:* http://www.depaul.edu/~soc/

■ DUKE UNIVERSITY

Graduate School, Department of Sociology, Durham, NC 27708-0586

AWARDS AM, PhD.

Faculty: 21 full-time, 5 part-time/adjunct.
Students: 48 full-time (30 women); includes 2 minority (both African Americans), 15 international. 89 applicants, 21% accepted, 8 enrolled. In 2001, 1 master's, 4 doctorates awarded. Terminal master's awarded for partial completion of doctoral program.
Degree requirements: For doctorate, thesis/dissertation.
Entrance requirements: For master's and doctorate, GRE General Test. *Application deadline:* For fall admission, 12/31. *Application fee:* $75.
Expenses: Tuition: Full-time $24,600.
Financial support: Fellowships, research assistantships, teaching assistantships, Federal Work-Study available. Financial award application deadline: 12/31.
Nan Lin, Director of Graduate Studies, 919-660-5617, *Fax:* 919-660-5623, *E-mail:* cpark@soc.duke.edu. *Web site:* http://www.soc.duke.edu/

■ EAST CAROLINA UNIVERSITY

Graduate School, College of Arts and Sciences, Department of Sociology, Greenville, NC 27858-4353

AWARDS MA. Part-time and evening/weekend programs available.

Faculty: 10 full-time (1 woman).
Students: 16 full-time (6 women), 12 part-time (8 women); includes 5 minority (all African Americans), 3 international. Average age 34. 7 applicants, 100% accepted. In 2001, 10 degrees awarded.
Degree requirements: For master's, one foreign language, thesis, comprehensive exam.
Entrance requirements: For master's, GRE General Test, TOEFL. *Application deadline:* For fall admission, 6/1 (priority date); for spring admission, 10/15. Applications are processed on a rolling basis. *Application fee:* $45.
Expenses: Tuition, state resident: full-time $2,636. Tuition, nonresident: full-time $11,365.
Financial support: Fellowships with partial tuition reimbursements, research assistantships with partial tuition reimbursements, teaching assistantships with partial tuition reimbursements, Federal Work-Study available. Support available to part-time students. Financial award application deadline: 6/1.
Dr. Richard Caston, Chairperson, 252-328-6768, *Fax:* 252-328-4837, *E-mail:* castonr@mail.ecu.edu.
Application contact: Dr. Robert Edwards, Director of Graduate Studies, 252-328-4863, *Fax:* 252-328-4837, *E-mail:* edwardsr@mail.ecu.edu.

■ EASTERN MICHIGAN UNIVERSITY

Graduate School, College of Arts and Sciences, Department of Sociology, Anthropology and Criminology, Program in Sociology, Ypsilanti, MI 48197

AWARDS MA. Evening/weekend programs available.

Degree requirements: For master's, thesis optional.
Entrance requirements: For master's, GRE General Test, TOEFL. *Application deadline:* For fall admission, 5/15; for spring admission, 3/15. Applications are processed on a rolling basis. *Application fee:* $30.
Expenses: Tuition, state resident: part-time $285 per credit hour. Tuition, nonresident: part-time $510 per credit hour.
Financial support: Fellowships, teaching assistantships available. Support available to part-time students. Financial award application deadline: 3/15; financial award applicants required to submit FAFSA.
Dr. Jay Weinstein, Coordinator, 734-487-0012.

■ EAST TENNESSEE STATE UNIVERSITY

School of Graduate Studies, College of Arts and Sciences, Department of Sociology and Anthropology, Johnson City, TN 37614

AWARDS Applied sociology (MA); general sociology (MA). Part-time and evening/weekend programs available.

Faculty: 10 full-time (4 women).
Students: 4 full-time (1 woman), 6 part-time (4 women). Average age 31. In 2001, 3 degrees awarded.
Degree requirements: For master's, thesis or alternative, internship, comprehensive exam.
Entrance requirements: For master's, GRE General Test, TOEFL, minimum GPA of 3.0 in major. *Application deadline:* For fall admission, 7/15 (priority date); for spring admission, 11/1. Applications are processed on a rolling basis. *Application fee:* $25 ($35 for international students).
Expenses: Tuition, state resident: part-time $181 per hour. Tuition, nonresident: part-time $270 per hour. Required fees: $220 per term.
Financial support: Research assistantships with full tuition reimbursements, teaching assistantships with full tuition reimbursements, career-related internships or

East Tennessee State University (continued)
fieldwork, Federal Work-Study, institutionally sponsored loans, scholarships/grants, and tuition waivers (full) available. Financial award application deadline: 3/15.
Faculty research: Medical belief systems, sociology of emotions, classical and contemporary social theory, folklore, Latin American ethnic identity. *Total annual research expenditures:* $635,933.
Dr. Scott H. Beck, Chair, 423-439-6648, *Fax:* 423-439-5313, *E-mail:* r30scott@etsu.edu.
Application contact: Dr. Martha Copp, Graduate Coordinator, 423-439-7056, *Fax:* 423-439-5313, *E-mail:* coppm@etsu.edu.
Web site: http://www.etsu.edu/

■ EMORY UNIVERSITY

Graduate School of Arts and Sciences, Department of Sociology, Atlanta, GA 30322-1100

AWARDS PhD.

Faculty: 15 full-time (7 women), 7 part-time/adjunct (3 women).
Students: 39 full-time (27 women); includes 10 minority (5 African Americans, 1 Asian American or Pacific Islander, 4 Hispanic Americans), 7 international. 89 applicants, 9% accepted, 8 enrolled. In 2001, 5 doctorates awarded.
Degree requirements: For doctorate, thesis/dissertation, 2 preliminary exams, paper presentation, research paper.
Entrance requirements: For doctorate, GRE General Test, TOEFL, minimum GPA of 3.0. *Application deadline:* For fall admission, 1/20 (priority date). *Application fee:* $50. Electronic applications accepted.
Expenses: Tuition: Full-time $24,770. Required fees: $100. Tuition and fees vary according to program and student level.
Financial support: In 2001–02, 24 fellowships were awarded; research assistantships, teaching assistantships, scholarships/grants and tuition waivers (full and partial) also available. Financial award application deadline: 1/20.
Faculty research: Political economy, culture, social psychology, criminology, gender.
Dr. Terry Boswell, Chair, 404-727-7510.
Application contact: Dr. Richard Rubinson, Director of Graduate Studies, 404-727-7530, *E-mail:* rrubin@emory.edu.
Web site: http://www.emory.edu/SOC/GRAD.html

Find an in-depth description at www.petersons.com/gradchannel.

■ FAYETTEVILLE STATE UNIVERSITY

Graduate School, Program in Sociology, Fayetteville, NC 28301-4298

AWARDS Sociology (MA). Part-time and evening/weekend programs available.

Faculty: 9.
Students: 2 full-time (both women), 4 part-time (2 women); includes 3 minority (all African Americans). Average age 35. 4 applicants, 100% accepted. In 2001, 3 degrees awarded.
Degree requirements: For master's, internship.
Application deadline: For fall admission, 8/1; for spring admission, 12/15. Applications are processed on a rolling basis. *Application fee:* $25.
Expenses: Tuition, state resident: full-time $810; part-time $426 per year. Tuition, nonresident: full-time $4,445; part-time $2,223 per year. Tuition and fees vary according to course load.
Dr. Kwaku Twumasi-Ankrah, Chairperson, 910-672-1122, *E-mail:* kankrah@uncfsu.edu.

■ FISK UNIVERSITY

Graduate Programs, Department of Sociology, Nashville, TN 37208-3051

AWARDS General sociology (MA). Part-time programs available.

Faculty: 3 full-time (1 woman).
Students: 7 full-time (4 women); all minorities (all African Americans). In 2001, 3 degrees awarded.
Degree requirements: For master's, thesis, comprehensive exam, registration.
Entrance requirements: For master's, GRE General Test, GRE Subject Test. *Application deadline:* For fall admission, 6/15 (priority date). Applications are processed on a rolling basis. *Application fee:* $25.
Expenses: Tuition: Full-time $9,790.
Faculty research: Criminal justice, mass media.
Dr. Dilip Kumar Bhowmik, Chair, 615-329-8611, *E-mail:* bhowmik@fisk.edu.
Application contact: William Carter, Director of Admissions, 615-329-8819, *Fax:* 615-329-8774, *E-mail:* bcarter@fisk.edu.

■ FLORIDA ATLANTIC UNIVERSITY

Dorothy F. Schmidt College of Arts and Letters, Department of Sociology, Boca Raton, FL 33431-0991

AWARDS MA, MAT.

Faculty: 12 full-time (7 women), 2 part-time/adjunct (1 woman).
Students: 5 full-time (4 women), 14 part-time (12 women); includes 6 minority (4 African Americans, 1 Asian American or Pacific Islander, 1 Hispanic American), 3 international. Average age 30. 19 applicants, 74% accepted, 10 enrolled. In 2001, 8 degrees awarded.
Degree requirements: For master's, thesis optional.
Entrance requirements: For master's, GRE General Test, minimum GPA of 3.0. *Application deadline:* For fall admission, 7/1; for spring admission, 10/20. Applications are processed on a rolling basis. *Application fee:* $20. Electronic applications accepted.
Expenses: Tuition, state resident: full-time $3,098; part-time $172 per credit. Tuition, nonresident: full-time $10,427; part-time $579 per credit.
Financial support: In 2001–02, 4 teaching assistantships with tuition reimbursements (averaging $7,374 per year) were awarded; Federal Work-Study also available.
Faculty research: Gender/race/class, globalization, theory, social control, social movements.
Dr. Anita Pritchard, Chair, 561-297-3212, *Fax:* 561-297-2997, *E-mail:* pritchar@fau.edu. *Web site:* http://www.fau.edu/divdept/soc.htm

■ FLORIDA INTERNATIONAL UNIVERSITY

College of Arts and Sciences, Department of Sociology/Anthropology, Miami, FL 33199

AWARDS Comparative sociology (MA); sociology (PhD). Part-time and evening/weekend programs available.

Faculty: 20 full-time (10 women).
Students: 28 full-time (14 women), 29 part-time (22 women); includes 23 minority (8 African Americans, 15 Hispanic Americans), 7 international. Average age 36. 26 applicants, 35% accepted, 6 enrolled. In 2001, 3 master's, 9 doctorates awarded.
Degree requirements: For master's and doctorate, thesis/dissertation.
Entrance requirements: For master's and doctorate, GRE General Test, TOEFL. *Application deadline:* For fall admission, 2/15 (priority date); for spring admission, 10/1. Applications are processed on a rolling basis. *Application fee:* $20.
Expenses: Tuition, state resident: full-time $2,916; part-time $162 per credit hour. Tuition, nonresident: full-time $10,245; part-time $569 per credit hour. Required fees: $168 per term.
Financial support: Teaching assistantships available. Financial award application deadline: 4/1.
Dr. Walter Peacock, Chairperson, 305-348-2247, *Fax:* 305-348-3605, *E-mail:* peacock@fiu.edu.

■ FLORIDA STATE UNIVERSITY

Graduate Studies, College of Social Sciences, Department of Sociology, Tallahassee, FL 32306

AWARDS MA, MS, PhD.

Faculty: 21 full-time (8 women).
Students: 24 full-time (16 women), 15 part-time (9 women); includes 4 minority (3 African Americans, 1 Asian American or Pacific Islander). Average age 31. 33 applicants, 70% accepted, 6 enrolled. In 2001, 5 master's, 5 doctorates awarded. Terminal master's awarded for partial completion of doctoral program.

Degree requirements: For master's, paper; for doctorate, thesis/dissertation. *Median time to degree:* Master's–1.9 years full-time; doctorate–6.3 years full-time.
Entrance requirements: For master's and doctorate, GRE General Test, minimum GPA of 3.0. *Application deadline:* For fall admission, 2/1 (priority date); for spring admission, 10/1 (priority date). Applications are processed on a rolling basis. *Application fee:* $20. Electronic applications accepted.
Expenses: Tuition, state resident: part-time $163 per credit hour. Tuition, nonresident: part-time $570 per credit hour. Tuition and fees vary according to program.
Financial support: In 2001–02, 24 students received support, including 1 fellowship with full tuition reimbursement available (averaging $13,000 per year), 10 research assistantships with full tuition reimbursements available (averaging $12,000 per year), 14 teaching assistantships with full tuition reimbursements available (averaging $12,000 per year); institutionally sponsored loans, scholarships/grants, and unspecified assistantships also available. Financial award application deadline: 2/1; financial award applicants required to submit FAFSA.
Faculty research: Social inequality (gender/race), demography, political sociology, work and organizations, age. *Total annual research expenditures:* $955,212.
Dr. Isaac Eberstein, Chairman, 850-644-6416, *Fax:* 850-644-6208, *E-mail:* ieberstn@garnet.fsu.edu.
Application contact: Jamie Yeargan, Graduate Studies Assistant, 850-644-6506, *Fax:* 850-644-6208, *E-mail:* jyeargan@mailer.fsu.edu. *Web site:* http://www.fsu.edu/~soc/

■ FORDHAM UNIVERSITY

Graduate School of Arts and Sciences, Department of Sociology, New York, NY 10458

AWARDS Criminology (MA); sociology (MA, PhD), including demography, ethnic minorities, sociology of religions. Part-time and evening/weekend programs available.

Faculty: 21 full-time (11 women).
Students: 14 full-time (10 women), 19 part-time (7 women); includes 8 minority (4 African Americans, 1 Asian American or Pacific Islander, 3 Hispanic Americans), 6 international. 35 applicants, 60% accepted. In 2001, 4 master's, 3 doctorates awarded. Terminal master's awarded for partial completion of doctoral program.
Degree requirements: For master's, one foreign language, comprehensive exam; for doctorate, 2 foreign languages, thesis/dissertation, comprehensive exam.
Entrance requirements: For master's and doctorate, GRE General Test. *Application deadline:* For fall admission, 1/15 (priority date); for spring admission, 12/1. *Application fee:* $65. Electronic applications accepted.
Expenses: Tuition: Part-time $720 per credit. Required fees: $135 per semester.
Financial support: In 2001–02, 13 students received support, including fellowships with tuition reimbursements available (averaging $15,000 per year), 1 research assistantship with tuition reimbursement available (averaging $12,000 per year), teaching assistantships with tuition reimbursements available (averaging $14,000 per year); career-related internships or fieldwork, Federal Work-Study, institutionally sponsored loans, tuition waivers (full and partial), and unspecified assistantships also available. Financial award application deadline: 1/16.
Dr. Orlando Rodriguez, Chair, 718-817-3853, *Fax:* 718-817-3846, *E-mail:* orodriguez@fordham.edu.
Application contact: Dr. Craig W. Pilant, Assistant Dean, 718-817-4420, *Fax:* 718-817-3566, *E-mail:* pilant@fordham.edu. *Web site:* http://www.fordham.edu/gsas/

■ GEORGE MASON UNIVERSITY

College of Arts and Sciences, Department of Sociology and Anthropology, Fairfax, VA 22030-4444

AWARDS Sociology (MA).

Faculty: 19 full-time (6 women), 8 part-time/adjunct (6 women).
Students: 3 full-time (all women), 23 part-time (20 women); includes 6 minority (3 African Americans, 1 Asian American or Pacific Islander, 2 Hispanic Americans), 3 international. Average age 29. 25 applicants, 56% accepted, 5 enrolled. In 2001, 5 degrees awarded.
Degree requirements: For master's, thesis.
Entrance requirements: For master's, GRE General Test, minimum GPA of 3.0 in last 60 hours; sample of written work; previous undergraduate course work in sociological theory, research methods, and social statistics. *Application deadline:* For fall admission, 5/1; for spring admission, 11/1. *Application fee:* $30. Electronic applications accepted.
Expenses: Tuition, state resident: full-time $3,168; part-time $132 per credit hour. Tuition, nonresident: full-time $11,280; part-time $470 per credit hour. Required fees: $1,416; $59 per credit hour.
Financial support: Research assistantships, teaching assistantships available. Support available to part-time students. Financial award application deadline: 3/1; financial award applicants required to submit FAFSA.
Dr. Joseph Scimecca, Chairman, 703-993-1441, *Fax:* 703-993-1446, *E-mail:* jscimecca@gmu.edu.
Application contact: Dr. John Stone, Information Contact, 703-993-1441, *E-mail:* socgrad@gmu.edu. *Web site:* http://www.gmu.edu/departments/soci/socframe.html

■ THE GEORGE WASHINGTON UNIVERSITY

Columbian College of Arts and Sciences, Department of Sociology, Washington, DC 20052

AWARDS MA. Part-time and evening/weekend programs available.

Faculty: 9 full-time (4 women), 1 (woman) part-time/adjunct.
Students: 7 full-time (all women), 4 part-time (3 women); includes 1 minority (Hispanic American). Average age 27. 39 applicants, 82% accepted. In 2001, 1 degree awarded.
Degree requirements: For master's, thesis or alternative, comprehensive exam.
Entrance requirements: For master's, GRE General Test, minimum GPA of 3.0. *Application deadline:* For fall admission, 5/1. *Application fee:* $55.
Expenses: Tuition: Part-time $810 per credit. Required fees: $1 per credit.
Financial support: In 2001–02, 3 fellowships with tuition reimbursements (averaging $5,500 per year), 4 teaching assistantships with tuition reimbursements (averaging $3,300 per year) were awarded. Career-related internships or fieldwork and Federal Work-Study also available. Financial award application deadline: 2/1.
Dr. Greg Squires, Chair, 202-994-6345. *Web site:* http://www.gwu.edu/~gradinfo/

■ GEORGIA SOUTHERN UNIVERSITY

Jack N. Averitt College of Graduate Studies, College of Liberal Arts and Social Sciences, Department of Sociology and Anthropology, Statesboro, GA 30460

AWARDS Sociology (MA). Part-time and evening/weekend programs available.

Faculty: 16 full-time (8 women).
Students: 3 full-time (2 women), 8 part-time (6 women); includes 2 minority (both African Americans), 2 international. Average age 35. 4 applicants, 100% accepted, 1 enrolled. In 2001, 2 degrees awarded.
Degree requirements: For master's, one foreign language, thesis, thesis or applied monograph.
Entrance requirements: For master's, GRE General Test, minimum GPA of 2.75, bachelor's degree in sociology. *Application deadline:* For fall admission, 7/1 (priority date); for spring admission, 11/15 (priority date). Applications are processed on a rolling basis. *Application fee:* $0. Electronic applications accepted.
Expenses: Tuition, state resident: full-time $1,746; part-time $97 per credit hour. Tuition, nonresident: full-time $6,966; part-time $387 per credit hour. Required fees: $294 per semester.

Georgia Southern University (continued)
Financial support: In 2001–02, 4 students received support, including 3 research assistantships with partial tuition reimbursements available (averaging $5,000 per year); career-related internships or fieldwork, Federal Work-Study, and unspecified assistantships also available. Support available to part-time students. Financial award application deadline: 4/15; financial award applicants required to submit FAFSA.
Faculty research: Work and family, gender roles, sociology of the South, social psychology, community. *Total annual research expenditures:* $35,000.
Dr. Sue M. Moore, Acting Chair, 912-681-5443, *Fax:* 912-681-0703, *E-mail:* smmoore@gasou.edu.
Application contact: Dr. John R. Diebolt, Associate Graduate Dean, 912-681-5384, *Fax:* 912-681-0740, *E-mail:* gradschool@gasou.edu. *Web site:* http://www2.gasou.edu/socianth/web-degr.html

■ GEORGIA STATE UNIVERSITY

College of Arts and Sciences, Department of Sociology, Atlanta, GA 30303-3083

AWARDS MA, PhD. Part-time and evening/weekend programs available. Terminal master's awarded for partial completion of doctoral program.

Degree requirements: For master's, one foreign language, thesis or alternative, exam; for doctorate, one foreign language, thesis/dissertation, exam.
Entrance requirements: For master's, GRE General Test, TOEFL, departmental supplemental form; for doctorate, GRE General Test, TOEFL, departmental supplemental form, sample of written work. Electronic applications accepted.
Faculty research: Aging, fatherhood, intimate violence, movements, diversity in the corporation. *Web site:* http://www.gsu.edu/~wwwsoc/

Find an in-depth description at www.petersons.com/gradchannel.

■ GRADUATE SCHOOL AND UNIVERSITY CENTER OF THE CITY UNIVERSITY OF NEW YORK

Graduate Studies, Program in Sociology, New York, NY 10016-4039

AWARDS PhD.

Faculty: 69 full-time (15 women).
Students: 112 full-time (72 women), 10 part-time (5 women); includes 35 minority (12 African Americans, 11 Asian Americans or Pacific Islanders, 11 Hispanic Americans, 1 Native American), 17 international. Average age 41. 106 applicants, 50% accepted, 19 enrolled. In 2001, 6 degrees awarded.
Degree requirements: For doctorate, one foreign language, thesis/dissertation.
Entrance requirements: For doctorate, GRE General Test. *Application deadline:* For fall admission, 4/15. *Application fee:* $40.
Expenses: Tuition, state resident: part-time $245 per credit. Tuition, nonresident: part-time $425 per credit. Required fees: $72 per semester.
Financial support: In 2001–02, 62 students received support, including 41 fellowships, 4 research assistantships, 1 teaching assistantship; career-related internships or fieldwork, Federal Work-Study, institutionally sponsored loans, and tuition waivers (full and partial) also available. Financial award application deadline: 2/1; financial award applicants required to submit FAFSA.
Dr. Philip Kasinitz, Executive Officer, 212-817-8787, *Fax:* 212-817-1536, *E-mail:* pkasinitz@gc.cuny.edu.

■ HARVARD UNIVERSITY

Graduate School of Arts and Sciences, Department of Sociology, Cambridge, MA 02138

AWARDS AM, PhD.

Degree requirements: For doctorate, thesis/dissertation, oral exams in 2 subfields.
Entrance requirements: For master's and doctorate, GRE General Test, TOEFL.
Expenses: Tuition: Full-time $23,370. Required fees: $816. Full-time tuition and fees vary according to program and student level.
Faculty research: Sociological theory, political theories, quantitative approaches to methodology.

■ HOWARD UNIVERSITY

Graduate School of Arts and Sciences, Department of Sociology and Anthropology, Washington, DC 20059-0002

AWARDS Sociology (MA, PhD). Part-time and evening/weekend programs available.

Faculty: 15 full-time (7 women).
Students: 46 full-time (30 women), 46 part-time (27 women); includes 78 minority (74 African Americans, 3 Asian Americans or Pacific Islanders, 1 Hispanic American), 11 international. Average age 28. 43 applicants, 77% accepted, 11 enrolled. In 2001, 4 master's, 9 doctorates awarded.
Degree requirements: For master's and doctorate, one foreign language, thesis/dissertation, comprehensive exam. *Median time to degree:* Master's–2.5 years full-time, 4 years part-time; doctorate–6 years full-time, 7 years part-time.
Entrance requirements: For master's, GRE General Test, minimum GPA of 3.0; for doctorate, GRE General Test, minimum GPA of 3.5. *Application deadline:* For fall admission, 4/1; for spring admission, 11/1. Applications are processed on a rolling basis. *Application fee:* $45.
Financial support: In 2001–02, 19 students received support, including 4 fellowships with tuition reimbursements available, 13 teaching assistantships with tuition reimbursements available; research assistantships, institutionally sponsored loans, traineeships, and unspecified assistantships also available. Financial award application deadline: 4/1.
Faculty research: Medical sociology; criminology; race, class and gender; urban sociology; political economy. *Total annual research expenditures:* $160,000.
Dr. Florence Bonner, Chair, 202-806-6853, *Fax:* 202-806-4893, *E-mail:* fbonner@howard.edu.
Application contact: Dr. Ralph Gomes, 1, 202-806-6853, *Fax:* 202-806-4893, *E-mail:* rgomes@howard.edu. *Web site:* http://www.howard.edu/CollegeArtsSciences/Socio

■ HUMBOLDT STATE UNIVERSITY

Graduate Studies, College of Arts, Humanities, and Social Sciences, Department of Sociology, Arcata, CA 95521-8299

AWARDS MA.

Students: 17 full-time (9 women), 12 part-time (8 women); includes 2 minority (both Hispanic Americans), 1 international. Average age 33. 24 applicants, 79% accepted, 11 enrolled. In 2001, 8 degrees awarded.
Degree requirements: For master's, thesis or alternative, qualifying exam.
Entrance requirements: For master's, TOEFL, minimum GPA of 2.5. *Application deadline:* Applications are processed on a rolling basis.
Expenses: Tuition, state resident: full-time $1,969. Tuition, nonresident: part-time $246 per unit.
Financial support: Application deadline: 3/1.
Faculty research: Sociology of women political activists, environmental dispute resolution, prosocial behavior.
Dr. Lee Bowker, Coordinator, 707-826-4446, *E-mail:* lhb3@humboldt.edu. *Web site:* http://www.humboldt.edu

■ HUNTER COLLEGE OF THE CITY UNIVERSITY OF NEW YORK

Graduate School, School of Arts and Sciences, Department of Sociology, New York, NY 10021-5085

AWARDS MSSR.

Faculty: 6 full-time (2 women), 1 part-time/adjunct (0 women).
Students: 5 full-time (4 women), 21 part-time (15 women); includes 10 minority (2 African Americans, 2 Asian Americans or Pacific Islanders, 6 Hispanic Americans), 3 international. In 2001, 3 degrees awarded.
Entrance requirements: For master's, GRE General Test, TOEFL. *Application fee:* $40.

Expenses: Tuition, state resident: full-time $2,175; part-time $185 per credit. Tuition, nonresident: full-time $3,800; part-time $320 per credit.
Dr. Charles Green, Chairperson, 212-772-5585, *Fax:* 212-772-5645.
Application contact: Dr. Naomi W. Kroeger, Graduate Adviser, 212-772-5580, *Fax:* 212-772-5581, *E-mail:* nkroeger@hunter.cuny.edu.

■ HUNTER COLLEGE OF THE CITY UNIVERSITY OF NEW YORK

Graduate School, School of Arts and Sciences, Program in Social Research, New York, NY 10021-5085

AWARDS Applied social research (MS). Part-time and evening/weekend programs available.

Faculty: 17 full-time (6 women).
Students: 16 full-time (all women), 26 part-time (16 women); includes 19 minority (6 African Americans, 4 Asian Americans or Pacific Islanders, 9 Hispanic Americans), 1 international. Average age 31. 22 applicants, 68% accepted. In 2001, 12 degrees awarded.
Degree requirements: For master's, internship, research reports.
Entrance requirements: For master's, GRE General Test, TOEFL, 3 credits in statistics. *Application deadline:* For fall admission, 4/1; for spring admission, 11/1. Applications are processed on a rolling basis. *Application fee:* $40.
Expenses: Tuition, state resident: full-time $2,175; part-time $185 per credit. Tuition, nonresident: full-time $3,800; part-time $320 per credit.
Financial support: Fellowships, research assistantships, teaching assistantships, career-related internships or fieldwork, Federal Work-Study, institutionally sponsored loans, and tuition waivers (full and partial) available. Support available to part-time students.
Faculty research: Consumer behavior, new electronic media, voting behavior, policy analysis, sociomedicine.
Dr. Naomi W. Kroeger, Director, 212-772-5580, *Fax:* 212-772-5581, *E-mail:* masters.socialresearch@hunter.cuny.edu.
Application contact: 212-772-5580, *Fax:* 212-772-5581, *E-mail:* grad.socialresearchadvisor@hunter.cuny.edu. *Web site:* http://www.hunter.cuny.edu/socialresearch/html

■ IDAHO STATE UNIVERSITY

Office of Graduate Studies, College of Arts and Sciences, Department of Sociology, Pocatello, ID 83209

AWARDS MA. Part-time programs available.

Faculty: 3 full-time (1 woman).
Students: 4 full-time (all women), 2 part-time (1 woman); includes 1 minority (Native American). Average age 39. In 2001, 1 degree awarded.
Degree requirements: For master's, thesis.
Entrance requirements: For master's, GRE General Test. *Application deadline:* For fall admission, 8/1. Applications are processed on a rolling basis. *Application fee:* $35.
Expenses: Tuition, area resident: Full-time $3,432. Tuition, state resident: part-time $172 per credit. Tuition, nonresident: full-time $10,196; part-time $262 per credit. International tuition: $9,672 full-time. Part-time tuition and fees vary according to course load, program and reciprocity agreements.
Financial support: In 2001–02, 3 teaching assistantships with full and partial tuition reimbursements (averaging $5,411 per year) were awarded; career-related internships or fieldwork, Federal Work-Study, institutionally sponsored loans, and tuition waivers (full and partial) also available. Support available to part-time students. *Total annual research expenditures:* $5,196.
Dr. Donald Pierson, Chairperson, 208-282-2929.
Application contact: Dr. James Aho, Program Director, 208-282-2576.

■ ILLINOIS STATE UNIVERSITY

Graduate School, College of Arts and Sciences, Department of Sociology, Normal, IL 61790-2200

AWARDS MA, MS.

Faculty: 21 full-time (7 women).
Students: 16 full-time (12 women), 18 part-time (14 women); includes 6 minority (5 African Americans, 1 Native American), 2 international. 5 applicants, 100% accepted. In 2001, 6 degrees awarded.
Degree requirements: For master's, thesis.
Entrance requirements: For master's, GRE General Test, GRE Subject Test, minimum GPA of 2.4 in last 60 hours. *Application deadline:* Applications are processed on a rolling basis. *Application fee:* $30.
Expenses: Tuition, state resident: full-time $2,691; part-time $112 per credit hour. Tuition, nonresident: full-time $5,880; part-time $245 per credit hour. Required fees: $1,146; $48 per credit hour.
Financial support: In 2001–02, 4 research assistantships (averaging $6,257 per year), 16 teaching assistantships (averaging $5,723 per year) were awarded. Career-related internships or fieldwork, Federal Work-Study, tuition waivers (full and partial), and unspecified assistantships also available. Financial award application deadline: 4/1.
Faculty research: Intergenerational service-learning archeological investigation of Gete Odena. *Total annual research expenditures:* $20,500.
Dr. Nick Maroules, Chairperson, 309-438-8668.
Application contact: Wilbert M. Leonard, Graduate Adviser, 309-438-8073. *Web site:* http://lilt.ilstu.edu/SOA/

■ INDIANA STATE UNIVERSITY

School of Graduate Studies, College of Arts and Sciences, Department of Sociology, Terre Haute, IN 47809-1401

AWARDS MA, MS.

Electronic applications accepted.

■ INDIANA UNIVERSITY BLOOMINGTON

Graduate School, College of Arts and Sciences, Department of Sociology, Bloomington, IN 47405

AWARDS MA, PhD. PhD offered through the University Graduate School. Part-time programs available.

Faculty: 27 full-time (7 women).
Students: 95 full-time (61 women), 103 part-time (61 women); includes 27 minority (9 African Americans, 7 Asian Americans or Pacific Islanders, 10 Hispanic Americans, 1 Native American), 25 international. Average age 35. 118 applicants, 18% accepted. In 2001, 21 master's, 20 doctorates awarded. Terminal master's awarded for partial completion of doctoral program.
Degree requirements: For master's and doctorate, thesis/dissertation.
Entrance requirements: For master's and doctorate, GRE General Test, TOEFL. *Application deadline:* For fall admission, 1/15. Applications are processed on a rolling basis. *Application fee:* $45 ($55 for international students).
Expenses: Tuition, state resident: full-time $4,720; part-time $197 per credit. Tuition, nonresident: full-time $13,748; part-time $573 per credit. Required fees: $642.
Financial support: In 2001–02, 84 students received support, including 20 fellowships with full tuition reimbursements available (averaging $12,000 per year), 35 research assistantships with full tuition reimbursements available (averaging $10,000 per year), 29 teaching assistantships with full tuition reimbursements available (averaging $10,500 per year); institutionally sponsored loans, scholarships/grants, traineeships, and unspecified assistantships also available. Financial award application deadline: 1/15; financial award applicants required to submit FAFSA.
Faculty research: Social psychology, social organization, political sociology, sociological research methods, stratification.
J. Scott Long, Chair, 812-855-4127, *Fax:* 812-855-0781, *E-mail:* jslong@ucs.indiana.edu.
Application contact: Mark G. Zacharias, Graduate Secretary, 812-855-2924, *Fax:* 812-855-0781, *E-mail:* mazachar@indiana.edu. *Web site:* http://www.indiana.edu/~soc/

■ INDIANA UNIVERSITY OF PENNSYLVANIA

Graduate School and Research, College of Humanities and Social Sciences, Department of Sociology, Program in Sociology, Indiana, PA 15705-1087

AWARDS MA. Part-time programs available.

Students: 11 full-time (8 women), 6 part-time (3 women); includes 3 minority (all African Americans), 1 international. Average age 29. 13 applicants, 69% accepted. In 2001, 8 degrees awarded.
Degree requirements: For master's, thesis optional.
Entrance requirements: For master's, TOEFL, GRE, letters of recommendation (2). *Application deadline:* For fall admission, 7/1 (priority date); for spring admission, 11/1. Applications are processed on a rolling basis. *Application fee:* $30.
Expenses: Tuition, state resident: full-time $4,600; part-time $256 per credit hour. Tuition, nonresident: full-time $7,554; part-time $420 per credit hour. Required fees: $800. Part-time tuition and fees vary according to course load.
Financial support: In 2001–02, 9 research assistantships (averaging $5,040 per year) were awarded. Financial award application deadline: 3/15; financial award applicants required to submit FAFSA.
Dr. Kay Snyder, Graduate Coordinator, 724-357-3931.

■ INDIANA UNIVERSITY–PURDUE UNIVERSITY FORT WAYNE

School of Arts and Sciences, Department of Sociology and Anthropology, Fort Wayne, IN 46805-1499

AWARDS Sociological practice (MA). Part-time programs available.

Faculty: 5 full-time (2 women).
Students: 3 full-time (2 women), 3 part-time (all women). Average age 37. 8 applicants, 75% accepted, 6 enrolled.
Degree requirements: For master's, practicum.
Entrance requirements: For master's, GRE General Test, minimum GPA of 3.0, transcripts. *Application deadline:* For fall admission, 8/1 (priority date); for spring admission, 11/1 (priority date). Applications are processed on a rolling basis. *Application fee:* $30.
Expenses: Tuition, state resident: full-time $2,845; part-time $158 per credit hour. Tuition, nonresident: full-time $6,323; part-time $351 per credit hour. Required fees: $9 per credit hour. Tuition and fees vary according to course load.
Financial support: In 2001–02, teaching assistantships with partial tuition reimbursements (averaging $7,350 per year); Federal Work-Study, scholarships/grants, and unspecified assistantships also available. Support available to part-time students. Financial award application deadline: 3/1; financial award applicants required to submit FAFSA. *Total annual research expenditures:* $244,016.
Dr. Peter Iadicola, Chairperson, 260-481-6842, *Fax:* 260-481-6985, *E-mail:* iadicola@ipfw.edu.
Application contact: Dr. Patrick J. Ashton, Director of Graduate Studies, 260-481-6669, *Fax:* 260-481-6985, *E-mail:* ashton@ipfw.edu. *Web site:* http://www.ipfw.edu/soca/socahome.htm

■ IOWA STATE UNIVERSITY OF SCIENCE AND TECHNOLOGY

Graduate College, College of Liberal Arts and Sciences, Department of Sociology, Ames, IA 50011

AWARDS Rural sociology (MS, PhD); sociology (MS, PhD).

Faculty: 41 full-time.
Students: 36 full-time (20 women), 18 part-time (12 women); includes 8 minority (5 African Americans, 1 Asian American or Pacific Islander, 1 Hispanic American, 1 Native American), 17 international. 38 applicants, 53% accepted, 9 enrolled. In 2001, 3 master's, 4 doctorates awarded.
Degree requirements: For master's and doctorate, thesis/dissertation. *Median time to degree:* Master's–1.9 years full-time; doctorate–4.9 years full-time.
Entrance requirements: For master's and doctorate, GRE General Test, TOEFL or IELTS. *Application deadline:* For fall admission, 2/1 (priority date); for spring admission, 10/1. *Application fee:* $20 ($50 for international students). Electronic applications accepted.
Expenses: Tuition, state resident: full-time $1,851. Tuition, nonresident: full-time $5,449. Tuition and fees vary according to program.
Financial support: In 2001–02, 27 research assistantships with partial tuition reimbursements (averaging $15,005 per year), 10 teaching assistantships with partial tuition reimbursements (averaging $12,204 per year) were awarded. Fellowships, scholarships/grants, health care benefits, and unspecified assistantships also available.
Dr. Robert Schafer, Chair, 515-294-8312, *Fax:* 515-294-8312, *E-mail:* rschafer@iastate.edu. *Web site:* http://socserver.soc.iastate.edu

■ JACKSON STATE UNIVERSITY

Graduate School, School of Liberal Arts, Department of Sociology, Jackson, MS 39217

AWARDS MA. Part-time and evening/weekend programs available.

Degree requirements: For master's, thesis or alternative, comprehensive exam.
Entrance requirements: For master's, GRE General Test, TOEFL.

■ JOHNS HOPKINS UNIVERSITY

Zanvyl Krieger School of Arts and Sciences, Department of Sociology, Baltimore, MD 21218-2699

AWARDS PhD.

Faculty: 8 full-time (3 women).
Students: 24 full-time (15 women); includes 4 minority (all African Americans), 10 international. Average age 33. 88 applicants, 14% accepted, 3 enrolled. In 2001, 7 doctorates awarded.
Degree requirements: For doctorate, one foreign language, thesis/dissertation, registration.
Entrance requirements: For doctorate, GRE General Test, sample of written work. *Application deadline:* For fall admission, 1/15. *Application fee:* $55. Electronic applications accepted.
Expenses: Tuition: Full-time $27,390.
Financial support: In 2001–02, 1 fellowship, 10 research assistantships, 12 teaching assistantships were awarded. Federal Work-Study and institutionally sponsored loans also available. Financial award application deadline: 4/15; financial award applicants required to submit CSS PROFILE or FAFSA.
Faculty research: Social inequality, comparative international development, sociology of education, sociology of family, migration and ethnicity. *Total annual research expenditures:* $3.9 million.
Dr. Andrew J. Cherlin, Chair, 410-516-7626, *Fax:* 410-516-7590.
Application contact: Dr. Karl Alexander, Director of Graduate Admissions, 410-516-7627, *Fax:* 410-516-7590, *E-mail:* sociology@jhu.edu. *Web site:* http://www.jhu.edu:80/~soc/

■ KANSAS STATE UNIVERSITY

Graduate School, College of Arts and Sciences, Department of Sociology, Anthropology and Social Work, Manhattan, KS 66506

AWARDS Sociology (MA, PhD). Part-time programs available.

Faculty: 15 full-time (6 women).
Students: 19 full-time (10 women), 7 part-time (3 women); includes 1 minority (Hispanic American), 6 international. 19 applicants, 58% accepted, 7 enrolled. In 2001, 2 master's, 2 doctorates awarded.
Degree requirements: For master's, thesis or alternative; for doctorate, thesis/dissertation.
Entrance requirements: For master's, GRE, TOEFL, minimum GPA of 3.0 (undergraduate); for doctorate, master's degree in sociology. *Application deadline:* For fall admission, 3/1 (priority date); for spring admission, 10/1 (priority date). Applications are processed on a rolling basis. *Application fee:* $0 ($25 for international students). Electronic applications accepted.

Expenses: Tuition, state resident: part-time $113 per credit hour. Tuition, nonresident: part-time $358 per credit hour.
Financial support: In 2001–02, 1 research assistantship with full tuition reimbursement (averaging $9,800 per year), 16 teaching assistantships with full tuition reimbursements (averaging $8,400 per year) were awarded. Institutionally sponsored loans and scholarships/grants also available. Support available to part-time students. Financial award application deadline: 3/1; financial award applicants required to submit FAFSA.
Faculty research: Demography, community, political economy, urban development, migration and immigration. *Total annual research expenditures:* $203,668.
Leonard Bloomquist, Head, 785-532-6865, *Fax:* 785-532-6978, *E-mail:* bloomqui@ksu.edu.
Application contact: Richard Goe, Graduate Program Director, 785-532-6865, *Fax:* 785-532-6978, *E-mail:* goe@ksu.edu. *Web site:* http://www.ksu.edu/sasw/

■ KENT STATE UNIVERSITY

College of Arts and Sciences, Department of Sociology, Kent, OH 44242-0001

AWARDS MA, PhD.

Degree requirements: For master's, thesis optional; for doctorate, variable foreign language requirement, thesis/dissertation.
Entrance requirements: For master's, GRE General Test or MAT, minimum GPA of 2.75; for doctorate, minimum GPA of 3.0. Electronic applications accepted.

■ LEHIGH UNIVERSITY

College of Arts and Sciences, Department of Sociology and Anthropology, Bethlehem, PA 18015-3094

AWARDS MA. Part-time programs available.

Faculty: 7 full-time (3 women).
Students: 12 full-time (10 women), 2 part-time (1 woman); includes 1 minority (Hispanic American). 20 applicants, 75% accepted, 11 enrolled. In 2001, 4 degrees awarded.
Degree requirements: For master's, thesis optional.
Entrance requirements: For master's, GRE, TOEFL. *Application deadline:* For fall admission, 7/15; for spring admission, 12/1. Applications are processed on a rolling basis. *Application fee:* $50. Electronic applications accepted.
Expenses: Tuition: Part-time $468 per credit hour. Required fees: $200; $100 per semester. Tuition and fees vary according to program.
Financial support: In 2001–02, 4 teaching assistantships with tuition reimbursements were awarded; fellowships, career-related internships or fieldwork, Federal Work-Study, and tuition waivers (full) also available. Financial award application deadline: 1/15.
Faculty research: Juvenile delinquency, parent-child relations, urban sociology, family, alcohol studies, communication, race and class.
Dr. James R. McIntosh, Chairperson, 610-758-3809, *Fax:* 610-758-6552, *E-mail:* ijm1@lehigh.edu.
Application contact: Dr. Judith N. Lasker, Graduate Coordinator, 610-758-3811, *Fax:* 610-758-6552, *E-mail:* jnl0@lehigh.edu. *Web site:* http://www.lehigh.edu/~insan/soc-ma.htm

Find an in-depth description at www.petersons.com/gradchannel.

■ LINCOLN UNIVERSITY

Graduate School, College of Liberal Arts, Science, and Agriculture, Division of Social and Behavioral Sciences, Jefferson City, MO 65102

AWARDS History (MA); sociology (MA); sociology/criminal justice (MA). Part-time and evening/weekend programs available.

Faculty: 10 part-time/adjunct (1 woman).
Students: 2 full-time (1 woman), 21 part-time (15 women); includes 7 minority (all African Americans), 2 international. Average age 36. 3 applicants, 100% accepted, 3 enrolled. In 2001, 12 degrees awarded.
Degree requirements: For master's, thesis or alternative.
Entrance requirements: For master's, GRE General Test or MAT, minimum GPA of 2.75 in major, 2.5 overall. *Application deadline:* For fall admission, 7/1; for spring admission, 12/1. *Application fee:* $17.
Expenses: Tuition, state resident: part-time $136 per credit hour. Tuition, nonresident: part-time $272 per credit hour. Required fees: $50 per term.
Financial support: Fellowships available.
Faculty research: Rural black elderly, international politics, convict labor, blacks in higher education.
Dr. Antonio Holland, Head, 573-681-5145.

■ LOUISIANA STATE UNIVERSITY AND AGRICULTURAL AND MECHANICAL COLLEGE

Graduate School, College of Arts and Sciences, Department of Sociology, Baton Rouge, LA 70803

AWARDS MA, PhD. Part-time programs available.

Faculty: 17 full-time (2 women).
Students: 33 full-time (17 women), 11 part-time (all women); includes 9 minority (4 African Americans, 1 Asian American or Pacific Islander, 4 Hispanic Americans), 4 international. Average age 33. 28 applicants, 57% accepted, 9 enrolled. In 2001, 1 master's, 5 doctorates awarded. Terminal master's awarded for partial completion of doctoral program.
Degree requirements: For master's and doctorate, thesis/dissertation.
Entrance requirements: For master's and doctorate, GRE General Test, minimum GPA of 3.0. *Application deadline:* For fall admission, 1/25 (priority date). Applications are processed on a rolling basis. *Application fee:* $25.
Expenses: Tuition, state resident: full-time $2,551. Tuition, nonresident: full-time $5,551. Required fees: $854. Part-time tuition and fees vary according to course load.
Financial support: In 2001–02, 1 fellowship (averaging $15,673 per year), 18 research assistantships with partial tuition reimbursements (averaging $11,875 per year), 5 teaching assistantships with partial tuition reimbursements (averaging $10,242 per year) were awarded. Unspecified assistantships also available. Financial award application deadline: 3/1; financial award applicants required to submit FAFSA.
Faculty research: Family, stratification, demography, rural sociology, criminology. *Total annual research expenditures:* $170,436.
Dr. Michael F. Grimes, Chair, 225-578-1645, *Fax:* 225-578-5102, *E-mail:* socgrm@lsu.edu.
Application contact: Dr. Wesley Shrum, Graduate Adviser, 225-578-1645, *E-mail:* shrum@lsu.edu. *Web site:* http://soc.lsu.edu/

■ LOYOLA UNIVERSITY CHICAGO

Graduate School, Department of Sociology, Chicago, IL 60611-2196

AWARDS Applied sociology (MA); sociology (MA, PhD). Part-time and evening/weekend programs available.

Faculty: 16 full-time (6 women).
Students: 53 full-time (33 women), 12 part-time (6 women); includes 15 minority (7 African Americans, 3 Asian Americans or Pacific Islanders, 4 Hispanic Americans, 1 Native American), 7 international. Average age 27. 71 applicants, 75% accepted. In 2001, 12 master's, 3 doctorates awarded. Terminal master's awarded for partial completion of doctoral program.
Degree requirements: For master's, thesis or alternative, comprehensive exam; for doctorate, thesis/dissertation, comprehensive exam.
Entrance requirements: For master's, GRE General Test, TOEFL; for doctorate, GRE General Test. *Application deadline:* For fall admission, 3/1 (priority date); for spring admission, 12/1. Applications are processed on a rolling basis. *Application fee:* $40.
Expenses: Tuition: Part-time $529 per credit hour.
Financial support: In 2001–02, 25 students received support, including 6 fellowships, 19 research assistantships; teaching assistantships, career-related

Loyola University Chicago (continued)
internships or fieldwork and Federal Work-Study also available. Financial award application deadline: 2/1; financial award applicants required to submit FAFSA.
Faculty research: Science and technology, religion, work, family and gender, urban sociology.
Dr. Peter Whalley, Chair, 773-508-3453, *Fax:* 773-508-7099.
Application contact: Dr. Judith Wittner, Graduate Program Director, 773-508-3473, *Fax:* 773-508-7099.

■ MARSHALL UNIVERSITY

Graduate College, College of Liberal Arts, Department of Sociology and Anthropology, Huntington, WV 25755

AWARDS MA.

Faculty: 6 full-time (2 women), 1 (woman) part-time/adjunct.
Students: 18 full-time (14 women), 6 part-time (4 women); includes 1 minority (African American). In 2001, 8 degrees awarded.
Degree requirements: For master's, thesis optional.
Expenses: Tuition, state resident: part-time $147 per credit. Tuition, nonresident: part-time $468 per credit. Tuition and fees vary according to campus/location and reciprocity agreements.
Dr. Kenneth P. Ambrose, Chairperson, 304-696-2788, *E-mail:* ambrose@marshall.edu.
Application contact: Ken O'Neal, Assistant Vice President, Adult Student Services, 304-746-2500 Ext. 1907, *Fax:* 304-746-1902, *E-mail:* oneal@marshall.edu.

■ MICHIGAN STATE UNIVERSITY

College of Human Medicine and Graduate School, Graduate Programs in Human Medicine, East Lansing, MI 48824

AWARDS Anatomy (MS); anthropology (MA); biochemistry (MS, PhD), including biochemistry, biochemistry-environmental toxicology (PhD); epidemiology (MS); human pathology (MS, PhD); microbiology (MS, PhD); pharmacology/toxicology (MS, PhD); physiology (MS, PhD); psychology (MA); sociology (MA); surgery (MS); zoology (MS). Part-time programs available.

Students: 63 (29 women); includes 7 minority (5 Asian Americans or Pacific Islanders, 2 Hispanic Americans) 7 international. Average age 26. In 2001, 14 master's, 2 doctorates awarded.
Entrance requirements: For master's and doctorate, GRE General Test, minimum GPA of 3.0. *Application deadline:* Applications are processed on a rolling basis. *Application fee:* $30 ($40 for international students). Electronic applications accepted.
Expenses: Contact institution.
Financial support: In 2001–02, 48 research assistantships with tuition reimbursements (averaging $12,058 per year), 1 teaching assistantship with tuition reimbursement (averaging $10,944 per year) were awarded. Fellowships with tuition reimbursements, institutionally sponsored loans also available. Support available to part-time students. Financial award applicants required to submit FAFSA.
Dr. Lynne Farquhar, Director, Medical Science Training Program, 517-353-8858, *Fax:* 517-432-0148, *E-mail:* mdadmissions@msu.edu. *Web site:* http://www.chm.msu.edu/chmhome/gradeducation/GMEWEB/

■ MICHIGAN STATE UNIVERSITY

Graduate School, College of Social Science, Department of Sociology, East Lansing, MI 48824

AWARDS Sociology (MA, PhD); sociology-urban studies (MA, PhD).

Faculty: 20.
Students: 48 full-time (32 women), 14 part-time (11 women); includes 9 minority (5 African Americans, 3 Asian Americans or Pacific Islanders, 1 Hispanic American), 21 international. Average age 34. 74 applicants, 30% accepted. In 2001, 2 master's, 5 doctorates awarded.
Degree requirements: For master's and doctorate, thesis/dissertation, comprehensive exam.
Entrance requirements: For master's, GRE General Test, minimum GPA of 3.0; for doctorate, master's degree in sociology or related field. *Application deadline:* For fall admission, 6/30. Applications are processed on a rolling basis. *Application fee:* $30 ($40 for international students). Electronic applications accepted.
Expenses: Tuition, state resident: part-time $244 per credit hour. Tuition, nonresident: part-time $494 per credit hour. Required fees: $268 per semester. Tuition and fees vary according to course load, degree level and program.
Financial support: In 2001–02, 13 fellowships (averaging $4,143 per year), 17 research assistantships with tuition reimbursements (averaging $11,004 per year), 24 teaching assistantships with tuition reimbursements (averaging $10,445 per year) were awarded. Career-related internships or fieldwork, Federal Work-Study, and institutionally sponsored loans also available. Financial award applicants required to submit FAFSA.
Faculty research: Family, race and ethnicity, rural sociology, sex and gender, well-being and health. *Total annual research expenditures:* $873,760.
Dr. Thomas L. Conner, Chair, 517-355-6640, *Fax:* 517-432-2856. *Web site:* http://www.soc.msu.edu/

■ MIDDLE TENNESSEE STATE UNIVERSITY

College of Graduate Studies, College of Liberal Arts, Department of Sociology and Anthropology, Murfreesboro, TN 37132

AWARDS Sociology (MA). Part-time and evening/weekend programs available.

Faculty: 10 full-time (3 women).
Students: 3 full-time (all women), 22 part-time (21 women); includes 5 minority (2 African Americans, 2 Asian Americans or Pacific Islanders, 1 Hispanic American). Average age 33. 6 applicants, 100% accepted. In 2001, 5 degrees awarded.
Degree requirements: For master's, thesis, comprehensive exam.
Entrance requirements: For master's, GRE. *Application deadline:* For fall admission, 8/1 (priority date). Applications are processed on a rolling basis. *Application fee:* $25. Electronic applications accepted.
Expenses: Tuition, state resident: full-time $1,716; part-time $191 per hour. Tuition, nonresident: full-time $4,952; part-time $461 per hour. Required fees: $14 per hour. $58 per semester.
Financial support: In 2001–02, 5 teaching assistantships were awarded; institutionally sponsored loans also available. Support available to part-time students. Financial award application deadline: 5/1; financial award applicants required to submit FAFSA.
Faculty research: Applied, crime/deviance, aging/social gerontology, social organization, social psychology. *Total annual research expenditures:* $8,175.
Dr. Edward Kick, Chair, 615-898-2508, *Fax:* 615-898-5428.

■ MINNESOTA STATE UNIVERSITY, MANKATO

College of Graduate Studies, College of Social and Behavioral Sciences, Department of Sociology, Mankato, MN 56001

AWARDS Sociology (MA, MT), including human services planning and administration (MA); sociology: corrections (MS). Part-time programs available.

Faculty: 17 full-time (4 women).
Students: 11 full-time (6 women), 37 part-time (25 women). Average age 32. In 2001, 9 degrees awarded.
Degree requirements: For master's, thesis or alternative, comprehensive exam.
Entrance requirements: For master's, minimum GPA of 3.0 during previous 2 years. *Application deadline:* For fall admission, 7/9 (priority date); for spring admission, 11/27. Applications are processed on a rolling basis. *Application fee:* $20.
Expenses: Tuition, state resident: full-time $3,253; part-time $157 per credit. Tuition, nonresident: full-time $4,893; part-time $248 per credit. Required fees: $24 per

credit. Tuition and fees vary according to reciprocity agreements.
Financial support: Research assistantships with full tuition reimbursements, teaching assistantships with full tuition reimbursements, career-related internships or fieldwork, Federal Work-Study, and institutionally sponsored loans available. Support available to part-time students. Financial award application deadline: 3/15; financial award applicants required to submit FAFSA.
Faculty research: Women's suffrage movements.
Dr. William Wagner, Chairperson, 507-389-1561.
Application contact: Joni Roberts, Admissions Coordinator, 507-389-5244, *Fax:* 507-389-5974, *E-mail:* grad@mankato.msus.edu.

■ MISSISSIPPI COLLEGE

Graduate School, College of Arts and Sciences, Department of History and Political Science, Department of Sociology, Clinton, MS 39058

AWARDS MSS.

Degree requirements: For master's, one foreign language, comprehensive exam.
Entrance requirements: For master's, GRE, minimum GPA of 2.5.

■ MISSISSIPPI STATE UNIVERSITY

College of Arts and Sciences, Department of Sociology, Anthropology, and Social Work, Mississippi State, MS 39762

AWARDS Sociology (MS, PhD). Part-time programs available.

Faculty: 22 full-time (4 women), 7 part-time/adjunct (2 women).
Students: 41 full-time (23 women), 23 part-time (15 women); includes 7 minority (3 African Americans, 1 Asian American or Pacific Islander, 2 Hispanic Americans, 1 Native American), 15 international. Average age 35. 30 applicants, 80% accepted. In 2001, 3 master's, 2 doctorates awarded.
Degree requirements: For master's, thesis (for some programs), comprehensive oral or written exam; for doctorate, thesis/dissertation, comprehensive oral and written exam.
Entrance requirements: For master's and doctorate, TOEFL, GRE. *Application deadline:* For fall admission, 4/15; for spring admission, 11/1. Applications are processed on a rolling basis. *Application fee:* $25 for international students.
Expenses: Tuition, state resident: full-time $3,586; part-time $150 per credit hour. Tuition, nonresident: full-time $8,128; part-time $339 per credit hour. Tuition and fees vary according to course load and campus/location.
Financial support: In 2001–02, 9 students received support, including 9 teaching assistantships with tuition reimbursements available (averaging $11,000 per year); Federal Work-Study, institutionally sponsored loans, scholarships/grants, and unspecified assistantships also available. Financial award application deadline: 3/15; financial award applicants required to submit FAFSA.
Faculty research: Community and regional development, criminology, natural resource development, family sociology, gender. *Total annual research expenditures:* $2.7 million.
Dr. Martin L. Levin, Head, 662-325-2495, *Fax:* 662-325-4564, *E-mail:* levin@soc.msstate.edu.
Application contact: Jerry B. Inmon, Director of Admissions, 662-325-2224, *Fax:* 662-325-7360, *E-mail:* admit@admissions.msstate.edu. *Web site:* http://www.msstate.edu/dept/sociology/

■ MONTCLAIR STATE UNIVERSITY

The School of Graduate, Professional and Continuing Education, College of Humanities and Social Sciences, Department of Sociology, Program in Applied Sociology, Upper Montclair, NJ 07043-1624

AWARDS MA. Part-time and evening/weekend programs available.

Degree requirements: For master's, comprehensive project.
Entrance requirements: For master's, GRE General Test, 30 credits in social sciences/history. Electronic applications accepted.

■ MOREHEAD STATE UNIVERSITY

Graduate Programs, Caudill College of Humanities, Department of Sociology, Social Work and Criminology, Morehead, KY 40351

AWARDS Criminology (MA); general sociology (MA); gerontology (MA). Part-time and evening/weekend programs available.

Faculty: 12 full-time (4 women).
Students: 7 full-time (5 women), 11 part-time (10 women), 2 international. Average age 25. 10 applicants, 60% accepted. In 2001, 2 degrees awarded.
Degree requirements: For master's, final comprehensive exam, thesis optional.
Entrance requirements: For master's, GRE General Test, TOFEL, minimum GPA of 3.0 in sociology, 2.5 overall; 18 hours in sociology. *Application deadline:* For fall admission, 8/1 (priority date); for spring admission, 12/1 (priority date). Applications are processed on a rolling basis. *Application fee:* $0.
Expenses: Tuition, state resident: part-time $176 per hour. Tuition, nonresident: full-time $1,584; part-time $472 per hour. International tuition: $4,247 full-time.
Financial support: In 2001–02, 5 teaching assistantships (averaging $5,000 per year) were awarded; career-related internships or fieldwork and Federal Work-Study also available. Financial award application deadline: 4/1; financial award applicants required to submit FAFSA.
Faculty research: Death and dying; aging, drinking, and drugs; economic development; adult children of alcoholics.
Dr. Edward Reeves, Chair, 606-783-2546, *Fax:* 606-783-5027, *E-mail:* e.reeves@moreheadstate.edu.
Application contact: Betty R. Cowsert, Graduate Admissions/Records Manager, 606-783-2039, *Fax:* 606-783-5061, *E-mail:* b.cowsert@moreheadstate.edu. *Web site:* http://www.moreheadstate.edu/

■ MORGAN STATE UNIVERSITY

School of Graduate Studies, College of Liberal Arts, Department of Sociology and Anthropology, Baltimore, MD 21251

AWARDS Sociology (MA, MS). Part-time and evening/weekend programs available.

Faculty: 5 full-time (1 woman).
Students: 10 (6 women); includes 6 minority (all African Americans) 3 international. Average age 25. 5 applicants, 60% accepted.
Degree requirements: For master's, comprehensive exam.
Application deadline: For fall admission, 2/1; for spring admission, 10/1. Applications are processed on a rolling basis. *Application fee:* $0.
Expenses: Tuition, state resident: part-time $193 per credit. Tuition, nonresident: part-time $364 per credit. Required fees: $40 per credit.
Financial support: Application deadline: 4/1.
Faculty research: Domestic violence, homelessness, social movements, marriage and family.
Dr. Maurice St. Pierre, Chair, 443-885-3518, *E-mail:* mstpierre@moac.morgan.edu.
Application contact: Dr. James E. Waller, Admissions and Programs Officer, 443-885-3185, *Fax:* 443-319-3837, *E-mail:* jwaller@moac.morgan.edu.

■ NEW MEXICO HIGHLANDS UNIVERSITY

Graduate Studies, College of Arts and Sciences, Program in Public Affairs, Las Vegas, NM 87701

AWARDS Administration (MA); applied sociology (MA); historical and cross-cultural perspective (MA); political and governmental processes (MA). Program is interdisciplinary.

Faculty: 16 full-time (5 women).
Students: 12 full-time (6 women), 14 part-time (6 women); includes 18 minority (4 African Americans, 2 Asian Americans or Pacific Islanders, 12 Hispanic Americans),

New Mexico Highlands University (continued)

1 international. Average age 35. In 2001, 3 degrees awarded.
Degree requirements: For master's, thesis or alternative.
Entrance requirements: For master's, minimum undergraduate GPA of 3.0. *Application deadline:* For fall admission, 8/1 (priority date). Applications are processed on a rolling basis. *Application fee:* $15.
Expenses: Tuition, state resident: full-time $2,238. Tuition, nonresident: full-time $9,366.
Financial support: Research assistantships with full and partial tuition reimbursements, Federal Work-Study available. Financial award application deadline: 3/1.
Dr. Tomas Salazar, Dean, 505-454-3080, *Fax:* 505-454-3389, *E-mail:* salazar_t@nmhu.edu.
Application contact: Dr. Linda LaGrange, Associate Dean of Graduate Studies, 505-454-3266, *Fax:* 505-454-3558, *E-mail:* lagrange_l@nmhu.edu.

■ NEW MEXICO STATE UNIVERSITY

Graduate School, College of Arts and Sciences, Department of Sociology and Anthropology, Las Cruces, NM 88003-8001

AWARDS Anthropology (MA); sociology (MA). Part-time programs available.

Faculty: 15 full-time (9 women), 4 part-time/adjunct (3 women).
Students: 33 full-time (23 women), 15 part-time (12 women); includes 9 minority (8 Hispanic Americans, 1 Native American), 2 international. Average age 28. 32 applicants, 78% accepted, 15 enrolled. In 2001, 7 degrees awarded.
Degree requirements: For master's, thesis (for some programs), comprehensive exam (anthropology), comprehensive exam. *Application deadline:* For fall admission, 2/15; for spring admission, 10/15. Applications are processed on a rolling basis. *Application fee:* $15 ($35 for international students). Electronic applications accepted.
Expenses: Tuition, state resident: full-time $3,234; part-time $135 per credit. Tuition, nonresident: full-time $9,420; part-time $428 per credit. Required fees: $858.
Financial support: In 2001–02, 12 students received support, including 1 research assistantship, 12 teaching assistantships with partial tuition reimbursements available; career-related internships or fieldwork and Federal Work-Study also available. Support available to part-time students. Financial award application deadline: 3/1.
Faculty research: Native American culture and society, Latin America and border studies, prehistoric and historic archaeology, demography, medical sociology and anthropology.
Dr. Wenda Trevathan, Head, 505-646-3821, *Fax:* 505-646-3725, *E-mail:* wtrevath@nmsu.edu. *Web site:* http://www.nmsu.edu/~anthro/

■ NEW SCHOOL UNIVERSITY

Graduate Faculty of Political and Social Science, Department of Sociology, New York, NY 10011-8603

AWARDS MA, DS Sc, PhD. Part-time and evening/weekend programs available.

Students: 127 full-time (70 women), 12 part-time (7 women); includes 28 minority (12 African Americans, 4 Asian Americans or Pacific Islanders, 11 Hispanic Americans, 1 Native American), 55 international. Average age 34. 97 applicants, 93% accepted. In 2001, 15 master's, 8 doctorates awarded. Terminal master's awarded for partial completion of doctoral program.
Degree requirements: For master's, exam; for doctorate, one foreign language, thesis/dissertation, qualifying exam.
Entrance requirements: For master's, GRE General Test; for doctorate, GRE General Test, MA. *Application deadline:* For fall admission, 1/15 (priority date). Applications are processed on a rolling basis. *Application fee:* $40.
Expenses: Tuition: Full-time $18,720; part-time $1,040 per credit. Required fees: $450; $115 per term. Tuition and fees vary according to program.
Financial support: In 2001–02, 78 students received support, including 13 fellowships with full and partial tuition reimbursements available (averaging $2,700 per year), 5 research assistantships with full and partial tuition reimbursements available (averaging $1,800 per year), 5 teaching assistantships with full and partial tuition reimbursements available (averaging $3,000 per year); career-related internships or fieldwork, Federal Work-Study, scholarships/grants, and tuition waivers (full and partial) also available. Financial award application deadline: 1/15; financial award applicants required to submit FAFSA.
Faculty research: Media, culture, urban sociology, democratic transitions, critical theory.
Dr. Terry Williams, Chair, 212-229-5737.
Application contact: Emanuel Lomax, Director of Admissions, 800-523-5411, *Fax:* 212-989-7102, *E-mail:* gfadmit@newschool.edu. *Web site:* http://www.newschool.edu/

Find an in-depth description at www.petersons.com/gradchannel.

■ NEW YORK UNIVERSITY

Graduate School of Arts and Science, Department of Sociology, New York, NY 10012-1019

AWARDS French studies and sociology (PhD); sociology (MA, PhD). Part-time programs available.

Faculty: 27 full-time (9 women), 1 part-time/adjunct.
Students: 69 full-time (41 women), 5 part-time (4 women); includes 7 minority (5 African Americans, 1 Asian American or Pacific Islander, 1 Hispanic American), 12 international. Average age 29. 264 applicants, 8% accepted, 8 enrolled. In 2001, 9 master's, 5 doctorates awarded. Terminal master's awarded for partial completion of doctoral program.
Degree requirements: For master's, thesis or alternative; for doctorate, thesis/dissertation, comprehensive exam.
Entrance requirements: For master's and doctorate, GRE General Test, TOEFL. *Application deadline:* For fall admission, 1/4 (priority date). *Application fee:* $60.
Expenses: Tuition: Full-time $19,536; part-time $814 per credit. Required fees: $1,330; $38 per credit. Tuition and fees vary according to course load and program.
Financial support: Fellowships with tuition reimbursements, research assistantships with tuition reimbursements, teaching assistantships with tuition reimbursements, Federal Work-Study, institutionally sponsored loans, and unspecified assistantships available. Financial award application deadline: 1/4; financial award applicants required to submit FAFSA.
Faculty research: Political sociology and social movements; gender and inequality; deviance, law, and crime; education; stratification and theory.
Kathleen Gerson, Chairman, 212-998-8340.
Application contact: Jeff Goodwin, Director of Graduate Studies, 212-998-8340, *Fax:* 212-995-4140, *E-mail:* gsas.admissions@nyu.edu. *Web site:* http://www.nyu.edu/gsas/dept/socio/

■ NEW YORK UNIVERSITY

The Steinhardt School of Education, Department of Humanities and Social Sciences, Program in Sociology of Education, New York, NY 10012-1019

AWARDS MA, PhD. Part-time and evening/weekend programs available.

Faculty: 3 full-time (0 women).
Students: 3 full-time (all women), 6 part-time (4 women); includes 2 minority (both African Americans). 14 applicants, 29% accepted, 4 enrolled. In 2001, 2 degrees awarded. Terminal master's awarded for partial completion of doctoral program.
Degree requirements: For master's, thesis (for some programs); for doctorate, thesis/dissertation.
Entrance requirements: For master's, TOEFL; for doctorate, GRE General Test, TOEFL, interview. *Application deadline:* For fall admission, 2/1 (priority date); for spring admission, 12/1. Applications are processed on a rolling basis. *Application fee:* $40 ($60 for international students).

Expenses: Tuition: Full-time $19,536; part-time $814 per credit. Required fees: $1,330; $38 per credit. Tuition and fees vary according to course load and program.
Financial support: Fellowships with full and partial tuition reimbursements, Federal Work-Study, institutionally sponsored loans, scholarships/grants, and tuition waivers (partial) available. Support available to part-time students. Financial award application deadline: 3/1; financial award applicants required to submit FAFSA.
Faculty research: Education's link with occupations, professions, and inequality; selective public high schools; planned educational change.
Dr. Floyd M. Hammack, Program Director, 212-992-9475, *Fax:* 212-995-4832.
Application contact: 212-998-5030, *Fax:* 212-995-4328, *E-mail:* grad.admissions@nyu.edu.

■ NORFOLK STATE UNIVERSITY

School of Graduate Studies, School of Liberal Arts, Department of Sociology, Program in Applied Sociology, Norfolk, VA 23504

AWARDS MS. Part-time programs available.

Application deadline: For fall admission, 3/1; for spring admission, 10/1. *Application fee:* $30.
Expenses: Tuition, area resident: Part-time $197 per credit. Tuition, nonresident: part-time $503 per credit.

■ NORTH CAROLINA CENTRAL UNIVERSITY

Division of Academic Affairs, College of Arts and Sciences, Department of Sociology, Durham, NC 27707-3129

AWARDS MA. Part-time and evening/weekend programs available.

Faculty: 7 full-time (1 woman), 1 part-time/adjunct (0 women).
Students: 4 full-time (3 women), 29 part-time (21 women); includes 31 minority (all African Americans). Average age 32. 10 applicants, 100% accepted. In 2001, 5 degrees awarded.
Degree requirements: For master's, one foreign language, thesis, comprehensive exam.
Entrance requirements: For master's, minimum GPA of 3.0 in major, 2.5 overall. *Application deadline:* For fall admission, 8/1. *Application fee:* $30.
Expenses: Tuition, state resident: full-time $1,424. Tuition, nonresident: full-time $9,492. Required fees: $1,054.
Financial support: Teaching assistantships, career-related internships or fieldwork, Federal Work-Study, and institutionally sponsored loans available. Support available to part-time students. Financial award application deadline: 5/1.
Faculty research: Urban demography, family, statistical methods.
Dr. James C. Davies, Chairperson, 919-560-6222, *Fax:* 919-530-7924, *E-mail:* jdavies@wpo.nccu.edu.
Application contact: Dr. Bernice D. Johnson, Dean, College of Arts and Sciences, 919-560-6368, *Fax:* 919-560-5361, *E-mail:* bjohnson@wpo.nccu.edu.

■ NORTH CAROLINA STATE UNIVERSITY

Graduate School, College of Humanities and Social Sciences and College of Agriculture and Life Sciences, Department of Sociology and Anthropology, Raleigh, NC 27695

AWARDS Rural sociology (MS); sociology (M Soc, PhD). Part-time programs available.

Faculty: 35 full-time (11 women), 12 part-time/adjunct (1 woman).
Students: 47 full-time (34 women), 31 part-time (23 women); includes 13 minority (12 African Americans, 1 Asian American or Pacific Islander), 1 international. Average age 34. 66 applicants, 48% accepted. In 2001, 6 master's, 5 doctorates awarded.
Degree requirements: For master's, practicum (M Soc), thesis (MS); for doctorate, thesis/dissertation, comprehensive exam.
Entrance requirements: For master's and doctorate, GRE General Test, sample of written work. *Application deadline:* For fall admission, 5/1 (priority date); for spring admission, 11/1. Applications are processed on a rolling basis. *Application fee:* $45.
Expenses: Tuition, state resident: full-time $1,748. Tuition, nonresident: full-time $6,904.
Financial support: In 2001–02, 2 fellowships (averaging $5,694 per year), 14 research assistantships (averaging $5,867 per year), 23 teaching assistantships (averaging $5,607 per year) were awarded. Career-related internships or fieldwork and minority grants also available. Support available to part-time students. Financial award application deadline: 2/1.
Faculty research: Gender and racial inequality, globalization and commodity chains, biotechnology and environment, poverty and economic development, work and families. *Total annual research expenditures:* $377,502.
Dr. William B. Clifford, Head, 919-515-3180, *Fax:* 919-515-2610, *E-mail:* william_clifford@ncsu.edu.
Application contact: Dr. Jeffrey C. Leiter, Director of Graduate Programs, 919-515-9009, *Fax:* 919-515-2610, *E-mail:* gradprog@server.sasw.ncsu.edu. *Web site:* http://sasw.chass.ncsu.edu/s&a/s&ahmpg.htm

■ NORTHEASTERN UNIVERSITY

College of Arts and Sciences, Department of Sociology and Anthropology, Boston, MA 02115-5096

AWARDS MA, PhD. Part-time programs available.

Faculty: 20 full-time (7 women).
Students: 48 full-time (34 women), 4 part-time (3 women); includes 8 minority (4 African Americans, 1 Asian American or Pacific Islander, 3 Hispanic Americans), 7 international. Average age 32. 49 applicants, 41% accepted. In 2001, 8 master's, 7 doctorates awarded.
Degree requirements: For doctorate, one foreign language, thesis/dissertation, teaching tutorial.
Entrance requirements: For master's and doctorate, GRE General Test or MAT, TOEFL. *Application deadline:* For fall admission, 2/1. *Application fee:* $50.
Expenses: Tuition: Part-time $535 per credit hour. Required fees: $56. Tuition and fees vary according to program.
Financial support: In 2001–02, 14 teaching assistantships with tuition reimbursements (averaging $12,000 per year) were awarded; research assistantships with tuition reimbursements, career-related internships or fieldwork, tuition waivers (full and partial), and unspecified assistantships also available. Financial award application deadline: 3/1; financial award applicants required to submit FAFSA.
Faculty research: Political economy, development, gender, work and occupations, social movements, Latino studies.
Dr. Luis M. Falcón, Acting Chair, 617-373-4988, *Fax:* 617-373-2688.
Application contact: Chrisie Halkett, Graduate Programs Assistant, 617-373-4940, *Fax:* 617-373-2688, *E-mail:* gradsoc@neu.edu. *Web site:* http://www.casdn.neu.edu/~socant/

■ NORTHERN ARIZONA UNIVERSITY

Graduate College, College of Social and Behavioral Sciences, Department of Sociology and Social Work, Flagstaff, AZ 86011

AWARDS Applied sociology (MA). Part-time programs available.

Students: 14 full-time (11 women), 10 part-time (9 women); includes 1 minority (Asian American or Pacific Islander), 2 international. Average age 33. 13 applicants, 46% accepted, 3 enrolled. In 2001, 6 degrees awarded.
Degree requirements: For master's, thesis or internship, thesis optional.
Application deadline: For fall admission, 3/1 (priority date). Applications are processed on a rolling basis. *Application fee:* $45.
Expenses: Tuition, state resident: full-time $2,488. Tuition, nonresident: full-time $10,354.

Northern Arizona University (continued)
Financial support: In 2001–02, 8 research assistantships were awarded; teaching assistantships, career-related internships or fieldwork, Federal Work-Study, and tuition waivers (full and partial) also available. Financial award application deadline: 3/1.
Faculty research: Demography, death and dying, criminology, social policy, divorce.
Dr. Karen Pugliesi, Chair, 928-523-9208.
Application contact: Dr. Warren Lucas, Graduate Program Coordinator, 928-523-2979, *E-mail:* warren.lucas@nau.edu. *Web site:* http://www.nau.edu/sociology/

■ NORTHERN ILLINOIS UNIVERSITY

Graduate School, College of Liberal Arts and Sciences, Department of Sociology, De Kalb, IL 60115-2854

AWARDS MA. Part-time programs available.

Faculty: 17 full-time (6 women).
Students: 25 full-time (22 women), 13 part-time (8 women); includes 3 minority (1 African American, 2 Hispanic Americans), 3 international. Average age 29. 19 applicants, 89% accepted, 14 enrolled. In 2001, 7 degrees awarded.
Degree requirements: For master's, thesis optional.
Entrance requirements: For master's, GRE General Test, TOEFL, minimum GPA of 2.75; previous course work in social theory, social methods, and statistics. *Application deadline:* For fall admission, 6/1; for spring admission, 11/1. Applications are processed on a rolling basis. *Application fee:* $30.
Expenses: Tuition, state resident: full-time $5,124; part-time $148 per credit hour. Tuition, nonresident: full-time $8,666; part-time $295 per credit hour. Required fees: $51 per term.
Financial support: In 2001–02, 23 research assistantships with full tuition reimbursements, 5 teaching assistantships with full tuition reimbursements were awarded. Fellowships with full tuition reimbursements, career-related internships or fieldwork, Federal Work-Study, tuition waivers (full), and unspecified assistantships also available. Support available to part-time students.
Dr. W. William Minor, Chair, 815-753-1194, *Fax:* 815-753-6302.
Application contact: Dr. Kay Forest, Director, Graduate Studies, 815-753-6429.

■ NORTHWESTERN UNIVERSITY

The Graduate School, Interdepartmental Degree Programs and Kellogg School of Management, Program in Management and Organizations and Sociology, Evanston, IL 60208

AWARDS PhD. Program requires admission to both The Graduate School and the Kellogg Graduate School of Management.

Faculty: 38 full-time (12 women).
Students: 8 full-time (2 women); includes 2 minority (both Asian Americans or Pacific Islanders), 1 international. Average age 27. 10 applicants, 0% accepted. In 2001, 1 degree awarded.
Degree requirements: For doctorate, thesis/dissertation, comprehensive exam, registration.
Entrance requirements: For doctorate, GRE General Test, TOEFL. *Application deadline:* For fall admission, 12/31. *Application fee:* $60 ($75 for international students). Electronic applications accepted.
Expenses: Tuition: Full-time $26,526.
Financial support: In 2001–02, 8 students received support, including 2 fellowships with full tuition reimbursements available; research assistantships, teaching assistantships, career-related internships or fieldwork, institutionally sponsored loans, scholarships/grants, and health care benefits also available. Financial award application deadline: 12/31; financial award applicants required to submit FAFSA.
Faculty research: Strategic alliances and organizational competitiveness, institutional change and the information of industries, social capital and the creation of financial capital, negotiation, organizational networks, diversity.
Brian Uzzi, Director, 847-491-3470, *Fax:* 847-491-8896, *E-mail:* kellogg-phd@northwestern.edu.
Application contact: Susan Jackman, Admission Contact, 847-491-2832, *Fax:* 847-467-6717, *E-mail:* s-jackman@northwestern.edu. *Web site:* http://www.kellogg.northwestern.edu/doctoral/programs/management/

■ NORTHWESTERN UNIVERSITY

The Graduate School, Judd A. and Marjorie Weinberg College of Arts and Sciences, Department of Sociology, Evanston, IL 60208

AWARDS PhD, JD/PhD. Admissions and degrees offered through The Graduate School.

Faculty: 19 full-time (5 women), 4 part-time/adjunct (2 women).
Students: 81 full-time (42 women); includes 28 minority (19 African Americans, 5 Asian Americans or Pacific Islanders, 3 Hispanic Americans, 1 Native American), 14 international. 159 applicants, 14% accepted. In 2001, 11 doctorates awarded.
Degree requirements: For doctorate, thesis/dissertation.
Entrance requirements: For doctorate, GRE General Test, TOEFL. *Application deadline:* For fall admission, 12/31. *Application fee:* $50 ($55 for international students). Electronic applications accepted.
Expenses: Tuition: Full-time $26,526.
Financial support: In 2001–02, 9 fellowships with full tuition reimbursements (averaging $16,080 per year), 9 research assistantships with tuition reimbursements (averaging $12,843 per year), 6 teaching assistantships with full tuition reimbursements (averaging $12,843 per year) were awarded. Career-related internships or fieldwork, Federal Work-Study, institutionally sponsored loans, and scholarships/grants also available. Financial award application deadline: 12/31; financial award applicants required to submit FAFSA.
Faculty research: Sociology of culture, social organizations, social inequality, comparative/historical sociology, economic sociology.
Carol Heimer, Chair, 847-491-2698, *Fax:* 847-491-9907, *E-mail:* c-heimer@northwestern.edu.
Application contact: Leslie Allen, Graduate Secretary, 847-467-1328, *Fax:* 847-491-9907, *E-mail:* socio1@northwestern.edu. *Web site:* http://www.northwestern.edu/sociology/

■ THE OHIO STATE UNIVERSITY

Graduate School, College of Social and Behavioral Sciences, Department of Sociology, Columbus, OH 43210

AWARDS MA, PhD.

Degree requirements: For master's and doctorate, thesis/dissertation.
Entrance requirements: For master's and doctorate, GRE General Test, TOEFL.

■ OHIO UNIVERSITY

Graduate Studies, College of Arts and Sciences, Department of Sociology and Anthropology, Athens, OH 45701-2979

AWARDS Sociology (MA). Part-time programs available.

Faculty: 21 full-time (8 women), 2 part-time/adjunct (0 women).
Students: 18 full-time (16 women), 21 part-time (12 women); includes 1 minority (African American), 11 international. Average age 25. 30 applicants, 83% accepted, 13 enrolled. In 2001, 8 degrees awarded.
Degree requirements: For master's, thesis or alternative.
Entrance requirements: For master's, minimum GPA of 3.0. *Application deadline:* For fall admission, 6/1 (priority date); for spring admission, 1/1. Applications are processed on a rolling basis. *Application fee:* $30.
Expenses: Tuition, state resident: full-time $6,585. Tuition, nonresident: full-time $12,254.
Financial support: In 2001–02, 11 students received support, including 8 research assistantships with tuition reimbursements available (averaging $7,339 per year), 4 teaching assistantships (averaging $8,500 per year); career-related internships or fieldwork, Federal Work-Study, institutionally sponsored loans, scholarships/grants, and tuition waivers (full) also available. Financial award application deadline: 3/1.

Faculty research: Criminology/deviance, gender studies, inequality, social psychology.
Dr. Leon Anderson, Graduate Chair, 740-593-1377, *Fax:* 740-593-1365, *E-mail:* anderson1@ohio.edu.
Application contact: Dr. Mary Beth Krouse, Graduate Chair, 740-593-1371, *Fax:* 740-593-1365, *E-mail:* krouse@ohiou.edu. *Web site:* http://wwwas.phy.ohiou.edu/departments/soc-anth/

■ OKLAHOMA STATE UNIVERSITY

Graduate College, College of Arts and Sciences, Department of Sociology, Stillwater, OK 74078

AWARDS Corrections (MS); sociology (MS, PhD).

Faculty: 14 full-time (3 women), 4 part-time/adjunct (3 women).
Students: 14 full-time (6 women), 17 part-time (10 women); includes 7 minority (3 African Americans, 1 Hispanic American, 3 Native Americans), 3 international. Average age 33. 12 applicants, 92% accepted. In 2001, 2 master's, 1 doctorate awarded.
Degree requirements: For master's, thesis; for doctorate, 2 foreign languages, thesis/dissertation.
Entrance requirements: For master's and doctorate, GRE General Test, TOEFL. *Application deadline:* For fall admission, 7/1 (priority date). *Application fee:* $25.
Expenses: Tuition, state resident: part-time $92 per credit hour. Tuition, nonresident: part-time $297 per credit hour. Required fees: $21 per credit hour. $14 per semester. One-time fee: $20. Tuition and fees vary according to course load.
Financial support: In 2001–02, 23 students received support, including 16 research assistantships (averaging $13,087 per year), 6 teaching assistantships (averaging $8,862 per year); career-related internships or fieldwork, Federal Work-Study, and tuition waivers (partial) also available. Support available to part-time students. Financial award application deadline: 3/1.
Faculty research: Criminology/correction/legal issues; race, ethnicity, and gender in American society; environmental conflict and population problems; international comparative research; social change and social movement in American culture.
Dr. Charles K. Edgley, Head, 405-744-6104, *E-mail:* edgley@okstate.edu.

■ OLD DOMINION UNIVERSITY

College of Arts and Letters, Program in Applied Sociology, Norfolk, VA 23529

AWARDS Applied sociology (MA). Part-time and evening/weekend programs available.

Faculty: 18 full-time (10 women).
Students: 3 full-time (all women), 17 part-time (14 women); includes 8 minority (7 African Americans, 1 Asian American or Pacific Islander), 2 international. Average age 29. 38 applicants, 89% accepted. In 2001, 10 degrees awarded.
Degree requirements: For master's, thesis.
Entrance requirements: For master's, GRE General Test, minimum GPA of 2.75, 12 credits in criminal justice, sociology, or women's studies. *Application deadline:* For fall admission, 4/1 (priority date); for spring admission, 11/1. Applications are processed on a rolling basis. *Application fee:* $30.
Expenses: Tuition, state resident: part-time $202 per credit. Tuition, nonresident: part-time $534 per credit. Required fees: $76 per semester.
Financial support: In 2001–02, 6 students received support, including 1 fellowship (averaging $2,000 per year), 6 research assistantships (averaging $8,000 per year), 3 teaching assistantships (averaging $8,000 per year); career-related internships or fieldwork, scholarships/grants, and tuition waivers (partial) also available. Support available to part-time students. Financial award application deadline: 2/15; financial award applicants required to submit CSS PROFILE or FAFSA.
Faculty research: Quantitative methodology, theory, family, gender/class/race. *Total annual research expenditures:* $78,206.
Dr. Randy Gainey, Graduate Program Director, 757-683-3791, *Fax:* 757-683-5634, *E-mail:* socgpd@odu.edu. *Web site:* http://www.odu.edu/al/soc-aj/appsocma.htm

■ OUR LADY OF THE LAKE UNIVERSITY OF SAN ANTONIO

School of Education and Clinical Studies, Program in Human Sciences and Sociology, San Antonio, TX 78207-4689

AWARDS Human sciences (MA); sociology (MA). Part-time and evening/weekend programs available.

Degree requirements: For master's, thesis optional.
Entrance requirements: For master's, GRE General Test or MAT.
Faculty research: Criminal justice, health care, family, Southwest studies.

■ THE PENNSYLVANIA STATE UNIVERSITY UNIVERSITY PARK CAMPUS

Graduate School, College of Liberal Arts, Department of Sociology, Program in Sociology, State College, University Park, PA 16802-1503

AWARDS MA, PhD.

Students: 40 full-time (27 women), 6 part-time (3 women). In 2001, 10 master's, 4 doctorates awarded.
Entrance requirements: For master's and doctorate, GRE General Test. *Application fee:* $45.
Expenses: Tuition, state resident: full-time $7,882; part-time $333 per credit. Tuition, nonresident: full-time $16,142; part-time $673 per credit. Required fees: $124 per semester.
John D. McCarthy, Graduate Officer, 814-865-6222.

■ PORTLAND STATE UNIVERSITY

Graduate Studies, College of Engineering and Computer Science, Systems Science Program, Portland, OR 97207-0751

AWARDS Systems science/anthropology (PhD); systems science/business administration (PhD); systems science/civil engineering (PhD); systems science/economics (PhD); systems science/engineering management (PhD); systems science/general (PhD); systems science/mathematical sciences (PhD); systems science/mechanical engineering (PhD); systems science/psychology (PhD); systems science/sociology (PhD).

Faculty: 4 full-time (0 women).
Students: 47 full-time (19 women), 32 part-time (10 women); includes 9 minority (4 Asian Americans or Pacific Islanders, 3 Hispanic Americans, 2 Native Americans), 15 international. Average age 36. 52 applicants, 38% accepted. In 2001, 8 degrees awarded.
Degree requirements: For doctorate, variable foreign language requirement, thesis/dissertation.
Entrance requirements: For doctorate, GMAT, GRE General Test, TOEFL, minimum undergraduate GPA of 3.0. *Application deadline:* For fall admission, 2/1; for spring admission, 11/1. *Application fee:* $50.
Financial support: In 2001–02, 1 research assistantship with full tuition reimbursement (averaging $6,839 per year) was awarded; teaching assistantships with full tuition reimbursements, career-related internships or fieldwork, Federal Work-Study, and institutionally sponsored loans also available. Support available to part-time students. Financial award application deadline: 3/1; financial award applicants required to submit FAFSA.
Faculty research: Systems theory and methodology, artificial intelligence neural networks, information theory, nonlinear dynamics/chaos, modeling and simulation. *Total annual research expenditures:* $106,413.
Dr. Nancy Perrin, Director, 503-725-4960, *E-mail:* perrinn@pdx.edu.
Application contact: Dawn Kuenle, Coordinator, 503-725-4960, *E-mail:* dawn@sysc.pdx.edu. *Web site:* http://www.sysc.pdx.edu/

■ PORTLAND STATE UNIVERSITY

Graduate Studies, College of Liberal Arts and Sciences, Department of Sociology, Portland, OR 97207-0751

AWARDS MA, MS, PhD. Part-time programs available.

Faculty: 12 full-time (5 women), 1 (woman) part-time/adjunct.
Students: 24 full-time (20 women), 12 part-time (10 women); includes 3 minority (1 Asian American or Pacific Islander, 2 Hispanic Americans), 4 international. Average age 30. 21 applicants, 71% accepted. In 2001, 9 degrees awarded.
Degree requirements: For master's, variable foreign language requirement, thesis, written exam; for doctorate, thesis/dissertation.
Entrance requirements: For master's, GRE General Test, GRE Subject Test, TOEFL, minimum GPA of 3.0 in upper-division course work or 2.75 overall. *Application deadline:* For fall admission, 4/1 (priority date). Applications are processed on a rolling basis. *Application fee:* $50.
Financial support: In 2001–02, 1 research assistantship with full tuition reimbursement (averaging $6,048 per year), 2 teaching assistantships with full tuition reimbursements (averaging $6,541 per year) were awarded. Fellowships with full tuition reimbursements, career-related internships or fieldwork, Federal Work-Study, and institutionally sponsored loans also available. Support available to part-time students. Financial award application deadline: 3/1; financial award applicants required to submit FAFSA.
Faculty research: Urban sociology, gender and class, development, social change, race/ethnic/minority relations. *Total annual research expenditures:* $8,589.
Dr. Grant M. Farr, Graduate Adviser, 503-725-3926, *E-mail:* farrg@pdx.edu.
Application contact: Information Contact, 503-725-3926, *E-mail:* htgf@odin.cc.pdx.edu. *Web site:* http://www.clas.pdx.edu/sociology/

■ PRAIRIE VIEW A&M UNIVERSITY

Graduate School, College of Arts and Sciences, Division of Social Work, Behavioral and Political Science, Prairie View, TX 77446-0188

AWARDS Sociology (MA). Part-time and evening/weekend programs available.

Faculty: 5 full-time (3 women).
Students: 3 full-time (all women), 8 part-time (7 women); includes 9 minority (all African Americans). Average age 36. 13 applicants, 100% accepted, 9 enrolled. In 2001, 7 degrees awarded.
Degree requirements: For master's, thesis optional.
Entrance requirements: For master's, GRE General Test, letters of recommendation (3). *Application deadline:* For fall admission, 7/1 (priority date); for spring admission, 11/1. Applications are processed on a rolling basis. *Application fee:* $25.
Expenses: Tuition, state resident: full-time $864; part-time $48 per credit hour. Tuition, nonresident: full-time $4,716; part-time $262 per credit hour. Required fees: $1,324; $59 per credit hour. $131 per term.
Financial support: In 2001–02, 3 students received support. Institutionally sponsored loans available. Financial award application deadline: 4/1.
Dr. Walle Engedayehu, Interim Division Head, 936-857-2192, *Fax:* 926-857-2101, *E-mail:* walle_engedayehu@pvamu.edu.
Application contact: Dr. Bernita C. Berry, Coordinator, Sociology Program, 936-857-2394, *Fax:* 936-857-2299, *E-mail:* bernita_berry@pvamu.edu. *Web site:* http://www.pvamu.edu/index.php

■ PRINCETON UNIVERSITY

Graduate School, Department of Sociology, Princeton, NJ 08544-1019

AWARDS Sociology (PhD); sociology and demography (PhD).

Degree requirements: For doctorate, variable foreign language requirement, thesis/dissertation.
Entrance requirements: For doctorate, GRE General Test, GRE Subject Test (recommended), sample of written work.

■ PRINCETON UNIVERSITY

Graduate School, Program in Population Studies and Department of Sociology, Concentration in Sociology and Demography, Princeton, NJ 08544-1019

AWARDS PhD.

Degree requirements: For doctorate, thesis/dissertation.
Entrance requirements: For doctorate, GRE General Test.

■ PURDUE UNIVERSITY

Graduate School, School of Liberal Arts, Department of Sociology and Anthropology, West Lafayette, IN 47907

AWARDS Anthropology (MS, PhD); sociology (MS, PhD).

Faculty: 32 full-time (8 women), 1 (woman) part-time/adjunct.
Students: 67 full-time (45 women), 1 (woman) part-time; includes 9 minority (1 African American, 2 Asian Americans or Pacific Islanders, 6 Hispanic Americans), 12 international. Average age 32. 73 applicants, 52% accepted. In 2001, 7 master's, 4 doctorates awarded. Terminal master's awarded for partial completion of doctoral program.
Degree requirements: For doctorate, thesis/dissertation.
Entrance requirements: For master's and doctorate, GRE General Test, TOEFL, TWE. *Application deadline:* For fall admission, 12/31 (priority date). Applications are processed on a rolling basis. *Application fee:* $30. Electronic applications accepted.
Expenses: Tuition, state resident: full-time $4,164; part-time $149 per credit hour. Tuition, nonresident: full-time $13,872; part-time $458 per credit hour. Tuition and fees vary according to campus/location and program.
Financial support: In 2001–02, 39 students received support, including 4 fellowships, 4 research assistantships, 31 teaching assistantships; tuition waivers (full) also available. Support available to part-time students. Financial award application deadline: 2/15; financial award applicants required to submit FAFSA.
Faculty research: Communiversity survey project, risk, fear, constrained behavior, archaeological services.
Dr. C. C. Perrucci, Head, 765-494-4666, *Fax:* 765-496-1476.
Application contact: Dr. H. R. Potter, Graduate Committee Chair, 765-494-4712, *Fax:* 765-496-1476, *E-mail:* potter@sri.soc.purdue.edu. *Web site:* http://www.sla.purdue.edu/academic/grad.prog/

■ QUEENS COLLEGE OF THE CITY UNIVERSITY OF NEW YORK

Division of Graduate Studies, Social Science Division, Department of Sociology, Flushing, NY 11367-1597

AWARDS MA. Part-time and evening/weekend programs available.

Faculty: 24 full-time (7 women).
Students: 5 full-time (4 women), 27 part-time (22 women). 29 applicants, 86% accepted. In 2001, 11 degrees awarded.
Degree requirements: For master's, thesis optional.
Entrance requirements: For master's, TOEFL, minimum GPA of 3.0. *Application deadline:* For fall admission, 4/1; for spring admission, 11/1. Applications are processed on a rolling basis. *Application fee:* $40.
Expenses: Tuition, state resident: full-time $2,175; part-time $185 per credit. Tuition, nonresident: full-time $3,800; part-time $320 per credit. Required fees: $114; $57 per semester. Tuition and fees vary according to course load.
Financial support: Career-related internships or fieldwork, Federal Work-Study, institutionally sponsored loans, and tuition waivers (partial) available. Support available to part-time students. Financial award application deadline: 4/1; financial award applicants required to submit FAFSA.
Dr. Dean Savage, Chairperson, 718-997-2800, *E-mail:* dean_savage@qc.edu.

■ ROOSEVELT UNIVERSITY

Graduate Division, College of Arts and Sciences, School of Policy Studies, Department of Sociology, Program in Sociology, Chicago, IL 60605-1394

AWARDS MA. Part-time and evening/weekend programs available.

Degree requirements: For master's, thesis, comprehensive exam.
Application deadline: For fall admission, 6/1 (priority date). Applications are processed on a rolling basis. *Application fee:* $25 ($35 for international students).
Expenses: Tuition: Full-time $9,090; part-time $505 per credit hour. Required fees: $100 per term.
Financial support: Teaching assistantships available. Financial award application deadline: 2/15.
Faculty research: Social theory, urban sociology, gerontology, social organizations.
Application contact: Joanne Canyon-Heller, Coordinator of Graduate Admissions, 312-281-3250, *Fax:* 312-341-3523, *E-mail:* applyru@roosevelt.edu.

■ ROOSEVELT UNIVERSITY

Graduate Division, College of Arts and Sciences, School of Policy Studies, Department of Sociology, Program in Sociology-Gerontology, Chicago, IL 60605-1394

AWARDS MA. Part-time and evening/weekend programs available.

Degree requirements: For master's, thesis or alternative, comprehensive exam.
Application deadline: For fall admission, 6/1 (priority date). Applications are processed on a rolling basis. *Application fee:* $25 ($35 for international students).
Expenses: Tuition: Full-time $9,090; part-time $505 per credit hour. Required fees: $100 per term.
Financial support: Teaching assistantships available. Financial award application deadline: 2/15.
Application contact: Joanne Canyon-Heller, Coordinator of Graduate Admissions, 312-281-3250, *Fax:* 312-341-3523, *E-mail:* applyru@roosevelt.edu.

■ RUTGERS, THE STATE UNIVERSITY OF NEW JERSEY, NEW BRUNSWICK

Graduate School, Program in Sociology, New Brunswick, NJ 08901-1281

AWARDS MA, PhD. Terminal master's awarded for partial completion of doctoral program.

Degree requirements: For master's, qualifying paper; for doctorate, thesis/dissertation, qualifying exam, qualifying papers.
Entrance requirements: For master's, GRE General Test; for doctorate, GRE General Test, sample of written work.
Faculty research: Comparative-historical, sex and gender, organizations and work, culture and cognition, economics, occupations/professions, religion. *Web site:* http://sociology.rutgers.edu/

■ ST. JOHN'S UNIVERSITY

St. John's College of Liberal Arts and Sciences, Department of Sociology and Anthropology, Jamaica, NY 11439

AWARDS Sociology (MA). Part-time and evening/weekend programs available.

Faculty: 11 full-time (4 women), 7 part-time/adjunct (5 women).
Students: 4 full-time (3 women), 19 part-time (11 women); includes 8 minority (5 African Americans, 2 Asian Americans or Pacific Islanders, 1 Hispanic American), 5 international. Average age 30. 14 applicants, 64% accepted, 4 enrolled. In 2001, 6 degrees awarded.
Degree requirements: For master's, thesis optional.
Entrance requirements: For master's, 18 undergraduate credits in social services, minimum GPA of 3.0. *Application deadline:* Applications are processed on a rolling basis. *Application fee:* $40.
Expenses: Tuition: Full-time $14,520; part-time $605 per credit. Required fees: $150; $75 per term. Tuition and fees vary according to class time, course load, degree level, campus/location, program and student level.
Financial support: Research assistantships with full tuition reimbursements, career-related internships or fieldwork and scholarships/grants available. Support available to part-time students. Financial award application deadline: 3/1; financial award applicants required to submit FAFSA.
Faculty research: Education and culture, criminology, addiction and gambling, health and illness, science and technology.
Dr. Dawn Esposito, Chair, 718-990-5184, *E-mail:* esposite@stjohns.edu.
Application contact: Matthew Whelan, Director, Office of Admission, 718-990-2000, *Fax:* 718-990-2096, *E-mail:* admissions@stjohns.edu. *Web site:* http://www.stjohns.edu/

■ SAM HOUSTON STATE UNIVERSITY

College of Arts and Sciences, Department of Sociology, Huntsville, TX 77341

AWARDS Social research (MA); sociology (MA). Part-time programs available.

Students: 5 full-time (4 women), 4 part-time (3 women); includes 1 minority (African American). Average age 30. In 2001, 1 degree awarded.
Degree requirements: For master's, thesis optional.
Entrance requirements: For master's, GRE General Test, TOEFL. *Application deadline:* For fall admission, 8/1; for spring admission, 12/1. Applications are processed on a rolling basis. *Application fee:* $20.
Expenses: Tuition, area resident: Part-time $69 per credit. Tuition, state resident: full-time $1,380; part-time $69 per credit. Tuition, nonresident: full-time $5,600; part-time $280 per credit. Required fees: $748. Tuition and fees vary according to course load.
Financial support: Teaching assistantships, Federal Work-Study available. Support available to part-time students. Financial award application deadline: 5/31; financial award applicants required to submit FAFSA.
Faculty research: Feminist approach to technology and nursing, gender differences in Japanese prisons, economic development and gender inequalities, social structural correlates of homelessness in Texas counties.
Dr. Alessandro Bonanno, Chair, 936-294-1512.
Application contact: Dr. David Bailey, Graduate Adviser, 936-294-1519, *Fax:* 936-294-3573. *Web site:* http://www/shsu.edu/~soc_www/

■ SAN DIEGO STATE UNIVERSITY

Graduate and Research Affairs, College of Arts and Letters, Department of Sociology, San Diego, CA 92182

AWARDS MA.

Entrance requirements: For master's, GRE General Test, TOEFL.
Faculty research: The homeless and mentally ill, medical data relating to the homeless.

■ SAN JOSE STATE UNIVERSITY

Graduate Studies, College of Social Sciences, Department of Sociology, San Jose, CA 95192-0001

AWARDS Criminology (MA); sociology (MA). Part-time and evening/weekend programs available.

Faculty: 19 full-time (0 women), 6 part-time/adjunct (3 women).
Students: 16 full-time (13 women), 28 part-time (22 women); includes 21 minority (4 African Americans, 6 Asian Americans or Pacific Islanders, 11 Hispanic Americans), 2 international. Average age 31. 29 applicants, 76% accepted. In 2001, 6 degrees awarded.
Degree requirements: For master's, comprehensive exams or thesis.
Entrance requirements: For master's, GRE Subject Test, minimum GPA of 3.0. *Application deadline:* For fall admission,

San Jose State University (continued)
6/29; for spring admission, 11/30. Applications are processed on a rolling basis. *Application fee:* $59. Electronic applications accepted.
Expenses: Tuition, nonresident: part-time $246 per unit. Required fees: $678 per semester. Tuition and fees vary according to course load.
Financial support: In 2001–02, 1 teaching assistantship was awarded; career-related internships or fieldwork, Federal Work-Study, and institutionally sponsored loans also available. Financial award application deadline: 3/1; financial award applicants required to submit FAFSA.
Faculty research: Theory construction, sexuality, sociology of the media, social causes of stress, social change.
Dr. Carol Ray, Chair, 408-924-5320, *Fax:* 408-924-5322.
Application contact: Yoko Baba, Graduate Coordinator, 408-924-5334.

■ SOUTHERN CONNECTICUT STATE UNIVERSITY

School of Graduate Studies, School of Arts and Sciences, Department of Sociology, New Haven, CT 06515-1355

AWARDS MS. Part-time and evening/weekend programs available.

Faculty: 7 full-time (2 women).
Students: 4 full-time (3 women), 14 part-time (9 women); includes 3 minority (2 African Americans, 1 Hispanic American). 41 applicants, 32% accepted. In 2001, 14 degrees awarded.
Degree requirements: For master's, thesis or alternative.
Entrance requirements: For master's, interview. *Application deadline:* For fall admission, 7/15 (priority date). Applications are processed on a rolling basis. *Application fee:* $40.
Financial support: Application deadline: 4/15.
Dr. Marie Selvaggio, Chairperson, 203-392-5683, *Fax:* 203-392-5670, *E-mail:* selvaggio@southernct.edu.
Application contact: Dr. Debra Emmelman, Graduate Coordinator, 203-392-5686, *Fax:* 203-392-5670, *E-mail:* emmelman@southernct.edu. *Web site:* http://www.southernct.edu

■ SOUTHERN ILLINOIS UNIVERSITY CARBONDALE

Graduate School, College of Liberal Arts, Department of Sociology, Carbondale, IL 62901-6806

AWARDS MA, PhD. Part-time programs available.

Faculty: 7 full-time (3 women), 1 (woman) part-time/adjunct.
Students: 36 full-time (19 women), 31 part-time (14 women); includes 6 minority (5 African Americans, 1 Native American), 12 international. Average age 32. 27 applicants, 63% accepted. In 2001, 2 master's, 3 doctorates awarded.
Degree requirements: For master's and doctorate, thesis/dissertation.
Entrance requirements: For master's, TOEFL, minimum GPA of 2.7; for doctorate, TOEFL, minimum GPA of 3.25. *Application deadline:* Applications are processed on a rolling basis. *Application fee:* $0.
Expenses: Tuition, state resident: full-time $3,794; part-time $154 per hour. Tuition, nonresident: full-time $6,566; part-time $308 per hour. Required fees: $277 per hour.
Financial support: In 2001–02, 33 students received support, including 1 fellowship with full tuition reimbursement available, 2 research assistantships with full tuition reimbursements available, 19 teaching assistantships with full tuition reimbursements available; Federal Work-Study, institutionally sponsored loans, and tuition waivers (full) also available. Support available to part-time students. Financial award application deadline: 2/10.
Faculty research: Deviance, family, social stratification, social change, theory methodology, culture. *Total annual research expenditures:* $10,000.
Dr. Robert Benford, Chair, 618-453-7614, *Fax:* 618-453-3253.
Application contact: Dr. Thomas Burger, Director of Graduate Studies, 618-453-2494, *Fax:* 618-453-3253, *E-mail:* sociology@siu.edu. *Web site:* http://www.siu.edu/~socio/

Find an in-depth description at www.petersons.com/gradchannel.

■ SOUTHERN ILLINOIS UNIVERSITY EDWARDSVILLE

Graduate Studies and Research, College of Arts and Sciences, Department of Sociology, Edwardsville, IL 62026-0001

AWARDS MA. Part-time programs available.

Students: 6 full-time (4 women), 18 part-time (14 women); includes 5 minority (4 African Americans, 1 Hispanic American), 3 international. Average age 33. 23 applicants, 83% accepted, 8 enrolled. In 2001, 3 degrees awarded.
Degree requirements: For master's, final exam, internship or thesis. *Median time to degree:* Master's–2.5 years full-time, 4 years part-time.
Entrance requirements: For master's, TOEFL. *Application deadline:* For fall admission, 7/24. *Application fee:* $25.
Expenses: Tuition, state resident: full-time $2,712; part-time $113 per credit hour. Tuition, nonresident: full-time $5,424; part-time $226 per credit hour. Required fees: $250; $125 per term. Tuition and fees vary according to course load, campus/location and reciprocity agreements.
Financial support: Fellowships with full tuition reimbursements, research assistantships with full tuition reimbursements, teaching assistantships with full tuition reimbursements, Federal Work-Study, institutionally sponsored loans, and unspecified assistantships available. Support available to part-time students. Financial award application deadline: 3/1.
Dr. Hugh Barlow, Chair, 618-650-3713, *E-mail:* hbarlow@siue.edu.
Application contact: Dr. Warren Handel, Graduate Director, 618-650-2945, *E-mail:* whandel@siue.edu.

■ SOUTHERN UNIVERSITY AND AGRICULTURAL AND MECHANICAL COLLEGE

Graduate School, College of Arts and Humanities, Department of Sociology, Baton Rouge, LA 70813

AWARDS Social sciences (MA). Part-time programs available.

Students: Average age 25.
Degree requirements: For master's, thesis.
Entrance requirements: For master's, GRE General Test, TOEFL. *Application deadline:* For fall admission, 6/1 (priority date); for spring admission, 11/1. Applications are processed on a rolling basis. *Application fee:* $25.
Expenses: Tuition, state resident: full-time $1,323. Tuition, nonresident: full-time $2,583. International tuition: $2,613 full-time. Tuition and fees vary according to program.
Financial support: In 2001–02, research assistantships (averaging $7,000 per year); scholarships/grants and unspecified assistantships also available. Financial award application deadline: 4/15; financial award applicants required to submit FAFSA. *Total annual research expenditures:* $230,000.
Dr. Christopher N. Hunte, Interim Chairperson, 225-771-5095, *E-mail:* drhunte@aol.com.

■ SOUTHWEST TEXAS STATE UNIVERSITY

Graduate School, College of Liberal Arts, Department of Sociology, San Marcos, TX 78666

AWARDS MA. Part-time and evening/weekend programs available.

Faculty: 7 full-time (5 women), 1 (woman) part-time/adjunct.
Students: 11 full-time (all women), 24 part-time (15 women); includes 10 minority (3 African Americans, 1 Asian American or Pacific Islander, 6 Hispanic Americans), 1 international. Average age 30. 10 applicants, 80% accepted, 7 enrolled. In 2001, 7 degrees awarded.
Degree requirements: For master's, essay or thesis.

Entrance requirements: For master's, GRE General Test, TOEFL, minimum GPA of 3.0 in last 60 hours. *Application deadline:* For fall admission, 6/15 (priority date); for spring admission, 10/15 (priority date). Applications are processed on a rolling basis. *Application fee:* $40 ($90 for international students).
Expenses: Tuition, state resident: full-time $1,512; part-time $84 per credit hour. Tuition, nonresident: full-time $5,310; part-time $295 per credit hour. Required fees: $864; $29 per credit hour. $195 per term. Full-time tuition and fees vary according to course load.
Financial support: In 2001–02, 6 teaching assistantships (averaging $8,723 per year) were awarded; research assistantships, career-related internships or fieldwork, Federal Work-Study, and institutionally sponsored loans also available. Support available to part-time students. Financial award application deadline: 4/1; financial award applicants required to submit FAFSA.
Faculty research: Substance abuse, ethnic and gender inequality, jury behavior, Native American women.
Dr. Susan Day, Chair, 512-245-2113, *Fax:* 512-245-8362, *E-mail:* sd01@swt.edu. *Web site:* http://www.soci.swt.edu/

■ SOUTHWEST TEXAS STATE UNIVERSITY

Graduate School, Interdisciplinary Studies Program in Applied Sociology, San Marcos, TX 78666

AWARDS MAIS. Part-time and evening/weekend programs available.

Students: Average age 51.
Degree requirements: For master's, comprehensive exam.
Application deadline: For fall admission, 6/15 (priority date); for spring admission, 10/15 (priority date). Applications are processed on a rolling basis. *Application fee:* $40 ($90 for international students).
Expenses: Tuition, state resident: full-time $1,512; part-time $84 per credit hour. Tuition, nonresident: full-time $5,310; part-time $295 per credit hour. Required fees: $864; $29 per credit hour. $195 per term. Full-time tuition and fees vary according to course load.
Financial support: Application deadline: 4/1.
Dr. Audwin Anderson, Head, 512-245-7606.

■ STANFORD UNIVERSITY

School of Humanities and Sciences, Department of Sociology, Stanford, CA 94305-9991

AWARDS PhD.

Faculty: 13 full-time (5 women).
Students: 74 full-time (36 women), 18 part-time (5 women); includes 32 minority (11 African Americans, 17 Asian Americans or Pacific Islanders, 4 Hispanic Americans), 25 international. Average age 26. 109 applicants, 17% accepted. In 2001, 12 doctorates awarded.
Degree requirements: For doctorate, thesis/dissertation, oral exam.
Entrance requirements: For doctorate, GRE General Test, TOEFL. *Application deadline:* For fall admission, 1/5. *Application fee:* $65 ($80 for international students). Electronic applications accepted.
Andrew Walder, Chair, 650-723-3956, *Fax:* 650-725-6471, *E-mail:* walder@stanford.edu.
Application contact: Graduate Administrator, 650-723-1205, *Fax:* 650-725-6471. *Web site:* http://www.stanford.edu/dept/soc/

■ STATE UNIVERSITY OF NEW YORK AT ALBANY

College of Arts and Sciences, Department of Communication, Albany, NY 12222-0001

AWARDS Communication (MA); sociology and communication (PhD). Part-time and evening/weekend programs available.

Students: 19 full-time (12 women), 30 part-time (19 women); includes 4 minority (2 African Americans, 1 Asian American or Pacific Islander, 1 Hispanic American), 8 international. Average age 30. 55 applicants, 71% accepted. In 2001, 9 degrees awarded.
Degree requirements: For master's, thesis or alternative, comprehensive exam; for doctorate, thesis/dissertation, comprehensive exam.
Entrance requirements: For master's, TOEFL, minimum GPA of 3.0; for doctorate, GRE, TOEFL, minimum GPA of 3.0. *Application deadline:* For fall admission, 8/1. *Application fee:* $50.
Expenses: Tuition, state resident: full-time $2,550; part-time $213 per credit. Tuition, nonresident: full-time $4,208; part-time $351 per credit. Required fees: $470; $470 per year.
Financial support: Fellowships, teaching assistantships, career-related internships or fieldwork and institutionally sponsored loans available. Financial award application deadline: 3/1.
Faculty research: Language and social interaction, campaign communication, media agenda-setting, high-speed management, organizational boundary-spanning.
Teresa Harrison, Chair, 518-442-4870.

■ STATE UNIVERSITY OF NEW YORK AT ALBANY

College of Arts and Sciences, Department of Sociology, Albany, NY 12222-0001

AWARDS Demography (Certificate); sociology (MA, PhD); urban policy (Certificate). Evening/weekend programs available.

Students: 46 full-time (19 women), 59 part-time (31 women); includes 13 minority (3 African Americans, 2 Asian Americans or Pacific Islanders, 8 Hispanic Americans), 13 international. Average age 31. 68 applicants, 56% accepted. In 2001, 4 master's, 7 doctorates, 1 other advanced degree awarded. Terminal master's awarded for partial completion of doctoral program.
Degree requirements: For master's, thesis; for doctorate, thesis/dissertation, 2 specialization exams, research tool.
Entrance requirements: For master's and doctorate, GRE General Test. *Application deadline:* For fall admission, 6/1 (priority date). Applications are processed on a rolling basis. *Application fee:* $50.
Expenses: Tuition, state resident: full-time $2,550; part-time $213 per credit. Tuition, nonresident: full-time $4,208; part-time $351 per credit. Required fees: $470; $470 per year.
Financial support: Fellowships, research assistantships, teaching assistantships, career-related internships or fieldwork and Federal Work-Study available. Financial award application deadline: 3/15.
Faculty research: Gender and equality, crime and deviance, aging, work and organizations.
Dr. Steve Messner, Chair, 518-442-4666.
Application contact: Richard W. Lockman, Graduate Committee Chair, 518-442-4682.

■ STATE UNIVERSITY OF NEW YORK AT BINGHAMTON

Graduate School, School of Arts and Sciences, Department of Sociology, Binghamton, NY 13902-6000

AWARDS MA, PhD.

Faculty: 13 full-time (4 women), 11 part-time/adjunct (4 women).
Students: 46 full-time (20 women), 56 part-time (23 women); includes 21 minority (5 African Americans, 5 Asian Americans or Pacific Islanders, 11 Hispanic Americans), 42 international. Average age 37. 46 applicants, 39% accepted, 7 enrolled. In 2001, 4 master's, 9 doctorates awarded. Terminal master's awarded for partial completion of doctoral program.
Degree requirements: For doctorate, thesis/dissertation.
Entrance requirements: For master's and doctorate, GRE General Test, GRE Subject Test, TOEFL. *Application deadline:* For fall admission, 4/15 (priority date); for spring admission, 11/1. Applications are processed on a rolling basis. Electronic applications accepted.
Expenses: Tuition, state resident: full-time $5,100; part-time $213 per credit. Tuition, nonresident: full-time $8,416; part-time $351 per credit. Required fees: $811.
Financial support: In 2001–02, 33 students received support, including 7 fellowships with full tuition reimbursements

State University of New York at Binghamton (continued)
available (averaging $7,558 per year), 20 teaching assistantships with full tuition reimbursements available (averaging $8,510 per year); research assistantships with full tuition reimbursements available, career-related internships or fieldwork, Federal Work-Study, institutionally sponsored loans, and unspecified assistantships also available. Support available to part-time students. Financial award application deadline: 2/15.
Dr. Dale Tomich, Chairperson, 607-777-2216.

■ STATE UNIVERSITY OF NEW YORK AT NEW PALTZ

Graduate School, Faculty of Liberal Arts and Sciences, Department of Sociology, New Paltz, NY 12561

AWARDS MA, MA/MSW.

Students: 3 full-time (2 women), 4 part-time (2 women). In 2001, 11 degrees awarded.
Degree requirements: For master's, thesis (for some programs), comprehensive exam.
Entrance requirements: For master's, GRE General Test, minimum GPA of 3.0. *Application deadline:* For fall admission, 3/15 (priority date). Applications are processed on a rolling basis. *Application fee:* $50.
Expenses: Tuition, state resident: full-time $5,100; part-time $213 per credit. Tuition, nonresident: full-time $8,416; part-time $351 per credit. Required fees: $624; $21 per credit. $60 per semester.
Financial support: Career-related internships or fieldwork, Federal Work-Study, and institutionally sponsored loans available.
Dr. Hal Jacobs, Chairman, 845-257-3505.

■ STATE UNIVERSITY OF NEW YORK INSTITUTE OF TECHNOLOGY AT UTICA/ROME

School of Arts and Sciences, Program in Applied Sociology, Utica, NY 13504-3050

AWARDS MS. Part-time and evening/weekend programs available.

Faculty: 5 full-time (1 woman).
Students: 7 applicants, 71% accepted.
Degree requirements: For master's, thesis or project.
Entrance requirements: For master's, minimum GPA of 3.0, letters of recommendation (3). *Application deadline:* For fall admission, 6/15 (priority date). Applications are processed on a rolling basis. *Application fee:* $50.
Expenses: Tuition, state resident: full-time $5,100; part-time $213 per credit hour. Tuition, nonresident: full-time $8,416; part-time $351 per credit hour. Required fees: $525; $21 per credit hour. Tuition and fees vary according to course load.
Financial support: Federal Work-Study, scholarships/grants, and unspecified assistantships available. Financial award applicants required to submit FAFSA.
Faculty research: Health promotion, creation of trust and at-risk youth, use of interactive multimedia in teaching criminology, drug education.
Dr. Linda Weber, Associate Professor, 315-792-7323, *Fax:* 315-792-7503, *E-mail:* flrw@sunyit.edu.
Application contact: Marybeth Lyons, Director of Admissions, 315-792-7500, *Fax:* 315-792-7837, *E-mail:* smbl@sunyit.edu.

■ STATE UNIVERSITY OF WEST GEORGIA

Graduate School, College of Arts and Sciences, Department of Sociology, Anthropology, and Criminology, Program of Sociology, Carrollton, GA 30118

AWARDS MA. Part-time programs available.

Faculty: 14 full-time (7 women).
Students: 6 full-time (3 women), 4 part-time (all women); includes 3 minority (all African Americans). Average age 35. 3 applicants, 100% accepted, 3 enrolled. In 2001, 3 degrees awarded.
Degree requirements: For master's, one foreign language, thesis (for some programs), comprehensive exam (for some programs), registration.
Entrance requirements: For master's, GRE, references, intellectual biography, minimum GPA of 2.5. *Application deadline:* For fall admission, 8/2 (priority date); for spring admission, 12/20. *Application fee:* $20. Electronic applications accepted.
Expenses: Tuition, state resident: full-time $232; part-time $97 per credit hour. Tuition, nonresident: full-time $928; part-time $387 per credit hour. Required fees: $536; $14 per credit. $100 per semester.
Financial support: Research assistantships with tuition reimbursements, career-related internships or fieldwork, scholarships/grants, and unspecified assistantships available. Support available to part-time students. Financial award applicants required to submit FAFSA.
Faculty research: Women studies, criminology, resources and methods.
Application contact: Dr. Jack O. Jenkins, Dean, Graduate School, 770-836-6419, *Fax:* 770-836-2301, *E-mail:* jjenkins@westga.edu.

■ STONY BROOK UNIVERSITY, STATE UNIVERSITY OF NEW YORK

Graduate School, College of Arts and Sciences, Department of Sociology, Stony Brook, NY 11794

AWARDS MA, PhD.

Faculty: 20 full-time (6 women).
Students: 37 full-time (22 women), 22 part-time (16 women); includes 10 minority (5 African Americans, 2 Asian Americans or Pacific Islanders, 3 Hispanic Americans), 15 international. Average age 34. 60 applicants, 40% accepted. In 2001, 1 master's, 6 doctorates awarded.
Degree requirements: For doctorate, thesis/dissertation, comprehensive exam or professional papers, field exam, teaching practicum.
Entrance requirements: For doctorate, GRE General Test, TOEFL, minimum GPA of 3.0. *Application deadline:* For fall admission, 1/15. *Application fee:* $50.
Expenses: Tuition, state resident: full-time $5,100; part-time $213 per credit. Tuition, nonresident: full-time $8,416; part-time $351 per credit. Required fees: $496.
Financial support: In 2001–02, 3 research assistantships, 34 teaching assistantships were awarded.
Faculty research: Deviant behavior, history of sociology/social thought, marriage and family sociology, political sociology. *Total annual research expenditures:* $180,350.
Dr. Norman Goodman, Interim Chair, 631-632-7700.
Application contact: Dr. Ivan Chase, Director, 631-632-7753, *E-mail:* ichase@notes.cc.sunysb.edu. *Web site:* http://www.sunysb.edu/sociology/

Find an in-depth description at www.petersons.com/gradchannel.

■ SYRACUSE UNIVERSITY

Graduate School, Maxwell School of Citizenship and Public Affairs, Department of Sociology, Syracuse, NY 13244-0003

AWARDS MA, PhD.

Faculty: 12.
Students: 25 full-time (21 women), 4 part-time (2 women); includes 10 minority (3 African Americans, 6 Asian Americans or Pacific Islanders, 1 Native American), 6 international. Average age 31. 38 applicants. In 2001, 9 master's, 3 doctorates awarded.
Degree requirements: For master's, thesis optional; for doctorate, thesis/dissertation.
Entrance requirements: For master's and doctorate, GRE General Test. *Application deadline:* Applications are processed on a rolling basis. *Application fee:* $50.
Expenses: Tuition: Full-time $15,528; part-time $647 per credit. Required fees: $420; $38 per term. Tuition and fees vary according to program.
Financial support: In 2001–02, 1 fellowship with full tuition reimbursement, 12 teaching assistantships with full tuition reimbursements (averaging $10,600 per year) were awarded. Research assistantships, Federal Work-Study, health care benefits, tuition waivers (full and partial),

and unspecified assistantships also available. Financial award application deadline: 1/1.
Faculty research: Qualitative methods and feminist methods, inequality studies, aging and the life course.
Julia Loughlin, Chair, 315-443-2347, *Fax:* 315-443-4597, *E-mail:* sociology@maxwell.syr.edu.
Application contact: Madonna Harrington-Meyer, Graduate Director, 315-443-9805, *E-mail:* mhm@maxwell.syr.edu. *Web site:* http://www.maxwell.syr.edu/soc/

Find an in-depth description at www.petersons.com/gradchannel.

■ TEACHERS COLLEGE COLUMBIA UNIVERSITY

Graduate Faculty of Education, Department of Human Development, Program in Sociology and Education, New York, NY 10027-6696

AWARDS Ed M, MA, Ed D, PhD.

Degree requirements: For doctorate, thesis/dissertation.
Entrance requirements: For master's, GRE (Ed M); for doctorate, GRE.
Expenses: Tuition: Full-time $19,080; part-time $780 per unit. Required fees: $170 per semester.
Faculty research: Stratification, race and evaluation, desegregation of schools and communities, quantitative research.

■ TEMPLE UNIVERSITY

Graduate School, College of Liberal Arts, Department of Sociology, Philadelphia, PA 19122-6096

AWARDS MA, PhD. Part-time and evening/weekend programs available. Terminal master's awarded for partial completion of doctoral program.

Degree requirements: For doctorate, thesis/dissertation.
Entrance requirements: For master's and doctorate, GRE General Test, TOEFL, minimum GPA of 3.0 during previous 2 years, 2.8 overall. Electronic applications accepted.
Expenses: Tuition, state resident: full-time $8,487; part-time $369 per credit hour. Tuition, nonresident: full-time $12,282; part-time $534 per credit hour. Required fees: $350. Tuition and fees vary according to course load, program and reciprocity agreements.
Faculty research: International development, race-ethnicity-gender inequality, urban structure, political economy. *Web site:* http://www.temple.edu/sociology/

■ TEXAS A&M INTERNATIONAL UNIVERSITY

Division of Graduate Studies, College of Arts and Humanities, Department of Psychology and Sociology, Laredo, TX 78041-1900

AWARDS Counseling psychology (MA); sociology (MA).

Students: 5 full-time (2 women), 30 part-time (21 women); includes 33 minority (all Hispanic Americans), 1 international. In 2001, 15 degrees awarded.
Degree requirements: For master's, thesis (for some programs).
Entrance requirements: For master's, GRE General Test. *Application deadline:* For fall admission, 7/15 (priority date); for spring admission, 11/12. Applications are processed on a rolling basis. *Application fee:* $0.
Expenses: Tuition, state resident: full-time $1,536; part-time $64 per credit. Tuition, nonresident: full-time $6,600; part-time $275 per credit. Required fees: $594; $9 per credit. $33 per term. One-time fee: $10 part-time.
Financial support: Application deadline: 11/1.
Dr. Marion Aguila, Chair, 956-326-2644, *Fax:* 956-326-2459, *E-mail:* maguilar@tamiu.edu.
Application contact: Veronica Gonzalez, Director of Enrollment Management and School Relations, 956-326-2270, *Fax:* 956-326-2269, *E-mail:* enroll@tamiu.edu.

■ TEXAS A&M UNIVERSITY

College of Liberal Arts, Department of Sociology, College Station, TX 77843

AWARDS MS, PhD.

Faculty: 31.
Students: 61 (35 women). Average age 32.
Degree requirements: For master's, thesis or alternative; for doctorate, thesis/dissertation.
Entrance requirements: For master's and doctorate, GRE General Test, TOEFL. *Application deadline:* For fall admission, 1/15 (priority date); for winter admission, 11/1 (priority date). Applications are processed on a rolling basis. *Application fee:* $50 ($75 for international students). Electronic applications accepted.
Expenses: Tuition, state resident: full-time $11,872. Tuition, nonresident: full-time $17,892.
Financial support: In 2001–02, fellowships (averaging $12,000 per year), research assistantships (averaging $9,795 per year), teaching assistantships (averaging $9,795 per year) were awarded. Institutionally sponsored loans and unspecified assistantships also available. Financial award application deadline: 1/15; financial award applicants required to submit FAFSA.
Faculty research: Demography and human ecology; ethnicity; law, deviance, and social control; social organization; rural sociology, culture.
Dr. Rogelio Saenz, Head, 979-845-4944, *Fax:* 979-862-4057, *E-mail:* rsaenz@unix.tamu.edu.
Application contact: Dr. Kathryn Henderson, Graduate Advisor, 979-845-9706, *Fax:* 979-862-4057, *E-mail:* hendrsn@acs.tamu.edu. *Web site:* http://sociweb.tamu.edu/

Find an in-depth description at www.petersons.com/gradchannel.

■ TEXAS A&M UNIVERSITY–COMMERCE

Graduate School, College of Arts and Sciences, Department of Sociology and Criminal Justice, Commerce, TX 75429-3011

AWARDS Sociology (MA, MS). Part-time programs available.

Faculty: 2 full-time (0 women).
Students: 14 full-time (9 women), 11 part-time (8 women); includes 9 minority (8 African Americans, 1 Native American), 1 international. Average age 36. 3 applicants, 100% accepted. In 2001, 3 degrees awarded.
Degree requirements: For master's, thesis (for some programs), comprehensive exam.
Entrance requirements: For master's, GRE General Test. *Application deadline:* For fall admission, 6/1 (priority date); for spring admission, 11/1 (priority date). Applications are processed on a rolling basis. *Application fee:* $0 ($25 for international students).
Expenses: Tuition, state resident: full-time $2,221. International tuition: $7,285 full-time.
Financial support: In 2001–02, research assistantships (averaging $7,875 per year), teaching assistantships (averaging $7,875 per year) were awarded. Federal Work-Study, institutionally sponsored loans, and scholarships/grants also available. Financial award application deadline: 5/1; financial award applicants required to submit FAFSA.
Faculty research: Marriage and family, drugs and society, criminal justice, delinquency.
Dr. Raghu Naath Singh, Interim Head, 903-886-5332, *Fax:* 903-886-5330, *E-mail:* raghu_singh@tamu-commerce.edu.
Application contact: Tammi Higginbotham, Graduate Admissions Adviser, 843-886-5167, *Fax:* 843-886-5165, *E-mail:* tammi_higginbotham@tamu-commerce.edu. *Web site:* http://www.tamu-commerce.edu/coas/

■ TEXAS A&M UNIVERSITY–KINGSVILLE

College of Graduate Studies, College of Arts and Sciences, Department of Psychology and Sociology, Kingsville, TX 78363

AWARDS Gerontology (MS); psychology (MA, MS); sociology (MA, MS). Part-time and evening/weekend programs available.

Faculty: 8 full-time (2 women).
Students: 23 full-time (19 women), 40 part-time (33 women); includes 41 minority (3 African Americans, 1 Asian American or Pacific Islander, 37 Hispanic Americans), 2 international. Average age 35. In 2001, 18 degrees awarded.
Degree requirements: For master's, thesis or alternative, comprehensive exam.
Entrance requirements: For master's, GRE General Test, TOEFL, minimum GPA of 2.5. *Application deadline:* For fall admission, 6/1; for spring admission, 11/15. Applications are processed on a rolling basis. *Application fee:* $15 ($25 for international students).
Expenses: Tuition, state resident: part-time $42 per hour. Tuition, nonresident: part-time $253 per hour. Required fees: $56 per hour. One-time fee: $46 part-time. Tuition and fees vary according to program.
Financial support: Federal Work-Study and institutionally sponsored loans available. Support available to part-time students. Financial award application deadline: 5/15.
Faculty research: Hispanic female voting behavior, attitudes toward criminal justice, immigration of aged into south Texas, folk medicine. *Total annual research expenditures:* $50,000.
Dr. Dorothy Pace, Graduate Coordinator, 361-593-2701, *Fax:* 361-593-3107.

■ TEXAS SOUTHERN UNIVERSITY

Graduate School, College of Liberal Arts and Behavioral Sciences, Department of Sociology, Houston, TX 77004-4584

AWARDS MA. Part-time and evening/weekend programs available.

Faculty: 5 full-time (3 women).
Students: 15 full-time (9 women), 21 part-time (15 women); includes 35 minority (all African Americans), 1 international. Average age 26. 8 applicants, 100% accepted. In 2001, 15 degrees awarded.
Degree requirements: For master's, thesis, comprehensive exam.
Entrance requirements: For master's, GRE General Test, TOEFL, minimum GPA of 2.5. *Application deadline:* For fall admission, 7/15 (priority date). Applications are processed on a rolling basis. *Application fee:* $35 ($75 for international students).
Expenses: Tuition, state resident: full-time $1,188. Tuition, nonresident: full-time $4,644. Required fees: $900. Tuition and fees vary according to degree level.
Financial support: Teaching assistantships, career-related internships or fieldwork, Federal Work-Study, and institutionally sponsored loans available. Financial award application deadline: 5/1.
Faculty research: Sociocultural systems, ethnic and regional studies, community sociology.
Dr. Betty Cox, Head, 713-313-7250.

■ TEXAS TECH UNIVERSITY

Graduate School, College of Arts and Sciences, Department of Sociology, Anthropology and Social Work, Lubbock, TX 79409

AWARDS Anthropology (MA); sociology (MA). Part-time programs available.

Faculty: 13 full-time (3 women), 2 part-time/adjunct (1 woman).
Students: 15 full-time (9 women), 14 part-time (9 women); includes 4 minority (1 African American, 2 Asian Americans or Pacific Islanders, 1 Hispanic American), 1 international. Average age 30. 15 applicants, 47% accepted, 4 enrolled. In 2001, 9 degrees awarded.
Degree requirements: For master's, one foreign language.
Entrance requirements: For master's, GRE General Test. *Application deadline:* Applications are processed on a rolling basis. *Application fee:* $25 ($50 for international students). Electronic applications accepted.
Expenses: Tuition, state resident: full-time $1,926; part-time $107 per credit hour. Tuition, nonresident: full-time $5,724; part-time $318 per credit hour. Required fees: $779; $737 per year. Tuition and fees vary according to course level, course load and program.
Financial support: In 2001–02, 15 students received support, including 2 research assistantships with partial tuition reimbursements available (averaging $9,250 per year), 13 teaching assistantships with partial tuition reimbursements available (averaging $9,308 per year); fellowships, Federal Work-Study and institutionally sponsored loans also available. Support available to part-time students. Financial award application deadline: 5/1; financial award applicants required to submit FAFSA.
Faculty research: Minority relations, social psychology, Texas and Southwest archaeology, Latin America, Native Americans. *Total annual research expenditures:* $29,331.
Dr. Doyle Paul Johnson, Chair, 806-742-2401, *Fax:* 806-742-1088.
Application contact: Graduate Adviser, 806-742-2401, *Fax:* 806-742-1088. *Web site:* http://www.ttu.edu/sasw/

■ TEXAS WOMAN'S UNIVERSITY

Graduate Studies and Research, College of Arts and Sciences, Department of Sociology and Social Work, Denton, TX 76201

AWARDS Sociology (MA, PhD); women's studies (MA). Evening/weekend programs available.

Faculty: 8 full-time (4 women), 2 part-time/adjunct (both women).
Students: 15 full-time (all women), 22 part-time (19 women); includes 11 minority (8 African Americans, 3 Hispanic Americans), 2 international. Average age 36. 9 applicants, 100% accepted. In 2001, 1 master's, 6 doctorates awarded. Terminal master's awarded for partial completion of doctoral program.
Degree requirements: For master's, thesis or professional paper; for doctorate, one foreign language, thesis/dissertation.
Entrance requirements: For master's, GRE General Test, minimum GPA of 3.0; for doctorate, GRE General Test, minimum GPA of 3.5, 12-18 hours prior work in sociology. *Application deadline:* For fall admission, 8/15 (priority date). Applications are processed on a rolling basis. *Application fee:* $30.
Expenses: Tuition, state resident: part-time $90 per semester hour. Tuition, nonresident: part-time $303 per semester hour. Required fees: $24 per credit hour. $79 per semester.
Financial support: In 2001–02, 18 students received support, including 1 research assistantship (averaging $7,245 per year), 13 teaching assistantships (averaging $7,245 per year); career-related internships or fieldwork, Federal Work-Study, and scholarships/grants also available. Financial award application deadline: 4/1.
Dr. Joyce E. Williams, Chair, 940-898-2052, *Fax:* 940-898-2067, *E-mail:* jwilliams@twu.edu.
Application contact: Dr. Lisa Garza, Graduate Adviser, 940-898-2058, *Fax:* 940-898-2067, *E-mail:* f_zgarza@twu.edu. *Web site:* http://www.twu.edu/as/socws/

■ TULANE UNIVERSITY

Graduate School, Department of Sociology, New Orleans, LA 70118-5669

AWARDS MA, MAD, PhD.

Degree requirements: For master's, thesis; for doctorate, thesis/dissertation, preliminary exams.
Entrance requirements: For master's, GRE General Test, TSE, minimum B average in undergraduate course work; for doctorate, GRE General Test, TSE.
Expenses: Tuition: Full-time $24,675. Required fees: $2,210.

■ UNIVERSITY AT BUFFALO, THE STATE UNIVERSITY OF NEW YORK

Graduate School, College of Arts and Sciences, Department of Sociology, Buffalo, NY 14260

AWARDS MA, PhD. Part-time programs available.

Faculty: 10 full-time (3 women).
Students: 35 full-time (21 women), 15 part-time (8 women). Average age 34. 34 applicants, 53% accepted, 10 enrolled. In 2001, 6 master's, 2 doctorates awarded. Terminal master's awarded for partial completion of doctoral program.
Degree requirements: For master's, project or thesis; for doctorate, thesis/dissertation, qualifying paper. *Median time to degree:* Master's–2 years full-time, 3 years part-time; doctorate–4 years full-time, 5 years part-time.
Entrance requirements: For master's and doctorate, GRE General Test, TOEFL. *Application deadline:* For fall admission, 1/1 (priority date). Applications are processed on a rolling basis. *Application fee:* $35. Electronic applications accepted.
Expenses: Tuition, state resident: full-time $6,118. Tuition, nonresident: full-time $9,434.
Financial support: In 2001–02, 24 students received support, including fellowships with full tuition reimbursements available (averaging $16,400 per year), 15 teaching assistantships with full tuition reimbursements available (averaging $8,400 per year); research assistantships, Federal Work-Study and unspecified assistantships also available. Financial award application deadline: 1/1; financial award applicants required to submit FAFSA.
Faculty research: Theory, culture, sociology of law/criminology, urban sociology, family. *Total annual research expenditures:* $34,566.
Dr. Michael P. Farrell, Chair, 716-645-2417 Ext. 438, *Fax:* 716-645-3934, *E-mail:* ofarrell@buffalo.edu.
Application contact: Dr. Jorge Arditi, Director of Graduate Studies, 716-645-2417 Ext. 409, *Fax:* 716-645-3934, *E-mail:* arditi@acsu.buffalo.edu. *Web site:* http://www.sociology.buffalo.edu/

■ THE UNIVERSITY OF AKRON

Graduate School, Buchtel College of Arts and Sciences, Department of Sociology, Akron, OH 44325-0001

AWARDS MA, PhD. Part-time programs available.

Faculty: 20 full-time (6 women), 8 part-time/adjunct (4 women).
Students: 20 full-time (15 women), 8 part-time (3 women), 7 international. Average age 32. 28 applicants, 68% accepted, 11 enrolled. In 2001, 4 master's, 3 doctorates awarded. Terminal master's awarded for partial completion of doctoral program.
Degree requirements: For master's, thesis, oral defense of thesis, paper or oral exam; for doctorate, one foreign language, thesis/dissertation, comprehensive exam.
Entrance requirements: For master's, GRE General Test, minimum GPA of 2.75; for doctorate, GRE General Test. *Application deadline:* For fall admission, 4/1. Applications are processed on a rolling basis. *Application fee:* $40 ($50 for international students).
Expenses: Tuition, state resident: full-time $6,562; part-time $219 per credit. Tuition, nonresident: full-time $9,027; part-time $383 per credit. Required fees: $272; $11 per credit. Tuition and fees vary according to course load.
Financial support: In 2001–02, 5 research assistantships with full tuition reimbursements, 14 teaching assistantships with full tuition reimbursements were awarded. Career-related internships or fieldwork, Federal Work-Study, and tuition waivers (full and partial) also available. Financial award application deadline: 2/1.
Faculty research: Social psychology, medical sociology, family, gerontology, social policy and program evaluation.
Dr. John Zipp, Chair, 330-972-7481, *E-mail:* jzipp@uakron.edu.
Application contact: Dr. Gay Kitson, Director of Graduate Studies, 330-972-7481, *E-mail:* kitson@uakron.edu. *Web site:* http://www.uakron.edu/artsci/

■ THE UNIVERSITY OF ALABAMA AT BIRMINGHAM

Graduate School, School of Social and Behavioral Sciences, Department of Sociology, Birmingham, AL 35294

AWARDS Medical sociology (PhD); sociology (MA). Evening/weekend programs available.

Students: 13 full-time (7 women), 12 part-time (8 women); includes 5 minority (4 African Americans, 1 Hispanic American), 2 international. 13 applicants, 69% accepted. In 2001, 3 master's, 1 doctorate awarded.
Degree requirements: For master's, thesis or alternative; for doctorate, thesis/dissertation.
Entrance requirements: For master's, GRE General Test or MAT; for doctorate, GRE General Test. *Application deadline:* Applications are processed on a rolling basis. *Application fee:* $35 ($60 for international students). Electronic applications accepted.
Expenses: Tuition, state resident: full-time $3,058. Tuition, nonresident: full-time $5,746. Tuition and fees vary according to course load, degree level and program.
Financial support: In 2001–02, 10 students received support, including 2 fellowships, 3 research assistantships; career-related internships or fieldwork, Federal Work-Study, and institutionally sponsored loans also available. Financial award application deadline: 3/1.
Faculty research: Gerontology, applied sociology, urban sociology.
Dr. Ferris J. Ritchey, Chair, 205-934-3307, *E-mail:* fritchey@uab.edu. *Web site:* http://www.sbs.uab.edu/socio.htm/

■ THE UNIVERSITY OF ARIZONA

Graduate College, College of Social and Behavioral Sciences, Department of Sociology, Tucson, AZ 85721

AWARDS MA, PhD.

Faculty: 18 full-time (6 women).
Students: 48 full-time (25 women), 9 part-time (4 women); includes 10 minority (3 African Americans, 1 Asian American or Pacific Islander, 3 Hispanic Americans, 3 Native Americans), 5 international. Average age 30. 126 applicants, 24% accepted, 12 enrolled. In 2001, 6 master's, 11 doctorates awarded.
Degree requirements: For master's, publishable paper/oral; for doctorate, thesis/dissertation, 2 preliminary exams. *Median time to degree:* Master's–2 years full-time; doctorate–5.5 years full-time.
Entrance requirements: For master's, GRE, TOEFL; for doctorate, GRE General Test, TOEFL. *Application deadline:* For fall admission, 1/15. Applications are processed on a rolling basis. *Application fee:* $45.
Expenses: Tuition, state resident: full-time $2,490; part-time $436 per unit. Tuition, nonresident: full-time $10,300; part-time $436 per unit. Full-time tuition and fees vary according to degree level and program.
Financial support: In 2001–02, 4 fellowships (averaging $5,000 per year), 48 teaching assistantships (averaging $13,973 per year) were awarded. Research assistantships, institutionally sponsored loans, scholarships/grants, health care benefits, tuition waivers (full), and unspecified assistantships also available. Financial award application deadline: 1/15.
Faculty research: Organizations, social psychology, social movement, stratification, religion.
Dr. Mark Chaves, Head, 520-626-2560, *E-mail:* mchaves@u.arizona.edu.
Application contact: Dr. Lynn Smith-Lovin, Director of Graduate Studies, 520-621-8744, *Fax:* 520-621-9875, *E-mail:* smithlou@u.arizona.edu. *Web site:* http://w3fp.arizona.edu/soc/

■ UNIVERSITY OF ARKANSAS

Graduate School, J. William Fulbright College of Arts and Sciences, Department of Sociology, Fayetteville, AR 72701-1201

AWARDS MA.

Students: 19 full-time (9 women), 6 part-time (4 women); includes 4 minority (2 African Americans, 1 Asian American or Pacific Islander, 1 Native American). 11

University of Arkansas (continued)
applicants, 91% accepted. In 2001, 4 degrees awarded.
Degree requirements: For master's, thesis.
Entrance requirements: For master's, GRE General Test. *Application fee:* $40 ($50 for international students).
Expenses: Tuition, state resident: full-time $3,553; part-time $197 per credit. Tuition, nonresident: full-time $8,411; part-time $467 per credit. Required fees: $42 per credit. Tuition and fees vary according to course load and program.
Financial support: In 2001–02, 15 teaching assistantships were awarded; research assistantships, career-related internships or fieldwork and Federal Work-Study also available. Support available to part-time students. Financial award application deadline: 4/1; financial award applicants required to submit FAFSA.
Dr. Bill Schwab, Chair, 479-575-3205.

■ UNIVERSITY OF CALIFORNIA, BERKELEY

Graduate Division, College of Letters and Science, Department of Sociology, Berkeley, CA 94720-1500

AWARDS MA, PhD.

Faculty: 16 full-time (5 women), 9 part-time/adjunct (5 women).
Students: 105 full-time (64 women); includes 29 minority (7 African Americans, 6 Asian Americans or Pacific Islanders, 14 Hispanic Americans, 2 Native Americans), 14 international. 256 applicants, 15% accepted, 14 enrolled. In 2001, 19 master's, 13 doctorates awarded.
Degree requirements: For doctorate, thesis/dissertation, qualifying exam.
Entrance requirements: For doctorate, GRE General Test, minimum GPA of 3.0, sample of academic written work. *Application deadline:* For fall admission, 12/15. *Application fee:* $60. Electronic applications accepted.
Expenses: Tuition, nonresident: full-time $10,704. Required fees: $4,349.
Financial support: In 2001–02, fellowships with full tuition reimbursements (averaging $16,000 per year), 30 research assistantships with partial tuition reimbursements (averaging $13,000 per year), 27 teaching assistantships with partial tuition reimbursements (averaging $14,400 per year) were awarded. Federal Work-Study and institutionally sponsored loans also available. Financial award application deadline: 12/15; financial award applicants required to submit FAFSA.
Faculty research: Race, gender, political, stratification theory.
Dr. Peter Evans, Chair, 510-642-4575.
Application contact: Elsa Tranter, Graduate Assistant for Admission, 510-642-1657, *Fax:* 510-642-0659, *E-mail:* etranter@uclink.berkeley.edu. *Web site:* http://www.sociology.berkeley.edu/

■ UNIVERSITY OF CALIFORNIA, BERKELEY

Graduate Division, Group in Sociology and Demography, Berkeley, CA 94720-1500

AWARDS PhD.

Degree requirements: For doctorate, thesis/dissertation, qualifying exam.
Entrance requirements: For doctorate, GRE General Test, minimum GPA of 3.0. *Application deadline:* For fall admission, 2/10. *Application fee:* $60.
Expenses: Tuition, nonresident: full-time $10,704. Required fees: $4,349.
Financial support: Fellowships with full and partial tuition reimbursements, research assistantships with full and partial tuition reimbursements, teaching assistantships with full and partial tuition reimbursements available. Financial award application deadline: 1/5.
Dr. Michael Hout, Chair, 510-643-6874.
Application contact: Liz Ozselcuk, Graduate Assistant for Admission, 510-642-9800, *Fax:* 510-643-8853, *E-mail:* office@demog.berkeley.edu. *Web site:* http://www.demog.berkeley.edu/

■ UNIVERSITY OF CALIFORNIA, DAVIS

Graduate Studies, Program in Sociology, Davis, CA 95616

AWARDS MA, PhD. Part-time programs available.

Faculty: 23 full-time (10 women), 12 part-time/adjunct (7 women).
Students: 47 full-time (29 women), 1 part-time; includes 5 minority (2 African Americans, 1 Asian American or Pacific Islander, 2 Hispanic Americans), 5 international. Average age 31. 81 applicants, 35% accepted, 8 enrolled. In 2001, 4 master's, 2 doctorates awarded. Terminal master's awarded for partial completion of doctoral program.
Degree requirements: For master's, written exam; for doctorate, thesis/dissertation, professional paper, qualifying exam.
Entrance requirements: For master's and doctorate, GRE General Test, minimum GPA of 3.0, sample of written work. *Application deadline:* For fall admission, 1/15. *Application fee:* $60. Electronic applications accepted.
Expenses: Tuition, state resident: full-time $4,831. Tuition, nonresident: full-time $15,725.
Financial support: In 2001–02, 43 students received support, including 13 fellowships with full and partial tuition reimbursements available (averaging $4,820 per year), 9 research assistantships with full and partial tuition reimbursements available (averaging $6,766 per year), 29 teaching assistantships with partial tuition reimbursements available (averaging $14,005 per year); career-related internships or fieldwork, Federal Work-Study, institutionally sponsored loans, scholarships/grants, and tuition waivers (full and partial) also available. Financial award application deadline: 1/15; financial award applicants required to submit FAFSA.
Faculty research: Collective behavior, social movements, comparative sociology, historical sociology, culture development, inequality.
Bill McCarthy, Graduate Chair, 530-752-1563, *Fax:* 530-752-0783, *E-mail:* bdmccarthy@ucdavis.edu.
Application contact: Mary Reid, Graduate Program Staff, 530-752-4147, *Fax:* 530-752-0783, *E-mail:* mmreid@ucdavis.edu. *Web site:* http://sociology.ucdavis.edu/

■ UNIVERSITY OF CALIFORNIA, IRVINE

Office of Research and Graduate Studies, School of Social Sciences, Department of Sociology, Irvine, CA 92697

AWARDS Social networks (PhD); social networks-social science (MA); social science (MA, PhD); sociology and social relations-social science (MA, PhD).

Faculty: 21.
Students: 53 full-time (38 women); includes 15 minority (4 African Americans, 5 Asian Americans or Pacific Islanders, 5 Hispanic Americans, 1 Native American), 7 international. 53 applicants, 45% accepted, 10 enrolled. In 2001, 9 master's, 6 doctorates awarded.
Degree requirements: For doctorate, one foreign language, thesis/dissertation.
Entrance requirements: For master's, minimum GPA of 3.0; for doctorate, GRE General Test. *Application deadline:* For fall and spring admission, 1/15 (priority date); for winter admission, 10/15 (priority date). Applications are processed on a rolling basis. *Application fee:* $60. Electronic applications accepted.
Expenses: Tuition, nonresident: full-time $10,704. Required fees: $8,396. Tuition and fees vary according to course load, program and student level.
Financial support: Fellowships, research assistantships, teaching assistantships, institutionally sponsored loans and tuition waivers (full and partial) available. Financial award application deadline: 3/2; financial award applicants required to submit FAFSA.
Faculty research: Cognitive anthropology, sociology of culture, social structure, family and gender.
Judith Stepan-Norris, Chair, 949-824-6043.
Application contact: Ivonne Maldonado, Graduate Counselor, 949-824-7352, *Fax:* 949-824-3548, *E-mail:* immaldon@uci.edu. *Web site:* http://hypatia.ss.uci.edu/sociology/

■ UNIVERSITY OF CALIFORNIA, LOS ANGELES

Graduate Division, College of Letters and Science, Department of Sociology, Los Angeles, CA 90095

AWARDS MA, PhD.

Students: 105 full-time (68 women); includes 33 minority (5 African Americans, 12 Asian Americans or Pacific Islanders, 15 Hispanic Americans, 1 Native American), 17 international. 180 applicants, 27% accepted, 21 enrolled. In 2001, 12 master's, 9 doctorates awarded. Terminal master's awarded for partial completion of doctoral program.
Degree requirements: For master's, thesis or alternative, final paper; for doctorate, thesis/dissertation, oral and written qualifying exams.
Entrance requirements: For master's, GRE General Test, TOEFL, minimum GPA of 3.0, sample of work; for doctorate, GRE General Test, TOEFL, minimum undergraduate GPA of 3.0, sample of work. *Application deadline:* For fall admission, 12/1. *Application fee:* $60. Electronic applications accepted.
Expenses: Tuition, nonresident: full-time $10,244. Required fees: $3,609. Full-time tuition and fees vary according to program.
Financial support: In 2001–02, 94 fellowships, 81 research assistantships, 80 teaching assistantships were awarded. Federal Work-Study, institutionally sponsored loans, scholarships/grants, and tuition waivers (full and partial) also available. Financial award application deadline: 3/1.
Dr. Roger Waldinger, Chair, 310-825-1026.
Application contact: Departmental Office, 310-825-1026, *E-mail:* dietrich@soc.ucla.edu.

■ UNIVERSITY OF CALIFORNIA, RIVERSIDE

Graduate Division, Department of Sociology, Riverside, CA 92521-0102

AWARDS PhD.

Faculty: 20 full-time (7 women), 3 part-time/adjunct (1 woman).
Students: 61 full-time (27 women), 1 (woman) part-time; includes 14 minority (3 African Americans, 3 Asian Americans or Pacific Islanders, 8 Hispanic Americans), 8 international. Average age 34. 63 applicants, 51% accepted, 12 enrolled. In 2001, 3 doctorates awarded.
Degree requirements: For doctorate, thesis/dissertation, 1 quarter of teaching experience, qualifying exams, professional paper. *Median time to degree:* Doctorate–7 years full-time.
Entrance requirements: For doctorate, GRE General Test, TOEFL, minimum GPA of 3.2. *Application deadline:* For fall admission, 5/1; for winter admission, 9/1; for spring admission, 12/1. Applications are processed on a rolling basis. *Application fee:* $40. Electronic applications accepted.
Expenses: Tuition, state resident: full-time $5,001. Tuition, nonresident: full-time $15,897.
Financial support: In 2001–02, 20 fellowships, 14 research assistantships, 29 teaching assistantships with partial tuition reimbursements were awarded. Career-related internships or fieldwork, Federal Work-Study, institutionally sponsored loans, health care benefits, and tuition waivers (full and partial) also available. Financial award application deadline: 2/1; financial award applicants required to submit FAFSA.
Faculty research: Crime/deviance, race/ethnic relations, family/gender, political economy/globalization, theory. *Total annual research expenditures:* $234,955.
Dr. Scott Coltrane, Chair, 909-787-3501, *Fax:* 909-787-3330, *E-mail:* scott.coltrane@ucr.edu.
Application contact: Anna M. Wire, Graduate Program Assistant, 909-787-5444, *Fax:* 909-787-3330, *E-mail:* socgrad@ucr.edu. *Web site:* http://wizard.ucr.edu/sociology/SocioGradInfo.html

■ UNIVERSITY OF CALIFORNIA, SAN DIEGO

Graduate Studies and Research, Department of Sociology, La Jolla, CA 92093

AWARDS Science studies (PhD); sociology (PhD).

Faculty: 22.
Students: 46 (33 women). 118 applicants, 25% accepted, 10 enrolled. In 2001, 9 doctorates awarded.
Degree requirements: For doctorate, thesis/dissertation.
Entrance requirements: For doctorate, GRE General Test. *Application deadline:* For fall admission, 1/18. *Application fee:* $40. Electronic applications accepted.
Expenses: Tuition, nonresident: full-time $10,434. Required fees: $4,883.
Carlos Waisman, Chair, 858-534-2779, *E-mail:* cwaisman@ucsd.edu.
Application contact: Graduate Coordinator, 858-534-4626.

■ UNIVERSITY OF CALIFORNIA, SAN DIEGO

Graduate Studies and Research, Interdisciplinary Program in Cognitive Science, La Jolla, CA 92093

AWARDS Cognitive science/anthropology (PhD); cognitive science/communication (PhD); cognitive science/computer science and engineering (PhD); cognitive science/linguistics (PhD); cognitive science/neuroscience (PhD); cognitive science/philosophy (PhD); cognitive science/psychology (PhD); cognitive science/sociology (PhD). Admissions through affiliated departments.

Faculty: 57 full-time (12 women).
Students: 8 full-time (4 women). Average age 26. 2 applicants. In 2001, 2 degrees awarded.
Degree requirements: For doctorate, thesis/dissertation.
Entrance requirements: For doctorate, GRE General Test. *Application deadline:* Applications are processed on a rolling basis. *Application fee:* $0.
Expenses: Tuition, nonresident: full-time $10,434. Required fees: $4,883.
Faculty research: Cognition, neurobiology of cognition, artificial intelligence, neural networks, psycholinguistics.
Gary Cottrell, Director, 858-534-7141, *Fax:* 858-534-1128, *E-mail:* gcottrell@ucsd.edu.
Application contact: Graduate Coordinator, 858-534-7141, *Fax:* 858-534-1128, *E-mail:* gradinfo@cogsci.ucsd.edu. *Web site:* http://cogsci.ucsd.edu/CURRENT/Cog-interdisciplinary.html

■ UNIVERSITY OF CALIFORNIA, SAN FRANCISCO

Graduate Division, School of Nursing, Department of Social and Behavioral Sciences, San Francisco, CA 94143

AWARDS Sociology (PhD).

Students: 27 (22 women); includes 10 minority (5 Asian Americans or Pacific Islanders, 4 Hispanic Americans, 1 Native American). In 2001, 4 degrees awarded.
Degree requirements: For doctorate, one foreign language, thesis/dissertation.
Entrance requirements: For doctorate, GRE General Test. *Application deadline:* For fall admission, 2/1. *Application fee:* $40.
Financial support: Career-related internships or fieldwork available. Financial award application deadline: 1/10.
Faculty research: Urban social relations; sociology of women's role in healing; sociology of work, occupations, and professions.
Chairperson, 415-476-3964.
Application contact: Ray Rudolph, Program Coordinator, 415-476-3047, *Fax:* 415-476-6552, *E-mail:* rgr@itsa.ucsf.edu. *Web site:* http://www.ucsf.edu/medsoc/

Find an in-depth description at www.petersons.com/gradchannel.

■ UNIVERSITY OF CALIFORNIA, SANTA BARBARA

Graduate Division, College of Letters and Sciences, Division of Social Science, Department of Sociology, Santa Barbara, CA 93106

AWARDS MA, PhD.

Degree requirements: For doctorate, variable foreign language requirement, thesis/dissertation.

University of California, Santa Barbara (continued)
Entrance requirements: For doctorate, GRE General Test, TOEFL, sample of written work.
Faculty research: Sociology of culture; economy and society; language/social linguistics; sex and gender; race, ethnicity, and nationality. *Web site:* http://www.soc.ucsb.edu/

■ UNIVERSITY OF CALIFORNIA, SANTA CRUZ

Division of Graduate Studies, Division of Social Sciences, Program in Sociology, Santa Cruz, CA 95064

AWARDS PhD.

Faculty: 17 full-time.
Students: 41 full-time (31 women); includes 13 minority (1 African American, 2 Asian Americans or Pacific Islanders, 7 Hispanic Americans, 3 Native Americans), 2 international. 112 applicants, 22% accepted. In 2001, 2 doctorates awarded.
Degree requirements: For doctorate, variable foreign language requirement, thesis/dissertation, qualifying exam. *Median time to degree:* Doctorate–1 year full-time.
Entrance requirements: For doctorate, GRE General Test. *Application deadline:* For fall admission, 1/15. *Application fee:* $40.
Expenses: Tuition: Full-time $19,857.
Financial support: Fellowships, research assistantships, teaching assistantships, career-related internships or fieldwork, Federal Work-Study, and institutionally sponsored loans available. Financial award application deadline: 1/15.
Faculty research: Marxism, feminism, ethnic studies, social theory.
Craig Reinarman, Chairperson, 831-459-2587.
Application contact: Graduate Admissions, 831-459-2301. *Web site:* http://www.ucsc.edu/

■ UNIVERSITY OF CENTRAL FLORIDA

College of Arts and Sciences, Department of Sociology, Orlando, FL 32816

AWARDS Applied sociology (MA); domestic violence (Certificate); gender studies (Certificate); Mayan studies (Certificate). Part-time and evening/weekend programs available.

Faculty: 25 full-time (12 women), 3 part-time/adjunct (2 women).
Students: 12 full-time (10 women), 40 part-time (33 women); includes 5 minority (3 African Americans, 2 Hispanic Americans). Average age 33. 34 applicants, 82% accepted, 22 enrolled. In 2001, 6 degrees awarded.
Degree requirements: For master's, comprehensive written exam or thesis.
Entrance requirements: For master's, GRE General Test, TOEFL, minimum GPA of 3.0 in last 60 hours. *Application deadline:* For fall admission, 7/15; for spring admission, 12/1. *Application fee:* $20. Electronic applications accepted.
Expenses: Tuition, state resident: part-time $162 per hour. Tuition, nonresident: part-time $569 per hour.
Financial support: In 2001–02, 5 fellowships with partial tuition reimbursements (averaging $2,500 per year), 15 research assistantships with partial tuition reimbursements (averaging $1,990 per year), 22 teaching assistantships with partial tuition reimbursements (averaging $2,681 per year) were awarded. Career-related internships or fieldwork, Federal Work-Study, institutionally sponsored loans, tuition waivers (partial), and unspecified assistantships also available. Financial award application deadline: 3/1; financial award applicants required to submit FAFSA.
Faculty research: Religious subcultures, attitudes toward abortion, population, sport research, stratification.
Dr. Jay Corzine, Chair, 407-823-2227, *Fax:* 407-823-5156, *E-mail:* hcorzine@mail.ucf.edu. *Web site:* http://www.ucf.edu/

■ UNIVERSITY OF CHICAGO

Division of Social Sciences, Department of Sociology, Chicago, IL 60637-1513

AWARDS PhD.

Students: 150.
Degree requirements: For doctorate, one foreign language, thesis/dissertation, 2 field exams.
Entrance requirements: For doctorate, GRE General Test, TOEFL. *Application deadline:* For fall admission, 12/28. *Application fee:* $55. Electronic applications accepted.
Expenses: Tuition: Full-time $16,548.
Financial support: Fellowships, research assistantships, teaching assistantships, Federal Work-Study and institutionally sponsored loans available. Financial award application deadline: 12/28.
Prof. Andrew Abbott, Chair, 773-702-8677.
Application contact: Office of the Dean of Students, 773-702-8415.

■ UNIVERSITY OF CINCINNATI

Division of Research and Advanced Studies, McMicken College of Arts and Sciences, Department of Sociology, Cincinnati, OH 45221

AWARDS MA, PhD.

Faculty: 12 full-time (7 women).
Students: 33 applicants, 55% accepted, 10 enrolled. In 2001, 3 master's, 1 doctorate awarded.
Degree requirements: For master's and doctorate, thesis/dissertation.
Entrance requirements: For master's and doctorate, GRE General Test. *Application deadline:* For fall admission, 2/1. *Application fee:* $30. Electronic applications accepted.
Expenses: Tuition, state resident: part-time $2,698 per quarter. Tuition, nonresident: part-time $4,977 per quarter.
Financial support: Fellowships with full tuition reimbursements, teaching assistantships with full tuition reimbursements, tuition waivers (partial) and unspecified assistantships available. Financial award application deadline: 2/1. *Total annual research expenditures:* $40,684.
Dr. Rhys Williams, Head, 513-556-4700, *Fax:* 513-556-0057, *E-mail:* rhys.williams@uc.edu.
Application contact: Dr. Paula Dubeck, Graduate Program Director, 513-556-4715, *Fax:* 513-556-0057, *E-mail:* paula.dubeck@uc.edu. *Web site:* http://www.artsci.uc.edu/sociology

■ UNIVERSITY OF COLORADO AT BOULDER

Graduate School, College of Arts and Sciences, Department of Sociology, Boulder, CO 80309

AWARDS MA, PhD.

Faculty: 21 full-time (10 women).
Students: 38 full-time (24 women), 23 part-time (14 women); includes 9 minority (2 African Americans, 1 Asian American or Pacific Islander, 6 Hispanic Americans), 2 international. Average age 33. 11 applicants, 91% accepted. In 2001, 4 master's, 7 doctorates awarded. Terminal master's awarded for partial completion of doctoral program.
Degree requirements: For master's and doctorate, thesis/dissertation, comprehensive exam.
Entrance requirements: For master's and doctorate, GRE General Test, GRE Subject Test, minimum undergraduate GPA of 3.0. *Application deadline:* For fall admission, 2/1. *Application fee:* $50 ($60 for international students).
Expenses: Tuition, state resident: full-time $3,474. Tuition, nonresident: full-time $16,624.
Financial support: In 2001–02, 5 fellowships (averaging $3,517 per year), 1 research assistantship (averaging $829 per year), 22 teaching assistantships (averaging $9,915 per year) were awarded. Federal Work-Study, institutionally sponsored loans, and scholarships/grants also available. Support available to part-time students. Financial award application deadline: 1/1; financial award applicants required to submit FAFSA.
Faculty research: Criminology, social control, law delinquency and deviance, population, health studies. *Total annual research expenditures:* $3 million.
Dennis Mileti, Chair, 303-492-8864, *Fax:* 303-492-8878, *E-mail:* dennis.mileti@colorado.edu.

Application contact: Michele Noe, Graduate Secretary, 303-735-2335, *Fax:* 303-492-8878, *E-mail:* michele.noe@colorado.edu. *Web site:* http://SOCSCI.colorado.edu/SOC/

■ UNIVERSITY OF COLORADO AT COLORADO SPRINGS

Graduate School, College of Letters, Arts and Sciences, Department of Sociology, Colorado Springs, CO 80933-7150

AWARDS MA. Part-time programs available.

Faculty: 4 full-time (1 woman).
Students: 12 full-time (10 women), 11 part-time (9 women); includes 6 minority (4 African Americans, 1 Hispanic American, 1 Native American). Average age 36. 78 applicants, 44% accepted. In 2001, 4 degrees awarded.
Degree requirements: For master's, thesis optional.
Entrance requirements: For master's, GRE, minimum GPA of 2.75. *Application deadline:* For fall admission, 5/1 (priority date); for spring admission, 11/1. Applications are processed on a rolling basis. *Application fee:* $60 ($75 for international students).
Expenses: Tuition, state resident: full-time $2,900; part-time $174 per credit. Tuition, nonresident: full-time $9,961; part-time $591 per credit. Required fees: $14 per credit. $141 per semester. Tuition and fees vary according to course load, program and student level.
Financial support: Teaching assistantships, career-related internships or fieldwork, Federal Work-Study, and institutionally sponsored loans available.
Faculty research: Environmental justice, gender, race and ethnicity, sport and popular culture, youth and deviant behavior.
Dr. Robert Hughes, Chair, 719-262-4141, *Fax:* 719-262-4450, *E-mail:* rhughes@uccs.edu.
Application contact: Dr. Abby Ferber, Graduate Student Adviser, 719-262-4139, *Fax:* 719-262-4450, *E-mail:* aferber@uccs.edu. *Web site:* http://www.uccs.edu/~sociolog/

■ UNIVERSITY OF COLORADO AT DENVER

Graduate School, College of Liberal Arts and Sciences, Program in Sociology, Denver, CO 80217-3364

AWARDS MA. Part-time and evening/weekend programs available.

Faculty: 8 full-time (2 women).
Students: 4 full-time (3 women), 10 part-time (8 women). Average age 27. 4 applicants, 75% accepted, 2 enrolled. In 2001, 3 degrees awarded.
Degree requirements: For master's, thesis or alternative.
Entrance requirements: For master's, GRE. *Application deadline:* For fall admission, 6/1; for spring admission, 11/1. Applications are processed on a rolling basis. *Application fee:* $50 ($60 for international students). Electronic applications accepted.
Expenses: Tuition, state resident: full-time $3,284; part-time $198 per credit hour. Tuition, nonresident: full-time $13,380; part-time $802 per credit hour. Required fees: $444; $222 per semester.
Financial support: Research assistantships, teaching assistantships, Federal Work-Study available. Financial award application deadline: 3/1; financial award applicants required to submit FAFSA.
Candan Duran, Chair, 303-556-8306, *Fax:* 303-556-3510, *E-mail:* cruranydint@carbon.cudenver.edu.
Application contact: Rachel Watson, Administrative Assistant, 303-556-3557, *Fax:* 303-556-3510, *E-mail:* rwatson@carbon.cudenver.edu. *Web site:* http://www.cudenver.edu/public/sociology/masters.html

■ UNIVERSITY OF CONNECTICUT

Graduate School, College of Liberal Arts and Sciences, Field of Sociology, Storrs, CT 06269

AWARDS MA, PhD.

Degree requirements: For doctorate, thesis/dissertation, 2 field exams.
Entrance requirements: For master's and doctorate, GRE General Test.
Expenses: Contact institution.

■ UNIVERSITY OF DELAWARE

College of Arts and Science, Department of Sociology and Criminal Justice, Newark, DE 19716

AWARDS Criminology (MA, PhD); sociology (MA, PhD).

Faculty: 29 full-time (13 women).
Students: 31 full-time (18 women), 2 part-time (both women); includes 6 minority (2 African Americans, 1 Asian American or Pacific Islander, 3 Hispanic Americans), 1 international. Average age 26. 44 applicants, 34% accepted, 5 enrolled. In 2001, 4 master's, 2 doctorates awarded.
Degree requirements: For master's, thesis/dissertation; for doctorate, thesis/dissertation, comprehensive exam.
Entrance requirements: For master's and doctorate, GRE, TOEFL, letters of recommendation (3). *Application deadline:* For fall admission, 2/1. *Application fee:* $50. Electronic applications accepted.
Expenses: Tuition, state resident: full-time $4,770; part-time $265 per credit. Tuition, nonresident: full-time $13,860; part-time $770 per credit. Required fees: $414.
Financial support: In 2001–02, 25 students received support, including 3 fellowships with full tuition reimbursements available (averaging $10,100 per year), 11 research assistantships with full tuition reimbursements available (averaging $10,450 per year), 14 teaching assistantships with full tuition reimbursements available (averaging $10,450 per year). Financial award application deadline: 2/1.
Faculty research: Sex and gender, criminology/deviance, theory, methods, collective behavior. *Total annual research expenditures:* $2.7 million.
Dr. Joel Best, Chairman, 302-831-2581, *Fax:* 302-831-2607, *E-mail:* joelbest@udel.edu.
Application contact: Dr. Ronet Bachman, Director of Graduate Studies, 302-831-2581, *Fax:* 302-831-2607, *E-mail:* ronet@udel.edu. *Web site:* http://www.udel.edu/soc/homepage.htm

■ UNIVERSITY OF FLORIDA

Graduate School, College of Liberal Arts and Sciences, Department of Sociology, Gainesville, FL 32611

AWARDS MA, PhD, JD/MA.

Degree requirements: For master's, thesis optional; for doctorate, thesis/dissertation.
Entrance requirements: For master's and doctorate, GRE General Test, minimum GPA of 3.0. Electronic applications accepted.
Expenses: Tuition, state resident: part-time $164 per hour. Tuition, nonresident: part-time $571 per hour. Tuition and fees vary according to course level and program.
Faculty research: Sociology of the family, social gerontology, criminology and deviance, race ethnicity. *Web site:* http://www.clas.ufl.edu/sociology/

■ UNIVERSITY OF GEORGIA

Graduate School, College of Arts and Sciences, Department of Sociology, Athens, GA 30602

AWARDS MA, PhD.

Faculty: 18 full-time (6 women).
Students: 26 full-time (21 women), 11 part-time (8 women); includes 4 minority (3 African Americans, 1 Hispanic American), 6 international. 71 applicants, 23% accepted. In 2001, 3 master's, 3 doctorates awarded.
Degree requirements: For master's, thesis; for doctorate, one foreign language, thesis/dissertation.
Entrance requirements: For master's and doctorate, GRE General Test. *Application deadline:* For fall admission, 7/1 (priority date); for spring admission, 11/15. *Application fee:* $30. Electronic applications accepted.
Expenses: Tuition, state resident: full-time $2,376; part-time $132 per credit hour. Tuition, nonresident: full-time $9,504; part-time $528 per credit hour. Required fees: $236 per semester.
Financial support: Fellowships, research assistantships, teaching assistantships, unspecified assistantships available.

University of Georgia (continued)
Dr. E. M. Beck, Head, 706-542-3175, *Fax:* 706-542-4320, *E-mail:* wbeck@uga.edu.
Application contact: Dr. William Finlay, Graduate Coordinator, 706-542-3207, *Fax:* 706-542-4320, *E-mail:* wfinlay@uga.edu.
Web site: http://www.uga.edu/~soc/

■ UNIVERSITY OF HAWAII AT MANOA

Graduate Division, College of Arts and Sciences, College of Social Sciences, Department of Sociology, Honolulu, HI 96822

AWARDS MA, PhD.

Faculty: 17 full-time (4 women), 17 part-time/adjunct (5 women).
Students: 43 full-time (29 women), 20 part-time (12 women); includes 13 minority (10 Asian Americans or Pacific Islanders, 3 Hispanic Americans), 29 international. Average age 32. 41 applicants, 71% accepted. In 2001, 2 master's, 3 doctorates awarded.
Degree requirements: For master's, thesis (for some programs); for doctorate, thesis/dissertation.
Entrance requirements: For master's and doctorate, GRE. *Application deadline:* For fall admission, 2/1; for spring admission, 9/1. Applications are processed on a rolling basis. *Application fee:* $25 ($50 for international students).
Expenses: Tuition, state resident: full-time $2,160; part-time $1,980 per year. Tuition, nonresident: full-time $5,190; part-time $4,829 per year.
Financial support: In 2001–02, 2 research assistantships (averaging $16,578 per year), 12 teaching assistantships (averaging $13,838 per year) were awarded. Federal Work-Study, institutionally sponsored loans, and tuition waivers (full and partial) also available.
Faculty research: Comparative sociology of Asia; population studies; crime, law, and deviance; health; aging and medical sociology.
Dr. Eldon Wegner, Chairperson, 808-956-7693, *Fax:* 808-956-3707.
Application contact: Dr. Patricia Steinhoff, Graduate Field Chairperson, 808-956-7676, *Fax:* 808-956-3707, *E-mail:* steinhof@hawaii.edu.

■ UNIVERSITY OF HOUSTON

College of Liberal Arts and Social Sciences, Department of Sociology, Houston, TX 77204

AWARDS MA. Part-time and evening/weekend programs available.

Faculty: 9 full-time (3 women).
Students: 10 full-time (all women), 9 part-time (5 women); includes 6 minority (3 African Americans, 3 Hispanic Americans), 1 international. Average age 29. 17 applicants, 65% accepted. In 2001, 13 degrees awarded.
Degree requirements: For master's, thesis.
Entrance requirements: For master's, GRE General Test, TOEFL, minimum GPA of 3.0. *Application deadline:* For fall admission, 8/1; for spring admission, 12/1. Applications are processed on a rolling basis. *Application fee:* $0 ($75 for international students).
Expenses: Tuition, state resident: full-time $1,512. Tuition, nonresident: full-time $5,310. Required fees: $1,308. Tuition and fees vary according to program.
Financial support: In 2001–02, 3 research assistantships, 6 teaching assistantships were awarded. Institutionally sponsored loans, scholarships/grants, and tuition waivers (full) also available. Support available to part-time students. Financial award application deadline: 6/1; financial award applicants required to submit FAFSA.
Faculty research: Gender, immigration, urban studies, religion, race/ethnicity, social psychology, medical sociology.
Dr. Janet Chafetz, Chair, 713-743-3953, *Fax:* 713-743-3943.
Application contact: Dr. Joseph A. Kotarba, Director of Graduate Studies, 713-743-3954, *Fax:* 713-743-3943, *E-mail:* jkotarba@uh.edu.

■ UNIVERSITY OF HOUSTON–CLEAR LAKE

School of Human Sciences and Humanities, Programs in Human Sciences, Houston, TX 77058-1098

AWARDS Behavioral sciences (MA), including behavioral sciences-general, behavioral sciences-psychology, behavioral sciences-sociology; clinical psychology (MA); cross-cultural studies (MA); family therapy (MA); fitness and human performance (MA); school psychology (MA); studies of the future (MS). Part-time and evening/weekend programs available.

Students: 562; includes 183 minority (95 African Americans, 16 Asian Americans or Pacific Islanders, 70 Hispanic Americans, 2 Native Americans), 16 international. Average age 34. In 2001, 152 degrees awarded.
Degree requirements: For master's, thesis or alternative.
Entrance requirements: For master's, GRE General Test. *Application deadline:* For fall admission, 8/1; for spring admission, 12/1. Applications are processed on a rolling basis. *Application fee:* $30 ($70 for international students). Electronic applications accepted.
Expenses: Tuition, state resident: full-time $2,016; part-time $84 per credit hour. Tuition, nonresident: full-time $6,072; part-time $253 per credit hour. Tuition and fees vary according to course load.
Financial support: Research assistantships, teaching assistantships, career-related internships or fieldwork, Federal Work-Study, institutionally sponsored loans, and scholarships/grants available. Support available to part-time students. Financial award application deadline: 5/1.
Dr. Hilary Karp, Division Co-Chair, 281-283-3383, *E-mail:* karp@cl.uh.edu.

■ UNIVERSITY OF ILLINOIS AT CHICAGO

Graduate College, College of Liberal Arts and Sciences, Department of Sociology, Chicago, IL 60607-7128

AWARDS MA, PhD.

Faculty: 22 full-time (8 women), 1 part-time/adjunct (0 women).
Students: 31 full-time (23 women), 12 part-time (8 women); includes 12 minority (7 African Americans, 2 Asian Americans or Pacific Islanders, 3 Hispanic Americans), 8 international. Average age 32. 84 applicants, 24% accepted, 12 enrolled. In 2001, 11 master's, 1 doctorate awarded. Terminal master's awarded for partial completion of doctoral program.
Degree requirements: For master's, thesis, comprehensive exam; for doctorate, thesis/dissertation, qualifying exam.
Entrance requirements: For master's, GRE General Test, TOEFL, minimum GPA of 4.0 on a 5.0 scale; for doctorate, GRE General Test, TOEFL, minimum GPA of 4.5 on a 5.0 scale. *Application deadline:* For fall admission, 6/1; for spring admission, 11/1. Applications are processed on a rolling basis. *Application fee:* $40 ($50 for international students). Electronic applications accepted.
Expenses: Tuition, state resident: full-time $3,060. Tuition, nonresident: full-time $6,688.
Financial support: In 2001–02, 28 students received support; fellowships with full tuition reimbursements available, research assistantships with full tuition reimbursements available, teaching assistantships with full tuition reimbursements available, career-related internships or fieldwork, Federal Work-Study, and tuition waivers (full) available. Financial award application deadline: 3/1; financial award applicants required to submit FAFSA.
Faculty research: Social psychology, social organization, applied sociology, demography and human ecology.
Pamela Popielarz, Head, 313-413-3757, *E-mail:* pamela@uic.edu.
Application contact: John Walsh, Director of Graduate Studies, 312-996-3009.

■ UNIVERSITY OF ILLINOIS AT URBANA–CHAMPAIGN

Graduate College, College of Liberal Arts and Sciences, Department of Sociology, Champaign, IL 61820

AWARDS Demography (AM, PhD); sociology (AM, PhD).

Faculty: 15 full-time, 1 part-time/adjunct.
Students: 48 full-time (28 women); includes 5 minority (2 Asian Americans or

Pacific Islanders, 3 Hispanic Americans), 30 international. 79 applicants, 15% accepted. In 2001, 1 master's, 1 doctorate awarded.
Degree requirements: For doctorate, thesis/dissertation.
Entrance requirements: For master's, GRE General Test, GRE Subject Test, minimum GPA of 3.0. *Application deadline:* For fall admission, 1/5. Applications are processed on a rolling basis. *Application fee:* $40 ($50 for international students). Electronic applications accepted.
Expenses: Tuition, state resident: part-time $3,227 per degree program. Tuition, nonresident: part-time $7,169 per degree program. Tuition and fees vary according to program.
Financial support: In 2001–02, 4 fellowships, 10 research assistantships, 25 teaching assistantships were awarded. Tuition waivers (full and partial) also available. Financial award application deadline: 2/15.
Andrew Pickering, Acting Head, 217-333-1950, *Fax:* 217-333-5225.
Application contact: Elizabeth Wilson, Administrative Secretary, 217-244-1808, *Fax:* 217-333-5225, *E-mail:* efleming@uiuc.edu. *Web site:* http://www.soc.uiuc.edu/

■ UNIVERSITY OF INDIANAPOLIS

Graduate School, College of Arts and Sciences, Department of Social Sciences, Indianapolis, IN 46227-3697

AWARDS Applied sociology (MA). Part-time and evening/weekend programs available.

Faculty: 1 full-time (0 women), 9 part-time/adjunct (4 women).
Students: 10 full-time (8 women), 8 part-time (5 women); includes 4 minority (all Asian Americans or Pacific Islanders). Average age 32. 3 applicants, 100% accepted. In 2001, 8 degrees awarded.
Entrance requirements: For master's, GRE Subject Test. *Application deadline:* Applications are processed on a rolling basis. *Application fee:* $30.
Expenses: Tuition: Part-time $260 per credit hour. Tuition and fees vary according to degree level.
Financial support: Federal Work-Study available. Financial award application deadline: 5/1; financial award applicants required to submit FAFSA.
Dr. Gregory Reinhardt, Chair, 317-788-3441, *Fax:* 317-788-3480, *E-mail:* reinhardt@uindy.edu.

■ THE UNIVERSITY OF IOWA

Graduate College, College of Liberal Arts and Sciences, Department of Sociology, Iowa City, IA 52242-1316

AWARDS Sociology (MA, PhD).

Faculty: 19 full-time, 1 part-time/adjunct.
Students: 17 full-time (15 women), 16 part-time (7 women), 9 international. 47 applicants, 47% accepted, 7 enrolled. In 2001, 3 master's, 3 doctorates awarded.
Degree requirements: For master's, exam, thesis optional; for doctorate, thesis/dissertation, comprehensive exam.
Entrance requirements: For master's, GRE General Test, TOEFL; for doctorate, GRE General Test, TOEFL, minimum GPA of 3.0. *Application deadline:* For fall admission, 1/1 (priority date); for spring admission, 11/1 (priority date). Applications are processed on a rolling basis. *Application fee:* $30 ($50 for international students). Electronic applications accepted.
Expenses: Tuition, state resident: full-time $3,702; part-time $206 per semester hour. Tuition, nonresident: full-time $11,924; part-time $206 per semester hour. Required fees: $101 per semester. Tuition and fees vary according to course load and program.
Financial support: In 2001–02, 1 fellowship, 10 research assistantships, 20 teaching assistantships were awarded. Financial award applicants required to submit FAFSA.
Jennifer Glass, Chair, 319-335-2502, *Fax:* 319-335-2509.

■ UNIVERSITY OF KANSAS

Graduate School, College of Liberal Arts and Sciences, Department of Sociology, Lawrence, KS 66045

AWARDS MA, PhD.

Faculty: 19.
Students: 32 full-time (22 women), 16 part-time (10 women); includes 3 minority (2 African Americans, 1 Hispanic American), 4 international. Average age 33. 45 applicants, 16% accepted, 6 enrolled. In 2001, 4 master's, 4 doctorates awarded.
Degree requirements: For master's, thesis or alternative; for doctorate, thesis/dissertation.
Entrance requirements: For master's and doctorate, GRE General Test, TOEFL. *Application deadline:* For fall admission, 4/15; for spring admission, 10/15. *Application fee:* $35.
Expenses: Tuition, state resident: full-time $2,722; part-time $113 per credit. Tuition, nonresident: full-time $8,586; part-time $358 per credit. Required fees: $551; $46 per credit. Tuition and fees vary according to campus/location, program and reciprocity agreements.
Financial support: In 2001–02, 7 fellowships (averaging $4,750 per year), 20 teaching assistantships with full and partial tuition reimbursements (averaging $10,546 per year) were awarded.
Faculty research: Comparative/historical sociology, gender, medical/legal systems, social change/social movements, theory.
William G. Staples, Chair, 785-864-4111, *Fax:* 785-864-5280.
Application contact: Shirley A. Hill, Graduate Director, 785-864-4111, *Fax:* 785-864-5280, *E-mail:* socdept@ku.edu. *Web site:* http://falcon.cc.ukans.edu/~socdept/

■ UNIVERSITY OF KENTUCKY

Graduate School, Graduate School Programs from the College of Arts and Sciences, Program in Sociology, Lexington, KY 40506-0032

AWARDS MA, MS Ag, PhD. Part-time programs available.

Faculty: 38 full-time (15 women).
Students: 32 full-time (21 women), 14 part-time (9 women); includes 5 minority (all African Americans), 7 international. 43 applicants, 49% accepted. In 2001, 2 master's, 9 doctorates awarded.
Degree requirements: For master's, thesis optional; for doctorate, thesis/dissertation, comprehensive exam.
Entrance requirements: For master's, GRE General Test, minimum undergraduate GPA of 2.5; for doctorate, GRE General Test, minimum graduate GPA of 3.0. *Application deadline:* For fall admission, 2/1; for spring admission, 10/1. Applications are processed on a rolling basis. *Application fee:* $30 ($35 for international students).
Expenses: Tuition, state resident: full-time $4,075; part-time $213 per credit hour. Tuition, nonresident: full-time $11,295; part-time $614 per credit hour.
Financial support: In 2001–02, 2 fellowships, 11 research assistantships, 14 teaching assistantships were awarded. Federal Work-Study and unspecified assistantships also available.
Faculty research: Work organizations, social inequalities, rural sociology, criminology/deviance, medical sociology.
Dr. Laurie Hatch, Director of Graduate Studies, 859-257-4413, *Fax:* 859-323-0272, *E-mail:* soc183@pop.uky.edu.
Application contact: Dr. Constance L. Wood, Associate Dean, 606-257-4613, *Fax:* 606-323-1928.

■ UNIVERSITY OF LOUISVILLE

Graduate School, College of Arts and Sciences, Department of Sociology, Louisville, KY 40292-0001

AWARDS MA.

Students: 14 full-time (10 women), 17 part-time (10 women); includes 5 minority (2 African Americans, 3 Asian Americans or Pacific Islanders), 4 international. Average age 33. In 2001, 6 degrees awarded.
Degree requirements: For master's, thesis optional.
Entrance requirements: For master's, GRE General Test. *Application deadline:* For fall admission, 3/1 (priority date); for spring admission, 10/15 (priority date). Applications are processed on a rolling basis. *Application fee:* $25.
Expenses: Tuition, state resident: full-time $4,134. Tuition, nonresident: full-time $11,486.
Financial support: In 2001–02, 4 teaching assistantships with full tuition reimbursements (averaging $10,000 per year) were awarded

University of Louisville (continued)
Dr. Wayne M. Usui, Chair, 502-852-6836, *Fax:* 502-852-0099, *E-mail:* wayne.usui@louisville.edu.

■ UNIVERSITY OF MARYLAND, BALTIMORE COUNTY

Graduate School, Department of Sociology and Anthropology, Baltimore, MD 21250-5398

AWARDS Applied sociology (MA, Certificate); medical sociology (MA). Part-time and evening/weekend programs available.

Degree requirements: For master's, thesis.
Entrance requirements: For master's, GRE General Test, GRE Subject Test, TOEFL, minimum GPA of 3.0.
Faculty research: Sociology of aging, gerontology, social stratification, medical sociology. *Web site:* http://www.umbc.edu/sociology/

Find an in-depth description at www.petersons.com/gradchannel.

■ UNIVERSITY OF MARYLAND, COLLEGE PARK

Graduate Studies and Research, College of Behavioral and Social Sciences, Department of Sociology, College Park, MD 20742

AWARDS MA, PhD.

Faculty: 31 full-time (12 women), 5 part-time/adjunct (3 women).
Students: 62 full-time (40 women), 26 part-time (16 women); includes 21 minority (12 African Americans, 5 Asian Americans or Pacific Islanders, 4 Hispanic Americans), 24 international. 166 applicants, 28% accepted, 24 enrolled. In 2001, 9 master's, 6 doctorates awarded.
Degree requirements: For master's, thesis; for doctorate, variable foreign language requirement, thesis/dissertation, 2 qualifying exams.
Entrance requirements: For master's, GRE General Test, minimum GPA of 3.0; for doctorate, GRE General Test. *Application deadline:* For fall admission, 5/1; for spring admission, 11/15. Applications are processed on a rolling basis. *Application fee:* $50 ($70 for international students). Electronic applications accepted.
Expenses: Tuition, state resident: part-time $289 per credit hour. Tuition, nonresident: part-time $448 per credit hour. One-time fee: $436 part-time. Full-time tuition and fees vary according to course load, campus/location and program.
Financial support: In 2001–02, 10 fellowships with full tuition reimbursements (averaging $1,080 per year), 58 teaching assistantships with tuition reimbursements (averaging $10,916 per year) were awarded. Research assistantships, Federal Work-Study and scholarships/grants also [illegible]upport available to part-time students. Financial award applicants required to submit FAFSA.
Faculty research: Social psychology, sociology of work, sociology of the military, population studies.
Dr. William Falk, Chairman, 301-405-6394, *Fax:* 301-314-6892.
Application contact: Trudy Lindsey, Director, Graduate Admissions and Records, 301-405-6991, *Fax:* 301-314-9305, *E-mail:* grschool@deans.umd.edu.

■ UNIVERSITY OF MASSACHUSETTS AMHERST

Graduate School, College of Social and Behavioral Sciences, Department of Sociology, Amherst, MA 01003

AWARDS MA, PhD. Part-time programs available.

Faculty: 24 full-time (6 women).
Students: 36 full-time (19 women), 29 part-time (23 women); includes 11 minority (4 African Americans, 3 Asian Americans or Pacific Islanders, 4 Hispanic Americans), 9 international. Average age 31. 148 applicants, 13% accepted. In 2001, 4 master's, 1 doctorate awarded. Terminal master's awarded for partial completion of doctoral program.
Degree requirements: For doctorate, thesis/dissertation.
Entrance requirements: For master's and doctorate, GRE General Test. *Application deadline:* For fall admission, 2/1 (priority date). Applications are processed on a rolling basis. *Application fee:* $40 ($50 for international students).
Expenses: Tuition, state resident: full-time $1,980; part-time $110 per credit. Tuition, nonresident: full-time $7,456; part-time $414 per credit. Required fees: $4,112. One-time fee: $115 full-time.
Financial support: In 2001–02, 25 fellowships with full tuition reimbursements (averaging $5,839 per year), 30 research assistantships with full tuition reimbursements (averaging $6,715 per year), 45 teaching assistantships with full tuition reimbursements (averaging $9,215 per year) were awarded. Career-related internships or fieldwork, Federal Work-Study, scholarships/grants, traineeships, and unspecified assistantships also available. Support available to part-time students. Financial award application deadline: 2/1.
Dr. Randall Stokes, Chair, 413-545-4059, *Fax:* 413-545-3204, *E-mail:* stokes@soc.umass.edu.

■ UNIVERSITY OF MASSACHUSETTS BOSTON

Office of Graduate Studies and Research, College of Arts and Sciences, Faculty of Arts, Program in Applied Sociology, Boston, MA 02125-3393

AWARDS MA. Part-time and evening/weekend programs available.

Degree requirements: For master's, thesis, thesis, comprehensive exam.
Entrance requirements: For master's, GRE or MAT, minimum GPA of 2.75.
Faculty research: Sociology of education, social deviance and control, women and development, race and ethnic group relations, criminology.

■ UNIVERSITY OF MASSACHUSETTS LOWELL

Graduate School, College of Arts and Sciences, Department of Regional Economic and Social Development, Lowell, MA 01854-2881

AWARDS MS.

Entrance requirements: For master's, GRE. Electronic applications accepted.

■ THE UNIVERSITY OF MEMPHIS

Graduate School, College of Arts and Sciences, Department of Sociology, Memphis, TN 38152

AWARDS MA. Part-time programs available.

Faculty: 11 full-time (5 women), 1 (woman) part-time/adjunct.
Students: 11 full-time (9 women), 21 part-time (16 women); includes 6 minority (all African Americans), 2 international. Average age 32. In 2001, 13 degrees awarded.
Degree requirements: For master's, thesis or alternative, comprehensive exam.
Entrance requirements: For master's, GRE General Test or MAT, 12 undergraduate hours in sociology. *Application deadline:* For fall admission, 8/1; for spring admission, 12/1. Applications are processed on a rolling basis. *Application fee:* $25 ($50 for international students). Electronic applications accepted.
Expenses: Tuition, state resident: full-time $2,026. Tuition, nonresident: full-time $4,528.
Financial support: In 2001–02, 9 research assistantships with full tuition reimbursements, 3 teaching assistantships with full tuition reimbursements were awarded.
Faculty research: Medical and health, deviant behavior, inequality, religion, globalization. *Total annual research expenditures:* $400,000.
Dr. York Bradshaw, Chair, 901-678-2611.
Application contact: Dr. Larry R. Petersen, Coordinator of Graduate Studies, 901-678-3341.

■ UNIVERSITY OF MIAMI

Graduate School, College of Arts and Sciences, Department of Sociology, Coral Gables, FL 33124

AWARDS MA, PhD. Part-time programs available.

Faculty: 8 full-time (4 women).
Students: 31 full-time (18 women), 7 part-time (4 women); includes 9 minority (6 African Americans, 3 Hispanic Americans), 4 international. Average age 30. 31

applicants, 48% accepted. In 2001, 13 master's, 2 doctorates awarded. Terminal master's awarded for partial completion of doctoral program.
Degree requirements: For master's and doctorate, thesis/dissertation.
Entrance requirements: For master's and doctorate, GRE General Test, TOEFL. *Application deadline:* For fall admission, 4/15 (priority date). Applications are processed on a rolling basis. *Application fee:* $50. Electronic applications accepted.
Expenses: Tuition: Part-time $960 per credit hour. Required fees: $85 per semester. Tuition and fees vary according to program.
Financial support: In 2001–02, 18 students received support, including 1 fellowship with full tuition reimbursement available (averaging $17,000 per year), 2 research assistantships with full tuition reimbursements available (averaging $11,572 per year), 15 teaching assistantships with full tuition reimbursements available (averaging $11,919 per year); career-related internships or fieldwork, Federal Work-Study, and unspecified assistantships also available. Financial award application deadline: 2/1; financial award applicants required to submit FAFSA.
Faculty research: Drug use of adolescents, AIDS, community mental health, inter-ethnic relations, sports research. *Total annual research expenditures:* $10,000.
Dr. Dale Chitwood, Chairman, 305-284-6768, *Fax:* 305-284-5310.
Application contact: Dr. Marvin P. Dawkins, Graduate Director, 305-284-6127, *Fax:* 305-284-5310, *E-mail:* socigrad@umiami.ir.miami.edu. *Web site:* http://www.as.miami.edu/sociology/

■ UNIVERSITY OF MICHIGAN

Horace H. Rackham School of Graduate Studies, College of Literature, Science, and the Arts, Department of Sociology, Ann Arbor, MI 48109

AWARDS Public policy and sociology (PhD); social work and sociology (PhD); sociology (PhD).

Faculty: 36 full-time (14 women), 11 part-time/adjunct (2 women).
Students: 153 full-time (102 women); includes 65 minority (32 African Americans, 11 Asian Americans or Pacific Islanders, 19 Hispanic Americans, 3 Native Americans), 18 international. 185 applicants, 30% accepted, 26 enrolled. In 2001, 17 doctorates awarded.
Degree requirements: For doctorate, thesis/dissertation, oral defense of dissertation, preliminary exam. *Median time to degree:* Doctorate–6.6 years full-time.
Entrance requirements: For doctorate, GRE General Test, letters of recommendation. *Application deadline:* For fall admission, 12/15. *Application fee:* $55. Electronic applications accepted.
Financial support: In 2001–02, 36 fellowships with tuition reimbursements (averaging $13,000 per year), 3 research assistantships with tuition reimbursements (averaging $14,000 per year), 37 teaching assistantships with tuition reimbursements (averaging $15,000 per year) were awarded. Health care benefits also available.
Faculty research: Power, history and social change; gender and sexuality; race and ethnicity; economic sociology; social demography.
Howard Kimeldorf, Chair, 734-764-5554, *Fax:* 734-763-6887, *E-mail:* hkimel@umich.edu.
Application contact: Cydne Friday, Graduate Program Office, 734-747-4428, *Fax:* 734-763-6887, *E-mail:* soc-gradprog@umich.edu. *Web site:* http://www.umich.edu/~socdept/

■ UNIVERSITY OF MINNESOTA, DULUTH

Graduate School, College of Liberal Arts, Department of Sociology/Anthropology, Duluth, MN 55812-2496

AWARDS MLS. Part-time programs available.

Faculty: 1 full-time (0 women), 21 part-time/adjunct (5 women).
Students: 5 full-time (all women), 11 part-time (8 women); includes 2 minority (1 African American, 1 Native American). Average age 38. 10 applicants, 80% accepted. In 2001, 4 degrees awarded.
Entrance requirements: For master's, interview, minimum GPA of 3.0. *Application deadline:* For fall admission, 7/15; for spring admission, 11/15. Applications are processed on a rolling basis. *Application fee:* $50 ($55 for international students).
Expenses: Tuition, state resident: full-time $2,932; part-time $489 per credit. Tuition, nonresident: full-time $5,758; part-time $960 per credit. Tuition and fees vary according to course load.
Financial support: Teaching assistantships with full tuition reimbursements, Federal Work-Study, institutionally sponsored loans, and scholarships/grants available. Financial award application deadline: 3/15.
Faculty research: Nature of knowledge, philosophy of science, ecology, cultural studies.
Dr. James Fetzer, Graduate Director, 218-726-7269, *Fax:* 218-726-7119, *E-mail:* jfetzer@d.umn.edu.
Application contact: Nancy Peterson, Assistant Director, 218-726-6149, *Fax:* 218-726-7119, *E-mail:* npeters3@d.umn.edu.

■ UNIVERSITY OF MINNESOTA, TWIN CITIES CAMPUS

Graduate School, College of Liberal Arts, Department of Sociology, Minneapolis, MN 55455-0213

AWARDS MA, PhD.

Faculty: 21 full-time (8 women), 15 part-time/adjunct (5 women).
Students: 62 full-time (40 women); includes 5 minority (3 African Americans, 1 Asian American or Pacific Islander, 1 Hispanic American), 18 international. Average age 31. 59 applicants, 51% accepted, 11 enrolled. In 2001, 5 master's, 12 doctorates awarded. Terminal master's awarded for partial completion of doctoral program.
Degree requirements: For master's, thesis optional; for doctorate, thesis/dissertation, preliminary and final written dissertation and oral defense. *Median time to degree:* Master's–4 years full-time; doctorate–8 years full-time.
Entrance requirements: For doctorate, GRE General Test, TOEFL, letters of recommendation (3), sample of written work. *Application deadline:* For fall admission, 1/1 (priority date). Applications are processed on a rolling basis. *Application fee:* $50 ($55 for international students). Electronic applications accepted.
Expenses: Tuition, state resident: full-time $2,932; part-time $489 per credit. Tuition, nonresident: full-time $5,758; part-time $960 per credit. Part-time tuition and fees vary according to course load, program and reciprocity agreements.
Financial support: In 2001–02, 57 students received support, including 9 fellowships with full tuition reimbursements available (averaging $13,000 per year), 9 research assistantships with full and partial tuition reimbursements available (averaging $10,233 per year), 35 teaching assistantships with full and partial tuition reimbursements available (averaging $10,233 per year); career-related internships or fieldwork, Federal Work-Study, scholarships/grants, traineeships, health care benefits, tuition waivers (full and partial), and unspecified assistantships also available. Financial award application deadline: 1/1.
Faculty research: Organizations, work, and markets; inequality; law, crime and deviance; family and life course; political sociology and social movements. *Total annual research expenditures:* $744,262.
Prof. Ronald Aminzade, Chair, 612-624-4300, *Fax:* 612-624-7020, *E-mail:* aminzade@umn.edu.
Application contact: Jessica Matteson, Graduate Program Assistant, 612-624-2093, *Fax:* 612-624-7020, *E-mail:* socdept@atlas.socsci.umn.edu. *Web site:* http://www.soc.umn.edu/

■ UNIVERSITY OF MISSISSIPPI

Graduate School, College of Liberal Arts, Department of Sociology and Anthropology, Oxford, University, MS 38677

AWARDS Anthropology (MA); sociology (MA, MSS).

Faculty: 11 full-time (3 women).
Students: 20 full-time (9 women), 2 part-time (1 woman); includes 3 minority (all Native Americans). In 2001, 4 degrees awarded.
Degree requirements: For master's, thesis (for some programs).
Entrance requirements: For master's, GRE General Test, TOEFL, minimum GPA of 3.0. *Application deadline:* For fall admission, 8/1. Applications are processed on a rolling basis. *Application fee:* $0 ($25 for international students).
Expenses: Tuition, state resident: full-time $3,626; part-time $202 per hour. Tuition, nonresident: full-time $8,172; part-time $454 per hour.
Financial support: Application deadline: 3/1.
Dr. Max Williams, Acting Chairman, 662-915-7288, *Fax:* 662-915-5372, *E-mail:* samax@olemiss.edu.

■ UNIVERSITY OF MISSOURI–COLUMBIA

Graduate School, College of Arts and Sciences, Department of Sociology, Columbia, MO 65211

AWARDS MA, PhD.

Faculty: 15 full-time (6 women).
Students: 17 full-time (13 women), 31 part-time (16 women); includes 6 minority (5 African Americans, 1 Asian American or Pacific Islander), 4 international. 13 applicants, 54% accepted. In 2001, 4 master's, 3 doctorates awarded.
Degree requirements: For doctorate, one foreign language, thesis/dissertation.
Entrance requirements: For master's and doctorate, GRE General Test, minimum GPA of 3.0. *Application deadline:* For fall admission, 2/1 (priority date). Applications are processed on a rolling basis. *Application fee:* $25 ($50 for international students).
Expenses: Tuition, state resident: part-time $179 per credit hour. Tuition, nonresident: part-time $539 per credit hour. Required fees: $122 per semester. Tuition and fees vary according to program.
Financial support: Research assistantships, teaching assistantships, institutionally sponsored loans available.
Dr. Ibitola Pearce, Director of Graduate Studies, 573-882-7265, *E-mail:* pearcei@missouri.edu. *Web site:* http://www.missouri.edu/%7Esocwww/gradpro.htm

■ UNIVERSITY OF MISSOURI–KANSAS CITY

College of Arts and Sciences, Department of Sociology, Program in Sociology, Kansas City, MO 64110-2499

AWARDS MA, PhD. PhD offered through the School of Graduate Studies. Part-time programs available.

Faculty: 9 full-time (3 women).
Students: 4 full-time (3 women), 16 part-time (14 women); includes 5 minority (4 African Americans, 1 Hispanic American), 1 international. Average age 38. 14 applicants, 57% accepted. In 2001, 5 degrees awarded.
Degree requirements: For master's, thesis optional.
Entrance requirements: For master's, minimum GPA of 3.0 in major, 2.6 overall. *Application deadline:* For fall admission, 4/30; for spring admission, 11/1. *Application fee:* $25.
Expenses: Tuition, state resident: part-time $233 per credit hour. Tuition, nonresident: part-time $623 per credit hour. Tuition and fees vary according to course load.
Financial support: In 2001–02, 7 teaching assistantships (averaging $7,600 per year) were awarded; career-related internships or fieldwork, Federal Work-Study, institutionally sponsored loans, and tuition waivers (partial) also available. Support available to part-time students. Financial award application deadline: 6/15.
Faculty research: Drug use, housing, stock quality, racial profiling, retirement.
Application contact: Prof. Peter Singlemann, Graduate Adviser, 816-235-2523, *Fax:* 816-235-1117, *E-mail:* singlemannp@umkc.edu.

■ UNIVERSITY OF MISSOURI–ST. LOUIS

Graduate School, College of Arts and Sciences, Department of Sociology, St. Louis, MO 63121-4499

AWARDS Advanced social perspective (MA); community conflict intervention (MA); program design and evaluation research (MA); social policy planning and administration (MA). Part-time and evening/weekend programs available.

Faculty: 5.
Students: 4 full-time (2 women), 6 part-time (4 women); includes 2 minority (1 African American, 1 Native American), 1 international. In 2001, 5 degrees awarded.
Degree requirements: For master's, thesis optional.
Entrance requirements: For master's, GRE General Test. *Application deadline:* For fall admission, 7/1 (priority date); for spring admission, 12/1 (priority date). Applications are processed on a rolling basis. *Application fee:* $25 ($40 for international students). Electronic applications accepted.
Expenses: Tuition, state resident: part-time $231 per credit hour. Tuition, nonresident: part-time $621 per credit hour.
Financial support: In 2001–02, 3 students received support, including 3 teaching assistantships with full and partial tuition reimbursements available (averaging $10,333 per year); research assistantships, career-related internships or fieldwork also available. Support available to part-time students.
Faculty research: Homeless populations, theory, social deviance, conflict resolution, Japan, Republic of South Africa, social change in East Germany. *Total annual research expenditures:* $30,040.
Dr. George McCall, Director of Graduate Studies, 314-516-6366, *Fax:* 314-516-5310.
Application contact: Jean Smith, Graduate Admissions, 314-516-6928, *Fax:* 314-516-5310, *E-mail:* gradadm@umsl.edu. *Web site:* http://www.umsl.edu/divisions/artscience/sociology/

■ THE UNIVERSITY OF MONTANA–MISSOULA

Graduate School, College of Arts and Sciences, Department of Sociology, Missoula, MT 59812-0002

AWARDS Criminology (MA); rural and environmental change (MA).

Faculty: 11 full-time (3 women).
Students: 15 full-time (11 women), 2 part-time (both women); includes 1 minority (Native American). 17 applicants, 88% accepted, 9 enrolled. In 2001, 4 degrees awarded.
Entrance requirements: For master's, GRE General Test. *Application deadline:* For fall admission, 3/15 (priority date). *Application fee:* $45.
Expenses: Tuition, state resident: full-time $2,482; part-time $1,700 per year. Tuition, nonresident: full-time $7,372; part-time $5,000 per year. Required fees: $1,900. Tuition and fees vary according to degree level.
Financial support: In 2001–02, 5 teaching assistantships with full tuition reimbursements (averaging $8,665 per year) were awarded; research assistantships, career-related internships or fieldwork, Federal Work-Study, and unspecified assistantships also available. Financial award application deadline: 3/1; financial award applicants required to submit FAFSA.
Faculty research: Housing, homelessness, hunger, infant mortality, work safety. *Total annual research expenditures:* $191,297.
Dr. Jill Belsky, Chair, 406-243-5281, *Fax:* 406-243-5951, *E-mail:* belsky@selway.umt.edu.
Application contact: Dr. Daniel P. Doyle, Graduate Coordinator, 406-243-2855, *Fax:* 406-243-5951, *E-mail:* ddoyle@selway.umt.edu. *Web site:* http://www.umt.edu/sociology/

■ UNIVERSITY OF NEBRASKA AT OMAHA

Graduate Studies and Research, College of Arts and Sciences, Department of Sociology, Omaha, NE 68182

AWARDS MA. Part-time programs available.

Faculty: 10 full-time (4 women).
Students: 4 full-time (2 women), 9 part-time (all women); includes 2 minority (1 African American, 1 Hispanic American), 3 international. Average age 31. 13 applicants, 100% accepted, 9 enrolled. In 2001, 1 degree awarded.
Degree requirements: For master's, thesis (for some programs), comprehensive exam.
Entrance requirements: For master's, GRE General Test, previous course work in sociology, statistics, and research methods; minimum GPA of 3.0. *Application deadline:* For fall admission, 7/1 (priority date); for spring admission, 12/1 (priority date). Applications are processed on a rolling basis. *Application fee:* $35. Electronic applications accepted.
Expenses: Tuition, state resident: part-time $116 per credit hour. Tuition, nonresident: part-time $291 per credit hour. Required fees: $13 per credit hour. $4 per semester. One-time fee: $52 part-time.
Financial support: In 2001–02, 11 students received support; teaching assistantships, Federal Work-Study, institutionally sponsored loans, scholarships/grants, tuition waivers (partial), and unspecified assistantships available. Support available to part-time students. Financial award application deadline: 3/1; financial award applicants required to submit FAFSA.
Dr. Mark Rousseau, Chairperson, 402-554-2626.

■ UNIVERSITY OF NEBRASKA–LINCOLN

Graduate College, College of Arts and Sciences, Department of Sociology, Lincoln, NE 68588

AWARDS MA, PhD.

Faculty: 17.
Students: 43 (27 women); includes 12 minority (7 African Americans, 1 Asian American or Pacific Islander, 4 Hispanic Americans) 1 international. Average age 36. 28 applicants, 25% accepted, 5 enrolled. In 2001, 6 master's, 7 doctorates awarded.
Degree requirements: For master's, thesis optional; for doctorate, thesis/dissertation, comprehensive exam.
Entrance requirements: For master's and doctorate, GRE General Test, TOEFL, writing sample. *Application deadline:* For fall admission, 1/15. *Application fee:* $35. Electronic applications accepted.
Expenses: Tuition, state resident: full-time $2,412; part-time $134 per credit. Tuition, nonresident: full-time $6,223; part-time $346 per credit. Tuition and fees vary according to course load.
Financial support: In 2001–02, 7 research assistantships, 18 teaching assistantships were awarded. Fellowships, Federal Work-Study, health care benefits, and unspecified assistantships also available. Support available to part-time students. Financial award application deadline: 1/15.
Faculty research: Family, deviance and social control, ethnic studies, inequality (gender, race, and class).
Dr. J. Allen Williams, Chair, 402-472-3631, *Fax:* 402-472-6070. *Web site:* http://www.unl.edu/unlsoc/

■ UNIVERSITY OF NEVADA, LAS VEGAS

Graduate College, College of Liberal Arts, Department of Sociology, Las Vegas, NV 89154-9900

AWARDS MA, PhD. Part-time programs available.

Faculty: 18 full-time (5 women).
Students: 19 full-time (8 women), 29 part-time (18 women); includes 5 minority (1 African American, 2 Asian Americans or Pacific Islanders, 2 Hispanic Americans), 1 international. 25 applicants, 72% accepted, 13 enrolled. In 2001, 3 master's, 2 doctorates awarded.
Degree requirements: For master's, thesis/dissertation, oral exams; for doctorate, thesis/dissertation, oral exams, comprehensive exam. *Median time to degree:* Doctorate–4.9 years full-time.
Entrance requirements: For master's, GRE General Test, minimum GPA of 3.0, 18 credits in sociology; for doctorate, GRE General Test, minimum GPA of 3.0. *Application deadline:* For fall admission, 6/1; for spring admission, 11/1. *Application fee:* $40 ($55 for international students).
Expenses: Tuition, state resident: full-time $1,926; part-time $107 per credit. Tuition, nonresident: full-time $9,376; part-time $220 per credit. Tuition and fees vary according to course load.
Financial support: In 2001–02, 1 research assistantship (averaging $4,900 per year), 16 teaching assistantships with partial tuition reimbursements (averaging $11,000 per year) were awarded. Financial award application deadline: 3/1.
Dr. Ronald Smith, Chair, 702-895-3322.
Application contact: Graduate College Admissions Evaluator, 702-895-3320, *Fax:* 702-895-4180, *E-mail:* gradcollege@ccmail.nevada.edu. *Web site:* http://www.unlv.edu/Colleges/Liberal_Arts/Sociology/

■ UNIVERSITY OF NEVADA, RENO

Graduate School, College of Arts and Science, Department of Sociology, Reno, NV 89557

AWARDS MA.

Faculty: 8.
Students: 6 full-time (5 women), 1 (woman) part-time; includes 3 minority (2 Asian Americans or Pacific Islanders, 1 Native American), 1 international. Average age 32. In 2001, 1 degree awarded.
Degree requirements: For master's, thesis optional.
Entrance requirements: For master's, GRE, TOEFL, minimum GPA of 3.0. *Application deadline:* For fall admission, 3/1 (priority date); for spring admission, 11/1. *Application fee:* $40.
Expenses: Tuition, state resident: full-time $2,067; part-time $108 per credit. Tuition, nonresident: full-time $9,282; part-time $109 per credit. Required fees: $57 per semester. Tuition and fees vary according to course load.
Financial support: In 2001–02, 4 teaching assistantships were awarded. Financial award application deadline: 3/1.
Faculty research: Statistics, politics and economics, religion and law, industry, theory stratification.
Dr. Berch Berberoglu, Graduate Program Director, 775-784-6647, *E-mail:* berchb@scs.unr.edu.

■ UNIVERSITY OF NEW HAMPSHIRE

Graduate School, College of Liberal Arts, Department of Sociology, Durham, NH 03824

AWARDS MA, PhD. Part-time programs available.

Faculty: 13 full-time.
Students: 27 full-time (19 women), 9 part-time (7 women); includes 3 minority (2 Hispanic Americans, 1 Native American), 1 international. Average age 34. 26 applicants, 50% accepted, 4 enrolled. In 2001, 3 master's, 1 doctorate awarded.
Degree requirements: For master's, thesis; for doctorate, one foreign language, thesis/dissertation.
Entrance requirements: For master's and doctorate, GRE General Test. *Application deadline:* For fall admission, 4/1 (priority date); for winter admission, 12/1. Applications are processed on a rolling basis. *Application fee:* $50. Electronic applications accepted.
Expenses: Tuition, state resident: full-time $6,300; part-time $350 per credit. Tuition, nonresident: full-time $15,720; part-time $643 per credit. Required fees: $560; $280 per term. One-time fee: $15 part-time. Tuition and fees vary according to course load.
Financial support: In 2001–02, 1 fellowship, 3 research assistantships, 17 teaching

University of New Hampshire (continued)
assistantships were awarded. Career-related internships or fieldwork, Federal Work-Study, scholarships/grants, and tuition waivers (full and partial) also available. Support available to part-time students. Financial award application deadline: 2/15.
Faculty research: Deviance, conflict and control, social psychology, comparative institutional analysis, family.
Dr. Lawrence Hamilton, Chairperson, 603-862-1859.
Application contact: Dr. James Tucker, Coordinator, 603-862-1814, *E-mail:* jetucker@cisunix.unh.edu. *Web site:* http://www.unh.edu/sociology/

■ UNIVERSITY OF NEW MEXICO

Graduate School, College of Arts and Sciences, Department of Sociology, Albuquerque, NM 87131-2039

AWARDS MA, PhD. Part-time programs available.

Faculty: 18 full-time (5 women), 2 part-time/adjunct (both women).
Students: 32 full-time (21 women), 13 part-time (8 women); includes 9 minority (1 African American, 1 Asian American or Pacific Islander, 6 Hispanic Americans, 1 Native American), 1 international. Average age 41. 19 applicants, 63% accepted, 3 enrolled. In 2001, 3 master's, 2 doctorates awarded.
Degree requirements: For master's and doctorate, thesis/dissertation.
Entrance requirements: For master's, GRE General Test, writing sample; for doctorate, GRE General Test. *Application deadline:* For fall admission, 2/1. *Application fee:* $40.
Expenses: Tuition, state resident: full-time $2,771; part-time $115 per credit hour. Tuition, nonresident: full-time $11,207; part-time $467 per credit hour. Required fees: $570; $24 per credit hour. Part-time tuition and fees vary according to course load and program.
Financial support: In 2001–02, 28 students received support, including 14 teaching assistantships with full tuition reimbursements available (averaging $12,000 per year); health care benefits, tuition waivers (full), and unspecified assistantships also available. Support available to part-time students. Financial award application deadline: 3/1; financial award applicants required to submit FAFSA.
Faculty research: Criminology/deviance, gender, Latin American/comparative sociology, political sociology, race and ethnicity. *Total annual research expenditures:* $5,633.
Dr. Susan B. Tiano, Chair, 505-277-2501, *Fax:* 505-277-8805, *E-mail:* stiano@unm.edu.
Application contact: Rose Muller, Administrator II, 505-277-2501, *Fax:* 505-277-8805, *E-mail:* rmuller@unm.edu. *Web site:* http://www.unm.edu/~socdept/

Find an in-depth description at www.petersons.com/gradchannel.

■ UNIVERSITY OF NEW ORLEANS

Graduate School, College of Liberal Arts, Department of Sociology, New Orleans, LA 70148

AWARDS Applied sociology (MA); sociology (MA). Part-time and evening/weekend programs available.

Faculty: 5 full-time (4 women).
Students: 14 full-time (9 women), 17 part-time (8 women); includes 7 minority (all African Americans), 4 international. Average age 30. 22 applicants, 77% accepted, 8 enrolled. In 2001, 11 degrees awarded.
Degree requirements: For master's, thesis (for some programs).
Entrance requirements: For master's, GRE General Test. *Application deadline:* For fall admission, 7/1 (priority date); for spring admission, 11/15 (priority date). Applications are processed on a rolling basis. *Application fee:* $20. Electronic applications accepted.
Expenses: Tuition, state resident: full-time $2,748; part-time $435 per credit. Tuition, nonresident: full-time $9,792; part-time $1,773 per credit.
Financial support: Research assistantships available. Financial award application deadline: 3/15; financial award applicants required to submit FAFSA.
Faculty research: Environment and gender.
Dr. David Allen, Chairperson, 504-280-6475, *E-mail:* hallen@uno.edu.
Application contact: Dr. Vern Baxter, Graduate Coordinator, 504-280-6476, *E-mail:* vbaxter@uno.edu.

■ THE UNIVERSITY OF NORTH CAROLINA AT CHAPEL HILL

Graduate School, College of Arts and Sciences, Department of Sociology, Chapel Hill, NC 27599

AWARDS MA, PhD.

Degree requirements: For master's and doctorate, thesis/dissertation, comprehensive exam.
Entrance requirements: For master's and doctorate, GRE General Test, minimum GPA of 3.0. Electronic applications accepted.
Expenses: Tuition, state resident: full-time $2,864. Tuition, nonresident: full-time $12,030.
Faculty research: Comparative historical, work/organizations, religion, demography, stratification. *Web site:* http://www.unc.edu/depts/soc/

■ THE UNIVERSITY OF NORTH CAROLINA AT CHARLOTTE

Graduate School, College of Arts and Sciences, Department of Sociology and Anthropology, Charlotte, NC 28223-0001

AWARDS Sociology (MA). Part-time and evening/weekend programs available.

Faculty: 17 full-time (10 women), 2 part-time/adjunct (1 woman).
Students: 6 full-time (5 women), 12 part-time (8 women); includes 7 minority (5 African Americans, 2 Hispanic Americans), 2 international. Average age 28. 5 applicants, 100% accepted, 4 enrolled. In 2001, 5 degrees awarded.
Degree requirements: For master's, thesis or comprehensive exam.
Entrance requirements: For master's, GRE or MAT, minimum GPA of 3.0 in last 2 years, 2.75 overall. *Application deadline:* For fall admission, 7/15; for spring admission, 11/15. Applications are processed on a rolling basis. *Application fee:* $35. Electronic applications accepted.
Expenses: Tuition, state resident: full-time $1,483; part-time $371 per year. Tuition, nonresident: full-time $9,850; part-time $2,463 per year. Required fees: $1,043; $277 per year. Tuition and fees vary according to course load.
Financial support: In 2001–02, 4 research assistantships, 4 teaching assistantships were awarded. Fellowships, career-related internships or fieldwork, Federal Work-Study, institutionally sponsored loans, scholarships/grants, and unspecified assistantships also available. Support available to part-time students. Financial award application deadline: 4/1; financial award applicants required to submit FAFSA.
Faculty research: Social psychology, sociology of education, social gerontology, quantitative methodology, medical sociology.
Dr. Charles J. Brody, Chair, 704-687-2252, *Fax:* 704-687-3091, *E-mail:* cbrody@email.uncc.edu.
Application contact: Kathy Barringer, Director of Graduate Admissions, 704-687-3366, *Fax:* 704-687-3279, *E-mail:* gradadm@email.uncc.edu. *Web site:* http://www.uncc.edu/gradmiss/

■ THE UNIVERSITY OF NORTH CAROLINA AT GREENSBORO

Graduate School, College of Arts and Sciences, Department of Sociology, Greensboro, NC 27412-5001

AWARDS MA. Part-time programs available.

Faculty: 12 full-time (5 women), 1 part-time/adjunct (0 women).
Students: 11 full-time (5 women), 25 part-time (19 women); includes 6 minority (5 African Americans, 1 Native American). 28 applicants, 43% accepted, 10 enrolled. In 2001, 12 degrees awarded.

Degree requirements: For master's, thesis, comprehensive exam.
Entrance requirements: For master's, GRE General Test, TOEFL. *Application deadline:* For fall admission, 3/15 (priority date); for spring admission, 11/1. Applications are processed on a rolling basis. *Application fee:* $35.
Expenses: Tuition, state resident: part-time $344 per course. Tuition, nonresident: part-time $2,457 per course.
Financial support: In 2001–02, 13 students received support, including 4 research assistantships with full tuition reimbursements available (averaging $7,125 per year); fellowships with full tuition reimbursements available, teaching assistantships with full tuition reimbursements available, career-related internships or fieldwork, Federal Work-Study, scholarships/grants, and traineeships also available. Support available to part-time students.
Dr. David Pratto, Head, 336-334-5295, *Fax:* 336-334-5283, *E-mail:* djpratto@uncg.edu.
Application contact: Dr. James Lynch, Director of Graduate Recruitment and Information Services, 336-334-4881, *Fax:* 336-334-4424. *Web site:* http://www.uncg.edu/soc/

■ UNIVERSITY OF NORTH DAKOTA

Graduate School, College of Arts and Sciences, Department of Sociology, Grand Forks, ND 58202

AWARDS MA.

Faculty: 11 full-time (4 women).
Students: 3 full-time (all women), 11 part-time (7 women). 4 applicants, 75% accepted, 1 enrolled. In 2001, 3 degrees awarded.
Degree requirements: For master's, thesis, final examination.
Entrance requirements: For master's, TOEFL, minimum GPA of 3.0. *Application deadline:* For fall admission, 3/1 (priority date); for spring admission, 10/15 (priority date). Applications are processed on a rolling basis. *Application fee:* $30.
Expenses: Tuition, state resident: full-time $3,298. Tuition, nonresident: full-time $7,998.
Financial support: In 2001–02, 3 research assistantships with full tuition reimbursements (averaging $8,775 per year), 13 teaching assistantships with full tuition reimbursements (averaging $8,775 per year) were awarded. Fellowships, Federal Work-Study, institutionally sponsored loans, scholarships/grants, tuition waivers (full and partial), and unspecified assistantships also available. Support available to part-time students. Financial award application deadline: 3/15; financial award applicants required to submit FAFSA.
Faculty research: Criminal justice studies, social psychology, research methods, corrections, social theory.
Dr. Clifford L. Staples, Director, 701-777-4417, *Fax:* 701-777-2468, *E-mail:* clifford_staples@und.nodak.edu. *Web site:* http://www.und.edu/dept/soc/socpage.htm

■ UNIVERSITY OF NORTHERN COLORADO

Graduate School, College of Arts and Sciences, Department of Sociology, Greeley, CO 80639

AWARDS MA.

Faculty: 9 full-time (6 women).
Students: 6 full-time (4 women), 1 part-time; includes 1 minority (Asian American or Pacific Islander). Average age 32. 5 applicants, 80% accepted. In 2001, 2 degrees awarded.
Degree requirements: For master's, comprehensive exam.
Application deadline: Applications are processed on a rolling basis. *Application fee:* $35.
Expenses: Tuition, state resident: full-time $2,549; part-time $546 per credit hour. Tuition, nonresident: full-time $10,459; part-time $581 per credit hour. Required fees: $631; $85 per year. Part-time tuition and fees vary according to course load.
Financial support: In 2001–02, 6 students received support, including 3 fellowships (averaging $667 per year), 1 research assistantship (averaging $10,339 per year), 2 teaching assistantships (averaging $3,323 per year); unspecified assistantships also available. Financial award application deadline: 3/1.
Dr. John Vonk, Chair, 970-351-2315.

■ UNIVERSITY OF NORTHERN IOWA

Graduate College, College of Social and Behavioral Sciences, Department of Sociology, Anthropology and Criminology, Cedar Falls, IA 50614

AWARDS Sociology (MA). Part-time and evening/weekend programs available.

Students: 8 full-time (6 women), 3 part-time (all women); includes 3 minority (2 African Americans, 1 Hispanic American), 1 international. 10 applicants, 100% accepted. In 2001, 2 degrees awarded.
Degree requirements: For master's, thesis.
Application deadline: For fall admission, 8/1 (priority date). Applications are processed on a rolling basis. *Application fee:* $20 ($50 for international students).
Expenses: Tuition, state resident: full-time $3,704; part-time $206 per credit hour. Tuition, nonresident: full-time $9,122; part-time $501 per credit hour. Required fees: $324; $108 per semester. Part-time tuition and fees vary according to course load.
Financial support: Career-related internships or fieldwork, Federal Work-Study, scholarships/grants, and tuition waivers (full and partial) available. Support available to part-time students. Financial award application deadline: 3/1.
Dr. B. Keith Crew, Head, 319-273-2786, *Fax:* 319-273-7104, *E-mail:* bk.crew@uni.edu. *Web site:* http://csbsnt.csbs.uni.edu/dept/sac/

■ UNIVERSITY OF NORTH TEXAS

Robert B. Toulouse School of Graduate Studies, School of Community Service, Department of Sociology, Denton, TX 76203

AWARDS MA, MS, PhD.

Faculty: 11 full-time (3 women).
Students: 16 full-time (8 women), 49 part-time (32 women); includes 8 minority (2 African Americans, 4 Hispanic Americans, 2 Native Americans), 8 international. Average age 27. In 2001, 12 master's, 8 doctorates awarded. Terminal master's awarded for partial completion of doctoral program.
Degree requirements: For master's, variable foreign language requirement, thesis, comprehensive exam; for doctorate, one foreign language, thesis/dissertation, comprehensive exam.
Entrance requirements: For master's, GRE General Test, minimum GPA of 2.8; for doctorate, GRE General Test, master's degree, minimum graduate GPA of 3.4. *Application deadline:* For fall admission, 7/17; for spring admission, 12/2. Applications are processed on a rolling basis. *Application fee:* $25 ($50 for international students).
Expenses: Tuition, state resident: part-time $186 per hour. Tuition, nonresident: part-time $319 per hour. Required fees: $88; $21 per hour.
Financial support: Research assistantships, teaching assistantships, career-related internships or fieldwork, Federal Work-Study, institutionally sponsored loans, and scholarships/grants available. Financial award application deadline: 6/1.
Faculty research: Sociological practice, aging, minorities, gender health. *Total annual research expenditures:* $147,000.
Dr. Dale Yeatts, Chair, 940-565-2296, *Fax:* 940-565-4663, *E-mail:* yeatts@scs.cmm.unt.edu.
Application contact: Dr. Rudy Ray Seward, Graduate Adviser, 940-565-2296, *Fax:* 940-565-4663, *E-mail:* seward@scs.cmm.unt.edu.

■ UNIVERSITY OF NOTRE DAME

Graduate School, College of Arts and Letters, Division of Social Science, Department of Sociology, Notre Dame, IN 46556

AWARDS PhD.

Faculty: 22 full-time (6 women), 6 part-time/adjunct (3 women).
Students: 53 full-time (28 women); includes 3 minority (all Asian Americans or Pacific Islanders), 15 international. 102

University of Notre Dame (continued)
applicants, 21% accepted, 10 enrolled. In 2001, 11 doctorates awarded.
Degree requirements: For doctorate, thesis/dissertation, 2 area specialty exams. *Median time to degree:* Doctorate–7 years full-time.
Entrance requirements: For doctorate, GRE General Test, GRE Subject Test (strongly recommended), TOEFL. *Application deadline:* For fall admission, 2/1 (priority date). Applications are processed on a rolling basis. *Application fee:* $50. Electronic applications accepted.
Expenses: Tuition: Full-time $24,220; part-time $1,346 per credit hour. Required fees: $155.
Financial support: In 2001–02, 49 students received support, including 19 fellowships with full tuition reimbursements available (averaging $14,000 per year), 15 research assistantships with full tuition reimbursements available (averaging $11,200 per year), 3 teaching assistantships with full tuition reimbursements available (averaging $11,200 per year); tuition waivers (full) also available. Support available to part-time students. Financial award application deadline: 2/1.
Faculty research: Family, education, religion, political sociology, research methods and statistics. *Total annual research expenditures:* $537,000.
Dr. Maureen T. Hallinan, Chair, Admissions Committee, 574-631-6463, *Fax:* 574-631-9238, *E-mail:* soc.1@nd.edu.
Application contact: Dr. Terrence J. Akai, Director of Graduate Admissions, 574-631-7706, *Fax:* 574-631-4183, *E-mail:* gradad@nd.edu. *Web site:* http://www.nd.edu/~soc/

■ UNIVERSITY OF OKLAHOMA

Graduate College, College of Arts and Sciences, Department of Sociology, Norman, OK 73019-0390

AWARDS MA, PhD. Part-time programs available.

Faculty: 10 full-time (5 women), 1 part-time/adjunct (0 women).
Students: 24 full-time (17 women), 10 part-time (7 women); includes 7 minority (4 African Americans, 1 Hispanic American, 2 Native Americans), 1 international. 11 applicants, 82% accepted, 6 enrolled. In 2001, 7 master's, 1 doctorate awarded.
Degree requirements: For master's, thesis or alternative; for doctorate, thesis/dissertation, general exams, qualifying exam.
Entrance requirements: For master's, GRE General Test, TOEFL; for doctorate, GRE General Test, TOEFL, MA. *Application deadline:* For fall admission, 3/1 (priority date). Applications are processed on a rolling basis. *Application fee:* $25 ($50 for international students).
Expenses: Tuition, state resident: full-time $2,208; part-time $92 per credit hour. Tuition, nonresident: part-time $297 per credit hour. Tuition and fees vary according to course level, course load and program.
Financial support: In 2001–02, 21 students received support, including 2 research assistantships with partial tuition reimbursements available (averaging $9,235 per year), 19 teaching assistantships with partial tuition reimbursements available (averaging $11,092 per year); fellowships, Federal Work-Study, scholarships/grants, tuition waivers (partial), and unspecified assistantships also available. Financial award application deadline: 3/15; financial award applicants required to submit FAFSA.
Faculty research: Criminology, demography and family, study of race, class and gender, historical/comparative/global sociology. *Total annual research expenditures:* $268,238.
Dr. Wilbur Scott, Chairperson, 405-325-1751, *Fax:* 405-325-7825, *E-mail:* wscott@ou.edu.
Application contact: Sonya Brindle, Secretary, 405-325-1751, *Fax:* 405-325-7825, *E-mail:* sbrindle@ou.edu.

■ UNIVERSITY OF OREGON

Graduate School, College of Arts and Sciences, Department of Sociology, Eugene, OR 97403

AWARDS MA, MS, PhD. Part-time programs available.

Faculty: 12 full-time (6 women), 5 part-time/adjunct (3 women).
Students: 42 full-time (23 women), 4 part-time (3 women); includes 7 minority (2 African Americans, 4 Hispanic Americans, 1 Native American), 8 international. 68 applicants, 15% accepted. In 2001, 5 master's, 2 doctorates awarded. Terminal master's awarded for partial completion of doctoral program.
Degree requirements: For doctorate, thesis/dissertation.
Entrance requirements: For master's and doctorate, GRE General Test, TOEFL, minimum GPA of 3.0. *Application deadline:* For fall admission, 2/1. *Application fee:* $50.
Expenses: Tuition, state resident: full-time $4,968; part-time $501 per credit hour. Tuition, nonresident: full-time $8,400; part-time $691 per credit hour.
Financial support: In 2001–02, 33 teaching assistantships were awarded; Federal Work-Study also available.
Faculty research: Criminology, environment, gender, labor, political economy.
Dr. Lawrence R. Carter, Head, 541-346-5002.
Application contact: Mary Redetzke, Admissions Contact, 541-346-1168, *Fax:* 541-346-5002. *Web site:* http://darkwing.uoregon.edu/~sociology/

■ UNIVERSITY OF PENNSYLVANIA

School of Arts and Sciences, Graduate Group in Sociology, Philadelphia, PA 19104

AWARDS AM, PhD. Terminal master's awarded for partial completion of doctoral program.

Degree requirements: For master's, thesis or alternative; for doctorate, one foreign language, thesis/dissertation.
Entrance requirements: For master's and doctorate, GRE General Test, TOEFL.
Expenses: Tuition: Part-time $12,875 per semester.

■ UNIVERSITY OF PITTSBURGH

Faculty of Arts and Sciences, Department of Sociology, Pittsburgh, PA 15260

AWARDS MA, PhD.

Faculty: 15 full-time (6 women).
Students: 25 full-time (20 women), 4 part-time (3 women); includes 5 minority (3 African Americans, 2 Asian Americans or Pacific Islanders), 7 international. 33 applicants, 39% accepted, 5 enrolled. In 2001, 4 degrees awarded. Terminal master's awarded for partial completion of doctoral program.
Degree requirements: For master's, thesis; for doctorate, thesis/dissertation, preliminary exam, comprehensive exam.
Entrance requirements: For master's and doctorate, GRE General Test, TOEFL, writing sample. *Application deadline:* For fall admission, 4/15. Applications are processed on a rolling basis. *Application fee:* $40. Electronic applications accepted.
Expenses: Tuition, state resident: full-time $9,410; part-time $385 per credit. Tuition, nonresident: full-time $19,376; part-time $797 per credit. Required fees: $480; $90 per term. Tuition and fees vary according to program.
Financial support: In 2001–02, 24 students received support, including 4 fellowships with full tuition reimbursements available (averaging $14,364 per year), 1 research assistantship with full tuition reimbursement available (averaging $12,465 per year), 19 teaching assistantships with full tuition reimbursements available (averaging $12,222 per year); scholarships/grants, tuition waivers (partial), and unspecified assistantships also available. Financial award application deadline: 3/15.
Faculty research: Global and comparative sociology, gender, race and class, social network process.
Patrick Doreian, Chairman, 412-648-7584, *Fax:* 412-648-2799, *E-mail:* pitpat@pitt.edu.
Application contact: Carol Choma, Graduate Administrator, 412-648-7585, *Fax:* 412-648-2799, *E-mail:* choma+@

pitt.edu. *Web site:* http://www.pitt.edu/~socdept/sociology.html

■ UNIVERSITY OF PUERTO RICO, RÍO PIEDRAS

College of Social Sciences, Department of Sociology, San Juan, PR 00931

AWARDS MA.

Students: 9 full-time (3 women), 19 part-time (10 women); all minorities (all Hispanic Americans). In 2001, 3 degrees awarded.
Degree requirements: For master's, thesis, comprehensive exam.
Entrance requirements: For master's, GRE, PAEG, interview, minimum GPA of 3.0. *Application deadline:* For fall admission, 2/1. *Application fee:* $17.
Expenses: Students that provide official evidence of private medicine insurance or service are exempt of the payment of $529 per academic year.
Financial support: Application deadline: 5/31.
Faculty research: Agroindustry of tobacco, sociology of the Dominican female population in Puerto Rico.
Dr. Jesús Tapia-Santamaría, Coordinator, 787-764-0000 Ext. 2471, *Fax:* 787-764-0000 Ext. 4325.
Application contact: Milagros Vázquez, Secretary, 787-764-0000 Ext. 3105, *Fax:* 787-764-0000 Ext. 4325.

■ UNIVERSITY OF SOUTH ALABAMA

Graduate School, College of Arts and Sciences, Department of Sociology, Mobile, AL 36688-0002

AWARDS MA. Part-time and evening/weekend programs available.

Faculty: 12 full-time (4 women).
Students: 4 full-time (3 women), 7 part-time (4 women); includes 4 minority (all African Americans). 12 applicants, 67% accepted. In 2001, 2 degrees awarded.
Degree requirements: For master's, thesis optional.
Entrance requirements: For master's, GRE General Test, GRE Subject Test, minimum GPA of 3.0. *Application deadline:* For fall admission, 9/1 (priority date). Applications are processed on a rolling basis. *Application fee:* $25.
Expenses: Tuition, state resident: full-time $3,048. Tuition, nonresident: full-time $6,096. Required fees: $320.
Financial support: In 2001–02, 5 research assistantships were awarded; fellowships Financial award application deadline: 4/1.
Faculty research: Cultural adaptation.
Dr. Steven Picou, Chair, 334-460-6347.

■ UNIVERSITY OF SOUTH CAROLINA

The Graduate School, College of Liberal Arts, Department of Sociology, Columbia, SC 29208

AWARDS MA, PhD. Part-time programs available.

Faculty: 11 full-time (2 women).
Students: 35 full-time (24 women), 5 part-time (3 women); includes 3 African Americans, 6 Asian Americans or Pacific Islanders. Average age 36. 30 applicants, 47% accepted, 11 enrolled. In 2001, 1 master's, 4 doctorates awarded.
Degree requirements: For master's, thesis/dissertation; for doctorate, thesis/dissertation, comprehensive exam.
Entrance requirements: For master's and doctorate, GRE General Test. *Application deadline:* For fall admission, 7/1; for spring admission, 11/15. Applications are processed on a rolling basis. *Application fee:* $40. Electronic applications accepted.
Expenses: Tuition, state resident: full-time $4,434. Tuition, nonresident: full-time $9,854. Tuition and fees vary according to program.
Financial support: In 2001–02, 1 fellowship with partial tuition reimbursement, 17 research assistantships with partial tuition reimbursements (averaging $8,000 per year) were awarded. Federal Work-Study also available. Support available to part-time students. Financial award application deadline: 4/1.
Faculty research: Social psychology, demography, social organization, social structure.
Dr. Barry Markovsky, Chair, 803-777-3123, *Fax:* 803-777-5251, *E-mail:* barry@sc.edu.
Application contact: Dr. J. M. Sanders, Graduate Director, 803-777-3123, *Fax:* 803-777-5251, *E-mail:* jimsand@sc.edu.

■ THE UNIVERSITY OF SOUTH DAKOTA

Graduate School, College of Arts and Sciences, Department of Social Behavior, Vermillion, SD 57069-2390

AWARDS Sociology (MA).

Faculty: 9 full-time (2 women), 1 part-time/adjunct (0 women).
Students: 7 full-time (6 women), 1 (woman) part-time; includes 1 minority (African American). 4 applicants, 100% accepted. In 2001, 1 degree awarded.
Degree requirements: For master's, thesis (for some programs).
Entrance requirements: For master's, GRE General Test. *Application deadline:* Applications are processed on a rolling basis. *Application fee:* $35.
Expenses: Tuition, state resident: full-time $1,700; part-time $95 per credit hour. Tuition, nonresident: full-time $5,027; part-time $279 per credit hour. Required fees: $1,062; $59 per credit hour.
Financial support: Teaching assistantships available. Financial award application deadline: 6/1; financial award applicants required to submit FAFSA.
Dr. Jon Flanagan, Chair, 605-677-5401. *Web site:* http://www.usd.edu/soc/

■ UNIVERSITY OF SOUTHERN CALIFORNIA

Graduate School, College of Letters, Arts and Sciences, Department of Sociology, Program in Sociology, Los Angeles, CA 90089

AWARDS MA, MS, PhD.

Degree requirements: For master's and doctorate, thesis/dissertation.
Entrance requirements: For master's and doctorate, GRE General Test.
Expenses: Tuition: Full-time $25,060; part-time $844 per unit. Required fees: $473.

■ UNIVERSITY OF SOUTH FLORIDA

College of Graduate Studies, College of Arts and Sciences, Department of Sociology, Tampa, FL 33620-9951

AWARDS MA. Part-time programs available.

Faculty: 11 full-time (7 women).
Students: 6 full-time (3 women), 12 part-time (9 women); includes 1 minority (African American), 1 international. Average age 29. 12 applicants, 100% accepted, 6 enrolled.
Entrance requirements: For master's, GRE General Test, minimum GPA of 3.0 in last 60 hours. *Application deadline:* For fall admission, 6/1; for spring admission, 10/15. *Application fee:* $20.
Expenses: Tuition, state resident: part-time $166 per credit hour. Tuition, nonresident: part-time $573 per credit hour. Required fees: $17 per term.
Financial support: Fellowships with full tuition reimbursements, research assistantships, teaching assistantships with full tuition reimbursements, Federal Work-Study and institutionally sponsored loans available. Support available to part-time students. Financial award applicants required to submit FAFSA. *Total annual research expenditures:* $15,402.
Maralee Mayberry, Chairperson, 813-974-2241, *Fax:* 813-974-6455, *E-mail:* mayberry@chuma1.cas.usf.edu. *Web site:* http://www.cas.usf.edu/sociology/index.html

■ THE UNIVERSITY OF TENNESSEE

Graduate School, College of Arts and Sciences, Department of Sociology, Knoxville, TN 37996

AWARDS Criminology (MA, PhD); energy, environment, and resource policy (MA, PhD);

The University of Tennessee (continued)
political economy (MA, PhD). Part-time programs available.

Faculty: 15 full-time (2 women), 1 (woman) part-time/adjunct.
Students: 22 full-time (14 women), 26 part-time (11 women); includes 7 minority (6 African Americans, 1 Asian American or Pacific Islander), 4 international. 30 applicants, 63% accepted. In 2001, 3 degrees awarded.
Degree requirements: For master's, thesis or alternative; for doctorate, thesis/dissertation.
Entrance requirements: For master's, GRE General Test, TOEFL, minimum GPA of 3.0; for doctorate, GRE General Test, TOEFL, minimum GPA of 3.5. *Application deadline:* For fall admission, 2/1 (priority date). Applications are processed on a rolling basis. *Application fee:* $35. Electronic applications accepted.
Expenses: Tuition, state resident: full-time $4,280; part-time $233 per hour. Tuition, nonresident: full-time $12,066; part-time $666 per hour. Tuition and fees vary according to program.
Financial support: In 2001–02, 1 fellowship, 2 research assistantships, 20 teaching assistantships were awarded. Federal Work-Study, institutionally sponsored loans, and unspecified assistantships also available. Financial award application deadline: 2/1; financial award applicants required to submit FAFSA.
Dr. Suzanne Kurth, Head, 865-974-6021, *Fax:* 865-974-7013, *E-mail:* skurth@utk.edu.
Application contact: Dr. T. C. Hood, Graduate Representative, 865-974-7032, *E-mail:* tomhood@utk.edu.

■ THE UNIVERSITY OF TEXAS AT ARLINGTON

Graduate School, College of Liberal Arts, Department of Sociology and Anthropology, Program in Sociology, Arlington, TX 76019

AWARDS MA. Part-time and evening/weekend programs available.

Students: 2 full-time (both women), 10 part-time (all women); includes 4 minority (1 African American, 1 Asian American or Pacific Islander, 2 Hispanic Americans), 2 international. 6 applicants, 100% accepted, 5 enrolled. In 2001, 4 degrees awarded.
Degree requirements: For master's, thesis or alternative.
Entrance requirements: For master's, GRE General Test, 12 hours of undergraduate course work in sociology. *Application deadline:* For fall admission, 6/16. Applications are processed on a rolling basis. *Application fee:* $25 ($50 for international students).
Expenses: Tuition, area resident: Full-time $2,268. Tuition, nonresident: full-time $6,264. Required fees: $839. Tuition and fees vary according to course load.
Financial support: In 2001–02, 3 students received support, including 1 fellowship (averaging $1,000 per year), 3 teaching assistantships (averaging $8,000 per year); research assistantships, Federal Work-Study also available. Financial award application deadline: 4/1.
Application contact: Dr. Frank J. Weed, Graduate Adviser, 817-272-3791, *Fax:* 817-272-3579, *E-mail:* fjweed@uta.edu.

■ THE UNIVERSITY OF TEXAS AT AUSTIN

Graduate School, College of Liberal Arts, Department of Sociology, Austin, TX 78712-1111

AWARDS MA, PhD.

Degree requirements: For master's and doctorate, thesis/dissertation.
Entrance requirements: For master's and doctorate, GRE General Test. Electronic applications accepted.
Expenses: Tuition, state resident: full-time $3,159. Tuition, nonresident: full-time $6,957. Tuition and fees vary according to program.
Faculty research: Criminology, demography, Latin America, race and ethnic relations, health. *Web site:* http://www.la.utexas.edu/

■ THE UNIVERSITY OF TEXAS AT DALLAS

School of Social Sciences, Program in Applied Sociology, Richardson, TX 75083-0688

AWARDS MA, MS.

Faculty: 8 full-time (3 women).
Students: 6 full-time (5 women), 6 part-time (3 women); includes 4 minority (2 African Americans, 2 Hispanic Americans), 2 international. Average age 28. 10 applicants, 50% accepted. In 2001, 2 degrees awarded.
Degree requirements: For master's, internship.
Entrance requirements: For master's, GRE General Test, TOEFL, minimum GPA of 3.0 in upper-level coursework in field. *Application deadline:* For fall admission, 7/15; for spring admission, 11/15. Applications are processed on a rolling basis. *Application fee:* $25 ($75 for international students). Electronic applications accepted.
Expenses: Tuition, state resident: full-time $1,440; part-time $84 per credit. Tuition, nonresident: full-time $5,310; part-time $295 per credit. Required fees: $1,835; $87 per credit. $138 per term.
Financial support: In 2001–02, 1 research assistantship (averaging $4,500 per year), 3 teaching assistantships with tuition reimbursements (averaging $3,750 per year) were awarded. Fellowships, career-related internships or fieldwork, Federal Work-Study, institutionally sponsored loans, and scholarships/grants also available. Support available to part-time students. Financial award application deadline: 4/30.
Faculty research: Social impact of alcohol in Latino families, reading one-to-one, Americorps, neighborhood evaluations.
Application contact: Program Coordinator, 972-883-2720, *Fax:* 972-883-2735, *E-mail:* ss-grad-info@utdallas.edu. *Web site:* http://www.utdallas.edu/dept/socsci/appsoc.htm

■ THE UNIVERSITY OF TEXAS AT EL PASO

Graduate School, College of Liberal Arts, Department of Sociology and Anthropology, El Paso, TX 79968-0001

AWARDS Sociology (MA). Part-time and evening/weekend programs available.

Students: 12 (4 women); includes 6 minority (1 African American, 5 Hispanic Americans). Average age 34. 1 applicant, 100% accepted. In 2001, 3 degrees awarded.
Degree requirements: For master's, thesis optional.
Entrance requirements: For master's, GRE General Test, TOEFL, minimum GPA of 3.0. *Application deadline:* For fall admission, 7/1 (priority date); for spring admission, 11/1 (priority date). Applications are processed on a rolling basis. *Application fee:* $15 ($65 for international students). Electronic applications accepted.
Expenses: Tuition, state resident: full-time $2,450. Tuition, nonresident: full-time $6,000.
Financial support: In 2001–02, research assistantships with partial tuition reimbursements (averaging $18,625 per year), teaching assistantships with partial tuition reimbursements (averaging $14,900 per year) were awarded. Career-related internships or fieldwork, Federal Work-Study, institutionally sponsored loans, and scholarships/grants also available. Financial award application deadline: 3/15; financial award applicants required to submit FAFSA.
Dr. S. Fernando Rodriguez, Chairperson, 915-747-5740, *Fax:* 915-747-5505, *E-mail:* fernando@miners.utep.edu.
Application contact: Dr. Charles H. Ambler, Dean of the Graduate School, 915-747-5491 Ext. 7886, *Fax:* 915-747-5788, *E-mail:* cambler@miners.utep.edu.

■ THE UNIVERSITY OF TEXAS AT SAN ANTONIO

College of Liberal and Fine Arts, Department of Sociology, San Antonio, TX 78249-0617

AWARDS MS. Part-time and evening/weekend programs available.

Faculty: 9 full-time (3 women).
Students: 3 full-time (2 women), 7 part-time (6 women); includes 6 minority (1

African American, 4 Hispanic Americans, 1 Native American). Average age 31. 7 applicants, 71% accepted, 3 enrolled. In 2001, 1 degree awarded.
Degree requirements: For master's, thesis optional. *Median time to degree:* Master's–3 years full-time.
Entrance requirements: For master's, GRE General Test, undergraduate course work in sociology. *Application deadline:* For fall admission, 7/1 (priority date); for spring admission, 11/1. Applications are processed on a rolling basis. *Application fee:* $25 ($50 for international students). Electronic applications accepted.
Expenses: Tuition, state resident: full-time $2,268; part-time $126 per credit hour. Tuition, nonresident: full-time $6,066; part-time $337 per credit hour. Required fees: $781. Tuition and fees vary according to course load.
Financial support: In 2001–02, 2 research assistantships (averaging $13,697 per year) were awarded; career-related internships or fieldwork, Federal Work-Study, scholarships/grants, and readers/graders also available.
Faculty research: Race and ethnic relations, qualitative research methods, complex organizations, gender stratification, social stratification, sociological theory.
Dr. Jeffrey Halley, Chair, 210-458-4626, *Fax:* 210-458-4629, *E-mail:* kbryan@utsa.edu.
Application contact: Kathleen McCleery, Secretary, 210-458-4620, *Fax:* 210-458-4629, *E-mail:* kmccleery@utsa.edu.

■ THE UNIVERSITY OF TEXAS AT TYLER

Graduate Studies, College of Arts and Sciences, Department of Social Sciences, Tyler, TX 75799-0001

AWARDS Criminal justice (MAIS, MS); economics (MAIS); political science (MA, MAIS, MAT); public administration (MPA); sociology (MAIS, MAT, MS). Part-time and evening/weekend programs available. Postbaccalaureate distance learning degree programs offered.

Faculty: 14 full-time (1 woman).
Students: 13 full-time (9 women), 54 part-time (34 women); includes 16 minority (14 African Americans, 1 Hispanic American, 1 Native American), 1 international. Average age 35. 8 applicants, 100% accepted, 8 enrolled. In 2001, 10 degrees awarded.
Degree requirements: For master's, thesis (for some programs), comprehensive exam.
Entrance requirements: For master's, GRE General Test, minimum GPA of 3.0. *Application deadline:* Applications are processed on a rolling basis. *Application fee:* $0.
Expenses: Tuition, state resident: part-time $44 per credit hour. Tuition, nonresident: part-time $262 per credit hour. Required fees: $58 per credit hour. $76 per semester.
Financial support: Teaching assistantships, career-related internships or fieldwork, Federal Work-Study, and scholarships/grants available. Support available to part-time students. Financial award application deadline: 7/1; financial award applicants required to submit FAFSA.
Faculty research: Urban segregation, minority business, violent crime, gender discrimination, Third World agriculture production.
Dr. Barbara L. Hart, Chair, 903-566-7426, *Fax:* 903-565-5537, *E-mail:* bhart@mail.uttyl.edu.
Application contact: Carol A. Hodge, Office of Graduate Studies, 903-566-5642, *Fax:* 903-566-7068, *E-mail:* chodge@mail.uttly.edu.

■ THE UNIVERSITY OF TEXAS–PAN AMERICAN

College of Social and Behavioral Sciences, Department of Sociology, Edinburg, TX 78539-2999

AWARDS MS. Part-time programs available.

Faculty: 6 full-time (1 woman).
Students: 5 full-time (1 woman), 7 part-time (2 women); includes 11 minority (1 Asian American or Pacific Islander, 10 Hispanic Americans). Average age 31. 6 applicants, 100% accepted. In 2001, 2 degrees awarded.
Degree requirements: For master's, thesis or journal article.
Entrance requirements: For master's, GRE General Test. *Application deadline:* For fall admission, 7/17 (priority date); for spring admission, 11/13. Applications are processed on a rolling basis. *Application fee:* $0.
Expenses: Tuition, state resident: part-time $212 per semester hour. Tuition, nonresident: part-time $367 per semester hour.
Financial support: In 2001–02, teaching assistantships (averaging $7,000 per year); fellowships, research assistantships, career-related internships or fieldwork, Federal Work-Study, institutionally sponsored loans, and tuition waivers (full and partial) also available. Support available to part-time students.
Faculty research: Border studies, U.S.-Mexico issues, Mexican-American peoples, aging and gerontology.
Dr. Kelly F. Himmel, Coordinator, 956-381-3579, *Fax:* 956-381-2343, *E-mail:* kellyh@panam.edu. *Web site:* http://www.panam.edu/

■ UNIVERSITY OF TOLEDO

Graduate School, College of Arts and Sciences, Department of Sociology, Anthropology, and Social Work, Toledo, OH 43606-3398

AWARDS Anthropology (MAE); sociology (MA, MAE). Part-time programs available.

Faculty: 10.
Students: 14 full-time (8 women), 6 part-time (5 women); includes 2 minority (1 African American, 1 Asian American or Pacific Islander), 2 international. Average age 32. 17 applicants, 71% accepted, 5 enrolled. In 2001, 5 degrees awarded.
Degree requirements: For master's, thesis or alternative.
Application deadline: For fall admission, 8/1 (priority date). Applications are processed on a rolling basis. *Application fee:* $30. Electronic applications accepted.
Expenses: Tuition, state resident: full-time $7,278; part-time $303 per hour. Tuition, nonresident: full-time $15,731; part-time $699 per hour. Required fees: $43 per hour.
Financial support: In 2001–02, 13 teaching assistantships were awarded; research assistantships, career-related internships or fieldwork, Federal Work-Study, institutionally sponsored loans, and tuition waivers (full) also available. Support available to part-time students. Financial award application deadline: 4/1; financial award applicants required to submit FAFSA.
Faculty research: Medical and social gerontology, population, social movements, socioeconomic development, corporations and work, race and ethnicity.
Dr. Barbara Chesney, Chair, 419-530-2791, *Fax:* 419-530-8406.
Application contact: Elias T. Nigem, Graduate Director, 419-530-4662, *Fax:* 419-530-8406, *E-mail:* enigem@utnet.utoledo.edu. *Web site:* http://uac.rdp.utoledo.edu/docs/socdept/soc.htm

■ UNIVERSITY OF VIRGINIA

College and Graduate School of Arts and Sciences, Department of Sociology, Charlottesville, VA 22903

AWARDS MA, PhD, JD/MA.

Faculty: 15 full-time (4 women), 7 part-time/adjunct (4 women).
Students: 34 full-time (24 women), 2 part-time (1 woman); includes 2 minority (both African Americans), 4 international. Average age 28. 58 applicants, 40% accepted, 8 enrolled. In 2001, 2 master's, 6 doctorates awarded.
Degree requirements: For master's, one foreign language, thesis; for doctorate, variable foreign language requirement, thesis/dissertation.
Entrance requirements: For master's and doctorate, GRE General Test, GRE Subject Test. *Application deadline:* For fall admission, 7/15; for spring admission,

University of Virginia (continued)
12/1. Applications are processed on a rolling basis. *Application fee:* $40. Electronic applications accepted.
Expenses: Tuition, state resident: full-time $3,988. Tuition, nonresident: full-time $17,078. Required fees: $1,190.
Financial support: Application deadline: 2/1.
James D. Hunter, Chairman, 434-924-7293, *Fax:* 434-924-7028, *E-mail:* sociology@virginia.edu.
Application contact: Duane J. Osheim, Associate Dean for Graduate Programs, 434-924-7184, *Fax:* 434-924-3084, *E-mail:* grad-a-s@virginia.edu. *Web site:* http://www.virginia.edu/sociology/

■ UNIVERSITY OF WASHINGTON

Graduate School, College of Arts and Sciences, Department of Sociology, Seattle, WA 98195

AWARDS MA, PhD.

Degree requirements: For master's and doctorate, thesis/dissertation.
Entrance requirements: For master's and doctorate, GRE General Test, TOEFL, TSE, minimum GPA of 3.0. Electronic applications accepted.
Expenses: Tuition, state resident: full-time $5,539. Tuition, nonresident: full-time $14,376. Required fees: $390. Tuition and fees vary according to course load and program.
Faculty research: Demography, criminology, social psychology, race/ethnicity/inequality, family. *Web site:* http://www.www.soc.washington.edu/

■ UNIVERSITY OF WISCONSIN–MADISON

Graduate School, College of Letters and Science, Department of Sociology, Madison, WI 53706-1380

AWARDS Rural sociology (MS); sociology (MS, PhD). Part-time programs available.

Faculty: 56 full-time (16 women), 2 part-time/adjunct (1 woman).
Students: 175 full-time (106 women), 2 part-time (both women); includes 20 minority (8 African Americans, 2 Asian Americans or Pacific Islanders, 10 Hispanic Americans), 27 international. Average age 32. 195 applicants, 46% accepted, 25 enrolled. In 2001, 21 master's, 19 doctorates awarded. Terminal master's awarded for partial completion of doctoral program.
Degree requirements: For master's, thesis, oral exam; for doctorate, thesis/dissertation, preliminary and final oral exams, 4 seminars. *Median time to degree:* Master's–3 years full-time; doctorate–7 years full-time.
Entrance requirements: For master's and doctorate, GRE General Test, TOEFL. *Application deadline:* For fall admission, 2/1; for spring admission, 9/1. Applications are processed on a rolling basis. *Application fee:* $45. Electronic applications accepted.
Expenses: Tuition, state resident: full-time $7,361; part-time $399 per credit. Tuition, nonresident: full-time $20,499; part-time $1,282 per credit. Required fees: $34 per credit. Full-time tuition and fees vary according to course load, program, reciprocity agreements and student level.
Financial support: In 2001–02, 96 students received support, including 17 fellowships with full tuition reimbursements available (averaging $13,446 per year), 23 research assistantships with full tuition reimbursements available (averaging $13,379 per year), 30 teaching assistantships with full tuition reimbursements available (averaging $10,476 per year); Federal Work-Study, institutionally sponsored loans, traineeships, and unspecified assistantships also available. Financial award application deadline: 12/15. *Total annual research expenditures:* $796,221.
Prof. Adam Gamoran, Chair, 608-262-1498, *Fax:* 608-265-5389.
Application contact: Mary E. Powers, Graduate Admissions, 608-262-4863, *Fax:* 608-265-5389, *E-mail:* gradinfo@ssc.wisc.edu. *Web site:* http://www.ssc.wisc.edu/soc/

■ UNIVERSITY OF WISCONSIN–MILWAUKEE

Graduate School, College of Letters and Sciences, Department of Sociology, Milwaukee, WI 53201-0413

AWARDS MA. Part-time programs available.

Faculty: 17 full-time (8 women).
Students: 7 full-time (6 women), 16 part-time (10 women); includes 3 minority (1 African American, 1 Hispanic American, 1 Native American). 16 applicants, 56% accepted. In 2001, 2 degrees awarded.
Degree requirements: For master's, thesis.
Application deadline: For fall admission, 1/1 (priority date); for spring admission, 9/1. Applications are processed on a rolling basis. *Application fee:* $45 ($75 for international students).
Expenses: Tuition, state resident: full-time $6,180; part-time $535 per credit. Tuition, nonresident: full-time $19,482; part-time $1,366 per credit. Tuition and fees vary according to course load, program and reciprocity agreements.
Financial support: In 2001–02, 10 teaching assistantships were awarded; fellowships, research assistantships, career-related internships or fieldwork and unspecified assistantships also available. Support available to part-time students. Financial award application deadline: 4/15.
Chava Frankfurt-Nachmias, Representative, 414-229-5319, *Fax:* 847-673-4122, *E-mail:* chava@uwm.edu. *Web site:* http://www.uwm.edu/dept/sociology/

■ UNIVERSITY OF WYOMING

Graduate School, College of Arts and Sciences, Department of Sociology, Laramie, WY 82071

AWARDS MA. Part-time programs available.

Faculty: 10 full-time (3 women), 2 part-time/adjunct (1 woman).
Students: 10 full-time (8 women), 5 part-time (2 women); includes 3 minority (all Hispanic Americans), 2 international. Average age 34. 7 applicants, 100% accepted. In 2001, 1 degree awarded.
Degree requirements: For master's, thesis.
Entrance requirements: For master's, GRE General Test, minimum GPA of 3.0. *Application deadline:* For fall admission, 3/1 (priority date); for spring admission, 12/1 (priority date). Applications are processed on a rolling basis. *Application fee:* $40. Electronic applications accepted.
Expenses: Tuition, state resident: full-time $2,895; part-time $161 per credit hour. Tuition, nonresident: full-time $8,367; part-time $465 per credit hour. Required fees: $491; $10 per credit hour. $2 per credit hour. Tuition and fees vary according to course load and program.
Financial support: In 2001–02, 11 students received support, including 6 teaching assistantships with full tuition reimbursements available (averaging $8,667 per year); Federal Work-Study and institutionally sponsored loans also available. Financial award application deadline: 3/1.
Faculty research: Gender, theory, international studies, law, social inequality. *Total annual research expenditures:* $40,000.
Dr. Audie D. Blevins, Head, 307-766-3342, *Fax:* 307-766-3812, *E-mail:* ablevins@uwyo.edu.
Application contact: Dr. Donna A. Barnes, Graduate Director, 307-766-3342, *Fax:* 307-766-3812, *E-mail:* dbarnes@uwyo.edu. *Web site:* http://august.uwyo.edu/sociology/index.html

■ UTAH STATE UNIVERSITY

School of Graduate Studies, College of Humanities, Arts and Social Sciences, Department of Sociology, Logan, UT 84322-0730

AWARDS MA, MS, MSS, PhD.

Faculty: 10 full-time (3 women), 11 part-time/adjunct (5 women).
Students: 18 full-time (14 women), 7 part-time (3 women); includes 2 minority (1 Hispanic American, 1 Native American), 3 international. Average age 24. 22 applicants, 59% accepted. In 2001, 5 master's, 2 doctorates awarded.
Degree requirements: For master's and doctorate, thesis/dissertation.
Entrance requirements: For master's, GRE General Test or MAT, TOEFL, minimum GPA of 3.0; for doctorate, GRE General Test, TOEFL, minimum GPA of 3.0. *Application deadline:* For fall admission,

2/1 (priority date); for spring admission, 10/15. Applications are processed on a rolling basis. *Application fee:* $40.
Expenses: Tuition, state resident: full-time $1,693. Tuition, nonresident: full-time $4,233. Required fees: $501. Tuition and fees vary according to program.
Financial support: In 2001–02, 24 students received support, including 1 fellowship with partial tuition reimbursement available (averaging $12,000 per year), 11 research assistantships with partial tuition reimbursements available (averaging $7,300 per year), 7 teaching assistantships with partial tuition reimbursements available (averaging $7,300 per year); career-related internships or fieldwork, Federal Work-Study, institutionally sponsored loans, and scholarships/grants also available. Financial award application deadline: 2/1.
Faculty research: Demography, environmental/natural resource sociology, rural community change, international development, health studies. *Total annual research expenditures:* $200,000.
Dr. Gary H. Kiger, Head, 435-797-1230, *Fax:* 435-797-1240.
Application contact: Dr. Richard Krannich, Director of Graduate Studies and Professor, 435-797-1241, *Fax:* 435-797-1240, *E-mail:* rkranich@hass.usu.edu. *Web site:* http://www.usu.edu/~sswa/

■ VALDOSTA STATE UNIVERSITY

Graduate School, College of Arts and Sciences, Department of Sociology and Criminal Justice, Valdosta, GA 31698

AWARDS Criminal justice (MS); marriage and family therapy (MS); sociology (MS). Part-time and evening/weekend programs available.

Faculty: 18 full-time (6 women).
Students: 35 full-time (30 women), 34 part-time (27 women); includes 7 minority (5 African Americans, 1 Asian American or Pacific Islander, 1 Hispanic American). Average age 27. 52 applicants, 90% accepted. In 2001, 27 degrees awarded.
Degree requirements: For master's, thesis or alternative, comprehensive written and/or oral exams.
Entrance requirements: For master's, GRE General Test, minimum GPA of 2.5. *Application deadline:* For fall admission, 7/1; for spring admission, 11/15. Applications are processed on a rolling basis. *Application fee:* $20. Electronic applications accepted.
Expenses: Tuition, state resident: full-time $1,746; part-time $97 per hour. Tuition, nonresident: full-time $6,966; part-time $387 per hour. Required fees: $594; $297 per semester.
Financial support: In 2001–02, 5 research assistantships with full tuition reimbursements (averaging $2,452 per year) were awarded; career-related internships or fieldwork, institutionally sponsored loans, scholarships/grants, and unspecified assistantships also available. Support available to part-time students. Financial award application deadline: 7/1; financial award applicants required to submit FAFSA.
Faculty research: Police-civilian ride-along project.
Dr. J. Michael Brooks, Head, 229-333-5943, *E-mail:* mbrooks@valdosta.edu.

■ VANDERBILT UNIVERSITY

Graduate School, Department of Sociology, Nashville, TN 37240-1001

AWARDS MA, PhD.

Faculty: 17 full-time (6 women).
Students: 34 full-time (27 women), 1 (woman) part-time; includes 7 minority (5 African Americans, 2 Asian Americans or Pacific Islanders), 3 international. Average age 30. 58 applicants, 47% accepted. In 2001, 1 master's, 4 doctorates awarded.
Degree requirements: For master's, general exam; for doctorate, thesis/dissertation, area, qualifying, and final exams.
Entrance requirements: For master's and doctorate, GRE General Test. *Application deadline:* For fall admission, 1/15. *Application fee:* $40. Electronic applications accepted.
Expenses: Tuition: Full-time $28,350.
Financial support: In 2001–02, 17 students received support, including 5 fellowships with full tuition reimbursements available (averaging $10,800 per year), 11 teaching assistantships with full tuition reimbursements available (averaging $10,800 per year); research assistantships, Federal Work-Study and institutionally sponsored loans also available. Financial award application deadline: 1/15.
Faculty research: Criminology; cultural sociology; gender, race, and ethics relations; deviant behavior and social control.
Daniel B. Cornfield, Chair, 615-322-7626, *Fax:* 615-322-7505, *E-mail:* daniel.b.cornfield@vanderbilt.edu.
Application contact: Karen E. Campbell, Director of Graduate Studies, 615-322-7626, *Fax:* 615-322-7505, *E-mail:* karen.e.campbell@vanderbilt.edu. *Web site:* http://www.vanderbilt.edu/AnS/sociology/

■ VIRGINIA COMMONWEALTH UNIVERSITY

School of Graduate Studies, College of Humanities and Sciences, Department of Sociology, Richmond, VA 23284-9005

AWARDS Applied social research (CASR); sociology (MS).

Students: 19 full-time, 9 part-time; includes 4 minority (3 African Americans, 1 Hispanic American). 18 applicants, 83% accepted. In 2001, 4 degrees awarded.
Degree requirements: For master's, thesis optional.
Entrance requirements: For master's, GRE General Test. *Application deadline:* For fall admission, 7/1; for spring admission, 11/15. *Application fee:* $30.
Expenses: Tuition, state resident: full-time $4,276; part-time $238 per credit. Tuition, nonresident: full-time $12,672; part-time $704 per credit. Required fees: $1,167; $43 per credit.
Financial support: Teaching assistantships, career-related internships or fieldwork, Federal Work-Study, institutionally sponsored loans, and tuition waivers (full and partial) available. Support available to part-time students.
Dr. Jimmie S. Williams, Chair, 804-828-1026, *Fax:* 804-828-1027.
Application contact: Dr. Stephen G. Lyng, Graduate Program Director, 804-828-6896, *Fax:* 804-828-1027, *E-mail:* slyng@vcu.edu. *Web site:* http://www.has.vcu.edu/soc/sochome.html

■ VIRGINIA POLYTECHNIC INSTITUTE AND STATE UNIVERSITY

Graduate School, College of Arts and Sciences, Department of Sociology, Blacksburg, VA 24061

AWARDS MS, PhD.

Faculty: 18 full-time (6 women), 3 part-time/adjunct (1 woman).
Students: 25 full-time (13 women), 1 part-time; includes 8 minority (6 African Americans, 1 Asian American or Pacific Islander, 1 Hispanic American), 6 international. 30 applicants, 87% accepted, 8 enrolled. In 2001, 9 master's, 2 doctorates awarded.
Degree requirements: For master's, thesis optional; for doctorate, thesis/dissertation, comprehensive exam.
Entrance requirements: For master's and doctorate, GRE General Test, TOEFL. *Application deadline:* For fall admission, 12/1 (priority date). Applications are processed on a rolling basis. *Application fee:* $45. Electronic applications accepted.
Expenses: Tuition, state resident: part-time $241 per hour. Tuition, nonresident: part-time $406 per hour. Tuition and fees vary according to program.
Financial support: In 2001–02, 20 students received support, including 17 teaching assistantships with full tuition reimbursements available (averaging $11,333 per year); research assistantships, unspecified assistantships also available. Financial award application deadline: 4/1.
Faculty research: Science and technology, deviance and criminology, social psychology, social organization, demography.
Dr. John W. Ryan, Department Chair, 540-231-9396, *Fax:* 540-231-3800, *E-mail:* johnryan@vt.edu.
Application contact: Lou Henderson, Graduate Secretary, 540-231-8972, *Fax:* 540-231-3860, *E-mail:* lohenderson@vt.edu. *Web site:* http://www.cas.vt.edu/sociology/

■ WASHINGTON STATE UNIVERSITY

Graduate School, College of Liberal Arts, Department of Sociology, Pullman, WA 99164

AWARDS MA, PhD.

Faculty: 21 full-time (5 women), 10 part-time/adjunct (8 women).
Students: 48 full-time (30 women); includes 10 minority (1 African American, 2 Asian Americans or Pacific Islanders, 6 Hispanic Americans, 1 Native American), 9 international. Average age 30. 48 applicants, 21% accepted. In 2001, 5 master's, 9 doctorates awarded. Terminal master's awarded for partial completion of doctoral program.
Degree requirements: For master's, thesis; for doctorate, thesis/dissertation, oral exam, comprehensive exam.
Entrance requirements: For master's, GRE General Test, minimum GPA of 3.0; for doctorate, GRE General Test, MA in sociology, minimum GPA of 3.0. *Application deadline:* For fall admission, 2/15 (priority date). *Application fee:* $35. Electronic applications accepted.
Expenses: Tuition, state resident: full-time $6,088; part-time $304 per semester. Tuition, nonresident: full-time $14,918; part-time $746 per semester. Tuition and fees vary according to program.
Financial support: In 2001–02, 1 research assistantship with tuition reimbursement (averaging $10,876 per year), 47 teaching assistantships with tuition reimbursements (averaging $11,200 per year) were awarded. Fellowships with tuition reimbursements, Federal Work-Study, institutionally sponsored loans, and scholarships/grants also available. Support available to part-time students. Financial award application deadline: 4/1; financial award applicants required to submit FAFSA.
Faculty research: Social organization, criminology, environmental sociology, social psychology, family. *Total annual research expenditures:* $189,746.
Dr. Gregory Hooks, Chair, 509-335-4595, *Fax:* 509-335-6419, *E-mail:* hooks@mail.wsu.edu.
Application contact: Louis Gray, Director of Graduate Studies, 509-335-4595, *Fax:* 509-335-6419, *E-mail:* grayln@wsu.edu. *Web site:* http://libarts.wsu.edu/soc/

■ WAYNE STATE UNIVERSITY

Graduate School, College of Liberal Arts, Department of Sociology, Detroit, MI 48202

AWARDS MA, PhD.

Faculty: 14 full-time.
Students: 68. 42 applicants, 50% accepted, 16 enrolled. In 2001, 6 master's, 6 doctorates awarded.
Degree requirements: For doctorate, thesis/dissertation.
Entrance requirements: For master's, GRE General Test, GRE Subject Test, minimum GPA of 3.3; for doctorate, GRE General Test, GRE Subject Test, minimum GPA of 3.5. *Application deadline:* For fall admission, 7/1. *Application fee:* $20 ($30 for international students). Electronic applications accepted.
Expenses: Tuition, state resident: full-time $3,764. Tuition and fees vary according to degree level and program.
Financial support: In 2001–02, 11 fellowships, 8 teaching assistantships were awarded.
Leon Wilson, Chairperson, 313-577-2157, *Fax:* 313-577-3276, *E-mail:* ab6077@wayne.edu.
Application contact: Mary Cay Sengstock, Graduate Director, 313-577-3282, *E-mail:* m.sengstock@wayne.edu.

■ WEST CHESTER UNIVERSITY OF PENNSYLVANIA

Graduate Studies, College of Arts and Sciences, Department of Anthropology and Sociology, West Chester, PA 19383

AWARDS Gerontology (Certificate); long term care (MSA). Part-time and evening/weekend programs available.

Faculty: 1.
Students: 2 full-time (both women), 3 part-time (all women); includes 1 minority (African American). Average age 43. 4 applicants, 75% accepted. In 2001, 3 degrees awarded.
Degree requirements: For master's, comprehensive exam.
Entrance requirements: For master's, MAT, GRE, or GMAT, interview. *Application deadline:* For fall admission, 4/15 (priority date); for spring admission, 10/15. Applications are processed on a rolling basis. *Application fee:* $25.
Expenses: Tuition, state resident: full-time $4,600; part-time $256 per credit. Tuition, nonresident: full-time $7,554; part-time $420 per credit. Required fees: $44 per credit.
Financial support: In 2001–02, research assistantships with full tuition reimbursements (averaging $5,000 per year); unspecified assistantships also available. Support available to part-time students. Financial award application deadline: 2/15; financial award applicants required to submit FAFSA.
Faculty research: West African communities in the U.S., life long learning-distance education, comparative religions.
Dr. Anthony Zumpetta, Chair, 610-436-2556.
Application contact: Dr. Douglas McConatha, Graduate Coordinator, 610-436-3125, *E-mail:* dmcconatha@wcupa.edu.

■ WESTERN ILLINOIS UNIVERSITY

School of Graduate Studies, College of Arts and Sciences, Department of Sociology, Macomb, IL 61455-1390

AWARDS MA. Part-time programs available.

Faculty: 19 full-time (7 women).
Students: 25 full-time (20 women), 8 part-time (5 women); includes 6 minority (5 African Americans, 1 Asian American or Pacific Islander), 2 international. Average age 28. 16 applicants, 100% accepted. In 2001, 8 degrees awarded.
Degree requirements: For master's, thesis or alternative.
Entrance requirements: For master's, minimum GPA of 2.75. *Application deadline:* Applications are processed on a rolling basis. *Application fee:* $0 ($25 for international students). Electronic applications accepted.
Expenses: Tuition, state resident: part-time $108 per credit hour. Tuition, nonresident: part-time $216 per credit hour. Required fees: $33 per credit hour.
Financial support: In 2001–02, 16 students received support, including 16 research assistantships with full tuition reimbursements available (averaging $5,720 per year). Financial award applicants required to submit FAFSA.
Faculty research: Testing/test evaluation, respite care evaluation, sociology of science, rural sociology.
Dr. John Wozniak, Chairperson, 309-298-1056.
Application contact: Dr. Barbara Baily, Director of Graduate Studies, 309-298-1806, *Fax:* 309-298-2345, *E-mail:* grad-office@wiu.edu. *Web site:* http://www.wiu.edu/

■ WESTERN KENTUCKY UNIVERSITY

Graduate Studies, Potter College of Arts, Humanities and Social Sciences, Department of Sociology, Bowling Green, KY 42101-3576

AWARDS MA, MA Ed.

Faculty: 12 full-time (4 women), 1 part-time/adjunct (0 women).
Students: In 2001, 3 degrees awarded.
Degree requirements: For master's, final exam, thesis optional.
Entrance requirements: For master's, GRE General Test, minimum GPA of 3.0. *Application deadline:* For fall admission, 7/1 (priority date); for spring admission, 11/1. Applications are processed on a rolling basis. *Application fee:* $30.
Expenses: Tuition, area resident: Part-time $167 per credit. Tuition, state resident: full-time $2,490. Tuition, nonresident: full-time $6,660; part-time $399 per credit. Required fees: $554. Part-time tuition and fees vary according to campus/location and reciprocity agreements.

Financial support: Teaching assistantships with partial tuition reimbursements, Federal Work-Study, institutionally sponsored loans, tuition waivers (partial), unspecified assistantships, and service awards available. Support available to part-time students. Financial award application deadline: 4/1; financial award applicants required to submit FAFSA.
Faculty research: Criminology/delinquency, quantitative and survey research methodology, occupations/professions, sex and gender, demography.
Dr. Paul Wozniak, Head, 270-745-3759, *Fax:* 270-745-6493, *E-mail:* paul.wozniak@wku.edu.

■ WESTERN MICHIGAN UNIVERSITY

Graduate College, College of Arts and Sciences, Department of Sociology, Kalamazoo, MI 49008-5202

AWARDS MA, PhD.

Faculty: 23 full-time (6 women).
Students: 51 full-time (30 women), 31 part-time (17 women); includes 15 minority (13 African Americans, 1 Hispanic American, 1 Native American), 5 international. 42 applicants, 90% accepted, 11 enrolled. In 2001, 6 master's, 5 doctorates awarded.
Degree requirements: For master's, thesis, oral exams; for doctorate, one foreign language, thesis/dissertation, oral exams, written exams.
Entrance requirements: For doctorate, GRE General Test. *Application deadline:* For fall admission, 2/15 (priority date). Applications are processed on a rolling basis. *Application fee:* $25.
Expenses: Tuition, state resident: part-time $186 per credit hour. Tuition, nonresident: part-time $442 per credit hour. Required fees: $602. One-time fee: $132 part-time. Tuition and fees vary according to course load.
Financial support: Fellowships, research assistantships, teaching assistantships, Federal Work-Study available. Financial award application deadline: 2/15; financial award applicants required to submit FAFSA.
Thomas Van Valey, Chair, 616-387-5270.
Application contact: Admissions and Orientation, 616-387-2000, *Fax:* 616-387-2355.

■ WESTERN WASHINGTON UNIVERSITY

Graduate School, College of Arts and Sciences, Department of Sociology, Bellingham, WA 98225-5996

AWARDS MA. Part-time programs available.

Degree requirements: For master's, thesis.
Entrance requirements: For master's, GRE General Test, TOEFL, minimum GPA of 3.0 in last 60 semester hours or last 90 quarter hours.

■ WEST VIRGINIA UNIVERSITY

Eberly College of Arts and Sciences, Department of Sociology and Anthropology, Morgantown, WV 26506

AWARDS Applied social research (MA). Part-time programs available.

Faculty: 10 full-time (2 women), 5 part-time/adjunct (2 women).
Students: 10 full-time (5 women), 7 part-time (all women); includes 1 minority (African American), 1 international. Average age 27. 28 applicants, 39% accepted. In 2001, 5 degrees awarded.
Degree requirements: For master's, thesis or alternative.
Entrance requirements: For master's, GRE General Test, TOEFL, minimum GPA of 2.5. *Application deadline:* For fall admission, 3/1. *Application fee:* $45.
Expenses: Tuition, state resident: full-time $2,791. Tuition, nonresident: full-time $8,659. Required fees: $1,002. Tuition and fees vary according to program.
Financial support: In 2001–02, 10 students received support, including 8 teaching assistantships; research assistantships, Federal Work-Study, institutionally sponsored loans, and tuition waivers (full and partial) also available. Financial award application deadline: 2/1; financial award applicants required to submit FAFSA.
Faculty research: Applied sociology, research methodology, stratification, social/complex organization.
Dr. F. Carson Mencken, Chair, 304-293-5801 Ext. 1627, *Fax:* 304-293-5994, *E-mail:* carson.mencken@wvu.edu. *Web site:* http://www.as.wvu.edu/soc_a/

■ WICHITA STATE UNIVERSITY

Graduate School, Fairmount College of Liberal Arts and Sciences, Department of Sociology, Wichita, KS 67260

AWARDS MA. Part-time programs available.

Faculty: 7 full-time (4 women).
Students: 14 full-time (9 women), 14 part-time (9 women); includes 2 minority (1 African American, 1 Native American). Average age 37. 14 applicants, 79% accepted, 9 enrolled. In 2001, 9 degrees awarded.
Degree requirements: For master's, thesis optional.
Entrance requirements: For master's, GRE, TOEFL. *Application deadline:* For fall admission, 7/1 (priority date); for spring admission, 1/1. Applications are processed on a rolling basis. *Application fee:* $25 ($40 for international students). Electronic applications accepted.
Expenses: Tuition, state resident: full-time $1,888; part-time $105 per credit. Tuition, nonresident: full-time $6,129; part-time $341 per credit. Required fees: $345; $19 per credit. $17 per semester. Tuition and fees vary according to course load and program.
Financial support: In 2001–02, 1 research assistantship (averaging $8,200 per year), 8 teaching assistantships with full tuition reimbursements (averaging $5,575 per year) were awarded. Federal Work-Study and institutionally sponsored loans also available. Financial award application deadline: 4/1.
Dr. Ronald R. Matson, Chairperson, 316-978-3280, *Fax:* 316-978-3281, *E-mail:* ron.matson@wichita.edu. *Web site:* http://www.wichita.edu/

■ WILLIAM PATERSON UNIVERSITY OF NEW JERSEY

College of the Humanities and Social Sciences, Department of Sociology, Wayne, NJ 07470-8420

AWARDS MA. Part-time and evening/weekend programs available.

Students: 4 full-time (all women), 8 part-time (4 women); includes 3 minority (1 African American, 2 Hispanic Americans). 22 applicants, 23% accepted, 3 enrolled. In 2001, 4 degrees awarded.
Degree requirements: For master's, thesis, comprehensive exam.
Entrance requirements: For master's, GRE or MAT. *Application deadline:* Applications are processed on a rolling basis. *Application fee:* $35. Electronic applications accepted.
Expenses: Tuition, state resident: part-time $322 per credit. Tuition, nonresident: part-time $468 per credit.
Financial support: Research assistantships with full tuition reimbursements, unspecified assistantships available. Financial award application deadline: 4/1.
Faculty research: Critical political theory, urban social/ethnic groups, family studies, human development.
Dr. Peter Stein, Program Director, 973-720-3429.
Application contact: Danielle Liautaud, Graduate Admissions Counselor, 973-720-3579, *Fax:* 973-720-2035, *E-mail:* liautaudd@wpunj.edu. *Web site:* http://www.wpunj.edu/

■ YALE UNIVERSITY

Graduate School of Arts and Sciences, Department of Sociology, New Haven, CT 06520

AWARDS PhD.

Degree requirements: For doctorate, thesis/dissertation.
Entrance requirements: For doctorate, GRE General Test.

SURVEY METHODOLOGY

■ UNIVERSITY OF MARYLAND, COLLEGE PARK

Graduate Studies and Research, College of Behavioral and Social Sciences, Joint Program in Survey Methodology, College Park, MD 20742

AWARDS MS, PhD.

Faculty: 2 full-time (both women).
Students: 9 full-time (7 women), 36 part-time (21 women); includes 6 minority (4 African Americans, 2 Asian Americans or Pacific Islanders), 2 international. 51 applicants, 49% accepted, 20 enrolled. In 2001, 6 degrees awarded.
Degree requirements: For master's, scholarly paper; for doctorate, thesis/dissertation.
Entrance requirements: For master's, GRE General Test (recommended), minimum GPA of 3.0; for doctorate, GRE General Test, minimum GPA of 3.0. *Application deadline:* For fall admission, 3/1. Applications are processed on a rolling basis. *Application fee:* $50 ($70 for international students). Electronic applications accepted.
Expenses: Tuition, state resident: part-time $289 per credit hour. Tuition, nonresident: part-time $448 per credit hour. One-time fee: $436 part-time. Full-time tuition and fees vary according to course load, campus/location and program.
Financial support: In 2001–02, 1 fellowship with full tuition reimbursement (averaging $12,131 per year), 10 research assistantships with tuition reimbursements (averaging $12,160 per year) were awarded. Teaching assistantships, Federal Work-Study also available. Support available to part-time students. Financial award applicants required to submit FAFSA.
Dr. Roger Tourangeau, Director, 301-314-7911, *Fax:* 301-314-7912.
Application contact: Trudy Lindsey, Director, Graduate Admissions and Records, 301-405-6991, *Fax:* 301-314-9305, *E-mail:* grschool@deans.umd.edu.

■ UNIVERSITY OF MICHIGAN

Horace H. Rackham School of Graduate Studies, Program in Survey Methodology, Ann Arbor, MI 48109

AWARDS MS, PhD, CGS.

Degree requirements: For master's and doctorate, thesis/dissertation, comprehensive exam, registration.
Entrance requirements: For master's and doctorate, GRE, 3 letters of recommendation. *Application deadline:* For fall admission, 1/15.
Faculty research: Survey methodology, statistics, psychology, sociology, social psychology.
Dr. James M. Lepkowski, Director, 734-936-0021, *Fax:* 734-764-8263, *E-mail:* jimlep@isr.umich.edu.
Application contact: Danielle A. Neilson, Coordinator, 734-947-5386, *Fax:* 734-764-8263, *E-mail:* neilsond@isr.umich.edu. *Web site:* http://www.isr.umich.edu/gradprogram/

■ UNIVERSITY OF NEBRASKA–LINCOLN

Graduate College, Interdepartmental Area of Survey Research and Methodology, Lincoln, NE 68588

AWARDS MS.

Students: 17 (10 women) 10 international. Average age 32. 13 applicants, 54% accepted, 6 enrolled. In 2001, 4 degrees awarded.
Degree requirements: For master's, comprehensive exam.
Entrance requirements: For master's, GRE General Test or GMAT, TOEFL. *Application deadline:* For fall admission, 3/15. *Application fee:* $35. Electronic applications accepted.
Expenses: Tuition, state resident: full-time $2,412; part-time $134 per credit. Tuition, nonresident: full-time $6,223; part-time $346 per credit. Tuition and fees vary according to course load.
Financial support: In 2001–02, 4 research assistantships, 1 teaching assistantship were awarded. Fellowships, Federal Work-Study, health care benefits, and unspecified assistantships also available. Financial award application deadline: 2/15.
Faculty research: Survey research and data analysis.
Dr. Allan McCutcheon, Graduate Chair, 402-472-6071, *Fax:* 402-477-3983. *Web site:* http://www.unl.edu/unl-srm/

Graduate Programs in Social Work

Social Work

HUMAN SERVICES

■ ABILENE CHRISTIAN UNIVERSITY

Graduate School, College of Arts and Sciences, Department of Sociology and Social Work, Abilene, TX 79699-9100

AWARDS Gerontology (MS); social services administration (MS). Part-time programs available.

Faculty: 7 part-time/adjunct (0 women).
Students: 4 full-time (3 women), 5 part-time (3 women); includes 1 minority (African American), 1 international. 5 applicants, 100% accepted, 4 enrolled. In 2001, 5 degrees awarded.
Degree requirements: For master's, comprehensive exam.
Entrance requirements: For master's, GRE General Test or MAT. *Application deadline:* For fall admission, 4/1 (priority date); for spring admission, 11/1. Applications are processed on a rolling basis. *Application fee:* $25 ($45 for international students).
Expenses: Tuition: Full-time $8,904; part-time $371 per hour. Required fees: $520; $17 per hour.
Financial support: Career-related internships or fieldwork and Federal Work-Study available. Support available to part-time students. Financial award application deadline: 4/1.
Bill Culp, Graduate Adviser, 915-674-2306, *Fax:* 915-674-6524, *E-mail:* culpb@acu.edu.
Application contact: Dr. Roger Gee, Graduate Dean, 915-674-2122, *Fax:* 915-674-2123, *E-mail:* gradinfo@education.acu.edu. *Web site:* http://www.acu.edu/academics/grad/ssaprog.html/

■ ANDREWS UNIVERSITY

School of Graduate Studies, College of Arts and Sciences, Department of Behavioral Science, Berrien Springs, MI 49104

AWARDS Community services management (MSA).

Students: 2 full-time (both women), 4 part-time (1 woman); includes 2 minority (both African Americans), 4 international. Average age 36. In 2001, 6 degrees awarded.
Application fee: $40.
Expenses: Tuition: Full-time $12,600; [illegible]525 per semester. Required [illegible] Tuition and fees vary according [illegible]evel.
Dr. Duane C. McBride, Chair, 616-471-3152.
Application contact: Carolyn Hurst, Supervisor of Graduate Admission, 800-253-2874, *Fax:* 616-471-3228, *E-mail:* enroll@andrews.edu.

■ ANTIOCH NEW ENGLAND GRADUATE SCHOOL

Graduate School, Department of Organization and Management, Program in Human Services Administration, Keene, NH 03431-3552

AWARDS MHSA.

Faculty: 1 full-time (0 women), 14 part-time/adjunct (6 women).
Students: 14 full-time (8 women), 1 (woman) part-time; includes 1 minority (Hispanic American). Average age 40. In 2001, 13 degrees awarded.
Degree requirements: For master's, practicum.
Entrance requirements: For master's, interview, previous course work and work experience in organization and management. *Application deadline:* For fall admission, 8/1; for spring admission, 12/1. Applications are processed on a rolling basis. *Application fee:* $40.
Expenses: Tuition: Full-time $15,150.
Financial support: In 2001–02, 6 students received support; fellowships, career-related internships or fieldwork and Federal Work-Study available. Financial award applicants required to submit FAFSA.
Faculty research: Leadership training for elected/nonelected municipal leaders, focus group research to determine community needs, work force stress related to aging.
Application contact: Robbie P. Hertneky, Director of Admissions, 603-357-6265, *Fax:* 603-357-0718, *E-mail:* rhertneky@antiochne.edu. *Web site:* http://www.antiochne.edu/

■ BELLEVUE UNIVERSITY

Graduate School, Bellevue, NE 68005-3098

AWARDS Business (MBA); computer information systems (MS); health care administration (MS); human services (MS); leadership (MA); management (MA). MA is delivered in an accelerated executive format. Part-time and evening/weekend programs available. Postbaccalaureate distance learning degree programs offered (no on-campus study).

Faculty: 62 full-time (24 women), 36 part-time/adjunct (10 women).
Students: 460 full-time (229 women), 260 part-time (105 women); includes 113 minority (70 African Americans, 24 Asian Americans or Pacific Islanders, 18 Hispanic Americans, 1 Native American), 73 international. Average age 33. 190 applicants, 95% accepted. In 2001, 205 degrees awarded.
Degree requirements: For master's, thesis or project.
Entrance requirements: For master's, TOEFL, minimum GPA of 2.5 in last 60 hours. *Application deadline:* For fall admission, 7/15 (priority date); for winter admission, 9/30 (priority date); for spring admission, 11/15 (priority date). Applications are processed on a rolling basis. *Application fee:* $50.
Expenses: Tuition, state resident: part-time $265 per credit. One-time fee: $50 part-time.
Financial support: In 2001–02, 324 students received support. Federal Work-Study and scholarships/grants available. Financial award applicants required to submit FAFSA.
Dr. Mary Hawkins, Provost, 402-293-2021, *Fax:* 402-293-2035, *E-mail:* mhawkins@bellevue.edu.
Application contact: Elizabeth A. Wall, Director of Marketing and Enrollment, 402-293-3702, *Fax:* 402-293-3730, *E-mail:* eaw@scholars.bellevue.edu.

■ BORICUA COLLEGE

Program in Human Services, New York, NY 10032-1560

AWARDS MS.

■ BRANDEIS UNIVERSITY

The Heller School for Social Policy and Management, Program in Management and Social Policy, Waltham, MA 02454-9110

AWARDS Child, youth, and family services (MBA, MM); elder and disabled services (MBA, MM); health care administration (MBA, MM); human services (MBA, MM). Part-time and evening/weekend programs available.

Faculty: 44 full-time (17 women), 16 part-time/adjunct (6 women).
Students: 45 full-time (32 women), 31 part-time (19 women). Average age 28. 72 applicants, 75% accepted. In 2001, 45 degrees awarded.
Degree requirements: For master's, team consulting project.
Entrance requirements: For master's, GRE General Test or GMAT (MM), GMAT (MBA). *Application deadline:* For fall admission, 6/1 (priority date); for winter admission, 11/1 (priority date); for spring admission, 2/15. Applications are processed on a rolling basis. *Application fee:* $50. Electronic applications accepted.

Expenses: Tuition: Full-time $27,392. Required fees: $35.
Financial support: Fellowships, institutionally sponsored loans, scholarships/grants, and tuition waivers (partial) available. Financial award application deadline: 2/15; financial award applicants required to submit CSS PROFILE or FAFSA.
Faculty research: Health care, child and family, elder and disabled services, general human services.
Barry Friedman, Director, 781-736-3783, *E-mail:* hfriedman@brandeis.edu.
Application contact: Lisa Hamlin Sherry, Assistant Director for Admissions and Financial Aid, 781-736-3835, *Fax:* 781-736-3881, *E-mail:* sherry@brandeis.edu. *Web site:* http://heller.brandeis.edu

Find an in-depth description at www.petersons.com/gradchannel.

■ BROOKLYN COLLEGE OF THE CITY UNIVERSITY OF NEW YORK

Division of Graduate Studies, Department of Health and Nutrition Science, Brooklyn, NY 11210-2889

AWARDS Community health (MA, MPH, MS), including community health (MA, MPH), computer science and health science (MS), health care management (MA, MPH), health care policy and administration (MA, MPH), thanatology (MA); nutrition sciences (MS), including nutrition. Part-time and evening/weekend programs available.

Students: 2 full-time (both women), 151 part-time (123 women); includes 65 minority (48 African Americans, 10 Asian Americans or Pacific Islanders, 7 Hispanic Americans), 3 international. In 2001, 39 degrees awarded.
Degree requirements: For master's, thesis or alternative.
Entrance requirements: For master's, TOEFL, GRE, 18 credits in health-related areas. *Application deadline:* For fall admission, 3/1; for spring admission, 11/1. *Application fee:* $40.
Expenses: Tuition, state resident: full-time $4,350; part-time $185 per credit. Tuition, nonresident: full-time $7,600; part-time $320 per credit.
Financial support: Career-related internships or fieldwork, Federal Work-Study, institutionally sponsored loans, and scholarships/grants available. Support available to part-time students. Financial award application deadline: 5/1; financial award applicants required to submit FAFSA.
Faculty research: Medical ethics, relocation stress, risk reduction, disease prevention, history of public health, computer applications.
Dr. Erika Friedmann, Chairperson, 718-951-5026, *Fax:* 718-951-4670, *E-mail:* erikaf@brooklyn.cuny.edu.
Application contact: Dr. Jerrold Mirotznik, Deputy Chairperson for Graduate Studies, 718-951-4197, *Fax:* 718-951-4670, *E-mail:* jerrym@brooklyn.cuny.edu.

■ CALIFORNIA STATE UNIVERSITY, SACRAMENTO

Graduate Studies, College of Health and Human Services, Division of Social Work, Sacramento, CA 95819-6048

AWARDS Family and children's services (MSW); health care (MSW); mental health (MSW); social justice and corrections (MSW).

Students: 297 full-time (257 women), 65 part-time (53 women); includes 134 minority (47 African Americans, 19 Asian Americans or Pacific Islanders, 61 Hispanic Americans, 7 Native Americans).
Degree requirements: For master's, thesis or alternative, writing proficiency exam.
Entrance requirements: For master's, TOEFL, minimum GPA of 2.5 during previous 2 years. *Application deadline:* For fall admission, 4/15; for spring admission, 11/1. *Application fee:* $55.
Expenses: Tuition, state resident: full-time $1,965; part-time $668 per semester. Tuition, nonresident: part-time $246 per unit.
Financial support: Career-related internships or fieldwork and Federal Work-Study available. Support available to part-time students. Financial award application deadline: 3/1.
Dr. Robin Carter, Chair, 916-278-6943.
Application contact: Dr. Santos Torres, Graduate Coordinator, 916-278-7064.

■ CAPELLA UNIVERSITY

Graduate School, School of Human Services, Minneapolis, MN 55402

AWARDS MS, PhD. Part-time and evening/weekend programs available. Postbaccalaureate distance learning degree programs offered (minimal on-campus study).

Faculty: 10 full-time, 30 part-time/adjunct.
Students: 742. Average age 42. 813 applicants, 80% accepted, 579 enrolled. In 2001, 34 master's, 14 doctorates awarded. Terminal master's awarded for partial completion of doctoral program.
Degree requirements: For master's, project, thesis optional; for doctorate, thesis/dissertation. *Median time to degree:* Master's–1.5 years full-time, 3 years part-time; doctorate–3 years full-time, 4 years part-time.
Entrance requirements: For master's, TOEFL, minimum GPA of 2.7; for doctorate, TOEFL, minimum GPA of 3.0. *Application deadline:* Applications are processed on a rolling basis. *Application fee:* $50 ($150 for international students). Electronic applications accepted.
Expenses: Tuition: Part-time $1,210 per course. Tuition and fees vary according to degree level and program.
Financial support: Institutionally sponsored loans and scholarships/grants available. Support available to part-time students. Financial award applicants required to submit FAFSA.
Faculty research: Compulsive and addictive behaviors, marriage and family therapy, psychology, substance abuse.
Dr. Pamela Patrick, Dean, 888-CAPELLA, *Fax:* 612-337-5396, *E-mail:* pksp@aol.com.
Application contact: Pam Gallagher, Associate Director of Enrollment Services, 800-987-1133 Ext. 220, *Fax:* 612-339-8022, *E-mail:* info@capella.edu. *Web site:* http://www.capellauniversity.edu/

■ CHESTNUT HILL COLLEGE

Graduate Division, Department of Professional Psychology, Program in Counseling Psychology and Human Services, Philadelphia, PA 19118-2693

AWARDS MA, MS, CAS.

Degree requirements: For master's, thesis.
Entrance requirements: For master's, GRE or MAT, TOEFL, TSE, and TWE; for CAS, Master's degree in counseling or a related discipline. *Web site:* http://www.chc.edu/graduate/Gpsych.html

■ CHESTNUT HILL COLLEGE

Graduate Division, Program in Administration of Human Services, Philadelphia, PA 19118-2693

AWARDS MS. Part-time and evening/weekend programs available.

Faculty: 1 (woman) full-time, 2 part-time/adjunct (both women).
Students: 1 (woman) full-time, 6 part-time (4 women); includes 3 minority (all African Americans).
Entrance requirements: For master's, 100 hours volunteer or 1 year work related human services experience.
Expenses: Contact institution.
Financial support: Career-related internships or fieldwork and unspecified assistantships available. Support available to part-time students. Financial award application deadline: 7/15; financial award applicants required to submit FAFSA.
Dr. Elaine Green, Coordinator, 215-248-7071, *Fax:* 215-248-7155, *E-mail:* green@chc.edu.
Application contact: Sr. Regina Raphael Smith, SSJ, Director of Graduate Admissions, 215-248-7020, *Fax:* 215-248-7161, *E-mail:* graddiv@chc.edu.

■ CONCORDIA UNIVERSITY

Graduate Studies, Program in Human Services, River Forest, IL 60305-1499

AWARDS Human services (MA, CAS), including administration (MA), exercise science

Concordia University (continued)
(MA). Part-time and evening/weekend programs available.
Degree requirements: For master's, thesis, comprehensive exam; for CAS, thesis, final project.
Entrance requirements: For master's, minimum GPA of 2.9; for CAS, master's degree.

■ CONCORDIA UNIVERSITY

College of Graduate and Continuing Studies, School of Human Services, St. Paul, MN 55104-5494

AWARDS Community education (MA Ed); criminal justice (MAHS); early childhood education (MA Ed); family studies (MAHS); leadership (MAHS); parish education (MA Ed); school-age care (MA Ed); youth development (MA Ed). Evening/weekend programs available. Postbaccalaureate distance learning degree programs offered (minimal on-campus study).

Faculty: 8 full-time (3 women), 98 part-time/adjunct (51 women).
Students: 161 full-time (136 women); includes 24 minority (20 African Americans, 2 Asian Americans or Pacific Islanders, 2 Hispanic Americans). Average age 34. 50 applicants, 90% accepted. In 2001, 18 degrees awarded.
Degree requirements: For master's, thesis or alternative, final project.
Entrance requirements: For master's, leadership portfolio, minimum GPA of 2.75. *Application deadline:* Applications are processed on a rolling basis. *Application fee:* $50. Electronic applications accepted.
Expenses: Tuition: Part-time $300 per semester hour. Tuition and fees vary according to program.
Financial support: Federal Work-Study available. Support available to part-time students. Financial award application deadline: 4/6.
James Ollhoff, Associate Dean, 651-603-6148, *E-mail:* ollhoff@csp.edu.
Application contact: Gail Ann Wells, Marketing Coordinator, 651-603-6186, *Fax:* 651-603-6144, *E-mail:* wells@csp.edu.
Web site: http://www.cshs.csp.edu/

■ DEPAUL UNIVERSITY

School of Education, Program in Human Services and Counseling, Chicago, IL 60604-2287

AWARDS Agencies, family concerns, and higher education (M Ed, MA); elementary schools (M Ed, MA); human services management (M Ed, MA); secondary schools (M Ed, MA).

Faculty: 3 full-time (1 woman).
Students: 60 full-time (54 women), 39 part-time (32 women); includes 30 minority (20 African Americans, 4 Asian Americans or Pacific Islanders, 6 Hispanic ...ns). 1 international. Average age ... 16 degrees awarded.
Degree requirements: For master's, oral exam or thesis.
Entrance requirements: For master's, interview, minimum GPA of 2.75, work experience. *Application deadline:* Applications are processed on a rolling basis. *Application fee:* $25.
Expenses: Tuition: Part-time $362 per credit hour. Tuition and fees vary according to program.
Financial support: Career-related internships or fieldwork available.
Sr. Frances Ryan, Coordinator, 773-325-4353, *Fax:* 773-325-7748, *E-mail:* fryan@wppost.depaul.edu.

■ DRURY UNIVERSITY

Graduate Programs in Education, Program in Human Services, Springfield, MO 65802-3791

AWARDS M Ed. Part-time and evening/weekend programs available.

Students: Average age 27.
Degree requirements: For master's, thesis.
Entrance requirements: For master's, GRE or MAT, minimum GPA of 2.75. *Application deadline:* For fall admission, 8/25 (priority date); for spring admission, 1/15 (priority date). Applications are processed on a rolling basis. *Application fee:* $15.
Expenses: Tuition: Part-time $214 per credit hour. Tuition and fees vary according to program.
Financial support: Career-related internships or fieldwork available. Financial award application deadline: 10/15; financial award applicants required to submit FAFSA.
Faculty research: Grant writing, multicultural education.
Dr. Protima Roy, Head, 417-873-7264, *Fax:* 417-873-7432, *E-mail:* proy@drury.edu.

■ FERRIS STATE UNIVERSITY

College of Education and Human Services, Big Rapids, MI 49307

AWARDS M Ed, MS, MSCTE. Part-time and evening/weekend programs available. Postbaccalaureate distance learning degree programs offered.

Faculty: 15 full-time (8 women), 13 part-time/adjunct (7 women).
Students: 169 (77 women); includes 22 minority (13 African Americans, 3 Asian Americans or Pacific Islanders, 3 Hispanic Americans, 3 Native Americans) 4 international. Average age 31. In 2001, 38 degrees awarded.
Entrance requirements: For master's, minimum GPA of 3.0. *Application deadline:* For fall admission, 8/31; for winter admission, 12/10. Applications are processed on a rolling basis. *Application fee:* $20.
Expenses: Tuition, state resident: full-time $2,335; part-time $196 per credit hour. Tuition, nonresident: full-time $4,945; part-time $414 per credit hour. Required fees: $200 per semester.
Financial support: In 2001–02, 8 students received support, including research assistantships with full tuition reimbursements available (averaging $3,960 per year), 1 teaching assistantship with partial tuition reimbursement available (averaging $3,800 per year); career-related internships or fieldwork and tuition waivers (full and partial) also available. Support available to part-time students.
Faculty research: Competency testing, teaching methodologies, assessment of teaching effectiveness, suicide prevention, women in education, special needs.
Michelle Johnston, Dean, 616-591-3646, *Fax:* 616-592-3792, *E-mail:* michelle_johnston@ferris.edu.

■ FIELDING GRADUATE INSTITUTE

Graduate Programs, Programs in Human and Organization Development, Santa Barbara, CA 93105-3538

AWARDS Human and organizational systems (PhD); human development (MA, PhD); human organization development (Ed D); human services (MA); organization development (MA). Evening/weekend programs available.

Faculty: 28 full-time (12 women), 15 part-time/adjunct (6 women).
Students: 464 full-time (299 women); includes 83 minority (53 African Americans, 10 Asian Americans or Pacific Islanders, 15 Hispanic Americans, 5 Native Americans), 10 international. Average age 47. 82 applicants, 78% accepted, 57 enrolled. In 2001, 42 master's, 51 doctorates awarded. Terminal master's awarded for partial completion of doctoral program.
Degree requirements: For doctorate, thesis/dissertation. *Median time to degree:* Master's–3.5 years full-time; doctorate–6 years full-time.
Application deadline: For fall admission, 3/5; for spring admission, 9/5. *Application fee:* $75.
Expenses: Tuition: Full-time $14,100.
Financial support: In 2001–02, 165 students received support. Career-related internships or fieldwork, institutionally sponsored loans, scholarships/grants, and diversity scholarships available. Financial award application deadline: 4/1; financial award applicants required to submit FAFSA.
Dr. Charles McClintock, Dean, 805-898-2930, *Fax:* 805-687-4590, *E-mail:* cmcclintock@fielding.edu.
Application contact: Alexis Long, Admissions Counselor, 805-898-4020, *Fax:* 805-687-9793, *E-mail:* along@fielding.edu.

■ FRAMINGHAM STATE COLLEGE

Graduate Programs, Program in Human Services Administration, Framingham, MA 01701-9101

AWARDS MA.

Dr. George Jarnis, Head, 508-626-4824.
Application contact: 508-626-4550.

■ FRANKLIN UNIVERSITY

Human Services Management Program, Columbus, OH 43215-5399

AWARDS MS. Part-time and evening/weekend programs available.

Faculty: 1 full-time (0 women), 4 part-time/adjunct (2 women).
Students: 52 full-time (36 women), 9 part-time (7 women); includes 23 minority (22 African Americans, 1 Asian American or Pacific Islander), 1 international. Average age 36. 41 applicants, 71% accepted, 22 enrolled. In 2001, 34 degrees awarded.
Degree requirements: For master's, thesis or alternative, registration.
Entrance requirements: For master's, minimum undergraduate GPA of 2.75. *Application deadline:* For fall admission, 7/15 (priority date); for winter admission, 11/6 (priority date); for spring admission, 2/26 (priority date). Applications are processed on a rolling basis. *Application fee:* $30. Electronic applications accepted.
Expenses: Tuition: Part-time $315 per credit hour. Tuition and fees vary according to program.
Financial support: In 2001–02, 16 students received support. Scholarships/grants available. Financial award application deadline: 6/30.
Dr. Terry Boyd, Program Chair, 614-797-4700, *Fax:* 614-224-4025, *E-mail:* boydf@franklin.edu.
Application contact: Graduate Services Office, 614-797-4700, *E-mail:* gradschl@franklin.edu. *Web site:* http://www.franklin.edu/

■ GEORGIA STATE UNIVERSITY

College of Health and Human Sciences, Department of Social Work, Atlanta, GA 30303-3083

AWARDS Community partnerships (MSW).

Degree requirements: For master's, community project.
Entrance requirements: For master's, GRE General Test, TOEFL.
Expenses: Tuition, state resident: full-time $8,156; part-time $132 per hour. Tuition, nonresident: full-time $12,624; part-time $526 per hour. Required fees: $660; $330 per semester.
Faculty research: Social work education, child welfare, labor unions and child care workers, secondary victimization in death penalty cases. *Web site:* http://www.gsu.edu/chhs/dept/soci/

■ INDIANA UNIVERSITY NORTHWEST

School of Public and Environmental Affairs, Gary, IN 46408-1197

AWARDS Criminal justice (MPA); health services administration (MPA); human services administration (MPA); management of public affairs (MPA); non-profit management (NPMC); public management (PMC). Part-time programs available.

Faculty: 2 full-time (1 woman).
Students: 11 full-time (9 women), 88 part-time (58 women); includes 55 minority (45 African Americans, 10 Hispanic Americans). Average age 38. In 2001, 25 master's, 13 other advanced degrees awarded.
Entrance requirements: For master's, GRE General Test. *Application deadline:* For fall admission, 8/15 (priority date). Applications are processed on a rolling basis. *Application fee:* $25.
Expenses: Tuition, state resident: full-time $3,827. Tuition, nonresident: full-time $8,567. Required fees: $416.
Financial support: Career-related internships or fieldwork, Federal Work-Study, and tuition waivers (partial) available. Support available to part-time students. Financial award application deadline: 3/1.
Faculty research: Employment in income security policies, evidence in criminal justice, equal employment law, social welfare policy and welfare reform, public finance in developing countries.
Joseph M. Pellicciotti, Director, 219-980-6695, *Fax:* 219-980-6737, *E-mail:* jpelli@iunhaw1.iun.indiana.edu.
Application contact: Suzanne Green, Recorder, 219-980-6695, *Fax:* 219-980-6737, *E-mail:* sgreen@iunhaw1.iun.indiana.edu.

■ KANSAS STATE UNIVERSITY

Graduate School, College of Human Ecology, School of Family Studies and Human Services, Manhattan, KS 66506

AWARDS Family studies and human services (MS); human ecology (PhD). Part-time programs available.

Faculty: 24 full-time (14 women).
Students: 69 full-time (58 women), 109 part-time (76 women); includes 22 minority (14 African Americans, 2 Asian Americans or Pacific Islanders, 4 Hispanic Americans, 2 Native Americans), 3 international. 88 applicants, 82% accepted, 48 enrolled. In 2001, 26 degrees awarded.
Degree requirements: For master's, thesis or alternative, oral exam, residency; for doctorate, thesis/dissertation, preliminary exam, residency.
Entrance requirements: For master's, GRE, TOEFL, minimum GPA of 3.0 in last 2 years of undergraduate study; for doctorate, GRE, TOEFL, minimum GPA of 3.5 in master's program. *Application deadline:* For fall admission, 2/1 (priority date); for spring admission, 10/1 (priority date). Applications are processed on a rolling basis. *Application fee:* $0 ($25 for international students).
Expenses: Tuition, state resident: part-time $113 per credit hour. Tuition, nonresident: part-time $358 per credit hour.
Financial support: In 2001–02, 15 research assistantships with partial tuition reimbursements (averaging $8,000 per year), 22 teaching assistantships with partial tuition reimbursements (averaging $8,000 per year) were awarded. Federal Work-Study, institutionally sponsored loans, scholarships/grants, and unspecified assistantships also available. Support available to part-time students. Financial award application deadline: 3/1; financial award applicants required to submit FAFSA.
Faculty research: Military families, neurogenic communication and swallowing disorders, child language and early literacy, communicative competence of people who use AAC systems, assessment of financial attitudes and financial risk tolerance. *Total annual research expenditures:* $2.8 million.
Dr. William Meredith, Department Head, 785-532-5510, *Fax:* 785-532-5505, *E-mail:* fshs@ksu.edu.
Application contact: Information Contact, 785-532-5510, *Fax:* 785-532-5505, *E-mail:* fshs@ksu.edu. *Web site:* http://www.ksu.edu/humec/fshs/

■ LEHIGH UNIVERSITY

College of Education, Department of Education and Human Services, Program in Counseling Psychology, Bethlehem, PA 18015-3094

AWARDS Counseling and human services (M Ed); counseling psychology (PhD); school counseling (M Ed, Certificate). Part-time and evening/weekend programs available.

Faculty: 4 full-time (2 women), 3 part-time/adjunct (1 woman).
Students: 34 full-time (27 women), 37 part-time (27 women). 132 applicants, 34% accepted, 13 enrolled. In 2001, 24 master's, 6 doctorates awarded.
Degree requirements: For doctorate, thesis/dissertation.
Entrance requirements: For master's, GRE General Test or MAT, TOEFL, minimum GPA of 2.75; for doctorate, GRE General Test or MAT, TOEFL; for Certificate, TOEFL. *Application deadline:* For fall admission, 2/1. *Application fee:* $50. Electronic applications accepted.
Expenses: Tuition: Part-time $468 per credit hour. Required fees: $200; $100 per semester. Tuition and fees vary according to program.
Financial support: Fellowships with full and partial tuition reimbursements, research assistantships with full and partial tuition reimbursements, career-related internships or fieldwork, Federal Work-Study, institutionally sponsored lo scholarships/grants, and tuition wa

Jniversity (continued)
(... d partial) available. Financial award application deadline: 1/31.
Faculty research: Multicultural counseling, career development, family systems.
Dr. Nicholas Ladany, Coordinator, 610-758-3250, *Fax:* 610-758-3227, *E-mail:* nil3@lehigh.edu.

■ LESLEY UNIVERSITY

Graduate School of Arts and Social Sciences, Program in Intercultural Relations, Cambridge, MA 02138-2790

AWARDS Development project administration (MA); individually designed (MA); intercultural conflict resolution (MA); intercultural health and human services (MA); intercultural relations (CAGS); intercultural training and consulting (MA); international education exchange (MA); international student advising (MA); managing culturally diverse human resources (MA); multicultural education (MA). Part-time and evening/weekend programs available.

Faculty: 3 full-time (2 women), 3 part-time/adjunct (all women).
Students: Average age 30. 35 applicants, 94% accepted, 4 enrolled. In 2001, 9 degrees awarded.
Degree requirements: For master's, one foreign language; for CAGS, one foreign language, thesis. *Median time to degree:* Master's–2 years part-time.
Entrance requirements: For master's, TOEFL, interview; for CAGS, interview, master's degree. *Application deadline:* Applications are processed on a rolling basis. *Application fee:* $50.
Expenses: Tuition: Part-time $330 per credit. Required fees: $15 per term. Part-time tuition and fees vary according to campus/location and program.
Financial support: In 2001–02, 8 students received support; research assistantships, teaching assistantships, career-related internships or fieldwork, Federal Work-Study, scholarships/grants, and unspecified assistantships available. Support available to part-time students. Financial award application deadline: 4/1; financial award applicants required to submit FAFSA.
Faculty research: Sociolinguistics, cross-cultural feminist theory, immigration and diaspora, intercultural business training.
Sylvia R. Cowan, Coordinator, 617-349-8978, *E-mail:* scowan@mail.lesley.edu.
Application contact: Hugh Norwood, Dean of Admissions and Enrollment Planning, 800-999-1959, *Fax:* 617-349-8366, *E-mail:* hnorwood@mail.lesley.edu.

■ LINCOLN UNIVERSITY

Graduate Program in Human Services, Lincoln University, PA 19352

AWARDS M Hum Svcs. Evening/weekend programs available.

Degree requirements: For master's, thesis.
Entrance requirements: For master's, 5 years of work experience in human services.
Faculty research: Gerontology/minority aging, computers in composition instruction.

■ LINDENWOOD UNIVERSITY

Graduate Programs, Programs in Individualized Education, St. Charles, MO 63301-1695

AWARDS Administration (MSA); business administration (MBA); corporate communication (MS); counseling psychology (MA); gerontology (MA); health management (MS); human resource management (MS); human service agency management (MS); management (MSA); marketing (MSA); mass communication (MS). Part-time and evening/weekend programs available.

Faculty: 11 full-time (6 women), 23 part-time/adjunct (6 women).
Students: 515 full-time (340 women), 266 part-time (232 women); includes 117 minority (107 African Americans, 1 Asian American or Pacific Islander, 5 Hispanic Americans, 4 Native Americans), 11 international. Average age 35. In 2001, 298 degrees awarded.
Degree requirements: For master's, thesis. *Median time to degree:* Master's–1.25 years full-time.
Entrance requirements: For master's, interview, minimum GPA of 3.0. *Application deadline:* For fall admission, 6/30 (priority date); for spring admission, 12/1. Applications are processed on a rolling basis. *Application fee:* $25.
Expenses: Tuition: Full-time $10,800; part-time $300 per hour. Tuition and fees vary according to course load and program.
Financial support: Career-related internships or fieldwork, institutionally sponsored loans, tuition waivers (partial), and unspecified assistantships available. Financial award application deadline: 6/30.
Dan Kemper, Director, 636-916-9125, *E-mail:* dkemper@lindenwood.edu.
Application contact: John Guffey, Dean of Admissions, 636-949-4934, *Fax:* 636-949-4910, *E-mail:* jguffey@lindenwood.edu.

■ LINDSEY WILSON COLLEGE

Department of Human Services and Counseling, Columbia, KY 42728-1298

AWARDS Counseling and human development (M Ed).

Expenses: Tuition: Part-time $396 per credit hour.

■ LOUISIANA STATE UNIVERSITY IN SHREVEPORT

College of Liberal Arts, Program in Human Services Administration, Shreveport, LA 71115-2399

AWARDS MS. Part-time and evening/weekend programs available. Postbaccalaureate distance learning degree programs offered.

Degree requirements: For master's, comprehensive exam.
Entrance requirements: For master's, interview, minimum GPA of 3.0.
Expenses: Tuition, area resident: Full-time $1,890; part-time $105 per credit. Tuition, nonresident: full-time $6,000; part-time $175 per credit. Required fees: $220; $55 per credit.
Faculty research: Collaboration, small nonprofits, volunteerism, financial management.

■ MINNESOTA STATE UNIVERSITY, MANKATO

College of Graduate Studies, College of Social and Behavioral Sciences, Department of Sociology, Mankato, MN 56001

AWARDS Sociology (MA, MT), including human services planning and administration (MA); sociology: corrections (MS). Part-time programs available.

Faculty: 17 full-time (4 women).
Students: 11 full-time (6 women), 37 part-time (25 women). Average age 32. In 2001, 9 degrees awarded.
Degree requirements: For master's, thesis or alternative, comprehensive exam.
Entrance requirements: For master's, minimum GPA of 3.0 during previous 2 years. *Application deadline:* For fall admission, 7/9 (priority date); for spring admission, 11/27. Applications are processed on a rolling basis. *Application fee:* $20.
Expenses: Tuition, state resident: full-time $3,253; part-time $157 per credit. Tuition, nonresident: full-time $4,893; part-time $248 per credit. Required fees: $24 per credit. Tuition and fees vary according to reciprocity agreements.
Financial support: Research assistantships with full tuition reimbursements, teaching assistantships with full tuition reimbursements, career-related internships or fieldwork, Federal Work-Study, and institutionally sponsored loans available. Support available to part-time students. Financial award application deadline: 3/15; financial award applicants required to submit FAFSA.
Faculty research: Women's suffrage movements.
Dr. William Wagner, Chairperson, 507-389-1561.
Application contact: Joni Roberts, Admissions Coordinator, 507-389-5244, *Fax:* 507-389-5974, *E-mail:* grad@mankato.msus.edu.

■ MINNESOTA STATE UNIVERSITY MOORHEAD

Graduate Studies, Department of Public, Human Services, and Health Administration, Moorhead, MN 56563-0002

AWARDS MS. Part-time and evening/weekend programs available.

Faculty: 6.
Students: 19 (11 women). 9 applicants, 100% accepted. In 2001, 7 degrees awarded.
Degree requirements: For master's, final oral exam, final project paper or thesis.
Entrance requirements: For master's, GRE General Test, TOEFL, minimum GPA of 2.75. *Application deadline:* For fall admission, 5/1 (priority date); for spring admission, 11/1. Applications are processed on a rolling basis. *Application fee:* $20 ($35 for international students). Electronic applications accepted.
Expenses: Tuition, area resident: Part-time $148 per credit. Tuition, nonresident: part-time $234 per credit.
Financial support: Career-related internships or fieldwork, Federal Work-Study, and unspecified assistantships available. Financial award application deadline: 7/15; financial award applicants required to submit FAFSA.
Dr. James Danielson, Coordinator, 218-236-2825, *E-mail:* daniels@mnstate.edu. *Web site:* http://www.mnstate.edu/phsha

■ MONTCLAIR STATE UNIVERSITY

The School of Graduate, Professional and Continuing Education, College of Education and Human Services, Department of Counseling, Human Development, and Educational Leadership, Program in Counseling and Guidance, Upper Montclair, NJ 07043-1624

AWARDS Human services (MA). Part-time and evening/weekend programs available.

Degree requirements: For master's, thesis or alternative, comprehensive exam.
Entrance requirements: For master's, GRE General Test or MAT, interview. Electronic applications accepted.

■ MURRAY STATE UNIVERSITY

College of Education, Department of Educational Studies, Leadership and Counseling, Program in Human Development and Leadership, Murray, KY 42071-0009

AWARDS MS. Part-time programs available.

Students: 21 full-time (15 women), 64 part-time (56 women); includes 24 minority (23 African Americans, 1 Asian American or Pacific Islander), 10 international. 28 applicants, 100% accepted.
Entrance requirements: For master's, GRE General Test or MAT, TOEFL. *Application deadline:* Applications are processed on a rolling basis. *Application fee:* $25.
Expenses: Tuition, state resident: full-time $1,440; part-time $169 per hour. Tuition, nonresident: full-time $4,004; part-time $450 per hour.
Financial support: Research assistantships, teaching assistantships, Federal Work-Study available. Financial award application deadline: 4/1.
Dr. Thomas Holcomb, Interim Chairman, 270-762-2795, *Fax:* 270-762-3799, *E-mail:* tom.holcomb@coe.murraystate.edu.

■ NATIONAL-LOUIS UNIVERSITY

College of Arts and Sciences, Division of Health and Human Services, Chicago, IL 60603

AWARDS Addictions counseling (MS, Certificate); addictions treatment (Certificate); career counseling and development studies (Certificate); community wellness and prevention (MS, Certificate); counseling (MS, Certificate); eating disorders counseling (Certificate); employee assistance programs (MS, Certificate); gerontology administration (Certificate); gerontology counseling (MS, Certificate); human services administration (MS, Certificate); long-term care administration (Certificate). Part-time programs available.

Degree requirements: For master's and Certificate, internship.
Entrance requirements: For master's and Certificate, GRE, MAT, or Watson-Glaser Critical Thinking Appraisal, interview, minimum GPA of 3.0.
Expenses: Tuition: Full-time $13,830; part-time $461 per credit hour.
Faculty research: Religion and aging, drug abuse prevention, hunger, homelessness, multicultural diversity.

■ NEW ENGLAND COLLEGE

Program in Organizational Management, Henniker, NH 03242-3293

AWARDS Business (MS); community mental health counseling (MS); health care (MS); health care management (Certificate); human resource management (Certificate); human services (MS). Part-time and evening/weekend programs available.

Degree requirements: For master's, independent research project.
Electronic applications accepted. *Web site:* http://www.nec.edu
Find an in-depth description at www.petersons.com/gradchannel.

■ PONTIFICAL CATHOLIC UNIVERSITY OF PUERTO RICO

Institute of Graduate Studies in Behavioral Science and Community Affairs, Ponce, PR 00717-0777

AWARDS Clinical psychology (MS); clinical social work (MSW); criminology (MA); industrial psychology (MS); psychology (PhD); public administration (MA). Part-time and evening/weekend programs available.

Faculty: 10 full-time (7 women), 17 part-time/adjunct (12 women).
Students: 86 full-time (56 women), 394 part-time (266 women); all minorities (all Hispanic Americans). 141 applicants, 83% accepted, 104 enrolled. In 2001, 35 degrees awarded.
Entrance requirements: For master's, GRE, 2 recommendation letters, interview, minimum GPA of 2.75. *Application deadline:* For fall admission, 4/30 (priority date). Applications are processed on a rolling basis. *Application fee:* $50. Electronic applications accepted.
Expenses: Tuition: Full-time $2,880; part-time $160 per credit. Required fees: $360. Tuition and fees vary according to degree level and program.
Financial support: Federal Work-Study and tuition waivers (partial) available. Support available to part-time students. Financial award application deadline: 7/15.
Dr. Nilde Cordoline, Director, 787-841-2000 Ext. 1024.
Application contact: Ana O. Bonilla, Director of Admissions, 787-841-2000 Ext. 1000, *Fax:* 787-840-4295. *Web site:* http://www.pucpr.edu/

■ RIDER UNIVERSITY

Department of Graduate Education and Human Services, Program in Human Services Administration, Lawrenceville, NJ 08648-3001

AWARDS MA. Part-time and evening/weekend programs available.

Faculty: 3 full-time (1 woman), 2 part-time/adjunct (0 women).
Students: 63 (53 women); includes 14 minority (all African Americans). Average age 36. In 2001, 18 degrees awarded.
Degree requirements: For master's, research project.
Entrance requirements: For master's, interview, minimum GPA of 2.5. *Application deadline:* For fall admission, 5/1 (priority date); for spring admission, 11/1 (priority date). Applications are processed on a rolling basis. *Application fee:* $35.
Expenses: Tuition, state resident: part-time $365 per credit hour. Required fees: $200. Tuition and fees vary according to campus/location and program.
Financial support: In 2001–02, 12 students received support. Career-related internships or fieldwork available. Support available to part-time students.

Rider University (continued)
Faculty research: Development of administrators in public, health/human services, and nonprofit areas.
Dr. Marcia Steinhauer, Coordinator, 609-896-5735, *Fax:* 609-896-5362, *E-mail:* msteinhauer@rider.edu.
Application contact: Dr. Christine Zelenak, Director of Graduate Admissions, 609-896-5036, *Fax:* 609-896-5261, *E-mail:* czelenak@rider.edu.

■ ROBERTS WESLEYAN COLLEGE

Division of Social Work and Social Sciences, Rochester, NY 14624-1997

AWARDS Child and family services (MSW); physical and mental health services (MSW).

Entrance requirements: For master's, minimum GPA of 2.75.
Faculty research: Religion and social work, family studies, values and ethics.

Find an in-depth description at www.petersons.com/gradchannel.

■ ROSEMONT COLLEGE

Graduate School, Program in Counseling Psychology, Rosemont, PA 19010-1699

AWARDS Human services (MA); school counseling (MA). Part-time programs available.

Faculty: 4 full-time (2 women), 5 part-time/adjunct (2 women).
Students: 78 (75 women). Average age 35. 21 applicants, 86% accepted. In 2001, 7 degrees awarded.
Degree requirements: For master's, thesis or alternative.
Entrance requirements: For master's, GRE or MAT. *Application deadline:* Applications are processed on a rolling basis. *Application fee:* $50.
Expenses: Contact institution.
Edward Samulewicz, Director, 610-527-0200 Ext. 2359, *Fax:* 610-526-2964.
Application contact: Karen Scales, Enrollment and Marketing Coordinator, 610-527-0200 Ext. 2187, *Fax:* 610-526-2964, *E-mail:* gradstudies@rosemont.edu. *Web site:* http://www.rosemont.edu/

■ SAGE GRADUATE SCHOOL

Graduate School, Division of Management, Communications and Legal Studies, Program in Public Administration, Troy, NY 12180-4115

AWARDS Communications (MS); gerontology (MS); human services administration (MS); nutrition and dietetics (MS); public management (MS). Part-time and evening/weekend programs available.

Students: 5 full-time (4 women), 21 part-time (16 women). Average age 31. 9 applicants, 100% accepted, 8 enrolled. In 2001, 12 degrees awarded.
Entrance requirements: For master's, minimum GPA of 2.75. *Application fee:* $40.
Expenses: Tuition: Full-time $7,600. Required fees: $100.
Financial support: Career-related internships or fieldwork available. Support available to part-time students. Financial award application deadline: 3/1; financial award applicants required to submit FAFSA. 518-292-1770.
Application contact: Melissa M. Robertson, Associate Director of Admissions, 518-244-6878, *Fax:* 518-244-6880, *E-mail:* sgsadm@sage.edu. *Web site:* http://www.sage.edu/

■ ST. EDWARD'S UNIVERSITY

College of Professional and Graduate Studies, Program in Human Services, Austin, TX 78704-6489

AWARDS Conflict resolution (Certificate); human services (MA), including administration, conflict resolution, human resource management, sports management; sports management (Certificate). Part-time and evening/weekend programs available.

Faculty: 4 full-time (1 woman), 12 part-time/adjunct (6 women).
Students: 12 full-time (11 women), 90 part-time (71 women); includes 28 minority (9 African Americans, 5 Asian Americans or Pacific Islanders, 13 Hispanic Americans, 1 Native American), 3 international. Average age 36. 22 applicants, 86% accepted, 16 enrolled. In 2001, 43 degrees awarded.
Degree requirements: For master's, minimum 24 resident hours.
Entrance requirements: For master's, GRE General Test, TOEFL, minimum GPA of 3.0 in last 60 hours or 2.75 overall. *Application deadline:* For fall admission, 8/1; for spring admission, 12/1. Applications are processed on a rolling basis. *Application fee:* $30 ($50 for international students). Electronic applications accepted.
Expenses: Tuition: Full-time $7,974; part-time $443 per credit hour.
Financial support: In 2001–02, 56 students received support. Career-related internships or fieldwork, institutionally sponsored loans, and scholarships/grants available. Support available to part-time students. Financial award application deadline: 4/15; financial award applicants required to submit FAFSA.
Dr. James A. Johnson, Dean, 512-416-5827, *Fax:* 512-448-8492, *E-mail:* jamesj@admin.stedwards.edu.
Application contact: Bridget Sowinski, Graduate Admissions Coordinator, 512-428-1061, *Fax:* 512-428-1032, *E-mail:* bridgets@admin.stewards.edu. *Web site:* http://www.stedwards.edu/

■ ST. MARY'S UNIVERSITY OF SAN ANTONIO

Graduate School, Department of Counseling and Human Services, San Antonio, TX 78228-8507

AWARDS Community counseling (MA); counseling (PhD, Sp C); marriage and family relations (Certificate); marriage and family therapy (MA, PhD); mental health (MA); mental health and substance abuse counseling (Certificate); substance abuse (MA). Postbaccalaureate distance learning degree programs offered (minimal on-campus study).

Faculty: 9 full-time (4 women), 5 part-time/adjunct (3 women).
Students: 125 (98 women); includes 48 minority (8 African Americans, 40 Hispanic Americans) 5 international. Average age 28. In 2001, 24 master's, 4 doctorates awarded.
Degree requirements: For master's, internship; for doctorate, thesis/dissertation, internship.
Entrance requirements: For master's, GRE General Test, MAT; for doctorate, GRE General Test. *Application deadline:* Applications are processed on a rolling basis. *Application fee:* $15. Electronic applications accepted.
Expenses: Tuition: Full-time $8,190; part-time $455 per credit hour. Required fees: $375.
Financial support: Career-related internships or fieldwork and Federal Work-Study available. Financial award application deadline: 2/15; financial award applicants required to submit FAFSA.
Dr. Dana Comstock, Graduate Program Director, 210-436-3226.

■ SOUTHERN OREGON UNIVERSITY

Graduate Office, School of Social Science, Health and Physical Education, Department of Psychology, Ashland, OR 97520

AWARDS Applied psychology (MAP); human service-organizational training and development (MA, MS); social science (MA, MS), including professional counseling, psychology. Part-time programs available.

Faculty: 10 full-time (5 women), 2 part-time/adjunct (1 woman).
Students: 37 full-time (27 women), 3 part-time (1 woman); includes 3 minority (1 Asian American or Pacific Islander, 1 Hispanic American, 1 Native American). Average age 33. 41 applicants, 39% accepted, 13 enrolled. In 2001, 6 degrees awarded.
Degree requirements: For master's, thesis, portfolio and oral defense. *Median time to degree:* Master's–2 years full-time.
Entrance requirements: For master's, GRE General Test, minimum GPA of 3.0. *Application deadline:* For fall admission, 2/15 (priority date). Applications are

processed on a rolling basis. *Application fee:* $50. Electronic applications accepted.
Expenses: Tuition, state resident: full-time $5,184; part-time $192 per credit. Tuition, nonresident: full-time $9,828; part-time $364 per credit. Required fees: $927. One-time fee: $75 full-time. Full-time tuition and fees vary according to course load, program and reciprocity agreements.
Financial support: Scholarships/grants and unspecified assistantships available. Financial award applicants required to submit FAFSA.
Dr. Josie Wilson, Chair, 541-552-6946, *E-mail:* jwilson@sou.edu.
Application contact: Wri Courtney, Graduate Coordinator, 541-552-6947, *E-mail:* map@sou.edu.

■ SPERTUS INSTITUTE OF JEWISH STUDIES

Judaica Studies Graduate Programs Institute of Advanced Judaica, Program in Human Services Administration, Chicago, IL 60605-1901

AWARDS MSHSA, MAJCS/MSHSA. Evening/weekend programs available.

Faculty: 33 part-time/adjunct (14 women).
Students: Average age 32. In 2001, 60 degrees awarded.
Degree requirements: For master's, one foreign language, thesis.
Entrance requirements: For master's, interview, minimum GPA of 2.75. *Application deadline:* Applications are processed on a rolling basis. *Application fee:* $50.
Expenses: Tuition: Part-time $200 per quarter hour. Tuition and fees vary according to degree level and program.
Financial support: In 2001–02, 85 students received support. Applicants required to submit FAFSA.
Dr. Kenneth Ehrensaft, Associate Dean, 312-322-1720, *Fax:* 312-922-6406, *E-mail:* kehren@spertus.edu.
Application contact: Suzann Lebda, Assistant Director, 312-322-1708, *Fax:* 312-922-8220, *E-mail:* slebda@spertus.edu.

■ SPERTUS INSTITUTE OF JEWISH STUDIES

Judaica Studies Graduate Programs Institute of Advanced Judaica, Program in Jewish Communal Studies, Chicago, IL 60605-1901

AWARDS MAJCS, MAJCS/MSHSA.

Degree requirements: For master's, one foreign language, thesis.
Entrance requirements: For master's, interview, minimum GPA of 3.0. *Application deadline:* Applications are processed on a rolling basis. *Application fee:* $50.
Expenses: Tuition: Part-time $200 per quarter hour. Tuition and fees vary according to degree level and program.
Financial support: Scholarships/grants available. Support available to part-time students. Financial award applicants required to submit FAFSA.
Dr. Dean Bell, Dean, 312-922-9012, *Fax:* 312-922-6406, *E-mail:* college@spertus.edu.
Application contact: Lisa Burnstein, Director of Student Services, 312-922-9012, *Fax:* 312-922-6406, *E-mail:* lisa@spertus.edu.

■ SPRINGFIELD COLLEGE

School of Graduate Studies, Program in Human Services, Springfield, MA 01109-3797

AWARDS MS. Part-time and evening/weekend programs available.

Faculty: 25 full-time (14 women), 146 part-time/adjunct (88 women).
Students: 401 full-time (272 women), 24 part-time (16 women); includes 218 minority (182 African Americans, 2 Asian Americans or Pacific Islanders, 33 Hispanic Americans, 1 Native American), 10 international. Average age 38. 220 applicants, 80% accepted. In 2001, 171 degrees awarded.
Degree requirements: For master's, project.
Application deadline: For fall admission, 7/15 (priority date); for spring admission, 11/15 (priority date). Applications are processed on a rolling basis. *Application fee:* $40. Electronic applications accepted.
Expenses: Contact institution.
Financial support: Fellowships with partial tuition reimbursements, Federal Work-Study available. Support available to part-time students. Financial award application deadline: 3/1.
Faculty research: Social justice, organizational management and leadership, counseling, education and criminal justice.
Dr. Daniel Nussbaum, Dean, 413-788-2441.
Application contact: Donald James Shaw, Director of Graduate Admissions, 413-748-3225, *Fax:* 413-748-3694, *E-mail:* donald_shaw_jr@spfldcol.edu.

■ STATE UNIVERSITY OF NEW YORK AT OSWEGO

Graduate Studies, School of Education, Department of Counseling and Psychological Services, Program in Human Services/Counseling, Oswego, NY 13126

AWARDS MS. Part-time programs available.

Faculty: 7 full-time, 6 part-time/adjunct.
Students: 7 full-time (3 women), 26 part-time (21 women); includes 3 minority (2 African Americans, 1 Asian American or Pacific Islander). Average age 31. 32 applicants, 66% accepted. In 2001, 12 degrees awarded.
Degree requirements: For master's, comprehensive exam.
Entrance requirements: For master's, GRE General Test, GRE Subject Test, interview, minimum GPA of 3.0. *Application deadline:* For fall admission, 2/1; for spring admission, 10/15. *Application fee:* $50.
Expenses: Tuition, state resident: full-time $5,100; part-time $213 per credit. Tuition, nonresident: full-time $8,416; part-time $351 per credit.
Financial support: Career-related internships or fieldwork, Federal Work-Study, institutionally sponsored loans, scholarships/grants, and tuition waivers (partial) available. Support available to part-time students. Financial award application deadline: 4/1.
Dr. Betsy Waterman, Chair, Department of Counseling and Psychological Services, 315-312-4051.

■ TEXAS SOUTHERN UNIVERSITY

Graduate School, College of Liberal Arts and Behavioral Sciences, Department of Human Services and Consumer Sciences, Houston, TX 77004-4584

AWARDS Human services and consumer sciences (MS), including child development, comprehensive human services and consumer sciences, foods and nutrition. Part-time and evening/weekend programs available.

Faculty: 3 full-time (all women), 1 (woman) part-time/adjunct.
Students: 3 full-time (all women), 22 part-time (18 women); includes 22 minority (21 African Americans, 1 Asian American or Pacific Islander), 3 international. 6 applicants, 100% accepted. In 2001, 10 degrees awarded.
Degree requirements: For master's, thesis (for some programs), comprehensive exam.
Entrance requirements: For master's, GRE General Test, TOEFL, minimum GPA of 2.5. *Application deadline:* For fall admission, 7/15 (priority date). Applications are processed on a rolling basis. *Application fee:* $35 ($75 for international students).
Expenses: Tuition, state resident: full-time $1,188. Tuition, nonresident: full-time $4,644. Required fees: $900. Tuition and fees vary according to degree level.
Financial support: In 2001–02, 1 research assistantship was awarded; teaching assistantships, career-related internships or fieldwork and institutionally sponsored loans also available. Financial award application deadline: 5/1.
Faculty research: Food radiation/food for space travel, adolescent parenting, gerontology/grandparenting. *Total annual research expenditures:* $185,000.
Dr. Shirley R. Nealy, Chair, 713-313-7638, *Fax:* 713-313-7228, *E-mail:* nealy_sr@tsu.edu.

■ UNIVERSIDAD DEL TURABO

Graduate Programs, Programs in Public Affairs, Program in Human Services Administration, Turabo, PR 00778-3030

AWARDS MPA.

Entrance requirements: For master's, GRE, PAEG, interview.

■ UNIVERSITY OF BALTIMORE

Graduate School, College of Liberal Arts, Program in Human Services Administration, Baltimore, MD 21201-5779

AWARDS MS. Part-time and evening/weekend programs available.

Faculty: 5 full-time (1 woman), 7 part-time/adjunct (1 woman).
Students: 12 full-time (7 women), 20 part-time (15 women); includes 23 minority (22 African Americans, 1 Hispanic American), 1 international. Average age 38. 9 applicants, 89% accepted. In 2001, 1 degree awarded.
Entrance requirements: For master's, interview. *Application deadline:* For fall admission, 7/15 (priority date); for spring admission, 12/15 (priority date). Applications are processed on a rolling basis. *Application fee:* $30. Electronic applications accepted.
Expenses: Tuition, state resident: full-time $5,508; part-time $306 per credit. Tuition, nonresident: full-time $8,352; part-time $464 per credit. Required fees: $37 per credit. $60 per semester. Tuition and fees vary according to course load and degree level.
Financial support: Career-related internships or fieldwork and Federal Work-Study available. Support available to part-time students. Financial award application deadline: 4/1; financial award applicants required to submit FAFSA.
Dr. Elaine Loebner, Director, 410-837-5315, *E-mail:* eloebner@ubalt.edu.
Application contact: Jeffrey Zavrotny, Assistant Director of Admissions, 410-837-4777, *Fax:* 410-837-4793, *E-mail:* jzavrotny@ubalt.edu.

■ UNIVERSITY OF BRIDGEPORT

School of Education and Human Resources, Division of Counseling and Human Resources, Bridgeport, CT 06601

AWARDS Community agency counseling (MS); human resource development and counseling (MS). Part-time and evening/weekend programs available.

Faculty: 4 full-time (1 woman), 9 part-time/adjunct (4 women).
Students: 11 full-time (8 women), 76 part-time (70 women); includes 42 minority (33 African Americans, 2 Asian Americans or Pacific Islanders, 7 Hispanic Americans), 5 international. Average age 35. 64 applicants, 83% accepted, 28 enrolled. In 2001, 11 degrees awarded.
Application deadline: For fall admission, 8/1 (priority date); for spring admission, 12/1 (priority date). Applications are processed on a rolling basis. *Application fee:* $25 ($35 for international students). Electronic applications accepted.
Expenses: Tuition: Part-time $385 per credit hour. Required fees: $50 per term. Tuition and fees vary according to degree level and program.
Financial support: In 2001–02, 27 students received support; fellowships, research assistantships, teaching assistantships, career-related internships or fieldwork, Federal Work-Study, and institutionally sponsored loans available. Support available to part-time students. Financial award application deadline: 6/1; financial award applicants required to submit FAFSA.
Faculty research: Corporate elder care programs.
Dr. Joseph E. Nechasek, Director, 203-576-4175, *Fax:* 203-576-4102, *E-mail:* nechasek@bridgeport.edu.

Find an in-depth description at www.petersons.com/gradchannel.

■ UNIVERSITY OF COLORADO AT COLORADO SPRINGS

Graduate School, College of Education, Colorado Springs, CO 80933-7150

AWARDS Counseling and human services (MA); curriculum and instruction (MA); educational administration (MA); educational leadership (MA); special education (MA). Part-time and evening/weekend programs available.

Faculty: 18 full-time (10 women), 26 part-time/adjunct (20 women).
Students: 302 full-time (216 women), 102 part-time (76 women); includes 57 minority (23 African Americans, 5 Asian Americans or Pacific Islanders, 26 Hispanic Americans, 3 Native Americans). Average age 36. In 2001, 134 degrees awarded.
Degree requirements: For master's, thesis or alternative, microcomputer proficiency, comprehensive exam.
Entrance requirements: For master's, GRE General Test, MAT. *Application deadline:* Applications are processed on a rolling basis. *Application fee:* $60 ($75 for international students).
Expenses: Tuition, state resident: full-time $2,900; part-time $174 per credit. Tuition, nonresident: full-time $9,961; part-time $591 per credit. Required fees: $14 per credit. $141 per semester. Tuition and fees vary according to course load, program and student level.
Financial support: Fellowships, career-related internships or fieldwork and Federal Work-Study available.
Faculty research: Job training for special populations, materials development for classroom.
Dr. David E. Nelson, Dean, 719-262-4111, *Fax:* 719-262-4110, *E-mail:* denelson@uccs.edu.
Application contact: Connie Wroten, Professional Assistant, 719-262-4102, *Fax:* 719-262-4110, *E-mail:* cwroten@uccs.edu.
Web site: http://web.uccs.edu/education/

■ UNIVERSITY OF GREAT FALLS

Graduate Studies Division, Program in Human Services, Great Falls, MT 59405

AWARDS Chemical dependent services (MHSA); family services (MHSA). Part-time and evening/weekend programs available. Postbaccalaureate distance learning degree programs offered (minimal on-campus study).

Faculty: 6 full-time (3 women), 10 part-time/adjunct (6 women).
Students: 6 full-time (4 women), 6 part-time (5 women); includes 4 minority (all Native Americans). Average age 41. 20 applicants, 100% accepted. In 2001, 6 degrees awarded. *Median time to degree:* Master's–1 year full-time, 1.5 years part-time.
Entrance requirements: For master's, GRE General Test or MAT. *Application deadline:* For fall admission, 8/15 (priority date); for winter admission, 11/15 (priority date); for spring admission, 12/15 (priority date). Applications are processed on a rolling basis. *Application fee:* $35.
Expenses: Tuition: Part-time $440 per credit. One-time fee: $35 full-time.
Financial support: In 2001–02, 2 research assistantships were awarded; fellowships, career-related internships or fieldwork, Federal Work-Study, and institutionally sponsored loans also available. Support available to part-time students. Financial award application deadline: 3/1.
Dr. Deborah J. Kottel, Dean, 406-791-5339, *Fax:* 406-793-5990, *E-mail:* dkottel@ugf.edu.

■ UNIVERSITY OF ILLINOIS AT SPRINGFIELD

Graduate Programs, College of Education and Human Services, Program in Human Services, Springfield, IL 62703-5404

AWARDS Alcoholism and substance abuse (MA); child and family studies (MA); gerontology (MA); social services administration (MA).

Faculty: 7 full-time (3 women), 10 part-time/adjunct (7 women).
Students: 44 full-time (32 women), 109 part-time (79 women); includes 32 minority (29 African Americans, 1 Asian American or Pacific Islander, 1 Hispanic American, 1 Native American), 2 international. Average age 37. 55

applicants, 85% accepted, 38 enrolled. In 2001, 16 degrees awarded.
Expenses: Tuition, state resident: full-time $2,680. Tuition, nonresident: full-time $8,064. Required fees: $626. One-time fee: $626.
Financial support: In 2001–02, 71 students received support, including 9 research assistantships (averaging $6,300 per year)
Rachell Anderson, Director, 217-206-7335.

■ UNIVERSITY OF MARYLAND, BALTIMORE COUNTY

Graduate School, Department of Psychology, Program in Psychology/ Human Services, Baltimore, MD 21250-5398

AWARDS Applied behavioral analysis (MA); psychology/human services (PhD). Terminal master's awarded for partial completion of doctoral program.

Degree requirements: For doctorate, thesis/dissertation.
Entrance requirements: For master's, GRE General Test, GPA of 3.06; for doctorate, GRE General Test, GRE Subject Test, TOEFL, minimum GPA of 3.57.
Faculty research: Addictive behaviors, cardiovascular and cerebrovascular disease, family violence, pediatric psychology, community prevention. *Web site:* http://www.umbc.edu/psyc/grad/hsp.html

■ UNIVERSITY OF MASSACHUSETTS BOSTON

Office of Graduate Studies and Research, College of Public and Community Service, Program in Human Services, Boston, MA 02125-3393

AWARDS MS. Part-time and evening/weekend programs available.

Degree requirements: For master's, practicum, final project.
Entrance requirements: For master's, MAT GRE, minimum GPA of 2.75.
Faculty research: Institutional and policy context of human services, ethics and social policy, public law and human services, social welfare, politics and human services.

■ UNIVERSITY OF OKLAHOMA

Graduate College, College of Arts and Sciences, Department of Human Relations, Norman, OK 73019-0390

AWARDS MHR. Part-time and evening/ weekend programs available.

Faculty: 13 full-time (7 women), 17 part-time/adjunct (6 women).
Students: 338 full-time (209 women), 954 part-time (630 women); includes 441 minority (298 African Americans, 61 Asian Americans or Pacific Islanders, 58 Hispanic Americans, 24 Native Americans), 15 international. 330 applicants, 96% accepted, 236 enrolled. In 2001, 497 degrees awarded.
Degree requirements: For master's, thesis optional.
Entrance requirements: For master's, TOEFL. *Application deadline:* For fall admission, 6/1 (priority date). Applications are processed on a rolling basis. *Application fee:* $25 ($50 for international students).
Expenses: Tuition, state resident: full-time $2,208; part-time $92 per credit hour. Tuition, nonresident: part-time $297 per credit hour. Tuition and fees vary according to course level, course load and program.
Financial support: In 2001–02, 229 students received support, including 7 research assistantships with partial tuition reimbursements available (averaging $9,521 per year); teaching assistantships, career-related internships or fieldwork and tuition waivers (partial) also available. Financial award applicants required to submit FAFSA.
Faculty research: Corrections, racial diversity, domestic violence, gangs, drugs and violence, international relations. *Total annual research expenditures:* $109,173.
Dr. Susan Marcus-Mandoza, Interim Chair, 405-325-1756, *Fax:* 405-325-4402, *E-mail:* smmendoza@ou.edu.

■ UNIVERSITY OF TOLEDO

Graduate School, College of Health and Human Services, Department of Counseling and Mental Health Services, Toledo, OH 43606-3398

AWARDS ME, PhD.

Faculty: 9.
Students: Average age 37. 80 applicants, 85% accepted, 55 enrolled. In 2001, 26 degrees awarded.
Degree requirements: For master's, seminar paper.
Entrance requirements: For master's, GRE General Test, interview, minimum GPA of 3.0. *Application deadline:* For fall admission, 6/15 (priority date). Applications are processed on a rolling basis. *Application fee:* $30. Electronic applications accepted.
Expenses: Tuition, state resident: full-time $7,278; part-time $303 per hour. Tuition, nonresident: full-time $15,731; part-time $699 per hour. Required fees: $43 per hour.
Financial support: In 2001–02, 2 research assistantships, 4 teaching assistantships were awarded. Career-related internships or fieldwork, Federal Work-Study, institutionally sponsored loans, and tuition waivers (full) also available. Support available to part-time students. Financial award application deadline: 4/1.
Faculty research: Training and supervision, ethics and standards, therapist development, multicultural issues, substance abuse screening.

■ WALDEN UNIVERSITY

Graduate Programs, Program in Human Services, Minneapolis, MN 55401

AWARDS PhD. Part-time and evening/ weekend programs available. Postbaccalaureate distance learning degree programs offered (minimal on-campus study).

Faculty: 20 part-time/adjunct (6 women).
Students: 140 full-time (83 women); includes 73 minority (59 African Americans, 4 Asian Americans or Pacific Islanders, 8 Hispanic Americans, 2 Native Americans), 3 international. Average age 45. 22 applicants, 77% accepted. In 2001, 7 degrees awarded.
Degree requirements: For doctorate, thesis/dissertation, brief dispersed residency sessions.
Entrance requirements: For doctorate, 3 years of professional experience, master's degree. *Application deadline:* For fall admission, 7/1; for winter admission, 10/1; for spring admission, 1/1. Applications are processed on a rolling basis. *Application fee:* $50. Electronic applications accepted.
Expenses: Tuition: Full-time $8,900. Tuition and fees vary according to degree level and program.
Financial support: In 2001–02, 88 students received support, including 4 fellowships with partial tuition reimbursements available (averaging $1,500 per year); tuition waivers (partial) also available. Support available to part-time students. Financial award applicants required to submit FAFSA.
Faculty research: Clinical social work, social policy, analysis, human services administration, counseling, social change.
Dr. Michael Graham, Director, 800-925-3368, *Fax:* 612-338-5092, *E-mail:* mgraham@waldenu.edu.
Application contact: 800-444-6795, *Fax:* 941-261-7695, *E-mail:* request@waldenu.edu. *Web site:* http://www.waldenu.edu/

■ WAYNE STATE UNIVERSITY

Graduate School, Interdisciplinary Program in Developmental Disabilities, Detroit, MI 48202

AWARDS Certificate.

Students: In 2001, 1 degree awarded.
Entrance requirements: For degree, master's degree. *Application deadline:* Applications are processed on a rolling basis. *Application fee:* $0. Electronic applications accepted.
Expenses: Tuition, state resident: full-time $3,764. Tuition and fees vary according to degree level and program.
Application contact: Dr. Barbara [illegible] Director, 313-577-2654, *Fa*[illegible] 3770.

■ WEST VIRGINIA UNIVERSITY

Eberly College of Arts and Sciences, School of Applied Social Science, Program in Social Work, Morgantown, WV 26506

AWARDS Aging and health care (MSW); children and families (MSW); mental health (MSW). Part-time programs available.

Faculty: 13 full-time (8 women), 10 part-time/adjunct (9 women).
Students: 113 full-time (86 women), 106 part-time (84 women). Average age 31. 253 applicants, 75% accepted. In 2001, 111 degrees awarded.
Degree requirements: For master's, fieldwork.
Entrance requirements: For master's, GRE, TOEFL, minimum GPA of 2.75. *Application deadline:* For fall admission, 3/1. *Application fee:* $45.
Expenses: Tuition, state resident: full-time $2,791. Tuition, nonresident: full-time $8,659. Required fees: $1,002. Tuition and fees vary according to program.
Financial support: In 2001–02, 35 students received support, including 7 research assistantships, 19 teaching assistantships; career-related internships or fieldwork, Federal Work-Study, institutionally sponsored loans, scholarships/grants, tuition waivers (full and partial), and stipends also available. Financial award application deadline: 3/1; financial award applicants required to submit FAFSA.
Faculty research: Rural and small town social work practice, gerontology, child abuse, health and mental health, welfare reform. *Total annual research expenditures:* $208,000.
Application contact: Dr. Nancy Lohmann, Head, 304-293-3501 Ext. 3107, *Fax:* 304-293-5936, *E-mail:* nancy.lohmann@mail.wvu.edu. *Web site:* http://www.wvu.edu/~socialwk/

■ WICHITA STATE UNIVERSITY

Graduate School, Fairmount College of Liberal Arts and Sciences, School of Community Affairs, Wichita, KS 67260

AWARDS Criminal justice (MA); gerontology (MA). Part-time programs available.

Faculty: 10 full-time (4 women), 2 part-time/adjunct (1 woman).
Students: 23 full-time (15 women), 44 part-time (26 women); includes 5 minority (2 African Americans, 1 Asian American or Pacific Islander, 2 Hispanic Americans), 1 international. Average age 35. 20 applicants, 60% accepted, 12 enrolled. In 2001, 25 degrees awarded.
Application deadline: For spring admission, 1/1. Applications are processed on a rolling basis. *Application fee:* $25 ($40 for international students). Electronic applications accepted.
Expenses: Tuition, state resident: full-time $1,888; part-time $105 per credit. Tuition, nonresident: full-time $6,129; part-time $341 per credit. Required fees: $345; $19 per credit. $17 per semester. Tuition and fees vary according to course load and program.
Financial support: In 2001–02, 8 research assistantships (averaging $1,941 per year), 8 teaching assistantships with full tuition reimbursements (averaging $4,879 per year) were awarded. Career-related internships or fieldwork, Federal Work-Study, institutionally sponsored loans, and unspecified assistantships also available. Financial award application deadline: 4/1; financial award applicants required to submit FAFSA.
Dr. Paul Cromwell, Director, 316-978-7200, *Fax:* 316-978-3626, *E-mail:* paul.cromwell@wichita.edu.

■ YOUNGSTOWN STATE UNIVERSITY

Graduate School, College of Health and Human Services, Department of Health Professions, Youngstown, OH 44555-0001

AWARDS Health and human services (MHHS). Part-time and evening/weekend programs available.

Degree requirements: For master's, thesis optional.
Entrance requirements: For master's, GRE General Test, TOEFL, minimum GPA of 3.0.
Faculty research: Drug prevention, multiskilling in health care, organizational behavior, health care management, health behaviors, research management.

SOCIAL WORK

■ ADELPHI UNIVERSITY

School of Social Work, Garden City, NY 11530

AWARDS Social welfare (DSW); social work (MSW). Part-time and evening/weekend programs available.

Students: 173 full-time (145 women), 501 part-time (432 women); includes 153 minority (109 African Americans, 5 Asian Americans or Pacific Islanders, 39 Hispanic Americans), 4 international. Average age 37. 548 applicants, 65% accepted, 214 enrolled. In 2001, 239 master's, 6 doctorates awarded.
Degree requirements: For doctorate, thesis/dissertation.
Entrance requirements: For master's, minimum undergraduate GPA of 3.0; for doctorate, master's in social work, 3 years post-MSW work experience, interview. *Application deadline:* For fall admission, 4/1 (priority date). Applications are processed on a rolling basis. *Application fee:* $50.
Expenses: Tuition: Full-time $12,960; part-time $540 per credit. One-time fee: $400 part-time. Tuition and fees vary according to course load, degree level and program.
Financial support: Research assistantships, career-related internships or fieldwork, Federal Work-Study, tuition waivers (full and partial), and unspecified assistantships available. Financial award application deadline: 2/15; financial award applicants required to submit FAFSA.
Faculty research: Services for rape victims, refugees, child welfare, international feminization of poverty, public welfare.
Dr. Brooke Spiro, Acting Dean, 516-877-4341.
Application contact: Muriel Levin, Admissions Coordinator, 516-877-4384.

■ ALABAMA AGRICULTURAL AND MECHANICAL UNIVERSITY

School of Graduate Studies, School of Arts and Sciences, Department of Social Work, Huntsville, AL 35811

AWARDS MSW.

Faculty: 8 full-time (4 women), 6 part-time/adjunct (3 women).
Students: 12 full-time (9 women), 46 part-time (38 women); includes 35 minority (all African Americans), 2 international. In 2001, 14 degrees awarded.
Degree requirements: For master's, thesis.
Entrance requirements: For master's, GRE General Test, portfolio. *Application deadline:* For fall admission, 5/1 (priority date). Applications are processed on a rolling basis. *Application fee:* $15 ($20 for international students).
Expenses: Tuition, state resident: full-time $1,380. Tuition, nonresident: full-time $2,500.
Financial support: Application deadline: 4/1.
Dr. Shelley Wyckoff, Chair, 256-851-5478, *Fax:* 256-851-5970.

■ ANDREWS UNIVERSITY

School of Graduate Studies, College of Arts and Sciences, Department of Social Work, Berrien Springs, MI 49104

AWARDS MSW.

Students: 33 full-time (30 women), 3 part-time (2 women); includes 18 minority (11 African Americans, 1 Asian American or Pacific Islander, 6 Hispanic Americans), 4 international. Average age 30. In 2001, 24 degrees awarded.
Application deadline: Applications are processed on a rolling basis. *Application fee:* $40.
Expenses: Tuition: Full-time $12,600; part-time $525 per semester. Required fees: $268. Tuition and fees vary according to degree level.
Dr. Sharon W. Pittman, Chair, 616-471-6196, *Fax:* 616-471-3868.

Application contact: Carolyn Hurst, Supervisor of Graduate Admission, 800-253-2874, *Fax:* 616-471-3228, *E-mail:* enroll@andrews.edu.

■ ARIZONA STATE UNIVERSITY

Graduate College, College of Public Programs, Department of Social Work, Tempe, AZ 85287

AWARDS MSW, PhD.

Degree requirements: For doctorate, thesis/dissertation.
Entrance requirements: For master's, GRE or MAT.
Faculty research: Management methods in social services, evaluation of day-care service delivery, evaluation of minority community mental health training.

■ ARIZONA STATE UNIVERSITY WEST

College of Human Services, Program in Social Work, Phoenix, AZ 85069-7100

AWARDS MSW. Part-time and evening/weekend programs available.

Faculty: 8 full-time (3 women), 2 part-time/adjunct (both women).
Students: 80 full-time (69 women), 32 part-time (26 women); includes 21 minority (8 African Americans, 3 Asian Americans or Pacific Islanders, 8 Hispanic Americans, 2 Native Americans), 2 international. Average age 37. 61 applicants, 82% accepted, 19 enrolled.
Entrance requirements: For master's, GRE or MAT. *Application deadline:* For fall admission, 5/1. Applications are processed on a rolling basis. *Application fee:* $45.
Expenses: Tuition, state resident: full-time $2,412; part-time $126 per credit hour. Tuition, nonresident: full-time $10,352; part-time $428 per credit hour. Tuition and fees vary according to program.
Financial support: Career-related internships or fieldwork, Federal Work-Study, scholarships/grants, and traineeships available. Support available to part-time students. Financial award applicants required to submit FAFSA.
Dr. Melissa Lavitt, Chair, 602-543-6615, *Fax:* 602-543-6612, *E-mail:* melissa.lavitt@asu.edu.
Application contact: Michele Johnson, Administrative Assistant, 602-543-4679, *Fax:* 602-543-6612, *E-mail:* michele.johnson@asu.edu.

■ AUGSBURG COLLEGE

Program in Social Work, Minneapolis, MN 55454-1351

AWARDS MSW. Part-time and evening/weekend programs available.

Faculty: 10 full-time (all women), 1 part-time/adjunct (0 women).
Students: 40 full-time (39 women), 8 part-time (7 women); includes 2 minority (1 African American, 1 Asian American or Pacific Islander), 2 international. Average age 32. 45 applicants, 98% accepted, 17 enrolled. In 2001, 52 degrees awarded.
Degree requirements: For master's, thesis.
Entrance requirements: For master's, previous course work in human biology and statistics. *Application deadline:* For fall admission, 1/15; for spring admission, 10/1. *Application fee:* $25.
Expenses: Tuition: Part-time $1,370 per course.
Financial support: In 2001–02, 38 students received support. Career-related internships or fieldwork, institutionally sponsored loans, and tuition waivers (partial) available. Support available to part-time students. Financial award application deadline: 4/15.
Dr. Tony Bibus, Director, 612-330-1746, *Fax:* 612-330-1493, *E-mail:* bibus@augsburg.edu.
Application contact: Janna Caywood, Program Assistant, 612-330-1763, *Fax:* 612-330-1493, *E-mail:* caywood@augsburg.edu.

■ AURORA UNIVERSITY

George Williams College, School of Social Work, Aurora, IL 60506-4892

AWARDS MSW. Part-time and evening/weekend programs available.

Degree requirements: For master's, thesis optional.
Entrance requirements: For master's, minimum GPA of 2.8. *Web site:* http://www.aurora.edu/

■ BARRY UNIVERSITY

School of Social Work, Doctoral Program in Social Work, Miami Shores, FL 33161-6695

AWARDS PhD. Part-time and evening/weekend programs available.

Faculty: 20 full-time (12 women).
Students: 42. Average age 44. In 2001, 2 degrees awarded.
Degree requirements: For doctorate, thesis/dissertation.
Entrance requirements: For doctorate, MSW from an accredited school of social work, 2 years of professional experience. *Application fee:* $30. Electronic applications accepted.
Expenses: Tuition: Full-time $12,480. Tuition and fees vary according to degree level and program.
Financial support: Tuition waivers (full) available.
Faculty research: Family and children services, homelessness, gerontology, school social work.
Dr. Elane Nuehring, Director, 305-899-3900, *Fax:* 305-899-3934, *E-mail:* nuehring@aquinas.barry.edu.
Application contact: Philip Mack, Director of Admissions, 305-899-3900, *Fax:* 305-899-3934, *E-mail:* sswadm@mail.barry.edu. *Web site:* http://www.barry.edu/

■ BARRY UNIVERSITY

School of Social Work, Master's Program in Social Work, Miami Shores, FL 33161-6695

AWARDS MSW. Part-time and evening/weekend programs available.

Faculty: 20 full-time (12 women).
Students: 339. Average age 35. In 2001, 149 degrees awarded.
Degree requirements: For master's, fieldwork.
Entrance requirements: For master's, minimum GPA of 3.0. *Application deadline:* For fall admission, 7/31. *Application fee:* $30. Electronic applications accepted.
Expenses: Tuition: Full-time $12,480. Tuition and fees vary according to degree level and program.
Financial support: In 2001–02, 75 fellowships with partial tuition reimbursements (averaging $4,500 per year), 5 research assistantships (averaging $7,500 per year) were awarded. Career-related internships or fieldwork, scholarships/grants, and tuition waivers (full) also available. Support available to part-time students. Financial award application deadline: 6/2.
Faculty research: Family and children services, homelessness, gerontology, school social work.
Application contact: Philip Mack, Director of Admissions, 305-899-3900, *Fax:* 305-899-3934, *E-mail:* sswadm@mail.barry.edu.

Find an in-depth description at www.petersons.com/gradchannel.

■ BAYLOR UNIVERSITY

Graduate School, College of Arts and Sciences, School of Social Work, Program in Social Work, Waco, TX 76798

AWARDS MSW, M Div/MSW.

Students: 34 full-time (26 women), 8 part-time (all women); includes 4 minority (3 African Americans, 1 Hispanic American), 1 international. In 2001, 17 degrees awarded.
Application fee: $25.
Expenses: Tuition: Part-time $379 per semester hour. Required fees: $42 per semester hour. $101 per semester. Tuition and fees vary according to program.
Dr. Dennis Myers, Director of Graduate Studies, 254-710-4417, *E-mail:* diana_garland@baylor.edu.
Application contact: Suzanne Keener, Administrative Assistant, 254-710-3588, *Fax:* 254-710-3870, *E-mail:* graduate_school@baylor.edu. *Web site:* http://www.baylor.edu/~Sociology/swo.htm

■ BOISE STATE UNIVERSITY

Graduate College, College of Social Science and Public Affairs, School of Social Work, Boise, ID 83725-0399

AWARDS MSW. Part-time programs available.

Entrance requirements: For master's, GRE General Test, minimum GPA of 3.0. Electronic applications accepted.

■ BOSTON COLLEGE

Graduate School of Social Work, Chestnut Hill, MA 02467-3800

AWARDS MSW, PhD, JD/MSW, MSW/MA, MSW/MBA. Part-time programs available.

Degree requirements: For master's, 2 internships; for doctorate, thesis/dissertation.
Entrance requirements: For doctorate, MAT, MSW.
Expenses: Contact institution.
Faculty research: Social Security utilization, women and employment, cross-cultural practice, gerontology, AIDS.
Find an in-depth description at www.petersons.com/gradchannel.

■ BOSTON UNIVERSITY

Graduate School of Arts and Sciences, Program in Sociology and Social Work, Boston, MA 02215

AWARDS PhD.

Students: 11 full-time (10 women), 7 part-time (6 women); includes 4 minority (2 African Americans, 2 Hispanic Americans). Average age 44. 13 applicants, 69% accepted, 4 enrolled.
Degree requirements: For doctorate, one foreign language, thesis/dissertation, critical essay.
Entrance requirements: For doctorate, GRE General Test or MAT, TOEFL, sample of written work. *Application deadline:* For fall admission, 1/15. *Application fee:* $60.
Expenses: Tuition: Full-time $25,872; part-time $340 per credit. Required fees: $40 per semester. Part-time tuition and fees vary according to class time, course level and program.
Financial support: In 2001–02, 5 students received support; fellowships, research assistantships, career-related internships or fieldwork, Federal Work-Study, and scholarships/grants available. Support available to part-time students. Financial award application deadline: 1/15; financial award applicants required to submit FAFSA.
Judith Gonyea, Acting Director, 617-343-3748, *Fax:* 617-353-5612, *E-mail:* jgonyea@bu.edu.
Application contact: Michelle Akemi ... Staff Coordinator, 617-353-3765, ...512, *E-mail:* sswphd@

■ BOSTON UNIVERSITY

School of Education, Dual Degree Program in Administration, Training, and Policy Studies and Social Work, Boston, MA 02215

AWARDS MSW/Ed M.

Electronic applications accepted.
Expenses: Tuition: Full-time $25,872; part-time $340 per credit. Required fees: $40 per semester. Part-time tuition and fees vary according to class time, course level and program.

■ BOSTON UNIVERSITY

School of Education, Dual Degree Program in Special Education and Social Work, Boston, MA 02215

AWARDS MSW/Ed M.

Expenses: Tuition: Full-time $25,872; part-time $340 per credit. Required fees: $40 per semester. Part-time tuition and fees vary according to class time, course level and program.

■ BOSTON UNIVERSITY

School of Social Work, Boston, MA 02215

AWARDS Clinical practice with groups (MSW); clinical practice with individuals and families (MSW); macro social work practice (MSW); social work and sociology (PhD). Part-time programs available.

Faculty: 26 full-time (18 women), 93 part-time/adjunct (74 women).
Students: 159 full-time (149 women), 164 part-time (144 women); includes 36 minority (14 African Americans, 11 Asian Americans or Pacific Islanders, 10 Hispanic Americans, 1 Native American), 6 international. Average age 30. 400 applicants, 68% accepted, 130 enrolled. In 2001, 177 master's, 3 doctorates awarded.
Degree requirements: For doctorate, one foreign language, thesis/dissertation, critical essay.
Entrance requirements: For master's, GRE General Test or MAT, minimum GPA of 3.0; for doctorate, GRE General Test or MAT, sample of written work. *Application deadline:* For fall admission, 3/2. *Application fee:* $60.
Expenses: Contact institution.
Financial support: In 2001–02, 90 students received support, including 3 research assistantships with tuition reimbursements available (averaging $4,000 per year); fellowships, career-related internships or fieldwork, Federal Work-Study, institutionally sponsored loans, and scholarships/grants also available. Support available to part-time students. Financial award application deadline: 3/1; financial award applicants required to submit FAFSA.
Faculty research: Health and aging, child and adolescent substance abuse, mental health. *Total annual research expenditures:* $1.3 million.
Wilma Peebles-Wilkins, Dean, 617-353-3760, *Fax:* 617-353-5612.
Application contact: Edward M. Greene, Director of Admissions, 617-353-3765, *Fax:* 617-353-5612, *E-mail:* busswad@bu.edu. *Web site:* http://www.bu.edu/ssw/
Find an in-depth description at www.petersons.com/gradchannel.

■ BRIGHAM YOUNG UNIVERSITY

Graduate Studies, College of Family, Home, and Social Sciences, School of Social Work, Provo, UT 84602-1001

AWARDS MSW.

Faculty: 12 full-time (6 women), 19 part-time/adjunct (11 women).
Students: 80 full-time (47 women); includes 17 minority (1 African American, 10 Asian Americans or Pacific Islanders, 5 Hispanic Americans, 1 Native American), 3 international. Average age 28. 131 applicants, 37% accepted. In 2001, 39 degrees awarded.
Application deadline: For fall admission, 1/15. *Application fee:* $50. Electronic applications accepted.
Expenses: Tuition: Full-time $3,860; part-time $214 per hour.
Financial support: In 2001–02, 5 fellowships with tuition reimbursements (averaging $3,460 per year), 14 research assistantships (averaging $1,820 per year), 5 teaching assistantships (averaging $3,640 per year) were awarded. Career-related internships or fieldwork, tuition waivers (partial), and administrative aides, paid field practicums also available. Financial award application deadline: 6/1.
Faculty research: Family abuse, depression, health, child welfare, marriage and family. *Total annual research expenditures:* $57,000.
Dr. Elaine Walton, Director, 801-422-3282, *Fax:* 801-378-4049, *E-mail:* socialwork@byu.edu.
Application contact: Lisa Willey, Graduate Secretary, 801-422-5681, *Fax:* 801-378-4049, *E-mail:* lisa_willey@byu.edu. *Web site:* http://fhss.byu.edu/socwork/

■ BRYN MAWR COLLEGE

Graduate School of Social Work and Social Research, Bryn Mawr, PA 19010-2899

AWARDS MLSP, MSS, PhD. Part-time programs available.

Faculty: 15 full-time (8 women), 19 part-time/adjunct (18 women).
Students: 158 full-time (138 women), 64 part-time (54 women); includes 47 minority (38 African Americans, 5 Asian Americans or Pacific Islanders, 4 Hispanic Americans), 5 international. Average age 34. 172 applicants, 85% accepted, 82 enrolled. In 2001, 67 master's, 4 doctorates awarded.

Degree requirements: For master's, fieldwork; for doctorate, thesis/dissertation, comprehensive exam.
Entrance requirements: For master's, TOEFL; for doctorate, GRE General Test, TOEFL. *Application deadline:* For fall admission, 3/1 (priority date). Applications are processed on a rolling basis. *Application fee:* $50.
Expenses: Contact institution.
Financial support: In 2001–02, 194 students received support, including 12 fellowships with full and partial tuition reimbursements available (averaging $3,517 per year), 4 research assistantships with full and partial tuition reimbursements available (averaging $9,382 per year), 8 teaching assistantships with full and partial tuition reimbursements available (averaging $9,121 per year); career-related internships or fieldwork, Federal Work-Study, institutionally sponsored loans, scholarships/grants, tuition waivers (full and partial), and PhD dissertation award also available. Support available to part-time students. Financial award application deadline: 3/1; financial award applicants required to submit FAFSA.
Faculty research: Aging, substance abuse, child and public welfare, occupational health and safety, children and adolescents. *Total annual research expenditures:* $1.5 million.
Ruth W. Mayden, Dean, 610-520-2600.
Application contact: Nancy J. Kirby, Assistant Dean and Director of Admissions, 610-520-2601, *Fax:* 610-520-2655, *E-mail:* swadmiss@brynmawr.edu. *Web site:* http://www.brynmawr.edu/gsswsr/

■ CALIFORNIA STATE UNIVERSITY, BAKERSFIELD

Division of Graduate Studies and Research, School of Humanities and Social Sciences, Program in Social Work, Bakersfield, CA 93311-1099

AWARDS MSW.

Expenses: Tuition, state resident: full-time $876; part-time $292. Tuition, nonresident: full-time $1,122; part-time $456.

■ CALIFORNIA STATE UNIVERSITY, CHICO

Graduate School, College of Behavioral and Social Sciences, School of Social Work, Chico, CA 95929-0722

AWARDS MSW.

Students: 20 full-time; includes 3 minority (1 African American, 1 Asian American or Pacific Islander, 1 Hispanic American). 22 applicants, 100% accepted, 20 enrolled.
Degree requirements: For master's, thesis or alternative, oral exam.
Entrance requirements: For master's, letters of recommendation on departmental form (3). *Application deadline:* For fall admission, 4/1. Applications are processed on a rolling basis. *Application fee:* $55. Electronic applications accepted.
Expenses: Tuition, state resident: full-time $2,148. Tuition, nonresident: full-time $6,576.
Jan O' Donnell, Graduate Coordinator, 530-898-6204.

■ CALIFORNIA STATE UNIVERSITY, FRESNO

Division of Graduate Studies, College of Health and Human Services, Department of Social Work Education, Fresno, CA 93740-8027

AWARDS MSW. Part-time and evening/weekend programs available.

Faculty: 15 full-time (8 women).
Students: 145 full-time (112 women), 42 part-time (33 women); includes 112 minority (14 African Americans, 20 Asian Americans or Pacific Islanders, 75 Hispanic Americans, 3 Native Americans), 1 international. Average age 31. 104 applicants, 88% accepted, 76 enrolled. In 2001, 69 degrees awarded.
Degree requirements: For master's, thesis or alternative. *Median time to degree:* Master's–2.5 years full-time, 3.5 years part-time.
Entrance requirements: For master's, GRE General Test, TOEFL, minimum GPA of 2.5. *Application deadline:* For fall admission, 2/23 (priority date). Applications are processed on a rolling basis. *Application fee:* $55. Electronic applications accepted.
Expenses: Tuition, nonresident: part-time $246 per unit. Required fees: $605 per semester. Tuition and fees vary according to course load.
Financial support: In 2001–02, 1 teaching assistantship (averaging $1,000 per year) was awarded; career-related internships or fieldwork, Federal Work-Study, and scholarships/grants also available. Support available to part-time students. Financial award application deadline: 3/1; financial award applicants required to submit FAFSA.
Faculty research: Children at risk, international cooperation, child welfare training.
Dr. Jane Middleton, Chair, 559-278-3992, *Fax:* 559-278-7191, *E-mail:* jane_middleton@csufresno.edu.

■ CALIFORNIA STATE UNIVERSITY, LONG BEACH

Graduate Studies, College of Health and Human Services, Department of Social Work, Long Beach, CA 90840

AWARDS MSW. Part-time and evening/weekend programs available. Postbaccalaureate distance learning degree programs offered (no on-campus study).

Students: 323 full-time (261 women), 183 part-time (146 women); includes 252 minority (51 African Americans, 52 Asian Americans or Pacific Islanders, 147 Hispanic Americans, 2 Native Americans), 11 international. Average age 33. 358 applicants, 63% accepted. In 2001, 162 degrees awarded.
Degree requirements: For master's, thesis.
Application deadline: For fall admission, 8/1; for spring admission, 12/1. Applications are processed on a rolling basis. *Application fee:* $55. Electronic applications accepted.
Financial support: Federal Work-Study, institutionally sponsored loans, and scholarships/grants available. Financial award application deadline: 3/2.
Dr. John Oliver, Acting Director, 562-985-4616, *Fax:* 562-985-5514, *E-mail:* joliver@csulb.edu.
Application contact: Dr. Linda McCracken, Graduate Coordinator, 562-985-8699, *Fax:* 562-985-5514, *E-mail:* lmccrack@csulb.edu.

■ CALIFORNIA STATE UNIVERSITY, LOS ANGELES

Graduate Studies, College of Health and Human Services, Department of Social Work, Los Angeles, CA 90032-8530

AWARDS MSW.

Faculty: 12 full-time, 19 part-time/adjunct.
Students: 82 full-time (68 women), 63 part-time (54 women); includes 110 minority (25 African Americans, 21 Asian Americans or Pacific Islanders, 62 Hispanic Americans, 2 Native Americans), 3 international. In 2001, 18 degrees awarded.
Entrance requirements: For master's, TOEFL. *Application deadline:* For fall admission, 6/30; for spring admission, 2/1. Applications are processed on a rolling basis. *Application fee:* $55.
Expenses: Tuition, nonresident: part-time $164 per unit.
Financial support: Application deadline: 3/1.
Thanh V. Tran, Director, 323-343-4680.

■ CALIFORNIA STATE UNIVERSITY, SACRAMENTO

Graduate Studies, College of Health and Human Services, Division of Social Work, Sacramento, CA 95819-6048

AWARDS Family and children's services (MSW); health care (MSW); mental health (MSW); social justice and corrections (MSW).

Students: 297 full-time (257 women), 65 part-time (53 women); includes 134 minority (47 African Americans, 19 Asian Americans or Pacific Islanders, 61 Hispanic Americans, 7 Native Americans).
Degree requirements: For master's, thesis or alternative, writing proficiency exam.

California State University, Sacramento (continued)
Entrance requirements: For master's, TOEFL, minimum GPA of 2.5 during previous 2 years. *Application deadline:* For fall admission, 4/15; for spring admission, 11/1. *Application fee:* $55.
Expenses: Tuition, state resident: full-time $1,965; part-time $668 per semester. Tuition, nonresident: part-time $246 per unit.
Financial support: Career-related internships or fieldwork and Federal Work-Study available. Support available to part-time students. Financial award application deadline: 3/1.
Dr. Robin Carter, Chair, 916-278-6943.
Application contact: Dr. Santos Torres, Graduate Coordinator, 916-278-7064.

■ CALIFORNIA STATE UNIVERSITY, SAN BERNARDINO

Graduate Studies, College of Social and Behavioral Sciences, Department of Social Work, San Bernardino, CA 92407-2397

AWARDS MSW. Part-time and evening/weekend programs available.

Faculty: 7 full-time (5 women), 2 part-time/adjunct (1 woman).
Students: 136 full-time (116 women), 7 part-time (5 women); includes 65 minority (18 African Americans, 3 Asian Americans or Pacific Islanders, 43 Hispanic Americans, 1 Native American), 1 international. Average age 37. 121 applicants, 51% accepted. In 2001, 76 degrees awarded.
Degree requirements: For master's, field practicum, research project.
Entrance requirements: For master's, minimum GPA of 2.75 in last 2 years, liberal arts background. *Application deadline:* For fall admission, 8/31 (priority date). *Application fee:* $55.
Expenses: Tuition, nonresident: full-time $4,428. Required fees: $1,733.
Financial support: Fellowships, research assistantships, career-related internships or fieldwork, Federal Work-Study, institutionally sponsored loans, and stipends for practicum available. Support available to part-time students. Financial award application deadline: 5/1.
Faculty research: Addiction, computers in social work practice, minority issues, gerontology.
Dr. Teresa Morris, Chair, 909-880-5501, *Fax:* 909-880-7029, *E-mail:* tmorris@csusb.edu.

■ CALIFORNIA STATE UNIVERSITY, STANISLAUS

Graduate Programs, College of Arts, Letters, and Sciences, Program in Social Work, Turlock, CA 95382

AWARDS MSW.

Faculty: 6 full-time (4 women), 5 part-time/adjunct (2 women).
Students: 122 (94 women); includes 47 minority (11 African Americans, 8 Asian Americans or Pacific Islanders, 24 Hispanic Americans, 4 Native Americans). 94 applicants, 95% accepted. In 2001, 62 degrees awarded.
Degree requirements: For master's, thesis.
Entrance requirements: For master's, minimum GPA of 3.0, letters of reference. *Application deadline:* For fall admission, 3/31. *Application fee:* $55. Electronic applications accepted.
Expenses: Tuition, nonresident: part-time $246 per unit. Required fees: $1,919. Tuition and fees vary according to campus/location and program.
Financial support: In 2001–02, 1 fellowship (averaging $2,500 per year) was awarded; career-related internships or fieldwork and Federal Work-Study also available. Financial award application deadline: 3/2; financial award applicants required to submit FAFSA.
Dr. Ellen Dunbar, Director, 209-667-3091, *E-mail:* edunbar@csustan.edu.

■ CALIFORNIA UNIVERSITY OF PENNSYLVANIA

School of Graduate Studies, School of Education, Department of Social Work and Gerontology, California, PA 15419-1394

AWARDS Social work (MSW).

Faculty: 3 full-time (all women), 2 part-time/adjunct (1 woman).
Students: 12 full-time (all women), 22 part-time (15 women); includes 5 minority (all African Americans).
Degree requirements: For master's, comprehensive exam.
Entrance requirements: For master's, TOEFL, GRE. *Application deadline:* Applications are processed on a rolling basis. *Application fee:* $25.
Expenses: Tuition, state resident: full-time $4,600. Tuition, nonresident: full-time $7,554.
Financial support: Tuition waivers (full) available.
Dr. Wilburn Hayden, Coordinator, 724-938-5910, *E-mail:* hayden@cup.edu.
Application contact: Coordinator, 724-938-5910. *Web site:* http://www.cup.edu/graduate

■ CASE WESTERN RESERVE UNIVERSITY

Mandel School of Applied Social Sciences, Cleveland, OH 44106

AWARDS Nonprofit organizations (MNO, CNM); social administration (MSSA); social welfare (PhD). Evening/weekend programs available.

Students: In 2001, 189 degrees awarded.
Degree requirements: For master's, fieldwork; for doctorate, thesis/dissertation.
Entrance requirements: For master's, GRE General Test, MAT, or minimum GPA of 2.7; for doctorate, GRE General Test or MAT, minimum GPA of 2.7. *Application deadline:* Applications are processed on a rolling basis. *Application fee:* $30.
Expenses: Contact institution.
Financial support: Career-related internships or fieldwork, Federal Work-Study, institutionally sponsored loans, and tuition waivers (partial) available. Support available to part-time students. Financial award application deadline: 4/27; financial award applicants required to submit FAFSA.
Faculty research: Models of social work practice, improved delivery in health and social services, evaluating community-based initiatives.
Dr. Grover Cleveland Gilmore, Dean, 216-368-2256, *E-mail:* gcg@po.cwru.edu.
Application contact: Director of Recruitment and Admissions, 800-863-6772 Ext. 2280, *Fax:* 216-368-5065, *E-mail:* msassadmit@po.cwru.edu. *Web site:* http://msass.cwru.edu/

Find an in-depth description at www.petersons.com/gradchannel.

■ THE CATHOLIC UNIVERSITY OF AMERICA

National Catholic School of Social Service, Washington, DC 20064

AWARDS MSW, PhD, JD/MSW. Part-time programs available.

Faculty: 15 full-time (12 women), 19 part-time/adjunct (17 women).
Students: 92 full-time (82 women), 115 part-time (96 women); includes 44 minority (31 African Americans, 4 Asian Americans or Pacific Islanders, 9 Hispanic Americans), 10 international. Average age 36. 145 applicants, 82% accepted, 80 enrolled. In 2001, 64 master's, 3 doctorates awarded.
Degree requirements: For master's, paper or thesis; for doctorate, one foreign language, thesis/dissertation, comprehensive exam.
Entrance requirements: For master's, GRE or MAT; for doctorate, GRE, MSW. *Application fee:* $55. Electronic applications accepted.
Expenses: Tuition: Full-time $20,050; part-time $770 per credit. Required fees: $430 per term. Tuition and fees vary according to program.
Financial support: In 2001–02, 100 students received support; fellowships, career-related internships or fieldwork, Federal Work-Study, institutionally sponsored loans, and scholarships/grants available. Support available to part-time students. Financial award applicants required to submit FAFSA.

Faculty research: Family and child services, social policy, health and mental health, ethics, spirituality and social work practice.
Dr. Ann Patrick Conrad, Dean, 202-319-5454, *Fax:* 202-319-5093.
Application contact: Christine Sabatino, Director of Admission, 202-319-5496, *Fax:* 202-319-5093, *E-mail:* cua-ncss@cua.edu. *Web site:* http://www.cua.edu/www/sss/

■ CHICAGO STATE UNIVERSITY

Graduate Studies, College of Arts and Sciences, Department of Social Work and Sociology, Chicago, IL 60628

AWARDS MSW.

Students: 40 applicants, 48% accepted. *Application deadline:* For fall admission, 3/15. *Application fee:* $25. Electronic applications accepted.
Dr. Doris Penny, Chairperson, 773-995-2207.

■ CLARK ATLANTA UNIVERSITY

School of Social Work, Atlanta, GA 30314

AWARDS MSW, PhD. Part-time programs available. Terminal master's awarded for partial completion of doctoral program.

Degree requirements: For master's, thesis; for doctorate, one foreign language, thesis/dissertation.

■ CLEVELAND STATE UNIVERSITY

College of Graduate Studies, College of Arts and Sciences, Department of Social Work, Cleveland, OH 44115

AWARDS MSW. Part-time programs available.

Faculty: 14 full-time (6 women).
Students: 53 full-time (47 women), 44 part-time (33 women); includes 28 minority (25 African Americans, 1 Asian American or Pacific Islander, 1 Hispanic American, 1 Native American). Average age 35. 58 applicants, 59% accepted. In 2001, 20 degrees awarded.
Entrance requirements: For master's, GRE. *Application deadline:* For fall admission, 3/15. *Application fee:* $25.
Expenses: Tuition, state resident: full-time $6,838; part-time $263 per credit hour. Tuition, nonresident: full-time $13,526; part-time $520 per credit hour.
Financial support: In 2001–02, 5 research assistantships (averaging $3,480 per year) were awarded; tuition waivers (full) also available.
Dr. Maggie Jackson, Chairperson, 216-687-4599, *Fax:* 216-687-5590, *E-mail:* mag.jackson@csuohio.edu.

■ COLLEGE OF ST. CATHERINE

Graduate Program, Program in Social Work, St. Paul, MN 55105-1789

AWARDS MSW. Part-time and evening/weekend programs available.

Faculty: 29 full-time (24 women).
Students: 128 full-time (114 women), 84 part-time (78 women); includes 22 minority (12 African Americans, 3 Asian Americans or Pacific Islanders, 3 Hispanic Americans, 4 Native Americans), 1 international. Average age 33. 175 applicants, 69% accepted, 80 enrolled. In 2001, 72 degrees awarded.
Degree requirements: For master's, clinical research paper.
Entrance requirements: For master's, Michigan English Language Assessment Battery or TOEFL, minimum GPA of 3.0. *Application deadline:* For fall admission, 2/1. *Application fee:* $25.
Expenses: Contact institution.
Financial support: Career-related internships or fieldwork and institutionally sponsored loans available. Support available to part-time students. Financial award application deadline: 4/1; financial award applicants required to submit FAFSA.
Barbara W. Shank, Department Chair, 651-962-5801.
Application contact: 651-690-6505.

■ COLORADO STATE UNIVERSITY

Graduate School, College of Applied Human Sciences, School of Social Work, Fort Collins, CO 80523-0015

AWARDS MSW.

Faculty: 11 full-time (4 women).
Students: 82 full-time (71 women), 8 part-time (7 women); includes 11 minority (4 African Americans, 3 Asian Americans or Pacific Islanders, 3 Hispanic Americans, 1 Native American), 1 international. Average age 36. 76 applicants, 80% accepted, 34 enrolled. In 2001, 44 degrees awarded.
Degree requirements: For master's, research paper.
Entrance requirements: For master's, GRE General Test, TOEFL, minimum GPA of 3.0, 18 credits in social or behavioral science, previous course work in human biology and statistics, human services experience. *Application deadline:* For fall admission, 1/31. *Application fee:* $30. Electronic applications accepted.
Expenses: Tuition, state resident: full-time $2,880; part-time $160 per credit. Tuition, nonresident: full-time $11,412; part-time $634 per credit. Required fees: $750; $34 per credit.
Financial support: In 2001–02, 4 fellowships, 3 research assistantships, 5 teaching assistantships were awarded. Career-related internships or fieldwork, Federal Work-Study, and institutionally sponsored loans also available.
Faculty research: Environmental health, child welfare, mental health, human-animal bond, international social work. *Total annual research expenditures:* $200,000.
Dr. Deborah P. Valentine, Director, 970-491-2536, *Fax:* 979-491-7280.
Application contact: Dawn Carlson, MSW Program Coordinator, 970-491-2536, *Fax:* 970-491-7280, *E-mail:* dcarlson@cahs.colostate.edu. *Web site:* http://www.cahs.colostate.edu/SW/

■ COLUMBIA UNIVERSITY

School of Social Work, New York, NY 10025

AWARDS MSSW, PhD, JD/MS, MBA/MS, MPA/MS, MPH/MS, MS/M Div, MS/MA, MS/MS, MS/MS Ed. PhD offered through the Graduate School of Arts and Sciences.

Degree requirements: For doctorate, thesis/dissertation.
Entrance requirements: For doctorate, GRE General Test.
Expenses: Contact institution. *Web site:* http://www.columbia.edu/cu/ssw/

Find an in-depth description at www.petersons.com/gradchannel.

■ CORNELL UNIVERSITY

Graduate School, Graduate Fields of Human Ecology, Field of Policy Analysis and Management, Ithaca, NY 14853-0001

AWARDS Consumer policy evaluation (PhD); family and social welfare policy (PhD); health administration (MHA); health management policy (PhD).

Faculty: 33 full-time.
Students: 52 full-time (36 women); includes 19 minority (9 African Americans, 7 Asian Americans or Pacific Islanders, 3 Hispanic Americans), 12 international. 88 applicants, 52% accepted.
Degree requirements: For master's, thesis.
Entrance requirements: For doctorate, GRE General Test, 2 letters of recommendation. *Application deadline:* For fall admission, 2/1. *Application fee:* $65. Electronic applications accepted.
Expenses: Tuition: Full-time $25,970. Required fees: $50.
Financial support: In 2001–02, 31 students received support, including 13 fellowships with full and partial tuition reimbursements available, 3 research assistantships with full and partial tuition reimbursements available, 15 teaching assistantships with full and partial tuition reimbursements available; institutionally sponsored loans, scholarships/grants, tuition waivers (full and partial), and unspecified assistantships also available. Financial award applicants required to submit FAFSA.
Faculty research: Health policy analysis and management, family and social welfare policy analysis and management, policy planning and evaluation, mixed methods research, applied research methods.
Application contact: Graduate Field Assistant, 607-255-7772, *Fax:* 607-255-4071, *E-mail:* PhDprogram-pam_phd@

Cornell University (continued)
cornell.edu. *Web site:* http://www.gradschool.cornell.edu/grad/fields_1/pam.html

■ DELAWARE STATE UNIVERSITY

Graduate Programs, Department of Social Work, Program in Social Work, Dover, DE 19901-2277

AWARDS MSW. Evening/weekend programs available.

Faculty: 6 full-time (2 women).
Students: 55 full-time (49 women), 50 part-time (36 women); includes 63 minority (61 African Americans, 1 Hispanic American, 1 Native American). Average age 36. In 2001, 35 degrees awarded.
Entrance requirements: For master's, GRE, minimum GPA of 3.0 in major, 2.75 overall. *Application deadline:* For fall admission, 6/30 (priority date); for winter admission, 9/4; for spring admission, 1/17. Applications are processed on a rolling basis. *Application fee:* $15. Electronic applications accepted.
Expenses: Tuition, area resident: Full-time $3,420; part-time $190 per credit hour. Required fees: $180; $90 per semester. Full-time tuition and fees vary according to degree level and program.
Financial support: In 2001–02, 4 fellowships, 1 research assistantship were awarded. Career-related internships or fieldwork, Federal Work-Study, institutionally sponsored loans, and tuition waivers (full and partial) also available. Support available to part-time students.
Faculty research: Gerontology, human behavior, corrections, child welfare, adolescent behavior policy.
Application contact: Jethro C. Williams, Director of Admissions, 302-857-6351, *Fax:* 302-857-6352, *E-mail:* jwilliam@dsc.edu.

■ DELTA STATE UNIVERSITY

Graduate Programs, College of Arts and Sciences, Department of Social Work, Cleveland, MS 38733-0001

AWARDS MSW. Part-time programs available.

Degree requirements: For master's, thesis or alternative.
Application deadline: For fall admission, 8/1 (priority date); for spring admission, 12/1 (priority date). Applications are processed on a rolling basis. *Application fee:* $0.
Expenses: Tuition, state resident: full-time $3,100; part-time $144 per hour. Tuition, nonresident: full-time $7,174; part-time $382 per hour.
Financial support: Research assistantships, career-related internships or fieldwork, Federal Work-Study, and institutionally sponsored loans available. Support available to part-time students. Financial award application deadline: 6/1.
Carol Boyd, Chairperson, 662-846-4407, *Fax:* 662-846-4403, *E-mail:* cboyd@dsu.deltast.edu. *Web site:* http://www.deltast.edu/

■ DOMINICAN UNIVERSITY

Graduate School of Social Work, River Forest, IL 60305-1099

AWARDS MSW.

Faculty: 3 full-time (all women), 1 part-time/adjunct (0 women).
Students: 14 full-time (11 women), 44 part-time (37 women); includes 30 minority (21 African Americans, 1 Asian American or Pacific Islander, 8 Hispanic Americans), 1 international. Average age 40. 72 applicants, 93% accepted, 55 enrolled.
Entrance requirements: For master's, minimum GPA of 3.0 in upper division courses.
Expenses: Tuition: Part-time $395 per credit hour.
Financial support: Career-related internships or fieldwork, institutionally sponsored loans, and scholarships/grants available.
Vimala Pillari, Dean, 708-366-3316, *E-mail:* vpillari@email.dom.edu.
Application contact: Maria Talarico, Administrative Assistant, 708-366-3463, *Fax:* 708-366-3446, *E-mail:* msw@email.dom.edu.

Find an in-depth description at www.petersons.com/gradchannel.

■ EAST CAROLINA UNIVERSITY

Graduate School, School of Social Work and Criminal Justice Studies, Department of Social Work, Greenville, NC 27858-4353

AWARDS MSW.

Students: 92 full-time (84 women), 57 part-time (50 women); includes 34 minority (27 African Americans, 3 Asian Americans or Pacific Islanders, 3 Hispanic Americans, 1 Native American), 1 international. Average age 32. 204 applicants, 57% accepted. In 2001, 63 degrees awarded.
Degree requirements: For master's, comprehensive exam.
Application deadline: For fall admission, 1/15 (priority date). *Application fee:* $45.
Expenses: Tuition, state resident: full-time $2,636. Tuition, nonresident: full-time $11,365.
Financial support: Application deadline: 6/1.
Dr. Brent Angell, Interim Dean, 252-328-4199, *Fax:* 252-328-4196, *E-mail:* angellg@mail.ecu.edu.

■ EASTERN MICHIGAN UNIVERSITY

Graduate School, College of Health and Human Services, Department of Social Work, Program in Social Work, Ypsilanti, MI 48197

AWARDS MSW.

Faculty: 14 full-time.
Students: 263 (220 women); includes 89 minority (81 African Americans, 4 Asian Americans or Pacific Islanders, 3 Hispanic Americans, 1 Native American) 1 international. 181 applicants, 48% accepted. In 2001, 59 degrees awarded.
Entrance requirements: For master's, TOEFL. *Application deadline:* For fall admission, 5/15; for spring admission, 3/15. Applications are processed on a rolling basis. *Application fee:* $30.
Expenses: Tuition, state resident: part-time $285 per credit hour. Tuition, nonresident: part-time $510 per credit hour.
Financial support: Application deadline: 3/15.
Dr. Lynn Nybell, Head, 734-487-0393.

■ EASTERN WASHINGTON UNIVERSITY

Graduate School Studies, School of Social Work and Human Services, Cheney, WA 99004-2431

AWARDS MSW, MPA/MSW. Part-time programs available.

Faculty: 49 full-time (29 women).
Students: 165 full-time (127 women), 78 part-time (64 women); includes 38 minority (6 African Americans, 6 Asian Americans or Pacific Islanders, 20 Hispanic Americans, 6 Native Americans), 2 international. 233 applicants, 73% accepted, 93 enrolled. In 2001, 213 degrees awarded.
Degree requirements: For master's, comprehensive exam.
Entrance requirements: For master's, minimum GPA of 3.0. *Application deadline:* Applications are processed on a rolling basis. *Application fee:* $35.
Expenses: Tuition, state resident: full-time $1,586; part-time $159 per credit hour. Tuition, nonresident: full-time $4,677; part-time $468 per credit hour. Required fees: $222; $159 per credit. $74 per quarter.
Financial support: In 2001–02, 4 teaching assistantships with partial tuition reimbursements (averaging $7,000 per year) were awarded; career-related internships or fieldwork, Federal Work-Study, institutionally sponsored loans, scholarships/grants, health care benefits, tuition waivers (partial), and unspecified assistantships also available. Support available to part-time students. Financial award application deadline: 2/1; financial award applicants required to submit FAFSA.

Dr. Michael Frumkin, Dean, 509-359-6885, *Fax:* 509-359-6475.
Application contact: Diane Somerday, Program Coordinator, 509-359-6482.

■ EAST TENNESSEE STATE UNIVERSITY

School of Graduate Studies, College of Arts and Sciences, Department of Social Work, Johnson City, TN 37614

AWARDS MSW.

Faculty: 3 full-time (all women).
Expenses: Tuition, state resident: part-time $181 per hour. Tuition, nonresident: part-time $270 per hour. Required fees: $220 per term.
Financial support: Research assistantships with full tuition reimbursements, teaching assistantships with full tuition reimbursements available.
Dr. Patty Gibbs Wahlberg, Interim Chair, 423-439-6663, *Fax:* 423-439-4471, *E-mail:* gibbs@etsu.edu. *Web site:* http://www.etsu.edu/

■ EDINBORO UNIVERSITY OF PENNSYLVANIA

Graduate Studies, School of Liberal Arts, Department of Social Work, Edinboro, PA 16444

AWARDS MSW. Evening/weekend programs available.

Faculty: 5 full-time (2 women).
Students: 27 full-time (24 women). Average age 31.
Degree requirements: For master's, competency exam.
Application deadline: Applications are processed on a rolling basis. *Application fee:* $25. Electronic applications accepted.
Expenses: Tuition, state resident: full-time $4,600; part-time $256 per credit. Tuition, nonresident: full-time $7,554; part-time $420 per credit. Required fees: $68 per credit.
Financial support: In 2001–02, 7 students received support. Career-related internships or fieldwork, Federal Work-Study, institutionally sponsored loans, scholarships/grants, and unspecified assistantships available. Support available to part-time students. Financial award application deadline: 5/1; financial award applicants required to submit FAFSA.
Dr. Michael Paulus, Chairperson, 814-732-1589, *E-mail:* mpaulus@edinboro.edu.
Application contact: Dr. Mary Margaret Bevevino, Dean of Graduate Studies, 814-732-2856, *Fax:* 814-732-2611, *E-mail:* mbevevino@edinboro.edu.

■ FLORIDA ATLANTIC UNIVERSITY

College of Architecture, Urban and Public Affairs, Department of Social Work, Boca Raton, FL 33431-0991

AWARDS MSW. Part-time and evening/weekend programs available.

Faculty: 15 full-time (8 women), 10 part-time/adjunct (7 women).
Students: 31 full-time (30 women), 28 part-time (22 women); includes 15 minority (10 African Americans, 1 Asian American or Pacific Islander, 4 Hispanic Americans). Average age 37. 77 applicants, 70% accepted, 43 enrolled.
Application deadline: For fall admission, 6/1 (priority date); for spring admission, 10/20 (priority date). Applications are processed on a rolling basis. *Application fee:* $20.
Expenses: Tuition, state resident: full-time $3,098; part-time $172 per credit. Tuition, nonresident: full-time $10,427; part-time $579 per credit.
Financial support: Career-related internships or fieldwork, Federal Work-Study, institutionally sponsored loans, and tuition waivers (partial) available. Financial award application deadline: 4/1.
Dr. Michele Hawkins, Head, 561-297-3234, *Fax:* 561-297-2866, *E-mail:* mhawkins@fau.edu. *Web site:* http://www.fau.edu/divdept/caupa/dsw/index.html

■ FLORIDA GULF COAST UNIVERSITY

College of Public and Social Services, Program in Social Work, Fort Myers, FL 33965-6565

AWARDS MSW. Part-time and evening/weekend programs available.

Faculty: 16 full-time (9 women), 7 part-time/adjunct (1 woman).
Students: 14 full-time (11 women), 5 part-time (4 women); includes 5 minority (2 African Americans, 1 Asian American or Pacific Islander, 2 Hispanic Americans), 1 international. Average age 36. 30 applicants, 97% accepted, 20 enrolled. In 2001, 16 degrees awarded.
Entrance requirements: For master's, GRE General Test, MAT, minimum GPA of 3.0. *Application deadline:* Applications are processed on a rolling basis. *Application fee:* $20. Electronic applications accepted.
Expenses: Tuition, state resident: part-time $164 per credit hour. Tuition, nonresident: part-time $571 per credit hour. Required fees: $36 per semester.
Financial support: In 2001–02, 6 research assistantships were awarded; career-related internships or fieldwork and tuition waivers (partial) also available. Support available to part-time students.
Faculty research: Gerontology, clinical case management.
Dr. Patricia Washington, Chair, 239-590-7826, *Fax:* 239-590-7842, *E-mail:* pwashing@fgcu.edu.

■ FLORIDA INTERNATIONAL UNIVERSITY

College of Health and Urban Affairs, School of Social Work, Miami, FL 33199

AWARDS MSW, PhD. Part-time and evening/weekend programs available.

Faculty: 11 full-time (3 women).
Students: 111 full-time (91 women), 90 part-time (77 women); includes 118 minority (40 African Americans, 3 Asian Americans or Pacific Islanders, 75 Hispanic Americans), 5 international. Average age 38. 104 applicants, 70% accepted, 40 enrolled. In 2001, 119 master's, 1 doctorate awarded.
Degree requirements: For doctorate, thesis/dissertation, comprehensive exam.
Entrance requirements: For master's, GRE General Test, TOEFL, minimum GPA of 3.0; for doctorate, GRE General Test, TOEFL, minimum graduate GPA of 3.5. *Application deadline:* For fall admission, 4/1 (priority date); for spring admission, 10/1. Applications are processed on a rolling basis. *Application fee:* $20.
Expenses: Tuition, state resident: full-time $2,916; part-time $162 per credit hour. Tuition, nonresident: full-time $10,245; part-time $569 per credit hour. Required fees: $168 per term.
Dr. Ray Thomlison, Director, 305-919-5880, *Fax:* 305-919-5313, *E-mail:* thomlisr@fiu.edu.

■ FLORIDA STATE UNIVERSITY

Graduate Studies, School of Social Work, Tallahassee, FL 32306

AWARDS Clinical social work (MSW); social policy and administration (MSW); social work (PhD). Part-time and evening/weekend programs available. Postbaccalaureate distance learning degree programs offered (no on-campus study).

Faculty: 31 full-time (18 women), 35 part-time/adjunct (22 women).
Students: 118 full-time (98 women), 120 part-time (104 women). Average age 28. 134 applicants, 72% accepted, 64 enrolled. In 2001, 198 master's, 3 doctorates awarded.
Degree requirements: For doctorate, thesis/dissertation, comprehensive exam.
Entrance requirements: For master's and doctorate, GRE General Test, minimum GPA of 3.0. *Application deadline:* For fall admission, 7/1; for spring admission, 11/1. Applications are processed on a rolling basis.
Expenses: Tuition, state resident: part-time $163 per credit hour. Tuition, nonresident: part-time $570 per credit hour. Tuition and fees vary according to program.
Financial support: In 2001–02, 5 fellowships with partial tuition reimbursements, 22 research assistantships with partial tuition reimbursements, 2 teaching

Florida State University (continued)
assistantships with partial tuition reimbursements were awarded. Career-related internships or fieldwork, Federal Work-Study, institutionally sponsored loans, scholarships/grants, and traineeships also available. Support available to part-time students. Financial award application deadline: 4/1; financial award applicants required to submit FAFSA.
Faculty research: Family violence, AIDS, aging, family therapy, trauma, substance abuse. *Total annual research expenditures:* $2.6 million.
Dr. Bruce A. Thyer, Dean, 850-644-4752, *Fax:* 850-644-9750.
Application contact: Craig Stanley, Coordinator of Recruitment and Admissions, 800-378-9550, *Fax:* 850-644-9750, *E-mail:* cstanley@mailer.fsu.edu. *Web site:* http://ssw.fsu.edu/

■ FORDHAM UNIVERSITY

Graduate School of Social Service, New York, NY 10023

AWARDS MSW, PhD, JD/MSW. Part-time programs available.

Faculty: 52 full-time (14 women), 129 part-time/adjunct (32 women).
Students: 922 full-time (810 women), 397 part-time (339 women); includes 541 minority (298 African Americans, 40 Asian Americans or Pacific Islanders, 203 Hispanic Americans). 1,846 applicants, 63% accepted, 673 enrolled. In 2001, 601 master's, 11 doctorates awarded.
Application deadline: For fall admission, 6/1 (priority date); for spring admission, 12/1. Applications are processed on a rolling basis. *Application fee:* $40.
Expenses: Contact institution.
Financial support: In 2001–02, 591 students received support; fellowships, research assistantships, career-related internships or fieldwork, tuition waivers (partial), and unspecified assistantships available. Support available to part-time students. Financial award applicants required to submit FAFSA.
Dr. Peter B. Vaughan, Dean, 212-636-6600, *Fax:* 212-636-6613, *E-mail:* gerald@fordham.edu.
Application contact: Elaine Gerald, Assistant Dean/Director of Admissions, 212-636-6600, *Fax:* 212-636-6613, *E-mail:* gerald@fordham.edu. *Web site:* http://www.fordham.edu/gss/

■ GALLAUDET UNIVERSITY

The Graduate School, College of Arts and Sciences, Department of Social Work, Washington, DC 20002-3625

AWARDS MSW.

Degree requirements: For master's, thesis optional.
Entrance requirements: For master's, GRE General Test or MAT.

■ GEORGIA STATE UNIVERSITY

College of Health and Human Sciences, Department of Social Work, Atlanta, GA 30303-3083

AWARDS Community partnerships (MSW).

Degree requirements: For master's, community project.
Entrance requirements: For master's, GRE General Test, TOEFL.
Expenses: Tuition, state resident: full-time $8,156; part-time $132 per hour. Tuition, nonresident: full-time $12,624; part-time $526 per hour. Required fees: $660; $330 per semester.
Faculty research: Social work education, child welfare, labor unions and child care workers, secondary victimization in death penalty cases. *Web site:* http://www.gsu.edu/chhs/dept/soci/

■ GOVERNORS STATE UNIVERSITY

College of Health Professions, Program in Social Work, University Park, IL 60466-0975

AWARDS MSW.

Students: 7 full-time, 59 part-time. Average age 36.
Application fee: $0.
Expenses: Tuition, state resident: part-time $111 per hour. Tuition, nonresident: part-time $333 per hour.
Financial support: Application deadline: 5/1.
Joan Porche, Head, 708-235-2179.

■ GRADUATE SCHOOL AND UNIVERSITY CENTER OF THE CITY UNIVERSITY OF NEW YORK

Graduate Studies, Program in Social Welfare, New York, NY 10016-4039

AWARDS DSW.

Faculty: 17 full-time (7 women).
Students: 76 full-time (55 women); includes 23 minority (13 African Americans, 1 Asian American or Pacific Islander, 9 Hispanic Americans), 4 international. Average age 44. 50 applicants, 40% accepted, 15 enrolled. In 2001, 4 degrees awarded.
Degree requirements: For doctorate, thesis/dissertation, project, qualifying exam.
Entrance requirements: For doctorate, GRE General Test, MSW or equivalent.
Application deadline: For fall admission, 3/1. *Application fee:* $40.
Expenses: Tuition, state resident: part-time $245 per credit. Tuition, nonresident: part-time $425 per credit. Required fees: $72 per semester.
Financial support: In 2001–02, 16 students received support, including 15 fellowships; research assistantships, career-related internships or fieldwork, Federal Work-Study, institutionally sponsored loans, and tuition waivers (full and partial) also available. Financial award application deadline: 2/1; financial award applicants required to submit FAFSA.
Dr. Michael Fabricant, Acting Executive Officer, 212-452-7023, *Fax:* 212-452-7440, *E-mail:* mfabrica@hunter.cuny.edu.

■ GRAMBLING STATE UNIVERSITY

Division of Graduate Studies, School of Social Work, Grambling, LA 71245

AWARDS MSW. Part-time and evening/weekend programs available.

Degree requirements: For master's, thesis or alternative.
Entrance requirements: For master's, GRE.
Faculty research: Welfare history, social services in Louisiana, stress and child abuse, the black family, rurality. *Web site:* http://www.gram.edu

■ GRAND VALLEY STATE UNIVERSITY

School of Social Work, Allendale, MI 49401-9403

AWARDS MSW. Part-time programs available.

Faculty: 24 full-time (15 women), 9 part-time/adjunct (6 women).
Students: 126 full-time (108 women), 197 part-time (170 women); includes 31 minority (19 African Americans, 1 Asian American or Pacific Islander, 5 Hispanic Americans, 6 Native Americans), 18 international. Average age 36. 136 applicants, 75% accepted. In 2001, 90 degrees awarded.
Application deadline: For fall admission, 5/1 (priority date); for winter admission, 10/1 (priority date); for spring admission, 3/15 (priority date). Applications are processed on a rolling basis. *Application fee:* $20. Electronic applications accepted.
Expenses: Tuition, state resident: part-time $202 per credit hour. Tuition, nonresident: part-time $437 per credit hour.
Financial support: In 2001–02, 20 research assistantships with partial tuition reimbursements (averaging $3,000 per year) were awarded; career-related internships or fieldwork, Federal Work-Study, and institutionally sponsored loans also available.
Faculty research: Drug addiction, aging, management, effectiveness of therapy.
Dr. Rodney Mulder, Dean, 616-771-6550, *Fax:* 616-771-6570.
Application contact: Dr. Lois Smith Owens, Chair, Admissions, 616-771-6550, *Fax:* 616-771-6570.

■ GRATZ COLLEGE

Graduate Programs, Program in Jewish Communal Studies, Melrose Park, PA 19027

AWARDS MA, Certificate, MA/Certificate, MBA/Certificate, MSW/Certificate. Part-time and evening/weekend programs available.

Faculty: 7 full-time (3 women), 11 part-time/adjunct (7 women).
Students: 2 full-time, 11 part-time. Average age 25. In 2001, 4 master's, 3 other advanced degrees awarded.
Degree requirements: For master's, one foreign language.
Application deadline: Applications are processed on a rolling basis. *Application fee:* $50.
Expenses: Tuition: Full-time $9,950; part-time $466 per credit.
Financial support: Fellowships, career-related internships or fieldwork, Federal Work-Study, and unspecified assistantships available. Support available to part-time students. Financial award application deadline: 4/15.
Dr. David Green, Coordinator, 215-646-5806 Ext. 135, *Fax:* 215-635-7320, *E-mail:* dgreen@bethor.org.
Application contact: Adena E. Johnston, Director of Admissions, 215-635-7300 Ext. 140, *Fax:* 215-635-7320, *E-mail:* admissions@gratz.edu.

■ HEBREW COLLEGE

Program in Jewish Studies, Newton Centre, MA 02459

AWARDS Jewish cantorial arts (Certificate); Jewish communal and clinical social work (Certificate); Jewish music (Certificate); Jewish studies (MA); management of Jewish philanthropic and community organizations (Certificate). Part-time and evening/weekend programs available. Postbaccalaureate distance learning degree programs offered.

Faculty: 6 full-time (1 woman), 19 part-time/adjunct (7 women).
Students: Average age 30. 20 applicants, 100% accepted, 19 enrolled.
Degree requirements: For master's, one foreign language.
Application deadline: For fall admission, 5/31 (priority date). Applications are processed on a rolling basis. *Application fee:* $40.
Expenses: Tuition: Part-time $550 per credit.
Financial support: Fellowships, teaching assistantships, tuition waivers (partial) available. Support available to part-time students. Financial award application deadline: 4/15.
Dr. Barry Mesch, Provost, 617-559-8600, *Fax:* 617-559-8601, *E-mail:* bmesch@hebrewcollege.edu.
Application contact: Melissa Roiter, Assistant to Dean of Students, 617-559-8610, *Fax:* 617-559-8601, *E-mail:* admissions@hebrewcollege.edu. *Web site:* http://www.hebrewcollege.edu/online/

■ HEBREW UNION COLLEGE–JEWISH INSTITUTE OF RELIGION

Irwin Daniels School of Jewish Communal Services, Los Angeles, CA 90007-3796

AWARDS MAJCS, Certificate, MAJCS/MAJS, MAJCS/MA, MAJCS/MAJE, MAJCS/MBA, MAJCS/MPA, MAJCS/MSG, MAJCS/MSW.

Faculty: 3 full-time (1 woman), 9 part-time/adjunct (2 women).
Students: 22 full-time (17 women), 1 (woman) part-time. Average age 26. 24 applicants, 71% accepted, 11 enrolled. In 2001, 10 degrees awarded.
Degree requirements: For master's, one foreign language. *Median time to degree:* Master's–2 years full-time.
Entrance requirements: For master's, GRE General Test, interview, minimum undergraduate GPA of 3.0. *Application deadline:* For fall admission, 2/15. *Application fee:* $55.
Expenses: Tuition: Full-time $8,500; part-time $355 per unit. Required fees: $373.
Financial support: Career-related internships or fieldwork and scholarships/grants available. Financial award application deadline: 3/1; financial award applicants required to submit FAFSA.
Dr. Steven Windmueller, Director, 213-749-3424, *Fax:* 213-747-6128, *E-mail:* swindmueller@huc.edu.
Application contact: Lisa Kaplan, Director of Admissions and Recruitment, 213-749-3424, *Fax:* 213-747-6128, *E-mail:* lkaplan@huc.edu.

■ HOWARD UNIVERSITY

School of Social Work, Washington, DC 20059-0002

AWARDS MSW, PhD. Part-time programs available.

Degree requirements: For doctorate, thesis/dissertation, qualifying exam, comprehensive exam.
Entrance requirements: For master's, TOEFL, minimum GPA of 2.5; for doctorate, GRE General Test, TOEFL, minimum GPA of 3.3, MSW or master's in related field.
Faculty research: Infant mortality, child and family services, displaced populations, social work practice, domestic violence, black males, mental health. *Web site:* http://www.socialwork.howard.edu

Find an in-depth description at www.petersons.com/gradchannel.

■ HUNTER COLLEGE OF THE CITY UNIVERSITY OF NEW YORK

Graduate School, School of Arts and Sciences, School of Social Work, New York, NY 10021-5085

AWARDS MSW, DSW.

Faculty: 36 full-time (23 women), 42 part-time/adjunct (30 women).
Students: 425 full-time (348 women), 317 part-time (237 women). Average age 34. 1,134 applicants, 52% accepted. In 2001, 270 degrees awarded.
Degree requirements: For master's, major paper; for doctorate, thesis/dissertation.
Entrance requirements: For master's, TOEFL. *Application deadline:* For fall admission, 1/15. Applications are processed on a rolling basis. *Application fee:* $40.
Expenses: Tuition, state resident: full-time $2,175; part-time $185 per credit. Tuition, nonresident: full-time $3,800; part-time $320 per credit.
Financial support: In 2001–02, 120 fellowships (averaging $1,000 per year) were awarded; career-related internships or fieldwork and Federal Work-Study also available.
Faculty research: Child welfare, AIDS, homeless, aging, mental health.
Dr. Bogart R. Leashore, Dean, 212-452-7085.
Application contact: Raymond Montero, Coordinator of Admissions, 212-452-7005, *E-mail:* grad.socworkadvisor@hunter.cuny.edu. *Web site:* http://www.hunter.cuny.edu/socwork/

■ ILLINOIS STATE UNIVERSITY

Graduate School, College of Arts and Sciences, School of Social Work, Normal, IL 61790-2200

AWARDS MSW.

Faculty: 9 full-time (7 women).
Students: 18 full-time (15 women), 15 part-time (11 women); includes 4 minority (2 African Americans, 2 Hispanic Americans). 28 applicants, 68% accepted.
Application fee: $30.
Expenses: Tuition, state resident: full-time $2,691; part-time $112 per credit hour. Tuition, nonresident: full-time $5,880; part-time $245 per credit hour. Required fees: $1,146; $48 per credit hour.
Financial support: Research assistantships, teaching assistantships available. Financial award application deadline: 4/1.
Faculty research: Adoption studies, Catholic social service promise pilot project, building bridges to child welfare careers. *Total annual research expenditures:* $974,714.
Dr. Richard Grimmell, 309-438-3631. *Web site:* http://www.socialwork.ilstu.edu/

■ INDIANA UNIVERSITY NORTHWEST

Program in Social Work, Gary, IN 46408-1197

AWARDS MSW. Part-time and evening/weekend programs available.

Students: 25 full-time (21 women), 84 part-time (74 women); includes 41 minority (31 African Americans, 10 Hispanic Americans). Average age 37.
Entrance requirements: For master's, minimum GPA of 2.5; previous

Indiana University Northwest (continued)
undergraduate course work in human biology, research methodology, and statistics. *Application deadline:* For fall admission, 2/1. *Application fee:* $25.
Expenses: Contact institution.
Financial support: In 2001–02, 43 students received support. Career-related internships or fieldwork, Federal Work-Study, tuition waivers (partial), and tuition remissions available. Support available to part-time students. Financial award application deadline: 6/1; financial award applicants required to submit FAFSA.
Faculty research: Educational outcomes, generalist practice, homelessness. *Total annual research expenditures:* $1,000.
Dr. Grafton Hull, Director, 219-980-7111, *Fax:* 219-981-4264, *E-mail:* ghull@iunhaw1.iun.indiana.edu. *Web site:* http://www.IUN.INDIANA.EDU/socio/wk/social.htm

■ INDIANA UNIVERSITY–PURDUE UNIVERSITY INDIANAPOLIS

School of Social Work, Doctoral Program in Social Work, Indianapolis, IN 46202-2896

AWARDS PhD. Part-time programs available.

Students: 2 full-time (1 woman), 7 part-time (6 women); includes 1 minority (African American). Average age 43.
Degree requirements: For doctorate, thesis/dissertation, residential internship.
Entrance requirements: For doctorate, GRE General Test. *Application deadline:* For fall admission, 4/1; for winter admission, 1/1 (priority date). *Application fee:* $45 ($55 for international students).
Expenses: Tuition, state resident: full-time $4,480; part-time $187 per credit. Tuition, nonresident: full-time $12,926; part-time $539 per credit. Required fees: $177.
Financial support: In 2001–02, fellowships with full tuition reimbursements (averaging $11,800 per year), research assistantships with partial tuition reimbursements (averaging $10,000 per year), teaching assistantships (averaging $3,000 per year) were awarded. Career-related internships or fieldwork, Federal Work-Study, institutionally sponsored loans, and tuition waivers (partial) also available. Support available to part-time students. Financial award application deadline: 6/1; financial award applicants required to submit FAFSA.
Faculty research: Diversity issues, mental health corrections, HIV/AIDS, gerontology. *Total annual research expenditures:* $120,000.
Dr. Gerald T. Powers, Director, 317-274-6724, *Fax:* 317-274-8630, *E-mail:* gpowers@indyvax.iupui.edu.
Application contact: MaDonna Taylor, Program Office, 317-274-4811, *Fax:* 317-274-8630. *Web site:* http://iussw.iupui.edu/

■ INDIANA UNIVERSITY–PURDUE UNIVERSITY INDIANAPOLIS

School of Social Work, Master's Program in Social Work, Indianapolis, IN 46202-2896

AWARDS MSW. Part-time and evening/weekend programs available.

Students: 240 full-time (213 women), 163 part-time (147 women); includes 68 minority (55 African Americans, 2 Asian Americans or Pacific Islanders, 11 Hispanic Americans). Average age 32. In 2001, 231 degrees awarded.
Degree requirements: For master's, field practicum.
Entrance requirements: For master's, minimum GPA of 2.5, previous course work in social behavior, statistics, research methodology, and human biology. *Application deadline:* For fall admission, 2/1. *Application fee:* $45 ($55 for international students).
Expenses: Tuition, state resident: full-time $4,480; part-time $187 per credit. Tuition, nonresident: full-time $12,926; part-time $539 per credit. Required fees: $177.
Financial support: Career-related internships or fieldwork, Federal Work-Study, institutionally sponsored loans, and tuition waivers (partial) available. Support available to part-time students. Financial award application deadline: 3/1; financial award applicants required to submit FAFSA.
Dr. Marion Wagner, Director, 317-274-6733, *Fax:* 317-274-8630.
Application contact: Rhonda Brock, Student Services Secretary, 317-274-8364, *Fax:* 317-274-8630, *E-mail:* rbrock@iupui.edu. *Web site:* http://www.iupui.edu/home/soc.html

■ INDIANA UNIVERSITY SOUTH BEND

Program in Social Work, South Bend, IN 46634-7111

AWARDS MSW. Part-time and evening/weekend programs available.

Faculty: 5 full-time (2 women).
Students: 34 full-time (31 women), 59 part-time (50 women); includes 12 minority (8 African Americans, 2 Asian Americans or Pacific Islanders, 2 Hispanic Americans), 1 international. Average age 35. In 2001, 25 degrees awarded.
Application deadline: For fall admission, 2/1. *Application fee:* $40 ($50 for international students).
Expenses: Contact institution.
Financial support: Career-related internships or fieldwork and Federal Work-Study available. Support available to part-time students. Financial award application deadline: 3/1; financial award applicants required to submit FAFSA.
Dr. Paul R. Newcomb, Director, 574-237-4464, *Fax:* 574-237-4876, *E-mail:* socw@iusb.edu. *Web site:* http://www.iusb.edu/

■ INSTITUTE FOR CLINICAL SOCIAL WORK

Graduate Programs, Chicago, IL 60601

AWARDS Clinical social work (PhD). Part-time programs available.

Faculty: 67 part-time/adjunct (40 women).
Students: 65 full-time (47 women), 19 part-time (15 women); includes 16 minority (9 African Americans, 2 Asian Americans or Pacific Islanders, 4 Hispanic Americans, 1 Native American). Average age 38. 20 applicants, 95% accepted. In 2001, 7 degrees awarded.
Degree requirements: For doctorate, thesis/dissertation, supervised practicum.
Entrance requirements: For doctorate, 2 years of experience, master's degree. *Application deadline:* For fall admission, 5/1 (priority date). Applications are processed on a rolling basis. *Application fee:* $50.
Expenses: Tuition: Full-time $11,000; part-time $880 per course.
Financial support: In 2001–02, 23 students received support. Institutionally sponsored loans available. Financial award application deadline: 9/1; financial award applicants required to submit FAFSA.
Faculty research: Impact of AIDS on partners, effects of learning disabilities on children and families, clinical social work issues.
Thomas K. Kenemore, President, 312-726-8480 Ext. 22, *Fax:* 312-726-7216, *E-mail:* tkenemore@aol.com.
Application contact: Dr. Barbara Berger, Dean of Admissions, 312-726-8480 Ext. 31, *Fax:* 312-726-7216. *Web site:* http://www.icsw.com/

■ INTER AMERICAN UNIVERSITY OF PUERTO RICO, METROPOLITAN CAMPUS

Graduate Programs, Division of Behavioral Science and Allied Professions, Program in Social Work, San Juan, PR 00919-1293

AWARDS MA. Evening/weekend programs available.

Degree requirements: For master's, comprehensive exam.
Entrance requirements: For master's, GRE or PAEG, interview. Electronic applications accepted.

■ JACKSON STATE UNIVERSITY

Graduate School, School of Social Work, Jackson, MS 39217

AWARDS MSW, PhD. Evening/weekend programs available.

Degree requirements: For master's, comprehensive exam; for doctorate, thesis/dissertation, comprehensive exam.
Entrance requirements: For master's, GRE General Test, TOEFL; for doctorate, MAT.

■ KEAN UNIVERSITY

College of Arts, Humanities and Social Sciences, Department of Social Work, Union, NJ 07083

AWARDS MSW.

Faculty: 10 full-time (7 women), 14 part-time/adjunct.
Students: 84 full-time (70 women), 14 part-time (10 women); includes 45 minority (24 African Americans, 21 Hispanic Americans), 5 international. Average age 32. 269 applicants, 55% accepted. In 2001, 42 degrees awarded.
Entrance requirements: For master's, GRE General Test. *Application deadline:* For fall admission, 6/15; for spring admission, 11/15. *Application fee:* $35.
Expenses: Tuition, state resident: full-time $7,372. Tuition, nonresident: full-time $9,004. Required fees: $1,006.
Financial support: In 2001–02, 22 fellowships (averaging $3,000 per year) were awarded
Dr. A. Lightfoot, Coordinator, 908-527-2835.
Application contact: Joanne Morris, Director of Graduate Admissions, 908-527-2665, *Fax:* 908-527-2286, *E-mail:* grad_adm@kean.edu.

■ LOMA LINDA UNIVERSITY

Graduate School, Department of Social Work, Loma Linda, CA 92350

AWARDS Social policy and research (PhD); social work (MSW).

Faculty: 8 full-time (4 women), 2 part-time/adjunct (both women).
Students: 69 full-time (67 women), 15 part-time (13 women).
Entrance requirements: For master's, GRE General Test. *Application fee:* $40.
Expenses: Tuition: Part-time $420 per unit.
Dr. Beverly Buckles, Chair, 909-478-8550.

■ LOUISIANA STATE UNIVERSITY AND AGRICULTURAL AND MECHANICAL COLLEGE

Graduate School, School of Social Work, Baton Rouge, LA 70803

AWARDS MSW, PhD. Part-time programs available.

Faculty: 14 full-time (8 women).
Students: 156 full-time (141 women), 61 part-time (49 women); includes 37 minority (31 African Americans, 2 Asian Americans or Pacific Islanders, 1 Hispanic American, 3 Native Americans), 4 international. Average age 30. 117 applicants, 67% accepted, 62 enrolled. In 2001, 80 master's, 4 doctorates awarded.
Degree requirements: For master's, field instruction.
Entrance requirements: For master's and doctorate, GRE General Test, minimum GPA of 3.0. *Application deadline:* For fall admission, 3/1. *Application fee:* $25.
Expenses: Tuition, state resident: full-time $2,551. Tuition, nonresident: full-time $5,551. Required fees: $854. Part-time tuition and fees vary according to course load.
Financial support: In 2001–02, 7 students received support, including 1 teaching assistantship with partial tuition reimbursement available (averaging $9,500 per year); fellowships, research assistantships with partial tuition reimbursements available, career-related internships or fieldwork and unspecified assistantships also available. Support available to part-time students. Financial award applicants required to submit FAFSA.
Faculty research: Methodology, child welfare, aging, social development, corrections, social work history. *Total annual research expenditures:* $911,973.
Dr. Steven Rose, Interim Director, 225-578-1351, *Fax:* 225-578-1357, *E-mail:* swrose@lsu.edu.
Application contact: Denise Chiasson Breaux, Director of Student Services, 225-578-1234, *E-mail:* dchiass@lsu.edu. *Web site:* http://www.socialwork.lsu.edu

■ LOYOLA UNIVERSITY CHICAGO

School of Social Work, Program in Social Work, Chicago, IL 60611-2196

AWARDS MSW. Program offered at Carthage College, Kenosha, WI.

Faculty: 32 full-time (14 women), 23 part-time/adjunct (18 women).
Degree requirements: For master's, 2 clinical practica.
Application deadline: For fall admission, 3/15. *Application fee:* $50.
Expenses: Tuition: Part-time $529 per credit hour.
Financial support: Fellowships, career-related internships or fieldwork, institutionally sponsored loans, and scholarships/grants available. Support available to part-time students. *Total annual research expenditures:* $850,000.
Application contact: Jude Gonzales, Director of Admissions, 312-915-7005, *Fax:* 312-915-7645, *E-mail:* socialwork@luc.edu.

■ LOYOLA UNIVERSITY CHICAGO

School of Social Work, Programs in Social Work, Chicago, IL 60611-2196

AWARDS MSW, PhD, JD/MSW, MJ/MSW, MSW/M Ed. Part-time programs available.

Faculty: 22 full-time (14 women), 23 part-time/adjunct (18 women).
Students: 212 full-time (185 women), 250 part-time (208 women); includes 108 minority (64 African Americans, 12 Asian Americans or Pacific Islanders, 29 Hispanic Americans, 3 Native Americans). 430 applicants, 83% accepted. In 2001, 204 master's, 6 doctorates awarded.
Degree requirements: For master's, 2 clinical practica; for doctorate, clinical practicum.
Application deadline: Applications are processed on a rolling basis. *Application fee:* $50.
Expenses: Tuition: Part-time $529 per credit hour.
Financial support: In 2001–02, 130 students received support, including 2 fellowships (averaging $10,000 per year), 31 research assistantships (averaging $4,050 per year); career-related internships or fieldwork, scholarships/grants, and tuition waivers (full and partial) also available. Support available to part-time students. Financial award application deadline: 2/28; financial award applicants required to submit FAFSA.
Faculty research: Clinical social work, ethics, health care, school social work. *Total annual research expenditures:* $850,000.
Application contact: Jude Gonzales, Director of Admissions, 312-915-7005, *Fax:* 312-915-7645, *E-mail:* socialwork@luc.edu.

■ MARYWOOD UNIVERSITY

Graduate School of Social Work, Scranton, PA 18509-1598

AWARDS MSW, MPA/MSW. Part-time and evening/weekend programs available.

Faculty: 14 full-time (10 women), 29 part-time/adjunct (21 women).
Students: 194 full-time (164 women), 175 part-time (143 women); includes 19 minority (7 African Americans, 2 Asian Americans or Pacific Islanders, 7 Hispanic Americans, 3 Native Americans), 1 international. 196 applicants, 62% accepted. In 2001, 149 degrees awarded.
Entrance requirements: For master's, minimum undergraduate GPA of 3.0. *Application deadline:* For fall admission, 5/15; for spring admission, 10/15. *Application fee:* $20.
Expenses: Contact institution.
Financial support: In 2001–02, 5 research assistantships were awarded; career-related internships or fieldwork, scholarships/grants, and tuition waivers (partial) also available. Support available to part-time students. Financial award application deadline: 5/1; financial award applicants required to submit FAFSA.
Faculty research: Impaired professionals, ethics, child welfare, communities, professional gatekeeping.
Dr. William Whitaker, Dean, 570-348-6282, *Fax:* 570-348-1817.
Application contact: Virginia Haskett, Director of Admissions, 717-348-6282, *Fax:* 717-961-4742.

Find an in-depth description at www.petersons.com/gradchannel.

■ MIAMI UNIVERSITY

Graduate School, School of Education and Allied Professions, Program in Social Work, Oxford, OH 45056

AWARDS Child and family studies (MS). Part-time programs available.

Faculty: 4 full-time (2 women), 1 (woman) part-time/adjunct.
Students: 15 full-time (11 women), 5 part-time (4 women); includes 6 minority (5 African Americans, 1 Asian American or Pacific Islander). 16 applicants, 100% accepted, 8 enrolled. In 2001, 1 degree awarded.
Degree requirements: For master's, thesis or alternative, final exam.
Entrance requirements: For master's, MAT, minimum undergraduate GPA of 3.0 during previous 2 years or 2.75 overall. *Application deadline:* For fall admission, 3/1 (priority date); for spring admission, 12/1. Applications are processed on a rolling basis. *Application fee:* $35.
Expenses: Tuition, state resident: full-time $7,155; part-time $295 per semester hour. Tuition, nonresident: full-time $14,829; part-time $615 per semester hour. Tuition and fees vary according to degree level and campus/location.
Financial support: In 2001–02, 4 fellowships (averaging $8,695 per year) were awarded; research assistantships, teaching assistantships, career-related internships or fieldwork, Federal Work-Study, and tuition waivers (full) also available. Financial award application deadline: 3/1.
Dr. Susan Cross Lipnickey, Chair, 513-529-2323. *Web site:* http://www.muohio.edu/~fswcwis/msreg.html

■ MICHIGAN STATE UNIVERSITY

Graduate School, College of Social Science, School of Social Work, East Lansing, MI 48824

AWARDS Administration and program evaluation (MSW); administration and program evaluation-urban studies (MSW); clinical social work (MSW); clinical social work-urban studies (MSW); interdisciplinary social science/social work (PhD); organizational and community practice (MSW); program evaluation-urban studies (MSW). Postbaccalaureate distance learning degree programs offered (minimal on-campus study).

Faculty: 17 full-time (9 women).
Students: 117 full-time (100 women), 148 part-time (129 women); includes 55 minority (38 African Americans, 6 Asian Americans or Pacific Islanders, 11 Hispanic Americans), 5 international. Average age 33. 215 applicants, 74% accepted. In 2001, 69 master's, 3 doctorates awarded.
Entrance requirements: For master's, minimum GPA of 3.0. *Application deadline:* For fall admission, 1/20. Applications are processed on a rolling basis. *Application fee:* $30 ($40 for international students).
Expenses: Tuition, state resident: part-time $244 per credit hour. Tuition, nonresident: part-time $494 per credit hour. Required fees: $268 per semester. Tuition and fees vary according to course load, degree level and program.
Financial support: In 2001–02, 33 fellowships with tuition reimbursements (averaging $2,808 per year), 11 research assistantships with tuition reimbursements (averaging $10,673 per year) were awarded. Teaching assistantships with tuition reimbursements, career-related internships or fieldwork and Federal Work-Study also available. Support available to part-time students. Financial award applicants required to submit FAFSA.
Faculty research: Women at risk, juvenile offenders, infant mental health, poverty, welfare reforms. *Total annual research expenditures:* $25,497.
Dr. Gary Anderson, Director, 517-353-8616, *Fax:* 517-353-3038, *E-mail:* socialwork@ssc.msu.edu.
Application contact: Prof. Rena Harold, Coordinator of Graduate Programs, 517-353-8260. *Web site:* http://www.msu.edu/~sw/

■ MONMOUTH UNIVERSITY

Graduate School, Department of Social Work, West Long Branch, NJ 07764-1898

AWARDS Community and international development (MSW); practice with families and children (MSW). Part-time and evening/weekend programs available.

Faculty: 9 full-time (5 women), 11 part-time/adjunct (9 women).
Students: 93 full-time (84 women), 96 part-time (86 women); includes 18 minority (12 African Americans, 6 Hispanic Americans). Average age 33. 185 applicants, 80% accepted, 81 enrolled. In 2001, 47 degrees awarded.
Degree requirements: For master's, thesis, internship.
Entrance requirements: For master's, minimum GPA of 3.0 in major, 2.75 overall. *Application deadline:* For fall admission, 3/15 (priority date). Applications are processed on a rolling basis. *Application fee:* $35. Electronic applications accepted.
Expenses: Tuition: Full-time $9,900; part-time $549 per credit. Required fees: $568.
Financial support: In 2001–02, 43 students received support, including 39 fellowships (averaging $2,635 per year), 6 research assistantships (averaging $5,260 per year); scholarships/grants and unspecified assistantships also available. Support available to part-time students. Financial award application deadline: 3/1.
Faculty research: Child welfare citizen participation, cultural diversity, diversity issues, employee help,.
Dr. Mark Rodgers, Chair, 732-571-3543, *Fax:* 732-263-5217, *E-mail:* swdept@monmouth.edu.
Application contact: Kevin Roane, Director, Office of Graduate Admissions, 732-571-3452, *Fax:* 732-263-5123, *E-mail:* gradadm@monmouth.edu. *Web site:* http://www.monmouth.edu/~swork/msw.html/

Find an in-depth description at www.petersons.com/gradchannel.

■ NAZARETH COLLEGE OF ROCHESTER

Graduate Studies, Department of Social Work, Rochester, NY 14618-3790

AWARDS MSW.

Students: 24 full-time (23 women), 44 part-time (38 women); includes 9 minority (5 African Americans, 1 Asian American or Pacific Islander, 3 Hispanic Americans). 34 applicants, 100% accepted, 28 enrolled.
Entrance requirements: For master's, minimum GPA of 3.0. *Application deadline:* For fall admission, 3/15.
Expenses: Tuition: Part-time $466 per credit hour. Required fees: $20 per semester.
Financial support: Applicants required to submit FAFSA.
Dr. Estella Norwood Evans, Director, 585-327-7450, *Fax:* 585-232-8603, *E-mail:* grcmsw@brockport.edu.
Application contact: Dr. Kay F. Marshman, Dean, 585-389-2815, *Fax:* 585-389-2817, *E-mail:* gradstudies@naz.edu. *Web site:* http://www.naz.edu/

■ NEWMAN UNIVERSITY

Graduate School of Social Work, Wichita, KS 67213-2097

AWARDS MSW.

Degree requirements: For master's, fieldwork.
Entrance requirements: For master's, interview, minimum GPA of 3.0.

■ NEW MEXICO HIGHLANDS UNIVERSITY

Graduate Studies, School of Social Work, Las Vegas, NM 87701

AWARDS MSW. Part-time programs available.

Faculty: 12 full-time (5 women), 13 part-time/adjunct (11 women).
Students: 166 full-time (137 women), 94 part-time (84 women); includes 125 minority (9 African Americans, 2 Asian Americans or Pacific Islanders, 79 Hispanic Americans, 35 Native Americans), 2 international. Average age 37. In 2001, 44 degrees awarded.
Degree requirements: For master's, thesis or alternative.
Entrance requirements: For master's, minimum undergraduate GPA of 3.0. *Application deadline:* For fall admission, 8/1 (priority date). Applications are processed on a rolling basis. *Application fee:* $15.

Expenses: Tuition, state resident: full-time $2,238. Tuition, nonresident: full-time $9,366.
Financial support: Research assistantships with full and partial tuition reimbursements, Federal Work-Study available. Financial award application deadline: 3/1.
Dr. Alfredo Garcia, Dean, 505-454-3307, *Fax:* 505-454-3290, *E-mail:* a_garcia@nmhu.edu.
Application contact: Dr. Linda LaGrange, Associate Dean of Graduate Studies, 505-454-3266, *Fax:* 505-454-3558, *E-mail:* lagrange_l@nmhu.edu.

■ NEW MEXICO STATE UNIVERSITY

Graduate School, College of Health and Social Services, School of Social Work, Las Cruces, NM 88003-8001

AWARDS MSW. Part-time and evening/weekend programs available.

Faculty: 7 full-time (2 women), 1 (woman) part-time/adjunct.
Students: 63 full-time (52 women), 25 part-time (22 women); includes 47 minority (4 African Americans, 2 Asian Americans or Pacific Islanders, 40 Hispanic Americans, 1 Native American), 3 international. Average age 34. 27 applicants, 56% accepted, 8 enrolled. In 2001, 35 degrees awarded.
Degree requirements: For master's, research project, oral exam, thesis optional.
Entrance requirements: For master's, minimum GPA of 3.0. *Application deadline:* For fall admission, 2/1 (priority date); for spring admission, 8/15 (priority date). Applications are processed on a rolling basis. *Application fee:* $15 ($35 for international students). Electronic applications accepted.
Expenses: Tuition, state resident: full-time $3,234; part-time $135 per credit. Tuition, nonresident: full-time $9,420; part-time $428 per credit. Required fees: $858.
Financial support: In 2001–02, 8 teaching assistantships were awarded; fellowships, research assistantships, career-related internships or fieldwork, traineeships, and unspecified assistantships also available. Financial award application deadline: 3/1.
Faculty research: Family centered, child abuse and neglect, women's issues, AIDS, multicultural issues.
Dr. Stephen Anderson, Director, School of Social Work, 505-646-2143, *Fax:* 505-646-4116, *E-mail:* stephean@nmsu.edu.
Application contact: Dr. Alice Chornesky, Graduate Program Coordinator, 505-646-2143, *Fax:* 505-646-4116, *E-mail:* achornes@nmsu.edu.

■ NEW YORK UNIVERSITY

Shirley M. Ehrenkranz School of Social Work, New York, NY 10012-1019

AWARDS MSW, PhD, JD/MSW, MSW/MS.

Faculty: 46 full-time (36 women), 128 part-time/adjunct (88 women).
Students: 570 full-time (503 women), 402 part-time (343 women); includes 332 minority (163 African Americans, 43 Asian Americans or Pacific Islanders, 124 Hispanic Americans, 2 Native Americans), 18 international. Average age 27. 1,532 applicants, 74% accepted, 523 enrolled. In 2001, 557 master's, 23 doctorates awarded.
Degree requirements: For doctorate, thesis/dissertation. *Median time to degree:* Master's–2 years full-time, 3 years part-time; doctorate–6 years part-time.
Application deadline: For fall admission, 7/1; for spring admission, 11/15. Applications are processed on a rolling basis. *Application fee:* $50.
Expenses: Contact institution.
Financial support: In 2001–02, 480 students received support, including 5 research assistantships with full tuition reimbursements available (averaging $5,000 per year); career-related internships or fieldwork, Federal Work-Study, scholarships/grants, and tuition waivers (partial) also available. Support available to part-time students. Financial award application deadline: 3/1; financial award applicants required to submit FAFSA.
Faculty research: Social welfare policies, foster care, aging.
Suzanne England, Dean, 212-998-5959, *Fax:* 212-995-4172.
Application contact: Stuart Gitlin, Director of Admissions, 212-998-5910, *Fax:* 212-995-4171, *E-mail:* essw.admissions@nyu.edu. *Web site:* http://www.nyu.edu/socialwork/

Find an in-depth description at www.petersons.com/gradchannel.

■ NORFOLK STATE UNIVERSITY

School of Graduate Studies, School of Social Work, Norfolk, VA 23504

AWARDS MSW, DSW. Part-time programs available.

Faculty: 21 full-time, 9 part-time/adjunct.
Students: 137 applicants, 74% accepted, 102 enrolled.
Degree requirements: For doctorate, thesis/dissertation.
Entrance requirements: For master's, TOEFL, minimum GPA of 2.7. *Application deadline:* For fall admission, 3/1; for spring admission, 10/1. *Application fee:* $30.
Expenses: Tuition, area resident: Part-time $197 per credit. Tuition, nonresident: part-time $503 per credit.
Financial support: Fellowships, research assistantships, teaching assistantships, career-related internships or fieldwork, Federal Work-Study, scholarships/grants, traineeships, and unspecified assistantships available. Financial award applicants required to submit FAFSA.
Dr. Marvin Feit, Dean, 757-823-8668.
Application contact: Margaret Kerekes, Coordinator, 757-823-8696, *E-mail:* mdkerekes@nsu.edu.

■ NORTH CAROLINA AGRICULTURAL AND TECHNICAL STATE UNIVERSITY

Graduate School, College of Arts and Sciences, Department of Sociology and Social Work, Greensboro, NC 27411

AWARDS MSW. Part-time and evening/weekend programs available.

Degree requirements: For master's, qualifying exam.
Entrance requirements: For master's, GRE General Test.

■ NORTHWEST NAZARENE UNIVERSITY

Graduate Studies, Program in Social Work, Nampa, ID 83686-5897

AWARDS MSW.

Faculty: 6 full-time (5 women), 2 part-time/adjunct (1 woman).
Students: 42 full-time (28 women), 21 part-time (14 women); includes 4 minority (1 African American, 3 Hispanic Americans).
Degree requirements: For master's, comprehensive exam.
Application deadline: Applications are processed on a rolling basis. *Application fee:* $25. Electronic applications accepted.
Expenses: Tuition: Full-time $1,770; part-time $295 per credit. One-time fee: $25. Tuition and fees vary according to program.
Mary Curran, Head, 208-467-8679, *E-mail:* msw@nnu.edu.

■ THE OHIO STATE UNIVERSITY

Graduate School, College of Social Work, Columbus, OH 43210

AWARDS MSW, PhD. Part-time programs available.

Degree requirements: For master's, thesis optional; for doctorate, thesis/dissertation.

■ OHIO UNIVERSITY

Graduate Studies, College of Arts and Sciences, Department of Social Work, Athens, OH 45701-2979

AWARDS MSW.

Faculty: 11 full-time (8 women), 2 part-time/adjunct (1 woman).
Students: 28 full-time (24 women), 9 international. 26 applicants, 73% accepted, 12 enrolled. In 2001, 14 degrees awarded.
Degree requirements: For master's, fieldwork. *Median time to degree:* Master's–2 years full-time.
Entrance requirements: For master's, GRE General Test, minimum GPA of 3.0. *Application deadline:* For spring admission, 2/1 (priority date). Applications are processed on a rolling basis. *Application fee:* $30. Electronic applications accepted.

Ohio University (continued)
Expenses: Tuition, state resident: full-time $6,585. Tuition, nonresident: full-time $12,254.
Financial support: In 2001–02, 15 students received support, including 9 research assistantships with tuition reimbursements available (averaging $8,000 per year); career-related internships or fieldwork also available. Financial award application deadline: 2/1.
Faculty research: Violence, suicide, ethics, technology, medical social work. *Total annual research expenditures:* $43,000.
Dr. Richard Greenlee, Chair, 740-593-1292, *Fax:* 740-593-0427.
Application contact: Dr. Susan Sarnoff, Graduate Chair, 740-593-1301, *Fax:* 740-593-0427, *E-mail:* sarnoff@ohio.edu. *Web site:* http://www-as.phy.ohiou.edu/Departments/SocWrk/grad.html

■ OUR LADY OF THE LAKE UNIVERSITY OF SAN ANTONIO

Worden School of Social Service, San Antonio, TX 78207-4689

AWARDS MSW. Part-time programs available.

Degree requirements: For master's, practicum, thesis optional.
Entrance requirements: For master's, GRE General Test or MAT.
Faculty research: Cross-cultural social work practice, mental health, adult literacy, spirituality, maternal health care, experiential learning.

■ PONTIFICAL CATHOLIC UNIVERSITY OF PUERTO RICO

Institute of Graduate Studies in Behavioral Science and Community Affairs, Ponce, PR 00717-0777

AWARDS Clinical psychology (MS); clinical social work (MSW); criminology (MA); industrial psychology (MS); psychology (PhD); public administration (MA). Part-time and evening/weekend programs available.

Faculty: 10 full-time (7 women), 17 part-time/adjunct (12 women).
Students: 86 full-time (56 women), 394 part-time (266 women); all minorities (all Hispanic Americans). 141 applicants, 83% accepted, 104 enrolled. In 2001, 35 degrees awarded.
Entrance requirements: For master's, GRE, 2 recommendation letters, interview, minimum GPA of 2.75. *Application deadline:* For fall admission, 4/30 (priority date). Applications are processed on a rolling basis. *Application fee:* $50. Electronic applications accepted.
Expenses: Tuition: Full-time $2,880; part-time $160 per credit. Required fees: $360. Tuition and fees vary according to degree level and program.
Financial support: Federal Work-Study and tuition waivers (partial) available. Support available to part-time students. Financial award application deadline: 7/15.
Dr. Nilde Cordoline, Director, 787-841-2000 Ext. 1024.
Application contact: Ana O. Bonilla, Director of Admissions, 787-841-2000 Ext. 1000, *Fax:* 787-840-4295. *Web site:* http://www.pucpr.edu/

■ PORTLAND STATE UNIVERSITY

Graduate Studies, Graduate School of Social Work, Portland, OR 97207-0751

AWARDS Social work (MSW); social work and social research (PhD). Part-time programs available.

Faculty: 33 full-time (24 women), 2 part-time/adjunct (1 woman).
Students: 298 full-time (255 women), 63 part-time (47 women); includes 57 minority (21 African Americans, 16 Asian Americans or Pacific Islanders, 14 Hispanic Americans, 6 Native Americans), 4 international. Average age 35. 433 applicants, 49% accepted. In 2001, 203 master's, 1 doctorate awarded.
Degree requirements: For doctorate, thesis/dissertation.
Entrance requirements: For master's, TOEFL, minimum GPA of 3.0 in upper-division course work or 2.75 overall. *Application deadline:* For fall admission, 3/1. *Application fee:* $50.
Financial support: In 2001–02, 12 research assistantships with full tuition reimbursements (averaging $9,543 per year) were awarded; teaching assistantships, career-related internships or fieldwork, Federal Work-Study, and institutionally sponsored loans also available. Support available to part-time students. Financial award application deadline: 3/1; financial award applicants required to submit FAFSA.
Faculty research: Child welfare; child mental health; social welfare policies and services; work, family, and dependent care; adult mental health. *Total annual research expenditures:* $5.4 million.
Dr. James Ward, Dean, 503-725-4712, *Fax:* 503-725-5545, *E-mail:* james@ssw.pdx.edu.
Application contact: Janet Putnam, Coordinator, 503-725-4712, *Fax:* 503-725-5545, *E-mail:* janet@ssw.pdx.edu. *Web site:* http://www.ssw.pdx.edu/

■ RADFORD UNIVERSITY

Graduate College, Waldron College of Health and Human Services, School of Social Work, Radford, VA 24142

AWARDS MSW. Part-time programs available. Postbaccalaureate distance learning degree programs offered (minimal on-campus study).

Faculty: 10 full-time (7 women), 6 part-time/adjunct (5 women).
Students: 47 full-time (44 women), 65 part-time (53 women); includes 7 minority (6 African Americans, 1 Asian American or Pacific Islander). Average age 33. 74 applicants, 72% accepted, 34 enrolled. In 2001, 53 degrees awarded.
Degree requirements: For master's, comprehensive exam.
Entrance requirements: For master's, GMAT, GRE General Test, MAT, or NTE; TOEFL. *Application deadline:* For fall admission, 2/1 (priority date); for spring admission, 10/1. Applications are processed on a rolling basis. *Application fee:* $25. Electronic applications accepted.
Expenses: Tuition, state resident: full-time $2,564; part-time $167 per credit hour. Tuition, nonresident: full-time $6,314; part-time $323 per credit hour. Required fees: $1,440.
Financial support: In 2001–02, 81 students received support, including 3 fellowships with tuition reimbursements available (averaging $3,410 per year), 16 research assistantships (averaging $3,391 per year); teaching assistantships with tuition reimbursements available, career-related internships or fieldwork, Federal Work-Study, institutionally sponsored loans, and scholarships/grants also available. Financial award application deadline: 2/1; financial award applicants required to submit FAFSA.
Dr. Marilyn Rigby, Director, 540-831-7689, *Fax:* 540-831-6053, *E-mail:* mrigby@radford.edu. *Web site:* http://www.radford.edu/

■ RHODE ISLAND COLLEGE

School of Graduate Studies, School of Social Work, Providence, RI 02908-1991

AWARDS MSW. Part-time programs available.

Faculty: 12 full-time (9 women), 12 part-time/adjunct (6 women).
Students: 121 full-time (107 women), 33 part-time (30 women); includes 12 minority (4 African Americans, 7 Hispanic Americans, 1 Native American). Average age 33. In 2001, 60 degrees awarded.
Degree requirements: For master's, thesis or alternative.
Application deadline: For fall admission, 2/1. Applications are processed on a rolling basis. *Application fee:* $25.
Expenses: Contact institution.
Financial support: Career-related internships or fieldwork available. Financial award application deadline: 4/1.
Dr. George Metrey, Dean, 401-456-8043, *E-mail:* gmetrey@ric.edu.

■ ROBERTS WESLEYAN COLLEGE

Division of Social Work and Social Sciences, Rochester, NY 14624-1997

AWARDS Child and family services (MSW); physical and mental health services (MSW).

Entrance requirements: For master's, minimum GPA of 2.75.

Faculty research: Religion and social work, family studies, values and ethics.

Find an in-depth description at www.petersons.com/gradchannel.

■ RUTGERS, THE STATE UNIVERSITY OF NEW JERSEY, NEW BRUNSWICK

Graduate School, Doctoral Program in Social Work, New Brunswick, NJ 08901-1281

AWARDS Direct intervention in interpersonal situations (PhD); social policy analysis and administration (PhD); social work (PhD). Part-time programs available.

Degree requirements: For doctorate, thesis/dissertation.
Entrance requirements: For doctorate, GRE General Test, MSW or related master's degree.
Faculty research: Women, substance abuse, aging, organizational behavior, social service needs assessment.

■ RUTGERS, THE STATE UNIVERSITY OF NEW JERSEY, NEW BRUNSWICK

School of Social Work, Program in Social Work, New Brunswick, NJ 08901-1281

AWARDS MSW, JD/MSW, M Div/MSW. Part-time programs available.

Entrance requirements: For master's, social work experience. Electronic applications accepted.
Faculty research: Children and families; alcohol and other drugs; health, mental health, and aging.

■ ST. AMBROSE UNIVERSITY

College of Arts and Sciences, Program in Social Work, Davenport, IA 52803-2898

AWARDS MSW. Part-time and evening/weekend programs available.

Faculty: 5 full-time (3 women), 5 part-time/adjunct (4 women).
Students: 51 full-time (42 women), 14 part-time (13 women); includes 5 minority (3 African Americans, 2 Hispanic Americans), 1 international. Average age 32. 35 applicants, 91% accepted, 28 enrolled. In 2001, 29 degrees awarded.
Degree requirements: For master's, thesis or alternative, integration projects, comprehensive exam (for some programs), registration. *Median time to degree:* Master's–2 years full-time, 4 years part-time.
Entrance requirements: For master's, minimum GPA of 3.0, previous course work in statistics, bachelor's degree in liberal arts. *Application deadline:* For fall admission, 8/1 (priority date); for winter admission, 12/15 (priority date); for spring admission, 1/1 (priority date). Applications are processed on a rolling basis. *Application fee:* $25. Electronic applications accepted.
Expenses: Tuition: Full-time $8,280; part-time $456 per credit. One-time fee: $100. Tuition and fees vary according to degree level and program.
Financial support: In 2001–02, 56 students received support, including 3 research assistantships with partial tuition reimbursements available (averaging $3,600 per year); career-related internships or fieldwork, scholarships/grants, and tuition waivers (partial) also available. Support available to part-time students. Financial award application deadline: 8/15; financial award applicants required to submit FAFSA.
Faculty research: Social work practice, cults/sects, family therapy, developmental disabilities.
Brenda DuBois, Associate Director, 563-333-6379, *Fax:* 563-333-6243, *E-mail:* bdubois@sau.edu. *Web site:* http://www.sau.edu/

■ SAINT LOUIS UNIVERSITY

School of Social Service, St. Louis, MO 63103-2097

AWARDS MSW, MPH/MSW, MSW/MAPS. Part-time and evening/weekend programs available.

Faculty: 20 full-time (10 women), 22 part-time/adjunct (14 women).
Students: 123 full-time (109 women), 147 part-time (126 women); includes 54 minority (44 African Americans, 7 Asian Americans or Pacific Islanders, 2 Hispanic Americans, 1 Native American), 6 international. Average age 31. 141 applicants, 91% accepted, 93 enrolled. In 2001, 109 degrees awarded.
Degree requirements: For master's, comprehensive exam. *Median time to degree:* Master's–2.5 years full-time, 3.5 years part-time.
Entrance requirements: For master's, minimum GPA of 3.0. *Application deadline:* For fall admission, 4/1 (priority date); for spring admission, 11/1 (priority date). Applications are processed on a rolling basis. *Application fee:* $40.
Expenses: Contact institution.
Financial support: In 2001–02, 211 students received support. Career-related internships or fieldwork, Federal Work-Study, scholarships/grants, traineeships, tuition waivers (partial), and unspecified assistantships available. Support available to part-time students. Financial award application deadline: 3/1; financial award applicants required to submit FAFSA.
Faculty research: Homelessness, child/maternal health, managed care, substance abuse, natural helping. *Total annual research expenditures:* $265,540.
Dr. Susan C. Tebb, Dean, 314-977-3460, *Fax:* 314-977-2731, *E-mail:* tebbsc@slu.edu.
Application contact: Dir sion, 314-977-2722, *Fax:* *Web site:* http://www.slu.edu/

■ SALEM STATE COLLEGE

Graduate School, Program in Social Work, Salem, MA 01970-5353

AWARDS MSW.

Faculty: 8 full-time (5 women), 6 part-time/adjunct (2 women).
Entrance requirements: For master's, GRE General Test or MAT. *Application deadline:* Applications are processed on a rolling basis. *Application fee:* $25.
Dr. Donald Riley, Director, School of Social Work, 978-542-6650, *Fax:* 978-542-6936, *E-mail:* donald.riley@salem.mass.edu.

■ SALISBURY UNIVERSITY

Graduate Division, Program in Social Work, Salisbury, MD 21801-6837

AWARDS MSW.

Expenses: Tuition, state resident: full-time $6,272; part-time $174 per credit. Tuition, nonresident: full-time $12,988; part-time $355 per credit. Required fees: $4 per term.

■ SAN DIEGO STATE UNIVERSITY

Graduate and Research Affairs, College of Health and Human Services, School of Social Work, San Diego, CA 92182

AWARDS MSW, JD/MSW, MSW/MPH. Part-time programs available.

Entrance requirements: For master's, GRE General Test, TOEFL.
Faculty research: Child maltreatment, substance abuse, neighborhood studies, child welfare. *Web site:* http://www-rohan.sdsu.edu/dept/chhs/su/su.html

■ SAN FRANCISCO STATE UNIVERSITY

Graduate Division, College of Health and Human Services, School of Social Work Education, San Francisco, CA 94132-1722

AWARDS MSW. Part-time programs available.

Degree requirements: For master's, thesis optional.
Entrance requirements: For master's, minimum GPA of 2.5 in last 60 units.
Faculty research: U.S. social policy alternatives, aging and health care, mental health in communities of color, community organizing in minority communities, racism and oppression.

■ SAN JOSE STATE UNIVERSITY

Graduate Studies, College of Social Work, School of Social Work, San Jose, CA 95192-0001

AWARDS MSW.

…an Jose State University (continued)
Faculty: 7 full-time (2 women), 5 part-time/adjunct (3 women).
Students: 203 full-time (169 women), 62 part-time (44 women); includes 137 minority (22 African Americans, 32 Asian Americans or Pacific Islanders, 78 Hispanic Americans, 5 Native Americans), 3 international. Average age 32. 315 applicants, 57% accepted. In 2001, 92 degrees awarded.
Application deadline: For fall admission, 6/29; for spring admission, 11/30. Applications are processed on a rolling basis. *Application fee:* $59. Electronic applications accepted.
Expenses: Tuition, nonresident: part-time $246 per unit. Required fees: $678 per semester. Tuition and fees vary according to course load.
Financial support: Application deadline: 5/31.
Dr. Joan Merdinger, Director, 408-924-5835, *Fax:* 408-924-5892.

■ SAVANNAH STATE UNIVERSITY

Program in Social Work, Savannah, GA 31404

AWARDS MSW.

Entrance requirements: For master's, GRE General Test, minimum GPA of 2.6.
Faculty research: Clinical and administrative social work.

■ SIMMONS COLLEGE

School of Social Work, Boston, MA 02115

AWARDS Clinical social work (MSW, PhD). Part-time programs available.

Faculty: 21 full-time (17 women), 56 part-time/adjunct (36 women).
Students: 278; includes 50 minority (23 African Americans, 9 Asian Americans or Pacific Islanders, 18 Hispanic Americans), 4 international. Average age 27. 397 applicants, 44% accepted, 175 enrolled. In 2001, 225 master's, 3 doctorates awarded.
Degree requirements: For master's, thesis or alternative; for doctorate, thesis/dissertation.
Entrance requirements: For master's, minimum GPA of 3.0 in last 2 years of undergraduate course work; for doctorate, MAT, interview, minimum GPA of 3.0 in last 2 years of undergraduate course work. *Application deadline:* For fall admission, 12/15 (priority date); for winter admission, 2/15. *Application fee:* $45.
Expenses: Contact institution.
Financial support: Fellowships, career-related internships or fieldwork, Federal Work-Study, institutionally sponsored loans, and tuition waivers (full) available. Support available to part-time students. Fi… …d application deadline: 3/1; … applicants required to
Faculty research: Adolescence and depression, multicultural social work, competence, domestic violence, narrative theory.
Dr. Joseph M. Regan, Dean, 617-521-3900.
Application contact: Deborah Sheehan, Director of Admissions, 617-521-3920, *Fax:* 617-521-3980, *E-mail:* ssw@simmons.edu. *Web site:* http://www.simmons.edu/

Find an in-depth description at www.petersons.com/gradchannel.

■ SMITH COLLEGE

School for Social Work, Northampton, MA 01063

AWARDS MSW, PhD.

Faculty: 13 full-time (9 women), 106 part-time/adjunct (77 women).
Students: 356 full-time (322 women); includes 50 minority (23 African Americans, 13 Asian Americans or Pacific Islanders, 13 Hispanic Americans, 1 Native American), 12 international. Average age 38. 328 applicants, 64% accepted. In 2001, 107 master's, 9 doctorates awarded.
Degree requirements: For master's and doctorate, thesis/dissertation.
Entrance requirements: For doctorate, MAT. *Application deadline:* For fall admission, 2/15. Applications are processed on a rolling basis. *Application fee:* $50.
Expenses: Contact institution.
Financial support: In 2001–02, 176 students received support. Institutionally sponsored loans and scholarships/grants available. Financial award application deadline: 5/15; financial award applicants required to submit FAFSA.
Dr. Carolyn Jacobs, Acting Dean, 413-585-7977, *E-mail:* cjacobs@smith.edu.
Application contact: Irene Rodriguez Martin, Director of Enrollment Management and Continuing Education, 413-585-7960, *Fax:* 413-585-7994, *E-mail:* imartin@smith.edu. *Web site:* http://www.smith.edu/ssw/

Find an in-depth description at www.petersons.com/gradchannel.

■ SOUTHERN CONNECTICUT STATE UNIVERSITY

School of Graduate Studies, School of Health and Human Services, Department of Social Work, New Haven, CT 06515-1355

AWARDS MSW, MSW/MS. Part-time and evening/weekend programs available.

Faculty: 14 full-time (7 women), 5 part-time/adjunct.
Students: 69 full-time (56 women), 111 part-time (84 women); includes 34 minority (24 African Americans, 2 Asian Americans or Pacific Islanders, 8 Hispanic Americans), 1 international. 366 applicants, 14% accepted. In 2001, 42 degrees awarded.
Degree requirements: For master's, thesis.
Entrance requirements: For master's, minimum undergraduate QPA of 3.0 in graduate major field or 2.5 overall, interview. *Application deadline:* For fall admission, 3/1; for spring admission, 12/1. *Application fee:* $40.
Financial support: Application deadline: 4/15;
Faculty research: Social work practice; social service development; services for women, the aging, children, and families in educational and health care systems.
Dr. Elbert Siegel, Chairperson, 203-392-6551, *Fax:* 203-392-6580, *E-mail:* siegel@southernct.edu.
Application contact: Dr. Valerie Dripchak, Director of Admissions, 203-392-6551, *Fax:* 203-392-6580, *E-mail:* dripchak@southernct.edu. *Web site:* http://www.southernct.edu/

■ SOUTHERN ILLINOIS UNIVERSITY CARBONDALE

Graduate School, College of Education, School of Social Work, Carbondale, IL 62901-6806

AWARDS MSW, JD/MSW.

Faculty: 10 full-time (6 women).
Students: 54 full-time (44 women), 6 part-time (all women); includes 7 minority (6 African Americans, 1 Asian American or Pacific Islander), 9 international. Average age 30. 35 applicants, 54% accepted. In 2001, 36 degrees awarded.
Entrance requirements: For master's, GRE General Test, TOEFL, minimum GPA of 2.7. *Application deadline:* For fall admission, 3/1. Applications are processed on a rolling basis. *Application fee:* $20.
Expenses: Tuition, state resident: full-time $3,794; part-time $154 per hour. Tuition, nonresident: full-time $6,566; part-time $308 per hour. Required fees: $277 per hour.
Financial support: In 2001–02, 19 students received support, including 6 research assistantships with full tuition reimbursements available; fellowships with full tuition reimbursements available, teaching assistantships with full tuition reimbursements available, career-related internships or fieldwork and tuition waivers (full) also available. Financial award application deadline: 5/1.
Faculty research: Service delivery systems, comparative race relations, advocacy research, gerontology, child welfare and health.
Dr. Sharon Krigher, Director, 618-453-3616.
Application contact: Sandy Schenk, Assistant to Graduate Director, 618-453-1202, *Fax:* 618-453-1219, *E-mail:* sandy@siu.edu. *Web site:* http://www.siu.edu/~socwork/index.html

Find an in-depth description at www.petersons.com/gradchannel.

637

■ SOUTHERN ILLINOIS UNIVERSITY EDWARDSVILLE

Graduate Studies and Research, College of Arts and Sciences, Department of Social Work, Edwardsville, IL 62026-0001

AWARDS MSW. Part-time programs available.

Students: 35 full-time (31 women), 10 part-time (4 women); includes 11 minority (all African Americans). Average age 33. 58 applicants, 66% accepted, 19 enrolled. In 2001, 16 degrees awarded.
Degree requirements: For master's, thesis or alternative, final exam. *Median time to degree:* Master's–2.5 years full-time, 4 years part-time.
Entrance requirements: For master's, GRE General Test or MAT, TOEFL. *Application deadline:* For fall admission, 7/20; for spring admission, 12/7. *Application fee:* $25.
Expenses: Tuition, state resident: full-time $2,712; part-time $113 per credit hour. Tuition, nonresident: full-time $5,424; part-time $226 per credit hour. Required fees: $250; $125 per term. Tuition and fees vary according to course load, campus/location and reciprocity agreements.
Financial support: Fellowships with full tuition reimbursements, research assistantships with full tuition reimbursements, teaching assistantships with full tuition reimbursements, unspecified assistantships available. Financial award application deadline: 3/1.
Dr. Thomas Regulus, Chair, 618-650-5758, *E-mail:* tregulu@siue.edu.

■ SOUTHERN UNIVERSITY AT NEW ORLEANS

School of Social Work, New Orleans, LA 70126-1009

AWARDS MSW. Part-time and evening/weekend programs available.

Faculty: 21 full-time (13 women).
Students: 140 full-time (121 women), 101 part-time (92 women); includes 190 minority (all African Americans). Average age 35.
Degree requirements: For master's, thesis.
Application deadline: For fall admission, 3/1. *Application fee:* $25.
Expenses: Tuition: Part-time $623 per unit. Tuition and fees vary according to course load.
Financial support: Fellowships, career-related internships or fieldwork and institutionally sponsored loans available.
Faculty research: Service needs of people with AIDS, suicidal rate of people with AIDS.
Mille M. Charles, Dean, 504-286-5376, *Fax:* 504-286-5387.
Application contact: James Donald Smith, Director of Student Affairs, 504-286-5376, *Fax:* 504-286-5387.

■ SOUTHWEST MISSOURI STATE UNIVERSITY

Graduate College, College of Health and Human Services, School of Social Work, Springfield, MO 65804-0094

AWARDS MSW. Part-time programs available.

Faculty: 9 full-time (6 women), 2 part-time/adjunct (0 women).
Students: 90 full-time (74 women), 16 part-time (11 women); includes 2 minority (1 African American, 1 Native American). In 2001, 38 degrees awarded.
Degree requirements: For master's, thesis or alternative, comprehensive exam.
Entrance requirements: For master's, GRE General Test, minimum GPA of 3.0. *Application deadline:* For fall admission, 3/2 (priority date). Applications are processed on a rolling basis. *Application fee:* $25. Electronic applications accepted.
Expenses: Tuition, state resident: full-time $2,286; part-time $127 per credit. Tuition, nonresident: full-time $4,572; part-time $254 per credit. Required fees: $151 per semester. Tuition and fees vary according to course level and program.
Financial support: In 2001–02, 3 research assistantships with full tuition reimbursements (averaging $6,150 per year), 1 teaching assistantship with full tuition reimbursement (averaging $6,150 per year) were awarded. Federal Work-Study, scholarships/grants, and unspecified assistantships also available. Financial award application deadline: 3/31.
Dr. Anne Summers, Acting Director, 417-836-6953, *Fax:* 417-836-6967, *E-mail:* socialwork@smsu.edu. *Web site:* http://www.smsu.edu/swk/index.html

■ SOUTHWEST TEXAS STATE UNIVERSITY

Graduate School, College of Health Professions, Department of Social Work, San Marcos, TX 78666

AWARDS MSW.

Faculty: 10 full-time (8 women), 2 part-time/adjunct (1 woman).
Students: 44 full-time (37 women), 46 part-time (44 women). Average age 35. 38 applicants, 71% accepted, 20 enrolled. In 2001, 45 degrees awarded.
Degree requirements: For master's, comprehensive exam.
Entrance requirements: For master's, GRE General Test, TOEFL, minimum GPA of 2.75 in last 60 hours. *Application deadline:* For fall admission, 6/15 (priority date); for spring admission, 10/15 (priority date). Applications are processed on a rolling basis. *Application fee:* $40 ($90 for international students).
Expenses: Tuition, state resident: full-time $1,512; part-time $84 per credit hour. Tuition, nonresident: full-time $5,310; part-time $295 per credit hour. Required fees: $864; $29 per credit hour. $195 per term. Full-time tuition and fees vary according to course load.
Financial support: In 2001–02, 4 research assistantships (averaging $9,814 per year), 1 teaching assistantship (averaging $8,535 per year) were awarded. Career-related internships or fieldwork, Federal Work-Study, institutionally sponsored loans, and unspecified assistantships also available. Support available to part-time students. Financial award application deadline: 4/1; financial award applicants required to submit FAFSA.
Faculty research: Domestic or workplace violence, parental participation and school social work, addictions and co-dependency.
Dr. Karen Brown, Chair, 512-245-2592, *Fax:* 512-245-8097, *E-mail:* kb01@swt.edu.
Application contact: Dr. Dorinda Nobel, Graduate Advisor, 512-245-2583, *Fax:* 512-245-8097, *E-mail:* dn12@swt.edu. *Web site:* http://www.swt.edu/

■ SPALDING UNIVERSITY

Graduate Studies, School of Social Work, Louisville, KY 40203-2188

AWARDS MSW. Evening/weekend programs available.

Faculty: 5 full-time (4 women), 4 part-time/adjunct (2 women).
Students: 27 full-time (all women), 7 part-time (1 woman); includes 7 minority (6 African Americans, 1 Native American), 2 international. Average age 35. 30 applicants, 80% accepted. In 2001, 23 degrees awarded.
Degree requirements: For master's, thesis or alternative, project presentation.
Entrance requirements: For master's, GRE General Test, 18 hours of course work in social sciences including methods and statistics, human biology. *Application deadline:* For fall admission, 4/1 (priority date). *Application fee:* $30.
Expenses: Tuition: Full-time $6,000; part-time $400 per credit hour. Required fees: $96.
Financial support: In 2001–02, 22 students received support, including 2 research assistantships (averaging $4,200 per year); career-related internships or fieldwork, Federal Work-Study, and scholarships/grants also available. Support available to part-time students. Financial award application deadline: 3/15; financial award applicants required to submit FAFSA.
Faculty research: AIDS, drug/alcohol, child welfare, critical thinking, reflective practice. *Total annual research expenditures:* $53,000.
Dr. Helen Deines, Dean, 502-585-7183, *Fax:* 502-585-7158.
Application contact: Graduate Office, 502-585-7105, *Fax:* 502-585-7158, *E-mail:* gradadmissions@spalding.edu. *Web site:* http://www.spalding.edu/

■ SPRINGFIELD COLLEGE

School of Graduate Studies, Program in Social Work, Springfield, MA 01109-3797

AWARDS MSW, JD/MSW. Part-time and evening/weekend programs available.

Faculty: 9 full-time (5 women), 28 part-time/adjunct (20 women).
Students: 117 full-time, 84 part-time. Average age 35. 208 applicants, 87% accepted. In 2001, 64 degrees awarded.
Degree requirements: For master's, fieldwork.
Entrance requirements: For master's, minimum GPA of 3.0 during previous 2 years. *Application deadline:* For fall admission, 3/15 (priority date). Applications are processed on a rolling basis. *Application fee:* $40. Electronic applications accepted.
Financial support: Fellowships with partial tuition reimbursements, teaching assistantships with partial tuition reimbursements, career-related internships or fieldwork, Federal Work-Study, institutionally sponsored loans, scholarships/grants, and unspecified assistantships available. Financial award application deadline: 3/1.
Faculty research: Community structure and social change, special services and program evaluation, evaluating social work practice.
Dr. Francine Vecchiolla, Dean, 413-748-3060.
Application contact: Donald James Shaw, Director of Graduate Admissions, 413-748-3225, *Fax:* 413-748-3694, *E-mail:* donald_shaw_jr@spfldcol.edu. *Web site:* http://www.spfldcol.edu/

■ STATE UNIVERSITY OF NEW YORK AT ALBANY

School of Social Welfare, Albany, NY 12222-0001

AWARDS MSW, PhD, MSW/MA. Part-time and evening/weekend programs available.

Students: 317 full-time (258 women), 151 part-time (125 women); includes 67 minority (35 African Americans, 6 Asian Americans or Pacific Islanders, 21 Hispanic Americans, 5 Native Americans), 10 international. Average age 34. 353 applicants, 84% accepted. In 2001, 156 master's, 7 doctorates awarded.
Degree requirements: For doctorate, thesis/dissertation.
Entrance requirements: For doctorate, GRE General Test. *Application deadline:* For fall admission, 2/15. *Application fee:* $50.
Expenses: Tuition, state resident: full-time $2,550; part-time $213 per credit. Tuition, nonresident: full-time $4,208; part-time $351 per credit. Required fees: $470; $470 per year.
Financial support: Fellowships, career-related internships or fieldwork and Federal Work-Study available. Financial award application deadline: 2/15.
Faculty research: Welfare reform, homelessness, children and families, mental health, substance abuse.
Katharine Briar-Lawson, Dean, 518-442-5324.
Application contact: Florance Bolton, Assistant to the Dean of Graduate Studies, 518-442-5200.

■ STATE UNIVERSITY OF NEW YORK COLLEGE AT BROCKPORT

School of Professions, Greater Rochester Collaborative Master of Social Work Program, Brockport, NY 14420-2997

AWARDS MSW. Part-time programs available.

Students: 15 full-time (14 women), 16 part-time (14 women); includes 3 minority (1 African American, 1 Asian American or Pacific Islander, 1 Native American), 1 international. 40 applicants, 83% accepted, 20 enrolled.
Degree requirements: For master's, thesis or alternative.
Entrance requirements: For master's, minimum GPA of 3.0. *Application deadline:* For fall admission, 3/15 (priority date). *Application fee:* $50.
Expenses: Contact institution.
Financial support: In 2001–02, 1 fellowship with tuition reimbursement (averaging $7,500 per year) was awarded; Federal Work-Study also available.
Faculty research: Family and community, health, collaboration, policy, diversity.
Dr. Estella Norwood Evans, Director, 585-327-7450, *E-mail:* enevans@naz.edu. *Web site:* http://www.brockport.edu/~grcmsw/main.html

■ STEPHEN F. AUSTIN STATE UNIVERSITY

Graduate School, College of Applied Arts and Science, School of Social Work, Nacogdoches, TX 75962

AWARDS MSW.

Faculty: 10 full-time (6 women).
Students: 35 full-time (32 women), 3 part-time (all women); includes 13 minority (11 African Americans, 2 Hispanic Americans). 30 applicants, 90% accepted. In 2001, 20 degrees awarded.
Degree requirements: For master's, thesis optional.
Entrance requirements: For master's, GRE General Test, TOEFL, interview. *Application deadline:* For fall admission, 4/1. Applications are processed on a rolling basis. *Application fee:* $25 ($50 for international students).
Expenses: Tuition, state resident: full-time $1,008; part-time $42 per credit. Tuition, nonresident: full-time $6,072; part-time $253 per credit. Required fees: $1,248; $52 per credit. Tuition and fees vary according to course load.
Financial support: In 2001–02, 2 research assistantships (averaging $6,600 per year) were awarded; career-related internships or fieldwork, Federal Work-Study, and institutionally sponsored loans also available. Support available to part-time students. Financial award application deadline: 3/1.
Dr. Michael Daley, Associate Dean, 936-468-5105.

■ STONY BROOK UNIVERSITY, STATE UNIVERSITY OF NEW YORK

Health Sciences Center, School of Social Welfare, Doctoral Program in Social Welfare, Stony Brook, NY 11794

AWARDS PhD.

Faculty: 17 full-time (10 women), 20 part-time/adjunct (12 women).
Students: 16 full-time (14 women), 10 part-time (6 women); includes 6 minority (4 African Americans, 1 Asian American or Pacific Islander, 1 Hispanic American), 1 international. 22 applicants, 36% accepted.
Degree requirements: For doctorate, thesis/dissertation.
Entrance requirements: For doctorate, GRE General Test. *Application deadline:* For fall admission, 2/1. *Application fee:* $50.
Expenses: Tuition, state resident: full-time $5,100; part-time $213 per credit. Tuition, nonresident: full-time $8,416; part-time $351 per credit. Required fees: $496.
Financial support: Fellowships available. Financial award application deadline: 2/1.
Dr. Joel Blau, Director, 631-444-3149, *Fax:* 631-444-7565, *E-mail:* jblau@ssw.hsc.sunysb.edu. *Web site:* http://uhmc.sunysb.edu/socwelf/phd.html

Find an in-depth description at www.petersons.com/gradchannel.

■ STONY BROOK UNIVERSITY, STATE UNIVERSITY OF NEW YORK

Health Sciences Center, School of Social Welfare, Master's Program in Social Work, Stony Brook, NY 11794

AWARDS MSW.

Students: 312 full-time (248 women), 26 part-time (21 women); includes 115 minority (74 African Americans, 3 Asian Americans or Pacific Islanders, 38 Hispanic Americans), 4 international. Average age 35. 322 applicants, 88% accepted. In 2001, 155 degrees awarded.
Degree requirements: For master's, project or thesis.
Entrance requirements: For master's, interview. *Application deadline:* For fall admission, 3/1. *Application fee:* $50.
Expenses: Tuition, state resident: full-time $5,100; part-time $213 per credit. Tuition,

nonresident: full-time $8,416; part-time $351 per credit. Required fees: $496.
Financial support: Application deadline: 3/1.
Application contact: Dr. Michael Lewis, Director, 631-444-3166, *Fax:* 631-444-7565, *E-mail:* michaell@ssw.hsc.sunysb.edu.

■ SYRACUSE UNIVERSITY

Graduate School, College of Human Services and Health Professions, School of Social Work, Syracuse, NY 13244-0003

AWARDS MSW, JD/MSW. Part-time and evening/weekend programs available.

Faculty: 18 full-time (8 women), 12 part-time/adjunct (7 women).
Students: 115 full-time (103 women), 104 part-time (89 women); includes 25 minority (16 African Americans, 2 Asian Americans or Pacific Islanders, 6 Hispanic Americans, 1 Native American). Average age 33. 132 applicants, 83% accepted. In 2001, 137 degrees awarded.
Entrance requirements: For master's, GRE General Test. *Application deadline:* For fall admission, 5/15; for spring admission, 11/1. Applications are processed on a rolling basis. *Application fee:* $50.
Expenses: Tuition: Full-time $15,528; part-time $647 per credit. Required fees: $420; $38 per term. Tuition and fees vary according to program.
Financial support: Fellowships, research assistantships, career-related internships or fieldwork, Federal Work-Study, scholarships/grants, tuition waivers (partial), and unspecified assistantships available. Financial award applicants required to submit FAFSA.
Faculty research: Aging policy, healthcare, criminal justice, disability, rights of passage, kinship care.
Dr. Bruce Lagay, Dean, 315-443-5582.
Application contact: Linda M. Littlejohn, Assistant Dean, Enrollment Management, 315-443-5555, *Fax:* 315-443-2562, *E-mail:* inquire@hshp.syr.edu. *Web site:* http://www.social.syr.edu/

■ TEMPLE UNIVERSITY

Graduate School, School of Social Administration, Program in Social Work, Philadelphia, PA 19122-6096

AWARDS MSW. Part-time and evening/weekend programs available.

Entrance requirements: For master's, minimum GPA of 3.0 during previous 2 years, 2.8 overall. Electronic applications accepted.
Expenses: Tuition, state resident: full-time $8,487; part-time $369 per credit hour. Tuition, nonresident: full-time $12,282; part-time $534 per credit hour. Required fees: $350. Tuition and fees vary according to course load, program and reciprocity agreements. *Web site:* http://www.temple.edu/social work/

■ TEXAS A&M UNIVERSITY–COMMERCE

Graduate School, College of Arts and Sciences, Department of Social Work, Commerce, TX 75429-3011

AWARDS MSW.

Students: 19 full-time (15 women), 13 part-time (11 women); includes 5 minority (3 African Americans, 2 Hispanic Americans).
Entrance requirements: For master's, GRE General Test. *Application deadline:* For fall admission, 6/1; for spring admission, 11/1. Applications are processed on a rolling basis. *Application fee:* $0 ($25 for international students).
Expenses: Tuition, state resident: full-time $2,221. International tuition: $7,285 full-time.
Dr. Ed Skarnulis, Department Head, 903-886-5029, *E-mail:* ed_skarnulis@tamu-commerce.edu.
Application contact: Tammi Higginbotham, Graduate Admissions Adviser, 843-886-5167, *Fax:* 843-886-5165, *E-mail:* tammi_higginbotham@tamu-commerce.edu.

■ TULANE UNIVERSITY

School of Social Work, New Orleans, LA 70118-5669

AWARDS MSW, PhD, JD/MSW, MSW/MPH. Part-time programs available.

Faculty: 19 full-time (14 women), 37 part-time/adjunct (22 women).
Students: 128 full-time, 31 part-time; includes 52 minority (45 African Americans, 1 Asian American or Pacific Islander, 5 Hispanic Americans, 1 Native American), 2 international. 186 applicants, 81% accepted. In 2001, 80 master's, 2 doctorates awarded.
Degree requirements: For master's and doctorate, thesis/dissertation.
Entrance requirements: For master's, GRE, TOEFL; for doctorate, GRE. *Application deadline:* For fall admission, 3/31 (priority date). Applications are processed on a rolling basis. *Application fee:* $25. Electronic applications accepted.
Expenses: Tuition: Full-time $24,675. Required fees: $2,210.
Financial support: Fellowships, Federal Work-Study available. Financial award applicants required to submit FAFSA.
Dr. Ronald Marks, Dean, 504-865-5314, *Fax:* 504-862-8727.
Application contact: Gail Brown, Admissions Coordinator, 504-865-5314, *Fax:* 504-862-8727.

■ UNIVERSITY AT BUFFALO, THE STATE UNIVERSITY OF NEW YORK

Graduate School, School of Social Work, Buffalo, NY 14260

AWARDS MSW, PhD, JD/MSW. MSW available in Buffalo, Rochester, Jamestown, and Corning, New York. Part-time programs available.

Faculty: 20 full-time (15 women), 4 part-time/adjunct (all women).
Students: 162 full-time (138 women), 212 part-time (183 women); includes 65 minority (34 African Americans, 5 Asian Americans or Pacific Islanders, 19 Hispanic Americans, 7 Native Americans), 8 international. Average age 32. 239 applicants, 86% accepted, 151 enrolled. In 2001, 130 master's, 1 doctorate awarded.
Degree requirements: For master's, 900 hours of field work; for doctorate, thesis/dissertation. *Median time to degree:* Master's–2 years full-time, 3 years part-time.
Entrance requirements: For master's, GRE General Test or MAT; for doctorate, GRE General Test, MSW. *Application deadline:* For fall admission, 3/1 (priority date). Applications are processed on a rolling basis. *Application fee:* $50. Electronic applications accepted.
Expenses: Tuition, state resident: full-time $6,118. Tuition, nonresident: full-time $9,434.
Financial support: In 2001–02, 5 research assistantships with tuition reimbursements (averaging $15,000 per year), 6 teaching assistantships with tuition reimbursements (averaging $15,000 per year) were awarded. Fellowships with tuition reimbursements, career-related internships or fieldwork, Federal Work-Study, institutionally sponsored loans, scholarships/grants, tuition waivers (partial), and unspecified assistantships also available. Support available to part-time students. Financial award application deadline: 2/1; financial award applicants required to submit FAFSA.
Faculty research: Social welfare policy, mental health, child welfare, alcoholism and other addictions, community. *Total annual research expenditures:* $1.9 million.
Dr. Lawrence Shulman, Dean, 716-645-3381 Ext. 221, *Fax:* 716-645-3883.
Application contact: Ann Still, Admissions Secretary, 716-645-3381 Ext. 246, *Fax:* 716-645-3456, *E-mail:* amls@acsu.buffalo.edu. *Web site:* http://www.socialwork.buffalo.edu/

■ THE UNIVERSITY OF AKRON

Graduate School, College of Fine and Applied Arts, School of Social Work, Akron, OH 44325-0001

AWARDS MS.

Faculty: 3 full-time (all women), 19 part-time/adjunct (13 women).

The University of Akron (continued)
Students: 70 full-time (66 women), 30 part-time (24 women); includes 26 minority (24 African Americans, 1 Asian American or Pacific Islander, 1 Hispanic American). Average age 36. 78 applicants, 86% accepted, 48 enrolled. In 2001, 21 degrees awarded.
Entrance requirements: For master's, undergraduate major in social work or related field. *Application deadline:* Applications are processed on a rolling basis. *Application fee:* $40 ($50 for international students).
Expenses: Tuition, state resident: full-time $6,562; part-time $219 per credit. Tuition, nonresident: full-time $9,027; part-time $383 per credit. Required fees: $272; $11 per credit. Tuition and fees vary according to course load.
Financial support: In 2001–02, 8 research assistantships with full tuition reimbursements were awarded; teaching assistantships, Federal Work-Study also available. Financial award application deadline: 3/1.
Dr. Virginia Fitch, Director, 330-972-5975, *E-mail:* vfitch@uakron.edu.

■ THE UNIVERSITY OF ALABAMA

Graduate School, School of Social Work, Tuscaloosa, AL 35487

AWARDS MSW, PhD. Postbaccalaureate distance learning degree programs offered.

Faculty: 18 full-time (10 women), 10 part-time/adjunct (6 women).
Students: 181 full-time (152 women), 35 part-time (30 women); includes 52 minority (47 African Americans, 1 Asian American or Pacific Islander, 2 Hispanic Americans, 2 Native Americans), 8 international. Average age 30. 110 applicants, 72% accepted, 50 enrolled. In 2001, 106 master's, 4 doctorates awarded.
Degree requirements: For doctorate, thesis/dissertation.
Entrance requirements: For master's, GRE General Test or MAT, minimum GPA of 2.5; for doctorate, GRE General Test, minimum GPA of 3.0. *Application deadline:* For fall admission, 2/1 (priority date). *Application fee:* $25. Electronic applications accepted.
Expenses: Tuition, state resident: full-time $3,292; part-time $183 per credit hour. Tuition, nonresident: full-time $8,912; part-time $495 per credit hour. Tuition and fees vary according to course load, campus/location and program.
Financial support: In 2001–02, 25 fellowships (averaging $7,500 per year), 6 research assistantships with partial tuition reimbursements (averaging $8,414 per year), 6 teaching assistantships with partial tuition reimbursements (averaging $8,414 per year) were awarded. Career-related internships or fieldwork, Federal Work-Study, scholarships/grants, traineeships, tuition waivers (partial), and unspecified assistantships also available. Financial award application deadline: 2/1.
Faculty research: Social service administration; direct clinical services with individuals, families, and groups; theory and practice development.
Dr. James P. Adams, Dean, 205-348-3924, *Fax:* 205-348-9419, *E-mail:* jadams@sw.ua.edu.
Application contact: Dr. Ginny Raymond, Associate Dean, 205-348-3943, *Fax:* 205-348-9419, *E-mail:* graymond@sw.ua.edu. *Web site:* http://www.socialwork.ua.edu/

■ UNIVERSITY OF ALASKA ANCHORAGE

College of Health, Education, and Social Welfare, School of Social Work, Anchorage, AK 99508-8060

AWARDS MSW.

Degree requirements: For master's, thesis or alternative, research project.
Entrance requirements: For master's, GRE General Test.
Expenses: Contact institution.

■ UNIVERSITY OF ARKANSAS AT LITTLE ROCK

Graduate School, College of Professional Studies, School of Social Work, Program in Social Work, Little Rock, AR 72204-1099

AWARDS Clinical social work (MSW); social program administration (MSW).

Entrance requirements: For master's, GRE General Test or MAT.
Expenses: Tuition, state resident: full-time $3,006; part-time $107 per credit. Tuition, nonresident: full-time $6,012; part-time $357 per credit. Required fees: $22 per credit. Tuition and fees vary according to program.

■ UNIVERSITY OF CALIFORNIA, BERKELEY

Graduate Division, School of Social Welfare, Berkeley, CA 94720-1500

AWARDS MSW, PhD, JD/MSW, MSW/PhD.

Students: 222 full-time (187 women); includes 68 minority (16 African Americans, 23 Asian Americans or Pacific Islanders, 22 Hispanic Americans, 7 Native Americans), 7 international. Average age 28. 438 applicants, 34% accepted, 98 enrolled. In 2001, 94 master's, 7 doctorates awarded. Terminal master's awarded for partial completion of doctoral program.
Degree requirements: For master's, thesis optional; for doctorate, thesis/dissertation, qualifying exam. *Median time to degree:* Master's–2 years full-time; doctorate–5 years full-time.
Entrance requirements: For master's, GRE General Test, TOEFL, minimum GPA of 3.0; for doctorate, GRE General Test, TOEFL, TSE, and TWE, minimum GPA of 3.0. *Application deadline:* Applications are processed on a rolling basis. *Application fee:* $60.
Expenses: Tuition, nonresident: full-time $10,704. Required fees: $4,349.
Financial support: Fellowships, research assistantships with partial tuition reimbursements, teaching assistantships with partial tuition reimbursements, career-related internships or fieldwork, Federal Work-Study, scholarships/grants, traineeships, health care benefits, and unspecified assistantships available. Financial award application deadline: 12/15; financial award applicants required to submit FAFSA.
Faculty research: Child welfare, law and social welfare, minority mental health, social welfare policy analysis, health services, psychopathology, gerontology.
Dr. James Midgley, Dean, 510-642-5039.
Application contact: Rafael Herrera, Director of Admissions, 510-642-9042, *Fax:* 510-643-6126, *E-mail:* socwelf@uclink4.berkeley.edu. *Web site:* http://www.hav54.socwel.berkeley.edu/

■ UNIVERSITY OF CALIFORNIA, LOS ANGELES

Graduate Division, School of Public Policy and Social Research, Program in Social Welfare, Los Angeles, CA 90095

AWARDS MSW, PhD, JD/MSW.

Faculty: 8.
Students: 206 full-time (186 women); includes 67 minority (10 African Americans, 23 Asian Americans or Pacific Islanders, 34 Hispanic Americans), 13 international. 392 applicants, 46% accepted, 96 enrolled. In 2001, 43 master's, 8 doctorates awarded.
Degree requirements: For master's, research project; for doctorate, thesis/dissertation, oral and written qualifying exams.
Entrance requirements: For master's, GRE General Test, TOEFL, minimum GPA of 3.0; for doctorate, GRE General Test, TOEFL, minimum undergraduate GPA of 3.0. *Application deadline:* For fall admission, 2/15. *Application fee:* $40. Electronic applications accepted.
Expenses: Tuition, nonresident: full-time $10,244. Required fees: $3,609. Full-time tuition and fees vary according to program.
Financial support: In 2001–02, 180 students received support, including 89 fellowships, 23 research assistantships, 24 teaching assistantships; Federal Work-Study, institutionally sponsored loans, scholarships/grants, and tuition waivers (full and partial) also available. Financial award application deadline: 3/1.
Dr. A. E. Benjamin, Chair, 310-825-7737.
Application contact: Departmental Office, 310-825-7737.

■ UNIVERSITY OF CENTRAL FLORIDA

College of Health and Public Affairs, School of Social Work, Orlando, FL 32816

AWARDS Gerontology (Certificate); non-profit management (Certificate); social work (MSW). Part-time and evening/weekend programs available.

Faculty: 15 full-time (10 women), 19 part-time/adjunct (12 women).
Students: 143 full-time (124 women), 69 part-time (65 women); includes 60 minority (27 African Americans, 3 Asian Americans or Pacific Islanders, 29 Hispanic Americans, 1 Native American), 2 international. Average age 32. 171 applicants, 90% accepted, 105 enrolled. In 2001, 73 degrees awarded.
Degree requirements: For master's, thesis or alternative, field education.
Entrance requirements: For master's, TOEFL, resumé. *Application deadline:* For fall admission, 3/1. *Application fee:* $20. Electronic applications accepted.
Expenses: Tuition, state resident: part-time $162 per hour. Tuition, nonresident: part-time $569 per hour.
Financial support: In 2001–02, 17 fellowships with partial tuition reimbursements (averaging $3,000 per year), 18 research assistantships with partial tuition reimbursements (averaging $1,752 per year), 16 teaching assistantships with partial tuition reimbursements (averaging $1,667 per year) were awarded. Career-related internships or fieldwork, Federal Work-Study, institutionally sponsored loans, and unspecified assistantships also available. Financial award application deadline: 3/1; financial award applicants required to submit FAFSA.
Dr. Mary Van Hook, Director, 407-823-2114, *E-mail:* mvanhook@pegasus.cc.ucf.edu.
Application contact: Dr. Ken Kazmerski, Coordinator, 407-823-2114, *Fax:* 407-823-5697, *E-mail:* kenkaz@aol.com. *Web site:* http://www.ucf.edu/

■ UNIVERSITY OF CHICAGO

School of Social Service Administration, Chicago, IL 60637-1513

AWARDS Social service administration (PhD); social work (AM). Part-time and evening/weekend programs available.

Faculty: 31 full-time (17 women), 51 part-time/adjunct (36 women).
Students: 313 full-time (260 women), 117 part-time (88 women); includes 134 minority (69 African Americans, 23 Asian Americans or Pacific Islanders, 40 Hispanic Americans, 2 Native Americans), 6 international. 525 applicants, 36% accepted, 173 enrolled. In 2001, 142 master's, 10 doctorates awarded.
Degree requirements: For master's, thesis (for some programs); for doctorate, thesis/dissertation, comprehensive exam. *Median time to degree:* Master's–2 years full-time, 3 years part-time.
Entrance requirements: For master's, personal statement, letters of recommendation (4); for doctorate, writing sample, letters of recommendation (4). *Application deadline:* For fall admission, 4/1 (priority date). Applications are processed on a rolling basis. *Application fee:* $60 ($70 for international students). Electronic applications accepted.
Expenses: Contact institution.
Financial support: In 2001–02, 415 students received support; fellowships, research assistantships with full tuition reimbursements available, teaching assistantships, career-related internships or fieldwork, Federal Work-Study, institutionally sponsored loans, and scholarships/grants available. Support available to part-time students. Financial award application deadline: 4/15; financial award applicants required to submit FAFSA.
Faculty research: Family treatment, mental health, the aged, child welfare, health administration.
Edward F. Lawlor, Dean, School of Social Service Administration, 773-834-3618, *Fax:* 773-702-1979, *E-mail:* e-lawlor@uchicago.edu.
Application contact: Madeleine Metzler, Director of Admissions, 773-702-1492, *Fax:* 773-702-0874, *E-mail:* mmetzler@uchicago.edu. *Web site:* http://www.ssa.uchicago.edu/

Find an in-depth description at www.petersons.com/gradchannel.

■ UNIVERSITY OF CINCINNATI

Division of Research and Advanced Studies, School of Social Work, Cincinnati, OH 45221

AWARDS MSW. Part-time programs available.

Entrance requirements: For master's, GRE General Test. *Application deadline:* For fall admission, 2/1. *Application fee:* $30. Electronic applications accepted.
Expenses: Tuition, state resident: part-time $2,698 per quarter. Tuition, nonresident: part-time $4,977 per quarter.
Financial support: Fellowships, career-related internships or fieldwork, tuition waivers (partial), and unspecified assistantships available. Financial award application deadline: 5/1.
Dr. Philip Jackson, Director, 513-556-4615, *Fax:* 513-556-2077, *E-mail:* philip.jackson@uc.edu.
Application contact: Gerald Bostwick, Graduate Program Director, 513-556-4624, *Fax:* 513-556-2077, *E-mail:* gerald.bostwick@uc.edu. *Web site:* http://blues.fd1.uc.edu/socialwork/

■ UNIVERSITY OF CONNECTICUT

Graduate School, School of Social Work, Storrs, CT 06269

AWARDS MSW, JD/MSW, MBA/MSW, MPA/MSW.

■ UNIVERSITY OF DENVER

Graduate School of Social Work, Denver, CO 80208

AWARDS MSW, PhD, JD/MSW, M Div/MSW, MSW/MA. Part-time and evening/weekend programs available.

Faculty: 22 full-time (14 women).
Students: 256 (230 women); includes 38 minority (11 African Americans, 5 Asian Americans or Pacific Islanders, 18 Hispanic Americans, 4 Native Americans) 7 international. Average age 34. 353 applicants, 86% accepted. In 2001, 179 master's, 7 doctorates awarded.
Degree requirements: For doctorate, thesis/dissertation.
Entrance requirements: For doctorate, GRE General Test or MAT, MSW. *Application deadline:* For fall admission, 5/1. Applications are processed on a rolling basis. *Application fee:* $50.
Expenses: Tuition: Full-time $21,456.
Financial support: In 2001–02, 230 students received support, including 6 fellowships with full and partial tuition reimbursements available, 3 research assistantships with full and partial tuition reimbursements available (averaging $8,199 per year), 6 teaching assistantships with full and partial tuition reimbursements available (averaging $8,199 per year); career-related internships or fieldwork, Federal Work-Study, institutionally sponsored loans, scholarships/grants, and tuition waivers (partial) also available. Support available to part-time students. Financial award application deadline: 2/1; financial award applicants required to submit FAFSA.
Faculty research: Children, youth, and families; community mental health; drug dependency; gerontology; health. *Total annual research expenditures:* $1.8 million.
Dr. Christian Molidor, Dean, 303-871-4652.
Application contact: Melodie Rahimi, Assistant Director, Graduate Admissions, 303-871-2841, *Fax:* 303-871-2845. *Web site:* http://www.du.edu/gssw/

Find an in-depth description at www.petersons.com/gradchannel.

■ UNIVERSITY OF GEORGIA

Graduate School, School of Social Work, Athens, GA 30602

AWARDS Nonprofit organizations (MA); social work (MSW, PhD).

Faculty: 19 full-time (9 women).
Students: 233 full-time (208 women), 43 part-time (32 women); includes 49 minority (38 African Americans, 3 Asian Americans or Pacific Islanders, 6 Hispanic

University of Georgia (continued)
Americans, 2 Native Americans), 12 international. 260 applicants, 53% accepted. In 2001, 99 master's, 5 doctorates awarded.
Degree requirements: For doctorate, one foreign language, thesis/dissertation.
Entrance requirements: For master's and doctorate, GRE General Test. *Application deadline:* For fall admission, 7/1 (priority date); for spring admission, 11/15. *Application fee:* $30. Electronic applications accepted.
Expenses: Tuition, state resident: full-time $2,376; part-time $132 per credit hour. Tuition, nonresident: full-time $9,504; part-time $528 per credit hour. Required fees: $236 per semester.
Financial support: Fellowships, research assistantships, teaching assistantships, unspecified assistantships available.
Dr. Bonnie L. Yegidis, Dean, 706-542-5424, *Fax:* 706-542-3845.
Application contact: Dr. Larry Nackerud, Graduate Coordinator, 706-542-5422, *Fax:* 706-542-5429, *E-mail:* nackerud@uga.edu. *Web site:* http://www.ssw.uga.edu/

■ UNIVERSITY OF HAWAII AT MANOA

Graduate Division, College of Health Sciences and Social Welfare, School of Social Work, Honolulu, HI 96822

AWARDS Social welfare (PhD); social work (MSW). Part-time programs available.

Faculty: 17 full-time (10 women), 2 part-time/adjunct (1 woman).
Students: 166 full-time (138 women), 36 part-time (29 women); includes 59 minority (4 African Americans, 49 Asian Americans or Pacific Islanders, 4 Hispanic Americans, 2 Native Americans). 39 applicants, 51% accepted, 10 enrolled.
Degree requirements: For doctorate, thesis/dissertation.
Entrance requirements: For doctorate, TOEFL, master's degree (MSW preferred), minimum GPA of 3.0. *Application deadline:* For fall admission, 3/1. Applications are processed on a rolling basis. *Application fee:* $25 ($50 for international students).
Expenses: Tuition, state resident: full-time $2,160; part-time $1,980 per year. Tuition, nonresident: full-time $5,190; part-time $4,829 per year.
Financial support: In 2001–02, 9 research assistantships with full and partial tuition reimbursements (averaging $15,380 per year), 1 teaching assistantship (averaging $12,786 per year) were awarded. Fellowships with full and partial tuition reimbursements, career-related internships or fieldwork, Federal Work-Study, institutionally sponsored loans, and tuition waivers (full) also available. Support available to part-time students. Financial award application deadline: 2/1; financial award applicants required to submit FAFSA.
Faculty research: Health, mental health, AIDS, substance abuse, rural health, community-based research, social policy.
Dr. Jon Matsuoka, Interim Dean, 808-956-3831.
Application contact: Toni Hathaway, Admissions Coordinator, 808-956-7182, *Fax:* 808-956-5964.

■ UNIVERSITY OF HOUSTON

Graduate School of Social Work, Houston, TX 77204

AWARDS MSW, PhD, MBA/MSW, MPH/MSW, MSW/PhD. Part-time programs available.

Faculty: 16 full-time (8 women), 21 part-time/adjunct (15 women).
Students: 178 full-time (157 women), 183 part-time (154 women); includes 166 minority (98 African Americans, 11 Asian Americans or Pacific Islanders, 57 Hispanic Americans), 6 international. Average age 35. 227 applicants, 72% accepted. In 2001, 95 master's, 2 doctorates awarded.
Degree requirements: For master's, field internship, thesis optional; for doctorate, thesis/dissertation, comprehensive exam.
Entrance requirements: For master's, TOEFL, GRE, minimum GPA of 3.0; for doctorate, TOEFL. *Application deadline:* For fall admission, 3/1 (priority date). Applications are processed on a rolling basis. *Application fee:* $50 ($125 for international students).
Expenses: Tuition, state resident: full-time $1,512. Tuition, nonresident: full-time $5,310. Required fees: $1,308. Tuition and fees vary according to program.
Financial support: In 2001–02, 9 fellowships with tuition reimbursements (averaging $8,000 per year), 1 research assistantship with tuition reimbursement (averaging $8,000 per year) were awarded. Career-related internships or fieldwork, Federal Work-Study, institutionally sponsored loans, and unspecified assistantships also available. Financial award application deadline: 4/1; financial award applicants required to submit FAFSA.
Faculty research: Health care, gerontology, political social work, mental health, children and families. *Total annual research expenditures:* $1.7 million.
Dr. Ira C. Colby, Dean, 713-743-8085, *Fax:* 713-743-3267, *E-mail:* icolby@uh.edu.
Application contact: Colen Skinner, Admissions Office, 713-743-8078, *Fax:* 713-743-8149, *E-mail:* cskinner@mail.uh.edu. *Web site:* http://www.sw.uh.edu/

■ UNIVERSITY OF ILLINOIS AT CHICAGO

Graduate College, Jane Addams College of Social Work, Chicago, IL 60607-7128

AWARDS MSW, PhD. Part-time programs available.

Faculty: 28 full-time (15 women).
Students: 299 full-time (253 women), 225 part-time (191 women); includes 194 minority (126 African Americans, 21 Asian Americans or Pacific Islanders, 46 Hispanic Americans, 1 Native American), 4 international. Average age 32. 626 applicants, 38% accepted, 206 enrolled. In 2001, 212 master's, 7 doctorates awarded.
Degree requirements: For doctorate, thesis/dissertation.
Entrance requirements: For master's, GMAT, TOEFL, minimum GPA of 3.75 on a 5.0 scale; for doctorate, GRE General Test or MAT, TOEFL, minimum GPA of 3.75 on a 5.0 scale. *Application deadline:* For fall admission, 2/1. *Application fee:* $40 ($50 for international students). Electronic applications accepted.
Expenses: Tuition, state resident: full-time $3,060. Tuition, nonresident: full-time $6,688.
Financial support: In 2001–02, 44 students received support; fellowships with full tuition reimbursements available, research assistantships with full tuition reimbursements available, teaching assistantships with full tuition reimbursements available, Federal Work-Study and tuition waivers (full) available. Financial award applicants required to submit FAFSA.
C. F. Hairston, Dean, 312-996-3219.
Application contact: Barbara Bergstrom, Director of Admissions, 312-996-3218.

■ UNIVERSITY OF ILLINOIS AT URBANA–CHAMPAIGN

Graduate College, School of Social Work, Champaign, IL 61820

AWARDS MSW, PhD.

Faculty: 14 full-time.
Students: 249 full-time (211 women); includes 39 minority (25 African Americans, 1 Asian American or Pacific Islander, 13 Hispanic Americans), 16 international. 181 applicants, 29% accepted. In 2001, 158 master's, 2 doctorates awarded.
Degree requirements: For doctorate, thesis/dissertation.
Entrance requirements: For master's and doctorate, GRE, minimum GPA of 3.0. *Application deadline:* For fall admission, 2/1. Applications are processed on a rolling basis. *Application fee:* $40 ($50 for international students).
Expenses: Tuition, state resident: part-time $3,227 per degree program. Tuition, nonresident: part-time $7,169 per degree program. Tuition and fees vary according to program.
Financial support: In 2001–02, 25 fellowships, 36 research assistantships, 8 teaching assistantships were awarded. Career-related internships or fieldwork and tuition waivers (full and partial) also available. Financial award application deadline: 2/15.

Jill Doner Kagle, Dean, 217-333-2260, *Fax:* 217-244-5220, *E-mail:* j-kagle@uiuc.edu.
Application contact: Michele Winfrey, Secretary, 217-244-5244, *Fax:* 217-244-5220, *E-mail:* mwinfrey@uiuc.edu. *Web site:* http://www.social.uiuc.edu/

■ THE UNIVERSITY OF IOWA

Graduate College, College of Liberal Arts and Sciences, School of Social Work, Iowa City, IA 52242-1316

AWARDS MSW, PhD, JD/MSW, MSW/MA, MSW/MS.

Faculty: 12 full-time, 5 part-time/adjunct.
Students: 87 full-time (72 women), 122 part-time (101 women); includes 7 minority (1 African American, 3 Asian Americans or Pacific Islanders, 1 Hispanic American, 2 Native Americans), 3 international. 173 applicants, 73% accepted, 93 enrolled. In 2001, 65 degrees awarded.
Degree requirements: For master's, exam, thesis optional; for doctorate, thesis/dissertation, comprehensive exam.
Entrance requirements: For master's, GRE General Test, TOEFL; for doctorate, GRE General Test, TOEFL, minimum GPA of 3.0. *Application fee:* $30 ($50 for international students). Electronic applications accepted.
Expenses: Tuition, state resident: full-time $3,702; part-time $206 per semester hour. Tuition, nonresident: full-time $11,924; part-time $206 per semester hour. Required fees: $101 per semester. Tuition and fees vary according to course load and program.
Financial support: In 2001–02, 2 fellowships, 9 research assistantships, 13 teaching assistantships were awarded. Financial award applicants required to submit FAFSA.
Salome Raheim, Director, 319-335-1250.

■ UNIVERSITY OF KENTUCKY

Graduate School, College of Social Work, Program in Social Work, Lexington, KY 40506-0032

AWARDS MSW, PhD.

Faculty: 24 full-time (16 women).
Students: 202 full-time (166 women), 66 part-time (51 women); includes 25 minority (22 African Americans, 1 Asian American or Pacific Islander, 2 Hispanic Americans), 1 international. 192 applicants, 80% accepted. In 2001, 97 degrees awarded.
Degree requirements: For master's, comprehensive exam; for doctorate, thesis/dissertation, comprehensive exam.
Entrance requirements: For master's, GRE General Test, minimum undergraduate GPA of 2.5. *Application deadline:* For fall admission, 4/15. Applications are processed on a rolling basis. *Application fee:* $30 ($35 for international students).
Expenses: Tuition, state resident: full-time $4,075; part-time $213 per credit hour. Tuition, nonresident: full-time $11,295; part-time $614 per credit hour.
Financial support: In 2001–02, 1 fellowship, 13 research assistantships, 16 teaching assistantships were awarded. Career-related internships or fieldwork, institutionally sponsored loans, and unspecified assistantships also available. Support available to part-time students.
Faculty research: Aging, family and children, domestic violence, delinquency, health and mental health. *Total annual research expenditures:* $93,993.
Dr. David Royse, Director of Graduate Studies, 859-257-6659, *Fax:* 859-323-1030, *E-mail:* droyse@pop.uky.edu.
Application contact: Dr. Jeannine Blackwell, Associate Dean, 859-257-4905, *Fax:* 859-323-1928.

■ UNIVERSITY OF LOUISVILLE

Graduate School, Raymond A. Kent School of Social Work, Louisville, KY 40292-0001

AWARDS MSSW, PhD.

Faculty: 24 full-time (14 women), 29 part-time/adjunct (18 women).
Students: 215 full-time (171 women), 123 part-time (82 women); includes 45 minority (36 African Americans, 2 Asian Americans or Pacific Islanders, 2 Hispanic Americans, 5 Native Americans), 4 international. Average age 34. In 2001, 139 master's, 1 doctorate awarded.
Degree requirements: For doctorate, thesis/dissertation.
Entrance requirements: For doctorate, GRE General Test, interview, sample of written work. *Application deadline:* Applications are processed on a rolling basis. *Application fee:* $25.
Expenses: Tuition, state resident: full-time $4,134. Tuition, nonresident: full-time $11,486.
Financial support: Research assistantships with full tuition reimbursements, tuition waivers (full) available. Financial award application deadline: 4/1.
Dr. Terry Singer, Dean, 502-852-6402, *Fax:* 502-852-0422, *E-mail:* terry.singer@louisville.edu.

■ UNIVERSITY OF MAINE

Graduate School, College of Business, Public Policy and Health, School of Social Work, Orono, ME 04469

AWARDS MSW.

Faculty: 8 full-time.
Students: 84 full-time (70 women), 4 part-time (3 women); includes 6 minority (3 African Americans, 1 Hispanic American, 2 Native Americans), 2 international. 72 applicants, 75% accepted, 44 enrolled. In 2001, 26 degrees awarded.
Entrance requirements: For master's, GRE General Test, TOEFL. *Application deadline:* For fall admission, 2/1 (priority date). Applications are processed on a rolling basis. *Application fee:* $50. Electronic applications accepted.
Expenses: Tuition, state resident: full-time $3,780; part-time $210 per credit hour. Tuition, nonresident: full-time $10,782; part-time $599 per credit hour. Required fees: $9.50 per credit hour. $32 per semester. Tuition and fees vary according to reciprocity agreements.
Financial support: Application deadline: 3/1.
Dr. Gail Werrbach, Director, 207-581-2387, *Fax:* 207-581-2396.
Application contact: Scott G. Delcourt, Director of the Graduate School, 207-581-3218, *Fax:* 207-581-3232, *E-mail:* graduate@maine.edu. *Web site:* http://www.umaine.edu/graduate/

■ UNIVERSITY OF MARYLAND

Graduate School, Graduate Programs in Social Work, Doctoral Program in Social Work, Baltimore, MD 21201-1627

AWARDS PhD. Part-time programs available.

Faculty: 45 full-time (23 women), 59 part-time/adjunct (35 women).
Students: 35 full-time (29 women), 10 part-time (8 women); includes 15 minority (9 African Americans, 4 Asian Americans or Pacific Islanders, 1 Hispanic American, 1 Native American). Average age 40. 21 applicants, 67% accepted. In 2001, 9 degrees awarded.
Degree requirements: For doctorate, thesis/dissertation.
Entrance requirements: For doctorate, GRE General Test, minimum GPA of 3.5, MSW. *Application deadline:* For fall admission, 2/1 (priority date). Applications are processed on a rolling basis. *Application fee:* $50.
Expenses: Tuition, state resident: part-time $281 per credit. Tuition, nonresident: part-time $503 per credit. Tuition and fees vary according to class time, course load, degree level and program.
Financial support: In 2001–02, 3 fellowships, 9 research assistantships, 4 teaching assistantships were awarded.
Faculty research: Breast cancer, child abuse, parental abduction, homelessness, elderly. *Total annual research expenditures:* $6 million.
Dr. Julianne S. Oktay, Director and Professor, 410-706-3831, *Fax:* 410-706-3448, *E-mail:* joktay@ssw.umaryland.edu.
Application contact: Tammy S. Fazenbaker, Administrative Assistant, 410-706-7960, *Fax:* 410-706-3448, *E-mail:* tderry@ssw.umaryland.edu. *Web site:* http://graduate.umaryland.edu/

Find an in-depth description at www.petersons.com/gradchannel.

■ UNIVERSITY OF MARYLAND

Graduate School, Graduate Programs in Social Work, Master's Program in Social Work, Baltimore, MD 21201-1627

AWARDS MSW, JD/MSW, MBA/MSW, MSW/MA, MSW/MPH.

Faculty: 45 full-time (23 women), 59 part-time/adjunct (35 women).
Students: 687 full-time (577 women), 187 part-time (155 women); includes 289 minority (252 African Americans, 3 Asian Americans or Pacific Islanders, 30 Hispanic Americans, 4 Native Americans), 3 international. Average age 29. 705 applicants, 86% accepted. In 2001, 360 degrees awarded. *Median time to degree:* Master's–2 years full-time, 3.5 years part-time.
Entrance requirements: For master's, minimum GPA of 3.0. *Application deadline:* For fall admission, 2/15 (priority date); for spring admission, 12/1 (priority date). Applications are processed on a rolling basis. *Application fee:* $55. Electronic applications accepted.
Expenses: Tuition, state resident: part-time $281 per credit. Tuition, nonresident: part-time $503 per credit. Tuition and fees vary according to class time, course load, degree level and program.
Financial support: In 2001–02, 15 fellowships (averaging $750 per year) were awarded; career-related internships or fieldwork, Federal Work-Study, and scholarships/grants also available. Support available to part-time students. Financial award application deadline: 3/15; financial award applicants required to submit FAFSA.
Faculty research: Child welfare, occupational social work, homelessness, community organization, multiculturalism. *Total annual research expenditures:* $6 million.
Dr. Geoffrey Greif, Associate Dean and Professor, 410-706-3567, *Fax:* 410-706-6046.
Application contact: Marianne Wood, Assistant Dean for Admissions, 410-706-7922, *Fax:* 410-706-6046, *E-mail:* mwood@ssw.umaryland.edu. *Web site:* http://ssw.umaryland.edu/

Find an in-depth description at www.petersons.com/gradchannel.

■ UNIVERSITY OF MICHIGAN

School of Social Work, Ann Arbor, MI 48109

AWARDS MSW, PhD, MSW/MBA, MSW/MPH, MSW/MPP, MSW/MUP. PhD offered through the Horace H. Rackham School of Graduate Studies.

Faculty: 53 full-time (26 women), 58 part-time/adjunct (37 women).
Students: 568 full-time (502 women), 18 part-time (15 women); includes 128 minority (72 African Americans, 29 Asian Americans or Pacific Islanders, 22 Hispanic Americans, 5 Native Americans), 22 international. Average age 29. 698 applicants, 84% accepted, 340 enrolled. In 2001, 279 degrees awarded.
Degree requirements: For doctorate, oral defense of dissertation, preliminary exam. *Median time to degree:* Master's–2 years full-time.
Entrance requirements: For doctorate, GRE General Test. *Application deadline:* For fall admission, 3/1 (priority date). Applications are processed on a rolling basis. *Application fee:* $50. Electronic applications accepted.
Expenses: Contact institution.
Financial support: Career-related internships or fieldwork, Federal Work-Study, scholarships/grants, and traineeships available. Financial award applicants required to submit FAFSA. *Total annual research expenditures:* $4.4 million.
Paula Allen-Meares, Dean, 734-764-5347, *Fax:* 734-764-9954, *E-mail:* pameares@umich.edu.
Application contact: Timothy Colenback, Assistant Dean of Student Services, 734-764-3309, *Fax:* 734-936-1961, *E-mail:* timot@umich.edu. *Web site:* http://www.ssw.umich.edu/

Find an in-depth description at www.petersons.com/gradchannel.

■ UNIVERSITY OF MINNESOTA, DULUTH

Graduate School, College of Education and Human Service Professions, Department of Social Work, Duluth, MN 55812-2496

AWARDS MSW. Part-time and evening/weekend programs available. Postbaccalaureate distance learning degree programs offered (minimal on-campus study).

Faculty: 9 full-time (7 women), 4 part-time/adjunct (2 women).
Students: 61 full-time (53 women), 21 part-time (19 women); includes 14 minority (2 Asian Americans or Pacific Islanders, 12 Native Americans), 3 international. Average age 35. 77 applicants, 82% accepted. In 2001, 32 degrees awarded.
Entrance requirements: For master's, minimum GPA of 3.0. *Application deadline:* For fall admission, 1/15 (priority date). *Application fee:* $50 ($55 for international students).
Expenses: Tuition, state resident: full-time $2,932; part-time $489 per credit. Tuition, nonresident: full-time $5,758; part-time $960 per credit. Tuition and fees vary according to course load.
Financial support: In 2001–02, 27 students received support, including 17 fellowships with partial tuition reimbursements available (averaging $2,195 per year), 5 research assistantships with partial tuition reimbursements available (averaging $6,500 per year), 5 teaching assistantships with partial tuition reimbursements available (averaging $6,500 per year); career-related internships or fieldwork, Federal Work-Study, institutionally sponsored loans, scholarships/grants, and traineeships also available. Support available to part-time students. Financial award application deadline: 1/15.
Faculty research: Domestic abuse, substance abuse, minority health, child welfare. *Total annual research expenditures:* $100,000.
Dr. Melanie Shepard, Director, 218-726-8859, *Fax:* 218-726-7185, *E-mail:* mshepard@d.umn.edu.
Application contact: Sandy Maturi, Admissions Secretary, 218-726-8497, *Fax:* 218-726-7185, *E-mail:* sw@d.umn.edu. *Web site:* http://www.d.umn.edu/~sw/

■ UNIVERSITY OF MINNESOTA, TWIN CITIES CAMPUS

Graduate School, College of Human Ecology, School of Social Work, Minneapolis, MN 55455-0213

AWARDS MSW, PhD, MSW/MPH, MSW/MPP. Part-time and evening/weekend programs available. Postbaccalaureate distance learning degree programs offered.

Degree requirements: For doctorate, thesis/dissertation.
Entrance requirements: For master's, minimum GPA of 3.0, 1 year of work experience; for doctorate, GRE, minimum GPA of 3.0, MSW.
Expenses: Tuition, state resident: full-time $2,932; part-time $489 per credit. Tuition, nonresident: full-time $5,758; part-time $960 per credit. Part-time tuition and fees vary according to course load, program and reciprocity agreements.
Faculty research: Child welfare, child sexual abuse, domestic violence, long-term care, community health.

■ UNIVERSITY OF MISSOURI–COLUMBIA

Graduate School, School of Social Work, Columbia, MO 65211

AWARDS MSW. Part-time programs available.

Faculty: 17 full-time (11 women).
Students: 92 full-time (82 women), 73 part-time (61 women); includes 15 minority (8 African Americans, 1 Asian American or Pacific Islander, 5 Hispanic Americans, 1 Native American), 2 international. 61 applicants, 48% accepted. In 2001, 57 degrees awarded.
Entrance requirements: For master's, GRE General Test, minimum GPA of 3.0. *Application deadline:* For fall admission, 1/15 (priority date). Applications are processed on a rolling basis. *Application fee:* $25 ($50 for international students).
Expenses: Tuition, state resident: part-time $179 per credit hour. Tuition, nonresident: part-time $539 per credit

hour. Required fees: $122 per semester. Tuition and fees vary according to program.
Financial support: Fellowships, research assistantships, teaching assistantships, institutionally sponsored loans available.
Dr. Michael Kelly, Director of Graduate Studies, 573-882-0922, *E-mail:* kellym@missouri.edu. *Web site:* http://web.missouri.edu/~sswmain

■ UNIVERSITY OF MISSOURI–KANSAS CITY

College of Arts and Sciences, Department of Social Work, Kansas City, MO 64110-2499

AWARDS MS.

Faculty: 5 full-time (3 women), 1 (woman) part-time/adjunct.
Students: 45 full-time (37 women), 47 part-time (38 women). In 2001, 11 degrees awarded.
Application deadline: For fall admission, 4/1 (priority date); for spring admission, 9/1 (priority date). Applications are processed on a rolling basis. *Application fee:* $25.
Expenses: Tuition, state resident: part-time $233 per credit hour. Tuition, nonresident: part-time $623 per credit hour. Tuition and fees vary according to course load.
Financial support: In 2001–02, 37 students received support, including 1 research assistantship with partial tuition reimbursement available (averaging $7,600 per year), 1 teaching assistantship with partial tuition reimbursement available (averaging $7,600 per year); career-related internships or fieldwork and institutionally sponsored loans also available.
Faculty research: Case management, women and substance abuse, children and families, bilingual clinical practice, African American urban youth.
Dr. Kathylene Sislca, Chair, 816-235-1025, *Fax:* 816-235-5193.

■ UNIVERSITY OF MISSOURI–ST. LOUIS

Graduate School, College of Arts and Sciences, Department of Social Work, St. Louis, MO 63121-4499

AWARDS MSW.

Faculty: 7.
Students: 45 full-time (40 women), 56 part-time (51 women); includes 27 minority (24 African Americans, 2 Asian Americans or Pacific Islanders, 1 Hispanic American). In 2001, 15 degrees awarded.
Application deadline: For fall admission, 3/15. *Application fee:* $25 ($40 for international students).
Expenses: Tuition, state resident: part-time $231 per credit hour. Tuition, nonresident: part-time $621 per credit hour.
Financial support: In 2001–02, 8 teaching assistantships with full tuition reimbursements (averaging $9,000 per year) were awarded *Total annual research expenditures:* $567,945.
Dr. Lois Pierce, Chairperson, 314-516-6364, *Fax:* 314-516-5816, *E-mail:* socialwork@umsl.edu.
Application contact: Graduate Admissions, 314-516-5458, *Fax:* 314-516-5310, *E-mail:* gradadm@umsl.edu. *Web site:* http://www.umsl.edu/~socialwk/

■ UNIVERSITY OF MISSOURI–ST. LOUIS

Graduate School, Program in Gerontology, St. Louis, MO 63121-4499

AWARDS Gerontological social work (Certificate); gerontology (MS, Certificate). Part-time and evening/weekend programs available.

Faculty: 11.
Students: 2 full-time (both women), 7 part-time (5 women); includes 2 minority (1 African American, 1 Asian American or Pacific Islander). In 2001, 8 degrees awarded.
Application deadline: For fall admission, 7/1 (priority date); for spring admission, 12/1 (priority date). Applications are processed on a rolling basis. *Application fee:* $25 ($40 for international students). Electronic applications accepted.
Expenses: Tuition, state resident: part-time $231 per credit hour. Tuition, nonresident: part-time $621 per credit hour.
Financial support: In 2001–02, 1 research assistantship with full tuition reimbursement (averaging $15,000 per year) was awarded; career-related internships or fieldwork and Federal Work-Study also available.
Faculty research: Health care policy, social support and stress, retirement policy health behavior, ethnic differences in aging. *Total annual research expenditures:* $896,161.
Dr. Robert Calsyn, Director, 314-516-5421.
Application contact: Jeff Headtke, Graduate Admissions, 314-516-6928, *Fax:* 314-516-5310, *E-mail:* gradadm@umsl.edu.

■ UNIVERSITY OF NEBRASKA AT OMAHA

Graduate Studies and Research, College of Public Affairs and Community Service, School of Social Work, Omaha, NE 68182

AWARDS MSW.

Faculty: 10 full-time (6 women).
Students: 90 full-time (83 women), 94 part-time (85 women); includes 12 minority (7 African Americans, 4 Hispanic Americans, 1 Native American), 2 international. Average age 30. 97 applicants, 71% accepted, 67 enrolled. In 2001, 50 degrees awarded.
Degree requirements: For master's, comprehensive exam.
Entrance requirements: For master's, GRE General Test or MAT, minimum GPA of 3.0. *Application deadline:* For fall admission, 3/1; for spring admission, 10/1 (priority date). Applications are processed on a rolling basis. *Application fee:* $35. Electronic applications accepted.
Expenses: Tuition, state resident: part-time $116 per credit hour. Tuition, nonresident: part-time $291 per credit hour. Required fees: $13 per credit hour. $4 per semester. One-time fee: $52 part-time.
Financial support: In 2001–02, 125 students received support, including 4 research assistantships; fellowships, career-related internships or fieldwork, Federal Work-Study, institutionally sponsored loans, scholarships/grants, tuition waivers (full), and unspecified assistantships also available. Support available to part-time students. Financial award application deadline: 3/1; financial award applicants required to submit FAFSA.
Dr. Sunny Andrews, Director, 402-554-2791.

■ UNIVERSITY OF NEVADA, LAS VEGAS

Graduate College, Greenspun College of Urban Affairs, School of Social Work, Las Vegas, NV 89154-9900

AWARDS MSW.

Faculty: 18 full-time (11 women).
Students: 84 full-time (65 women), 39 part-time (35 women); includes 29 minority (14 African Americans, 3 Asian Americans or Pacific Islanders, 10 Hispanic Americans, 2 Native Americans). 37 applicants, 81% accepted, 21 enrolled. In 2001, 44 degrees awarded.
Degree requirements: For master's, thesis optional. *Median time to degree:* Master's–2 years full-time, 3.5 years part-time.
Entrance requirements: For master's, GRE General Test, minimum GPA of 3.0 during previous 2 years, 2.75 overall, bachelor's degree in social work. *Application deadline:* For fall admission, 2/1. *Application fee:* $40 ($55 for international students).
Expenses: Tuition, state resident: full-time $1,926; part-time $107 per credit. Tuition, nonresident: full-time $9,376; part-time $220 per credit. Tuition and fees vary according to course load.
Financial support: In 2001–02, 3 teaching assistantships with partial tuition reimbursements (averaging $10,000 per year) were awarded; research assistantships Financial award application deadline: 3/1.
Dr. Esther Langston, Director, 702-895-3311.
Application contact: Graduate College Admissions Evaluator, 702-895-3320, *Fax:*

University of Nevada, Las Vegas (continued)
702-895-4180, *E-mail:* gradcollege@ccmail.nevada.edu. *Web site:* http://www.unlv.edu/Colleges/Urban/Social_Work/

■ UNIVERSITY OF NEVADA, RENO

Graduate School, College of Human and Community Sciences, School of Social Work, Reno, NV 89557

AWARDS MSW. Part-time and evening/weekend programs available.

Faculty: 12.
Students: 37 full-time (27 women); includes 3 minority (2 African Americans, 1 Native American). Average age 35. In 2001, 23 degrees awarded.
Degree requirements: For master's, thesis optional.
Entrance requirements: For master's, GRE General Test, TOEFL, minimum GPA of 2.75. *Application deadline:* For fall admission, 2/1 (priority date). Applications are processed on a rolling basis. *Application fee:* $40.
Expenses: Tuition, state resident: full-time $2,067; part-time $108 per credit. Tuition, nonresident: full-time $9,282; part-time $109 per credit. Required fees: $57 per semester. Tuition and fees vary according to course load.
Financial support: In 2001–02, 7 research assistantships were awarded; teaching assistantships, institutionally sponsored loans and tuition waivers (full) also available. Financial award application deadline: 3/1.
Faculty research: Policy practice, poverty, women's issues, race and diversity, vulnerable family.
Dr. Jill Jones, Graduate Program Director, 775-784-6542.

■ UNIVERSITY OF NEW ENGLAND

College of Health Professions, Program in Social Work, Biddeford, ME 04005-9526

AWARDS MSW. Part-time programs available.

Faculty: 13 full-time (10 women), 8 part-time/adjunct (5 women).
Students: 110 full-time (95 women), 77 part-time (68 women); includes 5 minority (3 African Americans, 2 Hispanic Americans). Average age 35. 125 applicants, 92% accepted, 76 enrolled. In 2001, 63 degrees awarded.
Application deadline: For fall admission, 1/15. Applications are processed on a rolling basis. *Application fee:* $40.
Expenses: Tuition: Full-time $13,440; part-time $420 per credit. Required fees: $240.
Financial support: Career-related internships or fieldwork and Federal Work-Study available. Support available to part-time students. Financial award application deadline: 5/1; financial award applicants required to submit FAFSA.
Faculty research: Domestic violence, solution focused practice, empowerment models.
Dr. JoAnne Thompson, Director, 207-283-0171 Ext. 2512, *Fax:* 207-294-5923, *E-mail:* jthompson@une.edu.
Application contact: Patricia T. Cribby, Dean of Admissions and Enrollment Management, 207-283-0171 Ext. 2297, *Fax:* 207-294-5900, *E-mail:* jshea@une.edu.

Find an in-depth description at www.petersons.com/gradchannel.

■ UNIVERSITY OF NEW HAMPSHIRE

Graduate School, School of Health and Human Services, Department of Social Work, Durham, NH 03824

AWARDS MSW. Part-time programs available.

Faculty: 10 full-time.
Students: 94 full-time (82 women), 49 part-time (43 women); includes 3 minority (1 Hispanic American, 2 Native Americans), 1 international. Average age 37. 136 applicants, 80% accepted, 58 enrolled. In 2001, 42 degrees awarded.
Application deadline: For fall admission, 2/1. Applications are processed on a rolling basis. *Application fee:* $50. Electronic applications accepted.
Expenses: Tuition, state resident: full-time $6,300; part-time $350 per credit. Tuition, nonresident: full-time $15,720; part-time $643 per credit. Required fees: $560; $280 per term. One-time fee: $15 part-time. Tuition and fees vary according to course load.
Financial support: In 2001–02, 3 fellowships, 7 teaching assistantships were awarded. Research assistantships, career-related internships or fieldwork, Federal Work-Study, and scholarships/grants also available. Support available to part-time students. Financial award application deadline: 2/15.
Dr. Robert Jolley, Chairperson, 603-862-1799, *E-mail:* rej@cisunix.unh.edu.
Application contact: Dr. Sharon Zunz, Coordinator, 603-862-0274. *Web site:* http://www.unh.edu/social-work/

■ THE UNIVERSITY OF NORTH CAROLINA AT CHAPEL HILL

Graduate School, School of Social Work, Chapel Hill, NC 27599

AWARDS MSW, PhD, JD/MSW, MPA/MSW, MSPH/MSW. Part-time programs available.

Faculty: 32 full-time (17 women), 25 part-time/adjunct (15 women).
Students: 246 full-time (203 women), 108 part-time (97 women); includes 64 minority (39 African Americans, 8 Asian Americans or Pacific Islanders, 12 Hispanic Americans, 5 Native Americans), 4 international. Average age 30. 437 applicants, 51% accepted, 152 enrolled. In 2001, 106 master's, 2 doctorates awarded. Terminal master's awarded for partial completion of doctoral program.
Degree requirements: For doctorate, thesis/dissertation, qualifying exam. *Median time to degree:* Master's–2 years full-time, 3 years part-time; doctorate–2 years full-time.
Entrance requirements: For master's and doctorate, GRE General Test, minimum GPA of 3.0. *Application deadline:* For fall admission, 1/1 (priority date). Applications are processed on a rolling basis. *Application fee:* $60. Electronic applications accepted.
Expenses: Tuition, state resident: full-time $2,864. Tuition, nonresident: full-time $12,030.
Financial support: In 2001–02, 316 students received support, including 3 fellowships with full tuition reimbursements available (averaging $7,500 per year), 40 research assistantships with full tuition reimbursements available (averaging $9,000 per year); teaching assistantships with full tuition reimbursements available, career-related internships or fieldwork, Federal Work-Study, institutionally sponsored loans, scholarships/grants, and unspecified assistantships also available. Support available to part-time students. Financial award application deadline: 2/15; financial award applicants required to submit FAFSA.
Faculty research: School success, risk and resiliency, welfare reform, aging, substance abuse. *Total annual research expenditures:* $10.3 million.
Dr. Jack Richman, Interim Dean, 919-962-5650, *Fax:* 919-962-0890, *E-mail:* jrichman@email.unc.edu.
Application contact: Prof. Dorothy N. Gamble, Assistant Dean for Student Services, 919-962-6446, *Fax:* 919-843-8562, *E-mail:* dee_gamble@unc.edu. *Web site:* http://www.ssw.unc.edu/

■ THE UNIVERSITY OF NORTH CAROLINA AT CHARLOTTE

Graduate School, College of Arts and Sciences, Department of Social Work, Charlotte, NC 28223-0001

AWARDS MSW. Part-time programs available.

Faculty: 6 full-time (3 women).
Students: 43 full-time (39 women), 11 part-time (9 women); includes 10 minority (8 African Americans, 2 Hispanic Americans). Average age 31. 53 applicants, 66% accepted, 30 enrolled.
Application deadline: For fall admission, 7/15; for spring admission, 11/15. Applications are processed on a rolling basis. *Application fee:* $35. Electronic applications accepted.
Expenses: Tuition, state resident: full-time $1,483; part-time $371 per year. Tuition, nonresident: full-time $9,850; part-time

$2,463 per year. Required fees: $1,043; $277 per year. Tuition and fees vary according to course load.
Financial support: Fellowships, research assistantships, teaching assistantships, career-related internships or fieldwork, Federal Work-Study, institutionally sponsored loans, scholarships/grants, and unspecified assistantships available. Support available to part-time students. Financial award application deadline: 4/1; financial award applicants required to submit FAFSA.
Faculty research: Social work practice with lesbian and gay youth, aging, welfare reform; non-custodial fathers, grandparents as caregivers of grandchildren.
Dr. Philip R. Popple, Chair, 704-687-4076, *Fax:* 704-687-2343, *E-mail:* prpopple@email.uncc.edu.
Application contact: Kathy Barringer, Director of Graduate Admissions, 704-687-3366, *Fax:* 704-687-3279, *E-mail:* gradadm@email.uncc.edu. *Web site:* http://www.uncc.edu/gradmiss/

■ THE UNIVERSITY OF NORTH CAROLINA AT GREENSBORO

Graduate School, School of Human Environmental Sciences, Department of Social Work, Greensboro, NC 27412-5001

AWARDS MSW.

Faculty: 8 full-time (6 women).
Students: 67 full-time (61 women); includes 25 African Americans, 1 Asian American or Pacific Islander, 1 Hispanic American. 105 applicants, 51% accepted, 35 enrolled. In 2001, 30 degrees awarded.
Entrance requirements: For master's, GRE General Test, TOEFL. *Application deadline:* For fall admission, 3/22. *Application fee:* $35.
Expenses: Tuition, state resident: part-time $344 per course. Tuition, nonresident: part-time $2,457 per course.
Financial support: In 2001–02, 13 research assistantships with full tuition reimbursements (averaging $1,962 per year) were awarded; fellowships with full tuition reimbursements, teaching assistantships with full tuition reimbursements, career-related internships or fieldwork, Federal Work-Study, scholarships/grants, and traineeships also available. Support available to part-time students.
Dr. John Rife, Chair, 336-334-4098, *Fax:* 336-334-5210, *E-mail:* jcrife@uncg.edu.
Application contact: Dr. James Lynch, Director of Graduate Recruitment and Information Services, 336-334-4881, *Fax:* 336-334-4424. *Web site:* http://www.uncg.edu/swk/

■ UNIVERSITY OF NORTH DAKOTA

Graduate School, College of Education and Human Development, School of Social Work, Grand Forks, ND 58202

AWARDS MSW.

Faculty: 13 full-time (6 women).
Students: 8 full-time (all women), 37 part-time (31 women). 32 applicants, 59% accepted, 8 enrolled. In 2001, 42 degrees awarded.
Degree requirements: For master's, thesis or alternative, comprehensive final examination.
Entrance requirements: For master's, TOEFL, minimum GPA of 3.0. *Application deadline:* For fall admission, 1/10. *Application fee:* $30.
Expenses: Tuition, state resident: full-time $3,298. Tuition, nonresident: full-time $7,998.
Financial support: In 2001–02, 30 teaching assistantships with full tuition reimbursements (averaging $8,775 per year) were awarded; fellowships, research assistantships, Federal Work-Study, institutionally sponsored loans, scholarships/grants, tuition waivers (full and partial), and unspecified assistantships also available. Support available to part-time students. Financial award application deadline: 3/15; financial award applicants required to submit FAFSA.
Faculty research: Mental health, gerontology, chemical abuse, children and families.
Dr. Ralph E. Woehle, Director, 701-777-2669, *Fax:* 701-777-4257, *E-mail:* ralph_woehle@mail.und.nodak.edu. *Web site:* http://www.und.edu/dept/socialwo/mainpage.htm

■ UNIVERSITY OF NORTHERN IOWA

Graduate College, College of Social and Behavioral Sciences, Department of Social Work, Cedar Falls, IA 50614

AWARDS MSW.

Students: 35 full-time (33 women); includes 3 minority (all African Americans), 1 international. 21 applicants, 71% accepted.
Application deadline: For fall admission, 8/1 (priority date). *Application fee:* $20 ($50 for international students).
Expenses: Tuition, state resident: full-time $3,704; part-time $206 per credit hour. Tuition, nonresident: full-time $9,122; part-time $501 per credit hour. Required fees: $324; $108 per semester. Part-time tuition and fees vary according to course load.
Financial support: Application deadline: 3/1.
Dr. Thomas W. Keefe, III, Head, 319-273-6249, *Fax:* 319-273-2738, *E-mail:* thomas.keefe@uni.edu. *Web site:* http://www.uni.edu/socialwork/

■ UNIVERSITY OF OKLAHOMA

Graduate College, College of Arts and Sciences, School of Social Work, Norman, OK 73019-0390

AWARDS MSW.

Faculty: 16 full-time (6 women), 4 part-time/adjunct (2 women).
Students: 125 full-time (108 women), 76 part-time (62 women); includes 60 minority (18 African Americans, 4 Asian Americans or Pacific Islanders, 4 Hispanic Americans, 34 Native Americans), 2 international. 113 applicants, 95% accepted, 95 enrolled. In 2001, 82 degrees awarded.
Entrance requirements: For master's, GRE, TOEFL. *Application deadline:* For fall admission, 3/1 (priority date). *Application fee:* $25 ($50 for international students).
Expenses: Tuition, state resident: full-time $2,208; part-time $92 per credit hour. Tuition, nonresident: part-time $297 per credit hour. Tuition and fees vary according to course level, course load and program.
Financial support: In 2001–02, 114 students received support, including 7 research assistantships with partial tuition reimbursements available (averaging $8,586 per year), 8 teaching assistantships with partial tuition reimbursements available (averaging $8,094 per year); career-related internships or fieldwork, scholarships/grants, and tuition waivers (partial) also available. Support available to part-time students. Financial award application deadline: 3/1; financial award applicants required to submit FAFSA.
Faculty research: Child welfare issues, social policy issues, public health, empowerment practice. *Total annual research expenditures:* $2 million.
Roosevelt Wright, Director, 405-325-2821, *Fax:* 405-325-7072, *E-mail:* roosevelt.wright-1@ou.edu.
Application contact: James Rosenthal, Graduate Coordinator, 405-325-1401, *Fax:* 405-325-7072, *E-mail:* jimar@ou.edu.

■ UNIVERSITY OF PENNSYLVANIA

School of Social Work, Graduate Group on Social Welfare, Philadelphia, PA 19104

AWARDS PhD.

Faculty: 29 full-time (12 women).
Students: 39 full-time (31 women), 4 part-time (all women). Average age 38. 48 applicants, 21% accepted.
Degree requirements: For doctorate, thesis/dissertation.
Entrance requirements: For doctorate, GRE General Test, TOEFL, MSW or master's degree in related field. *Application*

University of Pennsylvania (continued)

deadline: For fall admission, 2/1. Applications are processed on a rolling basis. *Application fee:* $65. Electronic applications accepted.
Expenses: Tuition: Part-time $12,875 per semester.
Financial support: In 2001–02, 23 students received support, including 2 fellowships with full tuition reimbursements available (averaging $12,500 per year), 22 research assistantships with full tuition reimbursements available (averaging $12,500 per year); teaching assistantships, career-related internships or fieldwork and institutionally sponsored loans also available. Financial award application deadline: 2/1; financial award applicants required to submit FAFSA.
Faculty research: Mental health, child welfare, organizational behavior, urban poverty, comparative social welfare.
Dr. Larry D. Icard, Director Doctoral Program, 215-573-7503, *Fax:* 215-573-2099, *E-mail:* licard@ssw.upenn.edu.
Application contact: Renee Joran-Barron, Information Contact, 215-898-5530, *Fax:* 215-573-2099. *Web site:* http://www.ssw.upenn.edu/

Find an in-depth description at www.petersons.com/gradchannel.

■ UNIVERSITY OF PENNSYLVANIA

School of Social Work, Program in Social Work, Philadelphia, PA 19104

AWARDS MSW, JD/MSW, MSW/Certificate, MSW/MBA, MSW/MCP, MSW/MS Ed, MSW/PhD. MSW/Certificate (Lutheran social ministry) offered jointly with Lutheran Theological Seminary at Philadelphia; MSW/Certificate (Catholic social ministry) offered jointly with St. Charles Borromeo Seminary; MSW/Certificate (Jewish communal services) offered jointly with Gratz College.

Degree requirements: For master's, fieldwork.
Entrance requirements: For master's, TOEFL.
Expenses: Tuition: Part-time $12,875 per semester.

Find an in-depth description at www.petersons.com/gradchannel.

■ UNIVERSITY OF PITTSBURGH

School of Social Work, Program in Social Work, Pittsburgh, PA 15260

AWARDS Gerontology (Certificate); social work (MSW, PhD). Part-time programs available. Postbaccalaureate distance learning degree programs offered (no on-campus study).

Faculty: 20 full-time (11 women), 32 part-time/adjunct (23 women).
Students: 350 full-time (300 women), 228 part-time (189 women); includes 83 minority (81 African Americans, 1 Hispanic American, 1 Native American), 19 international. Average age 31. 415 applicants, 54% accepted, 218 enrolled. In 2001, 171 master's, 4 doctorates awarded.
Degree requirements: For master's, practicum; for doctorate, thesis/dissertation, comprehensive exam, registration. *Median time to degree:* Master's–2 years full-time, 3.75 years part-time; doctorate–4 years full-time, 8 years part-time.
Entrance requirements: For master's, minimum QPA of 3.0, previous course work in descriptive statistics and human biology; for doctorate, MSW or related degree, previous course work in statistics. *Application deadline:* For fall admission, 3/31. Applications are processed on a rolling basis. *Application fee:* $40.
Expenses: Tuition, state resident: full-time $9,410; part-time $385 per credit. Tuition, nonresident: full-time $19,376; part-time $797 per credit. Required fees: $480; $90 per term. Tuition and fees vary according to program.
Financial support: In 2001–02, 79 students received support, including 2 research assistantships with full tuition reimbursements available (averaging $9,780 per year), 3 teaching assistantships with full tuition reimbursements available (averaging $11,980 per year); career-related internships or fieldwork, institutionally sponsored loans, scholarships/grants, traineeships, and unspecified assistantships also available. Financial award application deadline: 6/1; financial award applicants required to submit FAFSA.
Faculty research: Child abuse and neglect, poverty race relations and community empowerment, family preservation, welfare reform, mental health services research. *Total annual research expenditures:* $4 million.
Application contact: Dr. Grady H. Roberts, Associate Dean of Admissions, 412-624-6346, *Fax:* 412-624-6323. *Web site:* http://www.pitt.edu/~pittssw/

■ UNIVERSITY OF PUERTO RICO, RÍO PIEDRAS

College of Social Sciences, Beatriz Lassalle Graduate School of Social Work, San Juan, PR 00931

AWARDS MSW.

Students: 129 full-time (111 women), 34 part-time (27 women); all minorities (all Hispanic Americans). 61 applicants, 100% accepted. In 2001, 38 degrees awarded.
Degree requirements: For master's, thesis, comprehensive exam.
Entrance requirements: For master's, PAEG, interview, minimum GPA of 3.0. *Application deadline:* For fall admission, 2/1. *Application fee:* $17.
Expenses: Tuition, state resident: full-time $1,200; part-time $70 per credit. Tuition, nonresident: full-time $3,500; part-time $219 per credit. Required fees: $70; $35 per semester.
Financial support: Fellowships, research assistantships, teaching assistantships, career-related internships or fieldwork, Federal Work-Study, institutionally sponsored loans, and tuition waivers (partial) available. Financial award application deadline: 5/31.
Faculty research: Social work in Puerto Rico, Cuba, and the Dominican Republic, migration, poverty in Puerto Rico.
Dr. Norma Rodriguez, Acting Chairperson, 787-764-0000 Ext. 4256, *Fax:* 787-763-3725.
Application contact: Gladys N. Hernández, Student Affairs Officer, 787-764-0000 Ext. 5831, *Fax:* 787-763-3725.

■ UNIVERSITY OF ST. THOMAS

Graduate Studies, Program in Social Work, St. Paul, MN 55105-1096

AWARDS MSW. Part-time and evening/weekend programs available.

Faculty: 12 full-time (9 women), 14 part-time/adjunct (9 women).
Students: 128 full-time (114 women), 74 part-time (70 women); includes 22 minority (12 African Americans, 3 Asian Americans or Pacific Islanders, 3 Hispanic Americans, 4 Native Americans), 1 international. Average age 32. 175 applicants, 69% accepted, 78 enrolled. In 2001, 68 degrees awarded.
Degree requirements: For master's, thesis, fieldwork.
Entrance requirements: For master's, previous course work in developmental psychology, human biology, and statistics/methods. *Application deadline:* For fall admission, 1/10. *Application fee:* $25.
Expenses: Contact institution.
Financial support: In 2001–02, 151 students received support, including 18 research assistantships (averaging $944 per year); fellowships, career-related internships or fieldwork, institutionally sponsored loans, and scholarships/grants also available. Support available to part-time students. Financial award application deadline: 4/1.
Faculty research: Clinical supervision, group work, spirituality and social work.
Dr. Barbara W. Shank, Dean and Professor, 651-962-5801, *Fax:* 651-962-5819, *E-mail:* bwshank@stthomas.edu.
Application contact: Jon Ruzek, Coordinator of Student Services, 651-962-5810, *Fax:* 651-962-5819, *E-mail:* msw@stthomas.edu. *Web site:* http://department.stthomas.edu/sws1/index.html

■ UNIVERSITY OF SOUTH CAROLINA

The Graduate School, College of Social Work, Columbia, SC 29208

AWARDS MSW, PhD, JD/MSW, MSW/MPA, MSW/MPH.

Faculty: 27 full-time (16 women), 26 part-time/adjunct (17 women).
Students: 320 full-time, 132 part-time; includes 177 minority (131 African Americans, 39 Asian Americans or Pacific Islanders, 5 Hispanic Americans, 2 Native Americans). Average age 34. 550 applicants, 38% accepted. In 2001, 245 master's, 4 doctorates awarded.
Degree requirements: For doctorate, thesis/dissertation.
Entrance requirements: For master's, minimum undergraduate GPA of 3.0. *Application deadline:* For fall admission, 3/1. *Application fee:* $35. Electronic applications accepted.
Expenses: Contact institution.
Financial support: In 2001–02, 174 students received support, including 2 fellowships with partial tuition reimbursements available, 117 research assistantships with partial tuition reimbursements available; teaching assistantships, career-related internships or fieldwork, Federal Work-Study, and institutionally sponsored loans also available. Financial award application deadline: 5/1.
Faculty research: Victimization, child abuse and neglect, families.
Dr. Frank B. Raymond, Dean, 803-777-4886, *Fax:* 803-777-3498.
Application contact: Dr. John T. Gandy, Associate Dean, 803-777-5190, *Fax:* 803-777-3498.

■ UNIVERSITY OF SOUTHERN CALIFORNIA

Graduate School, School of Social Work, Los Angeles, CA 90089

AWARDS MSW, PhD, JD/MSW, M Pl/MSW, MPA/MSW, MSW/MAJCS, MSW/MS.

Degree requirements: For doctorate, thesis/dissertation.
Entrance requirements: For doctorate, GRE General Test.
Expenses: Tuition: Full-time $25,060; part-time $844 per unit. Required fees: $473.

■ UNIVERSITY OF SOUTHERN INDIANA

Graduate Studies, School of Education and Human Services, Department of Social Work, Evansville, IN 47712-3590

AWARDS MSW. Part-time and evening/weekend programs available.

Faculty: 9 full-time (5 women), 2 part-time/adjunct (0 women).
Students: 57 full-time (53 women), 40 part-time (35 women); includes 8 minority (6 African Americans, 1 Asian American or Pacific Islander, 1 Hispanic American), 1 international. Average age 29. 70 applicants, 74% accepted, 50 enrolled. In 2001, 34 degrees awarded.
Entrance requirements: For master's, minimum GPA of 2.8. *Application deadline:* For fall admission, 1/12. *Application fee:* $25.
Expenses: Tuition, state resident: full-time $1,361; part-time $151 per hour. Tuition, nonresident: full-time $2,732; part-time $304 per hour. Required fees: $60; $23 per semester. Tuition and fees vary according to course load.
Financial support: In 2001–02, 65 students received support. Federal Work-Study, institutionally sponsored loans, scholarships/grants, tuition waivers (full and partial), and unspecified assistantships available. Financial award application deadline: 3/1; financial award applicants required to submit FAFSA.
Dr. David J. Westhuis, Director, 812-464-1843, *E-mail:* westhuis@usi.edu. *Web site:* http://www.usi.edu/

■ UNIVERSITY OF SOUTHERN MISSISSIPPI

Graduate School, College of Health and Human Sciences, School of Social Work, Hattiesburg, MS 39406

AWARDS MSW. Part-time programs available.

Faculty: 9 full-time (8 women).
Students: 107 full-time (94 women), 21 part-time (17 women); includes 42 minority (38 African Americans, 1 Asian American or Pacific Islander, 3 Hispanic Americans). Average age 31. 133 applicants, 46% accepted. In 2001, 27 degrees awarded.
Degree requirements: For master's, practicum.
Entrance requirements: For master's, GRE General Test, minimum GPA of 2.75. *Application deadline:* For fall admission, 4/1 (priority date). Applications are processed on a rolling basis. *Application fee:* $0 ($25 for international students). Electronic applications accepted.
Expenses: Tuition, state resident: full-time $3,416; part-time $190 per credit hour. Tuition, nonresident: full-time $7,932; part-time $441 per credit hour.
Financial support: In 2001–02, teaching assistantships (averaging $3,000 per year); career-related internships or fieldwork, Federal Work-Study, and scholarships/grants also available. Financial award application deadline: 3/15.
Faculty research: Delinquency prevention, risk and resiliency in youth, successful aging, women in social service management, social work and the law.
Dr. Michael Forster, Director, 601-266-4171, *E-mail:* michael.forster@usm.edu.

■ UNIVERSITY OF SOUTH FLORIDA

College of Graduate Studies, College of Arts and Sciences, School of Social Work, Tampa, FL 33620-9951

AWARDS MSW. Part-time and evening/weekend programs available.

Faculty: 20 full-time (14 women), 1 (woman) part-time/adjunct.
Students: 70 full-time (59 women), 56 part-time (47 women); includes 30 minority (20 African Americans, 2 Asian Americans or Pacific Islanders, 8 Hispanic Americans), 1 international. Average age 34. 96 applicants, 66% accepted, 44 enrolled.
Degree requirements: For master's, comprehensive exam.
Entrance requirements: For master's, GRE General Test, minimum GPA of 3.0 in last 60 hours. *Application deadline:* For fall admission, 2/15 (priority date). Applications are processed on a rolling basis. *Application fee:* $20. Electronic applications accepted.
Expenses: Tuition, state resident: part-time $166 per credit hour. Tuition, nonresident: part-time $573 per credit hour. Required fees: $17 per term.
Financial support: Fellowships, research assistantships with partial tuition reimbursements, Federal Work-Study and institutionally sponsored loans available. Support available to part-time students. Financial award applicants required to submit FAFSA.
Faculty research: Posttraumatic stress disorder, substance abuse among social work, breast cancer telephone support groups, social service organization change. *Total annual research expenditures:* $529,305.
Jean Amuso, Chairperson, 813-974-1362, *Fax:* 813-974-4675, *E-mail:* amuso@chuma1.cas.usf.edu.
Application contact: Aaron A. Smith, Graduate Chair, 813-974-1356, *Fax:* 813-974-4675, *E-mail:* asmith@chuma1.cas.usf.edu. *Web site:* http://www.cas.usf.edu/social_work/index.html

■ THE UNIVERSITY OF TENNESSEE

Graduate School, College of Social Work, Knoxville, TN 37996

AWARDS Clinical social work practice (MSSW); social welfare management and community practice (MSSW); social work (PhD). Part-time programs available.

Faculty: 33 full-time (19 women).
Students: 305 full-time (263 women), 110 part-time (94 women); includes 72 minority (61 African Americans, 4 Asian Americans or Pacific Islanders, 5 Hispanic Americans, 2 Native Americans), 6 international. 356 applicants, 50% accepted. In 2001, 220 master's, 1 doctorate awarded.
Degree requirements: For master's, thesis or alternative; for doctorate, thesis/dissertation.
Entrance requirements: For master's and doctorate, GRE General Test, TOEFL, minimum GPA of 2.7. *Application deadline:* For fall admission, 2/1 (priority date). Applications are processed on a rolling basis. *Application fee:* $35. Electronic applications accepted.

The University of Tennessee (continued)
Expenses: Tuition, state resident: full-time $4,280; part-time $233 per hour. Tuition, nonresident: full-time $12,066; part-time $666 per hour. Tuition and fees vary according to program.
Financial support: In 2001–02, 8 fellowships, 9 research assistantships were awarded. Teaching assistantships, career-related internships or fieldwork, Federal Work-Study, institutionally sponsored loans, and unspecified assistantships also available. Financial award application deadline: 2/1; financial award applicants required to submit FAFSA.
Dr. Karen Sowers, Dean, 865-974-3175, *Fax:* 865-974-4803, *E-mail:* kmsowers@utk.edu.

■ THE UNIVERSITY OF TEXAS AT ARLINGTON

Graduate School, School of Social Work, Arlington, TX 76019

AWARDS MSSW, PhD. Part-time and evening/weekend programs available. Postbaccalaureate distance learning degree programs offered (minimal on-campus study).

Faculty: 25 full-time (13 women), 1 part-time/adjunct (0 women).
Students: 298 full-time (250 women), 247 part-time (209 women); includes 140 minority (73 African Americans, 14 Asian Americans or Pacific Islanders, 50 Hispanic Americans, 3 Native Americans), 6 international. Average age 34. 227 applicants, 98% accepted, 173 enrolled. In 2001, 201 master's, 8 doctorates awarded.
Degree requirements: For master's, thesis optional; for doctorate, thesis/dissertation.
Entrance requirements: For master's, TOEFL; for doctorate, GRE General Test, TOEFL, minimum graduate GPA of 3.4. *Application deadline:* For fall admission, 3/15. *Application fee:* $25 ($50 for international students).
Expenses: Tuition, area resident: Full-time $2,268. Tuition, nonresident: full-time $6,264. Required fees: $839. Tuition and fees vary according to course load.
Financial support: In 2001–02, 355 students received support, including 14 fellowships (averaging $1,000 per year), 10 teaching assistantships (averaging $8,000 per year); research assistantships, career-related internships or fieldwork, Federal Work-Study, institutionally sponsored loans, scholarships/grants, and unspecified assistantships also available. Financial award application deadline: 6/1; financial award applicants required to submit FAFSA.
Dr. Santos H. Hernandez, Dean, 817-272-3181, *Fax:* 817-272-5229, *E-mail:* herns@uta.edu.
Application contact: Dr. Donald K. Granvold, Graduate Adviser, 817-272-3613, *Fax:* 817-272-5229, *E-mail:* granvold@uta.edu.

■ THE UNIVERSITY OF TEXAS AT AUSTIN

Graduate School, School of Social Work, Austin, TX 78712-1111

AWARDS MSSW, PhD. Part-time programs available.

Faculty: 36 full-time (25 women), 15 part-time/adjunct (11 women).
Students: 205 full-time, 70 part-time. Average age 28. 190 applicants, 92 enrolled. In 2001, 126 master's, 4 doctorates awarded.
Degree requirements: For doctorate, thesis/dissertation.
Entrance requirements: For master's and doctorate, GRE General Test. *Application deadline:* For fall admission, 2/1 (priority date); for spring admission, 10/1. Applications are processed on a rolling basis. *Application fee:* $50 ($75 for international students).
Expenses: Tuition, state resident: full-time $3,159. Tuition, nonresident: full-time $6,957. Tuition and fees vary according to program.
Financial support: Fellowships, career-related internships or fieldwork, Federal Work-Study, institutionally sponsored loans, scholarships/grants, and unspecified assistantships available. Financial award application deadline: 2/1; financial award applicants required to submit FAFSA.
Faculty research: Substance abuse, child welfare, gerontology, mental health, public policy.
Dr. Barbara White, Dean, 512-471-1937.
Application contact: David Springer, Graduate Advisor, 512-471-9819, *E-mail:* sswinfo@utxums.cc.utexas.edu. *Web site:* http://www.utexas.edu/depts/sswork/

■ THE UNIVERSITY OF TEXAS–PAN AMERICAN

College of Health Sciences and Human Services, Department of Social Work, Edinburg, TX 78539-2999

AWARDS MSSW.

Faculty: 6 full-time (1 woman).
Students: 28 full-time (24 women); includes 26 minority (all Hispanic Americans). Average age 33. 26 applicants, 62% accepted, 16 enrolled. In 2001, 12 degrees awarded. *Median time to degree:* Master's–1 year full-time.
Entrance requirements: For master's, TOEFL, minimum GPA of 3.0, experience in social work, previous coursework in statistics. *Application deadline:* For fall admission, 3/30 (priority date). Applications are processed on a rolling basis.
Expenses: Tuition, state resident: part-time $212 per semester hour. Tuition, nonresident: part-time $367 per semester hour.
Financial support: In 2001–02, 5 students received support, including 4 fellowships (averaging $5,000 per year), 2 teaching assistantships (averaging $3,500 per year); career-related internships or fieldwork, Federal Work-Study, institutionally sponsored loans, scholarships/grants, and tuition waivers (partial) also available. Financial award applicants required to submit FAFSA.
Faculty research: Social work supervision, social work educational resources, post-traumatic stress disorder, Mexican/Americans in higher education, US/Mexico border issues.
Dr. Bruce D. Friedman, Chair, 956-381-3575, *Fax:* 956-381-3516, *E-mail:* friedm52@panam.edu.
Application contact: Dr. Gary L. Villereal, Director, 956-381-2555, *Fax:* 956-381-3516, *E-mail:* villerealg@panam.edu.

■ UNIVERSITY OF UTAH

Graduate School, Graduate School of Social Work, Salt Lake City, UT 84112-1107

AWARDS MSW, PhD, MPA/PhD. Part-time programs available.

Faculty: 17 full-time (11 women), 11 part-time/adjunct (5 women).
Students: 327 full-time (222 women), 25 part-time (16 women); includes 50 minority (7 African Americans, 14 Asian Americans or Pacific Islanders, 18 Hispanic Americans, 11 Native Americans), 2 international. Average age 35. 402 applicants, 58% accepted. In 2001, 144 master's, 4 doctorates awarded.
Degree requirements: For master's, thesis or alternative; for doctorate, thesis/dissertation, comprehensive exam.
Entrance requirements: For master's, TOEFL, GRE General Test, MAT, or minimum GPA of 3.0; for doctorate, GRE, TOEFL. *Application deadline:* For fall admission, 12/1. *Application fee:* $50.
Expenses: Tuition, state resident: part-time $320 per semester hour. Tuition, nonresident: part-time $1,135 per semester hour. Required fees: $143 per semester hour. Tuition and fees vary according to course load, degree level and program.
Financial support: Fellowships with full and partial tuition reimbursements, research assistantships with full and partial tuition reimbursements, teaching assistantships with full and partial tuition reimbursements, Federal Work-Study and institutionally sponsored loans available. Support available to part-time students. Financial award application deadline: 2/15; financial award applicants required to submit FAFSA.
Faculty research: Clinical/direct practice, health and mental health, gerontology, child welfare, prevention of substance abuse.
Jannah H. Mather, Dean, 801-581-6194, *Fax:* 801-587-7956, *E-mail:* jmather@socwk.utah.edu.
Application contact: Jeanette R. Drews, Associate Dean, 801-581-8828, *Fax:* 801-587-7956, *E-mail:* jdrews@socwk.utah.edu.

■ UNIVERSITY OF VERMONT

Graduate College, College of Education and Social Services, Department of Social Work, Burlington, VT 05405

AWARDS MSW.

Entrance requirements: For master's, GRE General Test, TOEFL.
Expenses: Tuition, state resident: part-time $335 per credit. Tuition, nonresident: part-time $838 per credit.

Find an in-depth description at www.petersons.com/gradchannel.

■ UNIVERSITY OF WASHINGTON

Graduate School, School of Social Work, Seattle, WA 98195

AWARDS MSW, PhD, MPH/MSW. Evening/weekend programs available. Postbaccalaureate distance learning degree programs offered (minimal on-campus study).

Degree requirements: For master's, thesis optional; for doctorate, thesis/dissertation.
Entrance requirements: For master's, GRE General Test, TOEFL, minimum GPA of 3.0; for doctorate, master's degree, sample of scholarly work, minimum GPA of 3.0.
Expenses: Tuition, state resident: full-time $5,539. Tuition, nonresident: full-time $14,376. Required fees: $390. Tuition and fees vary according to course load and program.
Faculty research: Health and mental health; children, youth, and families; multicultural issues; reducing risk and enhancing protective factors in children; etrology of substance use. *Web site:* http://depts.u.washington.edu/~sswweb/

■ UNIVERSITY OF WASHINGTON

Graduate School, School of Social Work, Tacoma Campus, Seattle, WA 98195

AWARDS MSW. Part-time and evening/weekend programs available.

Faculty: 6 full-time (4 women), 2 part-time/adjunct (both women).
Students: Average age 35. 72 applicants, 49% accepted, 29 enrolled. In 2001, 28 degrees awarded.
Degree requirements: For master's, registration. *Median time to degree:* Master's–3 years part-time.
Entrance requirements: For master's, GRE General Test, minimum GPA of 3.0 for last 90 undergraduate credits. *Application deadline:* For fall admission, 3/1 (priority date). *Application fee:* $50. Electronic applications accepted.
Expenses: Tuition, state resident: full-time $5,539. Tuition, nonresident: full-time $14,376. Required fees: $390. Tuition and fees vary according to course load and program.
Financial support: In 2001–02, 30 students received support. Institutionally sponsored loans and scholarships/grants available. Support available to part-time students. Financial award application deadline: 2/28; financial award applicants required to submit FAFSA.
Faculty research: Aging, diversity, feminism, spirituality, medical social work.
Dr. Marcie M. Lazzari, Director, 253-692-5828, *Fax:* 253-692-5825, *E-mail:* mlazzari@u.washington.edu.
Application contact: Terri M. Simonsen, Adviser and Administrator, 253-692-5822, *Fax:* 253-692-5825. *Web site:* http://www.tacoma.washington.edu/social/

■ UNIVERSITY OF WISCONSIN–MADISON

Graduate School, College of Letters and Science, School of Social Work, Madison, WI 53706-1380

AWARDS Social welfare (PhD); social work (MSSW).

Faculty: 21 full-time (14 women), 11 part-time/adjunct (6 women).
Students: 225 full-time (205 women); includes 32 minority (11 African Americans, 8 Asian Americans or Pacific Islanders, 7 Hispanic Americans, 6 Native Americans), 12 international. Average age 29. 290 applicants, 80% accepted, 128 enrolled. In 2001, 83 master's, 3 doctorates awarded. Terminal master's awarded for partial completion of doctoral program.
Degree requirements: For doctorate, thesis/dissertation.
Entrance requirements: For master's, 3.0 GPA on last 60 credits; for doctorate, GRE General Test, 3.0 GPA on last 60 credits. *Application deadline:* For fall admission, 2/1. *Application fee:* $45. Electronic applications accepted.
Expenses: Contact institution.
Financial support: In 2001–02, 22 fellowships with full tuition reimbursements (averaging $9,500 per year), 34 research assistantships with full tuition reimbursements (averaging $10,000 per year), 8 teaching assistantships with full tuition reimbursements (averaging $7,500 per year) were awarded. Career-related internships or fieldwork, scholarships/grants, traineeships, and unspecified assistantships also available.
Faculty research: Poverty, caregiving, child welfare, developmental disabilities, mental health, severe mental illnesses, adolescence, family, social policy, child support.
Dr. Daniel R. Meyer, Director, 608-263-3561, *Fax:* 608-263-3836.
Application contact: William A. Heiss, Assistant to the Director, 608-263-3660, *Fax:* 608-263-3836, *E-mail:* waheiss@facstaff.wisc.edu. *Web site:* http://polyglot.lss.wisc.edu/socwork/intro.html

■ UNIVERSITY OF WISCONSIN–MILWAUKEE

Graduate School, School of Social Welfare, Program in Social Work, Milwaukee, WI 53201-0413

AWARDS MSW. Part-time programs available.

Faculty: 17 full-time (9 women).
Students: 134 full-time (122 women), 140 part-time (117 women); includes 41 minority (32 African Americans, 1 Asian American or Pacific Islander, 6 Hispanic Americans, 2 Native Americans), 1 international. 275 applicants, 66% accepted. In 2001, 140 degrees awarded.
Degree requirements: For master's, thesis or alternative.
Application deadline: For fall admission, 1/1 (priority date); for spring admission, 9/1. Applications are processed on a rolling basis. *Application fee:* $45 ($75 for international students).
Expenses: Tuition, state resident: full-time $6,180; part-time $535 per credit. Tuition, nonresident: full-time $19,482; part-time $1,366 per credit. Tuition and fees vary according to course load, program and reciprocity agreements.
Financial support: In 2001–02, 4 fellowships, 1 teaching assistantship were awarded. Research assistantships, career-related internships or fieldwork and unspecified assistantships also available. Support available to part-time students. Financial award application deadline: 4/15.
Joan Jones, Representative, 414-229-4852, *Fax:* 414-229-5311, *E-mail:* jmj2@uwm.edu. *Web site:* http://www.uwm.edu/Dept/SSW/sw/

■ UNIVERSITY OF WYOMING

Graduate School, College of Health Sciences, Division of Social Work, Laramie, WY 82071

AWARDS MSW.

Faculty: 9 full-time (4 women), 6 part-time/adjunct (3 women).
Students: 40 full-time (27 women), 7 part-time (4 women); includes 4 minority (1 Hispanic American, 3 Native Americans), 2 international. 49 applicants, 78% accepted. In 2001, 28 degrees awarded.
Degree requirements: For master's, thesis or alternative.
Entrance requirements: For master's, GRE General Test, minimum GPA of 3.0. *Application deadline:* For spring admission, 3/1 (priority date). Applications are processed on a rolling basis. *Application fee:* $40. Electronic applications accepted.
Expenses: Contact institution.
Financial support: In 2001–02, 17 research assistantships with partial tuition reimbursements were awarded; career-related internships or fieldwork, Federal Work-Study, institutionally sponsored loans, scholarships/grants, and unspecified assistantships also available. Support available to part-time students. Financial award application deadline: 3/1.

University of Wyoming (continued)
Faculty research: Social work education, child welfare, mental health, diversity, school social work, rural social work.
Deborah P. Valentine, Director, 307-766-3904, *Fax:* 307-766-6839, *E-mail:* debval@uwyo.edu.
Application contact: Ruth A. Nielsen, Senior Office Associate, 307-766-5422, *Fax:* 307-766-6839, *E-mail:* rnielsen@uwyo.edu. *Web site:* http://www.uwyo.edu/

■ VALDOSTA STATE UNIVERSITY

Graduate School, Division of Social Work, Valdosta, GA 31698

AWARDS MSW.

Faculty: 4 full-time (2 women).
Students: 38 full-time (34 women), 26 part-time (19 women); includes 10 minority (all African Americans). Average age 28. 39 applicants, 77% accepted. In 2001, 38 degrees awarded.
Degree requirements: For master's, 5 practica.
Entrance requirements: For master's, GRE General Test, minimum GPA of 3.0 in last 2 years. *Application deadline:* For fall admission, 3/15. Applications are processed on a rolling basis. *Application fee:* $20.
Expenses: Tuition, state resident: full-time $1,746; part-time $97 per hour. Tuition, nonresident: full-time $6,966; part-time $387 per hour. Required fees: $594; $297 per semester.
Financial support: In 2001–02, 2 research assistantships with full tuition reimbursements (averaging $2,452 per year) were awarded; career-related internships or fieldwork, institutionally sponsored loans, scholarships/grants, and unspecified assistantships also available. Financial award application deadline: 7/1; financial award applicants required to submit FAFSA.
Dr. Peggy Cleveland, Director, 229-249-4864, *Fax:* 229-245-4341, *E-mail:* phclevel@valdosta.edu.

■ VIRGINIA COMMONWEALTH UNIVERSITY

School of Graduate Studies, School of Social Work, Doctoral Program in Social Work, Richmond, VA 23284-9005

AWARDS PhD.

Students: 10 full-time, 25 part-time; includes 10 minority (8 African Americans, 2 Hispanic Americans). 28 applicants, 54% accepted. In 2001, 1 degree awarded.
Degree requirements: For doctorate, thesis/dissertation, comprehensive exam.
Entrance requirements: For doctorate, GRE General Test, MSW or related degree. *Application deadline:* For fall admission, 3/1 (priority date). *Application fee:* $30.
Expenses: Tuition, state resident: full-time $4,276; part-time $238 per credit. Tuition, nonresident: full-time $12,672; part-time $704 per credit. Required fees: $1,167; $43 per credit.
Financial support: Fellowships, research assistantships, teaching assistantships, career-related internships or fieldwork, Federal Work-Study, institutionally sponsored loans, and tuition waivers (full and partial) available. Support available to part-time students. Financial award application deadline: 5/1.
Dr. Kia J. Bentley, Director, 804-828-0453, *E-mail:* kbentley@saturn.vcu.edu.
Application contact: Dr. Ann M. Nichols-Casebolt, Associate Dean, 804-828-0703, *Fax:* 804-828-0716, *E-mail:* acasebol@saturn.vcu.edu. *Web site:* http://www.vcu.edu/gradweb/slwhome.htm

■ VIRGINIA COMMONWEALTH UNIVERSITY

School of Graduate Studies, School of Social Work, Master's Program in Social Work, Richmond, VA 23284-9005

AWARDS MSW, JD/MSW, MSW/MA.

Students: 284 full-time, 230 part-time; includes 104 minority (82 African Americans, 14 Asian Americans or Pacific Islanders, 8 Hispanic Americans). 455 applicants, 82% accepted. In 2001, 202 degrees awarded.
Application deadline: For fall admission, 2/1. *Application fee:* $30.
Expenses: Tuition, state resident: full-time $4,276; part-time $238 per credit. Tuition, nonresident: full-time $12,672; part-time $704 per credit. Required fees: $1,167; $43 per credit.
Financial support: Fellowships, research assistantships, teaching assistantships, career-related internships or fieldwork, Federal Work-Study, institutionally sponsored loans, and tuition waivers (full and partial) available. Support available to part-time students. Financial award application deadline: 3/1.
Dr. Marcia P. Harrigan, Director, 804-828-0408, *E-mail:* mpharrig@vcu.edu.
Application contact: Dr. Ann M. Nichols-Casebolt, Associate Dean, 804-828-0703, *Fax:* 804-828-0716, *E-mail:* acasebol@saturn.vcu.edu. *Web site:* http://www.vcu.edu/gradweb/slwhome.htm

■ WALLA WALLA COLLEGE

Graduate School, School of Social Work, College Place, WA 99324-1198

AWARDS MSW. Part-time programs available.

Faculty: 19 full-time (15 women), 10 part-time/adjunct (5 women).
Students: 203 full-time (161 women), 12 part-time (11 women); includes 37 minority (5 African Americans, 3 Asian Americans or Pacific Islanders, 10 Hispanic Americans, 19 Native Americans). Average age 34. 177 applicants, 98% accepted. In 2001, 93 degrees awarded.
Entrance requirements: For master's, minimum GPA of 2.75. *Application deadline:* For fall admission, 7/15 (priority date). Applications are processed on a rolling basis. *Application fee:* $50. Electronic applications accepted.
Expenses: Tuition: Full-time $15,561; part-time $399 per credit.
Financial support: In 2001–02, 195 students received support. Career-related internships or fieldwork, Federal Work-Study, and scholarships/grants available. Support available to part-time students. Financial award application deadline: 4/1; financial award applicants required to submit FAFSA.
Dr. Wilma Hepker, Dean, 509-527-2273, *Fax:* 509-527-2253, *E-mail:* hepkwi@wwc.edu.
Application contact: Dr. Joe G. Galusha, Dean of Graduate Studies, 509-527-2421, *Fax:* 509-527-2253, *E-mail:* galujo@wwc.edu.

■ WASHINGTON UNIVERSITY IN ST. LOUIS

George Warren Brown School of Social Work, St. Louis, MO 63130-4899

AWARDS MSW, PhD, JD/MSW, M Arch/MSW, MAJCS/MSW, MAUD/MSW, MBA/MSW. Part-time and evening/weekend programs available.

Faculty: 28 full-time (14 women), 52 part-time/adjunct (32 women).
Students: 388 full-time (328 women), 52 part-time (40 women); includes 98 minority (56 African Americans, 18 Asian Americans or Pacific Islanders, 8 Hispanic Americans, 16 Native Americans), 92 international. Average age 29. 539 applicants, 87% accepted. In 2001, 190 master's, 6 doctorates awarded.
Degree requirements: For doctorate, thesis/dissertation. *Median time to degree:* Master's–2 years full-time, 4 years part-time; doctorate–5 years full-time.
Entrance requirements: For master's, minimum GPA of 3.0; for doctorate, GRE. *Application deadline:* Applications are processed on a rolling basis. *Application fee:* $35. Electronic applications accepted.
Expenses: Tuition: Full-time $26,900.
Financial support: In 2001–02, 334 students received support, including 166 fellowships with partial tuition reimbursements available (averaging $4,930 per year), 73 research assistantships with full tuition reimbursements available (averaging $3,000 per year), 49 teaching assistantships with full tuition reimbursements available (averaging $1,000 per year); career-related internships or fieldwork, Federal Work-Study, institutionally sponsored loans, and tuition waivers (partial) also available. Support available to part-time students.
Faculty research: Mental health services, social development, public child welfare,

at-risk teens, social development, dietary risks in African-American women.
Dr. Shanti K. Khinduka, Dean and George Warren Brown Distinguished Professor of Social Work, 314-935-6693, *Fax:* 314-935-8511, *E-mail:* khinduka@gwbmail.wustl.edu.
Application contact: Brian W. Legate, Director of Admissions, 314-935-6676, *Fax:* 314-935-4859, *E-mail:* msw@gwbmail.wustl.edu. *Web site:* http://gwbweb.wustl.edu/

Find an in-depth description at www.petersons.com/gradchannel.

■ WASHINGTON UNIVERSITY IN ST. LOUIS

Graduate School of Arts and Sciences, Program in Social Work, St. Louis, MO 63130-4899

AWARDS PhD.

Students: 55 full-time (39 women); includes 9 minority (4 African Americans, 1 Asian American or Pacific Islander, 1 Hispanic American, 3 Native Americans), 22 international. 60 applicants, 25% accepted. In 2001, 6 degrees awarded.
Application fee: $35.
Expenses: Tuition: Full-time $26,900.
Dr. Nancy Morrow-Howell, Head, 314-935-6605.

■ WAYNE STATE UNIVERSITY

Graduate School, School of Social Work, Detroit, MI 48202

AWARDS Social work (MSW); social work practice with families and couples (Certificate). Part-time and evening/weekend programs available.

Faculty: 13 full-time.
Students: 213 full-time (186 women), 332 part-time (296 women); includes 194 minority (170 African Americans, 9 Asian Americans or Pacific Islanders, 12 Hispanic Americans, 3 Native Americans), 29 international. Average age 34. 284 applicants, 68% accepted, 127 enrolled. In 2001, 293 master's, 8 other advanced degrees awarded.
Degree requirements: For master's, thesis optional.
Application deadline: For fall admission, 3/31; for spring admission, 2/28. *Application fee:* $20 ($30 for international students). Electronic applications accepted.
Expenses: Tuition, state resident: full-time $3,764. Tuition and fees vary according to degree level and program.
Financial support: Career-related internships or fieldwork, institutionally sponsored loans, scholarships/grants, and tuition waivers (partial) available. Support available to part-time students. Financial award application deadline: 5/1; financial award applicants required to submit FAFSA.
Faculty research: Violence prevention: domestic/intimate partner/dating/school; family policy/housing policy; community and social development: domestic/international; reintegration of ex-offenders and urban family development; social work treatment: children, adolescents, adults and families. *Total annual research expenditures:* $682,366.
Phyllis Vroom, Dean, 313-577-4409, *Fax:* 313-577-8770.
Application contact: Janet Clerk-Joiner, Director I, 313-577-4402.

■ WEST CHESTER UNIVERSITY OF PENNSYLVANIA

Graduate Studies, School of Business and Public Affairs, Department of Social Work, West Chester, PA 19383

AWARDS MSW. Part-time and evening/weekend programs available.

Faculty: 7.
Students: 19 full-time (18 women), 4 part-time (all women); includes 2 minority (both African Americans), 1 international. Average age 29. 35 applicants, 77% accepted. In 2001, 15 degrees awarded.
Degree requirements: For master's, thesis optional.
Entrance requirements: For master's, GRE, MAT, interview, minimum GPA of 3.0. *Application deadline:* For fall admission, 4/15 (priority date); for spring admission, 10/15. Applications are processed on a rolling basis. *Application fee:* $25.
Expenses: Tuition, state resident: full-time $4,600; part-time $256 per credit. Tuition, nonresident: full-time $7,554; part-time $420 per credit. Required fees: $44 per credit.
Financial support: In 2001–02, 2 research assistantships with full tuition reimbursements (averaging $5,000 per year) were awarded; unspecified assistantships also available. Support available to part-time students. Financial award application deadline: 2/15; financial award applicants required to submit FAFSA.
Faculty research: Teen pregnancy/parenting, adoption, health care advocacy, welfare-to-work, mentoring/alternative education.
Dr. Gwenelle O'Neal, Chair and Director, 610-436-2527.
Application contact: Dr. Ann Abbott, Graduate Coordinator, 610-436-0351, *E-mail:* aabbott@wcupa.edu.

■ WESTERN MICHIGAN UNIVERSITY

Graduate College, College of Health and Human Services, School of Social Work, Kalamazoo, MI 49008-5202

AWARDS MSW. Part-time programs available.

Faculty: 18 full-time (10 women), 1 part-time/adjunct.
Students: 219 full-time (183 women), 15 part-time (11 women); includes 39 minority (32 African Americans, 3 Asian Americans or Pacific Islanders, 4 Hispanic Americans), 2 international. 138 applicants, 88% accepted, 51 enrolled. In 2001, 83 degrees awarded.
Application deadline: For fall admission, 3/1. *Application fee:* $25.
Expenses: Tuition, state resident: part-time $186 per credit hour. Tuition, nonresident: part-time $442 per credit hour. Required fees: $602. One-time fee: $132 part-time. Tuition and fees vary according to course load.
Financial support: Fellowships, research assistantships, teaching assistantships, Federal Work-Study available. Financial award application deadline: 2/15; financial award applicants required to submit FAFSA.
Dr. Earlie Washington, Director, 616-387-3172.
Application contact: Admissions and Orientation, 616-387-2000, *Fax:* 616-387-2355.

■ WEST VIRGINIA UNIVERSITY

Eberly College of Arts and Sciences, School of Applied Social Science, Program in Social Work, Morgantown, WV 26506

AWARDS Aging and health care (MSW); children and families (MSW); mental health (MSW). Part-time programs available.

Faculty: 13 full-time (8 women), 10 part-time/adjunct (9 women).
Students: 113 full-time (86 women), 106 part-time (84 women). Average age 31. 253 applicants, 75% accepted. In 2001, 111 degrees awarded.
Degree requirements: For master's, fieldwork.
Entrance requirements: For master's, GRE, TOEFL, minimum GPA of 2.75. *Application deadline:* For fall admission, 3/1. *Application fee:* $45.
Expenses: Tuition, state resident: full-time $2,791. Tuition, nonresident: full-time $8,659. Required fees: $1,002. Tuition and fees vary according to program.
Financial support: In 2001–02, 35 students received support, including 7 research assistantships, 19 teaching assistantships; career-related internships or fieldwork, Federal Work-Study, institutionally sponsored loans, scholarships/grants, tuition waivers (full and partial), and stipends also available. Financial award application deadline: 3/1; financial award applicants required to submit FAFSA.
Faculty research: Rural and small town social work practice, gerontology, child abuse, health and mental health, welfare reform. *Total annual research expenditures:* $208,000.
Application contact: Dr. Nancy Lohmann, Head, 304-293-3501 Ext. 3107, *Fax:* 304-293-5936, *E-mail:* nancy.lohmann@mail.wvu.edu. *Web site:* http://www.wvu.edu/~socialwk/

■ WHEELOCK COLLEGE

Graduate School, Program in Social Work, Boston, MA 02215

AWARDS MSW.

Faculty: 5 full-time (all women).
Students: 31 full-time (27 women), 9 part-time (all women); includes 14 minority (10 African Americans, 4 Hispanic Americans). 42 applicants, 90% accepted, 26 enrolled.
Entrance requirements: For master's, minimum GPA 3.0; previous undergraduate coursework in human biology, statistics. *Application deadline:* For fall admission, 4/15. Applications are processed on a rolling basis. *Application fee:* $35 ($40 for international students). Electronic applications accepted.
Expenses: Tuition: Full-time $21,600; part-time $600 per credit.
Financial support: Application deadline: 4/1.
Dr. Kathleen Kirk, Dean of Social Work, 617-734-5200, *Fax:* 617-323-7127.
Application contact: Deborah A. Sheehan, Director of Graduate Admissions and Student Financial Planning, 617-879-2178, *Fax:* 617-232-7127, *E-mail:* dsheehan@wheelock.edu. *Web site:* http://www.wheelock.edu/

■ WICHITA STATE UNIVERSITY

Graduate School, Fairmount College of Liberal Arts and Sciences, School of Social Work, Wichita, KS 67260

AWARDS MSW.

Faculty: 9 full-time (6 women).
Students: 46 full-time (38 women), 30 part-time (26 women); includes 9 minority (7 African Americans, 2 Asian Americans or Pacific Islanders). Average age 37. 53 applicants, 51% accepted, 21 enrolled. In 2001, 23 degrees awarded.
Application deadline: For spring admission, 1/1. *Application fee:* $25 ($40 for international students).
Expenses: Tuition, state resident: full-time $1,888; part-time $105 per credit. Tuition, nonresident: full-time $6,129; part-time $341 per credit. Required fees: $345; $19 per credit. $17 per semester. Tuition and fees vary according to course load and program.
Financial support: In 2001–02, 1 research assistantship (averaging $3,500 per year) was awarded; teaching assistantships Financial award application deadline: 4/1; financial award applicants required to submit FAFSA.
Dr. Cathleen Lewandowski, Director, 316-978-7250, *Fax:* 316-978-3328, *E-mail:* cathleen.lewandowski@wichita.edu.

■ WIDENER UNIVERSITY

School of Human Service Professions, Center for Social Work Education, Chester, PA 19013-5792

AWARDS MSW. Part-time programs available.

Degree requirements: For master's, field practica.
Entrance requirements: For master's, minimum GPA of 3.0. Electronic applications accepted.
Expenses: Contact institution.
Faculty research: Clinical practice, clinical supervision, gerontology, child welfare, self-psychology, occupational/environmental health, women's issues.

■ YESHIVA UNIVERSITY

Wurzweiler School of Social Work, New York, NY 10033-3201

AWARDS MSW, PhD, MSW/Certificate. Part-time and evening/weekend programs available.

Faculty: 23 full-time (12 women), 32 part-time/adjunct (19 women).
Students: 179 full-time (134 women), 264 part-time (208 women); includes 137 minority (88 African Americans, 6 Asian Americans or Pacific Islanders, 42 Hispanic Americans, 1 Native American), 25 international. Average age 34. 505 applicants, 50% accepted, 199 enrolled. In 2001, 156 master's, 5 doctorates awarded.
Degree requirements: For master's and doctorate, thesis/dissertation.
Entrance requirements: For master's, interview; for doctorate, GRE, interview. *Application deadline:* For fall admission, 5/1 (priority date); for spring admission, 10/31. Applications are processed on a rolling basis. *Application fee:* $35.
Expenses: Contact institution.
Financial support: In 2001–02, 352 students received support. Career-related internships or fieldwork, institutionally sponsored loans, and scholarships/grants available. Financial award application deadline: 5/15; financial award applicants required to submit FAFSA.
Faculty research: Child abuse, AIDS, day care, nonprofits, gerontology, Jewish communal service. *Total annual research expenditures:* $208,000.
Dr. Sheldon R. Gelman, Dean, 212-960-0820.
Application contact: Michele Sarracco, Director of Admissions, 212-960-0811, *Fax:* 212-960-0822.

School Index

Index of Directories in This Book

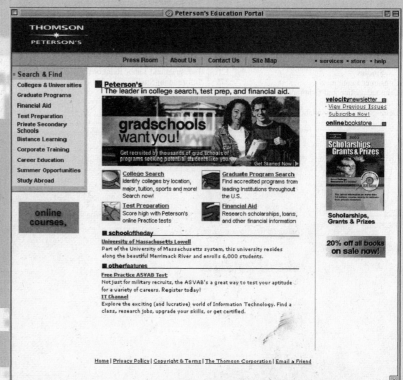